DICTIONARY of SCOTTISH CHURCH HISTORY & THEOLOGY

ORGANIZING EDITOR:
Nigel M. de S. Cameron
Associate Dean, Academic Doctoral Programs
Trinity Evangelical Divinity School, Deerfield, Illinois;
Formerly Warden, Rutherford House, Edinburgh

GENERAL EDITORS:
David F. Wright
Senior Lecturer in Ecclesiastical History
New College, University of Edinburgh

David C. Lachman	**Donald E. Meek**
Historian and Editor	*Professor of Celtic*
Philadelphia	*University of Aberdeen*

ADVISORY EDITORS:
Mark Dilworth, OSB
Abbot, Fort Augustus Abbey
Formerly Keeper, Scottish Catholic Archives
J. D. Douglas
Writer and Editor, St Andrews
Lecturer, Singapore Bible College
Henry R. Sefton
Formerly Master of Christ's College and
Senior Lecturer in Church History, University of Aberdeen
Andrew F. Walls
Director, Centre for the Study of Christianity
in the Non-Western World, New College, University of Edinburgh

ASSISTANT EDITORS:
Rachel J. Meek
Editor, Aberdeen
Nicholas R. Needham
Formerly Librarian, Rutherford House, Edinburgh

DICTIONARY of SCOTTISH CHURCH HISTORY & THEOLOGY

•ORGANIZING EDITOR•
Nigel M. de S. Cameron

•GENERAL EDITORS•
David F. Wright, David C. Lachman, Donald E. Meek

INTERVARSITY PRESS
DOWNERS GROVE, ILLINOIS 60515

Copyright © T & T Clark Ltd., 1993

T & T Clark Ltd., 59 George Street, Edinburgh EH2 2LQ, Scotland

This edition published in the United States of America under license from T & T Clark Ltd. by InterVarsity Press, P.O. Box 1400, Downers Grove, Illinois 60515.

All rights reserved. No part of this publication may be reproduced, stored in a retrieval system, or transmitted, in any form or by any means, electronic, mechanical, photocopying, recording or otherwise, without the prior permission of InterVarsity Press.

First published 1993.

Typeset by Rowland Phototypesetting Ltd., Bury St. Edmunds, Suffolk.

Printed and bound in Great Britain.

ISBN 0-8308-1407-8

Library of Congress Cataloging-in-Publication Data

Dictionary of Scottish church history and theology/edited by
  Nigel M. de S. Cameron.
      p.   cm.
  Includes bibliographical references.
  ISBN 0-8308-1407-8
  1. Scotland—Church history—Dictionaries.   2. Theology,
Doctrinal—Scotland—History—Dictionaries.   3. Christian biography—
Scotland—Dictionaries.   I. Cameron, Nigel M. de S.
  BR782.D43   1993
  274.11'003—dc20   93-3838
                                                  CIP

17	16	15	14	13	12	11	10	9	8	7	6	5	4	3	2	1
07	06	05	04	03	02	01	00	99	98	97	96	95	94	93		

Contents

Preface	vii
List of Abbreviations	ix
The Contributors	xi
Dictionary	1

Acknowledgement

The *Dictionary* was initiated and editorial and administrative facilities furnished by Rutherford House, Edinburgh.

Preface

The *Dictionary of Scottish Church History and Theology* was conceived in the mid-1980s, and its appearance after more than seven years of preparation is the fruit of energetic scholarship on the part of many. Its object is to make available to students, scholars, ministers, a variety of teachers and other interested readers an accurate and comprehensive account of Christianity in Scotland within the compass of a single volume. We have sought to produce a work which is representative of the best scholarship (many articles are by leading authorities on their subjects) and which offers a balanced treatment of Scotland's Christian past. We have sought also to make the *Dictionary* accessible, so writers assume little of their readers, and copious cross-references open up the context of material presented. In these and other matters (for example, the relative length of entries) we have been conscious of difficult choices, and are aware that some decisions could reasonably have been taken otherwise. The fact that so wide a spread of contributors has eagerly engaged in the project encourages us to have confidence in the principles we have followed.

Some of these principles invite explanation. The centre of gravity of the *Dictionary* lies within the Reformed tradition which has so dominated the modern religious life of Scotland. Yet we have been concerned to treat adequately the pre-Reformation period, including the Celtic Church; and, post-Reformation, to reflect Dissenting, Episcopalian and Roman Catholic traditions, as well as the mainstream. (We have even included, however briefly, religious groups on the fringes of Christianity that are commonly called 'sects'.) These concerns are carefully reflected in the distribution of editorial responsibility. An issue of another kind is that of our policy on biographical entries. Major figures include themselves, but it is one of the characteristics of the energetic history of the Scottish Church that it has spawned so many figures who were neither major nor insignificant. We have erred, perhaps, on the side of inclusion, in the interests of the usefulness of the *Dictionary* – in places remote from such resources as the *Fasti*. Sometimes we have sampled figures from a generation or a movement in which others might have equal call on our interest. We have tried to be especially generous with women, whose often near-absence from works of this kind is out of all proportion to their significance in the history itself (though that of course is partly the fruit of earlier, less equitable principles of history-writing). We struggled with the question of living persons, which after a failed experiment at generosity (ending when it resembled a man/woman most-likely-to exercise) resolved into a restricted list of figures deemed of major significance whose principal contribution, as we could judge, had already been made. A further problem concerns subjects who spent only part of their lives (perhaps only their early years, or a series of significant visits) in Scotland, and we are conscious that our principles of inclusion have (perhaps inevitably) had ragged edges.

Naturally, some of this material is controversial – both in matters of historical interpretation, and (especially) where it touches on questions of theology. While the centre of gravity of the *Dictionary* lies within the Reformed tradition, we have allowed our contributors considerable liberty in their exposition of their subjects. They were offered guidelines which we gladly share with their readers, including the following: 'Items of controversial character should be treated fairly. Where appropriate, different viewpoints should be covered. Contributors in disagreement with interpretations that are widely held must carefully justify their positions.' These standards of equity have been attempted and, though every reader may not agree, we hope we have done our best to see them attained.

It remains to thank some of those whose labour is not acknowledged in the lists of editors and contributors. Rutherford House, Edinburgh, as sponsor of the *Dictionary*, provided facilities and people to support the project over a number of years; of the staff, our warm thanks go to Janella Glover, Helen Short and, latterly and especially, Vivienne Goddard for the administration of a complex project.

Nigel M. de S. Cameron
Trinity Evangelical Divinity School,
Deerfield, Illinois

List of Abbreviations

A	Aberdeen
AFCS	*Annals of the Free Church of Scotland*, 2 vols, ed. W. Ewing (Edinburgh, 1914)
AGAFCS	*Acts of the General Assembly of the Free Church of Scotland*, 57 vols in 11 (Edinburgh, 1843–1900)
AGACS	*Acts of the General Assembly of the Church of Scotland, MDCXXXVIII–MDCCCXLII* (Edinburgh, 1843)
APCS	*Assembly Papers of the Church of Scotland*
APFCS	*Assembly Papers of the Free Church of Scotland*, 56 vols (Edinburgh, 1845–1900)
APS	*The Acts of the Parliaments of Scotland, 1124–1707*, 12 vols, eds T. Thomson and C. Innes (Edinburgh, 1844–75)
APUFC	*Assembly Papers of the United Free Church of Scotland*
ARG	*Archiv für Reformationsgeschichte*
ASOSC	*Annals and Statistics of the Original Secession Church*, ed. D. Scott (Edinburgh, [1886])
ASUPC	*Annals and Statistics of the United Presbyterian Church*, ed. W. Mackelvie (Edinburgh, 1873)
AUR	*Aberdeen University Review*
BCO	*Book of Common Order*
BCP	*Book of Common Prayer*
BQ	*Baptist Quarterly*
BUK	*The Booke of the Universall Kirk of Scotland, Acts and Proceedings of the General Assemblies of the Kirk of Scotland, 1560–1618*, 3 pts, ed. T. Thomson (Edinburgh, 1839–45)
Burleigh	J. H. S. Burleigh, *A Church History of Scotland* (Oxford, 1960)
BW	*British Weekly*
C	Cambridge
Calderwood	David Calderwood, *The History of the Kirk of Scotland*, 8 vols, ed. T. Thomson (Edinburgh, 1842–9)
CH	*Church Hymnary*
CHist	*Church History*
Chambers-Thomson	R. Chambers (ed.), *Biographical Dictionary of Eminent Scotsmen*, revd T. Thomson, 3 vols (L, 1875)
CofE	Church of England
CofS	Church of Scotland
Cox	J. T. Cox (ed.), *Practice and Procedure in the Church of Scotland*, ed. J. B. Longmuir (Edinburgh, 1964)
CSHFMR	*Church of Scotland Home and Foreign Missionary Record/Home and Foreign Missionary Record of the Church of Scotland*
D	Dundee
Disruption Worthies	J. B. Gillies (ed.), *Disruption Worthies, A Memorial of 1843*, with hist. introd. by J. A. Wylie (E, 1881)
DNB	*Dictionary of National Biography*, eds. L. Stephen, S. Lee et al. (London, 1885–)
Dowden	J. Dowden, *The Bishops of Scotland* (Glasgow, 1912)
E	Edinburgh
Easson-Cowan	D. E. Easson, *Medieval Religious Houses, Scotland*, revd I. B. Cowan (London, 1976)
EB	*Encyclopaedia Britannica*
EpCS	Episcopal Church of Scotland
EQ	*Evangelical Quarterly*
ERE	*Encyclopaedia of Religion and Ethics*, 13 vols, ed. J. Hastings (Edinburgh, 1908–26)
Est.C	Established Church
ET	English translation
Exp	*Expositor*
ExT	*Expository Times*
Farge	J. K. Farge, *Biographical Register of Paris Doctors of Theology 1500–1536* (Toronto, 1980)
FBD	*The First Book of Discipline*, ed. J. K. Cameron (Edinburgh, 1972)
FC/FCS	Free Church/Free Church of Scotland
FCM	*Free Church Magazine*
FCSR	*Home and Foreign Missionary Record for the Free Church of Scotland* (1843–50) / *Home and Foreign Record of the Free Church of Scotland* (1850–61) / *Free Church of Scotland Weekly* (1861–2) / *Free Church of Scotland Monthly Record* (1862–81) / *Free Church of Scotland Monthly and Record* (1882–1900) / *Free Church Monthly Record*

LIST OF ABBREVIATIONS

FES	*Fasti Ecclesiae Scoticanae*, ed. Hew Scott *et al.* (Edinburgh, 1866–)
FESMA	*Fasti Ecclesiae Scoticanae Medii Aevi*, ed. D. E. R. Watt (St. Andrews, 1969)
FP/FPC	Free Presbyterian/Free Presbyterian Church
FUFCS	*The Fasti of the United Free Church of Scotland, 1900–29*, ed. J. A. Lamb (Edinburgh, 1956)
G	Glasgow
IR	*Innes Review*
JEH	*Journal of Ecclesiastical History*
Knox, *History*	*John Knox's History of the Reformation in Scotland*, 2 vols, ed. W. C. Dickinson (London, 1949)
Knox, *Works*	*The Works of John Knox*, 6 vols, ed. D. Laing (Edinburgh, 1846–64)
L	London
LW	*Life and Work*
MRUFCS	*Missionary Record of the United Free Church of Scotland*
MRUPC	*Missionary Record of the United Presbyterian Church*
NLS	National Library of Scotland, Edinburgh
NSA	*The New Statistical Account of Scotland*, 15 vols, ed. J. Gordon (Edinburgh, 1845)
NY	New York
O	Oxford
PAGACS	*Principal Acts of the General Assembly of the Church of Scotland*
PAGAFCS	*Principal Acts of the General Assembly of the Free Church of Scotland (post-1900)* (Edinburgh, 1901–)
PGAFCS	*Proceedings of the General Assembly of the Free Church of Scotland*, 59 vols in 51 (Edinburgh, 1843–1900)
PGAUFCS	*Proceedings of the General Assembly of the United Free Church of Scotland*
PSAS	*Proceedings of the Society of Antiquaries of Scotland*
PUPS	*Proceedings of the United Presbyterian Synod*
RC/RCC	Roman Catholic/Roman Catholic Church
RGACS	*Reports to the General Assembly of the Church of Scotland* (from 1981 contains *Acts*, formerly published separately)
RGAUFCS	*Reports to the General Assembly of the United Free Church of Scotland*
RP/RPC	Reformed Presbyterian/Reformed Presbyterian Church
RPCS	*The Register of the Privy Council of Scotland*, ed. J. H. Burton *et al.* (Edinburgh, 1877–)
RSCHS	*Records of the Scottish Church History Society*
RSCS	*Reports of the Schemes of the Church of Scotland*
SAS	*The Statistical Account of Scotland 1791–1799*, 20 vols, eds I. R. Grant and D. J. Withrington (East Ardsley, Wakefield, 1973–83)
SBD	*The Second Book of Discipline*, ed. J. Kirk (Edinburgh, 1980)
SBET	*Scottish Bulletin of Evangelical Theology*
SBM	*Scottish Baptist Magazine*
SBYB	*Scottish Baptist Year Book*
SC	*Scottish Congregational Magazine* (1843–80) / *Scottish Congregationalist* (1881 ff.)
Scots Peerage	*The Scots Peerage*, 9 vols, ed. J. B. Paul (Edinburgh, 1904–14).
SGS	*Scottish Gaelic Studies*
SHR	*Scottish Historical Review*
SHS	Scottish History Society
SIMSB	*Scottish Institute of Missionary Studies Bulletin*
SJT	*Scottish Journal of Theology*
Small	R. Small, *History of the Congregations of the United Presbyterian Church*, 2 vols (Edinburgh, 1904)
Spottiswoode	John Spottiswoode, *History of the Church of Scotland*, 3 vols, eds M. Russell and M. Napier (Edinburgh, 1847–51)
SRO	Scottish Record Office
SRS	Scottish Record Society
SS	*Scottish Studies*
SSPCK	Scottish Society for the Promotion of Christian Knowledge
ST	*Stedfast. The Organ of the United Free Church* (1929 ff.)
STS	Scottish Text Society
TDGAS	*Transactions and Journal of the Proceedings of the Dumfriesshire and Galloway Natural History and Antiquarian Society*
TGSI	*Transactions of the Gaelic Society of Inverness*
TRE	*Theologische Realenzyklopädie*, eds. G. Krause *et al.* (Berlin, 1977–)
TSA	*Third Statistical Account of Scotland*, 29 vols in progress, various authors (Edinburgh, etc., 1951–)
UF/UFC	United Free/United Free Church
UP/UPC	United Presbyterian/United Presbyterian Church
USec./USec.C	United Secession/United Secession Church

The Contributors

ACKERMAN, Robert PhD
Director of Humanities, University of the Arts, Philadelphia
ADDINGTON, T. G. PhD
Assistant Professor, Department of Communication, University of Arkansas
ANDERSON, Andrew F. MA, BD
Minister, Greenside, Edinburgh
ANDERSON, G. W. MA, DD, TeolD, FRSE, FBA
Professor Emeritus of Hebrew and Old Testament Studies, University of Edinburgh
ANDREWS, J. S. MA, PhD, ALA
Formerly Sub-Librarian, University of Lancaster
ANGUS, R. J. MA
Auditor, Diocese of Moray, Ross and Caithness
ASPINWALL, Bernard BA, MA
Senior Lecturer in Modern History, University of Glasgow
BARBOUR, R. S. MC, DD
Professor Emeritus of New Testament Studies, University of Aberdeen
BARCLAY, I. C. MA, BD
Minister, Kilfinan with Kyles, Argyll
BARCLAY, Oliver R. MA, PhD
Formerly General Secretary of Inter-Varsity Fellowship (Universities' and Colleges' Christian Fellowship)
BARDGETT, Frank D. MA, BD, PhD
Minister, Strathy and Halladale, Caithness
BARROW, G. W. S. DLitt, FBA, FRSE
Sir William Fraser Professor Emeritus of Scottish History and Palaeography, University of Edinburgh
BAYLIS, Philippa J. MA, PhD
Honorary Research Fellow, Faculty of Divinity, University of Edinburgh
BEBBINGTON, D. W. MA, PhD, FRHistS
Reader in History, University of Stirling
BELL, John L. MA, BD
Worship Resource Worker, Iona Community
BINFIELD, Clyde MA, PhD, FRHistS, FSA
Reader in History, University of Sheffield
BISSET, Peter T. MA, BD
Formerly Warden/Evangelist, St Ninian's, Crieff
BLACKIE, Nansie MA
Formerly Tutor, St Colm's Education Centre and College, Edinburgh
BLACKWOOD, Roy BS, PhD
Pastor, Second Reformed Presbyterian Church, Indianapolis, Indiana
BOCK, Friedhart J.
School Principal, Aberdeen
BOWES, Harold R. BD, PhD
Methodist Minister, Worksop
BOYD, Robert
Researcher in Brethren History, Fort William
BRAY, Dorothy Ann BA, PhD
Lecturer, Department of English, McMaster University, Ontario, Canada
BREWARD, Ian MA, BD, PhD
Professor of Church History, United Faculty of Theology, Melbourne, Australia
BRIDGES, Roy BA, PhD
Professor of History, University of Aberdeen
BROCKIE, Colin G. F. BSc, BD
Minister, Grange Parish Church, Kilmarnock

THE CONTRIBUTORS

BROUN, Dauvit BA, PhD
Lecturer in Department of Scottish History, University of Glasgow

BROWN, Callum G. MA, PhD
Senior Lecturer in History, University of Strathclyde

BROWN, Eddie BA, BD, STM, ThD
Professor and Head of the Department of Ecclesiology, University of Stellenbosch, South Africa

BROWN, K. M. MA, PhD
British Academy Post-doctoral Fellow, Department of Scottish History, University of St Andrews

BROWN, R. G. BA, BD
Principal of St Colm's Education Centre and College, Edinburgh

BROWN, S. J. BA, MA, PhD
Professor of Ecclesiastical History, New College, University of Edinburgh

BROWN, William D. MA
Secretary of the Scottish Church Theology Society; formerly Minister, Thornlie, Wishaw

BRUCE, The late F. F. MA, DD, LittD, FBA
Formerly Rylands Professor of Biblical Criticism and Exegesis, University of Manchester

BUCHAN, John BD, MTh
Minister, Fodderty and Strathpeffer, Ross-shire

BURNS, J. H. MA, PhD
Professor Emeritus of the History of Political Thought, University of London

BUSCHKÜHL, M. PhD
Theology and History Librarian, Catholic University of Eichstatt, Bavaria, Germany

BUTLER, John M. F. DipTh, DipMS, MBIM, MIPM
Minister, Partick Congregational Church; formerly General Secretary, Scripture Union, Scotland

CALDWELL, David H. MA, PhD, FSA Scot
Curator in charge of the Scottish Medieval Collections, The Royal Museums of Scotland

CALHOUN, David B. BA, BD, ThM, PhD
Professor of Church History, Covenant Theological Seminary, St Louis, Missouri

CAMERON, Donald E. N.
Consultant in Christian Counselling, Edinburgh

CAMERON, Nigel M. de S. MA, BD, PhD
Associate Dean, Academic Doctoral Programs, Trinity Evangelical Divinity School, Deerfield, Illinois; formerly Warden, Rutherford House, Edinburgh

CAMPBELL, Ian MA, PhD
Professor of Scottish and Victorian Literature, University of Edinburgh

CAMPBELL, J. L. DLitt, LLD
Retired farmer; formerly President, Folklore Institute of Scotland

CAMPBELL, R. H. MA, PhD
Professsor Emeritus of Economic History, University of Stirling

CARSWELL, Joyce M.
Department of Social Responsibility, Church of Scotland

CARTWRIGHT, H. M. MA
Professor of Church History, Free Church of Scotland College, Edinburgh

CAVANAGH, Mary
Journalist and author

CHERRY, Alastair BA
Assistant Keeper, Department of Printed Books, National Library of Scotland

CHEYNE, Alexander C. MA, BLitt, BD, Hon DLitt
Professor Emeritus of Ecclesiastical History, New College, University of Edinburgh

CLARK, A. Benjamin R. BD, MTh
Minister, Westgate Chapel, Bury St Edmunds; Visiting Lecturer at Geneva Bible College

CLARK, Ian D. L. MA, PhD
Formerly Fellow of St Catherine's College, Cambridge

COLLINS, Kenneth E. PhD, MRCGP
Co-chairman, Scottish Jewish Archives Committee

COOK, E. D. BA, MA, PhD
Director, Whitefield Institute, and Fellow of Green College, Oxford

COWAN, The late Ian B. MA, PhD
Professor in Scottish History, University of Glasgow

THE CONTRIBUTORS

COWE, Alan W. MA, LLB
Secretary and Clerk, The Church of Scotland General Trustees

COX, James L. PhD, MDiv, BA
Lecturer in the Phenomenology of Religion, University of Zimbabwe

CRAIG, Maxwell BD, ThM
General Secretary of Action of Churches Together in Scotland

CRESSEY, M. H. MA, MA
Principal, Westminster College, Cambridge

CULBERTSON, Eric M. MA, DipMin, PhD
Northern Coordinator, Bible Churchmen's Missionary Society Crosslinks

CURRIE, David A. BA, MDiv, PhD
Pastor, Anchor Presbyterian Church, Penns Park, Pennyslvania

DARRAGH, James MA
Formerly Civil Servant

DAVIDSON, Allan K. MA, BD, PhD
Lecturer in Church History, St John's College, Auckland, New Zealand

DAWSON, Jane E. A. BA, PhD
John Laing Lecturer in Reformation History and Theology, University of Edinburgh

DEMPSTER, John A. H. MA, PhD, DipLib, ALA
Educational Librarian, Strathclyde Regional Council

DEMPSTER, The late W. M. OBE, MA, STM
Formerly Organizing Secretary of the Committee on Huts and Canteens; formerly Minister, The Scots Kirk, Paris

DICKSON, James A.
Antiquarian Bookseller, Edinburgh

DICKSON, Neil MA
English Teacher, Kilmarnock Academy

DILWORTH, Mark, OSB, MA, PhD, FRHistS
Abbot, Fort Augustus Abbey; formerly Keeper, Scottish Catholic Archives

DORAN, Wendy J. MA, MLitt, DipEd
Principal Teacher of History, Trinity Academy, Edinburgh

DORRIAN, George M. MA, BA
Research student, Strathclyde University

DOUGLAS, J. D. MA, BD, STM, PhD
Lecturer, Singapore Bible College

DUNCAN, A. A. M. MA, FBA, FRHistS, FRSE
Professor of Scottish History, University of Glasgow

DUNCAN, Denis MA, BD
Director, The Churches' Council on Health and Healing, London

DUNCAN, Gregor D. MA, BA, PhD
Rector, St Columba's Episcopal Church, Largs, Ayrshire

DUNLOP, A. I. TD, MA, BD
Formerly Minister, St Stephen's, Edinburgh

DURIE, Alastair J. PhD, FRHistS
Senior Lecturer in Economic History, University of Glasgow

DURIEZ, Colin BA
Editor, Inter-Varsity Press, Leicester

DURKAN, John MA, PhD, DLitt, FSA, FRHistS
Senior Research Fellow, Department of Scottish History, University of Glasgow

ELLINGWORTH, Paul BA, BA, MA, PhD
Translation Consultant, United Bible Societies, Aberdeen

ELLIOT, G. MA, BD, STM
Formerly Secretary, Board of Stewardship and Finance, Church of Scotland

EVANS, R. Lawrence W. BA
Research student, Keble College, Oxford

FAUPEL, D. William MS, MDiv, BA, AB
Associate Professor, Asbury Theological Seminary, Wilmore, Kentucky

FERGUSON, Ronald, MA, BD, ThM
Minister, St Magnus Cathedral, Kirkwall, Orkney

THE CONTRIBUTORS

FERGUSON, Sinclair B. MA, BD, PhD
Professor of Systematic Theology, Westminster Theological Seminary, Philadelphia, Pennsylvania

FORRESTER, Duncan B. MA, BD, DPhil
Professor of Christian Ethics and Practical Theology and Principal of New College, University of Edinburgh

FORSYTH, W. B.
Formerly Missionary with the Evangelical Union of South America in Brazil

FRANK, Albert H. BA, MDiv, DMin
Lecturer on Moravian Church History, Moravian Theological Seminary, Ohio

FULTON, Henry L. MA, PhD
Professor of English and Director, International Programs, Central Michigan University

GALLAGHER, Tom BA, PhD
Lecturer in Peace Studies, University of Bradford

GALLOWAY, Brenda Helen LLB, BD, MTh
Lecturer in Systematic Theology and Ethics, Adbi Sabda College, Medan, Indonesia

GIBLIN, Cathaldus OFM MA, DD
Research scholar in Irish-Continental History at Franciscan House of Studies, Killiney, Co. Dublin

GIBSON, Frank S. BL, BD, STM, DSWA
Minister, Kilarrow and Kilmeny, Islay

GILL, Robert A.
Minister, The New Jerusalem Church, Paisley

GILL, Stewart D. MA, MA, PhD
Lecturer in Church History, Presbyterian Theological College, Melbourne, Australia

GILLEY, Sheridan BA, PhD, FRHistS
Senior Lecturer in Theology, University of Durham

GRAHAM, Richard J. BA, PhD
Formerly Associate Professor, North West Theological Seminary, Vancouver, Canada

GRANT, B. J.
UK Press Officer, The Church of Jesus Christ of Latter Day Saints

GRANT, M. MA
Elder, Free St Columba's Church, Edinburgh

GRAY, Nelson OBE, MA, PhD
Formerly Producer in Religious Programmes, Scottish Television

GREENLESS, Ian
Elder in Glasgow (Cathcart) Congregation of Jehovah's Witnesses

GROGAN, Geoffrey W. BD, MTh
Formerly Principal, Bible Training Institute, Glasgow

HAIR, P. E. H. MA, DPhil, FRHistS
Ramsay Muir Professor of Modern History, University of Liverpool

HAMILTON, Ian BA, BD, MPhil
Minister, Loudoun Church, Newmilns, Ayrshire

HARDMAN MOORE, Susan MA, MAR, PhD
Lecturer in Church History, King's College, University of London

HARMAN, A. M. BA, BD, MLitt, ThM, ThD
Principal, Presbyterian Theological College, Melbourne, Australia

HARPER, Marjory MA, PhD, FRHistS
Lecturer, Department of History, University of Aberdeen

HAYES, Alan J. BSc, PhD, FRES, FCIFor
Formerly Senior Lecturer, sometime Associate Dean of Science, University of Edinburgh

HAZLETT, W. I. P. BA, BD, DrTheol
Senior Lecturer in Ecclesiastical History, University of Glasgow

HELM, Paul MA
Professor of History and Philosophy of Religion, King's College, University of London

HEMPTON, David BA, PhD, FRHistS
Reader in History, Queen's University, Belfast

HERBERT, Máire MA, PhD
Lecturer in Early Medieval Irish, University College, Cork

THE CONTRIBUTORS

HERON, Alasdair I. C. MA, BD, DrTheol
Professor of Reformed Theology, University of Erlangen-Nuremberg, Germany

HERRON, Andrew MA, BD, LLB, DD, LLD
Formerly Clerk to the Presbytery of Glasgow

HILL, Andrew M. BA
Minister, Unitarians in Edinburgh; Secretary, Unitarian Historical Society

HILL, Peter BA, FSAScot, MIFA
Excavation Director, The Whithorn Trust

HITCHEN, John Mason BA, BD, PhD
Principal, Bible College of New Zealand

HODGES, Louis Igou BA, MDiv, ThM, PhD
Professor of Systematic Theology, Columbia Biblical Seminary, Columbia, South Carolina

HOUSTON, Joseph MA, BD, DPhil
Senior Lecturer in Systematic Theology, University of Glasgow

HOWARD, John V. MA, FLA
Special Collections Librarian, Edinburgh University Library

HOWAT, Angus J. MA
Minister, Campbeltown Free Church of Scotland

ISBELL, Sherman MA, ThM
Minister in the Presbyterian Reformed Church, Oakton, Virginia

JAKI, Stanley L. PhD, STD
Distinguished University Professor, Seton Hall University, New Jersey

JAY, Elisabeth MA, MPhil, DPhil
Senior Lecturer in English, Westminster College, Oxford

JENKINS, Gordon F. C. MA, BD, PhD
Assistant Secretary, Department of Ministry, Church of Scotland

JOHNSON, Christine PhD
Keeper, Scottish Catholic Archives

JONES, R. Tudur DPhil, DD, DLitt
Honorary Professor, Department of Religion, University College of North Wales, Bangor

KEDDIE, Gordon J. BSc, DipEd, MDiv
Minister of the Reformed Presbyterian Church, State College, Pennsylvania

KELLING, F. H. BSc
Formerly Lecturer in Aeronautics and Fluid Mechanics, University of Glasgow

KELLY, Douglas F. BA, BD, PhD
Professor of Systematic Theology, Reformed Theological Seminary, Jackson, Mississippi

KERNOHAN, R. D. MA
Formerly Editor of *Life and Work, The Record of the Church of Scotland*

KERR, Philip J. PhB, STL
Vice-Rector, Gillis College, Edinburgh

KING, Fergus John MA, BD
Chaplain, St John's Episcopal Cathedral, Oban

KING, Robert MA, DipAED
Formerly General Secretary, Scottish National Council of YMCAs

KIRK, James MA, PhD, DLitt, FRHistS
Reader in Scottish History, University of Glasgow

KNOX, R. Buick, PhD, DD
Formerly Professor of Ecclesiastical History, Westminster College, Cambridge

KYLE, Richard G. BS, MA, MDiv, ThM, PhD
Professor of History and Religion, Tabor College, Hillsboro, Kansas

LACHMAN, David C. BA, MA, BD, ThM, PhD
Editor, *The Presbyterian Advocate*, Philadelphia, Pennsylvania

LAW, John E. MA, PhD, FRHistS
Senior Lecturer in History, University College, Swansea

LAWLOR, James BA
Assistant priest, Saint Kessog's, Balloch

THE CONTRIBUTORS

LENEMAN, Leah PhD
Research Fellow, Department of Scottish History, University of St Andrews
LETIS, Theodore P. BA, MTS
Research student, New College, University of Edinburgh
LEVISON, Mary I. BA, BD
Convener, Diaconate Committee, Church of Scotland
LITVACK, Leon B. BA, MA, PhD, AKC
Formerly Associate Professor of English Literature and Classics, Tokushima Bunri University, Kagawa, Japan
LIVINGSTONE, David N. BA, DipEd, PhD
Lecturer, School of Geosciences, Queen's University, Belfast
LOVEGROVE, Deryck W. MA, BD, PhD, FRHistS
Lecturer in Ecclesiastical History, University of St Andrews
LOW, Donald A. MA, BPhil, PhD, FRSE, FSAScot
Reader in English Studies, University of Stirling
LUGTON, George L. MA, BD
Minister, St Andrew's in the Grange, Guernsey
LYALL, Francis MA, LLB, LLM, PhD
Professor of Public Law, University of Aberdeen
McCABE, M. MA, MTh
Research student, New College, University of Edinburgh
McCAFFREY, John F. MA, PhD
Senior Lecturer, Department of Scottish History, University of Glasgow
McCORMACK, Bruce L. BA, MDiv, PhD
Weyerhaeuser Associate Professor of Systematic Theology, Princeton Theological Seminary
MacDONALD, A. A. MA, PhD
Professor of English, Rijksuniversiteit Groningen, The Netherlands
MacDONALD, Aidan D. S. MA
College Lecturer in Archaeology, University College, Cork
MACDONALD, Fergus MA, BD
General Secretary, National Bible Society of Scotland
MACDONALD, K. D. BA, MA
Senior Lecturer, Department of Celtic, University of Glasgow
MACDONALD, Lesley O. MA, BD
Research student, New College, University of Edinburgh
MACDONALD, Neil DipTh
Independent Evangelical Outreach to Homeless and Travelling People, Edinburgh
MACFARLANE, Leslie J. BA, PhD, DLitt, FRHistS, FSA
Honorary Reader in Medieval History, University of Aberdeen
McGOLDRICK, James E. BS, MA, PhD
Professor of History, Cedarville College, Ohio
McGOWAN, Andrew T. B. BD, STM, PhD
Minister, Trinity Possil and Henry Drummond, Glasgow
McGRATH, Stephen OFM
Vicar of Franciscan Community at St Patrick's, High St, Edinburgh
McHUGH, Mary BA, MLitt
Lecturer in Ecclesiastical History, Chesters College, Bearsden, Glasgow
MACINNES, Allan I. MA, PhD
Senior Lecturer in Scottish History, University of Glasgow
McINTOSH, John R. BA, MLitt, PhD
Free Church of Scotland Minister, Dollar
McINTOSH, G. Stewart MLitt, PhD
Director, MAC Research, Tayport
MACKINTOSH, Aeneas
Formerly Communication Advisor, Scottish Episcopal Church
MACLAREN, A. A. MA, PhD
Head of Sociology Unit, University of Strathclyde
MACLEAN, Allan M. MA
Provost, St John's Cathedral, Oban

THE CONTRIBUTORS

MACLEAN, Douglas BA, MA, PhD
Assistant Professor, Department of Art and History of Art and Architecture, Tufts University, Medford, Massachusetts

MACLEOD, Donald MA
Professor of Systematic Theology, Free Church of Scotland College, Edinburgh

MACLEOD, James Lachlan MA
Research student, New College, Edinburgh

MACLEOD, R. MA, BD, PhD
Minister, Cumlodden and Lochfyneside, Inveraray, Argyll

McLUCKIE, John M. BD
Curate, Inverness Episcopal Cathedral

MACMILLAN, Gilleasbuig MA, BD
Minister, St Giles, Edinburgh

MACMILLAN, The late J. Douglas MA
Formerly Professor of Church History and Principles, Free Church of Scotland College, Edinburgh

McMILLAN, James F. MA. DPhil
Lecturer in History, University of York

McNAUGHTON, William BA, ThD
Minister, West End Congregational Church, Kirkcaldy

MACQUARRIE, Alan MA, PhD
Department of Scottish History, University of Glasgow

MAGNUSSON, Sally MA
Journalist, Glasgow

MARSHALL, I. Howard MA, BD, PhD, BA
Professor of New Testament Exegesis, University of Aberdeen

MARSHALL, James S. MA, PhD
Formerly Associate Minister, South Leith

MASSEY, Richard D. MA, BD, PhD
Director, Deo Gloria Trust, South Croydon, Surrey

MAXWELL, Ian D. MA, BD
Research student, New College, University of Edinburgh

MEEK, Donald E. MA, PhD, FRHistS
Professor of Celtic, University of Aberdeen

MEEK, Rachel J. BA, PhD
Editor, Aberdeen

MILNE, Douglas W. MA, BD, ThM
Professor of New Testament, Presbyterian Theological College, Melbourne, Australia

MITCHELL, Christopher W. ThB, MA
Pastor, Bethany Chapel, Wheaton, Illinois

MITCHELL, William MA, MLitt, PhD
UBS Translations Consultant in South America, Quito

MIURA, Hiroshi BA, MA, MLitt
Research student, New College, University of Edinburgh

MOON, Norman S. BA, BD, MTh
Senior Tutor, Bristol Baptist College

MORRIS, W. J. DD
Minister, Glasgow Cathedral

MORRISON, Angus MA
Minister, Gilmore Place Church, Edinburgh

MORTON, Andrew R. MA, BD
Deputy General Secretary, Board of World Mission and Unity, Church of Scotland

MOYES, Sheila A.
General Secretary, YWCA of Great Britain, Scottish National Council

MUNRO, R. W.
Historian and writer, Edinburgh

MURRAY, Derek Boyd MA, BD, PhD
Part-time Tutor, Scottish Baptist College, Glasgow, and Chaplain, St Columba's Hospice, Edinburgh

THE CONTRIBUTORS

MURRAY, Douglas M. MA, BD, PhD
Lecturer in Church History, University of Glasgow
MURRAY, John J. DipTh
Minister, Free St Columba's, Edinburgh
MUSTARD, Andrew G. PhD
Senior Lecturer in Historical Theology, Newbold College, Bracknell, Berkshire
NEEDHAM, Nicholas R. BD, PhD
Formerly Librarian, Rutherford House, Edinburgh
NEWELL, Philip BA, BD, PhD
Formerly Warden, Iona Abbey; Assistant Minister, St Giles, Edinburgh
NICHOLLS, John
Minister, Cole Abbey Presbyterian Church, London
NIMMO, Alexander E. BD, MPhil
Rector, St Margaret's Episcopal Church, Aberdeen
NOBLE, Thomas A. MA, BD, PhD
Senior Lecturer in Theology, Nazarene Theological College, Didsbury, Manchester
NOLL, M. A. PhD
Professor of History, Wheaton College, Wheaton, Illinois
O'NEILL, J. C. BA, BD, PhD
Professor of New Testament Language, Literature and Theology, New College, University of Edinburgh
PATERSON, Lorna M. MA
General Secretary, Woman's Guild, Church of Scotland
PEAT, Michael D. BSc, BD
Lecturer in Apologetics and Systematic Theology, Oak Hill Theological College, London
PENNIE, G. N. MA, BD
Formerly Rector, St John's Episcopal Church, Greenock
PHILIP, James MA
Minister, Holyrood Abbey, Edinburgh
PHILIP, Mary Frances, MB, ChB, MRCPsych
Associate Specialist in Psychiatry, Gogarburn and Royal Edinburgh Hospitals, Edinburgh
PIERARD, Richard V. BA, MA, PhD
Professor of History, Indiana State University
PIGGIN, Stuart BA, DipEd, BD, PhD, AKC
Senior Lecturer in History, University of Wollongong, New South Wales, Australia
PRENTIS, Malcolm D. MA, PhD, FRHistS, FSAScot
Lecturer in History, Australian Catholic University, Sydney, Australia
PRIME, Derek MA, STh
Formerly Minister, Charlotte Baptist Chapel, Edinburgh
PYPER, Hugh S. BSc, BD
Research student, Department of Biblical Studies, University of Glasgow
QUINN, James S. J. MA
Roman Catholic Priest, Sacred Heart, Edinburgh
REID, Donald LLB, MPhil, BD
Curate in Charge, St John's Episcopal Church, Baillieston and St Serf's Shettleston, Glasgow
RENNIE, Ian S. BA, MA, PhD
Vice-President and Academic Dean, Ontario Theological Seminary, Toronto
RIESEN, Richard A. BA, MA, BD, PhD
Adjunct Faculty, Fuller Theological Seminary, California
ROBERTS Alasdair, MA, MEd
Lecturer in Educational Studies, Northern College, Aberdeen
ROBERTSON, Charles JP, MA
Minister, Canongate Kirk, Edinburgh
ROSS, Andrew C. MA, BD, STM, PhD
Senior Lecturer in History of Missions, New College, University of Edinburgh
ROSS, Kenneth R. BA, BD, PhD
Lecturer in Theology and Religious Studies, Chancellor College, University of Malawi
ROWDON, Harold H. BA, PhD
Formerly Lecturer in Church History, London Bible College

THE CONTRIBUTORS

ROXBOROGH, W. John, BE, BD, PhD
Lecturer in Missiology, Bible College of New Zealand, Auckland, New Zealand

ROY, Iain M. MA, BD
Minister, Livingstone Church, Stevenston

RUSSELL, Colin A. PhD, DSc, CChem, FRSC
Professor of History of Science and Technology, Open University

SANDERSON, Margaret H. B. MA, PhD
Archivist, Scottish Record Office

SCHLENTHER, Boyd Stanley BA, MA, PhD
Senior Lecturer in History, University College, Aberystwyth

SCHOLAN, Mary P. MA, MEd
Formerly Principal Teacher of English, St Thomas Aquinas School, Edinburgh

SCORGIE, Glen G. PhD
Assistant Professor of Theology, Canadian Bible College, Regina, Saskatchewan, Canada

SCOTT, James MA, BD
Minister, Northfield Parish Church, Aberdeen

SEFTON, Henry R. MA, BD, STM, PhD
Formerly Master of Christ's College and Senior Lecturer in Church History, University of Aberdeen

SELL, Alan P. F. BA, BD, MA, PhD, DD, FSA, FRHistS
Professor of Christian Doctrine, University of Wales, Aberystwyth

SHARP, John C. BSc, BD, PhD
Minister, East Kilbride South

SHER, Richard B. BA, MA, PhD
Associate Dean and Associate Professor of History, New Jersey Institute of Technology, Newark, New Jersey

SIMPSON, Murray C. T. MA, PhD
Librarian, New College, University of Edinburgh

SMITH, Brian MA
Archivist, Shetland Islands Council

SMITH, A. Christopher MA, BD, PhD
Religion Program, Pew Charitable Trusts, Philadelphia, Pennsylvania

SMITH, David W. MA, PhD
Principal, Northumbria Bible College, Berwick-on-Tweed

SMITH, Donald C. BA, BD, PhD
Professor of Church and Ministry, Knox College, University of Toronto, Canada

SMITH, Donald MA, PhD
Artistic Director, The Netherbow, Edinburgh

STEIN, Jock MA, BD
Joint Warden, Carberry Tower, Musselburgh

STEPHENS, W. P. MA, BD, DrèsScRel
Professor of Church History, University of Aberdeen

STEVENSON, David BA, PhD, DLitt
Professor of Scottish History, University of St Andrews

STEVENSON, The late Frederic Robert PhD, ARIBA, FRTPI, FRIAS
Formerly, Senior Lecturer in Architecture, University of Edinburgh

STEWART, Kenneth J. BA, MDiv, MTh, MPhil, PhD
Minister, Christian Reformed Church, Lethbridge, Alberta

STEWART, The late William MA, BD, DD
Formerly Minister, Lecropt, Stirling

STORRAR, William F. MA, BD, PhD
Lecturer in Practical Theology, University of Aberdeen

STUNT, Timothy C. F. MA
Teacher of History, Stowe School, Buckingham

SUTHERLAND, D. I. MA, BD
Minister, Hutchesontown, Glasgow

TARTAGLIA, Philip PhB, DD
Rector of Chesters College, Bearsden, Glasgow

TAYLOR, J. MA
Minister, Stirling Baptist Church

THE CONTRIBUTORS

TAYLOR, William Hey MA, MEd, MSc, PhD
Senior Lecturer in Education, University of Exeter

TELLINI, Gianfranco
Part-time Lecturer in Theology of Worship, New College, University of Edinburgh

TEMPLETON, D. A. BA, BD, PhD
Senior Lecturer in New Testament Language, Literature and Theology, New College, University of Edinburgh

TEMPLETON, Elizabeth MA, BD
Formerly Lecturer in Divinity, New College, University of Edinburgh

THOMPSON, David M. MA, PhD, BD, FRHistS
University Lecturer in Modern Church History, University of Cambridge

THOMPSON, Jack BA, PhD
Lecturer, Centre for the Study of Christianity in the Non-Western World, New College, University of Edinburgh

THOMSON, William P. L. MA, OBE
Rector, Kirkwall Grammar School, Orkney

TODD, A. Stewart MA, BD, DD
Minister, Cathedral Church of St Machar, Old Aberdeen

TORRANCE, Iain R. MA, BD, DPhil
Lecturer in Systematic Theology, University of Aberdeen

TULLOCH, Graham BA, PhD
Senior Lecturer in English, Flinders University of South Australia

WALKER, A. L.
Formerly Minister, Trinity Possil and Henry Drummond, Glasgow

WALLS, Andrew F. BA, MA, BLitt, DD, FSA, OBE
Director, Centre for the Study of Christianity in the Non-Western World, New College, University of Edinburgh

WAREING, Gordon BSc, LSE, PCE, MSc
Lecturer, Department of Communication, Glasgow College

WATERMAN, A. M. C. MA, BTh, PhD
Professor of Economics, University of Manitoba, Canada

WEATHERHEAD, James L. MA, LLB
Principal Clerk, General Assembly of the Church of Scotland

WHITE, Gavin BA, BD, STM, PhD
Formerly Lecturer, Department of Theology and Church History, University of Glasgow

WIEDERMANN, Gotthelf BD, DrTheol
Formerly Wissenschaftlicher Assistant to the Chair of Reformed Theology, University of Erlangen, Germany

WILKIE, G. D. OBE, PhD
Formerly Industrial Mission Organizer, Church of Scotland

WILKINSON, John BD, MD, FRCP
Formerly Community Medicine Specialist, Lothian Health Board, Edinburgh

WILLIAMS, Stephen N. MA, PhD
Assistant Director, Whitefield Institute, Oxford

WILLIS, G. W. MA, DipLib, ALA
Arts Librarian, University of Stirling

WITHRINGTON, D. J. MA, MEd, FRHistS
Senior Lecturer in Scottish History, University of Aberdeen

WOLFFE, John R. MA, DPhil
Lecturer in Religious Studies, Open University

WOOLSEY, Andrew A. MA, BD, PhD
Minister, Evangelical Presbyterian Church, Crumlin, Co. Antrim

WORMALD, Jenny MA, PhD
Fellow in History, St Hilda's College, Oxford

WRIGHT, D. F. MA
Senior Lecturer in Ecclesiastical History, New College, University of Edinburgh

WYSONG, J. M. MA, PhD
Research historian; formerly Lecturer, Trinity College, Washington DC

A

Aberdeen Breviary, published in 1510 under the direction of William Elphinstone,* Bishop of Aberdeen. It was intended as a service book for Scottish secular clergy and was one of the early productions of the Southgait Press of Walter Chepman and Andrew Myllar.

The purpose of a breviary is to provide the psalms, hymns, readings from Scripture and the Fathers, stories of the saints, prayers, responses and so on, needed to say or sing the seven (if matins and lauds are counted together) daily offices or services for the clergy. Two forms of the breviary had been available in medieval Scotland – the Roman and the Sarum. The Aberdeen Breviary is an adaptation of the Sarum Breviary with a distinctively Scottish flavour and capable of further adaptation for the needs of particular dioceses.

The Scottish element consists mainly in the provision of hymns, antiphons, collects and lessons for the services commemorating Scottish saints. These include not only the major ones like Ninian,* Columba* and Kentigern but also lesser known ones like Drostan, Donan and Moluag (*see* Celtic Saints). The main source material seems to have been collections made by Elphinstone himself.

Only four copies of the Aberdeen Breviary survive. Two of these show signs of adaptation for use in another diocese. There was no second edition, for it was replaced by the much more radically reconstructed breviary of Cardinal Quiñones (*d.*1540), eight copies of which survive from sixteenth-century Scotland.

There is an interesting parallel to Elphinstone's work in the breviary and missal issued in 1519 for the Church of Norway by Erik Walkendorf, Archbishop of Trondheim.

See also Liturgical books (pre-Reformation).

Ed. W. J. Blew, *Breviarium Aberdonense*, with preface by D. Laing, 2 vols (L, 1854–5 – and issued also by Bannatyne, Maitland and Spalding Clubs); D. McRoberts, 'The Scottish Church and Nationalism in the Fifteenth Century', *IR* 19 (1968), 3–14; W. J. Anderson, 'The Compassio Beate Marie in Manuscript and Print', *Edinburgh Bibliographical Society Transactions* 4:4 (1966), 139–47; L. J. Macfarlane, *William Elphinstone and the Kingdom of Scotland* (A, 1985), 231–46.

H. R. Sefton

Aberdeen Doctors, a group of six ministers who received the degree of Doctor of Divinity at King's College, Aberdeen, 1620–30 and who engaged in a pamphlet controversy with some leading Covenanters.*

Degrees in theology had fallen into disuse in the period after the Scottish Reformation as being associated with popery. The DD was revived by King James VI in 1616 as an encouragement to learning among ministers. The first award in Aberdeen was made in 1620 to David Rait, Principal of King's College 1592–1632 (*FES* VII, 364). That same year the degree was also awarded to John Forbes* on his appointment as the first Professor of Divinity at King's College.

The Aberdeen Doctors put their names to the *Generall Demands* and other pamphlets written against the position of the commissioners who visited Aberdeen on behalf of the National Covenant in 1638. William Leslie (*FES* VII, 365) had succeeded Rait as principal in 1632. Robert Barron (*FES* VII, 361–2) had been appointed in 1625 to the chair of Divinity at Marischal College,* Aberdeen, which had been founded in 1616 but had been hitherto unfilled. Alexander Scrogie had been minister at St Machar's, Old Aberdeen, since 1621 (*FES* VI, 36–7). James Sibbald was admitted as minister at St Nicholas (*FES* VI, 18–9), Aberdeen in 1625, where he was joined by Alexander Rose* in 1631 (*FES* VI, 14).

The National Covenant,* first signed in Greyfriars Kirk in Edinburgh on 28th February 1638, proved remarkably popular throughout Scotland and only in Aberdeen was there organized opposition to it. This opposition was regarded so seriously by the Covenanters that a strong deputation, headed by the Earl (later Marquis) of Montrose (*see* Graham, James) and including Alexander Henderson,* was sent north and arrived in Aberdeen on 20 July. The Provost and baillies sent an invitation to drink 'a cup of Bon-accord' but the commissioners refused until the Covenant should be signed. The civic leaders, in high dudgeon, distributed the refreshments to the inmates of the bede-house. The ministers of Aberdeen refused to allow the Covenanters to preach from their pulpits, but the balcony of the Earl Marischal's house in the Castlegate served as an open-air pulpit and some signatures were obtained for the Covenant.

There is no evidence that the Aberdeen Doctors and the Covenanting leaders ever actually met, but a brisk controversy was conducted in print. To the Doctors' *Generall Demands Concerning the Late Covenant* (A, 1638) the Covenanters issued *Answers* (A, 1638). The Doctors then sent replies which were also answered. Finally the Doctors issued elaborate *Duplyes* (A, 1638).

One of the notable features of the National Covenant is the ingenious use it makes of the Negative Confession of 1581 (*see* King's Confession). The Aberdeen Doctors strongly objected to the implication that a document designed as a recantation of the errors of Romanism could have any relevance to the current controversies about the Book of Canons and the *Book of Common Prayer* or could be interpreted as forbidding episcopacy and the Five Articles of Perth.* The Doctors were doubtful of the lawfulness of the Covenant, for all bands of mutual defence had been forbidden by an Act of Parliament in 1585. They asked whether it was right to swear to defend the King's person and authority but at the same time to add the qualification 'in defense and preservation of the true religion, Lawes, Libertyes of this Kingdome'. The Doctors asked whether it was possible to sign the Covenant without causing the scandal of dissenting from other Reformed Churches, from famous divines and the practice of the ancient Church.

A contemporary episcopalian historian claims that the Covenanting ministers were ill-matched for their abilities with the Doctors, but the debate began too late to have much influence on national opinion and the Covenanters either deposed the Doctors or forced them into exile. If in their own eyes the Doctors won the battle in Aberdeen, the general campaign in Scotland was won by the Covenanters.

D. Macmillan, *The Aberdeen Doctors* (L, 1909); D. Stewart, 'The Aberdeen Doctors and the Covenanters', *RSCHS* 22 (1984), 35–44; D. Stevenson, *King's College, Aberdeen 1560–1641* (A, 1990).

H. R. Sefton

Aberdeen Free Church/United Free Church College, *see* Christ's College.

Aberdeen, Marchioness of, *see* Gordon, Ishbel (1854–1939).

Abernethy, Thomas (*b.c.*1600), Jesuit* priest turned Covenanter.* Of the family of Mayen in Rothiemay (Banffshire), he fought in Germany until the Protestant collapse of 1623. He was received into the RCC in Florence and entered the Jesuit Order via the Scots College,* Rome, and seven years in French colleges. A relation of the Bishop of Caithness, John Abernethy (*FES* II, 125, VII, 337), in 1633 Abernethy became chaplain/chamberlain to Lord Berriedale, a RC like his father the Earl of Caithness. The Jesuit renounced his RCism secretly when Berriedale joined the Protestant party, returning to military life in Europe under Alexander Leslie, Earl of Leven (*c.*1580–1661). He signed the National Covenant* in Greyfriars Kirk on 24th August 1638, and supported Andrew Ramsay* in negotiating with the Privy Council* and drawing up evidence against the bishops. He was wounded outside Aberdeen in 1639, when his use of artillery helped Montrose, and is last heard of as a minister (*FES* II, 122).

A. Roberts, 'Thomas Abernethy, Jesuit and Covenanter', *RSCHS* 24 (1991), 141–60; P. F. Anson, *Underground Catholicism in Scotland, 1622–1878* (Montrose, 1970).

A. Roberts

Act of Grace (1742). The 'Act of the Associate Presbytery concerning the Doctrine of Grace' was its response to what it believed was a spirit of legalism generally prevailing in the CofS and, in particular, to the General Assembly's Acts of 1720 and 1722 condemning the *Marrow of Modern Divinity* (*see* Marrow controversy). In this Act the Presbytery defended the *Marrow*'s doctrine, and sought to counteract the charges of Arminianism and Antinomianism that had been levelled against it. The Act's preamble reveals the Associate Presbytery's* aim: 'to assert the Truth ... in opposition to the corrupt doctrine vented in some Acts of Assemblies, ... Errors and Mistakes anent the Nature of Faith ... the *absolute freedom* of the Covenant of Grace' (13).

The Act repudiates the claim that the *Marrow* taught either 'universal redemption as to purchase', or universal pardon, as claimed by the Acts of 1720 and 1722. It asserts that the *Marrow* teaches particular redemption while also teaching the free and unhampered offer of Christ to 'Mankind Sinners, as such' (23).

Three further areas in the Act reflect the Presbytery's concern. First, the Act asserts 'that justifying Faith has in it an appropriating *persuasion*, a Man's being persuaded that Christ is *his* in particular ... There can be no true Faith without this Persuasion in some Measure or Degree. For Faith is a believing the Promise' (29, 33).

Secondly, the Act condemns the injury done to the doctrine of God's grace by the Assembly's Acts enjoining ministers to preach the necessity of a holy life in order to the obtaining of everlasting happiness. The Presbytery did not dismiss the importance of holy living, but reflected its concern that repentance and good works were being brought in as part of the ground of our justification before God (40).

Thirdly, the Act asserts, as does the *Marrow*, that believers remain under the moral law, which forever binds all, but denies that they are to seek justification by such obedience.

Acts of the Associate Presbytery; viz. I. Act Concerning the Doctrine of Grace ... (E, 1744).

J. M'Kerrow, *History of the Secession Church* (E, 1841); A. Thomson, *Historical Sketch of the Origin of the Secession Church* (E, 1848).

I. Hamilton

Action of Churches Together in Scotland, successor to Scottish Churches Council as the national inter-church ecumenical* organization in Scotland. The modern journey towards Christian unity began at the Edinburgh Missionary Conference* in 1910, when leaders of many denominations met and agreed that the gospel of Jesus Christ would not be believed as long as Churches were in competition with each other.

The second stage of the movement for Christian unity in Britain and Ireland began in 1942, with the formation of the British Council of Churches. National groupings of Churches followed in Ireland, Wales and Scotland, the Scottish Churches Council being formed in 1964, 'to further the mission and manifest the unity of the Church by providing a national focus of inter-Church counsel and action'. Alongside the national initiatives, many towns and cities formed their own Councils of Churches to work together and better serve the local community.

Following these local and national initiatives, an important conference was held at Swanwick (Derbyshire) in 1987 which issued this declaration: 'It is our conviction that, as a matter of policy at all levels and in all places, our Churches must now move from *co-operation* to clear *commitment* to each other, in search for the unity for which Christ prayed.' As a result, Action of Churches Together in Scotland (ACTS) was inaugurated at a service in Dunblane Cathedral on 1 September 1990. New ecumenical 'instruments' came into being in the other countries also, and at a federal level for the British Isles. They are intended, more explicitly than their predecessors, to be a vehicle for co-operative inter-church activity.

The nine churches participating in ACTS are: CofS, RCC, EpCS, Congregational Union of Scotland, Methodist Church, Religious Society of Friends, Salvation Army, UFC, United Reformed Church. Unlike Scottish Churches Council, the RC Church is a full member, but the Baptist Union of Scotland has opted out.

The secretariat of ACTS is based at Scottish Churches House, Dunblane.

M. Craig

Adam of Dryburgh (d.1212), devotional writer. A native of south-east Scotland, he became a canon of the Premonstratensian* house of Dryburgh,* of which he was elected abbot in 1184. On a visit to Prémontré he was impressed also by the austerity of the Carthusian* order; he resigned his abbacy in 1188 and was admitted to the Carthusian house of Witham in Somerset, where he remained until his death.

His works consist of a large number of sermons for lay and religious audiences, including sermons on the religious life. He also wrote lengthy treatises, *De Tripartito Tabernaculo*, on the tabernacles of Moses, Christ, and the Holy Spirit, and *De Triplici Genere Contemplationis*, a meditation on God, man, and salvation. His *De Instructione Animae* is a short dialogue between reason and the soul. These were all written at Dryburgh. From his later years at Witham comes *De Quadripartito Exercitio Cellae*, a meditation in solitude.

His writings witness to great personal austerity and deep mystical devotion. His learning was wide but conventional, and he showed no striking originality. He was, however, heavily influenced by the Victorines, of whom Richard of St Victor* was also Scottish. A more personal influence came from St Hugh of Lincoln.

J. Bulloch, *Adam of Dryburgh* (L, 1958); *DNB* I, 81–3; G. Donaldson and R. S. Morpeth, *Who's Who in Scottish History* (O, 1973), 12–13.

A. Macquarrie

Adam (d.1222), Bishop of Caithness. Adam was a Cistercian monk, elected abbot of Melrose* in 1207. In 1213, probably under William the Lion's* influence, he was elected Bishop of Caithness, and consecrated in the following year by William Malvoisin, Bishop of St Andrews. Soon afterwards he visited Rome, probably to attend the Fourth Lateran Council. On his return to his diocese, he vigorously set about the collection of teinds,* thus arousing the hostility of the peasants or 'bondars' of Caithness. In 1222 a mob attacked him at the episcopal manor of Halkirk, near Thurso; the Bishop fled into the manor-house, which was then set on fire, and Adam perished in the flames.

King Alexander II expected a heavy punishment for the murder of his Bishop. The Earl of Orkney, who had been ineffective in restraining the mob, paid a large fine; so did the peasantry, and many of the perpetrators had their hands and feet cut off.

Adam's brief and tragic episcopate reflects local hostility to the Crown's attempt to extend its influence in remote areas under William and Alexander II. Subsequent bishops chose mostly to reside further south, at Dornoch.

A. O. Anderson, *Early Sources of Scottish History, AD 500 to 1286* (E, 1922), II, 449–52; *DNB* I, 77; Dowden, 233–4; A. P. Forbes, *Kalendars of Scottish Saints* (E, 1872), 261–3.

A. Macquarrie

Adam, John (1818–90), FC minister and administrator. Born at Kilsyth, he was ordained to Free West Church, Alloa, 1843, translated to Free South Church, Aberdeen, 1849, and to Wellpark FC, Glasgow, 1867, and appointed (full-time) Convener of the Home Mission Committee, 1875. He was Joint-Convenor of the Confession of Faith Committee 1889–90. His published works include:

ADAMSON (OR CONSTANE), PATRICK

An Exposition of the Epistle of James (E, 1867); *The Headship of Christ* (A, 1858); *Union on the Basis of the Standards* (E, 1870).

On his arrival in Glasgow in 1867 Adam was pitched into the FC Union controversy and quickly his lucid and effective public speaking made a mark. He became a bastion of Unionism in the west and was also prominent in the Disestablishment* campaign. He came to be a trusted guide of the Church's affairs, his influence perhaps second only to that of Robert Rainy.* Theologically conservative himself, he did not obstruct the rising liberal Evangelicalism. In the 'case' of 1890 he was not uncritical of Marcus Dods* but argued successfully that a place must be made in the FC for the new theological approach represented by Dods. Likewise he was open to confessional adjustment, but died during the early stages of the preparation of the Declaratory Act* of 1892.

AFCS I, 77.

K. R. Ross

Adamson (or Constane), Patrick (1537–92), Archbishop of St Andrews (1575–92). A baxter's son born in Perth, he was educated at Perth grammar school and St Mary's College, St Andrews University, where he enrolled in 1554. As a determinant in 1556, he was described as 'pauper'. He graduated MA in 1558, adhered to the Reformation, and was considered apt by the General Assembly in December 1560 for 'ministreing and teaching' in the kirk. By 1563, he served as minister at Ceres in Fife and acted as the Assembly's commissioner for planting kirks in north-east Scotland. Despite the Assembly's misgivings, he left his charge for France in 1566 as tutor to the eldest son of James Macgill of Rankeillor Nether, who had recently been dismissed as clerk register. Briefly imprisoned in Paris for publishing a work naming Mary Queen of Scots'* son and heir, James, as prince of Scotland, England, France and Ireland, Adamson travelled to Geneva, where he met Theodore Beza, and studied civil law at Bourges. On returning home, he re-entered the ministry, preaching first at court in 1570, before serving at Paisley from 1572 and acting as chaplain to the Regent Morton (*see* Douglas, James).

In 1572, he preached against John Douglas'* appointment to the archbishopric of Glasgow in a discourse on three sorts of bishop: 'my lord bishop', or papal prelate; 'my lord's bishop', or court bishop; and 'the Lord's bishop' or minister of the gospel; but he was already the client of the Regent Morton and James Macgill, the reinstated clerk register, and showed no reluctance, by 1576, in accepting the archbishopric on Douglas' death. As his appointment coincided with the General Assembly's resolution to dispense with diocesan episcopacy, Adamson found himself at variance with the Assembly's plans; he was repeatedly rebuked for declining to submit to the Assembly's jurisdiction, for usurping the office of visitor, for granting collation to benefices, for voting in Parliament without the Assembly's approval and for failing to undertake

ADAMSON, WILLIAM

a congregational ministry. In 1578, the Assembly threatened him with excommunication. In 1582, he was the intended victim of assassination by Patrick Lermonth, a son of the laird of Dairsie.

So long as the Presbyterians controlled the Assembly, Adamson's cause looked forlorn; indeed, he was obliged to assent to the *Second Book of Discipline** of 1578; but with the onset of the 'anti-Presbyterian dictatorship' of the Earl of Arran's (*see* Stewart, James *c*.1545–96) administration in 1583, Adamson returned to prominence as an apologist for episcopacy *iure divino* ('by divine right'), and for the King's supremacy over the Church. In the winter of 1583–4, on a visit to Lambeth Palace, he sought support for his ecclesiastical policies from Archbishop Whitgift; he also met the Archbishop of York and Bishop of London; and in a series of articles addressed to the churches of Geneva and Zürich, and to the French church in London, he denounced Presbyterian theories. On his return home by May 1584, Adamson's ideas were vindicated when Parliament overthrew presbyteries and entrusted supervision to bishops and other royal commissioners in ecclesiastical causes. On gaining access to the registers of the General Assembly, he removed sections of the minutes inimical to bishops. But, with Arran's downfall at the close of 1585 and the return of the Presbyterians, Adamson found himself on the defensive once more: he was censured in the Synod of Fife in 1586 but declined to acknowledge its jurisdiction over him. Excommunicated by the Synod, Adamson responded by excommunicating some Presbyterian leaders including Andrew* and James Melville.* The Assembly held in May 1586, at which King James VI was present, sought to reconcile the irreconcilable by combining bishops with presbyteries; and Adamson was absolved from excommunication. Further accusations against him led to his suspension from the ministry in 1587, his deposition in 1589 and, once more, his excommunication, which was lifted with his recantation in 1591. He died in poverty on 19 February 1592.

Catechismus latino carmine redditus (E, 1581), *De papistarum superstitiosis ineptis* (E, 1564), . . . *De sacro pastoris munere tractatio brevis* (L, 1619), . . . *Poëmata sacra* (L, 1619), *The Recitation of Master P. Adamson* (Middelburg, 1598).

BUK; Calderwood; J. Melville, *Diary* (E, 1842); *SBD*; T. M'Crie, *Life of Andrew Melville*, 2 vols (E, ²1824); *FES* III, 161; V, 130; VII, 325–6; G. Donaldson, 'The Attitude of Whitgift and Bancroft to the Scottish Church', *Trans. Royal Hist. Soc.*, 4th ser., 24 (1942), 95–115; J. M. Anderson (ed.), *Early Records of the University of St Andrews* (E, 1926); R. Chambers, *Eminent Scotsmen* (G, 1835), i, 19–22; *DNB* I, 111–15.

J. Kirk

Adamson, William (1863–1936), MP for West Fife (1910–31), and Secretary of State for Scotland in the Labour administrations of 1924 and 1929–31. A native of Fife and a one-time miner and miners' union leader, Adamson was a model of the late Victorian labour movement, believing that parliamentary democracy was the best means of pursuing social justice. He was chairman of the Parliamentary Labour Party and leader of the Labour Party in the Commons (1917–21). In the inter-war period he battled against Communism, especially in his native county. His social and political attitudes were inextricably bound up with his Christian convictions. He was a lifelong Baptist, latterly being a member of the West Baptist Church, Dunfermline, and serving as deacon, secretary and Sunday School Superintendent. He was also a founder member of the Dunfermline Temperance Council.

Dictionary of Labour Biography VII, 4–8; W. Knox (ed.), *Scottish Labour Leaders 1918–1939* (E, 1984), 58–61; *The Scottish Socialists* (L, 1931), chapter 4; *The Scotsman*, 24 February 1936; D. Bebbington, 'Baptist Members of Parliament in the Twentieth Century', *BQ* 31 (1986), 263.

M. McCabe

Adherents, officially those persons who, being parishioners of, or regular worshippers in, a congregation of the CofS, have, at the time of a vacancy, successfully claimed to have their names entered as adherents on the Electoral Roll of that congregation. For them to be so accepted the kirk session* has to be satisfied that they desire to be permanently connected with the congregation and must know of no reason why, were they to apply to be received as communicant members, such application would be refused (Act V of Assembly 1984). The decision of the kirk session on an application to be entered as an adherent is final and cannot be made the subject of appeal to the superior courts. For all purposes connected with the election of a minister, including membership of the Vacancy Committee, the adherent has precisely the same rights as a full member. This, however, does not extend to any other aspect of the congregation's life, such as voting at meetings called in connection with readjustment. Adherents may sign the substantive call once a minister has been elected, the paper of concurrence generally accompanying a call being for regular worshippers or parishioners who do not qualify either as members or as adherents.

Adherents have no voice in the management of the congregation's affairs and cannot act on the Kirk Session,* Congregational Board,* Deacons' Court or Board of Management. In 1963 a proposal was brought before the General Assembly 'to grant adherents a definite status within the Church'. The matter was remitted to a Committee which recommended that the tendency in certain areas to decline the commitment involved in Church membership, however sincere its motive, was not one to be encouraged, and that to grant status and recognition to such adherents would merely establish more firmly a tradition from which the Church should be seeking to break away. The Assembly agreed and took no further action. In many parts of the Highlands and Islands there are many more adherents attached to a congregation than there are members. The situation stems from a very literal application of Paul's warning in 1 Cor. 11:27 that 'anyone who eats the bread or drinks the cup of the Lord unworthily will be guilty of desecrating the body and blood of the Lord'. To avoid this danger the tradition has grown up of delaying full communicant membership until a very advanced age, even though at the same time adherents may be very fully involved in the life of the congregation. The custom still obtains today.

Cox, 19, 246; *RGACS 1984*, pt. II, 52–3, 68.

A. Herron

Admission to the Lord's Supper. From early times in the Eastern Churches baptism with chrismation has been regarded as the complete rite of Christian initiation, and baptised infants and children have accordingly received Communion. In the West the story is more complicated. For purely pragmatic reasons chrismation and blessing by the bishop became a post-baptismal rite, often administered many years after baptism. It was sometimes regarded as a completion of baptism, or as Spirit-baptism, as the reaffirmation of baptismal vows, or as a special strengthening by the Spirit. This 'confirmation'* was frequently regarded as a separate sacrament,* and was declared to be such by the Council of Trent.

The Scottish Reformers regarded confirmation as an 'idle ceremony', not instituted by Christ or authorised in Scripture. They stressed the completeness of baptism and strongly affirmed with Calvin that sacramental confirmation is 'an overt outrage against baptism' (*Inst.* 4:19:8). Calvin wished to restore what he believed to be the custom of the early Church, that the children of Christians when they reach years of maturity should profess their faith in public and be blessed with the laying on of hands (*Inst.* 4:19:4). This, however, Calvin did not clearly link with admission to the Lord's table.

The *First Book of Discipline** indicates that communicants were expected to know the Lord's Prayer, the Creed and the summary of the Law. From an early date, prior to admission to the Lord's Supper, members of the congregation were catechised by the minister and elders, and strenuous efforts were made to resolve disputes and tensions between members of the congregation. Tokens admitting to the Lord's table were issued to all those whose lives and doctrine were acceptable (*see* Communion Tokens). Visitors from other parishes who wished to receive Communion were expected to bring 'testimonials' as to their Christian faith and life from their own church. This examination of the congregation occupied a number of weeks prior to the Communion season, and each member had to be admitted afresh to the Lord's Supper.

In the CofS admission to the Lord's Supper for the first time was not marked by any special ceremony until the nineteenth century. The Assembly of 1570 had provided for the examination of children in 'the trew religion of Jesus Christ' at the ages of nine, twelve and fourteen. But such arrangements had no status as qualifications for admission to the Lord's table. In fact the age at which children or young people first received Communion varied widely. James Melville* records doing so when he was twelve, and Robert Blair when he was eleven. Walter Steuart of Pardovan mentions a French regulation that children should not be admitted until they 'be above twelve years of age'. He then continues, 'But I am sure, if children at nine years of age can express themselves piously and knowingly, shewing that they have the grace signified and promised, the seal of the promise cannot warrantably be denied unto them' (*Collections*, E, 1709, II.iv.2). St Andrews Kirk Session decreed in 1595 that no one younger than sixteen should be admitted. But there was no general legislation or binding convention on the matter.

The Five Articles of Perth* (1618) had required confirmation by a bishop, and services of confirmation closely modelled on the Anglican *BCP* were drafted and then one was included in 'Laud's*' Liturgy' (1637). But there is no evidence that confirmation services became established in the seventeenth century.

The Church Service Society* in the various editions of its *Euchologion** introduced an 'Order for the Admission of Catechumens to the Confirmation of their Baptismal Vows and to the Participation in the Lord's Supper', in which after a number of questions the minister admits the 'catechumens' to 'the participation in the Lord's Supper, and to all the privileges of the new covenant', and blesses them. The 1928 *BCO* has an 'Order for Admission to Full Communion' in which through the introduction of the strange concept of 'full communion' it is implied that baptism admits us to some unspecified kind of partial communion. The 1940 *BCO* has a service of 'Confirmation of Baptized Persons and ... Admission to the Lord's Supper' which sees the service as a confirmation of baptism, a strengthening through the Holy Spirit and admission to 'the fellowship of the Lord's Table'. The 1979 *BCO* treats the service as confirmation by the Holy Spirit rather than confirmation of baptism or of baptismal vows.

The old discipline of 'fencing the tables' was abandoned in most places in the late nineteenth century, partly because of a recognition that it placed Communion in a forbiddingly moralistic context, very different from the table fellowship of the Lord. For many years the CofS has welcomed to the Lord's table communicant members of other Churches. And in recent years there has been much discussion of the propriety of admitting baptized children to Communion, and in some congregations this is done, at least from time to time.

Today much confusion is evident about admission to the Lord's Supper in the CofS. There are various views on the significance and theology of services of admission and confirmation. While most agree on the psychological importance of providing an opportunity for the public profession of faith by those who have been baptised in infancy, there is uncertainty about the relation of this service to baptism, and to first Communion, and the theological significance of the service requires clarification.

W. McMillan, *The Worship of the Scottish Reformed Church 1550–1638* (L, 1931), 229–232; H. J. Wotherspoon and J. M. Kirkpatrick, *A Manual of Church Doctrine According to the Church of Scotland*, rev. T. F. Torrance and R. S. Wright (L, 1960), 31–6; J. D. C. Fisher, *Christian Initiation: The Reformation Period* (L, 1970); *id., Confirmation Then and Now* (L, 1978).

D. B. Forrester

Adomnán (*c.*624–704), abbot of Iona,* and biographer of Columba.* Adomnán was a kinsman of Columba, Iona's founder-saint, and, like his famous predecessor, was also of Irish royal lineage. Much of his early career appears to have been spent in Ireland. In the year 687 the Irish annals record the first public deed of his abbacy of Iona, a mission on behalf of his Irish kin to King Aldfrith of Northumbria. Bede,* our main source for Adomnán's Northumbrian contacts, relates that the Iona abbot presented to Aldfrith a copy of *De Locis Sanctis*, an account which he had written of *The Holy Places* of Christendom. Adomnán's scholarship first reveals itself in this work. His information is based on eyewitness testimony of a returning pilgrim bishop, but it is also checked against, and supplemented by, evidence from his reference books in Iona.

According to Bede it was in Northumbria also that Adomnán adopted the ecclesiastical observances of the universal Church. As his Columban community had long maintained its own traditional observances, particularly in the matter of the date of Easter (*see* Christian Year), the abbot's decision set him at variance with his Iona monks. Yet in the aftermath of these events Adomnán was in Iona, affirming his devotion to its monastic founder by compiling a new account of his life.

In the *Vita Columbae* (*Life of Columba*), Adomnán drew on previous reminiscences of Columba compiled by Cumméne* and added the fruits of his own researches, combining vivid accounts of Iona monastic life with literary representations derived from his scriptural and hagiographical reading. By depicting the universality of Columba's sanctity as well as the particularity of his life, the *Vita* stands both as a memorable account of its subject and as a testimony to the scholarly skill of its author.

In the year 697 Adomnán was in Ireland, securing the support of its notables in both Church and state for the proclamation of the 'Law of the Innocents'. This innovatory public measure was designed to protect noncombatants in times of strife. While the Columban community would benefit from the exaction of fines under the law, Adomnán's motivation seems to reflect genuine concern for the establishment of a more humane society. Penitential writings ascribed to Adomnán are of uncertain authorship.

His career is thus marked by broad vision, literary scholarship, and diplomatic and legislative abilities. The *Vita Columbae* seems particularly to express Adomnán's conviction that, as Iona's founder merited recognition throughout Christendom, so too his community should affirm its links with the universal Church. The single unachieved task at the time of his death in 704 was that Adomnán had not

AD VITAM AUT CULPAM

brought this about. Yet even in this he must be credited with having sown the seed of change. Just over a decade later, Iona joined in observance with the rest of Christendom (*see* Celtic Church; Whitby, Synod of).

D. Meehan (ed.), *De Locis Sanctis* (Dublin, 1958); A. O. and M. O. Anderson (eds and trs), *Adomnan's Life of Columba* (²O, 1991); K. Meyer (ed.), *Cáin Adamnáin* (O, 1905); S. MacAirt and G. MacNiocaill (eds), *The Annals of Ulster* (Dublin, 1983); M. Herbert, *Iona, Kells, and Derry* (O, 1988).

M. Herbert

Ad vitam aut culpam, a Latin phrase (literally, 'for life or until fault') that has traditionally defined the minister's tenure of a charge* in Scottish Presbyterianism. Even under patronage,* although the patron presented the nominee to the parish he had no power to terminate the incumbency. Only the Presbytery could do that, and then only on proof of *culpa*, which meant either heresy or serious moral delinquency. The phrase is still used, but in the CofS tenure now terminates automatically at age seventy. It may be terminated earlier when the Presbytery deems the congregation to be 'in an unsatisfactory state' or 'in changed circumstances' (by acts of the General Assembly of 1972, 1988, 1984), as well as in cases of *culpa*.

A. Herron

Africa, *see* Missions.

Agnew, Sir Andrew (Lochnaw) (1793–1849), politician and sabbatarian.* The posthumous son of Andrew Agnew, he succeeded to a baronetcy in 1809, attended Edinburgh University and married Magdalene Carnegie in 1816. He entered parliament in 1830 as a member for Wigtownshire, which seat he successfully defended twice, in 1831 and 1832, before failing in his candidature for the Wigtown boroughs in 1837. In politics he was a moderate reformer, but his parliamentary career was dominated by an unremitting campaign for sabbath observance. As the chief parliamentary spokesman for the Lord's Day Observance Society he introduced four bills designed to prohibit all unnecessary labour on Sunday, the last of which reached the committee stage before Parliament was dissolved on the death of William IV. Although unsuccessful, all four bills occasioned considerable controversy both inside and outside the House of Commons. His opponents, including Charles Dickens, alleged that his measures were exclusively directed against 'the amusements and recreations of the poor'. In response Sir Andrew stated that he was equally opposed to the casual amusements of the rich and that the poor would be the ultimate beneficiaries of a labour-free Sunday.

Although denied a parliamentary platform after 1837, Sir Andrew continued to promote the sabbatarian cause, particularly in the Scottish railroad industry, where he used his substantial financial influence to win important concessions. Renowned for his perseverance and consistency of purpose, he did as much as anyone to lay the foundations of the so-called Victorian Sunday.

T. M'Crie, *Memoirs of Sir Andrew Agnew* (L, 1850); *Hansard's Debates* (1832–7); *DNB* I, 178; *The Gentleman's Magazine* 31 (1849), 647–8; I. Bradley, *The Call to Seriousness* (L, 1976); J. Wigley, *The Rise and Fall of the Victorian Sunday* (Manchester, 1980).

D. Hempton

Aidan, *see* Celtic Saints.

Aikenhead, Thomas (1678–97), student hanged for blasphemy.* The son of an Edinburgh apothecary (once summoned before the Privy Council for selling dangerous aphrodisiacs), he was charged in December 1696 when aged 18 with flippantly scorning the Trinity, the incarnation and other Christian verities. He had adopted a blend of pantheism and deism, about which the General Assembly had lately expressed alarm. He admitted the charges (brought under an act of Charles II), pled the susceptibility of youth, but was not saved by repentance. He was hanged at Gallowlee on 8 January 1697, and buried at the foot of the gallows. His case aroused much public sympathy. The Privy Council might have spared him had ministers of the Kirk interceded for him.

R. Chambers, *Domestic Annals of Scotland from the Reformation to the Revolution* (E, 1874), III, 160–6; H. Arnot, *Collection and Abridgement of Celebrated Criminal Trials in Scotland* (E, 1785), 322–7; Munro Craig, *A Satyr Against Atheistical Deism* (E, 1696); J. Gordon, *Thomas Aikenhead. A Historical Review* (E, 1856).

D. F. Wright

Aikman, John (1770–1834), Edinburgh Congregational minister. Having resigned business interests in Jamaica and commenced preparatory study for the ministry, he relinquished his place at Edinburgh University's Divinity Hall to take up lay preaching. From 1797 he undertook a number of preaching tours with James Haldane,* becoming in time pastor of an overspill congregation from the Edinburgh Tabernacle. Together with pastoral duties, itinerancy and preaching to French prisoners of war, he lectured to the Haldane academy students and wrote articles for the *Missionary Magazine* (*see* Periodicals, Religious). Although his friendship with the Haldanes endured, their views on baptism and mutual exhortation by church members caused him to separate from them in 1808. Aikman believed that their ideas were destructive, 'both of the pastoral office and of all order in the house of God'. Despite periodic ill health he continued to itinerate, and remained as pastor of the North College Street congregation in Edinburgh until his death in 1834.

R. Kinniburgh, *Fathers of Independency in Scotland* (E, 1851), 152–65; G. Ewing, *A Sermon ... on the ... death of Mr John Aikman* (E, 1834).

D. W. Lovegrove

Aird, Gustavus (1813–98), distinguished Highland* minister and historian. Born at Kilmuir-Easter, Easter Ross, he studied at King's College, Aberdeen (MA, 1830) and was ordained to Croick, Strathcarron, Ross-shire, in 1841. After the Disruption* in 1843 he served Creich FC nearby until his death. His conspicuous intellectual powers, unfeigned Christian piety, striking personality and gifted pulpit eloquence put him in the front rank of Highland ministers. He was involved in the Temperance movement* and active in fund-raising for FC churches, schools and manses. He provided social relief for his parishioners and spoke out against the Clearances,* preaching on the duties of both tenants and proprietors.

Aird was also an historian of repute. John Noble's *Religious Life in Ross* (Inverness, 1909) used materials he had gathered, and he provided a sketch of James Fraser of Brea* for an edition of his *Memoirs* (Inverness, 1889), and an introduction to John Kennedy's* *The Days of the Fathers in Ross-shire* (Inverness, 1897). Aberdeen made him a DD in 1885, and the FC General Assembly elected him Moderator in 1888.

FES VII, 52; *AFCS* I, 78; A. MacRae, *The Life of Gustavus Aird* (Stirling, 1908).

G. Wareing

Alesius (Alane), **Alexander** (1500–65), Reformer and theologian. Born in Edinburgh, Alesius was sent to the University of St Andrews in 1512 and inscribed in St Leonard's College. In 1515 he graduated BA and joined the Augustinian priory. Continuing his academic career, he graduated MA and subsequently transferred to the theological faculty. Alesius was trained in the late nominalist tradition of scholastic theology as represented by John Major* and his pupils at the College of Montaigu in Paris. An acute mind and able debater, Alesius was in the forefront of the university's condemnation of the 'errors' of Luther's theology as it arrived in Scotland in the early 1520s. However, the encounter with the first Scottish Reformer, Patrick Hamilton,* and in particular the witness of his martyrdom in 1528, gradually undermined his convictions and eventually led to a complete change of mind. At the provincial synod in 1529 he attacked the state and leadership of the Church, thereby incurring the wrath of the prelates. The continued, at times brutal persecution by his prior finally (1530 or 1531) forced him into exile. Via Malmö, Brussels and Cologne he made his way to Wittenberg where, in October 1532, he matriculated at the university and established close contacts with Luther and Melanchthon. He eagerly absorbed the principles and methods of their teaching and from October 1533 lectured in the faculty of arts. In an attempt to further the cause of the Reformation in his home country he composed two tracts addressed to James V, urging the king to permit the circulation of the New Testament in the vernacular (*see* Bible (Versions, English)). In the summer of 1535 the Wittenberg Reformers sent Alesius to England in order to strengthen relations between Henry VIII and the German Protestants. While in England, Alesius made contact with Archbishop Cranmer and Thomas Cromwell, who perceived the Scot as an able ally in their endeavours for the English Reformation and invited him to stay. Alesius therefore returned to England in early 1536, whereupon Cromwell provided him with a theological lectureship in the University of Cambridge. His lectures on the Psalms, however, soon met with stiff opposition, and in April 1536 he was forced to leave Cambridge. During the following three years he worked as a physician in London, but with the passing of the Act of Six Articles in June 1539 was once again compelled to flee. On his return to Germany, Melanchthon procured him a professorship, first in Frankfurt-on-Oder (1540–2), then in Leipzig, where he remained until his death. Both these universities were in the process of being reformed at the time of his appointments, and Alesius played a significant part in that development.

Alesius' contribution to the Reformation in Germany still awaits thorough investigation. He was prominent as a negotiator with Catholic theologians at the various diets and colloquies, when his theological acumen and debating skills were much admired by Melanchthon and other Reformers. He was a prolific writer, producing numerous biblical commentaries of some substance as well as writing extensively against Catholic theologians, Osiander and the Antitrinitarians of his day. Theologically, he owed much to Melanchthon, but Luther's exposition of the Psalms equally left an indelible mark on his theology. In an age of controversy and strife, he never lost the vision of the one Church and, although firmly convinced of the truth behind the Reformers' theology, he was generally conciliatory towards his opponents.

DNB I, 254–9; A. F. Mitchell, *The Scottish Reformation* (E, 1900); A. F. S. Pearson, 'Alexander Alesius and the English Reformation', *RSCHS* 10 (1949), 57–87; J. T. McNeill, 'Alexander Alesius, Scottish Lutheran (1500–1565)', *ARG* 55 (1964), 161–91; *TRE* II, 231–5; G. Wiedermann, 'Martin Luther versus John Fisher: Some Ideas Concerning the Debate on Lutheran Theology at the University of St Andrews, 1525–30', *RSCHS* 22 (1984), 13–34; *id.*, 'Alexander Alesius' Lectures on the Psalms at Cambridge, 1536', *JEH* 37 (1986), 15–41; *id.*, 'Der Reformator Alexander Alesius als Ausleger der Psalmen' (PhD thesis, Erlangen, 1988) (contains an up-to-date biography as well as a complete list of Alesius' manuscripts and printed works).

G. Wiedermann

Alexander I (*c.*1077–1124), King of Scots 1107–24. He was one of the younger sons of Malcolm II and Queen Margaret.* Like his more famous brother David,* he shared in the family's tradition of piety and generosity to religious institutions. His name probably reflects his mother's admiration for the reforming Pope Alexander II (1061–73). Sometimes called 'the Fierce' because of his merciless harrying of thieves and brigands, he was remembered as a hard-working king. His religious policy combined generosity to the Augustinian* canons, whom he brought to Scone and probably intended to bring to Inchcolm and Loch Tay, with resistance to English claims to religious superiority. He secured the election of Turgot,* prior of Durham and his mother's hagiographer, as Bishop of St Andrews; when Turgot was consecrated by the Archbishop of York in 1109, the rights of both churches were reserved, but the question was unresolved at Turgot's death in 1115. Alexander then secured the election of Eadmer, a monk of Canterbury, in 1120, but when this raised the possibility of a Cantuarian claim to supremacy, Eadmer was allowed to withdraw without consecration. Shortly before his death in 1124 Alexander finally secured the election of Robert, prior of Scone, as Bishop of St Andrews; but it was not until 1128 that Robert was consecrated at York without profession of obedience to its archbishop.

During his later years Alexander seems to have been active mainly in central and northern Scotland while David ruled a large principality in Strathclyde and Lothian. The most significant ecclesiastical development of the reign, the introduction of reformed Benedictines* of the order of Tiron* to Selkirk c.1113 (later they moved to Kelso), was carried out by David.

Surviving *Acta* in A. C. Lawrie, *Early Scottish Charters Prior to 1153* (G, 1905), with supplement in G. W. S. Barrow, *The Acts of Malcolm IV, 1153-1165* (*Regesta Regum Scottorum* I; E, 1960); R. L. G. Ritchie, *The Normans in Scotland* (E, 1954); G. W. S. Barrow, 'The Royal House and the Religious Orders', in *The Kingdom of the Scots* (L, 1973), 165-87; A. A. M. Duncan, *Scotland: the Making of the Kingdom* (E, 1975), 128-32.

A. Macquarrie

Alexander, Henry (1883-1957), missionary to Switzerland. Born and reared in Edinburgh, in early life he was influenced by Dr George Wilson, minister of St Michael's CofS, Edinburgh, who was a founder of the Keswick Convention and helped organize the campaigns of R. A. Torrey and C. Alexander in Scotland (1838-1921; *FES* I, 115). Alexander was converted in Switzerland when aged seventeen, and returned to Edinburgh where he worked as a bank clerk. He was greatly influenced by the campaigns of Torrey and Alexander, and was later to reproduce their style and emphases in his own ministry. He studied at the Bible Training Institute,* Glasgow (1904-6), during a time when it was affected by the Welsh revival under Evan Roberts and Jessie Penn-Lewis, and he imbibed much of their theology. His baptism by immersion in Glasgow resulted in his rejection for missionary service with the CofS in India, and subsequently a visit to an aunt in Geneva opened the way to ministry in French-speaking Switzerland. Invitations to speak on what he considered experiences of revival at BTI led to an itinerant ministry around Lake Léman. Much blessing attended his preaching during the period 1912-18, and many from the moribund state Church were aroused to oppose the infiltration of rationalistic and liberal theology. Huge crowds attended his evangelistic campaigns throughout western Switzerland, but soon churches withdrew their support. Reluctantly he felt obliged to work outside the established Church, and converts were channelled into local groups collectively known as l'Alliance Biblique. He founded a Bible school near Bienne, but his fearless preaching drew many enemies who attempted to discredit him publicly. Intervention was made at the highest level of government, and he was totally vindicated. Meanwhile twelve assemblies had been planted. He returned to Geneva where he founded a large Bible school in 1928. From there the work was consolidated, and a new more positive direction was reflected in the change of name to l'Action Biblique. From then until his death in 1957 the work made remarkable progress, largely through evangelistic campaigns, colportage, conferences, youth and children's camps, the establishment of Geneva Bible Society, a chain of evangelical book shops and literature work. Churches were planted in Switzerland, France, Italy, Portugal, Brazil and areas of Africa. The work is strongest in French-speaking Switzerland and France, and now comprises some seventy churches and 150 full-time workers. Since Alexander's death the work of l'Action Biblique has had to face the challenge of developing from what was largely a missionary movement into a fellowship of churches. There is now a stronger Reformed emphasis in doctrine, and a greater tolerance of non-dispensational views.

H. and J. H. Alexander, *Contre Vents et Marées* (Geneva, 1983); H. Alexander, *Le Chemin Nouveau et Vivant* (Geneva, n.d.).

A. B. R. Clark

Alexander, William Lindsay (1808-84), Congregational minister. Born at Leith and educated there and at the Universities of Edinburgh (1822-5) and St Andrews (1825-7), he had a Baptist* upbringing. At St Andrews Thomas Chalmers* influenced him, but he joined Leith Congregational Church in 1826. Medicine, law and the ministry tugged at him. A chance preachment at Newington Chapel, Liverpool, helped to clarify his vocation. Two years and some pamphlet controversy at Newington, several months at Halle and Leipzig, and good London prospects, were consummated in Edinburgh, where he was ordained at North College Street Church in 1835.

During a notable pastorate (1835-77) North Street's dour buildings were improved into Argyle Square (1840), then abandoned after a sojourn in Queen Street Hall for the stately Augustine Church, George IV Bridge (1861). Alexander's preaching appealed to Edinburgh's professional and political intellects – with his multiple membership of the city's learned societies he was manifestly one of them. In days when 'elegance of diction ... a stately presence and a highly intellectual expression' worked wonders, he became Scotland's

ALEXANDER, WILLIAM MENZIES

best known minister outside Presbyterianism, announcing 'a conservative and rather aristocratic species of Congregationalism'. This representative role, recognized in doctorates from St Andrew's (1846) and Edinburgh (1884), also encompassed invaluable denominational services. When Glasgow's Congregational Theological Hall moved to Edinburgh (latterly in Augustine's basement), Alexander taught theology (1854–77) and became its full-time Principal (1877–81). With his *Selection of Hymns* (1849; better known as *The Augustine Hymn Book*, ^{5}1872) he contributed signally to Scottish Congregational hymnody, although it was 1863 before Augustine, reputedly Edinburgh's 'best sung congregation', installed an organ. The man who translated folk songs into Latin for fun and applied unavailingly for Edinburgh's Chair of Moral Philosophy (1852) was inevitably a prolific author. His *oeuvre* of sermons, biography, church history and theology included the editing of *Kitto's Cyclopaedia* (1861), the translating of Dorner's *History of the Doctrine of the Person of Christ* (1861) and collaboration in the Revised Version of the Old Testament (1870).

A System of Biblical Theology, 2 vols (E, 1888).

DNB Suppl. I, 32–3; *Congregational Year Book*, 1886, 146–9; J. Ross, *W. Lindsay Alexander, D.D., LL.D: His Life and Work* (L, 1887); A. Peel, *The Congregational Two Hundred 1530–1948* (L, 1948), 168–9; H. Escott, *A History of Scottish Congregationalism* (G, 1960).

J. C. G. Binfield

Alexander, William Menzies (1858–1929), FC professor. Born of Covenanter* stock near Glasgow and educated at its University and FC College, he was ordained in the FC in 1889. A highly qualified scholar (MA, BSc, MB and CM, BD, MD, DSc; Hon. DD of Edinburgh, 1927), Alexander taught scientific subjects in Wilson College, Bombay, and then briefly Apologetics and New Testament (1899–1900) at the Glasgow FC College before joining the UFC in 1900. He lectured at the Aberdeen UFC College for a period before rejoining the FC in 1904, becoming Professor of Apologetics and Natural Science in the (Edinburgh) FC College in the same year, and playing a key role in the College's reconstruction.

While still connected with the UFC, Alexander published *Demonic Possession in the New Testament* (E, 1902), which attracted criticism from several reviewers. Alexander admitted that it contained 'unnecessary speculations', and at the FC Assembly in 1905 it was announced that he had withdrawn his book. The controversy surrounding it, however, was another factor which influenced the FPC against closer relations with the FC after the House of Lords decision* in 1904. Alexander's later work in many fields of study betrays no evidence of deviation from confessional orthodoxy.

AFCS I, 80; G. N. M. Collins (ed.), *Annals of the Free Church of Scotland 1900–1986* (E, 1986), 6; A. McPherson (ed.), *History of the Free Presbyterian Church of Scotland (1893–1970)* (Inverness, 1974), 110–13; *History of the Free Presbyterian Church of Scotland (1893–1933)* (G, 1933), 151–6; *Who Was Who, 1929–1940*, 16.

A. M. Harman

Alison, William Pulteney (1790–1859), Professor of Medicine. Son of the Episcopalian minister, Archibald Alison, and brother of Sir Archibald Alison, historian, he studied arts and medicine at Edinburgh University. After working as a physician in the New Town Dispensary, he held various medical chairs at Edinburgh from 1820 to 1856. Alison, who studied under and admired Dugald Stewart,* was noted for the stress he laid on the links between his medical work and wider social problems. He was one of the most influential figures in the reform of the Scottish poor law and in the improvement of public health. He wrote *Observations on the Management of the Poor in Scotland* (E, 1840), and 'Observations on the Generation of Fever' in *Reports on the Sanitary Conditions of the Labouring Population in Scotland* (E, 1842).

Alison took issue with Thomas Chalmers* in the controversy over the poor law. He held that, while voluntary means of financing poor relief might suffice in a simple rural society, where rights and duties were recognized and upheld, it was inadequate to deal with the scale and complexity of destitution in an urban and industrial society. His medical experience among the poor of Edinburgh led Alison to hold that unrelieved poverty was behind much illness and premature death. In practice he rejected the Malthusian* ideas which often precluded others from supporting the provision of adequate relief for the poor. To Alison, more generous financial provision gave hope to the destitute, encouraged prudence, and so was more likely to check than encourage excessive growth of population.

DNB I, 290–2; S. J. Brown, *Thomas Chalmers and the Godly Commonwealth in Scotland* (O, 1982), 289–96; W. T. Gairdner, *Physician and Naturalist* (G, 1889), 388–425; R. A. Cage, *The Scottish Poor Law 1745–1845* (E, 1981), 125–30.

R. H. Campbell

Allan, Tom (1916–65), CofS evangelist. Born at Newmilns, Ayrshire, he studied at Glasgow University before and after World War II (MA, 1946). He was the minister of North Kelvinside, Glasgow, 1949–53, organizer of Tell Scotland* 1953–5, and minister of St George's Tron, Glasgow, 1955–64.

Allan was arguably the most significant figure in the story of Christian outreach in Scotland during the post-War years. Already committed to training for the ministry of the CofS, a conversion experience during wartime service in the RAF gave him new direction. Concerned for the advance of the Church's mission in post-War Scotland, various movements attracted him which sought to make it relevant to a new era, but while embracing the width of their concern the call to conversion remained central. A period as assistant to D. P. Thomson* schooled him in the organization of evangelistic programmes and led to the mission in the parish of North Kelvinside documented in *The Face of My Parish* (L, 1953). The experience of outreach gained, and the revolution in a congregation's life, brought him to public note and led to his appointment as Field Secretary/Organizer for Tell Scotland.* His skilful leadership brought together varied strands of Christian witness, but became controversial when he was instrumental in the invitation to Billy Graham* to share in Tell Scotland through the All Scotland Crusade.

The vision of Tell Scotland was expressed during the last years of his life in an effective ministry in central Glasgow, where a near redundant church found new life and creative outreach to the city's business community, social outcasts, and ordinary citizens. Allan's ministry was recognized by the city in the award of the St Mungo's Prize (1965). A CofS counselling centre in Glasgow bears his name.

The One Hope of the World (L, 1953); *Letter to a Layman* (E, 1952); *The Agent of Mission* (E, 1953); *The Secret of Life* (G, 1950).

FES IX, 284, X, 175; J. Highet, *The Scottish Churches* (L, 1960); R. Falconer, *The Kilt Beneath My Cassock* (E, 1978).

P. T. Bisset

America, *see* Missions; Emigration.

Amyraldianism, *see* Cameron, John.

Anderson, Christopher (1782–1852), a pioneer of Baptist* home missionary activity. Born in Edinburgh, Anderson worked initially in a Friendly Society. He was deeply influenced by the evangelistic enterprises of the Haldanes,* but became a Baptist in 1801. Following study at Edinburgh University, Sutcliff's Academy in Olney and Bristol Baptist College, he was unable to fulfil his desire to join William Carey in India, and turned to home mission. His missionary interests were encouraged by Andrew Fuller.* In 1806 he gathered the core of a Baptist church (on the 'English' single-pastor model) at Richmond Court, Edinburgh, becoming its pastor in 1808. This church (in a new setting) became Charlotte Baptist Chapel.

Anderson's home missionary interest was apparent as early as 1805, when he attended the constitution of Bellanoch Baptist Church (now Lochgilphead Baptist Church). In 1807–8, with George Barclay,* he set up an itinerant* society (*see* Baptist Home Missionary Society for Scotland), supporting missionaries in the Highlands (*see* Sinclair, Dugald), Kirkcudbrightshire, Falkirk and Aberdeen. He travelled in the Highlands and Ireland, and advocated the teaching of literacy in Gaelic* and Irish. Anderson became a founder and secretary of the Edinburgh Society for the Support of Gaelic Schools (1810) (*see* Gaelic School Societies), gathered support for the Carey mission, helped to found the Edinburgh Bible Society (*see* Bible Societies) (1809), and wrote *The Domestic Constitution* (E, 1826), annual reports (E, 1811–24) of the Edinburgh Gaelic School Society, memorials about the Irish and their language (E, 1815, 1818, 1819, 1828, 1830) and *The Annals of the English Bible* (L, 1845).

DNB I, 373; H. Anderson, *The Life and Letters of Christopher Anderson* (E, 1854); D. W. Bebbington (ed.), *The Baptists in Scotland* (G, 1988), 34–5, 44, 96–7, 284; D. E. Meek (ed.), *A Mind for Mission: Essays in Appreciation of the Rev. Christopher Anderson* (E, 1992).

D. E. Meek

Anderson, John (*c*.1668–1721), Presbyterian controversialist. He was minister of Dumbarton (1698–1718) and of Glasgow Ramshorn Parish (1718–21). Prior to ordination he acted as a tutor in the Argyll family. His controversialist inclinations were revealed in *A Dialogue between a Curat and a Countreyman concerning the English Service* (n.p., 1710), *The Countreyman's Letter to the Curat* (G, 1711), and *The Second Dialogue* on the same subject (G, 1711). In these he attacked the introduction of the English liturgy into Episcopalian services in Scotland and the contemporary historical criticism of Scottish Presbyterianism. The reply to these by the Episcopalian Robert Calder provoked a vitriolic response from Anderson entitled *Curat Calder Whipt* (E, 1712), which was viewed by some of his sympathizers as having done his case as much harm as good. The adversarial nature of his character was further revealed in his pursuing of a heresy case in 1718.

More important was his *A Defence of the Church – Government, Faith, Worship, and Spirit of the Presbyterians* (G, 1714), regarded as one of the ablest defences of Presbyterianism, in which Anderson attempted the disproof of prelacy and the support of Presbyterians from Scripture, the early Church Fathers and church history in general.

Inducted to the Glasgow Ramshorn parish, although not without the opposition of Glasgow ministers, he was censured for preaching a consecration sermon at the opening of his church. He was succeeded by the famous John Maclaurin.*

Papers of the Rev. John Anderson . . ., transcribed by A. W. Anderson (Dumbarton, 1914); *A History of the Introducing the Usage of the 'Lord's Prayer' in Dumbarton* (1705) (A, 1905).

FES III, 342, 438–9; DNB I, 382–3; J. Macleod, *Scottish Theology* (³E, 1974).

J. R. McIntosh

Anderson, John (*c*.1748–1830), Associate Synod* missionary, pastor and professor in the USA. Born just over the border in England of Scottish parents, from 1771 he attended the General Associate (Antiburgher*) Divinity Hall, studying under William Moncrieff.* Although licensed, he did not receive a call, probably because of his extreme shyness and weak voice. In 1783 he went as a missionary to America, where, after several years in the East, he was ordained to a charge near Pittsburgh. In 1792 he was appointed Professor of Theology to the Associate Church. He held this office until 1819, using the *Medulla* and *Compendium* of Johannes Marckius as his texts. He had great influence in the Church, being particularly esteemed for his publications, in which he emphasized the distinctive positions of the Secession* churches.

Essays on Various Subjects relative to the Present State of Religion (G, 1782); *The Scripture Doctrine of the Appropriation which is in the Nature of Saving Faith stated and illustrated* (Pittsburgh, 1793; ^{5}1875); *Precious Truth; or some points in Gospel Doctrine, vindicated...* (Pittsburgh, 1806); and three shorter works urging exclusive Psalmody.

J. B. Scouller, *A Manual of the United Presbyterian Church of North America* (Pittsburgh, 1887); W. B. Sprague, *Annals of the American Associate... Pulpit* (NY, 1869).

D. C. Lachman

Anderson, John (1805–55), missionary. He was born at Kirkpatrick-Durham, near Castle Douglas, Galloway, the son of a farmer. The family means were small; he did not reach Edinburgh University until his twenty-second year. Both his arts and divinity courses were so combined with school-teaching as to bring a breakdown from overwork. He became a family tutor in Nithsdale. Influenced by the General Assembly address of Alexander Duff* on his first furlough, he offered for missionary service. After licensing by Dumfries Presbytery in 1836, and a few weeks viewing the CofS institution in Calcutta, he arrived in Madras early in 1837, shaped by physical hardship and spiritual conflict.

Two CofS East India Company chaplains had begun a school in a suburb. Anderson took it over, and moved it into the heart of the city, convinced of the necessity to establish what Duff had done in Calcutta: a first-rate educational programme attractive to caste Hindus, with a philosophic content geared to introducing new ideas ('India must be brought to think') and the Bible a substantial part of the curriculum. This would provide a climate in which thorough conversions could occur and indigenous church leaders develop who alone could evangelize India. Anderson directed his whole ministry on this principle. (The English language newspaper he began was seen as part of the school enterprise.)

There was an early crisis over his refusal to expel 'untouchable' pupils, and recurrently over conversions. Baptisms were regularly followed by an exodus of pupils and Indian teachers. Baptized students often had no recourse but to live in the missionary's house. The first three such became the first ordained Indian ministers.

In 1839 Anderson was joined by his close friend from university days, Robert Johnston;* the signal for expanding the work to Kanchipuram and other branch schools. In 1841 another friend, John Braidwood, joined them in an unusually close and productive partnership. All three unhesitatingly joined the FC at the Disruption* (with consequent financial problems) and formed a presbytery of Madras.

Anderson never lost an interest in female education, for which Mrs Braidwood's arrival opened new possibilities. In 1847 he married Margaret Locher, a Swiss teacher of the Ladies' Association of the CofS now in the FC. She remained in Madras when Anderson was sent to Scotland, broken in health, in 1850, taking with him one of the new ministers, P. Rajagopal. When Anderson returned next year, Johnston left, already terminally ill, followed in 1852 by Braidwood. Anderson's own collapse was delayed until 1855. Though he had no immediate successors of comparable calibre, the institution he founded developed under William Miller* into Madras Christian College, which a century after Anderson's arrival was witnessing such thinkers as A. G. Hogg* in fundamental engagement with Hinduism.

See also Missions: South India.

DNB I, 386–7; *FES* VII, 687; *AFCS* I, 83; J. Braidwood, *True Yoke-Fellows in the Mission Field ... the Rev. John Anderson and the Rev. Robert Johnston* (L, 1862); S. Neill, *History of Christianity in India 1707–1858* (C, 1985), 319–23.

A. F. Walls

Anderson, William (1812–95), UP* missionary to Nigeria. Supported by his indefatigable wife Louisa, he dominated Presbyterian eastern Nigeria for over forty years. Born in Galashiels, he went via Jamaica (1840) to Calabar in 1848 with the Scottish Missionary Society (*see* Missions).

Committed to the value of education, he opened many schools and encouraged girls to attend. Baptism depended on attaining a high standard of Bible knowledge. Anxious to use the Efik language in school and church, he translated John's Gospel (G, 1857) and encouraged his colleagues' translation endeavours. As a social reformer, he co-founded the Society for the Abolition of Inhuman and Superstitious Customs, abhorring sacrificial deaths in particular. Despite Edinburgh opposition, he devised a formula to reconcile Efik church-membership and slave-ownership.

In 1848 he became the first moderator of the Presbytery of Biafra. In 1872 he gave the charge to Ukpabio, the first Nigerian to become an ordained minister. He developed constructive relationships with neighbouring Protestant missions. He regularly participated in palavers, usually siding with the Efik kings. He disliked Mary Slessor's* pioneering in Ibibio country, and resisted Edinburgh pressure (from 1876) to expand. In 1885 the British established a Consulate in Calabar, reducing Anderson's honest-broker role.

Having lost his youthful imagination and diplomatic skills, his ultimate stubbornness lost him respect and he had to resign in 1891 aged 79.

See also Missions.

W. Marwick, *William and Louisa Anderson* (E, 1897).

W. H. Taylor

Andrew (*d.c.*AD 60), apostle, patron saint of Scotland. One of the twelve disciples of Christ, Andrew was the brother of Simon Peter and, like him, a fisherman in Galilee. He is reported to have been a disciple of John the Baptist and was one of the first chosen by Jesus. In the New Testament, he is generally listed among the foremost of the apostles.

Stories of Andrew's travels and martyrdom are contained in works collected in the Apocryphal New Testament. According to these and other traditions, he preached in Scythia, Epirus and Achaia, and was martyred in Patras in Achaia (Greece). He was bound, not nailed, to a cross and suspended there for two days before he died. His supposed relics were translated to the Church of the Holy Apostles at Constantinople under Constantius II in the fourth century. This may have led the Byzantine Church to promote the cult of Andrew as a means of countering the claims to primacy by the Church in Rome. In 1204, when Constantinople was taken by crusaders, the relics were stolen and given to the cathedral of Amalfi in Italy.

St Andrew enjoyed a widespread cult in both East and West during the Middle Ages. A church dedication to him in Hexham by St Wilfrid and the OE poem *Andreas*, contained in the Vercelli book, attest to his cult in Anglo-Saxon England. His association with Scotland is preserved in the legend of St Regulus or Rule (*see* Celtic Saints), which exists in several, often conflicting, versions. According to an eighth-century legend, Regulus was a native of Patras and keeper of St Andrew's relics; he was told in a dream to take some of the relics to a place which would be shown to him. Regulus journeyed to Scotland, where he met the king of the Picts,* Angus, who had been promised in a dream victory over the Saxons in the name of St Andrew. Regulus was granted land where he built the monastery of Kilrymont, the present-day St Andrews,* and became the first bishop. This legend was the basis for the primacy of St Andrews among the churches of Scotland.

The saltire cross, with which St Andrew is associated, was first depicted in art in the tenth century at Autun in France. The earliest depictions of St Andrew's crucifixion show a Latin cross, but by the fourteenth century the saltire had become his symbol. St Andrew's cross, a white saltire on a blue field, is the emblem of Scotland and represents Scotland in the flag of the United Kingdom.

P. M. Peterson, *Andrew, Brother of Simon Peter* (Leiden, 1958); F. Dvornik, *The Idea of Apostolicity in Byzantium and the Legend of the Apostle Andrew* (Cambridge, MA, 1958); M. R. James (ed.), *The Apocryphal New Testament* (O, 1924); W. F. Skene, *Celtic Scotland* (E, 1876–80), I, 269, II, 296–99; D. H. Farmer, *The Oxford Dictionary of Saints* (O, ²1987); A. Butler, *Butler's Lives of the Saints*, rev. H. Thurston and D. Attwater (NY, 1963), IV.

D. A. Bray

Anglicanism, the beliefs of the CofE and of Churches in communion with it. The definition of Anglicanism raises acute problems, and is prone to reflect subjective conviction as much as cool historical judgment. The institutional origins of Anglicanism lay in the religious settlement of the reign of Elizabeth I, the Acts of Uniformity and Supremacy of 1559, the *Book of Common Prayer** of 1552 (revised in 1662) and the Thirty-nine Articles of 1563. These measures were a compromise intended to end the religious conflict of the mid-sixteenth century and were designed to bring the entire nation within the bounds of the CofE.

Subsequent definitions of Anglicanism have therefore been attempts to give theological coherence and legitimacy to a Church whose origins were political and national. The word 'Anglican' was not used at all in the Elizabethan period and only to a limited extent in the seventeenth century. Nevertheless it was in this era, in the view of later proponents of Anglicanism, that its intellectual foundations were laid, in the work of writers such as Richard Hooker (?1554–1600), Lancelot Andrewes (1555–1626) and Henry Hammond (1605–60). The position that emerged was one of firm Protestantism in the rejection of papal supremacy and 'Romanist' sacramentalism, and the advocacy of justification by faith alone. On the other hand bishops were retained and the Calvinist position, affirmed in Article XVII, was modified in practice. The authority of reason and patristic tradition was acknowledged alongside that of Scripture.* Hence Anglicanism has sometimes been presented as a *via media* (middle way). In the sixteenth and seventeenth centuries it was conceived as a middle way between Rome and Geneva that was still emphatically Protestant, but by the nineteenth century it came to be conceived more as a *via media* between Protestantism and RCism.

The legacy of Elizabethan comprehensiveness was the retention of a wide sphere of matters indifferent in which a diversity of belief was possible. This liberty was, however, during the eighteenth and nineteenth centuries pushed successively to the three extremes of Latitudinarianism,* Evangelicalism* and Anglo-Catholicism,* and divergent understandings of Anglicanism were thus generated. The liturgy of the *Book of Common Prayer* has, until recent years, served as something of a common reference point, but even this was interpreted in a variety of different ways, particularly from the Victorian period onwards.

During the first two centuries of the existence of the Church of England, Anglicanism was largely confined to England, Wales and Ireland. In the 1780s, however, the consecration of bishops for America began the process by which Anglicanism has developed a structure covering most of the world, loosely linked in the Anglican Communion, whose most visible expression is the decennial Lambeth Conferences.

The late eighteenth century was also a watershed in the relationship of Anglicanism to the EpCS (*see* Episcopalianism), which, up to that time, was wholly distinct from it. In the eighteenth century 'qualified' chapels existed in Scotland under the authority of English bishops. In 1784 the consecration of Samuel Seabury* by Scottish bishops began a process which continued with the subscription to the Thirty-nine Articles by the Episcopalian hierarchy in 1807, the gradual absorption of the qualified chapels by the EpCS, and the acceptance of Scottish orders in England in 1864. Hence in the twentieth century the EpCS has become a full constituent member of the Anglican Communion.

See also English Episcopal Churches; Episcopacy; Tractarianism.

Y. Brilioth, *The Anglican Revival* (L, 1933); H. R. McAdoo, *The Spirit of Anglicanism* (L, 1965); P. Lake, *Anglicans and Puritans?* (L, 1968); M. Lochhead, *Episcopal Scotland in the Nineteenth Century* (L, 1966); F. C. Mather, 'Church, Parliament and Penal Laws: Some Anglo-Scottish Interactions in the Eighteenth Century', *English Historical Review* 92 (1977), 540–72; G. White, 'The Consecration of Bishop Seabury', *SHR* 63 (1984), 37–49.

J. R. *Wolffe*

Anglican–Presbyterian relations could be said to have begun shortly after the Union of the Crowns in 1603 when the Stuart kings sought to impose unity of Church government, and latterly also of worship, on an episcopal basis throughout these islands. The attempt was stoutly resisted north of the border and for close on a century Scottish history was largely the story of these 'relations'. The term, however, is generally applied to conversations carried on between the two communions in course of the last half-century.

In 1932 the General Assembly of the CofS received an invitation to engage in conversations with the Anglicans with a view to closer union. The Assembly agreed and conversations began and continued in a desultory fashion without any very definite result until the wave of ecumenical fervour of the early 1950s lent fresh impetus, with the result that there was laid before the Assembly of 1957 a document popularly known as 'The Bishops Report' (*Relations between Anglican and Presbyterian Churches*, L, 1957). This document caused a considerable stir, not only within the courts of the Kirk, but throughout the country generally, featuring prominently in the media, particularly in the press. While the Report was received with interest in Church circles south of the border its impact there was in no way comparable.

The Report had been produced by a committee representative of the CofS, CofE, EpCS and Presbyterian Church of England. Its basic proposition was that the hope for the future lay in Presbyterianism accepting a system wherein bishops would be set apart to act as permanent Presidents of presbyteries.

> Bishops, chosen by each Presbytery, from its own membership or otherwise, would initially be consecrated by prayer with the laying on of hands by Bishops from one or more of the Episcopal Churches and by the Presbytery acting through appointed representatives. Thus consecrated, each Bishop would be within the apostolic succession as acknowledged by Anglicans on the one hand and as required by Presbyterians on the other. He would be President of the Presbytery and would act as its principal minister in every ordination and in the consecration of other Bishops.

The General Assembly would continue in its position of supremacy, the bishops being members but not forming an Upper House, but the reservation was made that decisions on doctrinal and constitutional matters *might* require their consent. Anglicans undertook that at some future time they would consider the possibility that 'lay persons might be solemnly "set apart" for some measure of pastoral responsibility towards their fellow-Christians in an office akin to the Presbyterian eldership'.

The Report had a fairly hostile reception in the Assembly, but was sent down to presbyteries for consideration and comment. In the light of returns received the Assembly rejected the proposals, but they appointed a Committee of Fifty to engage in a fresh series of discussions involving the same four denominations. These were to be directed towards resolving and clarifying certain issues – (a) the meaning of 'unity' in Church order, (b) the meaning of 'validity' as applied to ministerial orders, (c) the doctrine of Holy Communion, and (d) the meaning of apostolic succession* as applied to all these matters. At the request of the Anglicans the remit was later extended to include the Church as a royal priesthood, the place of the laity, and relations between church, state, and society. It was these conversations which produced the report, *The Anglican–Presbyterian Conversations* (E, L, 1966). Before this booklet appeared, however, a conference of all concerned in the conversations (120 of them) was held at Holland House, an Edinburgh University residence, in January 1966. Matters discussed at the conference went far beyond those embraced in the remit in so far as a very full debate was engaged in on a paper called 'Covenanting for Unity', doubtless inspired by the BCC Nottingham Conference of 1964. This recommended that the two Churches in Scotland should enter immediately into a binding agreement to unite on an episcopal basis – 'all future ordinations would be episcopal–presbyteral and within the succession hitherto acknowledged by the Churches of the Anglican communion'. When this was 'leaked' there was an outcry and it was later officially denied that it had been discussed at the conference.

The document *Anglican–Presbyterian Conversations* was sent down to presbyteries for study and comment and at the Assembly of 1968 it was reported that two comments had repeatedly appeared – (a) 'So long as mutual recognition of ministries as real and spiritually effective ministries in the one holy and apostolic Church is either implicitly or explicitly withheld, there can be no fruitful conversation'; and (b) 'Mutual intercommunion is a necessary early step in any advance towards closer unity.' That same Assembly of 1968 received a report on the conversations which had been inaugurated between the two Churches in Scotland. This made reference to a proposal in regard to intercommunion, which the Episcopal panel was prepared to put before its Church, 'welcoming' to its tables all baptised communicant members of Churches with which it was officially committed to seek union, but saying nothing about its members celebrating at non-episcopal services, and it was put forward 'only on the explicit understanding that nothing in it is taken as encouraging reciprocal intercommunion'. The report went on to say that this proposal had proved a disappointment to both sides; to the Anglicans because it was felt that its reception had been less than cordial, and to the Presbyterians because the advance seemed so small and so hedged about with 'elements of non-reciprocity and conditionality'.

In 1970 a novel suggestion was advanced from the side of the CofS to the effect that the Scottish Episcopal Church might form an 'Episcopalian Synod' within a united CofS. In November of the following year this came before the Episcopalian Provincial Synod when it was resolved that 'the proposal should not be further discussed as a possible way forward'. Since then no specific steps have been taken, and apart from the fact that both Anglican and Presbyterian communions are represented on the Multilateral Conversations* (as well as on the Anglican–Reformed International Commission, set up in 1978, which produced the report *God's Reign and Our Unity*, L, E, 1984, for discussion by the churches), the 'relations' are pretty much as they have always been.

See also Ecumenical Movement.

Ian Henderson, *Power Without Glory* (L, 1967); R. S. Louden, 'Anglican–Reformed Questions', *Reformed World* 35 (1978–9), 274–86.

A. Herron

Anglo-Catholicism, an extreme form of Anglicanism.* It is possible to discern the origins of Anglo-Catholicism in the High Church movements in the CofE in the seventeenth century, particularly as associated with William Laud,* but its more immediate origin was Tractarianism* in the mid-nineteenth century. Anglo-Catholics hold that Anglicanism is a branch of the Catholic Church and in practice have come to accept most RC doctrines and devotions, with the important exception of papal supremacy, but including a strong view of the distinctiveness of the priesthood and the reality of the apostolic succession.* The Reformed tradition* is rejected as not providing the essential marks of a Church.

The EpCS (*see* Episcopalianism) provided receptive soil for Anglo-Catholicism. An early achievement was the establishment of Trinity College, Glenalmond, Perthshire, in 1845, and subsequent advances were fostered by the Hon. G. F. Boyle (1825–90), later Earl of Glasgow, and A. P. Forbes,* Bishop of Brechin.

Anglo-Catholicism found particular expression in more elaborate worship and devotion, notably the use of vestments, the reservation of the sacrament and the introduction of auricular confession. It was also reflected in Gothic-revival ecclesiastical architecture, inspiring the building of cathedrals for the Episcopal Church, notably at Perth, Inverness and Edinburgh. Another distinctive development was the foundation of the collegiate church at Cumbrae in the Firth of Clyde in 1849. Parallel developments in worship in England gave rise to considerable litigation, but in the non-established EpCS, controversy was less far-reaching. However innovations encountered strong opposition, notably from Charles Wordsworth,* Bishop of St Andrews.

In the later nineteenth and twentieth centuries the influence of Anglo-Catholicism has been apparent in encouraging in some quarters more elaborate liturgy in the CofS, developments which were resisted by the National Church Association.* Meanwhile for others, the strength of Anglo-Catholicism both in the EpCS and the CofE itself has been seen as a substantial obstacle in the path of moves towards closer links between the Churches.

See also Catholic revival in worship.

G. Rowell, *The Vision Glorious* (O, 1983); M. Lochhead, *Episcopal Scotland in the Nineteenth Century* (L, 1966); W. Perry, *The Oxford Movement in Scotland* (C, 1933); A. L. Drummond and J. Bulloch, *The Church in Victorian Scotland 1843–1874* (E, 1975).

J. R. Wolffe

Anglo-Saxon Saints. The Anglo-Saxon saints of Scotland are to be found mainly among the leaders of the principal churches of that part of the early English kingdom of Northumbria which lay within modern Scotland: basically the lands between the Forth and the Tweed and Dumfries and Galloway. The principal Anglo-Saxon saints whose names are known to us are as follows:

Aebbe (Ebba, Abb): the sister of Kings Oswald and Oswiu and aunt of King Ecgfrith, she founded, or at least ruled, the monastery of *Urbs Coludi* at or near present-day Coldingham.* Here she was visited by St Cuthbert, between 661 and 664. When Ecgfrith's Queen Aethelthryth (St Etheldreda, who afterwards founded Ely) took the veil, she spent her first year as a nun under Aebbe in Coldingham, 672–3. Aebbe obtained the release from prison in Dunbar of St Wilfrid. She is said to have died on 25th August 683. She may not have been a very good administrator: contemporary opinion, in Bede's* account, attributed the subsequent accidental burning of the monastery to divine punishment for the lax discipline of the community, while apparently not wishing to implicate Aebbe herself. Bede seems favourably disposed towards Aebbe in his (prose) *Life of St Cuthbert*: see B. Colgrave (ed.), *Two Lives of Saint Cuthbert* (C, 1940), 188–9. (A. O. Anderson (ed.), *Scottish Annals from English Chroniclers, A.D. 500 to 1286* (L, 1908), 38–42; A. P. Forbes, *Kalendars of Scottish Saints* (E, 1872), 330.)

A later tradition of self-mutilation of an abbess, also called Aebbe, and of the martyrdom and destruction of the monastery at Coldingham at the hands of the Danes, in 870, may not be reliable.

Her feast-day is 2 April. (Anderson, *Scottish Annals*, 61–2; Forbes, *Kalendars*, 330.)

Baldred of Tyninghame: an anchorite, he is said to have died on 6 March 756. Traditionally, his three churches were Tyninghame, Auldhame and Preston (East Linton), all in E. Lothian. Auldhame and Tyninghame, among other places, are claimed for Lindisfarne in a Durham source under the year 854. Similarly, the *Historia de Sancto Cuthberto* (*c*.1050) claims for Lindisfarne extensive lands north of the Tweed, including all the land belonging to the monastery of St Baldred, called Tyninghame, 'from Lammermoor even to Eskmouth'. The church of St Baldred was devastated and Tyninghame burned by Norsemen in 941, according to later sources. The account of St Baldred preserved in the Aberdeen Breviary* (1509–10) is largely fabulous: but it is worth noticing his association with a hermitage on the Bass Rock.* (Anderson, *Scottish Annals*, 56, 60–1, 73; A. O. Anderson (ed.), *Early Sources of Scottish History A.D. 500–1286*, 2 vols (E, 1922), I, 242, 444; Forbes, *Kalendars*, 273.)

Cuthbert; he is among the foremost of Northumbrian saints. From his eighth year until manhood when he entered the service of God, he was reared by a foster-mother, Kenswith, a nun and widow in the village of 'Hruringaham' (presumably somewhere in the vicinity of the Leader Water and Melrose). He subsequently maintained a close relationship with her; and she was still alive when the anonymous *Life* of St Cuthbert was written, probably between 699 and 705 (Colgrave, *Two Lives*, 13, 88–91, 200–3, 322–3). He began his life in religion in the monastery of (Old) Melrose* during the abbacy of St Eata, entering the monastery in 651 after having a vision of the soul of St Aidan* of Lindisfarne (*see* Celtic saints) being conducted to heaven while herding his master's sheep on the hills near the Leader Water. He is said to have been attracted to Melrose rather than to Lindisfarne by the renowned sanctity of the prior, St Boisil* (after whom St Boswells is named). Cuthbert became Boisil's pupil. Later, after a period as guest-master under Eata in the newly-founded monastery of Ripon (Colgrave, *Two Lives*, 6–7, 174–9, 345–6), he succeeded Boisil as prior of Melrose on the latter's death of plague in 661. As prior, inspired by Boisil's example, he undertook the pastoral care of the country people in the hills around Melrose and apparently further afield, concentrating on the poorer and less accessible settlements and sometimes remaining away from the monastery for up to a month at a time. On one such journey he came by sea to the district of Niduari in Pictish* territory (possibly in Fife), though the reason for the visit is not given (Colgrave, *Two Lives*, 82–5, 192–5, 320–1; W. J. Watson, *History of the Celtic Place-Names of Scotland* E, 1926, 175–7). It was during this period also that he visited St Aebbe* at Coldingham. In 664, after the Synod of Whitby,* Bishop Colman* of Lindisfarne, about to leave Northumbria for Iona* and then Ireland, asked King Oswiu to appoint Eata Abbot of Lindisfarne. He did so because Eata had been one of the twelve English boys given to St Aidan at the beginning of his episcopate for training in the religious life. Eata transferred Cuthbert there as prior. Cuthbert's subsequent career is closely associated with Lindisfarne, of which church latterly he was bishop. He died on 20 March 687. (Anderson, *Scottish Annals*, 22–9, 32–3; Forbes, *Kalendars*, 317, 281, 329.)

Dryhthelm: Another saint of Melrose is Dryhthelm. After a disturbing vision of the rewards and punishments of the afterlife which is described at some length by Bede, he embraced the anchoritic life at Melrose *c*.696, during the abbacy of Aethelweald, Cuthbert's former attendant. There he devoted himself until his death to an austere regime of rigorous asceticism. His feast-day is 2 September. (Anderson, *Scottish Annals*, 40; Forbes, *Kalendars*, 326.)

Pechthelm: Whithorn* had been recently erected into a Northumbrian episcopal see in 731, according to Bede, with Pechthelm, previously a monk and deacon of Bishop Aldhelm of Sherborne, as its first (English) bishop. Pechthelm died in 735. He was succeeded in turn by Frithweald, Peohtwine and Aethelbeorht. Aethelbeorht was transferred to Hexham in 789 and succeeded at Whithorn in 790 by Bealdwulf. Bealdwulf assisted at royal and episcopal consecrations in 796 and 803. Some time thereafter, the English see of Whithorn apparently failed, as it is heard of no more. Pechthelm's feast-day is 15 July. (Anderson, *Scottish Annals*, 6–8, 52–5, 58–60; *Early Sources*, I, 246, 248, 254; Forbes, *Kalendars*, 434.)

Trumwine: he was consecrated to a see in the monastery of Abercorn by Archbishop Theodore (of Canterbury) in 681, to serve a Pictish province then under Northumbrian domination. He evacuated it in 685 after the Pictish victory over the Northumbrians at *Dún Nechtain*; and retired to Whitby, where he lived a monastic life for many years and where he died. (Anderson, *Scottish Annals*, 38, 42–4.)

See also Celtic Saints; Early Ecclesiastical Sites.

D. H. Farmer, *The Oxford Dictionary of Saints* (O, ²1987).

A. D. S. MacDonald

Angus, John (*c*.1515–*c*.1597), contributor to the music of the Reformed Kirk. Little is known of his life. By 1539 he was a Benedictine monk at Dunfermline,* and probably remained there after the Reformation of 1560, being presented to the vicarage of Inverkeithing (1562) and a prebend in the Chapel Royal, Stirling (1565). He was in receipt of other benefices or pensions in his latter years. His commitment to the Reformation was probably less than whole-hearted. 'Gude and meike Johne Angus' contributed a dozen canticles to Thomas Wood's (Wode's) (manuscript) compilation of 1566 known as St Andrews Psalter (*see* Psalms, Psalter). They include the Nativity canticles, the Lord's Prayer, and the Apostles' and Athanasian Creeds.

They are set in psalm tune style, 'ranging from ... a severe chordal idiom ... to a more gently decorative style ..., animated but not fussy'. Edward Millar's great Scottish Psalter of 1635 claims to draw on some of Angus's psalm tunes proper, but none can with certainty be attributed to him, although tradition has credited him with 'Dunfermline'.

K. Elliott in S. Sadie (ed.), *The New Grove Dictionary of Music and Musicians* (L, 1980), I, 435; *id.*, 'Scottish Music of the Early Reformed Church', *Trans. of Scott. Ecclesiological Soc.*15:2 (1961), 18–32; *id.*, *Fourteen Psalm-Settings of the Early Reformed Church in Scotland* (L, 1960); D. Laing, 'An Account of the Scottish Psalter of A.D. 1566', *PSAS* 7 (1870), 445–58; H. G. Farmer, *A History of Music in Scotland* (L, 1947); *FES* V, 42, VII, 379; M. Dilworth, 'Monks and Ministers after 1560', *RSCHS* 18 (1974), 217.

D. F. Wright

Angus, Joseph (1816–1902), Baptist theological educator, missionary society secretary and bibliographer. The only son of a Northumberland farmer and leather merchant, Angus gained the gold medal in moral philosophy under Thomas Chalmers* at Edinburgh University (MA, 1837). In *The Voluntary System* (L, 1839) he produced a reply to Chalmers' lectures on church establishments. While pastor at the New Park Street Chapel, Southwark, London, he served as secretary of the Baptist Theological College at Stepney (later Regent's Park College) 1838–44. He served the Baptist Missionary Society in secretarial roles 1840–9. As Principal of the College he equipped Baptist ministers and missionaries for forty-four years (1849–93). Awarded a DD from Brown University, Rhode Island (1852), Angus served on the 1881 English Bible New Testament Revision Committee and is best known to succeeding generations for *The Bible Handbook* (L, 1853). He exemplifies the wider influence of Scottish universities in the period when nonconformists had little access to those in England.

DNB Second Suppl. I, 44–5; E. A. Payne, 'The Development of Nonconformist Theological Education in the Nineteenth Century ...', in E. A. Payne (ed.), *Studies in History and Religion: Essays Presented to H. Wheeler Robinson* (L, 1942), 240–2; *id.*, *The Great Succession: the Leaders of the Baptist Missionary Society during the Nineteenth Century* (L, 1938), 11–25.

J. M. Hitchen

Ann (Annat), the half-year's stipend* vesting first after the death of a CofS minister who died in office. It fell to be divided equally between his widow and his next-of-kin, all going to the latter in the event of there not being a widow. The Law of Ann dates from an Act of the Scottish Parliament of 1547. Ann never formed part of a minister's estate but vested in the beneficiaries without the need for confirmation, and there was nothing the minister could do to alter its destination. Because of the dependence of stipend on the price of grain its payment was always back-dated, so that in effect Ann provided at the end of a minister's incumbency what he himself had not received at its outset. The CofS Property and Endowments Act (1925), while preserving existing rights, brought these payments to an end.

Cox 292, 294, 483–7.

A. Herron

Annuity Tax, a Church tax on the citizens of Edinburgh. The Burgh of Edinburgh, from the Reformation onwards, paid the stipends* of ministers, but by 1633 the ministers of the eight Burgh churches* were very poorly paid and Parliament provided for a 5 per cent rate (6 per cent from 1661) to be levied on the citizens (except members of the Court of Session). It was unpopular, and became more so when in 1767 the Burgh parish was extended to include the new town area. There, teinds* were due to St Cuthbert's as well, and in addition, after the Disruption,* FC members as well as others outside the Est.C were also supporting their own churches. From the early nineteenth century there were disputes and later angry criticism of the hated tax. When payment was refused, unseemly roups (sales of goods) followed. Acts of Parliament in 1860 and 1870 arranged for peace. The city paid over a sum of money, now administered by the General Trustees of the CofS, in lieu of the tax. The capital now provides an endowment, equally divided among the Burgh ministers.

J. Colston, *Trinity College and Trinity Hospital*, 2 vols (E, 1896); D. McLaren, *History of the Resistance to the Annuity Tax* ... (E, 1836).

A. I. Dunlop

Antiburghers, *see* General Associate Synod.

Anti-Catholic Societies, formed primarily in the mid-nineteenth century in order to resist legislative concessions to Roman Catholics, foster loyalty to Protestantism, and, in some cases, to engage in missions to Catholics. The earliest organization of this kind was the Protestant Association (1780) established in response to the Relief Act of 1778 in England. It was an important influence giving rise to the Gordon Riots in London in 1780. The Orange Order* originated in Ireland in 1795 and in 1813 the Protestant Union was formed in London to resist Catholic Emancipation,* but only survived for a short period.

A new phase began in 1827 with the formation of the British Society for Promoting the Religious Principles of the Reformation (later the Protestant Reformation Society), which initially sought to proselytise Roman Catholics in Ireland, but shortly came to confine its activities largely to the British mainland. This was followed by the Protestant Association in 1835, which had no continuity with the organisation of 1780. It had political objectives, contrasting with the religious purposes of the Reformation Society. Both organisations were based in London, but were active in Scotland. In 1835 and 1836 the Protestant Association held large meetings in Edinburgh, Glasgow, Perth, Aberdeen and other Scottish towns. The Glasgow branch was particularly active for a short period in the mid-1830s.

In general, however, Scottish Protestants were distracted from active anti-Catholicism by Non-Intrusionism* and Voluntaryism* and it was not until 1850 that the first specifically Scottish anti-Catholic society, the Scottish Reformation Society,* was formed. This was followed in 1854 by the Scottish Protestant Alliance and John Hope's* Scottish Protestant Association. Meanwhile a localized Glasgow Protestant Laymen's Society had been formed. (On James E. Gordon (?1788–1864) see *DNB Miss. Pers.* 261–2.)

Anti-Catholic societies remained small organizations in terms of their committed membership, which in no case was more than a few thousands, but they did draw substantial numbers to their meetings and their publications were widely circulated. From the mid-nineteenth century efforts were made to unite them in a single larger organization, notably by the Protestant Alliance of 1851. However its interdenominational constitution did not command universal support, so other organizations continued. They did however confer together from the 1850s onwards and, in 1897, a federal organization which became the United Protestant Council was formed.

In the twentieth century there have been a number of amalgamations of organizations, but several, notably the Scottish Reformation Society, the Protestant Reformation Society and the Protestant Alliance, continued in existence in the 1990s. Anti-Catholic movements have shown considerable continuing strength in Scotland, particularly in the inter-War period, when Alexander Ratcliffe's Scottish Protestant League and John Cormack's* Protestant Action had a significant impact on local politics in Glasgow and Edinburgh respectively. These Protestant parties were, however, viewed with considerable caution by many in the Churches.

See also Knox Club.

J. R. Wolffe, *The Protestant Crusade in Great Britain, 1829–1860* (O, 1991); S. Bruce, *No Pope of Rome* (E, 1985); T. Gallagher, *Edinburgh Divided* (E, 1987); *id.*, *Glasgow: the Uneasy Peace* (Manchester, 1987); J. E. Handley, *The Irish in Modern Scotland* (Cork, 1947); C. S. Carter and G. E. Alison Weeks (eds.), *The Protestant Dictionary*, new edn. (L, 1933).

J. R. Wolffe

Anti-slavery. Condemnation of slavery was one of the commonplace ideas of the Scottish Enlightenment,* though certain remarks in David Hume's* writings appear to affirm the racial inferiority of Africans and so support one of the stock arguments of the defenders of slavery. However, as in England and the United States, it was the Evangelical Revival that changed anti-slavery into a popular cause. In the subsequent campaigns in Britain that led first in 1807 to the abolition of the slave trade and then, in 1834, the abolition of slavery itself within the Empire, all the techniques of popular politics used later by the Anti-Corn Law League, by the Chartists* and many others were invented and perfected by this overwhelmingly evangelical movement. Among its leaders were three outstanding Scots, Zachary Macaulay,* James Stephen (*DNB* LIV, 161–3) and James Ramsay (*DNB* XLVII, 246–7). They, like many young Scots graduates of the eighteenth century, had sought fame and fortune in the West Indies. Unlike the majority of the others, this experience drove them into life-long opposition to slavery. Their later careers were in London where they became major figures in the British movement.

In Scotland itself the cause of anti-slavery had barely got off the ground when the savage government suppression of Scottish radicalism in 1793 brought it to a halt. It was not until 1814 that a meeting was held in Edinburgh which initiated the development of anti-slavery as a popular and evangelical movement in Scotland. This was a period when the Evangelical or 'Popular' Party* was gaining ground within the CofS, and Andrew Thomson* of St George's Edinburgh played a key role in making abolition a test of evangelical commitment. However the role of Kirk Evangelicals must not be overstated, because it is clear from the records of the various societies that it was dissenting* Presbyterianism and the Congregational* and Baptist* Churches of the Haldane* revival which produced most of the leaders. The Edinburgh Abolition Society was formed in 1823 and similar societies founded in Glasgow and Aberdeen. It is remarkable that Glasgow, whose initial wealth had been built on the West Indian and Virginian trade and where the West Indies 'lobby' was one of the strongest in Britain, could produce 38,000 signatures on a petition for abolition, compared with 17,000 from Edinburgh, with a much higher proportion of educated citizens, and 41,000 from Manchester, a comparably sized industrial city but with a much longer history of well-organized anti-slavery groups. This is explained, in part, because from around 1780 onwards Scottish Evangelicalism grew in strength of numbers and also in its influence on educated Scots. By the early years of the nineteenth century the educated leadership of Scotland had passed from the deists* and Moderates* to the Evangelicals. This movement, particularly among those influenced by the Haldanes, shared some important characteristics with the Second Awakening in the United States. One was the perception of slavery as a matter of national sin which, in consequence, meant that all needed liberation from it, both the slaves and the society which tolerated slavery. Another factor was explicitly pointed out by such diverse figures as William Innes,* the Baptist leader, and Thomas Chalmers.* Essential to the growth in holiness of a converted person was moral autonomy, something of which a slave was deprived. Thus slavery literally bound people in sin and was also the supreme symbol of the bondage of humanity in the power of sin.

APOCRYPHA CONTROVERSY

From 1833 the Scottish movement became very important to abolitionism in the United States. Scotland played a direct role in American affairs, and was not a satellite of London-based activity as it had been in the British campaign. In October 1833 the Edinburgh Emancipation Society was formed to support the American cause and before the year was out similar societies had been formed in Glasgow and elsewhere. How close Scotland and the USA were became clear in 1841, when the split between the Garrisonians and the rest of the abolitionist movement in the United States was paralleled in Scotland.

The central importance of the issue in Scottish Christian life is most clearly seen in the bitter 'send the money back' controversy. This was over the acceptance by the newly formed FC of money raised from Southern, and therefore slaveholding, Presbyterians. The subsequent conflict racked Scotland for years. The leading American abolitionists saw acceptance of the money as a terrible blow to their cause, apparently endorsing slavery as compatible with evangelical religion. Many Scots saw it in the same light and were enraged. However, enemies of the FC, who had little concern for slaves or slavery, leapt at the opportunity to attack this blatant 'hypocrisy'. As a result the controversy gradually shifted to become a purely Scottish conflict about Scottish issues. However, Scottish commitment to the abolitionist cause continued, and during the Civil War and the subsequent Reconstruction significant Scottish funds went to help the education and pastoral care of the freed slaves.

C. Duncan Rice, *The Scots Abolitionists* (Baton Rouge, 1981); G. A. Shepperson, 'The Free Church of Scotland and American Slavery', *SHR* 30 (1951), 126–43.

A. C. Ross

Apocrypha Controversy, a dispute in the 1820s as to whether the British and Foreign Bible Society should be involved with the circulation of Bibles containing the Old Testament Apocrypha.

When the British and Foreign Bible Society was founded in 1804 with the object of encouraging 'a wider circulation of the Holy Scriptures without note or comment', it was not anticipated that there might be argument about what constituted 'Holy Scripture'. Anglicans were used to readings from the Apocrypha, but the Thirty-Nine Articles made clear that they were not to be used 'to establish any doctrine', and the earlier practice of including the Apocrypha in English Bibles was already less common. The Westminster Confession* was more definite than the Articles in its rejection of the Apocrypha and this was reflected in Scottish attitudes. In Europe, Roman Catholics and Orthodox believers were frequently keen to obtain Bibles and insisted that the Apocrypha be included. More surprising to the British was an equally strong insistence from Lutheran and Reformed Protestants that a Bible without the Apocrypha was incomplete, even mutilated.

APOLOGETICS

Faced with a conflict between the concerns of supporters in Britain and the demands of societies in Europe, in 1813 the Society decided to allow European societies to make their own decisions. At the same time the Society's secretaries considered it prudent not to draw attention to the implications. It was only a matter of time before the situation became known and when it did in 1821, there was a range of reactions. Some were quite happy that Bibles should include the Apocrypha. 'Clapham' Evangelicals such as Charles Simeon* believed it was better to circulate the Bible with the Apocrypha than not circulate it at all. Others such as Andrew Thomson* and Robert and James Haldane* saw it as tampering with the canon of inspired Scripture. Europeans regarded British moves to withdraw support from the Apocrypha as unwarranted interference.

However by 1825 even supporters of the Apocrypha in Britain realized that the principle of 'without note or comment' must exclude the Apocrypha if for no other reason than that it could not be included without some explanation. The Society's annual meetings in 1826 and 1827 passed comprehensive resolutions to prevent any support for Bibles containing the Apocrypha, but it was soon apparent they satisfied the Scots no more than the Europeans. The Edinburgh Bible Society and the Glasgow Auxiliary Bible Society had already suspended donations and now demanded admission of wrongdoing, disciplinary action against those concerned and an absolute break with societies who circulated the Apocrypha, even at their own expense. In fact Scottish supporters were bitterly divided and many did not share the sense of indignation which Thomson and the Haldanes in particular brought to the affair. Nevertheless there were reasons enough for developing their own independent work, and the controversy thus became a distant though not insignificant factor in the formation of the National Bible Society for Scotland in 1861. Continental societies also developed a further measure of independence as they were forced to raise their funds for Bibles in the form their people still demanded.

See also Bible Societies.

R. B. Cox, 'The Nineteenth Century British Apocrypha Controversy' (PhD, Baylor University, Waco, TX, 1981); R. H. Martin, *Evangelicals United: Ecumenical Stirrings in Pre-Victorian Britain, 1795–1830* (Metuchen, NJ, 1983); G. Browne, *The History of the British and Foreign Bible Society*, 2 vols (L, 1859); W. Canton, *A History of the British and Foreign Bible Society*, 5 vols (L, 1904–10); A. Haldane, *The Lives of Robert Haldane of Airthrey and of His Brother, James Alexander Haldane* (L, ²1852); Lord Teignmouth (Charles John Shore), *Memoir of the Life and Correspondence of John Lord Teignmouth*, 2 vols (L, 1843).

W. J. Roxborogh

Apologetics, the defence of the faith by rational means. Since the Reformation period there has always been a strong polemical strain in Scottish theology; rival theologians have been keen to defend their respective positions both against the teachings of the Church of Rome and the various kinds of infidelity. Such exchanges have extended to controversies between the various Reformed Churches which have separated from the CofS, and between those Churches and their mother Church. But the tradition of apologetics, understood as the defence of the Christian religion by reason alone, or, more widely, by the removal of objections to the faith from whatever quarter, has not had a similar prominence. Among the likely reasons for this are the general Christian culture of Scotland, which made such apologetics unnecessary, and also an Augustinian distrust of the unaided human reason in matters of religion.

For these reasons, perhaps, it is difficult to find a systematic presentation of a Christian apologetic much before the rise of deism at the beginning of the eighteenth century, and in any case deism was not the potent religious force in Scotland that it became in England. This is not to say that before this time there were not theological developments which could – and later did – provide material for Christian apologetics. It is simply to emphasize the fact that since apologetics is essentially a practical activity, it is called forth not primarily in the classroom but by certain identifiable cultural and social conditions.

HISTORICAL DEVELOPMENT. During the eighteenth century apologetics almost exclusively took the form of presentations of various versions of the argument from design. The sources of this lay in the new science, the cosmological argument, and the general belief that in an age which prized reasonableness, the reasonableness of Christianity must be displayed. And so appeals were made to the orderliness and coherence of nature as providing evidence for a Creator-designer, and to the occurrence of miracles as validating the divine revelation in Scripture. This was the heyday of Moderatism* in the CofS, and of the Scottish Common-sense Philosophy.*

In the nineteenth century the picture becomes more variegated as the attacks upon the intellectual integrity of the Christian faith became more diverse. Besides almost traditional apologetic appeals of the sort already discussed, separate attempts were made to argue for the inspiration and authority of Scripture; to defend a theistic view of creation by an outright resistance to the naturalism of Charles Darwin; to use the findings of geology to corroborate what was taken to be the biblical view of the age of the universe, and the Flood. In this latter connection the writings of Hugh Miller,* for example *The Old Red Sandstone* (E, 1841) and *Footprints of the Creator* (L, E, 1849), were enormously popular, and Miller became for a time a national cult figure. At a rather different level the series of books known as *The Bridgewater Treatises*, published from 1833 to 1840 and written by authors such as Thomas Chalmers* and William Whewell, covered a variety of subjects from an apologetic standpoint. In a similar way the Gifford Lectures,* though devoted to natural theology, in practice provided a growing fund of matter for the apologete to present to the educated public.

While the main philosophical thrust of such apologetics, at whatever intellectual level, was *a posteriori* and inductive in character, there have been occasional attempts to present a case for God's existence on *a priori* grounds, for example that of W. H. Gillespie.*

While throughout the nineteenth century popular Christian apologetics centred around the argument for design and the increasingly sharp conflict between science and Christianity, the increasing influence of continental idealist thought from the mid-century onwards gave an impetus to an attempt to transcend these polarities. It was claimed that the sort of conflict that the more traditional apologetics addressed arose because of failure to appreciate the broader unity of all human thought. Instead of being understood in terms of sets of 'static' propositions in opposition to each other, the whole of human thought, including religious thought, ought to be seen in dynamic, dialectical fashion. And so the philosophy of religion aimed to provide an all-embracing, interpretative schema. The need for apologetics in the traditional sense was argued away. But except insofar as it discouraged the evangelical religion of the mass of the people, such an approach had relatively little popular impact.

THE THEOLOGY OF CRISIS. Such a confident, optimistic outlook, in which the distinctives of the Christian faith were submerged under a tide of idealist philosophy, was rudely awakened by the devastating experience of the First World War.* Through the influence of the theology of crisis, the thought that the Christian revelation can seek for any secular ally in an effort to commend itself to men and women became anathema. The stance of the word of God was *against* the prevailing culture, to sift and to judge. Grace needed no assistance from nature. The word of God had to be preached, not discussed and debated. Even the modest attempt made by Emil Brunner (1889–1966) to defend natural theology called forth a sharp rebuke from Karl Barth (1886–1968) (*see* Neo-Orthodoxy).

The influence of the theology of crisis, which was felt widely in Protestant Europe, was greater in Scotland than in the rest of the British Isles. This was due to the stronger cultural links with the continent, the greater emphasis upon theological thinking in Scotland than elsewhere and the personal influence of the crisis theologians, particularly Barth, both through visits to Scotland and through the influence of his students. This marked change in theological temper, which has had a profound effect upon apologetics, accorded to some extent with the more fideistic elements in traditional Scottish evangelicalism.

See also Natural Theology; Philosophy of Religion.

J. Baillie, *Our Knowledge of God* (L, 1939); A. B. Bruce, *Apologetics* (E, 1892); K. Barth and

APOSTOLIC CHURCH

E. Brunner, *Natural Theology* (1934; ET L, 1946); J. Buchanan, *Faith in God and Modern Atheism Compared*, 2 vols (E, 1855); A. P. F. Sell, *Defending and Declaring the Faith. Some Scottish Examples 1860–1920* (Exeter, 1987).

P. Helm

Apostolic Church, *see* Pentecostalism.

Apostolic Succession. The Scots Confession* of 1560 rejected as 'notes, signs and assured tokens' of the true Kirk 'antiquity, usurped title, lineal succession' (18). The Reformers saw no need for an episcopal system or for claims of unbroken continuity of ministerial orders deriving from the apostles themselves. Indeed, the *First Book of Discipline** dispensed even with the laying on of hands in ordination.* The discreditable lives of bishops in the old Church demonstrated that any true succession from the apostles had already broken down, and in that sense did not require to be breached (Knox, *History* II, 266, 286).

In his response to the Jesuit, James Tyrie,* Knox* shows the succession of the Kirk to have flowed directly and lawfully from the apostles in that it admits neither doctrine, rite nor ceremony not authorized in the apostles' writings (VI, 797–8). This remains the authentic note of the Reformed Church in Scotland, sounded by figures as diverse as Samuel Rutherford* ('we maintain only a succession to the true and apostolic doctrine') and Bishop Patrick Forbes* ('The succession of piety is properly to be holden succession, for who professes the same doctrine of faith he is partaker of the same chair'). 'Fidelity' rather than 'succession' more helpfully describes the Reformed teaching.

This insistence on adherence to apostolic doctrine as the true touchstone of apostolicity has been accompanied for most of the history of the Reformed Church by a concern for due order in the transmission of ministerial authority. The Scoto-Catholic* movement in the Kirk was inclined to inflate this into a Presbyterian apostolic succession (e.g. H. J. Wotherspoon* and J. M. Kirkpatrick,* *A Manual of Church Doctrine According to the Church of Scotland* (^{2}L, 1960), 94–8, 124–5; Wotherspoon and J. F. Leishman in *Reunion: The Necessary Requirements of the Church of Scotland* (Scott. Church. Soc. Confs., 4th ser., E, 1909), 17–57), but this remains a marginal position. The *Anglican–Presbyterian Conversations*, reporting on years of discussion between representatives of Presbyterians and Episcopalians in Scotland and England, failed to persuade the CofS to accept the Anglican insistence on episcopal succession (E, L, 1966, 30–6).

J. L. Ainslie, *The Doctrine of Ministerial Order in the Reformed Churches of the 16th and 17th Centuries* (E, 1940), 199–228; G. Donaldson, *The Scottish Reformation* (C, 1960), 104–18; Anon. ('John Knox'), 'Apostolical Succession', *Edinburgh Christian Instructor* n.s. 2 (1839), 135–52, 209–25, 379–97 (against the exclusive claims of Tractarians); J. Walker, *The Theology and Theologians of Scotland 1560–1750* (^{2}E, 1888), 188–200.

D. F. Wright

Appeals to Rome, *see* Papacy.

Arbroath, Tironensian abbey. Founded by King William* in 1177 with Tironensian* monks from Kelso,* it was dedicated to the recently martyred St Thomas Becket of Canterbury, whom William had known. William was buried there in 1214 and the church was consecrated in 1233. A dependent priory was founded at Fyvie, Aberdeenshire, in 1285. Four abbots became bishops: Ralph de Lamley (Aberdeen, 1239), William (Dunblane, 1284), Nicholas (Dunblane, 1301), Bernard de Linton* (Isles, 1328). The last-named, chancellor of Scotland 1308–28, is considered to have composed the Declaration of Arbroath* in 1320. Arbroath outstripped Kelso in importance; its revenues were the largest enjoyed by any religious house except St Andrews* and included forty appropriated parish churches.

Lying on the east coast, Arbroath was vulnerable to attack and suffered damage from English depredations in the fourteenth century; the church was also damaged by lightning in 1380. The impressive buildings were nevertheless rebuilt and extended. The abbot was granted *pontificalia* (i.e. episcopal insignia) by the Avignon pope in 1396.

In the fifteenth century, Arbroath's importance led to secular clerics rather than monks becoming abbot, and to the appointment of bishop-commendators. The Crown used Arbroath as a sustenance for important public figures. James Beaton I,* David Beaton* and James Beaton II* in turn were abbot or commendator.* A son of Châtelherault,* John Hamilton, was appointed commendator in 1551, aged twelve. Fyvie ceased to have a community in the fifteenth century. At Arbroath there were about twenty-seven monks until the 1540s and at least twenty-two in 1560. Four monks became ministers in the Reformed Church. The ruined church today is still imposing.

Liber S. Thome de Aberbrothoc (2 vols, Bannatyne Club, E, 1848–56); R. L. Mackie and S. Cruden, *Arbroath Abbey* (E, 1954); Easson-Cowan, 66–8; S. Cruden, *Scottish Medieval Churches* (E, 1986), 54–61; M. Dilworth, 'Monks and Ministers after 1560', *RSCHS* 18 (1974), 209–11.

M. Dilworth

Arbroath, Declaration of (1320), a letter subscribed by a large number of Scottish nobles and barons and 'the whole community of the realm', and sent to Pope John XXII who had declared against Robert Bruce.* It pointed out that Scotland, an ancient kingdom and among the first to embrace Christianity, had always been free of foreign interference until the reign of the English King Edward I. At that time churches had been spoiled, monasteries burnt, and their people oppressed until redeemed through the valour of Robert Bruce, whom the Declaration likened to Joshua or Judas Maccabeus. Bruce had been made their king by providence, the laws, the customs of the country, and the choice of the people. If he betrayed them they would elect another. They cared not 'for glory, or riches or honours, but only for liberty which no true man would yield save with his life'. The Pope accepted the letter favourably, and when the English did not answer a papal summons to defend their position, the Pope declared the Scots reconciled to the Church.

The document was quoted by Walter Bower* in *Scotichronicon*, a work compiled originally near the end of the fourteenth century by John of Fordun, and revised in the fifteenth century by Bower, Abbot of Inchholm. A good modern translation of the Declaration was given by Lord Cooper of Culross in *The Declaration of Arbroath Revisited* (E, 1950).

J. A. Duke, *The Church of Scotland to the Reformation* (E, 1937), 92–102; W. Nicholson, *Scotland: the Later Middle Ages* (E, 1974), 100–2.

J. D. Douglas

Arbuthnot, Alexander (1538–83), Aberdeenshire minister and Principal of King's College, Aberdeen. Born in Pitcarles, Angus, and educated at St Mary's College, St Andrews, he served after graduating as a regent in St Mary's, conformed to Protestantism at the Reformation,* and, with twenty others from St Andrews, was considered to be well-qualified for 'ministreing and teaching' by the General Assembly in December 1560. Among the College's students on the eve of the Reformation, when Arbuthnot was teaching, were Andrew Melville,* later his close friend, and James Lawson,* whom Arbuthnot accompanied to France in the early 1560s. Like Patrick Adamson,* Arbuthnot studied at Bourges, a famous legal school. Returning home in 1566, he served in the ministry at Logie-Buchan, whose benefice he obtained in 1568, and became Principal of King's College in 1569. A frequent member of the General Assembly and contributor to the *Second Book of Discipline*,* he was Moderator in 1573 and 1577. He conferred with Melville on reforming the structure and content of teaching at Aberdeen, but died before the projected re-foundation could take effect. He wrote a Latin work, *Orations on the Origin and Dignity of the Law* (E, 1572), of which no copy survives.

BUK; Calderwood; J. Melville, *Diary* (E, 1842); T. M'Crie, *Life of Andrew Melville*, 2 vols (E, ²1824); *SBD*; *FES* VI, 18, VII, 364, VIII, 516; J. Durkan and J. Kirk, *The University of Glasgow, 1451–1577* (G, 1977); Chambers–Thomson I, 44; *DNB* II, 660–1; *Selections from [Robert] Wodrow's Biographical Collections: Divines of the North-East of Scotland* (A, 1890), 179–92.

J. Kirk

Arbuthnott, Missal of, manuscript missal written for Arbuthnott Church, Kincardineshire, by James Sibbald, the parish priest. It is important as showing how the Sarum rite was adapted for Scottish use, by the commemoration of Scottish saints.

The Missal was commissioned by Sir Robert Arbuthnott in 1491 and it includes an obituary of the Arbuthnott family from 1314 to 1551. It is ornamented with flowers, leaves, scrolls and fruit and shows the beginnings of a Renaissance style. It includes masses for St Columba,* St Ternan (patron of Arbuthnott; *see* Celtic saints) and St Ninian.*

Sibbald had earlier written the Arbuthnott Book of Hours and the Arbuthnott Psalter. The Book of Hours is a manuscript of eighty pages containing the Office of Our Lady and is notable for its fine illuminations. One of these is especially interesting as it is the only extant painting of a Scottish medieval altar. According to the colophon the Psalter was completed in 1482 while the Book of Hours probably dates from between 1471 and 1484.

The service books were for long in the possession of the Arbuthnott family but were sold in 1897 to Archibald Coats (of the Paisley thread firm), who in turn presented them to the Paisley Art Galleries and Museum where they remain.

See also Liturgical books (pre-Reformation).

A. P. Forbes (ed.), *Liber Ecclesiae Beati Terrenani de Arbuthnott* (Burntisland, 1864); G. A. Henderson, *The Kirk of St Ternan, Arbuthnott* (E, 1962).

H. R. Sefton

Archaeology, Christian. Archaeology has not as yet made the contribution to Scottish Church history that it might and many opportunities have been missed. It is only since the Second World War that there has been any number of properly conducted excavations on ecclesiastical sites, the full published reports of which are still awaited. Many of the greater monuments, however, have been ruthlessly cleared in tidying up operations. The study of church furnishings has been severely hampered by the lack of surviving pieces from before the Reformation and serious interest in the more recent pieces has been slow in developing.

THE EARLY CHRISTIAN PERIOD. Two of the major homes of early Scottish Christianity, Iona* and Whithorn,* have been the focus of recent archaeological attention. At the former, fieldwork and excavation have led to the identification of much of the line of the enclosing vallum or rampart, a typical feature of early monastic sites, erected more to define the extent of the settlement than to be a serious defence. An area of as much as 8 ha (20 acres) may have been contained inside it. The earliest buildings may all have been of wood and more or less randomly arranged. Wooden buildings with wattle construction are implied from Adomnán's* *Life of Columba** and several post-holes for timber structures have also been recovered – also part of a building which may have had plank walls. Further light on life in early Christian communities has been shed by the recovery of debris from Iona workshops involved in wood-turning, leather-working, glass-making and metal-working, including broken wooden bowls and worn out shoes. There was evidence that cattle were raised but wild animals, fish and seashells formed a significant part of the diet. The earliest stone building surviving, the so-called St Columba's Shrine, is probably a small church of ninth- or tenth-century date.

Excavations at Whithorn have shown its continuing importance as a religious centre. The remains of a small stone building with plastered walls was uncovered to the east of the medieval church in 1949. While it is probably a chapel, initial identification of it with the *Candida Casa* of St Ninian* now appears to be unrealistic. It is probably no earlier in date than the seventh century. Nevertheless, more recent excavations have uncovered remains of the early Christian period (c.400–700), the Northumbrian Bishopric (c.700–900) and a Viking-type house and workshops of the eleventh century.

Archaeology may never shed any direct light on individuals like St Columba and St Ninian, but it can contribute to a more general picture of the spread and nature of early Christianity. Whithorn was an early diocesan centre, while Iona was a monastic settlement from its foundation. This latter, Irish, monastic tradition was dominant in the spread and development of the early Church of Scotland, and the sites of other early monasteries have been identified at, amongst other places, Applecross in Wester Ross, Old Melrose, Kingarth in Bute and Annait in Skye. Recent excavations at St Abb's Head, Berwickshire, suggest that the enclosure at Kirk Hill may be the vallum of the double monastery (Colodaesburg) founded by St Aebbe (Ebbe, *see* Anglo-Saxon Saints; Coldingham) in the seventh century (*see* Early Ecclesiastical Sites).

Some of the earliest Christian remains in Scotland are cemeteries, the bodies laid out in stone-lined graves – long cists – orientated east-west. Many of these have been thought to date as early as the sixth century but application of the radiocarbon technique of dating suggests that some around the 'Cat Stone' at Kirkliston in Midlothian belong to the previous century. In some cases there is evidence of non- or pre-Christian burials as well, and sometimes the cemeteries are enclosed by an earthen bank.

Also often associated with early cemeteries are sculptured stones and crosses, occasionally with inscriptions like the fifth-century ones from Kirkmadrine, one commemorating two *sacerdotes* (bishops), Viventius and Mavorius. The best sculpture dates from the eighth century onwards and includes such triumphs as the Northumbrian cross at Ruthwell* and several cross slabs in the lands of the Picts.* In the seventh and eighth centuries composite stone shrines for storing and displaying the bones of saints were erected at some churches, including Iona, St Andrews and St Ninian's and Papil in Shetland.*

The earliest chapels or oratories were of wooden construction and many probably sprang up at cemeteries throughout Scotland from the late sixth century onwards. The tenuous traces of such a structure have been uncovered on Ardwall Island off the coast of Kirkcudbright. The archaeological sequence demonstrated at Ardwall is of some interest as it is thought this might be typical of many other sites. First, there was a rural lay cemetery, possibly at first unenclosed, dating from the sixth or possibly the fifth century. Secondly, perhaps in the seventh century, the wooden chapel or oratory was erected. Thirdly, perhaps in the eighth century, this wooden building was replaced by a stone chapel of larger size. All this time the cemetery remained in use.

In the case of Ardwall the stone chapel fell out of use before 1000 and its ruined walls were later incorporated into the foundations of a medieval hall-house. In many other cases such cemeteries and chapels must have developed into parish churches.

There are few substantial remains of pre-twelfth-century stone churches anywhere in Scotland, but the plans of small unicameral (single-chamber) churches of tenth- or eleventh-century date have been recovered, for example at Chapel Finnian and Barhobble, both in Galloway. At the Hirsel in Berwickshire an apse and nave were added to such a small rectangular church, probably by the early twelfth century at latest. Excavation has also revealed the outlines of the church extended for St Margaret,* now covered by the nave of Dunfermline Abbey, and the eleventh-century cathedral and bishop's palace at Birsay in Orkney.*

THE MIDDLE AGES. The study of churches and other religious foundations from the twelfth century onwards has largely been a matter for architectural historians, though in recent years archaeologists have made important contributions. St John's in Ayr has been shown to have had an aisle nave in the twelfth or early thirteenth century, while a twelfth-century date has been confirmed for a fully developed cruciform plan at St Nicholas' in Aberdeen. A twelfth-century infirmary hall has been excavated at Kelso Abbey.* Part of the cloisters, including the refectory, of the Tironensian* Priory at Lesmahagow near Lanark have been dug and consolidated, and there have been excavations at the sites of several friaries in Aberdeen, Perth, Dunbar, Ayr, Jedburgh* and Linlithgow. At Linlithgow it has been shown how a thirteenth-century chapel was enlarged in the fifteenth century for use by White Friars (Carmelites*). Two ranges of claustral buildings were uncovered, including a sacristy, chapter-house, refectory and kitchen. The church of a small nunnery has been partially excavated at Elcho near Perth and part of the leper house of St Nicholas at St Andrews. Work in progress at the hospital at Soutra suggests that it was a substantial establishment before it was annexed to the college and hospital of the Holy Trinity in Edinburgh in 1460.

Archaeology has the potential to provide much more information on the fittings and furnishing of religious buildings and the lives of their users and occupants. This is important owing to the paucity of documentary sources and the almost complete destruction of fittings and equipment in the sixteenth century. Even altars, the most basic and fundamental part of pre-Reformation worship, scarcely survive. The *mensae*, or altar tops, however, might be re-used as grave-slabs, as at King's College in Aberdeen, where one was appropriated to commemorate Master Peter Udney. Sometimes altar tops were of wood with a recess for a small stone with the characteristic five consecration crosses, like a thirteenth-century one from Coldingham Priory.

Fragments of stone altar retables of late medieval date have survived at Paisley* Abbey, St Salvator's College in St Andrews and St Michael's Kirk in Linlithgow, amongst other places, and there are pieces of sculptured woodwork in the collections of the Royal Museum of Scotland which may have come from Scottish retables. The four painted panels by Hugo Van Der Goes in the National Gallery of Scotland are from an altar piece painted in the 1460s for Trinity College in Edinburgh. Represented on them are Edward Boncle, the provost of the church, the patrons of the college, James III and Queen Margaret,* and their two children. Only one altar frontal has survived. It is made from two fifteenth-century copes and was long preserved by the Hepburns of Smeaton as a relic of Mary Queen of Scots.* With the spectacular Fetternear Banner of *c*.1520, possibly a curtain from the Altar of the Holy Blood in St Giles,* Edinburgh, it is preserved in the Royal Museum.

Practically no pre-Reformation utensils have remained in use, though an important group of relics of early saints – the Breccbenach of St Columba, the crosier of St Moluag and a bell and crosier shrine associated with St Fillan (*see* Celtic Saints) – were preserved for many centuries in the care of families of hereditary keepers. Excavations at Whithorn Priory have uncovered the graves of fourteenth-century clerics (bishops?) buried with chalices and pattens of silver in two cases, and one with an exceptionally fine twelfth-century English crosier with an enamelled and gilt copper head. At Kirkwall and Rosemarkie other bishops' graves containing funerary copies of crosiers, chalices and pattens have been opened. Other pieces of equipment have turned up as casual finds at other churches, like an altar candlestick at Kinnoull by Perth and a Christ from a crucifix at Ceres in Fife. Both are thirteenth-century enamelled pieces from Limoges in France and it is evident from other surviving pieces that such work was not uncommon in Scotland. A fine fifteenth-century Flemish candelabra still hangs in St John's Kirk, Perth. An early sixteenth-century eagle lectern from Holyrood Abbey was in St Stephens Church in St Albans until a few years ago. A complete set of early sixteenth-century choir stalls survive *in situ* in King's College, Aberdeen, and other stalls or fragments come from St Nicholas in Aberdeen, Dunblane Cathedral, and the parish church of St Andrews. There is a fifteenth-century wooden screen at the small church of Foulis Easter in Perthshire and an ornate stone pulpitum or screen of *c*.1420 in Glasgow Cathedral.*

Some medieval fonts have been preserved, including a finely carved fifteenth-century one still in use in Inverkeithing Church, and also several medieval bells, some of foreign, others of Scottish manufacture. There is a fine twelfth-century holy water stoop from Herdmanston, now in the Royal Museum. Several medieval grave slabs and other funerary monuments, including effigies, have also survived, in particular a rich series in the West Highlands.

Archaeology has as yet contributed little to our knowledge of the internal decoration of churches. Window glass, however, has turned up at several sites in recent excavations, including friaries in Aberdeen and Linlithgow, Elgin Cathedral, St Giles Church in Edinburgh and Lesmahagow Priory, and although the pieces are mostly small, fragmentary and in poor condition, they nevertheless allow some idea of the schemes of decoration favoured. Most common is *grisaille* (clear glass with enamel paintwork) of the thirteenth and fourteenth centuries with foliage patterns. There is little evidence for figural representation except for fragments from Coldingham Priory and Holyrood Abbey. The only pre-Reformation decorated glass still *in situ* is four sixteenth-century heraldic roundels at the Magdalen Chapel* in Edinburgh.

In some churches there were colourful ceramic tile floors. Significant remains of thirteenth-century ones have been found at Newbattle and Melrose Abbeys and fifteenth-century ones at Glenluce Abbey near Stranraer and the Trinitarian Friary Church in Dunbar. The kiln for making the tiles for the adjacent nunnery in the thirteenth century has been excavated at North Berwick. They were glazed, green and brown, and embossed with animal and foliage patterns. Only fragments of the schemes of painting that must commonly have covered walls and ceilings have survived. Most important of these are the fifteenth-century Crucifixion at Foulis Easter Church and the Last Judgement from the Guthrie Burial Aisle in Angus. A twelfth-century voussoir (arch stone) was found incorporated in later work at Glasgow Cathedral, still covered with plaster painted with foliage patterns.

Excavations at religious establishments have produced quantities of bits and pieces illustrative of the daily life of the occupants. From Kelso Abbey there is an important group of twelfth-century pottery made from local clays. The introduction of good quality wares, and the professional potters to make them, may well be one of the many benefits Scotland reaped from the establishment of religious houses from the twelfth century onwards. The importance of learning has been hinted at by the discovery, at Elcho Nunnery, Crossraguel Abbey and the Carmelite Friary at Linlithgow, of book clasps, and from recent excavations at Jedburgh Abbey have come a bone parchment pricker and a twelfth-century gilt and gem set decoration from a book cover. It is also to be noted that many ecclesiastical seals survive, of individuals and institutions, in some cases the matrices themselves. They have yet to be adequately studied. Pieces of military equipment from Coldingham Priory, a dagger and fragments of armour, probably reflect the use of the building as a fort in the sixteenth century.

In recent excavations much material has been collected which should shed light on diet and health and the medieval environment in general. An assessment of the animal bones recovered from Elcho Nunnery led the bone specialist to suggest that the occupants of the house ate only the poorer offcuts of meat. It remains to be seen if the same can be said for the friaries and other houses from which substantial quantities of bone have been recovered, but the evidence from Lesmahagow Priory for the fourteenth/fifteenth century would suggest that the monks ate well from the better joints of meat, both mutton and beef. Preliminary reports on the excavations at Jedburgh Abbey suggest, on the one hand, that our ancestors were badly affected by whipworm, and that, on the other, the monastic community cultivated tormentil as an astringent. At Soutra Hospital 'infirmary waste' has been identified, containing traces of blood, presumably from the frequent medieval practice of blood letting, and pollen thought to be from cloves.

THE POST-REFORMATION PERIOD. There has been practically no archaeological investigation of any sort of the Church in Scotland after the Reformation. Much information on basic furnishings and pieces of equipment has still to be rescued and assessed, though some work has been done on grave monuments, Communion plate and tokens. An awakening interest in nineteenth- and twentieth-century window glass, especially produced in Glasgow, has come too late to prevent the loss or destruction of much work of the finest quality. A brief study has been made of the burials of a noble family, the Earls of Lauderdale, at St Mary's Church, Haddington, from the seventeenth to the nineteenth century, and the grave of an early eighteenth-century missionary priest, with chalice and crucifix, has been discovered at Dumbarton. Fieldwork could no doubt throw more light on the Covenanting* movement in the late seventeenth century. In Lochaber two 'mass stones' (out-door altars) used by priests in the seventeenth and eighteenth century have been identified.

See also Early Ecclesiastical Sites.

Much of the information on excavations is derived from more or less ephemeral interim reports or word-of-mouth information from the excavators. See also: C. Thomas, *The Early Christian Archaeology of North Britain* (G, 1971); *Argyll*, vol. 4: *Iona* (Royal Commission on Ancient and Historical Monuments of Scotland, E, 1982); D. H. Caldwell (ed.), *Angels, Nobles and Unicorns* (E, 1982); K. A. Steer and J. W. M. Bannerman, *Late Medieval Monumental Sculpture in the West Highlands* (E, 1977); J. S. Richardson, 'A Thirteenth-Century Tile Kiln At North Berwick', *PSAS* 63 (1928–9), 281–310; M. R. Apted and W. N. Robertson, 'Late Fifteenth Century Church Paintings from Guthrie and Foulis Easter', *PSAS* 95 (1961–2), 262–79; C. J. Tabraham, 'Excavations at Kelso Abbey', *PSAS* 114 (1984), 365–404.

D. H. Caldwell

Architecture, Scottish Church.

ORIGINS. As an outlying region partly occupied by frontier defences Scotland may have known those little gatherings of Roman Christians in adapted houses of which we have evidence in other frontier areas, pre-dating the building of churches. As early as the third century gravestones carrying within incised circles the *Chi Rho*, XP, sign for Χριστός, are evidence of a Christian presence, as at Kirkmadrine in Galloway. At nearby Whithorn* a church was built by St Ninian* probably towards the end of the fourth century, dedicated to St Martin of Tours. From later description it seems to have been of dressed stone, a tiny basilica carrying the name *Candida Casa* – white house. At the eastern end of remains of a later Romanesque cathedral replacing it, lower portions of rubble walls of a small rectangular building coated outside with light-coloured mortar have been uncovered. This could be St Ninian's building. Enclosure walls of Celtic monasteries (*see* Celtic Church) on other sites hint at architectural forms and ground arrangements, but little evidence of shapes of churches from that time has been found.

Meanwhile to the north the Picts were producing from the riches of Celtic art the occasional Christian symbol stone of which two cross-slabs found at Raasay, Skye, and now in the National Museum of Antiquities date from the sixth century. The cross is Greek, foliated, and by its geometrical skill in delineation must indicate a local capability to design churches. A contemporary granite slab at Elgin Cathedral of Irish pattern carries a glorified Latin cross accompanied by Celtic forms. This seems to say that Greek and Roman, Celtic and Irish, were competing architectural styles.

Two early medieval churches in the Isles display the same diversity with Scandinavian influence too. The ruin of a Norse cathedral at Birsay, Orkney* (1050?), with western tower, aisleless nave, apses for nave altars and an apsidal chancel reached through a narrow arch, is on the Roman model; while St Moluag's, Eorrapaidh, Lewis, recently restored, has a single-cell Byzantine plan with a triple eastern arrangement of prothesis, sanctuary and diakonikon. The free-standing Irish round tower appears earlier at Brechin (*c*.850) with an ornamental arch cut segmentally in a Celtic manner. A carved segmental arch found at Forteviot was presumably part of some ninth-century church. Taken together these could indicate the existence of a Celtic-Byzantine architecture, for a ninth-century sarcophagus of the same century at St Andrews and a cushion capital at St Bride's, Douglas, Lanarkshire, with another at Tyningham, East Lothian, have Byzantine origins, all within the Celtic cultural ambience. The well-known free-standing crosses, as in the island cathedral precinct on Iona* (*c*.1000), are a culmination of sculptural skills developed over some centuries in the English kingdoms and in Ireland. The cross at Ruthwell,* Dumfriesshire (*c*.700), is an early example in a pre-Romanesque style.

The kirks at Dalmeny, near Edinburgh, and Leuchars, Fife (*c*.1150), with the towered erstwhile Cathedral of St Rule at St Andrews, are near-complete Romanesque churches of the standardized western shape of nave, chancel and apse with arched side-entrances for men and women segregrated, north and south. At Dalmeny the south doorway has interlaced arches of three rings with grotesque masks, animals and interlacing serpents, the masks continued (as at Leuchars) on corbels round the apse, which has zig-zag-ornamented windows and is vaulted inside in rubble and plaster. St Magnus Cathedral, Kirkwall (1137), introduces via Scandinavia the tall European interior, completed later with pointed quadripartite vaulting over Romanesque walls, all on a cruciform plan with a Gothic central tower. Dunfermline* Abbey (1142), vaulted over the aisles, has drum columns reminiscent of Durham. English Norman appears at the ruined Tironensian* abbey church at Kelso* (1128) clothing a tall Burgundian interior, and at the Augustinian* abbey church at Jedburgh* (1138), where a notable triple-storey arcading is ready for a timber main roof with vaulted aisles.

GOTHIC ERA. The Gothic pointed arch appears about 1170 at Jedburgh, then by degrees at the other great Augustinian abbey at Holyrood,* where wall-ribs in the roofless ruin indicate that the whole was eventually vaulted; and full Gothic is magnificently displayed at the cathedrals of St Andrews, Dunblane, Dunkeld, Glasgow, Elgin, and Brechin. Of these St Andrews was the grandest, but in post-Reformation neglect became, with Elgin, a ruin. The others have been variously repaired, rebuilt and refurnished as parish churches. Glasgow (1233–1508), now the grandest, has a rectangular plan with central tower, spire, and short transepts, vaulted aisles and under the choir a large eastern lower church with chapter-house above and notable High-Gothic detailing of bases, capitals and ribs. Like these others, it was designed for a timber roof over nave, choir and transepts. Only St Machar's Cathedral, Aberdeen, curiously unstyled, retains its medieval timber ceiling, in panels with carved bosses (1520). At Holy Rude, Stirling, a collegiate* church, the open roof of adzed timbers remains. Elgin, roofless after a deliberate fire and later neglect, retains its octagonal vaulted chapter-house and, like St Machar's, its twin western towers. The Cluniac* abbey church at Paisley,* on a cathedral-like scale, also restored as a parish church, displays a versatile Gothic with Scottish and English features.

Cathedral rituals demanded a screened choir, and Glasgow retains at the crossing a fine stone screen with central door, loft, and to the left and right twin stone altars (or they may be platforms for altars now vanished). Inside the screen were choir stalls. The same requirements extended to collegiate churches intended, during the later Middle Ages, to bring the daily choral worship of the few cathedrals and abbeys to the many burghs. St Mary's, Haddington, a cruciform church, recently vaulted throughout in good imitation, with central tower, traceried windows and an elegant west door, is the largest and perhaps the best example. The rood screen and choir stallwork can be traced by damage caused when in the English raids and the Reformation it was destroyed. A complete set of choir stalls, with canopies, misericords, and a screen with return-stalls, central choir entrance and the base of a rood loft, remains at King's College Chapel, Aberdeen (1490). Recent research shows that *mutatis mutandis* this woodwork design fits into the Haddington church. Together, these two collegiate churches, with Glasgow Cathedral, Dunblane Cathedral and Paisley Abbey, illustrate what a Scottish interior looked like: a sumptuous display of Gothic art within a well-proportioned arcaded structure, vaulted overall where resources allowed; and outside a tower with a good stone spire. St Machar's towers have stone spires, Brechin an off-centre western spire, as also at St Salvator's College Chapel at St Andrews, and in parish churches such as St Monance and Inverkeithing (both Fife), which reflected all these characteristics where means afforded. Most parish churches were of modest size and low profile, as at Old Corstorphine, Edinburgh, collegiate in status but parochial in character, which is barrel-vaulted with solid stone-slabbed roof, and may be typical of many vanished or in ruins.

A specially northern alternative to a spire is the stonework crown at King's College Chapel, Aberdeen, repeated at St Giles',* Edinburgh, a collegiate church; and similar crowns built but later destroyed at Haddington and St Michael's, Linlithgow. This feature is a skeleton of arches, like diagonal vaulting ribs without infill, crowned with finial, the ribs thickened outwards at their base, like flying buttresses. The result is a beautiful pattern of open stonework against the sky.

Because Scottish Gothic churches are less than half the height of the great buttressed churches of France, the flying buttress is seldom seen. A French architect, Jean Moreau, constructed a set at Melrose,* spanning as in France a nave-aisle and transept aisles and a range of chapels. It afforded an opportunity for gargoyles and other embellishments not much seen elsewhere in Scotland. One flying buttress remains at Haddington, survivor of a set supporting the stone choir vault. Recent restoration of that vault in fibreglass did not need such support.

GREAT ABBEYS. The ruined border abbeys are a distinct group. International influence is present within the Roman obedience. Celtic influences are vestigial, though a continuing theme is structural rubble, deriving from ancient stonework skills, and a freedom to integrate it with the imported styles of dressed stonework. In all this Melrose is outstanding. Window tracery is first-class, especially the five-light south transept window with curvilinear work in which the main dividing members stand proud of the lesser, within an ordered system of mouldings. The vanished oak stallwork, ordered in 1441 from Bruges, completed this splendid church.

In plan these abbeys and others in Scotland follow the western tradition of conventual buildings grouped round a cloister, with water supply and drainage, nestling against an abbey church. The best remaining buildings are at the modest but beautiful Augustinian abbey on Inchcolm* in the Firth of Forth (c.1250), with cloister and vaulted octagonal chapter-house, closely rivalled by the more pretentious Premonstratensian* abbey at Dryburgh* where the buildings descend by steps towards the Tweed, indicating a strong sense of landscape. Sweetheart Abbey near Dumfries (1273; see Cistercians) combines Gothic elegance with a gabled central tower like a border stronghold. Nearby Dundrennan (c.1250; see Cistercians) has beautifully sophisticated Gothic features. Pluscarden, a Valliscaulian* priory in the north, recently roofed and taken into use by Benedictines* from Prinknash, exhibits a simple early Gothic character.

Dating Scottish Gothic involves overlaps of style. The Romanesque semi-circular arch survives into Gothic times, as at the triple-ringed arch at Dryburgh between nave and cloister, where the detail, including detached shafts – of red sandstone instead of dark marble – belongs to the pointed Early English style.

Similarly, the remarkable seven-light west window at St Machar's, Aberdeen, has rounded heads with Gothic 'cusping', as have the triple windows of the central tower at Haddington and at St Giles', Edinburgh. Another survival is the barrel-vault, which makes a late appearance at the sumptuous collegiate Church of St Matthew, Roslin* (1450), exuberant with carved work combining Scottish masonry styles with Hispanic and presaging the Renaissance.

Nearly all Scottish Gothic masonry is solid, little under-cut, and sensitive to the idea that stone surfaces should flow into one another. The English styles scarcely apply: the different window traceries appear fortuitously. The apse, French rather than English, is a deliberate choice at Holy Rude, Stirling, St Michael's, Linlithgow, the demolished Trinity College Church Edinburgh (1480s, re-erected in the nineteenth century and still the best example) and in one of the last Gothic parish churches at Ladykirk, Berwickshire (1520). The Border abbeys all have gabled east ends; combined at Melrose with an ingenious stellar vault with picturesquely carved bosses, piled with rubble to reach a low-pitched stone-slabbed roof over free interpretations of Perpendicular tracery and panelling. Loss through violence of whatever coloured glass filled these and other traceried windows in medieval Scotland leaves only fragmentary examples in private collections and a modest heraldic display in the Magdalen Chapel* in Edinburgh, a building which ushers in the Renaissance.

RENAISSANCE AND REFORMATION. That movement, coinciding with the Scottish Reformation, produced at Burntisland in Fife a new parish church (1592) using Italian ideas for a centralized church in contrast to the axially planned churches of the past. Exemplified by Bramante's St Peter's, Rome, with a central altar under a dome within a widening floor space, this type was discouraged by loyalist RC churchmen supporting the Counter-Reformation* but welcomed by the Protestants despite its papist taint. Burntisland Kirk is planned on two squares, an inner rising to a low tower over the area where Holy Communion and the ministry of the word took place, and a wider square under lean-to roofs for the congregation, standing on an earthen floor or seated on stools. Instead of an altar, one or more Communion tables were placed within a fenced enclosure into which communicants were admitted under elders' control. On Sundays when no Communion service was held, people were allowed into that area to 'sit under' a pulpit built on a pedestal as a permanent feature. The Burntisland architecture is modest: plain square columns support the tower at corners on unadorned semi-circular arches. Windows are those of the ordinary late-medieval house. The ceilings overhead were of uncarved timber, the pulpit a plain wooden construction. Later a carved and canopied pew for the lordly was inserted: it is still extant.

This potentially important prototype for a kirk of the Reformed religion was never directly copied or developed but its liturgical arrangements were much studied. Ignored or considered irrelevant was Scotland's miniature twenty-foot-diameter replica of the rotunda of the Church of the Holy Sepulchre, Jerusalem, erected at Orphir, Orkney, in Crusader times, when early centralized churches were briefly revived; today yet another ruin.

Haddington is again before us as the example of how an existing church, built for RC worship, was adapted to the new centralized form on Burntisland's principles. The choir, much damaged, was abandoned and a new church made of the nave. A pulpit, accepting now a trend for Renaissance ornament on Dutch and Scandinavian lines, was set up on two levels under an arch of the nave arcade halfway between west front and crossing. A Communion enclosure running east and west in front of it evolved from temporary joinery at Communion seasons* to a series of rectangular box-pews, each containing a table. The space where the first Reformed congregation stood, or sat on stools round about, became a circular series of pews, ignoring the old nave columns to create in effect a centralized auditorium church, as in contemporary theatre design.

This plan was shared with numerous new churches built to Reformed requirements in the next two centuries, by which time the semi-medieval architecture of Burntisland had evolved into a reflection of English Renaissance: fenestrated walls with classical details at windows and doors, and steeples (as towers with stone spires were being called). Two such, on a circular plan of walls and seating with theatre-like galleries above, are the church at Bowmore (1769), a new town designed to revive life on Islay, and St Andrew's, Edinburgh (1785). Logical developments of Burntisland, these follow St Andrew's-by-the-Green, Glasgow (1751), a 'qualified chapel' for Episcopalian use which, although also galleried, had rejected the centralized shape but vehemently introduced the

English-Baroque style. This style had been developed by Wren and others including James Gibbs (1682–1754), an expatriate Scot, whose St Martin's-in-the-Fields, London (1722) is in that context Scottish architecture. (Born in Aberdeen, he also designed part of King's College, Cambridge, and rebuilt the nave of St Nicholas', Aberdeen.) Numerous examples of this hybrid church all over Scotland with variations in furniture give us no complete specimen of a fully furnished, custom-built kirk of major size satisfying all the strivings of the Scottish Reformation. The best were earlier: the Scots Kirk* in Rotterdam (1697 – destroyed 1940), on a Greek cross plan like other churches in the Netherlands sharing the Reformed ideas. The best Scottish pulpit is in Stavanger Cathedral, Norway, gloriously carved and coloured for Lutheran clients by an expatriate Scot, Andreas Smith. The most satisfying interior at home may well be the Canongate Kirk, Edinburgh (1690), a simple basilica of early Christian form by James Smith (no relative; d.1731; he served James VII*). Intended perhaps for RC use, it has served the continuing cause of the Reformation with much acceptance, behind its Dutch-looking gabled façade.

REFORMED KIRKS. Meanwhile the village kirk had evolved from the nave-and-chancel arrangement of Gothic times. To this was added a transept, making a 'T' with pulpit and Communion table at the top of the T visible from each seat, as in the kirk at Lauder, built (under episcopacy but accepted by Presbyterians) by the royal Master of Works, Sir William Bruce of Kinross (1630–1710 – involved also in Holyrood Palace and Hopetoun House), in a vernacular style uniting Renaissance and Gothic elements (1673). Now there was serious doubt which arrangement to use: a small table from which Holy Communion was served, or long tables at which people helped to serve themselves. In large churches in towns pews convertible into Communion enclosures with hinged seats and table-tops sought to make arrangements flexible, but there was an inherent lack of dignity. The problem was unsolved. In the country the most significant development was the series of thirty-two Parliamentary churches* (1830), each with its manse, for general use in Highland* development. A single cell under a sloping slated and gabled roof which carries a sculpturesque bell-turret, contained a simple auditorium lit by tall arched windows with elementary medieval-vernacular tracery, as at Iona by the famous Scottish engineer, Thomas Telford (1757–1834). Between two windows rose the pulpit, with precentor's desk, flanked by the elders' pew, and down the centre ran one long Communion table. It was a simple, satisfactory arrangement. The heritors* provided many a kirk of similar simplicity, attracted by its low cost, and there are examples everywhere.

These and most other churches, classical or vernacular, urban or rural, were now finished inside with plaster, including ceilings, and timber wainscoting rising to pew-height. Heating by stoves was common; earthen floors gave place to stone slabs. Good oil lamps made reading easier. A somewhat pressurised display of feudal epitaphs and imagery adorned many a wall – the outward sign of the laird's patronage,* also expressed in a laird's gallery, usually facing the pulpit, with heraldry in gold-leaf, silver and bright colour. The Scandinavian custom of painting pews in bright colours may have been quite widespread, but the Enlightenment* and its accompaniment of pietism reduced such self-expression to impersonal colour 'schemes' in which strong bright colour gave way to controlled areas of muted colour degenerating into mere grey-brown monotone, or else just whitewash.

CLASSICAL REVIVAL. The Classical Revival accepted such disciplines and codified an architecture of its own. From the mild Baroque of James Gibbs we move to the severity of W. H. Playfair (1789–1857, architect of several major Edinburgh buildings) in the Edinburgh New Town, where St Stephen's Church (1828) has a diamond-shaped auditorium with pulpit-enclosure in one of the angles, six long Communion tables in the midst, an elders' pew, manse pew, separate entrances and staircases to galleries, a massive tower, and a monumental entrance stair. All of it expresses Edinburgh's neo-classical culture but also a secure national Church, based on Scripture, reason and enlightenment, and a loyal membership. With its confident but freely interpreted classicism, this is the model church of the later Scottish Reformation.

More beautiful, if more ordinary in liturgical arrangement, were the 1850s–1860s churches, many of them UPC, in Glasgow of Alexander 'Greek' Thomson (1817–75), with their romantic interpretation of classical and pre-classical forms, much asymmetry and many elements of surprise more akin to the Gothic Revival now under way in both cities.

GOTHIC REVIVAL. Gothic in Scotland had survived the invasion of Renaissance architecture, as in the Chapel Royal, Stirling (1594), which is in essence medieval, and in the hands of the lairds many a Gothic aisle was added to a Reformed kirk. At Kinfauns, Perthshire, the Gray aisle (1598) has a completely Gothic quadripartite vault. A tenacious Episcopalianism continued this attitude into the next century. Archbishop John Spottiswoode's* church at Dairsie, Fife (1621), reverted to the orientated medieval plan with traceried windows between buttresses, as did its contemporary, Greyfriars, Edinburgh (1620), both with strong vernacular characteristics. Even where churches vernacular in design and construction contained conscious elements of the Renaissance, Gothic was not left behind, still less eliminated, and somewhere a pointed window, with simple lancet tracery, would appear.

St George's Episcopal Chapel, Edinburgh (1794), by John Adam (1721–82, brother and associate of Robert and James), marks a serious return to Gothic, though built on an octagonal auditorium plan. A plaster Gothic vault appeared at Craig, Angus (1799), and complete English Gothic, including plaster fan-vaulting, at St John's, Edinburgh (1816), by William Burn (1789–1870, architect of other eminent Edinburgh buildings). His restoration of Dunfermline Abbey (1821) with a plaster stellar vault over the crossing, clustered piers and traceried windows, tower with corner turrets and a somewhat grotesque parapet, has some Scottish feeling, but Georgian liking for ashlar masonry marked these buildings and in restoring St Giles', Edinburgh (1820's), Burn refaced the original rubble exterior with smooth ashlar, leaving only the tower intact. The Tolbooth Church nearby (1844) by James Gillespie Graham (1776-1855; see J. Macaulay, *The Gothic Revival 1745-1845*, G, 1975) with an input by A. W. N. Pugin (1812-52, major inspirer of the Gothic Revival) and the adjacent complex of New College* by W. H. Playfair, continue this style, distancing the new Gothic from its medieval originals. So did two Catholic Apostolic* churches, at Glasgow and Dundee, under Pugin's aegis. William Butterfield (1814-1900), prolific and dedicated Gothic Revivalist working from London, did better. His Episcopal cathedral at Perth (1850) senses the older Scottish character, and his miniature cathedral and college at Millport, Bute, of great excellence, shows his interest in rough stonework and strong native detail.

The short-lived Catholic Apostolic churches, each with cathedral status, had an influence apart from architectural style. They were functionally planned round an up-to-date liturgy with active participation by a carefully structured team-ministry, and there were sets of rooms and a church hall for social work by deacons and deaconesses, to minister to the 'gathered' congregation but also beyond it. Here was material useful for the next century.

Parish boundaries were now of reduced importance as the several non-established Churches developed their own memberships, self-supporting and eager to express their faith in fine prestigious buildings. Glasgow in particular saw a new range of big Gothic churches raise their spires to punctuate the industrial skyline. Queen's Park Church (1883) by William Leiper (1839-1916; *Who Was Who, 1916-1928*, 620) in Normandy Gothic owes something to J. L. Pearson's (1817-97; *DNB Suppl.* III, 255-8) work in England, as does Barony Church by J. J. Burnet (1886), tall even without a spire (on Burnet, 1857-1938, see *Who Was Who, 1929-1940*, 193).

'CATHOLIC' REVIVAL. There was now a trend away from Reformed severity and from the Reformation rituals. Liturgies were written and older ceremonial revived. The altar re-appeared as a climax feature at the east end of the church, retaining in Presbyterian use the non-sacrificial name of Communion table. Tables set out lengthwise in the midst vanished and the new habit of facing east in rows of parallel pews towards a pulpit, with table close by, emptied the galleries. Reduction of membership in the Disruption* of 1843 had its effect and galleries began to be removed or not built. Choir stalls and organs arrived by English and Continental influence and added to the festive if crowded appearance of orientated chancels fitted to older churches and considered the norm in new designs.

Butterfield was followed by Sir Gilbert Scott (1811-78), whose heavy-handed Episcopal cathedrals in Edinburgh and Glasgow (1870s) retreated from Scottish tradition, and even at Dundee, with the redoubtable Bishop A. P. Forbes* as client, did not return to it, while the less famous John Henderson (1804-62; *DNB* XXV, 402-3) and others had produced for the emancipated Episcopalian congregations many fine neo-medieval churches of well-interpreted native Gothic, such as St Mary's, Dunblane (1845). Something is owed to J. T. Rochead (1814-78, designer of many Free Churches), whose Wallace Monument on the Abbey Craig at Stirling (1869) used with success a neo-medieval style, rugged and full of informality, which he had employed in a more restrained way at the Park Church, Glasgow (1858).

By that time architects venturing into Gothic had first to do sketching and measuring tours of England and France and thus learn the main source material. This produced a new generation of home-trained but accomplished and scholarly men, such as Peter MacGregor Chalmers (1859-1922, noted for his churches and author of *A Scots Medieval Architect*, G, 1895; *Who Was Who, 1916-1928*, 186), J. J. Burnet, Sir Robert Rowand Anderson (1835-1920, architect of leading Edinburgh buildings, including the MacEwan Hall) and Robert Lorimer (1864-1929; *DNB 1922-1930*, 520-2). Anderson's Catholic Apostolic Church in Edinburgh (1873), a grand essay in Transitional Romanesque, challenged the Gilbert Scott ascendancy by its simple form, freedom of expression and native spirit despite its plan borrowed from Gerona Cathedral, Spain, and its use of Burgundian detail. His simply-formed churches, using Gothic sparingly, also served the needs of Episcopalians and of high-church Presbyterians and extended to RCs through a disciple, Reginald Fairlie, who continued Pugin's struggle against Italian and Irish influences, to reach towards a truly Scottish grammar for churches and their appurtenances (1883-1952; *Who Was Who, 1951-1960*, 360).

Catholic emancipation* had begun well with a good vernacular building at St Ninian's, Tynet (Bellie, near Elgin, 1755), but foundered in a neo-Gothic of little native quality in the pro-cathedrals of Edinburgh and Glasgow (1816) by Gillespie Graham under conditions of poverty and stress. Fairlie's take-over of more sensitive neo-Romanesque works in progress at the Benedictine* Abbey of Fort Augustus* gave an opportunity to introduce native craftsmanship, a lead followed by others. Episcopalians, getting closer to Catholicism and distanced from the CofS, liked his work and their St Adrian's, Gullane, E. Lothian (1927), is one of his best churches. This compensated for their lack of support for Fairlie's contemporary, Ninian Comper, who from a Scottish Episcopalian origin made his name and fame as an expatriate in England, detached from main architectural fashions: a loner dedicated to Anglo-Catholic ideals and an entrenched medievalism (1864-1960; *DNB 1951-1960*, 244-5).

Meanwhile Lorimer had stolen the show with his

Thistle Chapel* at St Giles' (1911) complete with carved oak stalls, stained glass and a fine vaulted roof with a complex but scholarly apse. This marked a zenith for the new Scottish medieval style, containing a welcome participation by craftsmen of many kinds. Most of his subsequent church work was additions and furnishings, as at Dunblane Cathedral and Paisley Abbey, unless we include as an ecclesiastical building his Scottish National War Memorial at Edinburgh Castle (1926), with its wide effect in promoting mason-craft, wrought ironwork and the new manner in coloured glass exemplified by the work there of Douglas Strachan, whose windows appeared all over the country. Lorimer's head-draughtsman, Leslie Graham-McDougall, produced a notable follow-up at his Reid Memorial Church, Edinburgh (1932), with Lorimer-esque detail everywhere and the best choir-and-apse vaulting in stone since the Middle Ages. But the style was too expensive and unfunctional. It died there and then.

FUNCTIONALISM AND RESTORATION. Functionalism had made no entry yet. The distinguished Glasgow designer, Charles Rennie Mackintosh (1868–1928), never at home in churches, made only a shy contribution at Queen's Cross Church, Glasgow (1897), and his competition entry for Liverpool Cathedral, exciting in detail, had a humdrum plan. For any kind of building the modern movement reached Scotland late. For churches it was relegated to the Church Extension* charges in the spreading housing areas. There and in the New Towns which sprang up after World War II, another generation of architects, led by Jack Coia, a Mackintosh admirer (1898–1981; *DNB 1981–1985*, 92–3), and Alan Reiach, last of the Lorimer pupils (1910–92; *Who's Who 1992*, 1553), built interesting buildings under terrible restrictions of cost, using a building industry in which craftsmanship seemed also to have died. Coia worked for the RCs; Reiach and others were recruited by a CofS revitalized since its reunion in 1929 with a majority of the Disruption's dissidents, and now zealously extending its mission into the new areas. Reiach's two CofS churches in Cumbernauld and Coia's RC church there are outstanding. But few distinguished buildings resulted, partly because taste was indeterminate. The prototypes were Continental, from Le Corbusier's world-famous Ronchamp Chapel in the Vosges to the neat and elegant work of the Scandinavians, but few people knew about these sources of inspiration.

Contemporary with new churches, a series of restorations benefited from surer tastes about the antique. Ian Lindsay's (1906–66; *Who Was Who, 1961–1970*, 679) rescue of Iona Cathedral and his new buildings there (1950s) set a standard, as did the little ecumenical chapel at Dunblane by the author of this article (1965). Many face-lifts of old buildings created up-to-dateness where it was needed. Sir Basil Spence's (1907–76) new CofE cathedral at Coventry (1951), combining with the bombed-out ruin of the old, is full of Scottish aspirations and again, in the expatriate tradition, shows what could be done with adequate means to do it and a good Scottish training for the task.

The Extension churches may have their acceptance in the way they function. Many are dual-purpose, convertible into church or hall by mobile partition, marking a return to the medieval concept that the chancel is sacred, the nave secular. Livingston New Town made a notable achievement at the Lanthorn Centre (1972), where a complex community building accommodates on Sundays in a large secular room the main religious services of the different churches, joining together as they may. Two permanent chapels are incorporated, one for RC use. At the earlier St Paul's Church there (1969), a large space, recognizably a church, is used for secular functions, and much liked on Sundays when CofS, EpCS and RC congregations use it together or in succession, with one permanent chapel, also much used. Again the idiom is Scandinavian, adapted to a struggling economy.

An entirely new ecclesiastical building arrived within this period – the crematorium. Basil Spence's two chapels at Mortonhall, Edinburgh, are in the European front rank, but did not quite overcome the grimness of these places.

A new development related to modern secular interest in historic churches is catering for the visitor. St Giles', Edinburgh, has created by excavation a series of facilities within a sternly restricted city-centre site, all in emulation of such arrangements made by successively renamed government departments responsible for many of the ruined churches on tourist routes. Care of these ruins, structurally and cosmetically, is itself an important exposition of the Scottish architectural heritage.

Meanwhile care and restoration of churches not yet ruinous has become a major activity, supported by the Historic Buildings Council for Scotland with grant-aid and expert advice. The resultant rescue of many a church where the structure needs repair beyond the resources of its congregation points towards a future where new churches, competing with the old in popularity, now need a new standard of achievement. Progress is no longer a matter of replacement and novelty: it continues the search for lasting values.

S. Cruden, *Scottish Abbeys* (E, 1960); J. G. Dunbar, *The Historic Architecture of Scotland* (L, 1966); A. H. Gomme and D. M. Walker, *Architecture of Glasgow* (L, ^{2}1987); I. C. Hannah, *Story of Scotland in Stone* (E, 1934, 1988); G. Hay, *The Architecture of Scottish Post-Reformation Churches, 1560–1843* (O, 1957); I. G. Lindsay, *Georgian Edinburgh* (E, 1948); *id.*, *The Scottish Parish Kirk* (E, 1960); D. MacGibbon and T. Ross, *The Ecclesiastical Architecture of Scotland ... to the Seventeenth Century*, 3 vols (E, 1896–7); J. S. Richardson, *The Mediaeval Stone Carver in Scotland* (E, 1964); W. D. Simpson, *The Ancient Stones of Scotland* (L, 1965); G. I. S. Moncrieff, *The Stones of Scotland* (L, 1938); A. J. Youngson, *The Making of Classical Edinburgh, 1750–1840* (E, 1966).

For reference: Inventories of the Royal Commission on Ancient and Historical

ARGYLL, FIFTH EARL OF

Monuments (Scotland) – by counties; *Transactions of the Society of Antiquaries of Scotland*; *The Buildings of Scotland* – series by counties and cities, founded by N. Pevsner (Harmondsworth, 1978 ff.).

F. R. Stevenson

Argyll, fifth Earl of, *see* Campbell, Archibald (1530–73).

Argyll, first Marquis of, *see* Campbell, Archibald (1607–61).

Arminianism, a Protestant system of soteriology named after the Dutch theologian James Arminius (1560–1609). It originated as a deviant form of the Reformed* tradition, and is formally similar to Semi-Pelagianism. The term is often used to describe a historically recurring type of soteriology rather than the actual teaching of Arminius himself and those directly influenced by him. Its central features are a denial of divine monergism in regeneration and an assertion of human moral ability to co-operate savingly with God's grace ('synergism'). Election is understood as conditioned on a foreseen free human response, rather than decreeing that response.

Arminianism has taken three main forms, sacerdotal, rationalistic and evangelical. In Scotland it was in the guise of Laudian* sacerdotalism that it first made its appearance in the seventeenth century. It was associated with the Episcopalian* policies of James VI* and particularly Charles I.* In this variety of Arminianism, grace was conceived as flowing through the sacraments and episcopal Church order. The Aberdeen Doctors* were its most distinguished exponents. When the revolution of 1689 finally displaced Episcopalianism from the Est.C, the EpCS continued as a haven of Arminian soteriology. Episcopalian sympathies for Jacobitism* in the Risings* of 1715 and 1745 brought Arminianism under a severe political cloud and helped cement Calvinism* as the national religion. When in 1792 a bill was passed in Parliament to enable EpCS clergy to exercise their ministry, many clergy objected to a clause requiring them to assent to the Thirty-nine Articles of the CofE. The problem was the Calvinistic article seventeen on election. They were persuaded to give a general assent to the Articles, but the EpCS's non-juring* Arminian traditions continued unabated.

Some Moderates* in the eighteenth century had tendencies to rationalistic Arminianism, which downplayed original sin and exalted humanity's natural capacities, but they were largely held in check by their Church's Calvinistic confession of faith, which they could not afford to challenge openly. By the early nineteenth century the Moderates had returned to orthodoxy; their leader George Hill* wrote his *Lectures in Divinity* (3 vols, E, 1821), which taught an unqualified Calvinistic soteriology and were used by Calvinistic theology tutors all over the English-speaking world. After the Disruption,* however, Moderates increasingly conformed to the broad church theology of Anglicans like F. D.

ARNOT, FREDERICK STANLEY

Maurice, which was fundamentally Arminian in its concept of the human will.

Evangelical Arminianism in the form of John Wesley* and Methodism* never made much headway in Scotland. James Morison* (1816–93) and the Evangelical Union* were far more successful in the nineteenth century, although their soteriology was more rationalistic in tone than Wesley's. Their influence was probably more symptom than cause of a general drift from Calvinism in Scotland in the latter part of the nineteenth century, which ultimately led many Evangelicals to embrace substantially Arminian views of grace and free-will. The drift can be traced in most Scottish Churches, including the UPC, the pre-1900 FC, the Conregationalists and the Baptists. The process was aided by the popular evangelistic techniques introduced by Moody* and Sankey.

In consequence, much present-day Scottish Evangelicalism is Arminian in doctrinal ethos. However, there has been a renewal of interest in Reformed theology over the past three decades. The Banner of Truth publishing house, whose headquarters are in Edinburgh, has acted as the literary spearhead of this renaissance. The smaller Presbyterian Churches, such as the FPC and post-1900 FC, have swum against the tide and maintained an ongoing tradition of staunch Westminster Calvinism throughout the twentieth century.

B. B. Warfield, *The Plan of Salvation* (Grand Rapids, 1935); A. H. W. Harrison, *Arminianism* (L, 1937); D. MacMillan, *The Aberdeen Doctors* (L, 1909).

N. R. Needham

Arnot, Frederick Stanley (1858–1914), pioneer Brethren* missionary-traveller in Central Africa. He was born in Glasgow to a FC family which moved to Hamilton, Tayport (Fife), and back to Glasgow (1876). At Hamilton he heard David Livingstone* and played with his children. When he was ten, the family joined the Brethren. He was baptised in his teens, and developed a strong missionary vocation, for which he acquired several practical skills. In 1874 he attended the funeral in Westminster Abbey of his hero Livingstone, and in 1899 edited an edition of his *Missionary Travels and Researches in South Africa* (L).

In 1881 Arnot sailed for South Africa, aiming to reach the source of the Zambesi. From Durban he travelled north-west through Barotseland (where he won the confidence of King Lewanika) and the Kalahari to Bihé and Benguela on the coast of modern Angola (November 1884). After six months he set out eastwards, reaching Garenganze in modern Katanga (southern Zaire) in January 1886. Here he befriended another important ruler, Mushidi.

On his return to the UK in 1888 Arnot was greeted almost as a second Livingstone. He was honoured by the Royal Geographical Society for his explorations and discoveries, especially of the headwaters of the Zambesi and other rivers (*Proceedings of RGS* n.s. 11 (1889), 65–82). In 1889 he married Harriet Fisher and published *Garenganze;*

or, Seven Years Pioneer Mission Work in Central Africa (L), followed later by *Bihé and Garenganze* (L, 1893) and *Missionary Travels in Central Africa* (Bath, 1913; cf. also *Garenganze: West and East*, L, 1903 and H. Groves, ed., *From Natal to the Upper Zambezi: Extracts from the Letters and Diaries...*, G, 1883).

Arnot made nine journeys in all into Central Africa, being brought back from the last to die in Johannesburg. In the intervals between them (the longest was 1895–1900, based in Liverpool and Bristol) he travelled in America and Europe and met leading Christians – Lord Radstock, D. L. Moody* in Chicago, Andrew Murray.* His adventurous journeys (an estimated 29,000 miles) established schools, hospitals and churches. On his death he counted some sixty colleagues working in sixteen mission-stations in five fields.

E. Baker, *The Life and Explorations of Frederick Stanley Arnot* (L, 1921); T. Lawman, *From the Hands of the Wicked* (L, 1960).

D. F. Wright

Arnot, William (1808–75), FC minister and theological writer. Born in Scone, Perthshire, a farmer's son, he was trained as a gardener. A brother's death in 1828 confirmed his call to the ministry, and he gained entrance to Glasgow University (BA, 1836). Licensed by Glasgow Presbytery in 1837, he was ordained in 1839 to St Peter's, a new Church Extension* charge in Glasgow. He went out with the Disruption,* but was deprived of the church by civil action in 1849 and moved to a new building in Main Street. One of the most popular preachers in the city, he was called in 1863 as successor to Robert Rainy* in the Free High Church, Edinburgh. His ability as preacher, author, and editor of the *Family Treasury* (1867–76) gained him international status and he visited the USA three times, but declined honorary degrees from Glasgow and New York. His published works include: *Laws from Heaven for Life on Earth. Illustrations of the Book of Proverbs* (2 vols, L, 1857–58; 1 vol from 1864); *Roots and Fruits of the Christian Life* (L, 1860); *The Parables of Our Lord* (L, 1864); *Memoir of James Halley* (E, 1842); *Life of James Hamilton* (L, 1870).

DNB II, 119–20; *FES* III, 465–6; *Autobiography ... and Memoir* (by ... A. Fleming, daughter; L, 1877); *Disruption Worthies*, 7–14; C. G. M'Crie in *Brit. and Foreign Evang. Rev.* 27 (1878), 97–105.

J. D. MacMillan

Arran, second Earl of, *see* Hamilton, James (*c*.1516–75).

Arran, third Earl of, *see* Hamilton, James (*c*.1537–1609).

Arthur, John William (1881–1952), missionary. Born to a devoutly evangelical family in Glasgow, he decided for missionary service at the age of 12. He went from Glasgow Academy to study medicine at Glasgow (MB, ChB 1903; MD 1906) and joined the still young East African mission of the CofS, arriving at Kikuyu, Kenya, on New Year's Day 1907. He opened its first hospital, and was equally prominent in, *e.g.*, extending its hitherto restricted evangelistic operations and developing its first boarding school. In 1912, at the request of the mission staff, he was appointed to head the mission, in succession to Henry E. Scott (1864–1911; *FES* VII, 706). He led it for the next twenty-five years, greatly expanding its activities, and establishing Presbyterian structures and encouraging the African ministry, thus paving the way for an independent and indigenous Kenyan church. Ordained in 1915 (after licensing by Glasgow Presbytery), he eventually gave up medical work.

Among Protestant missionaries in Kenya Arthur achieved a sort of primacy; he was active in the alliance of evangelical missions (until its collapse in the early 1930s) and had much influence in the public sphere. His policy was one of discreetly critical co-operation with the colonial government. For instance, while avoiding rejection of the principle of forced labour, he worked steadily against its excesses and abuses. When these reached a climax in the degrading measures used to recruit a carrier corps for service in German East Africa in the First World War, Arthur raised and commanded a force of volunteer carriers from the missions which had better conditions, higher morale and far fewer casualties than the government conscripts. In the Kenya constitutional crisis of 1922 he accompanied the new Governor, Sir Richard Caryndon, to London as adviser on African interests; in 1924 he became a member of the Legislative Council to represent those same interests. He was forced to resign after the controversy of 1929–30 (in which he appeared less sure-footed than usual) over female circumcision. His subsequent years of leadership were spent in building up the developing church structures and promoting the notable Church of the Torch at Kikuyu. On retiral from Kenya he served as minister of Dunbog, Fife, 1938–48. He was made OBE in 1920 and DD (St Andrews) in 1946.

See also Missions: East Africa, Kenya.

FES VII, 888, VIII, 739, IX, 428, 728; Arthur papers, Edinburgh University Library; R. Macpherson, *The Presbyterian Church in Kenya* (Nairobi, 1970); J. Murray, 'The Kikuyu Female Circumcision Controversy' (PhD, University of California, Los Angeles, 1974).

A. F. Walls

Articles Declaratory of the Constitution of the Church of Scotland in Matters Spiritual, are contained in the Schedule to the Church of Scotland Act 1921* which gives them legal effect in the civil law.

The Articles Declaratory were negotiated between representatives of the CofS and the UFC* in the period 1912–17 to facilitate the union of these Churches through reflecting and accommodating the different attitudes and traditions of the Churches which were to unite on their basis. The resultant compromise was given statutory approval in 1921, was adopted by the Churches in 1926, and

ARTICLES DECLARATORY

union took place in 1929 (see Unions, Church, in Scotland).

Article I affirms that the CofS is part of the Catholic Church, narrates the orthodox Trinitarian doctrines which the Church professes, affirms its adherence to the Scottish Reformation,* its reception of the word of God contained in the Scriptures as its supreme rule of faith and life, and avows the fundamental doctrines which are founded on them. Any alteration to the Articles must be consistent with Article I, and adherence to it, as interpreted by the Church, is essential to its continuity and corporate life (art. VIII).

Article II confirms the place of the Westminster Confession of Faith* as principal subordinate standard of faith of the Church, affirms the Presbyterian nature of its government as exercised through Kirk Sessions,* Presbyteries,* Synods* and the General Assembly,* reference being made to various Westminster* documents. Article III affirms historical continuity with the Church as reformed in 1560, ratified in 1592 and protected in the civil Union arrangements of 1707 (see Union of Parliaments, 1707). It also acknowledges the call and duty to the Church as the national Church to provide a parochial ministry throughout Scotland.

Article IV states the freedom of the Church to determine its own affairs in matters spiritual, including the determination of the constitution and membership of its courts and defining the boundaries of the spheres of labour of its ministers and office-bearers. Article V claims the inherent right to legislate for the Church, always in agreement with the word of God and the fundamental doctrines as adjudged by the Church, while recognizing liberty of opinion in points which do not enter into the substance of the faith. Article VI recognizes the sphere of the civil magistrate, and the mutual benefit Church and state may afford each other. Article VII recognizes the duty to seek unity where the Word is purely preached and discipline exercised, and to enter such a union without prejudice to its own identity. Article VIII deals with the modification of the Articles Declaratory, and Article IX confirms the Constitution of the Church.

While there is doubt as to the extent to which the Church may alter itself, notably in the relationship with the Westminster Confession,* the statutory approval of the Articles Declaratory by the Church of Scotland Act, 1921* did considerably free the Church from state interference, and has allowed subsequent development and on occasion Church union. The Articles are, however, a compromise, and like all such documents should be treated with caution.

R. Sjölinder, *Presbyterian Reunion in Scotland, 1907–1921* (Uppsala, 1962); F. Lyall, *Of Presbyters and Kings* (A, 1980), 66–84; Lord Murray, 'Church and State' sec.6 of 'Constitutional Law' in *The Stair Memorial Encyclopedia of the Laws of Scotland* (1988), vol. 5, paras 695–700; D. Murray, *Freedom to Reform* (E, 1992).

F. Lyall

Arts and the Churches

THE CELTIC CHURCH. From its beginnings in Scotland (see Whithorn* and Iona*) the Celtic Church* employed artistic and craft skills as an integral part of its worship and mission. As the Church grew, its monastic organization allowed room for the regular exercise of skills such as carving in stone and wood and manuscript illumination, while for the arts of decorative metalwork the Church could look to the established achievements of Celtic smiths. Outstanding survivals include the Monymusk reliquary, the Guthrie bell-shrine and St Fillan's crozier (all in the Royal Museum of Scotland); Celtic crosses* such as St Martin's cross on Iona; and a manuscript tradition that stretches with increasing elaboration and complexity from the Cathach psalter $c.600$ (reputedly penned by Columba himself) to the Book of Kells* ($c.800$), which was probably made on Iona.

The art of the Celtic Church is remarkable for its continuity with pre-Christian Celtic culture. The Monymusk reliquary, dating from Columba's own lifetime, contains no Christian symbolism. Such symbols were integrated and developed through Celtic art rather than imposed upon it. This apparent harmony of spirit and imagination, which is also present in the poetry of the Celtic saints,* has been an object of admiration and imitation in the nineteenth and twentieth centuries.

THE MEDIEVAL AND RENAISSANCE CHURCH. Monastic orders* again provide the key to the growth of the Scottish Church between the twelfth and fourteenth centuries, but there is no evidence of any major order cultivating a distinctive Scottish ethos or culture. Both Benedictines* (including Tironensians* and Cluniacs*), who favoured artistic ornament and attracted artisans and craftsmen, and Cistercians,* who cultivated plainness and austerity, flourished in Scotland. Much of the medieval inheritance has been lost, but there is no reason to consider the Scottish medieval Church a lesser patron, albeit on a less lavish scale, than its sister Churches in Europe. Collegiate churches* brought a new source of patronage in the shape of sculptured ornament, stained glass (none of which survives), vestments, sacramental vessels, choral music and drama, which were all part of the Church's contribution to the cultural life of the expanding burghs.

Survivals from this period, which stretches into the prosperous early decades of the sixteenth century, include the rood-screen of Glasgow Cathedral, the stalls of King's College Chapel, Aberdeen, the carved ceiling of St Machar's Cathedral, Bishop James Kennedy's* tomb in St Salvator's Chapel, St Andrews, and the wall paintings in Foulis Easter Church near Dundee. In a class of their own are the side-panels from the Trinity College altarpiece (on loan to the National Gallery of Scotland) which were commissioned from the noted Flemish painter, Hugo Van der Goes.

Some medieval church music* has survived, notably the Mass of Robert Carver,* but of the mysteries, passions and pageants of the Scottish

ARTS AND THE CHURCHES

Church only a few titles survive (*see* Theatre, Christian attitudes to).

Despite the increased patronage of the later medieval period, its theological aesthetic remained unchanged; the arts were a means of illustrating Christian truth rather than a medium of truth in themselves. (A subtler philosophical basis for Christian art was later created by the Victorian Jesuit poet, Gerard Manley Hopkins, from the work of the medieval Scottish philosopher Duns Scotus.*)

In contrast to the Italian experience, the Scottish Renaissance extended naturally from the medieval period and produced a Northern, Gothic and often Christian reworking of the classical inheritance. This can be seen most clearly in the poetry of Robert Henryson (*c*.1420–90). The essential seriousness of the Scottish makars, their use of the vernacular, and their nationalism, reflect a similar spirit to that of the reforms of Bishop Elphinstone.*

THE REFORMATION. The impact of the Reformation* on the arts was less immediate and dramatic than is popularly supposed. Much of the physical damage ascribed to 'iconoclastic' Reformers is accountable to English armies or later neglect. Ecclesiastical music schools continued and poets such as Alexander Scott (?1530–84) kept writing. The Reformation itself had a major literary champion in George Buchanan,* and other writers such as Scott and Alexander Hume (*c*.1560–1609) drew inspiration from the new Protestant faith. The Reformers used popular song (*see Gude and Godlie Ballatis*) as an instrument of devotion and propaganda. Canonical plays however, were specifically barred by the General Assembly of 1575, and arts such as the decorative painting of churches discontinued, although a new tradition of domestic biblical painting began, inspired perhaps by engravings illustrating the early printed Bibles. Most serious of all, by establishing an English Bible (*see* Bible (Versions, English)), a *Book of Common Order* (1564*) in English, and metrical versions of the Psalms* in English, the Reformation, through political rather than cultural necessity, became a vehicle of anglicization in Scottish life.

THE SEVENTEENTH CENTURY. The loss of court patronage and a combination of civil and religious strife created a bleak environment for the imaginative and liturgical arts. For a time the older unities were preserved in the work of poets such as William Drummond of Hawthornden (1585–1649) and in the more settled conditions of Aberdeen (*see* Aberdeen Doctors), which fostered a scientific and cultural proto-Enlightenment, including a tradition of Scottish poetry in Latin which was to prove a cultural byway.

Church building did, however, continue, with interruptions, and a distinguished sequence of new Edinburgh churches (Greyfriars, the Tron Kirk, and the Canongate Kirk) spans this troubled century with harmonious order and functional dignity (*see* Architecture, Scottish Church). The same virtues are evident in the new silver and pewter Communion ware. Also underestimated in literary terms is the succession of devotional theologians, of different persuasions, that distinguishes the period (*see* Forbes, John; Bruce, Robert; Scougal, Henry; Rutherford, Samuel; Leighton, Robert, and Boston, Thomas).

In the Gaelic*-speaking Highlands,* an essentially medieval relationship between Christianity and culture continued through the seventeenth century. When in the eighteenth the 'evangelization' of the Highlands gathered pace, there was already in existence a Gaelic translation of the New Testament (*see* Bible (Versions, Gaelic)) and (since 1567) a Gaelic version of the *Book of Common Order* (*see* Carswell, John).

THE EIGHTEENTH AND NINETEENTH CENTURIES. The Scottish Churches played a full part in the explosion of social and economic energy in Scotland during these centuries when industrial revolution followed closely on intellectual enlightenment, but the relationship between Church and art was an uneasy one. It is hard to detect in the ecclesiastical luminaries of the Scottish Enlightenment, such as Hugh Blair,* Alexander Carlyle* and William Robertson,* much that is in cultural terms distinctively Christian, while within the Church itself the Moderates* produced little theology and no religious art.

There is on the other hand a close underlying relationship between the Evangelicals* and Romanticism that can be seen in the novels and stories of James Hogg* and in the paintings of David Wilkie (1785–1841; *DNB* LXI, 253–8), while, despite his criticisms of the Covenanters,* Sir Walter Scott* was imaginatively drawn to 'the religion of the heart', and can be fairly claimed, along with Robert Burns* and Robert Louis Stevenson, as a world-ranking author whose work is imbued with a distinctively Scottish and Christian ethos (*see* Literature, Religion in Scottish).

Yet the dilemma of the Evangelicals was that their undoubted energy and originality failed to discover new intellectual and cultural forms that were appropriate to the changing face of secular society and acceptable to the Reformed Church mainstream. Their outstanding literary figure, Hugh Miller,* was constantly embroiled in polemical argument and tragically committed suicide in 1856, while the departure of Thomas Carlyle* for London seemed to indicate that no contemporary synthesis of art, religion and philosophy could be achieved within the cultural and ecclesiastical environment of early Victorian Scotland.

Nonetheless, the Churches remained central to the cultural life of Scotland's people, and their influence is reflected in literature such as the Kailyard or rural, sentimental novels of the late nineteenth and early twentieth centuries.

THE MODERN AGE. It was in the period after 1850 that cultural change had a dramatic effect on Scottish Christians. The growth of the EpCS in mid-century and the general legacy of the Oxford Movement combined with the affective tenor of Evangelical worship and the expanding tastes of the prosperous middle classes to bring about the change in Reformed worship. In addition, the growth of the RCC in Scotland provoked a new awareness of liturgical variety and of the history of the Reformed tradition.

The controversial pioneer, Robert Lee,* provided both an historical rationale for a more artistic style of Reformed worship (in music, liturgy, architecture and the visual arts) and a practical example in his introduction to Greyfriars in Edinburgh of stained glass, a harmonium and responsive prayers. This work was taken up by the Church Service Society,* who created a new awareness of the aesthetic dimensions of worship. By 1900, outwith the continuing Secession and Free Churches and the Highlands, the Scottish Churches could no longer be described as 'puritan'.

Yet in 1900, even as these radical changes were being absorbed, the Churches were quite unprepared for the artistic revolution that would sweep through Europe in the early decades of the twentieth century. The restoration of Christian art in the Churches was essentially a revivalist movement imitating the medieval or the Celtic era – depending on taste. Only gradually and intermittently did Scottish Christianity become aware of the contemporary arts and ready to commission religious works in modern forms. Goodwill was not lacking, but there was no theological aesthetic capable of interpreting and utilizing the modern achievement.

After World War II the arts gained in social and educational importance with the development of organizations like the Scottish Community Drama Association, the Scottish Country Dance Society, the Saltire Society, the Edinburgh International Festival, the Royal Scottish Academy of Music and Drama and the Scottish Arts Council. The Churches played a full and active part in these developments, and in 1946 the CofS opened its own theatre, the Gateway, which was replaced in 1972 by the Netherbow Arts Centre (see Theatre, Christian attitudes to).

Meantime the Scottish renaissance movement in literature and the arts produced a flowering of twentieth-century national culture which, though severely critical of the perceived Calvinism of the Scottish Reformed Churches, is profoundly imbued with the moral seriousness and spiritual awareness that has characterized the Scottish arts through the centuries.

T. C. Smout, *A History of the Scottish People* (L, 1969); J. MacQueen, *Progress and Poetry* (E, 1982); A. C. Cheyne, *The Transforming of the Kirk* (E, 1983); I. Finlay, *Columba* (L, 1979); R. B. Sher, *Church and University in the Scottish Enlightenment* (E, 1987); D. Macmillan, *Painting in Scotland, The Golden Age* (O, 1986); id., *Scottish Art: 1460–1990* (E, 1990); C. Craig (ed.), *The History of Scottish Literature*, 4 vols (A, 1987 and 1988); D. F. Wright (ed.), *The Bible in Scottish Life and Literature* (E, 1988).

D. C. Smith

Assembly Council, a committee set up by the General Assembly of the CofS initially in 1978 on the report of the Committee of Forty,* but held in abeyance the following year in order to have its constitution sent to Presbyteries under the Barrier Act. After 28 Presbyteries approved and 21 disapproved, the General Assembly in 1980 voted by 583 to 365 to establish the Council, in terms which specify that it is entirely subject to and answerable to the Assembly. The opposition was based partly on the belief that the remit had been so widely drawn that the Council might at times usurp the authority of Courts of the Church, and partly also on the belief that the Council, as a co-ordinating body within the committee structure, was being interposed between committees and the General Assembly to whom they were directly responsible. In practice, it has negotiated a revised committee structure which was approved by the General Assembly, and advised the Assembly on questions of priority and availability of resources.

RGACS 1978, 505–9, and pt. II, 41; *PAGACS 1979*, 41–2, and *1980*, 31; and reports in *RGACS 1981 ff.*

J. L. Weatherhead

Assembly, General, see General Assembly.

Associate Presbytery, the name taken by Ebenezer Erskine,* William Wilson,* Alexander Moncrieff* and James Fisher* after seceding from the CofS* (see Associate Synod, General Associate Synod, United Secession Church, Original Secession Church, United Presbyterian Church). On being loosed from their charges in November 1733 by the General Assembly's* Commission, the four brethren (with Ralph Erskine* and Thomas Mair as observers) met in Gairney Bridge (south of Kinross) on 5 December. There they formed themselves into a Presbytery and protested against the prevailing party in the Church, making a secession from them until they repented, but holding it lawful to continue in communion with those of like mind. They agreed their meetings should at first be confined to prayer and religious conference, refraining from judicial acts until it became clear whether or not the CofS would be reformed. Early in 1734 they issued *A Testimony to the Doctrine, Worship, Government and Discipline of the Church of Scotland: or Reasons . . . for their Protestation . . .* (E, 1734), in which they complained of the Assembly's usurping Presbyteries' powers of ordination, toleration of doctrinal error and refusal to receive protests. Although at the instruction of the 1734 Assembly the Synod of Perth and Stirling restored the four and even elected Erskine its moderator, the brethren declined to return, because of the Assembly's failure to comment on its action in ejecting them and, as Erskine put it, the 'great difference between a positive reformation and a stop . . . given to a deformation'.

Just prior to the 1735 Assembly the Associate Presbytery (AP) issued a pamphlet giving *Reasons . . . why they have not acceded to the Judicatories of the Established Church* (E, 1735), acknowledging the good done in 1734 but pointing out that most of the evils of which they had complained persisted and even the Synod's Act rebuking Erskine had not been repealed. Although the Assembly's Acts were generally favourable, the Seceders did not consider the looked-for work of reformation to have taken place, and in August 1735 the AP voted unanimously to proceed to acts of jurisdiction, and began to comply with requests for ministerial supply. The 1736 Assembly enacted measures they thought praiseworthy, but sanctioned two violent settlements and gave Archibald Campbell* only a mild warning. In November Wilson was appointed to train youth for the ministry and the following spring began an annual three-month course of theological tuition (in Latin). In December the AP published its judicial testimony, condemning corruptions in the CofS. This publication widened considerably the breach between the Secession and their erstwhile friends in the CofS. Some, particularly John Currie,* wrote strongly against them. The ensuing enmity was, with few exceptions, never repaired. At the time of the Porteous Riots some even laid the blame for public unrest on the Seceders, though their loyalty was ultimately well established, particularly by their behaviour in the Rising of 1745.*

The AP took shape gradually. In January 1737 the sessions of Abernethy and Kinclaben (both Perthshire) formally joined and the first ruling elder sat in the Presbytery. In February Ralph Erskine and Thomas Mair joined, in October Thomas Nairn, and in June 1738 James Thomason. As even eight men could not supply the numerous requests for ministers, the AP began licensing young men to preach. In response, the 1738 Assembly urged that all means be used to reclaim 'these poor deluded people'. The AP gave in to the 1739 Assembly a formal declinature of its authority (*Acts and Proceedings of the Associate Presbytery, ... Containing their Declinature*..., E, 1739); after a final year's delay, in 1740 the eight were formally deposed.

The AP's concern for evangelism led them into correspondence with George Whitefield.* He came to Scotland at their invitation, but their first conference in August 1741 was a disaster. They wished to confine him to their church and he believed it his duty to preach the gospel wherever opportunity offered. They went their separate ways – Whitefield to take part in the Cambuslang Revival,* and the AP to denounce it, and him, as of the devil.

In October 1742 the AP passed an act maintaining the free grace of God (*Acts of the Associate Presbytery; viz. I. Act concerning the Doctrine of Grace; ... II. Act for renewing the National Covenant ... and the Solemn League and Covenant*..., E, 1744), paying particular attention to the doctrines at issue in the Marrow controversy.* In 1743 an act for renewing the Covenants* 'in a way and manner agreeable to our present situation and circumstances' was passed. Thomas Nairn* objected to condemnation of those who refused to acknowledge the present civil authority (as uncovenanted) and left the AP to join with John Macmillan* in constituting the Reformed Presbyterian Church.*

By 1742 there were twenty congregations with regular ministers, with some vacant congregations and a considerable number of requests for a minister or probationer, not only throughout Scotland, but in Ireland and America as well. In October 1744 the AP decided growth had been such that it was appropriate to constitute themselves into 'The Associate Synod',* with three Presbyteries. This was done in March 1745, though the Church so constituted lasted only two years, after which the breach over the Burgess Oath* led to the formation of the General Associate (Antiburgher) Synod* and Associate (Burgher) Synod.*

J. M'Kerrow, *History of the Secession Church* (E, 1848); A. Thomson, *Historical Sketch of the Origin of the Secession Church* (E, 1848).

D. C. Lachman

Associate Synod, popularly known as the 'Burgher' Synod (so-called after 'The Breach' occasioned by the Burgess Oath*), the continuation of the Synod constituted in 1745 by the Associate Presbytery.* The Burghers refused to make the condemnation of the Burgess Oath a term of communion and opposed the Synod's coming to any decision on the issue. After the separation they attempted reconciliation, but were refused. They authorized a day of fasting and solemn humiliation, but also granted 'supply of sermon' to various societies which had made application to them.

The Associate Synod grew steadily, the primary difficulty being the supply of a sufficient number of ministers rather than a dearth of call for their services. Theological training was given by a succession of ministers, with the 'theological hall' being located where the current professor served. After the separation, the Synod appointed Ebenezer Erskine* temporary theological professor, but required James Fisher* to prepare himself for future appointment. Fisher served from 1749 until 1764 and was followed by John Swanston* of Kinross, 1764–7, John Brown* of Haddington, 1767–87, George Lawson* of Selkirk, 1787–1820, and, just prior to the union, John Dick.* In 1786 the Synod urged that candidates for the ministry train in a university prior to attendance in the theological hall.

The Secession's* reputation for strictness in discipline as well as doctrine was not perhaps as fully merited by the Associate Synod as by the General Associate Synod.* Nevertheless, two cases before the Associate Synod in the early 1750s illustrate the degree to which the individual was expected to subject himself to his brethren. In each men were called by a congregation and the call was confirmed by Synod, but the man refused to accept the call. In both the call was ultimately withdrawn, but not without submission by and formal rebuke of the ministers involved; the principle that it was a matter of duty to submit one's private judgement and inclination to the decision of Synod being thus made clear.

That this principle was not as resolutely implemented as in the General Associate Synod* (Antiburgher) is evident in missionary work. Although in 1751 a presbytery was formed in Ireland and an application was received from Philadelphia for a

ASSOCIATE SYNOD

minister, the Associate Synod had considerable trouble complying with such requests, which came in large numbers from both home and abroad. Not until 1754 was anyone appointed to America, but no one went until 1764, and it was another five years before a permanent ministry was established there. There was considerable reluctance on the part of ministers and candidates to go off to the wilderness when there were congregations competing for their services in Scotland. As non-compliance with directives to go to America was not met with suspension, as it was in the Antiburgher church, the work of missions suffered.

The zeal for missionary work existed, however, and eventually the work went forward. The Associate Synod was happy to recognize the Associate Reformed Church in America, sent missionaries to Nova Scotia and supported the London Missionary Society* from its inception. As a result of a visit in 1801 by John M. Mason,* six men went with him to join in the work in the Associate Reformed Church.

The Associate Synod was careful to continue the work of the Associate Presbytery. It renewed the call for an explication of the Westminster Shorter Catechism. Initially Ebenezer and Ralph Erskine,* with James Fisher, began the work, but it was left to Fisher to complete and perfect it. In 1753 a carefully revised testimony* was approved and published, giving both a narrative of the history of the Secession* as they saw it and a testimony, reflecting the emphases of their theology. In 1778 they approved *A Re-Exhibition of the Testimony* (G, 1779), both denying the Secession to be a schism and affirming that the CofS was further than ever from the renovation which would warrant reunion.

Unlike the General Associate Synod, in the Old Light/New Light* controversy the Associate Synod did not revise its testimony or abjure the power of the civil magistrate in matters of religion. Rather it adopted in 1799 a 'preamble' prefixed to the formula* (questions asked of ministers prior to ordination), explaining that none was required to approve of compulsory measures in matters of religion. The continuing obligation of the covenants was also questioned. The less radical nature of the measures adopted failed to temper the heat of dispute or prevent the separation which followed. A number of ministers and congregations left and formed first 'The Associate Presbytery' and, in 1805, 'The Associate Synod', ordinarily known as 'The Original Burgher Synod' (*see* Original Secession Church).

The Associate Synod showed itself responsive to the trends of the times in making provision for the needs of its ministry. In 1779 a benevolent fund was established to provide for the widows and children of deceased ministers and in 1791 a general fund was established to assist weak congregations, sustain aged and infirm ministers and support theological training.

A petition from the London congregation to add a selection of spiritual songs and hymns to the Psalms of David for congregational worship was considered in 1811. It was agreed that this was 'a most desirable and necessary object', and a committee was appointed, but no report was ever submitted.

From the first, the Associate Synod deplored the separation from their brethren in the Synod. But, as is illustrated by the 1750 censure of a Glasgow mason for undertaking to build an Episcopal Chapel, it was not at first inclined to a wide recognition of other Churches. It remained more open to union than the General Associate Synod, however, trying, though failing, to negotiate a union with the Reformed Presbytery in 1788. When union finally came in 1820 the Associate Synod welcomed it warmly and gladly merged in the United Secession Church.*

J. M'Kerrow, *History of the Secession Church* (E, 1848).

D. C. Lachman

Associated Presbyterian Churches. The APC came into being in 1989 following a division within the Free Presbyterian Church.* The background lay in a growing difference of attitude in the Church to such issues as attendance at meetings of other denominations, relations with others outwith the FPC and membership of secular organizations. A number of 'hard-line' majority decisions and resolutions of Synod on these questions in recent years proved highly contentious.

Matters came to a head at the meeting of Synod in 1989 following the suspension, by majority decisions, of a minister and an elder, Alexander Murray and Lord MacKay of Clashfern.* A Protest (*see* Protest Question) was tabled and a Deed of Separation was drawn up and signed by fourteen ministers and about thirty elders. It held that by decisions and resolutions of a majority of Synod members over a number of years the Church had denied to its membership the right of private judgment 'in matters relating to the application of the Christian faith to daily living', despite this right being an explicit part of the Church's constitution. Signatories of the Deed of Separation proceeded to form a Presbytery calling itself the APC and claiming to represent, over against the Synod majority, the FPC as settled in 1893.

Approximately one-third of FP members and adherents in Scotland attached themselves to the APC. In Canada* two of the three FP congregations joined the APC. A separate Canadian Presbytery was formed and representatives of the Scottish and Canadian Presbyteries met as a Synod for the first time in 1990. The Church now calls itself the Associated Presbyterian Churches of Scotland and Canada.

Church property and assets belonging to the FPC are held by trustees for individual congregations. In the event of a separation they are held for the party which continues to adhere to the constitution of the Church. In this case both parties, the FPC and the APC, claim to be doing so. Neither party has initiated legal proceedings against the other in respect of its claim. In general, both sides continue to hold and use such property as they happened to possess in the aftermath of the 1989 meeting of Synod.

A. Morrison

Assurance, the conviction or persuasion that one has been saved by the grace of God and is a Christian believer. The debate on this doctrine in Scotland has largely taken place within the Calvinist* tradition. RCs do not believe that assurance is a normal element in Christian experience although it might well come as a result of a special revelation from God. This is possible but not to be expected. Protestants who do not accept Calvinist theology and believe that it is possible for a Christian to cease to be a Christian, to 'fall from grace', have difficulties with the doctrine of assurance. How can one speak of assurance of salvation if tomorrow salvation might be lost?

The debate within Scottish Calvinism concerning assurance is significant, although both sides in the debate believe that assurance is both possible and desirable. The doctrine was given prominence at the Reformation because of the necessary reaction against the Roman doctrine. This reaction led the Reformers, not least Calvin, normally to identify assurance with saving faith, although Calvin and Knox* both recognized that faith and doubt were often mingled in the true believer and that true believers did not always have a sense of assurance. The relationship between faith and assurance was not made explicit in the Scots Confession* but is perhaps implicit in chapter XII, where 'faith and its assurance' are said to be inspired by the Holy Spirit. William Cunningham* asserted that the tendency (erroneous, as he saw it) to assume that assurance was of the essence of saving faith continued for almost a century.

The men of the Second Reformation,* on the other hand, including Samuel Rutherford,* David Dickson* and William Guthrie,* tended to follow the Westminster Confession of Faith* in teaching that assurance was not necessary to saving faith, and that many true believers would wrestle long and hard before finding it.

The disagreement between those who believed assurance to be of the essence of saving faith and those who believed that it followed faith was given classic expression in the Marrow Controversy* in the early part of the eighteenth century. It was argued by some that the *Marrow of Modern Divinity* taught that assurance was of the essence of saving faith and was right to do so. But Principal James Hadow* of St Andrews objected to the use made of the doctrine of assurance in the *Marrow*. He argued that assurance could not be of the essence of saving faith except on the basis of a universal redemption, which was contrary to the Church's Confession, the Westminster Confession of Faith. In fact, the Westminster Confession's chapter on assurance is quite cautious. Assurance is possible, but not essential for salvation.

As the debate progressed, the exponents of the *Marrow* took a middle course. Ebenezer Erskine* distinguished between the assurance of faith and the assurance of sense, which follows upon faith. The assurance of faith is a direct, but the assurance of sense is a reflex, act of the soul. The former is of the essence of saving faith and is based on Christ and the gospel. The latter type of assurance is based on the work of God in the believer. Clearly the nature and character of God are unchangeable whereas our perception of our state is open to change due to a variety of personal and other circumstances. Thomas Boston* also stood between the two schools of thought within Calvinism on the question whether assurance is to be had by a 'direct act' or a 'reflex act'. He saw this as a false dichotomy, and argued that these are two aspects of the doctrine rather than incompatible expressions of it.

A century after this phase of debate the case of John Macleod Campbell* again brought the doctrine of assurance to the forefront. In 1831 he was deposed from the ministry of the CofS for teaching that the atonement* was universal in its extent, and that assurance was of the essence of saving faith. Faced with the problem of a lack of assurance among church members, Macleod Campbell traced it to uncertainty that God loved them since they might not be among the number of those for whom Christ died. He concluded that assurance would be possible only on the basis of a universal atonement. Assurance could then be linked with saving faith as a looking to Christ in faith, being fully persuaded of God's love. This debate continues to exercise minds today, with some scholars arguing that Macleod Campbell was correct and the General Assembly wrong.

R. T. Kendall argues that this is not simply a problem between two different groups within Calvinism, but a fundamental divergence between Calvin and the 'Calvinists' who followed. He posits two possible views. The one, which he attributes to Calvin, is that assurance of salvation may be enjoyed by a 'direct' act of faith. The second, attributed to the 'Calvinists', holds that assurance is a 'reflex' act which is subsequent to faith. It is on the basis of an alleged divergence of this kind that the doctrine of assurance has attained prominence in recent debate among Calvin scholars. R. W. A. Letham, in another recent thesis, has gone over much the same ground as Kendall and agrees that the two positions outlined above are the ones to be found in the Reformed Church, although he largely rejects the chasm which Kendall finds between them.

M. C. Bell, *Calvin and Scottish Theology* (E, 1985); W. Cunningham, *Historical Theology*, 2 vols (E, 1863); P. Helm, *Calvin and the Calvinists* (E, 1982); R. T. Kendall, *Calvin and English Calvinism to 1649* (O, 1979); D. C. Lachman, *The Marrow Controversy 1718–23* (E, 1988); A. N. S. Lane, 'Calvin's Doctrine of Assurance', *Vox Evangelica* 9 (1979), 32–54; R. W. A. Letham, 'Saving Faith and Assurance in Reformed Theology: Zwingli to the Synod of Dort' (PhD, Aberdeen University, 1979); W. Cunningham, *The Reformers and the Theology of the Reformation* (E, 1862), 111–48; J. R. Beeke, *Assurance of Faith* (NY, 1991).

A. T. B. McGowan

Atonement, The. The dominant view of the atonement in Scottish theology has been unashamedly Anselmic. This already appears in Patrick Hamilton's* *'Places'* ('Christ hath made satisfaction for us and for our sin') and in the Scots Confession* (Cap. IX). Surprisingly, however, few monographs on the subject appeared in the first three centuries of the Reformed Kirk. It was uncontroverted, and therefore assumed rather than inculcated. There are two extensive essays on the subject in James Durham's* *Commentary on Revelation.* Thomas Boston* discusses it thoroughly in his *View of the Covenant of Grace.* It is also prominent in the homiletical literature of the period, a fact which probably reflects the peculiar nature of the Presbyterian Communion service, where the 'action' (thanksgiving) sermon almost invariably focused on the cross.

Not until the nineteenth century do Scottish monographs appear in any number. Several of these came from Free Church* theologians: R. S. Candlish,* 1861; George Smeaton* and Hugh Martin,* 1882. Thomas Crawford* of Edinburgh University published his comprehensive study in 1871. The Dissenters* also contributed with such studies as Andrew Marshall's* *Catholic Doctrine of Redemption Vindicated* (1844) and William Symington's* *On the Atonement and Intercession of Christ* (1834).

MAIN CHARACTERISTICS. The characteristic features of this Scottish presentation of the atonement were as follows:

(i) *A sustained, reverent reflection on the sufferings of Christ.* Outstanding examples of this are Samuel Rutherford's* *Communion Sermons,* Hugh Martin's *The Shadow of Calvary* and R. A. Finlayson's* *The Cross in the Experience of our Lord.* In expounding this theme Scottish theologians sometimes came within a hair's breadth of denying the impassibility of God; 'But O what a fray was there!' cried Samuel Rutherford: 'God weeping, God sobbing under the water!'

(ii) *A perception of the work of Christ in sacerdotal terms.* The Mediator was simultaneously Priest and Victim, offering himself to God. Sustained treatments of this theme are found in such works as Alexander Stewart* of Cromarty's *Tree of Promise,* an exposition of the typological significance of the Mosaic sacrifices.

(iii) *An insistence that the sufferings of Christ were penal:* 'they were judicially inflicted in the execution of a law which denounced punishment on the sins of men' (Crawford, 190).

(iv) *A portrayal of the atonement as a satisfaction to divine justice.* Later theologians such as Crawford gave due emphasis to more specifically biblical concepts (*e.g.*, propitiation and reconciliation), but the primary emphasis was on satisfaction. Scottish theologians were strongly opposed to subjective theories of the atonement and stressed its objective, God-ward character.

(v) *The sufferings of Christ were vicarious.* The main concern here was to insist that he suffered *for* his people; and not only as their representative but as their substitute: 'in order to save men from sin and its consequences, Christ voluntarily took their place or position in relation to God and His law, and suffered and died in their room and stead' (William Cunningham,* *Sermons,* 405). Apart from all else, according to Scottish theologians, only the idea that Christ occupied our place could rescue the cross from the charge of caprice and immorality: 'The universe were one vast hell of suspense and horror, if God's wrath could alight elsewhere than where it is deserved' (Martin, 146). The answer to that was that by union with his people, Christ contracted their guilt.

(vi) *The setting of the cross in a covenant framework.* There was disagreement as to details, but all the old Scottish divines portrayed Christ as covenant head, his work as covenant obedience and his reward as covenant promise.

(vii) *The indispensable necessity of the atonement to salvation.* The earlier post-Reformation theologians hesitated about this, several, including Rutherford, holding that the atonement was entirely discretionary. But later Scottish theology insisted that God punished sin by necessity of nature. He could not dispense his pardons at the expense of the honour of his law.

(viii) *The unambiguous portrayal of the atonement as a fruit and consequence of the love of God.* In fact this was emphasized so clearly not only by the later but by the earlier theologians, that it is unpardonable to suggest that Scottish theology ever taught that the atonement caused or procured the love of God or changed his attitude from one of malice to (reluctant) benevolence. According to Samuel Rutherford, 'Christ's death only permits God to show the fruits of His eternal love out upon us, but after such a way as He thought convenient for His justice; and therefore *we* are said in Scripture "to be reconciled unto God", and not God to be reconciled unto us' (236).

(ix) *A prominence for the idea of victory not surpassed in any other Western tradition before Gustaf Aulén.* The most splendid statements are in Hugh Martin. 'His Cross was the instrument which, in the lowest ebb of His human strength, He wielded with Almightiness, through the Eternal Spirit, as the weapon of His warfare and the means of His victory' (250).

(x) *A belief in limited atonement, but stated very carefully.* The cross was not limited as to its intrinsic value or sufficiency. If it had been God's purpose to save each and every person, no other sacrifice would have been required. Scottish divines also accepted that many benefits accrued to the reprobate from the death of Christ and did so by God's conscious intention (see William Cunningham, *Historical Theology,* vol. II, 332f.). And they had no hesitation whatever about the universal offer of the gospel (*e.g.*, Cunningham, *Sermons,* 414). But, properly defined, they believed in limited atonement. To quote Cunningham: 'We have no doubt there is conclusive evidence in Scripture of a real limitation, not in the intrinsic value or sufficiency, but in the intended destination and actual application of the atoning work of Christ' (*Sermons*, 412).

Today, this discussion seems academic and sterile, if not indeed blasphemous. The real issue, however, was the *nature* of the atonement. We must either limit the constituency for which Christ died, or limit what he achieved for those for whom he did die. The essence of the Calvinist position – the evangelical core of the doctrine of particular redemption – was that the cross actually saved. It 'purchased not only reconciliation, but an everlasting inheritance in the kingdom of heaven' (Westminster Confession, VIII.v). It secured everything: the ontological, as well as the forensic; a change of nature as well as a change of status; faith, repentance, sanctification, adoption, Spirit-baptism, glorification, as well as redemption. Its extent coincided with its effects. It secured its own application.

Despite the confidence and competence of orthodox assertions on this question, it refused to go away. In one form or another it lay at the heart of all subsequent Scottish debate on the issue. Furthermore, subsequent developments confirmed that what was at stake was the nature, and not simply the extent, of the atonement.

The problem first surfaced dramatically in the Marrow controversy.* When the General Assembly of 1720 condemned *The Marrow of Modern Divinity* one of the errors attributed to the book was universal atonement. There were certainly some statements in *The Marrow* which lent plausibility to the charge, but it is improbable. For one thing, the men (such as Thomas Boston* and Adam Gib*) who so ardently espoused the teaching of *The Marrow* were themselves ardent advocates of limited atonement. Gib, in fact, accused the assembly of hypocrisy. In pretending to attack the doctrine of universal redemption, what they were really aiming at was 'the universal and unlimited offer of Christ to sinners as such' (*Display*, vol. I, 178). This was a basic tenet of Scottish theology as early as James Durham. Everyone, simply as a human being, has a warrant to believe in Christ. However, this warrant was based not on universal redemption but on a universal gospel call.

JAMES FRASER OF BREA. But if suspicions of *The Marrow* were groundless the same could not be said of James Fraser of Brea's* *Justifying Faith*. The offending part was 'An Appendix Concerning the Object of Christ's Death', where Fraser argued that Christ died in some sense for all, including reprobates. He maintained, however, that in doing so he was laying down nothing unorthodox. 'I abhor Arminianism,' he wrote, 'and the opinion of an equal, eternal good-will to all men, elect and reprobates' (207). While Fraser spoke of a two-fold redemption, special and common, he distinguished his position from that of the Amyraldians, asserting that Christ died for all, but with different ends in view (160–5).

The details of Fraser's position are as follows:

(i) As a result of the death of Christ, all, including reprobates, inherit the blessings of common grace. This was a standard view among Scottish theologians from Durham to Cunningham.

(ii) Christ died for all in the sense that he was united to all by community of nature: 'Surely there is a relation founded on the specific unity of that human nature which Christ did assume, to which every individual of that kind may challenge some relation' (184). Fraser did not argue, however, that in Christ human nature as such was redeemed.

(iii) Christ died for all in the sense that the price he paid makes him the Sovereign and Owner of every human being: Christ hath 'a right of purchase of their persons and fortunes, to do with them and to employ them as He pleases, and in this respect He is said to buy them' (187).

(iv) Christ died for all in the sense that his redemption is co-extensive with the Fall. More than once Fraser quotes Romans 5:20, 'But where sin abounded, grace did much more abound.'

(v) Christ died for all in the sense that reprobate sinners are in quite a different position from fallen angels: 'It may be said that all sinners of mankind have greater interest in Christ's death than Devils have, whose nature he did not assume' (184).

(vi) The gospel is preached to reprobates, which could not conceivably be true of devils. The concern to lay a foundation for the universal offer of the gospel was probably the dominant motive behind Fraser's treatise. There was nothing unusual in this stress, but he did push it to remarkable, though quite justifiable, lengths. It applied, he says, even to Judas and Cain.

The basis of this universal offer, according to Fraser, is that Christ has paid a sufficient redemption price for all. This is the really innovative feature of his doctrine. His predecessors had laid equal emphasis on the offer, but they had grounded it in the terms of the divine commission. Fraser, by contrast, grounded the gospel offer in an unequivocal doctrine of universal redemption: the price paid by Christ was a material price for the sins of the whole world. This meant, essentially, that all legal impediments had been removed: 'by the satisfaction and death of Christ the law is fundamentally satisfied for the sinner, be he what he will, if of Adam's posterity . . . and he hath such interest in the death of Christ as that in law it is competent to him to make use of the satisfaction of Christ for his liberation, and finally that there is no legal impediment in the way of his liberation' (190).

(vii) Christ died for all in order to ensure that reprobates would be without excuse. James Walker* asserts that this was the central feature of Fraser's position: 'It comes to this, in short – Fraser plainly states it – that Christ dies for reprobates that they may fall under a more tremendous doom' (*Scottish Theology and Theologians*, 82). There are certainly statements in Fraser to this effect, but it is still unfair to accuse him of holding that the primary motive behind universal atonement was to aggravate the guilt of the reprobate.

FRASER'S INFLUENCE. The publication of Fraser's treatise had immediate repercussions, especially in the Cameronian (*see* Societies, United) and Secession* churches. This was largely due to the book's connection with the Antiburgher* minister, Thomas Mair.* Mair was known to favour Fraser's doctrines and in 1753 the Associate Presbytery* of Edinburgh resolved to take the affair under consideration. Four years of controversy followed. In April 1754, the Presbytery presented an overture to the Associate Synod* in which it reported as a matter of public notoriety that the Arminian (*sic*) scheme of universal atonement and redemption as to purchase was lately revived and industriously promoted. After due deliberation, the Synod passed *An Act . . . in opposition to Arminian errors upon the head of Universal Redemption*. This Act made two key points: first, that Christ redeemed none others by his death but the elect only; secondly, that Christ died in one and the same sense for all those for whom he died in any respect.

Of the forty-eight ministers belonging to the Synod, Mair alone opposed the Act. He also gave in a paper of dissent in which he complained that the Act was directed against Fraser's treatise and indicated that he 'fully accepted the same in a general manner, without any exception'. A series of meetings and interviews followed over the next few years, but Mair's opposition did not falter. He was suspended from the ministry in August 1755, and deposed in April 1757.

To expel the man was easy. To expel his doctrines proved more difficult. When James Morison* of Kilmarnock was tried (and subsequently deposed) by the Synod of the United Secession Church* in 1841, it became clear that he had imbibed his ideas from his professors in the Theological Hall, Robert Balmer* and John Brown (of Edinburgh).* Attempts were then made (notably by Andrew Marshall*) to bring the professors under discipline. Before these proceedings could be concluded, however, Balmer died. A libel accusing Brown of heresy was debated at a meeting of Synod in July 1845. The charges were declared unfounded and Brown was acquitted.

But what did the acquittal mean? There is no doubt that Balmer and Brown held much the same views as Fraser of Brea. They were essentially Amyraldians. When the Synod concluded that the charges against them were 'unfounded' it did not mean they did not hold the views attributed to them. It meant that these views did not contravene the Church's Confession. On the face of things, this looks like sheer dishonesty and there is no doubt that after these developments the United Presbyterians* developed an uneasy conscience over their relation to the Confession. The fact that in 1879 they passed a Declaratory Act* which modified the terms of subscription is a clear symptom of this. The Church was trying to accommodate within its constitution the views of Fraser of Brea. When we recall that the UP Act was followed in 1892 by a similar FC Act and that this in turn paved the way for the Union of the two Churches in 1900 (and ultimately for the Union of 1929) we begin to appreciate how influential Fraser's treatise had been.

JOHN MCLEOD CAMPBELL. But if the Seceders were having their trials, equally dramatic events were taking place in the Est.C. John McLeod Campbell* was being tried for heresy.* Formal proceedings began in the Presbytery of Dumbarton in March 1830 and concluded with Campbell's deposition by the General Assembly in 1831.

There were two, closely related charges: first, that Campbell taught that assurance was of the essence of faith, and, secondly, that he taught universal redemption. Campbell did not deny the substance of the charges. On the contrary, he argued that the doctrines he was accused of constituted the very core of the gospel. What, then, was his defence?

(i) He insisted that he did not teach that all were saved. They were redeemed. Their sins were remitted. But: 'the appellant has uniformly taught that except a man be in Christ, as a member of his spiritual body, he neither has nor can have eternal life' (Lusk, *Proceedings*, II.168). In fact Campbell seems to have held a doctrine of 'gospel-wrath' very similar to that attributed to Brea. In his answers to the libel he declared that believers and unbelievers were in entirely different situations in respect of pardon: 'to the latter, the same pardon is the ground of condemnation, and is that precious talent committed to them of the Lord, for the folding up of which in a napkin, and failing to cultivate it for the fruits of righteousness, they shall, if they abide in unbelief, have their place assigned them in the lake which burneth with fire and brimstone' (*ibid.* I.38).

(ii) He insisted that his views on the extent of the atonement provided the only possible foundation for assurance: 'It soon appeared to me manifest that unless Christ had died *for all*, and unless the Gospel announce Him as *the gift of God to every human being*, so that there remained nothing to be done to give the individual a title to rejoice in Christ as his own Saviour, there was no foundation in the record of God for the assurance which I demanded (*sic*), and which I saw to be essential to true holiness' (*Reminiscences*, 24).

(iii) He argued that his doctrine of universal redemption was not inconsistent with the Westminster Confession: 'it is a decided error to hold that our present Confession of Faith denies the doctrine of Universal Atonement and Pardon through the death of Christ' (*Proceedings*, I.54).

But when, in 1856, Campbell published *The Nature of the Atonement* it became clear that any notion of loyalty to the Confession had been abandoned. He attacked the Westminster doctrine root and branch and proposed an alternative which had no precedent in Scottish theology and little anywhere else. He spoke scathingly of the idea of imputation, referring to 'its moral repulsiveness and intellectual contradiction' (1915 edit., 139). He was equally dismissive of the notion of substitution: 'the tasting of death for us was not as a substitute, – otherwise He alone would have died' (260). But where Campbell was at his sharpest (and where he cut himself off from the whole Reformation tradition) was in repudiating the idea that the sufferings of Christ were penal: 'while Christ suffered for our sins as an atoning sacrifice, what He suffered was not – because from its nature it could not be – a punishment' (101).

But if the sufferings of Christ were not penal, what were they? And where did their atoning value lie? In their moral and spiritual content, said Campbell, and particularly in the fact that they were the symptoms of Christ's sympathetic identification with sinners. More precisely, Christ's sufferings amounted to a vicarious repentance. Campbell appears to have caught this idea from a hint thrown out, almost casually, by Jonathan Edwards in his essay on *Satisfaction for Sin* (*Works*, 1834, II, 565). Campbell took it up enthusiastically: 'That oneness of mind with the Father, which, towards man, took the form of condemnation of sin, would in the Son's dealing with the Father in relation to our sins, take the form of a perfect confession of our sins. This confession, as to its own nature, would have been *a perfect Amen in humanity to the judgement of God on the sin of man* ... that response has all the elements of a perfect response in humanity for all the sin of man ... that due repentance for sin, could such repentance ever be, would expiate guilt, there is a strong testimony in the human heart ... such a repentance would be the true and proper satisfaction to offended justice, and there would be more atoning worth in one tear of the true and perfect sorrow which the memory of the past would awaken in this now holy spirit than in endless ages of penal woe' (116f., 124, 125).

Campbell ended up with what is essentially a subjective view of the atonement. Occasionally, Christ's vicarious repentance appears as a satisfaction to divine justice. But this is not the predominant note. What the atonement really secures is our faith and repentance; and he represents these as either the true ground of reconciliation or its very essence. He understands Luther as teaching that faith *is* our righteousness and heartily endorses that view. He even comes perilously close to a blatant theory of moral influence: 'The peace-speaking power of the blood of Christ is to be conceived of as a direct power on the spirit in its personal relation to the Father of spirits ... the shedding of the blood of Christ had its direct reference to the perfecting of the conscience' (185). Our righteousness, he writes elsewhere (150) 'is NOT the *past fact of legal obligation discharged*, but the *mind of sonship towards the Father*'. In fact what reconciles the Father to us is 'the quickening in us of the life of sonship' (291). Even more remarkable is Campbell's concept of the end of the atonement: 'the Amen of the individual human spirit to that divine Amen of the Son of God, is seen to be what the divine righteousness will necessarily acknowledge as the *end of the atonement accomplished*' (195).

TWENTIETH CENTURY. Among twentieth-century Scottish theologians the one who has given most attention to the atonement is James Denney.* There is considerable variation, however, in the doctrine set forth in his successive publications. *The Death of Christ* (L, 1902) sets forth in modern idiom the traditional doctrine of Anselm and the Re-formation. Hastings Rashdall deemed it worthy of extensive and detailed criticism, describing Denney as 'one of the very few scholarly theologians who in quite recent years have attempted to defend the old substitutionary view in a thoroughgoing and uncompromising manner' (*The Idea of Atonement in Christian Theology*, L, 1919, 439). But when Denney's second study, *The Atonement and the Modern Mind* (L, 1903) appeared, B. B. Warfield suspected that his position was already shifting: 'we cannot quite make out whether his theory of the Atonement rises essentially above what is known in history as the Grotian or Rectoral theory' (*Critical Reviews*, NY, 1932, 103).

Denney's third work on the atonement, *The Christian Doctrine of Reconciliation*, was published posthumously (L, 1917). Traces of the old doctrine still remain but the dominant impression is one of confusion. One critic called it an attempt to combine the rectoral (governmental) theory with that of McLeod Campbell. Campbell is certainly lauded, but so, too, is Bushnell; and Denney inclines to the latter as much as to the former. He rejects all notions of imputation and has little patience with satisfaction. Behind this there lies a profound methodological shift. Denney's concern is no longer to state the New Testament position and propose it as the Christian one. He seeks to derive his doctrine of reconciliation from Christian experience, frequently hints that the traditional view was non-moral and insists that we must see reconciliation as a personal relationship between the soul and its Saviour, rather than as a transaction between a Sin-bearer and God. The result is a book which contains many fine passages, but, overall, lacks not only coherence but evangelical conviction. The primary effect of the atonement is manward, not God-ward: 'Jesus in His death has been the supreme power by which men have been reconciled to God. It is as the crucified that He has been able to create in sinners God's thoughts of sin, to evoke penitence, to inspire faith, to bring men back to the Father' (17).

H. R. Mackintosh* is best known for his classic study in Christology, *The Person of Christ* (L, 1912), but his work, *The Christian Experience of Forgiveness* (L, 1927), is a significant contribution to soteriology. It is predictably critical of the evangelical doctrine of the atonement, although the criticism lacks credibility, being directed at a caricature. Such concepts as imputation and propitiation Mackintosh finds abhorrent. Yet his own alternative formulation, like Denney's, is confused. He takes seriously both sin and wrath and accepts that there can be no forgiveness without atonement. Yet he recoils from the orthodox Protestant doctrine of justification, dismissing it as 'a nakedly juristic imputation of Christ's merits'. This leaves him with no alternative but to argue that at the point of forgiveness man *is* righteous. The price of avoiding imputation is Baxterianism. Faith *is* righteousness. It *is* a new relationship with God.

How is this faith brought about? By the atonement! What is prominent for Mackintosh is the evocative power of the cross. It induces 'trustful and purifying penitence' and this is already a new (reconciled) relationship with God. The work of Jesus moves us to identify with him, and only as we do that are we reconciled and justified: 'We are saved only as in spirit we join ourselves to His act and suffering' (225). The interests of morality are thus safeguarded at the expense of the gospel.

Donald Baillie's* *God Was In Christ* (1948) is mainly concerned with Christology, but it also contains two chapters on the atonement. There is no denying the elevated tone and literary brilliance of Baillie's work. It fulfils Anselm's criterion of taking sin seriously; it vehemently rejects the idea that we should simply follow the parable of the Prodigal Son and dispense with the principle of atonement; and it recognizes that the cross does not fit easily into the categories of the Enlightenment.* 'The crucifixion,' he writes, 'might well seem to be the final *reductio ad absurdum* of the belief that the world is governed by a gracious providence' (184). Like Mackintosh, however, Baillie seems to know the evangelical doctrine only in caricature. In particular, he berates the idea of propitiation, as if it were inconsistent with the divine love and referred to a process by which wrath and justice were turned into mercy.

Baillie's own doctrine was distinguished by two features:

(i) His stress on the fact that God alone bears the cost: 'We contribute nothing to the process. God's forgiveness outruns all human attempts at expiation, because the expiation is made in the heart and life of God Himself' (178).

(ii) His emphasis on *eternal* atonement. He speaks of 'the eternal sin-bearing of the divine love', sees the incarnation and the cross as the outcropping of the divine passion and refers to God as bearing sin before the incarnation and as continuing to bear it still (190).

The doctrine of the atonement has also figured prominently in the work of Scotland's best known post-World War II theologian, T. F. Torrance.* The most accessible treatments are *The Mediation of Christ* (Grand Rapids, 1983), 'Justification: its Radical Nature and Place in Reformed Doctrine and Life' (in *Theology and Reconstruction*, L, 1965) and 'Karl Barth and the Latin Heresy' (*SJT* 39, 1986, 461–82). Significant material can also be found in his Introductions to Robert Bruce's *The Mystery of the Lord's Supper* (1958) and to *The School of Faith* (1959).

Torrance makes substantial use of traditional terminology. For example, he speaks of the active and passive obedience of Christ and of the three-fold division of the work of Christ (prophet, priest and king). But he quickly leads us into what from the standpoint of Reformed orthodoxy is totally unfamiliar territory. The key issue is the relation between incarnation and atonement. Torrance stresses that Christ took *fallen* humanity and insists that the person of the Mediator belongs to the essence of the atoning reconciliation: 'Christ took our fallen humanity including our depraved mind upon himself in order to redeem it from within' (*The Mediation of Christ*, 49). This involved several factors:

(i) In the very act of assuming it Christ *sanctified* our human nature. In effect, the incarnational union deals with original sin: 'In his holy assumption of our unholy humanity, his purity wipes away our impurity, his holiness overcomes our corruption, his nature heals our nature' (*Theology in Reconstruction*, 155). This 'healing' appears to arise directly from the effect of the divine nature on the human nature.

(ii) Christ *vanquished* our humanity. He came as *homoousios* with God, almighty, dwelling within the depth of our lost humanity in order to do away with everything that separates man from God: 'He laid hold upon our wayward human will, made it his very own, and bent it back into obedience to, and oneness with, the holy will of God' (*ibid.*, 157).

(iii) By the incarnation Christ *reconciled* our fallen humanity to God. In him, our humanity has been apprehended and converted back to union and communion with God. He has laid hold of the alienated human mind – our depraved mind – to redeem it from within, effecting reconciliation deep within the rational centre of human being. How? By judging (condemning) sin in order to redeem us from our carnal, hostile mind. This seems very close to McLeod Campbell's central idea that the atonement consists of Christ's 'Amen! in humanity' to God's condemnation of sin.

(iv) The incarnate Christ vicariously *appropriates* our reconciliation. This is what Torrance understands by subjective justification (*Theology in Reconstruction*, 157ff.). Jesus is not only the embodiment of God's justifying act but the embodiment also of our human appropriation of it: 'He was the great Believer – vicariously believing in our place and in our name.'

D. M. Baillie, *God Was In Christ* (L, 1948); J. McLeod Campbell, *The Nature of the Atonement* (C, 1855); R. S. Candlish, *The Atonement* (L, 1861); T. J. Crawford, *The Doctrine of Holy Scripture Respecting the Atonement* (E, 1880); J. Durham, *Commentary upon the Book of the Revelation* (E, 1658); J. Fraser, *A Treatise on Justifying Faith* (E, 1749); A. Gib, *A Display of the Secession Testimony* (2 vols, E, 1774); R. B. Lusk, *The Whole Proceedings ... in the case of the Rev John M'Leod Campbell* (Greenock, 1831); H. Martin, *The Atonement* (E, 1882); A. Robertson, *History of the Atonement Controversy in Connection with the Secession Church* (E, 1846); G. Smeaton, *The Doctrine of the Atonement as Taught by Christ Himself* (E, 1868); *id.*, *The Doctrine of the Atonement according to the Apostles* (E, 1870); G. M. Tuttle, *So Rich a Soil: John McLeod Campbell on Christian Atonement* (E, 1986); J. McIntyre, *The Shape of Soteriology* (E, 1992).

D. Macleod

Atonement Controversy. The Atonement* Controversy in the United Secession Church* (1841–5) revolved around two schools of thought,

ATONEMENT CONTROVERSY

both claiming to reflect the teaching of the Westminster Confession of Faith,* the United Secession Church's subordinate standard of faith. The initiator of the Controversy was Andrew Marshall* of Kirkintilloch. He charged the Church's two senior professors, John Brown (d.1858)* and Robert Balmer,* with departing from the Confession's teaching on the atonement, arguing that their emphasis upon the general and universal nature of the atonement contradicted the teaching of the church's doctrinal standards.

The immediate cause of the dispute was James Morison's suspension from ministerial duties by Kilmarnock Presbytery in 1841. The main charge against Morison (there were eight in all) was that he taught that 'election comes in the order of nature after the atonement'. Morison believed that Christ died for all indiscriminately, and that election refers to the application of Christ's atonement and not its provision.

Morison's removal from the ministry was opposed by John Brown. Marshall considered Brown's opposition to the Synod's decision to indicate his support, however qualified, for Morison's teaching. As Morison had studied under Brown, Marshall and his supporters looked upon Brown as the source of Morison's 'heretical' views.

During the next year, three publications crystallized the Controversy and polarized opinion in the Church: Brown's *Notes, Chiefly Historical, on the Question Respecting the Extent of the Reference of the Death of Christ* (E., 1841), Balmer's recommendatory preface to Edward Polhill's *Essay on the Extent of the Death of Christ* (Berwick, 1842), and Marshall's *The Death of Christ the Redemption of his People* (E., 1842).

In 1843, the Secession Presbytery of Paisley and Greenock overtured the Synod asking for clarification of the Church's relation to the 'new teaching'. Brown and Balmer explained their view of the atonement to a Synodical committee. While conceding that the Westminster Confession '... *prima facie* (seems) ... to teach that Christ made atonement only for the elect', Balmer argued that 'it is exceedingly problematical if the compilers of the Confession intended to deny a universal, and assert a limited atonement'. The Synodical committee concluded that the Controversy was substantially a misunderstanding over 'ambiguous language', and that scriptural harmony prevailed among the brethren.

The Synod's decision did not satisfy Marshall. In response he claimed that 'It may be found that a flood of Pelagianism has for years been issuing from our Divinity Halls ... (and) that missionaries tinctured with Pelagian and other kindred heresies have been going forth (from them)' (*The Catholic Doctrine of Redemption Vindicated* (G, 1844), 250). Brown and Balmer lodged a complaint with the 1844 Synod against Marshall's insinuations. The Controversy seemed all but over when Marshall intimated his purpose to suppress the offending Appendix in his book. However, in 1845 Marshall published a pamphlet accusing Brown and Balmer of 'unsound doctrine and heresy', of preaching 'a worthless gospel',

AUCHTERARDER CASES

and of peddling 'the vulgar doctrine of the new theology'. When the Synod met in May 1845, Brown registered his complaint against Marshall's charges. The Synod gave its 'undivided confidence' to Brown, and publicly censured Marshall for his charges against Brown. Marshall reacted by initiating a process of libel against Brown (Balmer had just died). He accused Brown of teaching five theological propositions contrary to the Church's Standards and Scripture. The most important was the third, 'that Christ has not died for the elect only, but that he has died for all men, and made atonement or satisfaction for the sins of all men'. The Synod acquitted Brown of every charge. Brown's 'double-reference theory' was accepted as not being contrary to the Church's Standards.

The conclusion of the Controversy paved the way for the United Secession Church to unite with the Relief Church* in 1847.

The effect of the Atonement Controversy was further to loosen the attachment of Scottish Presbyterianism to the theology of the Westminster Standards. It was not therefore surprising when the United Presbyterian Church* in 1879 framed and passed a Declaratory Act which effectively qualified its commitment to the precise Calvinism of the Westminster Standards. It was now accepted, at least in the Secession Churches, that total subscription to the Westminster Confession of Faith was an unreasonable burden to impose on its ministers.

A. Robertson, *History of the Atonement Controversy* (E, 1846); W. Cunningham, *Historical Theology*, II (E., ²1870); J. Cairns, *Memoir of John Brown* (E, 1860); J. Macleod, *Scottish Theology* (E, ³1974); A. C. Cheyne, 'The Westminster Standards: A Century of Re-appraisal', *RSCHS* 14 (1963), 199–214.

I. Hamilton

Auchterarder Cases, a series of legal cases about patrons' rights that paved the way for the Disruption.*

(i) The First Auchterarder Case represented a testing of the validity of the Veto Act* of 1834, that is, whether acceptability to a congregation was one of the 'qualifications' required before a Presbytery could induct a presentee. Robert Young (*FES* IV, 260), a man of good character and adequate learning, though a poor preacher, had been presented to the CofS parish of Auchterarder (Perthshire) by the Earl of Kinnoull. Only three people signed the call,* while 287 heads of families (of a possible 330) appeared to exercise their veto in terms of the Veto Act. The Presbytery having refused to proceed, the matter went to the Court of Session, where a full bench decided (eight to five) in favour of Young. The reporting of this to the Assembly in 1838 produced a strong reaction and it was decided to appeal to the House of Lords, which the following May found that the Veto Act was illegal and that the Presbytery was bound to make trial of Young's 'qualifications', that term referring exclusively to life, literature and doctrine.

(ii) The Second Auchterarder Case also ended in

the Lords. The decision in the first case having been reported to the Assembly, it was moved that Presbyteries deal with presentations as they had been used to do. This was heavily defeated in favour of a motion by Thomas Chalmers* that the Presbytery be instructed to offer no further resistance to the claims of Young or of the patron to the emoluments of the benefice, but that the Assembly further resolve that the principle of non-intrusion* 'cannot be abandoned' – in effect that Young was welcome to the stipend of Auchterarder so long as he did not attempt to minister to the people of Auchterarder. This was, predictably, rejected unanimously by the Lords. Lord Campbell commented: 'There can be nothing more dangerous than to allow the obligation to obey the law to depend upon the opinion entertained by individuals of its propriety.' The recalcitrant majority of the Presbytery was found liable in considerable damages.

(iii) The Third Auchterarder Case arose out of an effort to effect the admission of Young without involving the defeated majority. A Court order was obtained enabling the minority to constitute itself the Presbytery for this purpose. The Court also found that the remedies sought by laird and minister 'were appropriate to prevent and repair the wrongs which had been done to them'.

The Disruption which followed a couple of months later ensured that no further complications arose.

See also Stewarton Case; Strathbogie Cases.

F. Lyall, *Of Presbyters and Kings: Church and State in the Law of Scotland* (A, 1980), 30–5.
A. Herron

Auchterarder Creed, a series of propositions which the Presbytery of Auchterarder (Perthshire) required all candidates for licence or ordination to sign. These were additional to the prescribed questions and were designed by the Presbytery to guard against what it believed were prevalent doctrinal errors. One of the propositions, intended to guard against the preaching of the necessity of a preparation for grace, was: 'I believe that it is not sound and orthodox to teach, that we must forsake sin in order to our coming to Christ, and instating us in covenant with God.' A divinity student, William Craig, complained of this requirement to the 1717 General Assembly. The Assembly not only decided in Craig's favour and instructed the Presbytery to give him the requested extract of his licence, but went on to declare 'their abhorrence' of the proposition as 'unsound and most detestable', as it tended to 'encourage sloth in Christians and slacken people's obligation to gospel holiness'. After examining the Presbytery, the Assembly's Commission mitigated the force of the Assembly's Act by finding, in its report to the 1718 Assembly, that the Presbytery was 'sound and orthodox' in its meaning, though it found the 'words very unwarrantable and exceptionable', and the Presbytery was admonished not to use them again. It was in the context of the 1717 Assembly's debate that Thomas Boston* recommended *The Marrow of Modern Divinity* to a friend, thus setting in motion the events which led to the *Marrow*'s republication and the Marrow Controversy.*

D. C. Lachman, *The Marrow Controversy* (E, 1988).
D. C. Lachman

Augustinian Canons. These were canons regular (that is, priests under monastic vows belonging to a monastic community) who followed the Rule of St Augustine. Clerical status was of the essence, differentiating them from monks, and the rochet (surplice) formed part of their habit. They were the product of a long and complex process. Augustine (354–430) insisted on his clergy sharing a common life and wrote a Rule as a guide. Clergy living in community came to be called *canonici* (canons), which originally designated clergy closely attached to a church. From the tenth century *canonici regulares* (canons regular) were those who followed a rule of life. They were not bound by vows, however, nor were the communities co-ordinated.

Canons emerged as an organized monastic body in the mid-eleventh century. This development, greatly stimulated by the Gregorian reform insisting on clerical celibacy, originated in Italy and France and spread to other countries. They followed no particular rule, but by the mid-twelfth century Augustine's brief and unspecific Rule had been universally adopted. There was no commonly accepted code of observances until leading houses compiled their own, based partly on Benedictine* customs. As with Benedictines, some houses formed centralized congregations with frequent general chapters, and in 1215 the Fourth Lateran Council ordered unattached houses in each region to hold triennial chapters.

Augustinians, known as Black Canons, became one of the largest monastic families. The numerous small houses, such as collegiate churches* or hospitals,* were a source of weakness, while in the larger monasteries pastoral work was not easily compatible with community observance and complex liturgy. They declined in the later Middle Ages, and today only a few centralized congregations such as Premonstratensians* (White Canons) survive. Augustine's Rule made a particular contribution to Scottish life in the twelfth century, for it helped to assimilate the indigenous clergy to the new church structures. Culdees* and others lived together, whether bound by monastic vows or not, and many now adopted Augustine's Rule. In what follows, however, Augustinian Canons are understood as those under vows for life in a specific and permanent monastic house.

David I* was the chief founder and benefactor of such houses. The first two foundations, Scone* in Perthshire (c.1120) and Holyrood* next to Edinburgh (1128), were made from England. Two foundations from France followed soon: Jedburgh* (c.1138) and Cambuskenneth* near Stirling (c.1140). St Andrews* was established in 1144, Inchcolm* in the Firth of Forth c.1153. These all became abbeys, except for St Andrews, a cathedral

AULD KIRK

priory; St Andrews, Jedburgh and Holyrood founded dependent houses. Three independent houses were established in the thirteenth century: Inchaffray (1200) and Inchmahome (c.1238) in Perthshire, and Monymusk* (c.1245) in Aberdeenshire: Inchaffray became an abbey. Abernethy, a Culdee settlement in Perthshire, became Augustinian c.1172, but some decades later was made a secular college. Two small independent priories were later founded in the Highlands: Strathfillan in Perthshire, founded from Inchaffray c.1317, and Oronsay off the west coast c.1353. Pittenweem (or May) in Fife, having ceased to be Benedictine*, was dependent on St Andrews by 1318.

In number and importance, Scottish Augustinian houses were matched only by the Cistercians.* With time canons regular became more like monks although, unlike monks, they often served in appropriated parish churches. Small houses, such as Oronsay, Strathfillan and most of the dependent priories, ceased to have a community, but the larger monasteries survived until the Reformation.*

See also Crutched Friars.

The Catholic Encyclopedia III, 288–97; *New Catholic Encyclopedia* III, 62–4; J. C. Dickinson, *The Origins of the Austin Canons* (L, 1950); G. W. S. Barrow, *The Kingdom of the Scots* (L, 1973), 169–74; S. Cruden, *Scottish Medieval Churches* (E, 1986), 91–113; Easson-Cowan, 88–99.

M. Dilworth

Auld Kirk was originally a pejorative term denoting the Church of Scotland* which continued after the Disruption* and the formation of the UFC of Scotland.* As used in nineteenth- and early twentieth-century fiction and pamphlet, it implied that the members and ministers of the Auld Kirk were traditionalist, formal and subservient to the state to the extent of unfaithfulness to Christ. Latterly it has connoted the more beneficent elements of tradition which the former CofS brought into the Church as re-created in 1929, though an overtone of a lifeless formalism still attaches to the phrase.

See also Kirk.

F. Lyall

Auld Lichts, see New Light.

Australia, mission and emigration. Some half million Scots have emigrated to Australia. The first good evidence of Scottish Presbyterian worship in Australia is from 1793: political convicts Thomas Muir and William Skirving sang psalms and prayed in Sydney on Sabbath days. In 1802 some borderers settled on the Hawkesbury River, formed a congregation under layman James Mein, and built the first Presbyterian church in Australia in 1809. Presbyterians were unorganized and few until the 1820s, when the number of Scottish immigrants increased, and the first ministers arrived. It is significant that the first three ministers came from the three main branches of Scottish Presbyterianism. First was Archibald MacArthur, in Hobart in 1822, from the United Secession Church;* the second was John Dunmore Lang,* whose sympathies lay with the evangelical wing of the CofS and who arrived in Sydney the following year; finally there was the CofS Moderate* John McGarvie, who arrived in Sydney in 1826. Many problems stemmed from these differences.

The first Presbyterian worship on the frontiers was conducted at the homesteads of Scottish graziers. The first ministers in Victoria were James Clow and James Forbes, who arrived in 1837 and 1838 respectively. In South Australia, Ralph Drummond arrived in 1839. The first minister in Queensland was Thomas Mowbray, in 1847. Western Australia's first Presbyterian minister was ex-Congregationalist J. M. Innes, in 1869; David Shearer was sent out by the Scottish Churches in 1886. The cause was relatively strongest in Victoria (16.2 per cent in 1901), followed by Queensland (11.5 per cent) and New South Wales (9.9 per cent). The Free Church* tradition was stronger and the Establishment tradition weaker in Australia than in Scotland.

Within three years of the Disruption* there was an Australian 'Free Church'. By 1847 most colonies had three branches of the Kirk. Lang also operated his own quasi-UP* 'Synod of New South Wales'. The disruption of 1843–6 occurred against a strong minority protest that the issues were solely Scottish. Between 1859 and 1870, Presbyterian churches reunited in Victoria, Queensland, New South Wales and South Australia. The Tasmanian Kirk remained divided until 1896; there were never divisions in the West. Opposition to reunion was strongest from extreme Free Churchmen, mostly Highlanders, some of whom stayed out.

Presbyterians in Australia continued the old tradition of public worship. Between 1860 and 1890 all this changed, except in diehard Free Church congregations. At times, in the face of bitter opposition, hymns, choirs and organs were introduced (see Musical instruments in worship); the postures for singing and prayer were reversed, and so on. Family worship was maintained and the young continued to memorize the Shorter Catechism.* These traditions died out gradually in the early twentieth century.

When the challenges of modern science, philosophy and biblical scholarship faced Presbyterians in Australia, they responded like their brethren at home. Keen interest was shown by ministers and laity in issues such as Darwinism and the higher criticism. Immediately after the Robertson Smith* case in 1882, the Victorian Assembly modified the Church's relationship to the Confession by allowing liberty of opinion on matters not of the substance of the faith (see Declaratory Acts). Nevertheless, the clash between modernist and traditionalist came to a head in Victoria in 1883, when Charles Strong,* of the Scots Church in Melbourne, was deposed from the ministry for doctrinal unsoundness. There were also rumblings in other colonies. In New South Wales relative peace enabled a variety of opinions to coexist until the coming of Professor Samuel Angus* to the Theological Hall in 1915.

His theories about Christian origins and interpretations of Scripture were unorthodox, and he was accused of heresy from 1930 until his death in 1943.

Australian Presbyterians' social concern in the nineteenth century was by modern standards narrowly defined – sexual issues, gambling, alcohol and Sabbath observance were most prominent. Social reform would flow from personal sanctification. This theological stance reinforced the canniness of the Scot, to produce an occasionally harsh individualism which argued that poverty was an individual problem to be overcome by education and hard work. Nevertheless, the Church continued its welfare work and the depressions of the 1890s and 1930s stimulated more widespread questioning of the social order. But individualism was too deeply entrenched in the laity for the Church as a whole to stray too far into social activism.

The usual Scottish church organizations were founded in Australia, within and without the denominations, including Sunday schools and woman's guilds.* The Presbyterian Women's Missionary Union strongly supported Pacific, Korean, Indian and Aboriginal missions. From the 1870s the Presbyterian Fellowship movement, founded by a Scot, spread widely amongst youth. Interdenominational organizations of Scottish origin were also founded, such as the YMCA,* the YWCA* and the Boys'* and Girls' Brigades.

Most recruits to the Presbyterian ministry up to 1914 were born, if not trained, in Scotland. The first Theological Hall was founded in Victoria, in 1866. New South Wales followed in 1873 and Queensland in 1876 (closed 1891, recommenced 1912). South Australian students attended the ecumenical Union College (1872–85), after which they were mostly trained in Melbourne, as were Tasmanian candidates. After federation in 1901, theological training was also available in Perth. Victoria was first to become independent of overseas recruitment, in the 1880s. The other colonies' Churches had trouble attracting local recruits. New South Wales, especially, welcomed significant numbers of non-Presbyterian ministers; Queensland attracted a high proportion of its recruits from Ireland (about 24 per cent before 1900); the southern colonies were increasingly dependent on Victoria. Theological education,* dominated by Scots until the 1930s, was very much in the Scottish mould.

Even though local ministers were dominant by the 1920s, there was still a lay attitude that 'Scottish meant quality', and Scots Church, Melbourne, has had only one Australian minister in 153 years. Nevertheless, 'Scots Presbyterians in Australia' had decisively completed the transition to 'Australian Presbyterians' by the 1920s. 'Localization' took place earlier than in most denominations, but the Scottish links of Australian Presbyterians remained strong even after 1945.

Small Presbyterian Churches continue. The 'Wee Frees'* or Synod of Eastern Australia, the Free Presbyterians* and the Reformed Presbyterians'* all hold to strict Calvinistic traditions. The great majority of Presbyterians joined the Uniting Church in 1977. However, opposition to Church union in the 1920s and 1970s was to a certain extent associated with appeals to the need to preserve the Scottish heritage. The 'continuing' Presbyterian Church has been beset by doctrinal disputes in its determination to be biblical and reformed. In the Uniting Church, Scottish influences are mixed with many others.

Until the Second World War, non-Presbyterians were perhaps 15 per cent of Scots immigrants. Possibly less than 4 per cent of Scottish immigrants before 1939 were Roman Catholics, mostly Highlanders. There was a trickle of the Irish-descended from the 1860s, which increased significantly from the 1940s to 15 per cent. Mother Mary MacKillop made a great contribution to Roman Catholic education. Her brother Donald (SJ) and cousin, Duncan McNab, were both missionaries to the Aborigines.

There were Scottish Episcopalians in the colonies from the beginning and also some converts from Presbyterianism. At least two Anglican bishops have been of Scottish origin. Pioneer Congregational laity and ministers included a significant number of Scots, e.g. Robert Ross of Sydney and Alexander Gosman of Melbourne. The first Baptist preacher in Australia was John McKaeg, a Highlander in Sydney in the 1830s. The Scotch Baptists* were strongest in South Australia, where the Disciples (or Churches of Christ), who came from among the Scotch Baptists and Presbyterians, were also strongest. Very few Scots were Methodists, but there were many post-migration conversions, especially in South Australia and rural areas. Matthew Gilmore of nineteenth-century South Australia was a leading advocate of Christian socialism and theological modernism. The Salvation Army's ethos gave it a certain appeal to working-class Scots. The best known Scottish Salvationist was First World War chaplain W. L. ('Fighting Mac') McKenzie, MC.

M. D. Prentis, 'The Presbyterian Ministry in Australia, 1822—1900: Recruitment and Composition', *Journal of Religious History* 13 (1984), 46–65; *id*, 'Scottish Religious Influences in Colonial Australia, 1788–1900', *RSCHS* 21 (1981), 79–90; *id*., 'Scottish Roman Catholics in Nineteenth Century Australia', *IR* 33 (1982), 58–70; *id*., *The Scottish in Australia* (Blackburn, Vic., 1987), esp. ch. 10; R. S. Ward, *The Bush Still Burns: the Presbyterian and Reformed Faith in Australia 1788–1988* (Wantirna, Vic., 1989).

M. D. Prentis

Auxiliary ministry, an 'expression' or 'category' of ordained ministry of Word and sacrament in the CofS 'exercisable under supervision on a part-time and non-stipendiary basis'. Approved in 1980 (*RGACS 1980*, 487–91; *PAGACS 1980*, 57–8) following a proposal by the Committee of Forty* in 1977 (*RGACS 1978*, 492, 513–14), it was a response to shortfalls in both finance and ministerial recruitment, and to a need for 'new types of ministry', both urban and rural. The first auxiliary ministers were ordained in 1984–5. By comparison with other churches the scheme was late in coming; its welcome was lukewarm in some quarters and its implementation by Presbyteries (with whom lies the responsibility to 'promote' candidates (only) when they 'expect' to be able to use them within their bounds) was consequently limited. It needed early review and revision (*RGACS 1987*, 413–31; it is now governed by Act III 1987). All this reflects the CofS's rather inflexibly traditional approach to ministry. Although special attention has been given to preventing this Presbytery-restricted ministry appearing second-class, auxiliary ministers may not be inducted to a charge, and, if they wish to become full-time, stipendiary ministers, must apply and undergo selection *de novo*.

D. F. Wright

Ayrsmoss, a moor near Auchinleck, Ayrshire. On 22 July 1680, a month after the Sanquhar Declaration's* disowning of Charles II,* Richard Cameron* and his small band of armed followers encountered there a larger party of government troops. After Cameron's prayer, 'Lord, spare the green and take the ripe', the battle was joined. Although twenty-eight government troopers were killed to the Cameronians' nine, Cameron himself was among them and his party dispersed, thus putting an end to this insurrection. The five prisoners, including David Hackston, who had been present at the assassination of Archbishop Sharp,* were taken to Edinburgh and killed.

J. K. Hewison, *The Covenanters*, 2 vols (G, ²1913); P. Walker, *Six Saints of the Covenant*, ed. D. H. Fleming, 2 vols (L, 1901).

D. C. Lachman

B

Baikie, William Balfour (1825-64), Bible translator. The son of a naval captain and bank agent in Kirkwall, he qualified in medicine at Edinburgh (MD) and joined the Royal Navy as a surgeon (1848), serving in the Mediterranean and then at Haslar Hospital, near Portsmouth (1851-4). Through Roderick Murchison's influence appointed surgeon and naturalist to the Niger expedition of 1854, he ended up in command of *Pleiad*, the expedition's ship, which penetrated much further up the Niger than previous attempts (*Narrative of an Exploring Voyage Up the Rivers Kwóra and Bínue*, L, 1856 – respectively the Niger and Benue or Chadda).

After returning to Haslar, he joined a second expedition in 1857, which collapsed after the wreck of the *Pleiad*. He stayed on alone, founding a settlement at Lukoja at the confluence of the Niger and Benue where he held sway in every capacity and became British Consul. Within five years he had opened up the Niger to navigation, built roads, organized markets, continued exploration, recorded the vocabularies of numerous African dialects, and translated into Hausa the Epistles in the *BCP* and considerable parts of the Bible – Genesis to Leviticus, Psalms (published L, 1881), Jonah (in J. F. Schoen, *Dictionary of the Hausa Language*, L, 1876; omitted from rp. Farnborough, 1968), and Matthew to Romans. Of some 1400 MS pages very little was published. He also translated Genesis into Fula (in C. A. L. Reichardt, *Grammar of the Fulde Language*..., L, 1876). His varied achievements as traveller, naturalist and linguist earned him high regard among learned societies in Britain. He died in Sierra Leone while on his way home.

List of Books and Manuscripts Relating to Orkney and Zetland... (Kirkwall, 1847); with R. Heddle, *Historia Naturalis Orcadensis*, I (E, 1848); *Observations on the Háusa and Fulfúlde Languages* (L, 1861); with A. Adams et al., *A Manual of Natural History for the Use of Travellers*... (L, 1854); 'Notes of a Journey... to Kano... in 1862', ed. J. Kirk in *Journal of Royal Geographical Society* 37 (1867), 92-108.

DNB II, 406-7; *Gentleman's Magazine* n.s. 18 (1865), 375-6; R. N. Cust, *A Sketch of the Modern Languages of Africa*, 2 vols (L, 1883), esp. I, 205-40; *EB* (⁹1875-89), III, 241; P. E. H. Hair, *The Early Study of Nigerian Languages* (C, 1967).

D. F. Wright

Baillie, Alexander (1590-1655), abbot. From Carnbroe, Lanarkshire, he matriculated at Helmstedt University, but, having become a RC,* entered the Scots College,* Rome 1612 and took vows at Würzburg (see Schottenklöster) 1617. He was cellarer at Ratisbon 1633, and administrator 1634-6; abbot of Erfurt 1636-46, administrator of Ratisbon 1640-6, then abbot of Ratisbon 1646-55. He did much to restore the Scots abbeys in troubled times.

He published a polemical work, *A True Information of ... our Scottish-Calvinian Gospel* (Würzburg, 1628). At Ratisbon he produced a cartulary of the abbey and an account of contemporary events there.

M. Dilworth, *The Scots in Franconia* (E, 1974); T. G. Law (ed.), *Catholic Tractates* (STS, E, 1901), lx-lxii, 269-78.

M. Dilworth

Baillie, Donald Macpherson (1887-1954), distinguished UFC and CofS theologian. Like his brother, John,* Baillie studied philosophy at the University of Edinburgh (MA, 1909), followed by theology at New College* and in Germany (1909-13). Ordained in 1918 to the UFC ministry, he ministered in three pastoral charges (Inverbervie, Cupar and Kilmacolm) before appointment in 1934 to the Chair of Systematic Theology at St Andrews, which he occupied until his death. His publications included: *Faith in God and its Christian Consummation* (E, 1927; ²1964), *The Theology of the Sacraments* (L, 1957), and two volumes of sermons and lectures, *To Whom Shall We Go?* (E, 1955) and *Out of Nazareth* (E, 1958).

Baillie's greatest work, *God Was in Christ* (L, 1948), won acclaim for its mastery of both patristic scholarship and current New Testament debate, its spiritual sensitivity, and its much-discussed suggestion that the Christian's experience of the 'paradox of grace' (1 Cor. 15:10) may illuminate the Christological problems raised by 'that life which, being the perfection of humanity, is also, and even in a deeper and prior sense, the very life of God Himself' (*see* Christology). An outstanding preacher, he was also a life-long friend of the SCM* and the Iona Community* and a devoted servant of the ecumenical movement,* particularly in connection with its Faith and Order conferences at Edinburgh (1937) and Lund (1952).

See also Atonement, The.

FUFCS 370; *FES* IX, 768; J. Baillie, 'Donald: a Brother's Impression', in D. M. Baillie, *The Theology of Sacraments*, 13–36; J. Dow, 'Memoir', in D. M. Baillie, *To Whom Shall We Go?*, 1–19; A. C. Cheyne *et al.* in D. W. D. Shaw (ed.), *In Divers Manners* (St Andrews, 1990), 84–174; D. Fergusson (ed.), *Christ, Church and Society: Essays on John Baillie and Donald Baillie* (E, 1993).

A. C. Cheyne

Baillie, John (1886–1960), distinguished Presbyterian theologian. Born in the FC manse at Gairloch (Ross-shire), Baillie went from Inverness Royal Academy to the University of Edinburgh, where he graduated MA (in Philosophy) in 1908. He studied theology at New College,* Edinburgh, and in Germany. Two years as an assistant minister in Edinburgh and four with the YMCA in France (1915–19) were followed by fifteen in teaching appointments in North America, latterly (1930–4) at Union Seminary, New York. From 1934 until his retirement in 1956 he occupied the Chair of Divinity at Edinburgh. Moderator of the General Assembly of the CofS in 1943, he was convener of the special Commission for the Interpretation of God's Will in the Present Crisis* (1942–6), whose reports helped to shape post-War attitudes. He became one of the Presidents of the World Council of Churches in 1952, served as Dean of the Faculty of Divinity and Principal of New College 1950–6, took part in the negotiations which produced the 'Bishops Report' (*see* Anglican-Presbyterian relations), and was made a Companion of Honour by the Queen in 1957. His publications (all marked by exceptional lucidity and grace of style) included: *The Roots of Religion in the Human Soul* (L, 1926), *The Interpretation of Religion* (E, 1929), *The Place of Jesus Christ in Modern Christianity* (1929), *And the Life Everlasting* (NY, 1933), *Our Knowledge of God* (L, 1956), *The Belief in Progress* (L, 1950), *The Idea of Revelation in Recent Thought* (L, 1956), and his undelivered Gifford Lectures,* *The Sense of the Presence of God* (L, 1962).

Although his earliest writings bore a perceptibly Ritschlian imprint, for most of his life Baillie could not be identified with any philosophical or theological school. His strongly independent mind made him resistant to passing fashions, while his irenic spirit preferred to discover underlying unities rather than sharpen distinctions into conflicts. Even as a schoolboy he had sought to reconcile the religious insights of his Highland upbringing with the humanism of Renaissance and Enlightenment;* as an undergraduate he resisted the blandishments of idealistic philosophy; as a divinity student he favoured a notably liberal brand of Evangelicalism; as a young professor he steered a middle course between America's warring fundamentalists and modernists; and although he welcomed the Barthian movement in the 1930s as a salutary corrective of contemporary theology, he always – and increasingly – kept his distance from it. True to the substance of historic Christianity if uneasy with some of its traditional formulations, he demonstrated his essential fidelity in the eloquent apologetics of *Invitation to Pilgrimage* (1942) and in *A Diary of Private Prayer* (L, 1936), which rapidly became a devotional classic and has been often translated. After the deaths of H. R. Mackintosh* (1936) and W. P. Paterson* (1939) he was generally recognized as the doyen of Scottish theologians.

'Confessions of a Transplanted Scot', ed. V. Ferm, *Contemporary American Theology: Theological Autobiographies*, 2nd series (NY, 1933), 31–59.

FES IX, 768, X, 428; I. Forrester, 'John Baillie: A Cousin's Memories', in *Christian Devotion: Addresses by John Baillie* (L, 1962), ix–xxiv; D. S. Klinefelter, 'The Theology of John Baillie: A Biographical Introduction', *SJT* 22 (1969), 419–36; J. A. Mackay, 'John Baillie: A Lyrical Tribute and Appraisal', *SJT* 9 (1956), 225–35; J. Macquarrie, *Twentieth-Century Religious Thought* (L, 1963), 340–41; J. Mozley, *Some Tendencies in British Theology* (L, 1951), 149–53; A. C. Cheyne in D. W. D. Shaw (ed.), *In Divers Manners* (St. Andrews, 1990), 84–144; D. Fergusson (ed.), *Christ, Church and Society: Essays on John Baillie and Donald Baillie* (E, 1993).

A. C. Cheyne

Baillie, Lady Grisell (1665–1746), Presbyterian poetess. The daughter of Sir Patrick Hume of Polwarth (later first Earl of Marchmont), Grisell is said to have been sent by her father, at the age of twelve, to carry a letter to the imprisoned (1675–9) Robert Baillie of Jerviswood, in Edinburgh. The hope that a small child would attract less attention than an adult was well founded, and she accomplished her mission. Both Hume and Robert Baillie were opposed to the religious and civil policies of the regime of Charles II,* and both were suspected of being involved in the Rye House Plot against the king and his brother and heir James, Duke of York (*see* James VII and II). Fearing arrest after his outspoken defence of Robert Baillie, who was executed for treason in 1684, Hume hid in a vault beneath the church of Polwarth, Berwickshire, his daughter smuggling food to him at night. Later he fled to Holland, where Grisell and the rest of his family joined him, only returning to Scotland after the 1688 revolution. Grisell's exploits in helping her father led to her becoming a renowned heroine in

Presbyterian tradition. Grisell married George, the son of Robert Baillie, in 1692: she had first met him while smuggling the letter to his father. An avid writer of both poetry and prose, she later became noted for her Scottish songs.

Grisell, Lady Murray of Stanehope, 'Facts relating to my Mother's Life and Character', in R. Wodrow, *History of the Sufferings of the CofS* (²G, 1828–30), IV, 505–9; *DNB* II, 413–14; R. Scott-Moncrieff (ed.), *The Household Book of Lady Grisell Baillie, 1692–1733* (SHS, E, 1911), ix–lxxx; H. and K. Kelsall, *Scottish Lifestyle 300 Years Ago* (E, 1986), esp. 18–22.

D. Stevenson

Baillie, Lady Grisell (1822–91), the first CofS deaconess. The youngest daughter of George Baillie of Mellerstain, her family was pious and firm in its CofS churchmanship. For fifty years she taught in the Sabbath School of Bowden Church, Roxburgh. A generous and energetic philanthropist, she was involved in the YWCA,* the CofS Woman's Guild,* at whose first conference she presided, and from 1878 the temperance movement,* organizing a Band of Hope in Newtown, Roxburgh. She was the driving force behind the establishment of the Zenana Mission in 1881, a missionary association unique in uniting the efforts of the CofS, the FC and the UPC.

When the plans of A. H. Charteris* for inaugurating an order of deaconesses in the CofS came to fruition (*see* Diaconate), the honour fell on Lady Grisell Baillie to be the first woman to occupy the new office. She was appointed by Selkirk Presbytery in a service in Bowden Church on Sunday 9 December 1888.

Grisell Baillie spoke frequently on spiritual themes to mothers' meetings in Newtown Memorial Hall, often in an evangelistic strain. A selection of her addresses comprises the bulk of the Countess of Ashburnham's memoir, *Lady Grisell Baillie* (E, 1893).

D. P. Thomson, 'Scotland's First Deaconess', in *Women of the Scottish Church* (Perth, 1975).

N. R. Needham

Baillie, Robert (1599–1662), Professor of Divinity and Principal of the University of Glasgow. Born and educated at Glasgow (MA, 1620), he served as Regent there and as a tutor to the Earl of Eglinton's son before being episcopally ordained to Kilwinning (Ayrshire). Although at first in favour of limited episcopacy, careful study led him to oppose the imposition of Archbishop William Laud's* service-book and to the publication of his first book, *Ladensium Autokatakrisis, The Canterburians Self-Conviction* (?G, 1640). He was a member of the 1638 Glasgow Assembly* which re-established Presbyterianism as the church polity in Scotland, and in which he argued forcefully against what he saw as enroaching Arminianism.* Baillie was soon thereafter serving as chaplain in the covenanting forces which had taken to the field against Charles I. In 1642 he was appointed Professor of Divinity at Glasgow. From 1643 he spent much of the following three years as one of the Scots commissioners at the Westminster Assembly. In 1649 he was among those sent to Holland to invite Charles II to sign the Covenant, at which time he spoke out strongly against the recent execution of Charles I. Baillie took a most active part in the controversy between Resolutioners* and Protesters.* He believed the defence of king and country necessitated alliance with any who would help, and consequently thought the Protester position traitorous. Throughout the 1650s he did as much as he was able to advance the cause of the Resolutioners, including opposing overtures for peace put forward by James Durham* and Robert Blair* and joining in sending James Sharp* to London to plead the cause.

After the Restoration, having declined a bishopric, he was appointed Principal of Glasgow University. In 1661 he urged Lauderdale to be no party to foisting episcopacy on Scotland, a policy which, he warned, would involve 'persecution of the best persons and most loyal subjects that are in the three dominions', but Lauderdale never replied. When the following year Baillie's worst fears were realized and he saw the failure of his policies, he died (it was said) of a broken heart.

An erudite scholar who had mastered thirteen languages, including Chaldee and Ethiopic, Baillie had an engaging humility. Thomas Carlyle called him affectionately 'this headlong, warm-hearted, blundering, babbling, "sagacious jolterhead" of a Baillie!' Most of Baillie's writings concerned contemporary events. Among them were *A Parallel . . . of the Liturgy with the Masse-Book* (L, 1641); *An Historical Vindication of the Government of the Church of Scotland* (L, 1646); and *A Dissuasive from the Errours of the Time* (L, 1645–6), a two-volume polemic against Independents and sectaries). Robert Baillie is, however, best remembered for his *Letters and Journals* (ed. D. Laing, 3 vols, E, 1841–2) which cover the period 1637–62, offer racy accounts coupled with shrewd insights of those momentous years in Scottish church history, and are an especially valuable record of the proceedings of the Westminster Assembly.* A memoir of Baillie is included.

Baillie took great pains preparing his *Operis Historici et Chronologici* (Amsterdam, 1668) for the press. Although he regarded it as his *magnum opus* it is virtually unknown today.

FES VII, 395–6; James Reid, *Memoirs of . . . those Eminent Divines who Convened . . . at Westminster*, 2 vols (Paisley, 1811–15); Thomas Carlyle, 'Baillie the Covenanter', *Critical and Miscellaneous Essays*, vol. 4 (L, 1899); F. N. McCoy, *Robert Baillie and the Second Scots Reformation* (Berkeley, 1974); *DNB* II, 420–2.

J. D. Douglas

Baine, James (1710–90), probably the most influential minister of the Relief Church* in the latter decades of the eighteenth century. Minister successively of Killearn (1732–56), Paisley High (1756–66), and College Street Relief Church,

BAIRD LECTURES

Edinburgh (1766-90), he was widely regarded as one of the ablest preachers of his day. He resigned his Paisley charge, where he had been the colleague of John Witherspoon,* partly over the refusal of the church courts (including the General Assembly) to grant him his own Kirk Session* (Paisley at this time being administered by a General Session* for both congregations), since he felt himself physically incapable of coping with the demands of the large parish, and partly over his strong feelings about the treatment of Thomas Gillespie of Carnock,* for whom he had pleaded strongly in the 1752 Assembly. It seems that this latter factor would probably have led to his resignation sooner or later in any case.

In the Relief Church, he exerted considerable influence as the minister of a large city congregation, as a scholar and theologian of reputation, and as Clerk of the first Relief presbytery. In the estimation of Gavin Struthers, Baine 'had the moulding of the whole religious denomination in his hands; and unquestionably it was mainly due to his liberal and enlightened views of the constitution of the church of Christ, and his firmness in maintaining them, that the Relief Church, in the face of great opposition from every quarter, retained that catholic constitution on which it had been founded by Gillespie and Boston' (*The History of the Rise, Progress, and Principles of the Relief Church*, G, 1843, 368).

His most important work was his *Memoirs of Modern Church Reformation: or The History of the General Assembly, 1766* (E, 1766), in which he attacked the Moderates* over the Gillespie case and supported the Presbytery of Relief.

Select Sermons by Thomas Boston and James Baine (United Presbyterian Fathers) (E, 1850).

FES III, 171-2; *DNB* II, 437-8.

J. R. McIntosh

Baird Lectures, a series founded in 1872-3 by James Baird of Auchmedden and Cambusdoon (near Ayr), to be delivered annually by a minister of the CofS or any other Scottish Presbyterian church who had served for at least five years. Their subject was very broadly prescribed: 'Theology, Christian Evidences, Christian Work, Christian Missions, Church Work and Church Organisations, or such subject relative thereto'. Not less than six lectures were to be given in Glasgow, 'and, if required, at another Scottish University town'.

The first lecturer was William Smith of N. Leith (on whom see *FES* I, 157), *Endowed Territorial Work: Its Supreme Importance to the Church and Country* (E, 1875). Robert Flint* then served for two years: *Theism* and *Anti-Theistic Theories* (E and L, 1877, 1879). Others worthy of note include A. F. Mitchell,* *The Westminster Assembly. Its History and Standards* (L, 1883), and *The Scottish Reformation*, ed. D. Hay Fleming (E, 1900); W. Milligan,* *The Ascension and Heavenly Priesthood of Our Lord* (L, 1892); R. H. Story,* *The Apostolic Ministry in the Scottish Church* (E, 1897); G. A. Smith,* *Jeremiah* (L, 1923); James M. Black,* *New Forms of the Old Faith* (L, 1948); W. Manson,* *The Epistle to the Hebrews* (L, 1951); W. D. Maxwell,* *A History of Worship in the Church of Scotland* (L, 1955).

Names and some titles in *CofS Year Book* (annual), to 1962.

D. F. Wright

Balcanquhal, Walter (c.1548-1617), Presbyterian minister. Probably born in Fife, he studied at St Leonard's College, St Andrews, attained his baccalaureate in 1569, and his master's degree in 1570, was exhorter at Auchtertool in Fife but moved to Bothans and Baro in Lothian by May 1572, before becoming a minister at St Giles* in Edinburgh in 1574; he subsequently served Trinity Church from 1598 to his death. For preaching against French courtiers and popery, at a point when Esmé Stewart, on arriving from France, had won the affections of King James VI,* Balcanquhal and his fellow minister, John Durie,* were called before the Privy Council in 1580 but protested the council should not be judge of doctrine. King James referred the matter in 1581 to the General Assembly which upheld Balcanquhal's doctrine as 'solid, good and true'. In 1582, he opposed Robert Montgomery's* promotion by the Crown to the archbishopric of Glasgow, and announced from the pulpit Montgomery's excommunication. In 1582, the Assembly appointed him to a committee for censuring bishops. After preaching against the Earl of Arran's (James Stewart, c.1545-96) anti-Presbyterian administration and the 'Black Acts'* of 1584, he followed many of his colleagues into exile in England until Arran's fall from power at the end of 1585. Criticized by the King in 1586 for his opposition to bishops and the royal supremacy, he continued to play a prominent part in church affairs, fled to England after the riot in Edinburgh in 1596, returned in 1597, doubted the King's version of the Gowrie conspiracy in 1600, was removed from the capital for a spell, supported the stand taken by ministers at the Aberdeen Assembly of 1604, which King James had pronounced illegal, and condemned the Assembly of 1610 which reinstated episcopacy, twice being admonished by the Privy Council. Balcanquhal's sons included Robert, minister at Tranent, and Walter.*

BUK; Calderwood; J. Melville, *Diary* (E, 1842); *Registers of Ministers, Exhorters and Readers* (E, 1830), 10, 25; T. M'Crie, *Life of Andrew Melville*, 2 vols (E, ²1824); *SBD*, 264-6, 268; *FES* I, 52, 125-6, 396.

J. Kirk

Balcanquhal, Walter (c.1586-1645), son of Walter Balcanquhal,* the preceding. He took an opposing view to his father by supporting episcopacy and the royal supremacy. Graduating from Edinburgh University in 1609, he pursued divinity at Pembroke College, Oxford, was elected a fellow there in 1611, and a royal chaplain in 1617. He attended the Synod of Dort* in 1618, became dean of Rochester in 1624 and dean of Durham in 1639. As an executor of George Heriot's will, he helped establish Heriot's hospital in Edinburgh. His vindication of the royalist cause in *His Majestie's Large Declaration concerning the tumult in Scotland* (L, 1639), resulted in his denunciation by the Covenanters'* parliament of 1641.

A joynt Attestation, Avowing that the Discipline of the Church of England was not Imperilled by the Synod of Dort (L, 1626); *The Honour of Christian Churches* (L, 1633); and (see) *The Collegiat Suffrage of the Divines of Great Britaine, Concerning the Five Articles Controverted in the Low Countries* (L, 1629).

DNB III, 25–6; Chambers-Thomson I, 62; M. Dewar, 'The British Delegation at the Synod of Dort . . . ', *EQ* 46 (1974), 103–16.

J. Kirk

Baldred, *see* Anglo-Saxon Saints.

Balfour of Burleigh, Lord (1849–1921), Alexander Hugh Bruce, Sixth Baron, Conservative politician. The only son of Robert Bruce, MP (*d*.1864), and his wife Jane Hamilton Fergusson, he regained the barony, attained in 1716, in 1869. He was educated at Loretto, Eton and Oriel College, Oxford. On the 1875 Commission of the CofS General Assembly, he supported explorations towards Presbyterian reunion, a cause always dear to him. From 1882 he was joint convener of the Church Interests Committee, which co-ordinated opposition to the disestablishment* campaign. Sitting as a Conservative Scottish representative peer from 1876, he possessed influence with Lord Salisbury on Church defence tactics. He was Parliamentary Secretary to the Board of Trade (1889–92) and Secretary for Scotland in the cabinet (1895–1903). His wife, Lady Katherine Eliza Hamilton-Gordon (married 1876), was an Anglican, and he was friendly with several bishops. In 1910 he was president of the World Missionary Conference held in Edinburgh. He published *An Historical Account of the Rise and Development of Presbyterianism in Scotland* (C, 1911). A conscientious administrator, Balfour of Burleigh was stolidly loyal to established institutions.

DNB 1912–1921, 71; Lady Frances Balfour, *A Memoir of Lord Balfour of Burleigh, KT* (L, 1925); J. G. Kellas, 'The Liberal Party and the Scottish Disestablishment Crisis', *English Historical Review* 79 (1964), 31–46.

D. W. Bebbington

Balfour, Arthur James (1848–1930), first Earl of Balfour, Conservative statesman and philosopher. The eldest son of James Maitland Balfour, MP (*d*.1856), he was educated at Eton and Trinity College, Cambridge. An MP from 1874, he was successively Parliamentary Private Secretary to his uncle, Lord Salisbury (1878–80), President of the Local Government Board (1885–6), Secretary for Scotland (1886–7), Chief Secretary for Ireland (1887–91) and Leader of the Commons (1891–2, 1895 1902) before becoming Prime Minister (1902–5). Although he resigned as Conservative leader in 1911, Balfour became First Lord of the Admiralty (1915–16), Foreign Secretary (1916–19, issuing the Balfour Declaration in favour of Zionism) and Lord President of the Council (1919–22, 1925–9). Baptized and confirmed in the CofE, he attended the CofS when north of the border. His Scottish Churches Act (1905) removed the legal disabilities of the UFC and empowered the CofS to alter the form of subscription to the Westminster* Confession. His book, *A Defence of Philosophic Doubt* (L, 1879), argued that scientific knowledge is no better founded than religious knowledge. Similar themes were taken up in *The Foundations of Belief* (L, 1895) and in *Theism and Humanism* (L, 1915) and *Theism and Thought* (L, 1923), a series of Gifford Lectures.*

A. J. Balfour, *Chapters of Autobiography*, ed. B. E. C. Dugdale (L, 1930); B. E. C. Dugdale, *Arthur James Balfour*, 2 vols (L, 1936); K. Young, *Arthur James Balfour* (L, 1963); M. Egremont, *Balfour* (L, 1980); R. F. Mackay, *Balfour* (O, 1985).

D. W. Bebbington

Balfour, (Lady) Frances (1858–1931), churchwoman, suffragist and writer. The fifth daughter of the Duke of Argyll and granddaughter of Queen Victoria, she was brought up in Scotland and London. Along with her sister, Lady Victoria Campbell,* she was actively involved in both the CofS and the movement for women's suffrage.* In ecclesiastical matters, she was a firm supporter of established religion, and was passionate in her defence of the old order. But she was also committed to new ways of working within the Church (e.g. the Woman's Guild*), and was unequivocal in her criticism of institutional religion when it failed to offer equality of opportunity to women. She was the motivator and fundraiser (and her husband, Eustace Balfour, the architect) for the rebuilding of Crown Court Church, London. She and her sister were first Presidents of the Crown Court WG, and hoped that the Guild would promote active citizenship and leadership among Christian women. Lady Frances was especially pleased at the 1929 Union.*

In both ecclesiastical and political circles, Lady Frances – a zealous, flamboyant and combative public speaker – was able to exert some influence. But the restrictions in both spheres she found intensely frustrating. As Archibald Fleming wrote, 'For two generations, the Throne Gallery of the General Assembly knew her better than it knew many of its transitory occupants; and many an eternity she spent behind the grille in the House of Commons. It must have been torture to her that in neither conclave had she the right to speak' (*LW* n.s. 2 (1931), 151–2). Lady Balfour was a prolific writer of biographies and articles. In print as in speech, sarcasm and passion were her chosen weapons. An establishment aristocrat, she was also a woman of personal courage and vision who chastised the Church because of her loyalty to it. In 1919 she wrote, with characteristic urgency: 'The farther away the Church gets from the ideal that in

BALFOUR, ROBERT

Christ there is neither male nor female, and that there is a glorious liberty granted to the children of God, the less alive will be its hold on the Christianity of the world ... Which of us can afford to let the truth slip past us on the stream of time? The day is at hand!' (Introduction to *Christ and Woman's Power*, E. Picton-Turbervill, L, 1919).

Ne Obliviscaris, 2 vols (L, 1930) – autobiography; *Dr Elsie Inglis* (L, 1918; L, 1920 – different works); *Lady Victoria Campbell* (L, 1911).

Forthcoming biography by J. Huffman; *DNB 1931–1940*, 34–5.

L. O. Macdonald

Balfour, Robert (1748–1818), CofS evangelical minister. Born in Edinburgh, he studied at Edinburgh University and was licensed by Edinburgh Presbytery in 1773. In 1774 he was ordained to Lecropt, Stirling; in 1779 he moved to the Outer High Church, Glasgow. He attained celebrity as a powerful preacher, and was a zealous supporter of foreign missions and Bible societies.* He was one of the most eminent of the evangelical circle associated with Lady Glenorchy.* John Macleod* comments on Balfour that, 'He did not print much, but he impressed his generation' (*Scottish Theology*, E, ³1974, 214).

Balfour received a DD from Princeton, New Jersey, in 1802.

Three Occasional Sermons (L, 1798); *Sermons* (G, 1819).

'Memoir ...' in *Edinburgh Christian Instructor*, new ser. I (1838), 201–11; *FES* III, 463; funeral sermons by J. Campbell, *The Faithful Minister's Character and Reward* (E, 1818), R. Wardlaw, *The Duty of Imitating Departed Worth* (G, 1818), A. Ranken, *The Exhortation and Character of Barnabas* (G, 1818), J. Love, 'Communion with Saints in Heaven', in *Works*, vol. 1: *Sermons ...* (G, 1826), 161–94.

N. R. Needham

Balfour, Robert (?1550–?1625), RC philosopher and linguist. Born in Forfarshire, he attended St Andrews University and the University of Paris. He became Professor of Greek at the College of Guienne, Bordeaux, and was appointed principal c.1585. His high academic reputation is derived chiefly from his commentaries on Aristotle. His contemporaries also admired him for his mathematical skills and his knowledge of Greek and Latin. Balfour's edition of the Greek text of Gelasius of Cyzicus' history of the council of Nicaea, accompanied by his own Latin translation (Paris, 1599), has been reprinted in several editions of the ecumenical councils.

Commentarii in Organum Logicum Aristotelis (Bordeaux, 1618); *Commentarii in lib. Arist. de Philosophis tomus secundus* (Bordeaux, 1620); *Cleomedis Meteora Graece et Latine* (Bordeaux, 1605).

BALMER, ROBERT

Chambers-Thomson I, 68–9; *DNB* III, 977–8.

N. R. Needham

Balfour, Robert Gordon (1826–1905), FC* minister and writer. Born in Edinburgh, he was educated at Edinburgh University and New College.* Ordained to East Kilbride FC in 1852, he moved in 1858 to Rothesay FC, and in 1866 to New North FC, Edinburgh. He demitted his charge in 1897, but entered the UFC at the 1900 Union.

As a Free Churchman, Balfour was convener of several committees. He delivered the fifth series of Chalmers Lectures,* published as *Presbyterianism in the Colonies* (E, 1899). He was Moderator of the UF General Assembly in 1904.

Infant Baptism a Divine Institution (E, 1860); *Central Truths and Side Issues* (E, 1895).

AFCS I, 90; *FUFCS* 21.

N. R. Needham

Ballantyne, James Robert (1813–64), Sanskritist. He was brought up in Kelso and educated at Edinburgh University. For a time he taught oriental languages at the Edinburgh Naval and Military Academy. In 1845 he succeeded John Muir* as principal of the government's Sanskrit College. His literary work took three directions. To enlarge Hindu traditional learning he produced popular versions of Western philosophers – Francis Bacon, Richard Whateley, John Stuart Mill and others. To make Hindu philosophical systems more accessible to Europeans he produced both grammars and texts with commentaries. (*The Sānkya Aphorisms of Kapila* was posthumously republished in Trübner's Oriental Series; L, E, 1883.) Above all, like Muir, but more belligerently, he developed Christian apologetics, buttressed by Paleyite natural theology, in Sanskrit. Such works include *Candrabrahmaṇavicārah: Does the Moon Rotate? Argued in Sanskrit and English by the Pandits of the Benares Sanskrit College and James R. Ballantyne* (Benares, 1857), *Khṛstadharmakaumudī: Christianity Contrasted with Hindu Philosophy* (L, Benares, 1860), and *The Bible for Pandits: the First Three Chapters of Genesis Diffusely and Unreservedly Commented, in Sanskrit and English* (L, Benares, 1860). One of his pundits was Muir's adversary Nilakantha, who became the distinguished Christian, Nehemiah Goreh. In 1861 Ballantyne became Librarian of the India Office, London; his health was poor and his career there short.

DNB III, 81–2; *Dictionary of Indian Biography*, 24; R. F. Young, *Resistant Hinduism: Sanskrit Sources on Anti-Christian Apologetics in Early Nineteenth-century India* (Vienna, 1981).

A. F. Walls

Balmer, Robert (1787–1844), Professor of Theology, minister of the Associate Synod* and later of the USec.C. He entered Edinburgh University in 1802, and proceeded to the Theological Hall of the Associate Synod at Selkirk in 1806. Licensed in 1812 and inducted to the charge of Berwick-on-

Tweed, he remained there until his death. In 1834 he was also appointed Professor of Pastoral Theology by the USec.C, but by agreement transferred to the Chair of Systematic Theology. In 1842 he wrote a preface commending the re-publication of Edward Polhill's *Essay on the Extent of the Death of Christ*. During his last years, along with his more illustrious colleague John Brown of Edinburgh (*d*.1858),* he was embroiled in a controversy that shook the USec.C. They were accused by a fellow minister, Andrew Marshall,* of promoting Amyraldian,* and even Arminian,* views on the atonement (*see* Atonement Controversy). Balmer died before the issue was finally resolved. Although the Synod of 1845 fully vindicated the Calvinistic orthodoxy of Balmer's and Brown's views on the atonement, their use of universal categories helped to weaken the attachment of the USec.C, and after 1847 the UPC, to the Calvinism* of the Westminster Confession of Faith.* Glasgow made Balmer a DD in 1840.

Academical Lectures and Pulpit Discourses, with a Memoir ..., 2 vols (E, 1845).

DNB III, 89; I. Hamilton, *The Erosion of Calvinist Orthodoxy* (E, 1990), ch. 2.

I. Hamilton

Balmerino, *see* Cistercians.

Balnaves, Henry, of Halhill (?1502–70), an early Reformer and senator of the College of Justice. He was born in Kirkcaldy. He travelled through Flanders to Cologne, studied law and theology, on his return gained the patronage of Sir John Melville of Raith (in Fife), an early supporter of reform (*d*.1550), matriculated (though already a 'master') at St Salvator's College, St Andrews in 1527 and became a procurator in the consistorial court in St Andrews and in the Court of Session in Edinburgh. Appointed a lord of session in 1538, and secretary to the Queen in 1543, he was one of several who influenced the pro-Protestant policies of the Governor Arran (*see* Hamilton, James, *c*.1516–75), who 'appeared to be a true gospeller'; he supported reading the Bible in the vernacular, and took part in a diplomatic mission to England in 1543 to arrange the marriage of Mary, Queen of Scots* to Henry VIII's son, Edward. With Cardinal David Beaton's* ascendancy, Balnaves lost his secretary's office, was imprisoned in Blackness Castle in November 1543, but was freed by June 1544, and so resumed his judicial work. With Beaton's assassination in St Andrews Castle in May 1546, Balnaves joined the 'castilians', was taken prisoner by the French to Rouen where he composed in 1548 his treatise on *Justification by Faith*, which Knox* revised. An active supporter of the Reformation, he negotiated English support for the Lords of the Congregation*. With the Reformers' victory in 1560, he was appointed one of the General Assembly's commissioners in 1563 to revise the *First Book of Discipline*.* He was later present in the Regent Moray's party at the conference in York in 1568 to present the case against Mary, Queen of Scots. He died at Leith.

The Confession of Faith, conteining how the troubled man should seek refuge at his God (E, 1584), ed. C. Rogers; *Three Scottish Reformers ... with their Poetical Remains* (L, 1874).

Knox, *History* (via Index); Knox, *Works*, III, 405–543; Calderwood, *passim*; J. M. Anderson (ed.), *Early Records of the University of St Andrews* (E, 1926), 223; J. Melville, *Memoirs* (L, 1929); *DNB* III, 91–2; Chambers-Thomson I, 78–9.

J. Kirk

Band of Hope, *see* Temperance Movement.

Bannatyne, Colin Archibald (1849–1920), FC Professor. The son of Archibald Bannatyne, FC minister at Oban, and educated at the University and New College,* Edinburgh, he was ordained at Culter, Lanarkshire, in 1876. He became Professor of Church History and Church Principles in the FC College in 1906, resigning in the year of his death. He was Moderator of the FC (continuing) General Assembly in 1901 and again in 1905. A FC Constitutionalist,* Bannatyne played a leading role in the continuation of a separate FC after the Union of 1900.

See also Free Church of Scotland, post-1900; Free Church Case.

A. Stewart and J. K. Cameron, *The Free Church of Scotland 1843–1910* (E, 1910); *Who Was Who, 1916–1928*, 50.

K. R. Ross

Bannerman, Douglas David (1841–1903), FC writer on worship. The son of James Bannerman* of New College,* Edinburgh, he was educated at Edinburgh and studied at New College during his father's lifetime. He edited his father's lectures on the doctrine of the Church (*The Church of Christ*, 2 vols, E, 1868). He himself was also to lecture on the same doctrine in his Cunningham lectures* (*The Scriptural Doctrine of the Church Historically and Exegetically Considered*, E, 1889), though his presentation was more biblical than his father's systematic approach. After serving assistantships in Pilrig, Edinburgh, and Dundee, Bannerman was inducted as the FC minister in Dalkeith (1879), where he remained until his death (UFC from 1900). Bannerman had a deep interest in ecclesiology, and in addition to the Cunningham lectures he wrote several booklets concerning worship, Christian festivals, and admission to the sacraments (republished as a single volume *Worship, Order and Polity of the Presbyterian Church*, E, 1894). His concerns regarding worship also lay behind his part in the formation of the Public Worship Association of the FC. The aim of this Association was to improve public worship 'in accordance with the Word of God, and the example of the best Reformed Churches', not desiring anything approaching a compulsory liturgy and guarding jealously the duty and privilege of free prayer. Bannerman's part in the Association's work can be seen in *A New Directory for the Public Worship of God* (E, ²1898), to

BANNERMAN, JAMES

which he contributed the foreword. Edinburgh University made him a DD in 1890.

FUFCS 335.

A. M. Harman

Bannerman, James (1807–68), FC* divine. Born at Cargill, Perthshire, he studied arts at Edinburgh University 1822–6 and then theology until 1830, when he was licensed by the CofS Presbytery of Perth. He was ordained to Ormiston, Midlothian, in 1833. He played a leading role in the Ten Years' Conflict,* acting as convener of the General Assembly's Special Commission dealing with the supply of religious ordinances in Strathbogie*. Joining the FC at the Disruption*, in 1849 he was appointed Professor of Apologetics and Pastoral Theology in New College,* Edinburgh, a position he held until his death.

Bannerman produced several valuable works. The best-known is his *The Church of Christ* (2 vols, E, 1868), an elaborate exposition of Presbyterian ecclesiology which has had considerable influence and has been reprinted three times in recent decades. His *Inspiration* (E, 1865) is a magisterial presentation of the concept of the plenary verbal inspiration of Scripture. His publications include various pamphlets relating to the controversies of the period, including the Disruption and the proposed Union with the UPC,* which he favoured.

Bannerman received a DD from Princeton, New Jersey, in 1850. Together with James Buchanan,* he edited four volumes of the writings of William Cunningham* for the press.

Disruption Worthies, 15–22; *DNB* III, 139; *FES* I, 342; *AFCS* I, 49.

N. R. Needham

Banns, a procedure obsolete in law which was the formal proclamation among the intimations during a church service that two named and designated persons intended to marry at a specified date and place. The purpose of the procedure was to alert the community to the impending marriage, and allow any relevant objections to be prepared. Proclamation of banns was made in the church of the parish where each party was resident or a member. Certification of proclamation was required before a religious marriage ceremony might proceed. From the Marriage Notice (Scotland) Act 1878 (supplemented by later legislation) publication of notice through the local Registrar of Births, Deaths and Marriages was competent, though a minister of the Church of Scotland might refuse to solemnize a marriage on a registrar's certificate alone (*PAGACS 1880*, viii).

Since the Marriage (Scotland) Act 1976 all marriages, however celebrated, may be conducted only after a civil registrar's certificate has been produced to the person officiating. A 'marriage' not so conducted is invalid in law. The procedure for banns is irrelevant, and has become obsolete.

F. Lyall

Baptism, rite of admission to the Christian Church appointed by Jesus Christ.

BAPTISM

CELTIC PERIOD. Bede* (*Eccl. Hist.* 2:2) identifies the administration of baptism as one of the three issues on which *c*.600 Augustine of Canterbury demanded that the British (*i.e.* Celtic) bishops conform to universal (Roman) practice (*see* Celtic Church). How the Celtic observance differed has never been conclusively determined: possibilities include single immersion, not triple; omission of confirmation* or chrism as the 'completion' of baptism (although Patrick mentions both); most likely, their administration by presbyters or even deacons – in which case Celtic custom remained more primitive than the later reservation of confirmation-chrism for bishops (see F. E. Warren, *The Liturgy and Ritual of the Celtic Church*, ²Woodbridge, 1987, 64–7; H. Williams, *Christianity in Early Britain*, O, 1912, 473–5; C. Thomas, *Christianity in Roman Britain to AD 500*, L, 1981, 202–27, 'Baptism and Baptisteries'). A century later Celtic baptism might still be of questionable validity (Theodore of Canterbury, *Penit.* 2:19). An account of Kentigern's death (*see* Celtic saints) indicates he baptized not at Easter but at Epiphany – which in the East originally marked Christ's baptism (D. McRoberts in *IR* 24, 1973, 43–50).

Adomnán's* *Life of Columba* records a typical variety of subjects for baptism: two old men as new believers, one of them on his death-bed (1:33, 3:14), an infant brought by parents (2:10), and two households, one clearly including children (2:32, 3:14). It has been suggested that the Celtic Church used clinical baptism in place of extreme unction. Immersion was probably practised as well as affusion. But apart from Bede's enigmatic note, there is no reason to believe that medieval Scotland's baptismal belief and practice were at all peculiar.

REFORMATION. Nor in the sixteenth century did baptism prove as contentious as in most countries where the Reformation* took root and Protestantism* prevailed. The Reformation radicals'* rejection of infant baptism touched Scotland only marginally, and there was only a 'late and slow growth of Baptist* churches on Scottish soil'. To this day Baptists remain a small, albeit vigorous, body. For these and other reasons the Est.C has developed a more rigid attitude to baptism than most Reformed Churches, and now appears ecumenically out of step.

The essentials of the new Reformation understanding may be gathered from the *First Book of Discipline*,* the Scots Confession* (SC) and the *Book of Common Order* (1564).* Anabaptist errors are condemned but not specified (SC 23). Baptism and the Lord's Supper are treated together as 'the two chief sacraments* ... alone ... instituted by the Lord Jesus' and straitly denied, in the manner of Calvin or Bucer, to be merely 'naked and bare signs'. They distinguish God's covenant* people from outsiders and 'seal in their hearts the assurance of his promise, and of that most blessed conjunction, union and society, which the chosen have with their Head, Jesus Christ'. The language is sharply realist: 'by baptism we are engrafted into Christ Jesus, to be made partakers of his righteousness, by which our sins are covered and remitted' (SC 21).

Because sacraments are 'seales and visible confirmations of the spirituall promises contained in the Word', they must be 'annexed' to the true preaching of the gospel (*FBD* 90). The requirement that baptism be administered only at the time of preaching, whether Sunday or weekday, did not preclude variable practice. Sermon and sacraments should take place before noon, but afternoon baptisms were allowed when travel was involved (*FBD* 181–2). The noise factor might advance baptism before the sermon; the post-baptismal celebration was already a problem.

The normal expectation was that baptism should take place on the next preaching day after birth. This reflected the Calvinist insistence that it be administered 'in the face of the congregation' and also the rejection of the notion that babies dying unbaptized were consigned to hell or limbo and hence needed emergency baptism. The 1618 General Assembly at Perth allowed private baptism in emergency, but the Presbyterians never conceded this and the 1638 Glasgow Assembly* banned it. SC 22 restricted baptismal administration to 'lawful ministers', which meant those appointed to preach and 'lawfully called by some Kirk' (*see* Ordination). The *SBD* endorsed this (184–5). Concern was repeatedly expressed at baptism by unqualified persons – priests (perhaps still using the Latin, Sarum, rite); readers* (often ex-priests), although they were briefly authorized to baptize between 1572 and 1576; doctors* (*SBD* 189); laymen (the 1583 Assembly even declared that baptism by a layman was not baptism); and, of course, women (SC 22). The medieval Church had sanctioned lay baptism *in extremis* (see D. Patrick, *Statutes of the Scottish Church 1225–1559*, E, 1907, 30–2, 62, 186–7). The CofS still insists that only the ordained may baptize, but the reason – the rejection of quasi-magical notions about baptism – is often forgotten.

The SC declared Rome's sacraments to be 'so adulterated ... with their own additions that no part of Christ's original act remains in its original simplicity' (22). Yet the Reformed Church did not reject the validity of Roman baptism (*BUK* I, 75), although sundry accretions were purged and fonts mostly went out of use. Many were smashed because of their idolatrous carvings, others left unused at the church door. The *FBD* specifies that each church must have 'a basen for baptizing' (203), which was commonly bracketed to the pulpit (see G. Hay, *The Architecture of the Scottish Post-Reformation Churches 1560–1843*, O, 1957, 22, 185, 188–90). Baptism was normally administered from the pulpit, with the child held up by parent or sponsor, not taken by the minister as the *BCP* provided.

AFTER WESTMINSTER. The Westminster* *Directory* (1645) laid down the lines of baptismal practice and understanding that Scottish Presbyterianism would follow in the main. It assumed (unlike the other Westminster documents) that only infants would be baptized. Some of the *Directory*'s most basic provisions – only by a minister; 'in the face of the congregation'; a role for sponsors (not godparents) only in the father's 'necessary absence' – were to be frequently breached. Baptism in private houses became surprisingly common in the nineteenth century, and misconceptions still constrained unordained people to baptize ill babies on the spot.

The Old Church's response to the first Protestant baptisms had been to doubt their validity and order conditional re-baptism under pain of parental excommunication (council of 1559, Patrick, *ibid.*, 186–7). After the re-establishment of Presbyterianism in 1690, the nonconforming Episcopalians adopted various measures towards Presbyterian baptisms. Some rejected them altogether and, in a most uncatholic fashion, gave second baptism. Others re-baptized conditionally, while yet others treated Presbyterian sacraments (as Augustine had the Donatists') as valid but 'useless' unless the baptized joined their ranks. The extent of re-baptizing in Scotland, as elsewhere, has almost certainly been underestimated.

Although a sect of 'Waderdowpers' (Waterdippers) was recorded in Edinburgh in 1624, Baptist practice became clearly noticeable only in the 1650s when Cromwell's occupying armies during the Commonwealth included Baptists (cf. W. I. Hoy, 'The Entry of Sects into Scotland', in D. Shaw (ed.), *Reformation and Revolution*, E, 1967, 178–211). Some Kirk ministers even abandoned paedobaptism, but in 1672 toleration ended and the law required the baptism of all children within thirty days of birth. A permanent Baptist presence came only in the mid-eighteenth century (*see* Baptists). When the Haldane* brothers converted to believers' baptism early in the nineteenth century, for a time they followed a dual practice, baptizing both infants and believers in the embryonic Congregationalist* movement, but it proved divisive and was short-lived.

Presbyterian baptismal theology in Scotland has had little cause to take serious note of the case for believers' baptism. Despite the wide impact of his general theology, even Karl Barth's* rejection of infant baptism created little disturbance. As a consequence, baptism has rarely been high on theological agenda, and differences have not run deep until relatively recent years.

C OF S SPECIAL COMMISSION. The most extensive Scottish investigation of baptism came from the CofS Special Commission on Baptism set up under T. F. Torrance's* convenership in 1953, 'to carry out a fresh examination of the Doctrine of Baptism, and ... to stimulate and guide such a study throughout the Church as may lead to theological agreement and uniform practice' (*PAGACS 1953*, 372). Glasgow Presbytery had overtured the Assembly in dissatisfaction at diversity of administration and belief (*APCS 1953*, 44). The Commission hoped to report in 1956 (*RGACS 1954*, 591–2), but its work was finally wound up only in 1963. Its lengthy reports appeared in *RGACS*: on New Testament doctrine (*1955*, 609–62); the Fathers (*1956*, 605–46); medieval, Reformation and Anglican teaching (*1957*, 647–706); the CofS with particular attention to Knox,* Robert Bruce,* Rollock* and Boyd,* John Forbes (1593–1648)* and the Westminster* tradition (*1958*, 685–763); and the CofS since 1843, and CofS assessment of Baptist teaching (*1959*, 629–62).

In 1960 (677–92) the Commission presented a draft on 'The Doctrine of Baptism' and 'A Form of Instruction about Baptism'. 'The Doctrine' was revised in 1961 (715–31), but an overture sent down under the Barrier Act* proposing that it be recognized as 'an authoritative interpretation of the Biblical and Reformed doctrine of Baptism as contained in the primary and subordinate standards of the Church' (*1962*, 709–23; *1963*, 773–83) was frustrated. The Assembly merely noted its acceptance by a majority of Presbyteries as a valid statement of biblical and Reformed doctrine and commended it to general consideration (*PAGACS 1963*, 462). *The Doctrine of Baptism* was published in 1966, as had been *The Biblical Doctrine of Baptism* (1958).

However, the Commission's proposals for tidying up the administration of infant baptism did become Church law. In 1933 and in 1951 the Assembly had spelled out the conditions parents had to meet. The 1963 provisions required that one parent be a member of the CofS or a permanent adherent* or desirous of becoming a member. But the Commission failed to bring about uniformity of practice. Indiscipline has continued, and in 1990 the General Assembly re-opened the question whether one parent need normally be a member.

The Commission's labours, resting largely on T. F. Torrance's work, suffered from a density of expression. Its argument relied on some questionable linguistic analysis and focused on the theologically questionable notion that 'baptism' refers primarily to 'the one, all-inclusive, vicarious baptism of Christ for all men'. This basic conception, which could distinguish between 'the water rite' and 'the real baptism – Christ's', issued in a doctrine of sophisticated elusiveness which not surprisingly – since it sat loose to historical and contemporary baptismal realities – proved unequal to the demands of pastoral confusion and disorder.

ECUMENICAL DIMENSIONS. The ecumenical movement has been slow to give baptism the attention it deserves. In 1984 the CofS and the Baptist Union of Scotland appointed a group to study a report, *Baptists and Reformed in Dialogue*, that issued from conversations between the World Alliance of Reformed Churches* and the Baptist World Alliance. The group's findings (*RGACS 1986*, 279, 306–17) were largely ground-clearing, but even so the General Assembly faulted them for inadequately representing the Kirk's tradition (*PAGACS 1986*, 19), although it consented to continuing exchanges (*PAGACS 1987*, 21; cf. *RGACS 1987*, 380–9).

Though the CofS has agreed (*PGACS 1985*, 28), in response to *Baptism, Eucharist and Ministry* (Faith and Order Paper 111; Geneva, 1982), that in any future reunion infant and believers' baptism should be 'equivalent alternatives' in a so-called 'double-practice' arrangement (as implemented by several Reformed Churches), this commitment has scarcely affected its approach to domestic difficulties, whether doubts about the biblical warrant for infant baptism or requests for faith-baptism after conversion or charismatic experience later in life. In 1976, in a case of an elder's second baptism brought by Hamilton Presbytery (*APCS 1976*, 31–3; *PAGACS 1976*, 103), and in the 1983 Panel of Doctrine's review in the light of recent problems (*RGACS 1983*, 152–63), reaffirmation was the order of the day. The influence of the Special Commission is recognizable, e.g. in the assumption that infant baptism is the theological norm and in the particular interpretation of 'one baptism' in Eph. 4:5 and the Nicene Creed.

The Scottish Churches' sole ecumenical achievement on baptism is the adoption of a common baptismal certificate – apart from the incorporation of most of the Churches of Christ* into the United Reformed Church,* which resulted in some 'double-practice' URC congregations in Scotland. Further erosion of inherited divisions is likely. The sharp reduction in recent decades in infant baptisms in the CofS and other Churches has been accompanied by a slow increase in baptisms on profession of faith. The CofS now administers more believers' baptisms than Scottish Baptists, while the latter on rare occasions baptize, as believers, children of seven or so. The CofS in particular wrestles with the relationship of baptism to church membership, and whether baptized children should be admitted to the Lord's Supper. While some churchmen hanker after the indiscriminate general baptism of earlier ages, believers' baptism is likely to come increasingly to the fore, both ecumenically and with the rapid recession of Christendom, in Scotland as elsewhere in the West – for infant baptism came into its own only in the era of Christendom after Constantine.

W. McMillan, *The Worship of the Scottish Reformed Church, 1550–1638* (Dumfermline, 1931), 246–65; A. I. Dunlop, 'Baptism in Scotland after the Reformation', in D. Shaw (ed.), *Reformation and Revolution: Essays . . . Hugh Watt* (E, 1967), 82–99; G. D. Henderson, *Church and Ministry* (L, 1951), 46–50; J. MacInnes, 'Baptism in the Highlands', *RSCHS* 13 (1959), 1–24; D. W. Bebbington (ed.), *The Baptists in Scotland* (G, 1988); H. J. Wotherspoon and J. M. Kirkpatrick, *A Manual of Church Doctrine according to the Church of Scotland* (L, 1960), 21–38; Cox 53–9, 783–4; T. W. Moyes, 'Scottish Baptist Relations with the Church of Scotland in the Twentieth Century', *BQ* 33 (1989), 174–85.

D. F. Wright

Baptist Home Missionary Society for Scotland (BHMS), the organization which maintained Baptist home missionary activity principally in the Highlands* and Islands, northern Scotland, Orkney* and Shetland* (1827–1971). The society grew out of Baptist missionary interest in the rural areas of northern and western Scotland. This interest began in the 1790s and the early 1800s within the wider context of home missionary enterprise spearheaded by Robert and James Haldane.* The Haldanes' Society for Propagating the Gospel at Home* (SPGH), founded in 1797, supported itinerant* evangelists who toured the Highlands and planted Independent* churches in Perthshire, Strathspey and the coastal plain northwards to Thurso. The Perthshire churches were particularly influential, their pastors undertaking 'long tours' as far as Lewis. The Haldane impetus was maintained until the brothers became Baptists in 1808, when the SPGH collapsed (*see* Haldane Preachers).

Baptist home missionary activity was initially promoted by individual churches and pastors. In 1797 the Scotch Baptist,* James Watt, was active in rural Aberdeenshire, and the Scotch Baptists established a small fund which supported itinerancy in the early 1800s. Before 1805 the 'English' (single-pastor) Baptist church in Glasgow was supporting a small mission in the Highlands, which resulted in the foundation of a church at Bellanoch, Argyll. A desire for a wider programme of sustained evangelism appears to have developed from this. It was promoted by Christopher Anderson* and George Barclay,* who, by means of a small society, supported evangelists in the West Highlands (*see* Sinclair, Dugald), Perthshire and Kirkcudbrightshire. In Perthshire and Strathspey most of the earlier Independent churches were split by dissension after the Haldane débâcle in 1808, so that the area produced about ten Baptist churches with several itinerant pastors (*see* Grant, Peter). By 1816 the Baptist Highland Mission had been established in Perthshire by William Tulloch.* After 1808 the Haldanes' church at Leith Walk, Edinburgh, was supporting Baptist evangelists in the Highlands. By the 1820s there were therefore three Baptist 'groups' involved in Highland mission. By amalgamating the enterprises of Anderson and the Haldanes in 1823, and then by uniting this body with the Baptist Highland Mission, the BHMS was formed in 1827.

The BHMS was well organized, producing annual reports (E and G, 1827-1971) of the labours of its missionaries, who were active from Orkney and Shetland (*see* Thomson, Sinclair) to the Hebrides (*see* Grant, Alexander, and Fraser, William). A Travelling Agent was appointed to gather funds in Scotland and England, the English contribution amounting to more than half of the income in the mid-nineteenth century. Several churches were constituted in the period 1827-40, including those at Tobermory, Ross of Mull, Tiree and Lerwick. Church planting diminished after 1850, although a few causes emerged in the later nineteenth century, mainly in mainland towns (*e.g.*, Oban). While the BHMS was intended 'Chiefly for the Highlands and Islands', several Lowland churches were assisted at various times, including Ayr, Cumnock, Falkirk, Largo and Stirling.

Baptist missionaries worked sacrificially in very difficult conditions, especially in the Highlands and Islands. They acted as pastors of the churches, and visited remote communities, preaching in the fields and in cottages. Although their churches periodically experienced revivals,* their hard-won congregations were frequently depleted by emigration.* This led to the foundation of several Highland Baptist churches in Canada; Breadalbane Baptist Church, in Glengarry Co., Ontario, was established in 1817 by emigrants from Perthshire. By 1900 seven of the eight early Baptist churches in Highland Perthshire had been wiped out, mainly by depopulation. The last of the original Highland Baptist churches of Perthshire, Tullymet, was closed in 1969.

The twentieth century has witnessed the decline of most rural and island churches originally maintained by the BHMS, mainly because of depopulation, but small Baptist churches remain tenaciously in Orkney, Shetland, Mull, Islay, Colonsay and Tiree (*see* Taylor, F. W.). The churches in the larger towns (Oban, Lochgilphead and Inverness) have shown gradual growth.

The level of external support for the BHMS decreased in real terms after 1900. In 1931 the society was incorporated within the Baptist Union of Scotland,* and administered thereafter by the Home Mission Committee. The Committee was disbanded in 1971, and the work was integrated into the wider evangelism and sustentation programmes of the denomination.

See also Gaelic.

D. W. Bebbington (ed.), *The Baptists in Scoiland* (G, 1988), 35-7, 280-308, 317-35; G. Yuille (ed.), *History of the Baptists in Scotland* (G, 1926), 66-75, 89-120, 167-8; D. E. Meek, *Island Harvest: Tiree Baptist Church 1838-1988* (E, 1988); *id.*, 'Evangelicalism and Emigration: Aspects of the Role of Dissenting Evangelicalism in Highland Emigration to Canada', in G. MacLennan (ed.), *Proceedings of the First North American Congress of Celtic Studies* (Ottawa, 1988), 15-35; *id.*, *Sunshine and Shadow: The Story of the Baptists of Mull* (E, 1991).

D. E. Meek

Baptist Union of Scotland, a voluntary association embracing the majority of Baptist churches in Scotland. Baptist churches in Scotland preceded the Union by a hundred years and the Baptist Home Missionary Society for Scotland,* founded in 1827, was the senior body. The Particular Baptists in England formed a Union in 1812, but Scottish Baptists were slow to unite because of differences of church order, and a strongly held doctrine of the independency of the local church. An early attempt based on Edinburgh in 1827 foundered mainly on personal and doctrinal issues, and it was not until 1835 that a Baptist Association, developed into a Union by F. Johnstone* in 1843, was formed. It contained a minority of churches, was much influenced by James Morison's* theology, and its lively and aggressive evangelism made it suspect to the older leaders. This Union, which founded several churches and published a magazine, *The Evangelist*, became in the 1850s an association of individuals, and in 1856 dissolved.

In the aftermath of the 1859 revival,* evangelical unity was popular, and eventually in October 1869 in Hope Street Chapel, Glasgow, the present Baptist Union of Scotland was formed with the objects of disseminating the gospel of Christ in Scotland, giving aid to new and small churches, helping young men to train for the ministry, and sharing information and co-operative work. William Tulloch* was elected Secretary, Howard Bowser Treasurer, and Jonathan Watson* delivered the first Presidential address on 'Ecclesiastical Liberty, Fraternity and Equality'. James Culross and Oliver Flett instituted an educational committee, and Hugh Rose of Dublin Street, Edinburgh, initiated a fund for aged and infirm ministers. Fifty-one churches were represented and were joined by others as the Union became established. The Scotch Baptist* churches were the last to join, although pastors and members co-operated.

Soon new churches were being founded in the industrial areas of Scotland. The Union worked for many years on a tiny budget, but provided a stimulus for action and expansion. The status of the ministry was enhanced, and in 1903 an accredited list of pastors was agreed. Sunday School and missionary work was fostered. Relations with the Baptist Home Missionary Society for Scotland were increasingly close and in 1931 the two bodies amalgamated.

Education for the ministry proved a contentious issue, with several options being strongly advocated (*see* MacGregor, Duncan). In 1894 those who favoured a college closely linked with, but independent of, the Union triumphed and the Baptist Theological College of Scotland was founded; but relations remained difficult, especially when the college was charged with modernism in the 1940s. More recently the two bodies have drawn much closer.

After both World Wars changes in population distribution led to the founding of new churches in outlying areas and the New Towns, and the closing of some older causes, especially in central Glasgow. The Union has had an uneasy relationship with the ecumenical movement*, and several churches have withdrawn since the 1950s, although the Union is no longer in the World Council of Churches. In Christian education, youth work and church extension, much has been achieved, and in 1988 the membership stood at 16,241.

D. B. Murray, *The First Hundred Years* (G, 1969); *id.*, 'Baptists in Scotland before 1869', *BQ* 23 (1970), 251–65; D. W. Bebbington (ed.), *The Baptists in Scotland* (G, 1988).

D. B. Murray

Baptists. Baptists in Scotland, although occasionally called Anabaptists by parish ministers in the *SAS*, were originally firmly within the Calvinist tradition. The Scottish Reformers were strongly committed to paedobaptism, and it was only with the arrival of English soldiers during the 1650s that Baptist teaching effectively reached Scotland. Some of the army chaplains took part in debates with ministers, and in the garrison towns congregations of Baptists gathered. There are records of baptisms at Bonnington Mill near Leith, and at Cupar, and traces of congregations at Perth, Ayr and Aberdeen. E. Hickhorngill* ministered at Leith, briefly. There were some native converts, some of whom were excommunicated, and others returned to the church after 1659. With the political changes of 1659/60, the churches vanished and it is not until 1750 that anything more than a stray reference to an individual is found. The Keiss* church, founded 1750 (*see* Sinclair, Sir William), remained isolated, and it is with the Scotch Baptists* in Lowland towns that growth began, from 1765. A. McLean's* visits and writings laid a firm foundation for this body.

In the early nineteenth century two other strains of church life began. The Haldanes* became Baptists in 1808, and many of their converts followed them. In the same decade the first 'English' churches began, two of the earliest being at Kilwinning (and later at Irvine), 1803 (*see* Barclay, George), and Charlotte Chapel, Edinburgh, 1808 (*see* Anderson, Christopher). Meanwhile Baptist evangelists were itinerating in Perthshire, the Highlands, the Inner Hebrides and the Northern Isles (*see* Baptist Home Missionary Society for Scotland). After 1869 most churches were brought together in the Baptist Union of Scotland,* and a denominational consciousness emerged.

Scottish Baptists have always supported the BMS and other foreign missionary work, and have been enthusiastic evangelists in Scotland. The world family of Baptists, grouped in the Baptist World Alliance, is especially strong in the USA, with strong churches in USSR, Burma, and the Commonwealth countries. Scottish Baptists have gained from worldwide contacts.

Baptist principles derive from a biblically based theology of the gathered Church. The churches have been fiercely independent, gradually learning over the years the value of co-operation, but the Union is a voluntary association of churches without legislative power. Most Scottish churches restrict membership to believers immersed, at their own desire, in the name of the Trinity. Some will admit believers baptized by a different mode, and several practise open membership, admitting all credible believers but practising only 'believer's baptism'. Open communion is almost universal. Baptists encourage freedom from state control and uphold Christian liberty and toleration. While willing to co-operate in evangelism and mission, they have often been suspicious of the ecumenical movement.* Most churches have a trained pastorate, which in Scotland, although not in England and Wales, is exclusively male.

R. G. Torbet, *A History of the Baptists* (L, 1966); D. W. Bebbington (ed.), *The Baptists in Scotland* (G, 1988).

D. B. Murray

Barbour, George Freeland, of Bonskeid (1882–1946), philosopher, theologian, biographer and landowner, one of the most prominent laymen of

BARBOUR, JOHN

his generation in Scotland. Son of Robert Barbour (*AFCS* I, 91), a close friend of Henry Drummond* and Sir George Adam Smith,* Barbour came from a FC and Quaker background (see memoir of mother, *Charlotte Barbour*, E, 1935). Educated at Edinburgh and Morrison's Academies and at Edinburgh University, his major philosophical work was done when he was still in his twenties. His life of Alexander Whyte,* his uncle by marriage and minister of Free St George's, Edinburgh, has remained a classic of its kind. A busy life of public and church work curtailed his writing thereafter, but he continued to publish biographical, religious and political studies and essays. He served on the Scottish Housing Commission (1912–17) and for many years on the Perthshire Education Authority; he was a keen forester, and was twice Liberal candidate for West Perth and Kinross. From 1921 he did much work for the League of Nations Union and the YMCA;* from 1927, the year of the Faith and Order Conference at Lausanne, he was active as a CofS representative in the ecumenical movement*. In 1938 he was one of the two laymen appointed to the committee for the institution of the World Council of Churches; but the war years took a heavy toll from him and he did not live to see its birth.

Brought up in a tradition of open-hearted piety, political liberalism and philosophical idealism, a belief in progress and an ardent internationalism, Barbour might be thought to have spent many years as an advocate of lost causes. But like his friend John Baillie* he appreciated new and less 'liberal' movements in theology and other realms without altogether embracing them. 'Aefauld' his biographer called him; a man who retained to the end his simplicity, humility and vivid interest in every aspect of the life of the Scottish people.

A Philosophical Study of Christian Ethics (E, 1911); *The Life of Alexander Whyte* (L, 1923); *The Ethical Approach to Theism* (E, 1913); *Essays and Addresses*, with a biographical introduction by A. F. Giles (E, 1949).

R. S. Barbour

Barbour, John (*d*.1395), poet and churchman. He was archdeacon of Aberdeen by 1357, when he acted as his Bishop's commissioner in discussions regarding payment of David II's* ransom. He had safe-conducts to travel to Oxford and elsewhere in the 1350s and 1360s. In 1372–3 he held financial office under Robert II, and by 1377 he was in receipt of a crown pension, probably for his literary achievements.

He wrote a number of important long poems. *The Brus* [*Bruce*] (1375) is a vivid account of the reign of Robert I,* based in part at least on eyewitness accounts of those who took part in Robert's campaigns. As a historical source up to 1330 it is immeasurably valuable. The *Buik of Alexander* is a more conventional literary romance. Some of Barbour's poems are now lost, including *Troy Book* and the *Ballet of the Nine Nobles*, imaginary romances, and *Stewartis Orygenale*, an attempt to concoct for

BARCLAY, JOHN

the new dynasty of the Stewarts an august ancestry traceable to Brutus the Trojan.

Barbour's verse is fresh, vigorous and rhythmical, capable of sustaining a high theme through long passages; his descriptions are vivid and lively. He expresses an exalted view of national and personal freedom which equates national subjection with serfdom. Views like his may help to explain the very different relations between nobility and peasantry in England and Scotland in the later Middle Ages.

Editions of *Bruce* by W. W. Skeat, Early English Text Society (L, 1870–89) and STS (E, 1894); by W. M. Mackenzie (L, 1909); by M. P. McDiarmid and J. A. C. Stevenson, STS (E, 1980–5); *Buik of Alexander*, STS, ed. R. L. G. Ritchie (E, 1925–9). Also sometimes attributed to Barbour are the *Legends of the Saints*, ed. W. M. Metcalfe (STS, E, 1896).

A. Macquarrie

Barclay, George (1774–1838), a pioneer of Baptist* home missionary activity. A native of Kilwinning with an Est.C background, Barclay joined the Haldane* movement, trained as an Independent preacher at classes in Dundee and Glasgow, and returned to work in his native district in April 1802. Becoming a Baptist, he founded a Baptist church in December 1803 on the 'English' single-pastor model (now Irivine Baptist Church). He influenced Christopher Anderson,* whom he met when in Edinburgh, and with whom he later established an itinerant* society. In 1823 he became the secretary of this society, reconstituted as the Baptist Evangelical Society of Scotland, a precursor of the Baptist Home Missionary Society for Scotland.* His church supported candidates for Baptist home mission, sending the first Scottish student to Bradford Baptist Academy in 1804. Barclay had a strong supportive interest in William Carey's mission to India. He wrote a number of books and pamphlets, including *Memoirs of James Neil, Shipmaster, Irvine* (Irvine, 1821), *Essays on Doctrinal and Prophetic Subjects* (E, 1828) and *Strictures on Two Sermons by the Rev. McLeod Campbell of Row* (1829).

A. B. Thomson, 'Some Baptist Pioneers in Scotland during the Eighteenth Century and the Early Years of the Nineteenth', *SBYB 1902*, 24–31; D. W. Bebbington (ed.), *The Baptists in Scotland* (G, 1988), 33–5, 135, 284.

D. E. Meek

Barclay, John (1734–98), founder of the Bereans. Born in Muthill, Perthshire, he studied at St Andrews University (MA, 1755), and took divinity in St Mary's College,* where he espoused the contentious views of Professor Archibald Campbell (1691–1756; *DNB* VIII, 340–1; *FES* VII, 431–2) concerning the exclusive validity of the Bible in human knowledge of God. In an excess of antideistic zeal, Campbell denied that any knowledge of God's existence could be derived from creation by fallen reason. Barclay developed this into a repudiation of the objective validity of general revelation; the knowledge of God was produced by God's

BARCLAY, JOHN

sovereign act through the Scriptures alone. This knowledge he defined as passive and intellectual in nature, along Sandemanian* lines.

Licensed to preach by the Presbytery of Auchterarder in 1759, Barclay's career as a CofS licentiate was mixed. His preaching as assistant at Fettercairn, Kincardine, 1763–72, attracted unprecedented crowds and produced a sober, small-scale revival.* However, in 1766 he came into conflict with the Presbytery of Fordoun for his *Paraphrase of the Book of Psalms*, in a prefatory essay to which he argued that the speaker in all first-person psalms is Christ, an opinion reaffirmed in his *Rejoice Evermore* (G, 1767), which contained 196 hymns based on Scripture passages. In 1769 he argued in *Without Faith, Without God* (L, 1836), for his views on general and special revelation, and in 1774 published a letter maintaining that assurance* of personal salvation was essential to saving faith (*The Assurance of Faith Vindicated*, E).

When the minister died in 1772 the parishioners of Fettercairn almost unanimously desired Barclay to succeed him, but the hostile Presbytery preferred another candidate who was eventually appointed after congregational appeals to Synod and General Assembly had failed. The Presbytery also refused Barclay a certificate of character. He appealed against their decision, but it was upheld by General Assembly in May 1773; whereupon Barclay and most of the Fettercairn congregation left the CofS. They formed an Independent* church in nearby Sauchieburn, but Barclay chose to minister to another group of sympathizers in Edinburgh. James MacRae became pastor of the Sauchieburn congregation (or assembly).

Barclay spent the years 1776–8 in London where he founded several assemblies, and one in Bristol. By the time of his death there were also assemblies in Glasgow, Laurencekirk, Stirling, Kirkcaldy, Crieff, Dundee, Arbroath, Montrose and Brechin. Some Berean assemblies also sprang up in America.

The name 'Bereans' (from Acts 17:11) was promoted by Barclay himself, although his followers were sometimes called 'Barclayans' or 'Barclayites'. Barclay's distinctive opinions were adopted by the movement, e.g. regarding the psalms, faith, assurance and general revelation. Otherwise Bereans maintained an orthodox Reformed theology; Barclay attacked the Old Scotch Independents* for abandoning the doctrine of Christ's eternal Sonship; see his *The Eternal Generation of the Son of God* (n.p., 1769; L, 1836). Bereans had a Congregational* and paedobaptist Church order, and sang Barclay's hymns in public worship – a popular innovation, contrasting with the then standard Scottish Reformed practice of exclusive psalmody. No formal theological training was provided for, or expected of, their ministers.

By the 1840s only four pastored assemblies survived, in Edinburgh, Glasgow, Laurencekirk and Dundee, and the movement died out soon afterwards. The original assembly at Sauchieburn became a regular Congregationalist* church in 1809, continuing into the 1940s.

BARCLAY, WILLIAM

The Psalms, Paraphrased According to the New Testament Interpretation (E, 1776); *The Experience and Example of the Lord Jesus Christ* (E, 1783); *Works*, 8 vols (G, 1852).

D. Thom, preface to 1836 edition of *The Eternal Generation of the Son of God;* Chambers-Thomson I, 84–7; *ERE* II, 519–23; H. Escott, *A History of Scottish Congregationalism* (G, 1959), 37–42; *DNB* III, 164–6; *FES* V, 462.

N. R. Needham

Barclay, Robert (1648–90), Quaker 'Apologist'. Robert Barclay's mother was a Gordon and third cousin of Charles I. His father, David Barclay (a soldier), turned to Quakerism (*see* Friends, Society of) while in prison for his Commonwealth sympathies. Robert, who was educated at the (RC) Scots College* in Paris, also became a Quaker and experienced frequent ridicule, persecution, imprisonment and fines for his principles and for holding 'unlawful' meetings. He had access to the King through his relatives and friendship with the Duke of York (later James VII*), whom he had probably met in Paris. He was also a friend of William Penn, and together they had influence at Court for freedom of worship for dissenters and especially Quakers. Robert became a proprietor and then Governor of the American colony of East Jersey. He helped Quakers and some persecuted Covenanters* to emigrate there. He is best known for his *Apology for the ... principles and doctrines of the people called Quakers*, still a highly regarded theological work amongst the Society of Friends, which had considerable influence in gaining respect for them and articulating their theology.

Apology for the true Christian Divinity (L, 1678; Latin 1676); 'Truth Triumphant' in *Collected Works*, 3 vols (L, 1718).

H. F. Barclay and A. Wilson-Fox, *History of the Barclay Family*, vol. 3 (L, 1934); D. E. Trueblood, *Robert Barclay* (NY and L, 1968).

O. R. Barclay

Barclay, William (*c*.1546–1608), legal and political writer. The son of Alexander Barclay of Gartly (Aberdeenshire), he studied at King's College, Aberdeen, Paris and Bourges, and was invited by his Jesuit uncle, Edmund Hay*, to teach civil law at the new university at Pont-à-Mousson in Lorraine. (His course on testaments survives in MS 106 in Epinal.) He married a Frenchwoman (1581), their son John (1582–1621, *DNB* III, 162–4) becoming a famous poet. In *De Regno et Regali Potestate* (Paris, 1600) Barclay criticized George Buchanan's* *De Iure Regni* for equating people's power with an élite's deposing power. James VI* enlisted Barclay's support for divine right theory. Besides legal treatises, his *De Potestate Papae* (L.?, 1609) attacked papal power in temporal matters, provoking a reply by Robert Bellarmine. After returning to England and Paris (1603–4), he became professor and dean of law at Angers and died there.

DNB III, 173–4; J. H. Burns, 'Some Catholic

Critics of George Buchanan', *IR* 1 (1950), 92–109; C. Collot, *L'Ecole doctrinale de droit public de Pont à Mousson* (Paris, 1965).

J. Durkan

Barclay, William (1907–78), biblical scholar and communicator. Born in Wick and educated at the universities of Glasgow and Marburg, he was ordained in the CofS* in 1933, and for fourteen years was minister of Trinity Church, Renfrew. He was then lecturer (1947–63) and professor (1963–74) of New Testament at Glasgow. During his ministry on industrial Clydeside Barclay revealed a gift of communicating with ordinary people which was to be used in a remarkably successful television series to bring Christianity into the nation's living rooms. Yet Barclay held that preaching should be biblically and credally centred. 'This is far from saying,' he wrote in his *Testament of Faith*, 'that preaching should never deal with the social, political and economic situation, but it is to say that it should start from the Christian book and the Christian belief.' He also stressed the importance of pastoral visitation, and lamented the virtual disappearance of church discipline.* He was a great encourager of students, not least of those more conservative than he, and a supporter of numerous Christian organizations such as the Boys' Brigade,* Sunday School* Union and Bible Society.*

Doctrinally he was a universalist who rejected the substitutionary view of the atonement.* He was reticent about the authority of Scripture, rejected the Virgin Birth, and regarded miracles as symbolic of what God can still do. He called himself a liberal Evangelical, but in some things regarded himself as ultra-conservative: he once said he was the only member of his divinity faculty who believed that Matthew, Luke and John had written the gospels attributed to them.

Barclay is best remembered for his Daily Study Bible series that covered all the New Testament books, has sold to date about 3.5 million copies in English, and has been translated into many languages (including Estonian and Burmese). This project brought him a vast correspondence from all over the world. He had planned to complete the Old Testament also, but had barely begun the work when increasing ill health thwarted its progress. He was made CBE in 1969. Barclay's writing output was extensive. Among his many publications were *Ambassador for Christ* (E, 1950); *The Mind of St Paul* (G, 1957); *Many Witnesses, One Lord* (L, 1963); *A New Testament Wordbook* (L, 1964); *A New People's Life of Jesus* (L, 1965); *God's Young Church* (E, 1970); *Ethics in a Permissive Society* (E, 1972); *The Plain Man's Guide to Ethics* (G, 1973); *By What Authority* (L, 1974); *Testament of Faith* (autobiographical) (O, 1975).

R. D. Kernohan (ed.), *William Barclay* (L, 1980); C. L. Rawlins, *William Barclay* (Exeter, 1984); J. Martin, *William Barclay* (E, 1984).

J. D. Douglas

Barr, Elizabeth Brown (1905–), the first woman to be ordained as a Presbyterian* minister in Scotland. Daughter of James Barr,* she was educated at Glasgow University (MA, 1925) and was initially a schoolteacher in Glasgow (1926–30). Following training at the UFC College, Edinburgh (1930–3), she was ordained (1935) to the UF church which she had begun serving the previous year (Auchterarder, 1934–43). Further ministries followed at Clydebank (1943–55), Glasgow Central (1955–68) and Miller Memorial, Glasgow (1966–75). Miss Barr became Moderator of the General Assembly of the UFC in 1960 – the first woman Moderator of a Scottish Presbyterian Church.

UFCS Handbook (G, 1989), 4, 23; Glasgow University Register of Graduates.

D. E. Meek

Barr, James (1862–1949), Christian socialist and evangelist. Leader of the UFC minority which refused to enter the 1929 union with the CofS, he was Labour MP for Motherwell and Wishaw, 1924–31, and for Coatbridge and Airdrie, 1935–45.

Born near Kilmarnock, Barr graduated from Glasgow University in philosophy (MA, 1884), then studied for the ministry of the FC at the FC College, Glasgow. While in his first charge at Wamphray, Dumfriesshire, he completed the BD of Glasgow University. While serving Dennistoun FC (UFC), Glasgow (1896–1907), and St Mary's, Govan UFC (1907–20), he reached out to large numbers of unchurched working-class men in a way rare in nineteenth- or twentieth-century Scotland. In 1920 he became Secretary of the Home Board of the UF church. After the 1929 Union* he remained in the UFC (Moderator 1929 and 1943).

Pacifism,* temperance,* the abolition of capital punishment and 'Home Rule' for Scotland were the essential elements in his political life, which was rooted in his evangelistic concern. He believed the Kirk's integration with the social and political establishment of the day and its accommodation of class privilege were serious barriers between the people and the gospel.

The magazine of St Mary's UFC, Govan, 1907–20, is the best source for his ideas; his autobiography, *Lang Syne* (G, 1949), is less helpful.

The United Free Church of Scotland (L, 1934); *Christianity and War* (L, 1903); *The Scottish Covenanters* (G, 1946).

AFCS I, 82; *FUFCS* 571; *Who Was Who, 1941–1950*, 64; A. Bogle, 'James Barr, B.D., M.P.', *RSCHS* 21 (1983), 189–207; W. H. Marwick, 'James Barr: Modern Covenanter', *Scott. Journ. of Science* 1 (1973), 183–98.

A. C. Ross

Barratry, the offence of corruptly purchasing ecclesiastical offices or benefices. Derived from the French for 'bartering, cheating', it appeared first in the reign of James I (1406–37) in enactments banning unauthorized resort to Rome, which sought to restrict the export of money and control the movements of churchmen. Despite papal protests, the legislation remained in force, but barrators remained active, and James III* passed similar enactments. The Reformation Parliament* in 1560 condemned any who continued to acknowledge the jurisdiction of Rome to the penalties for barratry. The term also acquired wider meanings, *e.g.* the perversion of judicial verdicts by bribery.

See also Simony.

W. C. Dickinson *et al.* (eds), *A Source Book of Scottish History*, II (E, ²1958), 83–7.

D. F. Wright

Barrier Act (1697). After the Presbyterian form of government had been restored to the CofS by Act of Parliament with the accession of King William* in 1689, General Assemblies again met yearly. The 1697 Assembly brought in an Act 'Concerning innovation', 'to prevent any sudden alteration or innovation . . . in either doctrine, worship or discipline or government thereof . . .' 'Before any General Assembly of this Church shall pass any Acts which are to be binding Rules and Constitution to the Church', they were 'to be remitted to the consideration of the several Presbyteries of this Church' and 'their opinion and consent reported to the next General Assembly'. This is commonly called the Barrier Act (*AGACS* 260–1).

Delegating power from the superior court to the inferior, it was astonishing for its day and peculiar to Scottish Presbyterianism. Wherever Scottish Presbyterianism has had any influence the Barrier Act or a similar measure is to be found.

In the modern CofS, it is in constant use. The FCS, though less frequently, uses the Act from time to time. The UFC, the FPC and the RPC, though they have never used the Act, retain it as part of their constitutions.

The prevailing modern approach to the Act is that it arose from the enlightened influence of William and his advisers. But the Act itself refers to 'the frequent practice of former Assemblies of This Church'. It claims precedents. In 1639, to find the mind of the Church and to prevent 'innovations', the Assembly of that year introduced what was in all respects a Barrier Act. This was supplemented in 1641, and the Act continued in use until the Restoration* of Charles II* in 1660. These were 'the frequent practice of former Assemblies' appealed to by the Assembly of 1697.

The question then arises as to the ultimate inspiration of this Act. Claim can be made to an influence from Scottish constitutional law of the later middle ages. The Scottish government in the fifteenth century was markedly decentralized in comparison with European governments, with the practice of the Estates conferring with districts as to the suitability of proposed legislation.

Though the Act has been in general use in the churches in Scotland, its meaning and authority were never defined until the Free Church case.* In 1900, the majority in the FC united with the UPs. A minority did not and claimed to be the true continuing FC. Property and funds were in question. The case eventually came before the House of Lords in 1904 (*Bannatyne v Overtoun* 1904). Each side claimed, among other principles, the support of the Barrier Act – the majority that the Act allowed them to change their constitution and practice, the minority that the Act was there to prevent such 'innovations'. The House of Lords found for the minority. Lord Darey stated: 'That Act is a procedure Act, not an enabling Act.'

See also Innovations.

AGACS (as cited); Cox 385; *An Abridgement of the Acts of the Parliament in Scotland (1424–1707)* (E, 1841); W. Mair, *A Digest of Laws . . . Relating to . . . the Church of Scotland* (²E, 1923); A. Taylor-Innes, *The Law of Creeds in Scotland* (²E, 1902); D. H. MacNeill, *The Scottish Realm: An Approach to the Political and Constitutional History of Scotland* (G, 1947).

A. L. Walker

Barron, Robert, *see* Aberdeen Doctors.

Barthianism, *see* Neo-Orthodoxy.

Bass Rock, an island in the Firth of Forth about one and a quarter miles from the nearest land and three miles east-north-east of North Berwick, some 400 feet high and a mile in circumference. It was long used as a fortress and a prison and is best known in connection with the Covenanters* imprisoned there between 1672 and 1687. Purchased for use as a state prison in 1671, the Bass was appropriately garrisoned and at least thirty-nine Covenanters, mostly ministers, were imprisoned for such crimes as keeping conventicles.* The conditions there were substantially worse than average, even for the deplorable standards of the time. Among those so imprisoned were John Blackadder,* James Fraser of Brea* and Alexander Peden.*

T. M'Crie, Hugh Miller, James Anderson *et al.*, *The Bass Rock: its Civil and Ecclesiastic History . . . Geology . . . Martyrology . . .* (E, 1847).

D. C. Lachman

Bassendyne Bible, the first complete Bible published in Scotland, a reprint of the second (1562) edition of the Geneva Bible (*see* Bible (Versions, English)). A licence to print it had been granted to Robert Lekprevik in 1568, but had not been used. The Bassendyne Bible was published in Edinburgh in 1579 by Alexander Arbuthnot (possibly Arbuthnet), 'Printer to the Kingis Maiestie'; his associate Thomas Bassendyne, a Scot educated in Antwerp and trained in Leiden and Paris, had died earlier that year. In March 1575 the project had been approved by the General Assembly, which required each parish to pay £4.13s.4d in advance for a copy 'weel and sufficiently bund in paste or trimmer'. Bassendyne's name, with the date 1576, appears on the New Testament title page. Work on the Old Testament was delayed by disputes between Bassendyne, the compositor Salomon Kerknett of Magdeburg, and Arbuthnot. In 1579, the

Scots Parliament ordered every householder, yeoman or burgess of substance to have a copy of the Bible and Psalter 'in the vulgar language' in his house, on pain of fine. In the tradition of the Geneva Bible, the Bassendyne Bible contained copious reader's helps. The title page includes a dedication to 'Iames the Sext King of Scottis'.

[John Lee], *Memorial for the Bible Societies in Scotland* (E, 1824), 28–45; J. Eadie, *The English Bible* (L, 1876), II.43–51; W. T. Dobson, *History of the Bassendyne Bible* (E, 1887); A. S. Herbert, *Historical Catalogue of Printed Editions of the English Bible, 1525–1961* (L and NY, 1968), 88f.

P. Ellingworth

Bathan, *see* Celtic Saints.

Bayne, Margaret (1798–1835), wife of John Wilson (*see* Missions: India), Bombay missionary, pioneer of female education in India and inspirer of the first Scottish association to employ female missionaries. Born in Greenock and educated there and in Kilmarnock and Aberdeen, she was renowned for her learning and brilliant intellect. She married John Wilson in 1828. Within six months of their arrival in Bombay, and in the face of local prejudice, she had established six schools for Indian low- and outcaste girls. She later opened the first female boarding school in Western India. Until her death, she superintended the schools and trained teachers. A gifted linguist, she wrote textbooks, biographies and theological reviews for the Indian language press, and managed the general concerns of the mission during her husband's long absences. He described her work as 'no less rare and marvellous than estimable and exemplary' (J. Wilson, *A Memoir of Mrs Margaret Wilson*..., E, 1838).

Margaret Bayne quickly discerned the need for a distinctive mission to the women of India, which could only be engaged in by other women. She pleaded with her sisters to join her: 'Our whole hearts are set upon your coming to India ... Pious, well-principled ladies might do immense good ... Female society is so far from being so pure or so influential as it ought to be.' Bayne's pioneer work and witness at the beginning of the Scottish missionary enterprise helped to establish that women as well as men should share in the responsibilities and opportunities of spreading the gospel abroad. In 1837, Anna and Hay Bayne went to India to continue their sister's work; and inspired by her example, the Edinburgh Association of Ladies for the Advancement of Female Education in India was formed on 10 March 1837.

D. P. Thomson, *Women of the Scottish Church* (Perth, 1975), 181–92; E. G. K. Hewat, *Christ and Western India* (Bombay, 1950).

L. O. Macdonald

Beadle, church officer appointed by the Kirk Session* of a congregation in the CofS and other Presbyterian Churches as the personal attendant of the minister at services of worship. His is an old, responsible and honourable office, as the 'minister's man' and responsible for opening and closing the church. In earlier days, since he held the keys of the church, he was also responsible to the heritors* who had the care of the building, and then his appointment was properly made by heritors and elders. The beadle was often also the grave-digger in the churchyard. In the days when the Kirk Session disciplined members for sabbath-breaking and sexual impropriety, it was his duty to summon the parties to appear.

The beadle should be a member of the congregation in full communion and, if required, ought to be in attendance at meetings of the Kirk Session and also at meetings of the congregational board, deacons' court or board of management. His duty today is to bring in the Bible and other books to the pulpit and remove them after the service, to prepare water and napkin for baptisms, to assist in arranging the Communion tables and generally to superintend arrangements for public worship. His salary comes from congregational funds and any fees agreed at the time of his appointment.

J. M. Duncan and C. N. Johnston, *The Parochial Ecclesiastical Law of Scotland* (E, 1903); Cox 32, 34, 37–8, 43, 45, 119, 124; D. P. Thomson, *The Beadle Yesterday and Today* (Crieff, 1971).

A. I. Dunlop

Beaton, David (?1494–1546), Cardinal and Archbishop of St Andrews. From the family of Beaton of Balfour, Fife, he had an outstanding career in Church and state. Having studied at St Andrews and Glasgow universities, he proceeded to that of Orleans and then began his political career at the French court in the patronage of the French-born Duke of Albany, Governor of Scotland in the years after Flodden. He became Commendator* of Arbroath* in 1524, Bishop of Mirepoix, on Francis I's nomination, in 1537, a Cardinal in 1538 and Archbishop of St Andrews in succession to his uncle James Beaton* in 1539. In 1544 Pope Paul III made him Legate *a latere* in Scotland. Seven times between 1533 and 1542 he acted as Scottish ambassador to France, negotiating James V's* successive marriages to Princess Madeleine (1537) and Mary of Guise* (1538), and was made a French citizen.

His main preoccupations at home were with the maintenance of the Franco-Scottish alliance and the intimidation of increasingly articulate heretical opinions which were often combined with Anglophile political attitudes: 'the whole pollution and plague of Anglican impiety', as he called it. As a careerist prelate, he saw criticism of the Church as undermining her public authority and was afraid that, like Henry VIII, James V might lay hands on monastic revenues. Although he periodically prosecuted heretics* he failed to catch the most influential Anglophile-reformists, some of whom held government office and were among his own tenants in Fife and Angus. In 1544 Henry VIII became privy to a plot by some of them to kill him.

The Cardinal staunchly adhered to the French alliance and maintained an implacable antipathy to

England. He was blamed for the war policy that led to the defeat of Solway Moss in 1542. He was temporarily removed from power in a coup following the death of James V, during which the Anglophile party and Reformers encouraged the Governor, the Earl of Arran (*see* Hamilton, James, c.1516–75) to make a marriage treaty with England on behalf of the infant Queen Mary* and to appoint a number of Protestant preachers. On regaining power in 1543 Beaton had the treaty cancelled and carried out the prosecution of a number of heretics. He was blamed for the two English invasions that followed and for the failure of a Scottish invasion of England with French help in 1545. In order to revive his prestige he staged the arrest, trial and execution of the Reformer George Wishart* in March 1546. The resentment of those who had sympathized with Wishart, as well as private quarrels with some Fife lairds, led to the assassination of the Cardinal soon afterwards in his own castle at St Andrews. In international circles it was widely believed that his death had been in the interest of Henry VIII, who had long regarded him as the chief obstacle to his ambitions in Scotland.

The Cardinal gave little sign of being seriously interested in the internal reform of the Church. Like many prelates of his day he lived in open concubinage and provided lavishly for his family and the mother of his children from ecclesiastical and secular property. Some saw his stance against Henry VIII as patriotic while others remembered the extent of his own interests and material assets in France, calling him 'the best Frenchman' in Scotland.

M. H. B. Sanderson, *Cardinal of Scotland, David Beaton, c.1494–1546* (E, 1986); J. Herkless and R. K. Hannay, *The Archbishops of St Andrews*, IV (E, 1913).

M. H. B. Sanderson

Beaton, Donald (1872–1953), author and minister of the Free Presbyterian Church.* A native of Stirlingshire, he studied at Glasgow University. While a student for the ministry, he left the Free Church* after the passing of the Declaratory Act* in 1892 and joined the FPC at its inception in 1893. His first pastoral charge was at Wick where he was ordained in 1901. From 1930 until his resignation due to ill-health in 1948 he was minister of the Oban FP congregation.

Beaton served his Church as a theological tutor for many years and was a distinguished Clerk both of the Northern Presbytery and of the Church's supreme court, the Synod. For long periods he edited his Church's two journals, the *FP Magazine* and the *Young People's Magazine*. During his ministry he made several overseas trips on the Church's behalf, visiting the USA, Canada, Australia and New Zealand.

A respected scholar, Beaton wrote numerous books, mainly in the area of church history, and contributed substantial articles to learned journals including the *Princeton Theological Review* and the *RSCHS*. Among other published works were *Ec-*

clesiastical History of Caithness (Wick, 1909), *Some Foundation Truths of the Reformed Faith* (L, 1938), *Noted Ministers of the Northern Highlands* (1929; G, 1985), *History of the Free Presbyterian Church of Scotland* (ed., Inverness, 1933), *Memoir . . . of the Rev Donald Macfarlane** (ed., Inverness, 1929), *Memoir . . . of the Rev Neil Cameron** (ed., Inverness, 1932).

A. MacPherson (ed.), *History of the Free Presbyterian Church of Scotland 1893–1970* (Inverness, 1974).

A. Morrison

Beaton, James (c.1480–1539), Archbishop of Glasgow (1509–23) and of St Andrews (1523–39). A son of the laird of Balfour, Fife, he was educated at St Andrews University and held various benefices at an early age including the abbacies of Dunfermline* and Arbroath,* two of the richest monasteries in Scotland. He also held the government offices of Treasurer (1505) and Chancellor (1513). During James V's* minority (1513–28) and the ascendancy of the Anglophile Douglas family he championed the traditional Franco-Scottish alliance. He later led the clerical opposition to the King's 'great tax' of the Church, ostensibly to endow the civil court, but gave in for fear that James would lay hands directly on Church property. Said to have been lukewarm as a prosecutor of heretics, he nevertheless presided at several heresy trials* including that of Patrick Hamilton* in 1528. He used his patronage to advance the careers of his nephews, the most notable of whom was David Beaton,* who followed him as Archbishop of St Andrews in 1539.

J. Herkless and R. K. Hannay, *The Archbishops of St Andrews*, III (E, 1910).

M. H. B. Sanderson

Beaton, James (c.1524–1603), Archbishop of Glasgow. Of a well-known landed family in Fife, he studied in his teens at Paris and Poitou; then, returning to Scotland, he took minor orders and in 1546 succeeded his uncle, Cardinal David Beaton,* as abbot of Arbroath* (Tironensian*). In 1551, aged twenty-seven, he was appointed Archbishop of Glasgow* and in 1552 he received at Rome major orders and episcopal consecration. From 1553 he was a privy councillor. His policy was consistently pro-Catholic: he supported the provincial council* of 1558–9 and the Catholic regent, Mary of Guise.*

In 1560, after being with the French forces besieged in Leith, he went to France, taking with him treasures and muniments from Glasgow Cathedral.* For over forty years he was ambassador there for Mary, Queen of Scots,* and James VI.* He supported Scots Catholic students in Paris at Mary's expense and his own, and co-operated with efforts to restore Catholicism in Scotland. When he died in 1603, the last Scots Catholic bishop, he bequeathed a house and his whole estate to establish what became the Scots College* in Paris.

Beaton remained undisputed Archbishop of Glasgow 1560–70 and after Archbishop James Boyd's* death in 1581 gradually regained favour. Restored to the see in 1598, he remained abroad. He retained a reputation for probity in France and, despite his uncompromising Catholicism, in Scotland also.

M. Dilworth, 'Archbishop James Beaton II: a Career in Scotland and France', *RSCHS* 23 (1989), 301–16; Dowden, 349–52; [C. Eyre], *A Memoir of Archbishop James Beaton* (G, 1891).

M. Dilworth

Beauly, *see* Early Ecclesiastical Sites.

Bede (672/3–735), early English historian, hagiographer and commentator. Born probably near Jarrow in Northumbria, he was placed in religious life aged seven and soon thereafter entered the monastery of Jarrow, where he was to spend his life. He showed early promise as a scholar, and 'loved to learn or teach or write'. His literary production included commentaries on many books of the Bible, lives of the abbots of Jarrow, and prose and verse lives of St Cuthbert (*see* Celtic Saints). These latter are based upon an earlier anonymous life and show not only Bede's hagiographical method, but also the 'improvements' he could introduce, so that a Pictish* people in Fife, *Niuduera* (= Nith people), became the (classicised) *Niduarii*.

The Northumbrian church in Bede's lifetime was in close contact with Gaul and Italy and boasted libraries with both Christian and pagan classics. It produced four great biblical manuscripts of which the best known is the Lindisfarne Gospels, an 'Italian' text with superb 'Celtic' illumination, produced at the episcopal seat of Lindisfarne. This had been founded in 634, when, at the request of King Oswy, Aidan was sent from Iona* to be bishop of the Northumbrians (*see* Celtic Saints; Early Ecclesiastical Sites).

Bede's masterpiece, his *Ecclesiastical History of the Race of Angles*, completed in 731, followed earlier works on time, stimulated by the lack of uniformity within the Church in the calculation of Easter. Bede was a strong proponent of the Dionysian 532-year Easter cycle, which, under the influence of Greek popes, was accepted in Rome in the mid-seventh century, when more northerly churches used the Victorice cycle, and a residue of the Irish Church, including Iona, used a yet older 84-year-old cycle (*see* Christian Year). In 664 a council at Whitby* accepted the Dionysian Easter for Northumbria, and the dissenting minority left Lindisfarne for Iona (and eventually Inishbotin in Ireland), in order to adhere to the way of Columba* (*see* Celtic Church). The 'family' of Iona and its daughters, with the Welsh Church, in Bede's eyes, were a stain on the unity of observance necessary to make the Church catholic.

His *History*, modelled on the Bible, Eusebius and Gregory of Tours, was cast in five books, the first four of which deal with the peoples of Britain, the conversion through Augustine's mission, including its offshoot at York, the activities of Irish missionaries in England, the council at Whitby, the weakness of the Church in the south and its revival under Theodore and Hadrian, ending with the death of Cuthbert in 687. Hostile throughout to the Welsh Church because it made no effort to convert the Anglo-Saxons, Bede is significantly warmer in his attitude to Columba, 'distinguished by the life and habit of a monk', and his successors, 'distinguished for their great abstinence, their love of God, and their observance of the Rule'. He excuses their use of 'tables of doubtful accuracy in fixing the date of the chief festival because they were so far away at the ends of the earth'.

Bede sees Columba not as a pilgrim for God but as the missionary sent to convert the Picts, and so he immediately introduces us to Ninian* in a passage which is really our only literary source for that saint; a long time before, he claims, Ninian had converted the southern Picts. But epigraphic evidence suggests that in the fifth century Christianity spread only *south* of the Forth–Clyde line, perhaps under temporary Pictish control – or perhaps Bede misunderstood 'southern' in his source when he took it to refer to Picts. As he also says, 'the Picts . . . had received the faith of Christ through the preaching of the monks [of Iona]'. Unfortunately he never names any daughter monastery of Iona among the Picts, and the sites of such houses are unknown.

The fifth book of the *History* is a much less structured compilation, designed to carry the story forward to the second great triumph of catholicity, its acceptance (in the calculation of Easter) by the Picts soon after 710, and by Iona in 716, after what Bede calculated was 150 years of error from the foundation of Iona (wrongly placed in 565, not 563). The latter achievement, Bede knew, was the work of an Englishman, Egbert, brought up in Ireland, whom Bede honours by more striking epithets than those given to any other figure in the *History*.

But Bede consistently sees Iona through Pictish eyes, and shows himself remarkably well informed about Pictish society and rulers. He gives an origin legend of the Picts (including a version of 'matriliny'), but not of the Britons or Irish, ascribes the grant of Iona (to Columba) wrongly to a Pictish king, and quotes in full the reply from his abbot in response to a request from a Pictish king for instruction in catholic practices. It has been argued that all Bede's knowledge of Iona and the Picts comes from that letter of request, and that it was penned by Egbert, who is known to have been among the Picts in 712 and was responsible for converting them to the Dionysian Easter. The traditional and alternative view, that Bede learned of Iona from the tradition preserved at Lindisfarne, does not explain the pervasive Pictishness of his understanding.

At Easter 729 he celebrates the saintly death of Egbert, through whom God's purpose of converting the island of Britain to catholic faith was consummated; the remainder of Book Five is but a few desultory jottings.

Bede wrote on a framework of years calculated from the incarnation, a system which he did not invent but which undoubtedly spread into general use from his work; it alone made the writing of history possible as a secular exercise.

See also Anglo-Saxon Saints; Celtic Church; Monasticism, Celtic; Early Ecclesiastical Sites.

B. Colgrave and R. A. B. Mynors (eds), *Bede's Ecclesiastical History of the English People* (O, ²1992); A. A. M. Duncan, 'Bede, Iona and the Picts', *The Writing of History in the Middle Ages*, ed. R. H. C. Davis and J. M. Wallace-Hadrill (O, 1981), 1–42; J. M. Wallace-Hadrill, *Bede's Ecclesiastical History of the English People; a Historical Commentary* (O, 1988).

A. A. M. Duncan

Begg, James (1808–83), FC minister and churchman. Son of the parish minister of New Monkland, Lanarkshire, he was educated at Glasgow University, ordained at Maxwelltown, Dumfries, 1830, and translated to Lady Glenorchy's, Edinburgh (1830), then to Middle Parish Church, Paisley, 1831, and again to Liberton, near Edinburgh, 1835. A prominent Non-Intrusionist,* he took part in the Disruption* in 1843 and for the rest of his life was minister of Newington FC, Edinburgh. He was Moderator of the FC General Assembly in 1865. He founded the Scottish Reformation Society* and the Protestant Institute of Scotland* (*see* Anti-Catholic Societies) and launched and for twenty-one years edited the *Bulwark, or Reformation Journal*. He also edited the *Watchword** and the *Signal*, organs of the Constitutionalist* party within the FC of which Begg was the acknowledged leader. His works include: *Free Church Principles* (E, 1869); *Purity of Worship* (E, 1876); *A Handbook of Popery* (E, 1852); *Happy Homes for Working Men* (E, 1873); *Memorial in regard to the Constitution of the Free Church of Scotland* (E, 1874); *The Headship of Christ* (E, 1860); *National Education* (E, 1850); *The Use of Organs and other Instruments of Music in Christian Worship Indefensible* (G, 1866).

Begg rose to prominence as a right-hand man to Chalmers* during the Church Extension* and Non-Intrusion campaigns of the 1830s. He shared Chalmers' vision of a godly commonwealth sustained by an effective parochial system and carried that vision into a later period when it appeared anachronistic. Indeed it was his continued loyalty to the 'Establishment principle' which first signalled the opening of a rift between Begg and the later FC majority, which came to view Church and state more eclectically. However, differences over Union with the UPC, the Disestablishment* campaign and the use of hymns and organs in public worship reflected the basic difference between Begg's belief in a Church firmly tied to its constitution and the majority view in favour of the Church's liberty in regard to non-fundamentals. He maintained that to retain her identity the FC had to stand by the doctrine and practice enshrined in the Disruption documents.

Begg's identification with doctrinal and constitutional conservatism, together with his tireless anti-Romanism, has tended to obscure his earlier reputation as a radical social reformer. His robust Calvinism* involved commitment to a just social order. Campaigning for better conditions for working people, his concerns included housing, sanitation, land-law reform, education and devolution. He stood out as neither scholar nor preacher, but was distinguished among the FC leaders as an outstanding orator. 'What made him great was that he had something of the old heroic strain, a kinship with those who loved not their lives to the death,' remarked Robertson Nicoll.* For fifty years his abilities were employed in the interests of a combination of social radicalism and ecclesiastical conservatism which has puzzled modern commentators, but which may be identified as an authentic strand in Scotland's Calvinistic heritage.

See also Constitutionalists; Musical instruments in worship.

DNB IV, 127–8; *FES* I, 173; T. Smith, *Memoirs of James Begg*, 2 vols (E, 1885, 1888); P. C. Simpson, *The Life of Principal Rainy*, 2 vols (L, 1909); W. R. Nicoll, *Princes of the Church* (L, 1921), 12–15.

K. R. Ross

Beggars' Summons, The (1559), a broadsheet modelled on an English precedent, secretly printed, and nailed to the doors of Scottish friaries in January 1559 or earlier. In pseudo-legal language it warned the friars to quit their dwellings in favour of the truly poor.

As trained preachers, the friars* were leading opponents of Scottish Protestants. Initially part of a propaganda campaign, the Summons set a timetable for popular reformation by threatening forced eviction after Whitsun 1559. Mary of Guise's* pre-emptive strike after Easter against the Protestant preachers provoked the Reformation* crisis during which many friaries were in fact destroyed.

Knox, *History* II, 255–6; J. Durkan, 'The Care of the Poor: Pre-Reformation Hospitals', *IR* 10 (1959), 268–80; I. B. Cowan, *The Scottish Reformation* (L, 1983), 44–8, 111–20.

F. D. Bardgett

Belfrage, Henry (1774–1835), Associate Synod* minister and writer. Born at Falkirk, Stirlingshire, he attended Edinburgh University from 1786, and began studying theology in 1789 under George Lawson* at the Associate Divinity Hall in Selkirk. In 1794 he was ordained as colleague and successor to his father in the Associate congregation in Falkirk, where he ministered until his death. He helped found a ragged school in Falkirk in 1812, and a Sunday school (*see* Ragged Schools; Sunday School Movement).

Belfrage's many religious writings placed him on a pinnacle of high esteem among Evangelicals of his day. His *Practical Exposition of the Assembly's Shorter Catechism* (1832; ²enlarged, 2 vols, 1834) was particularly popular in Scotland and America.

Belfrage received a DD from St Andrews University in 1824 by the good offices of Sir Henry Moncrieff Wellwood.*

Practical Discourses (E, 1818); *Sacramental Addresses and Meditations* (E, 1815); *Select Essays* (Berwick,

1832); *History of the Assembly's Shorter Catechism* (E, 1834); *Memoir of Alexander Waugh* (E, 1839); *A Portrait of Job* (E, 1830); *The Sacred Fount Opened; or, Baptism Explained* (Berwick, 1836); *Sketches of Life and Character* (E, 1828).

J. M'Kerrow, *Life and Character of Henry Belfrage* (E, 1837); *DNB* IV, 147–8.

N. R. Needham

Believing Criticism, the acceptance of biblical 'higher criticism' by pious scholars in Scotland in the later nineteenth century.

This period saw the gradual diffusion among Evangelicals of approaches to biblical history and literature common on the continent yet more typically associated with rationalistic and 'unbelieving' criticism. There emerged a growing minority within the mainstream Churches who sought to retain both piety and substantial orthodoxy while accepting some version of the critical reconstruction of the Bible. They then adapted traditional doctrines of the inspiration and authority of Scripture accordingly. The emergence of this middle party between openly rationalistic critics and conventional, conservative rejection gave the new thinking credibility. This was a crucial development in the dissemination of the critical approach to Scripture within the conservative piety of nineteenth-century Scotland, and especially within the FC. Indeed, it was in the FC that it made most progress, since that was where the leading 'critics' were to be found.

A. B. Davidson* is widely credited with decisive influence on this development, as the 'power behind the throne' (George Adam Smith*). His pupil William Robertson Smith,* a brilliant orientalist and Old Testament scholar, brought the debate dramatically into the open. George Adam Smith, like the other Smith the subject of heresy* proceedings, sought consciously to articulate the struggle between old and new approaches: 'Modern criticism has won its war against the traditional theories. It only remains to fix the amount of the indemnity' (*Modern Criticism*, L, 1901, 72). The conversion of such able leaders of the FC to the continental methods created peculiar difficulties for conservatives who wished to argue for the fundamental incompatibility of these approaches with evangelical orthodoxy. Thomas Carlyle* wryly observed, 'Have my countrymen's heads become turnips when they think they can hold the premises of German unbelief and draw the conclusions of Scottish Evangelical Orthodoxy?'

R. A. Riesen, *Criticism and Faith in Late Victorian Scotland: A. B. Davidson, William Robertson Smith and George Adam Smith* (Lanham, MD, 1985); John Macleod, *Scottish Theology* (E, ³1974); N. R. Needham, *The Doctrine of Scripture in the Free Church Fathers* (E, 1991); Nigel M. de S. Cameron, *Biblical Higher Criticism and the Defense of Infallibilism in Nineteenth Century Britain* (Lewiston, NY, 1987).

N. M. de S. Cameron

Bell, Thomas (1733–1802), influential Relief* minister and author. Born in Moffat, he was educated at the University of Edinburgh and, when a student of theology there, joined the Relief Church as a matter of principle. He was ordained to Jedburgh in 1768, the year after the death of the younger Thomas Boston,* his predecessor. In 1776 he was called to Dovehill in Glasgow and, after being refused translation by the Synod in two successive years (out of concern for the Jedburgh congregation), went of his own accord. In 1780, after a time of separation, he and the congregation applied for and were granted readmission to the Presbytery. With one exception, the Relief Church never again exercised its authority to prohibit a minister from accepting a call.

Bell took an active part in the controversies of his day, preaching a course of sermons (*The Standard of the Spirit lifted up against the enemy . . .* , G, 1780) against the errors of 'popery', which helped prevent the repeal of the penal statutes against RCs. In response to William McGill's* *Practical Essay on the Death of Christ*, Bell translated a Dutch work on *The Satisfaction of Christ* by Peter Allinga (G, 1790; Utrecht, 1676), thinking thereby to cut 'the Sinews of Socinianism', and then a work by a Professor at Leiden, Dionysius Van de Wynpersse, *A Proof of the True and Eternal Godhead of our Lord Jesus Christ; against Modern Attacks* (E, 1795; The Hague, 1792). He opposed without success the introduction of paraphrases* and hymns* into the worship in the Relief Church, submitting a dissent and a paper to the Synod.

Two posthumous collections of his works were published: *Sermons . . .* (G, 1803) and *A View of the Covenants of Works and Grace and A Treatise on the Nature and Effects of Saving Faith* (G, 1814). He also translated Herman Witsius, *Conciliatory, or Irenical Animadversions, on the Controversies agitated in Britain, under the unhappy names of Antinomians and Neonomians* (G, 1807; Latin, Utrecht, 1696).

Small II, 260–1, 33–4; G. Struthers, *The History of the Rise, Progress, and Principles of the Relief Church* (G, 1843).

D. C. Lachman

Benedictines. St Benedict of Nursia (*c*.480–547) established several small monasteries at Monte Cassino (S. Italy) and composed a Rule for them. He deliberately turned away from the semi-eremitical and individualistic life-style of the Eastern monks, instituting instead an ordered and moderate life in community. The Rule envisages no specific enterprise; the chief activity is the communal choir office and the day is divided between prayer in public and private, *lectio* (reading aimed at spiritual formation) and work. The monks elect their abbot for life and owe him obedience, while he is to consult them on important matters.

The Rule was gradually accepted almost universally. There was great diversity between monasteries and each was more or less autonomous. Attempts were made in various places to reform and standardize observance, leading in the tenth to twelfth centuries to centralized groups of houses.

BEREANS

Some, such as Cluniacs* and Tironensians,* were still considered Benedictine (*see* Monastic Orders, Medieval). In 1215 the Fourth Lateran Council ordered 'black monks' (mainstream Benedictines, from the colour of their habits) to unite and meet regularly in general chapters.

As monasteries grew rich and their abbots became feudal lords, they became the target of ambition and greed. The papacy assumed the right of provision (appointing abbots) and in various regions commendators* were appointed; these were men given control of monasteries without being themselves monks. Some groups of Benedictines, from the fifteenth century on, resisted such encroachment by relinquishing abbatial dignity and establishing rule by general chapter. The Council of Trent (1545–63) decreed that monasteries were to arrange chapters and visitations among themselves; this led to the formation of homogeneous groups called congregations.

The Enlightenment and the French Revolution extinguished monastic life in most of Europe. From the mid-nineteenth century, however, Benedictines have expanded world-wide. Even now they do not constitute a religious order, for they have no central governing body or superior. Monasteries, mostly autonomous, are grouped in some twenty very diverse congregations. There are also many convents of enclosed nuns.

SCOTLAND. Black monks were never strong in Scotland. About 1070 Queen Margaret* brought some from Canterbury to Dunfermline.* Shortly after 1130 three priories were founded: Urquhart (Moray) subject to Dunfermline, Coldingham* subject to Durham, Isle of May subject to Reading. For a short time May had a cell at Rhynd (Perthshire). Iona* abbey was founded *c*.1203 (*see* Nunneries). The wars severed connections with England: May became Augustinian* and subject to St Andrews,* Coldingham was for a time subject to Dunfermline. Urquhart was merged with Pluscarden,* which became Benedictine. Four houses survived until the Reformation: the abbeys of Dunfermline and Iona, and the priories of Coldingham and Pluscarden. For all practical purposes the two priories were independent at this time and there is very little evidence that the Scottish houses ever met in chapter.

After the Reformation, the Schottenklöster* remained in Scottish hands until the nineteenth century. In modern times monasteries have been established at Fort Augustus* and Pluscarden. Two convents of nuns were founded: at Dumfries 1884 (moved to Largs 1988) and Fort Augustus 1892 (at Holme Eden, Carlisle 1920–84).

Catholic Encyclopedia II, 443–72; *New Catholic Encyclopedia* II, 283–303; E. C. Butler, *Benedictine Monachism* (L, ²1924); Easson-Cowan, 55–62.

M. Dilworth

Bereans (Barclayites), *see* Barclay, John.

Bernham, David de (*d*.1253), Bishop of St Andrews 1239–53. He was the first native Scotsman to hold that office since the death of Bishop Fothad in 1093. He was university trained, perhaps at Oxford or Paris. He served in the household of his predecessor, William Malvoisin (*d*.1238), under whom he held the vicarage of Haddington; later he was precentor of Glasgow before his royally influenced election to St Andrews in 1239.

The early years of Bernham's episcopate were remarkably active in his diocese. During 1240–9 he visited and dedicated over 140 parish churches. He issued constitutions governing clerical life in his diocese in the early 1240s. In 1245 he attended the crusading Council of Lyon. Later in the decade he mediated between the Augustinian* canons of St Andrews Priory* and the college of Culdees* or secular clerks; towards the end of the episcopate the latter moved out of the cathedral into the church of St Mary of the Rock beside the precinct.

After the death of his friend and patron King Alexander II in 1249, Bernham officiated at the enthronement of his successor, Alexander III. During the series of political crises of the new king's minority, Bernham associated himself with the party of Walter Comyn (*d*.1258) as opposed to that of Alan Durward (*d*.1268); it would be misleading to view this as a 'patriotic' party as opposed to a 'pro-English' grouping. He was present at the King's marriage at York at Christmas 1251. He was still actively travelling about his diocese at the time of his death.

He streamlined the episcopal administration of his diocese. For his vigour in caring for the pastoral needs of his diocese, he has been likened to his English contemporary Robert Grosseteste.

Acta mostly in *Liber Prioratus Sancti Andree in Scotia* (Bannatyne Club, E, 1841); constitutions in D. Patrick (tr.), *Statutes of the Scottish Church* (E, 1907); *Pontificale Ecclesiae S Andree: the Pontifical Offices used by David de Bernham* . . . , ed. C. Wordsworth (E, 1885); M. Ash, 'David Bernham, Bishop of St Andrews, 1239–1253' in D. McRoberts (ed.), *The Medieval Church of St Andrews* (G, 1976), 33–44; M. Ash, 'The Administration of the Diocese of St Andrews, 1202–1328' (PhD, University of Newcastle, 1972).

A. Macquarrie

Bethune, John (1751–1815), founder of Montreal's first Presbyterian church and the first Presbyterian preacher in Upper Canada (Ontario). He was born on Skye and educated at King's College, Aberdeen (BA, 1769; MA, 1772). In 1773 he emigrated to North Carolina as a licentiate* of the CofS. At the outbreak of the American War of Independence in 1776 the North Carolina Highlanders formed a regiment loyal to the King, and Bethune became their chaplain. After the war in 1786 he settled in Montreal along with other United Empire Loyalists and formed St Gabriel Street Church. In 1787 he moved to Upper Canada where he settled in Glengarry County and began a fruitful ministry to Scottish Highlanders.* He quickly organized churches in Williamstown, Martintown, Summerstown, Cornwall and Lancaster.

J. MacKenzie, 'John Bethune', *Called to Witness*, ed. W. S. Reid, 1 (Toronto, 1975), 95–110; R. Campbell, *A History of the Scotch Presbyterian Church, St. Gabriel Street, Montreal* (Montreal, 1887); *Dict. of Canadian Biography* V, 77–9.

S. D. Gill

Bible Board for Scotland, a body that authorizes printings of the Bible in Scotland. The controversy between the Bible Societies* in Scotland and the King's Printers for Scotland, who in 1823 sought to enforce a monopoly in Scripture production, was finally settled in 1839. Under the terms of the Warrant granted by Queen Victoria, the appointment of Her Majesty's Printers was given to a group of individuals now known as the Bible Board for Scotland, namely, the Lord Advocate for Scotland, the Solicitor-General for Scotland, the Moderator of the CofS General Assembly and four others. Any firm in Scotland may now print the Bible provided they first obtain the sanction of the Bible Board. The arrangement has worked smoothly and with universal acceptance.

F. Macdonald

Bible Societies. The first Bible Society in Scotland was formed in Glasgow in 1805 under the leadership of David Dale,* the Christian industrialist. But Dale died the following year and, deprived of his dynamic leadership, the new Society suspended activities in 1808.

Although Glasgow was first off the mark, it was Edinburgh which provided the first permanent Bible Society presence in Scotland, with the founding of the Edinburgh Bible Society and the Scottish Bible Society within days of one another in 1809. Soon other Bible societies sprang up and by 1812 were found in Aberdeen, Arbroath, Brechin, Dumfries, Forfar, Glasgow (Dale's Society was re-started that year) and Montrose.

The objective of all these local societies was to support to a greater or lesser extent the work of the British and Foreign Bible Society (BFBS) which had been founded in London in 1804. This Society was welcomed by Scottish Christians with considerably greater unanimity than by their English counterparts, and in 1806 received no less than 46 per cent of its income from Scotland.

Thomas Chalmers,* minister of Kilmany in Fife, was representative of many ministers who supported the new societies. He regarded them 'as the most magnificent scheme that ever was instituted for bettering the moral condition of the species'. In a pamphlet entitled *The Influence of Bible Societies on the Necessities of the Poor* (which reached four editions by 1818 and was published in America in 1826), he emphasized that the Bible Societies circulated 'the pure Christianity of the original record', and maintained that 'the Christianity of the Bible gains a readier access into the hearts of the ignorant than the Christianity of sermons and systems and human compositions.'

SCOTLAND AND BFBS. Some of the Scottish supporters of the BFBS desired a greater or lesser measure of devolution from London. While the Glasgow Society was content to see itself as 'a simple Auxiliary of the BFBS', the Edinburgh Society reserved the right 'to act ... separately as circumstances shall require'. The Scottish Bible Society went further and placed greater emphasis on its own circulation of the Scriptures than on co-operation with the BFBS. This led for a period to a dispute concerning the relative merits of the Scottish Bible Society and the others (most notably the Edinburgh Bible Society) which made support of the BFBS their priority.

The strong traditional attachment of Scots, from the Reformation onwards, to the Bible as a book which people should own, read and take to church, left the emerging societies with limited scope for supplying Bibles, apart from Gaelic-speaking areas. This was particularly so in the rural parishes. There was greater need among the growing numbers of urban poor. In Edinburgh, Bibles were supplied to Destitute Sick Societies, and in Glasgow the Catholic School Society received a total of 1,049 Bibles and 1,400 Testaments from 1815 until 1822.

The main focus of the Bible Societies in Scotland was the supply of Scriptures to Ireland, England, the Highlands and overseas. The Edinburgh Bible Society in particular always had broad horizons. Its Directors sought to 'excite compassion for the deplorable conditions of millions who have no Bible'. In addition to giving generously to the BFBS, it sent regular support to William Carey's* Serampore Press in India and to other missionary agencies. The Edinburgh and Glasgow societies (each the focal point of a network of smaller societies) distributed Scriptures among French, Danish and Dutch prisoners of war held in Scotland.

The area in which the Bible Societies made their greatest impact in Scotland was the Highlands,* where over 90 per cent of the 335,000 population spoke Gaelic only. In 1767 the SSPCK* had published the Gaelic New Testament translated by James Stuart,* minister of Killin; the full Bible followed in 1801. After 1804 responsibility for the Gaelic Scriptures passed to the BFBS and in 1809 to the Edinburgh Bible Society. These Scriptures received an extraordinary welcome from the Highlanders, whose religion had been 'a strange medley of half forgotten Catholicism and the fragments of a more ancient nature worship'. The deep spiritual impact remains in some parts until today.

A large part of the very generous support Scotland afforded to the early Bible Society movement came from ordinary people, many of whom were poor. Local Bible Societies and associations organized a system of regular donations of a penny per week. Inevitably they were accused of taxing the poor and indirectly placing a burden on the charitable poor relief which maintained them. In his pamphlet Chalmers rebutted this charge, arguing that the penny-a-week system helped to prevent poverty as it increased people's self-image by raising them to the status of givers and encouraging money management.

APOCRYPHA CONTROVERSY. The near-unanimous

BIBLE SOCIETIES

and harmonious support which the Bible Society cause enjoyed in Scotland came under great pressure during the Apocrypha Controversy,* which engulfed the Bible Societies of the UK and beyond between 1823 and 1826. This controversy, which was destined to influence Bible Society policy world-wide for almost a century and a half, had its storm centre in Scotland. In Britain there was little demand for Bibles containing the twelve additional books found in the Septuagint and regarded as canonical by the RCC. But the BFBS began to receive requests for the longer canon from Churches in continental Europe. The Edinburgh Bible Society took the view that publishing Bibles with the apocrypha (called the 'Deuterocanon' by RCs) was in breach of the rule in the BFBS constitution which limited its funds to the circulation of the Holy Scriptures exclusively, without note or comment. While officially the BFBS indicated agreement with the Edinburgh view, in practice the publication of Bibles with the deuterocanonical books continued, leading to very strained relations between Scotland and London and a pamphlet war between 'anti-Apocryphalists' and 'philo-Apocryphalists' which captured the attention of a wide public north and south of the Border.

There are some signs that the Edinburgh Bible Society would have settled for a pragmatic arrangement which would permit sponsoring Bibles with the apocrypha placed between the Old and New Testaments (an Anglican and Lutheran arrangement), provided that grants given by the BFBS would be restricted to meeting the costs of 'the Books of the Old and New Testaments as generally received in this country'. However, a subsequent decision of the BFBS to grant £500 towards a German Bible which had the deuterocanonical books interspersed hardened the Scottish position and fostered an atmosphere of distrust. As a result the Edinburgh Society intimated to the BFBS in 1826 its decision to withdraw from formal association with the parent society 'with much anxiety and deep regret'. The Glasgow Society followed Edinburgh's example, as did most of the societies and auxiliaries in Scotland, although some pro-BFBS groups continued for a short time.

Ironically, by the time Scotland broke with London the BFBS had decided 'not to print or circulate the Apocryphal books'. But this decision came too late to restore Scottish confidence. Though with the passage of time trust and co-operation were restored, Scotland retains to this day its Bible Society independence.

INDEPENDENCE AND CO-OPERATION. Going it alone proved to be no easy task for the Scottish societies. Almost immediately they had to fight a monopoly battle with the King's Printers (see Bible Board), and raising support was difficult in a period when cholera outbreaks, Chartist* riots and continental wars combined to unsettle society. Nevertheless the Edinburgh and Glasgow societies established work in Switzerland, France, Germany, Italy and Spain and in addition supplied Scriptures to the Caribbean, South America and Africa. Direct links were established with Scottish settlers in Canada, Australia and New Zealand, who received English and Gaelic Scriptures and gave strong financial support.

After the break with the BFBS the Glasgow Society was very conscious of the need for it and the Edinburgh Society to form 'a common Association, or a variety of Associations co-operating with one another'. Edinburgh appears to have been less enthusiastic, but serious discussions eventually got under way only to founder on petty rivalry about the location of the headquarters of the proposed new society. This inter-city squabble was in the end overcome by creating a new society which would be governed by *two* committees, Eastern and Western, each with its own sphere of responsibility. Thus it was that on 22 May 1861 The National Bible Society of Scotland (NBSS) was formed uniting Edinburgh and Glasgow as well as the smaller Bible societies (apart from the Scottish Bible Society, which did not merge with the NBSS until 1985, and the West of Scotland Bible Society which continues independent).

The creation of a genuinely national Bible Society made possible the rapid development of international work, especially in Africa and the Far East as well as on the Continent, and before long NBSS took its place alongside the BFBS, the American Bible Society and the Netherlands Bible Society as a partner in the team of Bible Societies which did much to support the missionary expansion of the Christian Church. NBSS gave sterling support to the Scots missionaries who played such a major role in planting the Bible in Africa, and it fulfilled a key commitment to Scripture production and distribution in China.

This extensive co-operation demonstrated the potential for a wider international fellowship of Bible Societies and in 1946 the four societies came together with eight European Bible societies to form the United Bible Societies (UBS). Since that year the UBS has provided the *modus operandi* for global Bible work and by 1988 had seventy-eight member societies.

G. A. F. Knight and W. C. Somerville, *The History of the National Bible Society of Scotland*, part 1: 1809–1900 (unpublished typescript, held in Bible House, Edinburgh); W. C. Somerville, *From Iona to Dunblane. The Story of the National Bible Society of Scotland* (E, 1948); W. J. Roxborogh, 'Thomas Chalmers and the Mission of the Church with Special Reference to the Rise of the Missionary Movement in Scotland' (PhD, University of Aberdeen, 1978), 93–104; F. Macdonald, 'The Bible Societies in Scotland', in D. F. Wright (ed.), *The Bible in Scottish Life and Literature* (E, 1988), ch. 2. Further details will be found in the Annual Reports (1810–61) of the Edinburgh Bible Society, and the Annual Reports (1861–) and Quarterly Records (1863–1963) of the National Bible Society of Scotland.

F. Macdonald

Bible Training Institute, Glasgow, an interdenominational theological college with a conservative evangelical ethos. It began in 1892 as an enterprise of the Glasgow United Evangelistic Association.* Men and women were trained over two years for overseas missions and Christian work at home. Numbers increased and in 1898 large premises in Bothwell Street were opened. Here the work was centred until the move to Great Western Road in 1980.

John Anderson superintended the college until 1913, when David McIntyre's* long principalship started. His deep devotion to Christ and ability to communicate good evangelical scholarship in a simple yet stimulating way became hallmarks of the college. Francis Davidson,* who succeeded him in 1938, steered the BTI through the difficult war years, having to do a great deal of the teaching himself. Andrew MacBeath took over in 1954. He was a missionary, and his fifteen years as Principal saw a strong emphasis on missionary training.

After the Second World War, London University certificate and diploma examinations were introduced. These were replaced by the Cambridge diploma/certificate examination and the London BD in the 1970s, and from 1992 by the College's own BA and diploma/certificate, under CNAA. The main course now lasts three years, and varied outreach training is provided in a city which has many evangelical churches. The evening and correspondence course programmes have also been extended. With a highly qualified staff, the college prepares Christian people at different levels for a wide range of Christian vocations. It was renamed the Glasgow Bible College from 1991.

G.W.Grogan

Bible (Versions, English) in Scotland. There is no evidence of Old English (Anglo-Saxon) Scriptures having circulated in Scotland, but Scots Lollards* had Wycliffite books from at least 1406, and it is likely that Wycliffite Scriptures were among them. John Purvey's revision of the Wycliffite New Testament was turned into Scots c.1520 by Murdoch Nisbet,* though not printed until 1901–5. William Tyndale's New Testament reached England in 1527 and probably entered Scottish ports almost simultaneously. A main charge against Patrick Hamilton,* burned in 1528, was that he taught that 'it is lawful for any man to read the word of God, and in special the New Testament'. In 1533 Henry Forrest of Linlithgow was burned for owning an English New Testament (see Heretics; Martyrs). In 1537 the free sale and distribution of the English New Testament were authorized in England, and its later prohibition in Scotland is evidence that it was read; many took refuge in England from punishment for this offence. In 1540 Sir John Borthwick was charged with having a New Testament *in vulgari Anglico impressum* ('printed in the common English tongue'). On 12 March 1543, on a proposal of Lord Maxwell, the Scottish Parliament resolved that 'all the lieges in this realm may read the Scriptures in our native tongue', the resolution applying to both English and Gaelic* Scriptures (see Bible (Versions, Gaelic)). Very large imports of English Scriptures took place, probably including not only Tyndale's New Testament but also Miles Coverdale's and 'Matthew's' (*i.e.* John Rogers') versions of the Bible, and the Great Bible (1539). John Knox* spoke at this time of 'the Bible lying upon almost every gentleman's table'. A short-lived reaction led to the burning of George Wishart* at St Andrews in 1546.

A group of Scottish Reformers wrote from Stirling to John Knox in 1557, the year in which the New Testament of the Geneva Bible was first published, saying that they would henceforth read the lessons in English. Knox himself may have used Tyndale's translation, perhaps not exclusively, until 1560, and thereafter the Geneva Bible, the English version produced by the Protestant exiles in 1560. The adoption of the Geneva Bible as the Bible of the Reformation in Scotland, its rapid adoption, together with the Catechism, as the most widely used school text-book, and the corresponding failure to produce a complete Scots Bible, are major factors in the gradual decline of Scots as a literary language (see Bible (Versions, Scottish)). 'The word of God in Scotland was enshrined in English as opposed to Latin as before [the Reformation] and not in Scots' (K. Williamson, 'Lowland Scots in Education: an Historical Survey', in *Scottish Language* 1, 1982, 57). In the Highlands,* the relation between the Gaelic and English Bibles is more complex; but even there, bodies promoting the use of Gaelic also often served indirectly as agents of Anglicization (C. W. J. Withers, *Gaelic in Scotland 1698–1981*, E, 1984; see also Gaelic School Societies; Scottish SPCK).

The first complete Bible printed in Scotland was the 1579 Bassendyne* edition of the Geneva Bible; but both before and long after that date English Bibles printed on the Continent and in England circulated freely in Scotland (F. F. Bruce, *History of the Bible in English*, Guildford, ³1979, 91–3). Editions of the New Testament for use in Scotland were printed in 1601 and 1603 at Dort.

The original 1560 edition of the Geneva Bible was 'as a whole generally Protestant in intention rather than specifically Calvinist' (S. L. Greenslade, 'English Versions of the Bible, 1525–1611' in Greenslade (ed.), *The Cambridge History of the Bible*, III, C, 1963, 158). The text, translation and notes of the New Testament revision by Laurence Tomson (1565) were strongly influenced by the more distinctively Reformed revision of the French New Testament (1560), prepared by Theodore Beza under Calvin's direction. To the English Geneva Bible were added in 1595 anti-RC comments on Revelation by Francis du Jon (Junius), a French Calvinist who later taught at the University of Leiden. The resultant Geneva–Tomson–Junius Bible was first published in London in 1599, and by Andrew Hart (*d.*1621; *DNB* XXV, 56) in Edinburgh in 1610. The Geneva Bible in both forms continued to be reprinted until 1644, though not in Scotland.

The first Scottish edition of the so-called Authorized (King James) Version New Testament was published in 1628 by the heirs of Andrew Hart; there is, in fact, no evidence that it was officially

BIBLE (VERSIONS, ENGLISH)

authorized either in England or in Scotland. It was followed in 1633 by the first complete Scottish Authorized Version Bible, published in Edinburgh by Robert Young, the King's Printer, possibly in connection with the Scottish coronation of Charles I.* The New Testament of this and some later editions aroused controversy because of the RC tendency of illustrations bound in some copies, notably one depicting the assumption of the Virgin Mary.

Twelve further editions of the Bible in the Authorized Version were published in Scotland, probably all in Edinburgh, between 1634 and 1700, some without the Apocrypha, and one, in 1696, containing marginal notes by the Brownist John Canne (d.1667), first published in Amsterdam in 1647. Editions of the New Testament were also published in Edinburgh and Glasgow. In 1650 there appeared, 'allowed by the authority of the Generall Assembly of the Kirk of Scotland', the first edition of the Scottish metrical Psalms, based on those by Francis Rous; later (e.g. in 1764) it was bound together with some editions of the Bible. A translation of Ostervald's annotated Bible was published in Edinburgh in 1770 for the SPCK. In the following year, an annotated and corrected *Family Bible* appeared in Aberdeen, where a school edition of Proverbs and four Psalms was published in 1780.

One of the first proposals for a revision of the Authorized Bible came from John Row of Aberdeen in 1655. He suggested among other things 'That all useles additions be lop't off, yt debase the wisdom of ye spirit: – to instance All ye Apocryphall writings: being meerly humane' (anticipating the later Apocrypha Controversy*), 'That Ingl[ish] words (not understood in Scotland) be idiomatiz'd'. Row was appointed a member of a revision committee, but the proposal fell through on the dissolution of the Long Parliament.

In 1792 there was published in Edinburgh an edition of the Reims-Douay RC translation prepared by an unknown scholar, and containing many variations, both in text and notes, from the standard text. This edition is now very rare.

Although the English Revised Version of 1881-5 originated in the (Anglican) Convocation of Canterbury, its various companies included strong Scottish (especially FC) representation, including for the Old Testament A. B. Davidson* of Edinburgh, †P. Fairbairn* and G. Douglas* of Glasgow, †J. McGill of St Andrews (*FES* VII, 427), and W. Roberston Smith* of Aberdeen; and for the New Testament †J. Eadie* of Glasgow, W. Milligan* and David Brown* of Aberdeen, and A. Roberts* of St Andrews. (The revisers whose names are marked † died before completion of the work.)

Probably the most widely read and influential translation of the English Bible by a single translator is the *New Translation* by James Moffatt* (NT 1913, OT 1924, Bible 1926, revised 1935), who had earlier published *The Historical New Testament* (1901), and who was later to serve as executive secretary, from 1937 until his death, of the American Standard Bible revision committee, whose work was published as the Revised Standard Version. The Scotticisms of Moffatt's *New Translation*, of

BIBLE (VERSIONS, GAELIC)

which the 'dishonest factor' of Luke 16:1-4 is the best-known example, have probably been exaggerated. They are best understood as part of an effort to find in each case the *mot juste*, whether exotic, learned or familiar, from within a rich and individual vocabulary; compare Moffatt's use of 'khan' (e.g. Exod. 4:24), 'fag-ends' (Isa. 7:4), 'catamite' (Deut. 23:18), 'cairngorm' (Exod. 28:19), 'blouse' of a man's garment (John 21:7), 'provost' (2 Kgs. 10:5; 2 Chr. 34:8) and 'sheriff' in the Scottish sense (Num. 25:5; 1 Chr. 23:4), but also 'Bedawin' (e.g. Judg. 5:24) and 'sheikh' (e.g. Gen. 25:16).

The initiative which led to the making of the New English Bible (NT 1961, Bible 1970) came from an overture from the Presbytery of Stirling and Dunblane to the 1946 General Assembly of the CofS. Among Scottish scholars who contributed to the work at various stages were William D. McHardy (OT and Apocrypha panels; Deputy Director), George W. Anderson (OT), William Barclay* (Apocrypha), Matthew Black (NT), John Mauchline (NT), Norman W. Porteous (OT and Joint Committee representative of the Church of Scotland), and J. K. S. Reid (secretary of the Joint Committee).

The Revised English Bible, a thorough revision of the New English Bible, was published in 1989. Scottish participants included W. D. McHardy (Director), J. K. S. Reid (Secretary of the Joint Committee to 1982), G. W. Anderson, R. S, Barbour, W. McKane, I. A. Moir (revisers), and successive General Secretaries of the National Bible Society of Scotland as members of the Joint Committee.

A. S. Herbert, *Historical Catalogue of Printed Editions of the English Bible 1525-1961* (L and NY, 1968), has an index of places of printing and publication; J. Eadie, *The English Bible*, 2 vols (L, 1876), pays special attention to developments in Scotland, and is still indispensable; see also D. F. Wright, ' "The Commoun Buke of the Kirke": The Bible in the Scottish Reformation', in D. F. Wright (ed.), *The Bible in Scottish Life and Literature* (E, 1988), 155-78; H. Wheeler Robinson, *The Bible in its Ancient and English Versions* (O, 1940); G. Hunt, *About the New English Bible* (O, C, 1970); R. Coleman, *New Light and Truth* (O, C, 1989); James Moffatt, *The Bible in Scots Literature* (L, n.d.).

P. Ellingworth

Bible (Versions, Gaelic). The need for a printed Gaelic* Bible for both Ireland and Scotland was first recognized by John Carswell,* Superintendent of Argyll, in 1567. However, the Gaelic Bible now used in the Highlands* was translated two centuries later, and financed by the SSPCK.* This translation, specifically aimed at a Scottish Gaelic readership, was made after the failure of other attempts to provide the Highland people with a version of the Scriptures which they could understand. These early attempts included the translation programme of the Synod of Argyll and the use of Classical Gaelic Bibles translated in Ireland.

THE TRANSLATION PROGRAMME OF THE SYNOD OF ARGYLL. Fifty years before the formation of the

SSPCK, efforts were made to produce a Gaelic translation of the Bible for Scottish use. In 1657 the Synod of Argyll, which was engaged in the provision of Gaelic catechisms and a Gaelic version of the metrical Psalter,* tried to expedite an existing plan to translate the Old Testament. The work was delayed by the struggle between Presbyterianism and Episcopacy, which led to the ejection of most of the translators from their parishes after 1660. Nevertheless, a complete Gaelic text of the Old Testament, the work of Dugald Campbell (1599–1673; FES IV, 15–16) of Knapdale, is said to have been available in manuscript by 1673, but it never reached print.

THE CLASSICAL GAELIC BIBLES. In the late 1680s Classical Gaelic Bibles were imported from Ireland as an interim solution, largely through the initiative of Episcopalians who had links with the (episcopal) Church of Ireland. In Ireland before 1700 considerable progress had been made with the translation of the Bible into formal Classical Gaelic, the language used by the trained *literati* of Ireland and Scotland mainly in the period 1200–1600. A translation of the New Testament had been completed by William O'Donnel (L, 1602–3), and William Bedell's translation of the Old Testament became available in 1686 (L, 1685–6). O'Donnell's translation of the New Testament may have been in use in Argyll in the earlier seventeenth century. Through the intervention of James Kirkwood,* 207 copies of Bedell's translation of the Old Testament and also some copies of O'Donnell's New Testament were acquired for Highland parishes. Distribution was slow and hardly effective. In 1688–90 Robert Kirk* undertook to modify the format of the Classical Gaelic versions for Scottish use, and thus produced 'Kirk's Bible' (L, 1690). After 1611, the King James Bible was available to those who became literate in English. Some ministers and lay readers made their own *ad hoc* translations from English into Scottish Gaelic.

THE SCOTTISH GAELIC BIBLE, 1767–1807. Although the evangelization of the Highlands was readily perceived as a priority by the SSPCK, antipathy towards the Gaelic language delayed its involvement in the provision of a specifically Scottish Gaelic Bible. The replacement of Gaelic by English was one of the aims of the Scottish crown and also of the SSPCK, and it was feared that the existence of a Scottish Gaelic Bible would prolong the life of the language. Indeed, the need for such a Bible was accepted only with reluctance by the Society, who hoped that it would be instrumental in promoting literacy, first in Gaelic and subsequently in English.

The role of the SSPCK in producing a Scottish Gaelic Bible reflected two important considerations. First, the Society had become aware of the lack of success with which it was pursuing its policy of eradicating Gaelic by enforced use of English in its schools. Thus it began to permit the gradual adoption of the 'comparative method' in the teaching of English in its Highland schools. This allowed some limited use of Gaelic to explain English words, and was employed as early as the 1720s.

By the mid-1750s the Society's policy had been modified sufficiently to allow some tentative steps to be taken towards the provision of a Scottish Gaelic Bible. Second, the perceived need for a specifically Scottish Gaelic Bible, rather than an Hiberno-Scottish Classical Gaelic Bible, acknowledged the fact that Scottish Gaelic speakers were having difficulties with the existing Classical Gaelic versions. Indeed, by 1700, if not earlier, Gaelic Scotland had developed its own distinctive form of Classical Gaelic, in which the verbal and syntactic structures had been modified to accord more closely with those of the spoken language.

In the early 1750s the SSPCK signalled its change of linguistic direction by trying to reproduce Kirk's version of the New Testament with Gaelic and English on facing pages, but, finding its way blocked, it commissioned its own translation of the New Testament. This was undertaken (from 1758) by James Stuart* of Killin, with the help of James Fraser,* Alness, and was printed (under the care of Dugald Buchanan*) in Edinburgh in 1767. Work on the Old Testament (in four volumes) continued thereafter. The first two volumes were translated under the supervision of John Stuart* of Luss, who also translated the third volume (completed last in 1801). The fourth volume was translated by John Smith* of Campbeltown.

The translators of the Scottish Gaelic Bible used the most recent scholarship in their understanding of the original Greek and Hebrew texts. This is particularly evident in their rendering of parts of the Old Testament. Smith made extensive use of the writings of Robert Lowth in his work on the Prophets, and his volume anticipates several of the readings of the English Revised Version of 1885. This was not appreciated at the time, and objections were raised to Smith's 'liberties', which became apparent when set alongside the King James Bible. Smith's volume was extensively revised by Alexander Stewart* for the 1807 edition. Several revisions of the Scottish Gaelic Bible, mainly affecting style and orthography, were made throughout the nineteenth century (*see* Cameron, Alexander; McLaughlan, Thomas; and Ross, Thomas). The process continued after 1900. A pocket Bible was produced by Malcolm MacLennan in 1911. Further orthographic revision was initiated by T. M. Murchison* about 1950, with the intention of producing a modern, clear-type edition. The task was taken over by D. E. Meek and completed in 1992 (*Am Bioball Gàidhlig*, E, 1992).

In its style the Scottish Gaelic Bible resembles its Classical Gaelic predecessors, and is to some extent indebted to 'Kirk's Bible' of 1690. It is also influenced by the King James Bible, which it matches in its overall tone. Although morphology and syntax are generally in keeping with the practice of spoken Scottish Gaelic, the language of the Gaelic Bible is formal 'differentiated register', with words and idioms which are today regarded as 'Bible Gaelic', in contrast to everyday, spoken Gaelic. It is best described as a form of 'Classical Scottish Gaelic'.

The translation of the Bible into Scottish Gaelic had great significance for the language and its speakers. It signalled the full emergence of a new phase in the literary life of Gaelic Scotland, in which Scotland was shown to be, to a large degree, independent of Ireland. Further literary development, especially of prose, was stimulated (*see* MacLeod, Norman). The translation also enhanced the status of Scottish Gaelic by providing a major text in 'upper register'. This, in turn, helped to stabilize the language, providing a standard for spelling and establishing a religious *lingua franca* which, after some initial reservations, came to be used throughout the Highlands. The Scottish Gaelic Bible made a major spiritual impact through the Gaelic School Societies.*

MACEACHEN'S GAELIC NEW TESTAMENT. The translation of the Scottish Gaelic Bible was undertaken by a Protestant society, and has been used pre-eminently in the Reformed Churches of the Highlands. The RCC did, however, produce a translation of the New Testament in the nineteenth century (A, 1875). This was evidently the work of Fr Ewen (or Evan) MacEachen of Arisaig (*d*.1849), and was based on the Vulgate. The style of this translation is noticeably closer to spoken Scottish Gaelic than that of the 1767–1807 Gaelic Bible (*see* Gaelic, Roman Catholic publications in).

'TODAY'S GAELIC VERSION'. The distinction between 'Bible Gaelic' and 'everyday Gaelic' has become more marked with time, especially among younger (post-1950) Gaelic speakers, who tend to be less familiar with 'pulpit Gaelic' than their forebears. As a result, the National Bible Society of Scotland (which has had responsibility for the text of the Scottish Gaelic Bible since the mid-nineteenth century) has initiated a 'modern Gaelic' translation of the New Testament. The first parts to be published are Mark's Gospel in *An Deagh Sgeul aig Marcus* ('Mark's Good News') (E, 1980), and Paul's Prison Epistles in *Facal as a Phriosan* ('A Word from Prison') (E, 1986). The project continues.

D. MacKinnon, *The Gaelic Bible and Psalter* (Dingwall, 1930); V. E. Durkacz, *The Decline of the Celtic Languages* (E, 1983), 52–72; C. W. Withers, *Gaelic in Scotland 1689–1981* (E, 1984), 116–37; D. E. Meek, 'The Gaelic Bible', and 'The Bible and Social Change in the Nineteenth-Century Highlands', in D. F. Wright (ed.), *The Bible in Scottish Life and Literature* (E, 1988), 9–23, 179–91.

D. E. Meek

Bible (Versions, Scottish), translations from the Bible into Scots. There is no complete translation of the Bible into Scots but there are three versions of the New Testament and a number of translations of individual books. Only two are directly translated from the original Greek or Hebrew; most are adaptations of English versions including the first, a version of the New Testament, made about 1520 by Murdoch Nisbet* and based on Purvey's revision of the Wycliffite Bible. Nisbet Scoticized the grammar and spelling but adopted a minimalist approach to the vocabulary, retaining Purvey's words wherever he could. His version has the virtues and defects of Purvey, a generally accurate and readable text with occasional nonsensical literalisms. It remained unpublished for nearly four centuries and was finally printed in 1901 by the STS.

There was no further translation of more than short passages into Scots until the mid-nineteenth century when Prince Louis Lucien Bonaparte commissioned versions of various books. He aimed to preserve information about the dying dialects of Europe and paid for the printing of versions of Matthew (L, 1856), the Psalms (L, 1857) and the Song of Solomon (L, 1860) by Henry Scott Riddell (1798–1870), of Matthew and the Song of Solomon (both L, 1862) by an unidentified George Henderson and two further translations of the Song of Solomon (both L, 1860) by Joseph Philip Robson (1808–70) and an anonymous translator. All were based on the Authorized Version; most retained non-Scots features from it and have little value as an historical record of spoken Scots. Robson, who was actually from northern England, was the only one to adopt a consistent style of more or less modern colloquial Scots. The Prince's aims were better fulfilled by James Murray (1837–1915) in the translation of Ruth he included in his *Dialect of the Southern Counties of Scotland* (L, 1873). Murray provided a version of the whole book in Teviotdale Scots plus phonetic transcripts of the first chapter of Ruth in Teviotdale, Buchan and Ayrshire Scots. Murray's work is unusual both in its use both of specific regional dialects and in attempting a faithful reproduction of contemporary spoken Scots. *The Psalms frae Hebrew intil Scottis* (E, 1871) and *Isaiah frae Hebrew intil Scottis* (E, 1879) of P. Hateley Waddell* are in a much more literary Scots, which includes many words created by Waddell himself. Working from the original text, Waddell produced new and vigorous translations full of passionate intensity. He also provided in Scots a full introduction, chapter headings and notes, thus attempting to supply a complete equivalent to the English Bibles of his time.

Twentieth-century translations begin with W. W. Smith's *New Testament in Braid Scots* (Paisley, 1901). Smith (1827–1917) made use of both the Authorized and Revised Versions and aimed to produce a fully colloquial version of the Bible. In fact his style is variable, sometimes successfully conveying the tones of colloquial Scots speech, at other times retaining English and archaic elements. *The Wyse Sayin's o' Solomon* (Paisley, 1917) by Thomas Whyte Paterson (*d*.1920) is much more consistently colloquial, with a real proverbial ring to it. He is the first of the Scots translators to adopt a modern layout of the text as poetry. Similarly, Henry Paterson Cameron (1852–1921) set out his *Genesis in Scots* (Paisley, 1921) in paragraphs rather than verses. Based on the Revised Version and slightly archaic in style, it is nevertheless very readable. Somewhat later in this century Alex Borrowman (*d*.1978) undertook a translation of Ruth which appeared posthumously in *The Buik o Ruth and Ither Wark in Lallans* (E, 1979). The 'ither wark' included sermons, metrical psalms and short Bible extracts in Scots. Borrowman based his Ruth on the New English Bible.

The highest point of Scots biblical translation is undoubtedly W. L. Lorimer's* *New Testament in Scots* (E, 1985). After a lifetime of teaching Greek in universities, Lorimer (1885-1967) undertook this translation in his retirement, bringing to it not only his redoubtable Greek scholarship but also a lifelong interest in Scots. This original and creative but also accurate translation brings the text alive in vivid colloquial Scots. Unlike Waddell, Lorimer avoided creating his own words and confined himself to words in actual use in the last three centuries. Consequently this is not only a brilliant translation but also a mine of information about Modern Scots. Lorimer's work was followed by Jamie Stuart's synoptic *Scots Gospel* (E, 1985), originally created by Stuart as an actor's script. Stuart makes good use of Smith, Lorimer, English versions and his own renditions to produce a script which is fast-moving and effective.

T. G. Law, Introduction to M. Nisbet (trans.), *The New Testament in Scots*, STS (E, 1901); G. Tulloch, Introduction to P. H. Waddell (trans.), *The Psalms in Scots* (A, 1987); G. Tulloch, 'The Language of Two Scots Versions of the New Testament', in T. L. and J. Burton (eds), *Lexicographical and Linguistic Studies* (C, 1988), 91-102; G. Tulloch, *A History of the Bible in Scots* (A, 1989); D. F. Wright (ed.), *The Bible in Scottish Life and Literature* (E, 1988).

G. Tulloch

Bible Women, *see* Fisherfolk.

Biblical Criticism, *see* Believing Criticism; Exegesis, Biblical.

Binnie, William (1823-86), RP/FC divine. Born in Glasgow and educated at its University and the RP Divinity Hall, he went on to study at Berlin under Neander and Hengstenberg. Ordained in 1849 to Stirling RP Church, he succeeded William Symington* in 1862 as Professor of Systematic Theology at the Divinity Hall. In 1876 he joined the FC and became the first Professor of Church History at the FC College Aberdeen (*see* Christ's College), where he laboured until his death. Glasgow gave him a DD in 1866. He published books on *The Psalms* (L, 1870) and *The Church* (E, 1882), as well as (posthumously) *Sermons* (L, 1887). *The Proposed Reconstruction of the Old Testament History* (E, 1880) shows him holding an intermediate position between supporters and opponents of his colleague William Robertson Smith.*

J. Robb, *Cameronian Fasti* (E, n.d.), 2; *AFCS* I, 49.

G. Wareing

Binning, Hugh (1627-53), minister in Govan. Son of a wealthy Ayrshire landowner, Binning showed an aptitude for studies and an interest in religious exercises at an early age. He was given a good education and after completing his course of philosophy at Glasgow (MA 1646) he began to study divinity. Later that year his name was put forward to fill a vacancy in the college and, in consequence of his acquitting himself well in the dispute set for the competitors, he was elected. After serving as regent for three years, he was called to Govan and ordained there in early January 1650. In his trials before presbytery he was given the common head '*De concursu et influxu divino cum actionibus creaturarum*' and was opposed by John Strang,* who had taught virtually the opposite of the (orthodox Reformed) opinion expressed by Binning. Despite Strang's high reputation, Binning more than maintained his ground in the debate.

When Oliver Cromwell entered Glasgow in 1651 he heard Binning preach and the following day invited him, with others, to a conference. Binning, who steadfastly opposed the intrusion of the English, is reported to have made an impression on Cromwell by the force of his reasoning. He took the side of the Protesters* in the division in the Church, but in that controversy as well as in that with the Independents* maintained a conciliatory spirit; in that context he wrote his *Treatise of Christian Love* (first published E, 1743).

Binning's reputation rests partly on the eminence he had as a preacher and partly on his printed works, which have long been circulated in spite of the disadvantages of being printed posthumously. His sermons were unlike those of most of his contemporaries (*see* Preachers and Preaching). 'Paul', Binning said, 'speaks of a right dividing of the word of truth . . . ; not that ordinary way of cutting it all in parcels and dismembering it by manifold divisions . . .' (*Works*, 213). Although much criticized, Binning's more simple and natural preaching, coupled with considerable eloquence, a warm practical piety and skilful application to his hearers' hearts, made him a most popular preacher. James Durham* commented: 'There is no speaking after Mr Binning.' Binning's preaching was warmly evangelical, urging sinners to come to Christ without previous preparations, which he described as a form of establishing our own righteousness and being ignorant of Christ's.

Works, ed. M. Leishman (E, 1851), with memoir. *FES* III, 411; *DNB* V, 59-60.

D. C. Lachman

Bishops Report (1957), *see* Anglican-Presbyterian Relations.

Bishops, *see* Episcopacy.

Bishops' Wars (1639-40), two series of confrontations between Charles I* and the Scottish Covenanters.* The General Assembly at Glasgow* in November 1638 had deposed the bishops, rejected steps taken by the King and Archbishop Laud* to consolidate the episcopal* system, and abolished the Courts of High Commission.* Both Scots and Royalists raised armies, but Charles found it prudent to back down, and the Pacification of Berwick in June 1639 satisfied Covenanting demands. This was, however, prevarication on the King's part; he delayed implementing the terms of the treaty, hoping that the English Parliament would finance another attempt to subdue the Scots (whose motives he had tried to misrepresent in London). When his fund-raising request was refused, Charles for the second time took to arms. A Covenanting army crossed the border and routed the Royalists at Newburn, four miles from Newcastle, in August 1640. The English 'Long Parliament', called by the King as a last resort, proved to be friendly to the Scots and took advantage of the King's dilemma to limit powers he had claimed and exercised in England.

J. K. Hewison, *The Covenanters* (G, ²1913) I, 317–53.

J. D. Douglas

Black Acts, series of Acts of Parliament of May 1584, which sought both to assert the supremacy of the Crown over all estates of the realm, including the Church, and to settle the latter's polity as episcopalian. A product of the short-lived political supremacy of James Stewart, Earl of Arran (Chancellor May 1584–November 1585), the Acts were resisted by Arran's political opponents and the Presbyterian portion of the Kirk.

The Reformation* of 1560 had been most effective at the parochial level; the question of the place of bishops or superintendents* within the Kirk remained unsettled during the personal reign of Mary* (1561–7) and the civil war that followed (1567–73). The debate involved several issues besides the biblical view of church government (*see* Second Book of Discipline). At the constitutional level, a proper parliament had included clerics as one of the three estates of the realm. More important was the problem of the extent of royal jurisdiction over the whole realm. Political factions taking opposing views on these matters sought support from foreign powers, from England and from Spain, thus embroiling the question of church government with James VI's* prospect of the English succession and reawakening fears of a Scottish counter-reformation.

Important in themselves for some, these biblical, ideological and constitutional issues were sometimes secondary to the political struggle to govern through the impressionable teenage King – who sought increasingly to establish his personal rule. Officially free from tutelage from 1578, James was not twenty-one until 1587. Between August 1582 and June 1583, he had been held captive by the pro-Presbyterian pro-English lords known as the Ruthven Raiders.* The Arran regime which followed his escape thus sought to re-establish royal and parliamentary sovereignty by outlawing Presbyteries as independent centres of jurisdiction and by governing the Church by bishops as royal commissioners. Always attracted by matters of principle, the King personally approved these policies of his Chancellor and of Patrick Adamson,* Archbishop of St Andrews. During the summer of 1584 all parish ministers were called upon to subscribe their assent to the Black Acts on pain of deprivation.

Most did so. Some assented 'as far as the word of God allows' – a concession won by John Erskine of Dun.* Andrew Melville's* small minority joined the banished Ruthven lords in exile in England (*see also* Durie, John, 1537–1600).

Arran's government was too ideological in tone and too narrowly-based to survive. He himself was an adventurer, ennobled only in 1581. Elizabeth I's* diplomats preferred to trust the exiled Protestant lords. They, on being allowed by London to return to Scotland in 1585, forced Arran into exile in his turn. James now sought more moderate, consensus administrations under which Presbyterianism revived and the 1584 Acts lapsed. He himself, however, did not surrender the beliefs on which they were based.

Historians debate how far the Black Acts followed or perverted the original principles of the Scottish Reformation.

G. Donaldson, *The Scottish Reformation* (C, 1960); id., *Scotland: James V–James VII* (E, 1978); *SBD*; D. G. Mullan, *Episcopacy in Scotland* (E, 1986).

F. D. Bardgett

Black, David (*c*.1550–1603), Presbyterian minister. He entered St Mary's College, St Andrews in 1561 and acted as a schoolmaster in England before his appointment as minister in St Andrews, on Andrew Melville's* recommendation, in 1590. He withheld his services for a spell with the town's failure to provide a second minister. Considered 'most antiprelatical', Black witnessed Archbishop Patrick Adamson's* recantation in 1591. Summoned before the King and Privy Council at Falkland in 1595 'for certain speeches uttered by him in his doctrine against the king's progenitors', Black declined their jurisdiction in spiritual matters. In 1596, he was again in trouble for preaching against the authority of princes, and warded north of the Tay. He was translated to Arbirlot near Arbroath in 1597.

BUK; Calderwood; J. Melville, *Diary* (E, 1842); J. Bain *et al.* (eds), *Calendar of State Papers relating to Scotland* (E, 1898–1969), X, no. 362; XI, no. 636; XII, no. 292; D. H. Fleming (ed.), *Register of the Minister, Elders and Deacons of the Christian Congregation of St Andrews* (E, 1889–90); J. H. Burton *et al.* (eds), *Register of the Privy Council of Scotland* (E, 1877–98), V; *FES* V, 231–2, 420; T. M'Crie, *Life of Andrew Melville*, 2 vols (E, ²1824).

J. Kirk

Black Friars, *see* Dominicans.

Black, Hugh (1868–1953), Professor of Practical Theology in Union Seminary,* New York. Born at Rothesay, Bute, he graduated MA from Glasgow University in 1887, attended Glasgow FC College (1887–91), and was ordained to Paisley Sherwood FC in 1891. He moved to St George's FC, Edinburgh, in 1896, and joined the UFC in 1900. In 1906 he accepted the call to a new chair at Union Seminary, where he taught until retirement in 1938.

BLACK, JAMES MACDOUGALL

He wrote several books, including *Christ or Caesar* (L, 1938), *Culture and Restraint* (L, 1902) and *Friendship* (L, 1897; S, 1899). He was a popular preacher, and various collections of his sermons appeared in *Edinburgh Sermons* (L, 1906), *Christ's Service of Love* (L, 1907), and *University Sermons* (L, 1908). Black had a poetic turn of mind, seen in his *Three Dreams* (L, n.d.). His theology was moderately liberal, lucidly argued in his sermon 'The Failure of God' in *University Sermons*. He was awarded the DD of Yale (1908), Princeton (1911) and Glasgow (1911), and the DLitt of Pittsburgh (1917).

AFCS I, 68; FUFCS 28; *Who Was Who, 1951– 1960*, 106–7.

N. R. Needham

Black, James Macdougall (1879–1949), one of the most distinguished Scottish preachers* of his day. After fourteen years as minister of Broughton Place UF Church, Edinburgh, in 1921 he became minister of Free St George's – known as St George's West after the Union* of 1929. His preaching attracted large congregations and he was a well-known visiting preacher on both sides of the Atlantic. He consolidated the reputation of St George's as probably the leading liberal evangelical* pulpit in Scotland. He was made a DD of Edinburgh (1924) and Moderator of the General Assembly in 1938. His most notable books were his Warrack Lectures,* *The Mystery of Preaching* (L, 1924), and a perceptive study of sects and heresies, *New Forms of the Old Faith* (L, 1948), his Baird Lectures.*

FUFCS 29; FES IX, 39; *Who Was Who, 1941– 1950*, 106.

D. B. Forrester

Blackader (or Blackadder), Robert (d.1508), Archbishop of Glasgow. Brother of Sir Robert Blackader of Tulliallan, a graduate of St Andrews and Paris, canon of Glasgow, rector of Lasswade and protonotary apostolic, he was provided to the see of Aberdeen when archdeacon, 14 July 1480. Apparently unconsecrated, he spent much of his short episcopate in a financial dispute with the burgesses. Translated to Glasgow, 19 March 1483, against the wishes of James III* who supported the election of George Carmichael, Blackader, who had been consecrated in Rome, eventually won the King's acceptance. In contention with William Scheves, Archbishop of St Andrews (d.1496), he gained exemption from his jurisdiction, 25 May 1488, and in June found favour with the newly-crowned James IV.* The campaign for archiepiscopal status for his see commenced almost immediately and was accomplished, 9th January 1492. Blackader became first Archbishop with the Bishops of Argyll, Dunkeld, Dunblane and Galloway as suffragans, although Dunkeld and Dunblane were later restored to St Andrews. During his archiepiscopate he played a prominent part in several embassies to France, Spain and England and officiated with the Archbishop of York at the marriage of James IV and Margaret Tudor in 1503. He

BLACKADDER, JOHN

was responsible for the building or completion of the Blackader aisle in Glasgow Cathedral,* and founded several chaplaincies in Glasgow. He died 28th July 1508 while on pilgrimage to the Holy Land, having previously visited Rome and Venice (D. MacRoberts, 'Scottish Pilgrims to the Holy Land', *IR* 20 (1969), 80–106).

J. Durkan, 'Archbishop Blackadder's Will', *IR* 24 (1972), 148–9; Dowden 127–8, 331–7.

I. B. Cowan

Blackadder, Adam, see Blackadder, John.

Blackadder, John (1615–86), Covenanting* field-preacher.* Born into the house of Tulliallan, he inherited, but did not assume, the baronetcy. Blackadder trained under his uncle, William Strang, in Glasgow (MA, 1650). He possibly spent the years prior to coming to the parish of Troqueer (near Dumfries) in 1653 as an itinerant preacher, but it is not known why he waited until he was thirty-seven before he became a parish minister. His ministry in Troqueer was notable. He first restored church discipline and then embarked on a regular course of instruction, including catechising,* all of which issued in a reformation in the lives of the people. Along with most ministers in south-west Scotland, Blackadder was removed from his parish for refusing to comply with the Act Rescissory in 1662. He moved to Glencairn, Dumfriesshire, and from early 1663 preached regularly there, with large numbers coming to hear him. He also commenced an itinerant ministry. In early 1666 he was forced to leave home and lived in seclusion in Edinburgh. In 1668 he recommenced field-preaching and for the next decade occupied a leading place among the field-preachers of his day, often joining with others such as Donald Cargill* and John Welsh of Irongray.* He was outlawed in 1674, but continued preaching. He fled to Rotterdam in 1678, but returned to Edinburgh the following year, taking up field-preaching yet again. He was again abroad briefly in 1680, but returned to the work after a short stay. In April 1681 he was arrested in Edinburgh, and was sent to the Bass Rock,* where he remained imprisoned until his death.

His second son, Adam (c.1659–c.1696; *DNB* V, 114–15), was arrested in 1674 for attending conventicles, and later imprisoned in Blackness Castle for attending his father's preaching. Fleeing to Sweden, he married a Swedish lady whom he won from Lutheranism to Calvinism. He returned to Edinburgh and was a subscriber to the Darien Scheme.* Andrew Crichton used his account in writing his father's life.

'Two Sermons' in Michael Shields, *Faithful Contendings Displayed...*, ed. John Howie (G, 1780).

FES II, 302; Andrew Crichton, *Memoirs of... John Blackadder* (E, 1826); *Select Passages from the Diary and Letters of John Blackadder* (E, 1806); John Anderson, 'Martyrology' in *The Bass Rock*, ed. T. M'Crie et al. (E, 1847).

I. Hamilton

Blackwell, Thomas (1660–1728), Principal and Professor of Divinity, Marischal College, Aberdeen and leader in the CofS. Born and educated in Glasgow, Blackwell was ordained to Paisley in 1694, translated to the second charge in Aberdeen in 1700 and to Greyfriars in 1711, a charge held in conjunction with his appointment as Professor of Divinity. He was appointed Principal in 1717.

He wrote a series of three books: *Ratio Sacra or an Appeal unto the Rational World about the Reasonableness of Revealed Religion* (E, 1710), to show that heresies and errors, such as atheism, deism* and Bourignonianism,* are not founded on solid reason as revealed religion is; *Schema Sacrum, or, A Sacred Scheme of Natural and Revealed Religion* (E, 1710), to declare positively the complex divine scheme of revealed religion; and *Methodus Evangelica: or, a Modest Essay Upon the True Scriptural-Rational Way of Preaching the Gospel* (L, 1712), showing how the gospel should be preached in the modern world. Influential for over a hundred years, they were reprinted at various times both in Scotland and in America.

FES VII, 358; *DNB* V, 147.

D. C. Lachman

Blackwood, Adam (1539–1613), legal writer. He went from school at Dunblane, Perthshire, to Paris, sent by his maternal uncle, Bishop Robert Reid.* After visiting Scotland (1558), he continued humanistic studies at Paris under the patronage of Mary Queen of Scots,* thence proceeding to do law at Toulouse. He then settled in Poitiers as a lawyer and counsellor to the parliament, marrying a Frenchwoman. His many writings (collected edition, Paris, 1644) include devotional treatises, Latin verse (e.g. *In novas asseclas carmen* in praise of Scots Catholic exiles), an invective against Elizabeth I* after Mary's execution (*Histoire de la Martyre...*, Paris, 1587), and works on political theory, especially an *Apologia...* (Poitiers, 1581) against George Buchanan's* *De Iure Regni*, which he declared irrelevant to Scotland.

DNB V, 149–50; J. H. Burns, 'Some Catholic Critics of George Buchanan', *IR* 1 (1950), 92–109.

J. Durkan

Blaikie, William Garden (1820–99), FC Professor and social reformer. Son of James Blaikie, Advocate and Provost of Aberdeen, and educated at Marischal College, Aberdeen, and Edinburgh University, he was ordained to Drumblade, Aberdeenshire, in 1842. After the Disruption* he was called to Pilrig FC, Edinburgh, 1844. From 1868 to 1897 he was Professor of Apologetics and Pastoral Theology at New College,* Edinburgh. He was Moderator of the FC General Assembly in 1892, and Convener of the Home Mission Committee, 1874–8. At different times he edited the *North British Review*, *Sunday Magazine*, *Catholic Presbyterian* and *Free Church Magazine*. His works include: *The Preachers of Scotland* (E, 1888); *For the Work of the Ministry* (L, 1873); *The Book of Joshua* (L, 1893); *The First Book of Samuel* (L, 1888); *The Second Book of Samuel* (L, 1888); *Better Days for Working People* (L, 1867); *After Fifty Years* (L, 1893); *An Autobiography* (L, 1901). His *Personal Life of David Livingstone* (L, 1880) was the standard biography for over half a century.

Blaikie was a Victorian polymath, appearing as churchman, biblical scholar, editor, biographer, educationalist and social reformer. Theologically he was in many respects conservative and was ill at ease with the liberalization of the FC. Yet he enthusiastically advocated the new view of Scripture which sprang from biblical criticism* and rejected the older theory of verbal inerrancy. As a social reformer he was active in improving housing and in temperance work. He advocated the old age pension and a conciliation service for industrial disputes. He was also a leader in the field of homiletics and was instrumental in the formation of the Pan-Presbyterian Alliance.

AFCS I, 49–50; *DNB Suppl.* I, 212–13; *Who Was Who, 1897–1916*, 67–8; N. L. Walker (ed.), *William Garden Blaikie: An Autobiography* (L, 1901); J. Silvester, *Dr. W. G. Blaikie* (Stirling, 1922).

K. R. Ross

Blair, Duncan MacCallum (1896–1944), physician and churchman. He was born at Ashington, Northumberland, of Scots parentage; from 1903 onwards he was brought up in Glasgow, where he was educated at Woodside School and then at the University. From the age of fourteen he decided on a medical career, and entered the Glasgow Faculty of Medicine in 1913. His studies were interrupted by the First World War, during part of which (1915–17) he served as medical officer on a minesweeper. In 1919 he graduated with honours, and was appointed Lecturer in Regional Anatomy in 1922. In 1927 he was invited to the Chair of Anatomy in King's College, London, from which he returned to Glasgow in 1935 as Regius Professor of Anatomy. During the Second World War he became commanding officer of the University Naval Division.

He was an active member of the FC, serving as an elder in Milton Free Church, Glasgow. He was firmly convinced of the truth of the Reformed faith, and gave unstinted help to a great number of evangelical causes. He was three times President of the Inter-Varsity Fellowship* (1936–6, 1936–7, 1942–3), Chairman of the *Evangelical Quarterly** Advisory Committee (1942–4), a board member of the Stirling Tract Enterprise,* a director of Glasgow United Evangelistic Association.*

A. Gammie (ed.), *Professor Duncan M. Blair: a Book of Remembrance* (G, 1945).

F. F. Bruce

Blair, Hugh (1718–1800), Moderate* divine. Professor of Rhetoric and Belles Lettres in the University of Edinburgh, Blair is remembered chiefly for the elegance of his sermons, which were and still are regarded as eighteenth-century stylistic models.

BLAIR, JAMES

The son of an Edinburgh merchant and the great-grandson of the Covenanter* Robert Blair,* Hugh, while still a student at the University of Edinburgh, was praised for an essay 'On the Good'. He graduated MA in 1739 and was licensed to preach in 1741. A sermon he preached at St Cuthbert's, Edinburgh, attracted the attention of the Earl of Leven, by whose good offices he was called to Collessie, Fife, and ordained in 1742. The following year he returned to Edinburgh where he ministered successively at Canongate 1743-54, Lady Yester's 1754-8, and St Giles'* (High) 1758-1800.

In 1759 Blair began to read lectures on composition in the University of Edinburgh and in 1760 the Town Council appointed him Professor of Rhetoric. When a Regius Chair of Rhetoric and Belles Lettres was established in 1762 Blair was the first incumbent. The two volumes of his *Lectures on Rhetoric and Belles Lettres* were not published until after his retirement (L, 1783). Although Blair acknowledged his debt to Adam Smith who had given the first lectures on rhetoric in Scotland, Smith and his friends felt that the indebtedness was insufficiently emphasized.

Blair's fame rests on his sermons, which came to be regarded as models of style, yet the first volume was initially declined by the publisher, William Strahan, a London publisher, who, however, showed it to Dr Johnson. Johnson's warm approbation changed Strahan's mind and between 1777 and 1801 he published five volumes. They were extraordinarily popular; by 1794 the first had reached its nineteenth edition and the second its fifteenth. They were also frequently printed in America and were translated into several languages. Curiously, Blair was unable to speak extempore and so refrained from prominent public appearances, declining the Moderatorship of the General Assembly.

Blair was a member, along with David Hume,* Alexander Carlyle,* Adam Fergusson, William Robertson,* Adam Smith and others, of the Poker Club and defended Lord Kames when he was accused of infidelity on account of his *Essays on Morality*. He was very willing to read manuscripts by young authors and encouraged James Macpherson (1738-96) to publish the *Fragments of Ancient Poetry* in 1760, praising their merits with more generosity than prudence in *A Critical Dissertation on the Poems of Ossian, the son of Fingal* (1763).

The Wrath of Man Praising God (E, 1746); *The Importance of Religious Knowledge to the Happiness of Mankind* (E, 1750).

John Hill, *Life of Hugh Blair* (E, 1807); *DNB* V, 160-1; *FES* I, 68; R. B. Sher, *Church and University in the Scottish Enlightenment: the Moderate Literati of Edinburgh* (E, 1985).

H. R. Sefton

Blair, James (1656-1743), Scottish Episcopal* clergyman, and founder of the College of William and Mary. Probably born in Edinburgh and educated in Scotland, he was episcopically ordained in 1679 and became rector of Cranston, but was ejected within two years for declining to take an oath supporting the Duke of York as heir-presumptive to the throne. In 1685 he went to Virginia at the instigation of Bishop Compton of London, who in 1689 appointed him commissary of the church in Virginia, which post gave him a seat in the colonial legislature. In 1690, deploring the low standard of education in the area, he was the leading figure in the move to establish a college. Commissioned by the Virginia authorities, he returned to England, and in 1692 received a charter and a grant from William and Mary, after whom the college was named. Blair was appointed its first president, but a series of setbacks delayed the consolidation of the college; though classes had been in progress for more than two decades it was not until 1729 that Blair officially took up his presidential office, a post he held until his death. He combined this rôle with the rectorship of Bruton parish in Williamsburg (1710-43). His only published work was *Our Saviour's Divine Sermon on the Mount*, 4 vols (L, 1722).

D. E. Motley, *The Life of Commissary James Blair* (Baltimore, 1901); *DNB* II, 623-4.

J. D. Douglas

Blair, Robert (1593-1666), Covenanter,* minister in St Andrews. Born in Irvine (Ayrshire), Blair studied in Glasgow (MA, 1612) and then served as assistant in a Glasgow school and later as regent in the university. He greatly admired Robert Boyd,* but had difficulties with John Cameron's* novelties in doctrine and fawning subservience to monarchy and episcopacy (H. M. B. Reid, *The Divinity Principals in the University of Glasgow*, G, 1917, 214-19). In consequence, Blair resigned and went to Ireland. Here he was ordained to Bangor in Presbyterian fashion, Bishop Echlin participating as one among the brethren, and laboured there with notable success. Possibly fearing the evident revival of religion would get out of hand, Echlin deposed Blair, despite the intervention of Archbishop Usher and Charles I.* To evade arrest, Blair escaped to Scotland. There he was admitted to the second charge in Ayr and then, in 1639, translated by the General Assembly, against his will, to St Andrews. He served as chaplain to a Scottish regiment in 1643 and as Moderator of the General Assembly in 1646. A mutual attachment arose between him and Charles I, whom he believed 'a good king, evil used' (*The Life of Mr Robert Blair*, ed. T. M'Crie, E, 1848, 261). In consequence he was appointed a royal chaplain. He developed what was perhaps a related antipathy for Oliver Cromwell.* Desiring earnestly the good both of religion and of the King, Blair attempted to mediate in the struggles between Resolutioners* and Protesters.* He thus earned the suspicions of both sides (his colleagues, Samuel Rutherford* and James Wood,* he used to say, cuffed him on both cheeks), but without achieving the desired results. Having joined with him in efforts for peace over the preceding decade, Blair wrote an introduction to and supervised through the press James Durham's* dying work (... *A Treatise* *concerning Scandal*), deploring division and urging unity.

Blair objected to Rutherford's *Lex Rex*, rejoiced in the Restoration,* but opposed James Sharp's* advancement. In 1661 he was sent by the Presbytery of St Andrews to admonish Sharp to repent of his wicked ways, enraging Sharp without accomplishing his object. He was compelled by the Privy Council* to leave St Andrews, and spent his retirement completing a commentary on Proverbs which was never published. He retained mediating views to the end.

FES V, 232–3; *DNB* V, 163–4; J. S. Reid, *History of the Presbyterian Church in Ireland*, I (Belfast, 1867); T. Witherow, *Historical and Literary Memorials of Presbyterianism in Ireland, 1623–1731* (L, 1879).

D. C. Lachman

Blair, Robert (1699–1746), poet and minister. Blair is chiefly remembered as the author of *The Grave*, a didactic poem in blank verse which was published in 1743 on the recommendation of his friends Isaac Watts and Philip Doddridge. It was several times reprinted and the 1808 edition was illustrated by William Blake. The 1927 edition is bound with Gray's *Elegy*, Porteous on Death and Dodd's *Prison Thoughts*. *The Grave* has been described as 'a long sombre, melancholy, sometimes morbid exploration of death's relentless and seemingly indiscriminate pursuit of human flesh' (R. B. Sher). Blair was a grandson of Robert Blair,* minister of St Andrews and the son of David Blair, Old Kirk, Edinburgh (*FES* I, 71). He was minister at Athelstaneford 1731–46 and was succeeded by the dramatist John Home.

FES I, 354; *DNB* V, 164–6.

H. R. Sefton

Blair's College, *see* Colleges and Seminaries, Catholic.

Blane, *see* Celtic Saints.

Blantyre, *see* Missions: Africa: Malawi.

Blasphemy, the scurrilous vilification of Christian doctrine and belief. It is said to be a crime at common law in Scotland, though it was regulated by statute when it was prosecuted. The death penalty was available in the case of any person who 'not being distracted in his wits, shall rail upon or curse God, or any of the persons of the blessed Trinity' by the civil Acts 1649 c.28, 1661 c.216 and 1695 c.14, and denial of the authority of Scripture was added by the Act 1695 c.14. Prosecutions were few, and only in the case of Aikenhead* (1697) was there an execution, under circumstances which do not reflect well on those involved. The statues were repealed by the Doctrine of the Trinity Act 1812, though retaining a common law criminal penalty for the offence, a penalty reduced to a fine by the Leasing Making (Scotland) Act 1825. In modern times blasphemy may be dealt with by the civil authorities as breach of the peace or obscenity. It does not figure as a crime in Scottish texts on criminal law. The *Gay News* trial (a celebrated recent English case) or similar private prosecution would not occur in Scotland.

In terms of Church discipline, blasphemy in an office-bearer may be a ground for process under Trial by Libel within the jurisdiction of the Church and subject only to the penalties which it may impose, such as suspension from office, or excommunication (*see* Discipline).

G. Maher, 'Blasphemy in Scots Law', *Scots Law Times* 1977, (News) 257–60; J. H. A. MacDonald, *The Criminal Law of Scotland* (⁵E, 1948) 153; *R. v. Lemon; R. v. Gay News, The Times* 5th–12th July 1977; [1978] 3 All England Reports 175; [1979] 1 All England Reports 898; (English) Law Commission, 'Offences against Religion and Public Worship', Working Paper No. 79 (L, 1980).

F. Lyall

Blythswood Tract Society, a charitable organization founded in 1966, whose work mainly involves the distribution of Bibles and other Christian literature. The BTS itself has published over sixty tracts, a number of which have been translated into several languages. Correspondence courses designed to encourage Bible study are produced and these are taken in many countries. The BTS also provides financial support for Christian workers in Italy and China, and is currently active in organizing supplies of medicines, clothing and other aid, including literature, for Romania and other Eastern European countries. BTS headquarters are at Lochcarron, Ross-shire.

D. Porter, *Go Deliver! The Blythswood Story* (Fearn, Ross-shire, 1992).

A. Morrison

Boece, Hector (*c*.1470–1536), humanist, historian and first Principal of the University of Aberdeen. Born at Dundee (his father was a burgess of Dundee and kinsman of the Boyis of Panbride, Angus) he was educated there and at the University of Paris (graduated MA, 1494). After teaching the liberal arts at Montaigu College, Paris, 1494–7, he was invited by William Elphinstone* to teach liberal arts at his newly founded University of Aberdeen in 1497. He studied medicine and theology there, and graduated as bachelor in both before 1506 (licentiate in theology 1516, doctor, 1528). He was installed as first principal of King's College, 1505. His *Murthlacensium et Aberdonensium Episcoporum Vitae* was basically a tribute to his patron Elphinstone. He was buried in King's College Chapel.

Boece absorbed his Christian neo-Platonism and love of classical learning at Montaigu College, along with his fellow student and lifelong friend, Erasmus. These qualities and interests he imparted to his Aberdeen students, so that before long King's College was producing elegant Renaissance* humanists in their own right like John Vaus, Adam Mure and Florentius Wilson. His reputation as an historian suffered badly when it was shown that the early sections of his *Scotorum Historiae* (Paris, 1527) were purely mythological. If he approached his sources uncritically, however, his subsequent condemnation by later critics is in need of revision. Renaissance historians wrote elegantly on the civic virtues of ancient Greece and Rome as they imagined them to be, and Boece's history is of this genre. It has, nevertheless, some rare prophetic qualities and original insights into the history of his country.

Murthlancensium et Aberdonensium Episcoporum Vitae, ed. J. Moir (A, 1894); *The History and Chronicles of Scotland*, trans. J. Bellenden, 2 vols (E, 1821).

L. J. Macfarlane, *William Elphinstone and the Kingdom of Scotland 1431–1514* (A, 1985); J. Durkan, 'Early Humanism and King's College, Aberdeen', *AUR* 48 (1979–80), 259–79; L. J. Macfarlane, 'Hector Boece and Early Scottish Humanism', *The Deeside Field* 18 (A, 1984), 65–9; A. M. Stewart, 'Hector Boece and "Claik" Geese', *Northern Scotland* 8 (1988), 17–23; *Quatercentenary of the Death of Hector Boece*, ed. W. D. Simpson (A, 1937).

L. J. Macfarlane

Bogue, David (1750–1825), Congregationalist minister and missionary educator. Born in Berwickshire and educated at the University of Edinburgh, he became minister in 1777 of the Independent church at Gosport near Portsmouth and in 1789 opened a seminary there for the ministry.

Bogue was an architect of the modern missionary movement. His appeal 'To the Evangelical Dissenters who practise Infant Baptism', a fine example of the genre, was published in September 1794 in the *Evangelical Magazine*, which he had helped to found. This letter led directly to the formation in 1795 of the London Missionary Society* at which he preached *Objections against a Mission to the Heathen, Stated and Considered* (L). With a zeal for learning, Bogue was a chief proponent of the view that missionaries should receive an education at least equal to that of ministers at home. He opposed the early LMS policy of sending unlettered artisans to the South Seas, preferring to see well-educated missionaries sent to the ancient civilizations of the East. By Bogue's death in 1825, 115 men had trained in his academy for missionary service, including fifty for India.

Bogue published anonymously in 1790 *Reasons for Seeking a Repeal of the Corporation and Test Acts* (L). A supporter of the ideals of the French Revolution, he prophesied in a 1791 sermon that 'this generation shall not pass away before the expiring groans of arbitrary power are heard through every country in Europe'. In 1796, with Robert Haldane,* in whose conversion he was instrumental, Bogue applied to establish a seminary in Benares for instructing the natives of India in the Christian religion. This was the only missionary proposal ever to be refused outright by the East India Company. Disappointed, Bogue consciously adapted his seminary at Gosport to serve the needs of India, and India was uppermost in the content of his missionary lectures.

Bogue was also committed to home missions. At the ordination of his pupil and biographer, James Bennett, Bogue advanced his 'plan for Promoting the Knowledge of the Gospel in Hampshire'. He was one of the architects of modern Congregationalism* in Scotland and was also instrumental in the formation of the British and Foreign Bible Society (*see* Bible Societies) and the Religious Tract Society, for whom he preached *The Diffusion of Divine Truth* (L, 1800). With James Bennett, he wrote *History of Dissenters*, 4 vols (L, 1808–12; 3 vols, rev. and ed. with a continuation, 1833, 1839), a standard work, although hardly impartial. In 1815 he was awarded the DD by Yale College. He published *Discourses on the Millennium* in 1818 (L). *The Theological Lectures*, which were published posthumously in New York in 1849, were sometimes used in missionary academies overseas.

An Essay on the Divine Authority of the New Testament (Portsea, 1801; ²L, 1804) was frequently reprinted and widely influential, as was his discourse *On Universal Peace* (L, 1819); *The Duty of Christians to seek the Salvation of the Jews* (L, 1806); *Objections against a Mission to the Heathen stated and considered* (L, 1795).

DNB V, 302–3; J. Bennett, *Memoirs of the life of the Rev. David Bogue, D.D.* (L, 1827); C. Terpstra, 'David Bogue, D.D., 1750–1825: Pioneer and Missionary Educator' (PhD, University of Edinburgh, 1959); S. Piggin, *Making Evangelical Missionaries* (Appleford, 1984); N. Gunson, *Messengers of Grace* (Melbourne, 1978); P. Carson, 'Soldiers of Christ: Evangelicals and India, 1784–1833' (PhD, London University, 1988); D. Reeves, 'David Bogue and Scotland', *The Banner of Truth* 134 (1974), 26–32.

S. Piggin

Bonar, Andrew Alexander (1810–92), FC preacher and writer. Born at Edinburgh, the brother of John, James (*FES* III, 204; *AFCS* I, 99) and Horatius,* also future ministers, he was educated at Edinburgh University and ordained to Collace, Perthshire, 1838. He visited Palestine as a member of the mission of inquiry to the Jews, 1839, and took part in the Disruption.* He was translated to Finnieston FC, Glasgow, 1856, and was Moderator of the FC General Assembly, 1878. He was noted principally as a central figure in the 'school of saints', which sought to promote experimental religion first in the Est.C and then in the FC and which fostered a passionate interest in revival.* His works include: *Memoir and Remains of R. M. M'Cheyne* (2 vols, D, 1844; ²1844; revised ed., E, 1892); *Narrative of a Mission of Inquiry to the Jews* (E, 1842); *A Commentary on Leviticus* (L, 1846); *Christ and His Church in the Book of Psalms* (L, 1859); *Redemption Drawing Nigh* (L, 1847); *Memoir of David Sandeman* (L, 1861); ed. *Letters of Samuel Rutherford* 2 vols (E, 1863; slightly revised in 1 vol., 1891); *Diary and Letters*, ed. by his daughter, Marjory Bonar (L, 1893).

BONAR, ARCHIBALD

Bonar's lasting influence has been exercised through his biography of his friend R. Murray McCheyne* and his own *Diary and Letters*. In these devotional classics desire for personal holiness and passion for the conversion of souls reach a height of intensity seldom equalled. These were the great emphases of the 'school of saints' which formed within the CofS Evangelical party in the 1830s and which helped to shape the character in the 1830s and which helped to shape the character of the FC (*see* Stuart, Alexander Moody). With frequent visits to one another and 'concerts for prayer', this group fostered a hunger for the revival of personal religion. They took a leading role in the revival movement of 1840–1. In 1859, when he heard of the revival in Ulster, Bonar hurried across the water and brought the flame back to Scotland. From 1873–5 he was at the forefront of the Moody* and Sankey campaign. Tireless in evangelistic endeavour, his career impressed upon the life of the Scottish Church the conviction which he had written in Hebrew letters above the entrance to his church in Glasgow: 'He that winneth souls is wise.'

The concern for personal religion which Bonar championed was exclusive. Social questions were not admitted to his pulpit. The question of where each individual stood with Christ was his all-absorbing theme. Indifference to social matters was reinforced by Bonar's lifelong premillennialism (*see* Millennialism) which also gave rise to his interest in the conversion of the Jews, a vision which was to be fruitful in the formation of mission policy. Doctrinally conservative, he held to the Westminster* Calvinism* in which he was reared, though in his preaching it was the psychological aspect which he stressed rather than the metaphysical. He rejected higher criticism and defended the infallibility of the Bible. Indeed, as a man of eighty, he led the conservative protest which followed the vindication of Marcus Dods* at the FC General Assembly of 1890.

M. Bonar, ed., *Andrew A. Bonar ... Diary and Letters* (L, 1893); F. Ferguson, *The Life of Andrew A. Bonar* (G, 1893); M. Bonar, ed., *Reminiscences of Andrew A. Bonar* (L, 1895); W. R. Nicoll, *Princes of the Church* (L, 1921), 55–61.

K. R. Ross

Bonar, Archibald (1753–1816), evangelical CofS minister. He was a member of a family that produced numerous CofS ministers over several generations, including his nephews Horatius* and Andrew Bonar.* He served briefly as the minister of churches in Fife and Glasgow before coming in 1785 to the parish of Cramond, near Edinburgh, where he spent the remainder of his life. He published three works: *Sermons* 2 vols (E, 1815–17), memoir by brother James prefixed to vol. 2; *Genuine Religion the Best Friend of the People* (E, 1796); *Sermon before the Society for the Benefit of the Sons of the Clergy* (E, 1800).

He was a strong proponent of revival* and missions* throughout his life. In his youth he was influenced by George Whitefield,* a family acquaintance. Bonar was a diligent parish minister, seeking to encourage spiritual renewal by preaching on the importance of 'vital religion' (see three sermons in *Sermons*, II) and through regular parochial visitation and catechising.* Although he was committed firmly to the CofS, he was also involved in interdenominational organizations like the Edinburgh Missionary and Bible societies (*see* Periodicals, Religious; Missions; Bible Societies) and was an early contributor to the *Missionary Magazine*.

Manuscript letters to Mrs Erskine of Edinburgh, 1792–1816, in Paul Papers, National Library of Scotland, MS. 5144.

FES I, 12f; *DNB* V, 335.

D. A. Currie

Bonar, Horatius (1808–89), FC hymnwriter and preacher. Descended from a long line of CofS ministers, he was the son of an Edinburgh solicitor of excise, James Bonar. Two of Horatius's brothers, Andrew Alexander* and John James, were (like himself) well-known preachers. He was educated at the Edinburgh High School and, under Thomas Chalmers,* at the University.

After a period as a CofS missionary assistant at St James's, Leith (near Edinburgh), he was in 1837 ordained parish minister in Kelso, Roxburghshire. At the Disruption* he remained in Kelso as minister of the FC, of which he became a leader. His many sermons, tracts and devotional and biblical books, notably the bestsellers *God's Way of Peace* (L, 1862), *God's Way of Holiness* (L, 1864) and *The Night of Weeping* (L, 1846), and his extensive correspondence gained him great influence. He edited John Gillies* *Historical Collections* (Kelso, 1845), demonstrating his great interest in revival in the Church, and *Catechisms of the Scottish Reformation* (L, 1866). In 1853 he became a DD of Aberdeen. In 1866 he was called to the Chalmers Memorial FC, Edinburgh, and in 1883 was Moderator of the FC General Assembly. He was a leading opponent in his Church of union with the UPC.

Most of his more ephemeral writing, including *The Border Watch*, *The Christian Treasury* and the other religious magazines that he edited, is now almost forgotten (*see* Periodicals, Religious). He was, however, one of the few Scottish hymn-writers to find widespread acceptance outside Scotland. At the outset of his ministry hymns* were not used in the regular services of his church in Leith. The metrical psalms* held little appeal for the young people, so he wrote hymns for them to popular tunes. Over his lifetime he wrote more than six hundred. Lack of revision left stylistic blemishes to which he was indifferent. Characteristic of his work as a whole is the simplicity and devotional warmth of two widely used hymns, one of evangelism and one on the Lord's Supper: 'I heard the voice of Jesus say' and 'Here, O my Lord, I see thee face to face'.

The influence of Edward Irving* when Bonar was young made the Second Advent a feature of his spoken and written ministry (*e.g., Prophetical Landmarks*, L, 1847). Premillennial sentiments in many of his hymns have militated against their wider circulation.

Nevertheless, eighty-five of his hymns were annotated and 110 more recorded as 'in common use' by J. Julian in his *Dictionary of Hymnology* (²L, 1907). Julian cited the collections in which they had been published or reprinted. Although most are now passing out of use, the 1927 *Church Hymnary** included fifteen, the 1973 *CH* only eight, but the Brethren collection, *Christian Worship* (Exeter, 1976), as many as eighteen. Besides the two already quoted, among the most enduring are: 'Fill thou, my life, O Lord my God'; 'Glory be to God the Father'; 'Go, labour on: spend and be spent'; 'Not what these hands have done'; and 'Thy way, not mine, O Lord'.

Hymns of Faith and Hope, 3 vols (L, 1856–7); *Family Sermons* (L, 1863); *Light and Truth: or Bible Thoughts and Themes*, 5 vols (L, 1868–72); *The Morning of Joy* (L, 1850).

New Cambridge Bibliog. of English Literature, ed. G. Watson (C, 1969–77), III, 511; *Hymns: Selected and Arranged by H. N. Bonar* (L, 1904); M. Bell in *The Poets and Poetry of the Century*, ed. A. H. Miles, XI, (²L,1907), 147ff.; H. Bonar in J. Julian, *Dictionary of Hymnology* (²L, 1907); *Horatius Bonar, D. D. A Memorial* (L, 1889) includes a list of Bonar's writings.

J. S. Andrews

Book of Common Order (1564). Printed in Edinburgh, it embodied the law of the CofS with regard to worship until it was replaced by the Westminster* *Directory of Public Worship* in 1645. Commonly known as 'John Knox's* Liturgy' it provides a common order for worship rather than common prayers which are obligatory. However, it could be, and probably was, used as a liturgy.

The origins of the *Book of Common Order* lay in Frankfurt. In 1554 a group of English Protestants who had fled from the persecution of Queen Mary Tudor obtained permission from the magistrates of Frankfurt to use the French church there on condition that they should follow as nearly as possible the French Reformed order of worship. In accordance with this an order of worship was drawn up by John Knox and other ministers of the congregation. This however did not find favour with many of the exiles who had become attached to the *Book of Common Prayer** of Edward VI. A compromise order failed to bring a reconciliation and Knox and those who sympathized with him went to Geneva. The order of service prepared in Frankfurt was published in Geneva in 1556 as *The Forme of Prayers and Ministration of the Sacraments, &c. used in the Englishe Congregation at Geneva*.

After Knox's final return to Scotland in 1559 this Geneva book began to be used by some of the Reformed congregations which were already in being. The *First Book of Discipline** refers to it as 'the book of our common order'. In 1562 the General Assembly enjoined its uniform use in 'the administration of the sacraments and solemnisation of marriages and burial of the dead', and with some additions it was reprinted in Edinburgh that year, still as *The Forme of Prayers*.

Between 1562 and 1564 the book was enlarged by the inclusion of a complete metrical Psalter* and additional prayers from continental and Scottish sources. Thus modified, it was printed in Edinburgh in 1564, still entitled *The Forme of Prayers...*, but now described as *...Approved and Received by the Churche of Scotland...* The General Assembly of that year 'ordained that every Minister, Exhorter and Reader shall have one of the Psalm-books lately printed in Edinburgh and use the Order contained therein in Prayers, Marriage and ministration of the Sacraments'. It was frequently known as the 'Psalm-Book', as the metrical Psalter formed the first part of it. It was kept in print until 1644. The prayers were translated into Gaelic* by John Carswell,* Superintendent of Argyll, and this version published in 1567 was the first book to be printed in Gaelic.

The *BCO* also provides guidance as to procedure in the election of ministers, elders* and superintendents,* in the exercise of discipline* and in the observance of fasting. Orders are given for the administration of the Lord's Supper* and baptism, and for the solemnization of marriage and the visitation of the sick. With regard to funerals the *Book* directs that the corpse should be reverently brought to the grave and buried without any further ceremonies, but that the minister, if he be present, may make some comfortable exhortation touching death and resurrection in the Church, if it be not far off. Full prayers, with alternatives, are provided for public worship. The service begins with a prayer of confession. A psalm is then sung 'in a plain tune' and the minister then prays for the assistance of God's Holy Spirit and proceeds to the sermon. There follows a prayer for the whole estate of Christ's Church, concluding with 'the Belief' or Apostles' Creed. Another psalm is sung and the minister pronounces a blessing. There is no mention of the public reading of Scripture, but this seems to have been included in a preliminary service by a reader.*

G. W. Sprott, *The Book of Common Order of the Church of Scotland, Commonly Known as John Knox's Liturgy* (E, 1901); W. D. Maxwell, *The Liturgical Portions of the Geneva Service Book* (E, 1931); W. Cowan, *A Bibliography of the Book of Common Order and Psalm Book of the Church of Scotland* (Public. of Edinb. Bibliograph. Soc.10, 1896; rp., E, 1913).

H. R. Sefton

Book of Common Order (modern editions). The Church Service Society* published in 1867 the first edition of *Euchologion or A Book of Common Order* (E). It was constantly revised and successive editions appeared for the next sixty years. To begin with, *Euchologion* largely reflected the order of worship commonly in use in Scotland, attempting to enrich the prayers from the classical treasury of Christian devotion as well as some modern compositions, and to encourage the more systematic use

BOOK OF COMMON ORDER

of Scripture in worship through the compilation of a lectionary. Later editions showed greater eagerness to change the structure of the Sunday services and in particular the order for Holy Communion. The sixth edition in 1890 attempted to model the Sunday morning service quite closely on the model of Anglican matins, and the two greatest influences on *Euchologion* were the *Liturgy* of the Catholic Apostolic Church*, and the Anglican *Book of Common Prayer*.* A *Book of Common Order* initially compiled by Cameron Lees* was used in St Giles* between 1884 and 1926, but this was not an authorized book and did not have the influence of *Euchologion*.

The General Assembly of the CofS in 1923 authorized *Prayers for Divine Service*, the first book of worship to receive such authority since the Westminster *Directory*.* This book was in most respects rather close to *Euchologion*, and was criticized for being an 'anglicanizing' book. Meanwhile the UFC was hard at work, and its *Book of Common Order* (1928) was published the year before the Union. 'It is not intended to be used as a liturgy,' wrote Millar Patrick,* the convener of the committee that compiled it, 'nor is there any obligation to follow, scrupulously or in exact detail, the orders it supplies. Its aim is to express the mind of the Church with regard to its offices of worship . . . .'

In 1936 the General Assembly of the reunited CofS commissioned its Committee on Public Worship and Aids to Devotion* to compile a new norm of worship, which finally appeared as *The Book of Common Order* (1940). Like its predecessors, this *BCO* was not a mandatory book. A consequence of this was that its compilers had an extraordinary amount of freedom and produced a fine and coherent book of worship. They were not required to make the awkward compromises and introduce the studied ambiguities which are almost inevitable when a liturgy is binding and every phrase and word has to be fought over by contending parties. It was deeply influenced by the insights of the liturgical movement, which could not yet find expression in the official orders of the Roman and the Anglican Churches. Its order for the Lord's Supper, in W. D. Maxwell's* judgement, 'represents a long tradition brought to a high perfection, indigenously Scottish and Reformed, and essentially Catholic. In its dignity of action, centrality of content, and felicity of expression, it provides a vehicle of worship entitling it to a place among the great rites of Christendom, and is rapidly being recognized as such.' For the decade until the appearance of the liturgy of the Church of South India it held a pre-eminent place. But in the period after the Second World War the pace of liturgical renewal quickened, especially with the reforms of liturgy authorized by the Second Vatican Council. The *BCO* (1940) began to appear to many a rather sedate and old-fashioned book. Accordingly work was started on a replacement, which finally appeared as the *Book of Common Order* (1979).

This new book goes further than any of its predecessors in affirming the centrality of the Lord's Supper. The *BCO* (1940) devotes its long first section to orders for non-sacramental services, on the assumption that the Lord's Supper would continue to be celebrated relatively infrequently. The *BCO* (1979) starts with three orders for the Lord's Supper, and gives only an outline structure for a non-sacramental service, apparently assuming that the Lord's Supper will quickly gain its proper place as the principal Sunday service in the congregations of the CofS. The *BCO* (1979) includes many fine things, but it has been much criticized, especially for its rather old-fashioned high-church emphasis (which provoked the *Reformed Book of Common Order**) and for its failure to grapple creatively with the distinctive problems of modern liturgical language. It has never been as highly regarded as a liturgical milestone as was the *BCO* (1940). Work is now complete on the compilation of another *Book of Common Order*.

D. B. Forrester, 'Recent Liturgical Work in Scotland', *ExT* 91 (1979), 39–44; D. B. Forrester and D. Murray, eds, *Studies in the History of Worship in Scotland* (E, 1984), chaps 6 and 11; W. D. Maxwell, *A History of Worship in the Church of Scotland* (L, 1955), 174–85; W. McMillan, 'Euchologion: The Book of Common Order', *Church Service Society Annual* 9 (1936–7), 24–33; A. S. Todd, 'The Ordering of Liturgical Worship', *Liturgical Review* 7/2 (1977), 11–19.

D. B. Forrester

Book of Common Order, Reformed, published in 1977 by the conservative National Church Association* in order to anticipate the 1979 *Book of Common Order* (see above). The Book claims to be based on Knox's *Book of Common Order** (1564) and the Westminster *Directory**, and attempts to provide an alternative norm to that presented by the allegedly Romanizing publications of the CofS's Public Worship Committee. It was in fact an old-fashioned book, strongly Victorian in ethos, archaic in language and uninfluenced by recent theology or by ecumenical developments. Its use of Knox's *BCO* and the *Directory* is selective and tones down their theological content in a memorialist and antisacramental direction.

D. B. Forrester

Book of Common Prayer. When the Roman rite was formally prohibited in Scotland in 1560 (*see* Reformation), experiments in worship were far from unknown, but the idea of conducting a service without written or printed guidance had not yet taken root. Many people longed for 'common prayers' in their own tongue and with books in their hands. Suitable material for the new services could be obtained from countries where the Reformation had been accepted earlier. Many Scots could, and did, translate from Latin, German, Danish and French sources, but much less trouble was to be had by making use of existing Protestant books from south of the border.

There are indications that the 1549 *BCP*, and perhaps more so that of 1552, were initially used, whole or in part, by Scottish Protestants of differing persuasions. Knox* himself, at whose insistence the 'Black Rubric' was inserted in the 1552 *BCP*, seems to have followed the Anglican book, in some respect, up to the last, though he did not approve of it as whole-heartedly as other Reformers, such as John Rough,* his colleague in St Andrews. Even after the publication of the *BCO** in 1562, those who so wished could still follow the *BCP* in its prayers and lessons. It would appear that, whilst Episcopalians were more likely to prefer the 1549 *BCP*, others would favour its more clearly Protestant-orientated version of 1552.

When Presbyterians gained ascendancy by the later 1580s, a distrust of bishops and of the forms of worship the English bishops upheld spread throughout the land. When Charles I* attempted a unification of the worship of the two kingdoms through the publication of the 1637 Scottish Prayer Book,* the climate for the enterprise was not at all favourable. Though it was read in a number of places, the book found little favour and was driven by law from both public and private worship after the triumph of the Covenanters* in 1638.

During the second episcopacy (1661–89), the *BCP* seems to have been used in some quarters, but in many places even Episcopalians continued to hold services without a book. The influence of the 1662 *BCP* revived a little only after Queen Anne made Scotland a gift of thousands of free copies, when some congregations, not all of them Episcopalian, adopted the book and started to use its form mostly for matins, evensong and the occasional offices.

To this day, there is nothing to prevent a CofS minister from using some of the *BCP*'s material in the preparation of services. The eighteenth-century worship revival among non-juring Episcopalians had encouraged them to look with favour to the Scottish *BCP* of 1637, whilst still striving to find their own form for the Eucharist (*see* Rattray, T.), whilst the so-called 'qualified congregations' of juring-Episcopalians (*i.e.* the CofE in Scotland) had little difficulty in adopting the English *BCP* in its entirety. The anglicization of the Church having become the fashion soon after the abolition of the Penal Laws, in 1863 the *BCP* was enforced in all ordinary services of the EpCS and the English form of liturgy was given pre-eminence over the Scottish, a state of affairs which was to continue in differing degrees until the modern days of liturgical reform.

G. Donaldson, 'Reformation to Covenant' in D. Forrester and D. Murray (eds), *Studies in the History of Worship in Scotland* (E, 1984), 33–51; W. McMillan, 'The Anglican Book of Common Prayer in the Church of Scotland', *RSCHS* 4 (1931), 138–49; A. Maclean, 'Episcopal Worship in the Nineteenth and Twentieth Centuries' in D. Forrester and D. Murray (eds), *Studies in the History of Worship in Scotland* (E, 1984), 96–112; C. J. Cuming, *A History of Anglican Liturgy* (L, ²1982).

G. Tellini

Booke of the Universall Kirk, title applied to the early registers of the proceedings of the General Assembly of the CofS from 1560. The minutes were held by the clerk who was also recognized as keeper of the register, but by 1584 the registers fell into the hands of Archbishop Patrick Adamson,* who destroyed portions of the Assembly's proceedings against bishops. In 1586, James VI agreed that the clerk should have custody of the registers during sittings of the Assembly, and that the keeper of the privy seal should retain the volumes at other times. Between 1618 and 1638, when no assemblies were held, the registers were neglected until Archibald Johnston* of Warriston recovered five volumes in time for the Covenanters'* Glasgow Assembly* of 1638. Four volumes of the original record covered the years 1560 to 1590 with gaps March 1573–March 1574, and July 1580–October 1583; the fifth volume, prepared in the 1590s by James Carmichael,* minister of Haddington, at the Assembly's behest, was an authenticated duplicate of the Assembly's proceedings to 1590. With the Cromwellian conquest in the 1650s, two volumes for 1590–1616 and Carmichael's text were entrusted to the Earl of Balcarres. Carmichael's work passed to the Earl of Cromarty and finally to Aberdeen University Library, and the registers passed through several hands before being deposited first in the library of Sion College, London, and then in the Houses of Parliament, where they perished in the fire of 1834. The other records not delivered to Balcarres were taken in 1652 by the Cromwellian regime from the Bass Rock* to the Tower of London. They may have perished at sea when records sent back to Scotland were lost at the Restoration* or subsequently were destroyed by fire in Edinburgh in 1701. None of the earliest registers of the General Assembly has therefore survived, and the printed compilation consists primarily of an abbreviate of (essentially extracts from) the original Acts, begun by John Craig* and continued by Carmichael and others in the late sixteenth and early seventeenth centuries.

In 1839 *The Booke of the Universall Kirk of Scotland*, edited by Alexander Peterkin, was printed from a manuscript in the Advocates' Library (now in the National Library of Scotland). At approximately the same time an edition, supplemented (and corrected) by extracts from other sources (particularly David Calderwood's* larger *History*), was printed 1839–45 in three volumes (but one pagination) by the combined efforts of the Bannatyne and Maitland clubs. Edited by Thomas Thomson, this is the most comprehensive record of the early General Assemblies of the CofS now extant.

BUK III, i–xvi; *BUK*, ed. Peterkin (E, 1839), vi–viii, 599–600.

J. Kirk

Borthwick, Jane Laurie (1813–97), **Sarah** (1823–1907), translators of German hymns. Daughters of James Borthwick, an insurance manager in Edinburgh, they were staunch members of the FC. Sarah married Eric John Findlater, the FC minister at Lochearnhead, Perthshire; their daugh-

BORTHWICK, (SIR) JOHN

ters were the novelists Jane H. and Mary Findlater.

The sisters published anonymously *Hymns from the Land of Luther*, 4 series (E, 1854-62). Many were published as *Thoughts for Thoughtful Hours* (L, 1859; ³L, 1867). A complete edition of the former (113 hymns) came out in 1862 (E); the 1884 (L) edition added thirty-three hymns headed 'Alpine Lyrics' from the German-Swiss Meta Heusser-Schweizer; these translations by Jane had been issued separately (L, 1875). Jane also wrote less well-known original poems: 'Still on the homeward journey' is in the 1927 *Church Hymnary*.* These and the hymns that she and her sister translated were pietistic in tone and concerned with the Christian life.

Jane Borthwick's translations include: 'Jesus, Sun of Righteousness' (Knorr von Rosenroth, 1636-89); 'Be still, my soul!' (K. A. D. Schlegel, *b*.1697); 'Jesus, still lead on' (N. L. von Zinzendorf, 1700-60, *et al.*). Sarah Findlater is best known for 'God calling yet!' (G. Tersteegen, 1697-1769) and 'O happy home' (K. J. P. Spitta, 1801-59), which reflects the type of homes enjoyed by the author and the translator. The translations are found mainly in FC and/or evangelical collections.

J. Julian, *Dictionary of Hymnology* (²L, 1907); *Handbook to the [Revised] Church Hymnary*, ed. J. Moffatt (²L, 1928) [fuller than *Handbook to CH3*, ed. J. M. Barkley (L, 1979)]; J. S. Andrews, 'The Borthwick Sisters as Translators of German Hymns', *ExT* 94 (1983), 329-33.

J. S. Andrews

Borthwick, (Sir) John (*d.*1569), early Protestant Reformer. A son of William, Third Lord Borthwick, he was probably the student of that name who matriculated at St Andrews in 1509 and 'determined' for his bachelorship in 1511. A visitor to England and France (and later to Denmark, Germany, and Switzerland), Captain Borthwick, a lieutenant of the French king's guard, escorted Sadler, the English ambassador, to Scotland in 1540, and supported Henry VIII's cause. Accused of heresy in 1540, he escaped to England and was condemned (in his absence), forfeited and excommunicated for allegedly claiming that the pope had no more authority than other bishops, indulgences had no effect, the pope was guilty of simony, the English heresies conformed to God's Word, the clergy should have no temporal property or jurisdiction, the king should appropriate church property, and canon law was contrary to God's law, and for possessing such heretical books as an English New Testament and the works of Oecolampadius, Melanchthon and Erasmus. After the Reformation, his sentence was reversed by the superintendent's court in St Andrews in 1561. As captain of the Regent Moray's (James Stewart,* Earl of Moray, 1531-70) horsemen, he was killed in a Border skirmish on 25 December 1569.

Knox, *Works* I, 61, 520, 533-4; Calderwood I, 114-23; II, 46; J. Foxe, *Acts and Monuments* (L, 1858), V, 607-21; D. H. Fleming (ed.), *Register of the Minister, Elders and Deacons of the Christian Congregation of St Andrews* (E, 1889-90), I, 89-104; J. M. Anderson (ed.), *Early Records of the University of St Andrews* (E, 1926), 99, 204.

J. Kirk

BOSTON, THOMAS

Boston, Thomas (1676-1732), CofS minister and author. Born in Duns of a father who was imprisoned for non-conformity (and whom he visited in prison as a child), Boston was greatly influenced in his youth by the ministry of Henry Erskine.* He was educated in Edinburgh (MA, 1694). After a term of divinity there under George Campbell* and a year as a domestic chaplain, he was ordained in 1699 to Simprin, a small country parish near Coldstream. After a diligent ministry there he was translated in 1707 to Ettrick, a country parish west of Selkirk which had been vacant four years and which was troubled with continuing Cameronian* (*see* Societies, United) influences. Although it took ten years of diligent pastoral labour, Boston's ministry was eventually so heartily received that it shaped the religious life of the parish for generations.

Temperamentally reticent and disinclined to public appearance, particularly debate in church courts, Boston was nevertheless compelled by conscience to take a stand on the issues of the day. In a sermon on 'The Evil and Danger of Schism' (*Works* VII, 593-613), he pleaded for unity and peace against the Cameronian position. He acknowledged the corruptions of the Church, but held that true strictness of practice is that which emulates Christ, who attended both temple and synagogue in spite of the corruptions of his day. He had scruples about the Abjuration Oath* and steadfastly refused to sign it. In 1719 he published an anonymous pamphlet giving *Reasons for refusing the Abjuration Oath in its latest form*. Although this was a popular position, the excessive penalties for non-compliance made refusal to take the oath a risk few were willing to take. He took an active part in the Marrow Controversy,* having 'relished [the *Marrow*] greatly' since first finding a copy in a cottage while engaged in pastoral visitation in Simprin. He and his close friends, Gabriel Wilson* of Maxton and Henry Davidson of Galashiels (*FES* II, 177-8), initiated the correspondence with James Hog* which led to the appeal of the 1720 Assembly's Act. The extensive notes he wrote to the *Marrow* (first edition 1726, but written 1721-2) have been reprinted with all but one of its many subsequent editions.

Although he did not take an active part in the second trial of John Simson,* Boston attracted much attention when he alone stood in the 1728 Assembly to protest at its decision, believing that Simson deserved deposition and holding any lesser sentence dishonouring to God.

John (Rabbi) Duncan* aptly characterized Boston as a 'commonplace genius'. In the early years of his ministry Boston had relatively few books, but did not shrink from conscientiously addressing – and answering – whatever questions came his way. His 'Miscellany Questions', published posthumously as the first part of *Sermons and Discourses* (2 vols, E,

1753), examines such questions as 'Whether or not all sins, past, present, and to come, are pardoned together and at once?' and 'Who have right to baptism, and are to be baptized?' In answer to the latter question (124–226) he takes issue with the position held by Samuel Rutherford* and earlier Reformed divines and asserts that only believers and children with at least one believing parent have a right to baptism (see J. Macpherson, *Doctrine of the Church in Scottish Theology*, E, 1903, 82–90). Boston also believed it better to speak of two covenants rather than three, as was then ordinary (*see* Covenant Theology). But he was not thereby led to reject Reformed orthodoxy. Rather he infused it with fresh life and warmth, influencing first his parish and eventually all of Scotland.

His theology can be characterized as what came to be known as 'Marrow theology'. From early in his ministry he emphasized a free offer of the gospel, an assurance focused on Christ and not in the believer himself, and the power of grace in the life of the believer rather than the threatenings of the law. These and like emphases are evident throughout his works. His first published book originated in a course of sermons preached in Simprin and again in Ettrick. After a series of mishaps *Human Nature in its Fourfold State* (E, 1720) was published anonymously. His most influential work, it has been reprinted perhaps 100 times and translated into a variety of languages. The Bible aside, it had an influence second to none in the religious life of Scotland for well over 100 years – and is still in print today.

A fine linguist, Boston taught himself Hebrew. After a time the accents caught his attention and attaining a full understanding of them became what he termed his 'darling' study. He came to believe them the key to the Hebrew text and of divine origin. Eventually, with the encouragement of friends, he completed a treatise on the subject, translated it into Latin and readied it for the press. Published posthumously as *Tractatus Stigmologicus, Hebraeo-Biblicus* (Amsterdam, 1738) it was favourably received by the learned of the day. With the light attained from this study, he prepared a new translation of Genesis and wrote an accompanying commentary, regrettably never published.

The first of many posthumous works, *A View of the Covenant of Grace* (E, 1734) was issued not long after his death. Its favourable reception led to the publication of other manuscripts, ranging from *An Illustration of the Doctrines of the Christian Religion, upon the plan of the Assembly's Shorter Catechism, comprehending A Complete Body of Divinity* (3 vols, E, 1773) and *A View of the Covenant of Works* (E, 1772; ²E, 1775) to *Sermons . . . on Communion Occasions* (G, 1814). His *Memoirs* is a classic; primarily a spiritual autobiography, it recounts his life with an endearing candour. Written as two overlapping accounts for the use of his descendants, without thought of possible publication, it was first edited for publication by Michael Boston, his grandson (*Memoirs of the Life, Time and Writings*, E, 1776; ed. G. H. Morrison, E, 1899; these combine *A General Account of My Life*, L, 1908, and *Passages of My Life*, otherwise unpublished). Boston's works were first collected as *The Whole Works* (E, 1767; Dundee, 1773); *The Complete Works* (12 vols, A, 1848–52; Wheaton, IL, 1980) is the definitive edition.

The Distinguishing Characters of True Believers, to which is prefixed, a Soliloquy on the Art of Man-fishing (E, 1773); *The Sovereignty and Wisdom of God Displayed in the Afflictions of Men* (the 'Crook in the Lot') (E, 1737); *The Beauties*, ed. S. McMillan (A, 1831).

FES II, 174–5; *DNB* V, 424–6; J. L. Watson, *The Pastor of Ettrick* (E, 1883); A. Thomson, *Thomas Boston of Ettrick* (E, 1895); W. Addison, *The Life and Writings of Thomas Boston of Ettrick* (E, 1936); D. J. Bruggink, 'The Theology of Thomas Boston' (PhD, Edinburgh University, 1956); A. T. B. McGowan, 'The Federal Theology of Thomas Boston' (PhD, Aberdeen University, 1990); D. M. G. Stalker, 'Boston of Ettrick as Old Testament Scholar', *RSCHS* 9 (1947), 61–8.

D. C. Lachman

Boston, Thomas (the younger) (1713–67), co-founder of the Relief Church.* The youngest son of Thomas Boston* of Ettrick, he was educated at the University of Edinburgh, licensed in 1732 and ordained in 1733 to Ettrick as his father's succesor. He was translated to Oxnam, near Jedburgh, in 1749, and in 1755 called to Jedburgh by the town council, elders and most of the people. The Crown, however, refused to present him. Although the first presentee, John Bonar, was not forced upon the church, the second, Robert Douglas, who was so unpopular that only five in the whole parish could be found to support his call, was forced. Unable to prevent his induction, the populace, with Boston's consent, erected a meeting-house and called him to become their minister. He was inducted in December 1757. Although the Presbytery of Jedburgh was unwilling to accept his demission from Oxnam, the General Assembly agreed to it, debarred him from any further presentation and prohibited all ministerial communion with him. While separating from the CofS,* Boston expressed himself willing to hold communion with all who were sound in faith and holy in practice. An immense crowd gathered for his first communion there. Next year he invited Thomas Gillespie,* and their continued fellowship led to the constitution of the Presbytery of Relief in 1761. Shortly before his death Boston was called to a newly formed congregation in Glasgow, but died before the matter was settled.

Three collections of Boston's works were published posthumously: *Select Discourses on a Variety of Practical Subjects* (G, 1768), *Essays . . . on Theological Subjects* (Falkirk, 1773), and *Select Sermons . . .* (E, 1850). He also prepared for the press several volumes of his father's works.

FES II, 136–7; *DNB* V, 426–7; Small II, 259–60; G. Struthers, *The History of the Rise, Progress, and Principles of The Relief Church* (G, 1843).

D. C. Lachman

Boswell (Boisil), *see* Celtic Saints.

Bothwell, Adam (c.1527–93), Bishop of Orkney. He was a younger son of Francis Bothwell, a lord of the Court of Session* and Provost of Edinburgh. Educated at the University of St Andrews and in France, Bothwell retained a lively interest in intellectual developments and his library and his reputation point towards a man of considerable breadth of learning and interests.

Bothwell's first charge was as rector of Ashkirk (near Selkirk), where he was serving by 1552, and at the same time he was a canon of Glasgow Cathedral. In 1559 he was appointed Bishop of Orkney, but soon after joined the Protestants. The depth of his commitment to Reformed ideas is unclear, but he did show some interest in reforming his diocese, and over the next few years was also prominent in the affairs of the General Assembly.* Simultaneously he pursued his legal interests and served on the Court of Session from 1563.

On 15 May 1567 Bothwell officiated at the Protestant marriage of Mary Queen of Scots* and the Earl of Bothwell, but by 29 July he was present in Stirling to anoint and crown James VI* following Mary's abdication. In December the General Assembly suspended him from exercising any ministry until he had satisfactorily explained his role in the marriage. Following his repentance he was restored in July 1568, but his rights to superintend the Orkney diocese were withheld. By 1570 he had extricated himself from Orkney, exchanging most of his temporalities for the abbacy of Holyrood*.

During the civil war of 1567–73 Bothwell sided with the King's Party, and in January 1572 was one of those responsible for negotiating a compromise over ecclesiastical revenues with the government at the Convention of Leith.* In spite of brief periods of imprisonment in 1578 and 1582, Bothwell continued as a Privy Councillor and Lord of Session throughout the vicissitudes of the next twenty years. He also had to endure criticism from the Presbyterians, first for neglect of his minsterial duties which he finally gave up in 1582, and then for his part as a Lord of the Articles in preparing Chancellor Arran's 1584 Black Acts,* which created an Erastian (see Church and State) episcopacy. He was not adversely affected by Arran's fall in 1585 and continued to enjoy royal favour until his death in 1593.

DNB V, 444–6; FES VII, 352–3; G. Donaldson, 'Bishop Adam Bothwell and the Reformation in Orkney', RSCHS 13 (1959), 85–100, rp. in id., Reformed by Bishops (E, 1987), 19–51; D. Shaw, 'Adam Bothwell: A Conserver of the Renaissance in Scotland' in I. B. Cowan and D. Shaw (eds), The Renaissance and Reformation in Scotland (E, 1983), 141–69; P. D. Anderson, Robert Stewart, Earl of Orkney, Lord of Shetland, 1533–1593 (E, 1982).

K. M. Brown

Bothwell Bridge (Lanarkshire), site of a battle between Covenanting* and government forces, 22 June 1679. Shortly after the assassination of Archbishop Sharp,* on 29 May 1679, some eighty horsemen rode into Rutherglen and read a Testimony against what they believed were the defections of the times, condemning the imposition of episcopacy* and the forsaking of the Covenants,* and deploring much of the work of the government of Charles II.* The commander of the government troops, John Graham of Claverhouse,* was sent to apprehend them. Hearing of a nearby conventicle,* he rode to give battle. The conventiclers, being warned of the approach of the enemy, gave command to Robert Hamilton. The two forces met at Drumclog and the government troops were routed, with Claverhouse making a narrow escape. Hamilton led the Covenanters in pursuit to Glasgow, but was unable to breach the city's defences.

They retreated to Bothwell Bridge, where many joined them, with their numbers fluctuating between five and eight thousand. But with numbers came disagreement. Hamilton, Donald Cargill* and others opposed the existing situation in Church and state root and branch; others, such as John Welsh of Irongray,* wished to restore freedom but on the basis of a broader Presbyterianism,* including even the Indulged (see Indulgence). To these incompatible groups were added those who thought that the Lord's people were called on to suffer rather than act for their own deliverance, and others who simply wanted a good fight. Instead of concentrating on preparations for war, the camp became a virtual theological debating chamber. On 13 June a declaration was affixed to the cross in Hamilton, justifying a defensive rising, but not specifying the public defections the stricter faction complained of. Hamilton's followers wished to dissociate themselves from the Indulged. The result of these wranglings was many desertions and an army of some four thousand ill-prepared for war.

The government, meanwhile, sent the Duke of Monmouth with some ten thousand men to quell the rebellion, but with instructions to act with moderation. Negotiations failed. After a stubborn defence of the bridge itself, Hamilton's inept leadership contributed substantially to a rout of the Covenanters. Some four or five hundred were killed and over 1,200 taken prisoner. Most were imprisoned in Greyfriars' Churchyard in Edinburgh. Although the majority of those who did not die while imprisoned were ultimately set free, those suspected of being the ringleaders and those who refused an oath to rise no more in arms were executed or sentenced to be transported. Of the 257 in the latter category, the majority died when their ship went down off Dearness.

J. K. Hewison, The Covenanters, 2 vols (G, ²1913).

J. A. Dickson

Bourignianism, the religious teachings of the Flemish mystic, Antoinette Bourignon (1616–80), once influential in Scotland. Madame Bourignon, professedly under divine guidance, elaborated a quasi-pantheistic conception of religion, in which Modalistic, Pelagian and Socinian elements all found a place. Ethically, she taught an extreme doctrine of 'resignation' to God's will, which involved extinction of desire and virtual independence of all external means of grace. She was condemned by all the established religious authorities of the day, RC and Protestant.

Bourignon's writings began to be translated into English in the 1670s. She had more followers in Scotland, it was said, than in any other country, especially in the first decade of the eighteenth century; chiefly a circle of Scottish Episcopalians* in the north-east, noted for their Jacobite* tendencies. These included Lord Forbes of Pitsligo, Lord Deskford, George Garden* and his brother James* (Professor of Divinity in Aberdeen University), and James Keith. By the succeeding decade, however, the movement seems to have faded, and Madame Bourignon's disciples had transferred their religious allegiance to Madame Guyon.

Concern about the spread of Bourignon's influence led the General Assembly of the CofS to pass deliverances against Bourignianism in 1701, 1709 and 1710. The particular tenets singled out for censure were: (i) Madame Bourignon's denial that God permits sin and punishes sinners with damnation; (ii) her attributing to Christ a twofold human nature, one sinless and derived from pre-fall Adam, reserved in heaven till the incarnation, the other sinful and derived from Mary; (iii) her denial of the Calvinistic doctrines of election and reprobation; (iv) her denial of divine prescience; (v) her belief in the existence of a good and evil spirit in every soul before birth; (vi) her ascription of spiritual free-will to fallen humanity and an infinite quality whereby he can unite himself to God; (vii) her belief in the fallenness of (one part of) Christ's human nature, and the consequent rebellion of his human will – in sentiment, though not in consent – against God's will; (viii) the possibility of perfection in this life, and several other errors.

In 1711 the General Assembly placed Bourignianism on the list of heresies to be abjured by all ordinands, together with Popish, Arian, Socinian and Arminian errors. This formula remained in force until repealed in 1889.

G. D. Henderson, *Mystics of the North-East* (A, 1934); A. R. MacEwen, *Antoinette Bourignon, Quietist* (L, 1910).

N. R. Needham

Bower, Walter (c.1385–1449), chronicler. He was an Augustinian* at St Andrews* and then abbot of Inchcolm* from 1418, known solely as compiler of the *Scotichronicon*, 1440–7. This chronicle* amplified the *Chronica Gentis Scotorum* (1384–7) of John of Fordun (ed. and tr. W. F. and F. J. H. Skene, E, 1871–2) and continued it down to 1437 (death of James I). Of Bower's sixteen books, the first five and more are mainly Fordun. The only complete edition of the *Scotichronicon* was produced by Walter Goodall (2 vols, E, 1759), but a new edition with ET is now in process, ed. D. E. R. Watt (A, 1987 –). Abridgements were composed by Bower himself (a MS known as the *Book of Cupar*, i.e. Coupar Angus, now in the National Library of Scotland)

and others (e.g. *Liber Pluscardensis*, 1461; ed. F. J. H. Skene, E, 1877–80).

D. F. Wright

Boyd, Andrew Kennedy Hutchison (1825–99), CofS minister and popular writer, son of James Boyd, minister of Auchinleck, Ayrshire. Educated at King's College and the Middle Temple, London, where he trained as a barrister, and at the University of Glasgow (BA, 1846) where he studied arts and divinity, he became minister of Newton-on-Ayr in 1851; of Kirkpatrick Irongay, Dumfriesshire, in 1854; of St Bernard's, Edinburgh, in 1859; and of the first charge of St Andrews in 1865. He was awarded honorary degrees by the universities of Edinburgh (DD) and St Andrews (LLD). He was elected Moderator of the General Assembly in 1890 and Fellow of King's College London in 1895. He became well known in both Scotland and England through his articles in *Fraser's Magazine* which were signed 'A.K.H.B.', and by his series of *Recreations of a Country Parson* (L, 1859, 1861, 1878). He had several friends among CofE clergy and strongly supported the establishment principle. He held a 'good Anglican Churchman' to be the brother to 'most men worth counting in the Scottish Kirk' (*Sermons and Stray Papers*, L, 1907, 41). He was a prominent advocate of liturgical change and promoted the introduction of organs, the use of hymns and the observance of the Christian year.* He was convener of the Committee on Psalmody and Hymns responsible for producing the *Scottish Hymnal* of 1870 (see Hymnology).

The Graver Thoughts of a Country Parson (L, 1862, 1865, 1875); *Twenty-Five Years of St Andrews*, 2 vols (L, 1892); *The Last Years of St Andrews* (L, 1896); *A Scotch Communion Sunday* (L, 1873).

FES V, 236; *DNB Suppl.* I, 244–5.

D. M. Murray

Boyd, James, of Trochrigg (Trochrague, near Girvan, Ayrshire) (*d*.1581), Protestant Archbishop of Glasgow. The second son of Adam Boyd of Pinkhill, brother of Lord Boyd, after studying civil law under Cujas in Bourges, he returned home to serve as minister at Kirkoswald in Ayrshire by 1572. He was appointed to the see of Glasgow in 1573, under procedures defined at the Convention of Leith* in 1572, though his uncle, Lord Boyd, was influential in securing his promotion. By 1575, he found the archdiocese too large to oversee without assistance from two commissioners of the Assembly. Moderator of the General Assembly in 1575, he contributed to drafting the *Second Book of Discipline** of 1578, was instructed in 1576 to assume a congregational ministry, and selected Kirkoswald and Glasgow. As Chancellor of Glasgow University, he helped secure Andrew Melville's* appointment as college principal in 1574, assigned to the college the Tron customs revenues of the city, and bequeathed over forty volumes to the college library. He was buried in the cathedral. His son, Robert,* was Principal of Glasgow and Edinburgh universities.

BUK; Calderwood III; J. Melville, *Diary* (E, 1842), 47, 55; Spottiswoode II, 172, 257; *SBD*; R. Wodrow, *Collections* (G, 1834–48), I, 205–30, 385–92, 521–35; J. Durkan and J. Kirk, *The University of Glasgow, 1451–1577* (G, 1977); *FESMA* 150; R. Keith, *Historical Catalogue of Scottish Bishops* (E, 1824), 261; *FES* III, 46, VII, 321, VIII, 708.

J. Kirk

Boyd, Robert, of Trochrigg (1578–1627), Principal of Glasgow and Edinburgh universities. Son of James Boyd,* tulchan* Archbishop of Glasgow, Boyd was educated at Ayr grammar school and at Edinburgh University (MA, 1595), where he studied under Charles Ferme* and Robert Rollock.* Graduating in 1594, he left for France in 1597, taught at Tours, and became a friend of André Rivet, who was minister there. He visited Poitiers, La Rochelle and Bordeaux and, from 1599, taught for five years at the Protestant academy of Montauban. Proficient in Greek and Hebrew, he taught philosophy and studied divinity. In September 1604 he left Montauban for Vertueil, where he was ordained to a pastoral charge. In 1606 he was invited through the influence of Du Plessis-Mornay to teach at the Protestant academy of Saumur and serve as one of the pastors there. By August 1607 he left Saumur for a spell to return home (during which period he was served heir to the Trochrigg estates), but was back by June 1608, and in September was appointed Professor of Divinity. He again paid a visit home in 1610. By December 1612 the services of his cousin, Zachary Boyd,* were secured for the academy with his appointment to teach in Arts. He declined an invitation in August 1606 to serve as minister at Montauban, and another to return home in April 1611; but by October 1614 he left Saumur for Glasgow, where he was appointed Principal of the University and minister of Govan in January 1615. Declining an invitation to return to Saumur in 1618, Boyd decided to demit his principalship at Glasgow in July 1621 when he found himself at variance with King James' liturgical innovations in the Church. In October 1622 he was chosen Principal of Edinburgh university and minister at Greyfriars, but demitted in early 1623 rather than conform to the King's 'Five Articles of Perth'.* He became minister at Paisley in 1626, but quarrelled with the RC Countess of Abercorn and resigned later that year. He died in Edinburgh, where he had gone to seek treatment for a malignant growth in his throat.

Subject to ill-health much of his life, Boyd was an austere and scholarly man who was not well-suited to the demands and intrigues his public position required. His posthumously published Latin commentary on Ephesians (... *in Epistolam Pauli Apostoli ad Ephesios Praelectiones* ... (L, 1652)) is an enduring monument to his learning. The work, however, is far more than a commentary and includes discussions of virtually every important *locus* of a systematic theology. Although his intention in this was to derive the chief heads of Christian doctrine from Scripture, Ephesians being deliberately chosen for the purpose, the result is a huge indiscriminate mass (the book is a large folio with 1236 pages of text) which is virtually unusable.

FES III, 162–3; H. M. B. Reid, *Divinity Principals in the University of Glasgow* (G, 1917); W. M. Campbell, 'Robert Boyd of Trochrigg', *RSCHS* 12 (1956), 220–34.

J. Kirk

Boyd, Zachary (*c*.1585–1653), minister of Barony Church, Glasgow. A cousin of Robert Boyd* of Trochrigg, he studied at the universities of Glasgow (1601–3) and St Andrews (1603–7, MA). He then went to France, studying and (from 1611) teaching at the Protestant Academy of Saumur, though he declined its principalship. Returning to Scotland in 1623, he became minister in 1625 of Glasgow's Barony parish. He also served as Glasgow University's Dean of Faculty (thrice), Rector (thrice) and Vice-chancellor (1644–53), and was a generous benefactor of the University. Hesitantly signing the National Covenant* in 1638, he was appointed to a commission for maintenance of Church discipline by the Glasgow Assembly.*

Boyd was a prolific writer, in both poetry and prose, but rarely attained literary qualities of any note. His deepest concern lay not in theology or public affairs, but in the spiritual and devotional well-being of the Kirk.

Selected Sermons (ed. D. W. Atkinson, A, 1989); *Crosses, Comforts and Councels* (G, 1643); *Cleare Forme of Catechising Before the Giving of the Lord's Supper* (G, 1639).

FES III, 392; *DNB* VI, 103–4; J. C. Johnston, *Treasury of the Scottish Covenant* (E, 1887), 319–20; D. W. Atkinson, 'Zachary Boyd as Minister of the Barony Parish ... ,' *RSCHS* 24 (1990), 19–32; biographies by G. Neil appended to his editions of Boyd's *The Last Battell of the Soule in Death* (G, 1838) and *Zion's Flowers* ... (G, 1855).

J. Kirk

Boys' Brigade, a religious, uniformed organization for boys. It began 4 October 1883 in Glasgow's North Woodside Mission when William Alexander Smith,* a young clothing exporter, determined to provide a religious organization for boys aged twelve to seventeen. Four influences moulded Smith's new brigade: the YMCA,* the Volunteer movement, the Moody* and Sankey revival* and the Free Church of Scotland.* Smith's pragmatic abilities transformed Woodside's brigade into a swiftly successful interdenominational movement. Its foundational pillars, tenaciously but sensitively sustained, were religion and discipline, the former ('the advancement of Christ's Kingdom among boys') focused in close association with a local congregation or Sunday school, the latter – firmly viewed as solely the means to the religious end – reflected in a uniform (probably derived from the Glasgow Foundry Boys Religious Society), bands (from 1885), drill (from 1886) and camps. It appealed to a lower-middle class and upper-working class constituency, sustained by grandees from the evangelical networks, notably Henry Drummond* and Lord Aberdeen (see Gordon, Ishbel).

It spread rapidly: fifteen companies and an English presence by 1885; then Wales (1887), Ireland (1888) and overseas – USA (1887), Canada (1891), Denmark (1902). It was copied: Church Lads' (1891), Jewish Lads' (1895), Catholic Boys' (1896), the fiercely non-militaristic Boys' Life Brigade (1899); also the Girls' (Ireland 1893), Girls' Life (England and Wales 1902) and Girls' Guildry* (Scotland 1900). With the YMCA it provided the seedbed for the Boy Scouts. Its organization was distinctive: individual Companies, officered by Captain and Lieutenants, grouped into local Battalions, gathered from 1913 into Districts and represented nationally by the Brigade and its executive. Smith was Brigade Secretary from 1885. There were 75,000 British boy members by 1900. Smith's unobtrusively guiding hand before 1914 (continued by his sons, of whom Stanley was Brigade Secretary 1925–54), kept the Brigade clear of involvement with national cadet forces. The wisdom of this was shown with the First World War. Although the Brigade emerged with numbers down and bankruptcy looming, the foundations were laid for post-War adaptation. From 1917 there was provision for the under-twelves. From 1921 the Boys' Brigade Week provided a sure-fire annual fund-raiser. In 1926 the Boys' and Boys' Life Brigade united and by 1934 the peak British membership (96,762) was reached. The Brigade was now, relatively, the most successful British uniformed youth movement, managing despite, perhaps because of, its social conservatism, to steer between the contemporary rocks of para-militarism and pacifism. After 1930 the London office (opened in 1902) became Brigade headquarters; the Glasgow office left George Square for Bath Street.

Already prominent in the growingly sophisticated (and government-influenced) youth service world, the Brigade opened training schools, notably Carronvale, near Larbert (1947), and commissioned reports, notably the Haynes Report (1963–4) and the Programme Study Group Report (1981). These profoundly affected Brigade style: the uniform was modified; Junior, Company and Senior Sections were introduced; General Wilson-Haffenden (Secretary 1954–65) brought in the breeze of Billy Graham's* evangelism; a woman (from Paisley) first addressed the Council in 1966; the sister organizations merged in 1965 and were housed in the Brigade's new Fulham headquarters (1966); a new constitution crowned the edifice in 1968. Even so, the Brigade lost a third of its boy members between 1949 and 1979.

Founded to exploit the efficient use of leisure for religious ends, the Brigade was uncannily representative of its time, product of a Protestant world open to Empire and Onward-Christian-Soldiering. Its survival makes it an accurate social barometer. Its suspicion of governmental engineering, fusion of voluntaryism and uniform, and intelligently conservative discipline made it a natural breeding ground for Labour MPs, Trade Union leaders and small businessmen. It is a tribute to the vitality of late-Victorian Glasgow and its evangelical culture. Its Scottish dimension remains strong, especially on the conservative side. Each President and Honorary President has been Scottish, and although by 1926 the Scottish and Irish membership was only 42 per cent of the British, in 1934 it retained 35,922 Scottish members and fifty years on it was relatively stronger in Scotland than in England.

John Springall, Brian Fraser, Michael Hoare, *Sure and Stedfast: A History of the Boys' Brigade 1883–1983* (L, 1983).

J. C. G. Binfield

Breach, The, see Burgess Oath.

Brechin, see Early Ecclesiastical Sites.

Brethren, a movement largely characterized by independent groups of believers, lay* leadership and a desire to emulate early New Testament practices. The Scottish Brethren had their origins in that Evangelicalism,* foreshadowed by the Haldanes* in Scotland, which began to make its presence felt throughout Britain in the 1830s. Small groups in Scotland which had seceded from Churches such as the Evangelical Union* or the Scotch Baptists* were moving towards a Brethren ecclesiology. In 1848 eight such groups entered into correspondence with each other. The earliest extant reference to Brethren in Scotland, however, is in Edinburgh in 1838. In a letter written that year J. N. Darby (1800–82), an Englishman resident in Ireland and one of the movement's founders, refers to a 'little fragment of a flock' which had already been depleted by two secessions – one over the issue of baptism (see 'Lettres de J.N.D.', *Messager Evangélique*, Vevey, Switzerland, 1897, 294).

The Brethren, formed in Ireland and England from 1829 onwards, were searching for primitive Church order and unity. They had no clergy and their weekly breaking of bread was open for contributions by the members. They refused any title other than those which could be applied to all Christians, and nomenclature among them has an informal status only. In 1848 they divided into 'Open' and 'Exclusive' wings in a controversy, 'the Bethesda Question', involving the influential assemblies in Plymouth (hence 'Plymouth Brethren') and Bristol. Henry Craik,* the only Scot among the early Brethren leaders, and his fellow elders in Bethesda Chapel, Bristol, insisted that while their assemblies sought to follow the ecclesiastical patterns of the New Testament, they should nevertheless welcome to the Lord's Supper all Christians regardless of their ecclesiastical associations. In contrast, 'Exclusive' Brethren followed Darby in holding that faithful believers have been called out from the ruined Church to testify against the errors of the last days. They maintained that a stricter rule was required: all Christians who failed to judge heresy or others associated with it could not be received. Both wings, however, were dominated by

Darbyite dispensational premillenialism (*see* Millennialism).

This division preceded any significant Brethren activity in Scotland, and both wings grew separately. The greater part of the Scottish movement traces its origins to the revival* of 1859–60. Before 1860 there were about six Exclusive assemblies in Scotland, but by 1880 there were around eighty. At least three of the independent corresponding churches made the transition to an Open Brethren identity, and by 1887 there were 187 such assemblies in Scotland. Some of them emerged spontaneously out of the fellowship groups formed after the revivals. Many English revival evangelists were Open Brethren and they helped spread the movement. Among mission halls and Baptists,* groups and sometimes whole churches became Brethren (see N. Dickson, 'Brethren and Baptists in Scotland', *BQ* 33 (1990), 372–87). This growth took place largely among artisans and the lower-middle class in industrialized and fishing communities (*see* Fisherfolk, Missions to).

The largest spontaneous movement was in the north-east. Donald Ross* had formed the Northern Evangelistic Society in 1870, and when relationships with existing churches became too strained he and others formed in 1871–3 some twenty new churches which later associated with Open Brethren. Ross's monthly magazine (later called *The Witness*) became the principal Brethren review in the United Kingdom. John Ritchie, one of the Society's converts, founded another important Brethren magazine, *The Believer's Magazine*, in Kilmarnock in 1891 (J. A. H. Dempster, 'Aspects of Brethren Publishing Enterprise in Late Nineteenth Century Scotland', *Publishing History* 20, 1986, 61–101; *see also* Periodicals, Religious).

From 1876 demands were made among Open Brethren for greater uniformity of practice and stricter procedures in receiving other Christians. Many had joined assemblies because of dissatisfaction with existing Churches, and the demands appealed to them. A journal, *Needed Truth*, was founded in 1888 to disseminate the new ideas. John Brown of Greenock, a founder editor, 'expected to carry all Scotland' with him, and leaders such as J. R. Caldwell, editor of *The Witness*, and Alexander Marshall* were swayed for a while. When Brown and others left to form the Church of God in 1892–3, many who remained sympathetic towards more restrictive practices, such as John Ritchie, did not secede. The new Brethren body adopted a form of Presbyterianism,* and a more centralized polity had little appeal for most. Within the Church of God some Scottish elders came to fear its increasingly authoritarian organization, and under the eponymous leadership of Frank Vernal formed an additional group almost entirely confined to Scotland. The controversy was critical for Scottish Open Brethren and it left them further isolated from other Churches.

By the later nineteenth century Scottish Exclusives were associated with moderate Brethren like Andrew Miller of Glasgow, writer of Church history, and Dr W. T. P. Wolston, whose medical practice in Edinburgh continued from 1864 to 1909. Their leadership probably ensured that the moderate 'Glanton Party', which seceded in 1908, was well represented in Scotland. The main Exclusive body lost its early impetus. It became increasingly occupied with internal matters, and to many in Scotland the Bethesda Question seemed remote. The Open Brethren, however, continued to evangelize vigorously until by the 1920s there was an assembly in almost every industrial and fishing community of substantial population in Lowland Scotland. In 1933 it was estimated there were 30,000 members.

For over a century the Scottish contribution to Open Brethren missionary* endeavour has been singularly striking. The pioneering work of F. S. Arnot* and Dan Crawford* aroused interest, and by 1900 some one-tenth of Brethren missionaries from the United Kingdom were commended from Scottish assemblies. The work of the Glasgow Missionary Council (established 1908) continues to foster interest and support at home on a remarkable scale.

Because of their uncentralized structure there have been considerable variations of attitude among Open Brethren, though most of them remained for a long time very conservative in their attitude to scriptural authority and in their traditional anticlericalism. Although most withdrew from the affairs of society, individuals such as Sir John Henderson, MP for Cathcart 1946–64, and Robert Rendall* engaged with political and cultural matters. Many eschewed association with other Christians, but the vision of Christian unity of the early leaders was maintained by individuals such as Henry Pickering* and F. F. Bruce.*

Numbers have declined sharply since 1960. The fissiparous tendencies of the Exclusives culminated in their division into several small splinter groups after an alleged scandal in Aberdeen in 1970 involving the American leader Jim Taylor Jnr.

The Glanton Party and the two divisions of the Church of God are now very small. Open Brethren have declined from 324 assemblies in 1959 to 242 at present. Since World War Two they have tended to become middle-class, and members can be found occupying positions of prominence in Scottish society. Many now prefer the title 'Christian Brethren'. More recently a number of assemblies have introduced new practices and forms of service, and they are hard to distinguish from independent evangelical churches.

N. Dickson, 'Scottish Brethren: Division and Wholeness 1838–1916', *Christian Brethren Review* 41 (1990), 5–41; *id*., 'Brethren and Baptists in Scotland', *BQ* 33 (1990), 372–87; H. H. Rowdon, *The Origins of the Brethren* (L, 1967); *ERE* II, 843–8; F. F. Bruce, 'The Origins of *The Witness*', *The Witness* (1970), 7–9; J. Cordiner, *Fragments of the Past* (L, 1961); W. T. Stunt, A. Pulleng, *et al*., *Turning the World Upside Down* (Eastbourne, Bath, 1972), 562–7.

T. C. F. Stunt and N. Dickson

Brewster, (Sir) David (1781–1868), scientist. A son of the Headmaster of Jedburgh Grammar School, he was early destined for the ministry, entering Edinburgh University for this purpose. Diverted from this vocation by nervousness in public speaking and a growing interest in natural science, he soon found a dual role as private tutor and scientific journalist, being specially associated with the *Edinburgh Philosophical Journal* and Blackwood's *Edinburgh Journal of Science*. He was a founding member of the British Association for the Advancement of Science in 1831 and author of an important biography of Isaac Newton. He was appointed Principal of the United Colleges at St Andrews in 1838, and of Edinburgh University from 1859 until his death. He became FRSE in 1808, FRS in 1815, and was knighted in 1832.

Brewster invented the kaleidoscope (1816) and extensively investigated polarized light. Agnostic as to the wave theory and other hypotheses, he considered speculation about nature (as opposed to empirical study) a manifestation of sinful pride. He early embraced Evangelicalism,* supporting the FC in the Disruption,* becoming one of its elders, and writing for *The Witness** and *North British Review**. Like other Scottish Evangelicals he questioned 'Mosaic' science, and cautiously approved natural theology. Highly critical of Chambers' *Vestiges of Creation* and Darwin's *Origin of Species*, he advocated the plurality of worlds and was one of the most eminent signatories of the *Scientists' Declaration* of 1865.

DNB VI, 299–303; *Dictionary of Scientific Biography* II, 451–3; *Proceedings of the Royal Society* 17 (1868–9), lxix; A. D. Morrison-Low and J. R. R. Christie (eds), *'Martyr of Science': Sir David Brewster, 1781–1868* (E, 1984); J. H. Brooke, 'Natural Theology and the Plurality of Worlds: Observations on the Brewster-Whewell Debate', *Annals of Science* 34 (1977), 221–86.

C. A. Russell

Brewster, Patrick (1788–1859), minister and campaigner for social and political reform. He grew up in Jedburgh, the younger brother of David, later Sir David Brewster,* scientist and Principal of Edinburgh University. After studying at Edinburgh for the ministry of the CofS he was to become minister of the second charge at Paisley Abbey, Renfrewshire, from 1818 to his death.

The first seventeen years of his ministry were spent uneventfully within the circle of his church and family life, except that Brewster was ministering in an industrial community that experienced the upheavals of political radicalism, disease and poverty in this period. Brewster first came into conflict with the church courts for his own radical political and social views in 1835, after attending a dinner and presiding at a meeting in honour of the Irish nationalist MP Daniel O'Connell. For that he was censured by the church. His involvement in the Chartist* movement, as a 'moral force' supporter of the 1838 People's Charter for political reforms, resulted in further disciplinary moves after he had preached in a Christian Chartist Church* in Glasgow in 1841. The Presbytery of Paisley referred him to the Commission of Assembly (*see* General Assembly) in 1842 for his Chartist preaching and for offending the local military commander by his political preaching in the Abbey. The matter was dropped in 1843 in the wake of the Disruption.* Though sympathetic to its cause, Brewster did not join the Free Church* because of the conservative social and political views of its leaders, especially Thomas Chalmers.*

Brewster was a unique, controversial figure in the nineteenth-century CofS, proclaiming a critical, prophetic Christianity and publicly campaigning for social and political reforms to benefit the working class while remaining a minister of the established church.

The Seven Chartist and Military Discourses (Paisley, 1843); *The Plague of Patronage* (Paisley, 1860).

S. Mechie, *The Church and Scottish Social Development 1780–1870* (L, 1960); D. C. Smith, *Passive Obedience and Prophetic Protest* (NY, 1987); A. C. Cheyne, *The Transforming of the Kirk* (E, 1983); W. Alexander, 'Patrick Brewster of Paisley Abbey (1788–1859)' (unpublished, n.d.); M. Fry, *Patronage and Principle* (A, 1987); W. H. Marwick, 'Social Heretics in the Scottish Churches', *RSCHS* 11 (1953), 227–39; *DNB* VI, 304; *FES* III, 169–70.

W. F. Storrar

British and Foreign Bible Society, *see* Bible Societies.

British and Foreign Evangelical Review. The first issue of the quarterly *Foreign Evangelical Review* appeared in May 1852, edited by Andrew Cameron* and printed and published by Johnstone and Hunter of Edinburgh. By making accessible to British readers articles in defence of the evangelical position which had appeared in American and continental journals such as the *Princeton Review* and the *Bibliotheca Sacra*, the publishers aimed to counter the threat which they believed RCism on the one hand, and a rationalistic scepticism on the other, posed to Evangelicalism. From the issue of March 1853 the journal was increased in size and scope to include original as well as reprinted material: the title became the *British and Foreign Evangelical Review*. The articles it contained covered philosophical, theological, biblical and historical themes: they were written to a high academic standard, and, until 1871, were anonymous. From that year, the *Review* became devoted almost entirely to original material, and authors' names were given. FC contributors predominated. Anonymity was restored in 1885. From 1857, the *Review* was published in London by James Nisbet, and printed in Edinburgh by, successively, John Greig (1857–78) and T. & A. Constable (1879–88). Cameron was succeeded as editor by, successively, William Cunningham,* George Smeaton,* Thomas M'Crie the younger (1797–1875),* James Oswald Dykes,* Hugh Sinclair Paterson (1831–1910) and (from

1887) Joseph Samuel Exell (1849–1910). The *Review* was continued as the *Theological Monthly* published by Nisbet between 1889 and 1891.

W. J. Couper, 'Bibliography of Edinburgh Periodical Literature', *Scottish Notes and Queries*, 2nd ser., 4 (July 1902), 3.

J. A. H. Dempster

British Weekly, a religious newspaper, founded in 1886. Published by Hodder and Stoughton, it was edited by (later Sir) William Robertson Nicoll.* Describing itself as 'A Journal of Social and Christian Progress', the first issue on 5 November 1886 laid out, in the Editor's opening article, its purpose under the heading, 'The Creed and the Hope of Progress': 'The creed we shall seek to express in this journal will be that of progress and, while independent of sect or party, we shall aim at the ends of what is known as Advanced Liberalism.'

The *BW*, born in the year of the first Home Rule Bill, with the Irish problem dominating and dividing the Liberal party, became known as 'The Nonconformist Conscience'. It represented the strength of the Liberal Party in the Free Churches in England. Nicoll saw the *BW* as an instrument to rally and re-unite Liberals. It was noted for the range of its contributors, Robertson Nicoll drawing on both ecclesiastical and literary names from his circle of influential friends and colleagues. He also maintained close contact with leading politicians, Lloyd George being one much influenced.

Church contributors included Marcus Dods,* Henry Drummond,* Alexander Whyte,* J. D. Jones, W. G. Elmslie* and James Denney.* J. M. Barrie and Robert Louis Stevenson contributed from the literary field. Nicoll himself wrote a regular and influential column under the name Claudius Clear.

The peak of circulation and influence was in Robertson Nicoll's best years, but during and after the First World War* it declined in strength. In 1923 Nicoll was succeeded by another Scot, J. M. E. Ross, but he was very soon succeeded by the great Scottish preacher, John Hutton*. By the end of Hutton's editorship a quarter of a century later, circulation had declined to around 14,000 copies weekly. After a brief interim editorship, Shaun Herron contributed seven dramatic editorial years developing the paper as 'a conversation between Christians all over the world'.

The Scottish tradition of editors continued between 1958 and 1970 with the appointment of the present writer, a minister of the CofS, which now owned the paper. He continued the crusading aspects of a radical and independent journal in the Nicoll tradition.

In the early 1960s, *BW* took over *Christian World*, thus extending its influence in the Nonconformist churches in England. It was also published in Scottish, Irish and Congregational editions. In 1970 the paper passed into the hands of Christian Weekly Newspapers, publishers of the *Church of England Newspaper*, with which it began to share some pages. In 1986 it celebrated its centenary but changed its name to *Christian Week*, under which title it continues.

D. Duncan

Brockie, Marianus (1687–1755), Benedictine* scholar. Donald Brockie, born in Edinburgh, was clothed as Brother Marianus at Ratisbon (*see* Schottenklöster) 1707, professed 1708, ordained priest 1713. From 1714 he taught philosophy at Erfurt University, graduated doctor in theology 1718 and was monastic superior 1719. His publication on Jansenism* in 1720 aroused bitter controversy with Jesuits.* He worked in Scotland 1727–39, then returned to Ratisbon, being prior from 1751, and compiled two monumental works of scholarship. His greatly enlarged edition of Holstenius' *Codex Regularum* appeared posthumously in 1759. His comprehensive work on Scottish monasticism (*Monasticon Scoticum*), never published, contains valuable as well as unscholarly or fabricated documentation.

L. Hammermayer, 'Marianus Brockie und Oliver Legipont', *Studien und Mitteilungen zur Geschichte des Benediktinerordens*, 71 (1961), 69–121; H. Docherty, 'The Brockie Forgeries', *IR* 16 (1965), 79–127.

M. Dilworth

Brodie, (Lord) Alexander (1617–80), Covenanting* statesman and Lord of Session. Brodie was prominent in public affairs before the Restoration* of Charles II,* but in later years he largely confined himself to his family estate in Morayshire, preferring to distance himself from a government with which he had little sympathy. His main legacy is his *Diary*, to which he committed an account of his spiritual experience and his thoughts on Church and state affairs. A touchingly human document, it well illustrates the tensions which beset him as he strove – not always successfully – to reconcile the claims of public duty with the demands of conscience.

The Diary of Alexander Brodie of Brodie (Spalding Club; A, 1863); G. Bain, *Alexander Brodie of Brodie: His Life and Times* (Nairn, 1904); *DNB* VI, 377–8.

M. Grant

Brown, Charles John (1806–84), influential FC minister and preacher. The brother of David Brown,* he was born in Aberdeen and educated at Marischal College there. He was minister of Anderston Chapel-of-Ease, Glasgow (1831–7) and of New North (CofS and FC), Edinburgh (1837–84). At the Disruption* he adhered to the FC, and was Moderator of the FC General Assembly in 1872. Princeton made him a DD in 1863. He took a significant part in Church controversies – on non-intrusion,* spiritual independence, establishment and union. He was particularly influential as a preacher and pastor. His publications mainly derived from sermons or dealt with preaching.

Divine Glory of Christ (L, 1868); *Church*

BROWN, DAVID

Establishments Defended (G, 1832); *The Ministry* (E, 1872); *The Word of Life* (L, 1874); 'Symptoms and Fruits of a Revival of Religion' in *Lectures on The Revival of Religion* (G, 1840); 'Preface' to R. Wodrow, *Suggestions for Daily Prayer* (E, 1848).

AFCS 103; *FES* I, 148; *Disruption Worthies*, 65–72.

H. M. Cartwright

Brown, David (1803–97), FC divine and Principal of the FC College, Aberdeen (*see* Christ's College). Born in Aberdeen, the son of a Lord Provost of the city and brother of Charles J. Brown,* he was educated at Aberdeen University (MA, 1821). He studied divinity for three sessions at Aberdeen, but for the last went to Edinburgh. Licensed in 1826, he was Edward Irving's* assistant in London for a time, but resigned when Irving began to encourage the exercise of 'gifts' such as tongue-speaking. Returning to Scotland, he became assistant at Dumbarton parish church, and in 1836 was ordained to the CofS parish of Ord, Banffshire. He joined the FC in 1843 and was appointed that year as minister of Free St James, Glasgow. In 1857 he became Professor of New Testament Exegesis, Church History and Apologetics in the FC College, Aberdeen, and in 1875 Principal. He resigned from his professorship in 1886 but remained Principal.

Brown was one of the founders of the Evangelical Alliance* and a director of the National Bible Society of Scotland (*see* Bible Societies). In 1885 he was Moderator of the FC General Assembly. He served on the Committee for the RV New Testament. He received a DD from Princeton, New Jersey, in 1852, and later from Aberdeen University, which also awarded him an LLD in 1895.

Brown was a prolific author. He is the Brown of R. Jamieson, A. R. Fausset and Brown's *Commentary Critical, Experimental and Practical on the Old and New Testaments*, 6 vols (G, 1871), to which he contributed the Gospels (originally *The Four Gospels*, G, 1863), Acts and Romans. He did more than anyone else to keep alive the memory of 'Rabbi' John Duncan* by writing a *Life of John Duncan* (E, 1872) and editing *The Rev. John Duncan, LL.D, in the Pulpit and at the Communion Table* (E, 1874). He contributed many articles to the *British and Foreign Evangelical Review*.* Brown's most enduring work, however, was his *Christ's Second Coming: Will It Be Premillennial?* (E, 1846; ²1847), which remains the classic evangelical polemic against premillennialism. Brown's own position was post-millennial.

Restoration of the Jews (E, 1861); *The Apocalypse* (L, 1891); *On United and Universal Prayers* (E, 1860); *Crushed Hopes Crowned in Death* (L, 1861); *To Whom Shall We Go?* (A, 1857); *Watchman, What of the Night?* (E, 1855).

W. G. Blaikie, *David Brown* (L, 1898); D. Cromarty, *Scottish Ministerial Miniatures* (L, 1892); *Disruption Worthies*, 73–8; *FES* VI, 290; *AFCS* I, 50.

N. R. Needham

BROWN, JAMES

Brown, George (1818–80), statesman in Canada (one of the architects of Canadian federation) and leading promoter of the Free Church* cause in Upper Canada (Ontario). Born in Alloa, in 1837 he emigrated to New York and with his father established a newspaper catering to British immigrants. They moved to Toronto in 1843 and commenced publication of *The Banner*, a weekly paper for Presbyterian readers. The religious column supported the Free Church* cause and emphasized the need for evangelical vigilance against the RC threat. Brown, as an elder of Knox Church, Toronto, signed the official protest in July 1844 that introduced the Disruption* to Upper Canada and led to the formation of the Presbyterian Church of Canada. In the same year he entered politics, and his involvement in the Reform Party was to dominate the remainder of his years. His last major contribution to the FC was to influence its move towards a voluntarist* stand over church–state relations which led eventually to its union with the United Presbyterian Church* in 1861.

Dictionary of Canadian Biography X, 91–103; J. M. S. Careless, *Brown of The Globe*, 2 vols (Toronto, 1959, 1963); *id.*, 'George Brown', *Our Living Tradition*, ed. R. L. McDougall (Toronto, 1959); J. S. Moir, 'George Brown, Christian Statesman', *Called to Witness* 2 (1980), 39–46.

S. D. Gill

Brown, Gilbert (*d*.1612), abbot. Of the family of Carsluith in Kirkcudbright, he was in 1559 a Cistercian* monk of New Abbey (or Sweetheart) near Dumfries. He studied at St Andrews 1562–5 and graduated in arts; while there, he conformed with Protestantism. In 1565 he received crown appointment as abbot of New Abbey in succession to John Brown, a kinsman. For thirty years, from *c*.1578, he was in almost continual trouble with Church and state authorities for actively promoting Catholicism. Supported by Lords Herries and Maxwell, he was very successful; New Abbey and Dumfries became centres of Catholic practice, and the English border authorities were seriously concerned by Brown's activities. He was ordained priest at Paris 1587 and engaged in written controversy with John Welsh,* *c*.1599. In 1605, despite local resistance, he was imprisoned, chose exile but soon returned. Arrested again 1608, he went abroad and died at Paris.

M. Dilworth, 'Abbot Gilbert Brown: a Sketch of his Career', *IR* 40 (1989), 153–8; W. Huyshe, *Dervorgilla, Lady of Galloway and her Abbey of the Sweet Heart* (E, 1913), 86–93.

M. Dilworth

Brown, James (*d*.1791), priest of the EpCS and (from 1788) irregular non-juring* bishop. He married Helen, daughter of the Revd Robert Taylor, and had two sons, of whom the younger was the famous Robert Brown, FRS (1773–1858, Keeper of Botany at the British Museum and discoverer of 'Brownian Motion'). He was Episcopal priest in Montrose from before 1773 until 1789. Suggested by Bishop Petrie of Moray as Bishop for English non-jurors 1783, he was willing to go if sent. He refused to accept the decision of the majority of Episcopalian bishops to pray for George III in 1788, and was consecrated bishop by Bishop Charles Rose* the same year. He removed to Monteith's Close, Edinburgh, 1789 and ministered to the non-juring congregation there and elsewhere (including Gask). He ordained Donald Macintosh* in 1789. He died in Edinburgh as Bishop of 'the Old Episcopal Church of Scotland'.

W. Walker, *The Life and Times of John Skinner, Bishop of Aberdeen and Primus of the Scottish Episcopal Church* (A, 1887); G. T. S. Farquhar, *Three Bishops of Dunkeld: Alexander, Rose and Watson 1743–1808* (Perth, 1915); J. Skinner, *Annals of Scottish Episcopacy* (E, 1818); G. Hatfield, *Robert Brown* (E, 1981); *Scots Magazine* LIII, 570 (E, 1791).

R. J. Angus

Brown, James (1862–1939), trade unionist and MP. The son of a weaver-cum-coalminer at Whitletts near Ayr, he received an elementary education at Annbank Public School before becoming a coalminer at the age of twelve. During his thirty years as a miner, Brown held various posts in the Ayrshire Mineworkers' Union serving as President in 1895 and as Secretary 1908–18. He was Secretary of the National Union of Scottish Mineworkers 1917–36. A convert from Liberalism to J. Keir Hardie's* ILP, Brown was Labour MP for South Ayrshire from 1918–31 and again from 1935 until his death. At Annbank Parish Church he served as elder, Sunday school superintendent and voluntary lay-preacher. Brown was a moderate Sabbatarian* and a strict teetotaller, active and influential in the Independent Order of Good Templars.*

He was appointed Lord High Commissioner* to the General Assembly* of the CofS in 1924, 1930 and 1931 (the Prime Minister on each occasion was J. Ramsay MacDonald); Brown was the first commoner to hold the post since the seventeenth century. He thus became an important symbol of the rise of the Labour Party.

The 'Ascension o' Jimmie Brown' from 'Pit to Palace' has become part of Labour mythology. Brown became especially well known in the 1920s and 1930s, but he was essentially a product of late Victorian religio-political culture.

Scottish Biographies 1938 (L, 1938), 80; J. Bellamy and J. Saville in W. Knox, *Scottish Labour Leaders: 1918–1939* (E, 1984); A. Gammie, *From Pit to Palace: The Life Story of the Right Hon. James Brown, MP* (L, 1931); J. H. Gillespie, *James Brown. A King o' Men* (E, 1939); R. Watson Kerr, *Annus Mirabilis, or the Ascension o' Jimmie Broon: A Satire in Verse* (E, 1924); *Ayrshire Post* (24 March 1939).

M. McCabe

Brown, John (of Wamphray) (c.1610–79), exiled CofS minister and theologian. Born in Kirkcudbright, Brown studied at Edinburgh (MA, 1630). In 1637 Samuel Rutherford* wrote that he 'always [had] . . . a great love to dear Mr John Brown because I thought I saw Christ in him more than in his brethren' (Letter 57). There is no firm evidence regarding the time of Brown's ordination or settlement in Wamphray, Dumfriesshire; *FES* puts it at 1655, but the preface to his *An Exposition of . . . Romans, with large Practical Observations* (E, 1766) implies it was considerably earlier, possibly shortly after 1637, appealing to dates in his manuscript sermons.

In 1662 he was imprisoned in Edinburgh for calling some neighbouring ministers 'perjured knaves and villains' for acknowledging the newly-appointed Archbishop of Glasgow, but was soon set free on condition of banishment. He accordingly left for Holland early in 1663, where he remained, living mostly in Rotterdam or Utrecht, until his death.

Although in Holland Brown had no pastoral call (he was on the short leet at Rotterdam in 1676 along with his friend Robert MacWard*), he was not idle. He soon began to write, with an abridged translation of a work previously written in Latin: *An Apologeticall Relation Of the particular sufferings of the faithfull Ministers & professours of the Church of Scotland, since 1660* (Rotterdam?, 1665; reprinted in *The Presbyterian's Armoury*, III, E, 1845). Extending and applying the principles regarding the relationship of Church and state previously enunciated by George Buchanan,* Samuel Rutherford* and George Gillespie,* Brown defends the Covenanters.*

James Walker* characterizes Brown as 'without doubt, the most important [Scottish] theologian of this period' (*The Theology and Theologians of Scotland*, ²E, 1888, 107). His *magnum opus* was his *De Causa Dei contra Antisabbatarios* (2 vols, Rotterdam, 1674–6). In addition to establishing the continuing obligation of the sabbath, it discusses a wide variety of questions concerning the law of God, 'great in length, great in learning, great in patient sifting of the subject, and in meeting of assertions and marshalling of arguments' (Walker, 25).

Brown's reply to Lambertus Velthuysius, which vindicates the orthodox Reformed doctrine of the Church against Erastianism, was issued with an answer to Ludovicus Wolzogius, a Socinian rationalist, on the interpretation of Scripture (*Libri Duo . . .* , Amsterdam, 1670). His interest in the affairs of Scotland continued with *The History of the Indulgence* (1678), demonstrating its unlawfulness and vindicating those who scrupled to hear those Presbyterian ministers who so compromised their principles. Shortly before his death Brown took part in the ordination of Richard Cameron.* Further, to oppose inroads of error in Scotland, he exposed the principles of *Quakerisme The Path-Way to Paganisme . . .* (1678). His *Christ the Way, and the Truth, and the Life* (Rotterdam, 1677, E, 1839), sermons on justification and sanctification, was the only other work issued in his lifetime.

Other works were issued posthumously. *The Life of Justification Opened* (1695) was written particularly against the corruptions of the doctrine by the late seventeenth century Anglicans and Richard Baxter, who, though 'purer in appearance', corrupted 'the true doctrine of Justification' nevertheless, making justification by repentance as well as by faith. As befits someone Robert Wodrow* described as 'a man of very great learning, warm zeal, and remarkable piety' (*The History of the Sufferings of the Church of Scotland*, G, 1838, I, 304), Brown's posthumous works display a combination of doctrinal weight with a real practical piety.

The Life of Faith In Time of Trial and Affliction...; *The Swan Song, or The Second Part* (1679–80; E, 1716); *Christ in Believers the Hope of Glory* (E, 1703, L, 1837); *A Treatise on Prayer and the Answer of Prayer* (1720; G, 1822); *A Vindication of Fellowship-Meetings, And of Hearing faithful suffering Ministers* (E, 1740); *Enoch's Testimony Opened* (E, 1771); *A Mirror: or, Looking-Glass for Saint and Sinner* (G, 1793).

FES II, 224–5; *DNB* VII, 9; Thomas Lockerby, *The Life of... John Brown* (E, 1839); I. B. Doyle, 'The Doctrine of the Church in the Later Covenanting Period', in *Reformation and Revolution*, ed. D. Shaw (E, 1967), 212–36.

D. C. Lachman

Brown, John (of Priesthill) (*c.*1627–85), a Covenanter* victim of the renewed persecution that followed the *Apologetical Declaration* published by James Renwick* and his followers in November 1684. A carrier and farmer, Brown had a remarkable ministry among children (perhaps we see here the first traces of a Sunday School* in Scotland), and conducted Sunday afternoon services to which people flocked on foot from miles around. Having regularly absented himself from Episcopalian worship, he was seized near his home by soldiers led by Claverhouse. He refused to take an oath renouncing Renwick's Declaration, and was shot – possibly by Claverhouse himself – in the presence of his pregnant wife and their children.

DNB III, 9–10.

J. D. Douglas

Brown, John (of Haddington) (1722–87), Associate Synod* minister and theological writer. Born of poor parents (who both died in his early youth) at Carpow near Abernethy (Perthshire), Brown had little formal education. He taught himself Latin, Greek and Hebrew – and much else – while successively a shepherd, pedlar, soldier (in 1745) and schoolmaster. In the 'Breach' (*see* Burgess Oath) in the Secession Church (*see* Associate Presbytery) he sided with the Burghers (the Associate Synod) and studied for the ministry under Ebenezer Erskine* and James Fisher.* In 1751 he became minister of the Associate congregation in Haddington (E. Lothian), which he served to his death (he strongly disapproved of ministers flitting from charge to charge). From 1767 he was also the Synod's professor, teaching all its ministerial candidates for the eight or nine weeks each year of their four- or five-year course. Brown crammed about 160 hours of instruction into these weeks, across the whole disciplinary span.

Brown had the makings – and even the aspirations – of a universal scholar. He learned also Arabic, Syriac, Persian and Ethiopic as well as the major modern European tongues. Of his thirty-odd publications, some embodied his lectures, such as *A General History of the Christian Church*, 2 vols (E, 1771) and *A Compendious View of Natural and Revealed Religion* (G, 1782; ^{2}1796) – his systematics. He attacked 'popery' and Catholic emancipation (*The Absurdity and Perfidy of all Authoritative Toleration*..., G, 1780). His posthumous *Apology for the Frequent Administration of the Lord's Supper* (E, 1804) also called for greater simplicity (against the extended Communion 'season'*); of those for whom infrequency alone safeguarded solemnity he asked, 'Why not pray seldom, preach seldom, read God's Word seldom, that they may become more solemn too?' He also welcomed the presence (but not participation) of children. Three collections of potted biographies were a kind of miracle-free counterpart to lives of saints; they included Fraser of Brea,* Thomas Halyburton* and John Nisbet's* son, James (*The Christian, the Student, and Pastor*, E, 1781; *Practical Piety exemplified*, G, 1783).

Brown's renown rests chiefly on *The Self-Interpreting Bible*, 2 vols (E, 1778), and to a lesser extent on *A Dictionary of the Holy Bible*, 2 vols (E, 1769). 'Brown's Bible' was repeatedly reprinted (in America as well as Britain, as were all his more popular works), with improvements by later editors, even into the twentieth century. Its numerous aids for 'the poorer and labouring parts of mankind' included a system of marginal cross-references novel in its extensiveness. This 'library in one volume' became as common as Bunyan's *Pilgrim's Progress* and Thomas Boston's* *Fourfold State*. It incorporated material from the *Dictionary*, which unlike modern counterparts, explained basic English vocabulary and grammar, and often went beyond making the Bible intelligible. The flea (only in 1 Sam. 24:11) 'is much given to haunt beds that are occupied in the summer season', while 'A platter of roasted onions and butter is a good remedy for the piles', and 'Antichrist' surveys papal history. Yet much of it is exemplary in its directness and accuracy.

Brown also founded a 'dynasty'. His numerous descendants developed a strong sense of corporate identity (some travelled from the USA to the 1987 commemoration), and included a galaxy of outstanding ministers, scholars and public servants (*see* John Brown (1754–1832) and William Brown (1783–1865), sons; John Brown (1784–1858), grandson; John (Rab) Brown (1918–82), great-grandson; John and David Cairns, great-great-grandsons). Other sons were Ebenezer (*d.*1836) (Small I, 364–5), minister of Inverkeithing (Fife) for fifty-six years and eminent preacher, and Samuel Brown,* pioneer of circulating libraries; Robert Johnston (*d.*1918; *FUFCS* 578), professor in the UP College, Edinburgh, and UFC College, Aberdeen, was a great-grandson.

Brown's theology was orthodox federal Calvinism. His first book, *An Help for the Ignorant* (E, 1758; ^{4}1781, expanded under the title *An Essay towards*

BROWN, JOHN

an easy ... explication of the Assembly's Shorter Catechism), was an exposition of the Westminster* Confession and Catechism. Yet he endeavoured to preach 'as if I had never read a book but the Bible', and ultimately his interest resided in Jesus Christ, 'that truly original *Book of God* ... that Original Bible'. His last recorded words were, 'my Christ'.

The Christian Journal; or, Common Incidents spiritual instructors (E, 1765) was frequently reprinted.

DNB VII, 12–14; Chambers-Thomson I, 176–80; R. Mackenzie, *John Brown of Haddington* (L, 1918; incomplete rp., L, 1964); W. Brown [son] (ed.), *Memoir and Select Remains* ... (E, 1856); J. Brown [son] (ed.), *Memoir* ... (²Berwick, 1828); J. Brown [grandson], *Letter to John Cairns*, bound with (some copies of) Cairns, *Memoir of John Brown, DD* [son] (E, 1860); J. C. Brown [grandson] (ed.), *Centenary Memorial* ... *A Family Record* (E, 1887); Small I, 516–8; *ASUPC*, 216–7.

D. F. Wright

Brown, John (of Whitburn) (1754–1832), devotional writer. The eldest son of John Brown* of Haddington, where he was born, he was educated at Edinburgh University and the divinity hall of the Associate (Burgher) Synod* taught by his father. Licensed to preach in 1776, he supplied for six months the pulpit of Archibald Hall* in London, who had an abiding influence on his ministry and theological views. Brown was ordained in Whitburn, Linlithgowshire, in 1777, and remained there for the rest of his life.

From his youth Brown was appreciative of the writings of Thomas Boston,* and later saw through the press five volumes of Boston's sermons. Brown's *Gospel Truth* (E, 1817, ²1831) gave a narrative of the Marrow Controversy,* with extracts from the writings of Boston and other defenders of the Marrow. In the *Memoirs of James Hervey* (E, 1806, ³1821), he chronicled the life of an English Nonconformist* whose understanding of the gospel was drawn from Marrow theology. He also edited his father's *Select Remains* (L, 1789), and popular digests of literature which adhered to the Marrow outlook.

On several occasions he preached in religiously destitute areas of the Highlands;* in 1799 he brought out a Gaelic* printing of his father's catechisms, and in 1811 a Gaelic translation of Boston's *Fourfold State*. He was a director of the London Missionary Society.*

Tour in the Highlands of Perthshire (E, 1818); *Memoir of Thomas Bradbury* (Berwick, 1831); *Religious Letters* (E, 1813); *Christian Experience* (E, 1825); *Descriptive List of Religious Books* (E, 1827); *Evangelical Beauties of Hugh Binning* * (E, 1828); *Evangelical Beauties of Archbishop Leighton* * (Berwick, 1828).

D. Smith, 'Memoir', in Brown, *Letters on Sanctification* (E, 1834); J. M'Kerrow, *History of Secession Church* (E, 1854); J. Cairns, *Memoir of John Brown* (E, 1860).

S. Isbell

Brown, John (1778–1848), CofS and FC minister in Langton, Berwickshire. Brown was born in Glasgow and educated under George Lawson.* When problems arose in connection with a call to the Associate (Burgher) Synod* congregation in Hamilton, he joined the CofS. He was ordained to Gartmore, Stirlingshire, in 1805 and translated to Langton in 1810. He came out at the Disruption* in 1843 and ministered in Langton FC until his death.

He is best known for his *Vindication of the Presbyterian Form of Church-Government* ... (E, 1805), written particularly against the 'ancient and modern independents', but wrote a variety of other works as well. He was a frequent contributor to the *Edinburgh Christian Instructor.* *

FES II, 23; Small II, 218; *AFCS* I, 104.

D. C. Lachman

Brown, John (1784–1858), minister of Broughton Place UPC, Edinburgh, and Professor of Exegetical Theology in USec. and UP College, Edinburgh.

Grandson of John Brown of Haddington* and eldest son of John Brown of Whitburn,* he studied at Glasgow University and under George Lawson* in the Burgher (*see* Associate Synod) branch of the Secession Church. He was ordained to the Burgher congregation at Biggar in 1806, translated to Rose Street, Edinburgh, in 1822, and to Broughton Place Church in 1829. In 1834 he was appointed to the new position of Professor of Exegetical Theology, a post which he filled in addition to his pastoral duties. His son, John (Rab) Brown*, was famous as an essayist and popular writer.

Brown was prominently involved in the Voluntary Controversy* of 1835–43, and in the Atonement Controversy* of 1840–5 within the USec.C. He defended James Morison* of Kilmarnock when the latter was expelled from the USec.C for teaching a doctrine of universal atonement. Brown himself taught an Amyraldian view of the extent of the atonement (*see* Cameron, John). Although the USec. Synod cleared him from a charge of unsound doctrine, his views marked a definite step in the process by which the Secession churches abandoned the teaching of the *Marrow* (*see* Marrow Controversy). His stress on the importance of basing preaching on careful and accurate exegesis led William Cunningham* to remark that the publication of Brown's *Expository Discourses on the First Epistle of Peter* (1848; rp. E, 1975) 'formed a marked era in the history of scriptural interpretation in this country'. He taught his students that 'it is of radical importance to you that your views be not only consistent *with*, but derived *from* a careful exegesis of the "words which the Holy Ghost teacheth." ... it has been my sincere desire to bring out of the inspired words what is really in them, and to put nothing into them that is not really there; impressed with the conviction that imginary exposition is one of the worst ways of adding to "the words of the prophecy of this book" ...' His expository lectures to his students were published from 1848 onwards and include *Exposition of the Discourses and Sayings*

BROWN, JOHN (RAB)

of our Lord (E, 1850, rp. L, 1967); *The Resurrection of Life* (E, 1851); *Analytical Expositions of Romans* (E, 1857); *An Exposition of the Epistle to the Hebrews* (E, 1862, rp. L, 1964); *An Exposition of the Epistle to the Galatians* (E, 1853); and *Parting Counsels, An Exposition of 2 Peter 1* (E, 1867, rp. E, 1980).

J. Cairns, *Memoirs of John Brown DD* (L, 1860); J. Brown, 'A Letter to John Cairns DD', in *Rab and his Friends* (E, 1860, rp. L, 1970); Small II, 407-8, I, 456, 438.

J. Nicholls

Brown, John (Rab) (1810–82), medical doctor and writer. Brown was born in Biggar, Lanarkshire, the son of the Secession (Burgher) minister, John Brown of Edinburgh.* His grandfather was John Brown of Whitburn* and his great-grandfather John Brown of Haddington,* famous for the *Self-Interpreting Bible*.

Brown's education was first with his father at Biggar, next at Steele's Classical School in Edinburgh, and then under Dr Carson at the High School. He began to study arts at Edinburgh University in 1826 and medicine in 1828. A pupil and apprentice of a surgeon called Mr Syme, he graduated in 1833 to start practising in Edinburgh, spending his whole life there.

Though he was an outstanding medical practitioner, his fame rests on his collections, *Horae Subsecivae* (3 vols, E, 1858, 1861, 1882) and *Rab and His Friends* (E, 1859). In these books he displayed a tender and imaginative understanding both of animals and people. His great loves were of dogs, children and the ordinary people with whom he came in contact through his work.

It was said of him that he read widely, held strong opinions, had the tenderness of a woman, with a powerful manly intellect. Yet he suffered from frequent bouts of depression, and during the last sixteen years of his life withdrew entirely from public life until six months before his death.

DNB VII, 20–1; J. T. Brown, *Dr. John Brown* (L, 1903); memoir in D. W. Forrest (ed.), *Letters* (L, 1907).

A. L. Walker

Brown, Samuel (1779–1839), pioneer of circulating libraries. The eighth son of John Brown* of Haddington, he was largely self-taught. After following his own quest to clear Christian faith, he was involved in several societies for promoting Christian knowledge in E. Lothian. During illness after his marriage in 1806 he conceived a scheme for itinerating libraries which he was the first – despite some antecedents – to make effective in 1817. By his death 3,850 volumes were distributed among 47 libraries, each moving on every two years. The system's advantages were cheapness and the urgency it lent to reading. It was adopted in other parts of Scotland, by the CofS and FCS among others, noted by parliament and copied abroad (cf. *EB* [11]1910–11, XVI, 564). Such libraries became the basis of some of the earliest 'mechanics' insti-

BROWN, WILLIAM

tutions', pioneering workers' education. Brown became provost of Haddington in 1833.

S. Brown [son], *Some Account of Itinerating Libraries and their Founder* (E, 1856) – revised version of 'Sketch...', *United Sec. Mag.* 7 (1839), 585–98; W. Brown [brother], *Memoir Relative to Itinerating Libraries* (E, ?1830); W. R. Aitken, *A History of the Public Library Movement in Scotland to 1955* (G, 1971).

D. F. Wright

Brown, Thomas (1811–93), FC minister. The son of John Brown (d.1848),* he studied at Edinburgh under Thomas Chalmers* before ordination to Kinneff, Kincardineshire, in 1837. After joining the FC in 1843 he moved to Dean FC, Edinburgh, in 1848, becoming senior minister in 1885. He was Moderator in 1890, and was awarded Edinburgh's DD in 1888.

Brown was a geologist and a Fellow of the Royal Society of Edinburgh. He delivered the third Chalmers lectures* (*Church and State in Scotland ... from 1560 to 1843*, E, 1891), was a leading figure in the FC Jewish and Continental Committee, but is best known as the compiler of *Annals of the Disruption* (E, 1883).

AFCS I, 105; *FCSR* May 1893, 107–8. Family papers in New College Library, Edinburgh.

D. F. Wright

Brown, William (1783–1863), historian of missions. A son of John Brown* of Haddington (who died when he was only four) and hence member of a distinguished 'dynasty' (cf. R. Mackenzie, *John Brown of Haddington*, L, 1918, ch. 28), he studied divinity from 1801 at Selkirk under George Lawson* and also graduated MD at Edinburgh. Ordained in the Associate (Burgher) Synod* in 1807, he married Isabella Taylor of Prestonpans but was frustrated in his intention to serve as a missionary in China. In 1820 he became Secretary of the Scottish Missionary Society (*see* Missions) and in 1821 Superintendent of its new training seminary, remaining in both capacities until the Society's dissolution in 1847.

Brown edited his father's Bible dictionary and collected his *Memoir and Select Remains...* (E, 1856), abridged Richard Baxter's *Reformed Pastor* (G, 1829), and compiled a *Memoir* on circulating libraries (*see* Brown, Samuel), an *Appeal to the Presbyterian Churches in Scotland on the Subject of Creeds and Confessions* (E, 1858) and catechetical materials for young children. His major work was *The History of the Propagation of Christianity Among the Heathen Since the Reformation* (2 vols, L, 1814; 3 vols, [3]E, L, 1854). Drawn largely from periodicals and society reports (with references), it was organized at first by nationality and then by society or denomination. The Moravians ('the United Brethren') received the fullest treatment. RC missions were excluded partly for space but also because RCism was 'antichristian in nature'. Brown affirmed that 'The propagation of Christianity in the world, is the most

BROWN, WILLIAM LAURENCE

important subject which can engage the attention of a historian.'

Small I, 517; *ASUPC* 671; *Annual Reports of Scottish Missionary Society*.

D. F. Wright

Brown, William Laurence (1755–1830), theologian and apologist. He was ordained minister of the English Church at Utrecht (where he was born) in 1788, and appointed Professor of Moral Philosophy and Ecclesiastical History at Utrecht in 1788 and Rector in 1790. He fled from Holland in 1795 as a result of the French invasion, and was appointed to the chair of Divinity in Marischal College, Aberdeen, becoming Principal in 1790. During the course of his academic career several of his essays won prestigious prizes both in Holland and in Britain. His writings, mainly of a theological and apologetical nature, were highly regarded at the time, possibly the most important being his *Essay on the Existence of a Supreme Creator* (A, 1816), but they have become dated and are not now perceived as significant. He was an influential spokesman of the 'Popular' party* in the General Assembly.

An Essay on the Natural Equality of Man (E, 1793; L, 1794); *The Proper Method of Defending Religious Truth in Times of Infidelity* (A, 1796); *The Salutary Effect of the British Constitution* (A, 1799); *The Nature, the Causes, and the Effects of Indifference with regard to Religion* (A, 1802); *Remarks on Certain Passages on 'An Examination of Mr. Dugald Stewart's Pamphlet by one of the Ministers of Edinburgh'* (A, 1806); *A Letter to Principal Hill* (E, 1807); *An Attempt towards a New Historical and Political Explanation of the Revelation* (A, 1812); *A Comparative View of Christianity and of the other Forms of Religion with regard to their Moral Tendency* (E, 1826).

DNB VII, 37–8; *FES* VII, 360–1, 555; *EB* (7th edit., 1841), V, 598–601.

J. R. McIntosh

Brownlie, John (1857–1925), UFC minister and hymnologist. Born in Glasgow, he was educated at Glasgow University and the Glasgow FC College. Licensed by the FC Presbytery of Glasgow in 1884, he became minister of Portpatrick Trinity Church in 1885. He received a DD from Glasgow University in 1908. During the First World War he served as chaplain to the armed forces, for which he was awarded a Volunteers' Decoration.

Brownlie was a prolific writer, almost exclusively on hymnology.*

Hymns of our Pilgrimage (L, 1889); *Zionward* (L, 1890); *Pilgrim Songs* (L, 1892); *Hymns of the Early Church* (L, 1896); *Hymns from East and West* (L, 1898); *Hymns and Hymn-Writers of the Church Hymnary* (L, 1899); *Hymns of the Greek Church* (E, 1900); *Hymns of the Holy Eastern Church* (Paisley, 1902); *Hymns from the Greek Office-Books* (Paisley, 1907); *Hymns from the East* (Paisley, 1907); *Hymns of the Apostolic Church* (Paisley, 1909); *Hymns from*

BRUCE, ALEXANDER BALMAIN

the Morning Land (Paisley, 1911); *Hymns of the Russian Church* (L, 1920).

FUFCS 118–19.

N. R. Needham

Bruce, Alexander Balmain (1831–99), distinguished FC New Testament scholar. Born in Aberargie, in Abernethy, Perthshire, he was educated at Edinburgh University 1845–9, proceeding to New College to study divinity in 1849.

Bruce suffered severe religious doubts as a student; Thomas Carlyle's* influence dominated his thinking for a time. This phase passed, however, and he became minister of the FC congregations in Cardross, Dunbartonshire (1859–68), and Broughty Ferry, Angus (1868–75). In 1875 he was appointed Professor of Apologetics and New Testament Exegesis in the FC Divinity Hall, Glasgow (*see* Trinity College), a position he occupied till his death.

Bruce ranks with A. B. Davidson* and William Robertson Smith* among the first Scottish biblical scholars whose views were highly esteemed by German critics. *St. Paul's Conception of Christianity* (E, 1894) and *The Epistle to the Hebrews: the First Apology for Christianity* (E, 1899) were notable contributions to New Testament studies. Unfortunately for Bruce, earlier productions of his pen had been noted with less than enthusiasm by conservative members of his own Church. His approach to Scripture was that of a liberal Evangelical: he had strongly defended Smith at his trial, and his *The Miraculous Elements in the Gospels* (L, 1886), while championing the basic historicity of Christ's miracles, denied that the Gospel accounts were free from all error. Similar sentiments were expressed in *The Kingdom of God* (E, 1889). This led to Bruce's being summoned before the FC General Assembly of 1890, which concluded that, while some of his statements had been unguarded, his teachings were not in breach of the Westminster* Confession.

Bruce was also Professor of Apologetics, and his services here have been criticized, *e.g.* by B. B. Warfield, as conceding too much to unbelief. Bruce's focus of concern in apologetics* (as in his personal piety) was the moral and spiritual glory of the man Jesus, on the basis that if he could but lead people to appreciate this, a sound Christology would naturally follow. What Bruce meant by a sound Christology may be gathered from *The Humiliation of Christ* (E, 1876; Cunningham Lectures* for 1874). Perhaps his most enduring work, Bruce here conducts a masterly historical survey of the doctrine of the incarnation, favouring the traditional Reformed Christology,* although not without some sympathy for Lutheran kenotic theories. His posthumously published article on 'Jesus' in the *Encyclopaedia Biblica* (L, 1901, II, 2435ff.), however, indicates a relinquishing of this high ground for a position substantially more liberal.

Bruce had a keen interest in music and the reform of worship. In the controversies in his Church over exclusive psalmody* and the use of instrumental

BRUCE, ARCHIBALD

music* in worship, he opposed the former and supported the latter. He was convener of the hymnal committees which issued the first *Free Church Hymn Book* in 1882, and the *Church Hymnary** for all Presbyterians in 1898 (*see* Hymnology, English).

Bruce made a profound and far-reaching impact as a teacher on a generation of FC students. Unhampered by respect for tradition, this bold and free-thinking individual, in the words of James Moffatt,* 'cut the cables and gave us a chance at the dangers and the glories of blue water' (quoted W. M. MacGregor, *Persons and Ideals*, E, 1939, 2).

Bruce was Ely lecturer at Union Seminary, New York, in 1886, and Gifford lecturer* for 1896–7.

The Parabolic Teaching of Christ (L, 1882); *F. C. Baur and his Theory of the Origin of Christianity and of the New Testament* (L, 1885); *Apologetics* (E, 1892); *The Providential Order of the World and The Moral Order of the World* (L, 1897, 1899 – Gifford lectures); *The Training of the Twelve* (E, 1871; ⁴1888, often reprinted).

W. Knight, *Some Nineteenth Century Scotsmen* (E, 1903), 203–14; *DNB Suppl.* I, 321–2; A. P. F. Sell, *Defending and Declaring the Faith: Some Scottish Examples, 1860–1920* (Exeter, 1987), 89–117; *AFCS* I, 50.

N. R. Needham

Bruce, Archibald (1746–1816), Secession author and Professor of Divinity. Born at Broomhall, near Denny, Stirlingshire, he studied philosophy and the classics at a private academy and Glasgow University. Taught divinity by William Moncrieff* of Alloa, he was ordained in 1768 in the Associate (Antiburgher) congregation at Whitburn, Linlithgowshire, which he served until his death. In 1786 he succeeded Moncreiff as Professor of Divinity for the General Associate Synod.* He protested against the New Narrative and Testimony of 1804 (*see* Testimonies), by which the Synod altered its teaching and denied that civil magistrates are obliged to exercise their authority in behalf of the true religion (*see* Church and State). When the Synod made the new document a term of communion, Thomas M'Crie* and three other ministers joined Bruce to form the Constitutional Associate Presbytery in 1806 (*see* Original Secession Church), and were deposed by their former colleagues. Bruce continued the theological hall at Whitburn on behalf of the new presbytery. Among his students were Thomas M'Crie, senior and junior,* George Stevenson,* Robert Shaw,* and 'Rabbi' John Duncan.* Bruce never married.

Bruce wrote extensively on the relationship of civil government to religion. When the British Parliament repealed the penal statutes against Roman Catholicism* in 1778, Bruce defended legal restraints in *Free Thoughts on the Toleration of Popery* (E, 1780), fearing RC threats to civil and religious liberties. His strictures on the monarch's supremacy in the CofE are contained in *A Dissertation of the Supremacy of Civil Powers in Matters of Religion* (E, 1802). *A Review of the Proceedings of the General Associate Synod* (E, 1808) traces the progress of New Light* in the events leading up to his deposition. These books, together with *True Patriotism* (E, 1785), contain his views on establishment of religion and toleration.*

In politics a Whig,* Bruce countered a government proclamation against seditious publications by issuing his *Reflections on the Freedom of Writing* (E, 1794), with its motto, 'What Britons dare to think, he dares to tell.' *A Statement and Declaration of the Genuine Principles of Seceders Respecting Civil Government* (E, 1799) defends the Secession Church's advocacy of parliamentary reform as consistent with subjection to lawful civil authority. Bruce taught the right of private judgment and freedom of inquiry, as illustrated in the second part of the *Introductory and Occasional Lectures* (E, 1797–1817).

Bruce was the author of several satirical poems: *The Kirkiad* (E, 1774) is a jibe at the formalism of the Moderate* party in the national Church; *The Catechism Modernized* (E, 1791) features the improprieties of patronage;* and *A Penitential Epistle to the Pope* (E, 1797) ridicules superstition in Roman Catholicism. *Annus Secularis, or the British Jubilee* (E, 1788) is a rejection of anniversary religious festivals; Bruce insists on a biblical warrant for any observance introduced into worship, reviews the history of opposition to religious holidays by the Reformed churches, and observes the effect of such commemorations in the decline of Churches into unscriptural symbolism and idolatry. He edited *Memoirs of James Hog** *of Carnock* (E, 1798) and wrote a *Life of Alexander Morus* (E, 1813).

J. M'Kerrow, *History of the Secession Church* (E, 1854); *ASOSC*; T. M'Crie, *Life of Thomas M'Crie* (E, 1840); *DNB* VII, 89; obituary by T. M'Crie, *Scots Magazine*, April 1816; *Small* II, 232–3.

S. Isbell

Bruce, Frederick Fyvie (1910–90), Biblical scholar. Son of a well-known Brethren* speaker, he was born in Elgin and educated at the universities of Aberdeen, Cambridge and Vienna. He lectured in Greek at Edinburgh (1935–8) and Leeds (1938–47), was lecturer (1947–55) and Professor (1955–9) in the Department of Biblical History and Literature at Sheffield, and Rylands Professor of Biblical Literature and Exegesis at Manchester (1959–78). A New Testament scholar of international repute and one of the foremost figures in the resurgence of evangelical scholarship in post-War Britain, Bruce was honoured by a DD from Aberdeen University and a Fellowship of the British Academy. He edited the *Evangelical Quarterly* (1949–80) and the *Palestine Exploration Quarterly* (1957–71), and encouraged younger writers in habits of meticulous research and presentation of material. A prolific writer, Bruce produced commentaries on nearly every New Testament book. His numerous other volumes included *Are the New Testament Documents Reliable?* (L, 1943); *Second Thoughts on the Dead Sea Scrolls* (L, 1956); *The Spreading Flame* (Exeter, 1958); *The English Bible* (³Guildford, 1979); *Israel and the Nations* (L, 1963); *New Testament History* (L, 1969); *The Message of the New Testament* (Exeter,

1972); *Paul: The Apostle of the Free Spirit* (Exeter, 1977); *Men and Movements in the Primitive Church* (Exeter, 1980); *Paternoster Bible History Atlas* (Exeter, 1982); and *The Pauline Circle* (Exeter, 1985).

F. F. Bruce, *In Retrospect* (L, 1980); *Who's Who 1991*, 244; I. H. Marshall, in *Proc. of Brit. Acad.* 80 (1993), 245–60.

J. D. Douglas

Bruce, John (1792–1872), General Associate Synod* and UP divine. Born in Glasgow, he graduated MA from Glasgow University in 1811 and then attended the General Associate Divinity Hall, Edinburgh. In 1815 he was licensed by Glasgow Presbytery, and ordained in 1816 to Newmilns, Kilmarnock, where he remained until his death, exercising a notable preaching ministry. His discourse on Voluntaryism,* *Christ on the Throne of His Father David* (G, 1835), gained him a DD from Washington College, Pennsylvania, in 1847.

Lectures and Sermons (n.p., 1841).

Small II, 296–7.

G. Wareing

Bruce Lectures, a series founded in 1900 in memory of A. B. Bruce.* The lectures have to deal with a New Testament subject and are delivered in the Divinity Faculty of Glasgow University (and formerly in the Glasgow UF College). A lecturer is appointed every third year by trustees who represent both CofS and Divinity Faculty interests. Many series appear not to have been published. Among the exceptions have been W. Manson,* *Christ's View of the Kingdom of God* (L, 1918), Matthew Black (see *An Aramaic Approach to the Gospels and Acts*, O, 1946), and George Johnston, *The Doctrine of the Church in the New Testament* (C, 1943).

Some details in *C of S Year Book* (annual), 1930–62.

D. F. Wright

Bruce, Michael (1746–67), poet. Born at Kinnesswood, Kinross-shire, a poor weaver's son, he studied at Edinburgh University (1762–5), where he met John Logan.* For some time Bruce kept a school, first nearby at Gairney Bridge, then near Tillicoultry (Clackmannanshire). To poverty were added sickness and melancholy until he died of consumption at Kinnesswood.

The authorship of a number of compositions, including some of the *Paraphrases*,* *The Ode to the Cuckoo* ('Hail, beauteous stranger of the grove') and the recasting of Doddridge's hymn, 'O God of Bethel', has been contested. Some have ascribed them to Bruce, others to Logan, who edited *Poems on Several Occasions*, by Michael Bruce (E, 1770), containing some (unspecified) said to be by other authors. In 1781 Logan published *Poems* under his own name, including some from the former book. The balance of the evidence is that Bruce composed the material and that Logan, as he did on at least one other occasion, appropriated it as his own after the author's death.

Life and Complete Works, ed. J. Mackenzie, (E, 1914); *Life and Works*, Bicentenary edn, ed. E. Vernon (Perth, 1951); T. G. Snoddy, *Michael Bruce* (E, 1947); *New Cambridge Bibliog. of English Literature*, ed. G. Watson (C, 1969–77), II, 2021; J. Julian, *Dictionary of Hymnology* (^{2}L, 1907), 187–9.

DNB VIII, 111–13.

J. S. Andrews

Bruce, Robert (c.1554–1631), Edinburgh minister and leading Reformed churchman. The second son of Sir Alexander Bruce of Airth and of Janet Livingstone, a great-granddaughter of James I, he initially studied law, in St Andrews, France and Louvain. After his return, he was provided by his father with the barony of Kinnaird, near Larbert, with a view to his becoming a Senator in the College of Justice. He decided, however, to devote himself to the Church, and returned to St Andrews. Here he was much influenced by Andrew Melville,* who brought him to Edinburgh in 1587.

The General Assembly of 1587 voted for Bruce to be appointed to the charge of Edinburgh (St Giles)*. He was chosen Moderator of the General Assembly in February 1588, a sign of the extraordinarily high regard with which he was held, both for his preaching and his personal integrity. A favourite of James VI*, he was appointed a Privy Councillor in 1589, and in 1590 he anointed Anne of Denmark at her coronation. In 1592 he was again Moderator of the General Assembly. After 1596, with a cooling of relations between the King and the Presbyterian Church, some of the royal discontent was focused on Bruce, the leading churchman in Edinburgh. There were several unhappy issues, including the fact that Bruce had not been regularly ordained 'by imposition of hands' until 1598 and the question of his income from Arbroath Abbey. After the Gowrie conspiracy in August 1600, Bruce refused to declare from the pulpit the King's version of what happened. Stung, the King ordered his banishment, and, scrupulously holding to his conscience, Bruce refused to submit. The King saw this as a means of silencing Bruce, who suffered the consequences for the rest of his life.

Banished to France in 1600, he was recalled in 1601, but ordered to keep to his house at Kinnaird. From 1605–13 he was banished to Inverness. From 1613–22 though nominally confined to Kinnaird, he had a little more freedom. From 1622–4 he was again banished to Inverness, but then returned to Kinnaird where he died in July 1631.

It was largely under Bruce's leadership that the Scottish Reformation found stability. His sermons on the Lord's Supper brought together Reformed doctrine and evangelical application in a way that helped to shape and became characteristic of the Scottish Reformed tradition.

Sermons upon the Sacrament of the Lords Supper (E, 1591?); *Sermons preached in the Kirk of Edinburgh* (E,

1591); the five sermons in the first volume and the eleven in the second were anglicized and reprinted as *The Way to True Peace and Rest* (L, 1617). Both were reprinted, in a slightly edited version of the original Scots, by William Cunningham,* *Sermons . . . with [R. Wodrow's] Collections for his Life* (Wodrow Society*, E, 1843). Further anglicized editions of the five sermons on the Lord's Supper were issued by John Laidlaw* (*Robert Bruce's Sermons on the Sacrament*, E, 1901) and T. F. Torrance* (*The Mystery of the Lord's Supper*, L, 1958).

MSS Sermons on the Epistle to the Hebrews, 1590-4, in New College Library, Edinburgh.

D. C. MacNicol, *Robert Bruce* (E, 1907, rp. L, 1961); *FES* I, 54-5.

I. R. Torrance

Brunton, Henry (c.1770-1813), missionary linguist in West Africa and southern Russia. Born at Selkirk and trained as a minister under the 'Burgher' Synod, in 1798-1800 Brunton served the Edinburgh Missionary Society* at Freetown, and on the Rio Pongas in Susuland (in modern Guinea), an Islamic area. On his return to Scotland, Brunton prepared for the Church Missionary Society a series of minor publications in and on the Susu language, including the first grammar of the language. In 1802, accompanied by Alexander Paterson,* he founded a mission station at Karass, in the northern Caucasus, among the Nogay Tatar, and there prepared and printed a series of works in and on Tatar, including the translated Gospels. The Karass station survived until the 1820s; the site is still known as Shotlandka ('Little Scotland'). Brunton's linguistic work, pioneering in both Susu and Tatar, deserves scholarly attention.

J. v. Klaproth, *Travels in the Caucasus* (L, 1814), 272-3; P. E. H. Hair, 'Susu literature', *Sierra Leone Lang. Rev.* 4 (1965), 38-9; id., 'Henry Brunton', *SIMSB* 13 (1973), 28-30; M. V. Jones, 'The Sad and Curious History of Karass 1802-35', *Oxford Slavonic Papers* 8 (1975), 54-81.

P. E. H. Hair

Buchan, Elspeth, see Buchanites.

Buchan, John (1875-1940), author and public figure. He was brought up in Kirkcaldy, Glasgow and Broughton, Peeblesshire, the son of a FC minister. Following a brilliant academic career at Glasgow and Oxford, Buchan quickly became an established author while pursuing a career as a colonial administrator, barrister, publisher and politician. Apart from his time as Conservative and Unionist MP for the Scottish Universities (1927-35), Buchan was Lord High Commissioner* to the General Assembly* of the CofS in 1933 and 1934 and Governor General of Canada from 1935 until his death.

It is, however, as a novelist and biographer that Buchan is principally remembered, with works including *John Burnet of Barns* (L, 1898), *A Lodge in the Wilderness* (E, 1906), *Prester John* (L, 1910), *The Thirty-Nine Steps* (E, 1915), *Greenmantle* (L, 1916), *Mr Standfast* (L, 1919), *The Path of the King* (L, 1921), *Huntingtower* (L, 1922), (ed.) *The Northern Muse* (L, 1924), *John MacNab* (L, 1925), *Witch Wood* (L, 1927), *Montrose* (L, 1928), *The Kirk in Scotland* (with George Adam Smith,* L, 1930), *Sir Walter Scott* (L, 1932), *The Free Fishers* (L, 1934), *Oliver Cromwell* (L, 1934), *The Island of Sheep* (L, 1936), *Augustus* (L, 1937), *Memory Hold-the-Door* (L, 1940) and *Sick Heart River* (L, 1941).

Buchan remained a devout Christian throughout his life. His Calvinist* upbringing was enriched by his delight in the physical world and a Platonic sense of the eternal and unseen (see particularly *Montrose*). His books are often popular in form but evoke serious concerns, particularly the conflict with evil and the regeneration of the self, both strongly Calvinist themes.

DNB 1931-40, 110-14; J. A. Smith, *John Buchan* (L, 1965); J. A. Smith, *John Buchan and His World* (L, 1979); D. Daniell, *The Interpreter's House* (L, 1975).

D. Smith

Buchanan, Claudius (1716-1814), Anglican* evangelical minister, East India Company Chaplain and missionary* publicist. Born at Cambuslang, Buchanan attended Inveraray Grammar School (1771-9), and Glasgow University (1782-4, 1786-7). Encouraged by John Newton to enter the CofE, he attended Queen's College Cambridge (BA, 1795). Ordained deacon in 1795 and priest in 1796, he served as Newton's curate. At Charles Simeon's* suggestion, Charles Grant* had him appointed a Chaplain in India. Stationed at Barrackpore (1797-9) and Calcutta (1799-1808), he helped organize the Company College of Fort William in 1800, serving as Vice-provost 1800-6 and as Professor of Greek, Latin and English Classics. He gave substantial sums for essays, poems and sermons at public schools and universities in Britain in 1803 and 1805 to publicize his concern for Christianity and civilization in India. He himself expressed his concern in his *Memoir of the Expediency of an Ecclesiastical Establishment for British India* (L, 1805). *Christian Researches in Asia* (L, 1810) resulted from two extensive journeys in India. His sermon *The Star in the East* (L, 1809) stimulated missionary interest in Britain and America. A curate at Ouseburn Yorkshire (1810-15), he was the leading publicist during the debate over the East Indian Company Charter, writing *Colonial Ecclesiastical Establishment* (L, 1813). His initiative resulted in the publication of the Syriac New Testament. He was awarded DDs by Glasgow, Aberdeen, St Andrews, Dublin and Cambridge. Buchanan was the outstanding missionary publicist of his day, at a time when interest in missionary activity was viewed by many as suspect.

DNB VII, 182-4; A. K. Davidson, *Evangelicals and Attitudes to India 1786-1813* (Appleford, 1988); H. Pearson, *Memoirs of the Life and Writings of the Rev. Claudius Buchanan*, 2 vols (L, 1817).

A. K. Davidson

BUCHANAN, DUGALD

Buchanan, Dugald (1716–68), celebrated Gaelic* religious poet, belonging to the foundational stage of the evangelical movement in the Highlands* (see Hymnology, Gaelic). Born at Ardoch, Strathyre, Perthshire, Buchanan was the son of a miller. He became a tutor to a local family, but moved to Stirling to continue his education. Apprenticed thereafter to a carpenter in Kippen and later in Dumbarton, he did not complete his apprenticeships, largely because of his restless nature. By the early 1740s, the religious impressions which were evident even in his boyhood had deepened noticeably, and he became conscious of his own sinfulness. In 1742 he heard George Whitefield* preaching at Cambuslang, during the revival,* but he did not find peace until his conversion in 1744. His spiritual search is documented in a diary which he wrote in English, following Puritan models. Marrying in 1749, he settled on his father's farm. A year later he abandoned farming, and became an itinerant teacher.

Buchanan's talent lay in teaching and preaching. In 1753 he was settled as a Scottish SPCK* teacher at Kinloch Rannoch in the estate of Strowan, forfeited after the Jacobite rising* of 1745. Combining the duties of teacher and catechist from 1755, Buchanan had a major role in 'civilizing' the estate after the 'Forty-five, and was instrumental in planting schools.

Buchanan's Gaelic poetry reflects his calling as preacher and teacher, since it has a strong didactic element. His eight surviving poems establish his reputation as a skilful craftsman of verse, although his themes are far from original. He is sometimes heavily indebted to Isaac Watts (1674–1748), whom he paraphrases *in extenso* in *Mòrachd Dhè* ('The Greatness of God'). The influence of the English 'Graveyard School' of poets (represented in England by Edward Young and in Scotland by Robert Blair*) is apparent, particularly in his poem *An Claigeann* ('The Skull'), in which he provides vignettes of possible owners of a skull found in a graveyard. His chief concerns as a poet are: (i) the majesty of God and the suffering of Christ; (ii) human accountability and impending judgment, a theme pursued in a long 'heroic ballad' on *Là a' Bhreitheanais* ('The Day of Judgment'); (iii) the transience of life and the need for timely repentance, developed with great skill in his 'symbolic' poem *An Geamhradh* ('The Winter'); and (iv) the practice of Christian virtues and spiritual, rather than physical, prowess, befitting the Christian warrior, whom he depicts in *An Gaisgeach* ('The Hero'), an adaptation of Watts' poem, 'True Monarchy, 1701'.

Buchanan's style is terse, conveying biblical teaching by means of vivid imagery, drawn mainly from the natural world of Perthshire. The effect is both homely and dramatic; the lightning accompanying Christ's Second Coming is 'like a moor-burn going up the steep slopes'. In *An Geamhradh*, the characteristics of a crisp Perthshire winter – feathery snowfalls, lead-like hailstones, blue slabs of ice – introduce his picture of death. Unlike the lazy flies, only those creatures that make adequate preparation beforehand can survive this last enemy.

Buchanan was also a notable Gaelic scholar, and supervised the printing of the Scottish Gaelic New Testament in 1767 (see Bible (Versions, Gaelic)).

D. MacLean (ed.), *The Spiritual Songs of Dugald Buchanan* (E, 1913); L. Macbean, *Buchanan, the Sacred Bard of the Scottish Highlands* (L, 1919); D. E. Meek, 'Ath-sgrùdadh: Dùghall Bochanan', *Gairm*, 147–8 (Summer–Autumn, 1989).

D. E. Meek

BUCHANAN, GEORGE

Buchanan, George (1506–82), Scottish humanist and writer. Born in a modest farmhouse near Killearn (Stirlingshire), in a largely Gaelic-speaking community, he was a student in Paris at fourteen, a soldier briefly at seventeen (to see what it was like), but then returned to studies and graduated at both St Andrews (1525) and Paris (1527). He was teacher and tutor in Paris before returning to Scotland about 1537. He sympathized with Reformed views, wrote against the Franciscans,* incurred the lasting enmity of Cardinal David Beaton* for exposing clerical corruption and hypocrisy, and was arrested and jailed as a heretic. He escaped to France, taught at Bordeaux and Paris, and was thereafter regent at the Portuguese university of Coimbra. There too he fell foul of ecclesiastical authority, was imprisoned, charged with heresy* before the Inquisition, and confined to a monastery under severe restrictions before acquittal in 1552 for lack of evidence. He was still a Catholic, albeit a critical one, and the Scottish Reformation* was eight years off.

He resumed tutoring in France, and all this time was furthering the classical studies that were to enhance his reputation as the most distinguished humanist from (what is now) Britain (see Renaissance). Buchanan was friend and tutor to Mary Queen of Scots* (they shared cultural interests) even after his return to Scotland in 1561. After Darnley's murder, however, convinced that she had a part in it (1567), he supported the Protestant lords against her, and Mary was to find him a more deadly enemy than was John Knox.* Buchanan held several distinguished offices: Member of Parliament, Lord Privy Seal, Principal of St Leonard's College, St Andrews, and, unusually for someone not a minister, Moderator of the General Assembly (*FES* VII, 437–8). In 1570 he became tutor to the child king James VI.*

Beza called Buchanan a greater man than himself – a remarkable tribute from one who might have been expected to frown upon the Scot's more earthy flights of poetic fancy, and his mingling of Christian and pagan tradition. Among Buchanan's numerous writings were *Baptistes* (1534), a dramatic presentation of the life of John the Baptist, and a history of Scotland up to 1572 which aimed to clear the record of 'Scottish vanity' and 'English lies'.

The publication of Buchanan's famous treatise *De Jure Regni apud Scotos* (E, 1579; On the Right of Kingship among the Scots) marked the real beginning of that conflict in Scotland which was to rend the country asunder and to end more than a century later with the overthrow of the House of Stuart and the subsequent fulfilment at every point of the political doctrines advocated by Buchanan in this work – with one exception to be mentioned below. Buchanan dedicated *De Jure Regni* to James VI '... that it may guide you beyond the rocks of flattery and not only give you advice, but also keep you in the road you are so happily entered, and in case of any deviation, replace you in the line of duty'. Writing in Latin, Buchanan taught that kings are chosen and continued in office by the people, that they are subject to both human and divine laws (he did not elaborate on how the true 'human' law was to be determined), and that the Scots had always claimed and exercised the right to call wicked rulers to account.

In his advocacy of tyrannicide, Buchanan trod a path followed in this era also by other Reformed churchmen, on the continent as well as in England and Scotland, and by Jesuits* too. He held that a manifest tyrant is a public enemy and may be lawfully slain by *any* subject whose conscience would justify the act. On the other hand, Buchanan tells of his ideal view of kingship. 'I wish,' he says, 'to see him beloved by his subjects; and guarded not by terror but by affection; the only armour that can render kings perfectly secure.' Having attracted much attention on the continent, the theories of government advanced by *De Jure Regni* were in the following century adopted and made popular by Samuel Rutherford,* Richard Cameron* and others, and became a potent force in the stand taken by the persecuted Covenanters* against the Stuart kings. Further publicized by John Locke in 1690, the doctrine came probably by way of Rousseau to immortality at the hands of Thomas Jefferson in 1776.

But James was now expressing very different views from those of his former tutor, teaching his own son that God had made him 'a little God to sit on his throne, and to rule over other men'. Thus Buchanan's book was condemned by Act of Parliament in 1584 as containing 'slanderous and untrue calumnies'. It was still considered dangerous enough to be singled out for public burning in 1683 by the University of Oxford, with other 'pernicious books ... destructive to the sacred persons of princes'. It was resuscitated and ran through three new editions in the eighteenth century.

When Buchanan's final illness was upon him in Edinburgh, Andrew Melville* and two others called to see him, and were surprised to find 'the greatest genius of the age' teaching a young valet to write. His visitors were concerned that Buchanan's history of Scotland, at that moment in the press, contained matter that might offend James VI and perhaps induce him to ban it. Convinced that he had told the truth, the dying scholar said, 'I will abide his feud, and all his kin's. Pray to God for me, and let him direct all.'

Long after Buchanan's death, tributes were coming even from improbable quarters. Pope Urban VIII, for instance, lamented that Buchanan was 'so great a heretic', for otherwise his version of the Psalms would have been made mandatory in Roman churches.

ET of *De Jure Regni* by D. H. MacNeill, *The Art and Science of Government among the Scots* (G, 1964); *Tragedies*, ed. and tr. P. Sharratt and P. G. Walsh (E, 1983); David Irving, *Memoirs of the Life and Writings of George Buchanan* (E, 1807); Robert Wallace, *George Buchanan* (E, 1899); I. D. McFarlane, *Buchanan* (L, 1981); *George Buchanan: Glasgow Quatercentenary Studies* (G, 1907); J. Durkan, *George Buchanan (1506–1582) Renaissance Scholar* (G, 1982) – incl. bibliography.

J. D. Douglas

Buchanan, James (1804–70), eminent FC divine. Born in Paisley, Renfrewshire, Buchanan was educated at Glasgow University and the Divinity Hall, Edinburgh. After a brief ministry in the CofS congregation of Roslin, Midlothian, in 1828 he became minister of North Leith Church, near Edinburgh, where his fame as a preacher soared. While at North Leith Buchanan published his popular *Comfort in Affliction* (E, 1837), a series of meditations born of his own frequent experiences of illness.

In 1840 Buchanan transferred to the High Church (St Giles)* in Edinburgh, a collegiate* charge which he shared with Robert Gordon.* This was of brief duration, since both men left the Est.C at the Disruption*. Buchanan became the first minister of St Stephen's FC, Edinburgh. He was soon called to be Professor of Apologetics in New College* in 1845, and then succeeded Thomas Chalmers* as Professor of Systematic Theology in 1847. This position he occupied until ill-health compelled retirement in 1868. He received a DD from Princeton in 1844, and later an LLD from Glasgow.

Buchanan was a Reformed* theologian of the old school. His *The Office and Work of the Holy Spirit* (E, 1842) and *The Doctrine of Justification* (E, 1867; Cunningham lectures* for 1866) contain lucid expositions of classical Calvinistic pneumatology and soteriology. He was, however, better known in his day as a metaphysical theologian, 'whose keen philosophic mind was at its best when showing the close connection that exists between "the best theology and the best philosophy"' (W. Knight, *Some Nineteenth Century Scotsmen*, E, 1903, 112). His productions in this field were *Faith in God and Modern Atheism Compared*, 2 vols (E, 1855) and *Analogy, Considered as a Guide to Truth* (E, 1864).

The former work is perhaps the more interesting of the two in the light of modern debates about apologetics.* It is divided into four sections: (i) 'Statement of the Evidence for the Being and Perfections of God'; (ii) 'Examination of the Rational Principles which are involved in the Process of Proof'; (iii) 'Modern Atheism'; (iv) 'Uses and Defects of the Natural Manifestations of God'. In section (i) Buchanan presents five arguments for God's existence – from existence in general, from mind, from conscience, from design in nature, and from the vestiges of the historic fact of creation.

Buchanan rejected the idea that humanity had any direct intuitive knowledge of God, arguing that theistic belief was grounded in the perception of phenomenal evidence. He admitted that the process from evidential perception to belief could be 'intuitional and spontaneous', but held it a proper task of the apologist to press home on men 'the natural evidences for the being and perfections of God'. He also observed that apologetics normally had more to do with exposing the fallacies of unbelievers than with positively proving the truth.

On the 'Tracts for the Times' (E, 1843); The 'Essays and Reviews' Examined (E, 1864); The Scriptural Argument for Non-Intrusion (E, 1840).

AFCS I, 50; Disruption Worthies, 101–10; DNB VII, 194–5; FES I, 69.

N. R. Needham

Buchanan, Robert (1802–75), a prominent leader in the evangelical party in the Disruption,* minister of Free Tron Church and Free College Church, Glasgow, and Convener of the Sustentation Committee of the FC (1847–75). Buchanan had studied at Glasgow and Edinburgh Universities and was ordained as parish minister of Gargunnock in 1827. In 1830 he was called to Saltoun, and in 1833 to the Tron Church, Glasgow, where Thomas Chalmers* had been minister from 1814 to 1818. He took an active part in the controversy surrounding the Veto Act* and its application, and by 1838 was a recognized spokesman and leader in the evangelical party. After the Disruption he was requested to write an account of the events, and the result was The Ten Years' Conflict, 2 vols (E, 1849), which traces the view of the legal relation between Church and state* in Scotland from the Reformation to the Disruption, giving detailed attention to the legal decisions in the Auchterarder Case* of 1838. The book confirmed his position as an ecclesiastical statesman within the FC, a position reinforced by his appointment in the Sustentation Committee which was charged with overseeing Chalmers' innovatory procedure for the funding of the ministry. He was Moderator of the FC General Assembly in 1860, and once more took a prominent role in legal disputes when the disciplined minister of Cardross FC initiated proceedings against the FC Presbytery in the Court of Session (see Cardross Case).

In 1862 Buchanan was appointed convener of the committee of the FC Assembly charged with working towards union with the UPC and other denominations. The initial enthusiasm for such a merger was later replaced by intense controversy within the FC, in which Buchanan and the majority were opposed by a strong minority led by James Begg.* The proposed union finally collapsed in 1873.

In Glasgow, before the Disruption, Buchanan had been involved with the movement for Church Extension.* His later ministry continued this emphasis, particularly in the Wynds district, where some 12,000 lived in squalid housing and social neglect in the centre of the rapidly growing city. Mission work was begun in 1845, and in 1851 a separate congregation was formed with 350 people. Further mission churches followed, accompanied by day schools and Sunday schools. Buchanan's research and principles are described in a leaflet, *The Spiritual Destitution of the Masses in Glasgow: its Alarming Increase, its Fearful Amount, and the Only Effectual Cure* (G, 1851). He took an active part in the development of the National Schools system, and in social improvements in Glasgow such as the Loch Katrine water scheme. His one published exegetical work was *Ecclesiastes: its Meaning and its Lessons, explained and illustrated* (L, 1859).

DNB VII, 196–7; N. L. Walker, Dr Robert Buchanan (L, 1877); FES III, 475–6; AFCS I, 108.

J. Nicholls

Buchanan, Walter (1755–1832), evangelical minister and writer of the CofS. Buchanan was born in Glasgow, son of a maltman. He received the MA from Glasgow University in 1774. Ordained at Stirling in 1780, he spent his later years in Edinburgh where he was minister of the Canongate Church. Buchanan was in the circle of such leading Evangelicals as John Erskine* of Greyfriars and John Colquhoun of Leith (FES I, 158). Together they encouraged two Scottish preaching tours by Charles Simeon* of Cambridge. Simeon said of Buchanan, 'it was one of the greatest blessings of my life ever to have known him' (Memoirs, 89).

Buchanan's sermon *The Beneficial Influence of the Gospel* (E, 1804) for the Scottish Society for the Propagation of Christian Knowledge* was widely distributed. He prepared 'An Account of the Life of John Witherspoon' (found in the Edinburgh edition of his *Works* I, 1804). Buchanan edited *The Religious Monitor* until it ceased publication in 1819.

FES I, 29; W. Carus, ed., *Memoirs of the Life of C. Simeon* (L, 1848), 89, 93, 118–19, 121; J. Macleod, *Scottish Theology* (E, ³1974), 219.

D. F. Kelly

Buchanites, small sect founded by Elspeth Buchan or Simpson (c.1738–91). Elspeth Simpson was born in Banffshire at Rothmackenzie(?). As a girl she came to Greenock, and later to Ayr, where she married(?) a potter, Robert Buchan. They quarrelled and she returned to Banffshire, coming later to Glasgow. There she heard Hugh White, Relief Church* minister in Irvine, preach. They began a correspondence in January 1783, and she visited him, persuading him of her novel interpretation of various Scripture passages. White, now a convert to her views, was swiftly removed by his Presbytery, whereupon she returned to him in Irvine, where they gained a following.

In May 1784 they were expelled from the town, and set up a community at New Cample, near Thornhill, Dumfriesshire. On Buchan's death the community quickly disintegrated. The poet Robert Burns gives a notable contemporary account: 'Their tenets are a strange jumble of enthusiastic jargon, among others, she pretends to give them the Holy Ghost by breathing on them, which she does with postures and practices that are scandalously indecent; they have likewise disposed of all their effects and hold a community of goods, and live nearly an idle life, carrying on a great farce of pretended devotion in barns, and woods, where they lodge and lye all together, and hold likewise a community of women, as it is another of their tenets that they can commit no mortal sin. I am personally acquainted with most of them, and can assure you the abovementioned are facts' (Letter to James Burness, 1784).

There are relevant contemporary volumes in the National Library of Scotland, the most important being *The Divine Dictionary or, A Treatise indicted by Holy Inspiration, Containing the Faith and Practice of that People (by this world) called Buchanites, who are actually waiting for the second coming of our Lord . . .* (c.1785). The work is in two 'numbers': the first is signed by Hugh White, and 'revised and approven of by Elespat Simson, alias Buchan', October 1785. The second contains their views on marriage, which incurred much contemporary hostility (70–71): 'The same law that finished the carnal services of the altar, and bestial sacrifices, put an end to carnal marriages' (71). It also contains a letter from Hugh White to 'a Countess of Great Britain', 1785 (80–3), and a number of hymns. (Burns' annotation to the song, 'The Beds of Sweet Roses', in Johnson's *Scots Musical Museum*, noted that the Buchanites sang 'some of their nonsensical rhymes . . . to this air'.) There is a collection of 'Eight Letters between the People called Buchanites and a Teacher near Edinburgh' (E, 1785), and a hostile pamphlet in ballad form: *The Western Delusion! Or an Account of the Buchanites, Who have lately raised an Uproar in the West of Scotland shewing, How one Mrs Buchan in the Town of Irvine, has deluded a number of . . . And amongst others, she has deluded one Mr White, a Relief Minister in that place.*

J. Cameron, *History of the Buchanite Delusion 1783–1846* (Dumfries, 1904); J. Train, *History of the Buchanites* (Irvine, 1883); *DNB* III, 178–9; Chambers-Thomson I, 226–7.

I. R. Torrance

Bulloch, James Boyd Prentice (1915–81), Church historian. Born in Belfast but educated in Glasgow (MA, 1935; BD, 1939), he was assistant at Glasgow Cathedral (1939–42), minister of Tranent Old, East Lothian (1942–53), and from 1953 of a Borders charge that grew to encompass Broughton, Glenholm and Kilbucho linked with Skirling linked with Stobo, and Drumelzier linked with Tweedsmuir. Such responsibilities did not prevent him becoming a prolific historical writer, with numerous papers in journals such as the *Records of the Scottish Church History Society,** the editing of the volume on Peeblesshire in *The Third Statistical Account of Scotland* (E, 1964), and several monographs, including *Adam of Dryburgh* (L, 1958), *The Life of the Celtic Church* (E, 1963) and *The Church in Celtic Scotland* (Inverness, 1971). He also completed for publication A. L. Drummond's* history of the modern Scottish Church. His distinctions included the degrees of PhD (Edinburgh, 1955) and DD (Glasgow, 1971).

FES IX, 74, X, 45–6; *LW* July 1981, 32.

D. F. Wright

Bunting, Jabez (1779–1858), Methodist churchman. He has been variously described as the indispensable ecclesiastical statesman, the Methodist Conference 'buttoned up in a single pair of breeches', the Methodist Pope, and the power-drunk minister of Christ (see Kent and Currie, below). A rising member of the Wesleyan Methodist hierarchy by 1820, one of his early acts was to lay the foundations of a form of Church government – not entirely successfully – to fill the vacuum following Wesley's death (*see* Wesley, John). Although this failed to prevent a number of schisms (Gregory), it preserved the broad bounds of Methodism intact. In Scotland, the Methodist decline after 1819 (*see* Ward, Valentine) led Bunting to pronounce that '. . . if Methodism were put up to auction it would be the best thing that could be done with it, except Glasgow, Edinburgh, Dalkeith and perhaps Ayr . . .' (Swift). In relation to the CofS, Bunting had corresponded with William Collins* and Thomas Chalmers* as early as 1821. The rapport with the latter was based on a shared appreciation of evangelical principles, a common interest in the missionary cause and coincident views on the nature and value of established Churches. While Bunting regarded Chalmers as one of the most illustrious men produced by Scotland, FC leaders praised Bunting and the Wesleyan Connexion at large. Wesleyan support for the Scots Evangelicals found full expression in a Bunting-inspired Parliamentary Petition in 1843, warning of the impending Disruption,* and in the principled and pecuniary support encouraged by the Wesleyan Conference later that same year.

R. Currie, *Methodism Divided* (L, 1968); B. Gregory, *Sidelights on the Conflicts of Methodism* (L, 1899); A. J. Hayes and D. A. Gowland, *Scottish Methodism in the Early Victorian Period* (E, 1981); J. Kent, *Jabez Bunting, The Last Wesleyan* (L, 1955); W. F. Swift, *Methodism in Scotland* (L, 1947).

A. J. Hayes

Burgess, Oath, oath of 1744 taken by citizens of Edinburgh, Glasgow and Perth, endorsing the religion professed in the realm. It occasioned a division (known as 'The Breach') in the Associate Synod* in 1747. Those who condemned the oath were known as Antiburghers. The issue was important to the Associate Synod because, within a burgh, none but burgesses were permitted to engage in commerce, belong to a trade guild, or enjoy the privilege of voting. Moreover, much of the Synod's strength lay in the three cities affected.

Some in the Synod interpreted the oath to include an endorsement of those practices in the established (*see* Church and State) CofS to which the recent Secession (*see* Associate Presbytery) had objected. Others construed the oath to be an approbation of the Protestant Reformed faith itself, and intended only to exclude Roman Catholics* from becoming burgesses. The religious clause of the oath was: 'Here I protest before God, and your Lordships, that I profess, and allow with my heart, the true religion presently professed within this realm, and authorized by the laws thereof: I shall abide thereat, and defend the same to my life's end; renouncing the Roman religion called papistry.'

The Synod met three times in 1745 to discuss the matter, with divinity professor Alexander Moncrieff* a leading voice in condemning the oath. At the April 1746 meeting a motion against the oath prevailed, thirteen to nine, but the decision was protested by some of the most eminent men in the Synod, including Ralph Erskine* and James Fisher.* The Synod seemed to reverse itself in April 1747 when it determined that the 1746 decision would not be a term of communion for ministers or members. But those opposed to the oath had protested against putting this question, and did not vote. Thomas Mair* then disclaimed the lawful authority of the Synod, and he and twenty-two others departed to the house of Adam Gib* where they constituted the General Associate Synod,* avowing that they were the rightful continuation of the Secession body.

The Antiburghers issued justifications of their action; these are found in Gib's *The Present Truth: A Display of the Secession Testimony*, 2 vols (E, 1774). They then proceeded to depose from the ministry and excommunicate men of the opposing party. The Burgher opinion concerning the oath is argued in Archibald Hall's* *Impartial Survey of the Religious Clause in some Burgess-Oaths* (E, 1771), and in six pamphlets by Ralph Erskine.* The controversy was a stormy and painful one; each of the rival synods privately censured themselves for excesses. The significance of the Oath was greatly diminished when both synods divided fifty years later over the New Light* denial that the magistrate was to exercise his authority on behalf of religion. The Burgess Oath was abolished in 1819, but by then negotiations were already in progress to form the United Secession Church* from New Light elements of the Burghers and the Antiburghers.

J. M'Kerrow, *History of the Secession Church* (E, 1854); D. Fraser, *Life and Diary of Ebenezer Erskine* (E, 1831); id., *Life and Diary of Ralph Erskine* (E, 1834); R. Mackenzie, *John Brown of Haddington* (L, 1918).

S. Isbell

Burgh Churches, the first effort of the Kirk to deal with the problem of church extension* when the population of the towns was steadily increasing. Normally the financial responsibility for the provision of the ordinances of religion rested on landowners and was met by a tax on the fruits of the earth – the tenth-part or tithe (*see* Teinds), which was a reflection of Jacob's vow at Bethel (Gen. 28:22). This gathering of teind had obtained from the fourteenth century. In the fast-growing burghs, however, there was no land on which to lay this burden, with the result that in the absence of heritors,* the municipal authorities had to assume the responsibility for building and maintaining church and manse and for providing stipend.* The causes so created were the Burgh Churches, and in 1925 there were still forty-five of them – fourteen in Edinburgh, eight in Glasgow, six in Aberdeen, four in Dundee, three in each of Paisley and Perth, two in each of Greenock and Stirling, and one each in Queensferry, Dumfries and Kilmarnock (listed Cox, 519f.).

The Edinburgh situation is interesting if not quite typical. At the time of the Reformation,* St Giles'* had been the only parochial charge in the capital, though it had carried a staff of about a hundred priests. At the Reformation it was taken over, along with Trinity College (not then a parish church) by the Provost, Baillies and Council to serve the needs of the people, and Queen Mary in 1566 disponed by charter to the Council to meet this responsibility the property in the city that had belonged to the RC Church – a charter later ratified by King James VI. By 1633 when Greyfriars was built by the town authorities, Parliament authorized a tax to be levied upon householders (the 'annuity tax'*) to provide the stipends and to maintain the buildings of the Burgh Churches. The Council were entitled also to charge rents for sittings in the churches, though provision was made whereby adequate sitting had to be reserved for the poor. The case of the Canongate is interesting in that it became a Burgh Church as recently as 1860, since it was only then that its parish became a part of Edinburgh. In the case of the three Paisley Burgh Churches, provision for their stipend is made in terms of a Cart Navigation Act. One additional duty which the ministers of Glasgow's Burgh Churches still undertake is that of opening with prayer the sittings of the High Court.

The Church of Scotland (Property and Endowments) Act of 1925 transferred to the General Trustees* of the CofS all rights in the heritable property of the Burgh Churches, reserving, however, to the local authority a right of pre-emption in case the property came on the market (Cox, 494–6). All provision for stipend was similarly transferred and now forms part of the statutory endowments of the parish. For all practical purposes only the name now differentiates a Burgh Church from any other.

A. J. Campbell, 'The Burgh Churches of Scotland', *RSCHS* 4 (1932), 185–94.

A. Herron

Burghers, *see* Associate Synod.

Burial. The Romans disposed of the human body by burning or interment, but as the Christian faith spread through the empire, burial became the norm, probably because Christ's body had been buried and he had risen again. When churches were built, it was usual to bury under the floor, or in any case near the place of worship. By about the ninth century it was normal to bury in churchyards outside the walls of churches, although the practice of burying under the floor of the church continued for centuries in some places. Sometimes burial aisles were attached to churches for the burial of members of noble and landowning families. By the seventeenth century churchyards and cemeteries were the legal responsibility of the heritors* in country parishes and the town council in urban areas. They were, however, to be situated not too far from the church. The Reformers in Scotland tried quite early to stop burials in churches, and this for obvious sanitary reasons. An Act of General Assembly in 1643 forbade the practice and, although there was no statute forbidding it, it was ruled in the Duddingston case of 1832 as not permissible. In a more recent church case even the ashes of a deceased minister were not permitted to be laid below the floor of a church. Those who had committed suicide and the excommunicated were in olden days buried apart, with none attending except grave-diggers.

Knox's *Book of Common Order* (1564)* stated that 'the corpse is reverently brought to the grave, accompanied with the congregation, without any further ceremonies; which being buried, the minister, if he be present and required, goeth to the church, if it be not far off, and maketh some comfortable exhortation to the people, touching death and resurrection.' The Reformers wished to discourage any RC observance of prayer for the dead or any mass (see *FBD*, 199-201). In the Covenanting* period of the seventeenth century there was renewed pressure against elaborate ceremonies at burial. Alexander Henderson's* account indicated that there were no funeral sermons (*Letters* II, 245). However, even Knox* preached at the funeral of the Regent Moray, and it is clear that discretion was given, within limits, to do what pastoral care demanded. The normal CofS (and generally Protestant) practice is for a minister to be present at house or church for a short service and then at the grave, after sentences and prayer, to commit the body to the ground with the words 'earth to earth, ashes to ashes and dust to dust, in sure and certain hope of everlasting life, through Jesus Christ Our Lord', and say the benediction.

In RC practice, burial is normally preceded by requiem mass. The body is received into the church; requiem mass follows and the priest then moves round the coffin, sprinkling blessed water and incensing in absolution. Thereafter the body is taken for interment. After initial hesitation, permission has now been given for cremation.

Sometimes it is appropriate to sing psalms and hymns in church and that tribute be paid to the work and life of the deceased, but churches of the Reformation allow no place for prayers for the dead. All make place for prayers for the bereaved. The FPC maintains the early Reformed position that there should be no ceremonies of any kind at the time of burial.

In former days, when the coffin was being carried to the grave, it used to be covered by a 'mortcloth' which was hired from the kirk session or a benevolent society and mortcloth fees went for the care of the poor of the parish. In recent years, cremation has largely replaced burial as the mode of disposal of the dead.

W. McMillan, *The Worship of the Scottish Reformed Church* (Dunfermline, 1931), *BCO* (1940).

A. I. Dunlop

Burleigh, John Henderson Seaforth (1894-1985), Church historian. Son of a Border manse, Burleigh graduated in classics and (after war service) theology at the University of Edinburgh, and undertook post-graduate research in Paris, Strasbourg, Prague and Oxford. Ordained in 1924, he ministered at Fyvie and Dundee St Enoch's before becoming Professor of Ecclesiastical History at Edinburgh in 1931. One-time co-editor of the *Evangelical Quarterly*,* and a keen Calvin* scholar, he contributed to patristic studies with *The City of God: A Study of St Augustine's Philosophy* (L, 1949) and *Augustine: Earlier Writings* (Library of Christian Classics, L, 1953). His best-known publication, however, was *A Church History of Scotland* (L, 1960), whose comprehensiveness, conciseness and balance made it a standard work. A devoted churchman, he helped to produce the 'Bishops Report' (1957), became Moderator of the General Assembly (1960), and ended his academic career as Dean of Divinity and Principal of New College,* Edinburgh (1956-64).

FES VI, 259, VIII, 489, IX, 514, 769, X, 429.

A. C. Cheyne

Burne, Nicol (*fl. c.*1580-90), Catholic polemical writer. Born about 1558, he graduated at St Andrews (1578), and was thereafter regent in St Leonard's College there. He became a RC after reading Domingo Soto. He invited disputation with Protestant opponents, and at Paisley faced Thomas Smeaton,* who, finding Burne immovable, proceeded to secure his excommunication. He was committed first to St Andrews Castle (1580), thereafter to Edinburgh tolbooth. Questioned by Andrew Melville* and others on behalf of the General Assembly, Burne stood his ground. Friends in high places secured his release on 31 January 1581, on payment of £500 security that he would leave Scotland for good. He offended his interrogators by personal attacks on Reformers, especially Beza, of whose pre-conversion verses Burne gave a scurrilous and defamatory rendering in Scots. His *Disputation* appeared with amendments in Paris (1581), a work of no great theological sophistication, though his Scottish background had given him some acquaintance with Hebrew and Greek philosophical commentators. *Ane Admonition* (Paris, 1581) was issued separately in a satirical verse attack on contemporary ministers, John Knox* and John Craig* being targeted in his prose. In 1581 Burne entered the Scots College* at Pont-à-Mousson (later transferred to Douai) and by 1598 he had become a Dominican* in Spain. His later history is unknown.

Disputation, ed. T. G. Law, *Catholic Tractates of the Sixteenth Century 1573-1600* (STS, E, L, 1901), 107-72, with introd. (xlix-liv); *DNB* VII, 383; D. McRoberts (ed.), *Essays on the Scottish Reformation* (G, 1962), 182, 273, 398-9.

J. Durkan

Burnet, Adam Wilson (1883-1962), minister, preacher and lecturer. Born at Cambuslang and

BURNET, ALEXANDER

educated at Glasgow's University (MA in Classics, 1906) and UF College, he served as minister at Tayport (Ferry-Port-on-Craig Queen Street), Fife (1911-14), Kilmarnock King Street (1914-20, interrupted by war service in France, 1917-18), Giffnock, Glasgow (1920-4), Glasgow Westbourne (1924-38, spanning the Union of 1929) and finally in the collegiate charge of St Cuthbert's, Edinburgh (1938-55). Honoured as one of the greatest preachers of his time, he delivered the Warrack lectures* (*Pleading with Men*, L, 1935) and the Russell lectures at Union Theological Seminary, New York (*The Lord Reigneth* L, 1946 – on the Revelation of John; delivered also at Chicago, Princeton and Northfield, MA). He made many other preaching and lecturing visits to the USA and also served as the Turnbull Trust Preacher in Melbourne (1950). Glasgow made him a DD in 1935. Burnet typified the common liberal Evangelicalism of his generation.

FUFCS 259; *FES* IX, 38; *LW* 17 (1962), 314; *Scotsman* Oct. 30, 1962, 5.

D. F. Wright

Burnet, Alexander (1614-84), Archbishop of St Andrews. He was the younger son of James Burnet, a minister, and Christian Dundas. Graduating at Edinburgh in 1633, he became chaplain to the Earl of Traquair before his abortive presentation to Coldingham in 1639. Appointed to the living of Burmash in Kent in 1641, he was ejected for his Royalist sympathies in 1650 and retired to the continent, becoming chaplain to the governor of Dunkirk and ministering to the English congregation there. In 1660, he became rector of Ivychurch (Kent) before returning to Scotland as Bishop of Aberdeen in 1663. Translated to the archbishopric of Glasgow in January, 1664, he also became a Privy Councillor and an extraordinary Lord of Session. As Archbishop he pursued a repressive policy against non-conformists who opposed the Episcopal Church, urging stern retribution for supporters of the Pentland Rising of 1666. In his pursuit of an Erastian episcopal establishment, his constant attempts to inform Charles II* of the inadequacy and self-interest of the Scottish nobility in dealing with ecclesiastical affairs, culminating in the Glasgow Remonstrance of September 1669, enraged both the King and his commissioner, the Earl of Lauderdale. Forced to resign his offices 'as one uselesse and unprofitable person', he retired to England where he remained for five years, but a return to repressive policies led to his reappointment to his former see in September 1674, thereafter resuming his campaign against conventiclers*. Translated to the archbishopric of St Andrews on 13 August 1679 following the assassination of Archbishop James Sharp,* he regularly attended Privy Council meetings and efficiently conducted diocesan and pastoral affairs. Married to Elizabeth Fleming who bore him a son who predeceased him, and two daughters, he died at St Andrews and was buried in St Salvator's chapel.

DNB VII, 392-3; J. A. Lamb, 'Archbishop Alexander Burnet, 1614-1684', *RSCHS* 11 (1955), 133-48; J. Buckroyd, 'The Dismissal of Archbishop Alexander Burnet, 1669', *RSCHS* 18 (1974), 149-55; *FES* VII, 327-8.

I. B. Cowan

Burnet, Gilbert (1643-1715), Bishop of Salisbury and church historian. Born in Edinburgh, he graduated at Aberdeen and in 1665 was episcopally ordained to Saltoun, East Lothian (1665-9). While there he published a pamphlet which contrasted the present ecclesiastical situation with that of the early Church. He accused the bishops of absenteeism, seldom preaching, preoccupation with affairs of state, arrogance, and theft of church property; and the clergy of pride, simony, worldliness and pubcrawling. This *Memorial of Diverse Grievances* (1668) incurred the ire of Archbishop Sharp,* and Burnet narrowly escaped excommunication. In 1669 he was appointed professor of divinity at Glasgow, but found his moderate stance resented by both Episcopalians* and Covenanters.* He went to London in 1674 and became chaplain of the Rolls Chapel and lecturer of St Clement's (1675-84), but was dismissed from his royal chaplaincy for rebuking Charles II's* way of life, and in 1687 outlawed by James II.* A strong supporter of William III, he was appointed by him as Bishop of Salisbury in 1689. Burnet preached at William's coronation and attended his deathbed. His writings include *History of the Reformation of the Church of England* (3 vols, L, 1679-1714); *A Vindication of the Authority, Constitution, and Laws of the Church and State of Scotland* (G, 1673); *An Exposition of the Thirty-Nine Articles* (L, 1699); and *History of His Own Time* (2 vols, L, 1723-34).

Lives by T. B. Burnet (his son) included in Burnet's *Works* (6 vols, O, 1833), and by T. E. S. Clarke and H. C. Foxcroft (C, 1907); *DNB* III, 394-405; *FES* I, 392-3.

J. D. Douglas

Burning Bush. In 1691 the Edinburgh printer, George Mossman, used the sign of the Burning Bush with the words '*nec tamen consumebatur*' ('and yet it was not consumed') on the cover of *The Principal Acts of the General Assembly*. The reference was to Exodus 3:2. The liberty that God, the 'I AM', had given to Israel, he had now brought to his suffering Church in the bloodless Revolution of 1689. It had been burned in fire but not consumed. Mossman may have had the idea from France or Holland. Although never officially authorized, the Burning Bush has become symbolic of the CofS and other Presbyterian churches.

G. D. Henderson, *The Burning Bush* (E, 1957).

A. I. Dunlop

Burns, (Sir) George (1795-1890), shipowner, youngest child of John Burns, minister of the Barony, Glasgow. After early employment in the cotton spinning mills at New Lanark (*see* Dale, David), he entered into partnership with his brother James as general merchants, but was soon in shipping, first as agent then as owner in Glasgow. He established the main services by steamship between Glasgow and Ireland and was associated with Samuel Cunard in the company formed to carry mail across the Atlantic. He was made baronet in 1889.

As a young man Burns was one of Thomas Chalmers'* supporters in Glasgow, but moved his allegiance to the Episcopal Church and became the leading layman among the English Episcopalians* in the dispute with the Scottish Episcopal Church.* Thereafter Burns was actively associated with the leading evangelical figures of the day, notably with Lord Shaftesbury.

E. Hodder, *Sir George Burns Bart.* (L, 1890); *DNB Suppl.* I, 344–5.

R. H. Campbell

Burns, Islay (1817–72), younger brother of the pioneer missionary to China, William Chalmers Burns.* After studies at Aberdeen University, Burns trained for the ministry at the Glasgow Divinity Hall. He was about to be ordained to St Peter's, Dundee, after R. M. M'Cheyne's* death, when the Disruption* interrupted the proceedings. Burns joined the new FC and was ordained by the FC Dundee presbytery to the charge of St Peter's FC, Dundee. In 1864 he became Professor of Apologetics and Systematic Theology at the Free Church College in Glasgow.

Burns' chief writings are *A History of the Church of Christ* (L, 1862) and biographies of his famous brother, *Memoir of William Chalmers Burns* (L, 1870), and father, *The Pastor of Kilsyth; or Memorials of ... W. H. Burns* (L, 1860).

AFCS I, 51; *DNB* VII, 422–3; memoir in *Select Remains* (L, 1874), ed. J. C. Burns.

I. Hamilton

Burns, Robert (1759–96), Scotland's national poet. The eldest son of a pious tenant farmer, his father produced for his use *A Manual Of Religious Belief, In a Dialogue Between Father And Son*. William Burns was extremely strict, but his theology was liberal for the time and place, a country parish in later eighteenth-century Ayrshire. His gifted son grew up with an excellent knowledge of Scripture and a keen interest in Kirk disputes, whether concerning matters of doctrine or the personalities of prominent local ministers and elders. He was a natural rebel and satirist, who found a subject ready to hand in divisive issues of the day concerning the CofS. 'Polemical divinity', he noted, 'was putting the country half-mad.' While still in his mid-twenties, he boldly attacked what he took to be life-denying attitudes in the Kirk, including the disciplinary role in sexual relationships exerted at parish level by 'the houghmagandie (fornication) pack' of elders, from whose corrective zeal he more than once suffered himself.

Poems, Chiefly In The Scottish Dialect, published at Kilmarnock in 1786, included 'The Holy Fair' and 'Address to the Deil', which deal respectively with amusing incidents observed at a country Communion,* and with the effects of superstitious religious belief. As J. G. Lockhart noted in his *Life of Burns* (1828), 'The Holy Fair' proved 'national manners were once more in the hands of a national poet'; while the 'Address to the Deil' was written in a familiar style calculated to rob traditional taboos of their force:

O THOU, whatever title
   suit thee!
Auld Hornie, Satan, Nick,
   or Clootie,   [*Cloven-hoof*
Wha in yon cavern grim
   an' sootie,
Clos'd under hatches,   [*bespatters*
Spairges about the brunstane   [*brimstone*
   cootie,   [*tub*
To scaud poor wretches!   [*scald*

An expanded edition of *Poems, Chiefly In The Scottish Dialect* (E, 1787) contained among other previously unpublished poems the 'Address to the Unco Guid'. This poem once again made use of the medium of satire to proclaim a characteristic Burnsian message about the need for respectable church-goers to show tolerance towards their imperfect neighbours, rather than be ruled by a habit of fault-finding:

O ye what are sae guid yoursel,
   Sae pious and sae holy,
Ye've nought to do but mark and tell
   Your Neebours' fauts and folly!
Whase life is like a weel-gaun mill,
   Supply'd wi' store o' water,
The heaped happer's ebbing still,
   And still the clap plays clatter ...

Then gently scan your brother Man,
   Still gentler sister Woman;
Tho' they may gang a kennin wrang,   [*trifle*
   To step aside is human:
One point must still be greatly dark,
   The moving *Why* they do it;
And just as lamely can ye mark,
   How far perhaps they rue it.

Who made the heart, 'tis *He* alone
   Decidedly can try us,
He knows each chord its various tone,
   Each spring its various bias:
Then at the balance let's be mute,
   We never can adjust it;
What's *done* we partly may compute,
   But know not what's *resisted*.

Too daring to publish for several years was 'Holy Willie's Prayer', an attack on Willie Fisher, a Mauchline elder whom Burns had certainly included among the least congenial 'unco guid' of his acquaintance. 'Holy Willie's Prayer' is a dramatic monologue in the form of an overheard prayer. As he prepared to heap curses on his parish enemy, Gavin Hamilton – as it happens, a good friend of the poet's – Willie gives away his true character. It is a mark of Burns's cutting edge in his poems about religious life that the terms 'unco guid' and 'Holy Willie' have both entered the language.

BURNS, ROBERT

Burns rejected the idea of original sin, writing to his friend Mrs Dunlop, 'I am in perpetual warfare with that doctrine of our Reverend Priesthood, that "we are born into this world bond slaves of iniquity and heirs of perdition..."' To his friend Clarinda (Nancy McLehose) he wrote, 'My creed is pretty nearly expressed in the last clause of Jamie Deans's grace, an honest weaver in Ayrshire: "Lord, grant that we may lead a gude life; for a gude life makes a gude end; at least, it helps weel!"'

The Poems And Songs of Robert Burns, ed. J. Kinsley, 3 vols (O, 1968); *Robert Burns, The Kilmarnock Poems (Poems, Chiefly in the Scottish Dialect, 1786)*, ed. D. A. Low (L, 1985); *The Letters of Robert Burns*, ed. J. De L. Ferguson and G. R. Roy, 2 vols (O, 1985).

T. Crawford, *Robert Burns: A Study of the Poems and Songs* (E, 1960); M. Lindsay, *The Burns Encyclopedia* (³L, 1980); D. A. Low, *Robert Burns* (E, 1986).

D. A. Low

Burns, Robert (1789–1869), minister and missionary* leader in Scotland and Canada. With his father converted by Whitefield,* he early imbibed Whitefieldian Evangelicalism,* with its stress on orthodox Calvinism,* intense religious experience, and involvement in evangelism, missions,* and social action. He was thus part of the evangelical surge that exercised such an important influence in the CofS* in the early nineteenth century.

Born in Bo'ness, Burns graduated from Edinburgh University in both arts and theology, and was ordained in 1811 to the Laigh Kirk (St George's) in Paisley, where he remained until the Disruption* and for two years after that in the reorganized FC congregation. In 1845 he became minister of Knox Church, Toronto, whose roots went back to the first Presbyterian congregation in the city, and also, briefly, Professor of Divinity in the newly founded Knox College, where he would later (1856–64) be Professor of Church History. Upon his arrival he was unanimously chosen as Moderator of the Synod of the Presbyterian Church in Canada in connection with the FCS. (He had toured British N. America in 1844 with a FC deputation. A Canadian Disruption took place that year.) Although this Church existed only in what would be known as the provinces of Ontario and Quebec, he was the most prominent individual in the FC in all the British North American colonies.

Burns was indefatigable. In his congregations he developed the apparatus for which nineteenth-century Evangelicals were famous – Sunday schools,* district visitation, fellowship groups, and various missionary and philanthropic organizations. He was interested in science, edited works in Church history (including Robert Wodrow's*), wrote on matters of social policy, especially poverty, and participated actively in the evangelical journal, *The Edinburgh Christian Instructor*.* With his opinionated and volatile temperament, he threw himself into the controversies of his day, which included the Apocrypha Controversy* in the Bible Society,* the Voluntary Controversy*, and the Non-Intrusion Controversy* in the CofS.

In spite of his many other involvements, Burns was above all a missionary enthusiast. He had taken the leading role in the Glasgow Colonial Society* from its founding in 1825. Once in Toronto, he gave priority to missionary work. He was frequently away encouraging the planting and organizing of new congregations, and there are still at least half-a-dozen in Ontario bearing his name. He secured John Black's move to Red River (Winnipeg) in 1851 as the first Presbyterian minister in W. Canada, while he also played a key role in the Buxton Mission as it ministered to former slaves at the end of the 'underground railway' in south-western Ontario. Burns epitomized and encouraged the dynamic, entrepreneurial Evangelicalism for which the mid-Victorian Canada Presbyterian Church was famous.

R. F. Burns, *The Life and Times of the Reverend Robert Burns, DD* (Toronto, 1871); *Dictionary of Canadian Biography* IX, 104–8; J. S. Moir, *Enduring Witness: A History of the Presbyterian Church in Canada* (Toronto, 1974); L. Stanley, *The Well-Watered Garden* (Sydney, 1983); P. Harrison, 'Robert Burns', *Called to Witness* 1 (1975), 144–61; R. W. Vaudry, *The Free Church in Victorian Canada* (Waterloo, Ont., 1989); *FES* III, 176–7; *AFCS* I, 109.

I. S. Rennie

Burns, Thomas (1796–1871), FC minister and nephew of Robert Burns* the poet. Born at Mossgiel, Mauchline, Burns was educated at Haddington (where he came under the influence of Edward Irving*) and the University of Edinburgh. He was licensed by the CofS Presbytery of Haddington in December 1822, and after a spell as a tutor for Sir Hew Dalrymple of North Berwick he was ordained to Ballantrae in April 1826.

Thomas Burns joined the FC at the Disruption,* and was the minister of Monkton FC from 1843 to 1846. He wrote an account of the Parish of Monkton and Prestwick for the New Statistical Account.* In 1846 he briefly moved to Portobello Church.

The remainder of his career was spent in New Zealand* (*see* Emigration). Initially (1847–54) he was the only Scottish minister in Otago. In 1860 he was awarded a DD by Edinburgh University, and in 1869 he became the first Chancellor of the University of Otago. A beautiful monument in Dunedin commemorates his Christian involvement in New Zealand.

AFCS I, 109–10; *Dict. of New Zealand Biography* I *(1769–1869)*, 58–60; E. N. Merrington, *A Great Coloniser ...* (Dunedin, 1929).

G. Wareing

Burns, William Chalmers (1815–68), missionary to China. Burns was one of the most remarkable figures in the history of the Scottish Church. Son of a parish minister, W. H. Burns (*FES* III, 480; *AFCS* I, 110), he was born at Duns (near Brechin). He was educated at Aberdeen Grammar School,

BURNS, WILLIAM CHALMERS

and entered Aberdeen University in 1829. His early thoughts of the law were quickly forgotten when he was converted in 1832. After graduating (MA, 1834), he started divinity studies at Glasgow University. A brilliant student, he excelled in Hebrew and Greek. In 1839 he was licensed as a probationer by the CofS Presbytery of Glasgow, and soon after supplied Robert Murray McCheyne's* pulpit in Dundee during the latter's visit to the Holy Land. While in Dundee he witnessed a remarkable spiritual awakening, and he also contributed to a revival* at Kilsyth while assisting his father at the parish Communion in August 1839. From this point until his departure for China in 1847 Burns travelled widely, usually preaching to great crowds.

Along with many of his evangelical contemporaries, he left the CofS at the Disruption* to join the FC. In 1844 he went to Canada, and returned two years later resolved to go overseas with the gospel. The English Presbyterian Church appointed him in 1847 as their first missionary to China. The advice of 'Rabbi' Duncan,* 'Take care of His cause, and He will take care of your interests', was exemplified in his life.

Burns had set his heart on reaching as yet unreached inland China, and in 1849 he left the security of the coastal mission stations to preach the gospel inland. The early years were marked by difficulties and discouragements. However, in 1854 he was involved in a remarkable work of God at Pechuia, near Amoy, when many native congregations were formed – his practice was to leave them in the care of others and press on to new regions.

Burns returned to Scotland in 1854 with a sick friend who died soon after he arrived home. Thus his first and only furlough ended within a month.

In 1864 Burns went to Peking, where he translated a number of hymns into Mandarin and also completed a translation of *The Pilgrim's Progress*. Next he began a translation of the Psalms.

Burns died of fever at Nieu-chwang. Few missionaries were more respected than he.

Islay Burns, *Memoir of William Chalmers Burns* (L, 1870); M. F. Barbour (ed.), *Revival Sermons: Notes of Addresses by William C. Burns* (E, 1869; rp., E, 1980); R. S. Miller, 'William C. Burns', in S. M. Houghton (ed.), *Five Pioneer Missionaries* (E, ²1987), 95–169.

I. Hamilton

Bute, Third Marquis of, *see* Stuart, John Patrick Crichton.

Butler, Dugald (1862–1926), CofS minister and writer. Born in Glasgow, he graduated MA from Glasgow University in 1883 and was licensed by Dunoon Presbytery in 1886. In 1890 he was ordained minister of Abernethy in Perthshire. He moved to the Tron, Edinburgh, in 1902, and then to Galashiels and Bolside, Selkirk, in 1907. The same year he received a DD from Glasgow University. He died in Peebles.

Butler wrote a number of books about the life and teaching of great Christians, usually with a Scottish emphasis, e.g. *Henry Scougal and the Oxford Methodists* (E, 1899), *John Wesley and George Whitefield in Scotland* (E, 1898), and *George Fox in Scotland* (E, 1913). Butler's own spiritual ideal, exemplified in his greatest hero Robert Leighton,* was a synthesis of 'Puritanism with a mystical Catholicism' – 'the quiet, meditative, mystic spirit of the cloister' with 'the manly Protestantism' of Reformed Scotland (*The Life and Letters of Archbishop Leighton*, L, 1903, 148–9).

Thomas à Kempis (E, 1913); *The Teaching of Emerson* (Newburgh-on-Tay, 1892); *Eternal Elements in the Christian Faith* (E, 1905); *Prayer in Experience* (E, 1922); *Woman and the Church in Scotland* (E, 1912); *Gothic Architecture* (E, 1910).

FES II, 180, VIII, 150.

N. R. Needham

C

Caird, Edward (1835–1908), philosopher and theologian. After study at Glasgow, St Andrews and Oxford Universities, Caird became tutor at Merton College, Oxford (1864–6) and then Professor of Moral Philosophy in Glasgow (1866–93). He was Master of Balliol College, Oxford, 1893–1907.

An exponent and popularizer of Hegelian idealism, founding, with his brother John,* but more especially with T. H. Green (1836–82), the Hegelian school in Britain, Caird contributed to the decline of the Realist Philosophy of his native Scotland (see Scottish Realism). As a teacher he was instrumental in moving his students away from Evangelicalism. He was greatly interested in the implications of idealism for metaphysics, and a devoted scholar of Immanuel Kant, writing two critical accounts of his philosophy, besides *The Evolution of Religion* (G, 1893) and *The Evolution of Theology in the Greek Philosophers* (G, 1904).

In Caird's view, the aim of the idealist philosophy is to transcend and integrate the otherwise fragmentary and opposing elements of experience into a higher unity. A failure to do this results in intellectual and spiritual disharmony. Human thought does not reflect experience, it constitutes it, driven on by a desire for the unity and coherence of all experience. Similarly in ethics the conflict between duty and initiation is resolved by ordering our conduct not in terms of the occurrence and satisfaction of transient desires, but by reference to the self, which is a centre of integration which transcends what is momentary and passing. The great religions of the world are united through being various stages in an upward evolution to a higher religious unity.

The Critical Philosophy of Immanuel Kant (G, 1889); *Hegel* (E, L, 1883).

Sir H. Jones and J. H. Muirhead, *The Life and Philosophy of Edward Caird* (G, 1921); *DNB Second Suppl.* I, 291–5.

P. Helm

Caird, John (1820–98), philosopher and theologian, was born in Greenock, the son of an engineer and was originally intended to enter his father's foundry. After study at Glasgow University, however, he was minister, successively, of Newton-on-Ayr (1845–7), Lady Yester's, Edinburgh (1847–9), Errol, Perthshire (1849–57), where he began the systematic study of the German thinkers which were to be so influential in later life, and Park Church, Glasgow (1857–62). He was appointed Professor of Theology at Glasgow in 1862. In his lectures he was one of the first in Scotland to advocate a version of Hegelian absolute idealism in opposition to the prevailing Scottish Realism.* He was active in University administration, becoming Principal of the University in 1873, continuing his theological studies and writing during his leisure time. His Croall lectures* (1878–9) were published as *Introduction to the Philosophy of Religion* (G, 1880), which was, in effect, a Hegelianized version of Christian theism, but his version was nearer to orthodoxy than that of his brother, Edward Caird.* This work was expanded in his Gifford lectures* which were published posthumously by his brother. He was renowned as a preacher.

The Fundamental Ideas of Christianity (G, 1899)–Giffords; *Spinoza* (E, L, 1888); *University Addresses* (G, 1898); *University Sermons 1873–1898* (G, 1898).

DNB Suppl. I, 368–9; *FES* VII, 397–8; Memoir by E. Caird prefaced to *Fundamental Ideas* I, ix–cxli; A. P. F. Sell, *Defending and Declaring the Faith. Some Scottish Examples 1860–1920* (Exeter, 1987).

P. Helm

Cairns, Adam (1802–81), Australian FC minister. Educated at St Andrews, Cairns was licensed in 1824 and after some years of ill-health inducted to Manor near Peebles in 1828. He moved to Dunbog in Fife in 1833, and then to the first charge in Cupar (Fife) in 1837. He was sent out to Victoria, Australia by the FC to help the Free Presbyterian Church of Victoria, formed in 1846 as a consequence of the Disruption* of 1843. He formed a new congregation, Chalmers Church, in East Melbourne, and remained minister of it until 1876. After some doubts, he was deeply involved in the move to unite all Presbyterians, which culminated in the formation of the Presbyterian Church of Victoria in 1859. He was prominent in the early training of theological students in Victoria, acting as part-time Principal of the Theological Hall from 1865 until his death in January 1881.

Disruption Worthies, 117–24; D. Chambers, *Theological Thought in the Theological Hall of the Presbyterian Church of Victoria 1865–1966* (Melbourne, 1967), 4–18; *Australian Dictionary of Biography* III, 329–30.

A. M. Harman

Cairns, David Smith (1862–1946), Presbyterian* teacher and writer. Born in Stitchel, Roxburghshire, son of a UP minister and a nephew of John Cairns,* he rebelled early against his father's Calvinism.* He commenced attendance at Edinburgh University in 1880, but was soon overwhelmed by a crisis of religious doubt under which his health broke down. A prolonged European vacation helped restore him physically, and he also began to reconstruct his faith with the poet Robert Browning as 'my main spiritual guide' (*David Cairns, An Autobiography*, L, 1950, 104).

Cairns resumed his university studies in 1886, proceeding to the UP Theological Hall in 1888. During his course he spent a summer at Marburg, where he came under the influence of the Ritschlian William Herrmann. Licensed in 1892, in 1895 he became minister of the UP congregation in Ayton, Berwickshire. In 1907 he was made Professor of Dogmatics and Apologetics in the UFC College, Aberdeen.

Cairns became intimately involved in the World Missionary Conference* held in Edinburgh in 1910, chairing its Commission on the Missionary Message. He drafted its influential report published as *The Missionary Message in Relation to Non-Christian Religions*. He also became involved at this period with the budding Student Christian Movement,* speaking frequently at SCM summer conferences.

After the War, Cairns visited America, delivering the Deems lectures in New York University and Lafayette College, and the Russell lectures in Auburn Theological Seminary in 1923. The same year he was elected Moderator of the UF General Assembly, which appointed him Principal of the Aberdeen College. 1927 saw Cairns touring and lecturing in China and Japan; in 1932 he delivered the Baird lectures,* later published as *The Riddle of the World* (L, 1937), his maturest exercise in apologetics. Retiring in 1937, in his last years he became a sponsor of the incipient Iona Community.* He received a DD from Aberdeen in 1909, from Debrecen (Hungary) in 1929, and from Edinburgh in 1933, and an LLD from St Andrews in 1937 and Aberdeen in 1938. He was awarded an OBE in 1918.

Cairns' most famous work was his *The Faith that Rebels* (L, 1928). Here he argued that Christ's miracles were not proofs of his message but part of it – manifestations of God's opposition to pain, disease and death, as having no place in his kingdom. Christ derived his miraculous powers from his perfect faith in God, and such power is always available to the Church as she imitates her Master's faith.

See Systematic Theology.

The Reasonableness of the Christian Faith (L, 1918); *Christianity in the Modern World* (L, 1906); *Life and Times of A. R. MacEwen* (L, 1925); *A System of Christian Doctrine* (E, 1979).

DNB 1941–50, 128; *FUFCS* 575; *FES* IX, 769.

N. R. Needham

Cairns, John (1818–92), outstanding UP divine. Born in Ayton Hill, Berwickshire, he was brought up in the USec.C. From 1834–40 he attended Edinburgh University where he excelled at philosophy and became Sir William Hamilton's* favourite pupil. In 1840 he commenced the study of theology at the USec. Hall in Edinburgh; here he was greatly influenced by Professor John Brown,* whose biography he later wrote (*Memoir of John Brown*, E, 1860).

Cairns was licensed by Edinburgh USec. Presbytery in February 1845, and in August became minister of Golden Square USec. Church in Berwick-on-Tweed, where he remained for the next thirty years. In 1867 he was appointed Professor of Apologetics in the UP Theological Hall, without relinquishing his pastorate. When the Hall was reorganized in 1875–6, however, its Professors were required to teach full-time; Cairns accordingly left Berwick-on-Tweed, becoming associate Professor of Dogmatics and Apologetics, and in 1879 Principal. He died a few days after ill-health compelled his retirement.

Cairns' literary output was largely in the form of pamphlets and magazine articles, and since these have never been collected he is virtually unknown today. However, the personal influence of this highly erudite, cultured and saintly man, especially among United Presbyterians, was immense in his own lifetime. Steeped in German philosophy and theology, Cairns admired most Germany's 'mediating school' of divines, and his account of their aims fairly describes his own – 'to build up, out of the data of Bible interpretation, counterchecked but not overruled by Christian consciousness, a system which may harmonize with the philosophic spirit of the present day' (A. R. MacEwen, *Life and Letters of John Cairns*, L, 1895, 334).

Cairns' theology was, in fact, quite conservative; he described himself as 'a fixed Calvinist' (*ibid.*, 779), defended the doctrine of eternal punishment, and accepted the plenary (although not verbal) inspiration of Scripture. He played a moderating role in his denomination's debates over the Westminster* Confession, approving of the Declaratory Act* of 1879. Cairns prized evangelical catholicity more than Reformed confessionalism – a fact which illuminates his zealous support for Moody* and Sankey and their evangelistic campaigns.

Cairns was an ardent proponent of disestablishment* and Church union (UPC and FC), and in latter years an increasingly vocal advocate of total abstinence (*see* Temperance Movement). He was Moderator of his Church's General Assembly in 1872, and in 1880 delivered the Cunningham lectures,* published as *Unbelief in the Eighteenth Century* (E, 1881).

Cairns received a DD from Edinburgh University in 1858.

Christ, the Morning Star, and Other Sermons (L, 1892). Cairns' many serial writings are listed in the appendix to MacEwen's *Life and Letters of John Cairns* (L, 1895).

J. Cairns, *Principal Cairns* (E, 1903); *DNB Suppl.* I, 369–71; *ASUPC*, 101.

N. R. Needham

Calderwood, David (1575–1650), church historian and apologist for Presbyterianism.* He was educated at the College of Edinburgh under Robert Rollock,* and ordained to Crailing in Roxburghshire in 1604. In 1608 he was confined to his parish and excluded from the church courts when he opposed Bishop James Law of Orkney's (*FES* VII, 322) substitution of royal supporters in place of the Presbytery's duly elected representatives to the General Assembly. But when King James VI* visited Scotland in 1617, Calderwood and fifty-four other ministers meeting in Edinburgh wrote a protest against the King's intention that the monarch and men of his preference should appoint forms of worship* and discipline in the Church. Calderwood was required to appear with Archibald Simson* before the King at St Andrews, where from his knees he boldly opposed the King's will and asserted the freedom of the General Assembly to control the Church's ceremonies and government.

Calderwood was deprived of his charge, imprisoned and banished. In 1619 he went to Holland, whence he issued anonymously his monumental critique of English episcopacy,* *The Altar of Damascus* (n.p., 1621), greatly enlarged in Latin under a pseudonym, Didoclavius (*Altare Damascenum*, Amsterdam 1623, reissued under Calderwood's name, Leiden, 1708). The title is a reference to the foreign altar which King Ahaz of Judah copied for the temple in Jerusalem. Calderwood's writings were erudite and widely persuasive, preparing the way for the restoration of Presbyterian practice at the 'Second Reformation'.* He returned to Scotland after the King's death in 1625. In 1640 he became the minister of Pencaitland in East Lothian. With Alexander Henderson* and David Dickson* he was appointed by the General Assembly of 1643 to draft a directory for public worship, to fill a need for guidelines after the episcopal conventions had been removed. In 1648 the General Assembly allowed him an annual pension while he laboured on *The True History of the Church of Scotland*. (Calderwood left three manuscripts. Of the largest only about a third has survived. A second large manuscript has been printed as *The History of the Kirk*..., ed. T. Thomson, Wodrow Society, 8 vols, E, 1842–9. A condensed version was prepared for the press by Calderwood. But although he completed it in 1631 it was not published until 1678 in Rotterdam (*History*, vol. VIII, 5–10 of appendix to preface). Calderwood intended the larger manuscripts, which were mainly collections of material, to be kept in reserve in the event of his history's loss.) It is a major source for the history of the CofS from the Reformation* until 1625. He died at Jedburgh. He seems never to have married, and offended some by his sharp speaking and obstinacy in argument.

Perth Assembly (Leiden, 1619) argues the unlawfulness of the General Assembly which passed the Five Articles of Perth,* at the King's behest, and against the Articles themselves; it was reissued as *Parasynagma Perthense* (St Andrews, 1620) and *A Re-Examination of Five Articles Enacted at Perth* (1636). *Course of Conformitie* (1622) traces the developing episcopal impositions in Scotland since 1597. Other publications include: *The Pastor and the Prelate* (1628; E, 1843); *Defence of our Arguments against Kneeling* (1620); *A Dialogue . . . Anent the Urging of New Ceremonies* (1620); *An Exhortation of the Particular Kirks in Scotland* (1624); *Dispute upon Communicating* (1624).

DNB VIII, 244–6; *FES* I, 384–5; Preface in *The History*, vol. VIII (E, 1849); R. Baillie, *Letters and Journals*, 3 vols (E, 1841–2); J. Row, *History of Kirk of Scotland* (E, 1842); D. G. Mullan, *Episcopacy in Scotland . . . 1560–1638* (E, 1986).

S. Isbell

Calderwood, Henry (1808–65), missionary, linguist and government official. Born at Peebles, he completed his MA at Edinburgh and his divinity training at Glasgow University. While minister of a Presbyterian congregation in Kendal, he was accepted for service in South Africa by the London Missionary Society.* Arriving in South Africa in 1838, he began a new mission at Blinkwater, then moved in 1845 to Healdtown (then Birklands). He was a brilliant linguist and published many evangelistic tracts in Xhosa. During the frontier war of 1846 he became an advisor on African affairs to the Governor of the Cape Colony. Thereafter he served as a colonial civil servant. He became the principal adviser on African affairs to four successive Governors, Maitland, Pottinger, Smith and Grey. He was the first administrator of the new District of Victoria East and was the Commissioner for the resettlement of the Mfengu people. Throughout this time he retained ministerial status, preaching every Sunday and founding a number of new congregations.

While still in the service of the LMS he was a bitter critic of its Resident Director, John Philip,* and Philip's closest colleague, James Read of Kat River, one of the original pioneers of South African missions, who had married an African woman. Calderwood allied himself with Robert Moffat* in attempting to reduce Philip's authority in the

CALDWELL, JOHN

Society, attacking the latter for his 'political activity'.

Although always seeking the good of Africans as he saw it, and a consistent opponent of crude injustice towards them, he unfailingly supported the English-speaking white settlers against their missionary critics and consistently took their side in dispute with the Xhosa people. For this he in turn was bitterly criticized by David Livingstone.* He died in Grahamstown in the Cape in June 1865.

Caffres and Caffre Missions (L, 1858); E. H. Brookes, *The History of Native Policy in South Africa* (Cape Town, 1924); R. H. W. Shepherd, *Lovedale, South Africa* (Lovedale, 1940).

A. C. Ross

Caldwell, John (fl.1765), founder of the Moravian mission in Ayrshire. Converted by John Cennick, the English Evangelical who became a Moravian, Caldwell established a Moravian community in Ayrshire in 1765. Initially a preaching station, it was constituted a regular church in 1778 after a visit from the Moravian Bishop de Watville. The movement spread from Ayrshire until it had preaching stations in Irvine, Tarbolton, Dumfries, Annan, Kilsyth, Kilmarnock, Glasgow, Edinburgh, and several other areas. See Moravians.

E. S. Towill, *People and Places in the Story of the Scottish Church* (E, 1976), 18.

N. R. Needham

Calendar, see Christian Year.

Call. This term is used in two quite different senses. It may refer to a sense of vocation.* A person feels a call to the ordained ministry – itself a 'calling' – or to some other form of service. Or it may be applied, in the CofS and similar Churches, to the document signed by members and adherents of a congregation and put into the hands of the person they have elected, inviting him (or her) to be their minister and promising 'all dutiful respect, encouragement and obedience in the Lord'. The call in this sense dates as far back as at least 1690. In days both of episcopacy and patronage* the congregation had no say in the choice of their minister, the call being the vehicle in which they could promise loyalty and support for the person chosen. It became the centre of bitter controversy in the nineteenth century when patronage was under attack, it being argued that in the absence of a well-signed call the Presbytery should refuse to induct. When patronage was at length abolished in 1874, congregations inclined to vote among a long list of candidates; and the Call provided a means whereby the member who had voted for Mr A could promise allegiance to Mr D who had topped the poll. In modern times, with sole nomination all but universal, the call has lost its original purpose. Considerable store, however, is still set upon a well-signed call in sustaining the appointment of a minister to a parish.

Both these senses of 'call' relate to an important emphasis in Reformation thought about ministry

CALVIN, CALVINISM

and congregation – the latter's act of choosing and calling a minister. The Scots Confession* insists that none may minister the Word and sacraments unless 'lawfully called by some Kirk'. This note frequently recurs, and even overshadows the need for ordination.* This call – regarded as recognition of God's calling – stresses the bond between minister and congregation.

Cox 257–64, 817–19; A. Herron, *A Guide to Congregational Affairs* (E, 1978); D. F. Wright, 'Word, Ministry and Congregation in the Reformation Confessions', in N. M. de S. Cameron and S. B. Ferguson (eds), *Pulpit and People* (E, 1986), 39–50.

A. Herron

Calvin, Calvinism. John Calvin (1509–64), French theologian and Reformer in Geneva, formulated a system of theology in his *Institutes of the Christian Religion* and in other writings, known even to contemporaries as 'Calvinism', which, with modifications over the decades, gained wide acceptance among Reformed churches after the Reformation, not least in Scotland.

Born at Noyon in Picardy, Calvin was intended for the priesthood. Studies at Paris in the 1520s, first in Latin grammar and then an arts course at Montaigu (where the Scot, John Major* taught), were followed not by theology but by civil law at Orléans and Bourges, where he also studied Greek. While at Bourges, Calvin was converted to Protestantism. To escape persecution in France, Calvin fled to Basel in 1535, where he issued his first edition of the *Institutes* in March 1536. In later years he produced a series of biblical commentaries which demonstrated his skills as probably the greatest biblical exegete of his day. The *Institutes*, as an exposition of the Christian faith, offered instruction in the Ten Commandments, the Apostles' Creed, the Lord's Prayer, the two sacraments of baptism and the Lord's Supper, and the powers of the magistracy. It met with outstanding success, and through successive editions became the most influential treatise produced by the Protestant Reformation. By the final editions of 1559 in Latin and 1560 in French, the slender work of 1536 had become a classic large-scale exposition of the Christian faith. Calvin's theology had come of age.

Accepting Guillaume Farel's invitation in 1536 for help in organizing the Reformation in Geneva, Calvin became by 1537 a full-time minister. Resistance from the civil authorities to their proposals for ecclesiastical discipline resulted in their expulsion. Invited by Martin Bucer and Wolfgang Capito to Strasbourg, Calvin ministered to the French church there. By 1540, however, the Genevans asked him to return; and in 1541 he secured the 'Ordonnances ecclésiastiques', which approved a fourfold ministry of pastors, doctors,* elders* and deacons* (on the model of Calvin's understanding of the New Testament church, and of his earlier association with Bucer's work at Strasbourg). This, in turn, became the pattern for church government among Calvinist churches in Europe.

With Calvin's death, his colleague and successor, Theodore Beza, became the systematizer of Calvin's theology, and the leader of international Calvinism which had spread in Switzerland, France, the Netherlands, Germany, Hungary, England and in Scotland, where a recognizably Calvinist polity was operational from the 1560s, as outlined in the *First Book of Discipline** of 1560 and reinvigorated in the *Second Book of Discipline** of 1578.

THE SCOTTISH REFORMATION. At the Scottish Reformation,* too, the 'Reformation Parliament'* in 1560 had approved a Reformed Confession of Faith (*see* Scots Confession) in which a firmly Calvinist contribution is detectable at the expense of the distinctively Lutheran tradition which had marked an earlier phase of reforming activity in Scotland. In doctrine, the characteristic Protestant emphases on original sin, atonement, justification by faith alone, predestination and the verbal inspiration of Scripture found homely expression in this hastily written work. The Confession focused on the cardinal themes of Christian understanding: God, the Trinity, creation, fall and redemption, the incarnation, Christ's passion, resurrection and ascension, and his return for judgment; on atonement through Christ, and sanctification through the Holy Spirit; on good works as the fruit of election; salvation through faith alone; and, briefly, on predestination, where God's double decree is suggested. Emphasis, too, was placed on the invisible Church of all ages, and on the necessity of discerning the true from the false church through true preaching of the Word, correct administration of the two sacraments, and ecclesiastical discipline properly executed. A high Calvinist understanding of Christ's presence in Communion is defended against the claims of Rome, Wittenberg and Zürich; and the magistrate's role is interpreted on Calvinist lines as defending, not dominating, the Reformed church.

Although the second Edwardine *Book of Common Prayer* (1552) had circulated in Scotland at the Reformation, by 1562 the General Assembly authorized use of the Genevan-inspired *Book of Common Order** ('Knox's Liturgy') in services. Changes in worship, themselves visible signs of new theological insights, meant that at the Scottish Reformation out went Latinity, sacerdotalism, altars and unleavened wafers, auricular confession, the cult of the saints, holy days and feast days, prayers for the dead, belief in purgatory, the use of responses, the sign of the cross, crucifixes, images and elaborate ritual, surplices or choir dress, and eucharistic vestments, organs and choristers, the plainsong of great churches and the silence of poor churches; and in their place came a simpler service focused on preaching, Bible study, prayers, and metrical psalms sung to popular tunes; and the active participation of congregations was encouraged in singing God's praise and in receiving, seated at tables, both wine and bread at the Lord's Supper.

LATER CONFESSIONS. At Beza's request, the General Assembly in 1566 endorsed the Second Helvetic Confession (apart from its discussion of holy days), prepared by Heinrich Bullinger for Calvinist and Zwinglian churches (*see* Confessions of Faith). In 1581, the King's Confession* (or Negative Confession), drafted by John Craig* and denying 'all contrary religion and doctrine, but chiefly all kind of papistry', was issued at a point when rumours of Catholic plots gained credence; and it was later to form the basis of the National Covenant* of 1638. In 1616, the General Assembly, by then under royal and episcopal direction, issued 'a new Confession of Faith', which reaffirmed the uncompromising Calvinist doctrine of God's omnipotence, the absoluteness of his divine will, the eternal decrees, before world and time, to 'elect some men in Christ' and 'others he did appoint for eternal condemnation, according to the counsel of his most free, most just and holy will', and of the certainty of salvation.

At the Synod of Dort* in the Netherlands, called in 1618 to condemn Arminian heresies of free will and universal atonement, King James' English representative, Walter Balcanquhal,* the son of the Scottish minister of the same name, adhered to the orthodox Calvinist view that Christ died for the elect alone. Yet John Cameron,* who taught briefly in his native Glasgow but mainly at Saumur in France, modified Calvinism in the direction which his pupil Moïse Amyraut (*see* Cameron, John), continued towards a semi-Arminianism.*

Concern in Scotland at the Arminian reaction against Calvinist theology focused on the activities of 'Laudians' or 'Canterburians' like William Forbes,* Bishop of Edinburgh, who favoured a more liberal theology and who readopted practices and ceremonial which had been jettisoned at the Reformation. In 1638, the Glasgow Assembly* decided to purge the church of suspected Arminians. The Calvinist Confession, devised by the Westminster Assembly* of Divines (1644–9), with its emphasis on 'federal theology', which the General Assembly approved in 1647, was also designed to combat Arminianism.

The rise, within the Reformed churches, of federal or covenant theology* (much in vogue by the mid-seventeenth century and anticipated in Scotland in the writings of Robert Rollock* in the late sixteenth century), placed particular emphasis on the nature of God's dealings with mankind, which took the form of a covenant: first, the covenant of works before the fall, and, thereafter, the covenant of grace which offered sinners salvation through Christ. The theology of the Westminster Confession was again approved at the 'Glorious Revolution', was reaffirmed by the Scottish parliament in 1693, and was employed as a religious and political test, even after the Treaty of Union* of 1707, which also recognized the Confession's standing in the Scottish church and so required all school and university teachers to subscribe it. In 1696 Calvinist discipline was still severe enough to punish the divinity student, Thomas Aikenhead,* with death for blasphemy*.

EROSION OF CALVINISM. Yet liberalizing attitudes detectable in the eighteenth century, associated with scientific discoveries, the rise of rationalism, the distaste for 'enthusiasm' and the lip-service paid to the Confession by many Moderate* ministers, began to undermine the dominance of Calvinism. One of the earliest speculative thinkers was John Simson,* professor of Divinity at Glasgow, whose elusive ideas seemed to some to smack of heresy. Charged with Arminianism, he disavowed the errors attributed to him, professed adherence to the Confession of Faith and was cautioned by the General Assembly in 1717; but by 1729, when charged with Arianism as taught by Samuel Clarke whose works he knew, Simson was suspended by the Assembly, despite his profession of orthodox Trinitarian teaching and his acceptance of the Confession. Further signs of incipient doctrinal controversy arose over the Auchterarder Creed,* devised by the presbytery for subscription by probationers, as a stand against Arminianism, but which could be interpreted as antinomian in wording.

A more serious dispute arose over the *Marrow of Modern Divinity** (*see* Marrow Controversy), a seventeenth-century work revived by Thomas Boston* and James Hog.* The work itself, which dealt with the relationship of law and grace, was intended to oppose both antinomianism and legalism. The attack on the *Marrow* by James Hadow,* principal of St Mary's College, St Andrews, led to the Assembly's condemnation of the *Marrow* in 1720 as antinomian. The 'Marrowmen' – including the Erskine* brothers – felt Hadow and the Assembly had misrepresented the work; and in the next great controversy they opted for secession. The Marrow Brethren did not object to Westminster Calvinism as such, but rather to what they believed a legalistic perversion of it, then prevalent in the CofS.

In the nineteenth century criticism of Westminster Calvinism grew. Thomas Erskine* of Linlathen rejected predestination, and influenced both Edward Irving,* who favoured the Scots Confession of 1560 and was deposed from the ministry by Annan presbytery for teaching that Christ had assumed fallen sinful nature, and John McLeod Campbell,* who was deprived for his views on universal atonement.

Though upheld in the divinity halls, Calvinism, as an intellectual system, showed signs of exhaustion; and Thomas Carlyle* in 1844 spoke of 'bare old Calvinism under penalty of death'. In 1866, seventy ministers, led by John Tulloch* of St Mary's College, St Andrews, contended that 'the old relation of our Church to the Confession cannot continue'. A distaste for dogmatic confessional statements and enforced subscription by ministers and elders to Westminster Calvinism, together with further heresy trials and the rise of rationalist biblical scholarship from Germany, strengthened the drift away from the old attachment to Calvinistic theology.

Within the United Presbyterian Church,* the Declaratory Act* of 1879 permitted ministers and elders some freedom in interpreting the Confession; the Free Church followed in 1892; and by 1910 the CofS, with parliament's approval, altered its formula of subscription. At the Union of 1929, the Confession was acknowledged as the Church's 'principal subordinate standard', and ministers were to profess 'the fundamental doctrines of the Christian faith contained in the Confession of Faith of this Church'. At the General Assembly of the CofS in 1974, an attempt to demote Westminster Calvinism from its status as a 'subordinate standard' to that of 'a historic document with a special place in the Presbyterian tradition' failed at the last hurdle. Some consider that adherence to the Confession is a necessary defence of the Church's faith and identity; others view it as a largely meaningless formality. Some have attempted to distinguish sharply between Calvin and Calvinism, to the discredit of the latter.

See also Subscription, Confessional; Heresy, Heresy Trials.

J. Kirk, 'The Influence of Calvinism on the Scottish Reformation', *RSCHS* 18 (1974), 157–79, revised in *Patterns of Reform* (E, 1989), 70–95; M. Lynch, 'Calvinism in Scotland, 1559–1638', in M. Prestwich (ed.), *International Calvinism 1541–1715* (O, 1985), 225–55; J. D. Douglas, 'Calvinism's Contribution to Scotland', in W. S. Reid (ed.), *John Calvin. His Influence in the Western World* (Grand Rapids, 1982), 217–37; I. Hamilton, *The Erosion of Calvinist Orthodoxy* (E, 1990); A. C. Cheyne, *The Transforming of the Kirk* (E, 1983); A. I. C. Heron (ed.), *The Westminster Confession in the Church Today* (E, 1982); J. Macleod, *Scottish Theology* (E, ³1974).

J. Kirk

Calvinism, Moderate, a form of Calvinism* developed chiefly in England as a reaction against hyper-Calvinism, which so stressed the divine decrees of election and reprobation that evangelistic endeavour was seriously hindered, if not stifled, in many churches. Its development was indebted to the views of Jonathan Edwards* and especially to the New England theology which took Edwards as its starting-point. The principal British exponent of moderate Calvinism was the Particular Baptist minister, Andrew Fuller,* who expounded the position in influential writings, mainly *The Gospel Worthy of All Acceptation* (1785). He found favour with certain Baptist and Independent leaders in Scotland, notably Christopher Anderson* and Ralph Wardlaw.*

The main characteristics of moderate Calvinism were as follows: (i) A renewed emphasis was placed on the obligation to preach the gospel to all people, with the expectation of response. Because of the contention that it was the duty of those who heard such preaching to respond with saving faith, this response was sometimes called 'duty faith'. (ii) With regard to particular redemption, Fuller argued that, while the blessings of redemption were imparted only to the elect, this did not deny the sufficiency of Christ's death as an atonement for the sins of the whole world. Moderate Calvinists were strongly opposed to the hyper-Calvinists' narrow interpretation of 'limited atonement'; it was the application, not the intrinsic adequacy, of the atonement which was limited. (iii) The atonement was explained in terms of God's moral government, within which Christ's death illustrated what all sin deserved (see Wardlaw, Ralph). (iv) Moderate Calvinists were inclined to reject a positive decree of reprobation, and to argue for a negative preterition, the view that God merely 'passes over' those not elected, leaving them in their sins.

The relationship of so-called moderate Calvinism to mainline Calvinism is debatable, as is the extent to which moderate Calvinists would have endorsed all its aspects. In England, and to a lesser extent in Wales and Scotland, it led to confused controversy. It invigorated many of the English Particular Baptists churches, tending to narrow the theological gap between them and the General (Arminian)* Baptists. In Scotland, Independent and Baptist churches (other than those within the Scotch Baptist* connexion) would have been inclined towards it. Its influence was also felt within the Relief and Secession churches. According to John Macleod (*Scottish Theology*, ³E, 1974, 241–57), the voluntaryist* aspirations of such men as John Brown (*d*.1858)* of Edinburgh promoted interaction with English Independents and Baptists, with the result that the new interpretation was absorbed within the Secession, particularly by the New Light* party. It was later accommodated in the USec.C and UPC, following the unions of 1820 and 1847.

A. Fuller, *Works*, 5 vols (L, 1837); E. F. Clipsham, 'Andrew Fuller and Fullerism: A Study in Evangelical Calvinism', *BQ* 20 (1963–4), 99–117, 146–54, 214–25, 268–76; H. Escott, *A History of Scottish Congregationalism* (G, 1960), 105–15.

D. E. Meek

Cambuskenneth, Augustinian abbey. Situated just outside Stirling, a royal residence, the abbey was founded *c*.1140 by David I* with Augustinian* canons of the strict congregation of Arrouaise (northern France). Its abbots were granted *pontificalia* (episcopal insignia) by the Avignon pope in 1406. The buildings, damaged in the fourteenth century, underwent extensive reconstruction. Later abbots served as treasurer and royal officials, the most notable being Alexander Myln,* first president of the court of session. The community, which numbered nineteen in 1588–60, made a considerable contribution to Protestantism: two canons were early Reformers and several served in the Reformed Church.

See aslo Early Ecclesiastical Sites.

Registrum Monasterii S. Marie de Cambuskenneth (E, 1872); Easson-Cowan, 88–90.

M. Dilworth

Cambuslang, *see* Revivals.

Cameron, Alexander (1827–88), Gaelic* scholar. Born in Badenoch, Inverness-shire, Cameron was a minister of the FC in Renton, Dunbartonshire (1859–74) and Brodick, Arran (1874–88). Developing an interest in Celtic scholarship, he studied under the continental scholars, Zeuss and Windisch. He became editor of the *Scottish Celtic Review*. His scholarly works were posthumously published as *Reliquiae Celticae* (ed. A. MacBain and J. Kennedy, 2 vols, Inverness, 1892–4). He was engaged in controversies about the revision of the Gaelic Bible (*see* Bible (Versions, Gaelic)).

AFCS I, 111; D. MacKinnon, *The Gaelic Bible and Psalter* (Dingwall, 1930), 99–101.

D. E. Meek

Cameron, Andrew (1823–77), FC minister, nicknamed 'the Prince of Editors' by C. H. Spurgeon.* He spoke of Charles Brown* as his spiritual father. Later in life he was ordained to Maryton FC, Angus (1866–70), serving thereafter in Melbourne, Australia (where he received Princeton's DD), as colleague and successor to Adam Cairns* (1870–3), and in the suburb of St Kilda (1873–7). His main contribution to church life, however, was literary. Initially on the staff of *The Witness*,* he edited successively the *Free Church Magazine*,* the Stirling Tracts,* the *Christian Treasury*ced* and the *Family Treasury* (both of which he founded). He was also involved with the inception of the *British and Foreign Evangelical Review*,* and of *News of the Churches and Journal of Missions* (1854–9, continued as *Christian Work*). He built up the colportage arm of the Religious Tract and Bible Society (*see* Scottish Colportage Society). In Melbourne he launched a new weekly, *The Southern Cross* (which continues to the present).

Cameron's religious ideals are set out in the opening number of the *Christian Treasury*, where he declares his purpose 'to lift up a standard' against popery and infidelity, and 'to exemplify and help forward that which in our day is so earnestly desired, and for many reasons so urgently needed, viz., the visible unity of Christians and their co-operation in those things on which they are agreed.' His work married conservative and progressive values.

The Free Church and Her Accusers in the Matter of American Slavery (n.p., 1846); *The Scripture Law of Marriage* (Melbourne, 1873).

AFCS I, 112; W. G. Blaikie in *FCSR* 189 (April 1878), 93–4.

N. R. Needham

Cameron, John (*d*.1446), Bishop of Glasgow. Probably the son of an Edinburgh burgess, he graduated at St Andrews in 1419. In 1420 he appears as official of Lothian, acting in Rome as nuncio of Robert, Duke of Albany, Governor of Scotland. In 1423 he occurs as secretary to the Earl of Wigtown, vicar of Kirkinner, and Provost of Lincluden, becoming first secretary to James I in April 1424. Elected Bishop of Glasgow in 1425, he countered papal objections which partially arose from legislation in 1424 which, by creating the crime of barratry,* forbade the purchase of benefices and the export of money. Provided on 22 April 1426 and consecrated on 12/13 January 1427,

CAMERON, JOHN

he was formally styled chancellor by May. Rapprochement with the papacy was short-lived when William Croyser, archdeacon of Teviotdale, claimed that Cameron was behind the barratry* legislation. He was threatened with deprivation, but matters were patched up before the pope's death in February 1431. Further disputes arose under his successor through royal support for the Council of Basel, in which Cameron was incorporated on 8 February 1434 on the day that Croyser again denounced James's ecclesiastical policies. Journeying to Florence to plead unavailingly before the curia, he remained at Basel until late 1436. King James I's assassination in 1437 shortly after the arrival of a papal legate resolved the ecclesiastical struggle in the pope's favour, but also ended Cameron's political career. Removed from the chancellorship in May 1439, he continued as an active diocesan administrator and as a generous benefactor of his cathedral until his death at Glasgow on Christmas Eve 1446.

E. W. M. Balfour-Melville, *James I, King of Scots* (L, 1936); J. H. Burns, *Scottish Churchmen at the Council of Basle* (G, 1962); R. K. Hannay, 'James I, Bishop Cameron and the Papacy', *SHR* 15 (1917–18), 190–200; Dowden, 319–22.

I. B. Cowan

Cameron, John (*c*.1579–1625), innovative Reformed theologian. Born in Glasgow, he obtained a bursary in 1595 to study at Glasgow University where, under Patrick Sharp's* principalship, he graduated in first place in 1599. As an arts student, he excelled in Greek and was said to have been 'addicted to the philosophy of Ramus and defended it with zeal'. After teaching in the College for a year, he left for France,where he taught from 1600 in the College of Bergerac in Bordeaux and then, by 1602, at the Protestant academy of Sedan (where Daniel Tilenus, the Professor of Divinity, was moving from Calvinism to Arminianism). He returned to Bordeaux as minister in 1604, and, financed by the Church as a travelling scholar, studied at Paris, Geneva (where he spent two years only to disagree with Beza's theology) and Heidelberg, where he expounded his covenantal ideas, affirming a threefold covenant between God and man (a covenant of nature, covenant of grace and the old covenant made at Sinai). This seemed at variance with the Calvinist emphasis on two covenants and gave rise to suspicions that Cameron favoured Arminianism.* His thinking influenced Moise Amyraut (or Amyrald, whence Amyraldianism), who believed that Calvinism had deviated from Calvin and who argued for universal atonement. After re-entering the ministry at Bordeaux in 1608 he was appointed in 1618 Professor of Divinity in the Protestant academy of Saumur in succession to the Calvinist Gomarus, and disputed with Tilenus (jointly Professor of Divinity with Andrew Melville* at Sedan) on grace and free will. (He was also acquainted with Melville, whom he had once visited in the Tower of London.) The religious strife in France resulted in his returning home, where after a year in London

CAMERON, LEWIS LEGERTWOOD LEGG

as a supporter of the Crown's prerogative powers, he was appointed Robert Boyd's* successor as Principal of Glasgow University in 1622. Meeting with opposition, he left Glasgow in 1623 and returned to France again, where he was appointed Professor of Divinity at Montauban in 1624. His early death, of injuries inflicted while he was trying to calm a riot, prevented the mature development of his thought. His collected works were issued as *Joannis Cameronis, Scoto-Britanni Theologi ... Opera ...* (Geneva, 1642).

R. Wodrow, *Collections upon the Lives of the Reformers*, ed. W. J. Duncan (G, 1834–48), II, 3–361; H. M. B. Reid, *The Divinity Principals in the University of Glasgow, 1545–1654* (G, 1917), 170–251; A. H. Swinne, *John Cameron, Philosoph und Theologe (1579–1625): Bibliographisch-kritische Analyse der Hand- und Druckschriften sowie der Cameron-Literatur* (Marburg, 1968); J. Durkan and J. Kirk, *The University of Glasgow, 1451–1577* (G, 1977), 350, 353–4, 371; B. G. Armstrong, *Calvinism and the Amyraut Heresy* (Madison, Wisconsin, 1969); *FES*, VII, 393–4; T. M'Crie, *Life of Andrew Melville* (E, ²1824), I, 258; II, 425–6.

J. Kirk

Cameron, John Kennedy (1860–1944), Professor of Systematic Theology, FC College, Edinburgh, 1906–44 (Principal, 1943–4); Moderator (1910) and Principal Clerk (1900–37) of the General Assembly. Ordained at Brodick, Arran, in 1890, he sided with the constitutionalist* party who opposed union with the UPs, and in 1900 was one of the twenty-six ministers who adhered to the FC. In 1901 he was largely instrumental in defusing a potentially dangerous situation at Ness, in Lewis, where the government had been provoked into sending a gunboat and force of police to compel compliance with an interdict granted against the local FC majority. He played a prominent part in the events surrounding the House of Lords appeal case and the subsequent allocation of the property. An able administrator, he earned widespread respect for his prudent handling of affairs at a time of particular difficulty and tension.

(With Alexander Stewart) *The Free Church of Scotland 1843–1910* (E, 1910); *The Church in Arran from the Earliest Period to the Present Day* (E, 1912); *Scottish Church Union of 1900; Reminiscences and Reflections* (Inverness, 1923); *The Clerkship of the General Assembly of the Free Church of Scotland* (Inverness, 1938).

FCSR, Nov. 1944; *Who Was Who, 1941–1950*, 182.

M. Grant

Cameron, Lewis Legertwood Legg (1896–1973), CofS Director of Social Service (*see* Social Responsibility, Board of). He was a brilliant innovator and expansionist in the field of social work.

After losing his mother when only ten days old, Cameron had a poverty-stricken childhood in Aberdeen and had to refuse a bursary for Robert Gordon's College because of the need to contribute to the family income. Employment in a pawnbroker's shop and on bakers' and dairy rounds was followed by a period as a farm-worker. After service with the 4th Gordon Highlanders in the First World War, he was invalided out in 1917 and entered Aberdeen University under ex-servicemen's regulations. He graduated BSc in agriculture and then lectured at a farm institute in Somerset and Leeds University. He returned to Aberdeen University in 1922 to study divinity. From 1925 to 1937 he ministered successively at St Ninian's, Aberdeen, at Mortlach (Banffshire), where he carried through a restoration of the ancient church, and at Bo'ness (West Lothian). Cameron's period as Director of Social Service from 1937 to 1963 was marked by rapid expansion, by an insistence on the highest possible standards and by a strong emphasis on care for the aged. In 1937 the CofS had three homes for the aged; when Cameron retired there were thirty-one (see Eventide Homes). In the same period the Committee on Social Service opened six homes for children and four approved schools for delinquents, and greatly improved its four hostels for young women and five hostels for young men.

Opportunity My Ally (L, 1965); *The Challenge of Need: A History of Social Service by the Church of Scotland, 1869–1969* (E, 1971); *A Badge to be Proud of: A History of the Church of Scotland Huts and Canteens 1939–1972* (E, 1972).

FES VI, 31, VIII, 532, 609, IX, 798, X, 453.

H. R. Sefton

Cameron, Neil (1854–1932), FPC minister. Born at Kilninver in Argyllshire, he spent his early years shepherding. Deep spiritual experiences at this time had an abiding influence on his life, and more immediately led to his leaving the CofS and joining the FC. In 1886 he entered Edinburgh University and later studied divinity at the FC's New College in Edinburgh. From the time of the Robertson Smith* case, Cameron was convinced of the need to combat rationalistic tendencies in the FC and to affirm the doctrines of the Westminster Confession of Faith. After the passing of the 1892 Declaratory Act* he joined the newly-formed FPC as a divinity student, completing his theological training at Glasgow University. In 1896 he was ordained and inducted to the congregation of St Jude's, Glasgow, where he remained until his death.

Throughout his ministry Cameron was a leader in his Church. He served as Convener of the Foreign Mission Committee and in 1921 visited the Church's expanding South African mission. After the post-1900 FC rescinded the Declaratory Act, he strongly opposed moves to bring the two Churches into a closer relationship. While not opposed to the principle of Church union, he feared that such proposals as were made would weaken his Church's adherence to the teachings of the Westminster Confession of Faith.

Cameron was an outstanding preacher. In his own charge he regularly preached five times each week to large congregations. His deep sense of the majesty of God and the authority of Scripture contributed to sermons which were unusually solemn and searching. In his later years the more gentle and winning notes of the gospel were given greater prominence.

D. Beaton (ed.), *Memoir . . . letters, lectures and sermons of Rev Neil Cameron, Glasgow* (Inverness, 1932); A. MacPherson (ed.), *History of the Free Presbyterian Church of Scotland 1893–1970* (Inverness, 1974).

A. Morrison

Cameron, Richard (c.1648–80), Covenanter* and field-preacher, born at Falkland in Fife. After graduating at St Andrews (MA, 1665) Cameron was employed for some time as a schoolmaster in his native Falkland, acting also as precentor* in the parish church. However, after hearing some of the persecuted field-preachers* he attached himself wholeheartedly to their cause, and became a convinced opponent of the ecclesiastical supremacy claimed by the state. On leaving Falkland he found employment as a private chaplain in the Border country, where he came to the notice of John Welsh* of Irongray, who prevailed upon him to accept licence to preach. For some months Cameron kept company with Welsh and his fellow-preachers, but his uncompromising views on public affairs increasingly isolated him. By the end of 1678 he had become identified with a new party in the Church which was ready to challenge the government's authority not merely in matters spiritual but in the realm of civil government itself.

In the spring of 1679 Cameron went over to Holland, where he received ordination at the hands of the exiled Robert MacWard* and John Brown (d.1679).* On his return he attempted to resume field-preaching, but because of the severity of the laws introduced following Bothwell Bridge* he could at first find no one to join him. Eventually he and Donald Cargill,* who had also returned from Holland, ventured to hold field-meetings in some of the most inaccessible parts of the country, taking stringent steps for their own defence. For some months in the summer of 1680 these meetings were frequented by thousands. Cameron, meantime, had been developing his thoughts on the need for a public testimony, and on 22 June 1680 he and a group of supporters issued the Sanquhar Declaration,* renouncing the authority of Charles II,* and declaring war upon him as a tyrant and usurper. For this he was proclaimed a traitor, and had a heavy price put on his head. A month later, at Ayrsmoss,* near Muirkirk in Ayrshire, Cameron and his party were attacked by a body of government forces and overcome by superior numbers. Cameron and eight others were killed, his head and hands being taken to Edinburgh and exhibited on the Netherbow Port.

Cameron's brief and meteoric career has made him the most celebrated of the martyrs of the Covenant. If at times he showed a degree of impulsiveness, particularly in state issues, it should be said that his actions merely anticipated what the country as a whole did in 1688. It was however as a preacher of the gospel that Cameron excelled. His sermons remain fresh and direct today. To those who heard them preached they were calculated to make a powerful appeal; and they had an undoubted influence in inspiring his followers to steadfastness and perseverance.

J. Herkless, *Richard Cameron* (E, 1896); J. Downie, *The Early Home of Richard Cameron* (Paisley, 1901); P. Walker, *Six Saints of the Covenant* (ed. D. Hay Fleming, E, 1901), I, 218–36; J. Howie, *Scots Worthies* (ed. W. H. Carslaw, E, 1871), 421–9; *Cloud of Witnesses* (ed. J. H. Thomson, E, 1871), 495–500; *DNB* VIII, 301–2.

M. Grant

Cameronians, *see* Societies, United.

Campbell, Alexander (*d*.1608), Bishop of Brechin. The brother of Campbell of Ardkinglas, while in his teens he was presented to the bishopric of Brechin by Queen Mary in May 1566, as tulchan* to his chief, Archibald Earl of Argyll.* When the young bishop went abroad after 1567, alienation of the bishopric's temporal lands (begun before 1560) was complete. Educated at St Andrews, and overseas at both Geneva and Paris, on his return Campbell served briefly as an apprentice-bishop under John Erskine of Dun,* but failed to make any real mark in ecclesiastical affairs. He did, however, exercise authority over the bishop's burgh of Brechin.

F. D. Bardgett, 'Faith, families and factions' (PhD, Edinburgh University, 1987); D. B. Thoms, *The Council of Brechin* (Brechin, 1971).

F. D. Bardgett

Campbell, Alexander (1788–1866), founder of the Campbellites, or Disciples (or Churches) of Christ. Alexander Campbell was born in Ballymena, N. Ireland, the eldest son of Thomas Campbell.* In 1808–9 he attended classes at Glasgow University and was greatly influenced by Greville Ewing,* minister of the Glasgow Tabernacle (one of the congregations established by James* and Robert Haldane*), and in particular by his weekly celebration of the Lord's Supper. Alexander joined his father in America in 1809 and began a new movement to restore unity among the churches on the basis of New Testament Christianity. In 1812 the Campbells adopted believers' baptism, and until 1830 were associated with the Baptists.

Alexander's theology combined an Enlightenment* critique of existing Church structures with a defence of revealed religion. He debated with Presbyterian ministers on baptism and in 1829 with Robert Owen (1771–1858; *see* Dale, David) on the evidences of Christianity. His assertion that baptism was for the remission of sins, and his understanding of the work of the Holy Spirit in salvation, made him suspect to many Baptists. He was best known through the magazines he edited, especially the *Christian Baptist* (1823–30) and the *Millennial Harbinger* (1830–66). His most influential book, *Christianity Restored* (1835), reissued in a second edition as *The Christian System* (Bethany, VA, 1839), contained articles from these magazines. Here he expounded his view of a primitive church order, in which independent local congregations chose their own elders, deacons and evangelists, co-operated in the work of evangelism, and practised believers' baptism by immersion and weekly celebration of the Lord's Supper. Campbell's congregations grew with the westward movement of the frontier, and in 1832 they joined with those of the Christian Connection, led by another ex-Presbyterian, Barton W. Stone (1772–1844). The new movement of 'Campbellites' became known as Disciples or Churches of Christ.* Campbell used the wealth he inherited from his first wife's father to found Bethany College, West Virginia, in 1840 and to support evangelistic work.

Campbell's writings became known in Britain in the early 1830s. During his visit to Britain in 1847 he was falsely accused by the Anti-Slavery Society of supporting slavery and spent several days in Glasgow prison. That October Campbell was chairman of the second General Meeting of Churches of Christ in Great Britain at Chester.

R. Richardson, *Memoirs of Alexander Campbell*, 2 vols (Philadelphia, 1868–70); T. Chalmers, *Alexander Campbell's Tour in Scotland* (Louisville, 1892); W. Garrison, *The Sources of Alexander Campbell's Theology* (St Louis, 1900); R. F. West, *Alexander Campbell and Natural Religion* (New Haven, 1948).

D. M. Thompson

Campbell, Andrew (1845–1919), missionary. He was born in Chorley, Lancashire. A mason, he was recruited to an industrial project initiated by the newly formed Santal (Eastern India) mission of the FC in 1872. In 1878, he was officially appointed to the mission as a lay evangelist, and was sent next year to open the new station in Tundi (Pokhuria), thereafter his principal home. He was ordained in 1880 by the Presbytery of Calcutta. His first furlough, in 1889, increased the Santal mission's visibility in Scotland, and gained new resources for it. In Pokhuria itself, Campbell held the post of honorary magistrate, and following the absorption of much of Santalia into Bihar, became an elected member of the Bihar Legislative Council in 1911. He received the Kaisar i Hind medal for his efforts to relieve and control the famine of 1897.

Despite his lack of formal education Campbell became a formidable Santal scholar. During 1899–1902 he produced a three-volume Santali dictionary, which is in effect also a compendium on Santal life. His work on Santal folk tales was used by Andrew Lang.* He made Santali translations for use by church and school (including the ubiquitous catechetical primer *Peep of Day*). He edited a magazine in Santali. In Bible translation, L. O. Skrefsrud, doyen of Santal missionaries, objected to Campbell's proclivity for using terms of Sanskrit origin, rather than a vernacular name, for the Godhead. But the Scandinavians accepted his orthography, under protest, and he seems to have been one of the few outside the Scandinavian mission who co-operated fully with them in revising their translation. St Andrews University made him DD in 1903.

Though involved in almost every aspect of the Santal mission, he never gave up his original 'industrial' interests. Besides building, designing water storage and training craftsmen, he attempted to introduce or extend cash crops (castor oil plant), establish new industries (silk production), and produce superior articles for the European market (textiles, fishing line gut). He sent more than 700 items to the Indian and Colonial Exhibition in London in 1885. In basic agricultural skills and techniques, however, he came to believe that the West had nothing to teach the Indian farmer.

Campbell seems to have neither married nor retired.

See also Missions: India: Bengal and Bihar.

AFCS I, 113; FUFCS 537; J. M. Macphail, *Andrew Campbell* (E, 1920); id., *Our Church's Work in Santalia* (E, 1907); O. Hodne, *L. O. Skrefsrud, Missionary among the Santals of Santal Parganas* (Oslo, 1966). Campbell's own writing, other than a substantial number of articles, appeared from the Santal Mission Press.

A. F. Walls

Campbell, Archibald (1530-73), fifth Earl of Argyll, Chancellor of Scotland. Argyll was converted to Protestantism in 1556, two years before succeeding his father, but remained a Protestant moderate and political trimmer who did not join the Lords of the Congregation* until 4 June 1559. Personal and family ambitions, particularly in Ireland, explain Argyll's subsequent record of repeated changes in allegiance to Queen Mary* and her enemies during the civil war of 1567-73. In 1571 he finally joined the King's Party, and was appointed Chancellor in November 1572.

See also Carswell, John.

DNB VIII, 314-18; J. E. A. Dawson, 'The Fifth Earl of Argyle, Gaelic Lordship and Political Power in Sixteenth Century Scotland', *SHR* 67 (1988), 1-27; id., 'Two Kingdoms or Three? Ireland in Anglo-Scottish Relations in the Middle of the Sixteenth Century', in R. A. Mason (ed.), *Scotland and England 1286-1815* (E, 1987), 120-31.

K. M. Brown

Campbell, Archibald (1607-61), eighth Earl and first Marquis, Covenanter* leader. Argyll was educated at the University of St Andrews (1622-5), and appointed a privy councillor in 1628 and an extra-ordinary Lord of Session in 1634. He did not sign the National Covenant* in February 1638, but did try to persuade Charles I* to compromise on the Covenanters' demands. However, at the Glasgow Assembly* in November, Argyll openly joined the Covenanters, inspired by a mixture of constitutional conservatism, religion, and clan politics.

Immediately Argyll became one of the Covenanters' leaders, and over the next year crushed his enemies in the Highlands, contributed to the King's defeat in the Bishops' Wars,* and swept aside the challenge from the envious and more moderate Montrose (see Graham, James).* During Charles's visit to Scotland in 1641 the King recognized Argyll's pre-eminence by creating him a marquis.

Argyll favoured an alliance with the English Parliament following the outbreak of civil war in England in the summer of 1642, and he helped draft and negotiate the Solemn League and Covenant,* as a result of which the Army of the Covenant was sent into England in January 1644. However, Montrose's successful Highland war in 1644-5, especially his defeats of Argyll at Inverlochy and Kilsyth, seriously undermined the Marquis's authority.

Following Charles's surrender to the Scottish army in 1646, Argyll failed to persuade the King to meet the Covenanters' demands. He was wholly opposed to the Engagement,* but after the defeat of the Engagers in England in August 1648 Argyll's radical Presbyterian allies seized power in the Whiggamore Raid. Argyll joined in the universal Scottish condemnation of the King's execution, and was head of the Committee of Estates throughout Charles II's* stay in Scotland, personally crowning Charles on 1 January, 1651.

However, Argyll was no longer the dominant figure he had once been, and played little part in the events leading to the final defeat of the Scots by Oliver Cromwell in 1651-2. Distrusted by Royalists, the English, and the dominant Protester* faction in the Church, Argyll was now a very isolated figure, although he did make his peace with the occupying regime. In 1660 he attempted to ingratiate himself with the restored Charles II, but was arrested and sent home to Scotland where he was found guilty of treason, and executed.

J. Willcock, *The Great Marquess* (E, 1903); *DNB* VIII, 319-29; D. Stevenson, *The Scottish Revolution, 1637-1644* (Newton Abbot, 1973); id., *Revolution and Counter Revolution in Scotland, 1644-1651* (L, 1977); E. Cowan, 'Montrose and Argyll' in G. Menzies (ed.), *The Scottish Nation* (L, 1972), 118-32.

K. M. Brown

Campbell, Donald, Abbot of Coupar Angus from c.1529 until his death in the winter of 1562-3, brother of Colin, third Earl of Argyll. His career, though associated with the politics of his clan, was of significance to the Reformation. Coupar was used as a base against the English invaders at Broughty Castle by Archibald fourth Earl of Argyll during the wars of 'The Rough Wooing' (1544-50) and the Abbot provided 150 soldiers. Campbell imperialism was behind Donald Campbell's unsuccessful candidatures for the bishoprics of Glasgow (1548), Dunkeld (1549-54) and Brechin (1557-9).

CAMPBELL, DUNCAN

During the Reformation crisis, he followed Archibald Campbell, fifth Earl of Argyll,* into the Protestant camp in May 1559. Clan politics was undoubtedly the chief motive, but his conversion was also necessary to save Coupar from violence. Though the Pope had refused to provide him to Brechin unless he renounced his abbey, he continued to exercise authority as bishop postulate.

Campbell had been appointed Keeper of the Privy Seal in 1554 and assisted the Protestant Lords of the Congregation* to maintain their usurping authority after October 1559 by issuing their writs under his Seal. This appearance of legality was vital in securing general obedience to the Lords after the death of the Queen-Regent, Mary of Guise,* and hence was important to the success of the Reformation in Scotland. The bishop's burgh of Brechin was probably reformed under his authority and that of his ward, Lord James Ogilvy of Airlie, whose election as Provost of Brechin he engineered early in 1560. Present at the Reformation Parliament* of 1560, Abbot Donald retained the Privy Seal until 1562.

The temporal affairs of Coupar Angus Abbey* were well handled by Donald Campbell until he began feuing lands c.1558. Initially caused by his need for cash to support his claim to the bishopric of Brechin, this dispersal of lands accelerated as the Reformation progressed. On his death, Archibald Earl of Argyll was gifted the temporalities of Coupar.

F. D. Bardgett, *Scotland Reformed: The Reformation in Angus and Mearns* (E, 1989); M. B. Sanderson, *Scottish Rural Society* (E, 1982); C. Rogers (ed.), *Rental Book of the Cistercian Abbey of Cupar-Angus*, 2 vols (L, 1879–80); D. E. Easson (ed.), *Charters of the Abbey of Coupar Angus*, 2 vols (E, 1947); R. K. Hannay, 'Some Papal Bulls among the Hamilton Papers', *SHR* 22 (1925), 25–41.

F. D. Bardgett

Campbell, Duncan (1898–1972), minister, evangelist and Bible College Principal, well known for his involvement in a spiritual awakening in the Outer Hebrides during the early 1950s. Born in Benderloch, Argyllshire, the son of a crofter/stonemason, Campbell served with the Argyll and Sutherland Highlanders during the First World War.* After demobilization he trained at the Faith Mission Bible College, Edinburgh, and became a Gaelic-speaking evangelist with the Faith Mission,* working mainly in the West Highlands and the Inner Hebrides with notable success. In 1925 he resigned from the Mission to take up a post as an ordained missionary with the UFC* in Ardvasar, Skye. When the Act of Union* was signed in 1929, he elected to remain in the UFC (Continuing) and devoted twenty years to pastoral ministry in Balintore and Falkirk. He was ordained as a minister in 1940.

A return to interdenominational evangelistic activity led to Campbell's participation in the revival* on the island of Lewis and Harris from December 1949–53. A brief account of this movement was written by him, entitled *The Lewis Awakening* (E, 1954). Appointed Principal of the Faith Mission Bible College (1958–66), he was also much in demand as a conference and convention speaker throughout the British Isles and further afield. He died in Switzerland while engaged in such ministry.

Preaching was the prominent feature of Campbell's career, and his emphasis was on the authority of the Word of God and prayer, and the need for personal holiness.

The Price and Power of Revival (L, 1956; ⁴E, 1968); *God's Answer* (E, 1960); *God's Standard* (E, 1964).

A. A. Woolsey, *Duncan Campbell* (L, 1974); ²*Channel of Revival* (E, 1982).

A. A. Woolsey

Campbell, George (?1635–1701), Professor of Divinity in the University of Edinburgh. Born in Inveray, Campbell was educated in Glasgow and Edinburgh (MA, 1656) and was ordained to Dumfries in 1658. Deprived in 1662, he refused the 1672 Indulgence.* After a brief imprisonment in 1684 he was released and fled to Holland. He returned in 1687 and ministered in a meeting-house in Dumfries before being restored to his charge there in 1690. Shortly afterward he was called both to the second or Old Kirk charge in Edinburgh and to the University. Although he published nothing, he taught a large portion of the first generation of ministers in the post-Revolution* CofS. Thomas Boston* speaks of him as 'the great Mr. George Campbell' and describes him as 'a man of great learning, but excessively modest' (*Life and Times*, ed. G. Morrison, E, 1899, 20–1). Campbell founded the University's theological library.

FES I, 75; A. Bower, *The History of the University of Edinburgh* (E, 1817), I, 384; II, 92; A. Grant, *The Story of the University of Edinburgh* (L, 1884), II, 258, 282.

D. C. Lachman

Campbell, George (1719–96), leading Moderate* and Principal (1759–96) and Professor of Divinity (1771–96) of Marischal College, Aberdeen. Educated at the Grammar School and King's College, Aberdeen, he was minister of Banchory Ternan, Kincardineshire (1748–57), Aberdeen (second charge, St Nicholas, 1757–71) and Aberdeen Greyfriars (1771–96). His appointment as Patron of the Incorporated Trades involved him in the commercial life of the city. He was a frequent member of the General Assembly, especially between 1762 and 1785.

Campbell was a prolific writer. His collected works published posthumously in 1840 run to six bulky volumes. His most notable publication was probably his *Dissertation on Miracles* (E, 1762; frequently reprinted). Campbell was at pains to point out that it was not his main intention 'to refute the reasoning and objections of Mr. Hume with regard to miracles'. He really wanted 'to set the principal argument for Christianity in its proper light'. His

CAMPBELL, GEORGE DOUGLAS

most significant argument was that the highest improbability of an event before its occurrence is counterbalanced by slight direct evidence after it. It was the only reply to David Hume* on which the sceptic philosopher commented.

Although Evangelicals have regarded Campbell with suspicion, not least for his criticisms of what he regarded as defects in the traditional Reformed attitudes to Church and doctrine, especially in his *Lectures on Ecclesiastical History* (L, 1800), his ability in a wide range of theological areas is usually admitted. His *Lectures* included a defence of Presbyterianism* which provoked at least two defences of episcopacy.* His *Philosophy of Rhetoric* (L, 1776) resembled Blair's* work on the subject, his 1789 *Translation of the Gospels* had run through seven editions by 1834. A few sermons demonstrated his Moderate sympathies, including *The Duty of Allegiance* (A, 1777), addressed in effect to the American colonists.

On occasion he followed an independent line in Church politics, being one of the leaders of the 1749 agitation for augmentation of ministerial stipends* (brought to heel only by a government threat of loss of his Royal Chaplaincy), and continuing his advocacy of RC relief legislation after the rest of the Moderates had fallen silent in the face of public opposition (*Address to the People of Scotland*, A, 1779). He learned German at the age of seventy in order to read Luther's translation of the Bible. He was one of the Scottish clergy identified by Alexander Carlyle* as the leading writers in their fields in the English-speaking world.

DNB VIII, 357–8; *FES* VII, 359; Life by G. S. Keith in A, 1815, edit. of *Lectures*; J. Valentine, *An Aberdeen Principal of Last Century* (A, 1896); D. R. Bormann, 'Some Common Sense about Campbell, Hume and Reid', *Quarterly Journal of Speech* 71 (1985), 395–421; H. R. Sefton, 'David Hume and Principal George Campbell', in J. J. Carter and J. H. Pittock (eds), *Aberdeen and the Enlightenment* (A, 1987), 123–8; R. B. Sher, *Church and University in the Scottish Enlightenment* (E, 1985).

J. R. McIntosh and H. R. Sefton

Campbell, George Douglas (1823–1900), eighth Duke of Argyll, laird, Kirk patron and Christian apologist. Educated by private tutors, Douglas succeeded in 1847 to the peerage. He soon championed agricultural and economic reform in Argyllshire and provided vicarious clan Campbell fame as Chancellor or Lord Rector of the Universities of St Andrews (1852), and Glasgow (1855), and as President of the Geological and Royal Geographical Societies. From Inveraray Castle he acted as patron of the Kirk, landlord of the Secession* chapel, well-loved laird of the tenantry, benefactor of parish and SSPCK* schools and a 'model of Victorian rectitude': 'This loud-voiced peer, confident and unselfconscious in public, but in private life gentle and modest ... seemed to epitomize the ideal of Victorian aristocracy: ... he and his girlish, fairy-like Duchess ... became close friends of

CAMPBELL, ISABELLA

Queen Victoria' (I. G. Lindsay and M. Cosh, *Inveraray and the Dukes of Argyll*, E, 1973, 322).

As politician the Duke served in every Liberal Cabinet 1852–81 and as Secretary of State for India 1868–74. Concerned ecclesiastically as early as 1842, he wrote to the peers and to Thomas Chalmers* seeking to avert the Disruption.* He kept informed on local church affairs and global missions. Missionaries David Livingstone* and local Glenaray lad, James Chalmers,* both planted trees in the castle grounds – an honour normally reserved for those of Queen Victoria's standing.

An active scholar with encyclopaedic interests, Campbell contributed to geology, economics, ornithology, geography, archaeology and particularly anthropology and philosophy of science. He saw Christianity as the only adequate integrative explanation of all knowledge. Hence in anthropology, for example, Campbell rebutted increasingly anti-Christian tendencies, challenging the Comtian presuppositions underlying his fellow-peer John Lubbock's popular approach.

The Duke continued his apologetic into the 1890s. His four-fold stress on loyalty to biblical revelation, the unity of all truth, the inexhaustible nature of knowledge, and the Christian duty to pursue new learning, was by then a lonely voice. A century later, perhaps it deserves a fresh hearing when the views he countered have run their inadequate course – as he predicted.

The Philosophy of Belief: or Law in Christian Theology (L, 1864); *Primeval Man* (L, 1969); *Letter to Peers from a Peer's Son on Church of Scotland* (E, 1942); *Letter to Thomas Chalmers on Church Affairs in Scotland* (E, 1842).

Ina Campbell (ed.), *George Douglas, Eighth Duke of Argyll, K.G., K.T., (1823–1900). Autobiography and Memoirs*, 2 vols (L, 1906); *DNB Suppl.* I, 385–90; J. M. Hitchen, 'Training Tamate: The Formation of the Nineteenth Century Missionary Worldview: the Case of James Chalmers of New Guinea' (PhD, Aberdeen University, 1984), 229–44.

J. M. Hitchen

Campbell, Isabella (c.1807–27) and **Mary** (d.1840), sisters whose religious experiences attracted excited attention. They grew up in a poor farm at Fernicarry in Robert Story's* Rosneath parish on the Clyde. Isabella's sanctity and ecstasies, preserved in Story's memoir *Peace in Believing* (Greenock, 1829) after her death from tuberculosis when only twenty, drew visitors to Fernicarry. The younger Mary, herself ill from consumption, inherited their fascination. Taught by Edward Irving* that illness was Satan's work, and by A. J. Scott* that Spirit-baptism was subsequent to regeneration, she came to expect, and in March 1830 received, the gift of glossolalia, the first in the Irvingite movement to do so. Moving to Helensburgh and then London, where she married W. R. Caird, an Edinburgh law clerk drawn to Fernicarry, she entered fully into Irvingite circles. The Cairds served for a time as lay chaplains to Lady Olivia Sparrow, a

CAMPBELL, JOHN

prominent supporter of Irvingism. Mary's charistmatic* experiences evoked widespread interest, *e.g.* from Thomas Erskine,* and sharply divergent assessments – not least because of her excitable mystical temperament. Story was deeply disillusioned, faulting her for reneging on a missionary call.

A. L. Drummond, *Edward Irving and His Circle* (L, 1937); A. Dallimore, *The Life of Edward Irving* (E, 1983); D. P. Thomson, *Women of the Scottish Church* (Perth, 1975), 161–80.

D. F. Wright

Campbell, John (1766–1840), 'philanthropic ironmonger' and London Independent minister. Educated at Edinburgh High School and brought up in the Relief Church,* he became an ironmonger in the city's Grassmarket in 1786. His correspondence and friendship with John Newton, Rector of St Mary Woolnoth, London, influenced his views and led in 1795 to a fresh awareness of the gospel. Thereafter, his shop became a principal clearing-house for evangelical activity in Scotland and for communication between the leaders of the Evangelical Revival in the south and those of a similar persuasion in the Scottish churches. His interests were broad, embracing children's literature and religious tract publication, Sunday schools, relief of the poor and orphans, and the reform of prostitutes. His early practice in exhorting those who attended the schools established in villages near Edinburgh led him in 1797 to become a lay preacher in conjunction with James Haldane.* The resulting attachment to itinerancy* continued throughout his life. Though his lay preaching was accepted by some Scottish ministers including David Black, the minister of Lady Yester's church in Edinburgh, and by his confidante, the aged Countess of Leven, it strained his relationship with the older generation of Scottish evangelicals represented by John Erskine.* Drawn towards Independency,* he left the CofS in 1799, studying at Greville Ewing's* Glasgow seminary and tutoring the following class of Haldane students before his ordination as pastor of Kingsland Chapel near London in 1802. Despite his continuing friendship and co-operation with the Haldanes, he showed no liking for the innovation and fissiparousness which characterized their movement. The new position, while not ending his interest in Scotland, encouraged him to pursue his long-standing enthusiasm for overseas missions. As a director of the London Missionary Society* he undertook two extensive tours of mission stations in Cape Colony and the interior of southern Africa between 1812–14 and 1818–21. As author and publisher of tracts and other religious works, founder of the Edinburgh-based *Missionary Magazine* (*see* Periodicals, Religious), compulsive traveller and preacher, and inveterate correspondent, Campbell's greatest significance lay in the realm of co-ordination and liaison.

R. Philip, *The Life, Times, and Missionary Enterprises, of the Rev. John Campbell* (L, 1841).

D. W. Lovegrove

CAMPBELL, JOHN MCLEOD

Campbell, John Gregorson (1836–91), collector of Gaelic folklore and parish minister of Tiree (1861–91). Born in Kingairloch, Argyll, Campbell initially studied law at Glasgow University. His presentation to Tiree (by the Duke of Argyll) was opposed at first by the parishioners. Campbell, however, won the confidence of the people to the extent that he collected substantial amounts of folklore in the island. His books include *The Fians* (L, 1891), *Clan Traditions and Popular Tales* (L, 1895), and two works on *Superstitions* (G, 1900) and *Witchcraft and Second Sight* (G, 1902) in the Highlands.

FES IV, 121–2.

D. E. Meek

Campbell, John McLeod (1800–72), outstanding if controversial innovator on the doctrine of the atonement.* Campbell was born in Armaddy House, near Kilninver, Argyllshire, the son of a Moderate* CofS minister. He studied at Glasgow University (1811–20), converted to evangelical views of salvation in 1824, and in 1825 was inducted to the CofS parish church of Row (modern spelling 'Rhu') on the Gareloch, Dunbartonshire.

Campbell's pastoral experience at Row formed the basis for his theological odyssey. Believing that a legalistic mentality among his parishioners was preventing them from living God-centred lives, he became convinced that sincere love for God could spring only from the assurance* of his love and forgiveness. Assurance was thus of the essence of faith. Further reflection led Campbell to conclude that such assurance could be founded only on a doctrine of 'universal pardon' – that Christ's death has secured forgiveness for all in this life (although not ultimate salvation in the next), and that faith means believing this.

Violent controversy ensued, and after lengthy and complex proceedings Campbell was deposed in 1831 by the General Assembly. From 1834 he pastored a Congregational church in Glasgow, until ill-health compelled retirement in 1859.

Campbell is best known, however, not for this early controversy, but for his mature and memorable restatement of the doctrine of the atonement. This is to be found in his classic treatise on *The Nature of the Atonement* (C, 1856; ²L, 1867; ³L, 1869; new ed. with introduction by E. P. Dickie, L, 1959), lauded by P. T. Forsyth as a 'great, fine, holy book' (*The Work of Christ*, L, 1938, 148).

Campbell's volume offers a sustained critique of traditional evangelical conceptions of the atonement. He rejected penal substitution on the basis that 'our relation to God as our righteous Lord is subordinate to our relation to Him as the Father of our spirits, – the original and root-relation, in the light of which alone all God's dealings with us can be understood'. The atonement was thus grounded not in any context of law, but in God's fatherhood – a father's desire to reclaim his erring children.

Salvation so conceived does not necessitate that God's retributive justice be satisfied as a prerequisite. This customary assumption had in Campbell's

CAMPBELL, PETER COLIN

view thrown up the doctrine of limited atonement: God could not justly punish those sinners whose penalty Christ had vicariously paid, so that he could not have been a substitute for the ultimately damned. This undermined Christ's manifestation of the Father's love for all humanity. Rather, Campbell maintained, repentance itself – if only true and perfect – would be adequate to restore spiritual relations between God and his sinful offspring. Christ's suffering Campbell interpreted as the perfect act of penitence, performed vicariously for impenitent humanity, which by sharing God's mind toward sin 'absorbed' his anger against it. The cross thus reveals God's grief and hatred for sin yet unceasing love for sinners, and discloses the nature of filial faith in the Father as exercised by Jesus himself in his death. Our repentance is our yielding ourselves to the Spirit of Christ, that he might utter in us his own 'Amen' to God's rejection of sin.

Campbell's criticisms of penal substitution have found more favour than his alternative doctrine of vicarious repentance. This presupposes that repentance as such can have atoning efficacy – a Roman and Socinian assumption foreign to the theology of the Reformation. The very notion of a vicarious repentance has failed to commend itself as meaningful to many. Further, Campbell's constant emphasis on God's universal fatherhood and grace has an inevitable tendency to eschatological universalism, which in his closing years he all but espoused (see *Memorials of John McLeod Campbell*, ed. D. Campbell, 2 vols, L, 1877, II, 294–5). These points constitute the cardinal difficulties in Campbell's highly influential reformulation of the doctrine of the atonement.

Reminiscences and Reflections (L, 1873); *Sermons and Lectures*, 2 vols (Greenock, 1832); *Christ the Bread of Life* (G, 1851); *Thoughts on Revelation* (C, 1862).

G. M. Tuttle, *So Rich a Soil* (E, 1986); R. H. Story, *Memoir of the Life of the Rev. Robert Story* (L, 1862); J. Tulloch, *Movements of Religious Thought in Britain during the Nineteenth Century* (L, 1885), 145–56; R. S. Franks, *A History of the Doctrine of the Work of Christ* (L, 1962), 665–72; J. B. Torrance, 'The Contribution of McLeod Campbell to Scottish Theology', *SJT* 26 (1973), 295–311; M. C. Bell, *Calvin and Scottish Theology* (E, 1985), 181–92; *FES* III, 366; *DNB* VIII, 840–1.

N. R. Needham

Campbell, Peter Colin (1810–76), first Principal of the University of Aberdeen. Born at Ardchattan, W. Argyll, he was educated at Edinburgh University (MA, 1829) and ordained by the Presbytery of Inverary, Argyll, in 1835 to serve, under the auspices of the Glasgow Colonial Society, at St John's Presbyterian Church, Brookville, Canada. In 1840 he became Professor of Classical Literature at Queen's College, Kingston, Ontario.

Returning to Scotland in 1845 he took up the charge of Caputh, Perthshire, whence in 1854 he was appointed Professor of Greek at King's College, Aberdeen. Next year he became Principal and was awarded the DD both of King's and of Edinburgh. In 1860 he became the first Principal of the newly united University of Aberdeen and served until his death.

Of a handful of works the most significant is *The Theory of Ruling Eldership* (E, 1866), which, with considerable learning, espouses the 'lay' view of the eldership.*

FES VII, 378–9.

G. Wareing

Campbell, Thomas (1763–1854), Secession minister and one of the original 'Campbellites'. Born in Newry, he studied at Glasgow University and the Antiburgher Divinity Hall under Archibald Bruce.* He became a schoolmaster and was minister of the Secession Presbyterian church in Ahorey, near Armagh, 1798–1807. He was a founder of the Evangelical Society of Ulster and worked for unity among the divided groups in the Secession Church. After emigrating to Pennsylvania in 1807 he was censured by the Associate Presbytery of Chartiers for admitting non-Seceders to communion. Campbell responded in his *Declaration and Address* (1809), pleading for the restoration of unity and peace to the Church by using as a test of fellowship only that which was enjoined in Scripture. With his son, Alexander,* he became one of the founders of the movement subsequently known as Disciples or Churches of Christ.*

Declaration and Address (1809), in D. M. Thompson (ed.), *Stating the Gospel* (E, 1989).

A. Campbell (ed.), *Memoirs of Elder Thomas Campbell* (Cincinnati, 1871); L. G. McAllister, *Thomas Campbell: Man of the Book* (St Louis, 1954); D. M. Thompson, 'The Irish Background to Thomas Campbell's Declaration and Address', *Journ. of the URC Hist. Soc.* 3 (1985), 215–25.

D. M. Thompson

Campbell, (Lady) Victoria (1854–1910), third daughter of George, eighth Duke of Argyll.* Born in London, Victoria was disabled from childhood by a form of rheumatism resulting in lameness. Reared in the cosmopolitan atmosphere of high society, she 'vowed her life to God' at a time of severe illness. Thereafter she combined an interest in social amelioration with a rather romantic evangelical commitment. Attending the churches of many of the best-known preachers in London and Edinburgh, and espousing proto-ecumenism,* she recoiled at the ecclesiastical divisions in the Highlands.* She had a special affection for the islands of the Argyll Estate, especially Iona,* Mull and Tiree. At a time (1884–6) when Tiree crofters, through the Land League, were agitating for land reform (*see* Clearances), she believed that islanders' minds could be 'improved' through sewing classes for the women and craft courses for the men. Promoting the YWCA,* foreign missions* and Woman's Guilds,* as well as the placement of Jubilee Nurses in the Highlands, Lady Victoria applied, in her own way, the ideals of Lady Kinnaird, Elizabeth Fry and Florence Nightingale.

CAMPBELL, WILLIAM HOWARD

Frances Balfour, *Lady Victoria Campbell* (L, 1911); M. MacArthur, *Iona* (E, 1990), 206–7.

D. E. Meek

Campbell, William Howard (1859–1910), missionary to India. Campbell was born in Londonderry. After arts, divinity and further study in Sanskrit and medicine in Edinburgh, he was ordained in a Congregationalist* church and went in 1884 as a missionary with the London Missionary Society* to South India, where he worked primarily in the Telugu country, being stationed successively at Cuddapah, Jammulamadugu (1895) and Gooty (1900). He was one of the founders of the South India United Church which brought together Presbyterians* and Congregationalists and was a forerunner of the Church of South India. He was appointed the first Principal of the United Theological College, Bangalore, but died before he could take up office. He was a leading authority on the Telugu language, and an expert entomologist.

DNB Second Suppl. I, 301–2; W. D. Mackenzie and W. R. Nicoll in *BW* 47 (1910), 584.

D. B. Forrester

Campbeltown Case (1835–9), an important legal case in Scottish church history. In 1835, at the height of the Voluntary controversy,* the minister of Campbeltown (or Campbelton) Relief* Church in Argyllshire, James Smith, attempted to take his congregation back into the Est.C. For this the Relief Synod declared him 'out of connection with the Relief body, and the Campbelton Relief church vacant' (G. Struthers, *The History of the Rise, Progress and Principles of the Relief Church*, G, 1843, 498). Smith challenged this decision in the civil courts. He argued that the Relief Synod's proceedings were in breach of its constitutional doctrines, since the Relief's Voluntary opposition to established Churches was a departure from original Relief principles.

The Campbeltown Case occasioned the first attempt ever made in Scottish law to apply the principle enunciated in the Craigdallie Case* (1803–19), that church property was tied to original doctrine. The judges in the Campbeltown Case determined that whereas civil courts could transfer the ownership of church property, on the grounds that its present occupiers had altered the doctrines for whose propagation the property had been erected, such transfer could be enforced only if that alteration had 'essentially changed the character of the tenets and faith originally professed' (*ibid.*, 545). The establishment principle was ruled not to constitute such an essential tenet in the case of the Relief. The Court of Session's final decision, therefore, given on 6 June 1839, vindicated the Relief, and awarded costs against Smith.

See also Church and State.

A. Taylor Innes, *The Law of Creeds in Scotland* (L, 1867), ch VI

N. R. Needham

CANADA

Camphill Village Trust, a charity caring for people with mental handicaps or other special needs. Camphill (near Aberdeen) was established to offer help to children and adults in need of special care in a community setting. Karl König with other Austrian refugees began this work in 1940, deriving their methods from Rudolf Steiner's anthroposophy, which informs Camphill's therapy, education and also social and Christian practice. An active exchange took place between König and George McLeod,* founder of the Iona Community,* during the pioneering phase of the 1940s.

The Christian festivals are an important tenet of community life in Camphill. Daily readings of a Gospel passage prepare for the Bible Evening held on a Saturday in every family unit. Lay services are held by co-workers for children, adolescents and adults. There are now many schools, training centres, hostels and adult communities run by the Trust in rural or urban settings, eleven in Scotland and seventy-eight world-wide.

A three-year diploma course in Curative Education and related courses in Social Therapy bring young people from many countries to Camphill.

C. Pietzner (ed.), *A Candle on the Hill* (E, 1990) and *Aspects in Curative Education* (A, 1966); K. König, *Being Human* (NY, 1989); T. J. Weihs, *Children in Need of Special Care* (L, 1971); W. Ferrants (ed.), *Camphill Villages* (Whitby, 1988).

F. J. Bock

Canada. Scottish religious bodies have had close links with Canada since the second half of the eighteenth century. These links were created principally through emigration from Scotland to the maritime provinces and the 'two Canadas', namely Upper and Lower Canada (as they were known before Confederation in 1867). Emigration led to the establishment of church structures on the model of the home country, and to the movement of clergy from Scotland. However, the relationship between Scotland and Canada can be too easily misunderstood at the ecclesiastical level. It needs to be underlined that the circumstances prevailing in Canada encouraged distinctive development and, in the case of certain churches, independence from Scotland at a relatively early stage. It is also noteworthy that, although the disputes that created division within the Scottish churches were reflected in their Canadian wings, the causes of contention (*e.g.* establishment) tended to be less relevant to the New World, and the struggles were fought on slightly different grounds. This, together with the challenge of the frontier, produced a more ecumenical climate, making church unions easier and much earlier than in Scotland.

Broadly, the following stages in the lives of the 'Scottish' churches in Canada can be observed: (1) the movement of people and ministers from Scotland; (2) a phase of re-rooting, in which religious groups and churches came to terms with their environment, and began to adapt to it; (3) the growth of independence, leading to the identification of the churches with Canada and labelling themselves (in the case of Presbyterians, for example) as being 'of Canada'; and (4) a willingness to examine the reasons for separate identity and to come together in broader groupings or in unions (as in the United Church of Canada, formed by the union of Methodists, Congregationalists and 65 per cent of Presbyterians in 1925). Yet in the case of smaller church bodies, which, for doctrinal or other reasons, stood rigidly apart from the main stream, Canada sometimes preserved (and continues to preserve) groups which had perished in Scotland in the early nineteenth century.

The first Scottish settlers in Canada had a strong Highland* element. Gaelic*-speaking RCs established themselves in Glengarry Co., Upper Canada, and in the Maritime Provinces from the 1780s. Following the end of the American War of Independence (1783), Loyalists of Scottish origin, including numerous RCs formerly resident in the province of New York, re-settled in Glengarry and Stormont Counties, thus reinforcing the Scottish presence. These colonies received their first Gaelic-speaking priest from Scotland, Roderick Macdonell, in 1785. With the assistance of Presbyterians (a point demonstrating the different religious climate in Canada) he built the church of St Andrew's, Stormont, in 1792. In 1786 another priest, Alexander 'Scotus' Macdonell, led emigrants from Knoydart to Glengarry Co. The first RC bishop of Upper Canada (appointed 1819) was a Gaelic-speaking Highland Scot, Alexander Macdonell,* whose name is commemorated in the town of Alexandria, Glengarry Co. Similarly, Angus Bernard MacEachern (1759–1835; *Dict. of Canad. Biogr.* VI, 447–51), arriving in 1790 in Prince Edward Island, where Highlanders had been settling since 1772, became the first RC bishop of Charlottetown (1829–35). In both Glengarry and eastern Nova Scotia, RC clergy of Scottish origin contributed to educational enterprises, and provided strong leadership in the social and political development of the colonies.

Settlement of Presbyterians in the Maritimes and in Upper and Lower Canada followed a broadly similar pattern. The Secession* Churches showed the way in adapting themselves to the New World. The Associate Synod* (Burgher) was the first Presbyterian body to provide Scottish emigrants with a minister, Samuel Kinloch, who came to Nova Scotia in 1766 (returning 1769). It was also the first to form a Synod in Canada, namely the Synod of Truro, Nova Scotia, in 1786. This was followed in 1795 by the formation of the General Associate Synod* (Antiburgher) of Pictou. As the Burgess Oath* was not of great significance in Canada, the two Synods merged as the Synod (or Presbyterian Church) of Nova Scotia in 1817 (*see* MacGregor, James, *d.*1820). In 1818 the Presbytery of the Canadas was formed, later becoming the United Synod. The early bodies of Seceders were drawn together by missionary and educational concerns, but initially remained estranged from the Est.C, whose first congregations were formed in Quebec (1765) and Montreal (*c.*1785) by George Henry (*d.*1795; *FES* VII, 637) and John Bethune* respectively.

The arrival of Presbyterian emigrants from Scotland led to requests for pastors, especially those of the Est.C. James MacGregor petitioned his own Synod, and tried to stimulate interest in Canada among CofS ministers. It was a hard struggle; only a comparatively small number of the latter were attracted across the Atlantic by the direct calls and entreaties of congregations (*see* MacLennan, John). The challenge was taken up by societies, particularly the Glasgow Colonial Society* (1825) and the Edinburgh Ladies' Association (*see* MacKay, Isabella). These societies were relatively successful in attracting ministers, but as they had a strongly evangelical commitment, they helped to sow the seeds of the Disruption* in Canada, an event which led to the formation of the Presbyterian Church of Canada in 1844. The protagonists who visited Canada to advocate Disruption principles included Robert Burns (*d.*1869),* Secretary of the Glasgow Colonial Society, while Norman MacLeod* (Caraid nan Gaidheal) advocated the cause of the Est.C.

Apart from the Seceders, the Presbyterian churches in Canada lacked initial missionary enthusiasm, and in the 'backwoods' they lost out to the endeavours of Methodists, Anglicans, Baptists and Independents. The last two bodies, in particular, were ready and willing to operate without the support of a parish system, and as they were prepared to utilize itinerant preachers and harness the pastoral gifts of laymen, they were better equipped to provide ministry to isolated groups of settlers.

Independents/Congregationalists and Baptists from Scotland began to enter Canada from the early 1800s. The Haldanes* sent a missionary, James Reid, to Martintown, Glengarry Co., in 1803, where he formed a Congregational church. Another Haldane missionary, Francis Dick, was active in Quebec (1805–12). In addition to missionaries specifically sent to Canada, several of the foundational pastors of the Independent and Baptist movement in Scotland emigrated to Canada, among them John Farquharson* (settling in Nova Scotia), Archibald MacCallum (from Kintyre, settling in New Brunswick in the 1820s), William McKillican (from Perthshire, settling in 1816 in Glengarry Co.) and Dugald Sinclair* (settling in Lobo, Ontario). Baptists from Perthshire formed a church in Lochiel Township, Glengarry Co., in 1817 (*see* Fraser, William). This remained a Baptist church. In south-western Ontario and Prince Edward Island, however, some Highland Baptists were influenced by the Disciples of Christ,* and helped to establish the Disciples (strong in the USA) in Canada. The dissenting bodies (including the Brethren,* some of whose early Scottish evangelists, like Donald Ross,* similarly emigrated to Canada) gained considerable followings at the expense of the larger denominations. They were also more liable to form close relationships with similar groups in the USA.

Although small independent missionary societies were active before 1840, missionary impetus among the Canadian churches developed most noticeably after 1844. In 1846 the Secession Synod of Nova Scotia sent John Geddie* and his wife as missionaries to the New Hebrides. Geddie was of Scottish parentage, and so too were a considerable number of Canada's earliest foreign missionaries. The visit of Alexander Duff* to Canada in 1854 had a 'startling' effect on missionary enthusiasm, which grew greatly into the 1870s and 1880s. Although early Presbyterian churches were established in Vancouver Island, British Columbia and Manitoba, the opening of what became western Canada (i.e. the prairie provinces and the North-west Territories) after 1867 provided a new stimulus to home mission. Scots helped to spearhead the western missions of several denominations. The westward expansion of the Presbyterian Church of Canada was led by James Robertson, from a FC background, who was appointed mission superintendent in 1881, remaining in post until his death in 1902. The Baptist thrust in the 1890s was led by Alexander Grant (d.1897), pastor latterly at Winnipeg, and a native of Strathspey. Both Robertson and Grant operated mainly in the North-west Territories.

The growing missionary interest of the Scottish–Canadian churches broadened their horizons (steering them away from an over-concern with 'Scottishness'), made them rub shoulders with the 'new Canadians' of non-Scottish origins, and produced a climate favourable to unions. In 1840 the United Synod of the Canadas merged with the CofS. In 1861 the Presbyterian Church of Canada (the largely independent equivalent of the Free Church of Scotland) joined with Canada's United Presbyterians (formed in 1847, as in Scotland, by the merging of the United Secession and Relief Churches) to constitute the Canada Presbyterian Church. In 1875 this body joined the majority of CofS congregations and the Presbyterian Church of the Lower Provinces, thereby forming the Presbyterian Church in Canada, based on the Westminster* standards but rejecting the concept of an established church (and thus losing some support). The union of 1875 was precipitated largely by Confederation, which called all prior Presbyterian configurations into question. The further union of 1925 (embracing Methodists, Congregationalists and Presbyterians) left a Presbyterian rump of 35 per cent, continuing as the Presbyterian Church in Canada.

The consequences of secessions, unions and 'continuing' bodies in both Scotland and Canada, with various surges of missionary interest, are reflected in the Canadian context before and after 1900. This makes the overall pattern complex, since denominations long since 'united' or indigenized re-emerge in new guises which owe little to their earlier forms. Thus, in 1834, United Secession missionaries from Scotland came to Canada, thereby adding another dimension to the Secession churches already in the country and introducing the United Presbyterians after 1847 (see Proudfoot, William). Since 1900, the FC of Scotland has replanted itself in Canada as a result of further emigration from Scotland, with FC churches presently in Vancouver and Toronto and formerly in Thunder Bay (Ontario). In 1953 the FC also received a group of congregations in Prince Edward Island which were formed originally by the ministry of Donald McDonald.* This has provided two associated FC presbyteries (Prince Edward Island, and Ontario and Western Canada). The Free Presbyterian Church* of Scotland had three congregations in Canada, but two of these are now identified with the Associated Presbyterian Churches.* Scots continue to serve in UCC and other Canadian pulpits, as well as in denominational colleges.

See also McCulloch, Thomas; Grant, George Monro.

J. W. Grant (ed.), *The Churches and the Canadian Experience* (Toronto, 1963); J. S. Moir, *Enduring Witness: A History of the Presbyterian Church in Canada* (Toronto, 1975); Richard W. Vaudry, *The Free Church in Victorian Canada 1844–61* (Waterloo, Ontario, 1989); W. S. Reid (ed.), *The Scottish Tradition in Canada* (Toronto, 1976), 93–126; G. N. M. Collins, *Annals of the Free Church of Scotland (1900–86)* (E, n.d.), 60–2; S. Ivison and F. Rosser, *The Baptists in Upper and Lower Canada before 1820* (Toronto, 1956); R. Butchart, *The Disciples of Christ in Canada since 1830* (Toronto, 1949); D. E. Meek, 'Evangelicalism and Emigration: Aspects of the Role of Dissenting Evangelicalism in Highland Emigration to Canada', in G. MacLennan (ed.), *Proceedings of the First North American Congress of Celtic Studies* (Ottawa, 1988), 15–35; W. S. Reid, *The Church of Scotland in Lower Canada* (Toronto, 1936).

D. E. Meek

Candida Casa, see Early Ecclesiastical Sites; Ninian; Whithorn.

Candlish, James Stuart (1835–97), theologian and FC leader. Born in Edinburgh, Candlish was the son of the great Disruption* leader, R. S. Candlish.* Educated at the University and New College,* Edinburgh, and in Erlangen and Berlin, he was ordained at Logiealmond, near Perth (1863), translated to Aberdeen East (1869), and elected Professor of Systematic Theology in the FC College, Glasgow, in 1872.

Regarded in his day as one of Scotland's most able theologians, he did not inherit his father's gifts for the public platform but quietly took his part in a theological revolution no less influential than the Disruption struggle. Until his appointment the Glasgow College had been a stronghold of conservatism but, along with A. B. Bruce,* Candlish turned it into a centre for the emerging liberal thought within the FC. He lent his energies to gaining acceptance for the new theological direction, being prominent as a proponent of biblical criticism during the Robertson Smith* case (*The Authority of Scripture Independent of Criticism*, E, 1877) and as an advocate of Confessional revision in the movement which led to the Declaratory Act* of 1892 (*The Relations of the Presbyterian Churches to the Confession of Faith*, G, 1886). His own writings owe much to the Calvinistic* theology in which he was reared,

CANDLISH, ROBERT SMITH

and include some outstanding exposition of the great evangelical themes. At the same time they are very sensitive to contemporary critical questions and candidly open up possible lines of reconstruction. Candlish's most important works were *The Kingdom of God Biblically and Historically Considered* (E, 1884), the Tenth Series of the Cunningham Lectures* and *The Christian Salvation* (E, 1899).

AFCS I, 51; *FCSR* May 1, 1897, 121-2.

K. R. Ross

Candlish, Robert Smith (1806-73), preacher and leader of the FC. Born in Edinburgh, the son of a medical teacher who died when his son was an infant, Candlish was educated at home by his mother and at Glasgow University. On graduation, he was a tutor at Eton for two years. Entering the CofS ministry he initially served assistantships at St Andrew's, Glasgow, and at Bonhill, and then in 1834 became minister of the leading Edinburgh church, St George's. He displayed great capacity as a preacher and furthered Church extension* in his large parish by using missionary assistants. He was instrumental in the formation of the *quoad sacra** parish of St Luke's.

In 1839 Candlish, who had not previously been active in ecclesiastical politics, made an outstanding speech in the General Assembly, rejecting compromise of the Church's spiritual liberty. In the following months he established himself as a major force among the Non-Intrusionists,* particularly through his speech in the Commission of Assembly on 11 December 1839 in which he proposed the suspension of the seven Strathbogie* ministers who had defied the General Assembly in the Marnoch Case. Candlish was also responsible for the important decision to appoint Hugh Miller* editor of *The Witness*.* By the summer of 1841 he considered the Disruption* inevitable and took a key part in the deliberations that led up to it.

After 1843 Candlish was second only to Thomas Chalmers* in his prestige in the new FC, and he was its most prominent figure between Chalmers' death in 1847 and his own a quarter of a century later, being Moderator in 1861. Candlish was an able administrator with a capacity for understanding and assimilating divergent viewpoints. In the early days of the FC he was a member of a deputation to England which sought to expound the principles of the new Church. In 1845 he toured the Highlands* and islands to investigate the position of the FC, and made forceful criticism of landlords who refused sites for churches. In 1846 he was appointed convener of the FC Education Committee, a post to which he devoted considerable energy, believing passionately in the importance of providing distinctively religious education. He also gave active support to a number of causes, notably sabbatarianism,* anti-Catholicism,* Christian missions* to the Jews, and union* between the FC and UPC. He took a leading part in the formation of the Evangelical Alliance,* but later lost enthusiasm for it. Candlish's *The Fatherhood of God* (E, 1865; ⁵1869-70, with a supplementary volume), the first

of the Cunningham Lectures,* created a considerable stir. He emphasized the sonship of believers in adoption and denied a universal fatherhood of God, properly speaking. Although many differences were largely verbal, he was severely criticized, particularly by T. J. Crawford.*

Candlish's theological prowess was recognized by his appointment to the Chair of Divinity at New College* in succession to Chalmers, although he later withdrew from this post in order to remain at St George's. In 1862 he was appointed Principal of New College. Some of his most notable writings were exegetical: *The Book of Genesis*, 2 vols (E, 1868); *The First Epistle of John* (E, 1877); *Life in a Risen Saviour* (E, 1858); *Paul's Epistle to the Ephesians* (E, 1875); *The Two Great Commandments* (L, 1860).

The Atonement (L, 1861); *Examination of Dr Maurice's Theological Essays* (L, 1854); *Reason and Revelation* (L, 1864); *Sermons* (E, 1874).

FES I, 106; *AFCS* I, 116-17; *DNB* VIII, 405; W. Wilson, *Memorials of Robert Smith Candlish, DD* (E, 1880); J. L. Watson, *Life of Robert Smith Candlish, DD* (E, 1882); *Disruption Worthies*, 139-46; R. Buchanan and R. Rainy, *In Memoriam R. S. Candlish, DD* (1873); A. L. Drummond and J. Bulloch, *The Church in Victorian Scotland, 1843-1874* (E, 1975); J. Macleod, *Scottish Theology* (E, ³1974), 271-5.

J. R. Wolffe

Canice, Kenneth, *see* Celtic Saints.

Canon Law, a term with several meanings. Its most usual modern signification is the canon law of the RC Church, epitomized in the *Code of Canon Law*, which governs within that Church. This was promulgated in 1917 and a revised Code in 1983 (ET, L, 1983 with Index, L, 1984). Canon law can also mean the law relating to the functioning of a denomination, but is usually restricted to an episcopal system.

Classical canon law was developed by the pre-Reformation RC Church, and as such the essence of many of its principles can be traced in Scottish church and civil legal history and principles. This systematization of the law and practice of the Church was in part modelled upon the codification of the Roman law embarked upon by the Emperor Justinian between AD 529 and 545 known collectively as the *Corpus Iuris Civilis* ('Body of Civil Law'). Amid the ruins of the disintegrating Empire and through the Dark Ages, the Church was the single fount of authority, though the sources of 'law' were many and inconsistent. In the twelfth century scholars (the Glossators) rediscovered and worked on the *Corpus*, seeking to produce a system of law for their own time. In parallel, the organization of the RC Church on the monarchical principle, which with the concept of bishoprics drew heavily on the Imperial constitutional model, also required systematization. The re-discovery of Roman law in the form of the Justinianic legislation, and notably the *Digest* of AD 533, provided a model which eventually resulted in the *Corpus Iuris Canonici* (many eds), although that was constantly added to by interpretation and further legislation. (The *Corpus Iuris Canonici* is really a bibliographical term used since 1671 for the body of various collections of papal and other decisions beginning with the *Decretum* of Gratian (1148) and including the fivebook *Compilationes* of Gregory IX (1234), the *Liber Sextus* of Boniface VIII (1298) and the Clementines (1317).) Thereafter the canonists discussed and extended the principles in the *Corpus*, seeking to make them more relevant and to infuse rule with theological principle.

Although, as indicated, much of canon law had to do with the organization of the Church, other matters where law and morality interact were also covered by it. These include marriage (including dowr and nullity of marriage as well as the related matter of succession), economic questions (including usury and the 'just price'), and concepts such as promise (unilateral obligation) and of good and bad faith in contract were developed. In criminal law the notion of intention was explored. Thus 'blame' was discussed by the canonists and prison came to be seen in part as a place of repentance rather than of vengeance.

Canon law was enforced through church courts, with the aid of the civil arm as required. So in Scotland marriage law and its accoutrements of status and inheritance were church matters, leading to the Commissary courts.

Even before the Reformation, and certainly after it, the direct impact of canon law was lessened, but most areas of law which have moral connotations contain more than traces of the concepts of canon law.

D. B. Smith, 'Canon Law', in *The Sources and Literature of Scots Law*, The Stair Society, vol. 1 (E, 1936), 183-92; *An Introduction to Scottish Legal History*, The Stair Society, vol. 28 (E, 1958), virtually *passim*; F. W. Maitland, *Roman Canon Law in the Church of England* (L, 1898); R. H. Helmholz, *Canon Law and the Law of England* (L, 1987).

F. Lyall

Canons, Book of (1636), a code of government for the CofS drawn up at the instigation of Charles I.* Its full title was, 'Canons and Constitutions Ecclesiastical gathered and put in Forme for the Government of the Church of Scotland. Ratified and approved by His Majesties Royall Warrand and ordained to be observed by the Clergie and all others whom they concerne.' Put together apparently by four Scottish bishops (Galloway, Aberdeen, Ross and Dunblane), who based them on the 1604 English model, and embodying the Five Articles of Perth,* the Canons were then edited by Archbishop Laud* and Bishop Juxon of London, and their nineteen chapters covering forty-three pages were authorized to be printed in 1635. They declared the King to be head of the CofS, and pronounced excommunication on those who denied this. The Book then deals with the training and ordination of presbyters and deacons, and rules for the conduct of worship and for general pastoral behaviour. There were to be synod meetings, but none in presbytery, session and conventicle. Extempore prayers, or prayers not in the Liturgy, were not to be used. Worshippers were commanded to kneel at prayer, stand at the Creed, and not leave before worship was ended. Ministers were banned from participating in civil affairs, private baptism was allowed in cases of necessity, and the confessional was sanctioned. The Canons reflected a drastic exercise of the royal power, and a misunderstanding of the Scottish situation by King and Archbishop. Reaction to the Canons helped pave the way for the National Covenant.* With the *Book of Common Prayer** of 1637, the Canons were condemned by the Glasgow Assembly* of 1638 and, with the King's agreement, rejected by the 1639 Assembly as containing 'Popish errors and establishing tyrannicall power over the Kirk, in the person of Bishops...' (*AGACS*, 36-7).

D. H. Fleming, *Scotland's Supplication* (E, 1927), 49-53.

J. D. Douglas

Cant, Andrew (the elder, 1590-1663), Covenanter.* Minister at St Nicholas, Aberdeen, 1641-60, Cant was an enthusiastic supporter of the National Covenant* and accompanied Alexander Henderson* on a delegation to Aberdeen to persuade the citizens to join.

Educated in Aberdeen at the Grammar School and King's College (MA, 1612), Cant was minister at Alford, Aberdeenshire, 1617-29. He demitted to become tutor to the son of Lord Forbes of Pitsligo, Aberdeenshire, by whom he was presented to the new parish of Pitsligo in 1633. He was a member of the Glasgow Assembly* of 1638. He was translated to Newbattle, Midlothian, in 1639 and served as chaplain with the Covenanting army at Newcastle in 1640. He is said to have been deposed for circulating Samuel Rutherford's* *Lex Rex*. He was Moderator of the General Assembly in 1650. His son Andrew (*d.*1685; *FES* I, 65) became Principal of Edinburgh University; his daughter Sarah married Alexander Jaffray.*

DNB VIII, 446; *FES* VI, 37-8.

H. R. Sefton

Carberry Tower, residential conference centre of the CofS. Formerly the home of the Elphinstone family and set in a woodland park of thirty-five acres near Musselburgh (Midlothian), it was gifted in 1961 to the CofS and opened by the Church's Department of Education in 1962 for use as a youth leadership and training centre. Responsibility passed to the Church's Mission Committee in 1986.

Courses are run each autumn and spring for church office-bearers and young people, and in the summer it is used for holiday weeks and the Carberry Festival. In addition courses are run for those about to retire, for young workers from industry, and also around a variety of themes relating Chris-

Cardross Case (1859–62), legal case in which the FC came into collision with the civil courts. A FC minister, John MacMillan, of Cardross in Dunbarton (*AFCS* I, 251), had been charged with immoral conduct on two counts. His Presbytery found him guilty on the second count. The case went by appeal to the General Assembly of 1859, in which the Assembly convicted MacMillan on both counts, despite his protest that the Church's constitution entitled it to rule only on the second count on which Presbytery had convicted him. He appealed to the civil courts, which issued an injunction preventing the Assembly, under penalty of libel, from publishing its censure against MacMillan on the first count. The Assembly deposed MacMillan from the ministry for resorting to the courts; he raised a civil action for damages.

MacMillan's claim for damages was ultimately dismissed on the grounds that no such action could be raised against an unincorporated body like the General Assembly. But the FC was compelled to face the fact that its ecclesiastical decisions could come under civil jurisdiction if those decisions had civil consequences, even to the extent of a party's right as to his social repute. The decisions of the Est.C's courts were not thus subject, since its established status gave them a co-ordinate jurisdiction with the civil courts.

See also Craigdallie Case; Church and State.

A. Taylor Innes, *The Law of Creeds in Scotland* (E, 1867), ch. V; A. M. Hunter, 'The Cardross Case', *RSCHS* 7 (1941), 247–58; F. Lyall, *Of Presbyters and Kings* (A, 1980), 90–101.

N. R. Needham

Carfin Grotto, RC shrine. In 1920 Thomas N. Taylor (1873–1963), RC parish priest of Carfin, a small mining town in Lanarkshire, decided to build a replica of Lourdes grotto. The work was done voluntarily by unemployed parishioners. It was opened 1922 and pilgrimages, small at first, were organized. Its popularity was astounding: 250,000 came in three months in 1923, and 50,000 worshippers on one occasion in 1924. More ground was acquired, and more shrines and replicas of pilgrimage places built. After the war 50,000 pilgrims came one day in 1948, and 35,000 children with 500 teachers on one pilgrimage in 1951.

An annual Corpus Christi procession through public streets attracted over 50,000 in 1923 but was banned in 1924 following an objection based on the Catholic Emancipation* Act of 1829. The resulting protests led to the Roman Catholic Relief Act (1926) removing such disabilities. From 1974, national pilgrimages in honour of St Margaret* and St John Ogilvie* have used Carfin Grotto.

See also Catholic Truth Society of Scotland.

T. N. Taylor, *The Carfin Grotto* (G, 1952); S. McGhee, 'Carfin and the Roman Catholic Relief Act of 1926', *IR* 16 (1965), 56–78.

M. Dilworth

Cargill, David (1806–43), Wesleyan missionary and linguist. He was born in Brechin, the son of a banker. Attending King's College, Aberdeen (MA, 1830), he came to evangelical conversion in the Methodist chapel. In 1831 he offered for ministerial service anywhere; next year he was appointed to Tonga, with an ultimate view to Fiji. He married Margaret Smith of Aberdeen. Unusually well educated for a Methodist missionary, and far beyond his immediate colleagues, he progressed well in Tongan language studies. In 1835 he was moved to Fiji, becoming with William Cross the first European missionary there. He worked first on Lakeba and then on Rewa, and was the first chairman of the Fiji district. While continuing comparative studies in Tongan he advanced the study of Fijian, leaving a manuscript grammar (Lakeba dialect) and dictionary and supervising early Bible translations. His most enduring memorial is the current Fijian orthography. In hard, and sometimes dangerous, situations, Cargill was often at odds with his colleagues; the culture gap between them frequently showed. In 1840 his wife, on whom he heavily depended, died in distressing circumstances. Grieving, he took his children to Britain for a year. While there he wrote a spirited defence of the Tonga missionaries against the published attacks of the Catholic seaman Peter Dillon. In London he remarried and was reappointed to Tonga in 1842. But he was a broken man, disillusioned by Christian declension in Tonga since his earlier sojourn, and drinking too much. His death on 25 April 1843 was interpreted at the time as suicide; evidence now suggests acute mental disorder brought on by dengue fever.

'A brief essay on the Feejeean language', *Report of the Wesleyan Methodist Missionary Society* (1840), appendix; *Memoirs of Mrs Margaret Cargill* (L, 1841); *A Refutation of Chevalier Dillon's Slanderous Attacks on the Wesleyan Missionaries in the Friendly Islands* (L, 1842).

A. J. Schütz (ed.), *The Diaries and Correspondence of David Cargill 1832–1843* (Canberra, 1977); Mora Dickson, *The Inseparable Grief: Margaret Cargill of Fiji* (L, 1976); N. Gunson, *Messengers of Grace: Evangelical Missionaries in the South Seas 1797–1860* (Melbourne, 1978).

A. F. Walls

Cargill, Donald (c.1627–81), Covenanter* and field-preacher.* Born at Rattray in Perthshire the son of a local notary, Cargill was educated to follow his father in the law, but an intense spiritual experience in early manhood determined him to devote himself to the work of the ministry. He studied divinity under Samuel Rutherford* at St Andrews, and was ordained to the Barony Church, Glasgow, in March 1655. In April 1656 he married Margaret Brown, widow of Andrew Beaton of Blebo in Fife, but she died within four months of their marriage.

CARLYLE, ALEXANDER

Cargill opposed the introduction of episcopacy* in the Church following the restoration of Charles II,* and his failure to conform to the new ecclesiastical order led to his expulsion from his charge in 1662 and to his banishment to the north of the Tay. When the banishment order was relaxed in 1669, Cargill took up residence near Glasgow, where he joined the growing band of ministers who were preaching in the fields (*see* Field Preaching). Cargill refused to accept the indulgences offered to ministers by the government, and as the persecution of the non-complying ministers intensified, he came increasingly into public prominence. After Bothwell Bridge,* where he was wounded, he went over briefly to Holland, but returned and joined Richard Cameron* for some months of field-preaching in the summer of 1680 until Cameron's death at Ayrsmoss.* In the following September he held a great meeting at Torwood, near Stirling, where he publicly excommunicated Charles II and some of his leading officers of state. This action greatly incensed the authorities against him, and a large reward was offered for his capture. After some further months of constant preaching, during which he escaped narrowly several times, he was finally captured at Covington Mill, near Lanark, and on being tried and convicted for treason was executed at the Cross of Edinburgh on 27 July 1681.

Though diffident and self-deprecating by nature, Cargill was nevertheless able to act decisively in any matter which he saw as a legitimate concern of the ministerial office. In his personal life he exercised the strictest discipline and self-control. As a preacher, he spoke searchingly to the consciences of his hearers, gaining immense respect. For many, his abiding legacy was the steadfast endurance he displayed in asserting the historic claims of the Church at a time of intense testing and trial.

FES III, 393–3; *DNB* IX, 79–80; M. Grant, *No King but Christ* (Darlington, 1988); W. H. Carlsaw, *Life and Times of Donald Cargill* (Paisley, 1900); P. Walker, *Six Saints of the Covenant* (ed. D. Hay Fleming, E, 1901) II, 1–62; J. Howie, *Scots Worthies* (ed. W. H. Carslaw, E, 1871), 439–53; *Cloud of Witnesses* (ed. J. H. Thomson, E, 1871), 1–26, 501–10.

M. Grant

Carlyle, Alexander (1722–1805), controversial parish minister and writer also known as 'Jupiter Carlyle' because of his commanding presence and white hair. Born in Prestonpans, Midlothian, he attended Edinburgh University (MA, 1743) and was licensed by Haddington Presbytery in 1746. For most of his life (from 1748) he was minister of Inveresk (or Musselburgh). A man of learning and witty conversation, open-minded and agreeable in polite company, he possessed an unrivalled opportunity to be a spectator and actor in nearby Edinburgh's literary scene at the time of the Enlightenment,* without being himself completely caught up in the capital and its ecclesiastical politics. In a lifetime of controversy, Carlyle was concerned with the politics of writing and of theatre:

CARLYLE, THOMAS

his practice gave a visible model to the Moderate* clergy who could reconcile participation in the Enlightenment and interest in creative (particularly theatrical) literature with the exercise of a Presbyterian* calling. A friend of Garrick's and of John Home's, he assisted the latter in the preparation of *Douglas* and endangered his career (though not fatally) by attending an early performance, earning the censure of many less liberal clergy in the Church. A lively friend also of Tobias Smollett, William Robertson, David Hume* and their circle, he was a minister who moved without embarrassment in aristocratic circles. Carlyle also participated in a vigorous climate of intellectual activity which he records with marvellous energy and humour in his autobiography. He travelled widely; his memoirs of Oxford life are witty and incisive. His memoirs were begun, he notes, on the first day of his seventy-ninth year but, as splendidly edited by James Kinsley in 1973, they emerge as an undoubted masterpiece of autobiography and literary memoir.

J. Kinsley (ed.), *Alexander Carlyle: Anecdotes and Characters of the Times* (O, 1973), previously published as *Autobiography*, ed. J. H. Burton (L, 1910); R. B. Sher, *Church and University in the Scottish Enlightenment* (Princeton and E, 1985); *FES* I, 326–7; *DNB* IX, 106–8.

I. Campbell

Carlyle, Thomas (1795–1881), Scotland's greatest Victorian, and one of its greatest writers. Born in Ecclefechan, Dumfriesshire, he studied in Edinburgh and worked there for many years as teacher, translator and writer. An early interest in science and mathematics gave way to German literature and thought, to a series of translations from Goethe and ground-breaking essays on German literature. A growing social consciousness at a time of hectic reform, sharpened by a peripheral viewpoint in Edinburgh and later in a hilly farm near Dumfries, led to a dazzling series of essays on his society, culminating with *Sartor Resartus* (1833), still underestimated for its innovation, with its incisive condemnation of a worn-out orthodoxy. The move to London in 1834 was followed by a series of books which propelled Carlyle to fame: *The French Revolution*, 3 vols (L, 1837), *Chartism* (L, 1839), *Heroes and Hero-Worship* (L, 1841), *Past and Present* (L, 1843), *Cromwell*, 2 vols (L, 1845), *Latter-Day Pamphlets* (L, 1850) and *Frederick the Great*, 6 vols (L, 1858–65). As he aged, he moved to a more conservative position, and the early radicalism gave way to a thunderous denunciation of the rottenness of his age. With his brilliant wife Jane (1801–66), Carlyle was Victorian London's outstanding conversationalist, and their letters are the masterpiece of their century. Possessing unforgettable style and pulsating energy in writing and speech, Carlyle captivated his age, and his death was treated as the end of an era. He outlived most of the eminent Victorian writers, and can fairly be said to have influenced most of them.

Carlyle's ideas are vivid and simple: an ordered universe reflected in an ordered society; duty and obedience within that order; the necessity of work; the inevitability of retribution when the order is flouted. Not himself a Christian after his Ecclefechan years despite the strength of his parents' piety, Carlyle never entirely threw off their Burgher (see Associate Synod) influence, though he mixed it liberally with features of German transcendentalism to produce a philosophy easily absorbed, easily understood (or giving the impression of being easily understood) and easily translated into strong, simple dictates. The result inspired an age; Carlyle's message emerges, transformed and often humanized, in the writings of almost all his contemporaries, perhaps most remarkably in the major fiction of the nineteenth century.

Essential Works (Santa Cruz: 1991–); *The Collected Letters of Thomas and Jane Welsh Carlyle* (Durham, NC: 21 vols, 1970–93; ongoing).
F. Kaplan, *Thomas Carlyle* (C, 1983); I. Campbell, *Thomas Carlyle* (L, 1974).

I. Campbell

Carmelite Friars. In origin they were hermits established at Mount Carmel in Palestine in the twelfth century. Brought to Europe, they were classed as mendicant friars* in 1229, which introduced tensions between their contemplative vocation and their new apostolate of teaching and preaching. The early history of their Scottish foundations is obscure. The first may have been at Tullilum near Perth in 1262, but this is unsubstantiated until the early fourteenth century. The house at Berwick, reputedly founded in 1270, was perhaps the first foundation, although Aberdeen (under construction in 1273) also vies for this honour. Others followed at Irvine, in Ayrshire (*c.*1273), Luffness in E. Lothian (*c.*1293); Banff (1321–3); Linlithgow (*c.*1403) and Queensferry on the Firth of Forth (1440–1). Inverbervie in Kincardineshire was founded before 1443, followed by Kingussie in Perthshire before 1501 and finally Edinburgh (1520–5).

The Carmelites were known as White Friars, from their white cloak worn over a brown habit, and their priories were dedicated to the Blessed Virgin Mary. Their communities averaged three or four friars and some may have been as tiny as a prior and a single friar. All told, there were probably no more than forty members of the order in Scotland, at least in the sixteenth century, although archaeological evidence at Aberdeen, Linlithgow and Tullilum suggests buildings designed for larger communities (J. Stones, ed., *Three Scottish Carmelite Friaries*, Society of Antiquaries of Scotland, E, 1989). The Scottish houses were in 1291–4 separated from the English province. In the sixteenth century they shared in the movement to raise the standard of religious life, and fear of their influence as orthodox preachers may have contributed to the destruction of their houses at the Reformation (D. McRoberts, ed., *Essays on the Scottish Reformation*, G, 1962, 209–11, 238, 446).

The great reform movement led by St Teresa of Avila and St John of the Cross led to the formation of the Discalced (barefoot) Carmelites, who now outnumber the original body. Both branches have come to Scotland in modern times: Carmelite friars in Glasgow 1978, discalced friars in Glasgow 1988, while there have been several communities of discalced nuns since 1918 (see Religious Orders).

New Catholic Encyclopedia III, 114–22; Easson-Cowan, 134–9; K. Egan, 'Medieval Carmelite Houses, Scotland', *Carmelus* 19 (1972), 107–12.

I. B. Cowan

Carment, David (1772–1856), FC minister. Born at Keiss in Caithness, he studied at King's College, Aberdeen, both arts (MA, 1795) and then theology, while supporting himself as a schoolmaster in Strath, on the Isle of Skye. From 1803–10 he was assistant minister to Hugh Calder at Croy in Nairn. As minister of Duke Street Gaelic Chapel, Glasgow, from 1810, he attained great popularity as a preacher. In 1822 he moved to Rosskeen, in Rossshire, as colleague and (1824) successor to John Ross. Here Carment fell out with 'The Men'* in his district. Such a rupture was usually lethal to a minister's reputation, but Carment carried his congregation with him.

Carment joined the FC in 1843, although not until a month after the Disruption;* he felt the Non-Intrusionists* should have continued their struggle longer against the civil courts. A new church was opened in 1845 for him and his congregation in Achnagarron.

Carment was a frequent and forceful speaker in Church courts, and one of the first in the CofS to argue for the admission of chapel-of-ease* ministers as members of Presbyteries.

Biographical sketch in his *Memoir of the Rev. James Carment* (Dalkeith, 1886); *Disruption Worthies*, 147–52; *FES* VII, 69; *AFCS* I, 117.

N. R. Needham

Carmichael, Alexander (1832–1912), Gaelic* folklorist. Born in Lismore, Argyll, he exploited the opportunities afforded by his employment as an exciseman, which included postings in Islay, Skye, Uist and Oban, to develop his interest in Gaelic antiquities, and between 1855 and 1899 amassed an enormous collection of varied Gaelic lore. He published papers on antiquarian topics in *Transactions of the Society of Antiquaries of Scotland*, *Transactions of the Gaelic Society of Inverness* and the *Celtic Review*, and contributed material to the published volumes of other collectors. He wrote a chapter on Highland land customs for W. F. Skene's *Celtic Scotland* (E, 1880) and the *Report on Crofting* (E, 1884).

His great monument, however, is the six volumes of *Carmina Gadelica* (E, 1900–71), which present a rich gleaning from the great harvest of his work as a collector. He personally edited the first two volumes, the reprint of 1928 being supervised by his daughter, Elizabeth. His grandson, James Carmichael Watson, edited volumes III and IV. Volumes V and VI were prepared by Angus Matheson,

CARMICHAEL, JAMES

whose work on volume VI was completed by William Matheson. Volume IV contains tributes to Carmichael by Professor Donald MacKinnon and Kenneth MacLeod.*

The material consists mainly of invocations, blessings and charms which relate to many aspects of the religious and daily life of Gaelic-speaking Highlanders, and which have, in many cases, clearly filtered down in the oral tradition from medieval times. Carmichael encountered in some informants a reluctance to divulge practices and traditions which later evangelical zeal had frowned on. The simplicity and directness of the piety expressed in these verse prayers have given them an enduring appeal to people who encounter them in English translation. Carmichael's own lavish volumes contain translations, and separate volumes of translation only have been published, notably A. Bittleston (ed.), *The Sun Dances* (E, 1960) and G. R. D. Maclean, *Poems of the Western Highlanders* (L, 1961). Items from Carmichael's collection continue to appear in popular manuals of devotion. Hamish Robertson, in 'Studies in Carmichael's *Carmina Gadelica*' (*Scottish Gaelic Studies* 12 (1976), 220–65) casts some doubt on Carmichael's integrity as an editor, but J. L. Campbell, in 'Notes on Hamish Robertson's "Studies in Carmichael's *Carmina Gadelica*"' (*Scottish Gaelic Studies* 13 (1978), 1–17) comes to his defence, pointing out that he was dealing with the debris of a long tradition, and was striving to produce tidy and literary versions of the items before him.

K. D. MacDonald

Carmichael, James (c.1543–1628), minister and Presbyterian Reformer. He graduated from St Leonard's College, St Andrews, c.1564, and was master of the grammar schools at St Andrews and then Haddington, where he became minister in 1570, being joined as assistant by Walter Balcanquhal* in 1573. He was one of the drafters of the *Second Book of Discipline*,* but in 1584–7 had to take refuge in England after supporting the Ruthven Raiders'* detention of James VI.* During his exile he remained active in the Presbyterian* cause (maintaining his English Puritan links after his return) and particularly in collecting an arsenal of documents. In the 1590s, at the General Assembly's request he compiled a record of all Assembly acts (now in MS in Aberdeen University Library). In 1607 the Assembly appointed him constant Moderator of Haddington Presbytery. Although he had had to give up his schoolmastership in 1576, he published a textbook on Latin grammar and etymology (*Grammaticae Latinae...*, C, 1587), collected Scots proverbs (M. L. Anderson, *The James Carmichael Collection of Proverbs in Scots*, E, 1957), proof-read Sir John Skene's edition of the Scots legal corpus, *Regiam Majestatem*, and on his death left a MS diary used in David Calderwood's* history. He was the brother-in-law of the more ardent Presbyterians, Archibald* and Patrick Simson.*

FES I, 369; J. Kirk, 'The Development of the Melvillian Movement in Late Sixteenth Century Scotland' (PhD, Edinburgh University, 1972), 586–9; *SBD* 154f.

D. F. Wright

Carmichael, Robert (d.1774), Antiburgher Secession minister and later a Scotch Baptist* elder. Carmichael was a schoolmaster in London in 1751, and later minister at Coupar Angus. In 1757 he read Sandeman's* *Letters on Theron and Aspasio*, and by 1761 was in touch with J. Glas,* and in trouble with Synod. He was deposed by the Associate Synod* in 1763 for holding Independent* views, and became an elder in the Glasgow Glasite church. He left with A. McLean* over a case of discipline and became an elder at the Independent church in Edinburgh in 1764. In 1765 he changed his views on baptism and was immersed in London by John Gill. On his return he baptized seven people at Canonmills, and was elder in the Edinburgh Scotch Baptist church, moving to Dundee in 1769. He preached at the first baptisms in Montrose, and returned to Edinburgh shortly before his death in 1774.

P. Wilson, *The Origin and Progress of the Scots Baptist Churches* (E, 1844); D. W. Bebbington (ed.), *The Baptists in Scotland* (G, 1988).

D. B. Murray

Carmina Gadelica, see Carmichael, Alexander.

Carnegie, Andrew (1835–1919), philanthropist. Carnegie was the son of a damask linen weaver in Dunfermline. He became legendary in his own lifetime for his remarkable wealth and, later, for his patronage of educational and other causes. His family emigrated to Allegheny, Pennsylvania, in 1848. Carnegie worked initially as a telegraph operator, but after some shrewd investments became increasingly interested in heavy industry, capitalizing on American railroad development after the Civil War. Carnegie Brothers and Company were estimated to have capital of around five million dollars by 1881. By 1888 his personal wealth had increased sixty times over. Carnegie retained his links with Scotland, and established various trusts. Buying the estate of Skibo in Sutherland he built a mansion and saw himself as a Scottish Highland laird.

Carnegie's father embraced the Swedenborgian faith (see New Jerusalem Church). His mother was a Unitarian* and the sister of one of Dunfermline's leading Chartists.* He espoused latterly a gospel of benevolence (expounded in his *Gospel of Wealth*, published in 1900), but appears to have had no formal religious commitment.

DNB 1912–21, 91–4; A. Wall, *Andrew Carnegie* (O, 1970); B. J. Hendrick, *The Life of Andrew Carnegie* (L, 1933).

G. F. C. Jenkins

Carslaw, William Henderson (1837–1926), FC minister and author. The son of John Carslaw, a RP minister in Airdrie, Carslaw studied at Glasgow

University (DD, 1901), the RP theological hall, the FC colleges in Glasgow and Edinburgh, and in Germany. He was ordained to the Free Park Church, Helensburgh, in 1862 as its first minister and remained there until his resignation in 1898.

He is best known for editing and writing a number of works relating to the Covenanters.* He edited J. Howie, *The Scots Worthies* (E, 1870) and *The Life and Letters of James Renwick the Last Scottish Martyr* (E, 1893). He wrote three volumes on *Heroes of the Covenant: Life and Times of Donald Cargill* (Paisley, 1900), *Life and Times of William Guthrie* (Paisley, 1900) and *Life and Times of James Renwick* (Paisley, 1900). Other works on the Covenanters include *Exiles of the Covenant* (Paisley, 1908) and *Covenanting Memorials in Glasgow & Neighbourhood* (G, 1912).

Six Martyrs of the Scottish Reformation (Paisley, 1907); *The Early Christian Apologists* (L, 1912).

AFCS I, 118, II, 86; *FUFCS* 272; W. J. Couper, *The Reformed Presbyterian Church in Scotland* (E, 1925), 108–9, 40–1.

D. C. Lachman

Carstares, William (1649–1715), CofS minister and confidant of William of Orange. Carstares was born on 11 February 1649, eleven days after the death of Charles I.* His father, John Carstairs (*sic*) was minister of Cathcart near Glasgow, an ardent Covenanter* and later Protester.* William was educated at Edinburgh College and then in Utrecht. In Holland, where there were many Presbyterian exiles, he was introduced to William of Orange and soon involved in under-cover relations with the discontented in Scotland and England. He spent the years 1675–79 in prison in Edinburgh Castle. In 1681 he became minister of a Presbyterian church at Theobalds in Hertfordshire. He probably played no part in the Rye House Plot to kill the King and Duke of York, but he knew of it and was believed to be involved. Captured at Tenterden, imprisoned in London, he was sent by ship with others to Scotland where torture was still legal. Thumbscrews and 'boot' were applied, after which he gave information on condition that it would never be used against any other; but it was, against Baillie of Jerviswood. Released after a confinement in Stirling Castle, Carstares returned to Holland and became Chaplain to William of Orange and a minister in Leiden. He accompanied the Prince to Torbay and was a close adviser and confidant, almost constantly with him, in Ireland, England and Holland until William's death in 1702. William III was never in Scotland and he relied heavily on Carstares for information and opinion on the situation north of the border. In spite of the King's personal desire for uniformity of Church order in both countries, he was persuaded that the Scottish bishops were Jacobite* and that his real friends were the Presbyterians who had suffered greatly during the Stewart period. He concurred in the decision to establish the CofS as Presbyterian and allow the General Assembly to meet.

The State Papers indicate the power Carstares wielded behind the scenes, leading some to call him 'The Cardinal'. When Queen Anne succeeded, Carstares settled in Scotland and became Principal of the 'Toun's College' in Edinburgh. In 1704 he was also minister of Greyfriars and in 1706 of the High Kirk. He was largely responsible for remodelling the College on the Dutch system of faculties and preparing the way for the University of Edinburgh to lead in the Enlightenment.* He was Moderator of the Assembly in 1705, 1708, 1711 and 1715 and Chaplain to Queen Anne and George I. Very influential in Church circles, he was strongly in favour of the Union of 1707.

Moderate, wise, strong and yet conciliatory, he saw it as his task to nurse the new Presbyterian Church government through the years of Queen Anne, when there was great pressure from England to restore episcopacy. He died on 23 December 1715 after George I had succeeded and the 1715 Rebellion had failed, knowing that his work had not been in vain.

R. H. Story, *William Carstares* (L, 1874); A. Ian Dunlop, *William Carstares and the Kirk by Law Established* (E, 1967); *DNB* IX, 187–90; *FES* I, 66–7; J. McCormick (ed.), *State Papers and Letters, addressed to William Carstares* (E, 1774).

A. I. Dunlop

Carswell, John (*d.c.*1572), translator and adapter of John Knox's *Book of Common Order*ticularly into Gaelic.* Carswell's family may have originated in Corsewall, Wigtownshire, and probably became established in Argyll through the Campbells, some of whom held land in Galloway. Carswell himself had close links with Archibald Campbell, fifth Earl of Argyll.* Graduating MA from St Andrews in 1544, he acted as a notary public in the diocese of the Isles. Becoming treasurer of the Cathedral Church of Lismore (in the diocese of Argyll) by 1550, he had succeeded to the parsonage of Kilmartin by 1553. Thereafter he received several significant grants of land from the Earl of Argyll, and also custody of Carnassery Castle in February 1559. He evidently supported his patron in his adoption of the Reformed faith, and in 1560 he became Superintendent* of Argyll. In 1565 Carswell obtained the bishopric of the Isles from Queen Mary, and became commendator* of Iona.*

Carswell's interests embraced literary matters. At some stage he received training in a bardic school, and learned to write Classical Common Gaelic, the language employed by the Gaelic literati of Ireland and Scotland. He translated the *Book of Common Order* into this literary dialect. Published in 1567, it was the first Gaelic printed book to appear in Ireland or Scotland. Carswell, however, modified parts of the original text, so that it reflected more closely the polity of the churches under the sway of the Earl of Argyll, to whom the book was dedicated.

See also Catechisms (Gaelic); Gaelic, Protestant Prose Publications in.

R. L. Thomson (ed.), *Foirm na n-Urrnuidheadh* (E, 1970); D. E. Meek and J. Kirk, 'John Carswell,

CARTHUSIANS

Superintendent of Argyll: A Reassessment,' *RSCHS* 19 (1975), 1–22; *FES* VII, 348.

D. E. Meek

Carthusians. In 1084 St Bruno (*c*.1030–1101) and six companions settled as hermits in the mountains of La Grande Chartreuse near Grenoble. (The Latin name of the place, Cartusia, gave the appellation Carthusian, while Charterhouse in English is a corruption of Chartreuse.) Similar colonies multiplied and the first chapter of superiors was held in 1140. Carthusian observance owes much to the Benedictine* rule but differs in two notable ways. It is uncompromisingly austere, whereas St Benedict aimed at moderation, and the emphasis is on solitude and silence rather than the common life. Its almost exclusive aim is to promote prayer and union with God.

During most of the year only one meal is taken. Meat is never allowed, and on Fridays only bread and water. A hair-shirt is always worn, and each night's sleep is split by the choir office. The monks go to the church three times daily, for mass, vespers and the night office. On Sundays and feast-days they have meals in the refectory, followed by recreation in common. Once a week they take a long walk together. Apart from these occasions they are in their cells, dividing their time between prayer, study and manual work. These cells are small two-storey houses with garden and covered walkway, built round the great cloister. Laybrothers, needed to serve the needs of the solitaries, follow a similar horarium but live more in common and work in various capacities.

There were in 1521 about 200 Charterhouses. After many suppressions over the last two centuries, they number about twenty today. The order is highly centralized, the general superior being the prior of the Grande Chartreuse. A general chapter has usually met there annually, which local priors were required to attend. The Carthusian order is said to have never been reformed, because never deformed. It never suffered from commendators.* In the eighteenth century successful action was taken against leanings towards Jansenism.*

The only Scottish Charterhouse was founded in 1429 just outside Perth for thirteen monks with attendant laybrothers. It at once attracted Scottish recruits and an abbot of Holyrood* resigned *c*.1497 to enter the house. In 1478 it had fifteen monks and two laybrothers, in 1529 and 1544 thirteen monks, in 1558 eleven monks. All the later names recorded are Scots.

The monastery was destroyed in 1559 by a reforming mob. Six monks went to Charterhouse abroad, two became Protestants in Perth. Six monks dying in the period 1519–69 were given the rare honour '*laudabiliter vixit*' (lived in a praiseworthy manner), indicating that for fifty years their cloistered life had been without reproach. This constitutes an almost unparalleled record in Carthusian history.

Long before the Perth foundation, Adam* of Dryburgh had become a Carthusian in England. William Chisholm II,* former bishop of Dunblane,

CASKIE, DONALD CURRIE

entered the Grande Chartreuse *c*.1584. The superiors of the Scots College,* Paris, were the priors of the local Charterhouse.

Catholic Encyclopedia III, 388–92; *New Catholic Encyclopedia* III, 161–8; E. M. Thompson, *The Carthusian Order in England* (L, 1930); J. Ferguson, 'The Carthusian Order in Scotland', *Trans. Scottish Ecclesiological Society* III (1910–11), 179–92; R. S. Fittis, *Ecclesiastical Annals of Perth* (E, 1885), 212–64; W. N. M. Beckett, 'The Perth Charterhouse before 1500', *Analecta Cartusiana* 128 (1988), i–xii, 1–74; A. Hogg, 'Sidelights on the Perth Charterhouse', *IR* 19 (1968), 168–9; M. Dilworth, 'Monks and Ministers after 1560', *RSCHS* 18 (1974), 204–6.

M. Dilworth

Carver, Robert (fl.1546), composer. Born between 1487 and 1490, he became an Augustinian* canon of Scone* when aged sixteen. He signed Scone documents 1544–66 (SRO, RH6); he also signed himself 'alias Arnat'. A manuscript volume in the National Library of Scotland (Adv. 5.1.15) contains his musical compositions. A Mass for ten voices, *Dum sacrum mysterium*, was probably composed for the coronation of James V at Stirling in 1513; Carver was very possibly connected with the Chapel Royal* there. Other compositions include a Mass dated 1546 and an impressive motet for nineteen voices, *O bone Jesu*. Carver's music, widely praised for its beauty, originality and technical skill, has recently, after long neglect, been published and performed.

K. Elliott in *The New Grove Dictionary of Music and Musicians* III, 842–3; *id.*, 'The Carver choir-book', *Music and Letters* 41 (1960), 349–57; D. Stevens (ed.), *Robert Carver: Collected Works*, I (*Corpus Mensurabilis Musicae*, XVI, Rome, 1959); I. Woods, 'The Carver Choirbook' (Ph.D., Princeton Univ., 1984); J. Purser, *Scotland's Music* (E, L, 1992); D. J. Ross, *Musick-Fyne: Robert Carver . . .* (E, 1993).

M. Dilworth and A. E. Nimmo

Caskie, Donald Currie (1902–83), minister of the Scots Kirk in Paris and the wartime 'Tartan Pimpernel'. He previously served in Gretna (1932–5) and later at Skelmorlie (1961–88). An Islay man and Edinburgh graduate, he was celebrated and honoured for his role in assisting British prisoners and escapees (said to number 2,000) during the Second World War.

After the German occupation of Paris in 1940 Caskie was cut off from Britain, but took over a seamen's mission in Marseilles through which British servicemen escaped from Vichy France into Spain. Later he co-operated with the French Resistance and moved to Grenoble.

Arrested by the Italians, he was handed over to the Germans and sentenced to death. Hesitation on the part of the German military authorities and the intercession of a Lutheran pastor, Hans Peters, serving as prison chaplain at Fresnes, saved him from execution. Caskie survived in internment until the liberation, resuming his ministry in a more conventional form and devoting himself to the rebuilding of the Paris Kirk in the Rue Bayard.

His modest and reluctantly written account of his wartime experiences, *The Tartan Pimpernel*, originally published in 1957, was a popular success and much reprinted, starting with Collins Fontana (L, 1960).

His remarkable deeds went with an inner shyness and nervous tension. He was awarded the OBE, and received a DD of Edinburgh University, but never held or sought any leading role in Kirk affairs in Scotland.

FES IX, 133, 722, X, 139, 413.

R. D. Kernohan

Catechisms (English and Scots), treatises for instruction in the principles of the Christian religion, generally by way of question and answer, usually designed for memorization by those young in the faith, particularly children. Although the ancient church put great emphasis on the oral instruction of the catechumen, the practice fell out of use and was revived only with the Reformation, the catechisms of Martin Luther and John Calvin being most influential.

Just prior to the Reformation in Scotland, Archbishop John Hamilton's* *Catechisme* (St Andrews, 1552) was issued, as the Provincial Council* of the Church explained it, to instruct both clergy and people in the rudiments of the Catholic faith. The *Catechisme* was a production of the mediating school of thought which in mid-century still hoped an accommodation could be reached with the Reformers. As such it reflects similar continental works of the period. There is no evidence that it was put into general use in Scotland. It is in the form of a few brief questions and very long answers.

Catechetical instruction was introduced in Scotland at the beginning of the Reformation, following the practice of other Reformed churches. *The First Book of Discipline** enjoins instruction of children and youth, 'especially in the Catechisme as we have it now translated in the booke of common order called the order of Geneva' (*FBD*, 130-1); 'after noone must the yong children be publickly examined in their Catechisme in the audience of the people, wherof the Minister must take great diligence as well to cause the people understand the questions proponed as answers', and the doctrines taught therein also (182). The catechism here referred to is a translation of Calvin's Genevan catechism (ET - Geneva, 1556; E, 1564, cf. T. F. Torrance, *The School of Faith*, E, 1959, 3-65). Calvin's 'Little Catechism', designed for brief instruction in the rudiments of the faith and printed along with the full catechism, was also commonly in use.

John Craig's* *A Shorte Summe of the Whole Catechisme* (E, 1581) was the first catechism of Scottish origin widely used in Scotland. Published with the King's, or Negative, Confession,* it was reprinted a number of times in London. A short version of this was produced for 'the forme of examination befor the Communioun'; the 1591 General Assembly 'thought it meitt to be imprintit' after being 'contractit in some shorter bounds' by the author (*BUK* II, 784).

The Heidelberg Catechism was printed in Edinburgh in Latin in 1591 and in English in 1615 and reprinted there and in Aberdeen several times. It was widely used in Scotland in both forms; popularly it was known as the Palatine Catechism. Latin catechisms were used in schools, enabling instruction in piety to be combined with grammar. Robert Pont's* *Parvus Catechismus* (St Andrews, 1573) and Patrick Adamson's* *Catechismus Latino Carmine Redditus* (E, 1581) had some use, but Andrew Duncan's* *Rudimenta Pietatis* (E, 1595) was most widely used (cf. Torrance, 279-81, and *Catechisms of the Scottish Reformation*, ed. H. Bonar, L, 1866, 287-98, 357-67). From the early seventeenth century other catechisms were produced and used in Scotland, though not in such abundance as in England. Generally for local use, none had wide circulation or influence. A manuscript catechism, said to be in Samuel Rutherford's* hand, is an example of this. 'Ane Catachisme conteining The Soume of Christian Religion' was probably begun at Anwoth and perhaps completed while Rutherford was a commissioner to the Westminster Assembly (*Catechisms of the Second Reformation*, ed. A. F. Mitchell, L, 1886, xiii-xxvii). In 1641 a little catechism, *The A.B.C. or A Catechism for Young Children* was published in Edinburgh. Only thirty-seven questions long, it was several times reprinted and widely used in Scotland in the 1640s.

Just prior to the Westminster Assembly's* work on a catechism, *The New Catechisme according to the Forme of the Kirk of Scotland* (L, 1644) was published. 'Very profitable and usefull for instructing of Children and Youth in the Principles of Religion [it was] Set forth for the generall good of both Kingdomes' (Mitchell, 277-96). This *New Catechisme* may have been designed for adoption by the Westminster Assembly, or intended to serve as a model. But although the Scottish commissioners took part in the discussions, the resultant catechisms were not primarily Scottish productions.

It is, however, difficult to underestimate the influence of the Westminster Standards in general, and the Shorter Catechism in particular, on Scotland. Though devoid of the 'homely imagery' of Rutherford, the Shorter Catechism is clear, logical and concise. As such it was generally used in Scotland well into the nineteenth century and, by some, is still used today. Its acceptance was such that it was almost continuously in print and almost universally used. Robert Smith even produced a metrical version: *The Assembly's Shorter Catechism in Metre* (E, 1729; E, 1872).

But the Shorter Catechism was not suitable for young children or, as it was sometimes put, those of weak capacity, and various works were produced to supply the need for more elementary instruction. A few were entirely independent of the Shorter Catechism: Alexander Hamilton's (*FES* IV, 321) *A Short Catechism concerning the three special Divine*

CATECHISMS (ENGLISH AND SCOTS)

Covenants, and two Gospel Sacraments (E, 1714), 'Calculated especially for the Use of those of Weaker Capacity', is a good example, though he was called before a Committee for Purity of Doctrine in 1719 to explain certain expressions in it (see D. C. Lachman, *The Marrow Controversy*, E, 1988, 259–67). But for the most part catechisms produced in Scotland tended to be explanatory of the Shorter Catechism, with a series of subordinate questions and answers, intended to be studied carefully but not memorized, elucidating the meaning as fully and clearly as possible. John Willison's* *The Mother's Catechism* (E, 1731, often reprinted) and Alexander Mair's (*FES* IV, 212) *A Brief Explication of the Assembly's Shorter Catechism* (E, 1752) are but two such. Two much larger works, going into considerably greater detail are James Fisher's* *The Assembly's Shorter Catechism Explained, By Way of Question and Answer* (G, 1753, 1760; G, ^{2}1763) and John Brown* of Haddington's *An Help for the Ignorant* (E, 1758; ^{2}E, 1761). Both, particularly the former, were frequently reprinted and had great influence in mediating the Shorter Catechism to the people, in England and America as well as Scotland. A variety of expositions of the Shorter Catechism were also composed, some as full systems of theology. Thomas Boston's* *An Illustration of the Doctrines of the Christian Religion, upon the plan of the Assembly's Shorter Catechism, comprehending A Complete Body of Divinity* (3 vols, E, 1773) and Alexander S. Paterson's *A Concise System of Theology, on the basis of the Shorter Catechism* (E, 1841; L, 1881) were but two of many.

In the nineteenth century a plethora of catechisms were composed. Some were based on the Shorter Catechism and continued to explain it to a new generation (*e.g.* Gavin Struthers, *Explanation of the Shorter Catechism on the Sacraments of Baptism and The Lord's Supper*, G, 1838). Others, also seeing the need for more elementary instruction, took a more independent approach. Quite a number focused their efforts on the preparation of parents about to bring their children for baptism or on preparing young communicants for the Lord's Supper (*e.g.* A Beith, *A Catechism on Baptism*, Stirling, 1842; Andrew Thomson,* *A Catechism for the Instruction of Communicants in the Nature and Uses of the Sacrament of our Lord's Supper*, E, 1807; ^{2}E, 1808). Many of these went through multiple editions, some twenty or more. Yet others attempted to fill the need for material more elementary than the Shorter Catechism (e.g. Matthew Frazer, *A Catechism designed for the Use of Children and Sabbath Evening Schools*, ^{10}E, 1842) or to add to it (e.g. James Gall, *A Sequel to the Shorter Catechism*, E, n.d.). Catechisms were used for other purposes as well: the Free Church Publications Committee issued a *Catechism on the Principles and Constitution of the Free Church of Scotland* (E, 1845) and David A. Sturrock wrote *A Catechism for the Times* (^{2}E, 1854), in which he addressed a variety of controversial questions, including 'When . . . will Christ's second coming take place?' (he gives as alternative answers the years 3470 or 493,410!). None of these catechisms was intended to be memorized. Rather the catechetical form was adopted as 'best calculated for conveying instruction to the generality of readers, with ease, distinctness, and effect' (Andrew Thomson).

The latter half of the nineteenth century, however, saw many voicing, as Horatius Bonar put it, 'a popular and high-sounding watchword: "Christianity a *life*, not a *dogma*" '. Although deplored by Bonar and Torrance (*School of Faith*, xiiff., xxiii–xli) and in opposition to Calvin, who believed 'the Church of God will never preserve itself without a Catechism', the writing, and to a large extent the use, of catechisms in Scotland has almost died out, though it is not yet extinct. *Faith and Understanding: Questions and Answers for Today* (E, 1990), by Howard Taylor, is a contemporary catechism.

See Catechizing.

D. C. *Lachman*

CATECHISMS (GAELIC)

Catechisms (Gaelic). The publication of catechetical texts in Scottish Gaelic* began shortly after the Reformation, when John Carswell* included a brief catechism in his translation of Knox's *Forme of Prayers* (E, 1567). R. L. Thomson, editor of the modern edition of Carswell's work, remarks: 'The Catechism which he substituted for Calvin's large one is, though based on Calvin's little catechism, almost entirely an original work, and the largest single piece of Carswell's own devising, about 500 lines of the present edition or about one eighth of the whole book'. In the National Library of Scotland is preserved the unique copy of the Gaelic version of John Calvin's *Catechismus Ecclesiae Genevensis*, the work of an unknown translator of perhaps the late sixteenth century and published *c*.1630. Both these works are couched in classical literary Gaelic, at some considerable remove from the contemporary vernacular. In 1649 the Synod of Argyll commissioned seven of its ministers to translate the Westminster Shorter Catechism into Gaelic, and the resulting document was in print by 1653, a second edition appearing along with the first fifty Metrical Psalms in 1659. An edition of this earliest Gaelic version of the Shorter Catechism is included by R. L. Thomson in his edition of the translation of Calvin's Catechism. In contrast to the two earlier catechisms, this work is more securely planted in the Scottish vernacular. Later translations of the Shorter Catechism, including versions by John Smith,* Thomas Ross* and John MacDonald,* have been frequently reprinted: in all, the *Scottish Gaelic Union Catalogue* lists almost 100 editions between 1659 and 1951.

With the appearance of the Gaelic translation of the Westminster Confession of Faith (E, 1725), a version of the Larger Catechism, '*An Cataichiosm Foirleathan*', was now in print, but was never separately issued. An instructional digest of the Westminster documents was published in 1767 as *Suim an Eòlais Shlàinteil*. As the eighteenth century progressed, catechetical works by individual authors also appeared in Gaelic translation. These included three works by John Willison* of Dundee: his *Mother's Catechism, Leabhar Ceist na Mathair do'n leanabh Og* (G, 1752), his *Eiseimpleir Shoilleir Ceas-*

CATECHISMS (GAELIC)

nuighe air Leabhar Aith-ghearr nan Ceist (E, 1773), a detailed application of the teaching of the Shorter Catechism running to 464 pp., and his catechism for young communicants, *Leabhar Ceist nan Og Luch[d]-Communachaidh* (G, 1798). A work by Isaac Watts appeared as *Da Leabhar Cheistin agus Urnuighean* (E, 1774), with Gaelic and English text on facing pages. This included 'The Young Child's First Catechism; or the Catechism for a Young Child, to be begun at three or four years old' and 'The Second Sett of Catechisms and Prayers; or, Some helps to the religion of Children, and their knowledge of the Scripture, from seven to twelve years of age'. The Reformed Catechism, *Leabhar Ceasnuighe Aithleasuighte* (E, 1779) was translated by Duncan Lothian of Glenlyon, author of another work of anti-Romanist polemic published in 1797. By the end of the eighteenth century, the Presbyterian monopoly in this area of Gaelic publishing had been broken with the appearance of the RC *Aithghearradh na Teagaisg Chriosduidh* (L, 1781), a catechism which went through several editions, including transatlantic ones, down to the mid-twentieth century, and the Anglican *Book of Common Prayer, Leabhar na H'Urnuigh Choitchionn* (E, 1794), which included its own catechism. *Da Leabhar Cheist Co-cheangailte r'a Cheile* (E, 1799) was a translation by 'Mr Mcdonald, teaching in Edinburgh' of *Two Short Catechisms Mutually Connected* by John Brown* of Haddington, 'translated and printed at the expense of some benevolent Christian [sic] who wish to spread the savour of Christ's name among our countrymen in the Highlands of Scotland'. Another Gaelic version of one of these catechisms appeared as *Leabhar-Cheistean Aithghearr airson Clann Og* (E, 1842).

The work of translating into Gaelic catechisms of one kind or another continued, though with reduced impetus, into the nineteenth century. Hugh Fraser of Oban translated Andrew Mitchell Thomson's *Catechism for the Instruction of Communicants* as *Leabhar Ceasnachaidh chum Luchd-comunachaidh Fhoghlum* (E, 1813). *Ceud Leabhar Ceasnachaidh air son Cloinne*, a children's catechism, appeared in 1827, and *Leth-Cheud Ceist mu Priomh Theagasgaibh agus Dhleasdanasaibh an t-Soisgeil* (E, 1828) was a translation by Francis Macbean* of Paul's *Fifty Scripture Questions*. It was probably the advent of Baptist teaching in the Highlands, through the labours of the brothers Haldane,* that led to the appearance in Gaelic of two catechisms on the subject, Alexander Beith's *Leabhar Cheistean mu Nadur a' Bhaistidh* (G, 1827) and John Barr's *Plain Catechetical Instructions on Christian Baptism*, translated by Neil Maclean as *Leabhar Ceasnachaidh mu Ordugh a' Bhaistidh* (G, 1836). Disruption* year saw *Leabhar Cheist air Uachdranachd agus Oideas na h-Eaglais Clèireachail* (G, 1843), a translation by MacIntosh MacKay* of *A Catechism on the Government and Discipline of the Presbyterian Church*. Beyond the mid-century point, only two works have been noted: Charles Forbes Buchan's *Catechism on Baptism and the Lord's Supper*, translated by Angus MacIntyre as *Leabhar-cheist mu Shacramaidean a' Bhaistidh agus Suipeir an Tighearna* (E, 1856), and the work en-

CATECHISMS (ROMAN CATHOLIC)

titled *Leabhar-Cheist gu bhi air Ionnsachadh roimh Leabhar-cheist na h-Eaglaise* (Inverness, 1863). The only work to make its first Gaelic appearance in the present century would seem to be the RC *Leabhar Cheist na Cloinne Bige* (Dublin, 1950) a translation of the First Communion Catechism.

See also Gaelic, Protestant Prose Publications in.

R. L. Thomson (ed.), *Foirm na n-Urrnuidheadh* (E, 1970); *id.* (ed.), *Adtimchiol an Chreidimh* (E, 1962); D. MacLean, *Typographia Scoto-Gadelica* (E, 1915); M. Ferguson and A. Matheson (eds), *Scottish Gaelic Union Catalogue* (E, 1984).

K. D. MacDonald

Catechisms (Roman Catholic). In the sixteenth century, two RC catechisms were published in Scots: that of Archbishop John Hamilton* in 1552 and Adam King's translation of Canisius (Paris, 1588; excerpts in T. G. Law (ed.), *Catholic Tractates*, STS, E, 1901). In 1580 the Jesuit* Robert Abercromby included catechisms among the books to be used for promoting Catholicism in Scotland (*IR* 7, 1956, 34, 45).

Little is known of the instruction given in the seventeenth century, but printed RC catechisms were available in English and in Irish Gaelic, while manuscript catechisms in English and Gaelic circulated freely, from the later decades at least. The Statutes of Bishop Thomas Nicolson* in 1700, reissued in 1782, stressed the duty of parents to instruct their children and ordered priests to instruct the young and ignorant not only on Sundays and feasts but also when visiting their homes. Three English catechisms were published by the priests James Carnegie and Andrew Hacket in 1724–5; Carnegie's was seized and publicly burned in Edinburgh but later reprinted, then all three were condemned by Rome in 1734–5 for their Jansenist* leanings. Bishop Alexander Smith therefore obtained Roman approval for his two catechisms, published in 1757 and 1760. In Gaelic, Robert Menzies produced his substantial *Aithghearradh na Teagaisg Chriosduidh* (*Abridgement of Christian Teaching*, L, 1781).

It was the custom at this time and in later decades to catechize the children at the altar rails on Sundays. Bishop George Hay* and Charles Gordon* did this in Aberdeen; so too did Robert Menzies in Edinburgh, as well as holding a catechism class on Saturday forenoons. In Glengairn Lachlan McIntosh would also call forward young adults and even older persons to give answers (*IR* 7, 1956, 13–17).

Bishop Hay made an outstanding contribution with his *Sincere Christian Instructed...* (L, 1781) and *Devout Christian Instructed...* (L, 1783). Both were in question-and-answer form and were summarized in *An Abridgement of Roman Catholic Doctrine* (A, 1795). His works went through numerous editions in Scotland, Ireland and America. The *Abridgement* was frequently published as an appendix to his *Pious Christian Instructed...* (L, 1786).

Throughout the nineteenth century a steady trickle of small paper-bound Gaelic catechisms appeared in Scotland and Canada. A variety of small English catechisms were published, following *A Short Abridgement of Christian Doctrine* (A, 1799). As in other countries, the proliferation of catechisms led to measures to impose uniformity; gradually *A Catechism of Christian Doctrine* (known as the penny catechism despite constant price increases through inflation) gained the monopoly, going through countless editions and being finally translated into Gaelic in 1940. It was superseded by the full (700 questions) and somewhat turgid *Scottish Catechism of Christian Doctrine* (L, G, 1954).

As the number of RC schools and Sunday schools increased, instruction became more systematized. Many parishes in the later nineteenth century had a Christian Doctrine Society. In more recent times, catechetical publications and conferences became common. From about 1950 it was apparent that instruction from a catechism at school was by no means entirely successful. Valiant efforts have been made to integrate instruction with the child's experience of life and liturgy and to use the insights of modern teaching methods. Catechetical centres, diocesan and national syllabuses and a stream of attractive children's books have resulted, though the more conservative lament the demise of the penny catechism.

See also Roman Catholicism; Gaelic, RC publications.

Catholic Encyclopedia V, 75–88; *New Catholic Encyclopedia* III, 208–32; J. F. S. Gordon, *The Catholic Church in Scotland* (A, 1874); collections in Scottish Catholic Archives, Edinburgh.

M. Dilworth

Catechizing, a method of instruction by the live recitation of questions and answers. The *First Book of Discipline** (1560) required that there be a Sabbath afternoon examination of the young children in the catechism, in the presence of the rest of the church, with the minister elucidating the doctrine. This afternoon service for the training of children had its precedent in Strasbourg and Geneva, was adopted by the English refugee church at Geneva, and so passed to Scotland when refugees like John Knox* returned home. From 1564 to 1611 Calvin's catechism was printed at Edinburgh with the *Book of Common Order,** and the *FBD* specified its use. Without knowledge of the main topics covered by the catechism, no one was to be admitted to the Lord's table. In 1570 the General Assembly instructed ministers and elders to examine children at the ages of nine, twelve and fourteen, to know how they are profiting from religious instructions.

Catechizing became a common feature in the church's life preceding the celebration of Communion. The Kirk Session at St Andrews ordained in 1595 that no one was to be admitted to the sacrament who absented himself from preaching and catechizing, but only those who could say the Lord's Prayer, the ten commandments, answer the questions of Calvin's brief 'Manner to Examine Children', and were at least sixteen years of age. A period of several weeks was set aside by the Session for the examination of all the people before each Communion, postponing the Communion if necessary in order to cover all the district.

Catechizing was also introduced into households at an early date. In 1596 the Presbytery of St Andrews, with burgesses present, solemnly renewed their covenant with God, and the first promise that was made engaged each father to read the Word and pray with the children and servants, and to catechize them. The General Assembly of 1592 urged the people to purchase John Craig's* abridged catechism, that it might be read in families (*see* Catechisms, English and Scots). The *FBD* mandated that catechetical instruction be given in the schools, and when the College of James VI was established at Edinburgh in 1583, Robert Rollock* trained his scholars in the Heidelberg Catechism on the Lord's Day afternoon

. As indicated by the General Assembly in 1649, the catechizing was an opportunity for the minister the present 'the chief heads of Saving Knowledge, in a short view' (*AGACS*, 211). A specimen of this instruction is the 'Sum of Saving Knowledge' composed about 1650 by David Dickson* and James Durham* and often printed with the Church's standards. The General Assembly of 1639 directed that every minister was to have weekly catechizing in some part of his parish, in addition to his Sabbath sermons. The universality of the practice was indicated by the observation of William Forbes* in 1633 that every minister had a catechetical manual of his own.

The Westminster Assembly's Shorter Catechism was approved by the CofS in 1648, and thereafter was the most common text for catechetical instruction. The method of teaching from it – by way of question and answer – is exemplified in Ebenezer Erskine* and James Fisher's* *The Assembly's Shorter Catechism Explained* (G,²1763). Such instruction lasted well into the nineteeth century and, in some quarters, into the twentieth.

FBD; J. Melville, *The Autobiography and Diary* (E, 1842); D. H. Fleming (ed.), *Register of the Ministers, Elders and Deacons of the Christian Congregation of St Andrews*, 2 vols (E, 1889–90); T. F. Torrance (ed.), *The School of Faith* (L, 1959); A. Edgar, *Old Church Life in Scotland* (Paisley, 1885); W. McMillan, *The Worship of the Scottish Reformed Church 1550–1638* (L, 1931); *BUK*; W. D. Maxwell, *The Liturgical Portions of the Genevan Service Book* (E, 1931).

S. Isbell

Cathedral Churches. Bishops existed within the Celtic Church but they were associated with the monastic communities and did not have cathedral churches. Cathedral foundations date from the period of the assimilation of the Church in Scotland to the Western pattern, and this owed much to the influence of Queen Margaret* and her sons, Alexander I* and David I.*

The system eventually included the following cathedrals:

Aberdeen. St Machar's (*see* Celtic Saints): The first

cathedral was begun in 1183; a new building was started in 1282 with further expansions beginning in 1370 and 1422. It was completed in 1531. The choir was destroyed in 1560 and the central tower collapsed in 1688. The nave in rugged granite with its western spires and splendid oak ceiling makes a fine parish church for Old Aberdeen. The heraldic decoration in the ceiling panels sets forth the shields of notable sovereigns and churchmen in Europe and Scotland.

Brechin. A cathedral was erected in the Norman style in the twelfth century, but was replaced by a cathedral in the early pointed style in the thirteenth century and this was further developed in the years after 1354. It suffered much after 1560. The choir was walled off and fell into decay. The transepts were removed in 1806 and 'much ruthless destruction was wrought in the name of modernisation'. Between 1900 and 1902 the choir and the transepts were rebuilt and a general restoration took place under the direction of John Honeyman, RSA. The building contains good woodwork and stained glass. The adjoining round tower links the site to the period of Celtic monasticism.

Dornoch. Under David's plan this became the seat of the bishop of Caithness. Building began in 1224 and continued spasmodically through the century. A clan feud led to its destruction by fire in 1570. In 1616 the choir and transepts were restored, but the nave was still ruinous in 1786. A thorough or, as some would have it, a 'ruthless' restoration took place between 1835 and 1837 under the direction of William Burn of Edinburgh and by the generosity of the Dowager Duchess of Sutherland. Many of the Sutherland family were buried in the cathedral. A further programme of restoration took place in 1924 and revealed the simple dignity of the building.

Dunblane. David made this the seat of a bishop and thus made it the ecclesiastical centre for the area instead of Abernethy. The lower storeys of the tower survive from the twelfth-century cathedral, which was rebuilt between 1238 and 1258, and there were later additions. The nave roof collapsed after the Reformation but the whole building was restored in the period from 1892 to 1914 under the guidance of Sir Rowand Anderson and Sir Robert Lorimer. The Gothic building is notable for its splendid proportions, its fine woodwork, medieval and modern, and for its stained glass, including a window by Douglas Strachan,* its furnishings and bells.

Dunkeld. Alexander I* founded this bishopric and an early church was replaced by a new cathedral begun in 1312. Expansion continued periodically until the completion in 1464. It incorporated Norman and Gothic styles. There was severe devastation at the Reformation and further demolition took place during the Jacobite resistance to the advent of William and Mary. Repairs to the choir took place in 1691, 1762 and 1803. A full restoration of the choir took place in 1908 through the generosity of Sir Donald Currie. It is the burial place of the son of Robert II, known as the Wolf of Badenoch, and of the Dukes of Atholl. The choir and the ruined nave are set in an idyllic setting around which sweeps the Tay.

Edinburgh. St Giles* began as the parish church of the city. An early church was devastated in 1385 by Richard II, but it was rebuilt in 1416 with an expansion later in the century. At the Reformation it was retained for Reformed worship and was later divided to form three churches. Under the Caroline plans it became the cathedral of the new diocese of Edinburgh from 1633 to 1637 and from 1661 to 1689. The building was restored and unified in the period 1870 to 1883 under the guidance of William Burn and by the generosity of Sir William Chambers. Liturgical changes across the centuries have been reflected in the internal arrangements and the present arrangement brings the focus of Word and Sacraments to the crossing under the tower. Further developments are in train. It is rich in memorials and the windows include a Douglas Strachan* window in his characteristic style and a recent splendid and startling window in memory of Robert Burns designed by Leifur Breidfjord of Iceland. Among the cathedral chapels is the sumptuous chapel of the Order of the Thistle* designed by Sir Robert Lorimer and opened in 1911.

Elgin. In the plan of Alexander for the see of Moray Elgin was chosen as the seat of its cathedral. Building began in 1224. About 1270 it was ruined by fire. It was rebuilt, but was burned again by the Wolf of Badenoch in 1390. Rebuilding began in 1422 and the tower was rebuilt in 1538. The lead was stripped from the roof by Mary's forces in 1568 and further demolition took place in the seventeenth century, some of this by Cromwell's forces. The ruins still give an impression of what must have been one of Scotland's most spacious and developed Gothic buildings.

Fortrose. In David's plan this was the site of a cathedral for the see of Ross. The building was erected in the fourteenth century but fell into decay in the sixteenth when the roof was removed by the Regent Morton. The devastation was completed when Cromwell used the stones to build the Inverness citadel. The surviving remains of the south nave aisle give an idea of the perpendicular style of the building.

Glasgow (St Mungo). A church has been on this site since the time of Mungo (*see* Celtic Saints), and in David's plan it was chosen as the seat of a bishop. The first cathedral was completed in 1136. A serious fire led to a rebuilding beginning in 1189. The crypt was completed in 1197 and the nave in 1232. The present choir and underchurch were built between 1233 and 1258 and the nave was reconstructed in the 1330s. The impressive aisle bearing the name of Archbishop Robert Blackadder* was erected at the beginning of his episcopate in 1484; the planned upper storey was not erected. The building survived the Reformation intact and the fabric has been well maintained, though two western towers were removed in the nineteenth century. The church was divided for use by two congregations with a third congregation in the underchurch, but in the nineteenth century the building was reunified. In its stately Gothic proportions it is the most spacious of Scottish cathedrals in present use. Its dignity is much enhanced by its furnishings, carpets, cloths and tapestries. Among its many fine windows there is one by Douglas Strachan* and several by more recent artists.

*Iona.** This had been the centre of monastic life from early times, but for a period from 1507 it was the cathedral of the bishops of the Isles. The Abbey Church and monastic buildings have been restored this century.

Kirkwall (St Magnus*). Bishops of Orkney* had a church on the island of Birsay but under David's plan Kirkwall became the seat of the bishop. Bishop William and Earl Rognvald* began to build the cathedral in 1137, and when it was completed the relics of Magnus were brought from Birsay. The predominant style is Norman and the cathedral has resemblances to Durham, where the Kirkwall masons probably learned their trade. The east end of the cathedral was extended in the thirteenth century and the ornate pointed western doorways belong to this period. The building did not suffer at the Reformation. The choir was cut off from the nave and was used as the parish church. The fabric was maintained by various grants from public and private sources until a major restoration between 1913 and 1930 brought the whole building into use. The building is now owned and maintained by the Orkney Islands Council, but major assistance in its upkeep has come from generous benefactors and from the Society of the Friends of the Cathedral. It has much fine wood carving, some good stained glass and many notable memorials. In 1965 the east end of the choir was transformed into the St Rognvald Chapel.

Lismore. The cathedral was built soon after 1236 when Lismore was made the seat of the bishop of Argyll. It was built on a simple plan and the surviving rectangular building is still in use as the parish church.

*St Andrews.** A bishopric was established here in the tenth century. Building began in 1158 and continued for a century. The west end was blown down during a storm and was rebuilt between 1272 and 1279. After further expansion the cathedral was completed in 1318. It was a striking example of Gothic architecture and was the largest of the Scottish cathedrals. It fell into disuse after the Reformation and its stones were used as a quarry for local buildings. The ruins are carefully preserved and indicate the great size of the building, 350 feet long.

*Whithorn.** This is an ancient Celtic foundation associated with Ninian.* It was designated by David as the seat of the bishop of Galloway. The buildings were erected as a Premonstratensian* priory. They are now ruinous. Extensive excavations have been carried out and further projects are in hand.

CATHEDRALS OF THE SCOTTISH EPISCOPAL CHURCH. The Episcopal Church has seven dioceses and eight cathedrals.

Aberdeen (St Andrew's). The interior decoration highlights the strong links between the Episcopal Church and the Episcopal Church in the United States of America. Built in 1817, it became a cathedral in 1914.

Cumbrae. This Collegiate Church of the Holy Spirit was built in 1849 to designs by William Butterfield and in 1876 was made the cathedral of the Isles in the diocese of Argyll and the Isles.

Oban (St John the Divine). This is also a cathedral, built 1910, in the diocese of Argyll and the Isles.

Dundee (St Paul's). This was built (1853–65) to designs by Sir Gilbert Scott for the diocese of Brechin.

Edinburgh (St Mary's). This, the largest Episcopal cathedral in Scotland, was built between 1874 and 1917 to designs by Sir Gilbert Scott. Its triple spires and ample scale make it a striking feature of the city skyline.

Glasgow (St Mary's). This was built for the diocese of Glasgow and Galloway and to the designs of Sir Gilbert Scott (1871–4) and J. O. Scott (1893).

Inverness (St Andrew's). This was built for the diocese of Moray, Ross and Caithness between 1866 and 1871 and to the designs of Alexander Ross.

Perth (St Ninian's). This is the cathedral, consecrated 1850, for the diocese of St Andrews, Dunkeld and Dunblane.

CATHEDRALS OF THE ROMAN CATHOLIC CHURCH. The RCC established a hierarchy in 1878 and designated dioceses and cathedrals.

Edinburgh (St Mary's, 1814, 1896), for the archdiocese of St Andrews and Edinburgh.

Aberdeen (St Mary of the Assumption), built in 1880 to cover the diocese of Aberdeen.

Ayr (The Good Shepherd, 1957), for the diocese of Galloway.

Dundee (St Andrew's, 1782, 1836), for the diocese of Dunkeld.

Glasgow (St Andrew's), for the archdiocese of Glasgow, built 1847–7.

Oban (St Columba's), built in 1927 to the design of Sir Gilbert Scott for the diocese of Argyll and the Isles.

In 1947 two new dioceses were carved out of the archdiocese of Glasgow with Cathedrals at *Motherwell* (Our Lady of Good Aid, built 1875, 1900) and at *Paisley* (St Mirin's, built 1808, 1932).

See also Architecture, Church; Early Ecclesiastical Sites.

D. MacGibbon and T. Ross, *The Ecclesiastical*

CATHOLIC APOSTOLIC CHURCH

Architecture of Scotland from the Earliest Times to the Seventeenth Century, 3 vols (E, 1896–7); Easson-Cowan, 201–12; *The Blue Guide* and many other travel handbooks provide much information; Cathedral histories and guidebooks provide detailed information on each building; Her Majesty's Stationery Office publish authoritative official guides to the buildings which are preserved as National Monuments by the Secretary of State for Scotland.

R. B. Knox

Catholic Apostolic Church, nineteenth-century religious group, in some ways a precursor of Pentecostalism* and the charismatic movement.* Its origins lay in the religious experiences of Mary Campbell* and James and George MacDonald,* Scots who in March 1830 began to exercise what they believed were the spiritual gifts of glossolalia, prophecy and healing. Their cause was championed by Edward Irving,* in whose London church the gifts appeared in 1831.

The first Catholic Apostolic congregation was formed from the six hundred communicants who adhered to Irving on his deposition in 1832. Irving was soon forced into a subordinate role, however, and control of the movement passed to a college of twelve 'apostles', headed by John Bate Cardale (1802–77; *DNB* IX, 36) and based at Albury, the Surrey home of the half-Scottish Henry Drummond,* another apostle. Other Scots among the apostles were Thomas Carlyle (1803–55; *DNB* IX, 110), William Dow (*d*.1855) and Duncan MacKenzie (*d*.1855).

The Catholic Apostolic Church had a fourfold ministry of apostles, prophets, evangelists and pastors. The chief pastor in each congregation, who had some episcopal powers, was known as an 'angel'. There was a strong emphasis on the doctrine of the incarnation, a conviction of the nearness of the Second Advent, and an acceptance as authentic of the contemporary manifestations of glossolalia and associated phenomena. The style of worship developed along richly ceremonial lines, and the dignified Catholic Apostolic liturgy had an important influence on other Churches.

The Church never had more than a few thousand adherents in Britain. The three Scottish congregations had in 1851 a total attendance of 588. In the later nineteenth century, as the apostles died, no successors were appointed. After the demise of the last apostle in 1901, the ministry died out, churches were closed, and their congregations generally joined the CofE. However, other groups including the New Apostolic Church in Germany and the Western Orthodox Church claim to continue the Catholic Apostolic tradition in the twentieth century.

P. E. Shaw, *The Catholic Apostolic Church* (NY, 1946); E. Miller, *The History and Doctrines of Irvingism*, 2 vols (L, 1878); A. L. Drummond, *Edward Irving and His Circle* (L, 1937); *The Years of Ferment* (Albury, 1980); *Western Orthodox Church, Yearbook for 1967*.

J. R. Wolffe

CATHOLIC DEVOTION

Catholic Devotion (pre-Reformation). Devotional practices in Celtic and medieval Scotland were closely related to the socio-religious ethos of their age, and have to be understood within that context. Thus the miracle stories of the seventh- and eighth-century Celtic annals, the prayers and lives of the Celtic saints,* and poems like the eighth-century *Dream of the Rood* incised on the Ruthwell Cross,* were devotional exercises which accurately reflect the current mental climate: the wonder and love of God's creation, the reality of the community of the saints and need for their intercession, of being exiles in a fallen world, pilgrims on their way to heaven (*see* Celtic Church). Such attitudes also help to explain the popularity of pilgrimages* from Celtic times onwards. These were undertaken with much hardship and at considerable danger, either to fulfil a vow or expiate a crime, but always to express sorrow for sin and gain remission from it at a holy shrine, such as the Holy Sepulchre at Jerusalem, those of the apostles Peter and Paul in Rome, of St James at Compostella in Spain, or more locally those of Columba* at Iona,* Ninian* at Whithorn* or Duthac in Tain. The influx of religious orders like the Benedictines* and Cistercians* in the eleventh and twelfth centuries, and of the Franciscans* and Dominicans* in the thirteenth, brought further devotions into the country, like the cult of the Blessed Virgin Mary and practical aids to prayer like the saying of the rosary, although it is important to remember that the Church's liturgy at the time remained firmly Christocentric with an increasing devotion to the eucharist. The devastating effects of the Black Death and of the wars of independence in the fourteenth century deeply affected the religious outlook of Scots in the later Middle Ages. It heightened their fear of death, best expressed perhaps in William Dunbar's* poem *Timor mortis conturbat me* ('fear of death disturbs me'), but it also increased their devotion to the Passion and Death of Christ, as may be seen in the introduction into Scotland of new feasts like the Crown of Thorns, the Holy Blood, the Five Wounds, and the Compassion of the Virgin at the Foot of the Cross, or of their pictorial representation in Books of Hours and Missals, on painted ceilings as in Aberdeen, and on banners like that at Fetternear, Aberdeenshire. On the positive side this led to a strongly individualistic piety, with private devotional reading of books like *The Imitation of Christ*. But this morbid interest in suffering and death also led many ordinary folk, and especially guilds and confraternities, to found altars and stipulate the number of masses for the dead which could be said at them, as if there were some arithmetical link between guilt and condign satisfaction. There was a pre-occupation with indulgences, relics and other outward forms of religious observance, emptied of their inner meaning. In consequence superstition became widespread. In justice it must be said that not only later Reformers like Luther, but also earlier Scottish bishops like Elphinstone* set their face against these false misconceptions of the faith, though with

CATHOLIC DEVOTION

little effect until the Council of Trent took such abuses seriously in hand.

Francis Oakley, *The Western Church in the later Middle Ages* (L, 1979); H. G. Beck, *From the High Middle Ages to the Eve of the Reformation* (*Handbook of Church History*, ed. H. Jedin and J. Dolan, vol. 4, L, 1970); *The Pursuit of Holiness in late Medieval and Renaissance Religion*, ed. C. Trinkaus with H. A. Oberman (Leiden, 1974); George Yule, 'Late Mediaeval Piety, Humanism and Luther's Theology', in *Religion and Humanism* (*Studies in Church History* 17), ed. K. Robbins (O, 1981), 167-79; J. T. Rosenthal, *The Purchase of Paradise: Gift Giving and the Aristocracy 1307-1485* (L, 1972); P. I. Kaufman, 'Piety and Proprietary Rights: James IV of Scotland', *The Sixteenth Century Journal* 13 (1982), 83-99; D. McRoberts, 'Scottish Pilgrims to the Holy Land', *IR* 20 (1969), 80-106; D. McRoberts, 'The Fetternear Banner', *IR* 7 (1956), 69-86; D. McRoberts, 'Provost Skene's House in Aberdeen and its Catholic Chapel', *IR* 5 (1954), 119-24; E. A. Macek, 'Fifteenth Century Lay Piety', in *Fifteenth Century Studies*, ed. G. R. Mermier and E. E. Du Bruck (Ann Arbor, MT, 1978-90); R. W. Pfaff, *New Liturgical Feasts in later Medieval England* (O, 1970).

L. J. Macfarlane

Catholic Devotion (post-Reformation), RC devotional life beyond minimum requirements of attendance at official worship, either more frequent participation or optional forms of prayer and worship.

In the period 1560-*c*.1700 many medieval practices continued. Special acts of worship took place at Christmas and Easter. Funeral rites were important and people prayed for their dead in kirkyards. Some practices were rooted in daily and local life, with no firm dividing line from folk customs or even superstition: visits and pilgrimages were made to wells, shrines and churches; objects such as crucifixes, paintings or statues were cherished; smaller objects like rosaries and medals were carried on the person, particularly by women.

In the eighteenth century, Jansenism* affected spirituality by making attitudes to God and worship more rigid and guilt-ridden. The results are still observable today. As Roman Catholicism* gradually established itself, devotional works in English and Gaelic* became more available, and RC Bibles were published in Edinburgh. Papal indulgences and jubilees were promulgated. Many received Communion three times a year, though only once was required.

From *c*.1800 Sunday worship became more elaborate. Catholics also rediscovered experiential religion, and numerous devotions were introduced: Way of the Cross, Sacred Heart, Exposition and Benediction of the Blessed Sacrament. Societies and pious practices proliferated; religious orders* brought continental spirituality. The rosary had never ceased to be popular. Later, *c*.1900, devotion

CATHOLIC EMANCIPATION

to Scottish saints was fostered, while pilgrimages within Scotland and abroad were revived.

In this century Scotland has shared in various profound reforms: frequent (even daily) Communion, interest in Scripture, active participation in liturgy. Vatican II has speeded and intensified the process, while movements like the charismatic renewal* are influential. Increasingly devotion is less a matter of particular practices than of commitment to renewal of the Church.

M. Dilworth

Catholic Emancipation, the ending of RC exclusion from Parliament. 'The Act for the Relief of His Majesty's Roman Catholic subjects' received the royal assent in April 1829, and effectively brought to an end the long period during which the operation of the penal laws had excluded RCs from the mainstream of national life. They were henceforward allowed to sit in Parliament and to hold all civil and military offices on taking an oath of allegiance to the Crown and disavowing any intent to subvert the Protestant religion. Some restrictions remained, notably exclusion from specified high offices (including High Commissioner to the General Assembly of the CofS) and from the universities. RC bishops were not permitted to assume territorial titles, priests were forbidden to wear habits or to perform ceremonies out of doors, and members of male religious orders, above all the Jesuits,* were forbidden to recruit and had to register with the authorities.

The Act of 1829 was the culmination of a long period of controversy over the position of RCs, which can be traced back at least to the late 1770s. Vigorous Scottish opposition prevented the extension of an English Relief Act of 1778 north of the Border and it was not until 1793 that Scottish RCs were granted the legal right to freedom of worship and to purchase and inherit land. The Union with Ireland in 1800 meant that the pressure for emancipation became considerably greater. Indeed the Prime Minister, William Pitt (1759-1806), had wanted to grant emancipation in association with the Union, but was frustrated by the opposition of George III (1738-1820, reigned 1760-1820). The issue was to remain at the centre of British politics for the next thirty years, until in 1828 the campaign of the Catholic Association led by Daniel O'Connell (1775-1847) became irresistible and the government of the Duke of Wellington (1769-1852) brought forward legislation in 1829.

In Scotland there was extensive opposition to emancipation, most apparent in areas in the west affected by Irish immigration* and in the parts of the north-east influenced by strong Evangelicalism.* In Edinburgh, on the other hand, opinion was more neutral, and there was even substantial support for the measure, articulated most notably by Thomas Chalmers* in speeches to a Whig* public meeting and to the Edinburgh Presbytery.

The opponents of emancipation were motivated in part by historic antagonism to RCism and by a belief that concession would open the door to subversion of the British political system. There was also an abstract sense that the constitution was inherently Protestant and that the admission of RCs would destabilize and endanger religious establishments. The pro-emancipation position was that political proscription was a counter-productive way of controlling religious error, that there was no warrant in Scripture for the state to control religious beliefs, and that the national establishment of religion was independent of the state.

In the event the passing of emancipation did not settle the issue of RC political involvement, but it did change the terms of the debate. The battle-lines were redrawn around issues such as the reform of the Church of Ireland and state endowment of the RC seminary at Maynooth, Co. Kildare. There were some calls for the repeal of emancipation, notably by John Hope,* but these made little headway. The measure thus secured a lasting extension of religious toleration, although a significant body of Scottish public opinion was to remain strongly hostile to RCs, supporting the anti-Catholic societies.*

The text of the Catholic Relief Act is printed in E. R. Norman, *Anti-Catholicism in Victorian England* (L, 1968), 131–9.

I. A. Muirhead, 'Catholic Emancipation: Scottish Reactions in 1829', *IR* 24 (1972), 26–42; I. A. Muirhead, 'Catholic Emancipation in Scotland: the Debate and the Aftermath', *IR* 24 (1973), 103–20; S. J. Brown, *Thomas Chalmers and the Godly Commonwealth in Scotland* (O, 1982); C. Johnson, *Developments in the Roman Catholic Church in Scotland, 1789–1829* (E, 1983); P. F. Anson, *Underground Catholicism in Scotland, 1622–1878* (Montrose, 1970); G. I. T. Machin, *The Catholic Question in English Politics 1820 to 1830* (O, 1964); J. C. D. Clark, *English Society 1688–1832* (C, 1985).

J. R. Wolffe

Catholic Revival in Worship (nineteenth century). The changes which took place in Presbyterian* worship in the late nineteenth century came about partly as a return to 'catholic' elements in the Church's tradition, but also as a result of dissatisfaction with what was considered to be a lack of dignity and order in public worship. Scholars such as G. W. Sprott* and Thomas Leishman* studied the historical basis of Presbyterian worship. They showed that the saying of the Lord's Prayer and the use of the Creed and the Doxology had been features of the worship in the post-Reformation CofS. In addition they pointed out that the services in both the *Book of Common Order** and the Westminster* Directory were based on the celebration of the Lord's Supper as the pattern for Sunday worship even on those Sundays when it was not celebrated. However, the pioneer of worship reform, Robert Lee* of Greyfriars, did not share their concern for 'catholic' tradition but simply wished to see a greater reverence in the services of the Church.

The Church Service Society* was formed in 1865 to promote the study of liturgy and the preparation of material for use in worship. In the CofS, and the UFC and UPC as well, hymns came to be sung instead of psalms alone and organs were introduced to accompany congregational singing, though not without controversy. Sermons tended to be shorter, Scripture was read without the lengthy addition of the 'lecture', prayers were read instead of being delivered extempore, and, in general, services came to be more formally structured. The main festivals of the Christian year* were observed in some parishes. Communion* was celebrated more frequently and service books were produced, first by unofficial societies and then by committees of the General Assembly.

See also Liturgy; Worship; Lord's Supper; Ecclesiological Societies; Scoto-Catholics; *Book of Common Order* (modern editions).

J. Kerr, *The Renascence of Worship* (E, 1909); D. M. Murray, 'Disruption to Union' in D. B. Forrester and D. M. Murray (eds), *Studies in the History of Worship in Scotland* (E, 1984), 79–95; A. C. Cheyne, *The Transforming of the Kirk* (E, 1983); A. L. Drummond and J. Bulloch, *The Church in Victorian Scotland, 1843–1874* (E, 1975).

D. M. Murray

Catholic Truth Society of Scotland. Established c.1893, its main role was publishing pamphlets with two purposes: to instruct RCs and to persuade or refute others. Almost 200 were printed 1894–1913 on a wide range of subjects. After a lull in the war years, it published somewhat more sparsely 1923–38, often jointly with the Catholic Truth Society, London. About seventy or eighty pamphlets were published 1940–76.

Diocesan branches were also active, some with lending libraries and shops. Other activities included lectures, conferences, exhibitions, rallies; the annual John Ogilvie* walk and St Margaret* pilgrimage to Dunfermline (later transferred to Carfin Grotto*). The Society ceased to exist 1977.

Collections in Scottish Catholic Archives, Edinburgh.

M. Dilworth

Celibacy. Within the Christian economy, as a permanent decision to observe sexual abstinence for gospel motives, celibacy is recognized to be a vocation,* alongside marriage, to which individuals are called for the sake of the kingdom of God (cf. Matt. 19:1–12; Mark 10:29; Luke 18:29). Celibacy is therefore first and foremost a gift (cf. Matt. 19:11; 1 Cor. 7:7).

Most commonly, celibacy denotes the discipline of the Latin-rite Roman Catholic Church whereby only unmarried men are ordained priest or bishop and may not thereafter contract marriage. In the West, the present discipline of celibacy dates from twelfth-century canonical legislation. Historians usually discuss the origins of the discipline in terms of a complex evolution from the early centuries towards compulsory celibacy.

By contrast, the Eastern Church continued to allow a married clergy. The Orthodox Churches maintain this practice and there is a married clergy also in the Eastern-rite RC Church. But though the oriental practice allows the ordination of married men, it does not allow ordained men to marry, and it elects bishops only from among celibate clergy.

The reasons advanced for maintaining priestly celibacy today are twofold: as a sign of freedom and commitment to service after the model of Christ (cf. 1 Cor. 7:32–5), and as a sign of the economy of the resurrection (cf. Matt. 22:30). Celibacy for priests is a matter of discipline, to be distinguished from the chastity which is an essential feature of religious (ascetic or monastic) life. There was, however, some confusion in the Celtic Church,* with monastic titles passing from father to son.

In Scottish civil law, clerics in major orders could not contract a valid marriage. Crown legitimations in the later Middle Ages, as well as Roman dispensations from the defect of illegitimacy, reveal breaches of celibacy among the more important clergy, and there are indications also of incelibacy among the lower clergy. The Scottish Reformation* permitted clerical marriage and indeed encouraged it (cf. *FBD* 88). In recent times Scottish RCs have shared in the debate about making celibacy optional for priests.

New Catholic Encyclopedia III, 366–74.

P. Tartaglia

Celtic Church, a general term used to describe the institutions and clergy of the Christian Church in Celtic-speaking lands, in particular Ireland, northern Britain (including Scotland) and Wales. The Celtic Church was not an organized ecclesiastical body, operating quite independently of the Catholic Church in the West led by Rome; the name was given to the many churches and monastic communities in Britain and Ireland which differed in certain practices from the Roman Church, owing to isolation, poor communication, and conservatism on the part of the Celtic clergy. The dates of this phase of Christianity in Celtic lands may be set between the fourth and the twelfth centuries.

CHARACTERISTICS. The differences between Celtic and Roman forms of Christianity were the main cause of contention between native Celtic Church leaders and Roman-trained clergy in the seventh century. For the northern Church this culminated in the Synod of Whitby* in AD 664. The major disputes were over the computation of the date of Easter,* the style of the tonsure* and the norm for the ordination of bishops.

The Celtic clergy calculated the date of Easter according to an older calendar method, different from that approved by the Roman Church (but formerly in use in Rome), which, by the seventh century, had adopted the Dionysian calendar reckoning as its standard. Bede* relates how the Celtic clergy consistently refused to celebrate Easter at the proper time, despite the pressures from the *Romani*. The confusion in Northumbria caused the king, who followed Celtic tradition, to be celebrating Easter while the queen, who followed Roman tradition, was still observing Lent (Bede's *Historia Ecclesiastica*, III, 25).

Priests and monks of the Celtic Church adopted a different style of tonsure, shaving the front of their heads from ear to ear, instead of the centre crown only. Celtic bishops were ordained by only one consecrated bishop, not by three, which was Roman practice. Bede also suggests that the rite of baptism* among the Celts differed from the Roman rite (*ibid.*, II, 2).

In his account of the Synod of Whitby, Bede implies that certain matters of doctrine were also at issue but does not elaborate (*ibid.*, III, 25). The conflict over the reckoning of Easter overshadowed the other issues at stake, and it is likely that the Celtic party's refusal to conform to Roman practices caused the *Romani* to call their orthodoxy into question.

In respect of doctrine, the adherents of the Celtic Church were not unorthodox; indeed, they were noted for their devotion and piety. Furthermore, Roman practices had been adopted by several Celtic churches in Wales, southern Ireland, and northern Britain before the Synod of Whitby. However, Christianity in Celtic lands did develop or preserve customs different from the Roman Church. The traditions of the Celtic Church show evidence of early Christian practices, long abandoned by Rome, but surviving in the Celtic outreaches of the later Roman Empire. Celtic customs also differed from one land, even one territory, to another, and not all of the Celtic churches followed the same usages.

The Celtic Church in Ireland was characterized by the development of a largely monastic organization and ethos and a devotion to extremes of asceticism, which suggest a direct acquaintance with early Syrian and Egyptian monasticism. It was never entirely monastic, but monasticism did play a preponderant role in its history, and likewise in Scotland (see Monasticism, Celtic). Individual churches and communities of Christians (not all of whom were in holy orders) also existed, borrowing their hierarchical structure from monastic models. Severe penitential discipline, propagated in a number of penitential books, also marked the Celtic Church (see Penance, Practice of).

Ecclesiastical boundaries tended to follow tribal territories, each with its own monastic centre, while elsewhere in the West a diocesan pattern developed around the town, the bishop's seat. In some cases, abbatial authority exceeded episcopal authority, another point of criticism on the part of the *Romani*. Bede comments that Iona was always ruled by a priest 'to whose authority the whole province, including the bishops, is subject', contrary to general custom (*ibid.*, III, 4). In this situation, the bishops retained functions of consecration *etc.*, not of church government.

ORIGINS AND DEVELOPMENT. Christianity had entered Britain under the Romans by the second century and had become sufficiently well established for the Church to send a delegation of British bishops to the Council of Arles in 314. Britain later

CELTIC CHURCH

attracted attention when Pelagianism, after being condemned throughout the Roman Empire, took root there. Pelagius denied the existence of original sin and heavily emphasized human effort and moral competence. He was probably a Celt from Britain, but was active in Rome and around the Mediterranean.

A mission to Britain, led by Germanus, Bishop of Auxerre (near Paris), was launched in 429 to halt the heresy but was not entirely successful; a second mission went out c.440, thus implying that Christianity in Britain was firmly established at that time, to the extent that Pelagianism posed a threat serious enough for the Church in Gaul to have to deal with it. The leaders of the British Church were most likely Romanized Celts; St Patrick, writing of his life in his *Confession*, indicates that he was of a British Christian family.

The British Church suffered a major setback in the late fifth century with the withdrawal of Roman troops, and invasions by Picts and Scots from the north and Germanic tribes from the continent. Christianity survived most strongly in the Celtic kingdoms of the west; the invasions of the Angles, Saxons, and Jutes undoubtedly contributed to the isolation of the Celtic Church and the preservation of its practices. Gildas, a Celtic monk of this period, blamed the troubles of the Britons on the laxity of British princes and priests. His indictment in *De Excidio . . . Britanniae . . . (The Fall and Conquest of Britain . . .)*, written c.540, is unreliable as history, but it does attest the tenacity of the Church in Britain as an organized body and as a power in social, political, and spiritual affairs.

When, in 597, Pope Gregory the Great sent a mission to the English headed by Augustine, the British Church was still in existence, with its own priests, bishops and customs. In 603, Augustine attempted to bring the British bishops into line with Roman practices, to enlist their aid in evangelizing the pagan English, and to have them submit to his authority. The bishops accused him of pride and refused his overtures (see Bede, *HE*, II, 2). The friction between the *Romani*, represented by Augustine and his followers, and the Celtic party continued thereafter. Nonconformity, to the Roman Church, was sinful, a denial of the authority of the universal Church; to the Celtic clergy, conformity meant the loss of their authority and long-standing traditions, an admission of error.

The Celtic Church in Ireland developed along its own lines. It is not known when Christianity reached Ireland, but it had certainly taken a foothold by the fifth century when Pope Celestine sent Palladius as bishop to the Christian Irish. According to tradition, on the death of Palladius, Patrick was chosen as his replacement and set out on a similar mission, but also to preach to the pagan Irish of the north, among whom he had lived for a time as a slave.

Patrick, called the apostle to the Irish, helped to establish an ecclesiastical organization in the north of Ireland; apparently, there was already an established Church in the south. It was the Church in northern Ireland, under the kings of Dál Riata, which was to affect profoundly the growth and development of the Celtic Church in Scotland and northern England in the sixth and seventh centuries.

The Church in Ireland, untouched by Germanic invasions, fostered Christian learning, letters and art during the sixth century. The Irish churches and monastic centres became known in Europe for their schools and their intellectual and artistic output. Numerous Irish missionaries made their way to the continent where they established monasteries and preached their brand of ascetic Christianity. By the seventh century, the Roman Church was pushing for conformity among the Irish, both on the continent and in Ireland.

In the late eighth century, a reform movement began under Mael-rúain of Tallaght (*d.*792) which sought a return to an earlier stage of the Irish Church, with an emphasis on anchoritism and austere living. The reformers called themselves *Céli Dé*, the 'servants of God', or Culdees.* The movement spread to Scotland, where it developed further in the ninth to the twelfth centuries.

THE CELTIC CHURCH IN SCOTLAND. Celtic Christianity entered Scotland largely through the work of St Columba* and his followers. The first recorded Christian missionary, however, was St Ninian,* a British bishop who preached to the Picts* of Scotland and founded a church at Whithorn* in Galloway (*see* Early Ecclesiastical Sites). By the time of Bede, the see of Whithorn, occupied by Pechthelm (*see* Celtic Saints), lay within the metropolitan province of York.

Ninian's foundation served as the centre of Christianity to the southern Picts. Although there is some evidence of links with Ireland (most notably Patrick's letter to Coroticus, a ruler of Strathclyde, regarding his sale of Irish Christian captives to the 'apostate' Picts), the Church of the southern Picts seems to have followed the Roman, rather than the Celtic, order.

Columba's mission was not initially to the Picts but to the people of Scottish Dalriada (Argyll). His disciples and successors extended his work to the northern Picts, and eventually the Columban Church dominated the Church in western Scotland and influenced the churches of south-east and north-east (e.g. Deer) Scotland and Northumbria. Iona* (*see also* Early Ecclesiastical Sites) became a centre of learning as well as worship, a sanctuary for penitents and exiles, and the focal point for Celtic Christianity in northern Britain. Oswald,* king of Northumbria, requested a bishop from the Scottish Church to preach the Christian faith to his people, and Aidan, a monk of Iona, was sent and was granted the island of Lindisfarne.

The Church established by Columba followed Celtic traditions and customs, a point on which Bede is continually critical. Other churches in southern Scotland also followed the Celtic order, such as the sixth-century foundation of St Kentigern at Glasgow in the Celtic kingdom of Strathclyde. The churches of south-east Scotland came under pressure from Northumbria and the Roman

CELTIC SAINTS

faction in the seveneth century. St Cuthbert, who had been a monk at Old Melrose* (originally a Celtic foundation; see Early Ecclesiastical Sites), followed Roman customs regarding the celebration of Easter and other forms, but showed tendencies toward Celtic Christianity and his ascetic practices.

THE END OF THE CELTIC CHURCH. The aftermath of the Synod of Whitby did not result in immediate conversion to Roman customs; acceptance among the Celtic churches was slow. Adomnán,* ninth abbot of Iona, failed to persuade the monks of his community to conform to the Roman date of Easter, although eventually it was accepted.

The terminal date for Celtic Christianity is arguable. The churches were ravaged but not destroyed by the Viking invasions of the late eighth and early ninth centuries; however, as a cultural entity Celtic Christianity had faded by the end of the twelfth century. In Ireland, the arrival of the Normans put paid to a distinctively Irish Church. In Scotland, the last traces of Celtic Christianity began to disappear after the succession of Malcolm III* in 1057/8. His queen, St Margaret* of Scotland, pressed for ecclesiastical reforms which were continued under her son, David I.* These reforms brought the Scottish Celtic Church more into line with the Church in England and the rest of western Europe. The Culdees in Scotland were by c.1300 assimilated into Roman monasticism by becoming Augustinians,* while Celtic monasteries on the continent gradually accepted Benedictine* elements and then, by the late eleventh century, the whole Rule.

See also Monasticism, Celtic.

B. Colgrave and R. A. B. Mynors (eds), Bede's Historia Ecclesiastica Gentis Anglorum (O, ²1992); K. Hughes, The Church in Early Irish Society (L, 1966); K. Hughes, 'The Celtic Church: Is This a Valid Concept?', Cambridge Medieval Celtic Studies 1 (1980), 1–20; W. D. Simpson, The Celtic Church in Scotland (A, 1935); A. P. Smyth, Warlords and Holy Men (L, 1984); A. C. Thomas, Christianity in Roman Britain (L, 1981); J. T. McNeill, The Celtic Churches (Chicago, 1974); R. Sharpe, 'Some Problems concerning the Organisation of the Church in Early Medieval Ireland', Peritia 3 (1984), 230–74; A. A. M. Duncan, Scotland: The Making of the Kingdom (E, 1975); A. C. Thomas, 'The Evidence from North Britain', in M. W. Barley and R. P. C. Hanson (eds), Christianity in Britain, 300–700 (Leicester, 1968), 93–121; L. Gougaud, Christianity in Celtic Lands (E, 1932); J. Ryan, Irish Monasticism (Dublin, 1931).

D. A. Bray

Celtic Saints. The saints* of the Celtic Church in Scotland are known mostly through legend. Few historical facts are available and, in some cases, the historicity of the saint is questionable. However, archaeological and place-name evidence point to the existence of saints' cults and a tradition of belief in their efficacy. The Celtic saints are those who flourished mainly in the fifth to the eighth centuries and adhered to, or were influenced by, Celtic ecclesiastical custom and tradition (see Celtic Church).

The majority of the early saints were from Ireland; they came as missionaries to the Picts* and to minister to Christians in Scottish Dalriada and northern Britain (see Gaelic). St Columba's* foundation on Iona* became the most influential centre of Christianity in western Scotland and northern Britain; although the extent of Columba's mission to the Picts is uncertain, the achievements of his disciples and successors point to an active Christian mission. The cults of certain Irish saints, St Bride for example, were probably imported by these early missionaries.

The legends of these saints are preserved in manuscript sources from Ireland (lives and martyrologies), as well as Scottish sources, such as calendars of saints and lectionaries, in particular the Breviary of Aberdeen.* The names and legends of several native-born saints are included in these sources. These were of Pictish or of British origin and would have been trained in the Irish Church or in the Church of northern Britain. Their influence was to be found mainly in parts of the north-east of Scotland and in the Lowlands.

The legends of the saints were recorded several centuries after their death, and consist largely of miracle stories and popular folk tradition. Miracle stories were a major part of a saint's tradition, designed to enhance the saint's holiness and to promote his or her cult. Many were local saints whose cults centred on a small area. They were commemorated by their churches as representatives of a Christian ideal and exemplary way of life.

LIST OF MAIN SAINTS.

Adomnán* (Adamnan) Irish; seventh century; feast-day 23 September. St Adomnán was the ninth abbot of Iona* and a distant relative of St Columba.* He succeeded to the office in 679. After a visit to the Northumbrian church, he accepted the Roman date of Easter and other Roman customs in favour of Celtic practices, but was unsuccessful in converting the monks of Iona. Adomnán is known for his scholarly works, especially his *Life of Columba*.

Aidán Irish; seventh century; feast-day 31 August. St Aidan was a monk of Iona* who became the first Bishop of Lindisfarne. Bede* relates how he was sent to Northumbria at the request of King Oswald,* and founded his monastery on Holy Island. This became second only to Iona as a centre of religion and learning. Aidan's mission extended throughout the north of England and south-west of Scotland. He died at Bamburgh in 651. Bede accords him high praise for his achievements and piety, despite his Celtic affiliation.

Bathán Irish; sixth–seventh century; feast-day 9 June. Also known as Baithene, St Bathan is mentioned in Adomnán's *Life of Columba*. He was a cousin of the saint and one of his companions to

Iona. He became abbot of Tiree and then succeeded Columba as abbot of Iona in 597.

Baya Irish; seventh century?; feast-day 3 November. St Baya, Begha or Vey, is commemorated on Little Cumbrae, but nothing is known of her life. She may have been a member of the community of St Maura (3rd November) whose cult centred on Kilmaurs. She is often identified with St Begha of Dunbar, although the connection is in doubt. St Bee (31st October) of St Bees Head in Cumberland was an Irish princess who was consecrated a nun by St Aidan and died *c*.681.

Blane Scottish; sixth century; feast-day 11 August. St Blane or *Bláán* (later *Blathan*) was born on Bute and studied in Ireland where he was a disciple of St Canice. Blane was ordained a bishop and preached in Scotland, often in the company of his uncle, St Catan, of whom nothing is known. He died at Kingarth *c*.590. The cathedral of Dunblane was built on the site of his monastery.

Boisil British; seventh century; feast-day 23 February. St Boisil or Boswell is mentioned by Bede as a monk of Lindisfarne. He was taught by St Aidan and succeeded St Eata as abbot of Melrose, where he later became teacher to the young St Cuthbert. He achieved considerable fame as a teacher and a biblical scholar, particularly on the Gospel of St John. He died of plague *c*.664 and is commemorated in St Boswell's, Roxburghshire.

Bride Irish; fifth century; feast-day 1 February. St Bride or *Brigit*, along with St Patrick and St Columba, is among the foremost saints of Celtic Ireland. Her legends have put her historicity in doubt; she is often associated with the Celtic goddess, Brigid. Her Life by Cogitosus is one of the earliest examples of Celtic hagiography and was composed for her community at Kildare. Her cult gained considerable popularity in Scotland, although there is no indication in her legends that she travelled there. She became known as 'Mary of the Gael' and is commemorated in place names throughout the British Isles (e.g. Kilbride, Bridewell). In Scottish legend, she is depicted as the midwife at the birth of Jesus.

Canice Irish; sixth century; feast-day 11 October. St Canice, Kenneth or *Cainnech* was born in Ireland *c*.515, and studied under St Cadoc of Wales and St Finnian of Clonard. He was said to have been a close friend of St Columba and to have accompanied him on his visit to the Pictish King, Brude. Cambuskenneth below Stirling and Kilchainnech (Cill Choinnich) on Iona attest to his tradition in Scotland, where he sometimes preached. He is also purported to have built the first church on the site of St Andrews. He died *c*.599.

Colmán Irish; seventh century; feast-day 18 February. St Colman was the third bishop of Lindisfarne. He was Irish by birth and a monk of Iona. Bede relates his role as the chief advocate for the Celtic faction at the Synod of Whitby. After the synod, he resigned his bishopric and returned to Ireland with several Irish and English monks. He founded a monastery on Inishboffin, off Connaught, and one at Mayo. Bede regrets his Celtic 'errors', but credits him with great Christian virtue.

Columba* (*Colum Cille*) Irish; sixth century; feast-day 9 June. St Columba was born into the nobility of Ulster but chose to enter the Church. He founded several monasteries in Ireland before his great foundation on Iona, which became the focal point of Christianity on the west coast of Scotland. Columba was renowned for his leadership and learning in both Ireland and Scotland. He died on Iona in 597.

Comgan Irish; eighth century; feast-day 13 October. St Comgan, Cowan or Cuan, was supposedly an Irish prince of Leinster who fled to Scotland with his sister and her children after a defeat in battle (*see also* Kentigerna and Fillan). He settled in Lochalsh and built a monastery, presumably having entered the Church in exile. His feast was celebrated in the diocese of Aberdeen.

Curitan Pictish; seventh century; feast-day 16 March. St Curitan is known as St Boniface in Bede, who tells that he was sent by abbot Ceolfrid of Wearmouth, at the request of King Nechtan, to preach among the Picts. Curitan introduced Roman usage to the Picts and Scots and was among the Scottish representatives at the Synod of Birr in 697. He was made Bishop of Ross, and established churches at Invergowrie, Restenneth, and elsewhere.

Cuthbert British; seventh century; feast-day 20 March. St Cuthbert is the patron saint of Northumbria and is known largely through the writings of Bede, both in his *History* and a *Life* of the saint. Cuthbert was probably born in Lowland Scotland; while a boy tending sheep, he received a vision which inspired him to enter the monastery at Melrose where he later became prior. He was appointed prior of Lindisfarne after the Synod of Whitby,* and was consecrated abbot and bishop in 685. Cuthbert preferred the life of a recluse, but under his leadership Lindisfarne flourished. He died in 687 and was buried on Lindisfarne, but Viking attacks forced the removal of his relics to a safer place. Eventually his body was deposited at Durham (*see* Anglo-Saxon Saints).

Donan (*Donnán*) Irish; sixth-century; feast-day 17 April. St Donan was a disciple of St Columba and accompanied him to Iona. With fifty-two companions, he founded a monastery on Eigg, but the entire community was massacred by raiders after Easter Mass. St Donnan's well on Eigg and Kildonan remain to commemorate one of the first martyrs of Scotland.

Drostán possibly Irish; sixth–seventh century; feast-day 11 July. St Drostan was supposedly of Irish royal blood, but he became a monk under St Columba. He lived as a hermit in Glenesk, then became the first abbot of Deer in Aberdeenshire. After his death (*c*.610), his body was removed to his shrine at Aberdour.

Duthac, *Dubhthach* Scottish, d.*c*.1068; feast-day 8

March. St Duthac, according to the Aberdeen Breviary,* was a native Scot who was educated in Ireland; upon his return, he was appointed Bishop of Ross. He was buried at Tain (in Gaelic, Baile Dhubhthaich, Duthac's Town), whose patron saint he became, and his shrine became an important place of pilgrimage. There is some question as to the date of his floruit. The Annals of Ulster mention an abbot of Iona, Dubthach, who died in 937, and a Dubthach Albanach who died in 1065. Other sources place him in the mid-thirteenth century.

Seven miracles are attributed to him; as a boy, he carried red-hot coals in his clothes without being singed. When a kite stole a piece of meat and a ring from his disciple, Duthac had the bird restore the ring, but allowed it to eat the meat. Duthac's body was found uncorrupted seven years after his death. He is commemorated in Kilduthie, Arduthie and Kilduich.

Fergus probably Pictish; eighth century; feast-day 15 November. The life of St Fergus is obscure. He has been identified with 'Fergustus, Bishop of Scotia, a Pict', who attended a synod held by Pope Gregory II in Rome in 721. His cult extended throughout the north-east of Scotland. By tradition he died and was buried at Glamis.

Fillan (Faolán) Irish; eighth century; feast-day January. In his tradition, St Fillan is the son of St Kentigerna and the nephew of St Comgan. For a while, he lived as a hermit at Glendochart, Perthshire. He then became abbot of St Andrews. Strathfillan commemorates the place of his death. His legends are confused with those of several other Irish Fillans.

Finan (Fíonán) Scottish? sixth century; feast-day 16 March. St Finan was supposedly a disciple of St Kentigern* who worked with him in Wales, then in Scotland, where he is said to have founded several churches in the Aberdeen area. There was a Finan born in Ireland, d.c.575, called Finan the Leper because he took a child's leprosy on himself. When he desired to visit Rome, St Columba* forbade it, but gave him a vision of the city. This saint may be identified with St Finan of Moville, the teacher of St Columba. Another St Finan (c.662, feast-day 17 February) is recorded. He was a Scottish monk of Iona who succeeded Aidan as bishop of Lindisfarne. There is a Finan commemorated at Kilwinning. St Wynnin or Gwynnin (in Latin Vynninus) was a Strathclyde saint who was born into a noble family, but left home to take up a religious life. He settled at Holywood, Dumfriesshire, and died 21 January 579.

Kentigern British/Scottish; sixth century; feast-day 14 January. St Kentigern is the patron saint of Glasgow, better known by his nickname, St Mungo. He was supposedly the first bishop to the Strathclyde Britons. His tradition has him driven into exile in Wales, where he met St David. He was later recalled to Scotland by King Rhydderch, and continued his mission in Glasgow where he died c.612. A legend which associates him with St Serf is highly dubious, although it is likely that he was a native of the Lothian region.

Kentigerna (Cáintighearnd) Irish; eighth century; feast-day 7 January. By tradition, St Kentigerna was an Irish princess of Leinster who fled to Scotland on her husband's death with her son and her brother (see above Fillan and Comgan). She withdrew to a hermitage on the island of Inchebroida in Loch Lomond, where she died c.734.

Kessog (Ceasóg) Irish; sixth century; feast-day 10 March. St Kessog or Mackessog is said in the Aberdeen Breviary* to have been born into the royal family of Munster, his father being the King of Cashel. He became a monk, went to Scotland, and joined the Culdees.* He was appointed Bishop in the provinces of Leven and Boyne, and took up residence on Monk's Island in Loch Lomond which became his base for evangelizing the surrounding territory. He was either murdered at Bandry or martyred abroad, and buried at Luss. The parish is fancifully said to have taken its name from the sweet herbs in which his body was embalmed (*lus* being Gaelic for 'herb'). Robert Bruce granted the church at Luss a three-mile sanctuary girth in 1313. Kessog became the patron of Lennox, where his bell was still venerated in the seventeenth century. He is depicted in art as an archer with a bow in his hand.

Machan Scottish; ? century; feast-day 28 September. The life of St Machan is largely unknown. He was supposedly a Scot trained in Ireland and is connected with Lennoxtown.

Machar possibly Irish; sixth century; feast-day 12 November. St Machar, or Macharius, was one of the companions of St Columba to Iona. He preached on Mull, was consecrated Bishop and preached among the Picts of Aberdeenshire. One tradition makes him the founder of Aberdeen; the church of Old Aberdeen is called *ecclesia Sancti Machorii*, 'St Machor's Church', in a papal bull of 1157.

Maelrubha Irish; seventh–eighth century; feast-day 21 April. St Maelrubha was of the same lineage as St Columba and was a pupil under St Comgall of Bangor. He went to Iona c.671 and became one of the foremost missionaries to the Picts. His most famous foundation was at Applecross, Ross-shire, which became the centre of his mission. His name (often in the form of *Ma-Ruibhe*) occurs in several place-names such as Eilean Maree, Mulruby, Murray, Summuruft, and others which attest to the breadth of his cult, if not his travels.

Modan (M'Aodhán) Irish; sixth century; feast-day 4 February. Little is known of the life of St Modan except that he preached along the Forth, in Stirling and Falkirk, and retired as a hermit near Dumbarton. There were evidently several other saints with this name.

Moluag (Mo-Luóc) Scottish; sixth century; feast-day 25 June. St Moluag was the founder of Lismore off Appin and, according to legend, a friend and rival to St Columba. A Scot educated in Ireland (perhaps at Bangor under St Comgall), his sphere of influence extended among the Picts of the north-west and the Hebrides, where his name is commemorated in the place-name Kilmaluaig (Skye and Tiree). He died at Rosmarkie (Ross-shire) in 572 and his relics were deposited at Murlach.

Mungo: see Kentigern.

Nathalan (otherwise *Nothlan, Nethalan*) Pictish?; seventh century; feast-day 19 January. Little is known of this saint. He was supposedly born at Tullicht near Aberdeen. He became an anchorite, supporting himself by farming; according to one legend, he was able to feed his entire people during a famine. On a pilgrimage to Rome, he was consecrated a bishop by the pope, then returned to Scotland where he founded several churches. He died at Tullicht in 678.

Pechthelm British?; eighth century; feast-day ?. St Pechthelm was known to Bede and may have been the main source for Bede's information on the see of Galloway when it was re-established by the Northumbrian Church. Pechthelm was consecrated the first Bishop of the see, whose centre was at Whithorn* (*see also* Anglo-Saxon Saints; Ninian).

Regulus, nationality unknown, fourth century?; feast-day 30 March. St Regulus or St Rule (Irish, *Riaghail*) is a legendary figure credited with bringing the relics of St Andrew* to Scotland. He was thought to be a native of Patras in Achaia, where Andrew was martyred, and brought the relics to Fife after receiving an angelic dream. He founded a monastery at the site of St Andrews and became the first Bishop. No *Life* exists for him before the ninth century, although his cult is thought to be ancient; his origins, however, are obscure.

Rónán Irish; eighth century; feast-day 7 February. St Ronan is an obscure figure, but a saint of this name is associated with Kingarth in Bute. He has left his name on Iona in Port Ronan and Teampull Ronain, but his real connection with the community is unknown. Nevertheless, several dedications exist over a wide area, from Islay to Lewis, attesting to the dissemination of his cult.

Serf Irish/British?; fifth–sixth century; feast-day 1 July. St Serf or Servanus is surrounded by legend. He has been associated with St Kentigern and given an exotic eastern origin. The earliest tradition makes him an Irishman who was consecrated by Palladius and founded a monastery at Culross.

Ternan (*Torannán* or *Mo-Dairen*) Scottish/Pictish; sixth century; feast-day 12 June. Sometimes confused with St Servanus, St Ternan is also purported to have been consecrated by Palladius and to have founded a monastery at Culross. He was a missionary among the Picts and resided at Abernethy, a Pictish capital, where he died. St Ternan is venerated in Aberdeenshire.

Triduanna British?; fourth–fifth century?; feast-day 8 October. Also known as Tredwell, St Triduanna has been associated with both St Regulus and St Curitan. She is a saint of Edinburgh, where she had a hermitage whose well was supposed to be efficacious in curing eye diseases. According to popular tradition, she plucked out her own eyes to discourage an importunate lover and preserve her virginity for Christ. Her name, apparently deriving originally from Latin, *triduanum ieiunium*, 'three days' fast', may reflect the rigour of her fasting.

See also Anglo-Saxon Saints; Early Ecclesiastical Sites.

A. P. Forbes, *Kalendars of Scottish Saints* (E, 1872); C. Plummer (ed.), *Vitae Sanctorum Hiberniae*, 2 vols (O, 1921, 1965); B. Colgrave and R. A. B. Mynors (eds), *Bede's Ecclesiastical History of the English People* (O, ²1992); A. Boyle, 'Notes on Scottish Saints', *IR* 32 (1981), 59–81; H. Thurston and D. Attwater (eds), *Butler's Lives of the Saints*, 4 vols (NY, 1963); J. J. Delaney, *Dictionary of Saints* (Surrey, 1982); M. O. Anderson, 'Columba and Other Irish Saints in Scotland', in J. L. McCracken (ed.), *Historical Studies* V (L, 1965), 26–36; E. S. Towill, *The Saints of Scotland* (E, 1983); W. J. Watson, *The History of the Celtic Place-Names of Scotland* (²Shannon, 1973), 270–338; M. Herbert, *Iona, Kells and Derry* (O, 1988); D. H. Farmer, *The Oxford Dictionary of Saints* (O, ²1987).

D. A. Bray

Census, Religious (1851). The Census of Religious Worship and Education, Scotland, contained two parts: first, a census of church accommodation and of church attenders on Sunday 30th March, matching a similar census taken in England and Wales on that day; and secondly, a census of educational provision at all kinds of day, Sunday and evening schools. The compiler of the Census, Horace Mann, caused controversy when in the introduction to the English and Welsh report, he drew attention to the extent of non-churchgoing (especially, he asserted without evidence, amongst the working classes), and the near equal size of attendance by Protestant Dissenters with that of the CofE. Controversy north of the border over denominational size (and principally the weakness of the CofS eleven years after the Disruption*) and day-school education led to an undertaking that the Census would not publish enumeration results for units smaller than counties or burghs, to prevent identification of individual returns. Local returns have been preserved for England and Wales, but the Scottish returns have never been found and were probably destroyed. Political pressure in 1854 to release the results quickly prevented Mann from including a detailed Scottish commentary.

The Scottish census also occasioned many difficulties. There were no local registrars in Scotland to enforce full enumeration by clergy. As a result, non-returns were significantly higher in Scotland (20 per cent for church attendances) than in England and Wales (4 per cent), and were more prevalent in the CofS (32 per cent of attendances) than the FC (12 per cent) or UPC (10 per cent). In addition, there were general statistical problems evident in all British results: figures were 'rounded'

CENSUS, RELIGIOUS (1851)

by enumerators (indicating at best negligence and at worst inflation); and attenders were counted at morning, afternoon and evening worship, without any satisfactory system (nor has one been devised since) to distinguish between single and multiple attenders ('oncers', 'twicers' and 'thricers'). Mann suggested in the English and Welsh Census that individual attenders could be estimated by adding morning attenders to half of afternoon attenders and to one-third of evening attenders, but this is statistically unjustified.

Despite these and other problems, the Census is an unique source of information on the denominational alignment of the population, church accommodation and *per capita* rates of churchgoing. The raw statistics for Scotland were presented in national and county tables, and in tables covering fifty-three burghs. In each there was set against every denomination the number of places of worship, the number of 'sittings' (broken down into 'appropriated' and 'free'), and the number of attenders at morning, afternoon and evening services. The results reveal many aspects of religion in mid-nineteenth-century Scotland. Contemporaries adduced conclusions from it to support current theories: such as the non-churchgoing of the working classes, and the lower rate of churchgoing in towns compared to the country. But recent historians have re-worked the data using modern statistical techniques and demonstrated errors in many long-standing interpretations. In terms of levels of churchgoing, the Census recorded a total number of 1,752,688 attendances on Census Sunday, 60.7 per cent of the population; allowing for 'twicers' and 'thricers', the true attendance rate was between that figure and 32.7 per cent, the proportion who attended the most popular (morning) service. Churchgoing was perceptibly higher *per capita* in the east of Scotland than the west, but the levels were not appreciably lower in industrial counties compared with agricultural. Indeed, unlike England and Wales, rates of churchgoing were higher in towns than in the country. In Britain as a whole there was no tendency for churchgoing to diminish as towns grew larger in size.

The Census showed that the denominational aligment of the population was very diffused. The CofS attracted the largest proportion of attendances (32.3 per cent), closely followed by the FC (31.7 per cent), with the UPC third (19.2 per cent). Taken together, Presbyterian Dissenters clearly outnumbered CofS with 53.5 per cent. Non-Presbyterians accounted for 13.78 per cent, the largest being RCC (4.6 per cent), the Congregationalists (3.9 per cent), and EpCS (2.5 per cent). The Census showed that these distributions were uneven across Scotland. FC dominated in the Highlands and Hebrides (95.9 per cent of recorded attendances in Sutherland) and was strong in the cities (taking 33 per cent in Edinburgh, almost double the CofS figure). UPC was strongest in Orkney and Shetland (where it was the largest Church), the south-east and urban districts of central Scotland (including Glasgow where it was the largest Church with 23 per cent of attendances). RCC was strongest in Glasgow (16 per cent of attendances) and neighbouring counties, with some adherents in Edinburgh, Inverness-shire and Banff. The Census showed that church accommodation (sittings *per capita* of population) was poorest in the most rapidly-expanding cities and industrial districts: in the counties of Lanarkshire, West Lothian, Ayrshire, Midlothian and Angus. The education section of the Census showed 10 per cent (292,549) of the population enrolled at Sunday schools; of these, 31 per cent were at FC schools, 26 per cent CofS, 19 per cent UPC, and 4 per cent RCC. Of 5,242 day schools, 937 were (statutory) parochial schools and a further 1,771 were supported by religious bodies. Over 13 per cent (368,517) of the population 'belonged' to day schools: of these, 21 per cent were in parochial schools, 17 per cent in FC schools, 10 per cent in CofS schools (with a further 7 per cent in schools supported to some degree by CofS), and 4 per cent at schools conducted by other Churches. A government religious census was never again taken in Britain.

Census of Great Britain, 1851: Religious Worship and Education, Scotland, *British Parliamentary Papers* 1854, lix; D. J. Withrington, 'The 1851 Census of Religious Worship and Education', *RSCHS* 18(1974), 133–48; C. G. Brown, *The Social History of Religion in Scotland* (L and NY, 1987), 57–84; C. G. Brown, 'Religion', in R. Pope (ed.), *Atlas of British Social and Economic History* (L, 1988); H. McLeod, 'Religion', in J. Langton and R. J. Morris (eds), *Atlas of Industrializing Britain* (L and NY, 1986); C. G. Brown, 'Did Urbanization Secularize Britain?', *Urban History Yearbook*, 1988.

C. G. *Brown*

Central African Federation (1953–63), federation which linked two British colonies, Northern Rhodesia and Nyasaland, with the autonomous 'colony' of Southern Rhodesia. The latter had been ruled by Cecil Rhodes' British South Africa Company until 1923, when the white settlers had gained *de facto* though not *de jure* independence from Britain. In 1929 and 1939 the British Government resisted settler agitation for the union of the three territories largely as a result of African and Scottish missionary opposition in Nyasaland, and, to a lesser degree, Northern Rhodesia, inspired by their fear of permanent white domination of the African population.

In 1945 the agitation started again and despite even more vehement and well-organized African opposition supported by the CofS, the Federation came into being in 1953. The only concession to its opponents was that it was a federal and not a unitary state. Opposition mounted in the north until a state of emergency was declared in March 1959. In May, the General Assembly of the CofS, profoundly influenced by the work of Kenneth Mackenzie,* by an overwhelming majority demanded that the British Government investigate what had been going on in Nyasaland. The Devlin Commission resulted from this Scottish Church pres-

CHALMERS, JAMES

sure. Its critical report began the changes in British policy which, by 1961, clearly were pointing to the dissolution of the Federation which came to a formal end in December 1963.

See also Missions.

R. I. Rotberg, *The Rise of Nationalism in Central Africa* (O, 1966); H. Franklin, *Unholy Wedlock: The Failure of the Central African Federation* (L, 1963).

A. C. Ross

Chalmers, James (1841-1901), missionary to Cook Islands and Papua New Guinea. Born at Ardrishaig, Argyllshire, he achieved well at Celtic Society and pupil-teacher examinations at Glen Aray SSPCK* school. Influenced by his 'Arminian'* UP pastor, Gilbert Meikle, in December 1854 Chalmers responded to a call to mission which proved seminal after his conversion experience during the 1859 Revival.

Missionary preparation included reading Wesleyan and Puritan theologians and missionary biography; serving eight months as a city missionary with Greyfriars'. UPC, Glasgow; two years, 1862-4, studying under gracious, godly Henry Robert Reynolds, Principal of Cheshunt College; and a final year of missions and linguistics at LMS* Farquhar House.

In 1865, Chalmers was ordained to the Congregational ministry. His voyage to the Cook Islands included two shipwrecks before the infamous sea-captain, Bully Hayes, landed him at Rarotonga in May 1867. From 1867-77 Chalmers trained Pacific Islanders as missionary teachers through the Rarotonga Institution and transferred church responsibilities to local leaders, while yearning personally for pioneer evangelism further west. In 1877 he joined the LMS New Guinea Mission. 'Tamate', as he was known locally, approached previously unreached village leaders, won their confidence and located teachers amongst them – Pacific Islanders initially, but from 1884-5, Papuans trained by his colleague, William George Lawes.* Chalmers established mission centres along the southern Papuan coast.

A well-known explorer, Chalmers' role in British Papua Protectorate negotiations, 1884-5, and his views opposing colonization and indenturing labour from New Guinea became widely respected. Chalmers published sixteen Papuan language vocabularies and ethnographic material on six Papuan societies, laying a significant base for later Melanesian anthropology.

Chalmers and his new colleague, Oliver Fellowes Tomkins, were killed contacting the still unreached people of Goaribari Island, Papua, on Eastern Sunday, 1901.

Pioneering in New Guinea (L, 1887); *Pioneer Life and Work in New Guinea, 1877-94* (L, 1895); 'New Guinea – Past, Present and Future', *Proc. of Royal Colonial Inst.* 18 (1886-7), 88-122.

R. Lovett, *James Chalmers: His Autobiography and Letters* (L, 1902); D. Langmore, *Tamate – A King* (Melbourne, 1974); J. M. Hitchen, 'Training

CHALMERS, THOMAS

Tamate: Formation of the Nineteenth Century Missionary Worldview: The Case of James Chalmers' (PhD, Aberdeen University, 1984).

J. M. Hitchen

Chalmers Lectures, a series established in memory of Thomas Chalmers* to uphold 'the Headship of Christ over His Church and its independent spiritual jurisdiction'. The four-year lectureship, open solely to ministers and professors of the FC, was founded with an endowment of £5,000 in 1880 by Robert Macfie of Airds and Oban, who was 'deeply interested in the maintenance of the principles' of the FC. He appointed the first lecturer, Sir Henry W. Moncreiff* (*The Free Church Principle: Its Character and History*, E, 1883). The lectures were to be delivered in successive years in the FC Colleges in Edinburgh, Glasgow and Aberdeen.

In the unions of 1900 and 1929, the lectureship passed via the UFC to the CofS. It could now deal also with 'the general doctrine of the Church and kingdom of Christ, or any subject cognate thereto', and could be delivered not only by a CofS minister or professor but by any adhering to CofS views on 'the Headship of Christ...'. It is controlled by a committee comprising the heads of the Colleges (now united with the University Divinity Faculties; *see* Education, Theological) and representatives of the CofS General Assembly. The committee is charged with securing publication. Originally all FC ministers and missionaries were provided with copies.

Volumes worthy of note have included C. G. M'Crie,* *The Confessions of the Church of Scotland. Their Evolution in History* (E, 1907); H. Watt,* *Thomas Chalmers and the Disruption* (E, 1943); G. D. Henderson,* *Presbyterianism* (A, 1954); A. I. Dunlop, *William Carstares and the Kirk by Law Established* (E, 1967); A. C. Cheyne, *The Transforming of the Kirk* (E, 1983).

PAGAFCS 1878-1883, 190-3; first seven listed in *AFCS* I, 65.

D. F. Wright

Chalmers, Thomas (1780-1847), preacher, theologian, Church leader and social reformer. Scotland's greatest nineteenth-century churchman was born in Anstruther (E. Fife) and educated in the local school and at the University of St Andrews (1791-9). In 1803 he became minister of Kilmany (N-E. Fife), and remained there until 1815, when he was presented to the prestigious charge of the Tron, Glasgow. Four years later he moved to the nearby parish of St John's, where he was given freedom to pursue his distinctive approach to religious and social questions. In 1823 he was appointed Professor of Moral Philosophy at St Andrews, and in 1828 Professor of Divinity at Edinburgh, gradually emerging as the leader of Evangelicalism* within the Kirk. Deeply involved in the Ten Years Conflict,* he took the Non-intrusionists* out of the Establishment in 1843 (*see* Disruption*). Father-figure and organizing genius of the emergent FC, he ended his days as Principal and Professor of Theology in New College,* Edinburgh.

While at Kilmany, Chalmers (like many other ministers of the period) felt able to divide his time between cultural pursuits and the care of his parishioners, and even the misgivings of Presbytery did not convince him that he had been neglecting essentials. Mathematics, natural science and economics engaged much of his attention. But a succession of deaths within the family circle, his own serious illness, and perhaps the changing climate of opinion in Church and nation, led to his conversion (*c.*1810/11) from conventional to enthusiastic Christianity. Though the imprint of Moderatism* never left him, he entered the evangelical camp and became an opponent of pluralities, an advocate of foreign missions and Bible societies,* and a proclaimer of the message that 'with a new principle and a new power, we become new creatures in Jesus Christ'. He also achieved fame as one of the greatest pulpit orators his country had ever known. From the time of his settlement in Glasgow he never left the centre of the national stage.

Chalmers' concern for the revival of religion and the reformation of society involved him in a series of arduous and controversial campaigns. All were inter-connected, and extended throughout his mature life; yet at different times one or other came to special prominence. The chief of them were these:

(i) *The revitalization of the parish** (notably during his years in the west). Glasgow in 1815 was not only racked by social distress and verging on revolution: it was also alienated from both gospel and Church, a menacing portent of what all Scotland might eventually become. The myriad evils of industrialism (secularization included) did not, however, dismay Chalmers. He believed that they could be cured by a recovery, within the new urban environment, of the traditional virtues of Scottish rural and small-town life – a recovery to be brought about by taking seriously the parochial organization inherited from Scotland's past but weakened or even obliterated by recent developments. A manageably small area encompassing some two thousand souls who lived, worked and worshipped together (the Anstruther model?), with a church and a school at its centre, a minister and Kirk Session* to attend to its spiritual and temporal necessities: here was the redemptive unit of Scottish society, the means of national regeneration. He set about making the Tron, and still more St John's, an example of what the revivified parish might mean for city and nation. Top priority was given to the needs of local inhabitants rather than the crowds of wealthy visitors drawn by his preaching fame; and the otherwise insuperable tasks of spiritual supervision, education and poor relief were tackled by the subdivision of the parish into manageable units ('proportions') and the devolution of responsibility to elders, deacons, Sunday- and day-school teachers. In many respects the experiment was a huge success. The church began to resume its place as the centre of the community and the guardian of the people's well-being; and the methods employed were not only copied elsewhere at the time but had their influence on subsequent generations. Even today, the parish ideal as Chalmers presented it still dominates the Scottish ecclesiastical scene.

(ii) *The defence of traditional approaches to poor relief** (particularly while in Glasgow). Whereas other social analysts and reformers were coming to believe that only innovations like the legal assessment of ratepayers could eliminate the worst evils of poverty, Chalmers adhered to the old remedies – not least because of the central role they gave to the Church. The self-help of the poor, the assistance of relatives, the kindness of neighbours, the discriminating charity of the rich, and the supervisory vigilance of the diaconate, with the offering-plate in the background as a last resort, could achieve far more than a compulsory poor-relief scheme with its bureaucracy, its impersonality, and its tendency to demoralize the recipients. He acted on his beliefs, and for a time his efforts really did appear successful: relief cost less, and the number of destitute folk within the parish declined. To the end of his days he defended his approach. But criticisms have been many. In his own time, it was argued that such effectiveness as his methods enjoyed was due not to their intrinsic excellence but to their author's exceptional gifts. W. P. Alison* suggested that he was lamentably deficient in understanding of the environmental, as opposed to the personal, factors in contemporary poverty – factors which called for Christian compassion rather than the somewhat censorious moralism displayed by his deacons. Later writers have accused him of undue veneration for the existing order, failure to subject the economic theories of Adam Smith and T. R. Malthus* to Christian scrutiny, anachronistic hankerings after a stratified and immobile society, fear of democracy (whether political or economic), paternalism, and even, occasionally, heartlessness. In any case, the verdict of events was unfavourable. In 1837 St John's ceased to be a peculiar enclave within the poor-law administration of Glasgow. In 1843 the Disruption intensified legislators' scepticism concerning Chalmers' approach. In 1845 the Poor Law Amendment Act finally took poor relief out of the Church's hands. The great experiment was over.

(iii) *The defence of Establishment.* Chalmers had always approved of the centuries-old alliance between Church and state;* but only when a Dissenting minister, Andrew Marshall,* called in 1829 for the abolition of every form of religious establishment throughout Great Britain did he feel obliged to support it publicly. In a number of speeches and writings he argued eloquently against leaving the provision of schools, colleges and churches to the mercies of the laws of supply and demand, and contended that the cure for both ignorance and impiety lay in state recognition and endowment of one particular religious body, with a Christian schoolmaster and a Christian minister in every parish to arouse a sense of spiritual need and offer the means of satisfying it. Pure 'Voluntaryism'* was incapable of reclaiming the heathenized masses for Christianity: only an adequately-endowed state Church could do so. Alas for Chalmers! The political circumstances of the 1830s prevented full realization of his ideal. Despite establishment, successive Westminster governments refused to finance his Church Extension* schemes; non-intrusion* brought the Kirk into damaging conflict with the state whose favour it presupposed; and the tragic Disruption* of 1843 marked the end of the order he had so passionately defended. Yet he never abandoned his faith in establishment. 'We are', he assured the first FC Assembly, 'the advocates for a national recognition and national support of religion – and we are not Voluntaries.'

(iv) *On behalf of Church Extension.** Valuing the parochial organization of the Church as he did, Chalmers desired to reduce over-large parishes to manageable proportions and create new ones wherever necessary. In 1834 he became convener of the Assembly's Church Accommodation* (soon, Church Extension) Committee, and launched a great crusade for multiplication of churches and subdivision of parishes so that 'there will not one poor family be found in our land who might not, if they will, have entry and accommodation in a place of worship and religious instruction'. Within four years he had raised 205,000 and added 187 churches to the strength of the Kirk. But even this unprecedented achievement was reckoned only a beginning. Churches had been provided: now ministers must be paid for. The ancient teinds* being inadequate, and the levying of seat-rents on the poor a denial of Chalmers' deepest convictions, the only way forward was to turn to the state for assistance. This he did – but regrettably neither Whigs nor Tories felt able to grant his request, and the increasing animosities of the Ten Years' Conflict* made any change of mind unlikely. The Kirk was forced to rely, like its Dissenting antagonists, on the free-will offerings of the faithful, and the Disruption finally extinguished Chalmers' hopes. Yet the parish churches created since 1834 remained as monuments to his faith and organizing genius, while the church-building programme of the youthful FC added a still more astonishing tally of new buildings to his already remarkable achievements in the field.

(v) *The defence of ecclesiastical freedom.* At the height of the Voluntary Controversy, Chalmers laid equal stress upon the Church-and-state alliance and the freedom of the Church to manage its own affairs. He was soon to discover the practical incompatibility of the two ideals. Hardly had government refused to subsidize the stipends of extension-charge ministers than lawcourts and legislature alike denied congregations the right to choose their ministers. By 1840 he feared the headship of Christ and the authority of the Bible and the Westminster Standards were all under threat from 'men who have put forth unhallowed hands upon them'. Only one response seemed possible. In May 1843 it fell to him to preside over the first General Assembly of those who, rejecting what they regarded as an irretrievably corrupt establishment, constituted themselves the Church of Scotland – Free. Then, with the catastrophe behind him, he did more than anyone else to determine the character of the new Church and set its finances on a firm footing. That it survived and flourished as a kind of alternative establishment throughout Scotland, undertaking an ambitious programme of church-, manse-, school- and college-building, setting up numerous mission stations overseas, defending and then restructuring the Calvinist inheritance in theology, was due to him above all others.

Chalmers the man combined immense drive with very considerable charm. Thomas Carlyle* and various politicians, Melbourne in particular, had their reservations about him; but William Collins (founder of the Glasgow publishing firm), Alexander Duff,* David Masson and Hugh Miller,* among others, well-nigh idolized him. Karl Marx might refer to him, dismissively, as 'the arch-parson', but Lord Cockburn spoke of him and the great Sir Walter Scott in one breath. He could be domineering, politically inept, perhaps unscrupulous and even mendacious, but the ideals whose publicist he was have proved remarkably durable. The evangelistic strategy of the re-united CofS still gives pride of place to the parish. Though the concept of establishment has been eroded by secularism and ecumenism, the Declaratory Articles* of 1926 clearly enunciated the reciprocal duties of Church and state – as well as affirming the principle of ecclesiastical independence. And recent research has shown how much he contributed to social thought in nineteenth- and twentieth-century Britain and America. He was indeed a star of the first magnitude; and the definitive modern biography by Stewart J. Brown closes, appropriately, with a tribute to one who was both 'an emphatically practical social reformer, with well-defined programmes for the reorganisation of the nation' and 'a visionary, who touched the conscience of his age'.

See also Systematic Theology.

The Collected Works of Thomas Chalmers, 25 vols (G, 1835–42); *Posthumous Works*, 10 vols (E, 1849); H. Watt, *The Collected Works of Thomas Chalmers: A Descriptive List* (E, 1943).

FES III, 446–7; AFCS I, 51–2; S. J. Brown, *Thomas Chalmers and the Godly Commonwealth in Scotland* (O, 1982) (contains an extensive bibliography); A. C. Cheyne (ed.), *The Practical and the Pious* (E, 1985) (essays, including J. McCaffrey, 'The Life of Thomas Chalmers', 31–64, and M. Butt, 'The Chalmers Papers', 186–95); W. Hanna, *Memoirs of Dr. Chalmers*, 4 vols (E, 1849–52); H. Watt, *Thomas Chalmers and the Disruption* (E, 1943); F. Voges, *Das Denken von Thomas Chalmers in Kirchen- und Sozialgeschichtlichen Kontext* (Frankfurt, 1984); L. J. Saunders, *Scottish Democracy, 1815–1840* (E, 1950), 208–21; R. A. Cage, *The Scottish Poor Law, 1745–1845* (E, 1981), 90–110; G. I. T. Machin, *Politics and the Churches in Great Britain 1832 to 1868* (O, 1977), 112–47; S. Mechie, *The Church and Scottish Social*

Development, 1780–1870 (L, 1960), 47–80; I. Henderson, 'Thomas Chalmers', R. S. Wright (ed.), Fathers of the Kirk (L, 1960), 129–42.

A. C. Cheyne

Chambers, Oswald (1874–1917), Bible teacher and preacher. Born in Aberdeen, the son of a Baptist* pastor, he became a Christian through the preaching of C. H. Spurgeon.* Following studies in Fine Art and Archaeology at Edinburgh University, he entered Dunoon Gospel Training College (see MacGregor, Duncan) in 1897 to study for the ministry, and soon became a tutor in Logic, Moral Philosophy and Psychology (1898–1906). There he was influenced by William Quarrier,* founder of Bridge of Weir Orphan Homes, and developed a strong faith in God and a zeal for evangelism. This zeal was intensified through 'the baptism of the Holy Ghost' while he was still at Dunoon. His mystical spirit and gift for Bible teaching led to a growing ministry, particularly under the auspices of the Pentecostal* League of Prayer, which he joined as a missioner in 1909. He visited Japan and made his first trip to the USA in 1907. In 1911 he became the first Principal of the Clapham Common Bible Training College, London. In 1915 he joined the staff of the YMCA,* and served among military personnel in Zeitoun and Ismailia in Egypt until his death in November 1917. His forty-five or so posthumously published writings were originally talks given to students and soldiers. These reflect his strong emphasis on practical, personal holiness. Among his best known works are: *My Utmost For His Highest* (L, 1937); *If Thou Wilt Be Perfect* (L, 1939); *God's Workmanship* (L, 1953); *Workmen of God* (L, 1937); *Baffled to Fight Better* (L, 1923); *Biblical Psychology* (L, n.d.); *The Shadow Of An Agony* (L, 1941).

Oswald Chambers, with foreword by Dinsdale T. Young (L, 1933); D. McCasland, *Oswald Chambers* (Grand Rapids, MI, 1993).

J. Taylor

Chambers, Robert (1802–71), author and publisher. His family, being in straitened circumstances, moved from Peebles, his birthplace, to Edinburgh in 1813. He left school in 1816, entered bookselling in a small way in 1818, and rapidly prospered. The success of *Chambers's Journal*, founded with his brother William (1800–83) in 1832 led to the establishment of the publishing house of W. & R. Chambers. Robert wrote and published numerous historical and literary works to meet a popular demand for 'useful knowledge' which, always an omnivorous reader himself, he perfectly understood. In churchmanship a Moderate* with Episcopalian* leanings, he wrote few religious works, but was eager to harmonize the faith and scientific discovery. His anonymous *Vestiges of the Natural History of Creation* (L, 1844) popularized Lamarck's evolutionary principles. While having many deficiencies, it generated vigorous debate, preparing the way for Darwin's analogous presentation in 1859.

See also Science and the Bible.

DNB X, 23–5; W. Chambers, *Memoir of Robert Chambers* (E, 1872).

J. A. H. Dempster

Channel Islands. The Reformed faith came to the Channel Islands from France and Geneva: by 1562 there were Presbyterian congregations in both Guernsey and Jersey, but by the middle of the seventeenth century Presbyterianism had been banished in both islands.

During the nineteenth century several Scottish regiments were posted for garrison duties at Fort George (Guernsey) and Fort Regent (Jersey), and through the influence of William Turnbull, an elder of the FC, who had taken up residence in Guernsey, and Mr Clark, a licentiate of the FC, who was tutor to the family of the Commanding Officer in Jersey, Presbyterian congregations were re-established in both islands (1850, Jersey; 1852, Guernsey).

In the initial years the congregations were administered from Edinburgh, but in 1876 they were received into the Presbyterian Church of England. Many of their ministers were Scots or had Scottish connections. In 1972 the Presbyterian CofE united with the Congregational Church in England and Wales to form the United Reformed Church* in England and Wales, but the congregations in Guernsey and Jersey exercised their right to opt out and successfully petitioned the General Assembly of the CofS to be received with their ministers as congregations of the CofS.

Both congregations, while having a strong nucleus of Scots, provide a spiritual home for island families whose roots are in the Presbyterian tradition and for others who find the Presbyterian form of government and style of worship meaningful and helpful.

J. Adamson, *The Story of the Presbyterian Church in Jersey* (Jersey, 1937); P. Johnston, *A Short History of Guernsey* (Guernsey, ³1987); A. J. Eagleston, *The Channel Islands Under Tudor Government* (C, 1949); B. A. Rankillor, *St. Andrew's in the Grange, Guernsey: A Brief History of the Church* (privately printed, 1978); *APCS 1972*, 31–8.

G. L. Lugton

Chapels Act, 1834, granting full status to 'chapels-of-ease'.* Evangelical zeal for church extension,* when thwarted by the refusal of heritors* to meet the costs of new churches, led to the erection by voluntary effort of 'chapels-of-ease' in populous districts. These congregations were often successful, but they lacked the customary privileges of the parish church. The Chapels Act gave them the same standing *quoad sacra** as the old parishes enjoyed *quoad omnia*:* they were to have their own kirk sessions,* parishes* were to be created for them, and their ministers were to have seats in the Church courts. This both increased evangelical strength in church courts and stimulated the work of church extension. The Court of Session, in the Stewarton* judgement of 1843, declared the Act incompetent (*see* Ten Years' Conflict).

CHAPELS OF EASE

AGACS, 1035-6; R. Buchanan, *The Ten Years' Conflict* (L, 1849), I, 317-48.

K. R. Ross

Chapels of Ease. In the third quarter of the eighteenth century the failure of the national Church to create additional places of worship for the growing population led to the creation of independent chapels. The first to be given an official constitution by the General Assembly was that of Dunfermline in 1779 when, after five years of litigation, some members of Thomas Gillespie's* Relief* congregation sought to adhere to the national Church. Opponents argued that this would lead to further division since, in contrast to the *quoad omnia** parishes, these maverick congregations had no elders and enjoyed a system of popular election in the choice of minister.

The growth of chapels during the period of the Haldanes* brought increasing fears of a class of independent congregations outside the scope of the 1712 Queen Anne's Act. The General Assembly of 1798, which was dominated by the Moderate* party, therefore passed an Act which permitted chapels to be erected only with the prior consent of that court, thus removing the initiative from Presbyteries (see W. Moodie, *Observations on the Overture respecting Chapels of Ease*, E, 1797; James Finlayson, *Heads of an Argument in support of the Overture transmitted to Presbytery respecting Chapels of Ease*, E, 1798). The creation of chapels introduced a two-tier ministry and set the Church on a collision course which was to become more obvious during the Ten Years' Conflict.*

These early chapels were the forerunners of Thomas Chalmers'* great Church Extension* drive. The Chapels Act* of 1834, passed by an Assembly dominated by the Evangelical Party,* gave chapels the same standing *quoad sacra** as the old parishes *quoad omnia* enjoyed, with Kirk Sessions* of their own and the right for their ministers to take their place in Church courts. The legality of this Act was challenged during the Ten Years' Conflict and the judgment arrived at in the Stewarton* case by the House of Lords made participation of chapel ministers in the proceedings of Church courts illegal. At the Disruption* well over 100 of the 451 who went out to form the FC were chapel ministers.

Some of the newly-formed Free congregations continued to meet in the chapels built under Chalmers' Extension scheme (*e.g.* Dunfermline North). However a House of Lords' Act in 1849 gave all such buildings back to the Est.C.

The successors of Chalmers' chapel congregations were the *quoad sacra* congregations created in the CofS by the Act 7 & 8 Victoria Chapter 44. This Act, piloted by Sir James Graham, gave to the CofS all the powers that the Chapel Act of 1834 had been designed to give, on condition that an endowment of 120 per annum were first secured. By the end of the nineteenth century, 400 *quoad sacra* congregations had been erected.

T. Hardy, *The Principles of Moderation* (E, 1782);

CHAPLAINCIES, ARMED SERVICES

Anon., 'A letter from a country gentleman to one of the ministers in Edinburgh on the subject of the regulations on an Overture respecting Chapels of Ease' (E, 1798).

G. F. C. Jenkins

Chaplaincies, Armed Services

The Army. In 1578 the CofS appointed through the Church courts ministers to serve in the army as chaplains. The General Assembly of 1642 further enacted that it was the responsibility of the colonel commanding a regiment to find a chaplain and to make financial provision for his maintenance. The chaplain's role in the Covenanting* armies often went beyond religious ministrations. The Cameronians (*see* Societies, United) raised a regiment which continued their name with Alexander Shields* its first chaplain. Other Scottish regiments constituted their own churches. During the seventeenth century ministers also served as Chaplains in Danzig, Sweden and the Netherlands as well as with Hepburn's Regiment in France. The Act of Union* provided that chaplains should be permanently stationed at the castles of Stirling, Edinburgh and Dumbarton, along with the fourteen Scottish regiments, whilst the barracks at Glasgow, Piershill (Edinburgh), Aberdeen and Dundee were to draw on the services of local clergy for the spiritual needs of their personnel.

The first Chaplain General, John Camble of the CofE, was appointed as a result of the Royal Warrant published on 23 September 1796, in which the system of regimental chaplaincies was abolished and a new organization was established – the Army Chaplains Department. Presbyterians were recognized as a separate branch of the Department in 1827, despite having served in Scottish regiments prior to this.

By Army Order No. 92, published on 22 January 1919, King George V gave approval for the designation 'Royal' to be applied to the Chaplains Department (RAChD), in view of the contribution made by Chaplains in their ministry during the First World War.

Royal Navy. Initially the appointment of chaplain in the navy was given only to Anglican clergy. But from 1870 onwards ministers were appointed to serve at various shore establishments and paid from naval funds on a capitation basis. From 1894 facilities were afforded to non-Anglican clergy to visit ships for the spiritual care of those of their denomination.

The first Scottish Presbyterian (UFC) chaplain to receive official recognition in the Navy List was R. Primrose (*FUFCS* 204) who was appointed as RNVR Chaplain on 18 February 1904. On 24 July 1915, the first Acting Presbyterian Chaplain took up his appointment. All CofS, UFC and FC chaplains still serving on 2 August, 1918 were given temporary commissions. The title refers to the fact that they were 'Ministers of Religious Bodies not in conformity with the Church of England rendering whole time service in the Royal Navy'. This title and the disadvantages which it brought were finally

CHAPLAINCIES, COLONIAL

removed by an Order in Council on 17 November 1943, establishing a permanent list of chaplains from 'Religious Bodies not in conformity with the Church of England'.

Royal Air Force. In 1919, Sir Hugh Trenchard's plan to establish a permanent peacetime RAF was approved, and with it a chaplains' branch. Chaplains had until then been drawn from the army and Royal Navy for service with the Royal Flying Corps. They were CofE, CofS, Wesleyan Methodists, United Board (Congregationalists, Baptists, Primitive and United Methodists) and RC. The union of all Methodists in 1932 left the United Board with only the Congregationalists and the Baptists grouped with others as PMUB (Presbyterian, Methodist, and United Board). They are now known as CofS and Free Churches (CSFC).

A. C. Dow, *Ministers to the Soldiers of Scotland* (E, 1962); J. Smyth, *In this Sign Conquer* (L, 1968); G. Taylor, *The Sea Chaplains* (O, 1978); E. Mantle, 'The Theological Significance of the PMUB Churches of the RAF and its Contribution to the Reunion of the Churches' (MA, Bristol University, 1965); T. B. S. Thomson, *The Chaplain in the Church of Scotland* (E, L, 1947); lists in *FES* VII, 448–53, VIII, 721, IX, 786–94.

I. C. Barclay

Chaplaincies, Colonial, ministries provided originally to serve Scots resident in British colonies. Bermuda had a Presbyterian congregation with a Scottish minister for some years from 1612, and chaplains were dispatched on the ill-fated Darien* venture at the end of the century. More lasting provision was pioneered in Canada* by different branches of the Secession* from the later eighteenth century. Similar developments followed in Australia* from 1823 (*see* Lang, John Dunmore), and in New Zealand* in the 1840s, while Cape Town had a Presbyterian church for Europeans from 1828 (*see* South Africa). Chaplaincies in some non-colonial territories, such as Argentina, were little different from the strictly colonial ones.

The Glasgow Colonial Society,* founded in 1825 and led energetically by Robert Burns (d.1869),* sent over forty CofS ministers to 'British North America' (*i.e.* Canada) within a decade. From 1818 the CofS had a committee to maintain communications with its ministers in the colonies, but not until 1836 was colonial mission adopted as one of the schemes of the Church under a standing Colonial Committee. In 1833 the General Assembly recommended ministers of fixed colonial congregations to form presbyteries; meantime they were not to license their own probationers but to ordain CofS licentiates.

The chaplains on the Indian Ecclesiastical Establishment, which dated from the Company's 1814 charter, included many serving military garrisons. These chaplains were appointed and paid by the East India Company, and later by the Indian government. The first Presbyterian chaplain appointed by the Company was James Clow in 1815 (*FES* VII, 570–1). In 1834 the Company's new charter made it imperative for the CofS to have a minister at each of the presidencies.

The colonial churches were inevitably affected by church divisions and reunions in Scotland, and after the Disruption* the FC, and later the UFC, had a major commitment to the chaplaincies. With the lapse of time they increasingly served local populations rather than Scots, and most of them were incorporated into the independent national churches that developed out of missionary foundations, although some former chaplaincies have remained specially dependent on Scottish support.

The CofS Colonial and Continental Committee submitted its last report in 1966 (*RGACS 1966*, 520–36); henceforth its work was incorporated into the Department of Overseas Mission and Inter-Church Relations. In 1991 the CofS had only half-a-dozen overseas congregations in former colonies (and one in Gibraltar, still a colony).

See also Missions; Emigration.

R. G. Balfour, *Presbyterianism in the Colonies* (E, 1899); A. Williamson, *What Has the Church of Scotland Done for Our Colonies?* (E, n.d.); *FES* VII, 556–680 and sections in subsequent vols.

D. F. Wright

Chaplaincies, Hospitals, Universities, Prisons

Hospitals. Christians have always seen the special importance of ministry to the physically and mentally sick, and monastic establishments provided hospital* and hospice care in the Middle Ages. When the great infirmaries developed in the eighteenth century there was chaplaincy provision. The Edinburgh Royal Infirmary may be typical. Shortly after its foundation, the ministers of the city and suburbs agreed to visit the sick by rotation, and in 1755 George Willis was appointed chaplain at an annual salary of £12. He agreed to preach once each Sunday, to visit the wards twice weekly, to attend dying patients, and to open with prayer the meetings of the Board of Management. Today all hospitals have either full-time or part-time chaplains, and since the early 1970s there has been close cooperation with Departments of Practical Theology in the Universities (cf. D. Lyall, 'Theological Education in a Clinical Setting', PhD thesis, Edinburgh University, 1979). Hospital chaplaincy has become a specialized ministry. In smaller hospitals local clergy continue to serve. Provision is made for RC and Episcopalian, and in some places chaplains from other Protestant bodies, to share the work.

Universities. City ministers have long had special concern for students. Full-time university chaplaincy, which began in Glasgow in the 1920s, with A. C. Craig* the first chaplain, is now available in all universities. D. H. C. Read* was the first chaplain to Edinburgh University. A distinction should be made between the University-appointed chaplains, who have generally but not invariably been CofS, and chaplains appointed by denominations, whether full-time or honorary. There are also Chaplains for overseas students.

CHAPLAINCIES, INDUSTRIAL

Prisons. All HM Prisons are served part-time by Protestant and RC clergy. There is also a long tradition of lay visiting by Christians, both in prisons and hospitals. More recently, Prison Fellowship Scotland has had an effective ministry to prisoners.

T. B. S. Thomson, *The Chaplain in the Church of Scotland* (E, L, 1947); D. P. Thomson (ed.), *The Church in the Modern Hospital* (Crieff, 1966); A. V. Campbell (ed.), *A Dictionary of Pastoral Care* (L, 1987); A. L. Turner, *The Story of a Great Hospital* (E, 1937); FES VII, 454–6, VIII, 722, IX, 795–7.

D. B. Murray

Chaplaincies, Industrial. During the Second World War* a number of ministers in Scotland began visiting men and women in factories, shipyards, steel mills and engineering shops which were supporting the war effort. If the armed forces had chaplains on the battle front, those serving on the 'home front' (often working seven days a week) needed chaplains too. Sometimes a short weekly service was held in the canteen; sometimes social facilities were organized; always there was access to men and women at the point of their work and, within limits, opportunities for conversation and pastoral support.

After the War it was discovered that nearly a hundred of these chaplains were still regularly visiting their workplaces, and although they were not very clear about their role, they felt that a door of opportunity had opened to them which should not be neglected. In 1948 the CofS appointed a full-time Organizer to stimulate and support them in their work.

At the same time Industrial Chaplains had begun visiting workplaces in England, most notably in Sheffield, where E. R. (Ted) Wickham pioneered a more intensive 'Industrial Mission' to the Sheffield steel-making community. During the 1950s there were eight full-time chaplains in Sheffield and over a hundred regular group meetings where questions of the faith and its relation to daily life were discussed.

It was this form of Industrial Mission which provided the pattern for development in Scotland with the appointment in 1962 of Cameron Wallace (*FES* IX, 452) as full-time chaplain to the shipbuilding community of the lower reaches of the Clyde. This was followed by similar appointments in the steel-making community of Motherwell, in the engineering works of Glasgow, in Dundee, in Falkirk/Grangemouth and more recently (1986) in the oil industry in Aberdeen. Part-time chaplains (about 100 of them) still undertake regular visitions to local works, but they go as part of a local team and have the backing of a programme of study and discussion (organized by the full-time chaplain) covering the industrial community as a whole.

From the start this has been an ecumenical venture among the Protestant Churches – with the CofS providing the full-time staff – and since the early 1970s the RC Church has become fully involved. Through Industrial Mission the churches have also been able to build up a network of relationships within the structures of industrial and commercial life, both among trades unions and management organizations. It is a mark of the trust which has thus been established that the church's voice is more and more sought and listened to when issues of justice and human relationships arise. Although it has always been maintained that chaplains should be seen to be financially independent of the firms in which they work – and indeed they are so today – since 1975 both firms and trades unions have been making annual contributions to an Industrial Mission Trust for the expansion of other facets of the work.

Reports of Home Board in *RGACS 1948–*; E. R. Wickham, *Church and People in an Industrial City* (L, 1957); G. D. Wilkie, *Christian Thinking about Industrial Life* (E, 1980).

G. D. Wilkie

Charge, the general term used in the CofS and other Reformed Churches to describe the responsibility laid upon a minister on induction – a 'charge of souls'. As a sphere of pastoral duty it normally refers to a parish.* At one time, because of the enormous increase in population following industrialization, certain urban parishes came to consist of two or more separate charges (generally known as first and second, *etc*.), each with its own provision for stipend,* *etc*. Today, in circumstances of rural depopulation, a charge may consist of as many as four parishes, the minister becoming minister of all in virtue of being inducted in one of them.

Cox 18.

A. Herron

Charismatic Movement. In 1960 a group of students in Edinburgh met to study the Bible in order to relate the Scriptures to teaching that came from the USA through *Trinity Magazine* on the use of spiritual gifts as defined in 1 Corinthians 12, and in particular the experience of 'baptism in the Holy Spirit'. In 1961 Brian Casebow, one of that group, experienced this baptism, and began to teach about the Holy Spirit in his church in Motherwell. Other leaders emerged, including Gordon Strachan, Douglas McBain and Tom Smail, who taught in their churches and at various ecumenical gatherings. Contact was made with Michael Harper of Fountain Trust, formed to disseminate teaching about the Holy Spirit in England and abroad, and meetings were held in Glasgow in the early 1970s, as more and more leaders and lay people sought renewal for themselves and their churches. The desire grew for a nationally organized fellowship, and in 1975 Fountain Trust encouraged David Black and others to form Scottish Churches Renewal with similar aims. Its work lasted until 1980, by which time the Movement had grown strong enough in some denominations for them to form their own groups. The Scottish Episcopal Renewal Fellowship and Baptist Renewal are two such groups, and at present the Scottish Churches Consultative Council (formed in 1975) meets from time to time to debate matters relating to renewal and revival. It is sponsored by the CofS. The Council now includes leaders of house churches that are fast emerging in many parts of the land, most of them with a bias towards the use of spiritual gifts. Some are beginning to coalesce into specific ministries, and there is today a slow momentum towards seeking wider spiritual if not organic unity.

The excitement of those who experienced the 'baptism in the Holy Spirit' in the 1960s, with the inevitable controversy it aroused, has today somewhat diminished. Early arguments among some Evangelicals that spiritual gifts, healings and miracles were solely for the first century, have long been discounted. Much theological debate has centred on the definition of the term 'baptism in the Holy Spirit' as taught in the Gospels and in Acts, and when this is experienced. The Pentecostal insistence that the 'baptism' is authentic only if speaking in tongues follows is not widely shared. The debate continues, but the Charismatic Movement has now found its way into all denominations (if least evidently among Presbyterians). Because of its very nature there is virtually no official literature of the movement in Scotland. The number of Christians who would call themselves 'charismatic' is still small, but growing. Very recently, the teaching of John Wimber, from the Vineyard Ministries in the USA, has made an impact with his thrust of evangelism through the employment of spiritual gifts. There is also a hunger not only for renewal through corporate prayer, but for revival in the land.

Minutes *etc.* at Scottish Churches House, Dunblane, and Smilam House, Lanark; *Trinity Magazine* (Van Nuys, CA); P. Hocken, *Streams of Renewal* (Exeter, 1986).

D. E. N. Cameron

Charismatic Movement (in RC Church). The movement which brought into being the Pentecostal Churches began to affect RCs in the USA in 1967. From there it spread rapidly through the RCC worldwide but everywhere remained within the institution. Because of the prominence of New Testament charisms, and to avoid confusion with classical Pentecostalism,* it was termed Charismatic Renewal. Since 1975 international leaders' conferences have been held in Rome, and each pope has given approval and encouragement.

The first stirrings among Scottish RCs were in 1973. From 1977 national conferences were held and there was a period of rapid growth. The many prayer groups are loosely co-ordinated through diocesan service teams and a national service committee with an episcopal advisor. Local day conferences and other events are a regular feature. Growth has been succeeded by consolidation, and Charismatic Renewal seems likely to remain a significant factor in the church renewal programmes now under way.

K. and D. Ranaghan, *Catholic Pentecostals* (NY, 1969); E. D. O'Connor, *The Pentecostal Movement in the Catholic Church* (Notre Dame, Indiana, rev. ed.1974); M. Dilworth, 'Renewal and Scottish Catholics', *Renewal* 86 (1980), 27–30; *The Vine* 1–6 (1981–7).

M. Dilworth

Charles I (1600–49), King of Scotland 1625–49. He was born at Dunfermline but left Scotland for London in 1604, returning only for brief visits in 1633 and 1641. When he succeeded his father, James VI and I,* on 27 March 1625, he inherited in Scotland an efficient administration which adequately coped with the underlying problems of absentee government. Unfortunately Charles squandered his initial popularity by reorganizing the membership of the Privy Council, clumsily introducing a radical and illegal Act of Revocation, dragging Scotland into England's costly wars with France and Spain, and increasing taxation.

Charles was also determined to go beyond his father's moderate Episcopalian policies and to exploit further the Erastian role of bishops in the state. More dangerously, he insisted on the enforcement of the Five Articles of Perth,* and on introducing Anglican- and Arminian-inspired liturgical innovations. What finally sparked off the orchestrated but popular riot in St Giles Cathedral, Edinburgh on 23 July 1637 was the enforcement on the Church of the highly publicised and easily misrepresented 'Laudian' Prayer Book (*see* Laud, William).

The King's refusal to compromise, and the weak and indecisive inactivity of his ministers, allowed government to fall into the hands of the opposition, who launched the signing of the National Covenant* on 28 February, 1638. At a meeting of the General Assembly in November (*see* Glasgow Assembly*) the Covenanters* committed themselves to a militant Presbyterian programme. Charles decided to subdue the Scots by force, but in the 'Bishops' Wars'* of 1639–40 his army was routed and the Scots occupied northern England. By the autumn of 1641 Charles had accepted defeat in Scotland, recognizing the Presbyterian gains and conceding constitutional reforms which greatly weakened Crown authority.

After the outbreak of the English Civil War in the summer of 1642, Charles tried to secure Scottish support, but distrust of the King's intentions helped ensure that the Covenanters joined the English Parliament instead. In the autumn of 1643 the Solemn League and Covenant* was agreed, and from January 1644 until his surrender to the Scottish army at Newark on 5 May 1646 Charles was faced by the combined strength of the English Parliament and the Scots.

In 1644–5 Charles's cause in Scotland was briefly revived by the highland campaign of James Graham,* first Marquis of Montrose, but it was not until after the Scots had 'sold' Charles to their allies, and the King had been seized by the English army, that support for Charles grew in Scotland. In December 1647 a secret agreement, the Engaged,* was contracted between Charles and the moderate Covenanters, but the Engagers' army was crushed by Oliver Cromwell at Preston on 17–19 August, 1648, and it was as a direct result of this renewal of the war that Charles was executed by the purged English Parliament on 30 January 1649.

Charles I inspired extremes of devotion and hatred. He was loved by his family and friends as a caring husband and father, and as a kind master. Charles was a very private man whose principal leisure interest was the appreciation of the arts, chiefly painting. There is no doubt that his religious beliefs were sincerely held, and his private life was above reproach. He was convinced also of the divine nature of his kingship. From this flowed a dogmatic, inflexible attitude to politics and religion, and a tenacious determination to have his own way by any means and regardless of the consequences. Being essentially shy and lacking in confidence, he created an aura of cold, aloof majesty which served to heighten the general impression of autocratic indifference. At his trial and execution, however, Charles was able to convey an image of an honourable, brave and dignified gentleman, which contributed enormously to the myth of the 'Royal Martyr'.

M. Lee, *The Road to Revolution* (Urbana and Chicago, 1984); D. Stevenson, *The Scottish Revolution 1637–44* (Newton Abbot, 1973); D. Stevenson, *Revolution and Counter Revolution in Scotland* (L, 1977); D. Mathew, *Scotland under Charles I* (L, 1955); G. Donaldson, *Scotland: James V–James VII* (E, 1965), 295–340; C. Carlton, *Charles I, The Personal Monarch* (L, 1983); P. H. Donald, *An Uncounselled King. Charles I and the Scottish Troubles, 1637–1641* (C, 1991); A. I. Macinnes, *Charles I and the Making of the Covenanting Movement 1625–1641* (E, 1991).

K. M. Brown

Charles II (1630–85), effectively king from 1660, though he acceded to the throne of Great Britain and Ireland in 1649. Six days after the execution of his father, Charles I,* he was proclaimed king in Edinburgh, but he was not to be allowed to exercise authority until he had accepted both Covenants,* and had sworn to establish Presbyterianism* in all his dominions. For a time Charles held out, but the failure of his cause elsewhere, the prospect of impoverished exile and his lack of religious scruples led to his acceptance of these terms in June 1650. 'He sinfully complied', said one of the Scots commissioners later, 'with what we most sinfully pressed upon him – *our* sin was more than his.' In August 1650 at Dunfermline he signed a paper in which he admitted the error of his father's ways, the idolatry of his RC mother, and his own sinfulness. At Scone on 1 January 1651, the occasion of the last coronation of a king in Scotland, he reaffirmed on oath his acceptance of the Covenants and of Presbyterian church government. It was of no avail: Scotland was lost to Charles when Cromwell triumphed at Worcester in September 1651, and Charles departed again into exile with convictions about the Scots and their religion that determined his hostility to them after he regained the throne in 1660.

While after the Restoration* Charles had no desire, in Patrick Walker's words, 'to mind his former engagements to God and his people', he had learned caution, for the monarchy had been shown to be vulnerable. The Divine Right theory (*see* Church and State) so dear to the Stuarts was no longer pushed, but Charles knew the power of Presbyterianism in his northern kingdom, and was resolved to defeat that threat to his supremacy. The Marquis of Argyll (*see* Campbell, Archibald) and James Guthrie,* powerful Covenanting leaders, were executed, and Episcopacy forced upon the country and maintained during a relentless campaign that ended only with the overthrow of a dynasty. The King's instruments in Scotland were often men of cruel and unscrupulous disposition, some of whom had old scores to settle, as he himself had. Charles was personally irreligious, mean and vindictive. He never visited Scotland after 1651 and referred to Presbyterianism as no religion for a gentleman. Whatever his reputation in England (he was a patron of arts and letters), Charles did not understand Scotland and its people, and his policies there, whether originating with himself or with his representatives subject to his approval, were almost wholly bad. Gilbert Burnet,* later Bishop of Salisbury, said of him, 'A secularist, he shook off Presbyterianism as a viper, utilized Episcopacy as the readiest political tool, and finally put on Popery as a comfortable shroud to die in.' Nothing illustrates Charles's rule so much as the contrast between the jubilant enthusiasm shown on his Restoration, and the low-keyed niggardly funeral accorded him by his brother and successor, the RC James.

G. Burnet, *History of His Own Time*, 2 vols (L, 1724–34); S. R. Gardiner, *Letters and Papers . . . Charles II and Scotland in 1650* (E, 1894); J. K. Hewison, *The Covenanters*, 2 vols (G, ²1913); *Lives* by O. Airy (L, 1901); A. Bryant (L, 1931); M. Ashley (L, 1971).

J. D. Douglas

Charleson, John (1862–1942), CofS minister who became a RC. Born in Inverness and brought up within the FC he became a member of the CofS before completing his training for the FC ministry. A graduate of the University of Edinburgh (MA, 1884; BD, 1888), he was minister at Thornliebank, south of Glasgow, from 1890 until being received into the RCC in 1901. He was ordained to the priesthood at Kirkintilloch, Dunbartonshire, in 1904 and later served at Croy, Dunbartonshire, and in Rome. He founded the Glasgow Ecclesiological Society (*see* Ecclesiastical Societies) in 1893 and was a member of the Scottish Church Society* until he was asked to leave because of his 'Romish proclivities'. In 1896 he encountered opposition in his congregation to certain of his advanced liturgical practices. In a pamphlet *Why I Left the Church of Scotland* (G, 1901) he said that he had been led to Rome by his search for absolute authority in doctrine and worship.

See also Graham, Henry Grey.

Church Services (G, 1890); 'Rationale and Symbolism of Christian Churches', *Transactions of the Glasgow Ecclesiological Society* 1 (1895),

CHARTERIS, ARCHIBALD HAMILTON

39–52; 'What to do with our Churches' *ibid*.4 (1898), 5–6.

FES III, 189, VIII, 245; Scottish Church Society, *Annual Report*, 1901–2, 18; Jacob Primmer, *Mr Charleson's 'Why I Left the Church of Scotland'* (Dunfermline, 1901).

D. M. Murray

Charteris, Archibald Hamilton (1835–1908), leading CofS divine in the post-Disruption* era. Born in Wamphray, Dumfriesshire, Charteris studied arts and divinity at Edinburgh University 1849–58. After a brief period at St Quivox, in Kyle, Ayrshire, he became minister of New Abbey, Galloway (1859) and then Park Church, Glasgow (1863). In 1868 he was appointed Professor of Biblical Criticism and Biblical Antiquities in Edinburgh University, a position he occupied until ill-health compelled retirement in 1898. He received a DD from Edinburgh University in 1868 and Aberdeen in 1906. He acted as Moderator of the General Assembly in 1892, and was a chaplain to both Queen Victoria and Edward VII.

Charteris defended conservative critical views throughout his professorship. He was accused of being the author of the anonymous review article in the *Edinburgh Evening Courant* of April 1875 which signalled the start of the case against William Robertson Smith* in the FC. The review criticized Smith's article on the Bible in the *Encyclopedia Britannica*. Charteris did not deny writing it, and his verdict on the kind of criticism practised by Smith was decidedly negative (*see* Believing Criticism; Exegesis, Biblical).

Theologically, Charteris espoused a mild form of Calvinism, taking a revisionist attitude to the Westminster* Confession; but it was as a churchman that he exercised his greatest influence. He was instrumental in establishing the CofS's Life and Work Committee in 1869 (*see* Social Responsibility, Board of), and in 1879 founded the *Life and Work* magazine; he pioneered the Young Men's Guild and Woman's Guild,* and was chief promoter of the restoration in his Church of the office of deaconess and of the founding of the Deaconess Institution (1887) and Deaconess Hospital (1894) (*see* Diaconate). As well as being a proponent of Presbyterian union in Scotland (*see* Church Unions) he was a moving spirit in the formation of the Alliance of Reformed Churches in 1875.

Canonicity (E, 1880); *The New Testament Scriptures* (Croall lectures for 1882, L, 1882); *The Church of Christ* (Baird lectures* for 1887, L, 1905); *The Present State of Criticism as regards the New Testament* (E, 1897); *Life of the Rev. James Robertson* (E, 1863).

A. Gordon, *The Life of Archibald Hamilton Charteris* (L, 1912); K. D. McLaren, *Memoir of the Very Reverend Professor Charteris* (L, 1914); *FES* VII, 388–9; *DNB Second Suppl.* I, 354–5; J. B. Logan, 'Archibald Hamilton Charteris...', *AUR* 50 (1983–4), 398–405, 51 (1985–6), 116–23.

N. R. Needham

CHARTERIS, LAWRENCE

Charteris, Catherine Morice Anderson (1835–1918), wife of A. H. Charteris* and 'Mother' of the CofS Woman's Guild.* Daughter of Sir Alexander Anderson, Lord Provost of Aberdeen, she married Charteris in 1863. Throughout forty-five years together, Katie not only supported her husband in his parish, university and committee work, but made her own practical, distinctive and forthright contribution to the development of women's work within the CofS.

In Glasgow and Edinburgh, she organized slum missions, Bible classes and mothers' meetings. She was directly involved in the promotion of the Woman's Guild,* founded in 1887 under the Life and Work committee chaired by Charteris. From 1891–1901, she was first editor of the WG supplement in *LW*, bringing the Guild concept to life for thousands of women. Her writing encouraged and challenged them to a life of confident action in the service of the Church, and brought to light some of the prejudice and injustice which women, working together, might alleviate. 'If the sight of the woes of others calls any of you to work beyond what have been hitherto the ordinary limits of women's work ... you need not fear surely to listen to the voice, nor think that it calls you beyond a woman's province. "Whatsoever He saith unto you, do it"' (*LW Woman's Guild Supplement*, 1901). Catherine Charteris served as WG national president until 1906, when there were over 40,000 members. She also initiated and helped fund the Home-House for children of missionaries, and a Rest House for deaconesses (*see* Diaconate). She was a woman of enthusiasm, intelligence, wit and common sense. 'Somewhat overshadowed in public life by her husband's forceful personality, only those who knew them well, realized how much Mrs Charteris really did to bring success to her beloved husband's many enterprises, and with what interest and self-forgetfulness she laboured in the Church's service' (*LW*, January 1919).

M. Magnusson, *Out of Silence: the Woman's Guild, 1887–1987* (E, 1987).

L. O. Macdonald

Charteris, Lawrence (1625–1700), CofS minister. He studied at Edinburgh (MA, 1646) and was ordained to St Bathan's in 1654. He conformed in 1662, but refused a bishopric because he disapproved of the methods used to enforce episcopacy. Charteris was one of the six preachers sent by Archbishop Robert Leighton* to advocate his plan of 'accommodating' the Presbyterians in 1670.

A son of Henry Charteris, Principal and Professor of Divinity at Edinburgh University, he held that chair 1675–81 but resigned because of the Test Act*. He became minister of Dirleton in 1688, but dissociated himself from the 1690 General Assembly's condemnation of prelacy.

The Difference between True and False Christianity (E, 1703); *The Corruption of this Age and the Remedy thereof* (E, 1704; reprinted 1761); *Spiritual Discourses* (E, 1704).

FES I, 360.

H. R. Sefton

Chartism. The Chartist movement in Scotland, like its English counterpart, expressed for the first time the unique political self-consciousness of the working classes. In many respects this movement, which reached its greatest strength in the period 1838 to 1842, anticipated the rise of the modern Labour Party. With the failure of the 1832 Reform Bill to extend the franchise to the working classes, the 'People's Charter' of 1838 contained six points: manhood suffrage, vote by ballot, annual parliaments, abolition of property qualifications for MPs, payment of members, and equal electoral districts. However, Scottish Chartism was much more than a political reform movement. It gave expression to a distinct working class ethos, embracing certain social, economic, ethical and religious attitudes. In addition to the political points of the Charter, Scottish Chartists normally supported repeal of the Corn Laws, a national system of education, temperance, and home rule for Ireland, and opposed capital punishment, militarism and war. Along with local political groups in virtually every important town in Scotland, there arose Chartist newspapers, Chartist churches* and Chartist schools, all committed to the advancement of the cause of civil rights and social justice for the working classes. Apart from Patrick Brewster* of Paisley Abbey, who was a leading figure in the movement, Chartism received virtually no support from the clergy of the day, and none from the churches, even those dissenting churches which were generally sympathetic to democratic movements. In these years most clergy preached 'passive obedience' to the working classes, which called for acceptance of the God-ordained social and economic *status quo*. Not surprisingly, in the face of this hostility to their cause, many Chartists withdrew from their churches and formed Christian Chartist congregations. At the height of the movement, there were some twenty to thirty such congregations in Scotland including four in Glasgow.

See also Chartist churches; Temperance Movement.

A. Wilson, *The Chartist Movement in Scotland* (Manchester, 1970); L. C. Wright, *Scottish Chartism* (E, 1953); D. C. Smith, *Passive Obedience and Prophetic Protest: Social Criticism in the Scottish Church 1830–1945* (NY, 1987).

D. C. Smith

Chartist churches, churches which endeavoured to combine Christian principles and Chartist ideals. These sprang up around 1839 when many Chartists were dismayed at the lack of social and political involvement, not only in the Est.C, but also among dissenters, chiefly in the Secession* and Relief* Churches. Among the main principles of the movement were the brotherhood of man, the need for Christians to be actively involved in matters of social concern, and the pursuit of universal suffrage. Most members of these churches stressed the moral aspects of Chartist reform. The movement floundered perhaps because, in their zeal, its leaders had no time to form a proper organization. Among the more radical claims made by some was that 'the man who is not a Chartist is not a Christian'. It is difficult to assess the claim made in the *Northern Star* in 1841 that a Chartist place of worship was to be found on the Lord's day in almost every town of note from Aberdeen to Ayr, but it was estimated by one observer that there were 'at least 20 Christian Chartist churches' in Scotland in that year.

The leading churchman to embrace Chartist principles was Patrick Brewster* of Paisley. Among the pamphlets and journals which carried their aims were the *Chartist Circular*, the *Scottish Patriot*, the *True Scotsman* and the *Northern Star*. It has been asked whether there would have been any place for Chartist churches if the Est.C had moved in response to the industrial revolution or Dissenters had not become so middle-class in outlook, but their spread indicates the deeply religious spirit which was part of the ethos of Scottish Chartism.

A. Wilson, *The Chartist Movement in Scotland* (Manchester, 1970); L. C. Wright, *Scottish Chartism* (E, 1953); D. C. Smith, *Passive Obedience and Prophetic Protest* (NY, 1987), 151–73.

G. F. C. Jenkins

Châtelherault, first Duke of, *see* Hamilton, James (*c.*1516–75).

Cheyne, Patrick (1794–1878), EpCS minister, incumbent of St John's, Aberdeen, from 1818 to 1858. During this time he became a protagonist of the Oxford Movement (*see* Tractarianism), which had provoked bitter controversy in the EpCS by teaching the real presence of Christ in the Eucharist. Cheyne published in 1858 six sermons, in which he expounded that doctrine, for which he was accused of teaching transubstantiation. He was tried before Thomas Suther, Bishop of Aberdeen, and the Diocesan Synod. Cheyne's chief accuser tried to make his teaching appear equivalent to that of Rome. Suther was hostile to Cheyne, and by bullying tactics tried to force an unanimous verdict against him. Cheyne was condemned, but by only twelve to eight, and dismissed from his charge. He appealed to the Episcopal Synod, which upheld the verdict by six to one. Several years later Cheyne made his peace with Suther.

Scottish Ecclesiastical Journal, June–November 1858.

G. N. Pennie

China, *see* Missions.

Chinnery-Haldane, James Robert Alexander (1842–1906), Bishop of Argyll and the Isles in EpCS. As a student at Trinity College, Cambridge, he had intended to become a barrister like his father, Alexander Haldane.* But following his marriage in 1864 to Anna Chinnery, the daughter of an Irish baronet, he entered Anglican orders, becoming a curate first at Calne in Wiltshire and sub-

CHISHOLM, WILLIAM I

sequently in Edinburgh. As a young ordinand his reflections on the inconsistent attitude towards the Prayer Book shown by Evangelicals led him to exchange the uncompromising Protestantism of his upbringing for a fervent and abiding Catholicism. His subsequent churchmanship combined an evangelical emphasis upon preaching and devotion to Christ with a firm adherence to Catholic usage in liturgy and sacraments. He was a member of the Society of the Holy Cross and the Confraternity of the Blessed Sacrament and enjoyed a lasting friendship with A. H. Mackonochie,* incumbent of St Alban's, Holborn, and other ritualist clergy. Having moved to the West Highlands in 1876 to become incumbent of St Bride's, Nether Lochaber (North Ballachulish), he attempted to learn Gaelic and established a reputation for assiduous pastoral work. Following his consecration in 1883 that was the characteristic feature of his twenty-three-year episcopate. His published writings included a collection of charges delivered to his diocesan clergy and a manual of eucharistic devotions designed for lay communicants.

T. I. Ball, *A Pastoral Bishop. A Memoir of Alexander Chinnery-Haldane, D.D. sometime Bishop of Argyll and the Isles* (L, 1907); J. A. L. Haldane, *The Haldanes of Gleneagles* (E, 1929).

D. W. Lovegrove

Chisholm, William I (c.1493-1564), Bishop of Dunblane. He was half-brother and successor as Bishop to James Chisholm. He matriculated at St Andrews in 1518 and graduated MA in 1521. He became a canon of Dunblane and then Bishop in 1526. He was present in St Andrews at the burning of Patrick Hamilton* for heresy* in 1528, and attended the execution of other heretics in 1534, 1539, 1540, 1544, 1550 and 1558. Appointed a Lord of Council in 1530, and Auditor of Exchequer in 1533 and 1558, a Lord of the Articles in 1535, and Privy Councillor by 1545, he supported Cardinal Beaton* against James Hamilton,* second Earl of Arran as governor in 1543, became a senator of the College of Justice by 1546 and took part in the Church's provincial council (*see* Councils, Provincial) of 1549. At the Reformation Parliament* in 1560, he was ready to do Argyll's bidding. He declined either to condemn or to approve the Reformed Confession of Faith (*see* Scots Confession), and was afraid to receive the papal envoy, Nicholas de Gouda, in 1562. Though often depicted as a confirmed papalist, he favoured in 1560 the proposed marriage of James, third Earl of Arran to Queen Elizabeth, a step at variance with Roman policy. He was said to have been at the point of death in December 1564. His nephew, William Chisholm (II),* was appointed coadjutor in 1561, and succeeded to the bishopric by 1565.

FESMA 78; *APS* II, 606; J. H. S. Cockburn, *The Medieval Bishops of Dunblane* (E, 1959), 199-214; *DNB* X, 262.

J. Kirk

Chisholm, William II (c.1526-93), Bishop of Dunblane. A canon of Dunblane and nephew and Bishop Chisholm I,* he was provided coadjutor to his uncle with succession in 1561 by Pius IV after nomination by the Crown, regardless of the 1560 Reformation Parliament's abrogation of papal jurisdiction in Scotland. He was also appointed titular Bishop of Massula in Numidia. In 1562 the papal envoy in Scotland commended his zeal, and in 1563 he was sent to Rome with a list of faithful Scottish Catholics. With his uncle's death, he returned from Flanders as Bishop of Dunblane in March 1565, and was again in Rome during the summer of 1565 to secure a dispensation for Queen Mary's* marriage to Darnley and in 1566 was appointed Mary's ambassador to the Vatican. After Mary's deposition, he was charged with massmongering and with favouring Darnley's murderers, but was found to be 'furth of this realm' and was deprived of his bishopric in 1569. Chisholm became administrator of the French see of Vaison near Avignon in 1570. He was rehabilitated as Bishop of Dunblane in July 1587 (at a point when James VI* was anxious to secure good relations with Catholic France and Spain), but his restoration was annulled in May 1589. He resigned his French bishopric in 1585, to be succeeded by his nephew, William Chisholm III. Having entered the Carthusian order, he became prior at Lyons and then at Rome, where he died.

FESMA 78; J. H. S. Cockburn, *The Medieval Bishops of Dunblane* (E, 1959), 215-34; *DNB* X, 262; J. H. Pollen (ed.), *Papal Negotiations with Mary Queen of Scots* (SHS, E, 1901).

J. Kirk

Christ's College, Aberdeen. Known previously as the Aberdeen College successively of the FC, UFC and the CofS, the name Christ's College was adopted in 1936 just before its association with the Faculty of Divinity in the University of Aberdeen.

The College originated in the need to provide instruction for the candidates for the ministry studying at Aberdeen who had come out of the CofS at the Disruption.* Classes were held during the winter of 1843-4 in a room in South Silver Street by Alexander Black (*FES* VII, 363; *DNB* V, 106), who had resigned his chair at Marischal College*. (He became Professor of New Testament at New College,* Edinburgh, 1844-56.) His resignation precipitated a long controversy over the desirability of the FC's having more than one theological college. The eventual recognition of the Aberdeen College encouraged the founding of a third at Glasgow (later known as Trinity College*).

Despite constant struggles to secure adequate staffing and endowment the College trained some 600 students between 1843 and 1936, including not a few from Europe and America. In the field of biblical studies its most distinguished scholar was William Robertson Smith,* while Stewart Salmond,* James Iverach* and David S. Cairns* made notable contributions to theological studies. Principal David Brown* was Moderator of the FC General Assembly in 1885 and Principals Iverach and

Cairns of the UF Assembly in 1913 and 1923 respectively. Since 1936 the head of the College has been known as Master, and the Senate was renamed the College Council. Of the Masters, G. D. Henderson* was CofS Moderator in 1955 and Robin Barbour in 1979.

R. A. Lendrum, R. G. Philip and D. S. Cairns, *The Church College in Aberdeen* (A, 1936).

H. R. Sefton

Christian Journal (Relief Church), *see* Periodicals, Religious.

Christian Treasury, The (1845–96), twelve-page weekly evangelical periodical. Originally published in Edinburgh by John Johnstone, its first editor was Andrew Cameron.* Its professed aims were to combat 'Popery and Infidelity' and to promote evangelical unity. It drew on a wide range of contributors, including Thomas Guthrie,* W. Lindsay Alexander,* J. H. Merle d'Aubigné, the Genevan historian of Reformation, and Friedrich W. Krummacher of Elberfeld, and achieved great popularity in its fifty-year span. 'There is abundant evidence to show that in the houses of the people its weekly and monthly appearance was eagerly looked for' (W. J. Couper in *Scottish Notes and Queries*, second series, 2, 1900–1, 133–4).

Cameron resigned from the editorship in 1859, and was succeeded by Horatius Bonar* until 1879. Later editors included J. H. Thomson and F. B. Meyer. It was latterly published in London by Marshall Bros.

J. A. H. Dempster

Christian Unity Association of Scotland, formed on 14 January 1904, to promote understanding chiefly between members of the CofS, UFC and EpCS. It grew out of a Reunion Conference that first met under the presidency of George H. Wilkinson, Bishop of St Andrews, on 30 June 1899, and later, by petitioning (with 2,225 signatures) the ecclesiastical authorities, secured the appointment of 13 October 1902 as a day of prayer for unity (cf. *Speeches of the Deputations...*, E, 1901). In its early days the Association (whose first officers were Canon Rowland Ellis, chairman, A. R. MacEwen,* secretary, and Alexander Crum Brown (1838–1922), Professor of Chemistry in Edinburgh University, treasurer) claimed 'practically all the leading churchmen in Scotland' in its ranks, which in 1917 numbered 190. By 1956, however, it had dwindled to nineteen – though including J. H. S. Burleigh,* Gordon Donaldson,* Kenneth Warner, Bishop of Edinburgh, and its last secretary, W. Montgomery Watt, later Professor of Arabic and Islamic Studies at Edinburgh. In that year its clerical members were absorbed by the Leighton Club* of Edinburgh, its lay members being accorded associate status. For a time the Association had at least one local branch (Aberdeen). *Historical Papers Submitted ... by its Special Committee 1911–1913* (E, 1914), by such as A. R. MacEwen, J. Dowden,* G. W. Sprott* and James Cooper,* concerned the historical claims of episcopacy and Presbyterianism.

R. W. Weir, *Notes on the History of the Christian Unity Association of Scotland* (privately, 1917); A. J. Mason, *Memoir of George Howard Wilkinson*, 2 vols (L, 1909), II, 364–405; MS papers in New College Library, Edinburgh.

D. F. Wright

Christian Year. The main festivals of the Church's year, including Christmas and Easter, were observed by the Church in Scotland from its beginnings, although in the Celtic Church* the date of Easter differed from the rest of Western Christendom. In the medieval period many local saints' days were added to the observance of the main festivals.

The Reformation. The 'keeping of holy dayes ..., all those that the papists have invented, as the feasts ... of Chrismasse ...: which things because in Gods Scriptures they neither have commandement nor assurance, we judge them utterly to be abolished from this realme' (*The First Book of Discipline*,* 88–9). Thus the Scottish Reformers abolished the observances of the Christian Year. In their view the Lord's Day alone had scriptural authority. Their attitude is further seen in the conditional acceptance by the General Assembly in 1566 of the Second Helvetic Confession of Faith: exception was taken to its support for the observance of the Christian Year. But the traditional festivals were also holidays and there was popular opposition to their abolition. The *Book of Common Order* (1564)* gave some support to the popular demand since it contained a Calendar. There were other reasons for such a Calendar since the fairs and markets of many burghs were held on saints' days and the law courts still based their terms on the Christian Year. But the Calendar contained, as well as a list of feasts required for dating purposes, a variety of other festivals, including 'The Assumption of Mary'. It is clear that some ministers continued to celebrate Communion at or about Easter and also held Christmas. Since there were regular services for preaching during the week, it meant that services could well be held on Christmas Day, Good Friday and Ascension Day. The season of Lent as a time of abstinence from the eating of meat continued to be observed for some years for economic reasons, to promote the fishing industry and to conserve stocks of cattle.

The Seventeenth and Eighteenth Centuries. An injunction to observe the main festivals of the Christian Year was one of the Five Articles of Perth* for which James VI* coerced the approval of the General Assembly. It is likely that this article had a measure of popularity, since the King proclaimed that the holy days were also to be holidays. But Presbyterians objected and, the Articles being made a term of communion, a number of ministers were deposed and some were imprisoned or exiled. David Calderwood's* *Altare Damascenum seu Politia Ecclesiae Anglicanae obtrusa Ecclesiae Scoticanae* (1623, reprinted Leiden, 1708) is the classic statement of the Presbyterian position. The Calendar included in Laud's* Liturgy, which Charles I* sought to foist on the Scottish Church, was much expanded. But the observance of the Christian Year was again 'utterly abolished' by the 1638 Glasgow Assembly* 'because they are neither commanded nor warranted by Scripture' (Act session 17). During the Restoration,* observances of Epiphany, Good Friday, Easter, Ascension, St Andrew's Day and Christmas were marked in some places. With the re-establishment of Presbyterianism after the Revolution the Christian Year ceased to be observed in the CofS for nearly 200 years.

The Nineteenth and Twentieth Centuries. The recovery of the observance of the Christian Year in Presbyterian worship took place in the late nineteenth century as part of the 'catholic revival' in worship.* Although the General Assembly in 1876 forbade the observance of 'Roman Catholic or Episcopal Feast or Festival Days' when considering the worship introduced by John Macleod* at Duns, ministers could not be prevented from mentioning the Incarnation, Resurrection and Ascension of Christ and Pentecost on certain Sundays of the year. The holding of Christmas and holy week services depended on the support of Kirk Sessions* and they came to be celebrated in some congregations. Four ministers in the CofS held Christmas Day services in 1873 and James Cooper* held holy week services at St Stephen's, Broughty Ferry, in 1878, the first such services to be held in a Presbyterian church in Scotland in the nineteenth century. The General Assembly of the CofS received favourably an overture advocating the observance of the more important festivals of the Christian Year in 1922. The observance of the Christian Year was also encouraged in the Kirk by the publication by the Committee on Public Worship and Aids to Devotion* of *Prayers for the Christian Year* in 1935. The *Book of Common Order** of 1940 contained a Calendar based on that of the Anglican Prayer Book except that all saints' days with the exception of St Andrew the patron saint of Scotland were omitted. Work of a scholarly nature on the origins and rationale of the Christian Year was published by Allan McArthur, *The Evolution of the Christian Year* (L, 1953). The general structure of the Christian Year is now widely accepted in the Sunday worship of many parishes in the CofS. Special weekday services on important Christian festivals, however, have not attained such widespread recognition, although watchnight services on Christmas Eve have attained a popularity not matched by those on Christmas Day, Ash Wednesday, during holy week or on Ascension Day.

Reasons for Observing the Christian Year. Many of those who advocated the greater observance of the Christian Year in the late nineteenth century saw it as a framework for teaching the fundamental doctrines of the Christian faith in a time of uncertainty and confusion. In the twentieth century the Iona Community* has also advocated a renewed emphasis on the Christian Year for this reason (A. A. Fleming, *The Christian Year*, G, 1948). Holy week services were seen by some of those who first intro-

duced them, such as John Macleod, as being both teaching and evangelistic opportunities. They were part of the catholic heritage of the Church, yet they also had an evangelical purpose.

See also Liturgy; Lectionary.

D. B. Forrester and D. M. Murray (eds), *Studies in the History of Worship in Scotland* (E, 1984).

D. M. Murray

Christie, Dugald (1855–1936), medical missionary. The ninth child of a Glencoe sheepfarmer, he was bilingual in Gaelic* and English. His parents dying early, he was apprenticed to a Glasgow draper. He was converted during D. L. Moody's* mission of 1874 and with the assistance of the Edinburgh Medical Missionary Society* qualified in medicine at Edinburgh in 1881, taking divinity classes also at New College* and the UP Divinity Hall. After a year as resident physician in the EMMS Cowgate Mission he was appointed to the Manchuria mission of the UP Church (though his previous affiliation had been with the FC). He arrived, with his wife Elizabeth Hastie Smith, in Newchang in 1882, and entered his life work in Mukden the next year. Christie provides his own account of the four necessary stages of medical missions: (1) itinerate, (2) open dispensaries, (3) open a hospital (where the best work, medically and spiritually, is done), (4) train a medical profession. His own work followed this pattern, beginning in an atmosphere where foreigners were unwelcome and Western medicine distrusted; in early years the death of a patient could have had a disastrous effect. After two years he opened Manchuria's first hospital; among those healed and converted through its agency was the famous evangelist Chang Shen ('Blind Chang'). The Mukden hospital was extended or replaced several times. One building was destroyed by the Boxers in 1900, another set up in 1907 with such substantial Chinese contributions that Scottish intervention proved unnecessary. Christie's desire for a professional medical college in Mukden was eventually fulfilled in 1911–12. The Foreign Mission Committee of the UFC, declaring medical education outwith its scope, stipulated that funds should be separately raised without appeal to congregations. The necessary subscription came, the Chinese Viceroy securing the teaching hospital site. Christie became principal of a medical school on Scottish lines with a five- (later seven-) year course. He retired in 1922 and died in Edinburgh.

Christie (who was ordained by the Presbytery of Manchuria in 1900) believed in medical missions as integral, not preparatory or supplementary, to Christian mission. As chairman of the medical section of the Shanghai Missions Conference of 1907 he secured the adoption of far-reaching resolutions on medical practice, including high professional standards and provision of Chinese medical schools. While critical of traditional Chinese medicine and of its undergirding metaphysic, he was scrupulously respectful of Chinese culture and courtesy; much of his success was due to the friendship and respect of high officials. He engaged in flood relief, served a Red Cross hospital in the Sino-Japanese War of 1894-95, was active in the Governor-General's relief committee in the Russo-Japanese War and in the organization of preventive measures in the plague of 1911-12. He was created CMG in 1911, and was FRCS and FRCP of Edinburgh.

Elizabeth Christie died in Scotland in 1888. In 1892 Christie married a UP missionary, Eliza Inglis, who wrote his biography, a life of his young colleague Arthur Jackson (who died in the plague) and a study called *The Chinese.*

Nine Years in Manchuria (Paisley, [1893]); *Thirty Years in Mukden,* edited by his wife (L, 1914).

[Eliza Inglis Christie], *Dugald Christie of Manchuria* (L, [1932]); A. Fulton, *Through Earthquake, Wind and Fire: Church and Mission in Manchuria 1867-1950* (E, 1967); *Records of China Centenary Missionary Conference* (Shanghai, 1907), 625-59; FUFCS, 549; *Who Was Who, 1929-1940,* 251.

A. F. Walls

Christmas, *see* Christian Year.

Christology. There was no distinctive Scottish Christology until the emergence of Edward Irving* in the middle of the nineteenth century. Nor was there much Christological controversy comparable, for example, to the Arianism which disturbed England in the late seventeenth and early eighteenth centuries. The closest parallel was the case of John Simson,* Professor of Divinity at Glasgow University, who was accused of denying in effect the essential deity of Christ. When the General Assembly of 1729 shrank from deposing Simson, Thomas Boston* dissented. The failure to deal with Simson's Arianism was also one of the grievances which led to the Secession* of 1733.

EDWARD IRVING. Not until 1828 was there any serious Christological controversy in Scotland. In that year Edward Irving published *The Doctrine of the Incarnation Opened in Six Sermons.* Irving's central tenet was that in becoming incarnate Christ took *fallen* human nature. Otherwise, he would not have been one with us; more particularly, he could not have been tempted. Further publications followed setting forth the same view: *The Orthodox and Catholic Doctrine of Our Lord's Human Nature* in 1830 and *Christ's Holiness in Flesh* in 1831. As a result Irving was charged with denying the sinlessness of Christ and deposed in 1833.

Many have questioned this judgment. It merits three comments. First, many of those who were most disturbed by Irving's teaching respected his piety. Robert McCheyne,* for example, noted in his Diary for 9 November 1834: 'Heard of Edward Irving's death. I look back upon him with awe, as on the saints and martyrs of old. A holy man in spite of all his delusions and errors. He is now with his God and Saviour, whom he wronged so much, yet, I am persuaded, loved so sincerely.'

Second, Irving himself vehemently affirmed his belief in the sinlessness of Jesus. 'I believe it to be necessary unto salvation that a man should believe that Christ's soul was so held in possession by the Holy Ghost, and so supported by the divine nature, as that it never assented unto a single evil suggestion' (*The Collected Writings of Edward Irving,* L, 1865, V, 126).

Third, Irving used extremely provocative language. One hearer complained of his referring to the humanity of Christ as 'that sinful substance'. His published statements are almost equally bold. God's scheme of redemption, he wrote, was that the Son of God 'should join Himself unto the fallen creation, and take up into His own eternal personality the human nature, after it had fallen, and become obnoxious to all the powers of sin and infirmity and rebellion' (115). Irving clearly meant by this that the Lord's own humanity was capable of sin and rebellion: 'the flesh of Christ, like my flesh, was in its proper nature mortal and corruptible' (116). The fact that this corruption did not erupt in actual sin was due entirely to the work of the Holy Spirit, restraining the fallen nature.

The early response to Irving was almost entirely critical. Marcus Dods* (*On The Incarnation of the Eternal Word,* L, 1831) accused him of Manicheism, Nestorianism and logical confusion. A. B. Bruce* (*The Humiliation of Christ,* E, 1876, 269ff.) pointed out the antecedents of Irving's teaching in the Spanish adoptionists of the eighth century and the preaching of Gottfried Menken of Bremen in the nineteenth; charged him with rhetorical inexactitude; and accused him of confusing sinless infirmities with vices. He also subjected Irving's view of temptation to a rigorous critique, pointing out, among other things, that temptation can come not only from lust but from its opposite – for example, from a holy shrinking from desertion by God.

It was left to Karl Barth* to bring Irving in from the cold. Barth (*Church Dogmatics,* I:2, 154) enthusiastically espoused the idea that Christ took a fallen humanity, taking this to mean a corrupt nature (*natura vitiata*), obnoxious to sin and existing in a vile and abject condition. Barth cites Irving, but he appears to know of his work only at second-hand, through H. R. Mackintosh's* *The Doctrine of the Person of Jesus Christ* (E, 1912).

H. R. MACKINTOSH. Mackintosh's own work is a reverent and magisterial survey of the biblical evidence and of post-biblical discussion. It is most notable today for its sympathetic treatment of kenoticism (based on the Greek of Phil. 2:7, 'emptied'). Mackintosh distanced himself, however, from the earlier forms of this theory put forward by such scholars as G. Thomasius (*Christi Person und Werke,* 3 vols, Erlangen, 1856-63; 2 vols, ³1886-8) and W. F. Gess (*Das Dogma von Christi Person und Werke,* Basel, 1887) and identified more closely with the work of his fellow Scots, D. W. Forrest* (*The Authority of Christ,* E, 1906) and P. T. Forsyth* (*The Person and Place of Jesus Christ,* L, 1909).

What particularly attracted Mackintosh was the religious value of *kenosis.* The main features of his exposition are as follows. First, he insisted on the need thoroughly to ethicize our concept of God, particularly our concept of immutability. Mackintosh feared that the idea of the changelessness of the Absolute could be – and often was – used to put the very idea of divine self-limitation out of court. 'Now it is not at all excessive to say that what Christ reveals in God is rather the infinite mobility of absolute grace bent on the redemption of the lost, the willingness to do and bear whatever is compatible with a moral nature. What is immutable in God is the holy love which makes His essence. We must let Infinitude be genuinely infinite in its moral expedients; we must credit God with infinite sacrifice based on His self-consciousness of omnipotence' (473).

Second, Mackintosh repudiated the notion that *kenosis* consisted in Christ's laying aside the *relative* attributes of deity, such as omnipresence and omniscience, while retaining such *essential* attributes as holiness and love. 'The distinction is not one which can be maintained... to talk of the abandonment of this or that attribute on the part of the Eternal Son is a conception too sharp and crude, too rough in shading, for our present problem. God ceases to be God not merely when (as with Gess) there is a self-renunciation actually of the divine consciousness, but even when such qualities as omnipotence are parted with' (476f.).

Third, he suggested that although the divine attributes of the Son were not laid aside they were modified ('transposed') 'to function in new ways, to assume new forms of activity... It is possible to conceive the Son, who has entered at love's behest on the region of growth and progress, as now possessing *all* the qualities of Godhead in the form of concentrated potency rather than of full actuality' (477). This applied particularly to omniscience, omnipotence and omnipresence. Christ had divine knowledge within reach, though he took only what was essential to his vocation: 'Though on many subjects He shared the ignorance as well as the knowledge of His contemporaries, yet He had at command all higher truth which can be assimilated by perfect human faculty' (477). The same was true with regard to power: 'in the historic Jesus there is a derived power over the souls of men, as over nature, which may be viewed as a modified form of the power of the Godhead' (478). Omnipresence, Mackintosh admits, is more baffling, but only at first sight. A transcending of spatial relationships is present and implicit in Christ's redemptive mission – 'in His triumphant capacity, that is, to accomplish in Palestine a universally and eternally valid work unhampered by the bounds of "here and there". As part of history, His work has a date and place, yet its power far transcends them' (478).

Fourth, Mackintosh asserts that the life which Jesus lived as a result of 'this divine act of self-abnegation' was 'a life wholly restrained within the bounds of manhood. Outside the conditions imposed by the choice of life as man the Son has no activity or knowledge' (479). This involved the possibility that 'His primary descent into the sphere of finitude had veiled in nescience His eternal relationship to the Father' (481). Pursuing this theme, Mackintosh suggests that, 'It can only have been in mature manhood and perhaps intermittently that Christ became aware of His divinity – which must have remained for Him an object of *faith* to the very end' (481). He even seems to limit Christ's awareness of his own divine sonship to 'high moments of visitation' in his experience.

This is the weakest link in Mackintosh's exposition. How could someone with no consistent sense of divine identity be the supreme revelation of God? At this point Mackintosh appears to have no defence against Albrecht Ritschl's objection that kenoticism, by definition, deprives us of the right to say that we find God in Jesus.

It may be that Mackintosh himself felt the force of such difficulties. It is at least very interesting that there are no traces of kenoticism in his later work. The idea is not mentioned at all in *The Christian Experience of Forgiveness* (L, 1927), nor are the kenotic theologians discussed in *Types of Modern Theology* (Welwyn, 1937). He also appears eventually to have dropped all reference to the kenotic theory from his class lectures (see 'H. R. Mackintosh's Contribution to Christology' by Robert R. Redman Jr., *SJT* 41, 1988, 517–34).

DONALD BAILLIE. Mackintosh's younger contemporary, Donald Baillie,* published his *God Was In Christ* in 1948. Baillie gave an enthusiastic welcome to what he called 'the End of Docetism': 'It may safely be said that practically all schools of theological thought today take the full humanity of our Lord more seriously than has ever been done before by Christian theologians' (11). He also recognized, however, that not all the results of twentieth-century scholarship had been positive. In particular, he was critical of the historical radicalism of such men as Rudolf Bultmann and R. H. Lightfoot. 'I cannot believe that there is any good reason for the defeatism of those who give up all hope of penetrating the tradition and reaching an assured knowledge of the historical personality of Jesus' (58).

Baillie devoted a substantial portion of his essay (85–105) to 'A Critique of Christologies'. This included a brilliant analysis of the kenotic theory, in which he argued that it had no answer to William Temple's question (posed in *Christus Veritas*, L, 1925, 142f.), What was happening to the rest of the universe during the period of our Lord's life? Was the world let loose from the control of the creative Word during the period of his depotentiation? He also argued that kenoticism implied a theophany rather than an incarnation; and that it seemed to leave no room at all for the traditional doctrine of the permanence of the manhood of Christ ('when the days of His flesh come to an end, Christ resumes His divine attribution and His *kenosis*, his humanity, comes to an end', 97).

Baillie was even more critical of the idea of *anhypostasia* (the notion that the Lord's human nature was 'impersonal'). In this he was following H. R. Mackintosh (390) and R. C. Moberly (*Atonement and Personality*, L, 1901, 92). It is not entirely clear, however, what Baillie was rejecting. Few would deny that Jesus was 'a man among men' (87); or that he was an individual man; or even that he had a human centre of consciousness. The question is whether Christ had a human centre of *self-*consciousness, and therefore two selves? True though it is that the man Christ Jesus was an individual human being over against others, the real issue is whether his human nature had an individual existence over against and independent of his divine nature. Baillie was sympathetic to the idea of *enhypostasia*, first proposed by Leontius of Byzantium and John of Damascus and reintroduced to English-speaking theology by H. M. Relton (*A Study in Christology*, L., 1922). He was not, however, quite convinced. Yet *enhypostasia* seems to meet all the difficulties. The humanity was *in*-personal: that is, from the very first moment of its existence it was the humanity of the Son of God and as such personalized in him. Yet he, and not merely his human nature (or his divine, for that matter) was always the subject of all his acts and experiences.

Baillie's own Christology was rooted firmly in the Nicene tradition, insisting that 'it is impossible to do justice to the incarnation without speaking of it as the coming into history of the eternally pre-existent Son of God' (151). His most distinctive contribution was his attempt to present the incarnation as a reflection of 'the paradox of grace', the fact that the good actions of a Christian are fully his own actions, yet whatever good there is in our lives is 'all of God'. 'This paradox in its fragmentary form in our own Christian lives is a reflection of that perfect union of God and man in the Incarnation on which our whole Christian life depends, and may therefore be our best clue to the understanding of it' (117). This is certainly worth exploring, although the obedience of a Christian is due rather to the indwelling of the Spirit than to a union of natures. But Baillie surely comes close to both Nestorianism and Adoptionism when he suggests that the incarnation of the divine Word in Christ was conditioned by his own continual response. It is indeed true that moment by moment Christ was choosing humiliation and adhering to *kenosis*. But it cannot be true that moment by moment he was choosing to be incarnate. The Gospels record his being tempted to abandon the path of service but we have no record of any attempt to go back on the enfleshment. It is also misleading to suggest that 'when at last God broke through into human life with full revelation and became incarnate, must we not say that in a sense it was because here at last a man was perfectly receptive?' (149). The man did not exist prior to the incarnation. This brings us back to the *enhypostasia*: the humanity did not exist for a single moment except as the humanity of God.

T. F. TORRANCE. T. F. Torrance* was a student of H. R. Mackintosh but seems to have imbibed little of his mentor's interest in *kenosis*. The real influences on his thought have been McLeod Campbell,* Edward Irving and Karl Barth. The Fathers and Reformers are read through the eyes of these later thinkers.

Torrance lays great stress on the *homoousion* ('of the same substance'), the 'king-pin of the Nicene-Constantinopolitan Creed'. The word itself is not sacrosanct, he admits, but the idea it encapsulates it absolutely vital to Christianity. Otherwise, what happens in Christ has nothing to do with any *self-*giving or *self*-revealing on the part of the eternal God (*The Incarnation*, E, 1981, xii). Jesus' acts are saving acts precisely because they are divine acts. If the *homoousion* is not true the cross is unintelligible. But if it is true, then 'Jesus Christ, even in the midst of our death which he made his own, even in the midst of our betrayal of him, is the Word and Hand of God stretched out to save us, the very heart of God Almighty beating with the pulse of his infinite love within the depth of our lost humanity in order to vanquish and do away with everything that separates man from God' (xv).

The *homoousion*, according to Torrance, is also of profound epistemological significance, because it means that the Father/Son and Son/Father relationship 'falls within the very being of God' (*The Mediation of Christ*, Grand Rapids, 1984, 64). It follows from this that we can be confident that what God is to us in Jesus he is in himself: the economic and the ontological Trinity are one and the same (*The Incarnation*, xx). 'There is no God,' he had written earlier (*The School of Faith*, L, 1959, lxxiii), 'except He who has shown us His face in Jesus Christ, so that we cannot go behind the back of Christ to find God, or know anything about Him apart from this God, for there is no other God than this God'.

Torrance's enthusiasm for the *homoousion* is paralleled by his aversion to Apollinarianism. This is set out particularly in his essay, 'The Mind of Christ in Worship: The problem of Apollinarianism in the Liturgy' (*Theology in Reconciliation*, L, 1975, 139–214). Torrance warmly endorses Athanasius' insistence that when we think of the Son becoming flesh 'we must include under that term all our human affections proper to human nature, including weakness, anxiety, agitation, passion, ignorance as well as the sentient characteristics of human beings, for the purpose of the economic condescension was to renew the whole man, not least his *mind*, in Christ' (152). He is equally enthusiastic about Cyril of Alexandria: 'Cyril considered it of the utmost importance that in his complete oneness with us Christ plumbed the depths of our most intense supplication and prayer to the Father, not only as an example for us to follow, important as that is for all our worship, but as the model of his vicarious mediation on our behalf' (174).

It is not always easy to disentangle the thinking of these Fathers from Torrance's exegetical interpolations. He does, however, make his own thinking plain elsewhere, constantly invoking the principle that 'the unassumed is the unhealed' and pushing the idea that Christ entered into our human mind to its furthest limits. In *The Mediation of Christ*, for example, he wrote: 'it is the alienated *mind* of man that God had laid hold of in Jesus Christ in order to redeem it and effect reconciliation deep within the rational centre of human being ... In Jesus

God himself descended to the very bottom of our human existence where we are alienated and antagonistic, into the very hell of our godlessness and despair, laying fast hold of us and taking our cursed condition upon himself, in order to embrace us for ever in his reconciling love' (48, 53).

In pursuance of this theme Torrance (encouraged, no doubt, by the example of Barth) went on to reintroduce to Scotland the peculiar Christology of Edward Irving: 'the Incarnation is to be understood as the coming of God to take upon himself our fallen human nature, our actual human existence laden with sin and guilt, our humanity diseased in mind and soul in its estrangement or alienation from the Creator' (*The Mediation of Christ*, 48f.). Torrance claims that such a conclusion is inevitable if we take seriously Paul's statement that God sent his Son 'in the likeness of flesh of sin' (Rom. 8:3). He also claims (*The Mediation of Christ*, 49) that the idea that Christ took our fallen humanity, including our depraved mind, prevailed generally among the Greek Fathers. This is extremely doubtful. Athanasius frequently speaks of Christ assuming flesh but (notwithstanding the impression created by Torrance, *Theology in Reconciliation*, 153) he never asserts that that meant Christ assuming our corruption and our sin; and true though it is that such Fathers as Gregory of Nazianzus constantly affirmed that 'what Christ has not assumed he was not healed', they never meant by this that Christ took fallen human nature. For the purposes of the Apollinarian controversy the 'unassumed' was not fallenness but the human mind of Christ. From this point of view the most ardent of Irving's opponents would have endorsed the principle that the unassumed is the unhealed, insisting that Christ took not simply a true human body but a reasonable human soul (*anima rationalis*). They would not have conceded, however, that a reasonable human soul was necessarily a fallen one; nor that it would in any way have furthered the work of redemption for Christ to have taken our corruption as well as our guilt.

There are three major objections to this Irving–Torrance theory. First, it does not pay sufficient attention to the extreme care with which Paul chooses his words in Romans 8:3. He does not say that Christ took sinful flesh (or flesh of sin). He says only that he took the *likeness* of sinful flesh. Second, it has no answer to the charge of Nestorianism. If Christ had a fallen human soul, does that mean that he, a divine person, was fallen? If not, was there another (human) person who was fallen? Third, it fails to take proper account of the historical meaning of 'fallen'. A fallen person is one who has lost his original righteousness and become corrupt in his whole nature (totally depraved). This is what Christ came to save us from. It is certainly not what he was.

INCARNATIONAL REDEMPTION. Torrance also shares with Irving a commitment to some form of the idea of incarnational redemption. He insists time and again that Christ sanctified the whole of human nature in the very act of assuming it. This idea occurs in such early works as *The School of Faith*, where Torrance speaks of the incarnational union as dealing with our original sin, 'or as sanctifying our fallen human nature through bringing it into healing and sanctifying union with holy divine nature' (lxxxvi). The same idea occurs in *Theology in Reconstruction*: 'In this union he both assumed our fallen human nature, taking it from the Virgin Mary, and sanctified it in the very act of assumption and all through his holy Life he lived in it from the beginning to the end. Thus our redemption begins from his very birth, so that we must regard the Incarnation, even in its narrower sense, as a redeeming event, reaching out to its full *telos* in the death and resurrection' (155).

Irving, too, held to a theory of incarnational redemption. One of the central concerns of *The Doctrine of the Incarnation Opened* was to 'open ... how God, by uniting the person of His Son to fallen flesh, doth thereby reconcile the whole lump of fallen humanity unto Himself, and is enabled, through Christ, to save as many as it pleaseth Him' (*Works* V, 115). But he would not have been happy with Torrance's way of expressing things. Irving completely repudiated the idea that the human nature of Christ was sanctified at birth by the power of the Holy Spirit. He makes this clear in the Preface to his treatise *On the Human Nature of Christ* where, having stated that the work which Christ did was to reconcile, sanctify, quicken and glorify this human nature of ours which is full of sin and death and rebellion he continues: 'The most part of those who are opposed to the truth agree in this; but differ from us in maintaining that the substance of human nature underwent a change in the miraculous conception. We maintain that it underwent no change, but was full of fellowship and community with us all His life long, and was not changed but by the resurrection' (*Collected Writings*, V, 563f.). Earlier, in his *Sermons on the Incarnation*, he had written to the same effect: 'With humility be it spoke, but yet with truth and verity, that the fallen humanity could not have been sanctified and redeemed by the union of the Son alone; which directly leadeth unto an inmixing and confusing of the Divine with the human nature, that pestilent heresy of Eutyches. The human nature is thoroughly fallen; and without a thorough communication, inhabitation, and empowering of a Divine substance, it cannot again be brought up pure and holy. The mere apprehension of it by the Son doth not make it holy. Such a union leads directly to the apotheosis or deification of the creature, and this again does away with the mystery of a trinity in the Godhead' (*Works* V, 123f.).

The truth is, as he himself recognized (566), that Irving's theory required not simply a humanity which was identical with ours in origin but one identical with ours in *life*. The two essentials for which he strove – the temptability of Jesus and his sympathy with his people – both demanded this. A humanity healed and sanctified in the very act of assumption would have been useless for his purposes because it would have differed from that of believers. As far as Irving was concerned, it was the living, struggling, suffering Jesus who had fallen, sinful flesh.

VICARIOUS HUMANITY. The remaining point in Torrance's Christology is his stress on the vicarious humanity of Christ. For example, Christ is not only the Word of God to humanity but humanity's perfect response to that word (*Theology in Reconstruction*, 157). He is also the one who vicariously believes; the one who was vicariously sanctified (so that sanctification, no less than justification, is *imputed* to us, 158); and the one in whom we enjoy a vicarious assurance – a subjective justification in which Christ, in our place, trusted in God's love towards us. 'We may summarise this,' writes Torrance, in language clearly reminiscent of McLeod Campbell, 'by saying that Jesus Christ was not only the fulfilment and embodiment of God's righteous and holy Act or *dikaioma*, but also the embodiment of our act of faith and trust and obedience toward God. He stood in our place, taking our cause upon him, also as Believer, as the Obedient One who was himself justified before God as his beloved Son in whom he was well pleased. He offered to God a perfect confidence and trust, a perfect faith and response which we are unable to offer, and he appropriated all God's blessings which we are unable to appropriate' (*Theology in Reconstruction*, 159).

Torrance also applies the idea of the vicarious humanity of Christ to the practice of Christian worship. The argument here is that if we do justice to the fullness of the Lord's humanity then we shall worship the Father not only *through* the Son but *along with* the Son; that is, we shall share in the Son's worship of the Father. 'Christian worship is properly a form of the life of Jesus Christ ascending to the Father in the life of those who are so intimately related to him through the Spirit, that when they pray to the Father through Christ, it is Christ the Incarnate Son who honours, worships and glorifies the Father in them' (*Theology in Reconciliation*, 139).

At first sight Torrance's exposition of this theme appears to involve a thorough-going Christomonism in which the work of Christ is everything and that of the believer nothing: we shall be saved regardless of our response because he responded for us. Yet so many qualifications are built into the exposition that a careful re-reading usually shows that the thinking is much less revolutionary than appears.

What has to be said, first of all, is that this stress on the vicarious humanity of Christ does not accord with the New Testament's portrayal of the distinctive roles of the Son and the Holy Spirit in the work of redemption. The Spirit is not the primary actor in the great drama of atonement; and the Son is not the primary enabler in the life of the believer. So far as Christian worship is concerned, for example, the stress falls on the role of the Holy Spirit, not on the role of Christ. We worship in Spirit and in truth. We sing in the Spirit. We pray in the Spirit.

Secondly, while the work of the Son is vicarious the work of the Holy Spirit is not. Christ died in our place, but the Spirit does not believe in our place. He enables us to believe but it is we who believe, just as it is we who repent, worship and mortify sin. All these activities occur by the aid of the Spirit but he does not perform them instead of us.

Thirdly, the term 'vicarious' cannot be used univocally even in relation to Christ. At one point – the cross – 'vicarious' means 'substitute'. In other instances, however, 'vicarious' indicates 'representative'; and in yet others it indicates 'solidarity'. When Torrance speaks of the vicarious humanity of Christ (particularly in relation to faith, assurance and worship) he is using the word in this last sense. Yet the impression of originality is due entirely to the fact that the reader instinctively takes it in the first sense. Christ is undoubtedly a believer *with* us (Heb. 12:2), but he is not a believer *instead of* us. He enjoys assurance with us, but he does not enjoy it instead of us. Even more important, while Christ worships with us he does not worship instead of us. In sum, while it is true that because Christ became a derelict we shall never be derelicts, it is not true that because he believed and worshipped we need not believe and worship.

However stimulating these modern Scottish essays in Christology, it is an enormous pity that they have so completely eclipsed their predecessors. The older writers may have lacked originality, in the sense that they never deviated from Chalcedonian orthodoxy. But they handled that orthodoxy itself with great sensitiveness and creativity. They certainly had no reservations about the humanity of Christ. In fact, the idea of our Lord's identification with humankind has never been better expressed than it was by Alexander Stewart of Cromarty* (*The Tree of Promise*, E, 1864, 31f.): 'Yet as the tabernacle after all was as truly a tent as the humblest in the camp of Israel, so Christ is as truly man as the meanest of our race. The blood which flows in the veins of the Hottentot, or springs under the lash from the back of an American slave, is that "one" same blood which flows in the veins of the Son of God.'

Stewart also spoke uninhibitively of the temptations of Christ. God, he wrote, perilled everything on his Son's absolute infallibility, 'as if He would say, "If He fail, let my throne be overturned, and I Myself cease to be God." The holy Son of God was tempted as if He could commit sin, and as if it were necessary that His principles should be put to the test' (78). In Stewart's judgment, the Son's deity in no way mitigated the force of the temptations. '"Ah, but," you say, "He was the divine Son of God, there was no fear for Him." We have no reason to think that His deity afforded Him the slightest relief from the pains of hunger. And thus He and all His suffering people are perfectly on a level. By the exercise of His divine power He might not turn the stones into bread. To do so would be sin; and just so is it sinful for you to resort to any unlawful means to supply your wants, even when they arise in the ordinary course of life. "But," you say, "He knew it would soon end, and I know not when relief may come." It does not appear from His answer to Satan that He knew this. His circumstances seem to have been much the same as those of any ordinary man suffering hunger and with nothing to eat. How entirely, then, is His fellow-feeling of infirmity under suffering unbroken by His deity!' (81).

This question of the Lord's temptability was also explored by James McLagan* in 'A Sermon on Hebrews IV.15' appended to Marcus Dods's *On the Incarnation of the Word* (289-306). 'It was not a few kinds only of our earthly struggles, apart from others, that he admitted into his heart, but he stood successively in all the main flood-gates of tribulation, and there made trial of the worst that mortal man can endure, whether from the hostility of a disordered world, or from the rage of fallen angels, or from the wrath of offended Heaven' (290). The resulting temptations, according to McLagan, were more sharp and terrible than those of any other man: 'What though he had no irregular or exaggerated passions to restrain? He had holy, just, pure, heavenly affections, strong in proportion to the greatness of his soul, and warm in proportion to the brightness and dignity of their objects; which he was called upon, by the nature of his undertaking, not only to control, but for a season to thwart so painfully, and to turn aside so violently from their natural courses, that he must have needed to exercise a persevering strength of self-denial altogether matchless; and must have had in his heart experience far beyond what mere mortality could have endured, of the profoundest sorrow, the keenest anguish and the harshest mortification' (297).

Like Stewart, McLagan recoiled from the idea that the fact of his being God cushioned the Lord against temptation. On the contrary, Christ had exactly the same resources as ourselves (300). McLagan also held that Jesus experienced a sense of weakness far beyond anything we can ever imagine. He illustrated this from the field of human conflict, where the leader feels a far greater sense of insufficiency than the common soldier precisely because he exercises far greater powers and bears greater responsibilities: '*He* saw the conjuncture in all its awful magnitude! He viewed the result in all its tremendous importance! He knew himself advancing to a post where his created and mortal nature, struck with the fiery darts of hell from beneath, and pierced from above by the arrows of the Almighty, must abide the shock and pressure of a falling world; and where the failure but for one moment of his *human* endurance and resolution, must effect not only the universal and eternal triumph of wickedness and misery; but what it is fearful to name, even while we know it can never happen – the defeat of his Father's counsel – the failure of his Father's truth – and the desecration of his Father's Godhead!' (302).

Equally impressive is Hugh Martin's* treatment of *kenosis* in *The Shadow of Calvary* (1875; G, 1954). 'This was the precise nature of his abasement, that though it was no robbery for him to be equal with God, he yet laid aside the reputation though never the reality thereof; and, remaining still, as he must ever remain, the same God unchangeable, he yet appeared in the form of a servant, not drawing on his divine might and energies, but denying himself their exercise and forth-putting – concealing, retiring out of view, withdrawing from the field of action, those prerogatives and powers of Deity, which in the twinkling of an eye might have scattered ten thousand worlds and hells of enemies. He withdrew them all from action that he might taste the weakness of created nature' (26).

What Martin was setting forth was not the idea of a mere *krupsis* (veiling) of Christ's divine powers but a genuine *kenosis*, involving a real self-denial and a real self-limitation. Christ assumed a nature and a position in which nothing but faith could have sustained him (63). Indeed, he entered so fully into our humanness that in Gethsemane he longed earnestly to escape from his sufferings (22); so fully that prayer was as indispensable to him as to any of his people: 'For in his resignation of all right to wield at pleasure the powers of his own Godhead, he "became poor" as his own poor and needy children, and left for himself only what *they* may ever draw upon – the fulness of the Father's Godhead and his promises' (55).

But perhaps no one epitomized the historic Christology of Scotland better than William Guthrie* of Fenwick, in his famous description of faith: 'now the heart is so enlarged for Him, as that less cannot satisfy, and more is not desired . . . The soul now resolves to die if He shall so command, yet at His door, and looking towards Him' (*The Christian's Great Interest*, 1658; rp. G, 1951, 43).

A. B. Bruce, *The Humiliation of Christ* (E, 1881); G. S. Hendry, *The Gospel of the Incarnation* (L, 1959); D. W. Forrest, *The Christ of History and of Experience* (E, 1897); *The Authority of Christ* (E, 1906); P. T. Forsyth, *The Person and Place of Jesus Christ* (L, 1909); J. Denney, *Jesus and the Gospel* (L, 1909); J. Orr, *The Virgin Birth of Christ* (L, 1907); M. Dods, *On the Incarnation of the Eternal Word* (L, 1831).

D. Macleod

Chronicles, Scottish Ecclesiastical. Chronicles were kept at several religious centres in Scotland for periods up to a thousand years. In their crudest form they were brief notices of events jotted on to a text such as a Calendar (for instance the *Calendar of Fearn* from the late fifteenth to the mid-seventeenth century) or more usually an Easter table (as in Iona* from maybe as early as its foundation in 563). Typically, though, they are a laconic account of events in a year-by-year series, recorded by a sequence of scribes over a number of generations. The earliest such chronicle was kept at Iona during the seventh century and first half of the eighth. The chronicle itself is now lost, but c.740 a copy was taken to Bangor (Ireland) where it was joined by a chronicle kept at Applecross (founded in 673): it is only because these chronicles eventually became the earliest stratum of all surviving Irish annals that any trace of them survives. The earliest chronicle of which a copy survives is the *Older Scottish Chronicle*, written perhaps in, or near, the royal monastery of Scone* c.975. It is not a straightforward chronicle, but is based on a king-list from Kenneth MacAlpin (d.858) with selections from a lost Scottish chronicle of this period. The only chronicle which survives as an original manuscript is the *Chronicle of Melrose*. Up to 1170 it is mainly a copy of Northumbrian texts, including a lost Scottish-Northumbrian chronicle, but thereafter until 1263 it is a continuous series of annals written at Melrose,* with a few entries added later in the century. The *Chronicle of Holyrood* from the same period survives only in copies. It, too, is written as a continuation of a Northumbrian text, and has annals written at Holyrood* and, later, at Coupar Angus (see Cistercians), which extend as a continuous series only as far as 1187 (with a few stragglers as late as 1356). Both the Melrose and Holyrood chroniclers used a lost St Andrews chronicle kept in the 1160s. No chronicles from major religious centres survive after the thirteenth century. Thereafter histories written by individual clergymen predominate (see Bower, Walter; Wyntoun, Andrew of). A late and more localized example of an ecclesiastical chronicle, however, was kept by successive incumbents at Fortingall (Perthshire) during the fifteenth and sixteenth centuries.

J. Bannerman, *Studies in the History of Dalriada* (E, 1974), 9–26; A. P. Smyth, 'The Earliest Irish Annals: their First Contemporary Entries, and the Earliest Centres of Recording', *Proc. Royal Irish Academy* 72 C (1972), 1–48; Isabel Henderson, 'North Pictland', in *The Dark Ages in the Highlands*, ed. E. Meldrum (Inverness, 1971), esp. 43–9; E. J. Cowan, 'The Scottish Chronicle in the Poppleton Manuscript', *IR* 32 (1981), 3–21; *The Chronicle of Melrose*, ed. A. O. and M. O. Anderson and index by W. Croft Dickinson (L, 1936); *A Scottish Chronicle known as the Chronicle of Holyrood*, ed. M. O. Anderson, (SHS, E, 1938).

D. Broun

Church Accommodation Committee. The Committee was formed by the General Assembly of the CofS in 1818, in the aftermath of Parliament's generous grant of 1,000,000 to the CofE for building new parish churches. It was instructed to negotiate a similar parliamentary grant for the Scottish Est.C. In presenting their case, the Committee put forward separate claims for new churches in the Lowlands and in the Highlands. In the Lowlands, they maintained, the problem was overcrowded parishes, especially in the new manufacturing districts where large numbers of people could not find accommodation in the parish church and were joining Secession* churches or drifting into irreligion. In the Highlands, on the other hand, the problem was overlarge parishes, too vast to be supervised by the parish minister and therefore providing inroads for the return of RCism. The Committee maintained that the need for churches was most urgent in the Highlands, and in 1823 Parliament granted 50,000 for erecting new Highland churches. But under pressure from Dissenters and those who favoured economic reform, the government decided against introducing the expected grant for Lowland church building. In 1834, disappointed over the unsuccessful negotiations with the government, the General Assembly enlarged and reorganized the Church Accommodation Committee under the new title of Church Extension* Committee, and instructed it to raise voluntary contributions for the required churches. It was also to continue working for the parliamentary grant, but now with more attention to mobilizing public opinion.

I. F. MacIver, 'The General Assembly of the Church, the State, and Society in Scotland, 1815–43' (MLitt, Edinburgh University, 1976); D. Chambers, 'The Church of Scotland's Parochial Extension Scheme and the Scottish Disruption', *Journal of Church and State* 16 (1974), 263–86.

S. J. Brown

Church and Nation Committee, of the CofS,* established in 1919 as a committee of the General Assembly, with the remit 'to watch over the developments of the Nation's life in which moral and spiritual considerations specially arise, and to consider what action the Church from time to time might be advised to take to further the highest interests of the people.'

The proposal to set up such a committee came from a Commission appointed by the General Assembly in 1916 to guide the Church in its response to the First World War.* The Commission's recommendation reflected a concern among leading churchmen like John White* and David Watson* about social and industrial problems and a recognition that the Church had to reform its own life to meet the challenges of the post-War era. The Church and Nation Committee was set up with a two-fold concern, for internal Church affairs as well as wider national affairs. In its first years, it had a sub-committee on the 'Life and Efficiency' of the Church, which studied such church matters as training for the ministry, the position of women in the Church, and ecumenical relations with other Churches. Its two other original sub-committees were concerned with domestic issues in 'Social and Industrial Life' and 'Empire Problems', covering constitutional and international affairs. Throughout the inter-war period, up to the outbreak of the Second World War* in 1939, the Committee reported regularly on such matters as gambling, Sunday* observance, marriage regulations, rural and industrial economic problems, education, the reform of the House of Lords, colonial affairs and support for the League of Nations. From 1924 onwards, it expressed a growing alarm at the effects of Irish immigration on its own racial conception of Scottish nationality. After the reunion of the CofS with the UFC in 1929, the Church and Nation Committee carried on both its own work and that of the 'Committee on Church Life and Social Problems' of the UFC, with a renewed commitment to safeguarding Church interests. In the 1930s its work responded to a worsening economic situation at home and the growing threat of war in Europe, with reports on the recurring topics of unemployment and the Church's attitudes to peace, war and disarmament (see Pacifism, Peace movement).

During the Second World War, 1939-45, the Committee was concerned primarily with the response of Church and nation to the issues raised by the conflict, including social conditions in war-time Scotland and occupied Europe, and plans for post-war national and international reconstruction (the Committee supported proposals for the Welfare state and United Nations). After 1945 the Committee's work did not include the internal Church concerns of the pre-war period. It divided its work among international, social, industrial and economic interests (and Scottish interests from 1948). Reports to the General Assembly in the post-War period considered a wide range of issues reflecting a period of profound social, economic and political change, including decolonization and third world development, nuclear weapons and disarmament, poverty, the social consequences of technological innovation, and the nationhood and government of Scotland,* as well as established concerns such as gambling and Sunday observance.

The Committee has functioned throughout its history without a full-time secretariat or research staff; relying on a series of able conveners, beginning with John White,* and the expertise of its fifty or so ministerial and lay members. Not without controversy, its work is a modern expression of the historic commitment of the Reformed Church to Christ's lordship over national life.

CofS, *RGACS* (E, 1919–), 'Report of the Commission on the War' (1919), and 'Report of the Committee on Church and Nation' (1920–); A. Muir, *John White* (L, 1958), 186–9; A. Elliot and D. B. Forrester, *The Scottish Churches and the Political Process Today* (E, 1986); J. Brand, *The National Movement in Scotland* (L, 1978), 127–35; H. Sefton, 'The Church of Scotland and Scottish Nationhood', in S. Mews (ed.), *Religion and National Identity* (Studies in Church History 18; O, 1982), 549–55; Burleigh, 415–16; A. C. Cheyne, *The Transforming of the Kirk* (E, 1983), 176–93.

W. F. Storrar

Church and State (Legal Questions). Difficulties and contentions about the legal relationship between Church and state have been present since the inception of the Church. Each institution tends to view the matter differently from the other. Scotland conforms to that pattern.

In Scotland the matter is complicated in part because the UK has no defined concept of 'the state', governmental authority being exercised by and in the name of the Crown. Conflicting and sometimes confused theologies (see Church and State (Theological Questions)) have therefore interacted with concepts of personal loyalty to a monarch and with theories of government ranging from the absolutist monarchical to that of democratic systems. A plethora of views exist as to positions tenable by a Church (or the Church) in relation to changing forms of civil government. Finally, earlier concepts have not necessarily been abandoned by some contestants as other theories and notions have gained ground.

As far as theory is concerned, the writings of George Buchanan* and Samuel Rutherford* were influential in the sixteen and seventeen centuries and did much to shape later thinking in the CofS as well, particularly that of the FC* fathers. Erastianism, the supremacy of state over Church, at one extreme, and the independent jurisdiction of the Church at the other, have been fully argued over the years since such matters came to be analysed in these terms. The Disruption* writings, particularly those of Thomas Chalmers,* William Cunningham,* Robert Rainy,* and John White,* are still not irrelevant, while in the legal arena those of Lord Sands* and A. T. Innes* bear scrutiny.

CHURCH OF SCOTLAND. The Reformation Parliament* was unconcerned with constitutional theory, and passed various Acts displacing the Pope's jurisdiction and that of RCC in Scotland. By the Act 1560 c.1 it ratified the Scots Confession* (1560), but refrained from settling ecclesiastical polity. The Church Act 1567 c.6 defined the CofS and gave it place as an institution of the realm, a step clarified by the Church Jurisdiction Act 1567 c.12. The Church itself adopted presbyterianism; this was ratified by the (civil) General Assembly Act 1592 c.8 following civil struggle (see Episcopacy).

In the next century rival theories of the relationship between Church and state were part of the contest between Crown and Parliament. The adoption of the Westminster Confession by the Westminster Assembly* in 1646, and the approval and ratification of the Confession and the Catechisms by the Scots Parliament in 1649, formed part of these events. Succeeding years saw further struggle between presbyterianism and episcopacy, ending with the coming of William and Mary and the passing of the Confession of Faith Ratification Act 1690 c.7 and related legislation.

At the Union of the Parliaments (1707)* steps were taken to preserve the CofS. Its presbyterian ascendancy was, however, soon dented by the new Union Parliament's enactment of toleration for episcopacy and the reintroduction of patronage.* Notwithstanding, the CofS continued pre-eminent and its parish system* was the major basis of local government, of education and of poor law administration for almost the next two centuries. The creation of a new parish with full powers (see *Quoad omnia*) was therefore a civil matter, requiring recourse to the Court of Session acting as Commissioners for the Plantation of Kirks.

In succeeding years dispute about Church and state gave rise to a number of independent churches (see Associate Presbytery; Associate Synod; General Associate Synod; Relief Church; New Light). Within the CofS the Moderates* established their ascendancy until the 1830s. Then a slim evangelical majority was in command and sought to address several problems. Patronage, and whether the Church itself had power to deal with it through the Veto Act,* and the question whether the Church could itself lawfully alter the membership of presbytery by adding the ministers of *quoad sacra** (chapels of ease*) charges, formed the battle-grounds of the Disruption* cases in the 1830s and 1840s. The majority in the courts held that civil law was the basis of the rights and duties of the Church in these matters, and that civil law did not permit what the Church had done. Some considered that such a restriction on the Church was Erastian, and contrary to the 'Crown Rights of the Redeemer' and the independent jurisdiction of his Church. Government took no action. The creation of the FC of Scotland* was the result.

On the basis of Articles Declaratory* of the Constitution of the Church of Scotland in Matters Spiritual, agreed between the CofS and the UFC,* declared lawful by the Church of Scotland Act 1921* and adopted by both Churches, the Union of 1929 took place. That settlement has been adhered to by other Churches which have subsequently joined the CofS. The constitutional basis of the relationship between the Church and the civil authority stated in the Articles Declaratory is that each recognizes the separate responsibilities of the other, and some matters are recognized as spiritual. However, the civil authority retains the power and duty to deal with matters of civil right, which could bring the courts into Church matters once more in ways which some in the Church may not understand.

The CofS is the 'established church', although this does not connote as close a connection between Church and state as does establishment south of the border. The Church is independent and the Lord High Commissioner* plays no part in its deliberations. Nor is the Crown or government involved in the appointment of ministers to charges. Ministers may not be elected to the House of Commons, though an appropriately qualified minister may sit in the House of Lords, but (unlike the 26 bishops) not by virtue of his ecclesiastical position. All that establishment means is that the civil authority has recognized the Church's self-imposed task to bring the ordinances of religion to all Scotland, and looks to the Church on suitable ceremonial occasions. (The inclusion of the Moderator* of the General Assembly of the CofS in Coronations is a recent development.)

OTHER CHURCHES. Churches other than the CofS may be incorporated bodies (though few are). Unincorporated Churches are in legal terms voluntary associations and are amenable to the jurisdiction of the courts through their trustees or those acting on their behalf. The courts will intervene in appropriate cases (*e.g.* in property matters) and to correct clamant error in their proceedings (*e.g.* by transgression of the rules of natural justice) once any remedy available through those proceedings has been exhausted. The property of these Churches is held in trust and departure from the terms of that trust can have major consequences. Thus in 1904 after the Union with the United Presbyterian Church* a remnant of the FC was held entitled to the whole assets of the FC, that part that had gone into the UFC of Scotland* having departed from the principles upon which the property was held (*see* Free Church of Scotland, post-1900).

OTHER MATTERS. In other respects conflict, compromise and a degree of mutual suspicion between Church and state continue in areas of social policy where the churches consider they have a role to play. These include medical matters (e.g. abortion and medical experiment), education, broadcasting, marriage and divorce.

A. Taylor Innes, *The Law of Creeds in Scotland* (E, 1867; 1904); Knox, *History*; F. Lyall, *Of Presbyters and Kings: Church and State in the Law of Scotland* (A, 1980); Lord Murray, 'Church and State' in *Constitutional Law* (*Stair Memorial Encyclopedia of the Laws of Scotland*, V, E, 1987); R. L. Orr (ed.), *The Free Church of Scotland Appeals, 1903–4* (E, 1905); T. M. Taylor, 'Church and State in Scotland', *Juridical Review* 121 (1957); Various authors, *Churches and Religious Bodies* (*Stair Memorial Encyclopedia of the Laws of Scotland*, IV, E, 1989).

F. Lyall

Church and State (Theological Questions). At the Reformation* in Scotland the civil magistrate was not accorded a supremacy over the Church, such as was claimed for the prince in England. In 1559 the Reformers told the Queen Regent that while she ruled in the temporal kingdom she was but a servant, and no Queen; in Christ's kingdom, she had no pre-eminence or authority above the Church – Christ being the Church's only lawgiver. And the *First Book of Discipline** (1560) placed in the hands of the Church's elders and ministers the authority to judge in the Church of God, and to oversee the manners of all men within their charge, including rulers as well as the other estates of the realm. This independence of the Church's discipline from control by the civil authorities was co-ordinated with a recognition in the Scots Confession* that the preservation and purification of religion is particularly the duty of magistrates, who are to suppress idolatry and superstition. Accordingly the Reformation Parliament* authorized the confession as doctrine grounded upon the word of God, abolished the jurisdiction of the Pope, and annulled past acts of Parliament not agreeing with the Scriptures and the new confession.

In the first chapter of the *Second Book of Discipline** (1578) ecclesiastical power is declared to be distinct from civil power, though both are given by God for the common end of advancing God's glory and for promoting godliness among the citizenry. Authority in the Church flows immediately from God and the Mediator Christ to the teachers and elders who exercise it, there being no temporal head of the Church on earth except Christ, whose voice is heard in the Scriptures. The civil power and the spiritual power are to assist one another, the magistrate not exercising Church censures or prescribing any rule how it should be done, but punishing transgressors by civil means, and commanding the ministers to follow the rule of Scripture in the application of discipline. Ministers are to teach a magistrate what God's word requires of him in the exercise of the civil function.

The tenth chapter calls upon the Christian magistrate to foster and defend the Church against enemies, to inflict civil punishments against those who do not obey the censures of the Church, and to see that sufficient provision is made for the ministry, the schools and the poor (see Poor Relief). When the Church is corrupt, the example of the godly kings of Judah sanctions intervention by the Christian magistrate, yet where the ministry is acting faithfully, godly princes are to respect their teaching of the Word of God.

Limitations to the King's power, and his accountability to the people he rules, were espoused in George Buchanan's* *De Jure Regni* (E, 1579; ET, 1680). The endeavour by James VI* and Charles I* to assert royal control over the CofS* (see Melville, Andrew), and to intrude ceremonies and bishops after the model of English episcopacy* (see Worship; Five Articles of Perth; Book of Canons), drew forth a large literature in protest. Moreover, at the Westminster Assembly* (1643), the Scottish commissioners George Gillespie* and Samuel Rutherford* responded to the Erastian argument that government and discipline in the Church are the prerogatives of the Christian magistrate rather than of Church officers. The Presbyterian claim for both the independent jurisdiction of ecclesiastical government, and also an obligation of nations and civil rulers to seek in their own sphere to promote the welfare of true religion and the prosperity of the Church of Christ, received classic expression in David Calderwood's* *Altare Damascenum* (1623; Leiden, 1708), George Gillespie's *Aaron's Rod Blossoming* (L, 1646), Samuel Rutherford's *The Divine Right of Church-Government and Excommunication* (L, 1646), *The Free Disputation Against A Pretended Liberty of Conscience* (E, 1649), and *Lex Rex* (E, 1644), James Durham's* *A Treatise concerning Scandal* (E, 1659), and John Brown of Wamphray's* *Libri Duo contra Volzogenium et Velthusium* (Amsterdam, 1670).

With the accession of William III,* the Revolution settlement of 1690 secured by Act of Parliament* 'the true Reformed Protestant religion', the government of the Church by presbyters on a parity, and the Westminster Confession of Faith as the avowed confession of the Church. This establishment was judged unsatisfactory by the Cameronians (see Societies, United), who desired to see the National Covenant* and the Solemn League and Covenant* restored as a test of loyalty (see Covenanting). Withdrawing from involvement in any responsibility for an uncovenanted establishment, they disowned the King, his courts, oaths of office and the payment of taxes.

Imperfections in the establishment continued to raise questions. In 1733 a secession* from the CofS occurred because of patronage;* the Associate Presbytery* was formed, pledging to restore the purity of a former time. Properly speaking, this body could not be classed with dissenters,* for their object was to maintain unimpaired the doctrine, discipline and worship of the Church's heritage. A second secession, the Relief Church,* which separated from the CofS in 1752, from the start took a greater interest in freedom of conscience and toleration of divergence from Presbyterian practice. But the first secession faced difficulties in defining its stance outside the Est.C; the Associate Synod* divided in 1747 over the oath required of burgesses in the larger towns, some finding it unacceptable to endorse the religion professed within the realm, as if this were to condone corruptions they had recently separated from (see Burgess Oath).

The Burghers and Antiburghers, in 1799 and 1804 respectively, changed their testimonies to allow a denial that the civil magistrate may use his authority on behalf of religion (see New Light). From the minority who adhered to the original testimony of the Seceders there emerged a careful restatement of the obligation of the civil magistrate towards religion, in which toleration* for the practice of other religions was acknowledged, while insisting on the positive role of the magistrate in promoting the true Reformed religion and Church (see Bruce, Archibald; M'Crie, Thomas the elder; Original Secession Church).

A sermon preached in 1829 by the USec.C minister Andrew Marshall* of Kirkintilloch sparked the Voluntary controversy,* in which the dissenting Seceders engaged in a pamphlet war with the Evangelicals within the Est.C. A campaign for Parliamentary reform was allied to the contention that a willing use of one's influence to advance the kingdom of Christ was appropriate only for individuals, and not for nations and their rulers. The call for disestablishment* was met by an eloquent argument in favour of the establishment principle in the lectures of Thomas Chalmers* and William Cunningham.* In 1843 Chalmers and Cunningham left the Est.C themselves, when the civil courts supported the intrusion of ministers under a system of patronage and forced the Disruption* in the CofS. Those who left to constitute the FC* embraced the establishment principle as part of their testimony, but acted to preserve the freedom of the Church when the civil magistrate invaded the jurisdiction of Church Courts.

Negotiations for union between the FC and the UPC* began in 1863, but opposition within the FC to an accommodation with the UPC's voluntary principles delayed such a union until 1900 (see Church Unions), the case for and against disestablishment being argued by such protagonists as Robert Rainy* and James Begg.* By the Churches (Scotland) Act of 1905, Parliament allowed a relaxation of the subscription* to the Westminster Confession in the Est.C. But the CofS did not surrender its endowments and civil connection when union was effected with the UFC* in 1929.

FBD; J. Kirk, 'Introduction', in *SBD*; A. T. Innes, *The Law of Creeds in Scotland* (E, 1902); T. M'Crie, *Statement of the Difference* (E, 1807, 1871); W. Cunningham, *Discussions of Church Principles* (E, 1863); W. Cunningham, *Historical Theology* (E, 1862); J. Bannerman, *The Church of Christ*, 2 vols

CHURCH EXTENSION

(E, 1868); W. Symington, *Messiah the Prince* (E, 1839); W. Graham, *Review of Ecclesiastical Establishments* (G, 1792); J. Kirk, 'Reformation and Revolution: Kirk and Crown 1560–1690', *History Today* 34 (1984), 14–21; I. B. Doyle, 'The Doctrine of the Church in the Later Covenanting Period', in D. Shaw (ed.), *Reformation and Revolution* (E, 1967), 212–36; M. Hutchison, *Reformed Presbyterian Church in Scotland* (Paisley, 1893); J. M'Kerrow, *History of the Secession Church* (E, 1854); H. Watt, *Thomas Chalmers and the Disruption* (E, 1943); G. N. M. Collins, *Heritage of our Fathers* (E, 1974); W. Wilson, *Free Church Principles* (E, 1880).

S. Isbell

Church Extension, the building and endowment of new churches. The background to the nineteenth-century Church Extension campaign, at its height in the mid- to late 1830s, was the enormous growth in population during the preceding decades. In 1755 there were 1,265,380 people in Scotland; in 1831 there were 2,364,386. On a more local level the relative increase was even more striking: the population of Glasgow, which had been 31,700 in 1755, was 83,700 in 1801 and 287,000 in 1841. Naturally the existing accommodation and pastoral resources of the CofS were quite unequal to the pressure.

Action on Church Extension was inspired by the Evangelical* party in the CofS led by Thomas Chalmers.* There was a recognition that the situation required not only the building of churches, but also active efforts to reach the poorer classes. In general these were not attending Christian worship, alienated by pew rents* and the social exclusiveness of existing churches.

The General Assembly appointed a Church Accommodation Committee* in 1828, but its initial operation was sluggish and it was not until Chalmers became its convener in 1834 that activity began to gather momentum. A structure of local and national committees was set up, which proved to be very successful. Between 1834 and 1841, 222 new churches were built, funded entirely from voluntary contributions.

Chalmers was much less successful in his efforts to obtain government money for Church Extension. In 1824 Parliament had granted 50,000, making possible the building of forty-three churches in the Highlands and Islands. It was hoped that this would be a prelude to further payments towards relieving the 'spiritual destitution' of the cities. In the event, although the Whig* government set up a Royal Commission on Religious Instruction in Scotland in 1835, the political influence of Voluntarism* precluded further concrete action.

The Church Extension campaign received a serious blow from Court of Session judgments in 1839 which severely constrained the operation of *quoad sacra** parishes, and the vision of bringing Christianity to working classes was only realized in a very qualified sense. Nevertheless much had been achieved. The issue had an important function in providing a focus for the Evangelical party in the Kirk, which turned during the next few years to support Non-Intrusionism* and hence formed the FC at the Disruption.* Indeed the experience and vision gained in the Church Extension campaign of the 1830s was translated in the mid-1840s into the task of creating the FC.

There were also broader and more long-term consequences. By means of his *Lectures on the Establishment and Extension of National Churches* delivered in London in 1838, Chalmers did much to bring Scottish Church issues to the attention of the English public and to stimulate campaigns for Church Extension south of the Border. In Scotland after the middle of the century the pace slackened but, although the Est.C was less energetic than other religious groups, the Kirk, FC and Dissenters all continued to build numerous churches until the 1880s. In the twentieth century the development of new housing has brought a continued need for Church Extension and substantial sums have again been raised for the purpose.

S. J. Brown, *Thomas Chalmers* (O, 1982); C. G. Brown, *The Social History of Religion in Scotland since 1730* (L, 1987); A. C. Cheyne (ed.), *The Practical and the Pious* (E, 1985); Burleigh; A. L. Drummond and J. Bulloch, *The Scottish Church 1688–1843* (E, 1973).

J. R. Wolffe

Church Hymnary. The first edition (E, 1898) was authorized for public worship by the CofS, the FCS, the UPC and the Presbyterian Church in Ireland. The last had had no recognized hymnbook, although hymns were sung in several of its congregations. The other Churches had each had experience of previous books (J. Mearns, 'Scottish Hymnody' in J. Julian, *Dictionary of Hymnology* (^{2}L, 1907), and J. Young, 'Scottish Hymn Books Antecedent to *CH*', *Hymn Soc. Bull.* 3 (1952), 58–66).

A. Henderson in J. Brownlie's* *Hymns and Hymn-Writers of the Church Hymnary* (L, 1899) described the preparation of the book, and also compared it with the books used in the Churches co-operating with the CofS. Excluding doxologies, *etc.*, there were in all 625 hymns, of which 172 were in all the books, 128 in two, 198 in one, leaving 127 completely new.

In the *CH* care was taken to verify the texts, and the authors' words were normally kept. Sir John Stainer was the musical editor (W. Cowan and J. Love, *The Music of the 'Church Hymnary' and the Psalter in Metre* (E, 1901)). The book was arranged thus: God – his attributes, works, and Word; the Christian life; the Church; for special occasions; for the young. A Scripture text prefixed each hymn.

CH eventually superseded all the earlier books listed by Young except two used by the CofS: *Translations and Paraphrases** (1781) and possibly *The Scottish Hymnal* (E, 1884).

In 1900 two of the Churches involved in the *CH*, the FC and the UPC, united in the UFC. When the *CH* became due for revision, the UFC shared in the work, as did (besides the CofS) the Presbyterian Churches of England, Wales, Ireland, Aus-

CHURCH HYMNARY

tralia, New Zealand and South Africa. The main sequence of the *[Revised] CH* (*RCH*; L, 1927) consisted of 728 items (including doxologies, *etc.*). The English and Welsh Churches added a joint Supplement of selected metrical and prose Psalms, canticles and Scripture sentences.

Great care was again taken over the words. The arrangement of the book was similar to that of its predecessor except that hymns on the Christian life followed those on the Church, and mission hymns (previously subsumed under 'Church') were relegated towards the end of the book. The revisers relented about excluding hymns for primary schoolchildren, but segregated them in a section for 'Home and School'.

The story of the revision of words and music was told in the *Handbook*, ed. J. Moffatt* (L, 1927) and *Supplement*, ed. M. Patrick* (L, 1935). Their historical and biographical information was much used in later handbooks, including (as acknowledged on an erratum slip) P. Dearmer's *'Songs of Praise' Discussed* (L, 1933). Patrick prepared a popular book on *RCH*, *The Story of the Church's Song* (E, 1927, ^{2}1947; rev. for American use J. R. Sydnor, Richmond, VA, 1962).

Despite general acclaim there were adverse comments, few as severe as the committee member who deplored the inclusion of some tunes 'beneath contempt' (*The Times*, 31 May 1927, 8).

The third edition of the *CH* (L, 1973) was compiled by the same Churches as had compiled the *RCH*, although in 1972 the Presbyterian Church of England merged with the Congregational Church in England and Wales to form the United Reformed Church.* *CH3* was more 'high church' than *RCH* and somewhat similar to *The English Hymnal* (^{2}L, 1933). Most of the 695 items were arranged in a 'eucharistic' order: I. The approach to God; II. The Word of God; and III. Response to that Word a separate sequence at the end of the book being confusingly reserved for 'personal faith and devotion'). One aim was to remove subjectivity. Psalms and paraphrases, formerly in a separate book, were placed (first) in the appropriate sections.

The overlap in the texts with *RCH* was rather more than 50%. Much of the new material, conservative in style, was for children and placed (last) in the appropriate sections. There were relatively few twentieth-century hymns and scarcely any on social aspects. *RCH* had had a Welshman, David Evans, as its musical editor; *CH3* had none, music and words being decided by the whole committee. Welsh and Victorian tunes were reduced in number. According to more than one reviewer, the book made exacting demands in its music but in its words was quite unadventurous. A cassette of twenty-one hymns from *CH3* was issued by St Andrew Press.

The *Handbook*, ed. J. M. Barkley (L, 1979) was only about two-thirds the length of its predecessor, which it largely followed (without superseding) in style, arrangement and detail, but the introductory essays now covered as many as seventy-five pages.

The United Reformed Church produced *New Church Praise* [*NCP*] (E, 1975) to supplement *Con-*

CHURCH OF SCOTLAND

gregational Praise (L, 1951), still used by some of its members, and *CH3*. Of its 112 items 71 were unique among the contents of hymnbook supplements then available. An order of worship for the Lord's Supper was appended. Most of the hymns were written during the previous twenty-five years. Not more than half a dozen appeared from earlier periods. A commentary by P. Cutts was published (L, 1981).

Most supplements to standard hymnbooks, including *NCP*, were arranged alphabetically by the first lines of the hymns. *Hymns for a Day* (E, 1982 [*i.e.* 1983]), intended to supplement *CH3*, followed the order of the Christian year. The 64 items offered one for each Sunday. Some items were traditional, others culled from the many post-1973 books and supplements.

The most recent supplement to *CH3* is *Songs of God's People* (O, 1988). Arranged alphabetically by first lines, it contains 120 items aimed at a diversity in worship and cultural tastes. The contents range from Victorian favourites to contemporary charismatic songs, with contributions from various countries including the French Taizé community. Particular attention has been paid to the needs of children. The contemporary material is rooted more in Bethlehem than Calvary. The book is a belated acknowledgement that *CH3* did not always let people sing 'in ways that were contemporary or upon subjects . . . of immediate concern to the Church' (D. Easton's review, *News of Hymnody* 26, April 1988, 1).

See also Hymnology, English.

L. H. Bunn, 'English Presbyterian Hymnology', *Hymn Society Bulletin* 3 (1953), 124–8; *id.*, 'Seventy Years of English Presbyterian Praise, 1857–1927', *Journal of the Presbyterian Historical Society of England* 11 (1959), 173–91. Reviews: E. Routley and D. Bruce, of *CH3*, *Hymn Soc. Bull.* 8 (1974), 41–51; N. Goldhawk, of *New Church Praise*, *Hymn Soc. Bull.* 8 (1975), 125–30.

New College Library, Edinburgh, houses the materials used for *RCH* and *CH3*.

J. S. Andrews

Church Music, *see* Music, Church.

Church of Scotland, the national Scottish Church. As the Scottish branch of the one holy Catholic or Universal Church it traces its roots to Ninian* and Columba,* and though a new era of its long history began when in August 1560 it was reformed by presbyters, that was not its beginning, nor did it (though completely transformed at that point) lose its identity. It is now Protestant and Reformed, owing much to the genius of John Knox* and set in the tradition of John Calvin,* who was said by 'Rabbi' John Duncan* to have pieced together the teaching of Augustine (salvation by grace and divine election), Remigius (particular redemption), Anselm (vicarious atonement), and Luther (justification by faith).

In its doctrine it is Trinitarian, adoring the Father,

confessing the Lord Jesus Christ and owing obedience to him in all things, and trusting in the promised renewal and guidance of the Holy Spirit. It adheres to the Scottish Reformation,* and receives the Word of God in the Scriptures of the Old and New Testaments as its supreme rule of life and faith, and avows the fundamental doctrines of the Christian faith founded on Scripture. It acknowledges a distinctive call and duty to bring the ordinances of religion to the people in every parish* of Scotland through a territorial ministry. It accepts the Westminster Confession of Faith* as its principal subordinate standard, recognizing liberty of opinion on such points of doctrine as do not enter into the substance of the faith (see Subscription, Confessional). Since 1966 and 1968 respectively women* have been eligible on terms of equality with men to be ordained to its eldership* and to its ministry.

A brief statement of the doctrinal position of the Church is incorporated in the first of the Articles Declaratory.* While provision is made, under elaborate safeguards, for modification of or addition to the Articles, that first Article is specifically excluded. Any proposed change in any of the others must be consistent with it, and adherence to it, as interpreted by the Church, is declared to be 'essential to its continuity and corporate life'.

During the eighteenth and nineteenth centuries the outward unity of the CofS was broken by various separations, particularly in the Disruption* of 1843. Most of the breakaway groups themselves suffered further schism, but all continued to claim adherence to the common traditions and standards of the Church. This era of division was followed by a period of healing, leading by 1929 to the coming together of most congregations in the re-united CofS (see Unions, Church). Minorities, however, elected in every case to stay apart, so that there remain in Scotland representatives of various Presbyterian denominations independent of the CofS (see Free Church of Scotland, post-1900; United Free Church of Scotland; Free Presbyterian Church of Scotland; Associated Presbyterian Churches; Reformed Presbyterians).

The government of the Church is Presbyterian,* being conciliar in character and exercised through courts,* that is, Kirk Sessions,* Presbyteries,* Synods,* and General Assemblies.* The system was initiated by John Knox* in the *First Book of Discipline*,* although it was Andrew Melville who in the *Second Book of Discipline** further developed and perfected it, and it was in the Act of 1592 ('the Magna Carta of the Kirk'; see Golden Act) that King and Parliament acknowledged and ratified the whole structure. In 1990 there were twelve Synods, forty-nine Presbyteries (forty-six in Scotland and the Presbyteries of England, Europe and Jerusalem), and 1685 Kirk Sessions (1343 charges*). Because of the inequality of the population spread, Presbyteries have come to vary enormously in size, the biggest (Glasgow) embracing 168 charges and having a membership of about 550 while the figures for the smallest (Uist) are 9 and 22 respectively. The right of the General Assembly, the supreme court of the Church, to meet annually, and more frequently if required, was explicitly recognized in the Act of 1592 referred to above and was ratified in the Treaty of Union of 1707.* Although in Stuart times the Church was prevented from so meeting in General Assembly, it has never abated its claim in this regard. The General Assembly consists of ministers and elders in equal numbers elected by Presbyteries, the number of such commissioners at the Assembly of 1991 being 1,276. It has been almost invariable practice that either the Sovereign in person or a Lord High Commissioner* acting as the Sovereign's representative has attended the Assembly, but not as a constituent member thereof. The total membership of the CofS is shown in 1991 as 786,787 out of a total adult population (1990) of 3,787,628, or under one in four.

The membership of the courts is essentially egalitarian in character and there is no respect of persons. Kirk Sessions inevitably consist predominantly of elders, but in all the other courts ministers and elders participate in practically equal numbers. In all the business of the courts elders vote on a basis of full equality with ministers. In the appointment of ministers to parishes the CofS has, since the abolition of patronage* in 1874, held to a system of free election by all the members and registered adherents* of the vacant charge,* although of recent years power has been assumed by Presbyteries to restrict choice in some cases to certain classes – e.g. persons of 55 years or over or probationers.

The support of the Church after the Scottish Reformation (see Thirds of Benefices) came from a tax on the fruits of the land – that is to say, the landowners or heritors* were under obligation to build and maintain a church and a manse, and out of the teind* to pay a stipend* which was assessed in terms of victual. In 1808 machinery was set up for converting the obligation into terms of cash by reference to Fiars' Prices* and requiring that it be so paid. The ordinances of religion thus became, and have remained, freely available to every citizen of the land. Collections taken at church services were all for the support of the poor. The emergence of the Secession* Churches led to the introduction of a 'voluntary' system involving the congregation being supported by the freewill offerings of its members (see Voluntaryism). Though a very limited income still accrues from the former teind (now a 'standard charge'), the expenses of the CofS today are almost wholly met out of what is subscribed by its members.

In the matter of worship* the official standard is the Directory of Public Worship, produced by the famous Westminster Assembly* and approved in 1645. The preaching* of the Word has occupied a prominent place in public worship as has the singing of the metrical psalms*. Holy Communion is usually celebrated only on occasion (quarterly in most kirks), but the tendency is toward more frequent celebration. While considerable freedom is permitted in the conduct of public worship, there is safeguard against unseemly or unwelcome innovation in the Formula* signed by a minister on induction, obliging himself 'to observe uniformity of worship and of all public ordinances as the same are at present performed and allowed, or shall hereafter be declared by authority of the same' (Act XIII, 1910).

In the matter of its constitution it is universally agreed that in Scotland there has been established a sound relationship between Church and state* through a formula which secures for the former freedom from control by the latter. This has been the result of many years of bitter struggle and even bloodshed. It finds expression in the Articles Declaratory of the Constitution of the Church of Scotland in Matters Spiritual, declared to be lawful by, and scheduled to, the Church of Scotland Act* of 1921. This settlement was prepared by the Kirk with a view to easing the way towards union by demythologizing the idea of 'establishment'. It is a declaration of the spiritual freedom of the Kirk, and is at pains to affirm that it is purely declaratory in character, asserting that it is not an attempt to regularize, recognize or authorize that position.

The position of the Church vis-à-vis the civil courts was put to the test when in 1936 certain members of a congregation raised an action in the Court of Session asking it to be declared that they had the right to call a minister, that being a civil right unaffected by the terms of the 1921 Act. In his judgment the Lord Justice Clerk (Aitchison) described Section I of the Act as 'a provision of the most far-reaching kind', going on to say, 'It is not for the civil authority to declare whether matters that are within the Articles are matters spiritual, for that the statute by Section I has already declared. Section I is a clear and unambiguous affirmation of the supremacy of the Articles in every conflict with existing laws or statutes touching the matters with which they deal. The primary purpose for which the Act was passed ... was to declare the right of the Church to self-government in all that concerned its life and activity ... The contrary view proceeds on the erroneous notion that all that the Act of 1921 accomplished was to declare the existing law and that it did nothing to recognize the wider claims of the Church to legislate and adjudicate finally in all matters of doctrine, worship, government and discipline as matters that lay peculiarly within its province' (*Ballantyne v. Presbytery of Wigtown*, Court of Session, 1936).

'Though as a Divine institution it must remain free to follow the guidance of the Spirit of God, as He interprets from one generation to another the Holy Scriptures, which form at once its royal charter and its supreme standard, from which there can be no deviation, yet as a human institution the Church requires a clear and authoritative statement of its principles and definite rules, according to which the affairs of the Church are to be transacted, that there may be neither injustice nor confusion. These principles and rules, framed as they have been in successive ages in accordance with the necessities of the time in the light of experience gained in the past, yet always liable to be modified by vision of future developments, may in their totality be said to form the Constitution of the Church of Scotland as we know it in our own day' (Cox 2–3). Along with the Articles Declaratory, Cox lists the UF Church Act of 1906 and the Act of Union of 1929 as 'leading documents' in determining the constitution (3–6). To these, he says, should be added the body of standing laws (apart from administrative regulations) which were brought in from both sides to the Union of 1929 and those which have subsequently been enacted.

The position of the CofS is further safeguarded by the Accession Oath taken by the Sovereign immediately on acceding to the throne, swearing to maintain and preserve in Scotland the true Protestant religion and the rights and privileges of the Church.

I. Henderson, *Scotland: Kirk and People* (L, 1969); A. Herron, *Kirk by Divine Right* (E, 1985); G. D. Henderson, *The Church of Scotland: A Short History* (E, 1939); *id., Why We Are Presbyterians* (E, n.d.); Burleigh; R. D. Kernohan, *Our Church: Guide to the Kirk of Scotland* (E, 1985); R. S. Louden, *The True Face of the Kirk* (L, 1963).

A. Herron

Church of Scotland Act, 1921. This Act (11 & 12 Geo. 5, c.29) was passed by Parliament to declare lawful the Articles Declaratory* of the Constitution of the CofS in Matters Spiritual agreed in order to promote the 1929 Union of the CofS and the UFC. The Articles prevail over prior law (s.1). Without the Act it is possible that, under the reasoning of the House of Lords in the FC case* (*Bannatyne v. Lord Overtoun* (1904) 7 Fraser (H.L.) 1; [1904] Appeal Cases 515), moves towards the 1929 union would have resulted in the loss of property held by the UFC to any minority of it staying out of the union. The Act, with the Declaratory Articles scheduled to it, is one half of the major reconstruction of relations between the CofS and the state, the other half being the Church of Scotland (Property and Endowments) Act 1925.* The Act also provides that it does not prejudice the protection of other Churches in the exercise of their spiritual function (s.2), and that subject to the recognition of matters in the Declaratory Articles as matters spiritual, the jurisdiction of the civil courts is not affected in matters of a civil nature (s.3). The Act was brought into effect in 1926 once the CofS and the UFC had approved the Articles by their own procedures.

F. Lyall, *Of Presbyters and Kings* (A, 1980), 66–84; R. King-Murray, 'The Church of Scotland', *Public Law* (1958), 155–68; Lord Murray, 'The Church of Scotland Act 1921' in his 'Church and State', in *Constitutional Law The Stair Memorial Encyclopedia of the Laws of Scotland*, V, E, 1987), paras 695–700.

F. Lyall

Church of Scotland (Property and Endowments) Act 1925. This Act (15 & 16 Geo. 5, c.33) radically altered the law under which the property and endowments of the CofS were held. Teinds* and stipends* were also affected. It set aside much of the earlier law and procedures, vesting appropri-

CHURCH OF THE NAZARENE

ate Church property in the CofS General Trustees* to be held either as investment or charges on land. The Trustees in law therefore hold the bulk of church property, including most church buildings, for the Church. In tandem with the Church of Scotland Act, 1921* this Act means, for example, that the Church can create a new church and parish without civil approval. Heritors* (property owners within parishes) were freed of duties in respect of the construction and upkeep of churches and stipend. Property and endowments, finance and organization were thus made matters for domestic arrangement within the Church, without state responsibility or intervention.

F. Lyall

Church of the Nazarene, an international evangelical denomination of about a million members in the Wesleyan 'holiness' tradition. The Scottish churches began independently in 1906, when George Sharpe, a Scot ordained in the Methodist Episcopal Church of America, was forced to leave Parkhead Congregational Church in Glasgow because of opposition to his doctrine. The minority supporting him formed an independent church, and the rapid growth of several other congregations led to the formation of the Pentecostal Church of Scotland in 1909. In 1915, the small denomination, now with ten congregations, united with the (till then American) Pentecostal Church of the Nazarene. (In 1919, 'Pentecostal' was dropped because it had become associated with speaking in tongues.) In the 1920s, Scottish missionaries led by David Hynd* established a hospital and schools in Swaziland. A theological college which was opened near Paisley in 1944 by George Frame moved to Manchester following the accession of two small English denominations in the 1950s. In Scotland there were in 1990 twenty congregations, mainly in Ayrshire, Lanarkshire, Renfrewshire and Glasgow, 1,200 members and eighteen ministers. The Church of the Nazarene is Methodist* in doctrine. In particular it follows John Wesley's* teaching on sanctification, including the teaching that a Christian may be 'wholly sanctified' (1 Thess. 5:23). This is regarded as a purification of the heart (Matt. 5:8; James 4:8) which integrates and unifies the motivation in a full and whole-hearted love for God ('perfect love', 1 John 4:17f). The Christian need no longer be characterized by 'the mind set on the flesh' (Rom. 8:5ff). While still recognizing and confessing his shortcomings, he is enabled to overcome temptation with consistency and to grow in Christian maturity. This Wesleyan understanding of 'full salvation' is also identified with being 'filled with the Spirit'.

The Church includes Baptists and paedo-baptists and combines congregationalism with elected district and general superintendents.

See also Winchester, Olive M.

J. Ford, *In the Steps of John Wesley: The Church of the Nazarene in Britain* (Kansas City, 1968).

T. A. Noble

CHURCH SERVICE SOCIETY

Church Review and Scottish Ecclesiastical Magazine (1836–8), short-lived monthly journal of Moderate* party in CofS. It was edited by George Cook,* and published between April 1836 and January 1838 by Fraser and Co. of North Bridge, Edinburgh. Its professed principal aim was to lay down 'those general principles by which an Established Church may be defended' and to show 'that it is the sacred duty of every wise and paternal government to uphold it' (I, 1836, 2). It also aimed to report proceedings in the Church courts, and to provide a platform for CofS ministers to display their scholarship. The *Review* was referred to by its detractors as 'the Cookery book', 'the Cookey-shine' and 'the Cook's oracle', after its editor.

J. A. H. Dempster

Church Service Society, formed by ministers and elders of the CofS in 1865 'for the study of liturgies – ancient and modern – of the Christian Church, with a view to the preparation and publication of forms of Prayer for Public Worship' (J. Kerr, *The Renascence of Worship*, E, 1909, 71). The principal way in which the Society carried out its aim was by the publication of its service book *Euchologion*,* the first edition of which appeared in 1867. The formation of the Society owed much to the stimulus provided by the controversial innovations* in worship* pioneered by Robert Lee,* but it was founded by those whose interest lay in recovering a 'catholic' basis for worship in the Kirk. G. W. Sprott* had suggested such a society but the actual formation was left to Robert H. Story,* minister of Rosneath and later Professor of Ecclesiastical History and Principal of Glasgow University, J. Cameron Lees,* minister of Paisley Abbey and later of St Giles' Cathedral,* and George Campbell, minister of Eastwood, near Glasgow. The Society aimed to further the 'practical improvement' of worship in the Kirk and was not to be connected to any particular point of view or position. In its early years, however, there were two definite 'parties', the broad church party and high church party. The former did not wish too much doctrinal content to be introduced into worship, while the latter group explicitly advocated a particular doctrinal basis. The controversy led to the high churchmen in the Society forming the Scottish Church Society,* which had a 'catholic' doctrinal basis (see Scoto-Catholics). Sister liturgical societies were formed in the FC and the UPC, which joined together when the Churches united in 1900 to form the Church Worship Association of the UFC. As a result of an approach from the Association, the Assembly of the UFC authorized the production of a *Book of Common Order** in 1928. In the reunited CofS the societies came together as the Church Service Society, and the General Assembly appointed a Committee on Public Worship and Aids to Devotion*, which produced a *Book of Common Order** in 1940. The work of the Society thus prepared the way for the Church itself to produce material for use in worship. In recent years the Society has not produced service books of its own but has published an *Annual*, a journal, *Liturgical Review*, from 1971 to 1981, and now produces the *Record* several times a year.

See also Catholic Revival in Worship (nineteenth century).

D. B. Nicol, 'The Church Service Society', *Church Service Society Annual* 1 (1928–9), 17–20; D. M. Murray, 'Disruption to Union' in D. B. Forrester and D. M. Murray (eds), *Studies in the History of Worship in Scotland* (E, 1984), 79–95; *id.*, 'Doctrine and Worship', *Liturgical Review* 7:1 (1977), 25–34.

D. M. Murray

Churches of Christ (in Scotland). The origins of Churches of Christ in Scotland lie in the Scotch Baptists* and the congregations founded by James and Robert Haldane.* Congregations, or groups of members, joined the new movement after reading the works of Alexander Campbell,* who preached a return to primitive Christianity on the basis of the New Testament. Campbell understood the primitive Church order to consist of independent local congregations, choosing their own elders, deacons and evangelists, co-operating with one another in the work of evangelism, and practising believers' baptism by immersion and weekly celebration of the Lord's Supper. John Dron, a leader of the Haldane Baptist church at Auchtermuchty, Fife (founded in 1809), visited Campbell in America in 1834. Campbell's works were first published in Britain by the Scotch Baptist, William Jones, in 1835–6; but Jones disagreed with Campbell's view that baptism was for the remission of sins, and divisions on this question followed in the south-west, Edinburgh, Fife and the north-east coast. In August 1842 the first Co-operative Meeting of Churches of Christ in Great Britain was held in Edinburgh, largely because of the initiative of G. C. Reid, a pastor in Dundee. Twenty-one Scottish congregations were represented.

Some congregations suffered division in the early 1850s because of adventist beliefs spread by John Thomas, founder of the Christadelphians and a former Campbellite. But the Scottish churches also took the lead in forming local associations for evangelistic work: by 1850 such associations existed in Fife and in the north of Scotland. In 1857, T. H. Milner began to publish a magazine for the Scottish churches, the *Christian Advocate*, and in 1861 an Annual Meeting for Churches of Christ in Scotland met for the first time.

The next twenty years saw development in two new areas – in the Slamannan coalfield villages following the 1859 revival,* and in the fishing villages along the Banffshire coast in the 1870s. Apart from these villages, Churches of Christ were to be found mainly in the towns. Several important national initiatives in the next half-century also had Scottish roots. The training scheme for evangelists established by the Scottish Conference in 1865 was merged with a national scheme the following year. When the British Churches of Christ sent their first overseas missionaries to Burma in 1892, two of them were Scots – A. E. Hudson of Glasgow and R. Halliday of Hamilton. The first full-time woman worker, Ethel Cranfield, began her ministry as a Home Missions Sister with the Glasgow churches in 1912. In the twentieth century, Scottish Churches of Christ were active in the ecumenical movement,* being founder members of the Scottish Churches Ecumenical Committee in 1950 and of the Multilateral Church Conversation* in Scotland in 1964.

Between 1842 and 1892 church membership in Scotland trebled from around 700 in twenty-one churches to 1,949 in thirty-seven churches. By 1917 there were forty-nine churches, though the peak membership of 2,809 came later, in 1933. Between 1945 and 1979 membership fell sharply from 2,231 to 725. In 1981 the majority of the thirteen Scottish Churches of Christ, with their colleagues in England and Wales, voted to unite with the United Reformed Church.*

W. Robinson, *What Churches of Christ Stand For* (Birmingham, 1926); A. C. Watters, *History of the British Churches of Christ* (Birmingham, 1948); L. Billington, 'The Churches of Christ in Britain: a Study in Nineteenth-Century Sectarianism', *Journ. of Rel. Hist.* 8 (1974–5), 21–48; D. M. Thompson, *Let Sects and Parties Fall* (Birmingham, 1980); D. W. Bebbington (ed.), *The Baptists in Scotland* (G, 1988).

D. M. Thompson

Cistercians. St Robert, the abbot of Molesme in Burgundy, with several of his monks founded a monastery at Cîteaux near Dijon in 1098, in order to observe the Benedictine* rule in its primitive austerity. They adopted a distinctive grey-white habit with a black scapular, whence their appellation of White Monks. Under St Stephen Harding (1109–33) the reform received a firm structure and expanded rapidly. In reaction against the Cluniacs,* it aimed at simplicity in the liturgy and church furnishings; the emphasis was rather on manual work, especially agriculture, carried out with the assistance of lay brothers. Discipline was to be maintained by regular visitations and general chapters. Following a decline in the late Middle Ages, there were vigorous efforts at reform in the seventeenth century, resulting in the 'Strict Observance'. Since 1892 Cistercians of the Strict and Common Observance have been quite separate orders.

The first Scottish house was founded by David I* at Melrose* (1136), which was colonized from Rievaulx in Yorkshire and in turn became the parent house of other royal foundations at Newbattle, south of Edinburgh (1140), and Kinloss in Moray (1150). A colony sent in this manner was expected to consist of at least thirteen monks, including an abbot, and usually with ten or more lay brothers. Another such community from Rievaulx colonized Dundrennan in Kirkcudbrightshire (1142), of which David was also the founder. The abbey of Coupar Angus, which may have been projected by David, was established under the patronage of Malcolm IV with monks of Melrose between

CISTERCIANS

1161 and 1164. Subsequent foundations, however, continued at a much slower pace, and it was not until the late twelfth century that Glenluce (Wigtownshire) (1191–2) was founded from Dundrennan by Roland of Galloway, whose generosity was quickly emulated by Reginald, son of Somerled, Lord of the Isles, with his foundation at Saddell in Kintyre (c.1207), which was colonized from Melifont in Ireland. Three further Cistercian foundations followed in the reign of Alexander II (1214–49): at Culross in Fife (c.1217), colonized from Kinloss at the instigation of Malcolm, earl of Fife; Deer in Aberdeenshire (1219), likewise a daughter-house of Kinloss, founded by William Buchan, earl of Buchan; and Balmerino in Fife (c.1227) founded by the king and his mother, Queen Ermengarde, with monks from Melrose. Finally, in 1273, the last of the eleven Cistercian foundations, the abbey of Sweetheart in Galloway, was founded from Dundrennan by Devorgilla de Balliol.

All of these were abbeys dedicated to the Blessed Virgin Mary and were autonomous in internal matters. In order to maintain strict observance, Cistercian abbeys had the right and duty of visiting their daughter-houses annually, no matter where they lay. All were bound by the decrees of the general chapter, which met yearly at Cîtreaux from 1119 and which all abbots were obliged to attend. As early as 1157, however, Scottish abbots were given leave to attend only once in four years. Nevertheless, Scottish affairs are reflected in statutes of the General Chapter at regular intervals until 1282. Thereafter the ties became looser, but the order, including seven or eight female houses (*see* Nunneries), remained high in royal esteem. Further expansion was restricted, for Cistercian abbeys did not normally have dependent houses. Balmerino, however, had a cell at Gadvan some miles away, recorded in 1475, and Melrose's twelfth-century grange at Mauchline in Ayrshire survived into the sixteenth century.

Although lay brothers were phased out in the fourteenth century, Cistercians continued to contribute to the country's economy through their coal-mining, pioneered at Newbattle, and wool production, as well as through agriculture. Perhaps because of economic difficulties, Saddell was suppressed c.1507. At that time, however, the Valliscaulian* priory of Beauly in Inverness-shire came under Cistercian control, though apparently never becoming fully Cistercian, and later had two abbots of Kinloss as commendators.* In 1531 the abbot of Chaalis was sent from Cîteaux at James V's request to conduct a visitation and restore weakened discipline. This bore little fruit but there are signs that Scottish Cistercians were making efforts at reform and resisting the imposition of unsuitable abbots (*see* Monasticism, medieval); indeed, at Kinloss under Thomas Crystal* and Robert Reid,* an Italian scholar conducted a school of humanities. After the Reformation,* Gilbert Brown* made Sweetheart a centre of Catholic resistance. In 1946 Cistercians of the Strict Observance founded a monastery at Nunraw, East Lothian (*see* Religious Orders, Roman Catholic, Modern).

New Catholic Encyclopedia III, 882–91; L. J. Lekai, *The White Monks* (Okanchee, Wisconsin, 1953); Easson-Cowan 5–31, 72–84; D. McRoberts (ed.), *Essays on the Scottish Reformation* (G, 1962), 212–40; G. W. S. Barrow, *Kingdom of the Scots* (L, 1973), 188–211; A. L. Brown, 'The Cistercian Abbey of Saddell', *IR* 20 (1969), 130–7; J. Campbell, *Balmerino and its Abbey* (E, 1978); J. C. Carrick, *The Abbey of St Mary Newbattle* (Selkirk, 1908); D. E. Easson (ed.), *Charters of the Abbey of Coupar Angus*, 2 vols (SHS, E, 1947); W. Huyshe, *Devorgilla, Lady of Galloway* (E, 1913); C. Innes (ed.), *Registrum S. Marie de Neubotle* (Bannatyne Club, E, 1849); C. Innes (ed.), *Liber Sancte Marie de Melros*, 2 vols (Bannatyne Club, E, 1837); D. McRoberts, 'Culross in the Diocese of Dunblane', *Journal of Soc. of Friends of Dunblane Cathedral* 10 (1968–9), 91–8; K. Stringer, 'Galloway and the Abbeys of Rievalux and Dundrennan', *TDGAS* 4 (1980), 174–7; J. Stuart, *Records of the Monastery of Kinloss* (E, 1872); R. C. Reid (ed.), *Wigtownshire Charters* (E, 1960).

I. B. Cowan

Claim of Right (1842). Adopted in 1842 by the General Assembly of the CofS, it was in essence a protest against the intrusion of the civil authorities into the principal domain of the Church, as its full title, the 'Claim, Declaration and Protest anent the Encroachments of the Court of Session', makes clear. The Claim was the Church's response to a series of Court of Session decisions which threatened to prevent the Church from exercising its spiritual authority as it saw fit. While recognizing that the civil courts had 'absolute' jurisdiction over the 'temporalities conferred by the State upon the Church', the Claim asserted the sole headship of Christ over his Church, and the independent jurisdiction of the Church's officers in spiritual matters. It is clear that the framers of the Claim of Right were on solid theological, biblical, and historical ground in making their protest. The government refused, however, to accede to the demands of the Claim, which in essence demanded the abolition of patronage.* The framing of the Claim of Right crystallized the issues at stake, and set the Church on a course which inevitably, as the Claim itself anticipated, led to the Disruption* of 1843.

See also Ten Years' Conflict.

Sir H. Wellwood Moncreiff, *Vindication of the Free Church Claim of Right* (E, 1877).

I. Hamilton

Clark, T. & T., *see* Publishing, Religious.

Clarke, John (1802–79), missionary* in Africa and the West Indies and African linguist. Born near Kelso, Clarke joined a Baptist* church while a schoolteacher and in 1829–39 and 1852–79 served the Baptist Missionary Society in Jamaica. Between 1840 and 1847, with assistance from Afro-Jamaicans, he helped to establish mission stations in West Africa, on the island of Fernando Po and in the Cameroons. Sound linguistic work was done by two colleagues, J. Merrick and Alfred Saker; Clarke's own work was less skilled. He returned from Africa because of ill-health, and in 1848 published an elementary but pioneering study of the Bubi language of Fernando Po, and a collection of *Specimens of African Languages* (Berwick-on-Tweed and L, 1848/9; reprinted with introduction by E. and S. Ardener, *Specimens of Dialects*, L, 1972). The latter work, containing a poorly-organized set of brief vocabularies of very many little-known languages, some collected by Clarke himself, has latterly attracted scholarly attention as historical documentation.

P. E. H. Hair, 'An Introduction to John Clarke's "Specimens of Dialects ... ", 1848–9' *Sierra Leone Lang. Rev.* 5 (1966), 72–82; *id.*, *The Early Study of Nigerian Languages* (C, 1967).

P. E. H. Hair

Claverhouse, *see* Graham, John, of Claverhouse.

Clearances, processes of population displacement, leading to migration and emigration,* principally from the Highlands* in the century after 1760. Population movements from the Lowlands were also attested in this period, but the Highland Clearances achieved a degree of notoriety unknown in the Lowland context, and controversy continues about their causes and consequences. The term 'clearance' is emotive, and is often used uncritically, being applied (wrongly) to gradual depopulation caused by adverse social and economic pressures before and after 1900. In practice clearing usually involved enforced removal or eviction.

The Clearances owe their origin primarily to changing attitudes to land and people, especially by their leaders, in the social and economic revolution after the 1745 Jacobite* rebellion. Land began to assume much greater importance as a commercial asset, while people became much less significant, particularly as a Highland fighting force. As Highland chiefs increasingly found themselves drawn towards the Lowland and English aristocracy – the result of a policy which was being pursued by the Crown from 1600 (*see also* Gaelic) – the bond between them and their clansmen was weakened substantially. New lifestyles demanded more money, and land, if rented as large single units to farmers, could yield profit. The earlier run-rig farms, maintained by tacksmen (holding land 'in tack' from clan chiefs) and sub-tenants, were gradually phased out. The 'redundant' population was then removed or resettled, sometimes in villages on poor land or by the sea, where some became fisherfolk* (as in Embo and Brora, Sutherland).

Tenurial reorganization in Argyll, favouring single tenants with leases and leading to emigration of old-style tacksmen, is attested as early as 1739. By 1770 tacksmen and tenants were emigrating from North Uist. Sheep became the principal economic units in the new milieu, with sheep-farmers entering the Highlands from 1760, and making their impact most noticeably on the mainland. Forced removal of the poorer population often preceded their advance, as in Glengarry in 1785 and on the Duke of Sutherland's estate in 1814. Patrick Sellar, the Duke's factor, was execrated when he allegedly removed Strathnaver people with force, including the firing of houses. Tried in 1816, he was acquitted of charges by a packed jury, and subsequently farmed sheep in Morvern.

The Clearances reached their height after 1800. Another wave of displacement, more severe and more rapid than the 'sheep clearances', was precipitated by the crop failures of the 1830s and especially the Potato Famine of 1846. A growing population, sustained mainly in the islands by the harvesting of kelp (sea-wrack) from the shoreline and living on units of land called 'crofts', suffered economic and social collapse, leading to massive emigration to Canada and Australia. Summonses of removal, backed up by the landlords' use of force, ensured the departure of the poorer classes. In addition, clearing of old townships to create and extend sheep-farms had reached the Hebrides by the 1830s, with stiff resistance at Borve, Harris, in 1839. Popular resistance, leading to arrest and imprisonment, is attested in individual localities in the 1830s and 1840s, although the prevailing view is that Highlanders were relatively tame.

The Highland Clearances have generated much debate about the culpability of landlords, the place of economic theory (*see* Malthusian Theory), the voluntary, involuntary or 'protesting' nature of emigration, and the role of the Est.C and its ministers. This last topic has drawn a mainly negative response from historians, who generally see ministers (*e.g.*, Donald Sage*) as hamstrung by 'passive obedience', allegedly believing that the process of displacement, however harsh, was within the providence of God (Donald C. Smith, *Passive Obedience and Prophetic Protest*, NY, 1987, 129–41).

Blanket conclusions overlook salient, but lonely, figures like Lachlan MacKenzie* (*d*.1819) of Lochcarron, who preached against the sheep-farmers. There was also much clerical ambivalence. Clergy who recognized injustice were torn by complex forces, including loyalty to their landowning patrons, a desire to see their oppressed flock prospering in more congenial circumstances, and the belief that God could bring good out of evil. In 1852 Norman MacLeod,* a friend of John Dunmore Lang,* preached in Greenock on board the 'Georgiana', bound for Melbourne with 300 Skye emigrants. Before preaching, he found that 'not one bitter word was spoken against landlord or factor. They declared, in very touching language, that they went forth trusting in God, as did Abraham of old' (*The Glasgow Constitutional*, 17 July 1852). MacLeod's sermon reinforced that trust. Yet in the 1820s he hinted in a Gaelic essay, *Long Mhòr nan Eilthireach* ('The Emigrant Ship'), that emigration was caused by 'covetousness and greed for gold' on the part of the landowning class (*Leabhar nan Cnoc*, Greenock 1834, 60–70). His relationship to that class through social standing and marriage prevented any stronger statement. FC leaders, however, were more outspoken; landlordism and clearing were roundly condemned by

Hugh Miller,* John Kennedy* and Thomas McLauchlan.*

Weaker reactions can be detected among the non-Presbyterian religious bodies. Coll MacDonald of Knoydart protested vigorously when a great proportion of his people were forcibly evicted in 1851-4, but other RC priests tended to act as leaders of emigrant groups. Baptist* and Independent* pastors were also inclined to follow their flocks overseas, recognizing the need for pastoral care in the New World and believing that emigration extended the range of Highland missionary endeavour (see Fraser, William, and Sinclair, Dugald).

The anti-clearance reaction, which emerged as the Land Agitation of the 1870s and 1880s, had a strong religious base. Revivals,* frequent in the nineteenth century, not only encouraged a belief in God's care for a rootless, migrating people, but also bore home the message that individuals mattered in God's eyes, and that his covenant people were not to be exploited. As Highlanders read the Bible (see Bible (Versions, Gaelic)) for themselves and became less bound to deterministic ministerial doctrine, proto-socialism fused with Evangelicalism to produce a brand of liberation theology preached vigorously by lay leaders and a few prominent ministers such as Donald MacCallum* (Est.C) and Duncan MacGregor* (Baptist) (see also MacAskill, Murdo). This perspective gained wide popular support and, coupled with strong political pressure, helped to achieve the Crofters' Holdings (Scotland) Act of 1886.

Eric Richards, *A History of the Highland Clearances*, 2 vols (L, 1982-5); James Hunter, *The Making of the Crofting Community* (E, 1976); J. M. Bumsted, *The People's Clearance* (E, 1982); T. Devine, *The Great Highland Famine* (E, 1988); D. E. Meek, 'The Bible and Social Change in the Nineteenth-Century Highlands', in D. F. Wright (ed.), *The Bible in Scottish Life and Literature* (E, 1988), 179-91.

D. E. Meek

Clerk, Archibald (1813-87), Est.C minister and Gaelic* scholar. Born in Glen Lonan, Lorn, he was Assistant at St Columba, Glasgow, to Norman MacLeod,* whose daughter he married, and minister, successively, at Acharacle, Diurinish in Skye, Ardnamurchan and Kilmallie. He was awarded the degree of LLD by Glasgow University in 1872. Clerk collaborated with his father-in-law in his literary labours, and edited the posthumous collection of his Gaelic writings. He was also editor of the Gaelic periodical *Fear-Tathaich nam Beann* (1848-50), the Gaelic supplement* of *Life and Work*,* the 1859 edition of the Gaelic Bible (see Bible, Versions, Gaelic), and *Poems of Ossian*, 2 vols (E, 1871).

FES IV, 136.

K. D. MacDonald

Clerk, Session, see Kirk Session.

Clerks, officials of courts of the church (Kirk session, presbytery, synod, General Assembly) in the Presbyterian system of church government. The term is to be understood by analogy with the clerks of civil courts, Parliament, etc., rather than with 'clerks in holy orders' or clergymen as distinct from laymen in episcopal systems. In the CofS the first clerk of the General Assembly of whom there is a record was John Gray, c.1572, but there are subsequent gaps in the records until the establishment of Presbyterianism in 1690. For most of the time since then the Assembly had more than one clerk – a Principal Clerk, and sub, depute, or junior clerks, one or more, the current term being Depute Clerk. In 1961 the Principal Clerk's position became a full-time appointment, combined with the secretaryship of the Committee on General Administration, now the Board of Practice and Procedure. He acts also as secretary to the Moderator.

Clerks need not be members of their courts, but they usually are, and Assembly clerks are members *ex officio*. Session clerks (see Kirk Session) are usually elders, since the minister is moderator* and the offices of moderator and clerk may not be held by the same person, but a person who is not an elder may hold this office. In practice, clerks of the superior courts are nearly always, but not invariably, ministers.

Clerks are responsible for the maintenance and custody of all court records, from which they are the only legal extractors. They make all necessary arrangements for meetings of their courts, advise on matters of procedure, and deal with correspondence. Clerks are warned to be careful about appending their official designations to their signatures, as this is deemed to give the signed letter or paper the authority of the court. Every clerk on taking office takes the oath *de fideli* (in full: *de fideli administratione officii*), which is a solemn oath to be faithful to the duties of the office.

Although the pastoral care of ministers is not among the official duties of presbytery clerks, and some presbyteries, in addition to having superintendence committees, have also appointed pastoral counsellors, these clerks frequently find that they are approached by their fellow ministers for advice and help.

Cox, 79-80, 118-19, 148, 186, 205-7, 777-81; FES VIII, 743-5, IX, 805, X, 1.

J. L. Weatherhead

Cloud of Witnesses, a collection of 'The Last Speeches and Testimonies' of Covenanter* martyrs* 'Who have Suffered for the Truth in Scotland' in the 1680s. The work was planned (from 1686) and the material subsequently carefully collected by the United Societies* and was first published, probably in Edinburgh, in 1714 (*A Cloud of Witnesses, for the Royal Prerogatives of Jesus Christ*; without identification of compiler, printer or publisher). Their grand object was owning 'Christ alone', as opposed to King Charles II,* 'as head and lawgiver to the Church', and the book a testimony to their willingness to suffer for the cause. It was intended as a continuation of the earlier compilation, *Naphtali* (1667), by James Stewart (1635-1713)* and

James Stirling. The *Cloud* was enlarged in successive editions (5th, E, 1751), the best with annotations by J. H. Thomson (E, 1871; rp. Harrisonburg, VA, 1989). William M'Gavin combined the *Cloud* and *Naphtali* as the second volume of *The Scots Worthies . . . Their Last Words and Dying Testimonies* (G, 1829; rp. separately 1846). The book had considerable influence in shaping the popular religious thought of Scotland for nearly two centuries.

J. C. Johnston, *Treasury of the Scottish Covenant* (E, 1887), 393–401.

D. C. Lachman

Clow, William Macallum (1853–1930), UFC divine and author. Born in Glasgow, he studied at Glasgow University (MA, 1878; BD, 1881). He also attended Glasgow FC College. Licensed by Glasgow FC Presbytery, he was ordained to Cambusnethan FC, Lanarkshire, in 1881. In 1886 he moved to Uddingston, Lanarkshire, in 1889 to Aberdeen South, and in 1897 to the Barclay Church, Edinburgh. He joined the UFC in 1900. In 1902 he moved to Glasgow Stevenson Memorial Church. He was appointed Professor of Practical Training and Christian Ethics in Glasgow UF College in 1911, and Principal in 1921. He resigned from the College in 1928.

For a time Clow was convener of both the UFC Home Mission Committee and its Glasgow Home Mission Executive. His many writings are marked by a deep evangelical faith, and include *In the Day of the Cross* (L, 1898); *The Cross in Christian Experience* (L, 1908); *The Secret of the Lord* (L, 1910) and *Christ in the Social Order* (L, 1913).

AFCS I, 122; *FUFCS*, 575; *Who Was Who, 1929–1940*, 265; *LW* new ser. 1 (1930), 95.

N. R. Needham

Clubs and Societies, Eighteenth Century. The eighteenth century was the great age of Scottish clubs and societies, and clergymen were instrumental in making it so. Not that ministers ever came close to matching lay members of the professional and landowning classes in sheer numbers of club men, but their influence was disproportionately great, particularly in organizations whose primary purpose was intellectual enrichment rather than mere conviviality. The beginnings of this development can be traced to a group of Edinburgh divinity students of the 1710s and 1720s who were among the leaders of the Rankenian Club. Half a century later one of their number, Robert Wallace,* boasted that 'he and his companions at the University of Edinburgh studied all the Controversies of that time & indeed all which were of real importance with great Care during a course of 6 years before and after 1720'; compared to this 'set of students', those who had written on Christian subjects since that time – including 'most part of the English Divines' – seemed to Wallace 'to be but bablers & half thinkers' (Wallace MSS, Edinburgh University Library). Besides Wallace, members of this circle included the brothers William* and George Wishart (1703–85)* and George Turnbull (later Professor of Philosophy at Marischal College, Aberdeen, 1721–7). Their preference for radical religious ideas, including opposition to credal formulae and confessions of faith, drew the ire of Robert Wodrow,* who also criticized a Glasgow divinity students' club, with which William Wishart was later associated, for opposing confessions and exalting reason 'under pretence of search after truth' (*Analecta*, G, 1842–3, III, 175, 178).

In subsequent decades Scottish divinity students continued to practise their skills at composition and public speaking in clubs of their own making. One such society at Edinburgh is said to have come to a fiery finish at a debate over the Cambuslang Revival (*see* Revivals) that featured the two future leaders of the Moderate* and Evangelical parties in the Kirk, William Robertson* and John Erskine,* in a heated exchange (H. Wellwood Moncrieff, *Account of John Erskine*, E, 1818, 16, 100). Around this same time, in the early 1740s, Alexander Carlyle* was a member of two clubs frequented by divinity students at Glasgow: at one, which met at the university, students 'criticized books and wrote abridgements of them, with critical essays'; at the other, which met at a tavern and included others besides divinity students, the 'conversation was almost entirely literary'. 'These societies contributed much to our improvement', Carlyle observed, 'and . . . they served to open and enlarge our minds' (*Autobiography*, ed. J. H. Burton, L and E, 1910, 85–7). The experience of an Edinburgh divinity student of the next generation, Thomas Somerville,* was similar to Carlyle's: in 1759 he joined a club intended specifically for divinity students, the Theological Society, and two years later joined another club with more general literary concerns, the Belles Lettres Society. 'To my attendance on these societies, more than to any branch of reading or study,' he later wrote, 'I impute any progress I have made in literature, in composition, and in solid intellectual improvement.' Even divinity students, however, could be lured into temptation: the Theological Society disbanded in 1764 because of too much 'excess and irregularity' (*My Own Life and Times*, E, 1861, 40).

Once their divinity school days were over, only clergymen whose parishes lay in or near large towns, or who pursued careers in universities, could continue to participate in the thriving club life of the Scottish Enlightenment.* Among these select few, however, were some of the foremost authors and speakers of the age. At Aberdeen, George Campbell,* Alexander Gerard* and Thomas Reid (*see* Scottish Realism) were among the mainstays of the formidable Aberdeen Philosophical Society, or Wise Club. The Literary Society of Glasgow numbered among its members not only clergymen-academics such as Reid and William Leechman* but also many non-academic ministers from the west of Scotland, including William Craig of Glasgow (one of only three non-academic constituent members; 1709–84, *FES* III, 433), John Walker* of Moffat, and the Ossianic controversialist Patrick Graham* of Aberfoyle. At Edinburgh, a number of ministers associated with the William Robertson-

CLUBS AND SOCIETIES

Alexander Carlyle circle of Moderate *literati*, as well as a few former Rankenians like Robert Wallace and George Wishart, were actively involved in the famous Select Society, and a core of Moderate divines provided the inspiration for the Poker or Militia Club. Though at first few clergymen belonged to the scientifically oriented Edinburgh Philosophical Society, by the time that body was transformed into the Royal Society of Edinburgh in 1783, ministers were among its leaders as well as among its most active scientific members (*e.g.* John Walker* and John Playfair*).

The subjects discussed at these and other intellectual clubs often touched on religion. At the Wise Club, for example, questions concerning scepticism and belief were treated on a high philosophical plane. Subjects debated at the Select Society were more topical, including issues such as the naturalization of foreign Protestants and the status of parochial decorum; however, the founders of the Select had from the outset explicitly banned topics dealing with revealed religion, and this stipulation may have discouraged attention to religious and ecclesiastical issues generally. But religious and ecclesiastical questions were quite popular at some other Edinburgh clubs, such as the Belles Lettres and Pantheon Societies. The following examples from the Pantheon, as recorded in the *Caledonian Mercury*, illustrate this point: Would Unlimited Toleration in Religion be advantageous to a State? (1775); Do the stipends of the clergy of Scotland require an augmentation? (1776); Is Patronage, or popular Election, the most eligible mode of settling vacant Churches? (1777); Are there just grounds to suspect, that fatal effects will arise to the nation from abolishing the Penal Statutes against the Papists? (1778); Is an attention to Secular Affairs consistent with the Office of a Clergyman? Were the Sufferings of Mary Queen of Scots, most owing to her Religious Principles, Personal Beauty, or the Rudeness of the Times? (*see* Patron, Patronage, Patronage Acts; General Assembly; Catholic Emancipation; Toleration; Mary Queen of Scots; Stool of Repentance).

Such questions reveal little concern with doctrinal matters but much with the social, political, economic and historical aspects of religion. In this way Scottish clergymen and laymen of the educated classes used clubs and societies to confront practical religious questions with rational arguments, in an effort to reach a polite consensus about the proper ordering of their Church and society.

D. D. McElroy, 'The Literary Clubs and Societies of Eighteenth-Century Scotland' (PhD, Edinburgh University, 1952); *id.*, *Scotland's Age of Improvement* (Washington, DC, 1969); R. B. Sher, *Church and University in the Scottish Enlightenment* (E, 1985); J. Dwyer, *Virtuous Discourse* (E, 1987); M. A. Stewart, 'Berkeley and the Rankenian Club', *Hermathena* 139 (1985), 25–45; R. L. Emerson, 'The Social Composition of Enlightened Scotland: The Select Society of Edinburgh', *Studies on Voltaire and the Eighteenth Century* 114 (1973), 291–329; *id.*, 'The Philosophical Society of Edinburgh, 1737–1783', *British Journal for the History of Science* 12 (1979), 154–91; 14 (1981), 133–76; 18 (1985), 255–302; S. Shapin, 'Property, Patronage and the Politics of Science: The Founding of the Royal Society of Edinburgh', *British Journal for the History of Science* 7 (1974), 1–14; S. A. Conrad, *Citizenship and Common Sense ... The Wise Club of Aberdeen* (NY and L, 1987).

R. B. Sher

Cluniacs. The abbey of Cluny, founded in 909 near Mâcon in Burgundy, embraced a reformed and strict variety of Benedictine* observance. Under a series of remarkable abbots, the reform spread quickly: new monasteries were founded and monasteries already existing accepted Cluny's observance. Two factors distinguished these Cluniac houses: the elaborate and lengthy choir offices which filled the monks' day, and the close juridical links with the mother-house at Cluny. Most daughter-houses were priories, with superiors appointed by the abbot of Cluny, while only he could receive the profession (monastic vows) of their monks, and indeed every monk was required to spend some time at Cluny itself. Cluny's success and influence were phenomenal, with four Cluniac monks becoming popes. Though its very success made such strict dependence impossible in practice (for instance, monks in distant houses often did not make their profession) and the regulations had to be modified, Cluniacs were a vast centralized order, undoubtedly Benedictine but very different from the other unattached and autonomous houses. In the later Middle Ages Cluny's influence declined, but it survived as a mother-house, much diminished in importance, until its suppression in the French Revolution.

In England the order attracted considerable support, but not so in Scotland, where the Cistercians* more readily found royal and private patronage. The Benedictine priory on the Isle of May, founded by David I,* was occasionally described as Cluniac, but not until the 1160s did Walter Fitzalan, Steward of Scotland, found within his land of Paisley a house of Cluniac monks, bringing thirteen monks from Wenlock in Shropshire. These monks were possibly already settled at Renfrew, where a priory may have already been established by Walter's father, Alan, *c.*1163. The transference of this community and their possessions to Paisley was effected about six years later. The establishment of a priory was consistent with Cluniac practice, but in 1219 Pope Honorius III permitted the prior and convent to elect an abbot. This move may have strained relations with Cluny, with which links continued to be indeterminate. Indeed, at some time between 1232 and 1241 there appears to have been an attempt by a successor and namesake of the founder to transform Paisley into a Cistercian house, but it was thwarted by William Bondington, the Bishop of Glasgow, who in 1240–1 took steps to regularize the relationship with Cluny, and secure Cluny's support for Paisley's struggle to remain Cluniac.

Paisley was further disturbed by a dispute over the foundation of another Cluniac house in Ayrshire.

COAST MISSION

This stemmed from a donation of Duncan, subsequently Earl of Carrick (1214-16), of lands and churches to the abbey of Paisley on condition that a religious house to which these possessions should pass should be founded by the monks. Instead they appear to have constructed a small oratory and it required a further judgment by the bishop of Glasgow in July 1244 that a 'religious house of monks of the order of Paisley' should be founded at Crossraguel with Paisley monks. The new house was to be exempt from the jurisdiction of Paisley 'save only in recognition of the order' (*i.e.* having the same habit and observance); and the abbot of Paisley was to visit it yearly. The property in Carrick was to be transferred to the house of Crossraguel by Paisley, to which an annual tribute of ten marks would be paid. Even then Paisley prevaricated and not until *c.*1270 were the conditions observed and a second Cluniac abbey brought into being. Thereafter relations between both houses appear to have been reasonably smooth, but little information is forthcoming about continuing links with Cluny between the resolution of this controversy and the Reformation, which brought both houses of the order to an end.

New Catholic Encyclopedia III, 966-70; Easson-Cowan 63-5; J. C. Lees, *The Abbey of Paisley* (New Club, Paisley, 1878); F. C. H. Blair (ed.), *Charters of the Abbey of Crosraguel*, 2 vols (Ayrshire and Galloway Archaeological Association, E, 1886); I. B. Cowan, 'Ayrshire Abbeys: Crossraguel and Kilwinning', *Ayrshire Collections* 14 (1986), 265-95.

I. B. Cowan

Coast Mission, *see* Fisherfolk, Missions to.

Coates Hall, *see* Episcopal Theological College.

Coats, Thomas (1809-83), businessman and Baptist* philanthropist. Thomas Coats was born in Paisley, the fourth of ten sons of James Coats, founder of J. and P. Coats, the thread manufacturers. Coats entered the family firm and joined in 1840, by baptism, the family church in Storie Street. He was a liberal supporter of all good causes, civic and church, and the Baptist Union of Scotland* in its early years owed much to his gifts. He gave donations to every new Baptist building in Scotland in the twenty years before his death, and supported Baptist ministerial education and the Baptist Missionary Society. He was chairman of Paisley School Board and also gave the town its observatory. He was President of the Baptist Union of Scotland in 1873-4. The magnificent new home of Storie Street Church, opened in 1894 as Thomas Coats Memorial Church, is a lasting tribute to his worth.

The Thomas Coats Memorial Church Paisley, Jubilee Book 1944 (Paisley, 1945); G. H. Coats, *Rambling Reminiscences* (Paisley, n.d.); *DNB* XI, 140; D. W. Bebbington (ed.), *The Baptists in Scotland* (G, 1988).

D. B. Murray

COLDINGHAM

Cochrane, Thomas (1866-1953), missionary. Born in Greenock in the family of a small merchant and orphaned at the age of thirteen, he was converted during D. L. Moody's* evangelistic tour of Scotland in 1882. A Congregationalist,* he volunteered for service with the London Missionary Society.* He received medical training at Glasgow and with his wife sailed for China in 1897. Cochrane engaged in a pioneer medical work at Chaoyang (Eastern Mongolia), and after the Boxer Rebellion he was assigned to rebuild the LMS hospital in Peking. In addition, he founded a medical college which with Rockefeller Foundation money was developed into the finest in China. He also maintained cordial relations with both Chinese regimes, the imperial and republican. He was firmly committed to ecumenical missionary endeavour and the formation of indigenous churches. He longed to see the establishment of one Chinese Christian Church by eliminating the sectarian nomenclatures that reflected the divisions of the Western societies. In 1915 he returned to London and worked with Sidney Clark and Roland Allen in the newly-formed National Laymen's Missionary Movement. They spoke of 'rethinking missions' by stressing world-wide witness based on the centrality of the cross and the Bible as the final authority in faith and practice, and urged that the younger churches witness and build after their own pattern. Through the World Dominion Press, *World Christian Handbook* and other means they promoted self-supporting, self-propagating churches and speedy indigenization of institutional works. The Survey Application Trust administered the World Dominion programme, and in 1931 the Movement for World Evangelization at the Mildmay Centre in North London was founded as an operations base. Cochrane remained involved in the work even after retirement. His writings include: *Survey of the Missionary Occupation of China* (Shanghai, 1913); *The Quest of Cathay: The South China Mission of the LMS* (Eastbourne, 1918); *The Task of the Christian Church: A World Survey* (L, 1926).

F. French, *Thomas Cochrane: Pioneer and Missionary Statesman* (L, 1956); M. Aitchison, *The Doctor and the Dragon* (Basingstoke, 1983).

R. V. Pierard

Coldingham, Benedictine priory. About 1098 King Edgar granted Coldingham (*see* Early Ecclesiastical Sites) and other lands to the Benedictine* monks of Durham. Eventually, *c.*1139, Durham founded a priory at Coldingham. It was richly endowed and supported thirty monks in the thirteenth century. The Anglo-Scottish wars put an end to Colingham's prosperity, for it was located near the border, on the Scottish side. It was the last 'alien priory' in Scotland. In the fourteenth century the monks abandoned the priory several times, and their number dropped to three or four.

In 1378 the Scottish king made Coldingham subject to Dunfermline.* This held good until 1424; from then until 1462 Durham monks were again in possession. The priory then became the object of a tangled dispute between the powerful Hume family and James III,* who erected it into a chapel royal. After James' defeat and murder in 1488, Coldingham became again a Scottish monastery, though not subject to Dunfermline. Its subsequent history was undistinguished but not peaceful, for it was involved in political struggles and suffered in the English invasions. Its commendator* from 1541 until after 1560 was a bastard son of James V.*

Easson-Cowan, 55–8; R. B. Dobson, 'The Last English Monks on Scottish Soil', *SHR* 46 (1967), 1–25; A. L. Brown, 'The Priory of Coldingham in the Late Fourteenth Century', *IR* 23 (1972), 91–101; N. Macdougall, 'The Struggle for the Priory of Coldingham, 1472–1488', *ibid.*, 102–14; M. Dilworth, 'Coldingham Priory and the Reformation', *ibid.*, 115–37.

M. Dilworth

Colleges and Seminaries (Roman Catholic). The practice of sending students for the priesthood to the Scots Colleges* on the continent had many drawbacks. An obvious answer was to open a seminary in Scotland which would prepare some boys for entry into the Scots Colleges abroad and give others a complete training for the priesthood. The first Scottish seminary opened in 1714. After the division of the Scottish Mission into two vicariates in 1731 there were in theory two seminaries, a Highland and a Lowland. These combined to form a national seminary in 1829 after the redivision of the Mission into three vicariates. Other seminaries were later founded, either minor (for boys up to the age of about eighteen) or major (for theological studies).

Loch Morar. The first seminary was opened in 1714 on Eilean Ban, Loch Morar, with a master and seven boys. It was abandoned after the 1715 Rising* and reopened at Scalan, in the Braes of Glenlivet, in 1716.

Scalan. Scalan was a small tenant farm with a house accommodating a master and about ten boys. To begin with, the seminary served the whole Mission; from 1732 just the Lowland Vicariate. During its first forty years various hostile attempts were made to suppress it, and in 1746 the house was burned by Cumberland's soldiers. The seminary, however, continued in makeshift accommodation until John Geddes* built the present house in 1762. In 1799 the seminary was moved to a less secret and more accessible location at Aquhorties on Donside.

Aquhorties. Penal Laws against Catholics were repealed in 1793. The French Revolution won sympathy in Britain for Catholics, while the French authorities and the Napoleonic Wars closed, either temporarily or permanently, all the Scots Colleges* abroad. The seminaries in Scotland were therefore of crucial importance to the Mission. The British government granted some funds towards their establishment.

Aquhorties was a farm of some 600 acres, supporting various sub-tenants. In 1796 Bishop George Hay* took a ninety-nine year lease on the farm and built a house large enough to accommodate about twenty-five boys, a procurator and three or four professors. It opened in 1799. It was intended that the seminary would be self-supporting once the farmland had been enclosed and improved. But by the time the improvements had been completed, at great cost, the house itself was proving inadequate. In 1829 the community moved to Blairs, just outside Aberdeen.

The Highland Seminary. Like Scalan, the Highland seminary was always situated on a tenant farm, but it did not have Scalan's continuity in place or time. It suffered from a chronic shortage of money. After Culloden the seminary was destroyed and the Highlands were unsafe. Between 1732 and 1803 the seminary was in five different locations; it was closed for twenty-six of the seventy-one years. It opened in 1732 on Eilean Ban, Loch Morar, with a master and eight students. Some time before 1738 it was transferred to Guidal on Loch nan Uamh, south of Arisaig. It was burned by soldiers in 1746 and closed down. In 1768 the seminary re-opened at Glenfinnan. Two years later it moved to Buorblach on Loch Morar, where it closed for a time due to lack of funds. In 1779 MacDonald of Sandaig terminated the lease. The seminary opened again at Samalaman, on Loch Ailort, in 1783. It could only support six to eight boys. In the 1790s there was crucial need to enlarge and improve the seminary, with the closure of the Scots Colleges abroad, and in 1803 it moved to the Island of Lismore, where Bishop Chisholm purchased the house of Kilcheran. The intention was to fund the seminary by producing lime, but the project was never economically viable owing to lack of local fuel. Lismore, which could support only about a dozen students, ranked a poor second educationally to Aquhorties.

Blairs. John Menzies of Pitfoddels, aware of the shortcomings of Lismore and Aquhorties, gifted his estate of Blairs to the Mission for a national seminary. In 1828 the Lismore boys transferred to Aquhorties, and in 1829 the combined seminary moved to Blairs. The original mansion house had been adapted to accommodate sixty boys. In time this became insufficient; the present building was completed in 1897, the chapel being added two years later. Blairs was the only Scottish seminary until 1874. Thereafter it continued as the national minor seminary, teaching normal school subjects. It closed in June 1986.

St Peter's College. This college was founded in 1874 by Archbishop Eyre as the major seminary for the Western District (later for the Archdiocese of Glasgow). It began at Partickhill, moving to New Kilpatrick in 1892, Cardross in 1946 and Newlands in 1980. In 1985 it was replaced by Chesters College, opened as an inter-diocesan major seminary for all the Scottish dioceses except Aberdeen and St Andrews & Edinburgh.

St Vincent's College, Langbank, opened in 1961 as

an inter-diocesan minor seminary to supplement Blairs. It amalgamated with Blairs in 1978.

St Andrew's College, Drygrange, and Gillis College. Opened at Drygrange in the Borders in 1953 as the major seminary for the Archdiocese of St Andrews and Edinburgh, it was transferred in 1986 to the former St Margaret's Convent, Edinburgh, and re-named Gillis College (*see* Gillis, James).

Various Religious Orders* have at times maintained colleges for their members.

C. Johnson, *Developments in the Roman Catholic Church in Scotland, 1789–1829* (E, 1983); *id., Scottish Catholic Secular Clergy 1879–1989* (E, 1991), 477–82; W. J. Anderson (ed.), 'The College for the Lowland District of Scotland at Scalan and Aquhorties: Registers and Documents', *IR* 14 (1963), 89–212; *Catholic Directory for Scotland* (annual) 1831–; 'Glenlivatensis' (i.e. A. S. MacWilliam), 'Scalan, 1717–1799', *St Peter's College Magazine* 17 (1946), 154–9; 18 (1947), 27–39; *id.,* 'The Highland Seminaries', *St Peter's College Magazine* 19 (1950), 133–9; 20 (1951), 20–4, 54–9, 119–23; A. S. MacWilliam, 'The Highland Seminary at Lismore 1803–1828', *IR* 8 (1957), 30–8; J. Ritchie, *Memorial of Centenary of St Mary's College, Blairs* (L, 1929); M. Ward (ed.), *St Vincent's College, Langbank, 1961–1978* (G, 1978).

C. Johnson

Collegiate Churches. In the Middle Ages, a college was a corporate body holding properties and endowments and associated for specific purposes, such as learning, justice or worship. Thence arose Colleges of Justice and University Colleges. In Europe, due to rivalry between regular and secular clergy, collegiate churches were founded. Somewhat late the idea came to Scotland. Secular clergy were then able to work together without taking monastic vows. Between 1250 and 1550, about forty collegiate churches were formed, the first being St Mary's on the Rock, St Andrews. The initiative in the earlier years usually came from powerful lords who wished to raise the status of churches in their domains. Dunbar (1325) was founded by the Earl of March, Bothwell (1398) by the Earl of Douglas, Corstorphine (1429) by Sir John Forrester, Crichton (1449) by Lord Crichton, Hamilton (1450) by Lord Hamilton, Dumbarton (1454) by the Duchess of Albany, all noticeably where there was no cathedral.

Trinity College, Edinburgh was founded (1460) by Mary of Guelders, Queen of James II, with a hospital nearby, with transfer of the friars from Soutra. Other royal foundations were Restalrig (1487) and the Chapel Royal, Stirling (1501).

Several later foundations were established by town councils, desiring to enhance the importance of their parish churches. St Giles' in Edinburgh, the largest town with no cathedral, where were the royal palace and the government, became collegiate by papal bull in 1467 after action by the provost, bailies, councillors and community of Edinburgh. Likewise collegiate churches were established in Haddington (*c.*1540), Peebles (1543) and Holy Rude, Stirling in 1546.

Other collegiate churches were at Abernethy (1325), Maybole (1384), Lincluden (1389), Dalkeith (1406), Kilmaurs (1413), Bothans (1421), Carnwath (1424), Methven (1433), Kilmun (1441), Dunglass (1443), Dirleton (1444), St Salvator's, St Andrews (1451), Guthrie (1479), Tain (1487), Seton (1492), Semple (1504), King's College, Aberdeen (1505), St Mary's-in-the-Fields, Edinburgh (*c.*1512), Crail (1517), Roslin (*c.*1521), Our Lady College, Glasgow (*c.*1523), St Nicholas, Aberdeen (*c.*1540) and Biggar (1546). There may have been several others. The collegiate church had a corporate life under statutes. The table, purse, chest, seal and chapter belonged to the community under the leadership of one called dean or provost or president. The total complement of personnel varied with place, size and period. St Giles' may have been typical. The vicar became the first provost and under him there were a curate to care for souls, a minister of the choir, a sacristan, fourteen canons or prebendaries and four chorister boys. The collegiate church was made independent of episcopal jurisdiction. Corstorphine had a provost, four chaplains and two boys. Tain had a provost, five prebendaries, two deacons and sub-deacons, a sacristan, his assistant clerk and two boys. The largest college was at the Chapel Royal at Stirling, where the dean was also bishop of Candida Casa (later Galloway) and there were sub-deacon, sacrist, sixteen canons, six boy choristers and a treasurer. Later ten lesser canons were added. A chancellor, arch-deacon and sub-chanter are also mentioned (see Easson).

After the Reformation, the term 'collegiate' has often been applied to churches where there were two colleagues in one charge, as in St Cuthbert's, Edinburgh until recently, or where a colleague and successor had been appointed. There were similar collegiate arrangements for many years in the Edinburgh Burgh churches* and in other towns.

D. E. Easson, 'The Collegiate Churches of Scotland', *RSCHS* 6 (1938), 193–215, 7 (1941), 30–47; J. Dowden, *The Medieval Church in Scotland* (G, 1910); J. Cameron Lees, *St. Giles' Edinburgh: Church, College and Cathedral* (E, 1889); Easson-Cowan.

A. I. Dunlop

Collins, William, *see* Publishing, Religious.

Colman, *see* Celtic Saints.

Colquhoun, (Lady) Janet (1781–1846), religious writer. Born in London to Scottish MP Sir John Sinclair, she was educated at Stoke Newington, north London. Converted in her teens by reading William Wilberforce's *Practical View*, she married Major James Colquhoun in 1799, who succeeded to his father's estate in Luss, on Loch Lomond, in 1805.

Lady Colquhoun patronized many religious and philanthropic societies, including the Luss and

Arrochar Bible Society, the Gaelic School Society, the Society for Female Education in India, and the Ladies' Society in Scotland in Aid of the Home Mission of the Presbyterian Church in Ireland. She began writing (anonymously) in 1822, with *Despair and Hope* (E, 1822). Other works followed. Her name was attached to them only after her father's death in 1836, in response to his dying wish.

Lady Colquhoun's spiritual experience was distinguished by its sobriety and tranquillity; she said she was first drawn to Christ more by the beauty of his character than by a sense of need. Her writings present practical religious truths in simple, unaffected prose.

In the Disruption* of 1843 Lady Colquhoun zealously adhered to the FC.

Thoughts on the Religious Profession of the Higher Classes of Society (E, 1823); *Impressions of the Heart* (E, 1825); *The Kingdom of God* (E, 1835); *The World's Religion* (E, 1839); *Works* (L, 1852).

J. Hamilton, *A Memoir of Lady Colquhoun* (L, 1849); D. P. Thomson, 'Lady Janet Colquhoun of Luss', in *Women of the Scottish Church* (Perth, 1975); *DNB* XI, 401–2.

N. R. Needham

Colquhoun, John (1748–1827), CofS minister and author. Born in the parish of Luss (Dunbartonshire), Colquhoun attributed his conversion to the answer to the Shorter Catechism's question, 'What is effectual calling?' Referred by a teacher to Thomas Boston's* *Fourfold State*, he began an acquaintance with Boston's writings which continued throughout his life. He studied at the University of Glasgow, was ordained to the New Church (St John's), South Leith, in 1781 and remained there until his death.

He was a popular and influential evangelical preacher, whose sermons and writings reflect in great measure those of the Marrow brethren (*see* Marrow Controversy) and whose theology was more in accord with that of the Secession* churches than that of his fellow Evangelicals* in the CofS. In advising the many students of divinity who frequented his ministry, he declined to recommend *The Marrow of Modern Divinity*, as the General Assembly had condemned it. But Boston's notes to the *Marrow* were not so condemned, and these he warmly recommended.

Colquhoun's works, all intensely practical, were widely influential: *A Treatise of Spiritual Comfort* (E, 1813; ³1822); *A Treatise on the Law and the Gospel* (E, 1816; ²1819); *A Treatise on the Covenant of Grace* (E, 1818); *A Catechism for the Instruction and Direction of Young Communicants* (E, 1821; ²1838); *A Treatise on the Covenant of Works* (E, 1821); *A View of Saving Faith* (E, 1824); *A Collection of the Promises of the Gospel* (E, 1825); *A View of Evangelical Repentance* (E, 1825); *Sermons, chiefly on Doctrinal Subjects* (E, 1836), includes a brief memoir.

FES I, 158.

D. C. Lachman

Colquhoun, John Campbell (1803–70), politician and Evangelical leader. Educated at Edinburgh and Oriel College, Oxford, Colquhoun entered Parliament as radical MP for Dumbarton in 1832. In 1834 he was responsible for the Act that permitted the CofS* to create *quoad sacra* parishes. Subsequently he played a major part in the anti-RC campaign in support of the Church of Ireland in 1834 and 1835, chairing an important public meeting in Glasgow in October 1835. When he returned to Parliament in 1837 he supported the Conservatives. At this time he was regarded as a possible successor to William Wilberforce (1759–1833) as leader of parliamentary Evangelicalism.* However, his early promise was not fulfilled and he retired from Parliament in 1847.

DNB XI, 403; J. R. Wolffe, *The Protestant Crusade in Great Britain, 1829–1860* (O, 1991); I. G. C. Hutchison, *A Political History of Scotland 1832–1914* (E, 1986).

J. R. Wolffe

Columba (*c*.521–597), founder of the monastery of Iona.* Though comparatively few sources survive from this early period of ecclesiastical history, Columba's life is well documented. We have two major early sources about him. The *Amra* or eulogy, a verse composition in the Irish language, appears to have been composed around the time of his death in the year 597. His Latin *Life*, the *Vita Columbae*, was written by his Iona successor Adomnán* at the close of the seventh century. Adomnán's work, moreover, incorporates an earlier account of Columba, compiled by Cumméne* from the testimonies of surviving contemporaries in the early decades after Columba's death.

As these memorials of Columba are literary works they have limitations as historical evidence. The *Amra* eulogizes its subject's moral, spiritual, and intellectual qualities, but provides tantalizingly few details about his public life. The *Vita* is concerned with manifestations of Columba's sanctity rather than with the chronology of his career. Yet, despite their limitations, these works provide valuable assistance in tracing the main outlines of his activities.

Both texts testify to Columba's noble ancestry. His kin, the Uí Néill, were acknowledged as Ireland's most powerful rulers. His immediate family were kings of Cenél Conaill in the north-west of Ireland. Little is known, however, of Columba's early life. The *Vita Columbae* places his departure from Ireland to Britain in his forty-second year, about 563. While we may infer that he was already a monk at this time, the circumstances of his departure from his homeland are unchronicled. Later Irish tradition viewed Columba's exile as an act of penitence for his part in instigating a battle. That his royal connections potentially involved Columba in Irish public affairs is certainly likely. The *Vita Columbae* statement, that his wish was to become 'a pilgrim for Christ', seems to imply a desire on Columba's part to pursue his monastic vocation in a setting more removed from secular concerns.

Yet his choice of settlement in Iona appears to have been facilitated by political contacts between his royal relatives and the rulers of Dál Riata, the Irish kingdom in western Scotland (see Gaelic; Highlands). While Columba's thirty-four years in Scotland were spent mainly in the island monastery, the *Vita Columbae* indicates that Dál Riata patronage enabled him to found monasteries throughout the kingdom. Mention is made, for instance, of monastic foundations subject to Iona in Tiree, and on an island called Hinba. Yet Columba's departure to Scotland did not sever his contacts with his native country. On one of his return journeys to Ireland he founded the monastery of Durrow in the Irish midlands.

Columba appears to have modelled his monastic organization on the secular model of overlordship practised by his royal kin. The *Vita Columbae* depicts a network of monasteries on both sides of the Irish Sea, each with its own ruler yet all united under the ultimate headship of the abbot of Iona himself. Moreover, kinship played a vital part in the choice of Columba's monastic abbots. His uncle, first cousin, and the son of another first cousin, were, respectively, abbots of Hinba, *Campus Lunge* in Tiree, and Durrow in Ireland.

Yet while we see a close-knit, Irish-focused community, primarily concerned with monastic establishment, this is not the complete picture. Though missionary activity does not appear to have been the prime motivating force of Columba's settlement in Scotland, his attention turned to the unchristianized Picts* beyond the border of Dál Riata. The *Vita Columbae* mentions journeys beyond the 'Spine of Britain', and Columba's meeting with the Pictish king, Brude. Whether the King himself was converted is unclear, but his toleration of Christian teaching in his kingdom seems to have been obtained. We learn of Columba's use of an interpreter in his preaching to the Picts, and of his baptism of believers. It is not clear whether monasteries were founded in the kingdom within his lifetime, but it is evident that Columba's activity laid the foundations for the establishment of Christianity in Pictland.

So by the time of his death at the close of the sixth century Columba, from his base on Iona, presided over a far-flung area of influence. Though he had renounced royal ambitions in Ireland, his social status seems to have afforded him easy access to rulers on both sides of the Irish Sea. In the political sphere, he appears to have helped to consolidate an alliance between his Irish kin, the Uí Néill, and his Scottish patrons, the rulers of Dál Riata. The *Vita Columbae* claims, moreover, that it was Columba who consecrated the newly-elected king of Dál Riata.

Yet his political involvement was subordinate to his role as churchman. Secular stability and royal support were necessary for the flourishing of an ever-growing confederation of monasteries. Iona had become the hub of a monastic enterprise which extended from Ireland to remote Pictland. Pilgrims, penitents and monks made their way to the island from west and east. This was Columba's visible achievement in his lifetime. Even more important was the fact that he provided his community with a system of organization, government and succession designed to ensure the continuity of his work. Until the disruption caused by Viking attacks at the beginning of the ninth century, Columba's legacy remained a dominating factor in both Irish and Scottish ecclesiastical life.

See also Celtic Saints; Celtic Church; Monasticism, Celtic.

W. Stokes (ed.), 'The Bodleian Amra Choluimb Chille', *Revue Celtique* 20 (1899), 31–55, 132–83, 400–37; W. Reeves (ed.), *The Life of St. Columba* (Dublin, 1857); A. O. and M. O. Anderson (ed.), *Adomnan's Life of Columba* (²O, 1991); M. Herbert *Iona, Kells, and Derry* (O, 1988).

M. Herbert

Colville, John (c.1542–1605), RC convert and agitator. Coming from Cleish (Kinross-shire) he studied at St Leonard's College, St Andrews (MA, 1565). As minister at East Kilbride (1567), he incurred complaints about his non-residence. At his wedding (1572) a play by John Davidson* of Prestonpans was performed. Turning to political activities, he was made master of requests (1578), attached himself to the Ruthven Raiders* (1583), became a Senator of the College of Justice and an ally of the rebel Earl of Bothwell. After years as an active English agent, proscribed in Scotland, suspected in England, he found patronage in Paris from John Fraser, the University rector. His *Palinod* (E, 1600) retracted his earlier efforts against James VI,* and his *Paraenesis* (Paris, 1601; in Scots, *Paraenese*, Paris, 1602) explained his conversion to RCism. He died in poverty in Paris, his widow seeking French clerical aid.

DNB XI, 420–2; *FES* III, 266; memoir by D. Laing in edition of *Original Letters, 1582–1603* with *Palinode* (Bannatyne Club, E, 1856); probably author of *The Historie and Life of King James the Sixth* (Bannatyne Club, E, 1825).

J. Durkan

Colville, William (d.1675), Principal of Edinburgh University. The son of a Kinross-shire laird, Colville graduated from St Andrews University in 1631, and became minister of Cramond, Midlothian, in 1635, the Trinity Church, Edinburgh, 1639, and the Tron Kirk, Edinburgh, 1641. In 1640 he was sent to France by the Covenanters* to seek the aid of Louis XIII against Charles I.* He was suspended in 1648 and deposed in 1649 for supporting the Engagement,* and was later minister of Perth, 1655, and principal at Edinburgh 1662–75.

Philosophia Moralis Christiana (E, 1670); *The Righteous Branch growing out of the Root of Jesse* (E, 1673).

FES I, 10, 126, 134–5, IV, 234, VII, 381; *DNB* XI, 422; D. Stevenson, *Scottish Revolution* (Newton

Abbot, 1973), 180–1, 184, 187; A. Grant, *The Story of the University of Edinburgh* (L, 1884), II, 252–3.

D. Stevenson

Comgan, *see* Celtic Saints.

Commendator, one entrusted temporarily with an office he did not hold by right. In time commendation became an extension of papal provision to monasteries (*see* Monastic Orders, Medieval): a commendator was one appointed abbot without being obliged to become a monk. Whereas a monk blessed as abbot held office *in titulum* (by entitlement), a non-monk was not blessed and held it *in commendam* (in trust). Laymen or children could be commendators. It was also a legal device permitting pluralism, the most usual commendator being a bishop holding an abbacy as well as his diocese.

Commendation became common in the fourteenth and fifteenth centuries but varied greatly according to country. In Scotland it arrived late and has often been confused with provision of non-monks obliging them to become monks. Until Flodden (1513) the relatively few commendators were all bishops. Subsequently others were appointed as either permanent or temporary commendators; the latter were minors too young for the abbatial blessing or adults given a period of grace. In Scotland commendators were never laymen or married but were secular clerics obliged to take major orders, while various safeguards limited the possibility of damage; in various other countries, however, commendation ruined monasteries completely. By 1560 only two-thirds of Scottish monasteries had commendators. As applied to men appointed by the Crown after 1560, the term 'commendator' denotes no church office but merely ownership.

R. Laprat in *Dictionnaire de Droit Canonique* III, 1029–85; P. Schmitz, *Histoire de l'Ordre de Saint-Benoît* (Maredsous, 1948–56), IV, 228–42; M. Dilworth, 'The Commendator System in Scotland', *IR* 37 (1986), 51–72.

M. Dilworth

Commission for Interpretation of God's Will. In May 1940, at the lowest point of Britain's fortunes in the Second World War, the General Assembly of the CofS appointed, under the convenership of John Baillie,* a 'Commission for the Interpretation of God's Will in the Present Crisis', charged with the task 'to seek reverently to guide the Church in the interpretation of the Holy Will and Purpose of God in present-day events, and to examine how the testimony of the Church to the Gospel may become more effective in our own land, overseas, and in the international order'.

The Commission, which included in its membership many of the most influential figures in the Church, covered a vast field of enquiry and submitted five reports to the Assembly between 1941 and 1945. Its main interests were in the area of Church and society, and it produced important statements on evangelism, Church and state, education, family life, and social and industrial issues. Despite its wide-ranging remit and grandiloquent title, the Commission managed to focus its work in such a way that its annual reports attracted considerable attention and comment outside as well as within the Churches. Under Baillie's influence the Commission adopted the 'middle axiom' method which had been developed in a series of ecumenical conferences in the 1930s. Much of the Commission's work looked towards post-War reconstruction, and its call for a more equal and just ordering of society, with industry and the economy accountable to the public, its proposals on education and its emphasis on the need for social security, made it a pillar of the post-War 'welfare consensus', as well as a contribution to social ethics of enduring significance.

The 1942, 1943 and 1944 Reports were published by SCM Press, L, as *God's Will in our Time*, *The Church Faces the Future*, and *Home, Community and Church*. In 1946 a composite volume, *God's Will for Church and Nation* (L) was published.

Donald C. Smith, *Passive Obedience and Prophetic Protest* (NY, 1987), 372–83; D. B. Forrester, *Christianity and the Future of Welfare* (L, 1985), 38–43.

D. B. Forrester

Commission of Assembly, *see* General Assembly.

'Committee of Forty', set up by the General Assembly of the CofS in 1971 on the proposal of the Church and Nation Committee with the remit 'to interpret for the Church the purpose towards which God is calling his people in Scotland, to investigate and assess the resources of the Church in persons and property, and to make recommendations for the reshaping of the life and structure of the Church and so to enable her to make her testimony to the Gospel more effective in the life of the changing world' (*PAGACS 1971*, 81, 84). The Committee's reports to succeeding General Assemblies indicate its attempts to achieve those very large aims. Reports in 1973, 1974 and 1978 dealt at some length with the first part of the remit, and those of 1975 to 1978 with the second and third. The Committee was discharged in 1978. Even if no profound or influential theological analysis emerged from the Committee's work, it seems probable that it did have a considerable effect on the Church's efforts throughout the 1970s and 1980s to adjust to the needs of the time. A number of the Committee's practical recommendations (e.g. with regard to the structure and functions of the General Assembly and of Presbyteries) were not accepted by the Church; of those which were, probably the institution of the Auxiliary Ministry* and of an Assembly Council* to guide the General Assembly in its business were the most significant.

RGACS 1973, 625–35; *1974*, 519–31; *1975*, 509–56; *1976*, 479–504; *1977*, 473–503; *1978*, 489–516, and pt. II, 40–2.

R.S. Barbour

COMMITTEE ON PUBLIC WORSHIP

Committee on Public Worship and Aids to Devotion, a Committee of the General Assembly of the CofS set up following the Union* of 1929. It undertook the work previously done by the Committee on Psalmody and Hymns and the Committee on Aids to Devotion of the CofS, and the Praise Committee and the 'Book of Common Order' Committee of the UFC. The amalgamation involved little change for the two committees concerned with praise, since for some years prior to 1929 they had carried out their work through a joint committee. A committee had been set up in the CofS in 1849 to produce material suitable for use in worship by 'soldiers, sailors, and other persons who are deprived of the ordinary services of the Christian ministry'. The resulting publication, *Prayers for Social and Family Worship*, first appeared in 1859 and was authorized for use by the General Assembly in 1863. Several editions were published and the book was revised in 1889. The Committee on Aids to Devotion also brought out *Prayers for Divine Service* in 1923, which differed from the earlier book in that it included material for the celebration of the sacraments and was intended as a guide to ministers in the conduct of worship. In the UFC the Church Worship Association, a parallel society to the Church Service Society* in the CofS, had been formed in 1900 as a result of the merger of the two societies concerned with worship in both the FC and the UPC. The Association produced a service book in 1909, *Directory and Forms for Public Worship*, and it approached the General Assembly in 1923 suggesting the production of a *Book of Common Order*. A committee was set up and the book was published in 1928. In the view of Millar Patrick,* who had first made the proposal, the publication meant that immediately prior to the union the UFC was reconciled to having an official service book and that the united Church would from the outset have a standing committee on public worship. Since 1929 the Committee has been responsible for many publications, most notably the *Book of Common Order** of 1940 and of 1979. In 1983 the Committee was renamed the Panel on Worship, and in the following year the Holy Tryst Committee, which had produced material for prayer for the overseas work of the Church, was merged with the Panel.

See also Hymnology; Liturgy.

D. B. Forrester and D. M. Murray (eds), *Studies in the History of Worship in Scotland* (E, 1984); M. Patrick, 'The Church Worship Association of the United Free Church', *Church Service Society Annual* 3 (1930–1), 79–82.

D. M. Murray

Common Order, *see Book of Common Order*.

Common-sense Philosophy, *see* Scottish Realism.

Commonwealth and Protectorate. In 1651, having conquered most of Scotland, the Parliament of the Commonwealth of England and Ireland (the republican regime dominated by Oliver Cromwell* which had been established in 1649 following the execution of Charles I* and the abolition of the English monarchy) resolved that Scotland should be united with it. Thus the Commonwealth of England, Scotland and Ireland came into being, though from 1653 the regime is often referred to as the Protectorate (reflecting constitutional changes which included Cromwell's assumption of the office of Lord Protector). After his death in 1658 the regime crumbled, and the union with Scotland was disowned by the English even before the Restoration* of 1660. Cromwell's attitude to the Scots was that they were a basically godly people who had been led astray – by their landlords and by the Presbyterian ministers of the CofS. England's mission was to free the Scots from these oppressors. In religion this meant that while the English were ready to support and encourage the Est.C as primarily godly in its teaching, they were determined to break the religious monopoly which allowed its ministers to persecute those who disagreed with them. The limited toleration* introduced by the English appears to have had very little popular appeal, though a few Scots did join sects sponsored by English officials and soldiers stationed in Scotland. In most parishes, whatever the intentions of the English, the minister and Kirk Session remained in dominant positions and thus few had any real opportunity to take advantage of the officially proclaimed toleration – though there is little sign that many wanted to. The principal of toleration was generally abhorrent to ministers and people alike, but the Church was in no position to force a change of policy, especially as it was weakened by division into the bitterly opposed factions of Resolutioners* and Protesters:* in 1653 the Church's humiliation was increased when the rival factions each tried to hold a General Assembly, only to have English soldiers disband both. However, while such divisions weakened resistance to English religious policies, they also complicated English attempts to establish a working relationship with Scots Presbyterians. The conquerors at first sought alliance with the Protesters, for though they were a minority, they had virtually disowned the cause of Charles II* and seemed in many other respects to have similarities to English Puritans. The Protesters were themselves divided as to how to react to tempting English offers of favour and support, but in the end their insistence on Presbyterianism as the only godly form of church government, and their refusal to accept any toleration outside it or fully to accept the legitimacy of the regime, made agreement impossible. The English therefore turned, in 1656, to the Resolutioners, and reached a tacit understanding with them whereby most stopped praying publicly for the exiled Charles II in return for a measure of official favour.

J. Buckroyd, 'Lord Broghill and the Scottish Church, 1655–1656', *JEH*, 27 (1976), 359–68; D. Stevenson, 'Cromwell, Scotland and Ireland', in J. S. Morrill (ed.), *Cromwell and the English Revolution* (L, 1990), 149–80.

D. Stevenson

Communion, Holy, see Lord's Supper.

Communion Seasons, special times in the year when the sacrament of the Lord's Supper* was celebrated within the Scottish Presbyterian* Churches. Although the *BCO* of 1564* (Knox, *Works* IV, 191) directed that the Supper be celebrated once a month, 'or so oft as the Congregation shall thinke expedient', the *First Book of Discipline** recommended a quarterly holding of the sacrament (183). In practice, it was celebrated much less frequently throughout Scotland, particularly in the Highlands,* where the lapse of celebration could extend for several years, for a variety of reasons: disruption caused by the Covenanting* troubles in the seventeenth century; poverty leading to a scarcity of bread and extreme hardship among the people; lack of qualified ministers; ministerial negligence; and the basic, practical difficulty of gathering the people of vast parishes. By the eighteenth century the CofS aspired to hold Communion annually in each parish, but in the nineteenth parishes aimed at twice-yearly celebrations (early and late in the year).

In spite of, and indeed possibly because of, infrequent celebration, Communion seasons assumed major significance within the Scottish Presbyterian calendar (*see* Christian Year). After 1600 the growing atmosphere of hostility between episcopacy and Presbyterianism stimulated the emergence of large outdoor Communion services, thus encouraging a distinctive popular piety dependent on mass gathering. As happened at Shotts in 1630, such 'Occasions' could sow the impulses of religious revival,* and Communions came to have great importance in this context. Nevertheless, the heightened sense of spirituality engendered by the Communion season was balanced by secular fellowship, which drew the community of several parishes into acts of rowdy celebration. Hawkers and traders set up stalls to take advantage of the traffic from neighbouring parishes, strong drink was dispensed, and charges of indecorous behaviour and immorality were laid against some of those attending the 'Holy Fairs'. Attempts to reform the Communion seasons were made from the eighteenth century, but traditional secular practices, doubtless drawing on earlier patterns, were modified (but not entirely eradicated) only with the emergence of Evangelicalism from the later eighteenth century.

Communion seasons had their own special ritual of events before and after the celebration of the Lord's Supper on the sabbath. A fast day was usually observed on Thursday, a preparatory service was held on Saturday, and a thanksgiving service on the Monday. In the Highlands the Friday of the Communion season came to be marked by the *Coinneamh Cheist*, 'Question Meeting', the focus of 'Men's Day' (*see* The Men), admission to the Supper was regulated by the dispensing of tokens (*see* Communion Tokens) and by the 'fencing' of the table, by which all potentially unworthy takers were debarred. Visiting ministers assisted the local minister in the services.

Even in a strictly evangelical context, the Communion seasons continued to be major social events in Scottish communities, although they have now been displaced in the Lowlands and southern Highlands by smaller, 'private' (indoor) Communions. In the northern Highlands, where the old tradition of extended services has survived longest, Communions are usually celebrated twice yearly, but indoors rather than in the open air. There they still provide a focus of fellowship, drawing together people from a number of parishes, and permitting a degree of human interaction at both sacred and secular levels.

L. E. Schmidt, *Holy Fairs* (Princeton, NJ, 1989); G. K. Neville, *Kinship and Pilgrimage* (O, 1987), 33–41; J. MacInnes, *The Evangelical Movement in the Highlands of Scotland* (A, 1951), 98–106.
D. E. Meek

Communion Tables, see Lord's Supper.

Communion Tokens. Calvin in Geneva tried to introduce the use of tickets for admission of true believers of good moral life to the Lord's Table, but it appears that it was in the Reformed Church of France that the practice first began. The use of tickets in Scotland began very soon after the Reformation*, probably in the form of stamped cards. In a few years the cards were replaced by metal tokens of lead and sometimes of tin or brass or pewter, but still often called 'tickets'. They were normally distributed by the minister or elders and deacons, either at catechizing* visits or at preparatory services before the sacrament of the Lord's Supper.* Tokens were withheld for disciplinary reasons and presentation of the token was obligatory for admission. In some parts of the Highlands* tokens are still used, being distributed at preparatory services. The metal tokens, often made locally in moulds, were roughly shaped in early Reformed times but became increasingly artistic with the passing of the years. The shape varied according to taste; some were square, some circular, some oblong. In size, the tokens were about three-quarters of an inch across. The name of the church or the initials of the minister was usually indicated and often the date of casting. There are several good collections of old tokens.

Metal tokens have generally been replaced by cards bearing the name of the comunicant and enabling attendance records to be kept, more to invite members to Communion than to authorize presence.

A. J. S. Brook, 'Communion Tokens of the Established Church of Scotland – Sixteenth, Seventeenth, and Eighteenth Centuries', *PSAS* 41 (1907), 453–604; R. Kerr, 'Unpublished Tokens of the Church of Scotland', *PSAS* 70 (1941), 144–83; *id.*, 'Communion Tokens of the Church of Scotland: Nineteenth and Twentieth Centuries', *PSAS* 77 (1943), 49–146; *id.*, 'Communion Tokens of the Free Church of Scotland', *PSAS* 79 (1946), 26–80; R. Dick, *Scottish Communion Tokens other than those of the Established Church* (E,

1902); M. Tenney, *Communion Tokens their origin, History, and use* (Grand Rapids, 1936); Thomas Burns, *Old Scottish Communion Plate* (E, 1892); W. McMillan, *The Worship of the Scottish Reformed Church* (L, 1931).

A. I. Dunlop

Comper, John (1825–1903), EpCS slum parson. He served at Nairn and Stonehaven before taking up the incumbency of St John's in 1861, and St Margaret's in 1871, both Aberdeen. Best remembered for his successful work in the latter, which he inaugurated as a mission station in the Gallowgate in 1864 and which, within fifteen years, received consecration as a church, Comper's success in creating a flourishing working-class congregation is all the more remarkable in the light of the failure of Presbyterian missionary efforts in the same area as well as the presence of another Episcopal church (St Paul's) in the Gallowgate. For the first time since the Reformation* uniformed sisters were introduced into the work of the EpCS (*see* Religious Communities, Episcopal Church). Alexander Gammie* records that 'considerable prejudice had to be overcome' (*The Churches of Aberdeen*, A, 1909, 288); given the dominance of Presbyterianism in the city this is not surprising. No doubt Comper caused further offence by introducing a surpliced choir to his services. He also opened other missions which denied entry to all those wearing a hat or bonnet, thus further flouting customary ideas of respectability. In this matter he may well have learned from earlier unconventional missionary efforts in the city (see A. A. MacLaren, *Religion and Social Class*, L, 1974, 167–207).

See also Anglicanism; Kidd, James (1761–1834); Episcopalianism.

A Popular Handbook . . . on Liturgies, 2 pts (E, 1891–8); *The Distinctive Teaching of the British Churches* (E, 1854), reissued as *Church Principles . . .* (L, 1904).

'Memoir' by J. Wiseman in *Church Principles*, xiii–xxxviii.

A. A. MacLaren

Comrie, Alexander (1708–74), Scottish-born minister of the Dutch Reformed Church. He went to Holland in his youth to pursue a mercantile career, but decided to enter the ministry, studying at Gröningen and Leiden. Having graduated MA and PhD from the latter in 1734, he was elected minister of the parish church of Woubrugge, which he pastored until 1773. He was a popular preacher.

Comrie spent much of his life opposing the progress of rationalism, latitudinarianism* and heresy in Holland, from the standpoint of traditional Calvinism. His most significant controversy was with Wilhelm Brakel on the nature of faith and justification. He also translated into Dutch many works of Anglo-Saxon theology and spirituality, such as Thomas Shepard's *Parable of the Ten Virgins* and Thomas Boston's* *Covenant of Grace*.

DNB XI, 454–5; A. Kuyper, *The Work of the Holy Spirit* (NY, 1900), 390–6; G. C. Berkouwer, *Faith and Justification* (Grand Rapids, 1954), 152–6; J. R. Beeke, *Assurance of Faith* (NY, 1991), 281–320.

N. R. Needham

Concern for the Kirk and the Reformed Faith, a movement launched in 1982 by the National Church Association,* dedicated to stirring up in the people of Scotland fresh interest in the great traditions of the national CofS, its faith, worship and government. That so many people in Scotland were lapsing from Church membership was seen as due to the Kirk's 'becoming increasingly an institution alien in polity and doctrine to our thinking and belief'. The movement opened with a massive rally in Edinburgh's Usher Hall which was disrupted by the intrusion of sectarian elements. Other public meetings and media statements have addressed controversial questions from this distinctive perspective.

A. Herron

Conciliarism, the doctrine and programme associated particularly with the Conciliar Movement of the fifteenth century. The basic notion that the faithful as a body (*universitas fidelium*), represented by a general or ecumenical council, have an essential place in the life and government of the Church has roots running back to the earliest phases of Christian history. Late-medieval conciliarism (much indebted to canon lawyers as well as to theologians) developed when it seemed that only a council could bring an end to the Great Schism (1378–1418), during which Latin Christendom was split between rival claimants to the papacy. The council of Constance (1414–18), besides achieving that goal, sought to institutionalize the conciliar principle by asserting the constitutional supremacy of council over pope and providing that councils should meet at regular ten-yearly intervals. Scottish contacts with Constance were limited and belated; but in the council of Basel (1431–49) Scottish churchmen played a substantial and in some cases a prominent part.

The most active Scots conciliarist was Thomas Livingston (*d*.1460), Cistercian* abbot of Dundrennan, whose surviving sermons illustrate the radical conciliarist principles upheld at Basel to the point of declaring Eugenius IV deposed and electing Felix V as anti-pope in 1439. Scottish ecclesiastical and political life was deeply marked by the resulting 'Little Schism' of the 1440s. Moreover, a 'conciliarist tradition' was established and was to be extended well into the next century by Scots trained in the deeply conciliarist theology faculty of Paris. Thus John Ireland (*d*.1495) took a firmly conciliarist position in his commentary on the *Sentences* of Peter Lombard, an early accession to the library of King's College, Aberdeen.

Most important, however, was the work of John Major* (Mair) in the early sixteenth century. Mair's elaborately argued statement of the conciliarist case in his 1518 commentary on St Matthew's

Gospel became a standard text in the literature of the subject. It was characteristic of Mair's thought to exploit the supposed analogy between the ecclesiastical and the civil polity. Like virtually all conciliarists Mair upheld the monarchical principle in Church government; but monarchy, he maintained, did not preclude, indeed it required, 'constitutional' limitations backed by the community's right to depose an unsatisfactory ruler. This scholastic, conciliarist theory of limited monarchy was an important factor in shaping the 'resistance theory' of Protestant controversy, notably in the case of Mair's former pupil George Buchanan.*

New Catholic Encyclopedia IV, 109–13; J. H. Burns, *Scottish Churchmen and the Council of Basle* (G, 1962); D. Shaw, 'Thomas Livingston, a Conciliarist', *RSCHS* 12 (1958), 120–35; J. H. Burns, 'The Conciliarist Tradition in Scotland', *SHR* 42 (1963), 89–104; F. Oakley, 'Almain and Major: Conciliar Theory on the Eve of the Reformation', *American Historical Review* 70 (1965), 673–90.

J. H. Burns

Concordat of Leith (1572), *see* Leith, Convention of (1572).

Concurrence/Congregational Assent, the right of the Christian people to concur in or assent to the call* of a minister, as an essential part of the call. A matter of contention from the Reformation,* it was debated most fully in the context of the Veto Act* prior to the Disruption* in 1843. Substantially, the issue has been one with that of patronage:* the assertion of the rights of patron and heritor* has led to the denial of the rights of the people, and the assertion of the rights of the people has brought calls for the abolition of patronage.

Presbyterians* in Scotland have generally maintained the congregation's right to call its minister and have not limited it to agreement with a call already extended. The *First Book of Discipline** asserts that 'It appertaineth to the people and to every severall Congregation to elect their Minister' (*FBD* 96), and that 'The Admission of Ministers to their offices must consist in consent of the people, and Church whereto they shall be appointed' (*FBD* 101). Care was taken for extraordinary situations in which the people did not act. A destitute church is judged unreasonable if it refuses one 'appointed and approved by the judgement of the godly and learned' and 'should be compelled by the censure of the Councell and Church' to take such a person. But should it even then present a candidate, unless he is judged 'unable', he is to be preferred (*FBD* 98–9).

Acting on this basic principle, the 1562 General Assembly ordained that none continue in the ministry who had not been 'presented be the peiple or ane pairt thereof' (*BUK* I, 27). The *Second Book of Discipline** took essentially the same view, though explicitly assigning to the eldership* a role in choosing a minister: 'Electioun is the chesing out of ane persone or personis maist able to the office that vaikis be the jugement of the eldarschip and consent of the congregatioun quhom to the persone or personis beis appointit' (*SBD* 179).

The 1638 Glasgow Assembly* reasserted the principle 'that no person be intruded in any office of the Kirke contrare to the will of the congregation to which they are appointed' (*AGACS* 26). A similar sentiment was expressed by George Gillespie.* He affirmed that the 'consent (tacit or expressed) of the major or better part of the Congregation' is 'necessarily required to the right vocation of a Pastor' (*A Treatise of Miscellany Questions*, E, 1649, 8–9). The abolition of patronage in 1649 led to the adoption of a Directory which gave the election of the pastor to the session, with the people to acquiesce and consent or dissent. Although the presbytery* was to have opportunity to deal with any 'causeless prejudices' of a majority and to require a minority to show relevant exceptions to the candidate, the congregational right to concur in the call of a pastor was clearly affirmed.

The Restoration* settlement restored patronage and imposed on ministers the obligation of seeking a presentation from the patron in order to retain their charges. Presbyterian objections were not answered until the Revolution, when patronage was again abolished. The call was to be proposed by heritors and elders, with the congregation to approve or disapprove with reasons. In the latter case, the presbytery was to conclude the matter. From contemporary explanatory documents, such as Pardovan's *Collections* and the Large Overtures of 1705, it is clear that in no instance was it expected that settlement would be made without the people's consent.

Parliament's restoration of patronage in 1712 engendered strenuous opposition in the church and considerable efforts were made to have the Act repealed. Throughout this period various works urged the right of the people, including John Currie's* *Jus Populi Divinum; or, The People's Right to Elect their Pastors* (E, 1727). The Secession* and Relief* churches were founded in consequence of the General Assembly's growing inclination to settle pastors against the will of the people. In time, as the Moderates* gained control over the church courts, such settlements became commonplace.

With the evangelical* resurgence of the 1820s and 1830s the question was revived, and the passage of the Veto Act* gave the Christian people the right of declining a presentee for whatever reason. The resultant establishment of the Free Church* left patronage intact in the CofS, but the uniform practice of the free churches in Scotland was the Congregational election of ministers.

With Parliament's passage of the Church Patronage (Scotland) Act, 1874, the right of electing and appointing ministers was vested in the congregation, subject to the regulation of the General Assembly and the reservation of the Assembly's right to 'try the qualifications' of such persons.

Comprehensive regulations governing the call and settlement of ministers were enacted by the General

Assembly in 1932, including provision for a congregational committee and a vote in a congregational meeting.

William Cunningham, *Defence of the Rights of the Christian People in the Appointment of Ministers* (E, 1840); *Select Anti-Patronage Library* (E, 1841); Cox 242-61, 576-80.

D. C. Lachman

Confessions of Faith, formal presentations of Church doctrine, especially those produced during and after the Reformation,* including writings not called 'confessions' (*e.g.* Heidelberg Catechism). Confession as the declaration of distinctive Christian convictions (*e.g.* 'Jesus is Lord') was constitutive of Christianity from its beginnings (cf. 1 Tim. 6:12-13). In the Reformation and post-Reformation eras, confessions commonly served as tests of orthodoxy, as well as distinguishing between different Protestant traditions.

The pre-Reformation Scottish Church acknowledged the credal statements of the rest of the Catholic Church. Of these the Apostles Creed was most clearly retained in the Reformed Church. Its use was provided for in the *Book of Common Order* (1564)* and in the *First Book of Discipline** (cf. *FBD* 184), and it appeared in a metrical version in some seventeenth-century *Psalters** (as it had in both prose and metrical forms in the *Gude and Godlie Ballates**). It served both as an instrument of basic Christian instruction and as a test of orthodox belief (G. D. Henderson, *Scots Confession*, E, 1937, 13-14). Its use was deliberately abandoned by the Westminster Assembly;* it was merely appended to the Shorter Catechism as 'a brief sum of the Christian faith, agreeable to the word of God, and anciently received in the churches of Christ'. Its reintroduction was the work of the nineteenth-century 'liturgical revolution' spearheaded by the Church Service Society* and its ilk. Hence it was included in the *Euchologion** of 1867, and has had a secure place in the various twentieth-century versions of the *BCO*,* as well as in the *Church Hymnary** from 1898.

The Nicene Creed appears in the 1940 *BCO* in the main order for the Lord's Supper, but although the early Reformed Church's adherence to the doctrine of this and other patristic creeds was never in doubt, it made no provision for the use of the Nicene Creed. Even in the modern CofS it enjoys only marginal usage.

Of the Reformation confessions acknowledged in Scotland a unique place belongs to the Confession of Faith drawn up by John Knox* and colleagues, known as the Scots Confession,* which was approved by Parliament in 1560. It remained the official confession of the Reformed Kirk until superseded by the Westminster Confession of Faith in 1647. Both Confessions clearly declared that they were provisional in character, and were in no sense to be thought of as supplying infallible compilations and interpretations of the faith. They were human products, and as such were open to revision and rejection when shown to be out of step with the Church's supreme standard, the Word of God. This is made clear in the justly famous preface to the Scots Confession, and in equally plain language in the opening chapter of the Westminster Confession, as well as in its unequivocal statement that 'God alone is Lord of the conscience'.

William Dunlop,* Professor of Church History in Edinburgh University, in the preliminary dissertation to his *Collection of Confessions of Faith*, highlighted three main purposes of 'such human composures'. First, they give a faithful account of Christian doctrine to the world. Second, they provide a standard of orthodoxy and a test for office-bearers. Third, they provide members of the Church with a useful summary of the faith. Philip Schaff (in his standard compilation of the *Creeds of Christendom*) adds a fourth use for creeds and confessions; they act as guards against false doctrine and practice (a use that was taken seriously by the Reformed CofS). James Bannerman* drew attention to the necessity of such human compilations: 'The unity of the Church as a society of believers requires and justifies human compilations of divine truth, if it is to be really a unity of faith and not merely a unity of form or formal words' (*The Church of Christ*, E, 1868, II, 298).

The Scots Confession was not the sole confession to feature in the Scottish Reformation and subsequent struggles. 1548 saw the publication of George Wishart's* translation of the First Swiss (Helvetic) Confession (ed. D. Laing, *The Miscellany of the Wodrow Society* I, E, 1844, 1-23), which was agreed in 1536 as the common confession of the Swiss Protestant cities. The new *BCO* (1564), which was largely an import from the English-speaking congregation in Geneva, included an English version of John Calvin's French Catechism of 1541. *FBD* prescribed its use in school and church (*FBD* 130f., 182), and it was printed with the *BCO* almost without exception until the early seventeenth century.

The *BCO* (1564) also included the Confession of Faith of the early days of the Genevan Reformation (1536), although this was never formally approved in Scotland except as part of the *BCO*. The Second Helvetic Confession, however, composed by Heinrich Bullinger in 1561 and adopted in 1566, was approved by the General Assembly in the same year after careful scrutiny. Only on the observance of the festivals of the Christian Year* did the Scots enter a reservation (Knox, *History* II, 190; *Works* VI, 544-50). This was perhaps the most mature of all the Reformation confessions (it included, for example, an explicit acknowledgement of the patristic creeds). A translation by Robert Pont* was ordered to be published, but no copy has survived – if indeed the printing took place. The Glasgow Assembly* of 1638 reaffirmed the Kirk's recognition of the Second Helvetic Confession.

Apart perhaps from the Westminster Shorter Catechism, the Heidelberg Catechism of 1563 enjoys the widest acceptance among Reformed catechisms. An English rendering of its Latin version, with accompanying notes, was issued by the authority of James VI* for the use of the CofS in 1591,

CONFESSIONS OF FAITH

and again in 1615. In Scotland it was often known as the Palatine Catechism and bound up with copies of the *BCO* and the *Psalter*.

The Reformer John Craig* was the compiler of the King's Confession* of 1581, so called because drawn up at the behest of, and first signed by, James VI. It was known also as the Negative Confession (from its strongly anti-Roman flavour) or the Second Confession of Faith (after the Scots Confession, the first, which it explicitly endorsed) or misleadingly as the National Covenant, for it formed the first of the three sections of the National Covenant* of 1638. Craig also composed a widely used Catechism often published along with the King's Confession.

In 1616, during the years of episcopal control of the CofS, the General Assembly at Aberdeen commissioned and approved a 'new Confession of Faith' (*BUK* III, 1132-3; Calderwood VII, 233-42). Largely the work of Robert Howie,* it enjoyed some authority until repealed by the 1638 Glasgow Assembly.* Although less stridently denunciatory than the Scots Confession, it was more unambiguously Calvinist, but its origins and subjection of the Church to the state ensured sparse recognition.

By its approval at the General Assembly of 1647 the Westminster* Confession became the subordinate standard of the Kirk, a position which it has retained to the present day. From 1661, following the Restoration* of Charles II,* until the re-establishment of Presbyterianism in 1690, Westminster Confession lost its official status, which by implication was regained by the Scots Confession. (It was certainly the basis of the Test Act of 1681.) But in usage the Confession (as it came to be often called, without qualification) remained the norm in the life of the churchpeople of Scotland.

It also continued to be, as it is still today, the subordinate doctrinal standard of all the other Presbyterian Churches in Scotland. Yet the parties from whom, and the occasions on which, and the terms under which, subscription* to the Confession has been required have undergone far-reaching and often controvesial changes (*see especially* Declaratory Acts). Moreover, the dissenting Presbyterian bodies have in nearly all cases approved statements, often known as testimonies,* giving expression to their own distinctive convictions and reasons for separation, whether from the Establishment or from one another. Thus in 1851 the FC General Assembly authorized the publication of the Church's 'subordinate standards, and other authoritative documents', which included, in addition to all the Westminster formularies, 'The Confession of Faith of the Kirk of Scotland: or, The National Covenant' (*i.e.* including the King's Confession) and the Solemn League and Covenant* of 1643.

Within the national Church, as earlier in the UFC, calls for the revision or more often the replacement of the Westminster Confession have sounded loud and long (cf. *Creed Revision in Scotland: its Necessity and Scope*, G, 1907). Attempts have been made to promote the first of the Declaratory Articles* as a kind of substitute, but they have fared no better than efforts at drafting a new statement. While the reasons for these failures are obvious enough – not least the doctrinal confusion and pluralism in the CofS – their price has been the perpetuation of a serious vacuum in the Kirk's confessional identity.

See also Catechisms; Subscription, Confessional.

C. G. M'Crie, *The Confessions of the Church of Scotland* (E, 1907); T. F. Torrance, *The School of Faith: The Catechisms of the Reformed Church* (L, 1959); H. Bonar, *Catechisms of the Scottish Reformation* (L, 1866); A. T. Innes, *The Law of Creeds in Scotland* (E, L, 1867); W. A. Curtis, *A History of the Creeds and Confessions of Faith* (E, 1911).

D. F. Wright and I. Hamilton

Confirmation, an ambiguous post-baptismal rite that developed in the medieval Church. It originated in the separation of one part of early Christian baptism – laying on of hands, with or without anointing (chrism) – and its reservation, in the West, for the bishop alone. This occurred for pragmatic, non-theological reasons, and the resultant ceremony (known as *confirmatio* from the fifth century) has always been a 'rite in search of theology'. It came to be associated with the giving of the Spirit (which in the New Testament belongs with baptism) and viewed as the 'completion' of baptism. Though regarded as one of the seven sacraments,* it did not always precede admission to Communion.

The Continental Reformers abandoned the late medieval rite (which centred on episcopal anointing). A fresh evangelical approach was developed (especially by Martin Bucer at Strasbourg, building on initiatives among Hussites and Waldensians picked up by Erasmus), and was propagated influentially by Calvin (*Institutes* 4:19:4-13 – with some erroneous reading of the rite back into the early Church). Confirmation became an occasion when those baptized in infancy, after instruction in the faith (*see* Catechisms; Catechizing), came forward to answer for themselves and, if satisfactory, might receive laying on of hands as a pastoral blessing and thereafter be eligible to share in the Lord's Supper.

The Scottish Reformers made only informal provision for the examination of the baptized prior to their first admission to the Supper. The *First Book of Discipline** merely asserted 'We think that none are to be admitted to this Mysterie who can not formally say the Lords prayer, the Articles of the Beliefe and declare the summe of the Law' (*FBD* 184). This in time developed into a service of admission* to the Lord's Supper.

Although the Five Articles of Perth,* William Cowper's* draft liturgy and Laud's* Liturgy all prescribed an order for confirmation akin to that in the *Book of Common Prayer*, evidence for confirmation by bishops in the seventeenth-century Kirk is lacking.

It was eventually the Scoto-Catholic* party that introduced 'confirmation' into CofS usage. The second edition of the *Euchologion** (1869) contained

'An Order for the Confirmation of Baptismal Vows and Admission to the Lord's Table', which by the 1940 *BCO** had become an 'Order for the Confirmation of Baptised Persons ...'. The titles reflect the confusion of Anglican practice, *e.g.* on whether the object of 'confirm' is the baptized, baptism, or baptismal promises (and hence whether God, the minister or the candidate 'confirms'). The 1940 order suggests the raising of the minister's hand in blessing over candidates as an alternative to laying on of hands.

In ecumenical discussions involving the CofS and Episcopalians, the traditional Anglican requirement of episcopal confirmation before admission to Communion has inevitably been raised (*Relations between Anglican and Presbyterian Churches*, L, 1958, 15; *The Anglican–Presbyterian Conversations*, E, L, 1966, 29). Anglicans increasingly regard confirmation as a domestic rite and stress that sacramental initiation is completed in baptism. In such a context, the infiltration of the language and even the practice of confirmation into the CofS in the last century or so is the source of regrettable confusion.

W. McMillan, *The Worship of the Scottish Reformed Church, 1550–1638* (L, 1931), 229–32; J. D. C. Fisher, *Christian Initiation: the Reformation Period* (L, 1970); J. M. Barkley, *The Worship of the Reformed Church* (L, 1966), 114–25.

D. F. Wright

Congregation, Lords of the, nobles and lords who came together at the Reformation* to effect a revolution against France and Rome. Hopes of incipient revolution were entertained as early as 1557 when a group of nobles, who invited John Knox* to return home from Geneva, organized themselves by drawing up their first band or covenant during December 1557, in which they promised to 'set forward and establish the most blessed Word of God and his Congregation', sustain and defend their ministers and to renounce Catholicism, 'the Congregation of Satan with all the superstition, abomination and idolatry thereof'. The signatories comprised the fourth Earl of Argyll and his son Lord Lorne (*see* Campbell, Archibald, *d.* 1573), the Earls of Glencairn* and Morton (*see* Douglas, James), and Erskine of Dun.* This was followed by a programme for reformed worship proposed by the 'lords and barons professing Christ Jesus', which provided for reading Edward VI's *Book of Common Prayer** weekly in every parish church and for Protestant preaching in private. By November 1558, the Protestants petitioned the Queen Regent, Mary of Guise,* for reading the common prayers in the vernacular, for interpreting Scripture by godly and learned persons, for baptism and the Lord's Supper (in both kinds) to be ministered in the vernacular, and for a reform of the clergy. When Mary of Guise suppressed their letter to Parliament attacking the hierarchy, the Congregation presented a 'protestation' to Parliament in December 1558 in favour of 'the reformation of abuses in religion only'. By May 1559, a fresh band was drawn up at Perth for the defence of Protestantism by 'the Congregations of the West Country with the Congregations of Fife, Perth, Dundee, Angus, Mearns and Montrose', and was signed by Argyll, Lord James Stewart (*d.*1570),* Glencairn, Lords Boyd and Ochiltree and Campbell of Loudoun.

As the Congregation began to mobilize its forces in defence of its preachers, churches were purged and religious houses attacked. The army of the Congregation had come into being to oppose the French forces of Mary of Guise. Further bands for the defence of Protestantism were concluded by the Congregation in August 1559 at Stirling and in April 1560 at Leith, where the insurgents counted among the signatories the Duke of Châtelherault,* his son the Earl of Arran (*see* Hamilton, James *d.*1609), the Earls of Argyll, Huntly, Glencairn, Rothes, Morton and Menteith, Lord James Stewart, Lords Ruthven, Boyd, Ogilvie, Ochiltree, Herries and Somerville, Lindsay of the Byres, the Bishop of Galloway and numerous lairds. As early as October 1559, the Lords of the Congregation had felt strong enough to 'depose' Mary of Guise from the regency, but the transfer of power to a Protestant government was fully effected only after English intervention in January 1560 and the death of the Queen Regent in June 1560. By July, the Treaty of Edinburgh provided for the withdrawal of English and French forces from Scotland, though the French commissioners refused to negotiate with the Lords of the Congregation, whom they regarded as rebels. The new provisional government, or 'great council of the realm', with Chatelherault at its head, was dominated by the Lords of the Congregation and functioned until Queen Mary's return from France in August 1561. With peace proclaimed in July 1560, a public thanksgiving was held at St Giles in Edinburgh, attended by 'the greatest part of the Congregation'. During the period when the Lords were temporarily in control, arrangements were made for nominating ministers to various charges, Parliament was petitioned, a Confession of Faith (*see* Scots Confession) approved by the Reformation Parliament,* and the *First Book of Discipline*,* drafted during 1560, was subscribed (with some qualifications on finance) in January 1561 by Châtelherault, Argyll, Rothes, Glencairn, Lord James Stewart, Lords Boyd, Crichton and Yester, the Bishop of Galloway, the Dean of Moray, the Abbot of Culross and a number of prominent lairds.

Knox, *History*; *Calendar of State Papers relating to Scotland and Mary, Queen of Scots*, ed. J. Bain, I (E, 1898).

J. Kirk

Congregational Board, a body managing the temporal business of a congregation in the CofS. The board is composed of the minister, all the elders or a number of them, and members of the congregation to a number equal to that of the elders serving on the board, elected at a congregational meeting. The minister is chairman *ex officio*, but if he or she declines to accept office the board elects one of its members. Its constitution is known as the 'Model Constitution', adopted by the General Assembly following the union of 1929. This replaced more complex arrangements in the CofS under the New Parishes (Scotland) Act, 1844. Parishes *quoad sacra** created under this Act were subject to control by the Court of Teinds* in the management of their property, but the changes brought about by the CofS (Property and Endowments) Act, 1925, vested such property in the General Trustees* and removed it from any kind of state control. The board appoints a clerk and a treasurer and is responsible for the management of the congregation's property and finances. Several other forms of constitution exist within the CofS, but the General Assembly has encouraged congregations to adopt this one. It has been modified from time to time in respect of accounting methods, etc., but not substantially amended. Some 1,500 constitutions have been issued since 1931 by the Delegations of Assembly appointed for this purpose. Due to readjustment, these are not all still in existence, but this is now the form in which the majority of congregations manage their temporal affairs.

RSCS 1828, 1054–7; Cox, 39–46, 610–17.

J. L. Weatherhead

Congregational Union of Scotland, a supportive confraternity of churches of Congregational* polity. It was formed in November 1812, out of the uncertainty caused among Scottish Congregationalists in 1808 by the withdrawal of the Haldane* brothers. Originating in Musselburgh, the suggestion for a union of Congregational churches crystallized in Edinburgh's Thistle Street Chapel when George Payne and John Watson* of Dalkeith, one of the fifth class (1803) of Robert Haldane's Seminary, became joint secretaries of a Union whose objects, focused in an annual meeting, were church aid and home mission. Fifty-five churches joined it. By 1822 their number was seventy-two, by 1896 ninety-six.

Constituted to avoid division in the aftermath of a disruptive controversy over baptism,* the Union's closest subsequent brush with it came in 1844, when seven of the nine students disciplined by Glasgow Theological Academy for advocating universal atonement* applied for Union recognition. They failed, but the conservative Lindsay Alexander's* masterly phraseology allowed the Union to stand aside from further involvement in doctrinal differences among member churches, a stance underlined in 1848 by the express statement that the Union was not 'in any sense, an ecclesiastical court or corporation'. It was, rather, a confraternity of churches 'in fellowship with each other'. Expressed thus in 1857, and again in 1873, their voting membership was regulated in 1878 and their admission – or separation – in 1883.

In 1896 the Congregational Union and the Evangelical Union* merged. The reconstituted Congregational Union of Scotland became responsible for home and foreign mission, ministerial and chapel-building funds, temperance,* publications, youth,

and church aid. (Only the united Theological Hall remained separate, for legal reasons.) It was thus a more significant denominational force than its predecessor, and the secretaryship of Charles Richardson* (1900–18, 1924–41) confirmed this. There was more sustained comment on social matters: the Temperance Committee evolved into the Temperance and Social Questions Committee. The role of women,* at issue from the 1890s, was expressed in the Women's Christian Union formed in 1898 (it was integrated into the Union in 1919), in the increasing number of women delegates (four in 1910, 162 – over half – in 1955), and in the ordination of Scotland's first woman minister in a mainstream Church, Vera Findlay* (1929). Six more Congregational women were ordained to Scottish pastorates in the next thirty years.

From 1924 the Union secretaryship was salaried. From 1934 there was an office (Bath Street, Glasgow, later West George Street). Economic exigencies also raised the Union's profile: church extension and ministerial settlement became increasingly Union concerns. So did strategic fundraising. The Central Fund, mooted in 1910, accepted in 1916 (prompted by the fact that in the Union's 180 churches seventy pastors received 150 at most), reached its enhanced target of £50,000 in 1926. Later funds had greater difficulty.

This provoked questions about the Union's separate role. Did the future lie with English Congregationalism (there were joint assemblies at Manchester in 1901 and Glasgow in 1902), or with the reunited CofS? Hence the Union's support from 1926 for the Scottish Churches Council, its commission into the Witness of Congregationalism (1932–3), its Ecumenical Committee (1945), issuing in a Statement of Belief (1949), and its participation since 1960 in a succession of conversations about unity with the CofS, URC and UFC. The most recent of these was with the United Reformed Church,* which had Scottish congregations. This scheme failed in 1988; although it gained majority support this fell short of the legal requirement of seventy-five per cent. Ironically, such conversations, although prompted by the Union's small size (12,000 members in ninety-six charges served by sixty-three ministers out of a ministerial roll of seventy-five), were hindered by a double disparity: numerical-cultural in the case of the CofS and cultural-national in that of the URC.

H. Escott, *A History of Scottish Congregationalism* (G, 1960); W. D. McNaughton, *The Scottish Congregational Ministry from 1794 to 1993* (G, 1993).

J. C. G. Binfield

Congregationalism, a form of church polity encapsulating the autonomy of duly constituted gathered congregations of believers. Regulated by church members' and deacons' meetings, and with varying emphases, their inspiration is biblical, their ancestry Calvinist,* their bias liberal evangelical. Their Scottish denominational expression is nineteenth-century, with a dual pre-history.

CONGREGATIONALISM

Congregationalism's first pre-history consists of visits by the Englishman Robert Browne (1583-4), and the Welshman John Penry (1589-90); and evidence of gathered congregations in 1624 and again in the 1650s, under the Cromwellian* impact. These left no posterity, although the letter (24 May 1652) of the future Quaker,* Provost Jaffray* of Aberdeen, has been called 'the first manifesto of Congregationalism in Scotland promulgated by Scots'.

Its second, entirely Scottish, pre-history bred a tenuous posterity from three eighteenth-century developments: the Glasites, the Old Scots Independents* and the Bereans. Each was biblically inspired, independent in polity, congenitally fissiparous (especially about baptism*), fired by distinctive personalities, and non-evangelistic but with some impact in England. John Glas* (1695-1773), though called 'the Father of Scottish Congregationalism', influenced it more through his writings, voluntaryism* and hymnody than through the dozen or so Glasite congregations or his emphases on weekly communion and plurality of elders (see Laity). With similar views, the Old Scots Independents, shaped by two Fifeshire ministers, James Smith* and Robert Ferrier,* reached a congregational position in 1768. Though best known through David Dale* (1739-1806) of New Lanark, the 'Benevolent Magistrate' who ministered to their Greyfriars Wynd church, Glasgow, their influence is traceable in the origins of Ward Chapel, Dundee. The Bereans began when John Barclay* (1734-98) left the CofS in 1773. They were extinct by the 1840s, although their mother church, Sauchieburn, Kincardineshire, was Congregational by 1809.

Congregationalism's mainstream, however, issues from the revival* generated between 1797 and 1808 by Robert and James Haldane.* Its impetus was evangelistic; a congregational polity developed in pragmatic consequence. From 1798 preaching centres similar to George Whitefield's* Tabernacles were opened in the major towns. In December 1798 the Haldanes' ablest coadjutor, Greville Ewing,* left the CofS. The following January he drafted the constitution for the Congregational church which moved in 1801 to Leith Walk, Edinburgh, under Robert Haldane's ministry. In August 1800 Ewing formed a church in Glasgow. Dundee followed in October. Other congregations, unconnected with the Haldanes, became associated with these churches. By 1800 there were fourteen; by 1807, eight-five. They were fused by Ewing's statesmanship, the Haldanes' evangelism and money, and a swift strategy for ministerial training.

The Haldanes, Congregationalists by circumstance rather than conviction, became Baptists* in 1808. Their churches split. Paedobaptist Congregationalism, however, was conserved through the institution in 1811 of the Glasgow Theological Academy and in 1812 of the Congregational Union.* The former, with Ewing and Ralph Wardlaw* as tutors, combined academic study and evangelism. The latter immediately attracted fifty-five churches.

Thus Congregationalism survived throughout Scotland, although most strongly in industrial areas. It was moderately Calvinistic (see Calvinism, Moderate), braced by revival in 1839 and by the theory of voluntaryism. The movement was jolted by the Disruption* of 1843 (having originally attracted many who were subsequently drawn to the FC) and by the controversy over universal atonement* caused within Congregationalism by John Kirk* of Hamilton and outside it by James Morison* of Kilmarnock. The chief result was the Evangelical Union,* formed in 1843. Nine of its thirteen founder churches were Congregational. While its partly United Secession* ancestry was reflected in its stronger Conference (which ordained its ministers and originated its agencies), it recognized congregational autonomy: each church was 'complete within itself'. For over fifty years these two denominations coexisted, geographically close, and increasingly sharing theology and polity as well as emphases in ministerial training, hymnody and social witness.

By mid-century Congregationalists had notably influential churches in Edinburgh and Dundee as well as their heartland, Glasgow. Ewing, Wardlaw and W. L. Alexander* were nationally known. The next generations – John and William Pulsford, John Hunter* – were fully their equals. Congregational agencies were well-established. *The Missionary Magazine* (1796), which became *The Scottish Congregationalist* after successive changes of name, was one of Britain's oldest religious periodicals. The college moved to Edinburgh in 1855, with premises in George Square from 1884.

Yet outsiders saw Scottish Congregationalism in an English shadow. Its overseas missionaries (see Livingstone, David; Legge, James; Gilmour, James; Chalmers, James) served the London Missionary Society,* English ministers occupied key Scottish pulpits, and English colleges attracted key Scottish scholars: P. T. Forsyth,* A. E. Garvie,* A. J. Grieve, C. S. Duthie and, from the Evangelical Union, A. M. Fairbairn.*

But Scottish Congregationalism was neither an English nor a Presbyterian mutant, and its distinctiveness was confirmed by the markedly successful merger, mooted from 1866 and consummated in 1896, of the Congregational and Evangelical Unions. Thereafter Scottish Congregationalism shared the history of its reconstituted Congregational Union, its role at once shaped by the seminal secretaryship of Charles Richardson* (1900-18, 1924-41) and questioned by the cumulative impact of war (7,000 from Congregational churches in the armed forces by late 1915), economic recession and ecumenism.* In 1929, during the Edinburgh International Congregational Council, J. D. Jones of Bournemouth raised the question of union with English Congregationalism. The response was dusty, and the issue was little nearer solution in 1986-7, when talks were held with English Congregationalism's largest successor, the United Reformed Church* (which had Scottish congregations of its own). For some the Scottish solution lay, if at all, in union with the CofS, whose very size and cultural hegemony has so far precluded any union on terms of parity.

H. Escott, *A History of Scottish Congregationalism* (G, 1960); W. D. McNaughton, *The Scottish Congregational Ministry from 1794 to 1993* (G, 1993).

J. C. G. Binfield

Conn, George (*c*.1598–1640), papal agent at the court of Charles I.* Born in Aberdeenshire the son of Patrick Conn of Auchry, he was educated at Douai, Paris, Rome and Bologna; certainly he was at the Scots College,* Rome, in 1619. He became tutor to the family of the Duke of Mirandola and then a member of the households of Cardinals Montalto and Francis Barberini. The latter was nephew of Pope Urban VIII, papal secretary of state and Cardinal Protector of Scotland and England. Conn took part in papal embassies to Paris and Spain and in 1629 became 'Latin secretary' (an important post) to Barberini. Having chosen the clerical state, he received major orders, although was never ordained priest, and was a canon of San Lorenzo in Damaso, Rome. He was familiar with Galileo and the Dominican philosopher, Tommaso Campanella (1568–1639). He published four works of controversy. *Praemetiae* (first-fruits) against the Irish (1621) is informative on his Scots contemporaries. It was followed by a life of Mary Stuart in 1624 and books of religious controversy in 1628 and 1629.

From 1633 the English court petitioned Rome to make Conn a cardinal and in 1636 he was sent to London as papal agent, technically on a mission to Charles I's RC Queen, Henrietta Maria. Over the next three years he was very influential and did much to alleviate the lot of English RCs, but was not successful in his major political objectives. This is apparently the reason for his never being in fact made cardinal. Conn never enjoyed good health. In late 1639 he returned to Rome, where he died and was buried in San Lorenzo in Damaso.

DNB XII, 20–1; G. Albion, *Charles I and the Court of Rome* (L, 1935); D. J. Harran, *The Catholics in Caroline England* (Stanford, 1962); E. Dubois, 'Un Ecossais, Légat à la Cour d'Angleterre; George Conn (1636–1640)', *Revue d'Histoire Diplomatique* 1–2 (1985), 5–20; T. Dempster, *Historia Ecclesiastica Gentis Scotorum* (E, 1829), 170–2.

J. Durkan

Constitutionalists, FC anti-Union party. The term 'Constitutionalist' was coined in the FC in the 1860s to describe the party which opposed union with the UPC on the ground that it was disallowed by the terms of the FC constitution. Led by James Begg* and including James Buchanan,* George Smeaton,* Hugh Martin,* John Kennedy,* the Bonar brothers,* and Alexander Moody Stuart,* they were successful in resisting the union though always in a minority. As the century progressed they lent their strength to opposing what they viewed as further violations of the Church's constitution: the disestablishment* campaign; the introduction of hymns and instrumental music (though the Bonars did not join in opposing these) (*see also* Musical Instruments in Worship); the acceptance of biblical criticism;* and the adjustment of the Church's Confessional position. Their numbers dwindled, however, and by the time the Declaratory Act* was passed in 1892, the Constitutionalists were a spent force in much of the country. Only in the Highlands did they retain popular support and there they were split between those who separated from the FC on account of the Declaratory Act, and those who separated seven years later on account of the 1900 Union (*see* Unions, Church, in Scotland). The former organized themselves as the FPC, the latter as the continuing FC. Between them they provided a lasting home for Constitutionalism.

The Constitutionalists held that the written constitution is supreme in church law. The General Assembly had administrative authority from which there is no appeal, but no majority of the supreme court has the right to alter the constitution. Should even an overwhelming majority wish to amend the constitution, they can do so only by founding a new church; the name and patrimony of the existing body belong to those who adhere to the original constitution. In support of this theory, Constitutionalists appealed to the terms of ordination vows, Assembly Commissions and the Treaty of Union, all of which appeared to enshrine loyalty to the existing constitution as a condition of office. It is possible that the constitution itself should provide for alteration and adjustment, but the Constitutionalists rejected the Unionist argument that this was so in the case of the FC. Furthermore, they held to the belief that whatever the Church had confessed to be scriptural was henceforth constitutional. The consuetude of the Church, in large measure, they held to be constitutionally binding. The Constitutionalist position did not appear to allow for *any* change in the Church's doctrine or practice.

See also Free Church of Scotland, 1843–1900; Free Church Case.

H. Bonar, *Statement Explanatory and Defensive* (E, 1867); J. Begg, *Memorial in regard to the Constitution of the Free Church of Scotland* (E, 1874); J. Gibson, *The Union Question* (G, 1870); J. Kennedy, *Unionism and the Union* (E, 1870); *The Watchword* (1866–73); *The Signal* (1881–9); N. L. Walker, *Robert Buchanan* (L, 1877); A. Stewart and J. K. Cameron, *The Free Church of Scotland 1843–1910* (E, 1910); P. C. Simpson, *The Life of Principal Rainy* (L, 1909); K. R. Ross, *Church and Creed in Scotland* (E, 1988).

K. R. Ross

Conventicles, unofficial and often illegal gatherings for worship. Originating in the Latin *conventiculum*, the conventicle in early Christianity was often no more than a synonym for 'church', and only gradually came to denote a meeting of religious dissenters. In 1624 Sir George Hay, Chancellor of Scotland, defined a conventicle as 'a private meeting of men and women to a private religious exercise in time of public sermon'. In Scotland, legislation against such gatherings was passed after the Restoration* of Charles II.* In December 1665 a proclamation against conventicles called them 'the ordinary seminaries of separation and rebellion' that threatened to undo Church and kingdom, and banned them under pain of fine, imprisonment, or corporal punishment. A second Act in July 1670, at a time when conventicles were increasing, charged all to reveal on oath whatever they knew about such meetings and those who frequented them. Any parent whose child was unbaptized by the 'curate' of the parish could be fined one-quarter of his annual income, and other severe penalties were both threatened and implemented. The Covenanters* took to meeting on hills and moors, and such 'field conventicles' became common and influential. One assembly in Carrick drew 7,000 people and 600 men in arms. Their worship was conducted after the Presbyterian manner, baptism was administered, Communion dispensed. In April 1681 a further proclamation decreed that death and the confiscation of goods was to be the punishment for preaching at field conventicles. In 1687 a letter of James VII* to the Scottish Privy Council urged that 'those enemies of Christianity' should be rooted out 'with the most rigorous prosecution of our forces'. Though earlier punctuated by offers of 'Indulgence',* the repressive campaign in the 1680s came to be known accurately as 'The Killing Times'.* It is said that some 18,000 people suffered in various ways for attendance at conventicles. Yet antinomianism had no part in their religious or political stance: the laws of the land were to be obeyed so far as conscience would allow, and active opposition to the magistrate was not lightly undertaken. In the words of Robert MacWard,* 'We never laid any ground for excess on the right hand, while we pleaded against evils on the left.' Those evils, supplemented latterly by a RC King in Reformed Scotland, continued until religious liberty was won after the flight of James VII in December 1688 and the advent of the Protestant William of Orange (see William II).

J. K. Hewison, *The Covenanters*, 2 vols (G, ²1913); A. Smellie, *Men of the Covenant* (L, 1909); *ERE* IV, 102–4; D. Stevenson, 'Conventicles in the Kirk, 1619–37', *RSCHS* 18 (1973), 99–114.

J. D. Douglas

Conventions, religious gatherings. From the 1880s on there have been several conventions in Scotland for the deepening of the spiritual life. They have been closely associated with the Keswick Convention in the English Lake District, whose teaching on sanctification by faith has been expounded by such Scottish speakers as Graham Scroggie.* A number of conventions on broader themes of Christian life and work prepared the way. From 1863 to 1868 there was a conference for Christian workers at Perth promoted by John Milne, a FC minister (*AFCS* I, 270). There were others in 1874 in Glasgow (addressed by D. L. Moody*) and Aberdeen.

The first annual Keswick-style convention in Scotland was organized in Edinburgh intermittently from 1881. Others followed in Glasgow (apparently from 1882), at Park Hall, Polmont, W. Lothian (from 1882), in Dundee (from 1890) and in Aberdeen (from 1891). The normal pattern was a sequence of addresses over several days urging greater consecration. Laymen prominent in the sponsorship of conventions included William Sloan, the son of a Glasgow shipowner, and Thomas Livingstone-Learmonth, who had bought Park Hall with a fortune from Australian sheepfarming. Ministers participated in the meetings but also organized their own denominational retreats to concentrate on the same teaching. UPs held retreats at Perth and then Bridge of Allan (near Stirling) from 1887 to 1899, once drawing 250 ministers. From 1900 they merged with the FC equivalent meeting at Dunblane. There was a similar CofS annual gathering in Edinburgh before the First World War, though its ethos was less distinctly shaped by Keswick.

From 1892 there was a 'Scottish National Convention' at Bridge of Allan. Held in June each year, its first convener was W. D. Moffat, an Edinburgh UP minister (Small I, 480, II, 710; *FUFCS* 18), and its committee included Lord Overtoun, the FC chemical manufacturer (*see* White, John Campbell). There was a regular choir and a fringe of house parties, often connected with overseas missions. The speakers were commonly the best known names in the international Keswick movement, such as F. B. Meyer and Andrew Murray.* In 1915 meetings were transferred to Crieff, Perthshire, where they continued for some years.

The 'Scottish Northern Convention' began at Strathpeffer, north of Inverness, in 1931. H. W. Oldham (*FUFCS* 485), UF minister in Tain and a man of great erudition and piety, launched the annual gatherings in co-operation with his father-in-law, R. B. Stewart, a Glasgow lawyer and chairman of the Keswick Council. Like Bridge of Allan, Strathpeffer was a spa town providing both accommodation and an atmosphere of retirement from the world. The convention, launched at a time of economic depression and explicitly modelled on Keswick, was held each September until it was suspended at the outbreak of the Second World War. It was resumed in 1949 and continues to the present day. Although there have been Keswick meetings in Edinburgh during recent years, Strathpeffer has long been the chief bastion of its distinctive holiness teaching in Scotland, under its banner 'All One in Christ' and with strong links also with the Protestant Convention in N. Ireland. Perth also hosts an annual convention.

N. C. Macfarlane, *Scotland's Keswick* (L, n.d.); A. MacVicar, *Scottish Northern Convention Jubilee* (n.p., 1981); H. Bonar, *Life of the Rev. John Milne of Perth* (L, 1868).

D. W. Bebbington and J. Buchan

Convocation, 1842, Non-Intrusionist* preparation for the Disruption.* As conflict between Church and state intensified, Thomas Chalmers* called a convocation of evangelical CofS ministers to meet in Edinburgh on 17 November, 1842. Not only did the convocation reject the claim of superiority over church courts involved in a recent decision of the civil courts, but 354 ministers pledged themselves to quit the Establishment if the state did not recognize the independent jurisdiction of the Church. Chalmers unveiled his ambitious plans for the organization and financing of the new 'Free Church'. The decision was presented as heartily unanimous, but it was later revealed that it was only after arguing with force for a stronger effort to retain Establishment that James Begg* fell in line with the majority. The minutes were recently discovered in the attic of the FC College, Edinburgh, and are currently being prepared for publication.

See also Ten Years' Conflict.

W. Wilson and R. Rainy, *Memorials of Robert Smith Candlish* (E, 1880), 219–59; R. Buchanan, *The Ten Years' Conflict* (L, 1849), II, 534–51.

K. R. Ross

Cook, Archibald (1789–1865) and **Finlay** (1778–1858), CofS and later FC ministers. Sons of Charles Cook, farmer in Glenscorradale, Arran, they came to faith during the revival* in Arran under the ministry of Neil MacBride* c.1812. Both studied at Glasgow University. As a student, Finlay was employed as a summer missionary at the Lanark Cotton Mills of Robert Owen. He was ordained to Achreny Mission, Halkirk (*see* Royal Bounty) in 1817, and translated to Cross, Lewis, in 1829; thereafter he served in Inverness East (1833–5) and Reay, Caithness (1835–58). Archibald was ordained as missionary-minister at Berriedale and Bruan, Caithness, in 1823, ministering subsequently at Inverness North (1837–44) and Daviot, Inverness-shire (1844–65). Both signed the Act of Separation and came out at the Disruption.*

The Cook brothers were well known for their down-to-earth and unpretentious evangelical ministries. They held their convictions firmly, even crossing swords with 'The Men'.* Finlay lost the support of two of the 'Men' in his parish when he joined the FC, while Archibald, holding traducian views of the origin of the soul (*i.e.* that it originated from procreation by parents) clashed with Joseph Mackay. Archibald was an eloquent preacher, and his sermons were later published individually and in collections (J. R. Mackay, ed., *Sermons: Gaelic and English*, G, 1907).

FES VII, 112, 134, 201; *AFCS* I, 124; A. Auld, *Ministers and Men of the Far North* (Wick, 1868), 100–33, with specimens of sermons 287–344; D. Beaton, *Some Noted Ministers of the Northern Highlands* (^{3}G, 1985).

D. E. Meek

Cook, George (1772–1845), Moderate* divine and church historian. Cook led the opposition to Thomas Chalmers* during the Ten Years' Conflict* which preceded the Disruption.* His advancement in the CofS owed as much to his connection with the Hill family (he was a nephew of George Hill*) as to his own considerable abilities. He was presented by the Principal and Masters of St Mary's College, St Andrews, to the parish of Laurencekirk (Kincardineshire) and ordained there in 1795. He was appointed to the Chair of Moral Philosophy at St Andrews in 1829 in succession to Chalmers and in preference to Thomas Carlyle.* It has, however, been suggested (by T. M. Knox, a twentieth-century successor in the chair) that Cook probably had a better acquaintance with the literature of philosophy proper than Carlyle.

Cook succeeded George Hill as leader of the Moderate party in the General Assembly, but was regarded with some distrust by many Moderates because of his stand against pluralities, the simultaneous holding of a chair and a parochial living. After two unsuccessful attempts he was elected Moderator of the General Assembly in 1825. Although no match for Chalmers in oratory, he consistently opposed the policies which led to the Ten Years' Conflict between Church and state.

His historical writings are clear and accurate but otherwise undistinguished. He also wrote the biography of his uncle, George Hill.

History of the Reformation in Scotland, 3 vols (E, 1811, ^{2}1819); *History of the Church of Scotland*, 3 vols (E, 1815); *Life of George Hill* (E, 1820); *A General and Historical View of Christianity* (E, 1822).

DNB XII, 65–6; *FES* V, 477–8.

H. R. Sefton

Cook, John (1807–74), Moderate* divine and churchman. The son of George Cook,* he was educated at St Andrews University, licensed in 1828 by the Presbytery of Fordoun and ordained and inducted to Cults, Fife, in 1832. He was translated to Haddington, serving the second charge 1833–43 and the first 1843–74.

He was keenly interested in education and published several pamphlets on the various government proposals for reform 1854 to 1871. Appointed convener of the General Assembly's committee on education in 1854, he was successively Deputy Clerk of Assembly (1859), Principal Clerk (1862), and Moderator in 1866. His *Styles of Writs, Forms of Procedure and Practice of the Church Courts of Scotland* was published in 1850 and ran to several editions.

DNB XII, 72; *FES* I, 370–1.

H. R. Sefton

Cooper, James (1846–1922), CofS minister and church historian. Born in Elgin, he studied at the University of Aberdeen where he was greatly influenced by Professor William Milligan* and at Heidelberg. He became minister of St Stephen's, Broughty Ferry, in 1873 and of the East Church of St Nicholas, Aberdeen (where he instituted a daily service), in 1881. He was Regius Professor of Ecclesiastical History in the University of Glasgow, 1898–1922, and Moderator of the General Assembly in 1917. Cooper was one of the leading Scoto-Catholics* of his day. A member of the Church Service Society,* he was a founding member and Secretary of the Scottish Church Society* and its President, 1900–1. He also founded the Aberdeen Ecclesiological Society.* He was influenced by the Oxford Movement and held a high regard for Pusey. For Cooper the unity of the Church was of the greatest importance and he wished above all to promote the union of the CofS and the Anglican Church, a 'United Church for the British Empire'. He was invited to lecture to Anglican clergymen on several occasions and received honorary degrees from the universities of Dublin (LittD), Durham (DCL) and Oxford (DD), as well as Aberdeen (DD) and Glasgow (LLD). Along with A. W. Wotherspoon* he was an influential member of the Church Union Committee with the UFC, and insisted that a formulation of the doctrines of the Trinity and the incarnation, which in his view was consistent with the catholic creeds, be included in the Articles Declaratory.* He became the best known public spokesman of Scoto-Catholicism. In the General Assembly he was noted for the unswerving faith and courage with which he defended his position. His doctrinal views and liturgical practices were challenged by eleven of his elders in the East Church in Aberdeen, 1882–3, but Cooper successfully defended himself by appealing to the Reformed standards of the Kirk.

Chartulary of the Church of St Nicholas, Aberdeen (New Spalding Club, 1888–1892); *A United Church for the British Empire* (Forres, 1902); *Confessions of Faith and Formulas of Subscription* (G, 1907); (ed.), *Laud's Liturgy* (E, 1904); *Reunion: A Voice from Scotland* (L, 1918); *The Revival of Church Principles in the Church of Scotland* (O, 1895); *Kindness to the Dead* (L, 1924). He co-operated with the Episcopalian A. J. MacLean* in an edition of the Syriac Liturgical document, *The Testament of Our Lord* (E, 1902).

H. J. Wotherspoon, *James Cooper: A Memoir* (L, 1926); D. M. Murray, 'James Cooper and the East Church Case at Aberdeen, 1882–3', *RSCHS* 19 (1977), 217–33; R. Sjölinder, *Presbyterian Reunion in Scotland 1907–1921* (E, 1962).

D. M. Murray

Cormack, John (1894–1978), anti-Catholic agitator. An ex-serviceman possessed of unusual oratorical skills, Cormack was able to reassert Scotland's militant Protestant heritage in an age when other loyalties and creeds were seeking to win over the masses.

In his native Edinburgh, his Protestant Action Society gave rise to the last serious upsurge of 'No-Popery' seen in Britain, during 1935–6. Following the disruption of the 1935 Catholic Eucharistic Congress in Edinburgh, his party won 31 per cent of the votes cast in the 1936 municipal elections. A populist programme that threatened to drive RCs from municipal and state employment, for a time appealed to churchless Protestants who were nevertheless hostile to RCism.

Cormack was a complex figure who diverged from the stereotypical anti-Catholic in a number of respects and whose personal appeal endured even after his movement ran out of steam in the later 1930s. He remained a popular open-air speaker for over thirty years and served a similar period on the city council, where he became a respected public representative in the post-War years.

His shortlived importance demonstrates how tense inter-communal relations occasionally were in 1930s Scotland, as much for educational, political or economic reasons as for straightforward religious ones.

See also Anti-Catholic Societies.

T. Gallagher, *Edinburgh Divided: John Cormack and No Popery in the 1930s* (E, 1987); id., *Glasgow: the Uneasy Peace* (Manchester, 1987); S. Bruce, *No Pope of Rome* (E, 1985).

T. Gallagher

Coronation. The first recorded coronation in Scotland was that of Aidan by Columba* in 578. The last took place on 1 January 1651 when Charles II* was crowned at Scone* in Perthshire by the Marquis of Argyll.

The distinctive features of the ancient Scottish coronation ceremony were the installation of the king on the Stone of Destiny at Scone, and the recital of the king's pedigree. The last Scottish king to be inaugurated on the Stone of Destiny was John Balliol in 1292. It was the custom for the king, once he had been placed on the Stone, to remain seated for the rest of the service. When Balliol was deposed in 1296 the Stone of Destiny was removed by Edward I of England and placed by him in a specially made coronation chair in Westminster Abbey, where it still remains. Despite this Robert the Bruce* decided to be crowned at Scone. It was the privilege of the Earls of Fife to place the crown on the king's head, but as the Earl was a follower of Edward I, his sister, the Countess of Buchan, took his place. Most, but not all, subsequent coronations took place at Scone. David II* was the first Scottish king (1329–71) to be anointed with holy oil. Several kings were crowned while still minors, and Mary Queen of Scots* and James VI* were only infants. Charles I* had been king for eight years when he was crowned at Holyrood in 1633. His coronation was described as 'the most glorious and magnifique coronation that ever was seen in this Kingdom'. The coronation of his son, Charles II,* was the only Presbyterian ceremony and included a long sermon by the minster of St Giles', Edinburgh, Robert Douglas.*

The regalia of 'Honours' of Scotland consist of the Crown, the Sceptre and the Sword of State. Because they were concealed in the church of Kinneff in Kincardineshire during the Cromwellian occupation, they escaped the destruction which overtook the English crown jewels. The Crown was remodelled in 1540 by order of James V. The Sceptre was presented in 1494 by Pope Alexander VI to

COUNCILS AND SYNODS

James IV and the same monarch received the Sword of State in 1507 from Pope Julius II.

John, Marquess of Bute, *Scottish Coronations* (Paisley, 1902).

H. R. Sefton

Councils and Synods (RC, post-Reformation). According to RC canon law, diocesan bishops meet on occasion in council. For three centuries after the demise of the post-Reformation bishops, there were no RC diocesan bishops in Scotland and thus no formal councils. From 1727, however, Scotland had two vicars-apostolic (Highland and Lowland) and from 1827 three (Northern, Western and Eastern Districts); often too these had coadjutors. These non-diocesan bishops met together regularly and annual meetings are recorded for some time after 1782. After the restoration of diocesan bishops in 1878, a plenary (national) council was held in August 1886 at Fort Augustus.* The six bishops, each accompanied by a theologian, with representatives of cathedral chapters and theologians from the religious orders, followed the example of the Councils of Westminster (England) and Baltimore (USA) in laying down norms for the RCC in Scotland. Subjects included seminaries and colleges, liturgy and the sacraments, the clergy and finance. The practice now is for the Scottish bishops to meet regularly in conference. From *c*.1881 there were also diocesan synods at irregular intervals, but none has been held in recent years.

Acta et Decreta Concilii Scotiae Plenarii Primi post Re-integratam Hierarchiam (E, 1888); J. Graham, 'The Council of Fort Augustus', *St. Peter's College Magazine* 20 (1952), 79–81; Acts of diocesan synods: collections (SS) in Scottish Catholic Archives, Edinburgh.

M. Buschkühl

Councils, Provincial, of Pre-Reformation Church. Scottish churchmen are occasionally found at early general councils of the Western Church, but while 'frequent councils' were held at a national level during the reign of Queen Margaret,* and provincial councils were summoned thereafter by papal legates, it was not until the Fourth Lateran Council of 1215, which enacted that metropolitans should hold provincial councils annually to correct abuses, that such meetings became obligatory. As Scotland had no metropolitan, special arrangements were made in 1225 by the bull *Quidam Vestrum* which allowed provincial councils to be held by apostolic authority, this being achieved by the appointment of one of the Scottish bishops as conservator of the statutes of the council. The frequency of such meetings may not have met the statutory requirement, and little over a hundred canons survive for the period before 1549. Most of these are very brief, and taken collectively they cover only fragmentary aspects of ecclesiastical life. The impetus of the Reformation* prompted further activity and on the initiative of Archbishop John Hamilton,* three provincial councils (in 1549, 1552 and 1559) passed a series of reforming statutes de-

COUNTER-REFORMATION

signed to promote social and economic justice, to remedy the moral laxity of the clergy, enhance spiritual ministrations and so ensure that the Church would recover its former vitality. These reforms came too late, and the last provincial council dispersed in alarm on 2nd May 1559 on hearing of the arrival in Edinburgh of John Knox.*

See also Conciliarism.

J. Robertson (ed.), *Concilia Scotiae*, 2 vols (Bannatyne Club, E, 1866), ET by D. Patrick, *Statutes of the Scottish Church, 1225–1559* (SHS, E, 1907); J. H. S. Burleigh, 'The Scottish Reforming Councils, 1549–59', *RSCHS* 11 (1951–3), 189–211; T. Winning, 'Church Councils in Sixteenth-Century Scotland', in D. McRoberts (ed.), *Essays on the Scottish Reformation* (G, 1962), 332–58.

I. B. Cowan

Counter-Reformation, the term given to the Roman Catholic revival of the sixteenth and seventeenth centuries, which, though not in origin a reaction against the Protestant Reformation, was greatly stimulated by it. In lands which remained RC, it usually denotes reform from within; in Protestant lands, it signifies chiefly Catholic efforts to regain lost ground. Catholic revival in Scotland before 1560 can be described as 'too little and too late'. Although several papal envoys were received, Scotland was not represented at any session of the Council of Trent (1545–63). The Scottish reforming councils* were largely ineffective, while the Catechism of Archbishop John Hamilton* did not have much influence.

After the Reformation Parliament* of 1560, Nicholas of Gouda was sent in 1562 as envoy to Mary Queen of Scots* by the pope, and in 1566–7 Edmund Hay* was in Scotland to prepare for the mission of another papal envoy. Mary's fall and exile in 1567–8 put an end to such moves. Thereafter the nominal leader of Scottish Catholics was Archbishop James Beaton II* in Paris, while Bishops John Leslie* and William Chisholm II* were likewise active on the continent.

There was some sporadic resistance to the Reformation in Scotland, notably the public but short-lived RC revival in Glasgow and towns nearby in 1563. Catholic practice continued under the protection of local magnates, chiefly in the north-east but also in the south-west, where Gilbert Brown* was active. Ninian Winzet,* however, who had protested against both Catholic abuses and Protestant usurpation, went into exile. Catholicism in Scotland lacked co-ordination and leadership.

Counter-Reformation initiatives from abroad were mostly at a political level, aimed at influencing or converting the young James VI* or indeed effecting a *coup d'état* with the help of Spanish forces. They were dependent on the fluctuating political situation in Europe and, apart from the limited success of converting James' wife, Anne of Denmark, they achieved little. The departure of James for London in 1603 put an end to this strategy.

The only sustained effort on a pastoral or spiritual

level was the mission of several Jesuit* priests in the 1580s. The Jesuits were a notable product of the sixteenth-century Catholic revival. Thereafter there were always a few Jesuits working in Scotland. Counter-Reformation vitality led also to re-establishing the Schottenklöster* for Scottish monks and to founding the Scots Colleges* for training priests. From c.1612 a few priests, either seculars or from religious orders other than the Jesuits, began to work in Scotland.

The most important initiative was the establishment in 1622 of the Roman Congregation of *Propaganda Fide*,* with the task of overseeing RC missionary work in pagan lands outwith Europe and European lands which had become Protestant. The new congregation at once concerned itself with Scotland, but had relatively little to show for its pains. Its most productive venture was to subsidize, on a very modest scale, the Irish Franciscan mission to the Gaelic-speaking Highlands,* begun in 1619, which achieved spectacular success.

A group of Scottish secular priests collaborated to set up their own mission, with William Leslie* as their agent in Rome and, from 1653, with a Prefect as superior. This initiative, supported by *Propaganda Fide*, led to the appointment in 1694 of a vicar-apostolic, that is, a bishop without a territorial diocese, deriving his authority from Rome and directly responsible to Rome. Vicars-apostolic were a Roman response to the situation created by the Reformation and the discovery of the New World.

The influx of Roman Catholics from Ireland in the nineteenth-century changed Scottish priorities entirely. No longer was it a matter of re-establishing a Church defeated by Protestantism but of providing for a large immigrant population. A body of territorial bishops was set up in 1878, marking the end of Scotland's status (in Roman eyes) as a mission country. It was a victory for the Counter-Reformation but also a compromise, for normal episcopal rule was restored not to a re-converted country, but to a RC minority in a still overwhelmingly Protestant land.

The Counter-Reformation in Scotland, especially in its earlier phases, is a story of missed opportunities and seemingly grudging support on the part of both Rome and the Jesuits, but it has to be seen in the context of competing claims for a share in missionary resources by all Protestant Europe and the whole New World.

See Roman Catholicism.

Catholic Encyclopedia IV, 437–45; *New Catholic Encyclopedia* IV, (1967), 384–9; A. G. Dickens, *The Counter Reformation* (L, 1968); J. H. Pollen (ed.), *Papal Negotiations with Mary Queen of Scots* (SHS, E, 1901); *id.*, *The Counter-Reformation in Scotland* (L, E, 1921); W. J. Anderson, 'Rome and Scotland, 1513–1625', *IR* 10 (1959), 173–93; J. H. Burns, 'The Political Background of the Scottish Reformation', *ibid.*, 216–34.

M. Dilworth

Coupar Angus, *see* Cistercians.

Court of High Commission, 1610–38. The Court of High Commission was established in 1610 by the royal prerogative of James VI.* There were two courts, one initially in St Andrews (moved to Edinburgh in 1611) and one in Glasgow. The courts were intended to form an integral part of the newly completed episcopal* structure of Church government – largely staffed by bishops and inspired by the King's desire to create uniformity with England. A single court was formed in 1615.

The court was empowered with jurisdiction in all cases of offence against religion, and from 1626 served as court of appeal from the lower Church courts. Moral offences and cases of expressed dissent, especially those involving ministers and teachers at university or school level, came before the High Commission. RC recusants also fell under the High Commission's remit, but it was the treatment of Protestant nonconformists, usually Presbyterian ministers, which earned the court a reputation for repressive activities. Presbyterians also attacked the court's 'unconstitutional' establishment. The High Commission attracted criticism from the nobility and from lay lawyers, who were worried by its growing power. In 1638 it was abolished by the Covenanters* at the Glasgow Assembly.*

G. I. R. McMahon, 'The Scottish Courts of High Commission, 1610–38', *RSCHS* 15 (1965), 193–209; W. R. Foster, *The Church before the Covenants* (E, 1975), 47–9.

K. M. Brown

Court of Session, the supreme civil court in Scotland. The Court of Session had its origins in the fifteenth-century parliamentary sessions and later lords of Council and Session. In September 1531 Pope Clement VII gave permission for Church revenues to be used to endow a college of justice for civil cases. In fact, James V had no intention of spending the £10,000 *p.a.* on judges' salaries, but the establishment of the College of Justice in 1532 is commonly considered to be the beginning of the modern Court of Session. From 1535 its members have been known as senators.

Until the Reformation* the president and half of the fourteen ordinary lords were clerics, and while the clergy were disqualified in 1584, clerics continued to be members of the court until 1668. The Court of Session also had until 1762 three or four extraordinary lords (none was appointed after 1723). It was subjected to a series of major reforms in the nineteenth century. The importance of the Court of Session lay in its role as a unitary court, its fostering of professionalism among lawyers, and its promotion and adaptation of civil law in Scotland, especially before 1707.

See also Mylne, Alexander.

R. K. Hannay, *The College of Justice* (E and G, 1933); G. C. H. Paton (ed.), *An Introduction to Scottish Legal History* (Stair Society 20; E, 1958), 341–6, 418–24; G. Donaldson, 'The Legal Profession in Scottish Society in the Sixteenth and

Seventeenth Centuries', *Juridical Review* n.s. 21 (1976), 1–19.

K. M. Brown

Courts of the Church, those bodies which under the Presbyterian system are responsible for the government of the Church at every level. In place of the hierarchy of individuals characteristic of Episcopal and some other systems, the CofS has a hierarchy of courts. 'Its government is Presbyterian and is exercised through Kirk Sessions, Presbyteries, Provincial Synods and General Assemblies' (Articles Declaratory* of the Church of Scotland in Matters Spiritual, The Church of Scotland Act* 1921). A Kirk Session* consists of the minister* and elders* of a parish; a Presbytery* consists of the minister and an elder from each Kirk Session within its bounds along with certain other ministers and elders and members of the diaconate;* a Synod* consists of all the members of Presbyteries within its Province; the General Assembly* consists of Commissioners appointed by Presbyteries to the number of one in four of their membership and six officials *ex officiis*. In a restricted number of matters finality of judgment is specifically conferred upon one of the courts, but in all other affairs cases may be taken either by appeal (by the party at the bar) or by dissent and complaint (by a member of the court sitting in judgment) to the next superior court and so to the Assembly itself. It is well established law that when a court of the CofS has passed judgment on some matter which is *intra vires* of it, no civil court has any jurisdiction.

At the time of writing, the CofS seems likely to dispense with Synods.

A. Herron

Cousin, Annie Ross (née Cundell, 1824–1906), hymn-writer. Born in Hull and raised an Episcopalian, she became a Presbyterian before marrying in 1847 William Cousin, a FC minister who served in Irvine and Melrose before retiring to Edinburgh (*AFCS* I, 126. He moved in the same FC circles as Moody Stuart* and the Bonars.*) She was a gifted linguist and from the 1850s published hymns and poems in several collections and periodicals. Her best-known hymn is 'The sands of time are sinking', originally in nineteen verses, based on the language of Samuel Rutherford's* letters. It is her only hymn to appear in *Church Hymnary* 2 and 3. Its refrain provided the title for her collection of one hundred and seven pieces, *Immanuel's Land* (L, 1876, ²1897). They are more meditative than doxological, reflecting a warm evangelical piety. She has been called 'a Scottish Christina Rossetti, with a more pronounced theology' (Campbell). She died in Edinburgh.

D. Campbell, *Hymns and Hymn Makers* (L, 1912), 146–7; J. Moffatt and M. Patrick, *Handbook to the Church Hymnary* (L, n.d.), 308.

D. F. Wright

Covenant, Solemn League and, *see* Solemn League and Covenant.

Covenant Theology (or federal theology), the use of the covenant concept as an architectonic principle for the systematizing of Christian truth. The seeds of this approach were sown by John Calvin (*Institutes* 2: 9–11) and there are already hints of it in Heinrich Bullinger and Zacharias Ursinus. But it took some time to develop fully, though by the early seventeenth century virtually all orthodox Reformed theologians came to accept it and work out their theology within its framework. Such theologians as Johannes Cocceius in his *Summa Doctrinae de Foedere et Testamento Dei Explicata* (Amsterdam, 1648) and Herman Witsius in his *De Oeconomia Foederum Dei cum Hominibus* (Leeuwarden, 1677; ET, 3 vols, L, 1763; ⁴1837, 2 vols) represent covenant theology in fully developed form. English divines also generally adopted the covenant theology. John Preston, *The New Covenant* (L, 1629), John Ball, *A Treatise of the Covenant of Grace* (L, 1645), Francis Roberts, *Mysterium & Medulla Bibliorum. The Mysterie and Marrow of the Bible: viz. God's Covenants with Man* (L, 1657), and William Strong, *A Discourse of the Two Covenants* (L, 1678), are but four examples. In keeping with this, the Westminster Assembly* used a covenant framework in drawing up the Confession of Faith and catechisms.

SCOTTISH COVENANT THEOLOGIANS. The phrase 'the covenant of works' occurs in Scottish theology as early as Robert Rollock's* *Quaestiones et Responsiones aliquot de Foedere Dei* (E, 1596) and *Tractatus De Vocatione Efficaci* (E, 1597; ET, *A Treatise of God's Effectual Calling*, L, 1603). Federalism quickly became a dominant influence in Scotland, so much so that James Walker* could comment, 'The old theology of Scotland might be emphatically described as a covenant theology' (*The Theology and Theologians of Scotland*, E, ²1888, 73). The widespread acceptance of this is illustrated by *The Sum of Saving Knowledge*, published in Edinburgh in 1650 and traditionally bound with copies of the Westminster Confession of Faith for centuries, even though it never received ecclesiastical sanction. According to Robert Wodrow* (*Analecta*, I, 166), the authors were David Dickson* and James Durham.* Dickson expounds covenant theology at some length, particularly emphasizing the Covenant of Redemption, in his *Therapeutica Sacra* (E, 1656; ET, by Dickson, E, 1664). Samuel Rutherford* advocates covenant theology in *The Tryal & Triumph of Faith* (L, 1645, E, 1845), Sermons VII and VIII, and more fully in *The Covenant of Life Opened: or, A Treatise of the Covenant of Grace* (E, 1655). But the most extensive work on the covenants was written by Patrick Gillespie,* though only the first two (of five) parts were published: *The Ark of the Testament Opened, or, ... a Treatise of the Covenant of Grace* (L, 1661) and *The Ark of The Covenant Opened: or, A Treatise Of the Covenant Of Redemption* (L, 1677).

In the eighteenth century both CofS and Secession* Church theologians propounded covenant theology: Thomas Boston* wrote both *A View of the Covenant of Works* (E, 1772) and *A View of the Coven-*

ant of Grace (E, 1734). Adam Gib's* *Sacred Contemplations* (E, 1786) is largely an exposition of the covenants of grace and works. Other works on the covenants include Thomas Bell's* *View of the Covenants of Works and of Grace* (G, 1814) and John Colquhoun's* *A Treatise on the Covenant of Grace* (E, 1818) and *A Treatise on the Covenant of Works* (E, 1821). James Fisher's* *The Assembly's Shorter Catechism Explained* (G, 1753, 1760) and Robert Shaw's* *Exposition of the Westminster Confession* (E, 1845) indicate loyal adherence to the covenant theology. FC theologians took a similar position. William Cunningham's* *Historical Theology* (2 vols, E, 1862) allocates no specific chapter to the covenant, but his treatment of both the fall (I, 502ff.) and the atonement (II, 261ff.) is strongly federalist. James McLagan,* FC Professor at Aberdeen, took a similar line (see *Lectures and Sermons*, A, 1853, especially Lecture xxx). But possibly the most enthusiastic nineteenth-century devotee of covenant theology was Hugh Martin,* who entitled his major work *The Atonement: in its Relations to the Covenant, the Priesthood, the Intercession of our Lord* (E, 1882).

THREE COVENANTS. Federal theology organizes Christian truth around three great covenants:

(i) *The covenant of works* (sometimes called the covenant of life or the covenant of nature). Federal theologians acknowledged that Scripture nowhere applied the term 'covenant' to the relationship between God and Adam. They also acknowledged that the relationship was asymmetrical: God and Adam were not equal partners in a mutually negotiated contract. On the contrary, God sovereignly imposed the conditions and graciously promised a reward for what Adam owed as a matter of duty. But all the elements of a covenant were there, they argued. There were two partners: God and Adam (as the representative of all mankind). There was a clear stipulation: perfect obedience, focused in the specific prohibition of one fruit. And there was a clear promise or threat. Obedience would mean life, disobedience would mean death.

Within the framework of this covenant, federal theology saw Adam as not simply a private individual but as the representative of the human race. Taking their cue from Rom. 5:14 they argued that Adam sustained the same relationship to all as Christ did to the Church. The justification for this lay in the fact that Adam and Eve were, organically, the root of all mankind. This oneness, at once federal and natural, legitimized the imputation to us of the guilt of Adam's first sin, explained the transmission to us of a corrupt nature, and accounted for the fact that even those who have never actually sinned (*e.g.*, infants) nevertheless suffer the very punishment denounced on Adam.

According to federal theology, the covenant of works is no longer in force as a probationary framework for mankind. Each stood probation in Adam and no longer stands each for himself. But in other important respects the covenant of works is still in force. In particular, the principle, 'Do this and live!' is still valid. If any could present himself at the bar of God and prove that he was free from sin, personal or imputed, actual or original, he would be acquitted. Similarly, the principle, 'The soul that sins shall die!' is still valid. This is clearly implied in the contrast between salvation by works and salvation by grace to which St Paul alludes so frequently. Salvation by works is impossible not because it is in principle inconceivable, but because we are morally and spiritually helpless. The weakness lies not in the law but in the flesh (Rom. 8:3).

(ii) *A covenant of redemption.* This was an eternal covenant between the Father and the Son, according to which the Son became surety for his people, undertook to obey and suffer in their place and was promised everything that pertains to grace and salvation. Express biblical warrant for this covenant (or counsel of peace, as it was sometimes called) was found in Ps. 2:7–9, 89:3, 2 Sam. 7:11–16 and especially Zech. 6:13 ('the counsel of peace shall be between them both'). But its real basis lay in broader biblico-theological considerations. Scripture constantly relates Christ's mission to the will of God the Father. He was sent from God, received his assignment from God and received certain promises from God. Such language, according to covenant theologians, clearly indicates that he did not come on his own initiative alone, but on terms agreed with the Father.

Some such covenant, in the view of federal theology, was also necessary to the union between Christ and his people. A union by mere divine decree would have rendered the obedience of Christ involuntary. Union by mere community of nature (*i.e.*, by incarnation) would have meant the saving identification of all mankind, simply as men, with Christ – a fact belied by the Bible's insistence that unbelievers perish. Union by means of the indwelling of the Spirit was itself the consequence of the work of atonement, and certainly could not have been its condition: at the moment when Christ bore their sins the vast majority of his people were completely alienated from him spiritually. The true basis of union then, according to the federal theologians, could only be the covenant of redemption.

There was no agreement among Scottish theologians, however, as to the need to posit a separate covenant of redemption. It is clearly promulgated in *The Sum of Saving Knowledge*. It is also asserted by Rutherford (see, for example, *Covenant of Life*, 282ff.). But other theologians insisted that it was simply part of the one covenant of grace (see below). This was particularly true of Thomas Boston: 'The covenant of redemption and the covenant of grace are not two distinct covenants, but one and the same covenant' (*Works* VIII, 396). They denote the same transaction under different considerations: 'By a covenant of redemption is meant a bargain of buying and selling: and such a covenant it was to Christ only; for as much as he alone engaged to pay the price of our redemption, 1 Pet. 1:18, 19. By a covenant of grace, is meant a bargain whereby all is to be had freely: and such a covenant it is to us only, to whom the whole of it is free grace; God Himself having paid the ransom, and thereupon made over life and salvation to us, by free promise, without respect to any work of ours, as the ground of our right thereto' (396f.).

This divergence between Dickson and Rutherford on the one hand and Boston (and Gib) on the other is probably not a substantive one. It is a matter simply of clarity. But clarity is not unimportant, and those who follow Boston find themselves having to distinguish constantly between the way the covenant of grace bears on Christ and the way it bears on believers. For them, it was pure grace; from him, it demanded perfect obedience. From them, it required faith; to him, it promised it. Besides, the archetypal covenant of grace is God's covenant with Abraham (see Gal. 3:15–18), and it is exceedingly difficult to subsume Christ under this covenant. There is no precedent for regarding Abraham as a type of Christ and in any case they diverge radically in their relation to the covenant. Abraham is a covenant-keeper as a non-worker: Christ is a covenant-keeper as a worker, obedient even to the point of death. The true fulfilment of the Abrahamic covenant is the bond between God and the individual believer, who becomes an heir according to the promise.

The older Scottish theologians believed it would be an impoverishment, therefore, to relinquish the covenant of redemption. It contributes significantly to a clearer and more comprehensive statement of the truth.

(iii) *A covenant of grace.* This concept was common to all federalists, but there was still room for considerable difference on matters of detail.

For example, who were the parties? Even the Westminster divines found this difficult to answer. The Shorter Catechism (Answer 20) is non-committal, saying merely: 'God having, out of his mere good pleasure, from all eternity, elected some to everlasting life, did enter into a covenant of grace to deliver them out of the state of sin and misery, and to bring them into an estate of salvation by a Redeemer.' This does not tell us with whom the covenant was made. The Westminster Confession is equally cautious: 'The Lord was pleased to make a second (covenant), commonly called the Covenant of Grace: whereby he freely offereth unto sinners life and salvation by Jesus Christ' (VIII.3). The Larger Catechism, however, attempts to be specific: 'The covenant of grace was made with Christ as the second Adam, and in him with all the elect as his seed' (Answer 31). This answer combines the covenant of grace with the covenant of redemption and well illustrates the confusion which results. There is no set of stipulations and promises which apply symmetrically to Christ and the elect. *The Sum of Saving Knowledge,* although speaking clearly of two covenants, is unspecific as to the parties. Thomas Boston was hampered by his refusal to distinguish between the covenant of grace and the covenant of redemption. The covenant of grace, he says, was made with Christ as the Last Adam, head and representative of his seed. But those 'contracted for' were the elect. In effect, this resolves everything into the covenant of redemption and virtually obliterates the covenant between God and the believer.

What is needed here is a firm commitment to seeing the covenant of grace in terms of the Abrahamic covenant. Abraham was not Christ (nor even a type of Christ). Nor was the covenant made with him as elect. Nor, again, was it made with him pre-temporally. It was made with him, in history, as a believer; and this warrants the conclusion that the parties to the covenant of grace are God on the one hand and the believer on the other. God's *diathēkē* (last will and testament) is made out in favour of faith.

The question of the promises of the covenant of grace provoked little discussion. Broadly, the covenant promised eternal life. But the stipulations were not so clear – they depended, again, on whether particular theologians distinguished between the covenant of redemption and the covenant of grace. Boston, who did not, took the view that the only condition of the covenant was Christ's fulfilling all righteousness (*Works* VIII, 438). From this point of view, faith was not a condition, but a promise. God produced faith in the elect because Christ, by his obedience, had fulfilled the conditions. Boston stressed, however, that faith was indispensable. A person is not in the covenant until he believes: 'He that believeth is within the covenant of grace personally and savingly: he that believeth not is still under the covenant of works, where the first Adam left him. Faith is the hand whereby one taketh hold of the covenant, signs it for himself, and closeth the bargain for his own salvation' (579).

Samuel Rutherford, on the other hand, asserted most strongly that faith was a condition: 'The condition of the covenant is faith … *This do* was the condition of the covenant of works. *This believe* is the condition of this covenant; because faith sendeth a person out of himself, and taketh him off his own bottom, that in Christ he may have his righteousness' (*The Trial and Triumph of Faith*, E, 1845, 87). The context in which Rutherford wrote was, of course, markedly different from that of Boston, and this probably explains the difference between the two men. For Boston, the great danger was the new legalism (Baxterianism), which turned faith itself into a 'work' and presented it as the ground of justification. For Rutherford, by contrast, the ogre was the antinomianism of Tobias Crisp (1600–43), which regarded justification as eternal and dismissed the human response to grace as of no importance.

There are two pressures on the theologian here. On the one hand, he must secure the gratuitousness of grace. On the other, he must maintain the reality of the covenant as bilateral. The first requires an avoidance of the language of conditionality. The second requires an insistence that the human response is both necessary and meaningful. The most appropriate way to secure these two objectives is to avoid speaking of faith as a condition while insisting that it is a requirement.

Covenant theologians were at great pains to stress the unity of the covenant of grace, while clearly recognizing that there were differences in administration. Essentially, this involved arguing that the Sinaitic covenant did not abrogate the Abrahamic but represented merely a different phase of its administration; and that the 'new (Christian) covenant' likewise perpetuated Abrahamic principles. Among other advantages, this insistence on the unity of the covenant enabled federal theologians to present a coherent theology of infant baptism. The Abrahamic covenant had clearly stipulated that the sign of the spiritual covenant be administered to the physical seed. Since this was the covenant under which the Church still existed (Gal. 3:14, 17) there was every reason to believe that this ordinance still stood; and that infant baptism, therefore, was not only a right, but a duty.

The twentieth century has seen a reaction to federal theology, even in relatively conservative theological circles. C. G. M'Crie,* writing in 1906, was already sharply critical of *The Sum of Saving Knowledge*, accusing it of reducing the gospel to a legal compact between two independent and equal partners: 'The blessedness of the mercy-seat is in danger of being lost sight of in the bargaining of the market-place' (*The Confessions of the Church of Scotland*, E, 1907, 72). John Murray,* a Scottish expatriate teaching in America, managed to combine a deep personal loyalty to the Westminster Confession with a detached attitude to federalism. Following the researches of such scholars as his own mentor, Geerhardus Vos, Murray took his cue from the biblical preference for *diathēkē* over *sunthēkē*, minimizing the two-sided nature of the covenant and viewing it as 'a sovereign dispensation of grace' (*The Covenant of Grace*, Phillipsburg, NJ, 1953, 18). But Murray's deepest reservations related to the idea of a covenant of works (*Works* II, 47ff.). He regarded the term itself as 'infelicitous' since it obscured the elements of grace which were prominent in the Adamic administration. But he also questioned the theological propriety of using the word 'covenant' in this connection. Scripture itself never called the Adamic administration a covenant: on the contrary, it limited this term to 'a provision that is redemptive or closely related to redemptive design' (49). In addition, 'covenant' involved a degree of security which the Adamic administration did not bestow.

Murray agreed, however, that the divine arrangements with Adam involved both conditions and promises, and traditional federal theologians would probably not have asked for more. He was also thoroughly conservative in his overall view, arguing, for example, that 'the Adamic administration with all its implications for racial solidarity' alone provided an explanation for original sin.

J. B. TORRANCE'S CRITIQUE. The most persistent Scottish critic of federal theology has been J. B. Torrance (1923–; *FES* IX, 519, X, 307, 439). Torrance set forth his position in an important article entitled, 'The Contribution of McLeod Campbell to Scottish Theology' (*SJT* 26, 1973, 295–311). He has frequently re-stated it in similar terms in several subsequent articles (for example, in 'Strengths and Weaknesses of the Westminster Theology', in *The Westminster Confession in the Church Today*, ed. A. I. C. Heron, E, 1982, 40–55). Besides his obvious debt to McLeod Campbell,* Torrance also reflects Barth's criticisms of federal theology (*Church Dogmatics* IV.1, 22–66); and he himself, in turn, has strongly influenced a whole generation of younger Scottish (and Scottish-trained) theologians (see, for example, M. C. Bell's *Calvin and Scottish Theology*, E, 1985).

Torrance's aversion to federal theology is not merely cerebral and academic but deep-seated and passionate. He clearly considers the gospel itself to be at stake. His main objections are as follows:

(i) The whole federal scheme is built on a deep-seated confusion between a covenant and a contract. These may mean the same in Scots law, but in theology they must be clearly distinguished. The edge of this criticism is rather blunted, however, by the fact that the Hebrew *berith* frequently means a contract.

(ii) The federal scheme involves a radical dichotomy between the sphere of nature (covenant of works) and the sphere of grace (covenant of grace). This, according to Torrance, makes nature (or law) prior to grace and thus represents a betrayal of the Reformation, which insisted that nothing was prior to grace. The obvious response to this is that there is always something (sin) which is prior to grace; and always something (law) which is prior to sin. To make grace prior to sin is to end up in the most unacceptable kind of supralapsarianism. Men and women must be related to God as sinners before they can be reconciled to him through a gracious adoption.

(iii) Federalism, according to Torrance, moves the focus away from what Christ has done for us to what we do for ourselves. It would, however, be very difficult to document this. In covenant theology faith itself is the gift of God, granted to the people of Christ in accordance with the covenant of redemption: and the object of faith was emphatically not anything we do for ourselves, but Christ crucified.

(iv) Federalism, according to Torrance, imperilled the very doctrine of God itself by suggesting that whereas justice was an essential attribute, mercy was a merely arbitrary or optional one. God was related to all men in terms of justice, but only to the elect in terms of love. But this antithesis between mercy and justice is a false one. A merciful judge and a loving father may sometimes show his true disposition not by forgoing punishment but by imposing it reluctantly. Besides, the whole gospel story is about God's provision of a just mercy.

(v) Federalism inverted the biblical order of the relation between forgiveness and atonement, teaching that God had to be conditioned into being gracious by the obedience and penal satisfaction of his Son. Scripture, by contrast (and here Torrance is closely following McLeod Campbell), insists that forgiveness always precedes atonement: in fact, it was because of his forgiveness that God provided a way of atonement.

Yet this argument rests on a confusion between love and graciousness on the one hand and forgiveness on the other. All federal theologians regarded God's love and graciousness as eternal, unearned and unconditioned. They were adamant that God's love preceded atonement, and indeed provided it. But they did not confuse love with forgiveness. The loving God proceeded directly not to forgiveness, but to atonement, making the One who knew no sin to be sin in our place (2 Cor. 5:21). Christ's death was not the ground of God loving us. But it was certainly the ground of his being reconciled to us: 'We were reconciled to God by the death of his son' (Rom. 5:10).

There are no signs today, even in the most conservative Scottish theological circles, of any return to a coherent federal theology. In this respect at least contemporary Evangelicalism has little organic connection with its past. Admittedly, all attempts to impose an artificial unity on Scripture should be treated with caution. But there is no doubt that large masses of biblical truth can be organized under the covenant principle; and that adherence to a covenant framework ensures close attention to the progressive, historical character of revelation. Ironically, to find a modern version of federal theology one has to turn to the work of the German Old Testament scholar, Walter Eichrodt, whose *Theology of the Old Testament* (1933; ET, L, 1961) uses covenant as its central concept, 'by which to illuminate the structural unity and the unchanging basic tendency of the message of the OT' (13). This shows that the idea is still viable and that attempts to relegate federalism to the museum of theological antiquities are premature.

G. D. Henderson, 'The Idea of the Covenant in Scotland', *EQ* 27 (1955), 2–14.

D. Macleod

Covenanters, supporters of the 1638 National Covenant* and the 1643 Solemn League and Covenant.* Their primary motivation was the preservation of the Reformed religion, particularly the spiritual independence of the Church and the sole headship of Christ within it. They can be broadly identified with the Presbyterians* during the period 1638–90. The Covenanters' roots lay in the political and theological thought of John Knox* and George Buchanan* (*see* Church and State (theological questions)), in the church polity of Knox and Andrew Melville,* and in the tradition of Presbyterian opposition to Crown interference in the Church since the Reformation.* Among the more influential Covenanters were Samuel Rutherford,* Alexander Henderson,* and George Gillespie.* During the early years many of the Covenanters' leaders were noblemen (*see e.g.* Campbell, Archibald, first Marquis of Argyll) whose own political conservatism drew them to a political theory which placed limitations on royal authority.

THE PERIOD 1638–60. By *c.*1620 many Presbyterians had been exiled or cowed into silence, but after 1625 Charles I's* liturgical innovations and his increasing reliance on bishops in government created widespread ill-feeling against the episcopate. In the summer of 1637 this resentment broke out in riots against the imposition of the 'Laudian' Prayer Book (*see* Laud, William). The National Covenant of February 1638 succeeded in giving the diverse opposition to the King a rallying point, but it was not until the Glasgow Assembly* of the following November that the Covenanters adopted a thoroughly Presbyterian programme.

The Covenanters' victory against the King in the Bishops' Wars* of 1639 and 1640, and the subsequent English Revolution of 1640–2, forced Charles I to accept Presbyterian church government and to concede constitutional changes which enhanced the power of the nobility. Some Covenanters, like James Graham, fifth Earl of Montrose,* were beginning to feel that their allegiance to the King was being compromised by the ongoing course of events and began to rethink their position. However, following the outbreak of civil war in England in the summer of 1642, the Covenanters were persuaded to give their support to the English Parliament. In August–September 1643 the Solemn League and Covenant was negotiated, and in return for the imposition of Presbyterianism on England and a constitutional settlement which ensured for the Scots a greater say in the regal union, the Covenanters promised to send an army into England to fight the King.

During 1644–6 the Covenanters fought as allies of the English Parliament, while at the same time the Westminster Assembly* sat to try to work out a religious settlement for the whole of Britain. However, Montrose's embarrassing campaign in Scotland in 1644–5, the lacklustre performance of the Army of the Covenant in England, and the growing strength of the English Parliament reduced the leverage the Scots had with their allies. Consequently there was little serious attempt made to impose Presbyterianism on England, especially as the New Model Army was predominantly made up of Independents.

Charles I surrendered to the Covenanters in May 1646, but they were unable to negotiate a satisfactory settlement and turned him over to the English in January 1647 rather than risk taking him home to Scotland, where Royalist support was growing. By December 1646 a number of nobles had already agreed to give Charles military support in return for a three-year trial introduction of Presbyterianism in England. The Engagement* was led by the Duke of Hamilton and had the support of Royalists and some aristocratic Covenanters, disillusioned with their English allies and resentful of the influence of the Presbyterian ministers in Scotland. However the Engager army was destroyed by Oliver Cromwell at Preston, 17–19 August 1648.

This defeat discredited the Engagers. Now it was the turn of the radicals who seized power in a coup, the Whiggamore Raid, and were sustained by English military aid. Power now lay with the ministers and the General Assembly, and the revolutionary nature of the new regime was underlined in January 1649 by the Act of Classes, which excluded from public office all who had been identified with the Engagement. Charles I's execution in the same month created widespread resentment throughout Scotland, but it was not until after Cromwell's conquest of Ireland in 1649–50 and Montrose's final defeat and execution in May 1650 had left Charles II no other option that he sought Scottish support and, in June, signed the Covenants. However, on 3 September the Army of the Covenant was crushed by Cromwell at Dunbar. Charles was nevertheless crowned at Scone on 1 January 1651. The Presbyterians now split into Remonstrants (see Protesters), who opposed any compromise with Engagers and Royalists, and Resolutioners,* who were prepared to co-operate with anyone who was not actually opposed to the Covenants and who rallied around the King.

But it was Cromwell and the English army who decided the fate of Scotland, conquering it after Charles' defeat at Worcester on 3 September, 1651. Until 1660 the kingdom was subject to English military occupation. This did not mean a total defeat for the Covenanting cause, as the CofS continued to be Presbyterian, although its ability to function was curtailed and it was forced to tolerate Protestant sects. At first Cromwell favoured the Remonstrants or Protesters, but latterly found the Resolutioners more amenable to control in spite of their latent royalism.

THE PERIOD 1660–90. It was the Restoration* which shattered the Covenanters' hopes, as Charles II's own prejudices and the resentment of the nobility combined to ensure the return of the bishops. The Act Rescissory of 1661 annulled all parliamentary legislation since 1633 (thus also sweeping away some of Charles I's more controversial laws), and a thoroughly Erastian episcopacy was established by 1662. As in all other religious upheavals of the sixteenth and seventeenth centuries, most of the clergy conformed; but some 270 ministers, over 25 per cent, were deprived of their livings for refusing to accept the new establishment. The resulting concentration of ousted ministers and people, particularly in Fife and in the south-west, met in open air conventicles* and constituted a challenge to both the Est.C and the King. From 1663 fines and quarterings were used to discourage dissent, but instead they provoked the November 1666 Pentland Rising, which ended with the defeat of the Covenanters at Rullion Green.*

Under John Maitland, second Earl of Lauderdale*, the government now swung towards conciliation, but Indulgences* in 1669 and 1672 were only moderately successful in encouraging conformity. Even harsher measures were simultaneously adopted against those who refused the Indulgences,* but popular support for the Covenanters continued to grow. By 1678 the government had lost control of the west, and in the face of large, armed conventicles and an untrustworthy militia, it quartered the army (the Highland Host) on the region. On 3 May 1679 Archbishop James Sharp* was assassinated by Covenanting activists, who followed this up with the Rutherglen Declaration condemning all violations of the Covenants since the Engagement. On 1 June a small government force was defeated by an armed conventicle at Drumclog in Ayrshire. The Covenanters then marched on Glasgow, but were crushed at Bothwell Bridge* on 22 June by an army under the command of the Duke of Monmouth.

This defeat and the subsequent repression under James, Duke of York (see James VII) ended any serious threat to the government from the Covenanters. Active opposition was now confined to the south-west, where a small band, who came to be called Cameronians (see Societies, United), renounced their allegiance to the King in the Sanquhar Declaration* of 22 June 1680. They too were defeated, at Airds Moss (see Ayrsmoss) on 22 July, but resistance continued, as did a more modest level of conventicling. For its part, the government reacted by deploying excessive and often illegal force, and the 'Killing Times'* only embittered the still very substantial numbers of Presbyterians in the country.

James VII's succession in 1685 initially guaranteed the continuation of repression. However, as a RC, James was determined to further the interests of his co-religionists, and he introduced religious toleration as part of his strategy. By June 1687 Presbyterians too were included, allowing them freedom to reorganize and to exploit the government's dangerously RC complexion by linking anti-Catholicism with the Presbyterian cause. The Revolution of 1688 was undoubtedly made in England, but the Scots were quick to exploit it, and the 1689 Convention which granted the Scottish Crown to William of Orange was influenced by Covenanting ideology. Furthermore, since the Scottish bishops refused to recognize its legitimacy, the new government had little choice but to turn to the Presbyterians. On 7 June 1690 Presbyterian government was restored in the Church, parliamentary approval was given to the Westminster Confession, and patronage was conditionally abolished. The ministry was then purged. The Covenants themselves were discreetly dropped from the revolutionary programme, but a substantial portion of the Covenanters' objectives had at last been achieved.

J. K. Hewison, *The Covenanters*, 2 vols (G, ²1913); D. Stevenson, *The Scottish Revolution, 1637–44* (Newton Abbot, 1973); id., *Revolution and Counter Revolution in Scotland, 1644–51* (L, 1977); W. H. Makey, *The Church of the Covenant, 1637–1651* (E, 1979); I. B. Cowan, *The Scottish Covenanters, 1660–88* (L, 1976); J. Buckroyd, *Church and State in Scotland, 1660–1681* (E, 1980); id., *The Life of James Sharp, Archbishop of St Andrews, 1618–1679* (E, 1987); F. D. Dow, *Cromwellian Scotland, 1651–1660* (E, 1979); G. Donaldson, *Scotland: James V to James VII* (E, 1971), 295–384.

K. M. Brown

Covenanting, the swearing of a pledge to support the Reformed religion. Covenanting is found in Scotland as early as 1557, when the gentlemen of Mearns 'band' (covenanted) themselves to maintain the true preaching of Jesus Christ, and 1560, when some nobles, barons and gentlemen professing Jesus Christ 'band' themselves to expel the French. But covenanting came to mean especially the renewal of the National Covenant* (1638) and the Solemn League and Covenant* (1643) by later generations. After the Revolution of 1689 covenanting was practised in parts of the Secession* tradition and in the RPC, which regarded the nation and the Church in Scotland as under a perpetual moral obligation to discharge the bonds sworn by their ancestors.

The RPs observed a swearing of the covenants at Auchensaugh in 1712, and the terms of this renewal continued as a qualification for membership until 1822. In time the covenant bond was seen as antiquated, and it was felt that the tiny Church could not plausibly renew what had been the transaction of the entire nation.

The Associate Presbytery* conducted a renewal of the covenants at Stirling in 1743, indicating its continuity with the persecuted Covenanters* whose sons were among its leading ministers. The next year covenanting was made a qualification for communion. Covenanting as a worship ordinance was observed only at rare intervals, such as in 1821 after the formation of the Original Secession Synod,* which preserved the custom longer than other bodies.

From the seventeenth century until the nineteenth, private or personal covenanting was also widespread. In such a covenant the individual commonly committed himself or herself to the service of God. D. Hay Fleming gives a 1693 example in which one Francis Wark acknowledged himself a sinner, deserving of God's wrath, betook himself to the righteousness and mercy of Jesus Christ, took God 'to be my God and my portion' and 'Jesus Christ for my Saviour . . .' and engaged 'to be for him and his glory, while I have a being upon the earth', subscribing it in his hand. These private documents helped sustain many an earnest Christian in times of trouble (*The Story of the Scottish Covenants in Outline*, E, 1904).

T. Houston, *A Memorial of Covenanting* (Paisley, 1857); James Morrison, *Present Duty: in Treatises relative to the duty of Covenant-Renovation* (E, 1789); J. Cunningham, *The Ordinance of Covenanting* (G, 1843); J. Muirhead, *Dissertations on Federal Transactions* (Kelso, 1782); A. Gib, *The Present Truth: A Display of Secession Testimony*, 2 vols (E, 1774); J. M'Kerrow, *History of the Secession Church* (E, 1854); D. Scott, *Annals and Statistics of the Original Secession Church* (E, 1886); J. C. Johnston, *Treasury of the Scottish Covenant* (E, 1887); M. Hutchison, *The Reformed Presbyterian Church in Scotland* (Paisley, 1893).

S. Isbell

Cowan, Henry (1844–1932), church historian. Born and schooled at Ayr, he studied at the Universities of Edinburgh (MA, 1864; BD, 1867), Bonn, Halle and Tübingen. Ordained to Aberdeen West (1869–73), he then served two Aberdeen suburban charges (Ferryhill, 1873–5; Rubislaw, 1875–82) and Edinburgh New Greyfriars (1882–9) before appointment to Aberdeen's Church History chair (1889–1924). He was widely honoured: DD (1888) and LLD (1925) of Aberdeen, DCL of Durham (1910) and DTh of Geneva (1910). His chief publications, still useful, are *The Influence of the Scottish Church in Christendom* (Baird lectures;* L, 1896) and *John Knox* (L, 1905). *Landmarks of Church History* (E, 1894) was more popular. He contributed to James Hastings'* *Dictionary of the Bible*.

He energetically led CofS church extension* for thirty-five years as vice-convener (1885–1908) and convener (1908–20) of the Endowment Scheme. He declined the Moderatorship more than once. His sermons were works of art. He was Patron of the Incorporated Trades of Aberdeen.

FES VII, 375; VIII, 714; *Who Was Who, 1929–1940*, 295; W. P. Paterson in *LW* n.s. 3 (1932), 517–18; *AUR* 20 (1932–3), 39.

D. F. Wright

Cowper, William (1568–1619), Bishop of Galloway. Born in Edinburgh, he studied arts at St Andrews University (1580–3). After some years in England as a school teacher, he returned to Scotland and was ordained to the parish church of Bothkennar, Stirlingshire, in 1587. Initially opposed to episcopacy, he was appointed Bishop of Galloway in 1612 and defended episcopacy against Presbyterianism as 'a lawful, ancient & necessary government' (*The Life and Death* in *The Workes*, L, 1629, 6).

Cowper was an eloquent and popular preacher and a prolific writer with a fine literary style. Thomas McCrie reckoned Cowper's discourses as 'perhaps superior to any sermons of that age' (*Life of Andrew Melville*, E, ²1824, II, 431–2).

Heaven Opened (L, 1632); *Pathmos: or, a Commentary on the Revelation of St John* (L, 1619); *Seven Days Conference, betweene a Catholicke Christian and a Catholic Romane* (L, 1613); *The Triumph of a Christian* (L, 1618); *A Holy Alphabet for Sion's Scholars* (L, 1613).

DNB XII, 387–8; *FES* VII, 345–6.

N. R. Needham

Cox, James Taylor (1865–1948), CofS minister and Church lawyer. He was born at Gardenstown, Aberdeen, and educated at the Grammar School of Old Aberdeen and at the University where he graduated in arts and divinity, and of which in 1928 he became a DD. His only charge was at Dyce in Aberdeenshire (1888–1936). He was Convener of the Assembly's Committees on Freewill Offerings and on Statistics. In 1928 he was appointed Principal Clerk* of Assembly, becoming Joint Senior Clerk of the united Assembly the following year and ten years later sole Principal Clerk, retiring in 1946. He assisted in revising the fourth edition of Mair's *Digest of Church Laws*, and in 1934 himself edited the work which has ever since been accepted as the law-book of the Kirk and with which his name has become inseparably linked, *Practice and Procedure in the Church of Scotland* (E, 1934).

FES VIII, 537-8.

A. Herron

Craig, Archibald Campbell (1888–1985), ecumenical churchman and theologian. The youngest of eleven children of Kelso FC manse, he studied arts at Edinburgh (1906–10) and divinity at New College* there (1912–14, 1918–20). War service in the Royal Scots and the Intelligence Corps won him an MC and made him a pacifist. After energetic ministries in Galston, Ayrshire (1921–6) and Gilmorehill, Glasgow (1926–9), both in the UFC, he became Glasgow University's first full-time chaplain (1929–39). He then worked in London, first as General Secretary to the Church's Commission on International Friendship and Social Responsibility (1939–42), and then to the newly-formed British Council of Churches (1942–6). His orchestration of the Religion and Life Weeks (1941–4) was seminal for local ecumenism in Britain. After a year as deputy-Leader of the Iona Community* (1946–7) he was appointed Lecturer in Biblical Studies in Glasgow University, where he taught till his retirement in 1957. He remained active as speaker, broadcaster, Church negotiator and ecumenical pioneer for more than two further decades. As Convenor of the Inter-Church Relations Committee (1957–9) he controversially championed proposals for a form of episcopacy* in the CofS (*see* Anglican-Presbyterian Relations). As CofS Moderator (1961–2), he made official visits to Pope John XXIII and to the oriental Patriarchs in Jerusalem.

His theological vitality, ethical commitment, ecumenical vision and robust churchmanship were acknowledged by DDs from Edinburgh (1938) and Glasgow and Dublin (1961). He was also widely loved for his lifelong zest, for his delight in music, literature, travel, gardening and above all people, and for his rich humour and unsanctimonious faith.

See also Chaplaincies, University; Ecumenical Movement.

University Sermons L, 1938); *Preaching in a Scientific Age* (L, 1954); *God Comes Four Times* (L, 1954); *The Church in the World* (E, 1961); *Jesus* (four Lenten talks – L, 1968); Foreword to D. S. Cairns, *A System of Christian Doctrine* (E, 1979).

FUFCS 137, 227; *FES* IX, 269, 778, 783, X, 434; obituary appreciations in *The Scotsman*, 30 August 1985, *The Times*, 28 August 1985, *LW* Oct. 1985, 36; E. Templeton, *God's February: a Life of Archie Craig* (L, 1991).

E. Templeton

Craig, John (*c*.1512–1600), Scottish Reformer. He left his native Aberdeenshire to enter St Andrews University. On completing his studies, he sought service in England as tutor to Lord Dacre's family for two years. Returning home, he entered the order of Dominican* friars, but after a spell of imprisonment on suspicion of heresy, he was released in 1536 and left first for England and later for France and Italy. At Bologna, he is said to have become master of the novices, but became a Protestant sympathizer after reading Calvin's *Institutes*. He left his order and served as tutor in Italy, but was delated for heresy, imprisoned in Rome by the Inquisition, tried and sentenced to be burned. In the confusion surrounding the death of Pope Paul IV in 1559, Craig managed to escape, reached Vienna and travelled through Germany to England and so north to Scotland in 1560, where he joined the Reformers, preached (in Latin) in the Magdalen Chapel* in the Cowgate, Edinburgh, was appointed minister of the Canongate in 1561 and became Knox's* colleague in St Giles in 1562. He supported Knox's arguments in 1564 on the limits of obedience by subjects to their rulers. His name, with Knox's, occurs in a list of persons said to have foreknowledge of Riccio's murder. During the civil war between supporters of Queen Mary and her son, King James VI, Craig remained in the capital (at a point when Knox retreated to St Andrews) and Marian lords attended his preaching. In 1571 he acted as intercessor between the rival parties. Three times moderator of the General Assembly (in March 1570, October 1576 and October 1581), Craig took part in the debates against diocesan episcopacy* in 1575, yet was ready to accept David Cunningham* as Bishop of Aberdeen in 1577 and to contribute to the *Second Book of Discipline** of 1578 (which condemned episcopacy). From 1571 he served for a spell as minister at Montrose and then from 1573 as minister in New Aberdeen. Appointed as a chaplain to James VI, Craig returned to Edinburgh in 1579 and prepared the King's Confession* of 1581 and a catechism, also printed in 1581. He condemned the 'Black Acts'* of 1584 which not only affirmed episcopacy and the royal supremacy, but proscribed Presbyteries* from meeting, and, for his opposition, was prohibited from preaching by the King until a compromise was reached. At the Assembly's request, he composed 'A Form of Examination before the Communion' in 1590.

BUK; Calderwood; Knox, *History*; J. Row, *History of the Kirk of Scotland*, ed. D. Laing (E, 1842); Spottiswoode; K. Hewat, *Makers of the Scottish Church at the Reformation* (E, 1920), 350–401; T. Angus Kerr, 'John Craig, Minister of Aberdeen and King's Chaplain', *Reformation and Revolution*, ed. D. Shaw (E, 1967), 100–23; *FES*, I, 23, 52, VI, 35–6; *DNB* XII, 445–7.

J. Kirk

Craigdallie Case (1803–19), one of the most important legal cases in Scottish church history. In 1795 a majority of the Associate Synod* voted to alter the Synod's formula of subscription, so as to bring the Church's confessional stance into harmony with newly prevailing views on religious liberty (*see* New Light). A minority protested and congregations were divided. One such division, in the Perth congregation, was brought before the civil courts, to decide which of the two parties should retain ownership of the church building. (The Old and New Lights shared the building for the duration of the case.)

Prior to this, Scottish civil courts had refused to judge the merits of such cases, remitting judgment to the Church itself – to a majority decision either by the congregation concerned, or by the whole Church through its ecclesiastical courts. This practice arose out of a feeling that civil courts should not intervene in the internal affairs of dissenting churches which were independent of state patronage.

The Craigdallie Case (or *Craigdallie vs. Aikman*, after two of the participants) revolutionized this attitude. After much legal wrangling, the House of Lords gave the following judgment in 1813: that a church building, erected in the interests of a particular set of religious tenets, was a trust recognizable in law, and that the use of the building therefore legally belonged to those who adhered to the tenets in whose interest the building was erected, not to a mere majority of the congregation or church. The principle was thus established that civil courts were competent to examine and pass judgment on the internal affairs of dissenting churches, insofar as civil consequences were involved (in this case, ownership of property).

The principle thus enunciated was not in fact applied to the Perth congregation, since the Court of Session in Edinburgh found in 1815 that no real difference of opinion had been shown to exist between the Old and New Light parties. The House of Lords confirmed this decision in 1819, and the Old Lights withdrew from the Perth meeting-house.

See also Campbeltown Case; Church and State.

A. Taylor Innes, *The Law of Creeds in Scotland* (E, 1867), 327–43, (²E, 1904), 222–31; *ASUPC*, 591–3.

N. R. Needham

Craik, Henry (1805–66), author and Bible teacher. Born at Prestonpans, East Lothian, he was educated at Kennoway, Fife, where his father was schoolmaster, and St Andrews University, 1820–6, where he was a member of the Missionary Society with Alexander Duff* and others. After service in Devon as a tutor at Teignmouth and as pastor at Shaldon, he began in 1832 his long association with the Brethren in Bristol sharing the principal preaching and pastoral responsibilities with G. F. Müller (1805–98) at Gideon, Bethesda and Salem Chapels. He studiously preserved a modest life-style, refusing any settled salary and twice declining a DD from St Andrews.

His lucid, earnest preaching attracted large numbers from neighbouring churches and the congregation rapidly grew with many conversions. Of a gentle, caring disposition, conscientious in work and study in spite of recurrent illness, he died at Bristol of stomach cancer. His works reflect a strong interest in the elucidation of biblical texts, and include: *Principia Hebraica* (L, 1831); *The Hebrew Language: its History and Characteristics* (L, 1860); *Improved Renderings ... of Passages in the English Version of the New Testament* (L, 1836); *Hints and Suggestions on the Proposed Revision of our English Bible* (L, 1860); *New Testament Church Order* (L, 1863); and *The Popery of Protestantism* (L, 1852).

W. E. Taylor, *Passages from the Diary and Letters of Henry Craik* (L, 1866); S. Piggin and J. Roxborogh, *The St. Andrews Seven* (E, 1985).

R. Boyd

Crawar, Paul, see Kravar, Paul.

Crawford, Daniel (1870–1926), missionary. Born in Gourock on the Clyde, he received a minimal education, worked as a book-keeper, and was a Sunday school teacher. In 1887 he was converted in a Brethren* meeting, baptized by immersion, and began to engage in itinerant preaching. Deeply influenced by an associate of David Livingstone,* 'Dan' Crawford felt called to serve overseas and sailed in March 1889 for Africa. He spent the remainder of his life in Central Africa as a pioneer 'faith' missionary, allowing himself only one three-year furlough, which he spent in Britain, America, and Australia promoting missions. He began working among the Nyamwezi in Katanga, and his ministry eventually extended through much of the upper Congo region. His residence was in Luanza on Lake Mweru. He was extremely effective, not least because he mastered ten languages and had a deep empathy for the culture of the people among whom he laboured. He preached widely, founded 'Bible schools' to train people in the Scriptures, and engaged in translation work. His monumental achievement was translating the entire Bible into the Luba-Sanga tongue.

Thinking Black: 22 Years without a Break in the Long Grass of Central Africa (L, 1913); *Back to the Long Grass: My Link with Livingstone* (L, 1923).

J. J. Ellis, *Dan Crawford of Luanza, or 37 Years Missionary Work in Darkest Africa* (Kilmarnock, 1927); G. E. Tilsley, *Dan Crawford, Missionary and Pioneer in Central Africa* (L, 1929); A. R. Evans, *Dan Crawford* (Grand Rapids, 1956).

R. V. Pierard

Crawford (Crauford), Matthew (c.1640–1700), CofS minister prominent in the 1690s. Born in Greenock and educated at Edinburgh (MA, 1662) and Utrecht, he was sought but not apprehended for attending conventicles.* Called by the parishioners of Eastwood (Presbytery of Paisley), he was privately ordained in Paisley in 1679. He took part in the first Synod after James VII's* toleration* in 1687 and was a member of the 1690 General Assembly. In addition to several brief published works he left a large manuscript history of the CofS to 1680.

FES III, 134–5.

D. C. Lachman

Crawford, Thomas Jackson (1812–75), CofS

theologian. Crawford was born and studied at St Andrews (MA, 1831; later DD, 1844). In 1831 he was licensed by the Presbytery of St Andrews and in 1834 became parish minister of Cults, Fife. He moved to Glamis, Perthshire (1838), and then to the second charge of St Andrew's, Edinburgh (1844).

His early writings were on presbytery and prelacy, but his main significance lies in his orthodox teaching and adherence to confessional theology as Professor of Divinity in the University of Edinburgh (1860-75). His major writings were *The Fatherhood of God* (E, 1866), *The Doctrine of Holy Scripture Respecting the Atonement* (E, 1871), and *The Mysteries of Christianity* (Baird lectures,* E, 1874). In all these there is a stress on divine revelation as the only source of saving knowledge of God. A deep interest in the atonement* lay behind his lectures on the fatherhood of God, and his position is stated explicitly in opposition to that of R. S. Candlish* in his Cunningham lectures.* He displays the inductive approach to theology especially in his treatment of the New Testament passages dealing with the atonement. *The Mysteries of Christianity* sets out his carefully stated positions on subjects such as the Trinity, the work of the Spirit and the divine decrees.

Under his convenership a manual of devotion entitled *Prayers for Social and Family Worship* was issued in 1859. He was Moderator of the General Assembly of the CofS in 1867, and in his closing address, emphasized the spiritual nature of Christian unity wherein 'true Christians, knot together by the bond of faith whereby they are all united to Christ their living Head and thus in Christ united to one another'.

FES VII, 383-4; *DNB* XIII, 55-6; H. Watt, *New College Edinburgh: A Centenary History* (E, 1946), 224-5; J. Macleod, *Scottish Theology* (E, ³1974).

A. M. Harman

Creeds, see Confessions of Faith.

Crichton, Robert (d.1585), Bishop of Dunkeld, 1554-71. He was the son of Patrick Crichton of Cranston-Riddell. Educated at St Andrews University where he matriculated in 1512 and graduated (in first place) MA in 1516, Crichton became parish clerk of the Canongate in 1515, was provost of St Giles, and parson of Tarbolton (Ayrshire) and prebendary of Glasgow cathedral. With his appointment as coadjutor to his uncle George Crichton, Bishop of Dunkeld (d.1544), Crichton sought the bishopric for himself in 1543, but his claims were contested first by John Hamilton,* abbot of Paisley, who with Governor Arran's (*see* Hamilton, James, d.1575) support gained the see, and then by Donald Campbell,* abbot of Coupar Angus. After Hamilton's appointment as Archbishop of St Andrews by 1549, the pope decided in Crichton's favour by 1554. As Bishop, he attended the burning of Walter Milne* for heresy in 1558 and, though present in the Reformation Parliament of 1560, was considered by Knox* to be one of the 'chief pillars of the papistical kirk'. He, in turn, refused to listen to 'an old condemned heretic' like Knox and declined either to condemn or consent to the Protestant (Scots) Confession* of 1560. He was ready, however, to support the marriage of the Protestant Third Earl of Arran (*see* Hamilton, James, d.1609) to Queen Elizabeth, a move hard to reconcile with Roman policy. At the same time, he was willing, almost alone, to receive the papal envoy, Nicholas de Gouda, who arrived disguised as an Italian banker in 1562, but the Bishop would only discuss money matters. He assisted at the baptism of Prince James, according to Roman rites, in 1566. In the civil war, he supported Queen Mary and the Hamiltons and, with the ascendancy of King James' supporters, was forfeited by Parliament in August 1571; a Protestant Bishop, James Paton (*FES* VII, 339), was elected in his place. With the onset of the conservative Arran administration, Crichton was restored to his bishopric by the Crown in 1584 (*see* Stewart, James, d.1596), and on his death permission was granted for his burial in St Giles.

Early Records of the University of St Andrews, ed. J. M. Anderson (E, 1926), 103, 105, 207; *The Protocol Book of James Young, 1485–1515*, ed. G. Donaldson (E, 1952), nos 2078-9; *Registrum Cartarum Ecclesie Sancti Egidii de Edinburgh*, ed. D. Laing (E, 1859) no. 124; *Register of the Privy Seal of Scotland*, ed. M. Livingstone et al. (E, 1908-82), II, no. 1296; Dowden, 91-4; R. Lindsay of Pitscottie, *The Historie and Cronicles of Scotland* (E, 1899-1911), II, 130-1; *FESMA*, 99-100; Knox, *History* II, 396; *Cal. Scot. Papers*, ed. J. Bain et al. (E, 1898-1969), I, nos 881, 885-6; *Papal Negotiations with Mary Queen of Scots*, ed. J. H. Pollen (E, 1901), 38-40; *Extracts from the Records of the Burgh of Edinburgh*, ed. J. D. Marwick (E, 1869-82), III, 405; Spottiswoode II, 42.

J. Kirk

Crieff Fraternal, principal gathering of conservative evangelical ministers in the CofS. The origins of this 'brotherhood' (as it likes to be called) may be traced long before the first meeting at Crieff, Perthshire, in 1970, to which William Still* invited a score of his colleagues, since the post-Second World War resurgence of conservative Evangelicalism within the Church had long since established bonds of friendship between a growing number of ministers and their congregations. Alongside the personal influence of Still, the brothers James and George Philip, Eric Alexander and others, the Inter-Varsity Fellowship (later UCCF)* and other agencies and societies offered points of contact.

The aim of the Fraternal, with which perhaps one-sixth of the ministers of the CofS are associated (together with students, and a handful of ministers of other denominations), is to offer fellowship and encouragement around an understanding of ministry in which the expository preaching* of Scripture and prayer are central. Eschewing formality and concerned to discourage party spirit, the Fraternal has not developed into a society but remains, as at first, largely a group of friends gathered (three times a year) by invitation.

N. M. de S. Cameron

Critical Review of Theological and Philosophical Literature, The. In 1886 the *Theological Review and Free Church Quarterly* was initiated, edited by S. D. F. Salmond,* and published by Macniven and Wallace of Edinburgh. It included original papers and assessments of European periodical literature, contributors being drawn largely from FC ranks. Proving unprofitable, it was taken over in 1890 by T. & T. Clark, and retitled as above. Salmond remained editor but now included literary as well as theological reviews, and provided a forum for scholars of all branches of the evangelical community. Selling just under 4,000 copies, the *Review* was widely circulated among British and American scholars. Despite its unprofitability, T. & T. Clark continued publication because of their commitment to academic theology, and because of the esteem in which the journal was held. However in 1899 it was sold to Williams and Norgate who published it (Salmond still editing) until its demise in 1904.

See also Periodicals, Religious.

Scottish Notes and Queries 3rd ser. 13 (1935), 156; J. A. H. Dempster, 'The Profitability of Progressive Theological Publishing' (PhD, University of Strathclyde, 1987), 339–46.

J. A. H. Dempster

Croall Lectures, a series given in the Faculty of Divinity of Edinburgh University established by the will of John Croall, member of an Edinburgh coach-building and undertaking family (of Southfield, Liberton) who died in 1872. The trustees comprise the divinity Professors, the Moderator, Principal Clerk and Procurator of the CofS General Assembly and the ministers of four city churches. The lecturers must be ministers of the Scottish Presbyterian Churches, or 'occasionally' of another non-Presbyterian Reformed Church. The subject is confined to: 'the Evidences of Natural and Revealed Religion; the Person, Work, Atonement, Divinity, and Resurrection of Christ; the Person and work of the Holy Spirit; the Doctrine of the Trinity'. The first series was John Tulloch's* *The Christian Doctrine of Sin* (E, 1876). Others have included: W. Milligan,* *The Resurrection of our Lord* (L, 1881); A. Hetherwick,* *The Gospel and the African* (E, 1932); H. R. Mackintosh,* *Types of Modern Theology* (L, 1937); John Mackay,* *God's Order: The Ephesian Letter and this Present Time* (NY, 1953); L. Hodgson, *The Doctrine of the Trinity* (L, 1943); John Burleigh,* *The City of God: A Study of Augustine's Philosophy* (L, 1949); G. S. Hendry, *The Gospel of the Incarnation* (L, 1959); J. Barr, *The Bible in the Modern World* (L, 1973).

The Centenary Lecture by M. Black, *A Survey of Christological Thought 1872–1972* (E, 1972), includes a list to 1975; details in *CofS Year Book* (annual), to 1962.

D. F. Wright

Cromwell, Oliver, *see* Commonwealth and Protectorate.

Crookshank, William (1712–69), Scottish Presbyterian minister in London. Born in Aberdeen and educated there at Marischal College 1732–5, he was ordained in 1735 to the London Scottish congregation which met in Swallow Street, Picadilly, where Richard Baxter's English Presbyterian congregation originally met, some of whom joined the new Scottish church when it moved there in 1710.

Crookshank is notable for his translation of Herman Witsius' classic work of federal theology, *The Oeconomy of the Covenants*, 3 vols (L, 1763), and for producing an abridgement of Robert Wodrow's* *History* (1721–2) entitled *The History of the State and Sufferings of the Church of Scotland*, 2 vols (E, 1749).

Crookshank received a DD from Aberdeen University in 1763. He ended his life under a cloud, however, dismissed in 1768 as minister and excommunicated for misconduct.

W. Wilson, *The History and Antiquities of Dissenting Churches ... in London, Westminster and Southwark*, 4 vols (L, 1808–14), IV, 46–8; *FES* VII, 500.

N. R. Needham

Crosbie, Andrew (*d*.1785), advocate and leader of the 'Popular' party* in the General Assembly of the CofS. Possibly the original of Walton Scott's Councillor Pleydell in *Guy Mannering*, he was involved in a bank failure and died in poverty. He rose to fame as the anonymous author of *Thoughts of a Layman concerning Patronage and Presentations* (E, 1769), the appearance of which coincided with the unsuccessful attempt in the years 1768–9 to persuade the middle-ranking gentry and heritors* to petition Parliament to change the laws relating to patronage.* Along with Henry Erskine* he was largely responsible for a more aggressive approach by the opponents of patronage to Assembly business which, through its mastery of ecclesiastical procedure and tactics, began to throw the Moderate* dominance of that body on the defensive. The *Thoughts of a Layman* marked a significant secularization of the polemic against patronage, abandoning, largely for pragmatic reasons, the attempt to argue against it on religious grounds. Such theological points as Crosbie made in the work embodied some similarity to Moderate emphases.

DNB XIII, 209–10; N. Morren, *Annals of the General Assembly of the Church of Scotland, 1739–1766*, II (E, 1840); R. Sher and A. Murdoch, 'Patronage and Party in the Church of Scotland, 1750–1800', in N. Macdougall (ed.), *Church, Politics and Society* (E, 1983), 197–220; R. B. Sher, *Church and University in the Scottish Enlightenment* (E, 1985).

J. R. McIntosh

Crosses, Celtic, free-standing sculptured stone crosses from an early Christian Celtic context. The ringed cross form, popularly recognized as Celtic, developed in Scotland through experimentation by a sculptural workshop or school based at Iona* between the mid-eighth and the early ninth century. A carpentry technique, suggestive of wooden precursors, was used to assemble the earliest Iona crosses: St Oran's cross, which was made of local stone, and St John's cross, which was carved in stone from the Argyll mainland. Damaged in an early fall, St John's cross was reconstructed with an open ring at the centre. The carpentry technique created unstable stone crosses, and St Martin's cross, Iona, is monolithic, although it has slots in the ends of its side arms for inserted terminals. The Iona sculptors also carved completely monolithic crosses: the ringed cross at Kildalton, Islay, and unringed crosses at Kilnave, Islay, and Keills in Knapdale.

The Iona school was influenced by contemporary metalwork and pictorial sources of Mediterranean origin. The 'serpents-and-bosses' decoration on the Iona and Kildalton crosses is related to similar ornament on Pictish* monuments at St Andrews and Nigg in Easter Ross. Virgin and Child scenes are carved on St Oran's and St Martin's crosses and on the Kildalton cross; the one on St Oran's cross is comparable to the Virgin and Child miniature in the Book of Kells.* Other Iona school figural scenes are from the Old Testament: Cain killing Abel, the sacrifice of Abraham, and Daniel in the lions' den. Iconography at Iona may have depended upon Pictish sources.

The Iona workshop's experimentation with different construction methods and cross forms ended with the Viking attack on Iona in 806. By then, ringed crosses had appeared in Ireland at Clonmacnois and along the Tipperary–Kilkenny border, in the old kingdom of Ossory. Figural scenes are mostly restricted to hunting themes on the early Clonmacnois crosses, which are carved in lower relief than the Iona school crosses. The ornament of the monolithic Ossory crosses is more clearly imitative of metalwork than was the case at Iona. Pictorial scenes are usually limited to cross-bases in Ossory, while the Iona school placed figures on the arms and shaft of the cross. The ringed cross form may have been used in eighth-century metalwork; it is found at Iona and in Ireland incised on burial slabs with eighth-century inscriptions.

The earliest Celtic crosses probably developed independently at Iona and in Ireland, although St John's cross, Iona, may be able to claim precedence. Free-standing crosses were erected in former Pictish territory after the unification of Picts and Scots in the mid-ninth century, but none is ringed. Further development of ringed crosses after 806 took place in Ireland.

Royal Commission on the Ancient and Historical Monuments of Scotland, *Argyll: An Inventory of the Monuments*, vol. 4, *Iona* (E, 1982), 17–19, 192–208; id., vol. 5, *Islay, Jura, Colonsay & Oronsay* (E, 1984), 28–9, 206–12, 220–22; R. B. K. Stevenson, 'The Chronology and Relationships of Some Irish and Scottish Crosses', *Journ. of the Roy. Soc. of Antiquaries of Ireland* 86 (1956), 84–93; I.

Henderson, 'The Book of Kells and the Snake-boss Motif on Pictish Cross-slabs and the Iona Crosses', in M. Ryan (ed.), *Ireland and Insular Art AD 500–1200* (Dublin, 1987), 56–65; D. MacLean, 'The Keills Cross in Knapdale, the Iona School and the Book of Kells', in J. Higgitt (ed.), *Early Medieval Sculpture in Britain and Ireland* (British Archaeological Reports, British Series 152) (O, 1986), 175–97; F. Henry, *Irish Art in the Early Christian Period to 800 AD* (L, 1965), 139–47, 151–7; N. Edwards, 'An Early Group of Crosses from the Kingdom of Ossory', *Journ. of the Roy. Soc. of Antiquaries of Ireland* 113 (1983), 5–41; C. Hicks, 'A Clonmacnois Workshop in Stone', *ibid.* 110 (1980), 5–35.

D. MacLean

Crossraguel, *see* Cluniacs; Paisley Abbey.

Cruden, Alexander (1699–1770), Bible concordance compiler. He was born in Aberdeen, graduated at Marischal College in that city and would have proceeded to ordination in the CofS but for the first of a series of mental breakdowns which punctuated his life (1721–2, 1738–9, 1753–4). In 1722 he moved to London where he became a tutor and later opened a bookstore. In 1735 he was appointed bookseller to Queen Caroline, to whom in 1737 he presented a copy of the first edition of his great work, *A Complete Concordance of the Holy Scriptures of the Old and New Testaments* (AV/KJV, including Apocrypha). The first edition was produced in eighteen months; it involved him in financial difficulties which led to an attack of lunacy and confinement in an asylum. He attempted unsuccessfully to prosecute the authorities for unlawful deprivation of liberty and published an indignant protest, *The London Citizen Exceeding Injured* (1739), dedicated to George II.

Two further editions of the *Concordance* appeared during his lifetime (1761, 1769). Many later editions have been abridgments, but the unabridged Cruden still gives pleasure because of the sometimes highly original definitions (soundly Calvinistic in theology) of key words which preceded the tabulation of their occurrences (e.g., under 'punishment', he describes thirteen different methods, including sawing a person through the middle, a method he assures the reader the Hebrews never used).

He donned the mantle of a guardian of public morality, especially in relation to profanity and sabbath-breaking, and dubbed himself Alexander the Corrector. In 1755 he petitioned Parliament unsuccessfully to confer this title on him officially. (The previous year he had offered himself, also unsuccessfully, for election as MP for the city of London.)

He was the author of a number of other works, including a word index to Milton's poetical works.

DNB XIII, 249–51.

F. F. Bruce

Cruickshank, Alexander (1854–1937), UP/UFC and latterly CofS missionary in Calabar,

CRUTCHED FRIARS

Nigeria. Born near Aberdeen, he attended evening school while an apprentice and proceeded to Aberdeen University. He left without graduating on being appointed to Calabar in 1881, but returned to undertake two years' study at the UP Divinity Hall in Edinburgh before being ordained by the Presbytery of Biafra in 1884. His base was Ikorofiong, an important market centre on the Efik–Ibibio frontier, where he served for over fifty years, retiring in 1936.

His avuncular warmth made him a revered pastor, earning him the coveted title of *etobum* (literally, 'father of the canoe'; really 'father of the Church community'). He kept a family of over fifty boys, clothing, feeding and educating them to take up professional occupations all over Nigeria, and teaching many to speak English with a strong Doric accent. He responded to countless invitations from chiefs to start schools in their villages. His strict, fair and professional supervision system was widely admired, particularly by the colonial government. For this he was honoured with an OBE, and later (1932) a DD from Aberdeen University. His excellence as an organizer was matched by his brilliance as a teacher of football as well as academic and pre-vocational subjects. Humanitarian, witty, patient and practical, he developed in-service training for teachers. His thoroughness contrasted with Mary Slessor's* less cautious approach (in putting ill-trained young teachers in charge of new schools), but they often co-operated to their mutual advantage.

He kept a diary, and edited and revised John Taylor Dean's* Obufa Efik New Testament (E, 1910). His Efik hymn-book is still in use.

FUFCS, 558; *FES* IX, 731; A. Gammie, *Cruickshank of Calabar* (L, n.d.); H. Goldie, *Calabar and its Mission* (²E, 1901).

W. H. Taylor

Crutched Friars, an order of friars* of uncertain origin so called from the cross on their habit (*cruciferi*, 'cross-bearing'). They followed a basically Augustinian* rule (as given to the Italian congregation in 1169 by Alexander III). One of several independent congregations, the Bethlehemites (whose general was the Bishop of Bethlehem, in the succession maintained at Clamecy in central east France) had a house near Tranent in East Lothian, St Germains. Founded c.1247 on a visit to Scotland by the Bishop of Bethlehem as a papal legate, it was a hospital* of unknown role. It functioned as a remote cell of the cathedral priory at Clamecy. By the mid-fifteenth century the distinctiveness of the order had been lost, and in 1497 William Elphinstone* annexed the revenues of St Germains for his new King's College at Aberdeen (*see* Universities).

J. P. B. Bulloch, 'The Crutched Friars', *RSCHS* 10 (1950), 89–106, 154–70.

D. F. Wright

Culdees (*Céli Dé*, 'clients of God'), communities of clergy attested at several places in Scotland dur-

CULDEES

ing the ninth to thirteenth centuries, but of somewhat uncertain origin and character. The origin of these *Céli Dé* has frequently been sought in Ireland, where the beginning of the Culdee movement has been attributed to the rule of Tallaght formulated by the monastic reformer Mael-rúain, who died in 792 and sought to create an elite of monks (*see* Celtic Church). Even there, however, few Culdee communities maintained their initial fervour, and many became the equivalent of groups of secular clerks living in a community or *muinter*.

In Scotland such clergy are first associated with an ecclesiastical centre at Dunkeld, to which the relics of St Columba* were brought before 849. More certainly, communities of *Céli Dé* appear at Kilrimont or St Andrews c.943, Loch Leven from the mid-tenth or eleventh centuries, Abernethy c.1100, and Iona,* Monifieth, Monymusk* and Muthil in the twelfth century. Dunblane and Turriff may also have housed similar communities.

Similar developments at Dunkeld may point to the existence of an early bishop with a group of non-monastic clerks as his *familia*. At Brechin likewise a community of *Céli Dé* associated with the bishops, who simply by change of name became canons of the cathedral, occurs in the mid-thirteenth century. So too at St Andrews, where two groups of clergy emerged to serve the bishop's cathedral. Of these, the community of *Céli Dé* had no rights connected with the church of St Andrew, c.1144, but still celebrated their offices at a side altar of that church. Similarly at Dunblane, where there was also a Culdee tradition, the early history of the church is closely tied to that of Muthil, which housed a Culdee community in the twelfth century.

Not all ministrations were provided from diocesan centres, and in the area north of the Forth–Clyde line, communities of secular priests, frequently but not invariably called Culdees, demonstrate marked similarities to minster-type communities south of that line, who served considerable areas which were deemed to be their *parochia*. If the communities at Abernethy and Muthil resemble those at episcopal centres, others such as Iona, Loch Leven, Monifieth, Monymusk and Turriff may have had monastic origins. At Loch Leven, however, the eleventh-century donation of churches points to their service by community members as clerks. The remaining Culdee communities cannot be assigned to any one category. Monifieth is an enigma, while at Monymusk the original foundation's status is questionable, but the brethren were evidently not following a strict monastic rule. Indeed, with the exception of Iona, the only hint of an older Columban-type monastery is found in the existence of a *fer-léginn* at Turriff. Iona alone provides positive proof of a monastic foundation with a Culdee community alongside. This is paralleled in an Irish tradition in which Culdee élite were often established alongside a larger community, not necessarily monastic, who respected them but did not share their devotions and austerities.

Significantly, as in England, in which minsters were reformed after 950, former Culdee communities which survived were reorganized as Benedictine* monks (cf. Iona); as canons under the Augustinian* rule (cf. Abernethy, Monymusk and Loch Leven), or (at cathedrals) as an efficient chapter (cf. Brechin, Dunblane and Dunkeld). In England a few monasteries survived as secular colleges, but in Scotland St Andrews alone followed this pattern (as the church of St Mary on the Rock). Whatever their origins, by the twelfth century the so-called Culdee monasteries approximated organizationally more closely to minsters than to monastic communities.

See also Early Ecclesiastical Sites.

I. B. Cowan, 'The Post-Columban Church', RSCHS 18 (1974), 245–60; Easson-Cowan, 2–4, 46–54; G. W. S. Barrow, *The Kingdom of the Scots* (L, 1973), 212–32; W. D. Simpson, 'The Augustinian Priory and Parish Church of Monymusk, Aberdeenshire', *PSAS* 59 (1925), 40–4; J. F. Kenney, *The Sources for the Early History of Ireland* (NY, 1929), 468–77.

I. B. Cowan

Culross, James (1824–99), Baptist* minister. Born in Blairgowrie, Perthshire, Culross studied at St Andrews University, graduating MA (1846) and later (in 1867) DD. He became minister of the Baptist churches at Stirling (1850–70), Highbury Hill, London (1870–8), and Adelaide Place, Glasgow (1878–83). Involved initially in training ministers on behalf of the Baptist Union of Scotland,* he moved south as Principal of Bristol Baptist College (1883–96). He combined a firm evangelical* faith with an appreciation of 'the widespread culture of science'. Developing relationships between his theological college and the newly formed University College of Bristol, he stimulated many students to serve with the Baptist Missionary Society. Culross was a friend of C. H. Spurgeon* and when President of the Baptist Union of Great Britain and Ireland (1887), he attempted (unsuccessfully) to reconcile his colleague to the Union. His publications include: *The Three Rylands* (L, 1897) and about twenty devotional books and missionary biographies.

G. Yuille (ed.), *History of Baptists in Scotland* (G, 1926), 250–5, 298; Baptist Union *Handbook*, 1888, 17–45; 1900, 209; N. S. Moon, *Education for Ministry* (Bristol, 1979), 53–7.

N. S. Moon

Culross, see Early Ecclesiastical Sites.

Cumbrae, see Cathedral Churches.

Cuming (Cumin), Patrick (1695–1776), minister at the Old Kirk of Edinburgh, 1732–76, and Professor of Ecclesiastical History in the University, 1732–62, Cuming was effectively 'leader' of the CofS 1736–42 and 1746–61, being Moderator three times (1749, 1752, 1756).

Cuming's influence in the Church was largely dependent on the support of the Earl of Ilay, later Third Duke of Argyll. When Ilay fell from power in 1742, so did Cuming, and Ilay's death in 1761 ended Cuming's power. Cuming valued good relations between Church and state so highly that he was prepared to support patronage* and to secure the settlement of unpopular presentees to parishes. He made extensive use of the 'riding committees'* which were specially appointed to carry out inductions when the local Presbytery was unwilling to act. This policy was abandoned in the Inverkeithing Case of 1752, when the Presbytery of Dunfermline was forced to act and Thomas Gillespie* was deposed.

Cuming hoped that this firmer line would persuade patrons to agree to the augmentation of ministerial stipends. He also played an active part in the proceedings against ministers who attended performances of the play *Douglas*, by John Home. The son of the laird of Relugas, Midlothian, Cuming was minister at Kirkmalue 1720–5 and Lochmaben 1725–32. His lectures seem to have been orthodox but dull and, according to Thomas Somerville, poorly attended. His son Robert held his chair after him (*FES* VII, 390), and another son, Patrick, was Professor of Oriental Languages at Glasgow 1761–1814.

FES I, 76, VII, 389; H. R. Sefton, 'Lord Ilay and Patrick Cuming: A Study in Eighteenth-Century Ecclesiastical Management', *RSCHS* 19 (1977), 203–16.

H. R. Sefton

Cumméne (d.669), sometimes described as *albus* ('white'), seventh abbot of Iona*. Cumméne, an Irishman, became abbot c.657. He was the author of a work on Columba* which is now lost. Its existence is known from Adomnán's* *Life of Columba*, where it is cited (f. 108a) as *Liber de virtutibus sancti Columbae* ('A book concerning the miraculous powers of saint Columba'). Eight years before his death Cumméne went back to Ireland and may not have returned to Iona. It is thought possible that he could have written his *Liber* during this period. Adomnán probably drew considerably from Cumméne's work. Cumméne was probably also the author of an extant penitential book (see J. T. McNeill and H. M. Gamer, *Medieval Handbooks of Penance*, NY, 1938, 98–117).

A. O. Anderson and M. O. Anderson (eds), *Adomnan's Life of Columba* (²O, 1991); A. P. Smyth, *Warlords and Holy Men. Scotland AD 80–1000* (L, 1984).

D. E. Meek

Cumming, John (1807–81), the most prominent Scottish Presbyterian minister in London in the mid-nineteenth century. Born at Fintray, Aberdeenshire and educated at Aberdeen Grammar School and University, Cumming was licensed to preach in 1832 and in August of that year was called to the National Scotch Church at Crown Court, London, a post in which he was to remain for the rest of his working life.

He established Crown Court as a major centre of fashionable London Evangelicalism, and his influence went far beyond Presbyterian circles. He held militant anti-RC views associated with detailed historicist premillennialist application of the prophetic books of Scripture. He was a staunch defender of the CofS against the FC.

In 1855 Cumming was the subject of a brilliant essay by the young George Eliot (1819–80) which linked an exposure of his intellectual limitations with a critique of the brand of Evangelicalism which he represented. His credibility was further undermined by the non-fulfilment of his confident predictions that the last vial of the Apocalypse would be poured out in 1867. Hence by the time he retired in 1879 his influence had been substantially reduced.

Apocalyptic Sketches (numerous editions, L, 1849–58).

FES VII, 468–9; *DNB* XIII, 297; G. Eliot, 'Evangelical Teaching: Dr. Cumming', *Westminster Review* LXIV (October 1855), 436–62, reprinted in T. Pinney, *Essays of George Eliot* (L, 1963); R. B. Knox, 'Dr. John Cumming and Crown Court Church, London', *RSCHS* 22 (1984), 57–84; G. G. Cameron, *The Scots Kirk in London* (O, 1979).

J. R. Wolffe

Cuninghame, William, of Lainshaw (c.1775–1849), writer on prophecy. Educated in Kensington, London, and Utrecht University, he was influenced by William Carey while in India with the Bengal Civil Service. On inheriting the Lainshaw estate, north of Kilmarnock, he returned to Scotland in 1804. In 1818 he started a sabbath school in nearby Stewarton, and withdrew from communion in the Kirk when his views on grace and the atonement were attacked. In 1826 he objected to the Kirk Session's* debarring Wesleyan Methodists* (teachers in his school) from the Lord's Supper (*Remarks . . .*, G, 1826), and next year became founder and pastor of a Congregational* church in Stewarton (*A Narrative of the Formation of a Church on Congregational Principles . . .*, G, 1827). In 1839 Cuninghame, as patron,* led the protest against Irvine Presbytery's proposed division of the parish that sparked off the celebrated Stewarton Case* (*Report of the Stewarton Case, William Cuninghame and Others . . .*, J. M. Bell *et al.*, E, 1843).

Cuninghame's main energies were devoted to prophetic and adventist literature – almost two dozen books (mostly listed in *The Fulfilling of the Times of the Gentiles*, L, 1847), and frequent contributions in the London *Christian Observer* and elsewhere, sometimes over the name of 'Talib' or 'Sophron'. He crossed swords with Edward Irving,* the church historian S. R. Maitland, J. H. Frere and others, and was a keen advocate of Jewish missions.

L. E. Froom, *The Prophetic Faith of Our Fathers*, III (Washington, DC, 1946), esp. 364–85.

D. F. Wright

Cunningham, Alexander, *see* Glencairn, 5th Earl.

Cunningham, David (d.1600), Bishop of Aberdeen, 1577–1600. He was the son of the laird of Cunninghamhead (Ayrshire). After finishing his studies at St Andrews amid the disruption of the Reformation, Cunningham left for the continent: in Paris he attended lectures in the Collège Royal in 1564, and was at Bourges, presumably studying civil law, in 1567. On returning home, he was appointed minister at Cadder (Lanarkshire) by 1572 (the prebend of the subdean of Glasgow), and elected dean of faculty at Glasgow University by 1576. He contributed to the *Second Book of Discipline** of 1578; but as a chaplain to the Regent Morton (*see* Douglas, James, d.1581), he was advanced to the bishopric of Aberdeen in 1577 only to discover that his Catholic predecessor, William Gordon,* had dilapidated the patrimony, leaving him merely 'a naked title'. In 1594, he baptized King James' elder son, Prince Henry.

BUK; Calderwood; J. Durkan and J. Kirk, *The University of Glasgow 1451–1577* (G, 1977); *SBD* 47, 55, 134; J. Melville, *Autobiography and Diary*, ed. R. Pitcairn (E, 1842), 56–7; J. Kirk, *Patterns of Reform* (E, 1989), 409–10; FES III, 372, VII, 329; *FESMA* 4.

J. Kirk

Cunningham, John (1819–93), CofS minister, academic and church historian. The son of Daniel Cunningham, he was born in Paisley, and educated at Paisley Grammar School and the Universities of Glasgow and Edinburgh. His incisive intellect enabled him to win the gold medals in both logic and moral philosophy. He was also a prize-winning poet.

In 1845 he was licensed to preach by the Presbytery of Paisley as assistant at Lanark, and in August 1845 was ordained to Crieff, remaining for forty-one years. During this period he acquired both a local and a national reputation. Crieff was becoming a fashionable resort, and Cunningham became the chaplain of the local Volunteers and a Trustee and Governor of Taylor's Educational Institute, Crieff. He promoted the use of instrumental music in the church, and was the centre of controversy in the 'Crieff Organ Case' of 1867.

Nationally, he was increasingly seen as one of the most brilliant CofS broad churchmen of liberal* theological persuasion. His reputation was established as a church historian with his authoritative *Church History of Scotland* (2 vols, E, 1859). He also wrote *New Theory of Knowing and Known* (E, 1874). He was a contributor of philosophical articles to both *The Westminster Review* and *The Edinburgh Review*.

Academic honours were bestowed on him, including a DD from Edinburgh University in 1860, an LLD from Glasgow University in 1886 and an LLD from Trinity College, Dublin, in 1887. In 1886 he became the Moderator of the General Assembly* of the CofS.

His academic career blossomed late in his life. In 1886 he was Croall Lecturer,* when his theme was *The Growth of the Church* (L, 1886), in which he attacked the divine right of ministers. The same year he succeeded John Tulloch* as the Principal of St Mary's College, St Andrews.

FES VII, 424-5; DNB Suppl. II, 96-7.

G. Wareing

Cunningham Lectures, a series in New College,* Edinburgh, endowed in 1862 in memory of William Cunningham* by William Binny Webster (d.1862), a surgeon in the East India Company. Webster also provided Cunningham Fellowships at New College, assistance for 'poor but pious' students and the Library, and for FC home missions, making him 'one of the greatest benefactors of the Free Church, as well as one of the most intelligent supporters of the cause of divine truth' (AGAFCS 1858–1863, 484).

The lectureship passed, with successive church unions, to the present New College. Appointments are made by a council comprising College and CofS General Assembly representatives. The subject must fall 'within the range of Apologetical, Doctrinal, Controversial, Exegetical, Pastoral or Historical Theology, including what bears on Missions, Home and Foreign'. Notable lectures have included: J. Buchanan,* The Doctrine of Justification (E, 1867); J. Walker,* The Theology and Theologians of Scotland ... (E, 1872); G. Smeaton,* The Doctrine of the Holy Spirit (E, 1882); S. D. F. Salmond,* The Christian Doctrine of Immortality (E, 1895); J. Moffatt,* 'The Theology of Tertullian' (1915); J. Denney,* The Christian Doctrine of Reconciliation (undelivered through death; L, 1917); J. Skinner, Prophecy and Religion: Studies in the Life of Jeremiah (C, 1922); W. Manson,* Jesus the Messiah (L, 1943); G. F. MacLeod,* Only One Way Left (G, 1958); S. Mechie, The Church and Scottish Social Development, 1780–1870 (L, 1960); A. Boesak, 'In the Eye of the Storm; The Church in South Africa Facing the Challenge of the Eighties' (1982).

List to date, H. Watt, New College Edinburgh. A Centenary History (E, 1946), 260; terms prefaced to published lectures.

D. F. Wright

Cunningham, William (1805–61), FC theologian. Born in Hamilton, he studied at Edinburgh University and began his ministry in the Middle Church, Greenock, in 1830. He was translated to Trinity College Church, Edinburgh, in 1834 and in 1844 became the FC's first Professor of Theology, transferring to the chair of Church History in 1845. In 1847 he succeeded Thomas Chalmers* as Principal of New College.* In 1859 he was elected Moderator of the FC General Assembly.

Cunningham published little during his life-time: he issued David Some's The Assembly's Shorter Catechism Explained with an introduction (G, 1836), edited Sermons by the Rev. Robert Bruce for the Wodrow Society* (E, 1843) and edited with extensive notes Edward Stillingfleet's Doctrines and Practices of the Church of Rome (E, 1837, ²1845). From 1855 to 1860 he was editor of the British and Foreign Evangelical Review;* many of his own contributions were published in The Reformers and the Theology of the Reformation (E, 1862). His Discussions on Church Principles (E, 1863) mostly comprised articles first published in the North British Review.* Otherwise Cunningham issued only pamphlets on contemporary questions. After his death a volume of Sermons was published (E, 1972), as was the Theological Lectures (L, 1878) of his first chair, dealing with natural theology, Christian evidences and the authenticity of Scripture.

Historical Theology, his lectures as Professor of Church History, is his magnum opus (2 vols, E, 1862, ²1864, ³1870). It is in effect a systematic theology,* using the major controversies as occasions for elaborate treatments of the main themes of Christian dogmatics: the Trinity, Christology,* sin and grace, justification, free will, predestination and the atonement.* The treatment is austere, and the documentation is minimal (the manuscripts contained only the substance of the lectures; in the actual delivery there were extensive extempore treatments of the literature). But the service performed for the student is immense, as Cunningham states the issue, summarizes the views of the various parties, indicates the evidence for the orthodox position and finally deals with the objections. The result is a superb training in theological method.

One striking feature is the stress on a sense of theological proportion. Taking his cue from Calvin, Cunningham insisted that there was a hierarchy among Christian truths: 'there is a great difference, in point of intrinsic importance, among the many truths of different kinds taught us in Scripture'. As a result, doughty Calvinist though he was, Cunningham repeatedly warned against giving the distinctives of Calvinism a prominence unwarranted by Scripture. He also insisted that 'the history of the church seems to indicate that somehow the prosperity of vital personal religion is more closely connected with correct views of the points involved in the Pelagian controversy, than even with correct views upon the subject of the Trinity and of the person of Christ.'

If there was a hierarchy of truths there was also a hierarchy of heresies. Cunningham devoted two hundred pages to the refutation of Arminianism. But Romanism ('the masterpiece of Satan') troubled him even more deeply, and Socinianism, with its denial of the deity of Christ and vicarious atonement, most of all. He recognized that it no longer existed in its classic form, but it flourished in 'the pantheistic infidelity of Germany' (the theology of Schleiermacher and his successors). Socinianism was 'a deliberate and determined rejection of the whole substance of the message which Christ and His apostles conveyed from God to men'.

Cunningham took a prominent role in events leading up to the Disruption.* His most important theological contribution was The Defence of the Rights of the Christian People (E, 1840). This pamphlet was issued in defence of the Veto Act* of 1834 and argued, with massive learning, that no pastor should be thrust on a congregation against their wishes. Cunningham's views on the rights of the people went beyond the terms of the Veto Act and even beyond those of Chalmers. He was an ardent believer in popular election and cited a host of witnesses from the early Church to the eighteenth century in support. This pamphlet probably changed the Ten Years' Conflict* from a movement for the control of patronage* into a struggle for its abolition.

Cunningham's peculiar strength lay in his grasp of the history of Christian opinion. But he was no mere historian; he made creative contributions in several key areas. His views on the doctrine of Scripture appear in his *Theological Lectures* (269–625). Of particular interest is his treatment of the *testimonium internum Spiritus Sancti* (320–42). He insisted that the author and sufficient cause of the conviction that the Bible is the Word of God is the Holy Spirit. This did not imply any by-passing of 'the rational evidences'. But the Spirit's witness is more than evidence – an inward work, changing the heart of the human subject, and enabling us to see the divinity of Scripture. Cunningham would obviously have repudiated vehemently the idea that orthodox belief in the authority of Scripture is a form of rationalism. In the last analysis it is a conviction produced by the Holy Spirit; and there can be no appeal to some other 'more compelling evidence' to prove the Spirit right.

The fruit of his reflections on the sacraments* is available in the essay 'Zwingle, and the Doctrine of the Sacraments' (*The Reformers*, 212–91). Cunningham professed himself completely mystified by Calvin's doctrine of the Lord's Supper: 'altogether unsuccessful ... as unintelligible as Luther's consubstantiation. This is, perhaps, the greatest blot in the history of Calvin's labours as a public instructor.' By contrast, Cunningham had considerable sympathy for Zwingli. Noting that virtually all the Reformed confessions* (including the Scots)* repudiate the doctrine that the sacraments are 'naked and bare signs', he doubted 'whether there be adequate grounds for alleging that Zwingle held the sacraments to be nothing else but naked and bare signs'. It was also very difficult, he thought, to work out what those who made this disclaimer meant to affirm. While accepting that Zwingle may have over-reacted to 'the mass of heresy, mysticism, and absurdity which had prevailed so long and so widely in the church on the subject of the sacraments', Cunningham went on to say that he 'rendered services of the very highest value to the church, by the light which he threw upon this important and intricate subject'.

The guiding principle of Cunningham's theology of the sacraments was that they were for believers only. This immediately ruled out both baptismal regeneration and the Lord's Supper's being a converting ordinance. No sharp distinction could be drawn between the significance of baptism and of the Lord's Supper. Both sacraments represented, sealed and applied Christ and all the benefits of the new covenant. Cunningham spoke very sharply on this issue because he suspected the motive behind the idea that baptism was a lesser sacrament which required a mere willingness to be instructed in the principles of Christianity. 'It furnishes an excuse,' he wrote, 'for baptising the infants of persons who could not be regarded as qualified to be members of the Christian church, in full standing, or as admissible to the Lord's Table.' On this point, Cunningham's view was the polar opposite of that of the Highland divine, John Kennedy* (see *The Days of the Fathers in Ross-shire*, 110ff.).

Another topic which engaged Cunningham's attention was the interface between predestination and determinism. 'Calvinism, and the Doctrine of Philosophical Necessity' (*The Reformers*, 471–524) was written in response to criticisms of the theology of Chalmers by Sir William Hamilton,* and is remarkable for its insistence that the theological doctrine of predestination and the philosophical notion of determinism must be kept separate. Cunningham admitted that some Calvinistic theologians (notably Chalmers and Jonathan Edwards)* had been determinists and that such a position was not inconsistent with the teaching of the Westminster Confession. On the other hand, nothing in the Calvinistic system of theology or in the Westminster Confession required the doctrine of philosophical necessity. Augustine and Calvin had no theory whatever on the psychological question 'as to what the laws are which regulate men's mental processes, and determine their volitions'; and in any case some degree of freedom must be acknowledged in the human will – otherwise there could be no moral responsibility. This means, at the very least, that no Calvinist can believe that people are so imprisoned in a causal nexus that they are compelled to do what their wills abhor. But Cunningham went further. There was nothing to prevent a Calvinist being a libertarian. Divine control over human affairs (through predestination and providence) was quite compatible with 'a liberty of indifference, or the self-regulating power of the will'.

Cunningham was deeply interested, too, in the relation between Calvin and later Protestant orthodoxy. The idea that Beza was *Calvino Calvinior* is, as Cunningham well knew, a very old one. Cunningham dealt with the issues in his essay 'Calvin and Beza' (*The Reformers*, 345–412). On the extent of the atonement he argued that it was unfair to quote Calvin on a question never formally put to him; that statements to the effect that Christ died in some sense for all could be gleaned not only from Calvin but from the writings of virtually all Calvinists; that Calvin, as a predestinarian, explicitly denied the doctrine of universal grace; that in his interpretation of such texts as 1 Tim. 2:4 and 1 John 2:2 Calvin took exactly the same line as later advocates of particular redemption; and that in his only statement resembling a formal deliverance on the subject, Calvin explicitly denied universal atonement, in *Concerning the True Partaking of the Flesh and Blood of Christ in the Holy Supper* (*Calvin: Theological Treatises*, ed. J. K. S. Reid, L, 1954, 285): 'I should like to know how the wicked can eat the flesh of Christ which was not crucified for them, and how they can drink the blood which was not shed to expiate their sins.'

Cunningham gave extensive attention to the doctrine of the atonement (*Historical Theology* II, 237–370). It was also the theme of one of his last sermons, preached at the opening of the General Assembly in May 1860 (*Sermons*, 393ff.). In this sermon, he did not shirk the issue of limited atonement but at the same time insisted on a clear presentation of the free offer of the gospel: 'it is right that these offers and invitations should be freely and indiscriminately addressed to men of all characters and in all circumstances, without exception, condition or qualification.' It is obvious from remarks in this sermon that Cunningham intended to develop it into a monograph. His premature death prevented this. What is sadder still is that what J. J. Bonar called 'the splendour that surrounds his name' was quickly eclipsed as Scottish churchmen opted for the theology of the Enlightenment in preference to that of the Reformation. If that situation is ever reversed people will once again take seriously Cunningham's claim to be considered Scotland's greatest theologian.

Works, 4 vols (E, 1863).

FES I, 129; *AFCS* I, 52; *DNB* XIII, 321–3; J. MacGregor, 'Dr. William Cunningham', *British and Foreign Evangelical Review* 20 (1871), 752–92; R. Rainy and J. Mackenzie, *Life* . . . (L, 1871); *Disruption Worthies*, 193–200.

D. Macleod

Curitan, *see* Celtic Saints.

Currie, John (1679–1765), CofS minister. Currie graduated MA from Edinburgh University in 1699, was licensed by Kirkcaldy Presbytery and became minister of Kinglassie, Fife, in 1705. He was a staunch Evangelical,* a friend and correspondent of Ralph and Ebenezer Erskine,* sharing their spiritual and ecclesiastical ideals but strongly opposed to securing them through secession. He regarded the Secession* of 1733 as an unwarranted violation of the unity of the CofS. He wrote in defence of the popular election of ministers in *Jus Populi Vindicatum* (E, 1720), *Jus Populi Divinum* (E, 1727) and *A Full Vindication of the People's Right to Elect their own Pastors* (E, 1733), and against the Seceders in *An Essay on Separation* (E, 1738) and *A Vindication of the Real Reformation – Principles of the Church of Scotland concerning Separation* (E, 1740).

J. Macleod, *Scottish Theology in Relation to Church History* (E, ³1974), 179–80; *FES* V, 97.

N. R. Needham

Curtis, William Alexander (1876–1961), theological professor and ecumenical churchman. Born at Thurso and educated with distinction at Edinburgh (MA, 1897; BD, 1901), Heidelberg, Leipzig and Oxford, he was elected (with no prior pastoral experience) to the Aberdeen chair of Systematic Theology when only twenty-seven (1903–15). He then became professor of Biblical Criticism and Antiquities (i.e. New Testament) at Edinburgh (1915–46), serving also as Dean of Divinity (1928–46) and, after the 1929 Union, as Principal of New College (1935–46). The scholarly promise of *A History of Creeds and Confessions in Christendom and Beyond* (E, 1911) was never quite fulfilled: *Jesus Christ the Teacher* (L, 1943) published his Croall lectures* of 1920–1, but his 1950–3 Cunningham lectures,* 'The Sequence of the Gospels' remain in MS in New College Library. College administration and ecclesiastical diplomacy preoccupied him throughout the Union negotiations and beyond – as CofS Inter-Church Relations convener and president of the World Presbyterian Alliance (1933–7). He was disappointed in 1931 when the General Assembly put an end to further discussions between the CofS and the CofE. He led the CofS delegation at the 1937 Faith and Order Conference at Edinburgh. He was showered with honorary degrees: DLitt and DD (Edinburgh, 1911 and 1914), DThéol (Paris, 1933), DTheol (Debrecen), LLD (Edinburgh, 1946). Neither 'an Assembly man' nor 'disturbed by Barthian dogmatics or eschatological thunder', he exemplified 'exact scholarship . . . at the service of warm piety'. Curtis' other writings were slight, including 'Reunion in the Scottish Church . . .', *Hibbert Journal* 18 (1919–20), 240–58.

FES VII, 389, VIII, 716, IX, 769; *Who Was Who 1961–1970*, 270; *LW* 16 (1961), 310; *Scotsman*, Nov. 4, 1961, 13.

D. F. Wright

Cuthbert, *see* Celtic Saints; Anglo-Saxon Saints.

D

Dale, David (1739–1806), trader and manufacturer, independent churchman and philanthropist. Born in Stewarton, Ayrshire, a grocer's son, he served a weaving apprenticeship in Paisley. He married Ann Caroline Campbell, a bank director's daughter in 1777; their daughter, Caroline, married Robert Owen, the utopian social reformer.

Dale set up shop as a textile merchant in Glasgow from 1763, and became the Glasgow agent of the Royal Bank in 1783. By then he was established as a successful businessman and civic leader in the city. From 1785 he became a cotton manufacturer, setting up several spinning mills, first at New Lanark, which was eventually bought by Robert Owen in 1799 and further developed as a model industrial community, with advanced social and educational provision for its workers. Dale devoted the wealth he made in business to Christian philanthropy, supporting schools, hospitals and aid to the poor. He retired to his estate near Cambuslang in 1800, where he died.

Dale was a devout Christian, originally within the CofS. He left it over the patronage* question, at first joining the Relief Church.* Later, influenced by John Barclay,* he became lay pastor and preacher of the Old Scots Independent* church in Greyfriars Wynd, Glasgow (*see* Ferrier, Robert), from 1769 to his death. Dale and this independent congregation are recognized as among the antecedents of the Congregationalists* in Scotland. His evangelical religious beliefs were reflected in his concern for his employees' social, educational and spiritual welfare, and in his generous support for charitable and religious bodies like the British and Foreign Bible Society (*see* Bible Societies).

Substance of a Discourse by David Dale, January 1792 (Glasgow University Library, n.d.).

S. Mechie, *The Church and Scottish Social Development 1780–1870* (L, 1960); A. L. Drummond and J. Bulloch, *The Scottish Church 1688–1843* (E, 1973); D. J. McLaren, *David Dale of New Lanark* (G, 1983); A. Liddell, *Memoir of David Dale Esq.* (G, 1854); H. Escott, *A History of Scottish Congregationalism* (G, 1960); *DNB* XIII, 384–5.

W. F. Storrar

Dall, Robert (1745–*c*.1828), Methodist preacher. A native of Dundee, he was converted by the preaching of the evangelist Thomas Hanby in 1763 and began to preach in 1772. His ministry was to last for fifty-six years, twenty-two of which were to be in Scotland. He travelled in a number of Scottish circuits including Glasgow, Edinburgh, Greenock, and Dumfries, but it would appear that his best work was done in his earlier years in the Northern Circuit, where he seems to have introduced Methodism in Old Meldrum, Peterhead, Fraserburgh, Forres, and Elgin. He was also responsible for the establishment of new societies in Kintyre and Campbeltown. He travelled widely, and on one occasion walked a return journey of over 600 miles from Glasgow to Ross and Cromarty. Having been sent by the Methodist Conference to Dumfries, in 1787 he obtained Wesley's approval for a preaching house there, 'larger than any in Scotland, except those in Glasgow and Edinburgh' (Wesley's *Journal*), and was commended by Wesley for its exceedingly cheap construction in 1788. By 1790, there were around forty members and a good-sized congregation. In Dumfries, he apparently enjoyed the support of the Established and Secession Church ministers but not, for some reason, that of the Relief Church. He is known to have written an autobiography but it was not published.

W. F. Swift, *Methodism in Scotland. The First Hundred Years* (L, 1947).

J. R. McIntosh

Darien Colony, abortive venture to found a Scottish settlement on the Isthmus of Panama by the Company of Scotland Trading to Africa and the Indies (founded 1695, dissolved by the Union of 1707). It proved disastrous for many reasons including the climate, Spanish hostility and English disapproval. Two CofS ministers accompanied the first expedition in July 1698, Thomas James (*FES* V, 61, VII, 663) and Adam Scott (*FES* VII, 665). Both died at sea. The General Assembly in January 1699 called for general prayer for success. Its Commission in July 1699 sent a letter to the new colony of Caledonia, together with four ministers for the second expedition that summer. Alexander Dalgleish (*FES* VII, 663) died on the voyage, the Covenanter* Alexander Shields* died in Jamaica in 1700 while sailing home after the break-up of Caledonia, Archibald Stobo (*FES* VII, 665) stayed in America after his returning ship was damaged at Charleston, South Carolina (he became a distant forebear of Theodore Roosevelt), and only Francis Borland made it home in 1701 to his parish of Glassford, Lanarkshire (*FES* III, 254, VII, 662). He wrote *Memoirs of Darien* (G, 1714; ²1779, *The History of Darien*), tracing the providence and judgement of God in the project's failures. With Shields and Stobo he had established the Presbytery of Caledonia, the first on the American continent. As the ministers were commissioned to evangelize the natives, it counts as the first attempt at overseas mission* by the CofS. In 1700 and 1701 the Assembly's calls for a solemn fast and humiliation noted the astonishing reverses it suffered.

J. Prebble, *The Darien Disaster* (L, 1968).

D. F. Wright

Darney, William (*d.c.*1774), independent Scots preacher in Yorkshire and Lancashire, known as 'Scotch Will'. His origins are obscure. A cobbler and pedlar, of massive build, he began preaching *c.*1742 in Rossendale, Lancashire, although unqualified and uncalled. Opposition made him waver between Methodism* and Moravianism. His raw Calvinism was frequently rebuked by John Wesley,* but William Grimshaw, the evangelical vicar of Haworth, and George Whitefield* acknowledged his gifts and fruitfulness. Through Grimshaw his independent group of 'William Darney's societies' were brought under Wesley's control, although Darney was recognized only as 'a preacher to assist only in one place'. In 1768 Wesley tried to return him to Scotland, to the Dunbar circuit, but he left the Methodists about then. He published *A Collection of Hymns* (Leeds, 1751) – his own doggerel efforts – and *The Fundamental Doctrines ... Laid Open to the Meanest Capacity ...* (G, 1755).

A. Fawcett, 'Scottish Lay Preachers in the Eighteenth Century', *RSCHS* 12 (1958), 111–14; F. Baker, *William Grimshaw* (L, 1963), 94f.

D. F. Wright

David I of Scotland (*c.*1085–53), King of Scots 1124–53. The youngest son of Malcolm III* and St Margaret,* he acquired from his mother a sincere religious piety and spirit of generosity to the Church which led his descendent James VI* to call him a 'sair sanct for the croun'. His reign saw the reorganization of the secular Church into bishoprics (*see* Episcopacy) and parishes, and the introduction of many orders of reformed Benedictines* into Scotland.

David first came to notice in 1097, when an English invasion overthrew his uncle Donald Bán and placed his brother Edgar on the Scottish throne; David was rewarded by Edgar with a promise of lands in southern Scotland, the great lordship of Strathclyde or Cumbria, Teviotdale and Lothian south of Lammermuir, which he secured *c.*1113 from his brother Alexander I,* who succeeded Edgar in 1107. He was at this time frequently resident at the English court, where his position as brother of the Queen brought him the favour of Henry I (1100–35), who *c.*1113 presented him with the marriage of the widowed countess of Huntingdon.

As lord of Strathclyde-Cumbria, he set about the task of reorganizing the ancient bishopric of Glasgow. The result was the appointment of his tutor John as Bishop of Glasgow and the holding of the 'Inquest of David' (1113/24) into the possessions of the church of Glasgow. *C.* 1113 David founded a house of the reformed Benedictine order of monks of Tiron (*see* Tironensians), at Selkirk, the first congregation of reformed Benedictines anywhere in Britain. An early source credits David with a visit to Tiron.

In 1124 David succeeded Alexander as King of Scots. Between then and his death in 1153 he founded many monasteries: Augustinian* canons at Holyrood* (1128) and Jedburgh* (1138), and in succession to *Céli Dé* (Culdee*) communities at Loch Leven and St Andrews* (the latter in 1144); Cluniac* monks at the Isle of May in the Firth of Forth (*c.*1140); Templar knights* at Balantrodoch in Midlothian (*c.*1128); Hospitaller knights* at Torphichen in E. Lothian; Cistercian monks at Melrose* (1136), Newbattle near Edinburgh (1140), and Kinloss in Moray (1150); Arrouaisians at Stirling (1140). Other monasteries, *e.g.* Inchcolm in the Forth, may have been founded by David. In some instances, such as Kinloss, the foundation seems to have gone hand-in-hand with feudal colonization. David encouraged his leading nobles to found monasteries; for example, Hugh de Morville brought Tironensians to Kilwinning in Ayrshire and Premonstratensians* to Dryburgh* during his reign.

David continued the reorganization of bishoprics which he had begun with Glasgow. In 1126 he unsuccessfully appealed for archiepiscopal status for St Andrews,* and throughout his reign he supported bishops of Glasgow and St Andrews in resistance to claims of superiority by English archbishops. It is uncertain how many bishops there were at the start of his reign, but by his death there were recognized episcopal sees at Glasgow, St Andrews, Dunkeld, Brechin and Aberdeen, and in the provinces of Strathearn, Moray, Ross and Caithness. (The diocese of Galloway, founded by Fergus of Galloway *c.*1126, gave its allegiance to the church of York, and the bishops of Orkney* and the Isles gave theirs to the archbishops of Trondheim in Norway; Argyll resulted from a later division of the diocese of Dunkeld; *see* Highlands.) David began the task of organizing cathedral chapters for his bishops, but this process, involving sometimes the conversion of *Céli Dé* and secular communities of Celtic* clerics, was not completed until long after his death.

David's piety and generosity won him the admiration of the reformed papacy* and such influential clerics as St Bernard of Clairvaux. But he was not afraid to come into conflict with the papacy over the independence of the Church in his kingdom when this was attacked by English archbishops; once he even threatened to transfer his allegiance to an anti-pope. The abbots and bishops appointed during his reign were men of exemplary life and learning, in contrast with some later times. David's personal life was devout and austere, although he enjoyed hunting. His introduction of reformed monasticism and reorganization of the bishoprics sought to bring Scotland into line with continental practice as approved by the reformed papacy; but he was sensitive also to the Celtic traditions of the Church as he found it, striving for what one scholar has called 'the balance of old and new'. He was by far the greatest lay benefactor of the medieval Church in Scotland.

Acta in A. C. Lawrie, *Early Scottish Charters Prior to AD 1153* (G, 1905), supplemented in G. W. S. Barrow, *The Acts of Malcolm IV King of Scots 1153–1165: Regesta Regum Scottorum*, I (E, 1960); on his reign, R. L. G. Ritchie, *The Normans in Scotland* (E, 1954); A. A. M. Duncan, *Scotland: the Making of the Kingdom* (E, 1975); on his ecclesiastical policy, G. W. S. Barrow, *The Kingdom of the Scots* (L, 1973); G. Donaldson, *Scottish Church History* (E, 1985); Easson-Cowan.

A. Macquarrie

David II (Bruce) of Scotland (1324–71), King of Scots from 1329. He became King when only five years old, in succession to his father Robert I, and the first king to be crowned and anointed with papal approval. Much of his early life was spent outside Scotland, in France (1334–41) and, after his defeat at Neville's Cross, in captivity in England (1346–57).

His reign was not marked by religious controversy, being prior to both the Great Schism and the Lollard* heresy. One of David's early acts on his return from France was the appointment of William Landallis as Bishop of St Andrews after a long vacancy. Landallis was to be prominent in diplomacy and affairs of state for over forty years, and led the Scottish Church in resistance to Edward III's attempts at ecclesiastical intrusion. David rewarded clerical followers with high Church office, for example when his secretary Walter Wardlaw* became Bishop of Glasgow in 1368. David's relationship with the papacy* was mostly good, owing to the anti-English bias of the Avignon papacy during the Hundred Years' War; but his attempt to divorce his Queen, Margaret Drummond, in 1369 brought conflict with Gregory XI and the threat of interdict, which was removed only by the King's death.

David was conventionally pious, going on pilgrimages,* encouraging Scottish crusaders, and building the church at St Monans in Fife. His private life, however, involved a degree of frivolity and immorality. His reign has been variously assessed by historians. Some have pointed to his successful financial and economic management after 1357 as a positive achievement; others have stressed the rashness of the Neville's Cross campaign, the apparent deviousness of the ransom negotiations before and after 1357, and his unsatisfactory relationship with his nobles. His apparent infertility was the source of many of his problems and the root cause of much of his less admirable conduct. In his treatment of the Church he was more circumspect than many of his successors.

Acta ed. A. B. Webster, *The Acts of David II, King of Scots 1329–1371: Regesta Regum Scottorum*, VI (E, 1982); R. Nicholson, *Scotland: the Later Middle Ages* (E, 1974); W. C. Dickinson and A. A. M. Duncan, *Scotland from the Earliest Times to 1603* (³O, 1977); A. Grant, *Independence and Nationhood: Scotland, 1306–1469* (L, 1984); A. B. Webster, 'David II and the Government of 14th-century Scotland', *Trans. of Royal Hist. Soc.* 5th ser. 16 (1966), 115–30; R. Nicholson, 'David II, the Historians and the Chroniclers', *SHR* 45 (1966), 59–78.

A. Macquarrie

Davidson, Alexander Dyce (1807–72), FC minister. Born in Aberdeen, he graduated MA from Marischal College* in 1825, was licensed by Aberdeen Presbytery in 1830, and became minister of Aberdeen's South Church in 1832. In 1836 he transferred to the West Church. He attained a remarkable ascendancy as a preacher over the students of the University and the more cultivated classes, almost single-handedly turning the tide of opinion in the city from the Moderate* to the Evangelical cause. At the Disruption* of 1843 he joined the FC. His congregation followed him, worshipping in Belmont Street from 1844 and moving to Union Street in 1869.

Davidson devoted himself to his own congregation and particularly to preaching. He played no part in the wider work of his Church, or in public and social affairs, and declined all suggestions that he should take up theological teaching or move to a more influential congregation. He published several books, e.g. *Lectures, Expository and Practical, on the Book of Esther* (E, 1859). A selection of his sermons, of which he left 2,000 fully written out, was published after his death, in *Lectures and Sermons* (E, 1872).

The Gospel, the Ministration of the Spirit (A, 1839); *The Position and Duty of Christ's Church* (A, 1844).

Disruption Worthies, 211–14; *FES* VI, 39; *DNB* XIV, 574.

N. R. Needham

Davidson, Andrew Bruce (1831–1902), outstanding Old Testament scholar who pioneered higher critical methods in Scottish biblical studies. Born in Kirkhill, Ellon, in Aberdeenshire, Davidson graduated from Aberdeen University in 1849

DAVIDSON, ANDREW BRUCE

with honours in mathematics. After three years as a schoolmaster at Ellon FC school, he took divinity at New College, Edinburgh, 1852-6. Licensed by Edinburgh FC Presbytery, he spent two years as a probationer without charge before being offered a Hebrew tutorship at New College as assistant to 'Rabbi' Duncan.* In 1863 he succeeded Duncan as Professor of Hebrew and Old Testament Exegesis, a position he held till his death.

Davidson early fell under the spell of the German critic H. G. A. Ewald, after a summer visit to Göttingen. Details are hard to trace, but certainly by the end of the 1860s Davidson had abandoned belief in the primacy of the Pentateuch over the prophets, redating Deuteronomy to Jeremiah's time. His greatest contribution to biblical studies, according to James Strahan, was that he 'shifted the centre of gravity of the Old Testament from the Law to the Prophets' (*ExT* 15, 1904, 453). Davidson also came greatly to admire the work of Julius Wellhausen, an admiration reciprocated by the German scholar, although the Scot's critical views were more conservative. Davidson's maturest expressions of these views are to be found in articles he contributed to the *Theological* (later *Critical*) *Review*, rather than in his posthumously published writings which were taken from early notebooks.

In matters theological Davidson distrusted logic, preferring intuition and experience, and is said to have been unsympathetic to certain aspects of the Westminster* Confession, e.g. its teaching on predestination. A powerful if occasional preacher, his sermons reveal an intense preoccupation with the struggles and enigmas of moral and spiritual life. The sermons of F. W. Robertson of Brighton were his own favourite homiletic reading.

Davidson's true gift was linguistic. His celebrated *Introductory Hebrew Grammar* (E, 1874; 19th ed. by J. E. McFadyen, 1914; 25th ed. by J. Mauchline, 1962; new edit. in preparation by J. D. Martin) went through seventeen editions in his own lifetime. He was a member of the Old Testament committee for the Revised Version of the Bible, in which his views on any matter of Hebrew translation were regarded as final.

Davidson was an overwhelmingly effective teacher, initiating an entire generation of FC students into the novelties of the critical method. He escaped ecclesiastical censure (unlike his brightest student, the swashbuckling William Robertson Smith*), probably because of the rather cryptic and undogmatic fashion in which he broached a contentious topic, and because of the immense affection and esteem which as a man he inspired in colleagues and pupils. Many, however, testified to an elusive quality in Davidson's personality. A. B. Bruce* nicknamed him, not unfittingly, the Erasmus rather than the Luther of Scottish criticism.

Davidson received the degree of DD from Edinburgh University and LLD from Aberdeen in 1868, LittD from Cambridge in 1900 and another DD from Glasgow in 1901.

See also Believing Criticism; Exegesis, Biblical.

Old Testament Prophecy (ed. J. A. Paterson, E,

DAVIDSON, JOHN

1903); *The Theology of the Old Testament* (ed. S. D. F. Salmond, E, 1904); *Biblical and Literary Essays* (ed. J. A. Paterson, L, 1902); *A Commentary on the Book of Job* (E, 1862); *Hebrews* (E, 1882); *Hebrew Syntax* (E, 1894); *The Called of God* (ed. J. A. Paterson, E, 1902); *Waiting Upon God* (ed. J. A. Paterson, E, 1904). Complete list of Davidson's writings in *ExT* 15 (1904), 450-5.

J. Strahan, *Andrew Bruce Davidson*, (L, 1917); A. T. Innes, 'Biographical Introduction' to Davidson's *The Called of God* (E, 1902); R. A. Riesen, *Criticism and Faith in Late Victorian Scotland* (Lanham, MD, and L, 1985); *DNB Second Suppl.* I, 471-2.

N. R. Needham

Davidson, Francis (1882-1953), evangelical teacher. Born in Hamilton but soon resident, for life, in Paisley, he was a graduate of Glasgow (MA, and later BD) and studied at the United Original Secession Church divinity hall. He served as a minister of this Church at Toberdoney, Co. Antrim (1909-21) and Paisley (1921-37, and thereafter senior minister), before becoming principal of the Bible Training Institute,* Glasgow, in 1938, having taught there part-time from 1934. He was also from 1923 his Church's Professor of Biblical Criticism. He held both offices until his death, which occurred on the publication day of the IVF's *New Bible Commentary* (L, 1953), of which he was at first sole editor.

At BTI he taught a wide range of subjects to the reduced student body during World War II. A genial, fatherly man, he was a gifted teacher, especially of doctrine. Based on good scholarship, his lectures were full of spiritual insight, well paced and enlivened by humour. His Paisley YMCA popular lectures were published as *The Faith that Lives* (Dumfermline, 1934), and his Tyndale lecture as *Pauline Predestination* (L, 1946). He contributed a memoir of D. M. McIntyre,* his predecessor at BTI, to McIntyre's *The Hidden Life of Prayer* (Stirling, 1945), and edited *The History and Doctrine of the United Original Secession Church of Scotland* (E, 1924). Aberdeen made him a DD in 1931.

Original Secession Magazine 13 (1953), 307-13.

G. W. Grogan

Davidson, John (c.1549-1604), Presbyterian minister. He was born in Dunfermline and educated at St Andrews University, entering St Leonard's College in 1566 and graduating MA in 1570. He remained to teach as regent in his college and study theology, meeting Knox* during his residence there. To celebrate the marriage of a college regent, he produced a play on the errors of Romanism, which Knox attended. By 1573, he had published *Ane Breif Commendatioun of Uprichtnes* (St Andrews) in praise of Knox; this accompanied another poem *Ane Schort Discurs of the Estaitis* lamenting Knox's death in 1572; his next poetical work, *Ane Dialog or Mutuall talking betuix a Clerk and ane Courteour concerning foure Parische Kirks till ane Minister*, printed anonymously (E, 1574), attacked the Regent Morton's (*see* Douglas, James) financial plans

DAVIDSON, JOHN

to link neighbouring churches under the service of a single minister with assistant readers. Prosecuted under an act of 1552 prohibiting the printing of unapproved 'books, ballads, songs, blasphemies, rhymes or tragedies', Davidson fled to the west, where Hew Campbell of Kinyeancleuch arranged his escape to England and, with Christopher Goodman's* help, to La Rochelle. Abroad, he visited Switzerland, matriculating at the university in Basel in 1575.

On returning home, Davidson was appointed minister at Liberton (near Edinburgh) in 1579, was active in the General Assembly, and executed the sentence of excommunication in 1582 against Robert Montgomery,* minister of Stirling, for accepting the Crown's nomination to the archbishopric of Glasgow in defiance of the Assembly. He spoke out against the removal of John Durie* in 1582 from the ministry in Edinburgh; in the Assembly of June 1582, Andrew Melville* as Moderator asked him 'to moderate his zeal'; and in 1583 others feared he would presume too far in his criticisms of James VI. He approved the *coup d'état* by the ultra-Protestant Ruthven* lords in 1582 and, with their downfall in 1583, and the onset of the conservative Arran regime (*see* Stewart, James, *d.*1596) which proscribed Presbyteries from meeting, he accompanied the Ruthven lords and leading Presbyterian ministers to England in 1584. For a spell, he acted as minister to the exiled lords at Newcastle, then visited the universities of Oxford and Cambridge, and attended the funeral in London of James Lawson.* Until prohibited by the Bishop of London, he preached in the winter of 1584–5 at St Olave in Old Jewry; and thereafter to the banished Scottish nobles in London.

With the downfall of Arran's government, Davidson returned home but declined to return to Liberton. Having witnessed in England 'the corruption of the bishops there', he continued to denounce at home 'that corruption at all times', and at Edinburgh Presbytery's request in 1589, wrote a reply to Bishop Bancroft's printed sermon against the Scottish church. In June 1589 he was appointed minister in Edinburgh, and in 1590 moved to the Canongate. In 1590 he opposed the coronation of Anne of Denmark on the sabbath, admonished James VI in 1591, and again offended him in a sermon in 1592. In December 1595, he accepted a call to Prestonpans, E. Lothian. Opposed to ecclesiastical representation in Parliament, Davidson firmly believed in the doctrine of 'two kingdoms' and reminded James VI that he sat in the General Assembly not as *imperator* but merely as a Christian and member of the Church. He voiced a strong protest when Melville was discharged by the Crown from attending the Assembly in 1598, and he himself was warded in 1601 for opposing royal policy. Before his death in 1604, he wrote *De Hostibus Ecclesiae Christi* (*On the Enemies of Christ's Church*) in which he affirmed that 'the erecting of bishops in this kirk is the most subtle and prevalent means to destroy and overthrow religion that ever could have been devised'.

DAVIDSON, LEWIS

Satirical Poems of the Scottish Reformation, ed. J. Cranston (E, 1891–3), I, 296–324; J. Melville, *Autobiography and Diary*, ed. R. Pitcairn (E, 1842); Calderwood; *BUK*; J. Row, *History of the Kirk*, ed. D. Laing (E, 1842); *Wodrow Society Miscellany*, ed. D. Laing (E, 1844), 467–520; R. M. Gillon, *John Davidson of Prestonpans* (L, 1936); *FES* I, 27, 53, 170, 387–8; F. D. Bardgett, 'Four Parische kirkis to Ane Preicheir', *RSCHS* 22 (1986), 195–209.

J. Kirk

Davidson, Katharine Helen (1845–1925), one of the first deaconesses of CofS. She was born at Inchmarlo, Aberdeenshire. Seeking to prepare herself for full-time Church work, she went to England to train and work at Mildmay and other institutions before responding, in 1887, to an appeal by the Life and Work Committee of the CofS for women to serve in a revived order of deaconesses (*see* Diaconate). She subsequently served the Church for thirty-eight years without remuneration. A. H. Charteris* appointed her to act as temporary head of the new Deaconess Training House. But it was as first official deputy for the Woman's Guild* that her gifts of enthusiasm and organization were effectively utilized. She travelled throughout Scotland, promoting the Guild concept, and helping women establish local branches. When she began this work, there were thirty-three branches with 2,000 members. By 1891, when she gave her report to the first national conference, there were 113 branches and 8,371 members. At the time of her death, the WG had become a major force in the CofS, with over 52,000 members.

Katie Davidson's other main contribution to the development of organized women's work was her pioneer mission to the fisher-girls (*see* Fisherfolk) who followed the herring fleet in Scottish ports, and to the south coast of England. In this distinctive witness, she combined nursing and welfare work with evangelism, and helped establish a tradition of imaginative, practical and efficient concern which characterized the growing contribution of women to the life of the Scottish Churches.

M. Magnusson, *Out of Silence: the Woman's Guild, 1887–1987* (E, 1987); D. P. Thomson, *Women of the Scottish Church* (Perth, 1975), 302–5.

L. O. Macdonald

Davidson, Lewis (1915–81), educationalist. Born in Glasgow and educated at its University (MA, 1937), he served with the Student Christian Movement* before becoming head of a boys' school in Kingston, Jamaica (1939–42). Appointed by the CofS Overseas board to the Presbyterian Church of Jamaica (which ordained him in 1946), he spearheaded the foundation of a church school, Knox College, at Spaldings in the centre of the island (1947). It grew into an influential centre for rural and industrial training and development, and Davidson himself was active in many areas of public life in Jamaica. In 1973 he was made CBE, and in 1974 DD of Glasgow. After leaving Knox College in 1977, he became minister of Christ Church (CofS), Bermuda, where he died.

J. Davidson [his wife], *Lewis Davidson. Man of Vision and Action* (Coupar Angus, 1992).

D. F. Wright

Davidson, Randall Thomas (1848–1930), Archbishop of Canterbury. Davidson was born in Edinburgh, his father the son, grandson, and great-grandson of Scots Presbyterian ministers. Confirmed at Harrow and a student at Trinity, Oxford, he was ordained an Anglican clergyman in 1875, and as resident chaplain to A. C. Tait, Archbishop of Canterbury, married the Archbishop's daughter Edith in 1878. He also impressed Queen Victoria, who had Gladstone* make him Dean of Windsor in 1883. As Archbishop Benson's confidant, and as Bishop of Rochester from 1891 and of Winchester from 1895, Davidson exercised great ecclesiastical power. He succeeded Frederick Temple to Canterbury in 1903.

Davidson was an administrator-Archbishop of genius and had a moderating political influence, trying to calm the turmoil over Lloyd George's budget and to mediate in the 1926 General Strike. From the Royal Commission on Ecclesiastical Discipline in 1904 to Parliament's rejection of the revised Prayer Book in 1928, he held the balance between irreconcilable high and low churchmen, and in 1919 won some freedom for the Church in the 'Enabling' Church of England Assembly (Powers) Act. He disarmed opposition to the episcopal consecration of the Modernist Hensley Henson, and achieved closer relations with the non-episcopal Churches and the Orthodox, though not with RCs. His twenty-five year primacy to 1928, the longest in post-Reformation history, saw the Edwardian zenith of the Anglican revival and its subsequent decline.

G. K. A. Bell, *Randall Davidson*, 2 vols (L, 1935); *DNB, 1922–1930*, 240–8.

S. Gilley

Deaconesses, *see* Diaconate.

Deacons, *see* Diaconate.

Dean, John Taylor (1866–1947), missionary and theological tutor in Calabar. Dean had been a pupil-teacher in Elgin before proceeding to Aberdeen University (MA, 1888) and being ordained in 1891 by the UP Presbytery of Elgin and Inverness. In that same year he and Muslim traders arrived in Calabar. The Muslim presence helped to shape his special contribution. Realizing that missionary strength lay in training indigenous pastors for the world they were to work in, he was ideally suited to be put in charge of the Hugh Goldie* Memorial (Theological) College in Creek Town.

He introduced Islamic studies but failed to get either African religions or the vernacular accepted. However, he insisted on the centrality of practical training for fostering preaching and pastoral skills. The scarcity of practice placements near Creek Town made him petition Edinburgh repeatedly for the re-location of the College; arguably, Edinburgh's lukewarmness hindered the UP mission's expansion.

Dean produced an important translation of the Obufa Efik New Testament (E, 1910), as well as a few other, mainly New Testament, studies. His imaginative work greatly benefited from his wives – Mary Chalmers and then, after her death, Mary Morrison, both already serving missionaries who supported him in adapting ministerial training to meet Nigerian circumstances. Because of ill health, Dean had returned to Scotland by 1899, when he became minister of Coldingham UP (formerly Burgher) church. Joining the UFC* in 1900, he was awarded a DD by Aberdeen University in 1923. He resigned from Coldingham UFC in 1919 to return to Calabar (having acted as Principal of the Hope Waddell Institute from 1917), retiring in 1936.

FUFCS, 69, 558; *FES* IX, 732; Small I, 422.

W. H. Taylor

Declaratory Acts, UP (1879) and FC (1892). The statements drawn up by these two churches, ostensibly to clarify their relation to the Westminster Confession of Faith,* in fact marked the end of unreserved subscription to the Confession's 'whole doctrine' (*see* Subscription, Confessional). The pattern of legislation was similar in both cases. As the Churches drifted from their earlier earnest and enthusiastic adherence to Westminster Calvinism, younger office-bearers began to call for a Confessional position which more honestly and authentically reflected the present faith of the Church. Committees were appointed to examine the matter and quickly rejected the idea of framing an entirely new Confession. Instead they proposed an explanatory statement, supposedly to guard against false interpretations of the Confession and to give what John Cairns* called 'here and there' liberty to those who had difficulty with relatively minor doctrinal points.

The greater part of both Acts consisted of an attempt to balance the Confession's predestinarian approach with affirmation of the universal love of God. While these paragraphs could be understood in a Calvinistic sense, conservative critics argued that they allowed for Arminian* and Amyraldian* views which were contrary to the Confession. Even more controversial were the clauses which allowed for liberty of opinion 'on such points in the Standards not entering into the substance of the faith' (UP) or 'on such points in the Confession as do not enter into the substance of the Reformed Faith' (FC). The difficulty was, and is, that nowhere in the legislation is there even a sketch of the parameters of the 'substance' of the faith. Cairns was confident that the clause would be treated in a gentlemanly way and not used to 'destroy the very faith it is brought in to strengthen and uphold'. While his confidence has often been justified, it has also been sorely abused. Subscription to an undefined 'substance' of the faith has not provided an evangelical bond of union for the Church.

Surprisingly, the UP Act was passed unanimously, and a pioneering Confessional adjustment occurred practically undebated. It was different in the FC, where the strong Highland* constituency remained loyal to Westminster Calvinism and vigorously defended the Confessional *status quo*. The Act was passed in face of furious resistance and, when calls for its rescinding were dismissed, a significant body of Highland people seceded to form the FPC* and many more became seriously disaffected. The Highlanders' perception was accurate. The provisions of the Act could be interpreted in a conservative sense and may have been so understood by their framers. Nevertheless, in the context of the religious and theological movement of the time, it signalled the exchange of the old Calvinistic doctrinal position for a more liberal understanding of the faith. The Acts were incorporated into the constitution of the UFC* in 1900 and the reunited CofS* in 1929.

PUPS, 1877–9; *PGAFCS*, 1889–94; J. S. Candlish, *The Relations of the Presbyterian Churches to the Confession of Faith* (G, 1886); C. G. M'Crie, *The Confessions of Faith of the Church of Scotland* (E, 1907), 279–302; A. R. MacEwen, *John Cairns* (L, 1898), 662–83; R. Rainy, *Explanatory Notes on the Declaratory Act* (E, 1894); *Free Church Declaratory Act: A Criticism and Protest* (G, 1892).

K. R. Ross

Declaratory Articles, *see* Articles Declaratory.

Deer, *see* Cistercians.

Deer, Book of, a small (154 mm × 107 mm) Gospel Book, now housed in Cambridge University Library. By *c*.1100 it was apparently in the possession of an early Columban* monastery (*see* Monasticism, Celtic) at Old Deer in north-east Aberdeenshire. This monastery has otherwise left no trace, although a Cistercian* abbey was founded nearby in 1219. The book contains, in Latin, the opening parts of the Gospels of Matthew, Mark and Luke, followed by a complete text of John. Between Mark and Luke is the final section of an Office for the Visitation of the Sick, and the manuscript concludes with the Apostles' Creed, the whole being rounded off with a colophon in Old Irish. The principal writings are apparently in a single hand of ninth-century date. The texts of the Gospels are derived from the Old Latin text of the Vulgate, but are badly written, with numerous instances of mis-spelling and general carelessness.

The manuscript is best known for six Gaelic* entries, and one Latin deed of David I* (1124–53), written in the blank spaces around the main items, and involving perhaps as many as five separate hands. These were probably drawn up and inserted towards the middle of the twelfth century. Because of their undeniably Scottish provenance and early date, the Gaelic entries are of great significance. The first item provides an origin-legend for a monastery at Aberdour and for the older monastery at Deer, said to have been given to Drostan (*see* Celtic Saints) by Columba, who received it from a landholder called Bede. The following four entries record later grants of land to the monastery, and the sixth concerns the 'quenching' or extinguishing (by the superior) of dues on certain lands received by it. Such writing demonstrates the value attached by Gaelic-speaking clerics to formal Gaelic deeds confirming (*c*.1100–50) their land-grants and immunities. The final, Latin deed of David I bestows on the monks of Deer a general immunity from 'all lay service and improper exaction', the latter phrase perhaps explaining their main concern at this time.

As the Gaelic entries come from a part of Scotland which was once under Pictish* sway, the customs of landholding and social convention reflected in them have both Pictish and early Gaelic associations. Place-names, legal terms and ecclesiastical and landholding designations are recorded in forms which are of special interest to linguists and social historians. The language of the entries is particularly important in showing the sporadic influence of spoken Scottish Gaelic on Middle Irish written in Scotland.

There is debate about the quality, significance and source-models of the artistry and illumination in the manuscript. The illumination includes decorated initials, arabesques and full-page drawings of what have been taken to be the Evangelists. Kathleen Hughes (*Celtic Britain in the Early Middle Ages*, ed. D. Dumville, Woodbridge, 1980, 22–37) regarded the art-work as degenerate, comparing unfavourably with Irish and other possible exemplars and suggesting that the artist was working from poor sketchbooks. More recently, Isobel Henderson (in D. E. Evans *et al.* (eds), *Proceedings of the Seventh International Congress of Celtic Studies*, O, 1986, 278) has claimed that the imagery is 'evidently modelled on a full-scale Gospel Book of some sophistication' and that the 'drastic reduction' of its forms conceals their skill and complexity.

K. Jackson, *The Gaelic Notes in the Book of Deer* (C, 1972).

D. E. Meek

Deism. 'Scotland received Deism, but made no substantial contribution to its literature, for she was to provide a sterner brand of scepticism in the writings of David Hume.' With these words A. L. Drummond* and J. Bulloch* concluded their discussion of deism, which impinged on Scotland significantly 1690–1760. And yet Gaskin, the equally judicious authority on Hume's* philosophy of religion, regards Hume's view as an attenuated deism. These differing verdicts are both defensible because deism is a loosely integrated constellation of claims and theses, which are characteristic, rather than precisely definitive of it, or essential to it (whether singly or in combination).

Characteristic of deism were beliefs respectively about God, about the way to knowledge of God, and about humanity. Typically deists held that there is a maker of the world, and (commonly) that this God is concerned that his creatures behave well;

but they eschewed further specific affirmations about God such as those made by Trinitarian orthodoxy, and there is at least a Unitarian* tendency in their thought. Relatedly they relied on reason as the means to knowledge of God, and tended to reject, or even ridicule, claims to special revelation supposed to have occurred at particular times and places. Human beings are thus capable, by their own capacities, of rising to knowledge of God, and also of rising to do God's will and to act well.

Many Scots were sympathetic to some of these ideas. There were influential figures outside of Scotland, such as the bookseller Thomas Johnson, who, through his businesses at The Hague and later at Rotterdam, supplied books of deistic tendency to many Scottish customers, students and others, over the first few decades of the eighteenth century. The extent of these views is hard to judge because those who held them used irony, or discussed them in dialogues with whose participants the authors could not be precisely identified, or kept rather quiet. Again, a moderate (or Moderate*) deist might have confidence in rational theology without denying all special revelation or biblical authority. Compared to more rational deists such as Toland, Hume was sceptical about our establishing the existence of some particular sort of deity with any confidence. Yet he seems to have thought that reason can take us so far as to attribute some probability to a heavily qualified belief in God, on the basis of an argument from design. It is difficult to find, in Scottish writing, any thoroughgoing deist. The arch-deist John Toland (1670–1722) was, it is true, a matriculated student at Glasgow University and a graduate of Edinburgh, but his intellectual debts lie elsewhere, in continental rationalism. His later life was not spent in Scotland and he can hardly be regarded as a Scottish writer.

The General Assembly of 1696 complained that some who posed as deists in fact taught atheism. How far this was true, it is now impossible, as it must then have been difficult, to determine. Both words, 'deist' and 'atheist', were often used of persons who were, in the eyes of the speaker or writer, rationalistically heterodox. In view of the impricese and multiple criteria for the use of 'deist', accusations of deism would more often (i.e. than accusations of atheism) have some justification.

D. Hume, *An Enquiry Concerning Human Understanding* (edited by L. A. Selby-Bigge) (²O, 1902), Section XI (entitled 'Of a Particular Providence and of a Future State'); D. Hume, *Dialogues Concerning Natural Religion* (edited by N. Kemp-Smith), (E, 1947); John Toland, *Christianity not Mysterious* (L, 1696); A. L. Drummond and J. Bulloch, *The Scottish Church 1688–1843* (E, 1973); J. C. A. Gaskin, *Hume's Philosophy of Religion* (L, 1978); P. Edwards (ed.), *Encyclopaedia of Philosophy* (L, 1967) II, 326–36.

J. Houston

Deliverances, decisions of church courts. In the practice of the General Assembly* of the CofS a committee publishes, with its report, a proposed deliverance, usually in numbered sections. The convener of the committee speaks to the report and then moves the deliverance, which becomes the motion before the Assembly. After debate, which may include amendments and counter-motions, the mind of the Assembly is ascertained by voting. What emerges from this process is the deliverance of the Assembly. In judicial cases the procedure is the same, except that there is no proposed deliverance, motions being called for after parties have been heard. Overtures* from members of Assembly or from inferior courts should have proposed deliverances, and the procedure is the same as for committee reports.

Standing Orders of the General Assembly of the Church of Scotland.

J. L. Weatherhead

Dempster, Thomas (1579–1625), RC scholar and academic. Born at Cliftbog, Aberdeenshire, he attended school at Turriff and Aberdeen, thereafter studying at Cambridge, Paris, the Scots College* of Douai, and Rome. After taking a degree in law at Paris (1601–3), he briefly renounced Catholicism at La Rochelle (1604). He then lectured at Catholic Toulouse and Protestant Nimes, but opposition compelled him to return to Scotland (1608). Fruitful years followed at Paris, until James VI* summoned him to London as Historiographer Royal. Finally he lectured on law in Pisa (1617) and humanities at Bologna (1619), where he died, the flight of his English wife hastening his early demise. His career was marked by continual dissensions. His *Ecclesiastical History*, a Scottish response to Irish claims, is in large part a patriotic invention. A capable Latin poet, he published editions of minor Latin writers that were much esteemed, while one posthumous work established his reputation as the pioneer of Etruscan studies. His notes on Justinian and on politics survive unpublished. In all his work, however, brilliant scholarship is vitiated by unreliable judgment.

DNB XIV, 335–40; J. Durkan, 'The French Connection' in T. C. Smout (ed.), *Scotland and Europe (1200–1850)* (E, 1986), 19–44; *id.*, 'Notes on Scots in Italy', *IR* 22 (1971), 12–18; J. H. Baxter in *Dict. d' Hist. et de Geogr. Eccl.* 14, 215–18; W. Murison, 'Sir Thomas Dempster', *AUR* 13 (1925), 118–32.

J. Durkan

Denney, James, (1856–1917), theologian and New Testament scholar. Born at Paisley into a Reformed Presbyterian family, Denney was educated in Glasgow at the University and FC College and ordained to Broughty Ferry East FC, 1886. He was elected Professor of Systematic Theology in the FC College, Glasgow, in 1897, Professor of New Testament Language, Literature and Theology in 1900, and Principal of the College, 1915. His works include: *Jesus and the Gospel* (L, 1908); *The Death of Christ* (L, 1902); *The Atonement and the Modern Mind* (L, 1903); *The Christian Doctrine of Reconcili-*

ation (L, 1917); *The Second Epistle to the Corinthians* (L, 1894); *The Epistles to the Thessalonians* (L, 1892); *Studies in Theology* (L, 1894); *The Way Everlasting* (L, 1911); *Letters to William Robertson Nicoll* (L, 1920); *Letters*, ed. James Moffatt (L, n.d.).

Denney was schooled in Calvinism as a child, but passed through a period of 'broad churchism', before emerging as a champion of the Pauline gospel of redemption after his wife had introduced him to the writings of C. H. Spurgeon.* His theology is passionately Christ-centred: 'Christ is the whole of Christianity – Christ crucified and risen.' He laboured to shift attention away from the quest for the historical Jesus to the 'reality' of the risen, present Christ. For speculative Christology, however, he had no time. He believed that Christ was known through what he had done. The atoning death was his absorbing theme and his great work was to defend its objective character. He expounded the reality and moral necessity of the wrath of God, and the propitiation in Christ's blood which alone forms the basis for divine reconciliation with mankind. He strikes his most sublime notes when speaking of the costliness of redemption.

While he based his theology on the historicity of the New Testament, Denney scorned the idea of the verbal inerrancy of Scripture in favour of an 'infallibility of power to save'. A further matter of controversy was that, while he was distinctly anti-Ritschlian, he eschewed metaphysics in his Christology and insisted that Christ could be described only with the language of religious faith. Regarding the work of Christ, Denney disliked the ideas of representation and mystical union which he considered inimical to a proper understanding of the atonement, but it remains a question whether he did justice to Paul's teaching on union with Christ. Nevertheless, he ranks high as an exegete of Paul. His notably lucid style gave him an accessibility often denied to the erudite, and his mastery of epigrammatic statement a timelessness to his writing. All his work was coloured by his conviction that 'I haven't the faintest interest in any theology which doesn't help us to evangelize.' The result is a *corpus* of theological writing that throbs with moral and spiritual power. Denney became increasingly involved in church administration and at the time of his death was becoming recognized as *the* ecclesiastical leader in Scotland.

See Systematic Theology.

J. R. Taylor, *God Loves Like That!* (L, 1962); T. H. Walker, *Principal James Denney* (L, 1918); A. P. F. Sell, *Defending and Declaring the Faith* (Exeter, 1987), 195–226; W. M. MacGregor, *Persons and Ideals* (E, 1939), 13–22.

K. R. Ross

Dewar, Daniel (1788–1867), CofS minister, scholar and latterly Principal of Marischal College, Aberdeen. A Gaelic* speaker born in Glen Dochart, Perthshire, Dewar was influenced initially by the Haldane movement, and studied at Robert Haldane's* seminary (1801). Thereafter he was an itinerant preacher with the Independents* (*see* Hal-

dane preachers), serving in the Aberfeldy district (1802–4). Educated further at Homerton Independent College (1804), he moved from Independency into the CofS and was licensed by the Presbytery of Mull in 1812. After a brief period as missionary at Strontian, in Ardnamurchan, he became minister of the College Church of Greyfriars, Aberdeen (1814–19). During this time he completed studies at Edinburgh University (MA, 1815). Glasgow University awarded him an LLD (1815), and later a DD (1833). He attained scholarly eminence, and was appointed Professor of Moral Philosophy at King's College, Aberdeen (1815). Translated to the Tron Church, Glasgow (1819–32), he assisted Norman MacLeod (1783–1862)* with the compilation of a Gaelic Dictionary (G, 1831). Demitting his Glasgow charge, he returned to Aberdeen as Principal of Marischal College (1832) and Professor of Church History (1833). He remained in the Est.C at the Disruption.* His works include *Elements of Moral Philosophy and Christian Ethics*, 2 vols (L, 1826), *Elements of Systematic Divinity*, 3 vols (G, 1867), and *The Nature and Obligations of Pastoral and Family Religion* (G, ^{2}1821).

FES III, 475, IV, 175, VI, 9, VII, 361, 363; J. Ross, *A History of Congregational Independency in Scotland* (G, 1900), 121, 228.

G. Wareing

Diaconate, Deacons, Deaconesses, a ministry of the Church, and those who serve in it. Its origins are found in the NT and the early centuries. The diaconate has taken different forms in the history and traditions of the Church, and has at times been in abeyance.

In Acts 6 the Seven represent the first differentiation of ministries. They are appointed with prayer and the laying on of hands to a practical ministry of serving those in need: the noun *diakonos* (deacon, servant) is not used here, but both *diakonia* (service) and *diakonein* (to serve) are. Later in the NT church deacons, twice coupled with bishops, seem to have been their helpers (Phil. 1:1; 1 Tim. 3), but it is impossible to be precise about their duties. Phoebe (Rom. 16:1) is described as *diakonos*, a helper. Whether the 'women' (1 Tim. 3:11) were wives of deacons or female deacons is not clear.

Soon in both the Eastern and Western Church, deacons and deaconesses are ambiguously found. Deacons exercised liturgical as well as charitable functions, *e.g.* assisting the bishop in the Eucharist, and leading the people's response in praise and prayer. Deaconesses had particular responsibilities among women, *e.g.* in preparing candidates for baptism, as well as serving the poor and needy. In the East, deacons have had a continuous history; in the West, by the Middle Ages the male diaconate had become a step towards the priesthood. In both East and West, by the sixth century, deaconesses were superseded by nuns.

Calvin observed that in the Roman Church 'the legitimate order of deacons has long ago been abolished' (*Institutes* 4:5:19). He intended to renew the primitive Catholic tradition of a diaconate engaged

DIACONATE, DEACONS, DEACONESSES

in pastoral care of the poor. The order of the diaconate should be restored to its integrity (*ibid*.4:5:15).

In Scotland the office of deacon was re-established at the Reformation. The *FBD* prescribed the election of and qualifications for deacons (along with elders*) and defined their duties as receiving rents of the teinds* (since the monies were to sustain not only the minister 'but also the poore and schooles' (158)), gathering alms and distributing them as appointed by the Session. They were also to be permitted to assist in judgement with the ministers and elders and to read in the assembly, if required and able to do so (178-9). The *SBD* followed the first in defining the deacon 'as a financial officer whose duties consisted in collecting the church's revenues and in distributing alms among the poor and needy' (97; cf. 174-6, 239-9). In addition, in practice to the end of the sixteenth century, deacons sat on the Kirk Session in some parishes (*e.g.* St Andrews), though not in others, and frequently, with the elders, assisted in serving Communion (98). The Westminster Assembly's* Form of Government affirmed the diaconate as practised in Scotland and both Alexander Henderson* (*The Government and Order of the Church of Scotland*, L, 1641) and James Guthrie* (*A Treatise of Ruling Elders and Deacons*, E, 1652) described the deacon's duties in much the same terms.

Although without a great deal of publicity, deacons were regularly elected by most congregations and their ministry continued without interruption through the end of the seventeenth century. It was not until the early eighteenth century that the office began to be neglected and its duties assumed by the eldership. Even then John Anderson* (*A Defence of the Church-Government, Faith, Worship, and Spirit of the Presbyterians*, G, 1714) affirmed that deacons were the rule in town churches and existed in many country parishes as well (212). And in 1719 the General Assembly recommended that deacons be ordained in such congregations where they were wanting (*AGACS*, 529).

A gradual decline led to an almost universal neglect of the office by the early nineteenth century, when first Thomas Chalmers* (*The Christian and Civic Economy of Large Towns*, 3 vols, G, 1821-6) suggested its revival as a temporary expedient and then John Lorimer (*The Deaconship*, E, 1842) argued for its reinstatement. Subsequently the FC elected and ordained deacons to serve on Deacons' Courts, whose duty was the administration of congregational finances (*AGAFCS 1842*, 22-4; *1847*, 26). That usage persists in a few congregations of the CofS.

In the CofS in 1887 Professor A. H. Charteris* proposed to the General Assembly the restoration of the scriptural office of the diaconate for women. In 1888 the General Assembly approved this step and the first deaconess, Lady Grisell Baillie,* was set apart by the Kirk Session of Bowden (near Melrose) to this office. Deaconesses and Parish Sisters (1906) in the Est.C and Church Sisters (1916) in the UFC existed side by side in the re-united CofS,

until in 1950 they came together to form a single Order of Deaconesses.

From the 1950s it came to be realized that the concept of an Order was not appropriate in a Presbyterian Church, and the term has fallen into disuse. Emphasis has since then been placed on the distinctive office held. In 1979 the General Assembly resolved that 'the office of the deaconess shall be renamed office of the diaconate', that 'the office of the diaconate shall be open to men and women', and that 'the holders of the office of the diaconate shall be known as deacons and deaconesses'. In 1988 the first men were recognized and commissioned as deacons, thus completing the realization of the 1888 vision of the restoration of the diaconate.

CofS deacons and deaconesses are trained at St Colm's.* They are commissioned by Presbytery, and are responsible to Presbytery for life and doctrine, and were admitted to membership of Presbyteries in 1990. They are at the disposal of the Church for appointment to the place of greatest need, such appointments being made in response to requests from Presbyteries. They have a corporate forum in the Diaconate Council, which is serviced by the Diaconate Committee of the General Assembly. Their function is to exercise a ministry in conformity with the gospel which may be expressed through evangelism, pastoral care, education or social service, in an appointment approved by the Diaconate Committee. There are currently about seventy-five deaconesses and deacons, of whom about one quarter are in appointments other than parishes.

In Baptist (and some other Independent) churches, the deacons constitute the corporate oversight of the congregation (cf. the Presbyterian eldership*). They are normally elected for a set period by the congregational meeting. Not all churches regard women as eligible. A few have full-time deaconesses, fulfilling a pastoral ministry, not only among women.

In the EpCS, deaconesses may be ordained but are not in holy orders; deacons, the third order of ordained ministry, have been probationers for the priesthood, but the restriction of the office to a transitional diaconate is now being questioned. Women have since 1986 been ordained deacons; and deacons, men and women, may now serve as permanent deacons with distinctive functions in liturgy and pastoral service.

In the RC Church, the decision was taken at the Second Vatican Council in 1964 to restore the diaconate as a permanent grade of ministry, since when it has been possible for married men of mature years to be ordained to the permanent diaconate. Women are not admitted. In Scotland the RC Church has ordained men to this office.

Ecumenically, there is considerable discussion on the restoration of the diaconate. 'Today there is a strong tendency in many churches to restore the diaconate as an ordained ministry with its own dignity and meant to be exercised for life' (*Baptism, Eucharist and Ministry*, commentary on Ministry, para. 31).

DICK, JOHN

The Multilateral Church Conversation* in Scotland has published a report *Deacons for Scotland?* On the initiative of the CofS a Scottish Ecumenical Encounter on the Diaconate was held in 1988.

A. H. Charteris, *The Church of Christ: its Life and Work* (L, 1905); *The Ministry of Deacons* (WCC Studies 2; Geneva, 1965); *The Deaconess: A Service of Women in the World Today* (WCC Studies 4; Geneva, 1966); *Baptism, Eucharist and Ministry* (Faith and Order Paper, 111; Geneva, 1982); *Deacons in the Ministry of the Church* (L, 1988) – CofE report; Multilateral Church Conversation in Scotland, *Deacons for Scotland?* (E, 1990).

M. I. Levison and the Editors

Dick, John (1764–1833), minister of Slateford (1786–1801) and of Shuttle Street, Glasgow (Greyfriars from 1821) (1801–33) USec. congregations, and Professor of Theology, USec.C (1820–33). He was awarded Princeton's DD in 1815. After a successful ministry at Slateford, near Edinburgh, he was inducted as colleague and successor to Alexander Pirie* in one of the oldest and wealthiest of the Secession congregations. Here he was successful in persuading a large portion of the congregation who regarded themselves as Old Lights (*see* New Light) to return to active membership. His sermons were regarded as models of clarity, conciseness, and simplicity of style. After he was appointed to the theological chair, which he accepted with much reluctance, at first only Burgher (*see* Associate Synod) students attended his lectures, but such was his ability and tact that the Antiburgher faction (*see* General Associate Synod) soon attended too. After his death his former students continued to meet as the 'Dick Association'.

He was very much involved in the attack mounted by several leading members of the Secession Church on the doctrines of William McGill of Ayr,* after the Est.C had failed effectively to prosecute McGill for the heretical socinian views he was widely regarded as holding, and he published a sermon on the subject entitled *The Conduct and Doom of False Teachers* (E, 1788). During the 1790s he contributed to the debate in the Secession Church over adherence to the Westminster Confession of Faith,* especially its teaching on the relationship of Church and state. His sermon *Confessions of Faith shown to be Necessary, and the Duty of Churches with Respect to them Explained* (E, 1796) led to a heated pamphlet war with some of the Old Light party. In the course of this, he supported the frequent revision of confessions of faith. He was a strong supporter, too, of the infant missionary movement, preaching on at least one occasion before the Edinburgh Missionary Society (*see* Missions).

His most influential work, published posthumously by his son Andrew Coventry Dick, *Lectures on Theology*, 4 vols (E, 1834; ²1838), was reprinted frequently and used widely in the Presbyterian Churches in the USA, where Archibald Alexander of Princeton commended it as the best systematics in English. Another important theological contribution was his *Essay on the Inspiration of*

DICK, THOMAS

the Holy Scriptures of the Old and New Testaments (E, 1800; ³G, 1813). In this work, which arose from the dispute in the Secession Church over continued adherence to the Covenants,* he defended the doctrine of plenary inspiration. However, he accepted varying kinds or degrees of inspiration as being required in the composition of different books of the Scriptures depending on the subject matter or previous states of mind of their authors. At the height of the Apocrypha Controversy* he was chosen President of the BFBS Glasgow Auxiliary (*see* Bible Societies). He had a high regard for the Scriptures, and a distrust of reason as a source of religious insight. In matters of Church politics, he was a strong opponent of the idea of establishment* but maintained cordial relations with members of other Churches.

See Systematic Theology.

A Sermon on the Qualifications and the Call of Missionaries (E, 1801); *Sermons* (G, 1816); *Lectures on Some Passages of the Acts of the Apostles*, 2 vols (G, 1805–8).

DNB XV, 14–16; 'Memoir' by A. C. Dick in *Lectures on Theology* (1834), vol. 1, ix–xl; W. Peddie, in *United Sec. Mag.* 1 (1833), 257–72; J. M'Kerrow, *History of the Secession Church* (²G, 1841); Small II, 25.

J. R. McIntosh

Dick, Robert (1811–66), baker and geologist. Although he spent most of his adult life as a baker in Thurso in Caithness, Robert Dick established himself as an amateur geologist and natural historian of considerable accomplishments. Besides accumulating an outstanding collection of British flora, he was stimulated by the appearance of Hugh Miller's* *Old Red Sandstone* in 1841 to turn more single-mindedly to questions of palaeontology, the consequence of which was a long correspondence with Miller, who benefited greatly from Dick's observations and assistance. Though Dick's career resembled Miller's, he published nothing and communicated his findings in letter. Sir Roderick Murchison, sometime President of the Royal Society, also gleaned much from his correspondence with him. Dick was a man of conspicuous religious and scientific culture, and Samuel Smiles found his life so inspirational that he told it as the final biography in his series on the virtues of self-help.

DNB XV, 16; C. C. Gillispie, *Genesis and Geology* (Cambridge, MA, 1951); S. Smiles, *Robert Dick*... (L, 1870).

D. N. Livingstone

Dick, Thomas (1774–1857), religious philosopher. Born in Dundee of parents belonging to the Antiburgher branch of the Secession* (*see* General Associate Synod), he studied at Edinburgh and then under the Synod's divinity professor, Archibald Bruce.* Ordained to Stirling in 1803, he was deposed and excommunicated in 1805 after serious personal disturbance. His membership was restored in 1806, but he turned to schoolteaching (at Methven, near Perth, 1807-17, and in Perth itself, 1817-27), making an important contribution to the development of adult education (cf. L. J. Saunders, *Scottish Democracy 1815-1840* (E, L, 1950), 256-8). His energies were thereafter devoted to science, especially astronomy (*The Practical Astronomer*, L, 1845), and writing. His works were frequently reprinted and had a large readership in Wales and the USA, where both collected and individual works were frequently reprinted. *The Christian Philosopher, or the Connection of Science and Philosophy with Religion*, 2 vols (G, 1823, ^{8}1842) made him widely known as 'the Christian Philosopher'. Other influential works were *The Philosophy of Religion, or an Illustration of the Moral Laws of the Universe* (G, 1826), and *The Philosophy of a Future State* (G, 1828) – dedicated to Thomas Chalmers* (David Livingstone* found both helpful).

Dick was a liberal thinker, impatient of technical theology and of Protestant disagreements. Opposed to war and the slave trade, he admired the benevolence of 'Quakers and Moravians' (*Christian Beneficence Contrasted with Covetousness*, L, 1838). He believed in a plurality of inhabited worlds, was sympathetic to emerging evolutionary theory and foresaw several modern discoveries and inventions. His natural theology has been called 'a theoloy of creative immanence'.

DNB XV, 18; W. Anderson, *The Scottish Nation* III (E, 1877), 704-7; H. Macpherson, 'Thomas Dick: "The Christian Philosopher"', *RSCHS* 11 (1955), 41-62.

D. F. Wright

Dickie, Edgar Primrose (1897-1991), theologian. Son of the editor of the *Dumfries and Galloway Standard*, he enlisted at 17 in the King's Own Scottish Borderers and won a Military Cross in World War I. After a brilliant career at Edinburgh and Oxford he was UF and then CofS minister in Lockerbie (1927-33) and Edinburgh (1933-5), and then till retirement in 1967 Professor of Divinity at St Andrews. Dickie was a great encourager of students, took full part in the Kirk's councils and wider work (notably as director of Huts and Canteens* in France in World War II), and was a royal chaplain. His published works include *Spirit and Truth* (L, 1935); *Revelation and Response* (E, 1938); *God is Light* (L, 1953); *The Unchanging Gospel* (E, 1960); and *The Father Everlasting* (Wallington, 1964). His great gift of humour found scope in a series of articles in *Punch* and three delightful volumes of stories for children.

FUFCS 99; *FES* IX, 10, 135, 769-70, X, 430; *Who's Who 1991*, 493.

J. D. Douglas

Dickson, David (*c.*1583-1663), eminent preacher, educator and federal theologian (*see* Covenant Theology), and defender of Presbyterian polity. He was the only son of John Dick, or Dickson, a wealthy and godly Glasgow merchant. After receiving the MA at the University of Glasgow and serving as Professor of Philosophy, he was ordained in 1618 to Irvine in Ayrshire. There he laboured with extraordinary fruitfulness (*see* Revivals) for about twenty-three years, though his ministry was interrupted between 1622 and 1623 when he was banished to Turriff in Aberdeenshire for his public opposition to the Articles of Perth* and the Episcopalian polity they imposed. Through his influence, the Presbytery of Irvine petitioned the Council in 1637 to suspend the prelatical service-book, and he was one of the three men sent by the Covenanters* to persuade the men of Aberdeen to join in the renewal of the Covenants. In the Glasgow Assembly* of 1638 Dickson demonstrated remarkable tact and learning and was chosen Moderator for the next Assembly in Edinburgh. About 1640 he was appointed to the newly created professorship of divinity in the University of Glasgow where he served with distinction; he also preached regularly in the High Church. In 1650 he was appointed Professor of Divinity in Edinburgh but was ejected from his chair for his refusal to take the oath of supremacy upon the return of Charles II* and the restoration of prelacy.* These hardships adversely affected his health and he fell ill in 1662 and died early the next year.

Dickson is best known through his writings. His most important theological work was his *Therapeutica Sacra . . .* (Latin, L, 1656; ET, by Dickson, E, 1664, ^{2}1695) which bore the English sub-title *The Method of Healing the Diseases of the Conscience Concerning Regeneration*. He wrote the first sympathetic and full commentary on the Westminster Confession* entitled *Praelectiones in Confessionem Fidei*, later published in English as *Truth's Victory Over Error . . .* (published under the name of a pirate author in E, 1684, but with Dickson's name in G, 1752). He is well known for his commentaries (*Hebrews*, A, 1635; *Expositio Analytica Omnium Apostolicarum Epistolarum*, G, 1645, translated as *An Exposition of all St. Paul's Epistles*, L, 1659; *Matthew*, L, 1647; *The Psalms*, L, 1653-4; ^{2}1655), which were part of a series begun at his initiation, whereby worthy divines were assigned particular books of the Bible considered difficult (*see* Exegesis, Biblical). He was co-author with Alexander Henderson* of 'Ansueris of Sum Bretheren of the Ministrie to the Replysis of the Ministeris and Professoris of Divinity at Abirdein', 1638. He also worked with Henderson and David Calderwood* on a Directory for Public Worship (*c.*1643) and was co-author with James Durham* of the famous The Sum of Saving Knowledge (*c.*1650, ed. J. Macpherson, E, 1886).

W. K. Tweedie (ed.), *Select Biographies*, 2, 1-14; DNB XV, 41-2; J. Howie, *The Scots Worthies* (^{2}E, ?1884), 288-97; Chambers-Thomson I, 446-9; J. Macleod, *Scottish Theology* (E, ^{3}1974), 83-7.

L. I. Hodges

Dickson, William Purdie (1823-1901), theological professor. Born in the CofS manse at Pettinain, Lanarkshire, he was an outstanding student at St Andrews (1837-44). After mission service at Grangemouth he was ordained to Cameron, Fife

(1851–63), where he was involved with his old University, especially its Library. He then became Professor of Biblical Criticism (1863–73) and of Divinity (1873–95) at Glasgow, where he was also Curator of the Library (1866–90). He twice declined nomination as Moderator, but received the DD of St Andrews (1864) and Glasgow (1896) and the LLD of Edinburgh (1885).

Dickson excelled as a translator from German – of Mommsen's *History of Rome* (4 vols, L, 1862–6) and *Provinces of the Roman Empire* (L, 1886), and of H. Meyer's *Commentary on the New Testament* (10 vols, E, 1873–80) – but was critical of much biblical criticism (*The Methods of the 'Higher Criticism' Illustrated...*, G, 1890; *The Newer Light of a Recent Book*, G, 1896). Another interest was evident in his lectures on *The Theological Chairs of the Scottish Universities* (G, 1883) and *The Universities in Relation to the Training of the Ministry...* (G, 1884). He gave the Baird lectures* on *St. Paul's Use of... 'Flesh' and 'Spirit'* (G, 1883). As a memorial, friends presented Glasgow University Library with a complete set of Migne's *Patrologia*.

DNB Second Suppl. I, 501; *FES* VII, 402–3; *Who Was Who, 1897–1916*, 197; J. L. Galbraith, *The Curator of Glasgow University Library* (G, 1909).

D. F. Wright

Dinwiddie, Melville (1892–1975), radio broadcaster. He was the BBC chief executive in Scotland from 1933 to 1957. After an outstanding First World War record (DSO and MC) he was minister of St Machar's Cathedral, Aberdeen (1925–33). He gave a Scottish dimension to the high-minded style of broadcasting favoured by another son of the manse, John Reith.* He had considerable influence on religious broadcasting,* for example in shaping 'Lift up your Hearts', which later became 'Thought for the Day'. After retiring from the BBC he was an Edinburgh town councillor.

FES VI, 24; VIII, 530; *LW* 31 (August, 1975), 16.

R. D. Kernohan

Dinwoodie, John Sharp (1904–80), Esperanto linguist. Born at Kelty, Fife, he studied at Edinburgh University (MA, 1925) and New College, Edinburgh, and served as minister (at first in the UFC) at Harthill, W. Lothian (1929–33), Thornhill, Dumfriesshire (1933–42) and Pittenweem, Fife (1942–70). Faithful in his modest way in Pittenweem, he achieved international renown as a speaker, translator and poet in Esperanto, earning a tribute even on Polish radio.

FUFCS 38; *FES* IX, 53, 149, 499; W. Auld *et al., Kvaropo* (La Laguna, Canary Isl., 1952), 115–56, 250 – poems in Esperanto, and portrait.

D. F. Wright

Directory for Public Worship, *see* Westminster Assembly and Documents.

Discipline, an authoritative expression of the common mind of the Church on matters of conduct and doctrine, and the teaching of it to members or intending members of the fellowship; the means, remedial and restorative, of winning them back from error; the guarding of the purity of the Church.

The early Scottish Church was mainly influenced by Celtic* practice in discipline, as in much else. The sixth-century *Poenitentiale Vinniai* (by the Irish monastic founder, Finnian of Clonard, who died *c.*550) appoints varying grades of penance* or acts of penitence for sins ranging from thoughts and desires to evil deeds of varying magnitude. Some of the prescriptions are very severe: to sing Psalm 119 seven times with arms extended 'in honest cross-vigil' is a feat which would test the stamina of the most practised ascetic. But the importance of this and the other Celtic penitential manuals is that confession of sins, assignment of penance and reconciliation are done in private, whereas in the rest of the Western church all were part of the public liturgy. Penitential rules attributed to Comméne* and to Adomnán* are extant (J. T. McNeill and H. M. Gamer, *Medieval Handbooks of Penance*, NY, 1935).

Under the influence of Queen Margaret* and her sons, most notably David I,* the Scottish Church conformed to the general pattern of the Western Church, but in the matter of discipline the rest of the Church changed its practice to a pattern similar to that of the Celtic Church. Scotland was represented by three bishops at the Fourth Lateran Council in 1215, whose chief work was of a disciplinary character. Over the period 1237–86 the Provincial Councils* of the Scottish Church framed or adopted some sixty canons which promulgated the decrees of the Lateran Council. The Catechism of Archbishop John Hamilton* issued by the Council of 1552 explains the sacrament of penance. Its three elements are contrition, confession and purpose of satisfaction. The priest is to absolve on a worthy confession and the penance is set not as something 'to deserve remission of sin by pain and punishment or to make God a recompense... for only Christ can do this. It is to cut away the occasions of sin and to give no entrance to their suggestions.' Because of the secrecy of the penitential system it is very difficult to assess how effective it was.

It is significant that the Scots Confession* of 1560 lists as the third of the notes by which the true Kirk is discerned from the false, 'ecclesiastical discipline uprightly ministered as God's word prescribeth whereby vice is repressed and virtue nourished.' This emphasis reflects the heightened importance attached to Church discipline in Reformed centres like Zürich, Strasbourg and Geneva. In view of this it is remarkable that the Scots Confession in another section concedes a very important role to the civil magistrate in the exercise of discipline. It is to kings, princes, rulers and magistrates that the conservation and purgation of religion chiefly appertains. They are not only appointed for civil policy but also for maintenance of true religion and for suppressing of idolatry and superstition. This was taken to mean the abrogation by the Church of her authority to make and administer laws relating to marriage, divorce, consanguinity, wills and testaments and usury, which up to 1560 had been largely in the hands of the Provincial Council of the Church.

The First Book of Discipline* of 1561 puts the power of discipline mainly into the hands of the ministers and elders.* The minister is to preach the Word and administer the sacraments, admonish his flock and pronounce the sentence of excommunication. The elders are to assist the ministers in determining and judging causes, in giving admonition to licentious livers and to have respect to the manners and customs of those in their charge. Elders were to be elected every year lest they should presume upon the liberty of the Church.

The procedures of discipline are set out with great detail in the 'Form and Order of Excommunication and of Public Repentance' of 1563. This document is often printed as part of the *Book of Common Order** and thus brings discipline back into the public liturgy. Much consideration is given to offences that 'fall not under the civil sword and yet are slanderous and offensive in the Church'. These include fornication, drunkenness, swearing, cursing, chiding, fighting, brawling, common contempt of the Church and breaking of the sabbath. Such offences can lead to excommunication if the offender shows no sign of repentance. Other less heinous offences, including wanton and vain words, uncomely gestures, negligence in hearing the preaching or abstaining from the Lord's Table, suspicion of avarice or of pride, superfluity of riotousness in food or raiment are said to deserve admonition among the members of Christ's body.

The first step is admonition by one or two members. If amendment is promised the matter is at an end. If not, the admonition is to be repeated before two or three other witnesses. If there is still no satisfaction the offender is to be brought before the ministers and elders. Upon amendment no further action is taken. The fourth step, if necessary, is to declare the offence to the church without naming the offender and to exhort the offender to satisfy in public what he refused to do privately. If the offender shows willingness to submit before the following Sunday he can be declared as having repented without appearing in public. If however he refuses, the fifth step is to publish both the offence and the name of the offender. He will now have to ask to be allowed to submit and declare his penitence in public. If he still does not do so there is a third public admonition with the warning of possible excommunication for his added contempt and disobedience. If after the fifth or sixth step the offender craves to be admitted to public repentance, the session have to see to it that he is instructed in the nature of sin, the fear of God and the meaning of repentance and grace. That is the seventh step and the eighth is his presentation before the congregation on a Sunday after sermon.

The 'Form and Order of Excommunication and Public Repentance' provides specimen exhortations and prayers to be used by the minister and also the following absolution: 'If thou unfeignedly repent thy former iniquity and believe in the Lord Jesus, then I, in his name, pronounce and affirm that thy sins are forgiven not only on earth, but also in heaven, according to the promises annexed with the preaching of his Word and to the power put in the ministry of his Church.' Then the elders and deacons in the name of the whole Church are to take the reconciled brother by the hand and embrace him. The service is concluded by the singing of Psalm 103 and the benediction.

But if after the sixth step (the third public admonition) the offender is still not penitent, the procedure for excommunication is set in train. On three succeeding Sundays the offender is given an opportunity to submit and repent. If he is still impenitent the minister invokes the name of the Lord Jesus Christ and says: 'Here I in thy name and at the command of this thy present congregation cut off, seclude and excommunicate from thy body and from our society, N., as a person slanderous, proud, contemner and a member for this present, altogether corrupted and pernicious to the body.' There is, however, an equally elaborate procedure for receiving the excommunicate again to the society of the Church should repentance occur.

The Second Book of Discipline* (1578) declares that the whole policy of the Kirk consists in three things, doctrine, discipline, distribution. The elders are for discipline and their office is to watch diligently upon the flock committed to their charge, both publicly and privately, 'that no corruption of religion or manners enter therein'. They are to hold assemblies with the pastors for establishing of good order and execution of discipline and to these assemblies all persons are subject that remain within their bounds.

The Westminster* Confession of Faith (1647) has a brief chapter on church censures and asserts that to church-officers 'the keys of the Kingdom of Heaven are committed, by virtue whereof they have power respectively to retain and remit sins'. The General Assembly of 1707 established a Form of Process in cases of discipline and ordered Kirk Sessions to refer certain serious sins directly to the Presbytery. These included incest, adultery, relapse into fornication, murder, atheism, idolatry, witchcraft, charming, heresy and error. The Toleration Act passed by the Parliament of Great Britain in 1712 deprived Church courts of the right to require sheriffs to enforce their decrees or to require offenders to appear before them. In spite of this, discipline remained the principal activity of Kirk Sessions during the eighteenth century. The most common offence was ante-nuptial fornication. The General Assembly of 1902 recognized that the rules of the Form of Process had largely become unworkable because of the changed spirit of the age, although the Form is acknowledged in the Articles Declaratory* of 1921. Much of the formality of the disciplinary law was set aside and much power of initiative in difficult cases was put into the hands of the ministry. It was also provided that cases of discipline should always be kept in a record apart from the principal minutes of the Kirk Session and after five years the names of the offenders are required to be blacked out so as to be illegible.

The exercise of discipline has largely lapsed in the modern CofS, even in the form of the Supplementary Roll for members not attending communion. Most disciplinary cases before the courts of the Church (*and see* Judicial Commission) concern ministers, and occasionally elders (see Cox, 314–27).

I. M. Clark, *A History of Church Discipline in Scotland* (A, 1929); J. T. McNeill, *A History of the Cure of Souls* (NY, 1951); *FBD*; *SBD*; G. W. Sprott (ed.), *The Book of Common Order* (E, 1901); G. D. Henderson, *The Scottish Ruling Elder* (L, 1935); W. Mair, *A Digest of Church Laws* (E, ³1904).

H. R. Sefton

Discipline, First Book of, *see First Book of Discipline*.

Discipline, Second Book of, *see Second Book of Discipline*.

Disestablishment, the termination of constitutional links between Church and state.* During the last third of the nineteenth century there was a strong campaign for the disestablishment of the CofS. This had its origins in the Voluntaryism* of the 1830s and the formation in 1844 of the British Anti-State-Church Association, later the Liberation Society, which sought to secure disestablishment throughout the United Kingdom.

Pressure for disestablishment in Scotland was stimulated by the enactment of Irish disestablishment in 1869. UPs* were the staunchest opponents of the CofS, while the FC,* where support for a cleansed establishment still continued, was divided. However the Patronage Act* of 1874 was followed by greater support for disestablishment from Free Churchmen.

Agitation was co-ordinated by the Scottish Council of the Liberation Society, set up in 1877, the Scottish Disestablishment and Disendowment Association, formed in 1871, and the Disestablishment Council for Scotland of 1886. In response, the CofS General Assembly appointed a Church Interests Committee in 1882. The issue was central to Scottish general elections between 1874 and 1892. Disestablishment bills were brought forward in Parliament on various occasions, but did not come close to success.

Scottish disestablishment never happened because the Liberal Party, its natural advocate, was divided on the issue. In the longer term disestablishment began to seem an irrelevance as religious issues receded from the centre of national politics and the Church became more concerned with social issues and home missionary endeavour. After the Union of 1900 the UFC* was too preoccupied with its legal battle with the continuing FC for it to attack the CofS. Progress towards general Presbyterian reunion provided a broader basis for the survival of the establishment. Hence, although the Church in Wales was disestablished in 1921, the CofS, like the Church of England, has retained its established status until the present day, but with a freedom from state control that is increasingly the envy of English churchmen.

G. I. T. Machin, 'Voluntaryism and Reunion, 1874–1929', in N. MacDougall (ed.), *Church, Politics and Society* (E, 1983), 221–38; G. I. T. Machin, *Politics and the Churches in Great Britain 1869 to 1921* (O, 1987); A. L. Drummond and J. Bulloch, *The Church in Late Victorian Scotland 1874–1900* (E, 1978); J. G. Kellas, 'The Liberal Party and the Scottish Church Disestablishment Crisis', *English Historical Review* 79 (1964), 31–46; I. G. C. Hutchison, *A Political History of Scotland 1832–1914* (E, 1986); W. H. Mackintosh, *Disestablishment and Liberation* (L, 1972).

J. R. Wolffe

Disruption, the secession of over 450 ministers from the CofS in 1843. It was preceded by a bitter Ten Years' Conflict* between those in the Est.C who wanted to assert the spiritual independence of the Church, and those who were content with the Church's relations with the civil powers. This conflict was initiated by the Evangelical party. In 1834, having assumed a majority in the General Assembly for the first time in approximately one hundred years, the Evangelicals passed a Veto Act,* which gave parishioners the right to reject the ministerial nominee of parish patrons. The desire of the Evangelicals was to restore significance to the call,* a once cherished aspect of Presbyterian polity, and to prevent the intrusion of ministers on an unwilling people. The Act polarized opinions within the Church, setting it on a collision course with the state. Both those who were in favour of the Act, and those who believed it denied the legal rights of patrons, appealed to the Scottish Reformers in defence of their position.

The first test of the Veto Act came in October 1834. The congregation of the parish of Auchterarder* in Perthshire almost unanimously rejected the patron's nominee. The Presbytery refused to proceed with the ordination and induction. The rejected nominee, Robert Young,* appealed against the decision to the Court of Session, which in March 1838 decided by a majority of eight to five that the Church had acted *ultra vires* in passing and operating the Veto Act. It stated that the Act infringed the statutory rights of patrons. Some of the Church's leaders, including Thomas Chalmers,* were in favour of rescinding the Act and pursuing a different course of action. However, the statement by the Court of Session that the Est.C was a creation of the State, and derived all its powers from certain Acts of Parliament, challenged the Church's Confession of Faith, and in particular its belief that within its own domain it exercised sovereignty. Burleigh has put it well: 'The notion of the Church as an independent community governed by its own officers and capable of entering into a compact with the State was repudiated' (Burleigh, 342).

The Auchterarder decision marked the point when the controversy shifted from the problem of

Non-Intrusion* to the deeper question of the Church's spiritual independence. The Church's appeal to the House of Lords in 1839 was rejected, the right of patrons being held to be absolute. The area of conflict widened when the Presbytery of Dunkeld was summoned before the bar of the Court of Session for proceeding with an ordination in disregard of an interdict. The situation was further complicated by the General Assembly suspending in 1839 seven ministers from the Presbytery of Strathbogie* for proceeding with an induction to the parish of Marnoch in Aberdeenshire in defiance of its orders. In 1841 the Assembly deposed the seven for acknowledging the secular court to be superior in spiritual matters to the judicatories of the Church.

The Evangelical party had further cause for concern when the 1834 Chapel Act* was deemed illegal by the Court of Session. In response to the threat to its spiritual independence, the Non-Intrusionists drew up and presented to Parliament their 'Claim, Declaration and Protest anent the Encroachments of the Court of Session'. The Claim recognized the jurisdiction of the civil courts in relation to all the temporalities conferred by the state on the Est.C. But rather than abandon the Church's cherished belief in its own sovereignty in spiritual matters it resolved to give up the privileges of establishment. The 'Crown Rights of the Redeemer' would not be sacrificed at any cost. The die was cast. The Crown's rejection of the Claim in January 1843 inevitably led to the Disruption in May of that year, when over 450 ministers left the CofS to form the FCS. Echoing Ebenezer Erskine's* comments in 1733, Chalmers declared, 'Though we quit the Establishment we go out on the Establishment principle; we quit a vitiated Establishment but would rejoice in returning to a pure one. We are advocates for a national recognition of religion – and we are not voluntaries.'

The principle that Chalmers and the other Evangelical leaders were contending for was that of 'sphere sovereignty'. The issue, however, was not exclusively one between Evangelicals and Moderates. A number of Evangelicals remained within the Est.C, believing it better to preserve the unity of the Church than provoke a schism. The leading figures of the 'Middle Party'* were Matthew Leishman,* Norman MacLeod,* and Alexander Simpson. But the leaders of the Non-Intrusionists, Chalmers, R. S. Candlish,* Robert Buchanan,* and Hugh Miller* among others, would not compromise. The issue was clear to them: Was Jesus Christ King in his own Church or not? The convictions and spirit which led to the Disruption are vividly seen in Hugh Miller's famous letter to Lord Brougham: 'We have but one Bible and one Confession of faith in our Scottish Establishment, but we have two religions in it; and these, though they bear exactly the same name and speak nearly the same language, are yet fundamentally and vitally different.'

The Ten Years' Conflict was not about the democratization of the Church. It was about the desire of the Church to be the Church, sovereign within its own domain. Although it was part of a European-wide movement of thought that sought to give new degrees of power to the ordinary people, the Disruption was essentially a spiritual phenomenon. Such a judgment does not preclude the considered view of many scholars that in the longer term this sundering of the national Church was fraught with gravely damaging consequences for the spiritual good of both Kirk and nation.

G. D. Henderson, *Heritage – A Study of the Disruption* (E, 1943); R. Buchanan, *The Ten Years' Conflict*, 2 vols (E, 1849); H. Miller, *The Headship of Christ* (E, 1861); W. Hanna, *Memoirs of the Life and Writings of Thomas Chalmers*, 4 vols (E, 1849–52); S. J. Brown, *Thomas Chalmers and the Godly Commonwealth in Scotland* (O, 1982); id. and M. Fry (eds), *Scotland in the Age of the Disruption* (E, 1993); T. Brown, *Annals of the Disruption* (E, 1893).

I. Hamilton

Dissenters. Presbyterian dissenters were, in the main, the children of the 1733 Secession (*see* Associate Presbytery; Secessions). The cause of dissent was basically disagreement with the 1712 Act of the General Assembly which reintroduced lay patronage.* Dissenters advocated the right of a congregation to have a determinative say in the choice of a minister. However, in practice their ideals were difficult to carry out, since the financial power exercised by leading laymen, many of whom had vested interests in the church property, proved as much a form of patronage as that of the lay patron within the Est.C. An interesting case of how divided a dissenting congregation could become is found in the pamphlet *The Spirit of the Union* (E, 1823). The new cause was soon divided over the Burgess Oath,* and an 'Antiburgher' Church (*see* General Associate Synod) was set up in 1747. By 1799 dissenters had divided into four main groups (*see* New Light). In 1820 the two more progressive groups, the New Lights, united to form the USec.C. In 1847 the more liberally-minded Relief Church* united with the USec. in the UPC.

Before 1790 the main body of Seceders had adhered to the concept of a state Church, but by the 1830s most of them, as the Relief Church had already, fully supported the Voluntary* principle.

The main stream of Scottish dissent differed from that of Independency or non-Calvinistic Methodism in England in that it remained Presbyterian with allegiance to the Westminster Confession of Faith. Divisions arose over patronage and Voluntaryism rather than doctrine, in which the Secession, Relief, UP and Free Churches retained essential similarities to the CofS. As J. R. Fleming says, 'External invasion has been more responsible than internal schism', and, 'The various forms have marvellously preserved the family likeness. The propensity to divide has never meant departure from the common ideal.'

There was, however, another stream of dissent emanating from the Presbyterian churches. This emerged primarily in the wake of the Haldane movement (see Haldane Preachers), and produced independent,* 'gathered' congregations (see Baptists; Congregationalism).

N. Morren, *Annals of the General Assembly* . . . [1739–66] (E, 1838–40); J. M'Kerrow, *History of the Secession Church* (G, 1841); A. R. MacEwen, *The Erskines* (E, 1900); G. Struthers, *The History of the Rise, Progress and Principles of the Relief Church* (G, 1843); Small; D. Scott, *Annals and Statistics of the Original Secession Church* (E, 1886); G. F. C. Jenkins, 'Establishment and Dissent in the Dunfermline Area 1733–1883' (PhD, University of Edinburgh, 1988).

G. F. C. Jenkins

Distributism, a radical political philosophy advocating restoration of liberty by distribution of property, opposed equally to monopoly capitalism and communism, and strongly influenced by papal social encyclicals. Its earliest advocates in Britain were G. K. Chesterton (1874–1936) and H. Belloc (1870–1953). The Distributist League, founded 1926, included a branch in Glasgow. Besides propaganda work, it encouraged craftsmen, small businesses and farms.

Distributists supported the already existing 'Back to the Land' movement. The Scottish Catholic Land Association, formed in 1929, soon had over 500 members. In 1931 Father John McQuillan (1889–1970) took over a 200-acre farm at Symington, Lanarkshire, to train men interested in farming their own land. A second farm was acquired and five similar centres, modelled on Symington, were opened in England. The Symington farm closed in 1936 in a period of agricultural depression.

The Distributist League did not survive the Second World War, but Glasgow University Distributist Club, founded 1930, still exists. Distributist ideas have found expression in the works of later writers such as E. F. Schumacher (1911–77), author of *Small is Beautiful*.

See also Phillimore, John S.

The Distributist Programme (1934); *G.K.s Weekly*, 1925–38; *Land for the People* [Glasgow], 1930–5; *Catholic Directory for Scotland*, 1971, 317–20.

J. Darragh

Divine Right of Kings, see Church and State.

Divine Right of Presbytery, the doctrine that the leading features of the Presbyterian form of government are revealed in the Scriptures as a rule permanently binding on the Church. The Westminster Assembly* asserted a divine right (Latin, *jus divinum*) for a government in the hands of Church officers distinct from the civil magistrate, and recognized a scriptural sanction for specific officers, for particular congregations, and for presbyterial and synodical assemblies governing many congregations. Two commissioners from the CofS, George Gillespie* and Samuel Rutherford,* contributed significantly to the Assembly's debate on the divine right of Presbytery.* In their published work preceding and concurrent with the Assembly, they vindicated the doctrine, particularly by examining the biblical evidence for the ruling elder* and for the Church courts* in which ministers* and elders on a parity exercised discipline.* An earlier exposition of a biblical mandate for Presbyterianism* is found in David Calderwood's influential *Altare Damascenum* (1623; Leiden, 1708).

Further extensive writing in behalf of the theory took place in the wake of the Revolution settlement of 1689 (see Church and State). The writers of this period, Gilbert Rule,* Thomas Forrester,* William Jameson* and John Anderson,* drew a comparison between episcopacy* and Presbyterianism in the light of apostolic practice and example. A more modern restatement of divine-right Presbyterianism was provided by the Edinburgh New College* professors William Cunningham* and James Bannerman.* Cunningham argued that in the Scriptures the worship ordinances and discipline are committed to the rulers rather than to the body of the Church, that biblical presbyters might be classed as some who both rule and teach while others only rule, and that a gradation of presbyterial assemblies is discernible in the scriptural record of Church order. Cunningham claimed an endorsement of these tenets is in the ordination* profession, that 'the Presbyterian government and discipline of this Church are founded upon the word of God, and agreeable thereto'. Involved in the notion of divine-right Presbyterianism is the conviction that apostolic example reflects a mandate from Christ to the apostles concerning how the Church should be organized, the belief that there are sufficient materials in the Scriptures for determining what the apostles practised, and the persuasion that Church government is not a matter left to expediency.

W. Cunningham, *Historical Theology*, 2 vols (E, 1862); id., *The Reformers and Theology of the Reformation* (E, 1862); J. Bannerman, *The Church of Christ*, 2 vols (E, 1868); G. Gillespie, *An Assertion of The Government of Church of Scotland* (E, 1641); id., *Aaron's Rod Blossoming* (L, 1646); S. Rutherford, *The Divine Right of Church-Government and Excommunication* (L, 1646); J. R. DeWitt, *Jus Divinum* (Kampen, 1969); J. MacPherson, *The Doctrine of The Church in Scottish Theology* (E, 1903).

S. Isbell

Divinity, see Education, Theological.

Divorce, see Marriage.

Dobson, Thomas (1878–1922), missionary. He was born in Tongland, Kirkcudbright. His family moved to Glasgow when he was nine; he became a printer. He was an Evangelical Union* member, influenced by George MacDonald's* theology, an active socialist and a vegetarian. He went to India in 1903 to manage the Pune printing works of the Scottish Mission Industries Company, the fruit of a former famine relief scheme. He rescued a flagging enterprise, while doing much for vulnerable groups (temple children, Eurasian boys) in the community, and for soldiers, and, through his explicitly Christian vegetarianism, finding a special place in local Hindu-Christian dialogue. He ceased to live in the European quarter, sharing the house of the local YMCA* secretary in order to help the young men of the Christian community. In 1920 he was appointed a missionary of the UFC in Jalna (see Missions: Western India) with special responsibility for the co-operative agricultural banks, which had come under strain through several years of famine. An exponent of 'the gospel of work', he applied capital raised by subscription in Scotland, introduced new farming methods, fought famine and assisted the growth in prosperity and dignity of the Mang 'untouchable' (now scheduled caste) group. He was murdered in circumstances that remain obscure.

E. G. K. Hewat, *Vision and Achievement* (E, 1960), 57–65; N. MacNicol, *Tom Dobson. A Champion of the Outcastes* (L, [1924]).

A. F. Walls

Doctors, one of the ministerial offices in the early Reformed Churches (not to be confused with the medieval designation of eminent Fathers – originally Ambrose, Jerome, Augustine and Gregory – as doctors of the Church). The doctors (Latin for 'teachers') were identified as a distinct office (in addition to pastors, elders and deacons) by Calvin* in the 1541 Genevan *Ecclesiastical Ordinances*, based on what he learned at Strasbourg (1538–41). Their role was the inculcation and defence of true doctrine, and the office could also be called 'the order of the schools', covering both grammar schools and the later Genevan Academy (1559). According to Calvin's *Institutes* from 1543 on, pastors and doctors were permanently necessary in the Church, corresponding respectively to the (temporary) apostles and prophets. Doctors were not to be involved in discipline or administering the sacraments but in scriptural interpretation (*Inst.* 4:3:4–5). In Geneva the public professors of the Academy, in subjects not restricted to theology proper, were associated with the pastors in the ministerial oversight of the Church.

In Scotland the *Forme of Prayers* (see *Book of Common Order*, 1564) spoke of doctors ('a fourth kind of minister') in terms very close to the 1541 Genevan *Ordinances*. The *First Book of Discipline** did not mention them, but proposed a system of parish schools as well as reform of the universities. The *Second Book of Discipline** has a section 'Off Doctouris and thair Office and of Scoles', which includes colleges and universities (*SBD*, 187–90). The doctors may also be called prophets, bishops, elders or catechizers. With other elders they assist the pastors in the government of the Kirk. The functions of doctors and pastors were differentiated as in Geneva, except that pastors might teach in the schools, but doctors did not preach. Somewhat as in Geneva, doctors and pastors shared in the corporate Bible study of the exercise,* harbinger of the Presbytery.* While schoolmasters might be called doctors, in the later sixteenth century the title chiefly belonged to university teachers like George Buchanan,* Andrew and James Melville,* Patrick Sharp,* Robert Rollock* and John Johnston.*

The royal ascendancy over the Church led to the eclipse of the doctoral office and the debarring of doctors, professors and regents from the Church courts. Although the 1638 Glasgow Assembly* reinstated the *SBD*, the Westminster Assembly's* Form of Presbyterial Church Government, after a sharp debate, depicted 'the teacher or doctor' as a special kind of congregational ministry not readily differentiated from the pastoral office and equally able to minister Word and sacraments. Only a brief tailpiece mentions the value of the teacher or doctor in schools and universities. Scottish opinions were by no means as clearcut as the *SBD*. James Guthrie* and George Gillespie* divided the eldership into preaching elders (pastors), teaching elders (doctors) and ruling elders, but others, such as Samuel Rutherford,* saw the doctor as a specialized pastor-minister. The teachers in the colleges of divinity were certainly doctors.

In the contemporary CofS, the title has not survived, but the office is reflected in the place assigned to university teachers in the Church courts and generally in the specialist work of committees. The Reformation doctor is best represented in the non-pastor teacher of theology.

The Aberdeen Doctors* were so called because they each had the DD of King's College.

R. W. Henderson, *The Teaching Office in the Reformed Tradition: A History of the Doctoral Ministry* (Philadelphia, 1962).

D. F. Wright

Dodds, George Theophilus (1850–83), FC missionary to France. Born in Dundee, where his father was a FC minister, he studied at St Andrews University (1866–70) and from 1871 at New College,* Edinburgh. In 1877 he proceeded to Paris where he worked with a Protestant missionary agency, the McAll mission. He was ordained by Edinburgh FC Presbytery in 1879, and devoted the remaining years of his life to the Paris mission. Dodds was the son-in-law of Horatius Bonar,* who wrote his biography, *The Life and Work of the Rev. G. Theophilus Dodds* (L, 1884).

N. R. Needham

Dods, Marcus (1786–1838), Presbyterian minister. Born in East Lothian, his only ministerial charge was at Belford in Northumberland, England, but his theological orientation was that of Andrew Thomson* and the *Edinburgh Christian Instructor*,* to which he was a contributor.

Amidst a rising pamphlet war over the extent of inspiration of the Scriptures, and the inclusion of the Apocrypha* in the canon, Dods' *Remarks on the Bible* (E, 1828) gave a careful defence of the doctrine of the plenary verbal inspiration. *On the Incarnation of the Eternal Word* (L, 1831) offered a sustained erudite critique of Edward Irving's* contention that the flesh Christ assumed was fallen and sinful. Dods argued that Christ's human nature was generated holy through the virgin birth.

DNB XV, 169; J. MacLeod, *Scottish Theology* (E, [3]1974), 260-5.

S. Isbell

Dods, Marcus (1834-1909), FC and UFC New Testament scholar. Born at Belford, Northumberland, the son of Marcus Dods (1786-1838),* and educated at Edinburgh University and New College, Edinburgh, he was ordained to Renfield Free Church, Glasgow (1864), elected to the chair of New Testament Exegesis, New College (1889), and Principal of the (by then UF) College in 1907.

Dods was a gifted writer and prolific editor, and left work of enduring value, such as the fifteen-volume translated *Works of Augustine* (E, 1871-6) which he edited, and the fifty volumes of *Handbooks for Bible Classes* which he co-edited with Alexander Whyte.* Historically, however, he stands out as the pioneer of a new understanding of Scripture and of a more liberal approach to the faith. While Robertson Smith* was challenging the FC with higher critical theories, Dods addressed himself directly to the question of biblical inspiration, in works such as *The Bible: its Origins and Nature* (E, 1905) and *Revelation and Inspiration* (G, 1877). He argued for a view which allowed for inaccuracies in matters of detail while preserving infallibility in matters of substance. His appointment in 1889 as Professor of New Testament Criticism and Exegesis in New College precipitated conservatives in the FC to libel him in the 1890 Assembly because of his liberalism on inspiration. Dods' triumph was a tacit sanctioning of his views by the FC. It also marked the advent of a new approach to Christianity, since Dods had distanced himself from the heavily doctrinal statement of the faith with which the FC had hitherto been identified. His new methods and emphases took him a long way from the FC 'orthodoxy' of an earlier day, but he was regarded as being steady on the essentials of the faith. His *Later Letters* (L, 1911; cf. *Early Letters*, L, 1910), however, seem to reveal a man who had lost his way. Whatever his personal position, he was certainly one of the most influential figures in the FC's movement towards a more liberal understanding of the faith (cf. his inaugural at New College, *Recent Progress in Theology*, E, 1889).

The Book of Genesis (E, 1882); *Introduction to the New Testament* (L, 1888); *I Corinthians* (L, 1889); *What is a Christian?* (E, 1889); *The Gospel of John*, 2 vols (L, 1891); *Erasmus and other Essays* (L, 1891); *Christ and Man* (L, 1909).

AFCS I, 53; FUFCS 576; DNB Second. Suppl. I, 510-12; W. R. Nicoll, *Princes of the Church* (L, 1921), 234-41; H. Watt, *New College Edinburgh* (E, 1946).

K. R. Ross

Dollarbeg Group, series of five ecumenical study conferences held 1947-50 near Dollar, Clackmannanshire. They involved a wide range of leading Scottish churchmen to deal with subjects of sharp contemporary importance. The group gathered first to respond to a questionnaire (from the World Council of Churches in formation) on 'The Life and Work of Women in the Church' (evoking E. G. K. Hewat's* booklet of that title), moving in 1948 to 'Christian Witness in a Revolutionary World'. It produced 'The Christian Challenge to Communism' in 1949 (with George MacLeod* and Donald Mackinnon*), 'The Work and Witness of the Laity' the same year (Hendrick Kraemer), and in 1950 'The Christian Doctrine of Work' (J. H. Oldham*). The group's activities paved the way for the Scottish Churches Ecumenical Association (see Ecumenical Movement). A leading activist throughout was Isobel Forrester, wife of Professor W. R. Forrester of St Andrews.

Mabel Small, *Growing Together. The Ecumenical Movement in Scotland 1924-1964* (typescript, Dunblane, n.d.), 17-25.

D. F. Wright

Dominicans. Known also as Black Friars (from the black cloak worn in public over their white habit) or Friars Preachers, they originated in the preaching mission conducted by St Dominic (c.1170-1221) among the Albigensians in southern France. The preachers, who practised evangelical poverty, became a permanent institute in 1215 and received papal approval in 1216. The motto of these friars,* *Contemplata tradere* (pass on what was learned in prayer), signified the contemplative and apostolic elements in their life. They became renowned as theologians and had close links with universities.

Dominicans were introduced to Scotland at Edinburgh in 1230, and a further eight foundations were made before 1249: at Aberdeen (1230-49), Ayr (c.1242), Berwick (c.1240/1), Elgin (1233-4), Glasgow (1246), Inverness (c.1240), Perth (c.1240) and Stirling (c.1249). Thereafter the pace slowed, with only six foundations – at Wigtown (1267 or c.1287), Montrose (c.1275), Cupar in Fife (1348), St Andrews (c.1364), Haddington (1471) and St Monans in Fife (1471) – taking place in the next two hundred years, during which period some of the earlier houses appear to have fallen into disarray.

However, the establishment of a Scottish province in 1481 and the appointment of John Adamson as provincial in 1511 initiated a new regime. With the support of the bishops, in 1519 he closed the friaries at Cupar and St Monans, which had each maintained only two friars, transferring their endowments to a revitalized house at St Andrews. Consolidation had, however, been preceded by plans in 1517 to found a new friary at Dundee, and this was achieved before 1521. The fervour of the friars brought them increased endowments, as the register of the Ayr Dominicans testifies (R. W. Cochran-Patrick (ed.), *Munimenta Fratrum Predictorum de Are*, Ayrshire and Galloway Archaeological Association, E, 1881). Gifts of arable or grazing land were particularly welcome; the Dominicans of Perth cultivated such lands and crofts, owned their privileges of mills and sold their crops and hides, but at least part of the profit was set aside for charity (R. Milne, *The Black Friars of Perth*, E, 1893). Gifts, whether in rents or kind, were dictated by piety, but the friary church could also act as a business centre, while many friars had contact with universities and their own libraries were well stocked (A. Ross, 'Libraries of the Scottish Blackfriars, 1481–1560', *IR* 20 (1969), 3–36). Their very intellectuality could, however, take them in the direction of heretical opinion, and in 1539 two Black Friars were burnt as heretics and several others fled to England. Others were equally staunch in their faith, and figured prominently in several trials for heresy. This factor, together with relative prosperity and apparent disregard for the poor, targeted them for exemplary treatment at the Reformation, when many of their houses were destroyed and their communities dispersed (D. McRoberts (ed.), *Essays on the Scottish Reformation*, G, 1962, 191–209).

After the Reformation Scots continued to become friars abroad, and some Dominicans worked as missioners in Scotland. Friaries were established at Edinburgh in 1931 and Glasgow in 1965 (*see* Religious Orders).

New Catholic Encyclopedia IV, 971–82; Easson-Cowan, 114–23; P. J. Anderson, *Aberdeen Friars: Red, Black, White, Gray* (A, 1909); W. M. Bryce, *The Black Friars of Edinburgh* (E, 1911); D. Currie, 'The Order of Friars Preachers in Scotland', *RSCHS* 10 (1950), 125–39; J. Robertson (ed.), *Munimenta Fratrum Predictorum de Glasgu* (Maitland Club, G, 1846); A. Ross, 'Dominicans and Scotland in the Seventeenth Century', *IR* 23 (1972), 40–75.

I. B. Cowan

Donaldson, Gordon (1913–93), eminent Scottish historian. A Shetlander by descent, he was born in Edinburgh and educated at its Royal High School, and the Universities of Edinburgh (MA, 1935) and London (PhD, 1938). He was appointed assistant, HM General Register House, Edinburgh, in 1938, Lecturer in Scottish History at Edinburgh University in 1947, Reader in 1955, and Sir William Fraser Professor of Scottish History and Palaeography, 1963–79. He served as a member of the Royal Commission on Ancient and Historical Monuments of Scotland, 1964–82, and the Scottish Records Advisory Council, 1964–87, and as president of the Scottish Ecclesiological Society, 1963–5, the Scottish Church History Society,* 1964–7, the Scottish History Society, 1968–72, the Scottish Record Society, 1981–93, and the Stair Society, 1968–93. He edited the *Scottish Historical Review*, 1972–7. Awarded Edinburgh's DLitt in 1954, he became FBA (1976), FRSE (1978), Hon. DLitt of Aberdeen (1976) and Hon. DUniv. of Stirling (1988), Historiographer Royal in Scotland (1979) and CBE (1988).

The author of over thirty books on Scottish history, and of innumerable articles in learned journals, Donaldson gained distinction for his prolific contributions to Scottish church history and to record scholarship. His early doctoral work on 'The Relations between the English and Scottish Presbyterian Movements' was followed by the seminal study *The Scottish Reformation* (the Birkbeck Lectures at Cambridge, 1958) in 1960. *Scotland: James V to James VII* appeared in 1965, a work indispensable to Scottish history students for over a generation. *All the Queen's Men*, in 1983, was highly influential in exploring the complexities of religion and politics in Mary Stewart's reign; *Scottish Church History* (1985) brought together selected essays, themselves the product of half a century's research and reflection, and *The Faith of the Scots* (1990) explores the hitherto neglected topic of religious thought and belief. Appropriately, he was the recipient of a *Festschrift*, *The Renaissance and Reformation in Scotland*, ed. I. B. Cowan and D. Shaw, in 1983.

As a member of the EpCS and a participant in several series of inter-Church discussions from 1950 to 1985, Donaldson contributed material to *The Anglican-Presbyterian Conversations* in 1966, was active in the Multilateral Conversation* (*see* Ecumenical Movement) which brought in the UFC and Congregationalists, and contributed to a working party on 'The reconciliation of ministries'.

Who's Who 1991, 506; *The Renaissance and Reformation in Scotland, Essays in Honour of Gordon Donaldson*, ed. I. B. Cowan and D. Shaw (E, 1983), 1–21, 236–44.

J. Kirk

Donan, *see* Celtic Saints.

Donnchad (Dunchad) (*d.*717), Abbot of Iona,* 707–17, succeeding Adomnán.* There appears to have been rivalry over the abbacy during his tenure, for the Irish annals mention other abbots at this time (Conamail, *d.*710; Dorbéne, *d.*713; Faelchú, 716–22). It is unlikely that the contest was related to the paschal controversy (*see* Christian Year), because Bede* states that Donnchad presided over the conversion to the Roman Easter in 716, while his contemporary Dorbéne made an early copy of Adomnán's *Life of Columba* and so could not have been opposed to Adomnán's Romanizing views. It has been suggested that the conflict was connected with warfare between the Cenél nGabráin and the Cenél Loairn, two tribes of the Dál Riata who were competing for the kingship of that people.

Bede associates the changes in celebration of Easter and shape of the tonsure* at Iona with Egbert, an English monk who came to Iona after years of study in Ireland in 716 and died there in 729. The Irish annals date the change of Easter to 716 and of the tonsure to 718, the year after Donnchad's death.

See also Celtic Church.

Bede, *Hist. Eccl.* 5:22; J. Bannerman, appendix to K. Hughes, 'The Church and the World in Early Christian Ireland', *Irish Historical Studies* 13 (1962–3), 113–16; M. Herbert, *Iona, Kells, and Derry* (O, 1988), 57–9.

A. Macquarrie

Dort, Synod of. Held in 1618–19 in the South Holland town of Dordrecht, this Synod was composed of three groups: fifty-six ministers and elders and five professors from the Netherlands; eighteen political commissioners, to supervise and to report to the Parliament; twenty-six delegates from foreign churches, though none from Scotland. No reference was made to Scotland in the invitation received by James I and VI,* who sent English delegates and instructed them how to act at the Synod. James did finally send a Scot, Walter Balcanquhal,* the son of a CofS minister, but himself a minister of the CofE.

The Synod was called as a consequence of the debate over the preaching of James Arminius (1560–1609) in Amsterdam and his teaching at the University of Leiden after his appointment there in 1603. Though committed to the Reformed confessions, Arminius' teaching in public, and more so in private, deviated from Reformed orthodoxy. His followers after his death composed a Remonstrance (hence their name the Remonstrants) which summarized the Arminian* teaching: (a) election on the basis of foreseen faith; (b) universal atonement securing the salvation of believers; (c) the necessity of regeneration (though with an understanding of human depravity which differed considerably from orthodox teaching); (d) resistible grace; (e) uncertain perseverance. The Calvinists produced their Counter-Remonstrance, and, after fruitless conferences achieved no consensus, the national synod was called.

After months of work and protracted conflict with the Remonstrants, the Synod produced its canons in ninety-three articles, in response to the five basic tenets of Arminian opposition and affirming: (a) the unconditional and gracious character of election; (b) an atonement limited in its extent and design to the elect; (c) human depravity which is total in extent so that we cannot do any saving good; (d) invincible divine grace; (e) the perseverance of God's saints. These canons did not profess to be a full statement of Reformed teaching, but only of these parts which bore upon the positions of the Remonstrants.

After the proclamation of the canons, forty of the Arminian ministers conformed and were restored to office. About 150 were either banished or agreed to refrain from their ministry. While it has often been claimed that this was a persecuting Synod, yet the ministers in question had been teaching contrary to their pledged adherence to the Reformed confessions.

The Synod of Dort had a considerable impact on the Scottish Church, reinforcing its Reformed (broadly Calvinistic) position. The discussions at Dort were well known in Scotland through books and teaching in the divinity faculties. In matters of Church order, appeal to procedures at Dort, such as occurred several times at the Glasgow Assembly of 1638,* was the best possible defence. The canons came to be regarded as a test of orthodoxy and at times subscription to them was either required or offered.

Their indirect influence on Scottish theology increased with the adoption of the Westminster Confession* in 1647, for the Westminster divines drew on the canons. The Confession did not reproduce Dort closely, but belonged to the same movement. Its adoption in Scotland further sharpened the distinction between orthodox Calvinism and Arminianism. Repudiation of Arminianism was required of CofS ministers from 1704 until 1889, and is still required in the smaller Calvinistic Churches.

P. Schaff, *The Creeds of Christendom*, I (NY, 1884), 508–23; W. Cunningham, *Historical Theology*, 2 vols (E, 1870), II, 371–513; M. W. Dewar, 'The British Delegation at the Synod of Dort – 1618–1619', *EQ* 46 (1974), 103–16; G. D. Henderson, *Religious Life in Seventeenth-Century Scotland* (C, 1937), 77–99; P. Y. De Jong (ed.), *Crisis in the Reformed Churches: Essays in Commemoration of the Great Synod of Dort, 1618–1619* (Grand Rapids, 1968).

N. R. *Needham*

Dougall, James Watson Cunningham (1896–1980), missionary and mission* strategist in Africa. Born in Auchterarder, Dougall attended Glasgow University where his studies were interrupted by war service, and he graduated MA in 1920. In 1920–1 he was inter-collegiate Secretary of the Student Christian Movement.* Licensed by the Presbytery of Auchterarder in 1923, he went to Africa as Secretary of the Phelps-Stokes Commission on education in East and Central Africa. In 1925 he was ordained for missionary service and proceeded to Kenya, where he was appointed first Principal of the Jeanes School, Kabete. In 1932 he became Education Adviser to the Protestant missions in Kenya and Uganda, a post he relinquished in 1936 to become Secretary of the Bible Churchmen's Missionary Society. In 1940 he became associate Secretary of the Foreign Missions Committee of the CofS and then General Secretary in 1946. He retired in 1960, after playing a key role in the merging of the missionary organization with the indigenous Church in a number of African countries.

Missionary Education in Kenya and Uganda (L, 1936); *Christians in the African Revolution* (E, 1963).

FES IX, 799, X, 453.

A. C. *Ross*

Douglas Affair. *The Tragedy of Douglas* by John Home,* minister of Athelstaneford, was first performed publicly in Edinburgh on 14 December 1756. The author of the play and several other ministers were present. During the following months, several Presbyteries attacked the theatre and theatre-going on both religious and social grounds, and action was taken against ministers who had attended. Only one, however, the most celebrated of those charged, Alexander Carlyle,* made any serious attempt to defend his actions, in a process which ended up at the General Assembly of 1767. Home resigned his charge shortly after the start of proceedings. The affair has been seen as of key significance in leading Scotland in the direction of cultural and intellectual freedom, but in view of the overwhelming dubiety with which ministerial attendance at the theatre was viewed, it is perhaps sounder to see it, as Carlyle did himself at the time, as an episode in the eighteenth-century conflict between the Moderates* and those he calls the 'High-flying set'.

Alexander Carlyle, *Autobiography* (L, 1910); *id., Anecdotes and Characters of the Times* (L, 1973); N. Morren, *Annals of the General Assembly of the Church of Scotland, 1739 to ... 1766* (E, 1838-40), II; R. Sher, *Church and University in the Scottish Enlightenment* (E, 1985).

J. R. McIntosh

Douglas, Gavin (*c.*1475–1522), bishop and poet. The son of Archibald Douglas, fifth earl of Angus, he was educated at St Andrews, and possibly Paris. He became Provost of St Giles', Edinburgh (1503) and later bishop of Dunkeld (1515). After Flodden (1513) Douglas became increasingly involved in political affairs, especially after his nephew married the widowed queen Margaret Tudor (1514). Family intrigues sent him to London (1521), and led to a charge of high treason. Death stopped his scheming to become archbishop of St Andrews. As a poet Douglas is numbered among the 'Scottish Chaucerians'. He is credited with the allegorical *Palice of Honour* (*c.*1501), but no longer with *King Hart*. His masterwork is his *Aeneid* translation (1513), one of the earliest complete renderings in any European vernacular; for each book there are original poetic prologues, several of which are celebrated for their descriptions of nature.

Virgil's Aeneid Translated, ed. D. F. C. Coldwell, STS, 4 vols (E, 1957–64); *Shorter Poems of Gavin Douglas*, ed. P. Bawcutt, STS (E, 1967); *Poetical Works of Gavin Douglas*, ed. J. Small, 4 vols (E, 1874).

P. Bawcutt, *Gavin Douglas* (E, 1976).

A. A. MacDonald

Douglas, (Blessed) George (*d.*1587), Roman Catholic martyr.* A Scottish priest, he was arrested in Yorkshire about 1585 for speaking against married priests and Protestant bishops and spent two years or more in confinement in Ripon and York. Condemned for 'persuading to popery', which was treason under an Elizabethan statute of 1581, he was hanged, drawn and quartered at York on 9 September 1587. English Catholics immediately venerated him as a martyr and he was beatified in 1987.

Almost certainly he was the secular priest interrogated at Rutland in 1584 and thus was the son of John Douglas, burgess of Edinburgh, and a kinsman of John Douglas (*d.*1574)*, Protestant Archbishop of St Andrews. Having graduated at St Andrews, he became a schoolmaster in Rutland and was ordained priest at Paris. He has sometimes been identified with Franciscan priests of the same name.

Sacred Congregation for the Causes of Saints, Historical Section, 92: Cause of Beatification of Ven. George Haydock and Companions (Rome, 1981), 2533–86; M. Dilworth, *George Douglas: Priest and Martyr* (G, 1987).

M. Dilworth

Douglas, George Cunninghame Monteath (1826–1904), Hebraist. He was born in Renfrewshire and graduated with distinction in languages from Glasgow University in the year of the Disruption* (1843). He then studied under Chalmers* at New College, Edinburgh, and was ordained FC minister at Bridge of Weir (1852). Appointed Hebrew tutor in the new FC College in Glasgow in 1856, he served as OT Professor 1857–92, and as Principal 1875–1902. He was awarded the degree of DD by Glasgow University (1867), and worked on the OT Committee for the RV revision of the AV (1870–84). He was a scholarly conservative, sceptical of higher critical views.

His publications include: *Joshua, Judges, Six Intermediate Minor Prophets*, Handbooks for Bible Classes (E, 1881); *Isaiah One and His Book One* (L, 1895); *Samuel and His Age* (L, 1901).

DNB Second Suppl. I, 517; *AFCS* I, 53.

J. D. MacMillan

Douglas, James, fourth Earl of Morton (*c.*1516–81), Regent of Scotland. Being only the younger son of Sir George Douglas of Pittendreich, he received only a very elementary education and much of his early life is obscure. However, in 1548 he inherited the earldom of Morton by marriage and by 1552 was appointed to the Privy Council. Already identifiable as a lukewarm Anglophile, Morton flirted with Protestantism, signing the First Band in 1557. But it was not until May 1560 that he clearly identified himself with the aims of the Lords of the Congregation.*

Morton was appointed Chancellor by Mary Queen of Scots* in January 1563, and he supported her against James Stewart, Earl of Moray* during the Chaseabout Raid in the autumn of 1565. However, a combination of personal rivalry, concern for his wealth, and unhappiness with the RC drift of Mary's policies led Morton to participate in the murder of David Rizzio on 9 March 1566. Flight into England and forfeiture followed, but Morton was pardoned on 24 December of that same year. Morton refused to commit himself to the murder of Darnley, but he did have foreknowledge of the murder, which was probably carried out by other Douglases in his employ. Morton initially gave public support to the Queen and the Earl of Bothwell following the murder, but he was a leading rebel in the campaign in May 1567 which led to Mary's defeat and enforced abdication. However, formal leadership of the King's Party (*see* James VI) did not fall to Morton until 1572 when he was elected Regent, and entrusted with bringing the civil war to a successful conclusion. This he did, with English aid, on 28 May 1573.

Morton's regency was marked by a very pro-

English foreign policy, although he was bitterly disappointed by Elizabeth I's refusal to sign a formal alliance, and by a determined crack-down on lawlessness. The final defeat of the Marians also provided the Protestant Church with a much-needed breathing space before the Counter-Reformation's* onslaught of the 1580s. However, he failed to meet the Church's financial expectations and he promoted the office of bishop against the wishes of the General Assembly. It was Morton's discussions with the Church which led to the writing of the *Second Book of Discipline*,* which was presented to him in 1578 (*SBD*, 35-42, 124-8).

Morton's greed and his monopolistic exercise of power finally led to his enforced demission of office in March 1578 following a palace coup. While he recovered control of the King, the next two years saw him fighting a losing battle against his personal enemies at court. On 31 December 1580 he was arrested, and was executed on 2 June following, having been convicted of 'art and part' of the murder of Darnley in 1567.

G. R. Hewitt, *Scotland Under Morton, 1572-80* (E, 1982); G. Donaldson, *Scotland, James V to James VII* (E, 1965), 165-70; M. Lee, 'The Fall of the Regent Morton: a Problem in Satellite Diplomacy', *Journ. of Mod. Hist.* 28 (1956), 111-29; *DNB* XV, 309-22.

K. M. Brown

Douglas, John (*c*.1494-1574), provost of St Mary's College, University of St Andrews. The natural son of Robert Douglas of Longnewton (Roxburghshire), he entered St Leonard's College, St Andrews in 1515 and graduated MA in 1517. He continued his studies at Paris where he became a bachelor of medicine (and possibly also a doctor of theology); as a teacher in Montaigu College, he received support from Archbishop James Beaton* in 1537. Attracted by the plans of Archibald Hay, himself a Paris teacher, to create a trilingual college in St Andrews, Douglas returned home, a clerk of Dunkeld diocese, and on Hay's death in 1547 was appointed provost of St Mary's College, a post he retained till his death. In 1550, he was appointed Rector of the university. According to Pitscottie (*see* Lindsay, Robert) (but not Foxe or Calderwood) he acted as judge with John Winram* and others at the trial of Walter Milne,* who was burned for heresy in 1558. Yet both he and Winram, once fellow-students, chose the Protestant path at the Reformation, and by 1560 were extracting recantations from former priests. A contributor to the *First Book of Discipline*,* Douglas had presumably particular responsibility for the section on the universities.* In December 1560, the General Assembly approved Douglas' aptitude to minister and teach; by 1561 he served as elder on St Andrews Kirk Session; and in 1566, with some fellow ministers, he wrote to Beza in Geneva to affirm the Scottish Church's support for the Second Helvetic Confession (except for a section on holy days). In 1564 he agreed with Winram that the nobility and estates might justifiably 'oppose' Queen Mary* as a RC in the defence of their religion. He subscribed a band drawn up by the General Assembly in 1567 for the defence of Protestantism; and was commissioner from St Andrews University to the Assembly in 1569. With the ascendancy of King James' party in the civil war, and the forfeiture and execution for treason in 1571 of John Hamilton,* the RC Archbishop of St Andrews, Douglas was provided by the Crown to the vacant see, but was inhibited by Winram, as Superintendent* of Fife, from accepting on pain of excommunication. With agreement reached at the Convention of Leith* in 1572 on procedures for appointments to the bishoprics, Douglas was finally elected as Archbishop, but retained his university offices amid much controversy, which led John Knox* to condemn the arrangements. Unable through age to discharge his archiepiscopal duties effectively, Douglas incurred the General Assembly's repeated censure.

Early Records of the University of St Andrews, ed. J. M. Anderson (E, 1926), 104, 106, 211; *BUK*; Calderwood; *FBD*, 4, 8, 57f, 88, 119; *SBD*, 3, 20-1, 29-31, 85, 289; J. Kirk, *Patterns of Reform* (E, 1989); W. A. McNeill, 'Scottish Entries in the *Acta Rectoria Universitatis Parisiensis* 1519 to *c*.1633', *SHR* 43 (1964), 71, 73, 79-81, 83; *Register of the Minister Elders and Deacons of the Christian Congregation of St Andrews* (E, 1889-90); *FESMA*, 299, 382; K. Hewat, *Makers of the Scottish Church at the Reformation* (E, 1920), 308-49.

J. Kirk

Douglas, John (1721-1807), Bishop of Salisbury. The son of a merchant of Pittenweem (Fife), he studied at Oxford University 1736-43, was ordained an Anglican deacon in 1744 and became a military chaplain. In 1747 he was ordained priest and was curate of Tilehurst, in Berkshire, and then Dunstew, Oxfordshire. This was the beginning of a long series of movements from one charge to another, although Douglas often held several simultaneously and was generally non-resident. In 1787 he was appointed Bishop of Carlisle, and in 1791 was translated to Salisbury.

Douglas's contemporary fame rested on his writings on literary, religious and (mostly) political matters. His contribution to theology was a work entitled *Criterion* (1754), in which he engaged with David Hume's* denial of the credibility of miracles. The most novel aspect of Douglas's strategy was to accentuate the differences between biblical and post-biblical miracles. He argued that the kind of evidence which validated the former was not available for the alleged miracles of RC saints, Jansenist relics or the English monarch's curative touch.

Select Works (Salisbury, 1820), with W. MacDonald's 'Biographical Memoir' prefixed; *DNB* XV, 337-8.

M. Dilworth

Douglas, Niel (*c*.1750-1823), radical preacher and politician. A Gaelic-speaking native of

Douglas, Robert

Glendaruel, Argyll, Douglas trained as a Relief Church* minister, with charges at Cupar (1785-92) and Dundee (1793-8). About 1784 he and another Relief preacher were dispatched to Luing and Seil, Argyll, where they attempted to participate in the revival* which had begun under John Smith.* With Daniel McNaught he preached throughout Kintyre, the Lochgilphead district and Cowal in 1797, and published an account in *Journal of a Mission to Part of the Highlands of Scotland* (E, 1799). Spiced with acerbic comments on ministers of other denominations, the journal provides a picture of the early years of dissenting Evangelicalism in Argyll, and shows that Douglas was somewhat outspoken, taking a strong stance against patronage*, and sympathizing with the French Revolution.* Allegedly associated with the Friends of the People, a radical political organization, he left the Relief Church about 1800 and espoused the cause of universalism. He preached latterly in the Andersonian Institution, Glasgow, where he gained a reputation as 'a most extraordinary character . . . in his huge brown wig, and ancient habiliments'. In his sensational lectures on 'Prophecies of Daniel', he identified the deranged George III with Nebuchadnezzar. As a result he stood trial for sedition before the High Court of Justiciary, Edinburgh, but was acquitted (J. Dow, *Trial of Niel Douglas*, E, 1817). Now regarded as a precursor of the Unitarians,* Douglas also championed abolitionism, publishing pamphlets under the pseudonym of *Brutus*.

L. B. Short, *Pioneers of Scottish Unitarianism* (Narberth, 1963), 58-64; G. Struthers, *The History of the Rise, Progress and Principles of the Relief Church* (G, 1843), 396-400; F. Worsdall, *A Glasgow Keek Show* (G, 1981), 160-3; D. E. Meek, 'Evangelical Missionaries in the Early Nineteenth-Century Highlands', *SS* 28 (1987), 13, 20, 22.

D. E. Meek

Douglas (Dowglas or Douglasse), Robert (1594-1674), minister in Edinburgh and a leading figure in the CofS in the 1640s and 1650s. He was said to have been the son of a child born to Queen Mary and Sir George Douglas while the Queen was imprisoned at Lochleven, a tradition which Douglas did not deny and perhaps even encouraged though there is no positive historical evidence for it. His father was an illegitimate son of Sir George. Douglas studied at St Andrews (MA, 1614) and served as a chaplain under Gustavus Adolphus in the Thirty Years War. He was ordained to Kirkcaldy in 1628, sat in the 1638 General Assembly (*see* Glasgow Assembly) and the following year was translated to St Giles in Edinburgh, serving in different charges there over the next twenty-three years. He was elected Moderator of the General Assembly in 1642 and in 1643 one of the Commissioners to the Westminster Assembly,* though he was the only minister elected who did not serve. He did serve as a chaplain in the Scottish army (*AGACS*, 94). It is a measure of the high esteem in which he was held that he was elected Moderator of the Assembly four further times: 1645, 1647, 1649 and 1651. His abilities were held in such esteem that, in 1645, Robert Baillie* wrote to Sir Archibald Johnston* of Wariston, saying 'It's necessar Mr. Robert Douglas be Moderator . . .' (*The Letters and Journals*, E, 1842, II, 255). After Alexander Henderson's* death in 1646, Douglas was regarded as the leading man in the Church. The last time he was elected Moderator it was in St Andrews, as the leader of the Resolutioners.* A man of majestic presence, Douglas was often chosen to represent the Church in its relations with the state; in 1651 he preached the sermon at the coronation of Charles II* at Scone. He spoke of the crowning of a king as a necessary duty, and of the many sins of the king and his family, desiring 'the king may be truly humbled for his own sins, and the sins of his father's house, which have been great' ('Coronation Sermon at Scone' in *The Covenants and the Covenanters*, ed. J. Kerr, E, 1895, 351-2; first edition *The Form and Order of the Coronation of Charles II*, A, 1651, reprinted G, 1741). The efforts made by Douglas to effect the Restoration* resulted in the offer of a bishopric, which offer was conveyed by James Sharp.* Douglas refused, but perceiving Sharp's intention to take the Archbishopric of St Andrews told him to 'take it, and the curse of God with it' (J. Kirkton, *The Secret and True History of the Church of Scotland*, E, 1817, 135). Douglas refused to conform and was deprived in 1662. In 1669 he was one who, at Gilbert Burnet's* instigation, wrote recommending the settlement of moderate Presbyterian ministers in vacant charges. He then accepted the resultant Indulgence* and was admitted to Pencaitland, in which parish he continued until his death.

FES I, 385-6; *DNB* XV, 346-7; John Kilpatrick, 'The Rev Robert Douglas' in *RSCHS* 12 (1954), 29-46.

J. A. Dickson

Dowden, John (1840-1910), Bishop of Edinburgh in the EpCS 1886-1910, an Irishman who made considerable contributions to Scottish historiography and liturgiology.

Born in Cork, the son of a Presbyterian father and a Church of Ireland mother, he learned the catechisms of both Churches but after graduating at Trinity College, Dublin he decided to seek ordination in the Church of Ireland. From 1864 to 1872 he ministered in Sligo and then spent two years as assistant curate at St Stephen's, Dublin.

In 1874 he was appointed by the Scottish bishops to the post of Pantonian Professor of Theology in the Theological College, which was then at Glenalmond, Perthshire. When Dowden arrived at Glenalmond he found that he had only one student. His disappointment was eased by the ample time this gave him for personal study and he embarked on the liturgical researches which resulted in the publication of *The Annotated Scottish Communion Office* in 1884. A considerably revised version of the same work was published posthumously in 1922 under the title, *The Scottish Communion Office 1764*. Dowden's work did much to commend the Scottish Lit-

DOWIE, JOHN ALEXANDER

urgy to a Church which was increasingly using the English office.

After a serious fire at Glenalmond, Dowden moved to Edinburgh and eventually persuaded the Bishop to establish the theological college there (*see* Episcopal Theological College). He continued as Pantonian Professor until his election as Bishop of Edinburgh. His duties as a diocesan during a period of considerable expansion in the EpCS did not prevent him from continuing his scholarly work. In 1894 he published *The Celtic Church in Scotland*, a small book which according to his daughter gained a popularity he never expected for it. In 1897, lectures which he had given in the General Theological Seminary, New York, were published under the title, *Outlines of the History of Theological Literature of the Church of England from the Reformation to the Close of the Eighteenth Century*. Two years later he published *The Workmanship of the Prayer Book* and *Further Studies in the Prayer Book* appeared in 1901.

Dowden played an active part in the foundation of the Scottish History Society in 1886 and edited for it *Correspondence of the Lauderdale family with Archbishop Sharp* (E, 1893) and *The Cartulary of the Abbey of Lindores* (E, 1903). He also collaborated in editing *Charters of Inchaffray Abbey* (1908). Dowden considered that he had begun the study of charters too late in life for him to produce a work of real service, but this is largely belied by two works of his which were published posthumously, *The Medieval Church in Scotland* (a revised version of the Rhind Lectures for 1901) and *The Bishops of Scotland* (1912). The latter work was intended to supplement the work of Bishop Robert Keith* who had published a catalogue of Scottish bishops to 1688 in 1755. Dowden's lists for most dioceses end at the Reformation.

Dowden's enthusiasm as an historian can be judged by a frequently made remark of his: 'To make *certain* of one fact in history gives more satisfaction to me now than all the metaphysical problems in the world.'

Alice Dowden, 'Biographical sketch ... ', prefixed to *The Medieval Church in Scotland* (G, 1910); *Who Was Who 1897–1916*, 206.

H. R. Sefton

Dowie, John Alexander (1847–1907), evangelist and charismatic founder of the Christian Catholic Apostolic Church (not to be confused with the Catholic Apostolic Church*). Born in Edinburgh, Dowie emigrated as a boy to Australia (but returned to study at Edinburgh for seven years) where he eventually became a minister in the Congregational* Church. After holding successful pastorates, he abruptly withdrew in 1878 to devote himself to independent evangelistic work, forming a congregation in Sydney. For ten years he held crusades throughout Australia, and advocated 'divine healing'.

Experiencing further success, Dowie began to think in terms of world-wide ministry. He reasoned that, with London as a centre, he could develop a following throughout the colonies. To that end he set sail in 1888, going by way of the USA. However, he received such a tremendous response to his ministry in North America that he decided to stay there. His flamboyant style and pointed tongue soon attracted several thousand followers. He established the Christian Catholic Apostolic Church in 1896. At its zenith, the Church claimed 25,000 members and 200,000 sympathizers.

Dowie was impressed by the Mormon* experiment at Salt Lake City, and in 1910 he founded Zion City, a utopian community, located forty miles north of Chicago. The city became a centre for banking, education, publishing, construction, fishing, and farming. His factories produced soap, candy, furniture, brick and lace. He formed smaller communities in Mexico, Switzerland, England and Australia.

His expanding empire was paralleled by the elevation of his status. Named General Overseer upon the formation of his Church, in 1899 he proclaimed himself 'Messenger of the Covenant' prophesied by the prophet Malachi. In 1901 he declared himself 'Elijah, the Restorer of All-things'. He was consecrated 'First Apostle' of a new apostolic order in 1904. Dowie summed up his message by stating: 'Zion stands for salvation, healing and Holy Living.' He was thus planted firmly in the Keswick tradition (*see* Conventions). What set him apart was the eschatological cast his message took. He believed that the miraculous gifts of the Spirit were to be restored and that a new apostolic order had been established to bring about the end of the age.

His downfall was as swift as his ascent. The Elijah declaration was difficult for adherents to accept. He was accused of financial mismanagement and of advocating polygamy. His vision of utopia shattered, Dowie died of a stroke in 1907. In retrospect, it is clear that he was a transitional figure connecting an emerging Pentecostalism* both to Keswick and to Irvingism.* The name of his church, the role of the Elijah ministry, his view of the gifts of the Spirit, and the restoration of apostolic authority, all found expression in Pentecostalism. Over a hundred of his adherents became Pentecostal leaders.

J. G. Melton, *Biographical Dictionary of American Cult and Sect Leaders* (NY, L, 1986), 73–4; G. Lindsey, *John Alexander Dowie* (Dallas, TX, 1980); A. Newcomb, *Dowie, Anointed of the Lord* (NY, 1930).

D. W. Faupel

Dr Graham's Homes, *see* Graham, J. A.

Dryhthelm, *see* Anglo-Saxon Saints.

Drostan, *see* Celtic Saints.

Druids, a learned class of men who were known in pre-Christian Britain (including Scotland), Ireland and Gaul as keepers of traditional knowledge. Along with bards and seers (*vates*), the druids constituted a priesthood in early Celtic society, although it is not known precisely what religious function they performed.

DRUMCLOG

The origin of the word 'druid' (O.Ir. *drui*, pl. *druid*) is in doubt; it is generally translated in Latin texts as *magus*, although Caesar writes of *druides*. The druids were described by classical writers such as Posidonius, Strabo, Diodorus Siculus, Caesar, Tacitus and Pliny, among others. Most of these writers were dealing with second-hand information and their accounts are coloured by Roman and Hellenic outlooks. The druids were perceived as philosophers and magicians who presided at sacrifices and other rituals, and who possessed arcane knowledge. Pomponius Mela made much of the information that druids believed in the immortality and transmigration of souls.

Caesar, in *The Gallic War*, describes two classes of Gallic society: the *equites*, the warrior class, and the *druides*, an intellectual class concerned with divine matters. He reports that druids were present at human sacrifices, where the victims were burned alive. However, his account may owe more to hearsay and previous writers (such as Posidonius and Strabo) than to eye-witness reports. Tacitus, in the *Annals*, relates how the druids on Anglesey cursed the army of Suetonius Paulinus across the Menai Straits. He later reports that the army destroyed their sacred groves, where human sacrifices were made. Accounts such as this gave rise to the modern idea of the druids as political nationalist leaders who incited the people to rebel against the Roman invaders. The suppression of the druids by Rome was more in accordance with the Roman imperial policy of absorbing conquered peoples into the Roman system of government, culture and beliefs, and eradicating non-Roman practices.

In popular tradition, the druids are closely associated with sacred groves and mysterious rituals. Pliny the Elder, in his *Natural History*, mentions the druids' expertise in medicine and magic, but only he describes the ritual cutting of mistletoe from an oak with a golden sickle. The druids possessed knowledge of the traditional history of their tribe, beliefs concerning the supernatural, customary laws, medicinal lore, divination, the interpretation of omens and, especially, calendrical computations by astronomy. They do not appear to have had a system of philosophy or religious dogma. Their numbers were drawn from the aristocratic class, but the status of druid was not necessarily hereditary. Novices were taught by oral tradition for a period which may have lasted up to twenty years, according to Posidonius and his successors.

In Christian writings, the druids degenerated into evil sorcerers who were the chief opponents of the early missionary saints (*e.g.*, Columba* is said to have battled with Broichan, the druid of the Pictish king Brude). Present-day manifestations of druids have little to do with the druids of antiquity.

S. Piggott, *The Druids* (L, 1971); N. Chadwick, *The Druids* (Cardiff, 1966); T. G. E. Powell, *The Celts* (L, 1968); A. Ross, *Pagan Celtic Britain* (L, 1967).

D. A. Bray

Drumclog, *see* Bothwell Bridge.

DRUMMOND, HENRY

Drummond, Andrew Alastair Lansdale (1902–66), church historian. Born in the manse of Jedburgh in the Borders, and schooled in Moffatt and Fleetwood (Lancashire), he studied at Edinburgh (MA, 1924; BD, 1927; PhD, 1930), Montpelier, Marburg and Hartford Seminary, Connecticut (STM, 1929). After spells of varying service in Edinburgh, Tiberias and Chicago, in 1932 he was ordained to the CofS charge of Alva Eadie, Clackmannanshire, where he remained until his death.

Drummond was an exemplar of an admired but threatened breed – the scholarly parish minister. Among his numerous writings were *The Church Architecture of Protestantism* (E, 1934), *Edward Irving and his Circle* (L, 1937), *The Churches Pictured by 'Punch'* (L, 1947), *The Churches in English Fiction* (Leicester, 1950), *German Protestantism since Luther* (L, 1951) and *The Kirk and the Continent* (E, 1956). Material he prepared for a history of the Scottish Church since 1688 was worked up by James Bulloch* and published (with a clear bias in favour of the Auld Kirk*) in their joint names (3 vols, E, 1973–8). He received St Andrews' DD in 1965.

FES IX, 441; X, 261; *LW* July 1966, 21.

D. F. Wright

Drummond, David Thomas Ker (1806–77), English Episcopal* minister and evangelical leader of the 'disruption' of 1842–4 in the EpCS. He was a graduate of Worcester College, Oxford. While incumbent of Holy Trinity, Edinburgh, he was reprimanded by Bishop Terrot* for holding non-liturgical services. In 1842 he withdrew himself and most of his congregation from the EpCS, founding St Thomas's, Rutland Street (now Glasgow Road), in 1843. He was incumbent until 1875. In his writings he asserted his chapel's communion with the united Church of England and Ireland and attacked Tractarianism* in the EpCS and the use of the Scottish Communion office.

Historical Sketch of Episcopacy in Scotland (E, 1845); other writings, pamphlets etc. in New College Library, Edinburgh.

R. Foskett, 'The Drummond Controversy 1842', *RSCHS* 16 (1967), 99–109.

E. M. Culbertson

Drummond, Henry (1786–1850), politician and founding member of Catholic Apostolic Church.* Born in Hampshire, England, Drummond spent his youth in Scotland with his maternal grandfather, the Tory politician Henry Dundas.* After studying at Oxford for two years but taking no degree, he became a banker, and 1810–13 was MP for Plympton Earle. In 1817 he visited Geneva *en route* to the Holy Land, and took a leading part in Robert Haldane's* crusade against the Socinianism of the Genevan Church. Back home, he established the Continental Society in 1819, and the Chair of Political Economy at Oxford in 1825.

Drummond's mansion in Albury, Surrey became the meeting place for a series of conferences on prophecy from 1826-30, at which Edward Irving* and the premillennial viewpoint assumed prominence, the seedbed for the Catholic Apostolic Church (founded 1832). A zealous supporter of Irving, he became the second of its twelve apostles. At great personal expense he built a church in Albury (the 'Apostles' Chapel') for the new denomination.

In 1847 Drummond was elected MP for West Surrey, holding the seat till his death. Although Tory by conviction, he acted with independence in the House of Commons, speaking frequently, criticizing all parties, and particularly addressing himself to Church issues.

A prolific author, most of Drummond's writings were political in nature, with a smaller number of religious works. These include: *Abstract Principles of Revealed Religion* (L, 1845); *Dialogues on Prophecy* (3 vols, L, 1827-9); *Candid Examination of the Controversy . . . respecting the Human Nature of the Lord Jesus Christ* (L, 1829); *Speeches in Parliament*, 2 vols (L, 1860). Thomas Carlyle* described him as 'a singular mixture of all things – of the saint, the wit, the philosopher – swimming, if I mistake not, in an element of dandyism'.

Lord Lovaine's biographical memoir, prefaced to Drummond's *Speeches in Parliament*; E. Miller, *The History and Doctrines of Irvingism* (L, 1878), I, 30ff.; P. E. Shaw, *The Catholic Apostolic Church* (NY, 1946), 73ff.; *DNB* XVI, 28-9.

N. R. Needham

Drummond, Henry (1851-97), essayist, geologist, visionary. Born in Stirling, Drummond has an established place in Christian intellectual history because of his essay *The Greatest Thing in the World* (L, 1890), on 1 Cor. 13, which is still widely published, individually and in collections such as *The Treasury of Christian Classics*.

Drummond was educated at Edinburgh University and FC College, and at Tübingen. He worked closely with Dwight L. Moody* and Ira D. Sankey in their great mission to Britain (1873-5), and again with Moody in 1882. He was assistant minister in the Barclay Church, Edinburgh, and later assisted Marcus Dods (1834-1909)* at Possilpark, Glasgow, a mission to working men.

Natural Law in the Spiritual World (L, 1883), often regarded as Drummond's principal work, was merely one of the best-sellers of his own time. Perceived as a reconciler of Darwinian and Christian thought, his emphasis throughout *Natural Law* and *The Ascent of Man* (L, 1894) is on the idea of progress, 'love' as the principle behind the universe, evolution (or 'advolution'), with the world ascending on an exponential curve toward the kingdom in heaven; the lines between earth and heaven being blurred by his concept of the 'identity' of natural and supernatural. Evolutionism, naturalism and Christianity shift and weave in kaleidoscopic fashion. The radical quality of his syncretism is, from the standpoint of the history of ideas, revolutionary rather than evolutionary, presaging both certain current types of evangelism, and the meta-physical writings of the New Age proliferating across the West today.

Tropical Africa (L, 1888), his geological report for the African Lakes Corporation on his exploration of Lakes Nyasa and Tanganyika, constitutes his only integrated full-scale book. *The Ascent of Man*, from the prestigious Lowell lectures, delivered in Boston in 1893, was published in 1894, under pressure, only because pirate copies were being circulated. Its evolutionism seemed to many a denial of any meaningful theistic concept of creation, and a motion was submitted to the FC General Assembly asking that a committee be appointed to examine the book's teachings. The motion was defeated by a two-to-one majority.

Drummond considered that his own major contribution had been in 1884-94, when he lectured to Glasgow divinity students as Professor of Natural Science on weekdays, and to Edinburgh students at weekends. Most summers he travelled extensively, lecturing in the USA in universities such as Harvard, Yale, and Princeton; at Chautauqua; and also in Germany, Australia, China and Japan. He introduced the Boys' Brigade* movement into Australia, and promoted it in the USA and Canada.

Drummond's works are available in various collections, including *The Greatest Thing in the World and 21 Other Addresses* (L, 1970); *The New Evangelism and Other Papers* (L, 1899); and *The Ideal Life and Other Addresses* (L, 1897).

J. M. Wysong, 'The "New" Evangelical Theology of Henry Drummond (1851-1897): An Historical Analysis' (PhD, University of Maryland, 1977); J. W. Kennedy, *Henry Drummond: An Anthology* (NY, 1953); G. A. Smith, *The Life of Henry Drummond* (L, 1899); J. Y. Simpson, *Henry Drummond* (E, 1901); *DNB Suppl.* II, 157-8.

J. M. Wysong

Drummond, Peter (1799-1877), *see* Stirling Tract Enterprise.

Drummond, Robert James. (1858-1951), UP, UF, and CofS minister. He was educated at Glasgow Academy, University of Glasgow and UP College, Edinburgh, and was minister of Lothian Road Church, Edinburgh, from 1890 until his death. As the first convener of the innovative UFC Social Problems Committee, Drummond was a pioneer in promoting his Church's involvement in social and industrial issues. He was a prominent speaker at church congresses, and was notably supportive of the growing labour movement and its social and political aspirations. Drummond was also a leading figure in the promotion of Presbyterian church union in Scotland. Among his best known works are: Kerr lectures, *The Relation of the Apostolic Teaching to the Teaching of Christ* (E, 1901); autobiography, *Lest We Forget – Reminiscences of a Nonagenarian* (L, 1951).

FUFCS, 18.

D. C. Smith

Drummond Trust, the name by which the former

Stirling Tract Enterprise* has been more generally known for the last twenty or so years. The Enterprise itself came into being in the early 1860s to perpetuate the work of the seedsman, Peter Drummond, who devoted much of his leisure time and fortune to publishing and distributing tracts to make known the gospel, primarily in and around Stirling and eventually in the whole country. With the increase in the cost of printing and other postwar conditions, the original function became less useful. So from about the year 1979, the Drummond Trust agreed to abandon the endeavour to continue publishing, and instead to offer subsidies to other organizations which proposed to publish books and other materials for sale. A few years earlier, the Drummond Trust undertook in conjunction with Stirling University to sponsor biennial lectures at the University, to examine the relevance of the gospel to modern science and other aspects of modern culture.

W. Stewart

Dryburgh. The abbey was founded in 1150 by Hugh de Moreville, Constable of Scotland, with canons from Alnwick, Northumberland. It was the first recorded Premonstratensian* foundation in Scotland, though Soulseat (Galloway) was later claimed as earlier. The writings of Adam* of Dryburgh conferred distinction on the abbey in its early years, and indeed were influential throughout the order. Two monasteries in Co. Antrim, Ireland, were considered daughter-houses of Dryburgh. Being situated near the Border, Dryburgh was vulnerable to English attacks. It was burned by English forces in 1322 and 1385, and damaged by fire in 1461, but underwent restoration.

Dryburgh suffered again in the sixteenth century, being seriously damaged in the English invasions of 1523, 1544 and 1545. From 1509 it was held by commendators,* apart from one regular abbot 1523–39; the commendators after 1539 belonged to the noble family of Erskine. In 1537–8 there were seventeen resident canons, and ten at the Reformation* in 1560; to these must be added canons serving as vicars in appropriated parishes. Dryburgh is known for its picturesque setting and the outstanding quality of its ruins. Sir Walter Scott* is buried there.

Liber S. Marie de Dryburgh (Bannatyne Club, E, 1847); J. S. Richardson and M. Wood, *Dryburgh Abbey* (E, ⁴1987); N. Backmund, 'The Premonstratensian Order in Scotland', *IR* 4 (1953), 25–37; M. Dilworth, 'The Border Abbeys in the Sixteenth Century', *RSCHS* 21 (1983), 233–47; Easson-Cowan, 100–2.

M. Dilworth

Drysdale Bustle, an episode in the patronage* controversy in 1762–4. It centred on the respective rights of Church courts and municipal corporations in the presentation of ministers to burgh* charges. The Moderate* leadership, in conjunction with various political factions within and without Edinburgh Town Council, attempted to place a Moderate minister, John Drysdale, in a vacant Edinburgh charge, Lady Yester's. The debate at first centred on the legality of the Town Council's claim to the sole right of presentation. This was contested by the 'Popular'* ministers and their supporters in the General Sessions of the city (*see* General (Kirk) Sessions). The Assembly of 1764 upheld the Council's right and Drysdale was settled in the charge. Other issues acquired prominence only later, with objections that such presentations would alienate the minds of the people from attending the regular ministry, lead to the erection of separate places of worship to the detriment of the morals of the people, and be destructive to the revenue of the Poor House. The General Sessions, which included both Moderate and Popular ministers and their supporters, disapproved unanimously of the exercise of the Council's right of patronage; and, on the other side, no exception was ever taken to the Moderate presentee by Popular members. The significance of this has so far gone unregarded. It was one of several instances of substantial agreement between members of the two parties away from the higher echelons of party leadership.

J. Cater, 'The Making of Principal Robertson in 1762...', *SHR* 49 (1970), 60–84; R. B. Sher, 'Moderates, Managers, and Popular Politics in Mid-Eighteenth Century Edinburgh: The "Drysdale Bustle" of the 1760s', in J. Dwyer, R. A. Mason and A. Murdoch (eds), *New Perspectives on the Politics and Culture of Early Modern Scotland* (E, 1982), 179–209.

J. R. McIntosh

Duff, Alexander (1806–78), missionary to India. Born in Moulin in the Perthshire Highlands* (*see* Stewart, Alexander), Duff was dux of Perth Grammar School and studied at St Andrews University, where he responded to Thomas Chalmers'* imaginative association of hitherto disparate disciplines. A deep conviction of the essential unity of all knowledge made Duff an impassioned educator. John Inglis,* convener of the CofS General Assembly's committee charged with the responsibility of establishing an educational mission in Bengal, offered the headship of the mission to Duff.

On arrival in Calcutta in 1830 Duff was befriended by Ram Mohan Roy, founder of the reformed Hindu 'Brahmo Samaj'; it won him immediate notice, as did the rapid conversion of some of his high-caste students. Later renamed Duff College, the school which he established was for a generation the largest and most successful missionary school in India. In 1837 it had 700 pupils; in 1862, 1,723. It left its mark on all subsequent missionary colleges.

Duff's missionary strategy was the higher education of the highest classes in biblical and Western knowledge through the medium of English. The conversion of high-caste Hindus would lead to the conversion of those below them, a strategy known as Duff's 'downward filtration' theory. The Bible, combined in the curriculum with Western science and literature, would undermine Hinduism.

Duff's influence was of decisive importance in the development of educational policy and, especially, the university system in India. Forced home by illness in 1834, Duff stirred both Church and state to recognize their respective responsibilities for the education of India. *Missions the Chief End of the Christian Church* (E, 1839) was first delivered in 1835 at the General Assembly; 20,000 copies of it were printed, and Marischal College, Aberdeen, awarded him the degree of DD. In 1835 Bentinck, Governor-General of India, issued an order which ensured, as Duff desired, that higher education would be in English. There was a similar response during his second furlough from 1850 to 1855. He was Moderator of the FC General Assembly in 1851. In 1854 he visited the USA and Canada, alerting the Church to its duty with a passion unequalled, it was said, since the days of George Whitefield.* The University of New York conferred on him the LLD degree. Duff was influential, too, in securing in 1854 the 'Wood Despatch' which established a university in each Indian presidency and guaranteed grants-in-aid to missionary colleges, thus ensuring the greatest period of expansion in the history of missionary education in India.

Duff left India for the last time in 1864. He became convener of the FC Foreign Missions Committee. In 1867 he was appointed the first Professor of Missions at New College,* Edinburgh. Apart from the *Calcutta Review*, of which he was a founder in 1841 and editor from 1845–9, Duff's numerous published works include *The Church of Scotland's India Mission* (E, 1835); *New Era of the English Language and Literature in India* (E, 1837); *The Mutual Duties and Responsibilities of Pastor and People* (E, 1836); *India and Indian Missions* (E, 1839); *Missionary Addresses* (E, L, 1850); *The Indian Rebellion: its Causes and Results* (L, E, 1858); and *The Proposed Mission to Lake Nyassa* (E?, 1875).

G. Smith, *Life of Alexander Duff*, 2 vols (L, 1879); L. B. Day, *Life of Alexander Duff* (L, 1878); W. Paton, *Alexander Duff* (NY, 1922); M. A. Laird, *Missionaries and Education in Bengal, 1793–1837* (O, 1972); S. Piggin and J. Roxborogh, *The St Andrews Seven* (E, 1985); S. Piggin, *Making Evangelical Missionaries, 1789–1858* (Appleford, 1984); *DNB* XVI, 125–8.

S. *Piggin*

Duff Lectures. The Duff Missionary Lectureship was established in accordance with the wishes of Alexander Duff* by his son William Pirie Duff in 1878. The first trustees included John Marshall Lang,* W. L. Alexander* and Andrew Thomson.* At least six lectures on a subject related to 'foreign missions' were to be delivered in Glasgow and Edinburgh every four years by a minister, professor or 'godly layman of any Evangelical Church'. Duff's daughter, Mrs Rebecca Jane Duff or Watson, was to be consulted to ensure justice was done to his 'very strong and earnestly held Evangelical sentiments'. The first lecturer was Thomas Smith, minister of Cowgatehead FC, Edinburgh, Duff's sole surviving Calcutta colleague. Since 1987 the Lectureship has, appropriately enough, been associated with the Centre for the Study of Christianity in the Non-Western World in New College,* Edinburgh. The first lecturer under this arrangement was Kwame Bediako of Ghana (1988–92). The lectureship has in effect passed from FC through UFC to CofS hands.

The following is a virtually complete list: T. Smith (*Mediaeval Missions*, E, 1880); W. F. Stevenson (*The Dawn of the Modern Mission*, E, 1887); Sir M. Monier-Williams (*Buddhism*, L, 1889); A. T. Pierson (*The New Acts of the Apostles*, L, 1894); J. M. Lang* (*The Expansion of the Christian Life*, E, 1897); J. Stewart* (*Dawn in the Dark Continent*, E, 1903); J. M. Mitchell (*The Great Religions of India*, L, 1905); R. E. Speer (*Christianity and the Nations*, NY, 1910); C. H. Brent (*The Commonwealth. Its Foundations and Pillars*, L, 1930); J. N. Ogilvie* (*Our Empire's Debt to Missions*, L, 1924); P. J. MacLagan (*Chinese Religious Ideas*, L, 1926); J. H. Oldham* (unpublished, 'The Christian Message in the New Era', 1933); D. Westermann (*Africa and Christianity*, L, 1937); V. S. Azariah, Bishop of Dornakal, India (unable to deliver the lectures, because of World War II); A. G. Hogg* (*The Christian Message to the Hindu*, L, 1947); A. M. Chirgwin (*The Decisive Decade*, L, 1949); J. S. Stewart* (*Thine is the Kingdom*, E, 1956); S. Neill (*Creative Tension*, L, 1959); J. W. C. Dougall* (*Christians in the African Revolution*, E, 1963); M. M. Thomas (*The Christian Response to the Asian Revolution*, L, 1966).

Papers in New College, Edinburgh.

D. F. *Wright*

Dunbar, Gavin (1455–1532), Bishop of Aberdeen. Like many younger sons of landed families, Dunbar followed a career in the Church, but by 1503 was a Privy Councillor, clerk register and was being employed by James IV* on diplomatic business. He continued to play a minor role in the factional politics of James V's* minority, but after his appointment as Bishop of Aberdeen in 1518 his energies were devoted largely to his episcopal responsibilities. Dunbar's most important monument is the magnificent heraldic ceiling which he gave to St Machar's Cathedral in Aberdeen, but he is honoured as the 'second founder' of King's College, Aberdeen, whose membership and endowments he increased considerably.

DNB XVI, 151; Dowden, 137–9.

K. M. *Brown*

Dunbar, Gavin (c.1490–1547), archbishop and chancellor. The son of Sir John Dunbar of Mochrum (Wigtonshire), and nephew of Gavin Dunbar*, Bishop of Aberdeen, he was educated at Paris and Angers. He became preceptor to King James V (1517–25) and Archbishop of Glasgow (1523–47). In these appointments Dunbar probably owed much to the patronage of John, Duke of Albany, Governor of Scotland. After the downfall of the Earl of Angus, Dunbar was appointed Chancellor (1528–43). Dunbar and Albany were associated with the Act (1532) which paved the way for the

College of Justice (1535, ratified 1541); the Court of Session* is thus often – somewhat misleadingly – said to date from 1532. Glasgow was erected into an archbishopric in 1492, with exemption from St Andrews in certain respects, but uncertainty in this matter led to continual friction between Dunbar and his archiepiscopal counterparts, James* and David* Beaton. This climaxed in unseemly fisticuffs in Glasgow Cathedral (1544), when the crosses of both Glasgow and St Andrews were damaged. Dunbar opposed the reading of the Scriptures in the vernacular, but in tackling heresy he lacked the persecuting zeal of Cardinal Beaton. Nonetheless he was present with the latter at the execution of George Wishart* (1546). Although ridiculed by Knox,* Dunbar was praised for his learning by George Buchanan,* and he was indubitably a highly competent clerical administrator.

D. E. Easson, *Gavin Dunbar* (E, 1947); R. K. Hannay, *The College of Justice* (E, 1933); J. Durkan and J. Kirk, *The University of Glasgow 1451–1577* (G, 1977); *Essays on the Scottish Reformation 1513–1625*, ed. D. McRoberts (G, 1962); Dowden, 343–9; M. H. B. Sanderson, *Cardinal of Scotland* (E, 1986); G. Brunton and D. Haig, *The Senators of the College of Justice* (E, 1836).

A. A. MacDonald

Dunbar, William (c.1460–before 1522), priest and poet. He was possibly related to the family of the Earls of Dunbar and March. He graduated MA at St Andrews in 1479, and may have been associated with the Franciscans,* but, if so, probably not beyond the novitiate. In 1500 King James IV granted him a pension of 10 for life (subsequently raised to 20, 1507, and 80, 1510), and in March 1504 made an offering at Dunbar's first celebrating mass. In 1501 Dunbar was in England, possibly in connection with the betrothal of James IV to Margaret Tudor. He has been thought to have travelled with diplomatic missions to Scandinavia, France and possibly Italy; precise documentation, however, is lacking. After Flodden (1513) there are no more certain records of the poet.

Dunbar is the author of some eighty-five poems (the canon has been the subject of scholarly debate); most survive only in manuscript, but three were printed by Chepman and Myllar (1508), and a further three by an unnamed printer of roughly the same date. Together with Robert Henryson* and Gavin Douglas,* Dunbar is usually considered one of the 'Scottish Chaucerians'; the influence on him of Chaucer, however, can be exaggerated, and is probably equalled by that of John Lydgate. Apart from the 'Tretis' and the 'Flyting' – each of over 500 lines, albeit that the latter was a joint composition with Walter Kennedy – nearly all Dunbar's poems consist of short lyrics. He wrote on a large number of subjects – religious, courtly, amorous, moral, satirical and comic – and his works are characterized by great stylistic versatility.

Dunbar is very much a court poet. He often records court events, and more than once appeals to the King for financial help. Elsewhere he writes of the officials, the artisans and the charlatans who profited from James's munificence. Several poems are marked by anti-bourgeois satire, which suggests that the intended audience was aristocratic. For rather different reasons this probably also applies to the religious poems, which may be classed as poems of meditation, celebration or argument. The 'Ballat of Our Lady' and the 'Passioun of Crist' fall into the first category: the former using extraordinarily aureate diction – in a vernacular elaboration on the opening words of the Angelic Salutation – to honour Mary and to communicate the poet's reverence; the latter narrating the harrowing events of the Passion to stimulate compunction and hence love. The Nativity lyric, '*Rorate celi desuper*', and the Resurrection lyric, 'Done is a battell on the dragon blak', are magnificent pieces of celebration, eminently suited for declamation or singing in James's refounded (1501) Chapel Royal. The remaining religious poems advise man to confession. In the 'Lament for the Makaris' Dunbar reflects sombrely on his position at the end of an English and Scottish literary tradition: his 'Tretis' is remarkable from a formal point of view in being almost the last poem in English to use unrhymed alliterative lines. Dunbar is the most brilliant, if not the most profound, of the mediaeval Scottish poets; his versatility, however, makes determination of his true personality difficult.

Poems of William Dunbar, ed. J. Kinsley (O, 1979). I. S. Ross, *William Dunbar* (Leiden, 1981); J. W. Baxter, *William Dunbar* (E, 1952); *History of Scottish Literature*, Vol. I, ed. R. D. S. Jack (A, 1988); J. J. Blanchot, 'William Dunbar, Rhétoriqueur Ecossais', 2 vols. (doct. diss., Univ. of Paris-Sorbonne, 1987); T. Scott, *Dunbar* (E, 1966); A. A. MacDonald, 'The Middle Scots Religious Lyrics' (PhD, University of Edinburgh, 1978).

A. A. MacDonald

Dunbar, (Sir) William (1804–81), Baronet, English Episcopal* minister and an evangelical leader of the Episcopal disruption of 1842–4. In 1841 the independent qualified chapel of St Paul's, Aberdeen united with the EpCS. Dunbar was appointed as minister. In 1843 Dunbar and his congregation left the Church in protest at Bishop Skinner's pressure on them to use the high church Scottish Communion* office. Skinner warned all Episcopalians to avoid communion with Dunbar. Leading CofE Evangelicals such as Edward Bickersteth and also C. P. Miles* supported him. Shortly afterwards he was instituted into the English living of Dummer, Hants.

D. T. K. Drummond, *Historical Sketch of Episcopacy in Scotland* (E, 1845).

E. M. Culbertson

Dunblane, *see* Early Ecclesiastical Sites; Cathedral Churches; Ecumenical Movement.

Duncan, Andrew (c.1560–1626), schoolmaster. A

DUNCAN, GEORGE SIMPSON

graduate and then regent of St Leonard's College, St Andrews, where he was deeply influenced by Andrew Melville,* he was rector of Dundee Grammar School from 1591 before being ordained to Crail, Fife, in 1597. His committed Presbyterianism (he attended the banned Aberdeen Assembly of 1605) brought him imprisonment and banishment for life in 1606. He became Professor of Theology at La Rochelle in France in 1607, but by July 1613 had returned to Scotland, submitted to James VI and resumed his charge at Crail. Further defiance earned him suspension, deposition in 1620, confinements in Dundee and in Dumbarton, and finally exile and penury in Berwick-on-Tweed.

Duncan was the author of some much-used school text-books on Latin (*Latinae Grammaticae* . . . , E, 1595; *etc.*) and of a brief simple Latin catechism, *Rudimenta Pietatis* (E, 1595), intended as a comparison to his grammars. The *Rudimenta* went through many printings, and after Duncan's death was commonly issued with the Latin manual of Andrew Simson (*see* Simson, Archibald). In this form it was called *Summula Catechismi* and Duncan's authorship was eventually lost from view.

Rudimenta, ed. T. F. Torrance, *The School of Faith* (L, 1959), 279–90.

FES V, 192; J. MacQueen (ed.), *Humanism in Renaissance Scotland* (E, 1990); J. Livingston(e), *Memorable Characteristics* . . . (G, 1754), 4–6.

D. F. Wright

Duncan, George Simpson (1884–1965), New Testament scholar. He was born in Forfar, educated at Forfar Academy, Edinburgh University, Trinity College, Cambridge, and also briefly at the Universities of Marburg, Jena and Heidelberg. During the First World War he served as chaplain to General Sir Douglas Haig (later Earl Haig of Bemersyde). In 1919 he became Professor of Biblical Criticism at St Andrews University and in 1940 Principal of St Mary's College; he retired from both posts in 1954, having been Vice-Chancellor of the University in 1952–3. In 1920 he was joint founder of St Andrews Summer School of Theology (still held annually). In 1949 he was Moderator of the General Assembly of the CofS. He died in Dundee.

His best known publication is *St. Paul's Ephesian Ministry* (L, 1929), a defence of the view that one or more imprisonments in or near Ephesus provide the historical setting for Paul's letters to the Philippians, Colossians, Philemon and Ephesians, and for the 'authentic' passages in the Pastoral Epistles (especially 2 Tim. 1:15–18; 4:6–22). This thesis he maintained (with refinements) to the end of his life.

His volume on *Galatians* in the Moffatt NT Commentary series (L, 1934) treated Galatians as the earliest of Paul's extant letters. *Jesus, Son of Man* (L, 1947) embodied his Croall Lectures* delivered in Edinburgh in 1937. In it he attempted to excavate the 'dark tunnel' separating the Jesus of history from the Jesus of early Christian faith. He continued the same exercise in his presidential address

DUNCAN, JOHN

to the Society for New Testament Studies, 'From Paul to Jesus' (*SJT* 2, 1949, 1–12). He played an active part on the translators' panel of the *New English Bible* (New Testament).

He was a man of great kindliness of spirit and is remembered with affection by successive generations of students.

FES VII, 431, VIII, 719, IX, 770, X, 430; *DNB* 1961–1970, 313–4.

F. F. Bruce

Duncan, Henry (1774–1846), credited with founding the trustee savings bank movement. Educated at St Andrews, Edinburgh and Glasgow, he was employed in Heywood's Bank, Liverpool, between his arts and divinity degrees. Ordained to Ruthwell (Dumfriesshire) CofS in 1799, he received a St Andrews DD in 1823 and was Moderator of the General Assembly in 1839. He was minister in the FC in Ruthwell from the Disruption* until his death.

Duncan was gifted in drawing, architecture, landscape gardening, science and literature, supported the anti-slavery movement and was known as a philanthropist. He founded and edited the *Dumfries and Galloway Courier* and wrote several books: *William Douglas or the Scottish Exiles*, *Sacred Philosophy of the Seasons* (4 vols, (E, 1838–41), and *Tales of Scottish Peasantry* (E, n.d.).

Inspired by John Bone's pamphlet, Duncan founded Ruthwell Savings Bank 1810. Earlier savings bank experiments had been made by Dr Heygarth in Bath, Priscilla Wakefield in Tottenham, and, unknown to Duncan, at West Calder in Scotland. But Duncan's bank created the real pattern for movement: self-help, non-profit-making, one penny minimum deposit, interest paid yearly, local notables as trustees. He lobbied political figures of both parties (*e.g.* Canning, Macaulay, Wilberforce) to secure the First Trustee Savings Bank Act (1817) against the opposition of *The Times* and Cobbett.

His claim to be 'father of the movement' was disputed in his own lifetime, but the *Quarterly Review* in 1817 asserted of his bank, 'It is in all fairness entitled to the appellation of the parent society.' In 1910 the trustee savings bank movement celebrated its centenary based on the Ruthwell foundation.

G. Duncan, *Memoir of Rev. Henry Duncan* (E, 1848); S. Hall, *Dr. Duncan, Founder of Savings Banks* (E, 1910); *FES* II, 255–6; *AFCS* I, 143; *DNB* XVI, 165–6.

I. M. Roy

Duncan, John (1796–1870), 'Rabbi' Duncan, CofS and FC Hebraist and missionary. Born in Aberdeen the son of a shoemaker, he was educated there at Marischal College* (MA, 1814). While at the divinity halls first of the Associate Presbytery* (at Whitburn under Archibald Bruce*) and then of the CofS (at Aberdeen), he was unable to find rest in orthodox Christianity, embracing pantheism, then Sabellianism. At first preferring a Christianity without its doctrines, he traced his conversion in 1826 to an encounter with César Malan of Geneva who taught him 'that God meant man to know his mind'. He called himself 'a philosophical sceptic who has taken refuge in theology'. Ordained to Milton Church, Glasgow (1836–41), in 1840 he received Aberdeen's LLD in recognition of his mastery of eastern languages. The CofS sent him in 1841 as a missionary to the Jews in Budapest, where he worked to invigorate the Hungarian Reformed Church to provide a lasting witness to the Jews. He worked also among Italian Jews at Leghorn (Livorno). At the Disruption* in 1843 he joined the FC and was elected Professor of Hebrew at New College,* Edinburgh, where he taught until 1863, and initiated a scholarship scheme for Hungarian students which continues to the present day (R. Hörcsik, 'The History of the Hungarian Scholarship at Edinburgh', MS, New College, E, 1989). His writings include *Pulpit and Communion Table* (E, 1874), and *Rich Gleanings* (L, 1925).

As a teacher 'Rabbi' Duncan was known for his original reflections presented in aphorisms reminiscent of the Talmud, his encyclopedic but unmethodical studies, his irregular habits and absentmindedness and his insatiable mental curiosity. A youth spent in philosophical speculation persuaded him that assurance of truth must be based on theology derived from the Scriptures rather than on the critical powers of reason. This persuasion gave him an anchor in his struggles for a personal assurance of salvation, and was central to the religious outlook he imparted to his students. In this conviction he stood apart from the emerging rationalism in the biblical criticism* of A. B. Davidson,* his successor in the Old Testament chair. After Duncan's death examples of his pulpit eloquence and epigrammatic wisdom were published by his friends.

D. Brown, *Life of John Duncan* (E, 1872); A. M. Stuart, *Recollections of John Duncan* (E, 1872); FES III, 425–6, VII, 715; *DNB* XVI, 167–8; J. MacLeod, *Scottish Theology* (E, ³1974); D. Chambers, 'The Church of Scotland's Mission to the Jews', *RSCHS* (1975), 43–58; W. A. Knight, *Colloquia Peripatetica* (E, ⁵1879) – notes of conversations with Duncan.

S. Isbell

Duncan, Mark (c.1570–1640), professor at the French Protestant Academy at Saumur 1606–40. The son of Thomas Duncan of Maxpoffle, Roxburghshire, he was educated partly in Scotland and partly abroad. By 1606 he was teaching Greek at the Academy of Sedan (where John Cameron* earlier taught) before moving, through the patronage of Philippe du Plessis-Mornay, to Saumur, which reached its zenith in Duncan's early years. Cameron, Robert Boyd* and Zachary Boyd* were among his Scottish colleagues there. He taught philosophy and oratory, later (1627) Greek as well, and was Regent (Principal) from 1616.

Duncan was an Aristotelian, a member of the last pre-Descartes generation. His main work was *Institutiones Logicae* (Saumur, 1612, with later editions). According to Thomas Dempster* he also published poems and speeches and wrote on ethics. He was also a much sought-after physician. In 1632 he intervened to defuse a case of alleged spirit-possession of a community of Ursuline nuns in nearby Loudun, attributing it to a combination of melancholy and hysteria (*Discours de la Possession...*, Paris, 1634), which brought the hostility of Cardinal Richelieu and others upon his head.

Apparently Duncan did not participate in the controversies concerning the broadening of Calvinism that disturbed Saumur (*see* Cameron, John). He was widely admired on all sides for his manners and his expertise in several fields.

M. Campbell, 'Mark Duncan...', *RSCHS* 5 (1935), 73–80; E. and E. Haag, *La France Protestante* V (Paris, ²1886), 834–5.

D. F. Wright

Dundas, Henry (1724–1811), First Viscount Melville, Lord Advocate 1775–83, created Viscount Melville 1802. Dundas was impeached in 1805 for alleged crimes and misdemeanours relating to fraud and irregularities in the Navy, of which he was Treasurer (1782–1800) and First Lord of the Admiralty (1804–5), but acquitted. As Keeper of the Scottish Signet from 1782 and of the Privy Seal of Scotland from 1800 he was in complete control of royal ecclesiastical and academic patronage in Scotland. In political terms he was the most powerful man in the country.

It was commonly assumed at the time, and has continued to be, that Dundas used his ecclesiastical influence in the interest of the Moderate party.* Recent research, however, has demonstrated that the picture was more complex than hitherto believed. Although he supported the Moderates in the General Assembly, of which he was a very frequent member (during the years 1762–85 he was absent only five times), his attitude towards them was ambiguous and did not always bring them the advantages they expected. For example, they complained that he consistently ignored their nephews in matters of preferment and often appointed members of the 'Popular' party* to ecclesiastical and academic posts in spite of their urgent protests. Royal presentations to parishes he distributed fairly equally to clergy of both parties, and the 'Popular' party gained about one-third of the royal chaplaincies, deaneries and almonerships. It seems, in fact, that Dundas dispensed patronage for political advantage rather than in the interests of the Moderates. He was willing to please them if it was not inconvenient, but he was far from following their dictates. It has been suggested, indeed, that strained relations with Principal William Robertson* was one of the main factors in the latter's retiral from ecclesiastical politics in 1780.

Yet it should not be assumed that he improperly used government influence to interfere in the affairs of the Church. The conservatism of the Moderates was mirrored in Dundas' political conservatism, so their interests often coincided, though for different reasons.

DNB XVI, 186–91; I. D. L. Clark, 'From Protest to Reaction: The Moderate Regime in the Church of Scotland, 1752–1805', in N. T. Phillipson and R. Mitchison (eds), *Scotland in the Age of Improvement* (E, 1970); R. B. Sher, *Church and University in the Scottish Enlightenment* (Princeton, E, 1985); M. Fry, *The Dundas Despotism* (E, 1992).

J. R. McIntosh

Dundrennan, *see* Cistercians.

Dunfermline Abbey. After her marriage to Malcolm III* in 1069, Queen Margaret* invited Benedictine* monks from Canterbury to Dunfermline. The foundation became an abbey *c*.1128 and was richly endowed by David I.* It was a prestigious 'palace monastery', one of the wealthiest in Scotland. Several kings were born in Dunfermline and the abbey church succeeded Iona* as the royal burial place: Malcolm, Margaret, Robert the Bruce* and other sovereigns were interred there. The abbot received the privilege of *pontificalia* (episcopal insignia) in 1245. Two abbots were notable in public life: Robert de Keldeleth* and Richard Bothwell.* Two monks became bishops: Andrew (Caithness *c*.1147–84) and George Crichton (Dunkeld 1526–44).

After becoming an abbey, Dunfermline was independent of Canterbury and from early times had a dependent priory of its own. Urquhart (Moray), founded *c*.1136, was eventually united in 1454 to Pluscarden,* which ceased to be Valliscaulian* and became dependent on Dunfermline. There was perhaps a cell at Dornoch (Sutherland) for a time *c*.1150. Coldingham,* a priory of Durham, was subject to Dunfermline *c*.1378–1424.

The abbey buildings were celebrated for their grandeur. The church, dedicated in 1150, was enlarged in preparation for Margaret's canonization in 1250. The destruction by English forces in 1303 was made good and extensive reconstruction was carried out in the fourteenth and fifteenth centuries. From 1500 the abbacy was held by a series of commendators* who were bishops or officers of state; they included James Beaton I,* Alexander Stewart,* Andrew Forman* and George Durie.* A community of twenty-five to twenty-eight monks is recorded in the period 1520–60. At the Reformation, some monks became Protestant readers* or ministers, notably John Durie,* while John Angus* composed music for use in Reformed worship. The buildings were damaged by the mob in 1560. Today the monastic buildings are in ruins but the magnificent nave still stands, joined to the modern parish church.

C. Innes (ed.), *Registrum de Dunfermelyn* (E, Bannatyne Club, 1842); Easson-Cowan, 58–9; M. Dilworth, 'Monks and Ministers after 1560', *RSCHS* 18 (1974), 216–20; J. M. Webster, *Dunfermline Abbey* (Dunfermline, 1948); G. W. S. Barrow, *The Kingdom of the Scots* (L, 1973), 188–99; S. Cruden, *Scottish Medieval Churches* (E, 1986), 26–38.

M. Dilworth

Dunkeld, *see* Early Ecclesiastical Sites.

Dunlop, John (1837–1909), influential theologian in New Zealand. From Fenwick (near Kilmarnock), he was a notable student at the University of Glasgow (1860–4) before attending Trinity College. Inducted to Free St David's, Dundee in 1870, he was active in civic affairs until appointed Professor of Theology by the Synod of Otago and Southland in 1887. A student rebel against aspects of Calvinism, he became a powerful apologist for that tradition, combining a deep knowledge of philosophy and the natural sciences with a powerful restatement of divine redemption. He was Moderator of Synod in 1893 and played an important part in debates on a Declaratory Act.* Students were deeply influenced by his combination of spiritual, moral and intellectual perception, which made him a national leader in overseas missions, education and ministry. He published little, but *Religious Certainty* (Dunedin, 1896) was important. Glasgow honoured him with a DD in 1887.

I. Breward, *Grace and Truth* (Dunedin, 1975); J. R. Elder, *History of the Presbyterian Church of New Zealand* (Christchurch, 1940).

I. Breward

Dunlop, William, the elder (1649?–1700), Principal of Glasgow University. Son of the Covenanting minister of Paisley, Renfrewshire, he inherited his father's Presbyterian zeal. He became a licentiate of the CofS, but emigrated in 1684 to Carolina, America, with a party of fellow-Scots in search of religious liberty. He stayed there as a planter and a major and chaplain to a militia regiment until the Glorious Revolution. On his return to Scotland, William III made him Principal of Glasgow University in 1690. He was ordained as a CofS minister in Glasgow without charge.

Dunlop was director of the Darien Company (*see* Darien Colony) in which Glasgow University had invested £500. He was the brother-in-law of William Carstares* and the father of William Dunlop* the younger.

FES VII, 376; *DNB* XVI, 209.

N. R. Needham

Dunlop, William (*c*.1692–1720), Professor of Ecclesiastical History at Edinburgh. The son of William Dunlop,* Principal of Glasgow University, and nephew of William Carstares,* Principal of Edinburgh, he was educated at Glasgow (MA, and theology under John Simson*), Edinburgh (under William Hamilton,* *d*.1732) and Utrecht (civil law). Appointed to the chair through Carstares' influence in 1715, he was by common testimony a highly gifted preacher and lecturer and a scholar of eminent promise. Besides two volumes of *Sermons Preached on Several Subjects* (E, 1722 – including some lectures) and a life of William Guthrie* (first published with *The Christian's Great Interest*, (L, 1733), his writings concern the place of confessions in the Church. He edited *A Collection of Confessions of Faith* (2 vols, E, 1719–22), with a long introduction also published separately as *A Preface to an Addition* [sic] *of the Westminster Confession of Faith*

... *Being A Full Account of All the Ends and Uses of Creeds and Confessions of Faith* .... (L, 1720; also ed. James Buchanan,* L, 1857), which he defended when controversy ensued. An early death silenced a voice and a pen spoken of in terms of genius.

FES VII, 389; DNB XVI 209–10; memoir prefaced to *Sermons*.

D. F. Wright

Duns, John (1820–1909), Professor of Natural Science at New College, Edinburgh. A native of Duns, Berwickshire, he graduated from the University of Edinburgh and was ordained in 1844 to the ministry of the FC, serving for twenty years (1844–64) as minister at Torphichen, near Bathgate, West Lothian. During these years he began publishing on the relationship between science and Christianity, and he was consequently appointed as lecturer in Natural Science at New College* in 1864. The Chair of Natural Science in the College had previously been occupied by John Fleming,* but had been vacant since Fleming's death in 1857. Initially there was some dispute as to whether Fleming's professorship should be abolished, some members of the 1864 General Assembly querying the propriety of retaining Natural Science as a *bona fide* constituent of a theological curriculum. Accordingly, Duns held his position at New College with the status of lecturer for some five years until the provision of a bequest provided for the endowment of a professorial chair in 1869. Duns occupied that position until his death. He joined the UFC in 1900.

Duns produced numerous works as a commentator on science and religion, notably *Biblical Natural Science, Being the Explanation of all References in Holy Scripture to Geology, Botany, Zoology, & Physical Geography*, 2 vols (L, 1863–68), *Science and Christian Thought* (L, 1866), and *Creation according to the Book of Genesis and the Confession of Faith* (E, 1877). He opposed Darwin's theory of evolution by natural selection and defended instead what he termed 'the theory of design'.

H. Watt, *New College Edinburgh: A Centenary History* (E, 1946), 55–7, 249; AFC I, 54; FUFCS, 576; UFC Monthly Record 99 (March, 1909), 105–6.

D. N. Livingstone

Duns Scotus, John (*c*.1266–1308), known as *Doctor Subtilis*, medieval theologian. Scotus was born around 1266 at Duns in Berwickshire (the view in many dictionaries that he was born at Maxton in Roxburghshire is now discounted: see Henry Docherty, 'The Brockie MSS and Duns Scotus', in *De Doctrina Ioannis Duns Scoti*, I, Rome, 1968, 327–60). He entered the Order of Friars Minor (Franciscans*) in 1278, and was ordained a priest in 1291. He seems to have studied at Paris from 1293 to 1296, and then went to Oxford, where he produced the *Oxford Commentary on the Sentences of Peter Lombard*. In 1302 he returned to Paris but was banished in 1303. From 1303–4 he was back in Oxford, and returned to Paris in 1304, where he again commented on the *Sentences*. In 1307 he went to Cologne, where he died in 1308.

Scotus is known as the great critic of Thomas Aquinas from the perspective of a realist epistemology. Very simply, according to St Thomas, the mind cannot know individual material things directly, because the mind only knows by reflecting on general ideas which are abstracted from particulars. Against this, Scotus insisted that the primary natural object of the mind is not the general idea of a thing (its essence or quiddity), abstracted from its existence, but being as such (actual knowledge of real things, material or spiritual). In consequence, he made 'intuitive' knowledge (the direct knowledge of an actually existent object) primary over 'abstractive' knowledge (the knowledge of an individual thing through its abstracted general idea). It followed from this that abstractive thinking (reflection on abstracted ideas, which was the basic activity of medieval theology) is limited and imperfect: we cannot argue logically from our logical abstractions to reality, and it is in the objective reference to a reality beyond our formalization that true knowledge arises. Scotus made a further vital distinction between a voluntary and a natural object. The human mind knows a natural object (a stone) necessarily through causality, but God is not known by us in this way. With a voluntary object, the human mind can know it only through its willed activity in making itself known, and this is the only way in which we can know God; our knowledge is contingent upon the divine will, which is always personal. From this realistic epistemology of Scotus there came a greater emphasis on personal obedience and prayer in response to God's self-revelation giving an immediate and straightforward knowledge of God. It was this teaching, together with his account of the Trinity, which through John Major* had immense impact on Calvin in Paris, and so for the Reformation. His beatification took place in March 1993.

Opera Omnia, ed. C. Balić (Rome, 1950).

F. Copleston, *A History of Philosophy* (NY, 1962), II, pt 2, 199ff.; T. F. Torrance, 'Intuitive and Abstractive Knowledge from Duns Scotus to John Calvin', *De Doctrina Ioannis Duns Scoti*, IV (Rome, 1968), 291–305; D. E. Sharp, *Franciscan Philosophy at Oxford* (L, 1930); J. B. Torrance and R. C. Walls, *Duns Scotus* (E, 1992).

I. R. Torrance

Durham, James (1622–58), Covenanter minister and author. The eldest son of the Laird of Easter Powrie, Angus (who was director of the Rolls of Exchequer and a decided Royalist), Durham studied at the University of St Andrews, but, without obtaining a degree, left to pursue the life of a country gentleman. Although moral and studious, it was not until some time after his marriage that he was converted. Experiences in the civil war and the influence of David Dickson* led him to study divinity at Glasgow with Dickson (MA, 1647), and he was ordained to Glasgow Blackfriars (the south quarter) in 1647. In 1650 he was called and trans-

DURHAM, JAMES

ported by the General Assembly to be Professor of Divinity in the University of Glasgow; but, being also instructed to serve as chaplain to the King, he was never admitted. In November 1650 he asked to be excused from this chaplaincy on account of indisposition and, despite the King's specific request, apparently never returned to what Robert Baillie* described as a 'grievous burden' (*Letters and Journals*, III, 150; cf. A. F. Mitchell and J. Christie (eds), *Records of the Commissions of the General Assemblies of the Church of Scotland* (E, 1892–9), II, 409; III, 117–18, 133, 234, 253, 335). Although he inquired about taking up his duties at the university, this was not welcomed (see Baillie, III, 146–8), and in September 1651 he was translated to the Glasgow High Church (St Mungo's, west quarter), where he remained until his death.

With Robert Blair,* Durham attempted to mediate in the Protester*/Resolutioner* controversy. From the first they were, as Baillie described them, 'a little ambiguous' (III, 126). In May 1651 Baillie feared Durham's 'accommodations' more than the violence of others (III, 171). He was not pleased with Durham's 1652 overtures for union, both urging others 'to guard against this assault' and writing a reply himself (III, 183, 185, 190–3). Baillie continued to fear Durham's influence, which he described as 'of exceeding great weight deservedly' (III, 222). Durham and Blair in 1655 came close to achieving their desired end, but their plans were eventually scuttled by the efforts of the more extreme of both parties, particularly James Guthrie* and Archibald Johnston* of Wariston of the Protesters, and Baillie and James Sharp* of the Resolutioners. Want of success did not lead Durham to despair. He spent his last days dictating the final part of *The Dying man's Testament to the Church of Scotland; Or, A Treatise concerning Scandal* (E, 1659), which urges union as a duty on the divided CofS.

Durham had a high reputation for great piety, great prudence and great learning. John Carstairs described him as 'a very candid and searching preacher', who in an instant was 'in the inmost corners of your bosoms', though with the utmost 'caution and meekness, without giving any of his hearers the smallest ground to fret and repine at his freedom in dealing with them'. Baillie concurred in this judgment, desiring Durham to write on cases of conscience, wherein he considered him 'excellent' (I, 222).

Durham is said, with David Dickson, to have written the influential *Sum of Saving Knowledge* (Robert Wodrow, *Analecta*, III, 10). He prepared *A Commentarie Upon the Book of the Revelation* (E, 1658; [7]G, 1766) for the press, but the rest of his published works were posthumous. His colleague, John Carstairs, edited most of them. Most went through several editions over the next 150 years, and some are still read, two having been reprinted recently. *An Exposition Of the Whole Book of Job* (G, 1759) was the last to be published; unpublished manuscripts are still extant.

The Blessedness of the Death of These that Die in the Lord (G, 1681); *Christ Crucified: or, The Marrow* *of the Gospel, ... on the whole 53. Chapter of Isaiah* (E, 1683); *Clavis Cantici: or, An Exposition of the Song of Solomon* (E, 1668); *The Great Corruption of Subtile Self* (E, 1686); *The Great Gain of Godliness* (E, 1685); *Heaven upon Earth* (E, 1685); *A Practical Exposition of the X. Commandements* (L, 1675; also issued under the title, *The Law Unsealed*, E, 1676); *The Unsearchable Riches of Christ* (G, 1685).

FES III, 456–7; *DNB* XVI, 255–6; R. Wodrow, *Analecta*, III, 104–9; G. Christie, 'James Durham as Courtier and Preacher', *RSCHS* 4 (1930), 66–80; 'A Collection of Some Memorable Things in the Life . . .', prefixed to *The Dying man's Testament* . . . (E, 1659); G. Christie, 'A Bibliography of James Durham: 1622–1658', *Publicns. of the Edinb. Bibliographical Soc.* 11 (1912–20, publ. 1921), 35–46.

D. C. Lachman

Durie, George (fl.1550), abbot of Dunfermline.* Son of the laird of Durie in Fife and Janet Beaton, sister of Archbishop James Beaton* (died 1539), he was the brother of Andrew Durie, bishop of Galloway, and first cousin of Cardinal David Beaton.* In 1526 his uncle, James Beaton, ceded the abbacy of Dunfermline to him, retaining for himself the revenues and certain rights. From c.1526 Durie was a claimant to be archdeacon of St Andrews* diocese and in 1534–6 gained undisputed possession. He also held other benefices.

In 1539, on his uncle's death, he became sole commendator* of Dunfermline and in 1553 ceded the abbacy to his own nephew, Robert Pitcairn, retaining the administration and revenues for himself. He ceded the archdeaconry of St Andrews to Pitcairn, on the same terms, in 1539. His career, however, was not in the Church but in public affairs. He attended Parliament constantly, was a Privy Councillor from the early 1540s and was often given particular remits, both routine offices and those meeting particular needs. He was made a Lord of Session in 1541 and was Keeper of the Privy Seal in 1552–5.

In early 1560 Durie joined the French forces in Scotland and in early 1561 he went to France. In 1570 he intended to return to Scotland and perhaps did so. At some time in the 1570s he died.

Durie's career needs to be demythologized. He was a clerical careerist, pluralist and nepotist and he sided with the RC forces at the Reformation; he was the father of at least four illegitimate children. His cruel anti-Protestant activities, however, in the accounts of John Knox,* David Calderwood* and John Spottiswoode* are uncorroborated. His martyrdom and beatification, related by Thomas Dempster,* lack any foundation. One son, John Durie, became a Jesuit,* and was an active missioner in south-west Scotland in the 1580s (*DNB* XVI, 260–1).

Registrum de Dunfermelyn (E, 1842); J. M. Webster and A. A. M. Duncan (eds), *Regality of Dunfermline Court Book 1531–1538* (Dunfermline, 1953); Durie's career can be followed in the public records, particularly *Registrum Magni Sigilli Regum*

DURIE, JOHN

Scotorum (E, 1882–8), *Register of the Privy Council of Scotland* (E, 1877), *Calendar of State Papers relating to Scotland* (E, 1898–1903); *DNB* XVI, 259–61.

A. L. Walker and M. Dilworth

Durie, John (*c*.1537–1600), Presbyterian minister. He was born at Mauchline, Ayrshire, and educated at Ayr before entering the Benedictine* order as a monk of Dunfermline, where his cousin George Durie* was abbot. According to Spottiswoode (III, 83), Durie was condemned for heresy and ordered 'to be shut up between two walls till he died', but was freed by Arran (*see* Hamilton, James, *d*, 1575), conformed to the Reformation* and was appointed first as exhorter* to Hailes (or Colinton), then as exhorter in 1568 and minister in 1570 to Restalrig (or Leith) and Penicuik, and finally to Edinburgh by 1573. In the General Assembly of August 1575, Durie raised objections to the 'office and name of a bishop' and the role of chapters in episcopal elections, which he 'and other brethren of his mind' entertained in the aftermath of the Convention of Leith* of 1572 and the appearance of bishops in the Kirk. His stand gained support from Andrew Melville,* and the Assembly agreed the word 'bishop' was applicable to all ministers, though some might be chosen by the Assembly to act not as diocesan bishops but as visitors of groups of parishes, a decision inimical to the survival of diocesan episcopacy. He contributed to the drafting of the *Second Book of Discipline*.* Called before the Privy Council in 1580 for preaching against French courtiers, Durie protested the council were not competent judges in spiritual matters. He was a fervent supporter of the Assembly's proceedings in 1582 against Robert Montgomery,* who had accepted the Crown's nomination to the vacant archbishopric of Glasgow. He was twice banished from Edinburgh by the King in 1582 and 1583 for his criticism of the Earl of Lennox and Arran and his approval of the ultra-Protestant Ruthven Raiders,* and subsequently served as minister at Montrose. With other Presbyterians, he strongly opposed the Assembly's decision in 1586 to absolve Patrick Adamson,* Archbishop of St Andrews, from his sentence of excommunication. His son Robert (1555–1616; *FES* V, 182–3, *DNB* XVI, 263–4) was minister in Fife (St Monans and Anstruther, 1588–1606) before being banished and becoming the first minister of the Scots Church in Leiden. John Durie (1596–1680)* was Robert's son.

BUK; Calderwood; *Accounts of the Collectors of Thirds of Benefices*, ed. G. Donaldson (E, 1949), 275–6, 291; *Register of Ministers, Exhorters and Readers*, ed. A. Macdonald (E, 1830), 7; *SBD*, 47, 53–4, 136; *FES* I, 2, 52, 164, 343, V, 409–10; *DNB* XVI, 261; R. Lippe (ed.), *Selections from Wodrow's Biographical Collections*, vol. I (New Spalding Club, A, 1860), 124–64.

J. Kirk

Durie (Dury), John (1596–1680), Scottish minister and pioneer of ecumenism. The son of Robert Durie, minister of Anstruther Wester, and grandson of John Durie,* minister in Edinburgh, he was born in Edinburgh. On his father's banishment in 1606, he pursued an education on the continent, first at Sedan, where his kinsman Andrew Melville* was Professor of Divinity, and then at Leiden, where his father was minister. In 1624 he went to Oxford, and by 1628 was appointed minister to the English Company of Merchants at Elbing in Prussia. Returning to England in 1630 he sought support for his schemes to unite the Lutheran and Reformed Churches, and on the continent enlisted the help of Gustavus Adolphus. After these endeavours, he entered the ministry of the CofE in 1634, but returned to the Netherlands in 1635, visited Sweden in 1636, Denmark in 1639 and Germany by 1640 to promote his ideas on religious unity. He was also in touch with the Churches of Switzerland and France. He supported the royalist cause in the English civil war, became chaplain at The Hague to Mary of Orange, and by 1643 was chosen minister of the English Merchants' church in Rotterdam. Present at the Westminster* Assembly of Divines, he contributed to the Confession of Faith and Catechisms. Between 1651 he wrote seven pamphlets in support of the Engagement,* including *Considerations Concerning the Present Engagement* (L, 1649). He renewed his tireless, if fruitless, efforts to re-unite Protestants with support from Cromwell and then, with the Restoration,* from the Earl of Clarendon, Edward Hyde. After further extensive travels in the Netherlands, Switzerland and Germany in pursuit of unity, he died at Cassel in Hesse. J. M. Batten, *John Dury: Advocate of Christian Re-union* (Chicago, 1944), includes a bibliography of Durie's numerous works.

T. M'Crie, *Life of Andrew Melville*, 2 vols (E, ²1824); R. S. Paul, *The Assembly of the Lord* (E, 1985); *DNB* XVI, 261–3; R. Rouse and S. C. Neill, *A History of the Ecumenical Movement 1517–1948* (²L, 1967).

J. Kirk

Dutch Reformed Church in S. Africa, Scottish influences on. The DRC in SA was influenced in its ministry and theological emphases by the Church of Scotland. This happened within a colonial context, because of cultural and theological motivations, and was effected by Scottish ministers and missionaries serving local congregations.

Occupied from 1795 to 1803 and taken over in 1806, the Cape of Good Hope became a British colony in 1814. Dissatisfied with the London Missionary Society* which sent them to the Cape, three Scottish missionaries, J. Evans (*d*.1823), J. Taylor (1788–1869) and G. Thom,* were appointed ministers of local congregations of the colonial DRC. In order to bring the colonial Reformed Church and its schools more closely into line with British practices, the governor requested Thom to recruit ministers and teachers in Scotland. With the help of Stevenson Macgill,* commissions were appointed in Glasgow and Aberdeen. In 1822

DUTCH REFORMED CHURCH

Thom brought Andrew Murray (1794–1866) and six teachers to the Cape. More teachers and the following ministers came thereafter: A. Smith (1823), C. Fraser (1824), H. Sutherland (1824), G. Morgan (1825), J. Edgar (1829), J. Cassie (1829), J. Pears (1830), W. R. Thompson (1830), W. Robertson (1822/31), A. Welsh (1833), R. Shand (1834), T. Reid (1836). Thus sixteen Scotsmen, along with eighteen Afrikaners, six Dutchmen and two Germans served the Reformed Church, which was recognized by the Dutch as having national status and also privileges from the British government.

The Scotsman A. J. Jardine (c.1790–1845), similarly secured by Thom, was the first to attempt a fragmentary description of *The Church History of the Cape of Good Hope* (1827). His main concerns are the 'General Principles of the Church of Scotland', as applied to 'The Colonial Church Establishment', which up to 1824, was merely the organized puppet of the state. In due time, the former DRC was partly shaped by a Presbyterian system typical of Scotland. The Scottish ministers also moulded the evangelical emphasis of the Church.

Because of their Scottish roots, the initial group of ministers around Thom were influenced by the events, developments, theologians and devotional literature of their mother country. They sided with, and related themselves to, the CofS. During the time of the Disruption,* the promising sons of the influential Andrew Murray, John* and Andrew,* stayed with their uncle John in Aberdeen. In their letters a detailed report is given of their experience of revival,* for which their father was praying at the Cape. His letters show a father guiding his children spiritually as if he were a nineteenth-century Puritan. Five of his sixteen children became ministers in the DRC, while four married ministers.

Suspected of pro-British activity, the Scottish ministers did not allow themselves to be used deliberately for political considerations. They did not turn the Afrikaners into Britishers. In addition, they did not always understand the culture of the members they served.

In the late 1830s, members, mostly from congregations served by the Scottish ministers, trekked or emigrated to the north. This resulted in the formation of three separate Dutch Churches. One reason is said to have been a desire to escape the influences of the Scottish ministers and also the Methodist* tenets introduced to the Cape Church. The ministers' children were, however, South Africans, though they retained something of the emphases and ministry of their Scottish fathers, in a pietistic mode influenced by the Murrays. This is especially evident in the devotional books they wrote. They were part of an evangelical majority who joined together as friends, instituting schools with Christian teachers, supplying Christian literature to educate the people, and proving themselves as leaders in official meetings. A characteristic ministerial and theological approach was thus formed. If the end-product is a South African fabric, increasingly identified with Afrikaner culture, it nevertheless has distinctive Scottish threads.

In 1859 the DRC opened its own indigenous theological seminary at Stellenbosch. One of the two professors, John Murray* (see above), was of Scottish descent. He taught dogmatics, in conjunction with the Bible-Apologete theologians of Utrecht, but also according to the Common-Sense philosophy of Scotland (*see* Scottish Realism). His later colleague, J. I. Marais (1848–1919), was a devout follower of Scottish moral philosophy. In teaching theology to divinity students, Murray and his close friend, N. J. Hofmeyr (1827–1909), who was of Dutch descent, concerned themselves particularly with improving the ministry of the Church.

The current revivals overseas were reported in detail at the Cape. The two professors, together with Andrew Murray (jnr)* and their friend, the local minister, J. H. Neethling, a brother-in-law of the Murrays, organized a conference in order to revive the church in South Africa. In 1860 a revival was indeed experienced. At the conference it was resolved to recruit more Scottish ministers, and, through the efforts of W. Robertson, eight more came to serve the DRC: A. McKidd (1860), the first foreign missionary of the DRC, W. Cormack, D. McMillan, T. McCarter, T. Gray, A. McGregor (1864), A. Ross (1863), and J. McCarter, who arrived in 1862 and was the first to write a fully-fledged history of the DRC, designed and interpreted on a Scottish score with a FC signature (1869). On this occasion, the Scottish ministers were needed to help withstand the influences of theologically liberal ministers who were trained in Holland. In the ensuing struggle the Scottish ministers stood firmly with the orthodox faith as formulated in the Heidelberg Catechism. Their faith was always practical with an emphasis on missionary activity. In extensive missionary work across the border in Central Africa, DRC missionaries co-operated with Scottish missionaries. Perhaps the best example is Malawi, where the Church of Central Africa, Presbyterian, was the result.

The Anglo-Boer War (1899–1902) severed the relationship of the DRC to the Scottish church and theology. Students of the DRC stopped visiting Scottish universities for postgraduate work. The prevailing Scottish tradition in the DRC received another severe blow with the heresy trial of Professor J. du Plessis in the late 1920s. Nevertheless, Scottish influence has left an indelible imprint on the ministry and theology of the DRC.

In the period after World War II, the DRC's support of apartheid led to its increasing isolation not only from Scottish Presbyterianism but also from the world-wide family of Reformed churches. Individual contacts were maintained chiefly with its non-white daughter churches. Most recently, as DRC theology began to distance itself from the apartheid system, leading CofS figures have been welcomed again in DRC circles.

F. W. Sass, *The Influence of the Church of Scotland on the Dutch Reformed Church of South Africa* (E, 1956); J. E. Orr, 'Evangelical Awakenings in South Africa in the 19th Century and their Antecedent Movements in the Motherlands' (DD, University of South Africa, 1969); J. Mackinnon, *South African Traits* (E, 1887); J. du Plessis, *The Life of Andrew Murray* (L, 1911); A. C. Ross in S. J. Brown and M. Fry (eds), *Scotland in the Age of the Disruption* (E, 1993), 151–64.

E. Brown

Duthac (*d*.1065), *see* Celtic Saints.

Dykes, James Oswald (1835–1912), Presbyterian theologian. Born in Port Glasgow, the son of the town clerk, he was educated at Dumfries Academy, Edinburgh University and New College, Heidelberg and Erlangen. Ordained in 1859 at East Kilbride he served at Free St George's, Edinburgh, 1861–4 with R. S. Candlish,* until his health broke down. After three years in Australia he ministered at Regent Square Presbyterian Church, London, 1869–88, after which he was until 1907 Principal and Barbour Professor of Divinity in the Theological College of the Presbyterian Church of England.

His many books included three on the kingdom of God, devotional works and *The Divine Worker in Creation and Providence* (E, 1909).

Who Was Who, 1897–1916, 217–8; *AFCS* I, 145; British Library, *General Catalogue*.

J. S. Andrews

E

Eadie, John (1810–76), USec. and UP biblical scholar. Born in 1810 in Alva, Stirlingshire, after a parish school education he completed university and divinity studies in Glasgow where he was to spend the rest of his life. He became in turn minister of Cambridge USec. Church (1835–63) and Lansdowne Street Extension Church (1863–76). For most of his ministry he was simultaneously Professor of Biblical Literature (1843–76) in the USec. (subsequently the UP) divinity hall.

He began his writing career in 1840 as editor of the *Voluntary Church Magazine*. He regularly submitted articles to scholarly journals and was to continue publishing to the very end of his life, mostly in the form of New Testament commentaries and a variety of Bible study aids. In 1870 he visited the Middle East with a group of friends to extend his knowledge of the world of the Bible. His writings were highly regarded in Britain and also widely known in the USA. In his last years his scholarship was publicly recognized when he was invited to be a member of the prestigious committee for revising the Authorized Version of the Bible. He died in 1876 having suffered from heart disease for several years. He had been awarded two university doctorates (LLD, Glasgow, 1844; DD, St Andrews, 1850).

Born and raised among the working classes of Lowland Scotland, Eadie never lost his interest in and ability to relate to the average person. He was a big man physically and surprisingly taciturn in conversation, but he was diligent as a pastor and affectionate in his manner. In his preaching Eadie favoured biblical expositions, very often on one of Paul's letters. His later commentaries grew out of some of these early discourses to his Glasgow congregations and Bible classes.

As a churchman Eadie's sympathies were both loyal to his Church and ecumenically broad. In his earlier years he wrote popular biographies of some of the founding fathers of the Secession Church, while in 1857 he was appointed Moderator of his Church's Synod and in 1873 was delegated to represent his Church among the Presbyterian Churches in the USA. Throughout his life he maintained contact with scholars and churchmen of different countries and churches.

Eadie is particularly remembered for his exegetical commentaries on some of Paul's shorter epistles. These were on Ephesians (L, 1854, ^{2}1883), Colossians (L, 1856, ^{2}1884), Philippians (L, 1859, ^{2}1884), Galatians (E, 1869, ^{2}1883) and Thessalonians (posthumously, L, 1877). His exegesis was characterized by erudition, clarity and sound judgment. Because Eadie held the highest view of the New Testament text as inspired by the Holy Spirit, he also had the highest conception of the task of the biblical exegete. For the same reason he rejected the subjectivism of much of the rationalistic scholarship of his day. One of his best known works is *Paul, the Preacher* (L, 1859).

See also Exegesis, Biblical.

The English Bible, 2 vols (L, 1876).

J. Brown, *Life of John Eadie* (L, 1878); *DNB* XVI, 307–9; *The Encyclopedia of Christianity* III (1972), 480f.; Small II, 67–8, 101–2.

D. J. W. Milne

Early Ecclesiastical Sites. There is a general predisposition to attribute great historical events and developments to outstanding individuals. Behind St Ninian* (Nynia), 'Apostle of the Picts',* and St Columba,* 'Apostle of the Scots', there must have been an anonymous legion of earlier preachers, proselytizers and simple witnesses to the Christian faith which, as James Bulloch* wrote, 'was carried by obscure men with more urgent tasks than the writing of records for posterity' – to which we need to add 'and obscure women too'. As early as the beginning of the third century Tertullian claimed that there were Christians north of the Roman *limes* in Britannia, *i.e.* north of Hadrian's Wall at least, if not north of Forth and Clyde. This outlying pocket of believers may not have survived, but we cannot doubt the existence of Christian communities in the 'sub-Roman' period. Charles Thomas states that 'Christianity in southern Scotland ... sprang from that early fifth-century see established at Whithorn',* yet he believes that the see was founded by and for Ninian (Nynia) precisely to serve the needs of an existing Christian community. Thomas would locate the powerhouse which generated the diocesan organization of Galloway at Carlisle (*Luguvalium, Luel*), and he sees a parallel between Ninian, set up as pastor of the Christians in Galloway, and his fellow-Briton Patrick, sent to be pastor, as Palladius had been before him, 'to those Irish believing in Christ'. It might be thought that a Christian community at Carlisle vigorous enough, c. 400–450, not only to preserve the faith locally but to oversee the supply and despatch of bishops who were effectively missionaries, would have left more traces in the archaeological record. Perhaps there has been too much physical disturbance and not enough archaeological activity. We must in any case bear in mind that none of the extremely jejune sources for Ninian claims that he founded the ecclesiastical establishment at Whithorn, merely that he built a church there at a location called *Candida Casa* ('the White House') by Bede;* it was constructed of stone or brick, something hitherto unknown to the local people. An alternative hypothesis would place Ninian in a late fifth-/earlier sixth-century context and would see him as one of an already established line of bishops in Galloway, who at one period in his career made it his special concern to bring Christianity to the still pagan Picts.

To see Patrick and Ninian as real-life figures we have to envisage Christian communities in northwestern England and southern Scotland. Their existence is to be inferred, regardless of Patrick or Ninian, from three distinct but related types of evidence.

(i) Carvings on stone (including native rock such as cave walls and boulders), comprising specifically Christian symbols (simple crosses, the chi–rho monogram, Latin formulae and personal names, alpha and omega *etc.*), are to be found, singly or in clusters, from Kirkmadrine in the Rhinns of Galloway to the Tweed basin and the Firth of Forth. They can seldom if ever be dated precisely, but the Latinus stone from Whithorn and two memorial stones from Stoneykirk are held to belong to the fifth century, and a date before 500 has also been suggested for the Catstane, still *in situ* in Kirkliston parish, west of Edinburgh, and commemorating Vetta son (or daughter?) of Victus. The tradition of carving memorial inscriptions in Latin died hard, if the Yarrowkirk stone dedicated to the memory of the 'famous princes Nudus and Dumnogenus, sons of Liberalis' (presumably chiefs among the Selgovae) is correctly attributed to the later sixth century. Latinized native names occur on stones discovered at and near Peebles, again probably of the sixth century. It is significant that all the stones mentioned, except perhaps for those at Peebles, are associated with early cemeteries, implying settled, and almost certainly Christian, communities which endured over appreciable periods.

(ii) Cemeteries or burial grounds containing full-length inhumations in long cists, *i.e.* roughly rectangular containers formed by flat stones or slabs inserted on their edges, capped by similar stone slabs. Diagnostic indications of the Christian nature of such burials are the absence of grave-goods, a marked tendency for the bodies to lie east–west, heads to the west, and a regular arrangement of graves in rows either end to end or side by side. Some of the graves of this type occur singly or in small numbers, but in a considerable number of cases there are graveyards containing scores or even hundreds of interments. The distribution of long-cist cemeteries is related to that of the stone carvings and inscriptions, but the territorial spread is considerably larger, for multiple burials are found in eastern Scotland from Berwickshire as far north as mid-Angus, while smaller sites and solitary burials occur from Galloway and south-west Roxburghshire to the north-east littoral. It is not seriously to be supposed that the Christianity implied by these cemeteries could be the result of the preaching of a single apostle, however eloquent. All early missionary preachers (including Ninian) would need to preach the faith in the first instance to kings and chiefs (and their wives); only after their conversion could Christianity have become firmly established among tribal and larger groups.

It is unlikely to be a coincidence that in Lothian three long-cist cemeteries are associated with ancient churches and church-sites, Tyninghame, Lasswade and Kirkliston, all of which belonged to the bishops of St Andrews in the twelfth century, while another was discovered immediately east of the twelfth-century abbey church of Holyrood and yet another on the abbey site of Jedburgh. Such association implies a degree of conscious continuity between the earliest phase of Christianity and later church foundations.

(iii) The third class of evidence consists of Christian and Christian-related place-names. Between these and the carved stones and cemeteries – especially the latter – there is a degree of correspondence. In Scotland, the early Celtic term *nemeton*, 'sacred place', 'place dedicated to a god', was carried over into the Christian period. Indeed, although there are instances of the term in Ireland and obsolete examples in southern Britain, *nemeton* in the British Isles may be regarded as a Scottish or at least north British phenomenon. Its use can be traced from Peebles-shire (Newholmhope alias Kirkhope in Manor) to Sutherland (Navidale), and in the great majority of cases the surviving place-name representing or embodying the term applies (or has applied) to an ecclesiastical site. The probability is that early Christian leaders deliberately sought out *nemeta* in order both to preserve continuity with popular reverence and also to reconsecrate sites for specifically Christian worship. The process cannot be dated, but for obvious reasons must have taken place at or soon after the conversion of a local pagan tribe or other grouping, since otherwise the significance of both term and site would have been lost. Examples where early religious connexions seem clear include Rosneath on the Gareloch, Nevay in Angus (close to Meigle with its cluster of early Pictish stones), Navar near Edzell, Newe in Strathdon and Nevie on the River Livet in Banffshire. At Newholmhope (formerly 'Newey') in the upper valley of the Manor Water, Peebles-shire, a fragment of a stone carved with apparently Brittonic names in Roman letters was discovered in 1891.

The imported term *eglēs*, assumed to have existed in early Brittonic and obviously borrowed from Latin *ecclesia* (itself a loanword from Greek), is found alone or embodied in compound place-names, in a number of regions of England (chiefly in the north west from Staffordshire to Cumberland) and has survived in some twenty-six or twenty-seven place-names in Scotland, distributed fairly widely across the southern counties and up the eastern seaboard as far north as the Aberdeenshire Don. Although the word *ecclesia* was borrowed into Old Irish (*eclais*), among the Irish or Scots, including those who from the fifth century settled the district of Argyll, this word did not become the normal element used in place-names to denote 'church'. The preferred word in Ireland and western Scotland was *cill*, and even in Wales the preferred word was not *eglwys* but *llan* ('enclosure'). The usage involving *eglēs* thus seems to be early, distinctively Brittonic and even markedly north Brittonic. It can only have found its way into Pictland on the lips of Brittonic-speakers, including missionaries and church leaders. Although many *eglēs* sites are lost or obsolete, several others belong to churches of considerable importance and apparent antiquity, *e.g.*, Eccles, Berwickshire, Falkirk ('Egglesbrech'), St Ninians ('Eccles'), 'Eglesnamin' (associated with St Andrews), 'Egglespether' (associated with Restenneth) and Ecclesgreig. In no Scottish instance can an *eglēs* name be closely associated with a known burial ground, unless the unlocated 'Eglesnamin' at St Andrews is represented by Hallowhill; but an early Christian cemetery has been discovered in Cumberland at Eaglesfield, which obviously belongs to the southern Scottish group of *eglēs* names. In a general way, however, there is a marked correlation between the distribution of *eglēs* names and orientated long-cist cemeteries.

According to Bede, Iona,* founded by Saint Columba in 563, long enjoyed hegemony over 'all the monasteries of the Picts'. This does not necessarily mean that every church, whether or not monastic, which had been established before 563 among the southern Picts simply ceased to exist, yielding place to new-founded 'Columban' monasteries. Rather it implies that the Columban clergy successfully asserted a supremacy throughout the Pictish kingdom which evidently endured till 717. Bede does not locate any of the monasteries of Pictland, whether Columban or pre-Columban. We are left to infer, partly from the notable concentrations of 'Class 2' sculptured stones, some of outstanding quality, which survive *in situ*, that there may have been early churches in the adjacent parishes of Tarbat and Nigg (Easter Ross), at Aberlemno and St Vigeans (Angus), Meigle (east Perthshire) and of course St Andrews, formerly Kinrimund, an old Pictish royal centre. It seems likely that these would have formed only a small proportion even of the prominent clerical centres, while across the whole of Scotland there would have come into existence innumerable burial grounds, rural shrines, chapels and small churches, most but by no means all of which may be dated to the period following Columba's death in 597.

If evidence from Orkney and Man be set beside that for the mainland province of Moray, it looks as though there was a deliberate policy of associating sites of worship and burial with well-established (and basically analogous or identical) territorial units, known locally as 'urislands' (Orkney), 'treens' (Man) and 'davochs' (mainland Scotland). Such, however, was probably not the case in southern Scotland. Bede, understandably, mentions only monasteries founded either by Aidan and his followers from Iona, such as Old Melrose, which had a *diseart* (hermitage) like any normal Irish monastery; or else by the Northumbrian Angles, such as Lindisfarne, Coldingham* and Abercorn. One probably early site which seems to have had no links with Scots or Angles was Glasgow, where tradition, of which the earliest record survives only from the twelfth century, relates that Saint Kentigern or Mungo (d. 612? see Celtic Saints) founded a church at a locality associated, perhaps falsely, with Ninian. Among many places connected with Mungo and Glasgow may be mentioned Stobo, Peebles-shire, in respect of which an accumulation of scattered evidence, including an apparent occurrence of the Brittonic term *clas*, points to ecclesiastical activity at an early period. Another seemingly purely Brittonic church site of early date is Paisley, a name derived from *basilica* and to be compared with Bassaleg in Gwent. Such a name is unlikely to have been formed much later than *c.* 600.

See also Cathedral Churches; Celtic Church; Celtic Saints; Culdees; Monasticism, Celtic.

C. A. R. Radford and G. Donaldson, *Whithorn and Kirkmadrine* (HMSO, E, 1957); A. S. Henshall, 'A Long Cist Cemetery at Parkburn Sand Pit, Lasswade, Midlothian', *PSAS* 89 (1958), 252–77; J. MacQueen, *St. Nynia* (E, 1990); J. Bulloch, *The Life of the Celtic Church* (E, 1963); A. D. S. Macdonald and Lloyd R. Laing, 'Early Ecclesiastical Sites in Scotland; a Field Survey', *PSAS* 100 (1969), 123–34, 102 (1973), 129–45; A. C. Thomas, *The Early Christian Archaeology of North Britain* (G, 1971); A. C. Thomas, *Christianity in Roman Britain to A.D. 500* (L, 1981); A. Macquarrie, 'The Date of Saint Ninian's Mission: a Reappraisal', *RSCHS* 23 (1987), 1–25.

G. W. S. Barrow

Easter, date and observance, *see* Christian Year.

Ebbe(a), *see* Anglo-Saxon Saints.

Ecclesiological Societies

Ecclesiological Societies. The first such society to be formed in the late nineteenth century was the Aberdeen Ecclesiological Society in 1886, mainly through the efforts of James Cooper,* then minister of the East Church of St Nicholas in Aberdeen. Its formation was inspired by the Cambridge Camden Society which performed a similar function in England. It was mainly concerned with the study of church architecture and furnishings and was interdenominational, open to members of any christian Church. It was one of the first meeting grounds between Presbyterians, Episcopalians and RCs in Scotland. Meetings were held monthly, papers were read and discussed and the annual *Transactions* of the Society were published. The Glasgow Ecclesiological Society was founded in 1893 by John Charleson* of Thornliebank, a minister of the CofS who was later to convert to RCism. The Aberdeen and Glasgow Societies joined together to form the Scottish Ecclesiological Society in 1903. Its objects were the study of the 'Principles of Christian Worship and of Church Architecture and its allied Arts, which are the handmaids of devotion', and the 'diffusion throughout Scotland of sound views, and a truer taste in such matters'. Cooper did not wish the societies to be merely gatherings of antiquarians but rather agencies to help members gain inspiration from the study of ancient buildings in order to provide for the religious needs of their own day. The societies tended to favour the Gothic style for church architecture and helped to influence opinion in this direction. Presbyterian churches in Scotland came to be built with chancels and side-pulpits and small 'altar' style Communion tables, as well as lecterns and prayer desks for the minister. The Scottish Ecclesiological Society continued to publish the *Transactions* of its proceedings until 1965 when it was discontinued. An Index of the *Transactions* was published in 1971.

D. M. Murray

Ecumenical Movement

PRESBYTERIAN REUNION. Scottish Presbyterianism* has shown a strong tendency to division, particularly in the eighteenth and nineteenth centuries, culminating in the Disruption* of 1843. But from the early nineteenth century there were also movements towards reunification, which became particularly urgent after 1843. The publication by Thomas Chalmers* and others of *Essays on Christian Reunion* (L, 1845) gave an impetus towards closer cooperation among evangelical Christians 'with a view to incorporation'. Chalmers in his essay in this volume looked forward with expectation to a larger union in which unity would ultimately be possible even with Rome and Orthodoxy. He was 'sanguine of union even still more comprehensive than that which we are immediately aiming at, and by which not only the smaller but the larger differences of the Christian world will at length be harmonised'. The Evangelical Alliance,* a fruit of the Evangelical Awakening, was founded in 1846, and although it was an organization of individuals rather than Churches, it was an ecumenical body which brought together Christians from a considerable number of denominations and gave impetus to the search for unity among Presbyterians in Scotland on the basis of a shared evangelical faith. In 1847 the Secession* and Relief* Churches came together to form the UPC. In 1900 the UPC and the FC united to form the UFC, and in 1929 the deepest remaining division was overcome by the union of the UFC and the CofS. The Articles Declaratory,* which were fundamental to the 1929 Union,* included a recognition of 'the obligation to seek and promote unity with other churches', and an affirmation that the CofS could unite without loss of identity (Article VII) (*see* Unions, Church, in Scotland).

THE WIDER ECUMENISM. The major Scottish Presbyterian Churches were also active in wider ecumenism. From the beginning the Scots were prominent in the establishment and leadership of what became the World Alliance of Reformed Churches.* J. H. Oldham* was probably the greatest Scottish ecumenical pioneer and leader of the twentieth century; he was a major architect of the World Council of Churches and British Council of Churches, and honorary President of the WCC from 1961. John* and Donald Baillie* were both prominent in the WCC and its commissions, Donald being a leading light in Faith and Order, and John in Life and Work. John Baillie was elected a President of the WCC at the Evanston Assembly (1954). T. F. Torrance* was a decisive theological influence at the Lund Conference of Faith and Order (1952) and for a number of years thereafter. Lesslie Newbigin,* J. H. Maclean (*FUFCS* 543; *FES* IX, 740), J. R. Macphail* and other Scots made an important contribution to the shaping of the Church of South India, and Newbigin became a world ecumenical leader as Secretary of the International Missionary Council and then, after its incorporation into the WCC (1961), as an Associate General Secretary of the WCC. At home the first General Secretary of the British Council of Churches, who decisively shaped this new ecumenical institution, was Archie Craig.*

DEVELOPMENT OF ECUMENISM IN SCOTLAND. At the end of the nineteenth century, Robert Lee,* William Milligan* and John Tulloch* of the CofS, with G. H. Wilkinson* of the EpCS, established the Christian Unity Association of Scotland,* which secured the agreement of the CofS, the UFC and the EpCS to set aside 13 October each year as a special day of prayer for Christian unity in Scotland. James Cooper* believed that the settlement of 1610 might suggest a way to unity between Presbyterians and Episcopalians, and both the Church Service Society* and the Scottish Church Society* were committed to the search for unity 'on a catholic basis'.

The World* Missionary Conference held in Edinburgh in 1910 gave a considerable impetus to the search for unity in Scotland. Its Continuation Committee promoted the formation in 1924 of a Scottish Churches Council, bringing together representatives of the CofS, UFC, EpCS, Congregationalist,

Baptist and Original Secession Churches. Its function was to suggest when concerted action was necessary on questions of national importance. It met quarterly until 1948 and co-operated with the various ecumenical bodies which preceded the establishment of the WCC and the BCC.

In 1948 a Scottish Churches Ecumenical Committee was established to co-ordinate and encourage ecumenical co-operation in Scotland. The Committee established the Scottish Committee on Inter-church Aid and Refugee Service, later to become Christian Aid, which flourishes under its secretary James Hodge. The Committee co-ordinated a wide range of activities and worked closely with the BCC. Its greatest achievement, however, was the establishment in Dunblane, Perthshire, of Scottish Churches House (1960). Under the imaginative leadership of its first Warden, Ian Fraser (*FES* IX, 469–70, X, 278), the House became a kind of 'Evangelical Academy' for Scotland. Numerous significant consultations were held, and the influence of the House was felt widely throughout Scotland.

Mention must also be made of the Dollarbeg Group,* so-called after the centre (near Dollar, Clackmannanshire) where they held a series of conferences between 1946 and 1950. These brought together leading figures and future leaders from all the Churches and from Scottish public life, to consider subjects such as 'Christian Witness in a Revolutionary World' (1948), 'The Christian Challenge to Communism' (1949), 'The Work and Witness of the Laity' (1949) and 'The Christian Doctrine of Work' (1950). Prominent figures in the Dollarbeg Group included a number of able women such as Mrs W. L. McKerrow, Elizabeth Hewat,* Mrs I. M. Forrester and Mrs Naomi Oates, and among the men deeply involved were Archie Craig, Donald Mackinnon,* George Macleod* and John Baillie. The Dollarbeg Group gave a wide range of people from all the major Scottish churches an exciting new sense of belonging together and sharing in the rapid growth of post-War ecumenism throughout the world.

The Dollarbeg Group took the initiative in establishing in 1950 the Scottish Churches Ecumenical Association, which thereafter continued the work of the Group both in promoting annual conferences and in encouraging local groups. The Association was loosely linked to the existing Scottish Churches Ecumenical Committee and several other important initiatives. The Tell Scotland* movement, founded in 1953 and led by Tom Allan* and D. P. Thomson,* co-operated closely with the Ecumenical Association, and tension was aroused when Tell Scotland invited Billy Graham* to lead a Crusade in Glasgow in 1955.

The Kirk Weeks* held between 1957 and 1965 were also organized by an independent committee which co-operated closely with the Ecumenical Association and the Ecumenical Committee. They were closely modelled on the German Kirchentag, although they never attracted equivalent participation. They gave an ecumenical vision and stimulated a variety of useful initiatives, particularly the Laity Forums and the Scottish Christian Industrial Order, spearheaded by W. S. Robertson and George Wilkie (*FES* IX, 237–8, X, 138, 456).

By the early 1960s there were a number of overlapping ecumenical agencies and organizations in Scotland, causing confusion in the public mind and some duplication of activity. On the initiative of Robert Mackie* and Nevile Davidson (1899–1976; *Who Was Who, 1971–1980*, 198), discussions were held between SCEA, SCEC, Tell Scotland, Kirk Week and Christian Aid in Scotland. As a result the Scottish Churches Council was inaugurated in 1964 'to further mission and manifest the unity of the Church Universal by providing a national focus of inter-church counsel and action'. Its Constitution was approved by the seven denominations that became members, together with the YMCA,* the YWCA,* the Student Christian Movement,* the National Bible Society of Scotland (*see* Bible Societies) and the United Society for Christian Literature. The first chairman was the Earl of Wemyss and March (who was also active on the world ecumenical scene), and the General Secretary Ian Fraser, Warden of Scottish Churches House.

The Scottish Churches Council encouraged closer relations between the Churches, and acted as a major link between Scotland, the BCC, and WCC.

During his visit to Scotland in May 1982, Pope John Paul II urged Scottish RCs to 'walk hand in hand' with other Christians. This, together with the new ecumenism engendered by the Second Vatican Council, made it possible for the first time to think of ecumenical structures which included the RCC. A grass-roots process of ecumenical encounter known by the cumbersome name of the 'Not Strangers but Pilgrims Inter-Church Process' was started in 1985. This was based on the willingness of the Churches at every level to enter into a commitment to one another – a particularly striking move for the RCC. The turning point of the process was the Swanwick (Derbyshire) Declaration of 1987, where representatives of the Churches proclaimed: 'It is our clear conviction that, as a matter of policy at all levels and in all places, our churches must now move from co-operation to clear commitment to each other, in search of the unity for which Christ prayed and in common evangelism and service of the world.'

A central part of the Inter-Church Process involved seeking new 'instruments' to replace the BCC, SCC and other existing ecumenical agencies in Britain and Ireland. A new body, Action of Churches Together in Scotland* (ACTS), has replaced the Scottish Churches Council. It will aim at greater unity, the growth of understanding and common action, particularly in evangelism and social responsibility. The new instruments incorporate a larger ecumenical constituency with the entry into full membership of the RCC and a range of Black churches which are mainly Pentecostal.

SCHEMES FOR ORGANIC UNION. The 1950s and 1960s were decades of great but fruitless optimism about possibilities of organic union in Scotland. Negotiations between the CofS, the CofE, the EpCS and the Presbyterian Church of England produced a scheme for union on a bishops-in-presbytery basis (see Anglican–Presbyterian Relations; Episcopacy). This was decisively rejected at the CofS General Assembly of 1957. Although conversations between the four Churches resumed in 1962, the Nottingham Faith and Order Conference in 1964 encouraged 'national unions'. A proposal that the EpCS should become an 'episcopal synod' in the CofS was rejected by the latter's General Assembly. Conversations with the UFC, the Congregational Union of Scotland and the Scottish Synod of the Methodist Church produced proposals which were turned down by one or both parties. The Multilateral Conversations* started in 1966 and still continue into the 1990s. They represent a gradual abandonment of hopes for successful bilateral schemes of organic union, and instead suggest a much slower process of growing together. Realism suggests that there is a moratorium on schemes for institutional unity, despite increasing co-operation and understanding between the Churches at every level.

M. Small, *Growing Together: The Ecumenical Movement in Scotland, 1924–1964* (typescript, Dunblane, n.d.); R. Rouse and S. Neill (eds), *A History of the Ecumenical Movement, 1517–1948* (L, 1967); J. R. Fleming, *The Story of the Church Union in Scotland* (L, 1929); W. A. Visser 't Hooft, *The Genesis and Formation of the World Council of Churches* (Geneva, 1982); R. Sjölinder, *Presbyterian Reunion in Scotland 1907–1921* (E, 1962).

D. B. Forrester

Edersheim, Alfred (1823/4–1889), biblical and Jewish historian. He was born of Jewish parents in Vienna, where he received his early education (being the first Jew to carry away a prize from the Gymnasium). He entered the University of Vienna in 1841, but soon had to interrupt his studies there because of his father's ill health. Moving to Budapest, he met 'Rabbi' John Duncan,* who was then serving as a missionary to Jews in that city, and under his influence he became a Christian. When Duncan returned to Scotland in 1843 to become first Professor of Hebrew in New College, Edinburgh,* Edersheim accompanied him and entered New College; he also studied theology in the University of Berlin.

In 1846 he was ordained to the FC ministry and went to Iasi, Romania, for missionary work among Jews. In 1849 he was called to the charge of Old Aberdeen FC (later St Mary's). He was compelled by ill health to move to the south of England, and settled in Torquay, where in 1861 St Andrew's Church was built for him. But ill health again forced him to give up preaching, and he lived for a time in Bournemouth, engaged in literary activity. In 1875 he took deacon's and priest's orders in the CofE, and served as vicar of Loders, Dorset, from 1876 to 1883. From 1880 to 1884 he was Warburtonian Lecturer at Lincoln's Inn, London: his lectures were published as *Prophecy and History in Relation to the Messiah* (L, 1885). In 1883 he resigned his living and took up residence at Oxford. There he lectured in the Honours School of Theology, and was select preacher to the University (1884–6). He received honorary doctorates from the Universities of Edinburgh, Berlin and Vienna.

He was a prolific author. He contributed the entries on Josephus and Philo to Smith and Wace's *Dictionary of Christian Biography*, III (L, 1882), IV (1887), and expounded Ecclesiasticus for the *Speaker's Commentary* (L, 1888). In three particularly helpful works he drew on his wide and detailed knowledge of Judaism in the Second Temple and tannaitic (especially the first centuries BC/AD) eras to illuminate the Gospel story: *The Temple: Its Ministry and Services as they were in the Time of Jesus Christ* (L, 1874), *Sketches of Jewish Social Life in the Days of Christ* (L, 1876) and, above all, *The Life and Times of Jesus the Messiah*, 2 vols (L, 1883, ³1886). The framework of the *Life and Times* is a continuous harmony of the four Gospels, in which there is little sign of influence from contemporary trends in Gospel criticism. In this respect the work exhibits a marked contrast to Emil Schürer's nearly contemporary *History of the Jewish People in the Age of Jesus Christ*; but Schürer was about twenty years younger than Edersheim and had received his theological education under quite different influences. Edersheim disclaimed any thought of writing a Life of Jesus in the usual sense of the words: 'the materials for it do not exist'. He conceived of the work as being 'more or less a Commentary on the Gospels', each passage in the fourfold record being treated separately. In addition to presenting the Christ of the Gospels in his contemporary setting he aimed to meet objections commonly raised to the Gospel narratives, especially those publicized in the work of David Friedrich Strauss. The work is still valuable (and in print), although its homiletical and moralizing tone may be alien to modern taste.

E. Edersheim (ed.), 'Memoir', in A. Edersheim, *Tohu Va-Vohu* (L, 1890), vii–xxxii; *DNB Suppl.* II, 175–6.

F. F. Bruce

Edinburgh Bible Society, *see* Bible Societies.

***Edinburgh Christian Instructor,* The.** Founded in 1810 by Andrew M. Thomson,* *The Instructor* was modelled on the Whig *Edinburgh Review** and the London *Christian Observer* (the journal of Wilberforce's Clapham Sect). It was the principal voice of the evangelical* party within the CofS under Thomson's vigorous editorship. It took a strong evangelical position on such issues as the Apocrypha controversy,* the anti-slavery* movement, patronage,* and the controversies surrounding Edward Irving* and J. McLeod Campbell.* *The Instructor* was continued for nine years after Thomson's death in 1831. Published initially by Oliphant and Balfour, it subsequently appeared under a variety of imprints, and was issued by Blackie and Son 1838-40.

J. A. H. Dempster

Edinburgh Christian Magazine (1849-59), monthly CofS periodical, printed in Edinburgh by Paton and Ritchie. It aimed to provide inexpensively a full spread of material (sermons, biographies, book reviews, home and foreign news), written from a CofS viewpoint but not aggressively so. The magazine was twenty-four monthly pages long in its first year of publication, expanded to thirty-two in its second. It achieved a circulation of 5,000 by the end of its first year (April 1849-March 1850).

W. J. Couper, in *Scottish Notes and Queries*, second ser., 3 (1901-2), 164.

J. A. H. Dempster and N. R. Needham

Edinburgh Conference (1937), the Second World Conference on Faith and Order (*see* Ecumenical Movement). Three hundred and forty-four delegates from 123 churches, including a significant number of Orthodox and oriental representatives, continued the pioneering ecumenical work initiated at the Lausanne Conference ten years before. There were no RC participants, and the German Evangelicals were unable to attend because of government restrictions. At Lausanne delegates had met as strangers and saw their task as the clear statement of their convictions and differences. At Edinburgh they met as friends; there was an atmosphere of trust and hope; and the work of the conference was more positive, confident and forward looking. The Second World Conference on Life and Work had taken place in Oxford immediately before.

The Conference concentrated on four themes: the doctrine of grace, ministry and sacraments, the Church of Christ and the Word of God, and the Church's unity in life and worship. In the report on unity the Conference endorsed the proposal to set up a World Council of Churches. The section on grace showed the greatest area of agreement, and it was concluded that in this matter there were no longer grounds for separation.

At its conclusion the Conference approved 'The Edinburgh Affirmation'. This strongly Christological statement declared that the delegates had discovered a profound unity in their common allegiance to the Lord Jesus Christ. They 'humbly acknowledge that our divisions are contrary to the will of Christ' and pray for the Spirit to guide 'into fullness of unity'. Christ, they declare, 'is the one hope for the world in face of the distractions and dissensions of this present time'.

A number of Scots were significant participants in the Conference. Donald Baillie* presented the report on 'The Ministry and Sacraments'. G. F. Barbour* became a member of the Continuation Committee, along with W. Manson* and W. A. Curtis.* E. J. Hagan served on the Executive Committee.

While its lasting results were not as apparent as those of Lund (1952), Edinburgh 1937 marks the coming of age of the Faith and Order movement. It contributed notably to the establishment of the World Council of Churches and provided an ecumenical trumpet call in the face of the challenge of Nazism.

L. Hodgson (ed.), *The Second World Conference on Faith and Order* (L, 1938); L. Vischer (ed.), *A Documentary History of the Faith and Order Movement 1927-1963* (St Louis, 1963).

D. B. Forrester

Edinburgh Medical Missionary Society. Founded on 30 November 1841, as the Edinburgh Association for Sending Medical Aid to Foreign Countries, the Edinburgh Medical Missionary Society (so named from 1843) was established after Dr Peter Parker, American pioneer of medical missions in China, held a meeting in Edinburgh to raise support for his work in China. In attendance was Dr John Abercrombie, a leader of the Scottish medical profession who became the first president of EMMS.

The Society's purpose was to 'circulate information on the subject [of medical missions] ... and to render assistance at missionary stations to as many professional agents as the funds placed at its disposal shall admit of'.

The Society was soon supporting medical work and personnel in China, Syria, Ireland and India, began assisting students in training and turned its attention also to the mission-field at home. The Cowgate Dispensary, later renamed the Livingstone Dispensary, was taken under the control of the Society in 1861, having been started by Dr Peter Handyside, an original member of the Society, in 1858, and was run for the poor in the heart of Edinburgh until 1952, soon after the advent of the National Health Service. Overseas, EMMS supported its own medical missions in Nazareth from 1866 and in Damascus from 1882.

Since it was founded the Society has financially supported over 400 students while training with the purpose of serving as medical missionaries. These men and women have served with many missionary societies and on every continent, over 80 with the FC, the UFC and the CofS, over 60 with the Council for World Mission and its predecessors, nearly 50 with the Church Missionary Society, and the remainder with the smaller missions.

The EMMS is no longer in Damascus but still supports the Nazareth Hospital. It no longer has its Malcolm Kerr Student Hostel in Edinburgh. Through the Student Elective Bursaries scheme, the Society helps place and finance medical students in suitable mission hospitals for their 'elective' periods. Through 'Medicines for Overseas', the Society processes, packs and despatches surplus medical and surgical supplies to mission hospitals. *See also* Lowe, John.

S. G. Browne, *Heralds of Health* (L, 1985); EMMS *Annual Report* 1988; E. V. Gulick, *Peter Parker and the Opening of China* (C, 1973); W. Hanna, *Memoirs of Dr. Chalmers*, 4 vols. (E, 1849-52); Record of Former EMMS Students; H. F. L. Taylor, *A*

EDINBURGH MISSIONARY CONFERENCE

Century of Service 1841–1941 (E, 1941); J. Wilkinson, *The Coogate Doctors* (E, 1991).
R. L. W. Evans

Edinburgh Missionary Conference (1910), *see* World Missionary Conference.

Edinburgh Missionary Society, *see* Missions.

Edinburgh Religious Tract and Book Society, *see* Scottish Colportage Society.

Edinburgh Review, *see* Periodicals, Religious.

Edinburgh Tract Society, *see* Scottish Colportage Society.

Education (Scotland) Acts, 1872 and 1918. The 1872 Education Act gave Scotland a comprehensive and tightly-organized national system: school boards for each parish, elected on a householder franchise, had the duty to provide universal elementary schooling, and parents were required to send their children until they reached certain standards; the boards were also enabled to promote secondary schooling and even to provide further education in evening schools. The old parochial schools were to be adopted at once into the new structure, to be supported from taxation and local rates. Voluntary schools, including those erected by Churches, were given every stimulus to transfer into the new system, for otherwise they would not receive government grants and rate-aid; except for a few RC schools, the vast bulk of non-parochial schools was quickly transferred. The new Scotch Education Department had very considerable control over the much-revised system.

That government should legislate for a coherent and truly national educational structure had been a long-standing demand. But English Dissenting MPs had been very wary of passing any Scottish bill which could be taken as a precedent for England, and, despite majorities of Scottish MPs in favour of some measures, had voted them down, as likely to widen the influence of the CofE. Also, the major non-established Presbyterian Churches in Scotland, the FC and especially the UPC, were determined not to allow public monies to be used to suport the extension of CofS influence. Why, then, did the Liberal government succeed in legislating in 1872?

There were some new factors. The Argyll Commission on Scottish schooling had confirmed that existing provision was very inadequate, especially in some industrial towns and in tracts of the Highlands; and once an English elementary education act had been passed in 1870, a distinctive Scottish bill, even with far wider powers, was no longer seen as threatening. Moreover, those same political and economic developments (e.g., extension of the franchise and Britain's weak market position) which had persuaded Parliament to legislate for English education were applicable in Scotland too. But there were other important reasons. The later 1860s had seen a sharpened public concern in Scot-

EDUCATION (SCOTLAND) ACTS

land over the 'moral condition' of the people, with a significant rise in demand on the poor-rates and a substantial increase in crime shown by prison statistics. Many in the middle and upper classes concluded, as had been argued by Thomas Chalmers* and other leading Church figures since the 1820s, that the debauchery and criminality of the lower orders would be reduced only by expanding the assured moralizing agency of the school throughout the entire population. Such was the level of the crisis that sectarian antagonisms which had thwarted previous attempts at reform had to be submerged.

The Churches were by the early 1870s much readier to compromise anyway. Church attendances had been falling badly, and the youth of the country were increasingly disengaged from any religious influence, so that a FC minister in 1872 concluded that 'the only likelihood of having them reared in Christian knowledge is to provide it in schools of daily instruction'. Meanwhile a rising tide of secularism, noisily attacking all Churches and organized religion, persuaded the major Scottish Churches that to reject the 1872 solution might result in the adoption of a purely secular system. As it was, the bills brought forward in 1871–2 ignored religion and religious training altogether. It was only at a very late stage that any move was made in respect of religion: not in the body of the act, but only in the preamble, a last-minute change gave school boards the opportunity to introduce religious instruction according to 'use and wont', but restricting it to the beginning or end of the school day, with parents having the right to withdraw their children. Only the most modest (and permissive) space for religious instruction was allowed, yet the 1872 Act inaugurated an expansion of religious influence in Scottish schooling.

The little that was offered soon came to be considered a substantial advance on the previous situation. Before 1872, even in the existing parochial system, the hold of the Est.C was often meagre, and vast numbers of private schools were only indirectly or nominally Church-connected. After 1872, however, at least in the earlier years, each contested election was generally dominated by the Churches and sectarian interests. The new management of the national schools thus afforded an unexpected opportunity to the Churches to give the teaching of religion a much securer place than previously. There was a general acceptance of simple Bible teaching, of a kind agreeable to all Protestants and, in some areas, to RC parents as well, and it became common for the Westminster* Shorter Catechism* to be added as a basic text. In addition, teacher-training was extended but left substantially in the hands of the major Churches. The usual judgment, that by the 1872 Act state control of education was substituted for Church control, is hardly satisfactory.

In 1918 the localized administration of education was replaced by county council committees. By then government, in the shape of the Scottish Education Department, was already in full control of the curriculum. Both the CofS and the UFC were suspicious of government policy. When small local boards, for long dominated by ministers and other Church folk, were disbanded, Church influence must diminish. So the Churches petitioned fervently for the new county education committees to be separately elected *ad hoc* rather than chosen from among councillors voted in on a general slate.

Of still greater concern was the proposal to transfer the remaining voluntary schools, mostly RC, to the new county authorities, *i.e.*, to incorporate Church schools within the state system and overturn the 1872 policy. These schools would retain the right to approve their teaching staff as regards religious belief and also rights over religious instruction. The very features which had been so vehemently opposed in the 1860s and 1870s in respect of schools in receipt of state grants or rate-aid were now to be part of the new legislation.

Yet reaction among the Protestant Churches was mixed. Many churchmen accepted the change as necessary because they so approved the other features of the legislation. Older Presbyterian antagonism to RCism had perceptibly weakened. Among others there was a deeper grievance – not so much that RCs had been granted these concessions as that their own Churches were not to have them. While RCism had been growing in strength, the major Presbyterian Churches had been visibly weakening since the turn of the century, and Church attendance and membership falling. These factors came together to force new attitudes. In 1872 the cry had gone up that the way to secure religion in the people was to provide religious teaching and observance in schools; by 1918 it was clear that that had not proved sufficient. Something more than 'use and wont' was needed, especially since it was known that the teaching of religion in most of the secondary schools was perfunctory or non-existent. Would the answer be to place the task in the Protestant schools in the hands of ministers or other Church-trained 'supervisors'? Even among some of the more hardened old Voluntaries* there was envy for the new position achieved by the RCs. If, as it turned out, the Protestant Churches in Scotland had not immediately lost control of schooling to the state in 1872, the last vestiges of their influence disappeared in 1918.

A. C. Cheyne, *The Transforming of the Kirk* (E, 1983); J. Scotland, *History of Scottish Education*, 2 vols (L, 1969); B. Lenman and J. Stocks, 'The Beginnings of State Education in Scotland, 1872–1885' and D. J. Withrington, 'Towards a National System, 1867–1872', in *Scottish Educational Studies* 4 (1972), 93–106, 107–24; Withrington, 'How the Churches Defended Religion in the 1872 Act', in *Times Educational Supplement (Scotland)*, 7 January 1972, and '"A Ferment of Change": Aspirations, Ideas and Ideals in Nineteenth-Century Scotland', in D. Gifford (ed.), *History of Scottish Literature*, vol. 3 (A, 1989), 43–63; 'Report on Education, Report on the Religious Instruction of Youth', in *RSCS 1918*, esp. 37ff., 335ff.; Debate on Education Committee Report (1918 Education Bill), in *PGAUFCS 1918*, 109–11, 229–33.

D. J. Withrington

Education, Theological. The study of theology, and especially its teaching to candidates for ordained service in the church, has in Scotland been more exclusively focused on the universities than elsewhere in the British Isles. The established Church has never had colleges or seminaries of its own separate from the university faculties of Divinity (but see St Colm's College: separate articles deal with Colleges and Seminaries, Roman Catholic; Episcopal Theological College). This identification with the universities has, for the CofS and also its derivative churches, set standards of theological education second to none.

1. MEDIEVAL PATTERNS. The monastery was the first setting for theological study in Scotland. Celtic* foundations from Columba's* time onwards translated to Scotland the role of the Irish monasteries (*e.g.* Bangor) as educational centres in the tradition of the country's bardic schools. Disciples attached themselves to 'fathers' or 'masters' as much for spiritual formation as intellectual endeavours. Iona,* Whithorn* and other communities served as seminaries for the training of many monastic leaders and missionaries who became eminent elsewhere. Yet Scottish medieval monasticism nowhere developed distinguished schools of theological learning, comparable to, say, the Northumbrian houses. Although the Franciscans produced, it seems, John of Duns (Duns Scotus*) to win renown abroad, other teachers of distinction, like Robert Richardson,* were rare.

Among the earlier Scoto-Irish churches, the ferleiginn, 'man of learning', had an educational responsibility akin to that of the chancellor in later Scoto-English churches. Such lecturers are attested at Iona and St Andrews in the twelfth and thirteenth centuries. In the newer diocesan episcopacy (from the time of David I*), the chancellor, *e.g.* of Moray, is found in charge of 'schools of theology'. On the continent such episcopal schools might become nuclei of future universities.

For some 250 years before the foundation of Scottish universities, Scots studied at universities abroad. Their destinations varied, especially according to the implications of papal politics. The divided allegiance of Scotland and England during the schism from 1378 diverted Scottish students from Oxford (where Balliol College had been virtually the earliest Scots college*) and Cambridge. During the conciliarist* controversy, papalist Scots gravitated towards Louvain, and anti-papalists to Cologne. Paris was a powerful attraction for much of the fifteenth century; a Scots College was established there early in the 1400s.

Scots graduates of universities furth of Scotland came to occupy a healthy proportion of the higher benefices of the Scottish church. As ecclesiastical administrators they would be qualified in canon law, while intermediate office-holders would often be graduates in arts. Most of the lower clergy would not have been graduates at all (and very rarely in theology), and some would not even have studied in universities. Indeed, the great majority who entered holy orders had little or no religious education as such. So if episcopal ranks embraced sufficient commitment to higher education to create universities, levels of theological – and linguistic – literacy among parochial clergy were dismally low.

2. THREE UNIVERSITIES. Scotland's medieval university foundations – St Andrews (1412), Glasgow (1450) and Aberdeen (1495) – were all creations of the church, by enlightened bishops keen to raise standards of clerical education and defend the true faith against errors like Lollardy* – Henry Wardlaw* at St Andrews, William Turnbull* at Glasgow and William Elphinstone* at Aberdeen. The curricular pattern, already firmly established in Europe's older universities, was for arts to be followed by theology or canon law; from matriculation to doctorate would take twelve years. The early faculty of theology at St Andrews was manned by the Priory;* the inquisitor Laurence of Lindores* taught there. The colleges of St Salvator's (1450), St Leonard's (1512) and St Mary's* (1538) were likewise all instituted to train parochial clergy.

Yet the universities seem to have had strictly limited success in meeting their chief goals. Despite remaining close to the bishop, Glasgow provided little theology before the Reformation. Humanism and in due course Lutheranism (especially in St Leonard's at St Andrews) took deep root. Despite some outstanding teachers (see Major, John; Boece, Hector), by the mid-sixteenth century disarray was extensive. The statutes of the Scottish provincial councils* revealed a sorry state of clerical ignorance. They stipulated that monks be sent to study at the universities (specifying numbers for named monasteries), that bishops provide canonists and theologians for every cathedral, episcopal households and monasteries each have a theologian, and ordered curricula be followed in arts and theology. Yet the requirement that only Latin-speaking students be admitted was quite unrealistic (David Lindsay's* 'Sir John Latinless' represented the average clergyman); even literacy in the vernacular could not be assumed.

3. REFORMATION IDEALS. From the outset the Protestant Reformers – some of them, like John Douglas* and John Winram*, products of the ferment of new teaching in the universities, especially St Andrews – placed a high premium on the renewal of theological education. The *First Book of Discipline** proposes a comprehensive and detailed reordering of the three universities (*FBD* 58–62, 137–55), including the radical step of assigning specific disciplines to individual colleges. One of St Andrews' three colleges should be responsible for 'the tongues' (Greek and Hebrew) and 'divinity', according to a curriculum lasting six years evidently based on Calvin's Academy in Geneva. Divinity would follow arts, of course, in Latin, and be taught by four lecturers in all – specializing (unlike the former regents) respectively in Hebrew, Greek, and Old and New Testaments. The Bible's domination of the curriculum is striking.

Vision, however, could not itself ensure realization, as the conservatively reformed St Andrews statutes of 1561–2 reveal. Glasgow and Aberdeen were much further adrift. The *FBD* assumed a decisive shift in the status of the universities from church agencies to more independent institutions supervised co-operatively by parliament, crown and General Assembly. By the 1570s greater political stability enabled Andrew Melville's* genius for educational reform to enact 'new foundations' for Glasgow and St Andrews – and soon even Aberdeen – that embodied large-scale acceptance of the ideals of the *FBD*. Furthermore, new colleges were instituted in Edinburgh (1583) and Aberdeen (Marischal College*, 1593) on unambiguously Reformed lines (cf. *FBD* 131).

Yet circumstances continued to frustrate the thorough observance of the educational programme laid down by the *FBD*. Shortage of ministers, not only in the decades after the Reformation but repeatedly in the seventeenth century's ecclesiastical vicissitudes, encouraged a lowering of standards. The requirement of competence in Latin was frequently departed from, and many were taken on trials (*see* Licensing) without completing the prescribed years of study.

In addition, the universities' provision developed only patchily. Under Glasgow's 'new foundation' of 1577 the University Principal was also Professor of Divinity (as well as minister of Govan). The two responsibilities were not legally separated until 1880, although the Principal had rarely taught divinity since the mid-seventeenth century. Other chairs were founded in 1640 (Divinity, second), 1709 (Oriental Languages), and 1716 (Ecclesiastical History).

At St Andrews, the 'New College' (St Mary's*) became by the 'new foundation' of 1579 exclusively a divinity college and was better provided with chairs, although not as generously as the *FBD* envisaged. A distinct professorship of Ecclesiastical History dates only from 1707. At Aberdeen the establishment of Marischal College supplemented the teaching given in King's (divinity students attended both), but additional chairs were erected only at intervals over centuries (Oriental Languages 1673 at King's, 1732 at Marischal; Church History at King's in 1843). Edinburgh acquired a chair of Hebrew in 1642 and of Ecclesiastical History in 1694.

In all four universities (King's and Marischal united in 1860), chairs of Biblical Criticism followed some years after they were recommended by the Royal Commission of 1826–30 (Edinburgh 1847, Aberdeen 1860, Glasgow 1861, St Andrews 1862). The Commission wanted to see chairs in four subjects – Divinity, Hebrew, Church History and Biblical Criticism – in every university. The introduction of pastoral or practical theology,* which would become a distinctive feature of academic theological study in Scotland, came later from church initiatives, extending, with varying effectiveness, over many decades.

But even when and where chairs existed, their holders differed markedly, in intellectual freshness, eloquence and sheer application to duty. Perhaps too many based their lectures too closely on a standard text-book, such as the *Theologia Christiana* of Benedict Pictet of Geneva. But if testimonies are easily found to teaching that was arid or tedious or perfunctory – or all three – the pages of this *Dictionary* are witness to numerous others who lent distinction to theological education in Scotland within the Establishment.

Each of the following is the subject of a separate article. They are listed here, without further information, in order to convey something of the remarkable strength and diversity of the principals and professors of divinity in the Scottish universities over the centuries. The dates indicate when they held office.

St Andrews: St Mary's College:* Andrew Melville* (1580–1606); John Johnstone* (1593–1611); Robert Howie* (1607–46); Samuel Rutherford* (1639–61); Thomas Forrester* (1698–1706); James Hadow* (1699–1747); Thomas Halyburton* (1710–12); George Hill* (1791–1819); Robert Haldane* (1820–54); A. F. Mitchell* (1848–99); John Tulloch* (1854–86); John Cunningham* (1886–93); George Galloway* (1915–33).

In *other St Andrews colleges*: John Rutherford* (1560–77); George Buchanan* (1568–78); John Herkless* (1915–20).

Aberdeen: King's College: Alexander Arbuthnot* (1569–83); John Forbes* (1620–41); William Leslie (*see* Aberdeen Doctors; 1632–40); William Guild* (1640–51); John Row* (1652–61); Henry Scougal* (1674–8); James Garden* (1680–97); Alexander Gerard* (1771–95, and at Marischal 1760–71); James Kidd* (1794–1834); Duncan Mearns* (1816–52); Peter C. Campbell* (1855–76).

Aberdeen: Marischal College:* Robert Howie* (1593–8); Robert Barron (*see* Aberdeen Doctors; 1625–39); John Menzies* (1649–84); Thomas Blackwell* (1711–28); George Campbell* (1759–96); William L. Brown* (1796–1830); Daniel Dewar* (1832–60); William R. Pirie* (1843–7, and 1860–85 after the union of the colleges).

King's and Marischal united as the single *University of Aberdeen* in 1860: William Milligan* (1860–93); John Forbes* (1870–87); Henry Cowan* (1889–1924); W. P. Paterson* (1894–1903, and thereafter at Edinburgh); John M. Lang* (1900–9); W. A. Curtis* (1903–15, and then at Edinburgh).

Glasgow: Andrew Melville* (1574–80); Thomas Smeaton* (1580–5); Patrick Sharp* (1585–1615); Robert Boyd* of Trochrigg (1615–22, and 1622–3 at Edinburgh); John Cameron* (1622–5); John Strang* (1626–50); David Dickson* (1640–50); Robert Baillie* (1642–62); Patrick Gillespie* (1653–60); Gilbert Burnet* (1669–74); Alexander Rose* (1682–6, and at St Mary's 1686–7); William Dunlop* (1690–1700); John Simson* (1708–40); William Leechman* (1744–85); Robert Findlay* (1783–1814); Stevenson McGill* (1814–40); Alexander Hill* (1840–62); James S. Reid* (1841–51); John Caird* (1862–98); W. P. Dickson* (1863–95); Robert H. Story* (1886–1907); William Hastie* (1895–1903); James Cooper* (1898–1922); H. M. B. Reid* (1903–27); George Milligan* (1910–32).

Edinburgh: Robert Rollock* (1585–99); Andrew Ramsay* (1620–6); John Sharp* (1630–48); David Dickson* (1650–62, after translation from Glasgow); Robert Leighton* (1653–62); William Colville* (1652–3, 1662–75); Alexander Monro* (1685–9, after 1682–5 at St Andrews); Gilbert Rule* (1690–1701); George Campbell* (1690–1701); George Meldrum* (1701–9); William Carstares* (1703–15); William Hamilton* (1709–32); William Dunlop* (1715–20); William Wishart* (1716–29); James Smith* (1732–6); John Gowdie* (1733–62); William Wishart* (1737–53); Patrick Cumin* (1737–62); William Robertson* (1762–93); Andrew Hunter* (1779–1809); Alexander Murray* (1812–13); Thomas Chalmers* (1828–43); David Welsh* (1831–43); John Lee* (1840–59); James Robertson* (1844–60); Robert Lee* (1847–68); Thomas J. Crawford* (1859–75); A. H. Charteris* (1868–98); Robert Wallace* (1873–6); Robert Flint* (1876–1903); W. P. Paterson* (1903–34); James MacKinnon* (1908–30).

4. COURSE ATTENDANCE. Another variable in theological education was student attendance. Although the formal requirement of six years' study (more precisely, six annual sessions, which rarely lasted as long as six months) proved remarkably durable, there is ample evidence of its frequent non-observance. An Assembly act first passed in 1582 allowing exceptions for 'singular and rare qualities' was often cited to justify evasions of various kinds, such as license below the minimum age. Increasingly the six-year stipulation applied only to students who attended none of the sessions full-time. The Royal Commission (1826–30) noted that the Church apparently required four years' regular attendance (over six years) which might actually be no attendance whatever. A similar double standard operated in respect of Hebrew.

Presbyteries had long been authorized to supervise private (non-attending) study. School-teaching kept many from being present at university classes; as late as 1868 the Assembly was reminded how it impeded both academic work and practical ministerial experience. There was no requirement of graduation in divinity (although by 1813 students embarking on divinity had to produce certification of an arts degree or the equivalent). Examination of candidates lay with the presbyteries, whose obligation to assess competence in the four disciplines – divinity, church history, Hebrew and Greek – was strengthened in 1827.

The Royal Commission recommended full-time attendance for four annual six-month sessions. (At the time Glasgow's session lasted six months, St Andrews' and Edinburgh's four, and Aberdeen's only three.) Two classes would be taught each session, for five days a week. Although in the following decades the Church tightened requirements, it continued to recognize combinations of full and partial attendance. Not until 1918 did the latter finally disappear. By then a session lasted twenty weeks.

The Commission of 1826–30 also proposed the introduction of the degree of Bachelor of Divinity (BD). No legislation ensued, and soon the student bodies in the new Free Church* divinity halls complicated the issue: were only CofS candidates (in the university faculties) to be eligible for the BD? The Commission of 1858 allowed the universities latitude in responding to the question, and by the time of the 1876 Commission the degree was available in all four without confessional or ecclesiastical restriction. The universities provided in quite different ways for students of the FC (later UFC) colleges to take the BD. In 1924 a General Ordinance of the four universities approved a uniform three-year curriculum, with two spent on systematic theology, church history and the two Testaments, and the third specializing in one discipline.

5. OTHER PRESBYTERIAN CHURCHES. The churches that withdrew from the Est.C or from earlier separations, but remained Presbyterian, all upheld the principle of a highly educated ministry, even when resources or constitution were inadequate to ensure provision for it separately from the universities' divinity halls. Most churches expected or required students to take a university arts curriculum prior to, or alongside, their theological course. A common pattern emerged whereby a serving minister would be also appointed professor of divinity and candidates would travel to wherever he had his charge for sessions of intensive teaching for several weeks each year over three or more years. The rest of the year they spent earning their livelihood but also under the supervision of their local presbytery.

Reformed Presbyterian. The RP Church,* heir to the faith of the Covenanters,* was unable to establish a theological hall until 1803, when John Macmillan of Stirling (1752–1819; J. Robb, *Cameronian Fasti,* E, n.d., 21) became professor (1803–19). His successors were the brothers Andrew* (at Paisley, 1819–53) and William Symington* (at Glasgow, 1853–62), William Goold* (at Edinburgh, 1854–76) and William Binnie* (at Stirling, 1862–75). When the professorships were doubled on Andrew Symington's death, his brother William, followed by Binnie, was assigned to systematic theology and Goold to biblical criticism and church history. At the same time the course was lengthened to five annual eight-week sessions. The RP theological succession was a distinguished one; for a church that was never numerous, it preserved exacting standards of divinity (cf. D. D. Ormond, *A Kirk and a College in the Craigs of Stirling,* Stirling, 1897). The majority of the RPC united with the FC in 1876, and Binnie moved to the Aberdeen FC college (*see* Christ's College) to teach church history.

Secession. Of the original seceding ministers who in 1733 created the Associate Presbytery,* William Wilson* of Perth began teaching students (six at first) in 1737, for three months each year, entirely in Latin, using the *Medulla* of Johannes Marckius of Leiden (Amsterdam, 1690; ³1705) as his text-book. He was succeeded in 1742 by Alexander Moncrieff* at Abernethy.

After the 'Breach' in the Secession in 1747 over the Burgess Oath,* the Associate (Burgher) Synod* had a succession of professors teaching where they were pastors: Ebenezer Erskine* at Stirling (1747–9), James Fisher* at Glasgow (1749–64), John Swanston* at Kinross (1764–7), John Brown* at Haddington (1767–87) and George Lawson* at Selkirk (1787–1820). Brown and Lawson were outstanding divines by any measure. In Brown's time a library was begun in his manse, and later moved to Selkirk. Brown took his oversight seriously enough to tour the students' lodgings at an early hour. The enrolment of new students fluctuated widely; hardly ever above twenty, it was normally nearer ten. In 1786 the Synod required that all applicants for the divinity hall first complete three sessions in philosophy and classics at a university.

Alexander Moncrieff continued as professor in the General Associate (Antiburgher) Synod* until his death in 1762. Previously, in the pre-'Breach' Associate Presbytery, Moncrieff had instituted a class in philosophy taught by selected students. This continued in the Antiburgher Synod, but not the Burgher Synod – which perhaps reflects the former's greater sensitivity to intellectual purity. One of these philosophical tutors, Alexander Pirie,* was sent packing for his impenitence on being found to have imbibed too much contemporary wisdom. Moncrieff was followed by his son William* at Alloa (1762–86), Archibald Bruce* at Whitburn, E. Lothian (1786–1805), and George Paxton* (1807–20). On appointment Paxton was released from his charge and moved to a settled divinity hall in Edinburgh without pastoral duties. This change partly respected Paxton's uncertain health, but also recognized the weight of the combined tasks for all minister-professors. During William Moncrieff's tenure, the session was reduced from three months to nine weeks, with six weeks, it seems, the minimum. Moncrieff was perhaps not quite the attraction that his father had been. Bruce taught larger classes, despite excelling more in literary than vocal gifts. (He was almost a professional author, with his own printer in Whitburn.) He was noted for close social contact with students and for promoting students' critiques of each other's work.

Paxton was still lecturing on Marckius' *Medulla*, over the whole five sessions. He also had the freedom to introduce a supplementary winter session, apparently not obligatory, for Hebrew in particular, and to assist the students prior to their attending the divinity hall.

When the Antiburghers divided over the New Light,* Archibald Bruce sided with the Auld Lichts and continued to teach for the Constitutional Associate Presbytery at Whitburn until his death in 1816. When the New Lights of both Burghers and Antiburghers united in 1820 to form the United Secession Church,* Paxton disapproved and moved, sideways in effect, into the Auld Licht Antiburghers, tutoring their students 1820–37.

United Secession. The USec.C theological course was taught by John Dick* in Glasgow 1820–33. By all accounts an outstanding and fresh lecturer, he excelled in systematic theology* and his published lectures would long enjoy favour. With students now numbering a hundred or more, Dick was given a colleague in 1825, John Mitchell,* also in a Glasgow charge, as professor of Biblical Literature and Criticism. Mitchell took the first two years, Dick the next three. In 1834, Dick was succeeded in the systematic theology chair by Alexander Duncan of Mid-Calder, W. Lothian (d.1844; Small I, 595–6; memoir in his *Discourses*..., E, 1845), and two further chairs were instituted, in pastoral theology (Robert Balmer* of Berwick-on-Tweed) and exegetical theology (John Brown* of Edinburgh, d.1858). Balmer and Duncan exchanged chairs by agreement. All four professors retained their pastoral commitments, so that the senior class (Balmer and Duncan) met in Edinburgh and the junior (Mitchell and Brown) alternated between Glasgow and Edinburgh. The session was fixed at two months in 1834. Mitchell, although sartorially impeccable, was too amiable to be intellectually formidable or to be aware of his students' delinquencies in Hebrew. John Brown exemplified exegetical principles in practice rather than expounding them in general terms, and was faulted for neglecting doctrinal implications. 'He never overlooked the *sense*; but he did sometimes miss the full *significance*. His critical had outgrown his theological habits' (Landreth, 233). Balmer was scarcely an elegant lecturer (he continually twisted his long neck and was said to 'circumnavigate' the clauses of a sentence), and adopted a more selective, less comprehensive treatment than Dick's.

Ill health forced the resignation of Mitchell and Duncan in 1843. They were replaced by James Harper* of Leith in pastoral theology and John Eadie* of Glasgow in biblical literature. Balmer (d.1844) had no successor, but Harper moved to systematic theology in 1846. The USec.C thus took three professors (Brown, Harper, Eadie) into the United Presbyterian Church.*

The small continuing Original Secession Church* trained its students at the hands of practising ministers. Among the last of these was Francis Davidson.*

Relief. Students of the Relief had, since its emergence in 1761, studied at the universities, chiefly Glasgow, under presbytery oversight. This arrangement became impracticable when university theological students were required to undergo examination by CofS presbyteries. Hence in 1824, James Thomson of Paisley became the first Relief divinity tutor (d.1841; Small II, 157, 521–2). He made the Westminster Confession his basic text and 'introduced some new exercises borrowed from the theological academies of English dissent' (Landreth, 257). Students had to report on Mondays on sermons heard on Sunday. Products of Thomson's course were noted for their rhetorical skills. Though by his death he was teaching less than fifty students, he was replaced by both William Lindsay* in exegetical theology and biblical criticism, and Neil McMichael of Dunfermline (d.1874; Small I, 359–60) in systematic theology. The divinity hall was now fixed at Glasgow.

United Presbyterian. The new UPC brought together five theological professors in its Synod Hall at 5 Queen Street, Edinburgh. When Brown died in 1858, Lindsay took over his teaching; four seemed the favoured number for professors. Hence John Cairns'* overdue appointment to a new chair of apologetic theology had to await Lindsay's death in 1866. Cairns was already the most eminent theologian in the Church.

The pattern of two-month sessions for five years taught by professors in pastoral charges continued until 1875, when a major reform took place. The capacious Synod Hall* in Edinburgh's Castle Terrace was purchased (ready for use 1880) to accommodate five full-time professors – no longer serving ministers – teaching six-month sessions each year. In 1876 Harper was made Principal and three new professors were appointed (McMichael died 1874 and Eadie 1876): John Ker from Glasgow (1819–86; *DNB* XXXI, 52) in pastoral training, James Alexander Paterson (1851–1915; *FUFCS* 582) in Hebrew, and David Duff of Helensburgh (1824–90; Small I, 237) in church history. Those teaching in the Edinburgh UP hall in 1900, at the UPC's union with the FC to form the UFC, moved to one or other of the former FC colleges: Paterson to New College, Edinburgh; the New Testament Professor since 1876, Robert Johnston, to Aberdeen (d.1918; Small II, 72; *FUFCS* 578); James Orr,* in the Church History chair since 1891, to Glasgow; Alexander Hislop, Professor of Practical Theology and Christian Ethics from 1892, also to Glasgow (1844–1906; Small I, 237; *FUFCS* 577); and James Wardrop, in the chair of Systematic Theology and Apologetics since 1892, to New College (1821–1909; Small I, 619, II, 564; *FUFCS* 584).

Free Presbyterian. The FP breakaway from the FC in 1892 never established its own college, reverting instead to the earlier practice of assigning students to minister-tutors. Among these Donald Beaton* gave influential long-term service, assisted in earlier years by John R. Mackay.* It is worth noting that in John A. Mackay* the FP bred a theological educator of international renown.

6. FREE CHURCH, UNITED FREE CHURCH AND THE 1929 UNION. The Disruption* of 1843 brought into being within a few years FC divinity halls at Edinburgh (New College*), Aberdeen (*see* Christ's College) and Glasgow (*see* Trinity College). At the 1900 union of the FC with the UPC, these became colleges of the new UFC.

EDUCATION, THEOLOGICAL

The continuing Free Church (post-1900)* established its own college, which continues in Edinburgh only a few yards from New College. Its curriculum remains strong in the biblical languages. Among its best known professors have been John Macleod,* A. M. Renwick* and R. A. Finlayson.*

It was in the era of the three non-university FC/UFC colleges that Scottish theology reached its greatest distinction. For much of the period they collectively outshone the university faculties, in Scotland and elsewhere in Britain. For example, in 1900 the Glasgow college assembled James Denney,* George Adam Smith,* James Orr,* and T. M. Lindsay* – all still names to conjure with. Between 1900 and the union New College's stars included A. B. Davidson,* H. A. A. Kennedy,* Marcus Dods,* Adam Welch,* William Manson,* and H. R. Mackintosh.*

The following lists of principals and professors of these colleges, with their dates of office, indicate their theological strength and breadth. Those named are all the subject of separate articles in this *Dictionary*.

New College, *Edinburgh*: Thomas Chalmers* (1843–7); David Welsh* (1843–5); John Duncan* (1843–63); William Cunningham* (1844–61); James Buchanan* (1845–68); John Fleming* (1845–57); Alexander Campbell Fraser* (1846–56, and thereafter a chair in the University, 1856–91); James Bannerman* (1849–68); George Smeaton* (1857–89); R. S. Candlish* (1862–73); Robert Rainy* (1862–1906); A. B. Davidson* (1863–1902); John Duns* (1864–1903); James MacGregor* (1868–81); W. G. Blaikie* (1868–97); John Laidlaw* (1881–1904); Marcus Dods* (1889–1909); Alexander Martin* (1897–1935); A. R. MacEwen* (1901–16); J. Y. Simpson* (1904–34); H. R. Mackintosh* (1904–36); H. A. A. Kennedy* (1909–25); A. C. Welch* (1913–34); Hugh Watt* (1919–50).

Aberdeen (*see* Christ's College): James MacLagan* (1845–52); Patrick Fairbairn* (1853–6); George Smeaton* (1853–7); James Lumsden* (1856–75); David Brown* (1857–97); William Robertson Smith* (1870–81); William Binnie* (1875–86, formerly RPC professor 1862–75); S. D. F. Salmond* (1876–1905); James Iverach* (1887–1920); James Stalker* (1902–24); David S. Cairns* (1907–37).

Glasgow (*see* Trinity College): Patrick Fairbairn* (1856–74); James Gibson* (1856–71); G. C. M. Douglas* (1857–1904); W. M. Hetherington* (1857–62); Islay Burns* (1864–72); J. S. Candlish* (1872–97); T. M. Lindsay* (1872–1914); A. B. Bruce* (1875–99); Henry Drummond* (1877–97); George Adam Smith* (1892–1910); James Denney* (1897–1917); James Orr* (1900–13; UP professor since 1891); J. E. MacFadyen* (1910–33); W. M. Clow* (1911–28); D. W. Forrest* (1914–18); James Moffatt* (1915–27); W. M. MacGregor* (1919–38).

Following the 1929 union,* the UF colleges merged with the university faculties in Edinburgh,

EDUCATION, THEOLOGICAL

Aberdeen and Glasgow. (For the college of the continuing UF Church (post-1929),* see below, on the Congregational college.) Co-operation and conference had prepared the ground well for a scheme that also affected St Andrews (*RGACS 1929*, xxxvii –xliv) – and still determines the pattern of university theology and CofS ministerial formation to the present day. The chief provisions were as follows:

i. All existing university chairs were to be freed from statutory (confessional-ecclesiastical) tests. (In 1853, legislation had enabled non-CofS persons to hold chairs except for theological professorships, which remained open only to licentiates or ministers of the CofS.)

ii. Appointments to these chairs were to be made by joint CofS–university boards. Other churches might in future be represented on these boards (which has not come to pass).

iii. The existing UF colleges' professors would become professors in the universities, but their stipends would be furnished by the Church and their successors appointed by the Church from its ordinand or ordained personnel.

iv. The Church would maintain the UF colleges' buildings. Those in Glasgow and Edinburgh, with their libraries, would be available for use by the faculties.

v. If the Church needed a college head, it would appoint a principal, who would become a member of the university faculty and senatus.

The Universities (Scotland) Act of 1932 enacted the scheme in the form of four separate Church–university agreements (*RGACS 1933*, 1197–1237). In addition to the above arrangements, these specified the church chairs added to the four existing university chairs in each faculty. This resulted in considerable duplication, which could in some cases be rationalized (*e.g.* by distinguishing between Old Testament and Semitic languages, or between divinity, *i.e.* apologetics and philosophy of religion, and dogmatics). In course of time, however, the professorial establishment would be reduced to the basic four or five.

Revised agreements came into force in 1950 (*RGACS 1950*, 484–95), effectively assimilating most of the 'church chairs' (the exceptions were those of practical theology at Aberdeen and Glasgow, which henceforth no longer enjoyed university recognition) to the other chairs, in respect of procedures for appointment and freedom from tests. The Church guaranteed a contribution towards their salaries – a fixed sum which inflation has since made nugatory.

These arrangements undergird the current teaching of theology in the four older Scottish universities (joined more recently in all except St Andrews, but also in Stirling University, by varying provision for religious studies). The distinctiveness is grounded in the dual character of the Edinburgh, Glasgow and Aberdeen faculties as also CofS colleges, each with its own Senate and Assembly-appointed principal or master. All appointments to established chairs in all four faculties are made by boards in which Church and university are equally represented. All CofS ordinands receive the whole of their college-based education in the faculties, with extensive Church-faculty co-operation in practical training and in supervision of candidates. Their whole training is overseen by the Church's Committee on Education for the Ministry, which began in 1884. The faculties as communities of teaching and learning have long been international (New College has welcomed Hungarian Reformed students for well over a century), and are now more ecumenical, with ordinands of several other churches (especially, in New College, of the Scottish Episcopal Church) also in training, and teaching staff drawn from varying traditions. The acids of secularization, affecting universities (by which the faculties are almost wholly financed, the CofS contribution now being minimal) no less than broader society, present sharp challenges to the faculties, as does religious pluralism. In most of them, ministerial students are clearly in a minority. Postgraduates, chiefly research, and many from overseas, are strongly represented.

For at least a century, education for the ministry in Scotland has been criticized for being excessively academic, with insufficient attention to spirituality and practical skills. (In 1897 John Macleod* of Govan averred that 'strictly speaking, the Church provides no ministerial training'.) Some would like to see the Church exercise greater control, or establish one or more church colleges for at least part of ministers' training. Yet it is a tradition not lightly to be discarded that the professional formation of ministers, as of doctors and teachers, remains an accepted function of the Scottish universities. And internationally the faculties maintain a reputation for promoting academically rigorous Christian theology in the service of the churches, in communities of study and worship.

The following theological teachers in the post-1929 Scottish divinity faculties are all treated in separate articles. Others still active after 1929 have been listed above.

Aberdeen: G. D. Henderson* (1924–57); G. T. Thomson* (1928–36, and then in Edinburgh); A. M. Hunter* (1945–71).

Edinburgh: W. A. Curtis* (1915–46); W. Manson* (1925–52); Daniel Lamont* (1927–45); J. H. S. Burleigh* (1931–64); John Baillie* (1934–56); G. T. Thomson* (1936–52); J. S. Stewart* (1947–66); T. F. Torrance* (1950–79).

Glasgow: W. M. MacGregor* (1919–38); A. J. Gossip* (1928–45); G. H. C. MacGregor* (1933–63); Ian Henderson* (1948–69); Ronald Gregor Smith* (1956–68); William Barclay* (1963–74).

St Andrews: G. S. Duncan* (1919–54); Donald Baillie* (1935–54); E. P. Dickie* (1935–67).

7. BAPTISTS, CONGREGATIONALISTS AND OTHERS. Among Baptists in Scotland the need for, or even the desirability of, separate theological education did not arise until the era of the Haldanes.* During 1799–1808 they had established two-year seminary courses in Edinburgh, Glasgow and Dundee (*see* Haldane Preachers). The pattern continued when the brothers became Baptists; Robert arranged tuition at Grantown under Lachlan McIntosh (whose students included John Leechman*). The 'English' Baptists at first made no special provision, the short-lived Baptist Academical Society for Scotland sending students to England for training.

Francis Johnstone's* attempt at a Baptist Union (1843–56) was accompanied by a theological academy (1845–56), which he taught first at Cupar, Fife, and then Edinburgh. The whole span of disciplines was covered in four nine-month terms. Both Union and academy lapsed when Johnstone left Scotland. During 1860–9 James Paterson, minister of Hope Street Chapel, Glasgow, provided theological classes alongside university study (*see* Yuille, George). After the present Baptist Union was formed in 1869, similar arrangements obtained for some years, involving James Culross,* Paterson and others. Different longer-term possibilities were sharply debated (a single tutor, as hitherto; use of existing institutions, whether Presbyterian in Scotland or Baptist in England; a new Scottish college). Duncan MacGregor's* Gospel Training College at Dunoon (1893–1915) trained many students.

Then in 1894 the Baptist Theological College of Scotland was founded, using Adelaide Place Church, Glasgow, staffed part-time by pastors and formally independent of the Baptist Union. In 1914 Jervis Coats (*d.*1921), hitherto minister of the Govan Church, became full-time Principal, succeeded by John T. Forbes* (1922–34). The College moved to its own premises, shared with the Union, in West Regent Street in 1925. Yet differences about the advantages – and dangers – of such a College persisted. Its independence invited suspicion, and in the 1940s it was attacked for alleged liberalism. John Shearer, former Union president, produced *The Downgrade of Modernism*, tarring the College with the English controversy involving Spurgeon.* When the Union refused to sever links with the College (and the College declined to amalgamate with the Union), the Evangelical Baptist Fellowship ran its own Bible College for some years in Glasgow.

Teaching at the College has expanded from a ten-week summer course to a three-year non-graduating qualification. Many students have taken Cambridge or London external degrees or diplomas, with the College's Diploma of Practical Theology following. A fully graduate ministry is an important ideal rather than a requirement. The Scottish Baptist College (renamed 1981) now works very closely with the Union, with premises next door on Aytoun Road, Glasgow, since 1980. (Hopes of a University link by moving to Oakfield Avenue in 1970 were not realized.) With only two full-time teaching staff, pastors make a major contribution. Among more recent principals, R. E. O. White was particularly distinguished as a scholar and author (1968–79).

Out of the confusion caused by the Haldanes' Baptist conversion (1808), their Glasgow seminary was re-founded as the Glasgow Theological Academy to serve the new Congregational Union,* formed by fifty-five churches in 1812. Greville

Ewing* (1811–36) and Ralph Wardlaw* (1811–53) combined tutoring with pastoral ministry. The curriculum included arts (covered partly in classes at Glasgow University) as well as theology, with a stress on practical evangelism that reflected the Haldane heritage. The college moved to Edinburgh in 1855 when W. L. Alexander* and Anthony Gowan, pastors respectively in Edinburgh and Dalkeith (where Gowan served 1843–72), were appointed to teach. Alexander became full-time Principal 1877–81, and in 1893 a second professor was set aside solely for lecturing. After using church premises, the theological hall acquired its own in George Square in 1884, moving to Hope Terrace in 1921 as the Scottish Congregational College. The college of the continuing UF Church (post-1929)* merged with the Congregational College, with Allan Barr, son of James Barr,* for many years the UF professor. Declining numbers made even the combined College unviable, and since 1984 the Congregational College with one full-time teacher has shared a home with the Episcopal* college in Coates Hall, Edinburgh. Its students, whenever qualified, take courses at New College. The UFC no longer has a college of its own, its candidates for ministry studying in the universities as well as training alongside ministers in charges.

In 1896, when the Congregational Union and the Evangelical Union* became one, their two colleges united also. The merger enlarged the staff, but the united institution was left independent of the new Congregational Union of Scotland. John Morison,* the architect of the Evangelical Union, was a keen advocate of a well-educated ministry. He was for long (1843–73) principal tutor of the EU's theological academy ('the first and dearest child of the Union'; Escott, 132), first at Kilmarnock and then from 1851 in Glasgow when he moved to a new charge there. The academy ended up in Regent Park, Glasgow. A. M. Fairbairn* and John Kirk* were two of its products, and Kirk taught practical theology there from 1859. All its tutors, like Morison, were serving ministers. Its curriculum was close to that of the USec.C college, in which Morison had trained.

Of the smaller non-Presbyterian churches, neither Methodists nor Pentecostalists have ever provided formal theological education in Scotland. The Methodist Conference, however, c.1990 approved arrangements for ordinands to study in the Edinburgh and Aberdeen faculties under local supervision. Early in the twentieth century the Pentecostal Church of Scotland, which later became the Church of the Nazarene,* ran Parkhead Holiness Bible school for some years in Glasgow. The Faith Mission's* Training College in Edinburgh and Glasgow's Bible Training Institute* (1892–; since 1991, Glasgow Bible College) have long histories of training students for evangelistic and missionary service. The latter now teaches for its own qualifications up to honours degree level (validated by the Open University), and is pioneering a practically-oriented marriage of academic study with training in evangelism and community care.

J. Robertson, 'On Scholastic Offices in the Scottish Church in the Twelfth and Thirteenth Centuries', in J. Stuart (ed.), *Miscellany of the Spalding Club* V (A, 1852), pref. app. 56–77; H. Rashdall, *The Universities of Europe in the Middle Ages* (O, ²1936), II, 301–24; D. E. R. Watt, 'University Graduates in Scottish Benefices before 1410', *RSCHS* 15 (1965), 77–88; *FESMA* 375–85; D. Patrick, *Statutes of the Scottish Church 1225–1559* (SHS; E, 1907); J. K. Cameron, 'The Church and the Universities in Scotland in the Era of the Reformation', in *The Church in a Changing Society* (Uppsala, 1978), 217–22; J. Durkan and J. Kirk, *The University of Glasgow, 1451–1577* (G, 1977); D. Stevenson, *King's College, Aberdeen, 1560–1641: From Protestant Reformation to Covenanting Revolution* (A, 1990); R. G. Cant, 'The Scottish Universities in the Seventeenth Century', *AUR* 43 (1970), 223–33; S. Mechie, 'Education for the Ministry in Scotland Since the Reformation', *RSCHS* 14 (1962), 115–33, 161–78, 15 (1965), 1–20; *FES* VII, 357–434, VIII, 711–19, IX, 767–82, X, 428–40; H. M. B. Reid, *The Divinity Principals in the University of Glasgow 1545–1654* (G, 1917); *id.*, *The Divinity Professors in the University of Glasgow 1640–1903* (G, 1923); *id.*, *A Scottish School of Theology* (G, 1904); G. Quig, 'The Divinity Staff at Glasgow University in 1903', *RSCHS* 3 (1929), 210–19; P. Landreth, *The United Presbyterian Divinity Hall* (E, 1876); *FUFCS* 574–85; W. MacKelvie, *Annals and Statistics of the United Presbyterian Church* (E, 1873), 652–705; G. Yuille (ed.), *History of the Baptists in Scotland* (G, 1926), 250–9; D. B. Murray, *The First 100 Years, The Baptist Union of Scotland* (G, 1969), 108–12; J. Ross, *A History of Congregational Independency in Scotland* (G, 1900); *The Story of the Scottish Congregational Theological Hall, 1811–1911* (E, 1911); J. Stein (ed.), *Ministers for the 1980s* (E, 1979).

D. F. Wright

Edwards, John (d. c. 1843), leader of Baptist* work in the Ottawa district of Ontario, Canada. Born in Morayshire, Edwards became a member of James Haldane's* Independent church in Edinburgh. Moving in 1808 to Portsea, England, he became a Baptist. He emigrated to Canada in 1818, and settled at Clarence, on the Ottawa river, in 1822. Three years later he formed a Baptist church there. Impressed by the spiritual destitution of the region and the need for leadership among the few existing Baptist churches, he sailed to Britain in 1829 to obtain support. He was able to persuade two Scotsmen, William Fraser* and John Gilmore, to join him in Canada. Gilmore, who had established a church in Aberdeen, settled in Montreal, where he founded the city's first Baptist church. In 1831 Edwards himself was ordained to the ministry. In 1839–41 he undertook another expedition to Britain, and raised substantial funds for the Canadian Baptist Missionary Society.

See also Emigration.

D. McPhail, *Churches of the Ottawa Baptist Association 1865* (Montreal, 1865), 19–25.

D. E. Meek

Edwards, Jonathan (1703–58), New England Congregationalist, President (briefly) of the College of New Jersey at Princeton, and influential Calvinist theologian. Edwards was best known in his lifetime as a promoter of revival.* In recent decades he has also been rediscovered as a first-rate philosopher who employed the learning of his day (including a stimulating engagement with Francis Hutcheson*) for the defence of traditional Calvinism.* Edwards sustained a long and intimate relationship with Scotland, and even considered Scottish offers of ministerial employment after being dismissed from his Northampton, Massachusetts, congregation in 1750. His *Humble Attempt* (1747), a work promoting prayer for revival, was a response to a similar memorial from Scotland. Throughout the 1740s he corresponded with James Robe* of Kilsyth, William McCulloch* of Cambuslang, and Thomas Gillespie* of Carnock on questions concerning conversion. Edwards's friendship with John Erskine* led to the Scottish publication of an important emendation to his *Freedom of the Will* that was designed to show how Edwards's form of determinism differed from that proposed by Henry Home, Lord Kames. Erskine and his colleagues also recommended Edwards' writings to other British Evangelicals, especially John Sutcliff and Andrew Fuller* of the Northamptonshire Baptist Association, where these works encouraged a more activist Calvinism. In the eighteenth and nineteenth centuries, Scottish publishers issued almost as many editions of Edwards's works as did the printers of New England.

Edwards continued long as a theological force in Scotland. Late in the eighteenth century, the Moderate* George Hill* spoke favourably of Edwards at St Andrews. Under Hill's tutelage, Thomas Chalmers* began a lifelong reading of Edwards. Chalmers' Calvinism was less precise than Edwards', yet in his *Institutes of Theology*, Chalmers testified that for him Edwards' treatment of predestination 'had succeeded not only in rationalizing, but in moralizing and evangelizing the whole of the argument'. A suggestion from Edwards' *The Necessity and Reasonableness of the Christian Doctrine of Satisfaction for Sin* also played a role in stimulating John McLeod Campbell's* belief that Christ's death opened up the possibility for divine reconciliation with all humanity. In this work Edwards suggested that the greatness of human evil required a recompense amounting to *either* an equivalent sorrow *or* (the orthodox view) an equivalent punishment. Although Edwards did not pursue the first possibility, Campbell used it as a springboard for arguing that the atonement was best explained by the infinite nature of Jesus's sorrow for sin. On the two-hundredth anniversary of Edwards' birth in 1903, James Orr* claimed that Edwards' *Freedom of the Will* had influenced his entire career. At the same time, Orr held that Edwards' piety possessed 'a certain strain' which had the unfortunate effect of limiting 'the range of his human sympathies'.

The Works of Jonathan Edwards (New Haven, Conn.): *Freedom of the Will*, ed. P. Ramsey (1957), 443–70; *A Treatise Concerning Religious Affections*, ed. J. E. Smith (1959), 465–513; *The Great Awakening*, ed. C. C. Goen (1972), 535–41, 558–66; *Apocalyptic Writings*, ed. S. S. Stein (1977), 444–60 (pages refer to Scottish correspondence).

I. H. Murray, *Jonathan Edwards* (E, 1987); H. P. Simonson, 'Jonathan Edwards and his Scottish Connections', *Journal of American Studies* 21 (Dec. 1987), 353–76; G. D. Henderson, 'Jonathan Edwards and Scotland', in *The Burning Bush* (E, 1957), 151–62; H. Wellwood Moncrieff, *Account of the Life and Writings of John Erskine* (E, 1818), 196–225; A. H. Kirkby, 'The Theology of Andrew Fuller and its Relation to Calvinism' (PhD., University of Edinburgh, 1956); J. Orr, 'The Influence of Edwards', in *Exercises Commemorating the Two-Hundredth Anniversary of the Birth of Jonathan Edwards*, ed. J. W. Platner (Andover, MA, 1904), 107–26.

M. A. Noll

Elder, Eldership, in Reformed churches the 'ruling elder', as distinguished from the 'teaching elder'. With the minister or pastor, the doctor* or teacher, and the deacon,* the Reformed asserted that the office of ruling elder was spiritual and ecclesiastical and, as prescribed in Scripture (1 Tim. 5: 17, Rom. 12: 8 and 1 Cor. 12: 28), permanent in the church. Ruling elders, with the minister, and sometimes the doctor, share the collective responsibility of governing the church and together comprise the eldership. On the parish level this is the kirk session,* more widely it is the presbytery* and the synod,* and nationally the general assembly.*

The Reformed church in Scotland began with worship in secret, in 'privy kirks',* and in assuming a definite structure deliberately emulated what it believed was the practice of the apostolic church in calling some as elders to 'exercise a godly discipline'. By 1559 in Dundee, when a stipend* was assigned to the town's preacher, the kirk session was already in operation (J. Kirk, *Patterns of Reform*, E, 1989, 12–13). Thus from the start, in accord with the doctrine and practice of the Reformed churches on the continent, the ruling elder was as integral a part of the church as was the minister or preacher (*BUK* I, 311, following Calvin, *Institutes* 4: 3: 8; see Kirk, 347).

The *First Book of Discipline** formally prescribed elders for the kirk. 'Men of best knowledge in Gods word and cleanest life' were to be nominated and, from such, elders and deacons chosen. Elders were to be elected yearly by a 'common and free election'. Duties consisted in assisting 'the ministers in all publike affaires of the kirk,' including 'determining and judging of causes,' ... 'giving of admonition to the licentious liver' and monitoring the lives of all under their charge. Likewise they were to take heed to their ministers, admonishing and correcting them as necessary (*FBD*, 174–6). A stipend was not judged necessary, both because election was only for a year (though re-election was permitted and became common) and because they would not be 'so occupied with the affaires of the kirk but that reasonably they may attend upon their domesticall business' (*FBD*, 179).

The *Second Book of Discipline** affirmed that the office of elder was one of the 'four ordinarie functionis or offices in the kirk of God' and that the office was clearly ecclesiastical. Admission to it was by election, with none to be chosen contrary to the will of the congregation or without the voice of the eldership (*SBD*, 178–80).

The ruling elder, both as delineated in the books of discipline and in a variety of subsequent writings, had as his principal office the holding of assemblies with the pastors and doctors 'for the establishing guid order and exercise of discipline'. This involved his being a shepherd of those under his care. As the *SBD* puts it, 'to watch diligentlie upone the flok committit unto thair charge, bayth publicklie and privatlie, that no corruptioun of religioun or maneris enter thairin', admonishing all men to their duties and seeking the fruit resulting from the pastor's sowing and the doctor's teaching of the Word (193). The elder was particularly to assist the pastor in the examination of those coming to the Lord's Table and in the visitation of the sick. This government of the local congregation by the eldership or kirk session, exercising spiritual care and jurisdiction over the parish, has so long been an integral part of Scottish life that it is difficult to imagine Scotland without it.

From the first, elders joined with ministers and doctors in the general assembly and took full part in exercising joint rule over the church. Although some have thought ruling elders not qualified to judge doctrinal questions (*e.g.*, R. Wodrow,* *Correspondence*, E, 1843, III, 47), most have asserted, as George Gillespie* put it, that 'ruling elders ought to have decisive voices, even in questions of faith and doctrine' (*An Assertion of the Government of the Church of Scotland*, E, 1846, 35), and in practice they have taken full part in all deliberations.

While the composition of kirk sessions generally included a cross-section of the people, chosen for the most part for spiritual and not secular qualifications, those sent to presbytery and, particularly, general assembly were the nobility and well-to-do. An examination of presbytery and assembly records shows that many were sent repeatedly. A goodly selection of the nobility, greater and lesser, professional men, particularly lawyers, and burgesses, was always in evidence. Reflecting the composition of the churches themselves, elders in the Secession* churches tended more to be successful tradesmen, artisans and, in more rural congregations, farmers. In more modern times, reflecting the democratization of society as a whole, a more broadly representative selection of the congregation has been sent.

Episcopalians have consistently opposed the participation of elders in the government of the church. Patrick Adamson,* writing against the *SBD*, wished to make assemblies 'a convention generall of clergie,' and to exclude elders as laymen (Calderwood IV, 53–5; Kirk, 366; *see* Laity), Archbishop John Spottiswoode* took essentially the same position as Adamson and his master, James VI,* characterizing ruling elders as a mere human device, without warrant in Scripture, and detrimental to church and state (Spottiswoode I, cxxxi, III, 211; Kirk, 432–3). Episcopalian opposition notwithstanding, the ruling elder had by the beginning of the seventeenth century become sufficiently integral to the life of the church that, in spite of long periods of Episcopal rule, the basic structure of government in the local church remained the kirk session, in which the eldership, the minister and ruling elders together, governed the church. This essential structure, with the teaching elder or minister acting as moderator and having considerable guiding influence, as is perhaps appropriate in and expected from one who is called as being 'apt to teach', has remained essentially unchanged to the present time.

Presbyterians themselves have been divided as to the warrant for and nature of the office of elder. Some have held there is one office of elder or presbyter, with all exercising rule, but some being specially set apart to preach or teach. Others have taught two or three more or less distinct offices, with the pastor (and teacher) holding distinct orders of ministry. Although a matter of some tension from the beginning of the Reformation, debate became particularly acute in the nineteenth century, with considerable input coming from America. William Cunningham* continued to incline to the single-office view, which was probably the position held by the large majority, in spite of attempts by Charles Hodge* to change his mind. On the other hand, taking a position not far from that of the Episcopalians, Peter Campbell,* in *The Theory of Ruling Eldership* (E, 1866), taught that the ruling elder is simply a layman and a representative of the people. In this he largely repeated the views of Thomas Smyth of Charleston, South Carolina (*The Name, Nature and Functions of Ruling Elders*, NY, 1845), virtually denying a New Testament warrant for the office, and separating it entirely from that of the minister.

Those like Campbell who have believed that the minister and elder hold entirely separate offices or who have denied that the ruling elder holds an *ecclesiastical* office at all, have tended towards a clergy/lay distinction, while those who have thought there is one office of elder or overseer, with some particularly called to preach or teach, have repudiated such a distinction. George Gillespie opposed those who 'nick-name and miscall them. Some reproachfully, and others ignorantly, call them lay elders. But the distinction of the clergy and laity is popish and anti-Christian; . . . Rather the office of ruling elder is apostolic and perpetual in the church' (*An Assertion*, 9).

Though agreeing with Gillespie in repudiating a clergy/lay distinction, Thomas Witherow* attempted to justify the very real division between minister and ruling elder by recognizing that, while no such distinction existed in Scripture, the demands of the modern age made it necessary that some be particularly trained so as to be able to teach adequately. Thus a distinction between the trained minister and the ruling elder, not needed in apostolic times, was now both beneficial and necessary. While today there is no real consensus as to a proper view of the subject, perhaps a majority tacitly support this position.

In recent years, some have argued that the eldership of the present-day CofS finds its closest NT counterpart in the diaconate.* This case is sometimes made for patently ecumenical motives – to demonstrate that the CofS possesses two orders of the 'threefold ministry', lacking only the episcopate. The argument ignores the ruling function of the eldership, as asserted by Reformed theologians and as practised in the CofS from the Reformation.

The 1966 General Assembly decreed the eligibility of women for the eldership on the same terms as men. In recent years, more women have been ordained as elders than men. In response to widespread uncertainty about the force of the 1966 Act and continued unhappiness with women's ordination on biblical grounds, the 1991 Assembly adopted an interpretation of the Act which makes 'any denial in practice of [women's] eligibility' a 'contravention of that Act'. In so doing the Assembly disallowed the claim that the conviction that 'the Word of God in Scripture' precluded the ordination of women was sufficient to excuse from obedience to the law of the church.

S. Miller, *An Essay, on the ... the Office of the Ruling Elder* (NY, ²1832); David King, *The Ruling Eldership of the Christian Church* (E, ²1846); John G. Lorimer, *The Eldership of the Church of Scotland* (G, 1841); John M'Kerrow, *The Office of Ruling Elder in the Christian Church* (E, 1846); David Dickson, *The Elder and His Work* (E, 1878); G. D. Henderson, *The Scottish Ruling Elder* (L, 1935); T. Witherow, 'The New Testament Elder', *British and Foreign Evangelical Review* 22 (1873), 201–28; I. H. Murray, 'Ruling Elders – A Sketch of a Controversy', *Banner of Truth* 235 (1983), 1–9; T. F. Torrance, *Eldership in the Reformed Church* (E, 1984).

D. C. Lachman

Elder, Robert (1808–92), FC minister. Born at Inveraray, Argyll, he was educated at Campbeltown Grammar School and Glasgow University (MA, 1825). He became minister at Kilbrandon and Kilchattan, south of Oban (1831–4), moving to Killin, Perthshire (1834–8) and St Paul's, Edinburgh (1838–47, Free St Paul's from the Disruption*). From 1847 he served Rothesay West FC, Isle of Bute (senior minister 1882). Moderator of the FC General Assembly and recipient of Glasgow's DD, both in 1871, he published a number of works – on the sacraments, the conversion of the Jews and other topics – as well as sermons.

FES I, 188; *AFCS* I, 147.

G. Wareing

Elim Pentecostal Church, *see* Pentecostalism.

Elizabeth I (1533–1603), Queen of England.

Elizabeth I, daughter of Henry VIII and Ann Boleyn, came to the throne in 1558, having lived in seclusion during the reign of her RC sister, Mary. The 'Elizabethan Settlement' of 1559, which declared England Protestant again, was once interpreted as a settlement forced on a reluctant Queen by a Protestant minority in the House of Commons (J. E. Neale); recently it has been argued that a Protestant Queen struggled for a majority in a conservative House of Lords (N. L. Jones). In light of this, Elizabethan Protestantism seems not a matter of 'Puritans' threatening an 'Anglican' establishment, but a long campaign to turn people to the new religion, by a Protestantism that went beyond the Queen's only as it became strident. Protestantism's success was not inevitable, but was secured by the stability Elizabeth achieved. Her foreign policy was shaped by her role as leading Protestant monarch in Europe, ranked against the RC powers of France and Spain, at a time when religious conflict was fierce. Mary, Queen of Scots,* was a challenge to stability: a RC heir for the unmarried Elizabeth. But though support for the Lords of the Congregation* against Mary and the French Queen Regent, Mary of Guise,* was in Elizabeth's political interest, their cause was rebellion against a royal cousin. When she overcame her reluctance and sent military aid in the spring of 1560, she gave the Scots ascendancy over the French. The danger of domination by France ended with Mary's return to Scotland and alliance with the Protestant party in 1561, her husband the French King dead. Elizabeth, keen to see Mary now marry an ally, put forward her favourite, the Earl of Leicester. Mary's disastrous marriage to Henry, Lord Darnley, disturbed the political equilibrium and brought fear of Scotland's involvement in a RC league. Elizabeth, though disturbed by Mary's weakness as a monarch, stood by her; Mary fled to England in 1568. Elizabeth equivocated about her fate: refusing to support Mary against her opponents, yet wanting her restored to the throne. The elapse of time allowed James VI* and the Protestant faction to prevent Mary's return. Her presence in England as a RC heir and focus for plots (particularly the Ridolfi and Babington plots, 1571 and 1586) led to pressure from Privy Council and Parliament to be rid of her. By 1587 Elizabeth could not avoid her execution. James VI was a stable prospect as heir: male, Protestant. But Elizabeth took a personal dislike to him: he thought too highly of himself, and impeded her influence in Scotland. She was infuriated by favours he demanded for giving help against the Spanish Armada in 1588, and by his reluctance to stop his RC earls dealing with Spain, 1589–92.

J. E. Neale, *Queen Elizabeth* (L, 1971); C. Erickson, *The First Elizabeth* (NY, 1983); C. Haigh (ed.), *The Reign of Elizabeth I* (L, 1984); J. Wormald, 'The Neighbour to the North' in S. Adams (ed.), *Queen Elizabeth I* (*History Today* special issue, L, 1988); N. L. Jones, *Faith by Statute* (L, 1983); J. Wormald, *Court, Kirk and Community, Scotland 1475–1625* (L, 1981); G. Donaldson, *James V to*

ELMSLIE, WALTER ANGUS

James VII (E, 1978); W. Ferguson, *Scotland's Relations with England, a Survey to 1707* (E, 1977).

S. Hardman Moore

Elmslie, Walter Angus (1856–1935), missionary of the Livingstonia Mission in Malawi, Central Africa, 1884–1924. Elsmlie began his service as a doctor at Njuyu. In 1889 he opened the new station of Ekwendeni where he was to spend most of his missionary career. He was ordained by Aberdeen FC Presbytery in 1897, later joining the UFC and the CofS.

He is chiefly remembered for his patient and pioneering work amongst M'mbelwa's Ngoni (building on the foundations already laid by William Mtusane Koyi, the Xhosa evangelist to the Ngoni, who died in 1886). Elmslie is also important for his early linguistic and historical studies. In 1886 he published *Izongoma zo'Mlungu* – a collection of hymns and Scripture selections, and the first printed book in the Ngoni language. He followed that in 1891 with a translation of Mark's Gospel and two books of chiNgoni grammar. A close ally of Robert Laws,* he represents the conservative stream in the Livingstonia tradition, fairly negative about African culture, and remembered with respect rather than affection by local Christians.

Introductory Grammar of the Ngoni (Zulu) Language (A, 1891); *Among the Wild Ngoni* (E, 1899, ³L, 1970).

AFCS I, 147; *FUFCS* 438; *FES* IX, 601; W. P. Livingstone, *Laws of Livingstonia* (L, 1923); K. J. McCracken, *Politics and Christianity in Malawi 1875–1940* (C, 1977).

J. Thompson

Elphinstone, William (1431–1514), bishop, Chancellor of Scotland, and founder of the University of Aberdeen. Born in Glasgow, he was educated at the Cathedral School and the University (MA, 1462). He studied and then taught canon law at the University of Paris 1465–70, followed by civil law at the University of Orleans 1470–1. He became the Official (i.e. judge in ecclesiastical court) of the diocese of Glasgow 1471–8, Rector of the University of Glasgow 1474–5, and the Official of Lothian 1478–83. He was nominated Bishop of Ross 1481, but never consecrated and transferred to Aberdeen 1483 (consecrated 1488). Made Chancellor of Scotland in February 1488, he was relieved of the office on the death of James III in June. In the 1480s and 1490s he was frequently involved in negotiations with England and continental powers. From 1478 he was a member of the King's Council, commissioner of crown lands and auditor of the Exchequer, and Keeper of the Privy Seal from 1492. He founded the University of Aberdeen in 1495, and King's College in 1505. Though nominated Archbishop of St Andrews in 1513, he was never provided. He died in Edinburgh.

As an auditor of causes, government administrator, statesman and liturgical reformer, Elphinstone probably had no equal in fifteenth-century Scot-

EMIGRATION

land. He sat longer and more frequently on Parliamentary Committees and the judicial Council than any of his contemporaries, and introduced statutes intended to remedy defective land law and improve the administration of civil and criminal justice. As Keeper of the Privy Seal, he brought order and registration to the office, thereby enabling the Crown to exercise control over its patronage and keep a regular check on its feudal casualties. The peace treaties he negotiated were designed to bring political stability to the realm, to forge a closer alliance with England, and to strengthen public international law. As a reforming bishop, he strove to select his own diocesan administrators rather than to have others thrust on him by the Crown and papacy. His constitutions for the clergy in 1506 sought to improve their stipends as well as their educational and moral training. He introduced printing into Scotland in 1507, among the first books off the press being his Aberdeen Breviary* in 1510, a compilation designed to become the national use for the Scottish Church, with diocesan variants. He inaugurated a massive building programme at his cathedral in Old Aberdeen, completed the choir of the parish church of St Nicholas, and built the first permanent stone bridge over the river Dee. The University he founded remains his lasting memorial. Its distinctive features included a chair of medicine from 1497 onwards, the academic excellence of its early teachers, a strong emphasis on Christian humanist learning led by its first principal, Hector Boece,* and its sound financial endowment, making possible, by 1514, the installation of six well salaried teachers and eight prebendary chaplains, all life tenured, twenty-two fully bursaried students and six choir boys, together with an elected, non-endowed Rector and Dean of the Faculty of Arts, with the Bishop of Aberdeen as its Chancellor.

Hector Boetii Murthlacensiuim et Aberdonensium Episcoporum Vitae, ed. J. Moir (A, 1894); *Fasti Aberdonenses 1494–1854*, ed. C. Innes (A, 1854); L. J. Macfarlane, *William Elphinstone and the Kingdom of Scotland 1431–1514* (A, 1985); *id.*, 'William Elphinstone's Library', *AUR* 37 (1958), 253–71.

L. J. Macfarlane

Emigration, the settlement of Scots abroad. From medieval times Scottish merchants, soldiers, students and churchmen sought advancement or refuge abroad, primarily in eastern Europe, the Baltic and at the papal court. In the 1620s there was an abortive attempt to establish a Scottish colony in Nova Scotia, and in the 1680s a few Scottish Quakers* and Presbyterians settled in New Jersey and South Carolina respectively. During and after the civil war with England, Scots were transported to the American and West Indian colonies. They included captured soldiers and (after 1666) about 1,700 Covenanters,* as well as beggars and criminals. Enforced emigration – of criminals, kidnap victims and Jacobites* – continued in the eighteenth century, at the same time as more free Scots also left for the colonies, taking advantage of opportunities created by the 1707 parliamentary union.

At this time emigration from the British Isles was almost exclusively a Scottish – and particularly a Highland* – phenomenon. From the late seventeenth century substantial numbers of Scots – and Scotch-Irish* – left for America, settling particularly in New York, New Jersey, Pennsylvania and South Carolina. In some cases entire congregations emigrated. Between 1763 (when the movement began to assume significant proportions) and 1815, it is estimated that approximately 27,000 Scots may have emigrated, setting a precedent for the much larger and broader-based nineteenth-century movement (see J. M. Bumsted, *The People's Clearance*, E, 1982, 224–9; I. C. C. Graham, *Colonists from Scotland*, NY, 1956, 188–9). From 1815 to 1913 at least 24 million emigrants left the British Isles, only 8 per cent of whom came from Scotland, although Scots accounted for 22 per cent of departures between 1914 and 1938.

MOTIVES IN EMIGRATION. Apart from the destitute and those who were forcibly removed, the decision to emigrate was rarely provoked by one isolated factor, but by a complex interaction of grievances and incentives, which varied according to location, period and individual circumstances. The upsurge in Scottish emigration after 1763 partly reflects the Highlanders' response to successive bad harvests, rising rents on their unimproved lands and fundamental changes in Highland society, and partly a reaction to commercial depression and unemployment in manufacturing centres in the early 1770s. Yet these economic and social grievances were generally combined with positive incentives to emigrate, particularly the offer of land or employment, and assurances in the correspondence of travellers or earlier emigrants that conditions in America were the opposite of those which were causing hardship and discontent in Scotland.

Extensive publicity on all aspects of emigration throughout the nineteenth century reminded Scots that many of their contemporaries were leaving home, and often encouraged them to do likewise. Information and advice appeared in guidebooks, press articles, advertisements and published correspondence, as well as in the very influential personal emigrant letters, which sometimes contained tangible aid in the form of a remittance or a prepaid ticket. A growing army of agents brought the attributes of different destinations to public notice, penetrating even the remotest districts to deliver lectures and arrange passages, and sometimes even to organize the emigrants' future employment or settlement on land. While lucrative employment opportunities increasingly attracted non-agriculturists and female domestic servants, the prospect of land ownership remained the main incentive for many emigrants from the rural Lowlands. When new farming policies led to the eradication of smallholdings and frustrated the landholding ambitions of modest agriculturists, many of them invested their savings in emigration, attracted by the promise of independence and security for themselves and their families, through the ownership of their own farms.

But while for some nineteenth-century emigrants discontent about conditions in Scotland interacted with the positive influences of precedent and personal persuasion, for many others the decision to leave was provoked entirely by adverse economic circumstances. After the Napoleonic Wars the character of emigration underwent a fundamental change, particularly from the Highlands, where emigrants, who had previously left on their own initiative, in order to preserve their culture in a new land, were increasingly pushed out in the face of famine and destitution in the 1830s and 1840s. In the West-Central Lowlands too, recurring economic crises in the 1820s, 1840s and 1850s led to the formation of several weavers' emigration societies, although only a small proportion of their members actually managed to raise sufficient funds to emigrate. Pauper emigration again became a topical issue during the widespread agricultural and commercial depression of the late nineteenth century, when there were renewed calls for a state-funded scheme to supplement the activities of charitable emigration agencies.

ATTITUDES TO EMIGRATION. Attitudes to emigration were moulded largely by economic imperatives. The eighteenth-century exodus was strongly opposed by Highland landowners and the government, on the mercantilist argument that national wealth was vested in the retention of a large population, particularly in order to implement fashionable policies of Highland development. The consequences of emigration were depicted in terms of enervating depopulation and the loss of not only economic but also military strength, especially in the 1770s, as the American colonies became increasingly rebellious. Throughout the War of Independence there was a prohibition against any ship carrying emigrants from Scotland to America, and further legislation imposed from 1782 to 1824 forbade the emigration of skilled artisans.

After the war the government's need to populate its remaining American territories for defensive reasons, together with its commitment to free enterprise, led to a modification of earlier mercantilist attitudes. It was only after the Napoleonic wars, however, that Highland landlords began to accept that their best interests were not served by opposing emigration, as their development schemes finally collapsed in the face of the 1820s depression, leaving them with hordes of redundant, impoverished tenants whom they could not afford to maintain. More systematic census-taking since 1800 had led to a new awareness of existing, and increasing, overpopulation, and once the notion had been discredited that the land should support the largest possible number of people, attitudes to emigration softened. In a direct reversal of earlier policies, Highland landlords now attempted to cut their losses by encouraging – and often financing – the emigration of tenants, converting the cleared lands into sheep walks and later into deer forests. While the relationship between clearance and emigration is somewhat ambiguous, it is evident that many of these Highlanders left unwillingly, particularly in cases where landlords provided only minimal aid in organizing their departure and relocation.

Like the Lowland weavers' emigration societies, Highland landlords repeatedly requested government assistance in implementing emigration policies, but to little avail. Despite the prevalence of Malthusian theories* in the 1820s – which advocated the state-funded emigration of excess population – the government was reluctant to provide financial backing for any such programme. Between 1815 and 1823 it gave limited assistance to Scots and Irish emigrants (including a group of impoverished Lanarkshire weavers) to settle in Canada, and in 1826–7 a parliamentary select committee considered the feasibility of extending this programme. But despite its positive recommendations, and the reports of subsequent select committees in 1841 and 1851 that Highland distress could be relieved only by widespread, state-financed emigration, the government took no further action, on the grounds of both expense and expediency. Throughout the nineteenth century it concentrated mainly on modernizing the Colonial Office to cope with the growing exodus, disseminating statistical information about various destinations, and implementing protective legislation through a series of passenger acts and the appointment of emigrant agents at the major ports. In the 1880s renewed pleas for state intervention nationally were compounded by the declaration of the Napier Commission that government-aided emigration remained the only solution to Highland overpopulation, but after spending 10,000 in establishing two small Highland colonies in Canada in 1888, the government in 1891 rejected the argument that it should provide funding on a larger or more permanent basis, and it continued to evade any large-scale financial responsibility for emigration until after the First World War.

Emigration was always a controversial issue and a frequent topic of parliamentary and public debate. State aid was opposed not only on financial grounds but also by adherents of *laissez-faire* doctrine, who disliked any prospect of centralization or the extension of state responsibility. They condemned government assistance to the able-bodied as indiscriminate charity which would corrupt the recipients and burden ratepayers, warning that those who were perfectly capable of emigrating unaided would cease to act for themselves and instead expect the state to finance their removal. Others claimed that state-aided emigration was a discreditable attempt to evade social reform at home by removing pauperized and potentially troublesome elements to the colonies, where they would form artificially concentrated pools of labour. Recipient countries objected to being treated as receptacles for Britain's redundant population, although advocates of emigration as a 'safety valve' argued that the objectives of relieving economic and social distress at home and meeting colonial labour needs were quite compatible.

A new concern then emerged in the early 1830s as the negative Malthusian doctrine of 'shovelling out the paupers' increasingly gave way to the settlement of Britain's Antipodean possessions under principles of selective colonization propounded by Edward Gibbon Wakefield. In a self-financing scheme, money from colonial land sales was used to assist the passages, not of paupers and radicals, but of hand-picked emigrants who met colonial manpower requirements. But since those requirements were often identical to the needs of British employers, increasing disquiet was expressed at the loss of the flower of the population, echoing old mercantilist arguments. Similar concern was felt about the calibre of many unassisted emigrants, particularly thrifty but disgruntled agriculturists, who invested their savings in land abroad, leaving behind only the most improvident – and therefore the least useful – of the rural population.

PHILANTHROPY AND EMIGRATION. Those who could not finance their own removal, and were ineligible for assistance from colonial land funds, could sometimes emigrate with the help of charitable societies or individuals. A few Scottish weavers managed to finance their emigration by a combination of church collections, private donations and small sums of their own, while impoverished Highlanders were enabled to leave through the efforts of distress committees, landlords and the Highland and Island Emigration Society, which from 1852 to 1858 despatched almost 5,000 recruits to Australia. The government's consistent refusal to undertake any major programme of state-aided emigration ensured a continuing – and expanding – role for charitable societies and individuals, particularly during the late nineteenth-century depression. In 1886 there were over sixty private emigration societies throughout Britain, most of which catered for specific categories of emigrants, particularly destitute children, single women and the unemployed.

William Quarrier* and Thomas Barnardo promoted juvenile emigration as part of a wider programme of rescue work among disadvantaged children, Quarrier sending almost 7,000 children from the Orphan Homes of Scotland to Canada between 1872 and 1933, in a scheme which predated the ultimately much larger exodus from Barnardo's Homes. Women like Lady Aberdeen (*see* Gordon, Ishbel) sponsored specifically female emigration, and her Aberdeen Ladies' Union, which despatched almost 400 emigrants from 1884 to 1913, was one of a number of societies devoted to redressing the imbalance of the sexes in Britain and her colonies, as well as offering recruits better economic and social prospects than were available at home. Carefully regulated emigration was an integral part of the social strategy of William Booth of the Salvation Army,* who favoured it on the grounds that it offered a viable means of relieving the twin pressures of overpopulation and unemployment in Britain, and by the early twentieth century the Salvation Army had become probably the largest emigration agency in the British Empire.

The philanthropists' activities did not go unchallenged. Colonial complaints highlighted careless selection, inadequate after-care facilities and mercenary motives, while opponents at home claimed that any reduction of the labour supply damaged national well-being and took away precisely those workers who were in greatest demand in Britain. The philanthropists – whose actions were often rooted in an evangelical Christian commitment to the needy – refuted these allegations, and argued that the offer of independence, employment and a new life abroad was the best way to provide practical and spiritual assistance to the destitute and disadvantaged.

EMIGRATION AND THE SCOTTISH CHURCHES. While philanthropists often sponsored emigration out of Christian concern, the Scottish Churches cannot be said to have adopted any consistent policy towards the movement. In the late eighteenth century a disproportionate number of Roman Catholic Highlanders emigrated to British America, in parties often led by priests, but not always with the acquiescence of the Church hierarchy. Thus in 1772 Father James MacDonald accompanied 210 emigrants from South Uist, Arisaig and Modart to Prince Edward Island, after the Uist tenants had been ordered to renounce their faith for Presbyterianism on pain of expulsion from their lands. The exodus was devised and financed clandestinely by two Scottish bishops, who hoped to stem the spread of Protestantism among Highland landlords by threatening to depopulate their estates, at a time when landlords still fiercely opposed emigration. It was hoped that the isolated location of their destination would help to preserve the Catholic faith of the settlers, whose removal was likened to the exodus to the Promised Land – a biblical metaphor frequently quoted in accounts of Highland emigration.

In 1786 a party of 540 Highlanders, having been evicted from their lands in Knoydart, emigrated under their priest, Alexander McDonell, to Glengarry County, near Montreal. Here they rejoined their countrymen, 600 of whom had emigrated in 1773, initially to the Mohawk Valley in New York. In 1804 there was a further substantial addition to the Glengarry community, when 1,000 Highlanders – members of the disbanded Glengarry Fencibles and their families – emigrated under the auspices of their chaplain, also Alexander McDonell, and took up land grants of 200 acres apiece. McDonell went on to become Bishop of Kingston in 1826, working alongside Aberdonian John Strachan,* first Episcopalian* Bishop of Toronto.

The Protestant Churches adopted a similarly ambivalent attitude. While they denounced the causes and effects of emigration, they ministered to departing emigrants and subsequently endeavoured to meet their spiritual needs. The finality of parting from friends and the prospect of settling in an alien environment often intensified emigrants' spiritual concerns and made them receptive to the exhortations of ministers who preached on board departing ships, urging their hearers to uphold the ordinances of religion even in the absence of churches and ministers. In fact, one of the primary concerns of many emigrants was to establish spiritual leadership in their new communities by securing the services of a minister from home, and with a few exceptions (notably Norman McLeod*) most emigrant ministers left in response to such pleas, rather than on their own initiative.

It was therefore against a background of popular demand that the Scottish Churches tackled colonial needs. It was relatively easy for pastors of independent churches to emigrate, for not only did they usually have a strong commitment to their people and to the missionary cause, but because they belonged to independent churches their removal did not have to be sanctioned and arranged by any higher central body; individual Baptist* or Congregationalist* ministers were free to decide for themselves whether or not to take up an invitation to emigrate.

The Church of Scotland* showed interest in emigrants shortly after the Revolution in sending two ministers with the first expedition to the Darien Colony* in 1698. From the early eighteenth century, ministers of the CofS emigrated to America. The presbytery formed under the guidance of Francis Makemie* in Philadelphia in 1706 grew, particularly as increasing numbers of Scots and Scotch-Irish arrived. They naturally looked to the General Assembly for support and received it, particularly as further ministers were sent.

From the first the Secession* churches received requests for ministerial supply from the colonies. Due to their inability to supply needs in Scotland it was not until 1753 that the first Antiburgher missionaries were sent (*see* General Associate Synod; Gellatly, Alexander). The first Burgher missionaries were not sent until the 1760's (*see* Associate Synod). Although under John Mason* both branches of the Secession joined with the Reformed Presbyterians* to form the Associate Reformed Church in 1782, missionary work continued unabated by the parent churches and each planted daughter churches again and continued to supply them. In 1836 the General Assembly appointed a Colonial Committee and recommended that parochial collections be taken up regularly for colonial missions. In 1837 the Committee was instructed to pay particular attention to current emigration, with a view to providing emigrants with church facilities, and by 1840 ten sub-committees had been formed throughout Scotland to raise funds, collect information and select candidates for the colonial ministry.

Evangelicals* in the Est.C generally had a more pronounced commitment to colonial missions than Moderates.* They carried this over into the Free Church,* which did not confine itself simply to supplying preachers or founding colonial theological colleges. The popularity of the New Zealand province of Otago with Scottish emigrants owed much to its establishment in the 1840s as a Scottish Presbyterian colony, created and conducted under Free Church auspices; a colony administered on principles of systematic colonization, but where careful attention was paid to the provision of religious and educational facilities, and where settlers were assured they would suffer no social dislocation.

DESTINATIONS. Such considerations, highlighted by enthusiastic agents, sometimes governed the choice of destination, and help to explain New Zealand's consistent popularity with Scottish emigrants. Agents were also active in the Australian colonies, but here they had to contend with the stigma of transportation, and warnings about Australia's uncivilized society, particularly in the wake of an indiscriminate influx of gold seekers in the 1850s. British fears that the USA would adopt a policy of territorial aggrandisement at Canada's expense were often embodied in criticism of the irreligion, immorality and egalitarianism of American society, but for most emigrants any political prejudices were outweighed by the promise of land or employment held out by advertisements, correspondents and professional agents. Between 1830 and 1913 46 per cent of Scottish emigrants went to the USA, 27 per cent to Canada and 15 per cent to Australasia. Canada, with its tradition of Scottish settlement and its advantages of proximity and accessibility (on timber-trading ships), was the Scots' favourite destination until 1847, and again in the early twentieth century, when it was the main receptacle for emigrants sent out by charitable organizations. Initially promoted by the British government for defensive reasons, after Confederation Canada's attributes were publicized by Dominion, provincial and railway company agents, who highlighted not only the ready availability of land, work and investment opportunities, but also the social advantages of settling amongst compatriots in a stable, well-ordered and Christian country.

See also Australia; Canada; Clearances; Highlands; Lang, John Dunmore; MacKay, Isabella; Missions.

G. Donaldson, *The Scots Overseas* (L, 1966); W. A. Carrothers, *Emigration from the British Isles* (L, 1965); D. E. Meek, 'Evangelicalism and Emigration: Aspects of the Role of Dissenting Evangelicalism in Highland Emigration to Canada' in G. W. MacLennan (ed.), *Proceedings of the First North American Congress of Celtic Studies* (Ottawa, 1988), 15–35; M. D. Harper, *Emigration from North-East Scotland*, 2 vols (A, 1988); M. Gray, 'Scottish Emigration: the Social Impact of Agrarian Change in the Rural Lowlands, 1775–1875', *Perspectives in American History* 7 (1973), 95–174; W. S. Shepperson, *British Emigration to North America* (O, 1957); D. S. MacMillan, *Scotland and Australia* (O, 1967).

M. Harper

Engagement, The, a treaty between Charles I* and some Scottish nobles, signed 26 December 1647 on the Isle of Wight. It bound the King to a limited support of the Covenants* and Presbyterianism,* with the suppression of Independents and sectaries (including Oliver Cromwell), and the nobles to restore the King to his throne by whatever means necessary. Though endorsed by the Estates and effectively implemented by Parliament, which passed an act denouncing English breaches of the Covenant in terms the English were bound to reject, the General Assembly condemned it as allowing 'no possibility of securing Religion so long as [it] is carried on'. In particular, the Engagement failed to declare 'the Popish, Prelaticall and Malignant party ... Enemies to the Cause', as well as the sectaries, endeavoured a breach between the two kingdoms, compelled unlawful oaths and encroached on the liberties of the Church (*AGACS*, 168–9). Ministers who did not oppose the Engagement as unlawful were to be disciplined, those who supported it deposed, and any who opposed ministers in this duty were to be excommunicated (*AGACS*, 188–9).

Notwithstanding the opposition of the Church, the Scottish army was raised and sent only to be routed and dispersed at Preston in Lancashire in August 1648. The Scottish Estates, with the Engagers out of power, forced the remnants of the Engager army to disband and excluded them from holding office. In January 1649 Parliament condemned the Engagement. Later that month it took action against those involved, passing an 'Act of Classes' (similar to one passed three years earlier), grouping offenders in four levels of punishment: the leaders who had plotted against the government by promoting the Engagement and general officers in the army were barred for life from public office; the malignants who had in some lesser way supported the Engagers were subject to ten or five years exclusion from office, depending on the severity of the offence; finally, frail brethren guilty of some moral offence were to be excluded for a year. Restoration to office at the end of the prescribed period was only permitted after appropriate repentance.

See also Protesters; Resolutioners.

Text in S. R. Gardiner, *The Constitutional Documents of the Puritan Revolution, 1625–1660* (O, ³1906); W. Makey, *The Church of the Covenant 1637–1651* (E, 1979), 73–7.

D. C. Lachman

English Episcopal Churches, evangelical Episcopal congregations formed after a minor disruption in the EpCS in 1842–4. At the General Synod of 1838 the word 'Protestant' was dropped from the Church's title, the high church Scottish Communion Office was upgraded in importance, and Canon XXVIII forbidding non-liturgical services was passed. After a dispute concerning the last in 1842, D. K. T. Drummond* left the EpCS to found an English Episcopal chapel. In 1843 Bishop Skinner of Aberdeen attempted to force Scottish services on St Paul's Chapel, Aberdeen, only recently united with the EpCS. Its minister, Sir William Dunbar,* and his congregation rescinded the union. In 1844 C. P. Miles* and his congregation also left the EpCS in support. These chapels were joined by others in Edinburgh, Glasgow, Dundee, Nairn, Huntly, Dunoon and Montrose, totalling eleven by 1880. They claimed legal status under an act of 1712 tolerating 'qualified' Episcopal chapels in Scotland (*see* Episcopalianism). Some evangelical

CofE bishops and retired colonial bishops were willing to conduct confirmations for them. In this century the remaining English Episcopal churches have joined the EpCS, the last, as a private chapel, being St Silas', Glasgow, in 1987.

E. M. Culbertson, *The Episcopal Disruption* (E, 1983); G. White, 'New Names for Old Things; Scottish Reaction to Early Tractarianism', in D. Baker (ed.), *Renaissance and Renewal in Christian History* (O, 1977), 329-37.

E. M. Culbertson

Enlightenment, the characteristic form of eighteenth-century intellectual expression that exalted human reason. Earlier usage normally restricted the term to later eighteenth-century German thought (as a translation of *Aufklärung*), but from the 1950s the word has been used as a synonym for 'the age of reason' in Western civilization. René Descartes (1596-1650) prepared the way, especially in France, by commending the ideal of mathematical certainty in human knowledge. More immediately influential was John Locke (1632-1704), whose dismissal of the traditional belief in innate ideas in *An Essay concerning Human Understanding* (1690) gave rise to the widespread Enlightenment supposition that all knowledge comes from experience. Equally significant was Sir Isaac Newton (1642-1727), whose scientific achievement brought prestige to the method of empirical investigation and inductive reasoning.

Enlightenment thinkers typically wished to discover the natural laws of a mechanistic universe. Strongly swayed by classical ideals, they hoped to achieve a balance in society that would reflect the order of the cosmos. A 'science of man' is possible, they held, because human nature is uniform in all times and places. Human benevolence should be harnessed for humanitarian ends such as anti-slavery.* A utilitarian ethic, judging actions by their tendency to augment human happiness, became widespread. The idea of progress, the supposition that humanity could improve its condition over time, emerged as the century proceeded. Nature was to be mastered, knowledge to be diffused and posts of influence flung open to men of talent. The obstacles to be overcome included government corruption, outdated metaphysics and frequently the benighted outlook of the clergy. Suspicions could extend to revealed religion, so that deism* was an early product of the Enlightenment. There was a general tendency to elevate toleration above dogma and, in some places, a desire to separate Church and state.* For all the prominence of reason, there remained an undercurrent of irrationalism. Rosicrucians, Swedenborgians, theosophists and Freemasons proliferated, and non-logical thought processes abound even in the high priest of reason, Denis Diderot (1713-84).

After early stirrings in England and the Netherlands, the efflorescence of the Enlightenment was in France. Diderot's *Encyclopaedia* (1751-72) was a joint enterprise by the *philosophes* of the Paris salons. It had been preceded by *The Spirit of the Laws* (2 vols, Geneva, L; ET, 2 vols, L, 1750), a pioneer exercise in political sociology by the Baron de Montesquieu (1689-1755), and the early writings of Voltaire (1694-1778), whose pungent wit made him the leading exponent of anti-clericalism. Others in the circle of Diderot adopted more advanced positions: the Baron d'Holbach (1723-89) upheld philosophical materialism. Jean-Jacques Rousseau (1712-78), though near the centre of the French Enlightenment, should be seen as a thinker reacting against many of its basic axioms.

Recent scholarship has contended (against Peter Gay) that the Enlightenment was not intrinsically irreligious and that the variety of its national forms must be appreciated. In Germany few writers were unsympathetic to religion, though Gotthold Lessing (1729-81) wished to dismiss revelation. Immanuel Kant (1724-1804), the greatest German philosopher of the age, similarly reduced Christianity to a system of ethics. In southern Europe the Enlightenment generated a wave of RC reform that was hostile to Jesuits but not to the Church. In England reason was employed, as by Bishop Butler (1692-1752), in defence of revealed religion far more than, as by the historian Edward Gibbon (1737-94), in an assault upon it. In America the appeal to reason led to deism in men such as Benjamin Franklin (1706-90), but equally it led Jonathan Edwards* (1703-58) to a brilliant synthesis of Calvinist orthodoxy with Enlightenment thought.

SCOTTISH ENLIGHTENMENT. Nowhere was the Enlightenment more fully assimilated by an established Church than in Scotland. Scholars were frequently ministers. William Robertson,* Principal of Edinburgh University, exemplified the enlightened temper in his historiography. Hugh Blair,* Regius Professor of Rhetoric and Belles Lettres at Edinburgh, was the leading exemplar of refined pulpit style in the English-speaking world. Both were deeply attached to the CofS. The teaching of the Moderates* as a whole tended to the moralism that was characteristic of enlightened religion. It has less often been recognized that the leaders of the Popular Party* were equally imbued with Enlightenment values. The writings of John Erskine* and John Witherspoon* were more traditional than those of the Moderates in their theological content, but equally enlightened in their expression.

The origins of the Scottish Enlightenment have been much debated. It has been argued that the civic humanism of the Renaissance was adapted to the fresh political circumstances after the Union of 1707.* A Whig culture of politeness gave rise to the achievements of the eighteenth century in the study of human society. More recently it has been suggested that there was greater continuity from the scholarly concerns of the late seventeenth century. Lord Stair's *Institutions of the Laws of Scotland* (E, 1681) already embodied the principle of rational reform. There was an enduring debt among eighteenth-century writers to the tradition of natural jurisprudence. It is equally apparent in the philosophical school of Scottish Realism* associated with Thomas Reid and in the seminal *Wealth of Nations* (2 vols, L, 1776) by Adam Smith.

Among the most notable intellectual achievements of the earlier phase of the Scottish Enlightenment was the work of Francis Hutcheson,* Professor of Moral Philosophy at Glasgow. His use of inductive method to postulate a moral sense and his advocacy of a Christian Stoicism deeply influenced subsequent thinkers. In the middle years of the century the most powerful mind was that of David Hume.* His veiled infidelity alarmed contemporary churchmen. His systematic empiricism has fascinated philosophers down to the present. Later writers are notable for their exposition of stages of human development produced by particular economic conditions. Thus Adam Ferguson (1723-1816), Professor of Moral Philosophy at Edinburgh, composed *An Essay on the History of Civil Society* (E, 1767); Sir James Steuart's *Inquiry into the Principles of Political Economy* (2 vols, L, 1767) elaborated similar themes and strongly influenced the German philosopher Hegel.

The thought of the Scottish Enlightenment was widely attractive because it blended progressive analysis with social conservatism. In Britain its legacy, popularized by Dugald Stewart* and *The Edinburgh Review* (*see* Periodicals, Religious), was powerful among early nineteenth-century Whig reformers. In America its teaching shaped the mind of the nation long into the nineteenth century.

R. Porter and M. Teich (eds), *The Enlightenment in National Context* (C, 1981); P. Gay, *The Enlightenment* (L, 1967); N. Hampson, *The Enlightenment* (Harmondsworth, 1968); H. F. May, *The Enlightenment in America* (NY, 1976); R. B. Sher, *Church and University in the Scottish Enlightenment* (E, 1985); I. Hont and M. Ignatieff (eds), *Wealth and Virtue* (C, 1983); R. H. Campbell and A. S. Skinner (eds), *The Origins and Nature of the Scottish Enlightenment* (E, 1982); J. J. Carter and J. H. Pittock (eds), *Aberdeen and the Enlightenment* (A, 1987).

D. W. Bebbington

Epiclesis, the petition in the prayer of consecration in the service of Holy Communion for the sending of the Holy Spirit upon the elements of bread and wine. Present in the early Eastern liturgies, there was no passage in the canon of the mass which was a clear epiclesis. Although included by Cranmer in the first *Book of Common Prayer* in England in 1549, it was subsequently omitted. It was not included in the *Book of Common Order** in Scotland, although it was regarded by some as an important element in the prayer of consecration. A form of epiclesis was included in the second draft liturgy prepared during the reign of James VI* and one was present in the Communion service of Laud's* Liturgy of 1637. The epiclesis was one of the features which distinguished the Scottish book from contemporary Anglican worship. An epiclesis was expressly enjoined in the Westminster* Directory. It has continued to be an important feature of the eucharistic liturgy of the EpCS and of the *Books of Common Order** of 1940 and 1979 produced in the CofS. An epiclesis is explicitly present in the eucharistic prayer of the RC mass prepared as a result of the Second Vatican Council.

D. B. Forrester and D. M. Murray (eds), *Studies in the History of Worship in Scotland* (E, 1984).

D. M. Murray

Episcopacy, the system of church government by bishops. This pattern is not discernible in the New Testament, but by *c.*200 the leadership of local churches by a single bishop (hence monepiscopacy, monarchical episcopate) assisted by presbyters and deacons was all but universal. This developed into a territorial episcopate, with the bishop of the town church presiding also over congregations in the surrounding countryside. This became the dominant order in the Christianization of Europe.

The Celtic Church* in Scotland was largely dependent on the Irish Church, whose organization had evolved along distinctive monastic lines. The abbot (who at Iona,* for example, was always a presbyter) was the supreme authority to whom bishops (who were essential for functions like ordination) were subject. Sometimes abbots were bishops, but the abbots of all Columban houses were answerable to Iona's presbyter-abbot. Thus much of Scottish Christianity began without an episcopal structure.

In the years following the Synod of Whitby* (664), the influence of Northumbria probably fostered the establishment of something akin to the territorial episcopate in parts of Pictland, e.g. at Abernethy, and at Whithorn.* But rule by abbot-bishops continued among the Scots, and spread further afield in the united kingdom of Alba from the mid-ninth century. The bishops first of Dunkeld* and then of St Andrews* seem to have held ecclesiastical primacy in Alba, but evidence is patchy.

The reorganization of the Scottish Church into territorial dioceses under bishops was largely the work of the sons of Queen Margaret* – Alexander I* and David II* – in the twelfth century. Thus Scotland was assimilated to English and Norman precedents, but the Scottish Church escaped subjection to York or Canterbury by becoming a 'special daughter' of Rome herself. The later medieval Roman Church in Scotland was divided into thirteen bishoprics. Archbishops were created, at St Andrews and Glasgow, late in the fifteenth century (see Burleigh, 64–70).

To the sixteenth-century Reformers the negligent and immoral bishops were largely self-condemned. (For some exceptions see David de Bernham,* William Elphinstone* and John Hamilton.*) A new order was called for, which had no need to preserve any apostolic succession* of bishops. From the *First Book of Discipline** (1560) to the final establishment of Presbyterianism* in 1690, the role of the bishops was one of the main issues in the lengthy struggles between the Kirk and the Crown. It has been claimed (especially by G. Donaldson,* *The Scottish Reformation 1560*, C, 1960) that the superintendents* provided for in the *FBD* were in effect reformed bishops, but the system has more the appearance of special provision for urgent nation-wide mission (see J. Kirk, *SBD*, 74–83; *id., Patterns of Reform*, E, 1989, 154–231). In any case, the aspirations of the Reformers found expression in the full-blooded Presbyterianism of the *Second Book of Discipline** (1578). Yet many vicissitudes lay ahead, with episcopacy and Presbyterianism in turn securing the ascendancy, until in 1690 the CofS was finally rid of episcopacy, and non-conforming Episcopalians set out on the road that would lead to the formation of the EpCS. In the preceding century or so, various accommodations between episcopacy and Presbyterianism were canvassed or implemented, but the former suffered all along from its inseparable association with royal authority.

And so Scottish Christianity became very largely Presbyterian for some two centuries. By comparison with the national CofS, the EpCS has always remained small but, in the later twentieth century, far from insignificant. In size it has long been overtaken by the RCC, by far the largest episcopal Church in Scotland.

Ecumenism made episcopacy a controversial subject once again in the post-World War II era. In 1957, representatives of Presbyterian and Anglican/Episcopalian churches in Scotland and England proposed that bishops 'in the apostolic succession' became permanent presidents of Presbyteries (*Relations between Anglican and Presbyterian Churches*, L, 1957). Such 'bishops-in-presbytery', possessing even a veto in the General Assembly, were decisively rejected by the CofS. Subsequent talks (see *The Anglican–Presbyterian Conversations*, E, 1966) made way for bilateral discussions between the CofS and the EpCS, which in turn fed into the Multilateral Church Conversation* in Scotland. Both its report, *Christian Unity: Now is the Time* (E, 1985), and the outcome of international Anglican–Reformed dialogue, *God's Reign and Our Unity* (L, 1984), picked up the proposal of the influential Faith and Order document, *Baptism, Eucharist and Ministry* (Geneva, 1982), for an individual regional ministry within a collegial (*e.g.* Presbyterial) context. The CofS has in effect been promoting such ministries, *e.g.* in evangelism and the pastoral support of ministers, without confusing them with 'the historic episcopate', thus securing some of the claimed pragmatic value of episcopacy without in any way acknowledging its pretensions to be essential for the proper ordering of the Church's life.

W. F. Skene, *Celtic Scotland* (E, 1876–80), II, 368–418; J. Dowden, *The Bishops of Scotland* (G, 1912) – prior to the Reformation; R. Keith, *A Historical Catalogue of the Scottish Bishops* (E, 1824) – to 1688; D. G. Mullan, *Episcopacy in Scotland, The History of An Idea 1560–1638* (E, 1986).
D. F. Wright

Episcopal Religious Orders, *see* Religious Communities, Episcopal.

Episcopal Theological College, from 1890–1 located in Coates Hall, Edinburgh. In the late eighteenth century, Bishop Arthur Petrie instructed students in his house at Folla (Meiklefolla) in the Aberdeen diocese, including Alexander Jolly* who later did likewise when Bishop in Fraserburgh. In 1810, Miss Kathrein Panton, one of Jolly's flock, provided for a 'Seminary of Learning or Theological Institution' for the EpCS, nominating James Walker* as the first (Pantonian) Professor (1824). Probably one of Jolly's pupils, he too taught at home in Edinburgh on becoming Bishop there in 1830. Charles Terrot succeeded him as Bishop and Professor (1841–63), teaching at 8 Hill Street and then St Andrew's Hall, High Street.

When Trinity College, Glenalmond, Perthshire, opened in 1847 (*see* Wordsworth, Charles), theological instruction became its 'Senior Department', but it failed to flourish. When John Dowden* assumed the Pantonian chair, he soon removed to Edinburgh in quest of students (1876), teaching at no fixed abode until 9 Rosebery Crescent was rented in 1880 with twelve students. Coates Hall nearby was purchased in 1890–1 – stability at last. Among various expansions, the chapel was extended by Robert Lorimer in 1923, when adjacent 21 Grosvenor Crescent was also acquired to house the libraries of Jolly and G. H. Forbes* (the latter now in Dundee University Library, the former in the National Library in Edinburgh).

The College now trains also non-Scottish Anglican ordinands, and since 1984 Coates Hall has also housed the small Scottish Congregational College. It has developed a close link with the University's Divinity Faculty. Its responsibility for training non-stipendiary ministers was in 1989 extended to lay training as the centre of the EpCS's Theological Institute. The College has had a succession of energetic principals (holding the Pantonian chair), several of whom have become Bishops.

F. Goldie, *A Short History of the Episcopal Church in Scotland* (²E, 1976); section in Church's *Year Book* to 1975–6 issue; College magazine (different titles) from at least 1947; P. Crosfield, *Coates Hall, A Short History 1892–1992* (E, 1992).
D. F. Wright

Episcopalianism, almost a synonym for episcopacy,* or Church government by bishops, but used particularly in distinction from Presbyterianism* or other forms of Church government. It normally refers to Churches belonging to the Anglican communion, *e.g.* the EpCS.

Episcopalianism has existed in Scotland from very early times. Ninian* who came to Whithorn* *c.*400 was a bishop, but his episcopal status has been cited as evidence that he came to an already well-established Christian community. During the Celtic* period bishops had a role subordinate to that of the abbots, but were the essential agents for the ordination of priests.

Episcopalianism in medieval Scotland broadly conformed to the pattern in western Europe, but had certain characteristic features. In the earlier period, there was a bishop for the whole kingdom based first at Dunkeld and from c.900 at St Andrews.* During the reigns of Alexander I* (1107–24) and David I* (1124–53) a number of other dioceses were established and eventually there were fourteen (the last, Edinburgh, founded in 1633). Not all were part of the CofS. The bishops of Galloway or Whithorn were suffragans of the archbishops of York, who also claimed jurisdiction over the bishops of the Isles and Orkney. Orkney* was assigned to the province of Nidaros (Frondhjein) in 1152.

The medieval Scottish Church had no archbishop until 1472, and the archbishops of York and Canterbury both claimed jurisdiction over it. But in 1188 Pope Clement III declared the Scottish Church to be the peculiar daughter (*filia specialis*) of the Roman Church and therefore independent of any archbishop (*see* Papacy). The provincial council of Scotland was therefore presided over by a bishop elected by his fellow bishops. The choice frequently, though not invariably, fell on the bishop of St Andrews. The inconvenience of cases having to be taken to Rome, instead of to an archbishop's court in Scotland, was one reason for the raising of St Andrews to an archbishopric in 1472. Rivalry rather than necessity achieved the same status for Glasgow in 1492.

The bishops of the medieval Church were important figures in secular affairs. They controlled vast areas of land and had a vital role in the Estates of Parliament* and the government of the kingdom. The great officers of state, such as the Chancellor or the Lord High Treasurer, were frequently bishops. With the connivance of the Pope, the King of Scots assumed control over the election of bishops and sometimes used bishoprics to provide for their illegitimate sons, *e.g.* Alexander Stewart,* Archbishop of St Andrews (1504–13). This royal exploitation of the episcopate was the seed of the later struggles between Church and state.*

The Reformation* Parliaments* of 1560 and 1567 abolished all authority derived from the pope, but did not abolish the office of bishop. The *First Book of Discipline** provided for superintendents* rather than bishops, but in 1572 the Concordat of Leith* provided for the filling of vacancies in the bishoprics (*see* Tulchan Bishops). The *Second Book of Discipline** called for the abolition of the episcopal office and the redistribution of the bishops' lands and rents, but James VI* annexed these to the Crown. The Golden Act* of 1592 transferred most episcopal functions to Presbyteries, but did not abolish the office itself. This enabled James VI to reintroduce bishops, first as parliamentary commisioners in 1599 and gradually with increased civil and ecclesiastical powers until 1610, when John Spottiswoode,* Archbishop of Glasgow, and the Bishops of Brechin and Galloway were consecrated by English bishops other than the two English archbishops. Episcopalianism was thus superimposed on Presbyterianism, and this combination lasted until the reaction against the attempted introduction of the Prayer Book in 1637 (*see* Laud, William). This led to the abolition of bishops by the Glasgow Assembly* in 1638 and subsequently by the Estates of Parliament.

The reintroduction of Episcopalianism in 1661 did not mean the abolition of the Presbyterian system of Church courts, though the General Assembly was not permitted to meet. The bishops presided over Synods and, when present, over Presbyteries and over the Kirk Sessions* of their cathedral towns. In many parts of the country the two systems continued quite well, partly because no prayer book was imposed, but especially in the south-west the opposition of the (largely Protester*) Covenanters* was implacable, and impervious either to coercion or concession. The episcopate was identified with the harsh legislation against conventicles* (or field gatherings for worship) and its brutal execution against those who participated. For many Scots the reputation of Episcopalianism was irretrievably tarnished. It was thus listed as a grievance in the Claim of Right* presented to William* and Mary in 1689.

Had the Scottish bishops been willing to transfer their allegiance from the fugitive James VII,* it is possible that William of Orange would have resisted the pressure for an exclusively Presbyterian system of Church government. The bishops also failed to give any clear guidance to their clergy and people, and Presbyterianism was fully reestablished in 1690.

By 1704 only five bishops were left and it became a matter of urgent concern to continue the episcopal succession. It was thought that only the exiled 'King' could nominate to the vacant sees but 'James VIII' showed no interest in doing so. The expedient was adopted of consecrating two new bishops, John Sage* and John Fullarton, without appointing them to any particular diocese. Links were formed with the non-jurors* in England, and a joint consecration of bishops took place in London in 1711.

The Act of Toleration (1712) gave legal recognition to the 'Episcopal Communion in that part of Great Britain called Scotland' and forbade the disturbing of its members in the exercise of their religious worship. It required, however, that Episcopal clergy should abjure the exiled Stuarts, take the oath of allegiance to Queen Anne and pray for her and her designated successor, the Electress Sophia of Hanover. Many clergy and all the bishops refused to 'qualify' in this way. The Jacobite* Rising of 1715* led to a period of increasing persecution of Episcopalians.

By 1720, the only diocesan bishop left was the Bishop of Edinburgh, Alexander Rose,* and when he died that year none of the remaining bishops possessed or claimed jurisdiction over any particular diocese. However, a meeting of the Edinburgh clergy resolved to fill the vacant see and elected Fullarton to do so. The other bishops ratified the election and appointed the new Bishop of Edinburgh to be their president with the title of Primus,* but without any metropolitan jurisdiction. These decisions were reported to 'James VIII' for approval. James gave his consent, but asked for prior consultation in future. The bishops hesitated to make further diocesan appointments, but informal arrangements were made for the clergy of certain areas to be supervised by particular bishops. When Fullarton died in 1727, the clergy of Edinburgh elected Arthur Millar as their diocesan and demanded that the bishops recover the rights of the Church to self-government.

There ensued a strong division between the bishops who were effectively diocesans and the 'College bishops' who had no specific jurisdictions. However in 1731 an agreement was reached whereby no-one was to be consecrated a bishop without the consent of the other bishops. The election of a bishop was to be by the presbyters of the diocese on the mandate of the Primus with the consent of the other bishops. The automatic appointment of the bishop of Edinburgh as Primus was replaced by an election. The Primus was to be convener and president of the College of Bishops, and all bishops were to have districts assigned to them. When this agreement was amplified into a code of canons in 1743 it was specifically stated that the bishops did not seek to encroach upon the rights and privileges of the competent secular powers. It would appear that the bishops still hoped for the re-establishment of Episcopalianism by Parliament. The Jacobite Rising of 1745* ended any such possibility and brought further restrictions upon Episcopal clergy.

All these difficulties had been further complicated by divisions over the 'Usages' at the celebration of the Eucharist. These included the mixing of a little water with the wine at the offertory, the commemoration of the faithful departed, the use of an express prayer of invocation and a formal prayer of oblation. This was linked to controversy over the revival of the Communion service in the *Book of Common Prayer* of 1637. The scholarly work of Thomas Rattray* did much to commend this Scottish liturgy, and a definitive edition was published under the authority of the bishops in 1764.

The accession of George III in 1760 and the deaths of 'James VIII' in 1766 and of Bonnie Prince Charlie in 1788 all eased the pressure on the Episcopalians, but the recovery of the Episcopal Church owed most to the able leadership of John Skinner.* It was he who facilitated the consecration of Samuel Seabury* for the Episcopal Church in the USA, who secured the repeal of the Penal Acts in 1792 and who reconciled the former non-jurors with the 'qualified' Episcopalians at a convocation at Laurencekirk in 1804.

The nineteenth century saw a notable revival in Episcopalianism. The fourteen former dioceses were grouped into seven: Aberdeen and Orkney; Moray, Ross and Caithness; Argyll and the Isles; Brechin; St Andrews, Dunkeld and Dunblane; Glasgow and Galloway; Edinburgh. Each diocese was provided with a cathedral situated in the main centre of population, and an extensive building programme increased the number of churches from 73 to 150 during the twenty years from 1837. During the same period clergy numbers increased from 78 to 163.

The century also saw the development of lay participation. The representative Church Council, which was set up in 1876 with responsibility for the whole finance of the Church, included with the clergy a lay representative from each congregation. In 1905, the Consultative Council on Church Legislation gave the laity* a voice in decisions on canons and liturgy. More recently the whole organization has been entrusted to a General Synod which also includes lay representatives along with the clergy and bishops.

F. Goldie, *A Short History of the Episcopal Church in Scotland* (E, 1976); G. Grub, *Ecclesiastical History of Scotland*, 4 vols (E, 1861); W. R. Foster, *Bishop and Presbytery* (L, 1958); M. Lochhead, *Episcopal Scotland in the Nineteenth Century* (L, 1966); W. Stephen, *History of the Scottish Church*, 2 vols (E, 1896).

H. R. Sefton

Erastianism, *see* Church and State.

Erskine, Charles (1739–1811) Cardinal, was born in Rome, grandson of Sir Alexander Erskine of Cambo, and protégé of Cardinal York.* He attended the Scots College,* Rome, 1748–53, going on to become one of Rome's leading advocates. He was made a domestic prelate (monsignor) in 1782 and ordained subdeacon in 1783. He held various important administrative posts in the Curia.

From 1793 to 1801 Erskine was in England as papal envoy, opening diplomatic channels between the Vatican and the British government. In 1793–4 he visited Scotland.

In 1803 he was made a Cardinal and succeeded Albani as Cardinal Protector of Scotland. In 1810, despite ill health, he was forcibly taken on Napoleon's orders to Paris, where he died.

W. M. Brady, *Anglo-Roman Papers* (Paisley, L, 1890), 121–268; B. Ward, *The Dawn of the Catholic Revival in England* (L, 1909), II.

C. Johnson

Erskine, Ebenezer (1680–1754), a founder of the Secession* church. Born in Dryburgh the son of Henry Erskine* (and older brother of Ralph*), he was educated at Edinburgh (MA, 1697). After serving as tutor and chaplain in the family of the Earl of Rothes (a prominent figure in both Church and state, serving as Commissioner to the General Assembly from 1715 to his death in 1721, and an earnest Christian who continued to show friendship to Erskine throughout his life), Erskine was licensed by the Presbytery of Kirkcaldy and ordained to Portmoak, near Kinross, in 1703.

In his first years at Portmoak, Erskine went through a spiritual struggle, being tempted to unbelief. It was not until he had been over two years in the ministry that he was brought to an acquaintance with what he termed 'the true grace of God', which transformed his ministry. (A record of his thoughts was deciphered from his shorthand and transcribed by Donald Fraser, *The Life and Diary of . . . Ebenezer Erskine*, E, 1831.) His diligence in preparation of sermons and zeal in delivery were greatly increased, and instead of fixing his attention on a stone in the rear wall of the church, he fixed his hearers in the eye! He was transformed into a preacher whom multitudes flocked to hear, particularly in Communion seasons,* from considerable distances. Many of the people of Portmoak, with encouragement from Erskine, habitually took notes of his sermons and discourses; so common was the practice that Erskine occasionally addressed them as the 'scribes'.

Erskine declined to take the Oath of Abjuration* and thereby gained the enmity of Alexander Anderson (of Falkland and St Andrews, later Moderator of the 1735 Assembly), among others. He took an active part in the Marrow Controversy,* joining with the other twelve brethren, particularly in drawing up *The Representation and Petition* . . . (E, 1721) and in preparing the first draft of their answers to the Assembly's commission (*Queries, . . . with the Answers* . . . , 1722). He encountered substantial personal abuse (particularly from Alexander Anderson), and friendships were severed. In 1724 he was considered for a call to the first charge in Kirkcaldy, but after opposition, essentially on the grounds of his participation in the Marrow Controversy, the 1725 Assembly's commission confirmed the Synod of Fife's refusal to allow his name to be put forward. Despite other calls, he remained in Portmoak until 1731, when he was called to a newly created third charge in Stirling.

Although Erskine had previously expressed his abhorrence of settlements according to the Act of Patronage* without or against a call* from the people of a parish, it was the action of the 1731 Assembly in transmitting an overture 'concerning the Method of Planting Vacant Churches' that set in motion the events leading to the Secession. The act overtured Presbyteries to send up their opinions in regard to a proposal that, when a call fell into the hands of Presbytery, *jure devoluto*, it meet with the heritors* and elders and proceed to elect and call someone to propose to the congregation for approval or disapproval, with the disapprovers to give reasons to Presbytery, which would then be free to conclude the matter at its discretion. The Assembly recommended that all take care not to violate this rule (*AGACS*, 614). Although the majority of Presbyteries responding expressed opinions hostile to this proposal, the 1732 Assembly mandated this procedure (*AGACS*, 620–1), thus violating the Barrier Act.* The same Assembly refused to receive a representation and petition (published as *A Publick Testimony; being the Representation and Petition of A considerable Number of Christian People . . . anent Grievances*, E, 1732) signed by some 2,000 people, and a similar document signed by forty-two ministers, of whom Erskine was one. Both complained of the evils of patronage. Erskine was one of fifteen who protested against the Assembly's refusal to hear the petitions and spoke against the Assembly's refusal to receive his dissent from its act on planting churches.

He preached against the 1732 Act on his return to Stirling, but did not consider this adequate to exonerate his conscience. As moderator, in October 1732 he preached a sermon before the Synod of Perth and Stirling against the Act and the growing defections in the Church in matters of both doctrine and government (*The Stone rejected by the Builders, exalted as the Head-Stone of the Corner*, E, 1732). Great offence was taken by some and, after heated debate, by a small majority the Synod voted to rebuke him for expressions used in his sermon. The 1733 Assembly confirmed the Synod's decision and rebuked and admonished Erskine. But after a protest, given in by Erskine and adhered to by William Wilson,* Alexander Moncrieff,* and James Fisher,* was read, the Assembly ordered the four to 'show their sorrow for their conduct and misbehaviour, in offering to protest', and authorized its commission to pass a higher censure in November if they refused to comply. This it did, by the casting vote of the Moderator, loosing them from their charges, declaring their churches vacant and prohibiting CofS ministers from communion with them. The four protested against this decision also.

Erskine joined with Wilson, Moncrieff and Fisher in December 1733 at Gairney Bridge, south of Kinross, in forming the Associate Presbytery,* at first without assuming judicial functions. He took a full part in the affairs of the Presbytery throughout the 1730s. His suspension had the effect predicted by the Presbytery of Stirling: rather than alienate the affections of the people from Erskine, it alienated them from the Church courts. Erskine continued performing his ministerial duties as if no sentence had been passed, but in 1735 declined to serve as Moderator of the Presbytery, judging that no positive reformation had occurred. He differentiated between the established CofS and the Church of Christ in Scotland, holding that 'the last is in a great Measure driven into the Wilderness by the first'. He believed that it would be much safer for brethren who pleaded with him to return to the CofS and help preserve the Lord's work and testimony, rather to come out as well (*The Testimony and Contendings of . . . Alexander Hamilton . . . [with] A Letter . . . from Ebenezer Erskine*, E, 1736, 69–80).

Erskine retained his position in Stirling until his deposition in 1740, on intimation of which he was immediately turned out of the church. Being of 'peaceable disposition', he prevented the congregation from breaking down the doors and retired to preach outdoors. A large congregation, from Stirling and neighbouring parishes, quickly gathered and Erskine ministered both to them and in a variety of other parishes as well, as the Secession cause grew.

With his brother Ralph, he carried on a correspondence with George Whitefield.* He joined in the renewal of the Covenants* in 1743. In the 1745 Rising* he was an ardent supporter of the government and was even appointed captain of a band of volunteers. He maintained that the religious clause in the Burgess Oath* was not such that it should be a term of communion (*The True State of the Question . . .* , E, 1747).

Alexander Moncrieff having gone with the General Associate (Antiburgher) Synod,* Erskine was

ERSKINE, HENRY

chosen to teach divinity. He served in this capacity only until 1749, when he resigned for health reasons. In January 1752 his nephew James Fisher was ordained his colleague and successor.

Erskine's preaching has been widely admired. After Erskine's death, Adam Gib* told a minister who had never heard Erskine, 'Sir, you have never heard the Gospel in its majesty.' The distinctive note of his preaching was an emphasis on God's gracious dealing with men in Christ – *God in Christ, a God of Love*, as the title of one of his sermons has it (E, 1752). His sermons were first published in controversial circumstances, to allow the public to judge of the justice of charges of erroneous or offensive content, and were often accompanied by an explanatory note or preface. Later editions met an increasing demand for their intrinsic value. *A Collection of Sermons*... by Ebenezer and his brother Ralph, edited by Thomas Bradbury, was issued in London in three volumes (1738–50) and several times reprinted. His *Sermons* were first collected by James Fisher (E, 1761, 4 vols) and a number of times reprinted (most recently, *The Whole Works*, 3 vols, L, 1871). A selection was made in *The Beauties*..., ed. S. Macmillan (G, 1830). He contributed to the first part of *The Assembly's Shorter Catechism Explained*... (G, 1753), which, as completed and revised by James Fisher, was widely influential for over a hundred years. His sermons were translated into Dutch and had (and to an extent still have) considerable influence in Holland.

FES IV, 328–9; *DNB* XVII, 404–7; A. R. MacEwen, *The Erskines* (E, 1900); J. Harper, 'Memoir' in *Lives of Ebenezer Erskine*... (E, 1849); Small, II, 663–4; J. M'Kerrow, *History of the Secession Church* (G, 1848).

D. C. Lachman

Erskine, Henry (1624–96), minister. Born in Dryburgh, Berwickshire, he studied at Edinburgh (MA, 1645) and was ordained to Cornhill in Northumberland. He was ejected in 1662 by the Act of Uniformity and moved to Dryburgh. In 1682 he was apprehended and sentenced to imprisonment on the Bass Rock* for exercising his ministerial office illegally, but his sentence was commuted to exile. He lived in England until the Revolution, from the Indulgence of 1687 preaching in the border parish of Whitsome. It was here that Thomas Boston* at age twelve heard him and was brought 'under exercise about [his] soul's state'. In 1690 Erskine was admitted to the parish of Chirnside, near Berwick, where he ministered until his death. He was the father of Ebenezer* and Ralph* Erskine.

FES II, 34.

D. C. Lachman

Erskine, Henry (1746–1817), a leader of the 'Popular' party* in CofS. The son of the tenth Earl of Buchan, he was Lord Advocate in 1783 and 1806–7 in short-lived coalition governments. He had an unsullied reputation for integrity and incorruptibility. With Andrew Crosbie,* with whom he

ERSKINE, JOHN

introduced an unsuccessful attempt to persuade the gentry and heritors to act against patronage,* and later with Sir Henry Wellwood Moncrieff,* he challenged the Moderate* domination of the General Assembly.

DNB XVII, 410–12; A. C. Chitnis, *The Scottish Enlightenment* (L, 1976); R. Sher and A. Murdoch, 'Patronage and Party in the Church of Scotland' in N. Macdougall (ed.), *Church, Politics and Society: Scotland 1408–1929* (E, 1983).

J. R. McIntosh

Erskine, John (1721–1803), leader of the Evangelicals in the CofS in the latter part of the eighteenth century. Born in Edinburgh, Erskine studied at its University from 1734–43, originally for the bar; but he experienced a change of heart and determined on the ministry instead, despite strong parental opposition. Licensed by Dunblane Presbytery in 1743, he was successively minister at Kirkintilloch, Dunbartonshire (1744–53); Culross, Fife (1753–8); New Greyfriars, Edinburgh (1758–67); and Old Greyfriars, Edinburgh (1767–1803). This last was a collegiate charge; Erskine's colleague, ironically, was William Robertson,* the distinguished historian and leading Moderate.*

As a minister, Erskine proved a zealous supporter of the Calvinistic wing of the Evangelical revival. He had been a warm admirer of George Whitefield* from student days, and in 1742 had published a pamphlet, *Signs of the Times* (E, 1742), defending Whitefield against his detractors. He even suggested in the pamphlet that the revival might be a prelude to the Second Coming. Conversely, Erskine opposed the teachings and influence of Wesley* (see his *Mr. Wesley's Principles Detected*, E, 1765), particularly Wesley's doctrine of Christian perfection. He helped prevent Wesley from attracting many followers north of the border.

A contemporary described Erskine thus: 'In his character were concentrated extensive learning; fervent piety; purity of doctrine; energy of sentiment; enlarged benevolence, uniformly animated by an ardent zeal for the glory of his Master and the salvation of men' (quoted in Sir Henry Wellwood Moncrieff's *Account of the Life and Writings of John Erskine*, E, 1818, 478). Erskine does not seem to have been a particularly eloquent preacher, but he had 'much learning, metaphysical acuteness and energy of argument', according to Sir Walter Scott, who portrayed him sympathetically in chapter 37 of his novel *Guy Mannering*.

By his preaching, literary output, church court activities, and personal influence among the upper classes, Erskine contributed powerfully to the evangelical cause in the CofS. His social rank and erudition imparted an air of respectability to his Evangelicalism, and although his relationship with his colleague Robertson was strained at times, especially over the preaching of Whitefield, the Evangelical and the Moderate usually maintained a generous friendship.

A many-faceted man, Erskine was among other things an early champion of the missionary movement; a precursor of the Disruption* fathers in his antagonism to intrusion;* a cordial correspondent of many foreign divines (including Jonathan Edwards*); an ardent Whig;* an opponent of war with the American colonies; and an adversary of Catholic emancipation,* the French Revolution* and the slave trade. He entertained Sandemanian* views of saving faith.

Erskine received a DD from Glasgow University in 1766. He was the uncle of Thomas Erskine of Linlathen.*

Theological Dissertations (L, 1765); *Discourses*, 2 vols (E, 1798-1804); *Dissertation on the Nature of Christian Faith* (E, 1804); *Shall I Go to War with My American Brethren?* (E, 1776). Erskine also edited and prefaced many writings by other theologians. For a complete list, see the article in Chambers-Thomson I, 549-54.

T. Davidson, *A Sketch of the Character of John Erskine* (E, 1803); J. Inglis, *The Memory of the Righteous* (E, 1803); *DNB* XVII, 432-3; *FES* I, 47-8.

N. R. Needham

Erskine, John of Dun (1509-90), laird of Dun (by Montrose), Protestant Reformer. He inherited as a minor after his father and grandfather were killed at Flodden (1513). First ward then client of his uncle, James V's Secretary, Sir Thomas Erskine of Brechin, John Erskine early developed Protestant sympathies, becoming one of Scotland's leading Reformers. Spiritual, principled, yet practical and able to compromise, his influence rivalled even Knox's.*

Though the laird of Dun was associated with George Wishart,* David Straiton* and others accused of heresy during the 1530s and 1540s, his influential uncle probably protected him from similar accusations. Sometimes described in modern writing as 'Lutheran', no hard evidence of John Erskine's pre-1550 doctrinal leanings survives. While his eldest son was reported to have studied under the German Reformer Melanchthon in 1542, the laird of Dun was host to the Swiss-influenced George Wishart in 1543.

Though increasingly supportive of confessed Protestants, John Erskine took care not to fall from favour at court. He married his French second wife, Barbara de Bierle, at an orthodox court ceremony in 1539. She had come to Scotland with Mary of Guise;* Dun was associated with the Queen-Regent until 1559. During the wars of 'The Rough Wooing' (1544-50), John Erskine as Constable of Montrose defended Angus against the Protestant English invasion force. He was part of the delegation sent to France to negotiate the marriage of Mary Queen of Scots* (1557).

His break with the RC Church did not come until 1555, during John Knox's* preaching tour. Erskine organized a debate on the mass in Edinburgh, during which Knox convinced him that believers should not participate in the RC sacrament. Subsequently, he invited Knox to Dun, where they celebrated the Lord's Supper with a group of Mearns lairds. From then John Erskine was a colleague of Knox and a leader among those gentry who maintained Protestant preachers. The Queen-Regent's 1559 attempt to arrest these precipitated the Scottish Reformation.

After 1560, John Erskine's known faith and abilities brought him both recognition as a preacher and appointment as Superintendent* of his home shires of Angus and the Mearns, which office he effectively held (despite changing titles) until his death. His province secured a favourable allocation of funds for stipends. Its parishes were among the best staffed in Scotland, though their ministers and readers were probably selected more for their local connections than for their spiritual credentials. Erskine's pragmatism made for administrative stability; his reformation endured.

John Erskine's few extant writings show concern for the spiritual jurisdiction of the Kirk without excluding that of the state; through life, his theology differed little from that of the First Helvetic Confession (1536). Erskine was also a student of Oecolampadius and preached from the Geneva Bible (*see* Bible (Versions, English)). Though his compromise episcopal national polity (*see* Leith Convention, 1572) was rejected, Erskine was nevertheless architect of a provincial Reformed Kirk suited to Scots society. Godly preacher and shire laird: he was uniquely placed so to do.

Miscellaneous minor tracts, 'Appendix to the Dun Papers' in *Spalding Club Miscellany* IV (A, 1849).

T. Crockett, 'The Life of John Erskine of Dun' (DLitt, Edinburgh University, 1924); F. D. Bardgett, *Scotland Reformed* (E, 1989); V. Jacob, *The Lairds of Dun* (L, 1931); R. S. Wright (ed.), *Fathers of the Kirk* (O, 1960); M. Lynch, 'Calvinism in Scotland, 1559-1638' in M. Prestwich (ed.), *International Calvinism* (O, 1985); A. H. Williamson, *Scottish National Consciousness* (E, 1979); D. G. Mullan, *Episcopacy in Scotland* (E, 1986).

F. D. Bardgett

Erskine, Ralph (1685-1752), minister in Dunfermline. Erskine was born in Monilaws (near Cornhill, Northumberland), son of Henry* and younger brother of Ebenezer.* He studied at Edinburgh (MA, 1704?). He showed evidence of early piety, according to notebooks he kept while a youth. From 1705 to 1709 he was tutor and chaplain in the family of Lieutenant-Colonel John Erskine, and taught John Erskine, the future Professor of Scots Law. He was ordained to the second charge in Dunfermline in 1711 and translated to the first charge in 1716. He exercised his parish responsibilities diligently, with his colleague undertaking an annual public examination and family visitation for the parish of over 5,000 examinable souls. He encouraged 'fellowship meetings' for prayer and religious conversation and occasionally attended himself. In 1715 his colleague in the first charge died. After two years of difficulty a united call was extended to James Wardlaw (*FES* V, 34-5), with whom he sustained a harmonious relationship for nearly twenty years.

He refused to take the Oath of Abjuration,* though a zealous supporter of George I against the claims of the Pretender. He took full part in the Marrow Controversy,* being the first to reply to Thomas Boston's* letter suggesting concerted action, and sharing in the ultimate rebuke. His published sermons from the time of the controversy, particularly in the 1720s, illustrate the doctrines of grace, guard against legalism and proclaim the 'Marrow' doctrine in general. His sermons are full of the love of God and offers of Christ in the gospel.

In his sermons he both opposed John Simson's* errors and spoke against the Arian heresy. He opposed the 1732 Assembly's act on planting churches and in 1733 was party to an unsuccessful appeal of a case involving the settlement of Robert Stark in Kinross against the will of the people. He took great interest in the case of his brother and his three colleagues, attending the meetings of the commission and signing the protest given in by Gabriel Wilson.* He was present at Gairney Bridge and, together with others, including John Willison* and John Currie* (who subsequently wrote with considerable zeal against the Seceders), continued in full fellowship with them. He spoke with fervour against the errors of Professor Archibald Campbell (of St Andrews; FES VII, 431–2) and, after the Assembly failed to take serious disciplinary measures against him, joined the Associate Presbytery,* adhering to the judicial testimony in February 1737, and thus shared in their deposition in 1740. Most of his elders and hearers seceded from the CofS, but not his colleague, James Wardlaw. A church seating some 2,000 was erected, but Erskine continued to take his turn in the parish church, unmolested by the civic authorities until after Wardlaw's death in 1742.

Erskine took full part in the work of the Associate Presbytery, including preaching tours throughout Scotland, and in the renewal of the Covenants,* when he preached *Covenanted Grace for Covenanting Work* (E, 1744).

The Secession attracted considerable interest outside Scotland, and Erskine corresponded with, among others, Gilbert Tennant, John Wesley* and George Whitefield.* Whitefield particularly expressed his gratitude for Erskine's sermons. But, on Whitefield's coming to Scotland, disagreements, particularly over church government, led to a breach. Erskine's most extensive publication was a contribution to the controversy with CofS ministers involved in the Cambuslang revival:* *Faith no Fancy: or, A Treatise of Mental Images* (E, 1745).

In the breach over the Burgess Oath* in 1747, Erskine was persuaded it was not unlawful to take the oath. He was the foremost of the first three names removed from the rolls by the General Associate (Antiburgher) Synod.* His son John was among those voting to censure him. It caused some soul-searching, particularly as to the previous conduct of the Seceders toward those left behind in the CofS. He wrote a number of pamphlets in this controversy, including *Fancy no Faith: or, A Seasonable Admonition* ... (G, 1747).

Erskine continued active until shortly before his death. An obituary characterized him as 'one of the most popular preachers in the church'. He had about forty separate sermons published in his lifetime. *A Collection of Sermons* ... by Ralph and his brother Ebenezer, edited by Thomas Bradbury, was issued in London in three volumes (1738–50). The *Sermons, and Other Practical Works* were issued in two folio volumes (G, 1764–5), and reprinted several times (last edition, 7 vols, L, 1863). A selection was published as *The Beauties* ..., ed. S. McMillan, 2 vols (L, 1812). He had a great reputation as a poet. *Gospel Sonnets* (first published as *Gospel Canticles, or Spiritual Songs*, E, 1720) was many times reprinted. *Scripture Songs* (G, 1754) was an attempt to turn appropriate passages of Scripture into metre for 'the same public use' as the Psalms of David, in accord with the Assembly Act of 1647 and as recommended by the Associate Synod in 1747. His 'Smoking Spiritualized', first appended to *An Elegy ... on the much-lamented Death of ... Alexander Hamilton* (E, 1739), has often been quoted – the refrain, 'Thus think, and smoke tobacco', far more frequently than the verses, 'And when the pipe grows foul within, Think on thy soul defil'd with sin'. Various of his works were printed in America and translations were made into Dutch from 1744, having great influence in the Netherlands. Erskine was noted for playing the violin, something most unusual for a minister in his day.

FES V, 30–2; DNB XVII, 435–6; D. Fraser, *The Life and Diary of ... Ralph Erskine* (E, 1834); A. R. MacEwen, *The Erskines* (E, 1900); J. M'Kerrow, *History of the Secession Church* (E, 1848).

D. C. Lachman

Erskine, Robert (*c*.1500–63), Dean of Aberdeen, uncle to John Erskine of Dun.* He held several benefices, including the parsonages of Glenbervie and Arbuthnott in the Mearns. Dean of Aberdeen from 1540, he was also on the Chapter of Brechin. During the 1550s he associated with the Protestant lairds of the Mearns, and in January 1559 headed a dubiously sincere appeal by the Chapter of Aberdeen to their Bishop, requesting him to set an example of the reformation of morals and practice agreed by the Provincial Councils.* Erskine's influence in Brechin helped to establish the Reformation* there.

'The Dun Papers', in *Spalding Club Miscellany* IV (A, 1849); F. D. Bardgett, *Scotland Reformed* (E, 1989); V. Jacob, *The Lairds of Dun* (L, 1931).

F. D. Bardgett

Erskine, Thomas (of Linlathen) (1788–1870), influential Scottish lay theological writer. Nephew of John Erskine,* leading CofS Evangelical, Thomas was brought up largely within the EpCS* through the influence of his mother and Jacobite* grandmother. Despite this Episcopalian background, his adult connections were mainly with Scottish Congregationalism* and the CofS.

ERSKINE, THOMAS

Erskine's religious awakening came around 1805 through the writings of John Foster, an English Calvinistic Baptist. A time of doubt some six years later impelled him to study the evidences of Christianity, from which ultimately emerged his first book, *Remarks on the Internal Evidence for the Truth of Revealed Religion* (E, 1820; 9th ed. rev., 1829), in which he argued that Christianity's truth was demonstrated by its correspondence with man's moral and spiritual needs (*see* Apologetics*). It was well received by the orthodox world, although its theology was that of a moderate moral government Calvinist.

Several minor works followed, but Erskine's next full-length book, *The Unconditional Freeness of the Gospel* (E, 1828; new ed. rev., 1873) provoked a storm of criticism for its advocacy of a doctrine of universal atonement* and pardon – that through Christ's death, all are in a state of forgiveness. The same year Erskine met John McLeod Campbell* of Row, and their names became joined as twin heresiarchs in the estimation of the orthodox during the 'Row controversy' of 1828–31, although Erskine took the brunt of the criticism. Erskine and Campbell became lifelong friends; Campbell's mature soteriology, including his doctrine of Christ's vicarious repentence, is seminally present in Erskine's *The Brazen Serpent* (E, 1831).

At this time Erskine also encountered Edward Irving,* and adopted his views on premillennialism, Christ's fallen humanity and the gifts of the Spirit. Initially he supported the 'Irvingite' charismatic movement, although never exercising any of the reputed gifts himself. His confidence, however, underwent a crisis in 1833–4, well documented in his published letters, and he abandoned the movement as delusive (*see* Catholic Apostolic Church).

The Doctrine of Election (L, 1837) concluded Erskine's breach with Calvinism. He repudiated the Calvinistic doctrine of election as inconsistent with God's love and justice. Christ, Erskine maintained, was the elect one, and men share in his election by freely yielding to the universal influences of his Spirit.

Erskine's theology shows an increasing preoccupation with conscience as the criterion of truth. He came to regard God as a universal Father who is educating all men into a filial relationship with himself through the indwelling of Christ the eternal Son in the human race, and from c.1840 he embraced the ultimate salvation of all as the quintessential gospel.

Erskine had a wide influence, both through his early writings (nothing more was published in his lifetime after 1837), and through his circle of friends, which included F. D. Maurice, Benjamin Jowett, Dean Stanley, Bishop Ewing,* and Alexander Scott.* In these ways Erskine contributed significantly to the liberalizing of nineteenth-century British theology.

Erskine derived his agnomen from his estate in Linlathen, near Dundee.

The Spiritual Order (E, 1871); *Essay on Faith* (E, 1822; 5th ed. revised 1829); *The Gifts of the Holy Spirit* (Greenock, 1830).

W. Hanna, *Letters of Thomas Erskine*, 2 vols (E, 1877); N. R. Needham, *Thomas Erskine of Linlathen* (E, 1989); H. F. Henderson, *Erskine of Linlathen* (E, 1899); J. S. Candlish, 'Thomas Erskine of Linlathen', *British and Foreign Evangelical Review* 22 (1873), 105–28; J. Tulloch, *Movements of Religious Thought in Britain during the Nineteenth Century* (L, 1885), 125–45; *DNB* XVII, 444–5; T. A. Hart, *The Teaching Father . . .* (E, 1993).

N. R. Needham

Esdaile School and Trust, for the education of daughters of ministers of the CofS. The School was instituted in 1863 by James Esdaile, Calcutta, and David Esdaile, minister of Rescobie, near Forfar (1811–80; *FES* V, 303), and was situated in Kilgraston Road, Edinburgh. In 1969 the Esdaile Trust Scheme empowered the governors to sell the school, and the funds were invested to provide educational grants. The School was originally open to daughters of professors in the Scottish universities, as well as to those of ministers. Daughters of ordained missionaries and widowed deaconesses, as well as of ministers, are included in the 1969 scheme.

RGACS, 1970, 12, 13; *CofS Year Books*.

J. L. Weatherhead

Establishment, *see* Church and State.

Ethics, Christian. The history of Christian ethics in Scotland cannot be separated from the development of moral philosophy,* especially the Scottish school of Common Sense (*see* Scottish Realism). Since the Reformation, Calvinism* undergirded theology and practice. Christian ethics was not seen as a separate discipline, but rather the inevitable concomitant of living the Christian life. In so far as Christian ethics did develop, it was through moral philosophers who, with the notable exception of David Hume,* found in nature evidence of design and a providential governor of the universe, who naturally revealed to us our duties to ourselves, each other and God.

Within a framework of natural law, the Scottish school of Common Sense stressed that reason was able to judge the first and necessary principles in logic, mathematics, morals, aesthetics and religion. These first principles were part of the constitution and structure of the human mind as a gift from heaven. Unless we could take for granted some immutable foundation to rely on in ethical matters and some basic principles of human character and conduct, moral decision-making would be impossible.

Within the Aberdeen Philosophical Society, the main body expressing the Common Sense philosophy, George Campbell,* Professor of Divinity, and Thomas Reid (1710–96) defended common sense against philosophical scepticism. Even the behaviour of those who tried to reject common sense was governed by the truths of common sense, which were so fundamentally part of human nature and determined the structure of our moral and everyday language that to offer an alternative view would require another language.

Moral principles are self-evident and a fundamental part of human nature. God is the author of human nature and the source of morality both in the design of the world and humanity. The fundamental moral principles are universal and known directly by intuition. Obviously, people's awareness and consciences can be developed or deadened. The appeal to self-evidence was to mature consciousness, rather than some simplistic naive realism. The objective nature of morals ensured both the possibility of moral discussion and the resolution of moral differences. Both Christian and non-Christian alike perceive the truth of moral principles by the process of intuition.

Dugald Stewart,* Professor of Moral Philosophy in Edinburgh, continued to study the fundamental principles and laws of human belief. Theism and morality were inevitably intertwined. On the basis of the argument from design, God's role in endowing human nature and the natural realm with morality was ensured. Human beings have an irreducible awareness of right and wrong. Moral principles have a universal appeal and force. Morality is objective and not a matter of taste or individual preference.

In all this the religious believer has the benefit not only of perceiving more clearly the nature of moral duties but, in Christ, has a new motivation to obey these demands. If Scripture commands new obligations, these are dependent on the more basic duties.

Christian ethics as a separate discipline waited until the mid-twentieth century for its birth.

T. Reid, *An Inquiry into the Human Mind, on the Principles of Common Sense* (E, 1764); D. Stewart, *Elements of the Philosophy of the Human Mind*, 3 vols (L, 1792–1827); T. Brown, *Lectures on the Philosophy of the Human Mind* (E, 1820); D. Stewart, *The Philosophy of the Active and Moral Powers of Man*, 2 vols (E, L, 1828); T. Martin, *The Instructed Vision. Scottish Common Sense Philosophy and the Origins of American Fiction* (Bloomington, 1961).

E. D. Cook

Eucharist, *see* Lord's Supper.

Euchologion, the service book produced by the Church Service Society* in the CofS in the late nineteenth century to provide forms of service and other material for the conduct of public worship. The first edition was brought out in 1867 and a total of eleven editions had been published by 1924. The first edition was in two parts, the first containing orders for the administration of the sacraments and the conduct of marriage and funeral services, the second containing a lectionary and material for use in Sunday services. Prayers were gathered from a variety of sources, from the Kirk's own traditions, but also from Eastern and Roman liturgies and from the *Liturgy and Divine Office* of the Catholic Apostolic Church.* The compilers stated that they did not wish to impose a liturgy on the Church. Rather they wished to offer forms of prayer which could be used within the existing forms of Presbyterian worship. *Euchologion* played an important part in preparing the way for the official service books produced by the Presbyterian Churches in the twentieth century.

See also Liturgy; *Book of Common Order* (modern editions).

Church Service Society, *Euchologion, A Book of Common Order* (E, 1867–1924); G. W. Sprott (ed.), *Euchologion* (E, 1905).

J. Kerr, *The Renascence of Worship* (E, 1909); D. M. Murray, 'Disruption to Union' in D. B. Forrester and D. M. Murray (eds), *Studies in the History of Worship in Scotland* (E, 1984), 79–95.

D. M. Murray

Evangelical Alliance, an interdenominational voluntary society. The Evangelical Alliance arose from a mood of millennial* expectation and associated yearning for unity among Evangelicals in a variety of countries and denominations in the early 1840s, reinforced by opposition to RCism. In Scotland a central impulse came from the newly-formed FC after the Disruption.* Thomas Chalmers* and Robert Candlish* were leading supporters. A preliminary meeting was held in Liverpool in October 1845 at the invitation of a group of Scottish Evangelicals. This was followed by an international conference in London in August 1846, attended by Evangelicals from America and Continental Europe. This formally established the organization. Its impact outside Britain was however limited by the hostility of the main Protestant Churches in Germany and Scandinavia, and initially by divisions over slavery in the USA. Moreover, after the early years support in Scotland itself became intermittent and lukewarm.

The Evangelical Alliance has sought to promote brotherly love between individual Evangelicals, international co-operation, vision, prayer and mission. It has also been a staunch advocate of religious liberty. After a period of stagnation in the early twentieth century it has recovered in the period since the Second World War* to become an important force in English Evangelicalism, and increasingly in Scotland, Wales and Ireland also. (A Scottish Evangelical Alliance was formed in 1992.) The FC and Baptist Union of Scotland are members. It is linked internationally, through the World Evangelical Fellowship.

J. Wolffe, 'The Evangelical Alliance in the 1840s', *Studies in Church History* 23 (1986), 333–46; R. Rouse and S. C. Neill (eds), *A History of the Ecumenical Movement, 1517–1948* (L, 1954); J. B. A. Kessler, *A Study of the Evangelical Alliance in Great Britain* (Goes, Netherlands, 1968); John W. Ewing, *Goodly Fellowship: A Centenary Tribute to the Life and Work of the World's Evangelical Alliance 1846–1946* (L, E, 1946).

J. R. Wolffe

Evangelical Quarterly, The, 'a theological review, international in scope and outlook, in defence of the historic Christian faith', founded in 1929 by J. R. Mackay* and D. Maclean,* professors in the FC College, Edinburgh. An editorial note which has appeared in each issue since April 1943 describes its purpose as 'the reverent exposition of the Reformed faith' – i.e. the faith expressed in the Thirty-Nine Articles, the Westminster* Confession of Faith and other standard documents of the Reformation.

In 1930 the editors were joined by two associate editors, G. C. Aalders and O. T. Allis (the latter had been editor of the *Princeton Theological Review* until its abrupt termination in April 1929). When illness forced Mackay's resignation in 1935, he was replaced by John Macleod* (with the title of consulting editor). About that time an attempt was made to expand the *Quarterly*'s scope and circulation by including anthropology; responsibility for this area fell to G. R. Gair, co-opted as directing editor. This experiment lasted barely three years. With the outbreak of World War II, existing resources could no longer sustain the financial maintenance of the *Quarterly*. In 1942 ownership was transferred to the Inter-Varsity Fellowship,* which agreed to sponsor it for a limited period. In 1956 the Paternoster Press undertook responsibility for its publication.

After Maclean's death (1943), J. H. S. Burleigh* served as editor for seven years; he was succeeded by F. F. Bruce* (1950) and he in turn by I. H. Marshall (1981). Changes in editorship may have been reflected in the areas of interest served by contributors and their contributions, but the *Quarterly*'s theological commitment remains unchanged.

A number of well-known writers made their literary debut in its pages: they include Lord Coggan, G. W. Bromiley, P. E. Hughes, T. F. Torrance,* J. K. S. Reid, J. Barr. One of its valuable services continues to be the introduction of younger scholars to a public that will be interested in their work. Its review pages have for long been a helpful feature.

See also Periodicals, Religious.

EQ, Editorials, 1 (1929), 1–2; 28 (1956), 1–4; 40 (1968), 193–6.

F. F. Bruce

Evangelical Repository, one of the three most significant periodicals of the Evangelical Union* (the others being the *Christian News*, founded 1846, and *Forward*, founded 1868). Established in 1854, the quarterly *Repository* was initially published by Lang, Adamson & Co. of Glasgow and edited by James Morison,* and aimed to propound the theological views of those Churches which had joined the Union, having 'recoiled from Scottish Calvinism' (*see* Atonement Controversy). For thirty-four years theological articles, book reviews, and Union news items appeared in its pages: it became a monthly in 1886, and was finally wound up because of unprofitability in 1888 by its then publisher, Thomas D. Morison. James Morison was succeeded in 1869 as editor by Fergus Ferguson (junior, 1824–97; *Memoirs*..., by T. C. Newall, G, n.d.; *Scottish Congregationalist* n.s. 10, 1897, 298–300), and he in turn gave way in 1886 to William Adamson (1830–1910; *Who Was Who, 1897–1916*, 5; *Scottish Congregationalist* n.s. 6, 1910, 84, 102).

W. Adamson, *The Life of the Rev. James Morison, D.D.* (L, 1898), 313ff.; H. Escott, *A History of Scottish Congregationalism* (G, 1960), 132f.

J. A. H. Dempster

Evangelical Union, an association of Arminian Congregational churches (sometimes called 'Morisonians'), which flourished in the latter part of the nineteenth century.

The Union was constituted in a series of meetings held in May 1843 by James Morison,* Robert Morison, John Guthrie* and A. C. Rutherford, four ministers who had been deposed from the USecC* over the period 1841–3 for their views on universal atonement. By the time of the Union's inception they were avowed Arminians,* holding to conditional election, Sandemanian* views of faith, and a pneumatology which made the Spirit's work as universal as they conceived the atonement to be, and dependent on human free-will for its effect. They had also relinquished Presbyterian views of church polity in favour of Congregationalism* (although retaining a plurality of elders, unlike Congregational Union* churches), and adopted an anti-credal stance – the Bible alone was their doctrinal standard (*see* Confessions of Faith).

The Evangelical Union was founded as a purely voluntary association of churches, for 'mutual countenance, counsel and co-operation in supporting and spreading the glorious, simple, soul-saving and heart-sanctifying gospel of the grace of God' (quoted J. Ross, *A History of Congregational Independency in Scotland*, G, 1900, 141). The language indicates the context of 'revival' preaching in which the Union was born, particularly the influence of Charles Finney, who was James Morison's theological mentor (*see* Revivals). This Finneyite emphasis was to characterize the Union throughout its life.

The Evangelical Union had thirteen parent congregations: the four Secession* churches of its ministerial founding fathers, and nine churches from the Congregational Union which adhered to it to escape the latter Union's then prevalent Calvinism.

The evangelistic zeal of the new movement had a powerful urban thrust. Working class people formed the bulk of its converts. Within thirty years eighty-two Evangelical Union churches had been established, and ninety by the time of the merger between the Evangelical and Congregational Unions in 1896, in areas as far apart as Shapinsay in the Orkneys and Dalbeattie in Dumfriesshire.

The Union movement was committed to the cause of temperance.* No one involved in the liquor trade was ever admitted into membership of a Union church. Ethical rigorism, however, coexisted with liturgical breadth, including the acceptance of hymns and organs. The first organ authorized in Scottish Presbyterian or Congregational worship

EVANGELICALISM

was introduced into North Dundas Street Evangelical Union Church, Glasgow, in 1851 (H. Escott, *A History of Scottish Congregationalism*, G, 1959, 159, n.1). Uninspired hymnody was accepted from the Union's commencement. James Morison edited its first hymnbook in 1844. *The Evangelical Union Hymnal* of 1878 became the hymnbook of the merged Evangelical and Congregational Unions, with some additions from the old *Scottish Congregational Hymnal*. (*See* Musical Instruments in Worship; Hymnology, English.)

The Union had an annual conference to which each member church could send two delegates. The conference controlled the Union's Theological Academy, Home Mission, Foreign Mission, Sabbath School, Publications and Temperance departments (all aspects of Union work except the Ministers' Provident Fund), but it had no jurisdiction over the internal business of individual churches.

James Morison zealously preserved the Presbyterian ideal of an educated ministry in the Union through its Theological Academy, which met in various places during its history, ending up in premises in Regent Park, Glasgow. Morison was its principal tutor; all teachers were pastors, and the curriculum was modelled on that of the USec.C.

On 1 January, 1897 the Evangelical Union ended its separate history by amalgamating with the Congregational Union.

See also Congregationalism; Fairbairn, A. M.; Kirk, John; Richardson, Charles.

Fergus, Ferguson, *A History of the Evangelical Union* (G, 1876); *The Worthies of the Evangelical Union* (G, 1883).

N. R. Needham

Evangelicalism, the movement emphasizing the need to pass on the gospel. The term 'Evangelical' was sometimes used in the sixteenth century as a synonym for 'Protestant', but by the end of the eighteenth century had become restricted to the groups within English-speaking Protestantism that continued to uphold orthodoxy and promote evangelism. Evangelicalism has become a worldwide interdenominational movement.

The characteristics of Evangelicalism begin with the need for conversion. Believing that human beings are sinners, Evangelicals have declared the need for a change of life when the gospel is received. They hold that justification* is by faith alone. They have differed about whether conversion must be sudden or may be gradual. Effort for the spread of the gospel makes Evangelicals notably activist. Commonly, but not consistently, activism has extended into the sphere of social concern.* Evangelicals have also been biblicist. They have regarded the Bible as the source of the gospel. In their theological scheme the cross is central. Although not all strands of the movement have maintained a substitutionary understanding of the atonement,* that view has been normal. Calvinists* have commonly held that Christ died only for the elect, whereas Arminians* have held that he died for all humanity. Beyond the basic characteristics there have been great variations over time and space.

EIGHTEENTH-CENTURY ORIGINS. The movement began, almost simultaneously but virtually independently, in America, Wales, England and Scotland. In the town of Northampton, Massachusetts, revival broke out in 1734–5. Jonathan Edwards* (1703–58), the Congregational minister, published an account, *A Faithful Narrative of the Surprizing Work of God, in the Conversion of Many Hundred Souls . . .* (Boston, 1737), which helped stir up 'the Great Awakening' in America of 1740–3. In 1735 Howel Harris (1714–73) and Daniel Rowlands (1713–90) were converted and began their preaching ministries in Wales. George Whitefield* and John Wesley* took the same path in England in 1735–7 and 1738 respectively. Whitefield roused parts of Scotland in 1741, and in the next year the Scottish sequence of revivals* was inaugurated at Cambuslang. The theological bond between these developments was the emergence of a strong doctrine of assurance.* Converts were encouraged to believe that trust in Christ normally issued in a vivid sense of personal salvation. The resulting conviction was the dynamic of Evangelicalism.

Wesley's Methodists,* who were few in Scotland, and Whitefield's Calvinistic Methodists, who never organized in Scotland at all, emerged as new denominations from the upsurge of spiritual life. In the CofE isolated clergy underwent conversion experiences and gradually formed a party professing Calvinistic views. English dissent was revitalized towards the end of the eighteenth century, and both Baptists* and Congregationalists* expanded rapidly. In America most denominations were affected by the new religious temper and engaged in vigorous evangelism on the expanding frontier.

In the CofS a section of the ministry led by John MacLaurin,* John Erskine* and John Gillies* fostered this teaching. When non-evangelical ministers were imposed on unwilling parishes, parishioners often responded by abandoning the CofS in order to form congregations of the Secession churches or the Relief Church.* Evangelicalism gave a powerful impetus to Presbyterian dissenters,* who by 1835 formed nearly one-third of the worshippers in the main cities. Nevertheless the movement also transformed the CofS under the leadership of Sir Henry Wellwood Moncreiff,* Andrew Thomson* and then Thomas Chalmers,* so that by the 1830s it had become the dominant party in the General Assembly.*

DEVELOPMENTS IN SCOTLAND AND BEYOND. The evangelistic impulse that in England generated Wesley's field preaching, led in Scotland to renewed efforts to carry the gospel to the Highlands.* The CofS, the Secession,* the Society for Propagating the Gospel at Home* of the Haldanes* and the itinerancy* promoted by Christopher Anderson* all contributed to home mission. Overseas missions,* though rejected by the General Assembly in 1796, were supported by the Baptists from 1792 and the London Missionary Society* from 1795. The CofS sent out its first missionary, Alexander Duff,* in 1830. Some of the best known Scottish Evangelicals, including David Livingstone,* were to be missionaries. Missions made Evangelicalism a cohesive worldwide movement.

In the years around 1830 leading Evangelicals were affected by the new intellectual currents associated with Romanticism. The effects were most marked in the circle of Edward Irving,* who in the 1820s concluded that the second advent of Christ would be personal and premillennial. The resulting premillennial adventism was taken up by Irving's Catholic Apostolic Church,* by Horatius Bonar,* its chief propagandist in Scotland, and by J. N. Darby (1800–82), whose dispensational brand of adventism was typical of the Brethren.* Another symptom of this intellectual ferment was the repristination by Robert Haldane* of the historic Protestant doctrine of verbal inspiration, as against the looser views which had been current in the eighteenth century. His views led him to provoke the Apocrypha Controversy* by questioning the inclusion of the Apocrypha in Bibles published for the continent by the British and Foreign Bible Society.

From the same period there was a broadening of evangelical theological attitudes. Thomas Erskine* of Linlathen and John McLeod Campbell* abandoned and criticized Calvinism, and in the second half of the century others, sometimes under German influence, were to adopt similarly softened doctrinal views. In America the evangelist Charles Finney (1792–1875) developed techniques for encouraging revivals that were associated with Arminian teaching and with a theology of conversion that minimized the supernatural element. In Scotland Finney's thought and practice were imitated by the Evangelical Union.* Not all revivalism, in Scotland in mid-century was of this type, however, for R. Murray McCheyne* and his circle remained loyal to Calvinism.

The Disruption* of 1843 created a wholly evangelical FCS, but left a significant and growing evangelical section in the Est.C. In the same year, D. T. K. Drummond* seceded from the EpCS, which had generated only a small evangelical presence, to set up St Thomas', Edinburgh, as an outpost of English evangelical Anglicanism. An effort to consolidate world evangelicalism from 1846 in the Evangelical Alliance,* though enthusiastically supported in Scotland, did not reverse the tendency to fragmentation. Far more was done for interdenominational co-operation by ongoing concerns such as the Sunday School Movement* and by the revival of 1859–60, inspired by a great revival in Ulster. Co-operation was further encouraged by the evangelistic campaigns of the Americans D. L. Moody* and I. D. Sankey in Edinburgh and Glasgow in 1873–4. Their efforts left a legacy of commitment to evangelism, subsequently nurtured by the Bible Training Institute, Glasgow,* and a dedication to advancing civic righteousness.

Social concern* in the form of organized philanthropy was a major feature of nineteenth-century Evangelicalism. Societies for charitable purposes proliferated. Anti-slavery* carried the mass evangelical public into the political arena and subsequently their major social concerns often had a political edge: that was true of the anti-Catholic societies* and the sabbatarianism* that reached the peak of their influence in the 1850s. Temperance,* at first frowned on as a diversion from the gospel, gathered momentum in the later nineteenth century and on into the twentieth. Individuals took up particular causes: James Begg* demanded housing reform and William Quarrier* set up a children's home. Gradually commitment to reform broadened into the social gospel, a supplement to, rather than a substitute for, the individual gospel, at least in its earlier years. Among the Scottish champions of this worldwide evangelical phenomenon was A. Scott Matheson.*

CHANGES SINCE THE 1870S. From the 1870s onwards international Evangelicalism was swept by a wave of holiness teaching, adapted from the early Wesleyan conviction that a believer could receive entire sanctification in this life. The main centre was the annual Keswick Convention, begun in 1875, but local holiness gatherings multiplied (*see* Conventions). A Scottish National Convention was regularly held at Bridge of Allan from 1892 and a Scottish Northern Convention at Strathpeffer from 1931. One of the chief exponents of Keswick teaching around 1900 was Andrew Murray,* and from the 1920s until the 1950s another was to be W. Graham Scroggie.* Other groups including the Salvation Army* and the Faith Mission* sprang up with evangelism and holiness teaching as their *raison d'être*. In America the numerous holiness churches formed the setting in which Pentecostalism* emerged at the beginning of the twentieth century, and soon it spread to Britain.

Biblical criticism* began to unsettle evangelical churches in the 1870s. The FC was racked by debate over the views of W. Robertson Smith,* but fears were mollified by the emergence of 'Believing Criticism',* which was widely disseminated in biblical commentaries by George Adam Smith.* The rise of evolutionary theory was less worrying, not least because of its integration in apologetic by Henry Drummond (1851–97).* The international broadening of views into theological liberalism* was challenged in the early twentieth century by the booklets called *The Fundamentals*.* In the wake of the First World War there emerged in America the phenomenon of Fundamentalism, a militant brand of Evangelicalism largely inspired by premillennial teaching that was hostile to liberalism ('Modernism'). There were echoes of the resulting uproar throughout the world, though they were at their faintest in Scotland. Not until the 1940s, and then only among the Baptists, was there a Scottish Fundamentalist controversy.

Community-based revivalism* continued into the twentieth century, conspicuous examples being the Jock Troup* revival of the early 1920s and the Hebrides revival of the early 1950s. For a while in the early 1930s a version of revivalism using novel techniques was organized by the Oxford Group, an early phase of Moral Rearmament.* Evangelism of and by students was undertaken by the Student Christian Movement* and the more conservative Inter-Varsity Fellowship,* supported (among others) by Duncan Blair* and Daniel Lamont.* The Scripture Union* promoted evangelism among children. The later 1940s and 1950s formed a golden age of co-operative evangelism led by Tom Allan* and D. P. Thomson.* Its focus was the Tell Scotland* campaign that included the visit of the American evangelist Billy Graham* to the Kelvin Hall, Glasgow, in 1955.

Suspicions of the ecumenical movement* set many post-war conservative Evangelicals apart from the mainstream of Scottish Church life. Yet there were signs of vigour in the work of William Still* and the Crieff Fraternal* in the CofS, in the inter-denominational Scottish Evangelical Theology Society* and in the foundation of Rutherford House.* The FPCS and post-1900 FCS stoutly championed Reformed theology, and the Baptists perpetuated a less theologically structured commitment to evangelism. From the 1960s the charismatic movement* began to have a notable impact on evangelical life, particularly in the sphere of worship.

D. W. Bebbington, *Evangelicalism in Modern Britain* (L, 1989); A. S. Wood, *The Inextinguishable Blaze* (L, 1960); J. MacInnes, *The Evangelical Movement in the Highlands of Scotland, 1688 to 1800* (A, 1951); S. J. Brown, *Thomas Chalmers and the Godly Commonwealth in Scotland* (O, 1982); G. M. Marsden, *Fundamentalism and American Culture* (NY, 1980); S. Bruce, *Firm in the Faith* (Aldershot, 1984); J. D. Allan, *The Evangelicals* (Exeter, 1989); K. G. Robbins (ed.), *Protestant Evangelicalism* (O, 1990).

D. W. Bebbington

Eventide Homes, communal residential provision for the elderly, made by several Churches in Scotland.

The CofS's traditional commitment to combining its evangelical message with a practical out-working of the gospel has been seen very clearly in caring for older people. The first Home opened by the CofS for old people was in 1926, a noticeable twenty-two years before the National Assistance Act which gave Local Authorities power to house old people. It offered accommodation to thirty-five residents in 'sparsely furnished rooms with little privacy – sittingrooms equipped with gifts of old chairs from interested donors, ill-assorted and rather dilapidated; bedrooms had a variety of iron bedsteads with flock mattresses and one large wardrobe'. Even at that early stage it was recognized that residential care was not an easy alternative to living on one's own, and the development of Homes was slow. Between 1926 and 1937 only four Homes were built, between 1937 and 1963 a further twenty-seven, indicating a growth in acceptance of residential care as a way of helping older people unable to live alone.

The Church has always sought to adapt and adjust to different forms of care. In the mid-1950s, cottages were built specially to accommodate elderly couples as an alternative to fully communal residential care, and in the mid-1960s two schemes of flatlets for ladies offered another alternative, in that only the mid-day meal was prepared by staff, and the ladies furnished their own large room and otherwise catered for themselves. While this may seem from the vantage point of the 1990s of little import, it should be noted that these developments were at least abreast, if not ahead, of the time.

In the more recent past, trends changed towards providing amenity housing. Kirk Care, which has grown into a major provider of 'sheltered' housing, has illustrated the CofS's willingness to adapt and diversify its caring. By the late 1970s and early 1980s the condition known as senile dementia was beginning to be diagnosed. The CofS through its Board of Social Responsibility* proved to be innovative and pioneering by providing the first Home specifically for sufferers of senile dementia.

During the period in which the CofS has sought to address the needs of older people, several beginnings have come full circle. The original flatlets, for example, have developed into sheltered housing, and the special care annexes, set up in the 1950s and 1960s to cater for frail ambulant people, no longer exist. Because over the years those coming into residential care have become older and frailer, the norm for residential care is now that which was once catered for in the special care annexe. While in the past it was usual for residents to remain in CofS care for thirty years, the average length of stay is now three years. As the Church values old people and seeks to meet the continuing demands, respite care, which offers short-term residence with relief for those who normally provide care in the home, is increasing.

These Eventide Homes, of which in 1991 there were forty-three throughout Scotland, represent a distinguished contribution by the CofS to the social welfare of the population. Similar provision for the elderly has also been made by other Scottish churches. The Baptists run four homes, the Salvation Army about ten, the Seventh-Day Adventists have one at Leven in Fife, the RCC has several catering for differing needs, the FC runs Maxwell House in Glasgow, and the FPC has two homes in N. Scotland.

RGACS 1976, 307–9; list of CofS Homes in current *Year-Book*.

F. S. Gibson

Ewart, David (1806–60), missionary to India. Born in Upper Balloch, Perthshire, on 24th September 1806, he entered St Andrews University in 1821, the same year as Alexander Duff,* his future co-worker. In 1823 he attended Thomas Chalmers's* first class at St Andrews, and, to finish his divinity course, followed Chalmers to Edinburgh for the 1829/30 session.

In 1834 Ewart accepted a teaching position at the CofS's Seminary in Calcutta and was ordained to that position, John Bruce* presiding. At the Disruption* he joined the FC and added to his seminary

EWING, ALEXANDER

labours the pastorate of Scots FC, Calcutta. After twenty-two years of continuous labours, he returned to Scotland in 1856. He returned to India in 1858 and died there of cholera.

Of robust physique and ruddy complexion, Ewart was an energetic teacher. Although awarded the DD by St Andrews, Ewart did not pretend to great scholarship. He was popular with weaker students, with whom he had inexhaustible patience.

S. Piggin and J. Roxborogh, *The St Andrews Seven* (E, 1985); *FES* VII, 693.

S. Piggin

Ewing, Alexander (1814–73), Bishop of Argyll and the Isles. Born in Edinburgh, he was educated at Aberdeen University. His lifelong antipathy to Calvinism,* then prevalent in all other Scottish Protestant Churches, impelled him to take refuge in the Arminian* traditions of the EpCS,* from which he received ordination in 1838. In 1842 he took charge of a new EpCS church at Forres in Moray. In 1847 he was consecrated Bishop of Argyll and the Isles.

Ewing's hostility to Calvinism was matched by his antagonism to the non-juring* high church theology favoured by many Scottish Episcopalians, and his career as a bishop was dogged by controversy. His outspoken disbelief in any corporeal presence of Christ in the Eucharist aroused considerable contention, while his rejection of apostolic succession* caused uproar. In truth, Ewing was closer to the liberal Anglican perspective of a man like F. D. Maurice than he was to any school of thought in his own Church. His gospel was the universal fatherhood of God and the ultimate salvation of all humanity. John McLeod Campbell* and Thomas Erskine* of Linlathen were his spiritual mentors.

Present Day Papers on Prominent Questions in Theology, 3 vols (L, 1870–5); *Revelation Considered as Light* (L, 1873); *Episcopacy in Scotland* (L, 1845); *The Celtic Church of the West Highlands* (E, 1864).

A. J. Ross, *Memoir of Alexander Ewing* (L, 1877); J. C. Lees, 'Bishop Ewing' in *St Giles Lectures, 3rd Series* (E, 1883), 353–89; *DNB Miss. Pers.* 215.

N. R. Needham

Ewing, Greville (1767–1841), a primary architect of Scottish Congregationalism* and pioneer statesman of Scottish foreign missions. Born at Edinburgh and educated at its High School, Ewing trained as an engraver before preparing for the CofS ministry at Edinburgh University. Ordained in 1793 as associate minister of Lady Glenorchy's* Chapel, Edinburgh, Ewing rapidly gained influence as an expository preacher and proponent of home and foreign missions. He helped to establish the *Missionary Magazine** (1796–8), Scotland's first missionary periodical (*see* Periodicals, Religious), and was the first secretary of the Edinburgh Missionary Society (*see* Missions). From 1796 he began an association with Robert and James Haldane* that lasted until 1808. It encompassed successively a failed attempt to mount a mission to

EXEGESIS, BIBLICAL

India, support for an itinerating ministry throughout Scotland, the establishment of the 'Tabernacle' preaching centres in Scotland's major cities, and the tutoring of the movement's theological students on the then-emerging 'academy' model. These enterprises illustrated his eclecticism in the interests of gospel proclamation and his growing impatience with the inelasticity of the CofS, whose ministry he left in 1798. When the Haldane-funded 'Tabernacle' movement, which had coalesced into early Congregationalism,* foundered due to changes in the donors' attitudes regarding baptism and Church order in 1807–8, Ewing, in company with Ralph Wardlaw* and others, followed through their principles with the establishment of Glasgow Theological Academy (1811) and the Congregational Union* (1812). The Haldane-initiated dissensions provoked Ewing's writings *An Attempt towards a Statement . . . on Some Disputed Points* (G, 1807), *Facts and Documents Respecting . . . Robert Haldane, Esq. and Greville Ewing* (G, 1809), and *An Essay on Baptism* (G, 1823). He combined theological lecturing with a Glasgow pastorate until 1836. Strongly Calvinistic in theology and honoured with a Princeton DD in 1821, Ewing imbued the first generations of Congregational ministers with his ideals of biblical exposition and ministry.

DNB XVIII, 95; *FES* I, 79–80; J. J. Matheson [daughter], *Memoir of Greville Ewing* (L, 1843); H. Escott, *A History of Scottish Congregationalism* (G, 1960).

K. J. Stewart

Excommunication, *see* Discipline.

Exegesis, Biblical. Before the Reformation, Scotland produced little of note in biblical exegesis. At the Abbey of St Victor in Paris (a school of biblical study of wide-ranging importance in medieval Christendom), the Scot Richard of St Victor* engaged in significant exegetical work. He defended the unity of the senses of Scripture and the reference of Isaiah 7:14 to Mary's virginal conception, and gave a literal description of the temple of Ezekiel.

POST-REFORMATION. Scottish contributions to biblical exegesis in the post-Reformation age may be said to have begun with Latin and English commentaries, published between 1591 and 1606, including works on John, several Pauline Epistles, and Daniel, by Robert Rollock,* first Principal of Edinburgh University. Robert Boyd's* massive later commentary on Ephesians, written but not published before his death in 1627, is not only an exhaustive commentary, but virtually a systematic theology as well.

David Dickson,* Professor of Divinity in Edinburgh, wrote highly esteemed commentaries on *Hebrews* (1635), *Matthew* (1647), *Psalms* (²1655) and *St. Paul's Epistles* (1659). In the same generation James Fergusson* commented on *Philippians and Colossians* (1656), *Galatians and Ephesians* (1659) and *Thessalonians* (1674), James Durham* on *Song of Solomon* (1668) and *Revelation* (1658), George Hutcheson* on *Job* (1669), the *Small*

Prophets (1654) and *John* (1657), Alexander Nisbet* on *Ecclesiastes* (1694) and *Peter* (1658). These works belonged to a co-operative effort inspired by Dickson to provide a series of expositions covering the whole Bible with concise, straightforward commentary for the ordinary reader. Unpublished collaborators included Robert Blair,* Robert Douglas* and Samuel Rutherford.*

This enterprise was marked by a remarkable unanimity of style. It would typically proceed by a brief synopsis of a chapter or passage, which would then be dealt with a few verses at a time. Each verse or two is then given a restatement, or a statement of why the material is present. Only infrequently are other possible interpretations discussed; the text is assumed, it seems, to be clear, and the major problem is to apply it. There follows a list of things to be learnt from the portion. The text is understood as the Word of God, such that it speaks directly to the Christian, every fragment inculcating some lesson. Underlying the restatement of the text can often be seen a concern to discern (or construct) a formal argument, behind the text if not in it. Scholasticism is visible here in the occasional overeagerness to make historical or rhetorical material serve as syllogistic matter. These commentaries live up to their design, and are often written in a connected, even flowing, prose which makes them easy to assimilate. This overcomes some of the fragmentation which the piecemeal treatment encourages, but, in spite of obvious attempts to avoid it, the large-scale development of the biblical book is sometimes slighted, and the natural thread and divisions of the text repressed. These are outstanding works for their period, of great practical usefulness.

Robert Leighton,* Archbishop of Glasgow, wrote a devotional exposition of *First Peter* (1693–4), a 'truly heavenly work' (C. H. Spurgeon*). The heavily doctrinal exposition of *Romans* by John Brown of Wamphray* remained unpublished until 1766, some 87 years after his death.

EIGHTEENTH AND NINETEENTH CENTURIES. The eighteenth century did not see so much expository work as the seventeenth, but mention must be made of the *Self-Interpreting Bible* (1778) by John Brown of Haddington,* which, though largely based on other writers, retained long and wide popularity. It expanded the practice of exegesis by a more deliberate comparison of the text under consideration with other texts, to aid in deciding on its interpretation, not merely to illuminate a meaning assumed to be readily discernible from the internal resources of the text. This was an indirect harbinger of later cross-reference Bibles, and also of the attitude which they reflect: that every reader can make up his own mind on a text, given the resources of Scripture, and is not to be dissuaded from using any part in it, including what seems confusing. That John Brown was the grandfather of John Brown of Edinburgh,* first Professor of Exegetical Theology in the UPC at its formation in 1847. His expository works included commentaries on *First ... Peter* (1848) and *Galatians* (1853). In his hands exegesis was less in bondage to dogmatic formulation than it had tended to be in his predecessors'. Reformed theology was firmly founded on Scripture, of course, so that it is not surprising to find Reformed theology emerging from exegetical study, but it should not have been necessary to turn the exposition of any one biblical book into a body of divinity. John Eadie's* commentaries on the Pauline epistles were of similar quality. Brown's colleague, William Lindsay (Small II, 34–5), produced a massive exposition of *Hebrews* (1867), while the Baptist Robert Haldane's* exposition of *Romans* (1835–9) 'ranks with those of Calvin and of Hodge' (J. Macleod,* *Scottish Theology*, E, ³1974, 228).

If Reformed exegesis was subject to dogmatic influence, much more was this so with RC exegesis, a notable exception being the work of Alexander Geddes.* His annotated translation of *The Holy Bible*, I, II (1792, 1797), was more significant critically than exegetically, like his *Critical Remarks on the Hebrew Scriptures*, I (1800); he pioneered the 'fragmentary' hypothesis of the composition of the Pentateuch.

The leading FC theologians of the first generation made greater contributions to systematics than exegesis. Patrick Fairbairn,* Principal of the Glasgow FC College, wrote a deservedly praised exposition of *Ezekiel* (1851) and a commentary on the *Pastoral Epistles* (1874); his *Typology of Scripture* (1845–7) and *Interpretation of Prophecy* (1856) should also be mentioned here. Andrew Bonar's* *Commentary on Leviticus* (1846) interprets the ceremonial law as an allegory of the work of Christ. Hugh Martin's* *The Prophet Jonah* (1866) retains its value, as a recent reprint testifies. James Morison,* founder of the Evangelical Union,* produced commentaries on *Matthew* (1870) and *Mark* (1873).

DISTINCTIVENESS. A number of traits in which Scottish exegesis had a certain degree of distinctiveness can tentatively be identified. A greater proportion of published Scottish exegesis than elsewhere has originated as sermons, or been produced in a sermonic style, and this tradition continues to the present. Often evident has been a strong interest in practical application, even doctrinal material being presented as possessing a moral thrust, requiring to be learned. A high proportion of commentary has been popular in nature, produced by learned exegetes but deliberately aimed at the keen and often well-schooled church member. A systematic theological interest, which asks how the passage under consideration integrates with the teaching of Scripture as a whole, crops up recurringly. This tradition of theological exegesis has not yet disappeared: one of its most illustrious representatives in recent times was John Murray,* author of a distinguished commentary on *Romans* (1959–65). Finally, it is perhaps not surprising if a high proportion of exegesis has been more or less strongly Reformed in theological character.

MODERN ERA. As elsewhere, Scotland experienced a shift in exegesis with the rise of biblical criticism* and critical theology. This expressed itself in two ways: a trend away from popular works and towards work written for the academy, and a trend towards the new theological attitude, which affected both methods and conclusions of exegesis. Yet Scottish exegesis seems to have been distinctive in two ways. First, the move seems to have been longer delayed. A. B. Davidson's* *Job* (1862, 1884) marks a watershed, with its detached rather than commendatory tone, its restrained but definite use of critical scholarship, and its wide acceptance. His *Ezekiel* (1892) similarly appeared in the Cambridge Bible series. His *Hebrews* (1882) remains one of the best popular treatments of that epistle. Secondly, the two trends have not been as closely linked. An excellent example is the work of William Barclay,* whose *Daily Study Bible* (1956–60) is so attractively addressed with easy presentation of first-century materials to the general reader, that its commitment to critical scholarship recedes into the background.

Scots exegetes figured prominently in expository series of the late nineteenth and early twentieth centuries. *The Expositor's Bible* (ed. W. R. Nicoll*) included George Adam Smith's* *Isaiah* (L, 1888, 1890) and *Twelve Prophets* (1896, 1898), and James Denney's* *Thessalonians* (1892) and *Second Corinthians* (1894). *The Expositor's Greek Testament*, ed. W. R. Nicoll (L, 1900–10), had contributions on the Synoptic Gospels by A. B. Bruce,* on John and Hebrews by Marcus Dods,* on Romans by J. Denney, on Ephesians by S. D. F. Salmond,* on Philippians by H. A. A. Kennedy,* on Thessalonians and Revelation by James Moffatt.* Denney was a specially able exegete of the Pauline letters: the excellence of his best known work, *The Death of Christ* (1902), is largely due to his exegetical treatment of the relevant biblical texts.

TWENTIETH CENTURY. G. A. Smith wrote the Cambridge Bible volume on *Deuteronomy* (1918) and an independent work on *Jeremiah* (1923). Moffatt wrote on *Hebrews* for the International Critical Commentary (E, 1924). To the Moffatt New Testament Commentary, based on his own translation, he himself contributed the volumes on *1 Corinthians* (L, 1938) and the *General Epistles* (1928), W. Manson* on *Luke* (1930), G. H. C. Macgregor* on *John* (1928), R. H. Strachan on *2 Corinthians* (1935), G. S. Duncan* on *Galatians* (1934), E. F. Scott on *Colossians, Philemon and Ephesians* (1930) and on the *Pastoral Epistles* (1936), W. Neil on *Thessalonians* (1950).

Scots contributors to the New International Commentary on the New Testament include, in addition to John Murray on *Romans*, F. F. Bruce* on *Acts* (Grand Rapids, 1954, ³1988), *Colossians–Philemon–Ephesians* (1984) and *Hebrews* (1964), A. Ross on *The Epistles of James and John* (1954), replaced by J. B. Adamson on *James* (1976) and I. H. Marshall on *The Epistles of John* (1978). The Tyndale New Testament Commentaries include I. H. Marshall on *Acts* (Leicester, 1980) and F. F. Bruce on *Romans* (1963, ²1985). To the New Century Bible J. Gray has contributed *Joshua, Judges, Ruth* (Grand Rapids/Basingstoke, 1986) and J. Mauchline *1 and 2 Samuel* (1971), H. Anderson *Mark* (1976), W. Neil *Acts* (1973), M. Black *Romans* (1973), F. F. Bruce *1 and 2 Corinthians* (1971), I. H. Marshall *1*

and 2 Thessalonians (1983), R. McL. Wilson *Hebrews* (1987).

George Milligan,* otherwise known as joint-editor with J. H. Moulton of *The Vocabulary of the Greek Testament* (E, 1930), contributed the volume on *1 and 2 Thessalonians* to the Macmillan series of New Testament Commentaries on the Greek text (1908). The same epistles have been treated by F. F. Bruce in Word Biblical Commentary (Waco, Texas, 1982), and *Romans* for the same series in two volumes by J. D. G. Dunn (1988), all on the Greek text.

The first Old Testament volume in the new series of the International Critical Commentary is on *Jeremiah 1–25* by W. McKane (E, 1986). I. H. Marshall is scheduled to deal with the *Pastoral Epistles* in this new series. Marshall is joint-editor (with W. W. Gasque) of the New International Greek Testament Commentary, which was launched with his own *Gospel of Luke* (Exeter/Grand Rapids, 1978); to the same series F. F. Bruce contributed *Galatians* (1982).

G. H. C. Macgregor wrote the section on Acts for *Interpreter's Bible*, IX (New York/Nashville, 1954), G. W. Grogan on Isaiah for *Expositor's Bible Commentary*, VI (Grand Rapids, 1986).

Outside special series must be mentioned commentaries on *1 and 2 Kings* by J. Gray (L, ²1970), and on *Daniel* by N. W. Porteous (L, ²1979).

W. Barclay* devoted his unusual skill as a communicator to New Testament exposition, especially in the *Daily Study Bible* (E, 1956–60, ²1975–6). The *Daily Study Bible* for the Old Testament has been edited by J. C. L. Gibson, with a variety of contributors (E, 1981–6).

A great service was rendered to biblical exegesis by James Hastings,* founder of the *Expository Times* (1889; see Periodicals, Religious) and editor until his death in 1922.

See also Believing Criticism.

C. H. Spurgeon, *Commenting and Commentaries* (L, 1876); J. Macleod, *Scottish Theology in Relation to Church History since the Reformation* (E, ³1974); G. D. Henderson, *Religious Life in Seventeenth-Century Scotland* (C, 1937), ch. 1; N. M. de S. Cameron, *Biblical Higher Criticism and the Defense of Infallibilism in 19th Century Britain* (Lewiston, NY, 1987).

F. F. Bruce and M. D. Peat

Exercise or Prophesying, initially public biblical conferences in Swiss Reformation churches designed to determine correct interpretation with sole reference to the Word of God in the original languages. In Scotland, the 'exercise' was used as a means both of testing the theological rectitude of ministers and of recruiting them. The scriptural paradigm was 1 Cor. 14 understood in terms of the 'teachers' or 'doctors' of Acts 13:1. An *ad hoc* organ such as prophesying was necessitated by various Reformation presuppositions, doctrines, and practical difficulties.

The *First Book of Discipline** envisages a weekly exercise in various localities. It facilitated the development of presbyteries,* which like the French 'Colloquies' had a dual purpose; but it could also function in Episcopalian polities. Despite Reformation ideals, the exercise's evolution consolidated the gap between ministry and ordinary church members, and it expired in the eighteenth century.

FBD 187–91; G. D. Henderson, *The Burning Bush* (E, 1957), 42–60; T. Güder, 'Prophezei' in *Realencycl. f. Prot. Theol. u. Kirche*³ XVI, 108–10; G. R. Potter, *Zwingli* (C, 1976), 221—4.

W. I. P. Hazlett

Exhorter, Office of. For a few years after the Scottish Reformation in 1560 exhorters were at work in parishes with ministers and readers.* There is no evidence of the origin of the office, but it seems that exhorters were able to conduct services and preach but not celebrate the sacraments, whereas readers were able only to read prayers and announce praise. The stipends of exhorters came from the thirds of teinds.* Some may have been later ordained to the ministry, and by 1570 there are few references to 'exhorters' in the CofS. The office does not seem to harmonize with Knox's* emphasis on the unity of Word and sacrament.

The word 'exhort' (παρακάλεω) is used extensively in the New Testament Acts and Epistles with the general meaning of 'preach'. Exhorter, then, is the equivalent of preacher or evangelist, interpreting the Scriptures, the word 'minister' being retained for a preacher ordained to preside at the sacraments of baptism and the Lord's Supper.

G. Donaldson, *The Scottish Reformation* (C, 1960).

A. I. Dunlop

Expository Times*, see* Periodicals, Religious.

Eyre, Charles Petrie (1817–1902), Archbishop of Glasgow. He was born at York, educated at Ushaw College, Durham, and the English College, Rome, and ordained at Rome in 1842. Having served in parishes in north-east England, he was made Vicar-General of Hexham and Newcastle in 1868. During these years he published his best-known work, *The History of St Cuthbert* (1849, ³1887). In 1868 he was nominated by Rome to settle affairs in the Western District of Scotland, was consecrated bishop and in April 1869 was appointed Apostolic Administrator of the District. On the restoration of a diocesan hierarchy in 1878, for which he had worked to prepare the ground, Eyre became Archbishop of Glasgow.

In his long episcopate there was rapid and sustained growth of clergy, churches and people. He founded St Peter's Seminary in 1874 (*see* Colleges and Seminaries, RC), and continued to write extensively, including *The Children of Holy Scripture* (1890–2) and papers on the medieval diocese and cathedral of Glasgow. His greatest achievement, however, was to restore peace between Scots and Irish Catholics in the west of Scotland. He is buried in St Andrew's Cathedral, Glasgow.

J. Darragh, *The Catholic Hierarchy of Scotland* (G, 1986), 22, 52–3; M. McHugh, 'The Glasgow Archdiocesan Archive', *Catholic Archives* 5 (1985), 19–33; *Catholic Directory for Scotland*, 1903 (A, 1903), 230–41; D. McRoberts, 'The Restoration of the Scottish Catholic Hierarchy in 1878', *IR* 29 (1978), 3–29; *DNB Miss. Pers.* 216–17.

M. McHugh

F

Fairbairn, Andrew Martin (1838–1912), Congregational minister. Fairbairn was born at Inverkeithing, Fife, the son of a miller. His schooling was minimal and he was earning before he was ten, but his memory and appetite for reading took him to Edinburgh University, although he left without taking a degree. The Fairbairns were United Secessionists* of Convenanting* stock but Andrew was drawn to the Evangelical Union,* attending its Duke Street Church, Leith. Called to its ministry, he entered the Union's theological college in Glasgow (1857), and his first pastorate followed in Bathgate (1860). There he was hit by agonizing intellectual and spiritual crisis, which he resolved in Germany by study under I. A. Dorner, F. A. G. Tholuck and E. W. Hengstenberg. Thereafter his mission was the passionately intelligent advocacy of a broad and contemporary theology. In 1871 he was President of the Evangelical Union and in 1872 he moved to St Paul Street Church, Aberdeen, where he consolidated his reputation as pastor and teacher, and made his scholarly name with *Studies in the Philosophy of Religion and History* (L, 1876). This development was reflected in his (unsuccessful) candidature for Aberdeen's Chair of Moral Philosophy and in the award of an Edinburgh doctorate (1878), the first of many.

By then he had left the Evangelical Union for English Congregationalism. From 1877 to 1886 he was Principal of Airedale College, Bradford, publishing *Studies in the Life of Christ* (L, 1881), and other works. From 1886 to 1909 he was Principal of the new Mansfield College, Oxford, which as community and building reflected his genius. There he formed Oxford's first Free Church ministerial generations. He lectured, latterly in India and the States as well as throughout Britain, and he wrote *The Place of Christ in Modern Theology* (L, 1893), *The Philosophy of the Christian Religion* (L, 1902), and *Studies in Religion and Theology* (L, 1910).

His power over young men was marked equally in Aberdeen, Bradford and Oxford. In each place he was inevitably an oppositional, and increasingly a public, figure. He was Chairman of the Congregational Union in 1883, served on two Royal Commissions (Education and the Welsh Church) and advised on theological education in the Welsh University colleges. His sermons, *Catholicism, Roman and Anglican* (L, 1899), issued from a controversy with J. H. Newman. In Fairbairn, who refused to be a 'dissenter', nonconformity became Free Church. He died in London.

Congregational Year Book, 1913, 165–6; *DNB 1912–1921*, 179–80; W. B. Selbie, *Life of Andrew Martin Fairbairn* (L, 1914); A. Peel, *The Congregational Two Hundred 1530–1948* (L, 1948), 221–2; J. W. Grant, *Free Churchmanship in England 1870–1940* (L, n.d.); H. Escott, *A History of Scottish Congregationalism* (G, 1960). R. S. Franks, 'The Theology of Andrew Martin Fairbairn,' *Trans. Cong. Hist. Soc.* 12 (1937–9), 140–50; A. P. F. Sell, 'An Englishman . . .', *SJT* 38 (1985), 41–83.

J. C. G. Binfield

Fairbairn, Patrick (1805–74), distinguished FC divine. Born at Halyburton, in Greenlaw, Berwickshire, he studied arts and divinity at Edinburgh University 1818–26. He was licensed by the Presbytery of Duns in 1826, and in 1830 became minister of North Ronaldsay, the most northerly of the Orkney Islands. There he mastered Hebrew and German through private study, laying the foundations of a thorough acquaintance with contemporary biblical and theological literature written in the latter tongue. In 1837 he moved to Bridgeton Church, Glasgow, and in 1840 to Saltoun, East Lothian. He joined the FC in the Disruption* of 1843.

1845 saw the publication of the first volume of Fairbairn's *magnum opus*, his *Typology of Scripture* (2 vols, E, 1845–7), still the standard Reformed text on the subject. Fairbairn argued that there were many more Old Testament types than were mentioned in the New Testament, although castigating the mentality which finds types everywhere. Most

FAIRFOUL, ANDREW

of the second volume is devoted to a detailed analysis of the typology of the Mosaic law, the tabernacle and the sacrificial system – probably the most valuable section of the work. His volume on *The Interpretation of Prophecy* (E, 1856; ²1865) was a sequel and supplement to this work.

Other writings followed, including translations of German religious literature (*e.g.* Hengstenberg's *Commentary on the Revelation of St. John*, 2 vols, 1851–2). In 1853 he was appointed Professor of Divinity in the FC College, Aberdeen. In 1856 he moved to the newly established Glasgow College, of which he became Principal in 1857.

In the closing decade of his life, Fairbairn supported both the movement for union between the FC and the UPC, and the evangelistic campaigns of Moody* and Sankey. He was an active member of the committee which ultimately produced the Revised Version of the Old Testament, and he edited *The Imperial Bible Dictionary*, 2 vols (L, 1864–6). In 1867 he visited America as part of a FC deputation to the General Assemblies of several American Presbyterian Churches. He delivered the Cunningham Lectures* for 1868 (*The Revelation of Law in Scripture*, E, 1868).

Fairbairn received a DD from Glasgow University (1854), and was Moderator of the FC General Assembly in 1864.

The Pastoral Epistles (E, 1874); *Ezekiel: An Exposition* (E, 1851); *Jonah* (E, 1849); *Hermeneutical Manual* (E, 1858); *Pastoral Theology* (E, 1875).

J. Dodds, *Biographical Sketch* in Fairbairn's *Pastoral Theology; Disruption Worthies*, 245–52; *DNB* XVIII, 122.

N. R. Needham

Fairfoul, Andrew (1606–63), Archbishop of Glasgow. He was born at Anstruther, graduated from St Andrews University, and later became minister at North Leith and at Duns. He was a signatory of the Covenant* and encouraged others to follow suit. Charles II,* having heard him preach several times in 1650, remembered him at the Restoration* and appointed him Archbishop of Glasgow. With James Sharp* (St Andrews), James Hamilton (Galloway), and Robert Leighton* (Dunblane) he was consecrated at Westminster in December 1661. In September 1662 Fairfoul complained to the King's Commissioner, the Earl of Middleton, that none of the ministers ordained since 1649 had owned him as Bishop. This led to an Act that demanded due acknowledgment of bishops from ministers on pain of banishment from manses, parishes and Presbyteries. Fairfoul said he did not believe more than ten ministers would abide by conscience, but the number exceeded 300. Wodrow* dismisses Fairfoul, whose episcopal career was short, as frivolous and insincere and sketches his repulsive personal habits. The more moderate Burnet describes him as 'insinuating and crafty . . . his life . . . scarce free of scandal'.

FES VII, 323; R. Keith, *Scottish Bishops* (²E, 1824);

FALAISE, TREATY OF

265; R. Wodrow, *History of the Sufferings*, ed. R. Burns, 4 vols (²G, 1828), I, 236ff., 282, 372f.

J. D. Douglas

Faith Mission, The, an interdenominational, evangelical organization committed to rural evangelism. Begun in Glasgow in October 1886, the Faith Mission was one of many societies formed in the wake of the Moody* campaigns in Scotland. The founder, John George Govan,* was the son of a Glasgow councillor and textile merchant.

The original idea of concentrated evangelism in the villages and country districts of Scotland was soon extended to Ireland and England, and later produced independent branches overseas: the Africa Evangelistic Band (1924), the Faith Mission in Canada (1929), and *Mission Foi Évangile* (1960) in France. A Training Home and Bible College was established in order to prepare young people for evangelistic work at home and abroad, and continues in Edinburgh.

Traditional Faith Mission policy of sending out workers ('Pilgrims') in pairs to conduct missions still continues. Team ministry is cultivated in open-air campaigns, and longer-term 'area work' has been developed in response to the increasing secularization of society. The 'faith principle' is the declared means of financial support. In practice this comes largely through Prayer Union groups set up following successful missions.

No basis of faith has ever been published by the Faith Mission. It is generally identified with the modern Holiness Movement. The theological orientation of Mission leaders has tended mainly to Wesleyanism (*see* Wesley, John), particularly in teaching the doctrine of sanctification as 'a second work of grace'. Evangelistic methods have been influenced by the works of C. G. Finney (*see* Revivals). The sacraments are not administered by the Mission.

I. R. Govan-Stewart, *Spirit of Revival* (E, 1938; ⁴1978); C. N. Peckham, *Heritage of Revival* (E, 1986).

A. A. Woolsey

Falaise, Treaty of (1174), a treaty imposed by King Henry II of England on King William I* of Scotland after his capture during the unsuccessful rising by William and Henry's sons against the Angevin ruler. The main ecclesiastical interest of the document lies in the provision that 'the church of Scotland shall henceforth owe such subjection to the church of England as it should do and was accustomed to do', and the acknowledgement by Scottish churchmen that 'the church of England shall have the right in the church of Scotland which it lawfully should'. The ambiguity of these phrases clearly shows the dubious nature of Henry's pretensions. In fact the Scottish churchmen were able to turn the treaty to their advantage by representing to Pope Alexander III (1159–81) that this was a new threat to ecclesiastical liberty by the king who had murdered Becket and imposed the Constitutions of Clarendon on the English Church. Alex-

FALCONER, RONALD HUGH WILSON

ander reacted by forbidding the Scottish bishops to offer subjection, and went far towards guaranteeing the independence of the Scottish Church, as confirmed by Pope Celestine III in 1192. Thus the ecclesiastical clauses in the treaty were a miscalculation by Henry which worked to the advantage of the Scottish Church in securing papal recognition of its independence.

Text in *Anglo-Scottish Relations, 1174–1328*, ed. E. L. G. Stones (O, 1965), no. 1; A. A. M. Duncan, *Scotland: the Making of the Kingdom* (E, 1975), 262ff.

A. Macquarrie

Falconer, Ronald Hugh Wilson (1911–77), religious broadcaster. It was within a deeply devout evangelical Christian home that Ronnie Falconer's commitment and conviction were formed, and on his father's deathbed that he knew the call to enter the ministry to which his father had given his life. After study at Aberdeen University (1931–7, MA and BD), conviction and call found sturdy expression in the work and witness of an industrial parish in Lanarkshire (Coatbridge: Trinity, 1939–45), were notably expressed in the radio and television ministry with BBC Scotland to which his creative energies were applied from 1945 for the major part of his ministry, and were resolutely upheld when in 1962 he refused appointment as Controller of BBC Scotland as alien to his ordination vows.

He contributed notably to the use of radio in mission, and promoted Radio Missions to Scotland in 1950 and 1952 which were foundational to the Tell Scotland Movement.* His creative ability won wide recognition, and in 1963 he became a founder member of the World Association for Christian Broadcasting. Aberdeen University awarded him the DD in 1960.

FES, IX 327, X 193; R. Falconer, *The Kilt Beneath my Cassock* (E, 1978); J. Highet, *The Scottish Churches* (L, 1960).

P. T. Bisset

Farquhar, John Nicol (1861–1929), missionary and Oriental scholar. Born in Aberdeen, he grew up in a devout Evangelical Union* home, and served apprenticeship as a draper before entering Aberdeen University in 1883. Transferring to Oxford with an exhibition at Christ Church, he took a first in Greats in 1889. He was accepted as a lay educational missionary of the London Missionary Society* and appointed to Bhowanipur College (Calcutta) in 1890. He found College work frustrating from a missionary viewpoint, and unsuccessfully sought release to work in student evangelism. In 1902 John R. Mott secured his appointment as a YMCA secretary to enable him to work with educated young Hindus in Calcutta. The increasingly anti-foreign climate of the national movement forced him to concentrate on literature (he produced a paper, *The Inquirer*, with questions and answers about Christianity), and on analysis of what young Hindus were reading. Discovery of the new

FARQUHARSON, ALEXANDER

significance given to the Bhagavad Gita led to his first substantial book, *Gita and Gospel* (Calcutta, 1903), and to progressively deeper study of both classical and modern Hindu literature. In 1907 he became National Student Secretary of the YMCA; his sympathy with the national movement increased, and he produced the still useful *Primer of Hinduism* (O, 1911). To set him free for such scholarship Mott devised in 1911 the post of Literary Secretary of the YMCAs of India, wherein Farquhar divided his time between India and Oxford. Three major works followed: *The Crown of Hinduism* (L, 1913), *Modern Religious Movements in India* (NY, 1915) and *An Outline of the Religious Literature of India* (O, 1920). He was also editor for three scholarly monograph series: The Religious Quest of India, The Heritage of India and The Religious Life of India. He returned from India in 1923, and became Professor of Comparative Religion at Manchester and Wilde Lecturer in Natural and Comparative Religion at Oxford. He was awarded Oxford's DLitt in 1916 and Aberdeen's DD in 1926. His widow received a civil list pension in 1931 in recognition of his services to scholarship.

Farquhar was the most considerable Indologist produced by the missionary movement. His scholarship (which has proved remarkably durable) was always missionary in intent; *The Crown of Hinduism* in particular has a direct apologetic purpose. His approach to Hindu literature was profoundly sympathetic (though he lamented deficiencies of historical foundation and moral consciousness). His liberal theology was simple, perhaps naive: Christ fulfils the highest longings of Hinduism; a providentially guided evolutionary process assures the continuing significance of Christ in India's development. Missiologically his work required complementing by that of his junior contemporary in India, A. G. Hogg.*

DNB 1922–1930, 296; J. Sibree, *LMS Register*, no. 909; E. J. Sharpe, *J. N. Farquhar: A Memoir* (Calcutta, 1963); *id., Not to Destroy but to Fulfil: the Contribution of J. N. Farquhar to Protestant Thought in India before 1914* (Lund, 1965); C. H. Hopkins, *John R. Mott 1865–1955* (Geneva, 1979).

A. F. Walls

Farquharson, Alexander (1793–1858), the architect of the original Presbyterian parish structure of Cape Breton. Born of sheep-farming stock in Straloch, Strathardle, Perthshire, Alexander and his brother Archibald were both influenced by the evangelical movement in their district. The latter trained for missionary work with the Independents, and was posted to Tiree, where he became pastor of the Independent church in the island (1835–78). Alexander trained for ministry with the CofS, and, supported by the Edinburgh Ladies' Association (*see* MacKay, Isabella), was sent to Cape Breton Island in 1833. Cape Breton had by then become the home of many settlers from the Scottish Highlands (*see* Emigration), but formal religious provision was extremely poor; the island had a bad name, and missionaries were reluctant to serve there.

Farquharson settled eventually at Middle River, finding more spiritual interest than had been reported. He itinerated extensively throughout the island, enduring 'many inconveniences ... which people in Scotland have no idea of'. He submitted to the Ladies' Association a plan for ten parishes, and the society worked to implement it. Their efforts bore fruit, as the first Presbytery of Cape Breton was constituted in 1836, and the number of ministers increased slowly. Strongly evangelical, the émigré ministers led their congregations effortlessly into the FCS.

L. Stanley, *The Well-Watered Garden* (²Sydney, Cape Breton, 1984).

D. E. Meek

Farquharson, John (1699–1782). Of the family of Auchindryne (Braemar), he entered the Scots College,* Douai, 1714 and the Jesuit* noviciate at Tournai 1718. Ordained priest, he returned to Scotland 1729 and ministered in Strathglass (Inverness-shire) for many years. Information on Farquharson is mostly from oral tradition and imprecise. At some point he was captured by government soldiers and taken to Fort Augustus but released. In 1746 he was captured, spent some months in a man-of-war off London and was conveyed to exile in Hanover, but soon returned to Strathglass. His position there was still insecure in 1753; soon after, he became prefect of studies in the Douai college. When Jesuits were banned in France in 1764, he went with colleagues and students to Dinant in Belgium; and on the Jesuits being suppressed in 1773, he returned to Scotland and lived with his nephew, Farquharson of Inverey, in Braemar.

While in Strathglass, he composed a poem, *Rabhadh MhicShimidh* (warning to Lord Lovat), and transcribed Gaelic* poetry, mostly Ossianic, from oral tradition. Having taken this large and valuable manuscript collection with him to Douai and Dinant, he left it at Douai in 1773. Eye-witnesses describe how the manuscript was ill-treated and disappeared.

The Celtic Magazine, 7 (1881–2), 49–52, 141–6, 191; 10 (1884–5), 65–6, 146; A. S. MacWilliam, 'A Highland Mission: Strathglass, 1671–1777', *IR* 24 (1973), 86–102; *The Poems of Ossian ... with a Dissertation on the Authenticity of the Poems by Sir John Sinclair*, 3 vols (L, 1807), I, xl–lviii.

M. Dilworth

Farquharson, John (*fl.c.*1800–10), itinerant evangelist with the Independents.* A native of Glen Tilt, Perthshire, Farquharson trained briefly at a Haldane* class in Dundee. Dispatched to Breadalbane, Perthshire, in 1800 as a Scripture reader, he displayed a devotion to Christ which deeply influenced the district. An awakening was evident by 1802, and Independent congregations were formed by him at Killin (Perthshire) and Acharn (Loch Tayside). Briefly imprisoned in Aberdeen for his preaching in Braemar, Farquharson emigrated afterwards (*c.*1806) to Nova Scotia. At some point (perhaps *en route* to Canada) he arrived in Skye, preached in the north end of the island, and was instrumental in the conversion of Donald Munro.*

A. Haldane, *Memoirs of the Lives of Robert Haldane of Airthrey, and of his brother, James Alexander Haldane* (L, 1852), 316–17; W. J. Couper, *Scottish Revivals* (Dundee, 1918), 96–7, 100–2.

D. E. Meek

Fasti Ecclesiae Scoticanae, a reference work, now in its tenth volume, the aim of which is to offer 'a comprehensive account of the succession of ministers of the Church of Scotland since the period of the Reformation'. Furthermore, an attempt is made 'to give some additional interest by furnishing incidental notices of their lives, writings and families' (quotations from the Preface to the first edition). Additionally, in a number of instances, there are notes about the history of the church buildings in a parish. The first edition (3 vols in 6 pts, E, 1866–71) was produced by Hew Scott, minister of Anstruther Wester in Fife (*FES* V, 185; *DNB* LI, 27). In a life-work of extraordinary diligence, he visited all the Presbyteries of the Church and about 760 different parishes to examine records, which he frequently cited. The result is a work of inestimable value: painstaking, anecdotal, witty, utterly fascinating, but with inevitable inaccuracies. Beginning in 1914, the General Assembly revised and updated Hew Scott's edition, turning it into a seven-volume work (E, 1915–28) under the convenership of W. S. Crockett, minister of Tweedsmuir (*FES* I, 297–8, VIII, 65). In 1950, under the convenership of Sir Francis J. Grant (*Who Was Who, 1951–1960*, 445), Vol. 8 covering 1914–29 was published with *Addenda* and *Corrigenda* of the earlier material. In 1961 Vol. 9 was produced under the editorship of John A. Lamb, librarian of New College, Edinburgh (*FES* IX, 785), covering 1929–54, and including reference to the *Fasti* of the UFC. In 1981 Donald F. M. Macdonald, Principal Clerk (*FES* IX, 328, X, 194, 458), edited Vol. 10 which brings the *Fasti* from 1955 to 1975.

I. R. Torrance

Faulds, Henry (1843–1930), medical missionary and pioneer of fingerprinting. Born in Beith, Ayrshire, where his father was a wholesaler, he studied arts at Glasgow (1864–7) and then qualified in medicine at Anderson's College there (1871). Influenced as a Sunday School teacher by Norman MacLeod* at the Barony, he served briefly (1872–3 – terminated by discord) at the CofS mission at Darjeeling, India. He then turned to the UPC (his father was an elder at Erskine, Glasgow), and was appointed the first Scottish medical missionary to Japan, reaching Yokohama in 1874.

Faulds soon attained prominence in Tokyo. He built and superintended a UP mission hospital in Tsukiji, the foreign concession, helped found an associated medical college (1876), introduced the milk-treatment of typhoid and Lister's new antiseptic methods and supervised anti-cholera measures, and declined a tempting offer to become royal physician. Faulds survived disagreement with the UP Home Board over his editorship of a medical journal, and overcame doubts about the continuation of the mission, which won few converts.

Faulds also gave and published in Japan popular anti-Darwinian lectures, and helped produce a Braille-type Japanese Bible and found Japan's first school for the blind. *Nine Years in Nipon. Sketches of Japanese Life and Manners* (L, 1885) was written the year before his wife's ill-health forced his return home (1885), after which he served as a local doctor in the Potteries in England. He edited the short-lived *East Asia*, a quarterly on lore and literature for the general reader (only vol. I: 1–3, 1897–8, Longton, Staffs.).

A chance observation c.1878 of fingerprints on prehistoric pottery led Faulds to investigate and experiment, often painfully on himself. His letter to *Nature*, 'On the Skin-Furrows of the Hand' (22, Oct. 28 1880, 605), constitutes his valid claim to be the first to establish by scientific experiments the unaltering persistence of fingerprints and to suggest their use in criminal identification. Faulds also cited the evidence of prehistoric fingerprints in his anti-evolution lectures.

After his return discussions with authorities in London failed to persuade them of the potential of fingerprinting, and when the London police set up a fingerprint bureau in 1901 the credit went elsewhere. Faulds' attempts to win recognition were in vain. His cause was taken up by George W. Wilton, a Sheriff-substitute in Lanarkshire (1862–1964; *Who Was Who, 1961–1970*, 1217), who in numerous writings and petitions over a quarter of a century sought in vain posthumous recognition for Faulds and civil-list pensions for his daughters. In Japan, however, on the fiftieth anniversary of police fingerprinting in 1961, a monument to Faulds was unveiled at his former residence after its site (and that of his hospital) had been re-established.

Dactylography, or the Study of Finger Prints (Halifax, 1912); *The Hidden Hand. A Contribution to the History of Finger Prints* (n.p., 1917).

G. W. Wilton, *Fingerprints. History, Law and Romance* (L, 1938); *id.*, *Fingerprints. Swan Song*... (N. Berwick, 1963); R. W. Stewart, '"Fingerprint" Faulds', *LW* n.s. 7 (1952), 75–6, 18 (1962), 276; S. Yasoshima, 'Henry Faulds – Pioneer in Dactyloscopy. His Life and Work in Japan', *Finger Print and Identification Magazine* (Chicago; May, 1960), 3–7, 23; H. Sekine, 'Erection of a Monument to the Memory of Henry Faulds...', *ibid.* (Apr., 1962), 3–7, 11–12.

H. Miura and D. F. Wright

Fellowship of Independent Evangelical Churches (FIEC), a fellowship of evangelical congregations which are either undenominational in constitution or, in a desire for doctrinal purity, detached from denominations with which they were once associated. The churches join together in area auxiliaries to promote united testimony to the gospel, to foster fellowship and mutual help, and to express evangelical church unity.

The conservative evangelical doctrinal basis of the Fellowship – to which both churches and ministers are required to reaffirm their agreement every year – concentrates on the primary truths of the faith, with the conviction that issues like baptism, forms of church government, and spiritual gifts should not be allowed to hinder church fellowship.

Established in 1922, the FIEC embraced 432 churches in 1988, of which twenty were in Scotland. The first church in Scotland to join the FIEC was Clarkston Baptist Church in 1942.

E. J. Poole-Connor, *Evangelical Unity* (L, 1941).

D. Prime

Fellowship of St Andrew. Following the interest created by the influx of Russian émigrés after the Russian Revolution, a number of conferences and events occurred throughout the British Isles where Orthodox Christians and Western Christians encountered one another. One such event was a conference held in Glasgow Cathedral on 28 October 1936, during which the Orthodox Divine Liturgy was celebrated in the ancient shrine. Dr Nicolas Zernov, the influential lay theologian of the émigré community, later described this as the beginning of the Fellowship of St Andrew. In fact the formation of the Fellowship dates from exploratory meetings held in 1961 in the Scottish Episcopal Theological College and the CofS offices, with the encouragement of Bishop Richard Wimbush and the Inter-Church Relations Committee of the CofS. At a subsequent conference of Eastern and Western Christians held at the new Scottish Churches House in Dunblane on 12–14 April 1961, the Fellowship was formed as a distinct Orthodox-Scottish Society and the name Fellowship of St Andrew* chosen in honour of the patron saint of Scotland, Russia and Greece. The Fellowship continues today with its original aim 'to promote mutual understanding and co-operation between divided Christians of East and West', believing that the worship and witness of the Eastern Churches must play an increasing part in the ecumenical movement.

N. Zernov, 'The Scoto-Russian Fellowship of St Andrew', *Sobornost* ser. 3/9 (1951), 423–4.

D. Reid

Fergus, *see* Celtic Saints.

Ferguson, Fergus (1832–1911), controversial UP and UF minister. After a brief business career, and with the encouragement of his minister John Ker (Small II, 223), he prepared for the ministry at Glasgow University (enrolled 1856) and the UP Hall before serving two UP churches: Buccleuch Street, Dalkeith (1864–75) and Queen's Park, Glasgow (1875–1905). Ferguson precipitated two major theological storms in the UPC: the 'Dalkeith Case' of 1871 and his heresy* trial of 1877–8. His survival in both instances indicated the UPC's willingness to tolerate theological diversity, and even anti-Calvinist doctrine, in its ranks.

In 1871, Ferguson was arraigned by his Presbytery (and eventually the UP Synod) for his pulpit musings on the intermediate state and the destiny of the heathen. He was acquitted after giving assent to several propositions which seemed to affirm the confessional view of human probation.

He campaigned vigorously for credal revision in the UPC (see his *Reconstruction of the Creed*, G, 1877) and was appointed in 1877 to the UP Synod's revision committee. Meanwhile, his inflammatory descriptions of the Westminster Confession (e.g., 'unworthy of God ... and an engine of spiritual oppression') outraged many, and the tenets of his alternative theology led to his libel trial by the Glasgow UP Presbytery in March 1878. Ferguson's theology was eclectic and heavily influenced by Hegelian thought, and the trial was considerably complicated by his enigmatic terminology. Eventually he was found guilty on five counts: his views of the atonement, justification, human depravity, the intermediate state and the destiny of the unconverted.

His case was carried by appeal to the Synod, which upheld the lower court's ruling. Widespread sympathy for Ferguson posed a serious threat to UP unity, however, and on Henry Calderwood's* suggestion it was agreed to give Ferguson 'an affectionate and solemn admonition' rather than remove him from the ministry. Thus 'the Synod did an amazing thing when it condemned a man for heresy, did not withdraw that condemnation, and yet refused to punish him' (J. H. Leckie, *Fergus Ferguson*, E, 1923, 274). When shortly afterwards Ferguson published *The Dilemma of Modern Orthodoxy* (1879) in support of the views of heretic David Macrae,* the Synod showed little will to prosecute.

Ferguson's career was relatively placid thereafter. He was awarded an honorary doctorate by Glasgow University (1885), and died beloved and respected. His works include: *The Law of the Sabbath* (E, 1865), *The Immortality of Man* (E, 1875), *Defence and Vindication* (G, 1878) and *The Redeemed in Glory* (G, 1890). He failed to publish the synthesis of philosophy and evangelical faith 'on which he brooded all his life' (J. R. Fleming, *History of the Church of Scotland*, 2 vols (E, 1927–33), II, 19–20).

Obituary, *Glasgow Herald*, 17 October 1911; FUFCS, 242.

G. G. Scorgie

Ferguson, James (1621–67), minister and biblical commentator. A member of an Ayrshire landed family, the Fergusons of Kilkerran, he graduated at Glasgow University in 1638. In 1643 he was presented to the Ayrshire parish of Kilwinning by its patron, the Earl of Eglinton. His reputation led to calls to move to Edinburgh (1648–9) and Glasgow (1658), which he successfully resisted with the Earl's help. In the 1650s he supported the Resolutioners* in controversy with the Protesters* in the Synod of Glasgow. He retained his parish after the Restoration,* though a proposal in 1661 to appoint him Professor of Divinity at Glasgow University came to nothing. His disapproval of the tendencies of the Restoration period was expressed obliquely in 1665 when, in giving notice to his congregation of a fast ordered to crave God's blessing on a war with the Dutch, he indicated that the fast should be regarded as being in repentance for the prevailing sins of the age as well. Ferguson contributed to David Dickson's* plan for producing a series of short expositions for the public of the books of the Bible, Ferguson's work being concentrated on the Epistles of St Paul (see Exegesis, Biblical).

A Brief Exposition Of The Epistles To The Philippians and Colossians (E, 1656); *... Galatians and Ephesians* (E, 1659); *... Thessalonians* (L, 1674); *A Brief Refutation of the Errors of Toleration, Erastianism, Independency and Separation* (E, 1692).

DNB XVIII, 342; *FES* III, 117; R. Wodrow, *History of the Sufferings of the C of S*, 4 vols (²G, 1828–30), III, 421.

D. Stevenson

Fergusson, David (*c.*1525–98), Reformation* minister. He was probably a Dundee glover before becoming a preacher in the privy kirks* and, after the Reformation, minister of Dunfermline and Moderator in 1572 and 1578. He was the author of three publications: *Ane Answer to ane Epistle written by Renat Benedict* (E, 1563); *Ane Sermon preichit befoir the Regent and Nobilitie* (St Andrews, 1572) and *Scottish Proverbs* (E, 1598, posthumously).

Fergusson was one of the most notable Reformation ministers. Having incurred Mary of Guise's* displeasure in 1558 for preaching in Dundee, he was appointed to Dunfermline by the July 1560 Assembly of the Kirk. He remained there to his death, by which time he was 'Father of the Kirk'. Approving notices of him are to be found in James Melville's* *Diary* and the *Histories* of David Calderwood* and John Row.*

In his *Answer* to Benedict, Queen Mary of Scots' confessor, Fergusson defended the Protestant attack on the mass as idolatry. He based his case on the Scots' Confession of Faith* (1560) and the Scriptures, arguing that he and the other ministers were teaching no new doctrine but ancient truths obscured during the thirteenth century.

Fergusson's *Sermon* on Malachi 3 likened the Scots Protestant nobility of 1572 to the Jews after the Exile attacked by the prophet for lukewarm devotion to God. Specifically, the minister blamed the turmoil of civil war and national distress on those who deprived the Kirk of the whole teind* and thus frustrated the programmes of the *First Book of Discipline.**

J. Lee (ed.), *Tracts by David Fergusson* (E, 1860); *SBD* 33, 48–50, 75, 76; D. G. Mullen, *Episcopacy in Scotland* (E, 1986), 84; *FES* V, 26–7; *DNB* XVIII, 341–2.

F. D. Bardgett

Ferme, Charles (1566–1617), Principal of the abortive university at Fraserburgh, Aberdeenshire.

FERRIER, ROBERT

He came of obscure parentage in Edinburgh (his name appears also as Fairholm, *etc.*). He studied at Edinburgh University under Robert Rollock* (MA, 1587), turned to study Hebrew and theology, and then assisted Rollock as regent in philosophy 1590-8, with David Calderwood* among his pupils.

In 1598 he accepted the charge of Philorth, Fraserburgh, to head the university planned by the patron, Sir Alexander Fraser of Philorth. In 1600 the General Assembly at Montrose appointed Ferme as Principal and agreed to his retaining his pastorate. His robust Presbyterianism brought him trouble on the restoration of episcopacy. He attended the banned Aberdeen Assembly of 1605, and was imprisoned at Doune and Stirling and confined to the Isle of Bute. In 1609 he was restored to his parish. The university continued until his death – such as it was, for there is no firm evidence of students or of the completion of building. He wrote a *Logical Analysis* of the Epistle to the Romans (Latin, with life by J. Adamson, E, 1651; ET W. Skae, Wodrow Society, E, 1850, with life by W. L. Alexander).

FES VI, 220-1; *DNB* XVIII, 368-9; R. Lippe, *Selections from Wodrow's Biographical Collections* (New Spalding Club; A, 1890), lxxvii-lxxix, 270-81.

D. F. Wright

Ferrier, Robert (1741-95), Independent/Glasite elder. He was the ninth son of the minister of Largo in Fife, and in 1764 joined his father as colleague and successor. He was made to think about church order by reading Glas's* *Testimony* on the advice of a dying neighbouring minister. He found that his neighbour, James Smith of Newburn (1708-75; *FES* V, 224-5), had also come to Glasite conclusions about the kingdom of Christ, and in 1768 they resigned their charges, gathering a small body of worshippers at nearby Balchrystie. Soon after this Ferrier went to Glasgow as colleague to David Dale,* but in 1770, on differing from him, became a member of the Glasite church. Ferrier, though earnest and sincere, was inclined to be dogmatic, insisting on unanimity of judgement. He disagreed with Dale over whether the Lord's Prayer should be said in public, whether the Amen should be audibly pronounced, and whether worshippers should stand to praise and pray. For a short time he was a Glasite elder, but, being widowed, he married a widow, Catherine Waterston, and had to relinquish the elder's office. Thereafter he became a teacher of the classics in Edinburgh until his death.

D. Beaton, 'The Old Scots Independents', in *RSCHS* 3 (1929), 135-45; R. Ferrier, preface to J. Glas, *The Testimony of the King of Martyrs* (E, 1777); J. Smith and R. Ferrier, *The Case of . . . Robert Ferrier . . . Truly Represented and Defended . . .* (E, 1768); *FES* V, 219.

D. B. Murray

Feuing. Title to land in most of Scotland is held by persons natural and artificial in a feudal structure, with feudal superiors retaining certain rights in the land which they 'feu' to their feudal inferiors, and imposing obligations which attach to the land irrespective of its transference from owner to owner. Using the feudal system, ownership of land in many parts of Scotland had obligations attached to it, including the payment of teinds.* While many burdens were so laid prior to the Reformation, the practice continued thereafter. One common restriction imposed through feuing was that an area feued for the erection of a church was not to be used thereafter for other purposes. Again, often the trustees of a church being sold seek to limit through the titles the use to which the building may be put. Unreasonable feudal burdens may now be discharged through the Lands Tribunal for Scotland, and no new monetary burden may be created in any new feuing of land nor may such existing burdens be increased.

A feuar was a heritor* of any parish within which he held land for the purposes of that classification.

J. Rankine, *The Law of Landownership in Scotland* (E, ⁴1909); J. Halliday, *Conveyancing Law and Practice in Scotland*, vol. 2 (E, 1986); J. Girvan, 'Feudal Law' in *An Introductory Survey of The Sources and Literature of Scots Law*, Stair Society, vol. 1 (E, 1936), 193-206.

F. Lyall

Fiars' Prices, the yardstick that made it possible for stipend,* which was assessed in terms of victual (that is, bolls of barley, chalders of meal, etc.), to be converted into cash terms, and an Act of Parliament of 1808 made it incumbent for all stipends to be so paid. Within each locality some time between 15th February and 3rd March (10th and 20th May in Orkney and Shetland), the Sheriff sat with a jury of fifteen men of knowledge living within the sheriffdom, to hear evidence regarding the prices that had obtained in the locality for the various commodities. Judgement had to be issued not later than 12th March. The stipend was in respect of a certain 'crop and year', but since the Fiars' Prices could not be struck until the crop had been sold, stipend was always paid in arrears.

A. Herron

Field Preaching, a method of popular evangelism. Neither the fugitive conventicles* of the Covenanting* period, nor the later use of outdoor preaching in the revivals* at Cambuslang and Kilsyth and in the Highland missionary work financed by the Royal Bounty,* bore any significant relationship to the spate of open-air or field preaching which began in the late 1790s. The earlier examples had either lacked an evangelical purpose or had accommodated their efforts to the normal parish structure. The new field preaching differed markedly, showing a range of distinctive features. No longer merely localized, it involved a strong element of itinerancy,* utilized the services of lay preachers, showed evidence of external organization, and in many cases adopted a critical stance towards existing religious structures and practices. The earliest examples of the new type of preaching were the mission conducted by Niel Douglas* and Daniel McNaught in Argyll in 1797 under the patronage of the Relief Church,* and James Haldane's* simultaneous tour through the northern counties of Scotland. Over the following decade the itinerant efforts of the young men trained by the Haldane academies led to field preaching becoming widespread. Audience size varied greatly: many open-air gatherings numbered no more than a few dozen hearers; in other cases as many as fifteen thousand were estimated to be present. Although criticism of the local parish ministry was voiced by some of the first itinerants, the majority of field preachers were concerned only to combat popular irreligion. They endeavoured to arouse spiritual anxiety among their hearers and to instruct their audiences in the principal themes of the gospel. From the side of the Est.C, the unwelcome novelty of open-air evangelism led the *Pastoral Admonition** to criticize the practice specifically for 'bringing together assemblies of people in the fields, or in places not intended for public worship'. The field preacher used places where people naturally met together, speaking not only to those working the land but also at quarries, ferry crossings, market places and to construction workers engaged on such projects as the Crinan Canal. In spite of the flexibility this afforded, the effects of an inhospitable climate coupled with harassment by landowners, magistrates and parish clergymen led most preachers to seek indoor accommodation, their venues including cottages, barns, inns and occasionally the pulpit of a friendly minister. The building between 1799 and 1803 of a series of large tabernacles in Edinburgh, Glasgow, Dundee and a number of other Scottish burghs, including Dumfries, Perth, Elgin and Wick, represented a not altogether successful attempt to combine provision for the institutional needs of converts, with a continuation of the ethos of the earlier undenominational open-air gatherings in a setting where preacher and audience were protected from the elements.

J. A. Haldane, *Journal of a Tour through the Northern Counties of Scotland and the Orkney Isles, in Autumn 1797* (E, 1798); N. Douglas, *Journal of a Mission to part of the Highlands of Scotland, in Summer and Harvest 1797, by appointment of the Relief Synod, in a series of letters to a friend*... (E, 1799); D. E. Meek, 'Dugald Sinclair: The Life and Work of a Highland Itinerant Missionary', *SS* 30 (1991), 59–91.

D. W. Lovegrove

Fillan, see Celtic Saints.

Finan, see Celtic Saints.

Findlater, Sarah, see Borthwick, Jane Laurie.

Findlay, David Jack (1858–1938), pastor of the St George's Cross Tabernacle, Glasgow. Born in Glasgow, Findlay was converted in 1874 during D. L. Moody's* campaign in the city. He was soon thrust to the forefront of a weekly mission meeting which evolved into a large independent Baptist* church. Findlay led the church at the same time as running a boot and shoe business. In 1894, the church settled in the newly built Tabernacle off Maryhill Road, and in 1899 Findlay relinquished his business to become full-time pastor. Serious illness in 1910 put an end to his regular preaching, but such was the force of his personality that he continued to control the Tabernacle's affairs while others preached.

According to his biographer, Findlay 'would not have resented being called a good old-fashioned Fundamentalist' (A. Gammie, *Pastor D. J. Findlay*, L, 1949, 97). He was hostile to biblical criticism, and the annual religious conference at the Tabernacle upheld a pronounced premillennialism. The Tabernacle church was ardently committed to mission,* sending dozens to the field; Findlay himself was President of the British section of the Poona and Indian Village Mission, and Vice-President of the British Council of the Africa Inland Mission.

N. R. Needham

Findlay, Robert (1721–1814), minister of Stevenston (1744–5), Galston (1745–54), Paisley (Laigh Church) (1754–6), and of Glasgow St David's (1756–83); Professor of Divinity, University of Glasgow (1783–1814). Between 1761 and 1762 he published anonymously as 'Philalethes' a series of 'Letters' on the divine inspiration of the Scriptures. He also wrote on prayer. He supported the authenticity and reliability of the works of Josephus, against the philosophical opinions of Voltaire, in *A Vindication of the Sacred Books and of Josephus, especially the former, from various Misrepresentations and Cavils of the celebrated M. de Voltaire* (G, 1770); he also advocated *The Divine Inspiration of the Jewish Scriptures* (L, 1803).

FES III, 40, 123, 174, 439, VII, 401; *DNB* XIX, 24; H. M. B. Reid, *The Divinity Professors*... (G, 1923), 270–84.

J. R. McIntosh

Findlay, Vera Mary Muir (1904–74), first woman ordained to a pastoral charge and in a mainstream denomination in Scotland (see Sharpe, Jane Brayton). Born in Glasgow, she was dux of Hillhead High School. A brilliant student, while taking honours in classics at Glasgow University she began seriously to consider the Congregational* ministry. She was encouraged by the Principal of the Scottish Congregational College, where she studied with distinction 1926–8. A gifted preacher, she so impressed the deacons of Partick Congregational Church, Glasgow, that they called her to be their pastor before she had completed her BD course. She was ordained at Partick in November 1928, and graduated BD in February 1929. That year she applied for recognition as a minister of the Congregational Union of Scotland – which stimulated considerable interest among both supporters and opponents within the Scottish religious community. On 29 April 1929 the Union carried a constitutional amendment to allow 'minister' to apply equally to women and men. She was minister at Partick 1928-34, and served three other Glasgow churches: Christchurch 1934-6; Hillhead 1936-45; Pollokshields 1954-68. During 1952-3, she was the first woman to serve as President of the Congregational Union of Scotland. In that capacity she was a representative to the CofS General Assembly in 1953, to which she was intially refused entrance on the grounds of her sex.

Theological education was one of her major concerns, and she chaired the management committee of the Scottish Congregational College. In 1933 she married Colin Kenmure. She was known as an eloquent preacher and helpful pastor, and enjoyed many friendships within and beyond the Congregational Union. Her obituary in the 1974-6 CUS Yearbook claimed: 'In the church family, which she loved and served – and beyond it – she will be remembered as the one who helped the CofS to realize that the gifts and service of a woman who has been called by God, whether she be unmarried or married, are an enrichment and not an embarrassment in the work of the ordinary ministry.'

Congregational Union of Scotland Yearbook 1974-6, 71.

L. O. Macdonald

Finlayson, Roderick Alexander (1895-1989), FC theologian and writer. Born in Lochcarron, Wester Ross, he studied at Aberdeen University (MA, 1919) and the FC College, Edinburgh (1919-22). He became minister at Urray, north of Inverness (1922-40), and then Hope Street, Glasgow (1940-6), before being elected Professor of Systematic Theology in the FC College (1946-66). He was Moderator of the FC General Assembly in 1945, and editor of its *Monthly Record** 1938-58. He was a founding member of the Scottish Tyndale Fellowship, which later became the Scottish Evangelical Theology Society* and established an annual Finlayson Lectureship in his honour. He was also active in the beginnings of the Inter-Varsity Fellowship.* During the Second World War he was Deputy Assistant Chaplain General, Scottish Command (1940-4). He was much in demand as a preacher and conference speaker, with a wit as sharp as his pen.

The Cross in the Experience of Our Lord (L, 1955); *God's Light on Man's Destiny* (E, n.d.); *The Story of Theology* (L, 1963).

Tribute by H. Cameron, *FCSR*, May 1989, 104-5.

J. D. MacMillan

First Book of Discipline (1560), one of the chief documents of the Scottish Reformation, designed to serve as a statement on doctrine, organization and endowment for the Reformed Church. As early as 29 April 1560, immediately following the band or contract by the Lords of the Congregation* to 'set forward the Reformation of Religion', the 'Great Council of the Realm' or Protestant provisional government commissioned some leading ministers to prepare a 'Book of Reformation', completed by 20 May. That early work (whose contents can be traced only in the final text of the *FBD*) underwent expansion later in 1560, to produce the much fuller *Book of Discipline*, whose text (first printed in 1621) was incorporated in Knox's manuscript 'History of the Reformation'. Although a Latin translation of the original 'Book of Reformation' was in preparation by August 1560, so that copies might be sent for approval to Calvin, Viret and Beza in Geneva, and to Peter Martyr, Bullinger and others in Zürich, it was evidently considered premature to submit the work to the Reformation Parliament,* whose meeting in August 1560 authorized a Reformed (Scots) Confession of Faith,* forbade the mass and abrogated papal authority. Parliament was followed by further discussion of ecclesiastical issues, and the granting of a commission to Winram,* Spottiswoode,* Willock,* Douglas,* Row* and Knox* – all six were John – to prepare a statement on polity and discipline, just as they had previously done on doctrine in their compilation of the Confession of Faith. In the revision and expansion of the earlier 'Book of Reformation', carried out between August and December 1560, three main interpolations were added on superintendents,* schools and universities.* Textual criticism also reveals that what looks like the original matter on doctrine, the sacraments, ministry, discipline, polity and endowment was subject to modification and change. The Book itself was ready for scrutiny by the General Assembly in December 1560, its contents confirm that it was examined by an ecclesiastical body, and in January 1560/1 it was presented for approval to a convention of nobles in Edinburgh, where the privy council* and many of the nobles present with some qualifications consented to the *FBD*, the implementation of whose programme became the Church's priority.

In their preface, the authors claimed for their proposals scriptural warrant, and urged the Protestant lords against sanctioning anything 'which God's plain Word shall not approve'. Section 1 on doctrine recognized the need for preaching the gospel 'truly and openly' in every church throughout the land, the suppression of false teaching and practice 'imposed on the consciences of men without the expressed commandments of God's Word' (deemed to include saints' days and feast days, obligatory celibacy and distinctive ecclesiastical attire). The two dominical sacraments* – baptism* and the Lord's Supper* – discussed in section 2, were to be administered (after congregations had been duly instructed) 'in such a tongue as the people do understand' (Scots or English, and presumably Gaelic) after the manner prescribed in 'the order of Geneva', which was already 'used in some of our churches'. Water alone was sanctioned in baptism, and punishment urged for those who continued to use 'oil, salt, wax, spittle, conjuration and crossing'. Communion in both kinds was affirmed, and 'sitting at a table' considered 'most convenient to that holy action'. A short chapter 3 on 'the abolition of idolatry', by which was understood 'the mass, invocation of saints, adoration of images' and 'all honouring of God not contained in his holy Word', called for the suppression of religious houses, cathedrals, chapels, chantries and collegiate kirks* where masses were said for the souls of the departed.

Parish churches, of course, were to be retained for congregational worship. The congregation's voice in selecting a minister was recognized; the candidate's examination was entrusted to 'men of soundest judgement' in the 'best reformed city and town' of the area; and the elders* (whose office is assumed, not defined, in chapter 4 of the book) were expected to contribute to that assessment. At a minister's inauguration, the imposition of hands or 'other ceremony' was considered unnecessary. Until such time as fully trained ministers were recruited for every parish, the authors proposed the temporary device of creating assistant readers,* equipped to instruct congregations in the common prayers and Scripture but not qualified to preach or minister the sacraments. Financial provision for the ministry, treated in chapter 5, led the authors to claim adequate and equitable (not equal) stipends* uplifted from the church's rightful patrimony,* and administered by the deacons* as financial officers. Assistant readers and those able to 'exhort' (see Exhorter) were also to receive recompense for their labours; the deserving poor, it was recognized, required sustenance from the church; and schoolmasters needed support from ecclesiastical resources. The extent of the church's patrimony and the means of securing sufficient finance for the work of the Reformed Church were not identified until chapter 6, and there are indications of revision in drafting. The claim that the Reformed Church should inherit all the teinds,* that is tithes, and at least part of the lands and rents of the pre-Reformation Church included a proposal to subvert the ancient structure of benefices and to redistribute resources in favour of the parishes. Such controversial and sweeping plans failed to attract unqualified support, for too many beneficiaries of ecclesiastical wealth and property – the Crown, nobles and lairds – stood to lose if the reforms were effected fully.

Inserted between chapters 6 on patrimony and 7 on discipline* are the three sections on superintendents,* schools and universities.* These interpolations arose as the Reformers gave further thought to the work of evangelization and oversight and to meeting the educational needs of society. The superintendent's work was justified as 'a thing most expedient for this time' on the practical ground that, with a shortage of ministers, 'ten or twelve' supervising, itinerant preachers were necessary to 'plant and erect kirks, to set order and appoint ministers' in those regions assigned them 'where none are now'. As schoolmasters were also to be sustained from ecclesiastical resources and subject to supervision by ministers and elders, the authors recommended the appointment of a schoolmaster for each congregation or parish, with Latin masters in the towns, and the creation of arts colleges in the larger burghs. The plans for reform of the three universities of St Andrews, Glasgow and Aberdeen are exceptionally detailed. Arts, medicine, law and divinity courses were proposed for the three existing colleges in St Andrews; Glasgow and Aberdeen were each to gain a second college, and teach in arts, law and divinity.

The essentially Calvinist* insistence on ecclesiastical discipline (to which princes and preachers are also subject, and whose administration is entrusted to the minister, elders and even deacons acting on behalf of the whole congregation) is distinguished in chapter 7 from the activities assigned to the civil magistracy, and the Church's right of excommunication is duly affirmed. The appointment for a term from each congregation of elders to assist the minister in exercising discipline, and of deacons to administer finances is outlined in chapter 8, where the Reformed practice of mutual censure and fraternal admonition is commended. Ecclesiastical administration (ch. 9) is largely focused on congregational activities: the need to establish good order for preaching the Word, administering the sacraments, public prayer, worship, matrimony, burials (to be held 'without all kind of ceremony' used in the past), religious instruction, correcting offenders, and the repair of church buildings.

In their conclusion, the authors commended their findings to the Protestant lords for endorsement and implementation. The unstable political situation, however, with the return from France in 1561 of Mary, Queen of Scots* to rule in person, coincided with continuing disagreement over the *FBD*'s radical financial proposals to frustrate efforts at implementing the authors' programme in its entirety. Yet, with singular tenacity, the General Assembly did its best to give effect to its proposals during the 1560s. The Convention of Leith* in 1572, it is true, marked a temporary deflection from achieving some of these aims, but the ideals were not abandoned, finding fresh expression in the *Second Book of Discipline** of 1578.

FBD; J. Kirk, *Patterns of Reform* (E, 1989).

J. Kirk

First World War (1914–18). In the initial stages of the War the Scottish Churches, like the Scottish people generally, tended to regard the conflict as a moral crusade. The overwhelming majority of Scots of all social classes and political persuasions rallied to the call to arm with hearty patriotism. The number of volunteers was far higher in Scotland than in Britain as a whole; some believed the conflict might well be over before the first troops reached the front. While a few Christian pacifists* – notably Keir Hardie* and several UFC ministers – and sections of the 'socialist left' opposed the War, the nation generally, including the major Churches, were caught up in the tide of patriotic fervour.

The temptation in wartime to identify the will of God with the nation's glory and destiny was evident in all the Churches. Not infrequently, the legacy of late Victorian optimism about the moral and spiritual evolution and perfectibility of mankind was linked to a shallow, idealistic liberal theology that saw the War as a providential and beneficial 'purifying fire' in the upward progress of the human race. Contemporary organs of Church opinion reflect the virtually unanimous conviction that the conflict had the full blessing of God. As the *British Weekly** expressed it: 'In fighting the war lords of Germany we are fighting anti-Christ' (17 September 1914, 586). A CofS minister, in a letter to soldiers at the front, was convinced that the bloodshed was part of God's plan: 'that nations, like souls, must first have their feet washed in blood ere they can stand erect' (*Life and Work,** January 1915, 11). The War, he claimed, was 'a holy war, more so than any Crusade of old, for in a cause so good and so imperative man never drew the sword'. George Adam Smith,* Principal of Aberdeen University, went so far as to call the War 'a sacrament, and a sacrament in the full sense of that name as we Scots have been brought up to understand it' (T. C. Smout, *A Century of the Scottish People 1830–1950*, L, 1986, 267).

Although the propagation of such views continued throughout the War, by early 1916, with the casualties mounting daily at an appalling rate, and with fresh revelations of incompetence among both generals and politicians, there were also signs in the Churches of a more realistic, penitent and self-critical attitude toward the War. One outcome was that in the two large Presbyterian Churches (CofS and UFC) special committees were formed in 1916 to study the implications of the War. Reports issued between 1917 and 1919 viewed the War as a judgment of God on the sins of both Church and nation, and summoned the Churches to promote the reformation of the nation's social and industrial life. Joint CofS and UFC congresses were held in the four large Scottish cities to address the issues of social reconstruction. Such joint events during the War, together with widespread local co-operation at the parish level, were key factors in preparing the way for the union of 1929.

W. P. Paterson and D. Watson (eds), *Social Evils and Problems – the CofS Commission on the War* (E, 1918); D. S. Cairns (ed.), *The Army and Religion* (L, 1919); C. Harvie, *No Gods and Precious Few Heroes: Scotland 1914–1980* (L, 1981); C. Brown, *The Social History of Religion in Scotland since 1730* (L, NY, 1987); P. C. Matheson, 'Scottish War Sermons, 1914–19', *RSCHS* 17 (1972), 203–13 (with bibliogr.); D. J. Withrington, 'The First World War: its Impact on the Churches in Scotland', *RSCHS* forthcoming.

D. C. Smith

Fisher, James (1697–1775), one of the founders of the Secession* Church. A son of Thomas Fisher (1669–1721) (*FES* IV, 244), minister of Rhynd, Perthshire, he was educated in Perth and at the Universities of Glasgow and St Andrews. He then studied divinity in Edinburgh. After his father's death in 1721 he was able to attend Ebenezer Erskine's* ministry at Portmoak, Kinross (later marrying one of Erskine's daughters). He was ordained to Kinclaven (in the Presbytery of Dunkeld) in 1725 with a unanimous call from the people, the presentation having devolved from the patron to the Presbytery.

Fisher was involved throughout in the petition and protests of 1732 that led to the Secession* of 1733. It was in Kinclaven that Erskine preached, in October 1732, what, tradition had it, was the same sermon he preached before the Synod a few days later. Fisher signed the protest in 1733, was duly loosed from his charge in November and took part in the December meeting at Gairney Bridge at which the Associate Presbytery* was formed. As clerk of the Presbytery he assisted William Wilson* in preparing the Presbytery's 'Testimony'.*

The congregation at Kinclaven formally acceded to the Presbytery in October 1736, though they continued in possession of both kirk and manse until August 1741. By then Fisher had already received a call from a newly formed congregation in Glasgow, where he ministered for the rest of his life.

Shortly after being called to Glasgow, Fisher took part in the controversy over the Cambuslang and Kilsyth revivals,* publishing *A Review of the Preface to a Narrative of the Extraordinary Work at Kilsyth . . .* (G, 1743), in which he called into question the genuineness of the supposed conversions. He joined his brethren in the Presbytery in renewing the Covenants* in 1743 and in supporting the government in the Rising* of 1745. He held that the Burgess Oath* was lawful, though views on the matter should not be imposed as a term of Communion. Consequently, in the split which followed he adhered to the Associate (Burgher) Synod.* He was appointed to succeed Ebenezer Erskine as the Synod's theological tutor (1749–64).

With initial contributions from Ebenezer and Ralph Erskine, Fisher wrote *The Assembly's Shorter Catechism Explained, By Way of Question and Answer* (G, 1753, 1760; revised and many times reprinted). Initially the project of the Church, Fisher perfected and completed it.

FES IV, 162; John Brown, *Memorials of . . . James Fisher* (E, 1849); J. M'Kerrow, *History of the Secession Church* (E, 1848).

D. C. Lachman

Fisherfolk, Missions to, missions aimed specifically at presenting the gospel to fishermen and fisherwomen, operated mainly by the Protestant Churches and by independent evangelists after 1850. The indigenous fisherfolk of the east and north-east coasts of Scotland, from Port Seton to Thurso, who were the main focus of attention, formed distinctive communities with strong religious affiliations, sometimes productive of deep spiritual movements. The major landing ports were also subject to large influxes of ancillary workers during the two annual herring seasons (spring and autumn). These workers included many 'hieland quines' (*i.e.* Highland girls) from the Outer Hebrides and the northern Highland mainland, who worked as gutters and packers of herring. In the wake of the fishing fleets they followed the herring round the western, northern and eastern coasts of Britain until they reached Yarmouth and Lowestoft in late autumn.

On the west coast, a Royal Bounty* missionary was stationed at Lochbroom as early as 1739. The fishing-ports of the north-east were visited regularly by itinerant and other preachers of various Churches from the early 1800s. A growing interest in the evangelization of the fishing communities emerged in the 1850s, and was reinforced by the series of revivals* associated with 1859. Evangelistic organizations aimed specifically at the fishing communities were established, mainly through the initiative of an Orcadian, Thomas Rosie (d. 1859), who founded the Edinburgh-based Scottish Coast Mission (1852), the Glasgow-based West Coast Mission (1855) and the Aberdeen-based North-East Coast Mission (1858), before moving to India as the missionary of the Bombay Harbour Mission. The North-East Coast Mission employed travelling evangelists such as the Gaelic*-speaking Donald Ross,* who was at the centre of strong revival movements in the fishing communities of Footdee and Fraserburgh in 1861. The Evangelicalism of these movements became indigenized in the fishing communities, so that 'out of men and women who could barely read or write, there arose men ... who became earnest preachers of the Gospel of God's grace'. Led by Ross and others they helped to lay the foundations of Scottish Brethrenism,* which was well suited to the traditions of the close-knit fisherfolk.

The movements in the fishing communities owed much to the FC, with which Ross was originally associated but from which he eventually dissented. It was believed by some that the formality of the FC tended to quench the liberating spirit of revival found among the fisherfolk. The FC, however, maintained its interest in the fisherfolk, and stationed missionaries in several of the ports. These men not only preached, but also provided some basic medical services, such as bone-setting.

By the end of the nineteenth century, most of the Scottish Protestant Churches were involved in missions to the fisherfolk, especially to the fishergirls, who formed a distinct group within the active communities. This required female workers, who often combined the dual role of 'Biblewomen' and nurses, attending to spiritual needs and bandaging sores caused by the knives and pickle essential to the work. The Biblewomen also distributed Christian literature such as tracts and Bibles. In 1898 the Highlands and Islands Committee of the FC appointed four Biblewomen to serve at the ports of Stornoway, Fraserburgh, Peterhead and Wick. Until the eve of the Second World War, Baptists* had an active interest in the fishing port of Lerwick, and for some years maintained a Baptist Mission to the Fishergirls, led by Miss Jane Henderson, who later became the pastor of Lossiemouth Baptist Church (1918–21). Her career shows how missions to the fishergirls aided the development of the concept of women's ministry, which had not normally been accepted within the Scottish Churches.

The mobility involved in fishing, especially during the herring seasons, meant that the fisherfolk could be influenced by preachers from other parts of Britain, particularly in the East Anglian seaports. The most prominent revivals experienced among the Scottish fishing communities since 1900, namely those of the early 1920s, were stimulated in part by the preaching of A. Douglas Brown, a Baptist pastor in London who held evangelistic campaigns initially in Lowestoft in the summer of 1921 (*Revival Addresses*, L, 1922). Brown's activities extended to Ipswich and Yarmouth, and converts included fisherfolk who had come south from Scotland. The Scottish fisherfolk at Yarmouth also heard powerful preaching from Jock Troup,* a Wick cooper. The impulses of this revival, which occurred during a very poor herring season, were taken north by the returning fisherfolk, and localized revivals broke out in many of the fishing ports. In December 1921 the *Glasgow Herald* reported that 'the prairie fire of religious revival is raging along the coasts from Wick to Peterhead'. The movement terminated in the Portsoy Revival of 1923, but its influence remained long afterwards.

Revivals in the fishing ports of Scotland have been less frequent since the 1920s. Nevertheless, the ports retain a strong, indigenized Evangelicalism which continues to produce preachers and evangelists. Regional hymnology* also preserves the spirit of mission and revival. The rugged, sea-going images of the fisherfolk's own hymns frequently portray the uncertainties and dangers of the voyage of life, and point to Jesus Christ as pilot, compass and anchor. The missionary work of individual bodies (*e.g.* the Faith Mission* and the Salvation Army*) is now supplemented in the larger ports by the Royal National Mission to Deep-Sea Fishermen. (*see* Seamen's Missions).

D. Fraser (ed.), *The Christian Watt Papers* (²Ellon, 1988); C. W. Ross (ed.), *Donald Ross* (G, 1987); J. Ritchie, *Floods Upon the Dry Ground* (Peterhead, 1983); S. Tracey, 'The Biblewomen and the Herring Trade', *FCSR*, January 1990, 9.

D. E. Meek

Fleming, David Hay (1849–1931), historian and antiquary. Born in St Andrews, Fleming attended Madras College and went directly into the family business. A substantial inheritance enabled him to devote himself to scholarly researches. His early literary endeavours, which included contributions to the *Watchword** and the *Original Secession Magazine*, exhibited much of the precision which characterized his work as a whole. From 1892 he contributed reviews to the *British Weekly*,* collected with others as *Critical Reviews Relating Chiefly to Scotland* (E, 1912).

Andrew Lang* described Fleming's scholarship as 'remarkable for accuracy, judicious treatment, and research', a judgment endorsed by the University of St Andrews, which conferred an LLD on him in 1898. His books include *Mary Queen of Scots, From her Birth to her Flight into England* (E, 1897), a work of meticulous scholarship in which the notes

FLEMING, JOHN

comprise over three-quarters of the whole, *The Reformation in Scotland* (E, 1910; Stone Lectures at Princeton Theological Seminary*), *The Martyrs and Confessors of St Andrews* (Cupar, 1887), and a *Hand-Book to St Andrews* (St Andrews, 1881; ²1924). He edited, with extensive introductions and notes, the *Register of the Minister Elders and Deacons of the Christian Congregation of St. Andrews ... 1559–1600* (E, 1889–90), the *Diary of Sir Archibald Johnston of Warriston, 1650–1654*, II (E, 1919), Patrick Walker,* *Six Saints of the Covenant*, 2 vols (E, 1901), *The Register of the Privy Seal of Scotland, 1529–42* (vol. II, E, 1921), and, at the author's request, A. F. Mitchell,* *The Scottish Reformation* (E, 1900).

He was vice-president of the Knox Club,* and president of the Scottish Reformation Society* from 1919 to his death, writing a number of pamphlets for each, particularly opposing the errors of Roman Catholicism. He was also a member of the Scottish History Society and a fellow of the Society of Antiquaries.

In protest at the introduction of instrumental music to Martyrs' Free Church, St Andrews, he joined the United Original Secession Church in Victoria Terrace, Edinburgh, and, in 1905, moved to Edinburgh. From 1927 to his death he was in intense pain from acute neuritis and, though he was able to complete his catalogue of the antiquities in the *St Andrews Cathedral Museum* (E, 1931), much contemplated work was left unfinished.

Over the years Fleming acquired a large, carefully selected library on the history and particularly the church history of Scotland. His will donated this collection to St Andrews, where it is still maintained and run by the Town Council as a reference library.

Henry M. Paton, *David Hay Fleming, Historian and Antiquary* (E, 1934); *DNB 1931–1940*, 282–3.

D. C. Lachman

Fleming, John (1785–1857), minister and zoologist. Born in Kirkroad near Bathgate, W. Lothian, the son of a tenant farmer, John Fleming achieved prominence as Scotland's foremost zoologist of his day. Graduating from the University of Edinburgh in 1805, he was licensed as a minister in the CofS and served in Shetland and Fife before assuming the chair of natural philosophy at King's College, Aberdeen in 1834. During the Disruption* he sided with the FC cause and in 1845 became Professor of Natural Science at New College,* Edinburgh.

Fleming's zoological work centred on freshwater and marine invertebrates. This led him to ponder questions of taxonomy and in 1822 he published *Philosophy of Zoology*, a treatise designed to counter some of the problems with Cuvier's taxonomic scheme. Later his *History of British Animals* (1828) added greatly to his scientific reputation. Fleming was a staunch proponent of uniformitarianism as the only viable method in geology, and accordingly he attacked William Buckland's violent-flood hypothesis, claiming it was compatible with neither Scripture nor science. Fleming's robust methodological concerns were later taken up by Charles Ly-

FLEMING, ROBERT

ell in his uniformitarian assault on catastrophism. At the same time Fleming was a tireless defender of the compatibility of science and religion and urged that zoology was nothing less than the study of 'the wisdom of the great plan of Providence'.

DNB XIX, 279–80; *FES* IV, 302–3; *AFCS*, I, 55; R. Laudan, *From Mineralogy to Geology* (Chicago, 1987); C. C. Gillispie, *Genesis and Geology* (Cambridge, MA, 1951); *Dictionary of Scientific Biography* V, 31–2.

D. N. Livingstone

Fleming, Placid (1642–1720), abbot. Thomas Fleming, descendant of the earls of Wigtown, was born at Kirkoswald, Ayrshire. Educated in Edinburgh, he became a RC* in Ireland; then, as a naval officer, he was a captive of Moorish pirates. Entering the Scots College,* Paris, 1667, he proceeded to Ratisbon (*see* Schottenklöster), took vows as Brother Placid 1669 and was ordained priest 1671. In December 1672 he was elected abbot, a position he held for forty-seven years.

His single-minded policy was to build up his monastery and thereby assist the RC mission in Scotland. He founded a seminary in 1713 to ensure a supply of novices and thus of missioner priests. At Erfurt he secured two permanent university professorships for his monks. He supported plans for a unified Scottish mission, with Benedictines* subject to the bishop. The benefits of his vigorous rule lasted into the Napoleonic anti-religious era.

M. Dilworth, *The Scots in Franconia* (E, 1974); W. R. Humphries, 'Abbot Placid', *AUR* 30 (1944), 315–19.

M. Dilworth

Fleming, Robert (1630–94), minister and theologian. Ordained at Cambuslang in 1653, he was deprived in 1662 for nonconformity. He was offered an indulgence* at Kilwinning in Ayrshire in 1672, but declined to accept. In 1677 he was admitted collegiate minister of the Scottish Church, Rotterdam, in succession to Robert MacWard.* On revisiting Scotland in the following year he preached at conventicles,* and was arrested and imprisoned. He was released in 1679 and returned to Rotterdam, where he remained until his death on a visit to London.

Fleming is best known for *The Fulfilling of the Scripture* (Rotterdam, 1669; ²1671), an elaborate work in three parts, in which he traces the outworking of Scripture truth in church history and Christian experience. In the ecclesiastical conflicts of the day he sought to exercise a moderating influence. His pleas for fellowship with the indulged ministers – in opposition to MacWard and others – occasioned considerable controversy, particularly among the exiles who sought refuge in Holland after Bothwell Bridge.*

Scripture Truth Confirmed and cleared (Rotterdam, 1678); *The Truth and Certainty of the Protestant Faith* (Rotterdam, 1678); *The Church Wounded and Rent by a Spirit of Division* (E?, 1681); *The Confirming

FLEMING, ROBERT

Work of Religion (Rotterdam, 1685); *The Present Aspect of our Times* (L, 1694).

FES III, 236-7; *DNB* XIX, 284-5; W. Stephen, *The History of the Scottish Church, Rotterdam* (E, 1833), 83-113.

M. Grant

Fleming, Robert (1660-1716), son of the above. He studied at Leiden and Utrecht, was privately ordained in Holland and, after serving four years as a tutor in England, was called in 1692 to the English Presbyterian church in Leiden and, in 1694, as his father's successor in Rotterdam. In 1698 he was called to the Founders' Hall (Scots Presbyterian) congregation in London, the oldest of the Presbyterian churches there. The call was favoured by both William Carstares* and William III, each of whom thought highly of him. Fleming continued in this charge until his death.

His works included: *Discourses on several subjects* (L, 1701), with a section enlarged as *Apocalyptical Key* (L, 1702; reprints include *Discourses*, E, 1793, and, with the fall of papal Rome, *The Rise and Fall of the Papacy*, L, 1848), *Christology*, 3 vols (L, 1705-8); *The Mirrour of Divine Lore Unvail'd, In A Poetical Paraphrase of the ... Song of Solomon* (L, 1691).

FES, VII, 489-90; *DNB* XIX, 285-6. W. Wilson, *The History and Antiquities of Dissenting Churches ... in London*, 4 vols (L, 1808), II, 468-87; W. Stephen, *The History of the Scottish Church, Rotterdam* (E, 1833), 114-37.

D. C. Lachman

Flint, John (1660-1730), minister and scholar. One of four young men chosen by the United Societies* for training for the ministry, Flint was sent to Holland and educated in Gröningen. On his return to Scotland he chose to unite with the CofS and was first ordained in 1688 to Lasswade (in the Presbytery of Dalkeith) and then, in 1710, translated to the New North Church in Edinburgh. He wrote against John Simson* (*Examen Doctrinae D. Johannis Simson*, E, 1717) and took part in the General Assembly's condemnation of the *Marrow*.* He had a considerable reputation as a scholar and linguist; Thomas Boston* solicited a testimonial when he was attempting to publish his work on the Hebrew accents.

FES I, 143.

D. C. Lachman

Flint, Robert (1838-1910), CofS minister and theologian. Born in Dumfriesshire the son of a farm overseer, he was educated at the University of Glasgow. He was minister of the East Church in Aberdeen 1859-62, and of Kilconquhar in Fife before becoming Professor of Moral Philosophy at St Andrews in 1864 and then Professor of Divinity at Edinburgh in 1876. He gave the Baird Lectures* in 1876 which were subsequently published as *Theism* (E, 1877) and ran into eleven editions between 1877 and 1905. His Croall Lectures* of 1887-8 were later published as *Agnosticism* (E,

FORBES, ALEXANDER PENROSE

1903). He also wrote extensively on the philosophy of history, including a monograph on the Italian thinker *Vico* (E and L, 1884) and a *History of the Philosophy of History* (E, 1893). He was made FRSE and FBA in 1901. He was appointed Gifford Lecturer* in 1908-9, but was unable to give the lectures due to ill health. A man of wide learning, Flint did not adopt the idealism fashionable at the time but continued to use rationalistic philosophy to defend theism. It could not prove the existence of God but could adduce arguments in favour of belief and counter polytheism. Flint also wished to use advances in science and in biblical criticism in the defence of the Christian faith. He was one of the first Scottish theologians to take an interest in socialism (*Socialism*, L, 1894). Flint's academic work occupied most of his time. He was unmarried and had few friends, but his patience and kindness made him popular with the students. He did not take much part in ecclesiastical affairs but he was a strong supporter of the Est.C. Although he did not become a member of the Scottish Church Society,* he spoke at several of its conferences and was sympathetic to its programme.

D. MacMillan, *The Life of Robert Flint, DD, LLD* (L, 1914); A. P. F. Sell, *Defending and Declaring the Faith. Some Scottish Examples, 1860-1920* (Exeter, 1987), 39-63.

D. M. Murray

Forbes, Alexander Penrose (1817-75), Bishop of Brechin in the Episcopal Church 1847-75. Forbes has been described as the Scottish Pusey. He met E. B. Pusey when on sick-leave from the East India Company, and it was Pusey who helped him to decide that his vocation was not to serve in India but in the ordained ministry of the Church. He was ordained in Oxford, but after a short ministry there offered his services to the EpCS, to which many of his family had made notable contributions. He was Rector of St James', Stonehaven, 1846-7 and in the summer of 1847 he ministered singlehanded at St Saviour's, Leeds, during a cholera epidemic.

At the age of thirty he was elected Bishop of Brechin and rector of the Episcopal congregation in Dundee. Forbes had a special concern for mission among the poor of Dundee and inspired his clergy to go to the most populous parts of the city to gather round them a congregation. As a result, there were three new Episcopal churches in Dundee. Forbes also decided to make Dundee the centre of the diocese and to build his cathedral there.

In a charge to the clergy of the diocese, he emphasized the real presence in, and the sacrificial character of, the eucharist and this led to a trial for alleged heresy by his brother bishops in 1860. He was censured but not found guilty. It was feared that he might follow Newman into the RC Church, and he was presented with an address signed by 6,386 working men in Dundee urging him to stay and continue his good work there. Pusey urged him to set out his views in *An Explanation of the Thirty-*

nine Articles (2 vols, O, 1867-8). In this he made a plea for the Pope to convene a council to heal the divisions of Christendom. He died bitterly disappointed with the First Vatican Council.

D. J. Mackey, *Bishop Forbes: A Memoir* (L, 1888); W. Perry, *A. P. Forbes* (L, 1939); R. G. W. Strong, 'Alexander Forbes of Brechin (1817-1875) . . .' (PhD, University of Edinburgh, 1992).

H. R. Sefton

Forbes, Archangel (*c.*1570-1606), Capuchin friar. He was the son of the Master of Forbes and Margaret Gordon, daughter of the fourth Earl of Huntly. To avoid a marriage arranged by his father, he fled to Belgium disguised as a shepherd and there, after various adventures, received the Capuchin (*see* Franciscans) habit in August 1593, taking the religious name of Archangel. A plan to send him to Scotland for pastoral work was apparently not implemented, though he was ordained priest and converted Scots in Belgium to RCism.

His elder brother, William, had also been a Capuchin in Belgium with the name Archangel but had died in 1592. Their mother, divorced in 1574, likewise went to Belgium and died there in 1606. Their father married again and, having succeeded as Lord Forbes in 1593, assigned the lordship and estates in 1598 to the eldest son of the second marriage, who assumed the title of Master of Forbes. When the father died on 29 June 1606, however, the Capuchin was the lawful Lord Forbes for some weeks until his own death in August. Much of his biography is unvouched for by public records but, like the more celebrated Scots Capuchin, Archangel Leslie* (with whom he is sometimes confused), he achieved a place in the printed literature of Europe.

A. Bellesheim, *History of the Catholic Church of Scotland* (E, L, 1887-90), III, 408-10, 576-7; Fr. Cuthbert, *The Capuchins* (L, 1928), II, 322-5; J. B. Paul (ed.), *The Scots Peerage* (E, 1904-14), IV, 57-61; T. G. Law, 'The Bibliography of . . . Two Scottish Capuchins', *Papers of the Edinburgh Bibliographical Society* 1 (1896), 1-12.

M. Dilworth

Forbes, George Hay (1821-75), Episcopalian* liturgist, brother of Alexander Forbes.* Paralysed in his legs from infancy, Forbes was a keen scholar with a lifelong passion for liturgical studies, particularly the Scottish Communion Office, whose superior 'catholicism' he championed against the English *Book of Common Prayer.** Ordained deacon in 1848, he commenced an Episcopalian mission at Burntisland, Fife. He was ordained priest in 1849.

In 1850 Forbes issued a controversial revised edition of the *BCP* which was suppressed on the orders of the Scottish bishops. When canons were enacted in 1863 enforcing the use of the English *BCP*, Forbes took the matter to the civil courts, claiming the Synod had acted *ultra vires*. The case lasted from 1863 to 1867, when the House of Lords gave judgment against Forbes.

Forbes established his own printing press in 1852, the Pitsligo Press, from which he issued an edition of Gregory of Nyssa's works, *S. Gregorii Nysseni Opera Omnia* (Burntisland, 1855-8), *The Ancient Liturgies of the Gallican Church* (with J. M. Neale, 3 vols, Burntisland, 1855-67), *The Arbuthnott Missal* (with A. P. Forbes, Burntisland, 1864), and two periodicals, the popular *Gospel Messenger* (1853-8) and the scholarly *Panoply* (1858-74).

Forbes had a powerfully independent mind, and sought in his writings, notably in the *Panoply*, to define a distinctively Scottish Episcopalian theology and worship, as against Presbyterianism, the RCC, Anglicanism and the new impetus of the Oxford Movement.

The Christian Sacrifice in the Eucharist, 3 vols (Burntisland, 1844-54). Forbes edited W. Forbes, *Considerationes Modestae*, 2 vols (O, 1850-6); T. Rattray, *Works* (Burntisland, 1854); *Missale Drummondiense* (Burntisland, 1882).

W. Perry, *George Hay Forbes. A Romance in Scholarship* (L, 1927); *DNB Miss. Pers.* 229-30.

N. R. Needham

Forbes, James (1813-51), Australian minister and educator. Educated in Aberdeen, Forbes served as a schoolteacher in Colchester, England. In 1837 he was ordained by the Presbytery of Glasgow and proceeded to Australia. He commenced his ministry in Melbourne on 3 February 1838, when the population was only about 300. At the Disruption* he sided with the FC, and when the Synod of Australia finally decided in 1846 to maintain the connection with the CofS, Forbes renounced his connection with the Synod. In June 1847 he led in the formation of the Free Presbyterian Church of Australia Felix (afterwards Victoria). Forbes' deep interest in education is shown by his opening of Scots' School (1838) and, after the break with the Synod of Australia, the John Knox School and Chalmers Free Church School. He planned the academy which opened shortly after his death, and which is the present Scotch College. He was involved in many religious and cultural enterprises, publishing the *Port Phillip Christian Herald* from 1846 to 1851, and editing the *Free Presbyterian Messenger* during 1847-9. At his death at the age of thirty-eight, Forbes had occupied for thirteen years an influential position during Melbourne's formative years.

Australian Dict. of Biogr. I, 399-400; E. Sweetman, *Victoria's First Public Educationalist* (Melbourne, 1939); J. C. Robinson, *Melbourne's First Settled Minister* (Melbourne, 1928).

A. M. Harman

Forbes, John (*c.*1568-1634), Presbyterian writer. Forbes graduated from the University of St Andrews in 1583, and was ordained minister of Alford, Aberdeenshire by 1593. An ardent Presbyterian, he acted as Moderator of the forbidden Aberdeen General Assembly of 1605 (*see* James VI),* and was subsequently banished for life. He was pastor of the English congregation in Middle-

FORBES, JOHN

burg from 1611, and Delft from 1621 to 1628, when he was dismissed following pressure from Charles I* and Archbishop William Laud.* He spent portions of his exile in France and died in Holland.

J. Forbes, *Certaine Records Touching the Estate of the Kirk* (1605), in D. Laing (ed.), *Scot's Narration and Forbes' Records* (Wodrow Society, E, 1846), xxxiii–lxiv, 345–558; *DNB* XIX, 401–2; *FES* VI, 117–18 (full list of his publications); C. G. F. de Jong, *John Forbes (ca. 1568–1634)* (Groningen, 1987); id., 'John Forbes ... ', *Nederl. Arch. v. Kerkgesch.* 69 (1989), 17–53.

K. M. Brown

Forbes, John (1593–1648), leader of the Aberdeen Doctors* and the first Professor of Divinity at King's College, Aberdeen. Forbes was one of the greatest patristic scholars and theologians Scotland has produced.

Second son of Patrick Forbes* of Corse who later became Bishop of Aberdeen, Forbes was educated at King's College, Aberdeen and on the continent at Heidelberg University and at Sedan, where he studied under his kinsman, Andrew Melville.* He was ordained by a Dutch classis in 1619 and the following year appointed to the new chair of Divinity at King's College. An academic competition preceded the appointment by the Synod of Aberdeen on this and all subsequent occasions until 1927.

Forbes defended the lawfulness of the Five Articles of Perth* in his *Irenicum* (A, 1629), and in April 1638 he attacked the National Covenant* in a pamphlet *A Peaceable Warning, to the Subjects in Scotland* (A, 1638). He led the Aberdeen Doctors in their dispute with the Covenanting* leaders and, in consequence, was deprived of his chair in 1641.

The death of his elder brother, Patrick,* meant that he succeeded as laird of Corse, and he retired to live on his estate. His refusal to sign the Solemn League and Covenant* forced him to seek refuge in the Netherlands. During his exile he published his monumental *Instructiones Historico-Theologicae* (Amsterdam, 1645). His devotional diary was translated into Latin by his friend George Garden* and included in his *Omnia Opera* (Amsterdam, 1702–3).

FES VII, 369–70; D. MacMillan, *The Aberdeen Doctors* (L, 1909); E. G. Selwyn (ed.), *The First Book of the Irenicum (of John Forbes)* (C, 1923); W. M. Low, *John Forbes of Corse and his Eucharistic Teaching* (E, n.d.).

H. R. Sefton

Forbes, John (1802–99), Professor of Hebrew at Aberdeen University 1870–87. Born at Boharm, Banffshire, he was a student at Marischal College, Aberdeen (MA, 1819). He met Goethe in 1829 while travelling on the Continent. From 1850 to 1870 he was House Governor and Headmaster of Donaldson's Hospital, Edinburgh, which in its handsome building by W. H. Playfair (1842–51) catered for poor and deaf children (later solely for the deaf). In Aberdeen he was a well-loved teacher

FORBES, PATRICK

– bright in manner, courteous, patient and respectful, retaining mental elasticity despite taking up the chair at sixty-eight years of age. He was deeply interested in the parallelism of Hebrew poetry, and believed its influence to be wide-ranging, as most of his works reveal: *The Symmetrical Structure of Scripture* (E, 1854), *Analytical Commentary on the Epistle of the Romans* (E, 1868), *The Servant of the Lord in Isaiah XL–LXVI Reclaimed to Isaiah* (E, 1873), *Predestination and Free-Will and the Westminster Confession of Faith* (E, 1878), and *Studies on the Book of Psalms* (E, 1888). King's College, Aberdeen, gave him an LLD in 1837 and Edinburgh a DD in 1873.

S. Ree in *Aurora Borealis Academica: Aberdeen University Appreciations 1860–1889* (A, 1899), 150–4; *FES* VII, 369.

G. Wareing

Forbes, John Thomas (1857–1936), Baptist minister and college principal. He was the son of Finlay Forbes (Baptist minister at Blairgowrie, 1873–80, and Alloa, 1880–95) and nephew of William Tulloch.* Educated at Edinburgh and Glasgow Universities, he served the Baptist churches at Cupar (1886–8); Newcastle (1888–95), Dublin Street, Edinburgh (1895–1901); and Hillhead, Glasgow (1901–28). From 1914 he lectured at the Baptist Theological College of Scotland in Glasgow and became its Principal in 1922, retiring in 1934. He was President of the Baptist Union of Scotland in 1904 and of the British Baptist Union in 1915. He published *God's Measure: Sermons* (E, 1901), and *Socrates* (E, 1905).

Obituary notices, *Scottish Baptist Magazine*, March 1936; A. Semple, *Hillhead Baptist Church 1883–1983* (G, 1983).

D. B. Murray

Forbes, Patrick (1564–1635), Bishop of Aberdeen. Born at Corse Castle, the eldest son of William Forbes of Corse (Aberdeenshire), he inherited the family estate on his father's death in 1598. Educated at Stirling grammar school under Thomas Buchanan, nephew of George Buchanan,* Forbes proceeded first to Glasgow University, where his second cousin, Andrew Melville,* was Principal, and then to St Andrews University, where he pursued his studies when Melville moved to become Principal of St Mary's College in 1580. Closely identified with the Presbyterian* cause at that stage, he followed Melville and the ultra-Protestant lords and ministers into exile in 1584 with the onset of the 'anti-Presbyterian dictatorship' of Arran's government (*see* Stewart, James, d.1596). He visited Oxford, was present in London at the funeral of James Lawson in October 1584, returned to Berwick by the close of 1585, and was considered 'a forward man for discipline and the banished'. With the collapse of the Arran regime, he accompanied Melville to St Andrews where he was offered a teaching post but declined. In 1589, he married Lucretia Spens, daughter of the laird of Wormiston in Fife, and lived at Montrose till his father's death.

FORBES, ROBERT

In 1612, he entered the ministry at Keith (Banffshire), and in 1617, with a view to mediating, visited the imprisoned Presbyterian minister, David Calderwood,* who had opposed royal policy. With the death of Bishop Alexander Forbes, he hesitantly accepted promotion to the see of Aberdeen in 1618. He considered King James' 'Five Articles of Perth'* of 1618 to be indifferent in themselves but argued for obeying the King's will and occupied his seat on the Court of High Commission* in 1622. Under Charles I,* Forbes attended conventions of estates in 1625, 1630 and 1631, but sat only occasionally on the privy council and took no prominent part in state affairs. Though obliged to suppress Presbyterian and RC nonconformity in his diocese, Forbes sought mediation and peaceful reconciliation. One of his sons, John (d. 1648),* became Professor of Divinity at King's College, Aberdeen.

An Exquisite Commentarie upon the Revelation of Saint John (L, 1613).

Calderwood; J. Melville, *Autobiography and Diary*, ed. R. Pitcairn (E, 1842), 18, 170, 260; W. G. S. Snow, *The Time, Life and Thought of Patrick Forbes, Bishop of Aberdeen* (L, 1952); J. Durkan and J. Kirk, *The University of Glasgow, 1451–1577* (G, 1977), 318, 376; R. Keith, *An Historical Catalogue of Scottish Bishops*, ed. M. Russel (L, 1824), 132; *FESMA* 4; *FES* VI, 319, VII, 337, VIII, 709; *DNB* XIX, 407–9.

J. Kirk

Forbes, Robert (1708–75), Episcopalian* clergyman and liturgiologist. Forbes began his ministry, first as assistant, and in 1736 as incumbent, of the Episcopalian congregation in Leith. An ardent Jacobite,* in 1745 he was arrested when attempting to join the Rising,* and imprisoned for several months. On release, he continued his ministry in Leith, apparently without persecution. In 1762 Forbes was consecrated Bishop of Ross and Caithness, while remaining incumbent in Leith. There had been no resident bishops in the north of Scotland since 1707, but non-resident bishops were always consecrated for those parts. Immediately Forbes set out to visit his diocese and its four remaining clergy. He kept a journal, describing people and places visited, services conducted, sermons preached, and recording that he confirmed 616 persons in chapels and private houses between Inverness and John O'Groats, with lists of names. In 1763, back in Leith, he was summoned by a colonel of the garrison to explain why he did not pray for the king, and why the chapel was unlicensed. Being warned that prosecution might follow, he left for London, where he visited Jacobite sympathizers and nonjuring* clergy, but soon returned on learning that he was safe from prosecution. In 1770 he made a journey through Inverness-shire, Ross-shire and Argyllshire encouraging the Episcopalians, about which he kept a further journal, in which he claimed to have confirmed 1,521 persons. His records show that these Episcopalians were native Scots, of all ranks in society, and that the Episcopal Church is not an exotic English importation, as it has been sometimes misrepresented. He compiled *The Lyon in Mourning*, a remarkable collection of speeches, letters and journals, relating to Prince Charles Edward Stewart and the 1745 Rising. Forbes was a learned liturgiologist, and helped to prepare the 1764 Scottish Liturgy.

J. B. Craven (ed.), *Journals of the Episcopal Visitations* ... (²L, 1923); *DNB* XIX, 409–10.

G. N. Pennie

Forbes, William (1585–1634), first Bishop of Edinburgh and leading high-church Arminian* divine. Born in Aberdeen, he graduated MA from Marischal College in 1601. He taught logic there until 1606, when he resigned in order to extend his education by travelling abroad. After five years in Poland, Germany and Holland, studying in various universities, he returned to Britain in 1611 and became minister at Alford and then Monymusk, both in Aberdeenshire. He was appointed minister of St Nicholas, Aberdeen, in 1616. In 1618 at the Perth General Assembly, he was chosen to vindicate the article requiring kneeling at communion (see Five Articles of Perth). The same year he maintained the lawfulness of prayers for the dead in a dispute with Principal Andrew Aidie (Adie; *FES* VII, 357) of Marishal College. On Aidie's enforced resignation Forbes was appointed Principal in his place.

In 1621 he became one of the ministers of Edinburgh, where his Arminianism and his enthusiasm for the Perth articles provoked much discontent. He returned to St Nicholas Church, Aberdeen, in 1626. In 1633 he preached before Charles I* at Holyrood; Charles was impressed, and decided to erect a new see in Edinburgh for him. Forbes was consecrated as Edinburgh's first Bishop in February 1634, but died in April that year.

Forbes was the outstanding Scottish representative of the Laudian* school of thought then in the ascendant in England. His piety, erudition and ability as a preacher, however, counted for little in the eyes of Scottish Presbyterians, when placed alongside his Arminianism and his zeal for episcopacy and reconciliation with Rome.

Forbes published nothing himself, but a posthumous work was put together from his manuscripts by Bishop Thomas Sydserf* (1587–1663) and entitled *Considerationes Modestae et Pacificae Controversiarum de Justificatione, Purgatorio, Invocatione Sanctorum, Christo Mediatore, et Eucharistia* (L, 1658). George Hay Forbes* of Burntisland edited an English translation as part of the Anglo-Catholic Library (Oxford, 1856).

R. Wodrow, 'Collections on ... William Forbes' in ed. Robert Lippe, *Selections from Wodrow's Biographical Collections* (A, 1890), 245–69; *FES* VII, 396; *DNB* XIX, 411–12.

N. R. Needham

Form of Presbyterian Government (1645), see Westminster Assembly and Documents.

Forman, Andrew (c.1465–1521), Archbishop of

FORM(E) OF PRAYERS

St Andrews. Little is known about his early life. He entered St Andrews University in 1479 and was a determinant in 1481, but did not take the Master's degree. He was attached to the household of the Earl of Angus before entering the royal service. In 1490 he was James IV's procurator in Rome, and was made apostolic protonotary by Innocent VIII. Forman was chiefly responsible for negotiating the marriage of Margaret Tudor, daughter of Henry VII of England, to James IV. He was appointed Bishop of Moray in 1501. Thereafter, records show that he attended meetings of parliament, was a Lord of Articles, a Lord of Session and a Lord of Council.

James sent Forman to congratulate Henry VIII of England on his accession in 1509. In 1510 he acted on behalf of James IV and Henry VIII on the continent, trying to secure peace among Christian rulers in order to make possible a new crusade in which James would hold naval command. Forman succeeded only in reconciling Louis XII of France and Pope Julius II, and making an alliance between Louis and James IV for a joint attack on England, which led to the disastrous Scottish defeat at Flodden (1513).

Archbishop Alexander Stewart of St Andrews was killed at Flodden, and this precipitated a convoluted struggle for the archbishopric between Forman, James Beaton,* William Elphinstone,* Gavin Douglas* and John Hepburn (*DNB* XXVI, 157–8). The new Pope Leo X initially appointed his young nephew, Cardinal Cibo, but struck a deal with Forman whereby the latter relinquished his archbishopric of Bourges to Cibo in exchange for St Andrews. Forman was not installed in the position, however, until 1516. His papal connections made him unpopular in Scotland in Flodden's aftermath, especially when Leo X tried to impose Cibo on St Andrews (a breach of the royal prerogative). Forman's pluralism had provoked general discontent among the Scottish nobility; he had held not merely the bishopric of Moray and archbishopric of Bourges, but the abbacies of Pittenweem, Dryburgh* and Arbroath,* and of Cottingham in England. He was compelled to resign everything except the abbacy of Dunfermline* in order to take up the archbishopric of St Andrews.

Despite his previous record, Forman made serious attempts as Archbishop of St Andrews to reform a number of abuses in the Scottish Church. His *Synodal Constitutions and Ordinances* gives invaluable information about the condition of Church and society in the early years of James V, just as the Reformation* was dawning.

A polemic against Martin Luther, *Contra Lutherum*, was ascribed to Forman, but this attribution is almost certainly a fabrication by Thomas Dempster.*

J. Herkless and R. K. Hannay, *The Archbishops of St Andrews* (E., 1909), vol. II; Dowden, 38–9; *DNB* XIX, 436–7.

N. R. Needham

Form(e) of Prayers, *see* Book of Common Order (1564).

FORREST, DAVID WILLIAM

Formula, The (always preceded by the definite article), an abridged statement of faith which everyone taking office in the CofS is required to subscribe. Act X of 1711 ordained that certain questions were to be put to the student who had completed his public trials, who was then to sign the Formula (prescribed by the same Act), adopting the Westminster* Confession of Faith (ratified in 1690) as a confession of his faith, owning the worship and government of the Church to be founded on the Word of God, promising to adhere to and defend the same, engaging not to endeavour to prejudice the same or to follow divisive courses (running in all to some 250 words). After the document had been signed, the Act against Simoniacal Practices (1759; *see* Simony) was to be read, after which the licensing would proceed.

In 1889 the terms of the Formula were silently amended so as 'not to present any unnecessary impediment to the acceptance of office by duly qualified persons'. Further Acts of 1901 and 1903 resulted in a much abbreviated Formula without any material alterations. The same legislation discontinued the reading of the Act against Simoniacal Practices. Some further adjustments were made in Act XIII of 1910.

The Basis and Plan of Union* of 1929 reduced the Formula to three simple statements: 'I believe the fundamental doctrines of the Christian faith contained in the Confession of Faith of this Church, I acknowledge the Presbyterian government of this Church to be agreeable to the Word of God, and promise that I will submit thereto and concur therewith. I promise to observe the order of worship and the administration of all public ordinances as these are or may be allowed in this Church.'

Most Presbyteries have a Formula Book maintained exclusively for signing on such occasions. The Presbytery of Glasgow has such a volume going back to the sixteenth century.

Cox 393, 434, 574.

A. Herron

Forrest, David William (1856–1918), minister and theologian. He was born in Glasgow, son of David Forrest, minister of St Rollox UPC. He was educated at Glasgow High School, Glasgow University, the UP Theological Hall, Edinburgh, and Leipzig, where he studied under F. J. Delitzsch. Licensed as a probationer in 1880, he served at Saffronhall, Hamilton (1882–87); Moffat (1887–94); Wellington, Glasgow (1894–9); Skelmorlie (1899–1903); North Morningside, Edinburgh (1903–14). He became Professor of Systematic Theology, Glasgow UF College, and was nominated to succeed James Denney* as Principal, but death intervened. In 1900 he moved the UP General Assembly resolution which committed the UPC to union with the FC. He became DD (Glasgow) in 1898.

Forrest established his reputation as a scholar with his Kerr Lectures,* *The Christ of History and of Experience* (E., 1897), and *The Authority of Christ* (E., 1906). In the former he expounded a subtle kenoticism, and in the latter he argued for the subjection of both individual and social concerns to Christ. His theology centres in the convictions that a direct relationship to the historical Jesus, which the simplest Christian experiences, may not be by-passed, and that the incarnation cannot be understood apart from the cross.

J. H. Leckie, Memoir in *David W. Forrest, DD* (L, 1919); A. P. F. Sell, *Defending and Declaring the Faith* (Exeter, 1987), ch. 8; Small II, 46, 210; *FUFCS* 577.

A. P. F. Sell

Forrester, Thomas (1588–1642), anti-Covenanting* clergyman and writer. Graduating from St Andrews in 1608, he was episcopally ordained, and in 1623, against the wishes of the kirk session, he was appointed minister of Ayr. Transferring to Melrose in 1627, he seems to have taken great pleasure in shocking Presbyterians, and it was no surprise when in 1638, when Presbyterianism* was re-established as the national polity, he was deposed for Arminianism* and popery. This merely developed further his satirical talents, and he publicly derided the Covenanting cause in 'A Satire in two parts, relating to public affairs, 1638–9', included in James Maidment's *Book of Scottish Pasquils* (E, 1868).

DNB XX, 9; *FES* II, 187–8.

J. D. Douglas

Forrester, Thomas (c.1635–1706), minister and controversialist. Ordained at Alva in 1664 he initially conformed to episcopacy, but on reading John Brown* of Wamphray's *Apologetical Relation* he became a convinced Presbyterian* and joined the ranks of the conventicle* preachers. He was arrested for irregular preaching in February 1674, but released a month later under a general indemnity. In April of the same year he was deposed for contumacy, and his charge declared vacant. Thereafter he preached frequently both in houses and in the fields. He took refuge for a time in Holland, and joined in Argyll's rebellion in 1685. After the Revolution he ministered at Killearn and St Andrews, and held the Principalship of St Mary's College, St Andrews, from 1698 to his death.

Forrester's experience in both camps well equipped him for the ecclesiastical controversies of the day. A prolific if painstaking writer, he became one of the ablest advocates of Presbyterianism.

Rectius Instruendum (n.p., 1684); *A Vindication and Assertion of Calvin and Beza's Presbyterian Judgment and Principles* (E, 1692); *The Hierarchical Bishops' Claim to a Divine Right, tried at the Scripture Bar* (E, 1699).

FES VII, 421; *DNB* XX, 9.

M. Grant

Forret, Thomas (d.1539), Protestant burned for heresy.* He was the son of Thomas Forret, master of the stables to King James IV. As Augustinian* canon of Inchcolm,* Forret served as vicar of Dollar (Stirlingshire), a parish appropriated to the abbey, and was rebuked by the Bishop of Dunkeld (George Crichton, 1526–44; Dowden, 87–8) for teaching his parishioners from the English New Testament (probably Tyndale's version) and for preaching every Sunday. He declined the customary clerical exactions, and would 'take not the cow nor the uppermost cloth' from his parishioners. He attended the marriage of Thomas Cocklaw, an Augustinian canon of Cambuskenneth* and vicar of Tullibody (Clackmannanshire), who was also condemned for heresy, and was one of the company, with which George Buchanan* seems to have been associated, who broke the fast at Lent by eating meat at the bridal. At Holyrood Abbey, Forret was condemned to death as a heretic by Cardinal David Beaton* and the Bishop of Dunkeld and was burned, with other heretics, on Castlehill in Edinburgh in the presence of King James V.*

Knox, *History* I, 26–7, 43; J. Foxe, *Acts and Monuments* (L, 1858), V, 621–3; Calderwood I, 124–9; J. Kirk, 'The Religion of Early Scottish Protestants', *Humanism and Reform*, ed. J. Kirk (O, 1991).

J. Kirk

Forsyth, Peter Taylor (1848–1921), Congregational* minister and theologian of Scottish birth and upbringing. He spent his working life in England in a series of congregations before becoming Principal of Hackney Congregational College, London. He was a notable author whose writings anticipated by some years the theology of Karl Barth.

Forsyth was born in Aberdeen, the eldest of five children. He went to Aberdeen Grammar School, and read classical literature and moral philosophy at Aberdeen University. Strictly brought up in the Congregational Church, he developed an interest in theology and, on the advice of his friend William Robertson Smith,* spent a year at Göttingen studying under Albrecht Ritschl. He returned to England, resolved upon the parish ministry, and entered the Congregational College at Hackney, London.

Over the next twenty-five years Forsyth served five English congregations: Shipley, Yorkshire (1876–80); St Thomas Square, Hackney, London (1880–5); Cheetham Hill, Manchester (1885–8); Clarendon Park, Leicester (1888–94); and Emmanuel Church, Cambridge (1894–1901).

In 1897 his first book, *The Holy Father and the Living Christ*, was published. In 1899 he visited the United States to address the International Congregational Council. In 1901 he was appointed Principal of Hackney College, later part of London University, a post he held until his death. In 1905 he was Chairman of the Congregational Union of England and Wales. In 1907 he lectured again in the United States. In 1910 he became Dean of the London Faculty of Theology. He started to write prodigiously and his main works date from this period. *Positive Preaching and the Modern Mind* (L, NY, 1907), comprising his Lyman Beecher lec-

FORT AUGUSTUS ABBEY

tures, are a recognized classic on preaching. Thereafter he produced almost a book a year for the next ten years. His last book, *This Life and the Next*, was published in 1918.

Forsyth's theological background reflected the orthodox Scottish Calvinism* of his upbringing. But his studies caused him to challenge much of this, and he came to accept some of what he considered the virtues of liberal theology, particularly biblical criticism. He developed distinctive doctrines on the Church and the sacraments. His writings reflect what came to be the main elements of his theology: the inadequacy of human reason, the infinite distinction between God and humanity, the reality of human sinfulness, the primacy of the objective over the subjective, the authority of Christ, the power and finality of the cross, the transcendent and prevenient grace of God. In his later years Forsyth restated and redefined orthodoxy, thereby acquiring the reputation as the prophet of what has come to be called 'neo-orthodoxy'.* Interest in his theology continues, and a number of his books have been published in recent years.

The Work of Christ (L, 1910); *The Holy Father and the Living Christ* (L, 1897); *The Principle of Authority* (L, 1913); *The Cruciality of the Cross* (L, 1909); *The Person and Place of Jesus Christ* (L, 1909); *Lectures on the Church and the Sacraments* (L, 1917); *The Soul of Prayer* (L, 1916).

W. L. Bradley, *P. T. Forsyth, the Man and His Work* (L, 1952); R. M. Brown, *P. T. Forsyth, Prophet for Today* (Philadelphia, 1952); G. O. Griffith, *The Theology of P. T. Forsyth* (L, 1948); A. M. Hunter, *P. T. Forsyth, Per Crucem Ad Lucem* (L, 1974); D. G. Miller, B. Barr, R. S. Paul, *P. T. Forsyth: The Man, The Preachers' Theologian, Prophet for the 20th Century* (Pittsburgh, 1981); J. H. Rodgers, *The Theology of P. T. Forsyth: The Cross of Christ and the Revelation of God* (L, 1965).

A. F. Anderson

Fort Augustus Abbey (1878–). The buildings and grounds of the Hanoverian fort at the southern end of Loch Ness (Inverness-shire) were presented by Lord Lovat in 1876 to the English Benedictine* Congregation. Adaptation and rebuilding went on 1876–80, monastic life began 1878, a solemn opening took place 1880. The new monastery, St Benedict's, was successor and continuation to the Scots abbey at Ratisbon (*see* Schottenklöster) and the English abbey at Lamspring, Hanover. It became fully independent and directly subject to Rome in 1882, but rejoined the English Congregation in 1910.

The adapted fort buildings comprised monastic quarter, boys' school and guest-house. The school, opened 1878, was closed 1894 but re-opened 1920. The church, built in stages 1890–1980, was dedicated 1981. The library, incorporating books and manuscripts from Ratisbon and other collections, contains 40,000 volumes. The printing-press has published many periodicals, pamphlets and books.

Contributions to scholarship were made, notably by Gregory Ould (hymnology) and Cyril Dieckhoff

FORWARD MOVEMENT, SCOTTISH

(Gaelic lexicography). Work was published on Scottish church history, in particular by Michael Barrett, Columba Edmonds and Odo Blundell. David Oswald Hunter-Blair translated Bellesheim's *History of the Catholic Church in Scotland* (4 vols, E, 1887–90).

Monastic cells were founded at Dornie (Wester Ross) 1899–1900, Letterfourie (Buckie) 1904–25, Nairn 1920–2. A dependent priory and school, in Edinburgh 1930–9, were refounded at North Berwick (1945–77). Two dependent priories in the USA, St Anselm's, Washington DC (1924) and St Gregory's, Portsmouth, Rhode Island (1926), became independent in 1949 and achieved abbatial status. A convent of Benedictine nuns, founded near Fort Augustus in 1894, moved to Holme Eden (Carlisle) 1920 and closed 1984.

The abbey hosted the national plenary Council of the RCC* in 1886 and the centenary celebrations of George Hay* in 1911. Three monks became bishops: Maurus Caruana (Malta 1915–43), Abbot Andrew Joseph McDonald (St Andrews and Edinburgh 1929–50), Ansgar Nelson (Stockholm 1947–62). The community, excluding the American priories, reached a peak of seventy-six professed monks in 1936.

Catholic Encyclopedia VI, 146; *Fort Augustus Abbey: Past and Present* (Fort Augustus, ⁵1963); *Catholic Directory for Scotland 1877–* (E, A, G, annually); *The Benedictine Almanack/Yearbook 1874–* (L, York, annually).

M. Dilworth

Forward Movement, a movement which expressed the changing theological and missiological perspectives within British Nonconformity during the last quarter of the nineteenth century. Influenced by the notion of 'progress' dominant within the wider culture, church leaders like Hugh Price Hughes, R. F. Horton and John Clifford attempted to redefine evangelical belief in the light of both 'modern thought' and social concerns. The Movement remained a rather vague concept, but the ideas it represented found frequent expression in the pages of the *Methodist Times* (founded 1885) and the *British Weekly** (founded 1886). Evangelistically, the Forward Movement reflected a growing concern for 'the vast uncared for masses' (Horton), which received visible expression in the building of some forty Methodist Central Halls, including that at Tollcross in Edinburgh in 1901.

C. Binfield, *So Down To Prayers* (L, 1977), 217; R. Currie, *Methodism Divided: A Study in the Sociology of Ecumenicalism* (L, 1968); R. Davies et al. (eds), *A History of the Methodist Church in Great Britain* III (L, 1983), 139, 276f.; N. Harmon (ed.), *The Encyclopedia of World Methodism* (Nashville, 1974), I, 867; K. Inglis, *Churches and the Working Class in Victorian England* (L, 1963), 70f.; J. Rogers, *The Forward Movement of the Christian Church* (L, 1893).

D. W. Smith

Forward Movement, Scottish, a campaign in

FRANCISCANS

1931-3 for the revival of the mission of the CofS, which followed close upon the Union* of 1929. The idea for the movement originated with Donald Fraser* of Livingstonia, a UFC missionary, and John White* of the CofS. It was intended to arouse zeal for home and foreign missions, and to define a purpose for the reunited national Church.

Preparations began in 1930, with the formation of an Executive Committee, headed by Fraser, and the creation of twelve commissions of experts assigned to investigate aspects of the Church's work. Their reports were published in 1931 as *The Call to the Church*. On 26-30 October 1931, the movement was formally opened with a Church congress in Glasgow, which brought together over 2,500 delegates from throughout Scotland for addresses, exhibits and discussion. During 1932-3, about a dozen revivalist 'Missions of the Kingdom' were conducted in different Presbyteries, intended to carry the Forward Movement to the Church as a whole.

The movement, however, was not successful in arousing the Church. The country was in the midst of economic depression and political crisis, which diverted public attention from the campaign. Furthermore, the organizers declined to define a specific programme, and many found the movement vague and lacking direction. This, in turn, raised doubts about the capacity of the reunited Church to provide leadership to a troubled nation.

[J. W. Stevenson (ed.)], *The Call to the Church* (E, 1931); J. A. Steele (ed.), *The Congress Message* (E, 1931; A. R. Fraser, *Donald Fraser of Livingstonia* (L, 1934).

S. J. Brown

Franciscans. Known also as Grey Friars or Friars Minor, they owe their origin to the dedication of St Francis of Assisi (*c.* 1182-1226) to uncompromising total poverty. The first papal approval was given in 1209. The order's rapid expansion caused irreconcilable tension between the friars'* wishing to imitate Francis' radical poverty and commitment and those willing to accept mitigations allowed by Rome. The latter friars were known as Conventuals, while the various more radical groups were termed Observants. Eventually in 1517, total separation ensued and Conventuals became a separate order.

The Friars Minor entered Scotland in 1231, when a house was established at Berwick. Friars appeared at Roxburgh (1232/4), Haddington (before 1242) and Dumfries (1234-66), but the date of the establishment of other houses is conjectural. Dundee appears before 1296, but Lanark (?1346) and Inverkeithing in Fife (before 1385) appear to date from the fourteenth century, and Kirkcudbright was founded between 1449 and 1467. A Scottish province of Conventuals existed *c.* 1231-9, again from 1260 to 1279 and from 1329 to 1359, when the Scottish vicariate was suppressed. This decree may have been ignored, for a Scottish vicar-general occurs in 1375. The Great Schism led to final separation from the English province.

FRASER, ALEXANDER CAMPBELL

A bull of Pope Pius II (9 June 1463) permitted the erection of three or four Observant friaries, and houses were founded at Edinburgh (*c.*1463), Aberdeen (1469), Glasgow (1473-9) and St Andrews (1463-6). On 19 March 1482 the Bishop of Dunkeld received papal permission to found two or three other Observant houses. This was seemingly put into effect by James IV, to whom the foundation at Stirling (1494) can certainly be attributed, while Ayr (1488-97), Perth (before 1496), Jedburgh (before 1505) and Elgin (before 1494), may also have been royal foundations.

Although Conventuals were not always unreceptive towards reform and renewal, their numbers seem to have diminished. However, the vitality which characterized the Observant branch counterbalanced such losses. Renewed fervour led to increased endowments; rents and ground annuals were increasingly accepted by the Conventuals, although the Observants still preferred to receive gifts in kind.

Though less active in preaching and teaching than their Dominican* counterparts, Friars Minor were nevertheless fairly active in both fields. Though their opinions were normally orthodox, one friar was burnt for heresy* in 1539. It does, however, appear that their relative prosperity and lack of concern for the poor, coupled with their defence of the old faith, led to the destruction of their houses at the Reformation.*

Irish Franciscans made an outstanding missionary effort in Scotland in the seventeenth century (*see* Irish Mission to Highlands). After the Reformation, the various branches of the Observant movement existed side by side until they were finally, in the nineteenth century, amalgamated as the main body of Friars Minor. They established houses at Glasgow (1868), Edinburgh (1926, 1938) and Dundee (1933-89). The Conventuals have not returned to Scotland, but a separate reformed branch of Franciscans, the Capuchins (founded 1532), had a friary in Lanarkshire 1949-80.

Franciscans of the EpCS have for some years worked in Edinbrgh and, more recently, Glasgow (*see* Religious Communities, Episcopal).

New Catholic Encyclopedia VI, 36-46, 65-71; Easson-Cowan, 124-33; P. J. Anderson (ed.), *Aberdeen Friars, Red, Black, White, Grey* (A, 1909); W. M. Bryce, *The Scottish Grey Friars*, 2 vols (E, 1909); W. R. Jones, 'Franciscan Education and Monastic Libraries', *Traditio* 30 (1974), 435-45.

I. B. Cowan

Fraser, Alexander Campbell (1819-1944), philosopher. He was the eldest son of Hugh and Maria Helen [Campbell] Fraser, Ardchattan, Argyllshire. He studied at Glasgow and Edinburgh Universities and was ordained to Cramond FC, near Edinburgh, 1844, soon becoming Professor of Logic, New College, Edinburgh (1846-57), and then Professor of Logic, Edinburgh University (1856-91). Gifford Lecturer* (1894-6) and recipient of five honorary doctorates, he was made FBA in 1903.

Over against positivistic/agnostic scepticism, and

FRASER, DONALD

in the wake of Thomas Reid (see Scottish Realism) and William Hamilton (1788–1856),* Fraser maintained both the reasonableness of the universe, and human inability fully to comprehend that reasonableness. To him idealist/'Gnostic' confidence in the possibility of such comprehension was for ever undermined by the fact of moral evil. Following Locke, he emphasized concrete experience, while in Berkeley's doctrine of causation as spiritual he found redemption from Humean* scepticism.

Fraser's ethical theism flowed from his presupposition of the trustworthiness of a morally perfect power. He charts a via media between deism* and pantheism, regarding personal relations as the essence of reality.

He specialized in Berkeley: ed. Works, 4 vols (O, 1871), Life, Letters and Unpublished Writings (O, 1871), Selections from Berkeley, 6th edit. (O, 1910), Berkeley (E, 1881), Berkeley and Spiritual Realism (L, 1908); and Locke: 'Locke' in EB, 9th edit., XIV, 751–62; Locke (E, 1890), and ed. Locke's Essay Concerning Human Understanding (O, 1894). His Gifford Lectures, The Philosophy of Theism (E, 1895–6), provide his constructive position. See also, Thomas Reid (E, 1898), Essays in Philosophy (E, 1856), Rational Philosophy in History and in Systems (E, 1858), Biographia Philosophica (E, 1905).

A. S. Pringle-Pattison, Proc. Brit. Acad. 1913–1914, 525–38; DNB 1912–1921, 195–7; A. P. F. Sell, Commemorations ... (Cardiff, 1993), ch. 10.

A. P. F. Sell

Fraser, Donald (1826–92), Presbyterian minister. Born in Inverness, he studied at King's College, Aberdeen (MA, 1842). He went to Canada in 1842 and pursued a commercial career, but the firm in which he was a junior partner collapsed. In 1848 he entered the Knox Theological Academy in Toronto, and in 1851 was ordained minister of Cote Street FC, Montreal. In 1859 he returned to Scotland to become minister of Free High Church, Inverness. In 1870 he moved to Marylebone Presbyterian Church, London, where he played a leading role in the Presbyterian Church of England, of whose synod he was Moderator in 1874 and 1880. He was also vice-president of the British and Foreign Bible Society.

Fraser wrote a number of religious works, of which his Synoptical Lectures on the Books of Holy Scripture (L, 1871–6) received C. H. Spurgeon's* highest commendation. He received a DD from Aberdeen Univesity in 1872.

Metaphors in the Gospels (L, 1885); The Speeches of the Holy Apostles (L, 1882); Seven Promises Expounded (L, 1889); Thomas Chalmers (L, 1881); The Church of God and the Apostasy (L, 1872); Sound Doctrine (L, 1892); Mary Jane Kinnaird (L, 1890).

J. O. Dykes (ed.), Autobiography of Donald Fraser (L, 1892); DNB Second Suppl. II, 244; ACFS I, 160.

N. R. Needham

Fraser, Donald (1870–1933), UF missionary to Livingstonia, Nyasaland (now Malawi), 1896–1925. The son of the FC minister of Lochgilphead, Argyll, he was educated at Glasgow High School, University and FC College. His commitment to overseas missionary work was confirmed at the Keswick Convention in 1891 and 1893, when he saw the potential for influencing students towards overseas service. As Travelling Secretary for the Student Volunteer missionary movement (1893–4) and Inter-University Christian Union (1894–5) (see Student Christian Movement), he travelled widely, founding Christian Unions and stimulating student commitment to mission service. He was Chairman of the Liverpool Conference of the Student Movement (1896). Ordained in 1896 in the FC (later UFC) for missionary service in Livingstonia (see Missions), he laboured at Ekwendeni (1896–1900), Hora (1901–2), and Loudon (1902–25), consolidating a great African movement into the Church. He was chairman of the Scottish Churches Missionary Campaign, uniting ten denominations (1921–3). In 1922 he became Moderator of the UFC General Assembly, one of only three missionaries to be so appointed. He received Glasgow's DD in 1922. He served as Joint Home Organization Secretary of the UF (later CofS) Foreign Missions Committee (1925–33), and also as chairman of the Forward Movement* (1931–3).

The Future of Africa (L, 1911); Winning a Primitive People (L, 1914); Livingstonia (E, 1915); African Idylls (L, 1923); Autobiography of an African (L, 1925); The New Africa (L, 1927); numerous magazine and newspaper articles.

FUFCS 571; DNB 1931–40, 295–6; A. R. Fraser, Donald Fraser (L, 1934); T. J. Thompson, 'The Growth of Christianity among the Northern Ngoni' (PhD, Edinburgh University, 1980); T. Tatlow, The Story of the Student Christian Movement ... (L, 1933).

B. H. Galloway

Fraser, James, of Brea (1638–98), persecuted Covenanter,* later minister in Culross, Fife. Fraser was born at Brea, the Ross-shire estate of his father, Sir James (who sat in the Glasgow Assembly* of 1638). The estate, which he inherited as a child, long proved a source of great difficulty, both legal and financial. After study at Marischal College, Aberdeen (MA, 1658), he turned to law. Although recently converted, he did not believe himself free to prepare for the ministry, because of legal entanglements and conscientious objection to the new Episcopalian Church government. But after briefly considering the principles of the Quakers (see Friends, Religious Society of), he began to expound the Scriptures and was ordained, in 1670 or 1672, by some ejected ministers. He preached regularly, without being apprehended. In July 1674 he was summoned to appear before the Privy Council* and, when he refused, denounced as a rebel. He was arrested in 1677 and, at the insistence of James Sharp,* imprisoned on the Bass Rock,* where he studied Hebrew and Greek and wrote his work on faith (see below).

FRASER, JAMES

Fraser was set free in 1679 in the general indulgence* given to all Nonconformists* not accessory to the rising which culminated at Bothwell Bridge.* He was arrested again in 1681 and confined to Blackness Castle. Released after six weeks, he was sent out of Scotland. After preaching and imprisonment in London, he returned to Scotland in 1687. After the Revolution he preached first in a meetinghouse in Culross and then became parish minister there until his death.

Fraser is chiefly remembered for his memoirs (*Memoirs of the Life...*, E, 1738), a record of the Lord's dealings with him in the course of his 'pilgrimage'. Alexander Whyte* said of it that Fraser 'will live in that remarkable book as long as a scholarly religion, and an evangelical religion, and a spiritual religion, and a profoundly experimental religion lives in his native land'. As a searching spiritual autobiography, it has, in Whyte's words, 'few, if any, equals' (*James Fraser, Laird of Brea*, E, 1911, 3).

Fraser's doctrinal views gained attention long after his death. The publication of the first part of his manuscript work on faith, *A Treatise on Justifying or Saving Faith* (E, 1722), created no stir, but the second part, *A Treatise on Justifying Faith* (E, 1749), which taught a form of universal redemption, brought about a division both in the Associate Synod (Antiburgher)* and in the Reformed Presbytery (*see* Reformed Presbyterian Church). Although Fraser's general teaching is evangelical and in harmony with the *Marrow** brethren, he taught that Christ died for all, but with different intentions for the elect and reprobate. Christ removed the legal impediments so that all might be saved, but died for the elect to bring them to glory and for the reprobate to purchase benefits in this life and, in particular, that they might be the recipients of gospel wrath or vengeance. Fraser's contemporaries viewed this as unsatisfactory and few since have been attracted to it. With the views of modern universalists it has virtually nothing in common (D. C. Lachman, *The Marrow Controversy*, E, 1988, 86–101).

The Lawfulness and Duty of Separation from Corrupt Ministers and Churches Explained and Vindicated (E, 1744) examined the duty of Christian people in regard to attending the ministry of those who had submitted to Episcopalian church government, but was printed by those who wished to see the principles applied to the Evangelicals who remained in the CofS after the Secession.*

Meditations on Several Subjects in Divinity (E, 1721); *Some Choice, Select Meditations...* (E, 1726; ²G, 1753); *Prelacy an Idol, and Prelates Idolators...* (1713; ²G, 1742).

FES V, 15–16; *DNB* XX, 207–8; J. Anderson, *The Bass Rock: 'Martyrs of the Bass'* (E, n.d.), 124–56; R. King, *The Covenanters in the North* (A, 1846).

D. C. Lachman

Fraser, James (1700–69), evangelical CofS minister. The son of John Fraser, minister of Alness in Ross-shire 1696–1711, he was licensed by the Presbytery of Chanonry in 1723 and ordained in 1726 to Alness, where he remained until his death.

Fraser's widely influential *The Scripture Doctrine of Sanctification* (E, 1774; ed. John Macpherson, with a biographical notice, L, 1898) is an anti-Arminian doctrinal exposition of Rom. 6:1–8:4. John Locke is faulted for abusing his own principles of biblical interpretation: he wrongly undestands chs. 5 and 6 to be addressed to Gentile converts to Christianity only, and ch. 7 to Jewish converts only. The last twelve verses of ch. 7 represent the case of a regenerate person.

Fraser was one of the most popular ministers in the Highlands.* His preaching was noted for producing great heart-searching and the conviction of sinners.

Sermons on Sacramental Occasions (E, 1785).

DNB XX, 208; *FES* V, 291–2; A. Fraser, preface to Fraser's *Sanctification*; J. Kennedy, *The Days of the Fathers in Ross-shire* (E, 1861); A. P. F. Sell, 'John Locke's Highland Critic', *RSCHS* 23 (1987), 65–76, rp. in Sell, *Dissenting Thought...* (Lewiston, NY, 1991), ch. 8.

A. P. F. Sell

Fraser, James (1913–59), FP missionary. He was born in Strathpeffer and died at Bulawayo, Rhodesia, being buried at Ingwenya. He had served there as a FP missionary for twenty years. Educated at Glasgow University and Jordanhill College, he left for Rhodesia in July 1935. There he worked as a teacher, as a teacher-trainer and, having been ordained as a minister in June 1947, as a preaching missionary. Fraser was a pivotal figure in the development of the FPC's Rhodesian mission and his achievements are still remembered there, where he earned the popular nickname 'The Man Who Loves the People'.

A. McPherson, *James Fraser* (L, 1967); A. McPherson (ed.), *History of the Free Presbyterian Church of Scotland* (Inverness, 1974).

J. L. MacLeod

Fraser, William (*d.* 1297), Bishop of St Andrews. A younger son of a knightly family with lands in Tweeddale, he became a master at Paris or Oxford, dean of Glasgow by 1273, chancellor in the same year, and Bishop of St Andrews in 1279. On the death of Alexander III in 1286 he was appointed one of the six guardians of the kingdom ruling in the name of the infant Queen Margaret ('maid of Norway'); on receiving rumours of her death in 1290 he adopted the cause of John Balliol (*c.* 1250–1313), and urged Edward I of England to favour him. For this he was censured by Robert Bruce.

Fraser was one of the council of twelve appointed in July 1295 to organize resistance to Edward's increasingly unreasonable demands; he led a commission sent to France which negotiated for aid against the English in November 1295. When Edward overran Scotland in 1296, Fraser remained in France and died near Paris. His body was buried in the Dominican church in Paris, but his heart was brought for burial in St Andrews Cathedral. He is said to have been opposed to Edward's intrusion of English clergy into Scottish benefices, and to have favoured William Wallace's rising in 1297.

Dowden, 19–21; *Anglo-Scottish Relations, 1174–1328*, ed. E. L. G. Stones (O, 1965); *Edward I and the Throne of Scotland, 1290–6*, eds E. L. G. Stones and G. G. Simpson (O, 1978); G. W. S. Barrow, *Robert Bruce* (E, ²1976); R. Nicholson, *Scotland: the Later Middle Ages* (E, 1974).

A. Macquarrie

Fraser, William (1801–83), influential Baptist pastor in the Highlands and in Ontario. Born in Strathspey, Fraser was converted through the preaching of Peter Grant,* and later became a member of the Baptist church at Grantown-on-Spey. Trained at Robert Haldane's* seminary, he began itinerant preaching in 1825. He settled a year later in Uig, Skye, where he was given charge of the local Baptist church. He was formally ordained to the pastorate in July 1828 (*see* Baptist Home Missionary Society for Scotland).
In response to a plea for Baptist leaders for the Canadian churches (*see* Edwards, John; Emigration), Fraser emigrated to Ontario in 1831, and became the pastor of Breadalbane Baptist Church, Lochiel Township, Glengarry Co., where he remained until 1850. While at Breadalbane, he sustained an itinerant ministry in eastern Ontario and southern Quebec, and served as superintendent of public schools in the counties of Glengarry, Stormont and Dundas. In 1850 he moved west to Bruce Co., Ontario, where he founded the Baptist church at Tiverton. This church grew rapidly as emigrants from the Hebrides settled in the area. A gifted preacher, leader and planter of churches, Fraser travelled to Manitoba in 1881 in the hope of gathering another congregation of Highland emigrants.

D. E. Meek, 'Evangelicalism and Emigration: Aspects of the Role of Dissenting Evangelicalism in Highland Emigration to Canada', in G. MacLennan (ed.), *Proceedings of the First North American Congress of Celtic Studies* (Ottawa, 1988), 29–31.

D. E. Meek

Frazer, James George (1854–1941), classical scholar and historian of religion. Born in Glasgow to a devout FC middle-class family, Frazer took degrees from Glasgow University (1874) and Trinity College, Cambridge (1878). In 1879 he won a Trinity fellowship that, renewed twice, became tenurable for life. He was befriended there by William Robertson Smith,* then in 'exile' from Scotland, who introduced him to comparative religion and anthropology and thereby determined the direction of his work.
Frazer's life was devoted to the study of primitive religion, as described in the ethnography of the time, and its relationship to that of classical antiquity. Although it is never mentioned, his real target was Christianity. In his view of human cultural evolution, religion had been progressive in its time but had since been superseded by science. The resemblances between Christianity and the religions of antiquity were therefore conclusive evidence that the former was the result of a mistaken world-view and was thus to be dismissed. Frazer's best known works are: *The Golden Bough* (L, 1890, ²1900, ³1911–15); *Pausanias's Travels in Greece* (L, 1898); *Folk-Lore in the Old Testament* (L, 1918).

R. Ackerman, *J. G. Frazer* (C, 1987); R. A. Downie, *Frazer and The Golden Bough* (L, 1975).

R. Ackerman

Free Assembly Uniting Act (1900), Act of FC approving Union of FC and UPC. Avoiding the mistaken policy of earlier negotiations when prior agreement had been sought on every point, the principle of the Act was that each Church would take the other as she found it. The Westminster Confession,* under the qualifications of the Declaratory Acts,* defined the common doctrinal commitment; all points not covered in the Confession were to be regarded as 'open questions'. A special FC General Assembly was called in October 1900 to pass the Act. A dissident Constitutionalist* minority argued that the Act was a violation of the FC constitution. It was passed by a majority of 643 to 27; the majority entered the Union and the minority continued the separate existence of the FC. No such problems were encountered by the UPC.

See also Free Church Case; Free Church of Scotland, 1843–1900; Free Church of Scotland, post-1900; Unions, Church, in Scotland.

J. K. Cameron, *Scottish Church Union of 1900* (Inverness, 1923); P. C. Simpson, *The Life of Principal Rainy* (L, 1909), II, 188–268; K. R. Ross, *Church and Creed in Scotland* (E, 1988).

K. R. Ross

Free Church Case (1900–4). The FC minority which opposed Union with the UPC had for many years held the proposed Union to be unconstitutional. When the Union was effected in 1900 they declined to enter the new UFC and took out a long-threatened legal action for payment and transfer of the whole assets of the property held in trust for the FC. The resultant case of *Bannatyne v. Overtoun* was twice dismissed by the Court of Session, but the final appeal to the House of Lords was successful, and the property and funds of the FC were declared to belong to the relatively small and largely provincial minority which had declined to enter the Union and firmly maintained the original principles of the Church. The case turned on two issues: whether the Union had effected substantial change in the FC constitution, and whether the Church was free to effect such change. It was dismissed in the Court of Session because the judges found that the Union did not involve any fundamental change in the creed or constitution of the Church, but was successful in the House of Lords. On 1 August 1904, the majority of the judges found that by entering the Union, especially through thus compromising the 'Establishment principle', the majority had departed from the original constitution of the FC and that they had no powers to effect such a change. This latter finding was regarded very seriously by churchmen in Scotland and led to the UF Act Anent Spiritual Independence of 1906, which was designed to state the Church's freedom to revise her constitution and laws in such a way that it could never again be questioned by a civil court. For those who had formed the continuing FC, the judgement vindicated their position. However, subsequent Parliamentary intervention led to an equitable division of the property involved.

See also Church and State (legal questions); Scottish Churches Act (1905).

R. L. Orr, *Free Church of Scotland Appeals 1903–4* (E, 1904); A. Stewart and J. K. Cameron, *The Free Church of Scotland 1843–1910* (E, 1910), 151–314; P. C. Simpson, *The Life of Principal Rainy* (L, 1909), II, 300–467; K. R. Ross, *Church and Creed in Scotland* (E, 1988).

K. R. Ross

Free Church Colleges, *see* Christ's College (Aberdeen), New College (Edinburgh), Trinity College (Glasgow).

Free Church of Scotland, 1843–1900, the body formed by the Evangelicals* who withdrew from the Est.C in 1843 in protest against the state's encroachment upon the spiritual independence of the Church (*see* Ten Years' Conflict; Disruption). While it can only be regretted that the Disruption led to the reduplication of ecclesiastical resources at the expense of a national movement of church extension,* nevertheless the speedy organization of a nationwide church was a remarkable and unexpected achievement. The FC's 500 ministers set about supplying ordinances for her supporters in every parish except in the Highlands,* where FC ministers were initially in very short supply. A church-building programme was undertaken which produced, within a year, 470 new churches and, by 1847, 700. A Manse Fund, under Thomas Guthrie,* assisted in the provision of a manse for each church. Robert MacDonald* spearheaded a campaign which led to the building of some 600 FC schools, educating 65,000 children. Hugh Miller* edited its periodical, *The Witness.**

The unprecedented financial generosity evoked by the Disruption is explained by the new wealth of the middle classes and by the evangelical awakening which won their allegiance. An entirely new approach to financing a nationwide ministry was the Sustentation Fund, brainchild of Thomas Chalmers,* to which congregations contributed according to their means and from which all ministers received the 'equal dividend'. The Fund was able to supply a modest income for 583 ministers in its first year and for almost 1200 by 1900. This centralized financial apparatus resulted in power and influence being transferred from parish level to the central organs of the FC. As Assembly Committees grew in power at the expense of Church courts, the affairs of the FC came to be guided largely by an Edinburgh leadership.

Great importance was attached to theological education and the FC ministry came to be regarded as the most learned in Christendom. When the New College* was opened in Edinburgh in 1850 with five theological chairs it became at once the leading theological college in the land. Later further colleges were set up at Aberdeen (*see* Christ's College) and Glasgow (*see* Trinity College). The first generation of teachers was united by enthusiastic adherence to Westminster Calvinism.* Indeed, among their ranks were some of its most distinguished exponents: William Cunningham,* Robert S. Candlish,* John Duncan,* James Buchanan,* and James Bannerman.* Nor were they merely conservative: they were not afraid to raise and pursue questions which pushed back the frontiers of Reformed theology. However, this fearless and adventurous approach had within it the seeds of its own undoing, for questions began to be raised to which the inherited standards gave no satisfying answers, and from the 1860s there was a palpable drift away from dogmatic Calvinism towards a more liberal understanding of the faith. The second generation of the FC produced theological teachers of the calibre of A. B. Davidson,* A. B. Bruce,* Marcus Dods,* and George Adam Smith.* These men possessed great evangelical and moral power, but took a much more liberal position than their fathers. It was in the FC that 'believing criticism'* of the Bible was developed, and William Robertson Smith* taught.

Another sphere in which the FC produced men of the first rank was that of foreign missions.* Alexander Duff,* John Wilson* and almost the whole staff of the India Mission adhered to the FC at the Disruption, and, though they lost their property, reorganized themselves to carry out strategic missionary and educational work. Work was begun in Africa, where the Lovedale Institution* under James Stewart* and the Livingstonia Mission under Robert Laws* were amongst the most effective of missionary centres. Evangelism among the Jews had been a particular concern since the Disruption. When missions to the New Hebrides under John G. Paton* and Aden under Ion Keith-Falconer* were added, the result was one of the largest missionary organizations in the world.

Home mission too was from the beginning given great prominence. Chalmers himself gave the lead with a territorial mission in Edinburgh's West Port. Efforts of this kind was continually made, notably in the 'Wynds' of Glasgow under Robert Buchanan.* Nonetheless, it appears that a complacency quickly settled upon the FC and she lost Chalmers' vision of a 'godly commonwealth'. Free churchmen were in the forefront of the 1859 Revival and the Moody* and Sankey campaign of 1873–5 (*see* Revivals), and were instrumental in many conversions, but on the whole, they failed to bridge the growing gulf between the Church and the urban masses. Only in the Highlands and Islands, where the vast majority were FC, was substantial progress made in evangelism and church extension.

The FC claim to be the authentic CofS was furthered by Unions with the Original Seceders* in 1852 and the Reformed Presbyterian Church* in 1876. The leadership was thwarted, however, in its attempt to unite with the UP Church when a determined minority under James Begg* maintained successfully that the FC was constitutionally unable to unite with a Voluntary* church. From that Union controversy of 1867–73 the FC was divided into progressive and conservative parties which were continually in conflict. The Disestablishment* campaign promoted from 1874 by the UPs and the FC majority further alienated the Constitutionalists.* Their disaffection was completed by the advent of biblical criticism,* hymns (see Hymnology, English) and organs (see Musical Instruments in Worship), and the Declaratory Act.* Robert Rainy,* who had succeeded Candlish in the leadership of the FC, needed all his considerable skills of diplomacy to prevent a further disruption and even he was powerless to halt the secession of (Highland*) Free Presbyterians* in 1893 and the further separation when Union with the UP Church was finally effected in 1900 (see Unions, Church, in Scotland; Free Church of Scotland, post-1900). The formation of the United Free Church* ended the independent history of the national FC, but the Disruption principle of spiritual independence was to be vindicated in the constitution of the reunited CofS of 1929, which inherited also much of the ethos of the pre-1900 FC.

PGAFCS, 1843–1900; T. Brown, Annals of the Disruption (E, 1893); W. G. Blaikie, After Fifty Years (L, 1893); R. Rainy and J. Mackenzie, William Cunningham (L, 1871); R. Rainy and W. Wilson, Robert Smith Candlish (E, 1880); P. C. Simpson, Principal Rainy, 2 vols (L, 1909); N. L. Walker, Chapters from the History of the Free Church of Scotland (E, n.d.); A. C. Cheyne, The Transforming of the Kirk (E, 1983); K. R. Ross, Church and Creed in Scotland (E, 1988); R. A. Riesen, Criticism and Faith in Late Victorian Scotland (Lanham, MD, 1985).

K. R. Ross

Free Church of Scotland, post-1900, a conservative Presbyterian Church claiming historical and theological continuity with the National Church reformed in 1560, and with the FC of 1843–1900 (see previous article).

ORIGINS. The roots of today's FC lie in two contentious ecclesiastical events – the Disruption* of 1843, which gave birth to the original FC, and the union between the FC and UPC in 1900 (and the ensuing legal struggle between the UFC and the non-uniting minority of the old FC for the property of the latter; see Free Church Case). The point at issue in 1843 had been the Church's right to freedom from state interference in spiritual affairs; in 1900, the dispute centred rather on the Church's commitment to the Westminster* Confession as its subordinate standard of faith, the propriety of the Declaratory Act* of 1892, and the abandonment of the establishment principle entailed in the merger with the staunchly Voluntary* UPs.

FOUNDATIONAL PRINCIPLES: THE 1904 WATERSHED. The twenty-seven FC ministers who remained outside the 1900 union were strongly conservative in their doctrine and Church principles, holding to an uncompromising Westminster theology and to the hallowed Scottish Presbyterian belief in the recognition of Christianity by the state through an established Church. They regarded the union as an abandonment of these principles. In stark contrast to their forebears of 1843, however, their views attracted little public attention and little sympathy. The spirit of the times was out of tune with the notion of confessional theology, especially where it appeared to hinder Christian fellowship.

It is unclear how many congregations initially adhered to the anti-union stance of the protesting ministers. However, by 1904, when the House of Lords finally ruled in favour of the anti-union minority in its claim to continuity with the Disruption Church and thus secured its legal right to that Church's property, there were calculated to be some 125 FC congregations and preaching stations and a membership of about 70,000. These were located mostly in the Highlands* and Gaelic*-speaking city charges in the south, where the FC is strongest to the present day.

1904–45: CONSOLIDATION AND RECONSTRUCTION. By 1906 a FC seminary had been re-established (in Edinburgh) and fully staffed, students were being trained for the ministry, and overseas mission work undertaken. By 1925 the FC had expanded to comprise ninety-one ministers and 170 congregations, organized into twelve Presbyteries over the whole country (though thinly spread in the south and south-east). FC missions were operating in central India, South Africa and Peru, involving medical, educational and evangelistic work. Two Presbyteries were also established in Canada.

This process of consolidation was not entirely smooth. The period from 1904 to the close of the First World War was to some extent marked in the FC by an exploratory attitude to its own precise bearings. Ministers who did not wholly share the FC's constitutive principles found entry into its pulpits, and between 1904–15 some seventeen of these left for other Churches. On the other hand, the FC's speedy repeal of the 1892 Declaratory Act encouraged a significant accession of strength from the FPC in this period, including such notable scholars as John Macleod* and John R. MacKay* who, together with Donald Maclean,* inaugurated the *Evangelical Quarterly*ced* in 1929. MacLean in particular did much to foster closer relations between the FC and other Reformed Churches in the Western world, and gave impetus to a general Reformed ecumenism.

POST-1945: THE FREE CHURCH TODAY. Post-War years saw the FC engaging in greater support for the wider evangelical cause. Such scholars as A. M. Renwick* and R. A. Finlayson* became familiar through their lecturing and writing for the Inter-Varsity Fellowship.* Several ministers, e.g. George MacKay of Fearn and Kenneth MacRae* of Stornoway, became widely known through their preaching ministries. After its growth in the early decades there had followed a slow statistical decline in the FC's membership, but this trend was for a time arrested and reversed in the 1980s.

The FC today maintains a strong commitment to the Westminster Confession and a conservative Reformed theology. It continues to practice the traditional Scottish Presbyterian style of worship,* chiefly distinguished by exclusive psalmody in sung praise, in the form of the Scottish Metrical Psalter, unaccompanied by musical instruments.* Its Church offices, bookshop, publishing agency (Knox Press) and seminary are situated on The Mound, Edinburgh. The seminary, which takes in private students as well as candidates for the FC ministry, is staffed by five full-time professors, and is under the jurisdiction of the General Assembly, which meets each May in Edinburgh. The FC issues a monthly periodical, *The Monthly Record.**

A. Stewart and J. K. Cameron, *The Free Church of Scotland 1843–1910* (E, 1910); W. MacLeod, *Steadfast in the Faith* (E, 1943); G. N. M. Collins, *The Heritage of Our Fathers* (E, 1974); id., *Annals of the Free Church of Scotland 1900–1986* (E, n.d.); J. Macleod et al., *Our Evangelical Heritage: the Work and Witness of the Free Church* (E, n.d.).

J. D. MacMillan

Free Presbyterian Church of Scotland. The FPC was formed in 1893 by two ministers, Donald Macfarlane* and Donald Macdonald,* together with a substantial number (estimated at 14,000) of elders, members and adherents of the FC. The immediate cause of the separation was the passing of a Declaratory Act* by a large majority at the FC General Assembly of 1892.

This Act was the outcome of a long controversy over the Church's relationship to the Westminster Confession of Faith, its subordinate standard (*see* Westminster Assembly and Documents; Subscription, Confessional). Its stated purpose was 'to remove difficulties and scruples which have been felt by some in reference to the declaration of belief required from persons who receive license or are admitted to office in this Church'. Those opposed to the Act (*see* Constitutionalists) believed that it seriously misrepresented the teaching of the Confession in a way detrimental to its distinctive Calvinism. The final paragraph of the Act made allowance for 'diversity of opinion ... on such points in the Confession as do not enter into the substance of the Reformed Faith', and the Church retained full authority to determine, as need arose, 'what points fall within this description'. No guidance was given as to which doctrines were of a substantial nature, and against the background of the growing influence of theological liberalism in the FC this omission was interpreted as significant and sinister.

At the 1893 General Assembly an attempt by the Constitutionalists to have the Declaratory Act rescinded failed. Donald Macfarlane tabled a protest (*see* Protest Question in FPC) and separated from the FC. At a meeting of the first FP Presbytery at Portree in Skye in August 1893 a Deed of Separation was approved and engrossed in the minutes. This division in the FC is unique in the history of Scottish secession* in that it hinged on a specifically doctrinal issue.

Since 1893 the FPC has maintained a separate stance in relation to other Churches. Although the post-1900 FC rescinded the offending Declaratory Act and sought closer relations, a majority of the Synod (the FPC's supreme court) considered that union would not strengthen the Church, especially in its witness to the authority of Scripture. Over the years the FPC has worked along with the FC and other Churches and organizations in promoting causes of mutual interest such as that of Lord's Day Observance and Bible distribution.

From the FPC's early years congregations have been concentrated mainly in the Highlands and Islands. Various approaches from expatriate Scots and others in sympathy with the Church's position led to the creation of congregations in Australia, New Zealand and Canada. There are also two FP congregations in England and one in Northern Ireland. The Church has a well-established and active Mission in Zimbabwe which has grown from small beginnings early this century. Over many years it has made a substantial contribution, particularly in the medical and educational fields. The FPC was one of the first in Britain to speak out against the policy of apartheid in South Africa. Its own first missionary in Rhodesia, John Radasi,* was a native African. More recently, other African ministers have served as Moderators of Synod. A small Mission was established in Italy in the 1960s and continues to receive Church support.

In FP congregational worship use is made of the Authorized Version of the Bible. Psalms are sung without instrumental accompaniment. In most congregations the Lord's Supper is administered twice each year and extra services are held from Thursday till Monday.

In the social sphere the FPC has shown special concern for the elderly. Since 1964 the Church has maintained a Home of Rest in Inverness and a second one was opened in Harris in the Outer Hebrides in 1988.

The total number of FP members and adherents has been estimated at 4,000, of whom almost half are in overseas congregations.

Recent decades have seen a growing division within the FPC, particularly concerning issues relating to liberty of conscience and relations with other Christian Churches. Two controversial discipline cases before the Synod in 1989 brought matters to a head (one involving Lord Mackay,* the Lord Chancellor). A Deed of Separation was signed by fourteen ministers and some thirty elders and the body known as the Associated Presbyterian Churches* (APC) was formed. About one third of the home membership of the FPC joined the APC. Both sides claim to have adhered to the constitution of the FPC. Such adherence has important legal implications for ownership of Church property and assets.

FREE PRESBYTERIAN RELIEF

A. MacPherson (ed.), *History of the Free Presbyterian Church of Scotland 1893–1970* (Inverness, 1974); G. N. M. Collins, *The Heritage of Our Fathers* (E, 1974); A. L. Drummond and J. Bulloch, *The Church in Late Victorian Scotland 1874–1900* (E, 1978); A. MacPherson, *James Fraser: A Record of Missionary Endeavour in Rhodesia in the Twentieth Century* (L, 1967).

A. Morrison

Free Presbyterian Relief Congregation, congregation formed in December 1945 by former elders, members and adherents of St Jude's congregation of the FPC, Glasgow. The background to the separation was a prolonged controversy on the meaning and effect of a protest against a decision of the supreme court of the Church. The Synod of the FPC held the view that persistence in such a protest may and usually does lead to the self-exclusion of the protester. Roderick MacKenzie, who was minister of St Jude's congregation from 1932 until his resignation due to ill-health in 1944, felt unable to accept the Synod's view. In May 1945 the Synod passed a resolution requiring unqualified subscription to the ruling of Synod with regard to protest. The resolution also stated that unless MacKenzie submitted by November 1945 he would no longer be considered a minister of the FPC. Since MacKenzie continued to adhere to his position the terms of the resolution took effect from 28 November 1945. The resolution of 1945 was the immediate cause of separation. Although MacKenzie took no active part in the separation which led to the formation of the Relief Congregation he preached to the congregation by invitation from the beginning of 1946 until his death in 1972. Thereafter the congregation had no permanent ministry, and was disbanded in 1986.

See also Protest Question in FPC.

A. MacPherson (ed.), *History of the Free Presbyterian Church of Scotland 1893–1970* (Inverness, 1974); *The Right of Protest* (G, 1975).

A. Morrison

Freemasons. The Grand Lodge of Scotland was founded in 1736, but lodges much like modern lodges existed in Scotland in the late seventeenth century. Freemasonry evolved from the guilds of stonemasons and cathedral builders of the Middle Ages. As work declined, some lodges of working ('operative') masons began to accept honorary members, which led to symbolic or 'speculative' Freemasonry. It was believed by some that 'operative' masons were aware of secrets handed down from antiquity. In 'speculative' Freemasonry it was believed that by adapting these existing rituals, using allegorically the symbols of a mason's trade, knowledge of the moral and spiritual world would be deepened. Freemasonry follows an elaborate mythology – elements include parts of the Old Testament (especially on Solomon's Temple), other religions and ancient chivalry.

Lodge meetings are private and candidates take oaths of secrecy. The first three degrees of Craft (Lodge) Masonry are Entered Apprentice, Fellow Craft, and Master Mason. Above that (Ancient and Accepted Scottish Rite) the degrees go up to the thirty-third degree. There are also other Masonic units in Scotland – including Royal Arch Chapter, which draws its recruits from Lodge Freemasonry. Freemasons undertake some charitable work.

Freemasons claim that Freemasonry is not a religion, nor a substitute for religion. However, meetings are in Masonic Temples. There is opened the 'Volume of Sacred Law' – usually the Bible. To join, one has to believe in a Supreme Being, who in the First Degree is identified as 'The Great Architect of the Universe'. As an integral part of the ritual, prayers are addressed to this Supreme Being. In the Third Degree there is a death and resurrection rite. In the Holy Royal Arch Degree (Chapter Freemasonry), the 'Sacred and Mysterious Name of the True and Living God Most High' is revealed to the initiate as 'JEHOVAH JAHBULON' – a syncretistic combination of Jahweh, Baal and the Egyptian god 'On' or 'Osiris' from the mystery religions. Freemasonry has therefore many elements of religion.

The historical reaction of the Christian Churches to Freemasonry is described in Walton Hannah's book *Darkness Visible*, where he concludes, 'the majority of Christians throughout the world have condemned Freemasonry as incompatible with the claims of our Lord and Saviour.' In recent years, reports by the Methodist Church (1985), the RC Congregation for the Doctrine of the Faith (1983), the CofE and the Baptist Union of Scotland (1987) have all affirmed or reaffirmed the incompatibility of Christianity and Freemasonry. In 1987, the General Assembly of the CofS instructed its Panel on Doctrine to consider the compatibility or otherwise of Freemasonry with Christianity. Its 1989 report invited members of the Church involved in Freemasonry to reconsider their position. The main Christian theological objections to Freemasonry, stated in the above works, are secrecy, gnosticism, deism,* the deliberate exclusion of the name of Jesus Christ from Craft Freemasonry prayers, justification* by works, and syncretism.

W. Hannah, *Darkness Visible* (Chulmleigh, 1985) and *Christian by Degrees* (Chulmleigh, 1984); J. Lawrence, *Freemasonry – a Religion?* (Eastbourne, 1987); S. Knight, *The Brotherhood* (L, 1985); *Freemasons and Christianity* – CofE Report (L, 1987); D. Stevenson, *The Origins of Freemasonry and Scotland's Century* (C, 1988); *RGACS 1989*, 182–90 (Panel of Doctrine report).

J. Scott

French Revolution. The French Revolution of 1789–99 sent shock waves throughout Europe, bringing down the remnants of the feudal order and ushering in an era of popular nationalism. The upheavals in France began as a result of bourgeois discontent with political absolutism combined with the financial collapse of the monarchical state. In the first phase of the Revolution, a constitutional monarchy was established and the French aristocracy and French Catholic Church were stripped of much of their power and influence. The Revolution, however, soon took a more radical direction, and in 1792 a faction of republican extremists, the Jacobins, seized power. After executing the King, they endeavoured to establish a Republic of Virtue through a Reign of Terror. They also proscribed Christianity, and sought to replace it with a state cult celebrating Reason and a Supreme Being. The Republic succumbed to disillusionment and corruption, and was overthrown in 1799 by Napoleon Bonaparte. By now, the contagion of revolution had spread, and across Europe the forces of revolution and reaction were locked in conflict.

In Scotland, the political nation was divided in its response to the Revolution in France. For some, the Revolution heralded a new era of liberty, equality and fraternity for all peoples, and even Jacobin excesses could not dampen their hopes. Probably the large majority, however, viewed events in France with a mixture of apprehension and hostility. Anti-revolutionary feeling was especially strong in the Scottish Churches. Fearing the spread of anti-Christian Jacobinism, many Scottish ministers became staunch supporters of the reactionary Pittite government. Propertied Church members expected their ministers to defend the existing social order as divinely ordained, and few ministers were prepared to risk disappointing them and being branded as dangerous radicals. Within the Est.C, the dominant Moderate* party was suspicious of any popular movements, including efforts to evangelize or educate the labouring poor. Some Presbyterian seceders were also apprehensive about the possible side-effects of popular Evangelicalism. The lay evangelists, Robert* and James Haldane,* encountered bitter opposition from Scottish Presbyterian ministers, both of the Est.C and, in some measure, of the Secession Churches, when after 1796 they carried the gospel to the unchurched masses through itinerant preaching. Fear of 'revolutionary' popular associations contributed in 1796 to the decision of the General Assembly of the CofS not to support the overseas mission movement. In 1799, the General Assembly passed a 'Pastoral Admonition', instructing parish ministers not to admit itinerants into their pulpits and condemning even sabbath schools as potentially subversive 'popular' associations. Not all ministers, to be sure, shared in the reaction, and the evangelical* minority in the CofS, along with the Secession Churches as a whole, retained their commitment to evangelize and educate the lower social orders. But those who worked to elevate the labouring poor often came under suspicion by the government and landed élites and their influence was limited.

The impact of the French Revolution in Scotland, however, was not only to strengthen the forces of social and political reaction. Fear of revolutionary republicanism brought the state to grant some modest extensions of individual rights at home, which contributed to the movement toward greater religious liberty. In 1792, to help ensure the loyalty of Scottish Episcopalians,* Parliament passed an act relieving them of many of the penal restrictions imposed after the Jacobite* risings. The following year, for similar reasons, Parliament passed a modest Scottish Catholic relief act. Presbyterian seceders, meanwhile, began questioning the principle of a state establishment for religion. Did not the anti-Christian state cult imposed on France by the Jacobin republic demonstrate the dangers implicit in any Church-state connection? A growing number of Presbyterian seceders experienced 'new light'* regarding the Westminster Confession's* teachings on the role of the magistrate in national religion. This resulted in fresh divisions within the Secession bodies after 1799, with New Light Burgher (see Associate Synod) and New Light Antiburgher (see General Associate Synod) Churches emerging to embrace a Voluntaryist* position. Threatened by the new social, political and religious challenges of the 1790s, the CofS became defensive and inward-looking, until revived by the evangelical party* early in the nineteenth century.

H. W. Meikle, *Scotland and the French Revolution* (G, 1912); I. D. L. Clark, 'From Protest to Reaction', in N. T. Phillipson and R. Mitchison (eds), *Scotland in the Age of Improvement* (E, 1970), 200–24; A. Haldane, *The Lives of Robert and James Haldane* (E, 1855); S. J. Brown, *Thomas Chalmers* (O, 1982); J. McManners, *The French Revolution and the Church* (L, 1969).

S. J. Brown

Friars. The thirteenth century saw the emergence of a new type of religious order. It was, at least in part, a response to the rise of an urban economy, in contrast to that of feudalism. These new religious, the friars ('brothers'), differed from the monastic orders in several ways: they had no corporate possessions (and hence were termed mendicants – i.e. beggars, living on alms); they were not bound by vow to a single monastery but rather were mobile; they were dedicated to apostolic work as well as to spirituality; their superiors were not elected for life but for a term of years. The Council of Lyons in 1274 restricted this new type to four orders: Dominicans,* Franciscans,* Carmelites,* and Augustinians.* The Council of Trent later modified the restriction on corporate possessions, and other similar orders were classed as mendicant friars. Such were the Trinitarians,* Servites (founded 1233), Friars of the Sack (founded 1251), Minims (founded 1435), Capuchins (founded 1525).

Of the orders which settled in Scotland, the Dominicans arrived in 1230 and eventually possessed sixteen houses, of which thirteen survived until the Reformation. The Franciscans arrived in 1231 and eventually possessed eight houses, including Berwick, which was ultimately lost to the Scottish province. To these were added houses of the reformed or Observant Franciscans, who arrived c.1463 and founded eight houses before 1500. The Carmelites reputedly arrived in 1262, eventually possessing eleven foundations. Augustinian friars, established by a papal decree of 1256 uniting several groups, preserved a tradition of eremetical life. One house

FRIENDS, RELIGIOUS SOCIETY OF

was established at Berwick before 1229, but attempts by James IV to found further houses at Haddington, Linlithgow and Manuel (W. Lothian) came to nothing. Trinitarians arrived in the mid-thirteenth century and founded eight houses, of which four survived until the Reformation. The Friars of the Sack had one short-lived house, at Berwick 1267–c.1285. Dominican and Franciscan nuns also established houses (see Nunneries).

At the Reformation,* following the threat contained in the Beggars' Summons* of 12 May, 1559, friars were ejected from their buildings, many of which were destroyed, but compensation, usually at the rate of 16 per annum, was paid to friars wishing to avail themselves of these bounties (commonly referred to as 'freiris wageis').

In the seventeenth century, Scots overseas entered orders of friars, including some which had never had houses in Scotland, e.g. Minims, Capuchins. Some friars, such as the Capuchin Archangel Leslie,* returned to work in Scotland. Houses of friars established in modern times have included Augustinians (Dundee 1948, Edinburgh 1986), Servites (Dundee 1950, Glasgow 1984), and Capuchins (Lanarkshire 1949–80).

See also Crutched Friars.

New Catholic Encyclopedia VI, 198, IX, 648–9; Easson-Cowan, 107–42, 152–5; J. Durkan, 'The Scottish Minims', IR 2 (1951), 77–81.

I. B. Cowan

Friends, Religious Society of (nicknamed 'Quakers'), a religious movement that arose out of the turmoil of the English civil war (see Commonwealth and Protectorate*). As new structures of political and ecclesiastical order evolved, small groups of Seekers (so-called) took to meeting in silence, waiting for the direct guidance of God, having lost faith in the leadership of the ministers. Such Seekers provided the seed-bed for the message of George Fox (1624–91), whose teaching centred on response to the Inner Light of Christ, and who bound groups together into a coherent religious body.

Quakerism spread to Scotland with Cromwell's army in the early 1650s. Fox himself visited the country in 1657, but the more radical form of the Reformation in Scotland and the link between Presbyterianism* and national identity meant that Quaker influence was limited. Some of those attracted by it, however, were people of standing, notably in Aberdeen, where Robert Barclay,* Alexander Jaffray* and George Keith* were active.

After its initial missionary surge, the Society became increasingly pietistic, and the particular forms of speech and dress which had arisen from a concern for simplicity and strict truthfulness became formal marks of distinction. In the present century most of these forms have been abandoned, but the Society retains its early commitment to pacifism and to the equality of men and women in its ministry and work.

There are currently some 600 members of the Society in Scotland in about twenty local Meetings.

FUNDAMENTALS, THE

Most Meetings gather weekly for worship based on silent waiting on God. Anyone present who feels so led, may make a vocal contribution to the worship. Each member is also entitled to attend the business meetings of the Society at local, regional and national levels. Decisions are reached without voting and the sense of the meeting is minuted there and then by the clerk. Worldwide, the Society has about 250,000 members, about half of whom are in the United States.

G. Fox, *Journal* (1694; ed. J. Nickalls, L, 1975); G. Burnet, *The Story of Quakerism in Scotland* (L, 1952); London Yearly Meeting, *Christian Faith and Practice in the Experience of the Society of Friends* (L, 1960); J. Punshon, *Portrait in Grey* (L, 1985).

H. S. Pyper

Fuller, Andrew (1754–1815), first secretary of the Baptist Missionary Society, which supported William Carey's mission to India. A native of Cambridgeshire, Fuller was pastor of Baptist churches at Soham (1775–83) and Kettering (1783–1815). A vigorous exponent of moderate Calvinism,* he wrote an influential book, *The Gospel Worthy of All Acceptation* (1785), in which he presented Calvinism* as a missionary theology. His interpretation, sometimes known as 'Fullerism', was challenged by hyper-Calvinists and Arminians;* it was important in the impetus it gave to the missionary movement. Fuller visited Scotland five times on behalf of the Baptist Missionary Society. Interested in both home and foreign missions, he encouraged the work of Scottish pastors who followed the 'English' (single-pastor) model of Baptist church polity. A particularly close friend of Christopher Anderson,* he controverted the views of the Scotch Baptist leader, Archibald McLean,* whose churches espoused Sandemanian* views of faith and were led by a plurality of elders.

J. W. Morris, *Memoirs of the Life and Writings of the Rev. Andrew Fuller* (L, 1816); D. Bebbington (ed.), *The Baptists in Scotland* (G, 1988), 27, 32–5, 283; G. F. Nuttall, 'The Modern Question: a Turning Point in Eighteenth-Century Dissent', *Journal of Theological Studies* n.s. 16 (1965), 101–23.

D. E. Meek

Fundamentals, The. Four Scots and two Scottish-born Canadians were among the sixty-four international contributors to *The Fundamentals*, a series of twelve pamphlets published in defence of conservative evangelical theology from 1910–15, funded by a California millionaire and circulated free of charge to some 250,000 religious leaders throughout the English-speaking world. The Scottish contributions, eleven of a total of ninety articles, reflect concern over rising secularism, rationalism and liberal theological reconstruction, and stress the viability of the supernatural and the reliability of Scripture.

James Orr,* Professor of Apologetics and Dogmatics at the UFC College, Glasgow, was author of the lead article for the entire series, 'The Virgin

Birth of Christ', and three others: 'Science and Christian Faith', 'The Early Narratives of Genesis' and 'Holy Scripture and Modern Negation'. All four of Orr's articles had been earlier published elsewhere. Another UF Churchman, Thomas Whitelaw* (Moderator of the UFC, 1912), contributed two apologetic articles, 'Christianity No Fable' and 'Is There a God?', and a third on 'The Biblical Concept of Sin'. T. W. Medhurst (1834–1917) of Glasgow offered a decidedly negative answer to his query, 'Is Romanism Christianity?', and the series' editor reprinted a brief essay by the long-deceased Thomas Boston* on 'The Nature of Regeneration'. William Caven (1830–1904), Principal of Knox College, Toronto, commended Christ's high view of the Old Testament, while another Scottish-born Canadian Presbyterian minister, E. J. Stobo, Jr (1867–1922), defended 'The Apologetic Value of Paul's Epistles'.

The Fundamentals, ed. A. C. Dixon and others (^{2}Los Angeles, 1917); E. Sandeen, *Roots of Fundamentalism* (Chicago, 1970), 188–207; C. G. Thorne, Jr, '*The Fundamentals* and their Place in Modern Protestant Church History' (MLitt, University of Dublin, 1971).

G. G. Scorgie

G

Gaelic, a Celtic language once spoken fairly generally in Scotland, but now used principally by crofting/fishing communities on the north-west Highland* mainland and in the Hebrides. Gaelic speakers are, however, found extensively in the Lowlands, especially in Glasgow and Clydeside, as a result of migration. The 1981 Census recorded 82,620 people in Scotland who could speak, read or write Gaelic, representing 1.6 per cent of the total Scottish population. All were bilingual in Gaelic and English. In 1891 there were 210,677 bilingual speakers of Gaelic in Scotland, and also 43,738 people capable of speaking Gaelic only.

ORIGIN AND DISTRIBUTION OF GAELIC. Gaelic, which is closely related to Irish, was brought to Scotland from Ireland by settlers (*Scoti*) mainly from the Irish kingdom of Dál Riata in north-east Ulster. Migration from Ireland was under way by the end of the fifth century, with initial settlements in present-day Galloway and Argyll, and was consolidated after AD 500, when a second kingdom called Dál Riata (Dalriada) was established within an area corresponding roughly to modern Argyll. The prestige of the Scottish kingdom was considerably enhanced in 563, when Columba* established a monastic house in Iona.* This led to a powerful alliance between the saint and the royal line, especially during the reign of Aedán mac Gabráin. The expansionist policies of Aedán and the missionary activity of Iona-based monks were influential in the first phase of the advance of the Gaelic language beyond Dál Riata. The name *Atholl* (from *Ath-Fhódla*, 'Second Ireland') bears witness to early Scotic settlement beyond Argyll.

The Scoti of Dál Riata were surrounded by neighbours who spoke other Celtic languages. Chief among them were the Picts,* whose principal language was essentially of Brittonic (*i.e.* Early Welsh) stock (and thus related to the ancestor-language of modern Welsh). The Picts held sway over territory from the Hebrides to southern Perthshire, where they have left enduring marks in place-names (beginning with the prefix *Pit-*) and in symbol-stones, often beautifully sculptured. The Picts appear to have been absorbed gradually during the expansion of the Scots of Dál Riata, and their culture was assimilated to that of their overlords. By 847 the Picts and the Scots were under a single king. To the south lay the kingdom of Strathclyde, whose inhabitants also spoke a P-Celtic language related to Pictish and to Welsh. Gaelic-speaking Scots appear to have been attempting to penetrate Strathclyde from the reign of Aedán mac Gabráin, but only in the tenth and eleventh centuries was that penetration sufficiently strong to overwhelm the original inhabitants and their rulers. By the early Middle Ages the Gaelic-speaking Scottish Crown, ruling over the united kingdoms of Dál Riata, Pictland and Strathclyde, was strong enough to establish its southern boundary at Carham (1018). Only in the west was its rule in jeopardy, largely because of the presence of Norsemen, who were eventually defeated at the battle of Largs (1263). The Norsemen left their mark on Gaelic, especially in areas of strong settlement such as Lewis, where Gaelic dialects still retain Norse intonation patterns.

The presence of Gaelic speakers by 1100 in most of present-day Scotland (excluding Orkney* and Shetland*) is demonstrated by literary remains and place-names, many of which have ecclesiastical connections. The Book of Deer* records, in Gaelic, land-grants associated with the monastery at Deer in Aberdeenshire. Place-names with the element *cill*, now represented as *Kil-*, bear more general witness to the spread of the language. This element (from Latin *cella*) meant 'monastic cell', and was commonly followed by the name of a Celtic saint.* Surviving *cill* place-names are concentrated in the west (from Kintyre to Skye and the Uists), but they extend up the Great Glen, and are attested in Fife and Galloway. They may date chiefly to the eighth century. (*See also* Monasticism, Celtic.)

Gaelic had begun its regression from what we now call the Lowlands by 1200. The language was probably weakest and most transient in Lothian; its gradual decay elsewhere in the south was hastened, even in areas of relative strength, by several factors, including English influences on the Scottish Crown, the coming of Norman French settlers, and the establishing of burghs. By 1500 Gaelic would have been spoken mainly in areas to the north of the 'Highland Line', but also in Kyle and Carrick, and in Galloway.

GAELIC AND THE MEDIEVAL CHURCH. Gaelic (in forms close to Old and Middle Irish) would have been used in the day-to-day conversation of the monks of the Celtic Church;* it would have been employed in the composition of early homilies (see Preaching, Celtic) and hymns (see Hymnology, Gaelic) and in the recording of land grants (as at Deer). Nevertheless, there is a scarcity of Gaelic writing from early Scottish scriptoria. Most writing would have been in Latin, since ecclesiastical documents would have had priority, both in their creation and in their preservation. This observation holds good for the pre-Reformation* Church of the early Middle Ages, but during the period 1200–1600 we find clear evidence that Gaelic-speaking churchmen were active in the recording of sacred and secular material. The most valuable Scottish collection of Gaelic (including Irish and Scottish) poetry to have survived from the Middle Ages is a manuscript called the 'Book of the Dean of Lismore' (National Library of Scotland, 72.1.37), compiled in the Fortingall district of Perthshire between 1512 and 1542, by James MacGregor, titular Dean of Lismore, and his brother, Duncan. The MacGregor brothers wrote their material in a spelling-system based on Middle Scots, and not on the 'normal' Gaelic system developed by the bardic schools of Scotland and Ireland.

In the West Highlands, especially in the region under the sway of the Lords of the Isles, the conventions of the bardic schools were more rigidly preserved. The Lords encouraged the development of a Gaelic 'civil service', consisting of clerics, medical men, judges, genealogists and sculptors who were capable of writing in Classical Common Gaelic, the *lingua franca* of a literary class in both Ireland and Scotland. There exists a Gaelic charter of 1408, granting lands in Kilchoman in Islay to a cleric, Brian Vicar MacKay (see J. and R. W. Munro (eds), *Acts of the Lords of the Isles 1336–1493*, E, 1986, 21–7).

The tradition of writing Classical Common Gaelic was transmitted to the Reformed Church through priests who had been trained in bardic schools, and who subsequently became ministers. The most prominent of these is John Carswell,* who translated the *Book of Common Order*ic into Classical Gaelic as *Foirm na n-Urrnuidheadh* ('The Form of Prayers'), published in 1567. As the first Gaelic printed book, it ensured that future publications would employ the spelling system of the bardic schools. The Classical Gaelic tradition, modified to suit vernacular Scottish Gaelic practice, is represented in the language of the Gaelic Bible (see Bible (Versions, Gaelic)) and the Gaelic Psalter.* Vernacular Scottish Gaelic (*i.e.*, Gaelic as spoken by the ordinary people) had begun to show features distinguishing it from vernacular Irish by at least 1300.

GAELIC AND THE CHURCHES 1500–1800. By 1600 Gaelic had lost much of its status under the patronage of the Lords of the Isles; the Lordship had become a threat to the Scottish Crown by the fifteenth century, and it was forfeited in 1493. As the Crown moved to suppress alleged lawlessness in the west, especially during the reign of James VI, Gaelic was equated with incivility. In the drive against 'these unhallowed people, with that unChristian language' (an official description of 21 December 1615), the equation of Gaelic with insurrection was doubtless (and paradoxically) increased by Highland support for the Royalist and Jacobite* causes in the course of the seventeenth century.

In 'civilizing' the Highlands the Presbyterian Church played an important role, reinforced by the erection of schools in Highland parishes, from Perthshire to Lewis, during the seventeenth century. Surviving records are meagre, and distribution patterns are uneven, but the number of such schools (established by heritors*) appears to have increased towards 1700. Their commitment to English and Latin, especially in grammar schools, would have been very much greater than their commitment to Gaelic, but Gaelic writing was apparently taught occasionally. In practice, too, the Jacobean Church recognized the importance of supplying Gaelic-speaking ministers for Highland parishes.

Schoolmasters were more potent than ministers in the thrust against Gaelic, but schools supported by heritors were probably less effective than those of a society with a direct policy. In 1709, the Scottish SPCK,* a very influential body whose schools initially taught English and aimed to eradicate Gaelic, began to work in the Highlands. It had financed the publication of the Gaelic New Testament by 1767 and the entire Bible by 1801 (see Bible (Versions, Gaelic)), signifying a change of strategy but not necessarily of overall policy. Scottish SPCK schools had a significant anglicizing effect in the parishes on the eastern and southern edges of the Highlands (C. W. J. Withers, *Gaelic in Scotland*, E, 1984, 120–33).

Protestant interest in the Highlands in the eighteenth century, through schoolmasters and ministers, established a strong tradition of printed Gaelic prose (see Gaelic, Protestant Prose Publications in). A very high proportion of early Gaelic prose texts were translations from English religious writings: eighty-six out of a total of 146 by 1800. Of the eighty-six, sixty-eight were produced in the period 1751–1800, suggesting that Gaelic was more favourably regarded in literary circles after the Jacobite Rising* of 1745. Poetry, especially of a hortatory or didactic nature, was stimulated also (see Buchanan, Dugald), and volumes of verse topped the list of original religious works appearing in Gaelic in 1741–99. Although the Episcopal Church of Scotland* published a Gaelic translation of its Communion office (E, 1797), the new literary movement was linked pre-eminently with Presbyterianism.

GAELIC AND EVANGELICALISM AFTER 1800. After 1800 Gaelic came to be identified very closely with the evangelical experience of many Highlanders. The foundation of Gaelic School Societies,* the first in Edinburgh in 1810, made the Gaelic Bible accessible to people who were taught to read it by travelling schoolmasters. Revivals* resulted in various districts, and there was a strong tradition of powerful evangelical preaching by ministers such as John MacDonald* of Ferintosh. The link between Gaelic and Evangelicalism was reinforced by the Disruption;* the FC of Scotland* became one of the chief bastions of Gaelic in the religious context. Missionary bodies active in the Highlands after 1800 (see Haldane Preachers; Baptist Home Missionary Society for Scotland) employed Gaelic-speaking missionaries of a similar status to the people themselves. Some missionaries translated English tracts into Gaelic (see McLaurin, Malcolm). The commitment of the Est.C to Gaelic was also strengthened, largely through the formation of General Assembly Schools and the literary labours of Norman MacLeod.*

Evangelical attitudes to Gaelic culture are difficult to summarize and need more careful consideration than they have received hitherto. Certain aspects of Gaelic culture, such as residual paganism and superstition, drew the wrath of all evangelical bodies, as did (increasingly) intemperance. Secular tales and music could sometimes be dismissed as vanity, but noted evangelical ministers (e.g., John MacDonald* of Ferintosh) and missionaries (e.g., Peter Grant*) were exponents of bagpipe and fiddle music. Evangelical conversion did not always result in renunciation of such interests. An organized campaign against Gaelic culture is nowhere attested. Rather, evangelical activity produced an alternative evangelical culture which drew selectively on secular models in several fields, such as hymnology, where popular secular tunes were widely used. Traditional forms of poetry, such as panegyric, were refashioned to honour the 'great divines' rather than clan chiefs (see Hymnology, Gaelic). Gaelic sermons must have owed something to indigenous rhetorical patterns (see Preaching, Gaelic and Highlands), and religious cottage-meetings were probably indebted to the concept of the cèilidh-house. Even the great open-air communions, attended by thousands of Highlanders, especially in times of revival,* may have drawn on earlier patterns of secular, communal gatherings (see Communion Seasons).

THE CHURCHES AND GAELIC SCHOLARSHIP. Ministers and members of all the main Churches active in the Highlands have made noteworthy contributions to Gaelic scholarship, in both the collection and the analysis of data. Within the Established Church, conspicuous collectors of Gaelic songs, traditions and stories include Alexander Pope,* James McLagan,* John Gregorson Campbell,* John MacDonald* of Ferintosh, Thomas Sinton (1855–1923; Gaelic poetry from Badenoch), Duncan MacInnes (d.1903; folktales), Duncan MacGregor Campbell (1854–1938; proverbs) and Kenneth MacLeod.* George Henderson (1866–1912, *FES* VII, 105–6) edited texts and studied the influence of the Norse on Celtic Scotland. The Free Church contained a distinguished group of evangelical scholars who contributed to the analysis and understanding of Gaelic language and poetry, notably Thomas McLauchlan,* Alexander Cameron* and Donald MacLean.* The Episcopal 'bishop', Donald Macintosh,* produced a collection of Gaelic proverbs (E, 1785). Roman Catholic scholars have placed an emphasis on the production of lexical resources, such as the dictionaries of Ewen MacEachen (Perth, 1842) and Henry Dieckhoff (E, 1932), and the word-book of Allan MacDonald* of Eriskay (1859–1905; *Gaelic Words and Expressions from South Uist and Eriskay*, Dublin, 1958). The Roman Catholic islands (Barra, Eriskay, South Uist) have furnished many Gaelic folksongs, of which a large number have been collected and made accessible through the outstanding work of John Lorne Campbell of Canna (with F. Collinson, *Hebridean Folksongs*, 3 vols, O, 1969–81) and his wife, Margaret Fay Shaw (*Folksongs and Folklore of South Uist*, A, ³1986). It is noticeable that the smaller missionary bodies, such as Baptists* and Congregationalists,* have contributed much less to Gaelic scholarship than the mainline Churches, although their pastors have produced numerous volumes of Gaelic hymns.

Since 1900, however, and more noticeably since 1945, the Gaelic scholarly activity of ministers of the larger Churches has diminished, and has probably been represented most saliently in the editorial work of T. M. Murchison.* The flowering of modern Gaelic literature since 1950 has owed more to the laity, but a lead was given by Donald Lamont,* and ministerial contributors (still active) include Colin N. MacKenzie (short stories) and Roderick MacDonald (poetry). Localized Gaelic publishing has occasionally been developed by parish ministers like Roderick MacLeod, formerly of Bernera, North Uist, and currently editor of *Life and Work*'s Gaelic supplement.*

CHURCHES' ATTITUDES TO GAELIC. The main denominations in the Highlands have generally always been aware of their obligation to provide appropriate means for the Gaelic-speaking people. The fulfilment of that obligation has, however, faced many practical difficulties over the years, and it is unfair to accuse the Churches of neglecting the language and its people. Unquestionably, there is evidence of an institutional lack of will to promote the language at particular periods; the delay in providing a Scottish Gaelic Bible represents that attitude at its worst (see Bible (Versions, Gaelic)). Nevertheless, the individual Churches have striven to find appropriate candidates for parishes and mission stations, and several ministers and priests have learned Gaelic for their parish duties. In 1831 the Episcopal Church of Scotland went so far as to form the Gaelic Episcopal Society for training Gaelic-speaking clergy (see Law, David).

GAELIC

Failure to provide Gaelic-speaking ministers can be caused by factors other than ill-will towards the language. Most obviously, the supply of candidates can decline or terminate, for reasons which reflect a wider malaise in the life of churches and their communities. The loss of Gaelic preaching in the Highland Baptist churches after 1965 was determined by failure of supply, matched by the decline of congregations and their increasing inability to evangelize their localities. The Baptists' evangelical emphasis on salvation, through the medium of the most expedient language, may also have hastened the eventual dominance of English. This model of language shift is already operating within the larger bodies, which face similar difficulties of recruitment; maintenance of regular services becomes more urgent than language loyalty. Hitherto the principal denominations have maintained Gaelic-speaking ministries most effectively in Skye and the Outer Hebrides; recently, however, the appointment of a non-Gaelic-speaking parish minister to the charge of Carloway was recognized as 'a new chapter in the ecclesiastical history of rural Lewis' (*LW*, February 1989, 27).

Institutional commitment to Gaelic can be measured beyond the parish in the space given to the language in the main organs of the Churches, such as the Established Church's *Life and Work*, which has had an influential Gaelic supplement* for many years (*see* Lamont, Donald and Murchison, T. M.), and the Gaelic page of the Free Church *Monthly Record*.* It is noticeable, however, that these Gaelic pages are parts of larger national organs, thus testifying that a fully self-sustaining and solely Gaelic denomination has never emerged in the Highlands, although there have been strong Highland wings of the main Scottish Churches.

The Churches active in the Highlands have become, with time, a major means of maintaining the Gaelic language in the prestigious areas of preaching and exposition. The role of the Presbyterian Churches has been particularly important. The future of Gaelic will therefore depend in no small measure on the extent of their continuing loyalty to the language and their success in recruiting Gaelic preachers.

D. S. Thomson (ed.), *The Companion to Gaelic Scotland* (O, 1983); W. J. Watson, *The History of the Celtic Place-Names of Scotland* (²Shannon, 1973); K. Steer and J. W. M. Bannerman, *Late Medieval Monumental Sculpture in the West Highlands* (E, 1977); J. MacInnes, *The Evangelical Movement in the Highlands of Scotland* (A, 1951); V. E. Durkacz, *The Decline of the Celtic Languages* (E, 1983); J. Kirk, 'The Jacobean Church in the Highlands, 1567–1625', in L. MacLean of Dochgarroch (ed.), *The Seventeenth Century in the Highlands* (Inverness, 1986), 24–51; D. Withrington, 'Education in the 17th Century Highlands', *ibid.*, 60–9; D. Bebbington (ed.), *The Baptists in Scotland* (G, 1988), 280–308; D. E. Meek, 'Baptists and Highland Culture', *BQ* 33, no. 4 (October 1989), 155–73.

D. E. Meek

GAELIC, PROTESTANT PROSE

Gaelic, Protestant Prose Publications in. The Protestant Churches have made a major contribution to the development of Scottish Gaelic* prose, beginning in 1567 with the publication of *Foirm na n-Urrnuidheadh* ('The Form of Prayers'), John Carswell's* translation of the *Book of Common Order*,* the first Gaelic printed book to appear in Ireland or Scotland. Carswell chose to use the ornate language of the classical bardic schools, and thus established a differentiated prose register for religious works in Gaelic. Carswell's style is characterized by periodic sentences; alliteration linking nouns, adjectives and phrases; and a syntactical precision which derives directly from the classical schools. Carswell's achievement was remarkable for its time, and unsurpassed in significance until the publication of the Scottish Gaelic New Testament (*Tiomnadh Nuadh*, E, 1767). The translation of the entire Bible (*Leabhraichean an t-Seann Tiomnaidh agus an Tiomnaidh Nuaidh*) into Scottish Gaelic followed (*see* Bible (Versions, Gaelic)), and numerous editions appeared after 1801. A translation of the Apocrypha was made by Alexander MacGregor (*Apocripha*, L, 1860) in response to L. L. Bonaparte (*see* Bible (Versions, Scots)). Although these are significant landmarks in Gaelic literature, other translators and writers were at work from at least 1630, and contributed greatly to the range of styles and topics available in Gaelic.

Original prose writing is apparent from the beginning: John Carswell prefaced his translation with his own dedicatory epistle to Archibald Campbell,* Fifth Earl of Argyll, and included an original catechism. Although the backbone of the Protestant prose tradition was formed by translations from English, the translators coined much new vocabulary for Gaelic religious expression, and to that extent their work is original. Overall, there is considerable diversity of material, but the broader groups are as follows:

(i) *Manuals of instruction and catechetical works.* These translations had the highest priority, and were produced initially by the CofS Synod of Argyll. Texts included: Calvin's* *Catechismus Ecclesiae Genevensis* (*Adtimchiol an Chreidimh*, E, *c.*1631); the Westminster* Confession of Faith (*Admhail an Chreidimh*, E, 1725); and the Westminster Shorter Catechism (*Foirceadul Aithghearr Cheasnuighe*, E, 1653), with around 100 subsequent editions, and new versions by John MacDonald* of Ferintosh (E, 1829) and Thomas Ross* of Lochbroom (E, 1820). With children in mind, John Willison's *Mother's Catechism* was translated (*Leabhar-ceist na Màthair*, G, 1752), with twenty later editions (the last being G, 1941). Willison's *Young Communicant's Catechism* was also translated (*Leabhar ceist nan Og Luchd-communachaidh*, G, 1798). The Episcopal Church of Scotland* produced a Gaelic version of its liturgy (*An Oifig chum Ceart Fhrithealadh an Comuin Naomh*, E, 1797) (*see* Catechisms, Gaelic).

(ii) *Large-scale hortatory and devotional works.* These are represented by Alexander MacFarlane's translation of Richard Baxter's *Call to the Unconverted* (*Gairm on Dé Mhóir*, G, 1750), with eight subsequent editions, and John Forbes' translation of his *Saints' Everlasting Rest* (*Fois Shiorruidh nan Naomh*, E, 1862?), with seven later editions. John Bunyan's works enjoyed a popularity unsurpassed by others, with several translations of *The Pilgrim's Progress*, the first by Patrick MacFarlane* (*Cuairt an Oilthirich; no, Turus a' Chriosduidh*, E, 1812), and thirteen later editions; *Grace Abounding* (*Gràs am Pailteas*, E, 1847) and *The Heavenly Footman* (*An Gille-ruith Nèamhaidh*, E, 1848) enjoyed five editions each. Other writers whose works were translated included Joseph Alleine, Thomas Boston,* Philip Doddridge, William Guthrie,* Robert McCheyne,* John Owen and Isaac Watts. After 1800, some substantial evangelistic works were translated by Malcolm McLaurin;* *see also* MacDonald, Robert; Smith, John.

(iii) *Tracts.* These were a very popular form of literature, transported easily by catechists, travelling schoolmasters (*see* Gaelic School Societies) and itinerant preachers (*see* Haldane Preachers). Their relatively small size and direct application attracted the creative interest of busy men, and many translations were made. The Scottish SPCK* (latterly) and the Edinburgh Gaelic School Society sought to establish libraries of tracts in various districts. Tracts were a major stimulus towards literacy in Gaelic, forming a sort of second stage for those already literate in the Gaelic Bible. The following categories are apparent:

(a) *Evangelistic.* These tracts emerged in great quantities after 1800, and are represented by such items as Gaelic versions of *Friendly Advice* and the *Life of John Covey*, a sailor who lost both his legs in the Battle of Camperdown (1797). Well over 100 different tracts appeared during the nineteenth century, occasionally with some original Gaelic contributions. *e.g. Ceil Mhor agus Maighstir Lachun* ('Big Kate and Mr Lachlan', G, 1848), 'Mr Lachlan' being Lachlan MacKenzie* of Lochcarron. Most are anonymous, and were published by several Tract Societies.*

(b) *Polemical.* The various ecclesiological debates in the Highland* Churches generated a large number of tracts, with different concerns at different times: thus the original anti-Baptist* works of Alexander Beith (G, 1824, 1827), the tracts published during the Ten Years' Conflict* preceding the Disruption* of 1843, and those promoting the debate preceding the formation of the United Free Church in 1900, e.g. James Begg's* attack on Voluntaryism,* translated by D. MacGregor (E, 1875/6).

(iv) *Homiletic works.* Individual Gaelic sermons by Highland ministers appeared in print occasionally, e.g. those of John MacDonald of Ferintosh. His sermon on the cholera epidemic (Dingwall, 1832?) is a practical piece, aimed at helping the readers to avoid the illness. Popular preachers whose sermons were translated included Jonathan Edwards,* Ralph Erskine* (E, 1836) and C. H. Spurgeon.* One senses a general Highland aversion to capturing the preached word in print (*see* Preaching, Highland/Gaelic), and there were surprisingly few collections of original Gaelic sermons before 1900; most had a commemorative aim, e.g. Angus McMillan's posthumously published *Searmoinean* (G, 1853). Archibald Cook's* sermons were published in several editions after 1900. A later example is Malcolm MacLeod, *An Iuchair Oir* ('The Golden Key', Stirling, 1950).

(v) *Educational pamphlets and books.* Each wave of educational interest in the Highlands produced appropriate school-books in the form of readers and instruction manuals. The Edinburgh Gaelic School Society produced primers by Alexander McLaurin (E, 1811, 1816) and Christopher Anderson.* Series of books were produced for the Free Church and General Assembly Schools. This flow of material was greatly reduced after 1872, with the passing of the Education Act, which nationalized education and marginalized the teaching of Gaelic.

(vi) *Periodicals.* A large number of relatively short-lived periodicals appeared after 1800, most with a strongly religious interest, including the Free Church's *An Fhianuis* ('The Witness', 36 issues, 1845–50), and Norman MacLeod's* *Teachdaire Gaelach* ('The Highland Messenger', 24 issues, 1829–30) and *Cuairtear nan Gleann* ('The Traveller of the Glens', 40 issues, 1840–3). The Disruption* probably removed the possibility of a sustainable Gaelic-only religious periodical by dividing the market and the resources; after 1850 Gaelic tended to find a place in bilingual denominational magazines and special supplements, which became the main outlet for original religious writing (*see Life and Work*, Gaelic supplement).

(vii) *Creative writing.* Educational interests and the flexibility of periodicals nourished Gaelic creative writing, which was often sober in subject-matter and style, but sometimes relieved with good humour. In developing his educational and other essays, Norman MacLeod was also seeking to increase the range of natural, idiomatic Gaelic, in contrast to the wooden prose of some translated sermons. Creative writing, often based on Gaelic folktales and popular story-telling, found its most natural outlet in secular periodicals such as *An Gàidheal* ('The Gael/Highlander'), first published in 1871.

(viii) *Commentaries and histories.* There are no Gaelic commentaries, perhaps because English works were accessible to ministers, who would have distilled their knowledge in sermons, so that there was no pressing need for such works for a general readership. Theological works by Highland ministers were invariably in English, reflecting the scholarly dominance of that language. Historical writings are sparsely represented in Gaelic by Mackintosh Mackay's* introduction to the ponderous Gaelic version of J. Howie's* *Scots Worthies* (L, 1872); D. MacCallum, *Eachdraidh na h-Eaglaise* ('The History of the Church', E, 1845); and D. MacGilliosa, *An Eaglais Shaor ann an Leòdhas* ('The Free Church in Lewis', E, 1981). Original biographies, even of and by Gaelic-speaking Highland divines (e.g. J. Kennedy, *The Apostle of the*

GAELIC, RC PUBLICATIONS IN

North, E, 1866), have tended to be written in English.

The Gaelic publishing of the Protestant Churches was at its height before 1900. In the twentieth century it has dwindled to a trickle; works by Baxter, Bunyan, Guthrie, McCheyne and Willison have been reprinted, but only Bunyan's *Pilgrim's Progress* has been translated afresh, by Malcolm MacLennan (L, 1929). The twentieth century has produced several volumes of sermons. The lively writings of Donald Lamont* are in many respects exceptional, but they paved the way for the emergence of post-1945 Gaelic literature. However, the challenge of pulling Gaelic prose towards modernity was faced only in 1952, with the publication of the all-Gaelic secular periodical *Gairm*, which continues under its founding editor, Professor Derick Thomson. Since then secular works have far outstripped religious works in quantity and quality.

D. MacLean, *Typographia Scoto-Gadelica* (G, 1915); M. Ferguson and A. Matheson, *Scottish Gaelic Union Catalogue* (E, 1984); D. MacLean, *The Literature of the Scottish Gael* (E, 1912); D. J. MacLeod, 'Gaelic Prose', *TGSI* 49 (1976), 198–230; D. S. Thomson, *The Companion to Gaelic Scotland* (Oxford, 1983), 240–3.

D. E. Meek

Gaelic,* RC publications in. Several factors lessened the need for printing. Liturgical texts were in Latin; instructional and devotional items were passed on orally or circulated in manuscript; perhaps, too, Irish Gaelic works were used.

Robert Menzies published a lengthy Catechism in 1781; many shorter ones followed, some in Canada. Eight editions, including two in Nova Scotia, of Ronald Rankin's prayer-book, *Iul a' Chriostaidh* ('Christian's Guide'), appeared 1834–1963. Other prayer-books were *Ordo Missae* ('Order of Mass', 1877) and *Lòchran an Anma* ('Lamp of the Soul', 1906). Devotional classics were few: the *Imitation of Christ* (*Leanmhuinn Chriost*) translated by Menzies (1785) and Evan MacEachen (1836); Scupoli's *Spiritual Combat* (*An Cath Spioradail*) translated by MacEachen (1835; 1908). MacEachen's translation of the New Testament appeared in 1875 (see Bible (Versions, Gaelic)). Allan McDonald's* hymn-book, *Comh-chruinneachadh de Laoidhean Spioradail* (1893), contained traditional songs, translations and new compositions.

The English and Scottish bishops' 'Declaration' was published (*Teisteanas nan Easbuigean Caitliceach*) in 1838. Some literary publications included RC spiritual songs circulating orally. The periodical *Guth na Bliadhna* ('Voice of the Year', 1904–25) propounded Roderick Erskine of Mar's amalgam of Celtic nationalism and Catholicism.

D. Maclean, *Typographia Scoto-Gadelica* (E, 1915; Shannon, 1972); M. Ferguson and A. Matheson, *Scottish Gaelic Union Catalogue* (E, 1984); D. J. Macleod, *Twentieth Century Publications in Scottish Gaelic* (E, 1980); J. L. Campbell, 'The Sources of the Gaelic Hymnal, 1893', *IR* 7 (1956), 101–11.

M. Dilworth

GAELIC SCHOOL SOCIETIES

Gaelic School Societies, societies which, by operating 'circulating' charity schools, taught the reading of the Gaelic Bible (*see* Bible (Versions, Gaelic)) chiefly in Highland* parishes. The use of Gaelic* as a medium of religious instruction in charity schools had been advocated by James Kirkwood* before 1709, but the Scottish SPCK* initially attempted to teach only English in its Highland schools. By the early nineteenth century literacy levels, in either English or Gaelic, were still extremely low in the Highlands. The completion of the Gaelic translation of the entire Bible in 1801 added urgency to the task of encouraging reading ability in the mother tongue. Influenced by the Welsh travelling schools of Griffith Jones and Thomas Charles, Christopher Anderson* convened a number of like-minded men from various denominations in Edinburgh in November 1810, and established the Edinburgh Society for the Support of Gaelic Schools. The Society issued its first Report in January 1811. Similar societies were also established in Glasgow (1812) and Inverness (1818), but these incorporated the teaching of English from the beginning. The Gaelic Bible was the main textbook of the Edinburgh Society. The Society also produced primers to assist learners; the first (E, 1811) was compiled by Alexander McLaurin, and two further volumes (E, 1816) appeared under the name of Christopher Anderson.*

The Edinburgh Society operated with the support of all the main Scottish Protestant denominations and during 1811–60 placed Gaelic schoolmasters in many Highland parishes. The Gaelic schools were concentrated in the western Highlands and Hebrides, in contrast to the earlier Scottish SPCK schools, which tended to be located on the eastern and southern edges of the Highlands. The schools moved around the parishes, spending several months in each location, and endeavouring to overcome the difficulty of providing education with limited resources in very extensive areas. The schoolmasters were forbidden to preach in the parishes, but some did so, and were disciplined by dismissal. Providing access to the Gaelic Bible, the schoolmasters became powerful figures in their localities, and deeply influenced the people, who sometimes maintained the schoolmasters at their own expense.

The Gaelic schools, known locally as *Sgoilean Chrìosd* ('Christ's Schools'), stimulated revivals* in parts of the Highlands, since teachers' 'observations' on Scripture texts could ignite spiritual fervour (as in Skye in 1842–3). Some schoolmasters (especially after dismissal from their societies) became popular leaders whose authority seriously challenged that of parish ministers. In Lewis in 1823, W. MacRae (*FES* VII, 200) complained bitterly to Mrs MacKenzie of Seaforth about two such teachers: 'It is easy to see that no good can arise to Society from the raving effusions of such ignorant men, who, with consummate effrontery, assume the character and office of public instructors, and expounders of Scripture...' (SRO: GD 46/17/62). Occasionally such foot-loose teachers became the founders of independent churches (*see* Grant,

Alexander), and the Gaelic schools generally helped to prepare the way for the Disruption* of 1843. They also created a taste for literacy in English in many areas, but overall they forged a lasting bond between Gaelic and Evangelicalism.

A. W. Harding, *'Sgoilean Chrìosd*: A Study of the Edinburgh Society for the Support of Gaelic Schools', (MLitt, University of Glasgow, 1979); C. W. Withers, *Gaelic in Scotland 1689–1981* (E, 1984), 137–50; V. E. Durkacz, *The Decline of the Celtic Languages* (E, 1983), 108–18; H. Anderson, *The Life and Letters of Christopher Anderson* (E, 1854), 125–34.

D. E. Meek

Galloway, George (1861–1933), CofS divine. Born in Stenton, Fife, he graduated MA from St Andrews in 1884 and BD from Edinburgh in 1887. Periods of further study at Göttingen and Berlin followed. Licensed by the Presbytery of Cupar, Fife, he became minister of Kelton in 1891. Further study gained him a DPhil from St Andrews in 1905.

Galloway's central interest lay in the philosophy of religion, on which he published a number of distinguished books beginning with *Studies in the Philosophy of Religion* (E, 1904). In 1915 he was appointed Professor of Divinity and Principal of St Mary's College, St Andrews. He delivered the Baird lectures* in 1916–17, *The Idea of Immortality* (E, 1919).

Galloway's conception of religion was evolutionary. He traced an upward development of human religious consciousness from tribal through national to universal religion. Christ he regarded as fundamentally revealer rather than redeemer; the 'religion of Jesus' was the greatest of the universal religions, summed up in the universal Fatherhood of God, the infinite worth of every human person, and the kingdom of God which reconciled individual and social values.

The Philosophy of Religion (E, 1914); *The Principles of Religious Development* (L, 1909); *Theological Doctrines and Philosophical Thought* (G, 1911); *Religion and Modern Thought* (E, 1922); *Faith and Reason in Religion* (L, 1927).

FES VII, 425; *Who Was Who, 1929–1940*, 489.

N. R. Needham

Galloway, Patrick (c.1551–1626), minister and royal chaplain. He was the son of a baker in Dundee and a student in the early 1570s at St Mary's College, St Andrews. Appointed minister first at Fowlis Easter (Perthshire) by 1576, then at Perth in 1581, Galloway became a critic of episcopacy and of Arran's government (*see* Stewart, James, *d*.1596) and so joined the Presbyterian exiles to England in 1584. In 1589, he became minister of the King's household and distanced himself from the Presbyterian cause. He was present at Falkland in 1596 when Andrew Melville* made his famous 'two kingdoms' speech before King James VI.* Appointed minister in Edinburgh in 1607, he accepted a seat on the King's new Court of High Commission* in 1610. Yet in 1617 he signed the 'protestation for the liberties of the kirk' against royal domination, but soon withdrew his protest. His second wife, Katherine, was the daughter of James Lawson.*

Calderwood; *BUK*; *Early Records of the University of St Andrews*, ed. J. M. Anderson (E, 1926), 172, 281; J. Melville, *Autobiography and Diary*, ed. R. Pitcairn (E, 1842); *The Historie and Life of King James the Sext*, ed. T. Thomson (E, 1825), 205; FES I, 53–4; IV, 229, 332; V, 351, 357.

J. Kirk

Galt, John (1779–1839), novelist, long known for one highly successful novel, *Annals of the Parish* (1821). Purporting to be the fifty years' diary of a parish minister, *Annals* charted the peaceful ministry of an unambitious CofS* pastor, Balwhidder, whose limited intelligence and selective world-view was offset by a keen observation of local affairs, and shrewd narration which took account, off-stage, of the Industrial Revolution, the French Revolution* and the other upheavals of 1760–1810. *Annals of the Parish* has many of Galt's own strengths: a strong local knowledge of Scottish affairs combined with a wide view, extensive experience in administration and commerce (particularly in Upper Canada where he was active in developing what is today the area of Toronto), a successful career as reviewer and public figure in Edinburgh and London, and an active political figure who contrived not to be typecast in the public eye. Galt moved widely in life; his output includes prose criticism, poetry and copious fiction of uneven quality. At its best – *The Ayrshire Legatees* (1820), *Annals* (1821), *The Provost* (1822), *The Entail* (1823), *Ringan Gilhaize* (1823), *The Last of the Lairds* (1826) – Galt's fiction combines the small-town with the metropolitan, the local with the wide-ranging, the shrewd peasant with the sophisticated, to produce an analysis of a changing society. The power of the laird is shown to be giving way to the Industrial Revolution, the balance of society is changing, and above all, the Kirk is giving ground as secularization and urbanization take their toll. His view of Balwhidder, the minister at the heart of his narrative, is at its sharpest at the time of his retirement in 1810, bewildered by an emptying church he has helped to empty by his loyal but inflexible ministry. This is a masterpiece; so, too, is his evocation of the real trials of the Covenanters* in *Ringan Gilhaize*, and his study of guilt and retribution in *The Entail*.

I. A. Gordon, *John Galt: the Life of a Writer* (E, 1972); C. Whatley (ed.), *John Galt 1779–1979* (E, 1979).

I. Campbell

Gammie, Alexander (d.1951), a leading Scottish religious journalist. He was Scottish correspondent of *The British Weekly** and even more widely read as 'Churchman' of the *Glasgow Evening Citizen*, being credited with a substantial contribution to its Saturday circulation. He was the author of numerous biographies and other books rich in personal anecdotes about ministers, with such titles as *Preachers*

GARDEN, GEORGE

I Have Heard (L, 1945). His biography of John White* (L, 1929) reveals much about how the CofS and White himself saw themselves at the time of Presbyterian reunion and shows Gammie at the peak of his powers, which depended on a stately clarity of style and sympathy with his subject. It was said that his love for the Church made him 'magnify the office' of the minister.

R. D. Kernohan

Garden, George (1649–1733), Episcopalian* CofS divine and Jacobite.* Born at Forgue, Aberdeenshire, he studied at King's College, Aberdeen, and was ordained as his father's successor in Forgue in 1677. In 1679 he moved to Old Machar, the cathedral* church of Aberdeen, and in 1683 became one of the ministers of St Nicholas, Aberdeen. He was deprived in 1692 by the Privy Council for refusing to pray for William II* and Mary. In 1700 a commission of the General Assembly suspended him from the ministry for Bourignianism;* Garden had translated some of Antoinette Bourignon's works and defended their doctrines before the commission (*An Apology for M. Antonia Bourignon*, L, 1699; *Preface and Translation of Bourignon's Light of the World*, L, 1696). He was cited to appear before the General Assembly of 1701 but refused to acknowledge its jurisdiction, failed to appear, and was deposed.

Garden continued to minister to his Episcopalian congregation. The accession of Queen Anne in 1702 restored his loyalty to the monarchy and he dedicated to Anne his edition of the works of John Forbes.* Reverting to Jacobitism on Anne's death he took part in the Rising* of 1715. The failure of the rebellion saw Garden imprisoned for a time, but he escaped to the continent. By 1720 he was back in Aberdeen, where his Bourignianism disqualified him from candidature for Aberdeen's vacant bishopric.

The Case of the Episcopal Clergy (n.p., 1703–5); *Queries and Protestations of the Scots Episcopal Clergy* (L, 1694).

G. D. Henderson, *Mystics of the North-East* (A, 1934), 32–8; *id., The Burning Bush* (E, 1957), 105–19; *FES* VI, 2; *DNB* XX, 409–10.

N. R. Needham

Garden, James (1647–1726), Episcopalian* CofS divine, brother of George.* Graduating MA in 1662 from King's College, Aberdeen, he was minister successively of New Machar in Aberdeenshire (1672–5), Maryculter in Kincardineshire (1675–6), and Balmerino in Fife (1676–80). He was appointed Professor of Divinity in King's College in 1680, Aberdeen, but deprived in 1697 for refusal to subscribe to the Westminster* Confession. Later he espoused the Jacobite* cause, but the government left him in peace after the collapse of the 1715 Rising.* He shared his brother's admiration for the mystical writings of Antoinette Bourignon (see Bourignianism), and his *Comparative Theology, or the True and Solid Grounds of a Pure and Peaceable Theology* (n.p., 1700) reflects this influence.

GARVIE, ALFRED ERNEST

Garden received a DD from King's College, Aberdeen, in 1681.

Theses Theologicae De Gratiae Efficacia (A, 1681).

G. D. Henderson, *Mystics of the North-East* (A, 1934), 61–4; *id., The Burning Bush* (E, 1957), 105–19; *FES* VII, 371; *DNB* XX, 410.

N. R. Needham

Garney Bridge, *see* Associate Presbytery.

Garvie, Alfred Ernest (1861–1945), Congregational minister. Garvie was born at Zyrardow, Poland, son of Peter Garvie, linen manufacturer, and Jane Kedslie, United Presbyterian Scots settled in Poland since the 1820s. He was educated at George Watson's College, Edinburgh (1874–8), and Edinburgh University, which poor eyesight forced him to leave for a Glasgow drapery warehouse. The call to ministry took him to Glasgow University (1885–9), a Logan gold medal and a First in Philosophy, followed by Mansfield College, Oxford (1889–93), and a First in Theology. Unwillingness to sign the Westminster* Confession determined his future as a Congregational minister, with pastorates in Macduff (1893–5) and Montrose (1895–1903), the General Secretaryship of the Scottish Congregational Ministers' Symposium and the Presidency of the Scottish Congregational Union* (1902–3). These and his first important book, *The Ritschlian Theology* (E, 1899), made his reputation, reflected in his Glasgow doctorate (1903) and his call to London. From 1903 he taught at Hackney and New Colleges, becoming Principal of New in 1907, of Hackney in 1922 and the united colleges in 1924, retiring in 1933. He wrote steadily (*A Guide to Preachers*, L, 1906; *Studies in the Inner Life of Jesus*, L, 1907; *The Holy Catholic Church*, L, 1920; *The Christian Doctrine of the Godhead*, L, 1925; *The Christian Ideal for Human Society*, L, 1930; *The Christian Belief in God*, L, 1933) and he became prominent beyond British Congregationalism (Chairman of the Congregational Union, 1920; President of the National Free Church Council, 1924; Moderator of the Free Church Federal Council, 1928).

Garvie's significance lay less as theologian or ecclesiastic than in his combination of those roles. He set Congregationalism in the context of the world Church. His Vice-Chairmanship of the Conference on Christian Politics, Economics and Citizenship (1924), his Deputy-Chairmanship of the Lausanne Conference on Faith and Order (1927) and doctorates from Berlin and London demonstrated his standing as Congregationalism's leading contemporary ecumenist. He died at Hendon, North London.

Memories and Meanings of My Life (L, 1938).

DNB 1941–1950, 289–90; *Congregational Year Book*, 1946, 440–1; A. Peel, *The Congregational Two Hundred 1530–1948* (L, 1948), 267–8; J. W. Grant, *Free Churchmanship in England 1870–*

GAU, JOHN

1940 (L., n.d.); H. Escott, *A History of Scottish Congregationalism* (G, 1960).

J. C. G. Binfield

Gau, John (*d.* 1553), early Scottish Lutheran. A student of St Salvator's College, St Andrews, he composed the first substantial Lutheran* treatise to be published in Scots, *The Richt Vay to the Kingdom of Heuine*, printed in 1533 at Malmö, and dedicated to King Frederick II of Denmark. Born in the 1490s, and apparently in major orders, Gau left home for Lutheran Scandinavia and settled in Copenhagen, where he served as a chaplain in the Church of Our Lady, marrying in 1536 Birgitta, a native of Malmö, who died in 1551. Gau himself died *c.* 1553. His work is substantially a Scots translation of a Danish Lutheran text composed by Christiern Pedersen, *Den rette vey till Hiemmerigis Rige* (1531), itself based on a German work by Urbanus Rhegius (the Reformer, of Augsburg), who borrowed material from Luther's own writings. As an aid to devotion, *The Richt Vay* expounded the Ten Commandments, the Apostles' Creed, the Lord's Prayer and angelic salutation. It stressed the supremacy of Scripture as the rule of faith and obedience, and the right of the laity to read the vernacular Bible, it recounted humanity's fall from grace, corrupt nature and need for redemption, the provision of redemption by the incarnation, work and passion of the eternal Son of God, justification by faith alone and sanctification by the Holy Spirit. Headship of the Church belonged to no mortal: Christ gave the keys of the kingdom to all Christians and not to Peter alone; all have the power to bind and loose, not just bishops, priests or monks; ministers of the Word should be chosen by Christian congregations; pilgrimages to holy places and journeys to Rome for papal pardons are unnecessary; instead of intercessory prayer to Mary and the saints, Christ alone should be worshipped for he 'alone made perfect satisfaction for all our sins and will mercifully forgive us through his own gracious goodness'. The work ends with a letter to the Scottish nobles and barons in which the false preaching of 'dreams and fables and the traditions of men' is contrasted with biblical teaching and the example of Patrick Hamilton,* martyred for confessing Christ.

J. Gau, *The Richt Vay to the Kingdom of Heuine*, ed. A. F. Mitchell (E, 1888).

J. Kirk

Geddes, Alexander (1737–1802), biblical critic. A cousin of Bishop John Geddes,* he was born near Buckie, Banffshire, and studied for the RC priesthood at Scalan (*see* Colleges and Seminaries, Roman Catholic), the Scots College,* Paris, and the University of Paris, where he encountered Enlightenment ideas. Ordained in 1764, he served as priest in various places in the Lowlands, but relations with Bishop George Hay* worsened, particularly when he attended a Protestant service at Banff (1780). He left the Scottish mission in 1781, and settled in London to devote himself to biblical studies.

GEDDES, JENNY

He is chiefly noted for his critical work in connection with his translation of the *Bible* (L, I (Gen.-Josh.), 1792; II (Judg., 1 Sam.–2 Chr., Ruth, Prayer of Manasseh), 1797; cf. *Prospectus*, 1786; *Proposals*, 1788; *Answers to Queries*, 1790; *Address to the Public*, 1793; *Critical Remarks* I, 1800; *Psalms 1–118* appeared posthumously). He is conventionally referred to as the originator of the 'fragment hypothesis' of the compilation of the Pentateuch: he rejected the view of J. Astruc (1753), refined by J. G. Eichhorn (1787), that Moses compiled Gen. 1–Exod.2 on the basis of two documents, and proposed that the Pentateuch represents an assemblage of discrete 'documents', written and oral, Israelite and non-Israelite, which is probably to be ascribed to the reign of Solomon (*Bible* I, xviii). Other issues raised by Geddes remain topical: his definition of the task of the critic 'to ascertain the genuine grammatical meaning of a genuine text' (*Bible* II, xiii); his principle of translation, which he termed 'equipollency' – not 'word for word' but the sense, semantically controlled by the sentence, idiomatically conveyed (*Answer*, 15). He anticipated later views on the importance of oral tradition. Through his probable influence on S. T. Coleridge he was instrumental in changing the climate of opinion. However, partly because of the incompleteness of his publications (the translation was never finished, only one volume of *Critical Remarks* was published, the promised *General Preface* never appeared), Geddes seems to have operated as biblical critic more by intuition than by thorough demonstration.

Geddes died under ecclesiastical censure, a circumstance not altogether surprising given the novelty of his views and the, at times, sharply polemical tone of his writing. But he never renounced Catholicism, and he defended Christ's divinity against Joseph Priestley. His non-scriptural writings were mostly verse, much of it humorous or satirical. Aberdeen's LLD rewarded his verse translation of *Select Satires of Horace* (L, 1779).

R. C. Fuller, *Alexander Geddes 1737–1802* (Sheffield, 1984); W. McKane, *Selected Christian Hebraists* (C, 1989), 151–90; J. W. Rogerson, *Old Testament Criticism in the Nineteenth Century* (L, 1984); E. S. Shaffer, *'Kubla Khan' and The Fall of Jerusalem* (C, 1975); J. F. S. Gordon, *The Catholic Church in Scotland* (A, 1874), 185–91.

M. Dilworth

Geddes, Jenny, Scottish 'herb-woman' of uncertain history and age who typified Presbyterian outrage at the new liturgy of William Laud.* According to the common tradition, she started a riot during the reading of the service on 23 July, 1637 in St Giles, Edinburgh, by throwing her stool at the bishop and shouting indignantly, 'Villain! do you say mass at my lug [ear]?' Strong opposition all over Scotland to Laud's service book led to the signing of the National Covenant.* In time Jenny Geddes became an important part of Scottish Protestant lore. A folding stool like the one that features in the tradition has been exhibited in the National

Museum of Antiquities in Edinburgh. Although the 1637 disturbance is well attested, a greengrocer named Jennie Geddes in the High Street, Edinburgh, is historically recorded only in 1660, when she contributed her stock and fittings to a bonfire to celebrate the restoration of the monarchy.

T. Royle, *MacMillan Companion to Scottish Literature* (L, 1983), 117.

D. B. Calhoun

Geddes, John (1735–99), RC Bishop of Morocco. Geddes was born at Mains of Corridoun, Enzie near Buckie, and taught (1748–9) by Alexander Godsman, Preshome. Sent to the Scots College,* Rome, in 1750, he was ordained at Rome in 1759.

He was stationed at Shenval (1759–62); became superior of Scalan (1762–7) (*see* Colleges and Seminaries, RC); and was later stationed at Preshome (1767–70). In 1770 he was sent to Spain to recover possession of the Scots College, Madrid, which he transferred to Valladolid.

After ten years as rector at Valladolid, Geddes was consecrated titular Bishop of Morocco and coadjutor to Bishop Hay* at Madrid. He was based at Edinburgh, acting also as Mission procurator. His popularity among people of all ranks and religious denominations greatly reduced anti-RC prejudice. In 1790 he visited Orkney, walking most of the way. In the winter of 1791–2 he was in Paris investigating the affairs of the Scots College. These two trips badly damaged his health and he retired in 1793. After a few months at Scalan, he moved to Aberdeen where he was nursed by his nephew, Charles Gordon.*

J. F. S. Gordon, *Journal and Appendix to Scotichronicon and Monasticon* (G, 1867);
C. Johnson, *Developments in the Roman Catholic Church in Scotland 1789–1829* (E, 1983).

C. Johnson

Geddie, John (1815–72), Canadian missionary. Born at Banff and reared in Nova Scotia, Geddie served as a minister on Prince Edward Island until 1846, when he was appointed by the Presbyterian Church in Nova Scotia as the first foreign missionary from Canada. Sent to the New Hebrides, he arrived on the island of Aneityum in 1848, where he did heroic service for nearly twenty years in evangelizing and educating the people. His last years were spent in Australia, where he supervised the translating and printing of the Bible in Aneityumese. He made yearly missionary voyages to the New Hebrides until his death. A memorial in the Aneityum church reads: 'In memory of John Geddie, D.D., born 1815. When he landed in 1848 there were no Christians here, and when he left in 1872 there were no heathen.'

G. Patterson, *Missionary Life ... Life of John Geddie* (Toronto, 1882); *Dictionary of Canadian Biography* X, 302–3; J. W. Falconer, *John Geddie* (Toronto, 1915).

D. B. Calhoun

Gellatly, Alexander (*c.*1720–61), first missionary of the Associate Synod* to America. Born in Perth, Gellatly studied theology in the General Associate Synod (Antiburgher)* theological hall. In response to requests from Pennsylvania he was ordained and, in 1753, sent as the first Secession* Church missionary. He was accompanied by Andrew Arnot (a minister who returned to Scotland the following year) and together they constituted themselves into the Associate Presbytery of Pennsylvania. They were attacked as schismatics and errorists by the New Light Presbyterians. In response, Gellatly published two works defending the Secession and its theology: *A Detection of Injurious Reasonings and Unjust Representations...* (Lancaster, PA, 1754) and *Some Observations...* (1758). Gellatly served churches in Chester and Lancaster counties until his early death.

J. B. Scouller, *A Manual of the United Presbyterian Church of North America* (Pittsburgh, 1887); W. B. Sprague, *Annals of the American Associate... Pulpit* (NY, 1869).

D. C. Lachman

General Assembly, the supreme court of the CofS (as of some other Presbyterian* Churches), combining judicial, legislative and administrative functions. It has jurisdiction over the inferior courts – Synods,* Presbyteries,* and Kirk Sessions,* and it has power to delegate specific functions, including finality of judgment in certain cases, to a Commission of Assembly composed of all the members of the General Assembly, or to a smaller Commission, such as a Judicial Commission.*

A restraint on legislative powers is imposed by the Barrier Act,* 1697, which provides that legislation which affects the constitution of the Church must be approved by a majority of Presbyteries before it can be enacted by the General Assembly; but approval by Presbyteries is permissive only, and it remains true that only the General Assembly has power to legislate.

The first General Assembly, though not known by that name, met in 1560. It had no legal precedent, and its constitutional authority, from a legal point of view, may be found in the medieval doctrine of necessity, or perhaps in the more modern concept of autochthony. Whatever the legal theory may be, the General Assembly was certainly established *de facto* before it was legally established by subsequent Acts of the Scottish Parliament; and theologically the position of the Church was always that which eventually found expression in the Declaratory Articles,* recognized by the Church of Scotland Act, 1921,* namely that the Church receives from Jesus Christ a government which he has appointed with 'the right and power subject to no civil authority to legislate, and to adjudicate finally, in all matters of worship, government and discipline in the Church'.

The significance of the General Assembly in Scottish history since the Reformation* arises not only from its place in Presbyterian polity but also from its place as the supreme court of a national Church.

For example, the conflicts between Church and state* were reflected in conflicts between Presbyterian and episcopal systems, because it was through bishops that monarchs sought to control the Church. When the Claim of Right,* 1689, declared that James VII* altered the constitution from 'a legal limited monarchy to an arbitrary despotic power', it highlighted a situation in which Church and people were naturally on the same side.

The conflict between Church and state was finally resolved by the 1921 Act and the combination of national recognition of religion and freedom of the Church, which is symbolized by the Queen or the Lord High Commissioner* attending the General Assembly, but sitting in a gallery which is outside the Assembly. However, the popular association of the General Assembly with democracy, and of episcopacy with aristocracy, persists to this day as one of the non-theological factors which ecumenism ignores at its peril.

In fact the General Assembly is not democratically constituted as the term is now understood politically. It is composed of commissioners appointed by Presbyteries, not by congregations; and its authority is derived from Christ, and not from any electorate. Nevertheless, the present membership of some 1,250 commissioners – ministers and elders in equal numbers, from every part of Scotland – is a significant cross-section of the population; so when the General Assembly debates political matters on the report of the Committee on Church and Nation* it attracts considerable public interest. It has to be stressed that these debates are intended to express a Christian view by the Church, rather than reflect the personal political opinions of its members.

Most of the business of the General Assembly, occupying a full week in May of each year, is Church business, and is conducted by hearing reports from the various committees and boards to which responsibilities have been remitted. These include mission, at home and overseas, finance, pay (stipend) and conditions of ministers, buildings, doctrine, social work, education, etc. Through these reports, and through the supervision of inferior courts and the hearing of appeals from them, the General Assembly supervises the whole life and work of the Church from year to year.

Since the first General Assembly met in 1560, it has evolved in various ways. It has grown numerically from an original six ministers and thirty-five others of whom two were elders, to its present size with equal numbers of ministers and elders; but for most of its life the number of ministers has exceeded the number of elders. It was at the Union of 1929 that the UFC concept of equal numbers was adopted, and the appointment of commissioners from burghs and universities was departed from.

Since the UFC, and the FC before it, were composed of those who had left the CofS over matters relating to Church and state, and not because of Church polity, their General Assemblies largely and deliberately duplicated that of the CofS,

so there are no substantial constitutional differences to be noted.

Not every Presbyterian Church has, or has had, a General Assembly. It is the conciliar system rather than any particular court which is the distinctive mark of Presbyterian polity. The *Second Book of Discipline*,* regarded as a definitive statement of Presbyterian Church government, specifies four kinds of 'assembly', none of which is called a Presbytery or easily identified with one; and our General Assembly is 'the national assemblie (quhilk is generall to us)' to distinguish it from 'the generall assemblie ... of the haill kirk of God' – i.e., an international assembly.

Although an international assembly was not possible at the time of the Reformation, the Reformers in Scotland knew that they were not founding a new national Church – they were reforming the catholic and apostolic Church within a particular realm. Aware of the international dimension, they looked back, through the ecumenical councils of the early Church to the council, or assembly, at Jerusalem (Acts 15), to find scriptural warrant for a conciliar system.

Thus the 1560 General Assembly would be fully aware of what the Scots Confession* of that year had said about the need for decrees of councils to be confirmed by the plain Word of God. Still today the General Assembly of the CofS is by its constitution expressly declared to be of a Church which is part of the holy catholic or universal Church, and which receives the Word of God as its supreme rule of faith and life. So, while free from interference by civil authority, it is constrained to act always in agreement with the Word of God.

SBD; G. D. Henderson (ed.), *The Scots Confession 1560* (E, 1960); S. Louden, *The True Face of the Kirk* (L, 1963); D. Shaw, *The General Assemblies of the Church of Scotland 1560–1600* (E, 1964); W. Mair, *Digest of the Laws and Decisions Relating to the Church of Scotland* (E, ^{5}1923); A. Herron, *A Guide to the General Assembly of the Church of Scotland* (E, 1976).

J. L. Weatherhead

General Associate Synod, popularly known as the 'Antiburgher' synod (so-called after 'The Breach' occasioned by the Burgess Oath*), claiming to be the continuation of the synod constituted in 1745 by the Associate Presbytery,* and at first (until 1788) using the same name, 'Associate Synod'. It was formed in 1747 by those who condemned the oath and wished to make their position a term of communion, but who withdrew after abstaining from voting. In 1748 they deposed and excommunicated their erstwhile brethren (*see* Associate Synod). They amended the questions in their formula* to make agreement with their position on the Burgess Oath a qualification for license and ordination. Although in 1749 the Synod rebuked itself for sinful conduct and temper in these proceedings, it regarded the sinfulness of the 'Burghers' in condoning the oath as precluding even a consideration of the restoration of fellowship.

GENERAL ASSOCIATE SYNOD

The Antiburghers grew from the first, with many congregations seeking the services of too few ministers. Alexander Moncrieff* continued as theological professor, having been appointed by the Associate Presbytery in 1742. He had instituted a philosophical class, which the Antiburghers continued, to provide the preparatory training normally acquired in a university. Latin and Greek were prerequisites, as was a reputation for personal piety. On Moncrieff's death in 1762 his son William* was appointed. He was followed by Archibald Bruce,* 1786–1805, and George Paxton,* 1807–20, who resigned rather than go into the union. With Paxton the theological hall was established in Edinburgh as a full-time position, rather than being held wherever the professor held a pastoral charge.

The Antiburghers shared in the Secession's* reputation for strictness in doctrine and discipline, and deservedly so. Much troubled by heresy and divisive teaching, perhaps because founded by those willing to separate over an issue like the Burgess Oath, from their early years the Antiburghers responded decisively. They took up the matter of Thomas Nairn,* who by then had joined John Macmillan* in forming the Reformed Presbytery (see Reformed Presbyterian Church). Though Nairn did not acknowledge the Synod's authority, it excommunicated him and several other members of the RPC. From 1754 the Synod engaged in debate with Thomas Mair* over the doctrine of universal redemption. Mair had had the second part of James Fraser of Brea's* *A Treatise on Justifying Faith* (E, 1749) reprinted, and adopted the doctrines propounded in it. With considerable reluctance, in 1757 the Synod deposed him. In 1766 Mair petitioned unsuccessfully for restoration. Others deposed for doctrinal error included Robert Carmichael* (1762) and Robert Imrie* (1806). When students were found to have embraced some of the philosophical thinking of the day, their teacher in the philosophical hall, Alexander Pirie,* was suspended and left the Church rather than comply. David Smyton, who petitioned for uniformity in the 'lifting' of the elements of the Lord's Supper before a prayer of consecration, was suspended for his unwillingness to accept the Synod's advice of mutual forebearance (see Lifters).

The stricter discipline exercised by the Antiburghers bore fruit in their considerably greater success in missionary work than the Burghers achieved. In 1751 application was made from Pennsylvania for ministers. Those appointed to go gave reasons for not complying, which were accepted. But the Synod decided that any entering on trials for license should be required to signify willingness to submit to any missionary appointment. Although a strict measure, it had the desired effect; unlike the Burgher synod, the Antiburghers had few further problems with sending men. Alexander Gellatly* and Andrew Arnot (of Midholm) had the honour of being the first Secession missionaries. A number of missionaries were sent to America in the 1760s, including John Mason,* who later was instrumental in uniting both branches of the Secession and the Reformed Presbyterian Church in America, forming the Associate Reformed Church. This was not welcomed by the Synod, though Adam Gib's* 1776 motion to remove Mason's name from the Synod's rolls was not acted upon until 1780. (Gib had a leading role in the Synod at first, but by 1770 had apparently lost much of his former influence.) The Synod continued to send missionaries to America (see Anderson, John), some of whom were among the first in Kentucky and Tennessee. Extensive work was done in Nova Scotia and monies were sent to further work among the Indians. Scotland was not neglected; Gaelic-speaking missionaries were sent to the Highlands. In 1788, as a means of accommodating growth, four synods (one in Ireland), subordinate to one general synod, were created. The name of the Church was changed from 'Associate Synod' to 'General Associate Synod' accordingly.

GENERAL (KIRK) SESSIONS

In 1763 a fund was formed to make provision for indigent ministers' widows and subsequently acts were passed to ensure adequate contribution to it, by both congregations and ministers. In 1788 the Synod declared its abhorrence of the slave-trade and urged efforts for emancipation, of both outward and spiritual bondage.

The controversy between Old Lights and New Lights* began in the Antiburgher synod when licentiates voiced their difficulties with the confessional teaching on the power of the civil magistrate in matters of religion. William Graham's* *A Review of Ecclesiastical Establishments* (L, 1792) was influential in changing opinion. In 1801 the Synod embraced the New Light in a new *Testimony* (E, 1801). After heated debate, in 1805 five ministers, including Thomas M'Crie* and Archibald Bruce,* the Synod's theological professor, withdrew to form the Constitutional Associate Presbytery (see Original Secession Church).

As one might expect of those who initiated the separation in 1747, the Antiburghers were unreceptive to proposals for union throughout the eighteenth century. In addition to objecting to the union in America, proposals for union in Ireland were rejected in 1784 and 1805. In 1798 the Synod declared itself against the practices of promiscuous Communion, particularly in relation to attending lay-preaching and sabbath evening schools, saying that no Antiburgher could attend such without being subject to discipline. The following year the prohibition was expressly applied to the public ministry of any bearing office in a church against which the Synod had lifted up a testimony. But the nineteenth century brought a different temper, and by the time proposals for union were advanced in 1818 the General Associate Synod was fully ready to receive them, joining with the Associate Synod in 1820 to form the United Secession Church.*

J. M'Kerrow, *History of the Secession Church* (E, 1848).

D. C. Lachman

General (Kirk) Sessions. After the Reformation, some Scottish towns had General Kirk Sessions, which met to discuss matters concerning the needs and life of the town – poverty, charity, discipline, 'penny bridals', fast days, etc. The minutes of Edinburgh's General Session are extant for 1574, and a residual form of General Session is evident in other towns where monies for the poor had to be distributed. In Edinburgh's Burgh churches* elders at their ordination still sign the formula* in a volume that has been used since 1690. Mair, however, states that there is no such term in CofS law as 'General Session'. After 1690, an Assembly committee set about codifying church law, and proposals came to the 1719 Assembly. A proposal to revive the General Session led to a bitter series of printed letters by John Anderson of Glasgow (1671–1721; *FES* III, 438–9) attacking the idea. Despite the support of William Dunlop,* William Carstares'* nephew, the 1720 Assembly had to give its mind to the Marrow* controversy, and the proposed General Session came to nothing. It is probable, nevertheless, that together with the exercise,* the General Session played a part in the development of the presbytery.*

A. I. Dunlop, 'The General Session: a Controversy of 1720', *RSCHS* 13 (1959), 223–39; W. Mair, *A Digest of the Laws and Decisions Relating to the Church of Scotland* (E, ⁵1923); 'Extracts from the Buik of the General Kirk of Edinburgh, in the Years 1574 and 1575', in *Miscellany of the Maitland Club* (E, 1833), 97–126.

A. I. Dunlop

General Trustees (Church of Scotland), a body corporate with perpetual succession set up by an Act of Parliament in 1921 as a holding body for properties and investments belonging to committees of the CofS. Trustees, who are appointed and may be removed by the General Assembly, must be either ministers or elders. Their role was extended in 1925 when further legislation provided for the transfer to them of *inter alia* (a) payments which were burdens on land and which replaced the old teind* stipend* and (b) the churches and almost all the manses and glebes* of the CofS. In respect of the properties and endowments transferred to them by this legislation the General Trustees are administrative trustees bound to apply the subjects primarily to meet the proper requirements of the parish or its neighbourhood and subject to directions from the General Assembly. For many years after the Union of the CofS and UFC in 1929 the General Trustees tended to be concerned almost exclusively with the old CofS properties vested in them, but since the late 1970s their role has become much more general following (a) the delegation to them by the General Assembly of powers in relation to heritable properties, (b) the setting up of the Central Fabric Fund and Consolidated Loan Fund, from which they give grants and loans to congregations facing fabric expenditure and (c) their being appointed the central body dealing with property maintenance. The number of members of the board varies, but the norm for some time has been thirty-two. The Trustees operate through a structure of executive committees at fortnightly intervals throughout most of the year. They own the Church of Scotland Insurance Company Ltd and are essentially the central CofS body involved in property.

The Church of Scotland (General Trustees) Order Confirmation Act 1921; The Church of Scotland (Property and Endowments) Acts 1925 to 1978.

PAGACS 1979, 30–1 (Act IX), 32–4 (Act XIV), 49–50 (Regul. 7); *RGACS 1989*, pt. II, Reguls. IV, V.

A. W. Cowe

Geneva, *see* Calvin, Calvinism; Haldanes.

Geneva Bible, *see* Bible (Versions, English).

Geneva Book, *see Book of Common Order* (1564).

Gerard, Alexander (1728–95), professor (lecturer) in Philosophy at Aberdeen in 1750, Professor of Divinity in Marischal College and minister of Aberdeen Greyfriars (1760–71), Professor of Divinity, King's College, Aberdeen (1771–95), and Moderator of the General Assembly of the CofS in 1764. He wrote extensively on the relationship between natural and revealed religion, and on the evidences for the truth of Christianity. He was the colleague of George Campbell,* Thomas Reid,* and other luminaries of Aberdeen University at the time. He took issue with David Hume* on the influence of the ministry on character in *The Influence of the Pastoral Office on the Character examined* (A, 1760). His most significant work was probably his *Dissertations on Subjects relating to the Genius and the Evidences of Christianity* (E, 1766), in which he defended the biblical presentation of the evidences for the Christian religion. He supported the Moderate party* in the patronage* controversy, though not especially actively, and revealed his Moderate inclinations in his works on taste and in his opposition to the colonial position in the American War of Independence.

The Influence of Piety on the Public Good (E, 1761); *An Essay on Taste* (E, 1764); *Liberty the Cloke of Maliciousness, both in the American Rebellion, and in the Manners of the Times* (A, 1778); *Sermons* (L, 1782).

FES VII, 372; *DNB* XXI, 210–11.

J. R. McIntosh

Gib, Adam (1714–88), theologian and churchman. He was born at Cowden Castle, the son of the laird of Castletown in the parish of Muckhart, Perthshire. Sent to study medicine at Edinburgh, the sight of an execution in the Grassmarket there led him to think seriously of religion, and the reading of Luther's commentary on Galatians brought him peace. He was appalled by the capricious dealings he observed in the CofS* General Assembly* and its commission, and when a minister was introduced (*see* Intrusion) in his home parish against the wishes of the population, Gib joined the Associate

GIB, ADAM

Presbytery* in 1735. His theological education was at the Secession* divinity hall under William Wilson* of Perth. In 1741 he was ordained as the first Secession minister in Edinburgh, and a large church assembled in Bristo Street, which he pastored until his death. During the Rising of 1745* most Presbyterian minister fled from Edinburgh at the approach of the Jacobites,* but Gib remained with his congregation of twelve hundred and in the presence of enemy soldiers defiantly prayed for the reigning King and for the survival of the Protestant succession to the throne.

In 1747 the Secession Church divided on the issue whether taking the Burgess Oath* was a ground for exclusion from the church. The party that insisted on exclusion rallied behind Gib, and the General Associate Synod* (Antiburgher) was constituted in his house. In the years that followed, Gib was the dominant figure in the Synod; sometimes withdrawing himself from its meetings and forcing the Synod to seek reconciliation with him. He was dubbed 'Pope Gib'.

Gib was a vigorous contender for the principles held by the Synod. When the Synod's Thomas Mair* published *A Treatise on Justifying Faith* (E, 1749) by James Fraser* of Brea and espoused its doctrine of universal redemption (*see* Atonement), Gib responded by reissuing John Owen's *Death of Death* (E, 1755), in defence of the teaching that Christ purchased remission of sins for the elect alone. The bulk of Gib's own *Sacred Contemplations* (E, 1786) is an exposition of the covenant of works and the covenent of grace (*see* Covenant Theology) in the tradition of Thomas Boston,* including the 'Marrow'* teaching about the warrant of faith in the gospel offer. The book also contains an astute refutation of the Synod's philosophy tutor, Alexander Pirie.* As a means of overthrowing the Arminian scheme of free will, Pirie had imbibed a theory which subjected both the will of God and the human will to a universal necessity in the laws of nature.

Gib was the author of many pamphlets; the positions espoused in these are digested in *The Present Truth: A Display of the Secession Testimony*, 2 vols (E, 1774). It contains his answer to Thomas Nairn* of Abbotshall, who in 1743 resisted the Associate Synod's act of public covenanting,* on the ground that swearing subjection to the present magistrates was questionable, seeing they had defected from the covenants of the Second Reformation.* Later, in 1759, Gib opposed a proposal by Alexander Moncrieff* that the Synod petition the King concerning the country's religious declension. In both these instances Gib seemed to think it improper for the Church to turn to the magistrate for help in promoting the Christian religion (*see* Church and State), and these statements were later appealed to by the advocates of Voluntaryism.*

Vindiciae Dominicae; A Defence of the Reformation-Standards of the Church of Scotland (E, 1778); *An Antidote Against a New Heresy concerning the True Sonship of Jesus Christ* (E, 1777); *Christ Has Other Sheep* (E, 1783); *Proceedings of the Associate Synod concerning Ministers who have Separated* (E, 1748); *Exposition of Reveries concerning Sonship of Christ* (E, 1778); *An Account of Burgher Re-exhibition of Secession Testimony* (E, 1780); *New Vocabulary of Modern Billingsgate Phrases* (E, 1784); *Warning against Countenancing the Ministrations of Mr. George Whitefield** (E, 1742).

DNB XXI, 246-7; Small I, 426-31; D. M. Forrester, 'Adam Gib, the Anti-Burgher', *RSCHS* 7 (1940), 141-69; J. M'Kerrow, *History of the Secession Church* (E, 1854); J. Macleod, *Scottish Theology* (E, ³1974); J. Thin, *Memorials of Bristo United Presbyterian Church* (E, 1888); J. Walker, *The Theology and Theologians of Scotland...* (E, ²1888).

S. Isbell

Gibb, John (1835-1915), Professor in Presbyterian CofE. He was born in Aberdeen, studied at Aberdeen and Heidelberg Universities and the FC College, Aberdeen, and was ordained by the FC Presbytery of Italy to Malta, as assistant to George Wisely (*AFCS* I, 360), ministering to Scottish troops (1863-7). After returning home on his father's death, he became resident tutor (1868) and later Professor of Church History and New Testament Exegesis (1877) at the English Presbyterian College in London, moving with it to Cambridge (Westminster College) in 1899. He resigned in 1913, having given up his NT responsibilities in 1907. Aberdeeen made him DD. Gibb translated *The Table-Talk of Doctor Martin Luther* (L, 1883), and Augustine's *Homelies on John* (E, 1871), but his best work, edited with W. Montgomery, was Augustine's Latin *Confessions* in the Cambridge Patristic Texts (C, 1908). He moved away from his earlier Evangelicalism to become 'a sincere lover of many-sided truth', impressed by the authority of religious experience. His closest friend was Meredith Townsend, editor of the *Spectator* (*DNB Second Suppl.* III, 531-3). He had a trenchant mind wide in its sympathies, with a certain dry detachment towards all traditions.

'Unbelief, Doubt and Faith', in J. O. Dykes (ed.), *Some Present Difficulties in Theology* (L, 1873), 121-74, and *Biblical Studies and Their Influence upon the Church* - inaugural (L, 1877).

AFCS I, 167; *Who Was Who 1898-1916*, 271; C. M. Townsend, *The Mind of John Gibb* (L, 1923).

D. F. Wright

Gibson, James (1799-1871), FC Professor, Glasgow. Born at Crieff, educated at the University and Theological Hall, Glasgow, he was ordained 1839 to Kingston (*quoad sacra*)* Church, Glasgow. He took part in the Disruption* and was elected Professor of Systematic Theology and Church History in the FC College, Glasgow, 1856. His works include: *The Inability of Man* (G, 1846); *Present Truths in Theology* (G, 1863); *The Church in Relation to the State* (E, 1872); *The Public Worship of God* (L, 1869); *The Marriage Affinity Question* (E, 1854); *The Deca-*

GIFFORD LECTURES

logue in the Old Testament Dispensation (G, 1866); The Union Question (G, 1868).

Gibson was one of the foremost spokesmen of the conservative wing of the FC. He was a staunch Non-Intrusionist* and Calvinistic theologian. He led the conservative forces in the Evangelical Alliance debate 1846, the Glasgow College case 1859 and the Australian Union case 1861. He was an early and outspoken opponent of union with the UP Church.

AFCS I, 55; FES III, 419–20; Disruption Worthies, 261–4.

K. R. Ross

Gifford Lectures, a series of lectures (usually ten) on natural theology that have been given almost annually since 1888 at each of the four ancient Scottish Universities: Edinburgh, Glasgow, St Andrews and Aberdeen. The lectureships were set up in 1885 by a munificent legacy of Adam Lord Gifford (1820–87), associate justice of the Court of Sessions of Scotland. Lord Gifford may also have wished to propagate his own convictions about the importance, for individuals as well as society, of a broadly theistic outlook on life. His own posthumously published lectures reveal his ecumenical religious interests, with no great emphasis on the positively supernatural. Although Lord Gifford provided for lectures on the popular level, they were from the start learned presentations that for the most part related to natural theology only in a broad sense. A reason for this lay in the prevailing trends (Neokantianism, pragmatism, logical positivism, linguistic analysis and existentialism in philosophy, liberalism, social gospel, demythologization, and neo-orthodoxy in theology) that were not supportive of studies in natural theology taken in the traditional sense. Only one Neothomist, Gilson, was a Gifford lecturer before the early 1970s. Since the four universities implemented their stewardship of their respective shares in Lord Gifford's bequest through committees of prominent faculty members, the invitations readily went to outstanding scholars. Excellence was all the easier to obtain as in the first decades of the lectureship the honorarium for a series, to be paid from the interest of the legacy, could be equivalent to a full year's professorial salary. The presence of Max Müller, Stokes, Frazer, Royce, and William James among the early lecturers did much to secure an international renown to the lectureship. Three-fourths of the 150 or so lecturers, more than half of whom gave two consecutive series of lectures, were British, with twelve Americans as the next largest group. Several of the lecturers were prominent scientists, such as Stokes, Driesch, Eddington, Sherrington, Bohr, Heisenberg and Eccles. Theological and philosophical trends in prominence in Scotland were voiced through the lectures of E. and J. Caird,* A. M. Fairbairn,* A. S. Pringle-Pattison, A. E. Taylor,* W. P. Paterson,* John Laird, Alexander M. Macbeath, C. A. Campbell, John Baillie,* D. M. Mackinnon* and John Macquarrie. Almost all the lecture-series have been published. Among promi-

GILBERTINES

nent invitees who could not come were Bergson, Cardinal Mercier, and Maritain.

S. L. Jaki, Lord Gifford and his Lectures: A Centenary Retrospect (E, 1986).

S. L. Jaki

Gilbert of Moray (de Moravia) (d. 1245), Bishop of Caithness from c.1223. He was a member of the powerful de Moravia familia, of Flemish origin, lords of Duffus and elsewhere in Moray, and had been Archdeacon of Moray before his election as Bishop.

His two predecessors had been the victims of violence by local laymen, so the new Bishop required tact, courage and the support of a powerful local family. He moved his cathedral from Halkirk to Dornoch, where he drew up a constitution for the chapter; Dornoch was closer to his family's lands across the Moray Firth. He had a reputation for sanctity, and although there is no record of his formal canonization he was locally venerated as a saint after his death (for which 1243 has also been suggested) with his feast-day on 1 April.

Dowden, 234–5; FESMA 58, 238; DNB XXI, 317–18; Easson-Cowan, 203–4; A. B. Scott, 'Gilbert of Moray, Bishop of Caithness', RSCHS 1 (1926), 135–42.

A. Macquarrie

Gilbertines, women's monastic order, peculiar to England, founded by Master Gilbert, parson of Sempringham in Lincolnshire, in 1131. The order's constitution provided for a community of nuns living according to the Rule of St Benedict, in conjunction with a smaller community of canons regular following the Augustinian* rule and further communities of lay sisters and lay brothers. The original concept was therefore of a house of religious women whose spiritual ministration was guaranteed by a resident body of priests and whose material needs were provided by a domestic and agricultural workforce of women and men in the manner familiar at contemporary Cistercian* and Premonstratensian* houses. Although the Gilbertines may be seen as essentially an order of women, at least by intention, in practice the direction of the order as a whole and of its individual houses rested with the male canons regular, the head of Sempringham being the Master of the order, while daughter-houses were in the charge of their priors. In the twelfth century the order spread quite widely across Lincolnshire and lowland Yorkshire. An attempt was made to establish it in Scotland, but this proved abortive. During the decade 1219–28 the hereditary Steward or Stewart of Scotland, Walter son of Alan, offered the Gilbertines of Sixhills (Lincolnshire) an attractive site at Dalmilling in Kyle Stewart, beside the River Ayr. Although the prior of Sixhills visited the site and two of his canons came to Dalmilling as an advance party, it seems clear that no church or monastery was established, nor were any nuns or lay sisters recruited. By 1238 the property acquired by the order in Scotland was handed over to the well-established Cluniac* abbey of Paisley.*

Easson-Cowan, 105-6; R. Graham, *S. Gilbert of Sempringham and the Gilbertines* (L, 1901); J. Edwards, 'The Order of Sempringham and its connexion with the West of Scotland', *Trans. Glasgow Archaeological Soc.*, new ser., 5 (1908), 66-95 (and separately, *The Gilbertines in Scotland*, G, 1904); G. W. S. Barrow, 'The Gilbertine House at Dalmilling' and 'Dalmilling Documents', *Collections of Ayrshire Arch. and Nat. Hist. Soc.*, 2nd ser., 4 (1955-7, publ. 1958), 50-7.

G. W. S. Barrow

Gilfillan, George (1813-78), minister and literary figure. Born at Comrie, Perthshire, and educated at Glasgow, he was ordained in 1836 to School Wynd Church, Dundee, where he remained until his death, moving with his USec.C into the new UP Church in 1847. An eloquent speaker and a prolific writer, he was prominent in literary circles for over thirty years. He compiled memoirs and introductions to an extensive series of editions of English poets. His publications included *Christianity and Our Era* (E, 1857), *The Martyrs: Heroes and Bards of the Scottish Covenant* (L, 1852; [10]E, 1914), and *The Bards of the Bible* (L, 1874). He supported Voluntaryism* but opposed ultra-sabbatarianism and the proposed union between the UPC and the FC. Further education was another cause he promoted. His doctrinal views, expressed, for example, in *Hades, or the Unseen* (Dundee, 1842) and in an attack on the UP standards in 1869, were controversial but he twice avoided censure by presbytery. He died at Brechin, and his funeral at Dundee was attended by huge crowds.

The History of a Man (L, 1856) – autobiography. *DNB* XXI, 350-1; *Small* I, 285-6; *ASUPC*, 160; W. Walsh, *George Gilfillan* (Dundee, 1898); D. Macrae, *George Gilfillan* (G, 1900); R. A. and E. S. Watson, *George Gilfillan; Letters and Journals, with Memoir* (L, 1892).

G. Wareing

Gilfillan, Samuel (1762-1826), General Associate Synod* minister and writer. Born in Buchlyvie, Stirlingshire, after attending Glasgow University (1782-4) he studied theology under first Alexander Moncrieff* of Alloa and then Archibald Bruce* of Whitburn. Licensed by the Presbytery of Perth in 1789, he was ordained to the General Associate congregation at Comrie, Perthshire in 1791, where he ministered for the rest of his life. He contributed many articles to the *Christian Magazine* under the name 'Leumas', and was one of the General Associate ministers responsible for the scheme initiated in 1819 to set up lending libraries, mainly of religious books, in the Highlands.

Gilfillan wrote a number of books, the most esteemed being his *Discourses on the Dignity, Grace, and Operations of the Holy Spirit* (E, 1826).

J. M'Kerrow, *History of the Secession Church* (G, 1841), 910-13; *DNB* XXI, 352-3.

N. R. Needham

Gillespie, George (1613-48), eminent divine. Noted for his erudition, keen mind, powerful debating skills and articulate speech and often called 'Great Mr Gillespie' in his day, he has been referred to as the prince of Scottish theologians and the supreme defender of Presbyterian church government.

He was the son of John Gillespie, minister of Kirkcaldy and described as a 'thundering preacher', and the older brother of Patrick Gillespie.* After finishing his studies at St Andrews University and being unwilling to receive ordination from a bishop, he became chaplain to Viscount Kenmure. Upon Kenmure's death in 1634 he became chaplain to the Earl of Cassilis. During this period he published anonymously his *A Dispute against The English-Popish Ceremonies, Obtruded Upon the Church of Scotland* (1637), which was critical of Episcopalian innovations* in worship imposed by Charles I* on the Church. Though the book was banned by the Scottish Privy Council, the cogency of the content and the unusual ability of its young author became well known. Robert Baillie* marvelled: 'I admire the man, though I mislyke much of his matter; yea, I think he may prove amongst the best witts of this Isle' (*The Letters and Journals*, E, 1841, I, 90).

Following the signing of the National Covenant* in 1638, Gillespie was ordained to Wemyss in Fife; his was one of the first non-episcopal ordinations since the imposition of bishops. Later that year he preached before the memorable General Assembly in Glasgow* which deposed them. Shortly afterward he was called to serve as a chaplain in the Scottish army and was then sent to London in 1640 as part of the commission charged to conclude peace. Following the re-establishment of Presbyterianism* in 1641, Gillespie preached before Charles I in Edinburgh and was given a pension by him. The next year he was translated by the General Assembly to Greyfriars Church, Edinburgh.

Gillespie was one of the ministers appointed in 1643 as Scottish commissioners to the Westminster Assembly.* Though he was the youngest member, he participated actively, including service on the committee which drafted the Confession of Faith, and distinguished himself by his clarity of thought, persuasiveness of argument, and control of spirit. Baillie described him as 'such an excellent disputer in our Assemblie, that our affaires would suffer if he were absent but for one moneth'. However, the stories regarding his composition of part or the whole of the Shorter Catechism are wholly unfounded (*op. cit.*, II, 161-2). Along with Baillie, Gillespie introduced the Directory to the Scottish Assembly in Edinburgh in 1645, and he presented the Confession of Faith to the Assembly in Edinburgh in 1647 and saw its formal approval.

In 1647 he was elected by the town council to the High Church of Edinburgh and in 1648 Moderator* of the General Assembly, as well as to the commission assigned to attempt religious conformity with England. But he fell victim to tuberculosis and died in Kirkcaldy where he had gone to recuperate.

Gillespie is most famous for his *Aaron's Rod*

Blossoming ... (L, 1646), called 'the *chef d'oeuvre* of Scottish ecclesiastical theology' (James Walker, *The Theology and Theologians of Scotland*, E, ²1888, 14), in which he discusses the nature and relationship of civil and ecclesiastical power. He also wrote *Nihil Respondes* ... (L, 1645) and *Male Audis*... (L, 1646), in which he defended more briefly Presbyterian polity against Erastianism (*see* Church and State). There are also his posthumous *A Treatise of Miscellany Questions*... (E, 1649), edited by his younger brother Patrick, published sermons preached before the House of Commons (L, 1644) and the House of Lords (L, 1645), *A Late Dialogue Betwixt a Civilian and a Divine, concerning the Church of England*... (1644), *Wholesome Severity Reconciled With Christian Liberty*... (1645), *CXI Propositions Concerning the Ministerie and Government of the Church* (L, 1647), *An Useful Case of Conscience, Discussed and Resolved*... (L, 1649), and *An Assertion Of the Government of the Church of Scotland*.. (E, 1641). His *Notes of Debates and Proceedings of Divines and Other Commissioners at Westminster, From February 1644 to January 1645* were edited by David Meek (E, 1846).

FES I, 58–9; *The Works of Mr. George Gillespie*... 2 vols (E, 1843), with W. H. Hetherington, 'Memoir'; *DNB* XXI, 359–61; J. Howie, *Biographia Scoticana: ... Scots Worthies* (G, 1775); Chambers-Thomson II, 109–110; J. Macleod, *Scottish Theology* (E, ³1974); W. D. J. McKay, 'The Nature of Church Government in the Writings of George Gillespie (1613–1648)' (PhD, Queen's University, Belfast, 1991).

L. I. Hodges

Gillespie, Patrick (1617–75), Covenanter,* Principal of Glasgow University and leading Protester.* A son of John Gillespie (minister in Kirkcaldy; *FES* V, 102) and younger brother of George,* Gillespie was educated at St Andrews (MA, 1635). In 1642 he was ordained to Kirkcaldy, and in 1648 translated to Glasgow High Church. He was appointed (by the English Commissioners) Principal of the University and admitted in February 1653, accepting as much of the charge as was compatible with his pastoral ministry, until a General Assembly rightly constituted could be consulted (R. Baillie, *The Letters and Journals*, E, 1842, III, 213).

From the first Gillespie opposed receiving Charles II* as king, requiring him first to subscribe the Covenants* and, with James Guthrie,* 'passionate against the proclaiming of the King, till his qualification for government has first been tryed and allowed' (*ibid.*, III, 114). In October 1650 he attended the gentlemen who presented the Western Remonstance (*The Life of Mr Robert Blair*, ed. T. M'Crie, E, 1848, 247), and was party to a Remonstance to much the same effect sent by the Synod of Glasgow and Ayr. In the following decade Gillespie was a leader of the Remonstrants or Protesters* and as such looms large as a villain in Baillie's *Letters and Journals*, particularly after he became Principal (*e.g.* III, 140). But while 'a most forward and zealous protester' (*Blair*, 266), Gillespie was at times willing to listen to and even encourage measures for peace proposed by James Durham* and Robert Blair.* If anything, a careful reading of Baillie shows him to be much less willing than Gillespie to make the concessions which would have made reunion possible (cf. III, 182, 200, 216–17, 276–7, 279, and *Blair*, 325).

Although not in agreement with the English Independents, Gillespie was willing to associate with the English (Baillie, III, 322). He was successful at obtaining substantial sums of money for the college, Baillie's frequent complaints about his administration and misuse of funds notwithstanding (III, 282, 384, 396–7, 412, etc.). He was one of the Protesters sent to court in London to seek to combat the influence of the perfidious Resolutioner* James Sharp.*

At the Restoration* Gillespie was imprisoned in Stirling Castle. Only by acknowledging his offences and casting himself on the King's mercy did he escape execution. Said by Robert Wodrow* to have been 'a man of considerable height of spirit' (*The History of the Sufferings of the Church of Scotland*, G, 1828, I, 203), Gillespie was much affected by this humiliation. In contrast to James Guthrie's refusal to make concessions, Gillespie's submission was considered disgraceful. He was removed from his positions and confined to within six miles of Ormiston, E. Lothian.

Gillespie was a man of considerable ability. His preaching was such that, when first in Glasgow, Baillie 'used to recommend him to his scollars as a pattern to imitate in their delivery and method' (Wodrow, *Analecta*, II, 4). Wodrow refers to him as having been esteemed 'a person of great learning, solidity, and piety' (*History*, I, 204). Baillie's objection that Gillespie was 'not furnished with that measure of learning which the place of our Principall does necessarily require' merely reflects his general prejudice against Protesters.

In addition to arranging his brother's papers (published as *Miscellany Questions*), Gillespie used his materials also for the beginning of the first of a five-volume work on the covenant. Only two were published: *The Ark of the Testament opened*... (L, 1661) and *The Ark of the Covenant opened:*... (L, 1677), respectively treating the nature and kinds of covenant and the Mediator of the covenant. The third, on the condition of the covenant and the instrumentality of faith in justification, was extant in 1707, when the remaining two, respectively on the privileges and duties of the covenant, were believed lost (*Analecta*, I, 168–9). John Owen, in his preface to the second part, commended the work highly.

FES III, 462; *DNB* XXI, 361–3.

D. C. Lachman

Gillespie, Thomas (1708–74), co-founder of the Relief Church.* Born in Duddingston, near Edinburgh, Gillespie was educated at the University of Edinburgh and then went to Perth to study under William Wilson* with a view to entering the Secession* Church. He stayed only ten days (probably

GILLESPIE, WILLIAM HONEYMAN

because he was dissatisfied with the teaching on terms of communion and the continued obligation of the Covenants*) and moved to the Dissenting Academy in Northampton (England) taught by Philip Doddridge. Early in 1741 he was ordained in England, but shortly afterwards returned to Scotland and was admitted to Carnock in Fife. In subscribing the Westminster Confession* he expressed some objection to its doctrine 'respecting the power of the civil magistrate in religion', but was allowed to sign with this exception. While at Carnock, Gillespie developed a reputation as an Evangelical* of note; he corresponded with, among others, Jonathan Edwards* and Henry Davidson, one of the Marrow* brethren.

A close friend of James Robe,* minister at Kilsyth, Gillespie frequently helped in the Revival* there. He testified that, whatever irregularities may have occurred, it was a real work of the Holy Spirit. Before 1744 he composed *A Treatise on Temptation* (E, 1774, with a preface and memoir by John Erskine*). His other published work (*An Essay on the Continuance of Immediate Revelations of Facts and Future Events in the Christian Church*, E, 1771) was written shortly afterwards. It denies the continuance of immediate divine revelations in the Church.

In 1752 the General Assembly ordered Dunfermline Presbytery to induct to Inverkeithing the patron's presentee despite the people's opposition. Among those whose refusal to comply left the Presbytery without a quorum and unable to act, the Assembly determined to depose Gillespie, the only one who gave in a further paper in support of his stand, by a vote of fifty-two to four, with 102 abstaining. (The following year a concerted attempt to reverse the decision was defeated by three votes.)

The Assembly's tyrannical procedure, coupled with Gillespie's meek response, produced considerable public indignation. He preached to a great gathering in the fields the next sabbath. By winter a meeting house was purchased in nearby Dunfermline, where he ministered to a large congregation for the rest of his life.

In 1761 the Presbytery of Relief was formed. After commencing fellowship with the younger Thomas Boston,* an obnoxious settlement in Colinsburgh, Fife, led to Gillespie's helping the congregation there. Gillespie, Boston and Thomas Colier constituted themselves into 'a Presbytery as Scripture directs ... to act for relief of oppressed Christian congregations – when called in providence'. As the Relief Church grew, Gillespie was a leading figure, though he was by no means deferred to in all matters. After his death it was claimed that, particularly in view of a recent controversy, he had planned to return with his congregation to the CofS, but there is no evidence of substance that this was the case.

FES V, 10–12; *DNB* XXI, 365–6; Small, I, 358–9; G. Struthers, *The History of the Rise, Progress, and Principles of The Relief Church* (G, 1843).

D. C. Lachman

Gillespie, William Honeyman (1808–75), philosophical apologist. Born in Glasgow and educated at its High School and University (and probably Edinburgh University), he became a lawyer in Edinburgh and a member of Nicolson Square Wesleyan Methodist* Church. In 1834 he married Elizabeth Honeyman, who later inherited the estate of Torbanehill, Linlithgowshire. Apart from a handful of publications on other topics (including *The Truth of the Evangelical History* ..., E, 1856, against the German critic David Strauss; *The Theology of Geologists*, E, 1859, especially on Hugh Miller;* and verse on *The Origin of Evil*, L, 1873), his energies were single-mindedly devoted to elaborating, propagating and defending a form of the ontological argument for the existence and nature of God (*see* Apologetics). First published in 1833, it was greatly enlarged by the time of its sixth and final version in 1872: *The Argument a Priori for the Being and the Attributes of the Lord God the Absolute One and First Cause* (L). His widow (*d.* 1886) took up the cause, and then her trustees, on whose behalf James Urquhart reissued Gillespie's main works (*The Argument* ..., E, 1906; *The Necessary Existence of God*, E, 1923; *The Parerga* ..., E, 1922), with comments or contributions from H. R. Mackintosh,* James Black* and other divines and ministers. Urquhart also compiled three accounts of Gillespie: *The Life and Teaching* ... (E, 1915), *William Honeyman Gillespie* ... *Scottish Metaphysical Theist* (E, 1920), and *Memorial* ... (E, 1926). The trustees still award a Gillespie scholarship in theology, and support work in medicine and homoeopathy.

D. F. Wright

Gillies, John (1712–96), evangelical CofS minister. He was born in Careston, near Brechin, and ordained a minister of the College (Blackfriars) Church in Glasgow in 1742, where he remained until his death. He is best known for his lengthy and influential pastoral ministry and his literary works – he preached three times each Sunday and for a time delivered mid-week lectures from which he published a weekly abstract called *Exhortation to the ... South Parish of Glasgow*, 2 vols (G, 1750–1). He sought to guide his people into true devotion free from the excesses of enthusiasm. To this end he published in 1769 his *Devotional Exercises on the New Testament* (L). In 1754 he issued his groundbreaking history of revival, *Historical Collections Relating to ... the Success of the Gospel* (2 vols, G; rp. E, 1981), which helped prepare the soil for the Scottish revivals* of the late eighteenth and early nineteenth centuries. Of an open temperament (although he opposed the repeal of legal restrictions on RCs in 1778), he was free from the prejudice of party spirit and opened his pulpit to John Wesley* and to George Whitefield.* He enjoyed Whitefield's friendship and wrote the first account of his life, *Memoirs of the Life of the Rev. G. Whitefield* (L, 1772).

A leading member of the 'Popular'* party in the General Assembly, he was also an important member of an international evangelical letter-writing network involving Jonathan Edwards,* Philip Doddridge, John Erskine* and others. He

GILLIES, KENNETH

joined the unsuccessful attempt to urge the Assembly to encourage a conciliatory government policy towards the American colonists in 1776–8. Edinburgh awarded him the LLD in 1778.

A Catechism upon the Suffering of the Redeemer . . . for the Use of Young Communicants (G, 1763).

J. Erskine, 'Account of the Revd Dr Gillies', in *Supplement to Historical Collections* (E, 1796); W. Nicol, 'Memoir', in *The New Testament . . . with Devotional Reflections*, by Gillies (L, 1810); *DNB* XXI, 367–8; *FES* III, 399; S. O'Brien, 'A Transatlantic Community of Saints: the Great Awakening and the First Evangelical Network, 1735–1755', *American Histor. Rev.* 91 (1986), 811–32.

C. W. Mitchell

Gillies, Kenneth (1887–1976), minister of the Gaelic charge of Partick Gardner Street UFC, later Gardner Street CofS, Glasgow (1924–76). Born in Applecross, Ross-shire, Gillies was converted while serving with Partick Burgh Police; he then studied at the Bible Training Institute,* Glasgow, and served as missionary with UFC in Lewis. Following service with the Royal Navy in the Great War, he studied for the ministry at Aberdeen University and Divinity College. During his remarkable fifty-two year ministry, he became a father figure to many younger Highland* preachers.

FUFCS 238; *FES* IX, 26; 159; tributes in *Life Indeed*, May 1974, and *Stornoway Gazette*, 14 August 1976.

K. D. MacDonald

Gillis, James (1802–64), RC Bishop. Born of a Scottish father in Montreal, Gillis came to Scotland in 1816 and entered the seminary at Aquhorties (*see* Colleges and Seminaries, Roman Catholic). He continued his studies in France 1818–26, and was ordained priest in 1827. Gillis took a leading part in the foundation in 1834–5 of St Margaret's Convent, Edinburgh (*see* Religious Orders; Trail, Ann). In 1837 he was appointed coadjutor to the Vicar-Apostolic of the Eastern District, whom he succeeded in 1852. He did much to form religious, educational and social organizations for the Catholic poor in Edinburgh, but was also at home in aristocratic society where he was instrumental in the conversion of several prominent individuals to RCism. Having gained a reputation for public eloquence, he travelled much, particularly in France, preaching and collecting money. At home he arranged spectacular religious functions and conceived grandiose plans which were often beyond his financial means. He wrote and published extensively and engaged readily in religious controversy. His name is commemorated in Gillis College, the RC seminary in Edinburgh (*see* Colleges and Seminaries, Roman Catholic).

J. F. S. Gordon, *The Catholic Church in Scotland* (A, 1874), 480–91; P. F. Anson, *Underground Catholicism in Scotland* (Montrose, 1970); B. Aspinwall and J. F. McCaffrey, 'A Comparative View of the Irish in Edinburgh in the Nineteenth Century' in R. Swift and S. Gilley (eds), *The Irish in the Victorian City* (L, 1985).

J. R. Wolffe

Gilmore, John, *see* Edwards, John.

Gilmour, James (1843–91), missionary to Mongolia. The child of godly Congregationalist parents (members of Ralph Wardlaw's* church) in Cathkin, Glasgow, he gained a distinguished MA at Glasgow (1865) and studied at the Congregational theological hall in Edinburgh (1865–7), prior to acceptance by the London Missionary Society,* for whose service he trained at Cheshunt College (1867–9) and its Highgate seminary (1869–70). Gilmour had experienced conversion early in his University course, numbering among his later friends there T. T. Matthews* and John Paterson of Airdrie.

In February 1870 he was ordained at Augustine Chapel, Edinburgh, to reopen LMS's Mongolian mission, inactive since 1841. In May 1870 he reached Peking, which became his base, but already in August–September journeyed far into Mongolia to the Siberian border. Most summers he itinerated among the tribes beyond Kalgan (on the Chinese–Mongolian frontier), and in winter contacted the numerous Mongols who visited Peking. In 1874 he married Emily Prankard there, a week after first meeting her. (He knew her sister in Peking and proposed to Emily by letter to England. 'Such is the romance of a matter of fact man', as he put it.) Wide interest was aroused by the Gilmours' first furlough in Britain 1882–3, and the publication of his *Among the Mongols* (L, 1883; extracts in *Adventures in Mongolia*, L, 1886), which got a 'rave' review in the *Spectator*. Its appeal derived from the remarkable degree to which Gilmour had shared ordinary Mongol life.

After his wife's death in Peking in 1885, Gilmour's attention shifted to eastern Mongolia's agricultural peoples. Chao Yang became his chief base, and he increasingly served as a lay physician. (He had medical colleagues for short periods.) His ministry won few converts (but contributed to the nuclei of three churches), and his rigorist views and policies created friction with fellow-missionaries. Yet his total acceptance of an extremely frugal indigenous life-style and endless sacrificial hardships made him something of a missionary hero. He died of typhus in Tientsin.

Gilmour left masses of MS material, from which his friend from college days, Richard Lovett, produced *More About the Mongols* (L, 1893), *James Gilmour of Mongolia. His Diaries, Letters and Reports* (L, ²1893), and *James Gilmour and His Boys* (L, 1894, 1905) – correspondence with his sons. He inspired several popular biographies, by W. G. Berry (L, 1908), N. Bitton (L, 1925), M. I. Bryson (L, 1894, ²1928), W. K. Greenland (L, 1920), D. E. Jenkins (Wrexham, 1908), W. P. Nairne (L, 1924, 1932), and H. F. Beach (*Princely Men in the Heavenly Kingdom*, NY, 1903, 77–106).

D. F. Wright

Girls' Association, UF and later CofS movement. It began in 1901 at a meeting in Lothian Road Church, Edinburgh, in support of foreign missions, and in 1905 sponsored its first GOM (Girls' Own Missionary), Bessie Hogg. Next year its mission study programme began summer schools at Bridge of Allan, using text-books written by J. H. Oldham* and others. By 1912 it counted twenty branches, had its own *GA Magazine* (1911) and had enlarged its scope to cover home missions also. The first national conference was held in 1915, and in 1920 its first full-time secretary, Gladys Dick, was appointed and involvement began in summer camps and missions alongside Divinity students. By 1922 it supported six GOMs. Strong educational emphasis, with the appointment of Educational Secretaries, made its youth character more difficult to maintain.

Co-operation developed with its CofS counterpart, the Girls' Guild (not to be confused with the Girls' Guildry*), soon after its inception in 1919. (The Fellow Workers' Union had previously united the female youth of the CofS, and several Glasgow churches had girls' guilds or societies.) Late in starting, the Girls' Guild grew more rapidly: 1920, *The Trailmaker* magazine; 1923, first general conference and the first GG missionary, Dr Toni Scott; 1927, membership of 6,000. The Guild had a particular commitment to Jewish missions, and raised funds for many overseas projects, often in league with the GA.

The two movements were well prepared for the Union of 1929:* by the end of 1928 a draft constitution was ready, with the GA's badge, the GG's magazine title and the name of the Girls' Association. (The GA in the continuing UFC became known as the Girls' Auxiliary.) The GA joined in the Forward Movement,* and was represented at major ecumenical youth conferences (Amsterdam 1939, Oslo 1947). The Second World War stimulated more intense study, and at its jubilee in 1951 the GA declared its immediate future very hopeful, despite losses to the burgeoning youth fellowships. By 1960, however, numerical decline and shortage of leaders for its predominantly youthful membership dimmed hopes (*RGAGS 1960*, 20–1) and next year the Assembly approved its dissolution (*RGACS 1961*, 21–4, 41).

M. G. Cowan *et al.*, *Chapters of Girls' Association History* (E, 1939); K. Young, *Our Sail We Lift. The Story of the Girls' Association 1901–1951* (E, 1950).

D. F. Wright

Girls' Brigade, *see* Girls' Guildry.

Girls' Guild, *see* Girls' Association.

Girls' Guildry, a Christian organization started in Anderston FC/UFC, Glasgow, in 1900 by W. F. Somerville (1858–1926), a doctor whose father had been minister of the Church. In many ways a counterpart to the Boys' Brigade,* it was the first uniformed movement for girls. Its object was 'to induce girls to become followers of the Lord Jesus Christ, and to develop in them capacities of womanly helpfulness'. It was interdenominational from the outset, and soon spread to England and Ireland, in 1914 to East Africa (Livingstonia) and later to Jamaica and elsewhere. Its companies had all to be linked to a church or mission. Somerville was the first editor of *The Girls' Guildry Gazette* (1909), which in 1932 became *The Lamp of the Girls' Guildry*.

In 1965 it merged with the Girls' Brigade (Ireland), which began in Dublin in 1893 with the aim of extending Christ's kingdom among girls (8,000 members), and with the Girls' Life Brigade, founded in England in 1902 by the National Sunday School Union (120,000 members worldwide), to form the Girls' Brigade, with aims and structure very similar to the Guildry's (which had 35,000 members in 1965). Its motto is 'Seek, serve and follow Christ'. In 1990 the Girls' Brigade in Scotland had 15,000 members in 350 companies. Its headquarters are in Glasgow, and its residential training centre in Ballinluig, Perthshire.

M. Lochhead, *A Lamp was Lit: the Girls' Guildry Through Fifty Years* (E, 1949); *Girls' Brigade (in Scotland). Annual Report 1989–90*.

D. F. Wright

Gladstone, William Ewart (1809–98), statesman. The fourth son of a Liverpool merchant, John Gladstone, he was educated at Eton and Christ Church, Oxford. Entering Parliament in 1832, he held office under the Conservative Sir Robert Peel* in junior posts (1834–5), as Vice-President (1841–3) and President (1843–5) of the Board of Trade and as Colonial Secretary (1845–6). He was a Peelite Chancellor of the Exchequer (1852–5, 1859–66) before becoming Liberal leader in 1867. He was four times Prime Minister (1868–74, 1880–5, 1886, 1892–4). His more substantial publications were *The State in its Relations with the Church* (L, 1838); *Church Principles considered in their Results* (L, 1841); *Studies on Homer and the Homeric Age*, 3 vols (O, 1858); *Juventus Mundi* (L, 1869); *The Impregnable Rock of Holy Scripture* (L, 1892); *The Works of Joseph Butler, D.C.L.*, 2 vols (O, 1896); and *Studies Subsidiary to the Works of Bishop Butler* (O, 1896).

Gladstone was brought up an evangelical Anglican. In the 1830s, largely independently of Tractarianism,* he developed High Church views. During the 1840s he erected an Episcopalian* church at Fasque, his father's Kincardineshire estate, and he promoted Trinity College, Glenalmond, as an Episcopalian school and seminary. Pained by the secession of friends such as H. E. Manning (1808–92) to the RCC, he remained staunchly Anglican. Although in 1869 he disestablished the Church of Ireland,* five years later he denounced the implications of papal infallibility for civil allegiance. Nonconformist political support helped confirm broader religious sympathies in his later years. He declared for Scottish disestablishment* in 1889. Gladstone was both a shrewd politician and a respected Christian apologist.

GLAS, JOHN

H. C. G. Matthew, *Gladstone, 1809–1874* (O, 1986); J. Morley, *The Life of William Ewart Gladstone*, 3 vols (L, 1903); P. Butler, *Gladstone: Church, State and Tractarianism* (O, 1982); D. C. Lathbury (ed.), *Letters on Church and Religion of William Ewart Gladstone*, 2 vols (L, 1910); A. R. Vidler, *The Orb and the Cross* (L, 1945); D. W. Bebbington, *W. E. Gladstone: Faith and Politics* ... (Grand Rapids, 1993).

D. W. Bebbington

Glas, John (1695–1773), Independent* pastor who gave his name to the Glasites. He was born in the CofS manse of Auchtermuchty, Fife, grew up in Perthshire, studied at St Andrews and Edinburgh, and was inducted to the parish of Tealing, near Dundee, in 1719. Confronted by controversy over the covenants,* he gradually came to an Independent position, and in 1725 gathered a group of seventy-four people within the parish, to exercise discipline and hold Communion monthly. In his most influential work, *The Testimony of the King of Martyrs* (D, 1725), based on the text, 'My Kingdom is not of this world', Glas asserted the independence of Church and magistrate. After long process, his views led first to his suspension by Synod and ultimately in 1730 to his deposition by the General Assembly for contumacy. In the same year he set up an Independent congregation in Dundee, supported by families from Tealing, including a manufacturer, Baxter. Practice developed with a fresh study of Scripture, and weekly Communion and a lay leadership were instituted. Churches were set up in Perth (1733), Edinburgh (1734), and in the growing textile towns such as Paisley, Kirkcaldy, Arbroath, Montrose, Galashiels and Dunkeld. While each church was self-governing, Glas kept close watch over doctrine, practice and leadership. After spending some time in Perth, he returned to Dundee, where he died, having survived his wife and fifteen children, and leaving a reputation for goodness and learning. For the distinctive doctrines and practices of Glasite churches, *see* Sandeman, Robert.

Through Sandeman, Glas's son-in-law, the churches spread into north-west England, London, Nottingham, and through the influence and interest of Benjamin Ingham and two of his preachers, James Allen and William Batty, into the Yorkshire Dales. Sandeman took the teaching to New England. The subsequent history of these small, non-aggressive churches, whose membership was about 1,000 in 1790, with many hearers in places like Dundee, is one of decline, schism and extraordinary powers of survival. Strong individuals were attracted, and there was much intermarriage. In 1798 the Perth church left the main body over a dispute concerning the doctrine of assurance and in 1853 and 1885 there were divisions over the question of blood-eating with reference to game birds. But in an 1888 correspondence about reunion it is matters of discipline and independency that are at the heart of the divisions. In 1896 Perth, Edinburgh and London reunited. Between the World Wars Perth, Glasgow and Dundee churches dissolved, leaving remnants now in Edinburgh (Barony Street) and London. The last ordination of an elder was in Edinburgh in 1967. Glas's influence was much wider than his own movement, and his views continue to be of interest and value.

The Works ..., 4 vols (E, 1761); *The Works* ..., 5 vols (²Perth, 1782–3).

J. T. Hornsby, 'The Case of Mr John Glas', *RSCHS* 6 (1938), 115–37; *id.*, 'John Glas: His Later Life and Work', *RSCHS* 7 (1941), 94–113; *id.*, 'John Glas and his Movement' (PhD, Edinburgh University, 1936); D. B. Murray, 'The Influence of John Glas', *RSCHS* 22 (1984), 45–56; *id.*, 'The Social and Religious Origins of Scottish Non-Presbyteryian Protestant Dissent from 1730–1800' (PhD, St Andrews University, 1977); L. A. McMillan, *Restoration Roots* (Dallas, TX, 1983).

D. B. Murray

Glasgow Assembly (28 November–20 December 1638), CofS General Assembly summoned by Charles I* at the insistence of the Covenanters,* who largely determined its membership by gaining control of the elections in the Presbyteries.* The King's Commissioner, the Marquis of Hamilton, tried to dissolve the Assembly when he found he had lost control of it, but it sat on in defiance of his orders. The main acts of the Assembly abolished Episcopacy* and declared it unlawful; rejected the Five Articles of Perth;* denounced the holding of civil offices by ministers; added the 'Glasgow Determination' to the National Covenant* stating that that document entailed acceptance of the above reforms; declared the Book of Canons and the *Book of Common Prayer** of 1637 unlawful; abolished the Court of High Commission;* deposed the bishops, excommunicating some of them; and declared that the government of the Church in future would be by Kirk Sessions,* Presbyteries,* Synods* and General Assemblies.*

These changes amounted to a revolution in the Church, destroying the whole apparatus of royal control through bishops built up by James VI* and Charles I and their reforms of worship, and substituting Presbyterian Church government and traditional forms of worship.

A. Peterkin (ed.), *Records of the Kirk of Scotland* (E, 1838), 21–193; R. Baillie, *Letters and Journals*, 3 vols (E, 1841–2), I, 118–76; J. Gordon, *History of Scots Affairs*, 3 vols (A, 1841), I, 139–93, II, 1–187; D. Stevenson, *The Scottish Revolution* (Newton Abbot, 1973), 102–26.

D. Stevenson

Glasgow Bible College, *see* Bible Training Institute, Glasgow.

Glasgow Bible Society, *see* Bible Societies.

Glasgow, Bishopric of. It was traditionally associated with St Kentigern (*see* Celtic Saints) as bishop of Cumbria in the sixth century. Early bishops ap-

GLASGOW CATHEDRAL (ST MUNGO'S)

pear to have been peripatetic, as Cadder, Hoddam and Govan were early ecclesiastical sites.* Although three eleventh- and twelfth-century bishops appear as bishop of Glasgow, they may have been suffragan bishops of the Archbishop of York (N. F. Shead, 'The Origins of the Medieval Diocese of Glasgow', *SHR* 48 (1969), 220–5). The see was apparently revived at Glasgow by the future David I,* c.1114/18, and a cathedral* was dedicated July 1136. The erection of a secular chapter (which consisted of thirty-two canons at the Reformation) commenced shortly thereafter (Easson-Cowan, 207–9). Early bishops were involved in resisting the metropolitan authority of York, an issue resolved by the acquisition of the status of a special daughter of the see of Rome in 1175, a concession extended to other bishoprics in 1176 and 1192. Placed under the metropolitan authority of St Andrews August 1472, Glasgow achieved archiepiscopal and metropolitan status January 1492, with the sees of Dunkeld, Dunblane, Galloway and Argyll within its jurisdiction. Dunblane was restored to the province of St Andrews January 1500 and Dunkeld was similarly re-transferred on or before May 1515 (*FESMA* 144). In terms of diocesan organization, the bishopric was divided into two archdeaconries of Glasgow (1126/7) and Teviotdale (1238) and eleven (originally twelve) deaneries – an indication of the extent of this vast diocese, which survived the Reformation* but was finally dissolved with the abolition of episcopacy in 1689 (*FESMA* 170–87).

See also Early Ecclesiastical Sites.

N. F. Shead, 'The Administration of the Diocese of Glasgow in the Twelfth and Thirteenth Centuries', *SHR* 55 (1976), 127–50.

I. B. Cowan

Glasgow Cathedral (St Mungo's). This impressive building which dates from the late thirteenth and early fourteenth centuries stands on the site of a monastic settlement traditionally founded by St Kentigern, or Mungo (*see* Celtic Saints), in the latter part of the sixth century. It is said that this site included a Christian burial ground dedicated earlier by Saint Ninian.*

The first stone-built cathedral was dedicated in 1136 in the presence of David I,* the first great benefactor of the cathedral. Fire extensively damaged this early building, and a second and larger edifice was consecrated in 1197. The present building is an extension eastwards, the downward-sloping site presenting a problem and an opportunity, resulting in an upper and lower church. The latter contains the tomb of St Kentigern, itself an object of pilgrimage* before the Reformation.*

After the Reformation, three Presbyterian congregations worshipped in the choir, the nave, and the lower church. Dividing walls and, later, galleries were inserted but were removed in the latter part of the nineteenth century. The old bell tower and consistory house were demolished in 1846 and 1848, only a decade before the building became officially crown property.

GLASGOW UNITED EVANG. ASSOC.

R. Fawcett, *Glasgow Cathedral* (E, 1985); C. A. R. Radford, *Glasgow Cathedral* (E, 1970);
R. Fawcett, *Scottish Mediaeval Churches* (E, 1985);
G. Eyre-Todd (ed.), *The Book of Glasgow Cathedral* (G, 1898).

W. J. Morris

Glasgow Colonial Society, CofS missionary agency in Canada. 'The Society for Promoting the Religious Interests of Scottish Settlers in British North America' was founded in 1825 by the Synod of Glasgow, at the suggestion of Robert Burns* of Paisley, later of Knox FC, Toronto. Although centred on Glasgow, the Society had branches all over Scotland which publicized the spiritual needs of Scottish emigrants and raised funds to send ministers, catechists and schoolmasters to settlers in British North America. For over a decade the Society was almost solely responsible for providing Presbyterian facilities in Canada, and by 1840 it maintained over forty ministers, primarily in the Upper Province. Thereafter it merged with the General Assembly's Colonial Committee (*see* Chaplaincies, Colonial), which had been appointed in 1836 as part of the CofS's greater commitment to overseas missions.*

See also Emigration.

Correspondence and reports, 1825–35 in United Church Archives, Knox College, Toronto; *Dictionary of Canadian Biography* IX (1861–70), 104–8; John Moir, 'Through Missionary Eyes: the Glasgow Colonial Society and the Immigrant Experience in British North America', in C. Kerrigan (ed.), *The Immigrant Experience* (Guelph, Ont., 1992), 95–109; R. F. Burns, *The Life and Times of the Rev Robert Burns* (Toronto, 1872).

M. Harper

Glasgow Ecclesiological Society, *see* Ecclesiological Societies.

Glasgow Educational Society, *see* Stow, David.

Glasgow Free Church/United Free Church College, *see* Trinity College; Education Theological.

Glasgow Missionary Society, *see* Missions.

Glasgow United Evangelistic Association, a body concerned with evangelism, social action and Christian education. Its spiritual origins lie in the evangelistic crusades of D. L. Moody,* and its work commenced in 1874 with evangelistic meetings in a tent on Glasgow Green. The Tent Hall, built nearby, opened its doors in 1876. It was the largest mission hall in the British Isles, and for much of its history, extending over more than one hundred years, its 2,200 seating capacity was extensively used. It was a great evangelistic power in the city, and also did much social work, including a weekly free breakfast and yearly Hogmanay supper. Evangelistic work has also been carried out under the auspices of GUEA in other buildings within the city.

Moody founded a Bible College in Chicago – later to be known as the Moody Bible Institute – in 1886, and so it was not surprising when, at the annual meeting of the GUEA in 1892, he issued a call for the establishment of such a college in Glasgow. This had been a concern of Christian leaders in the city for some time, and the GUEA took up the challenge, establishing the Bible Training Institute* later the same year. This interdenominational college (now Glasgow Bible College) has so far trained about five thousand men and women for many different forms of Christian service at home and overseas.

In 1912 the committee which superintended the Fresh Air Fortnight and the Glasgow Cripple League became part of the GUEA. The first of these activities was started in 1884 to provide seaside holidays for Glasgow's poor children. Homes for this purpose were opened in Dunoon and later in Troon. Glasgow Cripple Children's League of Kindness, as it was originally called, was established in 1899, largely under the inspiration of Alexander MacKeith. Sir Thomas Lipton gave a large sum of money to get the work started. At a later stage it provided employment training in crafts for disabled adults. The name was changed in 1984 to the Glasgow Centre for the Disabled. Its staff also visited handicapped people in their homes.

The GUEA, now renamed the Glasgow Bible College Association, is evangelical and interdenominational. It is concerned to win people for Christ, to express his love in social concern and to educate men and women for his service. These aims are reflected in its three branches.

R. W. Clark, *Moody and Sankey in Great Britain* (L, 1975).

G. W. Grogan

Glebe, land designated for the support of the incumbent of a church, instituted probably about the eighth century even before a manse* was provided or a parish* designated. Since the Reformation there has been much law about its extent and tenure. In 1572 it was designated as four acres Scots, i.e. about five imperial acres, and all ministers of landward parishes and town parishes with a landward area were provided with glebe. In 1593 it was ruled that glebe should be taken from 'church lands', lands which had belonged to the Church before the Reformation, and near the church of the parish. Church lands were usually the best land and in 1606 it was enacted that, if the land was not good arable land, four 'soums' of grass were to be substituted for each acre, a soum being enough to support ten sheep or one cow. This was known as 'grass-glebe'. In 1644 the glebe was to be not more than half a mile from the church and not necessarily from 'Church lands'.

In addition to his arable glebe, the minister was entitled to 'grass', normally further from the manse, to support his horse and two cows (1649). In lieu of 'grass' he might be provided by the heritors* with 20 pounds Scots per annum. After 1866, glebe might be feued by the minister with permission of the teind* court, Presbytery and heritors.

After the passing of the Church of Scotland (Property and Endowments) Act of 1925, in preparation for the union of the CofS and the UFC in 1929, the titles to all glebes were transferred to the CofS General Trustees.* Some few are worked by ministers or by Kirk Sessions,* some are let or leased to farmers and some have been sold for development. Rental of let or lease, and the proceeds of the income of investments from sale proceeds, are applied towards stipend.*

J. M. Duncan and C. N. Johnston, *The Parochial and Ecclesiastical Law of Scotland* (E, 1903); T. Burns, *Church Property* (The Benefice Lectures; E, 1905); J. Connell, *A Treatise ... on Tithes*, 3 vols (E, 1815).

A. I. Dunlop

Glegg, Alexander Lindsay (1882–1975), evangelist. Born in London of Scottish parents, Glegg obtained a diploma in electrical engineering and subsequently became a director of several companies. His great love, however, was evangelism. Converted at the 1905 Keswick Convention, he embarked on a pastoral association with Down Lodge Hall, Wandsworth, that lasted almost fifty years. He was a regular speaker at campaigns and conventions throughout the British Isles, actively supported numerous Christian societies, and spiritually and financially supported and encouraged young evangelists. During World War II he conducted well-supported meetings in the Albert Hall. He preached once in Westminster Abbey, and gave an appeal to which fifty people responded. An early supporter of Billy Graham* in Britain, Glegg was in his seventies when he began the annual Christian holiday camp at Filey, one of the most lively and rewarding Evangelical undertakings of modern times. He was still preaching after his ninetieth birthday. His written works, notably *Life with a Capital 'L'* (L, E, 1934) and *Four Score and More* (L, E, 1962), ran through many editions and went all over the world.

J. D. Douglas, *Completing the Course* (L, 1976).

J. D. Douglas

Gleig, George (1753–1840), Bishop of Brechin. Born at Boghall, Arbuthnott, Stonehaven, he attended King's College, Aberdeen. A brilliant student, Gleig could have aspired to assistant professorship but would not subscribe to the Westminster* Confession of Faith. He contributed to *Monthly Review, The Gentleman's Magazine, The British Critic, The Anti-Jacobin Review* and *The Scottish Episcopal Magazine* and wrote various theological and philosophical works and letters in defence of Episcopacy.

Ordained in 1773, he served first at Pittenweem and then at Stirling, his home for fifty-three years. In 1788 he became a regular and voluminous contributor to the *Encyclopaedia Britannica* (3rd edition) and later editor. His most important biography was 'A Life of Principal Robertson', prefixed to an edition of that author's works. He published sermons, delivered at the Episcopal Chapel at Stirling 1793-1803, edited Stackhouse's *History of the Bible* (L, 1817) (containing a most characteristic dissertation on original sin – mortality is at the root of original sin, not inherited guilt); and published *Directions for the Study of Theology* (L, 1827). He was elected Bishop of Dunkeld thrice, and of Brechin twice. Eventually consecrated Bishop of Brechin in 1808 at Aberdeen, and elected Primus of the Episcopal College in 1816, Aberdeen University conferred upon him the degree of LLD and he was elected member of the Royal Society in Edinburgh. He assisted in the repeal of the Penal Laws in 1792.

Gleig was an original thinker, not a 'party' man. He addressed himself to the problems of his time. Energetic and tactful, his biographer William Walker describes him as 'a robust genius, born to grapple with whole libraries', and claims that, 'As a metaphysician he deserves to take rank with Dr Reid and Dugald Stewart.'

Letters Containing an Apology for the Episcopal Church in Scotland (E, 1787).

DNB XXI, 423-4; W. Walker, *Memoirs of Bishops Jolly and Gleig* (E, 1878).

A. E. Nimmo

Glencairn, Alexander Cunningham, 5th Earl (d.1574), prominent Scottish Reformer. His father, the fourth Earl, was a Protestant, and Cunningham inherited his faith. As Lord Kilmaurs he was known as a supporter of the Reformed religion as early as 1540. About this time he wrote a satirical poem against the order of Grey Friars, reprinted by John Knox* in his *History of the Reformation*. He succeeded to the earldom on his father's death in 1547, after which he became one of the most outspoken proponents of reform. In 1557 he signed the covenant (the 'First Bond') by which he and several other nobles pledged themselves to promote the Reformation in Scotland, which placed him among the Lords of the Congregation.* He led a deputation to the Queen Regent, Mary of Guise,* in 1559 demanding freedom of worship, and when royal troops advanced on Perth in May to punish Protestant iconoclasts, Glencairn led a force of 2,500 to prevent the move. He participated closely in the military and diplomatic events which culminated in 1560 in the Treaties of Berwick and Leith (or Edinburgh), the expulsion of the French from Scotland, and the Reformation Parliament.*

Glencairn was elected to the Privy Council of Mary, Queen of Scots,* in 1561, but in 1565 joined the rebellion of the Earl of Moray (see Stewart, James, d. 1570) and was declared a traitor. In 1567 he held high command in the rebel army of the Earl of Morton (see Douglas, James), and led an iconoclastic assault on the royal chapel at Holyrood. He carried the sword at the coronation of James VI.* At the battle of Langside in May 1568, where Mary was finally defeated, Glencairn commanded a division. He was subsequently made Lord Semple Lieutenant of the West.

Glencairn was a close friend of Knox, and one of the most idealistically motivated of the Scottish Protestant nobility.

C. Rogers (ed.), *Three Scottish Reformers* (L, 1874); *DNB* XIII, 303-6.

N. R. Needham

Glenorchy, Lady (Campbell, Willielma) (1741-86), aristocratic patroness of evangelical causes. Born into the wealthy Maxwell family from Galloway, in 1761 she married John Lord Viscount Glenorchy, the heir of the Earl of Breadalbane, one of Scotland's major landowners. Four years later, while recovering from a serious illness, she underwent a conversion experience, primarily through the influence of the sister of Rowland Hill,* the eccentric evangelical Anglican preacher. After her husband's death in 1771, Lady Glenorchy devoted the remainder of her life and fortune to spreading vital religion.

She was the most influential woman of her time in Scottish religious affairs, her activities closely paralleling those of the Countess of Huntingdon in England. Lady Glenorchy held evangelistic services in her home near Edinburgh for rich and poor alike, and a number of her personal chaplains went on to become leading evangelical ministers in the CofS. She also established several chapels in both Scotland and England.

Encouraged by Alexander Webster,* one of her most trusted ministerial advisors, in 1770 she set up her first chapel in Edinburgh. This venture was a daring ecumenical enterprise for its time, intended to provide a place where Presbyterian, Episcopalian and Methodist ministers would preach regularly. Later that year, Lady Glenorchy met the leader of the Methodist movement, John Wesley,* who unsuccessfully attempted to persuade her to join his Society. The following year, as a result of both her own Calvinist leanings and the refusal of CofS ministers to preach in her new chapel, she closed her chapel to Methodists.* In 1774 she opened a new chapel, bearing her name, in connection with the CofS, which became a bulwark of Evangelicalism in Edinburgh for the next seventy years.

In 1773 Lady Glenorchy rebuilt a chapel in Strathfillan in Perthshire and provided the endowment for its minister and for two missionaries in the region, all three of whom were supervised by the Scottish SPCK.* During the last decade of her life, she travelled extensively in England seeking to restore her health. In her wake, she left a string of chapels: Exmouth (1777), Carlisle (1781), Matlock (1785), Bristol (1786), and Workington (1786). To ensure that her favourite religious causes would flourish after her death, Lady Glenorchy left large portions of her £30,000 estate to her chapels, to the Scottish SPCK., and to a fund for educating young men for the ministry.

DNB VIII, 397-8; T. S. Jones, *The Life of the Right Honourable Willielma, Viscountess Glenorchy* (E,

GLOAG, PATON JAMES

1822); D. P. Thomson, *Lady Glenorchy and Her Churches* (Perth, 1967); A. I, Dunlop, *The Kirks of Edinburgh 1560-1984* (SRS n.s. 15-16; E, 1988), 130-9, 359-74; G. W. Harvey, *Lady Glenorchy's North Church, Edinburgh* (E, 1946).

D. A. Currie

Gloag, Paton James (1823-1906), CofS minister and writer. Born in Perth, he studied arts at Edinburgh University from 1840 and theology at St Andrews after 1843. He was licensed in 1846 by Perth Presbytery, and became assistant to James Russell of Dunning, Perthshire (*FES* IV, 270). He was ordained minister of Blantyre, Lanarkshire, in 1860, and moved to Galashiels, Selkirk, in 1871. He resigned his charge in 1892 and retired to Edinburgh, serving however as interim Lecturer in Biblical Criticism in Aberdeen University 1896-8.

Gloag was a prolific theological writer. Profoundly influenced by F. D. Maurice, F. W. Robertson, Horace Bushnell and Germany's Mediating school, Gloag combined conservative and liberal elements in his theology. He disliked Calvinism and held a universalist eschatology, but his many exegetical writings were highly prized by such orthodox men as B. B. Warfield, with whom Gloag carried on a long friendly correspondence. His principal works were *A Critical and Exegetical Commentary on the Acts of the Apostles* (2 vols, E, 1870), *Introduction to the Pauline Epistles* (E, 1874), *Introduction to the Catholic Epistles* (E, 1887), *Introduction to the Johannine Writings* (L, 1891), and *Introduction to the Synoptic Gospels* (E, 1895). In 1879 he delivered the Baird Lectures,* published as *The Messianic Prophecies* (E, 1879).

Gloag received an LLD from Aberdeen University in 1898. He was Moderator of his Church's General Assembly in 1889.

Exegetical Studies (E, 1884); *A Treatise on the Assurance of Salvation* (E, 1853; ²1869); *A Treatise on Justification* (E, 1856); *A Treatise on the Resurrection* (E, 1862).

E. S. Gloag, *Paton J. Gloag DD, LLD. A Memoir* (E, 1908); *FES* II, 179, IV, 270; *DNB Second Suppl.* II, 119-20.

N. R. Needham

Golden Act (1592), act of Scottish Parliament* that first established the Presbyterian* character of the CofS, sometimes referred to also as the Great Charter of the Church. It was enacted by the administration of Sir John Maitland of Thirlestane (1543-95; Secretary, 1584, Chancellor, 1587), who had formed a moderating regime after the anti-Presbyterianism of the third Earl of Arran (*see* Hamilton, James, *d.*1609). The Act approved government of the Kirk by General Assembly* (though convened by the Crown), Synod,* Presbytery* and Kirk Session,* repeating statements from the *Second Book of Discipline*,* ch. VII. The Act was integrated into the constitution at the Union of 1707.*

APS III, 541-2; *BUK* II, 664-6; A. T. Innes, *The Law of Creeds in Scotland* (E, L, 1867), 51-4; F. Lyall, *Of Presbyters and Kings. Church and State in the Law of Scotland* (A, 1980), 17ff.

D. F. Wright

Goldie, Hugh (1815-95), UP missionary and scholar who made contributions to language study in West Africa. Born at Kilwinning (Ayrshire), Goldie first went to Jamaica in 1840 as a catechist. Following ordination in 1846, he sailed for Calabar with Hope M. Waddell* in 1847, settling first at Duke Town and then in 1855 at Creek Town.

His *Calabar and Its Mission* (1892; ²E, 1901) is our principal source of information about the Scottish team's missionary efforts in nineteenth-century Nigeria, even though it is uncritical. His *Principles of Efik Grammar* (Old Calabar, 1857) and his monumental *Dictionary of the Efik Language* (G, 1862; ²E, 1895) remain major contributions to lexicography. His Efik *Genesis* (G, 1862) and *Obufa Testament* (E, 1862) have not been surpassed. In his *Memoir of King Eyo VII of Old Calabar: A Christian King in Africa* (Old Calabar, 1894) we learn much about contemporary Efik society.

Missionary Record of the United Presbyterian Church, n.s. XVI (1895), 310-14; W. Dickie, *Story of the Mission in Old Calabar* (E, 1894).

W. H. Taylor

Good Words, popular religious monthly founded 1860 by Norman MacLeod (1812-72)* as a successor to his *Edinburgh Christian Magazine*,* published by Alexander Strahan, initially from Edinburgh and later from London. 25,000 copies of the first issue were sold, and circulation reached 80,000 by 1870. Though MacLeod's aim was 'the one end of leading souls to know and love God', he considered most religious magazines ineffective because of their narrowness and literary weakness. Despite extensive criticism, he aimed to produce in *Good Words* a periodical which, while having a distinctively Christian ethos, would include material on secular subjects, and sensitively-selected fiction from major writers. Their work, in contrast to the artificially pious tales issued by the tract societies,* would be genuinely appealing to working-class readers. This path towards breadth of appeal in religious periodicals led ultimately to the secularization of the popular religious press. After MacLeod's death, *Good Words* was edited by his brother Donald MacLeod* until its merger with the *Sunday Magazine* in 1906.

See also Periodicals, Religious.

'Good Words', *The Bookseller*, 10 December 1863, 711-13; D. MacLeod, *Memoir of Norman MacLeod* (L, 1876), 290-3, 301-2, 320-2; S. Smith, *Donald MacLeod of Glasgow* (L, [1926]), 110-17; J. Wellwood, *Norman MacLeod* (E, 1897), 88-90.

J. A. H. Dempster

Goodman, Christopher (1519-1603), close friend of John Knox* and a major figure in the

Scottish Reformation,* not least through his influence on Knox.

He was born in Chester and educated at Brasenose and Christ Church, Oxford, and became Lady Margaret Professor of Divinity at Oxford (1548-53). In exile (1553-8), he supported Knox during the Frankfurt 'Troubles'. While minister to the English church at Geneva, he wrote *How Superior Powers Ought to be Obeyed* (Geneva, 1558; ed. C. H. McIlwain, NY, 1931), advocating revolution. He subsequently served as minister in Ayr (1559-60) and St Andrews (1560-5), where his sermons on Revelation impressed John Napier.* He influenced the Scottish Church through his resistance theory and covenant* ideas, and contributed to the *Book of Common Order* (1564),* the Geneva Bible,* and the Metrical Psalter.* He returned to England late in 1565.

DNB XXII, 128-30; *FES* V, 230-1; Q. Skinner, *The Foundations of Modern Political Thought* (C, 1978), II, 221-38; D. G. Danner, 'Christopher Goodman and the English Protestant Tradition of Civil Disobedience', *Sixteenth Century Journ.* 8 (1977), 61-73; J. Dawson, 'The Early Career of Christopher Goodman and his Place in English Protestant Thought' (PhD, University of Durham, 1978); *id.*, 'Resistance and Revolution in Sixteenth-Century Thought; the Case of Christopher Goodman', in *The Church and Revolution*, ed. P. Hoftijzer (Leiden, 1990).

J. E. A. Dawson

Goold, William Henry (1815-97), minister of the Reformed Presbyterian Church,* best known today for his edition of John Owen's *Works* (E, 1850-3). Of Covenanter* stock, he was educated at the Royal High School, Edinburgh (dux, 1831), the University of Edinburgh (MA) and the RP Theological Hall (1836-9). He was awarded a DD (Edinburgh, 1852) and served the RPC as Professor of Biblical Criticism and Church History (1854-76).

Goold was prominent in RPC life, but never more so than as the architect of her effective disappearance from the Scottish scene. The Disruption* profoundly influenced him and stirred a desire within the RPC for union with the FC. This issued in a relaxation of the rigour with which the RPC had held her distinctive principles, so that in 1863 her prohibition of voting and taking the oath of allegiance was made a matter of liberty of conscience. The RPC divided and a minority RP Synod continued the older position. Goold chaired the RP union committee from 1864 and it fell to him in 1876 as the last Moderator of the (majority) RP Synod to lead that body from Martyrs Church, George IV Bridge, Edinburgh, to the FC Assembly Hall on the Mound for the enactment of the union. There, 'in an address of remarkable power and eloquence', he spoke 'on the normal condition of Presbyterianism as being that of unity, and on the doctrinal and historical bearings of the Union, in a strain which aroused the intense enthusiasm of the vast audience' (M. Hutchison, *The Reformed Presbyterian Church of Scotland, 1680-1876*, Paisley, 1893,

381). He was to serve as Moderator of the FC General Assembly in 1877. His significance in Scottish Church life lay in his commitment to a broadly Reformed ecumenism which insisted on confessional orthodoxy but turned its back on the finely-tuned controversies of the seventeenth century, which had so fragmented the Scottish Church.

Goold also served as the first Eastern Secretary of the newly formed National Bible Society of Scotland (1861-97; *see* Bible Societies), whose Bible House in Edinburgh has a Goold Hall named after him. His publications included *The Works of John Maclaurin** (E, 1860), controversial tracts and regular contributions to periodicals.

W. J. Couper, 'The Reformed Presbyterian Church in Scotland', *RSCHS* 2 (1925), 45-6, 116-17, 161; *AFCS* I, 170-1, II, 6; J. Robb, *Cameronian Fasti, 1680-1929* (E, 1975), 11; '*In Memoriam' Rev. William Henry Goold, D.D.* (E, 1897).

G. J. Keddie

Gordon, Alexander (*c.*1516-75), reforming Bishop of Galloway. He was the grandson of Alexander, third Earl of Huntly, and son of John, Lord Gordon and of Margaret Stewart, natural daughter of James V,* and from his designation 'Master' apparently received a university training in arts. A clerk of Glasgow diocese, he sought advancement to a bishopric: he was elected to Caithness in 1544, on Robert Stewart's* displacement. By 1548 he renounced his right to the bishopric to permit Stewart's reinstatement as bishop-elect, and as recompense was provided to the archbishopric of Glasgow in 1550, receiving consecration at Rome, only to be denounced at home as a barrator,* and resigned the see. In 1553, he obtained a gift of the bishopric of the Isles, and was still styled 'postulate' or elect of the Isles in 1562. Early in 1559, Gordon was nominated by the Crown to the bishopric of Galloway (and the annexed abbacy of Tongland as commendator*) but papal confirmation was not forthcoming; his title remained defective; and in January 1560 the Earl of Eglinton gained the temporality of the bishopric. This was perhaps the Crown's reaction to Gordon's open support for the Protestant Lords of the Congregation* whose ranks he had joined by September 1559. Earlier, as prelate, he had attended the burning of Walter Milne* for heresy in April 1558, but on renouncing papistry was admitted to the Reformers' inmost councils, and boasted, perhaps not idly, to have been 'the first that publicly preached Christ Jesus' in defiance of the government. In April 1560, he signed the Protestant band to 'set forward the Reformation of religion according to God's Word', was present in the Reformation Parliament* of July-August 1560, which repudiated papal authority, proscribed the mass and approved a Reformed (Scots) Confession,* was elected by the influential committee of the articles, preached earnestly and prayed for Elizabeth of England, and gave qualified assent to the *First Book of Discipline** in January 1561.

Gordon's attachment to the Reformed cause ex-

GORDON, ALEXANDER

tended to an active ministry in the Protestant Church, and he was instrumental in securing the services of many of his clergy in the diocese who conformed to the new regime as ministers, exhorters* and readers.* Although he retained his title in law as bishop-elect of Galloway (which the Reformation Parliament had confirmed), the General Assembly declined to recognize his title of bishop within the Reformed Church (and spoke grudgingly of the conforming bishops as 'them that are called bishops'), but it was prepared to appoint him as one of its commissioners to conduct visitations and fill vacant charges. His efforts to secure the better-paid office of superintendent,* by bribing the electors, were unsuccessful, and in later years, partly as a consequence of his support for Queen Mary in the civil wars, he incurred the General Assembly's censure for negligence in pastoral work and for devoting his time to affairs of state (as Privy Councillor and Lord of Session) 'which cannot agree with the office of pastor or bishop'. His commission of visitation was terminated in 1568, he himself suspended from the ministry in 1569 and 1573 and threatened with excommunication in 1574, before being reconciled in 1575, the year of his death. His son, John,* secured the bishopric.

Knox, *History*; *BUK*; Calderwood; J. Foxe, *Acts and Monuments* (L, 1858), V, 644; G. Donaldson, *Reformed by Bishops* (E, 1987), 1–18; J. Kirk, *Patterns of Reform* (E, 1989); *FESMA*, 61, 132, 149–50, 205; *DNB* XXII, 159–61; *FES* VII, 343–4.

J. Kirk

Gordon, Alexander (1587–1654), Covenanter.* Born at Earlston, near Dalry, Kirkcudbrightshire, he was the great-grandson of a namesake of Airds, Ayrshire (1479–1580), a pioneer of Protestantism in Galloway. Gordon and his family were correspondents of Samuel Rutherford* during his Aberdeen exile. As patron he declined episcopal instructions to present an Episcopalian curate to Earlston, and was therefore fined and warded in Montrose. He was a member of Parliament 1641–9, and of the General Assembly of 1641. Incapacitated by illness for some years before his death, he was, according to John Livingstone,* much affected by 'downcasting and uplifting'.

His Covenanting son William (1614–79) was a pious Presbyterian who studied for the ministry but was caught up in the civil war from 1639. He was banished (and withdrew to London) in 1663 for refusing to present an Episcopalian curate to Dalry. He was shot dead at Bothwell Bridge. His son Alexander (1650–1726) escaped in disguise. Condemned as a rebel in his absence (1680), Alexander spent periods in Holland but was captured and imprisoned, first on the Bass Rock* (1684) and then in Blackness Castle, W. Lothian, until the Revolution. He was a correspondent of Donald Cargill,* James Renwick* and other Covenanters.

DNB XXII, 161–3 (the Alexanders), 233–4 (William).

D. F. Wright

GORDON, CHARLES

Gordon, Alexander (1650–1726), *see* Gordon, Alexander (1587–1654).

Gordon, Andrew (1712–51), philosopher. George Gordon, of the family of Cofforach (Banffshire), entered Ratisbon seminary (*see* Schottenklöster) 1724. Having completed his humanities, he travelled extensively in Europe, then took the (Benedictine*) habit at Ratisbon as Brother Andrew 1732, was professed 1733 and ordained priest 1735. In 1737 he graduated in theology at Salzburg and was appointed Professor of Philosophy at Erfurt University. Besides writing on philosophy, he became known for pioneering experimental work on static electricity and published his findings in 1744. In 1745 he published a three-volume work on philosophy which gave much weight to modern writers and experimental sciences, following it with an open attack on traditional scholastic philosophy. Despite the ensuing bitter controversy with Jesuit* philosophers, Gordon's work received widespread acclaim. A key figure in 'Catholic Enlightenment', with an international reputation, he was important and influential in German cultural life. He died of consumption while not yet forty.

L. Hammermayer, 'Aufklärung im Katholischen Deutschland des 18. Jahrhunderts. Werk und Wirkung von Andreas Gordon O.S.B.', *Jahrbuch des Instituts für Deutsche Geschichte* 4 (1975), 53–109; J. M. Bulloch, *Bibliography of the Gordons* (A, 1924), 105–7.

M. Dilworth

Gordon, Charles (1772–1855), Aberdeen RC priest. He was born at Landends, Enzie, Banffshire, and educated at Scalan (*see* Colleges and Seminaries, RC) 1785–6, and in France at the Scots College,* Douai 1786–93, leaving at the Revolution and completing his studies under John Farquharson at Aberdeen. He was ordained then in 1795 and stayed on, assisting his brother, John Gordon, and nursing Geddes.* He was in sole charge at Aberdeen from 1799 to 1830. Thereafter he had a succession of assistants. He replaced the old chapel, the new building being dedicated in 1804 with high mass. He installed an organ in 1814, and organized a choir. His theological disputes with James Kidd* were famous.

From 1827 to 1829 he oversaw the conversion of Blairs to provide a national seminary (*see* Colleges and Seminaries, RC). In 1830–2 he built boys' and girls' schools in Constitution Street, Aberdeen, later adding an orphanage to each. In 1842 he opened a church at Woodside. In 1850, in declining health, he moved to Constitution Street, but retained the financial management of the Aberdeen Mission until 1854 even though he no longer carried out many pastoral duties. He is buried in the Snow Churchyard, Old Aberdeen.

C. Davidson, *Priest Gordon* (L, 1929); J. Stark, *Priest Gordon of Aberdeen* (A, 1909); A. S. MacWilliam, *St Peter's Church, Aberdeen* (A, 1979).

C. Johnson

GORDON, ELIZABETH

Gordon, Elizabeth (1794-1864), sixth Duchess of Gordon, FC lady. Born Elizabeth Brodie in London to a Scottish father, in 1813 she married George Gordon, Marquis of Huntly, heir of the fourth Duke of Gordon. She experienced a spiritual awakening in 1827 through reading the Bible and the writings of men like Robert Leighton* and Thomas Erskine of Linlathen.* When her husband died in 1836 she turned Huntly Lodge, her residence in Huntly, Aberdeenshire, into a centre of evangelical influence. Religious meetings and ministerial conferences were frequently held there.

The Duchess's own spiritual influence on her social peers was considerable; she disarmed hostility to evangelical religion and was instrumental in Brownlow North's* conversion. At the Disruption* she maintained her moral support for the evangelical ministers who left the CofS, although disapproving of their secession. She was at that time an Episcopalian and a staunch believer in the union of Church and state. She had a change of heart, however, in 1846, and joined the FC. In her latter years she allowed large religious and evangelistic meetings to be held in the parks around Huntly Lodge.

The Duchess made a great impression on the religious imagination of her day. She is the only woman to appear in the *Disruption Worthies*.

A. Moody Stuart, *Life and Letters of Elisabeth, Last Duchess of Gordon* (L, 1865); D. P. Thomson, *Women of the Scottish Church* (Perth, 1975), 204-16; *Disruption Worthies*, 271-8; *DNB* XXII, 177.

N. R. Needham

Gordon, George Angier (1853-1929), Congregational liberal churchman. He was born into a Scots Calvinist family in Pittodrie, Aberdeenshire. He was a classic example of the 'lad o' pairts' who came from a humble background, emigrated to Boston USA in 1871, and through education and ability achieved theological eminence. He was ordained in 1877, to Temple Church in Franklin County, Maine. He studied with distinction at Harvard College between 1878 and 1881.

In 1881 he was inducted into the Second Congregational Church, Greenwich, Connecticut, where he preached to a wealthy and literate congregation which at times included the Millbanks, the Benedicts, and the Rockefellers. It was however at the South Church in Boston, where he became minister in 1884, and remained until his death, that he achieved national eminence. He rejected the Calvinism of his childhood and became an eminent liberal churchman in the mould of Horace Bushnell and Harry Emerson Fosdick, though he defended the doctrine of the Trinity against New England's Unitarians.

The author of several books, some controversial, such as *Through Man to God* (1906), he was appointed to prestigious lectureships and received many honorary degrees.

My Education and Religion. An Autobiography (Boston, MA, 1925).

GORDON, JOHN

Dictionary of American Biography VII, 419-21; *Who Was Who in America 1897-1942*, 470; J. W. Buckham, *Progressive Religious Thought in America* (Boston, MA, 1919), 83-142.

G. Wareing

Gordon, Ishbel (1857-1939), Marchioness of Aberdeen, Christian advocate of women's* interests. She presented to the 1931 General Assembly of the CofS a petition signed by 336 women calling for the ordination of women to the ministry, the eldership* and the diaconate* (*APCS 1931*, 63-4). The resulting special committee appointed by the Assembly (*PAGACS 1931*, 557) was able to recommend only the eligibility of women for the diaconate. It was not until 1966 that women were declared eligible for the eldership, and not until 1968 for the ministry. The following year Catherine McConnachie was ordained by the Presbytery of Aberdeen.

Lady Aberdeen was for thirty-six years president of the International Council of Women, and a lifelong advocate of world peace. While her husband was Lord Lieutenant of Ireland, she founded the Women's National Health Association to combat tuberculosis, and, while he was Governor General of Canada, she founded the Victorian Order of Nurses for Canada. For girls employed in Aberdeenshire farmhouses, she set up the Onward and Upward Association. The hall which she and her husband built at Haddo House, Aberdeenshire, accommodates many musical, operatic and dramatic productions.

Her husband, John Campbell Gordon (originally Hamilton-Gordon; 1847-1934), the seventh Earl and the first Marquess of Aberdeen, had a distinguished public career and was a prominent Liberal. He was closely associated with Lord Shaftesbury and later with Henry Drummond,* and also with D. L. Moody,* whom he visited in the USA and invited to open a hall at Haddo House. He was Lord High Commissioner* to the CofS General Assembly in 1881-5 and 1915, and a patron of the Boys' Brigade.* On his mother's side he had links with covenanting* stock.

Lord and Lady Aberdeen, *We Twa*, 2 vols (L, 1925), *Women of the Bible* (L, 1927), and *More Cracks with 'We Twa'* (L, 1929); Lady Aberdeen, *The Musings of a Scottish Granny* (L, 1936).

D. P. Thomson, *Women of the Scottish Church* (Perth, 1975), 329-42; A. Gordon, *A Wild Flight of Gordons* (L, 1985); *DNB 1931-1940*, 347-9.

H. R. Sefton

Gordon, John (1644-1726), Bishop of Galloway, the last survivor of the pre-Revolution Scottish episcopate, having been appointed Bishop of Galloway in 1688. Born near Ellon in Aberdeenshire, he was a royal chaplain in New York when chosen as Bishop. After the Revolution he followed James VII* to Ireland and subsequently to France. At the exiled court of St Germain in Paris he read the English liturgy to such Protestants as attended him. However in 1702 he was re-ordained as a RC priest and took up residence in Rome. He was granted a pension by Pope Clement XI and given the honorary title of Abate Clemente.

DNB XXII, 216–17; T. F. Taylor, *A Profest Papist; Bishop John Gordon* (L, 1958).

H. R. Sefton

Gordon, Robert (1786–1853), a senior statesman of the rising evangelical party in the CofS before 1843 and a father of the Disruption.* A native of Glencairn, Dumfriesshire, Gordon was born into a pious family. Bereft of his schoolmaster father at the age of six, Gordon himself was a school-teacher prior to university. He studied arts at Edinburgh and divinity at Aberdeen, combining the latter with seasonal responsibilities as a tutor in Perthshire. He contributed articles on Geography, Euclid and Meteorology for *The Edinburgh Encyclopaedia* (ed. D. Brewster, E, 1830). His pastoral ministry began in Perthshire in 1816 and was followed by four pre-Disruption Edinburgh charges, the last being the High Church (from 1830). Gordon's pulpit ministry was of a consistently high order and numerous city students were deeply influenced by it; one (W. L. Alexander*) took Gordon for his model, and wrote, 'The golden mean above which Gordon seldom rises and beneath which he never sinks is the path in which every man who would be a good and useful preacher should ... walk.'

Gordon was an activist. From the 1820s, he was a keen supporter of foreign and continental missions. He was a vocal opponent of Catholic emancipation*. While not a controversialist, he was a steadfast and resolute upholder of the spiritual independence of the CofS during the Ten Years' Conflict,* supporting the use of the Veto Act.* As Moderator of the General Assembly of 1841, Gordon read the sentence of deposition for the Strathbogie* ministers who had deferred to the authority of the (civil) Court of Session and disobeyed the assembly. He was a forceful, though sagacious advocate of disruption from that year. Virtually the entire High Church congregation followed him into the FC and the Free High Kirk (now New College* Library) was shortly thereafter the scene of his ministry.

Sermons (E, 1825), and *Christ as Made Known to the Ancient Church*, 4 vols (E, 1854).

DNB XXII, 229; *FES* I, 61–2; *AFCS* I, 172; *FCM* n.s. 2 (1853), 554–60; R. Buchanan, *The Ten Years' Conflict* (2 vols, G, 1849); *Disruption Worthies*, 309–16.

K. J. Stewart

Gordon, William (*d*.1577), RC Bishop of Aberdeen (1545–77). He was the son of Alexander, third Earl of Huntly, and Jean Stewart, daughter of John, Earl of Atholl. After studying at Aberdeen and in Paris, Gordon pursued a clerical career as parson of Clatt and of Arbuthnot, chancellor of Moray by 1540 and in 1545 coadjutor to William Stewart,* Bishop of Aberdeen. Licentiate in both laws, Gordon was provided to the see in 1546 when he sat in Parliament and was appointed Privy Councillor and Lord of Session. Because he had no time to preach, he secured the services of a theologian in 1547 to refute heresies flourishing in his diocese. On the eve of the Reformation,* his chapter offered advice in January 1559 on achieving reform and 'stauncheing of hereseis pullelant within the diocie': Bishop and chapter were to set an example by reforming themselves and removing their concubines, preaching was to be undertaken, and Gordon was reminded 'not to be over familiar with them that are contrarious to the kirk'. With the outbreak of iconoclasm, the Bishop delivered silver from the cathedral to the canons for safekeeping, avoided attending the Reformation Parliament* and supported Queen Mary's party in the civil war. With the victory of King James' supporters, Gordon was forfeited in August 1571 but restored in February 1573, and dilapidated the patrimony extensively (including grants to Queen Mary).

Dowden, 141–3; *FESMA*, 4, 228; R. Keith, *An Historical Catalogue of the Scottish Bishops*, ed. M. Russel (E, 1824), 122–30; *Registrum Episcopatus Aberdonensis*, ed. C. Innes (E, 1845), I, lviii–lxvi, lxxxviii–xci, cxx–cxxiii; J. Kirk, *Patterns of Reform* (E, 1989); *DNB* XXII, 232–3.

J. Kirk

Gordon, William (1614–79), *see* Gordon, Alexander (1587–1654).

Gossip, Arthur John (1873–1954), preacher and writer. He held a succession of FC and UFC charges (St Columba's Liverpool, Forfar West, St Matthew's, Glasgow, and Beechgrove, Aberdeen) as well as acting as a Chaplain to the Forces in the last years of the First World War before being appointed to the chair of Practical Theology and Christian Ethics in Trinity College* (UF), Glasgow, in 1928. He occupied the chair until 1945, but it is as a preacher and author of popular religious books rather than a scholar or teacher that he is remembered. Of his many books *The Galilean Accent* (E, 1926), *The Hero in Thy Soul* (E, 1928) and *In the Secret Place of the Most High* (L, 1947) were the best known.

Who Was Who 1951–1960, 438–9; *FUFCS*, 577; *FES* IX, 771.

D. B. Forrester

Govan, John George (1861–1927), founder and leader of the Faith Mission.* Born in Glasgow, he was the son of William Govan, town councillor and businessman. After participating in mission work in Glasgow, Govan gave up business in 1885 to become an effective itinerant lay evangelist to villages and rural areas unpenetrated by ordinary Christian work. He founded the Faith Mission in 1886, promoting open-air meetings, house-to-house visitation and evening meetings. Govan's emphases were on conversion, personal holiness and spiritual power for all. He travelled widely, trained others, and guided and supervised the Mission. As a forceful speaker at public meetings and conferences, he

GOWDIE (GOUDIE), JOHN

combined the practical and the spiritual aspects of faith.

In the Train of His Triumph (E, 1932).

I. R. Govan, *Spirit of Revival* (L, 1938; ⁴E, 1978); C. N. Peckham, *Heritage of Revival* (E, 1986); I. R. Govan, *Spirit of Joy* (E, 1982).

B. H. Galloway

Gowdie (Goudie), John (1682-1762), Professor of Divinity and Principal in the University of Edinburgh. Probably born in Jedburgh, Gowdie was educated in Edinburgh (MA, 1700) and ordained to Earlston (Berwickshire) in 1704. He was a respected early friend of Thomas Boston,* who later wrote of Gowdie as 'a grave and learned man, upon the account of his candour and ingenuity, though joined with principles very contrary to mine' (*Life and Times*, ed. G. Morrison, E, 1899, 265).

Gowdie was translated to Lady Yester's in Edinburgh in 1730 and to the New North Church in 1732. In 1733 he was Moderator of the General Assembly and a few months later appointed Professor of Divinity. He was made Principal in 1754. Of pronounced Moderate* proclivities, he opposed the *Marrow** in both Synod and General Assembly, supported John Simson* in both processes, and in 1734, as Moderator of the Assembly's Commission, cast the deciding vote loosing Ebenezer Erskine* and the other Seceding brethren from their charges. Alexander Carlyle* (of Inveresk) characterized Gowdie as 'dull and tedious in his lectures' (*Autobiography*, ed. J. H. Burton, L, 1910, 63), and A. Bower (*History of the University of Edinburgh*, II, 283) says 'he was generally esteemed as a man of moderate abilities, but attentive to the discharge of his academic duties'.

FES VII, 382; J. Warrick, *Moderators of the Church of Scotland* (E, 1913), 305-11.

D. C. Lachman

Graham, Andrew (*d.* after 1594), Protestant Bishop of Dunblane (1573-94). He was the son of the laird of Morphie, a kinsman of the Earl of Montrose who was instrumental in securing Graham's appointment to the bishopric, vacant since the last RC bishop, William Chisholm,* had been outlawed in 1569. As yet, neither agreement nor machinery existed for the appointment of Protestant bishops, but in the aftermath of the Convention of Leith* in 1572 the way was open for the election of a Protestant Bishop. Andrew Graham was nominated by the Crown in 1573 and elected by a chapter of ministers, but the Crown's confirmation was forthcoming only in 1575. Graham's appointment proved controversial, for, although he was a Master of Arts, he had not previously served as a minister, and his earlier title as vicar of Wick had merely enabled him to draw the revenues through a factor without entailing any work. The General Assembly intervened in 1575 by appointing a committee, whose number included Andrew Melville,* to examine Graham's fitness, and ordered him to preach a trial sermon in the Magdalen Chapel*

GRAHAM, HENRY GREY

in Edinburgh. Once installed as Bishop, Graham played little part in diocesan administration, was criticized for his failure to preach, and dilapidated episcopal patrimony in favour of the Earl of Montrose, which caused the Bishop's tenants to complain to Parliament in 1578. When the General Assembly decided in 1576 that bishops should serve as parish ministers, Graham was assigned to Dunblane, but by 1580 the assembly heard complaints that he had failed to undertake a parish ministry and was negligent in his duties. His undistinguished career ended in 1594 with his deposition for non-residence and other irregularities.

BUK; Calderwood; *APS* III, 111-12; *SBD*; *Stirling Presbytery Records, 1581-1587*, ed. J. Kirk (E, 1981); *Visitation of the Diocese of Dunblane and Other Churches, 1586-1589*, ed. J. Kirk (E, 1984), ix-xlii; J. Kirk, *Patterns of Reform* (E, 1989); *FES* VII, 338.

J. Kirk

Graham, Henry Grey (1842-1906), historian and CofS minister, chiefly remembered for his *Social Life of Scotland in the Eighteenth Century*, 2 vols (L, 1900).

Graham was ordained in 1868 at Nenthorn in the Presbytery of Kelso, where his brother Manners Hamilton Nisbet Graham (father of his namesake Henry Grey Graham*) had been minister 1855-65. He was translated to Hyndland, Glasgow, where he ministered until his death. He gave the St Giles' Lectures on *The Lutheran Church* (E, 1882). His *Social Life* has valuable information on eighteenth-century Scottish Church life.

Literary and Historical Essays (L, 1908), with memoir; *FES* III, 417; *DNB Second Suppl.* II, 145.

H. R. Sefton

Graham, Henry Grey (1874-1959), the first and so far only ordained minister of the (Presbyterian) CofS to become a RC Bishop. Born at Maxton, Roxburghshire (his father, Manners H. Graham, was CofS minister, the first in Roxburghshire to introduce an organ), he was the nephew of his namesake.* He studied at St Andrews (MA, 1894; BD, 1896) and tutored there in Hebrew (1896-7) before being licensed (1897) and ordained to Avendale, Lanarkshire (1901). He was actively involved in the catholic revival* in worship* in the CofS spearheaded by the ecclesiological societies,* the Church Service Society* and the Scottish Church Society* (a leading light in these societies, John Charleson,* preceded him into the RC Church), and was attacked by Jacob Primmer.*

According to his memoir, *From the Kirk to the Catholic Church* (G, 1911), as a youth he tried in vain to reconcile Paul and James on justification.* Protestantism's disunity and theological diversity led him to consider the claims of the Roman communion, and he was received into the RC Church at Fort Augustus Abbey* on 15th August 1903 – the last of a family succession of CofS ministers unbroken for two centuries. He entered the Scots College* in Rome in 1903, and was ordained priest in Rome in 1906 for the archdiocese of Glasgow, serving as assistant priest at Motherwell (1907-15) and parish priest at Longriggend, Lanarkshire (1915-17). In 1917 he was made Bishop-auxiliary to the Archbishop of St Andrews and Edinburgh (and titular Bishop of Tipasa in Numidia). When the Archbishop died in 1929, he returned to Glasgow as a parish priest until his death.

Graham wrote several popular polemical works, including pamphlets for the Catholic Truth Society of Scotland* and its London counterpart: *Where We Got the Bible* (L, 1911; ^{2}1924); *What the Faith Really Means* (L, 1914); *The Church in Scotland, 1560-1913* (L, 1912; ^{2}1927); *Hindrances to Conversion to the Catholic Church and Their Removal* (L, 1913); *Prosperity, Catholic and Protestant* (G, 1912); *Cardinal Beaton* (L, 1913); *William Wallace* (G, 1951). Graham was portrayed as Andrew Gillespie, Bishop of Midlothian, in Bruce Marshall's novel, *Father Malachy's Miracle* (L, 1931; *The Devil, the World and the Flesh* in US edition).

H. G. McEwan, *Bishop Grey Graham 1874-1959* (G, 1973); *Catholic Directory for . . . Scotland, 1918* (G), 246-8, . . . 1960, 334-7; J. Darragh, *The Catholic Hierarchy of Scotland* (G, 1986), 29, 118; *FES* III, 224-5; *Scottish Biographies* (G, 1938), 295.

T. P Letis

Graham, James (1612-50), fifth Earl and first Marquis of Montrose, royalist general of the Covenanting civil war (*see* Covenanters). Montrose succeeded his father while still a minor in 1626, and matriculated at the University of St Andrews in the following year. He travelled on the continent throughout 1633-6, and included in his itinerary visits to a number of French military academies.

As an early enthusiast for the National Covenant,* Montrose was entrusted with military commands in the north-east in 1638 and 1639, and in the north of England in 1640. He appears to have been motivated by a mixture of adventurism, personal resentment against the court, and opposition to the growing influence of bishops in the state. However, by 1640 he had begun to distance himself from the Covenanters, as he felt that Charles I's* powers were being excessively reduced, and because of his personal jealousy of Archibald Campbell (*d.* 1661),* Eighth Earl of Argyll. He was a signator of the Cumbernauld Bond in August 1640 which claimed to support the 'public ends' of the National Covenant in contrast to the 'private practices' of Argyll. He was imprisoned from June to November 1642 when his secret plotting against the government was discovered.

After his release, Montrose tried to persuade the King to authorize a campaign in Scotland, but was thwarted by his rival, James, third Marquis of Hamilton. It was only after Hamilton's loss of favour, following his failure to prevent the alliance of the Solemn League and Covenant* in August 1643, that Charles sought Montrose's advice. Nevertheless it was not until August 1644 that Montrose, now a marquis, was able to enter Scotland and commence his brilliant Highland campaign. Between September 1644 and August 1645 he defeated six Covenanting armies in battle, and succeeded in occupying Glasgow. However, most of Montrose's Highland army refused to follow him further south, and he was unable to raise much support in the lowlands because of the reputation his part-Catholic and Irish army had for atrocities. Foolishly he attempted to reach the King, but was severely defeated by David Leslie at Philiphaugh on 13 September 1645. After unsuccessfully trying to continue the war, Montrose went into exile in August 1646.

He spent his exile trying to drum up support for Charles I and, after the King's execution in January 1649, for his son, Charles II.* However, the latter was negotiating with the Covenanters while simultaneously encouraging Montrose to launch another invasion of Scotland. In April 1650 Montrose landed in Caithness, but his pitifully small army was defeated at Carbisdale on 27 April. He was captured shortly afterwards, and was executed in Edinburgh on 21 May 1650.

M. Napier (ed.), *Memorials of Montrose and his Times*, 2 vols (E, 1850); E. J. Cowan, *Montrose, For Covenant and King* (L, 1977); D. Stevenson, *Alasdair MacColla and the Highland Problem in the Seventeenth Century* (E, 1980); *id., The Scottish Revolution, 1637-1644* (Newton Abbot, 1973); *id., Revolution and Counter Revolution in Scotland, 1644-1651* (L, 1977).

K. M. Brown

Graham, John Anderson (1861-1942), missionary to Kalimpong. He was born in W. Hackney, London, but his family soon returned to Cardross, Dunbartonshire. After schooling there and in Glasgow, he became a civil servant (like his father) in Edinburgh 1877-82. Influenced by John McMurtrie of St Bernards (*FES* I, 92), he studied for the CofS ministry at Edinburgh (MA 1885, BD 1888), during which period he was recruited by A. H. Charteris* as secretary of his Christian Life and Work Committee (Graham edited the first CofS Year Books, 1886-9) and of the Young Men's Guild. In 1889 he was ordained by Edinburgh Presbytery as the Guild's first missionary. Two days later he married Katherine McConachie and they travelled to Kalimpong, then a village in British Sikkim not far from Darjeeling. Through the labours of William Macfarlane* and W. S. Sutherland (*FES* VII, 708) it had a growing Christian community, but it was during Graham's long service that, with government development and a widening range of Christian agencies, it became an important regional centre.

Graham's initial efforts were devoted to church-planting around Kalimpong, chiefly among the Lepcha minority (for whom, with D. Macdonald, he translated Luke's Gospel; Calcutta, 1908). He developed a pattern of church leadership, involving heads of all households, which he likened to the *First Book of Discipline.** The Charteris Hospital was opened in 1893, and a leprosarium followed; Mrs

Graham started a girls' school (1889), her husband a credit society and silk farming, and the Scottish Universities Mission further upgraded its education for boys.

After an extended furlough (1895-8), Graham turned her energies to the needs of mixed-race children (Anglo-Indian - often the illegitimate offspring of Scottish tea planters), founding without CofS approval the St Andrews Colonial Homes in 1900. His model was William Quarrier's* in Scotland. The Homes, later renamed after Graham, grew into a veritable 'children's city', with training workshops, a farm and cottage 'arts and crafts' industries.

For their work in Kalimpong both Katherine Graham (who died there in 1919) and her husband received the Kaisar-i-Hind medal (and he its rare bar in 1935). He was made CIE (1911), DD of Edinburgh (1904) and LLD of Aberdeen (1932), and Moderator of the General Assembly in 1931. That year he retired from CofS missionary service but continued in the Homes and died at Kalimpong. He had got to know Rabindranath Tagore, and latterly dallied with *Stray Thoughts upon the Possibility of a Universal Religion* (1937).

On the Threshold of Three Closed Lands (E, 1897); *The Missionary Expansion of the Reformed Churches* (E, 1898).

FES VII, 694-5, VIII, 740; *DNB 1941-1950*, 312-13; J. R. Minto, *Graham of Kalimpong* (E, 1974).

D. F. Wright

Graham, John, of Claverhouse (*c.*1648-89), persecutor of the Covenanters,* usually known as Claverhouse. Of aristocratic lineage, he attended St Andrews University, though his letters are not those of an educated man. He served on the continent and after his return was appointed captain (later colonel) of a troop of horse assigned to Dumfriesshire. His well-deserved reputation over the next ten years was for taking delight in bloody cruelty. He wrote that in any service he undertook he never inquired further than the orders of his superior officers. From 1685, when he was admitted to the Privy Council,* he took part in setting policy as well as executing it. According to the widow of John Brown of Priesthill,* after having Brown shot Claverhouse told her that he could be answerable to man for the deed 'and for God, I will take him into my own hand'. He was created Viscount Dundee as a reward for his services. After the Revolution he led a force of Highlanders against the new government, but was shot and killed at the battle of Killiekrankie.

Memoirs of ... Viscount Dundee (L, 1711); ed. H. Jenner, L, 1903); *Letters ... with Illustrative Documents* (E, 1926); A. Taylor, *John Graham of Claverhouse* (L, 1939); C. S. Terry, *John Graham of Claverhouse* (L, 1905); M. J. Barrington, *Grahame of Claverhouse Viscount Dundee* (L, 1911); G. Daviot, *Claverhouse* (L, 1937).

D. C. Lachman

Graham, Patrick (*c.*1435-78), first Archbishop of St Andrews (1472-8). He was the son of Sir Robert Graham of Fintry (himself the grandson of Robert III's daughter Mary), and nephew of James Kennedy,* Bishop of St Andrews. He became canon of the sees of Glasgow and Aberdeen *c.*1450, MA of St Andrews University 1456, and Bishop of Brechin 1463-5. Transferred to St Andrews 1465, he was created metropolitan and first Archbishop of St Andrews in August 1472. Deprived of the archbishopric in January 1478, he died in confinement later that year.

Graham's rapid rise owed almost everything to his royal blood and his kinship with James Kennedy, Scotland's leading statesman during James III's minority. However, the manner in which he had personally persuaded Sixtus IV at the Roman curia in 1472 to elevate the bishopric of St Andrews to metropolitan status, with himself as its first Archbishop, scandalized the Scottish hierarchy and occasioned the indignation of James III, who had not been consulted. In consequence, Graham did not return to Scotland until September 1473, his goods and money meanwhile having been distrained. Discredited on his return, with his jurisdiction largely unrecognized, and powerless to pay his heavy dues to the apostolic camera, he suffered a breakdown, and by September 1476 a coadjutator Bishop of the King's choice, William Scheves, was appointed to deputize for him. By December 1476 a papal commission under a German canon lawyer was set up to enquire into his irregularities, the charges being made against him now including blasphemy and heresy. There is no evidence to show from the bull of condemnation, however, that Graham exhibited any heretical leanings or mental abnormality before 1472. Indeed there is considerable evidence to show that until then he was a hardworking and conscientious Bishop, however unfairly he had come by his office. But the lesson was clear. From 1478 onwards, no prelate, however well born and supported by the papacy, could hope successfully to secure his nomination against the combined opposition of the Scottish Crown and hierarchy, provided the king was not a minor.

L. J. Macfarlane, 'The Primacy of the Scottish Church, 1472-1521', *IR* 20 (1969), 111-29; *FESMA*, 40-1, 295; Dowden, 33, 186-7; A. Theiner, *Vetera Monumenta Hibernorum et Scotorum* (Rome, 1864), 465-8.

L. J. Macfarlane

Graham, William (1737-1801), minister of the General Associate* (Antiburgher) congregation at Whitehaven (1759-70) and at Newcastle-on-Tyne (1770-1801), writer against ecclesiastical establishments. After studying under Alexander Moncrieff* at Abernethy (Perthshire) he was appointed at the age of eighteen to conduct the philosophical class for Secession* divinity students. He was a strong supporter of foreign missions, but was best known for his *Review of the Ecclesiastical Establishments of Europe* (L, 1796). Of it, John M'Kerrow* said: 'It ... lent a most efficient aid in preparing the public

GRAHAM, WILLIAM FRANKLIN (BILLY)

mind for the formal consideration and free discussion of that great question to which it refers' (*History of the Secession Church*, G, 1841, 901).

John Baillie, *A Funeral Sermon ... An Elegy on the Death of the late Rev. Mr. Graham* (Newcastle, 1802).

J. R. McIntosh

Graham, William Franklin (Billy) (*b*.1918), the best-known modern evangelist. He was born at Charlotte, North Carolina, and educated at Florida Bible Seminary, Tampa, and Wheaton College near Chicago. Ordained as a minister of the Southern Baptist Convention, he was pastor of First Baptist Church, Western Springs, Illinois (1943–5), then Evangelist with Youth for Christ International (1945–8), and President of Northwestern College (1947–52). In 1950 he founded the Billy Graham Evangelistic Association, and embarked on his extensive evangelistic ministry. He also became an author, of *Peace With God* (NY, 1953), *World Aflame* (NY, 1954; ^{2}Waco, TX, 1984) and numerous other publications.

Billy Graham has exercised a remarkable ministry as an internationally renowned evangelist. Often criticized for his naiveté and lack of training in academic theology, his personal modesty, sincerity, integrity, and dedication have seldom been doubted. Critics who have attacked the BGEA have normally distinguished between the Association and its founder. In a world-wide ministry, he has exhibited a remarkable rapport and won wide respect among world leaders and statesmen. His leadership in the promotion of International Congresses on Evangelism at Berlin (1966), Amsterdam (1971), Lausanne (1974) and elsewhere, has done much to promote the concerns of world evangelization. In 1982 he was awarded the Templeton Prize for Progress in Religion.

His ministry was introduced to Scotland in 1955 when, amidst controversy, he brought the Tell Scotland* movement to a climax with the 'All Scotland Crusade'. A total attendance of 1,185,360 was recorded, and 26,547 enquiries registered. Response was unprecedented in the experience of the Graham team, but an upsurge in church attendance and membership was not maintained and was followed by major decline. When Billy Graham returned to Scotland for a two-day visit in 1961 there was sparse response.

Evaluation of Billy Graham's ministry in Scotland still arouses controversy. There is little doubt that the responsiveness owed much to the general climate of the years after the Second World War. Many future ministers owed their conversion or call to his preaching. It will remain a question of debate as to how far the Crusade contributed to or was simply a casualty of the tide of social change which by the mid-1950s was affecting all the churches.

Billy Graham returned to Scotland in 1991, with meetings in Glasgow, Aberdeen and Edinburgh.

T. Allan (ed.), *Crusade in Scotland ...* (L, 1955); J. C. Pollock, *Billy Graham* (L, 1966, and San Francisco 1979 – two works).

P. T. Bisset

GRANT, GEORGE MONRO

Grant, Alexander (1784–1874), a pioneer Baptist missionary in the Inner Hebrides. Born in Duthil, Inverness-shire, Grant was a schoolmaster with the Edinburgh Society for the Support of Gaelic Schools (*see* Gaelic School Societies), serving in the island of Shuna (1819–21) until he was removed for preaching in the parish. Supported by James Haldane,* he became a Baptist missionary in Mull. He established a Baptist church at Tobermory (1830), and contributed substantially to the formation of another in the Ross of Mull (1835). Ordained at Tobermory in 1833, Grant encouraged the growth of Baptist work in the surrounding islands.

See also Baptist Home Missionary Society for Scotland.

Annual Reports of the Edinburgh Society for the Support of Gaelic Schools, 8 (1819), 62; 10 (1821), 65; *Reports of the Baptist Home Missionary Society for Scotland*, 1831, 11–12; 1833, 14–15; G. Yuille (ed.), *History of the Baptists in Scotland* (G, 1926), 119–20.

D. E. Meek

Grant, Charles (1746–1823), evangelical Episcopalian* politician and philanthropist. Born at Dores, Inverness-shire, to a Jacobite* father killed at Culloden, he was adopted and raised by his uncle. He went to India in 1767, where he prospered as a merchant, supported a mission* at Malda, and was made a member of the board of trade at Calcutta by the Governor General, Cornwallis. He returned to England in 1790, and in 1792 wrote his *Observations on the State of Society among the Asiatic Subjects of Great Britain* (L, 1813), published by order of the House of Commons. Grant argued in this report for British toleration of missionary and educational work in the East.

His enthusiasm for philanthropic and evangelistic enterprises was manifest in various forms. He became one of the first directors of the Sierra Leone Company, chartered in 1791, which provided refuge for freed slaves. He was one of the first vice-presidents of the British and Foreign Bible Society, established in 1804. He also promoted the Church Missionary Society and the Society for the Propagation of the Gospel, and pioneered the introduction of Sunday schools in Scotland. In 1805 he became chairman of the East India Company, in which capacity he sent out Evangelicals like Henry Martyn as Company chaplains.

In 1802 Grant was elected MP for Inverness-shire, commencing a parliamentary career which lasted sixteen years. He was associated with such evangelical MPs as William Wilberforce and Henry Thornton and other members of the 'Clapham Sect'.

H. Morris, *The Life of Charles Grant* (L, 1904); *DNB* XXII, 378–80.

N. R. Needham

Grant, George Monro (1835–1902), Presbyterian educator in Canada. Born in Nova Scotia (his father emigrated from Banffshire in 1826), he won a bursary from Pictou Academy to Glasgow University, where he excelled in arts (MA, 1857) and divinity. In 1860 he was ordained by Glasgow Presbytery to serve as a missionary in Nova Scotia, declining an assistantship to Norman MacLeod* of the Barony. After serving in Nova Scotia and Prince Edward Island, he became minister of St Matthew's, the leading CofS congregation in Halifax (1863-77), and active in educational initiatives (an abortive plan for a theological college in Halifax) and reforms (of Dalhousie College, 1863). He was soon one of the most outstanding figures in Canada's ecclesiastical and educational life. He worked ardently for Presbyterian church union, consummated in 1875 (and was Moderator in 1889).

From 1877 to his death he was the brilliantly energetic Principal of Queen's University, Kingston, Ontario, a Presbyterian foundation. After failing to persuade the Church to fund its non-theological schools, he campaigned for their independence from the Church (finally achieved in 1911).

Grant enthusiastically supported Canadian federalism and was prominent in many public arenas. He was made DD of Glasgow (1877) and LLD of Dalhousie (1892), President of the Royal Society of Canada (1891), and CMG (1901).

His sole religious publication of note was *The Religions of the World in Relation to Christianity* (²L, 1895), written for the Church of Scotland textbook series for Guilds and Bible Classes. The attitude advocated to Islam, Confucianism, Hinduism and Buddhism is 'as a rich man should treat his poorer brothers ... getting on common ground and then sharing with them his rich inheritance'. His theological outlook was influenced by the Cairds, John* and Edward,* his attitude to religions by Max Müller. His progressivist, practical view of Christianity in turn influenced a whole generation of Canadian Presbyterianism, especially through an annual conference at Queen's.

FES VII, 636; *DNB Second Suppl.* II, 147-8; W. L. Grant and F. Hamilton, *Principal Grant* (Toronto, 1904); D. D. Calvin, *Queen's University at Kingston ... 1841-1941* (Kingston, 1941); H. Neatby, *Queen's University*, vol. I: *1841-1917* (Montreal, 1978).

D. F. Wright

Grant, Hay MacDowall (1806-70), lay evangelist prominent in the 1859 Revival.* Born in Arndilly, Banffshire, Grant was brought up an Episcopalian* and ever afterwards regarded himself as a member of the CofE. After attending Aberdeen University (MA, 1820), he joined the mercantile house of Baillie and represented its concerns in the West Indies from 1830-49. Here he became a zealous advocate of temperance,* anti-slavery* and popular education.

The estate of Arndilly fell to Grant in 1849 on his elder brother's death, and he returned to Scotland to manage it. A spiritual crisis induced him in 1856 to devote himself to evangelistic activities, and in the 1859 Revival he played a leading role as a preacher alongside Brownlow North* and Reginald Radcliffe. Despite his Episcopalianism, from whose Scottish clergy he received little encouragement, he co-operated freely with all denominations, particularly the FC. Indeed, his desire for spiritual sympathy led him to worship in the CofS and the FC more often than the Episcopal.

Theologically, Grant's Evangelicalism embraced lofty views of the necessity and possibility of personal assurance of salvation, and an idiosyncratic doctrine of Christian perfection (see M. M. Gordon, *Hay MacDowall Grant of Arndilly*, L, 1876, 270ff.).

Grant's latter years were clouded by ill-health and his wife's conversion to RCism, but he maintained his itinerant evangelism to the end, with remarkable success.

Forgiveness of Sins and Reconciliation to God (E, 1861); *Abounding in the Work of the Lord* (E, 1862); *The Temple of the Holy Ghost* (E, 1863).

N. R. Needham

Grant, Jean, *see* Women in Presbyterian Missions.

Grant, Peter (Abbé) (1708-84), RC agent. Of the family of Blairfindy (Glenlivet), he was educated at Scalan seminary (*see* Colleges and Seminaries, Roman Catholic) and in 1726 entered the Scots College,* Rome. Returning to Scotland 1735, he worked as a priest in Glengarry (Inverness-shire), but in 1738 was back in Rome as Scottish clergy agent, a post he held for forty-five years. His only lengthy absence from Rome was in 1783-4, when he revisited Scotland, and he returned to Rome to die.

Grant was influential and better known for fondness of society than devotion to duty. After the Jesuits* were suppressed, he declined the rectorship of the Douai and Rome colleges. While the Scots bishops complained of his procrastination and negligence, his services were avidly sought by British visitors. For them he acted as guide and provided liaison with artists and musicians; nicknamed *l'Introduttore* (the Introducer), he arranged papal audiences. Clement XIV (pope 1769-74), it was said, intended to create him a cardinal.

W. J. Anderson (ed.), 'Abbé Paul MacPherson's History of the Scots College, Rome', *IR* 12 (1961), 131-41, 153-4; J. F. S. Gordon (ed.), *The Catholic Church in Scotland* (A, 1974).

M. Dilworth

Grant, Peter (1783-1867), celebrated Gaelic* evangelical poet. Born of small-farming stock at Ballentua, Grantown-on-Spey, Grant became precentor in the local parish church when the Haldane* movement was beginning to affect certain parts of the Highlands.* He was later converted through the preaching of Lachlan Macintosh, the founder and first pastor of the Baptist church at Grantown-on-Spey. He then became an itinerant missionary. When Macintosh left Grantown in 1826, Grant succeeded him as pastor of the church and was formally ordained in 1829. He possessed considerable evangelistic gifts. Under his ministry the church achieved a membership of almost 300, and experienced intermittent revivals* (*see* Baptist Home Missionary Society for Scotland).

Of a musical disposition, and especially skilled in fiddle playing, Grant was first aroused spiritually by hearing the hymns of Dugald Buchanan.* His own hymns owe something to Buchanan, but are noticeably different in style and content. Their focus is the 'pilgrim's progress' in the life of faith. The Christian pilgrimage is followed from conversion until the believer's arrival in heaven. Grant extols the efficacy of Christ's blood, emphasizes the inevitability of death, and anticipates the joy of the eternal home. The world is depicted as a cold place, a vale of tears; the Christian hope compensates for the sorrow of believers' parting with loved ones. The experiential emphasis of Grant's hymns is reminiscent of Methodist hymnology. Set to well-known tunes, his pieces became extremely popular in the Highlands, and helped to establish a trend in the composition of Gaelic experiential hymns (*see* Hymnology, Gaelic).

H. MacDougall (ed.), *Spiritual Songs by Rev. Peter Grant* (G, 1926); D. W. Bebbington (ed.), *The Baptists in Scotland* (G, 1988), 265, 267, 286, 294.

D. E. Meek

Gray, Andrew (1633–56), preacher.* A son of Sir William of Pittendrum, Gray studied at St Andrews (MA, 1651). He was called and ordained to the High Kirk in Glasgow by the Protesters,* the objections of Robert Baillie* and others notwithstanding. Baillie's objections included Gray's having 'the new guyse of preaching, ... contemning the ordinary way of exponing and dividing a text, of raising doctrines and uses; bot runs out in a discourse on some common head, in a high, romancing unscripturall style, tickling the ear for the present, and moving the affections in some, bot leaving, as he confesses, little or nought to the memorie and understanding' (*The Letters and Journals*, E, 1842, III, 258–9). As Baillie did not object to the same style in his fellow Resolutioner* Robert Douglas,* it is probable that his chief objection to Gray was that he was a Protester. Other opinions of Gray were far more favourable. George Hutcheson* called him 'a spark of heaven' (Robert Wodrow, *Analecta*, E, 1842, III, 54), and James Durham* said he was so adept at pressing home his message on the consciences of his hearers that he caused the very hairs of their heads to stand up.

He was an exceedingly popular preacher, and his sermons proved equally popular after his death. First published from a student's notes, they were carefully revised from other sets of notes, including some from Gray's wife, and issued by Robert Trail* and John Stirling; they later edited and issued further collections (*The Mystery of Faith Opened Up . . .*; *Great and Precious Promises . . .*; *Directions and Instigations To the Duty of Prayer . . .*; *The Spiritual Warfare; Eleven Communion Sermons*). These went through numerous editions, being ultimately collected as *The Works* (e.g. A, 1839). A further collection was published as *Select Sermons* (E, 1765).

See also Preaching.

FES III, 465; DNB XXIII, 2–3.

D. C. Lachman

Gray, Andrew (1805–61), FC minister and writer. Born in Aberdeen, he graduated MA from Marischal College in 1824 and BD in 1828. Licensed by Aberdeen Presbytery in 1829, he was ordained to Woodside Chapel-of-Ease,* near Aberdeen, in 1831. In 1836 he moved to the West Church, Perth. A zealous Evangelical, during the Ten Years' Conflict* he opposed patronage* and promoted the Chapels Act* (1834), which admitted chapel-of-ease ministers to Presbyteries (see his *The Chapel Question*, E, 1834). His *The Present Conflict between Civil and Ecclesiastical Courts examined* (E, 1839) was regarded by Non-Intrusionists* as the most effective statement of their case to issue from the press. Most of Gray's congregation followed him out of the Est.C in 1843, to form the West FC.

At the request of FC leaders, Gray wrote *A Catechism of the Principles of the Free Church* (E, 1845). He visited Switzerland in 1851 on behalf of the FC, to express his Church's sympathy with the suspended evangelical ministers of Vaud. From 1855 he was convener of the FC Glasgow Evangelization Committee – urban evangelization was a cause in which he was ceaselessly active. He also promoted the establishment of a FC Divinity College in Aberdeen (*see* Christ's College), and built two parish schools in Perth, one before and one after the Disruption.*

Gospel Contrasts and Parallels: Sermons (E, 1862); *Persecution – the Lairds, the Lawyers and the Moderate Clergy against the Free Church* (Perth, 1843); *The Mary-worship of Rome* (Dundee, 1851).

R. S. Candlish, memoir prefixed to Gray's *Gospel Contrasts and Parallels*; DNB XXIII, 4; *Disruption Worthies*, 279–84; FES IV, 236; AFCS I, 176.

N. R. Needham

Gray, John (1866–1934), RC priest and poet. Born in London, son of a Scots carpenter, he left school at thirteen to work as a metal turner but educated himself assiduously and in 1888 entered the Foreign Office. He became known as a poet and man of fashion, the friend of Oscar Wilde and other literary figures. In 1890 he became a RC and in 1898 entered the Scots College,* Rome. Ordained priest in 1901, he worked in Edinburgh at St Patrick's 1902–5, then as parish priest of St Peter's, Morningside.

Early poetic works include *Silverpoints* (L, 1893; L, 1973) and *Spiritual Poems* (L, 1896). After ordination he produced some devotional poems (1903–5). In 1925 *Saint Peter's Hymns* appeared. Later publications were *The Long Road* (O, 1926), *Poems* (L, 1931) and his only novel, *Park* (L, 1932; Aylesford, Kent, 1966). He also translated and edited literary and devotional works.

His close friend in London and Edinburgh was

André Raffalovich, who financed the building of St Peter's church. As a 'half-hidden poet', and for his combination in later life of priestly zeal and impenetrable reserve, Gray remains an enigma.

B. Sewell (ed.), *Two Friends* (Aylesford, Kent, 1963); *id.*, *Footnote to the Nineties* (L, 1968); G. A. Cevasco, *John Gray* (Boston, MA, 1982).

M. Dilworth

Greenshields, James (*fl.*1700ff.), Episcopalian minister involved in a legal case after the Union* of 1707. Ordained after the abolition of episcopacy in 1690 by James Ramsay (*d.*1696), deprived Bishop of Ross, he returned to his native Scotland in 1709 after curacies in Ireland, and organized meetings in Edinburgh for worship according to the *Book of Common Prayer*. When the Presbytery ordered him to desist, he disclaimed its jurisdiction and was imprisoned by the magistrates. The Court of Session* ruled that the introduction of Presbyterian worship excluded, without need for explicit enactment, 'the English service'. The House of Lords, however, upheld Greenshields' appeal in 1711 – which was impossible before the Union and threw doubt on its provisions for the security of CofS interests. Greenshields, who was not a non-juror,* soon enjoyed the protection of the Act of Toleration of 1712.

R. Chambers, *Domestic Annals of Scotland from the Reformation to the Revolution* (E, ³1874), III, 350–2; T. Lathbury, *A History of the Nonjurors* (L, 1845), 446–55; [George Lockhart], *The Lockhart Papers* I (L, 1817), 345–8, 520–9.

D. F. Wright

Grey, Henry (1778–1859), FC minister. Born in Northumberland, his evangelical mother brought him to Edinburgh to study for the CofS ministry. Ordained to Stenton (E. Lothian, 1801), Sir Henry Wellwood Moncreiff's* promotion of Evangelicalism took him to a chapel of ease* of St Cuthbert's, Edinburgh (1813), whence he moved to New North (1821) and to the new town parish of St Mary's (1825). At the Disruption* he left to found Free St Mary's nearby. A member of the first FC deputation to England, he was Moderator in 1844, earning thereby the DD of New York University (1845). Grey's distinction lay in a cultivated refinement rare among Evangelicals, combined with the caution of a conciliator and catholicity of sympathy. He supported more frequent Communion, missions (influencing Duff*), Bible distribution (opposing Andrew Thomson* in the Apocrypha controversy*), anti-slavery,* temperance* and Earl Grey's reform party. A Grey Scholarship was endowed in his honour in New College, Edinburgh, where a bust by Patric Park is preserved.

FES I, 112–13; *DNB* XXIII, 188–9; *AFCS* I, 177–8, II, 11; C. M. Birrell, *Thoughts in the Evening... Sketch of the Life of Rev. Henry Grey...* (L, 1871); [J. Anderson], *Sketches of Edinburgh Clergy...* (E, 1832), 64–9; J. Kay, *A Series of Original Portraits...*, II:2 (E, 1842), 457 60.

D. F. Wright

Greyfriars, *see* Franciscans.

Grub, George (1812–92), Episcopalian* church historian. Born in Aberdeen, he studied at King's College in Aberdeen University and then trained as an advocate in an Aberdeen law-office. He qualified as an advocate in 1836. In 1841 he became librarian of the Society of Advocates; in 1843 he was appointed lecturer in Scots law at Marischal College, Aberdeen. Marischal united with King's College in 1860, and Grub became Professor of Law in Aberdeen University in 1881.

Grub's lasting reputation, however, lies in the field of church history. He was a founder member in 1839 of the Spalding Club, and an editor of its historical publications. When the New Spalding Club was formed in 1886, he was one of its vice-presidents. His own historical *magnum opus* was his *Ecclesiastical History of Scotland* (4 vols, E, 1861), which covers the period from the introduction of Christianity into Scotland down to 1857. Hailed in its own day as a masterpiece, it is distinguished by scholarship and relative impartiality.

Grub was a staunch Episcopalian and an erudite theologian. He was at first a keen follower of the Oxford movement, but his ardour cooled after Newman's secession to Rome in 1843. The permanent standard according to which he understood genuine Episcopalianism was the writings of the Caroline divines.

W. Walker, *Three Churchmen* (E, 1893); *DNB Suppl.* II, 373–4.

N. R. Needham

Gude and Godlie Ballatis, the familiar name (here *GGB*) for a collection of vernacular religious texts (nearly all verse), which did much to spread the basic ideas of Protestantism in Scotland. The book is also known as *Ane Compendious Book of Godly and Spiritual Songs*, the *Dundee Psalms*, and *Wedderburn's Psalms/Songs*. The last two names stem from the ascription of the book (as in James Melville's *Diary*, 23) to the Wedderburn* brothers of Dundee. The earliest edition now known is that of 1565 (printed at Edinburgh, probably by John Scot, for Thomas Bassandyne), and there were reprints in 1567, 1578, 1600 and 1621. In no edition is any author's name given. Despite the post-Reformation date, it is likely that many of the items in the *GGB* come from the two decades before 1560, and a few may be even older. These poems could have circulated by word of mouth, in manuscript, or in print; there are several enactments before the Reformation against the publishing of satirical ballads. John Knox* reports George Wishart* as singing the *GGB* version of Psalm 51 on the night before his arrest, 1546 (*Works*, I, 139–40).

There are two main sections in the book, and within each of these further groupings are discernible. The first section contains: (i) a prose catechism, with fundamental texts such as the Commandments, the Creed, the Lord's Prayer, the two sacraments – several are repeated in verse; (ii) 'spirituall sangis' – some sixteen poems heavily indebted to the Bible (some as paraphrases); (iii) 'certaine ballatis of the scripture' – some twenty poems, several being *contrafacta*, designed to replace the words of secular songs. The second section comprises: (i) 'psalmes of Dauid' – some twenty in number; (ii) 'uther new plesand ballatis' – approximately forty poems, many being *contrafacta*, satirical and propagandistic. There is some variation between the first three editions as to the total number of items: each was somewhat more compendious than its predecessor. The 1578 edition is unique in prefixing a calendar.

The theological influence in the *GGB* is Lutheran,* as one would expect of John Wedderburn.* Whether the latter was responsible for the entire collection is debatable: four items, for example, also appear in the *Goostely Psalmes* of Myles Coverdale (before 1546). All three Wedderburns were dead before 1565, and it seems likely that stray 'ballatis' were simply associated with the name of the Dundee family. The 'Proloug' reveals the purpose of the *GGB*. It was not designed for the theologically sophisticated, but for 'young personis and sick as ar nocht excersit in the scripturs'. The double advantage of the use of the vernacular and the reliance upon familiar melodies is also stressed, as is the moral purpose of supplanting 'bauldry sangis and unclene'. The *GGB* is a triumph of religious popularization.

A Compendious Book (*The Gude and Godlie Ballatis*), ed. A. F. Mitchell, STS (E, 1897); *A Compendious Book* (*The Gude and Godlie Ballatis*), ed. D. Laing (E, 1868); J. Melville, *The Autobiography and Diary*, ed. R. Pitcairn, Wodrow Society (E, 1842); *Essays on the Scottish Reformation 1513–1625*, ed. D. McRoberts (G, 1962); A. A. MacDonald, 'The Middle Scots Religious Lyrics' (PhD, Edinburgh University, 1978); *History of Scottish Literature*, vol. I, ed. R. D. S. Jack (A, 1988); B. Murdoch, 'The Hymns of Martin Luther in the *Gude and Godlie Ballatis*', *Studies in Scottish Literature* 12 (1974–5), 92–109.

A. A. MacDonald

Guild, William (1586–1657), Principal of King's College, Aberdeen, 1640–51, prolific writer, reluctant Covenanter* and generous benefactor of the Incorporated Trades of Aberdeen.

The son of an armourer, Guild was educated at Marischal College, Aberdeen, and was only twenty-two when his first treatise, *The New Sacrifice of Christian Incense or the true Entrie to the Tree of Life and the Gracious Gate of Glorious Paradise* was published in London. The same year (1608) he was ordained and inducted to the parish of King-Edward, i.e. Kinedward, Aberdeenshire. He signed a protestation to Parliament in support of the liberties of the Kirk in 1617, but he made three reservations when signing the National Covenant* of 1638. He promised only to disregard the Five Articles of Perth* of 1618, refused to condemn episcopacy and stood by his loyalty to the King, to whom he had been appointed a chaplain in 1631. That same year he had been elected to the second charge of St Nicholas, Aberdeen. He was an early recipient of Aberdeen's DD (*c.*1634). When William Leslie,* one of the Aberdeen Doctors,* was expelled from the principality of King's College for his refusal to sign the Covenant, Guild was appointed. He was dismissed in 1651 by Cromwell's military commissioners because of his royalist sympathies.

Guild was a generous benefactor to his native city. He gifted a house in Castle Street for the maintenance of three poor bursars at Marischal College and bequeathed 7,000 marks for the care of orphans. But his principal benefaction was his acquisition of the deserted friary and chapel of the Trinity Friars for the use of the Incorporated Trades as a meeting place and hospital for indigent craftsmen. The successor to this is still known as Trinity Hall. Guild was appointed Patron of the Trades, and a minister of the city is still invited to hold this office.

Several times reprinted, as late as the nineteenth century, was *Moses unvailed: or those figures pointing out Christ Jesus . . .* (L, 1619). Guild wrote a variety of other works, including a commentary on the Song of Solomon (*Love's entercours . . .* , L, 1658) and, particularly after he was forced to retire into private life, anti-papist treatises.

DNB XXIII, 323–4; *FES* VI, 2, 265, VII, 365–6; J. Shirrefs, *An Inquiry into the Life, Writings and Character of William Guild* (A, 1796); Alexander Keith, *A Thousand Years of Aberdeen* (A, 1972).

H. R. Sefton

Guilliame, Thomas (*fl.* 1540s), a former Black Friar (*see* Dominicans) through whom John Knox* was converted to Protestantism. Guilliame was a native of Athelstaneford in East Lothian and is said to have attained considerable distinction as a Prior of the Black Friar monastery at Inverness. After he became a Protestant, James Hamilton (*d.* 1575)* Earl of Arran, appointed Guilliame and John Rough* as his chaplains. Guilliame and Rough preached throughout Lothian, Fife, and Angus. One of the audience who heard Guilliame when he preached in Lothian was Knox, who was thereby converted to Protestantism. Little is known about Knox's conversion except that it was a definite decision based on John 17. Later Knox would write that Guilliame was of solid judgment, a fluent speaker, reasonably learned by the standards of 1543, and that his doctrine was wholesome. Nevertheless, Guilliame was too moderate in his opposition to Catholicism for Knox's liking.

Knox, *History* I, 42–3, 48; J. Ridley, *John Knox* (O, 1962); W. S. Reid, *Trumpeter of God* (NY, 1974).

R. G. Kyle

Gunning Victoria Jubilee Lectures, a series given in the Divinity Faculty of the University of Edinburgh and endowed by Robert H. Gunning in 1889 'to promote the study of Natural Science among candidates for the ministry, and to bring out among ministers the fruits of study in Science,

GUTHRIE, JAMES

Philosophy, Language, Antiquity and Sociology'. Gunning (1818-1900) was born in Ruthwell, Dumfriesshire, and taught anatomy at Marischal College, Aberdeen, and physiology at Edinburgh, before departing in 1849, for health reasons, for warmer climes in Brazil, where long medical service won him the accolade of Grand Dignitary of the Rose of Brazil. Queen Victoria allowed him to retain the title of 'His Excellency' in Britain. A man of wide accomplishments and one of the first elders (and lifelong supporter) of Chalmers* West Port Church, Edinburgh, Gunning endowed prizes and fellowships in the Royal Society of Edinburgh, the Society of Antiquaries of Scotland and the FC's New College,* Edinburgh (in memory of Hugh Miller*), as well as in different faculties of the University. He also contributed to other causes, including the Victoria Institute, London, and Waldensian missions.

Appointment to the Lectureship (which was preceded by a Fellowship with similar objectives, endowed in 1879 and first awarded after examination in 1883) has generally been made triennially, by the Faculty, but the restriction to 'any Scottish Presbyterian clergyman at home, or in the Mission field' has long since been departed from. Distinguished lecturers have included: John Baillie* (see *Our Knowledge of God*, L, 1939); N. Sykes, *Old Priest and New Presbyter* (C, 1956); Michael Foster, *Mystery and Philosophy* (L, 1957); Egon Wellesz, the Byzantine musicologist (1956); Hendrik Kraemer, Dutch missiologist and theologian (1958; only one lecture delivered through illness: *A Theology of the Laity*, L, 1958); Gustav Wingren, Swedish systematician (1959); Michael Polanyi, 'Perspectives of Personal Knowledge' (1960; MS in Chicago University Library); R. Hooykaas, *Religion and the Rise of Modern Science* (E, 1972); Bryan R. Wilson (1971; cf. *Magic and the Millennium*, L, 1973); G. H. Williams, 'Residues of Sacred Energies: The Reformation and the Counter Reform in Eastern Central Europe' (1987).

Obituary notice by J. Duns in *Proceedings of Royal Society of Edinburgh* 23 (1899-1901), 489-97 (and separately); *Edinburgh University Calendar 1889-90*, 251, 520; list to date in ... *Calendar 1962-1963*, xlii.

D. F. Wright

Guthrie, James (c.1612-61), Covenanting minister. Born the son of an Angus landowner who favoured Episcopacy, he too in his youth was 'prelatic and strong for the ceremonies'. At St Andrews University the friendship of Samuel Rutherford* was probably responsible for a change of outlook; when he left St Andrews it was for the Presbyterian ministry. He signed the Covenant* in 1638, and added, 'I know that I shall die for what I have done this day, but I cannot die in a better cause.' While minister of Lauder (1642-9) he was among Scottish delegates who in 1646 met Charles I* at Newcastle and pressed the claims of Presbyterianism.* As minister of Stirling (1649-61) he championed the cause of the Protesters,* who strongly upheld

GUTHRIE, THOMAS

the principles of the Covenant. He wrote many of the public papers for the Church from George Gillespie's* death until the breach and for the Protesters subsequent to it (R. Wodrow, *Analecta*, E, 1842, I, 168). Guthrie wanted the King's authority limited by a free parliament and a free assembly, and said so fearlessly. Moreover, he believed it sinful to give power to the King before Charles gave evidence he had been sincere in subscribing the Covenants. He carried out, despite Charles II's appeal, the excommunication pronounced by the Commission of Assembly against the Earl of Middleton, a royal favourite. Under Cromwell, whom he refused to meet, Guthrie defended the office of the king, but saw no contradiction in withholding support from King Charles II,* who had given no evidence his subscribing the Covenants was sincere.

In 1653 his *Causes of the Lord's Wrath against Scotland* spurned any suggestion of compromises and hailed as pre-eminent 'the duty of preserving and defending the true religion'. Scotland's ill he attributed to 'an arbitrary government and an illimited power'. The book was condemned and burnt with Rutherford's* *Lex Rex*. At the Restoration* Guthrie headed a band of twelve Protesters who congratulated the King, reminded him of his Covenant obligation, and urged him to fill key posts with those who had signed the Covenant and who loved God. The petitioners were flung into prison. Tried ostensibly with declining the King's authority in ecclesiastical affairs, he maintained that the conduct of the government released its subjects from their debt of obedience, declined to redeem his life with the loss of his integrity, and faced the gallows with equanimity.

Some Considerations contributing unto the Discoverie of the Dangers that Threaten Religion (E, 1660); *A Treatise of Ruling Elders and Deacons* (E, 1652).

FES IV, 318-19; T. Thomson, *Life of James Guthrie* (E, 1846); J. Kilpatrick, 'James Guthrie ...', *RSCHS* 11 (1955), 176-88; J. Howie, *Scots Worthies*, ed. W. H. Carslaw (E, 1870), 257-68; *DNB* XXIII, 377-9.

J. D. Douglas

Guthrie, Thomas (1803-73), preacher and social reformer. Born in Brechin, Angus, Guthrie attended Edinburgh University 1815-25 and was licensed by the CofS Presbytery of Brechin in 1825. In 1830 he became minister of Arbirlot, near Arbroath, in 1837 was called to Edinburgh, first to Old Greyfriars, and then from 1840 to the new church of St Johns, Victoria Street.

Guthrie played an important part in the Ten Years' Conflict* on the non-Intrusionist* side, advocating from the outset the complete abolition of patronage.* After the Disruption* he was minister of Free St Johns, Edinburgh, until a heart condition compelled retirement in 1864. Guthrie was principally responsible for raising the FC's manse fund through an itinerant campaign of appeals in 1845-6, but his health subsequently broke down and he was forced to give up preaching for several years.

GUTHRIE, WILLIAM

During this time Guthrie commenced his advocacy of Ragged Schools.* This philanthropic enterprise, for which he is chiefly remembered today, aimed at providing free food, education and vocational training for the multitudes of destitute children who begged for a living in Scotland's cities and often ended up as habitual criminals.

Guthrie was also an ardent champion of the temperance* movement. A total abstainer and prohibitionist, he was a founding member both of the FC Temperance Society and the Scottish Association for the Suppression of Drunkenness. One of his most effective literary productions, *The City, Its Sins and Sorrows* (E, 1857), was devoted to this topic.

In his closing years, Guthrie took up the cause of the union between the FC and the UPC. Although he had taken part in the Voluntary* controversy in defence of the Est.C before the Disruption, his later position was a virtual acceptance of the Voluntaryism of the United Presbyterians. His experience in the Ten Years' Conflict had led him to believe that establishment, although warrantable in principle, would always result in practice in state domination of the Church.

Guthrie's exalted reputation during his lifetime, however, rested mainly on his power as a preacher. After Chalmers* he was Scotland's most admired pulpit orator of the nineteenth century. Though without exceptional logical or theological ability, Guthrie's vivid pictorial imagination and sympathetic rapport with his audience enabled him to fashion men's emotions almost at will. His hearers became oblivious to their surroundings; a seaman, listening to Guthrie's description of a nautical disaster, leapt up and removed his coat, ready to dive in to save the drowning. James M'Cosh* called Guthrie 'the pictorial preacher of the age' (D. K. and C. J. Guthrie, *Autobiography of Thomas Guthrie, D.D. and Memoir*, L, 1877, 266). Needless to say, these qualities were exhibited not in his sermons alone but also in his public speeches on behalf of the various causes he supported. Guthrie himself particularly admired Charles Haddon Spurgeon.*

Guthrie received a DD from Edinburgh University in 1849, and served as Moderator of the FC General Assembly in 1862.

Christ and the Inheritance of the Saints (E, 1858); *The Gospel in Ezekiel* (E, 1856); *Man and the Gospel* (L, 1865); *Our Father's Business* (L, 1867); *The Parables, Read in the Light of the Present Day* (L, 1867); *Speaking to the Heart* (L, 1864); *The Way to Life* (E, 1862); *Plea for Ragged Schools* (E, 1847); *Second Plea* (E, 1848); *Seed-time and Harvest of Ragged Schools* (E, 1860); *Plea for Drunkards and against Drunkenness* (E, 1850).

O. Smeaton, *Thomas Guthrie* (E, 1900); C. J. Guthrie, *Thomas Guthrie, Preacher and Philanthropist* (E, 1899); *DNB* XXIII, 380-2; *FES* I, 48, 108; V, 422; *AFCS* I, 179.

N. R. Needham

Guthrie, William (1620-65), minister of Fenwick, Kilmarnock. The eldest son of the Laird of Pitforthie (near Brechin), and cousin of James Guthrie,*

GUTHRY, HENRY

under whom he studied at St Andrews, Guthrie studied divinity with Samuel Rutherford.* Before being licensed in 1642, Guthrie settled his estate on one of his brothers in exchange for a monetary consideration, so that he would be free to serve as a minister. He was tutor to Lord Mauchline, the eldest son of the Earl of Loudoun, a leading Covenanter,* and was then ordained in 1644 to Fenwick (newly disjoined from Kilmarnock). He was married the following year and served for a time as chaplain in the army. After the Engagement* he joined the Remonstrants or Protesters,* being one of the ministers who took part in the communion service at Mauchline Moor in June 1648. He was appointed one of the commissioners to visit the University of Glasgow in 1649. The same year he received the first of various calls to larger parishes, all of which he declined. He served as Moderator of the Protester Synod of Glasgow and Ayr in 1654 and was one of the Triers appointed by Cromwell* to 'take especial care none but godly and able men be authorized by them to enjoy livings appointed for the ministry in Scotland'.

In 1657 what Guthrie referred to as 'some imperfect notes' of his sermons were published in Aberdeen as *A Clear, Attractive, Warning Beam of Light*. In self-defence he published *The Christian's Great Interest* (G, 1658?), which he described as written in 'a Most homely and plain Stile' so as to consult the advantage of 'the Rude and Ignorant'. The book is divided into two parts: 'The Trial of a Saving Interest in Christ' and 'The Way how to attain it, first giving tests so one can know if he is a true Christian and then making known the way of Salvation'. From the first the book was well received; it has been many times reprinted and translated into a variety of languages. John Owen spoke of Guthrie as 'one of the greatest divines that ever wrote' and his book as containing 'more divinity' than all his own folios.

After the Restoration* Guthrie was unmolested in Fenwick until 1664, partly through the favour of the Earl of Glencairn,* then Chancellor. But the crowds who travelled to hear him excited the jealousy of Alexander Burnet,* the Archbishop of Glasgow, who suspended him from the ministry. Guthrie continued for about a year in the manse and died the following year while on a visit to Pitforthie.

Guthrie was known for his love of fishing, fowling and like sports. These, coupled with an amiable and witty personality and an earnest concern for their spiritual good, greatly endeared him to the people. He was described as 'the greatest practical preacher in Scotland'.

The Works (G, 1771).

FES III, 93-4; *DNB* XXIII, 382-3; *Memoir and Letters* ... , ed. W. Muir (E, 1827); W. H. Carslaw, *Life and Times* ... (Paisley, 1900).

D. C. Lachman

Guthry, Henry (1600-76), Bishop of Dunkeld, 1665-76. Guthry was a controversial figure during the early Covenanting period who was deposed for

GUTHRY, HENRY

'malignancy' or lack of fervour for the cause against the King in 1648. His *Memoirs of Scottish Affairs, Civil and Ecclesiastical* (L, 1702; reprinted 1748) was written long after the events described. The printed version varies significantly from extant manuscripts.

The son of Henry Guthry, minister of Bendochy, Guthry studied at St Andrews (MA, 1620) and was ordained to Guthrie, near Forfar, in 1625. His ministry at Stirling, 1632–48, was marked by a long-running dispute with the Laird of Leckie over private meetings for worship, which he alleged to be sectarian in character. Guthry deplored the lack of effective support from the General Assembly against Leckie and before long was an object of suspicion. He was restored to the ministry in 1655 and admitted minister of Kilspindie, near Perth, in 1656, where he remained until his elevation to the episcopate.

Guthry was described by George Crawford, in a 'Life' prefixed to the 1748 edition of the *Memoirs*, as being 'generally esteemed a wise man, moderate in his temper, regular and exemplary in the whole course of his life'.

Thomas Forrester,* however, describes him as one 'who loved always to swim with the stream and court the rising sun', being a man who had denounced the bishops in the late 1630s but who was quite ready to conform in 1660.

FES VII, 340; R. Baillie, *The Letters and Journals* (ed. D. Laing) (E, 1841–2), I, 248–58; D. H. Fleming, *The Subscribing of the National Covenant in 1638* (E, 1912).

H. R. *Sefton*

H

Hadow, James (*c.*1670–1747), Professor of Divinity and Principal of St Mary's College, St Andrews. After study in Utrecht, Hadow was ordained to Cupar (Fife) in 1692, called to the chair of Divinity in St Andrews in 1699 and, in 1707, to the Principalship. His participation in the CofS was almost exclusively confined to defence of what he considered to be orthodox doctrine. Robert Wodrow* characterized him as 'firm and sound as far as I knou in Doctrine, but ... dark and grimly in his appearance' (*Analecta*, E, 1843, IV, 486). Against the Episcopalian* clergy he defended Presbyterian* baptism,* in a work whose wealth of quotation shows him to have been a theologian of no little reading. He also published two pamphlets against John Simson.*

However, Hadow is chiefly remembered as the leading opponent of the *Marrow* in the Marrow Controversy.* The first to attack the *Marrow* in public, in April 1719 he preached a sermon before the Synod of Fife (printed as *The Record of God and the Duty of Faith Therein Required*, E, 1719) in which he charged the *Marrow* with doctrinal error. He played a key role in drawing up charges against the *Marrow* and subsequently wrote his most extensive work against it (*The Antinomianism of the Marrow of Modern Divinity Detected*, E, 1722).

Hadow's work was characterized by a narrow dogmatism, a tendency to wrest his opponents' arguments to fit his own preconceptions, and an inability to accept any terminology other than his own. His *Antinomianism* was effectively ridiculed by Robert Riccaltoun* in his *Politick Disputant* (E, 1722) and answered in his *Sober Enquiry* (E, 1723).

The Doctrine and Practice of the Church of Scotland, anent the Sacrament of Baptism vindicated... (E, 1704); *An Enquiry into Mr. Simson's Sentiments about the Trinity...* (E, 1730); *A Vindication of the Learned and Honourable Author of the History of the Apostles Creed, from the False Sentiment, which Mr. Simson has injuriously imputed to him* (E, 1731).

FES VII, 421; DNB XXIII, 437.

D. C. Lachman

Haining, Jane Mathison (1897–1944), CofS missionary to Jews in Budapest who died in Auschwitz. Born to a FC farming family near Dunscore, Dumfriesshire, she was educated at Dumfries Academy and took up secretarial work in the Coats thread business in Paisley. A meeting in Glasgow of CofS Jewish missions evoked a sense of call, and after further training (at Glasgow College of Domestic Science and St Colm's, Edinburgh), she arrived in Budapest in mid-1932 as matron of the girls' home of the Jewish mission. The school taught both Jewish and Christian pupils, the former including some from divided families, and soon (for Hitler became Chancellor in 1933) some refugees. In 1935 George A. F. Knight, later a well-known Old Testament scholar (*FES* IX, 292, 760, X, 172), became head of the mission.

When World War II broke out, she was on leave in Scotland, but hurried back to Budapest. As the situation in Europe rapidly deteriorated, she declined instructions to Scottish missionaries to return home. Amid increasing austerity and with the help of the Hungarian Reformed Church, she kept the work of home and school going. In March 1944 the Nazis invaded the country, and she was required to affix the yellow star of David to her Jewish children's clothing. In May she was arrested, on suspicion of espionage. (Other charges she admitted; she had wept when pinning on the yellow stars.) Soon she was in Auschwitz, where she died, probably gassed, on July 17. Memorials honour her martyrdom, in Budapest (Christian and Jewish) and in her (former UF) home church, Queen's Park West, Glasgow, now Strathbungo Queens's Park. She was the only Scot killed in a Nazi extermination camp.

D. McDougall, *Jane Haining of Budapest* (E, 1949); C. T. Walker (ed.), *A Legacy of Scots* (E, 1986), 242–53; D. P. Thomson, *Women of the Scottish Church* (Perth, 1975), 353–62.

D. F. Wright

Haldane, Alexander (1800–82), barrister and political-religious journalist. Second son and biographer of James Alexander Haldane,* he entered the English legal profession after studying at Edinburgh University, in due course being called to the bar. In 1822 he married the youngest daughter of Joseph Hardcastle, a London merchant and friend of his father, who until his death had been a leading dissenting supporter of evangelical ventures. A member of the Church of England and an uncompromising Evangelical, Alexander Haldane represented the anti-apocrypha viewpoint (see Apocrypha Controversy) on the committee of the Bible Society.* In 1828 he assumed an editorial liaison role for the proprietors of the *Record*, a newly formed but struggling Anglican periodical with a strong political flavour. Under his influence the journal prospered, though it established a reputation for pungency and controversialism in ecclesiastical matters, earning criticism from would-be sympathizers as being the cause of much of the dislike encountered by the evangelical party. As a close friend of Lord Shaftesbury, Haldane exercised a considerable influence on the ecclesiastical appointments made by Lord Palmerston during his time as Prime Minister.

A Biographical Sketch of Alexander Haldane (L, [1882]); G. R. Balleine, *A History of the Evangelical Party in the Church of England* (L, 1908); J. A. L. Haldane, *The Haldanes of Gleneagles* (E, 1929); I. S. Rennie, 'Evangelicalism and English Public Life, 1823–1850' (PhD, University of Toronto, 1962); *DNB Miss. Pers.*, 283.

D. W. Lovegrove

Haldane, James Alexander (1768–1851), itinerant evangelist, pastor and theological writer, brother of Robert Haldane.* Born in Dundee, he studied for a few years at Edinburgh University before commencing a maritime career in the service of the East India Company in 1785. In 1795 he settled with his wife in Edinburgh, and was converted following a period of religious enquiry initiated by David Bogue,* Independent minister of Gosport. Although he was still a member of the CofS, he began an unauthorized programme of evangelism in 1797 with a tour through the north of Scotland (see his *Journal of a Tour through the Northern Counties of Scotland and the Orkney Isles, in Autumn 1797*, E, 1798). Over the following eight summers he preached extensively, visiting many lowland areas as well as the remoter communities of Argyll, Orkney and Shetland.

As early as 1798, realizing the need for continuity, Haldane helped to found the Society for Propagating the Gospel at Home* as a permanent agency for organizing and supporting preachers and catechists. By his disregard of parish boundaries, open criticism of the Est.C's ministry, and encouragement of a network of itinerant preachers, he contributed notably to the sense of outrage which induced the 1799 General Assembly to issue the notorious Pastoral Admonition* against unqualified preachers.

By the beginning of 1799, however, Haldane had turned away from Presbyterianism and accepted ordination as pastor of an Independent* congregation meeting in the former Circus building in Edinburgh (the 'Tabernacle'). This move established Haldane as one of the pioneers of Scottish Congregationalism.* His willingness to review doctrine and polity in the light of Scripture produced an advocacy of weekly communion (see his *The Obligation of Christian Churches to Observe the Lord's Supper Every Lord's Day*, E, 1803), mutual public exhortation by church members (see his *A View of the Social Worship and Ordinances Observed by the First Christians*, E, 1805) and a plurality of elders, and led in 1808 to his embracing Baptist views (see his *Reasons for a Change of Sentiment and Practice on the Subject of Baptism*, E, 1808).

In his numerous writings, Haldane addressed himself to a wide range of subjects, from biblical exposition and doctrine to Church order and discipline. Many of his works were controversial in character; he wrote, for example, against Edward Irving* (*Refutation of Edward Irving's Doctrine respecting the Person and Atonement of Christ*, E, 1829), Thomas Erskine* (*Observations on Universal Pardon*, E, 1831), Thomas Chalmers* (*Two Letters to Dr Chalmers on his Proposal for Increasing the Number of Churches in Glasgow*, E, 1820), and Ralph Wardlaw* (*The Doctrine of the Atonement*, E, 1847). His own theology was that of an orthodox Calvinist. However, Haldane was essentially a practical Church leader rather than a controversialist. Together with his brother Robert, he laid the foundations for a broad acceptance of evangelical Calvinism* in Scotland in the early years of the nineteenth century.

An Exposition of the Epistle to the Galatians (E, 1848); *Notes Intended for an Exposition of the Epistle to the Hebrews* (L, 1860); *The Atonement* (E, n.d.); *The Foundation of the Observance of the Lord's Day, and of the Lord's Supper* (E, 1807); *The Change and Perpetuity of the Sabbath* (E, n.d.); *The Voluntary Question* (E, 1839); *Man's Responsibility; the Nature and Extent of the Atonement; and the Work of the Holy Spirit* (E, 1842); *The Doctrine and Duty of Self-examination* (E, 1806); *Judaism and Christianity* (E, 1849).

A. Haldane, *The Lives of Robert Haldane of Airthrey, and of his brother, James Alexander Haldane* (L, 1852); J. A. L. Haldane, *The Haldanes of Gleneagles* (E, 1829); DNB XXIV, 13–14; W. Landels, *The Haldanes* (L, 1854); D. MacGregor, 'The Haldanes', in W. Hanna (ed.), *Essays by Ministers of the Free Church of Scotland* (E, 1858), 113–47.

D. W. Lovegrove

Haldane Preachers, evangelists sponsored by Robert Haldane.* The creation in 1798 of the Society for Propagating the Gospel at Home* revealed a need for trained catechists and lay evangelists. Using money raised by the sale of his Stirlingshire estate, originally designated for the support of a mission to Bengal, Robert Haldane attempted to meet this demand by establishing a series of seminary classes under evangelical ministers in Glasgow, Dundee and Edinburgh. These classes, which functioned between 1799 and 1808 and offered a two-year course, provided a cadre of home missionary preachers nearly three hundred strong, equipped with basic biblical and literary skills. The young men, many of whom operated at some point under the auspices of the SPGH, acted as preachers and catechists in areas as widely separated as Caithness and Galloway. A number followed the example of John Cleghorn and William Ballantine who, having been sent by the society to Wick and Thurso respectively, settled as pastors over the congregations they had gathered. Others fulfilled more exactly their sponsor's intentions, remaining as itinerant evangelists and moving to other preaching centres once their work had achieved initial success. At a time when the Highland* line presented a sharp linguistic and cultural barrier resistant to the new wave of Evangelicalism, the enlistment of a number of native Gaelic speakers, including Archibald McCallum and John Farquharson,* allowed the Edinburgh-based society to penetrate the Highlands, establishing in mid-Argyll and Breadalbane (Perthshire) centres of strength for future Independency.*

See also Baptist Home Missionary Society for Scotland.

D. E. Meek, 'Evangelical Missionaries in the Early Nineteenth-Century Highlands', *SS* 28 (1987), 1–34.

D. W. Lovegrove

Haldane, Robert (1764–1842), evangelical philanthropist, theological writer and preacher, brother of James Haldane.* Born in London, he was raised and educated in Dundee and Edinburgh. After a brief naval career which ended in 1783, he married and settled on his estate at Airthrey near Stirling. The influence of David Bogue,* pastor of the independent church at Gosport, resulted in his conversion in 1795. Prior to this, Haldane had hoped for the renewal of society through radical politics, and had welcomed the French Revolution.* Haldane's reputation continued to be tarnished by this initial radicalism, even after his new-found evangelical faith had induced him to abandon it; an abortive missionary scheme to Bengal in 1796–7 and Haldane's ensuing support for itinerant evangelism in Scotland were seen as politically subversive. Not until his *Address to the Public concerning Political Opinions* (E, 1800) did Haldane persuade supporters of the establishment that he had no intention of undermining the status quo.

Convinced of the importance of home missionary work, Haldane expended 70,000 towards that end between 1798 and 1810. His financial sponsorship underpinned the entire activity of the Society for Propagating the Gospel at Home,* facilitating training courses for its future agents under evangelical ministers in Edinburgh, Glasgow and Dundee, the printing of religious tracts and Bibles for public circulation, and the initiation of a building programme designed to accommodate the crowds that gathered to hear the 'Haldane preachers'.* Until he and his brother became Baptists in 1808, Robert Haldane's generosity was a major factor behind the growth of Congregationalism* in early nineteenth-century Scotland.

Always more interested in developing the wider programme of evangelism than his own preaching, most of Haldane's remaining energies were directed towards writing on a range of theological subjects – apologetics in *The Evidence and Authority of Divine Revelation* (E, 1816; [3]L, 1839), the doctrine of scripture in *The Authenticity and Inspiration of the Holy Scriptures Considered* (E, 1827) and *The Books of the Old and New Testaments Proved to be Canonical, and their Verbal Inspiration Maintained and Established* (E, 1832; [7]1877), and exegesis in his classic *Exposition of the Epistle to the Romans*, 3 vols, L, 1836–9; [9]E, 1874). He was concerned above all with contemporary issues, engaging in turn with August Tholuck of Halle over his low views of biblical inspiration (see his *Remarks on Dr Tholuck's Exposition of St Paul's Epistle to the Romans*, E, 1838), with John Brown of Edinburgh* over payment of the city's annuity tax (see his *The Duty of Paying Tribute Enforced*, E, 1838), and with the North British Railway Company over its decision to run trains on Sunday (see his *Desecration of Sabbath by Edinburgh and Glasgow Railway*, E, 1842). His most protracted and celebrated conflict was with the British and Foreign Bible Society over its policy of including the Apocrypha in the Bibles it circulated in RC countries (see his *Review of the Conduct of the British and Foreign Bible Society*, E, 1825; *A Second Review of the Conduct of the Directors of the British and Foreign Bible Society*, E, 1826; *Summary View of the Conduct of the British and Foreign Bible Society*, L, 1831. See Apocrypha Controversy).

Haldane was not a merely academic polemicist. In his championship of evangelical Calvinism, at Geneva and Montauban in 1816–19 against the rationalism of the Vénérable Compagnie des Pasteurs, he provided an important stimulus to the nineteenth-century revival of continental Reformed Protestantism. Frederic Monod, Cesar Malan and Merle d'Aubigné – all notable figures in the revitalized evangelical movement in France and Switzerland – traced their conversion to the influence of Haldane.

By virtue of his wealth and talents, Haldane occupied a pivotal position in the revival of evangelical Calvinism within Scotland. He promoted the spread of the movement, encouraged the active participation of the laity,* and gave a new lease of life to the Congregationalist and Baptist churches.

Revival of Religion on the Continent (n.p., n.d.); *Permanent Obligation to observe the Sabbath Day* (E, 1842).

A. Haldane, *The Lives of Robert Haldane of Airthrey, and of his brother, James Alexander Haldane* (L, 1852); J. A. L. Haldane, *The Haldanes of Gleneagles* (E, 1929); *DNB* XXIV, 14–15; A. L. Drummond, 'Robert Haldane at Geneva (1816–17)', *RSCHS* 9 (1947), 69–82; T. Stunt, 'Geneva and British Evangelicals in the Early Nineteenth Century', *JEH* 32 (1981), 35–46; W. Landels, *The Haldanes* (L, 1854); D. MacGregor, 'The Haldanes', in

HALDANE, ROBERT

W. Hanna (ed.), *Essays by Ministers of the Free Church of Scotland* (E, 1858), 113–47.

D. W. Lovegrove

Haldane, Robert (1772–1854), CofS divine. Son of a Scottish farmer, after study at Glasgow University he became a private tutor. Licensed to preach in 1797 by the Presbytery of Auchterarder he served his church at Drumelzier, near Peebles, 1806–9, when he resigned to become Professor of Mathematics at the University of St Andrews. In 1820 he was appointed to the pastoral charge of St Andrews, succeeding Principal George Hill.* Haldane also served as Principal of St Mary's College and Professor of Divinity. He was Moderator of the General Assembly of the CofS in 1827. Despite close associations with dissenters in his early years, he remained with the Est.C at the Disruption* in 1843. He was a popular preacher, an evangelical theologian, a competent teacher, and a man of scientific learning, for which he was made a Fellow of the Royal Society of Edinburgh. He received St Andrews' DD in 1815.

DNB XXIV, 15–16; *FES* I, 269, VII, 423.

D. B. Calhoun

Haliburton, George (1616–65), Bishop of Dunkeld. Son of the CofS minister of Gleniala, Forfarshire, he graduated MA from King's College, Aberdeen, in 1636, and was licensed by the Presbytery of Meigle (Perthshire). He served as chaplain to the Scottish Covenanting army 1640–1 (see Covenanters); in 1642 he was ordained to Menmuir, Forfarshire; in 1644 he moved to Perth, second charge. He was deposed from the ministry in 1644 for conversing, eating and drinking with James Graham,* Earl of Montrose, but was reinstated in 1645 by the General Assembly on his repentance. In 1651 he was bound to silence by the English garrison at Perth for having preached in favour of Charles II.*

At the Restoration,* Haliburton was made Bishop of Dunkeld, in Perthshire, and enforced Charles II's ecclesiastical policy with great vigour. His Presbyterian opponents charged him with insincerity, as he had previously been an ardent Covenanter.

DNB XXIV, 42; *FES* VII, 339–40.

N. R. Needham

Haliburton, George (1628–1715), Bishop of Brechin and of Aberdeen. Born at Collace, Perthshire, he graduated MA from St Andrews University in 1646, and was ordained to Coupar-Angus in 1648. In 1650 he was suspended for Episcopalian* sympathies, but reinstated in 1652. The Restoration* brought him into favour; he became archdeacon of Dunkeld in 1664, Bishop of Brechin in 1678, and Bishop of Aberdeen and Chancellor of King's College, Aberdeen, in 1682. He received a DD from St Andrews in 1673. In 1689 he was forced into retirement on his estate at Dunhead, Coupar-Angus, but he illegally conducted Episcopalian services 1698–1710 at Halton of Newtyle in opposition to the Presbyterian appointee.

HALL, ROBERT

Dowden 403; *FES* VII, 332; *DNB* XXIV, 42–3.

N. R. Needham

Hall, Archibald (1736–78), Associate Synod* minister and writer. Born at Marfield, Penicuik, in Midlothian, he was taught Latin, Greek and Hebrew by John Brown of Haddington.* He studied mathematics, logic and philosophy at Edinburgh University, and then theology under James Fisher* of Glasgow. Licensed to preach in 1758, he was ordained to the Associate congregation in Torpichen, West Lothian. In 1765 he moved to the Associate congregation in Wall Street, London, where he exercised a widely influential evangelical ministry. He was, however, dogged by asthmatic illness, which culminated in his early death. His writings were highly regarded for their lucidity, vigour, good sense and doctrinal soundness.

Gospel-Worship (2 vols, E, 1770); *A Treatise on the Faith and Influence of the Gospel* (E, 1803; ²G, 1831, with introductory essay by Thomas Chalmers*); *An Humble Attempt to Exhibit a Scriptural View of the Constitution, Discipline and Fellowship of the Gospel-church* (L, 1795); *An Appeal to the Public wherein the Nature and Reasons of Covenanting are Explained* (E, 1769); *An Impartial Survey of the Religious Clause in some Burgess Oaths* (E, 1771).

Memoir prefixed to his *The Life of Faith Exhibited* (E, 1828); J. M'Kerrow, *History of the Secession Church* (G, 1841), 872–4; *DNB* XXIV, 56.

N. R. Needham

Hall, James (1755–1826), USec. minister. Born at Cathcart, near Glasgow, he attended Glasgow University, and then studied theology under John Brown* of Haddington. In 1777 he was ordained to the Associate Synod* congregation at Cumnock, Ayrshire, moving in 1786 to the Rose Street congregation in Edinburgh. He and most of his church moved to new premises in Broughton Place in 1821.

Hall was an eloquent and popular preacher, a masterly Church-court debater, and a leading progressive in the Old Light/New Light* controversy. He chaired the committee which effected the union of 1820 between New Light Burghers and Antiburghers, forming the USec.C. He received a DD from Columba College, New York, in 1812.

DNB XXIV, 68; Small I, 437–8.

N. R. Needham

Hall, Robert (1764–1831), Baptist* minister. The son of a scholarly Baptist minister at Arnesty, Leicestershire, he attended Bristol Baptist Academy (1778–81) and, as a Ward scholar, King's College, Aberdeen (1781–5), where his academic career was brilliant. He studied under the leading Moderate,* Alexander Gerard,* and formed a lifelong friendship with the Scottish philosopher (Sir) James Mackintosh (*DNB* XXXV, 173–7). In 1817 Marischal College, Aberdeen, awarded him a DD, but he declined to use the title. As Assistant Minister of Broadmead Baptist Church, Bristol (1784–91) his views broadened towards rationalism, but

HALYBURTON, THOMAS

in ministries at Cambridge (1791-1806), Harvey Lane, Leicester (1807-25), and Broadmead again (1826-31) he was a powerful evangelical preacher. His essay *On Terms of Communion* (Leicester, 1815) was influential in persuading Baptists to admit to Communion those not baptized as believers. Of his many published sermons, *Modern Infidelity Considered* (C, 1800) was the most widely circulated.

O. Gregory, 'A Brief Memoir' in O. Gregory (ed.), *The Works of Robert Hall, A.M.*, 6 vols (L, 1832); J. W. Greene, *Biographical Recollections of the Rev. Robert Hall, A.M.* (L, 1833); *DNB* XXIV, 85-7.

D. W. Bebbington

Halyburton, Thomas (1674-1712), Professor of Divinity in the University of St Andrews. The son of a minister deprived in 1662 (and denounced in 1676 by the Privy Council for keeping conventicles* [see *FES* IV, 193]), Halyburton was educated in Rotterdam, where his mother had fled to escape persecution after his father's death, and St Andrews (MA, 1696). He was ordained to Ceres, Fife, in 1700 and admitted Professor of Divinity at St Andrews in 1710, where he was colleague to Principal James Hadow.*

Halyburton's reputation rests chiefly on his *Memoirs of the Life...* (E, 1714; often reprinted) which, like all his works, was published posthumously. Largely taken from his private papers, not intended for publication, the *Memoirs* is a spiritual autobiography, detailing his thoughts and struggles. It had wide influence throughout Scotland, England (where it was printed with a warm recommendation by Isaac Watts) and America.

His *Natural Religion Insufficient, and Reveal'd Necessary... or, A Rational Enquiry into the Principles of the modern Deists* (E, 1714) was his *magnum opus*. Tempted by deism* in his younger years, Halyburton wrote against the English deists, particularly George Herbert. Long considered a standard work of apologetics,* it went through a number of editions over the next hundred years. John Newton said he would not part with it 'for its weight in gold' and termed it 'a masterpiece'. He also highly commended the essay on faith which was printed along with it.

Halyburton's doctrine as a whole is warmly evangelical; he expressly rejected the legalism of Richard Baxter, Daniel Williams and late seventeenth-century English Presbyterianism. His sermons were heart-searching and intensely practical (*The Great Concern of Salvation*, E, 1721; *Five Sermons Preached before and after the Lord's Supper*, E, 1721; *Other Five Sermons...*, E, 1723).

FES VII, 429; *DNB* XXIV, 129-30; the edition of *The Works...* by R. Burns (G, 1837) is heavily edited.

D. C. Lachman

Hamilton, Alexander (1663-1738), evangelical CofS minister. While a student at Edinburgh he removed James Guthrie's* head from Netherbow Port. Ordained to Ecclesmachan, W. Lothian (1694-1700), he ministered thereafter at Airth,

HAMILTON, JAMES

near Stirling (1700-25), and East Church, Stirling (1725 to his death). He was close to several of the Marrow* brethren and the Erskines:* Ebenezer supported his protest at the settlement of a minister in St Ninian's, Stirling, against the popular will (*The Testimony and Contendings...*, E, 1736), and Ralph composed a funeral poem (in *An Elegiack Poem...*, E, 1739, 13-22). With James Hog* and others Hamilton was summoned before the General Assembly's new Committee on Purity of Doctrine in 1720 to answer for statements in *A Short Catechism, Concerning the Three Special Divine Covenants...* (E, 1714). After several meetings he was discharged. He did not vote in the 1722 Assembly's decision to admonish the Marrow brethren.

FES IV, 321; D. C. Lachman, *The Marrow Controversy 1718-1723* (E, 1988), esp. 148-56, 259-67, 493 (for MSS at New College, Edinburgh).

D. F. Wright

Hamilton, Archibald (*d*.1596), Counter-Reformation RC. One of the Hamiltons of Orbiston (Bothwell, Lanarkshire), after education in France he entered St Andrews University in 1553, and in 1558 was appointed a regent there. A frequent office-bearer thereafter, he was Dean of the Faculty of Arts in 1566 and was described as Bachelor in Divinity in 1569. He was recommended for ministry in the Kirk and in 1572 was an elder. In summer 1572 he publicly opposed John Knox,* whose sermons had stigmatized the Hamiltons as murderers. His protest raised the wider issue of the place of academic institutions in the Kirk.

He is last recorded at St Andrews in November 1576. Embracing RCism, he published at Paris in 1577 *De confusione Calvinianae sectae* (*On the Confusion of the Calvinist Sect*). Thomas Smeaton,* urged by Andrew Melville,* wrote a reply in 1579, countered by Hamilton with *Calvinianae confusionis demonstratio* (*Demonstration of Calvinist Confusion*; Paris, 1581).

In the early 1580s he was in France, being described as a priest and *candidus* in theology. He subsequently went to Rome, where he was involved in Counter-Reformation* plans until his death on 30 January, 1596 (T. M'Crie, *Life of Andrew Melville*, various edns, App. VI).

A. I. Dunlop (ed.), *Acta Facultatis Artium Universitatis Sanctiandree* (SHS, E, 1964); Knox, *Works* VI; J. Durkan, 'James, Third Earl of Arran: The Hidden Years', *SHR* 65 (1986), 154-7.

M. Dilworth

Hamilton, James (*c*.1516-75), second Earl of Arran and first Duke of Châtelherault, Governor of Scotland. Following his appointment as Governor in 1543, Arran briefly flirted with Lutheran* reform, allowing, for example, vernacular Bible reading, and an English marriage alliance for the infant Mary, Queen of Scots.* Under pressure from Cardinal Beaton* he dramatically reversed these policies, precipitating war with England

(Henry VIII's 'Rough Wooing'). After his disastrous defeat at the Battle of Pinkie in September 1547, Arran was increasingly forced to accept French clientage. In 1554 he finally resigned office in exchange for a French duchy and pension. He re-emerged as the nominal leader of the Lords of the Congregation* in 1559. Although disgraced by Queen Mary in 1562 and exiled in 1566–9, Châtelherault helped lead the Marian party during the civil war, but made his peace with James VI's* government at the Pacification of Perth on 23 February 1573.

DNB, XXIV, 167–70; G. Donaldson, *Scotland: James V–James VII* (E, 1965), 63–166; M. Sanderson, *Cardinal of Scotland* (E, 1986); G. Donaldson, *All the Queen's Men* (L, 1983).

K. M. Brown

Hamilton, James (1537/8–1609), 3rd Earl of Arran (from 1549) and Protestant leader. The eldest son of the 2nd Earl (Châtelherault; *see* Hamilton, James, *d*.1575), he proved 'a convenient pawn for everybody from his youngest days' (Durkan). He was held hostage by Cardinal David Beaton,* then by Beaton's assassins in St Andrews Castle and from 1548 in France by Henry II. He probably became a Protestant there in the early 1550s (he helped found a Protestant congregation at Châtelherault) before escaping and returning to Scotland in 1559. He joined the Lords of the Congregation* and provoked his father to do likewise. He subscribed the *FBD** and was prominent in the Protestants' military campaigns. He was proposed for the hand of Elizabeth I* but was refused, and sued unsuccessfully for the hand of Mary Queen of Scots.* His machinations towards Mary in 1562 caused him to be declared insane, and he was henceforth confined first at Edinburgh Castle and then at Craignethan Castle, Lanarkshire.

DNB XXIV, 173–6; Knox, *History*; R. K. Hannay, 'The Earl of Arran and Queen Mary', *SHR* 18 (1921), 258–76; J. Durkan, 'James, Third Earl of Arran: The Hidden Years', *SHR* 65 (1986), 154–66.

D. F. Wright

Hamilton, James (*d*.1580), Bishop of Argyll (1553–80). He was an illegitimate son of James, first Earl of Arran, and half brother to his namesake,* the second Earl. He was probably a St Andrews graduate of 1540. He was presented to various benefices. He unsuccessfully sought Paisley Abbey when his brother, John,* was promoted to the see of Dunkeld, but gained the deanery of Brechin *c*.1545 and took his seat on the Privy Council in 1547. Nominated by the Crown, but rejected by the Pope, for the archbishopric of Glasgow in 1547, he became parson of Erskine (Renfrewshire) in 1549 and subdean of Glasgow in 1550. He sat in the Church's reforming provincial council* of 1549, was legitimized in 1551, and became Bishop elect of Argyll in 1553. He attended the Reformation Parliament* of 1560 and was accounted 'a good protestant', but although conforming to the Reformation,* he undertook no known ministry in the Reformed Church. In 1563, he leased the patrimony of the bishopric of Argyll and abbacy of Saddell (Kintyre), which he also held, to John Carswell,* the Reformed superintendent* of Argyll.

Early Records of the University of St Andrews, ed. J. M. Anderson (E, 1926), 140, 143, 242; *Register of the Privy Seal of Scotland*, ed. M. Livingstone *et al.* (E, 1908–82), III, nos. 621, 2410, 2511; IV, nos. 498, 921–2, 1404, 1548; *Calendar of Scottish Papers*, ed. W. K. Boyd *et al.* (E, 1898–1969), I, nos. 879, 891; *FESMA*, 27, 45, 149, 168; J. Kirk, *Patterns of Reform* (E, 1989); R. Keith, *Historical Catalogue of the Scottish Bishops*, ed. M. Russel (E, 1824), 289–90; Dowden, 391.

J. Kirk

Hamilton, James (1814–67), Presbyterian minister of the National Scotch Church, London, and prolific author. Born at Paisley, Renfrewshire, he graduated MA from Glasgow University in 1835, moved to Edinburgh to attend Thomas Chalmers' theology lectures, and was licensed by Edinburgh Presbytery in 1838. In 1841 he became minister of the National Scotch Church, Regent Square, London (built by Edward Irving*), which he pastored until his death. He zealously supported the FC in the Disruption* helping to popularize their cause in England. In 1849 he became editor of the *Presbyterian Messenger*, and in 1864 of *Evangelical Christendom*, the periodical of the Evangelical Alliance.* His literary output was extensive, writing and compiling many volumes. These included: *The Royal Preacher: Lectures on Ecclesiastes* (L, 1851); *A Memoir of Lady Colquhoun* (L, 1849); *Our Christian Classics*, 4 vols (ed., L, 1857–9); *Excelsior: Helps to Progress in Religion, Science and Literature*, 6 vols (L, 1854). His *Works* were published posthumously in six volumes (L, 1869–73). He wrote the botanical articles in Patrick Fairbairn's* *Imperial Biblical Dictionary* (L, 1866), and was particularly involved in the production of the *Book of Psalms and Hymns*, adopted after Hamilton's death by British Presbyterian churches.

Hamilton received a DD from the College of New Jersey (*see* Princeton Theological Seminary) in 1848.

The Pearl of Parables (L, 1868); *Life and Remains of the late Rev. William Hamilton*, 2 vols (G, 1836); *Moses the Man of God* (L, 1870); *China and the Chinese Mission* (L, 1847); *Memoir and Remains of J. D. Burns* (L, 1869).

W. Arnot, *Life of James Hamilton* (L, 1870); R. Naismith, *Memoir of the Rev. James Hamilton* (L, 1896); *FES* I, 187; *DNB* XXIV, 188.

N. R. Needham

Hamilton, John (*c*.1511–71), RC Archbishop of St Andrews. He was an illegitimate son of James, first Earl of Arran, and as monk of Kilwinning (*see* Tironensians) was provided in 1525 to the abbacy of Paisley* (*see* Cluniacs) which he, as a minor, was

HAMILTON, JOHN

to hold *in commendam* until he reached the age of twenty-two. In 1528, he entered St Leonard's College, St Andrews, acquired the parsonage of Innerwick (E. Lothian), took his seat in Parliament in 1535, and by 1541 visited France, where he was said to sympathize with Protestant opinions. Governor Arran, his half-brother (*see* Hamilton, James, *d*.1575), secured his appointment as Keeper of the Privy Seal and Treasurer of the Kingdom in 1543. In 1546 he exchanged his monastic habit for episcopal garb (though still in minor orders) with his consecration to the bishopric of Dunkeld, and was elected an extraordinary senator of the College of Justice. He retained Paisley, whose patrimony he dilapidated, until 1553, when he resigned the abbacy, the fruits being reserved to him for life. In 1545 he took his seat as a Privy Councillor, and in 1547 was provided to the archbishopric of St Andrews. He was also created papal legate *a latere*. In 1551 he was given a coadjutor on account of ill-health. Between 1549 and 1559, he presided over a series of reforming provincial councils* of the Scottish Church, and issued by his authority in 1552 a *Catechism* (largely written by Richard Marshall, an English Dominican at St Mary's College*) which appeared to make concessions to Protestant opinion: it spoke of the invisible Church and even of general councils but was silent on the papacy and hierarchy; it stressed justification by faith (seemingly at the expense of works) and denied that the mass itself was a sacrifice; at the same time, it contained much which was indisputably RC: transubstantiation, the seven sacraments, prayers for the dead, purgatory and a belief that the authority of Scripture derives from the authority of the Church. In August 1559 the Archbishop, it was said, candidly admitted his lack of practice in preaching.

At the Reformation Parliament* in 1560, Hamilton would neither approve nor utterly condemn the Protestant (Scots) Confession* of Faith. In October 1560, Arran considered the Archbishop to have given up the mass, received the common prayers and 'is like to become a good protestant', but with the return home of Queen Mary,* Hamilton celebrated mass at Easter 1562, and again in 1563, for which he was warded, and he responded to the letter of the papal envoy, Nicholas de Gouda. In 1564, he distributed ashes on Ash Wednesday, yet was anxious to speak to Knox,* and sent him a message recognizing the need for reformation in doctrine. Not only did he retain a legal title to his see, Hamilton intermittently exercised a consistorial jurisdiction, which Mary formally recognized in December 1566. A staunch supporter of Queen Mary, Hamilton baptized Prince James by Roman rites in December 1566, but was ready to attend Mary's marriage to Bothwell by Protestant rites in May 1567. While the Pope and RCs commended his constancy in religion, others considered him in August 1567 (after Mary's deposition) as 'a conformable man both in apparel and outward orders of religion', and in 1568 it was thought he 'would not be far' from approving conformity with the CofE. He himself explained his behaviour earlier

HAMILTON, PATRICK

in 1563 in his reported remark that he 'would change his religion for the duke's sake', for the welfare, that is, of his half-brother, then Duke of Châtelherault, and the house of Hamilton. He supported Mary's cause in the civil war, connived at the Regent Moray's murder in 1570, and he himself was hanged at Stirling in April 1571 for treason in denying King James' authority.

Calendar of Scottish Papers, ed. J. Bain (E, 1898–1900), I–II; Knox, *Works*; Calderwood; Spottiswoode; *Diurnal of Remarkable Occurrents*, ed. T. Thomson (E, 1833); J. Herkless and R. K. Hannay, *The Archbishops of St Andrews* (E, 1907–15), V; *Statutes of the Scottish Church*, ed. D. Patrick (E, 1907), 84–191; *The Catechism set forth by Archbishop Hamilton*, ed. A. F. Mitchell (E, 1882); J. C. Lees, *The Abbey of Paisley* (Paisley, 1878), 186–205 and appendix; *FESMA*, 99–100, 298–9; Dowden, 43–4, 88–91; *DNB* XXIV, 190–2; D. B. MacDonald, 'The Struggle to Reform: John Hamilton and His Kirk' (Ph.D, W. Virginia Univ., Morgantown, 1983).

J. Kirk

Hamilton, John (*c*.1540–1610), anti-Protestant writer. He was apparently born at Drumcairn (Perthshire). After graduating from St Andrews (1555) he studied for some years at Paris before being appointed regent in St Mary's College, St Andrews (1569). He embraced RCism (after being made an elder in the Kirk) and returned to Paris (1575) where he taught in different colleges in succession. His compendium on logic (1580) reflected the teaching of John Rutherford.* He was attacked by the Protestant, William Fowler (*fl*.1603; *DNB* XX, 89), and was a stormy partisan of the Catholic League. In 1584 he was elected Rector of Paris University, but on the arrival of Henry IV at Paris he fled to Flanders. *A Facile Traictise*... dedicated to James VI, was published at Louvain (1600). On entering Scotland with John Hay,* he was captured and sent to the Tower of London (1608), where 'the archpriest of Scotland' was interviewed by his fellow-prisoner, Andrew Melville.* He died in prison.

DNB XXIV, 195–6; J. Lee, *Lectures on the History of the Church of Scotland* (E, 1860); Paris University MS records; *A Facile Traictise*..., ed. T. G. Law, *Catholic Tractates of the Sixteenth Century* (*STS* 45, E, 1901).

J. Durkan

Hamilton, Patrick (1504(?)–28), the first martyr* of the Scottish Reformation.* Born possibly at Stanehouse, near Glasgow, he was the second son of Sir Patrick Hamilton of Kincavel and Stanehouse, the half-brother of the Earl of Arran, and of Catherine Stewart, the daughter of Alexander, Duke of Albany, the second son of James II. About 1517 he was appointed titular abbot of Fearn in Ross-shire, and possibly the same year went to the University of Paris, being registered a *Magister* in 1520. Here he came into contact with the teaching of Erasmus, and almost certainly the writings of

Martin Luther*. He may have studied at Louvain, but returned to Scotland, being incorporated into the University of St Andrews in 1523. Here, he was almost certainly taught by John Major,* who had been brought to St Andrews by James Beaton.* He seems to have excelled at choral music, and around 1526 probably became a priest. About the same time he first openly showed his support for the now banned teaching of Luther. Beaton ordered an inquiry into him in 1527, and early that year, Hamilton left Scotland for Germany. He visited Wittenberg and Marburg, where he came under the influence of Francis Lambert. With Lambert's encouragement, he wrote his only theological work, a set of common-places translated into English by John Frith and known as *'Patrick's Places'* (first published as *Dyvers frutful gatheriges of scrypture*..., L, ?1532). These short theses show a strongly Lutheran slant, with an emphasis upon justification by faith in Christ alone.

After only six months in Germany he returned to Scotland, to Kincavel near Linlithgow, where he began to preach the doctrines of the Reformation. (According to Alesius,* at this time he also married, becoming the father of a daughter, Isobel.) His teachings and family connections made him a considerable threat, and Beaton invited him to St Andrews in January 1528. He was examined, and then allowed to go free: he had an opportunity either to escape or to incriminate himself further. Here he met Alexander Alesius, who set out to refute him, but was himself refuted and convinced. After a month, he was again summoned before Beaton on a charge of heresy. He was swiftly found guilty and was burned at the stake on 29 February 1528. Many throughout Scotland were led by his cruel death – he was roasted rather than simply burned alive – to inquire why he had been condemned and some came to accept his teachings. Knox (I, 42) records a friend of Beaton as advising him against further public burnings, 'for the reik of Maister Patrik Hammyltoun hes infected as many as it blew upoun'.

Patrick's Places in Knox, *History* II, 219–29, and ed. R. Haas, 'Franz Lambert und Patrick Hamilton ...' (PhD, University of Marburg, 1973); *DNB* XXIV, 201–3; Peter Lorimer, *Patrick Hamilton, the first Preacher and Martyr of the Scottish Reformation* (E, 1857); Calderwood I, 73–86; I. R. Torrance, 'Patrick Hamilton and John Knox: A Study in the Doctrine of Justification by Faith', *ARG* 65 (1974), 171–84.

I. R. Torrance

Hamilton, William (1669–1732), Professor of Divinity at Edinburgh (1709–32), briefly Principal (1730–2), and teacher of many Moderate* divines. The son of Gavin Hamilton of Airdrie, a staunch Covenanter,* and baptized at an impressionable age at a Covenanting conventicle,* he nonetheless represents the transition from the religious wars of the seventeenth century to the verbal conflicts of the eighteenth. Ordained to Cramond, near Edinburgh, in 1694, he demitted on assuming the chair, which he resigned in 1732 to take up the charge of New North (West St Giles) for the last months of his life.

Five times Moderator between 1712 and 1730, chaplain to George II and highly esteemed by generations of students, he had great influence in the CofS. His material contribution to emergent Moderatism* remains an open question.

James Oswald* said of him, 'He taught us moderation and a liberal manner of thinking upon all subjects.' His teaching was important not in substance but in manner. It seems unlikely that it was heretical in content, though his silence on certain topics may have had more significance than a desire to set his students thinking. Robert Wodrow* expressed this suspicion: 'By severalls who knou him well, it's thought he is departed from the Calvinisticall doctrine and the ordinary doctrine taught in this Church, though he hath the wisdom to keep himself in the clouds' (*Analecta*, E, 1843, 139).

He was much involved in the controversies surrounding John Glas* and John Simson.* Hamilton probably had little sympathy with Glas's views, but he had no time for those who sought to drive this devout man from the Church. He was, however, outvoted in an attempt to reverse Glas's deposition. In the Simson case, Hamilton on two occasions urged the inadequacy of the proof, eventually supporting suspension, which would silence Simson as effectively as deposition. Although Thomas Boston* was unhappy with Hamilton's procedure, he was prevailed upon not to record his dissent, out of esteem for Hamilton as a scholar. In conversation with Boston in 1729, Hamilton agreed with the *Marrow*'s* use of 'deed of gift and grant'.

Hamilton's efforts to mitigate the effects of patronage* led to the passing of the Act anent Planting of Vacant Churches by the General Assembly of 1732. This was designed to guide presbyteries when the right of presentation devolved on them on the failure of the patron to act, but because it gave no effective voice to the people it sparked off the (original) Secession* of 1733.

The Truth and Excellency of the Christian Religion (E, 1732).

FES I, 146; J. Warrick, *The Moderators of the Church of Scotland 1690–1740* (E, 1913), 240–57.

H. R. Sefton

Hamilton, William (1780–1835), CofS theological writer. Born at Stonehouse, Lanarkshire, and educated at Edinburgh University he was ordained to St Andrew's, Dundee (1807), before moving to Strathblane, near Dumbarton, in 1809. He ministered there until his death. He was a scholarly Evangelical, a caring pastor, a temperance* reformer and a prolific writer. Two sons became ministers, and his daughter, Jane, married James Walker* of Carnwath.

His published works include: *The Establishment of the Law by the Gospel* (E, 1820); *A Dissertation on Election* (G, 1824); *Defence of the Second Advent* (L, 1828); *The Mourner in Sion Comforted* (G, 1828).

HAMILTON, (SIR) WILLIAM

FES III, 368; *DNB* XXIV, 227; James Hamilton (son), *Life and Remains of the late Rev. William Hamilton, D.D.*, 2 vols (G, 1836).

J. D. MacMillan

Hamilton, (Sir) William (1788–1856), distinguished Professor of Philosophy in Edinburgh University and one of the last major representatives of Scottish Realism.* Hamilton was born in Glasgow, son of a medical professor. He entered the University of Glasgow at age fifteen and in 1807 won a scholarship to Balliol College, Oxford, where he excelled in Greek and Latin philosophy, particularly the study of Aristotle and his *Organon*. He left Oxford after 1810 (BA and MA). Accepted as an advocate by the Scottish bar in 1813, he lived in Edinburgh for the rest of his life, inheriting a baronetcy in 1816. He visited Germany in 1817 and 1820 and became a student of its language and contemporary philosophy. In 1821 he was elected Professor of Civil History in Edinburgh University, a largely nominal post. His *Edinburgh Review* articles on Victor Cousin's Philosophy, 'The Philosophy of Perception', 'Logic' and 'The Study of Mathematics', established his reputation in 1829. They exhibited an unusual acquaintance for that period with continental philosophy. Hamilton was appointed Professor of Logic and Metaphysics in Edinburgh University in 1836, where he lectured to large classes. He suffered a stroke in 1844, but continued as Professor (with the help of assistants) and also did much writing, including editing and commenting on the works of his predecessors, Thomas Reid (*see* Scottish Realism) and Dugald Stewart.*

Hamilton followed traditional Scottish Realism, which taught that the mind can perceive external objects immediately and that ordinary human experience demonstrates the operation of general principles of common sense (or 'original and natural judgments'), such as the existence of external objects, the reality of a conscious mind, the validity of cause and effect, the difference between the knower and the known and the obligations of morality. He held that one had to use these principles even to argue against them, as did, for instance, David Hume* sceptically and Berkeley idealistically. Yet he was untraditional in trying to combine Kant's theory of the mind imposing forms on phenomena with intuitive *a posteriori* perception of objects. He denied the possibility of direct knowledge of the infinite. J. S. Mill's *An Examination of Sir William Hamilton's Philosophy* (L, 1865) greatly reduced his influence, though James Clark Maxwell* developed aspects of his thought, as did H. L. Mansel in his Bampton Lectures on *The Limits of Religious Thought* (L, 1858).

Lectures on Metaphysics and Logic, 4 vols (ed. H. L. Mansel and J. Veitch; E, 1859–60, ²1861–6).

DNB XXIV, 227–32; J. Veitch, *Sir William Hamilton: The Man and his Philosophy* (E, 1883); W. H. S. Monck, *Sir William Hamilton* (L, 1881).

D. F. Kelly

HARDIE, JAMES KEIR

Hanna, William (1808–82), FC minister and writer. Born in Belfast, the son of a Church of Ireland minister, he was educated at Glasgow and Edinburgh Universities, studying theology under Thomas Chalmers* at the latter. He became minister of the CofS congregation at East Kilbride, Lanark, in 1833, and moved to Skirling, Peebles, in 1837. At the Disruption* he joined the FC, and in 1850 became collegiate minister of Free St John's, Edinburgh, where his colleague was Thomas Guthrie.* He remained here until his retirement from active ministry in 1866.

Hanna had married Thomas Chalmers' daughter Anne in 1836, and on Chalmers' death in 1847 the task of writing his authorized biography was committed to him – *Memoirs of the Life and Writings of Thomas Chalmers* (4 vols, E, 1849–52). Hanna also edited Chalmers' *Select Works* (12 vols, E, 1854–79) and *Posthumous Works* (9 vols, E, 1847–9), and *A Selection from the Correspondence of the late Thomas Chalmers* (E, 1853). It was as a reward for his work in perpetuating Chalmers' memory that Hanna was awarded an LLD from Glasgow University.

Later in life Hanna edited the *Letters of Thomas Erskine of Linlathen* (2 vols, E, 1877 – *see* Erskine, Thomas), producing in effect a biography of the man. His evident sympathy with the liberal Erskine reveals the theological breadth of Hanna's own mature outlook.

Hanna received a DD from Edinburgh University in 1864.

Our Lord's Life on Earth (L, 1882); *Wycliffe and the Huguenots* (E, 1860); *The Resurrection of the Dead* (E, 1872).

AFCS I, 181; *DNB* XXIV, 301–2; *FES* III, 258–9.

N. R. Needham

Hardie, James Keir (1856–1915), Labour Party pioneer. Born an illegitimate son at Legbrannock, Lanarkshire, he was raised in circumstances of great poverty. He began work as a message boy at the age of eight and went down the pit at ten, where he worked till he was twenty-two. During this period he went to night school and, despite the committed atheism of his parents, became a devout Christian and active temperance* campaigner. He also began to organize a union among the miners; it cost him and his two brothers their jobs and led the Scottish mine owners to blacklist him. He never worked in the pit again after 1878, but began a new career as union organizer and journalist. In 1881 he moved to Cumnock, Ayrshire, which was to remain his home.

At this time he held himself to be a radical Liberal. However, the 1884 visit of the American Christian socialist, Henry George, led to a life-long socialist commitment. Through the columns of *Labour Leader* (which he founded) and by speeches across the country, he campaigned for real labour representation in Parliament and an end to the alliance of the Trades Union Congress (TUC) and the Liberals. In 1892 he was elected to Parliament for West

HARPER, JAMES

Ham, the first Labour MP, and the next year presided over the creation of the Independent Labour Party (ILP). His constant campaigning succeeded in 1899, when the TUC came together with the ILP to form the Labour Representation Council, which led in 1906 to the formation of the Parliamentary Labour Party with Hardie as leader of the twenty-nine members.

His health damaged in the pits, he was now an exhausted man. Yet he still campaigned vigorously, now on behalf of Indian self-government and civil rights for all in South Africa. The outbreak of the War in 1914 seemed to crush his spirit; neither socialism nor Christianity appeared able to check imperialist xenophobia.

Although Hardie was never a formal member of any congregation after a bitter dispute in the Cumnock Congregational Church in 1884, the gospel was always explicitly at the centre of his thought. He often criticized Churches and churchmen, but always for their failure to live out the faith.

E. Hughes, *Keir Hardie* (L, 1950); K. O. Morgan, *Keir Hardie: Radical and Socialist* (L, 1975); F. Reid, *Keir Hardie* (L, 1978).

A. C. Ross

Harper, James (1795–1879), leading UP divine. Born in Lanark, the son of an Associate Synod* minister, he attended Glasgow University 1810–13, and then the Associate Synod Divinity Hall in Selkirk. Licensed by Lanark Presbytery in 1818, in 1819 he was ordained to the Associate Synod congregation in North Leith, with which he was connected until his death. He and his congregation entered the USec.C in 1820, and in 1826 he became editor of the *Edinburgh Theological Magazine*, the USec.C's literary organ. In 1843 he was elected Professor of Pastoral Theology in the USec. Divinity Hall, and when Robert Balmer* died in 1844 Harper also took over the teaching of systematic theology.

Harper entered the UPC in 1847, and was appointed its Professor of Pastoral and Systematic Theology. He also became joint-editor of the *United Presbyterian Magazine*. In the period 1862–73 he was the acknowledged leader in the UPC of the movement for union with the FC. In 1876, when the UP Divinity Hall was reconstituted, he became Associate Professor (with John Cairns*) of Christian Apologetics and Systematic Theology, and Principal. His last contribution to his Church was to act as main architect of the 1879 Declaratory Act,* which aimed to broaden the frontiers of UP confessional Calvinism without revising the Westminster standards.

Harper wrote no books, and only a few pamphlets and reported speeches convey his mind to us today. But in his own day he stood second only to John Cairns in the esteem in which he was held in the UPC. Among his many talents – teacher, Church court debater, Liberal political activist – it was perhaps as a preacher that he excelled; Edward Irving* said of Harper that he 'approached nearer to the conception he had of the speeches of the ancient Greek orators, than anything else he had ever heard' (quoted A. Thomson, *Life of Principal Harper*, E, 1881, 40).

Harper was Moderator of the General Assemblies of the USec.C in 1840 and the UPC in 1860. He received a DD from Jefferson College, USA, in 1843.

The Difficulties of the Union Question (E, 1868); *Roman Catholic Endowment: a Correspondence between the Right Hon. the Lord Advocate and James Harper* (E, 1857); *The Mass, Transubstantiation, Adoration of the Host* (E, 1851); *The Voluntary Principle viewed in its relation to the Missionary Enterprise* (Liverpool, 1840); *The Credulity of Unbelief* (E, 1869); *Jesus Christ the only Foundation of the Church* (E, 1822).

DNB XXIV, 426–7; Small I, 505.

N. R. Needham

Harris, Margaret, Lectures on Religion, an annual series delivered in the University of Dundee. It was instituted unnamed in 1965 in the then Queen's College, Dundee, part of St Andrews University, the first lecturer being Alan Richardson, *Religion in Contemporary Debate* (L, 1966), but from 1974 was named after Miss Margaret Harris (1815–94), a notable benefactress of what was then the independent University College, Dundee. Her estate built the University's chaplaincy centre (1973). The lectureship has been held by a distinguished succession, including Owen Chadwick ('Science and Religion in England, the Origins of the Conflict', 1966); F. C. Copleston (cf. *Religion and Philosophy*, Dublin, 1974); Bryan R. Wilson (cf. *Magic and the Millennium*, L, 1973); John McIntyre (cf. *Faith, Theology and Imagination*, E, 1987); John Polkinghorne, *Science and Creation, The Search for Understanding* (L, 1988); and A. F. Walls, 'Two Centuries of Religion in Africa' (1989).

Full list in *University of Dundee Calendar* from 1978–9 issue on.

D. F. Wright

Hastie Lectures, a series given in the University of Glasgow for the encouragement of theological study among CofS ministers. The lectureship was founded by subscription in memory of William Hastie* (d.1903). The six trustees comprise the University Principal, the Dean of Divinity and the Professor of Divinity, and three elected often alternately by the Senatus and Glasgow Presbytery.

The first lecturer was Donald MacMillan (on whom see *FES* III, 419), *The Aberdeen Doctors* (L, 1909). Others worth particular note include A. J. Campbell, *Two Centuries of the Church of Scotland, 1707–1929* (L, 1930); W. McMillan, *The Worship of the Scottish Reformed Church* (L, 1931); G. S. Hendry, *God the Creator* (L, 1937); A. M. Hunter,* *Paul and His Predecessors* (L, 1940).

List of lecturers to date in *University of Glasgow Calendar 1976–77*, lxviii–lxix; names and some titles in *CofS Year Book* (annual), 1908–62.

D. F. Wright

Hastie, William (1842–1903), theological professor. He was born at Wanlockhead, graduated from Edinburgh (MA, 1867, BD, 1869), became a licentiate of the CofS in 1875, and was ordained to the Principalship of the CofS Institution at Calcutta in 1878. There he disagreed with the lady superintendent, Miss Pigot, and supported a letter from the wife of a colonel at Dum Dum encampment which accused her of immorality and other failings. This led to a libel case in 1883. Hastie was fined one anna, the smallest amount possible, and, on different grounds, deprived of his post. He appealed to General Assembly, speaking for eight hours; Pigot appealed to a higher court, which fined Hastie three thousand rupees and costs. Since he could not pay he was imprisoned in Calcutta for a month then discharged as a bankrupt. He returned to Scotland and after a flurry of lawsuits undertook literary hack work, translating learned works from various European languages and providing prefaces valuable for simplifying the arguments. It may be that his simplifications did not always do justice to those arguments, and the violence of his language all too often gave way to mere abuse. In 1875 he became Professor of Divinity at Glasgow University and pleased some, but not others, with his teaching. He also sued a Dutch professor; the circumstances suggest that Hastie had put his own views in the Dutchman's mouth. This strengthens the likelihood that the Calcutta scandals arose through Hastie persuading witnesses to assert things about which he himself remained silent. Some have considered Hastie an innocent victim of injustice; it is more realistic and more charitable to hold him not fully responsible for his actions.

The Theology of the Reformed Church in its Fundamental Principles (E, 1904).

D. MacMillan, *The Life of Professor Hastie* (E, 1926); G. White, 'William Hastie: Professor from Calcutta Gaol', *College Courant* 72 (1984), 26–9.

G. White

Hastings, Harry (d.1951), medical missionary. He was a prisoner of war in Germany, studied medicine at Edinburgh (MB, ChB 1922) and immediately on qualification was appointed to the CofS Calabar mission, Nigeria. After service at Itu he was appointed to Uburu hospital in 1924; he stayed there for 25 years. It had received only episodic medical direction since John Hitchcock* left in 1917, and no longer had much local impact. Under Hastings it became a place of almost legendary activity, due especially to his adoption of novoarsenobenzyl (NAB) to treat the local scourge of yaws, and his intensive campaigns of injection; to a network of leprosy settlements with clinics and dispensaries using hydnocarpus oil; and to his huge reputation as a surgeon. In 1928, the height of the anti-yaws campaigns, Uburu hospital (which a few years earlier faced abandonment) treated 60,401 outpatients. Hastings was known to perform as many as 36 operations in a day, and calculated that he conducted 10,000 major operations in all. He was usually the only professionally qualified person on his hospital staff; his wife (quite unqualified medically) was anaesthetist and assistant. Hastings established the supremacy locally of modern over traditional medicine, and undoubtedly contributed to the evangelization of the Cross River hinterland. In leprosy relief, he cooperated with and probably reinforced the local system of segregated leper camps – a less ambitious method, both medically and pastorally, than the leprosarium solution adopted by his colleague Andrew Macdonald* at Itu. Controversy long continued on their relative merits. Hastings (who was also Uburu's session clerk) was appointed OBE in 1945. In 1949, ill and worn out, he went on leave; he never recovered his health.

Minutes of CofS Foreign Mission Committee 22, 1950–51, no. 791; G. Johnston, *Of God and Maxim Guns* (Waterloo, Ontario, 1988), 196–206; D. M. McFarlan, *Calabar: the Church of Scotland and Mission founded 1846* (L, 1957²), 148–53; J. A. T. Beattie, *The River Highway* (E, n.d.), 48; M. Ross and N. Obini, *Presbyterian Joint Hospital Uburu 1913–1988* (Uburu, 1988).

A. F. Walls

Hastings, James (1852–1922), FC/UFC minister and theological editor. Born in Huntly, James was educated in Aberdeen at the Old Grammar School (c.1864–71), the University (MA Classics, 1876), and the FC College (from 1877). He held three charges – Kinneff FC (1884–98), Willison FC/UFC, Dundee (1898–1901), and St Cyrus UFC (1901–11) – and concurrently edited many significant theological works, almost all of which were published by T. & T. Clark of Edinburgh. He received honorary DD degrees from Aberdeen University in 1897 and Halifax University, Nova Scotia, in 1920, and was awarded the Dyke Acland medal for his work in popularizing biblical research in 1913. Retiring from the ministry in 1911, Hastings moved to Aberdeen, where he continued his editorial work until his death.

He conceived and was editor-in-chief of the following works: the *Expository Times* (founded 1889; *see* Periodicals, Religious); *Dictionary of the Bible*, 5 vols (E, 1898–1904); *Dictionary of Christ and the Gospels*, 2 vols (E, 1906–8); *Encyclopaedia of Religion and Ethics*, 13 vols (E, 1908–26); *Dictionary of the Bible*, 1 vol. edn (E, 1909); *Great Texts of the Bible*, 13 vols (E, 1910–26); *Greater Men and Women of the Bible*, 6 vols (E, 1913–16); *Dictionary of the Apostolic Church*, 2 vols (E, 1915–18); *Great Christian Doctrines*, 3 vols (E, 1915–22); *Sub Corona* (sermons preached by a variety of preachers at Aberdeen University Chapel) (E, 1915); *Children's Great Texts of the Bible*, 6 vols (E, 1920–1); *Speaker's Bible*, 36 vols (A, 1923–51), a posthumous publication prepared for press by Edward Hastings, his son.

James Hastings claimed that while he became an editor by choice, he was called to the ministry, and he conscientiously fulfilled that calling. Indeed, he viewed his editorial work not as a distracting addition to, but as an enriching extension of, his pastoral ministry. Among educated people he detected an increasing scepticism based on the perception that contemporary scholarship was undermining the fabric of Christian belief – as the authority of the Bible was eroded by higher criticism, and the uniqueness of Christ and his message challenged by comparative religious studies. Hastings contended that such scepticism was groundless. He saw moderate criticism as 'preparing the Bible for a renewed reign' (Robertson Nicoll's* phrase) by establishing the fundamentals of the faith on an unassailable footing. Further, believing that dimensions of truth were to be discerned in all world religions, he saw comparative studies not as diminishing Christ but as revealing him in his fullness. It was therefore his ambition to demonstrate that Christians had nothing to fear from academic research. He tried to mediate the results of scholarship to his own congregation, to his fellow-ministers, and through them to the Church at large, in such a way that the scholars would be clearly seen to be undergirding, not undermining, the faith. The wide acceptance which such views attained in the UK and USA during Hastings' lifetime was due in no small measure to the tireless commitment with which he edited his flood of works.

AFCS I, 182; *FUFCS* 390, 409; *DNB 1922–1930*, 409–10; J. A. H. Dempster, ' "Incomparable Encyclopaedist": the Life and Work of Dr James Hastings', *ExT* 100 (1988–9), 4–8; id., 'The Profitability of Progressive Theological Publishing ...' (PhD, University of Stirling, 1987), 525–85.

J. A. H. Dempster

Hay, Andrew (d.1593), minister of Renfrew (1560–93). The son of William Hay of Talla and brother of George,* he was a Glasgow graduate who studied Greek at Paris before becoming parson of Renfrew by 1556. He joined the Reformers at the Reformation* to serve as minister of Renfrew. His earlier training also equipped him to act as commissary of Hamilton in 1564, and, as an assiduous attender of assemblies, was frequently chosen by the General Assembly as its commissioner to conduct visitations. A supporter of James Stewart (d. 1570),* Earl of Moray, Hay was accused of complicity in the murder of Riccio in 1566. Described in 1574 as one 'who lyked never those bishopries', Hay supported Andrew Melville's* appointment as principal of Glasgow University, sided with the Presbyterians, and contributed to the drafting of the *Second Book of Discipline.* He remained a critic of the excommunicated Robert Montgomery,* minister of Stirling, who accepted the Crown's nomination in 1581 to the archbishopric of Glasgow. Twice Moderator of the General Assembly in March 1574 and October 1580, Hay was sentenced to be warded north of the Tay for his opposition to the 'antipresbyterian dictatorship' of Arran's (see Stewart, James, d.1596) administration in 1594. For much of the period between 1569 and 1586, he served as Rector of Glasgow University, was Dean of the Faculty of Arts in 1573 and sat as elder on Glasgow general Session. He was succeeded at Renfrew by his son John.

BUK; Calderwood; *SBD*, 47–51, 55, 109; J. Durkan and J. Kirk, *The University of Glasgow, 1451–1577* (G, 1977); *FES* III, 185.

J. Kirk

Hay, Edmund (c.1534–91), papal agent. He was a Hay of Megginch (Perthshire) and kinsman of the earls of Errol. Having graduated in arts at St Andrews* in 1553, he pursued an academic career there until c.1558. By 1562, however, he was a priest and bachelor of theology, living on the continent. In that year he went with the papal envoy, Nicholas of Gouda, to Scotland, where he acted as guide and interpreter and recruited some young men for the Jesuits.* Entering the Jesuits at Rome, he was in late 1564 appointed Rector of the prestigious Jesuit College in Paris. In the winter of 1566–7 he was again in Scotland, treating with Mary Queen of Scots* for the mission of a second papal envoy.

He was made superior of the French Jesuit province c.1568, was Rector 1574–81 of the Jesuit University at Pont-à-Mousson in Lorraine, then was Consultor of the French province. From 1585 to 1589 he was superior of the Jesuit mission in Scotland, where his activities were spiritual and not political. Recalled from Scotland, he ended his life at Rome as Assistant for France and Germany to the General of the Jesuits.

Catholic Encyclopedia VII, 157; J. H. Pollen (ed.), *Papal Negotiations with Mary Queen of Scots* (SHS, E, 1901); H. Chadwick, 'A Memoir of Fr Edmund Hay', *Archivum Historicum Societatis Iesu* 8 (1939), 66–85.

M. Dilworth

Hay, George (c.1530–88), minister of Rathven (Aberdeenshire) and Eddleston (Peeblesshire), whose benefices he held before conforming to the Reformation.* The son of William Hay of Talla and brother of Andrew,* as a youth he sided in 1544 with the pro-English Lennox rebellion, but after initial arts studies in Scotland, left for Paris where he enrolled, as a student from St Andrews diocese, in 1552. After studying Greek and 'eastern learning', which presumably included an acquaintance with Hebrew, Hay was directed to Rome to undertake litigation, and at the papal curia met John Row,* subsequently minister of Perth. His bad impression of Rome, which the Jesuit Edmund Hay* placed on record, seems to have lingered. After returning home, he not only conformed to the Reformation but undertook active service as minister. Considered by Knox* to be one of the 'principal ministers' at work in 1561, Hay agreed that Queen Mary should be denied her mass. When minister at Eddleston, he was employed by the General Assembly as one of its commissioners for visitation, first in Carrick (Ayrshire) in 1562 and then in the north-east. In 1562 he published a *Confutation* of Quintin Kennedy's* doctrines on the mass, after the abbot avoided a public disputation. By 1563 he was acting as chaplain to Moray (James Stewart, d. 1570*) and the Privy Council, and by 1564 was

HAY, GEORGE

described as 'minister of the court'. In his absence (for which he incurred the Assembly's rebuke in 1568), readers* undertook some of the routine work at Rathven and Eddleston. A friend of Knox, Hay declined the Earl of Morton's (James Douglas*) invitation in 1564 to argue against Knox on subjects' obedience to magistrates. He assisted in purging King's College, Aberdeen in 1569, when the Regent Moray deposed the surviving RC teachers, and delivered an *Oration* on 2 July 1569 justifying the government's intervention. By 1570 he was elected Moderator of the General Assembly, and undertook to debate with the Jesuit, James Tyrie* in 1573. He continued his work as commissioner, and was appointed by Parliament as a visitor of King's College in 1578.

Knox, *History* II, 23, 55, 57, 107–8, 115–16; *BUK*; Calderwood; *Accounts of the Collectors of the Thirds of Benefices*, ed. G. Donaldson (E, 1949); H. Chadwick, 'A Memoir of Edmund Hay S.J.', *Archivum Historicum Societatis Jesu* 8 (1939), 66–85; W. S. Watt and J. Durkan, 'George Hay's Oration', *Northern Scotland* 6 (1985), 91–112; J. Kirk, *Patterns of Reform* (E, 1989); *FES* I, 270; VI, 294, 298, 468.

J. Kirk

Hay, George (1729–1811), RC Bishop. He was born in Edinburgh of non-juring* Episcopalian* parents. At sixteen he was apprenticed to a surgeon and with him followed the Jacobite* army 1745–6. He was imprisoned 1746–7, and then completed his medical studies. He converted to RCism in 1748 and entered the Scots College,* Rome, in 1751. He was ordained priest in 1758, returning to Scotland in 1759, where he was stationed at Preshome (Banffshire) 1759–67, and thereafter at Edinburgh.

He was consecrated as Coadjutor Bishop in 1769, succeeding as Vicar Apostolic of the Lowland District in 1778. He saw his Edinburgh house burned in anti-RC riots in 1779. He moved to Aberdeen in 1780, to Scalan in 1788 and back to Edinburgh in 1793. He did much to secure the passage of the Scottish Catholic Relief Act in 1793. In 1799 Hay moved to establish Aquhorties (*see* Colleges and Seminaries, RC), and in 1805 resigned as Bishop. John Geddes* had been his coadjutor from 1780.

The greatest of the vicars apostolic, Hay succeeded in rehabilitating RCism after the setbacks of 1745. An able administrator, he was also a prolific devotional writer and controversialist. His most important works are *The Scripture Doctrine of Miracles Displayed*... (E, 1775); *The Sincere Christian* (E, 1781); *The Devout Christian* (E, 1783); *The Pious Christian* (E, 1786). All were frequently reprinted.

J. F. S. Gordon, *The Catholic Church in Scotland* (A, 1874); C. Kerr, *Bishop Hay* (L, n.d.); J. Darragh, *The Catholic Hierarchy of Scotland* (G, 1986), 10–12; C. Johnson, *Developments in the Roman Catholic Church in Scotland 1789–1929* (E, 1983); letters and MSS in Scottish Catholic Archives, Edinburgh.

C. Johnson

HAY, WILLIAM

Hay, John (1546–1608), Jesuit controversialist. He was born at Dalgety (Aberdeenshire), studied at King's College, Aberdeen, and graduated from Louvain (1563). He joined the Jesuits* in Rome (1566) and was assigned to the Vilnius academy in Lithuania. In philosophy he was a follower of Duns Scotus.* While recovering from illness he disputed with Lutherans at Strasbourg. A visit to Dundee was cut short (1579), and in Paris he submitted 166 questions to the Scots ministers (*Certaine demandes*..., 1580), evoking a response from Beza. His *Antimoine* answered an opponent who described him 'as a monk'. Further disputes in France with Protestants followed, and in 1606 he attempted a vain expedition to convert James VI. He died as Chancellor of the Scots College* at Pont-à-Mousson, near Metz, where he had taught earlier (1576–8). Hay took a keen interest in Jesuit missions in the New World.

Certain demandes, ed. T. G. Law, *Catholic Tractates of the Sixteenth Century* (STS 45; E, 1901).

DNB XXV, 267–8; W. Forbes-Leith, *Narratives of Scottish Catholics* (E, 1885); R. Darowski, 'John Hay SJ and the Origins of Philosophy in Lithuania', *IR* 31 (1980), 7–15; G. Lamdin, 'Un Professeur Ecossais a Tournon, John Hay', *Revue Vivarais* 59 (1955).

J. Durkan

Hay, Richard Augustine (1661–1736?), priest and antiquarian. Richard Hay, of the family of Barro, was at the Scots College,* Paris c.1673–7, entered the canons regular (taking the religious name Augustine) 1678, was professed 1679 and ordained priest 1685. Commissioned by his superiors to restore the canons regular (*see* Augustinians) in Britain, he returned to Scotland 1686 and treated with the Earl of Perth* for an establishment in Holyrood* (*see* Roman Catholicism; Jesuits). After the Revolution, he left for France 1689 and worked in various places as parish priest, with the title of prior. He was a friend and correspondent of the Benedictine* historian, Mabillon, and in 1714 graduated in arts at Bourges, where he was pastor. He was still in Bourges in May 1718, but was in Edinburgh by August 1719. He died there before September 1736.

Hay's later career in Edinburgh is obscure. In 1722–3 he published two historical works on the Stuart royal dynasty, describing himself as CR (Canon Regular), though apparently not active as a priest. He was said to be living in poverty and in 1730–1 sold some of the six large manuscript volumes of Scottish historical material described as his compilations, but dated 1696 or 1700 (when he was in France).

Genealogie of the Hayes of Tweeddale... including *memoirs of his own times* (E, 1835); MS collections in the National Library of Scotland.

M. Dilworth

Hay, William (fl. 1500–40), canonist. He was born c.1474 near Dundee, where he attended school with

Hector Boece.* He studied at St Andrews, graduated at Paris in 1494 and proceeded to theology and canon law. During 1505-36 he was Sub-principal and Principal of King's College, Aberdeen, where he gave a theology course on the seven sacraments. The first part is missing, and the section on anointing of the sick and ordination unpublished. The published part testifies to Scots marriage customs and to the infiltration of Lutheran* and anti-Lutheran ideas. Older authorities, like the conciliarist* Jean Gerson (d.1429), accompany newer ones like Heinrich Cornelius Agrippa (d.1535), a reformist scholar.

J. C. Barry (ed.), *William Hay's Lectures on Marriage* (Stair Society, E, 1967); J. Durkan, 'Scottish Universities in the Middle Ages' (PhD, University of Edinburgh, 1959).

J. Durkan

Heard, William Theodore (1884–1973), RC Cardinal. Born in Edinburgh where his father was headmaster of Fettes College, he was educated at Fettes and Balliol College, Oxford. Having graduated (BA, 1907), he qualified as a solicitor in London and did voluntary work with deprived youngsters. In 1910 he became a RC, and in 1913 entered the English College, Rome. Ordained priest 1918, he gained doctorates in theology and canon law, and in 1921 took up parish work in London. In 1927 he returned to Rome to be a judge in the Rota (legal tribunal). He became its dean (1958), was created a Cardinal (1959) and ordained a titular Archbishop (1962). After retirement he remained in Rome, and died there. The first Scots-born Cardinal since David Beaton,* at Rome he had close links with both English and Scots Colleges.*

Catholic Directory for Scotland, 1974 (G, 1974), 360-9.

M. Dilworth

Hebronites, *see* Hepburn, John.

Heidelberg Catechism, *see* Confessions of Faith.

Helvetic Confession (First, Second), *see* Confessions of Faith.

Henderson, Agnes, *see* Women in Presbyterian Missions.

Henderson, Alexander (1583–1646), Scottish minister, described as 'the Second Reformer'. Born probably in the Fife parish of Creich, he graduated with distinction at St Andrews (1603) and was appointed regent there. Favoured as a supporter of Episcopacy,* not later than 1614 he was given the parish of Leuchars, an induction carried out against the wishes of parishioners, who had secured the church doors. Soon afterwards, Henderson went secretly to hear Robert Bruce* preach at nearby Fergan Kirk, and was converted. Subsequently he publicly denounced Episcopacy as unauthorized by the Word of God and incompatible with the Reformed CofS's doctrine. In 1618 he was summoned before the Court of High Commission for speaking out against the Perth Articles,* but authority evidently found it imprudent to move against non-conformists of good reputation, and, though precluded from taking part in national Church affairs, Henderson continued his Leuchars ministry. In 1637 he petitioned the Privy Council in Edinburgh, pointing out that Laud's* Service Book had not been sanctioned by the General Assembly – a point conceded by the Council but ignored by Charles I,* who claimed a royal right to do what he thought fit.

Henderson was the prime architect of the National Covenant* (1638) and the Solemn League and Covenant* (1643), his primacy acknowledged by the 1638 Glasgow Assembly* which elected him as Moderator ('incomparably the ablest man of us all for all things'). During this Assembly and in the crucial few years that followed, his leadership cannot be overestimated, as modern commentators, Andrew Lang and John Buchan among them, have readily acknowledged. David Masson called him 'the greatest, wisest, and most liberal of the Scottish Presbyterians . . . a cabinet minister without office'. He was the leader of the Scottish commissioners to the Westminster Assembly,* and showed himself to be no ally of republicanism and religious independency. In 1641, having been chosen royal chaplain during Charles's visit to Edinburgh, he rebuked the King for playing golf on the Sabbath. Charles seems to have taken this in good part.

Henderson became minister of Greyfriars Church, Edinburgh in 1638, but a few months later was translated to the High Kirk (St Giles*). In the capital he was largely responsible for acquiring a building for the College library, and substantially contributed to its stock of books. One principal subsequently hailed him as 'the ablest educationist . . . of all who had to do with the College since its foundation' (Sir A. Grant, *The Story of the University of Edinburgh* (L, 1884), I, 209). Absorbed as he was by contemporary events and dogged by chronic ill health, Henderson published little; his tract, *The Government and Order of the Church of Scotland* (L, 1641), helped the English to understand Scottish affairs.

Sermons, Prayers, and Pulpit Addresses, ed. R. T. Martin (E, 1867).

FES I, 57-8; J. Aiton, *The Life and Times of Alexander Henderson* (E, 1836); T. M'Crie, 'Life of Alexander Henderson', in *Lives of Alexander Henderson and James Guthrie* (E, 1836); R. L. Orr, *Alexander Henderson* (L, 1919); J. B. Salmond and G. H. Bushnell (eds), *Henderson's Benefaction* (St Andrews, 1942); W. Makey, *The Church of the Covenant 1637–1651* (E, 1979).

J. D. Douglas

Henderson, Archibald (1837–1927), eminent UFC minister, Principal Clerk of the UF General Assembly. Born in Glasgow, he attended Glasgow University, Glasgow FC College and New College,* Edinburgh. He was ordained in 1862 to Crieff Free Church, South. In 1888 he was ap-

HENDERSON, EBENEZER

pointed Junior Principal Clerk of the FC General Assembly, and was Principal Clerk of the UF General Assembly 1900-16. After 1916 he was Clerk Emeritus. From 1918-21 he was Principal of Glasgow UF College.

Henderson was unsurpassed as a Church lawyer and Assembly speaker; looked upon by his Church as its acknowledged leader in no respect more prominently than in the movement for union with the CofS. He wrote very little, however.

Henderson received a DD from Glasgow University in 1890, and was Moderator of the UF General Assembly in 1909.

Palestine: Its Historical Geography (E, 1879); *The Analytical Arrangement of the Book of the Revelation* (E, 1893).

AFCS I, 184; *FUFCS* 342.

N. R. Needham

Henderson, Ebenezer (1784-1858), agent of the British and Foreign Bible Society (*see* Bible Societies), linguist and exegete. Born near Dunfermline, after attending the Congregational college in Edinburgh he was appointed as a missionary to India along with John Paterson (*d.*1855).* When the East India Company refused them entry to its territories this project was abandoned and they transferred the focus of their activities to Copenhagen. Using Denmark as a base Henderson travelled through Scandinavia, Russia and, eventually, Iceland, distributing vernacular Scriptures and encouraging the formation of local Bible societies. He founded the first Congregational church in Sweden in 1811. In 1821 Henderson was appointed to the Russian Bible Society in St Petersburg, from where he and Paterson completed a survey of the Crimea and Northern Caucasus with a view to extending their sphere of operations to Astrakhan. After a disagreement over the text of the BFBS-sponsored Turkish New Testament, Henderson and Paterson withdrew from the Society and Henderson was obliged to return to St Petersburg. Bible Society work had become increasingly difficult in the reactionary climate obtaining after the Decembrist revolt of 1825 and Henderson resigned. On his return home he was appointed to a lectureship at the new missionary institution at Hoxton and, latterly, to the Congregational Theological College in Highbury. In the closing period of his life he edited and revised a number of translations and exegetical works and published his own Old Testament commentaries.

T. Henderson, *Memoir of the Rev. E. Henderson, DD, PhD* (L, 1859); J. Paterson, *The Book for Every Land* (L, 1858); *DNB* XXV, 397-8.

I. D. Maxwell

Henderson, George David (1888-1957), scholar and minister of the CofS. Henderson made notable contributions to the historiography of the Scottish Church and to the committee work of the Church. He was Professor of Church History in the University of Aberdeen (1924-57), Master of Christ's

HENDERSON, IAN

College, Aberdeen (1947-57), and Moderator of the General Assembly of 1955.

Born in Ayr and brought up in Airdrie, Henderson was educated at the High School and University of Glasgow (MA, 1910; BD, 1914). After ordination in 1916 he had brief ministries at Greenock East (1916-22) and St Mary's, Partick (1922-4) before his appointment to the Regius Chair of Divinity and Church History at Aberdeen, where he remained until his sudden death during the General Assembly of 1957.

Henderson was a prolific writer. His major contribution was to seventeenth- and early eighteenth-century Scottish Church history, but his work ranges over a wide field. Some of his later writings are impaired by his reluctance to provide references to his sources, but his edition of *Mystics of the North East* (A, 1934) for the Third Spalding Club is a model of detailed annotation. His *Religious Life in Seventeenth Century Scotland* (C, 1937) is a magisterial work drawing on his vast knowledge of the period, while his *Chevalier Ramsay* (L, E, 1952) is an interesting biography of a little known figure. *The Scottish Ruling Elder* (L, 1935) is a remarkable compilation of interesting material, and he chose the subject of *Presbyterianism* (A, 1954) for his Chalmers lectures.* At a different level, he wrote a history for the Youth Committee entitled *The Church of Scotland* (E, 1939), which is still one of the best short accounts. He made several contributions to the history of the Universities* of Aberdeen, most notably *The Founding of Marischal College, Aberdeen* (A, 1947).

The Claims of the Church of Scotland (L, 1951) is a vigorous apologia. He had a keen interest in the links between the CofS and the continent and was fluent in Dutch. *The Burning Bush* (E, 1957) was published posthumously and includes a wide variety of articles including one under its title, the symbol of the CofS (*see* Burning Bush).

Heritage: A Study of the Disruption (E, 1943); *Church and Ministry* (L, 1951); *Why we are Presbyterians* (A, 1954).

Who Was Who, 1951-1960, 509; *FES* VII, 375, VIII, 714, IX, 767, 771, X, 430.

H. R. Sefton

Henderson, Ian (1910-69), Professor of Systematic Theology at the University of Glasgow from 1948 till his death. He was educated at Edinburgh and Oban, then in arts and divinity at the University of Edinburgh (MA, 1933; BD, 1936), and did further studies at Zürich and Basel with Emil Brunner and Karl Barth. Barth regarded him as his most promising pupil.

After ministering at Fraserburgh South (1938-42) and Kilmany, Fife (1942-8), he moved to the Glasgow chair. His main theological work was *Myth in the New Testament* (L, 1952), a critique of Bultmann's essay on the subject. He covered the ground thoroughly but one comment stands out and illustrates Henderson's remarkable ability for the telling phrase. Bultmann, an army chaplain in the First World War, said that he could not tell his

HENDERSON, JANE

German soldiers acquainted with modern science about the Resurrection and miracles. Henderson comments, 'They accepted the Nazi nonsense of "Blood and Soil".'

He wrote *Scotland: Kirk and People* (E, 1969), but the book he is best known for is *Power without Glory* (L, 1967), a caustic study in ecumenical politics. It was published before the 1967 General Assembly of the CofS and was to affect the discussion of the proposals for Anglican-Presbyterian* union before the Church at that time. He dedicated the book 'To the good Christians in every denomination who do not greatly care whether there is one Church or not'.

Can Two Walk Together? (L, 1948); *Rudolf Bultmann* (L, 1965).

FES IX, 771, X, 430; *Who Was Who, 1961–1970*, 517.

A. L. Walker

Henderson, Jane, *see* Fisherfolk, Missions to.

Hepburn, John (*c.*1649–1723), minister. The son of a landowner in Morayshire, Hepburn graduated from King's College, Aberdeen, in 1669. He stated that he was ordained in London in 1678 by Scots ministers there, and subsequently preached in Ross-shire. In 1680 he was invited to preach the gospel in Urr, Kirkcudbrightshire, by dissidents there, and in the years that followed he preached in Urr and other parishes in the area, as a result of which he was declared a fugitive in 1684. After the 1688 revolution he acted as minister of the Parish of Urr, though the Presbytery urged him to move to another parish. He was probably never formally admitted to Urr, but was tacitly accepted as minister. Hepburn's outlook was close to that of the Cameronians (*see* Societies, United), but whereas the latter disowned the government of both Church and state as unlawful, Hepburn accepted the authority of the Established Church now that Presbyterianism* had been restored, though rejecting the civil government as unlawful. His preaching won him the allegiance of a small band of followers, sometimes called the Hebronites, but led to conflict with the Church. He was suspended from the ministry in 1696 and imprisoned for a time for refusing the oath of allegiance to the King. His suspension was lifted in 1699, but he was again suspended in 1704, and deposed by the General Assembly the following year for 'erroneous seditions, and divisive doctrines, and schismatic courses, wherein he is obstinate, refusing to be reclaimed.' Restored to Urr in 1707, Hepburn was bitterly opposed to the Union of Parliaments* of that year. Nonetheless, during the Jacobite Rising of 1715* he led 320 of his supporters to occupy Dumfries in opposition to the rebels. Hepburn's outspoken denunciations of authority and the corrupt upper classes contributed to the rising in 1724 of the 'Levellers of Galloway', a popular movement resisting evictions by landlords.

W. McMillan, *John Hepburn and the Hebronites* (L,

HERESY, HERESY TRIALS

1934); *FES* II, 305; W. L. Mathieson, *Scotland and the Union* (G, 1905), 235, 312; T. C. Smout, *History of the Scottish People* (L, 1969), 325–30.

D. Stevenson

Hepburn, Patrick (*d.*1573), Bishop of Moray. The cousin of the Earl of Bothwell, after studying at St Andrews University, where he enrolled in 1509, he gained the parsonage of Whitsome (near Berwick) in 1521, was appointed coadjutor in 1524 to his uncle the prior of St Andrews, and became James V's secretary in 1525. On his uncle's death in 1526, he succeeded as prior, attended Patrick Hamilton's* execution in 1528, and was appointed Bishop of Moray and commendator* of Scone* Abbey in 1538. In 1547, he granted John Erskine of Dun* a lease of Scone for nineteen years, and was assiduous in dilapidating the patrimony of abbacy and bishopric. He sat in Parliament and Privy Council, was present at the provincial council* of 1549, and attended the burning of Adam Wallace* for heresy in 1550 and of Walter Milne* in 1558. By 1559 he declared himself ready to assist the reforming Lords of the Congregation,* if they saved his abbey from destruction, but withdrew his offer when the abbey was burned. He was absent from the Reformation Parliament,* but agreed in 1566 to pay for repairs to Elgin Cathedral for Protestant worship. A supporter of Queen Mary's* cause, he was forfeited by James VI's government in August 1571. He was notoriously profligate, fathering numerous children by different mothers.

Dowden, 171–2; J. Foxe, *Acts and Monuments* (L, 1858), V, 636, 644; Knox, *History*; *FESMA*, 217; Easson-Cowan, 98; *DNB* XXVI, 162–3; *Scots Peerage* II, 142–3.

J. Kirk

Heresy, Heresy Trials. Scotland was relatively little disturbed by medieval movements condemned as heretical by the Roman Church. James Resby, burned at Perth in 1407, was an English Wycliffite (*see* Lollards), and Paul Kravar,* burned at St Andrews in 1432 by Laurence of Lindores,* 'Inquisitor of Heretical Pravity', was a Bohemian Hussite.

During the Reformation decades, well over a hundred and fifty persons were accused of heresy (almost complete list for 1528–46 in M. H. B. Sanderson, *Cardinal of Scotland. David Beaton, c.1494–1546*, E, 1986, 270–84). Cardinal Beaton* is said to have identified 360 nobles and gentry deserving confiscation for heresy. The provincial councils* of 1549 and 1558–9 recognized its spread and took measures for its extirpation (D. Patrick, *Statutes of the Scottish Church 1225–1559*, SHS, E, 1907, 122–7, 150, 162, 219). Some fled to avoid prosecution (e.g. Alexander Alesius,* George Buchanan,* John MacAlpine*), but many suffered trial, and a good number were executed by burning, the last, Walter Milne,* in 1558 (*see* Fergusson, David; Forret, Thomas; Hamilton, Patrick; Straiton, David; Wallace, Adam; Wishart, George).

Their offences spanned a wide spectrum, from possessing Lutheran publications or vernacular Scriptures to anti-clericalism and attacking the mass or images. Only under Beaton were Protestant heretics pursued with vigour, but martyrdom,* as often in the church's history, boosted rather than dampened the Protestant cause.

The Reformation Parliament* annulled all the acts against heresy. The *First Book of Discipline* decreed perpetual deposition for heresy, now defined as 'pernicious doctrine plainly taught and openly defended against the foundations and principles of our faith' (*FBD* 177).

In the seventeenth century the church was largely preoccupied with ecclesiology. Although Principal John Strang* of Glasgow was forced to retire because of his pronounced sublapsarian views, deposition and exile (and, after 1662, imprisonment and execution) mostly resulted from deviation in theory and practice from the established church order of the time.

In the post-Revolution church – a church proud of its reputation for doctrinal orthodoxy – the first heresy trial was that of George Garden,* deposed in 1701 for espousing and spreading the heretical opinions of Antoinette Bourignon.*

John Simson,* Professor of Divinity at Glasgow, was accused of Arianism a second time in 1726, and suspended indefinitely – not deposed or deprived – in 1729. In 1736 Professor Archibald Campbell of St Andrews (d. 1756; *FES* VII, 431–2), and in 1743 Professor William Leechman* of Glasgow, easily secured acquittal on heresy charges prompted largely by the strongly rationalist flavour of their teachings. Alexander Ferguson (1689–1770; *FES* III, 117–18) was cleared in 1770 by Irvine Presbytery of seemingly blatant denial of central teachings of the Westminster Confession.* In 1786 William McGill's* Socinianism was examined more seriously, but he was given the benefit of the doubt when he clarified and apologized. John Leslie* was eventually appointed to the Edinburgh chair of mathematics in 1805 after escaping condemnation for apparently embracing the scepticism of David Hume.*

Several heresy cases related to contentious aspects of the Westminster Confession.* John McLeod Campbell* was condemned and deposed in 1831 for rejecting the Confession's doctrine of limited atonement, and Edward Irving* followed in 1833 for similar but broader unorthodoxy. In 1841 James Morison* was expelled by the United Secession Synod,* also for denying limited atonement. The dispute within the Synod also called into question the views on the same subject of Professor Robert Balmer* and John Brown (d. 1858).* Balmer died in 1844 and Brown was exonerated on all charges in 1845.

In 1878 Fergus Ferguson* was found guilty by the UP Presbytery of Glasgow and the Synod on several counts, in effect for espousing a universalism alien to the Confession. To general astonishment, then and now, he received only admonition, perhaps in anticipatory consideration of the UP Declaratory Act* passed in 1879. David Macrae's* explicit dissent from the doctrine of eternal punishment at the 1879 Synod brought him deposition.

Robert Wallace* survived an attempt to depose him in 1873 when nominated to the Edinburgh chair of Church History, but demitted his ministerial status in 1876. The influence of biblical criticism was a factor in his loss of vocation, and in a series of celebrated heresy proceedings around the turn of the century in the FC and UFC: William Robertson Smith,* removed from his chair in 1881; Marcus Dods* and A. B. Bruce,* both acquitted by the FC Assembly in 1890, but not without rebuke; George Adam Smith,* likewise acquitted by the UF Assembly in 1902. It remains remarkable that it was in the constitutional high orthodoxy of the FC tradition that such cases should be concentrated. William A. Knight* had earlier been accused of heresy after flirting with unitarianism* and other errors, whereupon he and his congregation flitted from the FC to the CofS.

The impact of the Declaratory Acts, and the doctrinal confusions and indifference of a post-liberal era have conspired to make prosecutions for heresy almost unthinkable in the contemporary CofS. Theological uncertainty has led, by compensation, to a more rigorous attitude towards pastoral and sacramental irregularities. In grotesque disproportion, a minister or elder is much more likely to be disciplined for re-baptizing than for denying the divinity of Christ.

Beyond Presbyterianism, independent churches which have not been inclined to define their theological position by credal statements have been less ready to recognize heresy or act against it. Congregational and Baptist churches have comparatively few major trials of 'deviant' preachers or teachers, although both movements have exhibited occasional tendencies towards unitarianism, universalism and the denial of Christ's divinity. Scottish Baptists have nevertheless removed from their Accredited List the names of men known to espouse doctrines incompatible with the Declaration of Principle of the Baptist Union of Scotland. Thus in 1932 E. J. Roberts, minister of the Baptist Church at Grantown-on-Spey, was deemed to hold erroneous views on the Virgin Birth of Christ and the need for atonement. His name was subsequently deleted from the roll of Scottish ministers, and 'the dispute is notable for having been almost the only one in which central theological matters were debated at the [Baptist] Assembly' (Derek B. Murray, *The First Hundred Years*, G, 1969, 102–3).

See also Atonement Controversy; Forbes, Alexander Penrose.

J. Kirk, *Patterns of Reform* (E, 1989); J. Durkan, 'Some Local Heretics', *TDGAS* .36 (1959), 66–77; R. Pitcairn, *Ancient Criminal Trials in Scotland* (E, 1829–33), I,* esp. 209–16; A. T. Innes, *The Law of Creeds in Scotland* (E, 1867), 210–18; H. F. Henderson, *The Religious Controversies of Scotland* (E, 1905); I. Hamilton, *The Erosion of Calvinist Orthodoxy* (E, 1990); A. C. Cheyne, *The Transforming of the Kirk* (E, 1983).

D. F. Wright

HERITOR

Heritor, a landowner possessing immovable or heritable property in a parish, described in 1866 as owner of land of at least 100 real rent *per annum*. The word began to be used widely in the time of Charles I.* Together heritors formed a 'quasi-corporation for the management and disposal of those parochial concerns to which they were entitled on their own to take action'. They had to provide and maintain the parish* church, manse,* church-yard and glebe.* When church door offerings were insufficient for care of the poor, heritors were responsible for assessments to increase the money available. The provision of schools was also a matter for them, but in the nineteenth century parliamentary acts passed responsibility for the poor and education to state-appointed bodies.

The work of heritors ended after the passing of the Church of Scotland (Property and Endowments) Act of 1925, in preparation for the Union of Churches in 1929.

J. M. Duncan and C. N. Johnston, *The Parochial and Ecclesiastical Law of Scotland* (E, 1903); T. Burns, *Church Property* (The Benefice Lectures; E, 1905); J. Connell, *A Treatise ... on Tithes*, 3 vols (E, 1815).

A. I. Dunlop

Herkless, Sir John (1855–1920), Scottish church historian and university principal. Educated at the universities of Glasgow and Jena, he was minister of Tannadice in Angus (1883–94), and Regius Professor of Ecclesiastical History of St Andrews (1894–1915), which office he combined from 1915 with that of principal of the university and of the United College of St Leonard and St Salvator. Among his publications were *Cardinal Beaton: Priest and Politician* (E, 1891); *Richard Cameron* (E, 1896); *The Church of Scotland* (L, 1897); *The Early Christian Martyrs* (L, 1904); and (with R. K. Hannay) *The Archbishops of St Andrews* (5 vols, E, 1907–16).

FES V, 306, VII, 416, 434.

J. D. Douglas

Hetherington, Irving (1809–75), Australian CofS minister. Hetherington came from the parish of Ruthwell, Dumfriesshire. In boyhood days he was friendly with Robert Murray McCheyne,* who used to spend his summer holidays there. Hetherington studied arts and divinity at Edinburgh and was licensed by the Presbytery of Lochmaben, but found it difficult to secure a parish. A published address of John Dunmore Lang* brought the need of Australia to his notice, and he was sent out by the Colonial Committee of the CofS in 1837. On arrival he was appointed to Singleton on the Hunter River in New South Wales and did excellent work as pastor and educationist. He was called to succeed James Forbes* at Scots' Church, Melbourne, in 1847. Although Hetherington showed sympathy with the FC position, he did not join the FC movement in Australia. He made the initial move for a general union of Presbyterian bodies in Victoria, which ultimately resulted in the formation of the Presbyterian Church of Victoria in 1859. His in-

HETHERWICK, ALEXANDER

fluence was strong in the early years of that denomination's life, especially as its clerk.

F. R. M. Wilson, *Memoir of the Rev. Irving Hetherington, Scots' Church* (Melbourne, 1876); *Australian Dictionary of Biography* IV, 387–8.

A. M. Harman

Hetherington, William Maxwell (1803–65), FC poet and divine. Born at Troqueer, in Kirkcudbright, he attended Edinburgh University from 1822, where he studied theology. Licensed by the CofS Presbytery of Linlithgow in 1830, in 1836 he was ordained to the charge of Torphichen, West Lothian. Joining the FC in 1843, he became minister of Free St Andrews in 1844, moving to Free St Paul's, Edinburgh, in 1848. In 1857 he was appointed Professor of Apologetics and Systematic Theology in the FC College in Glasgow, a position he held until stricken by paralysis in 1862. He produced *The Apologetics of the Christian Faith* (E, 1862).

Hetherington was a prolific writer. He founded the *FC Magazine* in 1844, editing it for four years, and was a frequent contributor to the *British and Foreign Evangelical Review*.* He produced several volumes of poetry, *e.g. Twelve Dramatic Sketches Founded on the Pastoral Poetry of Scotland* (E, 1829). He edited *The Works of Mr George Gillespie* (2 vols, E, 1846). His greatest prose works were his *History of the Westminster Assembly of Divines* (E, 1843; best edit. by Robert Williamson, E, 1878), and his *History of the Church of Scotland* (best edit., 2 vols, E, 1848). Both were widely circulated in America as well as in Britain.

Hetherington received a DD from Jefferson College, Pennsylvania, in 1855, and an LLD from New Brunswick, New Jersey.

DNB XXVI, 300–1; *FES* I, 232; *AFCS* I, 55–6.

N. R. Needham

Hetherwick, Alexander (1860–1939), African missionary. Educated at the Grammar School and University of Aberdeen, the best mathematician of his year, he trained at Aberdeen for the CofS ministry. Ordained for missionary service in Nyasaland, he went to Blantyre in 1885, where D. C. Scott* sent him to open a new mission at Domasi on the slopes of Zomba Mountain among hitherto antagonistic Yao chiefdoms. He rapidly became Scott's right-hand man and succeeded him as head of the Mission in 1898.

In 1900 he chaired the committee that produced the complete Nyanja Bible, used, until the 1970s, in Malawi, Zambia and Mozambique. For that his alma mater awarded him the DD in 1902. He represented African interests in the Legislative Assembly, 1908–13 and 1922–5. In 1925 he was awarded the CBE. His evidence before the Commission of Enquiry into the 'Chilembwe Rising' was a brilliant defence of African leadership in the Church and, for the time, an extraordinarily trenchant exposition of the potential equality of people of all races. He retired to Scotland in 1928.

HEWAT, E. G. K.

Robert Hellier Napier (E, 1926); *The Building of Blantyre Church, Nyasaland* (E, 1926); *The Gospel and the African* (E, 1932).

W. P. Livingstone, *A Prince of Missionaries* (L, 1931).

A. C. Ross

Hewat, Elizabeth Glendinning Kirkwood (1897–1968), CofS historian and missionary. The daughter of Kirkwood Hewat of Prestwick, Ayrshire (*FUFCS* 131), she graduated in history and philosophy at Edinburgh University and in 1926 was the first woman to graduate BD at Edinburgh. During 1922–6 she was on the staff at the UFC Women's Missionary Training College (*see* St Colm's College), before joining her sister as a missionary in China. After several years she returned to Scotland, and served as voluntary assistant at North Merchiston Church, Edinburgh.

From 1935 to 1955 Professor of History at Wilson College, Bombay, she also taught Scripture and was warden of the Women Students Hostel. An elder in the United Church of North India, she frequently conducted worship in the College Chapel, the Scots Kirk, and for other denominations. She believed that women* could not serve the Church fully unless they were admitted to the eldership* and ministry.

Her service in Scotland included a period as lecturer at St Andrews University, and the preparation of study and devotional material for the Woman's Guild.* For many years she was editorial assistant of the *International Review of Missions*, and she was chosen to write the history of CofS foreign missions, *Vision and Achievement, 1796–1956* (L, 1960).

In July 1966, she became the first woman to be awarded the honorary DD by Edinburgh University.

'A Comparison of Hebrew and Chinese Wisdom...' (PhD, Edinburgh University, 1933); *Christ and Western India* (Bombay, 1950); *The Life and Work of Women in the Church* (G, 1947); *Thine Own Secret* (³E, 1981); with G. A. Gollock, *An Introduction to Missionary Service* (L, 1921).

LW 23 (Dec.1968), 17.

L. O. Macdonald

Hewison, John King (1853–1941), church historian and antiquary. He was born in Morton, Dumfriesshire, educated at the University of Edinburgh (MA, 1874) and in Leipzig, and ordained to the parish of Stair, Ayrshire, in 1881. He was translated to Rothesay, Isle of Bute, in 1884 and ministered there until 1924. He received the DD of Edinburgh in 1900 and was Grand Chaplain to the Freemasons* of Scotland.

Hewison wrote many books and articles on the history and geography of Dumfriesshire, Galloway and Bute. He contributed to the *Proceedings of the Society of Antiquaries of Scotland*, of which he was a fellow, and wrote about the 'runic roods' at Ruthwell and Bewcastle. In 1888 he edited *Certain Tractates ... by Ninian Winzet*,* but is best remembered for the two volumes on *The Covenanters** (G, ²1913), dealing very fully with the history of the Scottish Church from the Reformation* to the 1689 Revolution.* Hewison amassed a vast quantity of material about the sufferings of those who resisted the authoritarianism of the Stewart kings. He gave a valuable collection of Covenanter material to the CofS Library, now in New College Library, Edinburgh.

FES IV, 42, VIII, 320.

A. I. Dunlop

Hickhorngill, Edward (*fl.*1652/3), soldier and chaplain. We have scanty information about this man, who may be regarded as the first Baptist* minister in Scotland. He was baptized at Hexham in northern England in June 1652, and appointed the Hexham church's messenger to Scotland in December 1652. He reported first to the garrison in Dalkeith and then to Leith, where he ministered to Cromwellian soldiers, and reported that some Scots 'longed to be gathered to the same Gospel'. By 1653 he was 'our sometimes precious but now alas deluded brother', and Thomas Stackhouse referred to him as 'a desperate atheist'. He was excommunicated, but later reconciled in Perth; and then disappears from view.

E. B. Underhill (ed.), *Records of the Churches of Christ gathered at Fenstanton, Warboys and Hexham* (L, 1854); D. Douglas, *History of the Baptist Churches in the North of England* (L, 1846).

D. B. Murray

Higher Criticism, *see* Biblical Criticism.

Highflyers, a term probably borrowed from the Anglican Church of the Reformation settlement and applied initially to the 'High Presbyterian' party in the CofS. In the middle of the eighteenth century, though, John Maclaurin* used it in reference to those of the Moderate party* who were determined rigorously to implement the law of patronage.* By the nineteenth century, however, it was being used to apply to the opposite position. This use of the term has been unjustifiably extended back to the previous century. On balance, it would seem to have been a term used somewhat indiscriminately by members of various ecclesiastical factions or parties to describe their opponents if they were deemed to be adopting positions felt to be extreme.

J. Maclaurin, *The Nature of Ecclesiastic Government* (G, 1754); J. Macleod, *Scottish Theology* (E, ³1974); A. L. Drummond and J. Bulloch, *The Scottish Church, 1688–1843* (E, 1973); R. B. Sher, *Church and University in the Scottish Enlightenment* (E, 1985), 17.

J. R. McIntosh

Highlands, that part of Scotland, about half of its land mass, generally recognized as lying to the north of the so-called Highland boundary fault, running approximately from Helensburgh to Stonehaven. The term, which excludes Orkney* and Shetland* and the coastal plain of the north-east, implies that high ground is the chief characteristic of the region, and this is certainly true of the mainland area. Nevertheless, the Highlands are by no means geologically or geographically uniform: the mainland includes much low-lying land, particularly towards the west coast, while the Islands, normally included within the 'Highland' designation, present a variety of geological formations, from the fertile 'raised beaches' of the Inner Hebrides to the Lewisian gneiss and rugged terrain of parts of the Outer Hebrides.

Patterns of human existence have been directed to a large degree by the regional differences within the geography and geology of the Highlands and also by the extent to which it has been possible to utilize the natural resources of the sub-areas. Such utilization has varied across the centuries, but the primary emphasis has been on pastoral and agricultural economies, with fishing as an important standby and, in some areas where there is poorer agricultural land and/or good harbours, as an economic mainstay.

The term 'system', as applied to patterns of life, is misleading in the Highland context, since various economic and ethnological 'systems' have interacted across the centuries. The 'clan system', stretching back into the Middle Ages, was probably much less systematic in practice than in theory, and came to be modified by feudalism; it functioned in terms of kin-based loyalties, a warrior lifestyle and, gradually, the emergence of an economy based on the rearing of 'black cattle'. Land cultivated in runrig, with strips of land allocated within open fields and worked by the tenants of individual townships, survived into the nineteenth century. Today the Highlands are identified predominantly with crofting, which provides individual families with pieces of land ('crofts'). Developed at the beginning of the nineteenth century in an attempt to retain the population during the kelp boom, when seawrack was harvested in abundance from the shorelines, crofting experienced considerable upheaval during the severe social dislocation caused by the Potato Famine (1846–7), leading to emigration* and clearance.* Nevertheless, it has provided a means of maintaining a small-holding population who have combined their agricultural interests with fishing and other forms of employment. Crofting is, however, associated mainly with the western Highlands and islands. In the east and north-east Highlands, and in mainland Argyll and Perthshire, larger farms are more common.

Apart from crofting, fishing and farming, industry has tended to be localized and transient (*e.g.*, slatequarrying at Ballachulish, diatomite mining in Skye), although there have also been more lasting industries (*e.g.*, Harris Tweed in the Outer Hebrides, especially Lewis, and whisky in various parts of the Highlands). Various bodies have been formed by government since 1900 to promote industry of different kinds, most notably the Highlands and Islands Development Board, established in 1965 and based at Inverness, the unofficial 'capital' of the Highlands. In the spring of 1991, the HIDB was superseded by a new government body, Highlands and Islands Enterprise.

The Highland interest of central government, whether from London or (before 1707) from Edinburgh, is a reminder that the region is by no means isolated from the rest of mainland Britain. Although frequently treated by writers and historians as if it were no more than a peripheral appendage of Scotland, it has been constantly influenced by movements originating beyond its boundaries, and it has contributed substantially to many of these movements. Nowhere is this more evident than in its religious history, which bears traces of interaction with most of the major European and British movements since the early Christian era. Penetration of the Highlands by non-indigenous bodies, often establishing themselves initially on the coastal fringe in the west or close to the 'Highland Line' in the east and moving with great effort into the heartlands, is the primary theme in the religious history of the region.

THE COLUMBAN ERA. The arrival of Columba* in Iona* in AD 563 marked the beginning of a significant Christian presence in the Highland area. Travelling across Druim Alban, the Columban monks, who belonged to the wider so-called Celtic Church,* established monasteries in land under the control of the Picts,* reaching as far east as Deer* in Aberdeenshire. Columba visited many of the islands of the Hebrides, including Skye and Tiree, where he had another monastery. The leadership of Columba was acknowledged in the political sphere, and greatly aided the expansion of the Scotic kingdom of Dalriada, in which Iona was situated. This had implications for the cultural and political development of what later became Scotland. The influence of the Celtic Church was carried eastwards as the Gaelic*-speaking Scots established themselves in Pictland and beyond, and is apparent at places such as Brechin, Abernethy and St Andrews, where houses of Culdees* were established.

The round towers still visible at Brechin and Abernethy preserve a distinctive architectural feature of the Celtic Church. Accommodation with Celtic culture is also evident at Iona, where the Celtic crosses* bear eloquent testimony to the interaction of native Celtic and Christian styles of art and iconography. The same interaction is apparent in the Book of Kells,* an illuminated manuscript almost certainly compiled at Iona.

THE MEDIEVAL CHURCH. The Celtic monasteries founded by Columba and his followers did not survive beyond the eleventh century. By then new influences were being felt in the west and south, and the structure of the Church was changing (*see* Margaret, Saint). In the west there was the presence of the Norsemen, who had come to occupy the Hebrides in the ninth century, left its mark on place-names and even on ecclesiastical organization. The Hebrides became the diocese of Sodor (from *Suðr eyjar*, Norse for 'Southern Isles'). Later known as the Isles, Sodor for a period included the Isle of Man (with bishops variously at Snizort, Man and Iona). In 1153 'Sodor and Man' was placed by the papacy under Trondheim as metropolitan, Norwegian control remaining until c.1350. With the reforms of the Scottish Church in the twelfth century, further dioceses were recognized in the Highlands, namely Caithness (seat at Halkirk, later at Dornoch; see Gilbert of Moray), Ross (Rosemarkie, later Fortrose), Moray (Elgin), Dunkeld, Dunblane and Argyll (Lismore), carved out of Dunkeld c.1190. These dioceses and Sodor maintained contact with Rome, and formed an integral part of western Christendom, while retaining regional differences of custom, such as the feast days of Celtic saints.* The European dimensions are apparent in the presence of the new monastic orders, represented rather sparsely in the Highlands by Augustinians,* Benedictines,* Cistercians,* and most prominently by the rather severe Valliscaulian* order at Ardchattan, Beauly and Pluscarden (see David I of Scotland).

The twelfth-century reforms of the Scottish Church included the development of a parish system, and, although details remain obscure, parishes gradually took shape in the Highlands. The Highland parishes were often of great size compared with those in the south of Scotland; in the whole of north-west Sutherland and Wester Ross, there were only eight parishes, while Fife and Dumfriesshire had about seventy parishes each. The vast extent of many Highland parishes, as well as their difficult terrain, posed problems for the Churches after 1200.

As in the Columban era, Gaelic culture interacted with the Christian culture of the medieval Church. The Lords of the Isles, who held sway from the twelfth century until 1493, patronized the Church. This alliance can still be viewed in the monumental sculpture preserved in the form of cross slabs, grave slabs, effigies and free-standing crosses like that at Oronsay, the site of an Augustinian priory founded (1325/53) by John, Lord of the Isles.

With the end of the Middle Ages and the forfeiture of the Lordship of the Isles, the great age of medieval patronage had passed, and the Reformation* brought new, unsympathetic views of iconography. John Carswell* praised the fifth Earl of Argyll (see Campbell, Archibald, d. 1573) for his iconoclasm. Nevertheless, the Protestant Church inherited much of the medieval culture through its links with the pre-Reformation clergy, who were sometimes trained in Lowland universities and Gaelic bardic schools. This is evident in the area of language and literature, suggesting strongly that the Protestant Churches became the patrons of the old, secular skills, transferred to another context. Gaelic preaching, employing Classical Scottish Gaelic as found in the Bible (see Bible (Versions, Gaelic)), helped to preserve a creative link with the medieval past.

THE ARRIVAL OF THE REFORMATION. The effort to provide a Reformed ministry in the Highlands after 1560 was evidently much stronger than has commonly been allowed. It has recently been estimated that 'in the essentially Highland dioceses of Caithness, Ross, Moray, a section of Dunkeld and also Dunblane, there were 215 kirks which, by 1574, were served by 65 ministers and 158 readers: a staff of 223 for 215 parishes' (J. Kirk, *Patterns of Reform*, E, 1989, 305–33). In Argyll and the Isles, the work of John Carswell suggests vigorous Protestant activity by 1567, at least in the southern mainland.

For reasons as much political as religious, the dominant phase of the RCC, whose supremacy stretched throughout the Middle Ages, was under severe threat by 1609 (see Iona, Statutes of) and was coming to an end by 1700. Even by the early 1600s there was an acute shortage of Gaelic-speaking priests (see Irish Mission to Highlands). A Scottish Mission, aimed at finding more priests and increasing membership, was therefore instituted in the seventeenth century, and a more specifically Highland Mission in 1727. After 1745 and the failure of the Jacobite* rebellion, in which RC and Episcopal sympathies were dominant, both Churches were further repressed.

Protestant allegiance to parish ministers of the Est.C gradually replaced allegiance to Rome, except for parts of mainland Inverness-shire, S. Uist and Barra. The transition from RCism was undoubtedly slow in many areas. Yet the Est.C, in replacing the earlier structure, cannot be wholly accused of neglect, although its coverage was far from complete; by 1626 there were nineteen ministers and two readers in the Isles, but of Lochaber in 1649 it was claimed that 'now since the Reformation never hath there been any care ... to fill these [three parish] churches with any minister at all'.

The progress of the Est.C in the Highlands was seriously hindered by lack of appropriate personnel, a problem exacerbated by the struggle between episcopacy* and Presbyterianism* (see Covenanters), especially after 1660, when many of its Protesting* and anti-episcopal ministers were ejected (see Hog, Thomas). Following the re-establishment of Presbyterianism in 1690, the EpCS retained an allegiance primarily in mainland Argyll, especially in Appin and Glencoe. After 1690 the Est.C's policy became noticeably more militant, with a strong attack on the 'popish parts' and a progressive extension into the mainland areas.

PENETRATING THE PARISHES. Although the Reformed Church employed the parish* system after 1560, the immense size of many Highland parishes made it necessary to utilize itinerant* catechists through agencies such as the Scottish SPCK.* The resources of the Royal Bounty* further helped to improve provision within the parishes, and brought the Presbyterian movement closer to the people by supporting missionary-ministers for the parts least accessible to the parish ministers. After 1800 the Independent* and Baptist* missionary* movement built itself on the momentum established by the SSPCK, and, as the gaps in the parish system were still apparent, further so-called Parliamentary

Churches* were built by Act of Parliament after 1824.

Notwithstanding the implications of 1690 and the support of various agencies, the effort to secure the Est.C firmly in the southern and western parishes was not completed much before 1800, and in the Outer Hebrides its triumph was merely an interim phase before the Disruption.* Evangelicalism, which was beginning to exert its presence powerfully in Lewis by the 1820s, had already added an ominous dimension to the struggle at the end of the eighteenth century, when the Est.C came under attack from some of its own supporters. The strength of Moderatism* in the Highlands in the eighteenth and early nineteenth centuries was variable, and not always inclined to contend with Evangelicalism, but evangelical ministers sometimes took control of the parishes against considerable opposition from some of their clerical contemporaries (*see* MacKenzie, Lachlan). Because of their battles against spiritual indifference, rather than their struggles with Moderatism, the great Popular* ministerial leaders of the northern Highlands and also the earliest evangelical ministers to occupy the parishes have achieved heroic status in later tradition. The epithet 'Mòr' ('Great') is duly applied to the physique and matching spirituality of such men as John Balfour of Nigg (*d.*1752), John MacDonald* of Ferintosh ('Ministear Mòr na Tòisidheachd', 'The Great Minister of Ferintosh') and the first evangelical minister in Lewis, Alexander MacLeod* (inducted 1824), who was known in Gaelic tradition as 'Alasdair Mòr an t-Soisgeil', 'Great Alexander of the Gospel', an appellation which recalls Alexander the Great of Macedonia.

Although such men were relatively rare in the Highlands, the difficulties of Highland ministry guaranteed that the Est.C had few rivals in the region before 1843. Even the Methodists,* who wished to establish a Highland mission in 1786, were unable to penetrate the area effectively (*see* McAllum, Duncan). The Orig. Sec. C. (*see* MacBean, Francis) and the Relief Church (*see* Douglas, Niel) made little impact on the Highlands. The main challenge to the Est.C came from within rather than from without.

NINETEENTH-CENTURY FRAGMENTATION. Having gained control of areas once under the sway of the RCC, the Est.C from 1800 gradually found its own authority being undermined by evangelical missionaries of Independent and Baptist persuasion (*see* Haldane Preachers), teachers of the Gaelic School Societies* and many of the catechists whom it had been happy to introduce to its parishes; as a result it had much ground cut from it by the development of allegiances to 'The Men'.* Tension, soon to erupt, was increased by the growing influence of the evangelical ministers, the continuing poor ministerial provision in the parishes and wider issues such as patronage.*

Highland Presbyterianism owed much to patronage, which had helped to build the parochial structure. Clan chiefs, tacksmen and other landed gentlemen acted (occasionally under duress) as patrons of the Church by sustaining the salaries of ministers, becoming commissioners (i.e. parish representatives) at the General Assembly, building and repairing churches, and protecting the Reformed faith within their bounds. Patronage sometimes aided the cause of Evangelicalism, and not least in Lewis, where Mrs MacKenzie of Seaforth presented Alexander MacLeod to the parish of Uig, and encouraged Baptist preachers to come to the island (temporarily) in the late 1820s. Nevertheless, patronage became progressively identified with the intrusion of patrons' candidates to parishes against the will of the people, and Highland Presbyterianism gradually turned against it. Disputes about presentation to vacant charges occurred after 1750, leading to the formation of Relief and Secession congregations at Campbeltown (1767) and Nigg (*c.*1756) respectively. This was one of the major issues in the Disruption* and the emergence of the FC.*

The FC received more than 80 per cent of existing Highland Presbyterian congregations, but less than 20 per cent of the ministers in the islands. To overcome this initial difficulty, a schooner, the 'Breadalbane', was built in 1844, and transported a small body of mainland-based FC ministers to and from vacant charges in the islands until 1854. Because unsympathetic landlords tended to favour the Est.C, the FC also faced great problems in securing church sites in certain areas, and took to preaching out of doors where no building was available, a practice long established by Baptist and other dissenters. The FC, however, eschewed Voluntaryism,* and adhered to the establishment principle, while insisting on the right of congregations to choose their own ministers.

Numerical growth for the Protestant bodies occurred chiefly before 1850, and again in the more settled decades of the 1870s and 1880s. After 1850, however, the implications of falling population (except in Lewis, where the population grew until 1911) were extremely serious. Phases of missionary activity, establishment and revival* were counterbalanced by periods of decay, frequently manifesting itself as chronic or acute decline in church life and membership. Some Churches weathered the storms better than others. The Presbyterian Churches, Established and Free, which put down firm territorial roots, to the extent of having very distinctive Highland branches, had the most noticeable staying power. Because of the breadth of their support and the size of their following, and perhaps because of their Covenant* theology, linking land and people in a powerful grip, they lived to witness the demise of almost 70 per cent of the thirty or so small, independent Baptist churches which emerged mainly before 1843, chiefly in Argyll, Perthshire, Strathspey and the Inner Hebrides. The latter demonstrate that independent gathered congregations are difficult to maintain successfully in rural areas with shifting populations (*see* Baptist Home Missionary Society for Scotland). All the Churches contributed to the tide of emigration,* their former members establishing new churches and chapels in the lands of their adoption. In the

Lowlands, Gaelic chapels were being built by 1760, and outreach missions for Highlanders were established thereafter (see MacColl, Duncan).

The RCC appears to have experienced some noteworthy recovery towards the end of the nineteenth century. Following the restoration of the Hierarchy in 1878, the Diocese of Argyll and the Isles was created. Its first Bishop was Angus MacDonald,* who built eight churches, opened three missions and established two convents before his elevation to Scottish metropolitan in 1892. The RC faithful recovered in numbers to about the level of 12,000 recorded in 1600.

Further theological and ecclesiological disputes made it difficult for the Presbyterian Churches to advance greatly in size. Controversy about the FC's Declaratory Act* of 1892 and the weakening of its adherence to the Westminster* Confession of Faith led to fragmentation, resulting in the emergence of the FPC from the FC in 1893. This occurred against the background of overtures for union between the FC and the Voluntaryist UPC. The eventual union of a large proportion of the FC and the UPC in 1900 caused a severe loss in the ministerial strength of the FC, with the majority of ministers in virtually all of its Presbyteries joining the new UFC. Only twenty-six ministers, predominantly in Highland charges, remained to form the FC (Continuing), which repealed the 1892 Declaratory Act, and reasserted its adherence to the Westminster Confession.

Although UFC congregations appeared in most parts of the Highlands, they were not as resilient or as strong as those of the FC, and they occupied a doctrinal middle ground which led to the loss of distinctiveness. The unification of most of the UFC with the CofS in 1929 greatly weakened the former, which eventually lost almost all of its 200 or so Highland congregations. The UFC has currently only four congregations within the whole Highland area. The FC, after a period of vacancies in most charges, gradually regained ground, and by 1905 was able to begin the process of refilling its pulpits. It has retained a pre-eminently Highland allegiance (currently ninety-five Highland congregations out of a total of 142), and this is evident in its loyalty to Gaelic.

THE HIGHLAND CHURCHES AND THE 'WORLD'. The use of Gaelic was a means to an end, but how far did the Presbyterian Churches embrace the Gaelic culture of the Highland people, especially in its secular form? A great deal of stereotyping is apparent in the perspectives commonly offered, especially in the rigid distinction drawn between the dogmatic and hostile attitude of the evangelical bodies and the more accommodating approach of the Moderate clergy and the RCC. The popular stereotype of total world-rejection by all Evangelicals is occasionally splendidly broken by the evidence; thus Evander MacIver alluded to the dances held in the house of no less a Highland Evangelical than John MacDonald of Ferintosh: 'I used to see as merry dancing in Dr MacDonald's house as anywhere, when many folks thought it was a sin to dance' (G. Hamilton (ed.), *Memoirs of a Highland Gentleman . . . Reminiscences of Evander MacIver*, E, 1905, 211). This may be the exception that proves the rule, but it is likely that there was considerable variation in the degree of austerity shown by different ministers in the Presbyterian Churches, from the warm humanity of MacDonald of Ferintosh to the severity of Roderick MacLeod,* the 'Bishop of Skye'. Secular renunciation may have intensified towards the end of the nineteenth century, especially as a greater theological conservatism took root and the Churches themselves became smaller as a result of fragmentation.

Within the Presbyterian Churches, especially the FC and the FPC, interaction between the world and the Church has been aided by various degrees of adherency. Adherents,* who enjoy some of the privileges of full members but who do not 'make a profession' which allows them to sit at the Lord's table, are a major part of the following of these Churches. In 1957, for example, the FC registered a total 'membership' of 5,909 full members and 18,377 adherents. The Churches thus preserve an 'outer shell' which allows them to penetrate secular society at various levels. Another significant link is maintained by ministers (as by priests in the RCC) who serve as councillors within their localities, and who sometimes act as office-bearers within Highland regional councils.

TWENTIETH-CENTURY PATTERNS. The Churches active in the Highlands, and especially the Presbyterian Churches, have had a major role to play in the development of the area throughout the centuries. Since 1900 their influence has diminished, but it is still potent, as can be seen in the strength of feeling against 'Sunday ferries' in Lewis and Harris. The Presbyterian Churches remain dominant, with smaller bodies such as Baptists in the Inner Hebrides and a Brethren* presence in Lewis. The Faith Mission* regularly conducts evangelistic missions in the region, and has a distinct Highland district.

As has happened in other parts of Britain, many individual churches are experiencing declining memberships. Falling membership is certainly attested among the conservative Presbyterian Churches (FC and FP) in Scotland generally (from a combined total of 27,550 in 1980 to 25,180 in 1984). In the Western Isles, these Churches have registered a 15 per cent decrease in membership in the same period, but a 3 per cent increase in the Highland mainland. Decline is also apparent in the attendance figures of churches offering Gaelic services in 1980-4. Declining membership in both districts is evident in the CofS, the loss being 2 per cent (P. Brierley and F. Macdonald, *Prospects for Scotland* (L, 1985), 40-1, 54-5, 74-5, 102-3).

Decline is caused by a variety of factors, including out-migration from certain areas (tending to favour the mainland churches), a preference for English rather than Gaelic as the language of worship among the younger age-groups (English being dominant in many Highland mainland churches), and perhaps a feeling that the Churches are too staid and too remote from the needs of modern society. There is, however, a growing awareness that the communities which they serve are economically fragile, especially in the Hebrides, and that the culture is changing as the Highlands experience immigration from the Lowlands and from England (*FCSR*, September 1989, 190–1). The Churches may thus need to face the challenge of adjustment to new demands and new contexts in the closing decade of the twentieth century. Their future viability may depend to no small degree on whether, and how, they make this adjustment.

See also Fisherfolk, Missions to; Preaching, Themes and Styles (Gaelic/Highland); Women in Highland Churches.

For an overview: A. C. O'Dell and K. Walton, *The Highlands and Islands of Scotland* (L, 1962); A. P. Smyth, *Warlords and Holy Men* (L, 1984); J. MacKay, *The Church in the Highlands* (L, 1914); J. MacInnes, *The Evangelical Movement in the Highlands of Scotland* (A, 1951); G. N. M. Collins, *The Heritage of Our Fathers* (E, 1974); J. Macleod, *By-paths of Highland Church History* (E, 1965); J. Highet, *The Scottish Churches* (L, 1960); C. W. J. Withers, *Gaelic in Scotland* (E, 1984) and V. E. Durkacz, *The Decline of the Celtic Languages* (E, 1983), both with excellent bibliographies.

For medieval culture: K. Steer and J. W. M. Bannerman, *Late Medieval Monumental Sculpture in the West Highlands* (E, 1977), and the Celtic background, G. W. S. Barrow, *Kingship and Unity: Scotland 1000–1306* (L, 1981); I. B. Cowan, 'The Medieval Church in Argyll and the Isles', *RSCHS* 20 (1978), 15–29.

On the Reformation: J. Kirk, *Patterns of Reform* (E, 1989).

Particular studies include: R. MacDonald, 'The Catholic Gaidhealtachd', *IR* 29 (1987), 56–72; D. Bebbington (ed.), *The Baptists in Scotland* (G, 1988), 280–308; D. E. Meek, 'Evangelical Missionaries in the Early Nineteenth-Century Highlands', *SS* 28 (1987), 1–34; id., 'The Independent and Baptist Churches of Highland Perthshire and Strathspey', *TGSI* 56 (1991), 269–343; R. MacLeod, 'The Progress of Evangelicalism in the Western Isles, 1800–1850' (PhD, University of Edinburgh, 1977); J. MacInnes, 'Religion in Gaelic Society', *TGSI* 52 (1980–2), 222–42; T. P. McCaughey, 'Protestantism and Scottish Highland Culture', in J. P. Mackey (ed.), *An Introduction to Celtic Christianity* (E, 1989), 172–205; A. I. Macinnes, 'Evangelical Protestantism in the Nineteenth-Century Highlands', in G. Walker and T. Gallagher (eds), *Sermons and Battle Hymns* (E, 1990), 43–68; G. Robb, 'Popular Religion and the Christianization of the Scottish Highlands in the Eighteenth and Nineteenth Centuries', *Journ. of Relig. Hist.* 16 (1990), 18–34. See also the bibliographies accompanying Celtic Saints; Monasticism, Celtic; Gaelic; Revivals.

D. E. Meek

Hill, Alexander (1785–1867), CofS divine, son of George Hill.* He was born in St Andrews, at whose University he studied, graduating in 1804. Licensed as a preacher in 1806, he did not obtain a charge till 1815, when he became minister of Colmonell, Ayrshire. The intervening period he spent as a private tutor. In 1816 he moved to the adjacent parish of Dailly. In 1840 he became Professor of Divinity at Glasgow, a position he occupied until his retirement in 1862. He remained loyal to the Est.C at the Disruption* of 1843 and played a leading part in endeavouring to rebuild its shattered fortunes.

Hill wrote a small number of works, including *The Practice in the Judicatories of the Church of Scotland* (E, 1830; ⁵enlarged, L, 1851), but his most valuable literary labour was his edition of his father's *Lectures in Divinity* (3 vols, E, 1821). He also edited his father's *A View of the Constitution of the Church of Scotland* (E, 1835), and *Counsels Respecting the Duties of the Pastoral Office* (E, 1862).

Hill was Moderator of the CofS General Assembly in 1845. He received a DD from St Andrews University in 1828.

FES VII, 402; *DNB* XXVI, 390–1; H. M. B. Reid, *The Divinity Professors in the University of Glasgow* (G, 1923), 310–7.

N. R. Needham

Hill, David Octavius (1802–70), FC painter and photographer. Born in Perth, he early developed a strong artistic talent, studying under Andrew Wilson in the Edinburgh School of Art. He became secretary to the Edinburgh Society of Artists (incorporated into the Royal Scottish Academy in 1838), occupying the position until a few months before his death. He was a founder of the Association for the Promotion of the Fine Arts in Scotland, and of the National Gallery of Scotland. His association with Robert Adamson of St Andrews and his pioneering work in photography led to Hill's novel application of photography to portraiture. Many of his 'calotype' portraits of distinguished men, including ministers and divines, can be seen today in the Scottish National Portrait Gallery. Hill's most famous painting is his 'The Signing of the Deed of Demission', begun in 1843 and finished in 1865. Its depiction of the first FC General Assembly contains some five hundred portraits of ministers and elders involved in the Disruption.*

H. Schwarz, *David Octavius Hill, Master of Photography* (L, 1932); S. Stevenson, *David Octavius Hill and Robert Anderson* (E, 1981); *DNB* XXVI, 391–2.

N. R. Needham

Hill, George (1750–1819), leading Moderate* divine. Minister of St Andrews 1780–1819, Hill was also a Professor in the University of St Andrews and led the Moderate party in the CofS General Assembly from the retirement of Principal William Robertson* in 1780.

His father, John Hill, minister of St Andrews (*FES* V, 235), died when George was only fourteen and

HILL, ROWLAND

his career was promoted by the Earl of Kinnoull, Chancellor of the University of St Andrews, and by Principal William Robertson* who recommended him to Pryse Campbell MP, one of the Lords of the treasury. After four years as tutor to the Campbell family, Hill was appointed Professor of Greek at the United College, St Andrews, in 1772. His uncle, Joseph McCormick, was minister at Prestonpans, and so it was the Presbytery of Haddington which licensed Hill in 1775 (ordained 1778, St Andrews). He was inducted to the second charge at St Andrews in 1780 and the first charge in 1808, and held his academic appointments along with his pastoral charges. He became Professor of Divinity at St Mary's College, St Andrews, in 1788 and Principal in 1791. He was Moderator of the General Assembly in 1789, and the friendship of Henry Dundas,* first Lord Melville, led to his appointment as Dean of the Thistle* in 1787 and as a Dean of the Chapel Royal* in 1799.

Hill was more than an ecclesiastical careerist. He was a competent teacher of Greek and is credited with raising standards in the teaching of theology. Notes on his lectures were published as *Theological Institutes* (E, 1803); a fuller version in three volumes was published after his death in 1821 as *Lectures in Divinity* (E, 1821) and reached a sixth edition by 1854. The *Lectures* teach orthodox Calvinistic theology. Thomas Chalmers* used them as a text book in New College* after the Disruption,* and they were popular among theological educators in America, *e.g.* R. L. Dabney.

Hill never reached Robertson's stature as an ecclesiastical statesman, for he was at once too dependent on the patronage of the Lord Advocate and too far from Edinburgh to be an effective force there.

See Systematic Theology.

G. Cook, *Life of George Hill* (E, 1820); C. G. M'Crie, 'George Hill', *British and Foreign Evangelical Review* 33 (1884), 669–719; E. Rodger, *A Book of Remembrance – the Descendants of the Rev. George Hill, D.D.* (G, 1913); *DNB* XXVI, 393–4; *FES* VII, 422–3.

H. R. Sefton

Hill, Rowland (1744–1833), author of *Journal of a Tour ... of Scotland*. In August 1798 and the following summer Rowland Hill, an irregular Anglican clergyman in deacon's orders who ministered at Surrey Chapel in Southwark, London, mounted two extensive preaching tours in Scotland. An aristocratic convert to Evangelicalism and an enthusiastic champion of itinerant preaching, Hill published the account of his first Scottish experiences early in 1799. With its amalgam of English Episcopalian distaste for the meanness of Scottish church buildings, pointed remarks about the coercive powers of the CofS General Assembly,* and disapproval of the spirit of bigotry and intolerance which seemed to characterize the smaller Presbyterian bodies, the *Journal* aroused the ire of many Scottish ministers, provoking a retort from amongst others John Jamieson,* a leading Edinburgh Anti-

HISLOP, STEPHEN

burgher* (*Remarks on the Rev. Rowland Hill's Journal, &c. ...*, 1799). The hostility engendered by Hill among the Moderate* clergy was one of the factors behind the decision of the 1799 General Assembly to close the pulpits of the national Church to those who, though ordained, were not licensed by the CofS.

Hill published other works – hymns, sermons, *etc.*, including *A Series of Letters, Occasioned by the Late Pastor of Admonition of the Church of Scotland ...* (E, 1799).

Journal of a Tour through the North of England and parts of Scotland with Remarks on the Present State of the Established Church of Scotland, and the Different Secessions Therefrom (L, 1799).

E. Sidney, *The Life of Rowland Hill* (L, ⁴1844); V. J. Charlesworth, *Rowland Hill* (L, 1877).

D. W. Lovegrove

Hislop, Stephen (1817–63), missionary and naturalist. He was born in Duns, Berwickshire, where his father was a Relief Church* elder, and educated at Edinburgh University, where a scientific and mathematical training sharpened his already well-developed interests in natural history. His divinity studies, between spells of teaching and tutoring, were at Glasgow under Stevenson MacGill* and at Edinburgh under Thomas Chalmers* and David Welsh.* Other intellectual and spiritual influences included Henry Duncan* of Ruthwell, Williams Chalmers Burns,* whose preaching at Kilsyth radically affected him, Erasma Hull his future wife (granddaughter of the English Evangelical Erasmus Middleton) and his entomologist brother Robert. John Wilson of Bombay (*see* Missions) turned his eyes to missionary service with his insistence that India needed teachers who could combine scientific excellence with theology. His divinity studies were concluding at the time of the Disruption;* he was accepted for India by the FC. Wilson had been arguing that the Western India field be extended to Nagpur, the centre of a Maratha princely state; a gift had become available for the purpose. Hislop was sent to open the mission.

He learned Marathi well, and gained a knowledge of several other Indian languages. He worked in India for 18 years with one break (which enabled him to assist with both the 1859–60 Revival and the Liverpool Conference on Missions, the former in fishing villages near Montrose).

For eight years he had as colleague Robert Hunter,* who shared his scientific interests; for most of the time he was single-handed. As with other Scottish India missions, education, in which secular learning was set in a Christian framework, was the main instrument; but, unlike the old Indian presidencies, Nagpur had no other schools. Hislop also combined education with itineration and vernacular preaching and a variety of pastoral oversight. Conversions came from diverse ethnic sources, including Indian soldiers and other incomers to the area. During the absence of John Anderson* he took over in Madras for a time, especially for the sake of the divinity students; with the support of

HITCHCOCK, JOHN WILLIAM

Alexander Duff* he successfully protested at plans to keep him there and close the Nagpur mission.

His itinerations included a month or so each year among the hitherto little known Gondh people. He learned the language and produced a form of writing it, compiled a compendium of information on Gondh life, and wrote down Gondh myths and traditions. This pioneer ethnographic survey of an Indian tribal people was near completion at Hislop's death, and was eventually published by Richard Temple, Chief Commissioner for the Central Provinces.

Hislop's home was in the East India Company settlement, and thus technically on British soil; but this did not preserve him from attacks on his person and property. His position as a British person independent of the Company's army and administration was unusual. He had various brushes with the administration, which, both Indian and British, he thought corrupt. He also criticized the participation of British officials and troops in Hindu festivals; the preparedness of the British Resident to hand over Christian converts as 'disobedient subjects' of the Raja; and the British administration's abandonment of Marathi as the language of the courts. His letters to, and briefing of, *The Friend of India* (then edited by George Smith*) may have affected the government decision in 1861 to establish the Central Provinces under a Chief Commissioner.

His scientific investigations covered archaeology, botany, zoology and above all geology, in which his scholarly papers and fossil collections provoked correspondence with specialists in Europe and India. He was the first to identify the region's coal seams, and a local mineral was named after him. He vigorously defended the Christian and missionary relevance of scientific study; seeking the truth by research was 'glorifying to the God of truth', and 'what is worthy of God to create is worthy of men to behold'.

He was accidentally drowned crossing a swollen stream. His main school became Hislop College, Nagpur.

See also Missions: South India.

Temptations of the Awakened and Converted (Montrose, 1860); R. Temple (ed.), *Papers Relating to the Aboriginal Tribes of the Central Provinces left in MSS by the Rev. Stephen Hislop* (Nagpur, 1866).

DNB XXVII, 12–13; *AFCS* I, 186; John Wilson, *Memorial Discourse on the Death of the Rev. Stephen Hislop of Nagpur* (Bombay, 1864); G. Smith, *Stephen Hislop, Pioneer Missionary and Naturalist in Central India* (L, 1888); S. Neill, *History of Christianity in India 1707–1858* (C, 1985), 316–19.

A. F. Walls

Hitchcock, John William (1882–1919), medical missionary. He was born at Bures St Mary, Suffolk, and worked as a clerk at his father's milling business. Baptized by F. B. Meyer at Westminster Bridge in 1899, he was accepted in 1905 by the Edinburgh Medical Missionary Society* with a view to service with the Sudan United Mission, but a spiritual conflict while a medical student at Edinburgh Royal Infirmary led to his withdrawal from that mission. While a houseman he met Dugald Christie* and was attracted to Mukden hospital, but agreed to a one-year locum position in the UF Calabar Mission in 1911. He was much stationed at Itu, and travelled widely, being much impressed by Mary Slessor.* Asked to make an investigative tour of the hinterland before departure, he recognized the strategic situation of Uburu, which he recommended as a hospital site. The UFC agreed, and Hitchcock was appointed to open it in 1912. Uburu proved decisive in the expansion of the mission up the Cross River. Hitchcock was an industrious Igbo-speaking evangelistic missionary. In 1917 staff shortage caused his transfer to Unwana as relief for the district missionary, and – after a vain struggle to supervise both – the closure of Uburu hospital. New staff shortages brought him to Itu again, and then the great influenza epidemic of 1917–18 hit the area. The consequent long hours, incessant work and hard travelling destroyed Hitchcock; he died soon after his 37th birthday. Hitchcock had brushes with colonial officials. He pressed for greater indigenous participation in church leadership. He seems to have made a deep impression on his colleagues: 'a superlatively great missionary, the greatest it has been my privilege to meet – and I except none', said A. W. Wilkie.*

Minutes of UFC Foreign Mission Committees 1919, no. 4543; W. P. Livingstone, *Dr Hitchcock of Uburu* (E, 1920); M. Ross and N. Obini, *Presbyterian Joint Hospital, Uburu 1913–1988* (Uburu, 1988).

A. F. Walls

Hog, James (c.1658–1734), leader of the Marrow* brethren and a prominent CofS minister. Educated in Edinburgh (MA, 1677) and Utrecht, Hog was ordained to Dalserf (near Hamilton) in 1691 and translated to Carnock (Fife) in 1699, where he remained the rest of his life. From his settlement in Carnock to the beginning of the Marrow Controversy* Hog wrote over twenty small books and pamphlets. They cover a variety of subjects, over half on the 'rooting' of grace in the soul. These include: *The Covenants of Redemption and Grace Displayed* (E, 1707), *Notes about The Spirit's Operations* (E, 1709) and *Remarks concerning the Rooting, Growth and Ripeness of a Work of Grace in the Soul* (E, 1715). The rest concern the encroaching deism* of the age, Church polity (the separation of the United Societies* from the CofS and the right of the people to choose their own minister), public prayer, the Lord's Supper and practical religion.

His 1717 preface to the *Marrow of Modern Divinity* embroiled him for the remainder of his life in the Marrow Controversy. He responded to criticism of the *Marrow* with several pamphlets and engaged in a pamphlet controversy with James Hadow* and James Adams (of Kinnaird) prior to the General Assembly's condemnation of the *Marrow*. Hog's inability, evident throughout his writings, to present his material in a clear, concise way, contributed substantially to the *Marrow*'s condemnation. At the same time he was called before the General Assembly's Committee for Purity of Doctrine, an examination which resulted in a considerable degree of mutual satisfaction.

Hog wrote two further dialogues on *The Controversie Concerning the Marrow*... (E, 1721–2), which were at best badly written. His defence of the *Marrow* made him the object of an inquiry and prosecution in the Synod of Fife, which lasted from 1719 to 1733 and concluded, the best efforts of his opponents notwithstanding, with a mild admonition.

FES III, 9–10; *Memoirs of... James Hog* (E, 1798); D. C. Lachman, *The Marrow Controversy* (E, 1988).

D. C. Lachman

Hog, Thomas (1628–92), influential Highland Covenanter.* Born in Tain, Ross-shire, and educated at Aberdeen, he was ordained to Kiltearn, Ross-shire, with which his name is associated, in 1654/5.

Although deposed in 1661 by the Synod of Ross, both for his sympathies with the Protesters* and his antipathy to prelacy, Hog had already gained considerable fame in the Highlands for his wise counsel as a pastor and his abilities as a preacher. Exiled first to Moray and then successively to Edinburgh, Berwick, London and Holland, he was repeatedly imprisoned (including thirty months on the Bass Rock*) for illicit preaching. He was one of the first of the ejected ministers to take young men on trial for license; one so trained by him was James Fraser of Brea.* He returned to Scotland in 1688 and was resettled at Kiltearn in 1691. William III* offered him the post of domestic chaplain, but Hog died without accepting it.

DNB XXVII, 81; FES VII, 41–2; Andrew Stevenson, *Memoirs of the Life of Mr. Thomas Hog* (E, 1756); *Memoirs of Mrs. William Veitch. Mr Thomas Hog,* ... (E, 1846); *The Banished Minister; or Scenes in the Life of Thomas Hog 1654–1692* (E, 1872).

J. A. Dickson

Hogg, Alfred George (1875–1954), missionary, theologian and philosopher. Born in Egypt, the son of the missionary John Hogg, he studied philosophy at Edinburgh University and entered the UP Divinity Hall, where he seems to have suffered a crisis of faith. Recovery was assisted by the friendship of D. S. Cairns,* who had been helped in a similar crisis by Hogg's father.

He went to India as a lay educational missionary of the UFC in 1903, to be Professor of Philosophy at Madras Christian College. He was licensed and ordained in 1915, and was Principal of the College through a time of major development, 1928–38. His Edinburgh philosophical mentor Andrew Seth Pringle-Pattison, a German Ritschlian theologian, and Cairns influenced his early thought. In *Karma and Redemption* (Madras, 1909), Hogg developed his critical distinction between faith and faiths, defining faith as the simple assurance or trust a person achieves through communion with God and faiths (beliefs) as the cognitive ways people achieve, maintain and interpret faith. He also introduced his missionary method of selective contrast, identifying karma as the pervasive Hindu belief most distinguishable from the Christian concept of redemption, a contrast through which he sought to impress Hindus with a religious need only Christ could satisfy. He developed this further in *Redemption from This World* (E, 1922).

Under Cairns' influence, Hogg expanded his understanding of moral and spiritual redemption to include immediate deliverance from physical affliction. As Chairman of Commission IV at the 1910 Edinburgh Missionary Conference,* Cairns made use of Hogg's thought in the Commission's final report, calling for the Church to return to the New Testament belief that God acts supernaturally to redeem the world from every form of evil.

Hogg published *Christ's Message of the Kingdom* (E, 1911; ²Madras, 1916) as a popular series of Bible study notes, but its chief purpose was to state the Christian message to the Hindu. Hogg believed that Hinduism offered an escape from a dissatisfying world made intolerable through suffering, whereas Christ's kingdom message promised deliverance through faith from all genuinely unredemptive suffering. Hogg's theology emerged into the world missionary debate at the 1938 Tambaram meeting of the International Missionary Council, where he was one of the chief critics of Hendrik Kraemer's theory of radical discontinuity (*The Authority of the Faith, The Tambaram Series* I, L, 1939). Hogg provided an alternative by drawing a line of continuity between Christian and non-Christian faith (something Kraemer did not allow), while emphasizing (with Kraemer) that a fundamental discontinuity exists between Christian and non-Christian beliefs. Hogg retired to Scotland in 1939, served several parishes during the Second World War and interpreted his life's work in numerous church and community meetings. His final contribution to missionary thought, *The Christian Message to the Hindu* (L, 1947), was originally delivered as the Duff Missionary Lecture* for 1945.

'The God that Must Needs Be Christ Jesus', *Intern. Rev. of Missions* 6 (1917), 62–73, 221–32, 383–94, 521–33; many significant articles in *Madras Christian College Magazine*.

FUFCS 543; FES IX, 438, 736, X, 420; J. L. Cox, 'The Development of A. G. Hogg's Theology' (PhD, Aberdeen University, 1977); E. J. Sharpe, *The Theology of A. G. Hogg* (Madras, 1971).

J. L. Cox

Hogg, James (1770–1835), satirist and poet, often remembered as the 'Ettrick Shepherd' of the *Blackwood's Edinburgh Magazine* parody. In reality he was a self-taught, often rough writer, but he was a genius, well-read and sophisticated, a keen parodist, a man who charmed society in Edinburgh and London, and who enjoyed the company of shepherds and farmers in the Scottish Borders (particularly his valley of Ettrick), whose oral tradition he knew intimately. A recent revival in interest has drawn attention to a prodigious output including *The Three Perils of Man* (L, E, 1822) and *The Domestic Manners and Private Life of Scott* (G, 1834). He has long been known as a splendid poet. Most of all he is now remembered for his extraordinary *The Private Memoirs and Confessions of a Justified Sinner* (L, 1824; ed. J. Carey, O, 1969), a satiric portrait of a rampant antinomian (*see* Marrow Controversy). The Sinner, Robert Wringhim, is convinced that no sin can call in question the salvation of an elect person; a suave devil-figure, Gil-Martin, easily corrupts Wringhim to the hell Wringhim threatens to others. Hogg's psychological insight into Wringhim's mind, the extraordinary portrait of a smiling, Bible-carrying devil, and the modernist narrative which overlays several plots, combine to create a unique atmosphere of evil and enigma. A sincere and churchgoing Christian, Hogg knew both his contemporaries' minds and speech-patterns and the antinomians whose reputation was still strong in the Borders during his formative years. Informed by such knowledge, *The Confessions* is undoubtedly one of the century's masterpieces.

D. Gifford, *James Hogg* (E, 1976).

I. Campbell

Holyrood, Augustinian abbey. David I* founded Holyrood (Edinburgh) in 1128 with Augustinian* canons from Merton, Surrey; the name derives from its notable relic of the true cross. The abbot was granted *pontificalia* (episcopal insignia) in 1379. A dependent priory was founded at Trail (Kirkcudbright) c.1170 and two Holyrood abbots became Bishops of Galloway: Henry c.1253, Simon de Wedale 1326. Thirty parishes were appropriated to Holyrood and Trail. The abbey was sacked by English forces in 1322, but much rebuilding was done in the fifteenth century.

As Edinburgh became the capital, Holyrood's prestige grew. Stewart kings made it their habitual residence, James II (1437–60) was born, crowned, married and buried there, and in 1501 the building of a royal palace in the outer court began. Its abbots were often royal officials. Robert Bellenden resigned as abbot c.1497 to become a Carthusian.* Robert Stewart, James V's natural son, became commendator* in 1539.

Holyrood was badly damaged by English forces in 1544 and 1547. The community, numbering twenty-four in 1537, was perhaps twenty in the 1550s. Andrew Blackhall, later a minister, helped to compose the Scottish Psalter (*see* Psalms). The abbey was used for Reformed worship, but in 1686–8 Holyrood became a RC chapel and Jesuit* college.

Liber Cartarum Sancte Crucis (Bannatyne Club, E, 1840); J. Harrison, *The History of the Monastery of the Holy-Rood* (E, L, 1919); *An Inventory of the Ancient and Historical Monuments of the City of Edinburgh* (E, 1951), 129–44; *The Bannatyne Miscellany* II (E, 1836), 9–31; Easson-Cowan, 88–97.

M. Dilworth

Home, John (1722–1808), minister of Athelstaneford (1747–57) and private secretary to Lord Bute. One of the Moderate* *literati* of Edinburgh, his claim to fame is his authorship of the tragedy *Douglas* which led to the famous Douglas Affair* of 1757, which was pursued from presbytery level to the General Assembly and which led to Home's resignation of his charge. He became the protégé of the Earl of Bute (Prime Minister, 1761–3), whose patronage secured for him the production of his subsequent plays, although they failed to gain critical acceptance. Bute also secured for him the post of Conservator of Scottish Privileges at Campvere in Holland, which gave him an *ex officio* seat at the General Assembly, which he used to support the Moderate party* in the patronage* controversy. He was the close friend and confidant of David Hume.*

R. B. Sher, *Church and University in the Scottish Enlightenment* (E, 1985); *DNB* XXVII, 235–8; *FES* I, 354.

J. R. McIntosh

Homiletics. The most significant period of homiletic discussion occurred in Scotland between 1740 and 1800, synthesizing classical rhetoric with contemporary understandings of nature and the mind. Developing a body of homiletic theory did not become a priority until the second quarter of the eighteenth century, though preaching* had been an important element of religious life at least since John Knox.* Two elements worked together to create a need for homiletic instruction. First, the Church became even more significant as a symbol of nationalism following the Union.* Second, there was a tremendous interest in rhetorical eloquence in Scottish society. Eloquence was understood as the pivot of all understanding, moulding together the divese fragments of knowledge into wholeness. It was only in the context of preaching that the two elements of Church and eloquence were fused together; preaching was eloquence in the context of the Church. Beginning around 1740 therefore, there was an almost insatiable interest in homiletic instruction, which spurred a sixty-year era of creative development in homiletic theory. After 1800, homiletic theory taught at Scottish universities was little more than a review of material from the preceding century.

Because professors of theology in eighteenth-century Scotland were mainly Moderates,* most homiletic theory was developed by the liberal constituents of the Church who, above all things were grieved 'that the Church was not in sympathy with ... the culture of the age'. It is therefore not surprising that their homiletics was essentially contemporary rhetorical theory with religious application. It was largely derived from society and applied to Scripture, rather than the reverse.

Homiletic theory in Scotland developed along two

basic lines. In the human-nature approach of William Leechman* and George Campbell,* an understanding of the workings of the mind was considered the key to effective communication.

The *belles lettres* approach to communication advocated by Hugh Blair* was, on the other hand, more literary in its emphasis. Blair deals with issues such as the sublime in writing, the rise, progress, and structure of language, as well as critical analysis of selected written texts.

Both the human-nature and belletristic homiletic orientations were ultimately grounded in the Greek and Roman rhetorical traditions. As deeply indebted to classical theories of rhetoric as homileticians were, however, they carefully selected and integrated traditional material of the past with the product of their own time. Besides the classical influence, all homiletic theories were commonly characterized by various mixes between the two elements of nature and the mind.

NATURE. To a greater or lesser degree, all eighteenth-century homileticians base their theories of communication on nature, using the terms 'nature', 'natural law' and acting 'natural' as a speaker, interchangeably. During the Enlightenment, 'nature' primarily signified uniformity. 'All the rules of criticism and morality,' contends Adam Smith in his lectures on rhetoric, 'when traced to their foundation, turn out to be some principles of common sense which every one assents to'. Smith's use of the term 'common sense' placed the emphasis on 'common', indicating that a particular idea or feeling was shared by most others (*see* Scottish Realism*). Information of value only to people of a certain era or condition was considered without truth or value. The object, therefore, of religious and social reformers was to homogenize individuals with regard to standards of belief and refinement, and one accomplished that through adherence to 'the light of nature'.

Leechman and Blair understood the communication enterprise, in its totality, as an attempt to meld the speaker's discourse in all its parts with natural law. According to Blair, 'The Art of Oratory proposes nothing more than to follow out that track which Nature has first pointed out to men.' For Leechman and Blair, the thought that mankind could improve on nature, in terms of effective communication, was absurd. A good rhetorician simply knew and understood the laws of nature well enough to apply them to communication. Division of a topic, methods of argument, the order of material, language, style and delivery all ought to conform to nature. And indeed, if one has a choice between naturalness and accuracy in delivery, Leechman admonishes students to be natural even if it brings some inaccuracy with it.

Although Campbell acknowledges the foundational quality of nature in contributing to an understanding of communication, he sees nature only as the springboard for homiletics, a necessary first step. The rest of rhetorical development is better left in human hands, to refine what was first observed in nature. *The Philosophy of Rhetoric* quickly leaves the discussion of nature to speak instead of the faculties of the mind.

MIND. All Scottish homileticians of the eighteenth century placed great emphasis on the mind, which was closely aligned with concepts of 'reason', 'rationality', and 'argument'. Thus Campbell clearly expresses his opinion that 'there is no art whatever that hath so close a connexion with all the faculties and powers of the mind, as eloquence, or the art of speaking.' He speaks throughout his work about the importance of the science of the mind, and spends a significant amount of space defining proper reasoning and arguments for rhetorical discourse.

Whereas the French preaching of the period evidenced a bent in the direction of influencing the passions, and the English toward influencing the understanding, Scottish homiletics attempted to find balance between the two. However, in Leechman's scheme the mind controls thinking, emotions, and behaviour. Indeed, when Leechman speaks of the passions, he does so in terms of exciting 'the passions *of the mind*', indicating the importance homileticians attached to the mind and reason as holding the key to whatever end the speaker wished to accomplish.

Homiletic theory in eighteenth-century Scotland was grounded in the classical tradition, mediated by major emphases on nature and the mind.

H. Blair, *Lectures on Rhetoric and Belles Lettres*, ed. H. F. Harding (Carbondale, IL, 1965); G. Campbell, *The Philosophy of Rhetoric*, ed. L. F. Bitzer (Carbondale, IL, 1988); H. Cohen, 'William Leechman's Anticipation of Campbell', *Western Journal of Speech Communication* 32 (1968), 92–9; D. Daiches, *The Paradox of Scottish Culture* (L, 1964); W. Leechman, 'Treatise of Rhetoric Especially as it Regards the Pulpit' (unpublished student notes, 1763, Glasgow University Library); A. O. Lovejoy, 'The Parallel of Deism and Classicism', *Modern Philology* 29 (1931), 281–99; A. Smith, *Lectures on Rhetoric and Belles Lettres*, ed. J.M. Lothian (Carbondale, IL, 1963).

T. G. *Addington*

Honyman, Andrew (1619–76), Bishop of Orkney.* Born in St Andrews, he was ordained to Ferryport-on-Craig, translated to St Andrews (1642 second charge, 1662 first charge) and served as archdeacon of St Andrews (1662) before being appointed Bishop of Orkney in 1664. Two years later he was wounded by a poisoned bullet intended for Archbishop James Sharp.* He never fully recovered and his early death was attributed to his injuries. Honyman undertook repairs to St Magnus Cathedral, Kirkwall, particularly after the steeple was destroyed by lightning in 1671. Although he was a zealous Covenanter* before the Restoration,* his publications included *The Seasonable Case of Submission to the Church Government Now Re-established by Law* (E, 1662) and *A Survey of the Insolent and Infamous Libel entitled Naphtali* (E, 1668 – see Stewart, Sir James).

See also Wood, James.

HOPE, JOHN

FES VII, 354; J. B. Craven, *Scots Worthies, 1560–1688* (E, 1894); id., *History of the Church in Orkney, 1662–1688* (Kirkwall, 1893).

W. P. L. Thomson

Hope, John (1807–93), philanthropist and founder of the Hope Trust.* He was born at Dalry, Midlothian, the son of James Hope, WS. After education at Edinburgh Royal High School and University he was himself admitted a WS in 1828. Following a Grand Tour he began in the early 1830s to develop his successful legal practice. This, in conjunction with substantial wealth inherited from his father, who died in 1842, provided the means to support his charitable activities.

In his early thirties Hope acquired distinctively evangelical convictions and began his half century of philanthropic endeavour. He supported numerous religious, social and political causes including sabbatarianism and home missions, but he particularly espoused total abstinence and 'anti-Popery'. He was generous with donations, but also sought to bring his influence to bear on government and the local authorities, especially in his capacity as an Edinburgh Town Councillor. He was prone to distrust organizations he did not control, and hence formed his own machinery to further his enthusiasms. Although a loyal son of the CofS, he had little patience with ecclesiastical politics and was anxious to foster co-operation between the Churches in relation to the causes he had at heart.

In connection with abstinence, Hope's most substantial achievement was the establishment in 1847 of the British League of Juvenile Abstainers, which in its heyday ran twenty weekly meetings in the Edinburgh area. Further classes were formed for apprentices and Hope took a great interest in the welfare of his young people, financing holidays and assisting them in the search for employment. In his later years his support for total abstinence led him to campaign for the use of unfermented wine at the Lord's Supper.

On the anti-Catholic front from 1850 onwards Hope developed a similar movement of Protestant classes, seeing it as his duty to teach children 'to avoid the mass house as the public house'. In this endeavour, as in his abstinence work, he commissioned numerous short tracts and other literature, and gave support to a number of relevant periodicals. Initially he also worked with the British Reformation Society and the Anti-Popery Committee of the CofS to establish missions to RCs in several towns, but the other organizations eventually withdrew. Hope was left to support operations on his own, and these became confined largely to Edinburgh. In the mid-1850s he founded the Scottish Protestant Association, which campaigned, with little hope of success, for the repeal of Catholic Emancipation.*

Hope never married and left his substantial fortune to form the Hope Trust.* This led to a celebrated court action in which his disappointed relatives claimed that he had not been of sound disposing mind, as he had delusions regarding abstinence and RCism. The House of Lords decided in July 1898 that there was a case to answer and the Trustees, uncertain of the prejudices of the jury and anxious to protect Hope's reputation, agreed to an out-of-court settlement. The incident illustrated the extent to which, at the time of this death, Hope's concerns had become unfashionable.

See also Anti-Catholic Societies; Temperance Movement.

D. Jamie, *John Hope* (E, 1900); J. B. Primmer (ed.), *Life of Jacob Primmer* (E, 1916); S. Bruce, *No Pope of Rome* (E, 1985); J. R. Wolffe, *The Protestant Crusade in Great Britain, 1829–1860* (O, 1991); Hope's extensive papers survive in the SRO.

J. R. Wolffe

Hope Trust, for the promotion of Protestantism, total abstinence and the use of unfermented wine at the Lord's Supper, set up by a deed of 22 April 1890 and endowed with the £400,000 estate of John Hope,* WS. The income was used to finance magic lantern lectures and circulation of appropriate literature. By the 1970s the terms of the original Trust were proving unrealistically restrictive, and the necessary legal measures were taken to allow a more flexible and positive interpretation of Hope's intentions. Part-time lecturers are employed and the Trust also gives support to a number of Protestant organizations, provides book grants to theological students and funds a postgraduate scholarship. The Trust is based in Hope's former house at 31 Moray Place, Edinburgh.

D. Jamie, *John Hope* (E, 1900).

J. R. Wolffe

HOPE-SCOTT, JAMES ROBERT

Hope-Scott, James Robert (1812–73), convert to RCism. He was educated at Eton and Christ Church, Oxford, and became a Fellow of Merton College. Excellently connected, he was a natural conservative of the *noblesse oblige* school. The owner of considerable estates in the Highlands, Borders, Ireland and France, he inherited Abbotsford through his first wife, Charlotte Lockhart, granddaughter of Sir Walter Scott. In 1860, two years after her death, he married Lady Victoria Fitzalan Howard, who died in 1870.

Extensively travelled on the continent, he was deeply influenced by German social romantic ideals and later by Frederic Le Play, *La Reforme Sociale*. His early philanthropy supported juvenile migration schemes to Canada and South Africa, the suppression of vagrancy, and Glenalmond College (Episcopalian).

A friend of Gladstone and of Newman, whose university schemes he supported, he converted to Catholicism in 1851. In his funeral oration Newman noted his 'lofty fastidiousness and keen wit'. Having given over 40,000 to help Catholic chapels, schools and charities, he was a model convert. In 1854–66 he built three churches in the Borders and two in Moidart. He was buried at St Margaret's Convent, Edinburgh.

Hope-Scott Papers, NLS, Edinburgh; *DNB* XXVII, 330–2; J. H. Newman, *Sermon Preached*

... at the Requiem Mass for ... J. R. Hope Scott, Esq (L, 1873); V. A. McClelland, English Roman Catholics and Higher Education, 1839–1903 (O, 1973); R. Ornsby, Memoirs of James Robert Hope-Scott 2 vols (L, ²1884).

B. Aspinwall

Hospitals, Medieval. Some 150 hospitals are recorded in medieval Scotland, Perth having as many as five. Their differing functions are reflected in different names, while their dedications or siting (e.g. on pilgrim routes) and their dependency on monastic or other patrons are often revealing. In addition to the early prevalent leprosy (a term covering several skin infections), they catered for geriatric or handicapped patients, widows (Dunfermline), seamen (Findhorn), casual poor (Glasgow). Responding to Lollard* criticism of neglect, collegiate churches* like Hamilton and Corstorphine provided hospital annexes, and royal supervision emerged. Richard Guthrie, James II's almoner-general, conducted inspections (e.g. Montrose) and reconstituted St Lawrence's, Haddington. Some hospitals came to be supported by confraternities or were converted to secular control, while a few suffered in the English wars or were terminated, wholly (like Aberdour) or partially (like Elgin). The effect of neglectful preceptors and wardens, economic decay and inflation was to provoke increased regulation from communal prayer to uniform dress. Hospital fare was plentiful though plain. Spiritual healing is amply attested as an aim, medical treatment less so. Some promising investigation of herbal gardens has begun, though the outcome of excavations at Soutra hospital in Midlothian (founded by Malcolm IV c.1164) awaits finalization.

See also Crutched Friars.

Easson-Cowan, 162–200; J. Durkan, 'Care of the Poor: Pre-Reformation Hospitals', IR 10 (1959), 268–80; J. H. Dickson and W. W. Gauld, 'Mark Jameson's Physic Plants', Scottish Medical Journal 32 (1987), 60–2; B. Tierney, Medieval Poor Law (Berkeley and Los Angeles, 1959).

J. Durkan

House Church Movement, the name given to charismatic churches which, in contrast to the wider 'renewal movement', operate outside existing denominational structures. The name is misleading in that few of the groups to which it refers now meet in homes. Alternative designations such as 'Restorationism' have been proposed, but leaders of the movement continue to describe their congregations as 'house churches' (e.g. J. Noble, House Churches: Will They Survive?, Eastbourne, 1988). 'New churches' is another designation. The house churches share certain convictions concerning the work of the Holy Spirit with the wider charismatic movement;* their distinctive beliefs are in the areas of eschatology and ecclesiology. They are generally separatist and have developed a doctrine of the Church which recognizes a restored apostolate. Since their emergence in the mid-1960s, house churches have demonstrated an impressive rate of growth. In so far as the movement is an expression of 'cultural Modernism' (D. Bebbington, Evangelicalism in Modern Britain, L, 1989, 248), its impact has been minimal in those areas of Scotland most resistant to contemporary culture. However, the ability of these churches to create a genuine sense of Christian community attracts people unsettled in a secular culture, with the result that they have become a growing force in urban contexts, often calling themselves 'Christian Fellowship'. The extension of the 'Spring Harvest' gatherings into Scotland (with annual meetings at Ayr) and a series of visits by the American charismatic leader John Wimber to Edinburgh have boosted such congregations, while their indirect influence on Scottish Christianity can be detected in changing styles of worship and hymnology within mainline denominations. There are some 150 fellowships associated with the movement in Scotland.

E. Barker, 'Religion in the UK Today' in P. Brierley (ed.), UK Christian Handbook (L, 1983), 5–9; J. Thurman, New Wineskins: A Study of the House Church Movement (Frankfurt, 1982); D. Tomlinson, 'Unity and Society', Tomorrow Today (October, 1988), 10–11; A. Walker, Restoring The Kingdom (L, 1985); B. Wilson, The Social Impact of New Religious Movements (NY, 1981), 221–3.

D. W. Smith

House of Lords Decision 1904, see Free Church Case.

Howie, John (1735–93), chronicler and biographer. Howie lived on his ancestral farm of Lochgoin, in Renfrewshire, which had been a noted place of refuge in Covenanting times. He early developed an interest in the Covenanters* and Reformers, and went on to amass a wealth of material from manuscript and published sources. This he used as a basis for a series of biographical sketches which in 1775 he published under the title of Biographia Scoticana or Scots Worthies. The work proved immediately popular, and a second enlarged edition was issued in 1781. Many other editions followed, and by the early nineteenth century the book had become a standard part of the library of many a pious Scottish household. Howie also edited collections of the sermons of the leading field-preachers,* the proceedings of the United Societies* which had met during persecution times, and various other pieces. He left a brief Life giving some account of his spiritual experience.

Though possessing only a basic education, Howie developed a distinctive and appealing literary style which was in peculiar sympathy with the subjects with which he dealt. While he contributed relatively little that was original, he performed valuable service by rescuing from oblivion much important material which, without his painstaking efforts, would certainly have perished. Not the least significant feature of his work was its appearance at a time when the memory of the Covenanters and Reformers was fast being forgotten. In his own way, Howie did much to rekindle Scottish public interest in its Reformed heritage and to pave the way for the evangelical revival of the next century.

Biographia Scoticana . . . Scots Worthies (G, 1775, many subseq. edns); *A Collections of Lectures and Sermons* (G, 1779; rep. as *Sermons in Time of Persecution in Scotland*, E, 1880); *Faithful Contendings Displayed* (G, 1780; incl. *A Collection of Very Valuable Sermons . . .* , G, 1780); *Faithful Witness-Bearing Exemplified* (Kilmarnock, 1783); *Reformation Principles, etc. Re-exhibited* (G, 1787); *Memoirs of the Life of John Howie* (G, 1796).

DNB XXVIII, 121; W. J. Couper, 'John Howie . . .', *RSCHS* 6 (1938), 55–65.

M. Grant

Howie, Robert (1568–?1646), CofS divine. Born in or near Aberdeen, Howie studied at King's College, Aberdeen, at Herborn in Hesse (under Caspar Olevianus), and at Basel. Most of his literary productions date from his time at Basel; these were works of standard Reformed divinity, including *De Justificatione Hominis coram Deo* (Basel, 1590), *De Reconciliatione Hominis cum Deo* (Basel, 1591) and *De Communione Fidelium cum Christo* (Basel, 1590).

Returning to Scotland, Howie became minister of St Nicholas (Third Charge), Aberdeen in 1591, and in 1594 was appointed the first Principal of Marischal College, Aberdeen. In 1598 he took a charge in Dundee, but was banned in 1605 by the Privy Council from exercising his ministry in the town or residing there. This was as a punishment for his having helped a political faction oppose the election of certain magistrates. After becoming minister of Keith, Banffshire in 1606, Howie was back in favour the following year when James VI* appointed him Principal of St Mary's College, St Andrews, in place of Andrew Melville.* Here Howie ingratiated himself with his royal patron by teaching an episcopal form of Church polity – for which, however, he was sharply rebuked by the Presbytery of St Andrews. His episcopal ardour was later replaced by opposition to royal attempts to conform the CofS to the government and worship of the English Church, and Howie was in danger of being dismissed. However, he remained Principal of St Mary's during the years of episcopacy* and for some time after the re-establishment of Presbyterianism* in 1638. It is not certain when he died.

Howie was one of the principal authors of the confession of faith adopted by the General Assembly at Aberdeen in 1616.

R. Lippe, *Selections from Wodrow's Biographical Selections* (A, 1890), lxix–lxxi, 235–44; *FES* VII, 418; J. Row, *The History of the Kirk of Scotland* (E, 1842), 248–9; J. K. Cameron (ed.), *Letters of John Johnston . . . and Robert Howie . . .* (E, 1963).

N. R. Needham

Huguenots, French Protestants, many of whom emigrated because of persecution. Huguenots were a minority in France but threatened political stability. During 1562–98 France suffered civil wars: half the aristocracy declared themselves Huguenot, reacting to weakness and ambition from the Crown. In the massacre of St Bartholomew's day, 1572, thousands lost their lives. (The aim was to assassinate a few militant Huguenot leaders, but discontented mobs escalated violence.) The Edict of Nantes (1598) gave Huguenots freedom of worship and civil liberties. Protestantism survived among skilled artisans; the nobility deserted the cause. The influence of the Counter-Reformation led to a diminishing of Huguenot rights. The Edict of Nantes was revoked in 1685: freedom of worship was impossible until the French Revolution.*

Huguenot emigration, following the pattern of persecution, was highest in the 1680s: 200,000–250,000 left, including many skilled workers. Most went to the nearby Calvinist Netherlands and southern England. Scotland received surprisingly few. Nevertheless, its reputation for Reformed religion led a number of Huguenots, publishing secretly in the 1570s, to disguise their tracts' origins by naming Edinburgh as the place of publication. Scottish concern was shown by collections for French churches in England (1576 and 1587), and for Huguenots in France (1622), when 80,424 6s. 8d. Scots was raised. But evidence is sparse for Huguenot settlement, apart from Frenchmen employed to teach the French language; even in Edinburgh few can be found before the 1680s. In 1586 the burgh granted 'the ministeris of the Fraynche kirk that is to cum heir' a place to worship, and permission for French exiles to practise trades: but no evidence survives of a Huguenot community at this time. Thomas Vautrollier, in London from 1562 and printer of Beza's Latin New Testament and Latin and English editions of Calvin's *Institutes*, worked in Edinburgh, 1584–6, with the General Assembly's approval. In 1587 he printed an edition of the *Book of Common Order** in London. Scattered references occur in burgh records, 1600–80, to French settlers plying trade. More arrived in the 1680s and 1690s when persecution was fiercest (including perfumiers, a mirror-maker and an ivory worker), and promised to teach Scottish apprentices their crafts. In 1729 a linen-weaving venture began, but soon failed (trace of it remains in the street-name 'Picardy Place'). A French church was formed in 1682: its ministers were paid by the burgh, from a tax on ale authorized by Parliament in 1690. The church survived until 1786.

The Confession and Discipline approved by the first national French Synod (1559) provided a model for the Scots Confession* and *First Book of Discipline*,* but were less influential than might be expected. The Burning Bush* symbol is said to have been used by the French church in 1583. Among Scots who had experience of French churches and Huguenot Academies were Andrew Melville,* Robert Boyd,* John Cameron,* and John Welsh.*

D. E. Easson, 'French Protestants in Edinburgh

(I)', *Proceedings of the Huguenot Society* 17 (1950), 325–44 [(II) never appeared]; A. W. C. Hallen, 'Huguenots in Scotland', *Proc. of the Huguenot Soc. of London* 2 (1887–8), 166–81; *Extracts from the Records of the Burgh of Edinburgh, 1573–1718* (Scottish Burgh Records Society, E, 1882–1967); D. Hay Fleming (ed.), 'Scottish Contributions to the Distressed Churches of France, 1622', *Miscellany of the Scottish History Society* 3 (second series, E, 1919); C. F. A. Marmoy, 'The Registers of the French Churches of Edinburgh and Cork', *Proc. of the Huguenot Soc.*22 (1970–6), 281–2; J. Mason, 'The Weavers of Picardy', *Book of the Old Edinburgh Club* 25 (1945), 1–33; *BUK*; J. Durkan, 'The French Connection in the 16th and early 17th centuries', in T. C. Smout, ed., *Scotland and Europe* (E, 1986); R. D. Gwynn, *Huguenot Heritage* (L, 1985); R. M. Kingdon, *Myths about the St Bartholomew's Day Massacre* (Cambridge, MA, 1988). J. A. Fleming, *Huguenot Influence in Scotland* (G, 1953) is unreliable.

S. Hardman Moore

Hume, David (1711–76), Scottish philosopher. Hume is a pivotal figure in the development of Western philosophy, including the philosophy of religion, on which he wrote a great deal, much of which has set the agenda for subsequent debate. Throughout his philosophical writings, but particularly in *An Enquiry Concerning Human Understanding* (1748), Hume developed philosophical ideas and arguments with avowedly anti-metaphysical and anti-theological consequences.

Destined for a career in the law, Hume's energies were soon captured by the study of philosophy and history. He published the major part of his first work *The Treatise of Human Nature* (L), designed to be an account of the mind on empirical principles, in 1739, the remainder appearing the following year. To his intense disappointment the book did not bring to Hume the prominence that he craved.

His life thereafter was devoted to tutoring and travel until he became librarian to the Faculty of Advocates in Edinburgh in 1752. Here he prepared his history of England, the work for which he was best known until the present century: *The History of Great Britain*, 4 vols, E, 1754–9; expanded, revised and corrected as *The History of England*, 8 vols, L, 1778. Later he became secretary to the British Embassy in Paris, and then Under-Secretary of State. As a person he was cheerful, charitable and tolerant, a witty raconteur, but reticent about his own personal religious views.

MAIN THEMES. The key to Hume's philosophy is his scepticism, his claim that experience does not disclose any connections of causal necessity between the events it experiences to enable us to reason with certainty either about the nature of the world disclosed in experience or to what the future will be like. Laws of nature are simply generalizations from past experience; they generate expectations, but they do not enable us to make rationally-based predictions. Similarly, experience does not disclose the existence of an enduring, substantial self, but only a 'bundle of sensations'. There can be no immortality of the soul if there are no souls. Hume claimed that moral distinctions are based not upon reason but upon the passions, or interests, and that action is the outcome not of belief but of desire. In taking this view Hume foreshadowed later subjectivist and emotivist accounts of ethics.

Paradoxically, perhaps, such radical views made Hume a practical conservative. As habit is the only available basis on which we can cope with the world in general, so custom is the best guide in ethics and politics. Besides being influential in his own right as a great philosopher, Hume is also noteworthy as the person responsible, on Kant's own admission, for awakening him from his 'dogmatic slumbers'.

While Hume is the foremost Scottish philosopher, he can hardly be said to be an exponent of Scottish Common-Sense realism,* even though some devotees of that philosophy, such as James M'Cosh,* have made such a claim for him. Hume had a high opinion of Thomas Reid (*see* Scottish Realism), however, writing to him on one occasion that he had 'learned more from your writings in this kind than from all others put together'.

MAIN ACHIEVEMENTS IN THE PHILOSOPHY OF RELIGION. In the philosophy of religion Hume is noteworthy for four distinct achievements. He provided a critique of the then-popular argument from design for God's existence, which, despite his critique, lived on well into the nineteenth century as the most frequently used apologetic* tool. Hume argued, in brief, that the hypothesis that the universe is the handiwork of an omnipotent designer is only one hypothesis among many that are consistent with the facts. The existence of evil, in particular, poses acute problems for the design argument.

He also undermined the apologetic use of the appeal to miracles to validate the Christian religion, maintaining that, while miracles are possible, there is never sufficient evidence to believe that one has taken place, since the degree of evidence needed would have to be such as to 'naturalize' the event in question. So miracles cannot be used to make religion credible *ab initio*, though Hume does not rule out there being evidence for miracles given certain other assumptions of a theological nature.

The third main influence lies in the impetus that Hume gave to naturalistic explanations of religious phenomena in *The Natural History of Religion* (L, 1757), paving the way for more thorough-going naturalisms, e.g. evolutionism.

Finally, throughout Hume's writings on theology and religion, there are repeated attacks upon the cognitive meaningfulness of language used about God when that language attempts to take us beyond experience. These views anticipate those of later logical positivists about theological and indeed all metaphysical language.

STYLE. Hume expressed his radical ideas on religion cautiously and obliquely, using irony and a professed fideism, in order to mask his own position and to soften the impact of his views. Hume's cautious style means that he is seldom, if ever, to be found directly controverting some theological position. More directly-expressed arguments, which were potentially more disturbing, for example his essays 'The Immortality of the Soul' and 'Of Suicide', were suppressed in his lifetime by Hume on the advice of his publisher. His *Dialogues Concerning Natural Religion* (L, 1779) discuss the standard arguments for the reasonableness of theistic belief.

Despite Hume's caution, opposition led to his being denied the chair of Moral Philosophy at the University of Edinburgh in 1745 and the chair of Logic at the University of Glasgow in 1752. In 1755 an attempt was made to excommunicate him from the CofS.

Hume's direct influence upon the religious thought of Scotland was less than his influence elsewhere. This was due, perhaps, to the success of efforts to suppress his views, and to their radical character. No doubt his writings contributed to the rise and strength of moderatism in the CofS, though precise lines of influence are hard to trace. The threat posed by his scepticism was a chief spur to the rise of Scottish Common-Sense philosophy.

The Life of David Hume, written by himself (L, 1777); *Life and Correspondence*, ed. J. H. Burton, 2 vols (E, 1846).

A. Flew, *Hume's Philosophy of Belief* (L, 1961); J. C. A. Gaskin, *Hume's Philosophy of Religion* (L, 1978); R. Wollheim (ed.), *Hume on Religion* (L, 1963); T. E. Jessop, *A Bibliography of David Hume* (L, 1938).

P. Helm

Hungary, *see* Missions (Jewish); Bonar, Andrew; Duncan, John; Edersheim, Alfred; Haining, Jane; Keith, Alexander; McCheyne, Robert M.; Somerville, Alexander N.

Hunter, Adam Mitchell (1871–1955), librarian of New College,* Edinburgh. Born in Edinburgh, he studied at Edinburgh University. In 1898 he entered the ministry of the FC (later UFC and CofS), as colleague and successor at Cardross Free Church, in Dunbartonshire. He wrote *The Age of Daniel and the Exile* (L, 1904) and *The Teaching of Calvin* (G, 1920), in which he surveyed the theology and churchmanship of Calvin from a sympathetic but not uncritical viewpoint. He became librarian of New College in 1922. In 1946 he wrote a section on New College library for Hugh Watt's *New College, Edinburgh: a Centenary History* (E, 1946).

FUFCS 585.

N. R. Needham

Hunter, Andrew (1744–1809), CofS evangelical divine. Born in Edinburgh of a well-to-do family, after private schooling he studied arts and divinity at the University before a year of theology at Utrecht. Remaining with his father until his death, he continued to study under Robert Walker (1716–83; *FES* I, 12, 25, 60, 137) and to participate in the Newtonian Society (precursor of the Royal Society of Edinburgh, of which he was a founding member in 1783), and other theological and literary societies (*see* Clubs and Societies) – a practice he later commended to his students. Soon after being ordained to New Church, Dumfries (1770), he sold the ancestral seat (Abbotshill, Ayrshire) and bought the Barjarg estate (near Thornhill, Dumfriesshire – still partly in the family's hands) which he 'improved' agriculturally with innovative technology (machinery from his limestone quarry has recently merited preservation).

In 1779 he was awarded Edinburgh's DD, translated to New Greyfriars, Edinburgh, appointed colleague and successor (1787) to his old teacher Robert Hamilton (1707–87; *FES* I, 46–7) in the Divinity chair – to the disappointment of James Macknight* (who had already written his lectures!) and his fellow-Moderates* – and married to Lord Napier's daughter. In 1786 he transferred to the Tron Church after the Presbytery disputed at length the Town Council's right of presentation. In 1793 he was Moderator, but declined a royal chaplaincy.

Hunter was a decided and prominent Evangelical, lecturing from the *Theologia Christiana* of Benedict Pictet of Geneva (1655–1724). Hardly a scintillating or original teacher ('dull and Dutch'), he was generous in friendship and material help for students, 'providing for young men of his own fanatical cast' (Alexander Carlyle*) – but also for Alexander Murray,* later a distinguished orientalist. He preserved untarnished the reputation of a Christian gentleman (he dined often with James Boswell), and his support for religious and charitable causes was extensive. His lecture notes (6 vols) survive in MS in Edinburgh University Library, as do his lectures on Romans, Ephesians and James.

DNB XXVIII, 284; *FES* I, 34, 137; VII, 383; H. M. Wellwood, *A Sermon . . . Following the Funeral of the Revd. A. Hunter* (E, 1809); J. Kay, *A Series of Original Portraits*, I (E, 1837), 298–302; A. Bower, *The History of the University of Edinburgh*, III (E, 1830), 204–9.

D. F. Wright

Hunter, Archibald Macbride (1906–91), minister in the CofS and New Testament scholar. He was born in Kilwinning, Ayrshire and educated at the Universities of Glasgow and Marburg. After holding a lectureship in Biblical Criticism and Elementary Greek in the University of Glasgow (1931–4) and a charge in Comrie (1934–7), he became Professor of New Testament in Mansfield College, Oxford (1937–42). After a further period of parish ministry in Kinnoull Church, Perth (1942–5), he was appointed to the Chair of Biblical Criticism in the University of Aberdeen (1945–71) and served as Master of Christ's College (1958–71). He died in Glasgow.

Like his contemporary William Barclay,* he was a writer of exceptional clarity who excelled at mediating the results of scholarship to the student and the ordinary reader. His numerous books included: *Paul and his Predecessors* (L, 1940, ²1961), *Introducing the New Testament* (L, 1945), *The Work and*

HUNTER, GEORGE W.

Words of Jesus (L., 1950, ²1973), *Introducing New Testament Theology* (L., 1957), *Interpreting the Parables* (L., 1960), *According to John* (L., 1968), and commentaries in the Torch series on *Mark* (L., 1948) and *Romans* (L., 1955).

Hunter would not have claimed to be an original scholar; nevertheless, his defence of *The Unity of the New Testament* (L., 1943) was pioneering in its thesis, and he introduced English-speaking students to the traditions used by Paul. An exponent of British 'critical orthodoxy' of such scholars as C. H. Dodd, T. W. Manson* and Vincent Taylor, Hunter was strongly conservative in his belief in the reliability of the Gospel tradition (notably of the Fourth Gospel) and in his affirmation of substitutionary atonement.

FES IX, 771f., X, 430; *Who's Who 1991*, 922.

I. H. Marshall

Hunter, George W. (1866–1946), missionary. Born in Kincardineshire and raised in Aberdeen, he spent some time in YMCA* work and in 1889 was accepted for service by the China Inland Mission. After language school he was posted to Kansu in northwest China where he became interested in reaching Muslims. After (his only) furlough during the Boxer Rebellion, he returned to take up a pioneer work in Chinese Turkestan (Sinkiang). He arrived in Urumtsi (Tihwa) in 1906 and quickly learned Turki. Not burdened with a family, he spent his life in incessant travel and gained an intimate knowledge of the people, languages, and culture of this vast, remote region. He was a rugged individualist who lived simply and completely detached from Western ways, and was known for sternness, obstinacy and single-minded commitment to spreading the gospel, distributing the Scriptures, and translation work. In 1914 Percy Mather joined him in Sinkiang and they worked together until Mather's death two decades later. As political turmoil swept the province his travels were increasingly restricted; he was jailed for thirteen months (accused of being a British spy), and then expelled. Hoping always to return, he spent his last days in Kansu.

M. Cable and F. French, *George Hunter: Apostle of Turkestan* (L., 1948).

R. V. Pierard

Hunter, John (1849–1917), Congregational minister and liturgist. Born and educated in Aberdeen, he trained for the ministry at Springfield College in Birmingham. He was ordained to the ministry at the Congregational Church in York in 1871 and became minister of Wycliffe Church, Hull, in 1882. He was minister of Trinity Church in Glasgow, 1887–1902, and again 1904–13 after an interlude at King's Weigh House Church in London. At Glasgow he observed the main festivals of the Christian year* and held daily services. His popular *Devotional Services for Public Worship* (L., 1886–1903) ran to eight editions and he served as secretary of the Congregational Church Service Society. His hymnbook compiled for Trinity Church, *Hymns*

HUTCHESON, FRANCIS

of Faith and Life (G, 1889, 1895) introduced several American and modern compositions which later reached the standard collections. In 1893 he was awarded a DD by Glasgow University and was the first non-CofS minister to be elected as president of the University's Theological Society. He was, after John Caird,* perhaps the most outstanding liberal preacher in Scotland. Active in social questions, he invited Keir Hardie* to preach, and predicted that the twentieth century would be 'the woman's century'.

See also Catholic Revival in Worship.

L. S. Hunter, *John Hunter, DD* (L., 1921); H. Escott, *History of Scottish Congregationalism* (G, 1960); R. T. Jones, *Congregationalism in England 1662–1962* (L., 1962).

D. M. Murray

Hunter, Robert (1823–97), FC minister and missionary. Born in Newburgh, Fife, he studied at Marischal College, Aberdeen (May 1841). He spent two years in Bermuda, where his work as a naturalist won him high commendation. He returned to Scotland, trained for the FC ministry in New College,* Edinburgh, and was ordained in 1846 as colleague of Stephen Hislop* in the FC mission at Nagpur, central India. A breakdown in health brought him home in 1855, where he helped Alexander Duff* to form missionary associations in the FC. He wrote a *History of India* (L., 1864), and a *History of the Missions of the Free Church of Scotland in India and Africa* (L., 1873).

During 1864–6 Hunter was tutor in the London Theological College of the Presbyterian Church of England. Although his association with that Church continued, in his founding of the Victoria Docks church and Sunday school, his main concerns became science and writing. He was a fellow of the Geological Society and a member of the British Archaeological Society, and acted for seventeen years as editor of the *Encyclopaedic Dictionary*, published in 1889 and reissued as *Lloyd's Encyclopaedic Dictionary* in 1895. He was also responsible for Cassell's *Concise Bible Dictionary* (L., 1901), and wrote many articles for the *British and Foreign Evangelical Review.**

Hunter received an LLD from Aberdeen University in 1883.

DNB Suppl. III, 14–15; *AFCS* I, 188.

N. R. Needham

Hutcheson, Francis (1694–1746), Professor of Moral Philosophy at the University of Glasgow 1729–46. By his teaching and writing Hutcheson exerted a profound influence on his students, many of them future ministers of the CofS.

The son of the Presbyterian minister of Armagh, Hutcheson entered Glasgow University in 1710 where for six years he studied philosophy, classics, literature and theology. On returning to Ireland he was licensed to preach and was about to accept a call from a congregation when he was persuaded to open a private academy in Dublin. His writings attacking Thomas Hobbes and Bernard Manderville were probably the reason for his being elected to the chair of Moral Philosophy at Glasgow, although he had not applied to be considered.

Hutcheson was the first professor at Glasgow to give up lecturing in Latin, even though he was himself an excellent classical scholar. He lectured five days a week on natural religion, morals, jurisprudence and government and three times a week on the Greek and Latin moralists. On Sunday evenings he spoke about the evidences of Christianity. The effect of his eloquent discourses, delivered often without notes as he walked to and fro, was described by Alexander Carlyle*, one of his students, as 'irresistible'. This opinion was echoed by William Leechman* and many other students who spoke of their former professor with veneration. David Hume* as a young man corresponded with Hutcheson on ethical questions and clearly regarded him with considerable respect.

Hutcheson was arraigned before the Presbytery of Glasgow in 1738 for teaching that the standard of moral goodness was the promotion of the happiness of others and that we could have a knowledge of good and evil without and prior to a knowledge of God. While both these propositions could be drawn from a superficial study of Hutcheson's writing they are not a fair representation of his teaching. For him the task of philosophy was 'to search accurately into the constitution of our nature, to see what sort of creatures we are; for what purposes nature has formed us; what character God our Creator requires us to maintain'.

Hutcheson's works were widely influential and include: *A System of Moral Philosophy*, 2 vols (L, 1755); *An Inquiry into the Original of our Ideas of Beauty and Virtue* (L, 1725); *Essay on the Nature and Conduct of the Passions and Affections* (L, 1730); *A Short Introduction to Moral Philosophy* (G, 1747) is a translation of *Philosophiae Moralis* (G, 1742).

W. R. Scott, *Francis Hutcheson* (C, 1900); Jane Rendall, *The Origins of the Scottish Enlightenment* (L, 1978); W. T. Blackstone, *Francis Hutcheson and Contemporary Ethical Theory* (Atlanta, GA, 1965).

H. R. Sefton

Hutcheson (or Hutchison), George (1615–74), Covenanting divine. After graduating from Edinburgh University in 1638, he became minister at Colmonell, Ayrshire, in 1642. In 1649 he moved to the Tolbooth, Edinburgh. In the debate between Resolutioners* and Protesters,* he was a leading light among the former.

On the Restoration* of Charles II,* Hutcheson attended the Marquis of Argyll (see Campbell, Archibald, *d.* 1661) at his execution in 1661, and was ejected from his charge in 1662 for refusing to conform to episcopacy. However, he received an indulgence from the Privy Council in 1669, and resumed his ministry in Irvine, Ayrshire, until his death five years later.

Hutcheson acquired a reputation as a great preacher, and his commentaries continue to be highly valued for their combination of orthodoxy, piety and lucidity. Charles Spurgeon* said, 'Whenever the student sees a Commentary by Hutcheson let him buy it, for we know of no other author who is more thoroughly helpful to the minister of the word' (*Commenting and Commentaries*, L, 1876, 79).

An Exposition of the Gospel of Jesus Christ According to John (L, 1657); *An Exposition of the Book of Job* (L, 1669); *A Briefe Exposition on the xii Small Prophets* (3 vols, L, 1655; 1 vol., L, 1657); *Forty-Five Sermons upon the CXXX Psalm* (E, 1691); *A Review and Examination of . . . 'Protesters no Subverters'* (E, 1659).

J. C. Johnston, *Treasury of the Scottish Covenant* (E, 1887), 334–6; *FES* I, 118, III, 99.

N. R. Needham

Hutchinsonianism, the teaching of John Hutchinson (1674–1737), a Yorkshireman who wrote twelve books against Newtonian science using a theological system based on the Hebrew Old Testament without vowel points. Behind the pedantry, he stood for revealed over natural religion, with a sacramental devotion. His later disciples used his system against deism, though in opposing unitarianism they went too far in the opposite direction. Duncan Forbes of Culloden (1685–1747; *DNB* XIX, 384–6) was Hutchinson's main exponent in the CofS, but in 1753 John Skinner* introduced the doctrines to the Episcopal clergy, of whom almost all those in the north became devotees.

Hutchinsonianism demanded a vast intellectual effort which was made by rural clergy fearful of new dangers, but it rested on a spurious interpretation of the Hebrew text and by the end of the century it was fading away.

R. Spearman and J. Bate (eds), *The Philosophical and Theological Works of John Hutchinson*, 12 vols (L, ³1748–9); D. Forbes, *The Works of the Right Hon. Duncan Forbes of Culloden* (L, 1816); G. White, 'Hutchinsonianism in Eighteenth-Century Scotland', *RSCHS* 21 (1982), 157–69.

G. White

Hutchison, Matthew (1828–1913), RP historian. Born at Loanhead, Midlothian, he studied at Edinburgh University and the RP Divinity Hall. Ordained in 1859 to Afton RP Church, New Cumnock, Ayrshire, he moved with the majority of the RP Church into the FC in 1876. His wide and accurate knowledge of ecclesiastical procedure and practice resulted in his becoming clerk of the FC Presbytery of Ayr in 1893. He remained in New Cumnock, becoming senior minister of Afton UFC in 1900 and dying there.

Hutchison's main distinction lay in Church history. *The Reformed Presbyterian Church in Scotland. Its Origins and History 1680–1876* (Paisley, 1893) became the standard text. Using original sources and stressing the RPC's adherence to scriptural principles, it is nevertheless written in a non-sectarian fashion. It made Hutchison *the* historian of the RPC.

HUTCHISON, PATRICK

J. Robb, *Cameronian Fasti* (E, n.d.), 13; *AFCS* I, 189; *FUFCS* 123.

G. Wareing

Hutchison, Patrick (*d.*1802), Relief Church minister and writer. Born in Dunblane, Perthshire, where his father was an elder in the General Associate Synod,* Hutchison was a zealous Seceder in his youth such that 'I scarcely could think that any person was a Christian who was not a Seceder' (quoted G. Struthers, *The History of the Rise, Progress and Principles of the Relief Church*, G, 1843, 257). While studying theology for the General Associate Synod ministry, however, he reacted against Secession narrowness, and joined the Relief Church.* He acted for a time as assistant to James Baine* in Edinburgh, and in 1774 became minister of the new Relief congregation in St Ninians, Stirling. In 1783 he moved to the Relief Church in Paisley, Renfrewshire, where he ministered until his death in 1802.

Hutchison was a forceful, eloquent apologist for Relief principles, and championed the causes of Voluntaryism,* religious toleration, the right of congregations to elect their own pastors, and free communion, in a series of writings occasioned by attacks on the Relief by Seceders. His most important works were *A Compendious View of the Religious System maintained by the Synod of Relief* (Falkirk, 1779), and *A Dissertation on the Nature and Genius of the Kingdom of Christ* (E, 1779). According to Struthers, 'To Mr. Hutchison, more than to any other author of the last century, the religious public of Scotland is indebted for correct and scriptural views of the constitution of the church of Christ' (*ibid.*, 417) – i.e., the Voluntary view.

Hutchison was also a keen supporter of the missionary cause, and one of the moving spirits behind the introduction of hymns (*see* Hymnology) into Relief worship. He acted as Moderator of the Relief Synod in 1781.

Sermons on Various and Important Subjects (E, 1803); *Animadversions on Two Pamphlets published by the Rev. Messrs. Ramsay and Walker* (E, 1781).

Small II, 510–20, 699–700.

N. R. Needham

Huts and Canteens, the CofS's welfare service to Scottish troops (and others) during and after World War II. In the First World War, the Scottish Churches' Huts – with CofS and UFC co-operating fully – provided a similar but less extensive service in Scotland and, from 1916, on the continent. Starting within hours of the declaration of war in 1939 and continuing until 1971 (when the last St Andrews Club at Dortmund in Germany closed; the Committee on Hut and Canteen Work for HM Forces was wound up at the General Assembly of 1972), the service developed under the War Office's co-ordinating Council of Voluntary War Work, reflecting the course of the war effort.

After the cessation of hostilities the work continued, especially in British-occupied Germany, with the provision of more permanent premises and a wider range of facilities wherever Scottish troops were stationed.

The service was funded by the CofS and by voluntary contributions. The aim was to provide, under the supervision of a CofS minister or deaconess wherever possible, a home from home, recreation and refreshment (without alcohol), facilities for letter-writing and opportunities for worship and spiritual counsel.

Of the personnel involved three can be mentioned. William Jamieson, killed by a land-mine in Cyprus in 1958, was the sole Huts and Canteens staff casualty. W. M. (Micky) Dempster (*FES* IX, 798–9, X, 414) opened the first canteen (in Portobello, Edinburgh) and was at the heart of the work and its aftermath (visits to war graves by bereaved Scots) until 1968. He died in Edinburgh in 1991. T. Hunter Thomson was Financial Adviser 1942–72.

L. L. Cameron, *A Badge to be Proud of: A History of the Church of Scotland Huts and Canteens 1939–1972* (E, 1972); E. P. Dickie, *Normandy to Nijmegen* ... (E, 1946).

W. M. Dempster

Hutton, George Clark (1825–1908), UP and UFC divine and ardent Voluntary. Born in Perth, Hutton studied at Edinburgh University 1843–6 and then at the USec. and UP Divinity Halls. He was licensed by Edinburgh UP Presbytery in 1851 and ordained to Canal Street UP Church, in Paisley, Renfrewshire, where he ministered until his death. He was Moderator of the UP Synod in 1884 and of the UF General Assembly in 1906. In 1892 he succeeded John Cairns* as Principal of the UP Theological Hall, and was Co-Principal with George Douglas of the UF College in Glasgow 1900–2.

Hutton's commitment to Voluntaryism* was uncompromising (see his *The Case for Disestablishment in Scotland*, L, 1878). He belonged to the Liberation Society and was on its executive from 1868; from 1872–90 he was convener of the UP Disestablishment Committee; in 1886 he helped create the Scottish disestablishment* council. He was chiefly responsible for drafting a bill for disestablishing the CofS which the Scottish MP John Peddie introduced in the Houses of Commons in 1883. Hutton was hesitant about union with the FC until convinced that freedom to express Voluntary views would not be curtailed, and he consistently opposed union between the UFC and CofS. In line with his Voluntaryism was his advocacy of a purely secular system of state education.

Among other causes he supported, Hutton was a zealous proponent of temperance* and prohibition, and acted as auxiliary secretary of the Scottish Bible Society.

Hutton's theology was strongly evangelical and conservative – he reacted negatively to higher criticism (see his *The Word and the Book*, Paisley, 1891). His Calvinism, however, did not prevent him supporting the 1879 Declaratory Act.* He was a colourful and dominating figure in the UPC, particularly after Cairns' death in 1892, and to a lesser degree in the UFC.

Hutton received a DD from Williams College, Massachusetts, in 1875.

Law and Gospel (E, 1860); *The Nature of Divine Truth* (Paisley, 1853); *The Rationale of Prayer* (Paisley, 1853); *The Irish Church: the wrong and the remedy* (L, 1868).

A. Oliver, *Life of George Clark Hutton* (Paisley, 1910); *DNB Second Suppl.* II, 334–5.

N. R. Needham

Hutton, John Alexander (1868–1947), liberal Evangelical. A product of Coatbridge, he studied at Glasgow University and became UP – later UF – minister at Alyth, Perthshire (1892–8), Bristo, Edinburgh (1898–1901) and Belhaven, Glasgow (1906–23). He served in the Presbyterian Church of England at Jesmond, Newcastle (1901–6), and in the Congregationalist Westminster Chapel from 1923, where 'he took London by storm'. He was also editor of the *British Weekly** 1925–46 and author of numerous books. A popular preacher on both sides of the Atlantic (e.g. at D. L. Moody's Northfield conferences), he espoused a broad Evangelicalism marked by wit, literary interests and social relevance, and controlled more by piety than doctrine.

Who Was Who 1941–1950, 583; Small I, 330, 433; *FUFCS* 4, 210; *BW* Jan. 23, 1947, 242.

D. F. Wright

Hymnology, Scottish. 'Scotland has its own way of performing Christian praise, and ... even the legitimizing of hymnody in Scotland in the mid-nineteenth century hardly disturbed this settled habit.' This observation applies to the period between the publication of the 1564 Psalter* and the 1973 edition of *The Church Hymnary** (*CH*) (E. Routley, *A Panorama of Christian Hymnody*, Collegeville, MN, 1979, 42). Moreover, 'until 1781 nothing but psalmody was permitted in any part of the Church of Scotland', and certain of the most conservative Scottish communions preserve this rule still.

According to J. Mearns* ('Scottish Hymnody', in J. Julian (ed.), *Dictionary of Hymnology*, L, ²1907, 1020–33), metrical psalmody* was the only part of worship in which Scottish congregations joined vocally until at least 1749. The singing of hymns, other than the Psalms and the *Paraphrases*,* was not general until after 1852 in the UPC,* after 1870 in the CofS, and after 1873 in the FC (*ibid.*, 1020). Whatever the precise dates, the general picture reflects the fact that, when Horatius Bonar* began his ministry in the 1830s, hymns were not used in the regular services of his church in Leith. J. Young ('Scottish Hymn Books antecedent to *CH* [1898]', *Hymn Society Bulletin*, 3 (1952), 58–66) has discussed the books used by the three main Presbyterian Churches and the Relief Church. (On the Glasite* 1749 book, *see* Sandeman, Robert).

C OF S HYMNALS. Eighty years after the *Paraphrases*, the CofS approved the use of *Hymns for Public Worship selected by the Committee of the General Assembly on Psalmody* (1861). It contained eighty-nine hymns, twenty-two doxologies, three thanksgivings, two dismissions, Hosanna, and four sanctuses. It included hymns by William Robertson (1820–64) and John Ross Macduff (1818–95) besides a translation by J. L. Borthwick.* There were eleven metres besides common and long, but no ordered arrangement of the hymns. An 1864 revision omitted twenty-two hymns and added fifty-three. The hymns were arranged by subject: God; Christ; the Holy Spirit and the Trinity; the Christian life, baptism, the Lord's Supper; the Lord's Day; missions; miscellaneous. Both editions amended the wording of a number of hymns. The need for a better selection with purer texts led to *The Scottish Hymnal* (E, 1870). Its good selection of 200 hymns owed only sixty-four to the 1864 book, and those were restored almost to their original forms. The *Hymnal* won general acceptance. A section, 'Hymns of Natural and Sacred Seasons', contained two on baptism, five on the Lord's Supper, and five on Church and ministry. Contributions from other countries and languages were drawn upon. Three of Bonar's compositions were included. An 1884 Appendix, which among other additions included eighty-six for children, brought the total to 442, each prefixed by a Scripture quotation. A music edition appeared in 1885.

For the *Church Hymnary* see the separate article. As supplements to *CH3*, the CofS has produced *Hymns for a Day* (E, 1982) and *Songs of God's People* (O, 1988).

FC HYMNALS. A selection from and additions to the *Paraphrases* was issued as *Psalm-Versions, Paraphrases, and Hymns* (E, 1873). It contained twenty-one Psalm-versions and 123 hymns, including forty of the *Paraphrases*, some curtailed. The selection of hymns was judicious, but their number small.

The Moody* and Sankey campaigns reconciled many in the FC to hymns and even organs. In 1882 the collection appeared, revised and enlarged, as *The FC Hymnbook*. It comprised 387 hymns (including twenty-three from the *Paraphrases*) with, in the larger edition, excellent indices by James Bonar. The hymns were arranged, oddly, by metre; but the many new hymns included fifty-three for the young. There was a full subject index. That year Edward John Hughes produced a music edition. One of the best collections of its time for both hymns and music, it owed much to A. B. Bruce* (Mearns, 1026).

RELIEF CHURCH HYMNALS. In 1786 James Steuart of Anderston Relief Church, Glasgow, published a collection of hymns for his congregation, the first such book in Scottish Presbyterianism. Like the 1781 *Paraphrases* the book opened with three hymns on creation. The only principle of arrangement was that works by the same authors were kept together, e.g. a large group by Watts was followed by a group from the *Paraphrases*. Apart from the authors of the *Paraphrases*, Young (60) found no Scottish author. Most of the hymns were in common or long metre.

In 1794 the Relief Church sanctioned a collection

comprising the Anderston book with fifty-one additions made by Patrick Hutchison* or Hutcheson (cf. Young, 61, and Mearns, 1026, 1029). In a preface he defended the use of hymns in worship. All his additions were in common or long metre. Although authors' names were not given, the only Scot (with fourteen hymns) seemed to be Alexander Pirie (*d.*1804)* (Mearns, 896, 1031). A full index of topics and a table of Scripture texts barely compensated for the lack of any classified arrangement in the book itself. James Dun combined 180 of Steuart's selections with the fifty-one additions and the preface and published the result as *Sacred Songs and Hymns on Various Passages of Scripture approved by the Synod of Relief* (G, 1794).

A revision was entitled *Hymns adapted for the Worship of God, Selected and Sanctioned by the Synod of Relief* (G, 1833). Items retained kept their old numbers, new ones replaced the omissions, and the total was increased. The preface was reprinted. There were many textual variations. Some missionary hymns and fifty Paraphrases were included. The index added authors' names. Among new authors were the son of an Ulster Scot, James Montgomery (1771–1854) ('According to thy gracious word'), and Sir Walter Scott,* whose *Ivanhoe* produced 'When Israel, of the Lord beloved'. There was more variety in metre than before.

UPC HYMNALS. When the Relief Church joined the USec.C to form the UPC, work began that resulted in the *Hymn-Book of the UPC* (E, 1852). It contained 468 hymns, including some by Andrew Young (1807–89), Ralph Wardlaw* and R. M. M'Cheyne,* fifty Paraphrases and twenty-three doxologies. There were thirty metres besides common and long. The hymns, each with a title and usually three Scripture references, were arranged in order of the first reference.

Since many of the hymns did not become popular and the wording had often been altered, a new book was prepared. *The Presbyterian Hymnal* (1876) comprised 366 hymns, eighteen doxologies, twenty-four Scripture sentences, but no Paraphrases. Fewer than half of the items in the 1852 book were kept. Titles were omitted, and references replaced by texts. The arrangement was by subject, and the whole elaborately classified. Scots included Bonar, William Bruce (1812–82), A. R. Cousin,* George Jacque (1804–92), and Hamilton Montgomerie Macgill (1807–80). Henry Smart compiled a music edition of the *Hymnal* (1877), the first Presbyterian collection with fixed tunes. In 1877 James Thin provided a large-type edition of the words and music with notes on the individual hymns, besides more Scripture sentences.

OTHER HYMNALS. For details of other nineteenth-century books, including many for denominations other than those already named, see Mearns (1028–32, 1699–1700). For Presbyterian collections for children see Young (63–4, 65). *CH* (1898, 1927, 1973 and supplements) superseded the earlier books of the main Presbyterian Churches. Many of the other Churches used the same books as their English counterparts.

EARLY HYMNWRITERS. Apart from Gaelic* hymns, some of which were rendered into English, there were few 'human hymns' as opposed to paraphrases of those in Scripture until the early nineteenth century. Some of the hymn-writers have already been mentioned.

Scotland had always had a tradition of RC hymnology. Among over 150 versions in English of *'Dies Irae'* (? Thomas of Celano), the greatest of the medieval hymns sung before the Gospel at mass, were those by William Drummond (1585–1649) of Hawthornden, Sir Walter Scott, George Walker (1783–1868), Hamilton Montgomerie Macgill (1807–80), and William Bruce Robertson* (1820–86).

It is not known whether Drummond was a RC, but his translation, 'O Trinity, O blessèd Light', appeared in an English *Primer of the Blessed Virgin* with eighteen other hymns and translations ascribed to him. Otherwise there was no poetry from English-speaking RC Scotland (Routley, 131–2) until recently.

Among early Protestant poets were Robert Boyd* (1578–1627), David Dickson* (*c.*1583–1663), Michael Bruce* (1746–67) and John Logan* (1748–88).

NINETEENTH-CENTURY HYMNWRITERS. With few exceptions most hymn-writers during the last century are remembered if at all by one or two hymns only, e.g. Sir Robert Grant (1779–1838), sometime MP for the Elgin Burghs and Inverness Burghs, is known for 'O worship the King, all glorious above'.

Increasing acceptance of hymn-singing led to many translations as well as original hymns. An American of Scottish descent, James Waddell Alexander (1804–59), translated much from German, notably 'O sacred Head, sore wounded'. So did the Borthwick* sisters. Jane Montgomery Campbell (1817–78) paraphrased 'We plough the fields and scatter'. Thomas Carlyle* gave us Luther's 'A safe stronghold'. Other translators from German were John Guthrie* (*b.*1814) and John Morrison Sloane.* John Stuart Blackie (1809–95) versified the *Benedicite* ('Angels holy, high and lowly'). Gilbert Rorison (1821–69) gave us from Latin, 'Three in One, and One in Three', and David Douglas Bannerman* from French, 'I greet thee, my Redeemer sure'.

Children's hymns were written by James Drummond Burns (1823–64), 'Hushed was the evening hymn'; Bonar's sister-in-law, Mrs Mary Duncan (1814–40), 'Jesus, tender Shepherd, hear me'; and Christian Henry Bateman (1813–89), 'Come, children, join to sing'. The American, Priscilla Jane Owens (1829–1907), of Scottish and Welsh descent, wrote 'We have heard the joyful sound'.

Besides J. D. Burns, CofS hymn-writers included: John Ross Macduff (1818–95), 'Christ is coming! let creation'; Norman MacLeod* of the Barony, 'Courage, brother! do not stumble'; and George Matheson,* 'Make me a captive, Lord' and 'O love that wilt not let me go'.

Besides Bonar,* FC writers included: Elizabeth Cecilia Douglas Clephane (1830–69), 'Beneath the cross of Jesus'; A. R. Cousin,* 'The sands of time are sinking' and 'O Christ, what burdens bowed thy head'; James Grindlay Small (1817–88), 'I've found a Friend'; and Walter Chalmers Smith,* 'Immortal, invisible, God only wise'.

The Edinburgh author of 'Lord, when thy kingdom comes', William Dalrymple Maclagan (1826–1910), became Archbishop of York.

With few exceptions Scottish hymn-writers have been ministers. The novelist George MacDonald* resigned as a Congregational* minister, but continued preaching. He wrote 'O Lord of life, thy quickening voice'. The Congregational founder of the circulating library, Charles Edward Mudie (1818–90), who had Scottish parents, wrote 'I lift my heart to thee'. Principal John Campbell Shairp (1819–85), wrote ' 'Twixt gleams of joy and clouds of doubt'. Margaret, Lady Cockburn-Campbell (1803–41), daughter of Sir John Malcolm, married a founder of the Brethren.* Her 'Praise ye Jehovah, praise the Lord most holy' appeared in the *Revised CH* (1927). Alexander Stewart (1843–1923) was one of the Brethren in Glasgow and Prestwick and author of 'Lord Jesus Christ, we seek thy face', which is included in at least four current non-Brethren collections.

MODERN HYMNOLOGISTS AND HYMNWRITERS. The late nineteenth and early twentieth centuries were noted for hymnologists: John Brownlie* (1859–1925), who edited *The Hymns and Hymn Writers of CH* (L, 1899); James Mearns;* James Moffatt;* Millar Patrick* and Lauchlan MacLean Watt.*

The *Revised CH* (1927) included hymns by: Patrick Miller Kirkland (1857–1943), 'Jesus, Lord, Redeemer'; Walter John Mathams (1851–1931), 'Jesus, Friend of little children'; and William Wright (1859–1924), 'March on, my soul, with strength'. Nicol MacNicol* (1870–1952) contributed a translation, 'One who is all unfit to count', of a hymn by an Indian, Narayan Vaman Tilak.

In Scottish hymnody, much of this century has been a time of consolidation. From 1969 onwards several English Churches supplemented their collections with small books of recent hymns. This development had been anticipated in Scotland. In 1962 in Dunblane poets and musicians had begun meeting under a CofS minister, Ian Fraser (b.1917). They published experimental new texts and tunes in two booklets entitled *Dunblane Praises* (1964–7).

Some of the hymns found their way into English and American hymnals; *CH3* (1973) was the only major hymnal that 'totally ignored' Dunblane, according to Routley (188). Routley overlooked 'God, your glory we have seen in your Son', by Sir Ronald Ernest Charles Johnson (b.1913) and Brian Arthur Wren (b.1936). This translation from the French, taken from *Dunblane Praises*, did appear there.

Nevertheless, few new texts of any kind were admitted in *CH3*. The following were included. James Neil Stewart Alexander (b.1921) paraphrased John 1:1–14 as 'Before all time the Word existed', and Archibald MacBride Hunter* Phil. 2:6–11 as 'Though in God's form he was'. Ian Robertson Pitt-Watson (b.1923) metricized three Psalms using the language of the New English Bible, *e.g.* 'Thou art before me, Lord, thou art behind.'

CH3 contained six hymns composed or translated by James Quinn (b.1919) of the Lauriston Jesuit Fathers in Edinburgh, who had produced *New Hymns for All Seasons* (L, 1969), the first major post-Vatican-II contribution to new hymn writing and, except for one hymn, the work of one author (R. Leaver, *A Hymn Book Survey, 1962–80* (Bramcote, Notts., 1980), 22). In 1980 Quinn announced a sequel to his book (Leaver, *News of Liturgy* 61 (Jan. 1980), 5). From another tradition have come the hymns of John Bell, Graham Maule and others under the Wild Goose imprint of the Iona Community,* of which several appear in *Songs of God's People*.

See also Church Hymnary; Music, Church.

E. Routley, *An English-Speaking Hymnal Guide* (Collegeville, MN, 1979) [companion to his *Panorama*]; CofS, Committee on Public Worship, *Draft of a Catalogue of Books of Psalters, Hymns, and Hymnology in National Library of Scotland, Edinburgh, Aberdeen University Library, New College Library, Edinburgh, Trinity College, Glasgow* (E, 1939); Hymn Society of GB & Ireland, *A Classified Index to the Society's 'Bulletin', vols I–X, 1937–1984* (Croydon, 1988); Sir R. Johnson, 'Hymnological Collections in Scotland', *Hymn Society Bulletin* 11:12 (October 1987), 269–71; J. Stein, *Singing a New Song* (E, 1988).

J. S. Andrews

Hymnology, Gaelic. There is a considerable body of religious verse in Scottish Gaelic,* and though some of it falls into the category of private contemplation, the greater part was certainly designed to be sung, though mostly in informal settings rather than in the worship of the church. There is a great dearth of evidence as to the place of Gaelic in the formal worship of the medieval church in Scotland, but it can be assumed that liturgical as well as more purely 'folk' items found their way into the oral tradition harvested by nineteenth-century collectors, notably Alexander Carmichael.* His *Carmina Gadelica*, vols II and III in particular, contain many pieces of devotion and supplication, whether to God, Christ or the saints, which are highly formulaic in character and may well have their origin in a church setting. Other items in this rich and varied collection seek the aid of divine power and saintly intercession at various points in the daily or yearly round, at critical junctures in human life and as an antidote to physical calamities or malign powers.

Post-Reformation Roman Catholic hymn writing in Gaelic is of comparatively small bulk. There survives a moving poem of resignation composed by Archibald, chief of Keppoch in Brae Lochaber, on his death-bed in 1682. His daughter, Sìleas, was a hymn-writer of some note (*see* Women in Highland Churches), and her compositions are interesting for their range of theme and imagery. Death occupies a prominent place in her thought, whether as the ravager who has deprived her of her husband and child, the stern claimant with whom she altercates, or the macabre dissolver of her physical body. She has a morning hymn in which spiritual discipline is presented in terms of household chores, the seven deadly sins seen as the heads of a monster, to be slain by the arrows of righteous living. She portrays the RC Church under the common medieval figure of an impregnable castle. Colin Chisholm published (in *TGSI* 11 (1885), 216–40) some RC hymns remembered in his native Strathglass, and in 1893 Father Allan MacDonald published a collection of sixty-three pieces, *Comh-chruinneachadh de Laoidhean Spioradail* (Oban, 1893).

The professional bardic poets had frequently turned to religious themes for their occasional compositions, an example being the seventeenth-century poet Cathal MacMhuirich castigating the body as the seat of sinful passions, and the bardic manner is still very much present in the 'sub-bardic' verse assembled in the late seventeenth-century Fernaig Manuscript by Duncan MacRae of Inverinate, though in this mainly Protestant company devotion to the Virgin and appeals for the intercession of saints are absent. A number of these poems express disillusionment with the world, and there are others on biblical themes such as the Creation, the Fall, the Day of Judgment. One poem dealing at length with the sinful misuse of the Lord's Day uses the medieval device of a conversation between the soul and the body.

With the steady advance of evangelical presbyterianism into the Highlands in the eighteenth century, religious song became an important buttress of biblical instruction and evangelistic appeal, especially at a time when the Bible was as yet untranslated into Scottish Gaelic and the population was largely illiterate. The most accomplished poet of the early phase of evangelical advance was Dugald Buchanan* (1716–68) of Perthshire, whose bilingual upbringing enabled him to borrow ideas and images from English poets such as Isaac Watts, Edward Young and Robert Blair, and accommodate them successfully to the native milieu of his Gaelic audience. Duncan Kennedy's *Co'chruinneachadh Laoidhe agus Dhantaichibh Spioradail* (G, 1786) presents a number of authors from the south-west Highlands. Iain Ban Maor ('Fair-haired John, the Officer') writes on the Incarnation, the Passion, the Judgment; Bean a' Bharra ('The Wife from Barr') links the Exodus and the atonement; and Ian Caimbeul Sgoilear ('John Campbell, the Scholar') summarizes the Gospel narrative. The versification of theological subjects is further developed in James MacGregor's* *Dain a Chòmhnadh Cràbhaidh* (G, 1819; Pictou, 1861). In verses set to the tunes of popular Gaelic songs, he handles such themes as the law, the covenant of works, the covenant of grace, sin, the gospel, faith, the work of the Holy Spirit, death, resurrection, heaven and hell. A northerly group of poets is represented in John Rose's *Metrical Reliques of the Men of the North* (Inverness, 1851). John MacKay of Mudale, Sutherland, dwells mainly on the cardinal doctrines of the Fall and redemption through Christ, while Donald Matheson of Kildonan, Sutherland, has a more subjective cast to his mind, contemplating his inner corruption and spiritual struggles, but he too summarizes the story of the Exodus as the exemplar of spiritual liberation.

Evangelical elegies emerge as a distinct subcategory of religious verse in the late eighteenth century and find their most accomplished practitioner in John MacDonald* of Ferintosh. His elegies for prominent ministers and his long poem on his own father's spiritual pilgrimage highlight the major crises of conversion and death, appraise the intervening preaching and pastoral labours, and bring the force of godly example to bear on the living audience. John Morrison* of Harris continues the tradition, and its momentum is not yet spent, for compositions of this type still appear from time to time in the pages of the *Stornoway Gazette*. John Maclean (1787–1848) of Tiree, emigrant to Canada, turned in later life to religious compositions, reflecting the influence of Bunyan in hymns on 'The Pilgrim's Progress' and 'The Holy War' (A. MacLean Sinclair (ed.), *Dàin Spioradail le Iain Mac-Gilleain*, E, 1880).

As the nineteenth century progressed, and revivals* spread throughout the Highlands,* less heavily doctrinal hymns with a higher emotional temperature became popular, making Peter Grant* of Strathspey perhaps the best known Gaelic hymnwriter of all. The compositions of Archibald Farquharson of Tiree and Murdo MacLeod of Lewis are similar in their breezy style. Contacts with religious life in the cities and the influence of the American evangelists Moody* and Sankey prompted the translation of popular English hymns into Gaelic, as evidenced by A. K. MacCallum's collection, *Laoidhean agus Dain Spioradail* (G, 1894), the St Columba Church Hymn Book, *Leabhar Laoidhean Eaglais Chaluim Chille* (G, 1906), Duncan MacColl's* *Leabhar Laoidh* (G, 1899), a collection of hymns for Gaelic missions, and the CofS's *Laoidheadair Gaidhlig* (G, 1902, 1904; E, 1935).

Four recent publications demonstrate both the traditional and innovative aspects of Gaelic hymnology. *A' Chulaidh as Fheàrr* ('The Best Cloak') (Stornoway, 1983) presents nearly forty compositions by Iain Smith (1857–1924) of Bernera, Lewis, catechist with the UFC. These are mainly biblical meditations, dwelling especially on the Person and work of Christ, and including a clutch of elegies for ministers. About 100 hymns by Hector MacKinnon* of Berneray, North Uist, appear in *An Neamhnaid Luachmhor* ('The Precious Jewel') (Stornoway, 1990). They combine contemplation of biblical themes with evangelistic appeal and tributes to departed saints. The RC collection, *Seinnibh dhan Tighearna*('Sing to the Lord') (Bury St Edmunds, 1986) draws on the Gaelic Catholic tradition, but also includes internationally popular items such as 'Amazing Grace' and 'Morning has Broken'. *Seinn an Duan Seo* ('Sing this Song') (Furnace, 1990) contains 101 popular hymns and choruses translated into Gaelic by Roderick Mac-

Donald. Gaelic RC congregations have long supported hymn-singing, as have Gaelic-speaking Baptists. Presbyterians, on the other hand, have used only Psalms in formal worship, reserving hymns for more informal gatherings. Such gatherings where Gaelic hymns are sung are probably now becoming rare, and Gaelic hymns are more likely to be heard through the recordings of individual singers.

J. MacInnes, *The Evangelical Movement in the Highlands of Scotland, 1688 to 1800* (A, 1951); id., 'Gaelic Spiritual Verse', *TGSI* 46 (1971), 308–52; D. Maclean (ed.), *The Spiritual Songs of Dugald Buchanan* (E, 1913); L. Macbean, *Buchanan the Sacred Bard of the Scottish Highlands* (L, 1919); D. Maclean, *The Literature of the Scottish Gael* (E, 1912).

K. D. MacDonald

Hynd, David (1895–1991), pioneer medical missionary. Born in Perth, the son of a railwayman, Hynd graduated in arts, science and medicine at Glasgow, was ordained in 1924, and went to Swaziland as a missionary of the Church of the Nazarene* in 1925. He operated at first on his kitchen table, and personally directed brickmaking, construction and plumbing for the first mission buildings at Manzini. Eventually he established a 200-bed hospital, a nursing college, leper colony, and (under the direction of Margaret K. Latta of Uddingston) schools and a teacher training college. Clinics, schools and churches were developed throughout Swaziland. The Swaziland Conference of Churches, a branch of the Red Cross, and the Swaziland Medical Association were among other institutions he established. Awarded the CBE in 1947, he was an honoured adviser of Sobhuza II of Swaziland and a member of the constitutional conference which led to independence in 1968.

Africa Emerging (Kansas City, 1959).

R. V. DeLong and M. Taylor, *Fifty Years of Nazarene Missions*, II (Kansas City, 1955); G. Frame, *Blood Brother of the Swazis* (Kansas City, 1952); J. F. Parker, *Into All the World* (Kansas City, 1983); J. S. M. Matsebula, *A History of Swaziland* (Cape Town, 1988).

T. A. Noble

I

Immigration, the arrival in Scotland of ethnically or nationally distinct groups. This process has served to shape the social and religious experience of the country in important ways, especially during the nineteenth and twentieth centuries. Some groups were only temporary settlers; others eventually merged into the mainstream of Scottish life; while yet others have maintained a distinctive identity.

Early Celtic migrants had an important role in shaping the political geography, culture and institutions of Scotland before 1066. The name of the country derives from the *Scoti* from north-eastern Ireland who crossed into Dalriada (approximately modern Argyll) from the fourth century (*see* Gaelic). Columba's* pilgrimage to Iona* made this phase of settlement of great significance for the Christianization of the land (*see* Celtic Church). From the late eighth century, Norsemen from Scandinavia, including Viking raiders, settled widely in northern and western regions, often after violent incursions (*see especially* Orkney* and Shetland*). In the twelfth century, Anglo-French barons and knights came northwards from England, and exerted strong and lasting influence on social, political and ecclesiastical conventions (*see* Monasticism).

Italians and Africans were to be found entertaining the court at Holyrood in the sixteenth century, but the first and largest modern immigration was that of the Irish in the early Victorian period. Initially, many of the Irish in Scotland were seasonal migrants in search of work, especially at harvest time, and they returned home in the winter. Increasingly, as industrialization gathered momentum in Scotland, they came to settle, and, as the deterioration of conditions in rural Ireland culminated in the Great Famine of 1847, the steady trickle swelled to a torrent. From the 1850s onwards immigration began to decrease, but it remained substantial for much of the rest of the century.

In 1851 7.2 per cent of the population of Scotland had been born in Ireland, a figure which underestimates the proportion of ethnically Irish, as it obviously does not include the Scottish-born children and descendants of immigrants. Moreover, the Irish were unevenly distributed over the country, being concentrated overwhelmingly in urban and industrial areas. The majority remained on Clydeside: in 1851 the Irish-born made up 18.2 per cent of the population in Glasgow and 12.7 per cent in Paisley. On the other hand, significant numbers moved east: there were 6 per cent Irish in Edinburgh, and in Dundee the expansion of the linen industry drew a higher proportion of Irish than in any other major Scottish town, at 18.9 per cent. In general the Irish were concentrated disproportionately in unskilled, low-paid occupations and they lived in the worst conditions found in overcrowded Victorian cities.

The majority of the arrivals, who came predominantly from Ulster and northern Connaught, were RCs, but a large minority, probably as much as a third, were Protestants. The latter were integrated fairly readily into the Scottish Churches, passing on in the process the militant religious sectarianism of Ulster, expressed most notably in the growth of the Orange Order.* Catholic immigrants were prone, however, to remain in a distinct subculture, having uneasy relations with native Scottish Catholics and frequently in tension with their Protestant compatriots, especially on Clydeside. Sectarianism was liable to be compounded by economic competition for work in periods of recession, and reinforced by residential segregation. Nevertheless, when the situation in Scotland is compared with that in Ulster and in Liverpool it is clear that the polarization of the communities was less extreme, finding expression in primarily non-violent means, such as the continuing rivalry between Celtic and Rangers football clubs in Glasgow.

As the Irish influx ebbed in the late nineteenth century, there was a new wave of immigrants from continental Europe, less numerous but more diverse in character. Poles, most of whom were Jews* escaping from Russian persecution, were the largest group. There was also a significant number of Lithuanians, who usually settled to work as miners in the Lanarkshire coalfield. These were RC in religion, but in the early twentieth century the Church had to struggle against socialist influence to maintain its hold on the community. Several thousand Italians also arrived in this period, making a living primarily in the ice-cream trade, thus stirring religious hostilities in which anti-Catholicism reinforced Sabbatarianism. The Second World War brought a fresh wave of Polish arrivals, and Edinburgh University hosted a Polish School of Medicine 1941-9.

In the twentieth century Scotland was relatively unaffected by immigrants from the Commonwealth, who in 1966 made up only 0.2 per cent of the population, as opposed to 1.1 per cent in the UK as a whole. More significant numerically has been the, often temporary, migration of English people northwards, generally in professional roles, which has contributed to the Anglicanization of the EpCS and, more generally, to the erosion of distinctively Scottish religious culture.

See also Ireland; Roman Catholicism.

A. A. M. Duncan, *Scotland: The Making of the Kingdom* (E, 1975); C. G. Brown, *The Social History of Religion in Scotland since 1730* (L, 1987); C. Holmes, *John Bull's Island: Immigration and British Society, 1871-1971* (L, 1988); J. E. Handley, *The Irish in Scotland 1798-1843* (Cork, 1945); id., *The Irish in Modern Scotland* (Cork, 1947); S. Gilley and R. Swift (eds), *The Irish in the Victorian City* (L, 1985); T. Gallagher, *Glasgow: The Uneasy Peace* (Manchester, 1987); W. M. Walker, 'Irish Immigrants in Scotland: Their Priests, Politics and Parochial Life', *Historical Journal* 15 (1972), 649-67; B. Collins, 'Irish Emigration to Dundee and Paisley during the First Half of the Nineteenth Century', in J. M. Goldstrom and L. A. Clarkson (eds), *Irish Population, Economy and Society* (O, 1981); R. D.. Lobban, 'The Irish Community in Greenock in the Nineteenth Century', *Irish Geography* 6 (1971), 270-81; M. Rodgers, 'The Lanarkshire Lithuanians', in B. Kay (ed.), *Odyssey* (E, 1980), 18-25; M. Rodgers, 'Italiani in Scozzia' and 'Glasgow Jewry' in B. Kay (ed.), *Odyssey: the Second Collection* (E, 1982), 12-21, 112-21.

J. R. Wolffe

Imrie, Robert (1770-1816), eccentric Antiburgher minister. He came from Perth. In 1792 he was ordained to Kinkell Antiburgher Church (*see* General Associate Synod) south of Perth, where his teaching provoked complaints not so much by heresy as by 'debasement of the pulpit through want of commonsense'. He insisted at length that Christ's physical blood was no different from an animal's, and required scriptural warrants in obsessive detail. Proceedings against him occupied Perth Presbytery, the provincial Synod and the General Synod intermittently from 1801 until his deposition in 1812. Suspended in 1807 for denying the covenant between the Father and Son and the merit of Christ's death, he was restored in 1810 only to question the Trinity unacceptably in 1811. The case gave rise to a number of pamphlets between 1809 and 1814, from the Synods, Imrie, 'Jeremiah Plaindealing', and A. Pringle.

The bulk of Imrie's congregation remained loyal and built him a church at Auchterarder, where he preached in unfettered independence until his death.

Small II, 608-9, 598-9; *ASUPC*, 603-4, 617-18.

D. F. Wright

Incarnation, *see* Christology.

Inchcolm, Augustinian* abbey. The foundation of this Augustinian house on an island in the Firth of Forth, projected by Kings Alexander I (1107-24) and David I,* was finally effected in the 1160s. It became an abbey in 1235. An outpost of the diocese of Dunkeld, Inchcolm was the favoured burial place of its bishops. Its location made it vulnerable to hostile action; it suffered English attacks in the fourteenth century and in 1421 the canons took refuge on the mainland. Its fortunes revived under the long rule of Abbot Walter Bower* 1417-49.

The community, numbering at least fourteen in 1541, included Thomas Forret,* executed for heresy in 1539. Inchcolm was attacked by English forces in 1542 and occupied by them 1547-8; the canons left the island and perhaps never resumed monastic life there. The buildings are the best preserved of any medieval monastery in Scotland today.

D. E. Easson and A. Macdonald (eds), *Charters of the Abbey of Inchcolm* (SHS, E, 1938); J. W. Paterson and D. McRoberts, *Inchcolm Abbey* (E, 1978); W. Ross, *Aberdour and Inchcolme* (E, 1885); Easson-Cowan, 88-91.

M. Dilworth

Independency, Church polity based on the autonomy of the individual congregation. (Most Independents, but not all, have been congregationalist* in church government.)

'The air of Scotland was alien to the growth of Independency', wrote Sir Walter Scott* in *The Heart of Midlothian*. John Knox* had warned his brethren in Scotland in 1557 of the excesses of the Anabaptists. When the English Independent Robert Browne landed at Dundee in 1584, he received little welcome, and John Penry had no better success between 1588 and 1590. In the early seventeenth century a few 'Brownists' were detected in Edinburgh, Stirling and Aberdeen, but until the Commonwealth* period no lasting effect can be claimed.

Oliver Cromwell wished to have gifted chaplains with his army who would proclaim ideas he found congenial, and there is evidence of Quaker,* Independent, and Baptist* activity during the 1650s, with debates, converts, believers' baptisms* at Leith and Cupar (Fife), and debates and condemnations by several Presbyteries. The Baptists of the garrison in Leith fell victim to rumours and plots, and after 1659 there are only a few scattered references to Independents, mainly to individuals, before the rise of native movements in the early eighteenth century.

In 1730 John Glas* was deposed from the ministry of the CofS and from his parish of Tealing near Dundee. In opposition to the Covenanting* prejudices of some of his flock, he had written the first Independent treatise in Scotland, *The Testimony of the King of Martyrs*. He followed this by a treatise, *A Congregation subject to no Jurisdiction under Heaven*. Glas and his friends formed small churches in several Scottish burghs, and his movement had a wider impact through the writings of his son-in-law, Robert Sandeman.* His peculiar ideas concerning the literal following of the Church polity found in Acts and his intellectualist view of faith influenced future generations of Scottish Independents, but his own followers remained few in number.

From 1760 onwards a second class of Independents grew slowly. Glasite in inspiration, these churches, whose best known leader was David Dale,* were wider in sympathy and co-operation. In 1765 the first small Scotch Baptist congregation was formed under Robert Carmichael,* in Edinburgh. He was soon joined by Archibald McLean,* whose influence and writings enabled a modest spread of Baptist ideas, with Glasite influences still evident in practice and doctrine.

In 1769 John Barclay,* assistant minister of Fettercairn, near Aberdeen, separated from the CofS, and a small group of followers, the Bereans, established themselves there, and in Edinburgh and Glasgow. Some of Barclay's views tended to Independency.

The real advance of Independency had to wait until the work of Robert* and James Haldane,* who turned from an aristocratic way of life to preach the gospel in rural as well as urban Scotland at the end of the eighteenth century. At first loyal to the national Church, the logic of their position, so often in opposition to parish ministers, drove them to establish Independent tabernacles, train preachers, and, almost disastrously, adopt some Glasite views of Church government, and in 1808 be baptized by immersion. From their work the modern Congregationalist* and Baptist denominations arose. Several of the old Scotch, McLeanite churches were strongly influenced by a newer Evangelicalism, and by 'English' Baptist churches, begun in the first decade of the century by George Barclay* and Christopher Anderson.* Until 1869, despite previous attempts at Union, Baptists remained largely isolated congregations, united mainly in support of the Home Missionary Societies, which evangelized the Highlands* and Islands and formed still-existing groups of Baptists from 1800 onwards.

By contrast, the Congregationalists formed a Union in 1812 with fifty-five churches, to aid weak churches and promote mission. Congregationalist missionaries also penetrated the Highland region, and Independency in both its main forms became firmly rooted until emigration weakened the churches. In Orkney* and Shetland,* there are still strong Congregationalist and Baptist communities.

Baptists finally formed a Union in 1869, and from then the two denominations proceeded side by side, occupying the growing towns in the Lowlands, colonizing the great cities, and taking root in fishing and mining communities. The more aggressive evangelism reaching Britain from America affected both denominations in the 1840s, and added a new dimension. The churches of the Evangelical Union,* sometimes known as Morisonians (*see* Morison, James), were driven from the Secession* in 1841. Although they retained many Presbyterian features, the EU gradually drew closer to the Congregational Union, and in 1896 they became one denomination.

In the twentieth century both Congregationalists and Baptists have enjoyed prosperity at times, and have suffered from the tensions of the modern world. Baptists have preserved their momentum in many areas, but have generally been suspicious of ecumenicity. Congregationalists have been involved in talks with the CofS and the United Reformed Church,* but as yet no basis of union has been found.

The Christian Brethren,* strong in many parts of Scotland from the mid-nineteenth century, should, at least in their Open groupings, be considered part of Independency, as may mission halls, Christian Unions (*see* Inter-Varsity Fellowship/UCCF), and other evangelistic agencies. Unitarianism* has never been strong, although in the past there have been more churches than the present four in the main cities.

In the last decades of the twentieth century, the charismatic* (renewal) and house church movements* have given birth to a scatter of Independent congregations.

W. I. Hoy, 'The Entry of Sects into Scotland', in D. Shaw (ed.), *Reformation and Revolution* (E, 1967), 178–211; H. Escott, *A History of Scottish Congregationalism* (G, 1960); G. Yuille (ed.), *History of Baptists in Scotland* (G, 1926); D. W. Bebbington (ed.), *The Baptists in Scotland* (G, 1988); A. L. Drummond and J. Bulloch, *The Scottish Church, 1680–1843* (E, 1973).

D. B. Murray

Independents, Old Scots. This body owed its beginning to two Fife ministers. James Smith of Newburn (1708–75) read Robert Sandeman's* *Letters on Theron and Aspasio* in 1757, and published *A Compendious Account ... of the form and order of the Church ...* (E, 1765), which was a statement of Independency* (*see* Congregationalism) and a vindication of weekly Communion. His neighbour Robert Ferrier* of Largo (1741–95) read John Glas's* *Testimony*, was convinced, and found Smith of the same opinion. They resigned their charges in 1768, began to meet at Balchrystie, a farm on the border of their parishes, and published *The Case of James Smith ... and of Robert Ferrier...* (E, 1768). They noted their dissent from the Westminster Confession* on these points: they disagree with the phrase 'eternal generation'; they reject the *filioque* clause; they hold faith to be a simple thing; they deny the civil magistrate's authority in church affairs; they believe discipline should be in the hands of the congregation; they advocate 'primitive' church customs, as adopted by the Glasites.* The body was greatly strengthened by the accession of David Dale* who brought to the group a more co-operative spirit. In Dundee a former Antiburgher congregation (see General Associate Synod) joined them in 1769. Later churches were formed in Paisley, Kirkcaldy, Edinburgh, Montrose, Methven, New Lanark and elsewhere. The movement was never large, and although a union was effected in 1814 with a group of churches in England associated with Benjamin Ingham, it seems to have had little effect in stopping a decline. Only the Glasgow church showed any strong life. In 1860 it was reported as having three elders, 143 members, and a congregation of 250, meeting in a church in Oswald Street. That church ceased to meet in the 1930s.

H. Escott, *A History of Scottish Congregationalism* (G, 1960); J. Brown, *Religious Denominations of Glasgow* (G, 1860).

D. B. Murray

India, see Missions.

Induction, a comparatively modern name for the service in which a minister in the CofS is installed in a parish.* (The term is also in use in other Scottish Churches.) The original term, 'admission', referred to a kind of investment. Time was when property was conveyed in the presence of witnesses by delivering 'sasines' – earth and stones for land, a clap and hammer for a mill, a net for salmon-fishing. So, the new minister was actually carried into the church and installed in the pulpit and thereby took 'actual, real and corporate possession' of teind,* manse,* glebe* and kirklands. This entry and installation are still the public symbol that the minister has entered into the rights and privileges and has accepted the responsibilities and obligations of the charge. The property aspect has today little significance, but induction still creates a unique tie between minister and congregation, a tie which cannot in any circumstances be severed by the latter and by the former only with consent of Presbytery.* It consists of a service of public worship conducted by the Presbytery at which the inductee makes profession of his faith, accepts responsibilities and signs the Formula;* and it is preceded by a meeting of Presbytery at which any member or parishioner may take exception, on cause shown, to the life or doctrine of the inductee.

Cox 52, 264–6; A. Herron, *A Guide to the Presbytery* (E, 1983).

A. Herron

Indulgence, Declarations of, 1669, 1672, 1679 and 1687, proclamations intended in part to conciliate the Covenanters.* The deprivation of around 270 ministers in 1662 and the defeat of the Pentland Rising in 1666 appeared to have broken the Covenanters. In June 1669 the government offered an amnesty conditional on future obedience which resulted in forty-two ministers returning to their vacant parishes. A second Indulgence in September 1672 extended the freedom to preach to a further ninety. Hand-in-hand with these measures the government increased its repression of the more unyielding Covenanters, provoking a rebellion in 1679. This was crushed by the Duke of Monmouth, who surprisingly followed up his victory at Bothwell Bridge* by issuing a third Indulgence on 4 July, offering an indemnity to the rebels and permitting house conventicles. However, the government soon resumed its harsh treatment and had some success in enforcing conformity. In June 1687 James VII* undermined the Est.C by extending freedom of worship to Presbyterians in an effort to deflect criticism from his decision to grant toleration to RCs.

J. Buckroyd, *Church and State in Scotland 1660–1681* (E, 1980); I. B. Cowan, *The Scottish Covenanters 1660–88* (L, 1976); G. Donaldson, *Scotland: James V to James VII* (E, 1971), 358–84.

K. M. Brown

Informatory Vindication (1687), a statement of principles issued by the Society People (see Societies, United) during James VII's* reign. Prepared mainly by James Renwick,* latterly in consultation with Alexander Shields,* it was published in Utrecht. Its full title reflects something of the contents: 'An Informatory Vindication of a Poor Wasted Misrepresented Remnant of the Suffering Anti-Popish Anti-Prelatic Anti-Erastian Anti-Sectarian True Presbyterian Church of Christ in Scotland united together in a General Correspondence. By Way of Reply to Various Accusations in Letters Informations and Conferences given forth against them.'

It refuted charges brought against the 'Remnant' of schism (in their eyes a great evil). They denied that their meetings constituted a Church, or were ecclesiastical judicatories. The Vindication mourned the estrangement from other Presbyterians who had accepted the government's Indulgences* or Edicts of Toleration, and expressed love for them as fellow-ministers 'with whom again we would desire to have communion in ordinances'. The separation had been forced upon the Society People by the tyranny and temper of the times, but it did not affect their position as being in the succession of the historic Kirk of Scotland. The document aimed to clear away the hostility and misunderstanding about them that had grown up in Scotland and Holland.

Alexander Shields, 'The Life and Death of . . . Mr. James Renwick' (E, 1724), reproduced in *Biographia Presbyteriana* II (E, 1827).

J. D. Douglas

Inglis, John (1762–1834), minister of Tibbermore, near Perth (1786–99), and of Old Greyfriars, Edinburgh (1799–1834). He became a DD (Edinburgh, 1804), Moderator of the General Assembly (1805) and one of the Deans of the Chapel Royal* (1810). Although he was one of the prime movers in the Moderate* attack on John Leslie* in 1805, he was instrumental in convincing the 1824 General

Assembly to appoint a committee for Foreign Missions and in establishing and carrying out the CofS's scheme for Indian missions from that time onwards. Apparently orthodox in doctrine (John Macleod characterized him as an 'Evangelical* Erastian'), he wrote in support of the establishment principle (*The Importance of Ecclesiastical Establishments*, E, 1821, and *A Vindication of Ecclesiastical Establishments*, E, 1833).

DNB XXIX, 3; *FES* I, 42; J. Macleod, *Scottish Theology* (E, ³1974).

J. R. McIntosh

Inglis, John (1807–91), missionary to Vanuatu (New Hebrides). Born at Moniaive, Dumfriesshire, he was a mason by trade. He entered Glasgow University and Paisley Theological Hall, 1838–41, before ordination in 1843 to the Reformed Presbyterian Church's* Maori mission. Marrying Jessie McClymont (1821–85) in 1844, they served eight years in New Zealand.* Deciding that Anglican and Wesleyan Maori missions were adequate, Ignlis joined forces with John Geddie,* a Nova Scotian Presbyterian missionary, on Aneityum, Vanuatu, in 1852. Locating at Aname, he and his wife concentrated on evangelist and teacher training, women's industrial school and Bible translation, and witnessed the evangelization of all Aneityum.

After retiring in 1877, Inglis published the Aneityumese Old Testament and three missiologically significant books. Awarded a Glasgow University DD in 1883, Inglis promoted missions until his death, at Kirkcowan, Wigtownshire.

A Dictionary of the Aneityumese Language (L, 1882); *In the New Hebrides: Reminiscences of Missionary Life and Work, Especially on the Island of Aneityum, from 1850 till 1877* (L, 1887); *Bible Illustrations from the New Hebrides with Notices of the Progress of the Mission* (L, 1890).

W. J. Couper, 'The Reformed Presbyterian Church in Scotland', *RSCHS* 2 (1926), 121; R. S. Miller, *Misi Gete: John Geddie: Pioneer Missionary to the New Hebrides* (Launceston, 1975); J. Graham Miller, *Live: A History of Church Planting in Vanuatu*, Books 1–7 (Port Villa and Sydney, 1978–90).

J. M. Hitchen

Innerpeffray, near Crieff, Perthshire, site of perhaps the oldest lending library in the country. Founded under the will (1680) of David Drummond, 3rd Lord Madertie, laird of Innerpeffray (*d.c.*1694), it is now housed in a building of 1750–1 erected by Robert Hay Drummond (Archbishop of York, 1761–76), adjacent to the Chapel of St Mary built by the first laird of 1506, on the site of an earlier chapel from the mid-fourteenth century. (It was a collegiate* church in the mid-sixteenth century.) The Library contains over 3000 books, 2000 of them pre-1800 (catalogued by W. M. Dickie), with a borrowing register extant from 1747. It is rich in Bibles, and has early printings of works by John Major,* Hector Boece* and Gavin Douglas.*

Innerpeffray Library and Chapel (Coupar Angus, 1955); W. M. Dickie, 'Innerpeffray Library', *Library Association Record* n.s. 6 (1928), 100–5.

D. F. Wright

Innes, Alexander Taylor (1833–1912), prominent FC lawyer. He was born at Tain, Easter Ross, and educated at Tain Academy and Edinburgh University. Scruples about confessional subscription* prevented him entering the ministry, but he became an authority on matters of Church and creed, wrote the standard Scottish work on the subject, and drafted the epochal United Free Church Act anent Spiritual Independence of 1906. He was also prominent in advocating disestablishment* and promoting higher criticism within the FC. His works include: *The Law of Creeds in Scotland* (E, 1867, ²1902); *Studies in Scottish History* (L, 1892); *Church and State* (E, n.d.); *Chapters of Reminiscence* (L, 1913).

Both friend and foe acknowledged that Taylor Innes, an Edinburgh advocate, wielded great influence in the counsels of the FC. Though an able speaker and gifted writer, his influence was exercised chiefly through personal friendships, as with R. S. Candlish,* Alexander Whyte,* and Marcus Dods.* Above all, he was the confidant of Principal Rainy.* Prominent Liberals and disestablishers, both Innes and Rainy combined simple, devout evangelical religion with passionate commitment to unfettered scientific and historical inquiry. Both were convinced from the days of the first FC Union controversy that the headship of Christ over the Church involved the duty of the Church, in obedience to her Lord, to revise or alter non-fundamental elements in her creed and constitution. This was challenged by an opposing party and was rejected by the House of Lords in the judgment of 1904 (*see* Free Church Case). That judgment, however, gave Innes and Rainy the opportunity to draft the Act of 1906 which asserted the right of the Church to 'alter, change, add to, or modify her constitution and laws'. The credal and constitutional freedom which Innes had long championed had been won, but was not counterbalanced in the UF constitution by a doctrinal pledge firm enough to prevent the Church from falling into laxity. Questions which Innes himself raised as to how the fundamentals of the Church's belief can be distinguished remained unanswered.

P. C. Simpson, *The Life of Principal Rainy* (L, 1909), G. F. Barbour, *The Life of Alexander Whyte* (L, 1923); M. Dods, ed., *Later Letters of Marcus Dods* (L, 1911); K. R. Ross, *Church and Creed in Scotland* (E, 1988).

K. R. Ross

Innes Review, historical journal. Named after Thomas Innes,* priest and historian, it has appeared half-yearly since its launch by the Scottish Catholic Historical Committee in 1950. Articles have covered the Scottish Church from early times to the Reformation,* and the RCC in Scotland from then to modern times. Many new avenues for research have been opened and, for the latter period, the holdings of the Scottish Catholic Archives (*see* Scots Colleges) have been much used. Special issues, also published separately, deal with Early Libraries (1958), the Reformation* (1959), St Andrews* (1974), Modern Catholicism (1978).

IR 1 (1950), 67, 77–8; 2 (1951), 110–11; and *passim.*

M. Dilworth

Innes, Thomas (1662–1744), Scottish missionary priest and historian. Born in Aberdeenshire, he studied for the priesthood at the Scots College* in Paris and also spent time with the French Oratorians. In the 1690s he established links with Port-Royal and prominent Jansenists* in France. He served on the Scottish mission between 1698 and 1702, before being recalled to the Paris College as Prefect of Studies. In that capacity he was undoubtedly the dominant intellectual and spiritual influence at the College in the first half of the eighteenth century and schooled his charges in the rigorist ideals of Port Royal. In the 1730s he was denounced as the main source of Jansenist 'error' on the Scottish mission, an accusation which caused him much suffering and disrupted his literary and historical work. The imputation of heresy was unjust, but Thomas Innes was undoubtedly a resolute opponent of the bull *Unigenitus,* strongly devoted to Quesnel and sympathetic to the French Appellants. His correspondence reveals a pronounced antipathy to the Jesuits,* whom he regarded as the chief authors of the bull. Apart from his involvement in the Jansenist quarrels, Thomas Innes is significant as a historian and antiquary, his two main works being *A Critical Essay on the Ancient Inhabitants of the Northern Parts of Britain or Scotland* (1729, rp. E, 1885) and *The Civil and Ecclesiastical History of Scotland,* published posthumously (Spalding Club, A, 1853).

J. F. McMillan, 'Thomas Innes and the Bull *Unigenitus', IR* 33 (1982), 23–30; R. Clark, *Strangers and Sojourners at Port Royal* (C, 1932), 230–40; memoir in *The Civil . . .* (1853), rp. in *A Critical . . .* (1885).

J. F. McMillan

Innes, William (1770–1855), Baptist minister and author. William Innes was the son of the minister of Yester, E. Lothian, and was ordained minister of the second charge at Stirling in 1793. He was associated with Greville Ewing* and James Haldane,* and in 1799 resigned his charge and became pastor of the Tabernacle in Dundee. He became founding pastor of the Open Membership Church in Elder Street, Edinburgh, which later built in Dublin Street. He was a partner for many years in the publishing house of Waugh and Innes. He was active in the Baptist Home Missionary Society* and in the Baptist Missionary Society and in early attempts at ministerial education for Scottish Baptists. He also co-operated in inter-church work. He was a prolific writer; amongst his publications are *Token of Regard for the Established Church at Stirling* (E, 1800); *Domestic Religion* (E, 1821); *The Christian Ministry* (E, 1824).

A. B. Thomson, 'Some Baptist Pioneers in Scotland', *SBYB,* 1902, 16–22; A. M. Baines, *History of Dublin Street Baptist Church, Edinburgh 1858–1958* (E, 1958).

D. B. Murray

Innovations (or Novations), changes in established use, especially in worship* or Church order, contested as unacceptable and hence the subject of several controversies in the CofS.

(i) The General Assembly of 1639 passed an 'Act anent advising with Synods and Presbyteries before determination in Novations' (*AGACS* 42–3; J. A. Lamb, 'Examination of Innovations', *RSCHS* 11, 1951, 23–5). Its professed aim was to safeguard the work of the Glasgow Assembly* of 1638 in recovering the Reformation settlement. It anticipated the Barrier Act* (see below).

(ii) Soon the 'novations' in contention were omissions or exclusions, advocated by many Scottish Presbyterians as well as English (Puritan or Independent) and Irish (mainly returning Scottish exiles) influences, of read prayers, the Lord's Prayer, the Doxology (the 'conclusion' of sung praise) and bowing or kneeling by ministers. Controversy involved David Dickson,* Robert Blair,* Samuel Rutherford,* Robert Baillie* and others. The 1641 Assembly's 'Act anent Novations' (*AGACS* 48) was couched in general terms; and agitation continued. The 1643 Assembly's plan for a Scottish 'Directory for Divine Worship' to regulate 'novations', to be drafted by Alexander Henderson,* David Calderwood* and Dickson (*AGACS* 79–80), was overtaken by the Westminster Assembly* (Lamb, 25–7; C. G. M'Crie, *The Public Worship of Presbyterian Scotland,* E, 1892, 178ff. 205ff. *See* Perth, Five Articles of).

(iii) After the final establishment of Presbyterianism in 1690, an overture 'anent Novations' of 1695 became the Barrier Act* of 1697, to provide against 'any sudden alteration, or innovation, or other prejudice to the Church, in either doctrine, or worship, or discipline, or government'.

(iv) In the year of the 1707 Union,* the Assembly passed an 'Act against Innovations in the Worship of God', directed especially against the use of the English *Book of Common Prayer* in some areas in the north and east. Among the salvoes in the pamphlet war was John Willison's* *Queries to the Scots Innovators in Divine Service . . .* of 1712 (Lamb, 29–33; M'Crie, 259ff.).

(v) In the mid-nineteenth century, the liturgical innovations of men like James Cooper,* John Macleod* and, most famously, Robert Lee* provoked years of controversy. An Assembly deliverance of 1865, known as the Pirie Act from its instigator, W. R. Pirie,* was intended as 'a decision against Innovations', but, with the assuaging of passions after Lee's death, its effect was as much to facilitate as to thwart change (Lamb, 33–7; M'Crie, 326ff.; A. C. Cheyne, *The Transforming of the Kirk*, E, 1983, 92ff.).

D. F. Wright

Instructor, The, *see* Edinburgh Christian Instructor.

Inter-Varsity Fellowship/Universities and Colleges Christian Fellowship. The Student Christian Movement* remained more conservative and evangelical in Scotland than in most other areas. As the theological colleges became increasingly dominated by liberalism, however, the speakers at student meetings followed suit and SCM branches ceased to provide a programme that could satisfy most Evangelicals. In 1919 the very large Cambridge group (Cambridge Inter-Collegiate Christian Union) disaffiliated from SCM on these grounds (the SCM started a new group alongside it at Cambridge). In London an evangelical London Inter-Hospital Christian Union was founded as a clearly evangelical body in 1912, and a new Christian Union was founded at Oxford. These three groups convened the first Inter-Varsity Conference in 1919. At the 1923 conference a contingent from Scotland joined the English Unions, and the annual conference gradually increased in size and scope. In 1928 the Inter-Varsity Fellowship of Evangelical Unions was formed by the evangelical university groups present, among them Aberdeen, Edinburgh and Glasgow, where groups independent of SCM had been formed in 1921, 1922 and 1923 respectively. Eric Liddell* was a founder member in Edinburgh.

With the help of students and staff of the London College of Divinity, an eight-point doctrinal basis was drawn up which all officers and committee members were required to sign. This was, and remains in its revised form, an influential statement of orthodox conservative evangelical Christianity. The most distinctive clauses were those asserting the substitutionary nature of the death of Christ and the 'divine inspiration and infallibility of Holy Scripture as originally given'. In Scotland the hostel of the Edinburgh Medical Missionary Society* and interest in the China Inland Mission had provided a focus of evangelical vigour with a strong missionary emphasis, but many of the early leaders of these groups came from FC, Brethren and other non-CofS backgrounds and knew one another through those connections. Medical students often played a prominent part. An annual Scottish conference was started in 1925.

Although most such groups had at first been called Evangelical Unions, they gradually changed their names to be known as Christian Unions (CU). After the Second World War, a growing number of students took the lead. Many members of the groups have entered the ministry, especially that of the CofS, so that strongly evangelical churches (especially in university towns) began to increase in number.

In the 1950s Christian Unions were also developed in the colleges of education and technical colleges. This development nationwide led to the change of name from 'Inter-Varsity Fellowship' to 'Universities and Colleges Christian Fellowship'. In both cases the full title added 'of Evangelical Unions'. The Inter-Varsity Press became an important focus in the 1940s and subsequently. A Graduates Fellowship was started during the war and included many Christian groups in various professions. It later became the UCCF Associates. Former leaders of the IVF/UCCF played an important part in the building up of similar work in many other countries, leading to the development of the International Fellowship of Evangelical Students.

Each CU is interdenominational and autonomous, being controlled by its own student committee. CU members are required to profess a personal faith in Christ and officers must sign a Doctrinal Basis 'substantially' similar to that of UCCF.

See also Scottish Evangelical Theological Society; Crieff Fraternal.

F. D. Coggan (ed.), *Christ and the Colleges* (L, 1934); D. Johnson, *Contending for the Faith* (L, 1979); *For the Faith of the Gospel, 1929–78: The IVF/UCCF Story* (L, 1978); T. Tatlow, *The Story of the Student Christian Movement of Great Britain and Ireland* (L, 1933).

O. R. Barclay

Intrusion, the imposition of a minister whom it had not called on a Presbyterian congregation. Intrusion was bound up with patronage.* For much of the history of the Presbyterian Est.C in Scotland, the patron, usually a local laird or aristocrat, had the legal right to present his own nominee as minister of the parish church, regardless of the wishes of the parishioners. The congregational call,* even in the form of a bare right of veto, was thus eliminated. Opponents of intrusion tended to be Evangelicals,* and were occasionally called the 'Popular Party'* in the eighteenth century and 'Non-Intrusionists'* in the nineteenth. The practice of intrusion occasioned the three great secessions* from the Est.C, resulting in the formation of dissenting Presbyterian Churches – the Associate Presbytery* in 1733 (*see also* Associate Synod; General Associate Synod), the Relief* Church in 1761, and the FC in 1843 (*see* Disruption). Intrusion was made impossible only when patronage was finally abolished in 1874.

N. R. Needham

Inverkeithing Case, *see* Gillespie, Thomas; Relief Church; Torphichen Case.

Iona, in Gaelic *Ì* or *Ì Choluim Chille*, an island in the Inner Hebrides off the southwest coast of Mull. It was here that St Columba* founded a monastery, soon after coming to Scotland in 563, which was the headquarters of his other monastic foundations and of the church among the Dál Riata in Scotland. Its position was assured when Aedán mac Gabráin, king of the Dál Riata, sought out Columba there for Christian inauguration to his kingship in 574.

IONA

From Iona Columba visited the Picts* in Skye and near Inverness, and was in contact with the king of Strathclyde; he also revisited Ireland.

Following Columba's death (597), Iona's reputation as a centre of scholarship, art and spirituality grew, culminating in the career of Adomnán (d.704), ninth abbot of Iona. He was the author of *The Holy Places*, a description of the Holy Land based on an eyewitness account, and the *Life of Columba*, an affectionate portrait of the saint's gentleness as well as of his power. Adomnán also sought to protect non-combatants in time of war, worked for the redemption of captives, and strove for Christian unity in the Easter controversy (*see* Christian Year). After his death Iona was racked by the controversy, and in 715–18 Nechtan, king of the Picts, imposed the Dionysian Easter and Roman tonsure on the monks. Despite this and the political eclipse of the Dál Riata, Iona remained a great centre of art and learning; to the eighth century probably belong its finest stone crosses (*see* Crosses, Celtic), and part at least of the Book of Kells.* (*See also* Celtic Saints.)

Repeated Viking raids starting in the 790s led the monks to transfer their headquarters in 807 to Kells in Co. Meath. A small staff remained to tend Columba's shrine, but in 849 this too was transferred to Kells, while Kenneth mac Alpin took some of the saint's relics to Dunkeld. A few monks still remained, however, and by the mid-twelfth century there was a flourishing Celtic monastery at Iona. In 1203 Reginald son of Somerled transformed this into a Benedictine* monastery, with a parallel foundation of Augustinian* canonesses. In the later Middle Ages Iona Abbey came to be dominated by the local Mackinnon family, not always with beneficial results. On the death of the last Mackinnon about *c.*1499, the abbacy passed *in commendam* to the bishops of the Isles, who used the abbey church as a *de facto* cathedral, but without the monks serving as a chapter.

At the Reformation, the Earl of Argyll (*see* Campbell, Archibald, *d.* 1573) was prominent among the Protestant lords, and his friend John Carswell* was appointed Superintendent* of Argyll and the Isles in 1560; in 1565 he added to this the titles and revenues of the bishopric of the Isles and commendatorship* of Iona. The most notable of the Protestant bishops of the Isles was Andrew Knox,* who promulgated the 'Statutes of Iona'* at a gathering of Island chiefs in 1609.

Iona declined in importance and the buildings fell into ruin, to the dismay of eighteenth- and nineteenth-century visitors (such as Samuel Johnson). Successive Dukes of Argyll attempted measures of conservation, until in 1899 the eighth Duke founded a trusteeship for the restoration of the abbey church for use by all Christian denominations. In 1938 George MacLeod* founded the Iona Community* to restore and occupy the monastic buildings. In 1979 the island was sold by the Argyll Estates and purchased by the Sir Hugh Fraser Foundation as a memorial to Lord Fraser of Allander, and vested in the care of the National Trust for Scotland.

M. Herbert, *Iona, Kells and Derry* (O, 1988); Royal Commission on the Ancient and Historical Monuments of Scotland, *Iona: an Inventory of the Monuments* (E, 1982); K. Steer and J. W. M. Bannerman, *Late Medieval Monumental Sculpture in the West Highlands* (E, 1977); J. G. Dunbar and I. Fisher, *Iona* (E, 1983); A. Macquarrie, *Iona through the Ages* (Coll, 1983); T. R. Morton, *The Iona Community* (E, 1977); D. A. Bullough, 'Columba, Adomnán and the Achievement of Iona', *SHR* 43 (1964), 111–30, and 44 (1965), 17–33; A. Macquarrie, 'Kings, Lords and Abbots: Power and Patronage at the Medieval Monastery of Iona', *TGSI* 54 (1987), 355–75; M. Dilworth, 'Iona Abbey and the Reformation', *SGS* 12 (1976), 77–109.

A. Macquarrie

Iona Community, an ecumenical fellowship of men and women, ordained and lay, seeking new and radical ways of living the gospel in today's world. Though the historic island of Iona* is its spiritual home, the Community's main work is elsewhere – particularly in what are regarded as difficult urban areas.

The Community was founded in 1938 by George MacLeod* when he was minister of Govan Old Parish Church, Glasgow. Deeply affected by the Church's lack of impact in working-class communities at a time of high unemployment, MacLeod initiated an experiment on Iona* – the Scottish Hebridean island from which St Columba had launched a great missionary movement in AD 563. The Iona Community, consisting of ministers and craftsmen, began to rebuild the ruins of the living quarters of the medieval Benedictine* abbey which had replaced the Celtic Columban foundation. MacLeod's intention was to train young ministers for work in the industrial parishes of inner-city and housing scheme areas of Scotland. He believed that clergy should work alongside industrial men, and learn to live together in Christian community. By 1967, when the rebuilding was completed, the Iona Community had provided many young ministers for work in urban areas.

The Iona Community today consists of 200 members, 800 Associates and 2,500 Friends. Its members – ordained and lay, Protestant and RC, men and women, married and celibate – share a fivefold Rule of prayer, economic sharing, planning of time, meeting together, and work for justice and peace. They live in many different parts of the world.

On Iona, the Community welcomes many people from all over the world every year. The pilgrims come as day visitors, or to live in the restored abbey and share in the Community's weekly programme of worship, work, recreation, healing and study. Young people come to the MacLeod Centre – a new international youth centre completed during the Iona Community's fiftieth anniversary celebrations in 1988 – and to Camas, an adventure centre on Mull. On the mainland of Britain, the Community has several 'Columban houses' – experimental communities living out the concerns of the

Iona Community – and has staff members engaged in peace and justice work, urban mission and renewal of worship.

The Community organizes a training scheme – the 'Peregrini Scheme' (named after the wandering Celtic monks) – in which young unemployed people are trained in theology and community leadership. It also has a share in Centrepeace, a justice and peace centre in Glasgow. Its publishing division, Wild Goose Publications, produces books, pamphlets, worship materials and cassettes, and its Wild Goose Worship Group helps introduce new methods of worship in local congregations.

G. F. MacLeod, *We Shall Rebuild* (G, 1944); T. R. Morton, *The Iona Community: Personal Impressions of the Early Years* (E, 1977); R. Ferguson, *Chasing the Wild Goose* (L, 1988).

R. Ferguson

Iona, 'Statutes' of (1609), measures for religious, social and cultural reform which Bishop Andrew Knox* of the Isles enjoined on leading Highland chiefs on board ship at a meeting at Iona. Part of a sustained attempt by King James VI* and I to bring the Highlands into line with more manageable parts of his realm, they aimed to secure: allegiance and support for the Reformed kirk; provision of inns; a reduction in the number of social parasites; control of alcohol; a Lowland education for the sons of the gentry; prohibition of firearms; and the suppression of Gaelic* bards.

D. Masson (ed.), *Register of the Privy Council of Scotland, 1610–13* (E, 1889), IX, xxv–xxx, 26–30; D. Gregory, *The History of the Western Highlands and Isles of Scotland* (L, G, ²1881), 329–33; D. Stevenson, *Alasdair MacColla and the Highland Problem in the 17th Century* (E, 1980), 28–30.

K. D. MacDonald

Ireland. Ireland has had many links with Scotland from early times. *Scotia* was for long one of the names by which Ireland was known to Latin writers such as Adomnán.* Tribesmen called *Scoti* had settled in Scotland by the beginning of the sixth century AD, and they established the kingdom of Dalriada, approximately coterminous with Argyll. The name *Scotia* was subsequently applied to Scotland north of the Forth, and by the twelfth century the *Scoti* had given their name to the whole of what is now Scotland (*see* Gaelic). Christian missionaries crossed to Scotland, Columba* making a pioneer journey in 563. There was much coming and going of Celtic monks in succeeding centuries (*see* Celtic Saints; Monasticism, Celtic).

English penetration of Ireland took place from the eleventh century, but contacts with Scotland persisted, and in the fifteenth century a branch of the MacDonalds, the Lords of the Isles, settled in north Antrim. Gaelic culture was common to Ireland and Scotland, and in the Middle Ages the Gaelic learned classes (poets, craftsmen etc.) of both countries maintained close contact.

The English government attempted to impose the Reformation upon the Church in Ireland, but with limited success. A rebellion against English rule broke out in Ireland in 1595; it was led by Hugh O'Neill, the Earl of Tyrone, and was not crushed until 1603. In that year James VI* became King of England, and he believed that the pacification of Ireland could be assisted if Scottish settlers were planted in the north of Ireland. He confirmed the MacDonalds in their holdings, though for a time they still remained RCs, and he also drew up a plan for a major plantation of Ulster.

As a prelude to this plan, Con O'Neill of Clandeboy in county Down solved his political and financial difficulties by selling a third of his lands to Hugh Montgomery and a third to James Hamilton, both Scots from south-east Scotland. These new landholders were ready to bring Scottish settlers to their lands and to the neighbouring lands of O'Neill. Due to economic hardship and ecclesiastical unrest in Scotland, many Scots were willing to venture to settle in Ulster, and, on the long view, they were returning to the land of their ancestors.

The King had the opportunity to put his major plan into operation in 1607 when O'Neill, the Earl of Tyrone, and O'Donnell, the Earl of Tyrconnell, fled from Ulster and vacated their lands. The plan envisaged 79,000 acres remaining in the possession of the native Irish, and after a time the Earls were allowed to return and occupy part of their lands; 155,000 acres were allocated to the English and the Scots. About eighty Scots were granted possession of large sections of these acres; they were known as 'undertakers', that is, persons who undertook the responsibility for defending their territory, planting settlers and cultivating the land. Most of these applicants were small lairds and gentry. Hamilton expanded his holdings far beyond his original holding in Down into Antrim, Armagh and Cavan. He also secured land for the support of the new Trinity College in Dublin, of which he had been one of the first Fellows. Another Hamilton, James, Earl of Abercorn, secured land in Tyrone. Montgomery also expanded his holdings, while his brother, George, who became Bishop of Clogher, brought some Scots into the western areas of Ulster. Scots also settled in areas held by English undertakers, notably those of Chichester in Belfast and south Antrim and of Clotworthy in mid-Antrim.

By 1611, sixty Scottish undertakers were in residence on the 80,000 acres they had been granted and there were about 700 adult Scottish settlers. By 1613 there were over 1,500 adult Scots, but only twenty-five of the undertakers had thoroughly developed their holdings. Many were retarded by lack of personal drive, by lack of capital, by difficulty of transport, by disputes with neighbours, and by the hostility of the native Irish. By 1619 a survey showed about 4,400 Scots in areas of Ulster beyond the river Bann, and by 1622 over 6,000. Between 4,000 and 5,000 were settled in Antrim and Down. Thereafter, the influx declined; some undertakers sold their holdings to others and some were ready to employ the native Irish, who worked for a lower wage than the Scots. However, there remained sufficient Scots to maintain their foothold, though Laud's* 1634 estimate of 40,000 able-bodied Scots in Ireland was probably an apprehensive exaggeration.

Most of the Scottish settlers retained their attachment to Presbyterianism, though early observers referred to many of the initial settlers as bankrupts and refugees from justice. However, resistance to the episcopalian policy of James VI* was strong in south-west Scotland and this was a factor in making many of them decide to leave Scotland.

At the start of the Plantation, the need for ministers and the pressure of the new landowners led to a compromise with the bishops of the established episcopal Church of Ireland. Scottish ministers were appointed to be ministers in the parish churches, though many of them had been ordained by Presbyteries in Scotland. The compliance of some Bishops, notably the Scots, Andrew Knox of Raphoe* and Robert Echlin of Down and Connor, allowed Scottish licentiates to be ordained in a manner which the ordinands regarded as ordination by Presbytery, with the bishop acting as a presbyter among the others, while the bishops could claim that their presence made it an episcopal ordination. Knox reported in 1622 that twelve of the fifteen ministers in his diocese were Scots. At least sixty-four Scots were ministers in parish churches in Ireland.

These accommodations were brought to an end when Wentworth became the Lord-Deputy. Supported by Bishop Bramhall of Derry, his policy led to the ejection of many Scottish ministers. Wentworth's policy led to an Irish rebellion in 1641 and many Scottish settlers were put to death. Many Scots fled to Scotland. A Scottish army was stationed at Carrickfergus to assist in crushing this rebellion and its Scottish chaplains along with some ministers and elders constituted the first Presbytery in Ireland in 1642. The Scots felt threatened until after Cromwell* had crushed the rebellion. Under his regime, as many as seventy Scots again ministered in parish churches and the Presbyterians re-grouped. In 1660 the Restoration* also restored a thorough policy of conformity to the re-established episcopacy. Bramhall, now Archbishop of Armagh, enforced the policy. The greatest concentration of Scottish ministers was in the dioceses of Down, Connor and Dromore, and the Bishop, Jeremy Taylor, ejected thirty-six ministers in one day.

Presbyterian congregations were now formed in a clandestine manner outside the established Church, and they suffered much harassment, though they were sheltered by some landholders. The disabilities continued until the grant of toleration by William III* in 1689. Even thereafter they suffered many civil disabilities. These led many Presbyterians to side with the RCs at the time of the 1798 rebellion, and they also drove many Presbyterians to emigrate to America, where they and their descendants had much influence upon the formation and growth of the United States.

Presbyterian congregations were organized into the Synod of Ulster. Scottish influence was also seen in the foundation of congregations linked to the Secession* in Scotland. These two strands came together in 1840 to form the Presbyterian Church in Ireland.

Scots gradually settled in every county in Ireland. They came as tenants in many estates and in time spread into commercial and public life. Churches were founded in many towns and were known as Scots churches. By 1870 there were sixty-three churches in the three southern provinces with a communicant membership of 4,269, while the churches in Ulster had a membership of 119,172. The partition of Ireland in 1922 transferred many Presbyterians from the old province of Ulster into the Republic of Ireland. There are now 10,639 communicant members in the Republic and 122,227 in N. Ireland. The estimated total community of Irish Presbyterians is 342,465.

This Church has been, and remains, conscious of its Scottish roots but it has also become an integral part of the Irish scene, and its Presbyterianism has been shaped by the environment of Anglican ascendancy and RC exclusiveness and numerical superiority.

The links with Scotland are further complicated by the consequences of the Irish potato famine in the 1840s when many Irish RCs emigrated to Scotland, and their offspring constitute a large proportion of the present Scottish RC population, estimated at over 800,000 persons (see Immigration).

R. F. G. Holmes, *Our Presbyterian Heritage* (Belfast, 1985); J. G. Leyburn, *The Scotch-Irish: A Social History* (Chapel Hill, NC, 1962); R. B. Knox, *James Ussher, Archbishop of Armagh* (Cardiff, 1967); M. Perceval-Maxwell, *The Scottish Migration to Ulster in the reign of James I* (L, 1973); R. Gillespie, *Colonial Ulster: The Settlement of East Ulster, 1640–1641* (Cork, 1985); C. A. Hanna, *The Scotch-Irish: The Scot in North Britain, Northern Ireland and North America*, 2 vols (NY and L, 1902) J. S. Reid, *History of the Presbyterian Church in Ireland*, ed. W. D. Killen (Belfast, 1867); T. Witherow, *Historical and Literary Memorials of Presbyterianism in Ireland*, 2 vols (L, 1879–80).

R. B. Knox

Ireland, John (*c.*1440–96), conciliarist, diplomat and writer. Of humble birth in St Andrews, he studied there (BA, 1455) before leaving under a cloud for Paris in 1458. There he remained until 1483 (apart from diplomatic missions to Scotland in 1479–80), serving as an academic politician for the German 'nation' to the University and twice (1469, 1476) as Rector of the University, teaching at first arts and then, after studying at the College of Navarre from 1466, theology, and writing in both fields. Extant but unpublished are his *Tractatus* on the immaculate conception of the Virgin Mary, endorsing the Scotist position in favour (1481; MS in Trinity College, Dublin), and his commentaries on books III–IV of Peter Lombard's *Sentences* (before 1483; MS in Aberdeen UL. Those on bks I–II are lost.) The latter show his conciliarism* (he had met Thomas Livingston* in his youth).

Back in Scotland from 1483, he was active in the

service of James III, but failed to secure the see of Dunkeld and the archdeaconry of St Andrews. He obtained other benefices, including the Rectory of Ettrick in the Borders, fell foul of Archbishop William Scheves of St Andrews, and earned repute as a preacher. His writings were now in Scots, on penance and confession (ed. W. A. Craigie, *The Asloan Manuscript*, STS, E, 1923–5, I, 1–80), and *The Meroure of Wyssdome* (1490), the earliest surviving original work in Scots (see J. H. Stevenson in *The Scottish Antiquary* 15, 1900–1, 1–14). It is both a 'mirror for princes' and a thorough presentation of the basics of Catholic faith (subtitlted 'A.B.C. of cristianite'). It argues against royal absolutism and gives evidence of vernacular heretical (Wycliffite; see Lollardy) literature in Scotland. About a third (bks 1–2) was edited by C. Macpherson (STS, E, 1926), the rest is in MS in NLS.

Macpherson, ix–xlvi; J. H. Burns, 'John Ireland and the Meroure of Wyssdome', *IR* 6 (1955), 77–98.

D. F. Wright

Irish Missions to the Highlands. At the beginning of the seventeenth century various appeals were made to Rome for priests to minister to the Catholics of the Highlands* and Islands of Scotland. As Gaelic* was in great part the language of those districts, it was only natural that the authorities at Rome turned to the Irish to supply the need. The first Irish priests to answer the call were Jesuits,* the best-known of whom, David Galwey, laboured in the Hebrides for short periods between 1611 and 1619. In 1619 three or four Irish Franciscans* went as missionaries and continued to work there until 1637; the most notable was Cornelius Ward. From 1626 the Franciscan friary of Bonamargy in Co. Antrim served as the headquarters of the mission. In 1650 Irish Vincentians* began to labour among the Gaelic-speaking Scots. In 1668 two Irish Franciscans, Francis MacDonnell and his brother Mark, volunteered as missionaries to the Highlands and Islands; Francis laboured there for fourteen years, and in conjunction with Oliver Plunkett, archbishop of Armagh, drew up a report on the mission which was forwarded to Rome in 1671. During the last twenty years of the seventeenth century a small number of Irish priests continued to work in the Highlands, but in a rather disorganized way. The Franciscan and Vincentian missions in particular were remarkably successful and thus instrumental in retaining whole districts for the RCC in Scotland.

C. Giblin, 'The "Acta" of Propaganda Archives and the Scottish Mission', *IR* 5 (1954), 39–76; *id.*, *Irish Franciscan Mission to Scotland 1619–1646* (Dublin, 1964); *id.*, 'St Oliver Plunkett, Francis MacDonnell, OFM, and the Mission to the Hebrides', *Collectanea Hibernica* 17 (1974–5), 69–102; J. Corboy, 'Father David Galwey (1579–1634)', *The Irish Monthly*, February 1944, 58–67.

C. Giblin

Irving, Edward (1792–1834), preacher, theologian, and one of the most colourful and controversial figures on the British religious scene in the early nineteenth century. A native of Annan, near Dumfries, Irving studied arts 1805–9 at Edinburgh University. He then took the divinity course while supporting himself through school-teaching in Haddington and Kirkcaldy, where he met and became a lifelong friend of Thomas Carlyle.* In 1815 he was licensed to preach by the CofS, and in 1819 became assistant to Thomas Chalmers* at St John's, Glasgow.

Three years later he accepted a call to one of London's Scottish congregations, in Hatton Garden. His subsequent rise to fame as a pulpit orator was meteoric. The Hatton Garden chapel, which had a congregation of fifty before Irving's arrival, was soon swamped by an influx of hearers which included 'statesmen, philosophers, poets, painters, and literary men; peers, merchants and fashionable ladies' in abundance (A. L. Drummond, *Edward Irving and his Circle*, L, 1934, 49), all captivated by Irving's brilliant rhetorical powers. Almost overnight Irving became the capital's latest sensation. To accommodate his hugely expanded congregation, a new church was built in Regent Square (1827).

By this time Irving had come to hold premillennial views about the Second Coming (*see* Millennialism). These he popularized, fervently and profusely, both in preaching and writing. Iain Murray attributes to Irving the turning of the tide in British evangelical circles to premillennialism from a previously postmillennial consensus (*The Puritan Hope*, E, 1971, 187–96).

In late 1827, controversy arose over Irving's doctrine of the humanity of Christ, culminating in 1833 in his official deposition from the ministry of the CofS. Irving maintained, in such works as *Christ's Holiness in the Flesh* (E, 1831), that the Saviour's humanity was identical with that of all other men since the fall, including innate sinful propensities. Jesus' human soul, however, was perfectly indwelt by the Spirit from the moment of conception, and this neutralized his sinful inclinations and empowered him to live a spotlessly holy life. Irving's opponents objected that if Jesus had sinful tendencies, he himself was in need of a Saviour, since God's law requires perfection in inward disposition as well as overt conduct. Irving responded sometimes by denying that sinful inclinations were strictly culpable, sometimes (apparently) by denying that Jesus had such tendencies at all.

Probably Irving's language was more at fault than his theology. In his friend S. T. Coleridge's words, 'Irving's expressions upon this subject are ill-judged, inconvenient, in bad taste, and in terms false ... It is Irving's error to use declamation, high and passionate rhetoric, not introduced by calm and clear logic' (*Tabletalk*, E, 1905, 278). Irving's intention was undoubtedly to remind the Church of the reality and relevance of Jesus' human brotherhood; his tragedy was to shipwreck such a noble enterprise by pushing language beyond the limits of catholic Christological reflection on the sinlessness of the Saviour (*see* Christology.)

Irving's name is probably most closely associated with the rise of the Catholic Apostolic Church,* a nineteenth-century precursor of Pentecostalism.* 'Irvingism' had its origins in the claim to possession of supernatural gifts by Mary Campbell* and James and George MacDonald.* Irving, influenced by his assistant Alexander Scott,* accepted the authenticity of these gifts, which included glossolalia, prophecies, and miraculous healing. Linking these phenomena with baptism in the Spirit as a distinct post-conversion experience, Irving welcomed their manifestation in his own church in 1831.

The results were bitterly divisive; Irving, opposed by his elders, was condemned by London Presbytery in 1832, and the trustees of Regent Square Church barred him and his followers from the building. The 'Irvingites' established themselves elsewhere and soon evolved into a new sect, complete with twelve apostles, as well as prophets and 'angels'.

Irving, who never personally exercised any of the spiritual gifts, was appointed an angel in the Catholic Apostolic Church, and played an increasingly insignificant role in the movement. His health, never excellent, gave way, and he died in Glasgow in 1834 a broken man.

The celebrated utterance of Robert Murray M'Cheyne* seems a fitting epitaph to Irving's grand, tragic life: 'I look back upon him with awe, as on the saints and martyrs of old. A holy man in spite of all his delusions and errors. He is now with his God and Saviour, whom he wronged so much, yet, I am persuaded, loved so sincerely' (A. A. Bonar, *Memoirs and Remains of the Rev. Robert Murray McCheyne*, E, 1892, 27).

Sermons on the Trinity (L, 1828); *Sermons on the Incarnation* (L, 1829); *The Orthodox and Catholic Doctrine of our Lord's Human Nature* (L, 1830); *For the Oracles of God, Four Orations* (L, 1823); *Exposition of the Book of Revelation* (4 vols, L, 1831); *Homilies on the Sacraments* (L, 1828); *The Works of Edward Irving*, ed. Gavin Carlyle (5 vols, L, 1865); *The Prophetical Works of Edward Irving*, ed. Gavin Carlyle (2 vols, L, 1867-70).

M. Oliphant, *The Life of Edward Irving* (2 vols, L, 1862; 5th ed., L, n.d.); R. Baxter, *Narrative of Facts* (L, 1833); *Irvingism* (L, 1836); E. Miller, *The History and Doctrines of Irvingism* (2 vols, L, 1878); G. Strachan, *The Pentecostal Theology of Edward Irving* (L, 1973); *FES* VII, 493-4; Chambers-Thomson II, 344-51; *DNB* XXIX, 52-6.

N. R. Needham

Itinerancy, peripatetic ministry not restricted to one parish or congregation. From the Revolution Settlement and the establishment of Presbyterianism, itinerancy played a part in the ministry of the CofS, especially in connection with remote communities and extensive Highland* parishes. The lay missionaries and schoolmasters employed by the Royal Bounty* and the Society in Scotland for Propagating Christian Knowledge* were the agents of a concerted attempt in the eighteenth century to secure and service the parochial structure of the church where it was weak or over-extended. Though this early application of the practice received official sanction, the term became synonymous during the French Revolution* with unauthorized lay evangelism which had every appearance of subversive intent. In spite of the firm control over agents exercised by the principal itinerant body, the Society for Propagating the Gospel at Home,* explicit rejections of politics and denials of animosity towards the Est.C failed to placate the critics of the new evangelism. Observers noted with alarm and distaste the spread of the movement, its connection with leaders such as David Bogue* and Robert Haldane* who had welcomed the overthrow of the *ancien régime* in France, and the pungent remarks on the national Church made by the eccentric Anglican advocate of itinerancy, Rowland Hill,* who undertook two preaching tours in Scotland. Yet apart from the declaratory act and Pastoral Admonition* issued by the 1799 General Assembly and isolated cases of arrest, opposition to itinerancy was confined to the realm of polemical literature and to local obstruction by landowners and employers. Pleas were made in 1799 for legislation to be used to control the practice, but no action was taken. In the decades following 1797 it became a feature of Scottish rural life, albeit more prominent in some areas than in others. Using this device, the lay missionaries trained by the Haldane seminary and a variety of ministers including William Ward (Episcopalian) of Old Deer, Aberdeenshire, Dugald Sinclair* (Baptist) of Bellanoch, Argyll, and John MacDonald* (CofS) of Ferintosh in the Black Isle, were able to spread an essentially undenominational concern for evangelical Christianity through many areas of the Lowlands and Gaelic-speaking Highlands, gaining access to ordinary hearers in parishes where the Church's home missionary task required serious attention. Although the practice of itinerancy was perpetuated well into the nineteenth century by a number of home missionary bodies, it gradually assumed a more institutional character as it addressed itself to the task of providing leadership for the isolated congregations of the Highlands and Islands.

See also Baptist Home Missionary Society for Scotland.

D. E. Meek, 'Evangelical Missionaries in the Early Nineteenth-Century Highlands', *SS* 28 (1987), 1-34; D. W. Lovegrove, *Established Church, Sectarian People: Itinerancy and the Transformation of English Dissent, 1780-1830* (C, 1988).

D. W. Lovegrove

Iverach, James (1839-1922), FC minister, professor and principal. He was born at Halkirk, Caithness. Excelling in mathematics and physics at Edinburgh University, he studied at New College, Edinburgh, and was ordained and inducted to West Calder FC, 1869. He served at Ferryhill, Aberdeen (1874-87) before holding various chairs at Aberdeen FC College (1887-1922). He was Principal 1905-22 and Moderator of the General Assembly of the UFC, 1912–13. He was DD of Aberdeen.

Iverach explored the frontier between science and religion: *Theism in the Light of Present Science and Philosophy* [the first Deems Lectures, New York] (L, 1900); evolutionary thought: *The Ethics of Evolution Examined* (L, 1886) and *Evolution and Christianity* (L, 1894); epistemological questions: *Is God Knowable?* (L, 1884), *The Truth of Christianity* (E, 1896). Other works included: *The Philosophy of Mr. Herbert Spencer Examined* (L, 1884); *Descartes, Spinoza and the New Philosophy* (E, 1904); *Jonathan Edwards* (E, 1884); *St. Paul: his Life and Times* (L, 1890); *Life of Moses* (E, 1881; in its twentieth thousand by 1947); and two collections of sermons and addresses: *The Other Side of Greatness* (L, 1906) and *The Christian Message* (L, 1920).

FUFCS 577; A. P. F. Sell, *Defending and Declaring the Faith* (Exeter, 1987), ch. 6.

A. P. F. Sell

J

Jacobites, the supporters of the exiled Stuart king, James VII,* and his son James and grandson Charles. They derived their name from Jacobus, the Latin form of James. Jacobitism was to some extent a religious movement as well as a political one, and profoundly affected the development of the EpCS.

Dissatisfaction at the dynastic, political and religious changes of 1689–90 was the main-spring of Jacobitism. The Convention Parliament of 1689 decided that James VII* had forfeited the crown of Scotland, and offered it jointly to William of Orange* and his wife Mary, daughter of King James. A small group in the Convention, led by John Graham* of Claverhouse, Viscount Dundee, dissented and the Jacobite movement in Scotland was born. The first rising began with the raising of King James' standard on Dundee Law in April 1689. The Jacobite victory at Killiecrankie was neutralized by the death of Claverhouse in the battle and the subsequent battle of Dunkeld effectively ended the rising.

There was, however, a considerable growth in Jacobite sentiment over the following twenty years or so. The Scottish bishops and quite a number of the clergy felt unable to transfer their allegiance from King James to William of Orange, which meant the abolition of prelacy and the establishment of Presbyterianism* in its fullness by the Estates of Parliament. These were by no means universally popular measures. People felt sorry for the clergy oppressed by Presbyterian commissions and the clergy encouraged their flocks to pray for and support the exiled King. The massacre of Glencoe and the Darien* colonial disaster added to the unpopularity of William's administration. The Union with England of 1707* also proved a gift to the Jacobite cause.

In 1708 Louis XIV of France provided a small fleet to convey the Pretender or James VIII to Scotland in the hope that James, having seized his northern kingdom, would invade England and force it to make peace with France. However Admiral Byng intercepted the Jacobite fleet and prevented James from even landing in Scotland.

The most famous Jacobite rising was in 1745 (see Rising of 1745) but there were also risings in 1715 (see Rising of 1715), and in 1719 there was the Little Rising sponsored by Cardinal Alberoni of Spain. A fleet of twenty-nine ships carrying 5,000 troops was sent to invade England but was destroyed by a storm. A smaller expedition landed in the Western Highlands but was routed at the head of Loch Duich.

Despite its military and political failure, Jacobitism continued to be used as a pretext for repressive measures against the Highlands and the EpCS up to the last decade of the eighteenth century.

F. McLynn, *The Jacobites* (L, 1985); I. and K. Whyte, *On the Trail of the Jacobites* (L, 1990).

H. R. *Sefton*

Jaffray, Alexander (1614–73), sometime Covenanter,* early Quaker and politician. Born and raised in Aberdeen, Jaffray became provost and represented the city in several parliaments. Under Cromwell, he was director of chancellery for Scotland. Widely respected for his personal piety, Jaffray's *Diary* (ed. J. Barclay, A, 1833) records his longing for the purification of religion and his later dissatisfaction with Presbyterianism. In 1662, he joined the small but vigorous Quaker group in Aberdeen (see Friends, Society of).. The conversion of such a prominent citizen alarmed the authorities and he was imprisoned for holding illegal meetings. He died at Kingswell.

DNB XXIX, 127–8.

H. S. *Pyper*

Jamaica, see Missions.

James III (1452–88), King of Scots 1460–88. The problems affecting the Scottish Church during his reign have to be seen within their European context. The papacy, having recently recovered from the debilitating effects of schism and conciliarism*, had already attempted to reassert its authority over the national churches by insisting on its right to nominate and provide to ecclesiastical benefices, particularly to those of the higher clergy. It also insisted on its right to resort to its own fiscal and legal expedients when taxing the clergy, in order to meet its loss of revenue from the papal states. James III, like his predecessors, geared his ecclesiastical policy to challenge these rights by nominating his own candidates to major benefices whenever possible, and to stem the export of gold and silver to Rome with antipapal legislation of his own. Given the frequency with which his legislation against simony* and barratry* had to be repeated throughout his reign, it is clear that he was unable to prevent Scottish clerics from purchasing benefices of all kinds at the Roman Curia, an abuse which was later to tell heavily against the papacy. He was more successful in *sede vacante* disputes, being able to reward a number of his most loyal administrators with key bishoprics and abbacies: a strategy which finally wrested from Innocent VIII, on 20 April 1487, an indult (special licence) by which the pope promised to refrain for eight months from providing to cathedrals and monasteries tax valued over 200 florins, in order to allow the Scottish Crown time to nominate its own candidates.

James III was prepared to defend the faith against heresy. He was careful not to interfere in the business of the ecclesiastical courts. He supported the religious orders, particularly the Dominicans* and Observant Franciscans.* After the death of his queen in 1486, he did not hesitate to supplicate the pope for permission to promote her canonization cause. On the other hand, his interference in the affairs of Coldingham Priory* could not fail to incur the lasting emnity of the Homes, who considered the priory their private preserve. On balance his ecclesiastical policy, which concentrated primarily on the interests of the Crown, did little to advance the cause of church reform.

Norman Macdougall, *James III: A Political Study* (E, 1982); L. J. Macfarlane, *William Elphinstone and the Kingdom of Scotland 1431–1514* (A, 1985); *APS* II (1424–1567); A. I. Cameron, *The Apostolic Camera and Scottish Benefices 1418–1488* (O, 1934); *Calendar of Entries in the Papal Registers relating to Gt Britain and Ireland*, XII–XIV, ed. J. Twemlow (L, 1933, 1955, 1960), and XV, ed. M. Haren (Dublin, 1978).

L. J. Macfarlane

James IV (1473–1513), King of Scots. He acceded to the throne 11 June 1488, married Margaret Tudor, sister of Henry VIII of England, 8 August 1503, and was killed at Flodden.

The Crown's attempt to control the Scottish Church reached a decisive phase during the reign of James IV. Although, like his predecessors, he recognized that his higher clergy had their own distinctive ecclesiastical responsibilities, James IV could not afford to dispense them from their political, judicial and other secular administrative duties deemed essential for national well-being. In consequence he strove to nominate men of his own choice, irrespective of their spiritual suitability for the task. Moreover, given that the Crown had already established its right to administer the temporalities of a bishopric during its technical vacancy, he used such occasions for his own personal profit with little regard for the well-being of the bishopric concerned. Thus, exploiting the opportunity presented by Innocent VIII's indult of 1487 (see above), he gained the archbishopric of St Andrews in 1497 for his brother James, then a layman aged twenty, and, on the latter's unexpected death in 1504, for his illegitimate son Alexander, aged eleven, with the full knowledge that neither could be consecrated before the age of twenty-seven, during which time he would have been able to pocket the profits on the temporalities of their estates for some twenty-three years. He persuaded Alexander VI to raise the bishopric of Glasgow to archiepiscopal and metropolitan status for his favourite, Robert Blackader,* in 1492, a promotion which could not fail to create disunity within the Scottish hierarchy when it needed to speak with one voice. His exploitation of the system of commendatory* abbacies by rewarding a number of them, often in plurality, to loyal servants of the Crown, was similarly bound to weaken the fabric of the Scottish monastic orders. Such moves were impossible without the consent of the papacy, which by this time could ill afford to challenge them. The truth was that the French invasion of Italy in 1494 compelled the papacy to seek all the political support it could muster throughout Europe, and the presentation of the Golden Rose to James IV by Innocent VIII in 1491, of the Sceptre to him by Alexander VI in 1494, and of the Sword and Hat by Julius II in 1507, as marks of their especial favour to the Scottish Crown, have to be seen in this light.

If James IV exploited the Scottish Church for his own political and financial ends, however, he was ready to support it in other ways. He was generous to the religious orders. He supplicated Alexander VI to allow Elphinstone* to found the University of Aberdeen in 1495. He used his authority to launch the Aberdeen Breviary* as a national breviary in 1510. As proof of his orthodoxy, he cherished the idea of leading a European crusade against the Turks, which Julius II fortunately recognized as wildly impractical. All in all, his reign illustrates the total inability of either Crown or papacy to concentrate on abuses within the Scottish Church calling urgently for reform.

Norman Macdougall, *James IV* (E, 1989); *The Letters of James IV 1505–1513*, ed. R. K. Hannay (E, 1953); C. Burns, 'Papal Gifts to Scottish Monarchs: the Golden Rose and the Blessed Sword', *IR* 20 (1969), 150–94; I. B. Cowan, 'Church and Society', in *Scottish Society in the Fifteenth Century*, ed. J. M. Brown (L, 1977), 112–35; L. Macfarlane, 'Was the Scottish Church Reformable by 1513?', in *Church, Politics and Society: Scotland 1408–1929*, ed. N. Macdougall (E, 1983), 23–43; D. McRoberts, 'The Scottish

Church and Nationalism in the Fifteenth Century', *IR* 19 (1968), 3–14.

L. J. Macfarlane

James VI (I) (1566–1625), King of Scotland. James was crowned on 29 July 1567, but civil war was waged in his name until the defeat of his mother's supporters in 1573 (*see* Mary, Queen of Scots). During his formal minority (1567–78) Scotland was governed by a succession of regents, including the formidable James Stewart (*d.* 1570)*, Earl of Moray, and James Douglas,* Earl of Morton.

James received a Calvinist education under George Buchanan,* and remained a Calvinist all his life. In the early 1580s he was seen by RCs as a potential convert, but he had no sympathy for RCism, although he was prepared to exploit religious divisions at home and abroad. However, he was offended by the radical Protestant politics espoused by Buchanan to justify rebellion against Mary, and to which he was exposed in the Ruthven Raid* of August 1582. Following James's escape from the Ruthven lords in 1583, Chancellor Arran (James Stewart, *d.* 1596) ruthlessly imposed an Erastian episcopacy on the Church in the form of the 'Black Acts'* of May 1584. Arran also laid much of the ground for the 1586 Protestant League* between James and Elizabeth I.

However, Arran's fall in 1585 was followed by the erosion of James's control over the Church, and he was forced to recognize a *de facto* Presbyterian system of church government in the 1592 'Golden Act'.* Presbyterian success during these years can be attributed to the support received from England and from Protestant noblemen worried by James's leniency towards Spanish-backed Catholic rebellions in the south-west and north-east during 1587–94.

Defeat of the Spanish faction in 1594 at last allowed James to acquire a tolerable level of control over his court and the localities. In pursuing domestic peace he had the support of the Church, which encouraged him to campaign against feuding and violent crime. James had already demonstrated his virtues as a godly prince in the persecution of witchcraft* which began in 1591 and culminated in the publication of his book, *Daemenologie* (E, 1597). All of this enhanced royal authority, but the divine-right monarchy described by James in *The True Lawe of Free Monarchies* (E, 1598) remained unattainable, as he admitted in the less theoretical *Basilikon Doron* (E, 1599).

Following Elizabeth I's* death on 24 March 1603, James succeeded to the English and Irish crowns as James I. The administration and law courts remained in Edinburgh, but the King and his court moved to London, returning only briefly in 1617. This 'government by pen' from London proved to be highly effective. The borders were pacified, the Highlands brought under closer royal supervision, crown patronage increased enormously, domestic politics grew uneventful, and, fortuitously, the economy improved dramatically. James's only failure lay in the refusal of the English and Scottish Parliaments to assent to a more complete union of the two kingdoms.

James seized the initiative in the Church in 1596 when a Protestant riot in Edinburgh allowed him to isolate the most militant Presbyterian ministers. Thereafter he exploited his control over the timing and meeting-place of the General Assembly to push the Presbyterians on to the defensive. The final blow fell when he arrested and imprisoned those leading ministers, including Andrew Melville,* who had attended a meeting of the General Assembly in Aberdeen in July 1605 contrary to James's order. The King's preference for bishops – summed up in his phrase 'no bishops, no King' – was already apparent before 1603, but was given added impetus by his desire for religious uniformity within his three kingdoms. By the end of 1610 an Erastian, diocesan episcopacy had been achieved.

James's interference in worship aroused more deep-seated opposition. His foisting on the Church of the Five Articles of Perth* in 1618 was extremely unpopular, even with his own bishops, and after Parliament gave the Articles statutory authority in 1621 James had the sense not to insist on their enforcement. By this time the disadvantages of the regal union were surfacing elsewhere, particularly over high taxation. Nevertheless, at his death on 27 March 1625 Scotland lost a King who had created a level of peace and prosperity unseen for generations.

James VI possessed many personal qualities which made him an extremely able king. He was a skilled politician whose devious scheming matched that of any of his subjects, but whose accessibility and gregarious nature allowed him to cultivate relationships with the nobility. James's learning and intellectual interests often displayed themselves in pedantry and arrogance, but they provided him with an informed awareness of the finer points of theological debate in an age of religious controversy. They also allowed him to propagate his own views on kingship. His tolerance, moderation, willingness to compromise, and his disapproval of war and violence all contributed to the more peaceful conditions of the latter half of his reign. James also had his faults. His high view of royal authority was in part inspired by his own vanity and pride, he was extremely irresponsible with money, and he presided over a court in which sexual licence (including his own deviant behaviour), financial corruption, drunkenness and vicious factionalism were in sharp contrast to the claims made for him in the preface to the King James Bible.

C. H. McIlwaine (ed.), *The Political Works of James I* (C, 1918); G. Donaldson, *Scotland: James V–James VII* (E, 1965), 157–291; M. Lee, *Government by Pen* (Urbana, 1980); K. M. Brown, *Bloodfeud in Scotland, 1573–1625* (E, 1986); M. Lee, *John Maitland of Thirlstane* (Perth, 1959); D. G. Mullan, *Episcopacy in Scotland* (E, 1986); A. H. Williamson, *Scottish National Consciousness in the age of James VI* (E, 1979); B. Galloway, *The Union of England and Scotland 1603–1608* (E, 1986).

K. M. Brown

James VII (II) (1633–1701), King of Scotland 1685–9. He was the second son of Charles I.* In 1679, while still Duke of York, he was sent to Scotland by his brother, Charles II.* This was done both to remove James from England, where his presence was an embarrassment during the Exclusion Crisis (an attempt to exclude him from the succession to the throne as he was a Roman Catholic), and so that he could act as the King's representative there in the aftermath of the 1679 rebellion (see Bothwell Bridge*), replacing the discredited Duke of Lauderdale (see Maitland, John, d. 1682). In spite of his RCism, James's arrival was widely welcomed, and his conciliatory policies towards Presbyterian dissenters led to a relaxation of repression. But the refusal of the more extreme dissenters to submit and James's determination to assert his right to the throne led by 1681 to harsher policies (see Killing Times*) and to a major controversy over the Test Act.* He returned to England in 1682. The majority of Scots were loyal to James when he became King in 1685, and in 1687 he introduced a new policy of offering toleration* to the worship of moderate Presbyterians. But similar toleration was also introduced for RC worship. This official favour to RCs, and James's increasingly arbitrary government in civil affairs, led to growing discontent. Therefore in 1688 many Scots were prepared to support the revolution which overthrew James (see William II*).

Conscientious and hard-working as King and sincere in his religious beliefs, James helped to bring about his own downfall through being a poor judge of men and inflexibly determined to have his own way. He was convinced that making concessions in the face of opposition would be fatal, but when events turned against him in 1688 his nerve failed and he fled to France. He maintained his claim to be rightful king until his death, but lapsed into melancholic piety, interpreting his misfortunes as punishments for his sins rather than as the effects of political ineptitude.

J. Miller, *James II* (Hove, 1978); I. B. Cowan, *The Scottish Covenanters, 1660–88* (L, 1976), 120–33; *DNB* XXIX, 181–99; F. C. Turner, *James II* (L, 1948).

D. Stevenson

Jameson, William (*fl.* 1689–1720), Presbyterian* historian and controversialist. His early life is surrounded in obscurity. Born blind, he was educated at Glasgow University, where he achieved great scholarly distinction, especially in secular and ecclesiastical history. The university senate appointed him to teach these subjects in 1692; after 1705 his salary was paid from central government funds. He was a staunch Presbyterian and wrote a number of anti-Episcopalian works, maintaining that the apostolic and primitive office of bishop was what Presbyterians rather than Episcopalians conceived it to be (particularly, *Nazianzeni Querela et Votum Justum* (G, 1697); *Cyprianus Isotimus* (E, 1705); *The Summ of the Episcopal Controversy*, E, 1712)). He also wrote against Quakers (*Verus Patroclus; or the Weapons of Quakerism the Weakness of Quakerism*, E, 1689), and against RCs and Socinians (*Roma Racoviana et Racovia Romana*, E, 1702). He attempted a harmony of sacred and secular history in his *Spicilegia Antiquitatum Aegypti* (G, 1720).

Mr. John Davidson's Catechism (E, 1708).

DNB XXIX, 235–6.

N. R. Needham

Jamieson, John (1759–1838), minister of the Associate congregation at Forfar (1780–97) and of Adam Gib's* divided Antiburgher congregation at Nicolson Street, Edinburgh (1797–1829). He was highly regarded as a theologian for his *Vindication of the Doctrine of Scripture . . . concerning the Deity of Christ* (E, 1794), which controverted Joseph Priestley, and his *Use of Sacred History* (2 vols, E, 1802). He was also a linguist of note and gained even more academic distinction for his *Etymological Dictionary of the Scottish Language* (2 vols, E, 1808), and for other linguistic works among the more than twenty publications to his credit. The College of New Jersey (Princeton) gave him its DD, and he was an honoured member of several learned societies.

Sermons on the heart (2 vols, E, 1789–90); *Socinianism unmasked . . . occasioned by Dr M'Gill's Practical Essay . . .* (E, 1790); *The Sorrows of Slavery, A Poem . . . [respecting] the African slave trade* (L, 1789); *Remarks on The Rev. Rowland Hill's Journal . . .* (E, 1799); *The Duty . . . of Brotherly Unity* (E, 1819).

DNB XXIX, 237–8; memoir in revd edit. (J. Longmuir and D. Donaldson, eds) of his *Etymological Dictionary*, 5 vols (Paisley, 1879–87), vol. 1; J. M'Kerrow, *History of the Secession Church* (G, 1841); Small I, 81–2, 429–30.

J. R. McIntosh

Jansenism, controversial movement in RCism. It used to be considered a heresy, a kind of RC Calvinism originating in the *Augustinus* (1640) of Cornelius Jansen, Bishop of Ypres. In reality, Jansenism was neither heretical nor monolithic, and underwent considerable change over time. Supporters of Jansen's theology of grace were to be found mainly at the University of Louvain. In France, the Jansenist 'party' was initially identified with the *dévots*, who, headed by Saint-Cyran, spiritual director of the abbey of Port-Royal, near Paris, opposed the foreign policy of Richelieu. Saint-Cyran advocated a moral rigorism which was meant to contrast with alleged Jesuit* 'laxity'. Jansenism as a movement was largely the creation of anti-Jansenists. Louis XIV regarded Port-Royal as a centre of subversion and ordered its destruction in 1710. In 1713 the Jansenist controversy shifted onto a new plane with the publication of Pope Clement XI's bull *Unigenitus*, which condemned 101 'Jansenist' propositions allegedly to be found in the 'Moral Reflections' (*Le Nouveau Testament . . . avec des réflexions morales . . .*, 2 vols, Paris, 1692; ET, L, 1719) of Pasquier Quesnel. The question of papal authority was now at stake along with the issue of truth and the matter of individual conscience.

The *Unigenitus* quarrels persisted in France through most of the eighteenth century, but they also came to Scotland in the 1730s and 1740s when a number of priests, including Thomas Innes,* mainly associated with the Scots College* in Paris, were denounced to Rome as opponents of the bull and therefore as heretics. The anti-Jansenist camp was headed by Colin Campbell, who along with John Tyrie left Scotland for Rome in 1735 to lay charges before the congregation of *propaganda fide*.* Propaganda ordered Monsignor Lercari, acting nuncio in Paris, to investigate. His report of 4th March 1737 seemed to vindicate the two 'Pilgrims' and to implicate the superiors of the Scots College. Recent research, however, has shown that the Lercari report cannot be accepted at face value (as older historians of Scottish RCism such as Bellesheim thought). The whole affair was fuelled by the frustrated episcopal ambitions of Colin Campbell, though it also involved long-standing rivalries between the secular and the regular clergy (the Jesuits in particular but also the Scottish Benedictines*). Above all, however, Campbell successfully represented himself as the spokesman for discontented secular clergymen in the Highlands, who thought that they were hardly done by in the distriction of the Mission's (meagre) funds. Money and a conflict of cultures, rather than doctrine, lay at the heart of the Scottish Jansenist quarrels.

J. F. McMillan, 'Scottish Catholics and the Jansenist Controversy: the Case Reopened', *IR* 32 (1981), 22–33; id., 'Jansenists and Anti-Jansenists in Eighteenth Century Scotland: the *Unigenitus* Quarrels on the Scottish Catholic Mission 1732–1746', *IR* 39 (1988), 12–45.

J. F. McMillan

Japan, *see* Missions; Faulds, Henry.

Jarvis, Ernest David (1888–1964), UF and CofS minister. Born in Forfar, he was educated at Forfar Academy, St Andrews University and New College Edinburgh, where he acted as sub-warden of the Settlement for a year before being caught up for four years in active military service in India, Mesopotamia and the Caucasus, achieving mention in despatches. In 1916 he was licensed by the Presbytery of Rajputana. On his return to civilian life he acted as assistant at Edinburgh New North for a year before being ordained at Penicuik North, south of Edinburgh. In 1924 he moved to Muswell Hill, London, returning in 1929 to succeed George Morrison* in Wellington, one of Glasgow's best known pulpits, a charge he was to fill with great distinction until his retirement in 1958. He was twice honoured with DDs (St Andrews 1943, Glasgow 1952) and was Moderator of the CofS General Assembly in 1954. His ministry combined elements of liberalism and Evangelicalism in a pattern fashionable in the Kirk in the inter-War decades.

More Than Conquerors (L, 1935); *If Any Man Minister* (Warrack Lectures,* L, 1950).

FUFCS 258; *FES* IX, 213, X, 183; *Who Was Who, 1961–1970*, 593; *An Account of the Retiral of . . . Ernest David Jarvis* (G, 1958).

A. Herron

Jedburgh, Augustinian* abbey. Augustinian canons were brought by David I* *c.*1138 from Beauvais (Northern France) to Jedworth, later called Jedburgh; an earlier foundation had existed nearby (*see* Early Ecclesiastical Sites). Having attained abbatial status *c.*1154, Jedburgh founded three dependent priories: Restennet (near Forfar), site of an earlier foundation, and Canonbie (Dumfriesshire) in the twelfth century, and Blantyre (Lanarkshire) *c.*1240. The abbey also administered local hospitals.* Jedburgh castle was used as a royal residence, thereby increasing the abbey's prestige. Being located near the Border, the monastery was abandoned at times during the English wars.

Further damage was done in the fifteenth century and, despite restoration, the buildings were ruinous in 1502. They were again burned by English forces in 1523, 1544 and 1545. From 1512 the abbots belonged to the powerful local family of Hume. Very little is known of the community at this time; probably not more than ten canons were resident. The surviving church building, although now a ruin, is most impressive. A structure within the abbey church was used for Protestant worship until 1875.

J. Watson, *Jedburgh Abbey* (E, 1894); *An Inventory of the Ancient and Historical Monuments of Roxburghshire* (E, 1956), 194–209; S. Cruden, *Scottish Medieval Churches* (E, 1986), 102–13; M. Dilworth, 'The Border Abbeys in the Sixteenth Century', *RSCHS* 21 (1983), 233–47; Easson-Cowan, 88–96.

M. Dilworth

Jeffrey, George Johnston (1881–1961), UF and CofS minister. Born at Alloa and educated locally and at Glasgow University and UF College, he was licensed by the Presbytery of Stirling in 1907 and served assistantships in Glasgow, Dowanhill, and Camphill, before being ordained to John Knox, Stewarton (Ayrshire) in 1908. In 1915 he was translated to Kirkcudbright St Mary's, devoting 1917 to work with CofS Huts and Canteens.* In 1922 he moved to Kilmarnock High, from there in 1928 to Helensburgh Park, and in 1937 to Sherbrooke in Glasgow (later Sherbrooke St Gilbert's), where he continued until his retiral in 1951. In 1945 he received a DD from Glasgow University, and in 1952 was elected Moderator of the CofS General Assembly. He represented the dominant liberal Evangelicalism – or evangelical liberalism – of the CofS during the era of the two World Wars.

Christian Intimacies (L, 1940); *Christian Resources* (L, 1943); *This Grace Wherein We Stand* (Warrack Lectures,* L, 1948).

FUFCS, 272–3; *FES* IX, 305, X, 180; *Who Was Who, 1961–1970*, 595.

A. Herron

Jehovah's Witnesses. Jehovah's Witnesses regard themselves as the latest in a long line of witnesses starting with Abel (Heb.11:4; 12:1) and including Christ Jesus (Rev. 3:14) and his apostles (Acts 1:8). All witness to the name and purpose of God, Jehovah. In Scotland, the modern organization started about 1890, with *Watchtower* readers in Glasgow and later in Edinburgh meeting together for worship. They became well known for their house-to-house visits. Numbers in Scotland, where they are now organized in over a hundred congregations, grew from 4,900 in 1978 to 7,400 by 1988. Meetings are held in 'Kingdom Halls' situated throughout Scotland, where 9,300 people regularly attend.

Witnesses believe that God's name, Jehovah, should be used and sanctified. They acknowledge Jesus as the Son of God and as their saviour, though they deny the Trinity. They believe that God's kingdom will soon restore the original paradise conditions to the earth.

Any Witness practising fornication, homosexuality, or drunkenness can be disfellowshipped from the congregation unless manifesting godly repentance and discontinuing such practices. Witnesses also reject abortion, and abstain from blood transfusions, smoking and drug abuse.

The Watchtower, magazine published by Watch Tower Bible and Tract Society of Pennsylvania, Brooklyn, New York.

I. Greenlees

Jerment, George (1759–1819), Antiburgher minister. Born at Peebles and educated at Edinburgh University and under William Moncrieff,* he was appointed by the Antiburgher General Associate* Synod as assistant minister of the dissenting congregation at Bow Lane, London in 1782, and soon became minister of the same charge (later removed to Oxenden Street) (1784–1816). He edited Archbishop Leighton's* *Works*, and published several of his own, mainly of a devotional nature. He was a strong supporter of the London Missionary Society* from its earliest days. In 1817 he was awarded a DD by an American institution.

J. M'Kerrow, *History of the Secession Church* (G, 1841), 874–6; *ASUPC* 494–5.

J. R. McIntosh

Jesuits, members of the Society of Jesus, a religious order founded by St Ignatius of Loyola (1491–1556) and approved by Pope Paul III in 1540. Their spirituality is based on the *Spiritual Exercises* of St Ignatius, a handbook for spiritual directors in the form of outlined meditations and instructions reflecting the experience of the author. The Society began as a movement of spiritual renewal within the Church; it soon became a powerful element in the so-called 'Counter-Reformation'.* Its distinctive characteristic is the vow of obedience to the Pope *circa missiones*, i.e. in particular assignments chosen by the Pope. It has always been a strongly missionary order. It has an enduring interest in education, scholarship and science.

The first Jesuit contact with Scotland was in 1542, when Fathers Broet and Salmeron, sent on a papal mission to Ireland, were received by James V at Stirling Castle. A papal mission to Scotland in 1562 was led by Father Nicholas de Gouda, a Dutch Jesuit. He was accompanied by Edmund Hay,* who later became a Jesuit and the first Superior of the Scottish Mission (1585–9): he died in Rome in 1591 as Assistant to the Jesuit General. Irish Jesuits worked in the Hebrides 1611–19 (*see* Irish Missions to Highlands).

The Scottish Jesuit Mission remained under a Superior until the suppression of the Society in 1773 (whereas the English Jesuit Mission became a Vice-Province in 1619 and a Province in 1623). Over 250 members of the Scottish Mission are known by name, and more than sixty are known to have died in Scotland. The most famous is John Ogilvie.*

In the Scottish Catholic Archives in Edinburgh there survives a large collection of letters from Scottish Jesuits: of individuals to their Superior, and to and from the Jesuit rectors of the Scots Colleges* in Rome, Douai and Madrid. They provide a primary source for events not only of religious but also of general contemporary interest.

Against the background of continuous persecution of Catholics in Scotland, one short-lived experiment in religious toleration deserves mention. In 1687 a Jesuit college was established in Edinburgh under the patronage of James VII and II. The 'Rules of the Schools of the Royal College at Holy-Rood-House' (*see* Holyrood) are preserved in the National Library of Scotland. This was recognizably a Catholic college, but with freedom of conscience for all students: '... although Youths of different Professions, whether Catholics or Protestants, come to these Schools, ... there shall not be, either by Masters or Scholars, any tampering or meddling to perswade any one from the Profession of his own Religion ...'. The Revolution of 1688 brought this interlude to an abrupt end.

The Brief of Suppression of the Society in 1773, signed by Pope Clement XIV under pressure, spelt the ruin of a vast network of missionary enterprise throughout the world. In Scotland, however, it had little effect on the Jesuits in Edinburgh, Aberdeen, Galloway (Kirkconnel, Terregles, Munches), Braemar, Glengairn, Glentanar, Buchan and Strathglass. The Scots Colleges with Jesuit rectors were taken over by secular priests.

The Society was restored throughout the world in 1814. The first Scottish foundations of the restored English Province were laid in 1859 when Jesuits were assigned a parish in Glasgow, opened a school there, and began the new parish of the Sacred Heart in Edinburgh (*see* Religious Orders).

The Jesuit presence in Scotland is now mainly in Glasgow (St Aloysius' College and parish), Edinburgh (Sacred Heart parish) and Bothwell, Lanarkshire (Craighead Retreat House), with individual Jesuits working in parishes in different parts of the country. Scottish Jesuits also maintain the worldwide tradition of the Society in Rome, Guyana, Zimbabwe, South Africa, as well as in England and Wales. England, Wales and Scotland form one

Province, known since 1985 as the British Province.

J. Brodrick, *The Origin of the Jesuits* (L, 1940); *id., The Progress of the Jesuits* (L, 1946); H. Foley, *Records of the English Province of the Society of Jesus* (L, 1877–83), especially Vol. VII, Parts I and II (1882–3) = *Collectanea*; W. Forbes-Leith, *Narratives of Scottish Catholics under Mary Stuart and James VI* (E, 1885); *id., Memoirs of Scottish Catholics during the XVIIth and XVIIIth Centuries*, 2 vols (L, 1909); M. V. Hay, *The Blairs Papers (1603–1660)* (L, E, 1929).

J. Quinn

Jews. Although there had been a Jewish community in England between 1066 and the expulsion in 1290, the story of Jews in Scotland does not begin until more recent times. A few Jews may have traded in Scotland before and just after the expulsion from England, but firm evidence for Jews in Scotland appears in Edinburgh only during the seventeenth century with the arrival of some Jewish converts to Christianity. The first, Julius Otto, born Naphtali Margolioth in Vienna, occupied the Chair of Hebrew and Oriental Languages at the University from 1641 (*FES* VII, 386). While some of these early Jews were ministers or academics, Jewish traders soon appeared also, and in 1691, after some debate at the Edinburgh Town Council, David Brown, a professing Jew, was given permission to carry on business.

We have few records of Jews in Scotland in the eighteenth century apart from the Jewish medical students attending Edinburgh University from the 1760s. Their presence confirms that Jews were taking advantage of the religious freedoms to study and graduate at the Scottish universities at a time when religious tests were still being applied at the universities in England.

EXPANSION. Jewish traders and residents became more numerous in Edinburgh and Glasgow from the end of the eighteenth century. The first Jewish cemetery in Scotland dates from 1795 with the purchase of ground on Calton Hill in Edinburgh by the Jewish dentist Herman Lion. Jewish communities were formally established in Edinburgh in 1816 and in Glasgow in 1823, though their numbers remained small. In 1847 there were only 107 Jews in Edinburgh and 128 in Glasgow, mainly of Central European origin, and growth continued slowly during the following decades.

In Glasgow the Jewish community began to expand in the 1870s with the arrival of some Jewish tailors, recruited by a Scottish firm to introduce new methods of production. Settling mainly in the Gorbals they laid the nucleus of its large and flourishing Yiddish-speaking community. With the growth in the number of Jews in Glasgow, a beautiful synagogue, situated at Garnethill and serving the West End of Glasgow, was opened in 1879 with E. P. Phillips as minister.

With developments in textiles, and the links between Scotland and the large commercial firms in Hamburg, some Jewish traders set up in Dundee from the middle of the nineteenth century and contributed to the commercial, economic and civil life of the town. In Aberdeen the newly established community in 1893 was able to defend successfully its practice of *shechita* (the Jewish method of slaughtering permitted animals or birds for food) against an attack by the Society for the Protection of Animals.

The unsettled conditions of Jewish life in Russia at the end of the nineteenth century, where millions were confined to a wretched existence in the 'Pale of Settlement', led to a wave of massive emigration westwards from the beginning of the 1880s. As Jews began to pass through Scotland on their way to North America, especially during the 1890s, many decided to settle in Scotland, whether temporarily or more permanently. By 1900 there were 8,000 Jews in Glasgow, about 1,500 in Edinburgh, and smaller communities grew up, not just in Aberdeen and Dundee, but also in towns like Falkirk, Dunfermline, Ayr, Inverness and Greenock.

ORGANIZATIONS. In Glasgow and Edinburgh the influx of Jews led to the formation of many new organizations. The Jewish welfare bodies were strengthened with many new agencies, including self-help groups and free-loan and friendly societies, formed to look after the poor, sick and needy. New Hebrew schools, *Talmud Torahs*, were formed, and synagogues were established both in the Glasgow Gorbals and hard by the Royal Mile in Edinburgh. The Jewish immigrants sought to pass on to their children something of the intense Jewish nature of the life they had left behind in Eastern Europe, while ensuring that they took full advantage of the Scottish educational system.

In Glasgow English evening classes for the immigrants were set up at the city's expense. Funds for Russian Jews were raised by the civic authorities in Dundee, and in Edinburgh practical support for weak and penniless trans-migrants passing through Scotland was organized by readers of *The Scotsman*.

With the Churches relations were cordial. The leadership of the CofS and the RC hierarchy supported Jewish attempts at self-sufficiency and helped in the political fight against anti-semitism, whether at home or abroad. The CofS also supported the Jewish claim to trade on Sunday, instead of Saturday, the Jewish Sabbath, seeing in the opponents to Jewish Society trading elements of anti-semitism.

Another side of Christian–Jewish relations focused on missionary activity toward the Jews through mission halls and welfare schemes. This could lead to problems in relations between the two communities, and was much resented by the Jews. The Jewish community came out of the encounter stronger, as the missionary challenge led to the creation of an extensive Jewish welfare network.

With the outbreak of World War I in 1914 Scottish Jews rallied to support the national cause. Many enlisted in the army and alien Jews became naturalized and helped the war effort in a variety of ways. Jewish organisational bodies, like the Jewish Representative Councils formed in Glasgow (1914) and Edinburgh (1915), looked after the rights of aliens during war-time conditions, and after the war defended the interests of the Jewish community in all its aspects.

AFTER THE WAR. In the inter-war years many new Jewish concerns emerged. Zionism, whose origins in Scotland dated back to 1890, became the leading Jewish political movement in Scotland, eclipsing socialism and other ideologies in the community. The 1930s saw the rise of Fascism and Nazism in Europe, and the Jewish community worked for the boycott of German goods and to try to resettle and absorb refugees. Scottish Jewry, never numbering more than 20,000 souls, was host to about 2,000 newcomers. During these years the Edinburgh community was led by Rabbi Salis Daiches, who sought a synthesis between Judaism and Scottish thought and was widely regarded as the 'Chief Rabbi of Scotland'. With the establishment of the State of Israel in 1949 Jewish efforts to raise funds and provide political support for the fledgling democracy were redoubled.

A group to promote Jewish-Christian understanding was launched in 1941 by David MacMahon (*FES* IX, 245, 762, X, 142) for the CofS and I. K. Cosgrove of the Garnethill Synagogue. Their activities over many years led to the eventual formation of the West Scotland Branch of the Council of Christians and Jews, which also involved the RC and other Churches, complementing the branch which has been running in Edinburgh for many years.

Today the Jews in Scotland have seen their numbers decline as members of the community have sought new oportunities in England or abroad. A substantial number have settled in Israel, enriching the life of that country and forging close bonds between Scottish Jewry and the Jewish State. Despite this, both Glasgow with about 11,000 Jews in 1990 and Edinburgh with about 1,000 have active and well-organized Jewish community structures which care for the social, cultural, welfare and educational needs of its members. Synagogue affiliation, with seven synagogues in Glasgow and one each in Edinburgh, Dundee and Aberdeen, remains mainly Orthodox in character, although there is a wide variety in the level of attachment to traditional Jewish practice. Members of the community participate actively in politics, law, medicine, education and the arts, and in a wide variety of other trades and crafts. While antisemitism has never been a major problem in Scotland, the Jewish community remains vigilant, keen to defend its interests and to play its full part in all aspects of modern Scotland.

A. Levy, 'The Origins of Scottish Jewry', *Trans. of Jewish Hist. Soc. of England* 19 (1960), 129–62; S. Daiches, 'The Jew in Scotland', *RSCHS* 3 (1929), 196–209; K. Collins, ed., *Aspects of Scottish Jewry* (G, 1987); *id.*, *Second City Jewry: the Jews of Glasgow in the Age of Expansion 1790–1919* (G, 1990).

K. E. Collins

Jews, Missions to, *see* Bonar, Andrew; Duncan, John; Edersheim, Alfred; Keith, Alexander; McCheyne, Murray; Millennialism; Missions; Saphir, Adolph.

Johnsone, John (*fl.c.*1530), Protestant writer. He is known only from *An Confortable Exhortation; of Oure Mooste Holy Christen Faith* (*c.*1533), of which imperfect copies survive in the British Library and Trinity College, Dublin. It was probably printed at Antwerp not long after Patrick Hamilton's* martyrdom, of which it gives an eye-witness account. The author was presumably a student at St Andrews. He clearly imbibed much of Luther's teaching on faith and works and his 'theology of the cross', and uses Tyndale's New Testament in English.

J. K. Cameron, 'John Johnsone's *An confortable exhortation* . . .', in D. Baker (ed.), *Reform and Reformation: England and the Continent c.1500–c.1750* (O, 1979), 133–47.

D. F. Wright

Johnston, (Sir) Archibald (Lord Wariston) (1611–63), Covenanter* politician. The son of an Edinburgh merchant, Wariston graduated at Glasgow University, studied for a time in France, and became an advocate in Edinburgh in 1633. He had considered becoming a minister, but realized that his temperament was unsuitable: he wrote that he could not endure the burden of more souls than his own, and his diary in the 1630s reveals the intense religious obsessions of a manic-depressive, swinging from the depths of despair to the heights of exaltation. From the start of the revolt against Charles I* in 1637 he was at its centre, frequently acting as secretary to the rebel leaders and drafting their declarations. He and Alexander Henderson* were joint authors of the National Covenant,* and he frequently took part in negotiations with the King and the English Parliament in the years that followed. In 1638 he was appointed clerk to the General Assembly and procurator of the Church, and in 1641 he was knighted and appointed a Lord of Session. In 1643 he became one of Scotland's representatives at the Westminster Assembly,* and in 1646 King's Advocate. He had from the start been identified with the most radical of the Covenanters,* and in 1648 he helped inspire opposition to the Engagement.* A leading figure in the Kirk Party regime of 1648–50, becoming Clerk Register in 1649, he was in the fore in demanding thorough purging and punishing of the ungodly in both Church and state. During the Cromwellian invasion of 1650–1 (*see* Commonwealth and Protectorate) he supported the Western Remonstrance* and the Protesters* in virtually disowning the cause of Charles II.* He refused to serve the regime of Oliver Cromwell at first, partly through opposition of the religious toleration* it imposed. Eventually he was tempted into accepting office as Clerk Register and a judge in 1657, through fear that Cromwell would turn to favouring the Resolutioners* if he was too unco-operative, and through financial anxiety for the future of his large family. Throughout his career Wariston displayed a feck-

JOHNSTON, CHRISTOPHER NICOLSON

lessness in financial matters based on the belief that as he was devoting himself to serving God's cause, God would provide for him, an attitude that led to repeated problems. After the Restoration* he was denounced as a traitor for having served Cromwell, and fled into hiding abroad. He was discovered in France, brought back to Edinburgh and executed, though he was both physically ill and mentally distressed. In many ways Wariston is one of the least attractive characters of his age, always in favour of extreme policies and harsh measures, and after the fall of the Covenanters, isolated, being generally hated and despised. Yet through his remarkable diaries one can gain much understanding of this troubled man.

G. M. Paul, *Diary of Sir Archibald Johnston of Wariston, 1632-9* (E, 1911); G. M. Paul (ed.), *Diary ... 1639...* (E, 1896); D. H. Fleming (ed.), *Diary ... 1650-4* (E, 1919); J. D. Ogilvie (ed.), *Diary ... 1655-60* (E, 1940).

W. Morison, *Johnston of Wariston* (E, 1901); *DNB* XXX, 56-8.

D. Stevenson

Johnston, Christopher Nicolson, *see* Sands, Lord.

Johnston, John (c.1565-1611), Latin poet and associate of Andrew Melville.* From childhood in Aberdeen, his career closely paralleled Robert Howie's.* Both graduated from King's College (1584), and then Johnston studied at Rostock (1584-5), Helmstedt (1585-7) and Heidelberg (1587-90), and visited Geneva and other Reformed centres in Switzerland (1590-1). After his return to Britain, through Melville's influence he was made Second Master (Professor) of Divinity in St Mary's College, St Andrews (1593). There, as well as corresponding with the numerous leading scholars (e.g. Justus Lipsius) and theologians (e.g. Beza) he had met on his travels, he participated in wider Church affairs, especially with Melville in resisting James VI's* encroachment upon Church prerogatives, e.g. in debarring professors from Church courts. Johnston fulfilled other ecclesiastical and educational commissions. With Melville's support he urged French Calvinists to compose their differences over the views on justification held by Piscator, one of his closest continental friends. Johnston's letters have only recently been collected and edited. All his writings were in Latin, concerned partly with Scottish kings, 'heroes' and martyrs, and partly with biblical kings. *Consolatio Christiana sub Cruce* (Leiden, 1609) reflected his experience of bereavement. In philosophy he strongly favoured Ramus over Aristotle.

FES VIII, 428; *DNB* XXX, 66-7; J. K. Cameron (ed.), *Letters of John Johnston c.1565-1611 and Robert Howie c.1565-c.1645* (E, 1963) – with introduction; T. M'Crie, *Life of Andrew Melville* (E, 1856).

D. F. Wright

JOHNSTONE, FRANCIS

Johnston, Robert (1807-53), missionary. He was born at Moffat, son of a farmer of modest means. He began at Edinburgh University in 1827, gaining distinction in Greek and mathematics, and worked as a tutor and schoolteacher before beginning divinity in 1831. He formed a student friendship with John Anderson* with whom he was associated for the rest of his life. After a time as a home missionary in Wallacetown, Ayrshire, he was licensed by Edinburgh Presbytery and sent to join Anderson in Madras, arriving early 1839. Together they built the CofS Madras mission, with its central institution and network of branch schools, and took them into the FC at the Disruption.* When he arrived on his first home leave in 1851 Johnston was in the grip of the tuberculosis which killed him. He addressed divinity students about missions, but was too weak to speak more than a few sentences at the General Assembly. Among his last activities were to publish an address on *The Conversion of the Jews* (E, 1853), and to dispose of property to the Madras mission. The first Indian ministers, whom he had helped bring to faith, endowed scholarships in his memory. Though somewhat overshadowed by his friend, Johnston's work is one of the early pillars of Scottish India missions.

See also Missions: South India.

FES VII, 696-7; *AFCS* I, 194; J. Braidwood, *True Yoke-Fellows in the Mission Field: ... Rev. John Anderson and Rev. Robert Johnston* (L, 1862).

A. F. Walls

Johnstone, Francis (1810-80), Baptist* minister. He was born into a Baptist family in Edinburgh, his parents being associated first with Christopher Anderson's* congregation, then with James Haldane's* Tabernacle. He was educated at the High School and the University, proceeding to Bradford College to study for the ministry. After short ministries in Yorkshire and Carlisle he returned to Scotland in 1842 to become minister of the Baptist Church in Cupar, Fife. In 1845 he formed a new church, later Marshall Street, in Edinburgh, where with a short interruption (1856-60), he remained until the end of his life.

He returned to Scotland at the time of the Disruption* and also the formation of the Evangelical Union.* Johnstone was in doctrinal agreement with James Morison,* and espoused a more liberal Calvinism* than did the older Baptist leaders. He eagerly took the leadership of a new association of Baptists, which became the Baptist Union in 1842. This small body sent out evangelists and church planters, published the *Evangelist* and the *Myrtle*, and sought to gather statistics and plan a Baptist advance. Johnstone incurred the wrath of the FC* in 1845 for distributing a Baptist tract and was also dropped from the Committee of the Baptist Home Missionary Society,* presumably for deviations from Calvinism. By the time of his death he had seen a more permanent Union established and his liberal views largely accepted.

The Work of God and the Work of Man in Conversion (E, 1848); *The Gospel Roll* (L, 1863).

JOLLY, ALEXANDER

A. Wylie, *Jubilee Handbook, Marshall Street Baptist Church* (E, 1896); D. W. Bebbington (ed.), *The Baptists in Scotland* (G, 1988).

D. B. Murray

Jolly, Alexander (1756–1838), in 1796 consecrated Episcopal bishop coadjutor for Moray and Ross, but continuing as priest at Fraserburgh. A man of deep spirituality and erudition, he 'did not know barley from oats'. Preaching the same sermons over and over, he celebrated the eucharist five times yearly but communicated himself weekly from the reserved sacrament. At a time when southern Episcopalians opposed Calvinism* with Latitudinarianism,* and northern ones with Hutchinsonianism,* Jolly was neither, but trained ordinands with English divinity largely of the non-jurors.* At the Synod of Laurencekirk in 1804 he convinced the clergy that they could accept the Thirty-nine Articles of the Church of England without any Calvinist interpretations. He is remembered for his work on the eucharist, *The Christian Sacrifice* (A, 1831).

W. Walker, *The Life of the Right Reverend Alexander Jolly, D.D., Bishop of Moray* (E, 1878).

G. White

Judicial Commission, a body exercising the judicial functions of the supreme court of some Presbyterian churches in certain cases and subject to certain restrictions. The large membership of the supreme court (in the case of the CofS the General Assembly*) makes it not a suitable or convenient body to hear evidence and determine fact, as a number of cases illustrate.

Within the CofS, following six years of discussion and consideration of models afforded by the Presbyterian Churches of England, Ireland, Australia, Canada and the United States, a Judicial Commission was first established by the Act VII, 1940, and its remit was extended by the Act XXII, 1960. Now under Act II, 1987, the Commission determines appeals in cases of Trial by Libel involving character or conduct (but not doctrine) of ministers and probationers, and in cases under the Act anent Congregations in an Unsatisfactory State. Only against the Commission's sentence may an appeal be made to the Assembly, which can no longer reopen and effectively re-try the case.

Under the 1987 Act and Assembly Standing Orders the forty-eight members (ministers and elders) of the Judicial Commission are appointed for four-year terms. The quorum is sixteen, but no case may begin unless twenty-four members are present. Only members present during the whole proceeding may vote on a case. Normal rules of natural justice apply. Parties may employ lawyers, and procedures largely mirror those of ordinary courts. The Judicial Commission has power to require witnesses to attend, and documents and other materials to be produced, and to examine on oath.

F. Lyall

Jus Devolutum, a term applied to the case where the right of a congregation to elect a new minister has passed to the local presbytery* by reason of the congregation's failure to act timeously, and no petition for an extension of time has been granted by the presbytery. By the present law of the CofS an appointment to a vacant charge must be made within six months of the congregation being given permission to elect a new minister. Thereafter, and unless the presbytery extends the time on the petition of the congregation, the right to appoint a minister to the charge* devolves upon the presbytery itself in accordance with its duty to see that the ordinances of religion are provided within the parishes for which it has responsibility. Procedure is regulated by Act of Assembly.

F. Lyall

JUSTIFICATION

Justification. The first theological standard of the Reformed CofS, the Scots Confession,* contained no separate chapter on justification. Yet the commitment to Luther's* doctrine is clear, even though it occurs under the heading 'The Perfection of the Law and the Imperfection of Man': 'For God the Father beholding us in the body of his Son Christ Jesus accepteth our imperfect obedience as it were perfect, and covereth our works, which are defiled with many spots, with the justice of his Son' (Chapter XV). Moreover in 1548 John Knox* produced a summary of Henry Balnaves'* work on justification (*Works* III, 3–28).

In the ensuing three centuries the subject received repeated attention from Scottish theologians, the outstanding contributions being those of James Durham* (*A Commentarie upon the Book of Revelation*, E, 1658, Discourse XI), John Brown* of Wamphray (*The Life of Justification Opened*, n.p., 1695), Robert Traill* (*A Vindication of the Protestant Doctrine Concerning Justification*, L, 1692), Thomas Halyburton*, in *Natural Religion Insufficient*, E, 1714, rp. *Works*, L, 1835, 559–67), and James Buchanan* (*The Doctrine of Justification*, E, 1867). There is a magisterial summary in William Cunningham's* *Historical Theology* (E, 1863), II, 1–120.

The doctrine set forth by these divines is essentially that of the Westminster Confession* (Chapter XI), which replaced the Scots Confession in 1646. The contours of both the Confession's statement and subsequent discussion were determined by the controversies of the period, particularly (although by no means exclusively) the debate with Roman Catholicism.

The most fundamental issue was the meaning of the word 'justification'. The medieval Church, misled by the Latin Vulgate's *justificare*, understood 'justify' as 'make righteous'. Over against this, the Reformers, followed by the Scottish theologians, argued that justification was forensic, a change of status, not of nature. They based this on the use of *dikaioō* in the New Testament. 'Wherever it is used with reference to our acceptance with God, it can only be understood in a juridical and forensic sense' (Buchanan, 241). The most common way of stating this was in terms of the antithesis between justification and condemnation: 'Justification and condemnation are opposites; every one is under condemnation that is not justified, and every justified man is freed from condemnation' (Traill, *Works*, E, 1810, IV, 162).

CONTENT. There is a typical summary of the content of justification in Brown of Wamphray: 'That change of state before God, which such as are made partakers of as lay hold of Christ by faith, through the imputation of the righteousness of Christ, whereby they are brought into an estate of favour and reconciliation with God, who were before under his wrath and curse; and upon which they have all their iniquities, whereof they are guilty, actually pardoned; are accepted of as righteous, and pronounced such through the Surety-Righteousness of Christ imputed to them; and freed from the sentence and curse of the Law, under which they were lying' (262).

According to this, justification includes two elements:

(i) pardon. This extends to all sins. There literally is no condemnation. As Robert Haldane* put it, in language clearly borrowed from John Owen, justification is at once complete, in the actual pardon of all past sins and the virtual pardon of all future sins (*Exposition of the Epistle to the Romans*, L, 1835–9; edit. of L, 1958, 144).

(ii) acceptance. Justification is never a mere pardon, affecting only the sentence. It also affects the verdict. The condemnation itself is revoked and the sinner is accepted into 'an estate of favour and reconciliation with God'. So complete is God's acceptance of the justified sinner that he is not content even with declaring him righteous. He adopts him. Scottish theologians distinguished carefully between justification and adoption: 'The privilege of adoption presupposes pardon and acceptance, but it is higher than either' (Buchanan, 277). The sinner might have been pardoned and even vindicated without being adopted. But in the divine plan of salvation justification and adoption are inseparably linked; 'This closer and more endearing relation to God, which is constituted by adoption, is necessary, in addition to that which is included in our Justification, to complete the view of our Christian privileges, and to enhance our enjoyment of them, by raising us above "the spirit of bondage, which is unto fear," and cherishing "the spirit of adoption, whereby we cry, Abba, Father".'

GROUND. But what probably occupied Scottish theologians more than anything else was the question of the ground of justification. What does God look to when he justifies a sinner? Protestant theology answered this largely with a series of negatives. There was good reason for this. People instinctively approach God on the basis of merit and personal achievement. 'There is a corrupt bias in the heart of men by nature,' wrote Brown of Wamphray, 'and a strong inclination to reject the gospel-doctrine of free justification, through faith in Christ; and to ascribe too much to themselves in that affair' (9). Hence the need for constant reiteration of what acceptance does not depend on.

(i) Our acceptance does not depend on what we do. If it did our case would be hopeless, because the law says, 'Do!' and nobody can do. All the classical theologians of Scotland accepted implicitly the position laid down in the Shorter Catechism (Answer 82): 'No mere man since the Fall is able in this life perfectly to keep the commandments of God, but doth daily break them in thought, word and deed.' Nor did they have any patience with the notion of substituting sincere for perfect obedience: 'Sincere obedience is as impossible to a dead unrenewed sinner as perfect obedience', wrote Robert Traill (*Works* I, 267). It was this perception of the unattainableness of any meaningful obedience which prompted the famous cry of St Bernard, quoted with approval by James Buchanan, 'So far from being able to answer for my sins, I cannot answer even for my righteousness' (106).

(ii) Justification does not depend on what is done in us. What is in view here is the more subtle form of legalism which tempts the sinner to build his confidence on the graces within him – such things as conviction of sin, love of the brethren, prayer, witness and spiritual growth. This differs little from the old medieval idea that justification depends on sanctification. The Gaelic hymn-writer, John MacDonald (*d.* 1849)*, put the evangelical position perfectly:

> What a Saviour did and suffered
> In His people's room and stead,
> That's the ground of my salvation,
> Not any grace conferred.

(iii) Our justification does not depend on the quality of our faith. The Westminster Confession gives a peculiar prominence to this: God does not justify 'by imputing faith itself, the act of believing, or any other evangelical obedience, to them as their righteousness' (XI.I). The background to this was the teaching of Socinus, Arminius and John Goodwin, all of whom denied the imputation of Christ's righteousness and regarded faith itself as the ground of our acceptance. This point of view later came to be identified with Richard Baxter (hence 'Baxterianism'), whose position can be seen in, for example, *Imputative Righteousness Truly Stated* (L, 1679). Baxter's eclectic mentality made it difficult for him to dissociate himself decisively from any point of view and it is sometimes difficult to make out precisely where he stood. But he was certainly unhappy that both the Westminster Confession and the Savoy Declaration repudiated the notion of the imputation of faith. In his view, this was a flagrant contradiction of Romans 4:3: 'If Scripture so oft say that faith is reckoned or imputed for righteousness it becometh not Christians to say, It is not' (28). More important, although Baxter accepted that the righteousness of Christ was imputed to the believer, he did not regard it as the ground of justification. It merely secured a modification of the terms of the divine covenant, so that whereas in the past God required perfect obedience now he requires only evangelical obedience (faith and repentance): 'The Day of Judgement is not to try and judge Jesus Christ or his merits, but us: He will judge us himself by his new Law or Covenant, the sum of which is, Except ye repent, ye shall all perish: and, He that believeth shall be saved; and he that believeth not shall be condemned' (31).

Baxter's theology deeply troubled Scottish theologians. In Brown of Wamphray's 563 pages it is scarcely ever out of sight. It occupies most of Durham's discussion and figures prominently in Traill. It was central to the Marrow controversy* and is alluded to frequently in Thomas Boston's* Notes to *The Marrow of Modern Divinity* (1726).

All the Scottish treatments are profoundly critical. Baxterianism, they said, was nothing but the old Socinianism; it turned the covenant of grace into a new covenant of works; it proposed something in ourselves (a personal righteousness) as the ground of justification; it meant that we are justified by an imperfect righteousness; it overturned the imputation of Christ's righteousness; it confused what is required for salvation with what is required merely for justification; and it placed the sinner in a hopeless position: 'Thus this poor convinced sinner, pursued by justice for a broken law, is called to lean his whole weight of acceptance with God, and found all his hope of pardon and justification, upon his own faith, or gospel righteousness, as the only righteousness wherewith he is to be covered and the only righteousness which is to be imputed to him' (Brown, 332).

FAITH AS INSTRUMENT. This discussion forced Scottish theologians to think carefully about the relation of faith to justification. If it was not the ground of acceptance with God, what was it? Brown (342ff.) and Durham (262ff.) were prepared to speak of it as a 'condition'. But they insisted on defining the term carefully. It was not a condition in the same sense as obedience had been a condition of the covenant of works. Nor did it give a legal title to justification. Nor again did it have intrinsic merit, as some kind of gospel righteousness. It was a condition only in the sense of being an indepensable requirement; in the sense of there being a fixed connection between justification and faith; in the sense that only to faith were the promises made; and above all in the sense that faith alone united to Christ.

But there was always a decided preference for speaking of faith as an instrument and this became the standard term among later theologians: 'This faith, in the office of justification, is neither condition nor qualification, nor our gospel-righteousness, but in its very act a renouncing of all such pretences' (Traill, 277). But the idea of faith as instrument was also carefully defined. It was not the instrument by which people laid hold on assurance* or even the instrument by which they laid hold on justification. What it laid hold of was Christ (complete with his righteousness). Its peculiar fitness with respect to justification was that it was a uniting grace.

This concern to ground justification entirely and exclusively on the righteousness of Christ was the driving passion of Scottish theologians and they affirmed it with unwearying emphasis: 'The minister dealing with the convinced sinner is not to bid him look inward to see whether he be regenerated and truly repents', wrote Thomas Halyburton* (*Works*, 557): 'the sinner, like the poor jailor, without any such previous enquiry for qualifications in himself, should directly cling to Christ for righteousness, as one altogether lost in himself, and destitute of any qualification that can avail him'. Robert Traill stated the position with characteristic simplicity: 'A convinced sinner seeking justification must have nothing in his eye but this righteousness of Christ' (257).

Despite their wide divergence from Baxter, however, Scottish theologians shared his fear of antinomianism and were at pains to defend their own doctrine against the charge of encouraging it. They offered two arguments:

(i) from experience: 'experience showeth that such as have fled to Christ for righteousness have another way of communion with God in all holy conversation; and their walking in all the way of God hath a spiritual lustre and heavenly beauty (by contrast) with the walk of others, strangers in practice and in opinion to the gospel way of being justified through faith in Christ' (Brown, 252).

(ii) from theology: justification took place only in union with Christ and that union led to moral and spiritual transformation as surely as it secured forgiveness and acceptance. Thomas Boston stressed this in his Notes on *The Marrow of Modern Divinity*: 'Christ is the only fountain of holiness, and the cause of good works, in these who are united to him: so that, where union with Christ is, there is personal holiness infallibly' (233).

The essential position of Scottish theology was this: In the moment of faith-union all the Saviour's righteousness becomes ours; and in that same instant the Spirit and power of Christ erupt into our lives to begin a process of transformation which moves on relentlessly until at last we are completely Christ-like.

In recent years, T. F. Torrance* has expounded justification in terms of his own distinctive emphases on 'the incarnational union of the Holy Son with our unholy nature' and on Jesus Christ as 'not only the embodiment of God's justifying act but the embodiment of our human appropriation of it' ('Justification: its Radical Nature and Place in Reformed Doctrine and Life', *SJT* 13, 1960, 225–46, citing Knox, Robert Bruce* and James Fraser* of Brea). In such a presentation justification also becomes a criterion, *e.g.*, in epistemology and ministry, as in Lutheranism.

D. *Macleod*

K

Kalimpong, *see* Graham, J. A.

Kalley, Robert Reid (1808–88), pioneer missionary in Madeira (1838–46) and Brazil (1855–76). He was born of wealthy parents in Glasgow, where he studied medicine, graduating in 1838. Converted from agnosticism (1834), he consecrated his many talents and wealth to Christ. Plans to serve in China with the London Missionary Society* did not come to fruition; family health reasons took him to Madeira instead. There mass conversions resulted from his three-pronged evangelism: medicine, schools, preaching. Incensed, the RC hierarchy persecuted the doctor and his converts, eventually securing their expulsion. Some 2,000 believers left to settle in the West Indies and Illinois. Kalley visited these Madeiran exiles, and also worked in Europe and the Middle East. His first wife, Margaret Crawford, an invalid, had shared his Madeira experience. On her death (1851) in Beirut, he married Sarah Poulton Wilson (1825–1907), a talented linguist, musician and hymnwriter.

In Brazil the Kalleys (later helped by co-workers from the 'Madeiran diaspora') adopted a multi-thrust policy: they trained national colporteurs, evangelists and pastors; compiled a hymn-book (Portuguese); influentially elucidated the Brazilian constitution's provision for freedom of worship and non-RC marriages and burials, and planted indigenous churches, leading to the establishment in Rio de Janeiro in 1858 on Congregational principles of what is today regarded as the oldest Brazilian Protestant church – Igreja Evangélica Fluminense. Socially, the Kalleys were friends of Emperor Pedro II, yet lived with and for the poor. They retired to Edinburgh, where they befriended university students and supported evangelical causes. Kalley was a lifelong member of the CofS. His funeral service was led by a friend of long standing, Hudson Taylor.

W. B. Forsyth, *The Wolf from Scotland* (Darlington, 1988); M. P. Testa, *O Apóstolo da Madeira* (Lisbon, 1963).

W. B. Forsyth

Keiss, *quoad sacra** parish in Caithness, north of Wick. Sir William Sinclair* gathered here the earliest surviving Baptist* congregation in Scotland in 1750. Despite his enforced departure to Edinburgh in 1763 the church continued, led by John Budge until 1803. He was succeeded by Donald Inrig until 1831, and Alexander Bain was the leader in 1847 when F. Johnstone investigated the church's history. The church used Sinclair's Hymns (Wick, 1750), and re-emerges into history as a station of the Baptist Home Missionary Society for Scotland.* It still continues, now linked with Wick, and has produced several ministers and missionaries, including A. B. Miller, principal (1950–67) of the Baptist Theological College of Scotland.

D. Beaton, *Ecclesiastical History of Caithness* (Wick, 1909), 219–26, 337; D. W. Bebbington (ed.), *The Baptists in Scotland* (G, 1988), 15–16, 312–13.

D. B. Murray

Keith, Alexander (1791–1880), FC minister and writer on prophecy. Born at Keith-Hall, Tulliallan, in Aberdeenshire, he studied arts at Marischal College, Aberdeen, 1805–9, and divinity 1809–13. Licensed by Garioch CofS Presbytery, he was ordained to St Cyrus, Kincardineshire, in 1816. His writings on prophecy soon brought him distinction, especially his *Evidence of the Truth of the Christian Religion from the Literal Fulfilment of Prophecy* (E, 1828), which went through nearly forty editions in his lifetime. Its most original feature was its use of the testimony of modern travellers to the present condition of Palestine and other Bible lands, showing the truth of fulfilled prophecies concerning them. See also his *The Signs of the Times* (E, 1832); *The Harmony of Prophecy* (E, 1851); *Sketch of the Evidence from Prophecy* (E, 1823); *The History and Destiny of the World and of the Church according to Scripture* (E, 1861).

KEITH, GEORGE

In 1839 Keith travelled with Andrew Bonar* and others to eastern Europe and Palestine at the behest of the General Assembly, to inquire into the state of the Jews. His friendship with the Archduchess Maria Dorothea paved the way for the establishment of the Jewish mission in Pest, Hungary. Keith was convener of the Jewish Mission Committee for some years, both in the CofS and the FC, which he joined in 1843.

Demonstration of the Truth of the Christian Religion (E, 1838); *The Land of Israel according to the Covenant with Abraham, with Isaac and with Jacob* (E, 1843); *Examination of Elliott's 'First Six Seals'* (E, 1847); *Scripture versus Stanley* (L, 1859).

DNB XXX, 315–16; FES V, 483; AFCS I, 196.

N. R. Needham

Keith, George (*c.* 1553–1623), fifth Earl Marischal, founder of Marischal College.* Educated at King's College, Aberdeen, he proved to be a good student, especially of languages. He completed his education on the continent, spending some of his time at Geneva under Theodore Beza. In 1581 he succeeded his grandfather to the richest inheritance in Scotland, and in 1582 was appointed to the Privy Council. His most prominent political role was his leading and financing of an embassy to Denmark in 1589,when he acted as James VI's* proxy in his marriage to Anne of Denmark. While he was keenly active in opposing the resurgence of RCism in the north-east in the 1580s and 1590s, Marischal took little interest in court politics or government office, and in 1599 was temporarily deprived of his place on the Privy Council for non-attendance. He was appointed a union commissioner in 1604 and was the King's Commissioner to Parliament in 1609, but his real interests lay elsewhere. In 1593 he founded Marischal College, Aberdeen, which was primarily intended to train ministers to serve in the region. In later life he lived quietly at Dunnottar Castle, pursuing his academic and religious studies.

DNB XXX, 316–18; Scots Peerage, VI, 51–3, VI, 51–4.

K. M. Brown

Keith, George (*c.*1639–1716), Quaker convert and dissident. Keith gave both great service and disservice to the Society of Friends.* Born in Aberdeen, he graduated MA at Marischal College and intended the ministry of the CofS. In 1662 he joined the Society of Friends and in consequence was imprisoned in Aberdeen for ten months. In 1675 he was associated with Robert Barclay* in a public disputation with three divinity students in Aberdeen. Barclay had been concerned at the misrepresentation of Quaker doctrines in Aberdeen pulpits and offered a public debate with the ministers concerned. The ministers refused and nominated the students in their place. A Quaker memoir records: 'The dispute was accordingly held for the appointed space of three hours, but terminated, as such disputes generally do, in tumult and disorder; the students handling serious subjects with levity,

KEITH, ROBERT

and at last triumphing in a victory which they had not obtained.' The students ended the debate by pelting the Quakers with clods and stones. However, four students who were spectators joined the Society of Friends.

Keith emigrated to Pennsylvania in 1688, but, according to John Barclay, 'imbibed notions subversive of all social order which led him to conduct himself with great disrespect towards the civil authorities in the state'. He was accused of denying the 'sufficiency of the light within', and forbidden to preach. He formed a group of followers who took the name of Christian Quakers.

In 1694 he left Pennsylvania for England, where for the next six years he celebrated the sacraments of baptism and the Lord's Supper while professing still to be a Quaker. He was ordained in the CofE in 1700 and was one of the first missionaries of the Society for Propagating the Gospel in America, 1702–4. He received the living of Edburton in Sussex in 1705. On his deathbed Keith told a visitor, 'I wish I had died when I was a Quaker; for then, I am sure, it would have been well with my soul.'

He wrote very extensively, first as a Quaker, but later to expose the error of their beliefs (e.g. *A General Epistle to Friends*, A(?), 1671; *The Christian Quaker*, Philadelphia, 1693; *George Keith's Complaint against the Quakers*, L, 1700).

J. Barclay (ed.), *Diary of Alexander Jaffray* (A, 1833); E. W. Kirby, *George Keith 1638–1716* (NY, 1942).

H. R. Sefton

Keith, Robert (1681–1756), Bishop in EpCS and church historian. He was born near Dunnottar, Kincardineshire, and educated at Marischal College, Aberdeen. After serving as tutor to George Keith, the future tenth Earl Marischal, and his brother James, later Field Marshall Keith, he became a deacon in the EpCS (1710). In 1713 he was ordained priest to serve a congregation in Edinburgh, and in 1727 was made bishop to assist the aged Bishop of Edinburgh, Arthur Millar. While still living in Edinburgh he was specifically entrusted with the episcopal care of Caithness, Orkney and the Isles, duties which he continued to fulfil after becoming Bishop of Fife in 1733. In 1743 he was elected Primus of the EpCS.

Keith's episcopate was passed during years of dispute in his Church. He was the mediator of a concordat on the question of 'usages'* in 1732, but his best contributions were made as a scholar. *The History of the Affairs of Church and State in Scotland* (E, 1734; ed. J. P. Lawson and J. C. Lyon, 3 vols, Spottiswoode Soc., E, 1844–50) covers 1527–68, drawing on original research and publishing numerous documents. Keith's *Catalogue of Scottish Bishops* (E, 1755) goes down to 1688 (enlarged and continued by M. Russel, E, 1824). A study of mystical divinity remains in manuscript. Keith was also a student of archaeology and numismatics.

DNB XXX, 326–8; memoirs by Russel (*Catalogue*, 1824, xvii–xliii) and Lawson (*History*, vol. I, ix–xc);

Keith-Falconer, Ion Grant Neville

J. F. S. Gordon, *Scotichronicon*, vol. II (G, 1867), 187-284.

D. F. Wright

Keith-Falconer, Ion Grant Neville (1856-87), Cambridge linguist and missionary to the Arabs. Keith-Falconer was born in Edinburgh, son of the eighth Earl of Kintore, a FC elder. From Keith Hall near Aberdeen he went to Harrow and then to Trinity College, Cambridge in 1874. There he read for the mathematical tripos, and then transferred to the tripos in theology, where he became particularly interested in Hebrew. Afterwards he was placed first in the newly organized tripos in Semitic languages (Hebrew, Syriac and Arabic).

A devout Christian from an early age, he helped form the Cambridge Inter-Collegiate Christian Union (*see* Inter-Varsity Fellowship) in 1877, conducted mission work among the poor, and was involved with the 'Cambridge Seven' missionaries to China. He translated from Syriac *The Kalilah and Dimnah* (C, 1885) and for a very brief period was Lord Almoner's Professor of Arabic in Cambridge University. In 1884 he went as a FC missionary to the Arabs at Sheik Othman, near Aden. There he set up a school and mission infirmary. He died of a fever.

M. L. Loane, *They Were Pilgrims* (L, 1970), 143-90; R. Sinker, *Memorials of the Hon. Ion Keith-Falconer* (L, 1888); G. Smith, 'The Hon. Ion G. N. Keith-Falconer', *Twelve Pioneer Missionaries* (L, E, 1900), 204-33.

D. F. Kelly

Kells, Book of, illuminated manuscript of the four Gospels. The Book of Kells (Dublin, Trinity College MS A.I.6) was probably made at Iona between the mid-eighth century and 806, when a Viking attack prompted the removal of most of the Iona monks to Kells in Ireland. It was stolen from Kells in 1007 but later recovered, minus its gold cover; the manuscript is missing its first and last folios, including some prefatory material and the text from John 17:13. A few internal folios are also lost. Its Canon Tables and those in early Carolingian manuscripts reflect common sources. The unique Virgin and Child miniature recalls the analogous scene on St Oran's cross, Iona (*see* Crosses, Celtic). Other full-page miniatures depict Christ on the Mount of Olives and the Temptation of Christ. A page displaying all four evangelist symbols and a full-page portrait of the appropriate evangelist preceded each Gospel, although only three of the four-symbol pages and two evangelist portraits survive. A full-page initial introduces the text of each Gospel. An unusual portrait of Christ faces the only carpet page, which precedes the magnificent Chi-Rho initial that begins Matt. 1:18. Iona had a large scriptorium when it created the Book of Kells; Henry detected it in the work of three scribes and three principal painters. It is the most elaborate of extant Insular Gospel books and marks the crescendo of the Insular style.

F. Henry, *The Book of Kells* (L, 1974);
G. Henderson, *From Durrow to Kells: Insular Gospel-books 650-800* (L, 1987), 131-98; J. J. G. Alexander, *Insular Manuscripts 6th to 9th Century* (L, 1978), 71-6.

D. MacLean

Kelman, John (1864-1929), liberal evangelical minister. Born in the FC manse in Dundonald, Ayrshire, he studied in Edinburgh, at the Royal High School, the University (MA, 1884) and New College, and at Ormond College, Melbourne. After assisting George Adam Smith* at Aberdeen Queen's Cross, he was ordained to Peterculter FC, Aberdeenshire, in 1891, and served thereafter at New North, Edinburgh (1897-1907), St George's UF, Edinburgh (1907-19), Fifth Avenue, New York (1919-24) and Frognal St Andrews, Hampstead (1924-5). For war service with the YMCA* in France he was awarded the OBE (1918). He was highly regarded as a preacher, with an effective ministry to students in Edinburgh. Many of his publications were sermons, and his Lyman Beecher Lectures at Yale were on *The War and Preaching* (L, 1919). He received the DD of Edinburgh (1907), Yale (1917) and Princeton. Typical of the evangelical liberalism dominant in the early twentieth century, Kelman had moved far from the theological stance of his brilliant FC father (*AFCS* I, 197). He accused the post-1900 FC* of Erastianism and of surrendering the right to preach the gospel freely to all. He died in Edinburgh.

AFCS I, 198; *FUFCS*, 29; *Who Was Who, 1929-1940*, 741; E. J. Hagan in *MRUFCS* n.s. 29 (1929), 257-9.

D. F. Wright

Kelso, a foundation of Tironensian* monks, made at Selkirk in 1113 by Earl David (later David I*), which moved to Kelso in 1128. Its early years were distinguished and important, as regards both Tiron and Scotland. David himself brought a second group of monks from Tiron in 1117. The first two abbots became, as immediate successors of the founder, abbots at Tiron itself; the third and fourth abbots became bishops in Scotland: Herbert at Glasgow 1147, Arnold at St Andrews 1160. A dependent priory was founded at Lesmahagow, Lanarkshire, in 1144. The heir to the throne was buried at Kelso in 1152.

The abbot of Kelso, the first in Scotland to be granted *pontificalia* (episcopal insignia; 1165), was able to dispute precedence with the abbot of Tiron in 1176. Kelso founded abbeys at Kilwinning (after 1162), Arbroath* (1178) and Lindores* (1191). Priors of Kelso and Lesmahagow became bishops of Aberdeen (1199) and Moray (1203). Another cell of Kelso was founded at Fogo, Berwickshire, in the thirteenth century. Kelso and Lesmahagow between them enjoyed the revenues of over forty appropriated parishes.

Being near the Border, Kelso suffered much in the English wars in the fourteenth century. Though diminished in importance, it still had a substantial community, and James III* was crowned there in

KELVIN, LORD (WILLIAM THOMSON)

1460. The abbey suffered again through English invasions in 1523 and, even more, in 1542-5. The community, numbering about twenty-four in the 1520s and 1530s, declined sharply; there were, however, also five monks at Lesmahagow. From 1468 the abbacy was held mostly by members of the powerful Border family of Ker, but a natural son of James V* was commendator* 1534-57.

Liber S. Marie de Calchou (2 vols, Bannatyne Club, E, 1846); G. W. S. Barrow, *The Kingdom of the Scots* (L, 1973), 174-7, 199-211; Easson-Cowan, 66-70; S. Cruden, *Scottish Medieval Churches* (E, 1986), 42-54; M. Dilworth, 'The Border Abbeys in the Sixteenth Century', *RSCHS* 21 (1983), 233-46.

M. Dilworth

Kelvin, Lord (William Thomson) (1824-1907), distinguished scientist and inventor. Born in Belfast, he was brought up in Glasgow where his father became a professor – and William a student when only ten. A spell at Peterhouse, Cambridge (1841-5), preceded his return to Glasgow as Professor of Natural Philosophy (1846-99). In 1892 he became Baron Kelvin of Largs (Ayrshire). For his contributions to thermodynamics, electricity and navigation, high honour attended him on every side – Order of Merit, Privy Councillor, President of the Royal Society, Chancellor of Glasgow University, etc.

Thomson was reared in the CofS (his father once trained for its ministry), in Cambridge conformed to the CofE, but in Largs attended the FC where his first wife's brother-in-law, Charles Watson (*AFCS* I, 352; *FUFCS*, 152) was minister. In later life he worshipped with the Episcopalians. He retained a confident, undogmatic faith, largely indifferent to denominational divisions but hostile to ritualism and sacerdotalism ('the High Church ... was high only in the sense that game is high') and to spiritualism. In addressing the Ladies' Protestant League (1902) he criticized perversions in the CofE. He was President of Largs and Fairlie Auxiliary of the National Bible Society of Scotland (1903-7), but declined office in sabbatarian bodies.

He frequently affirmed his belief in creative providence, rejecting evolutionism. In the annual address (1897) of the Victoria Institute he spoke of the 'miracle of the creation of living creatures', and clarified his convictions in the ensuing correspondence in *The Times*. He declined the Gifford lectureship,* uncertain whether he could improve much on William Paley's *Natural Theology*.

The house he built at Largs, Netherhall, was subsequently a Christian conference centre until the later 1980s.

DNB Second Suppl. III, 508-17; *Who Was Who, 1897-1916*, 392; A. G. King, *Kelvin the Man* (L, 1925), 28ff.; S. P. Thompson, *The Life of William Thomson...*, 2 vols (L, 1910), II, 1086-103; D. B. Wilson, *Kelvin and Stokes* (Bristol, 1987).

D. F. Wright

Kemp, Joseph William (1871-1933), evangelist and Baptist minister. He was born in Hull and edu-

KENNEDY, HARRY ANGUS ALEXANDER

cated there and at the Bible Training Institute,* Glasgow. In 1896-7 he served with Ayrshire Christian Union. In 1897 he was called as minister to Kelso Baptist Church, in 1898 moved to Hawick, and in 1902 to Charlotte Chapel, Edinburgh, at that time in a low state with membership down to 108. Revival, parallel to that in Wales, transformed the church between 1905 and 1907 to 830 by 1914. In 1912 the chapel was rebuilt to seat 1,000 people. In 1915 Kemp went to a pastorate in New York, and in 1919 to Auckland Tabernacle, New Zealand. He had outstanding gifts as a Bible teacher, evangelist and enabler. He published *The Soul Winner* (NY, 1916) and *Outline Studies on the Tabernacle* (L, 1913).

W. Kemp (his wife), *Joseph W. Kemp* (E, L, n.d.); *Charlotte Chapel Record* 1-10, 1906-15; W. Whyte, *Revival in Rose Street* (E, n.d.); G. Yuille, *History of the Baptists in Scotland* (G, 1927); D. W. Bebbington (ed.), *The Baptists in Scotland* (G, 1988).

D. B. Murray

Kenleith (or Kendeleth), Robert de (*d*.1273), a diplomat, courtier and churchman during the reigns of Alexander II (1214-49) and Alexander III (1249-86). He was abbot of Dunfermline* 1240-51, during which time he obtained the mitre and ring for his abbacy and canonization of St Margaret,* and a papal chaplaincy for himself. *C*.1247 he was made chancellor. He may have been at the papal court in 1251 seeking coronation and anointing for Alexander III, but if so was unsuccessful. The fall of Alan Durward's administration in that year cost him dear, for he lost both the chancellorship and his abbacy. He retired to the Cistercian* monastery of Newbattle. With the revival of Durward's party in the late 1250s and the King's majority, Kenleith's career recovered; he was engaged in diplomacy with England in 1260, and became abbot of Melrose* in 1268.

A. A. M. Duncan, *Scotland: the Making of the Kingdom* (E, 1975), 461, 559-62, 574, and sources there cited.

A. Macquarrie

Kennedy, Harry Angus Alexander (1866-1934), minister in the FC of Scotland and professor in New College, Edinburgh. Born in Dornoch, son of the FC minister, and educated in Edinburgh, Halle and Berlin, he was successively minister of the FC in Callander (1893); Professor of New Testament Language and Literature, Knox College, Toronto (1905); and Professor of New Testament Language and Literature, New College, Edinburgh (1909). He retired through ill-health in 1925. Kennedy wrote seven books, including *The Sources of New Testament Greek* (E, 1895); *St Paul's Conceptions of the Last Things* (Cunningham Lectures*, L, 1904); *St Paul and the Mystery Religions* (L, 1913); *The Theology of the Epistles* (L, 1919); *Philo's Contribution to Religion* (L, 1919). He contributed 'Philippians' to *The Expositor's Greek Testament*.

Kennedy was one of the outstanding group of

Scottish New Testament scholars who flourished at the turn of the century. He was fully abreast of the critical scholarship of his day, and his work represents a careful evaluation of the available evidence. He was a pioneer in arguing that New Testament Greek was essentially the common Greek of the time. His discussions of Paul's theology against its background retain their value, and his textbook on the theology of the Epistles remains a minor classic.

FUFCS, 578; DNB 1931–1940, 504f.

I. H. Marshall

Kennedy, Hugh (1698–1764), evangelical CofS minister. Born of Scottish parents in Northern Ireland, he graduated MA from Glasgow University in 1714 and was licensed by the Presbytery of Jedburgh in 1720. He was successively minister of Torthowald, Dumfriesshire (1721–3); Cavers, Jedburgh (1723–37); and the Scotch Church in Rotterdam (1737–64). He received a DD from Aberdeen University in 1762. His principal writings were *A Discourse Concerning the Nature, Author, Means and Manner of Conversion* (E, 1743), and *A Short Account of the Rise and Progress of a Remarkable Work of Grace in the United Netherlands* (L, 1752). Together with Alexander Comrie,* Kennedy 'was largely, if not mainly, responsible for the translation and circulation in Dutch of some of the best current Scots divinity of his age', *e.g.* Thomas Boston's* *View of the Covenant of Grace* (J. Macleod, *Scottish Theology*, E, ³1974, 130).

FES II, 106.

N. R. Needham

Kennedy, James (*c*.1406–65), churchman, politician and patron of scholarship. A grandson of King Robert III and so a nephew of James I, he studied at the young University of St Andrews in the 1420s, and then at Louvain, before returning to Scotland in the mid-1430s. He quickly rose to favour with the King, his uncle, one of whose last acts was to impose him on the chapter of Dunkeld at their bishop (1437). This Erastian appointment was confirmed by Pope Eugenius IV, and Kennedy responded by showing unswerving loyalty to the papacy in its struggle with conciliarism.* In 1439 he attended the Council of Florence, where the Pope rewarded his loyalty by appointing him commendator* of Scone;* in the following year he was translated to St Andrews.* But during the troubled later years of James II's minority he was out of favour with the Douglas/Livingston connection, and took little active part in politics 1444–50. In the latter year he travelled to Rome for the papal jubilee, returning to Scotland the following year via Flanders. Shortly before his departure he had founded the College of St Salvator at St Andrews, and its chapel with his magnificent tomb survives as his memorial. During the later years of James II's personal reign (1449–60) he was seldom at court, and it has been argued that his political influence has been overstated. After the death of James II, however, he returned to prominence in his support for the Queen Mother; and between her death in December 1463 and his own, Kennedy was undisputed leader of the regency government. During this period he promoted many of his own kin to positions of wealth and influence.

Kennedy's influence and personality have been debated. He is sometimes portrayed as a model churchman, scholarly, peace-loving, using his considerable influence to promote stability. On the other hand he has been viewed as a nepotist, egocentric, vain, politically ambitious but inept. The truth may lie somewhere in between.

A. I. Dunlop, *The Life and Times of James Kennedy, Bishop of St Andrews* (E, 1950) – standard account, criticized in N. A. T. Macdougall, 'Bishop James Kennedy of St Andrews ...' in *Church, Politics and Society*, ed. Macdougall (E, 1983), 1–22; R. Nicholson, *Scotland: the Later Middle Ages* (E, 1974).

A. Macquarrie

Kennedy, James (1777–1863), influential Independent* preacher. A native of the parish of Dull, Perthshire, Kennedy was trained by the Haldanes* and itinerated widely as a preacher in Perthshire, mainland Argyll and Lorn. He was pastor of the Independent church at Aberfeldy (1806–25), and of the Independent church in Inverness (1825–58). Though of small stature, he earned the soubriquet *An Ceanadach Mòr* ('Great Kennedy'), because he was a powerful preacher and fearless evangelist.

Inverness Chronicle, 17 July 1856; 1851 and 1861 Censuses for Inverness; D. E. Meek, 'Evangelical Missionaries in the Early Nineteenth-Century Highlands', *SS* 28 (1987), 11–12, 23; H. Escott, *A History of Scottish Congregationalism* (G, 1960), 279–80.

D. E. Meek

Kennedy, John (1819–84), the most influential Highland* minister of his time. His father was a close friend of John MacDonald* of Ferintosh (see our Kennedy's biography, *The Apostle of the North*, E, 1866). He studied at Aberdeen University, MA in 1840, and then at Aberdeen Theological Hall. He received a DD from Aberdeen in 1873.

Licensed with the Presbytery of Chanonry in September 1843, Kennedy sided with the Disruption* and in February 1844 was ordained and inducted to his only charge, Dingwall FC. Loved by young and old alike, Kennedy was much in demand as a preacher at Communion seasons.* While in London for recuperation following illness, he met C. H. Spurgeon,* who preached at the opening of the new FC building in Dingwall on 17 May 1870. Kennedy was Clerk to the Presbytery of Dingwall and to the Synod of Ross. He toured Europe in 1881, and died on the way home from a trip to Rome.

Kennedy was a reluctant, though doughty, controversialist. He joined James Begg* in opposing union with the UPC both because of his commitment to the establishment principle (see *Unionism and the Union*, E, 1870; *Unionism and its Last Phase*, E,

1873), and because of his fear that the UPs were unsound on the atonement (see *Man's Relations to God*, E, 1869). He was equally opposed to the disestablishment* of the CofS (see *The Distinctive Principles and Present Position and Duty of the Free Church*, E, 1875; *The Constitution of the Church of Scotland and Her Relations to Other Presbyterian Churches*, E, 1876; *A Letter to Members of the Free Church in the Highlands*, E, 1876). He rebuked the disestablishment party in his own Church in *A Plea in Self-Defence* (E, 1878) and in two lectures: *The Establishment Principle and the Disestablishment Movement* (E, n.d.) and *The Disestablishment Movement in the Free Church* (E, 1882).

Kennedy also objected to 'uninspired hymns'* and wrote *The Introduction of Instrumental Music into the Worship of the Free Church* (E, 1883). He opposed the organized temperance movement* (*Total Abstinence Schemes Examined*, E, 1879; *A Reply to Some Recent Defences of Total Abstinence Schemes*, E, 1879); and in *The Present Cast and Tendency of Religious Thought and Feeling in Scotland* (collected articles of 1879 from the *Perthshire Courier*, E, 1902), he faulted *inter alia* Sunday schools,* age- and sex-specific church organizations, soirées, and 'Plymouthism' – 'the slimiest of all isms'. He stood with Begg against William Robertson Smith's* views of Scripture (*A Purteekler Acoont o' the Last Assembly* [1881] *by Wan o' the Hielan' Host*, E, 1881); and in *The Doctrine of Inspiration in the Confession of Faith* (E, n.d.) he contended that the Westminster Confession* teaches verbal, plenary inspiration, and that this is what the Bible teaches.

A summary of Kennedy's theological position is found in *Man's Relations to God Traced in the Light of 'The Present Trends'* (E, 1869), his most sustained and least provocative tract. For his homiletic method see *Expository Lectures* (ed. John Kennedy Cameron, Inverness, 1911), and *Divine Religion Distinct from all Human Systems Ancient and Modern* (Dingwall, [1927]).

Kennedy determinedly adhered to 'the old paths'. As becomes clear from his first book, *The Days of the Fathers in Ross-shire* (E, 1861), there is sometimes a wistfulness in his attachment to the fathers and 'The Men',* but he valued their holding together of faith, experience and practice. He was no hyper-Calvinist who would offer the gospel to 'sensible sinners' only; and he was convinced that there is but one gospel for sinners of each succeeding age. He saw dangers, however, in certain evangelistic methods – hence his *Hyper-Evangelism 'Another Gospel' Though a Mighty Power* (E, 1874)

DNB XXX, 429–30; A. Auld, *Life of John Kennedy* (L, 1887); J. Noble, *Memoir* prefixed to *The Days of the Fathers* (Inverness, ⁵1897); A. P. F. Sell, *Defending and Declaring the Faith* (Exeter, 1987), ch. 2; G. N. M. Collins, *An Orchard of Pomegranates* (L, n.d.); centenary reappraisals in the *FCSR* by H. Cartwright (Oct., 1983) and D. MacLeod (May, 1984).

A. P. F. Sell

Kennedy, Quintin (1520–64), one of the foremost RC controversialists of the Scottish Reformation.* The fourth son of Gilbert, second Earl of Cassillis, he succeeded his uncle as Abbot of Crossraguel (Ayrshire) in 1547–8. He had been educated at the universities of St Andrews and Paris.

Little is known of Kennedy's early career (he was vicar of Girvan and Penpont, Nithsdale, before becoming abbot), though he was present at the 1549 provincial council.* By 1558 his stance was that of a reforming Catholic – as bitterly critical of abuses within the Church as many Protestants. For the ills of simony, pluralism and the dilapidation of benefices, he offered the remedy of a Church free from secular patronage, whose bishops and abbots were actually elected by their chapters. Reformation of life and morals would be attained once the ancient authorities of the Church had been restored to spiritual liberty.

Kennedy's *Ane Compendius Tractive* (E, 1558; in D. Laing, ed., *Miscellany of the Wodrow Society*, E, 1844, 95–174) is primarily important for its approach to the question of the authority of the Bible. He denied that the Scriptures were self-interpreting, or perspicuous in matters of controversy to the spiritual private reader. Rather, the Abbot saw the recognized leaders and councils of the Church as the God-given means for resolving disputes – including disputes on biblical interpretation. This restatement of the relationship between Scripture and tradition was of importance in 1558, when Scottish Protestants were pleading to be judged on the sole authority of the 'naked word of God' by Mary of Guise,* the Scots nobility and civil authorities. Knox* may have had Kennedy's arguments in mind when he complained of the Protestants' opponents that 'no judge would they admit but themselves, their Councils and Canon Law' (Knox, *History* I, 152, 155).

Carrick (southern Ayrshire) was Kennedy country and remained a RC stronghold for years after 1560. Monks of Crossraguel celebrated mass at Easter 1563 protected by Kennedy lairds. In 1562, the Abbot had engaged at Maybole in a three-day public disputation against John Knox on the validity of the sacrament (Knox, *Works* VI, 169–220). Though this debate was inconclusive, Kennedy's 'Ane Compendious Ressonyng' (ed. Kuipers – see below; cf.Knox's *Works* VI, 166–8) had sought to reject Knox's assertion that the mass was idolatry, being a human invention; and further argued that, though it was a sacrifice, it did not detract from Christ's sacrifice on the cross. Unafraid publicly to oppose both Knox and Willock,* Kennedy was staunch both in writing and in person.

C. A. Kuipers (ed.), *Quintin Kennedy (1520–1564): Two Eucharistic Tracts* (Nijmegen, 1964); Knox, *History* II, 54, 57, 70–1; M. Taylor, 'The Conflicting Doctrines of the Scottish Reformation', *IR* 10 (1959), 111–23; I. B. Cowan, *The Scottish Reformation* (L, 1982), 84–6; *Charters of the Abbey of Crossraguel* (E, 1886), I, xl–xlvi, 102–39.

F. D. Bardgett

Kennedy, Thomas (Ildephonse), (1722–1804). Thomas Kennedy, born in Perthshire, entered Ratisbon (*see* Schottenklöster) seminary 1735 and took Benedictine* vows as Brother Ildephonse 1742. After four years' study at Erfurt University, he was ordained priest 1747. At Ratisbon he taught mathematics and physics, became cellarer 1753 and seminary director 1756. A founder member of the Bavarian Academy of Sciences 1758, he was appointed permanent secretary 1761, a position he held until 1801.

Kennedy published scientific articles and was also a gifted administrator. He was influential in Bavaria, being an ecclesiastical councillor to the Elector and holding other offices, unusual for a foreigner. He had many international contacts. In the increasingly anti-religious climate, his influence benefited his monastery greatly.

L. Hammermayer, 'Academiae Scientiarum Boicae Secretarius Perpetuus: Ildephons Kennedy O.S.B.', in O. Kuhn (ed.), *Grossbritannien und Deutschland* (Munich, 1974), 195–246; id., *Gründungs- und Frühgeschichte der Bayerischen Akademie der Wissenschaften* (Munich, 1959).

M. Dilworth

Kenneth, *see* Celtic Saints.

Kentigern, *see* Celtic Saints.

Kentigerna, *see* Celtic Saints.

Kenya, *see* Missions.

Kerr, George McGlasham (1874–1950) and **Kerr, Isabel Gunn** (1875–1932), missionary leprosy specialists. George was born in Aberdeen, and seems to have worked first as a builder. Following an evangelical conversion at 16 he joined the Wesleyan Church, attracted by its class meetings. Through the local YMCA* he met Robert Laws* and decided for missionary service. He took classes (without graduating) at Aberdeen University, was trained for the Wesleyan ministry at Didsbury College, Manchester, and returned to Aberdeen to study medicine for two years. In 1901 he went to Southern Rhodesia under the Wesleyan Methodist Missionary Society, but pioneering work was closed to him, and he would not remain as chaplain to European settlers. In 1903 he married Isabel Gunn of Aberdeen who had just graduated MB, ChB. After a brief circuit appointment in Newbury they returned in 1907 to the mission field, to Nizamabad in the Indian princely state of Hyderabad. Here George ran an industrial school, while Isabel worked in two hospitals. Both were appalled at the incidence of leprosy and the attendant suffering, and challenged to action when a Hindu made them a substantial gift to establish a leprosy home. Eventually the Nizam of Hyderabad gifted a site at Dichpali, ten miles from Nizamabad, and a home was opened. At the time little could be done beyond restricting contagion and mitigating misery; and from 1914 the Kerrs also had pastoral responsibility for a mass movement which brought 60,000 people, in sixty villages, into the church. The discovery in Calcutta in 1920 of the hyndocarpus treatment for leprosy transformed the situation. Isabel worked closely with Ernest Muir, pioneer of the treatment, and introduced it at Dichpali in 1921. Thereafter it became one of the world's outstanding leprosy hospitals, supported by Isabel's medical skill and George's gifts in administration, finance raising, diplomacy with both British and Indian officials and development of occupational therapy. Isabel died suddenly in 1932; George continued at Dichpali until 1938. He retired to Cove, Kilcreggan, where he assisted the CofS parish church. The Government of India awarded both the Kerrs the Kaisar-i-Hind medal in 1923.

Kerr papers, Centre for the Study of Christianity in the Non-Western World, New College, University of Edinburgh; *Minutes of Methodist Conference* (L, 1950), 148; *Ministers and Probationers of the Methodist Church* (L, 1932), 237; D. Monahan, *The Story of Dichpali* (L, 1949); A. F. Walls, *Some Personalities of Aberdeen Methodism* (A, 1973).

A. F. Walls

Kerr Lectures, a series founded in 1887 from the gift of Miss Joan Kerr of Sanquhar, Dumfriesshire, to promote the study of 'Scientific Theology' in the UPC. The subject could in effect be any theological topic, including 'any important Phases of Modern Religious Thought or Scientific Theories in their bearing upon Evangelical Theology' – but 'the practical work of the Ministry' could not appear more than once in every five series. The lecturer should preferably be a graduate of a British university with a connection 'for some time' with a continental university, and a minister or licentiate of the UPC of no more than twenty-five years' standing. Between eight and twelve lectures were to be delivered in the Glasgow UP Hall, with the students examined on them thereafter.

Following the Church unions of 1900 and 1929 the lectureship is now administered by a committee of the CofS General Assembly, and preference is given to CofS ministers. When, 'occasionally', a scholar of another Church is appointed, the age restriction does not apply, although the aim is still the encouragement of theological study among younger ministers.

Among noteworthy series have been: James Orr,* *The Christian View of God and the World as Centring in the Incarnation* (E, 1893) – the first; J. W. Oman,* *The Problem of Faith and Freedom in the Last Two Centuries* (L, 1906); A. C. Welch,* *The Religion of Israel under the Kingdom* (E, 1912); D. M. Baillie,* *Faith in God and its Christian Consummation* (E, 1927); L. Newbigin,* *The Household of God* (L, 1953).

PUPS 1886–88, 489–90; *RGACS 1930*, 1187–9; details in *CofS Year Book* (annual), 1930–62.

D. F. Wright

Kerr, Mark (1517–84), commendator* of Newbattle* (south of Edinburgh; *see* Cistercians). The second son of Sir Andrew Kerr of Cessford, he was educated at St Andrews University. He was provided to the abbey of Newbattle in 1547 during the lifetime of the last regular abbot, gaining full possession in 1557. Having supported the Reformation he exchanged his clerical status for a secular career, becoming privy councillor and civil court judge. At the same time he transformed the abbey lands into a profitable private estate. His son Mark (*b.c.*1557) succeeded him as commendator, became Lord Newbattle in 1591 and Earl of Lothian in 1606. The Kerrs built a mansion house on the monastic site.

'Mark Kerr: Metamorphosis', in M. H. B. Sanderson, *Mary Stewart's People* (E, 1987).
M. H. B. Sanderson

Kessog, *see* Celtic Saints.

Keswick Teaching, *see* Evangelicalism; Conventions; Scroggie, W. Graham.

Kidd, James (1761–1834), CofS divine. Born at Loughbrickland, County Down, he studied at the College (now the University) of Pennsylvania, Philadelphia, and Edinburgh University. He was appointed in 1794 to the Chair of Oriental Languages at Marischal College, Aberdeen, while still completing his theological curriculum. Licensed to preach by the Presbytery of Aberdeen in 1796, he thereafter combined the duties of his Chair with those of evening lecturer at Trinity Chapel. He was ordained to Gilcomston Chapel-of-Ease* in 1801 (one of the largest congregations in Scotland) and continued as minister and professor until his death. He was a zealous opponent of patronage* and proponent of the popular election of ministers. The College of New Jersey (Princeton University) awarded him a DD in 1818.

A Course of Sermons explaining the Goodness of God (A, 1808); *A Catechism, for assisting the young preparing to approach the Lord's Table for the first time* (A, 1831); *Sermons* (A, 1835); *A Dissertation on the Eternal Sonship of Christ* (A, 1822); ed. R. S. Candlish, L, 1872).

James Stark, *Dr. Kidd of Aberdeen* (A, 1892); *FES* VII, 375–6; *DNB* XXXI, 90–1.
H. R. Sefton

Kilham, Alexander (1762–98), Methodist* reformer. Accepted by John Wesley as a preacher in 1785, he was already an advocate of greater liberty in the connexion, clear distinction from the established church ('our being so closely identified with the church cannot be looked on in any other light than as a species of trimming between God and the world'), and greater lay involvement in the appointment of leaders and preachers, when he was appointed to the Aberdeen circuit in 1792. His year in Scotland may have been decisive: the proposals set forth in his later writings, which brought about his expulsion from the Methodist Conference in 1796 and the establishment of the Methodist New Connexion the following year, are essentially Presbyterian in nature, and his main ally, William Thom,* was an Aberdonian. The records of the Aberdeen Methodist society of Kilham's time employ the terms 'minister' and 'elders'. Kilham died, worn out by his evangelistic labours as well as by the controversy, at 36. Most of what he advocated has since been adopted in Methodist polity.

DNB XXXI, 102–3; J. Blackwell, *Life of the Rev Alexander Kilham* (L, 1838); R. E. Davies, A. R. George and G. Rupp (eds), *History of the Methodist Church in Great Britain*, II (L, 1978), 276ff; A. F. Walls, 'English Bards and Scotch Reviewers: Some Early Interactions of Scottish and English Methodism', *Journal of the Scottish Branch of the Wesley Historical Society* 3 (1974), 8–14, 4 (1974), 2–13.
A. F. Walls

Killing Times, a term used to describe the peak of persecution at the end of the Restoration* period (1660–88). Some date the 'Times' from the 1679 rebellion (*see* Bothwell Bridge), others from August 1684 (Patrick Walker*) or from the accession of James VII* the following February (Alexander Shields*). Persecution was concentrated in the south-west, its aim being to destroy the small numbers of uncompromising Presbyterians* who had disowned the king and the state as uncovenanted. In practice, however, such action was often widened to include those suspected of sympathizing with them and helping them evade arrest. Such indiscriminate repression of the peasantry merely exacerbated the problem. The numbers who died were substantial, and comprised those tried and executed; those summarily shot for failing a simple test (such as refusing to repudiate the Sanquhar Declaration*); those killed in skirmishes; and prisoners who died through maltreatment or illness. One list of only 'the principal martyrs with the places where they were either publicly executed, or privately shot by troopers' produced a figure of 181 for 1680–8 (J. C. Johnston, *Treasury of the Covenant*, E, 1887, 597–601). Total estimates have been as high as 18,000; the real number was doubtless much smaller but still quite large. Many of those who died were active in resisting governmental oppression, but suffering of other sorts was much more widespread, with many enduring plundering; being driven from their homes and having to live on the run to avoid arrest, fining, imprisonment, and banishment to the plantations.

I. B. Cowan, *The Later Covenanters, 1660–88* (L, 1976); J. K. Hewison, *The Covenanters*, 2 vols (G, ²1913), II; R. Wodrow, *History of the Sufferings of the CofS*, 4 vols (²G, 1828–30), III–IV.
D. Stevenson and D. C. Lachman

Kilmartin Crosses, the three sculptured stone crosses at the Kilmartin church in mid-Argyll. The earliest dates from the tenth or eleventh century. Its side-arms are quite short and its decoration is related to late Pictish* sculpture and contemporary carvings on the islands of Canna and Eilean Mór in the Sound of Jura. Only the Crucifixion-bearing head survives of the second cross, which is a fifteenth-century product of the locally-based Loch Awe school of sculpture. The fragmentary third cross features a sensitive Crucifixion on one side and a seated Christ in Majesty on the other. Its itinerant sixteenth-century sculptor gave it a central open ring, the last of its kind in the West Highlands.

See also Crosses, Celtic.

J. Anderson and J. R. Allen, *The Early Christian Monuments of Scotland* (E, 1903), III, 394–5; R. B. K. Stevenson, 'The Inchyra Stone and Some Other Unpublished Early Christian Monuments', *PSAS* 92 (1958–9), 55; K. A. Steer and J. W. M. Bannerman, *Late Medieval Monumental Sculpture in the West Highlands* (E, 1977), 55–7, 77, pl. 36A; J. S. Richardson, 'The Campbell of Lerags Cross at Kilbride, Near Oban, With a Note On Cross-Heads of Late Mediaeval Date in the West Highlands', *PSAS* 61 (1926–7), 157–9.

D. MacLean

Kilsyth Revival, *see* Revivals.

King's Confession, or Negative Confession, or Second Confession of Faith, 1581, religious testimony designed to eliminate crypto-Catholicism in Scotland by enforced subscription. The impetus derived from acute anxiety about the Counter-Reformation* and the aggressive intentions of the Catholic powers, particularly Spain. Suspicions of Romanist infiltration into government circles, centring on the Regent, Esmé Stewart, Duke of Lennox, and fuelled chiefly by Queen Elizabeth I* of England, engendered a 'Popish scare'. The conflict between Presbytery and episcopacy was secondary to the need to flush out secret Romanists, who allegedly had received papal dispensations to subscribe to the Scots Confession.* The much more palpably anti-Roman King's Confession had a 'catch-all' intent, though Lennox signed. An anonymous RC reply was circulated.

Reputedly, the Confession appeared on the royal initiative. Its author was John Craig.* (It was to be included in all subsequent editions of Craig's catechism.) Published as *Ane shorte and generall confession*, it is composed of four parts: (i) a summary reaffirmation of the doctrine of the Scots Confession;* (ii) a vigorous and detailed denunciation of specifically RC doctrines, constitutions and practices; (iii) a form of oath disowning any Roman inclination; (iv) a declaration of loyalty to King, country and religion.

Within a few years Presbyterians had, in response to the onslaught of the Black Acts,* interpreted this oath as a covenant, binding posterity to maintain the Church as established in 1581. The Negative Confession resurfaced as a symbol of Protestant solidarity in 1590 in association with the general band to defend the faith. More controversially, it was used by Presbyterian apologists, like David Calderwood* and William Scott,* to challenge episcopal church government and liturgical changes. These innovations* were seen as breaches of the 1581 oath which, it was asserted, was perpetually binding on the Scottish people.

In February 1638 the Negative Confession was incorporated into the National Covenant,* of which it formed the opening section. Its inclusion was seen as a way to give the latter a broad Protestant appeal, but it was also intended unequivocally to place the Negative Confession on the side of the Presbyterians. In July 1638 Charles I* tried, unsuccessfully, to regain the initiative, authorizing the signing of the Negative Confession (the 'King's Covenant'), but without the additional text of the National Covenant. His supporters, including the Aberdeen Doctors,* denied the perpetual force of the Confession, while others like Archbishop John Spottiswoode* denied that the Church had been Presbyterian in 1581. However, the fate of the bishops and of the liturgy was settled at the Glasgow Assembly* in December 1638 when the Presbyterian interpretation of the Negative Confession was overwhelmingly endorsed.

BUK II, 515–18; G. Donaldson (ed.), *Scottish Historical Documents* (E, L, 1970), 150–3; G. D. Henderson (ed.), *The Scots Confession 1560 . . .* (E, G, A, 1937), 25–30, 101–11; Calderwood III, 488f.; G. Donaldson, *The Scottish Reformation* (C, 1960), 208–9; D. G. Mullan, *Episcopacy in Scotland* (E, 1986), 145, 156–7, 177–84, 189–90, 194.

W. I. P. Hazlett

King's College, Aberdeen, *see* Boece, Hector; Elphinstone, William; Universities; Education, Theological.

Kinloss, *see* Cistercians.

Kinnaird, George William Fox (1807–78), ninth Baron, Episcopalian social reformer and philanthropist. A conventional upper-class upbringing (Eton, the army, Freemasonry, title and Perthshire estate in 1826) was succeeded by an effective career as a 'radical laird'. He had many interests, but chief amongst his social concerns were temperance* and housing. He was also concerned with reform of the mint and mining conditions. His ends were achieved through the support of legislation such as the Forbes-MacKenzie Act of 1853 which limited drinking hours in Scotland; through pamphlets and letters (he wrote often and vigorously to advocate better working-class housing 'where health and decency can be preserved'), and in his book *Working Men's Houses* (Dundee, 1874). He also supported reformers such as James Begg* and social activists like James Scrymgeour, superintendent of the Dundee Band of Hope, whom Kinnaird accompanied in 'his adventures of charity'. Kinnaird was much involved in Dundee affairs, in, for example, the provision of the New Infirmary, public baths and model lodging houses, and he was much respected there.

Undoubtedly an important figure in the Scottish

KINNIBURGH, ROBERT

reform movement, his High Church Episcopalianism never inhibited his support of others of different religious persuasion but similar social objectives.

B. Lenman, C. Lythe and E. Gauldie, *Dundee and its Textile Industry* (Dundee, 1969); *DNB* XXXI, 191–2; *In Memoriam: Lord Kinnaird* (Dundee, 1878).

A. J. Durie

Kinniburgh, Robert (1780–1851), one of the most zealous and efficient supporters of the Congregational Union* of Scotland and its theological academy. Born near Kirkintilloch, Kinniburgh became a member of Greville Ewing's* church in Glasgow while serving in the army. He commenced studying for the ministry in 1805 in Robert Haldane's* theological seminary, and is believed to have been the last individual Haldane sent as a preacher to any of the Congregational churches in Scotland. Arriving in Dunkeld in autumn 1808, Kinniburgh was ordained minister of the Congregational church (1809). When the church adopted Baptist* sentiments he was compelled to leave (1810), and for a short time managed a factory in Kirkcaldy, prior to assisting John Braidwood teaching in the Institution for Deaf and Dumb, Edinburgh. Kinniburgh laboured as head teacher and superintendent of this institution 1811–47. The first historian of Scottish Congregationalism, Kinniburgh was one of a committee appointed in 1843 to collect information regarding the rise and progress of the Congregational churches in Scotland. A circular was issued to the churches containing some thirty questions and the answers were edited by Kinniburgh to produce the manuscript 'General Account of Congregationalism in Scotland from 1798 to 1848, and Particular Accounts Referring to Separate Counties'. (An edition is to be prepared by W. D. McNaughton, who is currently compiling a Scottish Congregational *Fasti* making use of it.)

(Editor) *Fathers of Independency in Scotland; or, Biographical Sketches of Early Scottish Congregational Ministers. A.D. 1798–1851* (E, 1851); 'A Historical Survey of Congregationalism in Scotland, from its rise in 1798 to 1812', in *The Jubilee Memorial of the Scottish Congregational Churches* (E, 1849), 41–93.

'Memoir...', *Scottish Congregational Magazine*, n.s. 2 (1852), 129–35, 169–75, 201–10.

W. D. McNaughton

Kirk, Scottish (and N. English) form of 'church', derived ultimately from the NT Greek adjective *kuriakos*, 'of the Lord'. It was used of the late medieval (i.e. RC) Scottish Church (as in many place-names) and likewise of the post-Reformation Church, even when temporarily episcopalian. When 'church' came into formal use from the late seventeenth century, 'Kirk session'* persisted (and cf. 'kirking', church attendance of new town council). Informally, 'kirk' increasingly distinguished the national CofS from non-Presbyterian nonconformists (RC, Episcopal, etc.). After the Disruption,* 'Auld Kirk'* denoted the continuing CofS. 'The Kirk' without qualification normally refers to the CofS (cf. 'Free Kirk').

M. Robinson (ed.), *The Concise Scots Dictionary* (A, 1985), 342–3; W. Grant and D. D. Murison (eds), *The Scottish National Dictionary*, V (E, 1960), 414–20; W. A. Craigie and A. J. Aitken, *A Dictionary of the Older Scottish Tongue*, III (Chicago, L, [1963]), 439–49 (incl. compounds).

D. F. Wright

Kirk, John (1813–86), leading Evangelical Union* minister. Born of poor parents in East Plean, Stirlingshire, Kirk was trained as a blacksmith. In 1835 he joined the Independent* congregation in Stirling, and in 1836 entered the Congregational Theological Academy in Glasgow. In 1839 he became minister of Hamilton Independent Church in Lanarkshire.

Initially a Calvinist, Kirk soon fell under Charles Finney's influence, adopting the American's revival* and temperance* ideals. He followed closely the controversy in the USec.C concerning another Finneyite, James Morison,* with whom he reformed a lifelong friendship.

In 1842 Kirk precipitated a similar controversy within the Congregational Union* by publishing *The Way of Life Made Plain* (G, 1842), in which he asserted universal atonement and taught that the Spirit exerts only a resistible influence on sinners. Kirk also undertook Finneyite-style itinerant evangelism, which produced much sensation. The controversy led to the expulsion in 1844 of nine students from the Glasgow Academy for their Kirkian views. The Glasgow Congregational churches suspended fellowship with Kirk's Hamilton congregation and several others sympathetic to his teaching.

In 1845 Kirk became pastor of a new Evangelical Union church in Edinburgh, which from 1846 met in Brighton Street Chapel. Here he exercised a powerful preaching and writing ministry until ill-health compelled retirement in 1876. He founded the newspaper *Christian News* in 1846, using it to promote temperance and prohibition. His church was the first in Edinburgh to use unfermented communion wine; he was first Grand Chaplain of the Scottish Good Templars Order (a temperance body).

Kirk had a keen interest in science, contributing a number of papers to the Victoria Institute. He was an outspoken critic of Darwinism and theories of the great antiquity of the human race and the earth (*Geological Theories*, L, 1867; *The Doctrine of Creation According to Darwin...*, L, 1869).

From 1859 Kirk was also Professor of Practical Theology in the Evangelical Union Theological Hall. In 1876 he received a DD from Waynesburg College (Cumberland Presbyterian), Pennsylvania.

H. Kirk, *Memoirs of Rev. John Kirk, DD* (E, 1888).

N. R. Needham

Kirk, Robert (?1644–92), Gaelic* scholar who

KIRK SESSION

transliterated the Classical Gaelic Bible into roman type. Kirk was the son of James Kirk, minister of the parish of Aberfoyle. Educated at the universities of Edinburgh and St Andrews, Kirk first became minister of Balquhidder (1664-85), and subsequently of Aberfoyle (1685-92). He acted as clerk to the Presbytery of Dunblane (1667-88), 'during which period the minutes were very carefully and beautifully written'. Remaining an 'unrepentant Episcopalian' until his death, he held his benefice unmolested after 1688. Kirk produced the first complete metrical Psalter* available in Gaelic (1684), but it was superseded by the 1694 edition of the Synod of Argyll.

Kirk's name is commemorated in 'Kirk's Bible'. This was a combination of the existing Classical Gaelic translations of the Old and New Testaments; these had been made by clergymen of the Church of Ireland (see Bible (Versions, Gaelic)). Although these translations were circulating in Scotland, they were printed in 'Gaelic script', which was by then generally unfamiliar in the Highlands. Their classical idiom was also a disadvantage. In the space of two years (1688-90), Kirk transformed these translations into a single volume in roman type, and modified some of the unfamiliar linguistic features. The work gradually earned esteem in the Highlands. Its production and distribution were promoted by James Kirkwood.* Kirk also wrote a 'strange but clever' book, *The Secret Commonwealth of Elves ... Faunes and Fairies* (E, 1815 first printing; written 1691), and compiled a short Scottish Gaelic Vocabulary (²L, 1893, 1702).

D. Maclean, 'The Life and Literary Labours of the Rev. Robert Kirk of Aberfoyle', *TGSI* 31 (1922-4), 328-66; J. L. Campbell, 'An Early Scottish Gaelic Vocabulary', *SGS* 5 (1938), 76-93; *FES* IV, 337, 334-5.

D. E. Meek

Kirk Session, the governing body of a Presbyterian congregation. In the CofS it is the lowest court under Presbytery,* Synod* and General Assembly.* It dates from the Reformation* and consists of the preaching elder (the minister) and a number of ruling elders.*

The session corresponds to the consistory of Calvin's Genevan church order and was the first court to appear when the CofS was reformed. Indeed St Andrews Kirk Session minutes begin in 1559, and from 1560 sessions were formed, with ministers, elders and (at first) deacons, as they became available, for the interpretation of Scripture, and oversight of parish and congregation and disciplinary action with regard to moral behaviour. In the *SBD* (1578) the 'particular eldership' is 'to keep religion and doctrine in purity without error and corruption and to keep comeliness and good order in the kirk'.

For centuries the session was responsible for the education of children, the care of the poor, the observance of the sabbath and the oversight of morals. Today the duties are almost entirely with the life and work of the local congregation.

The minister is *ex officio* moderator (chairman) with a casting but not deliberative vote. He is under authority of Presbytery and is responsible only to the Presbytery for life and doctrine, but elders may petition the Presbytery if they have cause to complain.

Another minister may act as moderator for specific business if properly mandated by the minister, but a minister must preside. Due notice of a meeting must be given by the minister from the pulpit, or with his authority, and a quorum is three. The session may not meet during the meeting of a superior court without that court's permission. Minutes must be kept, approved and signed by clerk and moderator.

The order of worship and administration of the sacraments of baptism and the Lord's Supper are the responsibility of the minister alone, but the session arranges the time of service and admits members by profession of faith. The service of admission to the Lord's Supper is conducted by the minister.

There is a roll of members in full communion to which the session adds the names of those who transfer from other congregations and from which the names of those who are disciplined or no longer fulfil their obligations as members of the church are removed.

The session is responsible for spiritual matters and, where there is no other body (e.g. Congregational Board*), for finance, property etc. in addition.

Elders assist the minister at the Lord's table in Holy Communion and are corporately responsible for the spiritual welfare and good order of the congregation. They have general responsibility with the minister for pastoral supervision and normally have districts to visit regularly.

The Kirk Session has other specific duties. It supervises all work among the young and all church societies. It is responsible for the use of buildings by other bodies. It appoints the church officer (or beadle*), the organist and leader of praise. It has to appoint an elder each year to represent it in Presbytery and Synod and, when called on by the Presbytery, to nominate an elder to be a commissioner to the General Assembly. It appoints days for collections in church for causes approved by the General Assembly or for special purposes. It should see that all acts of Assembly are properly implemented.

The session appoints a clerk* who takes the oath *de fideli*. He keeps all the session papers and records all the session minutes. Until the fairly recent legislation which removed the need for banns* of marriage, he was usually the person who dealt with the matter of banns. The session clerk holds an honourable and important appointment in every congregation and often for many years.

Cox 116-39; A. Herron, *A Guide to Congregational Affairs* (E, 1978), 1-34; G. D. Henderson, *The Scottish Ruling Elder* (L, 1935).

A. I. Dunlop

Kirk Weeks, ecumenical conferences of laity largely modelled on the German *Kirchentag* and forming part of the Tell Scotland* movement. The first was held in Aberdeen, 5–11 August 1957, the next in Dundee, 4–11 July 1959, the third in Ayr, 1st–18th August 1962, and the fourth in Perth, 24th–27th September 1965. Robert Mackie* chaired the planning of the first, and Colin Day, later Warden of Carberry Tower* (*FES* IX, 540, X, 316, 453), animated and organized from the outset. Despite eminent speakers, numbers never reached expectations (1,000 at Aberdeen instead of 3,000), and the effort remained a continental transplant that in the event failed to take successfully in Scotland. Particular frustration was felt at the refusal of a single Communion service. Some regional Kirk Weeks and Kirk Weekends were promoted, and the emphasis on lay responsibility in the world harmonized with other developments, e.g. in the Iona Community.* A series of smaller Laity Forums were held at St Andrews from 1963.

C. Day, *The Story of Kirk Week in Aberdeen*... (Arbroath, 1958); Mabel Small, *Growing Together: The Ecumenical Movement in Scotland 1924–64* (typescript, Dunblane, 1969).

D. F. Wright

Kirkmabreck Case (*Ballantyne and Others* v. *Presbytery of Wigtown* (1936) SC 625), case which helped clarify the relations of the civil courts to the right to call.* The parish of Kirkmabreck lies on Solway shore east of Newton Stewart. In the early 1930s, the parish having fallen vacant, the Presbytery initiated negotiations towards union with the former UF charge in the village of Creetown. Procedure in the vacancy was sisted while talking dragged on. In 1936 a group of elders raised an action in the Court of Session, arguing that the congregation's right to call a minister was a civil right conferred by the 1874 Act which had abolished patronage.* By a majority of two to one, the Second Division found for the Presbytery. The leading opinion says *inter alia*, 'The question must be, Is the particular matter complained of ... a matter which on a reasonable construction falls within the Declaratory Articles?* If so the matter is at an end, and neither the statute nor the common law, nor previous judicial decisions, whether upon statute or upon common law, can avail to bring the matter within the jurisdiction of the civil authority.' He had no difficulty finding that the right to call was such a matter. The important general principle here established has not since been challenged.

A. Herron

Kirkmadrine, *see* Early Ecclesiastical Sites.

Kirkpatrick, James Mackenzie (1868–1950), CofS minister. Educated at the University of Edinburgh (MA, 1888; BD, 1891), he was ordained in 1897 to St Bride's, Partick, in Glasgow, a church extension* charge of the parish of Govan. He was minister of Caddonfoot, Selkirkshire, 1926–40. He joined the Scottish Church Society* in 1897 and was its president, 1927–30. He collaborated with H. J. Wotherspoon* in writing *A Manual of Church Doctrine* (L, 1919; ed. T. F. Torrance and R. S. Wright, ²1960) a statement of the Scoto-Catholic* position on the doctrines of the Church, the ministry and the sacraments. His brother, Roger S. Kirkpatrick,* who succeeded John Macleod* as minister of Govan, was also a prominent member of the Scottish Church Society and one of its presidents.

FES III, 436, VII, 149.

D. M. Murray

Kirkpatrick, Roger Sandilands (1859–1943), CofS high-churchman. Born at Hamilton, he studied at Edinburgh University (MA, 1878; BD, 1881) and was minister of Dalbeattie, Kirkcudbrightshire (1886–96), Jedburgh (1896–9), Govan, Glasgow (1899–1912) and Yarrow, near Selkirk (1912–43). Edinburgh awarded him a DD in 1924. He was prominent in the National Church Defence Association* which opposed proposals for the 1929 Union,* and the Scottish Church Society.* His address on *The Jubilee* of the Society (E, 1942) proposed that its objects should be more selective – defence of the Catholic faith, affirmation of the divine basis of the Church, maintenance of the ordained apostolic ministry, and the efficacy and right observance of the sacraments.

The Church Question in the Stewartry (E, 1895), with H. M. B. Reid;* *The Ministry of Dr John Macleod in the Parish of Govan* (E, 1915); *The Ministry of Patrick Macdonald Playfair in St Andrews* (St Andrews, 1930); *The Blanket Preaching* (Galashiels, 1939).

FES II, 129, 198, 263, III, 414, VIII, 154.

D. F. Wright

Kirkton, James (1628–99), minister and historian. After holding charges at Lanark (1655–7) and at Mertoun in Berwickshire he was deprived in 1662 for nonconformity. He was offered an indulgence* at Carstairs in 1672, but refused to accept. In 1674 he was publicly denounced as a rebel, but apart from some minor brushes with the authorities he was able to avoid further persecution. Following the 1689 Revolution he ministered at the Tolbooth Church, Edinburgh, from 1691 to his death. His valuable *Church History*, though marred by an unsympathetic editor, gives insight into Church and state affairs at the Restoration* and after.

The History of Mr John Welsh, Minister at Ayr (E, 1703; rp. Wodrow Soc., *Select Biographies* (E, 1845), I, 1–61); *The Secret and True History of the Church of Scotland*, ed. C. Kirkpatrick Sharpe (E, 1817).

FES I, 119; *DNB* XXXI, 223–4.

M. Grant

Kirkwall, *see* Magnus, Saint; Orkney.

Kirkwood, James (c.1650–c.1709), assiduous advocate of Gaelic* literacy and distributor of Gaelic

Bibles (see Bible (Versions, Gaelic)). A native of Dunbar, Kirkwood trained at Edinburgh University and became a chaplain to the Earl of Breadalbane. An Episcopalian, he was briefly the incumbent of Minto parish (1679–81), but, refusing to take the Test Act* of 1681, he was 'outed', and settled as rector of Astwick, Bedfordshire. Failing to abjure in 1702, he returned to Scotland, where he apparently remained until his death.

Kirkwood's interest in Gaelic was probably kindled while acting as Breadalbane's chaplain. Thereafter he strove to provide Gaelic religious literature for the Highland* parishes, and he issued important memorials advocating the teaching of Gaelic through charity schools. He encountered considerable opposition, much of it within the Est.C,* and while his views contributed to the creation of the Scottish SPCK* in 1709, its initial policy of promoting English in its Highland schools was completely at variance with his life-long campaign.

Kirkwood was largely responsible for the introduction of Classical Gaelic Bibles to the Highlands. He obtained from the Irish philanthropist, Robert Boyle, surplus copies of Bedell's Old Testament and O'Donnell's New Testament, and tried to distribute these in Gaelic parishes. The scheme was only moderately successful. Kirkwood, again with Boyle's support, was also a prime mover in the making and distribution of 'Kirk's Bible' (see Kirk, Robert).

Kirkwood also enlisted the aid of the English SPCK in establishing parochial and presbyterial libraries throughout the Highlands, soliciting donations of both books and money in England. The libraries thus formed were a welcome addition to the meagre literary resources available to Highland ministers.

A Copy of a Letter anent a Project, for Erecting a Library, in every Presbytery . . . in the Highlands (E, 1702).

V. E. Durkacz, *The Decline of the Celtic Languages* (E, 1983), 17–30; D. MacKinnon, *The Gaelic Bible and Psalter* (Dingwall, 1930), 50–1.

D. E. Meek

Knight, George Angus Fulton (1909–), Presbyterian OT scholar. Born in Perth, he studied at Glasgow University 1927–35 (MA, 1930, with honours in Semitic languages, 1932; BD, 1935). Licensed by Glasgow CofS Presbytery in 1935, he was ordained the same year as a missionary to the Jews in Budapest. After serving as minister of Ruchill, Glasgow, from 1942, in 1947 he became Professor of OT Studies in Knox College, Dunedin, New Zealand. In 1959 he was appointed Lecturer in OT at St Andrews University, and then in 1960 took up the chair of OT in McCormick Theological Seminary, Chicago. In 1965 he became Principal of Pacific Theological College, Suva, Fiji. He retired from academic life in 1972, but was Moderator of the General Assembly of the Presbyterian Church of New Zealand in 1974. He continued to write, mostly on OT themes, but including an autobiography, *What Next? The Exciting Route Travelled* (E, 1980).

Knight's approach to the OT has been described as 'firmly in the orthodox liberal tradition of esteem for the Old Testament as the Word of God but insistence on a thoroughgoing reconstruction of the literature along critical lines as a necessary preliminary to theological assessment' (R. K. Harrison, *Introduction to the Old Testament*, n.p., 1969, 438). The distinguishing feature of Knight's OT theology (cf. *A Christian Theology of the Old Testament*, L, 1959) is its reluctance to interpret some portions of the OT as Christological over against others, since for Knight the OT is messianic in its totality.

A Biblical Approach to the Doctrine of the Trinity (E, 1953); *The Queen of the Danube: An Account of the Church of Scotland's Jewish Mission in Budapest* (E, 1937).

FES IX, 292, X, 172.

N. R. Needham

Knight, William Angus (1836–1916), Professor of Moral Philosophy in St Andrews, and Wordsworth scholar. Educated at Edinburgh University and New College, he was ordained in 1866 to St Enoch's FC, Dundee. In 1874 he and his congregation seceded from the FC and joined the CofS, after Dundee FC Presbytery had tried to discipline Knight for sentiments expressed in a discourse on prayer. In 1876 he was appointed Professor of Moral Philosophy in St Andrews. In 1879 he joined the EpCS.

Knight was a leading Wordsworth scholar. He founded the Wordsworth Society, edited eight volumes of its *Transactions* (1880–6), wrote and edited many books about Wordsworth, and donated his large collection of Wordsworthiana to the trustees of Dove Cottage, Grasmere (the Wordworths' old home). He performed a theological service to posterity by gathering and editing Rabbi Duncan's* conversations in *Colloquia Peripatetica* (E, 1870; ⁶1907). He received an LLD from Glasgow University in 1879.

FES V, 338–9, with list of works; AFCS I, 202.

N. R. Needham

Knights Hospitallers of St John. A military and religious order, the Knights of the Hospital of St John of Jerusalem are known also from places where they resided as 'Knights of Rhodes' and 'Knights of Malta'. Originally founded as a pilgrims' hospital at Jerusalem by Amalfitan merchants in the eleventh century, they soon became involved in the Crusades. Like the Knights Templars,* they came to Scotland in the reign of David I,* and were given by him Torphichen* (West Lothian) as the site of their 'preceptory'; it was ruled by a preceptor with a number of brothers, both knights and chaplains. They also had lands at Galtway in Galloway by gift of Fergus, lord of Galloway (d.1161), and a toft in each royal burgh by gift of King Malcolm IV (1153–65). During the twelfth and thirteenth centuries they built up a network of estates, tenements and churches, which was greatly increased on the suppression of the Templars (1312), with the rather greater wealth of the rival order passing to them before the end of Robert I's* reign (*d.* 1329). In the later Middle Ages the establishment became smaller, with, by the Reformation, a single knight brother ('Preceptor of Torphichen' or 'Lord of St Johns') administering the baronies, tenements and churches through a secular household. The main purposes of the Scottish preceptory were finance and recruitment; the latter was small-scale, but the preceptory continued to pay an annual cess (rate) to the Common Treasury of the Order until the Reformation. The Scottish preceptory was subject to the Priory of 'Tongue' of England; during the Great Schism (1378–1418) Scottish brothers attempted to break this relationship and establish a separate Scottish priory, but after the reunification of the Church the earlier dependence was restored. The last preceptor, James Sandilands, resigned all the Order's properties to Queen Mary in 1564, and (for a payment of 10,000 crowns) received back a grant of them as the hereditary barony of Torphichen.

I. B. Cowan *et al.* (eds), *Knights of St John of Jerusalem in Scotland* (SHS, E, 1983).

A. Macquarrie

Knights Templars, a military monastic order (cf. Knight Hospitallers of St John*) founded *c.* 1118 to defend the Holy Land from Islam. They adopted a form of the Cistercian* rule, and wore a white mantle with a red cross. The first master, Hugh de Paiens, visited Scotland in 1128 to recruit for the order and impressed David I,* who probably gave the Templars Balantrodoch (later Temple, Midlothian), which became its main Scottish preceptory (community). Under subsequent kings they were granted extensive lands throughout the country, notably the Maryculter estate, Kincardineshire. Other possessions included Aboyne on Deeside, Swanston (Midlothian), Temple Liston (now Kirkliston, W. Lothian) and Falkirk. Many Scots enlisted into the Templars' ranks in Palestine, but most Templars in the Scottish houses seem to have been English, for Scotland was part of the English province.

Templars often held positions in the royal household, but in Scotland as elsewhere they incurred increasing suspicion as a very wealthy society, rather secretive and independent of higher authority (their chaplains were subject to the Pope alone). The loss of the Holy Land after 1291 deprived them of their original *raison d'être*. Philip IV of France rounded up the French Templars in 1307 on a range of sinister charges, and helped persuade Pope Clement V to dissolve the order in 1312. The Scottish Templars were tried at Holyrood in November 1309, but the conflict between the English and the Scots frustrated an outcome until 1312. In time the Templars' properties passed to the Hospitallers, in whose ranks, as in other societies, many Templars continued to serve.

I. B. Cowan *et al.* (eds), *The Knights of St. John of Jerusalem in Scotland* (SHS, E, 1983), xvii–xxx;

41–8; J. Edwards, 'The Knights Templars in Scotland', *Trans. of Scott. Ecclesiol. Soc.* 4 (1912–15), 37–48; *id.*, 'The Templars in Scotland in the Thirteenth Century', *SHR* 5 (1908), 13–25; A. Coutts, 'The Knights Templars in Scotland', *RSCHS* 7 (1941), 126–40.

D. F. Wright

Knox, Andrew (1559–1633), Bishop of the Isles (1605–18). The second son of John Knox of Ranfurly in the parish of Kilbarchan (near Paisley), and educated under Andrew Melville's* new regime at Glasgow University (MA, 1579), Knox continued his theological studies there before entering the ministry at Lochwinnoch (Renfrewshire) by 1581 and at Paisley by 1585. He came to King James VI's* notice in 1592 when he discovered on Cumbrae a RC, George Kerr, bound for Spain, with certain blank papers signed by the conservative northern earls, which on Kerr's interrogation implicated them in a proposed Spanish invasion of Scotland. Knox's prominence in uncovering the 'Spanish blanks' no doubt assisted his promotion by the King to the bishopric of the Isles in 1605. As Bishop, he also gained the annexed abbacy of Iona* and priory of Ardchattan (Argyll) and from 1611 held the Irish bishopric of Raphoe (until his death). As Bishop of the Isles, which he demitted in 1618, Knox was one of the King's most strenuous servants in promoting royal policy in the Hebrides. At Iona a number of Hebridean chiefs met the Bishop in 1609 and accepted a series of measures designed to further the work of the Reformed Church in the Western Isles and schooling as a means of inculcating lowland values and culture. His son, Thomas, who succeeded as Bishop in 1619, continued to promote the 'statutes of Iona'* with some success.

BUK; Calderwood, V; J. Durkan and J. Kirk, *The University of Glasgow, 1451–1577* (G, 1977), 375, 379, 381; *FESMA*, 206; *FES* III, 152, 162; VII, 348; J. B. Craven, *Records of the Dioceses of Argyll and the Isles* (Kirkwall, 1907), 36; J. Kirk, *Patterns of Reform* (E, 1989), 485–6; *DNB* XXXI, 306–8.

J. Kirk

Knox Club, anti-RC society. It was founded in Edinburgh in 1909 with three aims: to promote the study of Scottish history, and especially the age of John Knox;* to maintain the Protestant succession to the throne; and to resist the efforts of the RCC to regain influence in Scotland. During 1909–23 it published fifty-six items, many reprints (e.g. D. Hay Fleming's *A Jesuit's Misconception of Scottish History...*, E, 1916, from the *BW**). With branches in Glasgow, Aberdeen and Belfast, its membership topped 3,000 by 1912. It kept a watchful eye on RC educational movements, and organized widespread protests against *Ne Temere*, the papal decree condemning mixed marriages. Its president was Dr Thomas Burns, FRSE, and its vice-president D. Hay Fleming.* Its honorary president was Lord Kinnaird (1847–1923; *Who Was Who, 1916–28*, 589), and honorary vice-presidents included the moderators or their counterparts in virtually all the Scottish Protestant churches, together with other eminent churchmen, such as H. R. Mackintosh,* Alexander Whyte* and George Adam Smith.*

See Anti-Catholic Societies.

D. F. Wright

Knox, John (*c.* 1514–72), Scottish Reformer. Born at Haddington, educated at St Andrews,* probably under the conciliarist and scholastic John Major,* Knox was ordained by the Bishop of Dunblane* (1536). Later he served as a notary (by 1540) in his native town and as a private tutor (by 1543). Thomas Guillaume* (Gilyem, Gwilliam) converted him to Protestantism and he subsequently came under the influence of John Rough* and George Wishart,* a student of Lutheran* and Swiss theology. It was probably through Wishart that Knox acquired his sense of prophetic vocation.

In 1547, after Wishart's martyrdom (1546), Knox went to St Andrews, where he received a call to preach the gospel. When the castle fell, he was sent to France where he became a galley slave for nineteen months. During this period, he wrote a summary of Henry Balnaves's* compendium of Protestant thought based on Luther's commentary on Galatians. In this early work, Knox demonstrated his acceptance of Luther's doctrine of justification.*

After his release in 1549, Knox went to England, where he stayed until 1554. He was appointed preacher at Berwick, where his attack on the mass as idolatry caused him to be called before the Council of the North (1550) to answer for his views. In 1551 he was made a chaplain to Edward VI and as such assisted in the revision of the *Book of Common Prayer*. He criticized the provision calling for kneeling during communion and appears to have been chiefly responsible for the inclusion of the declaration on kneeling – the 'Black Rubric'. Knox was offered the bishopric of Rochester, which he refused for reasons that are not completely clear. Though he criticized the details of English ecclesiastical policy, he generally approved of the religious climate that prevailed in Edwardian England.

The accession of the RC Mary Tudor to the throne of England brought many changes. Within a few months, events drove Knox into exile (January 1554). From this time until the deposition of Mary* Stewart in Scotland some thirteen years later, he was more or less preoccupied with the problems of the 'faithful Christian' confronted by 'idolatry' (i.e., RCism) and above all else by an 'idolatrous' sovereign. Shortly after arriving in Dieppe, Knox completed *An Admonition or Warning* (also printed as *A Godly Letter* . . . , L?, 1554), urging 'true Christians' not to participate in idolatry, that is, the RC mass. He then moved on to Switzerland where he met with Calvin,* Bullinger and other Reformed leaders, posing questions on rebellion against idolatrous monarchs and female sovereigns. Knox returned to Dieppe for a short while where he wrote *A Faythfull Admonition* (Emden, 1554), a long publication in which he attacked Mary Tudor directly and argued that England was repeating the idolatrous history of Israel.

In 1554 Knox left for Geneva, but at Calvin's urging, he soon headed for Frankfurt where he became pastor to the English congregation. A dispute over the *Book of Common Prayer* led to his departure and return to Geneva in 1555. But he did not stay long, returning the same year to Scotland. Here he openly preached Protestant doctrine with considerable success. Knox was summoned to appear in Edinburgh in May 1556 on a charge of heresy, but the intervention of the regent Mary of Guise* resulted in a quashing of the summons. But continuing persecution of Protestants led him in 1556 to accept a call to the English church at Geneva, where he published several tracts concerning problems in Scotland and England. Though he addressed several subjects, political issues received the most attention. In four pamphlets published in 1558, the Reformer set forth clearly his views on the rights of subjects against idolatrous and oppressive rulers. Most notable was *The First Blast of the Trumpet against the Monstrous Regiment of Women*, (Geneva, 1558), in which he argued that female sovereignty contravened natural and divine law. In a subsequent tract (*The Appellation . . . of Iohn Knoxe from the cruell and most injust sentence . . . with his supplication and exhortation to the nobilitie, estates, and communaltie* . . . , Geneva, 1558), Knox utilized OT models as a basis of his appeal to the nobles to compel religious reforms and as a summons to the common people to pressure the rulers toward the same objective. Knox stated unequivocally that the nobles had the right to remove an unrepentant monarch, while the commonality could set up their own 'reformed kirk' if their rulers failed to act. It was, however, *The First Blast* that gained for Knox a reputation among his contemporaries of being a revolutionary. Though he aimed *The First Blast* primarily at Mary Tudor, shortly after its appearance Elizabeth became Queen of England, making Knox's name odious in her court. During his sojourn in Geneva, Knox also addressed another subject – predestination. In this, his longest writing, he defended the Calvinist* doctrine against attack by 'an Anabaptist'.

The Protestant Lords of the Congregation* sought Knox's return to Scotland and he arrived in May 1559. Becoming minister of Edinburgh and a leader of the Reforming party, he devoted himself to preaching and to procuring money and troops from England. After the death of Mary of Guise, Knox, along with John Willock* and others, drew up a confession of faith (the Scots Confession*), which Parliament approved in August 1560. The authority of the pope was abolished and the celebration of the mass was proscribed. With Willock, John Douglas* and three others, Knox also drafted the *(First) Book of Discipline*,* which was in effect the Knoxian reform programme. After Mary's return to Scotland in 1561, Knox came into repeated conflicts with the Queen over her desire for the mass and the worldliness of her court. In 1561–2 he engaged in a controversy on ordination with Ninian

Winzet,* a RC priest and educator. Knox claimed that, like Amos and John the Baptist, he had an extraordinary calling, although he lacked the miraculous power to prove it. Knox also disputed with Quintin Kennedy,* abbot of Crossraguel (*see* Cluniacs), on the mass.

Meanwhile the conflict with Mary reached its conclusion. After Darnley's murder, she was captured and Knox demanded her execution. After her abdication, he preached at the coronation of her son, James VI.* Knox now became closely connected with the regent, James Stewart,* the Earl of Moray. After the murder of Moray in 1570, Knox's political power diminished, though his fundamental cause triumphed.

Knox did not see himself as an academic theologian or as a political theorist. His vocation was to be a preacher of the gospel and not a writer or an ecclesiastical organizer or official. Therefore, his main duty in life was 'to blow my master's trumpet'. Nevertheless, Knox wrote frequently and produced pamphlets, his *History of the Reformation of Religion in Scotland* ... (L, 1587; in effect his memoirs, with numerous documents), and numerous letters, filling in all six volumes in David Laing's edition. Yet his writings were not systematic, but were penned in response to concrete problems.

One exception is the *Book of Common Order, The Forme of Prayers* (E, 1564),* largely based on the *Forme of Prayers* prepared by Knox and others for the English-speaking congregations in Frankfurt and Geneva. Its austerely Reformed, didactic tone set an influential pattern for Scottish worship, with a simple order for the Lord's Supper in which scriptural reading, exhortation and exposition, together with extended extempore prayer, exclude any concern for traditional liturgical proprieties.

Though Knox adhered to basic Reformed principles, he particularly strove for a corporate return of Scottish religion to the ideal of spiritual Israel. He planned to use the 'Christian Commonwealth' as the primary instrument for restoring the purity of Scottish religion, with both civil and ecclesiastical powers co-operating in the cultivation of 'true religion'. He believed that government had a responsibility for establishing 'true religion' and abolishing everything contrary to it.

Knox's most distinctive positions concerned the purification of worship and resistance to idolatrous rulers. For these notions he was indebted to many sources, but first and foremost to the Bible, which he interpreted with both a considerable attention to the Old Testament and a pronounced literalness. Drawing from Deut. 12:32, he insisted that everything in worship be done according to the specifications of Scripture. All else Knox regarded as idolatry and to be resisted. Because of the mass in particular, he virtually equated RC religion with idolatry. The fight against the 'idolatrous' mass so dominated his thinking that virtually no major area of his thought was free from it. Increasingly, Knox developed his anti-idolatry theme in a political context and as a springboard to resistance against political authority. The obstacle to the reformation of religion in Scotland was the RCC established by law and promoted by the civil power. Thus Knox advocated the overthrow of established temporal authority (incurring the disapproval of continental Reformers), the seizure of political power, and the use of that power to establish the Reformed faith.

The exact extent of Knox's influence on his contemporaries and posterity is a matter of debate, but there can be no doubt that he came to be seen as the leading figure in the Scottish Reformation, playing a major role in the overthrow of RCism and the establishment of the Reformed Kirk. Although never formally made superintendent* (provided for in the *FBD*), Knox in effect acted as such – even as arch-superintendent. While Scotland might have had some form of Reformation without Knox, it was from him that the Scottish Reformation received much of its character and direction. What frustrated his particular blueprint of reform as much as any other factor was the vexed question of the 'patrimony' of the Kirk. The property-owning classes proved unwilling to accede to the demands of the Reformers for sufficient revenues to finance the wide-ranging programme set out in the *FBD*.

The Works of John Knox, ed. D. Laing, 6 vols (E, 1846–64); *John Knox's History of the Reformation in Scotland*, ed. W. C. Dickinson, 2 vols (E, 1949).

W. S. Reid, *Trumpeter of God* (NY, 1974); J. Ridley, *John Knox* (O, 1962); R. Kyle, *The Mind of John Knox* (Lawrence, Kansas, 1984); R. Greaves, *Theology and Revolution in the Scottish Reformation* (Grand Rapids, 1980); E. Percy, *John Knox* (^{2}L, 1964); P. Janton, *John Knox, l'homme et l'oeuvre* (Paris, 1972); I. Hazlett, 'A Working Bibliography of Writings by John Knox', in *Calviniana*, ed. R. V. Schnucker (*Sixteenth Century Essays and Studies* X; Kirksville, MO, 1988), 185–93; *TRE* 19, 281–7; *FES* I, 49–50; *DNB* XXXI, 308–28; H. R. Sefton, *John Knox* (E, 1993).

R. G. *Kyle*

Knox's Liturgy, *see Book of Common Order* (1564).

Knox, William, *see* Scottish School Book Association.

Korea, *see* Missions; Ross, John.

Kravar (Crawar, Craw, Cravar), Paul (*d.* 1433), Hussite and martyr.* A Moravian, he was educated at Paris and Montpellier, admitted in 1416 to the Faculty of Medicine in Prague and subsequently physician to Ladislas, king of Poland. Converted to the views of Wyclif and Hus, he joined the Praguites, one of the more moderate of the Bohemian reforming parties. Questioning the virtue of auricular confession and adoration of saints, he advocated Communion in both kinds, while denying transubstantiation. If authorship of *De Anatomia Antichristi* and *Sermones de Antichristo* is unlikely, his unorthodox opinions nevertheless cost him his position. About 1432 Kravar came to Scotland from Prague to seek support for the Hussite cause at the Council of Basel (and not directly in answer to an appeal to Prague in 1410 by the Scot, Quintin Folkhyrde).

After preaching at St Andrews he was accused by Laurence of Lindores,* inquisitor of heretical pravity, of the views noted above and was burned at the stake on 23 July 1433, a brass ball being allegedly placed in his mouth to prevent him addressing the onlookers.

T. M. A. MacNab, 'Bohemia and the Scottish Lollards', *RSCHS* 5 (1935), 10-22; L. Moonan, 'Pavel Kravar, and Some Writings Once Attributed to Him', *IR* 27 (1976), 3-23; M. Spinka, 'Paul Kravar and the Lollard-Hussite Relations', *CH* 25 (1956), 16-26.

I. B. Cowan

Kyle, James (1788-1869), RC Bishop and scholar. He was born in Edinburgh and educated at the Royal High School and at Aquhorties (*see* Colleges and Seminaries, RC). In 1808, too young for ordination, he joined the Aquhorties teaching staff, setting up a printing press. He attended Edinburgh University 1810-11 and was ordained priest at Aquhorties 1812. He continued teaching there, being prefect of studies from 1815. He also began collecting and organizing the surviving records of the Scottish Mission. In 1826 he was sent as assistant priest to Glasgow. In September 1828 he was consecrated Bishop of Germanicia and was first Vicar-apostolic of the northern vicariate. He settled at Preshome, Banffshire, rather than Aberdeen, owing to the intractability of Charles Gordon.*

During Kyle's forty-year episcopacy chapels were built, new mission stations founded, schools opened and communities of nuns established. His archival collection, begun at Aquhorties, expanded, and important documents were published. Kyle himself de-coded the cipher correspondence of Mary Queen of Scots.* His reputation as a churchman and scholar was considerable.

J. K. Robertson, 'Young Mr Kyle and his Circle', *IR* 1 (1950), 35-47; *id.*, 'The Bishop Looks at his Diocese', *IR* 3 (1952), 22-32; *Catholic Directory for Scotland*, 1870, 135-41.

C. Johnson

L

Laidlaw, John (1832–1906), FC divine. Born in Edinburgh, he studied arts at Edinburgh University 1851–4. He then attended the Reformed Presbyterian* divinity hall 1854–6, and New College,* Edinburgh, 1856–8. He was ordained to Bannockburn FC in 1859, moving to the West Church, Perth in 1863, and the West Church, Aberdeen in 1872. In 1881 he was appointed Professor of Systematic Theology at New College, a position he held until 1904.

Laidlaw adhered closely to the Westminster Confession* in his theology, and was not well-disposed towards higher criticism, although he counselled caution and moderation in the Robertson Smith* case. He was a zealous proponent of Presbyterian reunion, playing a leading part in the union between the Reformed Presbyterians and the FC in 1876. He entered the UFC in 1900.

Laidlaw's two principal works were *The Biblical Doctrine of Man* (E, 1879; ^{2}1895), the Cunningham lectures* for 1878, and *The Miracles of Our Lord* (E, 1890).

Laidlaw received a DD from Edinburgh University in 1880.

J. Laidlaw, *Studies in the Parables* (E, 1907); *Foundation Truths of Scripture as to Sin and Salvation* (E, 1897). He rendered into English and wrote a biographical introduction to Robert Bruce's* *Sermons on the Sacrament* (E, 1901).

H. R. Mackintosh, 'Memoir' prefaced to Laidlaw's *Studies in the Parables*; *DNB Second Suppl.* II, 411–12; *FUFCS* 578; *AFCS* I, 56.

N. R. Needham

Laing, David (1793–1878), historical editor. Thirty years a bookseller and forty-two years librarian of the Signet Library, Edinburgh (1837–78), Laing is now remembered as editor of over a hundred Scottish historical texts such as R. Baillie's* *Letters and Journals*, 3 vols (E, 1841–2); John Knox's* *Works*, 6 vols (E, 1846–64); and *The Gude and Godlie Ballates** (E, 1868). He was secretary and chief organizer of the Bannatyne Club throughout its life (1823–61). To Edinburgh University Library he bequeathed over 5,000 historical manuscripts which include illuminated books of hours as well as MSS of Burns,* Scott,* Wodrow* and Knox, and a collection of 3,300 Scottish charters.

DNB XXXI, 401–2; G. Goudie, *David Laing LL.D., a Memoir of his Life and Literary Work* (E, 1913); H. Paton, *Report on the Laing Manuscripts Preserved in the University of Edinburgh*, 2 vols (L, 1914–25); J. Anderson, *Calendar of the Laing Charters* (E, 1899); A. S. Bell (ed.), *The Scottish Antiquarian Tradition* (E, 1981), 69–81, 86–113.

J. V. Howard

Laing, John (1809–80), librarian and bibliographer. Born at Dalmeny, he studied at nearby Edinburgh and was ordained to Livingston CofS (1842), becoming FC minister there at the Disruption* (1843–6). Ill-health took him as military chaplain to Gibraltar and Malta (1846–50), but he suffered also from 'an invincible repugnance to appear in public'. From 1854 to his death, he was librarian of New College,* Edinburgh, producing a *Catalogue* of its printed and MS collections (E, 1868) and ordering the library with skill and enthusiasm. He completed the compilation, begun by Samuel Halkett (*d.* 1871), of *A Dictionary of Anonymous and Pseudonymous Literature of Great Britain*, finally produced by a daughter (4 vols, E, 1882–8). His successor, James Kennedy, oversaw a much enlarged edition (7 vols, E, 1926–34).

AFCS I, 203; *DNB* XXXI, 403–4; H. Watt, *New College Edinburgh. A Centenary History* (E, 1946).

D. F. Wright

Laity, a common designation of church members who are not ordained clergy that until recently had no secure place in Scottish Reformed usage. The word comes from the Greek *laos*, 'people', which is used in the New Testament of the whole people of God (e.g. 1 Pet. 2:9–10, where 'priesthood' likewise describes the whole body). 'Laity' has been most at home in traditions operating with a restricted 'priesthood', but its convenience as a way of referring to the un-ordained has earned it wider currency in Churches like the CofS. Theologically, however, it cannot be justified, for the ordained belong to the *laos* of God. Reformed churchmen who object to the clerical–lay distinction may nevertheless be found using a similarly questionable differentiation between ministers and members – as though ministers are not members of the Church. Some even argue that ministers are not, or should not be, members of the congregation they serve.

In all its manifestations the Reformation protested against the medieval relegation of the lay and the 'secular' to second-class status below the clerical and the 'religious' (monks and nuns). This protest found expression in various ways: an emphasis on the general priesthood of believers, a theology that spoke of Church before it spoke of ministry, the restoration of the Communion cup to all worshippers, the availability of vernacular Scriptures and service-books to the people, an insistence that all callings (vocations) are of equal dignity before God, and provision for the election of ministers by the whole congregation (e.g. *FBD* 96).

In the CofS and similar Presbyterian Churches the clergy–laity division is made more problematic still by the practice of ordaining non-teaching elders.* The epithet 'lay' probably first became common in the Kirk in the seventeenth-century controversy between 'presbyter-elder' and 'lay-elder' theories (G. D. Henderson, *The Scottish Ruling Elder*, L., 1935, 187–225). George Gillespie,* Samuel Rutherford,* Alexander Henderson,* James Renwick* and others rejected the 'lay-elder' view partly because the clerical–lay divide was Romanist. The argument continued and the two views were clearly distinguished in the nineteenth century, with P. C. Campbell* a forceful advocate of the lay-theory. A similar division of opinion has surfaced at intervals throughout the twentieth century. From 1900 to 1921 the Elders' Union of the CofS sponsored the annual publication of *The Layman's Book of the General Assembly*, 'a popular reproduction' of the proceedings for elders and Church members in general.

'Lay preachers' have played a less prominent role in the CofS than in many Reformation Churches, although the Men* were a remarkable exception – 'an ecclesiastically unofficial, but religiously significant order of evangelical laymen'. The Covenanting* cause fostered lay preaching, and through societies such as SSPCK* laymen fulfilled valuable ministries as missionaries, catechists and schoolmasters.

Today the CofS appoints 'lay-missionaries' (Cox 677) and employs other 'lay-agents' such as lay evangelists, yet its readers* are not 'lay-readers'. 'Laity' is often used to champion the essential contribution of the unordained, as in 'the ministry of the laity' (cf. H. Kraemer, *A Theology of the Laity*, L, 1958; G. D. Henderson, *The Burning Bush*, E, 1957, 206–18: 'The Witness of the Laity'). The leading aim of the Tell Scotland* movement was 'to recruit and train the lay forces of the Church for the task of witness through congregational groups', a task carried on by St Ninian's Crieff.* Nevertheless, a heading such as 'The Place of the Laity in the Church' in *The Anglican–Presbyterian Conversations* (E, L, 1966, 38–41) reflects an ethos alien to the CofS. The unfinished reformation of the Church calls for a recasting of the doctrines of Church and ministry that will guard against the ever-present lure of clericalism and sacerdotalism (seen especially in the restriction to clergy of activities that truly belong to God's whole people, e.g. ministry, priesthood, celebration) without resorting to terms like 'laity'.

This challenge is no less sharp for non-Presbyterian Churches, even though some have shown a greater willingness to perceive all (lay) members as an integral part of the 'total ministry' of the local church and its wider associations. Baptists,* who have laid great stress on the priesthood of all believers, have sometimes recognized teaching elders as part of a plurality of lay elders in the leadership of a church. This was the pattern adopted by the Scotch Baptists,* and remained characteristic of this body until its demise (in Scotland) in the 1920s (D. Bebbington, 'The Decline of the Scotch Baptist Plural Eldership', *The Ministry Today*, G, 1988, 30–4). Thereafter it was replaced by the single, full-time pastor, with deacons, a model followed from the early 1800s by the so-called 'English' Baptist churches and also by Independent* churches derived from the Haldane* movement. In the past (especially in the nineteenth century), both Baptists* and Independents have utilized lay missionaries, especially in rural evangelism (*see* Haldane Preachers), and have usually ordained them only after the formation of viable churches. The loss of missionary impetus after 1900 and the growing emphasis on the local congregation have been factors in the gradual removal of the concept of the lay missionary, leading to his replacement by the ordained minister. However, lay preachers are recognized within a specific Lay Preachers' Association within the Baptist Union of Scotland,* and the Presidency of the Union alternates between lay and ordained holders. Nevertheless, the tension between full recognition of 'lay ministry' and 'ordained ministry' remains problematic within the movement, and is probably most acute within gathered congregations of a strongly independent or separatist nature. Such independency may encourage a type of sacerdotalism, whereas connexionalism induces a wider range of support systems, with greater utilization of the laity. Within the Brethren* there is a growing tendency to appoint or recognzie Bible-teachers and men of pastoral gifts as leaders within churches, thus creating at least a practical distinction within their traditional framework of non-clerical ministry.

In Methodism* also lay, or local, preachers have always played a significant role. Prominent early figures included Duncan Wright (1736–91), Thomas Rankin (1738–1810) and Alexander Mather* (A. Fawcett, 'Scottish Lay Preachers in the Eighteenth Century', *RSCHS* 12, 1958, 97–119).

D. E. Meek and D. F. Wright

Lamberton, William de (*d.* 1328), Bishop of St Andrews 1298-1328. Lamberton was Chancellor of the diocese of Glasgow when he was elected Bishop of St Andrews in 1297. Edward I of England objected that the election had been forced on the cathedral chapter by William Wallace, but it was confirmed by Pope Boniface VIII. He was imprisoned by Edward at Winchester in 1306 but released to go to Rome in 1308. In 1310 he presided at a meeting of the Scottish bishops in Dundee which recognized Robert the Bruce* as King of Scots. Many charters survive bearing Lamberton's name. He consecrated the cathedral of St Andrews in the presence of King Robert, and was buried on the north side of the high altar.

D. McRoberts (ed.), *The Medieval Church of St Andrews* (G, 1976).

H. R. Sefton

Lamond, Mary (1860-1948), women's leader in the CofS. She was one of the first residents of Deaconess House, Edinburgh, and was set apart as a deaconess (*see* Diaconate) in 1894. Thereafter she devoted herself to the development of women's work and role within the CofS. In 1901 she became editor of the *Life and Work** Woman's Guild* Supplement, and 1905-11 was the full-time honorary Secretary of the WG. From 1911 she was Superintendent of Deaconess House. She was the most prominent woman in the Church as National President of the WG 1920-32. She reshaped its organization, strengthening its representative and Presbyterian character by introducing Presbyterial Councils, and linking all the women's organizations for missions and temperance under the aegis of the Guild. She was a dynamic and persuasive participant in negotiations leading to the 1929 Church Union,* so that the united CofS had at its heart a powerful and co-ordinated network to promote and utilize women's work. In 1948 it was written of her: 'Among all the succession of talented women who have contributed so largely to the success and growth of the Guild, there has been no one who played a more notable part than Miss Lamond. Indeed there are many now serving in the WG who were first won over to this work by her great and happy enthusiasm, deep sincerity, keen sense of humour, and unbounded faith in the future of the Guild' (quoted in D. P. Thomson, *Women of the Scottish Church*, 308).

But Lamond was not content simply to build up effective women's organizations – she sought real equality of office and opportunity. As the only female speaker at the 1929 Union Assembly, she had to respond, on behalf of all churchwomen, to paeans of praise for their 'selfless devotion': 'The women workers of the CofS thank the Assembly for recognition of their services ... I would say they are quite worthy of any encouragement. Perhaps they are also worthy of a greater share in Church counsels than you have yet given them.' She sought every chance to promote such an enlarged share, and was an Honorary Vice-President of the Fellowship of Equal Service, whose objects included the eligibility of women for ministry and eldership.

Lamond exemplified the qualities of intelligence, energy, faith and vision which characterized a succession of female Church leaders at a crucial period of change for women and for the Church.

See *LW Woman's Guild Supplement*, 1901-26, and *Women's Work in the Church*, 1926-9; M. Magnusson, *Out of Silence* (E, 1987), 96-100.

L. O. Macdonald

Lamont, Daniel (1869-1950), Scots theologian. He was born on the island of Bute. On graduating MA (Glasgow) in 1892 he spent four years as University Assistant in Mathematics before entering the FC College, Glasgow. In his fourth year there he assisted George Adam Smith* in teaching Hebrew. After filling UF pastorates in Kilmarnock, Newington (Edinburgh), Hillhead (Glasgow) and Helensburgh, he was elected (1927) to the Chair of Apologetics in New College,* Edinburgh. This was merged (1939) in a new University Chair of Christian Ethics and Practical Theology, from which he retired in 1945. His publications included *Christ and the World of Thought* (E, 1934), *The Anchorage of Life* (L, 1940), and the posthumously published *Studies in the Johannine Writings* (L, 1956).

He was Moderator of the General Assembly of the CofS in 1936. His evangelical sympathies were shown by his presidency of the Fourth Calvinistic Congress held in Edinburgh in 1938, his presidency of the Inter-Varsity Fellowship* (1945-5) and his vice-chairmanship of the *Evangelical Quarterly** Advisory Committee (1942-50). He was president of the Scottish National Dictionary Association.

G. R. Logan, 'Daniel Lamont: A Memoir of his Life', in D. Lamont, *Studies in the Johannine Writings* (L, 1956), 11-62; *FUFCS* 578; *FES* IX, 772.

F. F. Bruce

Lamont, Donald (1874-1958), distinguished Gaelic* writer. Born in Tiree, Lamont studied at Raining's School, Inverness, and Edinburgh University. He became a CofS minister, first (from 1902) in Glen Urquhart and later (1908-46) in Blair Atholl, Perthshire. From 1907 to 1950 Lamont was editor of the Gaelic Supplement to *Life and Work.** Besides sermons from different pens, it contained regular contributions from Lamont himself.

Lamont used two main literary forms, the essay and the short story, and contributed greatly to their development in Gaelic. An essay series entitled 'Anns a' Choille Bheithe' ('In the Birch Wood') drew lessons from the behaviour of animals. Other essays were more topical, ranging from MacBrayne steamers to 'alternative medicine'; contemporary matters were often discussed, and views vigorously expressed. Some of Lamont's short stories were set safely in an imaginary Highland village, Cille Sgumain. The foibles of its inhabitants were splen-

LANG, ANDREW

didly delineated, as in 'Taghadh a' Mhinisteir' ('Choosing the Minister'), a humorous satire on the criteria used by church folk on such occasions. Sometimes his satire could be more biting, and ministerial targets were not avoided. A rather verbose minister who received a civil decoration became the subject of an essay entitled 'The Reverend Theodore Boanerges Pom-Pom, OBE', explaining that the award had been given because he had used his voice as a fog-horn during the war. Under such lively editorship, the Gaelic Supplement achieved a level of creative wrting which has not been matched since.

T. M. Murchison (ed.), *The Prose Writings of Donald Lamont* (E, 1960).

D. E. Meek

Lang, Andrew (1844–1912), anthropologist, historian of religions and of Scotland and one of the most highly regarded literary figures of his age. Born in Selkirk in the Scottish Borders, after graduating he became Fellow of Merton College, Oxford. In 1873 he took up journalism and moved to London, continuing to pursue his anthropological interests in journal articles and books. During the latter half of the nineteenth century unilineal evolutionary theory dominated anthropological approaches to the study of religion. Scholars such as E. B. Tylor and J. F. McLennan* believed that the religions of non-literate peoples, characterized by animism and totemism, represented the lowest forms of religion. In *Myth, Ritual and Religion*, 2 vols (L, 1887) Lang used their ideas to develop a theory of myth in opposition to prevailing philological theories. Later, in *The Making of Religion* (L, 1898), Lang challenged anthropological theory itself. As a result of further researches into the reports of missionaries and others, Lang found that many of the least technologically advanced peoples, far from having the lowest religions, believe in a moral and creative High God. Although this was rejected by Lang's contemporaries, the High God is now recognized as a feature of many primal religions.

Lang was particularly well-known for his historical works. Although written for a broad audience, they were not devoid of genuine historical research. They included: *A History of Scotland from the Roman Occupation*, 4 vols (E, 1900–7); *John Knox and the Reformation* (L, 1905); *The Mystery of Mary Stuart* (L, 1902); *James VI and the Gowrie Mystery* (L, 1902); *Sir George Mackenzie, King's Advocate* (L, 1909); *Prince Charles Edward Stuart the Young Chevalier* (L, 1900).

DNB 1912–1921, 319–23; *Who Was Who, 1897–1916*, 409; P. J. Baylis, 'Andrew Lang and the Study of Religion in the Victorian Era' (PhD, Aberdeen University, 1987); R. L. Green, *Andrew Lang* (Leicester, 1946); E. J. Sharpe, *Comparative Religion* (L, 1975).

P. J. Baylis

Lang, John Dunmore (1799–1878), New South Wales's first Presbyterian minister; politician, journalist and emigration* agent. Born in Greenock and

LANG, JOHN MARSHALL

educated at Glasgow University (MA, 1820; DD, 1825), he was influenced by Thomas Chalmers's* Tron ministry. Ordained in the CofS in 1822, Lang emigrated on his brother's advice that Sydney's Scottish settlers required a Presbyterian minister, and from 1826 until his death he pastored the Scots Church which he founded.

An assiduous writer and traveller, Lang established three newspapers and published almost 300 books and pamphlets. His first major work, *An Historical and Statistical Account of New South Wales* (L, 1834, ⁴1874), was completed during the third of nine trips to Britain, undertaken to recruit ministers and Christian settlers and to seek public and government support for religious, educational and colonization projects. Lang advocated selective Protestant emigration to relieve poverty in Britain and effect the moral regeneration of Australian society, dominated by convicts and RCs. The success of his first recruits – fifty-four 'Scotch Mechanics' and their families who accompanied him to Sydney in 1831 to build a Presbyterian college – led him to organize several further emigrant parties, including nearly 4,000 impoverished Highlanders in 1837.

Lang's outspokenness in ecclesiastical and political affairs provoked hostility and he was four times imprisoned for debt and libel. Yet for fifty years he remained Australia's* best-known Scot, and his funeral – which attracted several thousand mourners – brought Sydney to a standstill.

FES VII, 591–2; *DNB* XXXII, 89–91; D. W. A. Baker, *Days of Wrath* (Melbourne, 1985); M. D. Prentis, *The Scots in Australia* (Sydney, 1983); I. F. McLaren, *John Dunmore Lang: a Comprehensive Bibliography* (Parkville, Victoria, 1985); I. H. Murray, *Australian Christian Life from 1788* (E, 1988).

M. Harper

Lang, John Marshall (1834–1909), CofS minister and educator. Lang was the son of Gavin Lang minister of Glasford, Lanarkshire. He was educated at the University of Glasgow. Following earlier ministries in Aberdeen (1856–8), Fyvie (1858–65), Anderston in Glasgow (1865–8) and Morningside (1868–73), Edinburgh, he was minister of the Barony Church, Glasgow (1873–1900), and Principal of the University of Aberdeen (1900–9). A man of broad interests and liberal sympathies, Lang was associated with the High Church party in the CofS, a member of Scottish Church Society,* and of the Scottish Christian Social Union.* In Glasgow he championed a minimum 'living wage' for the lowest paid workers, argued for an end to sweated labour, and became an advocate of state support for improved working-class housing. Along with other prominent Presbyterian churchmen such as Robert Rainy,* he took a leading role on the side of the workers in the famous Scottish Railway strike of 1890–1. While he was Principal in Aberdeen, Lang was instrumental in the completion of the new Marischal College.* His most notable works are his Duff lecture,* *The Ex-*

LANG, WILLIAM COSMO GORDON

pansion of the Christian Life (E, 1897), and his Baird lecture,* The Church and its Social Mission (E, 1902). He was awarded a DD (1873) and an LLD (1901) by Glasgow University.

FES I, 85, III, 390, 395, VI, 5, 258, VIII, 289, 715; DNB Second Suppl. II, 414-15.

D. C. Smith

Lang, William Cosmo Gordon (1864-1945), Archbishop of Canterbury. Lang was the son of John Marshall Lang.* Educated at Glasgow University and Balliol College, Oxford, he became President of the Union and was elected a Fellow of All Souls in 1888. Lang was confirmed an Anglican in 1889 and ordained in 1890, becoming Dean of Divinity at Magdalen College and vicar of St Mary's, Oxford. In 1896 he became vicar of Portsea, Portsmouth, where, assisted by sixteen curates, he demonstrated the strength of the CofE's parochial ministry.

In 1901 he was appointed Bishop of Stepney, a labour for the poor requiring his pastoral gifts. In 1908 he became Archbishop of York and in 1914 created the new diocese of Sheffield. In 1928 he was translated to Canterbury, and presided over the Lambeth Conference of 1930. His theology was Anglo-Catholic, tempered by his national conception of Anglicanism. He was a handsome, golden-tongued preacher, admired and consulted by Victoria and George V. Like his close colleague Randall Davidson,* whose moderate policies he shared and continued, he was an indefatigable administrator with ecumenical interests in the dissenters and Orthodox. He provoked two public controversies, the one by a favourable reference in 1914 to the Kaiser, and the other by his speech in 1936 on the abdication of Edward VIII, both informed by his heightened sense of history. He resigned in 1942.

J. G. Lockhart, Cosmo Gordon Lang (L, 1949); DNB 1941-50, 474-8.

S. Gilley

Latin America, see Missions; Free Church of Scotland; MacKay, John A.; Chaplaincies, Colonial; Thomson, James; Darien Colony; Kalley, Robert R.

Laud, William (1573-1645), Archbishop of Canterbury from 1633, held responsible for the imposition of 'Laud's Liturgy' on Scotland in 1637. A clothier's son from Reading, Berkshire, he was educated at St John's College, Oxford (BA, 1594; MA, 1598; BD, 1604; DD, 1608) and ordained priest in 1601. In 1608 he became chaplain to Richard Neile, Bishop of Rochester. Neile belonged to the emerging Arminian* party that found favour in the early 1620s with the ageing James VI and I,* and, significantly, with the future Charles I.* Neile's influence secured Laud's rise: President of St John's, 1611; a royal chaplain, 1614; Dean of Gloucester, 1616; Bishop of St David's, Wales, 1621. Under Charles I, helped by the political weakness of the Calvinist Archbishop of Canter-

LAUDER, ALEXANDER

bury, George Abbot, his power grew: Bishop of Bath and Wells, 1626; Privy Councillor, 1627; Bishop of London, 1628; Chancellor of Oxford University, 1629; Archbishop of Canterbury, 1633, following Abbott. Laud sought unity through uniformity in England, enforcing the Book of Common Prayer* and its ceremonies and suppressing Calvinist preaching and polemic. A turning point came in 1637, with attempts to bring the Book of Common Prayer to Scotland. Laud and Charles I wanted to impose the English liturgy without change, but Charles deferred to the Scottish Bishops' advice that revision was necessary. Laudian sympathizers, Bishops John Maxwell,* Thomas Sydserf* and James Wedderburn,* led the work; Laud was to repudiate the popular view that it was 'Laud's Liturgy'. The revision took some account of Scottish opinion: the word 'priest' was omitted, for example. But various elements proved a provocative reminder of Laudian policy in England, such as rubrics concerning the position of the table and celebrant at Communion. Laud and the bishops expected the Book to be introduced without difficulty. However, a riot greeted its first use in St Giles',* Edinburgh, on 23 July 1637. Robert Baillie* and John Row (1568-1646)* wrote vehemently against it. The King's failure to conciliate led to the Glasgow Assembly,* the National Covenant,* and the Bishops' Wars.* Laud was impeached by the English Parliament for treason in December 1641, and executed on 10 January 1645.

W. Scott, J. Bliss, eds, The Works of William Laud, 7 vols (O, 1847-60); C. Carlton, Archbishop William Laud (L, 1987); N. Tyacke, Anti-Calvinists (O, 1987); J. S. McGee, 'William Laud and the Outward Face of Religion', Leaders of the Reformation, ed. R. DeMolen (Susquehanna, PA, 1984), 318-44; H. Trevor-Roper, Archbishop Laud (O, 1940); G. Donaldson, The Making of the Scottish Prayer Book of 1637 (E, 1954); M. Lee, The Road to Revolution: Scotland under Charles I, 1625-37 (Urbana, IL, 1985); P. Donald, An Uncounselled King (C, 1991); DNB XXXII, 185-94.

S. Hardman Moore

Lauder, Alexander (1668-1719), Presbyterian apologist. Little is known of his background but he is thought to have been the brother of John Lauder, minister at Eccles, Berwickshire, 1691-1729. He was educated in Edinburgh (MA, 1684) and ordained in 1695 to the united (Border) parishes of Mordington and Lamberton.

Lauder was an apologist for Presbyterianism* during the pamphlet warfare which followed the Revolution of 1689-90. He published The Ancient Bishops considered, both with respect to the extent of their Jurisdiction and nature of their Power (E, 1707). Four years later The Divine Institution of Bishops having Churches consisting of many Congregations, examined by Scripture was published in London. An even more controversial work was Vindication of the Ministers and Ruling Elders who have taken the Abjuration, published anonymously (E, 1712). The Oath of Abjuration* was required by the Toleration* Act of 1712 and involved abjuring the exiled Stuarts as well as allegiance to Queen Anne. Many Presbyterians with no Jacobite* sympathies objected to swearing this oath.

FES II, 57-8.

H. R. Sefton

Laud's Liturgy, *see* Laud, William; Scottish Prayer Books (Episcopalian).

Laurence of Lindores (*c.*1373–1437), university teacher and papal inquisitor. Presumably born at Lindores in Fife, he graduated at Paris in arts (MA, *c.*1393; Regent, 1394–7, 1401–2) and theology (Bachelor, by 1403, Licentiate possibly by 1406). He was nominated inquisitor for Scotland by the papacy, possibly before returning to Scotland *c.*1406. He held various offices in the University of St Andrews from its inception in 1410 while teaching in the Arts Faculty (Dean 1416–25, 1432–7; Receptor before 1426, and 1430; possibly University's first Rector, before 1417). He attempted unsuccessfully to develop the College of St John into a single Pedagogy for arts and theology *c.*1430. His commentaries on Aristotle's *Physics* and *De Anima* written in Paris show him to have been a nominalist. This teaching aroused such controversy when introduced at St Andrews that by 1438 the Arts Faculty was forced to allow masters to teach the opposing moderate realist philosophy of St Albert the Great and others. A man of formidable intellect and will, as inquisitor Laurence was unswervingly orthodox, as can be seen in the trials of James Resby (*see* Lollards) and Paul Kravar,* and the recantation of Robert Gardiner, 1435.

D. E. R. Watt, *A Biographical Dictionary of Scottish Graduates to AD 1410* (O, 1977), 343–5; A. I. Dunlop, *Acta Facultatis Artium Universitatis S. Andree 1413–1588*, 2 vols (E, 1964); J. Durkan and J. Kirk, *The University of Glasgow 1451–1577* (G, 1977); J. Durkan, *William Turnbull, Bishop of Glasgow* (G, 1951); A. I. Dunlop, *The Life and Times of James Kennedy* (E, 1950).

L. J. Macfarlane

Lawes, William George (1839–1907), missionary in Pacific islands. Born in Berkshire, and trained at the Congregational Bedford College, Lawes with his bride, Fanny Wickham, reached Niue (Savage Island) in 1861. Consolidating earlier Pacific Islander evangelism, Lawes translated the Niuean New Testament and trained Niuean missionaries. He served the London Missionary Society* mainland New Guinea Mission 1874–1906. Assisted by James Chalmers* he translated the Motu Bible and equipped Papuan church leaders. Contributions to exploration and ethnology earned him the University of Glasgow DD in 1894, demonstrating Scots appreciation of the missionary role in Pacific development.

Grammar and Vocabulary of Language Spoken by the Motu Tribe, New Guinean (Sydney, 1885); 'Ethnological Notes on the Motu, Koitapu and Koiari Tribes of New Guinea', *Journ. of Royal Anthropological Inst.* 8 (1879), 369–77; 'Notes on New Guinea and its inhabitants', *Proc. of Royal Geographical Soc.* 2 (1880), 602–16.

J. King, *W. G. Lawes of Savage Island and New Guinea* (L, 1909); J. Garrett, *To Live Among the Stars* (Geneva and Suva, 1982), 136–7, 212–18.

J. M. Hitchen

Laws, Robert (1851–1934), leader of the Livingstonia Mission of the FC (later UFC) in northern Malawi and north-eastern Zambia from 1878 until he retired in 1927. His father was a cabinetmaker in Aberdeen, in which trade Robert was apprenticed on leaving primary school. He continued his education in the evenings and studied arts and medicine at Aberdeen University in 1868 (MA, 1872). Moving to the UP Seminary in Edinburgh, he also continued medical classes at Glasgow University and Anderson's College, passing his MB, ChB examinations at Aberdeen in 1875.

From a very early age he had wanted to be a missionary and was particularly fascinated by David Livingstone.* So when the FC planned a mission to the shores of Lake Malawi he was excited by the prospect but frustrated by a lack of interest on the part of his UP Church. However, by the efforts of James Stewart* and James Thin, a distinguished UP elder, the UP Church was persuaded to second Laws to the new venture. He was ordained for missionary work by the UP Presbytery of Edinburgh in 1875 and went out with the Livingstonia pioneers as medical officer and second in command to Lt E. D. Young. After the latter departed at the end of his contracted two years, Laws was made head of the mission in 1878.

The first site chosen for the mission, Cape Maclear, at the south end of Lake Malawi, was not suitable, being neither in ready contact with a large population nor healthy. In 1880, after exploratory journeys around the Lake, Laws decided to base the main station at Bandawe among the Tonga people of the Lakeshore. This was also a useful place from which to approach the Ngoni, who dominated central and northern Malawi. After the establishment of the British Protectorate in 1891, Laws began to plan a central institution modelled on Stewart's Lovedale to be situated on Khondowe mountain. This soon became the centre of the mission's activities in Malawi and north-eastern Zambia.

In 1894 he successfully negotiated with the Cape Synod of the Dutch Reformed Church to take over what is now the Central province of Malawi, so that, with the Blantyre Mission, all of Malawi was now served by a Presbyterian mission, and the foundations of the Church of Central Africa Presbyterian, which Laws helped to bring into being in 1924, were laid.

Laws was never able to enter into African society, but he had the talent to choose able men and women and eventually learned to give them autonomy. The most famous of them was David Kaunda, a pioneer preacher in Zambia and father of its first President, Kenneth Kaunda.

Perhaps Laws' most important contributions were his creation of a vast primary school network (so that as early as 1914, Livingstonia had more schools than all the other missions in Zambia and Malawi together) and his encouragement, after the First World War, of the mission's teachers, pastors and others to form Native Associations to help people cope with the new world breaking in on them. These associations in 1938 became the Nyasaland African National Congress.

Laws was Moderator of the UFC General Assembly in 1908.

See also Missions.

Reminiscences of Livingstonia (E, 1934).

DNB 1931–1940, 532–3; *AFCS* I, 206; *FUFCS* 562; *FES* IX, 737; W. P. Livingstone, *Laws of Livingstonia* (L, 1922); J. McCracken, *Politics and Christianity in Malawi, 1875–1940; The Impact of Livingstonia Mission...* (C, 1977); H. McIntosh, *Robert Laws* (E, 1993).

A. C. Ross

Lawson, George (1749–1820), Associate Synod Professor of Theology. Born in West Linton, Peeblesshire, of Associate Synod* parentage, he went to Edinburgh University in 1764, and in 1766 to the Associate Synod Divinity Hall, where he studied under John Brown of Haddington.* In 1769 he was licensed by Edinburgh Presbytery, and in 1771 became pastor of the Associate Synod church in Selkirk. In 1787 he succeeded his old tutor Brown as Professor of Theology in the Divinity Hall, which was henceforth situated at Selkirk to enable Lawson to continue as pastor there.

Lawson was loved by all who knew him for his transparent goodness – Thomas Carlyle* dubbed him the 'Scottish Socrates', declaring that 'no simple-minded more perfect lover of wisdom do I know of in that generation' (quoted in A. Thomson, *Life of Principal Harper*, E, 1881, 16). He was also admired for his vast erudition and apparently infallible memory, whose retentive powers, however, did not extend beyond matters academic. Many notable ministers were trained by him, including some who were to achieve distinction in other Churches, e.g. the Independent Ralph Wardlaw* and John Lee* of the CofS.

Lawson held progressive views on most subjects. He was a supporter of the missionary movement, an enemy of the slave trade, and an advocate of the use of uninspired hymns in worship. In the Old Light/New Light* controversy, he came forward as the leading proponent of New Light; his *Considerations on the Overture lying before the Associate Synod ... concerning the power of the Civil Magistrate in Matters of Religion* (E, 1797), advocating freedom of opinion on the subject, was regarded as a polemical masterpiece.

Lawson also wrote a number of sermons and commentaries. Spurgeon* praised his *Lectures on the Book of Ruth, with a few Discourses on the Sovereignty and Efficacy of Grace* (E, 1805) as being 'By a man of great genius. Simple, fresh and gracious' (*Commenting and Commentaries*, L, 1876, 66).

Lawson received a DD from Marischal College,* Aberdeen, in 1806.

Lectures on the History of Joseph (2 vols, E, 1807); *Discourses on the Book of Esther* (E, 1804); *Exposition of the Book of Proverbs* (2 vols, E, 1821); *Discourses on the History of David* (Berwick, 1833).

J. MacFarlane, *The Life and Times of George Lawson* (E, 1862); H. Belfrage, memoir of Lawson prefaced to Lawson's *Discourses on the History of David*; *DNB* XXXII, 701–1; Small II, 441–2.

N. R. Needham

Lawson, James (1538–84), Presbyterian minister. As a native of the town, he was educated at Perth Grammar School where the master, Andrew Simson (*see* Simson, Archibald), had taken him as a destitute child into his household, and he proceeded to St Andrews University, where he enrolled in St Mary's College at the same time as Andrew Melville,* his future associate, in 1559. On leaving St Andrews, he served as tutor in Paris to the Countess of Crawford's sons by 1567, and may have acquired his knowledge of Hebrew there, before the onset of fresh religious strife led to his returning to London, and on to Cambridge for further study in 1568. By 1569 he was appointed second master in St Mary's College, St Andrews, where he was said to have taught Hebrew, before his promotion later in the year as sub-principal of King's College, Aberdeen, and minister in St Machar's. In 1572, as John Knox's* chosen successor, Lawson was appointed minister in Edinburgh. In the General Assembly's debate on diocesan episcopacy* in 1575, he sided with Melville, and assisted in drafting the *Second Book of Discipline.** He served as an adviser in reconstituting St Mary's College in St Andrews as a theological college in 1579, and campaigned for a college in Edinburgh. As minister, he had custody for a spell of Clement Little's* theological library. Moderator of the Assembly which condemned episcopacy in July 1580, Lawson was later called before the Privy Council in 1582 and 1583 for opposing the government's policies for the Church. Praised by Melville in 1584, Lawson fled to England after condemning the Black Acts* which affirmed episcopacy and asserted the Crown's supremacy over the Church. After visiting Oxford and Cambridge universities, Lawson died in London. His funeral was 'the occasion of a gathering of English and Scottish presbyterians not only more impressive than any other recorded in the sixteenth century, but in a sense more representative than even the Westminster assembly'.

Calderwood, III–IV; *BUK*; J. Melville, *Autobiography and Diary*, ed. R. Pitcairn (E, 1842); W. A. C. Lindsay, *Lives of Lindsays* (L, 1849), I, 331–3; John Rylands University Library, Manchester: Crawford Muniments; Spottiswoode, II, 181–3, 315–19; *SBD*; J. Kirk, *Patterns of Reform* (E, 1989); G. Donaldson,

'Scottish Presbyterian Exiles in England, 1584–5', *RSCHS* 14 (1962), 67–80; *DNB* XXXII, 290–2; *FES* I, 51–2.

J. Kirk

Lay Patronage, *see* Patronage.

Lectionary, an ordered system of selected readings from Scripture appointed to be read on specific occasions during the Christian year.* In the medieval Church these readings were usually short selections chosen with a view to setting before the people the heart of the Scriptures. At the Reformation* the Scots abandoned the use of the Christian year. Scripture reading was still a vital part of Sunday worship, but according to the *First Book of Discipline*ered* the books of the Bible were to be read in order, a chapter from the OT and NT each Sunday, the sermon being an exposition of one of the lessons. There was an attempt to restore a lectionary based on the Christian year in Laud's* Liturgy in 1637, and lessons from the Apocrypha* were even included. The Westminster* Directory, however, in affirming that the reading of the Word was part of the public worship of God, stated that a chapter of each testament would normally be read at each service. The use of a lectionary based on the Christian year came into use gradually in Presbyterian worship as part of the Catholic revival of worship* of the nineteenth century. Although the table of lessons contained in *Euchologion*,* the service book of the Church Service Society,* was not based on the main festivals of the Christian year, such was not the case with the lectionary in *Prayers for Divine Service* produced by the CofS in 1923 or the *Book of Common Order* of 1940. The *Book of Common Order* (1979) has made use of the more recent lectionary prepared by the Joint Liturgical Group, which is made up of representatives of all the main British Churches. The lectionary has a two-year cycle, the OT lesson being additional to or alternative to that of the Epistle, with a controlling lesson based on the theme for that Sunday and the other two readings chosen in relation to it. This new lectionary is used in the EpCS and in the CofE. Since Vatican II the reading of Scripture occupies a prominent place in the RCC, which uses a lectionary on a three-year cycle with a homily based on the readings of the day.

D. B. Forrester and D. M. Murray (eds), *Studies in the History of Worship in Scotland* (E, 1984); R. C. D. Jasper (ed.), *The Calendar and Lectionary* (L, 1967).

D. M. Murray

Lee, John (1779–1859), Moderate* CofS divine, Principal of Edinburgh University. Born at Crannishills, Stow, in Midlothian, he was brought up in the Associate Synod.* In 1794 he entered Edinburgh University, and in 1797 attended the Associate Synod divinity hall in Selkirk under George Lawson.* From 1797–1801 he studied medicine at Edinburgh University, graduating MD, and for some years hesitated between medicine, law and the ministry. When he finally opted for the last, he joined the CofS, and was licensed by Dalkeith Presbytery in 1804. He acted as Alexander Carlyle's* amanuensis 1804–5, and Carlyle appointed him his literary executor. In 1807 he was ordained by Edinburgh Presbytery to the Scotch church in Hanover Street, London. In 1808 he moved to Peebles, and in 1812 was appointed Professor of Church History in St Mary's College, St Andrews. He was also appointed Professor of Moral Philosophy in King's College, Aberdeen, in 1820, but his lectures were delivered by proxy.

In 1821 Lee was presented by George IV to the Canongate Church, Edinburgh, although various problems prevented him from taking up the charge until 1823. In 1825 he moved to Lady Yester's Church, also in Edinburgh, and in 1835 to St Giles, the Old Kirk or South-East parish. In 1837 he became Principal of the United Colleges of St Salvator's and St Leonard's in St Andrews, and in 1839 Principal of St Andrews. He held each principalship alongside his ministry at St Giles. In 1840, however, he resigned his pastorate on being appointed Principal of Edinburgh University. After the Disruption* he replaced Thomas Chalmers* as the University's Professor of Divinity.

Orthodox in theology, Lee was a committed Moderate in church politics. He was probably the most distinguished and erudite divine who remained in the CofS in 1843. He led a campaign in the 1820s to overturn the exclusive right of His Majesty's Printers to print the Bible in Scotland, a privilege which led to Bibles being priced almost beyond the reach of the poorer classes. After several years of campaigning, the privilege was abrogated (*see* Bible Board; Bible Societies). An ardent bibliophile, he accumulated a library of some 20,000 volumes, catalogued and partly sold after his death.

Lee wrote little himself. His two major works are *Lectures on the History of the Church of Scotland* (E, 1860), and *The University of Edinburgh, 1583–1839* (E, 1884).

Lee was appointed Clerk* of the General Assembly in 1827, and was Moderator in 1844. He became a royal chaplain in 1830, and Dean of the Chapel Royal, Stirling, in 1840. He received a DD from St Andrews University and an LLD from Edinburgh.

Pastoral Addresses of the General Assembly (E, 1864); *Memorial for the Bible Societies of Scotland* (E, 1824); *Additional Memorial on Printing and Importing Bibles* (E, 1826); *Inaugural Addresses in the University of Edinburgh* (E, 1861).

D. P. Thomson, *The Lad from Torwoodlee* (Galashields, 1946); Lord Neaves, 'Memoir' prefixed to *Inaugural Addresses*; *DNB* XXXII, 361–2; *FES* I, 73.

N. R. Needham

Lee Lectureship, a single-lecture series instituted in 1886 to perpetuate the memory of Robert Lee* of Greyfriars, Edinburgh, the innovator in the CofS of stained glass and organ music and promoter of the more 'orderly' conduct of public worship. The

LEE, ROBERT

lecture is delivered in St Giles Cathedral,* Edinburgh, by 'a clergyman or layman' of the CofS or, 'in exceptional circumstances', an eminent CofE clergyman. The lecturer's theme, subject to the trustees' agreement, should deal with some question of 'Biblical Criticism, Theology or Ecclesiastical History or Policy', with particular reference to contemporary circumstances. In view of Lee's commitment to its enrichment, the lecture has commonly taken worship as its subject. The series has become less regular in recent decades.

The first lecturer was R. H. Story,* *The Reformed Ritual in Scotland* (E, 1886). Others of note have included John Cunningham,* *Is a Union of the Episcopal and Presbyterian Churches Possible?* (G, 1887); T. Leishman,* *The Moulding of the Scottish Reformation* (E, 1897); John Kerr, *The Renascence of Worship* (E, 1909) – on the Church Service Society;* H. H. Henson, *The Relation of the Church of England to the Other Reformed Churches* (E, 1911); Lord Sands,* *The Order and Conduct of Divine Service in the Church of Scotland* (E, 1923); John Baillie,* 'Secularistic and Demonic Forces in the World of Today' (1937); O. B. Milligan,* *The Scottish Communion Office and its Historical Background* (E, 1939); D. B. Forrester, 'Liberation of Worship' (1980). First six listed in *CofS Year Book* (1896), next seven in *Year Book* (1914), others in *Year Book* to 1962.

D. F. Wright

Lee, Robert (1804–68), CofS minister and liturgical pioneer. Born at Tweedmouth, Northumberland, the son of a boat-builder, he followed his father's trade before studying at the University of St Andrews. He became minister of Campsie in 1836 and then of Old Greyfriars in Edinburgh in 1843. He was awarded a DD by St Andrews in 1844 and was appointed the first Professor of Biblical Criticism in the University of Edinburgh in 1847, an appointment which at that time did not require him to give up his pastoral charge. He was also appointed Dean of the Chapel Royal.* Lee was concerned at the threat of the disestablishment* of the Kirk following the Disruption* and at the increasing number of those attracted by the EpCS because of dissatisfaction with Presbyterian forms of worship. He also thought that the worship of the Kirk was in need of reform. Unlike other liturgical reformers of the time, Lee was not greatly influenced by Catholic tradition. He was not involved in the formation of the Church Service Society* and became a vice-president only after some hesitation. According to Lee, worship should contain three elements: Word, prayer and praise. Services should be constructed to reflect this. He wished Presbyterian worship to be distinguished by 'good taste, decency, propriety and solemnity, as well as by purity of doctrine and fervour of devotion' (*Reform of the Church of Scotland*, E, 1866, 45). Lee took the opportunity for the reopening of Old Greyfriars for worship in 1857 after a fire to make several controversial changes in the services. The congregation stood to sing instead of sitting, and Lee read the prayers from a printed book which he had prepared, instead of delivering them extempore. A further innovation* was the introduction of a harmonium in 1863 to accompany the singing. A storm of controversy arose over his innovations and Lee was dubbed the 'Innovator' and criticized in the press and in the Presbyteries of the Kirk. After consideration by Edinburgh Presbytery, Lee was vindicated on all points at the Assembly of 1859, except that of reading prayers from a book. Lee defended his practices by maintaining that such changes were not expressly forbidden by the law of the Church. After several deliberations the Assembly in 1865 passed an Act on the motion of W. R. Pirie* of Dyce which in effect gave Presbyteries great latitude in considering changes in worship. Lee opposed the 'Pirie Act', thinking that it would stem the tide of liturgical reform, but in fact it led to changes being introduced gradually and without challenge in many parishes. Lee himself continued to create controversy. In 1865 he conducted a marriage service with read prayers, sung amens, and a *Te Deum* sung to a Gregorian chant. The case was indefinitely postponed in 1867 when Lee was paralysed as a result of a riding accident the day before he was due to defend himself at the bar of the General Assembly.

See also Catholic Revival in Worship.

The Reform of the Church of Scotland (E, 1866); *Prayers for Public Worship* (E, 1857–1873).

R. H. Story, *The Life and Remains of Robert Lee*, 2 vols (L, 1870).

D. M. Murray

Leechman, John (d. 1874), Baptist missionary to India and tutor at Serampore College (1832–7). Born in Glasgow, Leechman studied at Bristol Baptist College (1825–9) and Glasgow University (1829–31; MA). Supported by Christopher Anderson's* church (Charlotte Baptist Chapel) in Edinburgh, he assumed teaching duties at Serampore, and excelled at logic. A treatise compiled while he was at the College, entitled *Science and the Art of Reasoning*, was published after he returned to Britain, and Glasgow University awarded him the LLD in 1859 in recognition of his scholarship. On Carey's death in 1834, he became co-pastor (with John Mack* and Joshua Marshman) of the Baptist church at Serampore. Returning to Britain in 1837 because of his wife's ill health, he succeeded his father-in-law, George Barclay,* as pastor of the Baptist church at Irvine (1839–48), where he had a distinguished ministry, bringing revival* to the church. He later held pastorates in England, at Hammersmith (1848–67) and Hay Hill, Bath (1867–70).

G. Yuille (ed.), *History of Baptists in Scotland* (G, 1926), 61, 208; A. Swaine, *Faithful Men* (L, 1884), 305–7; Records of Bristol Baptist College.

D. E. Meek

Leechman (Leishman), William (1706–85), Professor of Divinity (from 1744) and Principal (from 1761) at the University of Glasgow to his death. Born in the parish of Dolphinton, Lanarkshire, he completed his theological training at Edinburgh under the direction of William Hamilton.* After thirteen years of ministry in the Presbyteries of Paisley and Irvine, he was elected professor at Glasgow.

Leechman studied in Glasgow soon after Francis Hutcheson* began teaching at the University, and attended his classes. Hutcheson recognized Leechman's superior ability, and when the theological chair became vacant immediately nominated his younger protégé, whom he describes in a letter to David Hume as 'one of my Scottish intimates who sees all as I do'.

As Professor of Divinity, Leechman was responsible for providing a rounded curriculum for students who planned to enter the Christian ministry. Following Hutcheson, he lectured in English, not Latin. He was sought after by students from every part of the theological spectrum – Seceders as well as Evangelicals* and Moderates.* That is significant, given the strong feelings generated by differences between the groups. According to the testimony of Leechman's biographer, 'The Divinity Hall at Glasgow was crowded in [Leechman's] time with a greater number of scholars than any other in Scotland' (Wodrow, 69).

Daiches understands Leechman's influence as a big 'step in the direction of moderating extremist opinion and intolerance in the Church of Scotland' (42). He received Glasgow's DD in 1754, and was Moderator in 1757.

James Wodrow, ed., *Sermons by William Leechman* (with a Life), 2 vols (L, 1789).

DNB XXXII, 391; *FES* VII, 397; J. F. Leishman, *A Son of Knox* (G, 1909), 65–87; David Daiches, *The Paradox of Scottish Culture* (L, 1964).

T. G. Addington

Lees, (Sir) James Cameron (1834–1913), CofS minister. The son of John Lees of London and Stornoway (*FES*, VII, 206–7), he was educated at the universities of Glasgow and Aberdeen. He was minister of Carnoch in Ross-shire before going to Paisley Abbey in 1859 and then St Giles* in Edinburgh in 1877. During his ministry the extensive refurbishment of St Giles both externally and internally was completed and the more liturgical worship which Lees introduced was given an appropriate setting. Lees was one of the founders of the Church Service Society* and was a member of its Editorial Committee, although he was in favour of more simple liturgical forms than the more Catholic members of the Society. He received several honorary degrees and was made CVO in 1906 and KCVO in 1909. He was appointed Dean of the Order of the Thistle* and of the Chapel Royal* of Scotland in 1886.

The Abbey of Paisley (Paisley, 1878); *St Giles' Edinburgh* (E, 1889).

N. Maclean, *Life of James Cameron Lees, KCVO, DD, LLD* (G, 1922); *FES* I, 62–3, III, 170.

D. M. Murray

Legge, James (1815–97), missionary and Chinese scholar. Born at Huntly, Aberdeenshire, and joining the Congregational church there, he studied at King's College, Aberdeen (MA, 1835), and Highbury College, London. In 1839 he was appointed to the Anglo-Chinese College at Malacca, then in effect a China mission-in-waiting. With the opening of China to missions after the Opium War of 1842, Legge moved the college to Hong Kong, changing its character from language institution to seminary. He also became the active pastor of Union Church. In 1875 a consortium of China merchants endowed a chair of Chinese at Oxford, and next year Legge, already 60, became the first incumbent. He never retired. He received doctorates from New York University (1841), Aberdeen (1870) and Edinburgh (1884). In family life he suffered much bereavement.

Probably the most important sinologist of the nineteenth century, Legge spans the period from the Western ignorance of China (at its height when Robert Morrison initiated Protestant missions) to the era of modern critical scholarship. At Malacca in 1841 he began to translate the Chinese classics; he completed his final contribution a few months before his death. While holding a simple evangelical faith (his theology was formed in the 1830s, and shows few signs of change), he evinced deep respect for the Chinese classics, reverenced Confucius and Mencius, advocated (like the Jesuits) the Christian use of the ancient terms Shang Ti and Ti'en for God, and believed the early religion of China to have been monotheistic. These positions disturbed some contemporary missionaries, and he was mistrusted and misrepresented by colleagues of less scholarship.

Legge had much effect on education in Hong Kong. Concluding that his college was failing in its professed object as a seminary, he closed it in 1856, and recommended a secular education system for the colony.

The Chinese Classics, first edit. Hong Kong, 1861–8 (most accessible Western version in Max Müller's Sacred Books of the East series); *The Notions of the Chinese Concerning God and Spirits* (Hong Kong and L, 1852); *The Religions of China . . . Compared with Christianity* (L, 1880); *The Nestorian Monument . . . Relating to the Diffusion of Christianity in China* (L, 1888).

DNB Suppl. III, 87–8; *Who Was Who, 1897–1915*, 308; W. Muirhead, obit. in *Chinese Recorder* 29 (3) 1898, 109–14; H. J. E. Legge, *James Legge, Missionary and Scholar* (L, 1905); A. Wylie, *Memories of Protestant Missionaries* (Shanghai, 1967), 117–22; L. T. Ride, 'Biographical note' attached to edition of *The Chinese Classics* I (Taipei, 1983), 1–25; R. R. Covell, *Confucius, the Buddha and Christ: a History of the Gospel in China* (Maryknoll, NY, 1986); L. Pfister, 'The "Failures" of James Legge's Fruitful Life for China', *Ching Feng* 31:4 (1988), 246–71.

A. F. Walls

Leighton, Alexander (c.1568–1649), persecuted

LEIGHTON CLUB

Presbyterian. Born of an ancient Forfar family, Leighton studied at St Andrews (MA, probably 1587), after which he taught and preached in England. After studying medicine at Leiden he was forbidden to practise in England, probably on account of his Puritan proclivities. However he apparently did so privately, and gathered a church in his house concurrently. In 1624 he published *Speculum Belli Sacri: or The Looking-glasse Of The Holy War* (Amsterdam), urging war with Spain; he was probably the author of a work against stage plays the following year. But his best known work, for which he suffered considerably, was *An Appeal To the Parliament; or Sions Plea against Prelacie* (Amsterdam, 1628; rp. E, 1842), demonstrating bishops 'to be intruders upon the Priviledges of Christ, of the King, and of the Common-weal'. Archbishop Laud* had Leighton apprehended, tried in the Star Chamber and sentenced. He had a nostril slit and one ear cut off, was branded on one cheek, received thirty-six lashes and was imprisoned until released, broken in health, by the Long Parliament in 1641. The following year he was appointed Keeper of Lambeth House, which had been turned into a state prison. Although he was in Scotland in 1643, visiting his son Robert,* and apparently signed the Covenant,* he seems to have spent the rest of his life in London.

D. Butler, *The Life and Letters of Robert Leighton* (L, 1903); *DNB* XXXIII, 1–2.

D. C. Lachman

Leighton Club, clerical ecumenical societies, in Glasgow and Edinburgh, uniting CofS and EpSC members and named after Archbishop Robert Leighton.* The Glasgow Club existed from c.1935 to 1965, the Edinburgh one from 1942 to 1976. They met regularly to hear papers and published leaflets. In 1965 the Edinburgh Club issued a manifesto (backed up by *Do We Still Want Unity?*), which admitted that primitive Christianity knew no normative church order, professed recognition of each other's ministries but insisted that church unity required some form of episcopacy. Such thinking reflected the heyday of Anglican–Presbyterian* conversations. The Club had its own Anglican-style printed office. In 1956 it absorbed the remnant, partly lay, of the Christian Unity Association.*

Edinburgh Club's papers in New College Library, Edinburgh.

D. F. Wright

Leighton Library, Dunblane. Founded on the bequest of Robert Leighton,* the library was opened in 1688 for the use of the clergy of the Diocese of Dunblane, which is situated some forty miles from Edinburgh and Glasgow and was the most poorly endowed see in Scotland. The task of setting up the library, including the transport of Leighton's books from his last home in Sussex, was undertaken by his executors and friends, notably his nephew, Edward Lightmaker (d.1708?), William Drummond (1617?–88), first Viscount of Strathallan, and James Fall (1647–1711), Principal of the University of Glasgow. Robert Douglas (1625?–1716), the last Bishop of Dunblane, co-ordinated their efforts (Douglas, 'An Account of the Foundation of the Leightonian Library', *The Bannatyne Miscellany*, E, 1827–55, III, 227–64). The founder's personal collection of 1,363 volumes and 149 pamphlets, many of which contain Leighton's marginalia, is one of the few surviving libraries of a seventeenth-century Scottish scholar. There are books in twelve languages, the Hebrew section being of particular interest. Strengths of Leighton's collection include works of the early Fathers; occult studies, religious and world history' geography and travel; and the classics. The library served as a public lending library from 1734 until about 1870. The collection, now numbering 4,000 volumes, has been carefully conserved, along with the building, which is the oldest purpose-built library to use traditional Scottish building techniques.

G. Willis, 'The Leighton Library, Dunblane', *The Bibliothek* 10 (1980–1), 139–57; W. J. Couper, *Bibliotheca Leightoniana, Dunblane* (G, 1917); J. M. Allan, *Only My Books* (Stirling, 1985); G. Willis, 'An Historic Library Conserved', *Library Review* 39:4 (1990), 28–32.

G. W. Willis

Leighton, Robert (1611–84), Archbishop of Glasgow. Son of Alexander Leighton,* he was reportedly born in London, graduated at Edinburgh in 1631, and spent the next ten years on the continent, probably near Paris, where his ecumenical tendencies were developed. In 1641 he became minister of Newbattle, near Edinburgh, and there delivered the sermons that were to form the basis of his renowned commentary on 1 Peter. In 1643 he signed the Solemn League and Covenant,* though he came increasingly to regret the intolerance found among its supporters. In 1653 he was appointed principal of Edinburgh University, and advised its students to follow charity and avoid 'that itch for polemical and controversial theology which is so prevalent and infectious'. With the reintroduction of Episcopacy at the Restoration* he reluctantly accepted the smallest and poorest of Scottish dioceses (Dunblane), allowing himself to be 'reordained' as well as consecrated in London. He became Archbishop of Glasgow in 1670, but would accept only one-fifth of the emoluments. Leighton's ruling passion was to achieve unity in the Church, taking the best features of Episcopacy and Presbytery. He strove earnestly for an accommodation with the Nonconformists, and regarded persecution as 'scaling heaven with ladders fetched out of hell'. The Covenanters* took his eirenic views for 'holy wobbling', a view not very different from that of his fellow bishops. Weary of all the wrangling, he resigned in 1674 and died in London, having declined Charles II's plea to return to Scotland after the assassination of Archbishop Sharp* in 1679. It is said that Coleridge held Leighton in such high regard that he based his *Aids to Reflection* on Leighton's aphorisms.

Leighton's best known work, frequently reprinted

to the present, is his highly regarded commentary on I Peter (*A Practical Commentary* ..., York, 1693; ... Vol. II, L, 1694). His works also include theological lectures (*Praelectiones Theologicae*, L, 1693), expositions of short portions of Scripture, and sermons. Editions of Leighton's works (with lives prefixed) were edited by J. N. Pearson (L, 1825) and J. Aikman, *The Whole Works* (E, 1832). The best edition, lacking a life which was never completed, is *The Whole Works as yet recovered*, ed. W. West (L, 1869–75), vols 2–7 only.

Lives by T. Murray (E, 1828); C. F. Secretan (L, 1866); D. Butler (L, 1903); E. A. Knox (L, 1930).

J. D. Douglas

Leishman, Matthew (1794–1874), leader of the 'Middle Party'* at the time of the Disruption.* Educated at Glasgow and Edinburgh, Leishman became minister of Govan in 1821, where he gained national recognition as an energetic parish minister and Church historian. With the beginning of the Ten Years' Conflict* in 1833, he found himself unable to back either party. He could not support the evangelical Non-Intrusionists,* as he believed that the Veto Act* based the selection of ministers on popular prejudice. Neither could he approve what he viewed as the Erastianism of the Moderate* party. In 1842, he became leader of a 'Middle Party'* of about forty ministers, many formerly associated with the evangelical party, who worked to achieve a last-minute compromise and preserve the unity of the Church – by giving Presbyteries the authority to review parish vetoes of patrons' candidates. Leishman and 'the Forty' failed to avert the Disruption,* and after 1843 he worked for the recovery of the CofS – as an active parish minister in his growing industrial parish, as a leader in temperance* reform and Church extension,* and as Moderator of the General Assembly of 1858. He edited Hugh Binning's* *Works* and Robert Wodrow's* *Analecta*, and wrote *A Brief Appeal to the Convocationists* (1843).

J. F. Leishman, *Matthew Leishman of Govan* (Paisley, 1924); *FES* III, 413.

S. J. Brown

Leishman, Thomas (1825–1904), CofS minister and liturgical scholar. The son of Matthew Leishman,* he was educated at Glasgow University (MA, 1843; DD, 1871), and was minister of Collace, Perthshire, 1852–5, and of Linton, near Kelso, 1855–1904. He was the Lecturer on Pastoral Theology to divinity students in the Scottish faculties of divinity, 1895–7, and Moderator of the General Assembly in 1898. A friend and colleague of George W. Sprott,* Leishman was in the forefront of the Catholic revival of worship* in the CofS in the late nineteenth century. He was a founding member of the Church Service Society* and served on the Editorial Committee and as a vice-president. He was also concerned with the place of doctrine in the life of the Church and was one of the founding members of the Scottish Church Society* and its president 1894–5 and 1901–2. He collaborated with Sprott in producing a new edition of *The Book of Common Order and the Westminster Directory* (E, 1868). His chapter, 'The Ritual of the Church', in R. H. Story (ed.), *The Church of Scotland, Past and Present* (L, 1890), V, 307–426, is an account of the history of the worship of the Kirk which is still a standard reference. He wished to recall the CofS to what he considered to be Reformed elements in its worship, such as the centrality of the Lord's Supper,* the saying of the Lord's Prayer* and the Creed (*see* Confessions) and the use of the doxology. He was succeeded as minister of Linton by his son, James F. Leishman.

See also Scoto-Catholics.

May the Kirk keep Pasche and Yule? (E, 1875); *The Moulding of the Scottish Reformation* (Lee Lecture,* E, 1897); *The State and Prospects of the Church of Scotland* (Moderator's Address, E, 1898); *The Church of Scotland as She Was and as She Is* (E, 1903).

FES II, 77; *DNB* Supplement II, 450–1; J. F. Leishman, *Linton Leaves* (E, 1937); G. W. Sprott, *The Character and Work of the late Very Rev. Thomas Leishman* (E, 1904).

D. M. Murray

Leith, Convention of, meeting between representatives of Kirk and Crown in January 1572 that reached a 'concordat' on a financial settlement for the 'prelacies' – bishoprics and abbacies – which had survived the Reformation* despite the Reformers' intention, outlined in the *FBD*,* of subverting the ancient structure of benefices. Already, by way of compromise, Queen Mary* in 1562 had given the Reformed Church a share in the 'thirds of benefices',* levied by the Crown's use. In 1566 she made further concessions to the Kirk by allowing its ministers access to the lesser benefices as they fell vacant, a measure which James VI's* first Parliament confirmed in 1567. No agreed solution was forthcoming for the greater benefices (most of which continued to be held by RC prelates, regardless of the Reformation) as the country drifted into civil war between supporters of Mary and her son James. The ascendancy of King James' cause allowed the regents to forfeit leading papalist or Marian bishops, to utilize episcopal patrimony as the government's patronage, and even to make appointments without consulting the Reformed Kirk, which duly protested at this misuse of power.

Amid the uproar, the government showed a readiness to compromise, and at Leith commissioners from the General Assembly and Crown provided the machinery for future episcopal and abbatial appointments. Having reached agreement that the 'prelacies' should remain as financial entities at least until the King's majority, the Convention proposed that as episcopal vacancies arose, qualified candidates, of at least thirty years of age, should be nominated by the Crown and examined by a chapter of ministers who had power to elect or reject candidates presented. On election, bishops were to swear their allegiance to the General Assembly in spiritual

LESLIE, GEORGE ('FATHER ARCHANGEL')

matters and to the Crown in temporal affairs; they were to enjoy no greater jurisdiction in the Church than that exercised by the existing superintendents,* at least until 'the same be agreed'; and they were expected to act collegiately with the advice of their chapter of ministers in admitting candidates to the ministry.

All this appeared to offer attractive endowment for a financially straitened Kirk. At the same time, it recognized the interests of the Crown in the disposal of abbatial property. The Crown might promote suitable candidates, perhaps the Crown's servants or senators of the College of Justice, as titular abbots or priors to enjoy monastic revenues. Although ministers serving the appropriated churches were to act in a capitular capacity in the disposition of monastic property (with the extinction of the old monastic chapters), the funds made available from this source, apart from teinds* allocated in stipend,* were devoted essentially for secular purposes.

From the outset, the operation of the agreement was subject to serious abuse; the Kirk did not gain proper access to the finances assigned for its use; and a series of disreputable episcopal appointments soon brought the system into disrepute. Such indeed was the General Assembly's dissatisfaction with the Leith settlement that the Regent Morton (see Douglas, James) conceded in 1576 that, if it were not prepared to adhere to the concordat of 1572, the Church should find an alternative solution. This was achieved in the *SDB** of 1578.

BUK I, 207ff.; J. Kirk, *Patterns of Reform* (G, 1989), 394–412; *SBD*, 18ff.

J. Kirk

Leslie, George ('Father Archangel') (c.1588–c.1637), RC missioner. Born of Protestant parents at Peterstown (Aberdeen), he entered the Scots College* in Rome in 1608. When twenty-six he became a Capuchin friar at Camerino (Italy), and was an associate of Thomas Dempster* at Pisa and Bologna 1617–18. He was a missionary in Scotland from c.1623, reporting to Rome on Scottish mission difficulties in 1626. He wrote three controversial treatises, one of which drew a response from Andrew Logie, minister of Rayne, Aberdeenshire (*Raine from the Clouds* ..., A, 1624; see *FES* VI, 183). Recalled to France by his superiors c.1629, he was cleared of charges made against him by his fellow-missioners. He was then assigned to the monastery of Monte Giorgio in the Italian diocese of Fermo, there enjoying the friendship of the local archbishop Rinuccini, whose uncritical biography (*Il Cappuccino Scozzese*, Bologna, 1644) gave a popular, vastly exaggerated account of Leslie's mission, echoed in a drama of Ignazio Fantozzi (1653; MS in Florence). Leslie returned to Scotland c.1634, and died there.

T. G. Law, 'The Bibliography of the Lives of Two Scottish Capuchins', *Papers of the Edinburgh Bibliographical Society* 1 (1890–1), 1–12; *id.*, *Collected Essays and Reviews* (E, 1904), 332–76; Colonel Leslie, *Historical Records of the Family of Leslie*, 3 vols (E, 1869), III, 415–35; F. Callaey, *Essai critique sur la vie du P. Archange Leslie* (Paris, 1914); C. J. Gossip, 'From Monymusk to Metz: Archangel Leslie on the European Stage', *AUR* 46 (1975), 137–50.

J. Durkan

Leslie, John (1527–96), RC bishop of Ross. The son of a priest, he graduated in arts at King's College, Aberdeen, studied theology at Paris and canon and civil law at Poitiers for four years. He received a licence in civil law at Toulouse, and a doctorate in law at Paris, where he taught (see *IR* 10, 1959, 388) before returning to Aberdeen to teach (1554). He was appointed official of Aberdeen and archdeacon of Moray.

At the Reformation* he refused to conform, becoming a champion of Catholic doctrine, Mary Queen of Scots* and the Counter-Reformation.* In 1561 he went to France to invite Mary to Scotland and returned with her. Support for her cause brought him several appointments, including in 1556 the commendatorship* of Lindores* and the bishopric of Ross. He was present at Mary's marriage to Bothwell. When deprived of his see in 1568, he left Scotland, never to return. He represented Mary at York, and was imprisoned by Queen Elizabeth in London (1571–4) for plotting against her. He became Mary's ambassador in Europe, moving from Paris (1574) to Rome (1575). With Ninian Winzet* he regained Schottenklöster for Scots (1576–8). In 1579 he was made suffragan bishop and vicar-general of Rouen. Although associated with James Beaton II* in Counter-Reformation measures, he was temporarily rehabilitated to Ross by James VI (1587–9). Provision to the see of Coutances in Normandy (1592) proved ineffectual. He died near Brussels.

Leslie was a brilliant lawyer and wrote several works vindicating Mary. In England he wrote a history of Scotland (in Scots: ed. T. Thomson, Bannatyne Club, E, 1830). An expanded Latin version (*De Origine, Moribus, et Rebus Gestis Scotorum* ..., Rome, 1578) was translated by James Dalrymple, a Ratisbon monk (1596; ed. E. G. Cody and W. Murison, 2 vols, STS, E, 1888–95).

FESMA 24, 25, 242, 246, 270; *DNB* XXXIII, 93–99; R. Keith, *Historical Catalogue of Scottish Bishops*, ed. M. Russel (E, 1824), 194–200; Dowden, 229–31; D. McN. Lockie, 'The Political Career of the Bishop of Ross, 1568–80', *Univ. of Birmingham Hist. Journ.* 4:2 (1954), 98–145; J. F. K. Johnstone and A. W. Robertson, *Bibliographia Aberdonensis*, 2 vols (Third Spalding Club, A, 1929–30).

I. B. Cowan

Leslie, John (1766–1832), scientist who was the subject of 'the Leslie case' in 1805. Born in Largo, Fife, he studied at St Andrews and Edinburgh Universities before forsaking divinity for science. He travelled, tutored, did literary work and experimented. When his candidacy for the Edinburgh chair of mathematics and natural philosophy gathered momentum, rumours of his heterodoxy were occasioned by his favourable comment on David Hume's* views of causation in (Leslie's) *An Experimental Inquiry into the Nature and Propagation of Heat* (L, 1804). The city ministers' opposition was defied by the town Council and University Senate, who claimed that the requirement of subscription* to the Westminster Confession had effectively lapsed in professorial appointments. In response, Leslie affirmed his orthodoxy and dissociated himself from Hume's religious views. Then the ministers split, and eventually in the 1805 General Assembly evangelical* support for Leslie prevailed over the Moderate* resistance.

The affair was notable as the Evangelicals' first Assembly victory over the Moderates, presaging a shift in the balance of parties, but also marked a theological turning-point. The Moderate opposition was rooted in their attachment to a rational natural theology requiring proofs and evidences, whereas Evangelicals would increasingly vindicate the faith on other, more subjective grounds.

Leslie was best known for his work on heat radiation. He was knighted in 1832.

DNB XXXIII, 105-7; I. D. Clark, 'The Leslie Controversy, 1805', *RSCHS* 14 (1962), 179-97; J. B. Morrell, 'The Leslie Affair...', *SHR* 54 (1975), 63-82.

D. F. Wright

Leslie, William (c.1621-1707), RC agent at Rome. Of the family of Conrack (Moray), he studied at the Scots Colleges* of Douai 1636-40 and Rome 1640-7. Ordained priest, he prepared at Paris for mission work in Scotland, but in 1650 was commissioned by fellow priests to work at Rome towards a Scottish establishment of secular (i.e. not religious) clergy. He was tutor in the household of the influential Cardinal Carlo Barberini. In 1653 Propaganda* appointed a secular prefect of the Scottish Mission, with stipends for ten priests (*see* Roman Catholicism). From 1661 Leslie was archivist at Propaganda. He remained at Rome until death, being Scottish agent under eight popes.

He strove single-mindedly for the ascendancy of secular clergy over Jesuits.* In 1694 Bishop Thomas Nicolson,* a secular, became superior of all priests in Scotland, including religious. The establishment of normal episcopal government in Scotland was due primarily to Leslie's efforts and influence.

P. F. Anson, *Underground Catholicism in Scotland, 1622-1878* (Montrose, 1970); W. J. Anderson (ed.), 'Abbé Paul MacPherson's History of the Scots College, Rome', *IR* 12 (1961), 3-172.

M. Dilworth

Lethington, *see* Maitland, William.

Levison, Mary, née Lusk (1923-), pioneer of women's ordination in the CofS. Born at Oxford, the daughter of the Revd David Lusk, she won a first in politics, philosophy and economics at Oxford and distinction in systematic theology at New College, Edinburgh, and then studied in Heidelberg and Basel. She was commissioned as a deaconess (*see* Diaconate) and licensed to preach the gospel, and in 1963 petitioned the General Assembly for ordination. She was the first woman to offer herself to the CofS for ordination and invite the Church to test her call. Although not herself ordained until 1978, and so preceded by several other women, she must count as the trail-blazer. She taught in St Colm's College* (1958-61), was Assistant Chaplain to Edinburgh University (1961-4), acted as Associate Minister in St Andrew's and St George's, Edinburgh (1978-83), where she developed the chaplaincy to shops and offices, and in 1988 was Moderator of Edinburgh Presbytery. She had married the Revd Fred Levison in 1965. She is also a well-known leader in the ecumenical movement,* having played a significant role in the World Alliance of Reformed Churches, the World Council of Churches and the Conference of European Churches. She served on the executive of the World Federation of Deaconess Associations for eleven years.

Wrestling with the Church (L, 1992).

D. B. Forrester

Liberalism, the growing doctrinal openness in later nineteenth- and early twentieth-century Christianity, arising from a widespread desire to adapt the faith to changing intellectual trends and cultural circumstances. It led in Scotland to the displacement of Westminster* Calvinism* (see Hamilton, below) as the central tradition of church and university theology, but in its wider threat to Trinitarian orthodoxy and the redemptive character of religion, it gained little ground at that time. The term has been used variously, and is best understood in relation to the prevailing orthodoxy (whether in Scotland, England, Germany or elsewhere). A classic nineteenth-century survey and welcome from Scotland is found in John Tulloch's* *Movements of Religious Thought in Britain* (L, 1885), which begins with Coleridge and notes, for example, 'a new outbreak of "Liberalism"' in *Essays and Reviews* (L, 1860). Burleigh pinpoints the significance for Scotland of 'English Broad Churchmen such as F. D. Maurice, Charles Kingsley and Dean Stanley'; Tulloch himself was 'the first Scottish Broad Churchman of note'. The impact of liberal theology on Scotland was tempered by 'Believing Criticism'.* The liberalism of Harnack's *What is Christianity?* (ET L, 1901) was altogether more radical, with its triple focus on the Fatherhood of God, the brotherhood of man, and the infinite value of the soul. Though the pervasive influence of neo-orthodoxy* in mid-twentieth-century Scotland was soon to set a neo-conservative context for a generation of theological discussion, the church union debates of the first three decades reveal how far even, for example, the UFC had departed from substantive commitment to the orthodoxy which had recently been fertile enough ground for heresy* proceedings.

Burleigh; I. Hamilton, *The Erosion of Calvinist*

LIBRARIES (CHURCH, THEOLOGICAL)
Orthodoxy (E, 1990); B. M. G. Reardon, *Liberal Protestantism* (L, 1968); R. Sjölinder, *Presbyterian Reunion in Scotland, 1907–21* (Uppsala, 1962); A. C. Cheyne, *The Transforming of the Kirk* (E, 1983).

N. M. de S. Cameron

Libraries (Church, Theological, etc.). Scotland is rich in library resources for Christian theology, church history, religious experience, and the study of other religions. Omitting those of local churches and congregations, there are some forty libraries, which can be considered in three main groups: first, those which exist for the education and training of ministers, priests and other church leaders; second, those whose bookstocks facilitate advanced theological and historical research; and third, those available for religious education and spiritual reading by the communities they serve, or for the general public.

COLLEGE LIBRARIES. This first group includes the libraries serving the Divinity Faculties (see Theological Education) of the four ancient universities,* St Andrews (founded 1411), Glasgow (1451), Aberdeen (1494) and Edinburgh (1583). Until recently, each also had a separate library in a separate building. St Andrews has St Mary's College (1579); Edinburgh and Aberdeen have the former FC Colleges of New College (1843) and Christ's College (1850). The large library of Trinity College, Glasgow (founded by the FC in 1856) was absorbed into Glasgow University Library after 1974. These four university faculties have arrangements with the CofS and some other churches for the education of candidates for their ordained ministries.

Other colleges whose libraries fulfil this function are St Colm's College,* Edinburgh (CofS mission and lay training); Gillis College, Edinburgh (RC, formerly St Andrew's College, Drygrange, Melrose); Chesters College, Bearsden, Glasgow (RC, formerly St Peter's College, Cardross); St Andrew's College of Education, Bearsden, Glasgow (RC, formerly Notre Dame College); the Free Church of Scotland College, Edinburgh; the Scottish Baptist College, Glasgow; the Edinburgh Theological College of the Scottish Episcopal Church (Coates Hall) which incorporates the library of the Scottish Congregational College (see Episcopal Theological College); the Bible Training Institute, Glasgow;* and the Faith Mission* Bible College, Edinburgh.

RESEARCH LIBRARIES. The National Library of Scotland, Edinburgh, originally the eighteenth-century Advocates' Library, has had the privilege of copyright deposit since 1710. Its strong historical collections on the Reformation* have been joined by the Bishop Jolly* Library from Coates Hall and the important Blairs College Library (RC; see Colleges and Seminaries, Roman Catholic) deposited in 1975. The Scottish Record Office, Edinburgh, should not be neglected by researchers into ecclesiastical history. Most of the surviving CofS Synod, Presbytery and Kirk Session records (formerly in the General Assembly Library) are deposited there

LIBRARIES (CHURCH, THEOLOGICAL)
(unless in regional record offices), as are the records of the EpCS. The Scottish Catholic Archives (Drummond Place, Edinburgh) preserve records which were taken to the continent at the Reformation, saved from the French Revolution, and ultimately transferred to Edinburgh with many later documents from Blairs College, Aberdeen, in 1958. The libraries of the four universities mentioned above (St Andrews, Glasgow, Aberdeen and Edinburgh) are also centres for theological and biblical research, having major collections of standard texts and current periodicals, as well as rare books and manuscripts. Special collections at St Andrews include the Von Hügel Collection of Philosophy and Theology, and (also from Coates Hall) the George Hay Forbes* Liturgical Collection. Glasgow University Library has the large biblical collection formed by John Eadie* (a substantial portion has recently been dispersed) and that of Constantin Tischendorf, discoverer of the Codex Siniaticus. At Glasgow are also large collections on hymnology and liturgy, including many medieval MSS. Edinburgh University's main library has substantial holdings of theological books, such as the libraries of Clement Little* (d.1580) and James Nairne* (1629–78). It has a collection of early editions of Martin Luther and other Reformers which complements those at the National Library and New College. It also has many Buddhist religious MSS on palm-leaves.

New College* Library, administratively part of Edinburgh University Library since 1962, is maintained in its distinctive 1850 buildings on the Mound as the largest separate theological library in the UK. It has absorbed parts of the UP College Library (1900); Edinburgh Theological Library (from the University's Divinity Faculty, 1936); the CofS General Assembly Library (1958); and the CofS Lending Library (from 121 George Street, Edinburgh, 1971). Reformed theology is naturally its greatest strength, but its holdings are ecumenical in breadth and exhaustive in depth. Major collections are its Ecumenical Collection; James Thin (Hymnology); W. F. Jackson (Biblical archaeology); Dalman-Christie (Judaica); English and Gaelic Bibles; Dumfries Presbytery Library (1714); Plato E. Shaw (Catholic Apostolic Church*); and Longforgan FC Minister's Library. Historical MSS include: seventeenth century – Robert Baillie;* eighteenth century – the Erskines;* nineteenth century – Thomas Chalmers;* twentieth century – Alexander Whyte;* John White;* John Baillie;* J. H. Oldham.* Also housed in New College is the library of the Centre for the Study of Christianity in the Non-Western World (formerly in Aberdeen University), an extensive collection of books, periodicals, ephemera and artefacts, with a strong concentration on missions.

Other research resources in Edinburgh are the National Bible Society of Scotland (see Bible Societies) and Rutherford House* (1982). In Glasgow, the Mitchell Library (HQ of the City Libraries) has strong historical collections; in Dundee, the University Library houses the former Brechin Diocesan Library, and in St Andrews the Hay Fleming* Library has an important church history collection. Stirling University Library also supports an active religious studies programme. Local historical libraries which also have resources for church history are the Innerpeffray* Library near Crieff (1680); the Leighton Library*, Dunblane (1687); the Allan Ramsay Library, Leadhills (1741), and the Miners' Library, Wanlockhead (1756), both in the Lowther Hills near Sanquhar.

COMMUNITY AND PUBLIC LIBRARIES. The libraries of religious communities are maintained primarily for the use of their members. The greatest of these is the Abbey of St Benedict at Fort Augustus,* which is also rich in historical books. The Abbeys of Pluscarden,* Elgin (re-founded 1948), and Sancta Maria, Nunraw, East Lothian (1946), have active collections. The Dominican Chaplaincy to Edinburgh University (1932) also has a large library. The Tibetan Buddhist community at Eskdalemuir, (Langholm) Karma Kagyu Samye-Ling (1967), is building a working collection of English and Tibetan books and MSS.

The public libraries of the cities, Edinburgh, Glasgow, Aberdeen and Dundee, and the regional and district libraries, are also a valuable source of religious and theological reading. All Scottish local authority secondary schools (including RC schools) and independent schools are obliged to teach religious education. Their libraries have therefore to provide materials on Christianity and other religions as appropriate to their local community.

J. A. Lamb, 'Theological and Philosophical Libraries in Scotland', *Library Association Record* 61 (1959), 327–33; J. Durkan and A. Ross, *Early Scottish Libraries* (G, 1961); M. I. Williams (ed.), *Directory of Rare Book and Special Collections* (L, 1985); E. Lea and A. Jesson (eds), *A Guide to the Theological Libraries* (L, 1986); *Scottish Library and Information Resources 1987–88* (Motherwell, 1987); P. Brierley and D. Longley (eds), *UK Christian Handbook, 1992/93 Edition* (L, 1991).

J. V. Howard

Licentiate, Licensing. When a candidate for the ministry in the CofS (and similar churches) has completed his studies to the satisfaction of the General Assembly's Committee on Education for the Ministry, he is granted an 'exit certificate' which entitles the Presbytery to whose supervision he belongs to take him on 'trials for licence'. These consist of an examination (oral, written, or both) and the conduct of worship at a principal service on a Sunday in presence of two ministers and two elders from the Presbytery, the object being to ensure that he is acquainted with the present legal and sacramental practice and the past traditions of the CofS (or other Church as appropriate), and that he is a fit person to proceed to the ministry. These trials having been sustained, the candidate may, at a service organized and conducted by the Presbytery, be licensed as a Probationer* for the holy ministry. At this service certain appointed questions are put to the candidate who is also required to sign the Formula.* He or she is then 'licensed to preach the Gospel of the Lord Jesus Christ and to exercise his gifts as a Probationer for the Holy Ministry', and as a symbolic act there is put into his hand a copy of the Holy Scriptures. Until the present century students of divinity were sternly discouraged from entering pulpits before licence. In 1854 a Declaratory Act was passed by the Assembly which did 'expressly discharge and prohibit all the Ministers of this Church from giving countenance or permission to any person or persons to engage in the public ministry of the Word, or lead the devotions ... except to such as have been ordained or admitted as Ministers of this Church, or to Probationers who have been regularly licensed ... to preach the Gospel' (*PAGACS 1854*, 35). But practice has completely changed today. (This has led to questions being raised about the point of licensing, at least at the *end* of the period of study, and even to proposals for discontinuance of the licentiate.) If the candidate is proposing to go forward to the parish ministry, he has to serve for a year in a charge to which he is directed, and during this period he is officially known as a Probationer. Titles that have also been employed are 'Preacher of the Gospel' and 'Expectant'. On being licensed the candidate is entitled to wear a clerical collar and to designate himself 'Reverend'.

Cox 154–5, 222–31, 571–2; A. Herron, *A Guide to the Ministry* (E, 1987), 33ff.; W. Mair, *A Digest of Laws ... Church of Scotland* (E, L, ⁴1923), 227–39, 675–700.

A. Herron

Liddell, Eric Henry (1902–45), Olympic athlete and missionary. Liddell was born in Tientsin, China, the son of Scots missionaries. His father was a Congregational minister with LMS.* He was educated at Eltham College in England and then Edinburgh University (BSc, 1924), where he emerged as an outstanding runner. He was selected for the Paris Olympics in 1924 to represent Britain in the 100-metre sprint, but refused to run when he discovered that the heats were to be on a Sunday, the day of rest (*see* Sabbatarianism). Instead he entered the 400 metres, a distance for which he had little time to train. Before the race he was handed a message: 'Them that honour me, I will honour.' He won, in a world record time of 47.6 seconds. Edinburgh University, at a special graduation ceremony, awarded him his degree and an olive wreath as his crown of victory.

After studying divinity at the Scottish Congregational* College in Edinburgh, Liddell returned to China in 1925 as a missionary himself with the London Missionary Society.* There he taught science at the Anglo-Chinese College in Tientsin and later moved to rural Siochang, where, in appalling conditions of poverty and war, he worked as an itinerant evangelist. In 1943 he was interned by the occupying Japanese army in Weihsien, where he died of a brain tumour in 1945. A man universally liked for his unaffected and practical Christianity, he was widely mourned in Scotland and China. In 1981 his Olympic exploits were celebrated in the hugely successful film *Chariots of Fire*. His published works include *The Disciplines of the Christian Life* (L, 1985); *Prayers for Daily Use* (Tientsin, 1942); *The Sermon on the Mount: For Sunday School Teachers* (Tientsin, 1937).

S. Magnusson, *The Flying Scotsman* (L, 1981); D. P. Thomson, *Scotland's Greatest Athlete* (Crieff, 1970); *DNB Miss. Pers.* 403-4; R. W. Ramsey, *God's Joyful Runner* (S. Plainfield, NJ, 1987).

S. Magnusson

Life and Work, the principal monthly magazine of the CofS since 1879. Founded by A. H. Charteris,* it incorporated the CofS *Mission Record* from 1900 and merged at the 1929 reunion with the UF *Record* as *Life and Work: the Record of the Church of Scotland*. Charteris was editor for the first year. Other notable editors included John McMurtrie (1880-98), R. H. Fisher (1902-25), W. P. Livingstone* (1930-4) and J. W. Stevenson* (1945-65). Livingstone, editor of the UF *Record* from 1912, was the first lay editor. At the 1929 reunion plans were considered but rejected for a switch to a weekly church newspaper.

Life and Work, one of many initiatives of the Committee on Christian Life and Work led by Charteris, was intended to 'speak with a Scottish tongue' and head off the challenge of Victorian English popular religious periodicals. It had a strong literary as well as religious emphasis, with serial stories by such popular writers as R. M. Ballantyne and Mrs Oliphant.* Notable Victorian contributions included much of the work of the hymn-writer George Matheson.* It also served as a major channel for Charteris' defence of the Auld Kirk* against threats of disestablishment,* though it was never closed to Free Kirk contributors. This made it seem pro-Conservative and hostile to Gladstonian Liberalism.

Despite its additional role after 1900 as a record of home and overseas mission activity, it remained more literary than its UF equivalent, which deployed more obvious journalistic skills. After 1929 the combined magazine circulation of more than 200,000 made it an effective advertising as well as communication medium, another circulation peak of 217,000 being reached in the 1950s.

In the 1960s problems of adjustment to new religious and cultural conditions were compounded by an acrimonious public dispute between the managing General Assembly committee and an editor, Leonard Bell, whose purported dismissal in 1970 was not upheld by the Assembly or a committee of enquiry. Efforts to restore the magazine's equilibrium included its use as a major channel for William Barclay's* popular biblical expositions and its development as a news magazine and forum for the wide range of opinions within the Church, and not merely opinions adopted by Church committees and ratified by the General Assembly.

At times in the 1970s and 1980s this revealed only too clearly the diversity of Kirk opinion (both in theology and politics), and the magazine's editorial stance was criticized from time to time for lack of enthusiasm for ecumenism and Church involvement in politics. In the 1950s, however, it had been criticized from the other direction, especially over the Suez crisis.

See also Life and Work: Gaelic Supplement.

R. D. Kernohan, *Scotland's Life and Work* (E, 1979); Arthur Gordon, *A. H. Charteris* (L, 1912).

R. D. Kernohan

Life and Work: Gaelic Supplement, available with each monthly issue of *Life and Work**, the record of the CofS. It was first published in January 1880, and its circulation has been unbroken since then. Known in Gaelic* as *Na Duilleagan Gaidhlig* ('The Gaelic Pages'), the *Supplement* has had only five editors in over a century – Archibald Clerk* (1880-7), John MacRury (1887-1907), Donald Lamont* (1907-51), Thomas M. Murchison* (1951-81), and Roderick MacLeod (since 1981). In 1930, following the union of the Churches, it was amalgamated with *An Fhianais* ('The Witness'), which had been the Gaelic Supplement of the UFC.* In 1930-1 Malcolm MacLennan, who had edited *An Fhianais*, acted as joint-editor with Lamont. (The predecessor of *An Fhianais* had been published by the FC* as early as 1845, but there were breaks in production.)

The *Gaelic Supplement* has published a wide variety of articles in poetry and prose. Sermons by living preachers and ministers from the past are a popular feature. Important essays on historical issues and on aspects of modern Highland church life have regularly been featured. Some of the work of the best known Gaelic hymn-writers of the twentieth century, such as Hector MacKinnon,* first appeared in the *Supplement*. News items from congregations, readers' letters, book reviews and material for children are among the other regular articles. In 1989 the *Gaelic Supplement* had a circulation of 4,500.

T. M. Murchison (ed.), *Prose Writings of Donald Lamont 1874-1958* (E, 1960); *id.*, 'A Century Completed and a Job Done', *LW* Jan. 1980, 18; *id.*, 'The Gaelic Supplement to the Red Book', *LW* Feb. 1979, 27.

R. MacLeod

Lifters, a short-lived Secession Church formed of those who believed it was essential that the minister should 'lift' the elements of bread and wine from the Communion table prior to the prayer of consecration. This view was set out in a pamphlet published in 1776 by Josiah Hunter, General Associate (Antiburgher) Synod* minister in Falkirk (*An Inquiry concerning the Scriptural Order and Method of Dispensing the Sacrament of the Lord's Supper*, Falkirk, 1776). David Smyton, Antiburgher minister in Kilmaurs, also took this view. Hunter was deposed in 1781 and Smyton was suspended in 1783 by the Synod. They formed the Associate Presbytery* and were joined in 1785 by John Proudfoot of Leith. At its peak the 'Lifter' Presbytery had six congregations, but its longest surviving, Falkirk, dispersed in 1827.

'Lifting' was unusual in the CofS after about 1740, but it was recommended by G.W. Sprott* in 1882 in his *The Worship and Offices of the Church of Scotland* (E).

H. Watt, 'David Smyton and the Lifters', *RSCHS* 13 (1959), 38–63; Small I, 661–3.

H. R. Sefton

Lindisfarne, *see* Early Ecclesiastical Sites.

Lindores Abbey. Situated on the Firth of Forth, the Tironensian* abbey was founded c.1191 by David, Earl of Huntingdon and grandson of David I;* the founding community came probably from Kelso.* In 1219 the monks numbered twenty-six. The abbot was granted *pontificalia* (i.e. episcopal insignia) by the Avignon pope in 1395, and a son of Robert III was buried there in 1402. Steps were taken in 1414 to repair the damaged fabric. The buildings were extended in the early sixteenth century. They were sacked by Reformers in 1543 and 1559, though there is no evidence of structural damage.

The last regular abbot was John Philp, who had been a monk of Lindores; he ruled 1532–65 and became a Protestant. His successor was the commendator* John Leslie,* bishop of Ross. The community numbered some twenty-five in the 1530s and twenty in the 1550s. Lindores made a substantial contribution to the Reformed Church: four monks became ministers, all the neighbouring parishes were served by Lindores monks as ministers or readers,* and the monk Thomas Wood* provided music for psalms and canticles in Reformed worship.

Liber Sancte Marie de Lundoris (Abbotsford Club, E, 1841); J. Dowden (ed.), *Chartulary of the Abbey of Lindores* (SHS, E, 1903); Easson-Cowan, 66–70; A. Laing, *Lindores Abbey and the Burgh of Newburgh* (E, 1876); M. Dilworth, 'Monks and Ministers after 1560', *RSCHS* 18 (1974), 211–16.

M. Dilworth

Lindsay, (Sir) David (c.1490–1555), poet and dramatist. He was the son of David Lindsay of the Mount (near Cupar-Fife). (It seems unlikely that he was the David Lindesay incorporated at St Andrews in 1508 or 1509.) In 1511 he was granted 3 4s. for a costume for a play performed before King James IV and Queen Margaret at Holyrood; Lindsay was then receiving a pension of 40, as a member of the Royal Household. On the birth of James V* (April 1512), he became the latter's personal servitor (usher), and later the Master Usher, and Master of the Household. Before 1522 Lindsay married Janet Douglas, a sempstress at the court. During the ascendancy of the Earl of Angus (1524–8), he was dismissed from office, but continued to receive payments from the King. By 1535 he had been appointed Lyon Herald, and in the early 1530s he was several times abroad (Burgundy, France) in connection with the marriage negotiations of James V. He probably attended the nuptials of James and Madeleine, daughter of King Francis I, in Notre-Dame, Paris, on New Year's day, 1537. After Madeleine's death, in July of the same year, James married Marie de Lorraine, who was welcomed to Scotland by a masque of Lindsay's devising, performed at St Andrews (June 1538). Lindsay was knighted in October 1542, and around the same date he, as Lyon King of Arms, compiled a list of the coats of arms of the Scottish nobility and gentry. Following the seizure of St Andrews castle by the assassins of Cardinal David Beaton* (1546), Lindsay negotiated with the rebels on behalf of the Crown forces, although he had no sympathy for Beaton. In late 1548 he went on a trade mission to Denmark. Lindsay died, without issue, in early 1555.

Lindsay was a true court-poet; many of his works – the *Dreme* (1528), the *Complaynt of Schir David Lindsay* (1529–30), the *Testament of the Papyngo* (1530) – reflect his intimate, avuncular relations with James V, and others commemorate events at court: e.g. the *Deploratioun of the Deith of Quene Magdalene* (1537). Lindsay had a strong satirical gift, seen in some shorter works – e.g. the *Tragedie of the Cardinall* (1547) – but especially in his play, *Ane Satyre of the Thrie Estaitis*, in which he castigated folly at court and corruption in the Church. The play was performed at Cupar (1552) and Edinburgh (1554). His last work is the lengthy *Dialogue betuix Experience and Ane Courteour* (1553), in which he reviews the miserable condition of the world, from Adam to the Last Judgement.

Virtually all Lindsay's works express outrage at the personal immorality of churchmen, yet the poet is also careful to commend the worthy. Saints Francis, Dominic, Bernard and Benedict, together with a small number of monks and friars, are given an honourable place in heaven at the end of the *Dialogue*, but too many of their followers, Lindsay believes, have failed to live up to the original standards. Lindsay also tended to emphasise the greed and rapacity of the clergy. Some specific points of Catholic doctrine and practice attacked by Lindsay include: purgatory – only grudgingly conceded in the *Dreme*; confession – denounced in *Kitteis Confessioun* (1543–50) as a mere human invention, and one characteristically abused for the sake of extorting sexual favours; idolatry – Lindsay's term for the cult of saints via images (often coupled with pilgrimages), impugned in the *Complaynt* and in the *Dialogue* (lines 2,279–2,708); and the efficacy of relics – ridiculed in the *Satyre*. The cause of corruption in the Church is traced to Pope Sylvester's acceptance of property from Emperor Constantine (*Papyngo*, 815; *Dialogue*, 4,409), and Lindsay views the papacy as a fifth monarchy, soon to give way to the realm of Antichrist. Lindsay's verse is more fluent than subtle, and his powerful combination of social satire, political comment and apocalyptic vision guaranteed success. For him religion was a public theme: he is not a poet of devotion or meditation. Though Lindsay was reformist in religion, it is debatable whether he was really a Protestant; but in any case he quickly acquired a posthumous reputation as a prophet of the Reformation.

LINDSAY, DAVID

The Works of Sir David Lindsay, ed. D. Hamer, STS, 4 vols (E, 1931–6); *Poetical Works of Sir David Lyndsay*, ed. D. Laing, 3 vols (E, 1879). W. Murison, *Sir David Lyndsay* (C, 1938); *History of Scottish Literature*, vol. I, ed. R. D. S. Jack (A, 1988); *Facsimile of an Ancient Heraldic Manuscript*, ed. D. Laing (E, 1878); Sir David Lindsay, *Ane Satyre of the Thrie Estaitis*, ed. Roderick Lyall (E, 1989).

A. A. MacDonald

Lindsay, David (c.1531–1613), Reformation minister. He was the son of Robert Lindsay of Kirkton, brother of David, ninth Earl of Crawford. If he served in the pre-Reformation Church, he may be identified with the graduate appointed chaplain of Woodside in Dunkeld diocese in 1552. He travelled in France and Switzerland, and may be the resident in Geneva in 1558 who was admitted to the congregation of English exiles there. He had evidently adopted Protestantism, and on returning home at the Reformation* was recognized as minister in Leith at a gathering of leading Protestants in July 1560. Present at the General Assembly in December 1560, he became a regular attender at some fifty Assemblies, was frequently selected to serve as one of the Assembly's commissioners or visitors, and was elected Moderator in February 1569, October 1577, October 1582, May 1586, April 1593, and March 1597. His labours for the Kirk were also recognized in the Crown's gift, with the consent of Erskine of Dun,* of the property of the Carmelite* friars in Inverbervie, which he received in 1570. In 1572 he approved the settlement achieved by the Convention of Leith,* but soon afterwards supported, and contributed to, the *Second Book of Discipline*.* In 1574 he was one of the Kirk's representatives at a meeting with the Regent Morton (*see* Douglas, James) who failed in his bid to gain the Church's acceptance of the royal supremacy. During the 'anti-Presbyterian dictatorship' of the Arran (*see* Stewart, James, d.1596) regime, he was imprisoned at Blackness for opposing royal policy in 1584. In later years, the moderate-minded Lindsay was apt to be dubbed a 'court minister' and was ready to comply with King James VI's* request to pray for his mother before her execution, though in 1592 he argued that James was not exempt from liability to excommunication if he disobeyed God's will, and in 1605 he spoke out in the Privy Council at the government's treatment of Presbyterian ministers who had approved the legality of the Aberdeen Assembly of 1605. In 1589, Lindsay conducted the proxy marriage of James VI to Anne of Denmark at Uppsala, and baptized Prince Henry at Stirling in 1594. For his services, he was advanced by James to the bishopric of Ross in November 1600, a post which then entailed no episcopal duties apart from power to vote in parliament;* he therefore continued his parish ministry in Leith. At the union of the crowns, he accompanied the King on his journey to England. He was succeeded at Leith by his son, David (*FES* I, 161). His son-in-law was Archbishop John Spottiswoode.*

LINDSAY, THOMAS MARTIN

Knox, *History*, I; *BUK*; Calderwood; Spottiswoode, III, 220; *Register of the Privy Council*, ed. P. H. Brown *et al.*, 1st ser. (E, 1877–98); *SBD*; *FES* I, 160–1, 165; J. Kirk, *Patterns of Reform* (E, 1989); *DNB* XXXIII, 297–8.

J. Kirk

Lindsay, Robert (c.1532–c.1580), Scotland's first vernacular prose historian. He was the laird of Piscottie, near Ceres, Fife, but little is known of his life. *The Historie and Cronicles of Scotland* (first published 1724; ed. E. J. G. Mackay, 3 vols, STS, E, 1898–1911) cover 1436–1575. For the earlier part he uses sources like Hector Boece,* but from 1542 he provides a valuable independent account. He writes as a son of the Reformation, not for scholars (he was probably not a graduate) but for his fellow-countrymen. He knew the Bible in English, and may well have borrowed from hearing Knox preach in Fife. He was a distant relative of Sir David Lindsay,* and connected to some of the Protestant nobles. Though even his contemporary record is far from faultless, he was a graphic and honest chronicler.*

Introduction to Mackay's edition.

D. F. Wright

Lindsay, Thomas Martin (1843–1914), FC/UF church historian. Born in the Relief* Church manse in Lesmahagow, Lanarkshire (Small II, 427–8), he was a brilliant student at Glasgow and Edinburgh where he became assistant to Professor A. C. Fraser* before training for the FC ministry at New College. He assisted R. S. Candlish* at Free St George's, Edinburgh, before being elected and ordained to the Chair of Church History at the Glasgow FC College in 1872. He served until his death, and from 1902 was also Principal of the, now UF, College.

Lindsay favoured a more liberal approach to confessional subscription,* and also actively supported William Robertson Smith* (although he affirmed biblical infallibility; 'The Critical Movement in the Free Church of Scotland', *Contemp. Review* 33, 1878, 22–34). He wrote extensively, with articles in the ninth edition of the *EB* (1875–88) and chapters in the Cambridge Modern and Medieval Histories. He is best known for his 1902 Cunningham lectures,* *The Church and the Ministry in the Early Centuries* (L, 1902), and above all for *A History of the Reformation*, 2 vols (E, 1906–7; ²1907–8). This work has remained in print, and represents one of the most substantial Scottish accounts of the Reformation, with a particular interest in its social and domestic aspects. Lindsay's social concern was evident in his involvement in crofting agitation and with labour leaders. He was convener of FC/UF Foreign Missions for fifteen years. He was a DD of Glasgow and LLD of St Andrews (1906). Other works include: *Luther and the German Reformation* (E, 1900); *Revivals* (L, 1909).

AFCS I, 56; *FUFCS* 574, 578; *DNB 1912–1921*, 338–9; *MRUFCS* 169 (Jan. 1915), 32–3; J. A. Ross, *The Fourth Generation: Reminiscences* (L,

1912), with Lindsay's *Letters ... to Janet Ross* (L, 1923).

D. F. Wright

Lindsay, William (1802–66), Relief* and UP professor. Born at Irvine, Ayrshire, he studied at Glasgow University and then at the Relief Church Theological Hall at Paisley (founded 1824) under James Thomson. Ordained to Johnstone Relief Church, Renfrewshire in 1830, he served from 1832 as minister of Dovehill Relief, Glasgow (as colleague to John Barr, and successor from 1839) which removed in 1844 to become Cathedral Street Relief (from 1847 UP) Church. He died suddenly after Sunday duty there.

From 1841 he was also Professor of Exegetical Theology and Biblical Criticism for the Relief Synod, continuing in the UP Theological Hall from 1847 until his death. Glasgow made him a DD in 1844.

He was a productive writer. He introduced Samuel Miller's *The Warrant, Nature and Duties ... of the Ruling Elder ...* (G, 1835), contributed to J. Taylor (ed.), *The Pictorial History of Scotland* (2 vols, L, n.d.) and a life of Thomas Gillespie* to *Lives of Ebenezer Erskine ...* , by James Harper et al. (E, 1849), and wrote *Miracles of Scripture* (E, 1850), *Duty of Submission to Civil Rulers* (G, 1838), *Inquiry into the Christian Law as to the Relationships which Bar Marriage* (G, 1855; ²L, 1871), and *Lectures on ... Hebrews* (2 vols, E, 1867). He served the whole UP community, without discrimination, but was not one to 'palter' with the truth.

DNB XXXIII, 315–16; Small II, 34–5, 537; *UP Magazine* n.s. 11 (1867), 351–6; *ASUPC*, 298.

D. F. Wright

Lismore, *see* Early Ecclesiastical Sites.

Literature, Religion in Scottish. Religion appears in the earliest surviving manuscripts, in the masterpieces of the Renaissance* such as Henryson's *Testament of Cresseid* and in many of Gavin Dunbar's* poems, in the attacks on the organizational shortcomings of the Church and churchmen in Gavin Douglas* and in David Lindsay's* *Satyre of the Thrie Estatis*. The Reformation* in the sixteenth century produced a flood of serious writing – John Knox* has been well known as a prose writer for centuries – and the CofS, with a literate graduate ministry, ensured a strong writing tradition, as did the survival of the learned professions (law, education, Church) after the Unions of 1603 and 1707. The Presbyterian* establishment co-existed with an increasing number of smaller, alternative Churches, including the Secession churches, the EpCS and the RCC; major events such as the Covenanting* wars, or the Disruption,* were to add substantially to the body of published literature.

In imaginative writing the results can be seen in several ways. Satiric or negative writing produced a series of sketches of unworthy Christians, the most celebrated being Robert Burns's* Holy Willie and James Hogg's* Robert Wringhim (in the *Confessions of a Justified Sinner*), and often of ambiguous churchmen such as Robert Louis Stevenson's Revd Soulis in *Thrawn Janet*, Sir Walter Scott's* fine suggestion of the timeserving clergyman in *Wandering Willie's Tale*. Presbyterians warped by inadequate understanding of religious ideas, or by character defects, are a frequent feature of Scottish writing; they inhabit the flinty Scottish towns of George MacDonald's* novels, they justify Clearances* in Fionn MacColla and Neil Gunn, they engage in sadism or worse in Lewis Grassic Gibbon's appalling John Guthrie in *Sunset Song*, and in George Mackay Brown's *Greenvoe* they still shelter behind the curtains of the most up-to-date manse. Burns' satiric verse kicks against the deadening hand of such clergymen, as does Hugh MacDiarmid's scorn in *A Drunk Man*. James Bridie's *Mr Bolfry* has little trouble in running circles round the slow-witted Revd McCrimmon; even John Galt's* much-loved Revd Balwhidder in *Annals of the Parish* empties his kirk while his preaching creaks, unchanging, from 1760 to 1810, as the world rages through revolution beyond his parish boundaries. The negative tradition goes from outright condemnation to a puzzled understanding; only rarely does the writer focus long enough on the clergyman trapped in his public and private role to explore – as does John Gibson Lockhart in *Adam Blair* – the contradictions between a public life of urgently-required blamelessness and the private demands of unsatisfied sexual longing. Adam Blair pays for one night's irregularity with a lifetime's remorse; a century later a Marxist novelist such as Grassic Gibbon could probe (in *Cloud Howe*) the mind of a socialist minister isolated in his parish and in his world, seeking to change a Church which regarded him with indifference or hostility.

Ambiguous or exploratory writing shades, as will be seen, into the previous category. Burns obviously felt able to combine personal belief and churchgoing with ferocious satire of individual clergymen and religious bigots, and Hogg's satiric portrait of perversion in the *Confessions* came from a man who sincerely practised religion in family and in public churchgoing. Perhaps the most conspicuous success in this ambiguous understanding was Scott who, in *The Heart of Midlothian*, combined the repellent features of the grimly inflexible Davie Deans with a delicate exploration of the hard times in the Covenanting wars that had made him the man he was, and the softening power of love in his daughter Jeanie who could accept him for what he was, while in herself demonstrating that such principle could co-exist with love and resilience. Many of Scotland's most attractive literary portraits of religious persons have had this quality of reconciling high principle with human character: Galt's Ringan Gilhaize, Stevenson's Archie Weir (contrasted with his appalling father) or his delicate probing of the psychology of Dr Jekyll, George MacDonald's Robert Falconer, Neil Gunn's Philosopher (in *The Serpent*) or J. MacDougall Hay's Mrs Galbraith (in *Gillespie*), Edwin Muir's honest but upsetting picture of his family in the *Autobiography*. The obvious formative features of the Church in the recent work of writers such as Alasdair Gray in *Lanark* indicate the continuing background importance of the CofS.

Kailyard writing in Scotland, which had its greatest impact in the late nineteenth century but continues in many forms, conspired to portray the country as one caught in a time-warp of contented peasantry, full churches, and basic decent Christian attitudes. (The term is Scottish for 'cabbage patch'. The movement sentimentally idealized humble village life.) Such portraits of Scotland – undoubtedly containing a great deal that is true – tended to postpone the attempt to explore the world of the cities and the slums, and factories and the post-Christian society. Douglas Brown's *The House with the Green Shutters* is a particularly scathing attack on this idyllic Scotland, long out of date if it ever existed; his Barbie is populated by two ministers (one a fool, one a glutton) but by no churches at all so far as the novel is concerned – neatly making the point about the marginalization of the Church in reality for many modern Scots. In the later parts of *A Scots Quair* Grassic Gibbon simply omits the Church; MacDiarmid, likewise, sees little need to mention it.

Throughout, religious writing in Scotland has sought to combine realistic description with analysis of the Church and its effect on society, from the courtly laughter of David Lindsay, the malice of 'Holy Willie's Prayer', the crude guying of *The House with the Green Shutters* to the real psychological brilliance of Hogg's exploration of the religious mind in the *Confessions*. Throughout, the Church has reformed, split, reunited – above all, changed. Fiction, poetry, drama, journalism have responded at the time with interest, but often only later with analysis. The influence of the kailyard has frequently perpetuated the attractive old features, while the recent influence of realism has accentuated the decline of the traditional features, including the Kirk. It has little place in the Glasgow of William McIlvanney's *Hard Man*, or Alasdair Gray's Duncan Thaw, the Edinburgh MacDiarmid scoffed at, the Aberdeen of Grassic Gibbon's *Grey Granite*. The finest writing has been an honest exploration of the ambiguities facing the sincere Christian, combined often with an attempt to educate reader and writer alike in the Church's position in doctrine and writing. Though the term 'Calvinist' is frequently used as a portmanteau term of abuse in Scottish writing, it has been left to few writers to explore Scotland's unique adaptation of Calvin* and sensitively to write about the balance between Church and life as it evolved over the centuries. The result has been to stimulate occasionally brilliant literature; and in Hogg, and in Scott above all, to generate enquiries about the possibilities of religious life at all in the perspective of the Scotland described.

D. F. Wright (ed.), *The Bible in Scottish Life and Literature* (E, 1988); D. Daiches (ed.), *Companion to Scottish Culture* (L, 1981); T. Royle (ed.), *Companion to Scottish Literature* (L, 1983);

I. Campbell, *Kailyard* (E, 1981). The most recent survey of Scottish literature is R. C. Craig (ed.), *History of Scottish Literature*, 4 vols (A, 1987–9).

I. Campbell

Little (Litill), Clement (*c.* 1527–80), advocate, commissary, and elder, lawyer, scholar and benefactor of the Reformed Kirk. He was a son of Clement Little, an Edinburgh merchant. Educated at Edinburgh's grammar school in the 1530s and St Andrews University, where he entered St Leonard's College in 1543, Little continued his scholarly pursuits overseas at Louvain, where he seems to have studied law after matriculating in 1546. On returning home by 1550, he served his legal apprenticeship in the courts, was sheriff by 1556 and practised as an advocate in the Court of Session by 1557. He conformed to the Reformation,* was already serving as elder on Edinburgh's Kirk Session* in 1561, donated £60 in 1562 to the Kirk Session's appeal for a new hospital for the poor, contributed to the financial support of the ministry in 1573, and was frequently a commissioner to the General Assembly. Appointed in 1564 as one of the four commissaries in Edinburgh, Little showed a readiness to place his legal expertise at the Kirk's disposal and by 1567 was chosen by the General Assembly to act as a lawyer for the Kirk. He approved of Queen Mary's enforced abdication in favour of her son in 1567, and was active in promoting educational facilities in the burgh. Not only was he appointed to examine the aptitude of the burgh's RC grammar master in 1562 (in a bid to secure the teacher's dismissal), but he was anxious to see a college or university established in the capital. Although he died several years before it was founded (1583), Little bequeathed to the town his outstanding theological library which became the nucleus of Edinburgh University library (1584). The collection of more than 270 volumes contains a remarkable range of theological literature from patristic studies, medieval commentaries and scholastic works to the humanist writings of the Renaissance and Reformation.

C. P. Finlayson, *Clement Litill and his Library* (E, 1980); J. Kirk, 'Clement Little's Edinburgh', in *Edinburgh University Library, 1580–1980*, ed. J. R. Guild and A. Law (E, 1982), 1–42 (also in Kirk, *Patterns of Reform*, E, 1989).

J. Kirk

Liturgical Books (Pre-Reformation). Over 140 liturgical books and fragments survive from pre-Reformation Scotland. They range in date from the sixth to the sixteenth centuries.

The earliest missionaries to Scotland almost certainly brought with them some form of the Gallican liturgy and from this was developed the distinctive Celtic rite. Only three liturgical fragments of Scottish origin illustrate this period: the sixth-century psalter of St Columba,* the office for the visitation and Communion of the sick in the Book of Deer* (tenth century) and the eleventh-century Drummond Missal (mass service-book).

LITURGY

The period between Queen Margaret* and the Wars of Independence (1100-1300) saw the gradual introduction into Scotland of the Sarum rite, which had originated in the diocese of Salisbury in England in an attempt to bring the local usage into closer conformity with that of Rome. It is known that the cathedrals of Glasgow, Moray and Dunkeld adopted this rite. The thirteenth-century manuscripts which survive all show English influence, but Scottish saints were included in the calendars. The most interesting survival from this period is the pontifical (bishop's service-book) of David de Bernham* (Bishop of St Andrews, 1239-53), which gives a list of eighty-nine churches and chapels consecrated by the bishop between 1240 and 1249.

The Wars of Independence led to some anti-English propaganda against the Sarum rite and Scottish liturgical writers turned increasingly to continental sources and native traditions. By the end of the fifteenth century, the text of the Sarum books in use in Scotland was sufficiently adapted to suggest that a distinctively Scottish rite was being developed. The Arbuthnott Missal* and the Missal of St Nicholas, Aberdeen, are the two most important survivals from this period.

The majority of the surviving liturgical books are concerned with the daily office or priest's services rather than the mass. One of the most beautiful is the Murthly Book of Hours (c.1270), which has twenty-three full-page and eleven small miniatures illuminated in gold and colours, but the Arbuthnott Book of Hours (1471-84) also has fine illuminations. The most famous of these books is the Aberdeen Breviary* of Bishop William Elphinstone,* printed in Edinburgh in 1510.

Early sixteenth-century Scotland was well aware of the radical reforms of both missal and breviary by the Spanish Cardinal Francisco de Quiñones (d.1540), and eight breviaries and two missals of this simplified type survive.

Some twenty-six inventories of vestments, vessels and furnishings, ranging in date from the twelfth to the sixteenth centuries, also give valuable information about medieval worship.

D. McRoberts, 'The Medieval Scottish Liturgy Illustrated by Surviving Documents', *Transactions of the Scottish Ecclesiological Society* 15 (1957), 24-40; id., *Catalogue of Scottish Medieval Liturgical Books and Fragments* (G, 1953); id., 'The Scottish Church and Nationalism in the Fifteenth Century', *IR* 19 (1968), 3-14; A. P. Forbes, *Kalendars of Scottish Saints* (E, 1872); L. C. Sheppard, *The Liturgical Books* (L, 1962).

H. R. Sefton

Liturgy. Liturgy can be used in the broad sense as the worship of the Church, but more particularly as the order of worship used in the celebration of Holy Communion. In the Episcopalian and RC traditions a fixed order has been followed, while in the Presbyterian churches directories have been used.

THE PRE-REFORMATION CHURCH. In the Celtic Church* the liturgy was that of the Latin Mass* with local variations, including the observance of certain saints' days. In the Middle Ages the 'use' of *Sarum* or Salisbury was largely followed (*see* Liturgical Books (Pre-Reformation)), the order for the mass most commonly found in England. After the Wars of Independence, and the Great Schism of the Western Church in which Scotland and England recognized different popes, there was a growth of continental influence and the observance of additional feasts, which made the liturgy rather cumbersome. A project to compose a revised 'Scottish use' was undertaken by Bishop William Elphinstone* of Aberdeen. The Aberdeen Breviary,* however, did not replace the Sarum book, which remained in fairly general use in Scotland until the Reformation.

THE REFORMATION. In the growing movement for reform, the English second *Book of Common Prayer** of Edward VI was most probably in general use in Scotland among Protestant worshippers. It was soon replaced after the Reformation* by the *Book of Common Order,** sometimes called 'Knox's Liturgy', which had been used by the English Protestant exiles to whom John Knox* had ministered in Geneva. It was authorized by the General Assembly for the celebration of the sacraments in 1562 and two years later for the 'common prayers' as well. It was not a fixed liturgy, but neither was it a mere directory, since some parts did not envisage deviation from the text. It was used for the reading of public prayers when ministers were not available (*see* Readers (Reformation Era)). The Lord's Supper,* however, did not come to be celebrated as frequently as the Reformers wished, although the people were not to be as passive as in the mass and were to take part in the singing of the psalms* and in the saying of the Lord's Prayer* and the Apostles Creed (*see* Confessions of Faith).

THE POST-REFORMATION PERIOD. Liturgical revision was attempted under King James VI and I* to bring the Churches in Scotland and England into greater uniformity. Several draft liturgies were prepared, but after obtaining the approval of the Five Articles of Perth* in 1618, James gave an undertaking that he would not press any further liturgical changes upon the Scottish Church. Charles I,* however, did not adopt the same caution as his father, and a new prayer book, popularly named after William Laud,* the Archbishop of Canterbury, was introduced in 1637, provoking a storm of protest associated with the legendary name of Jenny Geddes.* The protest was made formally in the National Covenant* of 1638, and the book was condemned by the General Assembly meeting at Glasgow* later that same year.

THE SEVENTEENTH AND EIGHTEENTH CENTURIES. In the civil war in England, the Scots supported the English Parliamentarians on the understanding that an attempt would be made to bring about a uniformity in religion in Scotland and England on the basis of Presbyterianism*. The Westminster* Directory for Public Worship was approved by both Parliament and General Assembly in 1645. It was intended as a replacement to the English and Scottish Prayer Books, but it was also different from the *BCO* in that there were no 'set forms' apart from the formulae for baptism and for the administration of Communion and the marriage vows. The only other traditional feature of Scottish worship to be retained was the Lord's Prayer, which in practice fell into disuse along with the Doxology, the Creed and the Ten Commandments. With the Restoration of Charles II* in 1660 the *BCO* theoretically resumed its lawful place in worship but there was a great deal of latitude in practice. There was little difference between Episcopalians and Presbyterians, although the Episcopalians tended to use the Doxology and the saying of the Lord's Prayer, features of worship in the post-Reformation period. Following the Glorious Revolution of 1688 and the expulsion of James VII and II,* the Westminster Directory resumed its place as the standard for worship in the Kirk.

After the case involving James Greenshields,* however, Episcopalians were able to worship using the *BCP* of the CofE. The non-juring* Episcopalians, who remained loyal to the house of Stuart, adhered to the Scottish liturgy of 1637, the Communion office of which was reprinted in what were called the 'wee bookies'. In the early twentieth century a revision of the Scottish Liturgy took place in the Episcopal Church and a new Prayer Book was published in 1928.

THE NINETEENTH AND TWENTIETH CENTURIES. With the 'Catholic revival'* of the late nineteenth century more liturgical forms were introduced into Presbyterian worship. One agency in this change was the Church Service Society* and its service book *Euchologion*,* the forerunner of official service books produced by the Presbyterian Churches. After the Union* of 1929 the *Book of Common Order** was published in 1940. It represents the combination of Reformed and 'catholic' elements in worship, as seen in the Order of Holy Communion which contains the 'warrant' for the sacrament from 1 Corinthians 11 as well as the *Sursum Corda, Sanctus, Benedictus* and *Agnus Dei*. The more recent *Book of Common Order* (1979) emphasizes the centrality of Communion in worship. The EpCS has also revised its liturgy and after *The Experimental Liturgy* (1971) has brought out the *Scottish Liturgy* (1982). Since Vatican II the mass of the RCC has been celebrated in English in a simpler form with the priest facing the people behind the altar. In all the main Churches in Scotland liturgy is now being assessed in very similar ways, by reference to the Bible and the practice of the early Church and by relating worship to the society in which the Church must witness to the gospel.

See also Worship; Lord's Supper; Christian Year.

W. D. Maxwell, *A History of Worship in Scotland* (L, 1955); D. B. Forrester and D. M. Murray (eds), *Studies in the History of Worship in Scotland* (E, 1984); W. McMillan, *The Worship of the Scottish Reformed Church, 1550–1638* (L, 1931); T. Leishman, 'The Ritual of the Church', in R. H. Story (ed.), *The Church of Scotland Past and Present* (L, 1890), V, 307–426; C. G. M'Crie, *The Public Worship of Presbyterian Scotland* (E and L, 1892); W. Perry, *The Scottish Liturgy* (E, ²1922); *id.*, *The Scottish Prayer Book* (C, 1929).

D. M. Murray

Livingston, Thomas (*d.* 1460), conciliarist,* the most influential Scot at the Council of Basel. Probably connected to the W. Lothian Livingstons, he studied under Laurence of Lindores* at St Andrews (BA, 1413; MA, 1414), and went abroad, perhaps to Paris, for theology. He became a Cistercian* of Newbattle (S. of Edinburgh) but visited Rome in vain to secure confirmation of appointment as abbot (1422–3). He became a doctor of theology at Cologne University (1423–5), where he may have met Nicholas of Cusa. He was (nonresident) abbot of Dundrennan (Kirkcudbrightshire) by the time he became the first Scot to join the Council of Basel in 1432, remaining until 1441.

Known as 'the Scottish abbot', Livingston fulfilled a range of commissions in pursuit of the Council's reformist policies, and was an elector in 1439 of its counter-pope, Felix V, who in 1440 appointed him, quite ineffectually, to the bishopric of Dunkeld. He later made him his legate to Scotland, but the conciliarist cause collapsed, and when Felix submitted to Pope Nicholas V in 1449, Livingston did likewise, receiving in return the parish of Kirkinner (near Wigtown) *in commendam* (*see* Commendator). In the service of Cardinal Nicholas of Cusa, legate for Germany, he reformed the German Benedictine houses (1450) and attended the provincial council of Mainz (1452). After 1454 he was granted the abbacy of Coupar Angus *in commendam*.

J. H. Burns, *Scottish Churchmen and the Council of Basle* (G, 1962); *id.*, 'The Conciliarist Tradition in Scotland', *SHR* 42 (1963), 89–104; D. Shaw, 'Thomas Livingston, A Conciliarist', *RSCHS* 12 (1958), 120–35.

D. F. Wright

Livingstone, David (1813–73), missionary, geographer, linguist and anti-slavery* campaigner. He was born at Blantyre, Lanarkshire. His grandparents were part of the large-scale migration from Gaeldom into central Scotland in the early nineteenth century, and the young David sometimes read the Gaelic Bible to his grandmother. Devout Christians, the family left the CofS to join an Independent* chapel in Hamilton. David entered the local cotton mill at the age of ten, but was determined enough to attend the mill's night school which operated after work ceased.

The first ever appeal by missionary societies for medical missionaries fired him, in 1834, with the determination to respond. Working at the mill in the long vacation, he studied at the Andersonian Medical School in Glasgow and also attended a Greek class at Glasgow University. He was accepted by the London Missionary Society* for service in 1838 and went to London for theological training. He continued medical training there, re-

LIVINGSTONE, DAVID

turning to Glasgow to complete the examinations of the Royal College.

He had hoped to go to China, but the Opium War made this impossible. A meeting with Robert Moffat,* his future father-in-law, turned him towards Africa. Ordained in London in 1840, he arrived in Cape Town in March 1841. It was on the slow 700-kilometre journey by ox-wagon from Port Elizabeth to Moffat's station at Kuruman that Livingstone decided that life 'in the bush' was the task for which God had prepared him. He was willing to do the conventional work on a mission station as a training programme, but pioneering was to be his long-term calling. He rapidly became fluent in Tswana, and on long journeys through the villages achieved an intimacy with Africans and an empathy with African culture unusual among Europeans in Africa. These journeys took him further into the Kalahari area than any other white on record. In 1845 he married Mary Moffat who, to the outrage of her parents, went with him on all his journeys, including the one where he and his friend Oswell were the first Europeans to see Lake Ngami.

Livingstone now decided to push northwards to open up new territory for the mission in areas where there was a reputedly much higher density of population than in what is now Botswana, and to get away from white settlers, Afrikaner or British. He accepted that such travel was impossible for Mary and the children, so they returned to Scotland. In 1852 he set off on an astonishing journey, northwards to what is now Zambia. Here he found his dense population, but the distance from South Africa was too long and arduous for the entry of 'Christianity and Commerce' which, he believed, would transform Africa and bring her 'into the community of nations'. A new route had to be found. With some companions from the Makololo people he walked to Loanda on the Angolan coast. But the increased activity of Portuguese slavers ruled out that route. With his Makololo companions he returned to the Zambesi and set off again, to Quilemane on the East coast, arriving in May 1856. A Royal Navy ship brought him to London. He received popular adulation for this astonishing feat, a march of over 5,000 kilometres. Despite the emphasis of later writers on the achievement of 'the lone white man', Livingstone always insisted on his debt to the support of the Makololo people.

In Britain he wrote *Missionary Travels and Researches in South Africa*, published in London in 1857, which sold over 70,000 copies and made his family financially secure. The LMS were unable to back his idea of a new, large-scale missionary effort into the Zambesi Valley. The Government decided to finance an expedition, which he would head, to explore the area 'in the interests of civilization and commerce'. The Universities Mission to Central Africa, inspired by his Cambridge lectures (W. Monk, ed., *Dr Livingstone's Cambridge Lectures*, C, 1858), would follow after.

The Zambesi Expedition lasted from March 1858 until July 1864. This well-equipped mission, with its European staff, was a disaster. Although much was learned about the area, and the Shire River

LIVINGSTONE, JOHN

and Lake Malawi partially explored, the loss of life among the UMCA mission (which withdrew to Zanzibar) and the bitter quarrels among the expedition members saw Livingstone's prestige and popularity plunge. The impossibility of using the Zambasi as a navigable entry to the area, and the increasing disruption caused by Portuguese and Arab slavers made his original plans seem impractical dreams. The failure was compounded by his deep grief over the death in 1862 of his wife Mary, who had insisted on joining him, and the death of their eldest son who fell in the American Civil War in 1864.

In Britain a few important people still backed him. With their help he returned to Africa in 1866, now determined to find the source of the Nile if possible, but above all to document the extent of the devastation of African society by the Portuguese and Arab slave-trade and to bring it to the attention of the world. Livingstone became increasingly famous during these extraordinary wanderings all over modern Western Tanzania, Zambia, Malawi and Zaire, no more so than when 'found' by H. M. Stanley of the *New York Herald*. He refused to return with Stanley and pressed on, desperately sick, but still mapping, learning Bemba and comparing it with Tswana and Swahili, making careful drawings of fauna and flora and always preaching.

When he died at Chitambo's village, Zambia, Chuma, Susi and a handful of his loyal Makololo eviscerated their friend's body, burying his heart there and carrying his embalmed remains on another extraordinary journey to Dar-es-Salaam. He was buried in Westminster Abbey.

So many words have been written about Livingstone, most in the late Victorian and Edwardian eras with little understanding. It can be argued that the Britain of the 'scramble for Africa' created its own Livingstone. Even the biographies by Jeal and Northcott have not entirely shaken off that influence. As with all previous writing, Livingstone's eleven years in South Africa were treated almost entirely as a preface to Central Africa, except, perhaps, for references to his quarrels with the Transvaal Boers. His bitter attacks on British policy in the Cape are entirely ignored, as are his defence of the rights of the Xhosa to fight for their land, and his justification of the 1851 rebellion of the 'Hottentots'.

When leading the hymn-singing at the dedication of Zambia's memorial to him, President Kenneth Kaunda called him 'first freedom-fighter'. That was a considerable oversimplification, but underlines a dimension of Livingstone's life-story little noticed in more conventional assessments.

T. Jeal, *Livingstone* (L, 1973); C. Northcott, *David Livingstone* (Guildford, 1973); A. C. Ross, *Livingstone: Scot and Doctor* (G, 1991).

A. C. Ross

Livingstone, John (1603–72), minister. Born in Kilsyth, Stirlingshire, where his father was minister, Livingstone graduated from Glasgow University in 1621 and then studied at St Andrews

LIVINGSTONE, WILLIAM PRINGLE

University. Licensed to preach in 1625, Livingstone quickly gained a reputation as a powerful preacher, but he refused to enter the parish ministry through opposition to the Five Articles of Perth.* In 1630, after being instrumental in a revival* at the Kirk of Shotts (Lanarkshire), he crossed to Ireland and became minister of Killinchy in County Down, but he was deposed for nonconformity in 1632. In 1638 Livingstone returned Scotland to support the Covenanters* against Charles I,* and became minister of Stranraer, Wigtownshire. He played a notable part in the tumultuous events of the following years. He joined those who demanded the abolition of some traditional practices in worship as unwarranted, and insisted on the right of the godly to hold prayer meetings in addition to attending public worship. In 1648 he became minister of Ancrum, Roxburghshire, and in 1650 was one of those who negotiated the return of the exiled Charles II.* Livingstone adhered to the Protester* faction in the Church, and took a prominent part in the controversies with the Resolutioners* and in negotiations with Cromwell (*see* Commonwealth and Protectorate). In 1662 he was deposed and banished for refusing the oath of allegiance to the restored Charles II. His exile was spent in Rotterdam.

'A Brief Historical Relation of the Life of Mr John Livingstone ... Written by himself' in W. K. Tweedie (ed.), *Select Biographies*, 2 vols (Wodrow Soc., E, 1845–7), I, 127–97, with papers by or concerning Livingstone, 199–370; T. M'Crie (ed.), *The Life of Mr Robert Blair* (Wodrow Soc., E, 1848); *RPCS, 1661–4*.

FES II, 99–100, 356; *DNB* XXXIII, 401–3; D. Stevenson, 'Conventicles and the Kirk, 1619–37', *RSCHS* 18 (1974), 99–114; D. Stevenson, 'The Radical Party in the Kirk, 1637–45', *JEH* 26 (1974), 135–65.

D. Stevenson

Livingstone, William Pringle (1865–1950), Scotland's foremost Church journalist, editor of the CofS magazine *Life and Work** and author of many books.

Born in North Queensferry, Fife, Livingstone worked in Edinburgh's assessor's office before being drawn to journalism in Jamaica and Haiti. He returned to Britain to be chief sub-editor on Fleet Street evening papers (*Evening News, Standard* and *Times*). As editor from 1912 he transformed the UFC *Record* into an effective news-magazine, at the 1929 Union becoming editor of the amalgamated Kirk magazine *Life and Work*. He also edited a missionary magazine *Other Lands*. He retired in 1934, but emerged in 1937 to serve the Kirk as 'press agent' and set up its press bureau.

His most popular books were biographies of missionaries. He carried into the twentieth century the fervour of Victorian missionary self-confidence. Caribbean interest has recently been shown in his early work, in which he showed sympathy with Jamaica's poor blacks and appeared hostile to the emerging mulatto middle-class. He saw Jamaica as a 'social and racial laboratory'.

Black Jamaica (L, 1899); *The Race Conflict* (L, 1911); *Mary Slessor* (E, 1915); *Dr. Laws of Livingstonia* (E, 1921).

LW n.s. 5 (1934), 475–8; *LW* n.s. 5 (1950), 228.

R. D. Kernohan

Livingstonia (Malawi), *see* Laws, Robert; Missions.

Lockhart (Lokert), George (c.1488–1547), logician and theologian and a leading figure in the circle of Scottish intellectuals around John Major* in Paris. Born at Ayr, he studied and taught at Paris from c.1504, in various colleges. Receiving his doctorate in 1520, he returned to Scotland c.1521, becoming provost of the Collegiate* Church of Crichton, near Edinburgh, and Rector of the University of St Andrews 1522–5. Back in Paris by 1526, he was overseer of the Scots College* and, as a fellow of the College of the Sorbonne, active in the faculty of theology. He took part in an investigation of Erasmus' writings, and is not known to have wavered in his allegiance to RC teaching. Returning to Scotland in 1533 while still holding Crichton, he devoted more time to his duties as dean of Glasgow from 1533 to his death. His writings on logic, if not original, exemplify the prominence of Scots among late-scholastic logicians.

A. Broadie, *George Lockert, Late-Scholastic Logician* (E, 1983); *FESMA*, 155–6, 178, 350; J. Durkan, 'The School of John Major, Bibliography', *IR* 1 (1950), 140–57; Farge 283–5.

D. F. Wright

Lockhart, George, of Carnwath (1673–1731), Jacobite* and Episcopalian. Lockhart was one of the commissioners appointed to negotiate for union* with England (1707) and supplied his allies with valuable information as to the course of the negotiations. He played a part (as a member of Parliament) in the passing of the patronage* and toleration* acts of 1712, but he was imprisoned during and after the 1715 rising*. Thereafter he took a leading part in Jacobite and Episcopalian intrigues until 1728, when he abandoned involvement in politics. He was killed in a duel. The *Lockhart Papers* (2 vols, L, 1817) include his memoirs and are a major source for events surrounding the union and Jacobite plots of the period.

DNB XXXIV, 45–7.

D. Stevenson

Lockhart, Robert (fl.c.1545–60), supporter of reform and religious middleman. He belonged to an Ayrshire family, the Lockharts of Barr. His early years remain hidden; he probably studied in Paris, and perhaps in Aberdeen, where he was a canon by 1543. By the late 1540s he had sided with the reform, spending 1547–9 in England on commissions with Somerset, Protector of Edward VI, and others. A letter survives that he wrote to Martin Bucer, the Strasbourg Reformer recently arrived in England, about Protestant responses to the policies of Mary of Guise.* In 1555, in the house of Erskine of Dun,* Lockhart heard Knox* call for a break with the mass; by 1558 he was a leader of 'the Privy Kirk'.* But when he volunteered to mediate between Mary of Guise and the Lords of Congregation,* he lost Knox's confidence. He never reappeared in reforming circles, although he lived on at least until 1581, for some years in the Edinburgh area. Lockhart's career may have been blighted by a fondness for negotiation coupled with an indecisive scrupulousness.

Knox, *History* I, 120, 148, 244–7; I. A. Muirhead, 'M. Robert Lokhart', *IR* 22 (1971), 85–100.

D. F. Wright

Lockhart, (Sir) William (1621–76), Commonwealth* soldier and diplomat. Born at Lee, Clydesdale, he saw service in the Dutch and French armies. After returning to Scotland in 1646 he became a colonel in the Scottish army and was knighted by Charles I.* He fought for Charles in the second civil war of 1648, and was present at the battle of Preston, where he surrendered to the victorious English Parliamentarians. He was held as a prisoner of war at Hull and Newcastle. Here he seems to have undergone a change in his religious outlook, adopting the more Puritan piety which henceforth stamped his character.

Released in 1649, Lockhart rejoined the Scottish army, now controlled by strict Presbyterians, but resigned his commission in 1650 after the recall of Charles II.* Henceforth he attached himself to Cromwell's rising star. He was one of the Scottish commissioners in arranging Cromwell's union of the English and Scottish Parliaments, married Cromwell's niece, became a member of the Scottish Council of State in 1655, and was appointed Commonwealth ambassador to France by Cromwell in 1656.

Lockhart's principal aim as British ambassador was twofold: (i) to cement the new Anglo-French alliance against Spain; (ii) to prevent French aid to Charles Stuart. He was eminently successful in both, and also acted as informal protector of French Protestant interests. In 1658 he commanded the English force at Dunkirk, where he routed the Spanish and captured the city. Cromwell made him its governor; Lockhart enforced a strict Puritan sabbath in the popish city.

After Cromwell's death, Lockhart resisted lucrative temptations by the French court and Charles II to betray the Commonwealth, but he accepted the fact of the Restoration.* Charles stripped him of office, and a decade of retirement and obscurity followed, spent partly in Huntingdon, Cambridge, partly in Lanark. His court connections saved him from further royalist revenge. He returned to favour in 1670, however, when he was made a Privy Councillor. In 1673 Charles II reappointed him British ambassador to France, where his outspoken Protestantism caused considerable offence to a court no longer afraid of England.

Thomas Carlyle* reckoned Lockhart 'the best ambassador of that age', while Gilbert Burnet* said, 'I ever looked on him as the greatest man that his country produced, next to Sir Robert Murray.'

DNB XXXIV, 50–2; J. Walker, 'Sir William Lockhart of Lee', in *James Walker, D.D.* (E, 1898); Chambers-Thomson II, 538–40; F. D. Dow, *Cromwellian Scotland 1651–1660* (E, 1979).

N. R. Needham

Logan, John (1748–88), poet and minister at South Leith, 1773–86. Logan is chiefly remembered for his contributions to the *Scottish Paraphrases*ial* of 1781. Born at Soutra, Midlothian, to parents who belonged to the Burgher (Associate Synod*) line of the Secession,* and educated at Musselburgh Grammar School and Edinburgh University, Logan was for a time tutor to Sir John Sinclair, later compiler of *The Statistical Account of Scotland*.* He had a considerable reputation as a preacher, but his intemperate habits forced him to resign his charge in 1786. His last years were spent as a hack writer in London. There is a still unresolved controversy about Logan's authorship of certain poems, also attributed to his friend from student days, Michael Bruce,* notably the *Ode to the Cuckoo*. However it is clear that he was the author and reviser of several of the paraphrases.

DNB XXXIV, 84–5; *FES* I, 167–8; life prefixed to E, 1805, edit. of *Poems*, and E, 1807, edit. of *Sermons*; J. Moffatt and M. Patrick, *Handbook to the Church Hymnary* (L, 1927).

H. R. Sefton

Logie, Gavin (d.1539), reforming Principal of St Leonard's College, St Andrews (1523–34, with a break c.1530). Not much is known of Logie's life. Educated at St Andrews, he was regent of St Leonard's from c.1518, and according to John Knox* (*History* I, 15) initiated reform there after the martyrdom of Patrick Hamilton.* His teaching of early Protestants like James and Robert Wedderburn* contributed to the College's reputation as a nursery of heretics;* they had 'drunk at St Leonard's well'. Logie's own beliefs remain obscure; shortly before his death he was active in a trial against heresy.

J. Herkless and R. K. Hannay, *The College of St Leonard* (E, L, 1905).

D. F. Wright

Lollards, a derogatory term for the English successors to John Wyclif (c.1329–84). By 1395 they had become a sufficiently large sect to draw up a programme for the Westminster Parliament. After the overthrow of Sir John Oldcastle's rising (1414) the movement went underground. Pockets of support survived to merge with growing Protestantism. Building on Wyclif's emphasis on biblical authority and on preaching, Lollards attacked the status of the clergy and the papacy, and denied RC doctrines of the mass and other sacraments.

Though Lollardy as an organized, even revolutionary, force remained essentially English, its impact was also felt north of the border. In 1407 James Resby was condemned and executed at Perth for preaching against the papacy and the current practices of penance and confession. Resby, an Englishman, derived his doctrines from Wyclif and had exercised an irregular preaching ministry in Scotland directed to the poor. Though unknown to Knox's *History*, Resby is reckoned the first of the Scottish proto-Protestant martyrs*.

The influence of Lollard beliefs in Scotland can also be measured by a growing hostility to heresy* in academic circles. A charter to the newly founded University of St Andrews emphasized the necessity to the church of higher education for confounding error. By 1417, the St Andrews' graduation oath included a promise to oppose Lollardy. Knox recounts that it was at St Andrews that the Hussite Paul Kravar* was tried and burnt *c*.1433 for denying transubstantiation, prayers for the dead and the sacrament of confession – all of which Lollards had also denied (Knox's *History* I, 7).

By the mid-fifteenth century, undercurrents of unorthodox belief and anticlericalism were sufficiently widespread to have made the term Lollard equivalent to heretic – as it was in the 1425 Act against heresy and in Abbot Walter Bower's* chronicles. The term no longer described a coherent movement but rather was one of general opprobrium for the dissident or for personal opponents.

Adam Reid of Barskimming and the other Ayrshire lairds known as the 'Lollards of Kyle' accused of heresy before James IV by Archbishop Robert Blackader* in 1494 (Knox's *History* I, 7–11) certainly took a low view of the sacraments and papal powers, but in other respects they had not seceded from the RCC. The doctrinal accusations against them may have stemmed from a desire to view opposition to the tithe in the worst possible light – to take venal anticlericalism as full-blown Lollardy (*see* Straiton, David). It seems that the King was not impressed by Blackader's prosecution.

While the Lollard movement never became truly domiciled in Scotland, its name came to be associated with a dissident, even heretical, mood of opposition to the clerical establishment and with a desire for simpler, more spiritual religion. Its myth, given added significance by persecution, appears to have prepared the way for sixteenth-century Protestantism. The lairds of Kyle were to be more receptive to Knox* than most before 1560.

See also Nisbet, Murdoch.

A. G. Dickens, *The English Reformation* (L, ²1989), 46–60; R. Nicholson, *Scotland: The Later Middle Ages* (E, 1974); I. B. Cowan, *The Scottish Reformation* (L, 1982); T. M. A. Macnab, 'The Beginnings of Lollardy in Scotland', *RSCHS* 11 (1955), 254–60; W. S. Reid, 'The Lollards in Pre-Reformation Scotland', *CH* 11 (1942), 3–17.
F. D. Bardgett

London Missionary Society. 'The Missionary Society' was established in 1795. Its founders adopted as its 'fundamental principle' the formulation of the Scottish minister, Alexander Waugh (1754–1827; *DNB* LX, 76–7): 'not to send Presbyterianism, Independency, Episcopacy or any other form of church order and government . . . but the glorious Gospel of the blessed God to the heathen'. LMS, as it was popularly known after 1814, swiftly became the preserve of Congregationalist* churches, but it retained its ecumenical emphasis, and converts were still left 'to assume for themselves such form of church government as to them shall appear most agreeable to the Word of God'.

Scotland made a major contribution to LMS. Scots were prominent among its founders: Waugh, John Love,* James Steven, and David Bogue.* Bogue trained the first generation of LMS missionaries. Up to 1850, ninety of 506 (18 per cent) LMS missionaries were Scots. From 1851 to 1900, when Scotland contributed the majority of the Society's medical missionaries, ninety-one of 614 (15 per cent) were Scots. Each of thirty-six nineteenth-century LMS Scots gave more than thirty years' service to the Society. By 1945 LMS had sent 1800 missionaries of whom 284 (15.7 per cent) were Scots.

The first LMS venture was an ambitious mission to Tahiti, which limped on until 1812 when Pomare, King of Tahiti, professed conversion. In 1817 John Williams arrived in Tahiti. He was martyred at Erromanga, New Hebrides, in 1839, after splendid evangelistic work which earned him the title of 'Apostle to Polynesia'. In the 1870s, James Chalmers* and others commenced LMS work in Papua which has led to the present self-governing 'Papua Ekalesia'.

Scots, usually better educated than other British missionaries, were more prominent in LMS missions to the East than to the South Seas. LMS work in India began in 1798 when Nathanael Forsyth, a Scot, commenced fourteen years' labour in the Dutch settlement of Chinsurah, near Calcutta. The mission at Surat, western India, was also started by two Scots, William Fyvie and James Skinner. Among LMS missionaries who worked in the South Indian mission, established in 1805 by three missionaries from the Scotch Church, Swallow Street, London, was Robert Caldwell, an Ulster-born Scot, who became Bishop of Tinnevelly and witnessed mass movements of converts into Hinduism into the Church. In J. N. Farquhar* the LMS produced one of the outstanding Protestant missionary scholars.

LMS work in China began in 1807 when Robert Morrison, born in Northumberland of a Scottish father and raised in Newcastle Presbyterianism, arrived in Canton at the beginning of his outstanding work of translation and dictionary compilation. China, destined to become for many years the largest of the LMS fields, also attracted the linguistic genius of James Legge,* William Milne and John Chalmers, all Scots. William Swan,* working in Siberia, translated the Scriptures into Mongolian and wrote the interesting *Lectures on Missions* (1830), although the LMS mission to Mongolia was not established until 1869, when a Glaswegian, James Gilmour,* pioneered the work.

In Africa, after an abortive start in Sierra Leone, LMS missions began in earnest in 1799 and indelibly influenced the development of the continent through the labours of three Scots, John Philip,* Robert Moffat,* and David Livingstone.* In 1807 LMS commenced work in the West Indies, and the Demerara mission enjoyed the long missionary service of James Scott and Charles Rattray. Work in Madagascar, sometimes affected by persecution, began in 1818. Here Perthshire-born James Cameron and the Aberdonian T. T. Matthews* were notable figures. LMS churches were eventually gathered together to form the Church of Christ in Madagascar.

In 1966 LMS became the Congregational Council for World Mission, made up of the seven Congregational Unions of the British Isles and of the Commonwealth, and combining the labours of LMS and the Commonwealth Missionary Society. In 1977 at a conference in Singapore, attended by representatives of all the churches who traced their origins to LMS and English Presbyterian influence, the Council for World Mission was established, with headquarters in London.

R. Lovett, *The History of the London Missionary Society, 1795–1895*, 2 vols (L, 1899); J. M. Calder, *Scotland's March Past: The Share of Scottish Churches in the London Missionary Society* (L, 1945); J. Sibree, *A Register of Missionaries, Deputations, Etc., 1796–1923* (LMS, L, 1923); N. Goodall, *The 'Fundamental Principle' of the London Missionary Society* (L, 1945); id., *A History of the London Missionary Society, 1895–1945* (O, 1954); C. S. Horne, *The Story of the LMS, 1795–1895* (L, 1894, ²1895); S. Piggin, *Making Evangelical Missionaries* (Appleford, 1984); N. Gunson, *Messengers of Grace* (Melbourne, 1978); R. H. Martin, *Evangelicals United: Ecumenical Stirrings in Pre-Victorian Britain, 1795–1830* (Metuchen, NJ, 1983); R. Turtas, *L'attività e la politica missionaria della direzione della London Missionary Society 1795–1820* (Rome, 1971).

S. Piggin

Lord High Commissioner, the Monarch's representative at the General Assembly of the CofS. The office of Lord High Commissioner may be traced back to the early years of the Scottish Reformation, its intention being to provide a channel of communication between the Church and the Crown. The regular appointment of a High Commissioner began only after James VI* moved to London in 1603, and since the end of that century Commissioners have been appointed by the Crown to every General Assembly, save that of 1978 when the Queen herself attended.

The Lord High Commissioner may not be a Roman Catholic (Roman Catholic Emancipation Act 1829, s.12), but need not be male. His allowance is regulated under the Lord High Commissioner (Church of Scotland) Act 1974, his suite including a Chaplain and Purse-bearer, while the Solicitor-General for Scotland is his legal adviser.

The Lord High Commissioner is not a member of the Assembly by virtue of his appointment (Plan of Union, 1929, para 4), although some Commissioners have been separately commissioned to the Assembly by their own presbyteries. The gallery in which he sits is technically not part of the Assembly Hall and is entered by a separate stair. Although neither the Crown nor the Commissioner has the right to initiate or control Assembly business, the Assembly is by custom addressed by the Commissioner. The Commissioner also makes a courtesy visit to the FC Assembly.

In early years a point of difficulty was whether any Assembly (ecclesiastical or not) might occur without the leave or summons of the Crown. Until 1927 it was customary for the Lord High Commissioner at his speech in the closing ceremonial of an Assembly to fix a day for the next Assembly which happened to be that already chosen by the Assembly itself. Since 1927 the Commissioner undertakes to inform the Crown of the date the Assembly has chosen.

S. Mechie, *The Office of Lord High Commissioner* (E, 1957).

F. Lyall

Lord's Day Observance Society, *see* Sabbatarianism.

Lord's Prayer. In the Reformed Church of Scotland the Lord's Prayer has traditionally performed three functions. In the first place, it provided the framework for the teaching on prayer in all the major Reformed catechisms* up to and including the Westminster Larger and Shorter Catechisms* of 1648. It was expected that everyone in the congregation should know, and be able to explain, the Lord's Prayer. Secondly, it was to be used regularly in worship, said either by the minister alone or by minister and people together. In Knox's *Book of Common Order* (1564)* it appears at the conclusion of the prayer after the sermon, while the Westminster Directory recommends its use in the same position as 'not only a pattern of prayer, but itself a most comprehensive prayer'. It is also to be used in personal prayer. In the third place, it is a pattern or criterion for all prayer. This emphasis on the prayer as a pattern probably contributed to its general abandonment in public worship in the seventeenth century in face of the onslaught on set forms and 'vain repetition'. Walter Steuart of Pardovan's *Collections* suggests that 'there are no public prayers used in our Church, wherein the petitions of the Lord's Prayer are not expressed throughout the prayers', and therefore its use is superfluous (II.1.21). It appears to have remained out of general use in public worship, despite attempts at the Restoration* to encourage its use, until the *Euchologion*'s* influence gradually restored it to a regular place in public worship, said by minister and people together. The *Euchologion* introduced the *Book of Common Prayer*'s* version (with 'trespasses'), but most congregations follow the majority tradition since the Westminster documents by using the AV of Matt. 6.9–13 (with 'debts').

D. B. Forrester

Lord's Supper, the name most commonly given to the sacrament of Holy Communion at the time of the Reformation.*

THE REFORMATION. The mass* was abolished, being in the view of John Knox* and his fellow Reformers idolatrous. They wished to emphasize the sole mediation of Christ in worship and the participation of the people in the sacrament. The Scots Confession* stated that Christ was really present in Communion by the Holy Spirit and condemned those who thought the sacraments were naked or bare signs. The service was in the vernacular and was to be preceded by the preaching of the Word. Only those authorized to minister the Word were to celebrate the sacrament. The Reformers wished to restore the Lord's Supper to the service for every Lord's day, following Calvin's* Genevan ideal, but this was not achieved in practice. The *Book of Common Order* (1564)* recommended a monthly celebration and the *First Book of Discipline** said that Communion should be celebrated quarterly in towns and twice-yearly in country areas. Although mass had been said frequently, the people had long been accustomed to communicate only once or twice a year at Christmas and Easter. There were also not enough ministers available to cover all the parishes of the land. Since the Christian year* was no longer observed, the Lord's Supper was celebrated at times other than the main Christian festivals. The Sunday service in the *BCO*, however, was based on the celebration of the Lord's Supper as the norm, with the prayers of intercession and the Lord's Prayer coming after the sermon, as would be the case on a Communion Sunday. Communion was received sitting round a table in the church to emphasize the aspect of fellowship. Discipline* was also to be exercised on those who would communicate and examination was made by the Kirk Session* (*see* Admission to the Lord's Supper).

THE SEVENTEENTH AND EIGHTEENTH CENTURIES. The Westminster* Confession reiterated the 'high' doctrine of the sacrament of the Reformers, and the order of service in the Westminster Directory was still based on the celebration of the Lord's Supper as the norm of Sunday worship. With the troubled times of the mid-seventeenth century, however, Communion was celebrated even less frequently than before, some parishes not having a Communion service for several years. The practice developed of parishes grouping together to celebrate the Lord's Supper, as did the observance of a fast day held beforehand to prepare for the sacrament. The 'fencing of the tables' was a common feature of the service whereby a warning was given to those who might communicate unworthily. More elaborate arrangements were made for the celebration of the Communion 'season',* with the emphasis on the minister's catechetical examination of the congregation and Communion tokens* being given to those considered eligible to participate. Two sermons would be delivered on the fast day preceding the sabbath, two on the Saturday, and then several 'sittings' of Communion would be held on the Sunday, with the minister assisted by visiting clergymen. A thanksgiving service with two sermons would be held on the Monday.

THE NINETEENTH AND TWENTIETH CENTURIES. Major changes gradually took place, partly as a result of the Catholic revival* of worship. Service books were produced by unofficial groups such as the Church Service Society* and then by the Churches themselves. The *BCO*s* of 1940 and 1979 provided Communion services which combined both Catholic and Reformed elements (*see* Liturgy). The congregation began to receive the sacrament sitting in their pews rather than going forward to the tables, although more Catholic churchmen wished to retain the traditional practice. The 'fencing of the table' began to disappear in the 1860s, and an exhortation was given by the minister instead. Session discipline became less severe and tokens were replaced by cards. The series of services before and after the Sunday were gradually reduced in number except in the Highlands, and in the FC and FPC, which have maintained both Communion seasons and infrequency of observance, and the fast days, which had become public holidays, began to disappear. The frequency of Communion was increased, especially in urban areas. A quarterly celebration became more common, although in rural areas a twice- or even once-yearly celebration remained the norm. Some congregations held a monthly celebration at a different time from, or immediately following, the morning service. John Macleod* at Govan, however, introduced a monthly Communion which was an integral part of the main service. The first CofS minister to introduce a weekly celebration was J. Cromarty Smith at Coatdyke in Coatbridge in 1906. It was held at 8.30 a.m. prior to the morning service. Some Presbyterian congregations, particularly those in historic churches in city centres, now celebrate a weekly Communion, but it is rarely the main service of the Sunday.

The rise of the temperance movement* and a concern for the problems of alcoholism led to a growing desire for the use of non-alcoholic wine at Communion. Its use was first discussed in the UPC and came to be widely accepted in the CofS and FC as well. Growing concern over hygiene led to a debate in the Churches over the use of individual glasses instead of the common cup. A committee of the Est.C's General Assembly was set up in 1907 to examine the issue. The Assembly agreed with the majority verdict of the committee in allowing the use of individual cups, with the condition that those who wished to partake in the common cup should be able to do so. These two developments have led some congregations to offer their members a choice of the way in which they receive Communion.

In Baptist and Brethren circles, the Lord's Supper has normally been held at least monthly, often weekly, usually as part of, or following, the Sunday morning service.

G. B. Burnet, *The Holy Communion in the Reformed Church of Scotland 1560–1960* (E and L, 1960); D. B. Forrester and D. M. Murray (eds), *Studies in the History of Worship in Scotland* (E, 1984).

D. M. Murray

LORDS OF THE CONGREGATION

Lords of the Congregation, *see* Congregation.

Lorimer, John Gordon (1804–68), FC minister and writer. Born in Haddington, East Lothian, he was educated at the Universities of Edinburgh and St Andrews, and licensed to preach by Haddington Presbytery in 1827. In 1829 he was ordained minister of Torryburn, Fife, and in 1832 moved to St David's, Glasgow. He played an active part in the Ten Years' Conflict* and adhered to the FC in the Disruption.* From then until his death he was minister of St David's Free, Glasgow.

Lorimer's literary output was considerable. A fair proportion of it was occasioned by the Ten Years' Conflict, in which his most notable production was his *The Statistics of Scottish Moderatism* (G, 1843), an attack on those who remained in the Est.C in 1843 as betrayers of the CofS. Lorimer also had a lively interest in foreign Protestant churches, and maintained constant correspondence with representatives thereof, contributing much in this way to eliciting sympathy for the FC cause abroad. Literary products of this interest included *The Past and Present Condition of Religion and Morality in the United States of America* (G, 1833), *Historical Sketch of the Protestant Church of France* (E, 1841), and *The Recent Great Religious Awakening in America* (G, 1859).

The Old Orthodox Faith Superior to Modern Opinions (G, 1847); *The Eldership of the Church of Scotland* (G, 1841); *The Deaconship* (E, 1842).

FES III, 440; AFCS I, 211.

N. R. Needham

Lorimer, Peter (1812–79), Presbyterian historian. A native of Edinburgh and educated there, conceiving a life-long indebtedness to Thomas Chalmers,* he was ordained to the Scots Church of Chadwell Street and Islington, London (1837), but seceded with his congregation at the Disruption.* He became one of the architects of the English Presbyterian Church (at the Berwick Synod which broke with the Kirk; Moderator, 1851), and a chief pillar of its new College in London (various addresses) – Professor from 1845 (his title varying from Syriac to modern church history) and latterly Principal (1878; L. Levi (ed.), *Digest ... Synod of the Presby. Church in England 1836–1876*, L, 1876, 117–48).

His writings chiefly concerned Christian evidences and Reformed Church history. Still valuable are *John Knox and the Church of England* (L, 1875), based on Knox* MSS he discovered, and *Precursors of Knox* (E, 1857), on Patrick Hamilton.* A founder member of the Wodrow Society,* and a DD (1857) of the College of New Jersey (later Princeton* University), he was deeply committed to both scholarship and 'a pure and thoroughly Evangelical creed', pursuing divergences from orthodoxy among his students.

DNB XXXIV, 138; FES VII, 495–6; A. H. Douglas, *Westminster College, Cambridge* ... (L, 1900), 6–10, 132–4; most works listed in Brit. Lib. Catal.; MSS and relics in Westminster

LORIMER, WILLIAM LAUGHTON

College. Lorimer was the model for Peters in the novel *Matthew Paxton*, 3 vols (L, 1854) by W. Wilson.

D. F. Wright

Lorimer, Robert (1765–1848), FC minister. Born at Kirkconnel, Dumfriesshire, and educated at Glasgow University, he was ordained by the Presbytery of Penpont (Dumfriesshire) as chaplain to the Hopetown Fencibles (1793) and inducted to the first charge of Haddington (1796). His long ministry greatly advanced evangelical strength in the area. According to his son, Alexander P. Lorimer (in *Disruption Worthies*, 339–42), but not others' accounts, he presided over the Convocation* of November 1842, which foreshadowed the Disruption.* Next year he withdrew with part of his congregation, becoming colleague to John W. Wright in Free St John's, Haddington. At his death he was 'Father' of the FC. In 1851 his son John (AFCS I, 211) donated his library (over 500 vols, listed in MS Ledger of Accessions) to New College Library.

FES I, 370; AFCS I, 211, II, 27; *The Witness*, 15 Nov., 1848.

J. D. MacMillan

Lorimer, Robert (1864–1929), *see* Architecture.

Lorimer, William Laughton (1885–1967), translator of Scots NT. Lorimer was the son of Robert Lorimer (AFCS I, 211), the grandson of Robert Lorimer of Haddington. He was educated at the High School in Dundee, Fettes College, Edinburgh, and Trinity College, Oxford. His academic career was spent in the University of St Andrews: Assistant and Lecturer in Greek (1910–29), Reader in Latin (Univ. Coll., Dundee, 1929–53) and Professor of Greek (1953–5). He was elected a Fellow of the British Academy (1953). Lorimer was also interested in the Scots language, becoming a contributor to the *Scottish National Dictionary* in 1946. Later he became a member of the *SND*'s Executive Council (1947) and held the office of Chairman (1953–67). For the last ten years of his life, Lorimer combined these two areas of study with his interest in theology, working on a translation of the New Testament into Scots. The final stages of revising this project were undertaken by his son, R. C. L. Lorimer. The *New Testament in Scots* was published posthumously in 1983 to widespread acclaim.

See also Bible (Versions, Scots).

The New Testament in Scots (E, 1983; revd edit., E and Harmondsworth, 1985, with introd. by R. C. L. Lorimer); *Who Was Who, 1961–70*, 691; K. J. Dover, 'William Laughton Lorimer', *Proceedings of the British Academy* 42 (1967), 437–8; D. Ogston, 'William Lorimer's *New Testament in Scots*: An Appreciation', in *The Bible in Scottish Life and Literature*, ed. D. F. Wright (E, 1988), 53–61; G. Tulloch, *A History of the Scots Bible* (A, 1989), 72–83.

F. J. King

Lothian, Andrew (1763–1831), Burgher minister of Portsburgh Chapel in Edinburgh from 1796. Born at Cowdenbeath, Fife, of poor parents, he spent four years at sea before studying at Edinburgh University and at the Associate Synod* Divinity Hall under George Lawson.* A supporter of the New Light,* he took a prominent part in the formation of the USec.C* and was Moderator of its Synod in 1828. He published a small volume entitled *The Christian Patriot and Seamen's Friend* (E, 1822). Various of his sermons appeared anonymously in *Edinburgh Christian Instructor.*

I. D. L. Clark, 'The Reverend Andrew Lothian, United Secession Minister', *RSCHS* 20 (1979), 143–62; Small I, 442, II, 294; J. M'Kerrow, *History of the Secession Church* (G, 1841), 924.

I. D. L. Clark

Love, John (1757–1825), promoter of foreign missions. Born at Paisley, he studied at Glasgow University. He served as minister of the Presbyterian congregation at Spitalfields, London (1788–1800) and of Anderston Chapel of Ease,* Glasgow (1800–25). He was granted the DD of Marischal College, Aberdeen, in 1816. He was one of the founders of, and a leading publicist for, the early foreign missions movement. He was an originator of the London Missionary Society* and secretary until 1800 and later of the Glasgow Missionary Society. He was a leading Evangelical in the CofS and a candidate for the chair of Divinity at Aberdeen in 1815. His *Memorials* (2 vols, G, 1857–8), published posthumously as were most of his works, were regarded as a model of deep but forthright evangelical devotion. Lovedale, in S. Africa, was named after him.

Addresses to the People of Otaheite, Designed to Assist the Labour of Missionaries (L, 1796); *A Serious Call respecting a Mission from Glasgow to the River Indus* (G, 1820); *The Character of the Wise Teachers of Righteousness and their Future Glory* (G, 1821).

DNB XXXIV, 158–9; FES III, 389; *Some Notices of the Character of . . . John Love* (G, 1827).

J. R. McIntosh

Lovi, Walter (1798–1878), RC clergyman. Born in Edinburgh of Italian-Scots parentage, he studied at the Scots College,* Rome 1823–5 and was ordained priest at Paris 1826. Appointed to Keith (Banffshire), he built a substantial church. While ministering at Wick to the herring fishers during the cholera epidemic of 1832, he had remarkable success in stemming mortality, and his ministrations were requested during cholera epidemics in Inverness and Ireland. From 1832 he undertook lengthy begging missions for his churches at Keith (opened 1831) and Wick (completed 1836). Having built a third church at Braemar 1839, he was thereafter mostly engaged in begging for funds on the continent. His ambitious entrepreneurial schemes in Vienna and Hungary came to nothing, and from 1848 he worked as a priest in the English Midlands.

Catholic Directory for Scotland 1831–44 (E, 1831–3; D, 1834–43); Blairs and Preshome Letters, Scottish Catholic Archives, Edinburgh.

M. Dilworth

Low, David (1768–1855), Bishop of Ross, Moray and Argyll. Born in Brechin, Angus, he studied at Marischal College, Aberdeen, and was ordained deacon in 1787, taking charge of the Episcopalian* congregation in Perth. In 1789 he was ordained priest and moved to Pittenweem, Fife. He was elected and consecrated Bishop of Ross and Argyll in 1819. In 1831 he was the prime mover in forming the Gaelic Episcopal Society for training Gaelic*-speaking clergy. He was also a leading campaigner for the repeal of legal restrictions imposed on Scottish Episcopalians after the Jacobite* rising* of 1745. Most of these had been lifted in 1792; the remainder were repealed by Parliament in 1840.

Low's episcopal jurisdiction was extended to Moray in 1838 on the death of Alexander Jolly,* but in 1847 Argyll and the Isles were divided from Ross and Moray, and a new bishopric created for the former, which Low endowed with £8,000. He resigned as Bishop of Ross and Moray in 1850 through ill-health.

Low received an LLD from Marischal College in 1820, and in 1848 a DD from Hartford College, Connecticut, and from Geneva College, New York.

W. Blatch, *A Memoir of the Right Rev. David Low* (L, 1855); M. F. Conolly, *A Biographical Sketch of David Low* (E, 1859); DNB XXXIV, 181–2.

N. R. Needham

Lowe, John (1835–92), medical missionary. Born in Banchory, Aberdeenshire, the son of an Independent minister from whom he inherited a passion for suffering humanity, he trained as a doctor and in 1861 sailed with his new wife to superintend the London Missionary Society's* medical mission at Neyoor, Travancore, S. India. He worked through a severe cholera epidemic, but after seven years his wife's ill-health took them back to Scotland and he resigned in 1871. Under Lowe's superintendency, Neyoor became LMS's most effective medical work in India, with a new medical training course, and enjoyed significant local patronage.

In 1871 he became superintendent of the Edinburgh Medical Missionary Society* training institution in the Cowgate, and the Society's secretary in 1883. These offices he held until his death. He increased the Society's income, transformed the Cowgate premises into the Livingstone Memorial Training Institution and greatly boosted the number of students it trained. (The Society also used the adjacent Magdalen Chapel* for services.) The Cowgate agencies touched the most deprived of Edinburgh's population. Lowe also became a much-consulted adviser on medical work to other missionary societies, and wrote the frequently reprinted *Medical Missions: Their Place and Power* (L, 1886). He also produced the *Jubilee Memorial Historic Sketch* of EMMS, and from the papers of William Jackson Elmslie of Kashmir the latter's view of *Medical Missions* (E, 1874).

Lumsden, James (1810–75), FC professor. Born at Dysart, Fife, he studied under Thomas Chalmers* at both St Andrews and Edinburgh. Ordained to Inverbrothock (CofS), Arbroath, in 1836, he moved to nearby Barry in 1838, remaining there in the FC after the Disruption* until elected Professor of Systematic and Pastoral Theology and Early Church History at the Aberdeen FC College in 1856. In 1864 he became its first Principal. St Andrews made him DD in 1869, but death forestalled his nomination as Moderator.

Lumsden's special interests included the YMCA,* foreign missions (he visited Lebanon in 1870 with Alexander Duff*), FC extension and especially Sweden. At Barry he met Swedish agricultural students and subsequently contributed in many ways to Swedish Evangelicalism, becoming known there as 'the Scotch Professor', being honoured as Knight of the North Star (1871) and writing *Sweden: its Religious State and Prospects* (L, 1855). His *Infant Baptism* (E, 1856) he agreed to withdraw after a critical response by A. H. Hislop (*AFCS* I, 186).

The Difference in Principle between the Free Church and the Establishment (A, 1858); *The Unity of the Church* (A, 1871).

FES V, 431; *AFCS* I, 56; *FCSR* n.s. 161 (Dec. 1875); 301–2; J. Rae, *Principal Lumsden...* (A, 1876); E. E. Eklund, 'The Scottish Free Church and its Relation to Nineteenth-Century Swedish... Lutheranism', *CH* 51 (1982), 405–18.

D. F. Wright

Lutheranism in Scotland, the first phase of Scottish Protestantism. As the Scots Confession of Faith* (1560) and the Westminster Confession of Faith* (1647) show clearly, the CofS adopted the Reformed expression of Protestant Christianity in which the influence of John Calvin* is paramount. The most significant of Calvin's Scottish disciples was John Knox,* whose leadership of the Reformation* of the Church left indelible marks of his subscription to the Reformed faith. Knox, however, acknowledged a debt to Martin Luther (1483–1546) as well as to Calvin, and it is apparent that Luther's teachings exerted considerable influence upon both Knox and the generation of Scottish Protestants which preceded him, among whom they made common cause with Lollard* influences.

LUTHERAN BEGINNINGS. It seems that a Monsieur de la Tour, a French Protestant, was the first agent of Lutheranism to appear in Scotland. He arrived in 1523 to work for the Duke of Albany, but there is scant information about his brief residence. Soon after his return to France he suffered martyrdom for his Lutheran beliefs. Although de la Tour was the Lutheran pioneer in Scotland, it is impossible to assess his precise contribution to the Reformation there.

Patrick Hamilton* was the first native Scotsman known to have embraced Luther's doctrine, and he therefore deserves recognition as the father of the Reformation in his homeland. Hamilton was related to the Stuart dynasty through both of his parents, and his family obtained an ecclesiastical benefice for him that made him titular abbot of Fearn (Ferne), Ross-shire, when he was about fourteen years old. Although Patrick was not a monk and discharged no abbatial duties, he enjoyed the income from the monastic property at Fearn. That revenue allowed him to study at the University of Paris (MA, 1520).

Although he did not become a Protestant during his stay in Paris, both Erasmian and Lutheran influences there were pronounced, so that he could not have failed to become acquainted with them. It is clear that the Christian humanism* of Erasmus affected him deeply, and when he returned to Scotland in 1523, he taught in St Andrews University. In that position he called for the adoption of humanist methods of scholarship, while he assailed corruption in the Catholic Church. Hamilton's bold criticisms aroused opposition from ecclesiastical authorities, Archbishop James Beaton* especially, and the young scholar fled to the continent to evade persecution for alleged Lutheran heresy.* Perhaps the accusation that he was a Lutheran led him to Wittenberg in 1527, and next to the University of Marburg, a new Protestant institution. There Francis Lambert, a former Franciscan friar, instructed him. Lambert was at that time an exponent of Luther's doctrine, which Hamilton assimilated readily. With Lambert's encouragement, the Scottish scholar composed *Dyvers Frutful Gatheryngs of Scripture Concerning Fayth and Workes*, which became known eventually as *Patrick's Places*. This treatise expounds the Lutheran understanding of salvation in accordance with the Wittenberg Reformer's distinction between the law and the gospel. Justification *sola fide*, through faith alone, is the theme of the work, the first theological writing by a Scottish Protestant.

Patrick's Places reflects the influence of Luther's *The Freedom of a Christian* (1520), Philipp Melanchthon's *Loci Communes* [*Common Places*] (1521), and William Tyndale's *Parable of the Wycked Mammon* (Antwerp, 1528), all of which extol the subject of justification through faith alone. Patrick Hamilton had by this time become a Lutheran champion of salvation *sola gratia*, by grace alone.

Late in 1527 Hamilton returned to St Andrews and boldly proclaimed Luther's teachings to both university scholars and people of the town. Archbishop Beaton apprehended him, and after a trial in which the accused heretic refused to recant he died in flames, the first Protestant martyr* of the Scottish Reformation. The transcript of his trial indicates that he espoused clearly the Lutheran doctrine of salvation.

OTHER EARLY SCOTTISH PROTESTANTS. From the death of Patrick Hamilton in 1528 to the return to Scotland of the Reformer George Wishart* in 1544, the first generation of Scottish Protestants laid the Lutheran foundation for the Reformation in their homeland. Their work has, however, gone largely unnoticed because Wishart, Knox and others erected a Reformed edifice upon that foundation.

The early successes of Lutheranism in Scotland were due in some degree to Patrick Hamilton's standing as a scholar and to the influence of his family. Hamilton found some Augustinian* friars quite receptive to his teachings, and prominent people in several of the country's larger towns embraced his cause. St Leonard's College at St Andrews became a centre for Lutheran activities as well as ongoing criticism of ecclesiastical corruption, as scholars inspired by Hamilton's courage spoke boldly in support of his concerns. East coast ports such as St Andrews, Dundee, Montrose and Leith were convenient entry points for Lutheran literature, despite Parliament's ban of 1525.

One of the first Scots to espouse Patrick Hamilton's theology was Alexander Seton (d.1542), a Dominican* friar and the father confessor to King James V. In 1527 he called for the reform of abuses in the church and in doing so revealed his subscription to the Lutheran doctrine of salvation *sola gratia, sola fide*. Seton criticized Catholic bishops for their failure to preach God's Word, and assailed the immoralities of his king. The royal and episcopal reactions placed him in danger, and so Seton fled to England, where he remained until his death.

About the time that Seton departed for England, RC authorities apprehended Henry Forrest or Forres (d.c.1533) for defending Patrick Hamilton. Forrest was a graduate of St Leonard's College who had become dean of an abbey on the Isle of May in the Firth of Forth. After listening to Hamilton's teaching and observing his painful death, Forrest contended that the recent martyr was not a heretic but a preacher of God's truth. This apology for Hamilton led to the execution of Forrest, perhaps as an example to deter others from adopting Luther's teachings. Other Scottish 'heretics' tainted with Lutheranism included Thomas Forret,* John Johnsone,* David Straiton,* Walter Milne* and John Willock.*

ALEXANDER ALESIUS. Alexander Alesius* also followed Patrick Hamilton into the Lutheran faith. Alesius had once tried to persuade Hamilton to abandon his beliefs, but finally he found them convincing. This graduate of St Leonard's College suffered imprisonment for embracing the doctrines he had earlier deplored, but escaped to the continent in 1532. He went to Wittenberg, where he studied theology and subscribed to the Augsburg Confession of Faith. From his exile Alesius implored James V to reform the Scottish Church and to support publication of a vernacular version of the Bible (*see* Bible (Versions, English)). Although his monarch did not comply with Alesius' request, the New Testament in William Tyndale's translation circulated illegally in Scotland, and RC authorities could not stop the distribution.

In 1535 Alesius went to England, where he enjoyed the favour of Archbishop Thomas Cranmer and Henry VIII's chief minister, Thomas Cromwell. For a time Alesius lectured on the Psalms at Cambridge University, but charges of heresy forced him to leave for London. There he aroused consternation when, in an address to the Convocation of the Clergy, he attacked the RC doctrine of the sacraments. After the English Parliament in 1540 adopted the Act of Six Articles, a categorical reaffirmation of traditional doctrines, Alesius left for the continent.

After a brief stay in Wittenberg he went to Frankfurt on the Oder and then to Leipzig, where he became a Doctor of Theology and remained until he died. Alesius associated regularly with such Protestant theologians as Philipp Melanchthon, Martin Bucer and John Calvin, and late in his career tried to mediate between Lutherans and Calvinists. In this effort he joined with Melanchthon, even at the cost of compromising Luther's teaching on some points of doctrine such as the presence of Christ in the eucharist.

Despite his eventual abandonment of some Lutheran teachings, for most of his career as a scholar Alesius promoted the Lutheran concept of reformation he had received initially from Patrick Hamilton. From his exile he sent his writings to Scotland and thereby encouraged the growth of Protestantism in his native land.

JOHN GAU AND HENRY BALNAVES. John Gau,* who was educated at St Andrews University at St Salvator's College, went to Denmark in 1533, where King Christian III had embraced Lutheranism. While there Gau produced *The Richt Vay to the Kingdom of Heuine*, the first thorough exposition of Luther's doctrine to come from the pen of a Scotsman, largely translated from a Danish version of a German Lutheran work. With *sola Scriptura*, Scripture only, as his basis, Gau affirmed the Lutheran teachings about sin and salvation, Christ as the sole head of the Church, and the proper distinction between the law and the gospel. *The Richt Vay* is similar to *Patrick's Places*, and reflects the influence of Luther's preface to his German New Testament. To Gau's chagrin, RC officials destroyed most copies of his work that he sent to Scotland. This Lutheran therefore exerted only a slight influence upon the Scottish Reformation.

Henry Balnaves* enjoyed considerable success as a transmitter of Luther's influence to Scotland. Balnaves studied at St Salvator's College, St Andrews, and then on the continent, where he seems to have received the Master of Arts at the University of Cologne. After returning to Scotland, Balnaves worked for the Earl of Arran (*see* Hamilton, James, d.1575), who governed the kingdom during Mary's minority. While engaged in a power struggle with Cardinal David Beaton,* the Regent Arran allowed the Protestants to proclaim their message. But in 1543 he returned to the RCC through the persuasion of John Hamilton,* his half-brother, the future archbishop. Repression of heretics ensued.

Henry Balnaves became a prominent preacher of Protestant doctrines during the time when the Earl of Arran allowed the Reformers considerable freedom. When the Regent initiated repression Balnaves joined those Protestants who had assassinated Cardinal Beaton in reprisal for his murder of George Wishart. When the killers of Beaton fell into RC hands, Balnaves became a prisoner of the French at Rouen, where he remained 1547–50.

Balnaves eventually returned to Scotland and joined the (Protestant) Lords of the Congregation,* nobles who resisted the Queen Mother (Mary of Guise* who had succeeded Arran as Regent in 1554). With English aid the Lords prevailed over the Regent and her French supporters, and a Protestant-dominated Scottish Parliament abolished papal jurisdiction in the kingdom and adopted the Scots Confession of Faith (1560), which is not unmarked by Lutheran emphases. Balnaves received due recognition when its General Assembly appointed him to participate in revising the *FBD*.*

While Balnaves was incarcerated at Rouen he composed *The Confession of Faith, containing how the troubled man should seek refuge at his God*, which is a major biblical-theological exposition of justification through faith alone, a work which Knox heartily approved. The treatment of salvation here is typically Lutheran and very similar to that which appears in Luther's 1535 commentary on the Epistle to the Galatians. Since Knox endorsed Balnaves' treatise, it is clear that he too had imbibed considerable influence from Wittenberg as well as from Geneva. Practically all of Luther's soteriological emphases are evident in this confession. Only on the extent of the atonement did Balnaves deviate from the German Reformer's doctrine. In this case the Scottish scholar contended that Christ died only for the elect, a position that eventually became a distinctive belief of Calvinism. The work of Henry Balnaves may therefore indicate that Scotland's transition from Lutheran to Reformed theology was already in progress when this confession appeared in 1548.

CONCLUSION. The movement toward Reformed Protestantism, to which Balnaves and Wishart contributed, became official when Knox achieved commanding influence in the CofS. Luther's legacy remained, nevertheless, evident in Knox's teaching about predestination, justification, assurance of salvation, and other aspects of Christian doctrine. In its music Luther's theology was spread through the singing of the (generally Lutheran) *Gude and Godlie Ballatis*,* produced by the Wedderburn* brothers of Dundee.

See also Nisbet, Murdoch; McAlpine, John; Zwinglianism.

Knox, *Works*; Knox, *History*; Spottiswoode; John Foxe, *Acts and Monuments...*, 8 vols, ed. S. R. Cattley (L, 1843–9); J. E. McGoldrick, *Luther's Scottish Connection* (Madison, NJ, 1989); *id.*, 'Patrick Hamilton, Luther's Scottish Disciple', *Sixteenth Century Journal* 17 (1986), 81–8; W. S. Reid, 'Lutheranism in the Scottish Reformation', *Westminster Theological Journal* 7 (1945), 91–111; J. K. Cameron, 'Aspects of the Lutheran Contribution to the Scottish Reformation, 1528–1552', *Lutheran Theological Journal* 19 (1985), 12–20 (and in *RSCHS* 22 (1984), 1–12); J. Kirk, *Patterns of Reform* (E, 1989); D. F. Wright, ' "The Commoun Buke of the Kirke": The Bible in the Scottish Reformation', in Wright (ed.), *The Bible in Scottish Life and Literature* (E, 1988), 155–78.

J. E. McGoldrick

M

McAllum, Duncan (1756–1834), Wesleyan Methodist* preacher from Argyll (commissioned 1775). McAllum apparently wanted to go to Africa as a missionary, but John Wesley* gave him an 'unlimited commission to visit the Highlands and adjacent Islands of Scotland', because of his fluency in Gaelic.* In 1786 Thomas Coke expected that McAllum would help to open up the Highlands* as a Methodist mission-field, and he was first assigned to Ayr, probably to preach to Gaelic-speaking immigrants. He was later active in Strathspey, but Methodism did not develop a Highland wing. In 1817–19 McAllum was Superintendent of the Dunbar Circuit. He was one of three known Gaelic-speaking Methodist preachers, the others being Hugh McKay (Inverness Circuit) and Duncan Wright (Perthshire, d.1791). McAllum's son, Daniel McAllum, MD (1794–1827), was also a Wesleyan Methodist minister (commissioned 1817). He served on the Haddington and Edinburgh Circuits, and visited Shetland* in 1822 to report on the possibility of a Methodist mission to these islands (see Methodism in Shetland).

J. H. Martin and J. B. Sheldon, *Ministers and Probationers of the Methodist Church* (L, 1965), 401–2, 431; A. J. Hayes and D. A. Gowland (eds), *Scottish Methodism in the Early Victorian Period* (E, 1981), 27–9, 39, 53; J. Crowther, *Remains of the late Rev. Daniel McAllum MD* (NY, 1840); J. Vickers, *Thomas Coke* (L, 1969), 132, 141–2.

D. E. Meek

MacAlpine (latinized as Macchabeus), John (d.1557), early Protestant. He was a bachelor of theology of Cologne and Dominican* prior at Perth in the early 1530s when he fled, suspected of heresy, to England, and like his fellow Dominican John Macdowell,* became a chaplain to Nicholas Shaxton, Bishop of Salisbury, and gained Thomas Cromwell's patronage. Naturalized and married in England, he later left for Germany, matriculated at the Lutheran University at Wittenberg in 1540 and on gaining a doctorate in theology, was invited by the Danish king, Christian III, to teach theology at the University of Copenhagen and was appointed a royal chaplain. He settled in Denmark, disputed on the mass, denied transubstantiation and also the views of the Protestant sacramentarians' in favour of Luther's doctrine, and as brother-in-law of Miles Coverdale's wife, sought the Danish king's intercession with Mary Tudor in 1554 to release the imprisoned Coverdale. He was active, too, as one of four translators into Danish of Luther's German Bible. In 1548, Sir David Lindsay* visited MacAlpine, who met the cost of printing one of Lindsay's works, 'The Monarchie', in 1553. Another Scot, Richard Melville of Baldovie, as tutor to James Erskine, younger of Dun, travelled with his pupil to Copenhagen to study under MacAlpine. MacAlpine died in Copenhagen.

M. A. F. Bredahl Petersen, 'Dr Johannes Macchabeus: Scotland's contribution to the Reformation in Denmark' (PhD, Edinburgh University, 1935); Spottiswoode, I, 131; J. Foxe, *Acts and Monuments* VI (L, 1859), 705; J. Melville, *Autobiography and Diary*, ed. R. Pitcairn (E, 1852), 14; Knox, *History* I, 23; *DNB* XXXIV, 398.

J. Kirk

McArthur, Donald (fl.1800–40), Gaelic*-speaking Baptist* evangelist and pastor of a Baptist church at Port Bannatyne, Bute. Born in Strachur, Argyll, McArthur was originally a shoemaker and fisherman. Following a visit to Glasgow, where he heard evangelical preaching by Angus Mackintosh at the Gaelic chapel, he experienced conversion and was later baptized by immersion in 1801. He established a following of 'McArthur Baptists' in Strachur parish, and evangelized extensively in Cowal and adjacent areas. In 1804 he was ordained to the ministry by Frederic MacFarlane in Edinburgh, and assumed the formal pastorate of the Port Bannatyne church, continuing his preaching as far afield as Perthshire, and stimulating localized awakenings (see Revivals). His activities roused opposition by lairds and heritors.* In October 1805, while preaching below the high-water mark at Colintraive Ferry, he was attacked and taken prisoner by men acting for Campbell of Southhall, the local landowner. Southhall conveyed him to Greenock, where he was handed over to the pressgang. Having served for five weeks, he was released by the Lords of the Admiralty after representations on his behalf. In 1808 his case came before the Court of Session, where he won damages, including a *solatium* of £105, against Southhall. The case made Scottish legal history, but local opposition did not cease, and McArthur emigrated to North America about 1810. He is said to have joined the Seventh Day Baptists in later life.

G. N. M. Collins, *Principal John Macleod D.D.* (E, 1951), 241-7; William Buchanan, *Reports of Certain Remarkable Cases in the Court of Session* (E, 1813), 60-72; D. Bebbington (ed.), *The Baptists in Scotland* (G, 1988), 281-2, 284.

D. E. Meek

MacArthur, Mary Flora, *see* Women in Highland Churches.

Macaskill, Murdoch (1838-1903), Highland* Church leader in the years before and after the 1900 Union. Born in Lewis, like many other divinity students he taught in FC schools during his university course. He ministered to Highlanders in Govan (1865-8), and served as FC minister in Glenlyon (1868-73) and the Gaelic Church, Greenock (1873-84), accepting a call to Dingwall in 1884. He led Highland opposition in the Marcus Dods* and A. B. Bruce* cases and in the debate on the Declaratory Act* at the 1891 FC General Assembly. Originally an opponent of the Union movement, he later served on the Committee negotiating union between the FC and the UPC. During the early years of his Dingwall ministry he was active in pressing for Highland land reform (*see* Clearances). He was a forceful and inspiring preacher in Gaelic* and English.

J. MacAskill, *A Highland Pulpit* (Inverness, 1907); A. Stewart and J. K. Cameron, *The Free Church of Scotland, 1843-1910* (E, 1910), 68-99, *passim*; FUFCS 480; AFCS I, 214.

R. MacLeod

Macaulay, Aulay (1758-1819), CofE minister and antiquarian. Macaulay was part of a truly remarkable family, the son of John Macaulay, minister of Cardross in Dunbartonshire (*FES* III, 336). His nephew was Lord Thomas B. Macaulay and his brother Zachary* was celebrated for his life-long crusade against slavery. Macaulay's life was largely spent in quiet country ministry and historical study after his graduation from Glasgow (MA, 1778). Initially he served as a curate at Claybrooke, leaving in 1789 to become rector of Frowlesworth from which he resigned in 1790. In 1796 he obtained the living of Rothley (in Leicestershire, like the above). The exceptions to this pattern were his extensive travels in Europe in 1793 (during which he tutored the future Queen Caroline in English) and again in 1815. He produced *Essays on Taste and ... Criticism* (L, 1780) and translated discourses from Prof. Noodt of Leyden (1781); his *The History and Antiquities of Claybrooke* appeared in 1790 (L). A long-projected life of Melanchthon never reached completion.

Joseph Irving, *The Book of Scotsmen* (Paisley, 1881), 295; W. Anderson, *Scottish Biographical Dictionary* (E, 1845), 512-13; *DNB* XXXIV, 406-7.

I. Campbell

Macaulay, Zachary (1768-1838), evangelical philanthropist and reformer. Son of John Macaulay of Cardross (*FES* III, 336), Zachary became a bookkeeper in 1783. From the age of sixteen he managed an estate in Jamaica, where he acquired a life-long loathing of slavery (*see* Anti-Slavery). On his return to England he was introduced by his brother-in-law, Thomas Babington, both to vital Christianity and to Clapham. William Wilberforce was impressed by his 'manly, collected mind', and in September 1792 Macaulay was appointed to the freed-slave experiment at Sierra Leone. He was governor from 1796 to 1799, returning to England with twenty-five African children for whom the Society for the Education of Africans was established.

In 1802 he was appointed to the Committee for the Abolition of the Slave Trade. He was its 'most laborious and most effective' member and, with James Stephen, Wilberforce's chief lieutenant in the campaign. In 1803 he moved to Clapham to be near Wilberforce. From 1802 until 1816 he was editor of the *Christian Observer*, using it to recruit Evangelicals to the abolition cause. He was secretary from 1807 to 1812 of the African Institution established for 'the civilization of Africa, and the Universal Abolition of the Slave Trade' in the wake of the Abolition Act of 1807.

In 1823 he joined with Thomas Fowell Buxton in the formation of the Anti-Slavery Society, for which he edited *The Anti-Slavery Reporter*. It presented an analysis of slave society of unprecedented sophistication and was a major factor in shaping anti-slavery feeling leading up to the 1833 Emancipation Act. Macaulay's prodigious accumulation and calm consideration of voluminous data resulted not only from the Protestant ethic of which he was an incarnation: he was serenely confident that Providence guarantees the congruity of religious duty with national economic interest. Supporters of the slave trade recognized in Macaulay their most dangerous foe and reserved for him their bitterest calumny.

Apart from his involvement in the prominent missionary, Bible, and charitable societies of his day, he also influenced the regulation of prisons, public houses and sabbath observance. He was Fellow of the Royal Society, promoted Sunday schools, and supported the educational system of Bell and, with reservations, that of Lancaster. He was a founder of the University of London. He favoured the Est.C over dissenting churches and, while committed to the value of voluntary associations, preferred

MACBEAN, FRANCIS

to approach the legislature with workable schemes where need was great and general.

Viscountess Knutsford, *Life and Letters of Zachary Macaulay* (L, 1900); 'Memoir of Z. Macaulay, Esq.', *Christian Observer*, 1839, 756–68, 796–817; J. Stephen, 'The Clapham Sect', *Essays in Ecclesiastical Biography* (L, 1849); E. M. Forster, *Marianne Thornton, 1797–1887* (L, 1956); E. M. Howse, *Saints in Politics* (L, 1953); F. J. Klingberg, *The Anti-Slavery Movement in England: A Study in English Humanitarianism* (New Haven, 1926); R. Anstey, *Anti-Slavery, Religion and Reform* (Folkestone, 1980); C. Bolt and S. Drescher (eds), *Anti-Slavery, Religion, and Reform* (Hamden, CN, 1980); *DNB* XXXIV, 418–20.

S. Piggin

Macbean, Francis (1793–1869), minister of the Original Secession Church* and later of the FC. Born in Corpach (near Fort William), Macbean was initially a schoolteacher in his native village, and then an Inspector, employed by the Edinburgh Society for the Support of Gaelic Schools (*see* Gaelic School Societies). He visited Lewis in this capacity in 1825/6, and is said to have presided over the first *Coinneamh Cheist* ('Question Meeting') held at a Communion season* in that island. He joined the Original Secession Church, and after training in Edinburgh was ordained in 1836 as a missionary-minister with responsibility for the whole area from Lochaber to Lewis. He almost succeeded in founding a Secession congregation in Harris, but a quarrel with the Harris poet-blacksmith, John Morrison,* impeded his progress. Leaving the Church some years before 1843, he lived in Stornaway and preached throughout Lewis. He joined the FC, and in 1844 became the first minister of the FC church at Fort Augustus and Glenmoriston. Macbean sympathized with Roderick MacLeod* of Bracadale in resisting indiscriminate admission to infant baptism,* and was inclined to admit only the children of full communicant members.

ASOSC 575–6; *AFCS* I, 215; J. Macleod, *By-paths of Highland Church History* (E, 1965), 22–40.

D. E. Meek

MacBride, Neil (1764–1814), CofS minister in the parish of Kilmorie, Arran, where his work was central to the revival* which had appeared by 1812. Born in Auchencairn, Kilbride (Arran), he was educated at Glasgow University and licensed by the Presbytery of Edinburgh. After serving as a missionary at Eriboll (from 1800), he became minister of Kilmorie in 1802. His settlement was opposed by the Presbytery of Kintyre, probably because of his strong evangelical identity. He co-operated with dissenters such as Alexander MacKay* and Dugald Sinclair,* who held him in the highest regard.

FES IV, 63; D. C. MacTavish (ed.), *The Gaelic Psalms 1694* (Lochgilphead, 1934), xxiii.

D. E. Meek

M'CHEYNE, ROBERT MURRAY

MacCallum, Donald (1849–1929), CofS minister and pro-crofter leader in the Highland Land Agitation of the 1880s. Born in Barravullin, Argyll, MacCallum observed the effect of the estate policy of local landlords, and inherited a strong tradition of resistance to 'improvements' (*see* Clearances). His critique appears to have developed while he was training at Glasgow University, probably through contact with pro-crofter activists. In 1880 he became assistant to John MacLeod in Morvern, north-west Argyllshire. His observation of conditions in Morvern, where there had been large-scale clearing and eviction of the people, helped to develop his anti-landlord radicalism, which grew still further when he was ordained to the mission station of Arisaig and South Morar, west Inverness-shire, in 1882.

MacCallum's tenure of the parish of Hallin, in Waternish, Skye (1884–7), brought him into the national headlines for his outspoken condemnation of, and conflict with, local landlords and enforcers of the law. Because of his provocative speeches, which combined proto-socialism with the language of the Old Testament prophets, he became known as the 'Prophet of Waternish'. His activism and proclamation of the 'land gospel' earned him the censure of the Presbytery of Skye in 1886. He was briefly imprisoned in Portree in November 1886, but no charges were pressed. Subsequently MacCallum was minister in Heylipol, Tiree (1887–9), and Lochs, Lewis (1889–1920), where he championed the cause of crofters and cottars. Much admired by the Highland crofting population, he retired to Glendale, Skye, and is buried there.

D. E. Meek, 'The Prophet of Waternish', *West Highland Free Press*, 8 July 1977; *id.*, ' "The Land Question Answered from the Bible": The Land Issue and the Development of a Highland Theology of Liberation', *The Scottish Geographical Magazine* 103 (1987), 84–9; *FES* IV, 127, VII, 204–5.

D. E. Meek

M'Cheyne, Robert Murray (1813–43), widely regarded as one of the most saintly and able young ministers of his day. Entering Edinburgh University in 1827, he gained prizes in all the classes he attended. In 1831 he commenced his divinity studies under Thomas Chalmers* at the Edinburgh Divinity Hall. M'Cheyne's early interests were modern languages, poetry, and gymnastics. The death of his older brother David in July 1831 made a deep impression on him spiritually. His reading soon after of the 'Sum of Saving Knowledge' (*see* Dickson, David) brought him into a new relationship of peace and acceptance with God.

In July 1835 M'Cheyne was licensed by the Presbytery of Annan, and in November became assistant to John Bonar at Larbert and Dunipace. In November 1836 he was ordained to the new charge of St Peter's Dundee, a largely industrial parish which did not help his delicate health. M'Cheyne's gifts as a preacher and as a godly man brought him increasing popularity. The Communion seasons* at St Peter's were especially noted for the sense of

God's presence and power. M'Cheyne took an active interest in the wider concerns of the Church. In 1837 he became Secretary to the Association for Church Extension* in the county of Forfar. This work was dear to M'Cheyne's heart. First and foremost he saw himself as an evangelist. He was grieved by the spiritual deadness in many of the parishes in Scotland and considered giving up his charge if the Church would set him apart as an evangelist. Writing to a friend in Ireland he revealed where his loyalties lay in the controversy that was then overtaking the Church: 'You don't know what Moderatism* is. It is a plant that our Heavenly Father never planted, and I trust it is now to be rooted out.'

Towards the close of 1838 M'Cheyne was advised to take a lengthy break from his parish work in Dundee because of ill-health. During this time it was suggested to him by Robert S. Candlish* that he consider going to Israel to make a personal enquiry on behalf of the Church's Mission to Israel*. Along with Alexander Keith* and Andrew Bonar, M'Cheyne set out for Israel (Palestine). The details of their visit were recorded and subsequently published in the *Narrative of a Mission of Enquiry to the Jews from the Church of Scotland, in 1839* (E, 1842). This did much to stimulate interest in Jewish Mission, and led to pioneer work among Jews in parts of Europe, most notably Hungary.

M'Cheyne returned to St Peter's to find that the work had flourished in his absence under the ministry of William Chalmers Burns.* M'Cheyne exercised a remarkably fruitful ministry in Dundee while in constant demand to minister in other places. Just prior to his death he had been preparing his congregation for the coming disruption in the CofS, which he thought inevitable after the Claim of Right* had been refused.

Memoir and Remains, ed. A. Bonar (2 vols, 1844; revd. ed. 1 vol., E, 1892); *Additional Remains* (E, 1847); *Basket of Fragments* (A, 1848); *Revival Truth* (L, 1860); *Why is God a Stranger in the Land?* (E, 1838); *Testimony against the Running of Railway Trains on the Sabbath* (Dundee, 1841); *Brief Expositions of the Epistles to the Seven Churches of Asia* (Dundee, 1845); *The Works* (NY, 1848–9).

FES V, 340–1; J. L. Watson, *Life of Robert Murray M'Cheyne* (^{2}E, 1882).

I. Hamilton

MacColl, Duncan (1846–1930), founder of the Glasgow Highland Mission (1898). Born on the island of Lismore, Argyll, MacColl moved with his family to a small farm on the mainland at Selma, near Benderloch, and later entered gentleman's service. Converted in 1872, he began open-air preaching, and joined the FC.* Moving to Glasgow and becoming an elder at the Wynd Church, he formed the Glasgow Open-Air Gospel Mission (later amalgamated with the Highland Mission) for the evangelization of towns and villages around the city. He also developed his particular interest in evangelistic activity among Highlanders, devoting his summer holidays to revival* missions throughout the Highlands.* Stimulated further by the Welsh Revival of 1904–5, MacColl consolidated his work at the Glasgow Highland Mission, on the site of St Peter's parish church, and attracted extensive inter-denominational congregations. The Mission published a popular *Gaelic Hymn Book* (G, ^{1}1899, ^{2}1913, ^{3}1922), containing original compositions, inspired by Highland and (increasingly) Hebridean revivals, and Gaelic* translations of popular English hymns.* After 1900 MacColl identified with the UFC.*

A. Stirling, *Duncan MacColl* (E., 1932).

D. E. Meek

M'Cosh, James (1811–94), philosopher and educator. After studying philosophy and theology under Sir William Hamilton* and Thomas Chalmers,* M'Cosh was ordained to Arbroath in 1835, translated to Brechin in 1839, and served the new East FC there from 1843. He rapidly gained a reputation as a natural theologian, particularly through the publication of *The Method of Divine Government, Physical and Moral* (E, L, 1850; ^{5}L, 1856). The favourable reception of this book led to his appointment to the Chair of Logic and Metaphysics at Queen's University, Belfast, in 1851.

He adopted the position of the Scottish Realist* school of philosophy, claiming that certain basic truths were known not *a posteriori* by experience but *a priori* by an intuitive process which relied a good deal upon evidence provided by self-conscious introspection. M'Cosh held that we have noninferential basic knowledge of the external world. Our beliefs about the world are not the product of sensation, but accompany sensation. Such beliefs are utterly reliable, recording reality directly, as it is. Unlike some later Scottish philosophers, for example his mentor Hamilton, M'Cosh rejected the influence of Immanuel Kant, and so was not driven to an agnosticism about God.

He defended this view against both positivism and empiricism on the one hand, and materialism on the other. He was a prolific and popular writer, in demand as a reliable apologist for orthodox, evangelical Christianity. Among his best known books are *The Supernatural in Relation to the Natural* (C, 1862), *An Examination of Mr. J. S. Mill's Philosophy* (NY, 1866), *Christianity and Positivism* (NY, 1871), and *The Scottish Philosophy* (L, 1874).

In 1868 M'Cosh was elected to the Presidency of Princeton College, combining this with the Chair of Philosophy. He was an able administrator, spearheading the expansion of Princeton, and an influential teacher and writer. He resigned the Presidency in 1888 but continued in the Chair of Philosophy until his death in 1894.

M'Cosh was one of the major voices disseminating Scottish Realist philosophy to the educated laity and ministers in the rapidly expanding Presbyterian Churches in the USA, both North and South. He was chiefly a popularizer and expositor and an apologist rather than a first-rank contributor to English-speaking philosophical thought. He adopted and defended a broadly theistic evolutionistic position, being in this almost a lone voice among orthodox Evangelicals. In his eyes the course of evolution was expressive of the wonder and intricacy of the creation. It was nothing more nor less than the way God had chosen to work in the development of the natural order.

M'Cosh was able to combine a commitment to Scottish Realism with evangelical convictions, while being fully aware of its Moderate* CofS antecedents. Yet there was in his eyes no opposition between the facts gathered by Scottish Realism and the truths taken out of God's Word by Scottish theology, even though, as he put it, 'the former tended to produce a legal, self-righteous spirit whereas the latter humbled men and exalted God'.

The Intuitions of the Mind (L, 1860, ³ NY, 1872); *Realistic Philosophy defended*, 2 vols (NY, 1887); *Gospel Sermons* (NY, 1888).

J. D. Hoeveler, Jr, *James McCosh and the Scottish Intellectual Tradition* (Princeton, 1981); *FES* V, 377–8; *AFCS* I, 218; W. M. Sloane, *The Life of James M'Cosh* (NY, 1896).

P. Helm

M'Crie, Charles Greig (1836–1910), FC minister and historian. Born in Edinburgh, he studied at Edinburgh University, the Presbyterian College of London and New College,* and was ordained to Barry FC, Forfarshire, in 1862. He moved to Blairgowrie South, Perthshire, in 1864; to St Mark's, Glasgow, in 1873; and to Ayr West in 1877.

M'Crie wrote a number of works on Scottish Church history, and edited a new edition of the Marrow of Modern Divinity (G, 1902) (*see* Marrow Controversy). He was the grandson of the elder Thomas M'Crie.*

The Public Worship of Presbyterian Scotland (E, 1892; Cunningham Lectures*); *The Church of Scotland, Her Divisions and Her Reunions* (E, 1901); *The Free Church of Scotland, her Ancestry, her Claims and her Conflicts* (E, 1896); *The Confessions of the Church of Scotland* (E, 1907, Chalmers Lectures*); *The Claim of Right* (E, 1886); *Scotland's Part and Place in the Revolution of 1688* (E, 1888).

AFCS I, 218–9; *FUFCS* 126.

M'Crie, Thomas (1772–1835), Presbyterian church historian. Born at Duns, Berwickshire, he entered Edinburgh University in 1788, but did not graduate. In 1791 he entered the divinity hall of the General Associate Synod* taught by Archibald Bruce* at Whitburn. In 1796 he was ordained to the Associate congregation in Potterrow, Edinburgh. New views were emerging in the Synod with respect to the power of the civil magistrate in spiritual matters, and the Synod responded to doubts M'Crie expressed at ordination by qualifying its subscription* to the Westminster* Confession. The Synod declared that it received the Confession with the exception of everything that seems to allow the civil magistrate to punish peaceable subjects on account of their religious opinions or observances. In 1804 the Synod revised its testimony* to make room for proponents of Voluntaryism,* who held it improper for the Christian ruler to exercise his authority and influence in behalf of religion. But in the meantime M'Crie had come to appreciate the doctrine of the Confession regarding the establishment of religion in the national life (*see* Church and state*). Bruce, M'Crie and two other ministers made protests against the new testimony's departure from the traditional views, and in 1806 they formed themselves into the Constitutional Associate Presbytery. They were popularly known as the Old Light Antiburghers (*see* New Light).

On behalf of the Presbytery M'Crie wrote his *Statement of the Difference* (E, 1807, 1871), which remains a standard exposition of the older Presbyterian teaching on the subject of a national acknowledgement of religion. But M'Crie did not stop at a contemporary apologia; he was drawn to lay bare the original historical setting of the nation's Church principles by making one of the first modern scholarly studies of the Scottish Reformation. For his biography of Knox,* M'Crie received the accolades of the literary world; in 1813 he became the first Scottish dissenting minister upon whom Edinburgh University conferred the DD. M'Crie's *Life of John Knox*, 2 vols (E, 1811, ²1813) contributed to the revival of the evangelical party in the CofS, and his discussion in *The Life of Andrew Melville*, 2 vols (E, 1819, ²1824) of the spiritual independence of Church courts from imposition by the civil authority anticipated the Disruption.*

After the death of Bruce in 1816, M'Crie conducted the Presbytery's divinity hall until 1818. In the pages of the *Edinburgh Christian Instructor** for 1817 he vindicated the religion of the Covenanters* from a hostile portrayal of it by Sir Walter Scott* in *Tales of My Landlord* in *A Vindication of the Scottish Convenanters* (G, 1824). After the union in 1820 of two New Light Secession bodies to form the USec.C, M'Crie expressed in print his apprehension about the further development of sentiment away from the original stance of the Secession fathers, and the impropriety of Church unions accomplished at the expense of abandoning the constitutional positions of the uniting Churches. *Two Discourses on the Unity of the Church* (E, 1821; Dallas, 1989) is a preview of the constitutional questions which would be raised in the Church union* discussions for the rest of the century. A union of M'Crie's presbytery with the Associate Synod of Protesters (another Antiburgher body) in 1827 formed the Original Secession Synod,* on a basis which M'Crie judged principled. In 1831–2 his historical narrative of the Marrow Controversy* in the CofS appeared in the *Edinburgh Christian Instructor*.

M'Crie died in Edinburgh, but Churches formed after his death found their conflicts on Church principles defined in his literary output. In 1871, amidst the union negotiations between the FC and the UPC, George Smeaton* reissued M'Crie's *Statement of the Difference* as the best presentation of the Confessional point of view on the relationship between Church and state.

M'CRIE, THOMAS

Miscellaneous Writings (E, 1841); *Sermons* (E, 1836); *History of the Reformation in Italy* (E, 1827); *History of the Reformation in Spain* (E, 1829); *Lectures on the Book of Esther* (E, 1838); *Memoirs of Mr. William Veitch and George Brysson* (E, 1825); *The Early Years of John Calvin* (E, 1880); *A Conversation Between John, a Baptist, and Ebenezer, a Seceder* (E, 1798-9, written with George Whytock*).

T. M'Crie, *Life of Thomas M'Crie* (E, 1840); *ASOSC*; J. M'Kerrow, *History of the Secession Church* (E, 1848); *DNB* XXXV, 12-14; J. Macleod, *Scottish Theology* (E, ³1974).

S. Isbell

M'Crie, Thomas (1797-1875), teacher and writer. Son of the historian of the Scottish Reformation (Thomas M'Crie*), M'Crie studied at the University of Edinburgh and the Theological Hall of the Original Secession Church.* Ordained in 1820, he served several congregations before succeeding his father as minister of the Davie Street Church in Edinburgh in 1836, at which time he also became professor of theology at the Theological Hall of the Original Secession Church. He promoted the union of the Original Seceders with the FC in 1852, and in 1856 was elected moderator of the FC General Assembly. In the same year he became Professor of Church History and Systematic Theology at the London College of the English Presbyterian Church. He edited a four-volume collection of his father's works (E, 1840), and *The Life of Mr. Robert Blair* (E, 1848); translated Pascal's *Provincial Letters* (E, 1847); and wrote numerous books, including the *Life of Thomas M'Crie* (E, 1840), *Sketches of Scottish Church History* (2 vols, E, 1841), *Lectures on Christian Baptism* (E, 1850), *Memoirs of Sir Andrew Agnew* (L, 1850), and the *Annals of English Presbytery from the Earliest Period to the Present Time* (L, 1872). For a short time he was editor of the *British and Foreign Evangelical Review.**

Disruption Worthies, 349; *DNB* XXXV, 14; *ASOSC*; *AFCS* I, 219.

D. B. Calhoun

McCulloch, James Duff (1836-1926), FC stalwart and College Principal. Born of solid evangelical stock in Logie Easter (Easter Ross), he studied at the University and New College, Edinburgh and was ordained to Latheron FC Caithness (1867-89). He moved to Glasgow Hope Street (1889-1926), electing to remain there rather than accept a chair in the Edinburgh FC College, although he did serve as Principal from 1905 to his death.

Prominent in the Constitutionalist* party opposed to the 1900 Union and in building up the post-1900 FC,* he was Moderator in 1901 and received Edinburgh's DD in 1917. He visited both South Africa and Princeton* in his early years as Principal, helping in the resumption of FC mission work in the former (1905, 1907). He had championed the crofters in Caithness and was never one to mince his words, although his preaching was scarcely popular. He lost four sons in their prime.

McCULLOCH, WILLIAM

AFCS I, 219; G. N. M. Collins, *The Heritage of Our Fathers* (E, 1974), 143-4; id., *Annals of the Free Church of Scotland 1900-1986* (E, n.d.), 18; *PAGAFCS 1927*, 510-11; *Glasgow Herald* (Dec. 13 1926), 16.

D. F. Wright

McCulloch, Thomas (1776-1843), Secession minister. Born in Neilston, Renfrewshire, he studied at Glasgow University and the General Associate Synod* divinity hall at Whitburn. Licensed by Kilmarnock Presbytery, he was ordained to the Antiburgher congregation in Stewarton, Ayrshire, in 1799. Having volunteered for overseas service, Synod sent him in 1803 to Prince Edward Island, Canada. However, on arriving in Pictou, Nova Scotia, he was persuaded to remain, being inducted to the Antiburgher congregation there in 1804. In 1805 he set up a grammar school to educate the children of dissenters.

McCulloch became involved in public controversy with a RC priest in 1808, and produced his *Popery Condemned by Scripture and the Fathers*, 2 vols (E, 1808-10). In 1817 he entered the Presbyterian Church of Nova Scotia, a union between the Burgher and Antiburgher Seceders in the province. In 1818 he became Principal of the Pictou Academy, a higher education college for dissenters, which he ran almost single-handed; in 1820 he was appointed as the Presbyterian Church of Nova Scotia's Professor of Divinity. These responsibilities proved too heavy to combine with his pastorate, which he relinquished in 1823.

The Pictou Academy had a turbulent existence, largely due to the internal politics of Nova Scotia, with its sharp Episcopalian-dissenter divide, and in 1838 McCulloch resigned as Principal to take up the Presidency of Dalhousie College in Halifax, where he taught till his death. He was a major figure in the Canadian educational scene.

McCulloch was Moderator of his Church's General Assembly in 1821, and the same year received a DD from Schenectady College, New York.

Calvinism, the Doctrine of the Scriptures (G, 1846).

Dict. of Canadian Biogr. VII, 529-41 (with further bibliogr.); W. McCulloch, *Life of Thomas McCulloch* (Truro, Nova Scotia, 1920); M. Whitelaw, *Thomas McCulloch: His Life and Times* (Halifax, Nova Scotia, 1985).

N. R. Needham

McCulloch, William (1691-1771), evangelical CofS minister. He was ordained to Cambuslang in 1731, where he spent the remainder of his life. Although he lacked eloquence, a great religious awakening known as the Cambuslang revival* occurred under his preaching in 1742. During the revival he preached five to six times a week, receiving assistance from neighbouring ministers and from the evangelist George Whitefield.* At the height of the revival as many as 30,000 were gathered at one time. McCulloch edited and published the first religious periodical in Scotland, *The Weekly History*. He also encouraged the growth of prayer societies and helped to foster renewed interest in foreign missions. His works include *An Account of Some Remarkable Events at Cambuslang* (G, 1742) and *Sermons on Several Subjects* (G, 1793), and MSS in New College Library, Edinburgh.

'Memoir' in *Sermons on Several Subjects* (G, 1793); A. Fawcett, *Cambuslang Revival* (L, 1971); *FES* III, 237-8.

C. W. Mitchell

McDonald, Allan (1859-1905), priest, poet and Gaelic* scholar and folklorist. He was born at Fort William and educated at Blair's College (*see* Colleges and Seminaries, RC) and at the Scots College* at Valladolid, Spain, where he pursued Gaelic studies in his spare time. He was ordained at Glasgow in 1882 and appointed to the Oban mission. He served as parish priest of Daliburgh, South Uist, from 1884, and transferred to Eriskay 1893, after a breakdown in health.

He commenced noting items from the rich oral tradition of South Uist in 1887, eventually filling eight quarto notebooks, of which two are still missing. He published a small Gaelic hymnal in 1889 (reprinted in 1936, expanded in 1893); this includes his Gaelic metrical version of the mass (*see* Gaelic, RC publications in). He was discovered by the Society for Psychical Research in connection with the enquiry into Highland second sight, in 1894, and Ada Goodrich Freer made free use of his folklore collection in her lectures and articles and in her book *Outer Isles* (Westminster, 1902). He was also a correspondent of Alexander Carmichael,* who consulted him while preparing *Carmina Gadelica* for publication. He was portrayed in fiction by Frederic Breton in *Heroine in Homespun* as 'Fr MacCrimmon' (L, 1893), and by Neil Munro in *Children of the Tempest* as 'Fr Ludovic' (L, 1903). In real life he is described by Neil Munro in *The Brave Days* (E, 1931); by Amy Murray in *Father Allan's Island* (E, 1920, 1936); by Frederick G. Rea in *A School in South Uist* (L, 1964).

Publication of his own writings and of material from his collection has been very largely posthumous. This includes his Gaelic diary for March 1897 (*Gairm*, Vol. I, 1952-3); his collection of Gaelic words and expressions from South Uist (Dublin, 1958); his ghost and second sight stories (ed. J. L. Campbell and T. H. Hall, *Strange Things*, L, 1968); his translations of some of the waulking songs in the MacCormick Collection (J. L. Campbell (ed.), *Hebridean Folksongs*, O, 1969); and *Bàrdachd Mhgr Ailein*, his Gaelic poetry, some of which had already appeared in *Gairm*, in E, 1965. A great deal of his collection remains unpublished.

J. L. Campbell, *Father Allan McDonald of Eriskay, 1859-1905, Priest, Poet and Folklorist* (E, ²1956).

J. L. Campbell

Macdonald, Andrew Buchanan (1892-1970), medical missionary. He was born in Stepps, Glasgow, and worked in his father's warehousing business. Seeking a form of Christian service that did not involve public speaking, he studied medicine at Glasgow University, interrupting his course for war service in the navy. He graduated MB, ChB in 1920 and after a year as a house surgeon was appointed to the Calabar Mission, Nigeria. He married Keeba Nisbet, a nursing sister. His long association with Itu hospital on the Cross River began in 1922 following a brief sojourn at Uburu. Like Harry Hastings* he was involved in the campaigns of the 1920s against yaws (financing the hospital from the proceeds); Mrs Macdonald was active in the rescue and care of abandoned twins. In 1926 he began to apply to local lepers a form of treatment developed in India, with marked success. An improvised settlement quickly proving inadequate, Macdonald led the development of Africa's first leprosarium. Direct action by women of the Church pressured reluctant chiefs to grant 168 acres of land; the colonial administration made a financial contribution. With John Paterson (a versatile lay missionary at Itu 1930-42), the Macdonalds devised an integrated medical, pastoral, evangelistic, industrial and agricultural programme fully engaging the skills and energies of leprosy-affected people. The leprosarium formed both a civil administrative unit (with its own chiefs, native court, and police) and an organized Presbyterian congregation. It produced its own cash crops and a river transport system, serving a bustling self-contained community. Macdonald frowned on outpatient treatment for leprosy, and his highly structured 'colony' contrasted with Hastings' network based on existing leper settlements outside villages. Itu was supported by the British Empire Leprosy Relief Association, the Leprosy Mission and Toc H; it was much visited and sometimes imitated. Macdonald became MBE in 1934 and CBE in 1957. He retired in 1952, but was recalled, and finally left in 1954.

Can Ghosts Arise? The Answer of Itu (n.p., 1946, 1957); *In His Name* (L, 1964).

Minutes of CofS Foreign Mission Committee 26 (1954-5), no. 2900, and Overseas Council 6 (1969-70), no. 3676; G. Johnston, *Of God and Maxim Guns* (Waterloo, Ont., 1988), 196-206; D. M. McFarlan, *Calabar. The Church of Scotland Mission founded 1846* (L, 1957); S. G. Browne, *Leprosy: New Hope and Continuing Challenges* (L, 1977); *id.*, F. Davey and W. A. R. Thomson (eds), *Herald of Health. The Saga of Christian Medical Initiatives* (L, 1985).

A. F. Walls

MacDonald, Angus (1844-1900), RC Archbishop of St Andrews and Edinburgh (1892-1900). Son of the laird of Glenaladale and grand-nephew of James Kyle,* he was born at Borrodale (Inverness-shire) and educated from the age of thirteen at Ushaw College, Durham. In 1865 he graduated BA at London University. Ordained priest at Ushaw in 1872, he served in Glasgow and Arisaig (Inverness-shire). On the establishment of normal RC territorial bishops in Scotland in 1878, he was appointed Bishop of the largely Gaelic*-speaking diocese of Argyll and the Isles. In 1892 he became Archbishop of St Andrews and Edinburgh. His

McDONALD, DONALD

elder brother, Hugh, was Bishop of Aberdeen 1890-8.

The restoration of pilgrimages* in Scotland was principally due to him and he initiated pilgrimages to Rome, Lourdes and Iona.* He was also largely responsible for the introduction of Scottish saints into the national liturgical calendar (*see* Christian Year). In 1883 he lobbied the Crofters Commission on behalf of the RC populations in the Western Isles who wanted RC teachers in their schools.

Statement of Certain Grievances of the Catholics in South Uist and Barra (G, 1883).

J. Darragh, *The Catholic Hierarchy of Scotland* (G, 1986), 27, 38, 121; *Catholic Directory for Scotland, 1901,* 276-81.

M. Dilworth

McDonald, Donald (1783-1867), Presbyterian minister, active chiefly in Prince Edward Island, Canada.* Born at Drumcastle in Rannoch (Perthshire), McDonald attended St Andrews University, completing studies in 1816. He was ordained a CofS minister and served as a missionary in Glengarry. He emigrated to Cape Breton Island in 1824, partly because of personal difficulties. Moving to PEI, he experienced evangelical conversion in 1827 and his ministry was transformed. Preaching and itinerating tirelessly, he participated in two intense revivals* in PEI (1830 and 1860), and believed himself to be an instrument of ingathering prior to the millennium. Despite his CofS ordination, McDonald founded an independent Presbyterian body in PEI, which by 1867 numbered some 5,000 members and adherents, and was sometimes known as 'Mr McDonald's Unattached Church' or 'the McDonaldites'. After 1843 some of his congregations joined the FCS. McDonald composed polemical pieces and Gaelic* hymns, found in *Spiritual Hymns* (Charlottetown, PEI, 1835).

See also MacLennan, John.

FES IV, 133; Murdoch Lamont, *Rev. Donald McDonald* (Charlottetown, PEI, 1902); *Dictionary of Canadian Biography* IX, 480-1.

D. E. Meek

Macdonald, Donald (1825-1901), Presbyterian minister and joint founder of the FPC*. Born in North Uist in the Outer Hebrides, he received his early education there. Following studies for the ministry he was ordained and inducted in 1872 to the FC charge of Shieldaig in Wester-Ross. Opposed to doctrinal changes in the FC he joined Donald Macfarlane* in leaving the denomination to form the FPC in 1893. From then until his death he was FP minister at Shieldaig. A man of deep Christian experience and a powerful preacher, Macdonald was highly respected as a spiritual instructor.

D. Macfarlane, *Memoir etc. of Rev. Donald Macdonald* (Inverness, 1957); A. MacPherson (ed.), *History of the Free Presbyterian Church of Scotland 1893-1970* (Inverness, 1974).

A. Morrison

MacDONALD, GEORGE

MacDonald, Duff (1850-1929), CofS missionary and parish minister. He was born in Keith, Banffshire, educated at Keith Grammar School and University of Aberdeen, and ordained to the parish of Pulteneytown near Wick in Caithness in 1877. In 1878 he became the sole ordained missionary to the newly founded mission at Blantyre, Nyasaland. There he faced an appallingly difficult situation. Some of the original staff had been unsuitable and had left the mission to become little more than bandits. The rest were running the mission and the associated freed-slave village as a colony, which created serious problems over the administration of justice. MacDonald, believing he had no authority in these 'civil' matters, concentrated on preaching and attempting to understand the local people. In 1881 a General Assembly commission recommended that the mission be restarted from scratch. Their report, most unfairly, made MacDonald a scapegoat, deflecting attention from the original errors in recruitment.

He returned to Scotland and, after a period of some distress and continuing controversy, was called to Dalziel South in Lanarkshire in 1883, where he was an outstanding and much loved minister till his death. His book *Africana, or The Heart of Heathen Africa,* 2 vols (E, 1885) is one of the earliest sympathetic accounts of the life and religion of an African people. MacDonald received the DD of Aberdeen in 1923.

FES III, 250; VII, 131, 698; VIII, 257; A. C. Ross, 'The Origins and Development of Church of Scotland Mission, Blantyre, Nyasaland, 1875-1926' (PhD, University of Edinburgh, 1968).

A. C. Ross

MacDonald, George (1824-1905), poet, fantasy writer, popular novelist, children's author and preacher. MacDonald was born in Huntly in rural Aberdeenshire, the son of a bleacher and weaver. In his lifetime he was classed as a writer with Charles Dickens, Anthony Trollope and Thomas Carlyle.* His roots lay in his clan identity as a MacDonald whose ancestors suffered at the massacre of Glencoe (1692).

MacDonald's childhood is beautifully captured in his semi-autobiographical *Ranald Bannerman's Boyhood* (L, 1871). He entered Aberdeen University in 1840, and had a scientific training. For a few years he worked as a tutor in London. Then he entered Highbury Theological College and married. He was called to a Congregational church in Arundel, Sussex, where his liberal views on the salvation of the heathen earned him disfavour with the deacons, who reduced his small salary to persuade him to leave. Some of the poorer members, however, rallied around with offerings they could ill afford. Then he moved to Manchester for some years, preaching to a small congregation and giving lectures. The rapidly growing family were always on the brink of poverty. Fortunately, the poet Byron's widow, recognizing MacDonald's literary gifts, started to provide financial help. The family moved down to London, living in a house then called 'The

MacDONALD, GEORGE

Retreat', near the Thames at Hammersmith, later owned by William Morris.

For a time MacDonald was Professor of Literature at Bedford College, London. Because of continued ill health the family eventually moved to Italy, where he and his wife were to remain for the rest of their lives. There were, however, frequent stays in Britain during the warmer months, and a long and successful visit to the USA on a lecture tour. One of his last books, *Lilith* (L, 1895), is among his greatest, a fantasy with the same power to move and to change a person's imaginative life as *Phantastes*.

C. S. Lewis regarded his theological debt to MacDonald as inestimable, and it is inevitable that he is interpreted through the eyes of his famous heir. Lewis, for example, wrestled with MacDonald's universalism in his book, *The Great Divorce* (L, 1945), where the Scot appears as a character. MacDonald's views on the imagination anticipated those of Lewis and J. R. R. Tolkien, and inspired G. K. Chesterton. His insights into the unconscious mind predated the rise of modern psychology.

MacDonald's sense that all imaginative meaning originates with God was the foundation of his work. Two key essays, 'The imagination: its functions and its culture' (1867) and 'The fantastic imagination' (1882) argue the central place of imagination in theology and devotion. The writer, MacDonald believed, dealt 'all the time with things that came from thoughts beyond his own', that is, from God.

MacDonald wrote nearly thirty novels, several books of sermons, a number of abiding fantasies for adults and children, short stories, and poetry. His novels can be divided into his Scottish and his English ones. His Scottish introduce dialect, lovingly captured. So effective is MacDonald's rendering of Scots that English readers can soon pick up its meaning. In his interest in dialect, he was running in parallel with writers like Mark Twain and 'Uncle Remus'.

MacDonald's main works are as follows: Scottish novels: *Alec Forbes* (L, 1865); *Malcolm* (L, 1875); *The Marquis of Lossie* (L, 1877); *Sir Gibbie* (L, 1879); English novels: *Annals of a Quiet Neighbourhood* (L, 1867); *Wilfred Cumbermead* (L, 1872); *Thomas Wingfold, Curate* (L, 1876); symbolic fiction and fantasy: *Phantastes* (L, 1858); *The Portent* (L, 1864); children's literature: *At the Back of the North Wind* (L, 1871); *The Princess and the Goblin* (L, 1872); *The Lost Princess* (L, 1895); *The Princess and Curdie* (L, 1883); also short stories, poetry, literary criticism, and sermons, including *Unspoken Sermons* (three series, L, 1867, L, 1885, L, 1889).

DNB Second Suppl. II, 513–15; Greville MacDonald, *George MacDonald and his Wife* (L, 1924); C. S. Lewis, *George MacDonald: an Anthology* (L, 1946); R. N. Hein, *The Harmony Within: The Spiritual Vision of George Macdonald* (Grand Rapids, 1982); Kathy Triggs, *The Stars and the Stillness: A Portrait of George MacDonald* (C, 1986); William Raeper, *George MacDonald* (Tring, 1987); Michael R. Phillips, *George MacDonald: Scotland's Beloved Storyteller* (Minneapolis, 1987).

C. Duriez

MacDonald, Hugh (1699–1773), the first vicar apostolic (*see* Propaganda Fide) of the Catholic Highland District, 1731. He was one of the first priests from Scalan (*see* Colleges and Seminaries, Roman Catholic), and was ordained in 1725. Son of the laird of Morar, he was related to many leading Jacobites* of 1745. Although critical of that Rising,* he blessed the Glenfinnan Standard and appointed Catholic chaplains. After Culloden he escaped to Paris, returning to Scotland 1749. Denounced and imprisoned 1755, but released 1756, he administered his District secretly. He died at Aberchalder, Glengarry.

He weathered the Jansenist* controversy, 1733–8, and the upheavals of the Forty Five, and contributed much to the survival of Gaelic Catholicism, notably by refounding the Highland seminary and assuring a supply of MacDonald priests.

J. Darragh, *The Catholic Hierarchy of Scotland* (G, 1986), 13–14, 121; J. F. S. Gordon, *The Catholic Church in Scotland* (A, 1874), 7–9.

G. M. Dorrian

MacDonald, James and George (1800–35), devout twin brothers, shipbuilders and proto-Irvingites (*see* Irving, Edward). The MacDonalds, of Port Glasgow, Greenock, were members of the CofS. Attracted to the preaching of McLeod Campbell* in nearby Row, they adopted the beliefs current in his and Edward Irving's circle concerning universal atonement, premillennialism, Christ's fallen humanity and the availability of supernatural gifts of tongue-speaking, healing and prophecy.

In March 1830, James MacDonald experienced what he believed to be baptism in the Spirit, accompanied by the gift of healing. A fortnight later, he and George both spoke in tongues. The interpretations of the tongues all referred to the Second Coming. Associating themselves with Mary Campbell* of nearby Fernicarry, who had experienced glossolalia a fortnight previously, the MacDonalds became the focus for much religious interest and excitement, particularly on the part of Henry Drummond's* Albury group.

After McLeod Campbell's deposition in 1831, the MacDonalds left the CofS, turning their own regular prayer meeting into a pastorless house-church. They broke with Irving and his London circle when the latter began appointing apostles in 1832, and were also critical of the London group for its placing prophecy on a level with Scripture. They thus played no part in the subsequent development of the Catholic Apostolic Church.*

James and George both died of pulmonary illness.

R. Norton, *Memoirs of James and George MacDonald of Port Glasgow* (L, 1840); W. Hanna, *Letters of Thomas Erskine of Linlathen*, 2 vols (E, 1877).

N. R. Needham

MacDonald, John (1779–1849), the 'Apostle of

MACDONALD, JOHN

the North'. He was the son of the catechist of Reay in Caithness, and was probably the most influential of early nineteenth-century Highland* preachers. Following licence in 1805, he served as missionary at Achrenie and Halladale and at Berriedale in Caithness before becoming minister of the Gaelic* Chapel, Edinburgh, in 1807. In 1813 he succeeded the saintly Charles Calder as minister of Urquhart (Ferintosh).

MacDonald's frequent evangelistic campaigns throughout the north of Scotland earned him the nickname of the 'Apostle of the North', and also raised questions at the General Assembly of 1818 about ministers preaching outwith their own parishes. Between 1822 and 1830 he visited St Kilda on four separate occasions, keeping a fascinating daily journal, and was partly responsible for having a church and manse built on that remote island under the auspices of the Scottish SPCK.* He also undertook a preaching tour of Ireland.

John MacDonald's powerful preaching resulted in one writer giving him the epithet, the 'Whitefield* of the Highlands and Islands of Scotland'. He often preached to congregations of many thousands, particularly at open-air services in connection with Communion seasons* (see Lord's Supper). He was at the centre of a number of revival* movements in the Highlands, e.g. Breadalbane (1816–17), Lewis (from the 1820s) and Syke (1840s).

Although not regarded by critics as in the first rank of Gaelic poetry, MacDonald's hymns (mostly elegies) contain some memorable lines which are still quoted (see Hymnology, Gaelic). His edition of the Gaelic Shorter Catechism had a wide circulation (see Gaelic, Protestant Prose Publications in). His teachings on theological subjects had a great influence on Highlanders – such as his assertion that applicants for baptism required an *uncontradicted*, while applicants for Communion must display an *accredited*, profession of faith.

A leader of Highland Evangelicalism at the time of the Disruption,* John MacDonald acted as 'Gaelic Moderator' at the FC General Assembly held in Inverness in 1845. In Gaelic he is known as *Dòmhnallach na Tòisidheachd* ('MacDonald of Ferintosh') or *Ministear Mòr na Tòisidheachd* ('The Big Minister of Ferintosh').

FES VII, 47–8; AFCS I, 222; J. MacDonald, *Marbhrainn agus Dàna Spioradail Eile* (E, 1897); J. Kennedy, *The Apostle of the North* (Inverness, 1932); D. Beaton, *Some Noted Ministers of the Northern Highlands* (Inverness, 1929), 157–70.
R. MacLeod

Macdonald, John (1807–47), missionary and colleague of Alexander Duff* in Calcutta. Born in Edinburgh the son of John MacDonald* (later of Ferintosh), he completed a prize-winning MA at King's College, Aberdeen, when only seventeen, and proceeded to divinity there, while also tutoring at Westerton, near Elgin. From there he was ordained to the Scots Kirk at Chadwell Street, Pentonville, London in 1830. Duff's visit to London Presbytery in 1835 stirred Macdonald, and

MACDONALD, WILLIAM CALDWELL

in 1837 (when he married Anne Mackenzie) he was appointed to Calcutta by the CofS Foreign Missions Committee. They arrived in 1838, and Macdonald took up his teaching in Duff's college, with occasional preaching. When at the Disruption* all the Calcutta missionaries joined the Free Church, Macdonald became acting minister of the Free Church in Calcutta, until shortly before his death.

Macdonald's diary reveals a spirit of intense piety. His writings show 'how zealously he embraced every opportunity for counteracting evil', his targets including the theatre, balls, duelling and even Haydn's 'The Creation'. Some of his works were edited posthumously by W. Clarkson.

Statements of Reasons for Accepting A Call to Go to India... (L, 1837); *Memorial of the late Koilas Chunder Mookerjee* (Calcutta, 1845); *A Pastor's Memorial to His Former Flock: Consisting of Sermons and Addresses* (L, 1842); *Memoirs and Manuscript of Isobel Hood*... (³E, 1848).

FES VII, 495, 698–9; AFCS I, 222; W. K. Tweedie, *The Life of the Rev. John Macdonald*... (E, 1949), with selections from diary and letters.
D. F. Wright

MacDonald, Mary (née MacDougall or Mac-Lucas) (1789 or 1800–1872), Gaelic* poetess from the Ross of Mull where she was born at Brolas. She was the composer of sacred and secular verse, but is best known for her hymn, 'Leanabh an Aigh' ('Infant of Splendour'), which Lachlan MacBean (1853–1931) translated rather freely into English as the carol, 'Child in the Manger'. Her family was closely associated with the Baptist church in the Ross of Mull and her brother, Duncan, became the first pastor (1838–50) of Tiree Baptist Church.

See also Hymnology, Gaelic; Baptist Home Missionary Society for Scotland.

Tocher 24 (1985), 304–12; D. E. Meek, *Island Harvest: Tiree Baptist Church 1838–1988* (E, 1988), 5–10, 24–6.
D. E. Meek

MacDonald, Robert (b.1795), Gaelic* school teacher and translator. He was born in Sutherland and taught in a number of places including Arnisdale, Inverness, Keils and Dingwall. His book of hymns, *Oranan Nuadh air Staid na Genealaich* (Inverness, 1836), contains some satirical 'sermons for asses'. He translated John Bunyan's *Life and Death of Mr Badman* and *Sighs from Hell* into Gaelic as *Beatha agus Bas Mhr. Droch-Dhuine* (Inverness, 1824) and *Osnaidhean 'o Ifrinn* (Inverness, 1829). He was one of several translators who published versions of Bunyan's books in the first half of the nineteenth century.

See also MacFarlane, Patrick.
R. MacLeod

MacDonald, William Caldwell (1891–1987), UF and CofS preacher. Born at Glasgow, he was edu-

MACDONELL, ALEXANDER

cated at Whitehill School, Glasgow University (MA, 1915) and Glasgow UFC College. In 1918 he went as assistant to Edinburgh Lothian Road, was ordained and inducted to Chirnside the following year and three years later translated to Kilmarnock, Portland Road. From 1927 to 1952 he conducted one of the most distinguished of Scotland's twentieth-century pulpit ministries at Edinburgh, Palmerston Place, from which he removed through ill-health to Chalmers, Bridge of Allan, where he was to serve for twenty-three years. When he demitted in 1975, he had been fifty-six years in the active ministry. He never married, his manse being shared by two sisters with whom, all three in their eighties, he retired to Dunblane, Perthshire, from where he continued his contributions to the *Expository Times* and local pulpits, encouraging younger men with offers of Palmerston Place manuscripts for their use and tips on voice production.

His published works include: *Modern Evangelism* (L, 1937), *Go Up Higher* (L, 1940), *Truth that Sings* (L, 1948) and *The Elder, His Character and Duties* (Stirling, 1958; ²E, 1982).

FUFCS 23; FES IX, 443, X, 262.

A. Herron

Macdonell, Alexander (1762–1840), RC Bishop of Kingston, Ontario. Born in Inverness-shire, he was educated at the Scots Colleges* in Paris and Valladolid. After ordination in 1787, he worked in Badenoch. In 1792, having obtained employment for Highlanders in Glasgow, he became the city's first resident priest. Then, after helping to form a RC regiment, the Glengarry Fencibles, he was in 1794 appointed their chaplain, the first RC chaplain* in the British army. He served with them in Guernsey 1795–8 and Ireland 1798–1802.

When the Fencibles were disbanded in 1802, Macdonell obtained land for them in Upper Canada (now Ontario) and followed them to Canada in 1804. The Bishop of Quebec in 1807 made him vicar-general of the entire province. In 1820 he was ordained as auxiliary Bishop; then, when Kingston diocese was erected in 1826, he became its Bishop. He died at Dumfries while on a visit to Scotland.

His labours in Canada were immense and successful: priests and people increased ten-fold under his leadership. He was also politically important. Profoundly conservative, he fostered loyalty to government and in 1831 became a member of the legislative assembly of Upper Canada. He was instrumental in raising a second Glengarry regiment, which saw action in the American war of 1812–14. The town of Alexandria, Ontario, was named after him.

K. M. Toomey, *Alexander Macdonell: the Scottish Years* (Toronto, 1985); J. A. Macdonell, *A Sketch of the Life of Alexander Macdonell* (Alexandria, Ontario, 1890); H. J. Somers, *The Life and Times of Alexander Macdonell* (Washington D.C., 1931); J. E. Rea, *Bishop Alexander Macdonell and the Politics of Upper Canada* (Toronto, 1974); *Dictionary of Canadian Biography* VII, 544–51.

M. Dilworth

McEWEN (OR McEWAN), WILLIAM

Macdowell, John (*fl*.1530–55), early Protestant. As Dominican* subprior in Glasgow, he was incorporated in Glasgow University in 1530 and seems to have been a bachelor in theology of Cologne in the 1520s. Appointed prior of Wigtown, Macdowell fled to England in 1534 when suspected of heresy, and was befriended by Thomas Cromwell. In England, he preached against the pope and gained the reputation of being a blasphemer of saints. He became a chaplain to Nicholas Shaxton, Bishop of Salisbury, who favoured the Reformation, and was naturalized in 1537. Archbishop Cranmer complained in 1537 how Macdowell 'damns all singing and reading and organ playing'. Presented to the parsonage of Hawkchurch in Dorset in 1537, Macdowell found himself imprisoned for a spell in Salisbury in 1538. In Edward VI's reign, he preached at a funeral in London and received a licence to preach, but fled abroad with the Protestant exiles on Mary Tudor's accession.

Knox, *History* I, 23; J. Durkan and J. Kirk, *University of Glasgow, 1451–1577* (G, 1977), 211–12; J. Durkan, 'Some Local Heretics', *TDGAS*, 3rd ser. 36 (1959), 67–71; J. Durkan, 'Scottish "Evangelicals" in the Patronage of Thomas Cromwell', *RSCHS* 21 (1982), 139–41.

J. Kirk

MacEwen, Alexander Robertson (1851–1916), UP/UF minister and church historian. Born at Edinburgh, he was educated at Glasgow (MA 1870; DD 1892), Oxford and Göttingen universities, and at the UP Hall, Glasgow. He taught Greek and Latin at Glasgow University (1875–7), was minister in Moffat (1880–6) and Glasgow (1886–1901), and then Professor of Church History in New College, Edinburgh. In theology MacEwen described himself as liberal and evangelical, and a 'resolute advocate of central and unifying beliefs'. His works included *Life and Letters of Principal Cairns* (L, 1894), *The Erskines* (E, 1900), and *A History of the Church in Scotland* – to 1560 only (2 vols, L, 1913–18).

FUFCS 579; *Who Was Who 1916–1928*, 668; Small II, 94.

J. D. Douglas

McEwen (or McEwan), William (1735–62), Associate Synod* minister and author. Born in Perth, he studied theology first under Ebenezer Erskine* at Stirling, then under James Fisher* at Glasgow. Licensed to preach by the Presbytery of Dunfermline in 1753, in 1754 he was ordained minister of the Associate congregation in Dundee. He died suddenly of a violent fever in Leith after a visit to Edinburgh, and was much lamented.

McEwen's distinction derives largely from two posthumous writings, *Grace and Truth* (E, 1763, often rp.), an exposition of Old Testament typology, and his *Select ... Essays* (2 vols, E, 1767, enlarged and rp. as *Select Essays*, E, ⁷1779), which covers the principal heads of Christian doctrine. Both works were edited by John Patison, minister of Edinburgh's Bristo Associate congregation. Patison also wrote a memoir of McEwen, which is prefixed to various editions of the latter's works.

J. M'Kerrow, *History of the Secession Church* (G, 1841), 868–71; *DNB* XXXV, 72, Small I, 274–80.

N. R. Needham

McFadyen, John Edgar (1870–1933), Presbyterian biblical scholar. McFadyen was born in Glasgow. After studying at the Universities of Glasgow, Oxford, and Marburg, and at the FC College in Glasgow, he was Professor of Old Testament at Knox College, Toronto (1898–1910) and at the UFC College in Glasgow (1910–33). He published many non-technical biblical handbooks and some translations of Old Testament books into modern speech. His influence as a teacher of theological students was deep and lasting. Among his best known works are his revision of A. B. Davidson's* *Introductory Hebrew Grammar* (E, ¹⁹1914, ²⁴1932); *The Problem of Pain: A Study in the Book of Job* (L, 1917); and *The Message of Israel* (L, 1931).

FUFCS 579–80; D. Lamont, 'John Edgar McFadyen, 1870–1933', *ExT* 45 (1933–4), 261–4.

G. W. Anderson

MacFarlan, Patrick (1781–1849), evangelical CofS and FC minister. Educated in Edinburgh and ordained to Kippen in 1806, in 1824 he succeeded Thomas Chalmers* as minister of St John's in Glasgow. This position proved too demanding, and in 1832 MacFarlan settled in Greenock, first as minister of the West parish (at that time the richest living in Scotland), and then from 1843 until his death as minister of the West FC. A leader of the Evangelical Party, he was elected Moderator of the General Assembly of the CofS in 1834, and of the FC in 1845. He wrote numerous pamphlets related to the Apocrypha Controversy* and the Disruption.* In addition he made frequent contributions to the *Edinburgh Christian Instructor,** of which he was an original proprietor. He paid particular attention to revivals* on the continent and was one of the original promoters of the Evangelical Alliance.*

A Vindication of the Church of Scotland (L, 1850); *The Past and Present State of Evangelical Religion in Switzerland* (E, 1845).

FES III, 207–8; *AFCS* I, 226–7; *Disruption Worthies*, 371–6; *FCM* VI (1849), 375f.

D. A. Currie

Macfarlane, Donald (1834–1926), Presbyterian minister and joint founder of the FPC. A native of North Uist in the Outer Hebrides, his early education was followed by teaching posts in various Hebridean schools. He then studied at Glasgow University and the Glasgow FC College. In 1874 he was licensed by the FC Presbytery of Skye and Uist and in January 1876 ordained to Strathconon. He later served in charges at Moy, Kilmallie and Raasay. During the earlier part of Macfarlane's ministry, the FC suffered serious internal disputes over its doctrinal position. In 1892 the General Assembly passed a Declaratory Act* which altered the Church's relationship to its subordinate standard, the Westminster* Confession of Faith (see Subscription, Confessional), thus, it has been argued, formally making space for theological liberals. Macfarlane protested and the following year left the FC (with Donald Macdonald* and others) and founded the FPC. He became FP minister at Raasay and from 1903 until his death he served the Church's Dingwall congregation.

A deeply prayerful man of gentle disposition, Macfarlane's bold action in 1893 was prompted by concern that a witness to the full authority of the Bible be maintained in the Scottish Church. Much esteemed as a preacher, his sermons combined clarity of presentation with depth of Christian experience. His published works included *Sermons on the Love of God and Cognate Themes* (G, 1986) and *Memoir, etc., of Rev. Donald Macdonald* (Inverness, ²1957).

D. Beaton, *Memoir ... of The Rev. Donald Macfarlane* (Inverness, 1929); A. MacPherson (ed.), *History of the Free Presbyterian Church of Scotland 1893–1970* (Inverness, 1974).

A. Morrison

MacFarlane, Patrick (or Peter) (1758–1832), influential Gaelic* translator. A schoolmaster in Appin, MacFarlane superintended the reprinting of the 1796 edition of the Gaelic New Testament (see Bible (Versions, Gaelic)). His Gaelic translations included some of the classics of English evangelical literature, notably Bunyan's *Pilgrim's Progress* (E, 1812), Doddridge's *Rise and Progress of Religion in the Christian Soul* (E, 1811) and *One Thing Needful* (E, 1811), and William Guthrie's* *Christian's Great Interest* (Falkirk, 1783). He compiled and translated a *Manual of Family Devotion* (E, 1829), collected a volume of Gaelic poetry (E, 1813), and produced a Gaelic Vocabulary (E, 1815).

D. MacKinnon, *The Gaelic Bible and Psalter* (Dingwall, 1930), 57.

D. E. Meek

MacFarlane, William (1840–87), missionary. The son of a farmer at Strathbraan, Perthshire, he was a brilliant student at St Andrews (MA, 1858). In 1865 he was ordained to serve in the mission (started 1859) in Gaya, Bihar, W. of Calcutta. But the fruitlessness of the preaching to which MacFarlane felt himself called led to the mission's closure and his removal to Darjeeling in 1870 – together with the Nepalese children originally sent by a godly tea-planter near Darjeeling to the Gaya orphanage. MacFarlane soon spotted the strategic position of Kalimpong for the unevangelized lands of Sikkim, Bhutan, Nepal and Tibet. When joined in 1879 by Archibald Turnbull (*FES* VII, 709–10) and W. S. Sutherland (*FES* VII, 708), he put the former in charge at Darjeeling and moved to Kalimpong. Unmarried, he was accompanied by his sister Margaret Ann.

Keenly committed to educational mission after his

Gaya disappointment, MacFarlane founded two teacher-training colleges as well as schools. Proving himself an adept linguist among the diversity of tongues in the area, he continued Bible-translation in Nepali and began it in Lepcha. His versatility extended also to printing and building. Under his lead the new mission enjoyed unusual success. After a generation it had several Indian ministers and twenty catechists with a baptized community of some 2,500. It has been called 'one of the wonder missions of the world', and MacFarlane 'the St Ninian* of the Eastern Himalayas'.

MacFarlane's extended furlough from 1881 stirred enormous interest in Scotland, and he returned with the backing of the new Scottish Universities' Missionary Association to initiate work in Sikkim. The Rajah's refusal of building permission meant that Kalimpong remained his base. He died there in his sleep after a day spent collecting timber.

See also Graham, John Anderson.

FES VII, 699; E. G. K. Hewat, *Vision and Achievement 1796–1956* (E, 1960), 157–62; J. A. Graham, *On the Threshold of Three Closed Lands* (E, 1897); J. Lindell, *Nepal and the Gospel of God* (Kathmandu, 1979).

D. F. Wright

McGavin, William (1773–1832), proponent of evangelical Protestantism and religious controversialist. From an Antiburgher (*see* General Associate Synod) farming family in Auchinlock, Ayrshire, he was apprenticed as a weaver and bookseller in Paisley, and then became a merchant and bank agent in Glasgow. He joined the Congregationalists* in 1802. His best known work is *The Protestant*, a weekly issued at Glasgow 1819–22. Statements in this led to his being tried for libel, successfully, in 1821. His interest in such polemic seems to have come from reading Thomas McCulloch* of Nova Scotia. McGavin's work, though prejudiced and narrow, derives its power from a forceful, satirical style. He published editions of John Knox's* Reformation history (G, 1831) and of John Howie's* *Scots Worthies* (G, 1827) and, as a second volume of the same work, *The Cloud of Witnesses** and *Naphtali* (G, 1729), attacked David Dale's* New Lanark scheme (G, 1824) and responded to Cobbett on the Reformation (G, 1825).

The Posthumous Works of the late William McGavin Esq., with a Memoir, including Autobiography, 2 vols (G, 1834).

DNB XXXV, 84–5; M. D. Peddie, *Biographical Sketch . . . Mr. W. McGavin* (E, 1887); W. Reid, *The Merchant Evangelist, being a Memoir of William McGavin* (E, 1884).

J. F. McCaffrey

MacGill, Stevenson (1765–1840), pastorally-minded Glasgow Divinity Professor who did much to raise the standard of ministerial earnestness and utility in the CofS prior to the Disruption*. Born at Port Glasgow, MacGill graduated from Glasgow University in 1781 with great distinction. Ordained to Eastwood, Glasgow, in 1791, a second pastorate at Tron Church in the city was commenced in 1797. A gifted writer, MacGill early wrote against the French Revolution* (1792) and on the formation of character (1796). Perhaps because of these books he was awarded the Aberdeen DD in 1803. The years of the Tron pastorate were characterized by zeal in evangelism and social improvement, *e.g.* prison reform and efforts at raising ministerial discussion of literature and theology. His popular essays, *Considerations Addressed to A Young Clergyman* (G, 1809), were originally delivered in this setting and proved widely influential. The Glasgow divinity chair was gained on the basis of such efforts and the backing of such well-placed Evangelicals as H. Wellwood Moncrieff* and Andrew Thomson.* While not always agreeing with his Tron successor, Thomas Chalmers,* he, like Chalmers, was a powerful influence upon students in the city and University.

DNB XXXV, 88–9; FES VII, 401–2; R. Burns, *Memoir of Stevenson MacGill* (E, 1842); H. M. B. Reid, *The Divinity Professors in the University of Glasgow, 1640–1903* (G, 1923), 285–309.

K. J. Stewart

McGill, William (1732–1807), CofS minister of Ayr (Second Charge) (1761–1807), subject of a famous heresy* case in 1789. Apparently under the influence of Joseph Priestley, he published his *Practical Essay on the Death of Christ* (E, 1786), which was commonly regarded as Socinian. This led to a heresy complaint in the Synod of Glasgow and Ayr in 1789. The action was shifted from Presbytery to General Assembly and back until a year later McGill offered an explanation and apology. The Seceders* were outraged by the CofS's failure to prosecute him effectively and a pamphlet war ensued. Burns* satirized the episode in 'The Kirk's Alarm'.

Scots Magazine, 51 (1789); FES III, 12–13; DNB XXXV, 89–90; A. McNair, *Scots Theology in the Eighteenth Century* (L, 1928).

J. R. McIntosh

MacGregor, Duncan (*d.*1915), Baptist* minister and founder of a Baptist College at Dunoon. Born in Easdale in the late 1830s, MacGregor studied for the Baptist ministry under James Paterson, Glasgow, and then emigrated to the pastorate of a Baptist church in Chicago. He became involved in radical politics among the city's Gaelic*-speaking immigrant population, and founded the Scottish Land League of America to support the land agitation movement in the Scottish Highlands in the 1880s (*see* Clearances).

Returning to Scotland in 1885, MacGregor appeared on political platforms in support of the candidature of Donald H. MacFarlane, who won the Argyll seat in that year. In November 1885 MacGregor became pastor of Dunoon Baptist Church, and in 1893, at a time of debate about Baptist ministerial training (*see* Baptist Union of Scotland), founded what was known initially as the Gospel

MacGREGOR, DUNCAN

Training College. Continuing until MacGregor's death, it attracted a substantial number of students, some of whom had a strong revivalist* emphasis (see Taylor, F. W.) and links with the Holiness movement, exemplified in Oswald Chambers,* who entered the College in 1897.

J. D. Wood, 'Transatlantic Land Reform: America and the Crofters' Revolt', *SHR* 63 (1984), 97–102; D. B. Murray, *The First Hundred Years* (G, 1969), 90.

D. E. Meek

MacGregor, Duncan (1854–1923), Gaelic* scholar, liturgiologist and poet. He was born at Fort Augustus, attended the University of Edinburgh, and after licensing by the CofS Presbytery of Aberdeen (1877) served on missions at Orkney, Drumoak, Kincardine and Gardenstown. He was ordained in 1881 and worked for the rest of his life as the much-loved minister of Inverallochy, near Fraserburgh.

MacGregor believed that 'A clergyman when officiating is higher than a King.' His several writings on worship, including his Lee Lecture* on *General Principles of Early Scottish Worship* (E, 1895), expressed his firm conviction that older forms of Christian worship had been richer. He preached at Iona* on the thirteenth centenary of Columba's* death. His poem, *The Scald, or the Northern Balladmonger* (A, 1874), enjoyed a reprint.

FES VI, 225; D. H. Edwards (ed.), *One Hundred Modern Scottish Poets* (Brechin, 1880–97), XI, 83–92.

G. Wareing

MacGregor, George Hogarth Carnaby (1864–1900), FC minister, popularizer of the aims and teachings of the Keswick Convention (see Scroggie, Graham). Born in the FC manse of Ferintosh, Ross-shire, MacGregor was educated at Inverness Academy and at Edinburgh University as an arts student (1884–8). This proved a seminal time, for MacGregor fell under the influence of the Hebrew Professor A. B. Davidson,* abandoning his belief in the strict verbal inspiration of the Bible and accepting the methods and results of a moderate biblical criticism.

In 1888 MacGregor became minister of the East FC, Aberdeen; in 1894 he moved to Trinity Presbyterian Church, Notting Hill, in London, where he remained till his early death six years later.

MacGregor soon became one of the foremost speakers at the Keswick Convention (see Conventions), which he first attended in 1889, and produced a steady stream of popular devotional books to promote the Keswick 'holiness' ethos. Some of his more unguarded utterances seemed to teach the possibility of sinless perfection in this life, but in other places he explicitly denounced this as erroneous. The burden of his message, expounded most notably in his *A Holy Life and How to Live It* (L, 1894), was that sanctification is as much Christ's work as justification, and that faith is as much instrumental in receiving the former as the latter.

MacGREGOR, JAMES

His views of Scripture apart, MacGregor remained loyal to the Calvinism* of his Presbyterian background, and was a keen student of the Puritans, especially John Owen. He had a lifelong passion for missionary* work – medical advice alone prevented him from becoming an overseas missionary. He was particularly concerned about Christian mission to the Jews, and in 1899 became joint-convener of the FC Jewish Mission.

So Great Salvation (E, 1892); *Praying in the Holy Ghost* (L, 1896).

D. C. MacGregor, *George H. C. MacGregor* (L, 1900); *AFCS* I, 229.

N. R. Needham

MacGregor, James (1759–1830), minister of the General Associate Synod* (Antiburgher) and a campaigner for the provision of Gaelic*-speaking ministers for Highland* settlers in the Canadian Maritimes. Born at Portmore, Comrie parish, Perthshire, MacGregor matriculated at Edinburgh University in 1779 and attended the Synod Hall in Edinburgh (1781–4). Serving as a probationer at Craigdon, Aberdeenshire, he was ordained by the Synod of Glasgow in 1786, and in that year emigrated to Pictou, Nova Scotia. His initially strict adherence to Antiburgher principles prevented his joining the Associate Presbytery of Truro (Nova Scotia), and in 1795 (following the arrival of two more Antiburgher ministers from Scotland) he formed the General Associate Presbytery of Pictou. Mellowing in later life, MacGregor became the first Moderator of the Presbyterian Church of Nova Scotia, formed in 1817 by the coming together of the two bodies. From the 1790s he travelled extensively in Nova Scotia, Cape Breton Island and Prince Edward Island, observing the condition of settlers and providing services. He corresponded with his Synod in Scotland to draw attention to the spiritual destitution of the settlements (*Letter from J.M. to the General Associate Synod*, Paisley, 1793). MacGregor campaigned vigorously for the establishment (1815) of Pictou Academy, to train native Presbyterian ministers in Nova Scotia. He was awarded a DD by Glasgow University in 1822, and his Gaelic hymns, *Dàin a Chomhnadh Cràbhuidh* ('Poems to Assist Devotion') were published (G, 1819, re-issued seven times).

G. Patterson, *A Few Remains of Rev. James MacGregor* (E, 1859); id., *Memoirs of James MacGregor* (Philadelphia, 1859); *Dictionary of Canadian Biography* VI, 457–62; J. M. MacLennan, *From Shore to Shore* (E, 1977), 14–16; L. Stanley, *The Well-Watered Garden: The Presbyterian Church in Cape Breton* (Sydney, Cape Breton, 1983), 36–8.

J. R. McIntosh and D. E. Meek

MacGregor, James (1830–94), theologian and apologist. Born at Callander, Perthshire, and educated at Edinburgh University and New College,* where he came to regard William Cunningham* as Scotland's greatest master of theology, he was

MACGREGOR, WILLIAM MALCOLM

ordained in the FC congregation at Barry, Angus, in 1857, and married the same year; he became the father of ten children. He was inducted to Free High Church, Paisley, in 1861. His *Sabbath Question* (E, 1866), written in response to the controversial views of Norman MacLeod* (of the Barony), is a comprehensive argument that the fourth commandment of the Decalogue is a moral law of permanent obligation. In 1868 he was called to the chair of systematic theology at New College, in succession to James Buchanan.*

MacGregor took part in the first union controversy involving the FC* and the UPC,* occasioning his refutation of Amyraldianism (*see* Cameron, John) in *The Question of Principle . . . regarding The Atonement* (E, ²1870). He was a frequent contributor to the *British and Foreign Evangelical Review.* Illness forced him to migrate to New Zealand* (*see* Emigration) in 1881, where he ministered to Columba Church in Oamuru from 1882 until his death. Here he wrote a trilogy on apologetics,* contending that 'the proof of Christianity is the whole historical phenomenon of this religion in the world'. Debates in the Synod of Otago and Southland elicited publications defending the Westminster Confession's* teaching on election and eternal punishment. Other works included biblical commentaries on Exodus and Galatians, memoirs and treatments of inspiration and the headship of Christ.

The Apology of the Christian Religion . . . (E, 1891); *The Revelation and the Record* (E, 1893); *Studies in the History of Christian Apologetics* (E, 1894).

AFCS I, 57; J. W. Keddie, 'James MacGregor' (unpublished, L, 1973); G. H. Schlefield (ed.), *Dictionary of New Zealand Biography* (Wellington, 1940), II, 16; obituary in *Oamuru Mail,* 9 Oct. 1894.

S. Isbell

MacGregor, William Malcolm (1861–1944), professor and churchman. Of Highland stock and a large clerical family, he was born in a FC manse in Glasgow and studied at Edinburgh University (MA, 1880) and Glasgow FC College. Ordained to Troon, Portland Road (1886–90), he served thereafter at Glasgow, Renfield (1890–8), Edinburgh St Andrews (1898–1919) and Glasgow UF College (*see* Trinity College), as Professor of New Testament (1919–35) and Principal (1928–38). He was the UFC Moderator in 1919, was appointed Baird lecturer* (*Christian Freedom,* L, 1914) and Warrack lecturer,* and won Glasgow's DD (1904) and St Andrews' LLD (1939).

His convenership of the UFC Highlands and Islands Committee made him widely known and respected in the Highlands* (cf. *Our Church in the Highlands,* E, 1907). He struck an impressive figure, but could be moody ('a difficult nature to manage' – A. K. Walton). He was more a preacher's preacher than a popular one. His sermons made good literature. He could be called a liberal Evangelical, and was active in the pre-Union* (1929) discussions.

His works include: *Some of God's Ministries* (E,

McINTOSH, HUGH

1910); *A Souvenir of the Union in 1929, with an Historical Sketch of the United Free Church College, Glasgow* (G, 1930).

AFCS I, 230; *FUFCS* 580; *FES* IX, 773; A. K. Walton in *LW* n.s. 15 (1944), 137; A. J. Gossip in MacGregor's *The Making of a Preacher* (Warrack lectures;* L, 1945), 7–20.

D. F. Wright

Machar, *see* Celtic Saints.

Macintosh, Donald (1743–1808), Gaelic* scholar and non-juring* priest (?bishop) of 'the old Scots Episcopal Church'. He was born at Orchilmore, Perthshire. Clerk (1785–9) for the Gaelic Language to the Society of Antiquaries in Scotland, and later Keeper of Gaelic Records to the Royal Highland Society of Scotland, he was made deacon in 1789 by Bishop James Brown,* and subsequently priest. Often referred to after his death as bishop, he allegedly described himself as a priest in his will (made 1808). He made annual tours ministering to remaining non-jurors through the Perthshire Highlands to Banffshire. In 1794, as 'Episcopal Minister in Baillie Fyfe's Close', he unsuccessfully petitioned the Court of Session for possession of a Fund for the Relief of Scots Episcopal Clergymen. He died, unmarried, in Edinburgh, the 'last of the non-jurant clergy in Scotland'.

A Collection of Gaelic Proverbs and Familiar Phrases (E, 1785); ed. A. Campbell, *Mackintosh's* [*sic*] *Collection of Gaelic Proverbs and Familiar Phrases* etc. (E, 1819) (prefaced by brief Life of Macintosh), subsequent ed. by A. Nicolson (E, 1881), reprinted with index by M. MacInnes (G, 1951); *Catalogue of the Mackintosh* [*sic*] *Library, Dunkeld* (E, 1823), being the catalogue of the Library (containing much scarce printed material on EpCS, English non-jurors, Jacobitism) left by Macintosh to the town of Dunkeld and now in Sandeman Library, Perth; *DNB,* XXXV, 113–4; Stephen's *Episcopal Magazine* (E, 1836), IV, 189–92; G. Grub, *An Ecclesiastical History of Scotland* (E, 1861), IV.

R. J. Angus

McIntosh, Hugh (1840–1921), FC minister. Born at Culloden, Inverness-shire, he studied at Aberdeen University (MA, 1869) and the Aberdeen FC College (*see* Christ's College). After ordination in 1872 he served as minister of Gartly FC, East Aberdeenshire (1872–7), London Road FC, Glasgow (1877–81), Brockley Presbyterian Church, London (1881–1911), and Kinlochleven UFC (1911–13). He was a prominent supporter of his teacher, William Robertson Smith,* delivering a notable speech in the FC Assembly on May 27, 1880, in which he commended Smith as a teacher of the doctrines of grace and professed no difficulty in reconciling his views with the strictest account of plenary inspiration (*PGAFCS May 1880,* 224–8). He presented his own beliefs – claimed to be in accord with Smith's – in *Is Christ Infallible and the Bible True?* (E, 1901; ³1902), perhaps the most thorough treatment of the subject in Britain in the twentieth century. It eschews 'absolute inerrancy' as apologetically vulnerable, but expounds a position – 'the truthfulness, trustworthiness and divine authority' of the whole Bible – not far short of it.

The Two Banners of the Old Battle (E, 1876); *The Philosophy of the Gospel* (L, 1887).

AFCS I, 232; *FUFCS* 299.

D. F. Wright

McIntyre, Alexander (c.1807–78), Presbyterian evangelist in Australia*. Hailing from the parish of Strontian, Argyll, McIntyre studied for the ministry and was licensed by the Presbytery of Mull in 1836. Much of his life was spent as an itinerant* evangelist in the Highlands* of Scotland, with the FC Colonial Committee in Canada in 1847–50, and in Australia from 1853 to his death. In the last twenty years of his life he was normally resident in Geelong, Victoria, but often went to the Clarence River in northern NSW in the winter. He also itinerated extensively in Victoria, especially among the Highland Scottish communities. McIntyre was a notable evangelistic preacher, especially in Gaelic.* His influence was very strong during the union movements among Presbyterians in the 1850s and 1860s in convincing the Highlanders to maintain an anti-union position, especially in NSW.

J. Macleod, *By-Paths of Highland Church History* (E, 1965), 41–9; J. C. Robinson, *The Rev. Alexander McIntyre* (Melbourne, 1929).

A. M. Harman

McIntyre, David Martin (1859–1938), Principal of the Bible Training Institute, Glasgow.* Born in Monikie, Angus, the son of a FC minister, he studied at Edinburgh University, New College* and the English Presbyterian College in London. In 1886 he was licensed by London North Presbytery and ordained to College Park Church, London. In 1891 he became the colleague of Andrew Bonar* in Finnieston, Glasgow, becoming sole minister on Bonar's death in 1892.

In 1913 McIntyre became Principal of the Bible Training Institute, Glasgow, without relinquishing his pastorate. This proved unworkable, and from 1915 he devoted himself wholly to the Institute, becoming senior honorary minister at Finnieston. He followed most of his church into the CofS in 1929.

McIntyre was a prolific author, mostly of books on practical religion. Francis Davidson,* his successor at the Institute, described him as 'staunch in his support of the evangelical fundamentals, yet not by any means an obscurantist. He was a progressive conservative in doctrine and no partisan to any labels of theology' (memoir prefaced to McIntyre's *The Hidden Life of Prayer*, ³L, n.d., xii). McIntyre's treatment of the doctrine of Scripture in *The Spirit in the Word* (L, 1908) reveals a largely negative evaluation of higher criticism, and a particularly dismissive attitude to A. B. Bruce,* coupled however with deep admiration for his old teacher A. B. Davidson.* McIntyre refused to call the Bible 'inerrant' on the grounds that 'that can apply only to the original documents, concerning which we are in fact altogether ignorant' (*The Spirit in the Word*, 4–5). His practical writings abound in quotations from classical spiritual writers, especially the Puritans.

McIntyre received a DD from Glasgow University in 1924.

The Divine Authority of the Scriptures of the Old Testament (Stirling, 1902); *Faith's Title Deeds* (L, 1924); *The Prayer Life of Our Lord* (L, 1927); *Christ the Lord* (L, 1932); *Christ the Crucified* (L, 1935); *Some Notes on the Gospels* (ed. F. F. Bruce, L, 1943).

AFCS I, 252; *FUFCS* 220.

N. R. Needham

McIntyre, Robert Edmond (1889–1961), UFC and CofS minister and preacher. Born at Leith and educated at Edinburgh University (MA, 1913) and New College, Edinburgh, after war service he became UF minister at Callander, Perthshire, 1920–5, and Giffnock (later Orchardhill), Glasgow, 1925–35. His most distinguished ministry was at Morningside High, Edinburgh, 1935–59. Edinburgh gave him its honorary DD (1950). He taught at St Colm's* and New College, and he enjoyed the repute of a fine expository preacher. His Warrack Lectures,* *The Ministry of the Word* (L, 1950), dotted with literary references, reflect the liberal Evangelicalism (or evangelical liberalism) of his day. His only publication was *Clue to the Old Testament* (E, 1947). He died at Inverness.

FUFCS 207; *FES* IX, 27–8; *Scotsman*, 14 April 1961, 7.

D. F. Wright

McIntyre, William (1806–70), leading Presbyterian in Australia. Born at Kilmonivaig near Fort William, and educated at the University of Glasgow, McIntyre sailed to Australia on 'The Midlothian' in 1837. He was the first Gaelic*-speaking minister in Australia and was very influential among the Highland community until his death in 1870. He was assistant to John Dunmore Lang* at Scots' Church in Sydney and also taught at the Australian College, and then became minister at West Maitland on the Hunter River in NSW (1840–62). He led those in the Synod of Australia who supported the FC* position at the Disruption,* and was the first Moderator of the Synod of Eastern Australia (1846). He was also the leader of those in the Synod of Eastern Australia who refused to enter the Presbyterian unions of 1864 and 1865 in NSW. Following the return of Mackintosh Mackay* to Scotland, McIntyre became the minister of St George's Church, Sydney, from 1862 to his death. He was an accomplished writer, editing *The Voice in the Wilderness* (1846–52) and *The Testimony* (1865–70). He wrote a significant booklet on baptism, *The Token of the Covenant* (1861), and others on *The Christian Sabbath* (1866) and *Faith* (1869).

MACK, JOHN

Australian Dictionary of Biography V, 166-7; *FES* VII, 594.

A. M. Harman

Mack, John (1797-1845), the first Scottish missionary recruited specifically to serve at Serampore, India, with William Carey. Born in Edinburgh, Mack was educated at the High School and Edinburgh University. He intended to enter the CofS ministry, and proceeded to Gloucester 'to acquire a thorough English style of speaking'. While there he became a Baptist, and joined a Baptist church at Shortwood. He then entered Bristol Baptist College for training (1818-21), where his potential was noted by Carey's colleague, William Ward, who was visiting Britain. The Serampore missionaries paid for his further training at Edinburgh University, this time in Natural Philosophy. Supported by Christopher Anderson's* church (Charlotte Baptist Chapel) in Edinburgh, he embarked with Ward for India in 1821. On his arrival at Serampore, he immediately took up duties as Professor of Natural Philosophy at the College. In 1832 he became co-pastor (with Carey and Joshua Marshman) of the Baptist church at Serampore. He had an interest in exploration, and prepared the first Bengali map, but he is best known for his scientific interests, especially in chemistry. He was latterly Principal of Serampore College.

E. A. Payne, *The First Generation* (L, [1936]), 128-32; M. A. Laird, *Missionaries and Education in Bengal 1793-1837* (O, 1972), 145-7, 191; Records of Bristol Baptist College.

D. E. Meek

McKail, Hugh (Hew) (1640-66), Covenanting* preacher. Born the son of Matthew McKail, minister at Bothwell, Lanarkshire (*FES* III, 230-1), McKail studied at the University of Edinburgh and was licensed by the Presbytery there in 1661. His last public sermon in Edinburgh, possibly preached in Trinity parish church, the charge being yet vacant after the death of his uncle (*FES* I, 126-7) in 1660, gave great offence. He said 'that the Church and People of God had been persecuted, both by a Pharaoh upon the Throne, a Haman in the State, and a Judas in the Church' (*Naphtali, or The Wrestlings of the Church of Scotland for the Kingdom of Christ*, 1667, 264). He escaped capture and spent the next four years in hiding, partly at his father's house and also 'in several places and with much uncertainty' (265), possibly on the continent.

In 1666 he joined part of the rising which culminated at Rullion Green,* but ill-health caused him to leave for home. He was apprehended, imprisoned, interrogated, tortured, tried and sentenced to be hanged. Attempts to obtain his release failed (T. M'Crie, *Memoirs of Mr. William Veitch, and George Brysson*, E, 1825, 35-8). His conduct and last speech and testimony had great effect and were much used by later martyrs* of the Covenant and in subsequent literature (cf. *Naphtali*, 283-6).

R. Wodrow, *The History of the Sufferings of the Church of Scotland*, ed. R. Burns, 4 vols

MACKAY, ALEXANDER MURDOCH

(?G, 1828); J. Howie, *The Scots Worthies*, ed. W. McGavin (G, 1838); *The Life of Mr. Robert Blair*, ed. T. M'Crie (E, 1848).

J. A. Dickson

MacKay, Alexander (1780-1856), an itinerant* preacher with the Independents. A native of Easdale, MacKay became pastor of the Independent church in Sannox, Arran, in 1806. He had an influential role in the founding (1817) of the Society in Paisley and its Vicinity for Gaelic Missions, which supported his itinerant preaching. He became a close friend of Dugald Sinclair,* whom he accompanied on some preaching tours. MacKay participated in and doubtless contributed to the revival* which had appeared in Arran by 1812. His church suffered greatly through mass emigration* of members to Megantic Co., Quebec, in 1829.

SC 1856, 127-8, 297-301; D. M. McKillop, *Annals of Megantic County, Quebec* (Inverness, Quebec, 1981 edn), 51-2, 170; D. E. Meek, 'Evangelical Missionaries in the Early Nineteenth-century Highlands', *SS* 28 (1987), 24.

D. E. Meek

Mackay, Alexander Murdoch (1849-90), missionary in Uganda. He was the son of the FC minister of Rhynie, Aberdeenshire (*AFCS* I, 233). Mackay's fervour was encouraged by Covenanting* traditions, and his desire to become an engineer missionary by David Livingstone's* idea that missions* should transform the material as well as moral and spiritual bases of African life. Training at Edinburgh University, plus practical engineering in Germany, preceded his joining the Church Missionary Society Uganda Mission in 1876, at the crucial period of the first evangelization of the Kingdom of Buganda and the political scramble for that part of Africa. Two years building a road from the East African coast followed. In Buganda from 1878 to 1887, he built up a strong following of ardent Protestant Christians among young men at the King's court. In 1879 the Roman Catholic White Fathers arrived and Mackay now began to denounce them as vehemently as he did pagans.

Christians were persecuted and martyred; pagans, Protestants, Roman Catholics and Muslims jockeyed for power and Mackay was forced to move to Usambiro on the other side of Lake Victoria in 1887. Now convinced that outside political control was necessary, Mackay created interest among British imperialists in the Uganda region. He died of malaria.

It is possible to argue that Mackay's extreme hostility to Roman Catholics and his linking the Protestant with the British imperial cause helped to foster religio-political factionalism of a type which led to further civil war in 1892 and which still plagues modern Uganda.

See also Missions.

DNB XXXV, 118; [J. W. Harrison – his sister], *A. M. Mackay* (L, 1890).

R. Bridges

MacKay, Donald Tulloch (1850–1932), minister of the FC and (after 1900) of the UFC, but pre-eminently an itinerant* evangelist. Born at Sallachy, Lochalsh, MacKay was licensed by the FC Presbytery of Mull, and ordained to Tiree (1882–1911). Known as *MacAidh Thiridhe* ('MacKay of Tiree'), he travelled throughout the Highlands,* and once to Canada. He preached in any available pulpit and frequently in the open air, even on board ship. His earnestness, idiosyncracies and impromptu appearances made him a legend in his own lifetime. He published two Gaelic* booklets, *Soldier's Help* (D, 1916) and *Gaelic Bible Promises* (Oban, 1927).

FUFCS, 301; Tormod Dòmhnallach, *MacAidh Thiridhe* (Stirling, ²1970).

D. E. Meek

MacKay, Isabella (1778–1851), patroness and promoter of missionary endeavour. Born in Sutherland as Isabella Gordon, she developed a special interest in the spiritual needs of Highland emigrants, partly through her involvement in the Glasgow Colonial Society* (*see* Emigration). Initially concerned to establish itinerating libraries, she dispatched large quantities of evangelical books and tracts to Upper Canada, Nova Scotia and Cape Breton Island. Hearing of its spiritual destitution, she later devoted her attention to Cape Breton, and mobilized the Edinburgh Ladies' Association to recruit ministers for that area, among them Alexander Farquharson.*

L. Stanley, *The Well-Watered Garden* (²Sydney, Cape Breton, 1984).

D. E. Meek

Mackay, John Alexander (1889–1983), missionary, theologian, educator, and ecumenical statesman. Born in Inverness of parents who joined the FP* in 1893, he studied philosophy at Aberdeen University (MA, 1912), and theology in the FP at Inverness (1910–11) and Wick (1912–13). In 1913 he went to Princeton Theological Seminary* (BD, 1915), and then resumed his study of philosophy at the University of Madrid, where he sat at the feet of the great Spanish existentialist, Miguel de Unamuno (one of the earliest proponents of Kierkegaard). It was during this time that he first developed the love for Hispanic culture which would be with him throughout his life. In 1910 he first met both John R. Mott and Robert E. Speer.

In 1916, Mackay married Jane Logan Wells, was ordained and sent by the FC (which he had joined) as a missionary to Lima in Peru, becoming the founding principal of the Colegio Anglo-Peruano (now San Andres). In his spare time, he attended the University of San Marcos, where he received a LittD for a thesis on Unamuno (1918), and was appointed to a chair in philosophy in 1925.

From 1926 to 1932, Mackay served the South American Federation of YMCAs as an itinerant evangelist and teacher, based first in Montevideo and later in Mexico City. During this period, he wrote three books, including his celebrated study of the history of Spanish spirituality, *The Other Spanish Christ* (NY, 1932), in which he contrasted the dead Christ of much of Spanish Catholic culture with the life-transforming 'Other Spanish Christ' of Raymond Lull, Teresa and Unamuno. In 1930 he secured a study leave in Bonn where he gave Karl Barth* his first lessons in the English language.

In 1932, at the invitation of Speer (General Secretary of the Board of Foreign Missions of the Presbyterian Church in the USA), Mackay became the Board's Secretary for Latin America and Africa. During his years in Latin America, he had become increasingly disillusioned with the institutional church, due in part to his study of the Hispanic Catholic Church, in part to sectarianism in his own church background. For a time, he had renounced membership in any denomination, but his faith in Christ even strengthened. His acceptance of a high-profile church post was made possible by his personal 'rediscovery of the church', which also constituted for him a personal mandate to become involved in the ecumenical movement. At the Oxford Conference on Life and Work (1937), he presided over Commission V, 'The Universal Church and the World of Nations', whose members included W. A. Visser 't Hooft, John Foster Dulles, and William Temple (then Archbishop of York). To this commission, Mackay presented his famous 'let the Church be the Church' study paper. 'Let the Church know herself, whose she is and what she is. ... This means concretely that the Church recognize herself to be the Church of Christ, the organ of God's purpose in Him. It must be her ceaseless concern to rid herself of all subjugation to a prevailing culture, an economic system, a social type, or a political order.'

From 1936 until his retirement in 1959, Mackay served as President and Professor of Ecumenics at Princeton. During these years his accomplishments included the following: founder and editor of *Theology Today* (1944); Chairman of the International Missionary Council (1947–57); Chairman of Commission II on 'The Church's Witness to God's Design' at the First Assembly of the World Council of Churches, Amsterdam, and Acting Chairman of the Committee on the Message of the Assembly (1948); member of the Central Committee of the World Council of Churches (1948–57); Chairman of the Joint Committee of the International Missionary Council and the World Council of Churches (1948–54); Moderator of the 165th General Assembly, Presbyterian Church in the USA (1953); President of the World Presbyterian Alliance (1954–9; *see* World Alliance of Reformed Churches). After his retirement, he served as an adjunct professor of Hispanic thought at American University in Washington, DC.

Mackay's tenure as Moderator of the PCUSA was marked by his courageous lead at the height of the McCarthyite anti-Communist hysteria. He himself was named as a 'top collaborationist' with Communism. His response was his famous 'Letter to Presbyterians' (issued with slight revisions by the General Council of the PCUSA in November

1953). It warned that the congressional investigations were in danger of becoming an 'inquisition', threatening basic human rights, dissent, and democracy itself. In response, the 'Letter' set forth three principles that should govern Christian political engagement. Most notable was the first: 'The Christian Church has a prophetic function to fulfil in every society and in every age.... While being patriotically loyal to the country within whose bounds it lives and works, the Church does not derive its authority from the nation but from Jesus Christ. Its supreme and ultimate allegiance is to Christ, its sole Head, and to His Kingdom, and not to any nation or race, to any class or culture.... [T]he Church owes to its own members and to people in general, to draw attention to violations of those spiritual bases of human relationships which have been established by God.' This clarion call was adopted unanimously by the 1954 General Assembly as its own.

Mackay's theology was a blend of many influences. The influence of Barth showed itself clearly in his christocentric ecclesiology. Unamuno, Dostoevsky, and Kierkegaard also figured prominently, and he could claim Theresa of Avila as 'his' saint. Mackay never forgot that he was a Scot. When asked to explain his gift for vivid images in his oratory, he would attribute it to his Celtic ancestry.

Mackay was the author of thirteen books and numerous articles. His achievements earned him many honorary degrees, including DDs from the Universities of Aberdeen, Princeton and Debrecen. He held some twenty-two lectureships during the course of his life, including the Croall Lectureship* at New College, Edinburgh, out of which emerged his unique commentary on Ephesians: *God's Order: The Ephesian Letter and the Present Time* (NY, 1953).

Works include: *A Preface to Christian Theology* (NY, 1941); *Christianity on the Frontier* (NY, 1950); *The Presbyterian Way of Life* (Englewood Cliffs, NJ, 1960).

E. J. Jurji (ed.), *The Ecumenical Era in Church and Society; A Symposium in Honor of John A. Mackay* (NY, 1959), incl. appreciation and bibliography; J. H. Smylie, 'Mackay and McCarthyism, 1953–54', *Journal of Church and State* (G, 1964), 352–65; D. A. Poling, 'Clergymen are Citizens, Too!', *The Saturday Evening Post* (24 April 1954), 70; E. A. Dowey, 'Poling and the Presbyterian Letter', *Christianity and Crisis* 14 (4 October 1954), 124–7; S. R. Wilson, 'Studies in the Life of an Ecumenical Churchman' (MTh, Princeton Theo. Seminary, 1958); A. Clemente-Vasquez, '*Communio Viatorum* ... The Understanding of the Church in ... John A. Mackay' (MTh, Edinburgh University, 1973); J. Harbison, 'John Mackay of Princeton', *Presbyterian Life* (15 September 1958), 7–11 (1 October 1958), 15–17, 34; 'Festschrift' edition of *Theology Today* 16 (1959), 301–75; *Who Was Who in America, 1982–85*, 225; *Who's Who 1983*, 1433; tributes in *Princeton Seminary Bulletin* 4 (1983), 161–7, 5 (1984), 41–3, 10 (1989), 167–92, *Theology Today* 40 (1984), 453–6, *Reformed World* 38 (1984), 177–81, *Intern. Rev. of Missions* 72 (1983), 672–3.

R. J. Graham and B. L. McCormack

MacKay, John Robertson (1865–1939), FP leader. A native of Strathy Point, Sutherland, he was one of the divinity students who left the FC in 1893 over the Declaratory Act* of 1893 to enter the new FPC. MacKay was the first person licensed to preach in the FPC. In October 1893 he was inducted to the Gairloch FP congregation. He went on to play a vital administrative role in the fledgling denomination, becoming the first Clerk of Synod (July 1896) and then, along with John Macleod,* the first theological tutor in July 1897. From early on, however, MacKay was keen to explore ways of getting closer to the continuing FC, especially after their removal of the Declaratory Act in 1905. He was gradually to come closer to the FC until in 1918 he and two other FP ministers joined that Church. He went on to become Professor of New Testament in the FC College in Edinburgh from 1919 to 1935, and Moderator in 1929.

The Free Church and the Free Presbyterian Church: The Question of Their Union Discussed (Inverness, 1918).

A. McPherson (ed.), *History of the Free Presbyterian Church of Scotland* (Inverness, 1973); G. N. M. Collins, *Annals of the Free Church of Scotland 1900–1986* (E, n.d.), 4, 23.

J. L. MacLeod

MacKay, Mackintosh (1793–1873), Gaelic* scholar, preacher, and Church leader. A native of Eddrachillis, Sutherland, he spent some years as a schoolmaster. He was ordained to Laggan (Inverness-shire) in 1825, where he became a friend of Sir Walter Scott* who visited the area. From 1832 he was minister of Dunoon, joining the FC at the Disruption.* From 1854 to 1861 he ministered among the Gaels of Australia, returning to Scotland as minister of Tarbert, Harris (1862–8). In 1849 he was Moderator of the FC General Assembly.

A fine Gaelic scholar, MacKay edited the FC periodical, *An Fhianuis* (1845–50), and wrote the Church history which accompanied the Gaelic version of *Scots Worthies* (see Gaelic, Protestant Prose Publications in). He was the first editor of the poems of Robert MacKay (*Rob Donn*). As Convener of the FC's Highland Committee, he was an influential figure.

FES IV, 24 (which lists publications), VII, 594; J. Greig (ed.), *Disruption Worthies of the Highlands* (E, 1877), 79–88; D. MacLean, *Typographia Scoto-Gadelica* (E, 1915), 236.

R. MacLeod

Mackay, Peggy (d. 1841), see Women in Highland Churches.

MacKay, William Sinclair (1807–65), FC missionary. Born in Thurso, Caithness, he was educated at King's College,* Aberdeen, and St

Andrews, and ordained as CofS missionary to Calcutta in 1831, where he worked alongside Alexander Duff.* In 1843 he joined the FC. He edited the *Calcutta Review*, carried out missionary work in Chinsurah, and retired to Scotland in 1862. He received a DD from St Andrews. His publications include: *The Missionary's Warrant and the Church's Duty* (E, 1850); *A Warning from the East* (L, 1845); *Explanatory Statement respecting the Recent Proceedings of the Missionaries of the Church of Scotland in Calcutta* (with A. Duff, D. Ewart, J. MacDonald and T. Smith, E, 1843).

AFCS I, 236; *FES* VII, 699.

N. R. Needham

MacKay of Clashfern, Lord (1927–), Lord High Chancellor of Great Britain. Born in Scourie, Sutherland, James Peter Hymers MacKay was educated at George Heriot's School, Edinburgh and at Edinburgh and Cambridge Universities. An able mathematician, he lectured in the subject at St Andrews University before studying law. He was admitted to the Scottish bar in 1955. In 1958 he married Elizabeth Gunn Hymers and they have one son and two daughters. Lord MacKay holds the unique distinction of having served in both of the country's two senior law offices, as Lord Advocate (1979–84) and since 1987 as Lord Chancellor. Marked features of Lord MacKay's career have been consistent Christian witness and loyalty to the FPC in which he was reared. He served as an elder of the FPC for over thirty years and, for a period, was assistant clerk of Synod.

In 1988, Lord MacKay was disciplined by the FPC's Southern Presbytery, on a majority decision, for attending a memorial service for a colleague at which requiem mass was said. A dissent and complaint by the Southern Presbytery minority and an appeal by Lord MacKay's Kirk Session were rejected by the Synod in 1989, by a majority decision. At the same meeting of Synod, a contentious case of discipline concerning Alexander Murray, minister in Lairg, was reviewed and the outcome of this case, together with that affecting Lord MacKay, was the immediate cause of a split in the FPC and the formation of the Associated Presbyterian Churches.* This outcome, however, must be seen in the light of a long and growing controversy in the Church regarding interpretation of the principles of liberty of conscience and the communion of saints enshrined in its constitution. In May, 1989, Lord MacKay ceased to be a member of the FPC.

Who's Who 1991, 1173.

A. Morrison

Mackenzie, John (1835–99), missionary in Southern Africa. Son of a farmer at Knockando, Morayshire, he was educated at the Anderson Institute in Elgin. He began work as a journalist on the local paper. His family were members of the CofS but John became a Congregationalist* and was accepted for service in South Africa by the London Missionary Society.* In 1858 he was ordained and sailed with four others to the Cape and then to Kuruman, the mission associated with Robert Moffat.* His wife's illness prevented him going on the ill-fated Makololo expedition. He settled to work among the Bamangwato in 1862 and stayed there for fourteen years, becoming the close friend of the new chief who emerged in this period, the great Seretse Khama, grandfather of the first President of Botswana.

Mackenzie then took up the mantle of John Philip.* He came to believe that uncontrolled expansion by whites was destructive of African life and created injustice that Christians must not tolerate. Only direct control by the imperial government in London could remedy the situation.

He dedicated the next years of his life to gaining imperial protection for as many of the Tswana people as he could, opposing the claims of Rhodes's British South Africa Company and of the Germans. His ideas were not at first acceptable in London, but he persevered and was even for a few months imperial administrator of what would in the twentieth century be Botswana. When the Bechuanaland Protectorate was guaranteed in 1891, he returned to ordinary mission work at Hankey (near Port Elizabeth), where he remained till his death at Kimberley.

Ten Years North of the Orange River (E, 1871); *Day-Dawn in Dark Places* (L, 1883); *Austral Africa, Losing It or Ruling It*, 2 vols (L, 1887).

W. D. Mackenzie, *John Mackenzie, South African Missionary and Statesman* (L, 1902); A. Sillery, *Founding a Protectorate* (The Hague, 1965); *id.*, *John Mackenzie of Bechuanaland* (Cape Town, 1971); Anthony Dachs (ed.), *Papers of John Mackenzie* (Johannesburg, 1975); *Dictionary of South African Biography* I, 487–9.

R. V. Pierard and A. C. Ross

Mackenzie, Kenneth (1920–71), missionary and spokesman for Africa. He was born in Strathpeffer and educated at Dingwall Academy and Aberdeen University. He began study for the ministry of the FC at their college in Edinburgh in 1940, but in 1942 he transferred to the CofS and completed his course at New College in 1944. In April 1945 he was ordained for missionary service and was posted to Nyasaland. There he served at Mulanje and Zomba and in 1948 was transferred to work in Northern Rhodesia. After two years' service at Lubwa he returned to Scotland and worked in the CofS Foriegn Mission offices 1950–2. He then returned to Northern Rhodesia where he worked at Chitambo until his return to Scotland in 1956. He was appointed missions tutor at St Colm's College* in 1957 and was called to Restalrig, Edinburgh, in June 1968.

He played a major role in organizing opposition to the Central African Federation* in the Churches, trades unions and political parties, particularly in Scotland, through the agency of the Scottish Council on African Questions. He was also one of the founders of an active anti-apartheid movement in Scotland.

MacKenzie, Lachlan

Collected Papers in Library of Edinburgh University; *FES* IX, 740, X, 20, 422.

A. C. Ross

MacKenzie, Lachlan (1754–1819), a native of Knockbain, Easter Ross, and parish minister of Lochcarron (1776–1819). Mackenzie's character was marked by eccentric habits, and unconventional but profound spirituality. He was outspoken in his reprimands of immorality or godlessness, but many of his best-known sayings and prayers are deeply mystical in their import and expression. He was much given to prayer and esteemed for his intimate relationship with God.

MacKenzie gained a reputation as a minor prophet in the Highlands,* where his name is still revered. His prophecies of the early death of those who opposed his ministry were widely regarded as having been fulfilled, and such threatenings appear to have had a deep effect on the lives of those with whom he came in contact. He prophesied that a time would come in Lochcarron when only one person would sit at a Communion table, an event fulfilled in the 1880s.

In the Church courts he took an aggressively anti-Moderate* line, and prophesied that the evils of Moderatism and Intrusion* would be ended sooner rather than later, but that the deliverance would be brief and would be succeeded by a great falling away from the faith marked by a plague of graceless ministers. He was well regarded in the Highlands for his opposition to the Clearances.* His sermons display a marked scriptural emphasis and a striking use of analogy. A notable example occurred when he used Isaiah 5:8 ('Woe unto them that join house to house, that lay field to field, till there be no place, that they may be placed alone in the midst of the earth . . .') to attack the sheep farmers in the Clearances.

MacKenzie was widely followed as a preacher, and some travelled to hear him from as far afield as Sutherland and Argyll. Thousands from Ross and Inverness-shire attended his preaching at Communion seasons*.

J. L. Campbell (ed.), *'The Rev. Mr Lachlan' of Lochcarron: Lectures, Sermons and Writings*, 2 vols (Inverness, 1928–30); I. Murray (ed.), *The Happy Man* (E, 1979); *FES* VII, 161.

J. R. McIntosh

MacKenzie, Murdo (1835–1911), FC minister at Kilcalmonell (1870–3), Kilmallie (1873–8), and Free North, Inverness (1887–1912). A native of Lochcarron, an area with a rich religious heritage, he was one of the twenty-seven ministers of the FC who remained outwith the Union with the UPC in 1900. MacKenzie took part in the Union debate in the General Assembly of 1899, and spoke against the Union at the 1900 Assembly. In 1907 he was Moderator of the FC General Assembly. A popular preacher in Gaelic and English, he was in great demand as an assistant at traditional Communion seasons* throughout the Highlands and Islands. His ministry at Inverness was particularly memor-

MacKenzie, William

able and influential. A former assistant referred to 'his kindness, his considerateness, his warm-hearted evangelicalism, his broad sympathies'.

E. S. MacKenzie, *Rev. Murdo MacKenzie: a Memory* (Inverness, 1914); *AFCS* I, 239.

R. MacLeod

Mackenzie, Peter (1824–95), Methodist preacher. Born in Glenshee, he worked as a farm servant in Fife and carter in Dundee. At the age of twenty he migrated to the Durham coalfield. Converted through a travelling evangelist, he became a Methodist local preacher. Preaching gradually replaced mining as his life's work. In 1855 he became circuit missionary in Bishop Auckland, and in 1858 was accepted for the Wesleyan ministry – exceptionally for the time, since he was nearly thirty-four and married. After a year at Didsbury College, Manchester, Mackenzie served various English circuits, especially in the North-East and Yorkshire, but came to be in national demand as a preacher. His early ministry was marked by revival* fervour and emotional scenes. In later life his lectures (really amplified sermons for weekdays) drew crowds and large cash collections for churches and societies all over the country. Mackenzie's exuberant wit, homely eloquence and unconventional style united the entertainer with the evangelist; his piety, warmth and generosity made a deeper impression. His retirement from circuit work in 1886 simply freed him for more travel, preaching and lectures, until such relentless activity brought about his death.

J. Dawson, *Peter Mackenzie, his Life and Labours* (L, 1896); *id.* (ed.), *Lectures and Sermons of Peter Mackenzie* (L, 1897); J. A. Noble, *From Coal Pit to Pulpit* (L, n.d. [c.1896]); D. Young, *Peter Mackenzie as I Knew Him* (L, 1904).

A. F. Walls

MacKenzie, William (1738–1834), first of a remarkable dynasty of evangelical ministers, father, son and grandson, who served the parish of Tongue in Sutherland from 1769 to 1845. A native of Kilmuir-Easter in Ross-shire, he was ordained as missionary at Achness in 1767. Two years later he was admitted to Tongue, where he was to spend the rest of his ministry, still preaching with vigour at the advanced age of ninety-three. When he moved to Tongue the religious life of the parish was at a low ebb. In 1773 a revival* began which was to transform the spiritual state of the congregation. MacKenzie noted that the subject which most affected his hearers during the course of the revival was 'the dying love of Christ'. His grandson, William MacKenzie, became colleague and successor to his son, Hugh M'Kay MacKenzie, and both joined the FC.

FES VII, 110–11; J. Greig (ed.), *Disruption Worthies of the Highlands* (E, 1877), 233–7; A. MacRae, *Revivals in the Highlands and Islands in the Nineteenth Century* (Stirling, 1905), 191–3.

R. MacLeod

Mackichan, Dugald (1851–1932), FC and UFC educational missionary who was Principal of Wilson College, Bombay (1878–1920), and three times Vice-Chancellor of Bombay University (1888–90, 1902–6, 1915–17). Born in Glasgow, Mackichan studied at Glasgow University (MA, 1869; BD, 1873), and was licensed and ordained by the FC Presbytery of Glasgow in 1874. Joining the UFC in 1900, he was Moderator of the UFC General Assembly in 1917–18. As a worthy successor to John Wilson,* Mackichan was an educationist of the first rank and a scholar of real depth. His Chalmers lectures,* *The Missionary Ideal in the Scottish Churches* (L, 1927), is a statesmanlike survey which is still worth reading although it shows little theological originality. He rejected the fulfilment approach as he believed it would make Hindus content with their own religion. Indian nationalism he saw as a major obstacle to the Christian mission. He was awarded the degree of LLD by Glasgow (1901) and Bombay (1916).

AFCS I, 240; *FUFCS* 539, 569, 585.
D. B. Forrester

Mackie, Robert Cuthbert (1899–1984), ecumenical leader. He was born at Bothwell, Lanarkshire, and studied at Glasgow University (MA, 1922; DD, 1948) and UF College (1922–5), with an interruption for World War I. From 1925 to 1938 he was Scottish, and then British General Secretary of the Student Christian Movement,* and from 1938 to 1948 was based in Geneva and Toronto as General Secretary of the World Student Christian Federation. He was Associate General Secretary of the World Council of Churches from 1948 to 1955, and also Director of its largest department – Inter-Church Aid and Refugee Service. For much of this time he was also minister of the Scots Kirk* in Geneva. Thereafter he became adviser and animator of the ecumenical movement* in Scotland, involved in Kirk Weeks,* the foundation of Scottish Churches' House, Dunblane, the Scottish Council of Churches, etc. For his generation he was probably the best known and respected Scottish churchman outside Scotland. A world vision sustained his outstanding talents as interpreter, administrator, pastor and reconciler. He was awarded a second honorary doctorate – by St Sergius' Orthodox Theological Academy, Paris.

FES IX, 722; *LW* April 1984, 30; forthcoming life by N. Blackie.
N. Blackie

McKillican (or McKilligen), John (c. 1630–89), minister of the Est.C. Born at Alves, near Elgin, McKillican was licensed by the Presbytery of Aberdeen on 28th March 1655. Called to Fodderty (Ross-shire) in 1655, he was ordained in February 1656. As a Protester* after the Restoration* of 1660, he was removed from his charge in 1662, and deposed by the Synod of Ross in 1663. Thereafter he held conventicles* in the district, and suffered imprisonment in Forres. In 1675 he conducted a memorable Communion* service at Obsdale, Rosskeen (Ross-shire) (*see* Revivals). Soldiers sent to arrest him were unsuccessful, but he was apprehended soon afterwards by the Earl of Seaforth's servants. He was then sent to the Edinburgh Tolbooth and imprisoned (1676–9) on the Bass Rock*, along with Thomas Hog* and James Fraser* of Brea. Liberated on bail, he resumed preaching, was re-arrested and again (1683) imprisoned on the Bass, but was later removed to Edinburgh because of poor health. Returning to Ross-shire in 1686, he preached at a meeting-house built on his own property at Alness. Called to Inverness (Second Charge) in 1688, he died before his induction.

D. Beaton, *Some Noted Ministers of the Northern Highlands* (Inverness, 1929), 13–23; R. G. W. Mackilligin, 'The Followers of St Fillan', *Journal of the Clan Chattan Association* 8 (1988), 318–22; *FES* VII, 26.
D. E. Meek

MacKinnon, Donald (1732–1831), CofS minister of the parish of Strath in Skye. A native of Strath, he studied at King's College, Aberdeen, graduating MA in 1746. Thereafter he served as missionary (*see* Royal Bounty) on the island of Benbecula and from 1770 at Strontian in Argyllshire. In 1779 he was presented to the parish of Strath by George III, and remained there until his death. MacKinnon was succeeded in the parish by his son, John MacKinnon (1786–1868). With a majority of his Kirk Session* and congregation he remained in the Est.C at the Disruption* in 1843. He, in turn, was succeeded by his son, Donald MacKinnon. Thus three successive generations of the same family ministered to the Strath parish for over 100 years.

FES VII, 183; D. Lamont, *Strath: In Isle of Skye* (G, 1913); A. Geikie, *Scottish Reminiscences* (G, 1904).
A. Morrison

MacKinnon, Donald MacKenzie (1913–), Norris Hulse Professor of Divinity of Cambridge, philosopher and theologian. He was born at Oban, the son of the Procurator Fiscal, and educated at Winchester and Oxford. He held academic appointments in philosophy at Edinburgh and Oxford before becoming Regius Professor of Moral Philosophy at Aberdeen in 1947. In 1960 he was appointed to the chair in Cambridge and retired in 1978. He now lives in Aberdeen.

MacKinnon is a remarkable polyhistor. His authorship is marked rather by wide-ranging reconnaissance and creative initiatives than the construction of a tight system. He is explicitly indebted to the philosophical work of Plato, Aristotle, Kant and Michael Dummett (1925–), both valuing their conclusions and even more entering into their intellectual struggles. But his work is informed almost as much by the perceptions and articulations of figures like Sophocles, Shakespeare and Hugh MacDiarmid; yet again, he seriously reckons with a different kind of contribution, that of Lenin.

Theologically, he has emphasized the disciplined use of concepts and attention to the existential, often tragic, contours of human life. In particular, he seeks to work towards a renewed appreciation of catholic Christology and Trinitarian theology, where he seeks to combine an ontological account with interpretation of the dramatic narrative. Repeatedly, his readers are brought through reflections which combine moral seriousness with metaphysical agnosticism to be recalled to Jesus Christ, his parables, his portrayal in the Fourth Gospel, his passion, death and resurrection. Here his endeavours may be fruitfully compared with those of the RC theologian, Hans Urs von Balthasar, whose work MacKinnon has long admired. Frequently MacKinnon explores historical instances, persons and periods to bring out the actual complexity of issues about right action or to show the points in human life from which doctrines and affirmations (theological or philosophical) take their rise, have their application and are renewed. Here again the leading case is the unique and extraordinary history of Jesus Christ.

Bibliography in B. Hebblethwaite and S. Sutherland (eds), *The Philosophical Frontiers of Christian Theology: Essays Presented to D. M. MacKinnon* (C, 1982); MacKinnon, *The Three-Fold Cord* (E, 1987), collected essays; K. Surin (ed.), *Christ, Ethics and Tragedy: Essays in Honour of Donald MacKinnon* (C, 1989); *Who's Who 1991*, 1180.

J. Houston and S. N. Williams

MacKinnon, Hector (1886–1954), Gaelic* hymn-writer. An elder and lay preacher of the CofS, MacKinnon composed about 100 Gaelic hymns,* a number of which, e.g. *An Neamhnaid Luachmhor* ('The Pearl Without Price'), have become extremely popular in the West Highlands. Some of his compositions are elegies on local church personalities. Others are virtually sermons in verse on biblical themes or inspired by scenes from the world of nature. His religious poems breathe a warm evangelical spirit, and are of a high poetic quality. All MacKinnon's hymns are sung to well-known Gaelic tunes, which adds to their appeal.

An Neamhnaid Luachmhor (Stornoway, 1990).

R. MacLeod

Mackinnon, James (1860–1945), Church historian. Born at Turriff, Aberdeenshire, he studied for health reasons in South Africa, graduating in arts and divinity from the Dutch Reformed Church College at Stellenbosch (1881–4), and ministered briefly to Presbyterian congregations there before being licensed by the CofS Presbytery of Turriff (1886 – he was never ordained). There followed locums (1886–8), further study at Edinburgh (MA, 1889), Bonn and Heidelberg (PhD, 1891) and teaching history in Queen Margaret College, Glasgow (1890–5) and the University of St Andrews (1896–1908), before his appointment to the Edinburgh chair of Ecclesiastical History (1908–30).

Mackinnon was a remarkably prolific writer, beginning with *South African Traits* (L, 1888) and his doctoral thesis in ET, *Culture in Early Scotland* (L, 1892). He wrote works on social, industrial, constitutional and royal history in Scotland, England, and France. *The Union of England and Scotland* (L, 1896) was provocatively sub-titled 'A study of international history'. His widest recognition came from *A History of Modern Liberty* in 4 volumes (L, 1906–41; a fifth volume was almost complete on his death), which was translated into German, Italian and French. His Church-historical productions were equally extensive: *Luther and the Reformation*, 4 vols (L, 1925–30) – still the most substantial study by a British scholar, *The Historic Jesus* (L, 1931), *The Gospel in the Early Church* (L, 1933), *From Christ to Constantine* (L, 1936), *Calvin and the Reformation* (L, 1936), and *The Origins of the Reformation* (L, 1939).

Mackinnon became FRS in 1911, DD of St Andrews in 1912 and LLD of Edinburgh. The DTheol. of Halle-Wittenberg University (1930) probably saluted his *Luther*. His fluency in German, French, and Dutch (cf. *Leisure Hours in the Study*, L, 1897, and *The British Journalists in Germany*, A, 1907) helped to win him a European reputation. Although none of his Church-historical works remains indispensable, he significantly influenced the discipline in Edinburgh by aligning it more clearly with history in the Arts Faculty. He competed unsuccessfully for the University's first professorship of history (1894), won a place for his chair in Arts as well as Divinity (1908), and set new standards (e.g. in his St Andrews inaugural, 'History as a subject of academic study', 1896, in *Leisure Hours*) for 'scientific methods of historical investigation and criticism'. In both St Andrews and Edinburgh he initiated a postgraduate research programme. Among his Edinburgh pupils was his successor, J. H. S. Burleigh.* He was an enthusiastic teacher, and was active in educational administration, especially on the Edinburgh Provincial Committee for the Training of Teachers.

FES VII, 391, VIII, 716, IX, 773; *Who Was Who, 1941–1950*, 735–6; *The Scotsman*, 13 July 1945, 4; *The Times*, 21 July 1945, 6; D. F. Wright in *New College Bulletin* 14 (1983), 26.

D. F. Wright

Mackintosh, Hugh Ross (1870–1936), minister and distinguished theologian, was born in Paisley, where his father held the FC Gaelic charge, and educated at John Neilson Institution, Paisley, Tain Royal Academy (Dux), and George Watson's Academy, Edinburgh. At Edinburgh University he was especially indebted to the philosophers A. S. Pringle-Pattison and R. P. Hardie. He proceeded to New College, Edinburgh, for divinity and was Cunningham Fellow, 1896. He took summer sessions at Freiburg, Halle and Marburg; Wilhelm Herrmann was a particular friend. He was DPhil (Edinburgh), DTh (Hesse-Nassau), DD (Edinburgh and Oxford).

Licensed in the FC in 1896, he was minister at

Tayport (1897–1901), and Beechgrove UF, Aberdeen (1901–4). He was Professor of Divinity, New College, Edinburgh (1904–36). 'Though unimpassioned in delivery [his lectures] were richly lit with Christian experience and the conviction of a soul resting on God's redeeming grace' (H. Watt*). His pupils included D. M. and J. Baillie,* E. P. Dickie,* John Dow, and H. Van Dusen. He was Moderator of the General Assembly, CofS, 1932, and an elder of Barclay Church, Edinburgh.

Mackintosh skilfully presented others' work: he translated (with A. B. Macaulay) Ritschl's *Justification and Reconciliation* (E, 1900); Loofs's *Haeckel's Riddle of the Universe* (L, 1903); and (with J. S. Stewart*) Schleiermacher's *The Christian Faith* (E, 1928). His *Selections from the Literature of Theism* (with A. Caldecott, E, 1904) long remained a standard text, and in his posthumously published Croall Lectures,* *Types of Modern Theology* (L, 1937), he lucidly expounded major theologians from Schleiermacher to Barth.

Mackintosh made his positive theological contribution most distinctively in *The Doctrine of the Person of Christ* (E, 1912), in which he espoused a judicious kenoticism (*see* Christology); *The Divine Initiative* (L, 1921), in terms of which initiative he treated the Incarnation and election; and *The Christian Experience of Forgiveness* (L, 1927), which was for him the central reality of the Christian life.

Mackintosh was a welcome and regular preacher who for thirty years, with the blessing of his colleagues in Pastoral Theology, conducted a sermon class. *Life on God's Plan* (L, 1909), *The Highway of God* (E, 1931) and *Sermons* (E, 1938) exemplify his homiletic style.

Many regarded Mackintosh as the greatest British theologian of his generation. 'I know that my Redeemer liveth' was inscribed upon his gravestone.

Studies in Christian Truth (L, 1916); *The Originality of the Christian Message* (L, 1920); *The Christian Apprehension of God* (L, 1929); *Some Aspects of Christian Belief* (L, 1923); *Immortality and the Future* (L, 1915); *The Person of Jesus Christ* (L, 1912).

Memoir by A. B. Macaulay, prefixed to *Sermons*; H. Watt *et al.*, *New College, Edinburgh* (E, 1946), *passim*; Robert R. Redman, Jr, 'H. R. Mackintosh's Contribution to Christology and Soteriology in the Twentieth Century', *SJT* 41 (1988), 517–34.

A. P. F. Sell

Mackintosh, Robert (1858–1933), Congregational minister and theologian. Son of the well-connected Charles Calder Mackintosh of Dunoon FC, Argyll, he declined a scholarship to Oxford, and studied philosophy and classics at Glasgow University and divinity at New College,* Edinburgh. Glasgow made him DD (1899).

His major early preoccupation was how to survive in the FC, which required subscription* to a Confession deemed unalterable. *Christ and the Jewish Law* (L, 1886), was followed by two provocative tracts, *The Obsoleteness of the Westminster Confession*

of Faith and *The Insufficiency of Revivalism as a Religious System* (both bound with *Essays Towards a New Theology*, G, 1889). After assisting at Withington Presbyterian Church, Manchester, in 1890 he accepted the Congregational charge at Dumfries. He had 'fled' to Congregationalism,* less a proselyte than a refugee. His quest of an honest faith inspired *A First Primer of Apologetics* (L, 1900). He served as Professor at Lancashire Independent College, Manchester (1894–1930).

He wrote on philosophy and ethics: *From Comte to Benjamin Kidd* (L, 1899), *Hegel and Hegelianism* (E, 1903), and *Christian Ethics* (L, 1909); on theology: *Christianity and Sin* (L, 1913); *Albrecht Ritschl and His School* (L, 1915), and *Historic Theories of Atonement* (L, 1920); a commentary on *Thessalonians and Corinthians* (L, 1909), and contributions to *EB* (11th edn), *ERE*, *Exp*, *ExT*, etc. Most of his writings display his critical aptitudes and his pungent literary style, directed notably against legalism and sacerdotalism. But his heart is there too – most clearly in *Values* (L, 1928) and *Some Central Things* (L, 1932). With Mackintosh, shibboleths tumble, but grace remains.

A. P. F. Sell, *Robert Mackintosh: Theologian of Integrity* (Berne, 1977); *Who Was Who, 1929–1940*, 872–3.

A. P. F. Sell

MacKnight, James (1721–1800), CofS minister. He served at Maybole (1753–69), Jedburgh (1769–71), Lady Yester's Church, Edinburgh (1771–3), and Edinburgh Old Church (1778–1800). He became a DD (Edinburgh, 1759), and Moderator of the General Assembly in 1769. An adherent of the Moderate party* in the CofS, he nevertheless moved the Declaratory Act of Assembly in 1782 which reaffirmed that a call* from a congregation was necessary as well as the nomination of the patron (*see* Patronage). His published works mainly concerned biblical criticism, and he translated the apostolic epistles.

A Harmony of the Four Gospels (L, 1756, 1763); *The Truth of Gospel History* (L, 1763); *A New Literal Translation from the Original Greek of all the Apostolic Epistles, with a Life of the Apostle Paul*, 4 vols (E, 1795).

FES I, 72; *DNB* XXXV, 184–5; Life, prefixed to *A New Literal Translation* ... in editions from 1806.

J. R. McIntosh

Mackonochie, Alexander (1825–87), Anglo-Catholic Anglican priest. Born to Scottish parents and raised in England, he attended Oxford, where he was influenced by E. B. Pusey. After serving as a curate in St George's-in-the-East, East London, where he endured rioting during services in reaction to worship innovations, Mackonochie became the first vicar of St Alban's, Holborn, a London slum. Although his sacrificial pastoral work won the affection of the poor, his ritualist practices incurred the wrath of the Protestant Church Association. After sixteen years of litigation, he resigned from active ministry in 1883, later dying tragically from exposure after becoming lost in the western Highlands.

Alexander Heriot Mackonochie, A Memoir by E.A.T., ed. E. F. Russell (L, 1890); J. Bentley, *Ritualism and Politics in Victorian Britain* (O, 1978).

D. A. Currie

McLagan, James (1728–1805), collector of Gaelic* poetry. Born in Logierait parish, Perthshire, McLagan became an Est.C missionary, probably based at Amulree, and then entered the Black Watch as chaplain (1764–81), seeing service in America. Latterly minister of Blair Atholl and Strowan (1781–1805), McLagan had a life-long interest in Gaelic songs and ballads, and gathered a major collection of verse (The McLagan MSS), now housed in Glasgow University Library. He supplied material to John Gillies of Perth, who published a significant collection of Gaelic poetry in 1786.

D. S. Thomson, 'A Catalogue and Indexes of the Ossianic Ballads in the McLagan MSS', *SGS* 8 (1958), 177–224; *FES* IV, 145.

D. E. Meek

McLaren, Agnes (1837–1913), RC medical mission pioneer. The daughter of a prominent Liberal family in Edinburgh, she was denied medical training at home, but became the first woman graduate in medicine at Montpellier, France. She practised in Nice, and at the age of sixty converted to RCism. A Vatican ban was in force on full medical training of priests and nuns. In 1910, when no professional RC medical missions existed in India, she founded St Catherine's Hospital at Rawalpindi and recruited women doctors. She died in 1913, after inspiring a young Austrian, Anna Dengel, with her sense of mission. Dengel gathered lay associates with the object of forming a religious society. When the Church ban was revoked in 1936, they became a religious order, the Medical Mission Sisters, within the RCC. Today they number over 700, working in over thirty countries. McLaren is venerated as the originator of RC medical missions.

M. Ryan, *Dr Agnes McLaren (1837–1913)* (L, 1915); K. Burton, *According to the Pattern* (NY, 1946); C. C. Martindale, *Medical Mission Sisters* (L, 1955).

M. Cavanagh

Maclaren, Alexander (1826–1910), Baptist preacher and expositor. Born in Glasgow to Baptist parents (though his mother, Mary Wingate, was the daughter of a Cameronian), Maclaren was educated at Glasgow High School, where he was a contemporary of Robert Rainy,* and at Glasgow University. When the family moved to London he began his studies for the ministry at Stepney Baptist College (later Regent's Park College), obtaining also a BA from London University. He was called to a pastorate at Portland Chapel, Southampton, before he finished college and ministered there 1846–58, steadily building up a strong congregation from a low and almost derelict state, drawing large numbers from many parts. Although his orthodoxy was at first questioned by some, his sermons were described by others as being in the Hebrew prophetic mould, with the directness of John Knox. He later said he was grateful to God for these 'early days of struggle and obscurity', which laid the foundations of his future ministry in Union Chapel, Manchester, to which he was called in 1858, and where he continued until his retirement in 1903. He declined invitations to move to Regent's Park Church in London in 1883 or to the Chair of Hebrew at Regent's Park College in 1886. He was President of the Baptist Union in 1875 and 1901 and the first President of the Baptist World Alliance in 1905. He tended, however, not to become greatly involved in commitments outwith his own preaching ministry in Manchester, and refused invitations to preach elsewhere, concentrating his attention and energy on establishing a ministry of exposition of Scripture. 'The secret of success for a minister', he once said, 'is that he should concentrate his intellectual force on the one work of preaching.' His ministry was interrupted by serious illness in 1881, leading to a long visit to Australia, which was said to have added twenty years to his life.

Two volumes of *Sermons Preached in Manchester* were published in 1860 and 1869. F. B. Meyer compared the sermons to 'a great cathedral, so exquisitely constructed were they, and so entirely complete in proportion'. He is best known for his *Expositions of Holy Scripture*, published after his retirement in 1903 at the suggestion of W. Robertson Nicoll,* founder and editor of the *British Weekly*,* who considered Maclaren to have 'a keener insight into the New Testament than anyone else I know'. The first volume on Genesis appeared in 1904 and other volumes being published regularly reaching a total of thirty-two. After Spurgeon's* sermons these were the most widely read of their time and are still greatly valued for the integrity and honesty of their exposition. His three volumes on the Psalms in *The Expositor's Bible* are a fine piece of scholarship.

D. Williamson, *Life of Dr Alexander Maclaren* (L, 1910); E. T. McLaren, *Dr McLaren of Manchester, A Sketch* (L, 1911); W. R. Nicoll, *Princes of the Church* (L, 1921); *BW* (issues from 12 May 1910 onwards).

J. Philip

McLaren, Duncan (1800–86), prominent dissenting* Liberal MP for Edinburgh 1865–81. The son of a farmer at Renton, Dumbartonshire, he lived from 1818 in Edinburgh where he was a long-term member of Bristo Street USec./UP Church, declining the eldership in 1838. The long ministry there of James Peddie (1758–1845; *DNB* XLIV, 203–4; Small I, 431–2) made it a leading centre of Liberal dissent in Scotland and shaped McLaren's later support for disestablishment* and Voluntaryism.* A draper by trade, McLaren entered political life around the time of the 1832 Reform Bill and set himself to marshall the voting power of the dissenting communities. He was the first chairman in 1834 of the Scottish Central Board of Dissenters which replaced the Voluntary Church Association and which soon headed a federation of Voluntaryist and dissenting societies. He opposed Thomas Chalmers'* church extension* scheme, and after the Disruption* widened his influence to take in the FC, helping to unite Scottish nonconformists* around the disestablishment cause.

McLaren was a successful Provost of Edinburgh in 1851–4. As an MP he became known as 'the member for Scotland' (in 1853 he joined the National Association for the Vindication of Scottish Rights). He was involved in the act for the commutation of the annuity tax,* and also the Irish Sunday Closing Act. He strove to Christianize legislation, in accord with the Decalogue.

DNB XXXV, 194–5; J. M. Mackie, *The Life and Work of Duncan McLaren*, 2 vols (L, 1888).

D. F. Wright

Maclaren, Ian (1850–1907), Presbyterian minister and writer, whose real name was John Watson. In his own name Watson was a successful pastor in Liverpool (where he had an enormous and wealthy Presbyterian CofE congregation in Sefton Park), also a well-known lecturer, particularly in North America. Of Highland stock, he was born in Maningtree, Essex (England) and educated at Edinburgh University. He trained at New College for the FC and in 1875 was ordained to Logiealmond FC (Perthshire), which was the source of the famous 'Drumtochty' of his kailyard fiction. He moved in 1877 to St Matthew's, Glasgow, and in 1880 to Liverpool. His *Beside the Bonnie Briar Bush* (1894) and *The Days of Auld Lang Syne* (L, 1895) were to make him famous at a time when literary taste welcomed these pastoral, essentially backward-looking sketches of a vanishing, pious Scotland. With J. M. Barrie and S. R. Crockett, Ian Maclaren is remembered as an enormously successful practitioner of a genre now almost universally deplored; his fiction, dispassionately read today, remains convincing and well-told in its realistic treatment of Scottish rural life seen from close-up. Watson was a shrewd communicator and had a good sense of public taste and mood; he published extensively in theology and in belles-lettres. He was DD of Yale University.

See also Literature, Religion in Scottish.

The Mind of the Maker (L, 1896); *The Life of the Master* (L, 1901); *The Doctrines of Grace* (L, 1900); *The Cure of Souls* (L, 1896).

W. R. Nicoll, *'Ian Maclaren': A Life of the Rev. John Watson* (L, 1903); I. Campbell, *Kailyard* (E, 1981); *DNB Second Suppl.* III, 605–7; *AFCS* I, 352.

I. Campbell

M'Laren, John (1667–1750), evangelical CofS minister. Educated at Glasgow University, M'Laren was ordained to Kippen (in Dunblane) in 1692, translated to Carstairs (Lanarkshire) in 1699 and to the Tolbooth Church (first charge) in Edinburgh in 1711, where he was colleague to James Webster.*

He refused to take the Oath of Allegiance* in 1712, and in 1733 was one of six who protested in the General Assembly's Commission against the loosing of Ebenezer Erskine* and his associates from their charges. He took no active part in the Marrow Controversy,* but his critique of John Simson's* doctrine (*The New System of Doctrine, contained in the Answers of Mr. John Simson, ...* E, 1717) shows him to have been an accomplished and well-read theologian.

Robert Wodrow* wrote that M'Laren was engaged in answering the (Arminian) Philip Limborch's system of divinity (*Theologia Christiana*, Amsterdam, 1686), but he did not think him the man for the job (*Analecta*, E, 1843, IV, 150). In the event, however, the work was never published.

The Spiritual Burgess (E, 1735).

FES I, 119.

D. C. Lachman

McLauchlan, Thomas (1815–86), Gaelic* scholar and eminent FC minister. Born in Moy, Inverness-shire, McLauchlan assisted and succeeded his father as parish minister of Moy (1838–43). Joining the FC in 1843, and serving a further year in Moy, he was minister successively in Stratherrick (1844–9) and Free St Columba's, Edinburgh. He was Moderator of the FC General Assembly in 1876. As Convener of the FC's Highland Committee, he was an outspoken critic of the clearance system (*see* Clearances). McLauchlan helped to lay the foundations of modern Gaelic scholarship, producing an edition of John Carswell's* Gaelic version of the *Book of Common Order* (E, 1873) and also (with the historian, W. F. Skene) an edition of the sixteenth-century manuscript, *The Book of the Dean of Lismore* (E, 1862). With Archibald Clerk, he produced the Gaelic Reference Bible (1860) (*see* Bible (Versions, Gaelic)).

AFCS I, 244; *FES* VI, 477; D. MacKinnon, *The Gaelic Bible and Psalter* (Dingwall, 1930), 98.

D. E. Meek

MacLaurin, John (1693–1754), minister of Glasgow, Ramshorn (North-West or St David's) (1723–54) and one of the ablest preachers and theologians of the eighteenth-century CofS. His sermon 'Glorying in the Cross of Christ' is widely regarded as the epitome of Scottish evangelical preaching of the century. Possibly his most important theological work was his 'Essay on the Nature of Christian Piety' (in *Sermons and Essays*, G, 1755), in the course of which he dealt extensively with the nature of faith. He played an important role in the disputes over patronage* in the latter part of his life, producing what was arguably the most effective defence of the 'Popular'* position in *The Nature of Ecclesiastic Government* (G, 1754). In this work, he advanced criticisms of the Moderate* position which were never answered, and displayed considerable acquaintance with the work of continental political and philosophical writers. He was also active in improving social conditions and in poor-law reform.

W. H. Goold (ed.), *The Works of the Rev. John MacLaurin*, 2 vols (E, 1860) – including life by J. Gillies; *DNB* XXXV, 198; *FES* III, 439; J. Macleod, *Scottish Theology* (E, ³1974).

J. R. McIntosh

McLaurin, Malcolm (1785–1859), itinerant* preacher with the Independents.* Born at Ardchattan, Argyll, and educated at Rotherham Independent Academy, Yorkshire, he became a full-time itinerant preacher in 1818, supported by the Society in Paisley and its Vicinity for Gaelic Missions, and making extensive tours of the West Highlands and Hebrides, reaching St Kilda. He settled in Islay in 1822 as pastor of the Independent church at Port Charlotte. He was the author of several Gaelic* works, including translations of William Dyer's *Golden Chain (Christ's Famous Titles)* (G, 1817), Legh Richmond's *Dairyman's Daughter* (G, 1822) and sermons by James Spence (G, 1825).

D. E. Meek, 'Evangelical Missionaries in the Early Nineteenth-Century Highlands', *SS* 28 (1987), 24–5, 30.

D. E. Meek

McLean, Archibald (1733–1812), Scotch Baptist* elder and author. McLean was born in East Kilbride into a Presbyterian family with roots in Mull. In 1746 he was articled to a printer in Glasgow. Spiritually influenced by Whitefield* and Malcolm McLaurin,* he taught himself Latin, Greek and Hebrew, married in 1759, and set up business in Glasgow until 1767, when he moved to Edinburgh to Donaldson and Co., Printers. He read Glas's* *Testimony* and joined the Glasite church in Glasgow in 1762, leaving next year on a point of discipline but remaining much in theological debt to Glas. He adopted Baptist* views, and became elder in the Edinburgh Scotch Baptist church in 1768, holding office until his death. He was instrumental in setting in order Scotch Baptist churches not only in Scottish towns, but also in the north of England, Nottingham and London. The church gave him a stipend from 1785, releasing him for travels to the churches and for writing. He faced many divisions in the fellowship, but with fellow-elders, W. Braidwood (*d.*1830) and H. D. Inglis (*d.*1806), he set the Edinburgh church on a firm foundation.

He wrote for Rippon's *Annual Register*, II (1795–6), 376–86, an 'Account of the Scots Baptists', and in his main work, *The Commission given by Jesus Christ to His Apostles, illustrated* (E, 1786), he set out the principles of the Scotch Baptists. He wrote much on baptism and on other controversial mattters; see his *Letters to John Glas* (E, 1767). He was an ardent supporter of the Baptist Missionary Society and a correspondent of Andrew Fuller.* His *Works* were published in 5 vols (E, 1817), 6 vols (L, 1823), and 7 vols (Elgin, 1847–53).

W. Jones, 'Memoir of the Author', in McLean, *Works* (L, 1823); M. I. Smith, *Bristo Baptist Church Bicentenary* (E, 1965); R. D. Mitchell, 'Archibald McLean, Baptist Pioneer in Scotland' (PhD, Edinburgh University, 1950); D. Bebbington (ed.), *The Baptists in Scotland* (G, 1988), 21–4.

D. B. Murray

Maclean, Arthur John (1858–1943), Bishop of Moray and distinguished liturgist. Born at Bath, Somerset, where his father was an Anglican rector, he studied at King's College, Cambridge (MA, 1880), and lectured there in mathematics. Conceiving a religious vocation, his Highland ancestry and love of Highland lore prompted him to offer himself for ordination (deacon, 1882; priest, 1883) to the Bishop of Argyll and the Isles. He served as chaplain of Cumbrae Cathedral (*see* Cathedral Churches) in Buteshire, and at St Columba's, Portree, Skye.

In 1886 Maclean led Archbishop Benson of Canterbury's mission to the Syrian Nestorian Christians on the Iran–Turkey borderland. Here he established schools for Syrian clergy and laity, was responsible for the first printed version of the Syriac Liturgy of St Adaeus and St Mari and other Syriac liturgies, and produced a Syriac grammar and other works for use in Nestorian schools. He and his team were known as 'the English Apostles'.

Returning to Scotland, Maclean was rector of St Columba's, Portree (1891–7), and St John's, Selkirk (1897–1903), and Principal of the Episcopal Theological College* (Coates Hall) in Edinburgh, 1903–5. In 1904 he had been appointed Bishop of Moray, and in 1931 was elected Primus.* As Bishop, Maclean championed the Scottish against the English Communion office, and was chief architect of the 1929 Scottish Prayer Book.*

Most of Maclean's writings were linguistic and liturgical. He appears most accessibly in his articles in James Hastings'* *Dictionary of the Bible*. His article on God exhibits a thorough acceptance of higher critical views of the evolution of Old Testament religion, whereas his article on Paul contains a careful exposition of the main themes of Pauline theology.

The Ancient Church Orders (C, 1910); *Church Services and Service-Books before the Reformation* (with H. B. Swete, L, 1896).

W. G. S. Snow, *Arthur John Maclean* (E, 1950); *Who Was Who, 1941–1950*, 738.

N. R. Needham

Maclean, Donald (1869–1943), noted FC minister and Gaelic* scholar. Born in Lochcarron, Wester Ross, Maclean was ordained and inducted to Moy, Inverness-shire (1897–1905), and translated to Free St Columba's Edinburgh (1905–18). He became Professor of Church History at the FC College, Edinburgh (1920–43), and Principal (1942). He was twice Moderator of the FC General Assembly (1919 and 1937). Maclean helped to steer the continuing FC through the crisis of 1900, became secretary of its Highlands and Islands Committee, and served on numerous national and international committees. A distinguished historian and Calvinist theologian, he was author of several books and articles which contributed greatly to the understanding of Scottish Church history. He wrote extensively on different aspects of Gaelic literature. Among his writings are a fine article on the work of Robert Kirk,* *The Counter-Reformation in Scotland* (E, 1931), *The Spiritual Songs of Dugald Buchanan* (E, 1913) and *The Literature of the Scottish Gael* (E, 1913). He was a founder, a co-editor (from 1929) and latterly the sole editor of the *Evangelical Quarterly*.*

L. MacBean, *The Celtic Who's Who* (Kirkcaldy, 1921), 102; *id.*, *Donald Maclean* (E, 1944); G. N. M. Collins, *Annals of the Free Church of Scotland 1900–1986* (E, n.d.), 25–6; W. H. Hamilton, in *EQ* 15 (1943), 85–90.

D. E. Meek

Maclean, Norman (1869–1952), CofS minister, popular preacher and writer. Born at the Braes in Skye, the son of a schoolmaster, he was educated at the Universities of St Andrews and Edinburgh. He was minister of Waternish on Skye (1892–7), Glengarry, Inverness-shire (1897–1903), Colinton, Edinburgh (1903–10), the Park Church, Glasgow (1910–15), and St Cuthbert's, Edinburgh (1915–37). He served as convener of the Life and Work Committee and was appointed a royal chaplain in 1926 and Moderator of the General Assembly in 1927. He acted as the religious affairs correspondent of *The Scotsman* and wrote a series of articles for the newspaper entitled 'In Our Parish'. His three-volume autobiography is a fascinating account of his own religious pilgrimage and of the Scottish Church during his lifetime (*The Former Days*, L, 1945; *Set Free*, L, 1949; *The Years of Fulfilment*, L, 1953).

FES I, 5, III, 471, VII, 170, 447.

D. M. Murray

MacLennan, John (1797–1852), the first CofS minister in Prince Edward Island, Canada. Born in Lochcarron, Wester Ross, MacLennan studied for the ministry at King's College, Aberdeen (1818–22), and was licensed by the Presbytery of Abernethy in 1822. Receiving a call from 'a considerable number of Free holders in Prince Edward Island, North America' in 1823, he emigrated and settled at Belfast, PEI. There he built the parish church of St John's, preached extensively throughout PEI, and travelled in other parts, notably Cape Breton Island and the adjacent mainland. He corresponded with the Glasgow Colonial Society* and the Edinburgh Bible Society (*see* Bible Societies), soliciting Gaelic* and English Bibles and Testaments, and attempting to recruit ministers for the settlements. After 1843, MacLennan remained in the Est.C, although his fellow ministers in Nova Scotia, Cape Breton (*see* Farquharson, Alexander) and Newfoundland joined the FCofS. Moving temporarily to Charlottetown, PEI, MacLennan found little support for his position, and returned to Scotland in 1849. He took charge of the Gaelic Chapel at Cromarty (1849–51) and then (in August 1851) of the parish church at Kilchrenan, Argyll, where he died less than a year later.

FES IV, 93; Jean M. MacLennan, *From Shore to Shore* (E, 1977); *Dictionary of Canadian Biography* VIII, 569–70.

D. E. Meek

McLennan, John Ferguson (1827–81), lawyer, anthropologist and historian of religions. Born in Inverness, he graduated from King's College, Aberdeen in 1849, then went to Trinity College, Cambridge. Returning to Scotland in 1857 he was called to the bar. In 1871 he became parliamentary draughtsman for Scotland, and for the rest of his life was involved in the legal profession. He became interested in non-literate societies while researching an article on 'Law' for the *Encyclopaedia Britannica* (⁸1857). A founding father of evolutionary anthropology, he later applied evolutionary theory to the study of religion. He elaborated a theory about early human institutions in *Primitive Marriage* (E, 1865, revised in *Studies in Ancient History*, first series, L, 1876). In a series of articles ('The worship of plants and animals', *Fortnightly Review* n.s. 12, 1869, 407–27, 562–82; 13, 1870, 194–216, reprinted in *Studies in Ancient History*, second series, L, 1896), he suggested that 'totemism', the worship of animals and plants, was the lowest form of religion, from which evolved all higher forms; and that contemporary non-literate peoples are still in the totemic stage. Although the evolutionary presuppositions of McLennan's work are no longer accepted, he stimulated the interest of his contemporaries in the study of religion, among them his friend William Robertson Smith,* and Andrew Lang.*

R. H. Lowie, *The History of Ethnological Theory* (L, 1937), 43–9; E. J. Sharpe, *Comparative Religion* (L, 1975), 75–7; *DNB* XXXV, 210–11; D. McLennan (ed.), *The Patriarchal Theory* (L, 1885).

P. J. Baylis

MacLeod, Alexander (1786–1869), reputedly the first evangelical Presbyterian minister in the island of Lewis. Born in Stoer, in the parish of Assynt, Sutherland, MacLeod was educated at King's College, Aberdeen (1808–12), and licensed by the Presbytery of Tongue in 1818. Ordained to the Gaelic* Chapel, Dundee, in 1819, he was translated to Cromarty Gaelic Chapel in 1821. In 1824 he was presented to the parish of Uig, Lewis, by Lady Mackenzie of Seaforth (*see* Highlands). Signing the Act of Separation and Deed of Demission in 1843, he joined the FC, but moved from Lewis shortly thereafter, being called to Lochalsh FC late in 1843. From 1846 until his death, he served as minister of Rogart FC.

MacLeod's ministry in Lewis was of strategic importance in establishing the course of nascent Evangelicalism in the island. He was appointed to Uig during a period of revival* fervour which reached

MACLEOD, ALEXANDER

a peak in 1823 and continued until 1830. Independents, Baptists and others participated. MacLeod's magisterial presence helped to channel this enthusiasm into the local Est.C, thus sowing the seed for the emergence of the FC in Lewis. His influence led to further revival movements in Uig – a 'calm, and deep, and prolonged flow' – particularly within the context of the Lord's Supper (*see* Communion Seasons), to which admission was strictly regulated. MacLeod visited several of the other islands to ascertain their spiritual condition. He came to be known in Gaelic tradition as *Alasdair Mòr an t-Soisgeil* ('Great Alexander of the Gospel').

AFCS I, 247; *FES* VII, 7; *Narratives of Revivals of Religion in Scotland, Ireland and Wales* (G, 1839), No. VIII; J. Greig (ed.), *Disruption Worthies of the Highlands* (E, 1877), 221–32.

D. E. Meek

Macleod, Alexander (1817–91), Presbyterian minister and writer. Born in Nairn, he attended Glasgow University (1835–9) and the Relief Church* theological hall (1839–44). He was ordained to the Relief congregation at Strathaven in 1844, moved to John Street UP church, Glasgow, in 1855, and then in 1864 became the first minister of Trinity Presbyterian church at Claughton, Birkenhead, in Cheshire (England). He received a DD from Glasgow University in 1865, and was Moderator of the Presbyterian Church of England in 1889.

Macleod's publications include: *Christus Consolator* (L, 1870); *Days of Heaven upon Earth and Other Sermons* (L, 1878); *A Man's Gift and Other Sermons* (L, 1895).

A. G. Fleming, 'Memorial Sketch', and A. M. Fairbairn, 'Personal Reminiscences', prefixed to Macleod's *A Man's Gift and Other Sermons*; *DNB* XXXV, 211–12.

N. R. Needham

MacLeod, Donald (1831–1916), CofS minister. The fifth son of Norman MacLeod, minister of St Columba's, Glasgow, and brother of Norman MacLeod* of the Barony, he was educated at the University of Glasgow (BA, 1851; DD, 1876) and became minister of Lauder in 1858 and of Linlithgow in 1862. He exercised a ministry of forty years at the Park Church in Glasgow, 1869–1909. He served as convener of the Home Mission Committee, was appointed a royal chaplain, and was Moderator of the General Assembly in 1895. He was the Editor of *Good Words** 1872–1905. Although he did not become a member of the Scottish Church Society* he shared many of the concerns of the Scoto-Catholics* in the Kirk. In his Baird Lectures,* *The Doctrine and Validity of the Ministry and Sacraments of the National Church of Scotland* (E, 1903), he defended the Kirk's ministerial orders and argued for the centrality of the Lord's Supper in worship*.

S. Smith, *Donald MacLeod of Glasgow* (E, 1926); *FES* III, 471.

D. M. Murray

MACLEOD, JOHN

MacLeod, George Fielden (1895–1991), Lord MacLeod of Fuinary, founder of the Iona Community.* Born in Glasgow the son of a Conservative MP, and grandson of Norman MacLeod* of the Barony, he was educated at Winchester, Oxford and Edinburgh. After service as a captain in the Argyll and Sutherland Highlanders during World War One, for which he received the Military Cross and the Croix de Guerre, he became a pacifist. A CofS minister in St Cuthbert's, Edinburgh (1926–30) and Govan Old, Glasgow (1930–8), MacLeod founded the Iona Community and began the rebuilding of the living quarters of the ruined medieval abbey on the historic island of Iona* in 1938. Under his direction the Community grew to become an ecumenical fellowship, eventually comprising men and women, ordained and lay, Protestant and RC.

MacLeod was the first Presbyterian since the seventeenth century to be Select Preacher at Cambridge and to occupy the pulpit of St Paul's Cathedral in London. In 1954 he became first Fosdick Visiting Professor at Union Theological Seminary, New York. In 1956 he was appointed a chaplain to the Queen, and became Moderator of the CofS General Assembly the following year. He was elevated to the House of Lords in 1967, resigning as Leader of the Iona Community, and became president of the International Fellowship of Reconciliation. He was Rector of Glasgow University 1968–71. In 1986, while in New York, he was awarded the Union Medal by Union Theological Seminary. The new international youth and reconciliation centre on Iona, opened in 1988, was named in his honour.

Lord MacLeod was one of the most influential and controversial figures in the CofS this century. His understanding of worship and his radical political views brought early criticism that his Iona Community was 'half way towards Rome and half way towards Moscow'. His book *We Shall Re-Build* (G, 1944) sold 20,000 copies in 1944–5, and his Cunningham lectures,* published as *Only One Way Left* (G, 1956), were widely quoted. He was awarded a DD by Glasgow University in 1937, and the degree of LLD by Iona College, USA, in 1968.

Govan Calling (L, 1934).

FES VIII, 19–20, IX, 38, 270; *Who's Who* 1990, 1174; R. Ferguson (ed.), *The Whole Earth Shall Cry Glory: Iona Prayers by Rev. George F. MacLeod* (G, 1986); id., *Chasing the Wild Goose* (L, 1988); R. Morton, *The Iona Community: Personal Impressions of the Early Years* (E, 1977); R. Ferguson, *George MacLeod* (L, 1990).

R. Ferguson

Macleod, John (1840–98), CofS minister. His father was John Macleod of Morven, Argyll (*FES* IV, 118), his uncle Norman MacLeod* of the Barony, and his brother Norman MacLeod* of Inverness. Educated at the University of Glasgow (BA, 1848; DD, 1883), he was minister of Newton-on-Ayr for a short time before becoming minister of Duns in Berwickshire in 1862 and of Govan near

MACLEOD, JOHN

Glasgow in 1875. One of the leaders of the Catholic revival of worship* in Scotland, the innovations* he made in the worship at Duns were later forbidden by the General Assembly, but he had comparatively little difficulty in conducting a similar type of liturgical worship at Govan. Macleod was a powerful preacher, had a forceful personality and a genius for organization. He was a founder of the Scottish Church Society,* being responsible for organizing its first successful conferences and acting as its president in 1896–7. His churchmanship was 'lower' than other Scoto-Catholics,* since he emphasized the immediate relation of the Church to Christ rather than ecclesiastical tradition. He was greatly influenced by Edward Irving* and became a 'presbyter, sealed' of the Catholic Apostolic Church* while still remaining a minister of the Kirk. He was convener of the Church Reform Committee set up by the General Assembly in 1896.

Holy Communion and Frequency of Celebration (E, 1887); *The Gospel of the Holy Communion* (n.p., 1927).

R. S. Kirkpatrick, *The Ministry of Dr John Macleod* (E, 1915); H. J. Wotherspoon, 'John Macleod of Govan', *The Constructive Quarterly* 8 (1920), 664–704; A. W. Williamson, *Dr John Macleod* (E, 1901); D. M. Murray, 'John Macleod of Govan', *Liturgical Review* 8:2 (1978), 27–32, and 'The Worship of Govan Parish Church', in J. Harvey (ed.), *Govan Old Parish Church 1888–1988* (G, 1988), 15–22; G. White, 'Dr John Macleod of Govan', *ibid.*, 9–12; *FES* III, 413–14.

D. M. Murray

Macleod, John (1872–1948), eminent Reformed scholar and churchman. Born of FC parentage in Fort William, he studied classics with distinction at Aberdeen University 1887–90, then spent a year at New College, Edinburgh, studying divinity. After schoolteaching in Stornoway, Lewis, he resumed divinity in 1894 at Belfast Theological College, having meanwhile left the FC over the Declaratory Act* controversy and thrown in his lot with the FPC. Licensed by his Church's Northern Presbytery in 1897, he was minister of Lochbroom, Ullapool, in Ross and Cromarty (1897–1901), and Kames in Argyll (1901–5).

In 1905, after the Constitutionalist* victory over the UFC in the House of Lords (see Free Church Case), Macleod moved that the FP Synod appoint a committee to consider the obstacles to union with the FC. When this motion was defeated, Macleod and several colleagues left the FPC and rejoined their old Church convinced that with the repeal of the Declaratory Act it had now returned to Reformed orthodoxy.

In 1906 Macleod became Professor of Greek and New Testament Exegesis in the FC College, Edinburgh. In 1913, however, he left to minister to the Free North Church, Inverness, and his connection with the College was not renewed until 1927, when he was appointed Principal. In 1929 he resumed

MACLEOD, NORMAN

full-time teaching as Professor of Apologetics. Ill-health forced his retirement in 1943.

Although Macleod's literary remains are meagre, he acquired during his lifetime a unique position of affection and respect in the international Reformed world, both for his profound knowledge of Reformed theology and his personal godliness. His ties with Princeton Seminary,* New Jersey, and after 1929 with Westminster Seminary, Philadelphia, were especially close. It was at Westminster in 1939 that he delivered in lecture form his magnum opus, *Scottish Theology in relation to Church History since the Reformation*, published on the centenary of the Disruption* (E, 1943; ³1974) – an opulent source of information and comment. Among other things, Macleod also helped to articulate the response of traditional Reformed theology to neo-orthodoxy as one of 'mingled hope and fear' (quoted G. N. M. Collins, *John Macleod DD*, E, 1951, 175).

Macleod was consulting editor of the *Evangelical Quarterly.** He acted as Moderator of the FC General Assembly in 1920, and received a DD from Aberdeen in 1927.

Lochaber and its Evangelical Traditions (Inverness, 1920); *The North Country Separatists* (Inverness, 1930); both revised, ed. G. N. M. Collins, *By-paths of Highland Church History* (E, 1965); *id.*, *Annals of the Free Church . . .* (E, n.d.), 28.

N. R. Needham

MacLeod, Kenneth (1871–1955), minister of Colonsay and Oronsay, 1917–23, and Gigha and Cara, 1923–47. Born in Eigg, and educated at Inverness and Glasgow, he served as CofS missionary in various places before becoming a minister. A noted Gaelic* folklorist and stylist, he collaborated with Marjory Kennedy-Fraser in *Songs of the Hebrides*, 3 vols (L, 1909–21). He published two volumes of Highland lore in English, *The Road to the Isles* (E, 1927) and *The Road to Iona* (E, 1933). His collected Gaelic prose, *The Gaelic Prose of Kenneth MacLeod* (E, 1988) has been edited by T. M. Murchison,* who supplies a full memoir.

FES IV, 69, VIII, 323, IX, 392.

K. D. MacDonald

MacLeod, Norman (1780–1866), separatist preacher and emigrant leader. Born at Stoer, Sutherland, MacLeod studied at Aberdeen to prepare for the ministry (MA, 1812), but after two sessions of theology at Edinburgh he was rusticated and in 1815 became parish schoolmaster in Ullapool. Talented but autocratic, MacLeod opposed the CofS's lack of zeal and discipline, and although unlicensed, expressed his views through preaching to separatist congregations which he established at Assynt and Ullapool. This irregularity angered the litigious minister of Lochbroom, who had his salary stopped, prompting MacLeod to emigrate to Nova Scotia in 1817.

Many of his 400 fellow-passengers shared his views and settled under his leadership at Pictou. In 1820 MacLeod embarked with 200 followers on a self-built boat, bound for a Highland colony in Ohio, but on being stormbound off Cape Breton Island they changed their plans and took up land there. The 'Normanites' established the first Presbyterian church in the Island, at St Ann's, and in 1826 MacLeod was ordained by Genesee Presbytery, New York.

Between 1851 and 1860 about 900 'Normanites' left Cape Breton for New Zealand, initially via Australia, in six self-built vessels. Following encouraging letters from MacLeod's son, the first two ships sailed for Adelaide in 1851 and 1852. Unimpressed with prospects there, the pioneers, led by MacLeod, halted briefly at Melbourne before settling finally on a 30,000-acre tract at Waipu, north of Auckland. They were subsequently joined by other shiploads direct from St Ann's and reconstituted the unique, co-operative Christian Socialist community which MacLeod had first created at Pictou fifty years earlier.

See also Emigration.

Dict. of Canadian Biogr. IX, 516–17; Dict. of New Zealand Biogr. II, 38–9; F. McPherson, *Watchman against the World* (Toronto, 1962); N. R. McKenzie, *The Gael Fares Forth* (Wellington, ²1942); G. Macdonald, *The Highlanders of Waipu* (Dunedin, 1928); N. Robinson, *Lion of Scotland* (L, 1952); A. J. Clark, 'The Scottish-Canadian Pilgrims of the Fifties', *Ontario Historical Society Papers & Records* 26 (1930), 5–15.

M. Harper

MacLeod, Norman (1783–1862), CofS minister and noted Gaelic* writer. Born in the Manse of Morvern, Argyll, and educated at Glasgow and Edinburgh Universities, he was successively minister of Campbeltown (1808–25), Campsie (1925–35), and St Columba, Glasgow (1835–62). He was Moderator of the General Assembly in 1836. His pastoral and philanthropic exertions on behalf of Highlanders, especially during the potato famine years of 1836–7 and 1846–7 (*see* Clearances), earned him the affectionate sobriquet *Caraid nan Gaidheal* ('Friend of the Gaels').

MacLeod was a strenuous campaigner for the extension of education and literacy in the Gaelic Highlands.* He was instrumental in having a large-format edition of the Gaelic Bible published in 1826 (*see* Bible (Versions, Gaelic)), and, with the support of Principal George Baird of Edinburgh, persuaded the General Assembly in 1824 to set up its own Gaelic schools (*see* Gaelic School Societies). This initiative was reinforced by a series of literary labours designed to provide reading matter for newly literate Gaelic speakers. He edited two anthologies for use in the General Assembly's schools, *Co'chruinneachadh* ('Anthology') (G, 1828) and *Leabhar nan Cnoc* ('The Book of the Hills') (Greenock, 1834). Along with Daniel Dewar* he compiled *A Dictionary of the Gaelic Language* (G, 1831).

More important was his establishing, and editing, of the first successful Gaelic periodical, *An Teachdaire Gae'lach* (1829–31), and a later title, *Guairtear nan Gleann* (1840–3). MacLeod aimed with these journals to supply Gaels at home and overseas with edifying, instructive and entertaining matter in their own language. In a variety of forms including essays, dialogues, spoof letters and short stories, he presented, as well as religious meditations, articles on current affairs, new scientific advances, countries overseas, and the social dislocation which many newly urbanized and emigrant Gaels were experiencing. As a Gaelic prose stylist, MacLeod has had a massive influence, though his personal style is by no means monolithic. It can range from the highly aureate in formal and emotional passages to the couthily colloquial in the dialogues, and also includes a lucid and businesslike prose of exposition. In broadening the base of Gaelic prose writing, he was a highly industrious and successful pioneer.

MacLeod supported the cause of Presbyterianism in Ulster (*see* Ireland) by personal visits, and by producing, in collaboration with the Irish scholar Thaddeus Connellan, an Irish version of the metrical psalter,* *Psalma Dhaibhí, Rígh Israel* (L, 1836). The most significant of his Gaelic writings were collected posthumously in the volume *Caraid nan Gaidheal* (G, 1867), edited by his son-in-law Archibald Clerk* and containing a memoir by his son, Norman MacLeod of the Barony,* grandfather of George F. MacLeod.* A further small selection, *The Highlanders' Friend: Second Series* (E, 1901), was edited by George Henderson.

See also Gaelic, Protestant prose publications in.

J. N. MacLeod, *Memorials of the Rev. Norman MacLeod* (E, 1898); *FES* III, 437; *DNB* XXXV, 216–17; Obituary in *Glasgow Herald*, 26 November 1862; C. Ó Baoill, 'Norman MacLeod, Cara na nGael', *SGS* 13 (1981), 159–68.

K. D. MacDonald

MacLeod, Norman (1812–72), distinguished CofS minister. Born in Campbeltown, the son of Norman MacLeod (1783–1862),* he studied arts at Glasgow University and divinity at Edinburgh, where Thomas Chalmers* made an ineradicable impression on him. He was successively minister of Loudoun, Ayrshire (1838–43), Dalkeith near Edinburgh (1843–51) and the Barony Church, Glasgow (1851–72). It was as 'MacLeod of the Barony' that he became, according to Dean A. P. Stanley of Westminster, 'the chief ecclesiastic of the Scottish Church. No other man . . . in all spiritual ministrations so nearly filled the place of Chalmers.' 'By the time of his death few Scottish ministers were better-known or more popular than he' (A. C. Cheyne). He was Queen Victoria's close adviser as chaplain. He made his mark in a remarkable range of activities. A leader of the 'Middle Party' at the Disruption* he remained in the Est.C and sought its revitalization.

As parish minister he came into close contact with urban poverty in the aftermath of industrialization, and strove to evangelize an unchurched working-class population. He became a champion of working men and a social reformer fired by the ignorance and squalor he encountered. At a time when the Churches were often criticized for their inability to communicate the gospel to the poorer sections of society, he held services in the Barony to which only people in working clothes were admitted. In his parish he encouraged the setting up of loan funds and savings banks, the erection of refreshment rooms, the provision of school buildings and the promotion of adult education and literacy.

Nationally his social activism encompassed also other causes, like temperance.* He was a very effective speaker and prominent at General Assemblies throughout his ministerial life. At the 1859 Assembly, for example, he spoke on the revival* of that year as well as on pressing economic and social issues. In 1865-6 he played a decisive and controversial part in defying sabbatarian* resistance to Sunday railway services – a role which reflected a more general departure from Westminster* Calvinism in his teaching and practice, although he always remained 'more of an Evangelical than a Moderate' (A. C. Cheyne).

MacLeod promoted Church extension* and home missions in general, including the London City Mission. Foreign missions* were also a strong commitment; he became convener of the Kirk's India Mission, and in one year (1844) helped to found thirty missionary associations for the support of female education in India.

He was also influential and distinguished as an author (especially of *Reminiscences of a Highland Parish*, L, 1867) and editor. He edited the *Edinburgh Christian Magazine** (1849-60) and also *Good Words** (1860-72), through which he sought to raise the standards of religious journalism.

A man of enormous capacity for work and considerable personal charisma, an outstanding preacher and a tireless proponent of congregational parochial mission, he challenges comparison with Chalmers, even in his political conservatism.

FES III, 394-5; *DNB* XXXV, 217-18; D. MacLeod, *Memoir of Norman MacLeod*, 2 vols (L, 1876); A. C. Cheyne, *The Transforming of the Kirk* (E, 1983), 157-62; J. Wellwood, *Norman MacLeod* (E, 1897).

G. Wareing

MacLeod, Roderick (1795-1868), popular preacher and religious leader in Skye and the Western Isles. The son of Malcolm MacLeod (1761-1832), minister of Snizort and chief of the MacLeods of Raasay, he was a cousin of John McLeod Campbell* and Norman MacLeod* of St Columba's. Licensed in 1818, MacLeod was ordained as Royal Bounty* missionary at Lyndale. In 1823 he became minister of Bracadale, and from 1838 until his death he was minister of Snizort, having spent his entire ministry in his native island.

Having been converted soon after his induction to Bracadale, MacLeod became the leader of Evangelicalism in Skye, which had begun as a lay movement. His uncompromising stand on admission to the sacraments* brought him into dispute with the majority of the members of Skye Presbytery, and from 1824 until shortly before the Disruption* the 'Bracadale Case' regularly came before the General Assembly. He also had strong views on temperance* matters and decidedly disapproved of alcohol and tobacco. In 1843 MacLeod joined the FC, about three quarters of his parishioners following him out of the Est.C. The fact that for many years he was the only FC minister in Skye gained him the title, 'The Bishop of Skye'.

M. MacKay, *Sermon Preached in the Free Church, Snizort, Skye* (E, 1869); D. Gillies, *The Life and Work of the Reverend Roderick MacLeod* (n.d.); D. Beaton, *Some Noted Ministers of the Northern Highlands* (Inverness, 1929); R. MacLeod, 'The Bishop of Skye', *TGSI* 53 (1982-4), 174-209; *FES* VII, 167, 180; *AFCS* I, 250.

R. MacLeod

Macmillan, John (1669-1753), first minister and principal founder of the RPC. Born in Barncaughlaw, near Newton Stewart, Galloway, his boyhood was spent under the shadows of persecution and the Killing Times.* Although his family appears to have adhered to the Est.C, from his youth his sympathies were with the Covenanters.* While a student at Edinburgh University (1695-97) he associated with their Societies, but on graduation (MA, 1697) returned to the CofS, took up theological studies and was subsequently licensed to preach in 1700 by the Presbytery of Kirkcudbright. He served as chaplain to the Laird of Broughton prior to ordination to Balmaghie, Kirkcudbrightshire, in 1701.

The death of William III* in 1702 reopened the question of the spiritual independence of the Church from the state. The Revolution Settlement had omitted any affirmation of the Divine Right of Presbytery* and the continuing obligation of the Covenants (National* and Solemn League*). Macmillan (and others) petitioned Presbytery with a list of 'Grievances' calling for a return to these historic expressions of the Church's spiritual independence. Presbytery was in sympathy with this basic perspective but cautioned against precipitate action. This did not satisfy Macmillan. Wodrow* comments that the 'Grievances' were 'whiggishly aboundantly' and suggests that Macmillan could 'desire noe more in reason' from the Presbytery (*Early Letters* . . . , SHS, E, 1937, 281). The discussion thereafter moved from agreed doctrine to disagreeable disputatiousness, and issued in the 'irregular and unjust' deposing of Macmillan (Reid), on 30 December 1703. Such was the devotion of his parishioners that he continued to preach unhindered in the church until 1715 and to occupy the manse until 1727.

Macmillan meanwhile renewed his association with the Covenanting Societies and on 9 October 1706 accepted a call to be their minister – their first since the martyrdom of James Renwick* (1688) and the defection of William Boyd, Thomas Lining and Alexander Shields* (1689). The 1707 Union* and the 1711 restoration of patronage* in the CofS confirmed him in his Covenanting principles: they were 'fresh instances of the apostacy of the nation' (*RP Testimony* [historical part], 201). The Covenants were renewed at Auchensaugh in 1712. Macmillan ministered tirelessly and with evident effectiveness to a scattered community of some 10,000 people. Worship was conducted in homes, barns and in the open air – there were no church buildings until well after his time. For thirty-seven years he was the only minister, but with the accession of Thomas Nairn* in 1743, the Reformed Presbytery was formed and an organized church took shape. He died at Broomhill, Lanarkshire.

More than any other single individual, Macmillan gave form and direction to the RP movement, including a Presbyterian structure and missionary plan which would in the course of time plant sister RP Churches in Ireland, the USA, Canada, Australia and Japan.

His son by his third wife, Grace Russell (his earlier wives bore no children), John Macmillan *secundus* (1729–1808), succeeded him in the RPC ministry, and his daughter Grizel married John Thorburn, RPC minister of Loanhead.

His published works are few. The *True Narrative of the case in the Presbytery* (n.p., 1704) is anonymous but almost certainly his. Other pieces include *Protestation, Declinature and Appeal* (n.p., 1708) and a poem, *An Elegy upon ... Mrs Mary Gordon* (E, 1723).

FES II, 392–3; *DNB* XXXV, 231–3; W. J. Couper, 'The Reformed Presbyterian Church in Scotland', *RSCHS* 2 (1925), 77–8; J. Robb (ed.), *Cameronian Fasti* (privately, E, 1975), 20; *AGACS*, esp. 332–3, 506; H. M. B. Reid, *A Cameronian Apostle* (Paisley, 1896); M. Hutchison, *The Reformed Presbyterian Church in Scotland, 1680–1876* (Paisley, 1893).

G. J. Keddie

MacMinn, Robert Donald (1870–1956), UFC and later CofS missionary. Born in Dalquharran, Dailly, in Ayrshire, MacMinn was appointed a FC lay missionary to Livingstonia, Nyasaland, in 1893. He adhered to the UFC in the union of 1900, and was ordained by the Presbytery of Livingstonia in 1906. He worked in a variety of locations in the Nyasa region, including Bandawe, Kasun, Loudoun, Ekwendeni, Mwenzo, Overtown Institution, and Labwa. He translated two-thirds of the New Testament into Tonga, a quarter into Tumbuka, and a number of theological and devotional writings into these languages and Bemba. He also compiled a Bemba hymnbook (Livingstonia, 1915).

MacMinn retired from missionary work in 1934.

FUFCS 563; *FES* IX, 740.

N. R. Needham

MacMurray, John (1891–1976), philosopher. Born in Maxwellton, Kirkcudbrightshire, MacMurray was educated in Aberdeen, Glasgow and Balliol College, Oxford. After war service for which he was awarded the Military Cross, he was John Locke lecturer in Mental Philosophy, Oxford University (1919). Following periods as lecturer at the University of Manchester (1919) and Professor at the University of Witswatersrand (1921) he became a Fellow of Balliol College, until 1928. In that year he was appointed Grote Professor of Mind and Logic at the University of London, holding the post until 1944, when he was elected to the Chair of Moral Philosophy at the University of Edinburgh, which he held until his retirement in 1958.

He was Gifford Lecturer* in 1953–4. The lectures were published (under the general title *The Form of the Personal*) as *The Self as Agent* (L, 1957) and *Persons in Relation* (L, 1961). He was a voluminous writer both of books and of papers, chiefly on the relation between science and religion, religious experience, and various studies of Communism. He was also an effective broadcaster in the years before World War II.

As the title of his Gifford Lectures reveals, MacMurray's philosophy centred upon the importance of interpersonal relations, particularly in love and in the sense of community.

MacMurray was influential as a lecturer and educator but his philosophical influence was rapidly eclipsed by the rise of analytic philosophy.

Interpreting the Universe (L, 1933); *Reason and Emotion* (L, 1935); *The Structure of Religious Experience* (L, 1936); *Challenge to the Churches* (L, 1941); *Science, Art and Religion* (Liverpool, 1961); *The Search for Reality in Religion* (L, 1965).

Who Was Who, 1971–80, 506.

P. Helm

McNeill, John (1854–1933), prominent Scots pastor-evangelist. Born the son of a pious FC quarryman at Houston (West of Glasgow) in 1857, McNeill underwent conversion in his late teens while working as a railway clerk in Greenock. This employment proved his training ground in dealing with common people. Having begun preaching with the YMCA,* he was encouraged to take arts and divinity only at age twenty-three. Continuing mission work with the FC during these studies, he graduated from the Glasgow FC College in 1886 an already-proven preacher and missioner, enjoying the highest approbation of his professors. Ordained in that year as minister of Edinburgh's McCrie-Roxburgh FC, he was translated, a successful evangelistic preacher, to London's Regent Square Church in 1889. He resigned in 1891, and from 1892 an itinerant* evangelistic ministry was commenced, initially in conjunction with D. L. Moody's* Scottish campaign* and later on four continents. This itineration came to a sudden halt in 1908 at the death of Lord Overtoun (*see* White, John Campbell), his major sponsor. British and North American pastorates bracketed an effective evangelistic ministry to troops during World War I. McNeill's stalwart evangelical convictions had been formulated prior to his college days with the help of the Westminster Shorter Catechism* and Charles Hodge's *Systematic Theology*, and were winsomely expounded in common dress.

From the 1890s he was in practice a freelance independent, under no Church's jurisdiction.

A. Gammie, *Rev. John McNeill* (L, 1934); *Regent Square Pulpit*, 3 vols (L, 1889–91); *Who Was Who, 1929–1940*, 883; *BW* 94 (27 Apr. 1933), 71; *AFCS* I, 254.

K. J. Stewart

MacNicol, Nicol (1870–1952), perhaps the leading scholar on Indian religion among Scottish missionaries in the first half of the twentieth century. Only J. N. Farquhar* could rival his knowledge and insight. After studying at Glasgow University and FC College, he was ordained in the FC in 1895. He served in Western India, first in Bombay and then in Poona, from 1895 to 1931, a period when the region was in the turmoil of far-reaching social, political and religious changes. Poona was a particularly lively intellectual centre and MacNicol was quickly recognized as a sympathetic scholar who valued the Hindu heritage but was also an honest and intelligent critic. He had many close friends among the Brahman intelligentsia and was in close touch with many of the new political and religious movements. He also had an unrivalled knowledge of the popular Hinduism of the villages. His *Indian Theism* (L, 1915) is a still valuable survey of the varieties of Hindu theistic belief, together with a critical assessment in which Christian faith is used as the standard and the ultimate judgement is that 'The faith of which [the Lord Jesus Christ] is the centre confirms the intuitions, and crowns the longings of the long centuries of Indian Theistic aspiration'. He thus stands shoulder to shoulder with J. N. Farquhar, whose *The Crown of Hinduism* had been published two years earlier. MacNicol's role as a sympathetic interpreter of Hinduism to Christianity and of Christianity to Hinduism was also shown in his numerous other writings, particularly his translation of *Psalms of Maratha Saints* (Calcutta, 1915), his life of the remarkable convert *Pandita Ramabai* (Calcutta, 1926), and his call in *The Making of Modern India* (L, 1924) for government to be more responsive to popular demands and aspirations. Glasgow made him a DLitt (1911) and DD (1928). He retired in 1931.

AFCS I, 254; *FUFCS* 539; *FES* IX, 741; *Who Was Who, 1951–1960*, 719; *LW* n.s. 76 (Apr. 1952), 76.

D. B. Forrester

Macphail, Alexandrina Matilda (1860–1946), first female medical missionary of the FC. Born in Skye, she studied at the London School of Medicine for Women (before Scottish universities would accept female students) and gained her triple qualification in 1887. She arrived in Madras in March 1888 to begin work among children, and women who would not allow male doctors to see or treat them. Macphail began to practise from the FC's existing dispensary, which was handed over to the Ladies Association. In 1891, she opened a twelve-bedded women's hospital in her own bungalow. In 1914, the purpose-built Christina Rainy Hospital was opened. Her main work was as its supervisor, but she also helped found the Union Mission Tuberculosis Sanatorium. Macphail was particularly concerned that Indian women should train and qualify as physicians, and she taught at the Medical School for Women at Vellore. During the First World War, she worked with Scottish Women's Hospitals as Chief Medical Officer of a unit for Serbian refugees.

Matilda Macphail was awarded the Kaiser-i-Hind Medal for services to India in 1912, with bar in 1918. She retired in 1929, and was awarded the OBE in 1930.

Of this greatly loved and admired pioneer medical missionary, Principal Meston of Madras Christian College wrote, 'Her care for those whom she attended was without bound ... Government doctors have spoken with glowing admiration of her marvellous powers ... Time and again Dr Macphail has been consulted by the Government ... In every endeavour to promote the medical education of women, she has taken an important part ... She has done a day's work which the most energetic of us might envy, and has used a great opportunity to magnificent purpose. In her there is a spirit which time and place do not bound' (*MRUFCS*, February 1929).

G. Pittendrigh and W. Meston, *Story of Our Madras Mission* (E, 1907).

L. O. Macdonald

MacPhail, Hector (1716–74), CofS minister. Born at Inverness, educated at King's College, Aberdeen, and licensed by the Presbytery of Inverness in 1746, MacPhail was ordained to the parish of Resolis (Black Isle) in 1748. He was married to a daughter of John Balfour, of Nigg, Easter Ross, who once had to return to her father's parish for spiritual sustenance because of the barrenness of her husband's preaching. Shamed by this, MacPhail wished to leave the ministry, but, through the preaching of James Fraser* of Alness, Ross-shire, who had come to intimate his resignation from his charge, he experienced evangelical conversion. Thereafter he was esteemed for his pastoral care and for the power of his preaching, although he sometimes found great difficulty in preparation. His ministry was mainly one of edification. He was among those who knew 'the secret of the Lord', and once acted on premonition to save a woman from suicide. On his death-bed, he had a beatific vision of the New Jerusalem.

FES VII, 19; J. Kennedy, *The Days of the Fathers in Ross-shire* (Inverness, ⁵1895); D. Beaton, *Some Noted Ministers of the Northern Highlands* (Inverness, 1929), 102–8.

D. E. Meek

MacPhail, James Merry (1863–1929), an ordained medical missionary in India. Born at Shaftesbury, Dorset, MacPhail was educated in Glasgow, and graduated from Glasgow University (MA, 1885; MB, CM, 1889; MD, 1906). After training at Glasgow FC College, he was appointed to Santalia in 1889, and ordained by the Presbytery of Calcutta in 1890. He pioneered medical work in Santalia (a tribal area in the modern Indian state of Bihar) with his headquarters at what became a great, if simple, eye hospital at Bamdah. Here from the 1890s a remarkably large number of eye operations were performed at extraordinarily low cost — in 1900 it was calculated that a cataract operation cost sixteen pence (see his *Eyes Right*, Calcutta, 1912). MacPhail was a committed evangelist, both in his hospital and as he moved around the villages. His work at Bamdah was continued by one of his sons; another, James Russell MacPhail,* became the Principal of Madras Christian College.

AFCS I, 255; *FUFCS*, 537–8.

D. B. Forrester

MacPhail, James Russell (1901–68), an educational missionary of the UFC and later the CofS, who served at Madras Christian College as lecturer and Professor in English Literature (1924–68) and, for a short time, as Principal. Born in Glasgow, MacPhail was educated at Glasgow University (MA, 1922) and ordained by the UF Presbytery of Edinburgh in 1928. The son of J. M. MacPhail,* he was a remarkable teacher who influenced deeply several generations of students and taught them a love for literature and a reverence for scholarship. He made a major contribution to the Church of South India through his convenership of the Liturgy Committee when *The Book of Common Worship* and its Supplement were being produced. His scholarly love of the Bible was shown particularly in his *The Way, the Truth and the Life* (L, 1954), *The Bright Cloud* (L, 1956) and his *Commentary on Matthew* (Madras, 1956), but above all in his splendid *Notes on the Daily Bible Readings of the Church of South India* (Madras, 1961). Parts of a large projected work *King and Teacher* appeared posthumously (Madras, 1976, 1977).

FUFCS, 543; *FES* IX, 741, X, 422.

D. B. Forrester

MacPhail's Edinburgh Ecclesiastical Journal (1846–63), see Periodicals, Religious.

MacPherson, John (1847–1902), FC minister, writer and translator of German theology. Born at Greenock, Renfrewshire, he attended Glasgow University (MA, 1867) and the Glasgow FC College. Licensed by Elgin Presbytery in 1871, he was assistant at Paisley St George's, Whithorn, in Wigtownshire, and then took charge of FC preaching stations at Carnwath, Lanarkshire, and Airth, Stirlingshire, before being ordained in 1878 as minister of Findhorn FC, Moray. He retired in 1900, and entered the UFC.

MacPherson was thoroughly familiar with the German theology of his century, and translated many volumes into English for T. and T. Clark (see bibliography; *see* Publishing, Religious). His own theology, set out in his *Christian Dogmatics* (E, 1898), was an Amyraldian (*see* Cameron, John) type of Reformed theology, defending the doctrines of total depravity, unconditional election and substitutionary atonement. He propounded a realist view of the relation between Adam and mankind, and held that the sources of Christian doctrine were (in descending order) Scripture, the ecumenical creeds and the Christian consciousness.

His *Doctrine of the Church in Scottish Theology* (Chalmers Lectures,* E, 1903) is still the standard work on the subject and his edition of the Westminster Confession (Handbooks for Bible Classes, E, 1881) was frequently reprinted well into the twentieth century.

A History of the Church in Scotland (Paisley, 1901); *The Sum of Saving Knowledge* (E, 1886). As translator: E. Schurer, *A History of the Jewish People in the Time of Jesus Christ* (6 vols, E, 1885–91); F. P. W. Buhl, *Canon and Text of the Old Testament* (E, 1892); J. H. Kurtz, *Church History* (3 vols, E, 1888–90); J. H. A. Ebrard, *Apologetics* (3 vols, E, 1886–8); J. F. Rabiger, *Encyclopaedia of Theology* (2 vols, E, 1884–5).

AFCS I, 256; *FUFCS* 470.

N. R. Needham

MacPherson, Paul (1756–1846), Rector of the Scots College, Rome. Born in Glenlivet, he was educated at Scalan (*see* Colleges and Seminaries, RC) 1767–9, and the Scots Colleges* at Rome, 1770–7, and Valladolid 1777–9.

Ordained priest, MacPherson served at Shenval, Banffshire, 1779–80; Aberdeen, 1780–3; Stobhall, Perthshire, 1783–91; and as Mission procurator at Edinburgh, 1791–3. In 1793 he was sent to Rome as Scots Agent, staying there until the French occupation. In 1798 he travelled home through France, bringing to safety the Scots, English and Irish students and valuable Scottish RC records from Rome and Paris. In 1800 he returned to Rome as Agent and was the first Scottish secular rector of the Scots College. Forced to leave again in 1811, he returned in 1812, taking part *en route* in the British plan to rescue the Pope. Having recovered and reopened the College, he continued as rector until 1827, when he returned to Scotland and founded the mission of Chapeltown, Glenlivet. In 1834, the College being again in a ruinous state and without a rector, he returned to Rome and remained as rector until his death. MacPherson's continuation of John Thomson's History of the RCC in Scotland has remained in manuscript.

D. McRoberts, *Abbé Paul MacPherson, 1756–1846*, (E, 1946); J. F. S. Gordon, *The Catholic Church in Scotland* (A, 1874), 341–446, 595–601.

C. Johnson

Macrae, David (1837–1907), UP heretic, journalist and Scottish nationalist. Born in Lathrones, Fife, he studied at Glasgow University and the UP Hall, and was minister of the UP Church in Gourock (1872–9). There he was an acerbic agitator in the campaign to alter the UPC's commitment to Westminster* orthodoxy, a campaign which led to the UP Declaratory Act of 1879 (*see* Declaratory Acts; Subscription, Confessional). However, Macrae's assertion in the course of debate, that the notion of everlasting torment of sinners was incompatible with the character of God and the teaching of Scripture, led to an investigation of his views. Also of concern was his strident demand for freedom to preach the options of conditional immortality and/or universal restoration. His position was judged (by a Synod majority of 288 to 29) to be incompatible with the Standards, and in excess of the amount of liberty intended by the fledgling Act. Following his removal from the UP ministry, he pastored the independent Gilfillan Memorial Church in Dundee (1879–97). His works include *The Americans at Home*, 2 vols (E, 1870), didactic novels *George Harrington* (G, 1863) and *Dunvarlich* (L, 1865), and a collection of ecclesiastical satires, *Diogenes Among the D.D.s* (1867; ^{2}G, 1883).

G. Eyre Todd, intro. to *Dunvarlich* (G, 1909); UPC, *Report of Committee Appointed to Deal with Rev. D. Macrae* (1879); Obituary, *Glasgow Herald*, 16 May, 1907, 7; R. Small II, 203–5; J. R. Fleming, *A History of the Church in Scotland 1843–1874* (E, 1927).

G. G. Scorgie

MacRae, John (1794–1876), Gaelic* preacher and Highland Disruption* leader. A native of Kintail, Ross-shire, he was for some time parish schoolmaster of Uig, Lewis, at the time the powerful religious revival* was at its height. Licensed as a preacher in 1830, he was assistant at Gairloch before becoming minister at Cross, Lewis, in 1830. From 1839 to 1849 he was minister of Knockbain, the parish with which his name is usually associated. His other ministries were the Gaelic Church, Greenock (1849–57), Lochs in Lewis (1857–66), and Carloway, Lewis, to which he transferred in 1866, retiring through ill-health in 1871.

MacRae, an effective orator, was one of the preachers chosen to tour the Highlands* before and after the Disruption, explaining the issues at stake. One of the outstanding Gaelic preachers of the period, his telling use of illustrative material meant that his sermons were remembered long after the service. In 1843 he led his congregation at Knockbain into the Free Church.* In Gaelic he is known as *MacRath Mòr* ('Big MacRae').

N. Nicolson, *An t-Urramach Iain MacRath* (G, 1939), containing biography and sermons of MacRae; G. N. M. Collins, *Big Macrae* (E, 1976); J. Greig (ed.), *Disruption Worthies of the Highlands* (E, 1877), 115–26.

R. MacLeod

MacRae, Kenneth Alexander (1883–1964), minister of the FC.* Born in Dingwall, Ross-shire, he was brought up in Edinburgh, where he entered the civil service. Converted under FC preaching in 1909, he joined that denomination and began studying for the ministry. He took his university arts and college divinity courses concurrently and was ordained in 1915. After pastorates at Lochgilphead, Argyll (1915–19) and Kilmuir, Skye (1919–31), he was called to the largest congregation of the FC, at Stornoway in the Isle of Lewis, where he exercised a powerful ministry for thirty-three years.

As a gifted preacher, he was in great demand throughout the FC. He strongly resisted all attempts to water down the Reformed* testimony of the Church and the spiritual heritage of Scotland, and was no stranger to controversy. Record of his life and ministry is preserved in his *Diary*, ed. I. H. Murray (E, 1980).

J. J. Murray

MacVicar, Neil (1871–1949), medical missionary. He was born in the manse of Manor, Peebleshire. While apprenticed to a law firm in Peebles he studied at night for entrance to Edinburgh University, where he graduated MB, ChB in 1893, the outstanding student of his year. In 1895 he went as medical officer to the Blantyre Mission, Malawi. There he was profoundly influenced by D. C. Scott* but after a disagreement with Scott's successor, Alexander Hetherwick,* he severed his connection with the mission in 1901.

James Stewart,* who had earlier met him on board ship, persuaded the FC to appoint him as medical superintendent of Stewart's new hospital at Lovedale in the Cape Colony. He spent the rest of his life in South Africa as a doctor, medical administrator and evangelist, this latter despite views deemed by some at the turn of the century to be less than orthodox.

He was the first person to train African nurses to qualify for state registration; for more than twenty years only at Lovedale could African women could receive such training. His early research work (*Tuberculosis Among the South African Bantu*, Cape Town, 1908) revolutionized the understanding of tuberculosis among Africans in South Africa and earned him the MD from Edinburgh, 1908. His later work on scurvy among African miners led to a transformation of the mine compounds on the Rand.

Above all he saw his role both as physician and Christian as the promotion of health. To the end of his life, he used his brilliant talents as a propagandist to encourage a healthier way of life both for Africans and the many poor whites in South Africa. In recognition of his achievements in this area, Witwatersrand University granted him the LLD in 1945.

Life and Work in British Central Africa (Blantyre), 1899–1901; *South African Outlook* (Lovedale, etc.), 1922–49; R. H. W. Shepherd, *A South African Medical Pioneer* (Lovedale, 1952).

A. C. Ross

MacWard, Robert (*d*.1681), CofS minister in Glasgow and Rotterdam. (Spellings of his name included M'Cuard and M'Vaird.) Born in Glenluce (Galloway), he studied at St Andrews where he was a favourite of Samuel Rutherford.* When Rutherford went to London as a Commissioner to the Westminster Assembly,* MacWard accompanied him as an amanuensis. After serving as a regent, first in St Andrews and then in Glasgow College in 1654, he was ordained to the Outer High Church in Glasgow in 1656, succeeding Andrew Gray.* As a protégé of Rutherford, MacWard was a zealous Protester* and was called to both Glasgow positions over Robert Baillie's* objections (*Letters and Journals*, E, 1842, III, 240-1, 285, 314). In 1661 he preached against an overturning of the Covenanted Reformation by Parliament, entering a protest in heaven that he desired to be free from the guilt thereof (Robert Wodrow, *The History of the Sufferings of the Church of Scotland*, G, 1828, I, 206ff.). He was imprisoned 'for sedition and treasonable preaching' and banished from the kingdom. Shortly afterward he left for Holland where he spent the rest of his life.

In Rotterdam MacWard collected and edited Rutherford's letters (*Joshua Redivivus, or Mr Rutherfoord's Letters*, 1664). Moving to Utrecht, he helped with the editing and publication of Rutherford's *Examen Arminianismi* (Utrecht, 1668). He kept himself acquainted with the situation in Scotland and wrote several tracts to encourage resistance to those whom he believed were usurpers of power in the CofS (*A Collection of Tracts*, Dalry, 1805). He asserted that it was not, as then constituted, 'of the *genus* Church at all, – that, by its mere physical force-raid on the real Church of Scotland, it has proved itself to be absolutely devoid of ecclesiastical rights' (J. Walker, *The Theology and Theologians of Scotland*, E, ²1888, 106; see *The true Non-Conformist*, n.p., 1671).

Such publications rendered MacWard, with his close friend, John Brown of Wamphray,* odious to the regime of Charles II,* and diligent efforts were made to have him expelled from Holland. He was forced to leave Rotterdam in 1677 only a year after having been called as second minister of the Scots Kirk* there. He returned, however, to Rotterdam in 1678 and remained there until his death.

He continued zealous against the Indulgences,* opposing the efforts of Robert Fleming, his successor, at conciliation (see *Epagōnismoi: or, Earnest Contendings for the Faith*, n.p. 1723). Wodrow characterized him as 'a person of great knowledge, zeal, learning, and remarkable ministerial abilities'.

FES III, 465; VII, 550; DNB XXXV, 286-7; W. Steven, *The History of the Scottish Church, Rotterdam* (E, 1832).

D. C. Lachman

Maelrubha, *see* Celtic Saints.

Magdalen Chapel, Edinburgh. The small chapel in Edinburgh Cowgate, 33 feet by 20 feet, was built for an almshouse about 1544, with money left by Michael McQuen and given by his widow, Janet Wynd, whose tomb is there. Put under care of the Hammermen's Incorporation in the early seventeenth century, the chapel became the Hammermen's Hall; the tower was built and other buildings were removed. The building is barrel-roofed and one window has roundels with the only pre-Reformation glass in Scotland.

It may have been used for the first General Assembly* in 1560 and was a meeting-place for Presbyterians before 1689 and Episcopalians afterwards. It is owned by the Protestant Institute of Scotland (*see* Scottish Reformation Society). From 1966 it was briefly used as a chapel by Heriot Watt University.

T. Ross, *Trans. of Scott. Ecclesiological Soc.* 4:1 (1913), 95-101; T. Ross and G. Baldwin Brown, 'The Magdalen Chapel...', *Book of the Old Edinburgh Club* 8 (1916), 1-78; J. Gifford *et al.*, *Edinburgh* (Buildings of Scotland; Harmondsworth, 1984), 163-6.

A. I. Dunlop

Magnus, Saint (*d.c.*1117), son of Jarl (i.e. Earl) Erlend of Orkney,* venerated after his death as a saint and martyr*. In fact, little is known of his life. His father had been joint jarl with his brother Paul or Pål, and *c.*1107 the earldom was divided between Magnus Erlendsson and Håkon Pålsson. According to the sagas, Håkon was aggressive and ambitious, while Magnus was mild and peace-loving, to the point of refusing to fight against men with whom he had no quarrel during King Magnus Barelegs' expedition to the Western Isles *c.*1098. A quarrel arose between the two cousins and joint jarls *c.*1117, prompted by Håkon's ambition and jealousy of Magnus's popularity; and in spite of his offers to undergo exile, imprisonment, or even mutilation, Magnus was murdered on the island of Egilsay by Håkon's men. His claim to the earldom was inherited by his sister's son Rognvald,* who built the great Cathedral at Kirkwall in his honour and translated his relics (about which miraculous stories had begun to develop) there from Christ's Church at Birsay *c.*1137. St Magnus Cathedral stands as one of the finest Romanesque/Gothic churches in northern Europe. The remains of St Magnus and Rognvald were uncovered in the Cathedral in 1926.

Orkneyinga Saga (various editions); J. S. Clouston, *A History of Orkney* (Kirkwall, 1932); *DNB Miss. Pers.* 439-40.

A. Macquarrie

Mair, Thomas (1701-68), General Associate Synod* divine. The son of George Mair of Culross, he was educated at Edinburgh University, licensed by the Presbytery of Kincardine O'Neil in 1722, and ordained to the charge of Orwell, Kinross, in 1725. Mair was a strong supporter of the 1733 seceders, but remained for several years in the CofS in the hope of reformation and reconciliation. By 1737 he had despaired and himself joined the Associate Presbytery.* The CofS General Assembly deposed him in 1740. A large congregation gathered round Mair and a new church was built.

In 1747 Mair took a leading part on the Antiburgher side in the controversy within the secession over the Burgess Oath;* he read the Antiburgher protest at the Associate Synod* and led the walkout which resulted in the formation of the General Associate Synod.

Mair, however, is best remembered for his own deposition from the General Associate Synod a decade later. This was precipitated by controversy over *A Treatise on Justifying Faith* (E, 1749) attributed to James Fraser of Brea.* The treatise taught a doctrine of universal atonement*, with the qualification that this was only intended to bring 'gospel wrath' on the non-elect for their rejection of it. The General Associate Synod condemned the work in 1754. Mair protested. His father had been Fraser's ministerial colleague, and Mair himself when a boy had written out a copy of Fraser's now published manuscript at his father's bidding. Mair argued before the Synod that 'in some sense Christ died for all mankind', thus purchasing 'the elect as his bride, and the rest of the world as his tools, for the glory of God and the good of the elect'. Pressed by the Synod to specify in what exact sense Christ died for all, Mair tended to repeat in a variety of phraseology that 'in some sense' Christ died for all, and that without this universal reference there was no basis for a universal gospel offer. He was eventually deposed in 1757. His congregation adhered to him, and after his death it joined the Associate Synod.

A Covenant of Duties no wise Inconsistent with a Covenant of Grace (E, 1768); *The Warrantableness of the Associate Synod's Sentence, Concerning the Religious Clause of some Burgess Oaths, Proved* (E, 1747); *Reasons of Dissent from the Act of the Associate Synod 1754* (E, 1756); *The Case Laid Open* (E, 1764).

Small, I, 373–5; J. M'Kerrow, *History of the Secession Church* (G, 1841), 260–6; *Proceedings of the Associate Synod at Edinburgh concerning Thomas Mair* (E, 1755); FES V, 71–2.

N. R. Needham

Mair, William (1830–1920), CofS minister, writer on church law and proponent of Church union. Mair was born at Savoch, Aberdeenshire, eldest son and fifth child of James Mair, the parochial schoolmaster. He was educated at Aberdeen Grammar School and at King's College and Marischal College, Aberdeen, graduating from the latter in 1849. Owing to ill-health which dogged him all his life, he did not take up his first minsterial charge (Lochgelly, Fife) until 1861, moving to Ardoch in 1864, and to Earlston, Berwickshire in 1869, from which he retired to Edinburgh in 1903. He was Moderator of the General Assembly in 1897.

Obituaries indicate that theologically Mair was a staunch traditionalist, simple, evangelical and direct in his preaching, and able to communicate with all sorts and conditions of men. His autobiography substantiates these statements. The obituaries all stress Mair's importance in pressing forward the cause of Church union, particularly that with the UFC (*see* Unions, Church, in Scotland). Much was effected through committee work, correspondence and persuasion. His role as an ecclesiastical lawyer now bulks larger. Mair was fascinated by Church law. He was adept at deploying and using it, as well as skilled in systematizing and explaining it. His *Digest of Church Laws*, went to four editions (E, 1887, 1895, 1904, 1912, with Supp. 1923) and quickly replaced the obsolete *Styles of Writs* by John Cook.* Mair's *Digest* collects its material from General Assembly Acts and cases, as well as from relevant civil law sources. As the authoritative text for the practice and law of the CofS prior to the 1929 Union it was a major source of *Practice and Procedure in the Church of Scotland* edited by J. T. Cox* (E, 1934), the sixth edition of which (E, 1976) still contains passages from Mair's first edition. Indeed, it is arguable that technically Mair's was the better law book; Cox does not generally refer to source material other than the Acts of Assembly.

W. Mair, *My Life* (L, 1911); FES II, 150–1.

F. Lyall

Maitland, (Sir) John (c.1545–95), first Lord Thirlstane, Chancellor of Scotland. He was the son of a Court of Session judge and the younger brother of William Maitland* of Lethington. After a legal training at the University of St Andrews and in France, Maitland's political career began with his appointment as Keeper of the Privy Seal in 1567 and as an extra-ordinary judge on the Court of Session in 1568. However, Maitland sided with the Queen's Party during the civil war of 1567–73 (*see* Mary Queen of Scots), and following its defeat was deprived of office.

The fall of James Douglas,* fourth Earl of Morton, in 1580 marked the beginning of Maitland's political rehabilitation under James VI.* In 1581 he was made an ordinary judge of the Court of Session, a privy councillor in 1583, he was knighted and appointed Secretary of State in 1584, Vice-Chancellor in 1586, was promoted to the Chancellorship itself in 1587, and was created Lord Thirlstane in 1590.

While Secretary, Maitland oversaw the negotiation of the Protestant League* with England in 1586. As Chancellor, he strove to increase royal authority, but his efforts were frustrated by intense feuding which left him politically vulnerable, and after 1592 his influence declined. Although a committed Protestant and not unsympathetic to the Presbyterians, Maitland was distrusted by the latter because of his early associations with Mary and with the Erastian* policies of the Arran government (*see* Black Acts).

M. Lee, *John Maitland of Thirlstane* (P. 1959); DNB XXXIV, 357–60; J. B. Paul (ed.), *The Scots Peerage* (E, 1904–14), V, 298–301.

K. M. Brown

Maitland, John (1616–82), second Earl and first Duke of Lauderdale, Secretary of State. Educated at the University of St Andrews, Lauderdale succeeded his father in 1645. He was an enthusiastic Covenanter,* helping to draft the Solemn League and Covenant,* attending the Westminster Assembly* as a lay commissioner, and sitting on the Committee of Both Kingdoms. However, he remained a Royalist and in 1647 negotiated the Engagement* with the imprisoned Charles I.* Thereafter he worked for the Royalist cause, but was captured at the Battle of Worcester and was imprisoned 1651–60.

At the Restoration* Charles II* appointed Lauderdale as his Scottish Secretary of State. He

MAITLAND, WILLIAM

lamely opposed the reimposition of an Erastian episcopacy, and tried unsuccessfully to moderate the Crown's policy towards Presbyterians. However, after the Pentland Rising of 1666 he was able to persuade the King to seek conciliation through the indulgences* of 1669 and 1672. These failed to secure peace, and Lauderdale embarked on more repressive measures, most notably the use of the 'Highland Host' in 1678.

This fuelled allegations of despotism from enemies in Scotland and in England, where the disintegration of the Cabal in 1673 had left him more vulnerable. His personal influence with the King was already in decline when the assassination of Archbishop Sharp* and the Covenanters' rebellion of 1679 discredited him, although he did not resign office until 1680.

W. C. Mackenzie, *The Life and Times of John Maitland, Duke of Lauderdale, 1616–1682* (L, 1923); J. Buckroyd, *Church and State in Scotland 1660–1681* (E, 1980); I. B. Cowan, *The Scottish Covenanters 1660–88* (L, 1976); M. Lee, *The Cabal* (Urbana, IL, 1965); *DNB* XXXV, 360–7.

K. M. Brown

Maitland, William, of Lethington (*c.* 1528–73), Secretary of State to Mary of Guise* and Mary, Queen of Scots.* His father was a judge of the Court of Session,* and at the University of St Andrews and on the continent he too was trained for a legal career.

From 1554 Maitland was in the employ of the Regent Guise, and was appointed Secretary of State in December 1558. Although sympathetic to Protestantism by 1556, Lethington did not join the Lords of the Congregation* until October 1559. Motivated largely by Francophobia, he became a committed Anglophile and negotiated the treaties of Berwick (27 February 1560) and Edinburgh (6 July 1560) which ensured English military assistance for the Protestants and a French withdrawal from Scotland (*see* Reformation).

After Queen Mary's return to Scotland in July 1561, Maitland continued in office and was appointed an extra-ordinary Lord of Session. Central to the policy devised by himself and James Stewart (*d.* 1570),* Earl of Moray, was peace with England as a prelude to persuading Elizabeth I* to recognize Mary as her heir. Maitland also led the negotiations for Mary's marriage to Don Carlos of Spain and then Robert Dudley, Elizabeth I's favourite. However, his pro-English policy was wrecked by Mary's marriage to Henry, Lord Darnley in July 1565, which infuriated Queen Elizabeth.

Maitland did not actively oppose Mary, and refused to join Moray when he rebelled in the autumn of 1565. But he was involved in devising the murder of David Rizzio in March 1566, and suffered a temporary loss of favour when Darnley revealed his part to the Queen. By the end of 1566 he was advising Mary to divorce Darnley, and he appears to have had some part in the plot which resulted in Darnley's murder on 8 February 1567. Maitland was not happy with Mary's marriage to

MAJOR (MAIR), JOHN

the Earl of Bothwell in May 1567, but he did not desert her until a week before her capture at Carberry on 15 June.

After Bothwell had fled abroad Maitland worked unsuccessfully to reconcile the Queen and her enemies. Even after her precipitate flight to England in May 1568 he hoped to arrange some accommodation acceptable to all parties. Behind this lay his desire to return to the situation before the Darnley marriage, and an adherence to legitimist principles. His sympathy for Mary eventually estranged him from the King's Party, and by the summer of 1570 he had openly committed himself to Mary's cause. On 1 April 1571 he retired to Edinburgh Castle in ill-health, and almost perversely refused to make peace with the Regent Morton (*see* Douglas, James). Deserted by most of his allies, he surrendered on 29 May 1573 following an English bombardment of the castle, and only escaped execution by dying or committing suicide on 9 June.

E. Russell, *Maitland of Lethington* (L, 1912); J. Skelton, *Maitland of Lethington and the Scotland of Mary Stuart*, 2 vols (E, 1887–8); *DNB* XXXV, 377–83; M. Lee, *John Maitland of Thirlstane* (Perth, 1959), 23–35; W. Blake, *William Maitland of Lethington, 1528–1573* (Lewiston, NY, 1990); M. Loughlin, 'The Career of Maitland of Lethington ... ' (PhD, Edinburgh University, 1991).

K. M. Brown

Major (Mair), John (*c.* 1467–1550), Professor of Theology at Paris, Principal of Glasgow University. Provost of St Salvator's College, St Andrews, colleague of Erasmus and teacher of John Knox.* Born at Gleghornie in East Lothian, he was educated, in preparation for the priesthood, at Haddington Grammar School, Christ's College ('God's House'), Cambridge, and the Colleges of Ste Barbe and Montaigu in Paris, where on graduating in 1495 he was appointed to teach scholastic philosophy. He studied theology under Jean Standonck, began to lecture on theology at Paris in 1499, and gained a DD by 1506. At Paris, he published at least forty-six separate editions of works in philosophy and theology. Returning home in 1518 to become Principal at Glasgow and teach divinity, Major produced a commentary on Matthew's Gospel, which he dedicated to his patron, Archbishop James Beaton,* whom he commended for opposing Lutheran heresy. Condemning the eucharistic doctrines of Wyclif, Luther, Oecolampadius and Zwingli, Major affirmed that transubstantiation was the doctrine of Scripture and the early fathers of the Church. While admitting the need for reform of the religious houses, he also defended the monastic life and clerical celibacy.

Although he attacked Luther's followers as a 'pestiferous sect', Major was a strong opponent of papal monarchy, favoured conciliarism,* subordinating the papacy to the authority of a general council, and attacked ecclesiastical abuses including indulgences, pluralism and non-residence. In repudiating papal supremacy, Major also helped to revive the debate on the location of political power in the commonwealth. A nominalist in philosophy, he borrowed from Ockham's theory on ecclesiastical and secular power. Insisting that 'kings were in no way subject to the Roman pontiff in temporal affairs', Major argued in favour of popular sovereignty: kings owed their authority to the people who had originally set them up; they were dependent on the people; and they might be rightfully deposed if they betrayed their trust. These views discussed at length in several of his writings also permeate his *Historia Maioris Britanniae* (Paris, 1521, ²E, 1740; ET *History of Greater Britain* by A. Constable, E, 1892), which carried a dedication to James V.* Here Major adopted a more critical approach to the study of history, rejecting much early mythology, and explored the benefits of a union of the Crowns of England and Scotland. After a brief visit to Paris in 1521, he moved from Glasgow to St Andrews in 1522, and by 1525 had returned to Paris, where he gained acclaim as 'the prince of Paris divines' (*see also* Lockhart, George). Returning to St Andrews in 1531, he was appointed provost of St Salvator's College, a post he held till his death. He was present in 1547 when Knox preached his first Protestant sermon, on the theme of Daniel and the four monarchies, in the parish church of St Andrews. As dean of the Faculty of Theology at St Andrews, he was summoned to attend the Church's provincial council* of 1549 but was excused on the ground of advanced age.

A History of Greater Britain (E, 1892), xix-cxxx; J. Durkan and J. Kirk, *The University of Glasgow, 1451-1577* (G, 1977), 155-78; A. Broadie, *George Lokert* (E, 1983), 1-31; *DNB* XXXV, 386-9; J. Durkan, 'John Major: After 400 Years', *IR* 1 (1950), 131-9, 140-57; Farge 304-11.

J. Kirk

Makemie, Francis (1658-1708), founder of American Presbyterianism. Makemie was born of Scotch-Irish parents in Donegal County, Ireland, and educated at the University of Glasgow. In 1682 he was ordained by the Presbytery of Laggan in Northern Ireland as a missionary to America. He preached in Barbados and in the middle colonies in America, where he organized some of the earliest American Presbyterian churches. In 1704 he went to London to recruit ministers and gain support for the Presbyterians in these colonies in their struggle for toleration. Two years later, with six other Presbyterian ministers (of Scottish, Scotch-Irish, and New England backgrounds), he formed at Philadelphia the first Presbytery in America and was elected moderator. Makemie preached Calvinistic doctrines and defended the right of free speech and Presbyterian meetings against the colonial authorities who attempted to restrict his work. In 1707 he was arrested on Long Island, New York, by Governor Cornbury, fined, and imprisoned for preaching without a licence. The governor described the versatile Makemie as 'a preacher, a doctor of physic, a merchant, an attorney, a counsellor-at-law, and, which is worst of all, a disturber of governments'. Makemie was acquitted, although he had to pay exorbitant court costs. His struggle gained new followers for his churches and furthered the ideal of religious freedom in America.

B. Schlenther (ed.), *The Life and Writings of Francis Makemie* (Philadelphia, 1971); I. M. Page, *Life of Francis Makemie* (Grand Rapids, 1938); L. P. Bowen, *The Days of Makemie* (Philadelphia, 1885); W. B. Sprague, *Annals of the American Pulpit* (NY, 1859-61), III, 1-4; H. Bowen, *Dictionary of American Religious Biography* (Westport, 1977), 283-4.

D. B. Calhoun

Malcolm III (*c*.1031-93), 'Canmore' (from Gaelic* *ceann mór*, 'great head'), King of Scots 1057-93. Malcolm fled to the English court for some fourteen years after his father, Duncan I, was killed by Macbeth in 1040. With English aid he regained southern Scotland from Macbeth, probably in 1054, and became full King of Scots after defeating Macbeth in 1057 and Lulach (Macbeth's stepson) in 1058. He first married Ingibjorg, daughter of Thorfinn, Earl of Orkney. Of their three sons, only Duncan II reigned briefly as King (in 1094). After Ingibjorg's death, the Norman Conquest of England in 1066 caused the flight of Edgar Atheling, dispossessed Saxon heir to the throne. Edgar, his mother and two sisters, Margaret* and Christina, took refuge at Malcolm's court in Dunfermline. By 1069 Malcolm married the cultured and pious Margaret (later canonized), who had a strong influence on his reign. Her influence helped dispose the court towards English ways and the Church towards general Roman procedure. Malcolm invaded the northern part of England five times and was invaded by its Norman kings three times in retaliation. He was killed at Alnwick in 1093. Of his and Margaret's six sons, Edgar, Alexander I* and David I* became Kings of Scotland.

G. Donaldson and R. S. Morpeth, *Who's Who in Scottish History* (O, 1973), 3-4; A. H. Dunbar, *Scottish Kings... 1005-1625* (E, ²1906), 25-34; A. A. M. Duncan, *Scotland: The Making of the Kingdom*, Vol. I (E, 1975), ch. 6.

D. F. Kelly

Malcolm IV (1141-65), King of Scots 1153-65. The eldest grandson of David I,* Malcolm IV, the last King of Scotland to bear a Scottish name, succeeded David immediately in May, 1153, at the age of twelve, because his father Henry, earl of Northumberland, died in 1152. The succession to full royal authority of the late King's grandson, scarcely yet adult, was a highly important landmark in the process by which the Scottish monarchy made the transition from collateral succession to primogeniture. Malcolm's twelve-year reign was dominated by persistent ill-health, leading to his early death; by the repudiation by Henry II of England of his oath to David I (1149) to leave the Scots in peaceable possession of Cumberland and Northumberland; and by the ambition of Somerled (*d*.1164), sub-king of Argyll, to break away from

Scottish overlordship. Nevertheless, the youthful Malcolm, deeply imbued with the spirit of Christian chivalry, overcame a serious revolt by the native nobility, subdued the province of Galloway, brought Somerled to peaceful submission, and although forced to yield the 'English' counties to Henry II (1157) did not thereby compromise the liberty of his realm. He himself was determined to remain celibate, but he married his elder sister Margaret to the duke of Brittany and his younger sister Ada to the count of Holland, strengthening Scotland's relations with principalities on the fringe of, or outwith, the menacing Norman-Angevin complex. He extended his grandfather's policy of feudalization, settling knights and barons in Moray, Clydesdale and Galloway. A sincere friend and patron of the Church, he founded the monasteries* of Coupar Angus and Manuel (W. Lothian), endowed many others, and made a strenuous though unsuccessful attempt to persuade the papacy* to make the see of St Andrews metropolitan. Above all, he left a reputation for vigorous government: Somerled was defeated and killed and wrongdoers were brought to justice.

G. W. S. Barrow (ed.), *The Acts of Malcolm IV King of Scots 1153–1165* (Regesta Regum Scottorum I; E, 1960).

G. W. S. Barrow

Malcolm, John (d. 1634), minister and opponent of episcopacy. A graduate of St Andrews and formerly regent in St Leonard's College there, Malcolm was minister of Perth from 1591, a close friend of Andrew Melville* and a stalwart defender of Presbyterian polity. In 1606, during Parliament's meeting at Perth, he helped organize the signing, in his own house, by over forty ministers, of a protestation against episcopacy. In 1615 he was summoned before the High Commission for championing the recall by James VI of ministers banished for holding a General Assembly at Aberdeen, contrary to James's will. This he argued in his Latin Commentary on the Acts of the Apostles (*Commentarius*..., Middleburg, 1615). He was honoured as 'a grave, godlie, and learned man'.

FES IV, 230; J. Kirk, 'The Development of the Melvillian Movement in Late Sixteenth-Century Scotland' (PhD, Edinburgh University, 1972), 636.
D. F. Wright

Malthusian Theory. The first *Essay on the Principle of Population* (L, 1798) of T. R. Malthus (1766–1834) was written to defend 'the established administration of property' from the 'Jacobin' attacks of Condorcet and Godwin. Population dynamics must defeat any attempt to equalize property and abolish social institutions. The latter emerge 'naturally' in society to maximize the economic surplus. The status quo is therefore both inevitable and superior to any other social order. However, a theodicy is required to justify the poverty and inequality associated with the status quo. Malthus's attempt at this in 1798 was a failure and in 1803 he published a drastically new recension (L, ^{2}1803) much influenced by William Paley's theodicy of 'social evil' in *Natural Theology* (L, 1802). The concept of 'moral restraint' was introduced in order to explain how social evil caused by population dynamics might be avoided without either 'vice' or 'misery'. Malthusian theory reached its final form in the fifth edition of the *Essay* (L, ^{5}1817), in response to J. B. Sumner's *Records of the Creation* (L, 1816).

From the first, Malthusian theory attracted keen attention in Scotland. Dugald Stewart* appraised the first *Essay* favourably in his Edinburgh University lectures of 1800–1, and early numbers of the *Edinburgh Review* (*see* Periodicals, Religious) (*e.g.* 1 (Oct. 1802), 83–90) trumpeted Malthus's annihilation of Jacobin ideas. Its importance for Scottish church history is due to Thomas Chalmers,* who attended Dugald Stewart's lectures, was the first to see the theoretical significance for political economy of Malthusian population dynamics and was later regarded by Malthus as his 'ablest and best ally'. Chalmers made Malthusian theory the centrepiece of an elaborate argument for a nationally established Church inculcating morality and self-restraint. The resulting deferment of marriage would reduce population and raise real wages at the expense of rents. The consequent prosperity of the working class would reduce social unrest, legitimatize property rights, reduce the burden of poor relief and hence more than recover the cost of church establishment (*Political Economy*, G, 1832). Chalmers's Malthusian theory of poor relief and church establishment was strongly attacked by the brothers W. P.* and A. Alison in the 1840s.

D. Winch, *Malthus* (O, 1987); A. M. C. Waterman, 'The Ideological Alliance of Political Economy and Christian Theology, 1798–1833', *JEH* 34 (1983), 231–44.
A. M. C. Waterman

Managers, members of the Committee of Management, the body with responsibility for temporal affairs in the congregations of the UPC and in those UFC and CofS churches which came from that denomination and which have not adopted the Model Constitution,* or which have adopted a form of constitution incorporating the Committee of Management. The number of managers is determined by the congregation, and all members of the congregation including the minister are eligible for election. Managers serve a three-year term and may be re-elected. The Committee of Management elects its own chairman (its *Preses*), the minister (if elected to the Committee) having no special claim to the position. It has no power in spiritual matters, that lying with the Kirk Session,* and is required to refer to a congregational meeting many matters, including the maximum to be spent on repairs and any question of securing finance through a charge on church property.

Cox, 35–9.
F. Lyall

Manchuria, *see* Missions.

Manse, the name given to the official residence of a minister in the CofS and most other Protestant churches (but not EpCS). In olden days the CofS manse was built and maintained by the heritors,* being such as is 'considered suitable at the time for others in the same class as ministers, with accommodation sufficient for an ordinary family and due hospitality'. It came under Presbytery jurisdiction. Today the manse is provided and maintained by the congregation, although increasingly ministers are authorized to live in their own property (being concerned particularly to provide for their retirement) and agreement is reached on the payment in lieu. It is still customary to refer to the minister's house as 'the manse' no matter by whom provided.

A. Herron

Manson, Thomas Walter (1893-1958), New Testament scholar. He was born of Shetland ancestry at North Shields, Northumberland, and graduated (1913) at the University of Glasgow with honours in mental and moral philosophy. After a period of war service he resumed studies at Christ's College, Cambridge, reading for the Oriental Tripos (Hebrew and Aramaic). He prepared simultaneously at Westminster College for the Presbyterian ministry; he was tutor there 1922-5. He was ordained in the Presbyterian Church of England, serving in its Jewish Mission Institute, Bethnal Green (1925-6), and as minister at Falstone, Northumberland (1926-32).

At Falstone he produced his greatest work, *The Teaching of Jesus* (C, 1931), which immediately marked him out as a distinguished scholar. In 1932 he became Yates Professor of New Testament Greek and Exegesis at Mansfield College, Oxford, and in 1936 Rylands Professor of Biblical Criticism and Exegesis in Manchester University, where he remained until his death.

The most distinctive element in his exposition of the teaching of Jesus was his corporate interpretation of 'the Son of man', a term which he equated with the prophetic 'remnant' of Israel. Jesus called his disciples to be associated with him in fulfilling the mission of the Son of man, but in the event he was left to fulfil it single-handed. Manson developed this thesis in later works, notably *The Servant-Messiah* (C, 1953).

He was awarded the Burkitt Medal for Biblical Studies by the British Academy (1950). In 1953 he was Moderator of his Church's General Assembly. He was a skilled and impressive teacher; his administrative gifts were greatly valued.

M. Black, 'Memoir of T. W. Manson', *Proceedings of the British Academy* 44 (1958), 325-7; *DNB 1951-1960*, 688-9; H. H. Rowley, appreciation in Manson, *Studies in the Gospels and Epistles* (Manchester, 1962), vii-xvi; bibliography etc. in A. J. B. Higgins (ed.), *New Testament Essays . . . in Memory of Thomas Walter Manson . . .* (Manchester, 1959).

F. F. Bruce

Manson, William (1882-1958), New Testament theologian. Born at Cambuslang, he was educated at Glasgow University, Oriel College, Oxford, and the UFC College (Trinity College), Glasgow. He was ordained in 1911, being minister of Oban, Dunollie Road, from 1911-14, and Glasgow, Pollokshields East, from 1914-19. From 1919 to 1925 he was Professor of New Testament at Knox College, Toronto, and in 1925 was appointed Professor of New Testament Language, Literature and Theology at New College,* Edinburgh. He remained there until he retired. His major works were: *Christ's View of the Kingdom of God* (L, 1918); *The Incarnate Glory: An Expository Study of St John's Gospel* (L, 1923); *The Gospel of Luke* [Moffatt Commentary] (L, 1930); *Jesus the Messiah* (L, 1943); *The Epistle to the Hebrews* (L, 1951); *The Way of the Cross* (L, 1958); and posthumously *Jesus and the Christian* (L, 1967). Manson was Vice-President of the British Council of Churches 1950-2, and Scottish Chairman of the Anglo-Scottish Conference on Intercommunion 1951. A convinced ecumenist, he worked for the reconciliation of the CofS and the CofE until his death. He was one of the major contributors to the 1940 *Book of Common Order*, especially stressing the notion of union with Christ in the Communion service. Deeply critical of the presuppositions of Dibelius and Bultmann, he was never convinced by form criticism. For him, the theological and the formal went together, and his call for 'depth exegesis' and theological interpretation was influential.

FUFCS 580; FES IX, 773; *Who Was Who 1951-60*, 730.

I. R. Torrance

Margaret, Saint (*c.* 1046-93), Queen of Scotland. The wife of Malcolm III,* she wielded strong influence on both the Scottish court and the Church. Descended from the old Saxon royal family, she was a daughter of Edward 'the Exile' (son of Edmund Ironside). Canute became King of England after Edmund's death and banished Edward, who went to Hungary where he married Agatha, a princess related to both the German Emperor and the Hungarian royal family. By her Edward had three children, Margaret, Christina and Edgar the Atheling. Probably born in Hungary before 1045, Margaret spent her early years in the fervently Christian court of the recently deceased Hungarian King Stephen (*d.* 1038). Margaret (and her family) were summoned in 1057 to yet another pious Christian court, that of Edward the Confessor, now King of England (an uncle of Edward the Exile). The family were under the Confessor's protection until 1066, when Harold II (successor of the Confessor) was slain in the Norman Conquest. Edgar the Atheling claimed the throne, but went into exile before William the Conqueror, taking with him his mother and two sisters. They took refuge in Scotland at the Court of Malcolm III in Dunfermline around 1067/8.

Around 1069 Malcolm, whose first wife had died earlier, married Margaret, who, according to the Anglo-Saxon Chronicle, had wished to dedicate her

MARGARET, SAINT

life to the service of God as a virgin. Her biographer (almost certainly her confessor, Turgot,* a Saxon who was prior of Durham and Bishop of St Andrews) chronicles her potent influence on the court and Church. Cultured and literate, she influenced the court in an English direction, emphasizing manners, the reading of devotional books, and needlework for the noblewomen. Her reforming interest was at least as great on certain practices of the Scottish Church. Having noted Scottish deviations from general Roman ecclesiastical procedures (perhaps more in line with ancient Eastern practices), she corresponded with Archbishop Lanfranc of Canterbury, who sent Benedictine* monks to Malcolm's court at Dunfermline to give Margaret advice. She is traditionally said to have summoned a council for the reform of the Scottish Church, in which (owing to her ignorance of Gaelic*) her husband served as Gaelic/English interpreter.

According to Turgot, the issues at stake were not those which were agitating the rest of Christian Europe at this time (such as lay investiture and clerical celibacy), but more of a regional and devotional concern. Apparently this council persuaded the Scottish clergy to determine the Lenten period according to Roman custom, to receive the sacrament at Easter, to recite the mass according to Rome rather than their 'barbarous rite' (perhaps a reference to use of the vernacular or to infant communion?), to cease from work on the Lord's Day, to abstain from marrying one's stepmother or brother's widow (these five points being traditionally known as the Five Articles of Margaret), and to return thanks after meals. But there is no evidence of her having changed the structure or organization of the Church.

Margaret surpassed ordinary devotional practice in fasting, praying, supporting orphans and the poor and patronizing the clergy, and especially monastic orders and hermits. Her Gospel Book is in the Bodleian Library, Oxford. She and Malcolm III donated the town of Balchristie to the Culdees* of Lochleven, erected an abbey church in Dunfermline,* repaired Iona,* and adorned the church at St Andrews.* She provided the Queen's Ferry to give free passage to pilgrims over the Firth of Forth on their way to St Andrews.

Margaret's strong piety bore long influence in the lives of her children whose education she closely supervised. By her Malcolm III had six sons, Edward, Edmund, Ethelred, Edgar, Alexander and David, and two daughters, Matilda (or Edith) and Mary. The medieval monastic, William of Malmesbury, asserted that 'No history has recorded three kings and brothers who were of equal sanctity or savoured so much of their mother's piety.' These three sons were successively King of Scots: Edgar (1097–1106/7), Alexander I* (1106/7–24), David I* (1124–53). The very fact of their English (rather than Celtic) names indicates something of their mother's influence. Their daughter Matilda married (secondly) Henry I, King of England (1100–35). Their second daughter, Mary, had a daughter, Matilda, who married Stephen, King of England. Of their sons, Ethelred was lay abbot of Dunkeld and Earl of Fife, and Edmund became a monk.

After an illness of some six months, Margaret died in Edinburgh Castle on 16 November 1093, not long after hearing of the defeat and death of her husband and her eldest son. According to her biographer, Margaret's priest reported that she died holding the cross, praying and praising God. Her body was taken to Dunfermline Abbey, where she was buried opposite the high altar. Nearly twenty years later her husband's body was moved to Dunfermline. Their bodies were placed together in a common tomb in the Abbey in the time of Alexander III. Pope Innocent IV canonized Queen Margaret in 1249. Her mortal remains seem to have been removed in the late sixteenth century to Antwerp, in the seventeenth to Douai, and after that possibly to the Escorial in Madrid, where they were lost.

A. Henderson-Howatt, *Royal Pearl* (E, 1948); J. R. Barnett, *Margaret of Scotland* (L, 1926); R. L. G. Ritchie, *The Normans in Scotland* (E, 1954); Turgot (?), *Life of St. Margaret*, trans. W. Forbes-Leith (E, ³1896); G. W. S. Barrow, *The Anglo-Norman Era in Scottish History* (O, 1980); D. McRoberts, *St Margaret, Queen of Scotland* (E, 1957).

D. F. Kelly

Marischal College, Aberdeen. Founded in 1593 by George Keith,* fifth Earl Marischal, this College was a separate degree-granting institution until its union in 1860 with King's College to form the University of Aberdeen.

There are uncertainties about the reasons for its foundation and its precise institutional character. Was it a *schola illustris* (liberal arts college), a college within the existing university (King's College), or a self-contained university? All three views have been held, but latterly Aberdonians were proud to claim that there were in Aberdeen as many universities as in the whole of England! The Earl Marischal's motives seem to have been a mixture of concern for educational reform, rivalry with the founder of the short-lived University of Fraserburgh (*see* Ferme, Charles), and the availability of lands and buildings formerly occupied by the Greyfriars and owned by him. Theories that Marischal was intended as an extreme Presbyterian foundation or as a rival to the more traditional King's are now largely discounted.

There was, however, considerable rivalry between the two colleges. Early in the seventeenth century the Principal of King's is recorded as refusing to acknowledge Marischal 'for schoole or college'. There was considerable competition for students, but the merchants tended to prefer Marischal for their sons while the landed gentry favoured King's. Students of divinity, however, studied in both colleges, for neither by itself was able to provide a complete theological curriculum. Apart from this there was considerable duplication between the colleges, and various attempts were made to unite them before the successful union of 1860 (see Thomson, Alexander).

At first Marischal employed the regent system whereby one teacher instructed a class in all subjects of the arts curriculum over a period of four years, but by the eighteenth century it had adopted the practice of appointing specialist professors. King's held to the old system until the end of the century.

The Marischal buildings were inferior to those at King's, but the mediaeval Greyfriars church survived until 1903 when it was demolished to make room for a range of new buildings in Kemnay granite. Behind these are buildings erected in 1837–44 to designs by Archibald Simpson to replace unsatisfactory older accommodation. Together they form the world's second largest granite building, inferior only to the Escorial in Madrid. Most of the University's recent development has been adjacent to King's College, and today only Anatomy, Geology, Physiology, Biochemistry and Pharmacology are taught in the Marischal College building.

G. D. Henderson, *The Founding of Marischal College, Aberdeen* (A, 1947); J. S. Smith, 'The Marischal College Story', *AUR* 50 (1984), 288–92, 380–6.

H. R. Sefton

Marriage. In the medieval church marriage was held to be a sacrament administered by the parties themselves. The Church insisted, however, that the private contract be followed by a public religious ceremony, and Tertullian refers to the custom of seeking permission to marry from bishops, priests and deacons. As time went on, barriers to marriage were multiplied. Charlemagne in 802 forbade marriage until inquiry had been made as to the consanguinity of the parties. This was the origin of the publication of banns,* which was made obligatory on the whole Church by Pope Innocent III. But the validity of clandestine marriage – unions effected by mutual consent without reference to a priest – was recognized by the Church, despite many evils associated with the practice, until the Council of Trent laid it down that a marriage could only be valid if consent was declared before a priest and at least three witnesses.

John Calvin submitted contemporary ideas on marriage to severe criticism (*Institutes* 4:19). The scriptural foundation claimed for the sacramental nature of marriage in Eph. 5:31f was based, he claimed, on a mistranslation in the Vulgate, where 'mystery' (*musterion*) was rendered as 'sacrament' (*sacramentum*). He also took issue with the rule of celibacy for the priesthood, asking on what authority the sacrament of marriage was denied to certain men. By the sixteenth century barriers to marriage had been increased to an absurd degree, although papal dispensations were usually available at a price. Marriage was also forbidden at certain seasons – from the third Sunday before Lent until Easter; for three weeks before the nativity of John the Baptist; and from Advent to Epiphany. Other regulations without apparent sense or reason had accumulated around the institution of marriage.

In the *First Book of Discipline** the Reformed Kirk directed that no persons should marry without consent of parents, unless no reasonable ground for refusal was adduced. The *Westminster Directory* qualified this by ruling that consent of parents should be obtained to first marriages, especially if the parties were under age. This presumably referred to the decree of the General Assembly of 1600 that, 'considering that there is no statute of the Kirk ... defining the age of persons who are to be married, ordain that no minister within this realm presume to join in matrimony any persons in time coming, except the man be fourteen years of age, and the woman twelve complete.'

Marriage might also be refused to persons under scandal. In 1565 the Assembly enacted that 'such as lie in sin under promise of marriage, deferring the solemnization, should satisfy publicly, in the place of repentance, upon the Lord's day before they be married.' In the early years of the Reformed Kirk, elders* on occasion introduced rules they considered appropriate. In many parishes couples contemplating marriage had to be able to repeat the Lord's Prayer, the Apostles' Creed and the Ten Commandments. In some places regular church attendance was made a prerequisite for marriage.

The General Assembly in 1581 forbade marriage in private houses; but since the establishment of Presbyterianism* marriage in a private house has not been regarded as irregular, and before that time private marriages were not infrequent. *FBD* directed that Sunday was the day 'most expedient' for weddings; but the Westminster Assembly* ruled that weddings should not be celebrated on the Lord's day, and the General Assembly in 1645 accepted this view, and marriages thereafter were usually solemnized on the day of the weekly lecture.

Many ministers of the Reformed Church held the pre-Reformation view that a religious ceremony was not necessary to constitute a valid marriage, and this was supported by the people at large, despite the opposition of kirk sessions. This was debated for many years. Lord Erskine argued that in Scotland the consent of parties was all that was necessary to constitute a valid marriage. In 1796 Lord Braxfield affirmed the opposite. Much later Lord Fraser said that Erskine's opinion was never judicially pronounced to be the law of Scotland until 1811. The matter was finally settled by the Marriage Act of 1856, by which the laws of Scotland and England on the subject were assimilated, and irregular marriage (i.e. marriage celebrated other than by a minister of religion, after due notice given) was severely limited.

Divorce was not recognized by the RC Church.* However, under canon law a judicial decree of nullity might be obtained. This did not imply the severance of the ties of a real marriage, but rather the declaration that the marriage had never existed. In other cases, separation 'from bed and board' was possible, but the separated parties were not free to remarry. Again, marriage was not regarded as a sacrament until it was consummated, so if non-consummation could be proved the marriage might

MARRIAGE

be dissolved. Luther's view, that marriage was 'a thing of this world, like food and raiment, house and yard, and subject to the civil power' was anathema to the RC Church; but the Protestant Church generally agreed that the ordinary courts of law should have power to grant divorces, leaving the parties free to marry again. From 1560 kirk sessions began to grant divorces, but in 1563 the Commissary Court was established at Edinburgh, with jurisdiction over all Scotland in questions of marriage, divorce and legitimacy. From this court there was an appeal to the Court of Session. The Commissary Court continued to function until 1830, when its powers were transferred to the Court of Session. In 1573 an act was passed declaring that if either husband or wife deserted the other for four years without reasonable cause, and refused to return to cohabitation, this should be a ground for divorce. After that, divorce in Scotland was granted on proof of adultery or desertion of either spouse.

Clandestine or irregular marriage was common both before and after the Reformation; but the Church never approved. The mere declaration of intent to marry before witnesses could never be sufficient to establish a sound and lasting relationship; but such a declaration in Scotland was legal and valid. For many years after the Reformation large areas of the country were ill-served by ministers. This was recognized, and the Church turned a blind eye to irregular unions in circumstances which could not be bettered for the time being.

When the initial shortage of ministers was overcome, clandestine marriages continued, and it became obvious that these signified a deliberate renunciation of the minister's services. The situation worsened after the Restoration* and the establishment of episcopal* rule. In 1661 an 'Act against clandestine and unlawful marriages' was passed, whereby any who got themselves married by anyone other than the parish minister would be fined or imprisoned; and the celebrator of such a marriage would be banished for life. Fines, ranging from 1,000 Scots for a nobleman to 100 merks for an ordinary person, were to be 'applyed to pious uses within the severall paroches wher the saids persones duells'.

This Act was largely disregarded. Presbyterians were not willing to be married by Episcopalian* ministers, and resorted to 'outed' men, for whom there was much sympathy. The establishment of Presbyterianism did nothing to remedy the matter, as the newly 'outed' Episcopalians similarly attracted their own followers who sought marriage with their blessing.

Towards the close of the seventeenth century kirk sessions began pursuing those believed to be irregularly married. These unions took place secretly, as the celebrator was anxious to avoid detection; but when the first child was born and the parents desired baptism the marriage had to be confessed to the kirk session. The parties were then rebuked for their misdemeanour, exhorted to be faithful to each other, ordered to pay the appropriate fine, and then required to pay the normal fee for the proclamation of banns.

MARROW CONTROVERSY

During the first half of the eighteenth century the number of clandestine marriages increased rapidly, and the Church's concern grew. A girl irregularly married had no proof of her marriage since no record was kept. If her husband died she had no proof of her widowhood and could not qualify for any benefit. If her husband later denied the marriage, the girl had no redress and would be left to bring up her children. Yet the practice continued among all classes.

The reintroduction of patronage* in 1712 gave great offence, and irregular marriage was one way of expressing disapproval. Marriages conducted by Episcopalian ministers for their own adherents were accounted regular, but not those celebrated by ministers of the Secession.* In England, 'An Act for the better preventing of Clandestine Marriages' was published in 1753, and this might have resolved the confused situation in Scotland, but the act only had effect in England, Wales and Berwick. It provided for the publishing of banns in places of worship other than the parish church, and for the celebration of matrimony in these places – such marriages to be deemed regular. 'Scotland, Quakers and Jews' were excepted. In 1784 these provisions were extended to Scotland and the effect on the number of irregular marriages was immediate. Clandestine unions ceased to be a problem.

The Marriage (Scotland) Act of 1939 put an end to the traditional distinction between regular and irregular marriage – with regular marriage conducted only by a minister of religion with due notice given. Henceforth marriage was either religious (Christian or Jewish) or civil (conducted by a registrar). A further Act of 1977 extended provision for religious marriage to other faiths, provided monogamy was in view, and also dispensed with the age-old proclamation of banns. Only a fortnight's notice was now required.

Christian marriage has found the acids of secularization deeply corrosive, even in ministerial marriages. The progressive liberalization of divorce, with breakdown of relationship replacing marital offence as the commonest ground, and the steep increase in the number of divorces tend to relativize promises of lifelong commitment. If church marriage retains its appeal, even alongside widespread pre-marital cohabitation, it does so less for religious than for sentimental or decorative reasons, and ministers are often asked to conduct marriages on non-church premises. By an Act of 1959 (revised in 1985), CofS ministers may solemnise the marriage of divorced persons, even while the divorced spouse is living. In this and in other respects the CofS is less restrictive than most other Scottish churches.

R. Mitchison and L. Leneman, *Sexuality and Social Control, Scotland 1660–1780* (O, 1989); K. M. Boyd, *Scottish Church Attitudes to Sex, Marriage and the Family, 1850–1914* (E, 1980); *EB* ([14]1929), XIV, 950–5.

J. S. *Marshall*

Marrow Controversy, a doctrinal controversy in

the CofS, 1718–23. Although the post-Revolution CofS thought of itself as particularly distinguished for doctrinal purity, by the second decade of the eighteenth century breaches in its doctrinal unity were becoming apparent. In addition to deciding the (John) Simson* heresy case, the 1717 General Assembly passed an Act condemning the Auchterarder Creed.* In that context, Thomas Boston* recommended the *Marrow of Modern Divinity* to a fellow minister. As a result, the *Marrow* was republished in 1718 with a recommendatory preface by James Hog.* Written by Edward Fisher, an English Presbyterian barber-surgeon, the *Marrow* (L, 1645) was a work of popular divinity which largely reflected the orthodox Reformed thought of its time. That it became the focus of theological controversy in early eighteenth-century Scotland indicates the extent of the changes which had occurred in Reformed thought over the previous century.

The controversy began with Hog defending the *Marrow* against rumours of verbal attacks. The next two years saw pamphlet warfare, largely between Hog and Principal James Hadow,* though with contributions from James Adams, a fiery though ignorant country minister (*FES* V, 345–6). Hadow argued that the *Marrow*'s phrases such as 'Christ is dead for him' and 'a deed of gift and grant' (taken respectively from the early seventeenth-century English Puritans John Preston and Ezekiel Culverwell) demonstrated that it taught a universal redemption. This, he claimed, was the necessary foundation for the *Marrow*'s making assurance* to be of the essence of saving faith. Hog's defence of the *Marrow* was woefully inadequate and, after charges were drawn up by a Committee for Purity of Doctrine, the 1720 General Assembly condemned the *Marrow*, both repeating the charges made by Hadow and, largely following Adams, charging it with teaching that 'holiness [is] not necessary to salvation', that 'fear of punishment and hope of Reward' are not motives to stimulate a believer to obedience, and that 'the believer is not under the Law as a rule of life'. Six so-called Antinomian paradoxes were also condemned. Little was said in the *Marrow*'s defence. The Assembly's Act prohibited all ministers of the Church from recommending the *Marrow* and required them to warn their people against it.

As might have been anticipated, the Act had the effect of drawing national attention to a previously obscure book. It also stimulated a small group of ministers to attempt to rectify the wrong done to 'precious gospel truths'. Three of them (Boston and Ralph and Ebenezer Erskine*) are still widely remembered – though none of their opponents is – but at the time all but Hog were relatively obscure. After acting without success on a presbytery level, they drafted a complaint to the 1721 Assembly. In their *Representation and Petition* (E, 1721), signed by twelve ministers, they complained that the 1720 Assembly, in condemning the *Marrow*, had condemned gospel truth, particularly in regard to the believer's freedom from the law as it is a covenant of works, and in regard to misunderstandings and misrepresentations of the *Marrow* which, they believed, involved a substantial measure of legalism.

After due and fair consideration by the Assembly's Commission, the 1722 Assembly confirmed the 1720 Act, vindicating it from the aspersions of the 'Marrow Brethren'. Although rebuked for their offences, both of erroneous doctrine and 'injurious reflections' against the Assembly, the brethren were allowed to return to their respective parishes. But both they and the theology of the *Marrow* alike suffered continuing rejection in the CofS. The brethren were kept from moving to more important parishes and some were pursued in Church courts with charges of doctrinal error. In some presbyteries approval of the Assemblies' Acts against the *Marrow* was even made a qualification for ordination. Nevertheless the brethren refused to submit, not only formally protesting at the Assembly's decision, but continuing to teach the doctrines the Assembly had condemned. Opportunity to do this freely and the desire to admit men of like mind to the ministry were important considerations in the founding of the Associate Presbytery.* 'Marrow theology', both in public acts and in private publications, became the theology of the Secession* churches and as such had continuing influence both in Scotland and in the colonies.

A considerable literature was produced in the course of the controversy, particularly after the 1722 reaffirmation of the *Marrow*'s condemnation. Few of the works are of enduring value: perhaps the best are the brethren's *Answers* to the Commission's Queries (E, 1722), Robert Riccaltoun's* *Sober Enquiry* (E, 1723) and Thomas Boston's 1726 edition of the *Marrow*, with copious notes.

Doctrinally, the controversy centred around various aspects of the relationship between God's sovereignty and human responsibility in the work of salvation, with the Marrow Brethren emphasizing God's grace and the majority insisting on what must be done in order to obtain salvation. The Brethren described the covenant of grace as a testament, containing God's promises of grace in Christ, who was to be freely offered to all. Assurance was founded in Christ and his work and a believer's motives to obedience were said to be love and gratitude. Their opponents conceived of the covenant as a contract, with mutual obligations. The gospel offer was made to the prepared or 'sensible' sinner and assurance focused on the good works of the believer. Obedience from God's people was said to be obtained by threatenings of wrath. Although accused of teaching universal redemption, all the Brethren except Hog clearly opposed it.

The theological divisions in the Marrow controversy reflected similar divisions in Reformed thought, with the *Marrow* and its defenders being more in harmony with the Reformed orthodoxy of the sixteenth and early seventeenth centuries and, on balance, with the Westminster* Confession of Faith and Catechisms.* Their opponents, though representative of the great majority of ministers in the early eighteenth-century CofS, reflected the legalizing tendencies of late seventeenth-century developments in Reformed theology, rather than Reformed thought as a whole.

See also Moncrieff, Alexander; Williamson, John; Wilson, Gabriel; Wodrow, Robert.

D. C. Lachman, *The Marrow Controversy* (E, 1988), with bibliography; D. Beaton, 'The "Marrow of Modern Divinity" and the Marrow Controversy', *RSCHS* 1 (1926), 112–34; J. Macleod, *Scottish Theology* (E, ³1974).

D. C. Lachman

Marshall, Alexander (1847–1928), Brethren* evangelist. Born in Stranraer, he was converted at the age of twenty through an address in Glasgow by the revivalist W. Gordon Forlong. In 1876 he became a full-time evangelist in association with Open Brethren. He had been brought up in the Evangelical Union,* and retained from that upbringing Arminian convictions which were in his day exceptional among Brethren preachers.

He was active as a counsellor in the Moody* campaign of 1874. In 1879 he moved to Ontario and engaged in pioneer evangelism there and elsewhere in North America. In 1904 he returned to Scotland and settled in Prestwick, Ayrshire. During World War I he served as an Army Scripture Reader. He was an energetic tract-distributor and tract-writer, his best known tract being *God's Way of Salvation*. To his last day he carried out an active ministry by correspondence.

J. Hawthorn, *Alexander Marshall* (G, 1930).

F. F. Bruce

Marshall, Andrew (?1779–1854), USec.C minister at Kirkintilloch (Dunbartonshire) and controversialist. After studying divinity under George Lawson,* Professor to the Associate Synod,* Marshall, who was from nearby Cadder, was ordained to Kirkintilloch (near Glasgow) in 1802. Under his ministry the congregation grew substantially.

Marshall was a chief figure in two major controversies. The first, the Voluntary Controversy,* was initiated by a sermon he preached in April 1829 in Greyfriars Church, Glasgow: *Ecclesiastical Establishments Considered* (G, 1829). It denied that religious establishments are among the institutions of Christ or found in the early Church. He pronounced it unjust and impolitic that the state should show partiality to some of its members over others. And he held the effect on the Church pernicious in that it tended to make the Church a political institution, supported by the state rather than by its members, who, he claimed, both could and should support the work of the Church themselves. The published sermon caused a great stir. To a review in the *Edinburgh Christian Instructor** (28, 1829, 569–94), Marshall answered with considerable vigour and asperity in *A Letter to the Rev. Andrew Thomson* (G, 1830). In the heated debate which lasted through much of the 1830s he took a prominent part. He served as Moderator of the USec.C in 1836 and was awarded a DD in 1841 by Jefferson College, and an LLD in 1842 by Washington College, both in western PA.

Marshall's popularity in the USec.C came to an abrupt end in the second of the controversies. He took the orthodox side in the trial of James Morison* in 1841 and the following year had published a small book in which he expounded the doctrine of particular redemption (*The Death of Christ the Redemption of His People; or the Atonement Regulated by the Divine Purpose*, E, 1842). The publication of Edward Polhill's *Essay on the Extent of the Death of Christ* (Berwick, 1842) with a preface by Robert Balmer,* endorsing universal atonement* in essentially Amyraldian (*see* Cameron, John) terms, drew a response from Marshall. *The Catholic Doctrine of Redemption Vindicated* (G, 1844) included an appendix charging Professors Balmer and John Brown (*d*. 1858)* with erroneous teaching. Marshall was censured by the Synod for this appendix and the libel he brought the following year against Brown (Balmer having died meantime) was not sustained in any point. Marshall responded by leaving the USec.C. In 1851 he met with the Original Secession Church,* but his ardent voluntaryism prevented his joining. The Kirkintilloch church seceeded with him and remained independent until 1855 when it joined the FC. Marshall left a thoroughly reworked treatise on the atonement which was eventually published in the context of the FC union discussions with the UPC, in order to demonstrate that the UPC was unorthodox on the atonement (*The Atonement: or, The Death of Christ the Redemption of His People*, ed. John Forbes, G, 1868).

Andrew Marshall's son William was ordained to the Kirkgate church, Leith, in 1839. He left the USec.C at the same time as his father for essentially the same reasons. In 1848 with two others he formed the Calvinistic Secession Presbytery, but later that year, with a portion of the Kirkgate congregation (the majority returned to the UPC), left and joined the Original Secession Church. In 1852, with the majority of the Original Secession Church, he joined the FC. In 1856 he succeeded his father in Kirkintilloch, but died on a trip to Israel in 1860.

See also Atonement Controversy.

Small II, 151–4, I, 499–501; *ASUPC*, 328–33, 209; J. M'Kerrow, *History of the Secession Church* (E, 1848).

D. C. Lachman

Marshall, Peter (1902–49), Presbyterian minister in the USA. Born in Coatbridge, where his education was furthered in the evenings at the Technical School and Mining College (1916–21), he turned from a naval career to a ministerial calling through influences like Eric Liddell,* the London Missionary Society* and his family's involvement in Buchanan Street Evangelical Union* Church.

Relatives and friends attracted him to the US in 1927 to study from 1928 at Columbia Theological Seminary, Decatur, Georgia (BD, 1931). Ordained in 1931 to Covington, Georgia, he moved to Atlanta (1933–7) (both in the Presbyterian Church in the US (Southern)), and finally to New York Avenue Presbyterian Church, Washington, DC (in the PC USA (Northern)), founded in 1803, where many Presidents had worshipped. He was also Chaplain to the US Senate for the last two years of his life. He married Catherine Wood in 1936 and was naturalized in 1938, when he also received the DD of Presbyterian College, Clinton, South Carolina.

By his preaching and Senate prayers Marshall became one of America's most popular ministers, not least after his death, when Catherine wrote his life and edited his sermons and prayers, beginning with *Mr Jones, Meet the Master* (NY, 1949).

Who Was Who in America II (*1943–1950*), 347; C. Marshall, *A Man Called Peter* (NY, 1951).

D. F. Wright

Marshall, William (*d*.1860), *see* Marshall, Andrew (?1779–1854).

Martin, Alexander (1857–1946), Principal of New College,* Edinburgh, and UF leader in the 1929 Union.* Born at Panbride, Angus, the son of Hugh Martin,* he had a brilliant student career at Edinburgh University and New College. He was ordained to Morningside FC, Edinburgh, in 1884, becoming Professor of Apologetics and Pastoral Theology in New College in 1897. He was also made Principal in 1918, demitted his chair in 1927, and retired 1935. His scholarly output did not fulfil his early promise: his Cunningham* lectures, *The Finality of Jesus for Faith* (E, 1933), and *Winning the Soul, and Other Sermons* (E, 1897), apart from several pamphlets, concerned chiefly with the Union.

Martin saw New College translated from FC to UFC and then to CofS, and was perhaps the key figure in the Union on the UF side. Already UF Moderator in 1920, he also presided at the first Assembly after the Union. (He signed the Union with the pen Chalmers* used to seal the Disruption.*) His theology was broadly evangelical, 'of a mediating kind', but it was as administrator, fundraiser (especially for the Library) and counsellor that he was chiefly distinguished. He was honoured with Edinburgh's DD (1898) and LLD (1929 – also Freeman of the city). The Martin Hall preserves his memory in New College.

AFCS I, 57; *FUFCS*, 581; *FES* IX, 773; *DNB 1941–1950*, 577–8; H. Watt, *New College Edinburgh. A Centenary History* (E, 1946).

D. F. Wright

Martin, Hugh (1822–85), FC minister and theologian. He early distinguished himself as a mathematician during his studies at Marischal College in his native Aberdeen. While reading theology at King's College, Aberdeen, he was won over to the principles of the Non-Intrusionists* by a speech of William Cunningham.* He was ordained to Panbride, near Carnoustie, in 1844, and served at Free Greyfriars, Edinburgh, from 1858 until poor health brought early retirement in 1865. He was an associate of James Begg* as a chief contributor to *The Watchword*,* and in the resistance to proposals of union with the UP Synod.* Edinburgh University made him DD in 1872. In his later years he published books and articles in both theology and mathematics. Much of his work appeared in the *British and Foreign Evangelical Review.**

Martin's writing on *The Atonement* (L, 1870) is reminiscent of David Dickson* and Thomas Boston* in its use of covenant theology* to describe Christ as a priest acting as the specific representative of the elect. The substitutionary nature of Christ's sacrifice is grounded in a covenant by which God the Son willingly accepts a commission from the Father; Christ undertakes the messianic role in order to secure the redemption of God's chosen. The covenant which God makes with his Son institutes a prior relation between the priest and the particular people on whose behalf the sacrifice is offered. Martin reviews an assortment of rival theories of the atonement* by his English contemporaries; in contrast to their depiction of Jesus' death as that of a victim's passive endurance, Martin writes of the crucifixion as an active death in which Christ with sovereign volition offers himself a sacrifice to God.

In 1877 Martin issued two incisive pamphlets unfavourably appraising the views of the younger Marcus Dods* on inspiration and biblical criticism.* Another category of Martin's literary output is his eloquent theological interpretations of Bible characters and of Christ's Gethsemane experience.

The Shadow of Calvary (E, 1875); *Christ's Presence in the Gospel History* (^{2}E, 1865); *The Prophet Jonah* (L, 1866); *The Westminster Doctrine of the Inspiration of Scripture* (L, 1877); *Letters to Marcus Dodds* (L, 1877); *Simon Peter* (L, 1967); *Free Church Declaratory Act* (G, 1892); *Ten Years' Conflict Misread by Historians* (E, 1869); *The Headship of Christ* (E, 1859); *Christ's 'Own House'* (L, 1859); *A Study of Trilinear Co-ordinates* (C, 1867).

DNB XXXVI, 279–80; J. Macleod, *Scottish Theology* (E, ^{3}1974).

S. Isbell

Martyrs, Christians who are put to death for their faith. The designation cannot always be confidently conferred. Should a pioneer missionary be declared a martyr if those who killed him knew him not as a servant of Christ but only as an alarming alien? Is the rebel or freedom-fighter who takes the sword, albeit for professedly Christian reasons, and then dies by the sword, a Christian martyr? Were the Crusaders who fell, martyrs? Magnus* of Orkney met a violent death for political rather than religious causes but was venerated as a martyr (cf. Peter Maxwell Davies' opera, *The Martyrdom of St Magnus*). The question of definition is important, for in Christian belief the martyr (from the Greek, meaning originally 'witness') dies not only for Christ, but like Christ. The theme of imitation of Christ invests the martyr with a special aura. The earliest 'saints' of the Church had been martyrs, and even traditions which do not confer canonization reverence martyrs with high honour.

Martyrdoms have been claimed for three main periods in Scottish church history: the age of the Celtic saints,* the Reformation,* and the Covenanting* era.

(i) During *the Celtic centuries* (*c*.500–*c*.1100), tra-

MARTYRS

ditions of varying reliability identify a number of Christians, mainly monks and nuns, who perished at the hands of pagan Picts or invading Norsemen. In 618 Donan was killed, probably by Picts, in his monastery on the island of Eigg in the Outer Hebrides, along with fifty-two (or perhaps 150) fellow-monks. Kessog was of Irish origin and became a monk and bishop near Luss in Dunbartonshire. He is said to have been killed by assassins c.600. Viking raiders attacked monasteries around the Scottish coasts. Early in the ninth century their slaughter of dozens of monks and laymen in Iona* led to its partial abandonment; a detailed account survives of Blathmac's martyrdom there in 825. When Norsemen destroyed Coldingham* c.870, the abbess Ebba (see Celtic Saints) and other nuns were slain.

Celtic Scotland produced no early martyrology like the Irish *Martyrology of Oengus the Culdee* (ed. W. Stokes, L, 1905) and *Martyrology of Tallaght* (eds R. I. Best and H. J. Lawlor, L, 1931), both compiled c.800. These and similar calendars included many saints who were not martyrs, and many from Celtic Scotland. Christians like Columba* who had chosen exile (*peregrinatio*) could be depicted as 'white martyrs', whereas Donan's separate mission was destined for 'red martyrdom'.

(ii) *The Reformation* witnessed the execution, normally by burning, of perhaps a score of early Scottish Protestants for the crime of heresy.* Patrick Hamilton* is commonly honoured as the first, in 1528, but mention should be made of the Wycliffite John Resby (see Lollards) who died at Perth in 1407 and the Hussite Paul Kravar,* burned at St Andrews probably in 1433. Most Protestant martyrs died in the 1530s: Henry Forrest of Linlithgow at St Andrews in 1533 (Knox, *History* I, 21–2), Norman Gourlay and David Straiton* at Edinburgh on 27 August 1534 (*ibid.*, 22–5), and Thomas Forret* with four others on 28 February 1539, on the Castle Hill in Edinburgh – Duncan Simson, two Dominican friars, John Kyllour, who had had his passion play performed before James V, and John Beveridge, and Robert Forster (*ibid.*, 26). The same year there died at Glasgow the Franciscan Jerome Russell, and Thomas Kennedy from Ayr (*ibid.*, 27–8). George Wishart* was martyred at St Andrews on 1 March, 1546, and Walter Milne* became the last Protestant martyr in 1558.

As a result of deaths like these, and the flight or exile whereby others escaped a similar fate, the literature of the Scottish Reformation was imbued with the hues of persecution, reflected, for example, in the Scots Confession.*

Knox* refers his readers for an account of Patrick Hamilton to 'that notable work, lately set forth by John Foxe, Englishman, of the Lives and Deaths of Martyrs within his isle in this our age' (*ibid.*, 11), *i.e.* Foxe's *Acts and Monuments* (L, 1563–4), popularly known as his *Book of Martyrs*. Knox reproduced Foxe's narrative on Wishart (*History* II, 233–45). If Scotland begot no Reformation martyrology, Knox's *History* in part served this purpose: the tone is set in the 'Preface' with mention of the shedding of 'the blood of innocents' and the 'terrible conflict that has been betwix the saints of God and the bloody wolves' (*ibid.*, I, 5–6).

On the RC side it is difficult to conceive of Cardinal David Beaton's* assassination as his martyrdom, nor the executions of Archbishop John Hamilton* and Mary Queen of Scots.* John Ogilvie* who was hanged in 1615 (and canonized in 1976) was the only unquestionable RC martyr of the Reformation era in Scotland.

(iii) *The Covenanting era* witnessed much more bloodshed, and a more intensively cultivated martyr-consciousness echoed in titles like *The History of the Sufferings of the Church of Scotland from the Restoration to the Revolution* by Robert Wodrow* (2 vols, E, 1721–2), and in the vivid imagery of the cross in Samuel Rutherford's* sermons and letters. Numerous accounts painted the Covenanters as martyrs and heroes. Their tombs and other sites associated with their escapades are marked with memorials and in several places still honoured on anniversaries (cf. J. H. Thomson, *The Martyr Graves of Scotland*, ²E, L, 1903, which counts 245 martyred Covenanters). They are found over wide areas of southern Scotland, urban and rural. (The Reformation martyrs all died in the major towns.)

One reckoning finds that over 18,000 Covenanters suffered banishment, being outlawed, death in battle or individual execution – the last category counting some 450 (*Tracts on the Martyrs and Covenanters*, E, 1843, no. 25: 'De Foe's Summary of the Sufferings of the Covenanters'). A recent survey, on the contrary, concludes that not many over 100 died in the 'Killing Times,'* *i.e.*, 1681–5, when persecution was at its height (I. B. Cowan, *The Scottish Covenanters 1660–1688*, L, 1976, 132–3). The times were violent, and some Covenanters justified killing and practised it, on the field of battle and even outside it. Those whom they viewed as persecutors in turn regarded them as rebels.

The noble army of Covenanting martyrs, even if its numbers have often been exaggerated, included both unknown and well-known (*e.g.* Alexander Peden,* Donald Cargill,* John Nisbet,* and Margaret Wilson and her fellow Wigtown martyrs*). It is perhaps less obvious in the age of the covenants than in the Reformation that 'the blood of the martyrs is seed'. The memory of the martyred Covenanters is perpetuated by various Protestant interests to the present day. Stamped less legibly on religious folk-memories is their legacy of contentiousness in controversy and uncompromising resistance to imposed (especially Episcopalian) ecclesiastical settlements.

D. F. *Wright*

Mary of Guise (1516–60), Regent of Scotland. The eldest daughter of Claude, Duke of Guise, in 1534 she married the Duke of Longueville, who died in 1537. In 1538 she married the recently widowed James V to whom she bore two sons, both of whom died in 1541. James himself died in December 1542, a few days after Mary had given birth to a daughter, Mary Queen of Scots.*

MARY OF GUISE

Mary opposed Governor Arran's (see Hamilton, James, d.1575) flirtations with a Protestant, Anglophile policy in 1543, and in 1544 an unsuccessful attempt was made to replace Arran with Mary. However, once Arran abandoned his policy, reconciliation became possible, and as Scotland came to rely increasingly on French aid her position strengthened. The removal of Queen Mary to France in 1548, the negotiation of a marriage contract with the Dauphin Francis, and the French victory over the English in Scotland by 1549, reduced Châtelherault to little more than a figure-head. In April 1554 he resigned and Parliament recognized Mary of Guise as Regent of Scotland.

Mary tried by a mixture of persuasion and bribery to keep Scotland within the bounds of French clientage, allowing the French to infiltrate the court and administration, building up a French military presence, and supporting the grant of the crown matrimonial on her daughter's husband, the Dauphin Francis who married Mary in April 1558. Mary also tried to defuse religious controversy by practising limited toleration towards Protestants, a policy which had the additional advantage of irritating Mary Tudor, the RC Queen of England.

However, during 1558 Mary abandoned conciliatory policies. The Church was becoming nervous about the growth of Protestantism, the Protestant Elizabeth I* succeeded to the English throne, and the crown matrimonial was conceded by Parliament. The Treaty of Cateau-Cambrésis between France and Spain in the spring of 1559 also reduced the need for France to be so cautious in Scotland. Almost simultaneously Scottish Protestants became more militant, and began to organize resistance to Mary's now pro-RC government.

Mary now found that her powerful French support turned to her disadvantage as the Reformers exploited it and identified their own cause with patriotic ideals. However, French involvement in Scotland only increased following the death of Henry II as the Guise family now dominated both the French and Scottish courts. On 21 October 1559 the Lords of the Congregation* suspended Mary from the regency, and only French troops allowed her to maintain her hold in Scotland. In the spring of 1560 an English army marched to the aid of the Protestants, and besieged the French garrison at Leith. With Guise power in France shaken by the Conspiracy of Amboise in March, further military commitment looked unlikely. On 11 June, in the midst of Anglo-French peace talks, Mary of Guise died, her policy of maintaining RCism with French arms having collapsed, thus bringing down both the RCC and the Auld Alliance.

A. I. Cameron (ed.), *The Scottish Correspondence of Mary of Lorraine, 1545–1560*, SHS 3rd series X (E, 1927); J. M. Wormald, *Mary Queen of Scots* (L, 1988), 43–101; R. K. Marshall, *Mary of Guise* (L, 1977); G. Donaldson, *Scotland: James V to James VII* (E, 1965), 63–99.

K. M. Brown

MARY, QUEEN OF SCOTS

Mary, Queen of Scots (1542–87). Mary succeeded her father, James V, when only six days old. Throughout her minority, government was in the hands of the Governor, James Hamilton (d. 1575)*, second Earl of Arran, and her mother, Mary of Guise.* From birth Mary was the subject of conflict, and Henry VIII's failure in 1543 to secure her as a bride for his son Edward resulted in war (the 'Rough Wooing'). Instead, in exchange for French military aid, Mary was promised in marriage to the Dauphin Francis and was sent to France in 1548. She married Francis in April 1558, granting him the crown matrimonial, and became Queen of France on 10 July 1559. In Scotland the Reformation* reached its climax with the overthrow of the RCC and the French-dominated government in the summer of 1560. Following the death of Francis II on 5 December 1560 Mary chose to return to Scotland, arriving there on 19 August 1561.

In accepting the new religious status quo while still refusing to ratify the legislation of the Reformation Parliament,* Mary opted for a *politique* policy. Her primary ambition was to persuade the Protestant Elizabeth I* of England to name herself (Mary) as her heir. Government was left in the hands of moderate Protestants like James Stewart (d. 1570)*, Earl of Moray and William Maitland* of Lethington, who pursued friendship with England, disgraced the powerful Hamilton family, and crushed a rebellion by the RC Earl of Huntly.

Mary's disastrous marriage to Henry Stewart, Lord Darnley, in the summer of 1565 marked a turning point in the reign. The marriage, which was not without advantages, infuriated Queen Elizabeth, and alienated Moray and the Hamiltons. However, Moray's rebellion in the autumn of 1565 ended in triumph for Mary, who embarked on modest pro-RC policies, which were abruptly halted by the murder of her secretary, David Rizzio, on 9 March 1566. Unfortunately her marriage to Darnley was soon in tatters. Darnley's murder on 8 February 1567 freed Mary, but she blundered into a political and personal relationship with the man thought to have killed her husband, James Hepburn, fourth Earl of Bothwell. Mary's marriage to Bothwell by Protestant rites in May 1567 finally destroyed her reputation at home and abroad. The marriage provoked a successful revolt which was followed by her enforced abdication on 24 July 1567. Five days later her infant son was crowned James VI* of Scotland.

On 2 May 1568 Mary escaped from Lochleven Castle, but her army was defeated at the Battle of Langside on 13 May. In spite of the fact that opinion in the country had swung towards her following the abdication, Mary made the catastrophic mistake of fleeing to England. She was imprisoned and became the focus of the fantasy plots of zealous English RCs. It was after the revelations of the government-infiltrated Babington Plot in 1586 that Mary was executed on 8 February 1587.

G. Donaldson, *Mary Queen of Scots* (L, 1974); M. Lynch (ed.), *Mary Stewart, Queen in Three*

MASON, JOHN

Kingdoms (L, 1988); G. Donaldson, *All The Queen's Men* (L, 1983); J. M. Wormald, *Mary Queen of Scots* (L, 1988); G. Donaldson, *Scotland: James V–James VII* (E, 1965), 63–106; A. Fraser, *Mary Queen of Scots* (L, 1969); D. Hay Fleming, *Mary, Queen of Scots* (L, 1897).

K. M. Brown

Mason, John (1734–92), leader in the Associate Reformed Church in the USA. Born near Mid-Calder, Linlithgow, Mason studied theology under Alexander Moncrieff* and subsequently assisted in the Associate Synod* (Antiburgher) theological hall, teaching logic and moral philosophy. In response to a petition from a small congregation of Scottish immigrants, he was ordained and sent by the Synod to New York in 1761. Soon after his arrival in America, believing 'the dry, the fruitless, the disgracing and pernicious controversy about the Burgess Oath'* a cause of needless division, he began to work for a union of the Secession Churches. After protracted negotiations, in which he took the leading part, the Reformed Presbyterian Church* and both branches of the Secession united, forming in 1782 The Associate Reformed Church. Mason was its first moderator. He had cordial relations with the other Presbyterian and Reformed Churches, but was unable to effect the further ecclesiastical union he desired. He served as a chaplain in the Continental Army and was highly esteemed in his adopted country. His son, John Mitchell Mason (1770–1829) was perhaps even more influential. (See his *The Complete Works*, 4 vols (NY, 1849).)

W. B. Sprague, *Annals of the American Pulpit*, vol. IX (NY, 1869); Jacob van Vechten, *Memoirs of John M. Mason* (NY, 1856).

M. A. Noll

Mather, Alexander (1733–1800), one of John Wesley's* closest confidants in the last years of his life and consequently an influential figure in the controversies over connectional government which rocked Methodism in the 1790s. Mather was born in Brechin, became involved in the Jacobite* Rising* of 1745, gained employment as a baker in London, and experienced an evangelical conversion under Wesley's preaching in 1754. He became an itinerant preacher in 1757 and travelled throughout the connection for forty-three years. During this period he built up a formidable reputation for courageous endurance of hardship and opposition. In 1788 he became the first Methodist preacher to be ordained by Wesley for service in England and was widely expected to assume an important role in the leadership of the connection after Wesley's death in 1791.

Although Mather became the second president of the Methodist conference in 1792 and was closely involved with both public and private discussions to determine the future shape of the Methodist polity, his declining health and lack of formal education imposed limitations on his contribution. He was among those who in 1794 proposed, unsuccess-

MATHESON, GEORGE

fully, an episcopal system for Methodism, and he was a leading opponent of greater lay participation in the government of the connection. Along with other senior Methodist preachers, Mather found it difficult to chart a clear and acceptable course in the 1790s when a combination of internal and external pressures unsettled the Methodist societies in the first decade after the death of their founder.

A. Mather and J. Pawson, *An Affectionate Address to the Members of the Methodist Societies* (L, 1796); A. Mather, J. Pawson and J. Benson, *A Defence of the Conduct of the Conference in the Expulsion of Alexander Kilham addressed to the Methodist Societies* (L, 1796).

T. Jackson, *The Lives of the Early Methodist Preachers* (L, 1837–8); *Minutes of the Wesleyan Methodist Conference* (L, 1801); *Wesleyan Methodist Magazine* (1845), 313–32; J. Vickers, *Thomas Coke* (L, 1969), 192–204.

D. N. Hempton

Matheson, Adam Scott (d. 1913), UP and UF minister. A product of Jedburgh, he studied arts at Edinburgh University and theology at the UP Divinity Hall before ordination in 1862. He ministered in Alloa (1862–73), Derby Road, Bootle, Liverpool (1873–7), Glasgow, Claremont (1877–88) and Dumbarton (1888–1909). His books were highly regarded in his day: *The Gospel and Modern Substitutes* (E, 1890), *The Church and Social Problems* (E, 1893), and *The City of Man* (L, Leipzig, 1910). They reflect wide reading and a sensitivity to contemporary social, economic and intellectual issues. Their radicalism was not untypical of the UPC in the late nineteenth century, just as his social Darwinism – seen especially in *The City of Man* – echoed the spirit of the age. His memoir of his wife, *Memorials of a Minister's Wife* (E, n.d.), included (203–91) remains of her addresses and writings, among them the funeral sermon she dictated in her last illness which was preached at her funeral.

FUFCS 271; *MRUFCS* 156 (Dec. 1913), 611; Small I, 232, II, 93–4, 682.

D. F. Wright

Matheson, George (1842–1906), influential liberal* CofS minister and hymn-writer. Born in Glasgow and almost blind before he was eighteen, he graduated in arts and divinity at Glasgow, and was minister at Innellan on the Firth of Clyde (1868–86) and St Bernard's, Edinburgh (1886–99). Dissatisfied with the Calvinism of his upbringing, he wrote sympathetically of German theology, which he acquitted of the charge of 'atheism' and which reportedly saved him from agnosticism. Generally tolerant of other views than his, he did not hold evolution to be incompatible with Christian doctrine (though he himself came to regard it as untrue). A most effective preacher and a writer whose works ranged over a wide field from the philosophical to the devotional, he is best remembered for two hymns: 'O love that wilt not let me go' and 'Make me a captive, Lord'. The former does not appear in his collection *Sacred Songs* (E, 1890). His other books included *Aids to the Study of German Theology* (E, 1874); *Natural Elements of Revealed Theology* (E, 1881); *The Psalmist and the Scientist* (E, 1887); *Studies of the Portrait of Christ* (2 vols, L, 1899–1900, often regarded as his best work); *The Representative Men of the Bible* (2 series, 1902–3); *The Representative Men of the New Testament* (L, 1905); and *The Representative Women of the Bible* (L, 1907). He wrote many other devotional books which sold well.

D. Macmillan, *The Life of George Matheson* (L, 1907); *FES* I, 92; *DNB Second Suppl.* II, 587–9.

J. D. Douglas

Matheson, Hugh Mackay (1821–98), prominent Presbyterian businessman. Born in Edinburgh, the son of an advocate, he joined a Glasgow mercantile house in 1836. In 1843 he moved to London. He became managing partner of Matheson and Co. in 1847, importing Chinese produce; in 1873 he founded the Rio Tinto company, which worked the mineral mines of the Sierra Morena hills in Huelva, Spain. Matheson also acted as chairman to the London Chamber of Commerce's East India and China section.

Matheson was a pious conservative Calvinist, committed to the work of the Presbyterian Church of England. From 1843 he was a deacon, then an elder, in Regent Square Presbyterian Church, London; in 1855 he moved to Hampstead, where he was an elder in Trinity Presbyterian Church. He championed many good causes, including the British and Foreign Bible Society (*see* Bible Societies), the Young Men's Christian Association (*see* YMCA), the London City Mission, Moody* and Sankey's campaigns, and various temperance* bodies.

Matheson is best remembered, however, for his involvement in the English Presbyterian Church's China mission (*see* Missions), of which he was treasurer from 1847–68 and committee convener from 1868 till his death. His influence here was vast. He largely selected the missionaries, maintained regular correspondence with them, and oversaw administrative details with close and comprehensive scrutiny.

See also Burns, William Chalmers.

A. Matheson (ed.), *Memorials of Hugh M. Matheson* (L, 1899).

N. R. Needham

Matthews, Thomas Trotter (1842–1928), missionary in Madagascar. Born in Aberdeen, he attended the East Free Church and was deeply influenced by the 1859 revival* in the area. He studied at Congregational colleges (Lancaster Independent and Highgate) in preparation for service with the London Missionary Society.* He was appointed with his wife, Mary Fiddes, to Madagascar in 1870, part of a strengthening of the mission in the light of the destruction of traditional cult symbols by the order of Ranavalona II in the previous year. After a short time in Antananarivo, he was appointed a country district missionary in Vonizongo, based in Fihaonana; after furlough in 1882 he served at Ambatonakanga, 'the mother church of Madagascar', until 1899. During the subsequent furlough he retired through ill health, but became a well known deputation speaker for the LMS until 1904. He received the DD of Aberdeen in 1911. The earlier part of his service coincided with the period of central government support for the LMS, the latter with French annexation and pressure on the Protestant missions. Matthews published widely in Malagasy (including works on biblical archaeology and the history of the Covenanters and the Camisards), and served on the revision committee of the Malagasy Bible.

Notes on Nine Years Mission Work in ... Madagascar, with historical introduction (L, 1881); *Thirty Years in Madagascar* (L, 1904); (ed.), *Reminiscences of the Revival of 1859, and the Sixties* (A, 1910).

J. Sibree, *London Missionary Society Register of Missionaries, Deputations, etc.* (L, 1923); *id.*, *Fifty Years in Madagascar* (L, 1924); B. A. Gow, *Madagascar and the Protestant Impact* (NY, 1979), *passim* (unsympathetic); *AUR* 15 (1927–8), 286–7.

A. F. Walls

Maxwell, Alice Maud (1856–1915), one of the first deaconesses of the CofS. Born in Cardoness, Galloway, she had a sheltered upbringing, and nursed her father, Sir William Maxwell. Her ministers recommended her to A. H. Charteris* as a suitable superintendent for a new institution to train women workers (*see* Diaconate; Woman's Guild). She reluctantly accepted the invitation, on condition that she was given time to prepare herself for the position. She returned to Scotland, after eighteen months in Australia and England, in 1888. On 13 January 1889, in St Cuthbert's Church, Edinburgh (*see* St. Colm's College), she and Katherine Davidson* became the second and third women to be set apart as deaconesses. From the new Deaconess Training House in George Square, Edinburgh, she initiated and developed training schemes and methods to develop the tremendous (but previously unorganized) potential of women's work for the Church. She was particularly successful in integrating practical experience with theoretical and biblical teaching, and took a leading part in the establishment of St Ninian's mission, the Deaconess Hospital and Charteris Memorial Church in the slums of the Pleasance area of Edinburgh. Poor health forced her retiral in 1911. She had given twenty-three years of unpaid service to the Church. At a service in Charteris Memorial Church to unveil a commemorative plaque, her good friend W. Robertson (*FES* III, 244) paid her this tribute: 'We recall her gracious presence and great personal charm ... her firm Christian faith that never failed, her loyalty that never swerved, her strong force of character combined with a gentle sympathy, and the ever ready helpfulness that made her beloved of all' (*LW*, June 1926).

Mrs H. (L.) Macrae, *Alice Maxwell, Deaconess* (L, 1919); M. Magnusson, *Out of Silence: The Woman's Guild, 1887–1987* (E, 1987).

L. O. Macdonald

Maxwell, James Clerk (1831–79), experimental physicist and pioneer in thermodynamics and electromagnetic field theory. He was the son of a landowner at Glenlair, Kirkcudbrightshire. Maxwell entered Edinburgh University to read natural philosophy and other scientific subjects. Three years later, in 1850, he became an undergraduate at Cambridge, first at Peterhouse and then at Trinity College, graduating as Second Wrangler in 1854. Rapid promotion followed to chairs of natural philosophy at Marischal College, Aberdeen (1856) and, following the union of the Aberdeen colleges, at King's College, London (1860). After the death of his father, he returned as laird to Glenlair in 1865. In 1871 he went to a new chair of experimental physics at Cambridge, and to design and direct the equally new Cavendish Laboratory.

Maxwell's scientific prowess is legendary. A brilliant mathematician, he sought to interpret mathematically Faraday's concept of the electromagnetic field. From this he was led to a unified theory embracing all known electromagnetic phenomena, in which light must now also be included. Equally fundamental was his work on the kinetic theory of gases and the second law of thermodynamics.

Maxwell maintained deep Christian convictions throughout his life, his papers revealing far more than conventional piety. He repudiated materialism and eschewed a wholly deterministic view of physics. This has been plausibly linked with his evangelical theology. However, he regarded certain contemporary attempts to harmonize science and Scripture as premature. He held lightly to denominational allegiances.

Some specific aspects of his scientific work have been attributed to his theology, not least the use of his famous 'demon' to illustrate the conclusion that the second law of thermodynamics has statistical validity only. For Maxwell, scientific research was almost an act of worship, though never adequate on its own. As he said, 'men of science as well as other men need to learn from Christ'.

L. Campbell and W. Garnett, *Life of James Clerk Maxwell* (L, 1882); I. Tolstoy, *James Clerk Maxwell, a Biography* (E, 1981); J. Hendry, *James Clerk Maxwell and the Theory of the Electromagnetic Fields* (Bristol and Boston, 1986); E. E. Daub, 'Maxwell's Demon', *Stud. Hist. Phil. Sci.* 1 (1970), 213–27.

C. A. Russell

Maxwell, John (1591–1647), Bishop of Ross (1633–8) and Archbishop of Tuam in Ireland (1645–7). Maxwell was educated at St Andrews (MA, 1611), ordained to Mortlach, Banffshire, in 1615 and subsequently served in three Edinburgh charges. As Bishop he was one of the Scottish 'Canterburians' associated with Archbishop Laud* and a principal compiler of the Book of Common Prayer of 1637 (Laud's Liturgy). While one of the ministers of Edinburgh, he was unsuccessful in persuading Charles I* and Laud of the wisdom of adopting a liturgy of Scottish origin for the CofS. Thereafter his efforts were directed to modifying the English *Book of Common Prayer* to make it more acceptable in Scotland. In this he was to some extent frustrated by James Wedderburn.* The Prayer Book which resulted caused a riot and the Covenanting* revolution. Maxwell fled to England and then to Ireland, where he served first as a Bishop and then as Archbishop of Tuam until his death.

Maxwell is chiefly remembered in that his *Sacrosancta Regum Majestas, or; The Sacred and Royall Prerogative of Christian Kings* (O, 1644) was the occasion of Samuel Rutherford's* *Lex Rex* (L, 1644). He also wrote *The Burden Of Issachar: Or, The Tyrannicall Power and Practices Of The Presbyteriall-Government* (O, 1646), answered by Robert Baillie's* *An Historicall Vindication Of The Government of the Church of Scotland* (L, 1646), and several other works defending Episcopacy against Presbyterianism.

FES VII, 355; G. Donaldson, *The Making of the Scottish Prayer Book of 1637* (E, 1954).

H. R. Sefton

Maxwell, Lady, of Pollok (c.1742–1810), leading lay Methodist. Born Darcy Brisbane, youngest daughter of Thomas, of Brisbane, Largs, in Ayrshire, she was educated in Edinburgh and in 1758 went to live in London with her aunt, the Marchioness of Lothian. She married Sir Walter Maxwell, fourth baronet of Pollok, but he died when she was only nineteen. This event had a deep and abiding religious impact on Lady Maxwell. She moved to Edinburgh, where she worshipped in St Cuthbert's, CofS, and in 1764 joined a Methodist society. Henceforth she was one of Scotland's foremost supporters of Wesleyan Methodism. She corresponded regularly with John Wesley,* and took his side in the controversy over his Arminianism,* which strained her relations with her Calvinist friend Lady Glenorchy.* She founded a charity school in Edinburgh, and championed the incipient Sunday school movement, founding two in Scotland and one in England.

J. Lancaster, *The Life of Darcy, Lady Maxwell, of Pollok* (^{3}L, 1839); R. Bourne, *A Christian Sketch of Lady Maxwell* (^{2}L, 1820); *Encyclopedia of World Methodism* (Nashville, TN, 1974), II, 1538–9.

N. R. Needham

Maxwell, William Delbert (1901–71), minister of the CofS and liturgical scholar. A son of the manse, he was born in Ontario, Canada, and was educated at the universities of Toronto and Edinburgh. He was awarded a DD by the University of Glasgow in 1952. After serving in Canada and England he became minister of Hillhead, Glasgow in 1934 and of Whitekirk and Tyninghame St Mary's in East Lothian in 1950, having served as an army chaplain during the Second World War. In 1956 he became Professor of Ecclesiastical History at Fort Hare University in South Africa and two years later was appointed Professor of Divinity at Rhodes University, Grahamstown. His first main publication, *The Liturgical Portions of the Genevan Service Book* (E, 1931; ²L, 1965) showed the influences behind 'Knox's Liturgy' (*see Book of Common Order*) and his Baird Lectures* of 1953, *A History of Worship in the Church of Scotland* (L, 1955), provided a much needed standard survey of that subject.

An Outline of Christian Worship (O, 1936); *Concerning Worship* (L, 1948); *The Book of Common Prayer and the Worship of the Non-Anglican Churches* (L, 1950).

FES IX, 95, X, 58, 423.

D. M. Murray

Mearns, Duncan (1779–1852), Moderate* CofS divine. Born at Cluny, Aberdeenshire, he graduated MA from King's College, Aberdeen, in 1795, and then studied theology under George Campbell,* 1795–9. He was ordained in 1799 as assistant at the parish of Tarves, Aberdeenshire, of which he became sole minister shortly afterwards. In 1816 he was appointed Professor of Divinity in King's College.

Mearns was one of the leaders of the Moderates during the Ten Years' Conflict.* He had early clashed with Thomas Chalmers* over the latter's views on apologetics; Mearns' *Principles of Christian Evidence* (E, 1818) expounds the internal moral evidence of Christianity against Chalmers' exclusive emphasis on historical evidence.

Mearns was Moderator of the General Assembly of 1821, and in 1823 was appointed a royal chaplain.

Lectures on Scripture Characters, 2 vols (E, 1853).

DNB XXXVII, 199; *FES* VII, 373.

N. R. Needham

Mearns, James (1855–1922), hymnologist*. Born on the Scottish border at Coldstream he studied at the University of Glasgow and the UPC Theological Hall in Edinburgh. He was licensed as a probationer but never called to a charge. Deciding to seek Anglican orders he was ordained priest in 1885, becoming in 1896 Vicar of Ashby de la Launde (Lincs.) and later Vicar of Rushden (Herts.) and Rector of Wallington.

Mearns helped with SPCK's *Church Hymns* (L, 1881) and the Scottish *FC Hymn Book* (E, 1882). This prepared him for his meticulous research as Assistant Editor of J. Julian's *Dictionary of Hymnology* (L, 1892; L, ²1907). Among many other articles, he wrote those on Latin, Greek and Scottish hymns and proof-read the whole work.

Durham offered him either a DD or an honorary MA. He chose the latter because he could not afford the fees for the former. His pay for work on Julian (1892) barely covered his expenses.

M. Patrick, 'James Mearns, Hymnologist', *Hymn Soc. Bull.* 35 (1946), 6–8; 36 (1946), 8.

J. S. Andrews

Meikle, James (1730–99), surgeon and religious writer. Born at Carnwath in upper Clydesdale, Lanarkshire, his father's death in 1748 left him responsible for his mother and two sisters. Poverty coupled with a weak voice compelled him to relinquish a desire to train for the ministry of the General Associate Synod* and to practise as a physician. He joined the Royal Navy in 1758 and was assigned as second surgeon's mate aboard the *Portland*. Discharged in 1762, he undertook further professional training and continued working as a physician. In 1789 he became an elder in the General Associate congregation in Biggar, Lanarkshire.

Meikle penned many devotional writings in his spare time, both poetry and prose. Extracts from these were published after his death as *Select Remains* (E, 1801). The popularity of this volume led to the publication of *Solitude Sweetened* (E, 1803; ²1804; ⁹1841 includes a memoir), and *The Traveller; or, Meditations on various subjects, written on board a man of war* (E, 1805). His works were popular in America and frequently reprinted there.

Metaphysical Maxims (E, 1797); *Miscellaneous Works* (E, 1807).

DNB XXXVII, 214–15.

N. R. Needham

Meldrum, George (1634–1709), prominent minister in the post-Revolution CofS. The son of an Aberdeen dyer, Meldrum graduated at Marischal College, Aberdeen, in 1651. He was ordained to the second charge in Aberdeen in 1658, suspended in 1662 (*see* Restoration), but restored in 1663, after agreeing to sit in presbytery and synod with a bishop presiding. He was deposed again in 1681 (for refusing the Test Act* oath). He was called to Kilwinning in 1688, and translated to the Tron Kirk, Edinburgh, 1692. He served as Moderator* of the General Assembly 1698 and 1703. In 1701 he became Professor of Divinity at Edinburgh University, but with the help of an assistant, continued in the Tron parish. He opposed Quakers and RCs, the former during his ministry in Aberdeen and the latter throughout his career, publishing pamphlets against them (and episcopalians) after the Revolution.

Selections from the Records of the Kirk Session, Presbytery and Synod of Aberdeen (Spalding Club, A, 1846), 146–8, 268–9; *FES* I, 139–40, III, 117, VI, 2, VII, 393; *DNB* XXXVII, 217; R. Wodrow, *History of the Sufferings of the CofS*, 4 vols (²G, 1828–30), I, 315–17, III, 310; J. Warrick, *The Moderators of the Church of Scotland from 1690 to 1740* (E, 1913), 92–112.

D. Stevenson

Melrose, Cistercian abbey. Cistercian* monks, brought by David I* in 1136 from Rievaulx (Yorkshire) to Old Melrose (*see* Early Ecclesiastical

MELROSE

Sites), moved almost at once to present-day Melrose. The foundation flourished and became important. The abbey church was dedicated in 1146. Abbot Waldef* (d.1159), step-son of David I, was venerated as a saint and miracle worker. Five early monks or abbots became bishops: Simon (Moray, 1171), Jocelin (Glasgow, 1174), Reginald (Ross, 1195), Adam* (Caithness, 1213), Gilbert (Galloway, 1235). Melrose founded monasteries at Newbattle (1140), Kinloss (1150), Coupar Angus (c.1161) and Balmerino (c.1227), as well as Holmcultram (1150) in Cumbria, at that time in Scotland. Kinloss in turn founded two more houses. Alexander II was buried at Melrose in 1249. The story of Robert I's* heart, brought back from the Crusades and buried in Melrose, is well known.

Although neither the richest monastery in Scotland nor the largest religious community, Melrose was well endowed and prospered materially because of its wool trade. It suffered in time of war through its nearness to the Border, being partially burnt 1300–7 by English forces, looted 1322 and again burnt 1385. Elaborate rebuilding took place in the fifteenth century, in a style far removed from early Cistercian simplicity: John Morow, the celebrated master-mason, has left his mark in the magnificent church.

The Avignon pope granted *pontificalia* (i.e. episcopal insignia) to the abbot in 1391. Melrose's standing remained high in the fifteenth century. Its monks obtained benefices and abbacies elsewhere, though no monk from elsewhere seems to have been made abbot of Melrose. Melrose abbots were often royal officials and ambassadors. Two became bishops: Robert Blackader* (never blessed as abbot) at Glasgow 1484, and Andrew Durie at Whithorn 1541.

Melrose was seriously affected by disputes over the abbacy 1486–1510 and again in 1524–6. James V's natural son, appointed commendator* 1541, governed for his own selfish ends, and the buildings were badly damaged in the English invasion of 1545. The community, numbering thirty-five in 1527, had dwindled to eleven in 1556; monks and commendator then agreed on having a community of sixteen. The alleged rack-renting of Drygrange by the abbey in 1537–41 is not supported by the evidence but is based on a misunderstanding of the canonical procedures for alienating monastic property.

The church was used as the CofS parish church from 1618 to 1810. The abbey ruins, made famous by Sir Walter Scott,* are among the most impressive in Scotland today.

A. O. Anderson *et al.* (ed.), *The Chronicle of Melrose* (L, 1936); *Liber Sancte Marie de Melros* (Bannatyne Club, E, 1837); *Selections from the Records of the Regality of Melrose* (SHS, E, 1914–17), III; J. S. Richardson *et al.*, *Melrose Abbey* (E, 1981); J. Hogg, 'Melrose Abbey', *The Scottish Border Abbeys* I, *Analecta Cartusiana* 35 (1986), 49–86; Easson-Cowan, 72–81; M. Dilworth, 'Monks and Ministers after 1560', *RSCHS* 18 (1974), 202–4; *id.*, 'The Border Abbeys in the Sixteenth Century', *RSCHS* 21 (1983), 233–46; S. Cruden, *Scottish Medieval Churches* (E, 1986), 64–76, 167–74.

M. Dilworth

Melville, Andrew (1545–1622), academic and Presbyterian* leader. He was born at Baldovie in Angus. With his father's death in 1547 and his mother's death when he was twelve, Melville was brought up by his eldest brother, Richard, later minister at Maryton and father of James Melville* the diarist. His brother Richard, who was a friend of Erskine of Dun,* had pursued theological studies at the Lutheran universities of Greifswald, Copenhagen and Wittenberg, and Andrew, after schooling at Montrose, where he acquired a knowledge of Greek, proceeded to St Mary's College, St Andrews, where he matriculated at the Reformation in 1559. There he was befriended by the College Principal, John Douglas,* co-author of the *FBD.** After finishing his arts course, it was said, 'with the commendation of the best philosopher, poet and Grecian of any young master in the land', Melville chose further study in France, first at Paris where he attended lectures in the Royal Trilingual College, including those of Peter Ramus, and then, by 1566, at Poitiers in law, before leaving in 1569 to study theology under Theodore Beza at Geneva, where he gained a teaching post in Humanity, not in the Academy but in the city's college. Finally responding to requests from his countrymen, Melville returned home by July 1574, not to assume the rôle of Presbyterian protagonist but to revitalize university* teaching in the aftermath of the Reformation.

As an outstanding young scholar equipped with a knowledge of the oriental tongues, Melville found competition for his services from St Andrews and Glasgow universities. In choosing Glasgow, where a fresh start could readily be effected, Melville as Principal pioneered reforms in the structure and content of university education. He swept aside the ancient system of 'regenting', whereby one teacher conducted the class through the entire curriculum, in favour of specialist teaching, and as an ardent humanist* he downgraded the philosophies in favour of a broadly based arts course taught on Ramist lines, to which he added instruction in theology. In the royal charter of 1577 annexing the benefice of Govan to the university, fresh endowment was forthcoming, and with that came an obligation on the Principal to preach each Sunday in the kirk of Govan. By 1580, however, Melville left Glasgow for St Andrews to become Principal of St Mary's College, reorganized as a divinity school.

Within the Church, Melville's services were soon sought by the General Assembly. He attended the Assembly of August 1574, at a point when renewed discussion focused on the Church's constitution in the aftermath of the Convention of Leith.* In March 1575, he was selected to serve on two committees of Assembly to investigate the abilities of the Bishop of Moray, George Douglas, and the Bishop elect of Dunblane, Andrew Graham,* but he is not known then to have voiced any disapproval of episcopacy.* At the next Assembly, however, in August 1575, when an Edinburgh minister, John Durie,* questioned the episcopal office, Melville illustrated how the New Testament bishop was 'not to be taken in the sense that the common sort did conceive, there being no superiority allowed by Christ amongst ministers', and, after his speech was 'applauded by many', the Assembly reiterated its position of 1565 that the name 'bishop' was common to all ministers, though some might still serve as visitors. Though not sole author of the SBD,* Melville was an active participant in its composition between 1576 and 1578. He quickly assumed the sort of leadership within the Church which John Knox* had supplied. Each stoutly defended the Church's independence from the Crown, its government through the General Assembly, and church discipline* exercised through the eldership.* Elected Moderator of the General Assembly in April 1578, April and June 1582, June 1587, and May 1594, Melville became spokesman for the anti-episcopal campaign. He was party to the Assembly's proceedings against Archbishop Patrick Adamson* of St Andrews and Robert Montgomery,* the Crown's nominee for the archbishopric of Glasgow, and was selected in 1581 to help establish presbyteries* in Fife. A critic of Arran's 'anti-presbyterian dictatorship' and of the legislation of May 1584 reviving episcopacy, prohibiting presbyteries and asserting the Crown's supremacy over the Church, Melville was summoned before the privy council* in February 1584 for alleged treasonable utterances in a sermon, and when sentenced to imprisonment at Blackness after declining the council's jurisdiction, Melville fled, with his brother Roger, to Berwick. The government, declaring the principalship of St Mary's College vacant, proceeded to make a fresh appointment in Melville's absence.

In England, Melville and other presbyterian exiles in June 1584 had an interview with Secretary Walsingham in London, and before visiting Oxford and Cambridge universities in July Melville wrote to Geneva and Zürich with his interpretation of events in Scotland, to counter Archbishop Adamson's propaganda to the Reformed churches abroad. In October, he attended the funeral in London of his fellow exile, James Lawson,* minister in Edinburgh. With Arran's fall from power by November 1585 and the return home of Melville and the presbyterian exiles, King James VI* was adamant that bishops should remain and negotiations ensued to effect a compromise along the lines of the 'bishop in presbytery'. For much of 1586 Melville in effect was confined in the north by the King, who ordered him first to remain at Baldovie in Angus and then to undertake a mission against Jesuits in the northeast. By the autumn, he was permitted to resume his duties in St Andrews, but was forbidden by the King from preaching to the people on Sundays in English. He also sat as an elder on St Andrews' kirk session.*

At the coronation of Queen Anne in 1590, Melville recited a Latin poem, which was published by royal command. In 1592, however, he defied the King by defending the reputation of Knox and George Buchanan,* and in 1593 sharply criticized the King for favouring RCs like Huntly. In 1595 and again in 1596 Melville made his famous 'two kingdoms' speech to the King on the separation of ecclesiastical and secular jurisdiction. Excluded by the King from attending presbyteries, Melville also found himself deprived of his office of rector of St Andrews University as James began his campaign to undermine Melville's influence. Opposed to ecclesiastical representation in Parliament, Melville was ordered by the King to leave the General Assembly at Dundee in 1598, and though commissioned by his presbytery to attend the Assembly he was again prohibited by the king from participating in the Assembly at Montrose in 1600. In 1602 he was confined to his College for critical remarks on the 'present corruptions in the kirk'. In 1606 he signed a protest against episcopacy, was summoned for interview with the King at Hampton Court, and imprisoned in the Tower of London from 1607 till 1611, when he was permitted to seek exile in France, where his services were sought at the academy of Sedan. As professor of biblical theology, he taught at Sedan until his death.

J. Melville,* *Diary*; Calderwood; *BUK*; T. M'Crie, *Life of Andrew Melville*, 2 vols (E, ²1824); J. Durkan and J. Kirk, *University of Glasgow, 1451–1577* (G, 1977); *SBD*; J. Kirk, *Patterns of Reform* (E, 1989); *DNB* XXXVII, 230–7; J. K. Cameron, 'Andrew Melville in St. Andrews', in *In Divers Manners* ... (St. Andrews, 1990), 58–72.

J. Kirk

Melville, Frances Helen (1873–1962), first woman to graduate BD in Scotland. Born in Edinburgh and educated at Edinburgh and St Andrews Universities, she was one of the first female students to be admitted to Edinburgh University. She graduated MA with first class honours in philosophy and was appointed lecturer in psychology at Cheltenham Ladies College, but returned to Scotland in 1900 to become warden of a residential college for women students at St Andrews. 'When I graduated BD in 1910, I thought I had broken new ground, and have been disappointed since at the few women who have felt called upon to equip themselves should ordination be granted ... I hold strongly that there should be no bar to women holding any office in the Church' ('Scotland's Pioneer Woman B.D.', *LW* n.s. 2 (1931), 142–3).

Unable to fulfil her own call to the ministry of the CofS, Melville had a distinguished career as an educationalist. From 1909 to 1935, she was first Mistress of Queen Margaret College, Glasgow University. On her retirement she was awarded the OBE. She was prominent in many organizations and societies concerned with the higher education and training of women, and was a lifelong activist in the cause of equal political rights. She was one of the five female graduates in whose name the Scottish Women Graduates lawsuit was conducted (claiming for women the right to vote for University

MPs), and she herself contested the Scottish Universities seat in the 1937 Parliamentary election.

This immensely gifted woman was herself an illustration of the complaint she sounded to the CofS in 1931: 'If ordination continues to be withheld and the Church does not accept the services of men and women on equal terms, there is a real and grave danger of our finest, most energetic and intellectual young women throwing their energies into the work of organizations which may have a Christian basis, but which are nevertheless outside the Church' (*ibid*.).

See also Women's Suffrage.

University Education for Women in Scotland (pamphlet, 1902); 'Queen Margaret College', in *College Courant* (Glasgow University), Vol. I, 99–107.
Who Was Who, 1961–1970, 774.

L. O. Macdonald

Melville, James (*fl*.1525–35), Franciscan* who became a Lutheran* sympathizer. He is most clearly recognizable as the Scottish author of a Latin refutation of Lutheranism (presented as the argument of a disputation held at Wittenberg) published at Bologna in January 1530, *i.e.* 1531 (*Certamen cum Lutheranis*..., ed. D. Laing, *The Miscellany of the Wodrow Society* I (E, 1844), 25–47). He was probably the Observant Franciscan who *c*.1526 was summoned before the Archbishop of St Andrews for Lutheran heresy* and, after counter-accusing the 'bishop of Moray', fled to Rome. Pope Clement VII may have been persuaded by him at first, but in 1527 confirmed his banishment from Scotland. The *Certamen* was perhaps written in self-vindication, for it reads like the work of a semi-Lutheran accused of Lutheranism. In exile in Germany Melville probably became more zealously Lutheran. He apparently revisited Scotland in 1535, spreading the Lutheran 'contagion'.

H. Watt, 'The Three James Melvilles', *RSCHS* 3 (1929), 101–11; W. M. Bryce, *The Scottish Grey Friars* (E, L, 1909), I, 104–6.

D. F. Wright

Melville, James (1556–1614), Reformed minister and nephew of Andrew Melville.* He was a son of Richard Melville of Baldovie, minister of Maryton near Montrose. Educated at Montrose and St Leonard's College, St Andrews (matriculated, 1569; BA, 1572), Melville as a student was attracted to John Knox's* weekly preaching in St Andrews in 1571, and resolved to enter the ministry rather than pursue a career in law as his father intended. With Andrew Melville's appointment as Principal of Glasgow University in 1574, James accompanied him thither for further study and was elected a regent or teacher in the arts course. When Andrew Melville became Principal of St Mary's College, St Andrews in 1580, James joined him to provide instruction in Hebrew. With the flight of Presbyterian ministers and lords to England during Arran's regime in 1584, James followed his uncle into exile, seeking sanctuary in Berwick, Newcastle and London. On Arran's downfall, the Melvilles resumed their divinity teaching in St Andrews by 1586. At the synod of Fife, in April 1586, James Melville bitterly attacked Archbishop Patrick Adamson* for subverting the Church's polity approved by the Assembly; Adamson, on being excommunicated, retorted by excommunicating the Melvilles, and James VI intervened in an effort to settle the dispute. Appointed minister of Anstruther and Kilrenny in Fife in 1586, Melville by 1590 had his charge reduced to Kilrenny. Elected Moderator of the General Assembly in June 1589, he preached against attempts at introducing conformity with the English Church, and after obtaining Adamson's repentance in 1591, he recommended to the synod of Fife the archbishop's release from excommunication. In 1594, with his uncle, he accompanied King James on an expedition against the northern 'Catholic' earls; but by 1598 he opposed the King's plans for ecclesiastical representation in parliament as a device for reviving episcopacy.* He strongly supported the ministers prosecuted for holding the Aberdeen assembly in 1605 in defiance of the King, and signed the protest against episcopacy in 1606. Summoned with his uncle and six other ministers to meet King James at Hampton Court in 1606, he was forbidden to return to Scotland, being ordered to remain at Newcastle. He declined the offer of a bishopric in 1607, and was removed to Berwick-upon-Tweed in 1610, where he died. A committed supporter of the Presbyterian* cause, he was author of numerous publications and, as his *Diary* shows, was enthusiastic in his admiration of Andrew Melville.

The Autobiography and Diary of Mr James Melvill, ed. R. Pitcairn (E, 1842); Calderwood; J. Durkan and J. Kirk, *The University of Glasgow, 1451–1577* (E, 1977); *FES* V, 182, 212; *DNB* XXXVII, 240–4.

J. Kirk

Men, The, a spiritual élite who acted as the custodians and leaders of experiential religion among Presbyterians* in the Highlands,* especially after 1700. It is unlikely that the term merely distinguishes 'the men' from 'the ministers'. In Gaelic* they are known as *Na Daoine*, literally 'The People', but implying a quasi-aristocratic differentiation; the tacksmen and 'gentle' class of Highland society were called *Na Daoine Uaisle* ('The Noble People'), and the Gaelic term for 'The Men' appears to echo such secular appellations. The emergence of this distinctive class of leaders, embracing elders, catechists, schoolmasters and missionaries (*see* Gaelic School Societies; Royal Bounty; Scottish SPCK), may have been indebted to earlier secular models, perhaps deriving ultimately from the medieval Gaelic learned orders (judges, craftsmen, poets, etc.) who regulated the Gaelic communities. Such men would have belonged to the 'free' (and thus 'noble') grades in medieval Gaelic society. 'The Men' in Highland communities acted as regulators of spiritual taste, directing the overall religious tone of their districts.

'The Men' were latterly particularly distinguished for their participation in the *Coinneamh Cheist*, or 'Question Meeting', on the Friday preceding the Communion in Presbyterian churches (*see* Communion Seasons). At this meeting, they 'spoke to the question', set by one of 'The Men' and expounded by the minister as a topic for spiritual examination, and gave their views of its implementation and significance in their own lives. They thus set the standards for spirituality and also for differentiating between the 'godly' and the 'ungodly'. The 'Question Meeting' was a public development of the private, and somewhat exclusive, 'Fellowship Meeting' which, under the leadership of 'The Men', had become a powerful means of nurturing spiritual life in different parts of the Highlands, especially in times of revival.* Admitting communicants and 'anxious inquirers' seeking further instruction, it may well have replaced, or been grafted on to, earlier secular 'moots' at which the social affairs of the community were the focus of discussion.

The origin of 'The Men' as a spiritual force in Highland society can be traced back to the mid-seventeenth century and to the influence of the Covenanting* ministers who came to occupy parishes in the northern Highlands, especially in Easter Ross. One of the first representatives of the class was John Munro, the 'caird' of Kiltearn (from the Gaelic term *ceàrd*, 'craftsman', originally one of the 'free' grades of early Gaelic society, but latterly equated with 'tinker'). Munro's spiritual father and mentor was Thomas Hog,* parish minister of Kiltearn (1654/5–92), ejected at the Restoration.* Hog appears to have implanted in his parish the concept of the prayer meeting, already known beyond the Highlands. From this the Fellowship Meeting and the sway of 'The Men' evidently developed, fusing with Gaelic culture and spreading gradually as Presbyterian Evangelicalism penetrated other parts of the Highlands.

'The Men' wielded very considerable power in the parishes, and could oppose successfully movements and practices to which they objected. Thus, by 1757, they were able to counteract an attempt by the Synod of Caithness and Sutherland to suppress public Fellowship Meetings. Their role in opposing Moderatism* and the abuse of patronage* was similarly of great importance in the late eighteenth century, and resulted in the Separatist* movement (*see* MacLeod, Norman, of Assynt). Sometimes 'The Men' would distance themselves even from evangelical ministers who did not come up to their standards. Although influenced to some extent by the work of Robert and James Haldane,* which favoured the use of lay preachers, 'The Men' were already (by 1790) well established in the northern Highland parishes, and this was almost certainly one of the reasons that the Independent* and Baptist* movement failed to make a lasting impression in the north-west. In parishes where there was little or no evangelical ministry, 'The Men' acted as potent evangelists, and in many areas their flocks were ready and waiting to receive the FC* in 1843. In later controversies, 'The Men' were strongly conservative.

'The Men' were revered among their followers. Besides their qualities of leadership, they were distinguished for their deep knowledge of the Bible, eloquent expression, prayerful lives and intimacy with God. Some were said to possess gifts of prophecy. Others were noted for their eccentricities of dress and manner.

J. MacInnes, *The Evangelical Movement in the Highlands of Scotland* (A, 1951), 211–20; R. MacCowan, *The Men of Skye* (G, 1902); J. Kennedy, *The Days of the Fathers in Ross-shire* (Inverness, 1979 edn), 74–97; G. MacDonald, *Sketches of Some of the Men of Sutherland* (Inverness, 1937); N. C. MacFarlane, *The 'Men' of the Lews* (Stornoway, c.1925).

D. E. Meek

Menteith (Monteith, Mentet), Robert (1603–c.1660), minister and historian. The son of an Edinburgh merchant, Menteith graduated from Edinburgh University in 1621 and spent four years in France as Professor of Philosophy at the Huguenot University of Saumur. Returning to Scotland, he was ordained, as an Episcopalian, minister of Duddingston, Midlothian, in 1630. In 1633 he was apparently accused of adultery with the wife of a local laird and fled to France. There he became an RC and gained the favour of Cardinal Richelieu. Later he became secretary to Cardinal de Retz, who appointed him a canon of Notre Dame Cathedral. It is not known whether he was ordained (his wife had died by now). Menteith is mainly remembered for the history he wrote of the civil wars in Britain, *Histoire des Troubles de la Grand' Bretagne* (Paris, 1649; [2]1661; ET, *The History of the Troubles of Great Britain*, L, [3]1735).

FES I, 18; *DNB* XXXVII, 257–8; *SAS* II, 240–1.

D. Stevenson

Menzies, John (1624–84), Professor of Divinity. The son of an Aberdeen burgess, Menzies graduated from Marischal College, Aberdeen, in 1638, and was a regent there by 1644. In 1649 he became minister of the second charge in St Nicholas's Church in the city, but moved in the same year to Greyfriars Church and the professorship of Divinity at Marischal College. In 1650 he supported the Protesters,* but in 1652 he became an Independent,* switching back to Presbyterianism* in 1658. After the Restoration* he complied with Episcopacy when threatened with deprivation; similarly in 1681 he refused the Test Act* oath, but took it the following year. Indecision also characterized his academic career: he moved to the chair of Divinity at King's College, Aberdeen, in 1678, but resigned two years later and returned to the Marischal College chair and the ministry of Greyfriars. Menzies was noted as a preacher and for his attacks on Catholics and Quakers, but was notorious for his vacillations – which he himself bitterly repented.

Britannia Rediviva (A, 1660); *Papismus Lucifugus* (A, 1668); *Roma Mendax* (L, 1675).

FES VI, 2, 8, VII, 362–3, 371; *DNB* XXXVII, 258–9; G. D. Henderson, *Religious Life in Seventeenth-Century Scotland* (Cambridge, 1937), esp. 106–8, 112–24; R. Wodrow, *History of the Sufferings of the CofS*, 4 vols (²G, 1828–30); R. Wodrow, *Analecta*, 4 vols (Maitland Club, E, 1842–3), III, 123–5.

D. Stevenson

Methodism. Though Methodism differs radically from Presbyterianism in matters of doctrine, ministry and membership, it displays many superficial similarities in the broad outlines of its discipline and polity. The Church Councils (formerly Leader's Meetings) correspond to Kirk Sessions;* Circuit (formerly Quarterly) Meetings to those of Presbytery* and Synods (District) Meetings to Synods* in the CofS. In Methodism, the highest Church court, the Annual Conference, is similar to the General Assembly* in form, but not entirely in composition or powers. Doctrinally, the adherence of Methodism to the beliefs of Arminius,* with their emphases on universal redemption and Christian perfection, stands in stark contrast to the traditional Calvinism* of Presbyterianism. There are also three great contrasts in organization. First, the itinerant and imposed ministry of Methodism (ministers being appointed to Circuits by the Stationing Committee, but in the last analysis by the Conference) contrasts directly with the settled ministry of the CofS. The basic unit in Methodism is the Circuit, rather than the individual charge. Second, the dependence of Methodism upon Local (or lay) Preachers long had little appeal in Scotland (*see* Laity), where the ordained, academically qualified ministry of the Kirk was universal. Third, the insistence in Methodism of a weekly meeting in Class as a test of membership was a unique and strengthening feature in the early years.

John Wesley* came to Scotland against the advice of his friends. Nevertheless, Wesley was to make twenty-two visits to Scotland; he was befriended by members of the nobility and of the CofS (*e.g.* Sir Archibald Grant of Monymusk; the Earl and Countess of Haddington; Lady Glenorchy;* John Gilles;* Alexander Webster*). For the first few years all went well. However, the Erskine controversy (*see* Erskine, John; Hervey, James) in the 1750s and 1760s did incalculable damage to the infant Methodist cause; large numbers of adherents melted away: Lady Glenorchy became estranged from Wesley and circumstances were never again so favourable for Methodist work in Scotland.

The early Methodist Preachers did not relish the prospect of a Scottish Station – often synonymous with misery and banishment (for the contrary view see Swift, *Methodism in Scotland*) and a hard field for the pioneers. Travelling was rough and difficult, roads were much worse than in England and Circuits were much more extensive. Naturally, the most popular of the early Preachers were Scots, including Thomas Rankin (Dunbar), Alexander Mather,* Alexander Coats, Alexander McNab, Peter McOwan and William Darney.* Duncan McAllum* laboured long and hard in Inverness and on Speyside, as did Duncan Wright in Aberdeen, Perth and Greenock. Robert Dall's* best work was probably when he travelled the Northern Circuit, including Peterhead, Fraserburgh, Forres and Elgin, with forays to Cromarty and Dingwall. By 1790, there were four major Circuits, with other chapels built at Dalkeith, Dumfries, Dunbar and Inverurie. In addition, preaching rooms had been bought or rented in Elgin, Inverness and Newburgh, Banff, Fraserburgh, Peterhead, Brechin, Greenock, Ayr, Kelso and Montrose, supported by sixteen Preachers ministering to 1,179 members. The increasing antagonism of the CofS to the Methodists and the refusal by some ministers to allow the Methodists the Lord's Supper, led Wesley to ordain eleven of his Preachers for Scotland, similar to his provisions for Methodists in America. This action resulted in a major expansion in membership during 1790–1819, but the number of Travelling Preachers remained inadequate and many Societies succumbed. Nevertheless, there were spectacular advances between 1820 and 1840 in the Moray Firth area and in Central Scotland, together with the establishment of Methodism in Orkney and Shetland in the 1820's (*see* Methodism in Shetland). During this period, the Primitive Methodists began their work in Scotland. From 1819, numbers slowly declined; this decline becoming progressively sharper post-1826 and lasting until the 1860s. Economic problems following the end of the Napoleonic Wars were undoubtedly responsible and it is unreasonable to blame Valentine Ward* for 'so rashly straining to breaking point the slender financial resources of Scottish Methodism'. Problems in the Connexion as a whole during 1830–50, with the Warrenite and Reform separations, had a ripple effect in Scotland.

From the 1860s Scottish Methodism generally enjoyed a relatively stable existence until the end of the Second World War, since when, as a result of the decline of traditional industries and population movements in the Central Belt, there has been a second cycle of chapel closures and Circuit amalgamations. This has been balanced by a number of new extensions, *e.g.* in East Kilbride, and by active participation in the Livingston Ecumenical Experiment, so that the future again seems bright.

Despite its numerical weakness, Methodism has had a disproportionately large influence upon religious affairs in Scotland. In 1898 D. Butler could write: '[Wesley] has helped most efficiently in pervading the churches with a more spiritual atmosphere, with greater endeavours towards a personal religion, towards a belief in God as a living Spirit, acting directly upon the soul, as the redeemer of the human will, as giving in Christ a present redemption from the power of sin. If theology shut the door against him, Scottish piety opened its door to him and every time Scottish congregations sing his hymns, they are admitting the Wesleyan influence.' It is safe to say that this influence has been maintained to the present day.

METHODISM IN SHETLAND

O. A. Beckerlegge, 'In Search of Forgotten Methodism', *Proceedings of the Wesley Historical Society* 32 (1960), 109–14; D. Butler, *Wesley and Whitefield in Scotland* (L, 1898); B. Gregory, *Sidelights on the Conflicts of Methodism* (L, 1899); A. J. Hayes, 'A Warrenite Secession in Edinburgh', *Journal of the Scottish Branch, Wesley Historical Society* 10 (1977), 3–17, 11 (1978), 3–6; *id.*, 'The Extinct Methodist Societies of South-East Scotland. I–IV', *Proceedings of the Wesley Historical Society* 51 (1977–8), 12–21, 43–52, 77–85, 105–17; A. J. Hayes and D. W. Gowland, *Scottish Methodism in the Early Victorian Period* (E, 1981); Methodist Church, *The Constitutional Practice and Discipline of the Methodist Church* (L, 1951–); W. Pierce, *The Ecclesiastical Principles and Polity of the Wesleyan Methodists* (L, 1873); W. F. Swift, *The Romance of Banffshire Methodism* (Banff, 1927); *id.*, *Methodism in Scotland* (L, 1947); W. R. Ward, 'Scottish Methodism in the Age of Jabez Bunting', *RSCHS* 20 (1979), 47–63.

A. J. Hayes

Methodism in Shetland,* second largest and most widespread denomination in the islands after the CofS,* with whom in several places worship and witness is now shared.

Methodism* has chapels in most areas of Mainland, and in Unst, Yell, Burra, and Fair Isle. Though causes like Aith, Bressay, Fetlar, and Whalsay have closed, in 1988 – with Home Mission Division support – about 550 members comprise two circuits, with twenty-four congregations, three ministers and a lay worker, a dozen or so local preachers, and other lay leaders.

Started unofficially about 1819 by John Nicolson,* Methodism's energetic pioneers from October 1822 were John Raby and Samuel Dunn. They endured great hardship. Finding finance and preachers, Adam Clarke gave close supervision during ten years of rapid growth and careful consolidation. He twice visited the islands, in 1826 and 1828. The Wesleyan-Methodist community reached a peak of 6,000 in 1866, one-third being communicant members. It included public figures like Archibald Sutherland, Sheriff Clerk, and humble, talented islanders like Robert Georgeson of West Burrafirth, and Robert Strong Wilson, keen ornithologist of Fair Isle. Shetland-born ministers such as William and James Goudie, missionaries in India, served Wesley's 'world parish'.

Methodism in Orkney* – mainly in Stronsay, 1835–41 – proved short-lived, but in the 1980s a small 'House Congregation' in South Ronaldsay became a recognized offshoot of Shetland Methodism.

H. R. Bowes, 'Revival and Survival' (MTh, University of Aberdeen, 1988); *id.*, 'The Launching of Methodism in Shetland', *Proceedings of Wesleyan Historical Society* 38 (1972), 136–46; A. Clarke, *Collected Works* XIII (L, 1837); H. R. Bowes (ed.), *Samuel Dunn's Shetland and Orkney Journal, 1822–1825* (Sheffield, 1976); J. Lewis, *William Goudie* (L, 1923); A. S. Wood, 'Methodism in Scotland', in R. Davies, A. R. George and G. Rupp (eds), *A History of the Methodist Church in Great Britain* (L, 1965–88), III, 271f.

H. R. Bowes

Methven, Paul (*d.*1606), Protestant preacher at the Reformation.* A baker by trade born at Falkland in Fife, he was instructed in Protestantism by Miles Coverdale in England. Banished under Mary Tudor, he returned home by 1558, preaching publicly in Dundee and elsewhere in Angus and at the homes of Fife lairds. At Lundie in Angus he ministered the sacraments, was active in destroying images, and fostered the 'privy kirk'* in Cupar, whose meetings were held 'in the Lady Brakmonth's house', where Methven administered the Lord's Supper. Dundee, the first town openly to appoint a Protestant preacher, chose Methven as its minister in 1558 and a kirk session* was at work, under the magistrates' protection, by the summer of 1559. Summoned by Mary of Guise,* the Queen Regent, Methven was advised by the provost to avoid Dundee. In May 1559, he was called before the justiciary court at Stirling for usurping the ministerial office and for preaching 'erroneous and seditious doctrines and heresies', and was denounced as a rebel. He subsequently served as one of two Protestant preachers in Aberdeen. Depicted by Robert Maule of Panmure, who supported his work, as a 'more mild man, preaching the Evangel of grace and the remission of sins in the blood of Christ', Methven was appointed minister of Jedburgh in the Borders by 1560. Accused of adultery in 1562, after trial he was sentenced in 1563 to be deposed from the ministry and excommunicated. Thereafter, to the irritation of the General Assembly, Methven entered the service of the CofE. He gained naturalization in 1570, was in touch with exiled Scottish ministers in 1584, and held several benefices in south-west England.

When he petitioned the General Assembly in 1564 and 1566 to be received again into the Scottish Church, the repentance prescribed was that he stand for an hour in sackcloth at St Giles in Edinburgh, before declaring his penitence to the congregation, and to repeat the prescription in Dundee and Jedburgh. After complying in Edinburgh and Jedburgh, he failed to complete the requirements in Dundee, and returned to England where he ended his days as prebendary of Wells.

Knox, *History*; *Wodrow Society Miscellany*, ed. D. Laing (E, 1844), I, 55, 425, 428; R. Lindesay of Pitscottie, *Historie and Cronicles of Scotland*, ed. A. J. G. Mackay (E, 1899–1911), II, 136–7; *Criminal Trials*, ed. R. Pitcairn (E, 1833), I: i, 406–7; Calderwood, I–II; *BUK*; J. Kirk, *Patterns of Reform* (E, 1989); *FES* II, 124–5.

J. Kirk

Metrical Psalms, *see* Psalms, Psalter.

Middle Party, a group of Evangelicals in the CofS who did not leave the Est.C at the Disruption* in 1843. Led by Matthew Leishman,* minister of

Govan, and including Robert Story* and Norman MacLeod,* they were nicknamed 'the Forty Thieves', although in fact they numbered forty-five. If they had not withdrawn their support the Evangelicals might have enjoyed a majority at the General Assembly of 1843, had they chosen to remain in the CofS. They did not accept the invitation to join the Convocation* held during the previous winter to prepare for the coming division of the Church but instead held their own meeting in Edinburgh. The Middle Party did not wish to endanger the unity of the Church or its establishment. Their stance was outlined in a *Declaration* made by Leishman at the Synod of Glasgow and Ayr in 1842. They were willing to accept the measure outlined by Sir George Sinclair (1790–1868; *DNB* LII, 295–6) in relation to the presentation of ministers to parishes. This proposal would have left the church courts free to reject a patron's presentee if they considered the objections made to him to be valid or held by such a proportion of the parishioners as to preclude that minister's usefulness in the parish.

J. F. Leishman, *Matthew Leishman of Govan and the Middle Party of 1843* (Paisley, 1921).

D. M. Murray

Miles, Charles Popham (1810–91), English Episcopal* minister and an evangelical leader of the Episcopal 'disruption' of 1842–4. A graduate of Caius College, Cambridge, in 1843 he became incumbent of St Jude's, Glasgow, and in the same year preached to support the Revd Sir William Dunbar* and his English Episcopal congregation. Rebuked by his own diocesan, Bishop Michael Russell, in 1844, he and St Jude's left the EpCS. He remained incumbent until 1858. In his writings he upheld the legitimacy of Protestant and evangelical Episcopalianism in Scotland and attacked the territorial and exclusive claims of the EpCS.

An Address to the Members of St Jude's Congregation, Glasgow (G, 1844); *The Voice of the Glorious Reformation* (L, 1844).

E. M. Culbertson

Millar, Robert (1672–1752), apologist and historian. Born in Dailly or Neilston, Ayrshire, and educated at Glasgow University, he was ordained at Greenock in 1697 and translated to Paisley Abbey in 1709, where he served until his death. Millar was the author of two essays in historical apologetics, *A History of the Propagation of Christianity* (2 vols, E, 1723) and *A History of the Church under the Old Testament* (E, 1730). In both, as an apologetic argument against the natural religion of the English deists,* Millar attempted to demonstrate the course of providence in history by means of a chronology ordered and reinterpreted theologically.

Millar's progressivist philosophy of history, derived from French and English Calvinist apologetics,* is most apparent in *Propagation*. Devoting the bulk of ch. I to a recapitulation of a range of arguments from the classic apologetical canon of the early eighteenth century, Millar draws on an extensive range of historical and contemporary sources in chh. II, III, V, and VII to characterize natural religion as demonstrably irrational and socially retrogressive. By contrast, in chh. III, IV, VI and VIII he argues for the progressive and, consequently, providential expansion of Christianity. Millar's advocacy of missions* in ch. IX, therefore, is best understood within the context of the argument for the superior moral rationality and assured progress of Christianity.

This combination of apologetic with progressivist, eschatological and missionary motifs accounts for the wide influence of the work in the first half of the eighteenth century. It was published in a Dutch translation, and two further editions appeared in London in 1726 and 1731. While later writers generally ignored the apologetic framework of the *Propagation*, and Gibbon's *Decline and Fall* put into question the direct correlation of progress and providence, theologians and ecclesiastical historians continued to make use of Millar's historical extracts.

FES III, 166; J. Foster, 'A Scottish Contributor to the Missionary Awakening: Robert Millar of Paisley', *International Review of Missions* 37 (1948), 138–45; R. E. Davies, 'Robert Millar – An Eighteenth Century Scottish Latourette', *EQ* 62 (1990), 143–56; R. S. Crane, 'Anglican Apologetics and the Idea of Progress, 1699–1745', *Modern Philology* 31 (1933), 273–306, 349–82; O. G. Myklebust, *The Study of Missions in Theological Education* (Oslo, 1955); J. van den Berg, *Constrained by Jesus' Love* (Kampen, 1956); J. A. De Jong, *As the Waters Cover the Sea* (Kampen, 1970); A. Fawcett, *The Cambuslang Revival* (L, 1971).

I. D. Maxwell

Millennialism, a term sometimes used to signify belief in a thousand-year reign of Christ on earth prior to the Last Judgment. In this sense it is synonymous with premillennialism. However, it is taken here in the broader sense to indicate the full spectrum of views of those for whom the 'thousand years' (millennium) is significant.

MIDDLE AGES. In common with other West European lands prior to the Reformation, medieval Scotland accepted the Augustinian view of the millennium. This was a form of amillennialism which interpreted the thousand years of Rev. 20:2–6 as the era of the Church and its spiritual influence between the first and second comings of Christ. No future conversion of the Jews was anticipated in this scheme, nor any future millennium, literal or figurative.

THE REFORMATION. Many of the Reformers (e.g. Calvin) adopted a modified version of the Augustinian amillennialism. New eschatological horizons, however, were explored by Martin Bucer, Peter Martyr Vermigli and Theodore Beza, all of whom anticipated a future conversion of Israel. Martyr's Commentary on Romans (ET, L, 1568) was particularly influential in transmitting this view to Eng-

MILLENNIALISM

lish and Scottish Protestants. Martyr placed the conversion of Israel at the end of history, ushering in the Last Judgment rather than any further calling of Gentiles. The English Puritan William Perkins also popularized this view.

A genuine postmillennial perspective also gained adherents among English-speaking Protestants in the sixteenth century. It appeared most significantly in the Geneva Bible (1560) (see Bible (Versions, English)), whose marginal notes to Rom. 11:15 and 25 taught that Israel's conversion would occasion not the Last Judgment but an unparalleled time of spiritual blessing among Gentiles.

SEVENTEENTH CENTURY. This postmillennial understanding had triumphed over the Martyr–Perkins view among English and Scottish Puritans by the time of the Covenants* and civil wars of the 1640s. It was enshrined in the Westminster Assembly's* Larger Catechism in the answer to question 191, 'What do we pray for in the second petition [of the Lord's prayer]?' 'In the second petition . . . we pray, that the kingdom of sin and Satan may be destroyed, the gospel propagated throughout the world, the Jews called, the fulness of the Gentiles brought in . . .' The Directory for the Publick Worship of God also expressed this view, advising ministers to pray publicly 'for the conversion of the Jews, the fulness of the Gentiles, the fall of Antichrist'.

Among the Scottish divines of this period to advocate postmillennialism were Samuel Rutherford,* George Gillespie,* David Dickson,* James Durham,* George Hutcheson,* Robert Baillie,* Robert Leighton,* Richard Cameron* and John Brown of Wamphray* (see his *An Exposition of . . . Romans*, E, 1776). Alexander Petrie* was almost a lone voice in advocating the old amillennialism.

EIGHTEENTH CENTURY. In the eighteenth century, postmillennialism lived on among the Evangelicals* in the CofS, e.g. Thomas Boston,* from whom it flowed into the Secession* tradition. In the CofS the Evangelical Revival gave fresh impetus to postmillennial optimism about the conversion of the nations. John Erskine of Edinburgh* and James Robe* of Kilsyth were of this mind, influenced by Jonathan Edwards'* *Humble Attempt to Promote Explicit Agreement and Visible Union of God's People in Extraordinary Prayer . . . for the Revival of Religion and the Advancement of Christ's Kingdom on Earth, Pursuant to Scripture Promises and Prophecies concerning the Last Time* (Boston, MA, 1747). The second wave of revival* in the 1790s, spearheaded by the Haldanes,* led to the establishment of many missionary societies resolved on spreading the gospel beyond the English-speaking lands. These societies were cradled in postmillennial expectation, and often had auxiliaries devoted to evangelizing the Jews. The Haldane brothers were postmillennialists (see Robert's *Exposition of The Epistle to the Romans*, 3 vols, L, 1836–9).

NINETEENTH CENTURY: POSTMILLENNIAL NOON. The first half of the nineteenth century saw the rise of postmillennialism to its zenith of influence, and paradoxically the sowing of the seeds of its virtually total eclipse. Great names, such as Thomas Chalmers,* John Brown (d. 1858)* of Edinburgh, Patrick Fairbairn,* 'Rabbi' John Duncan* and Robert Murray M'Cheyne* added their weight to the postmillennial interpretation of Scripture and world history. David Bogue,* the Independent minister of Gosport, near Portsmouth, impressed a generation of students in his theology classes with a postmillennial vision of missionary enterprise and expansion. Many Scottish missionaries were sustained in their labours by the same vision: Alexander Duff,* David Livingstone,* J. G. Paton,* Alexander Somerville,* Robert Johnston* (see his *The Conversion of the Jews and its Bearings on the Conversion of the Gentiles*, E, 1853).

It is doubly ironic that the classic exposition in Scotland (indeed, in the English language) of postmillennial eschatology, David Brown's *Christ's Second Coming: Will It Be Premillennial?* (E, 1846), should have devoted its bulk to polemic against a resurgent premillennialism, and been authored by the erstwhile ministerial assistant to the man chiefly responsible for that resurgence – Edward Irving.*

NINETEENTH CENTURY: PREMILLENNIAL DAWN. Irving derived his premillennialism from James Hatley Frere, and disseminated it in the 1820s in a flood of books and lectures. Henry Drummond (1786–1860)* added impetus by hosting premillennial prophetic conferences in his Albury mansion in Surrey, 1826–30. Irving and Drummond were soon diverted into the bypaths of the Catholic Apostolic Church,* but their influence lived on among the Brethren.* J. N. Darby was present at the premillennial Powerscourt conference in Ireland in 1831, an Irish version of Albury. Other leading Brethren pioneers, such as Henry Craik* and Anthony Norris Groves, were also influenced by Irving's premillennialism. The Brethren movement became the single most potent channel through which premillennialism spread among British Evangelicals in the middle decades of the nineteenth century, undermining the old postmillennial consensus.

Through Darby's influence the Brethren's premillennialism soon became dispensational. In Scotland, however, premillennialism was popularized, in book, hymn and sermon, mainly by two FC ministers, Horatius and Andrew Bonar.* The Bonars were converted to premillennialism by Irving, but adhered to the traditional historicist premillennialism rather than the new and more influential Darbyite dispensationalism. Horatius edited *The Quarterly Journal of Prophecy*. The Bonars also stood apart from the mainstream of premillennial resurgence in their hostility to the Keswick Convention teaching on sanctification. The Keswick message had early become intertwined with premillennialism, and its influence outstripped the Brethren in attracting British Evangelicals to the new eschatology in the nineteenth century's latter decades.

TWENTIETH CENTURY. The liberal Evangelicalism which came to dominate Scottish Presbyterianism

MILLER, EUPHEMIA

at the close of the nineteenth century and into the twentieth led to a loss of interest in millennial questions. Leading thinkers of this school in the first part of the twentieth century, such as H. R. Mackintosh* and John Baillie,* were concerned to question the doctrine of eternal punishment and reconsider the annihilationist and universalist options, rather than debate prophetic timetables. To the degree that liberal Evangelicalism was strong, millennialism in any form was weak. Premillennialism, however, flourished among Brethren, Pentecostalists and Baptists (among the last, especially through Graham Scroggie*), helped by the dispensationalist Scofield Bible. Postmillennialism survived in the FC and FPC.

The present Scottish evangelical scene offers no consensus millennial view. Premillennialism is still strongest among Brethren, Pentecostalists and Baptists. Amillennialism has gained ground among the more academically minded. Postmillennialism, however, has seen something of a resurgence as part of the broader renewal of interest in Reformed theology, and was ably expounded by John Murray* in his *The Epistle to the Romans*, 2 vols (Grand Rapids, 1960–65).

I. Murray, *The Puritan Hope* (E, 1971);
D. Bebbington, *Evangelicalism in Modern Britain* (L, 1989); L. R. Froom, *The Prophetic Faith of Our Fathers*, 4 vols (Washington, DC, 1946–54), II–III.

N. R. Needham

Miller, Euphemia, *see* Women in Presbyterian Missions.

Miller, Hugh (1802–56), crusading Free Churchman, editor and geologist. Born in Cromarty, he was the son of Hugh Miller, a sailor lost at sea in 1807, and Harriet Wright, whose Gaelic* mysticism influenced him deeply. Educated locally, he showed early interest in geology and literature, but disruptive behaviour abruptly terminated his formal schooling. He served as an apprentice stonemason (1820–2), thereafter (1823–34) working as a journeyman in Cromarty and elsewhere, including Edinburgh. His discoveries in the stone quarries deepened his interest in geology. By 1834 he had established a local reputation as poet, antiquarian and journalist, which led to his being appointed accountant at a Cromarty bank, a post he held until 1839. His interest in theology, and the relationship between Church and state*, was growing. When Lord Brougham ruled against the Non-Intrusionists* in the Auchterarder Case* (*see* Ten Years' Conflict), Miller produced a *Letter . . . to the Right Honourable Brougham* (E, 1839), powerfully arguing the anti-patronage case. So impressed were the evangelical leaders that they invited Miller to edit *The Witness*,* the bi-weekly newspaper which they were about to launch. Sacrificing (as he saw it) his literary and scientific aspirations, Miller accepted, moving to Edinburgh in late 1839. His remaining years were spent in unremitting labour: apart from his editorial duties, he published many

MILLER, WILLIAM

books, including his autobiography *My Schools and Schoolmasters* (E, 1854), and defended the creationist position from a scientific standpoint in print and on the podium. Miller was always highly-strung, his periodic morbid depressiveness exacerbated by the effects of silicosis. Excessive stress and brain disease led to his suicide.

Miller is chiefly remembered for his editorship of *The Witness* and his geological writings. He was a brilliant editor, stamping each page with his highly individualistic personality. The part played by *The Witness* in generating the groundswell of opinion against patronage,* which led eventually to the Disruption,* cannot be over-estimated, nor can its later influence in marshalling support for the new FC. Miller's trenchantly expressed views were not always shared by the FC leadership: however, he skilfully circumvented attempts to undermine his editorial independence, and in fact won more freedom. He was a gifted popularizer of geology, combining the logical approach of the scientist with a rare creative imagination, and was thus uniquely gifted 'to stand as interpreter between nature and the public', as he put it. The serious contribution to geology made by works such as *The Old Red Sandstone* (E, 1841), which describes fossils found in the Cromarty sandstone quarries, was widely recognized. Miller was especially concerned to uphold by scientific method the idea of God as Creator at a time when evolutionary views such as those put forward by Robert Chambers* in the anonymous *Vestiges of . . . Creation* (L, 1844) were gaining ground. Miller responded with *Footprints of the Creator* (L, 1849) and the posthumous *Testimony of the Rocks* (E, 1857): for him, science unveiled in creation a vastness undreamed of by the theologians.

P. Bayne, *The Life and Letters of Hugh Miller* (L, 1871); G. Rosie, *Hugh Miller: Outrage and Order* (E, 1981).

J. A. H. Dempster

Miller, William (1838–1923), the most influential educational missionary of his day in India. Born in Thurso, Miller was educated at Aberdeen University (MA, 1856). Ordained by the FC Presbytery of Edinburgh, he was appointed in 1862 to teach in Madras Christian College, which he served as Principal from 1877 until his retirement in 1907. He acted for a period as Vice-Chancellor of the University of Madras, was a member of the Madras Presidency Legislative Council, and was Moderator (1896) of the General Assembly of the FCS.

As a missionary strategist and statesman he showed himself the natural successor of Alexander Duff,* concentrating as had Duff on higher education as a way to India's heart. His personal influence on generations of students was immense. Miller saw the task of the Christian college as the spreading of Christian thought and influence throughout India rather than the conversion of individuals. Missions* are not, he taught, primarily or exclusively concerned with the numerical and rapid expansion of the Church. Preaching and conversion have their place. Christian education involves a sowing which others will reap, years or decades later. Education must not be used as a bribe for converts. It is rather a way of diffusing Christian ideas and values which will gradually transform the Hindu mind and Hindu society. While Duff held that Christian influence would be spread by his converts, Miller believed that the validity and truth of Christianity was such that it would and could make its own way.

Miller differed from Duff also in his more positive assessment of Hinduism. He taught that Christ was the source of all that was good and true in Hinduism as in Christianity, and was capable of purifying any system of error and evil. For him, as for J. N. Farquhar,* Christ was the Fulfiller.

Miller was awarded the degree of LLD by Edinburgh University and later by Madras University, and the DD degree by Edinburgh.

AFCS I, 269; *FUFCS* 544; *Who Was Who, 1916-1928*, 732; O.K. Chetty, *Dr. William Miller* (Madras, 1924).

D. B. Forrester

Miller, William Douglas, of Ruchill (1868-1924), UFC minister. Born at Dreghorn, Ayrshire, he studied at Edinburgh University, graduating MA in 1889, and then at New College. Licensed by Edinburgh FC Presbytery in 1893, he was assistant at Largs FC, Ayrshire, 1893-5, and then in 1895 was ordained to Denny Dunipace FC, Stirlingshire. In 1905 he moved to Ruchill UFC, Glasgow, where he spent the remainder of his ministry, and from which he derived his sobriquet 'Miller of Ruchill'. He did war service in the YMCA in France 1916-17. In his last years he became one of the UFC's most outspoken opponents of union with the CofS, an opposition rooted in his ardent Voluntaryism.*

Miller was a celebrated preacher and evangelist, and a zealous proponent of sabbath schools and the temperance movement.* His theological and spiritual mentors were Wilhelm Herrmann of Marburg and Alexander Whyte.*

J. S. Smith, *Miller of Ruchill* (G, 1924); *AFCS* I, 269; *FUFCS*, 245.

N. R. Needham

Milligan, George (1860-1934), CofS minister and biblical scholar. The son of Professor William Milligan* of Aberdeen, he followed his father into the ministry and into the field of biblical studies. A graduate of the University of Aberdeen (MA, 1879; BD, 1883), he also studied at the universities of Edinburgh, Göttingen and Bonn. He was minister of St Matthew's Church in Edinburgh, 1883-94, and of Caputh in Perthshire, 1894-1910, before becoming Regius Professor of Biblical Criticism in the University of Glasgow, 1910-32. In his commentary on the *Epistles to the Thessalonians* (L, 1908) he used his study of Greek papyri to re-examine Paul's grammar and vocabulary. His major work, *The Vocabulary of the Greek Testament* (L, 1914-29), was written in collaboration with the English Methodist scholar, J. H. Moulton. He was convener of the Committee on the Religious Instruction of Youth, 1913-24, and was Moderator of the General Assembly in 1923. Although not a member of the Scottish Church Society,* of which his father had been the first president, he was sympathetic to its aims.

FES VII, 405; *DNB, 1931-40*, 616-17.

D. M. Murray

Milligan, Oswald Bell (1879-1940), leading representative of the 'high church' school in CofS. The son of William* and brother of George,* he was a student at Edinburgh (MA, 1899; BD, 1902), Göttingen, Halle and Berlin. He was parish minister successively at Wallacetown, Ayr (1906-9), St Leonard's, Ayr (1909-19, interrupted by chaplaincy service during World War I (1914-17; MC, 1916), Jedburgh (1919-27) and Corstorphine Old (from 1927). Death overtook him at the height of recognition and influence: DD (Edinburgh, 1939); Lee Lecturer,* 1939 (*The Scottish Communion Office and its Historical Background*, E, 1939); Warrack Lecturer* at Aberdeen and Glasgow, 1940 (*The Ministry of Worship*, L, 1941); President of the Church Service Society,* 1938-40; and Convener of the Committee on Public Worship and Aids to Devotion* which produced the 1940 *Book of Common Order*.* His responsibility for this monument to the ascendancy of Scoto-Catholicism* in the CofS has proved a lasting legacy. He also published *The Practice of Prayer* (E, 1938), histories of St Leonard's, Ayr, and Corstorphine Old, and pamphlets on baptism and communion.

FES III, 15-16, VIII, 3, 139, IX, 10; appreciations by M. Patrick in *LW* n.s. 11 (1940), 153, and by 'T.M.' in *Church Service Soc. Annual* 12 (1941-2), 22-3; A. C. Cheyne, *The Transforming of the Kirk* (E, 1983), 195-8.

D. F. Wright

Milligan, William (1821-93), CofS minister, biblical scholar and theologian. He was the son of George Milligan, minister of Elie in Fife and was educated at the universities of St Andrews (MA, 1839; DD, 1860), Edinburgh, and Halle. He was minister of Cameron, 1844-50, and then of Kilconquhar, Fife, 1850-61, before being appointed Professor of Biblical Criticism in the University of Aberdeen in 1860. He became Depute Clerk of the General Assembly in 1875, Principal Clerk in 1886 and Moderator in 1882. He was a member of the Revision Committee of the New Testament. As a scholar his chief interest lay in the Johannine literature and in the Epistle to the Hebrews. In collaboration with W. F. Moulton he published *A Popular Commentary on the Gospel of St John* (E, 1880). He wrote a *Commentary on the Revelation of St John* (E, 1883) and for the Expositor's Bible (L, 1889). A commentary on Hebrews remained unpublished at his death. His principal theological works were *The Resurrection of our Lord* (L, ^{3}1884) and *The Ascension and Heavenly Priesthood of our Lord* (L, 1892). He wished to supplement what he accepted as a proper emphasis in much nineteenth-century theology on the Incarnation by expounding the doctrines of the Resurrection and Ascension. He also stressed the continuing heavenly ministry of Christ as high priest. He believed the priesthood of Christ had been forgotten in Scotland. In spite of the Reformation* emphasis on the 'priesthood of all believers', the Reformers' rejection of the priesthood of the clergy had led to neglect of the priestly calling of the Church. Milligan did not wish to encourage sacerdotalism; the Church's priesthood could not be exercised in its own right but only in union with Christ. He therefore stressed the importance of the Lord's Supper* in worship, since it is in the eucharist that the one offering of Christ as priest is most fully set forth. He favoured a weekly celebration of Communion. He was one of the founders of the Scottish Church Society,* its first president, 1892–3, and profoundly influenced the thinking of Scoto-Catholics* such as James Cooper,* John Macleod* (d.1898) and H. J. Wotherspoon.* His son George Milligan* also became a biblical scholar.

FES VII, 376–7; A. M. Milligan, *In Memoriam William Milligan, D.D.* (A, 1894); W. F. Moulton, 'In Memoriam, the Rev. William Milligan, D.D.', *ExT* 5 (1893–4), 247–51; P. J. Anderson (ed.), *Aurora Borealis Academica* (A, 1899), 185–8.

D. M. Murray

Milne, John (1807–68), evangelical CofS and FC minister. Within months of his ordination in 1839 as minister of St Leonard's in Perth, revival* broke out in his congregation through the preaching of William Chalmers Burns* and soon spread throughout the city and surrounding area. Milne developed close ties with other revival leaders such as Horatius* and Andrew Bonar* and Robert Murray McCheyne.* In 1843 he became minister of St Leonard's FC, where he remained, except for a brief tenure as minister of a FC congregation in Calcutta during the mid-1850s, until his death.

Gatherings from a Ministry (L, 1868).

FES IV, 239; AFCS I, 270; H. Bonar, *Life of the Rev. John Milne* (L, 1869).

D. A. Currie

Milne (or Mille, Mylne), Walter (c.1476–1558), heretic* and martyr*. Milne was said to have held the mass as idolatry, to accept clerical marriage, private preaching and other such heresies. He had been priest in the parish of Lunan, Angus, and fled during the 1530s when accused by David Beaton,* abbot of Arbroath. Sentenced to be burnt whenever apprehended, he was the last Protestant martyr in Scotland, burnt at St Andrews at the age of c.82.

Knox affirmed that this cruelty backfired. When the Protestant preachers were summoned for trial in 1559, their patrons defended them with arms, thus initiating the Reformation.*

Knox, *History* I, 153, 190; A. Petrie, *A Compendious History of the Catholick Church* (The Hague, 1662),

189; M. H. B. Sanderson, *Cardinal of Scotland* (E, 1986).

F. D. Bardgett

Ministry. The Scottish Reformers emphatically rejected the medieval understanding of ministry as primarily or exclusively that of priests who had received a *character indelebilis* through the sacrament of orders and took their place in a hierarchically structured ministry. Instead, within a strong theological reaffirmation of the continuing priestly ministry of Christ, in which the whole Church participates as a royal priesthood, the Reformers stressed the importance of a lawful ministry, properly constituted. This was a matter of good order, but it was necessary for the being of the Church. Such ordained ministers are understood first of all as Christ's ministers, and his gift to the Church, in which capacity they act in Christ's name and represent him to the Church. All their work is for the equipment of the saints for the work of ministry and for building up the body of Christ (Eph. 4:12). It is, in other words, to enable the broader ministry of the whole royal priesthood.

The essential, or perhaps the only, ministry is that of Word and sacrament. In this, as in other ways, seeking to follow the precedents of the early Church, Scottish Reformed theologians discerned in their 'ministers' both the presbyters and the bishops of the NT documents. Although to begin with there was neither the later phobia of 'episcopacy',* nor a stress on 'parity of ministers',* when superintendents* or bishops were recognized it was not as a separate or distinct order of ministry.

The primary functions of ministers were to proclaim the gospel, to administer the sacraments and other ordinances, to catechize, to exercise discipline* (under which head was assumed much of what we would today call pastoral care), and to lead and govern the congregation. The elders,* commonly known as 'ruling' elders, shared with the minister, particularly in pastoral care, governing and leading. They did not administer the sacraments, nor did they preach. They were regarded by the Westminster Assembly* as representatives of the people who assisted, particularly in the pastoral work of ministry. In the courts* of the Church they have the same powers as ministers, and in all courts above the Kirk Session* there are equal numbers of ministers and elders. Elders are ordained, but not by the laying on of hands, and some challenge whether the term 'ordination' is properly to be used of elders at all. Indeed there are profound and deep-rooted differences within the CofS as to how the eldership is to be understood. Yet, for largely pragmatic reasons, the eldership has commended itself in recent years widely outside the Presbyterian Churches as an effective way of structuring the ministry of the whole congregation.

For some decades there has been considerable uncertainty in the CofS about the ministry, arising mainly from an unplanned and unco-ordinated proliferation of recognized forms of ministry, and an increasing emphasis on the ministry of the whole people of God in such a way that there seems little place for the ordained ministry. These problems have been exacerbated by role uncertainty among ministers and a declining supply of ministers. The Panel on Doctrine issued a Statement on the Office of Elder in 1963 and a Statement on the Ministry of Word and Sacrament in 1965. In 1982 the General Assembly gave the following remit to the Panel: 'Aware of the great diversity of ministries exercised within the Church, instruct the Panel on Doctrine to clarify the Church's theology of ministry in general, and particularly to offer guidance as to how these various ministries relate to each other and to the ministry of the Church as a whole.' An imaginative Interim Report was submitted to the General Assembly of 1985 which, grounding the ministry of the whole Church in the ministry of Christ, discerned two 'clusters' of specific but not exclusive ministries within the Church – one the ministry of Word and sacrament, the other the ministry of service. This report has been extensively discussed throughout the Church, but there is as yet little sign of a consensus emerging.

Another major influence on the CofS's thinking on ministry has been the development of ecumenical views on ministry. Up to the 1950s the major endeavour had been to provide coherent and reasoned statements of the traditional Reformed understanding of ministry as a contribution to 'comparative ecclesiology'. Recently we have seen the production of 'convergence texts', of which two have been specially influential on CofS thinking of ministry – *Baptism Eucharist and Ministry (Faith and Order Paper* 111, Geneva, 1982), and the Report of the Anglican-Reformed International Commission, *God's Reign and our Unity* (E, 1984). These both stimulate and indicate a widespread search for a renewed understanding of the ministry of the Church. For the CofS, as for other Churches, this will involve a far more profound reconsideration than anything that has yet taken place.

G. D. Henderson, *Church and Ministry* (L, 1951); T. F. Torrance, *Royal Priesthood* (E, 1955); T. F. Torrance, 'The Meaning of Order' and 'Consecration and Ordination', in *Conflict and Agreement in the Church*, vol. 2 (L, 1960); H. J. Wotherspoon and J. M. Kirkpatrick, *A Manual of Church Doctrine*, new edn (L, 1960).

D. B. Forrester

Missionary Magazine, The, *see* Periodicals, Religious.

Missions: Origins

A. GENERAL INTRODUCTION.
I. Origins. On the title page of the Scots Confession* of 1560 are the words of Matthew 24:14: 'And this glaid tydinges of the kingdom shall be preached throught the hole world for a witnes to all nations and then shall the end cum'. The worldview of the Reformers was largely bounded by Europe, and the text was probably chosen to point to the preaching of the Reformation faith throughout Christendom, rather than to indicate a worldwide mission. The Larger Catechism (the Shorter Catechism is silent on the subject; *see* Catechisms; Westminster Assembly) enjoins prayer for the propagation of the gospel and the bringing in of the fulness of the Gentiles; and the Directory of Public Worship, for the preaching to all nations, the fall of Antichrist and the hastening of Christ's return. Thus the great documents of the period link their rare references to the world beyond Christendom to God's action in the last times rather than to the Church's mission in the present.

Seventeenth-century Scotland had parallels to those Puritan theocratic ideals and post-millennial eschatology that are often identified as sources of the missionary movement in England and America. But the missionary vision emerged more slowly, perhaps because seventeenth-century Scotland consolidated its European relationships rather than opened inter-continental ones. The first Scottish writer to set out a comprehensive missionary programme is Robert Millar* of Paisley Abbey (1723). Millar traces the parallel themes of the propagation of Christianity and the downfall of paganism, one age of evangelization ending with the completion of the Christianizing of Europe. He then describes the state of paganism in the contemporary world, in parallel with a new age of evangelization beginning with 'the reviving of arts and sciences, knowledge and learning'.

The disastrous Darien* scheme (1698, not mentioned by Millar), the first major Scottish venture overseas, included several ministers for the pastoral care of the settlers, while allowing that one day 'the poor heathens' might hear the gospel. Some ministers (one of them Robert Wodrow's* father-in-law) are known to have gone to India in the late seventeenth century, but again to the cure of European souls. A Scot, the ex-Quaker George Keith,* became in 1702 the first missionary of the (Anglican) Society for the Propagation of the Gospel, organizing its early work in the American colonies. Early SPG missionaries included Scottish non-jurors* seeking a religious climate more hospitable than at home. In its early phase the SPG was primarily concerned with the European population of the colonies, though its charter provided for the spread of the faith to non-Christian peoples.

John Wesley, himself a former SPG missionary, had at least one Scottish preacher, Duncan MacAllum,* who expressed a desire to be a missionary. Wesley's answer was 'You have nothing at present to do in Africa. Convert the heathen in Scotland.'

The true origins of Scottish overseas mission lie in the confluence of two streams, each emerging from activity directed to Scotland but transformed by transatlantic influences. One flows from the Scottish Society for Propagating Christian Knowledge.* In the Highlands* and Islands, eighteenth-century Scotland had a mission field in a sense that England did not, and churchmen of many persuasions could unite in the objects of the Society. Founded in 1709, it sought to instruct the people of the Highlands 'in the Christian Reformed Protestant Religion', including in its charter also provision for 'the advancement of the Christian religion to heathen countries'. It combined preaching by

MISSIONS: ORIGINS

licensed itinerants with regular schools, teaching from the Bible, and support by libraries, in English and in Gaelic. Millar notes that the SSPCK schoolmaster sent to St Kilda in 1710 encountered virtual paganism. In 1735 SSPCK work was extended to the Highland diaspora when John Macleod (*FES* VII, 664) was appointed to Georgia from Skye. A legacy from the English dissenter Daniel Williams enabled SSPCK to implement the wider provisions of its charter. It did so much more by funding the New England churches to undertake missions to the Native American peoples than by sending missionaries from Scotland. Thus the appointment of David Brainerd in 1742 was made possible by the SSPCK; and the story of Brainerd, who never saw Scotland, raised missionary consciousness in Scotland as elsewhere. The preaching tour in Britain in 1766–8 of the Native American Samson Occum, another SSPCK missionary, gave further impetus, and the 1767 General Assembly approved a collection for the mission work in America.

A second stream comes from the evangelical awakening of 1742 (*see* Revivals). Observers of the Cambuslang revival noted the prevalence of prayer for the spread of the knowledge of Christ throughout the world. In 1744 John MacLaurin* and other ministers entered a two-year covenant to pray that God would 'revive true religion in all parts of Christendom ... and fill the whole earth with his glory'. Jonathan Edwards* seized on the idea of a wider 'Concert of Prayer' for the advancement of Christ's kingdom. In *An Humble Attempt to Promote Explicit Agreement and Visible Union of God's People in Extraordinary Prayer* (1747) Edwards, Brainerd's mentor and a pillar of the New England Native American mission, set the Scottish experience of prayer, the contemporary experience of revival, and biblical prophecies of the kingdom within a history of redemption which pointed to an approaching time of the spread of the gospel. His Scottish correspondent John Erskine* sent the book to the group of English Baptists which included Andrew Fuller,* who had already been influenced by Millar. This issued in the prayer meetings which led to the foundation of the Baptist Missionary Society (BMS) and a new phase of the missionary movement.

Thus in the formative period of Scottish missionary thought, concern for the kingdom in Scotland was interwoven with concern for the kingdom overseas. The association long continued. John Gillies'* *Historical Collections* (1754), as much as their continuation by Horatius Bonar* (1845), identify 'remarkable periods of the success of the Gospel' in evangelical awakenings and missionary enterprise alike. The result of the frustration of the Haldane* mission to India was the Haldane mission to the Highlands. The response of the Relief Church* in 1798 to a debate about overseas missions was to open a mission to the Highlands. Thomas Chalmers* is emblematic in holding together a mission in Scotland and overseas as inseparable companions. But even such an archetypal Moderate* as William Robertson* could respond to Millar's vision of the propagation of Christianity and the downfall of modern paganism, and like him link it

MISSIONS: EARLY SOCIETIES

with the progress of learning. A generation later, George Hill,* Chalmers' Moderate teacher, could look to the eventual worldwide acceptance of Christianity, divinely prepared for by 'a long intercourse with the nations of Europe' to remove 'the prejudices of idolatry and ignorance'. The gospel and education had marched together in the Scottish Reformation,* and again in the eighteenth-century mission to the Highlands. Evangelical and Moderate alike, despite their different understandings of the gospel process, expected the companionship to continue.

II. The early Societies. By the end of the eighteenth century the growing strength of evangelical* religion and its increasing diversity found new expression. Within the CofS evangelical power and influence increased: evangelical alternatives to Presbyterianism appeared in the Congregational* and Baptist* movements; and many in the older churches found traditional grounds of separation to matter less than evangelical fraternity and obligation. Increasingly, voluntary societies were accepted as a mode of Christian activity. These united people of similar outlook across denominational boundaries. Without challenging the individual's denominational allegiance, they by-passed the churches' structures and procedures.

Social changes enhanced Scottish Evangelicals' consciousness of their counterparts in England who likewise had adopted the voluntary society. In missionary matters, Scottish and English influences intermingled. As already indicated, Scottish developments played a part in the formation in 1792 of the BMS. Its *Periodical Accounts* of work in India circulated in Scotland, but its earliest subscription lists contain few Scottish names (though David Dale* was a regular donor from 1796). The Baptist movement in Scotland was new and highly controversial. Nevertheless from about 1804 there was noticeable Scottish support for the BMS, and not only from Baptists: several Secession, Methodist and Independent congregations contributed, and some CofS ministers. Many gifts were earmarked for the Serampore missionaries' translation work; and the Serampore fire of 1812 evoked a generous response. The Moravians,* pioneers of Protestant missions, also received Scottish support.

Relations were still closer with the Missionary Society, founded in London in 1795 and later called the London Missionary Society.* Its immediate inspiration was an appeal in the *Evangelical Magazine* by David Bogue,* an expatriate Scot. All four London-based CofS ministers were active in the Society. One, John Love,* was among the first secretaries, and almost half the original committee were Scots. Alexander Waugh, a London-based Secession minister, devised the 'fundamental principle' whereby the Society pledged itself to send only the gospel, leaving polity to the decision of the churches that would emerge. Twenty-eight Scottish ministers (half of them CofS) served as Directors of the LMS during its first five years. The names of the earliest missionaries suggest a strong Scottish element. The LMS records do not record the birthplaces of missionaries until about 1812; from then until the 1880s the high proportion of Scottish candidates is evident, and Scotland provides some of the most eminent names. As in England, Congregational churches produced many; without the historical antecedents of English Independency, Scottish Congregationalism was often essentially an expression of fervent Evangelicalism. But many candidates came from Presbyterian backgrounds. For at least half a century the LMS was a major, perhaps the predominant, influence in thought about missions in Scotland.

It was widely imitated. In 1796 the Glasgow Missionary Society (GMS) was established, and a few weeks later the Edinburgh Missionary Society (EMS), John Erskine preaching the first sermon. The range of enthusiasm, however, is shown in the profusion of local mission societies – at least another sixty-one between 1796 and 1825, and this apart from the many branches of the Bible Society* movement which appeared from 1804 onwards. Some of these were auxiliaries of larger societies, but many were independent, gathering and diffusing information about missions and contributing to the various missionary causes (often at home as well as abroad) at their discretion. Each of the universities had a student missionary society: Aberdeen (1820), Glasgow (1821), St Andrews (1824) and Edinburgh (1825). The Edinburgh society, founded by the future eminent missionary John Wilson, was particularly influential. That at St Andrews, where Chalmers as professor gave inspiration and encouragement, was still more significant; its student founders included John Adam, Alexander Duff,* David Ewart,* William Sinclair Mackay,* Robert Nesbit,* all to be notable missionaries, and John Urquhart* who, despite his early death, was their pathfinder.

One casualty of the new missionary activity was the SSPCK, which had enjoyed the support of Moderates and Evangelicals. All continued to speak well of it, but the ardour and subscriptions went into the new societies.

Official church responses to the societies were guarded. The hardier denominationalists, well represented in the Antiburgher (General Associate*) and Reformed Presbyterian* Synods, would not accept mechanisms involving co-operation with those of other bodies. The Relief Church* recorded goodwill to the missionary societies, and the Burgher (Associate*) Synod of 1796 even appointed a committee to correspond with the LMS. But none voted funds, and some were conscious of the need for ministers of the new Scottish diaspora in Canada,* and the difficulty of getting recruits for such inhospitable locations. The crucial decision was that of the CofS. The 1796 General Assembly received overtures from the Synods of Fife and Moray, one calling on the Church to consider the best way of contributing to 'the diffusion of the Gospel among the heathen nations', the other seeking general collection on behalf of the new societies. Combining the overtures ensured that the debate would follow party lines of Moderate and Evangelical, and that the latter would lose. In the event, the margin (58-44) against appointing a committee to review the matter further was not great; but the terms of the decision approved overseas missions in principle while precluding any immediate supporting action in practice.

The debate seems to have brought together various arguments against missions: proponents of natural theology insisted on civilization as a precondition of evangelization to enable rational assent to the demonstrable truths of the gospel; champions of the political order feared the radical opinions of many of the friends of missions, such as the Haldanes, not to mention English dissenters; and guardians of the ecclesiastical order feared the consequences of entrusting so much to societies that were not subject to the courts of the CofS and included in their leadership many who were in secession from the Est.C. It was the societies, not any projected mission activity on the part of the CofS, that lay at the heart of the debate; but its outcome kept the topic of overseas mission off the Assembly's agenda for almost two decades, and left the societies the only organ of Scottish missions for longer. By the same token, overseas missions remained, as in England, essentially a concern of Evangelicals.

Even some of those sympathetic to missions may have accepted the Assembly's wisdom, since none of the earliest ventures of the LMS, EMS and GMS showed much fruit, and some were utter disasters. Furthermore, the now explicitly Congregational or Baptist allegiance of such advocates as Haldane and Greville Ewing* confirmed the view that missions were subversive of church order and the constitution. As late as 1815, Chalmers complained that a great proportion of nobility, gentry and clergy regarded missions as 'a very low and drivelling concern ... that no good can come out of'. But the societies had reached, through the local societies and auxiliaries, a range of concern and support that did not depend on nobility, gentry or clergy.

Interest was fed by periodicals* which were circulated and read aloud. The *Missionary Magazine* appeared in Edinburgh in 1796, with Ewing as editor. This magazine moved with its sponsors, the Haldanes, in a Congregational direction. From 1819 the Scottish Missionary Society (see below) published the *Scottish Missionary Register*, in imitation of the well known English publication of the Church Missionary Society, and like it covering mission news from many sources. It evidently had a healthy effect on the society's support. The Baptist Christopher Anderson* used to read the *Periodical Accounts* from the pulpit. At St John's, Glasgow, Chalmers (who at one time had a network of missionary societies covering the whole parish) maintained a monthly meeting at which he read out missionary news for an hour.

By such means the societies weathered the storm, and new churches began to appear as the fruit of missionary work. By the 1820s the mission cause was respectable enough for the home churches to seek to reclaim it from the voluntary societies. Meanwhile, the same societies, so long abused for visionary enthusiasm, were now criticized by the new radical Evangelicals, such as Edward Irving,* for excessive caution and worldly prudence. The dominical missionary charter was not for organized societies, but for apostolic bands without purse or scrip.

One of the earliest attempts at a mission from Scotland was proposed by the laird of Airthrey, Robert Haldane,* who sold his estate to finance a mission to the heart of Hinduism at Benares, which was intended to include Bogue and Greville Ewing* and to set up printing and educational establishments. Despite sympathy from William Wilberforce and others, the East India Company vetoed the scheme. The scheme for an India mission was revived by the Edinburgh Congregational churches in 1803, and John Paterson* and Ebenezer Henderson* were appointed as missionaries. Again the Company refused entrance, a circumstance which led Paterson and Henderson to their life work in Scandinavia and Russia.

Of the Scottish-based organizations, only GMS and EMS actually sent out missionaries on a regular basis. Both were largely modelled on the LMS with an interdenominational constituency and a committee of directors. (When Love moved from London to Anderston in 1800 he became secretary of GMS.) The societies comprised people of various denominations, but voluntaryists* were prominent. The directors tried to maintain close oversight (the EMS directors met weekly) but were frustrated by the difficulty of communication, and, increasingly, financial weakness. Meagre resources and voluntaryist principle combined to stress self-support; but, to the directors' occasional chagrin, self-support enabled the more viable missions to act independently.

Both societies began their work in West Africa using the new Sierra Leone colony as a base, EMS working in co-operation with LMS. Of the earliest missionaries only one, Henry Brunton,* had received the theological education the societies looked for in candidates, reflected in an unattainable requirement that missionaries be ordained by the churches to which they belonged. After initial disaster (one of their missionaries got involved in slave trading and another became an atheist lecturer), GMS decided against sending more artisan missionaries. EMS (called the Scottish Missionary Society [SMS] from 1819) early decided (as LMS had already done) on a missionary training centre; but only in 1821 could this be implemented, with William Brown,* the historian of missions, as tutor.

In 1800, GMS initiated a Jamaica mission; it was soon taken over by EMS, which appointed two missionaries to an abortive Pacific mission. In 1800 EMS closed its W. African mission and centred its activities on the Russian Empire (see B.IV below). These activities in turn were transferred to the Basel Mission, or given up altogether, in 1825–6; though two British and Foreign Bible Society (BFBS) agents in Russia were briefly seconded to SMS in 1835. Work in New Zealand, Malacca and Madagascar was apparently contemplated at different times, but the only other work actually established by SMS was in the Bombay Presidency of Western India in 1823. Meanwhile, GMS decided in 1820 to appoint a minister to a settler party going to the Cape of Good Hope. The shipwreck of the settlers diverted the effort to 'Kaffraria', where the GMS mission first joined with John Brownlee (d. 1871) of LMS. The appointment to the mission of John Ross (1799–1878; FES VII, 564) in 1823 marked the first time a CofS presbytery (Hamilton) ordained a minister specifically for missionary work.

Such a development reflected the growth of mission concern within the Est.C. When after 1829 the CofS had its own missions, followed in 1835 by the Associate (Burgher) Synod, the resource base of the societies shrank significantly. The Ten Years Conflict* took evangelical attention elsewhere. In 1835 the Bombay missionaries were transferred from the SMS to the CofS, with a subvention for their support (on which it had to default from 1840). The Jamaica presbytery, already self-supporting and largely independent, was transferred to the USec.C in 1847 and SMS dissolved next year. The voluntaryist* question had already split GMS in 1837, resulting in 'the Glasgow Missionary Society adhering to the Principles of the Church of Scotland' and 'the Glasgow South African Missionary Society'. The former joined the FC at the Disruption;* the latter the UPC at the 1847 union.

III. Christian concern about India. The social and religious condition of India, and British responsibility for it, made an impact both in and beyond evangelical circles through the writings of an East India Company chaplain, Claudius Buchanan,* a Scot in English orders. (To promote such concern Buchanan endowed prizes at and donated books to the Scottish universities; he received doctorates from three of them.) Public concern found a channel in Parliamentary debates over the renewal of the Company's charter in 1813, leading to the establishment of a bishopric in India, the strengthening of the chaplaincy system and recognition of the right of missionary residence. The Burgher Synod was among the petitioners for the 'pious clauses'; and the CofS declared its right as an established church to chaplaincies alongside those of the CofE. Chaplains were appointed to the three Presidencies of Bengal, Madras and Bombay, the Presbytery of Edinburgh exercising oversight and thereby gaining some knowledge of India affairs. In Bengal James Bryce (1785–1866; FES VI, 112), a former Buchanan prizeman and a Moderate, foresaw the possibility of a Scottish mission to India. With the backing of the key Moderate figure John Inglis,* Bryce prepared a memorial on the subject for the 1824 General Assembly. There were sympathetic overtures from several synods and presbyteries, including Edinburgh. The Assembly appointed a committee, convened by Inglis, to bring forward proposals for a Church mission to India.

IV. The origin of Church of Scotland missions. The 1825 Assembly adopted a report proposing a central Church school in India, with branch schools, headed by an ordained minister, primarily for

Indians who had already received some liberal education. The Assembly authorized a collection for this mission and Inglis drafted a 'letter to the people of Scotland' in support. Neither Moderate nor Evangelical could object on principle, since the proposed mission was in line with accepted practice towards the Highlands as exemplified in the SSPCK. Inglis (who was associated with the Edinburgh Sessional School set up by churchmen in alarm at the barbarism of the Edinburgh slums) retained the Moderate conviction that rational assent to Christianity was best prepared for by 'civilization', *i.e.* education; by stressing this aspect he brought round other Moderates. The political dissidence of missions was no longer an issue; by the 1813 charter decision, the government itself was involved in the Christian presence in India. Further, missions had seen modest successes round the world. It was not desirable that the Church should be outflanked by voluntary societies any more than that chaplaincy privileges should be preempted by the English establishment. Just as some Moderates disliked missions as an evangelical activity, some Evangelicals feared that the societies would suffer, or distrusted the stress on 'civilization'. Other Evangelicals such as James Douglas of Cavers (*d.*1861), whose *Hints on Missions* (E, 1822) proved influential, argued that, while conversion was the end, education was the providential means.

The scheme was slow to take shape. Not until 1829 was a suitable headmaster found: Alexander Duff,* disciple of Chalmers, keen scholar and newly graduated product of the St Andrews student missionary society. In May 1830 he arrived in Calcutta.

V. The development of Scottish mission theory. An outline of the subsequent events in India is given below. Duff did in fact obey the spirit, if not the letter, of his consensual instructions, and what he did set the pattern for Scottish missions, at least of the Established and Free churches, for the rest of the century. Mission by education, even by higher education in English, was not uniquely Scottish. What was characteristic of Scottish missions was the primacy given to it, its use not for short-term tactics but for long-term effect. 'We thought' says Duff, 'not of individuals merely.... We directed our view not merely to the present but to future generations. While you [other missions] engage individually separating as many precious atoms from the mass as the stubborn resistance to ordinary appliances can admit, we shall, with the blessing of God, devote our time and strength to the preparing of a mine, and the setting of a train, which shall one day explode and tear up the whole from its lowest depths.'

The mine which he conceived as one day blowing up Hinduism was a new world-view, based on the Bible taught in the context of the whole encyclopedia of knowledge – philosophy, natural science, mathematics, astronomy, and more – just the vision he had received as a student from Thomas Chalmers,* his teacher in moral philosophy. Science and astronomy undermined traditional Hindu learning, exposing received ideas of the constitution of the universe. Such teaching took place, certainly, in the government's own entirely secular college, but Duff argued that it only tore down without building anew. He desired not simply to destroy an integrated world view but to transform it.

In order to be able to hear the gospel, people must be brought to think. His teaching method was essentially dialectical – he never dictated notes, lest pupils memorized them. Lal Behari Day, a pupil who became a convert, said, 'The ideas of the pupils were enlarged; their power of thinking was developed; they were encouraged to observe; they were taught to express their ideas in words; and as learning was made pleasant to them, their affections were drawn to the acquisition of learning.'

This was in essence the method developed not only by Duff and his Bengal colleagues but, with some differences of emphasis, by John Anderson* and Robert Johnston* in Madras, John Wilson* and Robert Nesbit* in Bombay, and Stephen Hislop* in Nagpur. This first generation caught the tide of Hindu reform and opened relations and exchange with 'enlightened' Hindus and Muslims. It also, especially in Calcutta, brought a stream of conversions of young men from the heart of the caste system, who came to faith after searching intellectual and spiritual pilgrimage, and were trained and equipped as Christian leaders.

As a missionary method it was, however, heavily criticized throughout the century. Some of the criticisms came from Scotland itself, on three main grounds: it wasted scarce resources; it pandered to high-caste pride; and it denied the New Testament priority of the gospel to the poor. The criticism intensified after the Indian Mutiny, which drew popular rhetoric against caste and Islam as its source; especially when the stream of conversions appeared to have dried up.

Duff's mine had manifestly exploded, but the impact was not as shattering as he had predicted. It is striking, however, to find the next Scottish missionary generation in India continuing and developing this method, while refining the rationale and avoiding prescription of time scales. For William Miller,* the architect of Madras Christian College, education was pre-evangelism. The function of a Christian college was 'to draw out and revive those longings, yearnings and strivings for the good they comprehend not'. Christian education was to open minds, to awaken moral responsibility and the living apprehension of the spiritual world, and to create awareness of the power of choice. In other words, it was to create the conditions in which Hindus could actually hear the gospel, to introduce the mental and volitional components which made evangelical conversion possible. At present it was well nigh impossible: conviction of sin had no way of entering. His assessment of the general missionary situation in India was that almost all the missions except the Scottish had in effect given up trying to evangelize Hindus; they were concentrating all their efforts on the depressed classes and tribal peoples who were for practical purposes outside Hinduism. The emergent church in India was not able to touch Hindus either, for the same reason. With all the faults of the Scots colleges, more true Hindus had come to Christ through them than through all the other means taken together.

The emphasis had changed since Duff's day; Miller was expecting a long, organic process rather than an explosion. What Duff and Miller had in common was a providential view of corporate intellectual development under the influence of consistent Christian teaching relating to every aspect of life and learning.

This conviction of a total Christian world-view in which Christian faith should be joined with sound education was frequently expressed and striven for in missions of Scottish origin all over the world. This is displayed even in the UP's Calabar mission, most of whose early staff had nothing approaching the educational attainments of the India missionaries. Their underlying assumptions still allowed the mission to work simultaneously for social reform in the Calabar state, the enhancement of education and the gathering of a church. It is still more manifest in the Scottish missions in Malawi, within the Est.C at Blantyre and the FC at Livingstonia; these are seen as communities in which education, agriculture, technology and medicine all derive from the Christian gospel and belong together in its proclamation. Dan Crawford,* of Brethren background, doubted whether education was any part of a missionary's duty – until he saw Livingstonia. In those schools, he decided, Scripture bears fruit.

It is significant that the first chair of mission studies to be established anywhere was set up in Scotland. In 1867 Duff persuaded the Assembly of the FC to establish a chair of Evangelistic Theology at New College,* Edinburgh. The plan was to integrate missions ('the chief end of the Christian Church', according to Duff) into all the theological disciplines, as well as to introduce theological students to the history, culture and religions of the non-Western world. It was part of an even more ambitious plan for an Institute which would conduct research and teaching in Oriental and African languages and cultures. Duff was not afraid to say that a model already existed – he wanted a Protestant version of the Roman *Propaganda Fide*. The Institute was soon forgotten, and the chair did not prosper; Duff and Thomas Smith (1817–1906; *DNB Second Suppl.* III, 347–8) were the only incumbents, and Scottish theological education* abandoned what might have been its most innovative contribution to theological discourse. The study of the significance of missions in Christian history had to be pursued by other means. It was not entirely by accident that the watershed World Missionary Conference* of 1910 was held in Edinburgh, nor that its unobtrusive executive was J. H. Oldham* whose life was spent grappling with the transformation of the Christian world brought about by the missionary movement.

VI. Missions and Scottish Church development. The establishment of its overseas mission could be envisaged in Church terms as a success. This was certainly the verdict in 1835, when illness forced Duff to recuperate in Scotland, and he transfixed the General Assembly with his exposition on India and the missionary task. The Assembly ordered it to be printed, and 40,000 copies were circulated in Europe and America. That year the Assembly had no difficulty in taking over the Indian work of the SMS. By 1839 Duff was proclaiming *Missions the Chief End of the Christian Church*, and no one came forward to contradict the statement. But though missions were by now generally acceptable, it is hard to see that the Ten Years' Conflict* brought them much enhanced attention or direct benefit. At the Disruption* every serving missionary (except for one lady) identified with the FC (East India Company chaplains saw things differently). But all mission property (except where special local arrangements were in force) belonged to the CofS. Much mission activity was thus dislocated or driven to unsatisfactory premises, while other premises remained empty or underused. The CofS determined to rebuild its missions, and stationed some new missionaries as early as 1844; but in view of the characteristic Scottish mode of mission activity through education this usually meant opening a new, and potentially rival, institution. Pre-Disruption missionary stipends had been reasonably generous; the new situation brought real financial difficulties. It is clear that missions in India survived and expanded in the immediate post-Disruption period through money donated in India (often by devout or sympathetic soldiers or officials) or raised through local sources.

On another home visit Duff brought to the FC Assembly a plan of home organization for foreign missions, reporting how he had used the Synod of Perth ('an average Synod') for a pilot scheme of quarterly missionary subscriptions for missionary work and quarterly congregational meetings for prayer and 'missionary intelligence'. This had resulted in increased giving of between three and six times as much as the average giving for missions over the last six years. Certainly the FC did produce marked and regular liberality for missions even when Duff was not present; the CofS had more difficulty raising missionary income. Per head of membership, the UP gave much more than either.

From the viewpoint of the mission field, however, straitened resources were the rule of life. New developments – *e.g.* the Nagpur and Punjab missions – happened because of concerned individuals, rather than through regular supplies being made available by the home church. Even the impression made on the Scottish nation by the death of David Livingstone,* despite the creation of two missions in Central Africa associated with his memory, did not produce a large increase to mission funds. Certainly there were liberal donors to missions among the wealthy; but Lord Overtoun (*see* White, John Campbell) and other merchant princes were interested in directing as well as resourcing, and some of the new missions of the later nineteenth century had their own committees apart from the Foreign Mission Committee (*e.g.* Livingstonia) or were completely independent of it (*e.g.* East Africa Scottish Mission).

The last decades of the century saw relations healing between the disrupted churches (on the mission field co-operation was common, and there were some union congregations), the heyday of imperial consciousness, and increasing numbers of missionaries. But the union of the FC and UP in 1900, or rather, the uncertainties arising from the associated litigation, blighted more than one hope of missionary expansion at a time when new opportunities were beckoning. For instance, the Calabar Mission was at a crossroads in 1900, but the resources needed to carry it forward were not available. And in a curious echo of 1843, the continuing FC lost all its serving missionaries in 1900 and had to build its overseas work afresh. The 1929 union took place in a time of economic depression which critically affected missions all over the world. The missionary movement is arguably the single most important event in the history of Western Christianity; certainly no other so profoundly altered the form of Christian presence in the world. Scotland played its full share within that movement. But while the Scottish perception of missions has sometimes (not always) been a high one, it is hard to escape the conclusion that the missionary project, whether forwarded by the abundance of the rich or the tithes of the poor, was always a peripheral one, always on the edge of the home church's vision, always the direct concern of the few.

VII. Scots and non-Scottish missions. The outline regional survey which follows relates purely to the missions of the Scottish churches. However the story of the missionary movement in Scotland does not relate only to these specifically Scottish bodies. Reference has already been made to the remarkably large number of Scots in the early records of the SPG, and of the high degree of Scottish involvement in the formation of the LMS and its high Scottish recruitment throughout its history. Not only was the LMS the natural outlet for Scottish Congregationalists and members of the EU; its roll includes many members of the larger Presbyterian bodies. The best known Scottish missionary to serve with the LMS was David Livingstone, whose roots were in an independent congregation in Hamilton. There is a long catalogue of others. William Milne (1785–1822; *DNB* XXXVIII, 9) is the first important figure in Protestant China missions after Robert Morrison; Robert Moffat,* in both his grandeur and his deficiencies, is one of the seminal figures in S. African Christian history. William Swan (1791–1866) appears in one of the most remarkable of early nineteenth-century missions, that directed to the Siberian Buriats. How the Scottish background of John Philip,* champion of the oppressed in the Cape, shaped his whole missionary and humanitarian approach has been demonstrated by Andrew Ross. James Legge* was one of the most outstanding of all scholars to come from the missionary movement; contemporaries always respected his learning, even if it has taken a later generation to realize its missionary relevance. George Turner's (1818–91) forty-two years in the Pacific encompassed a critical period of Samoan church history and he is linked with that church's outstanding possession, the Samoan Bible. The work of Alexander Wylie (whose later service was with the British and Foreign Bible Society in China; 1815–87, *DNB* LXIII, 235–6) on Chinese Christian literature and its authors remains an important resource today. John Mackenzie* is the most important missionary figure in the history of Botswana, and close study of his work is a corrective to facile assessments of the relations of missions and imperialism. James Chalmers* is likewise crucial to the early Christian history of what is now Papua New Guinea. James Gilmour* remains the person first thought of in the modern history of Christian encounter with the Mongolian peoples. T. T. Matthews* did much to make Madagascar and Malagasy Christianity known in the Western world. In John Nicol Farquhar* the missionary movement had one of its most learned and sensitive interpreters of India; in Thomas Cochrane,* one of the missionary elder statesmen of the early twentieth century and one of the pioneers of the survey type of missionary research; and in Eric Liddell,* a hero figure for a modern generation.

The CMS, with its evangelical Anglican tradition, includes Scots among its most distinguished names. These are not restricted to people who, while linked with Scotland, belonged naturally to the circle from which CMS recruited, such as W. H. Temple Gairdner, a characteristic product of the Student Volunteer period of missions and one of the most significant missionaries to Muslims of modern times (*Life* by C. E. Padwick, L, 1929). Alexander Mackay,* the central figure in the establishment of the Uganda mission of the CMS, was a member of the FC; it was natural even for an Anglican society to look to Scotland when someone of Mackay's engineering skills was required to handle steamers for inland waterways. In the previous decade the CMS had appointed a medical missionary, an unusual step for that society at that period. Again it recruited from the FC (via the EMMS). W. J. Elmslie from Aberdeen (1832–72; memoir *Seedtime in Kashmir* by M. Elmslie and W. B. Thomson, L, 1875), who thus began the CMS Kashmir mission, had cause, he tells, to rejoice that he had attended J. Y. Simpson's* classes; anaesthesia was thus introduced into a hospital in Kashmir before it was in regular practice in Britain. Duncan Main (1856–1934; *Dr Apricot of 'Heaven-Below'*, by K. De Gruchè, L, 1910) was another eminent Scottish medical missionary who came to the CMS, in this case in China, through the EMMS.

The contribution of Scottish Methodism,* always a rare flower in Scotland, to the (Wesleyan) Methodist Missionary include the tragic figures of David Cargill,* whose work has had permanent significance for Fiji and the Fijian language, and his wife Margaret. They include also a later husband and wife partnership with fewer elements of drama but a great deal of influence in transforming lives, George and Isobel Kerr,* who together compiled a chapter of Christian service for leprosy sufferers. Scottish influence in the earliest period of Baptist missions has already been noted. It was continued in Carey's successor John Mack,* who from 1821 to 1845 maintained the tradition at Serampore College, through to Elizabeth Sale (1818–98) of Helensburgh, the founder of the Baptist Zenana Missions in India. George Yuille's* *History of the Baptists in Scotland* lists some 180 Scottish Baptists then (1926) in missionary service with various agencies. The list includes some well known names – Andrew MacBeath, of the Baptist Missionary Society in Congo (later of the Bible Training Institute,* Glasgow), Alexander Mair of the China Inland Mission, Herbert Dickson, who had extraordinarily long service with the Qua Iboe Mission in Nigeria – and some surprises, such as J. W. Arthur,* leader of the CofS Kikuyu Mission, whose antecedents included Hillhead Baptist Church, Glasgow. The 'faith missions' – the China Inland Mission (and its development, the Overseas Missionary Fellowship), the Regions Beyond Missionary Union and the other activities associated with Grattan Guinness and his family, the Evangelical Union of South America, and many others – had an undoubted impact in Scotland. Some Scottish congregations – Charlotte Chapel, Edinburgh, is an example – have supplied the faith missions and other interdenominational agencies with large numbers of candidates over many years, and the Bible Training Institute,* Glasgow, and numerous smaller training centres (such as that organized for women by Miss Forrester Paton in Glasgow) were available for their preparation.

The Brethren* movement represented a new (or as it would be seen within the movement, a renewed) missiological reading of the New Testament. Scottish Brethren who put these principles to the test had in F. S. Arnot* at least one figure of major significance in the Christian history of the Central African territories he traversed, and who, because of his understanding of New Testament principles, carefully avoided the political impact he might easily have had. Dan Crawford,* the Greenock bookkeeper whose missionary work began in the wake of Arnot's, took those principles further. He refused the opportunity to seek missionary recruits – because he did not think they would learn the language properly, nor sufficiently identify with African life. It was better to work directly through Africans.

Many Scots found themselves in the service of missionary agencies other than British. Sometimes this was by marriage; the wife of François Coillard, the towering figure of the Paris Mission in South-Central Africa, was Christina Mackintosh; Mrs Ruthqvist, the singing missionary of the Swedish Evangeliska Fosterlands Stiftelsen in Central Africa, was born Alexina Mackay in Fordyce, Aberdeenshire (she was in fact the cousin of Alexander Mackay). A range of other circumstances brought Scots into the service of North American missions, especially, but not only, Presbyterian agencies. The work of John Hogg (1833–85; *A Master-Builder in the Nile*, R. L. Hogg, Pittsburgh, 1914) was important in the American Presbyterian mission in Egypt, whose approach was in nice counterpoint to that of the Scottish Anglican, Temple Gairdner. In the movement of the Kuki people of N.-E. India towards Christianity, a Scot called William Pettigrew (1869–1934) played a prominent part. For most of his career he was in the service of the American Baptist Mission. In many parts of the world where Presbyterian missionaries worked together, North American missions, still growing at the point where British missions were becoming overstretched, subsumed Scottish mission work (as with the UP mission in Japan) and sometimes also the remaining Scottish personnel (as with the FC in Lebanon). And the missions of Canada, Australia and New Zealand, burgeoning in the second half of the century, contained many people of Scottish birth or upbringing, such as John Geddie,* born in Banff, missionary of the Presbyterian Church of Nova Scotia, and a key figure in Melanesian missions. Emigrants from Scotland sometimes became missionaries in the next generation: Peter Cameron Scott (1867–96) was born near Glasgow, emigrated to North America with his family in 1879, and went on to found the Africa Inland Mission (C. S. Miller, *Peter Cameron Scott*, L, 1955). Perhaps the strangest of all is the story of J. A. Dowie,* emigrant to the Antipodes and North America, the patriarch of Zion City, Illinois, which gave its name to hundreds of independent 'Zionist' churches across Southern Africa. And there are various cases of Scottish missions (CofS in Madras, RP in Vanuatu) handing over missionary responsibility to the expatriate Scots Presbyterians of Canada or the Antipodes.

(*See also* Lumsden, James; Kalley, Robert; Robertson, Alexander; Thomson, James; Stewart, James Alexander; Strachan, Harry.)

B. REGIONAL SURVEY.

I. Africa. 1. West Africa

Sierra Leone (EMS, GMS, United Pentecostal Mission). The establishment of an African 'province of freedom' in 1787, and still more its reorganization under evangelical auspices by the Sierra Leone Company in 1792, offered a natural early starting point for missions to Africa. Sierra Leone ('the morning star of Africa', Wilberforce called it) with its Christian population of former slaves in Freetown, was envisaged as a base for missions to the interior. The GMS's first two extremely ill-prepared representatives arrived in March 1797, and went to Temne country, 100 miles from the colony. Neither learned Temne, and by 1799 one had returned to Scotland and the other turned trader. In September 1797 EMS, GMS and LMS combined in a more ambitious programme, supported by the Sierra Leone Company, to the Muslim Fulani. By the time the missionary party reached Freetown its internal theological disputes were so bitter that Zachary Macaulay,* then Governor, dispersed it. The Glasgow pair went to the Banana Islands and later crossed to the Sherbro mainland; the Edinburgh pair, Henry Brunton* and Peter Greig (1775–1800), went to Susu country. All suffered heavily from disease, and the Glasgow men soon succumbed. Brunton and Greig got vernacular work started, but Greig was murdered by robbers in 1800 and Brunton returned to Scotland.

He composed a Susu grammar (one of the earliest of an African language), with a preface which reveals how the experience of SSPCK in the Highlands informed his missionary theory. The CMS endeavoured for a time to build a Susu mission on the EMS foundation.

After these early disasters (which seem almost to have paralysed the GMS for two decades), no Scottish mission essayed Sierra Leone or its hinterland until 1920, when Matthew Sinclair (1896–1971), an ex-miner supported by an independent Pentecostal assembly in Kilsyth (which had sent a missionary to Liberia as early as 1912), began work in Freetown. The Kilsyth-based United Pentecostal Mission which developed from this later established a Temne church with several congregations in northern Sierra Leone.

Nigeria (SMS, UP, UFC, CofS). The origins of the Calabar mission lie not in Scotland but Jamaica and in the vision of the years following emancipation of the slaves of the redemption of Africa through converted Africans. The Presbytery of Jamaica (in which both SMS and USec. missionaries sat) discussed a mission to Africa in several meetings from 1839, noting the enthusiasm for it in its congregations. T. F. Buxton's *The African Slave Trade and its Remedy* (L, 1839–40) added impetus, rationale and practical information. The languishing SMS could neither assist the project (which in fact it discouraged) nor prevent Presbytery pursuing it. Sympathetic commercial men made contact with the leaders of the Efik community of (Old) Calabar on the Cross River, an established African ocean trading centre, once for slaves, now for palm oil. This produced an invitation for a mission, and in 1846 a party arrived from Jamaica led by H. M. Waddell,* a SMS missionary, with one European catechist and his wife and three Jamaican assistants. The union of the Secession Churches of 1847, and the demise of the SMS, brought the mission under UP supervision.

The Efik commercial aristocracy, already in trading contact with the West, recognized the commercial advantages of Western education, and were prepared to consider other changes; but they were anxious to maintain their local trade monopoly. This restricted the mission to the immediate area of Calabar until the 1880s. During this early period the mission worked partly through schools, which combined the vocational expertise the Efik wanted with the dissemination of Christian teaching, and partly through preaching, aimed not only at building a church but at influencing opinion in Calabar in favour of religious and social change. Missionaries could sometimes combine preaching against such institutions as ritual killing at funerals of important persons, destruction of twins, and poison ordeals, with pressure from the international trading community in the harbour. A crucial, if unpredictable ally was the wealthy aristocrat King Eyo Honesty of Creek Town; though he never became a Christian, he allowed his son, Eyo VII, to do so. Changes that took place (even the abandonment of particular cults) were decided and proclaimed through Calabar's central social and religious institution, the Ekpe society.

The mission's early decades were dominated by three figures: Waddell, who stayed until 1859, William Anderson,* who was at Duke Town for forty years, and Hugh Goldie,* who became the mission's leading Efik scholar and translator. All began their missionary service in Jamaica, and Jamaica continued to supply teachers and workers for Calabar until the 1950s.

Church membership remained small in the early decades, even when the mission was effecting notable social changes; and it tended to consist mainly of marginal people. Closure of the mission was several times contemplated. By the 1880s, growth in numbers and influence was evident, and the Scriptures, now available in Efik through Goldie's efforts, were having an impact. The same period saw geographical expansion up the Cross River; Jamaican missionaries trained by Alexander Robb* (who had gone from Calabar to Jamaica when his health broke down) and African teachers produced by the Calabar church made this possible. The appointment of Mary Slessor* to Okoyong was part of the same expansion.

In 1901, steadily increasing British overrule culminated in a military expedition which destroyed the oracle at Arochukwu and broke the political and economic power of the Aro people in the territory to the north of Calabar. The British 'pacification' of Igboland followed. Such drastic political, economic and social change shattered much of the traditional world-view. Some places saw rapid movements towards Christianity as a means of coping with the upheaval. The mission, and notably Mary Slessor, who had already prepared the way for expansion along the Enyong Creek, begged for increased resources; the Scottish church (UP/UFC), caught up in the 1900 union and the subsequent law suit, was reluctant to take risks. The situation was saved by young African teachers coming forward from Ikorofiong, trained through the work of Alexander Cruickshank.* Western medicine was part of the new order offered by the mission; doctors such as J. W. Hitchcock* and Harry Hastings* were also important figures in evangelism and pastoral care.

Waddell, Goldie and Anderson had functioned like local parish ministers; the new district missionaries superintended networks of congregations (some self-supporting with their own ministers), preaching posts, schools, clinics, preachers and teachers.

By the early 1920s the Christian impact on Efik, Ibibio and southern Igbo society was wide and pronounced. Around 1927 an indigenous 'Spirit movement' affected parts of the area, seen by some missionaries as revival, by others as a source of perversion and confusion. One result was the emergence of numbers of African Independent churches of the prophet-healing type. (Assistance to these churches, and bridge-building between them and the older churches, came mainly with the work of an American Mennonite, E. I. Weaver, in the 1960s; it was the CofS mission which provided the guarantees enabling him to work.) Christian

MISSIONS: WEST AFRICA

expansion to the north-eastern Igbo hardly began before the 1930s, and accelerated only in the 1950s. Increasing mobility among Nigerians caused Presbyterian churches also to appear in cities elsewhere in Nigeria, such as Lagos, Kaduna and Enugu.

In 1858 the missionaries had constituted (against Edinburgh's wishes) the Presbytery of Biafra, consisting of the five ordained men and one Jamaican elder. The first Efik minister, E. E. Ukpabio, who had also been the first baptized convert, joined it on his ordination in 1873.

The most fundamental change in government thereafter occurred following the 1900 union: the erection of a mission council, consisting of the ministerial and medical missionaries (women missionaries gained a qualified entrée in 1917). The council controlled policy and the educational, medical and other institutions, thus greatly reducing the role of presbytery. The balance of power shifted as African ministers increased in number, and powerful educated laymen appeared; in 1934 a local man, Francis Akanu Ibiam (1906–; *Who's Who 1992*, 946) became a medical missionary of the CofS, with outstanding results. He was to become a major figure in independent Nigeria, and in the international church. In 1935 Presbytery made clear that missionaries might intervene in congregational matters only if invited. There was pressure from Edinburgh (induced by a lawsuit) for the church to become a legal entity, and in 1945 the Presbyterian Church of Nigeria was constituted. With an eye to the future, the standards adopted were the Apostles' and Nicene creeds, not those of Westminster.* The mission council was formally abandoned in 1960, by which time the Church was opening other overseas links, *e.g.* with Canada and the Netherlands.

Inter-mission cooperation began early in the twentieth century with agreements on respective areas of expansion, developing into shared activities and resources in areas such as theological education, literature, urban mission and hospitals. A Nigeria-wide union of the Anglican, Methodist and Presbyterian churches collapsed on the eve of implementation in 1965.

Between 1966 and 1970 Nigeria was engulfed in civil war. Historic and personal associations of the area fuelled sympathy in Scotland for the secessionist Biafra, which used as its national anthem the hymn 'Be still my soul: the Lord is on thy side', known in both countries from the *Church Hymnary*.* Nigeria's appalling wartime sufferings, and the complexity of the issues surrounding humanitarian relief, confronted the CofS and other British churches with unusual moral dilemmas.

Ghana (UFC, CofS). Scottish involvement in Gold Coast missions arose from the circumstances of World War I. The missionary staff, mostly German, of the Basel Mission in the colony were interned or deported, as were those of the Bremen (Norddeutsche) Mission here and in the adjacent German colony of Togo. The British government invited the CofS to fill the vacancy; it declined. The UFC proved more amenable, and A. W. Wilkie* made a reconnaissance from Calabar in 1916.

MISSIONS: EAST AFRICA

The first mission party arrived in 1918. Its small size – two ministers and three lady missionaries where the Basel Mission alone had stationed nearly fifty – dictated the shape of future development. Neither the Basel network of district missionaries nor its distinctive stress on economic development was now possible. Scottish missionaries would concentrate on superintendence and institutional work. The indigenization of church government was thus forced. A synod (with an African majority on the Synod committee) was established in 1918; reserve powers of veto held in Scotland were never used and eventually given up. J. H. Oldham,* meanwhile, by now a key figure in British inter-mission co-operation and the International Missionary Council, sought the return of the continental missions. By 1926 Basel missionaries were admitted, and the Presbyterian Church of the Gold Coast was established. Basel and Scottish missionaries now worked in parallel; the Church resisted any arrangement that would have given either mission *de facto* territorial control in any area. A similar development in the Bremen Mission area, where the peace settlement brought part of Togo into the Gold Coast boundaries, produced the Ewe Presbyterian Church (from 1954 the Evangelical Presbyterian Church). Scottish support here could not be maintained to the extent desired, leading to the introduction of the (USA) Evangelical and Reformed Church.

Under the Presbyterian Church of the Gold Coast much mission effort was invested in schools. The results were mixed. Schoolchildren, with the full consent of non-Christian parents, regularly became 'first-stage Christians'; but the resultant increased number of schools made it harder to secure enough teachers with the necessary degree of Christian commitment. Further, while from 1925 the colonial government provided 80% of teachers' salaries, it also exercised increasing control. As early as 1922 Wilkie raised the question whether education was deflecting the Church's energies from its main task; if education was training for the whole of life, its religious character should be central. For such a view, the quality of teachers was crucial. The college at Akropong (1924) brought together the training of teachers and catechists (from whom ministers were usually recruited). Whatever the difficulties of rapid primary school expansion, the Scottish contribution to the development of the educated elite which made the Gold Coast (as Ghana) the pioneer of the new African nationhood is undoubted. So is the special place given to women's education (*e.g.* the Aburi and Krobo institutions). Scottish resources were never sufficient to maintain the Basel Mission's institutional medical work; the last clinics were closed in 1928. A personal initiative by two Scottish missionaries (F. D. (1902–66) and Margaret Harker; *FES* X, 419)) produced in 1943 West Africa's first special school for blind people.

Since 1960 a decreasing number of CofS missionaries have been 'fraternal workers' of the Presbyterian Church of Ghana.

2. East Africa

Kenya (East Africa Scottish Mission, CofS). In

1886 the Sultan of Zanzibar, titular ruler of much of East Africa, conceded rights of administration over part of his claimed territory to a company formed by Sir William Mackinnon, a Scottish businessman who combined Livingstone's interests in African commerce and missions. Between 1890 and 1900 British rule was established over what became known as Kenya Colony, first in the name of the company (from 1888 called the Imperial British East Africa Company) and then of the Crown, African resistance crumbling under superior firepower and a series of natural disasters. In 1891 Mackinnon and other wealthy Glasgow laymen set up their own East Africa Scottish Mission to combine religious, medical, educational and industrial activities – a pattern inspired by the example of Malawi. The first missionaries, all laymen, were despatched in 1891, under the temporary care of James Stewart,* borrowed from the FC mission at Lovedale, South Africa. The pioneer years saw a catalogue of disasters: unsuitable sites, misjudgements from inexperience and devastating loss of missionary life and health. Of the early missionaries, Thomas Watson (an evangelist who received FC ordination and died in 1900), stands out for perseverance in adversity and for the decision to move the mission to the territory of the Kikuyu, Kenya's most numerous people. (Both the mission and its principal station, were commonly called 'Kikuyu'.)

In 1901 the ailing mission was handed over to the CofS, on condition that its fourfold aspect be maintained. David Clement Scott,* the outstanding figure of the Blantyre mission, came to lead it. He envisaged a chain of self-supporting missions on the Blantyre model across East Africa, and looked to achieve self-support by establishing a commercially viable mission estate.

The attempt proved financially ruinous. More seriously, the estate was established without regard to Kikuyu custom on land tenure; and the priority given to it inhibited extension of the mission for some years. However, three young missionaries arrived who were to shape future advance: J. W. Arthur,* a doctor of energy and versatility, A. R. Barlow (1886/7–1965; *LW* Jan. 1966, 17), and Marion Scott Stevenson.* Barlow, a relative of Scott, became a notable translator and defender of Kikuyu land rights; he and Stevenson were probably the missionaries with the fullest understanding of Kikuyu culture. Scott died in 1907; another senior Blantyre missionary, Henry Edwin Scott (1864–1911; *FES* VII, 706), came to the mission, bringing a new sense of direction. Extended evangelistic and educational activity displaced estate management; H. E. Scott also involved the mission in the English-speaking congregation of St Andrews, Nairobi, and initiated cordial co-operation with other missions in Kenya. After his death, Arthur, the new leader, took these policies further.

In the sphere of mission relations this led to the Kikuyu Conference of 1913, with its plan for a federal union of the churches arising from the work of the CofS, CMS, United Methodist Missionary Society and African Inland Mission, and its famous concluding interdenominational Communion. Norman Maclean, a visitor from the CofS (1869–1952; *FES* III, 471–2, VIII, 19), enthusiastically drew British press attention to the proceedings, resulting in the outraged intervention of Bishop Frank Weston of Zanzibar. The conference became a *cause célèbre*, involving Canterbury and the Lambeth Conference which effectively closed that route to church union. A later, more modest, structure for closer mission co-operation foundered on the requirement of the Africa Inland Mission of firmer assurances about particular formulations of doctrine and about teetotalism than CofS could unconditionally give.

In 1913 the CofS mission had still only 87 full members; with World War I began a period of sustained growth of church and schools. Young Kikuyu (exemplified in the future Jomo Kenyatta) increasingly recognized mission education as the best means of coping with a white-dominated world; and if the mission was an organic part of the white presence, other parts – government's harsh use of forced labour and the accelerated post-War white settlement which appropriated vast areas of African land – made it appear relatively benevolent. The mission could sometimes obtain redress or relief for land and labour abuses. Visiting London following the 1922 crisis in the colony, the Governor took Arthur as adviser; the Devonshire Declaration which ensued made African interest paramount in colonial policy leading to increased government aid for mission education (*see* Dougall, J. W. C.). The Kikuyu Scriptures (much used in schools) became available to an African church able to appropriate them in its own way. Africans were now the primary evangelists. The structure of kirk sessions and presbytery was in place by 1916 (though not recognized by Edinburgh until 1920), and a body of church law emerged by local consensus.

The year 1926 saw the publication of the complete Kikuyu New Testament (a joint effort of the missions) and the ordination of the first Kikuyu Presbyterian ministers. 1928 brought unprecedently large numbers into the church. Alliance High School, the colony's premier educational institution, though the product of an 'alliance' of missions, was very much Arthur's project and located in the CofS area. But in 1929–30 events occurred which caused a recession from the church which it took nearly a decade to make up.

The controversy over the traditional Kikuyu practice of female circumcision (clitoridectomy) affected all the missions, but the CofS most of all. Mission attitudes to the practice (an initiation to womanhood, performed at puberty) varied in emphasis over the years; the mission sought generally to discourage it, but sometimes to reform, sanitize or even christianize it, and above all to protect the right of girls to choose not to undergo it. The events of 1929–30 have, however, to be seen in the broader context of mounting Kikuyu anger over land loss to whites, the emergence of the Kikuyu Central Association (KCA) to articulate Kikuyu grievances, and conservative reaction among traditionalist leaders in Kikuyu society against the accelerating rate of social change. The clitoridectomy issue served to unite KCA radicals and traditionalist conservatives on a matter which seemed to involve white dictation of the parameters of Kikuyu life. Stung by the poor decision of a European judge in a case of forced circumcision, the missions intensified their campaign for Christians to reject the practice. Tension mounted; and at a meeting in Chogoria, a new Christian community, in 1929, Arthur called not only for church discipline to be enforced against those involved in the practice but also for all Christians to repudiate the KCA. But the KCA was the vehicle of the political aspirations of the very people most likely to be attracted to Christianity. Presbytery adopted the call with obvious reluctance, and dropped it in 1931; but the damage was done. Attendance not only at Chogoria, but at the central Kikuyu station itself, was halved. The nascent nationalist movement identified the mission, and by implication the church, as its enemy. Government, dodging the land issue, blamed the unrest on injudicious mission interference with social life, Arthur had to resign from the colony's Legislative Council, and, arguably, the cause of Kikuyu identity became unnecessarily involved with a regressive custom.

But the storm alerted missionaries to the urgency of the land issue. Barlow investigated land claims against the mission estate, and secured the return of almost half of it to the legitimate owners. The government's Land Commission was less receptive of his research about valid claims on other estates.

The union of churches in Scotland in 1929 brought division to the Church in Kenya. An 'overseas presbytery' was constituted (though opposition from Kenya delayed implementation for several years) to include the session of St Andrew's Nairobi plus all the missionaries, thus effectively setting up separate black and white churches. The measure may, however, have hastened the emergence in 1943 of the Presbyterian Church of East Africa, based on the African church. In 1946 the church incorporated, as a presbytery, the Gospel Mission Church, which arose from a North American faith mission with advanced principles about indigenization; and in 1956, with the advocacy of David Steel (1910–; *FES* IX, 750, X, 41), minister of St Andrew's Nairobi, the European presbytery was absorbed into the African church – well ahead of political independence. Much subsequent Scottish involvement in the Kenyan church has been in its ecumenical institutions, such as departments of the Christian Council of Kenya and the union theological college (now university) at St Paul's Limuru.

The other major developments of the post-War period – the massive impact on Kikuyu Presbyterians of the East African Revival; the Mau Mau emergency of 1952–7 which took many lives and faced Christians with searching questions; the steady spread of Christianity to become the normal profession of faith in Kikuyuland; new patterns of church relations; and above all new patterns of Christian responsibility in an independent and multi-ethnic state – belong to the history of the African church rather than that of the Scottish mission.

Mauritius (CofS). The island was annexed from the French in 1810, with a promise to preserve all its 'religious establishments' intact, and retained after the Napoleonic War. A small British element was added to a population of French, African and Indian, and later Chinese origin, with a corresponding variety of religions. Scottish interest is first manifest in 1851, with the appointment of a young minister, Patrick Beaton, who established St Andrew's Church, Port Louis, before leaving for an army chaplaincy in 1858 (1825–1904; *FES* VII, 535). Another charge, St John's, was established later. Though conceived initially as a mission, the CofS in Mauritius was not usually under the direction of the Foreign Mission Committee. Moreover, it held a place in the colonial establishment, alongside the RC and Anglican churches, by extension of the terms of the 1810 treaty. The missionary function was exercised from time to time, notably by the brothers Samuel and James Anderson, born in Mauritius to Scottish and French parents. Samuel (1845–1923; *FES* VII, 559), who was ordained in 1870 and left in 1883 to undertake long service in Paris, had 19 churches and outstations, established a new Indian congregation, and translated most of the New Testament into Mauritian Krio; James (1852–1926; *FES* VII, 558–9), entering the ministry in 1903 when he was over 50, is the historian of Mauritian Protestantism. The CofS subsumed what remained of the work of the LMS, begun in 1814, getting a new lease of life in the 1840s through Malagasy refugees, and finally abandoned by the LMS in 1871. John Joseph Le Brun, who had worked in Mauritius for the LMS since 1844, and was the son of the first missionary there, was admitted by the General Assembly in 1877 (cf. *FES* VII, 559). The CofS work is largely overlooked in statistical surveys of missions made in the nineteenth and early twentieth centuries.

When Mauritius became independent in 1968 the constitutional status of the churches had to be resolved, and Neil C. Bernard, lately African Secretary (1909–91; *FES* IX, 729, X, 416), was sent to negotiate on behalf of the CofS. The present constitution recognizes no state church or religion, but the Presbyterian Church receives an annual payment from the state, though at a lower level than that accorded to the RC and Anglican churches.

3. Central Africa

Malawi (FC, UFC, CofS). Two Scottish missions began in Central Africa at much the same time, each conceived as a memorial to David Livingstone. They had been preceded by the survey made in 1861 by James Stewart,* still at the time a student at New College, Edinburgh, with the backing of a committee of businessmen and academics. He withdrew in disgust after two years, and the committee disbanded. In the 1870s the FC Foreign Missions Committee was considering ideas, favoured by Duff and John Wilson, for an East African Mission on the Ethiopian coast (some Ethiopian Galla had studied in Bombay). Stewart re-

MISSIONS: CENTRAL AFRICA

turned to the Central African theme as a better proposal. Again a committee, Glasgow-based, was formed in 1874, to direct a new Central African ('Livingstonia') mission. In line with Livingstone's own thought it was assumed that missions would promote honest trading, which would benefit Africa, and work against slave trading and war. After a false start at Cape Maclear, at the south end of Lake Malawi, in 1875, the mission moved in 1880 to Bandawe, on the west side of the lake, and began to make an impact on Tonga and Ngoni peoples. The dominating figure was Robert Laws,* an ordained doctor, who came with the first party and directed the work for fifty-two years. In 1894 an 'Institution' was founded at Khondowe (frequently called Livingstonia) for training teachers, pastors, health workers and craftsmen; the mission from the beginning had all these aspects in mind. The teachers and preachers of the Livingstonia Institution formed an army of evangelists who established community churches over wide areas of what is now Malawi. The first ordination was in 1914; a strong ministry and church structure developed. W. A. Elmslie* was especially associated with the Ngoni; but the key to relations with the Ngoni was the Lovedale-trained minister from South Africa, William Koyi. In the development of the church Donald Fraser* played a vital part; he was also known in Scotland as a particularly forceful speaker and writer. T. Cullen Young* was a good example of the missionary as anthropologist.

Meanwhile the CofS, launching a nationwide appeal to its membership, established in 1876 a mission in southern Malawi, named Blantyre (for Livingstone's birthplace). It, too, was to have a strong industrial-practical component (most of the first missionaries were artisans); it was another example of the recurrent Scottish concern with the nexus of Christianity and civilization. After a disastrous start (the mission found itself exercising civil jurisdiction but not equipped to do so), under the leadership of David Clement Scott* it produced what many visitors took to be a model Christian community. The mission's relationships with the African Lakes Company (intended as a philanthropically-minded commercial venture) did not bring the expected benefits to either side.

The Blantyre mission's first head was Duff MacDonald,* withdrawn as scapegoat for the early disasters but one of the first writers to describe the religion of an African society in detail. After Scott, the figure of Alexander Hetherwick* is of particular significance.

The relations of the two missions with the local power structures – African, Portuguese, British and commercial – were complex; the very presence of the mission set them in inescapable tensions. The Church of Central Africa (Presbyterian) emerged in 1926, with Blantyre and Livingstonia each forming a synod, and Nkhoma, of Dutch Reformed Church origin, providing a third. The close association of Scotland and Malawi caused the issue of Central African Federation* to be of public concern in Scotland, and Scottish Christians have continued to show special concern in issues relating to Malawi.

MISSIONS: SOUTHERN AFRICA

Zambia (UFC, CofS). Livingstonia-trained evangelists extended their activities beyond the bounds of what was then Nyasaland and into the neighbouring territory of Northern Rhodesia. In 1904 they came into close contact with the eastern Bemba. David Kaunda (the father of the future President of Zambia) took charge of the work, though he was not ordained until 1930. The Bemba population was scattered and the work never had the strong indigenous leadership characteristic of Livingstonia itself. This may explain why the movement of the prophetess Alice Lenshina (Lumpa Church) had such a deep effect on the church. The development of the Copperbelt industrial zone induced early mission and church cooperation in the territory which emerged as Zambia in 1964, and the United Church of Zambia was formed in 1965.

4. Southern Africa

South Africa (GMS, FC, UP, CofS, FC continuing, EpCS). The first missionaries of the GMS, sent in 1821, joined forces with a fellow Scot already established among Xhosa people, John Brownlee of LMS (1791–1871; *Chronicle of LMS 1872*, 62). The group (augmented in 1823) worked together, and to some effect, for several decades. Evangelization of the Xhosa included conscious acculturation; not only the recommendation of Western clothing but the expectation that men, and not only women, would do regular farm work. Lovedale, named after John Love,* secretary of the GMS, was opened in 1824, but destroyed as a result of the war of 1834.

In 1838, the GMS split between establishmentarians and voluntaries split the missionaries also, though they continued to meet together in a single Synod. The Disruption hardened matters; the establishmentarians all declared for the FC, while the voluntaries, after the 1847 union, joined the UP. The matter was to arise again with more serious undertones than those of the establishment principle.

Lovedale Seminary was established in 1841, under William Govan (1804–75; *FES* VII, 562; *AFCS* I, 173), who sought the advice of both Alexander Duff* and John Wilson. Under their guidance the principle enunciated in India was transferred to Africa: the whole discourse of higher education in English would be opened to Africans. The result was that Lovedale offered the same ministerial training to all students, black or white; by contrast with many situations in South Africa, they studied and ate together. Lovedale was more than a theological seminary, however; it gave a sound liberal education and a practical, technological one also. Tiyo Soga* was an early student; when the institution was closed by war, Govan took him for theological study in Scotland, before resuming his remarkable ministry in South Africa. The Mfengu people requested, and largely paid for, a Lovedale of their own, the Blythswood Missionary Institute, on their movement into the Transkei.

The FC committee decided in 1848 to close the South Africa mission; this was avoided, but only by acquiring separate funding for Lovedale. James Stewart* became its head in 1866 and began to

MISSIONS: SOUTHERN AFRICA

turn it into an institution to prepare leadership for an African, not a multiracial, church. This reflected tensions that were to become a permanent part of the existence of the South African church. In Scottish terms, it was reflected in UP insistence on a single church for black and white, and FC stress on the development of black leadership in the black church, which inevitably led to the emergence of parallel black and white churches. The union of 1900 complicated matters further. Needless to say, this was the beginning rather than the end of a complex chapter, throughout which the overwhelming majority of South African Presbyterians have been black.

Scotland entered the South African story at another point, with momentous consequences, when it sent out ministers to Afrikaner congregations (see Dutch Reformed Church; Murray, Andrew).

The FC (continuing) sent a missionary to resume work in South Africa in 1908; a Xhosa synod developed, with continuing FC support.

(See further MacVicar, Neil; Shepherd, R. H. W.)

In Natal Anglican missions were torn apart by the conflicts between Bishop Robert Gray of Cape Town and Bishop Colenso of Natal. Colenso had become starved of funds and support but the judicial apparatus of the English establishment had largely found in his favour. It was to the EpCS, where he could expect sympathy in doctrine and churchmanship, that Gray now turned. In 1871, a letter in the name of the bishops in South Africa invited the Primus and bishops of the EpCS to turn their attention to 'a province of heathendom partly within and partly adjoining the border of British territory which, whether as regards population or extent of soil exceeds that of any other possession of the British crown, India alone excepted'.

The result was the establishment of the EpCS's Board of Missions and an undertaking to supply, in cooperation with SPG, a bishop and staff for a new diocese of 'Kaffraria'. The SPG would put its existing missionaries in the area under the bishop. In 1873 the arrangement was put into effect with the consecration in Edinburgh as missionary bishop for Independent Kaffraria of Henry Callaway (1817–90; DNB Suppl. I, 378–9), a distinguished missionary scholar who had served with, and was respected by, Colenso. The association of the EpCS with the diocese of St John's (as the diocese soon became known) continued, leading in recent times to close Scottish involvement with the Church of the Province of South Africa.

Botswana (UF (continuing)). The minority of UPC who remained out of the 1929 union had no missions or missionaries. In 1932 the church took over part of the LMS field in Botswana. A hospital was built in Molepolole which is the centre of the area served.

Zimbabwe (FP). The FPC mission began in Ingwenya in 1904 with the commissioning of John Radasi,* who had received theological training in Scotland. The first European missionary arrived in 1924.

There are also various churches of indirectly Scot-

MISSIONS: SOUTH ASIA

tish origin – white Presbyterian congregations with S. African connexions and Malawian congregations of the Church of Central Africa Presbyterian.

II. The Americas. 1. Caribbean
The history of the Scottish Churches in the Caribbean defies brief summary. Antigua, Bahamas, Grenada, Jamaica, St Vincent, Tobago and Trinidad have all had churches of Scottish origin with various changes of affiliation and status. The early field of the SMS in Jamaica, extended later to the Cayman Islands and Trinidad, was the most substantial, and led to the mission to Calabar (see above).

On the Caribbean coasts there have been churches in Belize and Guyana, the latter with local mission to Native American peoples.

2. Latin America
Peru (FC continuing). John A. Mackay* was ordained for service in South America by the FC Presbytery of Inverness in 1916. He had already concluded that in the Peruvian context a school in Lima of high quality was the best method of procedure; not to act directly as an evangelizing agency but as an 'evangelical influence'. Evangelistic and (for a time) medical work followed. The FC's involvement continues to the present day.

Mackay's book *The Other Spanish Christ* (L, 1932) opened to many a new view of the Christian significance of Latin America.

(See also Darien Colony.)

III. Asia. 1. South Asia
Western India (SMS, CofS, FC, UFC). The earliest Scottish missionary efforts in Asia were directed to the Bombay Presidency. Over the course of the nineteenth century they were extended from the coastal strip south of Bombay, to the city itself and its immediate hinterland to Pune, the other great city of Western India, one of the traditional Hindu intellectual centres; and even into the northern part of the princely state of Hyderabad. Bombay was also the base for the mission to Nagpur, at the geographical heart of India; and for the survey which led to the establishment of the Rajputana mission. In addition, Bombay being at this time the entrepot for the whole of the Western Indian Ocean and Arabian sea, it was for Scottish missions a centre of strategic thinking about East Africa and Arabia.

Yet the local church was never large – there were few substantial group movements to Christianity, of the sort seen elsewhere – and early missionaries often believed that they operated in a climate of greater hostility than their colleagues in Bengal and Madras. This was attributed to the fact that in W. India, the British had overcome a local power, the Marathas, and not simply replaced another conqueror. It may be noticed, however, that Bombay was hardly touched by the great Mutiny of 1857. What stands out is the extraordinarily high calibre of some of the W. India missionaries and the outstanding quality of much of the Indian church leadership.

The minds of the SMS directors were turned to

Bombay by an offer of service from one Donald Mitchell (1792–1823; *FES* VII, 701–2). He had lost his faith when a divinity student, gone to India, taken a commission in the Bengal army, and there undergone an evangelical conversion. He returned to Scotland, was ordained by Nairn presbytery, and in 1823 came back to India as the first missionary there of the SMS. Within a year he was dead, but the society sent another batch of missionaries who, denied access to Pune by the East India Company, developed a school system in the south Konkan coastal area. The schools were too many to supervise adequately and the only clear result seems to have been to show that Western education, for which the Bombay government did very little, was a desirable product. The Konkan mission was closed, and the remaining missionaries moved to the cities of Bombay and Pune. In 1827 there arrived in Bombay Robert Nesbit,* Duff's fellow-student who reached India before Duff himself and attained a legendary command of spoken Marathi. In 1829 came John Wilson, a towering figure in Bombay life for most of the next half-century (1804–75; *DNB* LXII, 113–15, *FES* VII, 711–12, Life by G. Smith, I, 1878, 1879). On these two, with John Murray Mitchell* who arrived in 1838, the Scottish work in Bombay city was established.

As we have seen, the SMS work in India was taken over by the CofS in 1835; most of its serving missionaries had already been ordained by presbyteries of the Est.C. The missionaries joined the FC at the Disruption, and accordingly lost the mission property, including a newly constructed school. The CofS thereupon opened a new Bombay mission, but it was always hard to staff, and closed in 1891. CofS missionaries continued, however, to work in Pune.

Wilson was second only to Duff in the missionary reputation he had both in India and in Scotland. He was more aware than Duff of the significance of the Indian ancient languages and modern vernaculars (and he was unusually good at them), and had a greater intellectual curiosity. This took him into Indian and Middle Eastern antiquities and serious study of the background of the various religious communities of Bombay, both the Parsis and the Bene Israel, the Bombay Jews. He was one of the first Western scholars to tackle Zend, the language of the Zoroastrian scriptures, and to identify the significance of the Asokan inscriptions. One of his early ventures was a paper, *The Oriental Christian Spectator*, which discussed such things at length, and which led to a series of set-piece debates between Wilson and Parsi (and later Hindu and Muslim) religious leaders.

In his early years he organized a tiny congregation, engaged in open-air preaching and began vernacular schools. He does not seem at first to have aimed at the sort of educational institution that Duff was building in Calcutta. He arrived there, however, by another route. Some 'pious European gentlemen' asked him to take over an English school they had begun. With Nesbit and (later) Murray Mitchell he developed it along lines similar to those adopted by Duff and by John Anderson* in Madras, and with similarly dramatic effects. The first impact was on the well-to-do Parsi community; in 1839 several Parsi boys in the school sought baptism, and two, Dhanjibhai Nauroji and Hormazdi Pestonji, were actually baptized. The subsequent uproar drastically reduced the school roll, and ensured that no more Parsi pupils attended for many years; but incidents of the same sort occurred from time to time. The request for baptism by a Brahmin, Naraya Sheshadri, and his young brother (the latter refused by the court to which the issue was taken) raised controversy between liberal and conservative proponents of the caste laws. In cosmopolitan Bombay the school covered the unusually wide range of religious communities characteristic of the city and provoked intense inter-religious debate. There were even two young Galla men from Ethiopia, introduced by C. W. Isenberg of the CMS with a view to their establishing a Christian school in East Africa. It was to Bombay that David Livingstone* came to recruit assistants for his last African journey. Among those brought into evangelical Christianity through Wilson and his colleagues we hear not only of Parsis and Hindus but Muslims, Sikhs, Goanese Catholics, Armenians, an Assyrian and a merchant from Milan.

When in 1857 the University of Bombay was established (originally as an examining body) the Bombay missionaries were better prepared than their colleagues in Madras. The relationship between the FC institution and the University blossomed; the College department was affiliated to the University in 1861. Wilson took a lively part in university life and served as Vice-Chancellor 1868–70. When a testimonial (subscribed across the city's religious spectrum) was awarded to mark his forty years in Bombay, he devoted it to a lectureship in Oriental philology. Relations were cemented further when Dugald Mackichan* became principal of the institution (which took the new name of Wilson College), a post he held 1877–1920. Wilson College continued to represent a high proportion of the Scottish missionary presence in Bombay long after MacKichan's time. It was not an easy atmosphere in which to maintain the original goals of the institution; as the national movement built up, the political agenda shifted the debate away from the old type of religious enquiry and debate, and Christianity, especially when propounded by missionaries, was easily identified with the maintenance of the British raj. There was an assassination attempt on N.G. Velinkar, a professor at Wilson College who had become a Christian under the influence of Bible studies when a student there.

In Bombay, as in Calcutta and Madras, early converts who had gone through the fire like Nauroji, Pestonji and Sheshadri, became the earliest indigenous ministers. Nauroji came to Scotland to train in 1843; one of his first duties was to brief the new missionary candidate Stephen Hislop.*

Women's education developed along lines parallel to men's, even to occasional crises over conversion. Wilson's first wife, Margaret Bayne,* was an effective pioneer; after her early death her two sisters took over her schools. It was the need in Bombay which in 1837 produced the Scottish Ladies' Association for Female Education in India, the forerunner of the Women's Foreign Mission.

The special character of Scottish missionary work in Bombay inevitably directed its activity to the educated middle class. It was the Brahmin convert Sheshadri, now teaching at the Institute, who set up a school for the sweeper class. Rural evangelism in Konkan, in which the mission had originated in the 1820s, was resumed in the 1870s and strengthened in the 1890s, with some response from groups at the bottom of or outside the caste system, whose movement to Christianity did not bring the disruption and rejection known by high-caste converts. As Wilson College moved into the social sciences, surveys made there began to display the harsh conditions under which most of Bombay's Christian community (which grew significantly in the first half of the twentieth century) lived and were housed. Concern for both the urban and rural poor was particularly expressed in the deployment of the last generation of Scottish missionaries to work in the area.

Early attempts at mission work in Pune were restricted, as much by cautious British officials as by Hindu hostility. When work was established, it was on the usual pattern of schools, though the FC closed down its institution, much against the missionaries' desire, after a visitation from Edinburgh in 1889. Both CofS and FC missionaries served in Pune, and the congregation there was a union one. Among those who served in the Pune area were Nicol MacNicol,* a sympathetic student of Indian religions and an interpreter of India to the West, and the redoubtable Miss Annie Small,* later Principal of the Women's Missionary College that became St Colm's.* John Small (1833–99; *AFCS* I, 318), who became something of an institution in Pune, developed an orphanage for famine relief that was the nucleus of a printing and binding complex of local importance. It was to this that Tom Dobson* came in 1910 to place such 'industrial' enterprises on a different footing.

As early as 1832 Wilson had visited Jalna and Indapur, in the dominions of the Nizam of Hyderabad. After two or three aborted beginnings, regular work was instituted following a visit from Murray Mitchell in 1861. A couple from Jalna were baptized in Bombay in 1862, and returned there. They were followed by Narayan Sheshadri, the Brahmin convert of 1843, now an ordained minister. He worked at Jalna till his death at sea in 1891, with remarkable response. Converts came from the lowly Mang group in particular; their Brahmin pastor secured a new settlement for them and established the Christian village of Bethel. The economic peril of the Christian communities and of their neighbours continued, and was exacerbated by recurrent drought and famine. Tom Dobson's later years were spent wrestling with one of the inbuilt problems of the Indian church – the grinding poverty of so many of its members. The story of Scottish missionary effort embraces both Wilson College and Tom Dobson; but the greater number of Indian Christians belong to the groups that Dobson – and Sheshadri – knew.

Bengal (CofS, FC, UFC). Duff's instructions had been to set up his school in a rural area. Having examined the situation, he defied them and established it in Calcutta itself. He also decided to work in English – good and meticulously taught. When he made this decision, the debate between those who favoured English as the language of administration and those who favoured the old languages used under the Moghul empire was not yet settled. That the Anglicists eventually won was certainly to his advantage. He got encouragement from William Carey, and the more immediately valuable support of the Hindu reformer Ram Mohun Roy, a close student of the Scriptures, a staunch monotheist, a devotee of Jesus, but not a Christian. His backing reassured caste Hindu families who might have feared to entrust their children to the missionary. The school was intellectually stimulating, and in descriptions of conversion there was regularly an intellectual progression, before the spiritual conflict and then the awesome choice of baptism, the public outcry, the family cleavage. There were converts of the quality of Mohesh Chunder Ghose ('my progress was not that of earnest enquiry but of earnest opposition'), Krishna Mohun Banerjea, a reforming activist who went on to proclaim pointers to Christ in the classical Hindu scriptures, and Lal Behari Day, pastor, professor and author. Others held back from the step of baptism; others stopped at points along the way, such as the theistic Brahmo Samaj. There was no doubt about the impact of the Scottish Institution.

Duff's colleagues included two of his fellow-students at St Andrews, W. S. Mackay* and David Ewart,* and Thomas Smith, who was to succeed him as professor at Edinburgh (1817–1906; *FES* VII, 707–8; *DNB Second Suppl.* III, 347–8).

As in Bombay the Disruption meant for the missionaries the loss of their building; to which the newly appointed CofS missionaries succeeded on arrival in 1846. The two institutions continued side by side until they joined in 1908 as the Scottish Churches' College. There was, however, no continuing parallel to the early stream of conversions, which ceased before Duff left India. But the institutions had made their mark on both Christian and Hindu history.

South India (Madras) (CofS, FC, UFC, EMMS). 'Madras' in the nineteenth century stood not only for the great city of that name, but for the Madras Presidency, a thousand miles long, occupying much of S. India. The origins of the Scottish missions there lie in the establishment of a Christian school in the city by G. J. Laurie (1796–1878; *FES* III, 57–8) and Matthew Bowie (1800–69; *FES* V, 95–6), CofS chaplains of the East India Company in 1835. They asked the CofS to provide a missionary to develop it on the model already operating in Calcutta; the Church sent the ebullient, talkative, single-minded John Anderson.* He arrived in 1837; in 1839 he was joined by his close friend Robert Johnston* and in 1841 by John Braidwood (1810–75), the future biographer of the two.

By immense labour and conviction the trio built up the school, which, with its provincial network of subsidiary schools, was to be the cornerstone of the Scottish mission. The aim was to supply first-rate general education in a Christian setting; the object, to lay an intellectual and spiritual foundation that would allow conversions in depth to take place from within the heart of caste Hinduism. A second object was to provide a thorough training for an indigenous ministry. Anderson and his colleagues sought also to demonstrate the integrity of sacred and scientific learning; to promote such intellectual ferment among Hindus and Muslims as could lead to profitable discussion. Though directed to young men within the caste system, the school insisted on the eligibility of pupils from outside it. This provoked one of its earliest crises, when many caste pupils were withdrawn from the school in outrage. More serious, however, were the recurrent outbursts, usually resulting in a massive withdrawal of pupils, which attended successive requests for baptism. The school recovered, but the only possibility open to the converts, when cut off from family and society, was to continue at the school, as part of the missionary family. Inevitably this meant assimilation to Western lifestyle, and opened the danger of later disorientation. The first three young men baptized in 1841 did indeed, five years later, become the first licensed preachers, and five years after that, the first ordained ministers. One of them at least, P. Rajagopal, became an effective and innovative leader, well known to Scottish audiences through visits.

A network of branch schools – Kanchipuram, Nellore, Chingleput, Triplicane, Tiruvallur – depended on the central school in Madras. The first three, all important for the future, were offered to the mission, together with financial support, by sympathetic British officials, sometimes with backing from Indian notables. It is typical of the Madras mission story (and of some other Indian missions) that both initiatives and resources tended to be from local, rather than Scottish, origin.

At the Disruption, all the missionaries joined the FC, breaking the link with the Scottish chaplaincy which had brought the mission to birth. Within a year, the CofS had sent three missionaries (one of whom was soon sent to head the Calcutta Institute) to start another school.

Both Scottish missions had lean times in the 1850s. Johnston left, sick, in 1850; Anderson died in 1855. Other missionaries came and went, but direction flagged. The FC school failed to maintain educational excellence; staffing suffered in numbers and morale, and it fell into debt. The most notable development of these years was in the work of Rajagopal, who assumed charge of the Madras congregation. In 1863, William Miller,* 25 years old, found himself in sole charge of the disintegrating school. He reclaimed its standards, morale and finances, and gave it a new direction, albeit in continuity with that of the founders. The University of Madras had been founded in 1857. Miller urged that, instead of leaving higher education to Hindu and secular influence, the College should be a Christian institution of the highest academic excellence, not only eligible for affiliation to the new university, but able to 'influence the corporate thought of Hinduism'. He opened a university class in 1865, and successfully presented candidates for the degree examinations in 1869. By 1873 he was able to propose a united Christian college for S. India, with the FC institution as its nucleus, and to get support from the main English missions (and friendly sympathy from the CofS). In 1877 the project blossomed as Madras Christian College, with six established chairs. The FC retained responsibility for the school department, a preparatory institution, until 1900. In 1911 the CofS college was merged with Madras Christian College. Miller remained as principal until 1907; among his successors A. G. Hogg* particularly demonstrated the role Miller sought for the College in relation to Hindu thought. He also oversaw the College's move to Tambaram outside Madras, where it hosted the famous International Missionary Council conference of 1938, at which Hendrik Kraemer presented his thesis on *The Christian Message in a Non-Christian World* (L, 1938), of which Hogg's was perhaps the most searching critique.

Though the College continued to lie at the heart of the mission (fourteen of the twenty ordained UF missionaries who served in the Madras mission between 1900 and 1929 were attached to it), its progress was accompanied by an extension and diversification of the mission's work. In 1870 Rajagopal opened a 'Poor School' for children outside the caste system, which had an immense roll. A school directed to caste women, parallel to the central school, had begun in 1841 under Mrs Braidwood; while Anderson's widow, a teacher, headed until 1872 the boarding school that had begun in the 1840s as a shelter for converts rejected by their families and for orphans. Under impetus from the Women's Foreign Mission, women's education developed considerably in the later nineteenth century, the schools producing a corps of women teachers and church workers. (Zenana evangelism developed directly out of school work.) A training centre for lace manufacture attached to the school system was intended to provide women with a means for independent subsistence later in life.

The EMMS set up work in Madras in 1854. The first doctor was a FC elder, which brought the work, though independent, into association with the FC, who eventually took it over through the Women's Foreign Mission. A training institution was set up for medical personnel; the Rayapuram church was the result of the medical and evangelistic work of one of its trainees.

The first expansion of the work beyond Madras city had been based on schools; a resident missionary was not feasible before the 1860s. The appointment to Chingleput of Andrew Adam (1851–1921) with a staff of catechists in 1879 opened a new stage of development, with the organization of the Chingleput congregation and evangelistic efforts extended to towns such as Sriperumbudur (Ramanuja's birthplace), which did not have a single Christian in 1883. For several years from 1890 there was a movement in that area of village groups of very poor non-caste peoples towards the Christian faith. Their already harsh conditions of life were compounded by the hostility to them generated by the conversion movement. Adam secured their transfer to new lands and three new Christian villages emerged (Lord Overtoun (*see* White, John Campbell) paid the land price for one settlement, thereafter named Overtounpetta).

Throughout India a feature of the twentieth century has been the movement for closer union. The core institution of the Scottish work in Madras became, as we have seen, a union institution; other union institutions – the Women's Christian College, the Vellore Medical College – became theatres of inter-mission and inter-church co-operation. Territorial adjustments between missions were frequent. The FC took over (though it could not properly staff) evangelistic work from the Danish mission, and gave up Vellore to the American Baptists and Tiruvallur to the Wesleyans; the CofS ceded their work in Arkonam to the Presbyterian Church of New South Wales. The earliest institutional moves to church union concerned the Scottish missions, perhaps not unrelated to the union movement going on in Scotland. In 1901 the Indian congregations of the FC united with the larger Arcot Mission of the Reformed Church in America. The CofS mission joined in the conversations, but more cautiously. The resultant South India United Church adopted a modified form of the Westminster* standards. The same year the decision was taken to form a single Presbyterian Church of India. The South India United Church joined, but only on condition that it might withdraw if a prospect arose of a South Indian union on a wider than Presbyterian basis. This occurred when in 1907 the Congregational churches arising from the work of the LMS and the American Board (a much larger constituency than that of the Scottish churches) joined the South India United Church in a form of federal union with a basic confession that allowed for other more detailed standards in addition. Increasingly the need was recognized for the development of a self-consciously Indian church. The developments which led in 1947 to the birth of the Church of South India (and in which at least one Scottish missionary, J. H. MacLean, played a crucial part; 1868–1944; *FUFCS* 543, *FES* IX, 740) lie outside our scope here; the churches of Scottish mission origin form a small, if highly significant, part of it.

Central India (Nagpur) (FC, CofS; EpCS). Nagpur lies at the geographical centre of India. John Wilson identified it, despite its distance from Bombay, as a natural field of expansion from the Western India mission. A start was made possible by a gift from an army officer and his wife. The Disruption delayed implementation; the bequest was secured by the FC, and a new missionary, Stephen Hislop,* appointed to establish it.

The pattern followed that of the earlier Scottish missions, with a school, explicitly Christian but at the highest level of education, as its centrepiece. Once again the aim was the intellectual penetration of the heart of Hindu society through the gospel. ('I am persuaded that they [schools] are preparing the way for a great moral revolution in a future age,' said Hislop.) The difference from the older missions in Bengal, Bombay and Madras was that here there were no other schools. When Hislop began his work Nagpur was a princely state; when he died, it was the centre of the Central Provinces, administered by a British Chief Commissioner. The change induced a greater desire for English, but for a long time the Commissioner preferred to support Hislop's school rather than institute a new one. When in 1868 a government school was established, it had an effect on the church school roll. There seem to have been fewer dramatic conversions than in the older schools, but they occurred among a wide range of people, many of them incomers to Nagpur, and so did not make a great local stir. The most threatening crisis seems to have occurred in the last year of Hislop's life, when the admission of boys from the *chambar* community, the leatherworkers, caused a walk-out of high-caste pupils.

The main problem of the Nagpur mission was always shortage of staff. Hislop found an excellent colleague in Robert Hunter,* who also shared his scientific interests; but Hunter was badly traumatized by the death of his brother Thomas during the mutiny of 1857, and eventually left India. For much of the time Hislop worked alone. He made close acquaintance with the Gondh (Kond) tribal people of the area, but the demands of a Gondh mission, however pressing, were incompatible with those of the school, which he still saw as the heart of the Nagpur mission. A Gondh mission at last began, with a Tamil catechist, in 1865; a missionary was assigned in 1869. The Gondh work was handed over to the Swedish mission in 1884.

Meanwhile Hislop's principal work, the school, was extending its scope. It had, like its predecessors, a 'college department' which became the nucleus of Hislop College, affiliated to the University of Calcutta. It became important for the small Christian community which grew up in the towns and villages around Nagpur, Seoni and other places in the Central Provinces from the last years of the century onwards.

One of the best known aspects of the Nagpur mission was its medical work, begun in the 1880s and repeatedly strengthened. Dr Agnes Henderson's work (*see* Women in Presbyterian Missions) was secured by a family endowment; two Ayrshire ladies provided the funds for the Mure Hospital. As in other parts of central India, the hospitals touched more people than any other aspect of the mission.

In Chandrapur, south of Nagpur, the EpCS has had a mission involvement since the 1870s (C. M. Copland, *The Chandra Mission* ..., n.p., 1988).

Central India (Seoni) (Original Secession, FC continuing). The United Original Secession* (*i.e.*, that minority of the Original Secession Church which did not join the FC in 1852) first committed itself to the missionary movement in 1868. Inspired partly by an account by J. Murray Mitchell* of missionary possibilities among the Gondh tribal people, the church agreed with the FC to take over the northern part of its Nagpur field. The first missionaries, George Anderson (1841–1914; *Orig. Soc. Mag.* 4th. ser. 13, 1915, 44–53) and his wife, arrived in 1871 and established themselves in Seoni, a minor administrative centre lying north of Nagpur and south of Jabalpur. A start was made by engaging as salaried evangelist a Christian who was working in the administration, the missionary preaching to a small English congregation in the Anglican church. The work developed along lines characteristic of North and Central Indian missions: village itineration with vernacular preaching as opportunity arose, preaching and discussion at markets and fairs, school provision, and orphan care. Initially the school was for the Eurasian community but by 1876 the mission had adopted the regular Scottish mission pattern, offering high school education as a means of introducing the Hindu community to Christian teaching, while supplying a commodity that was valued. It also provided a less popular and prestigious girls' school. Neither preaching nor education brought many open conversions; the orphanages, on the other hand, where the mission undertook the whole formation of abandoned children, came to provide many of the local staff.

Medical work began in 1901. The area, like the rest of the region, suffered heavily from famine and plague in the early decades of the twentieth century, and from the influenza epidemic following World War I. The mission was heavily involved in famine relief and the government-sponsored plague camps. There is little sign that the Gondh, the original inspiration for the mission, ever became its special target.

The expatriate staff was always very small, and its two best known figures originated outside the Original Secession. The American Associate Presbyterian Church (which had Antiburgher origins) joined with it in sending John McNeel (1868–1954), a student at the Secession Divinity Hall, to Seoni in 1898; he stayed for the next fifty-six years. Dr Jeannie Grant, of FC background, began Seoni's medical work in 1901, gave it a formidable reputation, and served until her death in 1953 (*see* Women in Presbyterian Missions).

From 1902, all serving FC missionaries having entered the UFC at the union, the continuing FC maintained its overseas concern by sending staff to Seoni. It was the intention from the beginning that the church would take over from the Original Secession the northern part of the area it sought to cover; but the separate mission was established only in 1924. In 1957, the United Original Secession remnant joined the CofS, by which means the original Seoni mission passed into the United Church of North India, and in 1970 to the Church of North India.

The division of the mission in 1924 gave the FC the administrative area of which Lakhnadon was the centre; Lakhnadon and Chhapara were the main foci of activity. Inevitably much of the practice of Seoni was carried over. Though the evangelistic aim remained primary (hospital provision was deliberately modest to emphasize this), far more people were reached by medical (including community health) work than in any other way. Some four-fifths of missionaries (some of whom came from Ireland or Australia) were doctors, nurses or other diaconal workers; and most of them were women. (It is also clear that the Women's Foreign Missionary Association was an essential arm of support.)

In 1974 the medical work at Lakhnadon and Chhapara was incorporated in the Emmanuel Hospital Association, an Indian organization, in order to secure its future.

Education had a more chequered history, with long closures. The Chhapara Middle School closed for lack of qualified staff. Orphan care was for long informal (with Scottish and Australian congregations sometimes sponsoring individual orphans). The home board authorized an orphanage in 1955, but no more entrants were accepted after 1969. As at Seoni, however, many Christian leaders and staff workers were orphans. A new enterprise in 1976 gathered a church, based originally on Christians far from their own congregations, in a lower middle class suburb of Jabalpur.

The congregation of Lakhnadon and Chhapara was constituted in 1956. In 1985, with the days of missionary presence clearly numbered, the Free Church of Central India was recognized, with two ministers and four congregations (two in Jabalpur suburbs). Ministers give adherence to the Westminster Confession, modified in the section on the state to allow for the Indian constitution. Since there is no Hindi version of the Westminster Confession, elders acknowledge the Shorter Catechism. The regulative principle is maintained for public worship.

The last missionaries withdrew in 1988, and visas are no longer granted. The FC in Scotland sends an official visitor every second year.

Punjab (CofS). The Punjab mission of the CofS was begun with a gift from an army officer, General Murray, in 1857. It was led by Thomas Hunter, brother of Robert Hunter* of the FC in Bombay (1827–57; *FES* VII, 695–6). He and his family were killed in Sialkot in the 1857 war. The mission, originally addressed to Sikhs, saw largescale movements of Chuhras, descended from the aboriginal tribes of India, in the late nineteenth and early twentieth centuries. The resultant church is now part of the Church of Pakistan.

Rajputana (UP, UFC, CofS). The Rajputana mission of the UP church arose as a Scottish response to the Indian War of 1857. The area of work was chosen with the advice of John Wilson* and Murray Mitchell* of the FC, and the first missionaries arrived in 1860. Its workers included James Shepherd,* particularly linked with Udaipur. As in much of N. India, famine and consequent relief operations and orphan care played a large part in early mission history, the orphans proving of importance to the church. Rajputana saw no large group movements to Christianity.

Bihar (Santalia) (FC, UFC, CofS). Though the aboriginal tribal peoples of the subcontinent represent a significant proportion of Indian Christians, they were late on the agenda of Scottish missions. John Wilson,* always prescient, saw their importance, and Stephen Hislop's* posthumous account of the Gondh is an early systematic study; but organized mission emerged only in the last third of the nineteenth century.

The Santal are a Munda-speaking group scattered over a wide area of Chota Nagpur, now in Bihar state. They attracted no great attention until 1855, when a large-scale revolt, aimed in the first instance at Hindu landlords and money-lenders, issued in bloody confrontation with the British army of the Bengal administration. Thereafter a large section of the Santal heartland was administered as a sort of reserve, through local headmen, with a minimal British presence. 'Santalia' however, has never been a single geographical entity; there is a long history of migration, and Santal and other peoples frequently live side by side.

Alexander Duff* visited the area in 1861–2, and recommended that the FC envisage work there. By 1868 there was a prospect of resources for a mission, and Murray Mitchell* undertook a further reconnaissance. The available finances were mostly within India itself, and an Anglo-Indian agent of the Calcutta Bible Society was the first missionary sent in 1869. The FMC of the FC became directly involved only in 1872, with the dispatch of an ordained medical missionary, Archibald Templeton (1843–1923; *AFCS* I, 339). By this time there was considerable Scottish awareness of the Santal, much of it stirred by A. Graham, a retired Indian government medical officer. Through his influence the Indian Home Mission to the Santals, a Scandinavian group of which L. O. Skrefsrud was the leading figure, developed a strong Scottish base (it even had a Scottish missionary), with local committees in Edinburgh, Glasgow, Aberdeen and Dundee. But Graham was a FC elder, and among his services to the FC Santal mission was his recruitment of Andrew Campbell,* a lay artisan who was to become its outstanding missionary.

Templeton began at Pachamba, then an administrative centre, though it later ceased to be such. Campbell extended the mission to another police district, Tundi, in 1879. He arrived in the village of Pokhuria with two catechists; under a great tree they celebrated the event by singing Psalm 100. Undesirable spirit activity at the site ceased forthwith, and a welcome at Pokhuria was secured. A further extension to Bamdah in the Chakai police district came next year, and another to Tisri in 1908. Meanwhile Campbell, aware that large numbers of Santal migrant workers went to the tea plantations in Assam, visited Sylhet, and eventually negotiated with a Scottish tea importer to pay for an appendix to the mission there. A missionary served as chaplain to the (mainly Scottish) tea planters and oversaw the work of two teachers among their Santal labourers.

From the beginning there was a strong medical thrust to the Santal mission. Pachamba under Templeton saw the creation of the first FC mission hospital anywhere, and three of the four mission centres had hospitals. Campbell apart, most of the leading early missionaries were ordained doctors. The first Christian contact with many Santal villages came through the hospitals; that at Bamdah (on a main pilgrim route, attracting many non-Santal) attained celebrity in the twentieth century for its ophthalmic work. 'Industrial' mission (which today might be called 'development' work) was also present from the beginning. An immediate aim was to provide a livelihood for orphans and other unfortunates and for Christians dispossessed as a result of their profession; a longer-term one to bring economic betterment to marginal cultivators who lived near the edge of ruin and were often subject to extortion and exploitation. Famine, especially severe in 1874 and 1897, stimulated provision of a permanent water supply. New cash crops were introduced, as were new forms of production of silk and cotton. It proved easier, however, to establish industrial activities in mission institutions than secure their widespread adoption as cottage industries.

Education, the traditional mainstay of Scottish missions in India, was not at first a commodity particularly attractive to the Santal. Its importance naturally grew with the growth of the church. One of the earliest missionaries was a certificated teacher, and in Pachamba the government handed over its own schools to the mission in 1883.

Inevitably linguistic and translation work, in which Campbell was again pre-eminent, was a vital aspect of mission activity. Bible translation gave rise both to co-operation and controversy with other missions. (The Scandinavians were wont to complain that the Scots missionaries were defective in Santali and even more so in Greek.) The establishment of the Santal Mission Press (a fruit of Campbell's furlough advocacy in Scotland) allowed the development of a corpus of Santal literature, including a vernacular newspaper.

A curiosity of the Santal mission is the unusually small number of women missionaries, whose presence was vital to most other Indian missions. The Women's Foreign Mission had staff in Pachamba 1887–99, but, despite the substantial growth of women's education in the Santal mission, Scottish women missionaries seem not to have been appointed to it again until the 1950s.

The first major movement towards Christianity followed the famine of 1874. Inevitably there was anxiety, among both friends and critics of missions, about 'rice Christianity'; but there were permanent results, and it was long noted that the orphans of 1874 later provided many leaders for the Santal church. There were some significant early conversions among village headmen, and patterns developed of traditional social units moving towards the Christian faith. The Santal Christian population is substantial, though without Christianity becoming the universal profession as was once predicted, and as is seen in tribal groups in N.-E. India. Santal people sought to maintain their identity in relation to all the outside forces. Attitudes to the British raj, with which the mission was inevitably associated, were ambiguous. Christian practice could sometimes appear as abandonment of

Santal tradition, but the emergence of Santal Christian communities with vernacular Scriptures, literature and music could equally be seen as preserving and enhancing that identity. The other available identity was a Hindu or 'Sanskritized' one, adapted from the universe of the neighbouring, and in the long term, the dominant culture. Some Santal have found a Sanskritized and others a Christian identity; since independence, the Indian authorities have been highly sensitive about the latter.

Related tensions occurred in church organization. Like other fruits of Scottish missionary work, the Santal congregations moved into the United Church of North India and then the Church of North India (Diocese of Chota Nagpur); but equally important developments were the establishment of the Santal Christian Council in 1935 and the indigenous spiritual movement, the Santal Convention. The CofS mission council was dissolved in 1956, and its assets transferred to the Church.

Eastern Himalaya (CofS). A mission was begun in 1859 in Gaya, in Bihar. William Macfarlane* joined it in 1865; he had dissented from the received wisdom about the primacy of education in India missions, but came to adopt it after arrival. The hill children sent by a tea planter to an orphanage attached to the mission attracted his attention and he decided to close the Gaya mission and transfer to Darjeeling. This placed the mission at a crossing of routes to Bhutan, Nepal and Tibet. The church saw unusual early success from a wide variety of ethnic groups. The mission attracted considerable attention in Scotland (which had other links with the area through Scottish tea planters); both the Scottish Universities' Mission (directed to Sikkim) and the Young Men's Guild adopted projects related to it. The guild missionary, John A. Graham,* and his homes at Kalimpong for the children of tea planters, gave the area even greater Scottish celebrity.

Nepal (CofS). The CofS was one of the original group of missions to form the United Mission to Nepal in 1954, and its involvement continues.

2. East Asia

North China and Manchuria (UP, UFC, CofS). In 1862 the UP Synod accepted the offer from a Glasgow committee of laymen to establish a mission in the treaty port of Ningpo, taking over the medical missionary, himself a Glaswegian, of an aborted English mission. He died, the work languished, and though extended in 1870 to Chefoo, was wound up in 1872. The National Bible Society of Scotland was also involved in China; the services of its agent, Alexander Williamson (1829–90; *DNB* LXII, 2), were eventually shared with the UP. Between 1866 and 1868 Williamson reconnoitred Manchuria and distributed Chinese Bibles there (cf. his *Journeys in North China...*, 2 vols, L, 1870). Meanwhile William Chalmers Burns* undertook his influential mission under English Presbyterian auspices. Burns died in Manchuria, beseeching the Presbyterian Church of Ireland to take up work there. Irish missionaries arrived in 1869, by which time the UP Church (through Williamson) was also considering Manchuria. John Ross* was appointed there in 1870, and John Macintyre (1837–1905; Small II, 135; *FVFCS* 550) transferred from Chefoo next year. Thereafter Manchuria was the main centre of Scottish church involvement in China until 1950. Chinese in language and (principally) in population, the experience of Manchuria during the missionary period often differed from that of China 'within the wall'. It was a frequent theatre of war: between China, Japan and Russia, between different Chinese factions, between Nationalists and Communists. War brought agricultural and economic dislocation, deprivation and, in 1912, plague. The Japanese made Manchuria the puppet state of Manchukuo in 1932. From then until 1945 Manchurian Christians were isolated from the rest of the Chinese church; during the war the Japanese created a United Protestant church in Manchuria under Japanese leadership.

Mission polity was also unusual. Irish irritation at Scottish intervention gave way, first to division of the field (Irish west, Scots east of the Liao river) and then to co-operation. A single Chinese church emerged, organized from 1891 on a presbytery basis and from 1907 as the Presbyterian Church of China. While Edinburgh and Belfast recognized distinct field mission councils, the missionary forum in practice was a conference (from 1890, formalized 1912) composed of the personnel of both missions. The best-known mission institution, Dugald Christie's* Mukden Medical College, was independent of Edinburgh, raised its own funds, and had from 1924 its own 'home committee', chaired by Christie. A proposal in 1938 that the missions, like the church, should formally amalgamate, did not find favour in Scotland or Ireland.

Japan's entry into World War II brought internment of mission staff (except for one CofS missionary, a Hungarian national). In 1945 a joint commission from Scotland and Ireland proposed a limited missionary presence, which responded to specific invitations from the Chinese church. Communist control was established in Manchuria in 1948 and all missionaries were withdrawn in 1950.

Missions in Manchuria began amid militant anti-foreign feeling, and so early converts were often dissenters from the prevailing ethos. A reaction in favour of Western institutions, buttressed by the good reputation of Christian humanitarian activity, promoted church growth. Membership multiplied more than threefold between 1896 and 1899. The growth reflected both indigenous activity and mission infrastructure. (The famous 'Blind' Chang Shen, for instance, began his evangelistic tours without completing the pre-baptismal catechumenate but had become a Christian as a mission hospital patient.) In 1900 the Boxer Rising brought missionary withdrawal and persecution of the church, with many (including Chang) killed, others lapsing, and consequent pastoral problems. A revival movement, apparently sparked off from Korea and marked by public confession of sins, arose in 1908. The rough-tongued Canadian Jonathan Goforth was prominent, but missionaries in general were surprised observers of an indigenous movement. A second movement in 1932 took less dramatic forms. The church developed its own structures and extension work (with an indigenous missionary society by 1905) and congregational self-support (periodically inhibited by national disasters). There was little chance, however, of its being able to support the missionary medical and educational institutions.

Manchurian circumstances posed political dilemmas for missionaries. Under Boxers, Japanese and Communists, association with foreigners could harm the church; on the other hand, in the police state of Manchukuo where the church could not discuss government policy, missionaries, simply as foreigners, could sometimes exert helpful influence. Thus in the 1930s the church devolved certain powers to the missionary conference. By 1938 government restrictions had made Christian schools virtually unworkable. The Manchurian church, held together in good measure by its womenfolk, survived occupation, war and the Japanese imposition of state cult. The small-scale postwar missionary return was speedily followed by the Communist takeover and the final eclipse of missionary institutions. The Manchurian church story then merges with that of China as a whole.

Central China (CofS). The China field was the last extensive nineteenth-century overseas undertaking of the CofS. Its basis was a tied donation; its first Chinese staff was borrowed from the LMS; its first lay missionaries were shared with the NBSS; its most innovative branch, the women's work, arose from the initiative of a retired LMS missionary and long depended on staff from New Zealand. Alexander Williamson of the NBSS was responsible for the location: Ichang (Yijang), 500 miles up the Yangtze, newly declared a treaty port, and thus open to foreigners, the most westerly town in that category. In 1878, the recently ordained George Cockburn, from Aberdeen (1853–98; *FES* VII, 690), with the Chinese evangelists and his NBSS colleagues, established preaching and colportage. Medical work, seen as integral to the mission from early days, was hampered by the early deaths of several successive doctors. Educational effort included the important St Andrews secondary school and the pioneering of female education. Women's work, embracing evangelism, education and medicine was initiated in 1897 through the Women's Association for Foreign Mission. It proved one of the more prosperous aspects of the mission. After the Boxer Rising, women missionaries from New Zealand introduced lace-making which gave local girls a source of income for school fees and provided resources to build the girls' school.

Treaty-port status brought disabilities as well as privileges. The foundation work was done amid intense anti-foreign feeling. Subsequent fluctuations of hostility and response reflected the changing conditions in Central China surrounding the Boxer Rising, the republican revolution and the nationalist movement. The church was never large – fifteen congregations in the 1920s, down to eight by 1935 – though the mission's medical and educational work was influential. In 1927 missionaries were withdrawn for a time; on their return it was clear that Chinese must take over senior institutional posts. (This soon led to those Chinese leaders becoming full members of the mission council.) The Japanese war brought new responsibilities for refugee relief. The secondary schools, with their teachers, moved westward to 'Free China'; missionaries who stayed behind were interned by the Japanese in 1942. Resumption of activities after 1945 was interrupted by the civil war (in which the mission hospital was destroyed), the Communist victory, and the recognition by 1950 that continued missionary presence would be a millstone for the Chinese church.

The presbytery of Ichang was established in 1922 as a constituent part of the Presbyterian Church in China (which represented churches arising from the work of various Presbyterian missions) and of the Hupeh Synod of the Church of Christian China (which reflected a provincial union of Presbyterians with LMS Congregationalists). A subsequent wider union involving the American Presbyterian mission produced a single synod for Hupeh and Hunan. Women elders were in place by 1946.

South China and Taiwan. When China opened to missionary activity in the 1840s, Scotland was in the midst of ecclesiastical turmoil and its churches were slow to accept official involvement. However, the Presbyterian CofE (constituted 1842) established a FMC in 1855 which focused attention on China and became the channel whereby FC resources were directed to China. It sponsored William Burns,* whose mission the FC had declined to support; and at his urging a 'Scotland Association' for the mission was founded in 1854. G. F. Barbour* was a vigorous supporter. The Association raised funds and recruited missionaries, mainly from FC sources. For its first fifty years the English Presbyterian Mission drew most of its missionaries (including eminent names such as Thomas Barclay (1849–1935; *Who Was Who 1929–1940*, 63; E. Band, *Barclay of Formosa*, Tokyo, 1936), J. C. Gibson (1848–1919; *Who Was Who 1916–1928*, 402–3) and Campbell Moody (1865–1940; *Int. Rev. of Miss.* 29, 1940, 506–18)) and much of its finance from the Association, which (by then renamed 'the Scottish Auxiliary') survived the union of 1900. Following up Burns' lone journeys, missionary work was established in S. China, first in Amoy, then in Swatow (George Smith (1833–91; *Chinese Recorder* Sept. 1891, 417–23), 1858) then in Taiwan (J. L. Maxwell (1837–1921; *Presb. Messenger* May 1921, 102), 1865). A mission to the mountain Hakka, funded by Barbour, began in 1879. The basis of the S. China mission was itinerant evangelism, supported by medical work, the latter often providing the point of entry. Education at first aimed to produce a literate Bible-reading community; that concern led the mission, with some notable leadership from women missionaries, to promote the use of romanized script for more rapid learning. With the opening to Western influence after the Boxer Rising there was some development of good-quality secondary education. Response on the mainland was slow, but the speed of church development relatively fast; both Amoy and Swatow had fully constituted presbyteries some 20 years from the first preaching, and the principles of self-government, self-support and self-propagation were widely recognized. Greatest response came in the special conditions of Taiwan, where the missionaries developed a modus vivendi with the Japanese colonial government. Language (three forms of Chinese, all distinct from Mandarin and Cantonese) helped to give a distinctive character within China to the S. China mission and the resultant church. Missionaries withdrew from Taiwan in 1940, and from the mainland in 1951.

Japan (UP, EMMS, NBSS). Protestant missions in Japan began as an American enterprise, while Christianity was still illegal there. The 1868 revolution, resulting in greater religious toleration and openness to Western influences, encouraged the entry of many more missions. In Scotland Hamilton MacGill (1807–80; *DNB* XXXV, 88) urged the claims of Japan on the UPC, at much the same time as he was rescuing and reconstructing the UP China mission. Simultaneously the EMMS designated Japan as a field for medical pioneering. Both sent their first missionaries in 1874. Alexander Williamson, as so often, was consulted about arrangements. The UP missionaries found their most hopeful contacts among the new Westward-leaning young intelligentsia; interest among the Tokyo middle class encouraged the foundation of a girls' secondary school in Tokyo. The innovative, if prickly, UP mission doctor, Henry Faulds,* started a hospital, medical school, scientific magazine, and Japan's first programme for education of blind people. T. A. Palm of the EMMS (1848–1928), who had Dutch and Scottish connexions, established his hospital at Niijita, then the only treaty port with no missionary, and started such open evangelism as to attract physical opposition. The presence of Scottish missions introduced the NBSS to Japan, producing some tensions with the American Bible Society. The more successful NBSS ventures included colportage organization and the production of Scriptures for the blind, using a process invented by Faulds.

From the beginning, the UP co-operated with the larger and more established missions of the Presbyterian Church in the USA and the Reformed Church in America, and joined these churches in a single Presbyterian Church in 1877, enlarged by the participation of other American Reformed missions in 1887. The response of the Western-influenced intelligentsia in this period, and the emergence of a vigorous Japanese leadership, induced a 'brief dream' of a Japanese national movement to Christianity. After this faded, Japan missions seem to have left little mark on Scottish consciousness; perhaps their small size and special history left no room for the sense of Scottish identity. At any rate, the Scottish contribution to Japanese Presbyterianism was discontinued after the 1900 union of the UPC with the FC. The EMMS did not replace Palm.

Korea maintained strict exclusion of foreigners and proscription of Christianity long after the establishment of missions in China. Robert Thomas, a Welsh LMS missionary attached to the NBSS, was killed attempting to enter Korea by sea in 1866. Alexander Williamson of the NBSS also conceived of Christian expansion into Korea from his base in Chefoo. The opening of the Manchurian mission, however, suggested another route. As early as 1874 John Ross* visited Funghwan (now Kaoli-mên), 'The Korean Gate', whose four annual markets gave Koreans trading opportunities in China. Ross set himself to learn Korean, and, with his colleague John Macintyre, to supervise a Bible translation. A few visitors were converted, and a Korean Bible class begun. The translation of the New Testament, however (first parts published 1882, complete in 1887), led to many more conversions, first among Korean settlers in north Manchuria and then (partly through returning traders, partly through Korean colporteurs) in Korea itself. By the time missions were established there (mainly from USA), it already had a self-supporting church and a widespread movement to Christianity. Despite Ross's pleas, the UP Church would not extend its work into Korea, and with a new American translation, the Ross version, the seedbed of Korean Protestantism, dropped out of use.

South-East Asia. After the withdrawal of missionaries from China, many went to work in Malaysia in the 'new villages' of Chinese forcibly moved during the Emergency of the 1950s. It seems, however, that while the CofS was invited to participate, only one couple did so.

3. **Middle East**

Palestine and Israel (EMMS, FC, UFC, CofS). An Armenian former student of the EMMS* opened a clinic in Nazareth in 1861. It developed into a major hospital. The FC/UFC/CofS has been associated with Tabeetha and Jaffa, and the churches and hospices at Tiberias and Jerusalem. (For Dr David W. Torrance, 1862–1923, see *AFCS* I, 345, *FUFCS* 533, W. P. Livingstone, *A Galilee Doctor*..., L, 1923.)

See also Jewish Missions (below).

Syria and Lebanon (FC, RP). A FC Mission in Lebanon was transferred to the Presbyterian Church of America in 1899.

RP missionaries worked in Syria in conjunction with the Reformed Presbyterian Synod in Ireland.

Yemen (FC, UFC, CofS). The S. Arabian mission was essentially the work of Ion Keith-Falconer.* When already drawn to Arabia, and influenced by John Wilson's* writings, he realized that the Protectorate was the one part of Arabia where missions might be possible. After a six-month reconnaissance in 1885, he persuaded the FC next year to accept him as an honorary missionary and to appoint a medical missionary. The FMC would have preferred to begin operations from Bombay; but Keith-Falconer chose Sheikh Othman, on the caravan route to the Arabian interior. He envisaged a school and hospital, an industrial school for orphans and outcasts to produce a force of evangelists, personal conversation and discreet distribution of Arabic Scriptures. His death so soon after his arrival inspired missionary response among the students of New College,* Edinburgh, and in the USA, where the Arabian Mission of the Reformed Church in America associated with Samuel Zwemer was the result. The FC therefore retained the Sheikh Othman mission, and the hospital's influence spread far into Arabia, for a time playing a crucial role in the Protectorate's medical services. The school was less popular; for twenty years education was surrendered to the Danish mission under a comity agreement, and though the school was restarted, it did not survive World War II.

British troops in Aden, and other foreigners, became a sphere of ministry – not intended by Keith-Falconer. Several attempts were made at an industrial school, but one based on a cargo of liberated Galla slaves had to be transferred to the Lovedale mission in S. Africa. The mission saw numbers of individual conversions over the years, including the distinguished Dr Ahmed Sa'eed Affara who in 1931 became a medical missionary of the CofS. But no Arab congregation emerged; often the only security for converts was to leave.

The end of the Aden Protectorate changed the conditions under which the mission operated. Though small, the S. Arabian mission was important as a centre of Scottish Christian encounter, and sometimes dialogue, with Muslims.

IV. Europe

Russian Empire. One of the principal early projects of the EMS (later SMS) was directed to the Russian Empire. The imperial authorities hoped it might have some effect on the Muslim Tatars; the mission's fate was sealed when it became interested in Orthodox believers.

The mission has to be seen in relation to the Bible Society* movement which had the support of Tsar Alexander I in the years following the Napoleonic Wars (*see also* Brunton, Henry; Paterson, John; Henderson, Ebenezer).

For Hungary, *see* Jewish Missions (below).

V. Pacific

Vanuatu (RP, FC, UFC, CofS). Many Scots missionaries served in the Pacific, especially in the service of the LMS; only in Vanuatu (New Hebrides), however, and only for a short time, was a Scottish mission involved. The first Protestant contact with the islands was made by the LMS; the Presbyterians from Canada under John Geddie* were brought in friendly alliance. In 1852 Geddie introduced John Inglis,* of the RP Church, who had originally been sent to New Zealand. Inglis worked on Anyeitum until 1876, compiling an Anyeitumese dictionary and becoming known in Scotland for his *Bible Illustrations from the New Hebrides* (L, 1890). John G. Paton* came to Tanna in 1858. His books and deputation tours created a vivid picture not only of the island peoples but of the depredations of European traders, the iniquities of the Australian labour traffic, and the nefarious designs of the French in the Pacific. The union of the RP majority and FC in 1876 brought the mission into connexion with the FC and UFC. Two missionaries of the UFC came: the long-serving F. G. Bowie (1869–1933; *FUFCS* 568, *FES* IX, 729) and William Gunn (1853–1935; *FUFCS* 568), another missionary with a literary reputation. Gunn's popular accounts of the conversion of the people of Futuna (*The Gospel in Futuna*..., L, 1914; *Heralds of Dawn*..., L, 1924), maintained the themes popularized by Paton himself, who had long seen Australian Presbyterians as the proper custodians of the New Hebrides mission, and who campaigned vigorously in Australia for funds, transferred to the Presbyterian Church of Victoria. Though Australian involvement increased, Scottish responsibility in the New Hebrides ceased only with the death of Bowie in 1934.

VI. Jewish Missions

In 1838 the General Assembly appointed a committee to consider a mission to the Jews, and a deputation to visit Jewish communities in Europe and the Middle East. Part of the interest came from the fact that contemporary Evangelicals were rethinking their eschatology and seeing new significance in Israel's restoration within the scheme of redemption. Andrew Bonar,* Robert Murray M'Cheyne* and Alexander Keith* were all members of the deputation. Two of the deputies fell seriously ill in Budapest; the Archduchess Marie Dorothea, a Protestant, urged them to establish a Jewish mission there. In 1841 Budapest became the first Jewish mission of the CofS. One of its missionaries was John ('Rabbi') Duncan,* who, with the other three Jewish missionaries, declared for the FC at the Disruption. Among those converted through the mission were Alfred Edersheim* and Adolph Saphir.* The CofS maintained its Jewish work for a time with German missionaries in India, Persia and the Middle East, as well as in London and Germany. In the period after the Crimean War the focus moved to the E. Mediterranean, and, briefly, among the Falasha in Ethiopia. The original Budapest mission has proved the most durable (*see* Haining, Jane). The UP synod opened its own Jewish mission in 1857 to work in Continental Europe.

The several Scottish churches seem to have found it easier to co-operate in Jewish matters than in many other fields. Jewish missions were generally conceived as being in a different category from 'overseas missions'. An express link was made in 1964, when the Church and Israel Committee of the CofS was brought together with the FMC and the Christian Aid Committee, under the newly formed Overseas Council.

The FPC has had a small Jewish mission, in Palestine and the UK.

See also Somerville, Alexander; Millennialism; and Palestine and Israel (above, B.III.3).

See also Australia; Canada; Chaplaincies, Colonial; Emigration; New Zealand; Scots Kirks; Women in Presbyterian Missions.

A. GENERAL INTRODUCTION.

[See also bibliographies in separate biographical entries]

I–VI: I. G. Andrew, *A Brief Survey of the Society*

in Scotland for Propagating Christian Knowledge (E, 1957); R. G. Balfour, *Presbyterianism in the Colonies with Special Reference to the Principles and Influences of the Free Church of Scotland* (E, 1899); J. van den Berg, *Constrained by Jesus' Love. An Enquiry Into the Motives of the Missionary Awakening in Great Britain in the Period between 1698 and 1815* (Kampen, 1956); W. Brown, *History of the Propagation of Christianity among the Heathen since the Reformation* (E, 1854); J. A. De Jong, *As the Waters Cover the Sea. Millennial Expectations in the Rise of Anglo-American Missions, 1640–1810* (Kampen, 1970); A. Duff, *Missions the Chief End of the Christian Church* (E, 1839); id., *Foreign Missions: Being the Substance of an Address Delivered before the General Assembly of the FC of Scotland* (E, 1866); id., *Evangelistic Theology* (E, 1868); A. Fawcett, *The Cambuslang Revival* (E, 1971); N. Goodall, *A History of the London Missionary Society 1895–1945* (L, 1954); J. A. Graham, *The Missionary Expansion of the Reformed Churches* (E, 1898); E. G. K. Hewat, *Vision and Achievement 1796–1956. A History of the Foreign Missions of the Churches United in the Church of Scotland* (E, 1960); J. A. Huie, *History of Christian Missions, from the Reformation to the Present Time* (E, 1842); R. Hunter, *History of the Missions of the Free Church of Scotland in India and Africa* (L, 1873); J. Inglis, *The Grounds of Christian Hope in the Universal Prevalence of the Gospel ...* (E, 1818); E. Irving, *Missionaries after the Apostolical School* (L, 1825); J. Kilpatrick, 'The Records of the Scottish Missionary Society (1796–1848)', *RSCHS* 10 (1950), 196–210; R. Lovett, *The History of the London Missionary Society 1795–1895* (L, 1899); C. H. MacGill, *Memories of the Rev. Dr Hamilton MacGill* (E, 1880); J. M'Kerrow, *History of the Foreign Missions of the Secession and United Presbyterian Church* (E, 1867); D. MacKichan, *The Missionary Ideal of the Scottish Churches* (L, 1927); D. E. Meek, 'Evangelical Missionaries in the Early Nineteenth-Century Highlands', *SS* 28 (1987), 1–34; R. Millar, *The History of the Propagation of Christianity ...* (E, 1723); O. G. Myklebust, *The Study of Missions in Theological Education ... with Particular Reference to Alexander Duff's Chair of Evangelistic Theology* (Oslo, 1955); S. Piggin and J. Roxborogh, *The St Andrews Seven* (E, 1985); S. H. Rooy, *The Theology of Missions in the Puritan Tradition* (Grand Rapids, MI, 1965); A. C. Ross, 'Scottish Missionary Concern 1874–1914; a Golden Era?', *SHR* 51 (1972), 52–72; W. J. Roxborogh, 'Thomas Chalmers and the Mission of the Church with Special Reference to the Rise of the Missionary Movement in Scotland' (PhD, Aberdeen University, 1978); G. Smith, *Short History of Christian Missions from Abraham and Paul to Carey, Livingstone and Duff* (E, ^{6}1904); T. Smith, *Medieval Missions* (E, 1880; the first Duff Missionary Lectures*); A. S. Swan, *Seed Time and Harvest. The Story of the Hundred Years Work of the Women's Foreign Mission of the Church of Scotland* (L, 1937); H. Watt, '"Moderator, rax me that Bible"', *RSCHS* 10 (1948), 54–5; R. W. Weir, *A History of the Foreign Missions of the Church of Scotland* (E, 1900); G. White, '"Highly preposterous": Origins of Scottish Missions', *RSCHS* 19 (1977), 111–24.

VII. H. W. Dickson, *All the Days of my Life* (Belfast, 1981); A. Gammie, *Duncan Main of Hangchow* (L, n.d.); J. W. H[arrison], *A. Mackay Ruthquist, or Singing the Gospel among Hindus and Gonds* (L, 1893); J. M. Hitchen, 'Training "Tamate": Formation of the Nineteenth-Century World View: the Case of James Chalmers' (PhD, Aberdeen University, 1984); [John Lowe], *Medical Missions: as Illustrated by some Letters and Notices of the late Dr [W J] Elmslie* (E, 1874); R. S. Miller, *Misi Gete. Pioneer Missionary to the New Hebrides* (Launceston, Tasmania, 1975); J. Sibree, *London Missionary Society. A Register of Missionaries, Deputations, etc from 1796 to 1923* (L, 1923); W. B. Thomson, *A Memoir of W. Jackson Elmslie, MD* (L, 1875); T. Torrance, *China's First Missionaries. Ancient 'Israelites'* (L, 1937; Chicago, 1988); G. Turner, *Nineteen Years in Polynesia: Missionary Life, Travel, and Researches in the Islands of the Pacific* (L, 1861); id., *Samoa a Hundred Years Ago and Long Before* (L, 1884).

B. REGIONAL SURVEY.

I. **Africa.** 1. **West Africa: Sierra Leone**: H. Brunton, *Grammar of the Susoo Language ...* (E, 1802), preface; E. Sinclair, *The Wee Man with the Big Heart. The Story of the Life of Matthew Sinclair and of the United Pentecostal Mission, Sierra Leone* (Kilsyth, 1973); G. Smith, *Twelve Pioneer Missionaries* (L, 1900), 122–36. **Nigeria**: J. F. A. Ajayi, *Christian Missions in Nigeria 1841–1891. The Making of a New Elite* (L, 1965); W. Daniel, 'Missionary Preaching in the Scottish Calabar Mission 1846–1930' (PhD, Edinburgh University, 1993); F. K. Ekechi, *Missionary Enterprise and Rivalry in Igboland 1857–1914* (L, 1971); H. Goldie, *Calabar and its Mission*, revd. J. T. Dean (E, 1901); G. Johnston, *Of God and Maxim Guns. Presbyterianism in Nigeria 1846–1946* (Waterloo, Ontario, 1988); id., 'Some Aspects of Early Church History in Ohahafia', *Bulletin of the Society for African Church History* 2 (1967), 139–54; O. Kalu, *Divided People of God. Church Union Involvement in Nigeria, 1867–1966* (NY, 1978); J. Luke, *Pioneering in Mary Slessor's Country* (L, 1929); D. M. McFarlan, *Calabar. The Church of Scotland Mission 1846–1946* (L, 1957); H. M. Waddell, *Twenty-nine Years in the West Indies and Central Africa* (L, 1863); E. and I. Weaver, *The Uyo Story* (Elkhart, IN, 1970). **Ghana**: H. Debrunner, *A History of Christianity in Ghana* (Accra, 1967); S. Prempeh, 'The Basel and Bremen Missions and their Successors in the Gold Coast and Togoland, 1914–1926' (PhD, Aberdeen University, 1977); N. Smith, *The Presbyterian Church of Ghana, 1835–1960* (Accra, 1966).

2. **East Africa: Kenya**: J. Anderson, *The Struggle for the School. The Interaction of Missionary, Colonial Government and Nationalist Enterprise in the Development of Formal Education in Kenya* (Nairobi, 1970); D. B. Barrett et al., *Kenya Churches' Handbook. The Development of Kenyan Christianity 1498–1973* (Kisumu, 1973); J. W. C. Dougall,

Christians in the African Revolution (E, 1963); K. J. King, *Pan-Africanism and Education* (L, 1973); R. Macpherson, *The Presbyterian Church in Kenya. An Account of the Presbyterian Church of East Africa* (Nairobi, 1970); H. R. A. Philip, *A New Day in Kenya* (L, 1936); J. S. Smith, *The History of Alliance High School* (Nairobi, 1973). **Mauritius**: *FES* VII, 558–60; J. F. Anderson, *Esquisse de l'histoire du Protestantisme à l'île de Maurice et aux îles Mascaregnes, 1505 à 1902* (Paris, 1903); P. Beaton, *Creoles and Coolies, or Five Years in Mauritius* (L, 1859); *id.*, *Six Months in Réunion* (L, 1860).
3. **Central Africa: Malawi**: M. M. S. Ballantyne and R. H. W. Shepherd (eds), *Forerunners of Modern Malawi. The Early Missionary Adventures of Dr James Henderson* (Lovedale, 1968); W. A. Elmslie, *Among the Wild Ngoni. Being Some Chapters in the History of the Livingstonia Mission in British Central Africa* (E, 1899, 1901); P. Forster, 'Missionaries and Anthropology: the Case of the Scots of Northern Malawi', *Journal of Religion in Africa* 16 (1986), 101–20; D. Fraser, *Winning a Primitive People* (L, 1914); *id.*, *African Idylls* (L, 1923); *id.*, *Livingstonia. The Story of our Mission* (E, 1915); A. Hetherwick, *The Romance of Blantyre. How Livingstone's Dream Came True* (L, n.d.); *id.*, *The Gospel and the African* (E, 1932); J. W. Jack, *Daybreak in Livingstonia*, revd. R. Laws (E, 1901); R. Laws, *Reminiscences of Livingstonia* (E, 1934); J. McCracken, *Politics and Christianity in Malawi, 1875–1940. The Impact of the Livingstonia Mission in the Northern Province* (C, 1977); D. MacDonald, *Africana, or the Heart of Heathen Africa* (L, 1882); H. McIntosh, *Robert Laws* (E, 1993); *id.*, 'The Effect of the War of 1914–1918 on the Livingstonia Mission', *SIMSB* n.s. 4–5 (1988–9), 1–15; K. N. Mufuka, *Missions and Politics in Malawi* (Kingston, Ontario, 1977); R. Oliver, *The Missionary Factor in East Africa* (L, 1952); A. C. Ross, 'The Origins and Development of the Church of Scotland Mission, Blantyre, Nyasaland' (PhD, Edinburgh University, 1968); G. Shepperson and T. Price, *Independent African. John Chilembwe and the Origins, Setting and Significance of the Nyasaland Native Rising of 1915* (E, 1958); J. Stewart, *Livingstonia: its Origin* (E, 1894); T. J. Thompson. 'Fraser and the Ngoni: a Study in the Growth of Christianity among the Ngoni of Northern Malawi' (PhD, Edinburgh University, 1980); H. J. Sindima, *The Legacy of Scottish Missionaries in Malawi* (Lewiston, NY, 1992). **Zambia**: P. Bolink, *Towards Church Union in Zambia. A Study of Missionary Co-operation and Church Union Efforts in Central Africa* (Franeker, 1967); P. B. Mushindo, *The Life of a Zambian Evangelist* (Lusaka, 1973); L. Oger, *'Where a scattered flock gathered'. A Catholic Mission in a Protestant area (Free Church of Scotland, Chinsali District), 1934–1984* (Ndola, 1991); A. D. Roberts, *A History of the Bemba* (L, 1973); W. V. Stone, 'The Livingstonia Mission and the Bemba', *Bulletin of the Society for African Church History* 2 (1968), 211–322; J. V. Taylor and D. Lehmann, *Christians of the Copperbelt. The Growth of the Church in Northern Rhodesia* (L, 1961).

4. **Southern Africa: South Africa**: M. S. Benham, *Henry Calloway MD DD, First Bishop for Kaffraria* (L, 1896); E. H. Brookes and C. B. Webb, *A History of Natal* (Durham, 1960); D. Bruno, *South African Homeland. St John's Diocese 1873–1973* (E, 1973); W. P. Livingstone, *Christina Forsyth of Fingoland. The Story of the Loneliest Woman in Africa* (L, 1918); J. McCarter, *The Dutch Reformed Church in South Africa* (E, 1869); D. W. Semple, *A Scots Missionary in the Transkei. Recollections of Field Work* (Lovedale, 1965); R. H. W. Shepherd, *Lovedale, South Africa. The Story of a Century 1841–1941* (Lovedale, [1940]); J. Stewart, *Lovedale South Africa* (E, 1894). **Botswana**: A. M. Merriweather, *Molepolole. A Pictorial Record* (E, 1954); P. M. Shepherd, *Molepolole, A Missionary Record* (E, n.d.).

II. **The Americas**. 1. **Caribbean**: L. Davidson, *First Things First: a Study of the Presbyterian Church in Jamaica* (E, 1945); W. P. Livingstone, *Black Jamaica. A Study in Evolution* (L, 1899); F. J. Osborne and G. Johnston, *Coastlands and Islands. First Thoughts on Caribbean Church History* (Kingston, Jamaica, 1972); A. Robb, *The Gospel to the Africans: a Narrative of the Life and Labours of the Rev. William Jameson* (E, 1861); G. Robson, *Missions of the United Presbyterian Church: the Story of our Jamaica Mission with Sketch of our Trinidad Mission* (E, 1894); H. M. Waddell, see under Nigeria above.

2 **Latin America**: W. E. Browning, J. Ritchie and K. G. Grubb, *The West Coast Republics of South America. Chile, Peru and Bolivia* (L, 1930); J. B. A. Kessler, *A Study of the Older Protestant Churches in Peru and Chile* (Goes, 1957); J. A. Mackay, 'An Introduction to Christian Work among South American Students', *International Review of Missions* 17 (1928), 278–90.

III. **Asia**. 1. **South Asia: India and Pakistan**: M. Moher Ali, *The Bengal Reaction to Christian Missionary Activities 1833–1857* (Chittagong, 1965); F. Ashcroft, *The Story of our Rajputana Mission* (E, 1907); K. A. Ballhatchet, *Social Policy and Social Change in Western India, 1817–1830* (L, 1957); G. D. Bearce, *British Attitudes towards India 1784–1858* (O, 1961); J. Bryce, *A Sketch of the State of British India, with a View of Pointing out the Best Means of Civilising its Inhabitants and Diffusing the Knowledge of Christianity* (E, 1810); C. Buchanan, *Christian Researches in Asia* (L, 1811); E. Y. Campbell, *The Church in the Punjab. Some Aspects of its Life and Growth* (Nagpur, 1961) – also in V. E. W. Hayward (ed.), *The Church as Christian Community. Three Studies of North Indian Districts* (L, 1966); C. Crawford, *Women's Work in the Maratha Country* (E, 1908); W. B. Davis, 'A Study of Missionary Policy and Methods in Bengal: 1793–1905' (PhD, Edinburgh University, 1942); Lal Behari Day, *Recollections of Alexander Duff, DD, LLD, and of the Mission College which he Founded in Calcutta* (L, 1879); S. R. Dongerkery, *A History of the University of Bombay 1857–1957* (Bombay, 1957); A. Duff, *The Church* of Scotland's India Mission: . . . Being the Substance of an Address Delivered before the General Assembly . . . (E, 1835); id., India and India Missions: including Sketches of the Gigantic System of Hinduism . . . (E, 1839, 1840); id., India and its Evangelization (L, 1851); id., The Indian Rebellion: its Causes and Results (L, 1858); [A. Graham] = 'An old Indian', The Gospel in Santalistan (L, 1875); J. A. Graham, On the Threshold of Three Closed Lands. The Guild Outpost in the Eastern Himalayas (E, 1897, 1905); Dr Agnes Henderson of Nagpur. A Story of Medical Pioneer Work (E, 1927); E. G. K. Hewat, Christ and Western India. A Study of the Growth of the Indian Church in Bombay City from 1813 (Bombay, 1950, 1953); O. Hodne, L. O. Skrefsrud, Missionary and Social Reformer among the Santals of Santal Parganas (Oslo, 1966); T. A. Jeyasekaram, 'William Miller and the Meaning of Christian Education in India', SIMSB n.s. 4–5 (1988–9), 42–53; J. Kellock, Breakthrough for Church Union in North India and Pakistan (Madras, 1965); D. Kopf, British Orientalism and the Bengal Renaissance (Berkeley, CA, 1969); M. A. Laird, Missionaries and Education in Bengal 1793–1837 (O, 1972); A. J. Langdon, 'Wilson College and the University of Bombay', in Thoughts on Indian Education (Bombay, 1961); J. M. Macphail, Santalia. The Story of our Mission (E, 1908); G. Macpherson, Life of Lal Behari Day, Convert, Pastor, Professor, and Author (E, 1900); D. G. Manuel, A Gladdening River. Twenty-five Years' Guild Influence among the Himalayas (E, 1914); W. Miller, Indian Missions, and How to View Them (E, 1878); id., Scottish Missions in India (E, 1868); id., The Madras Christian College. A Short Account of its History and Influence (E, 1905); H. Morris, The Life of John Murdoch, LLD, the Literary Evangelist of India (L, 1906); S. Neill, A History of Christianity in India 1707–1858 (C, 1985); T. V. Philip, Krishna Mohan Banerjea, Christian Apologist (Madras, 1982); G. Pittendrigh and W. Meston, The Story of our Madras Mission (E, 1908); K. P. Sen Gupta, 'The Christian Missionaries in Bengal, 1795–1871' (PhD, London University, 1966); G. Smith, The Conversion of India from Pantaenus to the Present Time (L, 1893); B. Sundkler, Church of South India. The Movement towards Union, 1900–1947 (L, 1954); A. Tomory and Mrs K. S. MacDonald, The Story of our Bengal Missions (E, 1907); J. Torrance, The Story of our Maratha Missions (Western and Central India, with Aden) (E, 1908); A. M. Urquhart, Near India's Heart. An Account of the Free Church of Scotland Mission Work in India during the 20th Century (E, 1990); D. Williamson (ed.), Forty-five Years in India. Memoir and Reminiscences of Principal MacKichan (L, 1934); J. Wilson, The Evangelization of India: Considered with Reference to the Duties of the Christian Church at Home and of its Missionary Agents Abroad (E, 1849); id., The Independent Eastern Churches (E, 1845); id., Indian Caste (Bombay, 1877); id., The Parsi Religion as Contained in the Zand Avasta, and Propounded and Defended by the Zoroastrians of India and Persia . . . (Bombay, 1843); J. F. W. Youngson,

Forty Years of the Panjab Mission of the Church of Scotland, 1855–1895 (E, 1896). **Nepal**: C. Perry, A Biographical History of the Church in Nepal (Kathmandu, 1990, 1993); M. Foyle, Nepal: the Early Years (L, n.d.); United Mission to Nepal, Nepal on the Potter's Wheel (L, n.d.).
2. **East Asia: China**: W. Campbell, Formosa under the Dutch . . . (L, 1903); id., Sketches from Formosa (L, 1915); D. Christie, Thirty Years in Moukden 1883–1913 (L, 1914); G. Cockburn, John Chinaman, his Ways and Notions (E, 1896); A. Fulton, Through Earthquake, Wind and Fire. Church and Mission in Manchuria 1867–1950 (E, 1967); A. Hood, Mission Accomplished? The English Presbyterian Mission in Lingtung, South China (Frankfurt, 1986); T. R. Kearney, The Jubilee Book of our Mission in Ichang, 1878–1928 (E, 1929); C. Moody, The Heathen Heart: an Account of the Reception of the Gospel among the Chinese of Formosa (E, 1907); T. R. Morton, Today in Manchuria. The Young Church in Crisis (L, 1939); D. T. Robertson, Manchuria. The Story of our Mission (E, 1913); J. Ross, Mission Methods in Manchuria (E, 1905); J. Webster, 'Times of blessing' in Manchuria (Shanghai and E, 1908, 1909). **Japan**: A. H. Ion, The Cross and the Rising Sun, vol. 2: The British Protestant Missionary Movement in Japan, Korea and Taiwan 1865–1945 (Waterloo, Ontario, 1993); T. A. Palm, 'The Position of Medical Missions', Proceedings of the General Conference of the Protestant Missionaries in Japan held at Osaka, Japan 1883 (Yokohama, 1883), 310–24. **Korea**: J. H. Grayson, Korea: A Religious History (O, 1989); J. N. Mackenzie, An Autobiography, ed. E. Mackerchar (L, n.d.); J. Ross, History of Corea, Ancient and Modern: with Description of Manners and Customs, Language and Geography (Paisley, 1879).
South-East Asia: G. Hood, Neither Bang nor Whimper. The End of a Missionary Era in China (Singapore, 1991); J. Roxborogh, 'Presbyterianism in Malaysia', SIMSB n.s. 4–5 (1988–9), 69–92.
3. **Middle East** (see also Jewish Missions below): W. Ewing, Paterson of Hebron. 'The Hakim'. Missionary Life in the Mountain of Judah (L, n.d.); N. A. Homer, A Guide to Christian Churches in the Middle East. Present-day Christianity in the Middle East and North East and North Africa (n.p., n.d.); J. Richter, A History of Protestant Missions in the Near East (ET: E, 1910); J. H. Wilson and James Wells, The Sea of Galilee Mission of the Free Church of Scotland (E, 1895). **Yemen**: Ahmed Sa'eed Affara, How I Found Christ (E, n.d.); J. Robson, Ian Keith-Falconer of Arabia (L, n.d.); R. Sinker, Memorials of the Hon. Ion Keith-Falconer . . . with the Subsequent History of the Mission (C, 1903); W. H. Storm, Whither Arabia? A Survey of Missionary Opportunity (L, 1938).

IV. Europe. **Russian Empire**: C. R. Bawden, Shamas, Lamas and Evangelicals. The English Missionaries in Siberia (L, 1985); M. V. Jones, 'The Sad and Curious History of Karass, 1802–35', Oxford Slavonic Studies n.s. 8 (1975), 54–81.

V. Pacific. **Vanuatu**: J. Garrett, To Live among the Stars. Christian Origins in Oceania (Geneva and

Suva, 1982); H. R. Gillan, *Vanuatu Victory. Four Generations of Sharing Christian Faith in the Pacific* (Richmond, Victoria, 1988); J. Kay (ed.), *The Slave Trade in the New Hebrides* (E, 1872); F. H. L. Paton, *The Triumph of the Gospel in the New Hebrides. The Life Story of Lomai of Lenakel* (L, 1903, 1908); M. W. Paton, *Letters and Sketches from the New Hebrides* (L, 1894, 1896).

VI. *Jewish Missions* (see also Middle East above)
A. A. Bonar and R. M. McCheyne, *Narrative of a Mission of Inquiry to the Jews from the Church of Scotland in 1839* (E, 1842); D. Chambers, 'Prelude to the Last Things: the Church of Scotland's Mission to the Jews', *RSCHS* 19 (1977), 43–58; W. Ewing, *Our Jewish Missions I. The Holy Land and Glasgow* (E, n.d.); J. Hall, *Our Jewish Missions II. Israel in Europe* (E, 1914); F. Levison, *Christian and Jew. The Life of Leon Levison 1881–1936* (E, 1989); D. McDougall, *In Search of Israel. A Chronicle of the Jewish Missions of the Church of Scotland* (L, 1941).

A. F. Walls

Mitchell, Alexander Ferrier (1822–99), CofS ecclesiastical historian. Born at Brechin, he studied arts at St Mary's College, St Andrews (1837–41), and was licensed to preach in 1844. In 1847 he was ordained minister of Dunnichen in Perthshire. In 1848 he was appointed Professor of Hebrew in St Mary's College, St Andrews, moving in 1868 to the Chair of Divinity and Ecclesiastical History, from which he retired in 1892.

Mitchell's most valuable contributions to church history were his studies of the Westminster Assembly* and Confession: *The Westminster Confession of Faith* (E, 1866; ³1867), *The Westminster Assembly* (L, 1883 – the Baird Lecture* for 1882), his edition, with J. Struthers, of the *Minutes of the ... Westminster Assembly* (E, 1874), and *Catechisms of the Second Reformation* (L, 1886).

During 1856–75, Mitchell was convener of the CofS committee on mission to the Jews. He was Moderator of the General Assembly in 1885, and received a DD from St Andrews University in 1862, and an LLD from Glasgow University in 1892.

The Scottish Reformation (E, 1900 – Baird Lectures* for 1899); *The Wedderburns and their Work* (E, 1867); editions of *The Records of the Commissions of the General Assemblies of the Church of Scotland, 1646–49* (with J. Christie; 2 vols, E, 1892–96), *Gude and Godlie Ballatis* (E, 1897), and *The Catechism Set Forth by Archbishop Hamilton, 1551* (E, 1882).

Biographical sketch by John Christie, prefixed to *The Scottish Reformation*; *DNB Second Suppl.* III, 177–8; *FES* VII, 433–4.

N. R. Needham

Mitchell, Anthony (1869–1917), Episcopal Bishop of Aberdeen. Born into a poor family in Aberdeen in 1869, Mitchell had a brilliant career at Aberdeen University and Edinburgh Theological College (see Episcopal Theological College). After ordination in 1892, he spent thirteen years with congregations of varied types, in which he proved to be an outstanding preacher, sympathetic pastor and evangelist. In 1905 he was appointed Principal of Edinburgh Theological College, and was soon recognized as a priest of intellectual distinction, a gifted teacher and a wise trainer of future clergy. He also wrote *A Short History of the Church in Scotland* (L, 1907 – on the EpCS), and took part in the revision of canon law and liturgy. In 1912 he was consecrated Bishop of Aberdeen and Orkney. Though hindered by ill-health, he showed spiritual gifts in preaching and exceptional administrative ability. He published one other work, *Biographical Studies in Scottish Church History* (Milwaukee, 1914).

In early life he wrote some verse, of which a translation of St Columba's* *Altus Prosator* is memorable. His early death was widely mourned.

W. Perry, *Anthony Mitchell* (L, 1920); *Who Was Who, 1916–1928*, 736.

G. N. Pennie

Mitchell, John (1768–1844), General Associate Synod* and USec. minister. From 1793 to his death he was minister of the congregation known from 1828 as Wellington Street Church, Glasgow. From 1825 to 1842 he was the USec.C's Professor of Biblical Literature. He earned distinction among Secession ministers for his cultivated, classical eloquence as a preacher. In 1804 he won first prize in a competition sponsored by Claudius Buchanan* for his *An Essay on the best means of civilising the subjects of the British Empire in India, and of diffusing the light of Christian religion throughout the eastern world* (E, 1805).

Mitchell received a DD from Princeton, New Jersey, in 1807, and from Glasgow University in 1837.

Sermon on the death of Dr. John Dick (G, 1833);

J. Brown and J. Robson, *John Mitchell, Funeral Sermons on his Death* (G, 1844); Small II, 44–5; J. M'Kerrow, *History of the Secession Church* (G, 1841), 927–8; *Pastoral Address of the United Associate Synod* (G, 1820, following the union of the Secession branches).

N. R. Needham

Mitchell, John Murray (1815–1904), missionary. He was born in Aberdeen and brought up in Kinneff in the Mearns. He performed with distinction in the MA of Marischal College, Aberdeen, where his interest in the mission field was aroused. While a theological student at Aberdeen he met Alexander Duff,* who tried to attract him to Calcutta. Mitchell, however, sought further theological studies in Edinburgh, and when ordained in 1838, he was appointed to Bombay. Here he worked in the school of John Wilson* and Robert Nesbit.* He became particularly close to the latter, and eventually wrote his memoir (L, 1858). He also made extensive tours, preaching in Marathi. With the other missionaries, he joined the FC in 1843.

Mitchell's missionary service was unusually long and varied. Though working mainly in Bombay, he spent much time in Pune, where he even served as Visitor (in practice, interim principal) of the Government College. He established Stephen Hislop* in his work in Nagpur, surveyed the missionary potential of Indapur and Jalna, leading to the establishment of the FC work in the latter, and turned the attention of the UP Synod to Rajputana and assisted the establishment of the mission there. He retired from Western India in 1863, and took charge of the FC congregation at Broughty Ferry; but in 1868, at Duff's request, he transferred to Calcutta, where he worked in Duff's former college, established the union congregation at Simla, and carried out the survey that led to the FC Santal mission. In 1873 he became secretary of the FC's Foreign Mission Committee; but in 1880 he was back in India preaching and lecturing. His retiral in 1888 took him to the ministry of the Scots Kirk* in Nice for ten more years. He was in sight of ninety when he accepted the Duff Missionary Lectureship,* of which his posthumous book *The Great Religions of India* (E, 1905) is the fruit.

Mitchell loved Marathi poetry, and attempted metrical translations of it; he was particularly attracted by the mystic Tukaram. He also studied Sanskrit, including the Bhagavad Gita, learned Zend, was interested in tribal peoples, and was indefatigable in investigating popular Hinduism, for which he had less sympathy. His book *Hinduism Past and Present* (L, 1885, 1897) reflects both his belief in the declension of Hinduism since Vedic times and his awareness of contemporary reform movements. He assisted in the revision of the Marathi Bible translation, and even translated parts of the Anglican *Book of Common Prayer*.

His wife, Maria Hay Flyter (d.1907) of Alness, wrote several accounts of Indian life, including *Sketches of Indian Life and Travel* (L, 1876), *In Southern India* (L, 1885) and *Sixty Years Ago* (E, 1905).

In Western India (E, 1899).

FES VII, 702–3; *DNB Second Suppl.* II, 623–4; *The Scotsman*, 16 Nov., 1904.

A. F. Walls

Mitchell, William (1670–1727), five times Moderator of the General Assembly of the CofS (between 1710 and 1726). The son of William Mitchell of Footdee, Aberdeen, he was successively minister in three Edinburgh parishes: ordained in 1695 to the second charge, Canongate, he then served in the Old Kirk, St Giles and the second charge of St Giles. A chaplain to George I, he had influence at court, where he went from time to time on Church business. Robert Wodrow* (*Analecta*, E, 1842, IV, 447) described him as the man 'in whose hands the affairs of the Church . . . have been very much since Mr. Carstaires' death'. Mitchell presided in the 1722 Assembly, administering the rebuke to the Marrow brethren (*see* Marrow Controversy), and firmly opposed John Simson* in the second process against him. He was commended as a preacher by both Elizabeth West and Robert Wodrow.* He was said to have been not only the most influential but also the wealthiest minister in the CofS at the time.

FES I, 67; J. Warrick, *Moderators of the Church of Scotland* (E, 1913), 225–39; 'Diary of . . . William Mitchell', *Spalding Club Miscellany* (A, 1841), 227–53.

D. C. Lachman

Mixed marriages, *see* Marriage.

Modan, *see* Celtic Saints.

Model Constitution. Acts of Parliament of 1844, 1868 and 1876 made provision for the erection of parishes *quoad sacra** in the rapidly expanding Scotland of the time, and by 1903 no fewer than 426 had been created. Power to erect lay with the Court of Teinds,* acting on application from local parties, with the concurrence of the Presbytery, which had to delimit the parish. Another requirement was the existence of a constitution which took account of the ownership of the heritable property and made provision for the management of temporal affairs. Though differing in detail, these conformed to a common pattern, and so models came to be prepared for guidance, that of 1901 having been 'prepared with unusual care and fullness in the light of all past experience'. On the Union of the Churches in 1929 a Model Constitution was prepared and widely adopted. In 1965 an amended Model Constitution was approved and all congregations were 'recommended and urged' by the General Assembly to adopt it. More than 70 per cent of all congregations now operate under this Model Constitution.

A. Herron

Moderates, a term used, frequently pejoratively, of various groups of Scottish divines in the eighteenth and early nineteenth centuries. It was not in general use until the nineteenth century. In a pamphlet published in 1841 (*The Two Parties in the Church of Scotland*, E), Hugh Miller* discusses the two parties and claims that Moderatism enjoys the advantage of not being thoroughly known. Miller implies that a Moderate is not only a highly objectionable ecclesiastic but also a readily recognizable one. However there is a considerable diversity of opinion among historians about the origins of the Moderates and the definition of the term.

One view is that the term originates in William II's* message to the General Assembly of 1690: 'Moderation is what religion requires, neighbouring churches expect from you, and we recommend to you.' R. H. Story* claims that by 1708 the predominating control of the Moderate party had already been established under the leadership of William Carstares,* but several modern scholars would apply the term Moderate only to the party of churchmen that emerged shortly after 1750 under the leadership of William Robertson* and his friends. It is therefore necessary to distinguish between 'moderate' trends in the CofS and the Moderates perceived as a party by nineteenth-century opponents.

Dean Stanley traced 'the Moderation of the Church of Scotland' right back to George Buchanan* – a view attacked by Robert Rainy* as inaccurate and tendentious. Several scholars however trace the origins of the Moderates to the attitudes of men like Robert Leighton* and Henry Scougal.* Gavin Struthers* alleged that Moderatism originated in Dutch theology imported along with a Dutch king.

Moderatism can be regarded as the attitude of those who were so satisfied with the ecclesiastical settlement secured by the Revolution of 1690 that they were prepared to endure hardships such as the presentation of ministers to parishes by patrons (*see* Patronage) and the necessity of subscribing to the Westminster* Confession of Faith. Their opponents regarded patronage as an intolerable infringement of the rights of the church and many seceded from 'the prevailing party' in the CofS in 1733, 1761 and 1843 (*see* Secessions; Disruption). In the first half of the eighteenth century there was a distinguishable group, all students of William Hamilton,* Professor of Divinity at Edinburgh, who held 'moderate' views of this kind. They include Patrick Cuming,* Robert Wallace* and William* and George* Wishart. They were very critical of 'manmade creeds and confessions' but even when in positions of influence did not press for a revision of the terms of subscription* to the Confession of Faith. Cuming was the informal but influential leader of the CofS from 1736 to 1761, apart from a brief period 1742–6 when Wallace was in power.

Cuming's leadership ended in 1761 with the death of his patron, the third Duke of Argyll (better known as Islay). William Robertson's subsequent leadership was independent of a patron but insisted on the enforcement of patronage in settlements to parishes and on the obedience of inferior courts to the orders of the superior. During this period the ministers of the CofS played a notable part in the intellectual activity associated with the Scottish Enlightenment,* but did not contribute much to theology and resisted all attempts to relax the doctrinal requirements of the Revolution settlement.

George Hill* succeeded Robertson as leader in 1780 but owed his position largely to the influence of Henry Dundas,* the government 'manager' in Scotland. The Leslie Case of 1805 not only ended Hill's power but also marked a radical change in Moderate attitudes. John Leslie,* the better qualified candidate for the chair of Mathematics at Edinburgh and a layman, was opposed unsuccessfully by the Moderates who wished to appoint a minister from their own group. The case proved to be the beginning of the end of the Moderates.

R. B. Sher, *Church and University in the Scottish Enlightenment* (E, 1985); A. L. Drummond and J. Bulloch, *The Scottish Church 1688–1843: The Age of the Moderates* (E, 1973); G. E. Davie, *The Scottish Enlightenment* (L, 1981); N. Macdougall (ed.), *Church, Politics and Society: Scotland 1408–1929* (E, 1983), chs 10–11; F. Voges, 'Moderate and Evangelical Thinking in the later Eighteenth Century: Differences and Shared Attitudes', *RSCHS* 22 (1986), 141–57; I. D. L. Clark, 'From Protest to Reaction: The Moderate Regime in the Church of Scotland 1752–1805', in N. Phillipson and R. Mitchison (eds), *Scotland in the Age of Improvement* (E, 1970), 200–24.

H. R. Sefton

Moderator, the distinctive title in the CofS and most other Presbyterian Churches for the member of any of its courts who acts as its chairman, his powers and duties being essentially those of a normal chairman except that he has a casting but not a deliberative vote. It is for him to constitute all meetings with prayer and to close them with the benediction, to cause good order to be kept, to rule on points of order, to refuse to accept motions that are incompetent, irrelevant or offensive, to take the vote and to declare the result thereof. In all of these matters he is vested with complete authority – a position which obtains only while the court is in session.

There cannot be a Kirk Session* unless with a minister as its Moderator. He will normally be the minister of the charge. During a vacancy or when the minister is on leave of absence the Presbytery will appoint one of its ministerial members to act as Interim Moderator. If for any reason the regular or Interim Moderator cannot be present, he may appoint another minister to act as Moderator *pro tempore* on giving a written mandate specifying the business to be undertaken. It is the duty of the Moderator to convene meetings of Session, and he is bound to do so on being requisitioned by at least two-thirds of the elders.

The Moderator of the Presbytery is chosen by free election from among the ministerial members of the court and holds office for one year, being eligible for re-election. (Until 1944 it had been customary for the Moderator to be chosen by rota and to hold office for six months.) In the absence of the Moderator the chair is taken by a predecessor or by the senior minister present. It is the duty of the Moderator to call, or to decline to call, a *pro re nata* (literally, 'for the issue raised') meeting of Presbytery when asked by three members.

What has been said about the Moderator of Presbytery applies *mutatis mutandis* to the Moderator of Synod.

The Moderator of the General Assembly is nominated by a special committee in the October before he is due to assume office, though in earlier times there were free and often contested elections. He is Moderator of the General Assembly and not, as is often misrepresented, Moderator of the CofS. His duties at the General Assembly are those of the Moderator of any other court. When he rules on a point of order his ruling becomes a judgment of the court. A convention has been established that after the Assembly has risen he should visit within some of the Presbyteries and in some of the overseas fields where the Church is active, conveying greetings from the Assembly. He is not a minister plenipotentiary, a 'Church Leader', or an author-

MOFFATT, JAMES

ized spokesman of the Church. By custom, during his period in office he is designated 'Right Reverend' and afterwards 'Very Reverend'. When in the chair he is properly addressed as 'Moderator' – not as 'Mr Moderator'.

Comparable arrangements obtain in the other Presbyterian Churches in Scotland.

Moderators of General Assembly of CofS to 1975 listed in *FES* VII, 436–47, VIII, 720, IX, 804, X, 457.

A. Herron

Moffatt, James (1870–1944), biblical scholar. Moffatt was born in Glasgow and educated there, at the Academy, the University, and the FC College, where he was deeply influenced by A. B. Bruce.* After serving as FC/UFC minister at Dundonald, near Kilmarnock (1896–1907), and Broughty Ferry, near Dundee (1907–11), he was appointed Professor of Greek and New Testament Exegesis at Mansfield College, Oxford. In 1915 he succeeded T. M. Lindsay* as Church History Professor in the UFC College in Glasgow. From 1927 till 1939 he held the Washburn Chair of Church History at Union Theological Seminary, New York.

Although Moffatt spent almost all his teaching career as a Church historian, he was first and foremost a biblical scholar. The only book on Church history which he published was a short textbook (*The First Five Centuries of the Christian Church*, L, 1938). By contrast, his contributions to New Testament scholarship and to biblical translation were substantial and distinguished. While still at Dundonald he published *The Historical New Testament* (E, ^{1,2}1901), containing an independent translation of the New Testament writings, arranged in what Moffatt held to be their historical order, accompanied by a mass of introductory and critical comment. His immense erudition was further displayed in *An Introduction to the Literature of the New Testament* (E, 1911, ^{3}1918), and his gifts as a translator in *The New Testament: A New Translation* (L, 1913), *The Old Testament: A New Translation*, 2 vols (L, 1924), and *The Complete Moffatt Bible* (L, 1926, revised 1935). The style of these later translations, though criticized by some, undoubtedly illumined the meaning of Scripture for many (*see* Bible (Versions, English)). He edited The Moffatt New Testament Commentary, based on his translation, contributing *Corinthians* (L, 1938) and the *General Epistles* (L, 1928). In his later years Moffatt was executive secretary of the translation committee of the Revised Standard Version.

Commentary on the Epistle to the Hebrews (ICC, E, 1924); *Love in the New Testament* (L, 1929); *Grace in the New Testament* (L, 1931).

AFCS I, 273; FUFCS 581; DNB *1941–1950*, 602–3; G. W. Anderson, 'James Moffatt: Bible Translator', in D. F. Wright (ed.), *The Bible in Scottish Life and Literature* (E, 1988), 41–51.

G. W. Anderson

Moffat, Malcolm (1870–1939), UF missionary.

MOFFAT, ROBERT

Born at Kuruman, Botswana, Moffat was the son of John Smith Moffat, and grandson of Robert Moffat.* Educated at St Andrew's College, Grahamstown (South Africa), he was appointed missionary to Livingstonia (1894) and senior missionary to Chitambo, Zambia (1906). Ordained by the Presbytery of Livingstonia in 1908, by authority of the Commission of the UF General Assembly, Moffat served at Livingstonia as an agriculturist in the Overtoun Institute founded by Robert Laws.* His most significant work was in pioneering a new station at Chitambo, near where his famous uncle David Livingstone* had died. There his practical skills and understanding of the African people equipped him to establish schools and a church, and to begin the reduction of the language to writing and the translation of the Scriptures. In 1911 he set up a small printing press, turning out hymn books, catechisms and Testaments. Widely respected by both Africans and Europeans, he was appointed by the British Government as a Commissioner to take evidence during the Copperbelt Riots. He retired to farm at Kalwa, Zambia, in 1930. In 1960 the Malcolm Moffat Training College, Serenge, was opened in his memory.

Obituary in *LW*, April 1940; *FUFCS*, 563; *FES* IX, 743; UFCS, Livingstonia Mission Committee Minutes, 1906; CofS Foreign Mission Committee Minutes, 1931.

M. F. Philip

Moffat, Robert (1795–1883), missionary. Born at Ormiston, E. Lothian, he grew up in Falkirk and Inverkeithing, Fife. He served an apprenticeship as a gardener and in 1813 got work in Cheshire, where he was deeply influenced by some Methodist friends and decided to become a missionary. In 1815 he moved to work in Manchester for James Smith from Perth, whose daughter Mary would later join Moffat in South Africa as his wife.

In 1816 he was accepted for service by the London Missionary Society* and was ordained at the Surrey Chapel the same year. Early in 1817 he arrived in Cape Town. He began work on the northern frontier of the Colony with Jager Afrikaner and his people, notorious frontier raiders. In early 1819, Moffat brought Afrikaner as his Christian friend to Cape Town. On that visit Moffat married and was posted north to the Tswana peoples. He settled among the Thlaping division of the Tswana. The Thlaping and Moffat finally settled together at Kuruman, which was to be Moffat's home for the rest of his time in Africa.

Moffat very quickly began his long and fruitful work of translation into Setswana. He had his Gospel of Luke published in 1830, and in 1840 the complete New Testament, the first in any southern African language. With a new colleague, William Ashton, he began the enormous task of translating the whole of the Old Testament. This time the printing was done on a press that he had brought to Kuruman. In 1857, the whole Bible in Setswana was published. Moffat also published successfully in English, including *Missionary Labours and Scenes* in *Southern Africa* (L, 1842), which was frequently reprinted. Many of his addresses were published and sold in vast numbers. In the eyes of the interested public and of the LMS Directors, Moffat was now the leading missionary in southern Africa.

One extraordinary aspect of Moffat's life was his friendship with Mzilikazi of the Ndebele. He first visited this breakaway Zulu nation when they were in the Transvaal in 1829 and 1835, then three times at the new capital Bulawayo in 1854, 1857 and 1859.

In 1870 Moffat retired to live in London where his wife died in 1871. He remained a very popular propagandist for the missionary cause. In 1874, on its arrival in London, he formally identified the body of his son-in-law, David Livingstone,* whom he had steered to serve Africa. In 1881 the Lord Mayor gave a dinner in his honour with a guest list which was a 'Who's Who' of British society at the time.

Moffat always opposed John Philip's* commitment to justice as a distraction from the true missionary vocation. However, his work as a translator was of enormous importance to the growth of Christianity in southern Africa.

DNB XXXVIII, 97–101; J. S. Moffat, *The Lives of Robert and Mary Moffat* (L, ²1886); E. W. Smith, *Robert Moffat* (L, 1925); C. Northcott, *Robert Moffat* (NY, 1961).

A. C. Ross

Monastic Orders, Medieval. Monasticism, was apparently first introduced into Scotland in the fifth century, following in the footsteps of the first Christian missionaries, but by the mid-eleventh century communities survived at best at Iona* and possibly Turriff in Aberdeenshire. Elsewhere so-called monasteries approximated more closely to minsters, consisting of secular clerks, sometimes designated as Culdees.* The arrival in Scotland of the Saxon princess, Margaret,* paved the way for the introduction of medieval-type monasticism. Before 1089, Lanfranc, Archbishop of Canterbury, at Margaret's request, sent three Benedictine* monks to Dunfermline,* where they established a priory. By this step, the Queen inaugurated a policy of encouraging the establishment of monastic orders, to be developed by her sons and successors, especially David I.*

Traditional (i.e. Black Monk) Benedictine monasticism, which prescribed that monks should spend their time in manual labour and study as well as prayer, found early favour, with Coldingham* becoming a Benedictine monastery before 1137. But the number of Benedictine monks was to remain small, possibly due to the chronology of the monastic revival in Scotland and the preference shown for reformed Benedictine orders. In consequence, although a dependent priory of Dunfermline at Urquhart in Moray was founded c.1136, other foundations were restricted to the Isle of May in the Firth of Forth (perhaps subsuming an earlier foundation at Rindalgros in Perthshire) and Iona.*

The scarcity of Black Benedictine houses was more than compensated for by the emergence of new orders at Tiron and Cîteaux, each following the Benedictine Rule, but with a strict code and supervisory machinery calculated to maintain discipline and keep fervour alive. Of these orders the first to arrive, the Tironensians,* were introduced at Selkirk by Earl David, Margaret's sixth son, in whose reign the community was transferred to Kelso* and achieved abbatial status. A dependent priory at Lesmahagow followed in 1144, with further foundations following in the reigns of his successors at Kilwinning, Arbroath,* Lindores,* Fogo and Fyrie.

If the Tironensian abbeys were richly endowed, the Cistercians,* founded by St Robert and monks of Molesme in Burgundy in 1098, attained many more foundations. In 1136 Cistercians from Rievaulx colonized an abbey founded by David I* at Melrose,* parent house of a monastic-type grange at Mauchline in Ayrshire and four other abbeys, including Newbattle and Kinloss. Another community from Rievaulx went to Dundrennan in Kirkcudbrightshire, which became the mother house of two later houses in Galloway. Successive rulers and magnates followed King David's example, with foundations at Coupar-Angus, Balmerino and Culross in Fife, and Deer in Aberdeenshire. Foundations also took place in outlying parts of the kingdom through the initiative of local potentates – at Glenluce in Wigtownshire and Saddell in Kintyre. By the thirteenth century, as the age of major monastic foundations was drawing to a close, the abbey of Sweetheart in Kirkcudbrightshire brought the major era in Scottish monasticism to a close.

Of the other reformed Benedictine groups, however, the Cluniacs,* although founded almost two centuries before either the Cistercians or the Tironensians, did not reach Scotland (with the possible exception of a short-lived priory on the Isle of May) until c.1163, when monks arrived at Renfrew from Wenlock in Shropshire, transferring to Paisley* some six years later. Relations with Cluny, however, were indeterminate, and were further disturbed by a dispute over the foundation of a second Cluniac house at Crossraguel in Ayrshire. Although after c.1270 relations between the two houses appear to have been smooth, little information is forthcoming about continuing links with Cluny. Both houses were dissolved at the Reformation.

Although the above Benedictine orders were most prolific, the other main rule, the Augustinian,* was also widely followed in Scotland from the twelfth century onwards. No fewer than nineteen houses of this order were founded, commencing with a priory at Scone c.1120. With the exception of Holyrood near Edinburgh and Cambuskenneth in Stirlingshire, all were founded as priories, although some, including Scone and Jedburgh, subsequently became abbeys.

Less enthusiasm was shown for a new institute of regular canons founded by St Norbert at Prémontré in N. France in 1120. The Premonstratensians* (White Canons) followed the Augustinian rule but were organized on Cistercian lines. The history of the Scottish houses of this order is difficult to reconstruct. The foundation of the abbey of Dryburgh* in 1150 is usually reckoned as the earliest, but a case can be mounted in support of Soulseat in Wigtownshire, which subsequently colonized Whithorn.* The remaining houses do not appear on record until the thirteenth century – Fearn in Ross-shire and Tongland and Holywood in Wigtownshire.

Of the remaining monastic orders present in Scotland, the Valliscaulians* had three priories, Ardchattan in Argyll, Beauly (N. of Inverness) and Pluscarden in Morayshire. Pluscarden later became Benedictine and Beauly Cistercian.

Other orders were less well represented in Scotland, such as the Carthusians,* founded by Bruno as a group of hermits at La Grande Chartreuse near Grenoble in 1084. In 1426, the prior of Grande Chartreuse, at the request of James I, authorized the erection of a house near Perth for a prior and twelve monks; the foundation was completed in 1429 – the sole charterhouse in Scotland.

If the Carthusians were late arrivals, they were successfully established. Not so the Gilbertines,* representative of an order founded in 1131 by St Gilbert, the rector of Sempringham in Lincolnshire, and designed to provide a monastic life for women following the Benedictine rule, in association with canons observing the rule and customs of the Augustinian and Premonstratensian orders. The one attempt to extend the order to Dalmilling in Ayrshire (1219–28) proved short-lived.

More success was enjoyed by the Trinitarians,* a non-mendicant order of friars following the Augustinian rule founded in Paris in 1198. Scotland possessed eight houses: Berwick, Dunbar, Scotlandwell in Kinross-shire, Houston in E. Lothian, Aberdeen, Peebles, Fail in Ayrshire and Dirleton in E. Lothian. Amalgamations in the fifteenth and sixteenth centuries reduced these houses to four small communities at Aberdeen, Fail, Peebles and Scotlandwell.

With the exception of the Gilbertines, all these orders, several of which had their female counterparts (see Nunneries), continued to flourish until the Reformation, which brought their presence in Scotland to an end. By then their period of greatest activity in the twelfth and thirteenth centuries lay far behind them but, although surpassed in popular esteem by the collegiate churches* founded from the fourteenth century, they never entirely lost the vitality which had characterized their introduction.

After a long interval, the monastic orders returned to Scotland. The Benedictines settled at Fort Augustus* in 1876 and Pluscarden* in 1948, while the Cistercians arrived in Nunraw in E. Lothian in 1946. The Premonstratensians had a number of short-lived communities from 1889 but finally settled at Kilmarnock in 1971 (M. Dilworth, 'Religious Orders in Scotland 1878–1978', *IR* 39 (1978), 92–109).

G. W. S. Barrow, 'The Royal House and the Religious Orders', and 'Benedictines, Tironensians and Cistercians', *The Kingdom of the Scots* (L., 1973), 165–87, 188–211; G. C. Coulton, *Scottish Abbeys and Social Life* (Cambridge, 1933).

I. B. Cowan

Monasticism, Celtic. Monasticism arrived in Britain and Ireland with the establishment of Christianity (see Celtic Church). In its broadest definition, monasticism refers to the communal efforts of consecrated Christians to dedicate themselves to a life of prayer and devotion, free of worldly ties.

The earliest form of monasticism was begun by St Antony in the Egyptian deserts at the beginning of the fourth century. St Antony retired to the desert as a hermit, where he followed a strict regime of prayer and fasting. As his reputation grew, disciples sought him out in order to join his eremitical life. Each was assigned a separate cell and was expected to spend his day in solitary meditation. The community as a whole met together occasionally under the auspices of the founder. This type of monasticism emphasized individual devotion and asceticism.

The cenobitical form of monasticism, which is the most commonly known and accepted form, was begun by Pachomius in the early fourth century, also in Egypt. Pachomius established a community of monks who lived and worked together under one rule. The emphasis was on communality, rather than solitude, but ascetic practices were still followed. At the same time, communities for women ascetics were also established.

Monasticism in Europe gradually came under the influence of the civil organization of the later Roman Empire; communities under one rule became the accepted form. Celtic monasticism, however, developed outside the Roman order and retained several of the characteristics of the early desert form of monasticism.

In general, the ideal of desert monasticism was to overcome all physical desires in pursuit of perfection in holiness. Monks were enjoined to abandon all earthly possessions and to commit themselves to a life of poverty and chastity. In order to subdue the flesh, various types of asceticism were practised, usually fasting, abstinence and self-mortification. Although the climate of Ireland and northern Britain prevented some of the extremes of the desert monks, the 'Scoti' were known for their rigorous acts of asceticism.

What distinguished Celtic monks from the eastern ascetes was their high regard for learning and letters, and their missionary efforts abroad. Education was an important aspect of Celtic monasticism and few communities were without a school. Monasteries such as Clonard, Iona,* and Lindisfarne* became famous as centres of learning. Several Irish monks crossed the sea in '*peregrinatio*', following literally the injunction to forsake all for Christ, where they lived in self-imposed exile and preached to the pagans; Irish foundations were established in Scotland (see Celtic Saints). Irish monks were also active on the continent, where several Celtic houses were organized (e.g. Bobbio, by St Columbanus, originally from Bangor).

MONASTICISM, CELTIC

CELTIC FOUNDATIONS. The first monastic foundation in Scotland is not known. One of the earliest ecclesiastical sites is attributed to St Ninian* at Whithorn* in Galloway during the fifth century (see Early Ecclesiastical Sites). Whether or not this was a monastic site, later legends relate that a school once existed there where many monks from Ireland received their education, among them St Enda of Aran and St Finnian of Clonard. This was likely to be the work of hagiographers who wished to establish a link with the community. In the eighth century, it became a bishopric under the Northumbrian Church and its first bishop, Pechthelm, was known to Bede* (see Anglo-Saxon Saints).

The period of great monastic growth in the Celtic Church was the sixth century. Most of the major foundations of Celtic Ireland and Scotland were established at this time, including Clonard (c.530), Clonfert, founded by St Brendan (c.552), and Derry and Durrow, founded by St Columba* (c.546 and 552). It was St Columba who founded the first great Irish monastic community in Scotland when he settled on Iona c.563 (see Early Ecclesiastical Sites). Other foundations followed, including an important foundation at Applecross established by St Maelrubha c.671 (see Celtic Saints). The British Church as well as the Irish Church moved into Scotland. Monastic centres were set up as far north as Aberdeen, but many more were founded in southern Scotland, most notably Abercorn, whose bishop, Trumwine (see Anglo-Saxon Saints), is mentioned by Bede as a missionary to the Picts,* and Old Melrose, where St Cuthbert received his training (see Early Ecclesiastical Sites; Anglo-Saxon Saints).

FOUNDATIONS FOR WOMEN. There are almost no records of religious communities for women in early Scotland. The earliest female house recorded in Ireland is Kildare, whose legendary foundress, St Brigit, is celebrated as St Bride (see Celtic Saints). Kildare was a double monastery in which men and women resided side by side (but in separate dwellings) and met together only for prayer and mass. Double monasteries were a feature of Celtic monasticism, although little is known of them. They provided not only a monastic home for women who wished to enter religion, but also protection to women and a place where married couples might enter a religious order together. Celtic monasteries, as they grew, admitted lay clergy, many of whom were married.

Double monasteries were ruled by an abbess. The monastery of St Hild at Whitby was a double house and was almost certainly influenced by Celtic monasticism. Other double monasteries are recorded for the Anglo-Saxon Church. With regard to the Church in Scotland, Adomnán,* in his *Life of St Columba*, indicates that there were women associated with the community on Iona, although there is no evidence that a separate female house existed. Coldingham* was a double monastery.

However, the custom of *virgines subintroductae* continued in the Celtic Church long after it was condemned by the Roman Church. This kind of 'spiritual marriage' allowed unmarried Christian men and women to live and work together in chastity and celibacy, if they were unattached to any community. In the legends of St Kentigern (see Celtic Saints) there is an allusion to his housekeeper who was a kinswoman and a consecrated nun. While women were excluded from any priestly function, they were necessary to the running of large communities and double houses. The custom of having *virgines subintroductae* died out through censure from the Church and the establishment of houses for women.

STRUCTURE AND ORGANIZATION. The monasteries were built within an enclosure of stone or earth, and consisted of separate cells for the monks (in the desert fashion), a church, a refectory and kitchen (in the cenobitical fashion), and a guesthouse. The wealthier monasteries were able to support a scriptorium for the production of books. Insular illuminated manuscripts from Celtic monasteries were highly prized for their quality and beauty (see Kells, Book of). The wealth of the monasteries was acquired through gifts and donations of land. The buildings were constructed of wood or wattle and daub; stone structures, such as St Ninian's church, were rare enough to invite comment.

Some monasteries were situated on islands or in remote areas, in adherence to the eremetical ideal; however, most monasteries were situated near enough to secular communities to allow regular traffic and communication. Like monasteries on the continent, Celtic monasteries were places of refuge and sanctuary, and offered hospitality to travellers. The size of the monasteries varied; some contained a handful of monks, while others housed a few hundred, including lay members.

The monasteries were independent communities under the rule of their founder. The abbot was supreme head of the monastery and was considered the heir, or *coarb*, to the founder's *paruchia*. The *paruchia* of a saint included all the monasteries and churches founded by him or by his followers in his name and which observed his rule. The position of abbot was essentially hereditary; he was usually chosen from the same family or tribe as the founder. After the Viking period, the abbot became known as the *erenagh*. The abbot had considerably more influence than a bishop in monastic affairs, a feature of Celtic monasticism quite alien to the Roman Church. Most founder saints were recorded as both abbots and bishops, a notable exception being St Columba.

The abbot had charge of a community which included a steward, a porter, a guest-master, artisans, craftsmen, cooks, scribes and labourers. Monks were expected to do manual labour for the monastery as well as to observe the hours for prayer, fast, do penance and study.

By the eighth century, the major monasteries had grown considerably in size and wealth. The Céli Dé ('Culdee'*) reform movement (represented in Scotland by communities at Abernethy, Loch Leven, Muthil and St Andrews) advocated a return to the solitary life of prayer and asceticism favoured by the saints of the fifth and sixth centuries, but the coming of the Vikings put a halt to any attempt at reform. With the arrival of the great medieval orders, Celtic monasticism ceased to be. On the continent, monasteries could follow a rule which was a mixture of Celtic and Benedictine. Everywhere the latter became the norm, because of its twin virtues (as seen) of order and moderation (see Schottenklöster). In Scotland in the eleventh and twelfth centuries, Roman monasticism was introduced at the same time as other Roman features. The new monks made their settlements independently of existing Celtic monasteries, though they tended to choose already hallowed spots. The only Celtic monasteries which were reorganized were those which adopted Augustinian* rule, such as St Andrews and Loch Leven.

C. Thomas, *Christianity in Roman Britain to AD 500* (L, 1981); J. T. McNeill, *The Celtic Churches* (Chicago, 1974); J. F. Kenney, *The Sources for the Early History of Ireland* (NY, 1929; rp. Dublin, 1965); L. Bieler, *Ireland, Harbinger of the Middle Ages* (L, 1963); W. D. Simpson, *The Celtic Church in Scotland* (A, 1935); M. W. Barley and R. Hanson (eds), *Christianity in Britain 300–700* (Leicester, 1968); K. Hughes, *The Church in Early Irish Society* (L, 1966); J. Ryan, *Irish Monasticism* (Dublin, 1931); A. P. Smyth, *Warlords and Holy Men* (L, 1984); M. Herbert, *Iona, Kells and Derry* (O, 1988); A. Macdonald, 'Major Early Monasteries . . .', in D. J. Breeze (ed.), *Studies in Scottish Antiquity* (E, 1984), 69–86.

D. A. Bray

Monasticism, Medieval. This form of Christian life was common to Western Christendom, but it is impossible to say when it was first introduced into Scotland. The foundation of a monastery at Iona* in 565 initiated a period of Celtic monasticism* which was mainly short-lived. By the mid-eleventh century monastic traditions of an Irish type had almost entirely disappeared, to be replaced by western-style monasticism dominated by the rule of St Benedict. In the course of the twelfth and thirteenth centuries a variety of monastic orders* were introduced by rulers and magnates whose endowments facilitated the erection of religious houses which, if modest by continental standards, were visible signs of the strength of monasticism.

Spiritual vitality cannot, however, be judged in stone; the lifestyle of the religious alone attests to the maintenance of the monastic ideal. Divine service was to be conducted regularly and devoutly, beginning with Vigils or Nocturns during the night hours followed by Matins or Lauds at dawn and Prime an hour later. Thereafter services were held at regular intervals, ending with Compline just before bedtime. Whatever the initial zeal, by the fourteenth century individual monks and canons were already irregular in their devotions, absent at times from the monastery and guilty of frequenting booths and taverns. Nevertheless, the tradition of community choir service was, even in adversity, firmly rooted in the consciousness of the most lax monastic body.

When not engaged in communal or private prayer, the religious were expected to engage in manual labour or study, but although one abbot of Kinloss is said to have worked even to perspiration in the garden, not many similar examples are recorded. Nevertheless monastic houses often acted as sympathetic landlords, and although some monastic granges may have been initially served by lay brothers, they too were gradually phased out in favour of tenants or hired labour. Study prompted a very different attitude, as many monasteries had adequate libraries and each possessed a scriptorium in which the religious could employ their talents. If few chose to write chronicles,* that of Melrose* survives for most of the eighth to thirteenth centuries, while in the sixteenth century John Smyth wrote a short but interesting chronicle at Kinloss, and at St Andrews* a more substantial piece was produced by John Law. Scholars and men of outstanding sanctity are, however, few and far between. St Waldef,* abbot of Melrose, and Adam* of Dryburgh remain isolated figures. Simpler skills were, however, apparent: the scriptorium at Culross produced a late fifteenth-century psalter, and the brethren copied service books. Monks at Kinloss and Dunfermline* also acted as copyists, as did a monk of Newbattle who in 1528 transcribed the Cistercians'* *Institutions*. Illumination of manuscripts was less developed, but the beautiful floral designs in the Cambuskenneth* cartulary indicate that this art was not unknown. Book-binding and repairing also engaged the religious. Several were also distinguished musicians, and Robert Carver,* a sixteenth-century canon of Scone,* displayed exceptional talents as a composer of a nineteen-part mass, its composition underlining the importance still placed upon the sung mass.

Study for some religious meant university; monks from Kilwinning attended Glasgow from its foundation, and at St Andrews canons of the cathedral priory were involved in teaching and studying. In an effort to improve further the educational standard of the monks, communities were instructed in 1549 to send some of their members to university to pursue studies in theology and Scripture, who on return were expected to educate novices. Occasionally educational ability was turned to wider use and at Arbroath* a monk taught not only novices but also children of lay people who had letters of confraternity. On the whole, however, extramural activity was limited, although the almoneries at Arbroath and Dunfermline were, significantly, situated outside the monastic precinct. Normally, however, concern for the poor was restricted to a niggardly dole.

Provision by the monks for themselves was more lavish. From an early period, strict common life had been modified by the allotting of individual 'portions' in money and provisions. Although, with the exception of commendators* and outsiders appointed as abbots, there is relatively little hint of immorality among the religious, monks and canons were reputed to be gluttons, and criticisms of their life of ease and comfort were commonplace in the late Middle Ages.

Such accusations were furthered by the changing character of monastic superiors from the mid-fifteenth century. Until then all abbots and priors had made their monastic profession before advancement; thereafter, it gradually became more common to nominate secular clergy who did not assume the habit and take monastic vows until after appointment. Such appointees frequently belonged to local families and their attitude towards monastic life was naturally affected by this fact. Opportunities in this direction were extended by a papal indult in 1487 stipulating that, on the occurrence of vacancies in elective benefices worth more than two hundred gold florins, the pope would postpone provision for eight months while awaiting nominations from the Scottish king. Bishops appointed to abbacies did not take the monastic habit and vows, but ruled their monasteries as commendators (that is, non-monks). After the carnage of Flodden (1513), appointment of commendators became increasingly common, but these were never laymen. They were clerics in major orders obliged to celibacy, and those under age were destined for a clerical career. By 1560 only a third of the monasteries were ruled by monks, and some of these had not been monks before their advancement.

The average commendator may have felt little responsibility for the welfare of his monastery, but his bulls of appointment obliged him to keep the fabric in good repair, maintain choir office and keep up community numbers. Indeed, novices are evident in several abbeys in the immediate pre-Reformation era. At Kinloss the number of monks, which had drifted to a dozen or so, was increased to about twenty, while in 1543 at Paisley,* of a community of nineteen, four were novices. The steady influx of novices helped to maintain and retain stability. At Lindores,* where twenty-six monks are recorded in 1219, there was only one less in 1532 and nineteen or twenty in 1558, with possibly five other novices. St Andrews recruited well in the 1550s. On the other hand, the Border abbeys, which suffered the effects of war, inevitably declined in numbers.

Numbers alone, however, do not justify the existence of a religious community but, as noted above, favourable as well as unfavourable signs can be discussed. Indeed reforms were being mooted. James V ostensibly promoted monastic discipline and in 1530–1 requested the abbot of Cîteaux to provide a visitor to reform Cistercian* houses in his kingdom. In consequence, the abbot of Chaalis came to Scotland in 1531, and in the following year a Premonstratensian* visitation was proposed. Although little success ensued, the abbot of Melrose was censured over the vice of private ownership, and attempts at internal reform followed. In 1537 the abbot and convent of Deer agreed that they should lead a fully regular life and hold their fruits in common. A similar compact is recorded in 1553 by the community of Coupar-Angus, who chose 'to lead a regular life . . . according to the reforms of the Cistercian order' (Easson-Cowan, 1–31).

Although these efforts towards reformation were unavailing, sixteenth-century monasticism was in better shape than has sometimes been allowed. Reforms of obvious abuses were being implemented; numbers were on the whole being maintained and the monastic ideals of prayer and study were still foremost. But for the intervention of the Reformation, reformed monasteries, bereft of many of their former endowments but spiritually more alive, might have emerged. It was not to be: the monastic ideal was extinguished in Scotland (though kept alive on the continent by the Schottenklöster*), not to return until the second half of the nineteenth century (M. Dilworth, 'Religious Orders in Scotland, 1878–1978', *IR* 29 (1978), 92–109).

See also Early Ecclesiastical Sites; Monastic Orders, Medieval.

Easson-Cowan; I. B. Cowan, *The Scottish Reformation* (L, 1982), 27–48; A. Ross, 'Some Notes on the Religious Orders in Pre-Reformation Scotland', in D. McRoberts (ed.), *Essays on the Scottish Reformation 1513–1625* (G, 1962), 185–244.

I. B. Cowan

Moncrieff, Alexander (1695–1761), one of the founders of the Secession* Church. Moncrieff was grandson and namesake of a Covenanter* who was arrested with James Guthrie* and almost shared Guthrie's fate, and the heir to the substantial estate of Culfargie, in the parish of Abernethy (Perthshire). He attended St Andrews (MA, 1714), studied divinity under James Hadow* there, and then, for a year, at Leiden, studying with Johannes Marckius. He was ordained to Abernethy in 1720.

Although he attended one of the meetings held by the Marrow brethren prior to their giving their Representation and Petition to the Committee of Bills and Overtures, being one of the two persons Thomas Boston* names as turning a meeting designed for prayer into an all-night disputation, Moncrieff took no further part in the Marrow Controversy.* Subsequently, however, he fully approved of the brethren's theological position. He took great interest in the first and second processes against John Simson* and even requested permission to speak in an Assembly of which he was not a member, charging the Assembly with dereliction of duty in not deposing Simson.

In 1732 Moncrieff supported Ebenezer Erskine* in Synod and through the subsequent process, being loosed from his charge in November 1733. He was one of the four who met at Gairney Bridge and established the Associate Presbytery.* He was deposed in 1740, but apparently occupied the pulpit until 1744 and the churchyard until 1746 (his successor was not ordained until June 1747), after which the congregation moved to a new building, a considerable portion of the cost of which he contributed himself. In the course of his subsequent ministry he refused to take a stipend from his congregation.

In 1742 he was chosen, as successor to William Wilson,* as tutor to candidates for the ministry in the Church, a position he filled until the breach five years later; afterwards he filled the same position in the General Associate (Antiburgher) Synod* until his death. His son William followed him in this office. He had a hand in composing various Church testimonies. With Adam Gib* he was largely responsible for the breach over the Burgess Oath* (cf. *The Artifices of the Burghers, To hide their Defection, considered*, G, 1761).

Moncrieff was generally referred to as 'Culfargie', his patrimonial estate. The 'lion' of the four seceding brethren, he was a bold and resolute man. He was best known, however, as a man of prayer, and the story is frequently repeated of a woman in the congregation saying of him, on his pausing in the middle of a sermon: 'See! Culfargie is away to heaven, and has left us all sitting here.'

The countenancing of Mr. Whitefield's Administrations, and the Secession of the Burghers, considered (G, 1759); *The Warrantableness of the Associate Synod's Sentence, concerning the religious Clause of some Burgess-Oaths, proved* (E, 1747); *The Practical Works*, 2 vols (E, 1779; this includes *The Duty of National Covenanting* and *Christ's Call to the Rising Generation*).

David Young, *Memorials of Alexander Moncrieff* (E, 1849); J. M'Kerrow, *History of the Secession Church* (E, 1848); *FES* IV, 197–8; Small II, 583–4.

D. C. Lachman

Moncreiff (Moncrieff), (Sir) Henry Wellwood (1809–83), FC minister, grandson of Sir Henry Moncrieff Wellwood.* Born in Edinburgh, he studied arts at Edinburgh University (1823–6) and at New College, Oxford (1827–31). He then studied theology at Edinburgh University under Thomas Chalmers.* In 1836 he was ordained minister of Baldernock, Stirlingshire, moving in 1837 to East Kilbride, Lanarkshire. An active Non-Intrusionist* in the Ten Years' Conflict,* he joined the FC at the Disruption.* Thereafter he was minister of Free East Kilbride. In 1852 he became minister of Free St Cuthbert's, Edinburgh, and he was appointed principal clerk to the FC General Assembly in 1855, where his knowledge of Church law was put to good use.

In the debates of 1863–73 over union with the UPC, Moncreiff was a leading proponent of union. His views of Church-state relations approximated to the Voluntaryism* of the UPC. Accordingly he submitted a motion to the FC Assembly of 1871 that the establishment principle should be declared not to be part of the distinctive testimony of the FC; the motion was passed. He was more conservative, however, on such matters as higher criticism, submitting motions to the Assembly during the Robertson Smith* case for the relevance of the libel against Smith and for his dismissal from the Aberdeen College.

Moncreiff delivered the first series of Chalmers Lectures* in 1881, on *The Free Church Principle, Its Character and History* (E, 1883). He also wrote the important *Creeds and Churches in Scotland* (E, 1869). He received a DD from Glasgow University in 1860, and was Moderator of the FC General Assembly in 1869.

On succeeding to the baronetcy on his father's death (1851), he assumed the name Wellwood.

The Practice of the Free Church (L, 1871); *History of the Case of Professor William Robertson Smith* (E, 1879); *Christian Union and Visible Churches* (E, 1860); *A Vindication of the Free Church Claim of Right* (E, 1877).

Disruption Worthies, 419–28; *FES* III, 269; *DNB* XXXVIII, 168; *AFCS* I, 274.

N. R. Needham

Moncrieff, William (?1729–86), Professor of Theology to the General Associate (Antiburgher) Synod.* Son of Alexander Moncrieff,* Moncrieff was ordained in 1749 to Alloa (near Stirling). In 1762 he succeeded his father as Professor of Theology, holding this office in conjunction with his pastoral charge until his death. Although his influence in the church was considerable, he published only two single sermons and *Observations on a Pamphlet entitled 'An Essay on National Covenanting'* (E, 1766).

Small II, 680–1.

D. C. Lachman

Monro, Alexander (d. 1698), staunch Episcopalian. Monro had a distinguished career culminating in his nomination to the see of Argyll in October 1688. He was suspected of a leaning towards Romanism.

The fourth son of Hugh Monro of Fyresh (Ross and Cromarty), Monro served as minister of the second charge of Dunfermline 1673–6, Kinglassie 1676–8 and Wemyss 1678–82, all in Fife. He was Professor of Divinity at St Mary's College, St Andrews, 1682–5 (and DD, 1682), and then Principal of Edinburgh University and minister of the second charge at St Giles', in both succeeding Andrew Cant (d. 1685; *FES* I, 65). The Revolution prevented his consecration as a bishop and the last ten years of his life were spent in writing pamphlets attacking the 'Presbyterian Inquisition'. He died in London.

DNB XXXVIII, 179; *FES* I, 66; VII, 334, 381.

H. R. Sefton

Monro, Donald (fl. 1550), clergyman and topographical writer. One of the Kiltearn branch of the Munros (Monros) of Foulis in Ross-shire, and nephew of Donald Monro, provost of Tain collegiate church, he served in the pre-Reformation ministry, probably as vicar of Snizort and Raasay in Skye (1526), and was appointed archdeacon of the diocese of Sodor or the Isles c. 1548. After the Reformation* he was minister of Kiltearn, also serving the neighbouring parishes of Lemlair and Alness, and was chosen by successive General Assemblies* as Commissioner (*see* Superintendent) of Ross from June 1563 to March 1574, after which Alexander Hepburn became bishop. Thereafter Monro's name disappears from the surviving records. By 1574 the thirty-five parishes in Ross were served by eight ministers and twenty-five readers* in addition to Monro – a considerable increase since his appointment to 'plant kirks' there. Monro wrote a description of the Western Isles of Scotland, through many of which he is said to have travelled in 1549, and a short genealogy of the chief families of Clan Donald. His description of the Hebrides, although lacking in detail, is the earliest known to be written from personal observation, and George Buchanan* (who called Monro a learned, godly and diligent man) made use of it in the topographical introduction to *Rerum Scoticarum Historia* (E, 1582); the description itself was first published from an incomplete MS in 1774 (*Description of the Western Isles of Scotland, called Hybrides* ..., E), and the full text appeared in 1961: *Monro's Western Isles of Scotland* (E).

R. W. Munro (ed.), *Monro's Western Isles of Scotland and Genealogies of the Clans, 1549* (E, 1961); *BUK*, I; J. Kirk, 'The Kirk and the Highlands at the Reformation', in *Northern Scotland* 7 (1986), 1–22.

R. W. Munro

Monteith of Carstairs, Robert (1812–84), activist in Scottish Catholic resurgence. The only male heir of Henry Monteith, an immensely wealthy Glasgow textile magnate, Robert was well connected with Tory and mercantile interests. Educated at Glasgow and Cambridge Universities, he was a friend of Monckton Milnes, later Lord Houghton, Tennyson and Gladstone. Twice defeated as a Tory parliamentary candidate, he turned down later offers of seats. Influenced by David Urquhart, the Russophobe, he sought to infiltrate and influence the Chartists* in a more conservative direction. He supported the Urquhartite Workingmen's Foreign Policy Association, its *Free Press* and its correspondent Karl Marx. Under the influence of John Henry Newman, he became an RC in 1846. He subsequently provided considerable financial and social support for the Scottish Catholic revival. His close interest and generosity sustained religious orders of men and women. At the First Vatican Council Monteith pressed for a reassertion of the Law of Nations under papal leadership to promote international peace.

B. Aspinwall, 'Robert Monteith, 1812–84', *Clergy Review*, 63 (1978), 265–72; *id.*, 'The Scottish Dimension: Robert Monteith and the Origins of Modern British Catholic Social Thought', *Downside Review* 97 (1979), 46–68; *id.*, 'David Urquhart, Robert Monteith and the Catholic Church: A Search for Justice and Peace', *IR* 31 (1980), 57–70; *id.*, 'Another Part of the Island: Robert Monteith and the Roman Catholic Revival in Nineteenth Century Scotland', in D. A. Bellinger (ed.), *Opening the Scrolls: Essays in Catholic History*... (Bath, 1987), 199–215.

B. Aspinwall

Montgomerie, Alexander (c.1545–98), poet. He was a younger son of John Montgomerie, Laird of Hessilhead (Ayrshire), and a distant relation of King James VI.* He may have spent time in Spain; there or elsewhere he forsook his Protestant upbringing for RCism. He was present at the Scottish court from (probably) the mid-1560s; under James VI he attained high favour, becoming the 'Master poet' of the group of poets and musicians known as the 'Castalian band'. He was involved in obscure political intrigues, and in 1586, while on a mission from James to King Philip of Spain, was captured at sea by the English, and imprisoned for over three years. After 1595 he may have visited the Scottish Benedictine abbey at Würzburg (*see* Schottenklöster). In 1597 he was involved in the seizure of Ailsa Craig (in the Firth of Clyde) by RC forces, and was outlawed, and died the following year. After intervention by the King, he was buried in the Canongate Church, Edinburgh.

As a poet Montgomerie was influenced by the French styles of Marot and the Pléiade. He wrote many lyrics (often to existing song tunes), sonnets, moral and religious verse, and court entertainments. His longest poem is *The Cherrie and the Slae* (E, 1597), a religious dream allegory probably intended to contrast the sweetness of the RC faith with the sourness of the Reformed; with its neat turns of phrase and copious use of proverbs, this work remained popular for more than two centuries. To the stanza (and for the tune) of the love poem, 'Lyk as the dum / Solsequium', Montgomerie composed elegant versions of fifteen psalms, *Nunc dimittis* and *Gloria Patri*, published in 1605 as *The Mindes Melodie* (E).

The Poems of Alexander Montgomerie, ed. James Cranstoun, STS (E and L, 1887); *Poems of Alexander Montgomerie* (Suppl. Vol.), ed. George Stevenson, STS (E and L, 1910); *A Choice of Scottish Verse 1560–1660*, ed. R. D. S. Jack (L, 1978); H. M. Shire, *Song, Dance and Poetry of the Court of Scotland under King James VI* (C, 1969); R. D. S. Jack, *Alexander Montgomerie* (E, 1985); *The History of Scottish Literature* I, ed. R. D. S. Jack (A, 1988).

A. A. MacDonald

Montgomery, Robert (*d.c.*1609), titular Archbishop of Glasgow. Born at Hesselhead, Ayrshire, he was among the first list of persons found 'apt and able to minister' by the Reformation* Assembly in 1560. He was appointed minister successively of Cupar, Fife (1562), Dunblane (1567) and Stirling (1572), and in the 1570s was involved in various Assembly commissions. In 1581 James VI nominated him Archbishop of Glasgow, an appointment strenuously opposed by the Kirk (the Assembly of 1582 deposed him) but upheld by the court and Privy Council (which barred his disposition). The Presbytery of Stirling also subjected him to a stringent examination (*SBD* 132–5). He finally resigned the archbishopric in 1587, and the Assembly lifted its sentence in 1588, allowing him to be appointed to Symington, Ayrshire (1588) and then to Ayr (1589).

FES III, 124–5; *DNB* XXXVIII, 309–10; Calderwood III.

D. F. Wright

Monthly Record of the Free Church of Scot-

land, journal of the FC from 1900. From June 1843 the FC published the *Home and Foreign Missionary Record* to give information on its missionary activities at home and abroad, particularly by the publication of letters from missionaries on the field. It was in direct continuation to the magazine of the same title produced under the aegis of R. S. Candlish* in the pre-Disruption* CofS. Its continued appearance immediately after the Disruption (referred to by Candlish in the General Assembly in May 1843) points to the FC's commitment from the very start to overseas missionary effort and the support of missionary workers who had joined its ranks. The General Assembly of 1850 amalgamated it with two other FC serials in order to widen its field of reference and popular appeal, at the same time dropping the word 'Missionary' from its title. Its initial popularity, however, was not maintained, and circulation declined until the publication became the responsibility of Thomas Nelson, who, after experimenting unsuccessfully with a weekly issue in 1861–2, succeeded in increasing the circulation from 30,000 to 80,000 in twenty years. Its editors were: J. A. Wylie* (1853–60); James Mackenzie (1863–9); and N. L. Walker* (1869–1900). After 1862 the title *Free Church of Scotland Monthly* was adopted with occasional slight variations and the magazine became increasingly the denominational magazine of general religious interest, which it remains to this day.

After the Union of 1900 the magazine combined with the *United Presbyterian Witness*, but the continuing FC maintained production of the *Monthly Record* under that name. The first editor, Alexander MacNeilage, brought his considerable professional expertise as editor of the *Scottish Farmer* to the production of a journal which contributed in no small way to the consolidation of the FC and the maintenance of its distinctive witness after 1900. Subsequent editors have been: Alexander Stewart (1917–37); R. A. Finlayson* (1937–58); G. N. M. Collins* (1958–73); Professor J. W. Fraser (1973–7); Professor Donald Macleod (1977–90); and Ronald Christie (1990–). Present circulation is 7,200 including a sizeable readership outside Scotland.

N. L. Walker, *Chapters from the History of the Free Church of Scotland* (E, 1895), 323–6.

A. J. Howat

Montrose, Earl of, *see* Graham, James.

Monymusk, Augustinian* priory. Situated in Aberdeenshire, it was originally a Culdee* foundation (*see* Early Ecclesiastical Sites) but became a priory of Augustinian canons; the transformation took place in the period *c.* 1200–45. The bishop of St Andrews* was regarded as the founder of the Culdee establishment and remained the feudal superior of Monymusk. The priory, however, was never a dependency of the Augustinian priory in St Andrews. The Monymusk canons nominated their prior to the Bishop of St Andrews, who then presented him for installation to the local bishop in Aberdeen. In 1445 Monymusk parish church (not the priory) was made a prebend of Aberdeen cathedral; the Bishop of St Andrews consented and retained certain revenues.

The priory declined in the fifteenth century. There were about six canons in 1535, but internal troubles and the ruinous state of the buildings brought about virtual dissolution, even before the Reformation* in 1560.

W. M. Macpherson, *Church and Priory of Monymusk* (A, 1895); W. D. Simpson, 'The Augustinian Priory and Parish Church of Monymusk, Aberdeenshire', *PSAS* 59 (1925), 34–71; M. Dilworth, 'The Dependent Priories of St Andrews', in D. McRoberts (ed.), *The Medieval Church of St Andrews* (G, 1976), 157–66; Easson-Cowan, 88, 93–4.

M. Dilworth

Moody, Dwight Lyman (1837–99), American evangelist and hymn-writer. Moody arrived in Scotland in November 1873 with his colleague Ira D. Sankey. Soon he was preaching to vast crowds. Support for Moody's work was forthcoming across the denominational spectrum, although some ministers objected to this 'band of unordained and unauthorized preachers going forth on their evangelistic crusade ... without any pastoral or presbyterial supervision'.

After an initial few weeks in Edinburgh, Moody visited Glasgow for a series of meetings, followed by visits to other towns in the west of Scotland. During this period Moody was almost universally praised. A leading churchman, W. G. Blaikie,* declared, 'Never, probably, was Scotland so stirred; never was there so much expectation.' Horatius Bonar* also commended Moody: 'These American brethren bring us no new Gospel ... save perhaps that of giving greater prominence to the singing of hymns.' Bonar's comment highlights two issues that brought a measure of controversy to Moody's missions. First, his use of 'uninspired' hymns and a small portable organ caused an initial stir in some circles, but his 'kist o' whistles' was soon generally accepted. The use of music* in worship had been a source of recent controversy in the Church in Scotland (*see* Lee, Robert), and Moody's use of the organ helped to prepare the way for the more widespread use of musical instruments in the Scottish Church. Secondly, while Horatius Bonar and most other Evangelicals did not see any novelty in Moody's preaching, there was a reaction, especially in the Highlands, to Moody's Arminianism.* John Kennedy* of Dingwall refused to support his meetings, and published a pamphlet condemning his preaching as 'hyper-evangelism'.

Moody's visits to Scotland (he returned in 1881–2 and 1891–2) helped to transform the face of the Church in Scotland. At a time when higher criticism was beginning to make its mark on academic theology in Scotland, Moody's mission seemed to bring a new lease of life and give a new confidence to the Scottish Church. A new stimulus was given to social philanthropic work, with the impetus given to the newly founded Quarrier's Homes.*

The verdict by P. Carnegie Simpson* on Moody's impact on Scottish Church life highlights the 'new spirit' of Evangelicalism he helped to disseminate: 'Moody's preaching of a "free Gospel" to all sinners did more to relieve Scotland generally . . . of the old hyper-Calvinistic doctrine of election and of what theologians call "a limited atonement" and to bring home the sense of the love and grace of God towards all men, than did even the teaching of John Macleod Campbell'* (Rainy, L, 1909, I, 408).

W. R. Moody, *D. L. Moody* (NY, 1930); R. W. Clark, *Moody and Sankey in Great Britain* (L, 1975); A. L. Drummond and J. Bulloch, *The Church in Late Victorian Scotland 1874–1900* (E, 1978); J. M., *Recollections of D. L. Moody and His Work in Britain 1874–1892* (priv., 1905); K. R. Ross, 'Calvinists in Controversy: John Kennedy, Horatius Bonar and the Moody Mission of 1873–74', *SBET* 9 (1991), 51–63.

I. Hamilton

Moore (Muir), Charles (c.1683–1736), early Moderate.* Born in Ireland, the second son of Captain Charles Moore of the Mures of Polkelly, Ayrshire, he matriculated at Glasgow under Gershom Carmichael (1702) and then studied divinity under William Hamilton* in Edinburgh. Licensed at Dunfermline (1713), he was ordained as associate at Culross in Fife (1715) and then called to Stirling (1718) through the influence of the Duke of Argyll, whose family had long been patrons of the Moores. His Stirling call proved unpopular – ultimately prompting the call of Ebenezer Erskine in 1731.*

Described by his eldest son as 'a tall man, of a pale complexion, of a pleasing mild countenance and remarkably genteel', Moore has been depicted as an early representative of Moderatism. In 1722 he alone of the General Assembly Commission voted against the overture on the Marrow* – which reflected his tolerance rather than Marrow sympathies. He allied himself with Argathelian politics (followers of the second and third Dukes of Argyll).

In 1727 Moore married Marion, daughter of John Anderson the Younger of Dowhill (Glasgow). Illustrious descendants included Sir John Moore of Corunna and Charles Macintosh the chemist.

FES IV, 325; H. L. Fulton, 'The Managed Career of the Reverend Charles Moore of Stirling', *RSCHS* 20 (1980), 231–47; *id.*, 'A Scottish Middle-Class Family and Patronage: The Ancestors of Sir John Moore', *Studies in Eighteenth-Century Culture* 15 (1985), 145–60.

H. L. Fulton

Moral Philosophy. Moral philosophy in Scotland was most influenced by the natural-law theorists Hugo Grotius (1583–1645) and Samuel Pufendorf (1632–94) and by Calvinism.* Francis Hutcheson,* an Ulster Presbyterian who became Professor of Moral Philosophy in Glasgow, tried to ease the Calvinistic emphasis. He introduced the notion of moral sense. In presenting a psychological map of this universal faculty, he stressed the operation of moral sense in the perception, approval or disapproval and motivation towards moral actions.

The best known Scottish moral philosopher was the empiricist David Hume.* A sceptic in religion and metaphysics, Hume believed that reason alone could not decide moral questions, but only a moral sentiment, moved by what is pleasant or useful. Reason, then, is and ought to be the slave of passions, which alone produce or prevent action. Morality is thus a matter of the expression of feelings. Hume believed (some scholarly interpretation notwithstanding) that one cannot get an 'ought' from an 'is'. The realm of morality is that of subjective feelings and not one of objective facts. As social creatures our passions develop in moral communities, so we share common goals and desire common goods. Sympathy is a key to making appropriate moral decisions based on our feelings.

Hume's subjectivism has been highly influential in modern empiricist philosophy, especially in the emotive theory of ethics, which reduces moral judgement to expressions of feelings and taste and attempts at arousing the same emotions in others. But Hume's moral philosophy was severely attacked in Scotland by the Scottish school of Common Sense (*see* Scottish Realism). This has been a major influence on philosophy not only in its day, but in the USA and the continent. Based on 'The Wise Club' – the Aberdeen Philosophical Society – its key figure was Thomas Reid (1710–96). It defended common sense against philosophical scepticism and paradoxes, especially as expressed in Hume. It was based on common-sense intuitionism. Our moral sense and conscience enable us to distinguish between right and wrong by a combination of rational intuition and benevolent emotion. Our moral principles do not require and cannot have any justification. They are natural to human beings. Morality, like science, is a matter of objective fact. Its principles are self-evident and discovered by common sense.

For Reid the principles of common sense were obviously true. They were embedded in our common language and understanding, were basic convictions for most people, and were ultimately founded on God. With George Campbell* and Alexander Gerard,* James Beattie (1753–1803) supported Reid with a vicious attack rebutting Hume's scepticism. Beattie stressed that humankind possessed the faculty of common sense which perceives truth by an instantaneous, instinctive and irresistible impulse.

The Common Sense School continued under Thomas Brown (1778–1820) and Dugald Stewart,* both professors of moral philosophy in Edinburgh, who stressed the study of human nature as a whole. This reveals the intuitive truth of our moral beliefs, the objectivity of right and wrong, and the universality of moral principles. William Hamilton (1788–1856)* and H. L. Mansel (1820–71) continued the realistic school of intuition well into the nineteenth century.

F. Hutcheson, *A System of Moral Philosophy*

(G, 1755); D. Hume, *A Treatise of Human Nature*, I–III (L, 1739–60); D. Hume, *Enquiries Concerning the Principles of Morals* (L, 1751); T. Reid, *An Inquiry into the Human Mind, on the Principles of Common Sense* (E, 1764); J. Beattie, *An Essay on the Nature and Immutability of Truth* (E, 1770); W. Hamilton, *Discussions on Philosophy, Literature, Education and University Reform* (L, 1852); D. S. Robinson, *The Story of Scottish Philosophy* (NY, 1961).

E. D. Cook

Moral Re-Armament (MRA), a movement designed to make Christian living appeal to people of the twentieth century. Before the title 'MRA' was adopted in 1938, it was normally called the Oxford Group, under which title it was licensed in Britain in 1939. Its founder was Frank Buchman (1878–1961), a Pennsylvanian Lutheran minister who specialized in student evangelism, originally in America. After operating in Cambridge (1920–1), he concentrated on Oxford, where annual houseparties made a national impact (1930–5). The movement attracted criticism from conservative Christians, but exerted considerable influence in more liberal circles. After 1935 it enjoyed greater success on the continent, where a conference centre was established at Caux in Switzerland (1946), and in America, where it was projected as an anti-Communist crusade. By the 1950s it claimed to vitalize the faith of anyone acknowledging a Higher Power, and it still has its appeal today.

A student campaign in Edinburgh churches (1930) led to the adherence of several Scottish churchmen, and its Scottish supporters have included prominent clergy and laity. In 1989 two Scots (one a minister) served on its UK Council, and in 1988 a recent CofS Moderator took part in its fiftieth anniversary service in London. MRA has no Scottish office, but in recent years has had up to twenty full-time (but unsalaried) workers active in Scotland. MRA has characteristically used drama to further its message. Among Scottish productions have been *Keir Hardie: the Man They Could Not Buy*, by Henry Macnicol and *Columba* by Juliet Boobbyer and others.

G. Lean, *Frank Buchman* (L, 1985); A. W. Eister, *Drawing-Room Conversion* (Durham, North Carolina, 1950); W. H. Clark, *The Oxford Group* (NY, 1951); 'The Church's Task' (by CofS ministers) in R. C. Mowat (ed.), *Report on Moral Re-Armament* (L, 1955); K. D. Belden, *Reflections on Moral Re-Armament* (L, 1983); D. W. Bebbington, 'The Oxford Group Movement between the Wars', in W. J. Shields (ed.), *Voluntary Religion* (O, 1986).

D. W. Bebbington

Moravians, the name commonly given to the Church which derives from the followers of the Bohemian reformer John Hus (1369–1415), which was formed in 1457. Establishing their own ministry in 1467 with the orders of deacon, presbyter and bishop, the Unity of the Brethren (*Unitas Fratrum*) has maintained an unbroken succession since that time. Their principles include the centrality of the Scriptures, Communion under both kinds (bread and wine), a moral clergy, and insistence on practical Christian living. John Amos Comenius (1592–1670), Moravian bishop and educator, was recognized throughout Europe for work in educational reform including graded curriculum, illustrated texts, and co-educational schools.

Following the Thirty Years War, the Unity was renewed on the estate of Count N. L. von Zinzendorf in Saxony in 1727. Foreign mission work was started in 1732 when two men went to St Thomas in the West Indies, followed by missions to Greenland in 1733, to South America in 1735 and to South Africa in 1737. Work today is on five continents with a total membership of 513,300, and local leadership is now emerging in all areas.

Theologically the Moravian Church (*Unitas Fratrum*) is in the mainstream of Protestant thought, utilizing the major creeds of Christendom as well as a body of liturgical material which sets forth the focus of belief which is highly Christocentric. A large body of chorale-type hymns and anthems also express the faith and tradition. Worship services are semi-liturgical with much music, and include such unique features as the lovefeast, cup of covenant, and Passion Week Reading services.

Beginning work in England in 1738, congregational centres were established in London, Yorkshire, Lancashire, Bath, Wales and Northern Ireland. Numerous societies and preaching places flourished from time to time, although membership growth was hampered by an insistence on the casting of the lot to approve all applications for membership. Today there are thirty-eight congregations in England and Ireland, which constitute the British Province. Mission work in Africa, Jamaica, the Holy Land and North India is directly supported by these congregations.

Work in Scotland was started by John Caldwell, a protégé of the former Methodist, John Cennick, and a congregation was organized at Ayr in 1778. This work lasted some 150 years. Societies were active in Ayrshire at Irvine and Tarbolton, with some thirty additional preaching places. Reluctance to proselytize and insistence on the use of the lot led to the gradual decline of the work. James Montgomery,* poet and editor, was born at Irvine while his father served as pastor of that society.

J. T. and K. G. Hamilton, *History of the Moravian Church* (Bethlehem, PA, 1967); J. E. Hutton, *A History of the Moravian Church* (L, 1909).

A. H. Frank

Morison, James (1816–63), principal founder of the Evangelical Union,* and Scotland's most prominent Arminian* preacher and theologian. Born in Bathgate, West Lothian, he was the son of Robert Morison, a New Light* Antiburgher minister (*see* Burgess Oath). Morison attended Edinburgh University (1830–4), and the USec. Theological Hall thereafter. While a theology student he delivered a paper denying the eternal

MORISON, JAMES

Sonship of Christ, a denial he maintained the rest of his life. In 1839 he was licensed by Edinburgh Presbytery and sent north to preach for the Presbytery of Elgin.

During this secondment Morison read Charles Finney's *Lectures on the Revivals of Religion* (NY, 1835), which had a great effect on him (*see* Revivals). He adopted Finney's views and methods of evangelism, which produced a widespread impact and much sensation, and also came to accept an Amyraldian and moral government conception of the atonement. His doctrine of saving faith was strongly Sandemanian.* These views are reflected in his *What Must I Do To Be Saved?* (E, 1840). In October 1840 he became minister of the USec. congregation in Clerk's Lane, Kilmarnock, in Ayrshire. His moral government views of the atonement were published in a popular tract, *The Nature of the Atonement* (E, 1841; new ed. L, 1890).

By now, opposition had been aroused in the USec.C to Morison's doctrines and style of evangelism. This culminated in his trial before Kilmarnock Presbytery in March 1841, where he was charged among other things with Amyraldianism (*see* Cameron, John), denying that unbelievers should pray for faith, and equivocating over original sin. Presbytery suspended him from the ministry; Morison appealed to the USec. Synod, its supreme judicatory. Meanwhile he published *The Extent of the Atonement* (Kilmarnock, 1841), in which he reiterated his views on the universality of God's love and Christ's death.

Synod met in Glasgow in June amid much public excitement and upheld the suspension, appointing a committee to confer with Morison. Morison, however, defied the sentence of suspension and continued to act as minister of Clerk's Lane Church. He was consequently deposed. Most of his church adhered to him.

By 1843 Morison had abandoned his modified Calvinism in favour of Arminianism, and along with three other deposed USec. ministers formed the Evangelical Union, of whose annual conference he was president in 1845 and 1868. He commenced as Professor of the Evangelical Union Academy also in 1843, where he taught until 1873. In 1851 he transferred from Kilmarnock to the Evangelical Union church in Glasgow, which from 1853 met in North Dundas Street. His ministry here lasted until ill-health compelled retirement in 1884.

Morison was an erudite scholar, particularly in languages, being proficient in Greek, Hebrew, Latin, Syriac, Chaldee, Ethiopic and Arabic. His exegetical writings, notably his commentaries on *Matthew* (L, 1870) and *Mark* (L, 1873), were highly prized by Evangelicals of all persuasions. Other commentaries included *A Critical Exposition of the Third Chapter of Paul's Epistle to the Romans* (L, 1862), and *An Exposition of the Ninth Chapter of Paul's Epistle to the Romans* (Kilmarnock, 1849). He edited, and largely wrote, the Evangelical Union's periodical, the *Evangelical Repository*, 1854–68.

By the time of Morison's death, Scottish theology had generally followed his lead in abandoning the Calvinism of the Reformers* and Covenanters* for what was considered a more humane theology, emphasizing God's universal love. Morison was one of the foremost pioneers in this movement, although he did not share its increasingly negative attitude to the authority of Scripture.

Morison received a DD from Adrian University, Michigan, in 1863, and from Glasgow University in 1882.

St. Paul's Teaching on Sanctification (L, 1886); *Vindication of the Universality of the Atonement* (G, 1861).

W. Adamson, *The Life of the Rev. James Morison, DD* (L, 1898); O. Smeaton, *Principal James Morison* (E, 1902); *Report of the Proceedings in the Cases of Rev. James Morison and the Rev. Robert T. Walker* (E, 1841); *DNB* XXXVIII, 954–5.

N. R. Needham

Morisonians, *see* Morison, James; Evangelical Union.

Mormons (Church of Jesus Christ of Latter-day Saints), founded in 1830 by Joseph Smith in New York, after the discovery of the 'Book of Mormon'. This, and other sacred books additional to the Bible, account for Mormonism's divergencies from orthodox Christianity.

The story of Mormonism in Scotland begins in Canada, a second homeland for many thousands of Scots in the nineteenth century. Alexander Wright, of Banffshire, and Samuel Mulliner, of Midlothian, had settled in the Ontario area in the mid-1830s. Shortly thereafter they were converted to Mormonism and in 1839 returned to Scotland as missionaries. Mulliner began his work in Edinburgh, where he had family and friends; Wright started his labours in Marnoch, Banffshire.

The first public preaching of Mormonism in Scotland took place in a small rented room in Bishopton, near Paisley, on 10 January 1840. Four days later the first Scottish baptisms took place, in the River Clyde – the first of more than 9,000 Scots to join the Church during the nineteenth century. Notable amongst these were Richard Ballantyne, founder of the Church's first Sunday school, born near Galashiels, and Charles W. Nibley, who became a member of the First Presidency in 1925, and was born in Hunterfield, Midlothian.

Emigration* took its toll, and by the mid-1950s there were only 500 Church members in Scotland. Today, there are five 'stakes' (dioceses) and over 11,000 members.

V. B. Bloxham, J. R. Moss and L. C. Porter (eds), *Truth Will Prevail* (C, 1987); D. A. Cuthbert, *The Second Century: Latter-day Saints in Great Britain, I: 1937–1987* (C, 1987); R. L. Evans, *A Century of 'Mormonism' in Great Britain* (Salt Lake City, 1937).

B. J. Grant

Morrison, George Herbert (1866–1928), UFC minister and writer. Born in Glasgow, he was edu-

MORRISON, JAMES HORNE

cated at Glasgow University (MA, 1888) and Glasgow FC College. From 1888-9 he was assistant editor of the *Oxford New English Dictionary*. He was licensed by Glasgow FC Presbytery in 1893, assistant at Free St George's, Edinburgh, 1893-4, and ordained colleague and successor at Thurso First, Caithness, in 1894. In 1898 he moved to Free St John's, Dundee. He entered the UFC in 1900, and in 1902 moved to Wellington Church, Glasgow, the largest UF congregation in the city.

Morrison was a celebrated preacher and a prolific author. Most of his writings were sermonic and devotional in nature, and he wrote many articles and poems for periodicals. George Reith described him as having 'the mind of a poet, the pen of an artist in words, and a rare touch of that indefinable quality which our forefathers called "unction"' (*Reminiscences of the United Free Church General Assembly*, E, 1933, 290). Morrison also produced a number of interesting historical and literary studies: *Memoir of the Life and Writings of Thomas Boston* (E, 1899), *St Columba* (E, 1900), and *Christ in Shakespeare* (L, 1928). His evangelical theology is perhaps most clearly and economically stated in his *The Significance of the Cross* (G, 1923), which expounds and defends the penal substitutionary nature of the atonement.

Morrison received a DD from Glasgow University in 1913, and was Moderator of the UF General Assembly in 1926.

FUFCS 257; introd. by G. M. Docherty to Morrison, *The Incomparable Christ* (L, 1959); A. Gammie, *Dr. George H. Morrison, The Man and His Work* (L, 1928); C. M. Morrison (wife), *Morrison of Wellington* (L, 1930).

N. R. Needham

Morrison, James Horne (1872-1947), UFC minister and promoter of missions.* Born in Aberdeenshire, Morrison was educated at Gordon Schools, Huntly, Aberdeenshire, and graduated from Aberdeen University (1892) in classics and philosophy. He entered New College,* Edinburgh, in 1892, and became president of the college missionary society.

From April 1894 to April 1895 he served as student missionary in the Canadian North West Territory. He kept a diary, colourfully portraying settlers' lives. Graduating from New College in 1897, he became Assistant at the South FC, Aberdeen (1897-9), and St Leonard's UF Church, Perth (1899-1901), being ordained to the UFC ministry at Falkland, Fife, in 1901. Maintaining his interest in missions, he travelled to central Africa in 1914 as a delegate to the UFC General Assembly missions. Thereafter he was minister at Newhills UF Church, Bucksburn, Aberdeen (1917-42). He delivered the Cunningham lectures* at New College in 1936, lecturing on the relationship of faith and science. He was awarded a DD by Aberdeen University in 1937. His publications include: *On the Trail of the Pioneers* (L, 1913); *Streams in the Desert* (L, 1919); *Missionary Heroes of Africa* (NY, 1922); *William Carey* (L, 1924); *The Scottish Churches' Work Abroad* (E, 1927); *Christian Faith and Science of To-day* (L, 1936).

FUFCS, 371, 425; B. S. Schlenther, 'James Horne Morrison', *RSCHS* 21 (1983), 263-74.

B. S. Schlenther

Morrison (or Morison), John (c.1796-1852), blacksmith and noted Gaelic* religious poet. Born in Rodel, Harris, Morrison was brought to Christian assurance under the preaching of John MacDonald* of Ferintosh, for whom he later composed a long elegy. He became a leading figure in local revival* movements, and served as catechist, first with the SSPCK* and later the FC. He was a prominent ambassador for the Disruption* cause.

He was the major religious poet of the West Highlands in the nineteenth century. Though sometimes of undisciplined length, his compositions are linguistically rich and robust, and have had an enduring vogue. They deal with major theological themes such as our innate spiritual inability, the effectiveness of God's grace, the new birth, Christian conflict and victory. Others reflect on some of the principal personalities and controversies of the Disruption era in the Highlands,* and his elegies commemorate some of the leading laymen he had known. There are also lighter pieces, some of them of a vituperative nature, including a vivid portrayal of the physical and moral degradation caused by drunkenness. Some individual pieces were published as separate pamphlets, and a collected edition by Alastair Maclean appeared in Toronto in 1861. The fullest edition - G. Henderson (ed.), *Dain Iain Ghobha*, 2 vols (G, 1893-6); 1 vol. (E, n.d.) - incorporates a memoir in English.

See also Hymnology, Gaelic.

K. D. MacDonald

Morton, fourth Earl of, *see* Douglas, James.

Morton, Robert (1849-1932), Original Secession* professor. Born near Quarter, Lanarkshire, amid Covenanting* traditions, he was educated at Carluke, Glasgow University (not graduating, though later he was made DD) and the Original Secession Theological Hall (1869-72). He ministered at Kilmarnock (1872-5), Perth (1875-1902) and Mains Street, Glasgow (from 1902 to his death). He edited the *Original Secession Magazine* 1884-96, and from 1895 was Professor of Systematic Theology and Church History in the denomination's Theological Hall in Glasgow. For many years he served the Scottish Reformation Society* and the Lord's Day Observance Association of Scotland (*see* Sabbatarianism) - he was president of both - and likewise the City of Glasgow Society of Social Service, editing unnamed its magazine *Organised Help*. He also supported Glasgow's Bible Training Institute.* He was not a prolific author (although he overcame the loss of both hands in a boyhood accident), but was a dominant figure in his Church and influential in wider Evangelicalism.*

MUIR, GEORGE

'Principal John Lee and His Memorials for the Bible Societies', *Records of the Glasgow Bibliographical Society* 4 (1914–15, published 1918), 12–37; 'The Literature of Dissent in Glasgow in the Latter Half of the Eighteenth Century', *ibid.* 11 (1933), 56–72.

Who Was Who, 1929–1940, 974; *Original Secession Magazine*, 4th ser. 31 (1933), 6–12, 41–53, 140–3, 340–2.

D. F. Wright

Muir, George (1723–71), evangelical CofS minister. Born in Spott, Haddington, his original career was in law, serving in the office of a writer to the signet in Edinburgh. Attracted out of curiosity to Cambuslang during the revival* of 1742, he was converted, and decided to study for the ministry. Licensed by the Presbytery of Dunfermline in 1750, he was ordained to Old Cumnock, Ayrshire, in 1752, moving in 1766 to the High Kirk in Paisley, Renfrewshire. His life and ministry were cut short by a cancerous growth in the foot; for some time Muir was carried about in a chair, but finally the foot had to be amputated and he died through loss of blood.

A number of published writings testify to Muir's zealous Evangelicalism. His *Christ's Cross and Crown* (E, 1759) was republished in Paisley with some additional sermons in 1769, and is said to have been the first book published there. Other works included *The Parable of the Sower Illustrated and Applied* (L, 1769) and *The Parable of the Tares: In Twenty-One Sermons* (Paisley, 1771). Muir had several miscellaneous sermons published; see *The Substance of Four Table Sermons...* (E, 1794). He also wrote against Independents (*The Synod of Jerusalem: or, Courts of Review in the Christian Church considered*, G, 1768) and on the proper relationship of the church to the civil magistrate (*The Christian's Duty toward Kings and those in authority*, G, 1760).

Muir received a DD from Princeton, New Jersey, in 1768.

Edinburgh Christian Instructor n.s. 1 (1838), 153–9; *FES* III, 172.

N. R. Needham

Muir, John (1810–82), Sanskrit scholar and Christian apologist in India. He was born in Glasgow, son of a merchant and brother of William Muir.* He was an Episcopalian.* He interrupted his studies at Glasgow University to join the East India Company, involving preparatory study at Haileybury College, where he excelled academically. Between 1830 and 1850 he served in a succession of administrative posts in the North Western Provinces, interrupted by a short but critical time in charge of the reorganization of the Sanskrit College at Benares (1844–5). From 1850 until retiral in 1854 he was a judge at Fatehpur. Muir was an unremarkable administrator, but an outstanding Sanskritist. A devout, but not a crusading, Christian, he sought to develop a Christian apologetic in Sanskrit and to engage in debate with classical Indian metaphysics. He saw mission largely in

MUNRO, DONALD

terms of imparting knowledge in appropriate forms. He drew the fire of Alexander Duff,* but his treatise *On Conciliation in Matters of Religion: the Proper Adaptation of Instruction to the Character of the People Taught* (Calcutta, 1849) became a manual for missionaries. His *Matapariksa: a Sketch of Arguments for Christianity and against Hinduism* (Calcutta, 1839, 1840) was a landmark in Hindu-Christian controversy, provoking vigorous Hindu response. On retirement he advanced oriental learning and the comparative study of religion in Scotland, founding the chair of Sanskrit and Comparative Philology at Edinburgh University in 1862. His widely acclaimed five-volume series *Original Sanskrit Texts on the Origin and History of the People of India* was published between 1868 and 1870. He wrote hymns in Sanskrit and translated Sanskrit poetry. His later writings, influenced by continental models, display non-traditional views on biblical inspiration and the fate of the heathen. He received doctorates from Oxford, Edinburgh and Bonn and was made CIE in 1878.

DNB XXXIX, 267–8; *Athenaeum* 1882, 1, 318, 346; *Academy* 21 (1882), 196; *Journal Royal Asiatic Society* 14 (1882), i–xiv; *Edinburgh Courant*, 9 March 1882; R. F. Young, *Resistant Hinduism. Sanskrit Sources on anti-Christian Apologetics in Early Nineteenth-century India* (Vienna, 1981); E. J. Sharpe, *Not to Destroy but to Fulfil* (Uppsala, 1956).

I. D. Maxwell

Multilateral Church Conversation, an ecumenical process involving most Scottish Churches – the CofS, the UFC, the Congregational Union, the EpCS, the Methodists, and latterly the URC (formerly the Churches of Christ). The RCs and the Baptists participate as observers. It started in 1967 on the initiative of the CofS in the aftermath of the failure of several bilateral union projects. The Conversation has produced a series of agreements on issues such as Church and state, ministry, baptism, and the Lord's Supper. It has given considerable impetus to the establishment of 'ecumenical parishes', and is laying the groundwork for a plan of union which it is hoped the major participants will endorse.

See also Ecumenical Movement.

The main productions of the Conversation have been: The Controlling Principles for a Basis of Union (1969); *Interim Report* on Witness and Service, the Faith of the Church and Ministry for Scotland (E, 1972); *Worship and Sacraments* (E, 1974); *Church and State* (1977); *The Next Step* (on ecumenical parishes; 1979); *Christian Unity: Now is the Time* (1985); *Deacons for Scotland?* (E, 1990).

D. B. Forrester

Mungo, *see* Celtic Saints.

Munro, Donald (1773–1830), catechist. Munro was born in the parish of Portree, Skye. Having lost his sight through smallpox in his youth, he became a catechist with the Scottish SPCK,* one of several remarkable blind Highland* catechists. In 1805 he was converted as a result of the preaching of John Farquharson,* a visiting Haldanite* missionary. Spoken of as the 'Father of Evangelical Religion in the Isle of Skye', Munro was at the centre of the great Skye revival* of 1812-14. The blind catechist was a friend and supporter of Roderick MacLeod* of Bracadale and Snizort, the leading ministerial figure in nineteenth-century Skye Evangelicalism. Munro's influence spread beyond Skye to the Outer Hebrides, and he was visited by many of the leaders of the Hebridean evangelical movement. Known in Gaelic* as *An Dall Munro*, it is said that he had memorized the entire Gaelic Bible.

D. MacKinnon, *Domhnall 'Munro', An Dall* (Portree, n.d.); R. MacCowan, *The Men of Skye* (G, 1902), 1-30; G. Henderson (ed.), *Dain Iain Ghobha* (G, 1893-6), 61-83.

R. MacLeod

Munro, Robert (c.1645-1704), RC mission priest. Born in Ross, he became an RC and studied at the Scots Colleges* in Douai 1663-8 and Rome 1668-71. From 1671 he worked as a priest in mainland Inverness-shire. He was with Dundee's army in 1689. Captured c.1696, he was imprisoned in Edinburgh and exiled to Flanders. Returning to Scotland 1698, and having been imprisoned in London on the way, he served in Strathglass and Glengarry and was Bishop Thomas Nicolson's* vicar for the mainland Highlands. In January 1704 he was captured by soldiers while seriously ill, thrown into a dungeon in Invergarry Castle without any attention, and died.

J. Ritchie, *Robert Munro* (G, c.1931); A. S. MacWilliam, 'A Highland mission: Strathglass, 1671-1777', *IR* 24 (1973), 75-86.

M. Dilworth

Murchison, Thomas Moffat (1907-84), minister at Glenelg (1932-7), and the Gaelic* charge of St Columba-Copland Road, later St Columba-Summertown, Glasgow (1937-72). He was Moderator of the General Assembly of CofS in 1969.

Born in Glasgow and reared in Skye, Murchison studied for the ministry at Glasgow University and Trinity College. He was awarded an honorary DD by Glasgow University in 1964.

Involved in 1935 in setting up the Highland Development League, he published *The Plight of the Smallholders* (E, 1935). Closely involved with the work of An Comunn Gaidhealach, he edited its magazine, *An Gaidheal* (1946-58). He helped set up the Folklore Institute in Scotland in 1947.

He articulated his passionate interest in Highland* culture and tradition in a phenomenal journalistic output, notably his 'Highland Causerie' column in the *Perthshire Advertiser*, his editorship of the Gaelic supplement to *Life and Work* (1951-80), and his weekly Gaelic column in the *Stornoway Gazette* (1955-83).

He contributed scholarly papers to the *Transactions of the Gaelic Society of Inverness*, notably 'The Synod of Glenelg' in Vol. 38; 'Glenelg, Inverness-shire: Notes for a Parish History' and 'Notes on the Murchisons' in Vol. 39/40; 'The Presbytery of Gairloch, 1724-50' in Vol. 44; 'The Presbytery of Gairloch (or Lochcarron), 1751-1827' in Vol. 47. For the Scottish Gaelic Texts Society, he edited *The Prose Writings of Donald Lamont* (E, 1960) and *The Gaelic Prose of Kenneth MacLeod* (E, 1988).

See also Bible (Versions, Gaelic).

FES IX, 294, X, 174; *Who's Who 1984*, 1644.

R. MacLeod

Murray, Alexander (1775-1813), orientalist. Murray was born at Dunkitterick in Galloway, the son of a shepherd. He had little schooling, but at an early age showed an intense love of books and of languages. He studied arts and divinity at Edinburgh (1793-1802) and became CofS minister of Urr in Kirkcudbrightshire in 1806. His election to the chair of Oriental Languages at Edinburgh (1812) was a recognition of his vast linguistic erudition. Edinburgh awarded him its DD in 1812. He retained his charge at Urr. His pioneering work on comparative philology was posthumously published (1823).

History of the European Languages, 2 vols (E, 1823) (including a life of Murray by Sir Henry Moncrieff Wellwood*); *FES* II, 306-7; *DNB* XXXIX, 346-7; J. Reith, *The Life and Writings of Rev. Alex. Murray* (Dumfries, 1903); *From Shepherd's Cot to Professor's Chair: Centenary Celebrations*... (Newton Stewart, 1913).

G. W. Anderson

Murray, Andrew (1828-1917), churchman, spiritual leader, writer, educationalist. He was the second of the sixteen children of Andrew Murray (1794-1866; *FES* VII, 563). With his elder brother John* he was sent in 1838 to Aberdeen for his education. The two brothers moved to Utrecht in the Netherlands in 1845 to complete their theological training. With other South African students they associated themselves with followers of the *Réveil*, a religious revival directed against the prevailing rationalistic theology. In the year of his arrival Andrew experienced conversion, an event he often emphasized in his preaching. At the age of twenty-one he was appointed the first and only minister of the Orange River Sovereignty. He travelled extensively in this vast territory and did much to mitigate the feelings of the emigrants against the English regime and Cape Church. In Bloemfontein he was instrumental in founding Grey College (1856) which gave birth to the University of the Free State. He was to establish a succession of educational institutions aimed at 'the growth of a spiritual and Christian character', and recruited teachers in the Netherlands, Scotland and America. Famous are the seminaries for girls he opened and staffed with teachers from Mt Holyoke in Massachusetts. But he also did more than anyone else to advance domestic and foreign missionary work and helped the

MURRAY, JOHN

Dutch Reformed Church more than double its membership.

He became internationally known for his many books, which have been widely translated and many of which remain in print. The 1860 revival which he helped to foster stimulated his ministry as author. *Abide in Christ* (1864), 'regarded abroad as his most influential work', is perhaps the best example. As churchman, six times Moderator of the Synod, and writer, he opposed liberal theology and advanced an evangelical view of ministry. In a practical and personal way he emphasized conversion, sanctification, prayer, the Holy Spirit, the missionary call, though without a concern to reconcile them according to his Reformed theology. He had to defend himself from accusations of teaching free will and that God wills the redemption of all. He was an abstainer and advocated a qualified faith-healing. W. J. Hollenweger (*The Pentecostals*, L, 1972, 111ff.) considers him as the forerunner of the Pentecostals. In 1898 he was awarded an honorary doctorate by Aberdeen and in 1907 by the University of Cape of Good Hope. He was a legendary figure in his own time and remains a 'spiritual father' for many in the DRC, South Africa and across the world.

Versamelde Werke (*Collected Works*) (Stellenbosch, 1945).

J. du Plessis, *The Life of Andrew Murray* (L, 1919); *Dictionary of South African Biography* I, 574–83; W. M. Douglas, *Andrew Murray and his Message* (E, n.d.); L. F. Choy, *Andrew Murray, Apostle of Abiding Love* (Fort Washington, 1978).

E. Brown

Murray, John (1826–82), first Professor of Theology in the Dutch Reformed Church in South Africa. He was the eldest son of Andrew Murray (1794–1866; *FES* VII, 563), the Scottish minister who arived at the Cape in 1822 to serve in the Dutch Reformed Church until his death. With his younger and more famous brother Andrew,* John was sent to Aberdeen for his education. Both completed their training for the ministry in Utrecht (Holland) and returned to South Africa. With like-minded ministers he helped to shape an evangelical Reformed ministry. From 1849 to 1858 he served as local minister in Burgersdorp, and realized the need for sound Christian literature, especially for the rural population. A co-founder of the South African Christian Book Society, he himself wrote books, two of which, a Childrens' Bible (1856) and a Catechism (1857), excel in simplicity and clarity and were used until recently. Along with N. J. Hofmeyr (1827–1909), who had a Dutch-Cape background, he was called to start the Theological Seminary in Stellenbosch (1858). Evangelically minded, they trained ministers for the Dutch Reformed Church, prescribing the works of the 'Bible Apologetic' school of thought developed at Utrecht, and with reference to authors of the Free Church of Scotland. With the local minister J. H. Neethling (1826–1904), the three of them established educational institutions at Stellenbosch, including the university.

P. B. van der Walt, *John Murray, 1826–1882* (Pretoria, 1979); *Dictionary of South African Biography* II, 502–4.

E. Brown

Murray, John (1898–1975), theologian. Born at Migdale, near Bonar Bridge, Murray was reared in the FPC, educated at Dornoch Academy, Glasgow University and Princeton Theological Seminary.* He taught at Princeton (1929–30) and Westminster Theological Seminary, Philadelphia (1930–66), and was ordained in 1937 by the Orthodox Presbyterian Church, USA. Murray was influential in Scotland largely through his published works, especially from c. 1960.

Committed to Reformed orthodoxy, Murray's scholarly interests lay in the relationship of exegesis and biblical theology to the development of Systematic Theology. His exegetical strength is evident in his *The Epistle to The Romans* (Grand Rapids, 2 vols, 1960–5). Characteristic of his biblical-theological sensitivity are his rooting of ethics in the creation ordinances, his reservations about the 'covenant of works' and his exposition of definitive (as well as progressive) sanctification. His semi-popular study *Redemption – Accomplished and Applied* (Grand Rapids, 1955), expounds particular redemption, stresses union with Christ, and sees adoption as the apex of redemptive privileges. The profound influence of his Princeton mentor, Geerhardus Vos (1862–1947), is everywhere evident.

Murray's work was accomplished despite the physical handicap of the loss of one eye during service in the First World War. At his death he was a minister of the FC.

Collected Writings, 4 vols (E, 1976–83), including I. H. Murray, 'The Life of John Murray', vol. 3, 1–158; bibliography, vol. 4, 361–75.

S. B. Ferguson

Music, Church, music which enhances and enables the corporate worship of the Church in a manner appropriate to that worship.

THE CELTIC PERIOD. There is little or no information about the music of the Celtic Church* in Scotland, though it is conjectured that the chant in use may have resembled the elaborate chant of Gaul, which was wedded to liturgies of the Gallican family, to which the liturgy (or more probably liturgies) of Celtic Scotland almost certainly belonged. Bede* states that Gregorian Chant was not introduced into Britain until AD 678. Praise for the Eucharist* and for the Divine Office was drawn mainly from the Psalms, but use was also made of canticles and hymns. Adomnán* speaks of a 'book of hymns for the seven days of the week' written by St Columba* himself. The attribution to various Celtic saints* of an outstanding ability to sing suggests that the servant role of music may have been held in considerable honour. There is, moreover, evidence from Ireland that music had academic status among the Celts at a time when it and other liberal arts were being neglected in non-Celtic Europe. The Welsh historian Giraldus Cambrensis (1147–1223) names the *cithara* (harp) as the chief instrument in use in Ireland, Scotland and Wales.

THE MEDIEVAL PERIOD. The history of church music in Scotland in the medieval period is the history of church music in RC Europe with only minor local modification. Scotland was a sovereign, but European, nation, and in Europe the Church was the largest single organization, the largest employer of labour and the sole arbiter in artistic questions. Its worship was a highly professional vocation. The cathedrals* and collegiate churches* sang the increasingly complex polyphonic music of the age. In Aberdeen, for example, twenty-nine canons sat in the choir of the Cathedral by the end of the fourteenth century, and in 1506 Bishop Elphinstone* ruled that, complementing the canons, eleven singing boys should be maintained in the Sang Schule. The Latin Sarum (Salisbury) rite being used in Scotland, certainly by the late fifteenth century, it may be supposed that English music, for which Salisbury was renowned, was known and sung in Scotland. Information on the contribution of Scottish composers to the corpus of medieval music is scanty, and not many compositions survived the destruction of music books at the Reformation.* Of the few names which survive, that of Robert Carver* of Scone is the best known. A mass in ten parts by this composer has found champions among a few skilled choirs in recent times.

THE REFORMATION PERIOD. The increasing elaboration of church music, the long tradition of using Latin as the language of worship, and the resolute refusal of the papacy to make any concessions, either in terms of partial use of the vernacular or in terms of music fitted to the ability of the people to sing it, fuelled fires of discontent. The restoration of the psalter to the people in their own tongue, furnished with music within their competence, was one of the most popular and significant contributions of the Reformation* to the Church in Scotland.

The source from which the great stream of metrical psalmody* flowed was Calvin's* *Strasbourg Psalter* of 1539. Thereafter *The French Psalter*, produced in the period 1541–62, The *Book of Common Order*,* produced by John Knox* and his colleagues for use in the English-speaking congregation in Geneva, *The Anglo-Genevan Psalter* of 1561 and *The English Psalter* of 1562, led to the first *Scottish Psalter* of 1564. Acceptance of metrical psalmody in Scotland was probably facilitated to some degree by the popularity of the *Gude and Godlie Ballatis*,* of the Dundee brothers Wedderburn,* first published between 1542 and 1546. These included twenty-two psalm-versions and, while they were never used in public worship, they were sung by people in their homes and were greatly treasured.

By the end of the sixteenth century metrical psalmody was firmly established in Scottish worship and a rich heritage of tunes had been absorbed. Much of this appeared in *The Scottish Psalter* 1615. The full flowering of Scottish psalmody came in *The Scottish Psalter* of 1635. 'Proper Tunes', attached to specific psalms, including many of the fine compositions of Louis Bourgeois (c. 1510–61) are found here, as are the 'Common Tunes' of the 1615 psalter and 'Tunes in Reports'. The next psalter published, that of 1650, had no music, and when tunes were provided in 1666 it was a collection of twelve common-metre tunes (with Bon Accord in reports as an extra). Other older tunes were used as well and many new ones were added. *The Scottish Psalter 1929*, a music edition, breathed new life into the metrical psalms of the 1650 psalter, and a further enhancement of the contribution psalms can make to worship was essayed in the inclusion of fifty-seven selected portions of metrical psalmody, with appropriate tunes, sometimes the 'proper tune', in the third edition of the *Church Hymnary*,* published in 1973.

The strong emphasis in the Reformed tradition on scriptural material (psalms and New Testament canticles) as the suitable medium of praise led in time to *The Scottish Paraphrases* (1781) – Holy Scripture rendered into verse, following the model of *The Scottish Psalter* of 1650.

THE MODERN ERA. Modern hymns were introduced into Scottish worship in the middle years of the nineteenth century, but only gradually. The *Church Hymnary*,* was first published in 1898: it was revised in 1927 and again in 1973 (*CH3*). This third edition contains, besides the psalm portions mentioned above, a few prose psalms, a selection of paraphrases, liturgical material, hymns from the treasury of the Church's hymnody, some hymns and tunes written this century and a number of specially commissioned tunes. The FC, FPC and Associated Presbyterian Churches* still use psalms exclusively. Within the CofS some congregations supplement the hymnary by drawing on musical material in an idiom lighter than that favoured by *CH3*.

For the Reformers respect for the Word of God implied restraint, even gravity in the music to be wedded to it. Calvin found no place in worship for instrumental music, organ or choral singing. On the other hand it was clearly recognized that the voice of the people, silent for so long, ought to be heard in worship. Happily, within the severe limits within which they had to work, some of the composers of psalm-tunes managed to achieve considerable rhythmic variety and austere splendour: and singing in parts was permitted.

While the arrival of hymnody (*see* Hymnology) eventually brought greater musical interest to Scottish worship, the Reformation ideal of restraint in use of artistic form and regard for the nature of worship, in which the human and divine interpenetrate, has not been forgotten. The introduction to *CH3* speaks of music being 'true to' the words, and taking account of the activity of Christ in the midst of his worshipping people: it also speaks of this concern being balanced by a concern that the music be appropriate to the variety of the people's emotions as well as to their musical ability. The influence of the Church Service Society* from the middle of the nineteenth century, and more recently of church committees responsible for worship, has done much to promote the catholicity of worship in the CofS and to direct attention to the full repertoire of choral music, classical and modern.

The close association of music with the liturgy* and its ancillary function have been given clear expression in the arrangement of the contents of the *Church Hymnary* of 1973, where for the first time a hymn book is arranged on a liturgical pattern, in this case a eucharistic pattern, matching the models for worship in the CofS's *Book of Common Order* of 1979.

While, as was noted above, singing in parts was permitted in Scotland after the Reformation, this is not to be taken as implying the presence of a choir. The continuance of the Sang Schules for some time after the Reformation meant that there was, here and there at least, a fair degree of musical competence in singing psalms, and 'psalms in reports', also mentioned above, were offered as a concession, but leadership fell to the 'uptaker of the psalm' or, as he was later known (certainly by 1653), the precentor.* In a very few places he was joined by three or four 'sangsters'. The custom of 'lining', recommended by the Westminster Assembly of Divines* and reluctantly accepted by the Scots present, greatly detracted from his musical contribution: he was in fact required to read or intone each line of the psalm before it was sung. The General Assembly of 1746 recommended 'the ancient practice of singing without reading the line', but 'lining' continued well into the next century.

CHOIRS. Something which can be identified as 'the choir movement' begins around the middle of the eighteenth century. Colourful credit for its inception is given to an Englishman, Thomas Channon, a soldier in General Wolfe's army quartered in Aberdeen in 1753. He showed such expertise in teaching singing that, upon discharge from the army, he was persuaded to devote himself to choir training. His work began not, as one might expect in Aberdeen itself, but in Monymusk, almost certainly financed by Sir Archibald Grant, a singularly enlightened and progressive laird. The choir movement spread and a revival of church singing began, though not without much initial conservative opposition. Where the movement flourished choirs became so large that 'singing lofts' had to be built for them. In 1754 such a loft provided for Kintore (Aberdeenshire) contained seating for 120 persons. When John Wesley* paid the first of two visits to Sir Archibald Grant in 1761 he made this entry in his diary: 'About six we went to church. It was pretty well filled with such persons as we did not look for so near the Highlands. But if we were surprised at their appearance, we were more so at their singing. Thirty or forty sang an anthem after sermon, with such voice as well as judgment, that I doubt whether they could have been excelled at any cathedral in England.'

The renewed interest in choral singing brought with it a demand for new tunes, few of which, sadly, matched the older Reformation tunes in quality; it may also be said to have given impetus to the production of the paraphrases* and in due course hymnody (*see* Hymnology).

It is not clear how typical Wesley's experience of an anthem in the service would have been. Certainly throughout the eighteenth and nineteenth centuries choirs had access to anthems and to Handel choruses, but the use of these as part of a service of worship was not widespread until the latter part of the nineteenth century.

The contribution of choirs to worship in Scotland in the latter part of the twentieth century is very slender, though in the cathedrals, abbeys and parish churches where there are choirs the standard is often very high. The reason for the decline may be the church's equivocation about what it really wants from the arts; it may be also that so many non-church choirs, choral and operatic societies offer seasonal opportunities for singing which are more acceptable than the weekly commitment upon which church worship depends.

While a great deal of the music offered to choirs in the early stages of the choir movement consisted of tune-books for psalmody, collections of anthems begin to appear by the beginning of the nineteenth century. A few were included in a publication called *Sacred Harmony* which appeared in E, 1820. The CofS issued a collection in 1875 and *The Scottish Anthem Book* in L, 1891. The UPC issued in E, 1886 *Scripture Sentences and Chants*, which contained 107 anthems. The UFC published an authorized collection of 166 in 1905. Few of these collections proved to be of lasting value. With the appearance of *The Church Anthem Book* in L, 1934, however, the prospects for choir music in Scottish worship improved considerably. This collection of 100 anthems, edited by Sir Walford Davies and Henry G. Ley and authorized by the CofS General Assembly for use in public worship, brought to the attention of choirs anthems from the classical repertoire as well as from contemporary composers. Many of these, being of proved workmanship as well as of initial inspiration, have stood the test of time, and the book is still used by competent choirs. Undoubtedly some choirs found *The Church Anthem Book* beyond their powers, and with this in mind Oxford University Press in conjunction with the Church of Scotland's Committee on Public Worship and Aids to Devotion* published *The Oxford Easy Anthem Book* (L, 1964).

In many congregations, within and beyond the CofS, informal music groups, comprising vocalists and instrumentalists and singing a variety of compositions (*see* next article), have become common, often in place of more traditional choirs. In others, the deliberate demise of choir and anthem has facilitated the recovery of truly congregational praise. Unaccompanied psalmody thrives in Highland areas (*see* Precentor).

MUSICAL COMPOSITIONS. Until recent times the record of musical compositions in Scotland for use in the church was rather inglorious. The large output in the late nineteenth and early twentieth centuries is best forgotten. The small but significant contribution of Cedric Thorpe Davie (1913–83) deserves honourable mention, however – especially three popular anthems and many acceptable carols – as does that of Martin Dalby (1942–). Magisterial modern compositions of considerable complexity and demanding a high standard of choral competence have come from the hand of Kenneth Leighton (1929–88). These include many settings of canticles, numerous anthems and a major work entitled *Crucifixus Pro Nobis*. The fact that these works are sung and appreciated is evidence that in the last decade of the twentieth century the verdict on church music of musical and theological integrity must be that 'the maid is not dead but sleepeth'.

J. Bulloch, *The Life of the Celtic Church* (E, 1963); A. Robertson, *Music of the Catholic Church* (L, 1961); M. Patrick, *Four Centuries of Scottish Psalmody* (L, 1949); J. M. Barkley (ed.), *Handbook to the Church Hymnary* (O, 1979); Church of Scotland Committee on Publication, *Manual of Church Praise* (E, 1932); D. Fraser, *The Passing of the Precentor* (E, 1916); H. G. Farmer, *Music Making in the Olden Days* (L, 1950); articles in publications of the Church Service Society, called first *The Annual*, subsequently *Liturgical Studies* and presently *The Church Service Society Record*; J. Stein, *Singing a New Song* (E, 1988).

A. S. Todd

Music, Church, Recent Developments in. In the late sixties, Britain experienced a 'hymn explosion', a profusion of new writing which broke some of the standard moulds of hymnody. What is not well known is that this movement found its cradle in Dunblane, Scotland, where at the Scottish Churches House (*see* Ecumenical Movement) in 1961 a group of ministers and musicians met to discuss the state of church music in Scotland and to write and commission new songs for worship. Reginald Barrett Ayres and Erik Routley were two of the prime movers, and the group they headed produced numerous publications, the first of which, *Dunblane Praises* No 1, appeared in 1965. It was produced at a time when Scotland was undergoing something of a renaissance in the folk arts, and that is reflected both in the idiomatic language of some of the songs and the evident folk antecedents in the style and music of others.

The Dunblane enterprise, though not a long-lasting project, inspired new writing throughout Britain and, in Scotland, was crucial to the production of *Songs of the Seventies*, a St Andrew Press (E, 1972) publication which almost became the supplement to *CH3* but for being slated in the General Assembly for including a song of Sydney Carter's which some commissioners dubbed blasphemous.

It was not until 1988 that the CofS Panel on Worship* produced a supplement to the 1973 Hymnary (*CH3*). *Songs of God's People* was maligned in the press by irate organists who feared it would spread banality throughout the Church. Yet within two years it had sold over 160,000 copies and was being used extensively. It was an eclectic assortment of material from evangelical, charismatic, radical and new liturgical sources. Its 120 songs originate in a wide spectrum of denominations and encompass Taizé chants, songs from the world church and a number of items written in Scotland.

Shortly before its publication, the Iona Community* began to produce a series of collections of songs written in Scotland, reflecting both biblical faith and contemporary social concerns. These home productions have been supplemented by a second series of books using material from across the globe.

At the same time as Dunblane was spawning new materials and writers, and Iona was promulgating songs from abroad, an Edinburgh Jesuit, James Quinn, encouraged by the liturgical reforms of Vatican II, emerged as the foremost RC hymnwriter in Scotland, producing scriptural and liturgical songs which draw on ancient Scots and Irish Celtic traditions.

The Christian rock music scene, while not perhaps as lively as in England, has nevertheless enjoyed a profile in Scottish churches, much aided by the Street Level festivals begun in Dundee in 1979. Jock Stein, sometime minister of the Steeple Church there, and a Brethren musician, Ricky Ross (later to become lead singer with the prestigious rock group Deacon Blue), inspired these annual festivals, where young people from different backgrounds and denominations were made aware of how the Lord's song could be sung with guitars, synthesizers and backing vocals. While inevitably drawing on the experience of similar English and American musicians, many of the Scottish writers and performers have evolved distinctive styles, as is the case with Ian White, whose new settings of the Psalms have gained recognition throughout Britain.

The combined effect of these several developments in church music has been that in Sunday worship, as in conference worship, reliance on the organ and choir has been broken. Instrumental groups and *a capella* singers have opened up new possibilities in the leadership of the church's music, at the same time as chants from the Taizé and Iona communities and the world Church, and the Celtic or folk-based contemporary hymns have become tools for contemporary liturgical innovation. This does not so much mark the demise of traditional hymnody and worship leadership, as offer alternative materials and models which may be more pertinent to the Church's mission in the third millennium.

J. Stein, *Singing a New Song: Fresh Resources for Christian Praise* (E, 1988).

J. L. Bell

Musical Instruments in Worship. The Scottish Reformation* saw the discontinuance of the later medieval practice of instrumental music in church worship. In line with Reformed teaching, this practice was seen as a breach of the 'regulative principle' that the constituent parts of Christian worship must be authorized by New Testament precept or

MUSICAL INSTRUMENTS IN WORSHIP

example. Consequently instrumental music in worship was 'unknown in the [Scottish] Church since the Reformation' (T. Leishman, 'The Ritual of the Church of Scotland', in *The Church of Scotland Past and Present*, ed. R. H. Story, V, 423). Unaccompanied singing led by a precentor* became the norm in Presbyterian Scotland.

The first recorded incident of a musical instrument being used in Presbyterian worship was in 1807, when William Ritchie, minister of St Andrew's Church, Glasgow, introduced a chamber organ. The Lord Provost of the city reported the matter to the presbytery, which declared organ music in worship to be 'contrary to the law of the land, and to the law and constitution of our Established Church' (quoted R. S. Candlish, *The Organ Question*, E, 1856, 26). A similar incident took place in the Relief Church* in 1829, with similar results (see G. Struthers, *The History of the Rise, Progress and Principles of the Relief Church*, G, 1843, 442–3).

The first organ ever authorized in the worship of a Scottish Presbyterian or Congregational church seems to have been in the North Dundas Street Evangelical Union* Church, Glasgow, in 1851. Organs also began to make their appearance in Congregational Union* churches around this period, championed by W. Lindsay Alexander.*

In the CofS the question was reopened in 1863, when Robert Lee* introduced a harmonium into Old Greyfriars, Edinburgh, and then in 1865 an organ, as part of his liturgical reform programme. Much opposition was aroused, but the General Assembly effectively authorized the practice in 1866 by remitting such matters to the discretion of Presbyteries. The 'organ movement' gathered momentum, and by the 1870s the use of an organ in worship had ceased to be an innovation* as far as the CofS was concerned.

The most vigorous debate on the subject took place in the FCS. When two Glasgow congregations petitioned the Assembly of 1882 for the liberty to use organs, James Begg* submitted a formal protest, indicative of his view that such a step would be unconstitutional. Begg and the Constitutionalists* held to the old Reformed position that instrumental music in worship was precluded by the regulative principle. To the majority who voted in the 1883 Assembly to permit instrumental music, however, no substantial innovation was being made. They argued that an organ was merely a means of sustaining and regulating congregational singing, comparable to the role of a precentor, a tuning-pipe and music books.

Apart from uncompromising conservatives, Lowland Scots proved ready for instrumental music in worship, and by 1900 there were few congregations without an organ of some sort. It was different in the Highlands, where FC Constitutionalist strength ensured that organs continued to be regarded with antipathy. This made Highland worship distinctive in its adherence to the original Scottish Reformed pattern of unaccompanied singing, which remains the practice of the FC, FPC, RPC and the Associated Presbyterian Churches (*see* Precentor).

Organs have remained the standard accompaniment of congregational praise in Scottish churches throughout the twentieth century. However, since the 1960s, increasing use has been made of other instruments, such as pianos, guitars and synthesizers, and sometimes in a way which oversteps the description 'accompaniment'.

D. B. Forrester and D. M. Murray (eds), *Studies in the History of Worship in Scotland* (E, 1984); J. Inglis, 'The Scottish Churches and the Organ', (PhD, University of Glasgow, 1987).

K. R. Ross

Mylne, Alexander (1474–1548), abbot of Cambuskenneth* (Stirlingshire) from 1517. The son of an Angus mason, he studied arts and perhaps law at St Andrews, and held various benefices and offices in the diocese of Dunkeld. While canon of Dunkeld (1505–14) he also had charge of the monks building Dunkeld bridge, and while abbot of the wealthy Augustinian* abbey of Cambuskenneth served also as master mason to James V (*c.*1517–*c.*1529). He was an outstanding abbot, extending the buildings, educating the novices (sending some for training to the abbey of St Victor in Paris (where in 1530 Robert Richardson* dedicated his commentary on the Rule of St Augustine to Mylne), preaching frequently and having Scripture read during meals. He compiled an account of the lives of the bishops of Dunkeld (*Vitae...*; Bannatyne Club, E, 1831; transl. by R. K. Hannay in *Rentale Dunkeldense...*, SHS, E, 1915), giving a far from bleak picture of Dunkeld's secular clergy. Active also in the service of court, from 1532 he was the first Lord President of the College of Justice (later Court of Session), in which capacity he excelled as a draughtsman of rules and procedure. He was a notable exemplar of the learned and pious churchman-administrator.

DNB XL, 2–3; W. Fraser (ed.), *Registrum Monasterii S. Mariae de Cambuskenneth A.D. 1147–1535* (Grampian Club, E, 1872), lxxxviii–xcvi; R. S. Mylne, *The Master Masons to the Crown of Scotland and Their Works* (E, 1893), 17–35; G. Brunton and D. Haig, *An Historical Account of the Senators of the College of Justice* (E, L, 1832), 5–10.

D. F. Wright

Mylne, Andrew (1776–1856), minister of Dollar (1816–56) and first rector of Dollar Academy (1818–50), DD (Glasgow, 1821), Member of the Royal Physical Society and Fellow of the Society of Scottish Antiquaries, the author of several highly regarded school textbooks. Before he entered Edinburgh University in 1807 at the age of thirty-one, he ran a school in his native Haddington, E. Lothian. Around 1803 he was engaged as an occasional tutor by Craufard Tait of Harvieston. One of Tait's sons, Archibald,* was to become Archbishop of Canterbury. In 1812 he was licensed by the Presbytery of Edinburgh but continued to run a school in the city until 1816, when Tait presented him to the charge of Dollar. He thereby became chief trustee of the fortune left by John McNabb (1732–1802), in connection with which he was instrumental in introducing a plan to establish a 'great Academy or Seminary of Education', in which the poor of the village were to be educated free and the rich 'privileged' to share in their education by payment of a sliding scale of fees. Although it was successfully implemented, the scheme met local opposition, and Mylne's unpopularity led to significant numbers in the parish joining the FC in 1843.

FES IV, 307.

J. R. McIntosh

Mylne, Walter, *see* Milne, Walter.

N

Nairn(e), James (1629–78), cleric and book collector. A graduate of Edinburgh (1650) and University Librarian (1652–3), he became minister of Canongate/Holyroodhouse (1656–62), Bolton, E. Lothian (1662–5), Wemyss, in Fife (1665–78), and royal chaplain-in-ordinary (1675–8).

Although conforming to episcopacy* in 1662, Nairn was essentially a moderate. In 1670 he was one of six clergymen appointed by Robert Leighton* to preach in the south-west; in 1672 he refused the bishopric of Dunblane after election proceedings had begun.

Nairn's preoccupations were pastoral duties, study and private spirituality. Robert Wodrow* described him as having 'very considerable learning and gifts, but inclinable to the Pelagian tenets'. Gilbert Burnet,* whom Nairn influenced in the early 1660s, admired his preaching.

Nairn bequeathed to Edinburgh University 4,000 Scots for divinity bursaries and his wide-ranging library numbering over 1,900 items, which, apart from particular strengths in devotional literature, patristics, Latin classics and history, also contains important contemporary philosophical and scientific works, for example by Spinoza, Boyle, Hobbes and Pufendorf.

M. C. T. Simpson, *A Catalogue of the Library of the Revd. James Nairn* . . . (E, 1990).

M. C. T. Simpson

Nairn, Thomas (1680–1764), Presbyterian minister whose career was peppered with controversy. Born in Errol, Perthshire, he graduated MA from St Andrews in 1702, was licensed by Cupar Presbytery in 1708, and was ordained to Abbotshall, Kirkcaldy, in 1710. In 1737 Nairn seceded from the CofS and joined the Associate Presbytery;* the CofS General Assembly deposed him in 1740, upon which a new church was built for him.

In 1743 Nairn became involved in controversy with his fellow seceders over the National Covenant* and Solemn League and Covenant.* The Presbytery drafted an act for renewing the Covenants in which it condemned those who wished to employ force of arms to overturn Britain's uncovenanted government. Nairn objected to this clause, having embraced the views of the 'old dissenters' or Cameronians (*see* Societies, United) on this point. Finding himself isolated, he seceded from the Associate Presbytery at the end of the year and joined the Cameronians. Together with their other minister John Macmillan* he established the Reformed Presbytery (*see* Reformed Presbyterian Church). In 1745, however, he seceded from this body, and in 1751 re-entered the CofS, confessing his sin in having left her communion in the first place.

A Short Account of Mr. T. Nairn . . . his secession from the Associate Presbytery (n.p., 1743); *A sermon preached at Braehead . . . together with a short account of the constitution, and some of the proceedings of the Reformed Presbytery* (G, 1745).

Small I, 352–3; J. M'Kerrow, *History of the Secession Church* (G, 1841), 174ff.; FES V, 99.

N. R. Needham

Naphtali, *see* Stewart, Sir James.

Napier (or Neper), John (1550–1617), mathematician and inventor of logarithms. Born at Merchiston Castle, near Edinburgh, he studied for a time in St Andrews University, but completed his education on the continent. During 1573–1608 he lived at Gartnes, in Stirlingshire, moving into Merchiston Castle on his father's death. He was a zealous Protestant; his *Plaine Discoverie of the Whole Revelation of St John* (E, 1593, ²L, 1611) was substantially an anti-RC polemic, aimed at proving that the great whore of Babylon was the RCC.

Napier's epoch-making book on logarithms, *Mirifici Logarithmorum Canonis Descriptio* (E, 1614), made him famous throughout the European academic world. It was translated into English in 1616 as *A Description of the Admirable Table of Logarithms* (L), and elaborated in his *Mirifici Logarithmorum Canonis Constructio*, published posthumously (E, 1619). Napier was also interested in many other branches of science, such as astronomy. He invented a hydraulic screw for pumping water out of mines and a burning mirror for destroying ships, and introduced the use of salt as a fertilizer. 'Napier's bones', a device he invented to simplify multiplication and division, were in use for about a century.

De Arte Logistica (E, 1839).

C. G. Knott (ed.), *Napier Tercentenary Volume* (L, 1915); W. R. Thomas, *John Napier* (L, 1935); D. S. Erskine, *An Account of the Life, Writings and Inventions of John Napier of Merchiston* (1787); M. Napier, *Memoirs of John Napier of Merchiston* (E, 1834); *DNB* XLI, 59-65.

N. R. Needham

Nathalan, *see* Celtic Saints.

National Bible Society of Scotland, *see* Bible Societies.

National Church Association, an organization formed in 1932 'for the safeguarding of the Protestant and Presbyterian witness of the Church of Scotland'. The Association was a reaction against the decision of the 1932 General Assembly to engage in conversations with the CofE. It criticized the subsequent Statement of Agreements approved by the General Assembly in 1934.

The NCA's concern for the purity of Presbyterianism* led it to oppose the Scoto-Catholics* and associated architectural trends. The *Book of Common Order* (1940)* was thought to be too liturgical and to contain doctrinal errors. The NCA later itself published a *Reformed Book of Common Order** (E, 1977), based primarily on Knox's* original work of 1562 (*see Book of Common Order*, 1564), with a view to pre-empting the further official version to be published in 1979. It also played a prominent part in the controversy stirred by renewed contacts between Anglicans and the CofS in the 1950s (*see* Anglican-Presbyterian Relations). Proposals for the introduction of a form of episcopacy* into the Kirk were criticized as inconsistent with the New Testament and the traditions of the Scottish Church.

The NCA was led in the 1940s and 1950s by Thomas M. Donn (*FES* IX, 634), and a revival in the 1960s was headed by George M. Dale (*FES* IX, 449). Membership has always been small, ranging from forty in the 1930s to two hundred in the 1980s, but the Association has served as a focus for a more widespread body of opinion in the Kirk.

'The National Church Association' [An account of the circumstances which led to its formation], typescript in the National Library, 1933; *The National Church Association*, a statement of its aims and policy (n.p., 1953); 'The National Church Association: Origin and History 1932-1984' (NCA, typescript); T. M. Donn, *The Unity of the Church* (Inverness, 1957?); Burleigh.

J. R. Wolffe

National Church Defence Association, a pressure group in the CofS formed after the General Assembly of 1919 to oppose the looming Union* with the UFC. Among its leaders were A. G. Mitchell of Killearn, Stirlingshire, its secretary (1864-1943; *FES* III, 350, VIII, 279), R. S. Kirkpatrick,* Donald MacMillan of Prestonfield, Edinburgh (1866-1944; *FES* I, 87, VIII, 14) and John MacGilchrist of Govan and Old Machar, Aberdeenshire (1866-1928; *FES* III, 414, VIII, 530). In 1920 MacMillan, Kirkpatrick and others (including A. W. Wotherspoon* and H. M. B. Reid*) left the CofS Union Committee because they found the Declaratory Articles* unsatisfactory. The Association lobbied the government and secured publicity through various outlets – Mitchell in the *Spectator*, MacMillan in the *Hibbert Journal* ('Presbyterian Reunion in Scotland: the Draft Articles', 17, 1918-19, 309-18), and pamphlets (*e.g. The Church of Scotland in Danger...*, Peterhead, 1919, by J. M. Finlayson of Lonmay, near Fraserburgh; 1883-1945, *FES* VI, 230, VIII, 583).

Its counterpart in the UFC was the United Free Church Association, set up at the same time to resist any scheme based on a continued establishment of religion. The two Associations reflected divergent interpretations of the Declaratory Articles. Leaders in the UFC body included James Barr* and W. D. Miller of Ruchill, Glasgow (1868-1924; *FUFCS* 245). In their lobbying of government they made common cause with proponents of disestablishment* among leading Scottish Congregationalists* and Baptists.*

R. Sjölinder, *Presbyterian Reunion in Scotland 1907-1921* (E, 1962); J. Barr, *The United Free Church of Scotland* (L, 1934).

D. F. Wright

National Church Union, a society for upholding the right and duty of free theological enquiry. It originated from a meeting in Glasgow on 19 October 1896, called by a circular from James Murray of Kilmacolm, who became its secretary (*FES* III, 213, VIII, 249). Its object was to resist attempts to limit liberty of teaching in the CofS and to uphold the right to continue to study and propagate biblical criticism. It also sought to apply Christian teaching to modern life and to engage in discussion of social questions. Prominent among the membership were liberal Evangelicals who felt that the Westminster Confession (*see* Westminster Assembly) no longer served as an adequate doctrinal basis for the modern church. The president was Allan Menzies (1845-1916), Professor of Divinity and Biblical Criticism at St Andrews (*FES* VII, 430-1), and the vice-presidents Alexander Mcquisten of Inverkip (*FES* III, 210) and John Herkless,* later Principal of St Andrews University. The first conference was held in Glasgow in 1897 and heard papers on the substance of the Christian faith, the modern attitude towards Scripture, the creeds, and the social office of religion.

National Church Union, Record of Proceedings (E,

National Covenant (1638), a document prepared by Scottish Presbyterians, primarily Alexander Henderson* and Archibald Johnston of Wariston,* against the policies of Charles I.* Written in the context of the riots resulting from the imposition of 'Laud's Liturgy' (*see* Laud, William) in 1637 and the King's refusal to receive the petitions of supplicants for redress, the National Covenant was an appeal to the people for support. It began by repeating the King's Confession* of 1581, otherwise known as the Negative Confession (to avoid confusion with Knox's Affirmative Scots Confession* of 1560). This had condemned RC errors and 'the usurped authority of that Roman antichrist upon the Scriptures of God, upon the Kirk, the civil magistrate, and consciences of men; all his tyrannous laws made upon indifferent things against our Christian liberty'.

The Covenant then went on to detail numerous Acts of Parliament which had established the Reformed faith and Church government. Thereafter, more specifically, the subscribers bound themselves to maintain the freedom of the Church from civil control, to defend the true Reformed religion, and to decline the recent innovations* in worship decreed by the King until the General Assembly had ruled on them. There was no attempt to denigrate the King's position; indeed, the signatories swore to defend him 'in the preservation of the foresaid true religion, liberties, and laws of the kingdom'.

Although it had omitted any explicit condemnation of Episcopacy, Charles was alarmed and resentful. But the Scots were not to be moved. This was for them an assertion by the Kirk of freedom from royal or state control, a personal oath of allegiance to Jesus Christ, the only Head of the Church, King of kings, and a dedication of life to him.

It stemmed directly from God's covenant of grace, was in the succession of those earlier bonds the Scots had made with God for his people's defence and deliverance, and represented a call in the Pauline sense to 'conduct themselves as citizens'. What Andrew Melville* had told James VI about Scotland's two kings and two kingdoms (and which took priority) found an echo in the Covenant provoked by James's son.

What Charles I called 'those impertinent and damnable demands' constituted no violation of statue law, and the King's legal experts told him so. Archibald Johnston* of Wariston cited more than sixty Acts of Parliament in defence of the Covenanters' action. Signed initially in Greyfriars church, the National Covenant found supporters all over the land. It won a temporary victory for its supporters, but half a century was to pass before its essential position was finally vindicated and the war against royal tyranny won.

A. Peterkin, *Records of the Kirk of Scotland* (E, 1838); J. Gordon, *History of Scots Affairs (1637–41)* (A, 1841); J. K. Hewison, *The Covenanters*, 2 vols (G, ²1913); R. L. Orr, *Alexander Henderson* (L, 1919); *Tercentenary of the National Covenant* (L, 1939); H. Watt, *Recalling the Scottish Covenants* (L, 1946); D. Stevenson, 'The National Covenant: A List of Known Copies', *RSCHS* 23 (1988), 255–99; D. H. Fleming, *The Subscribing of the National Covenant in 1638* (E, 1912); E. Whitley, *The Two Kingdoms* (E, 1977); J. Morill (ed.), *The Scottish National Covenant in its British Context 1638–51* (E, 1990).

J. D. Douglas

Natural Theology, the derivation of theological conclusions from premises accepted by all rational men. The phrases 'natural theology', 'philosophy of religion', 'philosophical theology' and even 'apologetics' are often used interchangeably. But it is more accurate to reserve 'natural theology' (sometimes also referred to as 'rational theology') for the programme of establishing theological conclusions – usually the claim that God exists – from premises which any rational person would accept. By contrast the philosophy of religion is the philosophical treatment of certain human states, those produced by belief in God, but including the study of that belief itself; philosophical theology is the study of metaphysical, moral and epistemological claims about God himself; while Christian apologetics is the rational defence of Christianity against its intellectual opponents and detractors.

So understood, 'natural theology' in Scotland is characterized less by its distinctive ideas – unless one makes an exception of the theological voluntarism of Duns Scotus* (*c*.1264–1308), whose influence was felt chiefly outside his native Scotland – than by its relative lack of prominence. A sustained treatment of any theme of natural theology is hard to find before the end of the seventeenth century. The reason for this is twofold. There was until this period an intense preoccupation with the fight for survival by the Reformed Church in Scotland. Not only was there no time for natural theology, there was no need, since all participants in the theological controversies of the period were united in their belief in the God whose existence natural theology attempts to establish. To engage in natural theology would have been a wasteful extravagance, like fiddling while Rome burned.

THE INFLUENCE OF DEISM AND SCEPTICISM. It was not until the influence of religious minimalism and scepticism was felt that thinkers had need to confront the question of how natural theology is to be valued and used. Two waves of such influence can be identified. The first is the rise of deism,* the chief effect of which was felt in England, but which washed on Scottish shores as well. Thus a writer such as Thomas Halyburton* (1674–1712) wrote against the deism of Lord Herbert of Cherbury more to keep the influence of the later deism at bay in Scotland than because it was present as an active religious force. In his *Natural Religion Insufficient and Revealed Necessary to Man's Happiness in his Present State* (E, 1714), Halyburton argues that natural religion is insufficient, but he does not question either the necessity of natural theology or of natural religion. Yet it is fair to say that the amount and quality of natural theology called forth in Scotland by the deistic movement was small and confined to a very few thinkers.

Of considerably more importance was the scepticism of David Hume,* the theological challenge of which was answered by the Realism of Thomas Reid and his followers (see Scottish Realism). Reid's influence went in two directions. On the one hand the stock of common-sense ideas to which he appealed against Hume's scepticism included belief in the existence of a Supreme Being. This is a species of theological innatism, though rather different in character from the *sensus divinitatis* of John Calvin. But more importantly Reid's Realism supported the development of varieties of *a posteriori* arguments for God's existence, variants of the cosmological arguments of Thomas Aquinas and the argument from design of William Paley (1743–1805) and others. Through the influence of Reid upon the theological world, not only the Moderate* party of which he was a member, but also upon the Evangelicals,* a firm but rather muted commitment to *a posteriori* natural theology became standard fare.

Alongside this positive view of natural theology one finds theologians with a less sanguine approach. Robert Riccaltoun's* *Inquiry* (L, G, E, 1762) is largely dismissive of natural theology. John Dick's* *Lectures on Theology* 4 vols (²E, 1838) is also restrained, though this aspect of his work cannot be said to be of a very high order.

Under the influence of Reid, and collateral influence of English theologians such as Butler and Paley, a host of nineteenth-century Scottish theologians, *e.g.* William Cunningham* and James Buchanan,* lectured and published on natural theology. The positions that they defended became the orthodoxy of much of the nineteenth century, and found their way into the prolegomena of many treatises on systematic theology. This prevailing orthodoxy was reinforced by other factors, for example the publication of the *Bridgewater Treatises* (1833–40) on various aspects of 'the power, wisdom and goodness of God as manifested in the creation'. Thomas Chalmers* was perhaps the best-known of the Bridgewater authors.

THE ONSET OF IDEALISM. This position changed markedly to the extent that Kantian and post-Kantian modes of thought became influential in Scotland. This development occurred from the middle years of the nineteenth century and onwards until the outbreak of the First World War. Natural theology, which derived sustenance from Scottish Realism, came to be regarded by many as parochial, and as psychological rather than truly philosophical in character. The emphasis of the natural theologian upon *reason* gave way to a stress upon *understanding*. Kant's rejection of natural theology in all its forms except the moral argument for God's existence, was reflected in a shift in Scottish theological thought away from rigorous argument to theological conclusions, to an emphasis upon *re-ligion* as an organic whole, a higher unity which both embraced and overcame scepticism and materialism. A chief influence here was James Ferrier (1808–64), who after a period of study in Germany became Professor of Moral Philosophy and Political Economy at the University of St Andrews. His influence was reinforced by the better known John and Edward Caird,* and the importance of the influence of a Church-statesman such as Robert Rainy* ought not to be underestimated.

Occasional individuals stood apart from both the common-sense and the idealistic streams of influence. A notable figure in this respect is W. H. Gillespie* who in *The Argument a priori for the Being and Attributes of God* (E, 1833; ⁶1872) provided an elaborate version of the ontological argument. It is doubtful whether the influence of Gillespie extended very far. The agnosticism about God which was embedded in the post-Kantianism of Sir William Hamilton* and (in England) H. L. Mansel (1820–71) was challenged by Henry Calderwood* in *The Philosophy of the Infinite* (L, 1854).

BARTHIANISM. While after the First World War the theological temper changed markedly, the validity of the Kantian and post-Kantian arguments against natural theology were taken for granted. Instead of the emphasis being upon the human conscience and religious consciousness, however, the stress fell upon the word of God. Under the influence of Barth and others the 'vertical' dimension of the Word of God, its power to break in upon and to break up human complacencies, was stressed. In this 'positivism of revelation' there was no place for natural theology, as Barth's controversy with Brunner over the status of natural theology, published in England in 1954, made clear (*see* Neo-Orthodoxy). This Barthian emphasis has been continued in the writing of a number of Scottish theologians for example, H. R. Mackintosh,* but more notably in the work of T. F. Torrance* and J. K. S. Reid (1910–; *FES* IX, 11–12, X, 431). Insofar as Torrance stresses the *sui generis* character of Christian theology, and is distrustful of human rationality, he likewise can allow no place for natural theology in a developed Christian theology.

See also Apologetics; Philosophy of Religion.

R. Wollheim (ed.), *Hume on Religion* (L, 1963); W. Cunningham, *Theological Lectures* (L, 1878); J. Buchanan, *Analogy* (E, 1864); J. F. Ferrier, *Institute of Metaphysics* (E, L, 1854); J. Caird, *Introduction to the Philosophy of Religion* (G, 1880); T. F. Torrance, *Theological Science* (L, 1969); *id.*, *God and Rationality* (L, 1971).

P. Helm

Nazarene, see Church of Nazarene.

Neale, John Mason (1818–66), Anglican priest, church historian, ecumenist, hymnologist. He was raised as an Evangelical, but while at Trinity College, Cambridge (1836–40), was influenced by Tractarianism* and became an Anglo-Catholic, founding in the process the Cambridge Camden

NEGATIVE CONFESSION

Society (1839). Subsequent illness precluded parish work; instead he became warden of Sackville College, East Grinstead (1846), where he spent the rest of his life, writing and tending to the Sisterhood of St Margaret, of which he was founder (1854).

Neale had great energy. His publications include the carefully researched *History of the Holy Eastern Church* (L, 1847–73), *A Commentary on the Psalms*, 4 vols (L, 1860–74), and over 400 hymns, mostly translations from Latin and Greek including 'Christ is made the sure Foundation' and 'Jerusalem the golden'. He is also noted for promoting ecumenical dialogue between Anglicans and Orthodox through the Eastern Church Association (1863).

Neale's interest in the EpCS led to his defending her liturgy from alteration through CofE pressure. As a reward Bishop Patrick Torry* offered him the Perth Cathedral deanery, which he turned down (1850). Neale's other Scottish endeavours include planning, with Bishop Alexander Forbes,* an Episcopalian mission to Orkney* (1849), and establishing St Margaret's Convent, Aberdeen (1863).

An Earnest Plea for the Retention of the Scotch Liturgy (L, 1862); *The Life and Times of Patrick Torry* (L, 1856); *Ecclesiological Notes on the Isle of Man, Ross, Sutherland, and the Orkneys* (L, 1848).

M. S. Lawson (ed.), *Letters of J. M. Neale, DD* (L, 1910); A. G. Lough, *The Influence of J. M. Neale* (L, 1962); L. B. Litvack, 'All for Love: J. M. Neale and the Perth Deanery Refusal', *Churchman* 101 (1987), 36–48; Sister Miriam, *J. M. Neale: A Memoir* (East Grinstead, 1887–95).

L. B. Litvack

Negative Confession (1581), *see* King's Confession.

Neo-Orthodoxy, a term originally coined to label the new movement in continental Protestant theology in the late 1920s represented by Karl Barth and Emil Brunner on the Reformed side and by Friedrich Gogarten and Georg Merz on the Lutheran. After an earlier 'dialectical' phase ushered in by Barth's *The Epistle to the Romans* (^{2}1922; ET, O, 1935), with its rejection of liberal theology, the movement turned increasingly towards a critical reappropriation of the theology of the Reformation and of subsequent Protestant orthodoxy: hence 'Neo-Orthodoxy'.

The movement was a turbulent one and by no means unified; in the early 1930s its representatives came to follow very different paths, not least in their different reactions to German National Socialism (which Gogarten supported) and to the question of natural theology (on which from 1934 onwards Barth and Brunner found themselves on opposite sides). Barth's conviction was expressed in the Theological Declaration of Barmen (1934) which affirmed in its first thesis: 'Jesus Christ, as he is attested for us in Holy Scripture, is the one Word of God which we have to hear and which we have to trust and obey in life and in death.' This Declaration was of major significance in stating and stiffening the resistance of the German Confessing Church to the ideology

NEO-ORTHODOXY

of the 'German Christians', whose aim it was to make the German Protestant Church subservient to the National Socialist programme.

In Scotland, as in England, the challenge to radical theological reorientation around God's self-revelation in Jesus Christ had been anticipated in some measure by P. T. Forsyth.* By the 1930s, Barth had found ready hearers and advocates, e.g. in G. S. Hendry, *God the Creator* (L, 1937), and H. R. Mackintosh,* *Types of Modern Theology* (L, 1937). Among the very earliest to appreciate *The Significance of Karl Barth* (L, 1931) was John McConnachie, minister of St Johns CofS, Dundee, author also of *The Barthian Theology* (L, 1933).

The situation in Scotland was not, however, the same as in Germany. Liberal theology (*see* Liberalism) had not made such deep inroads at the turn of the century, nor had British churchmanship and theology been so drastically shaken by the events of the First World War* and its consequences. Scottish theological thinking was still in many respects more conservative than in Europe (or in England) and marked by its own nineteenth-century history, which was characterized by the struggle with the internal difficulties of classical Calvinism* as expressed in the Decrees of Dort (1619) (*see* Synod of Dort) and the Westminster Confession (1646) (*see* Westminster Assembly), as also by the recovery of a 'high' doctrine of the Church and of the value of dignified liturgical order (*see* Church Service Society). Scottish Barthianism tended as a result to be more theologically and politically conservative than Barth himself, though appreciative of Barth's contribution and stimulus. Both Barth, at Aberdeen in 1937–8 (*The Knowledge of God and the Service of God*, L, 1938) and Brunner, at St Andrews in 1947–8 (*Christianity and Civilization*, 2 vols, L, 1948–9), gave series of Gifford lectures.*

In the decades following the Second World War 'Post-Liberal' Scottish theology (to use the term employed by J. Macquarrie) reacted in a variety of ways to Barth. Some of its leading representatives – the brothers John and Donald Baillie* and Macquarrie himself – sought to achieve a balance between Neo-Orthodox and liberal concerns. Others inclined more to Brunner than to Barth, as also did the American Reinhold Niebuhr. Yet others stood avowedly closer to Barth, but developed the impulses given by him in diverse ways, as three examples illustrate. In Trinity College, Glasgow,* Ian Henderson* followed Barth in insisting upon the importance of the gathered congregation, the local and the national Church. This led him in his later years to a negative, polemical stance over against the whole ecumenical movement,* articulated in his *Power without Glory*. His Glasgow colleague Ronald G. Smith* combined influences from Barth, Martin Buber and Gogarten to develop a poetical 'secular theology'. By contrast, John K. S. Reid in King's College, Aberdeen was both strongly Barthian in his thought and deeply committed to ecumenism.

The outstanding Barthian, 'Post-Liberal' or Neo-Orthodox theologian in the last decades has been Thomas F. Torrance,* for nearly thirty years Professor of Christian Dogmatics in New College,*

Edinburgh. His voluminous writings deal with many aspects of historical, dogmatic and ecumenical theology (see Systematic Theology) and reflect an industry unparalleled by any other Scottish theologian of the last two or three generations. Torrance shares with Barth the conviction that theological thinking, teaching and writing matters deeply, and he has exerted a corresponding influence on many generations of students. Since the late 1960s he has given particular attention to the connection and interaction between theological thinking and the new thought imposed upon us by the advances of natural science, especially in physics (see Science and Religion). In doing so, he has driven the frontiers of theology forward beyond what Barth could envisage. This too, however, can be seen as the consistent development of an earlier Scottish theological tradition represented by Henry Drummond* and James Y. Simpson.* Whether this can properly be called 'Neo-Orthodoxy' depends on how the term itself – never a very fortunate one – is understood. What Torrance's work makes clear is that 'Orthodoxy' in the proper sense is not merely a matter of traditionalist reassertion of past theological formulations, but rather their fresh re-appropriation and re-appreciation in their bearing on our understanding of the reality of the creation to which we belong – and therefore always 'new'. In that sense, to be 'Neo-Orthodox' is to be a member of what Calvin called 'the company of the faithful' and the Second Vatican Council 'the pilgrim people of God'. It is not simply to belong to a particular theological school.

H. R. Mackintosh, 'Karl Barth', ExT 39 (1927–8), 536–40; J. G. Riddell, What we Believe (E, 1937); Karl Barth and Emil Brunner, Natural Theology (L, 1946); J. K. S. Reid, The Authority of Scripture (L, 1957); J. Macquarrie, Twentieth Century Religious Thought (L, 1971); A. I. C. Heron, A Century of Protestant Theology (L, 1980).

A. I. C. Heron

Nesbit, Robert (1803–55), missionary in India. Born to an English Presbyterian family in Bowsden, near Berwick-on-Tweed, he studied arts and divinity with distinction at St Andrews. By nature serious, he was converted in 1823 through reading Jeremy Taylor's Holy Living and Holy Dying after his brother's death by drowning. Thomas Chalmers* arrived at the University the same year and deeply influenced Nesbit and others (see Duff, Alexander; Urquhart, John) active in the University Missionary Association formed in 1824. After leaving St Andrews in 1825, Nesbit tutored in Caithness and Exeter before being accepted by the Scottish Missionary Society for India, being ordained by the CofS Presbytery of St Andrews and travelling to Bombay in 1827. He was stationed at Hurnee to the south. He developed into a sensitive pastoral evangelist and a highly fluent Marathi scholar, helping to revise the Marathi New Testament.

In 1831 he moved to Poona for health reasons, which in 1834 took him to South Africa. On his return to Bombay he became Secretary of the Book and Tract Society. He wrote several tracts in Marathi. In 1835 he was among a group of missionaries transferred at their own request from the SMS to the CofS, but they all joined the FC at the Disruption,* thereby losing their mission buildings. A voyage home in 1848 was not soon enough to prevent his wife dying at sea. He returned to Bombay in 1851 and remarried a few months before his own death from cholera.

AFCS I, 282; FES VII, 703–4; J. M. Mitchell, Memoir of the Rev. Robert Nesbit (L, 1858); R. Hunter, History of the Missions of the Free Church of Scotland in India and Africa (L, 1873); S. Piggin and J. Roxborogh, The St Andrews Seven (E, 1985); Piggin, Making Evangelical Missionaries 1789–1858 (Appleford, 1984).

D. F. Wright

Netherlands. Scottish connection with the Netherlands arose in several different ways. First, trading patterns between Scotland and the continent necessitated close links with the Low Countries. In particular Campvere (now known as Veere near Middleburg) served as the stapling port for Scotland. Scottish products were shipped to the continent via Veere, and the ships returned with purchases from the continent. The link with the small ports on the East Neuk of Fife was very strong. Secondly, many Scottish students made their way to Dutch universities, especially to study medicine and law at Leiden. The Dutch theologians also attracted Scottish students, and in the period of the Covenanters* a considerable number of men (including John Livingstone,* Richard Cameron* and James Renwick*) were trained in the Netherlands and ordained there. Others, such as John Brown of Wamphray* and Robert MacWard,* spent many years there in exile (see also Carstares, William). Thirdly, the presence of Scottish soldiers, especially the Scottish brigade raised by the Earl of Leicester in 1572, also meant frequent links with Scotland as well as the presence of many Scots in the country.

Scottish churches developed in Amsterdam, Campvere, Delft, Dordrecht, Flushing, the Hague, Middleburg, Rotterdam, and Utrecht (see FES VII, 537–55). Some of these were originally congregations associated with the English refugees, but afterwards became more Scottish in orientation. The Amsterdam and Rotterdam congregations still exist (see Scots Kirks).

The impact of Dutch theologians such as Gisbert Voetius and Hermann Witsius is apparent on Scottish theology. The Medulla of the English Puritan William Ames, adviser to the president at the Synod of Dort* and afterwards professor at Franeker, continued to be used in Scottish theological courses until the end of the nineteenth century. In turn the 'old writers' (such as Samuel Rutherford,* Thomas Boston* and Ralph and Ebenezer Erskine*) continue to be read widely in the Netherlands. The ministry and writings of Alexander Comrie* from Perth, who studied at Leiden and settled nearby at Woubrugge, were influential in transporting Marrow* and Secession* theology to the Dutch scene. The ecclesiastical inter-connection between the Netherlands and Scotland had passed its peak by the mid-eighteenth century. The following century saw both countries intensely involved in national Church conflicts (the Dutch Secession of 1834 and the Scottish Disruption* of 1843), and the close links have never been restored.

See also Spang, William.

W. Steven, *The History of the Scottish Church, Rotterdam* (E, 1833); A. L. Drummond, *The Kirk and the Continent* (E, 1956), 76–168.

A. M. Harman

New College, Edinburgh, successively a FC, UFC and CofS theological college, united since the Union* of 1929 with the University's Divinity Faculty. Planned from the outset of the Disruption* of 1843, the College met in temporary premises (Free St George's, 80 George Street, 25 George Street) until the building on the Mound, designed by William Playfair (1789–1857), was ready for use in 1850. The Free High Church, built as an integral part of the complex, became New College Library in 1936. It now houses the largest separate theological library in Britain (*see* Libraries). Some years after the Union, in 1961, the CofS agreed to cede the buildings to the University, under careful conditions. The Church's Assembly Hall is adjacent, and fruitful Church–University co-operation over use and development continues.

Despite early aspirations for an institution more like a university than a divinity hall, the College never expanded beyond the classical languages, philosophy and logic (all for a few years only) and natural science (to J. Y. Simpson's* death in 1934). Nevertheless, it grew rapidly, with 168 students in its first year and a peak of 257 in 1850. Thereafter numbers were normally well over a hundred, dipping to the 70s in the early 1900s. With a strong postgraduate presence (as earlier in 1920s and 1930s), recent growth has lifted the community to over 500. The student body is richly international (New College has about a thousand alumni/ae in N. America) and ecumenical. Ordinands from several churches, especially the EpCS (*see* Episcopal Theological College), study alongside CofS students, and an historical link continues with the nearby FC College. Religious studies degrees began in 1971 and have a growing inter-disciplinary appeal.

New College under its founding Principal, Thomas Chalmers,* soon outshone the University Faculty. He was followed in office by William Cunningham,* R. S. Candlish,* Robert Rainy,* Marcus Dods* and Alexander Whyte.* Other distinguished teachers have included James Buchanan,* James Bannerman,* Alexander Duff* (*see* Practical Theology), John (Rabbi) Duncan,* A. B. Davidson,* Adam Welch,* H. A. A. Kennedy,* James Mackinnon,* H. R. Mackintosh,* William Manson,* John Baillie,* J. S. Stewart,* J. H. S. Burleigh,* T. F. Torrance* and John McIntyre (1916–; *FES* IX, 190, X, 430–1; *Who's Who 1991*, 1171–2). Among other influential churchmen on the staff were A. H. Charteris,* W. G. Blaikie,* Alexander Martin,* and William Curtis.*

New College escaped the heresy proceedings that agitated the Glasgow and Aberdeen FC/UFC colleges (*see* Christ's College; Trinity College) in the late nineteenth century. Much later it became the leading British home of Neo-orthodoxy.* The *Scottish Journal of Theology** still retains links with the College. In addition to the traditional divinity disciplines, together with religious studies, the College now embraces the Centre for the Study of Christianity in the Non-Western World. New College seeks to do justice to its dual identity, as church college and university faculty, with its inevitable tensions.

See also Education, Theological.

H. Watt, *New College Edinburgh: A Centenary History* (E, 1946); '1583–1983', *New College Bulletin* 14 (1983).

D. F. Wright

New Jerusalem Church, The, looks to the vision of the Holy City of New Jerusalem (in Revelation 21) as its model. The Church's teachings are drawn from the Bible and are expounded in the theological writings of the Swedish scientist and seer, Emanuel Swedenborg (1688–1772). The Church was founded in 1787 by followers of his distinctive mystical teachings. The Church worships the Lord Jesus Christ as the one God, in whom is the Trinity of Father, Son and Holy Spirit.

Although it has never been numerically strong, the New Jerusalem Church has existed continuously in Scotland since the 1790s. It began with a few scattered people who were readers of the teachings published in the books of Swedenborg, which had begun to circulate in Scotland even in his lifetime. The Church started to organize itself in the early nineteenth century, after missionary visits by English ministers, including Robert Hindmarsh. By the mid-nineteenth century, there were congregations in Alloa, Dundee, Edinburgh, Glasgow and Paisley. This was the greatest extent of the denomination in Scotland, and the twentieth century has seen a decline in numbers. One eminent Scotsman who was influenced by Swedenborg's teaching was Thomas Carlyle.*

The Church in Scotland is a constituent part of the General Conference of the New Church in Great Britain, which holds an Annual Meeting to conduct business and formulate policy. Over the years, ten of its Annual Meetings have been held in Scotland. The Church in Scotland today consists of a congregation in Paisley and a group in Edinburgh. There is a comprehensive collection of the Church's literature in the Mitchell Library in Glasgow.

A. Macwhirter, 'The Church of the New Jerusalem in Scotland', *RSCHS* 12 (1956), 202–19.

R. A. Gill

New Lanark, *see* Dale, David.

New Light, a change of sentiment in the Secession* Churches on the question of government support of the church (*see* Church and State) which led to conflict between Old Light and New Light. This shift at the close of the eighteenth century also opened the way to a wider toleration* of theological diversity within the Church. The Enlightenment* advocacy of reason and the right of free inquiry disposed people to assert the liberty to think, speak, write and publish as they pleased; as a corollary, some objected to the civil government acting as patron to any form of religion. When the French Revolution* transformed the civil constitution of France and removed RC* domination, hopes were aroused in Scotland that the British constitution would undergo reforms well.

New Light had a Scottish precursor in John Glas,* deposed by the CofS in 1730 for his resistance to national covenants and their implied uniformity (*see* Covenanting), and the right of the state to interfere in matters of religion. The Relief Church* adopted the Glasite outlook, its protagonist Patrick Hutchison* of St Ninian's objecting in 1779 that any association with the kingdoms of this world would imperil the nature of the Church as a purely voluntary society.

The Associate (Burgher) Synod* in 1799 adopted a preamble to its formula of subscription* allowing divergent views with respect to the magistrate's power in matters of religion and the nature of the obligation which national covenants have on posterity. John Dick* pleaded that a Church's views were not to displace the individual's right to judge for himself what the Scriptures teach. This forbearance was endorsed by George Lawson* in his *Considerations on the overture ... respecting some Alterations in the Formula* (E, 1797). A minority departed and formed the Original Burgher Presbytery, which continued an Old Light testimony until, as the Original Burgher Synod, it united with the CofS in 1839. Their chief pamphleteer was William Willis of Greenock, who wrote *A Smooth Stone from the Brook* (G, 1799).

In the General Associate (Antiburgher) Synod,* William Graham's* *A Review of Ecclesiastical Establishments in Europe* (L, 1792) was influential in leading many to question the propriety and usefulness of a national establishment. New Light was embraced in the Synod's New Testimony of 1804 (*see* Testimonies), which declared that 'the power competent to worldly kingdoms is wholly temporal, respecting only the secular interests of society'. Aversion to persecution for the sake of conscience was cited as reason enough to oppose national establishments of religion altogether. Five Old Light ministers – disavowing persecuting principles, yet maintaining the propriety of an alliance between Church and state – withdrew in 1806 to organize the Constitutional Associate Presbytery (*see* Original Secession Church). A cogent exposition of Old Light principles was given by Thomas M'Crie* in *Statement of the Difference* (E, 1807). His colleague Archibald Bruce* narrated the progress of New Light in the Secession Churches, in his *A Review of the Proceedings of the General Associate Synod* (E, 1808).

New Light was full grown in the Voluntaryism* advocated when the two New Light synods merged to create the USec.C* in 1820, and the addition of the Relief Church* in 1847 produced the UPC.* In the Voluntary controversy* (1829), the dissenters* contended with Old Light proponents in the CofS, and the dispute was fuelled by concurrent agitation for parliamentary reform. But the moral dilemma of New Light appeared when Church officers used their positions to release themselves from the pledges they had formerly given concerning confessional teaching. And its wider bearing became evident in the atonement controversy,* when the pleas for indulging dissimilar views within the USec.C reached to questions other than Church and state.

J. M'Kerrow, *History of the Secession Church* (E, 1854); G. Struthers, *History of Relief Church* (G, 1843); D. Scott, *Annals and Statistics of Original Secession Church* (E, 1886); J. Macleod, *Scottish Theology* (E, ³1974); J. MacFarlane, *Life and Times of George Lawson* (E, 1880); T. M'Crie, *Life of Thomas M'Crie* (E, 1840); J. Cairns, *Memoir of John Brown* (E, 1860).

S. Isbell

New Zealand, Missions and Emigration. Early missionary work amongst Maoris was pioneered by English Anglicans and Methodists and French RCs. J. D. Lang,* the pioneer Presbyterian minister in Australia, after a brief visit in 1839 wrote *New Zealand in 1839* (L, 1839). It was a critical account of this missionary work and called for colonization founded on Christian principles. Scots came to New Zealand as migrants and Presbyterians were largely involved from 1840 in establishing a settler Church. John Macfarlane, the first resident Presbyterian minister, learnt Maori and made some initial attempts to undertake missionary work. He unsuccessfully challenged the CofS to take up this work.

James Duncan (1813–1908) and John Inglis* from the RPC were sent as missionaries to the Maori in 1843. They worked in the Manawatu area but had little success. Duncan became a minister to settlers at Foxton 1861–97. Inglis, after ministries in Wellington and Auckland, went to the New Hebrides, where he made a notable contribution on Aneityum 1852–79.

Scots, after the English, were the second largest migrant group to come to New Zealand. The Otago Association established in 1847 brought together the concerns of the New Zealand Company and the Lay Association of members of the FC. Led by Thomas Burns,* William Cargill (1784–1860) and John McGlashan (1802–64), they hoped to establish a FC settlement, 'a Geneva of the Antipodes'. The first settlers arrived at Port Chalmers in 1848 and Dunedin was developed as the main centre. Scottish interests in the availability of education were fulfilled in the country's first university and boys' and girls' high schools established in Dunedin. Scottish migrants and their Church made a strong imprint on the southern part of the country in particular. Scots took a leading part in business, education and politics throughout the country.

Presbyterian energy went into 'home missions', establishing parishes, setting up sustentation funds, recruiting ministers, building manses and churches. David Bruce of the FC (1824–1911), born at Cramond and brother of A. B. Bruce,* served as minister of St Andrew's Auckland (1853–76) and as Church Agent (1877–81). More than anyone else he was responsible for establishing the Presbyterian Church north of the Waitaki River. His counterpart in the south, also from the FC, was D. M. Stuart (1819–94), minister of Knox Church Dunedin 1860–94. The first superintendent of home mission work (1911–14) was P. B. Fraser (1852–1940) from Lerwick, a controversial figure who helped Presbyterians develop parishes covering the whole country.

The Presbyterian Church of New Zealand, or Northern Church, established in 1862, began overseas missionary work in the New Hebrides in 1869 when William (1843–1926) and Agnes Watt (d.1894), who had been recruited from Scotland, went to Tanna. The Synod of Otago and Southland, or Southern Church, established in 1866, recruited Peter Milne (1834–1924) from the FC, who with his wife Mary began work in the New Hebrides on Nguna, also in 1869.

The New Hebrides was the main focus for New Zealand Presbyterian overseas missionary work. After the union of the two Churches in 1901 they became involved in supporting work in China and North India and much later in Indonesia and Papua New Guinea. The missionary work in China had its origins in the ministry of Alexander Don to Chinese miners on the Otago goldfields.

Sustained Presbyterian Maori work did not begin until H. J. Fletcher (1868–1923) was stationed at Taupo in the 1890s. Work amongst the Tuhoe in the Urewera became the major focus for their mission. J. G. Laughton (1891–1965), born in the Orkney Islands, gave outstanding leadership. His understanding of Maori culture and fluency in the language made him a respected figure in Maoridom and a key figure in interpreting the Maori world to the Church. Significant contributions were made by women teachers and nurses such as Annie Henry (1879–1971) and Edith Walker (1886–1969). The first Presbyterian Maori ministers, Timu Teoke and Hemi Potatau, were ordained in 1931 and 1933 respectively. Greater autonomy was given to Maori Presbyterians through the establishment of the Maori Synod in 1956. Because Presbyterians were much later than other Churches in beginning missionary work amongst Maori, the number of Maori identifying with the Presbyterian Church has remained small.

Successive waves of migrants and the recruitment of ministers from Scotland reinforced strong Scottish characteristics within the Presbyterian Church. The new context, however, and the need to work together, resulted in greater unity amongst the different Presbyterian groups who came to the country than was the case in Scotland. Ecumenical relationships, union ventures and the influx since 1970s of a large group of Pacific Islanders from a Congregational background have reshaped Presbyterian identity.

The contribution of Scottish migrants to other denominations tended to be absorbed by the dominant majority ethos in these churches. Amongst the most noteworthy of these Scots was Joseph Kemp,* minister of the Baptist Tabernacle Auckland, 1902–33. A student at the Glasgow Bible Training Institute* 1893–5, Kemp founded the New Zealand Bible Training Institute in Auckland in 1926, which had a strong missionary focus in its work.

D. McEldowney (ed.), *Presbyterians in Aotearoa 1840–1990* (Wellington, 1990); entries on John Inglis, Thomas Burns, David Bruce in *AFCS* I; on James Duncan and Inglis in J. Robb, *Cameronian Fasti* (E, n.d.); on William Cargill, John McGlashan, Burns, Bruce, D. M. Stewart in G. H. Scholefield (ed.), *A Dictionary of New Zealand Biography*, 2 vols (Wellington, 1940); on all except Cargill, McGlashan and Kemp in I. W. Fraser, *Register of Ministers 1840 to 1989* [of Presbyterian Church of New Zealand] (Lower Hutt, 1990); *FES* VII, 602–5, VIII, 734.

A. K. Davidson

Newbattle, *see* Cistercians.

Newbigin, James Lesslie Edward (1909–), ecumenical leader and theologian. Born in Newcastle-upon-Tyne, he studied at Cambridge (1928–31) and Westminster College there (1933–5). He served as CofS missionary in South India from 1936, was consecrated as one of the original bishops of the Church of South India at its inauguration in 1947, and became the leading defender of the CSI way to unity through mutual recognition of ministries (see *The Reunion of the Church* (L, 1948) and *The Household of God* (L, 1953)). As an ecumenical* statesman and theologian of mission, he chaired the committee on the main theme for the Second Assembly of the WCC (Evanston, 1954), was vice-chairman of the Faith and Order Commission, and as Chairman and then General Secretary of the International Missionary Council led its incorporation into the WCC at New Delhi in 1961. He acted as an Associate General Secretary of the WCC from 1959 to 1965, when he returned to India as Bishop in Madras. After his retirement from India in 1974, he lectured in Selly Oak Colleges and acted as minister of a small United Reformed Church* congregation in Birmingham, becoming quickly recognized as one of the most creative and imaginative Church leaders in Britain. Among his many important publications in this period are a theology of mission, *The Open Secret* (L, 1978), and a penetrating critique of post-Enlightenment western Christianity in *The Other Side of 1984* (Geneva, 1983) and *Foolishness to the Greeks* (L, 1986).

Unfinished Agenda: An Autobiography (Geneva, 1985).

NIC(H)OLSON, JOHN

FES IX, 744-5; Who's Who 1992, 1363.
D. B. Forrester

Nic(h)olson, John (1790-1828), pioneer of Methodism* in Shetland.* Born in a crofting family at Queensetter, Aithsting, near Lerwick, serving in the Royal Artillery Company during the Napoleonic Wars, converted in the Tower of London through the witness of a Methodist fellow-soldier, Bombardier Nicolson worshipped at Wesley's Chapel, City Road, and enjoyed class-meeting fellowship at Slater's Court and Woolwich. An army general encouraged his education. Medical experience in the Convalescent Hospital and clerical work with the East India Company followed.

Breakdown of both his health and his marriage precipitated his return to Shetland around 1819. Continuing to preach as he had done in London, he formed a West Side circuit with two prayer meetings and three unofficial classes. Letters to several leading Methodists sought advice and approval. His persistence was rewarded when, in 1822, Conference appointed two itinerant ministers, the first of many.

By the time Nicolson died at Gruting, upwards of 4,000 Shetlanders attended the seven chapels and many other regular preaching places, large and small, Sunday and weekday, including well over 1,000 Wesleyan-Methodist members meeting in weekly classes.

H. R. Bowes, 'Revival and Survival' (MTh, University of Aberdeen, 1988), 32-62; id., 'The Launching of Methodism in Shetland', *Proc. of Wesley Hist. Soc.* 38 (1972), 136-46; J. Austen, 'John Nicolson', *ibid.* 19 (1935), 126f.; P. Goodlad, 'John Nicolson', *The New Shetlander* 72 (1965), 12-14.
H. R. Bowes

Nicholson, William Patteson (1876-1959), Irish evangelist. A Belfast Presbyterian, he was converted in 1899 after deep conviction of sin. Trained at the Bible Training Institute,* Glasgow (1901-3), he evangelized with the Lanarkshire Christian Union (1903-8). After assisting the American evangelist Wilbur Chapman (1908-10) and deputizing for D. J. Findlay* at St George's Cross Tabernacle, Glasgow (1911), he was ordained an evangelist by the Carlisle presbytery of the Presbyterian Church in the United States (1914) and worked under the Bible Institute of Los Angeles (1918-20).

His most successful missions followed an invitation by the Glasgow United Evangelistic Association* to return to Scotland and Ireland. Against a background of intense political and civil strife, his Irish missions (1920-3) resulted in small-scale revival,* with 12,409 enquirers and an increase in the number of first communicants in the Presbyterian Church alone from 4,741 (1920) to 6,059 (1923). Subsequent missions in Ireland (1924-6) secured less support and success. His denunciation of established religion, as well as of liberal theology and biblical criticism, increased. He addressed the Keswick Convention, and his sensational preaching at

NICOLL, WILLIAM ROBERTSON

a Cambridge University CU Mission resulted in about 100 professions of faith. Evangelism continued to be his life, in the USA, the British Isles, Australasia and South Africa. An effective evangelist, Nicholson's rugged style of preaching, direct, blunt and sometimes offensive to the cultured ear, communicated with working men to an unusual degree. His style and preaching can still be savoured in his published works, *On Towards the Goal!* (E, 1925), *The Evangelist* (L, 1937), and *God's Hell* (L, 1938).

S. W. Murray, *W. P. Nicholson* (Belfast, 1973).
H. H. Rowdon

Nicoll, William Robertson (1851-1923), minister and journalist. The son of Henry Nicoll, FC minister of Lumsden, Aberdeenshire, he lost his mother in 1859. He was educated at Achindoir Parish School, Aberdeen Grammar School, Aberdeen University and Aberdeen FC Divinity School, before becoming FC minister of Dufftown, Banffshire (1874-7), and Kelso, Roxburghshire (1877-85). He was twice married, to Isa Dunlop (1878-94) and Catherine Pollard (from 1897). Resigning his charge because of ill health, he went to London to become editor of *The Expositor* (1885-1923), *The British Weekly** (1886-1923) and *The Bookman* (1891-1923). His industry and range of interests are indicated by a selective list of his publications: *Songs of Rest* (E, 1879; L, 1885); *The Incarnate Saviour* (E, 1881); *James Macdonell, Journalist* (L, 1890); *Prof. W. G. Elmslie, D.D.*, edited with A. N. Macnicoll (L, 1890); *Literary Anecdotes of the Nineteenth Century*, with T. J. Wise, 2 vols (L, 1895-6); *The Return to the Cross* (L, 1897); *Letters on Life* (L, 1901); *The Church's One Foundation* (L, 1901); *The Day Book of Claudius Clear* (L, 1905); *A History of English Literature*, with T. Seccombe, 3 vols (L, 1906); *My Father* (L, 1908); *The Problem of 'Edwin Drood'* (L, 1912); *A Bookman's Letters* (L, 1912); *Reunion in Eternity* (L, 1918); *Letters of Principal James Denney to W. Robertson Nicoll* (L, 1920); *Princes of the Church* (L, 1921); *Dickens's Own Story* (L, 1923); *Memories of Mark Rutherford* (L, 1924). In addition he edited several series including *The Expositor's Bible* (L, 1887-96) and *The Expositor's Greek Testament* (L, 1897-1911).

Through *The British Weekly*, which had a separate Scottish edition, Nicoll exerted a significant influence on public affairs. Suspicious of Gladstone and favourable to empire, he advocated passive resistance against the Education Act of 1902 for England and Wales and subsequently supported Lloyd George. He was knighted in 1909 and made CH in 1921. With enormous literary erudition and considerable theological acuteness, he did much to broaden the taste of the evangelical public.

See also Swan, Annie S.

T. H. Darlow, *William Robertson Nicoll* (L, 1925); *DNB 1922-1930*, 636-7; A. S. Peake, *Recollections and Appreciations* (L, 1938), 11-28; D. Carswell, *Brother Scots* (L, 1929), 212-37.
D. W. Bebbington

Nicolson, Thomas (c.1645–1718), first post-Reformation RC Bishop in Scotland. Son of Thomas Nicolson, later of Kemnay, he matriculated at Marischal College, Aberdeen in 1660. He was regent at Glasgow University from 1666 until his refusal to take the Test Act* oath in 1681. Having embraced RCism, he entered the Scots College,* Douai, in 1682 but went on to Padua, where he taught in the diocesan seminary and was prefect of studies 1685–7. In March 1686 he was ordained priest at Padua.

He returned to Scotland as a missioner in 1687 but was exiled after the Revolution. The appointment of a bishop for Scotland had long been mooted. Nicolson was made Vicar-Apostolic (see Propaganda Fide) 1694 and received episcopal consecration 1695; then in 1697 he arrived in Scotland and resided at Preshome, Banffshire. His episcopal administration was vigorous and successful. He united Scottish RCism under his rule, making long journeys to the West Highlands and Islands to administer confirmation. The religious priests in Scotland, notably the Jesuits,* submitted to his authority. His 'Statutes' laid down guidelines for the Scottish mission for the next eighty years, and the first seminary in Scotland was founded in 1714 (see Colleges and Seminaries, RC).

J. Darragh, *The Catholic Hierarchy of Scotland* (G, 1986), 6–7; W. Doran, 'Bishop Thomas Nicolson', *IR* 39 (1988), 109–32.

W. J. Doran

Ninian, traditionally regarded as the earliest Christian missionary in Scotland. Bede* (*d.*734) says that he converted Pictish* tribes south of the Mounth, adding that he was a British bishop who had studied at Rome and who built a stone church at *Candida Casa* ('White House', Whithorn*), which he dedicated to St Martin, Bishop of Tours in Gaul (France) (*d.*397), and where he was buried together with many saints. Apart from stating that he was active 'a long time before' St Columba's* visits to the Northern Picts (between 563 and 597), Bede gives no indication as to when he lived. The twelfth-century assertion that he was a contemporary of Martin is now widely rejected, and some scholars consider that he may have been one of a succession of bishops in Galloway; certainly Bede's details do not fit easily into a fifth-century context, and the archaeological record does not give confidence for a fifth-century conversion of the Picts. Place-name evidence, however, does suggest British missionary activity among the Southern Picts, and it is probable that Ninian's name is to be associated with this, and that Whithorn was the base from which he and his companions came. This may have been in the later fifth century, or the first half of the sixth, rather than the traditional dating c.400.

There was an Anglian diocese at Whithorn in the eighth century, and evidence of Norse occupation thereafter. Fergus, lord of Galloway, revived the see c.1126, and it became the site of a medieval bishopric. The cult of St Ninian was strong in the Middle Ages, and the cathedral at Whithorn became a centre of pilgrimage. An archaeological investigation is under way at Whithorn.

See also Anglo-Saxon Saints.

Sources: B. Colgrave and R. A. B. Mynors (eds), *Bede's Historia Ecclesiastica Gentis Anglorum* (O, ²1992), iii, 4; a twelfth-century life by Ailred of Rievaulx in A. P. Forbes (ed.), *Lives of S. Ninian and S. Kentigern* (E, 1874). Modern studies: W. D. Simpson, *St Ninian and the Origins of the Christian Church in Scotland* (E, 1940); N. K. Chadwick, 'St Ninian: a Preliminary Study of Sources', *TDGAS* 3rd. ser. 27 (1950), 9–53; P. Grosjean, 'Les Pictes apostats dans l'Épître de S. Patrice', *Analecta Bollandiana* 76 (1958), 354–78; J. MacQueen, *St Nynia* (E, 1990); A. A. M. Duncan, 'Bede, Iona and the Picts', in R. H. C. Davis and J. M. Wallace-Hadrill (eds), *The Writing of History in the Middle Ages* (O, 1981), 1–42; A. Macquarrie, 'The Date of St Ninian's Mission: a Reappraisal', *RSCHS* 23 (1987), 1–25.

A. Macquarrie

Nisbet (Nesbitt), Alexander (1623–69), Covenanting* minister. Little is known of Nisbet's life. He graduated MA from Edinburgh University in 1643, and was ordained to the Second Charge of Irvine, Ayrshire, before or during 1646. In 1650 he moved to Irvine's First Charge. He was ejected in 1662 on the re-establishment of Episcopacy. He is remembered today for *A Brief Exposition of the First and Second Epistles General of Peter* (E, 1658), and *Exposition with Practical Observations upon the Book of Ecclesiastes* (E, 1694). These were parts of a series of biblical commentaries inspired by David Dickson* (see Exegesis, Biblical). C. H. Spurgeon praised Nisbet's commentary on Peter as 'judicious and gracious' (*Commenting and Commentaries*, L, 1876, 192).

FES III, 99, 101.

N. R. Needham

Nisbet, John (c.1627–1685), soldier. The son of James Nisbet of Hardhill in Ayrshire, John served as a soldier in Europe for some time before returning to Scotland about 1650, taking the covenants and settling on his family's farm. Steadfast in his resistance to the Restoration* settlement of religion, Nisbet took part in the rebellion of 1666, being severely wounded and left for dead on the battlefield of Rullion Green.* He was also active in the 1679 rebellion, fighting in the skirmish at Drumclog that sparked off the rising and serving as a captain at Bothwell Bridge.* He escaped after the defeat and was outlawed in 1684, a reward being offered for his arrest. When he and three others were captured by a party of soldiers his companions were summarily shot, but Nisbet was taken to Edinburgh, where he was tried and executed in the Grassmarket, thus becoming one of the martyrs* of the Killing Times.*

A True Relation of the Life and Suffering of John Nisbet in Hardhill (E, 1718), in W. K. Tweedie (ed.),

NISBET, MURDOCH

Select Biographies, II (E, 1847), 371–409; *DNB* XLI, 70; R. Wodrow, *History of the Sufferings of the CofS*, 4 vols (²G, 1828–30), IV, 235–7.

D. Stevenson

Nisbet, Murdoch (*d.c.*1545), reputed Lollard* who merged in the Reformation,* and representative of the pre-Reformation tradition of vernacular biblical translation. From Hardhill, Loudon, in Ayrshire, he was a diocesan official and notary public. The trial of Kyle Lollards in 1494 may have occasioned his attraction to dissent and departure from Scotland, probably around 1513, returning possibly before 1525. Association with other returned Ayrshire exiles executed for heresy* at Glasgow in 1539 drove Nisbet underground. Re-emerging after 1542, he participated in Reformation agitation in Ayrshire though died soon afterwards. Discovered in 1893, the MS Scots recension of the Wycliffite New Testament (*see* Bible (Versions, Scottish)) is attributed to him while in exile. See text in T. G. Law (ed.), *The New Testament in Scots . . . by Murdoch Nisbet*, STS, 1st ser., 46, 49, 52 (E, L, 1901–5).

Nisbet sources are sparse, the chief one being an eighteenth-century family memoir. Unresolved is whether Nisbet sojourned in England or on the continent. That his MS provides an independent translation of Luther's New Testament Preface may suggest the latter. As a Vulgate-based text, Nisbet's New Testament had no future in Reformation circles.

J. Nisbet, *A True Relation* (²1719) in W. K. Tweedie (ed.), *Select Biographies*, II (E, 1847), 377–409; J. Anderson (ed.), *Calendar of the Laing Charters* (E, 1899), nr. 102; T. M. Lindsay, 'A Literary Relic of Scottish Lollardy', *SHR* 1 (1904), 260–75; T. M. A. Macnab, 'The New Testament in Scots', *RSCHS* 11 (1951), 82–103; G. Tulloch, *A History of the Scots Bible* (A, 1989).

W. I. P. Hazlett

Nonconformity. This term, so commonly used and widely understood in English Church history, is difficult to handle in a Scottish context. During the troubles of the 1650s James Durham* wrote *The Dying Man's Testament* (E, 1659), arguing firmly for the unity of the Kirk in Scotland: 'That as Union is ever a duty, so, we conceive, if men interested will do their duty, there can be no division amongst orthodox divines or ministers, but it is possible also to compose it, and union is a thing attainable.' In this statement he spoke for most Presbyterians, who had a horror of schism. Yet unity was not evident, from the times of episcopacy* to the present day. There have been protesters against the prevailing form of Church government, or against the current trends in the Est.C, who may be described as nonconformists, ranging from adherents of the unreformed Church to devotees of modern sects, but the word nonconformist is applied, in Ian Cowan, *The Scottish Covenanters 1660–1688*, only to the Protester* party, to the Cameronians (*see* Societies, United),* and to the Episcopalians 'outed' in 1688–9. There is a 1679 pamphlet in the National Library of Scotland entitled *The Humble Supplication of the Nonconformists in the West and other Parts of Scotland* (L), addressed to the Duke of Monmouth.

A word used more frequently in Scotland is dissent.* In the eighteenth century three secessions from the Est.C were often referred to in this way: the Glasite movement (*see* Glas, John*), beginning in 1730, the first Secession* in 1733, and the Relief* Presbytery in 1761. Presbyterian dissent has played a large part in Scottish life, increasingly after the Disruption* in 1843, but it did not take on the characteristics of English nonconformity. In its attitudes to the Est.C, at least until the Voluntary Controversy* in the early nineteenth century, it differed considerably from English Baptists and Congregationalists, and it did not bear the burden of legal disabilities which English dissent had to carry.

Those bodies in Scotland which had the same names as their English counterparts, the Baptists,* Independents,* Methodists,* and Unitarians,* were small, and in no position to pose the threat to the Est.C that English nonconformity sometimes did. In the later nineteenth and early twentieth century, there are signs of a nonconformist conscience. It is notable that Members of Parliament who were Baptists, such as Sir Thomas Glen-Coats (see *Who Was Who, 1916–1928*, 412), were members of the Liberal Party, and later Keir Hardie* was associated with the Evangelical Union,* and William Adamson,* a Baptist, was the first Labour Secretary of State for Scotland in 1924. While classical nonconformity has not been a feature of Scottish history, those who have been unwilling to conform to the Est.C, or to Presbyterianism in any form, have played an important part in her life.

G. Yuille (ed.), *History of the Baptists in Scotland* (G, 1926); H. Escott, *A History of Scottish Congregationalism* (G, 1960).

D. B. Murray

Non-Intrusionists, evangelical defenders of popular rights and Church independence in the CofS 1834–43. The Non-Intrusionist (*see* Intrusion) controversy broke out when the legitimacy of the Veto Act* was contested in the civil courts. The Evangelicals who had promoted the congregational 'veto' were not prepared to allow the Court of Session to 'intrude' unwelcome ministers upon defenceless congregations (*see* Ten Years' Conflict). They continued to champion the belief that congregations must have some say in the choice of their ministers and finally, in 1842, they passed a resolution in the General Assembly calling for the outright abolition of patronage.* By that time, however, the ground of the conflict was wider and deeper. In finding the Veto Act incompetent, the civil courts had enunciated the theory that the Church was a creature of statute, subordinate to the legislature and the courts, having no independent jurisdiction. By contrast, the Non-Intrusionist theory was that the Church was a spiritual creation, recognized by statute but with its own independent existence and sphere of jurisdiction. The interference of the civil courts in the matter of ministerial appointment they regarded as an unwarranted 'intrusion' into the 'spiritual independence' of the Church. Their position was based on the *Second Book of Discipline** and they considered themselves profoundly conservative, defending the traditional prerogatives of the Church from the encroachments of an expanding State. Faced with government defiance, they did not shrink from leaving the Establishment in the interests of the spiritual independence of the Church (*see* Disruption).

Thomas Chalmers* was the Non-Intrusionist leader but much of the driving force in the movement came from younger men such as William Cunningham,* Robert S. Candlish,* Robert Buchanan* and James Begg.* They may have lacked maturity, but the cause was also adopted by such experienced churchmen as Patrick Macfarlan,* David Welsh,* Robert Gordon* and Lord Moncreiff (1776–1851). There may be something in the suggestion that ecclesiastical power went to the heads of the young Evangelicals, but few would now dispute that what they were defending was, substantially, the historic position of the Scottish Church. Nor should it be forgotten that it was a genuinely national movement. The outstanding figure in the popularizing of Non-Intrusion was Hugh Miller,* whose journalistic flair, exercised in the columns of *The Witness*,* gave a currency to the ideas of the Non-Intrusionists which was integral to their success. Another factor not to be underestimated was the religious awakening of the time, in which almost all the prominent preachers were Non-Intrusionist. Candlish in Edinburgh, Buchanan in Glasgow, Robert Murray M'Cheyne* in Dundee, John MacDonald* throughout the Highlands and Roderick MacLeod* in Skye: the powerful evangelical preaching of such men gained for Non-Intrusion the allegiance of thousands. The movement was characterized theologically by the recovery of Calvinistic theology with which its leading protagonists were identified. Conservatism in polity was reinforced by conservatism in doctrine.

H. W. Moncreiff, *The Free Church Principle* (E, 1883); H. Miller, *Letter to Lord Brougham* (E, 1839); J. Mackenzie and R. Rainy, *William Cunningham* (L, 1871), 61–201; N. L. Walker, *Robert Buchanan* (L, 1877), 120–257; W. Wilson and R. Rainy, *Robert Smith Candlish* (E, 1880), 77–335; S. J. Brown, *Thomas Chalmers and the Godly Commonwealth in Scotland* (O, 1982), 211–340.

K. R. Ross

Non-jurors (*i.e.* 'non-swearers'), Episcopalians* who refused to take an oath of allegiance to William II* and Mary after the Revolution* of 1689 when the Scottish Convention of Estates declared James VII* to have forfeited the crown and recognized William and Mary. All of the Scottish bishops refused this oath, and with the re-establishment of Presbyterianism* in 1690 some clergy followed them into Episcopalian nonconformity.* In the following years other oaths were prescribed – in 1693 an oath of 'assurance' that William was King not only *de facto* but also *de jure*, and in 1712, as part of the Act of Toleration,* an oath of abjuration of the pretensions of James' son, the 'Old Pretender'. This Act granted toleration to Episcopalians who used 'the liturgy of the Church of England', provided they also swore allegiance to Queen Anne and in worship prayed by name for her and the royal family. Some who had hitherto been non-jurors conformed to the terms of this Act; the rest would soon take up the Jacobite* cause.

A. L. Drummond and J. Bulloch, *The Scottish Church 1688–1843* (E, 1973); J. H. Overton, *The Nonjurors* (L, 1902), ch. 10; G. Grub, *An Ecclesiastical History of Scotland*, III (E, 1861).

D. F. Wright

North British Review, The. Published by W. P. Kennedy, the *Review* was founded in 1844 by a group of FCS men dissatisfied with the *Edinburgh** and *Quarterly Reviews*, considering the first too secular and the second too Tory. They aimed to examine all areas of human activity from the standpoint of evangelical Christianity and of political liberalism. Initially, the *Review* sold well (up to 4,000 copies), but declining circulation persuaded successive editors that if it were to succeed, it must be freed both from its provincialism, and from the dominance of Scottish theology. Though the *Review* was not an official FC journal, successive editors found themselves under pressure from the proprietor and the FC to adhere to the FC position on social and political issues. Tension culminated during the editorship of Alexander C. Fraser* between 1850 and 1857. He increased the national reputation of the *Review*, but in so doing antagonized its FC readership. When he published a review critical of Thomas Chalmers'* standing as a writer, he was forced to resign, and the *Review* thereafter took a narrower FC line and circulation declined. In 1860, the journal was purchased by T. & T. Clark, who appointed William G. Blaikie* as editor. He resigned in 1863, and around the same time, the Clarks sold the *North British* to Edmonston and Douglas. Issued by their London partners Williams and Norgate from 1869, it was sold by Douglas in 1871 to Lord Acton, becoming a liberal RC journal, and finally ceasing publication in 1875.

W. G. Blaikie, *Recollections of a Busy Life* (L, 1901), 136–47; *Scottish Notes and Queries*, 2nd. ser., 3 (1901), 24–5; 3rd ser., 11 (1933), 37–9; J. Shattock, 'Editorial Policy and the Quarterlies: the Case of the North British Review', *Victorian Periodicals Newsletter* 10 (1977), 130–9; *id.*, 'Problems of Parentage: the North British Review and the Free Church of Scotland', in J. Shattock and M. Wolff (eds), *The Victorian Periodical Press* (Leicester, 1982), 145–66; 'The Story of the North British Review', *The Scottish Review*, 3rd January 1907, 20.

J. A. H. Dempster

North, Brownlow (1810–75), evangelist. Born in

London, North was the son of a minister, grandson of the Bishop of Winchester, and great-grandson of Lord North, the eighteenth-century Prime Minister. He studied at Eton, where he was known as 'Gentleman Jack', and distinguished himself as an athlete and travelled on the Continent, but exerted little effort in serious study. Financial pressures after the death of his father led to gambling and a stint in Portugal as a soldier in Don Pedro's army in 1832. He returned home in 1833 and led a carefree, pleasure-filled life, dedicated largely to hunting and fishing in Scotland. In 1839 he decided to enter the ministry and went to Magdalen College, Oxford, where he graduated in 1842. North's misgivings about his call and the reluctance of the bishop to ordain him led to the abandonment of his plans and a return to his old life. In 1854, impressed with the wastefulness of his life and startled by a sudden illness, he was converted at Dallas Moors in Scotland. He wrote: 'For forty-four years of my life, my object was to pass time pleasantly; so long as the day was spent agreeably I was satisfied ... In the end of 1854 it pleased God to bring home with power to my heart, that it would profit me nothing if I gained the whole world and lost my own soul.' He began to study the Bible avidly, and to visit the sick, distribute tracts, and conduct religious meetings in homes, churches, and out-of-doors. He soon became known as an earnest and gifted preacher, and in 1859 the General Assembly of the FCS formally recognized him as an evangelist (*AGAFCS 1858–1863*, 124–5, 147). That same year during July and August he preached to thousands throughout Northern Ireland and the next year in Scotland, as revival* came to both countries. North wrote *Ourselves a Picture* (L, 1866), *The Rich Man and Lazarus* (L, 1869), and *The Way and the Word* (E, 1862). He died on a preaching mission at Tullichewan, Dunbartonshire.

K. Moody Stuart, *Brownlow North* (L, 1878); W. Gibson, *Year of Grace* (E, 1860).

D. B. *Calhoun*

Nova Scotia, *see* Canada; Emigration.

Novations, *see* Innovations.

Nunneries, Medieval. Female religious houses appear to have been unknown in Scotland before the twelfth century. Their foundation is imperfectly documented and uncertainty prevails regarding the order they belonged to. The earliest foundations were probably Benedictine,* becoming Cistercian* at a later date. This is true of Berwick, founded by David I* before 1153, and may also apply to North Berwick, founded by Duncan I, Earl of Fife, *c.*1150. The three or more undisputed Cistercian nunneries, Manuel in W. Lothian (*c.*1164), Eccles (1156), and possibly Coldstream (*c.*1166), both in Berwickshire, the latter the largest of the Scottish houses of women, appeared in the reign of Malcolm IV (1153–65). Other foundations followed in quick succession, but Lincluden in Kirkcudbrightshire (*c.*1174) remained Scotland's only indisputably Benedictine nunnery until its suppression in 1389. Two further Cistercian priories, Elcho in Perthshire (*c.*1241) and St Bothans in Berwickshire, followed in the thirteenth century; a ninth, situated in Galloway and dedicated to St Evoca, is not known of until 1423, when it was derelict. By this time Berwick had also succumbed to the ravages of war. The remaining seven Cistercian priories, all of which appear to have been dedicated to St Mary, were to survive until the Reformation; by then, however, most of them had fallen into the hands of local families, who provided a succession of prioresses.

Of other orders, two houses of Augustinian* canonesses were founded, one at Iona (*c.*1208) and another in the thirteenth century at Perth, the latter being suppressed *c.*1434. An attempt was made to found a Gilbertine* house for women at Dalmilling in Ayrshire between 1219 and 1228. Communities at all Scottish nunneries, all of which ranked as priories, were small. Like all female religious until the seventeenth century, the nuns were bound by strict enclosure. In addition to their life of prayer, they produced embroidered religious artefacts, cared for the aged, and provided elementary schooling for gentlewomen. Though little sign of an active community life is evident, some injection of vitality was provided from the late fifteenth century by the foundation of two houses of Franciscan* nuns (otherwise known as Gray Sisters or Poor Clares) at Aberdour in Fife in 1486 and Dundee in 1501–2, and the establishment of a house of Dominican* nuns at Sciennes near Edinburgh in 1517. This last, one of the most vigorous of Scottish nunneries, with a prioress and at least eleven nuns in 1556, was short lived. It was dedicated to St Catherine of Siena (hence Sciennes).

Easson-Cowan, 143–56; for general information on individual orders see *New Cath. Encyclop.* and *Cath. Encyclop.* IV, 60–4.

I. B. *Cowan*

Nunraw, *see* Cistercians.

O

Oaths. Apart from the irrelevant use of God's name or other religious language in conversation (which may amount to blasphemy*), the oath is important as a solemn statement calling on God (or other deity) to witness the truth of what is being stated or the intention to engage on a course of conduct, and as the form in which that statement is made.

In the past oath-taking was proscribed, for example in relation to incipient trade-unionism under the Combination Acts. Many have considered that Masonic oaths (*see* Freemasonry) are undesirable for similar reasons, but such matters are now of minor importance.

Oaths of office are required of office-bearers in many denominations, and of public officials including judges. By the Security Act, 1707,* on accession to the throne the Sovereign takes an oath to preserve the True Protestant Religion and the Worship, Government, Discipline, Rights and Privileges of the CofS, with a similar oath for English purposes. Under the Nationality Acts, persons becoming naturalized take an Oath of Allegiance.

Oaths have important consequences in legal proceedings, most witnesses still swearing in Scottish form with uplifted hand, a procedure competent throughout the UK under s.3 of the Oaths Act 1978 (c.19). The procedure has been found to increase the telling of the truth by witnesses, not only because it also marks the point at which their words may be open to questions of perjury.

Two major problems have been encountered. First, for religious reasons some decline to 'swear'. This problem originally crystallized in the case of Quakers (*see* Friends, Society of), but is not unknown among other denominations. Secondly, a religious oath makes little sense in the case of one who professes atheism, and perhaps even agnosticism. Charles Bradlaugh, the noted atheist, was barred from the House of Commons, though elected, on the ground that he could not properly take the appropriate oath. The Oaths Act 1888 elided that difficulty.

The Oaths Act 1978 presently regulates most oathtaking in the UK. Under it an oath binds a person to whom it is administered if administered in a form he declares is binding on him (s.4(1)), and is not vitiated by an absence of religious belief (s.4(2)). Christian belief is not required, and Scottish courts deal equally with such beliefs as they can accommodate, or may require affirmation instead. Affirmation is open to those who wish to affirm rather than swear, and may be required by a court (ss. 5 and 6. Oaths Act 1978).

See also Burgess Oath; Non-jurors.

F. Lyall, *Of Presbyters and Kings* (A, 1980), 140–2.

F. Lyall

Ogilvie, James (1695–1776), CofS minister at St Nicholas', Aberdeen, 1729–76. Apart from a brief ministry at Inchtyre, Perthshire, 1726–9, Ogilvie spent nearly all his life in Aberdeen. He was educated at both King's College and Marischal College and was licensed by the Presbytery of Aberdeen in 1719. In 1720 he was ordained by the same Presbytery and inducted to Footdee, whence he was translated briefly to Inchtyre. Ogilvie's reputation as an evangelical preacher went far beyond Aberdeen. His advice was sought by William McCulloch* when preparing for publication the testimonies of those who had been converted in the Cambuslang Wark of 1742 (*see* Revivals). Ogilvie was an admirer of George Whitefield* with whom he corresponded, and he was host to John Wesley* when he visited Aberdeen. He was described as 'a sweet-blooded man' with 'a very taking gift'.

A. Fawcett, *The Cambuslang Revival* (L, 1971); *FES* VI, 38.

H. R. Sefton

Ogilvie, John (Saint) (*c.* 1579–1615), RC martyr*. Son, most probably, of Walter Ogilvie of Milton (Keith, Banffshire), he went abroad in 1592. Converted to Catholicism, he entered the Scots College* of Douai (then at Louvain) in 1596 and the

OGILVIE, JAMES NICOLL

Jesuit* college at Olmutz (Bohemia) in 1598. He became a Jesuit novice in 1599 and studied or taught in Central Europe in 1610; then, ordained priest at Paris, he taught at Rouen.

Returning to Scotland in late 1613, he ministered as a priest in the north-east and Edinburgh. In spring 1614, for reasons unknown, he journeyed to London and Paris. Having resumed missionary work in Scotland, he was captured in Glasgow in October 1614. There followed months of interrogation and disputation, his chief antagonist being Archbishop John Spottiswoode.* In December he was examined in Edinburgh before lords of council and tortured by eight days of enforced sleeplessness to extort names of associates. Finally, after interrogation concerning papal and royal jurisdiction, he was condemned for treason and hanged at Glasgow Cross on 10 March (N.S.) 1615.

A process for beatification begun in 1628–9 soon lapsed, but a new process resulted in his beatification in December 1929. Canonization, following acceptance of a miraculous healing, took place on 17 October 1976. Ogilvie is the only RC judicially condemned and executed in Scotland for his religion, doubtless because he impugned royal prerogative during a period of episcopacy.

W. E. Brown, *John Ogilvie* (L, 1925); T. Collins, *Martyr in Scotland* (L, 1955), 231–64; *St John Ogilvie SJ 1579–1615* (G, 1979); W. J. Anderson, 'A Jesuit that Calls Himself Ogilvy', *IR* 15 (1964), 56–65; M. Dilworth, 'Three Documents relating to St John Ogilvie', *IR* 34 (1983), 51–65.

M. Dilworth

Ogilvie, James Nicoll (1860–1926), CofS missionary statesman. Born at Monymusk, the son of the head of Gordon's Hospital, Aberdeen, he studied at the Universities of Aberdeen (MA, 1881; DD, 1911), Edinburgh and Leipzig. In 1885 Edinburgh Presbytery ordained him to serve as chaplain in the Indian Ecclesiastical Establishment in Madras. After twenty years' service in India, he became minister of New Greyfriars, Edinburgh (1905–19), but his most influential work was done as convener of the Foreign Missions Committee 1909–25. During this period he served on the 1910 World Missions Conference* Continuation Committee (1911), delivered Croall* (1914), Baird* (*The Apostles of India*, L, 1915), and Duff* lectures (1923; *Our Empire's Debt to Missions*, L, 1924), and was Vice-President (1921–5) and President (1926) of the (later World) Alliance of Reformed Churches.* He was the elder statesman of CofS missions, in an era of continuing buoyancy of missions in the Kirk.

'*Afric's Sunny Fountains*'. *Travel Notes*... (E, 1921); *An India Pilgrimage. Travel Notes*... (E, 1922).

FES I, 36, VII, 579; *Who Was Who, 1916–1928*, 791.

D. F. Wright

Old Light, *see* New Light.

OLIPHANT, MARGARET

Oldham, Joseph Houldsworth (1874–1969), missionary and Church statesman. Born in India, he was educated at Edinburgh Academy and Oxford University. He returned to India in 1897 with the YMCA. Invalided home in 1901, he entered New College, Edinburgh. Though licensed by the UFC he was never ordained.

In 1908 he became Organizing Secretary of the forthcoming World Missionary Conference of 1910 (*see* Edinburgh Conference). He was so successful that he became the Secretary of the Continuation Committee, and also first editor of the *International Review of Missions* in 1912. His was a key role in founding the International Missionary Council in 1921. Oldham also played an important part in the 'Life and Work' movement; as chairman he shaped the 1937 International Congress, Oxford.

Throughout the twenties and thirties he was a very influential lobbyist on African affairs. He made important contributions to ending forced labour in Kenya and obtaining the Devonshire Declaration (1923), whereby Westminster made African interests paramount in East Africa. In 1931, after the publication of the Hilton-Young Commission's *Report on Closer Union of the East and Central Africa Territories*, he was the organizer again of public pressure to prevent Britain handing over autonomy to the white settlers in these territories.

Increasingly after 1930 he turned his attention to awakening the laity to their missionary task in the modern world. In retirement in the fifties he actively aided the Capricorn Society in the new Central African Federation. This brought him into conflict with the majority of Christians and missionaries in Northern Rhodesia and Nyasaland who had been his allies in the pre-war years. Oldham was a DD of Edinburgh (1931) and Oxford (1937), and a CBE (1951).

The World and the Gospel (L, 1916); *Christianity and the Race Problem* (L, 1924); *The New Christian Adventure* (NY, 1929); *Life is Commitment* (L, 1953); *New Hope in Africa* (L, 1955).

Who Was Who, 1961–1970, 853; *DNB 1961–1970*, 806–8. Oldham's papers are now in New College Library, Edinburgh.

A. C. Ross

Oliphant, Margaret Oliphant Wilson (1828–97), novelist, biographer, literary historian and mainstay of *Blackwood's Edinburgh Magazine*. Born in Wallyford, Midlothian, at the age of ten she moved to Liverpool with her parents, where she was educated at home. The first of her ninety-eight novels was published in 1849. Oliphant's work soon had to support an elder brother, 'shipwrecked' by drink, and then her artist husband's ventures. After only seven years of marriage (1852–9) she became the breadwinner for her surviving children and a host of other relatives. She tried her hand at kailyard fiction (*see* Literature, Religion in Scottish), 'romans à thèse', domestic romance and melodrama, before lighting upon her most successful formula in the nine-volume *Chronicles of Carlingford* series (1863–6), which clearly owed much to

George Eliot and Trollope in their imagined provincial setting and the importance of religion in defining social boundaries. The complicating sense of irony that plays over *The Perpetual Curate* (3 vols, E, 1864) and *Miss Marjoribanks* (3 vols, E, 1866) is, however, distinctively her own. Her own 'outsider' status as a woman and a Scot drew her to become the biographer of such unorthodox religious figures as Edward Irving,* Montalembert and Laurence Oliphant. She also shared with them a mystical streak which surfaced in her stories of the occult and of the afterlife. She also compiled biographies of John Tulloch* and Thomas Chalmers.* Predeceased by all her children, she died in London.

The Autobiography and Letters (E, 1899), contains list of *Blackwood's* contributions, ed. E. Jay (O, 1990); J. S. Clarke, *Margaret Oliphant: A Bibliography* (U. of Queensland St Lucia, 1986), lists fiction; *DNB Suppl.* III, 230–4; V. and R. A. Colby, *The Equivocal Virtue: Mrs Oliphant and the Victorian Literary Market Place* (NY, 1966); M. Williams, *Margaret Oliphant: A Critical Biography* (Basingstoke, 1986).

E. Jay

Oman, John Wood (1860–1939), philosophical theologian. Brought up in Orkney,* he was privately tutored until university entrance. He prepared for ministry in the UPC and was ordained to Alnwick, Northumberland, by the Presbyterian Church of England, of whose General Assembly he was Moderator in 1931. He served that Church's Westminster College, Cambridge, from 1907 as Professor of Systematic Theology and Apologetics, and from 1922 also as Principal.

As an Edinburgh student he was moved by the debates on biblical criticism* (*see* Smith, William Robertson). The key notes of his life and thought were recognized as reverence, freedom and sincerity. He made and perceptively introduced the first English translation of Schleiermacher's 1799 speeches *On Religion* (L, 1893). Self-confessedly no orator, Oman struggled to express difficult thinking in ordinary language. While his chief work, in strong contrast with emerging Neo-orthodoxy,* was *The Natural and the Supernatural* (C, 1931), his most enduring contribution has been *Grace and Personality* (C, 1917, ³L, 1925), which persuasively presents grace and faith in what Oman believed to be the absence of any infallible authority.

DNB 1931–1940, 657–9; G. Alexander and H. H. Farmer in Oman's *Honest Religion* (C, 1941), xv–xxxii; F. G. Healey, *Religion and Reality: The Theology of John Oman* (E, L, 1965); Y. Woodfin, 'John Wood Oman ... A Critical Study ...' (PhD, Edinburgh University, 1962).

M. H. Cressey

Orange Order, a militant Protestant organization. The tradition on which the Orange Order is based originated in the events in Ireland* following the Revolution of 1688 and the accession of William of Orange as William II.* In particular, the decisive defeat of the forces of ex-King James VII* at the Battle of the Boyne on 1 July 1690 (12 July new style) was regularly commemorated by Protestants.

However, as an institution the Orange Order was founded a century later in 1795 as part of the sequence of reaction and counter-reaction which characterized the troubled sectarian relations in County Armagh in the 1790s. It developed a lodge structure and elaborate hierarchy, with functions that blended the social, political and religious. The organization was transmitted to Britain through military units which had served in Ireland and by Protestant migrants. By 1807 there were several lodges in Scotland.

Orangemen took an active part in resistance to Catholic Emancipation* but in general, while Orangeism attracted a degree of working class support, it did not in the early nineteenth century become a mass movement in Britain. In the early 1830s there were a number of outbreaks of sectarian violence in south-west Scotland in which Orangemen were implicated. Meanwhile a vigorous but largely unsuccessful attempt was made by Colonel W. B. Fairman to establish the Order as a basis for a revived populist Toryism. Radical criticism of Orangeism led to its proscription by the government in 1836.

The Order gradually revived during the next few decades, the 1870s being years of particularly rapid growth. In 1878 there were an estimated 15,000 Orangemen in Glasgow alone. Up to the early 1920s there were close links with the Conservative Party, but thereafter Tory Irish policy tended to alienate the Orangemen. In the twentieth century the Orange Order has remained a significant force in western Scotland, and has been directly linked with Protestants in Northern Ireland. However, it has generally been a force for relative moderation, eschewing Ratcliffe's Scottish Protestant League in the 1930s and, after the renewal of conflict in Northern Ireland in 1969, distancing itself from Ulster Protestant paramilitary organizations.

See also Anti-Catholic Societies; Immigration; Roman Catholicism.

H. Senior, *Orangeism in Ireland and Britain 1795–1836* (L, 1966); T. Gallagher, *Glasgow: The Uneasy Peace* (Manchester, 1987); S. Bruce, *No Pope of Rome* (E, 1985); I. G. C. Hutchison, *A Political History of Scotland 1832–1914* (E, 1986); R. M. Sibbett, *Orangeism in Ireland and throughout the Empire* (2 vols, L, 1939); G. Walker and T. Gallagher (eds), *Sermons and Battle Hymns. Protestant Popular Culture in Modern Scotland* (E, 1990); E. W. McFarland, *Protestants First: Orangeism in Nineteenth Century Scotland* (E, 1990).

J. R. Wolffe

Ordinal and Service Book, The, of the CofS (1931, ²1952, ³1962), book containing rites for the ordination* and induction* of ministers, and services for the admission of readers* and the commissioning of deacons and deaconesses, together with various orders for the dedication of a church, and an order for Holy Communion for use in courts of the Church. This last was to appear with some modification and expansion in the 1940 *Book of Common Order*.* The Ordination Service contains parts which are mandatory – the narrative, the splendid Preamble concerning the faith of the Church which was part of the 1929 Basis of Union, the questions to the ordinand, the Formula,* and the stipulation that ordination should be by prayer and the laying on of hands. The full service in the *Ordinal* is, however, followed closely in most Presbyteries, although its authority is simply that it has been recommended by the General Assembly's Committee on Public Worship and Aids to Devotion.* This service, and in particular its prayer of ordination, has been much admired, and influential outside Scotland. It was used as a model by the Church of South India and the Church of North India in the production of their own ordinals. A new *Form and Order for the Ordination of a Minister* was published in 1988 for experimental use. This uses modern and inclusive language and makes only minor modifications in the mandatory elements. The ordination prayer and the charges to minister and congregation are fresh and dignified. There is a stronger emphasis on ministry as being shared between congregation and minister, and the congregation has a slightly larger role in the service. The sacramental responsibilities of the minister are more stressed than previously, and there is a suggestion that the Lord's Supper may be celebrated as part of the service, the newly ordained minister presiding; failing which the new minister should preside at Communion as soon as possible after ordination.

The EpCS produced an impressive new Ordinal in 1984.

D. B. *Forrester*

Ordination. In medieval Scotland, as in the rest of Christendom, ordination was regarded as an unrepeatable sacrament* which conferred a *character indelebilis* ('indelible character') and special authority on the ordained person. In the rite of ordination, which became increasingly complex, the heart was prayer invoking the Spirit, together with the laying on of the hands of the bishop. This was understood as placing the ordained person within an historic apostolic succession in a hierarchically organized ministry.

In the early years of the Scottish Reformation* the medieval rite, the understanding of ordination as a sacrament, and the very term 'ordination' were all rejected as irretrievably involved with superstition. The laying on of hands was specifically discountenanced: 'for albeit the Apostles used imposition of hands, yet seeing the miracle is ceased, the using of the ceremonie we judge not necessarie' (*FBD* 102). There is plentiful evidence that many ministers were 'inaugurated' without the imposition of hands. It is impossible to sustain the argument that (re)ordination was unnecessary as all the initial ministers were already in Roman orders; indeed Roman priests had to renounce their orders before becoming ministers. The ingenious argument that the lifting up of hands in prayer and the imposition of hands are in effect the same is hardly convincing (T. F. Torrance, 'Consecration and Ordination', *SJT* 11, 1958, 251–2). The Scottish Reformers saw themselves as making a clean break with medieval understandings of ministry and ordination.

Yet in the Scottish Reformation there was a constant stress on the necessity for a 'lawful ministry'.* The central functions of this ministry were preaching, the administration of the sacraments of baptism and the Lord's Supper, and the exercise of discipline:* 'In a Church reformed or tending to reformation, none ought to presume either to preach, either yet to minister the sacraments till that orderly they be called to the same' (*FBD* 96; *see* Call). In place of ordination, services of inauguration and admission are enjoined. The nature of these services is clear from the Genevan *Forme of Prayers* (W. D. Maxwell, *The Liturgical Portions of the Genevan Service Book*, E, 1931, 164–8; Maxwell adds the term ordination to the heading), *FBD* (96–105, 204–7), and the order used by Knox in 1560 for the election of John Spottiswoode* as Superintendent* of Lothian and printed in successive editions of *BCO** as a model for all 'elections' of ministers. Here, after the sermon, the people are first asked if they will receive the new minister, and then a series of questions are addressed to the minister-elect. Then comes a prayer asking for the Holy Spirit to be sent upon the new minister to guide and strengthen him in his duties. The other ministers and elders take the new minister by the hand, and the blessing and Psalm 23 conclude the service.

SBD (1578) restored the term 'ordination' and the practice of laying on of hands, although there is much evidence that it was some time before uniformity of practice was established. Ministers are called by God and elected by the eldership with the consent of the congregation. Ordination follows, which is 'the separation and sanctifying of the person appointed by God and his kirk after he be well tried and found qualified'. The service consists of 'fasting and earnest prayer, and imposition of hands of the eldership' (cf. *SBD* 180). There is still little, if any, interest shown in ordination as providing the essential links in ministerial succession, or as conferring a special grace or character. A further effort to ensure uniformity of practice was the publication in 1620 of *The Forme and Maner of Ordaining Ministers; and Consecrating of Arch-Bishops and Bishops used in the Church of Scotland*.

The Directory for the Ordination of Ministers in the Westminster Form of Presbyterial Church-Government (1645) has provided the structure for all modern Scottish Presbyterian ordination rites. In all it is strongly stressed that Christ is the minister of ordination through the Presbytery, that prayer with fasting and the laying on of hands is essential, and that a minister is given to a congregation.

An increasingly 'high' doctrine of ordination became influential as a result of the work of the Scottish Church Society* and the high church movement (*see* Scoto-Catholics) and as a response to ecumenical discussions. This is best represented today in the work of T. F. Torrance,* who sees ordination as a special form of participation in Christ's self-consecration on our behalf: 'Those ordained are to be regarded as drawn in a special way within the sphere of Christ's Self-consecration so that it is only as they share in His Self-consecration that they can minister the Word to others in His Name.' Torrance also strongly emphasizes historical succession: 'The historical Jesus still commissions His ministers through that eternal and historical succession, and therefore the historical mediation of ordination is of fundamental importance as attesting the binding of the Church to the historical Jesus and the historical Revelation.'

But it must be said that there is great diversity in the way ordination is understood today within the CofS and the other Scottish Presbyterian churches, although the practice of ordination is remarkably uniform and unchanging. Yet elders* continue to be ordained for life, though normally without laying on of hands.

In non-Presbyterian Protestant churches, ordination of pastors is generally observed for the maintenance of good order. In Baptist churches since the early nineteenth century, ordination has usually involved 'the laying on of hands', and is thereby distinguished from the 'setting apart' of candidates for other areas of service. In Brethren and other independent bodies which do not practise ordination, there is an increasing awareness of the value of 'setting apart' of members for particular roles within the fellowship.

H. J. Wotherspoon and J. M. Kirkpatrick, *A Manual of Church Doctrine according to the Church of Scotland*, rev. T. F. Torrance and R. S. Wright (L, 1960), ch. IV; D. Shaw, 'The Inauguration of Ministers in Scotland, 1560–1620', *RSCHS* 16 (1966), 35–62; W. McMillan, *The Worship of the Scottish Reformed Church, 1550–1638* (L, 1931), ch. 27.

D. B. Forrester

Ordination Vows, the affirmative answers given by the candidate to the questions put on the occasion of his or her ordination.* In the case of ordination to the ministry in the present-day CofS, they are found as an Appendix to the Act of Union, 1929. The first three concern basic Christian verities (the Trinity, and Christ as saviour and Lord; the Word of God as 'the supreme rule of faith and life'; 'the fundamental doctrines' in the Westminster* Confession – the modified subscription* resulting from the Declaratory Acts*). Two deal with acceptance of Presbyterian* Church order and commitment to build up the Church, and the last two with the candidate's motives and dedication. An eighth question, about acceptance of the call* and the pledge to fulfil it, is added when a person is also being inducted to a pastoral charge.* The satisfactory answering of the questions is followed by the signing of the Formula.* On every induction* to a charge or admission to an ecclesiastical office the candidate has to declare his or her continued adherence to these vows.

In the pre-Union* CofS the vows, though differently phrased, were substantially identical except that the first question was omitted and that the last included a requirement 'to rule well your own family'. In the former UFC the questions were again practically the same, but here there was included a declaration that Christ is King and Head of the Church and that civil rulers possess no jurisdiction in spiritual affairs.

In the case of ordination of elders* in the present-day CofS one question is put: 'Do you believe the fundamental doctrines of the Christian faith; do you promise to seek the unity and peace of this Church; to uphold the doctrine, worship, government and discipline thereof; and to take your due part in the administration of its affairs?' They then, like ministers, sign the Formula.

Cox, 569, 573–4.

A. Herron

Ordo Salutis, Latin for 'order of salvation', the systematic ordering of the aspects of salvation.

It was Reformed theologians in the sixteenth and seventeenth centuries who gave most attention to the development of an *ordo salutis*. (The term itself first appeared early in the eighteenth century.) There has, however, been much disagreement over the centuries on the 'order' of doctrines, and more recently some Reformed scholars have questioned the value of the exercise. This criticism has been particularly marked in comments on the Westminster Confession.*

Whatever form may be developed, however, it is necessary to give some analysis and description of the process by which the Christian believer comes to and goes on in faith.

The process by which this is accomplished is described in terms of various doctrines. Some describe the change in the sinner's status: justification and adoption; others the change in the sinner's condition: regeneration, conversion, repentance and sanctification. And several doctrines overlap, including effectual calling and union with Christ. The *ordo salutis* is the construct whereby these are related together in a logical (although not chronological) manner, relating to the Christian experience of the believer. It is based particularly on Romans 8:28–30.

Calvin was slightly unusual in that he treated most of salvation under the broad general heading of sanctification in order to make the point that the entire purpose of God in salvation is to make us holy. By contrast, RC theologians encompassed everything under justification.

In Scottish theology the main discussions on the *ordo salutis* have centred on where election, repentance and assurance should fit into the scheme. For example, Calvin deals with the doctrine of election in the *Institutes* after he has dealt with the doctrine of Christ. Is there a natural progression from this, through the major work of John Knox* on the subject, to the covenant theology* of Robert Rollock* and on still further to the high predestinarian emphasis of the developed federal theology in Samuel Rutherford* and David Dickson?* Or, as some argue, was this development a reversal of Calvin's *ordo salutis*?

The arguments about the relationship between faith and assurance* at the beginning of the eighteenth century in the Marrow controversy* are another case in point. Is assurance of the essence of saving faith or does it follow after faith? The precise relationship between these doctrines has many implications both for the understanding of other doctrines and for the preaching of the gospel. Or what about the debates in the late seventeenth and early eighteenth centuries in the CofS and then in the Secession Church* on whether repentance was a condition of faith or a consequence of faith? There were also parallel discussions as to the difference between legal repentance and evangelical repentance.

In all these controversies, the key issue was the *ordo salutis*, that is, how precisely these doctrines related to what goes before and what comes after in God's *schema*.

L. Berkhof, *Systematic Theology* (L, 1971), 415–22; H. Hoeksema, *Reformed Dogmatics* (Grand Rapids, 1966), 446–51; J. Murray, *Redemption Accomplished and Applied* (Grand Rapids, 1955); J. Calvin, *Institutes* 3.

A. T. B. McGowan

Organs, see Musical Instruments in Worship.

Original Secession Church, formed of various Secession* Churches which maintained the establishment principle (*see* Church and State*) and the obligation of the national covenants. These Old Light elements from both the Antiburgher and Burgher wings of the Secession (*see* Burgess Oath) merged in 1842.

One of these components was the Antiburgher Constitutional Associate Presbytery, formed by five ministers who under the guidance of Archibald Bruce* withdrew in 1806 from the General Associate Synod* when it embraced Voluntaryism.* Another departure from the General Associate Synod took place in 1820, when the minority protested against the Synod's union with the New Light* Burghers to form the USec.C. The minority called themselves the Associate Synod* of Protesters.* From the first they sought to negotiate a union with the Constitutional Presbytery, and this was effected in 1827 on the basis of an Original Secession Testimony (*see* Testimonies), the historical part of which was composed by Thomas M'Crie* of the Constitutional Presbytery, and the doctrinal segment by George Stevenson* of the Synod of Protesters. The resulting Original Secession Synod (properly, the Associate Synod of Original Seceders) observed in the following year a solemn renewal of the National Covenant* and the Solemn League and Covenant.*

The Burgher component in the Original Secession Church was the Remanent Synod, which resisted a union by the majority of the Original Burgher Synod with the CofS in 1839 (*see* Associate Synod). The Original Burgher Synod had explored union with the Constitutional Presbytery since 1819, but had become attracted to the rising evangelical party in the CofS. In 1832 negotiations were opened with the Original Secession Synod, but the Burgess Oath stood in the way for conservative patriarch George Paxton* of the Antiburgher body. Paxton died in 1835 and the Original Secession Synod joined in 1842 with the Remanent Synod to create the Original Secession Church, more properly 'The Synod of United Original Seceders'. The union took place upon an acknowledgement that, because of the defects which had existed in the national Church, the swearing of the Burgess Oath to defend the established religion had been sinful.

Many in the Original Secession Church were sympathetic with the Non-Intrusionists* during the Ten Years' Conflict* in the CofS, hailed the adherence of the FC to the establishment principle, and saw the Disruption* as similar to the departure of the Secession brethren a century earlier. The primary question at issue in proposals for union between the new FC and the Original Secession Church was whether the FC's standards should be extended beyond those of the Revolution settlement (*see* Church and State) to include the continued obligation of the national covenants of the Second Reformation* period (*see* Covenanters). Responding to these concerns, the FC in 1851 adopted an act and declaration identifying herself as the same Church which had espoused the Second Reformation. The next year most Original Secession ministers joined the FC. The Original Secession Church's minority – thirteen ministers led by James Anderson of Carluke and John Aitken of Aberdeen – contended that since acknowledging the obligation of the covenants on posterity was a qualification for Church fellowship in the unions of 1827 and 1842, it should continue to be a fundamental article in any union. The Church's majority acknowledged the obligation of the covenants, but did not consider that the Scriptures warranted making such historical considerations an obstacle to Church fellowship. The Original Secession Church survived until 1956, when it joined the CofS, and one congregation was received into the FC.

ASOSC; T. M'Crie, *Life of Thomas M'Crie* (E, 1840); *Testimony of Associate Synod of Original Seceders* (1827); J. M'Kerrow, *History of the Secession Church* (E, 1848); J. Macleod, *Scottish Theology* (E, ³1974).

S. Isbell

Orkney, Early Christianity in. The earliest known Christian contacts with Orkney are described in Adomnan's* account of St Columba's* visit to the court of Brude (Bridei mac Maelchon, *c.*561). Columba commanded the Pictish King to issue instructions to his under-king in Orkney that no evil should befall Christian missionaries then in northern waters. As a result Cormac was saved from almost certain death when later he arrived in the islands.

Contacts at a similar date, if not even earlier, are

implied by the life of St Ailbe (early sixth century), who desired to escape from the cares of a busy monastery in Ireland to live as a hermit in Thule. In the event Ailbe was prevented from leaving, but the story suggests that, even at that date, others may have sought solitude in the Northern Isles. A number of sites have been identified on headlands and rocky sea-stacks which illustrate the austerity of these eremetical retreats.

Despite these contacts, it seems unlikely that there was an organized Christian Church before the early eighth century. It has recently been suggested that a network of St Peter-dedications relate to the Northumbrian initiative in Pictland c.715 and that these churches provided centres from which clergy served numerous field chapels. These *urisland* chapels, so called because they were often distributed one per urisland or ounceland, are actually of uncertain date. It is possible that the system was revitalized by the Norse following their conversion, but before the establishment of regular parishes. Dedications to St Boniface and St Tredwell in Papa Westray also point to a cult of Northumbrian provenance. On the basis of these dedications, and substantial unexplored remains, it has been suggested that Papa Westray may have provided the site of a Pictish bishopric of Orkney and Shetland.

The relationship between the early Norse settlers (early ninth century) and the Christian Church is not clear. Immediate destruction of the Church by Viking marauders may have taken place, but is by no means certain. A number of points suggest the possibility of Christian survival, at least for a time. Certainly the Norse, who seem to have retained no real recollection of the lay inhabitants, preserved memories of the *Papae*, the white-robed clergy of the Celtic Church. Seven place-names incorporating the element *Papa* commemorate the sites of communities which appear to have been monastic rather than eremetical. One possible interpretation of the Life of St Findan, an Irish saint who escaped in Orkney while being carried off into slavery in Norway, is that a bishop and a Pictish monastic house still existed in Orkney as late as the middle of the ninth century.

The evidence of Norse graves suggests that the Norse adopted Christian practices at a relatively early date, so their conversion may not have been so sudden and dramatic as the *Orkneyinga Saga* implies. This work describes how Olaf Trygvasson, King of Norway, on his homeward voyage, captured the Orkney Earl, Sigurd Digre, at Osmundwall, and presented him with the stark choice of accepting Christianity or seeing the islands put to fire and sword. The saga suggests that Sigurd was a reluctant convert, and seems to imply that he died an obdurate heathen when his magic banner of Odin failed him at the battle of Clontarf (1014).

Perhaps Odinism indeed continued as an aristocratic cult, or perhaps the saga merely uses Sigurd's supposed heathenism as a literary contrast to the Christian innovations of his son, Earl Thorfinn* the Mighty. After a long and bitter struggle to gain sole possession of the earldom, Thorfinn made a pilgrimage to Rome (c.1050) during which he probably made the arrangements which resulted in the appointment of Orkney's first post-Pictish Bishop, Turolf. In the later part of Earl Thorfinn's life he settled in Birsay, where he built the cathedral of Christchurch for his Bishop (the actual site is disputed). Turolf and his immediate successors were Hamburg-Bremen consecrations, but the right to consecrate Orkney bishops was contested by the archbishops of York, with the result that there was a period in the early twelfth century when rival bishops asserted their claims to the bishopric.

The martyrdom of Earl Magnus* Erlendsson, executed c.1115 on the island of Egilsay by his cousin Earl Hakon Palsson, provided Orkney with its patron saint. The promotion of Magnus's sainthood had much to do with the claims of Magnus's nephew and heir, Rognvald Kalisson, who encouraged the cult and emphasized his own relationship to the saint. Preparatory to launching an invasion from Norway, Rognvald was also keen to secure an alliance with the Bishop. The sequence of events suggest the political motives for Magnus's canonization. First, Bishop William pronounced Magnus's sainthood (c.1135), then Rognvald successfully invaded the islands (c.1136). Thereafter work began on the building of St Magnus Cathedral (c.1137) in which the saint's relics were installed. Bishops had previously been 'court bishops' living under the shadow of the earls, but now they became leading figures in their own right. The bishopric was endowed with large blocks of former earldom territory, and it may be assumed that rapid progress was made in parochial organization. The building of the cathedral symbolized the end of the Viking isolation and the emergence of Orkney into full membership of Western European Christendom.

B. E. Crawford, *Scandinavian Scotland* (Leicester, 1987); id., *St Magnus Cathedral* (A, 1988); H. Löwe, 'Findan von Rheinau', *Studi Medievali*, 3rd ser., xxxvi (Spoleto, 1985); *Orkney Heritage*, II (Kirkwall, 1983); H. Palsson and P. Edwards, *Orkneyinga Saga* (L, 1981); W. P. L. Thomson, *History of Orkney* (E, 1987).

W. P. L. Thomson

Orr, James (1844–1913), theologian, apologist and polemicist. Born in Glasgow, he studied at the UP Divinity Hall, Edinburgh (1868–72), and Glasgow University where, under the tutelage of John Veitch (one of Scotland's last Common-Sense* philosophers) and John* and Edward Caird,* he acquired a respect for reason's role in theology. After a pastoral ministry at East Bank UP Church, Hawick (1874–91), he delivered a lecture series which was afterwards published as *The Christian View of God and the World* (E, 1893). This work, which proved to be his greatest, was widely acclaimed and launched him on a prolific academic career. He was appointed to the church history chair at the UP College (1891–1900), and soon succeeded John Cairns* as the UPC's leading theologian. He had a key role in the UFC union of 1900, thereafter teaching systematic theology and apologetics at the UFC College, Glasgow (1900–

13). He also came to exercise a significant influence in North America.

While retreating from strict Calvinism (he campaigned in the 1870s for modified subscription* to the Westminster Confession, and helped to draft the UP Declaratory Statement of 1879), he defended the central tenets of evangelical orthodoxy with wide-ranging scholarship. He was one of the earliest and principal British critics of Albrecht Ritschl's thought. In *The Ritschlian Theology and the Evangelical Faith* (L, 1897) and elsewhere, Orr insisted that Ritschlianism was opposed to genuine Christianity, and was intellectually untenable because of its limitation of the role of reason in Christian thought and experience. In *The Progress of Dogma* (L, 1901), Orr tried to counter Ritschlian Adolf Harnack's negative verdict on the history of dogma by arguing that it has unfolded according to a recognizable inner logic. By regarding this logical movement as a manifestation of God's hand in history, Orr sought to vindicate the orthodox doctrines that the movement produced.

In *The Problem of the Old Testament* (L, 1906), which was prompted partly by his Glasgow colleague George Adam Smith's* advocacy of the documentary hypothesis, Orr argued for the 'essential Mosaicity' of the Pentateuch, and for a traditional construction of Old Testament history. With respect to Scripture generally, Orr affirmed its plenary inspiration and remarkable accuracy, but regarded inerrancy as apologetically 'suicidal' (see his *Revelation and Inspiration*, L, 1910).

Orr treated Charles Darwin's theory of humanity's origin as a serious threat to the Christian doctrines of humanity and sin. Initially he appeared comfortable with theistic evolution, but later, in *God's Image in Man* (L, 1905), he stressed the necessity of supernatural interruptions of the evolutionary process to account for the human being as an embodied soul, and still later, in *Sin as a Problem of Today* (L, 1910), he argued that the idea of moral evolution (as articulated by F. R. Tennant and others) undermined the seriousness of sin and humanity's accountability for it. Finally, he held firmly to orthodox Christological formulations in the face of alternative assessments of the historical Jesus. In such works as *The Virgin Birth of Christ* (L, 1907), he defended theologically as well as biblically the virginal conception of the Mediator.

A general lack of support for his views within the scholarly community, combined with his own deep-seated populist instincts and common-sense convictions, led Orr in later years to direct his appeals primarily toward the Christian public (see, e.g. his *The Bible Under Trial*, L, 1907 and his contributions to *The Fundamentals*,* 1910–15). His last great work as general editor of the five-volume *International Standard Bible Encyclopaedia* (Chicago, 1915) constituted a substantial and enduring means of extending conservative orthodoxy's line of defence.

Orr's contribution was decisively shaped by the convictions that evangelical orthodoxy is ultimately self-authenticating, that truth comprises a unity of interconnected whole, and that genuine Christian belief implies a two-storey supernaturalist cosmology. The significance of Orr's theological contribution lies in neither its brilliance nor its originality, but in the breadth of his grasp of orthodox theology, the exhaustiveness of the reading upon which his conclusions were based, and the vigour with which he defended and diffused his views.

See Systematic Theology.

G. Scorgie, *A Call for Continuity: The Theological Contribution of James Orr* (Macon, GA, 1989); A. Sell, *Defending and Declaring the Faith* (Exeter, 1987); A. Neely, 'James Orr' (PhD, Southwestern Baptist Sem., Forth Worth, TX, 1960); J. Rogers and D. McKim, *The Authority and Interpretation of the Bible* (San Francisco, 1979); P. Toon, *The Development of Doctrine in the Church* (Grand Rapids, 1979); *FUFCS* 581–2; Small II, 459.

G. G. *Scorgie*

Oswald (*c*.605–42) King of Northumbria. Born into the Bernician royal family, Oswald was the son of Ethelfrith, King of Northumbria. When Edwin of Deira seized the Northumbrian throne in 616, Oswald with other members of the royal family fled into exile among the Picts* and Scots, where they were converted to Christianity and baptized. Oswald and his brothers returned to Bernicia after the death of Edwin in 634. The British king Cadwalla slew the elder two, Eanfric and Osric, and ruled Bernicia for a year before Oswald, with a small force, defeated him in 635 at a battle near Hexham. Oswald then succeeded to the throne and reunited Bernicia and Deira as the kingdom of Northumbria. He married Cyneburga, daughter of Cynegils, King of Wessex, for whom he stood as godfather.

Oswald was anxious to promote Christianity in his realm and evidently favoured the Celtic form, owing to his instruction in Scotland (*see* Celtic Church). He sent for a bishop from Iona,* which led to the arrival of St Aidan (*see* Celtic Saints) who was given the island of Lindisfarne as his episcopal seat (*see* Early Ecclesiastical Sites).

Oswald's reign was cut short after only eight years, when he was killed in battle at Maserfield by the pagan king, Penda of Mercia. His body was mutilated on Penda's orders; the head and arms were raised on stakes on the battlefield, to be recovered later by his brother Oswy, who had the head buried on Lindisfarne and the arms at Bamburgh. Oswald's body was eventually translated to the monastery of Bardney by his niece Osthryd, wife of Ethelbert of Mercia, then moved again in the tenth century to Gloucester by Ethelfled, Lady of the Mercians.

Bede* commemorates Oswald as a pre-eminent Christian king and martyr.* He reports that his relics caused several miracles of healing, even the very ground on which his blood had spilled. Before his battle with Cadwalla, Oswald had erected a cross on the field, the remains of which were said to have curative powers. Oswald's head was supposedly buried with the body of St Cuthbert and was

OSWALD, JAMES

discovered at the opening of Cuthbert's tomb in Durham in 1827 (*see* Celtic Saints; Anglo-Saxon Saints). His cult grew up almost immediately; his feast day, 5 August, has been kept in the English Church from the eighth century and there are several churches dedicated to him.

Although Oswald is venerated as an Anglo-Saxon king and saint, he clearly had strong connections with the northern Scottish kingdoms. Bede hints that his political influence extended to overlordship of Scottish Dál Riata and the Lothian region; very probably Oswald laid the foundations for his successors to expand the kingdom into lowland Scotland. By supporting St Aidan and the church of Iona, he opened Northumbria to the influence of Celtic Christianity and its promulgation in the north, as opposed to the Roman form in the southern kingdoms. Despite the political and religious controversies which ensued, Oswald's actions had a significant effect on the development of the Church in both northern England and southern Scotland.

B. Colgrave and R. A. B. Mynors (eds), *Bede's Ecclesiastical History of the English People* (O, 1969); Alcuin, *The Bishops, Kings and Saints*, ed. P. Godman (O, 1982); H. Moisl, 'The Bernician Royal Dynasty and the Irish in the Seventh Century', *Peritia* 2 (1983), 103–26; A. P. Smyth, *Warlords and Holy Men* (L, 1984); P. H. Blair, *An Introduction to Anglo-Saxon England* (C, ²1977).

D. A. Bray

Oswald, James (1703–93), Moderate* divine and philosopher of the Scottish Realist* school. Oswald was minister at Dunnet, Caithness (1726–30), and at Methven, Perthshire (1730–83). He was Moderator of the General Assembly in 1765. After his retirement in 1783 he became one of the founders of the Glasgow Society of the Sons of the Clergy, to which he bequeathed £100. He was awarded Glasgow's DD in 1765. In 1766 he opened the debate on the 'Schism Overture'* on patronage* and secession* in the General Assembly.

An Appeal to Common Sense on Behalf of Religion,

OVERTURE

2 vols (E, 1766, 1772); *Letters concerning the Present State of the Church of Scotland*... (E, 1767).

FES IV, 223; G. Ardley, *The Common Sense Philosophy of James Oswald* (A, 1980); J. Cooper, 'James Oswald 1703–93 and the Application of the Common Sense Philosophy to Religion' (PhD, University of Edinburgh, 1948).

H. R. Sefton

Overture, the instrument by which in the CofS and other Churches a court may submit to a superior court a formal proposal for executive or legislative action of a general kind – the particular business of parties being promoted by petition. Overture may similarly be employed by members of the court itself, though today this is found in the CofS only in the General Assembly,* the method in the lower courts being by simple motion, preceded if appropriate by notice of motion. Where a Presbytery* resolves to overture the General Assembly, the document has to be forwarded through the Synod,* which is bound to transmit and may do so *simpliciter* or *cum nota* (i.e., with or without comment) and which may indicate either approval or disapproval. An overture will not be received by the Assembly if its subject-matter is covered in a deliverance of one of its committees.

The Assembly may itself send overtures for the consideration of Presbyteries. In particular, in terms of the Barrier Act* any Act which is to become a 'binding rule and constitution to the Church' must be proposed as an Overture to the Assembly and then passed by them to Presbyteries, and only if a majority of all the Presbyteries of the Church indicate approval may a subsequent Assembly pass the Act. If the proposal is to amend the terms of the Articles Declaratory,* the overture must be sent down in two successive years and must each time obtain the approval of at least two-thirds of all the Presbyteries of the Church, and only then may be approved, if so resolved, by the Assembly.

Cox, 102–6, 181, 191, 584; A. Herron, *A Guide to the Presbytery* (E, 1983), 150; *id.*, A Guide to the General Assembly, (E, 1976), 32.

A. Herron

P

Pacifism, Peace Movement. Only a tiny minority in the Scottish Churches have been pacifists, but a larger number have supported anti-war movements for peace since the advent of modern warfare. The main Reformed and Catholic traditions have accepted the 'just war' arguments justifying the limited use of force by the state. Among the few early pacifist groups in Scotland, excepting the medieval religious orders, was the Society of Friends,* or Quakers. Founded by George Fox (1624–91), the Quakers opposed military service and the use of arms. The movement spread to Scotland but suffered persecution and remained small in number. The Scottish Quaker theologian Robert Barclay* was an eloquent apologist for Christian pacifism. He stated in his *Apology for the True Christian Divinity* (L, 1678): 'It is not lawful for Christians to resist evil, or to fight or war in any case.' The Quakers were almost alone in their pacifist testimony in Scotland until the nineteenth century.

The founding of the London Peace Society in 1816, in the aftermath of the Napoleonic wars, marked a growing concern among British Christians, especially Evangelicals, with the peace issue. The Peace Society opposed all war on Christian grounds and was largely a pacifist body. It had individual supporters in Scotland, especially among Evangelicals in the radical Seceding tradition found in the UPC. They formed an overlapping social world with the supporters of non-violent abolition in the Scottish anti-slavery movement.* Individual churchmen expressed their opposition to the Crimean and Boer Wars. The pacifist, anti-war position of James Barr* during the First World War* was in contrast to the support given to the War by most church leaders, like James Denney,* and the lack of sympathy in the Churches for conscientious objectors to military service.

Christian pacifist arguments were put forward during the 1930s in the CofS as one viewpoint within the 1937 General Assembly Report on Christian attitudes to war and peace, especially by G. H. C. Macgregor.* The Iona Community,* formed in 1938, committed its members to peace-making, if not to the pacifist position held by its founder George MacLeod,* although the Community adopted a position of nuclear pacifism in 1966. Some Scottish Christians, including ministers, were active in the peace movement from the 1950s, including the Campaign for Nuclear Disarmament and Christian CND, especially in protests against nuclear military bases in Scotland. In 1982 the RC Justice and Peace Commission was constituted with a peace-making concern, reflected in the 1982 Scottish Catholic Bishops' Conference Easter letter, questioning the morality of nuclear weapons. The 1983 CofS General Assembly adopted a position of moral and theological opposition to nuclear weapons and their threatened use. In the 1980s there was a growing concern in the Scottish Churches to link peace-making to questions of justice and environmental stewardship.

G. B. Burnett and W. H. Marwick, *The Story of Quakerism in Scotland* (L, 1952); P. Brock, *Pacifism in Europe to 1914* (Princeton, 1972), 272–4, 367–406; C. D. Rice, *The Scots Abolitionists 1833–1861* (Baton Rouge, 1981); P. C. Matheson, 'Scottish War Sermons 1914–1919', *RSCHS* 17 (1972), 203–13; A. Bogle, 'James Barr B.D., M.P.', *RSCHS* 21 (1982), 189–207; R. Ferguson, *Geoff* (Gartocharn, 1979), 109–15; J. Muir, *Christian Non-Pacifism* (E, 1938); G. H. C. MacGregor, *The Relevance of the Impossible* (L, 1941); R. Ferguson, *Chasing the Wild Goose* (L, 1988), 123–7; A. Muir, *John White* (L, 1958), 359–65.

W. F. Storrar

Paisley Abbey. Cluniac* monks, brought from England by Walter Fitzalan, steward of Scotland, settled at Renfrew *c.* 1163 and then at Paisley *c.* 1169. The latter site probably incorporated the church containing the tomb of St Mirin. Although Cluniac houses, even the more important, were usually priories, Paisley became an abbey in 1219–20, and its abbot was granted *pontificalia* (episcopal insignia) by the Avignon pope in 1395. It remained a Cluniac house, but abbatial status gave Paisley almost complete autonomy. One abbot, Thomas Morow (c.1424–44), played a part in the conciliarist* movement. In the thirteenth century Paisley founded a house at Crossraguel (Ayrshire), which itself became an autonomous abbey though remaining subject to Paisley in certain matters.

Paisley was important both as a monastery and as a place of pilgrimage;* it received the revenues of about thirty appropriated parishes. Stewart notables, including King Robert III, were buried there. It was burned by English forces in 1307, but extensive rebuilding took place in the fifteenth century. The complement of monks was twenty-five and in the 1540s there were over twenty. From 1525 the abbacy was in the hands of the powerful Hamilton family, notably Archbishop John Hamilton.* Partly at least because of this influence, the monks remained faithful to RCism at the Reformation,* and Paisley Abbey in 1563 witnessed a short-lived resurgence of RC worship. Nevertheless the abbey has served as a Protestant parish church from 1572 to the present day. Extensive restoration of the buildings has been carried out in modern times, especially by Robert Lorimer (*see* Architecture) and Peter MacGregor Chalmers (1859–1922).

Registrum Monasterii de Passelet (Maitland Club, E, 1832); J. C. Lees, *The Abbey of Paisley* (Paisley, 1878); Easson-Cowan, 63–5; J. Durkan, 'Paisley Abbey: Attempt to Make it Cistercian', *IR* 7 (1956), 60–2; *id*., 'Paisley Abbey and Glasgow Archives: Some New Directions', *IR* 14 (1963), 46–53; *id*., 'Paisley Abbey in the Sixteenth Century', *IR* 27 (1976), 110–26.

M. Dilworth

Pakistan, *see* Missions.

Palmer, Thomas Fyshe (1747–1802), Unitarian* minister and political martyr. Born in Northill, Bedfordshire, he studied at Queen's College, Cambridge (BA, 1769; MA, 1772; BD, 1781). For a year he was Anglican curate of Leatherhead, Surrey, but was converted to Unitarianism by the writings of Joseph Priestley. Leaving the CofE, in 1783 he was invited to minister to a Unitarian society recently formed in Montrose and preached there for two years. In 1785 he went to Dundee and founded a Unitarian church, but also preached frequently in the surrounding area, forming Unitarian societies in Edinburgh, Glasgow, Arbroath and Forfar.

In 1793 Palmer revised a speech made by a Dundee political reformer and had a thousand copies printed. He was arrested, convicted of sedition and sentenced to seven years' transportation. All attempts by Charles Fox and other Whigs* to have the sentence reversed were rebuffed by Pitt's government.

Palmer spent his sentence in New South Wales' penal colony, Botany Bay. After his release he had various adventures before dying on one of the Ladrone Islands south of Hong Kong. Two years later an American captain had Palmer's body reinterred in Boston, Massachusetts. A monument was erected in Edinburgh's Calton cemetery in 1844 in memory of Palmer and other political martyrs of that era.

DNB XLIII, 162–4; *The Trial of the Rev. Thomas Fyshe Palmer* (E, 1793); E. S. Towill, *People and Places in the Story of the Scottish Church* (E, 1976), 74–5.

N. R. Needham

Panel on Worship, *see* Public Worship and Aids to Devotion, Committee on.

Papacy, Scottish Relations with (pre-Reformation). The relationship between the early Scottish Church and the papacy was tenuous but unambiguous. Some of its bishops were present in Rome in the eighth century; Donald, king of Strathclyde, died on pilgrimage there in 975 and Macbeth made a more successful visit as king of Scots in 1050. By the early twelfth century contact had become more regular: Scottish bishops, such as Turgot,* Bishop of St Andrews (1107–15), sought papal guidance about a number of apparent deviations, while the popes on their side not only offered advice, but from 1119 onwards commanded the Scottish bishops to desist from admonishing one another and to submit to the archbishop of York as their rightful metropolitan. This successive kings were unwilling to accept, although their pleas for the erection of an archbishopric at St Andrews were equally unsuccessful. The controversy continued unresolved, but though the feudal subjections of William the Lion* to Henry II at Falaise* in 1174 appeared likely to lead to the ecclesiastical subjection of the Scottish Church, this was averted by quarrels between York and Canterbury. The falsification of Scottish royal letters by York led in turn to Pope Alexander III issuing the bull *Super Anxietatibus* in 1176, forbidding York to exercise any metropolitical authority over the Scottish bishops until he had proved his case in the Roman curia. A dispute between the papacy and William the Lion over an appointment to the bishopric of St Andrews in 1178 raged for ten years, and appeared to threaten this compromise when York was allowed legatine power in Scotland, but this further threat to the liberty of the Scottish Church was averted, and the bishops' privilege of direct subjection to the apostolic see as a special daughter confirmed, by the bull *Cum Universi* of 1192. The Church was not, however, equipped with any organ of government as a province, until in 1225 the bull *Quidam Vestrum* provided the machinery for holding provincial councils and appointing one of the bishops as conservator of their statutes (A. A. M. Duncan, *The Kingdom of the Scots* (E, 1975), 256–80).

For some time thereafter relations with the papacy remained relatively cordial, if occasionally characterized by disputes over appointments (Dowden, 13, 15, 150, 195, 126–9, 304–6), but the Wars of Independence produced new difficulties with the excommunication of Robert the Bruce.* This papal injunction was ignored by most Scottish churchmen, while the Scottish barons made their historic appeal to the pope, since 1306 resident at Avignon, in the Declaration of Arbroath (1320).* With the resolution of this conflict by a bull of 13th June 1329 authorizing the episcopal anointing of the kings of Scotland, signs for better relations between the papacy and Scotland appeared propitious. However, another source of dispute arose as successive fourteenth-century popes reserved elective benefices, thus threatening to eliminate chapter elections and, more importantly, royal influence over them, and also non-elective benefices, thus threatening the rights of patrons. By the time of the Great Schism (1378–1417), when Scotland resolutely supported the Avignon popes, Clement VII and Benedict XIII, against the claims of their rivals, this system to which were tied the payment of annates (first-year revenues) in the case of lesser benefices and common services for greater benefices was threatening to become controversial (F. McGurk, *Calendar of Papal Letters to Scotland of Benedict XI of Avignon, 1394–1419* (SHS, E, 1976), xv–xxxi). However, it was not until the reign of James I, after the schism ended, that matters came to a head when legislation in 1424 created the crime of barratry and forbade the purchase of benefices or pensions at the curia. It was aimed at preventing multiple petitions for reserved benefices, as they led to expensive litigation in the curia. Though he did not deny the legitimacy of promotion taxes, the king and his supporter John Cameron,* Bishop of Glasgow, nevertheless encountered determined opposition from the papacy, which after James's assassination in 1437 was able to secure its own ends. Though further conflict in the reign of James II over the right of bishops to bequeath their personal possessions, and over royal rights *sede vacante*, was resolved against the wishes of the papacy, a more serious conflict over provision to elective benefices was to occupy much of the reign of James III. Initially victory lay with the Crown as successive papal efforts to provide Patrick Graham,* Bishop of St Andrews, to the commend (*see* Commendator) of three religious houses were thwarted; in the course of the struggle his see was raised to archiepiscopal status in 1472 (J. A. F. Thomson, 'Some New Light on the Elevation of Patrick Graham', *SHR* 40 (1961), 83). (The presence of metropolitan authority in Scotland lessened the need for recourse to Rome, and when later archbishops received legatine powers, this decreased even further.) In 1483, however, papal provisions to the bishoprics of Dunkeld and Glasgow countermanding royal wishes were successful. This set-back led to an agreement between Crown and papacy whereby, according to an indult of 1487, the pope promised, in the case of elective benefices worth over 200 gold crowns, to await royal recommendations for at least eight months before making provision (R. K. Hannay, *The Scottish Crown and the Papacy, 1424–1560* (E, 1931); J. A. F. Thomson, 'Innocent VIII and the Scottish Church', *IR* 19 (1968), 23–31). Papal rights to reserve and provide and receive the taxes due were thereby recognized, but the right to recommend was increasingly interpreted by Scottish rulers as one of nomination and was eventually recognized as such in 1536. In consequence few disputes over elective benefices occurred thereafter, but the standard of nominees dropped sharply and the number of non-episcopal commendators* rose. By the early sixteenth century, with the advent of Protestantism, successive popes were making concessions of a financial and administrative nature in order to retain the allegiance of Catholic rulers. In Scotland, after decades of struggle between Crown and papacy in this area, the situation was brought to an end by the Reformation, and the consequent abrogation of papal authority. A week before the Reformation Parliament* abolished papal jurisdiction in Scotland in 1560, Mary Queen of Scots received the papal gift of a golden rose, which, with the blessed sword and hat, was the most coveted mark of papal favour and had been bestowed on Scottish kings since William I (1165–1214).

C. Burns, 'Papal Gifts to Scottish Monarchs: The Golden Rose and the Blessed Sword', *IR* 20 (1969), 150–94; A. I. Cameron, *The Apostolic Camera and Scottish Benefices 1418–1488* (St Andrews, 1934); W. J. Anderson, 'Rome and Scotland, 1513–1625', *IR* 10 (1959), 173–93; R. Somerville, *Scotia Pontificia* (O, 1982).

I. B. Cowan

Paraphrases, metrical versions of Scripture passages other than Psalms. The first complete Scottish Psalter* appeared in 1564. In 1575 and later editions a few 'spiritual songs', i.e. metrical versions of other Scripture passages, were added. None appeared in Rous's Psalter of 1650, even though the General Assembly authorizing the work had recommended that translations of 'Scriptural songs' should be submitted to it.

No progress was made until 1741, when an overture* to the General Assembly led to the appointment in 1742 of a committee to collect such songs. In 1745 the committee, enlarged, produced forty-five *Translations and Paraphrases*, which were sent to Presbyteries for consideration. Presbyteries were, however, preoccupied with the Jacobites.* Little happened until 1775, when the Assembly appointed another committee to revise and expand the 1745 book. This committee was enlarged in 1777.

In 1781 a draft of the committee's collection was submitted to the General Assembly, which after making amendments sent copies to Presbyteries for their opinions and meanwhile allowed temporary use in congregations if ministers approved. No formal authorization was ever given to these *Translations and Paraphrases, in Verse, of several Passages of Sacred Scripture* (E, 1781). The book consisted of forty-five much revised paraphrases from the 1745 edition, twenty-two new ones, and five hymns. The custom arose of printing what became commonly known simply as the *Paraphrases* (i.e. including the hymns) at the end of Scottish Bibles, following the Scottish Psalter.

The committee responsible for the final shape of the 1781 book included Hugh Blair* and Alexander Carlyle.* Much of the work fell upon John Logan* and a non-committee member, William Cameron (?1751–1811).

The *Paraphrases*, based on extracts from nine Old Testament books and fifteen New Testament ones, were arranged in Scripture order. They were all in common metre except six in long metre (including two of the hymns). Although no authors' names were given, only three non-Scots were represented among the traceable authors: Nahum Tate (*see* Psalms), Isaac Watts and Philip Doddridge (on both of whom *see* Hymnology, English). The other authors seemed to be all Scots, the best known being Thomas Blacklock (1721–91), Hugh Blair, Robert Blair (1699–1746),* John Morison and Michael Bruce.* The Paraphrases were translated into Gaelic,* first by Alexander MacFarlane (published G, 1753) and then by John Smith* (published E, 1787). The present Gaelic versions derive directly from Smith.

The first three of the five hymns had appeared in *The Spectator* for 1712 and were composed by Joseph Addison (1672–1719): 'When all thy mercies, O my God!' 'The spacious firmament on high' and 'When rising from the bed of death'. The fourth was a recast of Watts's 'Bless'd morning, whose young dawning rays'. The last, 'The hour of my departure's come', was by either Logan or Bruce.

The 1929 Scottish Psalter recommended for public worship forty-two of the *Paraphrases*. The 1927 *Church Hymnary** contained thirteen, and the 1973 *CH* twenty-two. Among the best known were 'How bright these glorious spirits shine!' 'I'm not ashamed to own my Lord', and 'O God of Bethel!'

D. J. Maclagan, *The Scottish Paraphrases* (E, 1889); T. Young, *The Metrical Psalms and Paraphrases* (L, 1909); J. Julian, *Dictionary of Hymnology* (²L, 1907), 1024–5, 1033, *et passim*; *Handbook to the [Revised] Church Hymnary*, ed. J. Moffatt (²L, 1928), s.v. 'Scottish Paraphrases'; G. V. R. Grant in *New Grove Dictionary of Music and Musicians* (L, 1980), XIV, 179.

J. S. Andrews

Parish System. It is unknown when 'parish' came to be understood as the area round a church for which a priest was responsible in spiritual things. In Scotland, clear demarcation of parishes probably became necessary when churches with their teinds* passed into the hands of monasteries and cathedrals, and poorly paid vicars were appointed to minister in the parishes. By about 1200 it appears that bishops had completed the task.

When the monastic system was swept away at the Reformation, the Reformers sought to establish a true parish system; every parish should have an educated parish minister with elders and sometimes a reader.* There should be proper care for the poor and education of children in the faith. The seizure of old RCC funds, however, meant that their ideal could never be attained in its fullness.

In the early nineteenth century, agricultural and industrial changes began to cause movement of the population into the towns. To meet the need for places of worship, chapels of ease* were erected in some *quoad omnia** parishes, served by parish ministers. Destitution was increasing in the towns, especially in Edinburgh and Glasgow, and the Est.C was quite unable to cope with the situation. In 1815 Thomas Chalmers* moved to the Tron parish in Glasgow and attempted to organize a parish system on the model he had known in rural Kilmany, a self-caring community. The population numbered ten thousand, many of whom were very poor. He was able to interest business men in his work and made detailed arrangements for relief of the 'worthy poor' with small gifts. He worked diligently at visitation himself and divided up the parish into small units, each with an elder to visit regularly. The problems were tremendous. Chalmers believed the experiment successful, but many critics from his time to the present have, in varying measures, disagreed. Chalmers then took up the case for church extension.* The idea was to create *quoad sacra** parishes where there were chapels of ease,* and where the government might be persuaded to build new churches. The government did build about forty-three new churches, mostly in the Highland area (*see* Parliamentary Churches), but nothing was done for the cities where it was considered that there were enough churches if Secession* congregations were taken into account. The Evangelicals then set about raising the money themselves and many new buildings were erected. The General Assembly in 1834 passed the Chapels Act* which gave new churches parish areas *quoad sacra*. However the Chapels Act was declared illegal by the civil courts and after the Disruption* it was repealed. Most of the churches were later given *quoad sacra* status by the Court of Teinds.

The FCS built churches in most parishes and as cities spread, new *quoad sacra* parishes were created from the large *quoad omnia** ones. After the Union in 1929 of the CofS and the UFC, the whole parish system had to be rearranged so that each congregation had an area of responsibility. From 1921 parish boundaries have been entirely a matter for the Church itself through Presbyteries, and there is readjustment at any union of congregations or dissolution or for any good reason, by the Presbytery.

Responsibility for education and the care of the poor passed from the Church's hands in the nineteenth century, but pastoral care of church members and evangelism among non-members in a parish remain the responsibility of minister and Kirk Session.* The CofS still sees its duty to preach and teach the gospel to the whole population of every parish in Scotland. In the larger towns and cities, mobility and other factors, *e.g.* rehousing, have seriously eroded the recognition of the parish church in favour of more 'gathered' congregations.

W. Mair, *A Digest of Laws . . . Church of Scotland* (⁴E, 1923); C. Innes (ed.), *Origines Parochiales Scotiae*, 2 vols in 3 (Bannatyne Club, E, 1850–5); S. J. Brown, *Thomas Chalmers and the Godly Commonwealth* (O, 1982).

A. I. Dunlop

PARITY OF MINISTERS

Parity of Ministers, a doctrine dear to the hearts of Presbyterians* and central in their whole conception of the ministry. It was spelt out in several of the Reformed confessions, was a major factor in resistance to prelacy and hierarchy in Scotland in the sixteenth and seventeenth centuries, and is a presupposition of government by Church courts.* There is in Presbyterian Churches no office more exalted than that of ministering to a parish, and no parish minister has any power, authority or control over any other and is sternly forbidden to intrude into the territory of another. There are those who would go so far as to claim that there are bishops in the Presbyterian Church – only they are called parish ministers. For in them, individually or corporately, have been vested all the peculiar powers that traditionally belong to the bishop – they lay on hands at ordinations, they receive new members into the fellowship of the Church, they vote and determine on all doctrinal and constitutional issues.

Any complaint against a minister must be made to his or her Presbytery which, if satisfied that there is a case to answer, will institute a trial by libel. The resultant judgment may be made the subject of appeal or of dissent and complaint to the Synod and thence to the General Assembly. In all of these courts elders* sit and judge on the same terms as ministers, and indeed the two have often been seen as belonging to a single order of elders or presbyters, as ruling and teaching elders respectively.

For the purpose of occupying the chair at meetings of any of the courts, a minister is appointed to act as Moderator,* generally for only one year but in most cases carrying eligibility for re-election (though this rarely happens), and vested with an authority that obtains only during the sessions of the court concerned and that extends only to the keeping of good order thereat. This is true of the Moderator of the General Assembly no less than of a Presbytery.

In the Kirk Sessions* the minister may introduce business and speak to it, but he may not propose a motion, and he has no deliberative vote. A Kirk Session decision on any matter within its competence is binding on the minister as completely as on any other, the only difference being that disobedience on his part can be dealt with only by the Presbytery.

Equality of status belongs also to those ministers who have demitted their charges on grounds of age or ill health or in the interest of readjustment, and to others who, being holders of offices specified in Act II 1970 as amended, are entitled to a seat in Presbytery. On the other hand ministers who have completely left the service of the Church, though they will normally retain their status as ministers, do not sit in the courts and may not discharge the normal duties of the ministry unless they hold a current certificate authorizing them to do so from the Presbytery within whose bounds they reside, and they can be called to a charge only on securing a Certificate of Eligibility from the Committee on Admission of Ministers. So long as they retain their ministerial status they are prevented from sitting in the courts as elders.

J. L. Ainslie, *The Doctrines of Ministerial Order in the Reformed Churches of the 16th and 17th Centuries* (E, 1940), ch. 4.

A. Herron

PARLIAMENT, SCOTTISH

Parliament, Scottish, in origin, a 'talking together', an occasion when kings sought advice from important men. Advice might be forthcoming from the king's small council composed of members of his immediate entourage or it might be offered by a larger assembly, a *colloquium*, the word used in the reigns of Alexander II (1214–49) and III (1249–86) or, through English influence, a *parliamentum*, as in the *parliamentum Scocie* held at Birgham (Berwickshire) in March 1290 and others called in King John's reign (1292–6). The king's advisers who sat in Parliament were the great lords spiritual and temporal, the key elements in the politically articulate 'community of the realm'; but the Crown's financial needs under Robert I (1306–29), who asked Parliament to approve a substantial tax in 1326, led to the appearance in Parliament of representatives from the burghs. During the reign of David II* (1329–71), Parliament had three groups, three 'communities' or 'estates': nobles who held their lands directly of the Crown, the prelates (bishops and abbots), and burgesses. Parliament met on a summons of forty days, sat in a single chamber, and might discuss all great issues of state. Besides, Parliament remained the chief law court, a court of appeal where wrongs might be righted. James I* (1406–37), who used Parliament to particular advantage in reminding subjects of the king's will, sought to widen its composition to include lesser landholders in the shires, but these measures, despite an act of 1428 for electing shire commissioners, remained ineffective until the Reformation Parliament,* when an unprecedented number of lairds clamoured for representation on the basis of James I's legislation.

As it was, throughout the Middle Ages, some found attendance irksome and expensive, and from the later fourteenth century, Parliament (whose meetings were of short duration, perhaps a fortnight or so, at infrequent intervals, though sometimes annually under David II) began to delegate powers to committees to expedite business or, again, to commissions composed of certain members enabling the rest to return home. Out of this practice developed the 'committee of the articles', which drew up Parliament's agenda, and with it the potential to exert a stranglehold over business. Under James VI* (1567–1625), appointments to this influential committee were conducted in a manner designed to ensure that the king's will would prevail. For much of its history, Parliament displayed no great tradition of independence from the Crown, largely because medieval kings had usually managed to live within their means, without raising large armies for expensive foreign wars or resorting to regular taxation. As a consequence, before the seventeenth century, Parliament was seldom able to exercise financial pressure on the Crown by withholding supply. Besides, the Crown had the option of summoning not a full Parliament but a general council, and later a convention of estates, smaller, less formal gatherings which might meet at shorter notice and, though lacking Parliament's judicial powers, had power to raise taxes as well as legislate. There again, the Privy Council* which emerged from the king's ordinary or undifferentiated council in 1545, became an omnicompetent executive organ of government.

In the sixteenth and seventeenth centuries, Parliament's broadening membership, already apparent in the composition of the irregular Reformation Parliament, was the subject of a series of enactments. The role of the 'lairds', those small barons and freeholders from the shires who claimed representation in 1560, was regularized in an act of 1587 which revived the legislation of 1428 and permitted two commissioners, annually elected by the freeholders of each shire (except Clackmannan and Kinross which each gained one), to sit in Parliament. Later electoral changes were forthcoming in 1661 and 1681. After the Reformation too, the spiritual estate was subject to modification: the existing RC bishops and abbots retained their seats; the Reformed Church advanced no claims in the 1560s for its superintendents* or ministers to assume this lordly role; but during James VI's minority, it was recognized at the Convention of Leith* in 1572 that Protestant bishops should take the place of their Roman predecessors with a right to sit in Parliament, and that the Crown's nominees to the abbacies might also vote as titular abbots in Parliament. The subsequent transformation of abbacies into temporal lordships under James VI removed the holders of these properties from the spiritual estate in Parliament to that of the nobility.

At the same time, the General Assembly's campaign, under Presbyterian pressure, for the abolition of episcopacy raised the issue of ecclesiastical representation in Parliament. In 1597 a compromise was reached whereby ministers appointed as titular bishops – 'parliamentary bishops' (with no other episcopal duties) – would represent the Church in Parliament; this in turn, through manipulation by the Crown, prepared the way for the restoration of episcopacy by 1606; but in Charles I's* reign (1625–49) the Covenanters* succeeded in abolishing the office of bishop in the Glasgow General Assembly* of 1638 and in the Parliament of 1640, which also removed the clerical estate in Parliament. Both were revived after the Restoration* in 1662 and abolished again at the 'Glorious Revolution' in 1689. Similarly, in 1640 the Covenanters dispensed with the committee of the articles, which was restored by 1663 and removed in 1690. The constitutional checks on the Crown secured by the Covenanters in the 1640s when Parliament gained control of the executive and judiciary proved short-lived; the Cromwellian conquest of the 1650s not only abolished Scottish institutions but created a united Parliament at Westminster for the Commonwealth* of England, Scotland and Ireland. Yet with the Restoration of the monarchy and a Scottish Parliament after 1660, despite all the shackles of royal control, signs emerged of a growing assertiveness in parliamentary opinion, which was given free rein at the Revolution of 1689–90 when a convention-parliament adopted the Claim of Right* and Articles of Grievances, affirmed that James VII by his misdemeanours had forfeited the Scottish throne, embarked on a programme of constitutional reform and established Presbyterian government in the Church. However, with the Treaty of Union* in 1707, Parliament in Edinburgh voted itself out of existence by accepting the terms of an incorporating union with England, in which Scotland was to receive forty-five members in the British House of Commons and sixteen elected peers in the Lords, and with safeguards for the Presbyterian constitution of the Scottish Church.

Throughout its history, Parliament showed a readiness to legislate on ecclesiastical issues. Traditionally, in the Middle Ages, one of Parliament's first enactments on meeting was to confirm the privileges and freedoms of 'holy kirk', but none of that prevented the estates from proceeding to curb papal powers in ecclesiastical appointments, impose taxation, demand a reform of clerical morals, legislate on heresy and for the repair of churches, and authorize vernacular Scriptures. After the Reformation too, though the Church formulated its own programme in its General Assembly,* Parliament had its role to play in repudiating papal authority, prohibiting the mass and approving a Protestant (Scots) Confession of Faith* in 1560 and again in 1567, in affirming episcopacy in 1584, 1612 and 1662, and in ratifying a Presbyterian* constitution in 1592, 1640, 1690 and in 1707. It also legislated on patronage,* presentations to benefices, ecclesiastical property and teinds.*

See Church and State.

APS, vols I–XII; R. S. Rait, *The Parliaments of Scotland* (G, 1924); C. S. Terry, *The Scottish Parliament, its Constitution and Procedure, 1603– 1707* (G, 1905); A. A. M. Duncan, 'The Early Parliaments of Scotland', *SHR* 45 (1966), 36–58.

J. Kirk

Parliamentary Churches, churches built by Act of Parliament (1824) to improve provision in CofS parishes, mainly in the Highlands* and Islands. As a Thanksgiving for Peace after the Napoleonic Wars, the Government granted funds to build churches and manses for the CofS in remote but populous parts of the Highlands and Islands, and to endow them. After protracted negotiations, led by John Inglis* of Greyfriars Church, Edinburgh, on behalf of the General Assembly, the final (amended) act was passed on 21 June 1824 (5 Geo. IV c.90). Thirty-two churches and forty-one manses were built at a cost of £54,442; eleven churches were to be repaired by the heritors;* and stipends* of £150 were to be provided for forty-two ministers, in perpetuity.

The Commissioners for Highland Roads and Bridges were responsible for choosing the sites, from those offered by heritors, and for the erection of the buildings, which were all completed by July 1830. The designs were made by three surveyors, and then amended by Thomas Telford, whose name they often bear. The church design could be altered to meet local requirements by the addition of galleries (at the heritor's expense) or an aisle; the plan was of the most simple and traditional form, but with gothic detail to the windows and doors. The best known example is the parish church of Iona. The manse could be of one or two storeys.

Future upkeep was to be financed from seat rents, by the heritor and the minister. Controversy arose over the appointment of the first ministers, the patronage* being with the Crown, who on the first occasion followed the heritor's advice; yet in some places a Royal Bounty* missionary had been stationed, often for many years. All these places were made *quoad sacra** parishes in 1833. A Bill of 1825, along similar lines, to build new churches and manses in the Lowlands at a cost of £50,000, but without stipends, was not passed.

Sixth Report of the Commissioners, *P.P.* 1831 (330) IX, 19; A. M. Maclean, *Telford's Highland Churches and Manses* (Coll, 1988); S. Hackett and N. Livingston, 'Scottish Parliamentary Churches and their Manses', in D. Breeze (ed.), *Studies in Scottish Antiquity* (E, 1984), 302–36.

A. M. Maclean

Pastoral Admonition (1799). Copies of this pastoral letter, issued by the General Assembly* together with a declaratory act concerning unqualified ministers and preachers, were sent to parishes throughout Scotland in June 1799. Written by Hugh Blair* at the request of George Hill,* it outlined the hostility of the Moderate* leadership of the CofS to the contemporary upsurge in itinerancy,* and unauthorized Sunday schools.* Overtures from the synods of Aberdeen, and Angus and Mearns, expressing local concern, had been received by the Assembly following the appearance of itinerant preachers in those areas during 1797. At the heart of the letter's strictures concerning self-assumed authority and the threat to political stability (accusations directed specifically against the agents of the newly formed Society for Propagating the Gospel at Home*) lay a jealousy for the prerogatives of the Est.C and its ministry, a distrust of religious enthusiasm and a fear of the social consequences of unregulated lay activity. Although it was ordered to be read from the pulpit of every parish church, the document achieved little apart from the alienation of evangelical church members and the embarrassment of those within the Church's ministry who embraced evangelical sentiments.

AGACS, 870–3; A. Haldane, *The Lives and Robert Haldane of Airthrey, and of his Brother, James Alexander Haldane* (L, 1852).

D. W. Lovegrove

Paterson, Alexander (1766–1831), RC Bishop and Vicar-apostolic. Born at Pathhead, Banffshire, he went to the RC Scots College* in Douai, France, in 1779, where he remained until its dissolution by the revolutionary government in 1793. Returning to Scotland, he was stationed at the RC missions in Glenlivet, Banffshire (1793–1812), and Paisley, Renfrewshire (1912–16). In 1816 he was appointed Bishop of Cybistra *in partibus* and coadjutor to Bishop Alexander Cameron, Vicar-apostolic of the Lowlands. In 1821 he went to Paris and regained possession of all Scottish college properties which had remained unsold during the revolutionary period. He succeeded Cameron as Vicar-apostolic of the Lowlands in 1825; in 1827 he became Vicar-apostolic of the new eastern district.

The two RC seminaries of Aquhorties (near Inverurie, Aberdeenshire) and Lismore (on the island of Lismore in the Firth of Lorne) were united by Paterson and re-established at Blairs, Kincardineshire (*see* Colleges and Seminaries, RC).

DNB XLIV, 15–16.

N. R. Needham

Paterson, John (1632–1708), last Archbishop of Glasgow. Paterson's enthusiastic espousal of the Stuart cause at the time of the Revolution of 1688–9 prevented him exercising the kind of leadership which might have been expected of him.

The eldest son of John Paterson (*c.*1604–79), Bishop of Ross, Paterson was educated at King's College, Aberdeen, and St Mary's College, St Andrews. He was called to Ellon near Aberdeen in succession to his father and ordained in 1660. He was translated to the Tron, Edinburgh, in 1663 and appointed a chaplain to the King in 1668. He was Dean of Edinburgh 1672–4 and consecrated as Bishop of Galloway in 1675. Appointed a Privy Councillor, he was translated to Edinburgh in 1679 and to the archbishopric of Glasgow in 1687, being deprived at the ensuing Revolution.

After the Revolution, Paterson seems to have been involved in various Jacobite* activities, but he personally solicited the sympathy of Queen Anne for the dispossessed Episcopal clergy. It was in the chapel of Paterson's house in Edinburgh that the first consecration of bishops after the Revolution took place in 1705. John Fullarton and John Sage* were consecrated to preserve the Episcopal succession, but were not assigned to dioceses. Paterson's death in 1708 made necessary further consecrations in 1709.

DNB XLIV, 18–20; *FES* VII, 324; J. B. Craven, *Scots Worthies, 1560–1688* (E, 1894).

H. R. Sefton

Paterson, John (1776–1855), Congregationalist* missionary. Born at Duntocher, near Glasgow, he went to Glasgow University in 1798. Coming under the influence of James Haldane's* preaching, he decided to become a Congregationalist minister, and trained for a time under William Innes* of Dundee. In 1803 he was set apart as the minister of a church he had gathered in Cambuslang, Lanarkshire. He resigned the following year in favour of missionary work in India, and left Britain with his fellow Congregationalist Ebenezer Henderson.* Stopping off in Denmark, however, conditions made it impossible for them to obtain passage for India. Paterson remained in Copenhagen until 1807, carrying out evangelism, until war forced him to move to Stockholm. Assisted financially by the British and Foreign Bible Society (see Bible Societies), he did missionary work in Scandinavia. He also commenced translating the Bible into several northern languages, including Swedish, Finnish and Icelandic.

In 1812 he transferred his sphere of labours to St Petersburg. Having withdrawn from the British and Foreign Bible Society in 1822, he assumed responsibility for the Russian Bible Society, the Emperor Alexander paying him a yearly salary. On Alexander's death, the new Emperor Nicholas gave the running of the society to the Greek Church, and Paterson returned to Scotland. Settling in Edinburgh, he became Scottish secretary of the London Missionary Society* and chairman of the committee of the Congregational Union of Scotland.* He moved to Dundee in 1850.

Paterson received a doctorate in theology from the Finnish University of Abo in 1817.

The Book For Every Land (L, 1858), with memoir by W. L. Alexander.

DNB XLIV, 20-1.

N. R. Needham

Paterson, William Paterson (1860-1939), CofS divine. Born at Skirling Mains, Peeblesshire, he studied arts and divinity at Edinburgh University, and absorbed German theology at Leipzig, Erlangen and Berlin 1883-5. Ordained to St Michael's, Crieff, Perthshire, in 1887, in 1894 he became Professor of Systematic Theology in Aberdeen University. He moved to Edinburgh as Professor of Divinity (1903-34), and was Dean of the Divinity Faculty 1912-28. He gave the Gifford lectures* in 1924 (*The Nature of Religion*, L, 1925). He played a prominent role in the movement that led to the Union* of the CofS and UFC in 1929.

Paterson's theology was an eclectic synthesis of Reformed and liberal elements. He accepted the deity of Christ and an Augustinian understanding of grace, but rejected penal substitution and displayed syncretistic tendencies in his evaluations of non-Christian religious experience. His writing is characterized by clarity, energy and a fine breadth of scholarship.

Paterson was Moderator of the CofS General Assembly in 1919. He received DDs from Edinburgh (1897), Pennsylvania (1905), Trinity College Dublin (1920), Glasgow (1926) and St Andrews (1937), and an LLD from Edinburgh (1937).

Conversion (L, 1939); *Outline of the History of Dogmatic Theology* (E, 1916); *The Rule of Faith* (^{4}L, 1932); *The Position and Prospects of Theology* (E, 1903).

DNB 1931-40, 675-7; *FES* VII, 385; VIII, 716; IX, 774; *The Diaries...*, ed. C. L. Rawlins (E, 1987), with bibliography *etc*.

N. R. Needham

Paton, John Gibson (1824-1907), missionary to Vanuatu (New Hebrides). Born at Kirkmahoe, Dumfries, Paton was the son of a stocking-maker. His meagre education stimulated a thirst for learning. Ten years of city mission work, university and theological studies in Glasgow preceded his ordination as a RPC* missionary in March 1858. Paton married Ann Robson, and reached Vanuatu in August 1858.

Discounting the experiences of his Pacific Islander missionary predecessors on Tanna during 1839-58, Paton endured physical hardships and the loss of his wife and infant son in March 1859. He was blamed for local illnesses, before fleeing Tanna with his intrepid Aneityumese assistant, Abraham, in 1862.

After remarkably successful promotional tours in Australia and Scotland during 1862-6, and remarriage, to Margaret Whitecross in 1864, Paton, with Australian Presbyterian backing, established the church of Aniwa, Tanna's tiny neighbour, during 1866-81.

Often controversial, Paton endorsed British man-of-war retaliatory raids, campaigned against the Pacific labour trade, and opposed growing French influence, but lacked the cultural sensitivity of his colleagues John Geddie* and John Inglis.*

Leaving Aniwa in 1881, Paton wrote his influential autobiography, received a Cambridge DD in 1891, and promoted missions globally. He died in Melbourne. Three generations of his children served in Vanuatu till 1970.

James Paton (ed.), *John G. Paton, DD, Missionary to the New Hebrides: An Autobiography*, 2 vols (L, 1889); A. K. Langridge and F. H. L. Paton, *John G. Paton, Later Years and Farewell: A Sequel* (L, 1910); M. W. Paton, *Letters and Sketches from the New Hebrides* (L, 1894); *DNB Second Suppl.* III, 77-8; J. G. Miller, *Live: A History of Church Planting in Vanuatu*, Books 1-7 (Port Vila and Sydney, 1978-90); J. Garrett, *To Live Among the Stars: Christian Origins in Oceania* (Geneva and Suva, 1982).

J. M. Hitchen

Patrick, Millar (1868-1951), hymnologist.* Born in Ladybank, Fife, he studied at St Andrews, where he was chief editor of *The Scottish Students' Song Book* (L, 1891) and later of *The University Song Book* (L, 1901). After ordination in the UPC he served five pastorates. He was on the committee of *The [Revised] Church Hymnary.** The collection belies his *Story of the Church's Song* (E, 1927, ^{2}1947; rev. for American use J. R. Sydnor, Richmond, 1962). He edited the UFC *Book of Common Order* (1928) and produced an edition of the *Scottish Psalter of 1635* (L, 1935). He edited the *Supplement* to the *Handbook* to *RCH* (L, 1935) and served on the Public Worship and Aids to Devotion Committee of the Scottish Churches. In 1937 he became the first editor of the [British] Hymn Society's *Bulletin*. His *magnum opus* was *Four Centuries of Scottish Psalmody** (L, 1949).

Biography in *The Scottish Students' Song Book*, 1897; *Scottish Biographies 1938* (L, 1938); W. H.

Hamilton in *Hymn Soc. Bull.*, 2 (1951), 249–51; *The Times* (18 August 1951), 6 and (25 August 1951), 6; *St Andrews Alumnus Chronicle* 20 (1937), 11–17; *FUFCS* 7; *FES* IX, 11.

J. S. Andrews

Patrimony of the Kirk, *see* Stipends; Teinds; Thirds of Benefices.

Patron, Patronage, Patronage Acts, the role of landowners in the appointment of ministers. A system of patronage was haphazardly developed during the Middle Ages as pious lairds built and endowed churches for which they appointed priests. Much endowment went to the monasteries, and parishes* were neglected as the system became subject to the classical abuses of non-residence, plurality and nepotism. At the Reformation* the attempt was made, through the *First Book of Discipline*,* to abolish patronage outright, as part of a radical redistribution of the patrimony of the Kirk. The *Second Book of Discipline** went further and condemned the medieval system of presentations to benefices as a papal corruption. It called for pastors to be elected by the people. Patronage, however, was defended by powerful vested interests. The landowners, who supplied church accommodation and ministerial stipends, retained, as a right of property, their positions as patrons. Often the patron, through informal consultation, presented a candidate acceptable to the people, but difficulties arose when the patron was out of sympathy with parochial opinion. There was also the theoretical difficulty that patronage appeared to interfere with the Kirk's independent jurisdiction, though the Church guarded its prerogatives by maintaining exclusive control over the licensing and induction of ministers.

Still, dissatisfaction with patronage continued until 1649, when it was abolished by Parliament and the General Assembly vested the election of ministers in Kirk Sessions.* All this, however, was swept away by the Act Rescissory of 1662 which annulled all Parliamentary Acts of 1649. When the Presbyterians again gained the upper hand in 1690 they secured once more the abolition of patronage. This time the heritors* and elders of vacant parishes were to nominate a minister to the congregation for approval or disapproval, with reasons for disapproval to be submitted to the Presbytery which had final decision. There remained ample scope for conflict between heritors and congregations and there was much 'heat and division' in vacant parishes in the twenty-two years of this arrangement.

It was abruptly brought to a close with the restoration of patronage in the Act of 1712 which flagrantly violated the terms of the Treaty of Union* of 1707. Consultation with the Church was avoided and the Act was patently aimed at advancing Episcopal opinion within the Church with a view to facilitating a Stewart return. The General Assembly deplored it as 'grievous and prejudicial to this Church' and called for its repeal, a call repeated annually until 1784. Until its repeal a century and a half later the Act was to be productive of more mischief in Scottish ecclesiastical life than any other single piece of legislation. Initially patrons' presentations did not greatly conflict with the popular desire for congregational election but from the 1730s patrons increasingly insisted upon their rights. The result was vigorous congregational resistance to unwelcome presentations. Presbyteries, moreover, were often reluctant to proceed with an induction where local opposition was strong, so the General Assembly appointed 'riding' committees* to carry out inductions. As a result, the Secession,* which began in 1733 as a defence of popular right of call, gained widespread support. From 1751 'riding committees' were discontinued but Presbyteries were compelled to act in accordance with the Moderate* doctrine of subordination of judicatories. Resistance to this resulted in a second patronage-related secession and the formation of the Relief Church* in 1761.

The Moderates, however, came to terms with patronage, in the first instance because it was the law of the land and secondly because they believed the system produced a ministry of higher calibre than could be expected from the operation of popular call. By the early nineteenth century these assumptions had also come to be held by a number of Evangelicals. Patronage was generally working through consultation and Thomas Chalmers* hoped that popular rights could be reasserted by a gradual restitution and reinvigoration of the congregational call,* which had fallen into desuetude under the Moderates. However, evangelical zeal for 'Non-Intrusion'* led to the Veto Act* of 1834, which gave congregations an unconditional veto of patrons' presentees. There was a wing of the evangelical party which was dismayed by this attempt to curb the abuses of patronage, holding that abolition alone was the answer. After the vain attempt to defend the Veto Act from rejection by the civil courts (*see* Ten Years' Conflict), the evangelical majority in the Assembly of 1842 finally came out in favour of total abolition and petitioned Parliament to that end.

After the Disruption,* Lord Aberdeen's Benefices Act of 1843 granted congregations the right to object to any presentee, with final decision vested in the Church courts. This right of objection was freely exercised and led to such an untidy and unsatisfactory situation that after twenty years fresh calls for the abolition of patronage were being made within the Est.C. The hope was also expressed that the removal of patronage would pave the way for a reunion of Scotland's fragmented Presbyterian Church. Approaches to the Government were made from 1869. Gladstone could not afford politically to do the Est.C any favours, but when the Conservative government of Disraeli took office in 1874, it was ready to oblige. The Church Patronage (Scotland) Act of 1874 abolished patronage once and for all. It gave congregations the right to elect their own ministers and recognized the authority of Church courts to decide all questions as to the appointment of ministers. Ironically, this led not to closer relations between the Churches but to bitter division, as the non-Established Churches, sensing a threat, launched a disestablishment* crusade which was to postpone reunion well into the next century. Nevertheless, the Act of 1874 did remove a serious obstacle in the path of reunion and rooted out a source of endless conflict and division.

See Call; Concurrence/Congregational Assent.

A. J. Campbell, *Two Centuries of the Church of Scotland* (Paisley, 1930); T. Brown, *Church and State in Scotland* (E, 1892); G. I. T. Machin, *Politics and the Churches in Great Britain* (O, 1977), 112–47; W. Cunningham, *Defence of the Rights of the Christian People* (E, 1840); J. Begg, *A Violation of the Treaty of Union* (E, 1871); G. D. Campbell, *The Patronage Act of 1874* (E, 1874); A. T. Innes, *The Church of Scotland Crisis 1843 and 1874* (E, 1874).

K. R. Ross

Paxton, George (1762–1837), General Associate Synod* divine. Born at Dalgourie, Bolton, in East Lothian, after studying at Edinburgh University he went in 1784 to Alloa to learn theology under William Moncrieff,* the General Associate Synod's Divinity Professor. In 1789 he was ordained to the united General Associate congregations of Kilmaurs and Stewarton, Ayrshire. In 1807 he was appointed as the Synod's Professor of Divinity, and moved to the divinity hall in Edinburgh. When the Synod entered the USec.C in 1820, Paxton resigned and joined the Constitutional Associate Presbytery* (Old Light Antiburghers), becoming their Divinity Professor. He also pastored a congregation of fellow dissenters from the USec.C, which met in Infirmary Street. He took part in the apocrypha controversy,* writing *The Sin and Danger of Circulating the Apocrypha in connection with the Holy Scriptures* (E, 1828). He received a DD from St Andrews shortly before his death.

See Original Secession Church.

Illustrations of the Holy Scriptures in Three Parts (2 vols, E, 1819; 4 vols, ^{3}1841–3); *An Inquiry into the Obligation of Religious Covenants upon Posterity* (E, 1801); *Letter to the Rev. W. Taylor on Healing the Divisions in our Church* (E, 1802).

J. Mitchell, 'Brief Memoir' prefixed to *Illustrations* (1841), vol. I; J. M'Kerrow, *History of the Secession Church* (G, 1841), 918–19; *DNB* XLIV, 102; Small II, 279.

N. R. Needham

Peace Movement, see Pacifism.

Pechthelm, see Celtic Saints.

Peden, Alexander (*c.*1626–86), Covenanting* preacher. He was born in Ayrshire, probably near Sorn (accounts differ), studied at Glasgow University (1643–8) and served as schoolmaster, precentor and session clerk at Tarbolton and then Fenwick (both Ayrshire). In 1660 he was ordained to New Luce, Galloway, but was ejected in 1662 for refusing to conform to episcopacy. (His farewell sermon, on Acts 15:31–2, lasted until midnight.) He took to preaching at conventicles,* and became one of the most illustrious and revered of all Covenanting preachers, frequently spoken of as a 'prophet', as were various Scottish preachers from the Reformation on. Peden's gift seems to have combined foresight, insight and impassioned utterance in circumstances of heightened tension, often in warning of impending menace or unglimpsed hope – e.g., 'Though there be wrath in (God's) face, there is love in His heart, and He will return to thee, O Scotland, and there shall be as glorious days in thee, O Scotland, as ever there were in the world' (from *The Lord's Trumpet Sounding an Alarm G?*, 1720?; often rp.). Other prophecies took the form of specific, personalized predictions, especially of misfortune or death for the ungodly or hypocrites. He was declared a rebel, and excluded from the pardon of October 1667. After fleeing to Ireland, he returned only to be arrested and confined to the Bass Rock* (1673–7). After further imprisonment in Edinburgh's Tolbooth, he was released on condition he leave Britain for good, but avoided exile after the ship's captain refused to transport religious offenders. Further fugitive adventures in Scotland and Ireland ended with his death near his birthplace, and his burial in Auchinleck Church. Troops subsequently disinterred his body, which was finally left to rest beneath the gallows of Cumnock. Only a few sermons and letters of Peden's survive (especially *The Lord's Trumpet*). His experiences and prophecies were collected in the *Life of Alexander Peden* (E, 1724; ^{3}1728), perhaps not always with strictest historical accuracy, by Patrick Walker,* and subsequently published under several titles and in two collections: *Biographia Presbyteriana* (2 vols, E, 1827) and *Six Saints of the Covenant* (2 vols, L, 1901).

DNB XLIV, 205–6; *FES* II, 345–6; K. Hewat, *Peden the Prophet* (Ayr, 1911); J. C. Johnston, *Alexander Peden, the Prophet of the Covenant* (G, 1902).

D. F. Wright

Peebles, David (*fl.*1530–76), composer of tunes for the St Andrews Psalter (*see* Psalms). Little is known of his life. Around 1530 he set a canticle *Si quis diligit me* in four parts and presented it to James V.* It displays a striking melodic gift. Other early works are lost. Although a canon of St Andrews Priory,* he was commissioned after the Reformation (1560)* by James Stewart (*d.*1570)* to compose 'plain and dulce' psalm-tune settings for the new Reformed psalmody. The St Andrews Psalter compiled by Thomas Wood* contains 106 of Peebles' compositions. Wood described him as 'one of the principall musitians in all this land in his tyme'. His music is written in a simple chordal style, but as a skilled polyphonist he made the individual parts always of interest.

Peebles had died by 1592. He may have remained a RC (although he and his wife were granted land by the Priory commendator* in 1571), for in 1576 Robert Stewart (*d.*1586)* commissioned from him a four-part motet setting of *Quam multi, Domine* (Psalm 3) which displays awareness of European developments in sacred music.

M. Patrick, *Four Centuries of Scottish Psalmody* (L, 1949), 57–9; S. Sadie (ed.), *The New Grove Dictionary of Music and Musicians* (L, 1980), XIV, 333; K. Elliott (ed.), *Music of Scotland 1500–1700* (*Musica Britannica* 15; L, ^{2}1964); *id.*, 'Scottish Music of the Early Reformed Church', *Trans. of Scott. Ecclesiological Soc.* 15:2 (1961), 18–32.

D. F. Wright

Peel, (Sir) Robert (1788–1850), statesman, the son of a manufacturer and MP. Educated at Harrow and Christ Church, Oxford, he entered Parliament in 1809. He was Under-Secretary for War and the Colonies (1810–12), Chief Secretary for Ireland (1812–18) and a reforming Home Secretary (1822–7, 1828–30). In 1829 he carried Catholic Emancipation.* He was Conservative Prime Minister (1834–5, 1841–6), in 1846 repealing the Corn Laws and splitting his party.

When installed as Rector of the University of Glasgow in 1837, Peel expounded his vision of a providentially ordered universe. Although normally undemonstrative in religion, he read family prayers and warmed to writings of Evangelicals, including Thomas Chalmers.* Peel declined, however, to support a measure canvassed by Chalmers and the Non-Intrusionists* in 1840. He gave much time to the developing crisis in the CofS. His insistence on the existing rights of patrons* was one of the factors contributing to the Disruption.*

N. Gash, *Mr Secretary Peel* (L, 1961); *id.*, *Sir Robert Peel* (L, 1972); B. Hilton, 'Peel: a reappraisal', *Historical Journal* 22 (1979), 585–614; C. S. Parker (ed.), *Peel*, 3 vols (L, 1891–9); *The Speeches of . . . Sir Robert Peel*, 4 vols (L, 1853).

D. W. Bebbington

Pemberton, John (1727–95), Quaker. He came from an influential Quaker family in Philadelphia (*see* Friends, Religious Society of). On a voyage to Europe in 1750 he met John Churchman, an older Quaker minister, and joined him in a preaching tour of Great Britain and Ireland. On his return to Philadelphia, he founded an association to promote peaceful approaches to the Delaware Indians. He was arrested in 1777 for opposing armed resistance to Great Britain in the War of Independence. In 1781 he undertook another journey through the British Isles which lasted five years and included two extensive tours through Scotland between 1785 and 1786. The records of these offer fascinating glimpses of religious life in then little-known parts of the country, particularly in the Orkneys.* His aim was to kindle a living faith in his hearers rather than to proselytise, and his journeys had little effect on the position of Quakers in Scotland. Pemberton returned to the United States in 1786, but once again felt called to travel through Europe, setting out for Holland in 1794 at the age of sixty-seven.

On this journey his always delicate health gave way and he died at Pyrmont in Westphalia.

The Life and Travels of John Pemberton, ed. W[illiam] H[odgson], Jun. (L, 1844).

H. S. Pyper

Penance, Practice of, the external expression of repentance. Ascetical practices have traditionally been accomplished in three ways, prayer, fasting (self-denial) and works of charity, for sin offends God, harms the sinner and hurts our neighbour. Although they should ideally be a personal expression of conversion, in early and medieval times severe penances were imposed on the penitent that he might demonstrate his sincerity and make satisfaction. The Celtic Church* produced a number of penitential books (*see* Adomnán; Cummene), and was distinguished by the harshness of its penitential discipline.

Penances were also imposed in a general way on all Christians, e.g. Scottish Catholics 200 years ago were to fast and abstain from meat throughout Lent and on twenty-three other days in the year. Today penitential practices are normally left to the individual's discretion: Catholics are asked to keep Friday as a day of penance in commemoration of the cross.

J. T. McNeill and H. M. Gamer, *Medieval Handbooks of Penance* (NY, 1938); R. Rader, 'Asceticism', in G. S. Wakefield (ed.), *A Dictionary of Christian Spirituality* (L, 1983), 24–8; K. Rahner, 'Asceticism', in *The Practice of Faith* (L, 1985), 211–16; M. Dilworth, 'Roman Catholic Worship . . .' (*cited under* Penance, Sacrament of).

P. J. Kerr

Penance, Sacrament of, commonly known as Confession. The favoured title since Vatican II is Sacrament of Reconciliation, as it celebrates reconciliation with God and the Church. Its form has altered greatly over the centuries. In the patristic period it was reserved for very grave offences and the penitent was required to spend a lengthy time in public penance before being readmitted by the bishop to full communion. This severe practice was gradually replaced by a custom originating in Celtic monasteries and continuing until today whereby one regularly confessed one's sins to a confessor and received from him advice, penance and absolution. In the Middle Ages most received this sacrament prior to each reception of Holy Communion, often only at Easter. In eighteenth-century Scotland one might also have confessed and communicated at Christmas and the feast of the Assumption (15 August; *see* Catholic Devotion). Only in this century have most Catholics communicated again more frequently: consequently many confess weekly/monthly, although since Vatican II it has become common to confess more rarely, but when so doing to spend more time in preparation. The *Rite of . . . Penance* (1974) makes provision for communal services in preparation for individual confession and absolution and for general absolution in case of necessity.

M. Hebblethwaite and K. Donovan, *The Theology of Penance* (Dublin, 1979); L. Orsy, *The Evolving Church and the Sacrament of Penance* (Denville, New Jersey, 1978); M. Dilworth, 'Roman Catholic Worship' in D. Forrester and D. Murray, *Studies in the History of Worship in Scotland* (E, 1984), 113–31.

P. J. Kerr

Pentecostal Church of Scotland, *see* Church of the Nazarene.

Pentecostalism. Pentecostalism began in America in 1906 and current statistics estimate some 60 million adherents worldwide. Its roots lie in the nineteenth-century holiness and evangelical movements, but it is distinguished by an emphasis upon a baptism in the Holy Spirit (Acts 1:5) which results in power for mission (Acts 1:8) and an exercising of spiritual gifts, especially speaking with tongues (Acts 2:4; 1 Cor. 12:8–10).

The movement came to Britain in 1907 where, for several years, it was centred on Sunderland under the leadership of an Anglican vicar, Alexander Boddy (1851–1930). Boddy introduced Pentecostalism to Scotland when invited to speak at the Faith Mission* Conference in Edinburgh during January 1908, although it is interesting to note that the nineteenth-century Irvingite movement (*see* Irving, Edward) had been a forerunner of the phenomena of glossolalia and prophecy. A group led by William Hutchinson (1864–1937) from Westport Hall, Kilsyth, heard Boddy speak and during that year some two hundred professed to have been baptized in the Spirit. Kilsyth became a focal point, with eleven Pentecostal groups being established in central Scotland in 1908. Similarly Eilif Beruldsen (1855–1948), an elder at Charlotte Baptist Chapel, Edinburgh, had travelled to Sunderland to meet Boddy and returned to commence a Pentecostal assembly in Leith.

During the first two decades of the twentieth century various independent Pentecostal assemblies continued to emerge in Scotland, which were later to join the denominational groups of the Apostolic Church, the Assemblies of God and the Elim Pentecostal Church, which were formed in Britain during the 1920s. However some, notably Westport Hall, Kilsyth, which developed into a large and vigorous church with a strong overseas mission interest, remained independent.

The Apostolic Church was formed out of the assemblies which put an emphasis on prophecy as a contemporary means of revelation and personal guidance. They also recognized apostles and prophets within their pattern of church government, who exercised leadership through prophetic revelation. The Burning Bush* Assembly in Glasgow, led by Andrew Turnbull (1872–1937), was such a group. In 1919 he joined his assembly to the main Apostolic Church centre in Penygroes, South Wales, and in the following year was appointed as the Apostle of the Scottish assemblies. In 1922 the Apostolic Church amalgamated its four main centres of Penygroes, Glasgow, Bradford and Hereford, with Penygroes eventually becoming the denominational headquarters. During the 1920s the Apostolic Church flourished in Scotland with some fifty assemblies being formed, albeit some were small and many members were proselytized from existing Pentecostal churches. However it was not unusual for several thousand people to gather for the Apostolic conventions in St Andrew's Hall, Glasgow.

The Assemblies of God came into being in Britain in 1924, partly to safeguard small independent Pentecostal assemblies from what they regarded as the unscriptural prophetic practices and proselytizing methods of the Apostolic Church. However, the distinguishing features of the Assemblies of God were its insistence upon glossalalia as the 'initial evidence' of baptism in the Spirit and the maintenance of local autonomy for each of the member churches. Only a few Scottish Pentecostal assemblies originally joined the new denomination, but among them was a key figure in the formation of the group and a future international leader of the Pentecostal movement, Donald Gee (1891–1966), pastor of the Leith assembly. Gee had moved from London to Leith in 1920 and was instrumental in bringing several leading Pentecostal preachers to visit Scotland, for example, George (1899–1943) and Stephen (1876–1962) Jeffreys and Smith Wigglesworth (1859–1946). Several small assemblies were commenced by him in the Edinburgh district. Following the formation of the Assemblies of God there was a major increase in their numbers in Scotland, especially after a visit by Stephen Jeffreys in 1926 to conduct the largest healing crusade so far held, at the Alhambra Theatre in Edinburgh. Gee later described this event as a 'turning point for Pentecostalism in Scotland'.

In contrast to the other groups, the Elim Pentecostal Church revolved around the personality of its leader, George Jeffreys. Originating from Wales and possessing remarkable evangelistic and organizational gifts, he had first begun his Elim movement in Ireland in 1915. When Jeffreys established his headquarters in Clapham, London, in 1924, Elim churches began to be formed in mainland Britain. They were similar in belief and practice to the Assemblies of God, except that their polity was one of central government under the control of Jeffreys. A major series of campaigns was conducted by him in Scotland during 1927, and churches began in Glasgow, Paisley, Greenock, Edinburgh, Dundee and Aberdeen. The early Elim leadership in Scotland lay with W. G. Hathaway (1892–1969) and P. G. Parker (1890–1959), whose talents soon attracted appointments for them in the London headquarters.

Prior to the Second World War all of the Pentecostal denominations saw steady growth and consolidation, especially in the working-class urban areas of Scotland. Apart from some of the small fishing ports, there was little progress in the more rural and religiously conservative regions. Following that era there was a levelling off, especially as some of the outstanding early leaders died. Nevertheless in the 1960s the historic denominations began to be affected by the Charismatic Renewal* movement and Scotland produced some new theological leaders, such as Tom Smail (1928–). This in turn stimulated a more balanced and less introspective development of the traditional Pentecostal churches of which, including the independent groups, there are some seventy in total at present in Scotland.

See also Church of the Nazarene.

D. S. Barrett, *World Christian Encyclopaedia* (Nairobi, 1982); D. Cartwright, *The Great Evangelists* (Basingstoke, 1986); D. Gee, *Bonnington Toll: The Story of a First Pastorate* (L, 1943), *Wind and Flame* (Croydon, L, 1967) (incorporating the earlier work *The Pentecostal Movement*), *These Men I Knew* – personal memoirs of Pentecostal pioneers (Nottingham, 1980); M. Harper, 'As At The Beginning': The Twentieth Century Pentecostal Revival (L, 1965); P. Hocken, *Streams Of Renewal. Origins and Early Development of the Charismatic Movement in Britain* (Exeter, 1986); W. J. Hollenweger, *The Pentecostals* (L, 1972); J. Hutchinson, *Weavers, Miners and the Open Book* – a history of Kilsyth (Cumbernauld), 1986); A. E. Missen, *The Sound of a Going* – the story of Assemblies of God (Nottingham, 1973); T. N. Turnbull, *What God Hath Wrought* – a short history of the Apostolic Church (Bradford, 1959); G. Strachan, *The Pentecostal Theology of Edward Irving* (L, 1973).

R. D. Massey

Pentland Rising, see Rullion Green.

Periodicals, Religious. At its zenith in the late nineteenth century, the Scottish religious periodical press was performing several important functions. Periodicals represented specific viewpoints, whether those of a Church or a minority faction. Some acted as channels for news and advertising. Others were used as tools for social amelioration and evangelism, and as a means of promoting, and raising funds for, the work of Churches and organizations. Furthermore, subscribing to a particular title was often a means by which a reader could define his personal position in a changing ecclesiastical climate, and gain a sense of identity with a common cause.

The religious press in Scotland was in its infancy in the eighteenth century. Of 153 periodicals that appeared prior to 1800, only ten (most, including the *Missionary Magazine,** dating from the 1790s) were specifically religious in content. Possibly the earliest was published in Glasgow during 1750–1: each issue of the weekly *Exhortation* . . . contained a sermon by a leading Evangelical, John Gillies.*

In the nineteenth century, just as there was a sustained increase in the total number of periodicals issued, so too specifically religious titles comprised a greater proportion of that total. There were five reasons for this. (i) Ecclesiastical. Factionalism and controversy increased within existing Churches, resulting in the establishment of new Churches and of para-Church organizations such as tract and temperance* societies; (ii) Social. There was increasing literacy, and (for many people) more time available for reading due to social improvements. (iii) Political. This period saw the progressive abolition (completed by 1861) of restrictive taxes on the press, initially imposed to obstruct the spread of radical literature; (iv) Economic. There was the growth of a fast, efficient distribution system as the railway network was expanded, and the postal service improved; (v) Technical. Rapid advances in printing technology were made.

The nineteenth-century religious periodicals which emerged in the light of these developments can be broadly categorized as follows:

(i) *Denominational.* All major Churches issued their own periodicals (*e.g.*, for Congregational organs see H. Escott, *A History of Scottish Congregationalism*, G, 1960, 143–4). Furthermore, publishing firms occasionally issued periodicals which, while not the official mouthpiece of a given Church, nevertheless gave strong support to its position. For example, there were from the very first three periodicals officially connected with the FC: these were combined in the *Monthly Record*ced first three periodicals Monthly from 1850. On the other hand, the *North British Review,** while not an official organ of the CofS, nevertheless gave it strong support. If periodicals were important to highly-centralized Churches, they were even more so to decentralized groupings such as the Brethren.* Titles such as the *Northern Witness* and the *Believers Magazine* provided vital channels of communication among scattered assemblies later in the century.

(ii) *Factional.* As controversies arose within Churches, so periodicals were issued in support of conflicting party positions. Early in the century, for example, the first *Scottish Guardian** and the *Edinburgh Christian Instructor** both supported the evangelical* party within the CofS: the *Scottish Ecclesiastical Journal** took an opposing view. Later, controversies over Church union, Voluntaryism and theological liberalization generated their own periodical literature.

(iii) *Theological and Philosophical.* A number of notable periodicals of this type were issued, including the *British and Foreign Evangelical Review,** the *Expository Times** and the *Critical Review.*

(iv) *Para-Church Organizations.* Periodicals provided the new para-Church organizations with instruments of communication and fund-raising. The *Missionary Magazine,** for example, focused attention on missionary enterprise. The temperance movement* had its *Temperance Society Record*, while the Stirling Tract Enterprise* published the *British Messenger.*

(v) *Evangelistic.* Periodicals which were very often series of tracts issued on a regular basis under a common title were widely sold for free distribution as an evangelistic medium. Great quantities of these, targeted at every conceivable audience, were produced, particularly by the Stirling Tract Enterprise and by Brethren publishers, notably John

PERIODICALS, RELIGIOUS

Ritchie of Kilmarnock, and Pickering and Inglis of Glasgow (see Publishing, Religious).

(vi) *Literary and Family*. The sale of denominational magazines was slowly undermined by the development of general literary journals. Initially, many of these were strongly religious in content, but this religious element was progressively diluted. The *Scottish Christian Herald** (1836) was one of the earliest cheap religious magazines. It took a pro-Evangelical stance, and sold 40,000 copies monthly at its peak. The *Christian Treasury** was selling 30,000 monthly by 1860. Most such journals excluded fiction, which was viewed with suspicion by Evangelicals. On the other hand, Norman MacLeod's* *Edinburgh Christian Magazine** eschewed narrow theological positions, included fiction, and aimed at a broad working-class audience. MacLeod was later to edit the highly successful *Good Words*,* in which the narrowly religious content was further reduced. By the early twentieth century, the popular periodical press had been essentially secularized.

The Scottish religious periodical press has, in general, declined throughout the twentieth century. Many Church publications were reduced in influence by family magazines, which became indistinguishable from the secular press. CofS periodicals and those of para-Church organizations continued, however, to have a modest circulation, and some new titles have been published. Although there has been a significant upturn since the 1960s in the number of religious (especially evangelical) periodical titles being sold in Scotland, the majority of these are produced south of the border. Arguably, this is as much due to the fact that Scottish Evangelicals look for the most part to London for leadership as it is to Scotland's decline in importance as a print centre.

Only for a short segment of Church history was the Scottish religious periodical press a dominant medium: within those decades, however, its influence was immense.

See also: *British Weekly*; *Christian Journal*; *Church Review and Scottish Ecclesiastical Magazine*; *Edinburgh Review*; *Evangelical Quarterly*; *Evangelical Repository*; *Instructor*; *Life and Work*; *MacPhail's Edinburgh Ecclesiastical Journal and Literary Review*; *Presbyterian Magazine*; *Presbyterian*; *Presbyterian Review and Religious Journal*; *Reformed Presbyterian Magazine*; *Scottish Christian Journal*; *Scottish Catholic Herald*; *Scottish Journal of Theology*; *Scottish Pulpit*; *Watchword*; *Witness*.

R. D. Altick, *The English Common Reader* (Chicago, 1957); W. J. Couper, *The Edinburgh Periodical Press* [to 1800], 2 vols (Stirling, 1908); R. M. W. Cowan, *The Newspaper in Scotland* (G, 1946); R. S. Crane and F. B. Kaye, 'A Census of British Newspapers and Periodicals 1620–1800', *Studies in Philology* 24 (1927), 1–205; M. E. Craig, *The Scottish Periodical Press 1750–1789* (E, 1931); *The Waterloo Directory of Scottish Newspapers and Periodicals, 1800–1900*, 2 vols (Waterloo, 1989).

J. A. H. Dempster

PERTH, FIVE ARTICLES OF

Perth, Five Articles of, devised by King James VI* to impose episcopalian worship ceremonies on a reluctant CofS at the 1618 General Assembly. At the 1616 Assembly in Aberdeen, it was ordered that a liturgy and book of canons be drafted. The King desired to have five articles of his own included in the book of canons, requiring: kneeling rather than sitting at the Lord's Supper,* private communion, baptism* not withheld longer than one Sunday and administered privately where necessary, the participation of bishops in confirmation,* and the observance of church holy days such as Christmas and Easter (see Christian Year).

The King visited Scotland in 1617 in the company of his persuasive chaplain, William Laud,* the better to cajole the Church into submission to the ceremonies of English episcopacy.* But a body of ministers meeting in Edinburgh asserted the Church's freedom from domination by the King and a committee of his favourites. James demanded that an Assembly be held to ratify his five canons. After that Assembly hesitated, the King cut off the stipends of recalcitrant ministers.

Another Assembly was called by the King for August 25 1618, at Perth. The new primate, John Spottiswoode,* presided over a gathering at which many were present at the King's request. After the reading of the King's letter requiring compliance, eighty-six voted to receive the articles, and forty-two opposed them. But the articles were not well received among the population, and apprehension grew when the King's *Book of Sports* (1618) promoted the use of the sabbath day for dancing and games. The articles were confirmed by Parliament* in 1621. Defiance by the Church's ministers was curbed; Robert Bruce* was imprisoned and David Dickson* was divested of his charge.

Resistance to the articles reflected a series of Reformed convictions: a rejection of worship* forms not commanded in Scripture;* kneeling at communion pre-supposes the RC adoration of the host in the mass; the sacraments are not to be separated from the preaching of the Word in the congregation; the baptism of dying infants and the reception of the host at death are not necessary for salvation; confirmation implies that baptism is defective without the bishop; and religious festivals, as revivals of the Old Testament ceremonial law superseded by the work of Christ, diminish respect for God's appointment of the Christian sabbath.

David Calderwood* wrote trenchant assessments of the Perth articles and the policy of imposing English ceremonies on the CofS, and issued his books from Dutch presses. George Gillespie* followed with his *Dispute against English Popish Ceremonies* (Leiden, 1637). These writings articulated with scholarly arguments the Presbyterian opposition to episcopacy, and prepared the ground for the Glasgow Assembly (1638)* which condemned the Perth Assembly of 1618 as unfree and null, and refuted and repealed each of the Five Articles.

Calderwood VII; J. Row, *History of the Kirk of Scotland* (E, 1842); P. H. R. Mackay, 'The Reception Given to the Five Articles of Perth',

RSCHS 19 (1977), 185–201; W. McMillan, *The Worship of the Scottish Reformed Church 1550–1638* (L, 1931); Spottiswoode III; I. B. Cowan, 'The Five Articles of Perth', in D. Shaw (ed.), *Reformation and Revolution* (E, 1967), 160–77.

S. Isbell

Perth, fourth Earl of (1648–1716). James Drummond succeeded to the title 1675 and was Lord Chancellor 1684–8. After James VII's* accession, he became a RC and was James's chief agent in Scotland. Having been over four years in confinement 1688–93, he went into exile. In late 1694 he began a slow journey south and spent ten months in Rome conducting business for James. In 1696 he joined the Jacobite* court at St Germain, Paris, where he remained until death. He was buried in the Scots College,* Paris.

Despite the opportune timing, his conversion was undoubtedly sincere, being due primarily to reading works by Bossuet, with whom he maintained cordial relations. His letters reveal him as a fervent RC, disenchanted with the politics and atmosphere of Rome itself. As governor 1696–1706 of James's young son, the Old Pretender, his influence was important. In 1701 he was created Duke.

A. Joly, *Un converti de Bossuet: James Drummond, Duc de Perth 1648–1716* (Lille, 1933); W. Jerdan (ed.), *Letters from James Earl of Perth* (L, Camden Society, 1845).

M. Dilworth

Petrie, Alexander (1594?–1662), Covenanting* divine. Born at Montrose, Angus, he graduated MA from St Andrews University in 1615, and during 1620–30 was master of Montrose's grammar school. He was ordained to the parish church of Rhynd, Perthshire, in 1632. He zealously supported the Covenanting movement, and was a member of the Glasgow Assembly of 1638* and of various committees in subsequent assemblies. In 1643 he went to Rotterdam to pastor a Scottish church formed the previous year. Here he published his *Chiliasto-Mastix, or, the prophecies of the Old and New Testament* (Rotterdam, 1644), an attack on millenarian views, especially those of Robert Maton's *Israel's Redemption* (L, 1642), then popular among Independents and Baptists (*see* Millennialism). A large part of his remaining years was taken up with preparing his *Compendious History of the Catholick Church from the year 600 to the year 1600* (The Hague, 1662). This contains valuable extracts from early CofS General Assemblies, records of which were lost by fire in 1834.

DNB XLV, 97–8; *FES* IV, 243.

N. R. Needham

Pew Rents, an obsolete method of gathering church funds. The system of renting pews grew with the installation of fixed seats in burgh* churches in the seventeenth century, in rural churches c.1720–1800, and was ubiquitous in Victorian Church life (except Baptist* and Chartist* churches). It was often regulated by burgh councils to allow access by all social groups, but by the mid-eighteenth century heritors* in rural and urban parishes appropriated a proportion of the parish kirk equal to their landholdings in the parish and erected palatial pews for themselves and their retainers. The remainder was rented out at varying prices or sold by 'roup', with the revenues passing to the poor-relief* fund.

The pew rent system added to grievances with patronage* and teinds,* promoting defection from the Est.C to the Secession* and Relief* Churches. But pew-renting imparted social status within congregations and, with sustained population growth, developed greatly in the nineteenth century. Though regarded by many Evangelicals as a cause of non-churchgoing, it remained widespread in Scottish Presbyterianism until the 1950s, when it rapidly declined.

C. G. Brown, 'The Costs of Pew-Renting', *JEH* 38 (1987), 347–61; W. G. Black, *Handbook of the Parochial Ecclesiastical Law of Scotland* (E, ²1891), 64–71, (⁴1928), 194–208.

C. G. Brown

Philanthropy, doing good to others without thought of return. It can involve more but is conventionally focussed on financial assistance. Its extent is determined by the interaction of four factors. The first is human need, the awareness of that through personal contact or publicity or whatever; the second, the responsiveness of the individual, sensitized by religious or secular concern; the third, the economic resources available on which to draw, and the fourth, the organizational or individual skill to bring need and response together. In pre-industrial Scotland, philanthropy mostly took the form of almsgiving, or bequests to education,* and it was on a limited scale. As the economy developed, however, and awareness of poverty and other related problems became more widespread, philanthropic activity burgeoned, aided by the social emphasis of much evangelical preaching. Thomas Chalmers* said, 'The great use of wealth is to do good with it,' and philanthropy flowered in the nineteenth century as the wealthy were persuaded to part with their money. In a world where the state took a very limited part in social relief, philanthropy took a bewildering variety of forms; outside the poor relief system* much attention went into causes such as education, libraries, lunatic asylums, dispensaries, homes for the destitute or disabled and so on. Some of the activity was long term, but other funds were a response to an immediate crisis, such as the potato famine of 1846–7 in the Highlands* (*see* Clearances).

Dynamic individuals like William Quarrier* of the Bridge of Weir Orphan Homes or Sir William Smith,* founder of the Boys Brigade,* played a leading part. But a glance at any nineteenth-century directory will show how many charitable and benevolent funds there were, and how many upper- and middle-class people were involved. Philanthropy was not, however, as altruistic as the biblical injunction (Matt. 6:2) to give alms in secret required.

PHILLIMORE, JOHN SWINNERTON

Subscription lists were published by charities to highlight who had given what, and wealthy patrons found their role carried kudos. By the end of the nineteenth century philanthropy as a system came under fire, particularly from socialist critics who argued that it merely dealt with symptoms, not causes. What was needed was not patronage, but state-funded rights for the poor and disadvantaged. And increasingly the state took over responsibility. The philanthropic tide retreated within Scotland and many local charitable societies became defunct. But that the benevolent impulse in the Churches or society at large is far from dead is seen in recent fundraising of Christian Aid, War on Want, or Band Aid.

O. Checkland, *Philanthropy in Victorian Scotland* (E, 1980); N. Masterman, *Chalmers on Charity* (L, 1900).

A. J. Durie

Phillimore, John Swinnerton (1873–1926), professor of classics. Born in Cornwall of a distinguished upper-class family, he had a brilliant career at Westminster School and Oxford University. After graduation 1895, he became a don at Christ Church and in 1899 Professor of Greek at Glasgow University. Although widely expected to enter politics or return to Oxbridge, he became a RC 1905 and in 1906 transferred to the chair of Humanity (Latin), which he occupied until death.

His reputation for classical scholarship was international; his interests were wide, embracing medieval Latin, European literature and Elizabethan prose. He published poetry, both translations and original work with a considerable religious element. He became an acknowledged leader in Glasgow RC circles and wrote for the Catholic Truth Society of Scotland.* His intimate friendship with Hilaire Belloc and G. K. Chesterton was a factor in introducing Distributism* to Scotland. Endowed with exceptional charisma as a teacher, he influenced greatly the embryonic RC middle class in the west of Scotland.

S. N. Miller, 'John Swinnerton Phillimore: a Memoir', *Dublin/Wiseman Review* 234 (1960), 316–34, 235 (1961), 23–47; *DNB 1922–1930*, 675–7.

M. Dilworth

Philip, John (1777–1851), Congregational* minister and missionary strategist. Born in Kirkcaldy of weaving stock, Philip was converted during the Haldane* revival and gave up a managerial career in a new spinning factory to study for the Congregational ministry at Hoxton College. In 1802 he was called to a church in Newbury, Berkshire, and then in 1804 to Belmont congregation in Aberdeen. There he soon established himself as a leading evangelical figure in Aberdeen and the north-east. A warm supporter of the London Missionary Society,* he was called by it to go to South Africa on a commission of enquiry and then stay as the resident director of the Society. It was only after long negotiations that his congregation at last agreed to free him, and he arrived in Cape Town in February 1819.

A dedicated Evangelical, Philip belonged to that stream in the tradition which was dedicated to the transformation of society as well as the conversion of individuals. After two years of patient reorganization of the society's work and careful observation of life in the Colony, Philip was convinced that fundamental reform of governmental policy was necessary if Christian mission was to flourish and its ends be achieved.

In 1827, unable to effect change locally and in despair over the unjust treatment of the indigenous peoples, he returned to lobby for change in Britain. There he published his two-volume *Researches in South Africa* (L, 1828). Meanwhile, to forestall potentially more drastic reform, the Colonial Government passed Ordinance 50 which, in effect, gave equal civil rights to all free people in the Colony, a vital change with the freeing of the slaves soon to take place. From this time on, Philip was unpopular with a majority of white colonists, English-speakers as well as Afrikaners. He nevertheless continued to campaign against injustice wherever he saw it. This meant that he took very unpopular stands over the frontier wars with the Xhosa and the independence of the Griqua, who by the 1840s were an almost wholly Christian people. Meanwhile he had also personally persuaded both the Paris Evangelical Mission and the American Board to work in South Africa, and had become official adviser to both societies as well as to the newly arrived Rhenish Mission.

By the 1840s, Philip had lost the confidence of his fellow directors in London, who now looked to the pietist element in the mission staff led by Robert Moffat,* though they refused Philip's resignation, needing his administrative talents and influence with other missions and white liberal opinion in Britain and in the Colony. In 1847 he retired to Hankey to live with one of his minister sons in a congregation of his loyal 'Cape Coloured' people. It was there that he died.

P. Robert, *The Elijah of South Africa* (L, 1851); A. C. Ross, *John Philip (1775–1851)* (A, 1986).

A. C. Ross

Philip, Robert (c.1583–1647), RC priest. Born in Sanquhar (Dumfriesshire), he left Scotland in 1599 and was among the first entrants to the Scots College* at Rome in 1602. Ordained priest, he secured a master's degree in Paris before embarking on the Scottish Mission in 1613. His active ministry lasted three months. Tried and convicted for saying masses in and around Edinburgh and Dumfries, Philip was banished from Scotland. Having entered the Parisian Oratory for secular clergy, he accompanied Henrietta Maria to the court of Charles I in 1625. Remaining as the Queen's confessor when her French entourage was expelled, he was an unassuming force for moderation during the 1630s. He cultivated influential politicians rather than work for the formal concession of toleration. Intercepted overtures to the papacy led to his parliamentary impeachment in 1641 and his expulsion from England. Despite a brief return to the Royalist camp in 1643-4, he was an exiled observer of the civil wars, dying in Paris in 1647.

DNB XLV, 181-2; W. McMillan, 'Robert Philip, Father Confessor to Henrietta Maria', *RSCHS* 9 (1946-7), 83-96, 142-54; G. Albion, *Charles I and the Count of Rome* (L, 1935).

A. I. Macinnes

Philosophy of Religion, the philosophical treatment of responses to God. The philosophy of religion was not recognized as such in Scottish theology (or in theology more generally) until the nineteenth century. Until the onset of idealist forms of thought, derived from the epoch-making influence of Immanuel Kant (1724-1804), the focus of attention fell on the metaphysical underpinnings of the Christian revelation, on questions of theological method, on the scope and limits of natural theology, and (since the time of Descartes, 1596-1650) on problems of religious knowledge. During this period, the Christian religion was not considered as a product of the constructive ability of the human mind to postulate or project God but rather as embracing the varied responses to the Word of God in personal religious experience, prayer and public worship.

As a result, matters which were later regarded as phenomena capable of being studied in their own right were, until the nineteenth century, treated as sets of intentionally-directed responses to revealed truth. The essential difference is that before Kant, for example throughout the medieval and Reformation periods, the human mind was regarded as being essentially receptive to all truth, including revealed truth, whereas after Kant the mind is said, one way or another, to contribute to what it experiences in accordance with *a priori* forms of intuition. Yet it is possible to discern at least four different epochs in the history of Scottish theology in which at least some of the issues of what is now known as the philosophy of religion were addressed.

REFORMATION AND POST-REFORMATION. Prior to the Reformation it is not easy to discover any distinctive intellectual currents in Scottish thought. But from the period of the Reformation until the end of the seventeenth century, a time dominated by the Reformation conflict and struggles for the rights of the Church against Erastianism, theologians such as Samuel Rutherford* were absorbed in the elaboration and defence of the doctrines of grace against Arminian* and antinomian perversions of it, and concurrently with the development of covenant theology* as both an interpretative scheme for Scripture and an ecclesiastical ideology. Both developments involved the theologians in philosophical discussions, the one on the perennial issues of grace, free will and divine providence, including proposed mediating positions such as the *scientia media* ('middle knowledge') of Luis de Molina (1535-1600), the other on the relationship between natural law and the original covenant. Besides Rutherford, another representative figure is Robert Boyd,* whose commentary on Ephesians contains elaborate discussions of metaphysical issues in Christian dogmatics. The method of treatment of the issues is essentially scholastic, owing more to Aquinas and Bradwardine than to Calvin and the more humanist-inspired strand of the Reformation, although the medieval influences on Calvin, and through him on the Reformed theologians, ought not to be underestimated. There was little natural theology* at this period.

The turn of the seventeenth century saw the onset of three important changes lasting into the next century. One was the rise of deism* (or Socinianism, as earlier versions were called; *see* Unitarians) as a distinct movement. The earlier deistic influences, emanating from Lord Herbert of Cherbury (1583-1648), felt to a degree in England, did not get a hand-hold in Scotland. But deism, inspired by a rationalistic, undogmatic temper and propelled by the new science, required of Christian theologians a greater awareness than hitherto of the rational basis of Christian theism, and of the needful distinction between on the one hand the use of reason as a theological tool, and rationalism on the other. Thomas Halyburton* is an example of an orthodox Calvinist ('Rabbi' Duncan* called him an 'Owenian') who wrestled in an able and informed way with these problems at an early phase of the deistic controversy. It is possible, also, to find able discussions of philosophical themes of religion in surprising places. Thus Ralph Erskine's* *Faith no Fancy, or a Treatise of Mental Images* (E, 1745) contains an informed critique of John Locke's (1632-1704) account of ideas as mental images.

MODERATISM. A second influence was the rise of the Moderate* party in the CofS, following the settlement of 1688-90. It laid much emphasis on the preaching of morality and little on the atonement, the need for conversion and spiritual warfare. The morality was usually a version of what came later to be known as utilitarianism, or the ethical institutionism of the 'moral sense' theorists such as Francis Hutcheson.* At this period, the middle of the eighteenth century, the influence of the Scottish Enlightenment,* of Hutcheson, Adam Fergusson (1723-1816), Adam Smith (1723-90), and David Hume,* was at its height.

One product of the Scottish Enlightenment which was destined to have an influence beyond the borders of Scotland, in France as well as in North America, was the Scottish Realism* or commonsense philosophy of Thomas Reid (1710-96) and his immediate followers, such as Dugald Stewart* and Thomas Brown (1778-1820). In response to David Hume's* radical scepticism, Reid claimed that the human mind had a natural endowment of certain common-sense beliefs which were not derived from the 'ideas' of the empiricist philosophers (Reid argued that the introduction of such ideas was in any case unwarranted), but which provided a basic understanding of reality which could not be gainsaid.

The philosophical influence of Reid was not confined to the Moderate party of the CofS but extended through Thomas Chalmers,* for example, to the Evangelicals of that Church and through John Witherspoon* to the evangelical Presbyterians of North America. Another important philosophical influence at this period and subsequently was Jonathan Edwards,* who during his lifetime corresponded with a number of Scottish clergymen and at one period thought of emigrating to Scotland.

While Reid's influence persisted at the popular level, it was brought to a fairly abrupt end among thinkers and educators in Scotland by a new set of philosophical influences, those of post-Kantian German idealism, the influence of which was felt not only on the recurring issues in philosophy and theology but also on the study of the biblical text, e.g. through the work of William Robertson Smith.* Important early figures in this transition were James Ferrier (1808–64), and the Caird* brothers, James and Edward, and Henry Mansel (1820–71) in England.

CONTINENTAL IDEALISM. The coming of continental idealism to Scotland produced two crucial changes. Whereas Reid had appealed to naturally-endowed principles of the mind which receive the data of experience and interpret it to provide knowledge of the world as it is, for the idealists the mind had a crucial role in interpreting and harmonizing fragmentary and seemingly contradictory elements of experience into a wider, all-embracing unity. Later in the century evolutionary ways of thinking inspired by Charles Darwin's *Origin of Species* and a general optimism about human progress provided further impetus to the view that, at the highest theoretical level, reality was not given but made.

The second crucial change concerned the knowledge of God. Reid had relied upon various *a posteriori* arguments to establish the existence of God. Kant and the idealists were agnostic about God because they held that any attempt to think about God leads to *antinomies*, apparently incompatible lines of thought. While God cannot be known, however, he is still needed; in particular, he is needed to provide a rational grounding for morality, morality rooted not in the moral law of Scripture nor even in natural law, and not in the theological dogma of any one religion, but in human autonomy and rationality.

The net result of the influence of idealism on Scottish theology was a stress on theological indefinites, on the understanding of religion in mainly moral terms, and on the need to develop all-embracing philosophical systems to overcome the various conflicts generated by different aspects of human experience, for example the conflict between religion and science, and between the theologies of different historical religions. One representative and influential later idealist is Seth Pringle-Pattison (1856–1931), whose *Idea of God* (O, 1917) was widely circulated. A. Campbell Fraser's* *The Philosophy of Theism* (2 vols, E, 1895–6) is also representative.

NEO-ORTHODOXY. The sentiments which undergirded this liberal-minded, undogmatic, optimistic, philosophical approach to religion were rudely shattered by the horror of the First World War. This abrupt change heralded a deep theological change, the rise of the 'theology of crisis' or the 'theology of the word' of Karl Barth (1886–1968) and Emil Brunner (1889–1966; *see* Neo-Orthodoxy). Although they differed sharply from each other on the question of natural theology, the two theologians were united in turning their backs upon theological liberalism and optimism, and giving prominence to biblical categories. Barth, in particular, was emphatic that the only way to engage the culture was not to seek common ground but to confront it with the message of Scripture. Barth's connections with Scotland were fairly close, both through his students and his lectures. He delivered the Gifford lectures* in 1937–8, published as *The Knowledge of God and the Service of God* (L, 1938). The extent to which Barth's theology is truly biblical, and not another variant on the German post-Kantian tradition, remains a matter of debate. T. F. Torrance* has maintained the Barthian emphasis upon both the objectivity of theology and its distinctiveness from other endeavours. A rather different emphasis, reflecting increasing reaction against Neo-Orthodoxy, is represented by John Baillie,* whose *Invitation to Pilgrimage* (L, 1942) has been widely read (*see* Apologetics; Natural Theology). Existentialism has only marginally influenced Scottish philosophical theology, as in Ronald Gregor-Smith.*

The Gifford lectures have since 1888 provided an often distinguished platform for the discussion of fundamental issues in the philosophy of religion.

J. Baillie, *Our Knowledge of God* (L, 1939); J. Caird, *An Introduction to the Philosophy of Religion* (G, 1880); C. A. Campbell, *Selfhood and Godhood* (L, 1957); J. Macleod, *Scottish Theology* (E, ³1974); A. S. Pringle-Pattison, *The Idea of God in the Light of Recent Philosophy* (O, 1917); A. E. Taylor, *The Faith of a Moralist* (L, 1930); J. Walker, *The Theology and Theologians of Scotland* (E, ²1888).

P. Helm

Pickering, Henry (1858–1941), Brethren publisher. He was born at Kenton, near Newcastle-upon-Tyne. He planned to become a schoolmaster, but turned to printing. He moved to Glasgow in 1886 to take charge of a tract depot; in 1895, with William Inglis, he established the printing, publishing and bookselling firm of Pickering and Inglis. He was a pithy and pointed speaker on Christian subjects, especially to young people. He published several volumes of his addresses, outlines and illustrations. He edited *Chief Men among the Brethren* (G, 1918, ²1931), a collection of sixty-five, later raised to 100, short biographies. From 1914 to his death he was editor of *The Witness*, in its day the most influential periodical among Open Brethren. His considerable gifts for religious journalism raised its circulation to record heights. His last eighteen years were spent in London, but he died and was buried in Largs, Ayrshire.

H. J., 'Henry Pickering', *The Believer's Pathway* 62 (1941), 22–3.

F. F. Bruce

Picts. The term *Picti*, 'painted folk', first occurs in Latin literary sources, referring to a people allied to the Irish and hostile to the romanized Britons of southern Britain at the end of the third and beginning of the fourth century AD. From one of the earliest references it may be deduced that the Caledonians, whose territory lay in the central highlands of Scotland and especially the higher glens and straths of Perthshire, were included among the *Picti*. The term was surely a nickname, probably coined by Roman troops. It is not a translation of, but may be thought to bear some relation to, the name Priteni (OIr. *Cruithin*), apparently applied to the natives of northern Britain and meaning literally 'figured', 'tattooed'.

There are no grounds for supposing that the historical Picts were anything other than the descendants of the people dwelling in Britain to the north of the Clyde–Forth isthmus at the period when Roman armies first penetrated into what is now southern Scotland, *c.*AD 79. According to the geographer Ptolemy, Scotland north of Forth and Clyde was occupied by twelve or thirteen tribes, to which we may add the Boresti mentioned by Tacitus and the Maeatae and Verturiones of later writers. The generally accepted view among modern scholars is that these peoples, collectively called Picts, had two languages, one non-Indo-European and not now recoverable, the other Indo-European and recognizably classifiable as belonging to the P-Celtic branch of the Celtic family of languages. In the absence of literature and of all but a few inscriptions, much of what we know of the languages in use in northern Britain on the eve of the historic period and during its earliest centuries must be derived from surviving or recorded place-names.

Apart from a handful of difficult names, mostly of rivers although occasionally of inhabited localities such as Elgin and Forfar or districts such as Buchan, by far the largest number of these names betray a P-Celtic origin even where they are no longer fully P-Celtic in form. Thus from the area around the upper Moray Firth eastward to Aberdeenshire and then southward to the southern lowlands, a common generic for 'stream' (often but by no means exclusively sluggish or slow-running) is *pol*, of which the reflex in modern Scots is often *pow*; this term is by definition P-Celtic. Again, a P-Celtic term found in modern Welsh as *mynydd*, 'hill', but also specifically 'hill grazing', 'rough pasture', can be traced with precisely the same range of meaning in numerous place-names of northern and north-eastern Scotland and, like *pol*, was well established in southern Scotland (e.g., compare Welsh *penmynydd*, *penfynydd*, 'end of the hill grazing', with the numerous Scottish Kinmundies, Kinminities, Kinmonths, etc., where P-Celtic *pen* has become Q-Celtic *cend* (*ceann*) of identical meaning). Other P-Celtic terms found in the north include *carden*, 'thicket' (Kincardine), *lanerc*, 'grove' (Lanrick), *aber*, 'confluence' (Applecross, Abertarff, Aberdeen, etc.) and *pefr*, 'beautiful', used of a stream (Strathpeffer, Innerpeffray). This vocabulary was shared with Lothian and Cumbria, but notably distinctive of Pictish territory is the element *pett*, literally a 'piece', 'share' or 'portion', but in practice meaning a farm(stead), equivalent to Gaelic *baile*, Old English *tun*. From Sutherland in the north to just south of the Forth many hundreds of crofts, farms (large and small), hamlets, villages, even small towns, bear 'pett-' names, the modern reflex being normally Pit- or (with the article) Pitten-, followed by a qualifying word or name, e.g. Pitsligo, Pitfoddels, Pittengardner, Pitlochry and Pittenweem. Unless Pitcon, Ayrshire, and Pettinain, Lanarkshire, are outlying exceptions, *pett-* is not found south of the Forth's southern littoral, and may be seen as essentially Pictish. 'Pictish' place-names are noticeably rare in both the Northern and the Western Isles, and even along the west Highland seaboard. In the former case they have probably been elbowed out by Norse names, but their scarcity in the Hebrides and west is harder to explain, and probably points to a decline in Pictish population numbers in this region.

A considerable degree of political organization is implied by accounts of the Pictish monarchy from the mid-sixth century onward. Brude (Bridei mac Maelchon), a pagan who nevertheless permitted St Columba* to preach in his realm, is called a 'very powerful king' by Bede; Bruide son of Bile inflicted a total defeat on the Northumbrians in 685, thus ensuring the future independence of Scotland *vis à vis* the English kings; Onuist (Angus) son of Urguist (Fergus) established a Pictish hegemony in the period 730–50; and even after the successful takeover bid by Kenneth MacAlpin in the 840s, the combined Scoto-Pictish realm continued to be the kingdom of the Picts till *c.*900. All this was achieved despite an apparently unique succession rule whereby no king of the Picts could be the son or paternal grandson of any previous king: the claim to kingship was derived from the mother, who was presumably of royal lineage. It is a testimony to the political cohesion and military skills of the Picts that this rule did not make for unduly weak government, although by *c.*800 the Picts came under extremely heavy pressure from both the Scots of Dalriada and the Vikings infiltrating into and soon acquiring for permanent settlement the Northern Isles and adjacent mainland of Caithness, together with eastern Sutherland and Ross.

The Picts south of the Grampians or 'Mounth' (itself a Pictish name) seem to have been converted to Christianity by the early sixth century, while their northern and western kindreds adopted the Christian faith during and following the Scottish sojourn of St Columba. While still pagan, the Picts had begun to develop a remarkable art style expressed, as far as surviving examples go, in carvings on stone and metalwork. Christianity undoubtedly gave this vigorous art a fresh stimulus and provided fruitful links with Ireland and Northumbria. The artists made much use of what seems to be a universal standardized language or code of symbols, embracing animal forms, domestic objects, geometrical shapes and unexplained devices such as 'V-' and 'Z-rods'. So far this code has defied all attempts to decipher it, although certain symbols, such as comb and mirror (for a woman) or a sword or spear (for a fighting man), seem self-explanatory. After the Picts became Christian, their symbols began to be combined with bas-relief crosses of Hiberno-Anglian character, and motifs were incorporated which have much in common with those found in Northumbrian and Irish stone-carvings and manuscripts. Just as the Picts did not suddenly come into existence when the name *Picti* was coined, so also they did not suddenly vanish when 'Scotland' appeared on the scene. Rather, they and their descendants remained as the inhabitants of Scotland north of Forth and Clyde, doubtless with a steadily increasing admixture of Dalriadan Scots, whose language (Old or Middle Irish or Gaelic*), conveniently cognate with Pictish and sharing a sizeable common vocabulary, replaced Pictish very gradually during the ninth and tenth centuries. Even in the far north it is doubtful whether the Norse settlers totally displaced the Picts, while in parts of Fife and Angus there was evidently some Anglian penetration from c.750.

F. T. Wainwright (ed.), *The Problem of the Picts* (E, 1955); S. Cruden, *The Early Christian and Pictish Monuments of Scotland* (E, 1957); Isabel Henderson, *The Picts* (L, 1967); A. A. M. Duncan, *Scotland: the Making of the Kingdom* (E, 1975); J. G. P. Friell and W. G. Watson (eds), *Pictish Studies: Settlement, Burial and Art in Dark Age Northern Britain* (BAR British Series 125, O, 1984); A. P. Smyth, *Warlords and Holy Men: Scotland, 80–1000* (L, 1984).

G. W. S. Barrow

Pilgrimage. Journeying to a sacred place for a religious purpose, e.g. to Jerusalem (in OT), Mecca, Benares, is a feature of many religions. From early centuries, Christians visited the Holy Land and, in Rome, the reputed tombs of the apostles Peter and Paul. The tomb of St Martin (d.397) at Tours also attracted pilgrims.

Pilgrimages were a conspicuous feature of medieval life. They were undertaken for a variety of reasons: penance for misdeeds, thanksgiving, fulfilment of a vow, to seek healing or spiritual benefit, to gain a rich indulgence, or simply out of devotion. Pilgrimage routes came into being, with hospices along the way; religious orders tended to and protected the pilgrims. Before departure the pilgrim's garb was donned and a liturgical blessing received. A lengthy pilgrimage also offered release from ties for the unstable, the irresponsible and the mere sightseer.

After the Holy Land and Rome, the traditional site of St James' tomb at Compostela in Spain was the most popular shrine. Particular relics or statues also drew pilgrims, with legends playing a great part, and each country had its popular shrines (*see* Saints). In modern times, pilgrimages are again popular. Places of Marian apparitions, particularly Lourdes, draw immense numbers, Scots included, as does Rome during a holy year. Modern transport and the amenities offered by hotels and travel agencies have, however, made pilgrimages speedy and removed the physical hardship.

Scotland too was addicted to pilgrimage and gave legal protection to the pilgrim's property and household. Early pilgrims to Rome included an abbot of Iona* (854), Kings Donald (975) and Macbeth (1050), and the earl of Orkney who slew St Magnus* (1120). Adomnán* wrote a treatise on pilgrimage places in the Holy Land (c.670). A national hospice for Scots pilgrims was established in Rome, probably in 1450; it was the forerunner of the Scots College* there. Archbishop Robert Blackader,* having visited Rome, died on his way to Jerusalem in 1508. In the sixteenth century, Scots were pilgrims to Compostela, Germany and even Mount Sinai.

Scotland had its own shrines. Apostolic relics drew foreign pilgrims to St Andrews.* The future Pope Pius II walked barefoot to Whitekirk (East Lothian) in 1435, while James IV went often to Whithorn* and St Duthac's shrine at Tain (Ross-shire) (*see* Celtic Saints). James V in 1536 went on foot to the Lady Chapel of Loretto at Musselburgh outside Edinburgh (*IR* 16, 1965, 209). Visiting the main pilgrimage places in Scotland was a common reparation for homicide. In modern times, favourite spots have included Iona, Dunfermline* (St Margaret's* shrine), Whithorn and Carfin.* An inter-church pilgrimage takes place annually at Haddington. Visits to the Holy Land by Protestants, which have greatly increased in recent years, are often informally conceived of as pilgrimages, and the growth of 'heritage' tourism has begun to attract similar sentiments.

Catholic Encyclopedia XII, 85–99; *New Catholic Encyclopedia* XI, 362–74; D. McRoberts, 'Scottish Pilgrims to the Holy Land', *IR* 20 (1969), 80–106; *id.*, 'The Scottish National Churches in Rome', *IR* 1 (1950), 110–30; M. Dilworth, 'Two Scottish Pilgrims in Germany', *IR* 18 (1967), 19–24; D. McKay, 'The Four Heid Pilgrimages of Scotland', *IR* 19 (1968), 76–7.

M. Dilworth

Pirie, Alexander (1737–1804), controversial Secession* and Independent minister. Prior to licence, he was appointed in 1760 by the Antiburgher (General Associate)* Synod to conduct the philosophical class for divinity students under Alexander Moncrieff* at Abernethy, Perthshire. He was then suspended and excommunicated for his contumacious spirit, after the synod rebuked him for using and recommending Lord Kames's *Essays on the Principles of Morality and Natural Religion* (E, 1751). He was ordained in 1765 as minister to a new Burgher congregation in Abernethy but in 1766 he attacked the principle of national covenanting* in his *Essay* on the subject, and was suspended by the Presbytery for this and for denial of the perfect humanity of Christ. Although the Synod in 1768 dismissed the case as informal, he became convinced of the unscriptural nature of Secession principles and left the Church in 1769. In 1770 the Relief* congregation at Blairlogie near Stirling called him and entered into an arrangement with him whereby he became their minister but without

PIRIE, WILLIAM ROBINSON

Presbytery approval. By 1776, the congregation wished to return to the authority of the Relief Synod, but Pirie seems to have had no desire to be part of the proposal, and left in 1778. He became a merchant in medicines at Newburgh where he ministered to a small Glasite* congregation. His *Miscellaneous and Posthumous Works* were published in 6 vols, E, 1805-6.

J. M'Kerrow, *History of the Secession Church* (G, 1841), 289-91; Small II, 586-8.

J. R. McIntosh

Pirie, William Robinson (1804-85), leading CofS divine in the post-Disruption* era. Born in Slains, Aberdeenshire, the son of its parish minister, he studied arts at Aberdeen University (1817-21), and then divinity (1821-5). Licensed by the Presbytery of Ellon in 1825, in 1830 he became minister of Dyce, Aberdeenshire.

Although an admirer of Thomas Chalmers,* Pirie espoused the Moderate* cause during the Ten Years' Conflict.* In 1843 he was appointed Professor of Divinity in Marischal College, Aberdeen; when Marischal and King's Colleges were united in 1860, he became Professor of Church History. In 1877 he was elected Principal of Aberdeen University. He acted as convener of the General Assembly Business Committee (1862-77).

Pirie's reputation lay chiefly in his vast knowledge of Church law (cf. his *Position, Principles and Duties of the Church of Scotland*, E, 1864), and his supreme ability as a General Assembly debater. His greatest contribution to the CofS combined these abilities when he launched a crusade for the abolition of patronage.* After several defeats in successive Assemblies, Pirie finally won in 1869. Parliament was petitioned, and the necessary legislation abolishing patronage was passed in 1874.

Pirie received a DD from Marischal College and from King's College, Aberdeen, in 1844. In 1864 he was Moderator of his Church's General Assembly.

P. Pirie, *William Robinson Pirie. In Memoriam* (A, 1888); *DNB* XLV, 327-8; *FES* VII, 363, 374, 379-80.

N. R. Needham

Playfair, James (1736-1819), CofS minister and college principal. Born in Perthshire, he graduated at St Andrews and was minister of Newtyle (1770-7) and Meigle (1777-1800), then Principal of United College, St Andrews (from 1799) and minister of St Leonard's Church to his death. Several times he declined nomination as Moderator of the General Assembly. Apart from compiling Statistical Accounts of three Perthshire parishes, his published works were mostly on geographical subjects. He was also historiographer to the Prince of Wales (later George VI).

A Complete System of Geography, Ancient and Modern, 6 vols (E, 1808-14).

FES VII, 415.

J. D. Douglas

PLAYFAIR, PATRICK MACDONALD

Playfair, John (1748-1819), mathematician and geologist. Born at Benvie, near Dundee, Playfair was the eldest son of the Revd James Playfair (*FES* V, 348). During his studies at the University of St Andrews (MA, 1765), where he was preparing for the CofS ministry, he showed great mathematical flair. After a period of parish ministry (at Liff and Benvie, 1773-83) and private tutoring (1783-5), he was appointed in 1785 to a joint Professorship in Mathematics at the University of Edinburgh, a position which he exchanged in 1805 for a Chair in Natural Philosophy. He was for many years editor of the *Transactions of the Royal Society of Edinburgh*, where he published papers.

After the death in 1797 of his friend James Hutton, the pioneer geologist (*DNB* XXVIII, 354-6), Playfair undertook to elucidate Hutton's *Theory of the Earth* (E, 1785), and consequently published his *Illustrations of the Huttonian Theory of the Earth* (E, 1802). It is for this work that he is most remembered, even though his professional field of scientific competence was mathematics. As well as presenting Hutton's work in a coherent form, Playfair defended it from theological censure by dissociating Huttonian geology from deistic* natural theology.* In so doing Playfair suppressed Hutton's teleological deism and went on to suggest that, correctly understood, uniformitarian geology was actually more conducive to a reverent attitude towards the workings of God in the natural order than the catastrophic convolutions to which Mosaic critics resorted. Playfair's *Illustrations* thus constitutes a landmark in the history of geological science.

J. G. Playfair (ed.), *Works of John Playfair*, 4 vols (E, 1822).

Dict. of Scientific Biogr. XI, 34-6; *DNB* XLV, 413-14; *FES* V, 348-9.

D. N. Livingstone

Playfair, Patrick MacDonald (1858-1924), CofS minister, restorer of St Andrews Town Church. Born at Abercorn, West Lothian, son of the parish minister, he attended Edinburgh University (MA, 1877). He then studied science at Edinburgh for two years, and then theology. He was licensed in 1882 by Edinburgh Presbytery, and became assistant to Norman Macleod of St Stephen's, Edinburgh. In 1886 he was ordained to the parish church of Glencairn, in Dumfriesshire. In 1899 he moved to St Andrews. Here he devoted the first ten years of his ministry to restoring the historic Town or Parish Church, built in 1412, where John Knox* preached his first sermon. The restoration was a great success, and Playfair is remembered chiefly for this.

Playfair was an eloquent and powerful preacher. He promoted many local causes in St Andrews, particularly education as a member of the councils of St Katharines and St Leonards girls' schools. He received a DD from St Andrews, and was offered the Moderatorship of the General Assembly in 1922 and 1924, but declined for health reasons.

PLUSCARDEN

R. S. Kirkpatrick, *The Ministry of Patrick MacDonald Playfair in St Andrews* (St Andrews, 1930); *FES* II, 316; V, 237-8.

N. R. Needham

Pluscarden, Scottish abbey belonging to the Subiaco Congregation of the Benedictine* order, situated six miles south-west of Elgin, Morayshire. Founded as a priory in 1230 by Alexander II for an austere, Order of Valliscaulian* monks from Burgundy, it was united to Urquhart Priory, itself a dependency of Dunfermline Abbey,* in 1454, and erected into a free barony for Alexander Seaton in 1587. The fourth Earl of Fife began restoration of its ruins in the 1820s, the third Marquess of Bute bought it in 1897, and his son Lord Calum Crichton-Stuart gave it to Prinknash Abbey, Gloucester in 1943. Re-established as a Benedictine monastery from Prinknash April 1948, it became an independent Priory in 1966, and was raised to the status of Abbey 1974. Much of the original building has now been handsomely restored, with a thriving contemplative community whose daily life is equally divided between singing the divine office, spiritual reading and manual work, specializing in the latter in stained glass, stone carving and market gardening.

S. R. Macphail, *History of the Religious House of Pluscardyn* (E, 1881); Easson-Cowan; R. Hamilton, *The Pluscarden Story* (Inverness, 1977); P. F. Anson, *A Monastery in Moray* (L, 1959).

L. J. Macfarlane

Pollok, Robert (1798–1827), religious writer and poet. Born in Eaglesham, Renfrewshire, he was educated at Glasgow University 1817–22, and then studied theology at the USec. Hall in Edinburgh. Here from 1824-5 he wrote his oft-reprinted *Tales of the Covenanters*, consisting of *Helen of the Glen*, *Ralph Gemmell* and *The Persecuted Family*, originally published separately and anonymously. These celebrate the Covenanting* heroes and martyrs* of the Killing Times.* In December 1824, he began to write the poem on which his literary fame chiefly rests, *The Course of Time* (2 vols, L, 1827), a religious meditation on human existence, in ten books of blank verse. It was finished by July 1826 and published early in 1827. Influenced in theme and style both by Milton (Pollok's favourite poet) and William Cowper, it was widely acclaimed, reaching its twenty-fifth edition in 1867.

Pollok was licensed by the USec.C in spring 1827, but developed consumption. A planned recuperative holiday to Italy was cut short by a worsening of his condition when he reached London; he died in Shirley Common, near Southampton, in September 1827. The inscription over Pollok's grave in Millbrook churchyard says, 'His immortal Poem is his monument.'

Tales of the Covenanters (E, 1833; new ed., E, 1884, with biogr. sketch by A. Thomson); D. Pollok, *The Life of Robert Pollok* (E, 1843); *DNB* XLVI, 69-70.

N. R. Needham

PONT (KILPONT, KINPONT), ROBERT

Polwarth, Lord (1864–1944), pioneer of social work in the CofS. His father was a farmer and landowner at Mertoun in the Borders, who became Lord Polwarth in 1867, whereupon his son, Walter George Scott (Hepburne-Scott), became Master of Polwarth. Both parents were strong Evangelicals. As Walter's tutor they chose Clement Scott,* the missionary to Nyasaland. From Eton he went to Trinity College, Cambridge (BA, 1885), where he made lasting friendships among the 'Cambridge Seven' (in 1888 he married the sister of one of them, Edith Frances Buxton) and other Evangelicals. A tour of India laid the basis for a long-term commitment to the Kirk's Foreign Missions. (His sister, Mary, served in J. A. Graham's* Kalimpong mission, and was the first woman to receive a Scottish University's DD, from St Andrews.)

Soon after their marriage, the Scotts moved to Humbie in E. Lothian, where he farmed and embarked on an extraordinarily active career in local government (having failed to win a seat in Parliament as a Tory) and public service, especially from 1909 as Chairman of the Prison Commissioners for Scotland, but also in other organizations concerned with children, youth and offenders. There were many links with his energetic twenty-one-year convenership of the Kirk's Committee on Social Work (*see* Social Responsibility, Board of), which assumed in 1904 in its second year (perhaps the first convener of a major CofS committee who was not a minister). Under his lead it developed an impressive range of homes (for girls' training, rehabilitation, children in special need, the elderly – *see* Eventide Homes – and other schemes, e.g. emigration*).

He succeeded as the ninth Lord Polwarth on his father's death in 1920 (*Who Was Who, 1916–1928*, 845), and after retirement in 1929 was elected to the House of Lords as Scottish representative peer. He became Lord Lieutenant of E. Lothian (1937) and received Edinburgh's LLD (1937). Among other causes he supported was the National Bible Society of Scotland (*see* Bible Societies). His wife served as President of the Woman's Guild* (A. H. Charteris* was a friend) and of the Scottish Mothers' Union. The Polwarths gave the land for the Humbie Children's Village started by the Edinburgh Children's Holiday Fund spearheaded by Mrs Stirling Boyd.

In 1945 the CofS opened in Edinburgh the Lord and Lady Polwarth Memorial Home for homeless children; more recently it has been devoted to other Church uses.

Who Was Who, 1941–1950, 925; G. F. Barbour, *Lord Polwarth 1864–1944* (E, n.d.); *LW* n.s. 15 (1944), 152.

D. F. Wright

Pont (Kilpont, Kinpont), Robert (1524–1606), Reformer and minister. Born in or near Culross in Fife, where he attended school before entering St Leonard's College, St Andrews in 1544, by the Reformation* he had settled in St Andrews, had opted for Protestantism and was already serving as an elder on St Andrews Kirk Session* in 1559. He attended the General Assembly in December 1560 as a commissioner from St Andrews, and was approved by the Assembly for the ministry and teaching. Appointed minister of Dunblane in 1562, he was soon transferred to Dunkeld and subsequently served as the General Assembly's commissioner for Inverness, Moray and Banff. Elected Moderator of the General Assembly in 1570, 1575, 1581, 1583 and 1596, he was appointed provost of Trinity College, Edinburgh in 1571, participated in the Convention of Leith* in 1572, and gained the Assembly's dispensation to serve as a senator of the College of Justice while remaining a minister. He was active in drafting the *Second Book of Discipline*,* and was appointed minister of St Cuthbert's, Edinburgh in 1578. An associate of Andrew Melville* and the Presbyterians, Pont opposed the Crown's efforts to appoint Robert Montgomery* as Archbishop of Glasgow in 1581, protested at the anti-Presbyterian 'Black Acts'* of 1584, was deposed from the College of Justice and fled to England. On his return, he opposed releasing Archbishop Patrick Adamson* from his sentence of excommunication in 1586. When James VI nominated him Bishop of Caithness by 1587, Pont referred the matter to the Assembly which censured the office; but he was later prepared to serve as the Assembly's commissioner for Orkney. He was the author of several works.

Register of the Minister, Elders and Deacons of the Christian Congregation of St Andrews, ed. D. H. Fleming (E, 1889–90); *BUK*; Calderwood; *SBD*; J. Kirk, *Patterns of Reform* (E, 1989); *FES* I, 93, 99, IV, 154, 342; *DNB* XLVI, 91–4.

J. Kirk

Poor Relief. Early legislation to deal with the poor in the fifteenth century was often an attempt to remove vagabonds and beggars as much as to relieve those who needed the charity of society for their subsistence. A major statute of 1574 identified those, such as the sick and the aged, who were incapable of providing for themselves, and charged local officials with the responsibility of taxing residents in the parish* for their relief. In 1597 responsibility was passed to the Kirk Sessions,* which shared it with the heritors* on whom fell the burden of any assessment raised. Magistrates were in charge of relief in the burghs. A statute of 1672, which consolidated the provision, remained the foundation of poor relief until 1845.

Parochial devolution led to local diversity, which meant that for most people, especially the recipients of relief, the Kirk Session was the body with which they dealt. Two general characteristics of the poor law remain amid the local diversity. First, even though an early statute permitted an assessment for the relief of the poor, the source of funds was assumed to be voluntary contributions. Second, those who were unable to look after themselves in any circumstances were distinguished from the able-bodied poor; relief was to be confined to the former. These two characteristics of the traditional system of poor relief were subject in practice to qualification. Assessments were sometimes raised, though only in a minority of parishes, and relief was sometimes given to the able-bodied. The rule that the able-bodied should not be given relief was recognized formally only in the late eighteenth century, and even then in practice the distinction was often reflected more in the amount given: the able-bodied had to rely on spasmodic and not very generous subscriptions.

The effectiveness of the two formal characteristics could be defended in the small, tightly-knit state of many Scottish rural parishes. On such the greatest defender of the Scottish poor law, Thomas Chalmers,* based his belief that adherence to the traditional principles ensured spontaneous Christian charity and the moral resilience of its recipients. Practice differed from the ideal. Even in rural communities the individual care and attention to which the poor law was supposed to lead according to Chalmers was marred by petty investigation and the inevitable stinginess when funds had to be provided by parsimonious heritors*. Behind much of the moral discipline* exercised by Kirk Sessions* was a simple desire to ensure that the financial responsibility of paternity did not fall on the parish.

The inadequacy of the provision was most acute in the towns, the larger of which had to make special provision for the poor early in the eighteenth century. Thereafter dissent, the advent of Irish RCs, and above all the massive movements of population within Scotland and from Ireland which accompanied industrialization, destroyed any possibility of relieving the poor in their parishes of origin. Cyclical or technological unemployment, notably among the handloom weavers in the 1830s and 1840s, gave rise to large numbers of highly localized able-bodied poor, the group for whom the poor law made even less provision as their numbers grew.

Chalmers remained wedded to the old parochial system dependent on voluntary finance, and made a controversial effort to apply it in the new parish of St John's in Glasgow in the early 1820s. Opposition grew, especially from medical critics led by W. P. Alison,* who held that unrelieved poverty lay behind rising death rates in the towns. Ironically, Chalmers helped to ensure that the old system of poor relief could not continue. The relief of dissenters had always been difficult to fit into a system administered by the Est.C. The Disruption* of 1843 finally broke the old parochial structure and the possibility of continuing with the old methods. The legislation of 1845, which followed the investigations of a Royal Commission, tried to build on the old methods, but assimilation to practice based on the assumptions behind the English reforms of 1845 gained ground.

R. A. Cage, *The Scottish Poor Law 1745–1845* (E, 1981); R. Mitchison, 'The Making of the Old Scottish Poor Law', *Past and Present* 63 (1974), 58–93; *id.*, 'The Creation of the Disablement Rule in the Scottish Poor Law', in T. C. Smout (ed.), *The Search for Wealth and Stability* (L, 1979); J. Lindsay, *The Scottish Poor Law* (Ilfracombe,

POPE, ALEXANDER

1975); L. J. Saunders, *Scottish Democracy 1815–1840* (E, 1950).

R. H. Campbell

Pope, Alexander (*c.* 1706–82), CofS minister who made an important collection of Gaelic* heroic ballads, *c.* 1739. Born at Loth, Sutherland, and educated at King's College, Aberdeen, he served initially as a parish schoolmaster in Reay. He was licensed by the Presbytery of Dornoch and ordained to the parish of Reay in 1734. He was alleged to have carried a cudgel because of the disaffection shown towards Presbyterianism in the parish. Nevertheless, he was popular with the people. He and his namesake, Alexander Pope, the English poet, met at Twickenham in 1732. He was interested in local history and archaeology.

FES VII, 132–3.

D. E. Meek

Popular Party, a name used to describe those in the eighteenth-century CofS who opposed the implementation of the law of patronage.* The name was given on the grounds that the opposition represented the views of the ordinary members, who were generally regarded as favouring the election of ministers by popular vote. It was rarely organized as a 'party' in any coherent manner and rarely controlled the General Assembly, although it almost certainly represented the views of the majority of both ministers and members. Although it is generally assumed that it was an evangelical* party, it was a complex grouping and encompassed some whose views had much in common with Moderatism.* Virtually all Evangelicals advocated the right of the people to choose their own ministers, but not all who did so were Evangelicals. The concept of a clearly recognizable 'Popular Party' has, therefore, limited value beyond the patronage dispute proper.

See Crosbie, Andrew; Erskine, Henry; Erskine, John; MacLaurin, John; Webster, Alexander; Moncrieff, Sir Henry Wellwood; Witherspoon, John.

R. B. Sher, *Church and University in the Scottish Enlightenment* (E, 1985); J. McIntosh, 'The Popular Party in the Church of Scotland, 1740–1800' (PhD, University of Glasgow, 1989).

J. R. McIntosh

Practical Theology, Teaching of. Presbyterian Scotland has always stressed the need for a learned ministry. For centuries this involved a highly academic form of education in the classical theological disciplines – dogmatics, apologetics, biblical studies with the appropriate languages, and Church history – with no place in the curriculum for any kind of practical theology. Prior to the nineteenth century, subjects such as pastoral care and mission were not taught, although prior to licensing students were required to demonstrate to Presbytery their ability at least in preaching (*see* Homiletics) and the conduct of worship. But since all theological teachers were ordained and most had been in the pastoral ministry (and some remained in a pastoral charge alongside their tasks in the divinity hall), there is no doubt that a good deal in the way of 'hints and tips' based on past experience was incorporated into theological teaching. This lack of any systematic attention to 'ministerial formation' and practical theology was increasingly recognized as a lack in the course of the nineteenth century. In 1849 the Countess of Effingham offered an endowment for a chaplain-cum-professor of practical theology in New College, Edinburgh, but after much controversy the offer was declined. The chair of Mission, which was established for Alexander Duff* and involved delivering lectures in all three FC divinity halls, was in a real sense the first chair in practical theology in Scotland. Duff was the founder of the theological study of missiology, which is of fundamental importance as the context for practical theology. Duff emphasized the need for students to shape their practice, wherever their work might lie, to a careful theological assessment of the context. Later in the century some responsibility for teaching practical theology was often allocated to one of the divinity chairs. But the subject was hardly regarded as a theological discipline on a level with the others, and in practice it was a hotch-potch of advice on preaching, pastoral visitation and Church government, with 'sacred elocution' and Church music added from time to time.

From the early nineteenth century, various projects were established involving divinity students in pastoral ministry in slum areas of the cities. These were important opportunities to acquire skills and understanding and practise the craft of ministry. Some of these projects were essentially student initiatives under the auspices of the missionary societies. Others, such as Thomas Chalmers'* involvement of students in the West Port Territorial Church, or A. H. Charteris'* project based on the Tolbooth parish in Edinburgh, were more official, and seen by many as a significant aspect of preparation for ministry. The New College Missionary Society eventually established a settlement in the Pleasance which became a major influence on many generations of students. Especially when Harry Miller (1869–1940; *FUFCS* 24, *FES* IX, 32) was Warden (1908–34) and Lecturer in Christian Sociology (1923–34), the work of the settlement was what we would call today supervised field education and a recognized and important part of the New College offering. As the students themselves declared, 'It gives the students an opportunity to study actual social conditions and to prepare themselves for the ministry under the direction of the warden.'

The first systematic teaching of practical theology in Edinburgh University began in 1924, when D. Bruce Nicol (1886–1930; *FES* III, 219), minister of St Margaret's and warden of the 'Pastoral Institute' based there, offered a course which appeared in the University Calendar. Similar institutes were soon founded in Glasgow, Aberdeen and St Andrews. Nicol outlined the scope of his subject as covering preaching, public worship, pastoral theology, religious education, Church law, and missions. This was closely reflected in the content of the discipline agreed at the time of the 1929 Union:* homiletics; public worship, pastoral duties, and Church music; government and discipline of the Church; principles and methods of religious education and care of the young; Christian missions; and practical application of Christian principles (Basis and Plan of Union 1929). To this end chairs in practical theology (sometimes linked with Christian ethics) were to be maintained in all four centres. As a consequence of the work of professors such as Daniel Lamont* and William Tindal in New College (1899–1965; *FES* IX, 775), W. R. Forrester in St Andrews (1892–1984; *FUFCS* 5, *FES* IX, 770), David Cairns in Aberdeen (1904–92; *FES* IX, 769), and James Pitt Watson in Trinity College, Glasgow (1893–1962; *FES* VIII, 386–7, IX, 776), the subject gradually became an accepted part of the theological scene in Scotland.

The next major development is associated particularly with the work of Professor James Whyte in St Andrews (1958–86; *FES* X, 433) and Professor James Blackie in Edinburgh (1966–76; *FES* IX, 457; X, 429). They led a transformation of the subject from being a rather unco-ordinated collection of 'hints and tips' to being a critical and rigorous 'theology of practice': 'This is a *theoretical* enquiry, in so far as it seeks to *understand* practice, to evaluate, to criticize, to look at the relationships between what is done and what is said or professed. It is a *practical* enquiry, not only in the sense that it seeks to understand practice, but that the understanding has the aim of guiding practice in the future.' (J. A. Whyte). Within this general understanding, special attention is given to ministerial practice, and supervised field education is an integral part of the programme in all four centres.

Practical theology in Scotland, while it has learned much from developments in North America, is less psychologically based; working with a theological foundation, it has pioneered an interdisciplinary approach to its subject matter.

A. V. Campbell, 'Is Practical Theology Possible?', *SJT* 25 (1972), 217–27; Duncan B. Forrester, 'Practical Theology', in P. Avis (ed.), *The Threshold of Theology* (Basingstoke, 1988), 125–39; *id.* (ed.), *Theology and Practice*, (L, 1990); R. Gill, *Theology and Social Structure* (L, 1977); David Lyall, 'Theological Education in a Clinical Setting' (PhD, Edinburgh University, 1979); J. A. Whyte, 'New Directions in Practical Theology', *Theology* 76 (1973), 228–38.

D. B. Forrester

Preachers. Christian preaching has an ancient lineage. The principal antecedents of New Testament preaching as the exposition of Scripture lie in the ministry of the Old Testament prophets and, more immediately, in the service and worship of the synagogue, which came into its own during the exile. Nehemiah 8 records how Ezra the scribe 'stood upon a pulpit of wood ... and read in the book of the law of God distinctly and gave the sense and caused (the people) to understand the reading'. Jesus stood in this tradition when he ministered in the synagogue in Nazareth and expounded Isaiah 61 (Luke 4:16ff.). Paul and Barnabas did likewise in the synagogue in Antioch in Pisidia (Acts 13:15). The apostolic preaching often consisted of a brief account of the life, ministry, death and resurrection of Christ according to the Old Testament Scriptures, amply demonstrated in the description of Paul's habitual practice in Acts 17:2,3. This was the legacy left by the early Church to posterity.

In Scotland, the Celtic church* produced a number of great missionaries, but we know relatively little about their preaching. Men like Ninian* in Whithorn (probably about the turn of the fifth century), Mungo (Kentigern), and Columba* (*d*.597) exercised preaching in their evangelism of parts of Scotland. After the twelfth century, there is little trace of true Christian preaching, apart from some activity among itinerant friars,* until the time of Wyclif and his Lollard* preachers in the late fourteenth century, whose influence spread to Scotland through people like James Resby, burned at the stake (*c*.1407), as was Paul Kravar,* a Bohemian physician in St Andrews, in 1431. Efforts to suppress the new teaching proved unavailing, and the Wycliffite translations of the Bible, and later Tyndale's, found their way to Scotland, giving momentum to the movement that was to usher in the Reformation. Patrick Hamilton (1504–28)* came under the influence of Erasmus and later of Luther and Tyndale. His eloquent advocacy of the biblical doctrines of grace and the doctrine of justification by faith alone led to his condemnation as a heretic* in St Andrews in 1528.

Another vigorous preacher was George Wishart (1513–46).* Greatly influenced by the continental Reformers, he returned to his native Scotland to preach with effectiveness and widespread influence, proclaiming God's way of life for sinners through the sole work of Jesus Christ, in a wide-ranging expository ministry. His preaching influenced John Knox (*c*.1514–72),* who became his bodyguard for a time. When Wishart was arrested and burned at the stake, his mantle fell on Knox, who became the acknowledged leader of the Reformation in Scotland, although but one of a number of prominent and powerful preachers at the time, such as John Rough,* under whose preaching Knox responded to a call to the ministry, and Thomas Guilliame,* whose ministry first awakened in Knox an interest in the teaching of the Reformers.

Knox's power as a prophetic preacher was formidable, and he followed Calvin's and Wishart's method of consecutive exposition of books of Scripture in the pulpit. Contemporary with Knox were men such as William Harlow (1500–75), John Willock (1512–85),* John Craig (1512–1600),* author of the first Scottish catechism* to come into widespread use in the Kirk, David Fergusson (1525–98),* James Lawson (1538–84),* Knox's successor at St Giles. Greater than all these, however, was Andrew Melville (1545–1622),* scholar, administrator and preacher, easily the most influential minister of his day, and instrumental in the establishing and triumph of Presbyterianism in Scotland. Another gifted preacher of these times was Robert

PREACHERS

Bruce (1554–1631),* who, in his nine years at St Giles in Edinburgh, rose to national prominence. His sermons on the sacrament of the Lord's Supper are one of Scotland's religious classics.

Alexander Henderson (1583–1646),* one of Bruce's spiritual children and the intellectual force behind the National Covenant* (1638), was a powerful expository preacher and leading member of the Westminster Assembly.* Other notable figures of this period were David Dickson (c. 1583–1663),* who exercised a profound influence on the ministry of the time by his devotion to biblical studies and the promotion of commentaries on many parts of Scripture, Robert Blair (1593–1666)* of St Andrews, a man of majestic appearance and great personality in the pulpit, and Samuel Rutherford (1600–61),* one of the most famous names among the Covenanters.* His *Letters* reflect the most characteristic theme of his preaching, the love and the loveliness of Christ.

The post-Restoration period saw the emergence of the field-preachers. Among the most eminent were Donald Cargill (c. 1619–80),* Alexander Peden (c. 1626–86),* John Welch of Irongay (c. 1624–81),* Gabriel Semple (1632–1706; *FES* II, 126–7), Richard Cameron (c. 1648–80)* and James Renwick (1662–88).* All alike men of courage, deep piety and powerful preaching, they nurtured and sustained evangelical faith in the people of Scotland in a time of suffering and persecution.

The eighteenth century saw a decline in the evangelical spirit of the covenanting times with the growing ascendancy of Moderatism* in the life of the Church. Two notable factors marked this period and characterized its preaching, the Marrow Controversy* and the Secession* movement. The *Marrow of Modern Divinity* stressed the unconditional offer of salvation to all, and that true repentance was a part of salvation, itself the gift of the Lord Jesus Christ. In spite of its condemnation by the General Assembly and the subsequent harassment of the Marrowmen, their preaching attracted great numbers and their influence was far-reaching. Prominent among them were Ebenezer Erskine (1680–1754),* his brother Ralph (1685–1752),* Thomas Boston (1677–1732),* James Hog of Carnock (1658–1734)* and James Wardlaw of Dunfermline (1669–1742). Boston and the Erskines in particular exercised a deep influence in Scotland. Boston's best-known work, *Human Nature in its Fourfold State* (E, 1720), did more to shape the thought of his countrymen than anything except the Westminster Shorter Catechism. In the Secession movement, John Brown of Haddington (1722–87)* was decisively influenced by Ralph Erskine's preaching and became himself a preacher of great distinction.

Evangelical preaching was also maintained, however, within the established Church. James Robb* of Kilsyth (1688–1753) and William McCulloch* of Cambuslang (1691–1771) were greatly used in the Cambuslang Revival (*see* Revivals) in 1742, and George Whitefield (1714–1770)* was also involved in this work. Other prominent preachers included George Campbell (1719–96)* of Banchory, later Principal of Marischal College and Professor of Theology, John Erskine (1721–1803)* of Old Greyfriars in Edinburgh, leader of the evangelical party in the established Church, and George Lawson (1749–1820)* of Selkirk, noted for his exceptional ability as an expositor of the Scriptures, and for preaching through the entire Bible. Late in the century the Haldane brothers, James (1768–1851)* and Robert (1764–1842),* laymen of great eloquence, stirred Scotland by their evangelical fervour and their preaching tours, particularly in the Highlands.

The early years of the nineteenth century saw a steady development in evangelical ministry. Andrew Thomson (1778–1831)* of St George's, Edinburgh, had a far-reaching impact as an evangelical leader in the movement that led to the Disruption* of 1843. John McDonald of Ferintosh (1779–1849),* the 'Apostle of the North', exercised a prodigious influence throughout the Highlands and the Western Isles. Robert M. M'Cheyne* (1813–43), brief though his ministry was, was one of the best-known preachers of his day, evoking spiritual awakening in St Peter's Church, Dundee. William C. Burns (1815–68),* associated with the revival work in Dundee, exercised a notable ministry in various parts of Scotland before going to China as a pioneer missionary. The Bonar brothers, Horatius (1808–89)* and Andrew (1810–92),* close associates of M'Cheyne's, and both Moderators of the FC General Assembly, became household names throughout the land.

The Disruption of 1843,* which marked the birth of the Free Church of Scotland,* was a movement of great spiritual fervour, with a far-reaching impact upon preaching through men such as Thomas Chalmers (1780–1847),* Robert Candlish (1806–73),* Robert Buchanan (1802–75),* Thomas Guthrie (1803–73),* William Cunningham (1805–61),* John Kennedy of Dingwall (1819–84), Alexander Stuart (1809–98),* Alexander Stewart of Cromarty (1794–1847)* and others, such as Norman Macleod of the Barony in Glasgow (1812–72),* whose ministry depended, in John Kennedy's words, upon 'a profound experience of the power of God, a clear view of the doctrines of grace, peculiar nearness to God, a holy life, and a blessed ministry'.

The second half of the nineteenth century was dominated by two very diverse movements, one a widespread spiritual awakening, beginning in 1859 and continuing until the turn of the century, and the other the growing influence of biblical criticism and liberal theology. The spiritual awakening threw up some great preachers, both lay and ordained, and names such as Brownlow North (1810–75)* and Hay Macdowall Grant of Arndilly,* gentlemen evangelists, exercised remarkably fruitful ministries. James Orr (1844–1913)* and Alexander Whyte (1836–1921),* who were later to attain great eminence in the Church, were decisively influenced by the revival movement, as was William Robertson Nicoll (1851–1923),* founder and editor of the *British Weekly*, himself a notable preacher, and one of the most influential churchmen in nineteenth-century Britain. The influence of the new theology steadily increased, however, and there was a progressive departure from the Calvinistic orthodoxy of the earlier FC, which inevitably had an effect on the pulpit ministry of the later nineteenth and early twentieth centuries.

Typical of this transition period were men like Robert Rainy (1826–1906),* Principal of New College and architect of the 1900 union between the FC and the UPC, A. B. Davidson (1831–1902),* famous at one time for his expository sermons on great Bible characters, A. B. Bruce (1831–99),* whose book *The Training of the Twelve* enhanced his reputation as a preacher, James Stalker (1848–1928),* Professor of Church History at Aberdeen, Henry Drummond (1851–97),* noted for his leadership of the Student Movement, George Adam Smith (1856–1942),* a man of brilliant scholarship and outstanding preaching gifts, and J. P. Struthers of Greenock (1855–1915),* a preacher of unusual talents and friend of James Denney (1856–1917),* a New Testament scholar of distinguished preaching abilities.

Alexander Whyte* of Free St George's, Edinburgh, was regarded by many as the greatest preacher of his generation. Graphic and compelling in the pulpit, he drew enormous crowds Sunday by Sunday over many years. Prominent among his colleagues and associates were men like Hugh Black* (1868–1953) and John Kelman* (1864–1929). He was succeeded in 1921 by James Black* (1879–1949), author of a fine book on *The Mystery of Preaching*. G. H. Morrison* (1866–1928) of Wellington Church did in Glasgow what Whyte had done in Edinburgh, gathering crowded congregations to hear a ministry marked by skilled exegesis and meticulous and thorough preparation.

More clearly evangelical preachers in the next generation included D. P. Thomson,* W. C. MacDonald* of Palmerston Place, Edinburgh, and James S. Stewart,* widely regarded as the finest Scottish preacher of the twentieth century.

In the post-World War II years a renewed emphasis on systematic and continuous exposition of the Scriptures, in line with the practice of the early Reformers, constitutes one of the most hopeful signs of renewal. The outstanding figure has been William Still (*b*.1911)* of Gilcomston South, Aberdeen, the impact of whose ministry (1945–) throughout the second half of the century has been far-reaching in the recovery of the centrality of such preaching.

The Warrack lectures* are devoted to preaching in particular, although their scope has been interpreted very loosely by some recent lecturers.

Y. T. Brilioth, *A Brief History of Preaching* (Philadelphia, 1965); E. C. Dargan, *A History of Preaching*, 2 vols (NY, 1905); F. R. Webber, *A History of Preaching in Britain and America*, 3 vols (Milwaukee, 1955); C. Smyth, *The Art of Preaching: A Practical Survey of Preaching in the Church of England 747–1939* (NY, 1940); W. G. Blaikie, *The Preachers of Scotland from the Sixth to the Nineteenth Century* (E, 1888); J. A. Broadus, *Lectures on the History of Preaching* (NY, 1876); D. M. Lloyd Jones,

Preaching and Preachers (L, 1971); W. F. Mitchell, *English Pulpit Oratory* (L, 1932); A. Milroy, *Scottish Theologians and Preachers 1610–1638* (E, 1891).

J. Philip

Preaching: Themes and Styles

CELTIC AND EARLY MEDIEVAL. Of the literary remains of the early Church in Scotland, there are few texts which point to actual styles of preaching. However, the broader literary evidence demonstrates the importance of sermons in a Church which, in the Celtic period at least, was vigorously evangelistic and intellectual.

Old Irish (*see* Gaelic) glosses on scriptural passages contain many allusions to preaching, which was often in the vernacular language. Approaches vary from brief elucidation of Scripture (with some application) to fully-fledged homilies addressing particular themes, such as thankfulness to God for all his blessings (J. Strachan, 'An Old Irish Homily', *Eriu* 3 (1907), 1–10). Appropriate homilies were also prepared for saints' days and other festivals. Preachers aimed at simplicity and directness of style, although perorations sometimes show a fondness for adjectival elaboration in the manner of secular poems and prose tales (e.g. 'Blessed is he who shall reach the kingdom where God is himself, a King, great, fair, powerful, strong, holy, pure, righteous, keen, ... merciful, beneficent, charitable ...'). Such preaching must have been common at Iona* and other Columban monasteries, although Adomnán* casts Columba* more in the role of prophet (uttering imprecations and prognostications), and less in the role of homilete.

Besides native culture, Latin literary culture also influenced preaching in the early medieval period, drawing heavily on early Church writings for its themes and style. The art of rhetoric from classical handbooks formed part of the curriculum in monastic education. Patristic sermons in particular influenced homiletic and exegetical texts. Biblical themes, such as the renunciation of the world and the life to come, were popular exemplar subjects in saints' legends and other devotional texts. While the hortatory style of the early Church Fathers provided a model for preaching in the early Church, the style of later medieval homilists tended more obviously towards the florid mannerism and bombastic rhetoric beloved of Irish clergy. By the twelfth century, the Church, feeling the effect of the Cistercian* movement, had absorbed the homiletic themes of Christian humanism of the later Middle Ages.

See also: Celtic Church; Celtic Saints; Monasticism, Celtic.

L. Hardinge, *The Celtic Church in Britain* (L, 1972), 29–51; R. Atkinson (ed.), *The Passions and Homilies from Leabhar Breac* (Dublin, 1887).

LATER MEDIEVAL. The fundamentally sacramental role of the parish clergy in this period diminished the preaching ministry. Very little evidence is available for the period before the sixteenth century. Resident clergy were ill-paid and ill-educated. On important state occasions prelates would preach, as when Thomas Rossy, Bishop of Whithorn (Dowden, 364–6), preached at the coronation of Robert III in 1390, but the more usual work was done by the mendicant friars.* Notable among these were the Order of Preachers (Dominicans*), the Franciscans* and the Carmelites.* These were employed as diocesan preachers, as in Dunkeld, but were encouraged to preach only once a year in any one place. The content of their sermons, informed by their respective spiritualities, revolved around the traditional devotion to the Virgin Mary, the Passion and the mass.

The Council of Trent (1545–63) attempted to address this widespread malaise by ordering the inclusion of a general instruction on the Epistle and the Gospel during the liturgy. There seems to have been an effort in the Scottish Church to put this directive into practice. A benefice was to be provided to support a preacher in every diocese and monastery, and these were encouraged to give theological and spiritual instruction. Each church had to have its pulpit and its 'pulpit clayth'; the saying of mass during the sermon was forbidden at St Nicholas' in Aberdeen. Thus the homily became more integrated into the liturgy.

To help provide such preachers, both a theological education and a handbook were required. The content of the homilies of John Annand, first principal of St Leonard's College, St Andrews (c. 1512), can be inferred from John Eck's *Sermones* and from the *Sermones 'Dormi Secure' Dominicales* which were in his possession. A specifically Scottish response to this need was provided by Archbishop John Hamilton's* *Catechism* of 1552. The re-foundation of St Mary's College* for theological study at St Andrews and Hamilton's handbook place Scotland in the context of continental, and specifically German, reform movements.

The content of the homily in the later part of this period was more concerned with impugned doctrines such as the mass, the sacraments and good works. The presence of a summary of the teaching on the eucharist by Bengît Vernier of Bourges among the books of John Watson (*fl.* 1540–60), canon and preacher at Aberdeen, bears this out. Watson also owned the commentaries on the Gospels, Epistles and feast-days of the saints of John Royaerts (Royardus, *d.* 1547), a Franciscan and eminent preacher in Belgium, as can be seen from his preaching schedule, a rare glimpse of the late medieval homilist's mind.

It is well nigh impossible to gauge the influence of the sermon on the average worshipper. For while Knox* could say that some in the past 'would occupye the pulpete and trewly preach Jesus Christ', undoubtedly many others in 1559 still did not, or could not, preach.

J. H. Baxter, 'Four "New" Medieval Scottish Authors', *SHR* 25 (1928), 90–7; J. K. Cameron, ' "Catholic Reform" in Germany and in the Pre-1560 Church in Scotland', *RSCHS* 20 (1980), 105–17; J. A. W. Hellman, 'The Spirituality of the Franciscans' and S. Tugwell, 'The Spirituality of the Dominicans', J. Raitt (ed.), *Christian Spirituality* II (NY, 1989); G. Hill, 'The Sermons of John Watson, Canon of Aberdeen', *IR* 15 (1964), 3–34; D. McRoberts (ed.), *Essays on the Scottish Reformation* (G, 1952).

REFORMATION. Any description of Scottish preaching of the Reformation* era must be impressionistic, because very few actual sermons have come down to us. The Protestant Reformers in principle gave pride of place to the sermon within the weekly diet of worship.* Services were described as 'the time of sermon' or 'of prayers and preaching'. 'Preaching the Word' was the prime, almost the only, duty of the minister (Calderwood III, 14). It was the hearing of the Word that was the source of spiritual life: 'spirituall fude' was one minister's description of preaching – a 'Spirituall Feist' to be enjoyed weekly (John Davidson,* 'Ane Dialog or Mutuall Talking', ed. J. Cranstoun, *Satirical Poems*... (E, 1891) I, 296–324, lines 635–75). A sharp contrast was thus made to the sacrament of the mass. Due to the extreme shortage of ministers, this ideal took many years to achieve in most of Scotland's parishes. For years after 1560, in many churches preaching was at most monthly, supplemented at other times by the reader's* service of common prayers and the *Book of Homilies* of the Church of England.

Even among the few early preachers of the era of the 'privy kirk',* different personalities led to different emphases. One John Brabner was said to be 'ane vehement man for inculcating the Law and pain thereof'; his contemporary Paul Methven,* however, was 'ane more myld man, preaching the Evangel of Grace and remission of sins in the blood of Christ' (SRO, Dalhousie MSS).

John Knox* provides examples of his own sermons in his *History of the Reformation in Scotland*, but his preaching at St Andrews in 1571–2 was probably more typical of his regular style. Knox preached weekly from a single chosen text – Daniel 9. He sought to apply prophecy regarding God's judgment on Israel to the Scotland of his day, preaching 'according to the tyme and stait of the people; whairby the wicked and trublers of Godis kirk mycht be knowin and painted out in thair collouris!' (R. Pitcairn (ed.), *Memorials ... by Richard Bannatyne* (E, 1836), 70f.). To his disciples, it was insufficient to expound the general meaning of Scripture; particular application, if necessary to named individuals, was true preaching of the Word.

Less politically radical were the sermons of John Erskine of Dun.* The few surviving examples of his writing (*Spalding Club Miscellany* IV, A, 1849) suggest a man concerned to preach from the text of the Gospels: first explaining his passage, then expounding its spiritual challenge to his hearers.

Whether directed to a particular political situation or not, Scottish Protestant preaching took as its sole authority the teaching of the Bible. Above all, a 'true Kirk' was marked by 'trew preaching' from 'the written Worde of God' (Scots Confession 18).

F. D. Bardgett, 'Four Parische Kirkis to ane Preicheir', *RSCHS* 22 (1986), 195–209; G. Donaldson, 'Reformation to Covenant', in D. Forrester and D. Murray (eds), *Studies in the History of Worship in Scotland* (E, 1984); D. F. Wright (ed.), *The Bible in Scottish Life and Literature* (E, 1988); Bannatyne Club (ed.), *Tracts by David Fergusson* (E, 1860).

SEVENTEENTH CENTURY. The ordinary seventeenth-century sermon had for a text something between a portion of a verse and, at most, several verses. This text was handled, not only by dividing it into points, but by dividing it into points of doctrine, uses and application, with, where appropriate, points of controversy against adversaries (generally the papists) as well. This meant a fairly artificial and complex structure. But at the same time it made it easier to remember – and easier for the not infrequent hearer who took notes. Indeed the only extant sermons of a number of eminent preachers of this period are those taken down in such a way. This practice was encouraged, for in a period of relatively few books the preacher's desire was that his auditors might be able to remember – and meditate on – his message. Thus when some deviated from this practice – Robert Douglas,* Hugh Binning,* Andrew Gray* and Robert Leighton* are a notable few – and began preaching without heads of doctrine, a practice referred to by contemporaries as 'skimming the text', there were loud objections to this new method. Robert Baillie,* opposing Gray's use of 'the new guyse of preaching', said that Gray condemned 'the ordinarie way of exponing and dividing a text, of raising doctrines and uses', but ran out 'in a discourse on some common head, in a high, romancing, unscripturall style, tickling the ear for the present, and moving the affections in some, bot leaving, as he confesses, little or nought to the memorie and understanding' (*Letters and Journals*, E, 1842, III, 258–9). It should be observed that such sermons are nevertheless full of doctrine and include divisions as well; what they lack is the formal division between 'doctrines' and 'uses'. These exceptions, however, prove the rule and the ordinary way of preaching described above remained common.

The General Assembly's Commission aptly summarized the ideal of preaching in the period: setting forth 'the excellency of Christ in His person, offices, and the unsearchable riches of His grace; the new covenant, and the way of living by faith in Him'; making this the main theme of preaching and 'preaching other things with a relation to Christ and urging all by the authority of God's commands, the love of Christ and the grace of the Gospel, directing people to Jesus Christ that they might receive from him the grace to enable them to comply'. Though this was said in warning against the very beginnings of the legalizing tendencies which developed in the eighteenth century into the legalism and formalism of Moderatism (*see* Moderates), it reflects aptly the ideals, and to a considerable degree the practice, of seventeenth-century preaching. It is what might today be termed a warm evangelical religion, though without the coldness and indifference which first elicited the use of the term 'evangelical' by way of contrast. The story of an Englishman, previously largely a stranger to religious impressions, come to Scotland on business is often told. He heard first a stately man, Robert Blair,* who showed him the majesty of God, then a little fair man, Samuel Rutherford,* who showed him the loveliness of Christ, and finally a well-favoured old man, David Dickson,* who showed him all his heart. He returned to England an earnest Christian.

There was, to be sure, a certain amount of what has been called 'preaching to the times' and this was perhaps inevitable in such a turbulent period. But the sermon preached by Robert Douglas* at the coronation of Charles II* at Scone shows remarkable attention to the text and practical application to the situation in a measure virtually unknown today. And the sermons preached on the hills and moors by the field preachers* in the times of persecution (*see* Conventicles*) display a remarkable affinity to the Commission's ideal and pay relatively little attention to the evils of the time (see *Sermons Delivered in Times of Persecution in Scotland*, ed. J. Howie, G, 1779; E, 1880; J. Walker, *Scottish Theology and Theologians*, E, ²1888, 175–81). Indeed, as Walker points out, the preaching was richly Christocentric, not only fostering the Covenanter's desire to see King Jesus head of his Church, but exhibiting a warm personal love for him and union, by faith, with him.

Mention should be made of *The Scotch Presbyterian Eloquence;* or the Foolishness of their Teaching Discovered* (L, 1692; ²1693 and many times reprinted), an attempt by an Episcopalian, who styled himself 'Jacob Curate' (identified both as Robert Calder and as Gilbert Crockat) and who had been ejected at the Revolution, to cull all that seemed to him offensive from Presbyterian preaching. As such it contains much that demonstrates that Presbyterians were accustomed to speak in the homely language of the people. Much of the rest includes figures of speech familiar to those who have read Samuel Rutherford's* *Letters*. But taken as a whole the excerpts given are not remotely representative of those they purport to portray, but can aptly be described as 'silly yet mischievous' and even a 'collection of profanity and obscenity' (Matthew Leishman, in Preface to H. Binning, *Works*, E, 1846, xx). Several replies were made, in part in kind (*e.g. An Answer to the Scottish Presbyterian Eloquence*, L, 1693). But it would be a serious mistake to characterize any of the preaching of the age, except perhaps that of the time-serving curates hastily thrust in to replace those ministers ejected in 1662, by the representations found in these pamphlets.

G. D. Henderson, 'The Scottish Pulpit in the Seventeenth Century', in *Religious Life in Seventeenth-Century Scotland* (C, 1937), 190–219.

MODERATES AND EVANGELICALS. As yet, little systematic analysis of Moderate* preaching has been undertaken, and what is known relates to the preaching of Moderates among the Edinburgh *literati*, in particular Hugh Blair* and Alexander Carlyle.* Blair defined Christianity chiefly in terms of virtue or benevolence based on faith in Christ. The Moderates combined Christian and Stoic principles and stressed virtue and submission to the will of God as the way to happiness in this life and the next. In general, as the publications of ministers listed in the *Fasti* indicate, Moderates were more prepared than Evangelicals* to preach on secular topics. Carlyle in particular preached on political topics and in support of the government of the day. Central to this theme lay the concept of the covenanted nation. Published Moderate sermons exemplified the ornamented style of which Blair was the exemplar, and sought to rid their expression of 'Scotticisms'.

Much preaching in the middle to late eighteenth century cannot be described as clearly Moderate or Evangelical. Many preachers are best seen as orthodox Calvinists who saw little need or justification for diverging from traditional forms of doctrinal expression. After the 1760s, however, a group became dominant who were orthodox but also concerned to apply contemporary ideas in a constructive way. The watershed was marked by the publication of John Erskine's* *Dissertation on the Nature of Christian Faith* (E, 1765). For the first time it was unequivocally asserted that the majority of those professing Christianity in Scotland had no experience of 'saving faith'. Hitherto, the problem had been seen as one of 'infidelity' or backsliding. Thereafter, preaching for conversion became more prominent in non-Moderate pulpits, and sermons increasingly dealt with the pursuit of holiness in contrast to what Evangelicals believed was Moderate preaching for virtuous living.

Evangelical preaching, to judge from published sermons, embodied simplicity of style. It has worn much better than that of the Moderates. Its perceptions of the nature of saving faith, and of such central doctrines as the atonement,* were oriented towards an intellectual as well as an experiential conception of conversion and faith. This was true of Thomas Boston,* Ebenezer and Ralph Erskine,* John Willison,* and John Erskine,* in ascending order. During the eighteenth century, though, there was an increasing stress on the love of God and of the blessings of the redeemed as a means of motivating people to renounce sin. Overall, then, in the course of the later eighteenth century, there developed an increasingly confident evangelicalism which paved the way for the appearance of the nineteenth-century evangelical revival in Scotland.

J. Macleod, *Scottish Theology in Relation to Church History* (E, ³1974); R. B. Sher, *Church and University in the Scottish Enlightenment* (E, 1985), 40–4, 182–6, 206–12.

THE MODERN ERA. Sermons in the English-speaking world never concentrated more on the central evangelical themes of sin and salvation than in the mid-nineteenth century. Protestant pulpits, not least in Scotland, preached Christ crucified. There were fewer numbered points or formal arguments than in the past. A florid rhetorical style was in vogue, especially in more prosperous congregations. At a time when sermons remained the most popular form of reading material, they were often constructed as contributions to literature. Manner was thought important: stance and action, eye as well as voice, were carefully evaluated by discriminating hearers.

There were several related trends in the later nineteenth century. As educational standards rose, there was an increase of intellectual preaching. More sermons were read, and as college homiletics classes became more rigorous and published sermon aids multiplied, the craft of preaching established its own conventions. Poetry was more frequently quoted. Illustrations were more often drawn from nature, especially outdoor scenery. There was more sentimentality – what was called the 'wooing note' – in the preacher's language. The most striking thematic change was the decline of references to everlasting punishment.

A counter-current among those affected by revivalism* tended to make preaching more popular in style. The revival of 1859 encouraged preaching outside traditional channels. The visit of D. L. Moody* in 1874 put a premium on a more homely, businesslike manner in the pulpit. Humour was often introduced, sometimes in imitation of C. H. Spurgeon.* Sentences were short, simple and direct. Teaching on holiness as a second work of grace and on the premillennial advent of Christ (*see* Millennialism) was common in such circles.

In March 1896 the *British Weekly** invited readers to notify the editor of subjects and lengths of sermons on a particular Sunday. The result is an unusual survey of British preaching. Three-quarters of all texts were from the New Testament, with John's Gospel the favourite. One-fifth of Old Testament texts were from the Psalms. The preaching commonly lasted about half an hour, Presbyterian sermons usually exceeding their Anglican equivalents. The joint longest was preached in John O'Groats Free Church, lasting 1 hour 28 minutes.

The early twentieth century witnessed a broadening of themes in many pulpits. The immanence of God and the humanity of Jesus were dwelt on. There was less theology and more ethical teaching. Social issues were examined, though party political statements were rare in Scotland. In terms of technique there was a growing tendency to open a sermon with a contemporary story rather than information about the background of the text. Illustrations sometimes crowded out content, and applications were left imprecise. As amongst statesmen, oratory was on the decline. From the 1920s broadcasting encouraged a more conversational pulpit style.

Liturgical revival, fostered by ecumenical contacts, led to more widespread acceptance of the Christian Year* among Presbyterians. There was also a stronger awareness of corresponding views of the doctrine of the Church and the significance of its sacraments. Psychological insights started to be appropriated by more progressive preachers. From the 1930s Neo-Orthodoxy* began to make themes such as grace, sin and eschatology more frequently heard. The Second World War* reinforced a tendency to return to basic doctrines. Expository preaching, a tradition never extinguished in Scotland, once more grew in favour. Conservative Presbyterians still clung to undemonstrative discourses. RCs retained brief homilies except when visiting preachers, often Dominicans,* took congregations by storm. In the mid-twentieth century, however, it was generally considered that the quiet intensity of James S. Stewart* represented the finest Scottish preaching.

E. C. Dargan, *A History of Preaching* II (NY, 1912); R. G. Turnbull, *A History of Preaching* III (Grand Rapids, 1974); H. Davies, *Worship and Theology in England: from Newman to Martineau, 1850–1900* (Princeton, 1962); H. Davies, *Varieties of English Preaching, 1900–1960* (L, 1963); *British Weekly*, 19 March 1896, 355–6, 26 March 1896, 379; W. G. Enright, 'Preaching and Theology in the Nineteenth Century: A Study of the Context and Content of the Evangelical Sermon' (PhD, Edinburgh University, 1968); W. M. Taylor, *The Scottish Pulpit. From the Reformation to the Present Day* (L, 1887).

GAELIC AND HIGHLANDS. In the Gaelic*-speaking Highlands* preaching has had a pre-eminent role in the life of the Protestant Churches. The sermon, within the ecclesiastical domain, came to have a prestige which rivalled that of the folk-tale in the secular domain, but the two shared common ground. First, the oral tradition which flourished in the Gaelic areas and had the folk-tale as its centrepiece, probably helped to determine the preferred view of the sermon as an oral artifact, delivered by the minister without the use of manuscript; *ministear pàipeir* ('minister of paper', i.e., a manuscript-bound minister) was a term of severe disapproval for a minister who was dependent on reading his sermon to the detriment of spontaneity (*see* 'Stickit Minister'). The evangelical* stress on inspirational delivery reinforced traditional perspectives. Secondly, the Gaelic sermon was sometimes delivered in a form of monotone or recitative which was called a *duan* ('song': cf. the Welsh *hwyl*), reflecting emotional animation and resembling the tradition of indigenous chant used to transmit Gaelic heroic ballads; in practical terms, this form of chant overcame acoustic difficulties, especially in the open air. Thirdly, Gaelic sermons were often liberally sprinkled with *exempla*, reflecting an older medieval tradition which was preserved within the oral context for reasons of memorability. Certain Highland ministers were particularly famed for their apposite illustrations. Fourthly, the average Highland listener had a remarkable capacity for remembering sermon content and illustration, and, in company, would readily resort to swapping sermons and memorable *exempla*. In short, Highland preaching and sermon delivery were, and still are, firmly contextualized in cultural terms.

As Evangelicalism* took firm root in the Highlands after 1800, popular dislike of Moderatism* may have been based to some degree on the manner in which its homiletic principles conflicted with traditional expectations. Finely tuned moral or ethical argument, delivered from a manuscript, was the hallmark of Highland Moderate preaching, and, while common in parishes before 1800, it was generally rejected by the people. The conversion to Evangelicalism of Moderate ministers such as Alexander Stewart* of Moulin was followed by a marked change in the content and style of their preaching. Nevertheless, certain ministers who were Moderate in terms of ecclesiastical politics (*e.g.* Norman MacLeod,* '*Caraid nan Gàidheal*') could, and did, preach in a manner consistent with evangelical sentiments.

The thematic concerns of Gaelic sermons preached by Evangelicals fell broadly within three categories, which were described in Gaelic as *comhfhurtachd* ('consolation'), *earal* ('instruction' or 'advice') and *rabhadh* ('warning', i.e., of spiritual danger). Although most ministers would cover all three categories in the course of their preaching, some were famed for their special skills in particular areas. *Rabhadh*, which applied to sinners the righteous demands of God's law, found its exponents in such men as Thomas Hog* of Kiltearn; *earal* could embrace a wide homiletic category, but would probably typify the oratory of men such as John Kennedy* of Dingwall; while Charles Calder of Ferintosh (1748–1812; *FES* VII, 47), predecessor of John MacDonald,* was widely known for his gracious preaching within the category of *comhfhurtachd*. MacDonald of Ferintosh, noted for his itinerant ministry, was distinguished for his presentation of the atonement and the free offer of salvation through the death of Christ.

Nevertheless, thematic categorization is perhaps misleading as a guide to the dynamism of Gaelic preaching, since the themes themselves usually arose from the verses of Scripture which were spiritually impressed on the preacher's mind. Some ministers, massively erudite in the Gaelic Bible (*see* Bible (Versions, Gaelic)), would use individual, and humanly unpredictable, 'texts' for regular preaching; others would engage in systematic exposition of sections of Scripture or entire books of the Bible. In the early 1850s, Peter Grant* of Grantown-on-Spey preached systematically through Mark's Gospel at his morning services (Manuscript Notebook of Grant's sermons, preserved at Grantown).

Special occasions also determined the nature of Highland preaching, not least at Communion seasons,* where the different stages in the celebration required sensitive focal points – for preparation before participation, the 'action sermon' prior to the Supper itself, and the thanksgiving on the Monday immediately following the sacrament. MacDonald of Ferintosh excelled in his preaching at such services. The nature of Highland communities and the needs of particular social groups were similarly significant in the choice of an appropriate homiletic approach. Thus, itinerant preachers of Baptist and Independent persuasion (*see* Haldane Preachers), who were active chiefly after 1800, had a penchant for employing a text or passage of Scripture which

PRECENTOR

matched the immediate physical circumstances of their hearers. An itinerant preacher in Perthshire in 1817 applied the theme of Psalm 65 to the body of people who, at harvest time, gathered to listen to him in Glenlyon (W. McGlashan, *Letters on the State of Religion in the Highlands of Scotland*, G, 1818, 8-9).

Gaelic preaching, embracing a rich variety of themes and styles, functioned primarily on the upper linguistic register provided by the Gaelic Bible. It encouraged eloquence in both ministers and hearers, and its influence can be detected in the work of poets, writers and speakers to the present day. Although the Gaelic language has receded in strength, Gaelic preaching continues to be a powerful vehicle for the spiritual and cultural protection of the Gaelic people.

J. MacInnes, *The Evangelical Movement in the Highlands of Scotland* (A, 1951), 167-96; D. Beaton (ed.), *Sermons of Noted Ministers of the Northern Highlands* (Inverness, 1930); M. Campbell, *Gleanings of Highland Harvest*, ed. J. D. MacMillan (Tain, 1989), 145-8.

D. A. Bray, J. M. Lawlor, F. D. Bardgett, D. C. Lachman, J. R. McIntosh, D. W. Bebbington, D. E. Meek

Precentor, the leader of singing in church, a person who, in the absence of a musical instrument or choir, strikes up the tune for the congregation. In the early days of Reformed worship* in Scotland, the reader* was probably the precentor, and he often combined these offices with those of session clerk* and schoolmaster. The name 'precentor' was not at first in common use, the more familiar terms being the 'up-taker of the psalm', 'raiser of the psalm', 'letter-gae'. After the acceptance of the Westminster* Directory for the Public Worship of God (1645), the precentor 'read' each line of the psalm before the congregation sang it, but it is not clear from the terms of the direction whether this 'lining' was in fact read or sung. Singing the line (or sometimes two lines at a time) came to be the common practice, and continues to this day in Gaelic psalmody. In 1746 the General Assembly recommended 'the ancient practice of singing without reading the line', and this change encouraged precentors in the early nineteenth century, such as R. A. Smith of Paisley Abbey (later of St George's, Edinburgh), to foster improvements in congregational singing; they became instructors of psalmody classes, and later choirmasters. Precentors still lead the praise unaccompanied in the worship of the FC and FPC, and in the meetings of Presbyteries and the General Assembly of the CofS.

M. Patrick, *Four Centuries of Scottish Psalmody* (O, 1949), 126-35, 190-208; W. D. Maxwell, *Worship in the Church of Scotland* (O, 1955), 94, 124, 129; Walter Steuart (of Pardovan) *Collection ... Concerning the Worship, Discipline, and Government of the Church of Scotland* (E, 1709), Book I Title X para 5, Book II Title I para 26; Cox, 123, 746; Duncan Fraser, *The Passing of the Precentor* (E, 1906).

C. Robertson

PREMONSTRATENSIANS

Prelacy, government of the Church by prelates – ecclesiastical dignitaries, bishops, archbishops, cardinals, metropolitans, patriarchs. Literally, a prelate is a person 'placed before, preferred before' others in honour or jurisdiction. (In the Lower House of Convocation in the Church of England the *praelati* were the archdeacons.) Prelacy may then be the position, power or dignity of office, and the word can be used in a hostile sense with the idea of self-conscious pride or haughtiness in the holding of the appointment. In the historical dramas of Shakespeare the word is almost always used in that sense.

It may be that it was the fear of prelacy as seen in men like Cardinal David Beaton* and Archbishop James Sharp* in the folk-history of Scotland that led to an extreme aversion on the part of many Scottish Christians to any higher office in the Church than that of minister (*see* Parity). Perhaps it might be fair to define a prelate as a bishop etc. viewed in the exercise of his power rather than his ministry. Prelacy was used pejoratively for episcopal government during the Covenanting* era, and an Act abolishing prelacy was passed in 1689.

A. I. Dunlop

Premonstratensians, religious order. Known also as Norbertines or White Canons, they were founded by St Norbert (c.1081-1134) at Prémontré, near Laon (northern France) in 1120. Their aim was to combine strict monastic life with pastoral care. The Rule of St Augustine was adopted, together with Benedictine* customs and considerable austerity. Originally considered simply strict Augustinian* canons, they became an autonomous order with a constitutional framework modelled on the Cistercians.* Annual general chapters were held at Prémontré, where the abbot general resided; houses in each region formed groups, called circaries.

After spectacular success and expansion in the twelfth and thirteenth centuries, the order declined. Two weaknesses were difficulty of communication with Prémontré and the numerous very small houses, including the parishes administered by canons. Commendators* and the Reformation* made great inroads; then, despite a revival in the seventeenth century, the French Revolution all but extinguished the order. Following a revival in the nineteenth century, there are today circaries in northern Europe and a number of houses overseas.

There were six Premonstratensian houses in Scotland: Dryburgh,* Soulseat, Whithorn,* founded c.1150-77; Tongland, Fearn, Holywood, founded c.1218-27. All except Dryburgh and Fearn (Rossshire) were near the Galloway coast; all were abbeys except Whithorn, a cathedral priory. Although c.1300 they were in a circary with northern England, they later formed a Scottish circary. Relations with Prémontré, originally close but later disrupted for a lengthy period, were resumed in 1505. Adam* of Dryburgh made an important contribution to Premonstratensian spirituality. Since the Reformation,* a few canons have worked in southwest Scotland, in 1889-96 and again from 1957.

PRESBYTER

Catholic Encyclopedia XII, 387–92; *New Catholic Encyclopedia* XI, 737–41; H. M. Colvin, *The White Canons in England* (O, 1951); N. Backmund, *Monasticon Praemonstratense*, 3 vols (Straubing, 1949–56); *id.*, 'The Premonstratensian Order in Scotland', *IR* 4 (1953), 25–41; S. Cruden *Scottish Medieval Churches* (E, 1986), 82–90; Easson-Cowan, 100–4.

M. Dilworth

Presbyter, see Elder; Presbyterianism.

Presbyterian Review and Religious Journal, see Periodicals, Religious.

Presbyterian, The. Two nineteenth-century periodicals bore this title. The first was published monthly by James Adam of Arbroath between January 1843 and January 1845. In its final issue, its aims were summarized thus: 'The leading object of our labours has been, first, to prepare the minds of our readers for the Disruption, and since that event to vindicate and illustrate the principles on which it was based.' The second, also a monthly, was founded at the height of the FC/UPC union controversy in May 1868. The anti-union case was being forcefully stated by *The Watchword*,* and *The Presbyterian* (edited by Robert Rainy* until pressure of work forced his resignation in November 1869) gave a platform to those who favoured union. The journal, a stylishly contemporary production, was published successively by Thomas Nelson and Sons (until June 1870), John Greig and Son (until October 1870), and John Maclaren. *The Presbyterian* reflected changing attitudes within the FC to the feasibility of union, latterly aiming merely to cultivate unity among all Scottish Presbyterians as the goal of ultimate incorporation receded. Attempts to promote union, and the 'mutal eligibility' of ministers having finally collapsed, *The Presbyterian* ceased publication, in common with *The Watchword* in July 1873.

J. A. H. Dempster

Presbyterianism, the form of church government by presbyters (elders) which has been dominant in Scotland since the Reformation.* It was a logical application of certain Reformation principles discernible in and after 1560, first, in the Reformers' disinclination to vest final authority over the Church in parliament,* privy council* or prince; and, secondly, in their emphasis on devising a system of representative government which subordinated the work of individual administrators to the supervision of a series of courts* or councils, from the local kirk session* (functioning from 1559) of minister and elected elders* and deacons,* to the court of the superintendent* (from 1561), the provincial synod* (from 1561–2) and to the General Assembly* (from 1560) of the whole Church, presided over by an elected moderator* (by 1563) as temporary chairman, where decisions were reached by majority of votes. The importance which Scottish Reformers attached to conciliar government, exercised through a graded series of courts (with an

PRESBYTERIANISM

appellate jurisdiction), on which elected elders were expected to have a voice at every level, was a conscious attempt to apply Reformed understanding of the rôle of the New Testament eldership (*presbyterium*) towards meeting the needs of a Protestant church organized for a nation.

Nor was government through the Church's courts considered incompatible with assigning particular duties of superintendence to individual overseers: to superintendents, commissioners (including three conforming bishops) and visitors, so long as these powers were understood to be exercised on behalf of the whole Church, to which the overseers were accountable, and not to be exercised as an intrinsic part of an episcopal office, which the Reformers had eschewed at the Reformation. All this, at any rate, was consistent with the Assembly's verdict in 1565 that 'every true preacher of Jesus Christ is a Christian bishop'.

POST-REFORMATION VICISSITUDES. These arrangements of the 1560s were modified at the Convention of Leith* in January 1572, which assigned to the Reformed church the ancient diocesan structure and introduced Protestant bishops, who were to acknowledge their subordination to the General Assembly; but soon one newly appointed archbishop declined to submit to the Assembly, and the disreputable financial transactions surrounding episcopal appointments went far in the Assembly's eyes towards bringing the system into disrepute. In August 1572, the General Assembly declined to accept the settlement as lasting, and in 1575, after debating whether 'the bishops, as they are now in the Kirk of Scotland, have their function in the word of God or not', it decided to replace this unsuccessful experiment in episcopal administration by reverting to a system of visitation by ministers commissioned by the Assembly. This device, adhering to practices from the 1560s, was endorsed in the *Second Book of Discipline*,* of 1578, which is usually regarded as an authentic statement of presbyterian principles. At the same time, the Assembly's determination to eliminate diocesan episcopacy reinforced the Reformers' original emphasis on conciliar government and led to a differentiation between the congregational eldership, or kirk session, and the district eldership, or presbytery,* which assumed many of the functions exercised in an episcopal system by bishops.

This 'anti-episcopal' movement in the Church, led by Andrew Melville,* incurred the Crown's hostility. The ascendancy of the Presbyterians suffered a severe setback in 1584 when parliament affirmed the powers of bishops, prohibited presbyteries and asserted the authority of king and parliament over all estates, spiritual and temporal. Yet by 1586 the Crown was forced to make concessions to the Presbyterians; and in 1592 parliament recognized presbyteries and approved Presbyterian government in the Church.

After a riot in Edinburgh in 1596, James VI* launched a fresh assault on the Presbyterians and renewed his campaign for the restoration of episcopacy.* Through bishops, James hoped to gain effec-

673

tive control of Church and commonwealth, and so become a 'universal king' free from faction. His first step in 1596 was to gain the Assembly's approval for ministers to represent the ecclesiastical estate in parliament. These 'parliamentary bishops' were denied any ecclesiastical rôle as bishops; but James' next step was to frustrate the work of General Assemblies, to terrorize the Presbyterian leadership through imprisonment and banishment, and to curb the activities of presbyteries and synods by appointing 'constant moderators'. By 1606, episcopal endowment was revived; and in 1610 the king prevailed on the Assembly to recognize diocesan episcopacy. At that point, too, two courts of High Commission* were established to punish Presbyterian nonconformity;* and in 1612 parliament ratified episcopal government. Success seemed almost within James' grasp had he not undertaken a programme of liturgical revision, which the bishops were obliged to implement, and of tampering with patterns of worship amid mounting hostility.

COVENANTS AND RESTORATION. This was the legacy bequeathed to his son, Charles I,* who, at best an imperfect politician, allowed disgruntled Presbyterians to make common cause with disaffected nobles distrustful of the political power of bishops and fearful that royal policies to improve the finances of Crown and Kirk would be achieved at their expense. The combination of constitutional and ecclesiastical grievances found expression in the National Covenant* of 1638 which called for 'free' General Assemblies and parliaments. At the General Assembly in Glasgow* in 1638 – the first to have met since 1618 – episcopacy was abjured and the bishops excommunicated. In 1640, parliament abolished the ecclesiastical estate in parliament, made subscription to the Covenant compulsory, approved the abolition of episcopacy and revived the Presbyterian legislation of 1592.

As the 'Presbyterian revolution' of the 1640s gained momentum, moderate and anti-Covenanting elements became increasingly alienated by the course of events. With the outbreak of the English civil war in 1642, the Covenanters believed that their own revolution could best be secured by supporting the English parliamentarians in their struggle against the king. This was achieved in the Solemn League and Covenant* of 1643, which was a military alliance concluded in time of emergency, but it also provided that the churches of England, Scotland and Ireland should adopt uniformity in doctrine, worship, discipline and government, 'according to the Word of God and the example of the best reformed churches', which the Presbyterians took to mean an endorsement of their own system. Scottish representatives attended the Westminster Assembly of Divines* in 1643 which issued a Confession of Faith, a Shorter and a Larger Catechism, a Directory of Public Worship and a Presbyterian Form of Church Government. Though they proved unacceptable in England, the Westminster standards were adopted by the Church of Scotland.

Opposition to these developments led to the emergence of a royalist party in Scotland under Montrose (see Graham, James) and to concluding an 'Engagement'* with Charles I. As Scotland also drifted into civil war, Presbyterians from the southwest marched on Edinburgh and seized power in the Whiggamore raid of 1648. Charles' execution in England led Scots to rally in accepting Charles II* as king; but this, in turn, invited retaliation from Cromwell in the form of a military occupation and enforced union of the kingdoms. Though the General Assembly was dissolved in 1653, the rest of the Presbyterian system remained intact, but divisions among Presbyterians between the theocratic Protesters* and more moderate Resolutioners* meant that at the Restoration* of the monarch in 1660 the Presbyterians were poorly placed to win concessions from the new regime.

Though representing a slight majority within the nation, the Presbyterians had weakened their position by quarrelling; while the Episcopalians proved to be particularly strong north of the Tay, and had powerful friends at court. In devising a settlement for the Church, Charles II, who disliked Presbyterianism intensely, was inclined to expediency. He chose to ignore his earlier promises to support the Covenants and thereby Presbyterianism. Yet the revival of Episcopacy was achieved in an underhand manner; and the Presbyterians felt betrayed by their own representative, James Sharp,* minister at Crail, who emerged as Archbishop of St Andrews.

In 1661, the Act Rescissory annulled all legislation – including that of the Covenanters – since 1633. Charles had no wish to perpetuate a Presbyterian ascendancy. Another act on religion and church government indicated that Charles would maintain the Church's doctrine and worship as it had been under James VI and Charles I, and would settle its polity in a form agreeable to God's Word and appropriate to the monarchy and peace of the kingdom; kirk sessions, presbyteries and synods were to continue for the present; but there was silence on the return of the General Assembly. The restoration of episcopacy and a revival of lay patronage quickly followed, and in 1662 the bishops took their seats in parliament. The settlement so devised for political ends notoriously led to trouble. Further legislation in 1662 denounced the Covenants, prohibited conventicles* for private worship and imposed a rigorous penal code.

INDULGENCES AND REVOLUTION. Efforts by the regime to dragoon Presbyterians into an Episcopal church led to the Pentland rising of 1666 and to the outbreak of sporadic guerrilla warfare in the south-west. Attempts at conciliation took the form of a Declaration of Indulgence* issued in 1669, but it proved no more fruitful and was replaced by renewed repression in 1670. The situation deteriorated; a second Indulgence, offered in 1672, offered little in positive results, and fresh repression followed. In 1679 the assassination of Archbishop Sharp was the prelude to a further armed rising, suppressed at Bothwell Bridge.* A short interlude of conciliation under the Duke of Monmouth saw the offer of a third Indulgence in June 1679.

With the failure of the rebellion, many dissident Presbyterians accepted their lot; but a remnant still refused all compromise, and at a point when Monmouth had been replaced in Scotland by James, Duke of York, an open RC, uncompromising Presbyterians or Cameronians (later to become the Reformed Presbyterian Church* by 1712), in their Queensferry Paper* and Sanquhar Declaration* of 1680, affirmed their belief in the divine right of Presbyterian government, in ecclesiastical independence and the Covenants, renounced their allegiance to the king, and rejected the claim to the throne of James, Duke of York. After he became king in 1685, James' decision to grant toleration, first to Roman Catholics and Quakers, and then to Presbyterians by 1687 transformed the ecclesiastical situation, for his action undid all the work since 1660 in forcing Presbyterians to accept the established Episcopal church.

At the Revolution,* William of Orange* favoured comprehension and reconciliation between the two rival parties in the Church. He would have preferred to retain Episcopacy, but finding the episcopalians largely Jacobite* in sympathy, he was obliged to restore moderate Presbyterianism. In 1689 parliament abolished Episcopacy and in 1690 established Presbyterian government on the model of the Golden Act* of 1592. The Treaty of Union* with England in 1707 also secured the Presbyterian worship, discipline and government of the CofS 'in all succeeding generations'.

By 1710, a Tory ministry – high church and sympathetic to the Scottish Episcopalians – found a useful political weapon in the Greenshields* case. The House of Lords in 1711 found in favour of Greenshields as an Episcopalian minister, thereby overturning the Court of Session's decision that he had been improperly ordained. This was made the basis of several acts of the British parliament – the Toleration, Patronage and Yule Vacance Acts of 1712 – which were designed to create mischief and to weaken the Presbyterian establishment in Scotland.

The protest against patronage* voiced by Ebenezer Erskine* and other evangelical* ministers in 1732 led them to form the Associate Presbytery* in 1733 and, when deposed by the CofS in 1740, to found the Original Secession Church,* an influential body of Presbyterian seceders, who split in 1744 on the issue of the Burgess Oath* into the Burghers and Antiburghers, and then later split again, at the end of the century, into the Old Lights and New Lights (*see* New Light)* over the magistrate's role in the Church.

DIVISIONS AND REUNIONS. The divisive tendencies in Presbyterianism remained strong. As disputes over patronage grew in intensity, a second secession, led by Thomas Gillespie* in protest at patronage, created the Relief Presbytery* in 1761, which grew into the Relief Church, which upheld the voluntary* principle that the Church should not seek help from the state, and later united with the United Secession Church* (New Lights) in 1847 to form the United Presbyterian Church.* Within the Established Church, the rise of rationalism and 'enlightened' ideas helped sustain the Moderate* party's ascendancy in the General Assembly from 1752; but by the end of the century the Evangelicals were again to the fore, and were active in church extension. Increasingly, the Assembly, under evangelical leadership from 1833, challenged statute law on patronage,* and the secular courts, in turn, interpreted the Assembly's decisions as illegal. 'Non-intrusionists',* opposing patronage, appealed to the *First Book of Discipline** which upheld congregational rights.

The ensuing struggle – the Ten Years' Conflict* (1833–43) – to free the Church from political and judicial domination saw the Assembly ready in 1834 to amend the Church's constitution in the Veto and the Chapel Acts, without seeking parliament's consent. As the conflict deepened, a majority of Old Light Burghers who had formed the Original Associate Synod (*see* Associate Synod) rejoined the CofS in 1839, so strengthening the evangelical party, whose leaders by 1843 resolved to secure a Church free from political domination by separating from the Establishment. The Disruption* of 1843 saw the formation of the FCS* when around a third of the ministers and members seceded from the Est.C. By 1852, the FC attracted a majority of the Original Secession Church, and in 1876 most in the Reformed Presbyterian Church joined the FC.

By the end of the century, the three large presbyterian churches were the CofS, the FC and the UPC, though smaller presbyterian denominations persisted among the minorities in dissenting churches who had declined any union, and in 1893 the Free Presbyterians* split from the FC, whose theology they considered too liberal. When a majority of the FC and the UPC united in 1900 to form the UFC* (which possessed more ministers than the CofS), a dissenting minority continued to regard itself as the true FC.

Although patronage had been abolished in 1874, it was not until 1921 that parliament recognized the CofS's 'right and power, subject to no civil authority, to legislate and to adjudicate finally in all matters of doctrine, worship, government and discipline'. This facilitated the union in 1929 of the UFC and CofS; and in 1956 the small United Original Secession Church joined the establishment.

In an era of falling church attendance and of ecumenical dialogue with other churches, including the RCC, the CofS has had discussions for union with the Congregationalists, the Scottish Episcopal Church and the Methodists, but without success. While adjustments have been made to its machinery for government, the CofS has so far shown no serious inclination to jettison the substance of its Presbyterian heritage.

Bibliographies by J. Kirk (Reformation and James VI), *RSCHS* 23:1 (1987), 113–55, D. Stevenson (1600–60), *ibid.* 21:2 (1982), 209–20, J. F. McCaffrey (nineteenth century), *ibid.* 23:3 (1989), 417–36.

Burleigh; A. L. Drummond and J. Bulloch, *The Scottish Church 1688–1843*, *The Church in Victorian Scotland 1843–74*, *The Church in Late Victorian Scotland 1874–1900* (E, 1973, 1975, 1978); W. M. Campbell, *The Triumph of Presbyterianism* (E, 1958); R. Sjölinder, *Presbyterian Reunion in Scotland 1907–21* (E, 1962); G. D. Henderson, *The Claims of the Church of Scotland* (L, 1951), *Presbyterianism* (A, 1954), *Why We Are Presbyterians* (E, n.d.).

J. Kirk

Presbytery, the court standing midway between General Assembly* (or Synod*) and Kirk Session* in the hierarchy of courts that constitute the Presbyterian* system of Church government. The following account applies to the current CofS, but similar arrangements obtain in other Presbyterian Churches, within and without Scotland.

As a Kirk Session has a parish,* so a Presbytery has a geographical area – its 'bounds'. These areas vary considerably in size, normally in inverse ratio to the number of its charges, ranging in the present CofS from Glasgow with 169 (85,228 members) to Uist with 9 (709). Most are around the 40–50 mark.

Each charge* in the CofS is represented in Presbytery by its minister and one of its elders, though in the case of linkings each Kirk Session appoints an elder.* In recent years seats in Presbytery have been awarded to an increasing number of other ministers – chaplains, ordained assistants, community ministers, teachers of religious education in schools and of theology in universities – as well as to retired ministers. To maintain parity the Presbytery itself appoints additional elders. All members of the diaconate* serving within the bounds are members.

Meetings of Presbytery are held regularly (usually monthly). The date has to be determined and publicly announced before the previous meeting adjourns. Thus a Presbytery is always either in session or appointed to meet. Otherwise it is held to have lapsed and its reconstitution involves a complicated process. Ordinary meetings are in public, though for special reason the court may resolve to meet in private. It may also meet *in hunc effectum* or *pro re nata*, the former for some specific item of business such as an induction,* and the latter to deal with some emergency situation, in which case the Moderator* summons the meeting by a letter addressed to each member, the approval of his conduct being the first item of business.

Like other courts a Presbytery has a Moderator to preside over its deliberations, to see that good order is maintained, and generally to act as chairman. He or she is elected from among the ministerial members, holds office for a year and may be re-elected. The Presbytery appoints a Clerk* to keep the record of its affairs, almost always a minister, though not necessarily so, and not necessarily a member of the court. Having no funds of its own, the Presbytery has to impose a tax on its constituent congregations to meet its outlays. To oversee its finances a treasurer is appointed, almost always an elder.

The duties of the Presbytery are both extensive and varied. It has to exercise careful oversight over all its congregations, ensuring that the laws of the Kirk are being observed and the work of God's kingdom advanced. On the occurrence of a vacancy, the responsibility for the ongoing work of the congregation falls on the Presbytery, which immediately appoints one of its ministers to be interim moderator. It has then to consider the future of the charge, whether, and if so what kind of, readjustment should be involved, and when that question has been resolved, to give leave to the congregation to call a minister. In due course it adjudges the call* and makes the necessary arrangements for and carries through the resultant translation or induction. If a union or other readjustment is to be effected, it is the Presbytery that has to prepare and get agreement for an appropriate basis. It has also to secure for all of this the concurrence of the appropriate Assembly committee.

The Presbytery is bound to arrange visitation of each of its congregations once in every five years to satisfy itself as to the health of the cause, to ensure that the regulations regarding building maintenance are being observed, and, if need be in extreme cases, to take action to deal with a congregation in an 'unsatisfactory state' or 'in changed circumstances'.

A further duty of the Presbytery is to care for the personal well-being of its ministers and their families, e.g. in sickness or other special need. In the case of allegations of serious moral aberrations, it is for the Presbytery to institute formal examination of fact, and, if appropriate, carry through a process of libel. It is not true that a minister can be tried only by his peers; he has to be tried in the first place by his Presbytery from whose judgment appeal may be taken to the General Assembly. In the case of an elder, on the other hand, any serious allegation would first be reported to the Kirk Session concerned, whose judgment could, of course, be appealed to the Presbytery and thence to the Assembly.

The nomination of candidates for the ministry is the business of the Presbytery in which their congregations lie, and that Presbytery has the responsibility of looking after aspirants throughout their study. After its completion, the Presbytery takes them on trials for licence and, in due course, licenses them as preachers of the gospel at a special service which is also a meeting of the court. The overall duty of caring for their welfare continues with the Presbytery throughout the probationary period and until a call to a parish or appointment to some comparable post has been received. The same general pattern of supervision applies in the case of members of the diaconate and of readers.*

As part of the Kirk's judicial machine the Presbytery deals with appeals against judgments of Kirk Sessions on practically every matter that can come before them, its decisions being subject to review only by the Assembly. Any disgruntled member of a Kirk Session may bring a matter to the Presbytery, though in this case the instrument is officially known as 'dissent and complaint'.

PRESBYTERY CLERK

Presbytery also has a vital role in determining the Kirk's doctrine and practice. Any matter that is to become a 'binding rule and constitution for the Church' must, in terms of the Barrier Act* of 1697, be submitted to Presbyteries and receive the support of more than half of these. Presbytery may also institute consideration of some major issue by itself introducing it to the Assembly as an overture.*

Cox 140–84; A. Herron, *A Guide to the Presbytery* (E, 1983).

A. Herron

Presbytery Clerk, *see* Clerks; Presbytery.

Presbytery, Origins of. From the Reformation, the Reformed church developed a system of conciliar government in which discipline* was exercised primarily through the eldership.* At congregational level this took the form of 'kirk sessions',* the kirk, or its representatives – the minister, elders and (sometimes) deacons – sitting to hear disciplinary cases. With the General Assembly's resolve by 1576 to end its experiment with diocesan episcopacy, introduced at the Convention of Leith,* a renewed emphasis was placed on government through courts. Such a trend was evident in England, too, where supporters of the anti-episcopal cause pressed for the elimination of bishops and the adoption of the 'presbytery', or congregational eldership, and of the 'classis', or district court, both to be subordinate to the provincial synod and national assembly. In Scotland, however, where 'presbyteries' (in the English sense) had existed from 1559, there was less need for adopting an entirely new court modelled on the English 'classis'. Instead, what did emerge by the later 1570s was the decision that not every congregation need have an eldership of its own, and that in rural areas, particularly where kirk sessions may not have been fully established, several adjacent churches might share a common eldership on a basis similar to the 'general sessions'* which had emerged in some of the larger towns. This solution of the communal eldership, or presbytery in its Latinized form, was adopted in the *Second Book of Discipline** of 1578. At that point too, the General Assembly used 'presbytery' as a synonym for 'eldership' when it warned bishops 'to usurp not the power of presbyteries'. By 1579 the Assembly determined that the 'exercise'* for interpreting Scripture 'may be judged a presbytery', and in 1581 the Assembly, with help from the privy council,* decided to set up thirteen model presbyteries in the main towns of the central lowlands 'as exemplars to the rest' of the country. The earliest extant register – that of Stirling presbytery – records the creation of the presbytery on 8 August 1581, with ministers and selected elders from the constituent kirk sessions (which continued to function) in attendance.

SBD, 102ff.; *Stirling Presbytery Records, 1581–1587*, ed. J. Kirk (E, 1981), ix ff.; J. Kirk, *Patterns of Reform* (E, 1989).

J. Kirk

PRINCETON THEOLOGICAL SEMINARY

Primmer, Jacob (1842–1914), minister of the CofS and prominent anti-Romanist campaigner. Born in Leith the son of a merchant seaman, he was an apprentice in the printing trade before he trained as a minister at the University of Edinburgh. He was minister of Townhill, Dunfermline, 1876–1904. He was a low churchman, preferring the title 'Pastor' to 'Reverend', and was greatly influenced by the Edinburgh lawyer John Hope* in his opposition to RCism. He was the chief instigator in the Dunfermline Protestant Defence Association and held a series of Protestant meetings throughout Scotland at which he spoke out against popery. He used his grasp of Church law and his skill as a debater to great effect when he opposed what he considered to be ritualism in the CofS. He protested against the annual General Assembly service in St Giles', and drew the attention of the courts of the Church to the advanced liturgical practices of T. N. Adamson at Barnhill, Broughty Ferry. When ministers such as Henry Grey Graham* of Strathaven and John Charleson* of Thornliebank became RCs he saw clear evidence of a Romanizing conspiracy in the Kirk.

Jacob Primmer in Rome (L, 1921).

J. B. Primmer, *Life of Pastor Jacob Primmer* (E, 1916); *FES* V, 36–7.

D. M. Murray

Primus, the title of the Presiding Bishop of the EpCS's College of Bishops, a short form of *Primus inter pares* ('first among equals') or a deliberate revival of an early Scottish title *Primus Episcopus* ('first bishop'). The office and college were introduced in 1720, following the death of Bishop Alexander Ross (Rose)* of Edinburgh, to avoid the appointment of a metropolitan, whose authority thereafter was vested corporately in the college. Moves to reintroduce a metropolitan failed, but since 1890 the Primus has had the courtesy prefix 'the Most Revd'. Various Episcopal Churches have copied the idea, including the American Episcopal Church.

Canons and Digest of Resolutions (EpCS, E, 1988); F. Goldie, *Short History of the Episcopal Church in Scotland* (E, ²1976); R. Keith, *Historical Catalogue of the Scottish Bishops*, ed. M. Russel (E, 1824).

A. Maclean

Princeton Theological Seminary, founded in 1812 as the first seminary of the Presbyterian Church in the United States. During the first century of its existence, it was the centre of 'Old School' Calvinism. Princeton's first three professors – Archibald Alexander (1772–1851), Samuel Miller (1769–1850) and Charles Hodge (1797–1878) – were all descended from Scottish stock. Yet Princeton's ties to Scotland were even stronger intellectually. The ethos of Princeton was shaped decisively by the Scottish Common-Sense philosophy associated with Thomas Reid (*see* Scottish Realism). Under this influence the theology of Hodge, especially, stressed the foundational character of self-evident mental axioms and the indispensability of rational proofs for the existence of God. Hodge followed the events leading up to the Disruption* closely, and especially after meeting William Cunningham,* who had come to the States to solicit support for the FC, became a champion of the new body. The friendship was reciprocated by Cunningham, who regarded Hodge as the greatest advocate of Calvinism in the new world. The *Princeton Review*, which Hodge edited, took full notice of Thomas Chalmers'* works, approving Chalmers' educational, social and ecclesiastical convictions enthusiastically, but expressing doubts about Chalmers' opinions on the will.

Later Princetonians wrote extensively on developments in Scottish theology. One of the first extended critiques of William Robertson Smith's* use of biblical criticism came from the Old Testament scholar William Henry Green (1825–1900). B. B. Warfield (1851–1921), the leading theologian of the generation after Hodge, wrote critically of the work of Edward Irving,* John McLeod Campbell* and Marcus Dods.* He found greater sympathy with the views of James Denney* and James Orr.*

Princeton Seminary was reorganized in 1929 to achieve greater theological pluralism. As a result, several professors (led by J. Gresham Machen*) left Princeton and established Westminster Theological Seminary in Philadelphia to maintain and defend the 'Old School' Calvinism with which Princeton had so long been associated.

The reorganization opened a new chapter in the history of the influence of Scottish churches and theology on Princeton Seminary. It was above all through the direction given by Inverness native John A. Mackay* (President of Princeton 1936–59 and a person of immense stature in the ecumenical movement) that Princeton became a major centre of the movement known as Neo-orthodoxy.* Mackay's own theology had been strongly influenced by the Spanish existentialist, Miguel de Unamuno, and through him by Soren Kierkegaard, as well as by the theology of Karl Barth. Through a series of striking appointments, Mackay contributed greatly to Princeton's continued international standing. Emil Brunner came for a year (1938–9). Joseph Hromadka, the great Czech Reformed theologian, fled Prague (and the Gestapo) in 1939 and was given a home in exile at Princeton, serving as guest professor of ethics and theology until 1946. Otto Piper (also an exile from Nazi Germany) was made professor of New Testament literature and exegesis in 1942. In 1944, Princeton's role in shaping contemporary theology was further strengthened when Mackay founded *Theology Today*, soon hailed as the leading Protestant publication of its kind. In the years following the war Scottish influence was furthered by the appointment of Norman V. Hope (*FES* IX, 241) to the Archibald Alexander chair in church history (in 1946), and of George S. Hendry (*FES* IX, 433) to the Charles Hodge chair in systematic theology (in 1949). More recently, the connection between Princeton Seminary and the Scottish churches and divinity schools has remained strong, with a regular interchange of students and faculty.

C. Hodge, 'The General Assembly of the Free Church of Scotland', in *Biblical Repertory and Princeton Review* 16 (1844), 86–119; C. Hodge, 'The Claims of the Free Church', *ibid.*, 229–61; A. A. Hodge, *The Life of Charles Hodge* (NY, 1880); T. M. Lindsay, 'The Doctrine of Scripture: The Reformers and the Princeton School', *The Expositor* 5th ser., 1 (1895), 278–93; W. H. Green, 'Professor W. Robertson Smith on the Pentateuch', *Presbyterian Review* 3 (1882), 108–56; B. B. Warfield, *Critical Reviews* (NY, 1932); M. A. Noll (ed.), *The Princeton Theology, 1812–1921* (Grand Rapids, MI, 1983); R. T. Clutter, 'The Reorientation of Princeton Theological Seminary, 1900–29' (ThD, Dallas Theological Seminary, 1982); G. L. Haines, 'The Princeton Theological Seminary, 1925–60' (PhD, New York University, 1966); B. J. Longfield, 'The Presbyterian Controversy, 1922–36: Christianity, Culture, and Ecclesiastical Conflict' (PhD, Duke University, 1988); J. C. Vanderstelt, *Philosophy and Scripture: A Study in Old Princeton and Westminster* (Marlton, NJ, 1978).

M. A. Noll and B. McCormack

Principal Clerk, *see* Clerks.

Pringle, Alexander (1752–1839), Secession minister. He was ordained as minister of the North Antiburgher congregation, Perth, in 1777, where he remained until his death. He showed strong interest in Christian unity, serving on the committee that formed the USec.C in 1820 from the New Light* branches of the Antiburghers (*see* General Associate Synod) and Burghers (*see* Associate Synod), and encouraging Christians of all Churches to unite in prayer for revival and missions, especially in small group prayer meetings.

Sermons and Letters, with a memoir by D. Young (Perth, 1840); *Prayer for the Revival of Religion and for the Spread of the Gospel* (E, 1796); *The Duty of Prayer Recommended* (Perth, 1781).

D. A. Currie

Privy Council, i.e. secret council, the monarch's ordinary council, readily convened on an informal basis in the Middle Ages and composed of such advisers as the King found it useful to consult on routine matters of government without recourse to a full-scale council or to a Parliament formally summoned at infrequent intervals. The councillors, consisting of invited household officials and such magnates as happened to be at court, were sworn to secrecy, hence 'privy council', a phrase which occurs in 1369 in the reign of David II.* The council's competence was exceedingly wide-ranging, with legislative, judicial and administrative functions. Developing into the main executive instrument of government, it became virtually omnicompetent, tackling almost any issue as it arose, and its decrees had the full force of law. Any

PRIVY KIRK

continuity in government is very largely attributable to the work of the privy council, which came to sit more or less continuously. Even with James VI's* accession to the English throne in 1603, the privy council continued to meet in Edinburgh as the instrument of the King's authority. From the Reformation* it increasingly concerned itself with religious and ecclesiastical issues, ranging from matters affecting benefices and stipends* to issues of overlapping jurisdiction: on occasion, it sought to overturn the General Assembly's sentence of excommunication, and even after the creation of two Courts of High Commission* in 1610 it continued to act against Presbyterian and RC nonconformity during much of the seventeenth century. By then the council's nominal membership could be as large as fifty, but seven members formed a quorum, and regular attendance was confined to a small core of officials, lairds, lawyers and some bishops, who were all nominees of the Crown and took their orders from the King. Placed in abeyance during the Cromwellian occupation 1653–60, the Scottish privy council was abolished in 1708 after the Treaty of Union with England.

Register of the Privy Council of Scotland, ed. J. H. Burton et al., 38 vols (E, 1877–1970).

J. Kirk

Privy Kirk, a feature of Protestant organization in its earlier phase as an underground movement before the Reformers' victory of 1559/60. As clandestine meetings for Bible study and worship, the privy kirks afforded contact and protection for Protestants harried by the authorities. They also assisted in developing a network of Protestant cells, at first isolated and dispersed, but soon well-organized and militant, as Reformers seized the initiative in the revolution against Rome and France. The problem of religious dissidents meeting for private worship in conventicles,* where literate laymen might read passages from the vernacular Bible* to those assembled and discuss controverted passages, had led Parliament in 1541 to ban 'the private congregation and conventicles of heretics where their errors are spread'. The measure was less than fruitful, for conventicling persisted and was fortified in the 1550s through the efforts of itinerant Protestant preachers, who began to administer Reformed Communion to those gathered in the privy kirks. In 1556, John Knox* had counselled that Protestants of one household or several should meet together each week as a 'congregation' for 'reading, exhorting and in making common prayers'. The structure of Edinburgh's privy kirk, where believers gathered secretly in the large houses of merchants in winter or in the fields during summer, reveals how some were called 'to occupy the supreme place of exhortation and reading', and how others were elected as elders* to maintain discipline* or as deacons (see Diaconate) to provide for the poor within the group. The formation of these clandestine congregations greatly assisted the transition of Protestantism at the Reformation from a mere network of underground cells to a recognized Church intent on claiming the allegiance of the nation.

J. Kirk, 'The "Privy Kirks" and their Antecedents: the Hidden Face of Scottish Protestantism', *Voluntary Religion*, ed. W. J. Sheils and D. Woods (O, 1986), 155–70; J. Kirk, *Patterns of Reform* (E, 1989), 1–15.

J. Kirk

Probationer, the name given to a candidate for the ministry in the CofS who has satisfactorily completed his course of study, had his trials for licence sustained and been licensed* by his Presbytery, and who is serving his 'probationary period' as assistant in a charge* to which he has been directed by the Committee on Education for the Ministry. This is the official definition as set forth in Act VII of the General Assembly of 1985. Until then the custom had been to apply the term 'probationer' to the candidate who, having been licensed, was proceeding towards the ministry, the term 'licentiate' being reserved for those who had achieved that status but who, for whatever reason, were not immediately seeking ordination.

It was in 1973 that the idea of a period of compulsory probation was introduced with the object of providing 'a long and intensive period of practical training and experience for candidates for the ministry to complement the academic training provided and the experience gained in attachments during the university course and to form an immediate preparation for the parish ministry'. Exemption from the probationary period may be granted in exceptional circumstances, but of recent years this has rarely been done. The period lasts between nine and eighteen months. In any case where the work of the probationary period has not been sustained, a second period of service will be required. Towards the end of the period the probationer is at liberty to preach in a vacancy with a view to election, but he may not be inducted to a charge until the full period has expired.

Cox, espec. 223–32; *RGACS 1985*, pt. II, 47–50.

A. Herron

Procurator, the 'Advocate for the Church'. The Procurator is an official and *ex officio* member of the General Assembly of the CofS. He is a senior member of the Faculty of Advocates appointed to advise the General Assembly on legal matters and to conduct litigation on behalf of the Church. In litigation he is instructed through the Solicitor of the Church of Scotland, who is a full-time official, but requests for advice from inferior courts and Assembly committees are transmitted to him through the Principal Clerks (see Clerks). The first Advocates for the Church were appointed by the General Assembly of 1564. At that time there were three, but the practice of having only one was established by the end of the sixteenth century. The change from the title 'Advocate for the Church' occurred after the appointment of Archibald Johnston* of Wariston, who was also Clerk, in 1638, no doubt to distinguish the office from that of Lord

Advocate, to which he was appointed in 1646. The name is derived from the Latin *procurator*, and reached Scotland from the *Corpus Iuris Civilis* through canon law and the pre-Reformation Church, in which the advocates in the Court of the Bishop's Official were known as procurators.

Cox, 207–8, 779; D. Shaw, *The General Assemblies of the Church of Scotland 1560–1600* (E, 1964); S. Ollivant, *The Court of the Official in Pre-Reformation Scotland* (E, 1982).

J. L. Weatherhead

Propaganda Fide. The Sacred Congregation of *Propaganda Fide* (for the Propagation of the Faith) was established in 1622 to administer the RCC's missionary work in Protestant lands in Europe and non-Christian territories of the New World. Its college was founded at Rome in 1627 to educate secular priests for mission lands. *Propaganda*'s powers were extensive. In a lengthy struggle with RC colonial powers, it imposed its authority as a supranational body and appointed bishops subject to itself, called vicars-apostolic, in Spanish and Portuguese territories. Similarly it brought missionary work by religious orders, Jesuits* in particular, under its control. Its early progress was marred by bitter controversies over jurisdiction and indigenous rites. In 1967 *Propaganda* was renamed Congregation for the Evangelization of the Nations.

Scotland's development under *Propaganda* followed a classical pattern. A non-episcopal superior, called a prefect, was appointed 1653; Thomas Nicolson* became vicar-apostolic 1694; the one vicariate became two in 1727 and three in 1827; normal diocesan bishops were instituted 1878. For almost two centuries Scottish vicars-apostolic had close and cordial links with *Propaganda*. William Leslie* was one of its most notable archivists. In 1908 countries with an episcopal hierarchy, Scotland included, were withdrawn from *Propaganda*'s authority.

Catholic Encyclopedia XII, 456–61; *New Catholic Encyclopedia* XI, 840–4, XIV, 638–9; P. F. Anson, *Underground Catholicism in Scotland* (Montrose, 1970).

M. Dilworth

Protectorate, *see* Commonwealth and Protectorate.

Protest Question, a prolonged controversy in the FP Church over the effect of a protest against a decision of the Church's supreme court. In its most recent ruling the Synod holds that a protest – in contrast to a dissent, which may be tendered simply to relieve the dissenter from involvement in the decision – implies non-acquiescence or disobedience and usually leads to the protester's self-exclusion from the Church. The Synod view holds that it was by means of a protest in the FC General Assembly of 1893 that Donald Macfarlane* separated from the FC, thus preserving inviolate the historic constitution of the reformed CofS.

These views have been challenged. In 1938 Ewen MacQueen protested against a Synod decision in a case of discipline and was held to have separated himself. In 1944 Roderick MacKenzie expressed disagreement with the Synod view of protest. This led to his separation and to the formation of the FP Relief Congregation.* In 1980 John Brentnall and Moshe Radcliff disagreed with the Synod's view and, in the ecclesiastical procedure which followed, were suspended from office. At their instance the matter came under the review of the civil courts, but recent attempts to have the basis of the right of protest reviewed by the Synod have been unsuccessful.

A. MacPherson (ed.), *History of the Free Presbyterian Church of Scotland 1893–1970* (Inverness, 1974); *The Right of Protest* (G, 1975); S. F. Tallach, *The Ides of May* (E, 1981).

A. Morrison

Protestant League (1586). Since the Reformation* in 1560 there had been strong pressure from Anglophile Protestants in Scotland for an English alliance. However, Elizabeth I* was reluctant to offend France, and besides, an alliance was impossible during the personal reign of Mary Queen of Scots.* The successive governments of James VI's* minority were treated as English clients, and it was not until the government of Chancellor Arran (1583–5) that Elizabeth was forced to negotiate, although agreement was not reached until after his fall.

Serious talks finally began in February 1586, when the major stumbling-blocks were James VI's claim to the English succession, the size of pension he could expect to receive from Elizabeth, and the privileges Scottish merchants should enjoy in England. James was able to extract modest concessions to the first two of these, but Elizabeth would only admit to James's 'pretended' claim in the treaty, tricked him over the size of the pension, and refused all Scottish demands for rights of naturalization in England. On 5 July, 1586 the League was finally signed. In essence it was an alliance against RC aggression, although Elizabeth insisted that the phrase stating that the League was 'for causes of religion' be deleted. James hoped to draw other Protestant princes into the League, but while his grand vision never materialized the alliance with England endured until he succeeded to the English throne in 1603.

J. Bain *et al.* (eds), *Calendar of State Papers relating to Scotland and Mary, Queen of Scots, 1547–1603*, 13 vols (L, 1898–1969), VIII, 43–6; M. Lee, *John Maitland of Thirlstane* (Perth, 1959), 87–97; C. Read, *Mr Secretary Walsingham and the Policy of Queen Elizabeth*, 3 vols (O, 1925), II, 118–257.

K. M. Brown

Protestant Religion and Presbyterian Church Act, *see* Security Act (1707).

Protestation, a motion from the Reformation* party in the Scottish Parliament in December 1558 claiming interim toleration. The Protestation

PROTESTERS

occurred within the distinctive period in Scottish religious affairs which began with the 'Common Band' or covenant made in December 1557, and ended in May 1559 with the lurch to open confrontation.

During this period, there existed a religious *modus vivendi*. The Reformation movement, led by the Lords of the Congregation,* balanced optimism and boldness with discretion. This was due to the Governor of Scotland, Mary of Guise,* whose policy has been variously characterized as lenient, temporizing, conciliatory, vacillating, and duplicitous. Needing maximum support for Mary Queen of Scots'* diplomatic marriage, she granted religious concessions.

Further rigorous actions by the Church authorities led the Reformation party to petition for the provisional suspension of anti-heresy legislation. Though expressing sympathy, Mary of Guise was reluctant to propose this to Parliament. In response, Reformation supporters delivered a parliamentary 'protestation', but failed to have it minuted. The statement urged provisional freedom of worship and conscience, exemption from civil disabilities, disclaiming responsibility for further disorder, and expressing concern for the reform of religious abuses. While promising consideration, Mary's subsequent but unsuccessful policy was to encourage RC reform in the hope of diminishing Reformation activism and avoiding a Scottish schism.

Knox, *History* I, 147f.; *Calendar of State Papers, Foreign Ser., of the Reign of Q. Elizabeth*, I, nr. 66; D. H. Fleming, *The Scottish Reformation* (E, 1903), 29f.; G. Donaldson, *Scotland: James V to James VII* (E, L, 1965), 85f.

W. I. P. Hazlett

Protesters, also called Remonstrants, those in the CofS who supported a Remonstrance presented to the Commission of the General Assembly in October 1650, which complained of the hasty admission of Charles II* to the Covenants*. They believed that '. . . to promise any power to the King before he had evidenced the change of his principles, and the continuing of that power in his hand was sinfull till that change did appear' (R. Baillie, *The Letters and Journals*, E, 1842, III, 122). The Resolutioners,* for their part, believed this to be 'high treason' (*ibid.*, 123).

Censured and barred from election to the 1651 General Assembly, twenty-two ministers including Samuel Rutherford* and James Guthrie* handed in a Protestation. They complained 'against the validity and constitution of this Assembly, as not being free and lawful', of 'the allowing and carrying on of a conjunction with the Malignant Party', contrary to the Word of God and the Covenant, and protested that any actions taken by such an Assembly were 'void and null'. When the Assembly reconstituted itself in Dundee, it deposed Guthrie, Patrick Gillespie* and James Simson, and called on presbyteries and synods to censure all signers of the Protestation.

Although the Protesters acknowledged the claims of Charles II, they differed from their brethren in having a more realistic view of the King. They believed it sinful to require and accept what was obviously insincere compliance, and thought the combination of Royalists, Engagers* and other enemies of the Covenant and Reformed religion more of a threat to the Church – and thus to the best interests of Scotland – than the English Independents and sectaries. They interpreted the disaster at Dunbar (September, 1650) as a want of God's favour due to compromises already made.

The resultant separation lasted through the Restoration,* with considerable hostility on both sides. The Protesters referred to themselves as the 'godly party', and demanded repentance by the Resolutioners as the price of union. While some were more amenable to peace, the more extreme (such as Archibald Johnston of Wariston* and Guthrie), with full cooperation from the more violent Resolutioners, opposed any concessions. Separate presbyteries and synods were held, and in 1653 opposing General Assemblies were planned; the two sides even ordained rival ministers in the same parish.

Although the minority in the 1650 Assembly's Commission and the 1651 Assembly, it is difficult to determine the strength of the Protesters. They were strong in the west, and with the accession of most new ordinations through the 1650s, they were probably a majority by the end of the decade.

The Protesters were more inclined at first to cooperate with the English, and in consequence received better treatment. But as Scots and Presbyterians they soon recognized underlying obstacles to real co-operation. They sent representatives to London to counteract those of the Resolutioners, and after each side had presented its case Cromwell sent them home to agree among themselves (*The Life of Mr Robert Blair*, E, 1848, 330–4).

After the Restoration a few prominent Protesters were executed (*e.g.* Guthrie) and some went into exile. On balance they remained more constant to Presbyterian principles through the persecution, and they constituted the core of the re-established, Presbyterian, Church after the Revolution.

See also Resolutioners; Commonwealth and Protectorate; Douglas, Robert; Baillie, Robert; Cant, Andrew; Guthrie, William.

The Records of the Commissions of the General Assemblies of the Church of Scotland, ed. A. F. Mitchell and J. Christie, vols 2 and 3 (E, 1896, 1909); *Register of the Consultations of the Ministers of Edinburgh . . . 1652–1657* and *1657–1660*, ed. W. Stephen, 2 vols (E, 1921, 1930); *Diary of Sir Archibald Johnston of Wariston, 1650–1654*, ed. D. H. Fleming (E, 1919) and *. . . 1655–1660*, ed. J. D. Ogilvie (E, 1940); James Beattie, *History of the Church of Scotland during the Commonwealth* (E, 1842).

D. C. Lachman

Protesters, (Associate) Synod of, *see* Paxton, George; Original Secession Church; United Secession Church.

Proudfoot, William (1788–1851), one of the founders of the USec.C in Upper Canada and its first Professor of Theology. Born in Manor parish near Peebles and educated at Lanark grammar school and Edinburgh University, he gained his theological training under George Lawson* of Selkirk. Licensed by the Associate Presbytery of Edinburgh, in 1813 he was ordained and inducted into the charge of Pitrodie in the Carse of Gowrie. In 1832 he went as one of the USec.C's missionaries to Upper Canada and settled in London, Upper Canada. His main contribution to the Church lay in the field of theological education, as he established a college in London in 1844 in order to train Canadian ministers. This college eventually become part of Knox College as a result of the union of 1861 with the FC.

S. D. Gill, 'We are too Scotch', *RSCHS* 22 (1985), 175–94; *id.*, 'A Scottish Divine on the Canadian Frontier', *Bulletin of Canadian Studies*, 8 (1984), 162–82.

S. D. Gill

Provinces, Ecclesiastical. Following the practice of the Roman Empire, the administrative structure of the Western Church throughout the Middle Ages was arranged by provinces, not by national territories. Provinces in turn were divided into dioceses, each under a bishop, the province itself being ruled over normally by an archbishop metropolitan. The papal bull *Cum universi* of 1192 constituted the Scottish Church as an independent province, but without a metropolitan, which gave Scotland a special relationship to Rome. On 17 August 1472 Sixtus IV erected St Andrews* into an archbishopric and metropolitan see, with the other twelve Scottish dioceses subject to its jurisdiction, but on 9 January 1492 Innocent VIII erected Glasgow into an archbishopric and metropolitan see, taking under its jurisdiction the sees of Argyll, Candida Casa, Dunblane and Dunkeld. This arrangement proved to be unsatisfactory even before the Reformation of 1560, which abolished both provinces. Today the RCC in Scotland consists of two provinces, the metropolitan sees being St Andrews and Edinburgh, and Glasgow, but archiepiscopal status today is little more than honorific. The EpCS is constituted as a single province with seven dioceses, none of them an archbishopric.

FESMA; A. Theiner, *Vetera Monumenta Hibernorum et Scotorum* (Rome, 1864); *The Catholic Directory for Scotland, 1989* (G, 1989); F. Goldie, *A Short History of the Episcopal Church in Scotland* (²E, 1976).

L. J. Macfarlane

Psalms, Psalter. In some form the Psalter, the Church's first book of praise, has always played an important role in worship. The Psalms were the basis of medieval church services; but the rediscovery of them as a living part of the people's corporate worship dates from the Reformation. Both Luther and Calvin insisted that singing should no longer be confined to professionals. While Calvin gave the greatest impetus to singing metrical Psalms, i.e. the words translated into metrical and strophic form so that they might be sung to hymn tunes, it was Luther who first composed such versions.

In England Myles Coverdale's *Goostly Psalmes and Spirituall Songes* (*c.* 1536) consisted largely of translations from Luther. Coverdale's prose version of the Psalms, based on various predecessors and revised for the Great Bible (1539), was included in the *Book of Common Prayer*.

The first Psalms sung by the Scots were translations of Luther published between 1542 and 1546 by the Wedderburn brothers* as *Ane Compendious Buik of Godlie Psalmes and Spirituall Sangis. The Gude and Godlie Ballatis,* as the book was commonly known, never received any ecclesiastical sanction.

THE FRENCH-GENEVAN AND ANGLO-GENEVAN PSALTERS. In France the first metrical Psalter adopted by Protestants was *Aulcuns pseaulmes et cantiques mys en chant* (Strasburg, 1539). This contained seventeen versions by Calvin, the rest by Clément Marot. Encouraged by Calvin, Marot translated and published more Psalms in several editions. In 1562 the complete Psalter appeared in Geneva with versions by Marot and Theodore Beza, most of the melodies being by Louis Bourgeois.

During the Marian persecutions many English exiles formed a congregation in Geneva under John Knox.* In 1556 they published *The Forme of Prayers and Ministration of the Sacraments*, the second section of which comprised fifty-one metrical Psalms, each with a tune. These had been published in England (without tunes) by Thomas Sternhold, John Hopkins and William Whittingham. A second edition (1558) contained sixty-two Psalms. A 1561 edition included additional ones by William Kethe, a Scot, best known for his paraphrase of Ps. 100: 'All people that on earth do dwell'. Many of his versions and the tunes were founded on those that were to appear in the 1562 French collection. These Anglo-Genevan Psalters contained the nucleus of the words and music in the complete metrical Psalters later adopted in England and Scotland.

THE ENGLISH PSALTER, 1560 ONWARDS. The earliest metrical Psalter with tunes issued for use in England was dated 1560. It reprints the Anglo-Genevan Psalter of 1558 with three additional Psalms. Another edition in 1561 had eighteen more Psalms, mainly by Sternhold or Hopkins. This book is independent of the 1561 Anglo-Genevan edition. *The Whole Book of Psalmes Collected into English Metre* was printed by John Daye in 1562, the versions still required being supplied by Hopkins, Kethe and others. The book contained only forty-six 'proper' tunes, and these re-appear in nearly all later books. The book became known as the 'Old Version'.

In 1592 Thomas Este published a Psalter with additional tunes, the four-part harmonies being by eminent contemporary musicians. A fourth edition appeared in 1611. A similar Psalter, edited and with tunes often arranged by Thomas Ravenscroft, appeared in 1621 and 1633. Many of the tunes are still used.

PSALMS, PSALTER

The 'Old Version' held sway until 1696, when *A New Version* by Nahum Tate and Nicholas Brady appeared. To this we owe 'As pants the hart' and 'Through all the changing scenes'. After 1696 hymnody gained acceptance among dissenters and eventually among Anglicans. Metrical Psalms largely gave way to Psalm paraphrases* used as hymns (particularly those by Isaac Watts) or to non-metrical chants.

The 'Old' and 'New Versions' co-existed until c.1870. Since then a number of unofficial versions of the Psalms for singing have appeared, e.g. in recent years the compositions of Père Joseph Gelineau and *Psalms for Today*, edited by Michael Baughen (L, 1973).

THE SCOTTISH PSALTER, 1560 ONWARDS. Unlike the English Reformers, those in Scotland adopted the Anglo-Genevan 1561 edition as it stood, with eighty-seven Psalms and many French tunes. In 1564 the complete Psalter, known as the St. Andrews Psalter, was issued as part of the *Book of Common Order*, containing forty-two additional versions from the English 1562 Psalter, twenty-one by Robert Pont* and John Craig* and 105 different tunes (*see also* Peebles, David; Wood, Thomas). In 1615 and later editions a number of 'common' tunes appeared. In 1635 an edition giving all the tunes in harmony was produced by Edward Millar.

In 1643 the House of Commons resolved on the advice of the Westminster Assembly* to authorize one version of the Psalter throughout the kingdom. The version, by Francis Rous, Provost of Eton, much revised by himself and two committees of the General Assembly,* was authorized in 1650 and is still in use. No tunes were provided. The first collection of tunes for use with it was published in Aberdeen in 1666.

The first additional material for worship permitted in many Scottish churches was Scripture set to metre after the style of the 1650 book: *The Scottish Paraphrases* (1781).* Modern hymns were introduced in Scotland by the Relief Church* in the late eighteenth century, but were not widespread in Scottish Presbyterianism until roughly between 1850 and 1875. *The Church Hymnary* first appeared in 1898. A new music edition of the 1650 *Scottish Psalter* was published in 1929. Many of its metrical-Psalm portions and their settings are now included in the 1973 *CH³*, which has also taken a few items from *The Psalter in Metre: a Revised Version ... published by ... the Presbyterian Church in Ireland, with Tunes* (1880). (*See* Hymnology.)

The Prose Psalter (Authorized Version), pointed to Anglican chanting, has been used by some CofS congregations since the end of the last century. An improved version of a similar prose Psalter was published as *The Scottish Psalter, 1929: Authorized Version Pointed with Chants*. The 1973 *CH³* includes a number of Psalms set to chants.

J. Julian, *Dictionary of Hymnology* (²L, 1907), 916–36, 1020–33, 1541–7, 1699, *et passim*;
M. Patrick,* *Four Centuries of Scottish Psalmody* (L, 1949); *id.*, *The Story of the Church's Song* (E, 1927); M. Munck, 'Psalms, metrical, IV, 1:

PSALMS, PSALTER (GAELIC)

Scotland' in *New Grove Dictionary of Music and Musicians* (L, 1980 XV), 371–6; *Handbook to the [Revised] Church Hymnary*, ed. J. Moffatt (²L, 1928), *s.v.* 'Psalters, Early Metrical'; R. S. Louden, 'Psalmody in the Church' in *Handbook to CH³*, ed. J. M. Barkley (L, 1979); K. J. Kraan, 'Calvin and Hymn-singing', *EQ* 26 (1954), 167–70; D. F. Wright (ed.), *The Bible in Scottish Life and Literature* (E, 1988), 140–54.

J. S. Andrews

Psalms, Psalter (Gaelic). Scotland owes the Gaelic* Psalter to the labours of the Synod of Argyll, which regarded a metrical translation of the Psalms into Gaelic as a major priority. Indeed, it appears to have pursued the project with more vigour than its proposed translation of the Old Testament, mainly because of the importance attached to the Psalms within the Reformed tradition (*see* previous entry) and the complete lack of any earlier 'Irish' version (*see* Bible (Versions, Gaelic)). In 1653 the Synod decided to translate the Psalms 'so as they may be sung with the common tunes'. Exerting considerable pressure on the initial translators (Dugald Campbell, John Stewart and Alexander MacLaine), it had procured a Gaelic rendering of the first fifty psalms by May 1658, but the translation needed to be revised immediately as it was found to be 'defective in syllabization'; common metre was 'strange and unknown to the Gaelic tongue' and had posed problems. The adjustments were undertaken by David Simpson and John McMarquess, 'ane old man able in the Irish (i.e. Gaelic) song'. *An Ceud Chaogad do Shalmaibh Dhaibhidh* ('The First Fifty of the Psalms of David') was duly published in Glasgow, 1659.

A programme for translating the remainder of the Psalter was immediately drawn up, and it is probable that some work was carried out. However, the post-1660 struggle with episcopacy intervened, and the project was delayed still further by the competitive appearance of a translation by Robert Kirk,* Episcopalian incumbent of Aberfoyle. This work, which supplemented the Synod's 'First Fifty' Psalms with Kirk's rendering of the remainder, was published in Edinburgh in 1684 with an eleven-year privilege. The Synod of Argyll nevertheless retained its interest, and a manuscript of the remaining 100 Psalms was procured in 1691. The entire Psalter, incorporating revisions of the 'First Fifty', was published by the Synod in 1694 (only ²E, 1702 survives), and gained great popular esteem, eclipsing Kirk's rendering.

Revision of the Psalter then became an important issue, involving an element of competition and the appearance of rival versions. First in the field was Alexander MacFarlane (*see* Gaelic), whose mainly orthographic revision was published in 1753, and subsequently adjusted by Thomas Ross* (E, 1807). A revision which affected vocabulary, style and phrasing was produced by John Smith* (E, 1787). In 1826 the General Assembly of the CofS issued an edition which attempted to combine the best features of MacFarlane and Smith – and thus produced a third main version (E, 1826).

Given the syntactic structures of the Gaelic language, it is understandable that the first translators had difficulty with common metre. However, the use of a Scottish form of Classical Gaelic allowed flexibility, and provided a supply of monosyllabic preverbs and adverbs to satisfy the metre. The overall style is less contrived and contorted than that of the Scottish Metrical Psalter, and subsequent revision has gently removed older morphology and arcane vocabulary, while keeping much of the 1694 texts.

The Gaelic metrical psalms have retained their central position in the Highland Presbyterian Churches. 'Long tune' psalm-singing, with the precentor* 'giving out' the line, is still a standard feature of services in the main Gaelic-speaking areas.

D. MacKinnon, *The Gaelic Bible and Psalter* (Dingwall, 1930); D. C. MacTavish (ed.), *The Gaelic Psalms 1694* (Lochgilphead, 1934).

D. E. Meek

Public Worship and Aids to Devotion, Committee on, set up by the Basis and Plan of Union* in 1929. It combined the Committee on Aids to Devotion appointed by the CofS General Assembly in 1849 to draw up forms of social worship according to the usage of the national Church for 'soldiers, sailors, colonists, and other persons, who are deprived of the ordinary services of a Christian ministry', and the *Book of Common Order* Committee of the UFC. In 1983 it became The Panel on Worship. Its task is to witness to the importance of worship* as a primary function of the Church, and to prepare service books and other resources for worship, prayer and devotion. Its work, at least until quite recently, was much influenced by the Scoto-Catholic* element in the CofS (A. C. Cheyne, *The Transforming of the Kirk*, E, 1983, 195ff.).

The Committee has produced a series of books, the best known of which are *The Ordinal and Service Book for Use in the Courts of the Church* (1931; additional material 1954, 1962), *Prayers for the Christian Year* (1935, 1952), and *The Book of Common Order* (1940). The influence of these books has spread far beyond the CofS: both the Church of South India and the Church of North India, for example, used the *Ordinal* as a model. None of the books is mandatory, though they have usually been authorized by the General Assembly. A revision of *The Book of Common Order* was published in 1979, with its companion volume for non-sacramental services, *Prayers for Sunday Services*, following in 1980. A completely new *Book of Common Order* is in course of preparation, and the *Ordinal* is being revised.

C. Robertson

Publishing, Religious. It is impossible to overestimate the influence of the press on the religious life of Scotland. The wide and rapid spread of Reformation theology in Europe and no less in Scotland was due to Gutenberg's invention of c.1450. Subsequently, every significant development in the history of the Scottish Church was both shaped and accompanied by a torrent of print.

SIXTEENTH CENTURY AND BEFORE. 'Publishing', in a broad sense, pre-dated the introduction of the press into Scotland. For centuries, MS works had been circulated, and copied in the monasteries, and it remained not uncommon throughout the sixteenth century for works to be circulated in MS form. As early as 1470, books were being imported from continental presses. This practice, too, continued after the establishment of an indigenous press: the 1520s and 1530s saw significant numbers of Protestant works and copies of Tyndale's Bible being imported despite the vigorous opposition of the Scottish Parliament, and later the General Assembly found it equally difficult to curb the import of RC works. Throughout the century, many works by Scottish authors whose views were out of favour were printed on the continent, where, in any case, the pressmanship was of superior quality.

The book trade developed gradually, the early printers often combining the roles of printer, publisher and bookseller. The first Scottish printers were Walter Chepman and Andrew Myllar (1507-8: unless otherwise stated, dates throughout refer to the individuals' period of activity. Chepman issued the *Aberdeen Breviary** in 1509-10.) There followed a hiatus until Thomas Davidson's emergence (c.1532-42); significant printers throughout the rest of the century included John Scot (1552-71), who, although he later printed David Lindsay's* satires, was responsible for the issue of RC works aiming to strengthen the Church in the immediate pre-Reformation period, such as Hamilton's *Catechism* (1552). Robert Lekpreuik (1561-82) issued many works, including the 1561 *Confession of Faith*, with the encouragement of the Reformers and the financial support of the General Assembly, which also authorized Thomas Bassandyne (1564-77) and Alexander Arbuthnet (1576-85) to print the first Bible issued in Scotland, a folio edition of the Geneva Bible (1579; *see* Bassandyne Bible). John Ross (1574-80), Henry Charteris (1568-99), and Robert Waldegrave (active in Edinburgh 1589-1603) also issued Presbyterian works. Some of these printers were deeply committed to the theology of the works they handled. Others accepted work as expediency dictated.

The power of the press to influence, whether by theological treatise or popular broadsheet (which would reach even the illiterate), was recognized from the first, and attempts made to control it. Political regulation, as successive monarchs tried to outlaw unlicensed printing, was coupled, especially perhaps between 1563 and the start of James VI's personal reign, with ecclesiastical regulation. Constraints proved difficult to enforce, but in the rapidly-shifting politico-ecclesiastical climate it was not unusual for a printer to find himself temporarily imprisoned.

By 1600 there had been printing in Edinburgh, St Andrews and (briefly) in Stirling. Four hundred titles, many of them theological, are known to have been issued by around fifteen printers.

PUBLISHING, RELIGIOUS

SEVENTEENTH CENTURY. This century of political and ecclesiastical ferment saw presses and their output multiplying. There was, however, some stagnation following the union of the Crowns, and thereafter fear of incurring penalties for unlicensed printing somewhat inhibited the spread of the press, which still operated under many constraints. Extensive monopolies were granted to the Kings' Printers, and the upheavals of the century brought varying pressures to bear. Thus, for example, in c.1637 Robert Young, a Londoner, was temporarily driven from Scotland by the Covenanters* for printing the *Book of Common Prayer*, while in the 1680s, as James VII was introducing James Watson (Senior's) RC press into Holyrood, the Privy Council proscribed the issue of unlicensed anti-RC works. Works by Scottish authors were printed abroad throughout the century, sometimes in London, more frequently on the continent.

These very upheavals, however, also stimulated the spread of the press: while many of the flood of publications were ephemeral, little theological writing of quality being produced and printed in Scotland throughout the century, some English theological works were 'pirated' in Scotland. Printing reached Aberdeen in 1622 on Edward Raban's arrival (1620–c.50), and Glasgow in 1638, when George Anderson (1637–47) moved there in time to print for the crucial 1638 General Assembly.* Significant numbers of Presbyterian works were issued by, among others, Andro Hart (1587–1621), John Wreittoun (c.1621–40), Evan Tyler (c.1633–72) and John Reid (1680–c.1716) in Edinburgh, and Robert Sanders (1661–96) in Glasgow.

In 1671 Andrew Anderson (1653–76), possibly through corruption, secured the gift of King's Printer for forty-one years, with extensive monopolies including theological works, and claimed to be the sole authorized printer in Scotland. Other printers could continue operating only under licence from Anderson. His wife (1676–1716) succeeded him, and, while vigorously defending her monopolies, issued many books, some very carelessly printed. The latter part of the century has seen a decline in Scottish printing standards, which reached a nadir with Mrs Anderson's output. Bible publishing was not unaffected: although excellent editions had been issued in 1610 by Hart (Geneva version), and by Andrew Anderson in 1676 (KJV), Mrs Anderson's edition of 1698 (KJV) was full of errors. Robert Young (active in Scotland with interruptions 1632–43) printed the first Scottish edition of the KJV in 1633, while the Scottish metrical psalms were first issued by Tyler in 1650.

EIGHTEENTH CENTURY. The eighteenth century saw a gradual increase both in the number of prints and the quality and the quantity of their output. With the work of James Watson (Junior) (1695–1722), Thomas Ruddiman (1715–57), and William Smellie (1752–95) in Edinburgh, and Robert and Andrew Foulis (c.1741–76) in Glasgow, the quality of Scottish pressmanship improved significantly. In a century which saw the Scottish Enlightenment* and a rapid increase in the sales of general literature, Watson was the only one of these printers to be deeply involved in religious publishing, but their elegant productions set new standards, influencing the trade as a whole.

Reasons for the expansion of the indigenous Scottish religious press, and for the start of significant importation from London booksellers, included theological disputes. The Marrow* and Simson* controversies, for example, generated substantial literatures. Other factors were religious revivals, such as that accompanying Whitefield's* visits, and ecclesiastical division. Seceders from the CofS had much recourse to the press. For example, the Morisons of Perth (active from c.1774) printed for the Glasites (*see* Glas, John), while James Pillans (active in Edinburgh from 1775) issued works for Adam Gib's* Antiburgher Church. There was also an Episcopal literature. Political upheaval was a further cause of proliferating literature. The fact, for example, that the 1790s saw the issue of more religious works than any other decade, may have been due to current international tension. Political uncertainty has always stimulated the religious book trade. The spread of literacy must also be taken into account. The work of SSPCK* and parish schools created a demand for Bibles and other literature. Reading was generally taught using the Shorter Catechism and the Bible, special editions being produced. A Family Bible came widely to be regarded as a necessity. (The Bible printing monopoly was still held by the King's Printers.) Increased literacy also fostered the demand for chapbooks, often crudely written and printed leaflets, tailored to popular taste, and distributed by itinerant pedlars. An estimated 200,000 chapbooks, a substantial proportion of which were religious, were sold annually.

The first Gaelic* printed book dates from 1567, but not until the eighteenth century were Gaelic works produced in any numbers. Most were religious titles sponsored by interested parties such as the Church for a still largely illiterate Gaelic-speaking population.

By the end of the century, religious works were being issued in fifteen Scottish towns. Edinburgh remained the dominant centre, with Glasgow in second place. Perth, due to the activities of the Morisons, ranked third.

NINETEENTH CENTURY. All the factors which stimulated Scottish religious publishing in the eighteenth century remained influential in the nineteenth. Publishing developed as a separate operation distinct from printing and bookselling (although some of the religious publishers established their own printing capacity). The centre of gravity of religious, as of general publishing, became more firmly rooted in Edinburgh. Local printers proliferated, but in general came to have only local significance. There were changes in the mode of distribution: retail outlets dedicated to religious bookselling were established, and there was an increase in the door-to-door selling of works in parts, both by the Scottish Colportage* and similar societies, and by canvassers employed by publishing firms. In 1831 in Glasgow alone 126 were employed.

Whereas at the start of the century there was a large market for theological titles among working-class Evangelicals, increasingly they came to be satisfied with religious fiction. As the Westminster Confession declined in influence, works of academic theology espousing liberal continental thinking were increasingly issued. The market for sermons and religious chapbooks was undermined by the rise of mass-circulation religious periodicals.

The publishers can be categorized as follows: (i) Houses such as that of William Blackwood (founded 1804) and A. & C. Black (founded 1807) were general, literary publishers who issued some theology. Blackwood published regularly for the CofS; most of the firm's other religious issues were published at the authors' expense. (ii) Firms such as Nelson in Edinburgh (founded 1798), and Blackie (founded 1809) and Collins (founded 1819) in Glasgow all concentrated initially on religious works (Nelson and Blackie especially aiming to produce cheap books for a mass audience) and then diversified into educational, reward-book and general publishing as the century progressed. All three developed large printing capacities and, when the Queen's Printer lost the monopoly in Bible publishing in 1839 (see Bible Board), they were among the firms to issue Bibles under licence. (300,000 Bibles were being produced annually in Scotland by 1860: W. R. McPhun of Glasgow, who specialized in cheap Family Bibles, was claiming annual sales of 12,000 in 1864.) (iii) T. & T. Clark (founded 1821) became by the 1890s the most significant Scottish publishers of academic theology. Concentrating from the first on theology and law, they did not diversify. (iv) Official publications were issued by all Churches represented in Scotland, including Baptists, RCs and Episcopalians. In addition, a commercial house might align itself with a particular denomination. Thus in Edinburgh, Johnstone and Hunter (founded 1843) supported the FC cause. The decentralized Brethren* were served by two amicably-competing firms, Pickering* and Inglis (founded c.1893) in Glasgow, and John Ritchie (founded c.1883) in Kilmarnock. (v) There remained some significant local firms, such as George Miller's East Lothian Press (founded 1795), which issued cheap tracts and periodicals, and Alexander Gardner's Paisley enterprise (founded c.1828), which in its early years distributed cheap books and Bibles Scotland-wide. (vi) The tract and colportage societies and the Stirling Tract Enterprise* produced vast quantities of tracts (seeing them as a more wholesome substitute for chapbooks than cheap fiction) which were, however, largely sold to the middle classes for distribution.

In the nineteenth century print was still the dominant medium; technological advances and the spread of literacy increased its potency, and Scottish religious publishing reached its zenith.

TWENTIETH CENTURY. The early twentieth century saw a decline in the importance of Scotland as a publishing centre, as firms moved their head offices to London, and a UK-wide decline in evangelical publishing in an age of increasing scepticism. Some firms continued to operate in Scotland, such as T. & T. Clark, which issued important works including James Hastings'* *Encyclopaedia of Religion and Ethics*. Collins, though publishing from London, maintained their religious list and continued to print in Scotland. There was much denominational publishing: two Glasgow firms, John S. Burns (founded 1926) and Sands and Co. (founded 1913) issued RC works.

While the years since 1950 have seen an upsurge in the activities of both indigenous Scottish general publishers and British evangelical publishers, there has not been a corresponding blossoming of Scottish religious publishing. However, some notable theological firms have been established, such as the CofS's St Andrew Press (founded 1954), which has sold six million copies of the New Testament volumes of William Barclay's* *Daily Study Bible* worldwide, the Banner of Truth Trust (moved to Edinburgh in 1973), the Handsel Press (founded 1975), and Rutherford House* (founded 1983), which is initiating ambitious projects. Christian Focus Publications (Fearn, Ross-shire) is another active newcomer.

Other media have proliferated, but though they are of crucial importance, print on paper remains influential, and, for the present, indispensable to the Church in Scotland.

There have been no systematic surveys of Scottish religious publishing. A starting point for further study is provided by relevant material listed in the following:

H. R. Plomer, et al., *Dictionaries of the Printers and Booksellers who were at work in England, Scotland and Ireland 1557–1775* (L, 1977; initially published in four volumes 1910, 1907, 1922 and 1932); *New Cambridge Bibliography of English Literature*: 'Scottish Literature: Introduction' in I (600–1600) ed. G. Watson (C, 1974), cols 2419–22; 'Scottish Printing and Bookselling' and 'Scottish Literature: General Introduction' in II (1660–1800), ed. G. Watson (C, 1971), cols 271–2, 1955–8; 'Book Production and Distribution' in IV (1900–50), ed. I. R. Willison (C, 1972), cols 33–130; R. Myers, *The British Book Trade: from Caxton to the Present Days – a Bibliographical Guide*... (L, 1973); J. A. H. Dempster, *The History of T. & T. Clark* (Soham, Cambs., 1992).

J. A. H. Dempster

Q

Quakers, see Friends, Religious Society of.

Qualified Chapels, places of Episcopalian worship in Scotland whose clergy 'qualified' to minister under various Acts of Parliament (1712, 1718, 1746, 1748) which laid down conditions for lawful Episcopalian worship, especially after the Jacobite* risings* of 1715 and 1745. The clergy serving these chapels were not under the jurisdiction of the Scottish bishops and were in English or Irish orders. They were required to pray in public worship for the sovereign and the royal family. By 1792, when the Penal Laws against the EpCS were repealed, there were twenty-four such chapels in existence, including six in and around Edinburgh. After that date it became the policy of the Scottish bishops to bring the qualified chapels into the EpCS; all but one (St Peter's Montrose) had come in by 1850. The qualified chapels were particularly associated with the use of the English *Book of Common Prayer* and remained aloof from the contemporary developments in the Scottish Liturgy.

F. Goldie, *A Short History of the Episcopal Church in Scotland* (E, ²1976).

G. D. Duncan

Quarrier, William (1829–1903), founder of Quarrier's Homes. Born into a humble home in Greenock, fatherless at three, starving Glasgow slum-dweller at five, he evidently had no schooling, and from age six worked twelve hours a day. He was converted when seventeen, and later became a deacon in Hope Street Baptist* Church, Glasgow. Successful in business, he never forgot the plight of children such as he had known. He initiated a Shoe-Black Brigade, Newspaper Brigade, Parcels Brigade, an orphanage in Glasgow, and the sending of residents to new lives in Canada. In 1878 the first cottage homes were opened at Bridge of Weir; then came the first tuberculosis sanatorium in Scotland, 'to provide for Lazarus the pure air, warmth, nourishment, and comfort hitherto monopolized by Dives'. Quarrier rejected appeals, collectors, bazaars for raising funds – the work was the Lord's, and he would supply. When Quarrier died, having arranged for the country's first epileptic colony, 1,526 children were in care at Bridge of Weir, with kindred work in Glasgow, Argyll and Canada.

James Ross, *The Power I Pledge* (G, 1973); *DNB Second Suppl.* III, 146–7; lives by J. Climie (G, 1905), A. Gammie (L, 1936, 1951), E. M. Sawyer (G, 1962), J. Urquhart (L, 1901).

J. D. Douglas

Queensferry Paper (1680), Covenanting* manifesto, evidently the work of Henry Hall of Haughhead and Donald Cargill.* Found in the former's possession when he was arrested at South Queensferry, it bound and obliged them to defend their rights and liberties, including the spiritual independency of the church, the right of the people to 'root out' a tyrannical government, and the continuing and binding obligation of the Covenants* on Scotland. While the Queensferry Paper was incomplete, it was a stepping-stone to the historic Sanquhar Declaration.*

Text in J. C. Johnston, *Treasury of the Scottish Covenant* (E, 1887), 134–41.

J. D. Douglas

Quoad Omnia, a Latin technical term (literally, 'with respect to all things') applied to a parish,* originally signifying that it was constituted as a governmental unit for both ecclesiastical and civil purposes. For ecclesiastical purposes the parish was the territorial unit within which a particular charge* and ministry was responsible for the preaching of the Word, the administration of discipline, supervision of the parochial school and giving of relief to the poor. For civil purposes, the parish was the unit for poor relief,* for schooling and for certain purposes of representation and voting, as well as the division within which a register of births, deaths and marriages and of landholding was maintained. (The land register, the Register of Sasines, is kept in Edinburgh: parochial records have also been transferred mostly to Register House, Edinburgh.) In time the reorganization of local government and the removal of a statutory role in poor relief and school supervision has left the Church with only its ecclesiastical responsibilities. A mark of a previous *quoad omnia* function is that both the spiritual and temporal affairs of a congregation are still governed by the Kirk Session, with no separate financial body, but many previous *quoad omnia* congregations have adopted the Model Constitution.*

W. G. Black, *A Handbook of the Parochial Ecclesiastical Law of Scotland* (E, ³1901); id., *A Handbook of Scottish Parochial Law Other than Ecclesiastical* (E, 1893); id. and J. R. Christie, *The Parochial Ecclesiastical Law of Scotland* (E, 1928); J. M. Duncan, *Parochial Ecclesiastical Law of Scotland* (E, ³1903); A. Dunlop, *Parochial Law* (E, ³1841); W. Mair, *Digest of Church Law* (E, ⁵1923).

F. Lyall

Quoad Sacra, a Latin technical term (literally, 'in respect of sacred things') referring to a parish* constituted for ecclesiastical purposes only, and without civil responsibilities, jurisdiction or significance. The function of such a parish was to subdivide a parish *quoad omnia** either because it was too big, or because the church associated with it was remote from the actual residences of the bulk of its parishioners. Occasionally a preaching station would first be constituted, serviced by the parish church, then, when it had rooted, it would be constituted as an independent entity by whatever procedure was required at the time. The creation of parishes *quoad sacra* and the giving of their ministers status in presbytery without the consent of the civil authorities was a major element of the disputes which resulted in the Disruption.*

N. Eliot, *Erection of Parishes Quoad Sacra and the Feuing of Glebes* (E, 1879).

See also bibliography for Quoad Omnia.

F. Lyall

R

Radasi, John Boyani (d. 1924), FP missionary. Born in the Cape Colony, South Africa, he became acquainted with the FPC in Scotland in 1900 and was ordained in Glasgow in 1904. In Rhodesia he established the first FP mission, at Ingwenya, and worked there virtually unassisted for nineteen years. He always valued education highly and laid the foundations of the FP mission schools, as well as being instrumental in establishing the medical side of the mission. In October 1924, on his way to meet the FPC's first Scottish missionary, John Tallach,* Radasi was struck by a train and tragically killed.

M. Macpherson, *The Life and Labours of a Native African Missionary* (Gisborne, 1966);
A. McPherson (ed.), *History of the Free Presbyterian Church of Scotland* (Inverness, 1974).

J. L. Macleod

Radical Reformation. Besides those movements for Reformation associated with the magisterial Reformers Luther, Calvin and Zwingli, and besides the Catholic Reformation following the Council of Trent, historians identify a so-called Radical Reformation. The term covers a wide array of incidents and trends (for too long described simplistically as Anabaptist), often based on the lower orders of craftsmen and peasants. In general, the radicals followed the practice of believers' baptism and sought a church that would be a fellowship of committed Christians, separated from the world and distinct from their host nations.

Extreme paucity of documentation makes it virtually impossible to identify the beliefs of members of the Scots nobility – much less craftsmen. The policies of the major Reformers in Scotland assumed a national Church and advocated infant baptism. Those who had had experience of ministry before 1560 had been connected, like Knox* or Willock,* with Geneva or England – with the magisterial Reformers. Knox knew of 'Anabaptist' activities from his years in both England and Geneva; his treatise on predestination, written in Geneva in 1559, was occasioned by an English radical's attack on the doctrine. Some evidence does exist that implies the acquaintance of a few with the European radicals. Knox's *Letter to his Brethren in Scotland* (*Works* IV, 270–1) warned against 'thair opinionis, maist horribill and absurd'. The *First Book of Discipline** argued strongly against those who celebrated the Lord's Supper in private houses, without preaching and without a minister, warning the Privy Council* that unless preventative measures were taken, 'ye shall find them pernicious enemies ere it be long' (*FBD* 204–7). The authors of the Scots Confession* explicitly condemned the 'errors of the Anabaptists' (G. D. Henderson (ed.), *The Scots Confession*, E, 1960, 78). The household nature of the privy kirks* before 1560 was ground in which radicalism could flourish and the magisterial Reformers of Scotland took successful preventative measures against that eventuality.

H. Willmer, 'Radical Reformation' in J. D. Douglas (ed.), *New International Dictionary of the Christian Church* (Exeter, 1974), 822–3; R. Kyle, 'The Nature of the Church in the Thought of John Knox', *SJT* 37 (1987), 485–503.

F. D. Bardgett

Ragged Schools, educational institutions for poor children which (in Scotland) provided *gratis* food, clothing, vocational training and religious instruction. The Scottish ragged schools as developed by FC minister Thomas Guthrie* were also called 'industrial schools'. The idea originated in England with John Pounds of Portsmouth, and in Scotland in 1841 with Sheriff Watson of Aberdeen. Guthrie, however, came to be the main driving force behind the Scottish movement. Stimulated by the example of Pounds, Guthrie appealed for public backing in his *Plea for Ragged Schools* (E, 1847), which went through eleven editions in one year. He met with a good response from a wide spectrum of supporters, and secured premises for his first ragged school on the Castlehill, Edinburgh, in 1847. From this the movement grew throughout Scotland.

There was some dissension over the religious

aspect of the education provided. Guthrie and most of his backers argued that they were acting *in loco parentis* to the children and so were entitled to instruct them in Protestant Christianity; a minority established a separate school, the United Industrial School, where religious instruction was given on a segregated denominational basis supported by separate funds.

Guthrie continued to publicize the cause of ragged schools, with a *Second* and *Third Appeal* in 1849 and 1859. He gave evidence before a House of Commons committee in 1852, which resulted in Dunlop's Act in 1854. This empowered Scottish magistrates to commit vagrant children aged fourteen and under to industrial schools, even if not guilty of any crime. A government grant of five shillings per head was withdrawn in 1861, although an allowance for committed children was increased. A later Act (1866) broadened the category of children who could be committed by magistrates. The Education (Scotland) Act, 1872,* empowered the newly established school boards to found and maintain industrial schools.

See also Education (Scotland) Acts, 1872 and 1918; Stow, David.

S. Mechie, *The Church and Scottish Social Development* (L, 1960), 154–9; D. K. and C. J. Guthrie, *Autobiography of Thomas Guthrie, D.D. and Memoir* (L, 1877), 436–96.

N. R. Needham

Rainy, Robert (1826–1906), Principal of New College,* Edinburgh, FC leader and architect of the 1900 Union. Born at Glasgow into a prominent evangelical family of Highland descent, Rainy was educated at Glasgow High School, Glasgow University and New College, Edinburgh. He was ordained at Huntly in 1851; transferred to the Free High Church, Edinburgh, 1854; elected to the chair of Church History in the New College, 1862. In 1874 he succeeded R. S. Candlish* as Principal of the College, having already begun to occupy his unofficial position as 'leader' of the General Assembly. From that year he was prominent in the disestablishment* campaign; in 1876–81 he was taxed by the Robertson Smith* case; and from 1889 he convened the Confession of Faith Committee which resulted in the Declaratory Act* of 1892. In 1900 came the crowning achievement of his life when the FC and UPC united. He was Moderator of the FC General Assembly in 1887 and of the UF Assembly in 1900 and 1905. His works include: *Delivery and Development of Christian Doctrine* (E, 1874); *The Bible and Criticism* (L, 1878); (with James Mackenzie) *Life of William Cunningham* (L, 1871); (with William Wilson) *Memorials of Robert Smith Candlish* (E, 1880); *The Ancient Catholic Church* (E, 1902); *Three Lectures on the Church of Scotland* (E, 1872; ²1883).

RAINY'S LEADERSHIP. Rainy's attempt to retain the evangelical heritage of the FC while keeping pace with rapid contemporary developments made him a controversial figure: 'black Rainy' in parts of the Highlands* where Constitutionalist* strength lay; 'this unprincipled Principal' to the CofS; and 'Dr Misty as well as Dr Rainy' to much of the secular press. Yet in much of his own Church the Principal was loved and revered and followed in a manner almost unexampled in the history of Presbyterianism. His influence owed much to towering intellectual stature, perhaps more to the rare and deep spirituality to which all who knew him bore witness. He had the distinction of being named by Gladstone* as the greatest living Scotsman.

HIS ECCLESIASTICAL POLICY. Rainy's promotion of disestablishment was widely condemned as self-interested and vindictive, but he professed to be motivated simply by a desire for the justice which he considered the only true foundation for a reconstructed national Church. What remains open to question is whether his policy of restricting his vision to disestablishment and the union of the FC and UPC was the one which best served the cause of Scottish Christianity. Probably the most influential policy he adopted was that of offering unlimited hospitality to biblical criticism.* In the Robertson Smith* case he decided that the particular critic must be sacrificed in order to safeguard the principle of critical liberty. In the later heresy trials of Marcus Dods (1834–1909),* A. B. Bruce,* and G. A. Smith,* he was able to protect both the men and the principle. Personally, he did not find criticism a major issue and he underestimated the degree to which it provoked questions regarding biblical authority. Likewise, he considered the Declaratory Act of 1892 to be a minor confessional adjustment when, in fact, it marked the tidal change as the FC moved from dogmatic Calvinism* to liberal Evangelicalism.* Characteristically, the Act appeared conservative, but was devised to give a long rope to those who were straying from Reformed theology. Rainy's credal reform was completed by the Act Anent Spiritual Independence of 1906, which embedded in the Church's constitution an undefined reserved right to change her doctrinal position. He made the Church master of her creed, but raised the question whether her doctrinal commitment was altogether elusive and ephemeral.

The greatest question posed by Rainy's career is how a man who was sufficiently representative of the Disruption* to be the natural sucecssor to Candlish came to preside over the dramatic liberalization of the FC. It may be that his serene confidence in the integrity of the Reformed faith, born of the evangelical buoyancy of the early FC, prevented him from seeing how undermining the movements of biblical criticism and credal revision might be. Certainly he seems to have been too easily satisfied with building a consensus within the FC, when something more prophetic was needed. The fact that his leadership was characterized by complacency and opportunism, rather than initiative and conviction, accounts in part for the loss of ground which the FC suffered in his time.

AFCS I, 57; *FUFCS*, 569, 574, 582; *DNB Second Suppl.* III, 152–5; *PGAFCS*, 1862–1900; P. C. Simpson, *The Life of Principal Rainy*, 2 vols. (L,

1909); A. T. Innes, *Chapters of Reminiscence* (L, 1913), 177–253; J. S. Black and G. Chrystal, *The Life of William Robertson Smith* (L, 1912), 179–451; A. C. Cheyne, *The Transforming of the Kirk* (E, 1983); A. L. Drummond and J. Bulloch, *The Church in late Victorian Scotland 1874–1900* (E, 1978); W. R. Nicoll, *Princes of the Church* (L, 1921), 192–203.

K. R. Ross

Ramsay, Andrew (1574–1659), Covenanting* divine. Son of David Ramsay of Balmain, Kincardineshire, he was probably educated at St Andrews, and taught for a time at the French Protestant Academy at Saumur. In 1606 he became minister of Arbuthnott, Kincardineshire, moving to Edinburgh in 1614. In 1620 he was appointed rector and Professor of Divinity of the College of Edinburgh. In 1626 he resigned and became one of the ministers of the Greyfriars church. In 1629 he was made sub-dean of the Chapel Royal at Holyrood, and in 1634 became a member of the chapter of the newly erected see of Edinburgh.

Ramsay now fell out with the episcopal* regime, and was the only Edinburgh minister who refused to read Laud's liturgy in 1637 (*see* Laud, William). In 1638 he preached in Greyfriars preparatory to the signing of the National Covenant.* He played a leading role in the Glasgow* Assembly that year, and was Moderator in the 1640 Assembly which deposed the Aberdeen Doctors.*

In 1649 Ramsay was himself deposed by the General Assembly for refusing to preach against the Engagement.* This prompted him to write an apologia, in which he criticized alterations in Scottish worship introduced by the Westminster Assembly,* *e.g.* the discontinuance of the Lord's Prayer in public worship. He was restored to the ministry in 1655 by the Resolutioners.*

Ramsay was a highly erudite man and a Latin poet of some distinction.

Poemata Sacra (E, 1633); *A Warning to Come Out of Babell* (E, 1638).

DNB XLVII, 234–5; *FES* I, 70.

N. R. Needham

Ramsay, Edward Bannerman (1793–1872), Episcopalian Dean of Edinburgh. Ramsay was born in Aberdeen as Edward Bannerman Burnett. His father, Alexander, was advocate sheriff of Kincardineshire, where the family estates lay. In 1806, however, Alexander Burnett inherited the estates of Sir Alexander Ramsay in Balmain and Fasque, and assumed the name of Ramsay. He was educated in Halsey (Yorkshire), Durham and St John's College, Cambridge (1811–14). Ordained to the CofE ministry, in 1816 he became curate of Rodden, in Somerset.

In 1824 Ramsay moved to Edinburgh as curate of St George's Episcopal Church, York Place. In 1826 he became sole minister of St Paul's, Carrubber's Close; in 1827, he was appointed curate to Bishop Daniel Sandford* of St John's, on the junction of Princes Street and Lothian Road. When Sandford died in 1830, Ramsay took sole charge of the church. He was appointed Dean of Edinburgh in 1846.

Ramsay was a staunch Episcopalian* in his views of Church government, but his evangelical outlook gave him wide cross-denominational sympathies. He was, for instance, an ardent admirer of Thomas Chalmers,* contributing a memoir of the FC leader to the proceedings of the Royal Society of Edinburgh (*A Biographical Notice of Thomas Chalmers*, E, 1850), and being largely responsible for the erection of Chalmers' statue in Edinburgh's George Street. His breadth of outlook was also revealed in his phenomenally popular *Reminiscences of Scottish Life and Character* (E, 1858, [22]1874), which went through twenty-one editions in his lifetime. The second chapter on 'Scottish Religious Feelings and Observances' evinces a warm appreciation of Scotland's Presbyterian heritage.

Ramsay was an eloquent preacher and much respected by the Scottish public. On his death an Iona cross was erected by public subscription as a memorial in St John's cemetery, facing Princes Street. Ramsay was Vice-President of the Royal Society of Edinburgh and chief founder of the Scottish Episcopal Church Society.*

C. Innes, 'Memoir' in Ramsay's *Reminiscences* ([22]E, 1874); *DNB* XLVII, 241–2.

N. R. Needham

Ramsay, James, *see* Anti-slavery.

Ramsay, William Mitchell (1851–1939), Anatolian archaeologist and New Testament historian. He was born in Glasgow, educated at Aberdeen University, where he graduated with classical honours in 1871, and at Oxford, where (having gained a scholarship at St John's College) he took a first in Moderations (1874) and Litterae Humaniores (1876). In 1879 he was awarded a three years' travelling scholarship by Exeter College, Oxford, and paid the first of many archaeological visits to Asia Minor (the last in 1914).

He was Fellow successively of Exeter and Lincoln Colleges, Oxford, first Professor of Classical Art and Archaeology at Oxford (1885–6) and Regius Professor of Humanity (Latin) in Aberdeen University (1886–1911). He was a founder-member of the British Academy in 1903 and was knighted in 1906. He spent his last years in Edinburgh.

Ramsay quickly established his reputation as a leading authority in Anatolian archaeology. His *Historical Geography of Asia Minor* (L, 1890), and *Cities and Bishoprics of Phrygia* (2 vols, O, 1895, 1897), were his main scholarly contributions in this field. Other contributions appeared as articles in periodicals and dictionaries, notably 'Roads and Travel (in NT)', Hastings' *Dictionary of the Bible*, V (E, 1904), 375–402. The chief academic productions of his later years were his Gifford Lectures,* *Asianic Elements in Greek Civilization* (L, 1928), and his posthumously published *Social Basis of Roman Power in Asia Minor* (A, 1941).

At an early stage in his historical research Ramsay

became convinced, against the then influential Tübingen school, that Acts was a product of the first century, not of the second, and also that Paul's letter to the Galatians was sent to churches in the southern regions of the Roman province of Galatia (those whose planting is recorded in Acts 13:14–14:23). He applied his specialist knowledge to New Testament studies in a succession of more popular works, the best known of which is *St Paul the Traveller and the Roman Citizen* (L, 1895, ¹⁴1920). These procured for him the reputation of an apologist for conservative views in New Testament criticism, but his motivation was not apologetic but a determination to test critical theories by historical evidence. His *Historical Commentary on St Paul's Epistle to the Galatians* (L, 1899) was followed by fragmentary historical commentaries on Corinthians (*Exp*, 1900–1) and 1 Timothy (*Exp*, 1909–11).

DNB 1931–40, 727–8; W. W. Gasque, *Sir William M. Ramsay* (Grand Rapids, 1966).

F. F. Bruce

Rattray, Thomas (1684–1743), bishop and liturgical writer, laird of Craighall (Perthshire) and eldest son of James Rattray and Elizabeth Hay of Megginch. As a young man he translated into Greek (1716) the text of the proposed concordat between the non-juring* bishops and the Patriarchs of Moscow and Constantinople. While still a layman, he was heavily involved in the controversy between the 'usagers' (the non-jurors who observed the usages* of prayer for the dead, eucharistic epiclesis, etc.) and their opponents, 'non-usagers' (who also largely stood for government by the college of bishops against the 'usagers'' preference for rule by individual bishops). Later in life he became Bishop of Brechin (1727) and Dunkeld (1731). In 1739, he was elected Primus* and Bishop of Edinburgh. The election was contested and he did not take control of the diocese until a few months before his death.

His entire theological outlook was greatly influenced by his contact with the Christian East. His major contribution to liturgical scholarship was the posthumous publication (1744) of a critical edition and translation of the ancient Liturgy of St James, together with an adaptation for local use of its eucharistic prayer, with additions from other eastern sources. His complete eucharistic office (of which a mutilated copy is in the Scottish Record Office and a full manuscript in the Church of St John's, Pittenweem, Fife) did not appear until 1748. In both works, the structure and theology of the adapted eucharistic prayer pointed forward to modern ecumenical formulations, but a combination of political circumstances (the defeat of the Jacobites* at Culloden) and the unfamiliarity of clergy and people with eastern models of worship prevented the adoption of his liturgical models.

The Ancient Liturgy of the Church of Jerusalem, being the Liturgy of St James, with English Translation and Notes, as also an Appendix containing some other Ancient Prayers (L, 1744); *An Office for the Sacrifice of the Holy Eucharist* (L, 1748).

DNB XLVII, 312–14; H. Sefton, 'Revolution to Disruption', in D. Forrester and D. Murray (eds), *Studies in the History of Worship in Scotland* (E, 1984), 66–7; J. Dowden, *The Scottish Communion Office of 1764* (L, 1922), 71ff.; G. Grub, *Ecclesiastical History of Scotland* (E, 1860), III, 388ff., IV, 1ff.

G. Tellini

Read, David Haxton Carswell (1910–), Fife-born Scottish and American minister and writer. He was a CofS parish minister in Coldstream and Edinburgh and a Second World War army chaplain (prisoner of war in Germany from 1940 after capture at St Valery), before becoming first official chaplain* to Edinburgh University in 1949. He moved to the USA as minister of Madison Avenue Presbyterian Church, New York in 1956, becoming a leading Christian preacher and publicist there for thirty years. He put a strong emphasis, within Reformed doctrine and tradition, on the sacraments, ordination, and the distinctive office of the ministry.

Although he was most influential as a preacher, his books spanned half a century, among them *The Communication of the Gospel* (L, 1952) and two volumes of autobiography, *This Grace Given* and *Grace thus Far* (Grand Rapids, 1985 and 1987).

FES IX, 783, X, 442; *Who's Who 1991*, 1520.

R. D. Kernohan

Reader (Modern), an office instituted by the CofS in 1918 (Act VII; *PAGACS 1918*, 52) to provide authorized persons to conduct public worship in response to the shortage of ministerial manpower caused by the First World War.* Commended somewhat misleadingly as the recovery of a Reformation precedent (see below), the reader was to function only 'in an emergency, when the services of an ordained minister or licentiate* are not available'. The office was to lapse after five years (Act VI; *PAGACS 1919*, 22–3). Although it escaped such a rapid demise (*PAGACS 1923*, 70–1; Act IX, *PAGACS 1927*, 24–5; Act XIII, *PAGACS 1933*, 42–3), the role of lay readers (simply 'readers' from Act X, *PAGACS 1958*, 375) has never wholly thrown off the initial restrictions. The limitation to 'in an emergency' was dropped in 1967 (Act XX; *PAGACS 1967*, 199–200), but proposals to develop the readership into a regular supplementary ministry, not solely for pulpit supply, have been frustrated (cf. *RGACS 1956*, 762–3, with the 1958 Act cited above). The introduction of the auxiliary ministry* may well have sealed that frustration.

The standing of the office long suffered from inadequate standards of training, which was not regulated until 1974 (Act XXVIII; *PAGACS 1974*, 40–1). Women became eligible in 1970. The use of the present three hundred readers varies markedly between Presbyteries; in some they are rarely used (even Divinity students have priority over them for pulpit supply), but in others their service exceeds the statutory position. The history of the modern readership well illustrates the CofS's conservatism in fostering non-ordained ministry.

Cox 162-5, 575; *RGACS 1978*, 456-8.
D. F. Wright

Readers (Reformation), persons authorized to read to Reformed congregations the common prayers, homilies and passages of Scripture, but not to compose sermons. Such a function, familiar in the privy kirks* before 1560, was commended in the *First Book of Discipline** of 1560 as a temporary device for instructing congregations lacking preachers. Readers who applied themselves to further theological study, the *FBD* envisaged, might be admitted ministers after due examination, though readers not so promoted were forbidden to preach or minister the sacraments. A distinction was also recognized between those who were to 'content themselves with reading' and others who, though not qualifying as ministers, possessed the 'gift of exhortation', the ability, that is, to 'exhort and explain the scriptures'. This prepared the way for the appointment of exhorters,* who occupied an intermediate position between readers and ministers, permitted to preach, conduct marriage ceremonies and even the sacrament of baptism, but denied the right of administering the Lord's Supper. During the 1570s, the exhorter's office disappeared, with some promoted to the ministry and others demoted to reader. The *FBD* recommended that readers able to serve as teachers in the parishes should receive a starting salary of 40 merks. Schoolmasters and notaries public often figured among recruits as readers at the Reformation, though remuneration was usually poor. The General Assembly in December 1560 approved the appointment of readers in various localities; and by 1574 over 700 were employed in parishes. At the Convention of Leith* in 1572, readers, if found qualified, were permitted to baptize and officiate at marriages; but by 1576, the General Assembly decided to reserve such duties to those able to 'exhort' or preach, and in 1580 it decreed that, as the reader's office was 'no ordinary office within the kirk of God', existing readers, on examination, should either become ministers or be deposed. In 1581 the Assembly prohibited the appointment of further readers, but it took longer to eliminate the office, which survived, on a much diminished scale, into the seventeenth century.

BUK; *FBD*; *SBD*; J. Kirk, *Patterns of Reform* (E, 1989).
J. Kirk

Reformation Parliament, held in Edinburgh during July and August 1560. It was a product of the Treaty of Edinburgh in July 1560, which provided for the withdrawal of French and English forces from Scotland in the aftermath of the Protestant revolution. Although they were unwilling to negotiate a treaty with the insurgent Lords of the Congregation,* the French commissioners offered the Scots certain 'concessions' from King Francis and Queen Mary, who authorized the summoning of Parliament according to use and custom. Parliament was not specifically forbidden to discuss the religious issue; the 'concessions' merely recognized that certain articles on religion already submitted should be remitted to the King and Queen in France. The announcement that Parliament was to meet on 10 July was duly made by the privy council* for 'all such as by law and ancient custom had or might claim to have title therein'. In a house well attended by fourteen earls, six bishops, nineteen lords, twenty-one abbots or commendators,* and commissions from twenty-two burghs, over a hundred named lairds or lesser barons, with 'many other barons, freeholders and landed men', appeared, claiming a right to sit. After Parliament's adjournment for three weeks, the committee of the articles was elected, and a petition received seeking a condemnation of transubstantiation, justification by works, indulgences, purgatory, invocation of saints, papal authority and profanation of the sacraments, and favouring a restoration of the discipline of the early Church and a redistribution of the Church's patrimony in favour of the ministry, schools and poor. On 17 August, Parliament approved a Reformed Confession of Faith (*see* Scots Confession), and on 24 August abolished the mass, prescribed punishments for offenders, recognized the Reformed preachers as alone competent to minister the sacraments (of baptism and communion alone), and repudiated papal jurisdiction within the realm, rescinding all earlier statutes at variance with the Reformed Confession of Faith. Parliament assigned to others the details of a settlement on the Church's polity and endowment. Although Queen Mary declined to approve this legislation, ratification was forthcoming in the first Parliament of James VI's reign in 1567.

APS II, 525-35; R. Keith, *History of the Affairs of Church and State in Scotland* (E, 1844-55), I, 296ff.
J. Kirk

Reformation, Scottish, the formal break with Rome which may be said to have occurred in 1560 when the Reformation Parliament* severed official links with the papacy, and with Roman Catholicism as the established faith, by repudiating the pope's authority, forbidding the celebration of mass, and by approving a Protestant Confession of Faith (*see* Scots Confession). Such legislative action was made possible in the aftermath of the Protestant revolution against France and Rome in 1559, which took the form of a rebellion against the regime of Mary of Guise,* who governed Scotland in the absence of her daughter, Mary, Queen of Scots,* who then was also Queen of France. As a decisive act, the Reformation in Scotland came late in the day; but there had been ample opportunity during four decades for Scots at almost every level to discover the evangelical message proclaimed by the Protestant Reformers.

Renaissance* humanism had contributed a spirit of critical reappraisal which encouraged educational reform and ecclesiastical renewal; and within a few years of Luther's doctrinal revolt in 1517, action in Scotland was considered necessary to stem the invasion of Lutheran* heresy* from the continent through east-coast ports, and, with it, the threat of doctrinal turmoil and confusion. In July 1525 Parliament banned the importation of 'any books or works of the said Luther, his disciples or servants', and it strove to suppress the recitation of 'his heresies or opinions' throughout the realm; the lords of council strengthened the measure in 1527; and Parliament, in ratifying the statute in 1535, required all who harboured Lutheran literature to hand it over to their bishops. Such action was less than fruitful. Despite James V's* orders to his sheriffs in Aberdeenshire in August 1525, at his bishop's behest, to search out 'sundry strangers and others within his diocese' who possessed 'books of that heretic Luther and favoured his errors and false opinions', Reformation literature continued to be smuggled into east-coast ports: from Antwerp and Bergen-op-Zoom, it was reported in 1527, Scottish merchants readily shipped home Protestant works and English New Testaments, particularly to the university town of St Andrews and to Edinburgh, by far the largest burgh, with a claim to recognition as the capital. This subversive literature, imported at a cost – and at an even greater cost were the authorities to detect it – evidently had a ready market among scholars and the literate.

PATRICK HAMILTON. At that point, too, in scholarly circles in St Andrews, doctrinal controversy erupted with the arrival, fresh from the continent, of Patrick Hamilton,* who became the first martyr* of the Scottish Reformation. When accused of heresy, he had left St Andrews for the Lutheran universities of Wittenberg and Marburg, where he composed his *Loci Communes*, or 'Patrick's Places', on faith and good works. Returning to St Andrews in 1528 to renew his appeal for a doctrinal reformation, he was tried for heresy and executed. In his academic disputations, Hamilton had challenged the medieval system (and won converts for so doing); his burning for heresy made international news; and his evangelical teaching was perpetuated with the swift publication by 1529 of *Patrick's Places*.

The spread, in scholarly circles and clandestinely through familial ties, of Luther's theology of grace, his denial of the 'treasury of merit' and of human ability to earn salvation, and his emphasis on the sufficiency of faith alone, went far towards undermining the clerical domination of religion. Apart from personal association, the wider circulation of Lutheran doctrine was achieved through printing several devotional works. John Gau's* *The Richt Vay to the Kingdome of Heuine*, written in Scots and published at Malmö in 1533, warned of the futility of intercessory prayer to Mary and the saints, and of purchasing earthly remission from the pains of purgatory; transubstantiation was repudiated in favour of Luther's teaching on the real presence in the consecrated elements of bread and wine; tradition was contrasted with the biblical message; papal headship was denied; the power of the keys to bind and loosen was not entrusted to pope or bishop; and the fortitude of Patrick Hamilton, who perished for confessing Christ, was commended to the reader.

Another devotional work circulating at this point by a Scottish Lutheran exile was John Johnsone's* *An Confortable Exhortation to our mooste Holy Christen Faith and her Frutes written unto the Christen brethern in Scotland after the pure word of God*, printed at Antwerp or Malmö in the early 1530s. An eyewitness to Patrick Hamilton's execution and an expositor of Tyndale's New Testament, Johnsone accepted Luther's teaching on faith and works, and sought to inculcate a sense of Lutheran piety and perseverance in the face of adversity; suffering, he explained, was a mark of the Christian's life on earth, from which there is final deliverance and reward for the steadfast in faith.

Works such as these (to which may be added a list of prohibited English books published abroad) comprised the sort of subversive literature, it seems, which James V had in mind in 1534 when he attacked the circulation in Leith, Edinburgh, Dundee, St Andrews, Montrose, Aberdeen and Kirkcaldy of 'diverse tracts and books translated out of Latin in our Scots tongue by heretics, and favourers of the sect of Luther'. Reaction to this spate of Lutheran activity was forthcoming in a series of prosecutions designed to suppress incipient Protestantism. With a further conviction for heresy of a graduate by 1531, arrangements were put in place in 1532 for 'the accusation of the Lutherans'; by 1534, nine people from Lothian, including a priest, a schoolmaster, and a sheriff were also charged; a St Andrews graduate was burned for denying the existence of purgatory, identifying the pope with antichrist and repudiating papal jurisdiction in Scotland; another layman who refused to pay his teinds (tithes)* – at a point when the Church experienced difficulty in collecting its dues – was executed for heretical opinions involving a denial of purgatory; and a priest from Brechin diocese fled to Lutheran Germany when charged with heresy in 1534. By 1536, two iconoclasts were pursued by the authorities in Dundee and Perth; action in 1537 was intensified for 'searching of the heretics in the westland', where Luther's doctrines circulated 'both in public and in private', English New Testaments were read, and sporadic acts of iconoclasm occurred in Ayr from 1534. Further prosecutions of townspeople followed in the late 1530s and early 1540s in Dundee, Perth, Stirling and Edinburgh; two noblemen's sons stood among the condemned; and a bailie of Haddington had abandoned Catholicism by 1538.

CLERICAL HERETICS. Even more revealing were the signs that doctrinal heterodoxy was rife among the clergy. One Dominican* prior, who disapproved of Lenten fasting, argued that priests should marry; and with such advice on offer, one vicar entered the estate of matrimony, and with others ate meat at Lent; the Dominican priors of Wigtown and Perth, four other Dominican friars and three Franciscans* escaped in the 1530s to English or continental centres, there to proclaim their Lutheranism; a fifth Dominican friar was burned in 1539; and another four Dominicans turned Protestant preachers by the 1540s; by that date, too, five Augustinian* canons defected, and suspicion fell on a Premonstratensian;* two monks, a Cistercian* and a Carthusian,* also fled to Lutheran lands; and a handful of secular priests figured among the detected heretics in the 1540s. Ecclesiastical disaffection, in short, could no longer be concealed.

Nor did it prove possible to check the spread of Protestant ideas. Indeed, the magnitude of the task facing the authorities in combating reforming views is again apparent in the spate of statutes issued in 1541, which pointed to the futility of earlier legislation and action. Parliament now ordered the sacraments to be honoured 'to the confusion of all heresy'; the Virgin to be the object of worship and prayer; the pope's authority to be upheld; the 'negligence of divine service' to be remedied; private conventicles 'of heretics where their errors are spread' to be prohibited; informers to be rewarded; heretics, even the abjured, to be incapable of holding public office; and the images of saints not to be broken, dishonoured or irreverently treated. These enactments are testimony to the thrust of Protestant attacks focused on the mass, the sacraments, auricular confession, free will, papal authority and the cult of Mary and the saints, and an indication of the rise in clandestine meetings – conventicles and privy kirks* – for Protestant worship and study of the vernacular Scriptures.

The legislation can hardly have had the desired effect: in Perth a group of burgesses defied the statutes and were arrested in 1544 for holding a secret assembly for biblical study, at which they disputed scriptural texts to the 'dishonouring of the glorious Virgin Mary and the communion of saints'; and in the same year some thirty landowners in the north-east were pardoned by the crown for assorted offences which included disputing on Scripture and reading prohibited literature. The futility of further coercion was appreciated by Lord Methven, who considered in 1545 that too many powerful men favoured heresy. At this point, too, the preparation by the clergy of a list for the king's use of over a hundred landowners disaffected to the church suggests that the friends of reform could hope for influential backing; and when opportunity arose, with James V's death in 1542, sympathizers with the Reformation were sufficiently strong to form a government (under the Earl of Arran, who at that point favoured the English and reforming causes; see Hamilton, James d.1575) which permitted the reading of the Bible in the native tongue, in defiance of the Church's stand. Besides, ever since Henry VIII's break with Rome and his excommunication, English policy had aimed at detaching Scotland from its traditional ties with France and Rome, in the hope of achieving Anglo-Scottish conformity through a marriage treaty between the infant Queen Mary and Edward, who was Henry's heir. This, in turn, encouraged the spread of 'English heresies' in Scotland, as Henry tried to secure the collaboration of Scots ready to side with the English cause, as a counterpoise to those, led by Cardinal David Beaton,* who favoured the Roman and French connection.

SPREAD OF PROTESTANT BELIEFS. The charges already advanced in 1540 against John Borthwick,* who had visited both England and France and who favoured Henry's cause, indicate a widening of reforming beliefs beyond the strictly Lutheran to embrace Swiss and English views. Besides a repudiation of papal powers, canon law, indulgences, good works for salvation, intercession through the saints, and the Catholic faith professed in Scotland, Borthwick advocated clerical marriage, the crown's appropriation of clerical property and the abolition, on the English model, of monastic houses. He also approved the reading of the English New Testament and the works of Oecolampadius, the Reformer at Basel, Melanchthon and Erasmus, copies of whose texts he possessed (He was later to become a resident of Geneva in 1556.)

Even so, Cardinal Beaton's political ascendancy in 1543, at Arran's expense, undermined support for the English match and spelt an end to Arran's reforming policy. It also invited English retaliation in the form of the 'Rough Wooing' during 1544 and 1545, which saw widespread destruction in south-east Scotland. At that point, too, a fresh emphasis on Swiss reforming thought is apparent, both in the action taken by the authorities in 1543 and 1547 against 'sacramentarians', who stressed the commemorative and symbolic aspects of the Lord's Supper, and in the preaching tours of George Wishart* from Montrose, student of St Andrews, Louvain and Cambridge and translator of the first Swiss Confession of Faith, whose evangelism in 1544–5 reinvigorated the message of the Reformation in Angus, Ayrshire and the Lothians and won the admiration of a renegade priest, John Knox,* who acted as his bodyguard. Wishart's arrest, condemnation and burning at the stake in 1546 invited retribution. This took the form of assassinating the persecuting cardinal, David Beaton, whose castle in St Andrews the rebels seized, perhaps in the expectation of precipitating a wider Protestant revolt. John Knox associated himself with the rebel 'Castilians', who held out until forced to surrender to the French in 1547, only to be imprisoned or assigned as galley slaves.

Although English intervention in 1547 arrived too late to save the 'Castilians', Somerset continued the policy of Henry VIII (who had died in January 1547) of occupying south-east Scotland north to Dundee. To counter English military action, the Scots again secured French help but only after conceding that the infant Mary, Queen of Scots, should leave for France to become the Dauphin's bride. The period of English invasion from 1547 to 1549 assisted the reforming cause to make headway; the services of Protestant preachers were again in demand; several earls promised 'to cause the Word of God to be taught and preached'; and English Bibles and New Testaments circulated freely. Yet the prospect of further advances receded with the departure of the English and with the ascendancy of Mary of Guise, who wished to maintain the links with France and Rome and who gained the regency from 1554 till 1559.

Even so, at a popular level, satirical plays, poetry and religious songs – such as the compendium of *Gude and Godlie Ballatis** – produced by the Wedderburn* brothers in the 1540s – helped to sustain the message of the Reformation. In 1543 the Privy Council, to little effect, had ordered the destruction of 'slanderous bills, writings, ballads and books that are daily made, written and printed to the defamation of all estates both spiritual and temporal'; in 1549 the provincial council* lamented the circulation of 'books of rhymes or popular songs containing calumnies and slanders defamatory of churchmen and church institutions'; and in 1552 Parliament tried to ban unapproved 'books, ballads, songs, blasphemies, rhymes or tragedies in Latin or English'. Yet the efforts were less than fruitful, and even in the capital, as Mary of Guise reminded the town council in 1556, there freely circulated 'certain odious ballads and rhymes lately set forth by some evil–inclined persons of your town, who have also taken down diverse images and contemptuously broken the same'. The new theology had reached minds and hearts in a way which ordinary folk could understand.

REFORMING COUNCILS. Within the Church, the sustained assault of Renaissance humanism, with its moral concern for improving educational and ecclesiastical standards, helped shape a programme for internal reform, which Archbishop John Hamilton* of St Andrews initiated in a period which witnessed an advance in literacy and in expectations among laymen on an unprecedented scale. Hamilton's plans for Catholic reform, to be effected through a series of provincial councils* which met between 1549 and 1559, followed the examples set by the provincial council at Cologne summoned by Archbishop Hermann von Wied in 1536, the provincial council at Mainz in 1549, and the reforming Council of Trent which met intermittently between 1545 and 1563. Observing how 'many heresies cruelly assail the Lord's flocks', the Scottish council of 1549, in calling for a reformation of morals, attributed much of the blame to 'the corruption of morals and profane lewdness of life in churchmen of almost all ranks, together with crass ignorance of literature and of all the liberal arts'.

A code of statutes, intended to curb such irregularities as concubinage, non-residence, pluralism, unqualified office-holders, the trading activities of clerics, and improper clerical attire and diet, also attempted to foster scriptural devotions among churchmen; to improve preaching by bishops and parsons (who were charged to preach 'at least four times a year') and by 'others who are skilled' (by placing a theologian in each cathedral, as Trent had decreed, and a lecturer on Scripture in each college, and by ensuring instruction in the faith was offered); to encourage visitations of parishes and religious houses; and to halt the secularization of property belonging to glebes and parochial livings. Within the religious orders, too, educational standards were to be improved by sending one or two monks from each house to university and by appointing a theologian for each monastery; apostate monks and nuns were to be disciplined.

Effective reform, however, was not achieved. The statutes of 1549 were reiterated in 1552 by the next council, which candidly admitted the decrees of the former had not been properly executed. It voiced concern, too, that 'the greatest neglect of the divine mysteries has prevailed among the subjects of the realm within these last few years so that very few indeed out of the most populous parishes deign to be present at the sacrifice of holy mass on the Sundays and other double festivals appointed by the Church, or to attend preaching of God's word'. If its message on church attendance was stark, the council's sombre verdict, that 'the inferior clergy of this realm and the prelates have not, for the most part, attained such proficiency in the knowledge of the holy Scriptures as to be able, by their own efforts, rightly to instruct the people in the Catholic faith and other things necessary to salvation or to convert the erring', reads like a damning indictment of existing practice.

In an effort to remedy clerical ignorance, the council approved the printing of a Catechism*, prepared under Hamilton's auspices, to be issued to churches for the instruction of priests 'in at least the first elements of the Catholic faith' and for parishioners who would hear it read aloud in church. The clergy were therefore exhorted to make thorough preparations, 'lest they expose themselves to the ridicule of their hearers when through want of preparation, they stammer and stumble in mid-course of reading'. In certain passages, the Catechism showed signs of a readiness to meet Reformers half-way, and it was silent on the papacy. The defeatist tone of the final council in 1559 is apparent in its recognition of 'this turbulent time when Lutheranism, Calvinism and very many other nefarious heresies are being propagated everywhere in this realm'. A petition by 'lords and barons' to Mary of Guise submitted to the council pointedly observed that the exhortations of earlier councils had borne 'no or little fruit as yet'; worse still, the clerical estate had 'deteriorated' without sign of amendment; the call was reiterated for well-qualified preachers in the parishes, for the 'Common Prayers' to be read in English, and for alleviation from certain exactions by the clergy. Though proposing a modest improvement in the salaries of parish priests and ordering the repair of churches, the council made no effort to reform the Church's top-heavy financial structure in favour of the parishes; and its plans to improve oversight of the lower clergy hinged on the ability, or otherwise, of the higher clergy to provide that supervision. On doctrine, the traditions of the Church, the veneration and invocation of saints, the 'right use of images', belief in purgatory, transubstantiation and the 'sacrifice of the mass' as beneficial to the living and the dead were all reiterated with approval; and, for instruction in the faith, the council ordered the publication of 'Ane Godlie Exhortation' on the eucharist, a leaflet popularly known as the 'Twapenny Faith'.*

The emphasis which the provincial councils

placed on reformation of morals stood in contrast to the stress which Protestant Reformers laid on a doctrinal Reformation which excluded the papacy, the mass and a sacrificing priesthood. Some conservatives, it is true, like Ninian Winzet,* Linlithgow schoolmaster and later abbot of Ratisbon, conceived a 'reformation of doctrine and manners', presumably in the sense of Trent's clarification of Catholic doctrine. Between Scottish Protestants and Catholics, divergence centred not on the necessity of reform but on whether reform would be achieved from inside or outside the existing ecclesiastical establishment. Hamilton's well-intentioned attempts at moderate, internal reform (which looked like too little, too late) proved no substitute for the religious radicalism of Protestant Reformers who had already taken the initiative in advocating drastic change in the Church's doctrine, endowment and government. Indeed in 1558 'the first oration and petition of the Protestants of Scotland', addressed to Mary of Guise, had urged a root-and-branch reform so that Christianity in Scotland might be restored on the model of the New Testament.

MARY OF GUISE. At first the response of Mary of Guise to the activities of Protestant preachers in the 1550s had been one of leniency, for they could expect no sympathy from Mary Tudor in England, and she needed as much support as she could win for her pro-French policies; but Scottish resentment at French domination carried with it the danger for the regime that anti-French feeling might find an outlet in Protestant protest at a government intent on fortifying the links with France and Rome. Besides, the marriage of Queen Mary to the heir to the French throne in 1558 heightened fears that Scotland would be governed as a French province, ruled by Francis and Mary and their descendants. Already in 1557, some Scottish lords had contemplated an outbreak of revolutionary activity and invited Knox to return from Geneva, but then they considered the time was not yet ripe and so changed their plans. Instead, the first band or covenant was drawn up in December 1557 'to maintain, set forward and establish the most blessed word of God and his Congregation' and to renounce all superstition and idolatry. This was followed by outbreaks of iconoclasm, of increasing severity, in 1558 and 1559. At the same time, preparations were made early in 1558 for a Reformed programme of worship and preaching in the parishes, as communities began the search for Protestant ministers and readers of the English BCP.*

The burning of a Protestant preacher, Walter Milne,* in April 1558 served as a reminder that the authorities were still prepared to react to criticism by burning the critics; but it also demonstrated the folly of such a policy. The Regent's summons of Protestant preachers in July 1558 to answer for their activities was cancelled after a show of force by west-country lairds as the Protestant offensive gathered momentum, and iconoclastic rioting erupted in the capital itself. The accession of Elizabeth in November 1558 also meant that Scottish Protestants might again look in hope to England for assistance. Threats of violent action against the friars were forthcoming in January 1559 with the appearance of the 'Beggars' Summons',* which warned the friars to quit their houses in favour of the infirm and needy by Whitsunday in May. At this point Knox returned home from Geneva to preach in Dundee and Perth which publicly opted to support the Reformation; and in the same month, on the west coast, the town of Ayr also adopted the Reformation. When Mary of Guise proceeded against the preachers, the Protestant mobilization was swift: the 'Congregation' of the Mearns, Angus, Fife and Strathearn, with the towns of Dundee and Montrose, gathered in force to defend their preachers, and reinforcements were forthcoming from the Congregation of Kyle and Cunningham in the west. A truce was called and the insurgents finally dispersed, having sacked Scone abbey and the friaries in Dundee, Perth, Stirling, Linlithgow and Edinburgh, and having purged of Catholic symbolism all the kirks they came across.

Despite the success the Reformers enjoyed, Mary of Guise had still the advantage of professional troops and the prospect of French reinforcements. With support from the duke of Châtelherault,* heir presumptive to the Scottish throne, who accepted leadership of the increasingly militant 'Lords of the Congregation',* the Protestants negotiated help from the English government, which advanced them £3,000 but declined any commitment to military aid, and in October 1559 they carried through their plans to 'depose' Mary of Guise and transfer power to a 'great council of the realm', a provisional government headed by the duke and dominated by Protestant lords. The French forces garrisoned at Leith proved more than a match for their opponents; but the appearance of the English fleet in the Firth of Forth in January 1560 was followed in February by the treaty of Berwick between Elizabeth and Châtelherault, as second person in the kingdom, permitting the arrival of an English army in April, which went far towards tipping the balance of forces in the other direction. If Catholicism had been sustained by French military might, Protestantism was to be permitted to gain the ascendancy through English intervention.

In June, Mary of Guise died; and in July, the Treaty of Edinburgh secured the withdrawal of French and English forces from Scotland. In France, Francis and Mary conceded the right for their subjects to hold a parliament – the Reformation Parliament* meeting in July and August – which accepted a Protestant Confession of Faith and broke official links with Rome by forbidding the celebration of mass and abrogating papal authority within the realm. Far from marking the starting point of the Reformation, the proceedings of this parliament were a belated reflection of the work of Reformation already undertaken in local communities. Earlier, in April, at a point when the outcome of the Protestant revolt was still in doubt, the Reformers had begun the task, apparently at the invitation of the 'great council of the realm', of preparing a statement of their programme for the polity and endowment of the reformed church. This took final shape in the *First Book of Discipline** of 1560. While much still required to be done to safeguard the Protestant victory of 1559–60 and to extend evangelization across the land, the work of the Reformation Parliament and *Book of Discipline*, both of which were denied royal sanction, helped shape the nature and outcome of the Reformation settlement.

See also Bible (Versions, English, Scottish); Calvin, Calvinism; Lollards; Martyrs; Zwinglianism.

Full bibliography to date by J. Kirk in *RSCHS* 23 (1987), 113–55. Among recent works: J. Kirk, *Patterns of Reform: Continuity and Change in the Reformation Kirk* (E, 1989); *id.* (ed.), *Humanism and Reform* (O, 1991), esp. 361–435; G. Donaldson, *The Faith of the Scots* (L, 1990); I. B. Cowan, *The Scottish Reformation* (L, 1982); *id.*, *Regional Aspects of the Scottish Reformation* (L, 1978); J. Wormald, *Court, Kirk and Community: Scotland 1470–1625* (L, 1981); F. D. Bardgett, *Scotland Reformed. The Reformation in Angus and the Mearns* (E, 1989); M. Lynch, *Edinburgh and the Reformation* (E, 1981).

Earlier works: G. Donaldson, *The Scottish Reformation* (C, 1960); D. McRoberts (ed.), *Essays on the Scottish Reformation, 1513–1625* (G, 1962).

J. Kirk

Reformed Ecumenical Synod, Council, 'a venture in confessional ecumenism'. The idea of an ecumenical synod for Churches adhering to the Reformed confessions* in a normative sense was vented by the Dutch theologian, H. H. Kuyper, and decided on by the Reformed Church in South Africa in 1924. After years of official correspondence, delegates from the Reformed Churches in the Netherlands and in South Africa and the Christian Reformed Church of America met in 1946 at Grand Rapids to plan a Reformed Ecumenical Synod. A 'call to authentic ecumenism' went out to Churches which understood the Old and the New Testament in accordance with the following Reformed confessions: the Second Helvetic Confession; the Belgic Confession; the Westminster Confession; the Gallican Confession; the Heidelberg Catechism; the Canons of Dort and the Thirty-nine Articles. The Church of Amsterdam called for the meeting which took place at Amsterdam in 1949. Thereafter, delegates of member Churches have gathered once every three to five years to discuss issues of common concern and decide on joint action. Paul G. Schrotenboer has been a distinguished secretary. In one of many study reports issued, the scriptural 'nature of the Church and its ecumenical calling' is stressed. The quest for a scriptural concept of race relations remains on the agenda. In 1980 the issues concerned were argued in the report, 'The Church and its Social Calling'. Several consultations on race relations in South Africa have been held. The Harare meeting in 1988 was attended by thirty-three member Churches from twenty countries, representing six million Christians, and proved a watershed. Being only an advisory council, the name was changed to 'Reformed Ecumenical Council'. Several Churches resigned, being convinced that member Churches have drifted away from the Reformed articles of faith. The fact that some member Churches also joined the World Council of Churches is another point of dispute.

RES, *RES Handbook* (Grand Rapids, issued after each meeting); P. G. Schrotenboer, *RES, a Venture in Confessional Ecumenism* (E, 1965); P. Rossouw, *Ecumenical Panorama* (Pretoria, 1989), 88–100; *Acts of the First [Second etc.] Reformed Ecumenical Synod* (Grand Rapids, 1946–); J. H. Krominga, 'The WCC and the RES: Dutch Influence within Ecumenism', *Reformed World* 38 (1985), 140–7.

The RES/REC issues several serials: *News Exchanger* (1964–); *Mission Bulletin* (1981–); *Theological Forum*, quarterly (1973–).

E. Brown

Reformed Presbyterian Church, founded by those Covenanters* who remained aloof from the re-established CofS after the Revolution Settlement (1690).

Following the Rutherglen Testimony (29th May 1679), the stricter Covenanters, led by Richard Cameron* and Donald Cargill,* coalesced as a distinct entity, still within the CofS, but upholding the principles of the National Covenant,* which asserted the *jus divinum* of a free, Presbyterian and Reformed Church in a covenanted nation which acknowledged the kingship of Jesus Christ. This stance was sealed by the formation of the United Societies* on 15 December 1681 and found expression in the Queensferry Paper,* the Sanquhar Declaration* and the Torwood Declaration* (1680); the Declaration at Lanark (1682); and 'The Apologetical Declaration' and 'An Informatory Vindication'* (1684). The Societies were served by other ministers including: James Renwick,* William Boyd, Thomas Lining and Alexander Shields.*

The Revolution CofS was established on the basis of the will of king and nation and the legislation of 1692, rather than the *jus divinum* principle, the perpetual binding obligation of the 1638 Covenant* and the legislation of the Second Reformation period (see Act 15, par. I.2, Charles II, 7 February 1649, as quoted in the 'Protestation and Apologetic Declaration', Sanquhar, 21 May 1703, in *Testimony-bearing Exemplified*, Paisley, 1791, 315). Boyd, Lining and Shields joined the CofS, but the Societies remained separate. Guided by Sir Robert Hamilton of Preston (1650–1701), who had fought at Drumclog and Bothwell Bridge,* they maintained their fellowship as a quasi-Church without ministers or sacraments. The accession of John Macmillan* (1706) and Thomas Nairn* (1743) permitted the constituting of the Reformed Presbytery (Braehead, 1 August 1743). Ministers could now be

REFORMED PRESBYTERIAN CHURCH

regularly ordained. The Presbytery duly expanded, although only after 1761 was the 'Community' – scattered across Lowland Scotland – divided into pastoral charges. In 1751 John Cuthbertson (1718–91) was sent to minister to Covenanter emigrants in the American Colonies.

The polemic against a covenant-breaking national government continued unabated. The 1707 Union of the Parliaments* raised the spectre of renewed Episcopalian hegemony, awakened painful memories of the Killing Times* and drew a 'Protestation and Testimony' against 'the sinful incorporating union with England, and their British Parliament' (*Testimony-bearing Exemplified*, 347). When the Covenants were renewed at Auchensaugh in August 1712, care was taken to note in the margin, at each mention of the monarch, the words 'the lawful supreme magistrate when obtained', thus ensuring that no-one conclude that they recognised Queen Anne. They successively protested against the 1733 Secession,* the preaching of George Whitefield,* and the Cambuslang revival,* all on grounds relating to defective views of the Covenants. They were, however, warm to the Marrow* teaching over against that of the Moderates.*

In 1753, a 'Breach' in the RPC resulted from the posthumous publication of *A Treatise on Justifying Faith* (E, 1749) by James Fraser of Brea.* Presbytery issued a pronouncement against Fraser's view that Christ's atonement not only secured salvation for the elect, but also won something called 'gospel wrath' for the reprobate. Two ministers, James Hall and Hugh Innes, favoured this doctrine, and withdrew to form a dissentient 'Reformed Presbytery of Edinburgh', which disappeared about 1817 (W. J. Couper, 'A Breach...', *RSCHS* 1 (1926), 1–28).

The century after 'the Breach' saw the Community transformed from an assemblage of societies with a collegiate ministry into a highly organized Presbyterian Church. A Synod was organized in 1811, and by 1863 this comprised six Presbyteries with forty-six congregations and *c.*6,700 communicants. The definitive 'Testimony' of the RPC – a doctrinal and historical statement, explaining and expanding upon the RPC's commitment to the Westminster Standards,* the National Covenant* and the Solemn League and Covenant* – was adopted in 1837. Mission work was done in Canada, New Zealand and among the Jews in England, but it was the New Hebrides mission, begun in 1852 by John G. Paton,* which was to become one of the great missionary sagas of modern times.

In 1803 a Theological Hall was founded, at first at Stirling, with John Macmillan *tertius* as Professor. His successors were all theologians of repute: Andrew Symington* (1820–53); William Symington* (1853–62); William Goold* (1854–76) and William Binnie* (1862–75), later of the FC College, Aberdeen (1876–86). For a Church never more than 10,000 strong, the RPC produced a remarkable volume of literature, mostly controversial and on Church–state relations. John Howie's* *Biographica Scoticana* (1775; revd. E, 1870 as *The Scots Worthies*) is one of the great works on the Coven-

REFORMED TRADITION

anters, while John Laidlaw's* *The Bible Doctrine of Man* (E, 1895) became a standard work of Reformed theology.

The Reform Act (1832) greatly extended the electoral franchise. This agitated the RPC because her protest of 'political dissent' from the covenant-breaking British Constitution was held to require separation from actions implying approval of the state's failure to recognize the mediatorial kingship of Christ. Voting was seen as 'incorporating' with a corrupt Constitution and, in 1833, was declared incompatible with Church membership. After thirty years of further debate, the 1863 Synod relaxed Church censures on voting, and a minority, led by William Anderson, Loanhead, withdrew to form the present RPC. The majority RPC united with the FC in 1876, although the Stranraer congregation returned to the minority RPC.

The continuing RPC, twelve congregations and *c.*1,100 members in 1876, maintained the former testimony for 'the perpetual obligation of the covenants' and 'political dissent', but in 1960 removed Church discipline for voting, thereby adopting the position of the majority in 1863 (*R.P. Witness*, LXXX, August 1960, 122). Of her ministers, J. P. Struthers,* through his magazine *The Morning Watch* (1887–1915), and A. Sinclair Horne, presently heading the Scottish Reformation Society,* have exercised nation-wide ministries. The RPC is a conservative evangelical body, with an unmodified commitment to confessional theology. In worship only the psalms are sung, unaccompanied. Close relations are maintained with the RPC of Ireland. In 1988 the Scottish body had five congregations with *c.*150 members.

Testimony-bearing Exemplified (Paisley, 1791; NY, 1834) – RP source documents; A. Symington *et al.*, *Principles of the Second Reformation* (G, 1841); *Testimony of the Reformed Presbyterian Church of Scotland*, 2 pts (Paisley, 1837, doctrinal; G, 1839, historical); *The Disruption of the Reformed Presbyterian Church of Scotland* (G, 1863); M. Hutchison, *The Reformed Presbyterian Church in Scotland, its Origin and History 1680–1876* (Paisley, 1893); W. J. Couper, 'The Reformed Presbyterian Church in Scotland', *RSCHS* 2 (1925), 3–179; also in book form, E, 1925; *id.*, 'The Literature of the Reformed Presbyterian Church', *RSCHS* 5 (1935), 227–37, 6 (1938), 68–79, 183–92, 299–304; J. Robb, *Cameronian Fasti, 1680–1929* (E, 1975).

G. J. Keddie

Reformed Presbyterian Magazine, see Periodicals, Religious.

Reformed Tradition. There is no unanimity about the identity of the authentic interpreters of this tradition. Minority groups which uncompromisingly adhere to Reformation confessions* (*see, e.g.* Scots Confession) argue for their normative character, even when they disagree among themselves. The major representatives of the Reformed tradition in Europe and America cherish their confessional heritage, but embody its variety and historicity and believe that they are called to continue the confessional task in their own context.

Defining the boundaries of the Reformed tradition has become increasingly difficult because of changes in Churches which were once strongly Reformed, like Anglicans, Baptists and Congregationalists. Reunions have removed Reformed landmarks into new positions, and the success of missions has brought genuinely international cultural diversity. Many rejoice in these changes as a sign of healthy diversity, while others continue to pursue the ideal of a unitary theology recognizably continuous with classic Calvinism.*

Hearing and obeying the Word of the sovereign God lies at the heart of the Reformed tradition. Its historical roots are found in the Imperial and Swiss cities of the sixteenth century, where leaders like Zwingli,* Bucer, Bullinger, Calvin* and Peter Martyr contributed to reform of Church and society, by calling their community to forsake every human addition to the gospel. They shared with Lutherans fundamental convictions about Scripture, faith and grace, and a common critique of the Roman version of catholicity and Anabaptist enthusiasm. Yet significant disagreements between Reformed and Lutherans emerged on the relation of law and gospel, on worship and on the ordering of the Church, even though some Lutherans called themselves 'reformed'.

The Reformed Churches developed a variety of polities (see Presbyterianism; Congregationalism; Independency), but all insisted on the sole headship of Christ, parity* of ministry and equality of vocation. Such commitment often spilled over into rejection of political authority which denied freedom of worship. France, Holland, England and Scotland (see Covenanters) all experienced civil wars. Theologians like Theodore Beza, Samuel Rutherford* and Hugo Grotius made important contributions to political thought. Potent minorities of Reformed Christians in Britain and America were involved in political revolution, for they had a strong popular base of commitment to a Christian social order and world view. The relation between the Reformed tradition and economic development (especially capitalism) is complex, but has been of permanent importance.

Loyalty to Scripture alone, without an agreed hermeneutic, soon caused division theologically, and led some Reformed groups to reject Trinitarian theology (see Unitarians*). In Britain and Holland there were bitter disputes over predestination; the Synod of Dort* and the Westminster Assembly* marked the parting of the ways between Reformed theology and Arminianism.* Evangelical awakenings (see Revivals) created further tensions, which remain to this day. There were also conflicts over the authority of the magistrate in matters of religion that led to divisions in Scotland (see Church and State; Voluntaryism; Secessions; UPC; UFC) and Holland and to revision of classic confessions in the USA.

Reformed Christians sought to hold together Word and Spirit with the best human knowledge of their day. Such a synthesis became increasingly difficult in the nineteenth century and almost impossible in the twentieth, because of the enormous growth in knowledge and intellectual pluralism. Attempts to find fresh foundations for faith by theologians like Schleiermacher and his liberal heirs led to heresy trials,* polemic and the attempt to banish new approaches to Scripture and foundational doctrines like the atonement.* Many Reformed Churches painfully moved towards a modest comprehensiveness in doctrine (see Declaratory Acts) and worship,* but serious questions have remained over how far the Reformed tradition can leave classical formulations behind without surrendering to secularism and pluralism.

Similar tensions have persisted since the seventeenth century over the relation of dogma and personal piety. British Puritans and their counterparts in Europe and America insisted that theology and experience of God as Trinity could not be separated. That emphasis has been reinforced by evangelical renewal, and by theologians like Jonathan Edwards,* but others within the Reformed tradition have been very critical of such emphasis on personal experience as subversive of Church order. They insist that such an approach reduces Reformed Christianity to a set of untestable private convictions with no influence in the public domain.

Like all major traditions in Europe and America, the Reformed heritage has been seriously weakened by massive decline in membership in the later twentieth century, though the situation in Asia and Africa is very different. Reformed Churches in Indonesia, Korea and Southern Africa have grown rapidly and produced significant leaders. Finding credible identity for the Reformed tradition is proving a challenging task. Bilateral dialogues with Rome and the Orthodox have reminded some Reformed theologians of their Catholic heritage.

Discovering what it means to be continually reformed according to the Word of God is never completed. That process has led many heirs of the Reformed tradition in the twentieth century to a commitment to ecumenical partnership in mission, evangelism and mutual service. Such involvement can arguably help free the Reformed tradition from its tendency to legalism and to depreciation of the gifts of God in creation and what may be a too monolithic understanding of unity in Christ. Some sister Churches suspect flaws in our Trinitarian theology and our understanding of incarnation and resurrection and limitations in our eschatology. Exponents of the Reformed tradition are sometimes regarded as over-emphasizing the verbalness of the Word and reducing the language of praise to propositions, which are used to try to create a pure theology free from the corruptions of historicity. More Catholic and Pentecostal styles of worship have had a great impact in many Reformed Churches in recent years.

Being credible confessors of the sovereign God revealed in Word and Spirit is challenging in such a constantly changing world. The Reformed tradition still has resources to enable its heirs to honour the freedom of others in religion and morality without compromising their own witness to divine order by living an ethic of gratitude to a gracious God.

J. W. Beardslee, *Reformed Dogmatics* (NY, 1965); A. C. Cochrane, *Reformed Confessions* (Philadelphia, 1966); I. J. Hesselink, *On Being Reformed* (Ann Arbor, 1983); J. H. Leith, *Introduction to the Reformed Tradition* (Atlanta, ²1981); M. E. Osterhaven, *The Spirit of the Reformed Tradition* (Grand Rapids, 1971); W. K. B. Stoever, 'The Calvinist Theological Tradition', in C. H. Lippy and P. Williams (eds), *Encyclopaedia of the American Religious Experience*, vol. 2 (NY, 1988); D. K. McKim (ed.), *Encyclopedia of the Reformed Faith* (Louisville, 1992).

I. Breward

Regulus, *see* Celtic Saints.

Reid, Henry Martyn Beckwith (1856-1927), CofS divine. Born in Glasgow, he studied at St Andrews University (MA, 1876; BD, 1879). He was ordained to Balmaghie, Kirkcudbright, in 1882, and in 1903 was appointed Professor of Divinity in Glasgow University.

Reid wrote a considerable number of books. His *Text-book of Dogmatics* (L, 1919) outlines his theology in the most accessible form, presenting an eclectic synthesis of Calvinism and modernism. He defended penal substitution, for example, as the best interpretation of the atonement, but restricted the inspiration and inerrancy of Scripture to its 'spiritual truth' and was inclined towards a universalist eschatology.

Reid received a DD from St Andrews in 1903.

The Divinity Principals in the University of Glasgow 1545-1654 (G, 1917); *The Divinity Professors in the University of Glasgow 1640-1903* (G, 1923); *The Holy Spirit and the Mystics* (Croall Lectures,* L, 1925); *The Historic Significance of Episcopacy in Scotland* (Lee Lecture,* E, 1899); *Lost Habits of the Religious Life* (E, 1896); *Books that Help the Religious Life* (E, 1897); *The Layman's Book of the General Assembly* (E, 1900-11).

FES VII, 404; *Who Was Who, 1916-1928*, 878-9.

N. R. Needham

Reid, James Seaton (1798-1851), Irish Presbyterian divine, Professor of Church History in Glasgow University. Born at Lurgan, county Armagh, he studied arts at Glasgow University 1813-16 and then divinity. Licensed by the Presbytery of Letterkenny in 1818, he was ordained the following year to the Irish Presbyterian congregation at Donegore, county Antrim. In 1823 he moved to the church at Carrickfergus. He defended the doctrine of the Trinity against Arians in the controversy which split the Synod of Ulster, and was Moderator of the Synod in its decisive anti-Arian session of 1827. He was one of the founders of the periodical *Orthodox Presbyterian* in 1829. In 1837 he was appointed Professor of Church History and Polity and Pastoral Theology in the Royal Belfast College. In 1841 he became Professor of Church History in Glasgow University.

Reid wrote a *History of the Presbyterian Church in Ireland*, 3 vols (E, 1834-53; ed. W. D. Killen, Belfast, 1867), still a standard work. He also edited and annotated Murdock's translation of Mosheim's *Institutes of Ecclesiastical History* (L, 1848), then widely used as a college textbook.

R. Allen, *James Seaton Reid* (Belfast, 1951); *DNB* XLVII, 429; *FES* VII, 408.

N. R. Needham

Reid, Robert (d.1558), Bishop of Orkney* (1541-58). Born in Clackmannan, he was educated at St Andrews University, entering St Salvator's College in 1511 (MA, 1515). He was granted several offices and benefices in Moray and Fife. Entrusted with the rule of Kinloss Abbey (*see* Cistercians) in 1526, Reid visited Rome in 1528 to secure his title as abbot (forthcoming in 1529), and in Paris he met the Piedmontese scholar, Giovanni Ferrerio, whom he encouraged to settle at Kinloss and to introduce a programme of humanist teaching (*see* Renaissance). By 1530 he had taken his seat as a lord of council, and was provided *in commendam* (*see* Comendator) to the priory of Beauly in 1531. He also sat in Parliament as abbot from 1532, and served the Crown on several diplomatic missions to England and France. He concluded the marriage contract between King James V and Mary, daughter of the Duke of Vendôme (which did not ensue), and retained the confidence of the King, who nominated him as Bishop of Orkney in 1541. A supporter of Cardinal David Beaton,* Reid attended the condemnation for heresy of John Borthwick* in 1540, served as vicar general of the archbishopric of St Andrews during the Cardinal's absence in France in 1541, was appointed president of the College of Justice by 1549, and in 1550 resigned the commendatorship of Kinloss in favour of his nephew, Walter Reid. He was present at the trial of heretics in Perth in 1544, attended the provincial council* of the Scottish Church in 1549, and participated in the trial of Adam Wallace.* Appointed as one of Queen Mary's commissioners in 1558 to treat with the French king for her marriage to the Dauphin, Reid was party to the marriage contract and attended the wedding at Notre Dame. Falling ill at Dieppe, Reid, on his deathbed, was visited by Lord James Stewart (d.1570),* with whom he used to debate religious issues and to whom he is said to have confided 'My lord, long have you and I been in play for purgatory: I think that I shall know or it be long whether there be such a place or not.'

A patron of learning, Reid maintained several students at universities in France. Within his own diocese of Orkney, where religion was said at his appointment to have been neglected through the carelessness of bishops, Reid, though often an absentee, set about reforming the constitution of his cathedral chapter in 1544. The emphasis was on improving the educational standards of the clergy and on increasing services for worship, where some modest provision was made for preaching.

REID, THOMAS

The chaplain of St Peter was recognized as master of the grammar school, and the chaplain of St Augustine master of the song school. Beyond his diocese, Reid planned to establish a college of Arts and Law in Edinburgh and bequeathed 8,000 merks as endowment in 1558. Though not immediately effected due partly to the Reformation and partly to difficulties in securing the funds, Reid's vision found fresh expression in renewed efforts by the Reformed church to create in the capital a college or university which came to fruition by 1583.

FESMA 232, 244, 254; DNB XLVII, 433–4; Dowden, 265–7; J. Kirk, *Patterns of Reform* (E, 1989), 25ff.

J. Kirk

Reid, Thomas, see Scottish Realism.

Reith, John Charles Walsham (1889–1971), first Baron Reith, pioneer in the development of British broadcasting. Born at Stonehaven, son of a FC* minister, he was trained as an engineer at the Royal Technical College, Glasgow. After serving in military and civil posts during the First World War he became general manager (1922–3), managing director (1923–7), and then the first director-general (1927–38) of the British Broadcasting Corporation, during which time he oversaw the inauguration of British television. At the suggestion of the Prime Minister, Neville Chamberlain, he entered political life, but basically distrusted politicians, and after he had successively held the ministries of Information, Transport and Works he was dropped by Churchill in 1942. He then proved to be a highly efficient director of Combined Operations at the Admiralty. He served in a number of post-war commercial positions, notably in the field of aviation, but the long-hoped-for invitation to a key governmental job that would 'stretch' him never came. He came to regret leaving the BBC and regarded his subsequent career as an anti-climax.

It was as a pioneer of broadcasting that he made his mark. A man incapable of compromise, he was determined to build a worthy institution whose staff would maintain high moral standards both professionally and personally. He restricted Sunday broadcasting. He brought together a religious advisory committee, and rebuked absentees from its meetings as failing in imagination. He soon clashed with the BBC's new governors. Knighted in 1927 and the recipient of numerous honours, he was Lord Rector of Glasgow University (1965–8), and Lord High Commissioner to the CofS General Assembly (1967 and 1968). He was the author of the autobiographical *Into the Wind* (L, 1949) and of *Wearing Spurs* (L, 1966).

Charles Stuart (ed.), *The Reith Diaries* (L, 1975); *DNB 1971–1980*, 713–5.

J. D. Douglas

Relief Church, dissenting Presbyterian Church, founded in 1761, notable for its non-sectarian spirit and commitment to religious liberty.

RELIEF CHURCH

ORIGINS. The Relief Church came into being largely as a reaction against the dominance of the Moderate* party in the CofS. Two of the Relief's three pioneers, Thomas Gillespie* of Dunfermline and Thomas Boston* of Jedburgh, were CofS ministers who had fallen foul of the patronage* laws as enforced by the Moderates. Gillespie had been deposed in 1752, and Boston had seceded in 1757. The third pioneer, Thomas Colier, was an English dissenting minister called by a newly-established Independent church in Colinsburgh, Fife – the result of another anti-patronage secession.

In October 1761 these three ministers and their congregations formed themselves into a Presbytery 'for the relief of Christians oppressed in their Christian privileges' (G. Struthers, *The History of the Rise, Progress and Principles of the Relief Church*, G, 1843, 160). The 'Presbytery of Relief' was the title they adopted.

RELIEF PRINCIPLES. The primary 'relief' the new Presbytery determined to provide was liberty for its churches to elect their own pastors – an ideal shared by the Seceders of 1733 (*see* Associate Presbytery). Unlike the Seceders, however, the Relief repudiated the binding obligation of the National Covenant* (1638) and Solemn League and Covenant* (1643), and their imposition as terms of communion. It maintained instead the principle of 'free communion', given classic expression in Gillespie's declaration: 'I hold communion with all that visibly hold the Head, and with such only' (*ibid.*, 123). This meant that Relief ministers were free to share pulpits and services with orthodox ministers of other Churches (although the Relief definition of orthodoxy excluded Arminians*), and that all 'visible saints', of whatever Church, were admitted to the Lord's Supper. Ironically, this catholic attitude isolated the Relief from its fellow dissenting Presbyterian Churches, which denounced it for 'latitudinarian,* unscriptural terms of communion' (*ibid.*, 250).

Other distinctive characteristics of the Relief as a Presbyterian body were the early acceptance of Voluntary* views of Church–state* relations by most of its teachers, and the way in which its Church courts acted more as 'consultative meetings' than 'legislative and authoritative judicatories' (*ibid.*, 123), affording maximum liberty to individual ministers and congregations.

GROWTH, EVANGELISM AND MISSIONS. The Relief movement grew in its first few decades by the steady addition of congregations which had seceded from the CofS. In 1772 it formally divided into two Presbyteries, the 'eastern' and the 'western', which henceforth met as the Relief Synod. The progress of the Relief in the Fife area led to the constitution of a third Presbytery, that of Dysart, in 1776.

The Relief sought to grow not only by 'church-stealing', and its uncharacteristically narrow reaction to the lay preaching of the Haldanes* in the 1790s was no sign of antagonism to evangelism as such. Indeed, in 1796 the Relief became the first Presbyterian body in Scotland officially to espouse

RELIEF CHURCH

the missionary cause, when its Synod passed a declaration strongly supporting foreign missions,* and encouraging 'all the members of this synod [to] unite their exertions with any society that may be formed to promote such a good and great design' (*ibid.*, 394).

The Relief also undertook its own missions to the Scottish Highlands.* In July 1797 it appointed its first two Highland evangelists, Niel Douglas* of Dundee and Daniel McNaught of Dumbarton, who laboured with considerable success in Argyllshire. The missions, however, came to an untimely demise in 1804. Lack of Gaelic-speaking evangelists was one problem. Another was Douglas, who was found to have acted as president of a political reform society; in the days of conservative reaction in Britain against the French Revolution this was enough to cause all Relief missionaries to be stigmatized as agitators. The Synod suspended the missions, and its surplus funds were given to the Scottish SPCK* for the printing of a Gaelic Bible (*see* Bible (Versions, Gaelic)).

THE SLAVE TRADE AND PSALMODY. The same sympathetic consciousness of human need which prompted the Relief's missionary concern lay behind the stand it took against the slave trade. As early as 1788, it petitioned the Burgher and Antiburgher Seceders to join it in fighting 'the inhuman system of the slave-trade'. One of the most effective polemics against the trade to be published in Britain was produced by Niel Douglas, in the shape of a lengthy pamphlet entitled *The African Slave Trade* (E, 1792), which speedily achieved a country-wide circulation (*ibid.*, 348–9).

It was about this time that a reformation of Relief psalmody was effected. James Stewart of Anderston, having compiled a selection of 180 hymns, introduced them into the worship of his congregation; Patrick Hutchison* of Paisley and James Dun of Glasgow followed suit. The Synod of 1794 approved in principle, and accepted a report recommending the adoption of Stewart's compilation. A minor controversy resulted when Thomas Bell* of Dovehill, Glasgow, wrote a lengthy protest in favour of the traditional Scottish Presbyterian practice of exclusive psalmody. Synod, however, went ahead, prefacing the new hymnbook with a defence of uninspired hymnody in worship (*see* Hymnology, English).

The hymnbook was composed mostly of material by Watts, with additions by Newton and Doddridge. It was soon in general use in the Relief churches, and a revised version was issued in 1832.

THE NEW CENTURY. The new century ushered the Relief into a period of steady growth. Beginning with sixty congregations and some 36,000 members, by the time of the union with the USec.C in 1847 they had 136 congregations, among them some of the largest in Scotland. Nor was this process only numerical. The Relief's ecclesiastical laws were codified for the first time in the 1820s, and in 1824 its first divinity hall was opened in Paisley, with James Thomson as theological tutor. Relief students had previously trained for the minis-

RELIGIOUS BROADCASTING

try in the Scottish university divinity halls, chiefly in Glasgow, but this avenue was closed to dissenters by new enactments which required theology students to submit to examination by the CofS Presbytery in whose bounds they resided. This was symptomatic of a widening rift between Scottish dissent and CofS Evangelicals.* As the latter grew in strength, they drew closer to the Moderates* and away from their old dissenting brethren. This, however, contributed to a spirit of rapprochement among dissenters, and hence, indirectly, to the union between the Relief and the Secession.

THE UNION OF 1847. The possibility of union was mooted in the Relief Synod of 1834, via an overture from the Presbytery of Dysart. The two 'New Light' branches of the Burgher and Antiburgher Seceders had united in 1820 to form the USec.C (*see* New Light), which like the Relief held Voluntary views on Church–state relations and had abandoned the custom of renewing the Covenants. The Secession's more traditional Presbyterian ethos and model of church government proved no insurmountable barrier to union between the two bodies; 118 of the 136 Relief churches entered the union, and their principles and influence continued within the UPC.

See also Baine, James; Campbeltown Case; Dissenters; Pirie, Alexander; Secessions; Struthers, Gavin.

P. Hutchison, *A Compendious View of the Religious System Maintained by the Relief Synod* (Falkirk, 1779); Small; *ASUPC*; R. Logan, *The United Free Church, 1681–1906* (E, 1906), 54–64; J. Barr, *The United Free Church of Scotland* (L, 1934), 67–82.

N. R. Needham

Religious Broadcasting. On 28 January 1923 G. H. Morrison* of Wellington Church, Glasgow gave the first religious broadcast on radio in Scotland. BBC began transmission from Scotland (Glasgow) on 6 March of that year, and in May 1924 the proceedings of the General Assembly of the CofS were relayed from the Assembly Hall.

Until 1939, religious broadcasting was organized from London for the whole of Britain. In 1933, Melville Dinwiddie* of Aberdeen was appointed Head of BBC Scotland and took a special interest in religious broadcasting. During the War years (1939–45) R. Selby Wright of the Kirk of the Canongate in Edinburgh became familiar to millions as the Radio Padre.

In 1946, Ronald Falconer* was appointed Head of Religious Broadcasting in Scotland, and six months later was joined by Stanley Pritchard as Assistant Head. They introduced a varied pattern of local and network programmes, in spite of the lack of enthusiasm in London for regional broadcasting. Falconer was responsible for the Radio Mission (1950–2), out of which developed the Tell Scotland* movement.

1952 saw the advent of television in Scotland and the enlargement of the religious department to in-

RELIGIOUS COMMUNITIES

clude Father Hugh Mackay, Ralph Smith and Wilson Anderson. During 1962-70 William Barclay* presented several highly popular series of Bible teaching programmes. After Ronald Falconer's retiral in 1968, James Deay, a Congregational minister, was briefly Head of Religious Broadcasting in Scotland and was followed in 1974 by Iain Mackenzie, in 1990 by Ian Bradley, and in 1992 by Andrew Barr. In 1957 commercial television came to Scotland. In 1962 Robert McPherson was appointed Head of educational and religious programmes on STV, and in 1967 Nelson Gray, a Congregational minister, was appointed to oversee the Company's religious output. During the following years, STV made more religious programmes than any other company in the Independent Television network. Gray retired in 1988 and was succeeded by Alistair Moffat.

In 1961 Grampian Television obtained its franchise. The Head of Programmes, James Buchan, was responsible for Grampian's religious output and he concentrated on documentaries about Christian action worldwide. Although Border Television has never made religious programmes for its Scottish sector, it has a policy of including items of religious interest in its daily programming. Independent Radio began in 1974 with the emergence of Radio Clyde, and with Radio Forth the following year. Then came a number of lesser regional companies, all of which transmit a variety of religious programmes, produced by part-time staff. Both the BBC and the ITV companies, both TV and radio, are served by religious advisory committees, appointed by the companies from the churches, on an ecumenical basis. Radio, and in particular television, have probably been the most effective agents of ecumenical development in Scotland.

Earliest Days of Broadcasting in Scotland. Fiftieth Anniversary (1923-73) (G, 1973); M. Dinwiddie, *Religion by Radio* (L, 1968); R. H. W. Falconer, *The Kilt Beneath My Cassock* (E, 1978); id., *Message, Media, Mission* (Baird Lectures* for 1975, E, 1977).

N. Gray

Religious Communities, Episcopal Church. From time to time the mission work of the EpCS has been and continues to be enriched by the contributions of members of religious orders.

The Community of St Margaret of Scotland, Aberdeen, is a daughter house of the East Grinstead Community in Sussex, founded by John Mason Neale* in 1854 and established in Aberdeen at the request of John Comper,* Rector of St Margaret's in the city in 1862. In the past the Sisters have worked in Fraserburgh, Stirling, Kirkwall, Lerwick and Oban. Their present work is focused at St Margaret's and is mainly of a parochial nature.

Other short-lived communities were set up in the same years, especially at the initiative of A. P. Forbes* and under the impact of the Oxford Movement – the Sisterhood of St Mary and St Modwenna, devoted to visiting and nursing among the poor of Dundee (nine sisters were in residence

RELIGIOUS ORDERS

in 1871), the Community of St Andrew of Scotland in Edinburgh (1858), and the Sisterhood of the House of Bethany in Aberdeen.

The Community of the Transfiguration at Roslin, near Edinburgh, was founded in Scotland in 1965 (at nearby Loanhead). Roslin is a community of men and women drawn from different ecclesiastical traditions who seek to foster the contemplative life and the life of prayer. The members do all that they can to foster and deepen ecumenical relationships. The Manual of the Community states that 'the rule and office are designed to support a vocation to live in solitude, in community and in the world, and to manifest the joy, simplicity and compassion of the Gospel'.

The Brothers of the Society of St Francis work among the poor in a variety of ways in both Glasgow and Edinburgh. For the last few years four or five brothers have been available to serve where special needs are discerned and also to educate ordinary members of the Church about the nature and manner of the religious life. The Society of St Francis (Anglican) was founded in 1921 and comprises a First Order for men (SSF) and women (Community of St Francis), active orders called to the Franciscan* life under the vows of poverty, chastity and obedience. The brothers and sisters of the First Order engage in active work for the under-privileged, receive casual visits from the homeless unemployed, care for men recently released from prison and Borstal, work in universities, schools, colleges, parishes, parish missions and retreats.

Sisters of the Order of the Holy Paraclete (OHP) have served for some years on the staff of Scottish Churches' House at Dunblane in Perthshire (*see* Ecumenical Movement) and have done much to help members of all the Churches appreciate the dedication and quality of life of religious sisters. The mother house of the Order is at Whitby, Yorkshire. Founded in 1915 and based on the rule of St Benedict, the main undertakings of the Order are listed as teaching, hospital and university chaplaincies, retreats, conferences and missions.

Sisters of the Community of St Peter the Apostle, Westminster, worked for many years in Scotland; for example for more than thirty years sisters ran the St Andrews Home for Girls at Joppa, Midlothian, and the Retreat House at Walkerburn in Peeblesshire.

Other communities like the Society of St John the Evangelist (SSJE), commonly known as the Cowley Fathers, from near Oxford, have undertaken work for shorter periods in order to meet particular needs.

Information in Year Book of the EpCS annually.

A. Mackintosh

Religious Orders, Roman Catholic, Modern. Religious life in the RCC in recent centuries has been increasingly varied. Communities in modern

RELIGIOUS ORDERS

Scotland bear little resemblance to those existing before 1560, for most belong to orders founded more recently and, in sharp contrast to pre-Reformation times (see Nunneries), women religious far outnumber men and are mostly active and unenclosed. Following Catholic Emancipation (1829),* the first to come were Ursulines (see Trail, Ann) at St Margaret's Convent, Edinburgh, in 1834. Three other women's orders came 1847–50, and a further three 1860–2. Six men's orders came 1858–67. The first medieval order to return was the Franciscans* (1868), followed by Benedictines* at Fort Augustus* (1876).

The following table covers the period 1878–1978. Figures cannot be exact, while those for women and brothers (i.e. not priests) are not available (see further below). The term 'order' is used for all, though technically it refers only to institutes of pre-Reformation type. Men living in community but not taking vows (e.g., some missionary institutes) are counted as religious.

	MEN			WOMEN	
	Orders	Houses	Priests	Orders	Houses
1878	8	15	55	8	24
1914	8	15	94	22	65
1945	13	30	167	26	82
1978	31	60	257	57	137

There was steady if not uniform growth until, after the Second World War, more rapid expansion took place. Houses are mostly concentrated in the urbanized central belt, with only a few in the less populous north and west. Some orders have a variety of large institutions and numerous members, while others have one simple dwelling-house. Some have exercised a variety of apostolates, others have concentrated on one field of work. Some orders are centuries old, others (e.g. Mother Teresa's Missionaries of Charity) are recent.

ROLE AND APOSTOLATE. The first religious came in response to two urgent needs: in the Lowland slums, to provide elementary education and to care for the sick and destitute. It is largely due to their efforts that the immigrant poor remained faithful to their Church. Religious priests helped to provide pastoral care for the ever-increasing Irish immigrants. Work in education has continued. The sisters' contribution in primary schools was immense, and for decades they provided secondary education for girls. Two orders established training colleges for women teachers. In Glasgow, Marist Brothers and Jesuits* conducted boys' schools which helped to build up a RC middle class. More recently Jesuits and Dominicans* have established university chaplaincies*.

Almost the whole field of human need and distress has been catered for by men and women religious. Only the briefest summary can be given: rehabilitation centres and schools; orphanages; homes and schools for the handicapped; homes for the sick and elderly; hospitals and nursing homes; hostels and guest houses meeting various needs. Some institutions have gained a reputation for pioneering work or as models of their kind.

RELIGIOUS ORDERS

Religious priests have manned large urban parishes and conducted parish missions. Religious houses have offered retreats and courses. Since the 1930s missionary orders have recruited young men and women for service abroad. Monasteries (see Benedictines, Cistercians) provide the whole public liturgy and places for quiet retreat. Enclosed women's communities exercise a hidden apostolate of prayer. Religious have also been influential in introducing ideas and spiritualities from abroad.

CONSTITUTION AND GOVERNMENT. The relationship of religious to local bishops is regulated by canon law;* their internal government depends on canon law and their statutes approved by Rome. As regards constitution, there are roughly two groups. For monks and enclosed women, the community is the unit: members normally remain in one house and elect their own superior. For most, however, the unit is the province: individuals are moved between houses, and local superiors appointed by the provincial authorities. This is of crucial importance, as Scotland is usually included in a province with England or Ireland or both; and since Scotland has a far smaller RC population, the centre of gravity in almost every province lies elsewhere. Although Scotland has its autonomous bishops' conference, jurisdiction over most religious is exercised by provincial superiors resident in England or Ireland.

There are of course exceptions. The Franciscan Sisters of the Immaculate Conception (Glasgow) have founded houses in several countries and have their generalate (supreme authority) in Scotland. The provincials of the Marist Brothers and Xaverian Fathers reside in Scotland, as does the Sisters of Nazareth's regional superior. The Ursulines in Edinburgh became a diocesan institute (i.e. under the local bishop's jurisdiction) and founded daughter houses, but since 1920 they have been part of a British province. Jericho Benedictines, founded recently, are an indigenous growth.

A consequence of this provincial organization is that probably less than half of the religious in Scotland are Scots. Missionary orders have recruited well in Scotland and in 1987 up to 200 Scots missionaries were working abroad. Young Scots also freely enter orders with no Scottish house. Margaret Sinclair,* a candidate for beatification, entered an enclosed community in England. Probably two out of three Scottish religious live outwith Scotland.

RECENT DEVELOPMENTS. In post-war Britain, comprehensivization of schools and the National Health Service have affected religious greatly. If they remain in the private sector, the education and medical care originally intended for the poor are, ironically, priced beyond the latter's reach. At the same time, the stimulus to reappraisal given by Vatican II has led religious to move away from traditional institutions to small communities and more informal apostolates. Many larger establishments (schools, hospitals, retreat houses, etc.) have been closed recently, while small communities of three or four sisters have been set up in council houses.

Increasingly sisters work as pastoral assistants in parishes.

In the early 1960s Councils of Major Religious Superiors (CMRS) were formed. The Scottish CMRS, the first in the world to have men and women in a single council, elected its first woman president in 1977. Provincial superiors usually appoint a delegate resident in Scotland to the CMRS. A centre for fostering communication and a counselling service for religious were established. Numerous conferences have been organized, including a week-long national conference in 1984. A joint commission of bishops and CMRS meets regularly, and several dioceses have an 'episcopal vicar' to liaise with religious.

Women's houses increased slowly in the 1950s and 1960s, then in 1967–74 seventeen new orders entered Scotland and in 1969–77 over fifty new houses were founded. The following table (an amalgam from different sources) covers the years for which statistics of personnel are readily available.

	MEN		
	Orders	Houses	Priests	Brothers
1975		57	235	146
1977–8	31	61	253	130
1982	31	57	236	127
1985–6	30	57	222	119

	WOMEN			Total
	Orders	Houses	Sisters	Religious
1975		128	1293	1674
1977–8	57	135	1297	1680
1982	58	151	1191	1554
1985–6	56	157	1163	1504

Several factors may be noted. Though orders and houses of men remained stable, the number of brothers declined, while priests are reduced by 23 per cent from a peak of 288 in 1965. Women's houses continued to increase while the number of sisters declined. As elsewhere in the western world, recruitment is insufficient to maintain numbers, and the proportion of elderly religious increases. Present trends seem likely to continue and accelerate rather than diminish.

M. Dilworth, 'Religious Orders in Scotland, 1878–1978', *IR* 29 (1978), 92–109; *Catholic Directory for Scotland* (annual) 1835–; *Religious Order Centre News* (later *CMRS Bulletin*) (E/G) 1971–; *Directory of Catholic Religious Communities in Scotland* (published by CMRS Scotland) 1982, 1986.

M. Dilworth

Religious Tract and Book Society, *see* Scottish Colportage Society.

Remanent Synod, *see* Original Secession Church.

Remonstrants, *see* Protesters.

Renaissance. The study of the Renaissance in Scotland faces problems, due to the occasional nature of surviving evidence. Some scholars even go so far as to deny its presence. Little exists to indicate Italian influence before 1500, the visit of Aeneas Sylvius Piccolomini (later Pope Pius II) in 1435 being politically motivated. (He wrote an account of Scotland in his *Commentaries*..., tr. F. A. Gragg, Northampton, MA, 1937–57.) One survivor from the Greek diaspora after the Fall of Constantinople in 1453 was Serapion, physician of the court of James II* (J. Durkan, *William Turnbull*, G, 1951, 56). Numerous Scots visited Italy to seek benefices in Rome, some perhaps catching the humanist contagion. Manuscripts in a fine Roman hand were executed in Italy in the 1450s by George Kinninmont (J. Durkan and J. Kirk, *The University of Glasgow, 1451–1577*, G, 1977, 10). New discoveries of lost classical manuscripts seem to have been slow to reach Scotland, except through later printed editions. Thomas Lowrie, archdeacon of Brechin (1467–92), whose 'humanity' was honoured in 1476 at St Andrews, owned a rediscovered text of Cicero, the *De Oratore*. The Archbishop of St Andrews, William Scheves (*d*.1496; *DNB* L, 416–17), and Alexander Inglis (in 1496; *FESMA*, 13, etc.) both bequeathed classical works to that university: a fine medal of Scheves by Quentin Metays is preserved in Edinburgh. At Aberdeen a new university for the north was in the making, its founder, Bishop William Elphinstone* being styled 'another Cusa', after Nicholas of Cusa, a cultural hero of the humanists: among other things, Elphinstone donated a copy of Lorenzo Valla's *Elegantiae* to King's College Library.

INFLUENCE OF ERASMUS. Meantime Desiderius Erasmus, the greatest of the northern humanists, was surrounded in Paris by many Scots, notably Hector Boece,* the historian, and William Hay,* Boece's successor as Principal at King's. The Erasmian passion for tranquillity and peace was communicated through Boece as an Aberdeen theme to Florence Wilson (*c*.1504–*c*.1555; *DNB* LVIII, 389–91), John Leslie* and Alexander Arbuthnot.* The natural son of James IV,* Alexander Stewart (*d*.1513),* studied law at Padua before joining Erasmus for Greek and Latin tuition in Siena. He was joined in 1508 by another Stewart, James, Earl of Moray, whose death in 1544 was commemorated by a poetic dialogue composed by a monk of Glenluce (*see* Cistercians), the interlocutors being Bishop Robert Reid* and the Italian tutor at Kinloss Abbey (*see* Cistercians), Giovanni Ferrerio (*fl*.1528–40), a native of Piedmont who wrote a continuation of Boece's history of Scotland (see J. Durkan in K. Robbins (ed.), *Religion and Humanism*, O, 1981, 181–94).

As yet Scotland had produced no Latin poet of note, although verses sent from Paris to the King by John Ireland* had a classical tincture. However in 1512 appeared James Foulis' long Latin elegy on the late Edinburgh plague in which is portrayed the total disaster affecting Scotland, and with it a happy Sapphic ode celebrating St Margaret.* Foulis (*d*.1549; *DNB* XX, 70) became a royal secretary, one of a succession of classically moulded secretaries from Archibald Whitelaw's (d.1498) time under James III.* Some Latin letters by Foulis remain unprinted. It could indeed be said that the Renaissance upgrading of rhetoric most notably served this epistolary revival in court and school: the later correspondence of John Johnston* and Robert Howie* exemplified this. However, the verbal lushness of Walter Ogilvie's oration praising the English King Henry VII echoes the Ciceronianism of the secretaries.

Contributions to contemporary legal debate came from Edward Henryson (c.1510–c.1590; DNB XXVI, 129–30) in the 1550s. His treatises on jurisdiction and testaments exhibit the philological approach to law rather than syllogistic reasoning as in medieval masters like Bartolus (1314–57), the Italian jurist of Perugia. Here Henryson followed Guillaume Budé. The latter was also prime mover in establishing royal lectureships in Paris, and lectures were established by Mary of Lorraine in Edinburgh with Henryson's collaboration. The latter's colleague at Bourges, Henry Scrimgeour (1505–72; cf. J. Durkan in Edinb. Bibliogr. Soc. Trans. 5, 1978, 1–31), became manuscript collector for the Fuggers at Augsburg, an editor of Justinian's Novellae and Professor of Civil Law at Geneva. Thomas Craig of Riccarton's (1538–1608; DNB XII, 448–51) subsequent contribution to feudal theory seems a backward step, though in fact it followed the lead of French legal humanists. Wittenberg inspired the antiquarianism of John Skene's (c.1543–1617; DNB LII, 336–8) Regiam Majestatem and the brief forays into Church law of William Welwood (fl.1578–1622; DNB LX, 245–6).

LANGUAGES AND GRAMMAR. With theologians, the new interest in 'the Tongues' revolutionized higher studies. Before that happened, there were solitary pioneers like Florence Wilson and Alexander Alesius* in the 1530s and Archibald Hay (1540; DNB XXV, 252), while Robert Hamilton (FES V, 231) and Archibald Hamilton* were scheduled to begin public Hebrew lectures at St Andrews. Principal John Davidson* at Glasgow read Hebrew, though the arrival from Geneva of Andrew Melville* was needed to give Hebrew-related studies a solid university footing. Interest in Arabic manuscripts took George Strachan* as far as Persia; oriental studies led David Colville to become librarian at the Escorial in Spain.

This philological approach had its basis in Scottish schooling, with the abandonment of medieval grammars and establishment of the Louvain grammarian, Joannes Despauterius (c.1480–1520; Biogr. Nation. de Belgique XXIII, 304–12), as prime model, followed notably by Andrew Simson, father figure (d.1590; see Simson, Archibald), whose grammars in adapted form persisted till the days of the Enlightenment: even George Buchanan's* Latinized version of Thomas Linacre's Rudimenta could not compete, though some Scots editions of Despauterius were laced with borrowings from Linacre. An original grammar inspired by Petrus Ramus was that of Alexander Hume (c.1557–1609, poet and minister of Logie, near Stirling; DNB XXVIII, 210–11), correspondent of Andrew Melville, another Ramist enthusiast, but that failed to secure the country-wide monopoly Hume sought. The utilization of Ramus in theology is most visible in the commentary of Charles Ferme,* appointed first head of the projected but failed university at Fraserburgh.

George Buchanan* is Scotland's most notable renaissance man because of the diversity of his contribution and his European reputation. Here only brief reference can be made to his lyrical mastery, especially in the epigrams echoing the Greek anthology, his psalm paraphrases modelled on Horace which were popular in continental countries, his humanist dramas replacing medieval mystery plays, his quasi-scientific epic The Sphere, his radical political theories very soon overtaken by the absolutist practice of contemporary monarchs including his pupil, James VI,* his pamphleteering in Scots against Queen Mary,* his ambitious history of Scotland, and his theorizing on educational reform.

EDUCATION. The university* foundations of the fifteenth and sixteenth centuries catered for an élite, though St Leonard's College at St Andrews was founded as a 'college of the poor'. Yet already pre-Reformation Church councils* envisaged schools even in less wealthy parishes, while the First Book of Discipline* took advantage of the religious revolution to put flesh on such ideas despite financial stringency and initial setbacks. The objective of a 'school in every parish' was striven for with more early success than is commonly realised, the gap between élite and populace being ironed out. Vernacular literature never regained the commanding heights of Robert Henryson,* William Dunbar* and Gavin Douglas,* and though King James's 'Castalian' school of poets updates their approach, they lost the assurance and verbal vigour of their predecessors. Against encroaching anglicization, verse writers turned to the Latin of Europe's 'republic of letters'.

The Reformation's* rejection of the elaborate church music characteristic of Robert Carver* in favour of understandable texts and singable tunes led to musical decline, as by contrast it helped popular appreciation of biblical prose rhythms. John Black (fl.1546–87), of the Aberdeen song school, soon provided the theoretical foundation of the new approach. Though teachers like Duncan Burnett (fl.c.1615–52) in Glasgow still cherished the polyphonic music of Byrd, the metrical psalms* remain the central heritage of the period. Court dance music, while it lasted, turned to customary French models. Reformers also removed the curtained altars and painted or sculpted images, while wall embroideries in primary colours and painted ceilings utilizing Greek and Roman mythology invaded private houses: the chorally dominated plans of cathedral* and collegiate* kirks gave way to some like Burntisland in Fife, with its central focus (see Architecture). Crichton Castle, Midlothian (1590), is an astonishing late response to Stirling Palace with its renaissance 'medallions'. Typical of northern Europe is the Gothic detail that beds down happily in architecture with new Renaissance motifs. Externally, Edzell in Angus (1606) is the best known of our landscaped gardens.

HISTORY AND GEOGRAPHY. In historiography, advance is less easy to chart. Hector Boece's* Scots history (1527) is finer as a sample of Roman eloquence than of documented fact. It was preceded by John Major's* history of Britain, where Renaissance prefaces are side by side with scholastic text – a history informed by a soberer patriotism than Boece's. While throwing some fables overboard and deploying a wide range of classical learning, Buchanan writes 'eloquent' history like Boece. In Church history, John Knox* and David Calderwood* make ample use of documentation, even if it is polemically handled, while John Leslie, on the RC side and in his vernacular history, eschews rhetorical colouring.

Some geographical indications are given in Boece, but no map. Friar Alexander Lindsay produced a chart for James V's* famous round-Scotland voyage. Jean Rotz (or John Ross), French-born son of an expatriate Scot, hydrographer to Henry VIII, charted some coastal areas of America. The key figure in native cartography was Timothy Pont (c.1565–1614; DNB XLVI, 94, FES VII, 119), whose maps were ready for printing (in Holland, perhaps) by 1596, maps based on ground surveys mostly not available till 1654. Robert Gordon (1580–1661; DNB XXII, 226–7) of Straloch, Perthshire, and his son James (1615–86; DNB XXII, 206–7) later followed Pont's example. Scots ships were not equipped for voyages of discovery, and Dunbar's poetic reference to the 'new found Yle' has been questioned as a reference to northwest America, though John Major was discussing Spanish New World policies as early as 1510 and later pointed to the 'oceanic flow' in eastern seas discovered by Portuguese navigators. Other indications of an early Scottish interest in South America need investigation, but there is no doubt about John Black's presence in New Mexico from 1535.

Scottish attention to antiquities is observable in Boece and Buchanan, the latter noting inscriptions as a philologist, not as an archaeologist. Yet the desire to preserve the Roman site at Inveresk near Edinburgh goes back to Queen Mary's reign, while later foreign visitors indicated sites in print. John Napier* renewed interest in Inveresk in his commentary on Revelation. Napier's vernacular was replaced by Latin in his mathematical works. In 1614 he introduced the famous logarithms, which Johann Kepler immediately utilized to check astronomical tables he held before proceeding to extend Napier's theory on his own. Napier also developed algebraic theory, while in France Alexander Anderson (1582–?1619; DNB I, 371–2) advanced the mathematical progress made by François Viète (1540–1603). In Italy, the young Galileo's discovery of the 'Medicean' planets rallied some Scots to his cause. In the interim, more traditional professors concentrated on more accurate texts of Greek mathematicians as bases for further advance.

PHILOSOPHY. Philosophy took a decisive turn in the sixteenth century. Considerable advances in logical theory were still being made in its early years, to which the school of John Major contributed ideas of continuing interest to contemporary logicians. This new medieval accretion was rejected by humanists as an unworthy appendix to Aristotle, the first signs of rejection being evident even before the slimmed-down textbook (*Dialecticae Compendium*, Paris, 1540) of William Cranston (c.1513–62, Provost of St Salvator's, St Andrews), with its acknowledgement to Rudolph Agricola, which was followed by the expanded text in Ciceronian Latin (1557) of John Rutherford* (d.1577), based on ancient Greek commentators rather than medieval, and issued as Rutherford tutored in the household of Michel de Montaigne. Andrew Melville* ignored Rutherford's work in Glasgow, replacing it with the new system of Petrus Ramus, though elsewhere in philosophy Melville too followed Aristotle when his thought did not clash with biblical teaching. An influential pupil of Rutherford, Robert Balfour (c.1550–c.1625, philosopher and mathematician, DNB III, 57–8), taught at Bordeaux, an anti-Ramist who used classical citations as starting points for argument in the way Ramus himself had pioneered.

In a sense the claim that Scotland's Renaissance was a mainly literary one is defensible, but only if literature is understood in its widest sense to cover all areas of scholarship. In this connection, Principal Robert Boyd's* learning programme bequeathed to his son is instructive. Besides being a reader of Protestant divinity, he was expected to be a 'universal man'. He was to study Despauterius in grammar, followed by poetry and rhetoric; to practise calligraphy, with daily linguistic exercise in Latin, Greek and the Scots and French vernaculars, turning later to Hebrew. History was to involve ancillary disciplines like textual criticism and archaeology and not confine itself to chronology, while geography included not only ancient place names but modern mapmakers like Ortelius. Study models included Erasmus, the two Scaligers, father and son, Justus Lipsius, Isaac Casaubon, Beza, plus German and Dutch scholars. Several Hebraists from Sebastian Munster to Thomas Erpenius (1584–1624, Dutch orientalist) were to be studied. Musical theory, 'logistic' (algebra), geometry, mechanics, geology, the *Sphere*, astrology (omitting futurology) and astronomy, anatomy, physics, agriculture, painting, sculpture, moral and political theory and jurisprudence, alongside the current university curriculum, completed an encyclopaedic round of studies.

I. B. Cowan and D. Shaw (eds), *The Renaissance and Reformation in Scotland* (E, 1983); T. C. Smout (ed.), *Scotland and Europe* (E, 1986); A. Broadie, *The Circle of John Mair* (O, 1985); G. Hay, 'Scottish Renaissance Architecture', in D. J. Breeze (ed.), *Studies in Scottish Antiquity* (E, 1984), 196–231; J. MacQueen, *Humanism in*

RENDALL, ROBERT

Renaissance Scotland (E, 1990); R. D. S. Jack (ed.), *The History of Scottish Literature* I (A, 1988); *The New Grove Dictionary of Music and Musicians* (ed. S. Sadie), II, 769 (John Black), III, 488 (Duncan Burnett), XV, 371-6 (Metrical Psalms), XVII, 68-70 (Scotland); J. K. Cameron, 'The Renaissance Tradition in the Reformed Church of Scotland' in D. Baker (ed.), *Renaissance and Renewal in Christian History* (O, 1977), 251-69; J. MacQueen, 'Some Aspects of the Early Renaissance in Scotland', *Forum for Modern Language Studies* 3 (1967), 201-22 (on Whitelaw, Ogilvie, *etc.*); J. Durkan, 'The Cultural Background – Sixteenth Century Scotland', in D. McRoberts (ed.), *Essays on the Scottish Reformation 1513-1625* (G, 1962), 274-331; J. Durkan, *The Renaissance in Scotland* (forthcoming).

J. Durkan

Rendall, Robert (1898-1967), Orkney poet and naturalist. He was born in Glasgow of Orcadian parents who moved back to Orkney* in 1905. Although he left school at thirteen, he continued his study of natural history. In the Thirties he wrote several papers on his archaeological explorations and discovered the Broch of Gurness. His first published poems, *Country Sonnets* (Kirkwall, 1946), came from his experience of farming in World War II. His finest poetry, in the Orkney dialect, appeared next in *Orkney Variants* (Kirkwall, 1951). A life-long member of the Brethren,* he wrote for *The Witness** and for the *Evangelical Quarterly*;* papers written for both journals appeared in *History, Prophecy and God* (L, 1954) and *The Greatness and Glory of Christ* (L, 1956). *Mollusca Orcadensia* (*Proc. of Royal Soc. of Edinb.* (B), E, 1956) brought his forty-year study of molluscs to completion. His best religious poems appeared in *Shore Poems* (Kirkwall, 1957) and his autobiography is *Orkney Shore* (Kirkwall, 1960). A lyric poet, Rendall depicted the Orkney crofter-fisherman as representing the enduring human condition. The poet George Mackay Brown testifies his regard for Rendall. His immersion in Orkney culture was informed by his understanding of God's creative ingenuity and the ways humanity can reflect it.

G. M. Brown, 'Robert Rendall', in *An Orkney Tapestry* (L, 1967); N. Dickson (ed.), *Island Shore: Life and Work of Robert Rendall* (Kirkwall, 1990).

N. Dickson

Renwick, Alexander MacDonald (1888-1965), FC minister, missionary, professor and writer. Born in Kintail, Wester Ross, Renwick left a promising career in the civil service for the FC ministry. He graduated MA from Edinburgh University in 1911 and BD in 1913. Completing studies in the FC College in 1913, he was ordained to St Columba FC, Aberdeen. He served as Chaplain in the First World War and then became minister of Free High, Dumbarton (1918-26). He was next appointed Principal of the FC Mission College, Lima, where he opened a new complex, Colegio San Andres, in

RENWICK, JAMES

1932. While in Lima he gained a DLitt by archaeological/historical studies at the University of San Marcos, Lima (1931). His appointment as Professor of Church History in the FC College followed (1943-63). Moderator of the FC General Assembly in 1931, Renwick had the rare distinction of being chosen to the same office in 1960, the tercentenary year of the Scottish Reformation. He supported the Inter-Varsity Fellowship,* and was a popular lecturer and preacher at university centres throughout the UK, specializing in early and Celtic Church* studies. He was awarded a DD by Edinburgh University in 1945. His published works include *The Story of the Church* (L, 1958, ²Leicester, 1985) and *The Story of the Scottish Reformation* (L, 1960).

G. N. M. Collins, *Annals of the Free Church of Scotland 1900-1986* (E, n.d.), 36; *FCSR*, March, 1965.

J. D. MacMillan

Renwick, James (1662-88), Scottish Covenanter* and field-preacher.* Born at Moniaive in Dumfries-shire, the only surviving son of godly parents, he was given a good education, graduating at Edinburgh University in 1681. In the same year the execution of Donald Cargill,* at which he was present, prompted him to cast in his lot unreservedly with the adherents of Cargill and Richard Cameron,* and to join with them in forming their United Societies* for mutual support and correspondence. Through their instrumentality he was sent to Holland, where he studied divinity at the University of Groningen and received ordination in May 1683. On his return to Scotland he was formally called by the Societies as their minister, and despite the severity of the laws against irregular preaching he immediately commenced a career of preaching in the fields. He was soon noticed by the government, and proclaimed a traitor and rebel. In the face of constant dangers, and often fragile health, he continued to pursue an active ministry, preaching wherever he could find opportunity, and framing statements and declarations vindicating the Societies' position. The publication of the Societies' *Apologetical Declaration* in 1684, about which Renwick is said to have expressed misgivings, led the government to intensify the persecution to almost unparalleled severity. Renwick also came under attack from extremists on his own side, some of whom disputed the validity of his ordination. Others criticized him for refusing to support the Earl of Argyll's uprising in 1685, which in Renwick's view was not based on conformity to the Covenants.* To vindicate himself and the Societies, he produced in 1687 the *Informatory Vindication*,* giving a brief compendium of the Societies' principles, and justifying their stand. After many hair-breadth escapes, Renwick was finally captured in Edinburgh, and on being tried and convicted for treason was executed in the Grassmarket on 17 February 1688.

Renwick was the last to suffer during the twenty-eight years of the persecution in Scotland. Though firm and uncompromising in his views of public affairs, he was kindly and sensitive in his personal relationships, inspiring intense loyalty among his followers and dealing courteously at all times with opponents. Possessed of an active and vigorous mind, and a maturity of judgment beyond his years, he was responsible more than anyone for guiding the forces of resistance during the sharpest period of the persecution.

A. Shields, *Life* in *Biographia Presbyteriana* (E, 1827), II; (ed.) T. Houston, *Spiritual Support and Consolation in Difficult Times* (Paisley, 1865); W. H. Carslaw, *The Life and Letters of James Renwick* (E, 1893); *id.*, *The Life and Times of James Renwick* (Paisley, 1901); J. Howie, *Scots Worthies* (ed. W. H. Carslaw, E, 1871), 525–49; *Cloud of Witnesses* (ed. J. H. Thomson, E, 1871), 471–91; *DNB* XLVIII, 23–5.

M. Grant

Resby, James, *see* Lollards.

Rescissory Act (1661), *see* Restoration.

Resolutioners, those in the CofS who approved of the 'Public Resolutions' of Parliament (December 1650), repealing laws obstructing the raising of an army for the defence of the kingdom.

Most Scots were horrified at the execution of Charles I* and quickly proclaimed Charles II* king. He agreed 'for the outward part' to subscribe the Covenants* and establish Presbyterianism.* The Scots army was partly purged of 'Malignants' (enemies to the Covenants* and Reformed religion) and was routed by Cromwell at Dunbar on 3 September 1650. The Church now divided as to the appropriate course of action. Patriotism and a considerable amount of credulity in regard to Charles II's sincerity led some to rethink the exclusion of those driven from government and army by the Act of Classes (*see* Engagement). They hoped Charles would be more amenable to the Covenants and to presbytery after the defeat of the English.

The Remonstrants (*see* Protesters), on the other hand, deplored the hasty admission of Charles II to the Covenants, the toleration of Malignants, backsliding, etc. The 1650 Commission of the General Assembly acknowledged the Remonstrance contained some 'sadd truethts', but it nevertheless urged the Church not to give comfort to the enemy by 'speaking disrespectfully of the public, just, and necessarie Resolutions', and justified their support of allowing all but a few to join in the defence of the kingdom by various arguments from Scripture and 'sanctified prudence'. They believed the English 'sectaries' to be the main threat.

In response to some 'Public Resolutions' to this effect, with a question from the Estates if the Act of Classes might be repealed, the Commission answered affirmatively, and advised presbyteries to 'censure any who persuade or preach contrary' to the Resolutions. The actions of the General Assembly of summer 1651 against the Protesters effectively split the CofS. In spite of efforts for peace and union by some, notably James Durham* and Robert Blair,* the Church remained divided until overtaken by the Restoration* and the reimposition of episcopacy.*

Robert Baillie* perhaps typifies the Resolutioner line of thought. He was inclined to a naive trust in the King, believed that 'a defence of our life and countrey in extreame necessitie' was justified, and that 'our former strickness had been unadvysed and unjust' (*Letters and Journals*, E, 1842, III, 126). He considered the Protesters* in formal rebellion against Church and state (*ibid.*, 132). On behalf of the Resolutioners he attempted in 1657 to enlist the support of some of his English friends, giving a rather one-sided summary of the state of affairs, but received scant encouragement in reply (*ibid.*, 346). The Resolutioners sent James Sharp* to London, a move which had a measure of success, but Sharp betrayed their trust (*ibid.*, 484; R. Wodrow,* *Analecta*, E, 1842, I, 21).

After the Restoration and disillusionment with Sharp, James Wood* reputedly confessed: 'Alace [alas], I see nou the Remonstrants wer in the right; the Resolutions have ruined us! For my oun part, I still hated breaches and separation, and that made me doe as I did' (*ibid.*, II, 118–19).

See also Protesters; Commonwealth and Protectorate; Douglas, Robert.

The Records of the Commissions of the General Assemblies of the Church of Scotland, vols II and III, ed. A. F. Mitchell and J. Christie (E, 1896, 1909); *Register of the Consultations of the Ministers of Edinburgh ... 1652–1657* and *... 1657–1660*, 2 vols (E, 1921, 1930); *Diary of Sir Archibald Johnston of Wariston, 1650–1654*, ed. D. H. Fleming (E, 1919) and *... 1655–1660*, ed. J. D. Ogilvie (E, 1940); James Beattie, *History of the Church of Scotland During the Commonwealth* (E, 1842).

D. C. Lachman

Restoration, the return of monarchy, in the person of Charles II,* in 1660. The Restoration was welcomed in Scotland, but since it was unconditional there was apprehension about what sort of settlement would follow. The Church was deeply split between the Resolutioner* and the Protester* factions, each hoping for royal favour. The Protesters based their hopes on the fact that Charles II had signed the Covenants* in 1650, but when some of them attempted to meet to remind him of his obligations as a covenanted King they were arrested: the fact that they had virtually disowned the King's cause in 1650–1 meant that he would never trust them. Action against the Protesters encouraged the Resolutioners, and they also took heart from a promise by Charles in August 1661 that he would maintain Church government in Scotland as it was established by law. Since Charles I* had ratified the work of the Glasgow Assembly,* surely his son's promise meant that Presbyterianism* would be maintained. But in March 1661 Parliament passed the Act Rescissory, declaring all public legislation passed in the Covenanters' parliaments up to 1649 null and void, and though legislation ratified by Charles II in 1650-1 was not mentioned, it too was in practice regarded as null.

The Act Rescissory was the basis for the Restoration Settlement of religion in Scotland, and if fully implemented would have returned the Church to the position it had been in at the time of the rebellion against Charles I. Moves were soon made in this direction. The appointment of bishops began, and in 1662 acts formally re-established Episcopacy,* outlawed the Covenants, banned conventicles,* and re-introduced patronage.* However, the more provocative of Charles I's innovations were quietly abandoned. The employment of bishops in leading roles in civil government, which had alienated the nobility, was not revived: though the two archbishops were made members of the Privy Council,* only one other bishop was appointed to it in Charles II's reign, and it was made clear to all bishops that they were to keep out of politics and avoid upsetting the nobility. When in 1669 an Act of Supremacy was passed asserting the power of the Crown in ecclesiastical matters, it was aimed as much at the pretensions of a few bishops as against Presbyterian dissidents. The Restoration settlement also abandoned Arminian* theology (which had threatened Calvinist* orthodoxy under Charles I), the Five Articles of Perth,* the 1636 Book of Canons* and the 1637 *Book of Common Prayer.*

Thus there was a good deal of moderation shown. But why was Episcopacy restored, a deeply unpopular move that did much to undermine the whole settlement? Charles's motives were mixed. Some of his most ardent supporters had suffered from Presbyterian persecution in the past, and were determined on revenge. The King himself found it hard to forget the humiliations inflicted on him in 1650-1. Events since 1637 seemed to confirm the argument that Presbyterianism was incompatible with monarchy. Finally, establishing Episcopacy in Scotland maintained uniformity with England.

No settlement could have been contrived which would be acceptable to all. It was virtually inevitable that the Protesters would be purged. It was hoped, however, that nearly all the Resolutioner ministers could be reconciled to the settlement, and at first it seemed that this would be the case. They had wanted to retain Presbyterianism, but many were ready to accept moderate Episcopacy: all thought of resistance to the Crown was discredited. A final blow to Resolutioner morale was the acceptance of an archbishopric by James Sharp.*

However, the expectation that only relatively small numbers of ministers would refuse to accept the settlement and have to be purged was thwarted, primarily by retrospective aspects of the act restoring patronage. Instead of just ruling that in future appointments the rights of patrons would be restored, it specified that all existing ministers whose appointments had been made ignoring the rights of patrons must now, humiliatingly, seek presentation from the restored patron and collation from the bishop of the diocese. This was the last straw for many ministers, concentrated in the Western Lowlands and, to a lesser extent, in Fife. About 270 were therefore deprived of their parishes in 1662-3 – well over a quarter of the total number of ministers. Moreover, most of these ministers retained the support of many of their parishioners. Attempts to prevent the former ministers holding worship in conventicles* for their supporters and to force the latter to attend their parish churches led to escalating bitterness and violent resistance, with the army being used to enforce religious conformity.

The blunder over the way in which patronage was introduced undermined the whole Restoration settlement, turning what might have been a limited, containable problem of religious dissent into a major challenge to the regime. It showed some flexibility in trying to deal with the problem: when harsh persecution led to rebellion, as in 1666 and 1679 (*see* Rullion Green; Bothwell Bridge), more conciliatory policies were tried. The First and Second Indulgences* of 1669 and 1672 sought to 'comprehend' dissident ministers in the Est.C by offering them easy terms for returning to it; and the Third Indulgence of 1679 offered toleration* (under state supervision) for Presbyterians to worship outside the establishment. But neither repression or moderation worked: the former increased bitterness and drove dissidents to adopt more inflexible positions, while the latter allowed the conventicles of the dissidents to spread more widely than ever. Thus the Restoration period (1660-88) culminated in the Killing Times* of the 1680s. The pro-RC policies of James VII(II)* exacerbated the problem, and the running sore of religious dissent increasingly discredited the regime, contributing to its collapse in 1688.

J. Buckroyd, *Church and State in Scotland, 1660-81* (E, 1980); G. Donaldson, *Scotland. James V to James VII* (E, 1965), 358-84; G. Davies, *The Restoration of Charles II* (L, 1955), 215-33; G. Davies and P. H. Hardacre, 'The Restoration of the Scottish Episcopacy, 1660-1', *Jrnl. of British Stud.*, (1961), 32-51.

D. Stevenson

Revivals, spiritual movements of unusual power which have manifested themselves mainly in the Protestant Churches of the land. 'Revival', which has been an important dimension of Scottish Church history, can be defined in a number of different ways.

First, the term can be applied to the revitalization of a body which once possessed spiritual life, but which has lost its former vigour. 'Revival' in this sense presumes that there has already been some degree of vitality in the body. Thus, Christian believers in a church may be stimulated in such a way that their new, reinforced commitment to Christ begins to energize the church in a dramatic fashion, leading to a deep concern for the unconverted, and spilling out into the community, with the result that spiritual concern is aroused widely, and people who have been 'awakened' seek spiritual counsel.

The second definition of 'revival', as a movement which 'awakens' the unregenerate to a sense of sin and spiritual lostness, is the best known application of the word. In this context, the term is imprecisely used in English, since the unregenerate possess no earlier spiritual vitality. The application is, however, entirely valid if the movement has begun in a revitalized body of earlier believers. Nevertheless, the English term is used with increasing imprecision with the passage of time and the introduction of new 'techniques'; it eventually shades into 'renewal' (*see* Charismatic Movement) or even 'spiritual response in a small group of people'. In Gaelic* the term regularly used of a major movement in a community is *dùsgadh* ('awakening', in the same sense as 'wakening from sleep'). Those who have experienced revival movements in the Highlands* frequently testify to a time of 'awakening' preceding their conversion. Such 'awakening' might require the institution of regular meetings to counsel those who were *fo chùram anama* ('under concern for the soul'), and further 'fellowship meetings' are sometimes provided to nurture new converts. As people are brought into churches from unbelief, revival makes new demands of these churches in instructing the converts, many of whom will have had little or no previous contact with the Christian faith.

Third, the term has come to be used more recently of the reassertion or rediscovery of aspects of doctrine or practice which have been neglected in the life of a congregation or Church. Thus it could be argued that the Reformation* was a 'revival' in the sense that it included the rediscovery of the primacy of the Scriptures and the reassertion of certain doctrines which were once more prominent in the life of the pre-Reformation Church. Similarly, it may be argued that the Evangelical Revival of the eighteenth century, which was particularly marked in England (A. S. Wood, *The Inextinguishable Blaze*, Exeter, ²1967) and Wales (D. Ll. Morgan, *The Great Awakening in Wales*, L, 1988) and influenced Scotland, was grounded in a return to a practical pietism and to a more personalized expression of the Christian faith than was fashionable in the institutional Church. Even in the context of smaller, localized spiritual movements in Scotland which are popularly termed 'revivals', it is sometimes possible to detect a rediscovery of apparently 'forgotten' or 'discarded' doctrines (e.g. the sovereignty of God, human accountability). 'Revival' may thus include an element of reasserted doctrinal conservatism which, when given due emphasis, becomes a potent force within a congregation, Church, or a community. Nevertheless, 'revival' is generally identified in terms of the first two definitions.

Revival operates most powerfully within communities in which people are linked or bonded together by similar cultural aspirations and by similar occupations, whether coal-mining, fishing, farming or crofting. The importance of the community is emphasized by Duncan Campbell,* who was instrumental in the Lewis Revival of 1949–53: 'Revival is a going of God among His people, and an awareness of God laying hold of the community. Here we see the difference between a successful campaign and revival; in the former we may see many brought to a saving knowledge of the truth . . . but in revival the fear of God lays hold upon the community, moving men and women, who until then had no concern for spiritual things, to seek after God' (C. N. Peckham, *Heritage of Revival*, E, 1986, 165).

The profound sense of the immanence of the Almighty in a community during a revival is further described by James Packer: 'Times of revival bring a deep sense of being always in God's sight; spiritual things become overwhelmingly real, and God's truth becomes overwhelmingly powerful, both to wound and to heal; conviction of sin becomes intolerable; repentance goes deep; faith springs up strong and assured; spiritual understanding grows quick and keen; and converts mature in a very short time. Christians become fearless in witness and tireless in their Saviour's service' (J. I. Packer, *Keep in Step with the Spirit*, L, 1984, 256–7).

These, of course, are the characteristics of 'ideal' revival, but revivals can also produce their share of spurious 'conversions' and they can be profoundly disturbing experiences for 'saint' and 'sinner' alike. While congregations and Churches may indeed be revitalized in such circumstances, they may also be fragmented, and revival, which often provokes strong opposition, is not always the panacea of popular evangelical thought. It releases impulses which create new modes of expression, new allegiances to influential leaders and new alignments within denominations. The creative power of revival movements generally requires to be controlled and structured. This may result in the formation of yet another denomination, which in due time experiences further waves of revival.

ROOTS OF REVIVAL. The earliest recorded revivals in Scotland occurred immediately before and soon after 1600, at a time when Europe generally was settling into 'established' post-Reformation ecclesiastical patterns, which were not always regarded as beneficial or desirable by certain Reformed Christians. In the face of conflict with unacceptable forms of Church polity or practice, imposed by government or the Crown, devotion was strengthened among dissident groups who felt that they must preserve the old and true order. Scottish revivals in Ayrshire at Stewarton and Irvine in 1625, and at the Kirk of Shotts in Lanarkshire in 1630, occurred among Presbyterian bodies who were opposed to Erastianism (*see* Church and State) and episcopacy* (John Gillies, *Historical Collections relating to Remarkable Periods of the Success of the Gospel*, ²Kelso, 1845, 197–8). Ministers who were associated with these revivals, such as David Dickson* of Irvine, became prominent figures among the Covenanters* after 1638, and they wrote influential books and tracts, which not only stimulated Presbyterian piety, but also preserved the memory of great 'warks' of God. The signing of the National Covenant* in various parts of the country and its adoption by individual Presbyterian churches often generated scenes of deep emotion and soul-searching, as signatories examined their lives in the light of their 'covenant' with God. The sense of danger also deepened spiritual impressions, as happened at a celebration of the Lord's Supper at Obsdale, Kiltearn, E. Ross-shire, in 1675, when 'there was a plentiful effusion of the Spirit upon a great many present; and the oldest Christians there declared that they had not been witnesses to the like' (J. MacInnes, *The Evangelical Movement in the Highlands of Scotland*, A, 1951, 155). Links between earlier Covenanting experience and the revivals of the eighteenth and nineteenth centuries can be discerned in both the Highlands and the Lowlands.

Although Scottish revivals have a native root, they must nevertheless be placed in a wider international context of religious experience. After 1600 the population of Europe was becoming more mobile, as exploration opened up the possibility of emigration* to a New World across the Atlantic. Persecution could stimulate emigration, as happened in 1620 when the Pilgrim Fathers left England and established a colony in New England. As early as 1625 hard-pressed Scottish Presbyterians were making attempts to reach America. Persecution and emigration together could lead to apocalyptic views of the New World, thus strengthening the resolve of Christians to emulate and recreate biblical patterns for Church and state. In both Europe and North America before 1700 the concept of a 'peculiar people', specially singled out for God's blessing, fused with new political aspirations. When God was believed to be among his people, especially at times of religious or political stress, revivals could emerge (R. Bloch, *Visionary Republic*, C, 1985).

From the eighteenth century, Scottish revivals can be seen as part of a North Atlantic phenomenon, in which spiritual impulses were transmitted from Britain to America and vice versa, and also between countries within the British Isles (R. Carwardine, *Transatlantic Revivalism*, Westport, CN, 1978). Scottish divines were closely informed about events in North America, especially in New England, through letters and publications, and interest increased as emigration from Scotland led to the provision of Presbyterian ministers for the colonies. The revival or 'surprising work of God' which had emerged in 1734-5 in Jonathan Edwards'* church at Northampton, Massachusetts, and was at its height during 1740-2, was publicized through his writings (reissued as *Jonathan Edwards on Revival*, E, 1984). The events of the American 'Great Awakening' in general probably served to heighten spiritual expectancy in Scotland, and strengthened indigenous Scottish desires for revival. John Sutherland, minister of Golspie, gave his parishioners regular information about 'the blessed and wonderful success of the Gospel in the British colonies in America' (MacInnes, *Evangelical Movement*, 160). Already in the 1720s spiritual movements were apparent in the northern Highlands, and in 1739 in the parish of Nigg, E. Ross, during the ministry of John Balfour, an awakening took place. In 1742 a major revival began in the Lowland parish of Cambuslang, and combined several influences, including the Covenanting traditions known to the minister, William McCulloch,* the example of the Great Awakening and the potency of the Evangelical Revival, proceeding in England and Wales. The British and American dimensions were bound together in the person of the great itinerant evangelist, George Whitefield,* who preached at Cambuslang. Ministers from Highland and Lowland parishes who visited Cambuslang spread its influence farther afield. American and Scottish connections were reinforced by the establishment of the 'Convert for Prayer' in the wake of the Cambuslang Revival (A. Fawcett, *The Cambuslang Revival*, E, 1971).

Further interaction of American and Scottish influences can be observed in the nineteenth century. Since 1800 American preachers have continued to stimulate the currents of revival in Scotland, most noticeably through the campaigns of D. L. Moody* in the 1870s, and their contribution extends into the twentieth century, although with less conspicuous results. It is apparent too that Scottish revivals not infrequently occur at the same time as, and are influenced by, movements elsewhere in the British Isles. For instance, in addition to its American dimensions, the so-called '1859 revival' in Scotland (in effect a sequence of revivals, lasting into the early 1860s) needs to be seen in the context of contemporaneous movements in Ulster and Wales* (J. E. Orr, *The Second Evangelical Awakening*, L, 1949). The Welsh Revival of 1904-5 (E. Evans, *The Welsh Revival of 1904*, Bridgend, 1969) also contributed directly to a small surge of evangelical activity in Scotland.

The influence of Scottish revivals on other lands should not be underestimated. The Cambuslang Revival of 1742 had a catalytic effect on movements in America, England and Germany. Emigration* from the Scottish Highlands, especially in the nineteenth century, took place against a background of intermittent awakenings, and Highland settlers in colonies from North Carolina to Ontario were well aware of events in the mother country. Highland preachers who had experienced revivals in their native areas sometimes took their fervour overseas to their fellow-countrymen in Canada and America. Foreign missionary* endeavour after 1800 gained strength and personnel in consequence of Scottish revivals.

PATTERNS OF REVIVAL. The earliest recorded revivals in Scotland were usually associated with the celebration of the Lord's Supper.* In the seventeenth and eighteenth centuries this was a relatively rare event, sometimes known in the Lowlands as the 'Occasion'. Attracting participants from far and near, it created a sense of spiritual expectancy, especially when notable ministers presided (see Communion Seasons). The revival at the Kirk of Shotts occurred during the weekend of the Supper, and impressions were particularly deep on the Monday thereafter, when John Livingstone* was preaching. The Cambuslang Revival incorporated the celebration of two large Communions, which were attended by many thousands. The Lord's Supper was a focal point of the revivals which were directly influenced by that at Cambuslang, principally those at Kilsyth, Stirlingshire, and Muthill, Perthshire, although it is important to note that the revivals in these parishes had begun before the Communions were celebrated. The Communions drew vast audiences, and spread the impulses of revival farther afield. The Lowland Communions and associated revivals attracted Highland participants, and were one of the means by which the seeds of Evangelicalism* were implanted in the Highlands. Dugald Buchanan* attended the revivals at Cambuslang, Kilsyth and Muthill, and John Porteous, minister of Kilmuir Easter, Ross-shire, visited Kilsyth. Gaelic-speaking people from Cowal, Argyll, were in the habit of attending the Communions in Greenock and Glasgow, and, filled with spiritual enthusiasm, returned to parishes which, at the end of the eighteenth century, were held by Moderate* ministers. The importance of the Lord's Supper, although diminishing in the Lowland revival context after 1800, is again attested at Kilsyth in 1839, under the preaching of William Chalmers Burns.*

In the Highlands the pattern of sacrament-based revivals had begun to emerge in certain parts, chiefly the northern mainland, by the end of the seventeenth century, but it spread most vigorously in the nineteenth century (A. MacRae, *Revivals in the Highlands and Islands in the Nineteenth Century*, Stirling, 1905). The sacrament-based revivals were then closely linked with the growing body of evangelical Presbyterian ministers who came to Highland parishes after 1800, and who continued the practice of earlier ministers like Thomas Hog* of Kiltearn in seeking clear signs of 'a work of grace upon the souls' of those who partook. The Lord's Supper, often celebrated in natural amphitheatres in the open air, was thus transformed from a time of secular sport and merriment to an occasion of soul-searching solemnity, suffused in vibrant expectancy. Communion rolls were reduced drastically in certain parishes such as Uig, Lewis, where Alexander MacLeod* (admitted 1824) ensured that the roll was cut from 800 to six. The Lord's table thus came to be 'fenced' against those who would partake 'unworthily', and only those with credible professions of faith participated. In this way, the significance of the Supper was heightened, and participation became one of the hall-marks of saving faith in individual lives. The demarcation between the 'worthy' and the 'unworthy' could create a tension which would be ignited into revival by the diet of preaching during the Communion weekend. Certain evangelical ministers became famous for their powerful preaching at the time of the Lord's Supper, and they would frequently travel from their own parishes to assist at Communions in other areas. None was more famous than John MacDonald* of Ferintosh, whose great Gaelic oratory became one of the highlights of Highland Communions in the period before 1850. In September 1816, for example, MacDonald was the preacher at the Communion at Ardeonaig, on the south side of Loch Tay, Perthshire. Deep spiritual interest was already emerging in the district, due to the labours of dissenting preachers and the Royal Bounty* missionary, Robert Findlater, but MacDonald's preaching on the Sunday brought matters to a climax: 'Mr Macdonald himself seemed to be in raptures. There were several people who cried aloud, but the general impression seemed to be a universal melting under the Word. The people of God themselves were as deeply affected as others, and many have confessed they never witnessed such a scene' (W. J. Couper, *Scottish Revivals*, D, 1918, 104-5).

The efforts of evangelical ministers in encouraging revivals in the Highlands were augmented by the contribution of itinerant preachers (*see* Itinerancy), predominantly of dissenting persuasion, who began to penetrate the region from the end of the eighteenth century. The first such preachers were sent to the parish of Kilbrandon and Kilchattan, Argyll, by the Relief* Church about 1784 to gather the fruit of a revival initiated by John Smith.* Relief missionaries were subsequently active in Kintyre and mainland Argyll in 1797, with signs of deep spiritual interest (*see* Douglas, Niel). The itinerant preachers of the Haldane* movement brought further revival enthusiasm to the southern parts of the Highlands, where John Farquharson* was at the centre of a revival in Breadalbane, Perthshire, in 1800-4. Soon afterwards he was active in Skye, and laid the foundation of a vigorous Evangelicalism which contributed to the emergence of Baptist* churches and a strong evangelical presence within the CofS (D. E. Meek, 'Evangelical Missionaries in the Early Nineteenth-Century Highlands', *Scottish Studies*, 28 (1987), 1-34). A similar development occurred in Arran, where Baptist, Independent* and CofS preachers co-operated in the movement which had appeared in the island by 1812. Spiritual impulses were transmitted to other islands (Islay, Colonsay, Mull and Tiree) before 1820, frequently by itinerant preachers who passed through Arran on their westward journeys. Revival movements emanating from the southern isles and from the western mainland converged in Lewis in 1823, when an intense awakening was initiated, lasting until the early 1830s.

A major development of the nineteenth century was the growth of Highland revival movements which were not so closely associated with the celebration of the Lord's Supper. Independents and other dissenters, who contributed greatly to this new pattern, generally attributed less significance to this sacrament, offering it only to members of their churches as a sign of their Christian unity, but doing so much more frequently than in the Presbyterian Churches. Itinerant preachers spread evangelical fervour more evenly throughout the countryside, since they did not depend on assembling the people in mass gatherings, but would gather small bodies together in corn-fields, barns and cottages at any time of the week. Revival impulses were also transmitted powerfully by the itinerant schoolmasters of the Gaelic School Societies;* some urged their pupils to examine their lives in the light of what they had learnt from their reading of the Gaelic Bible,* while others took to preaching in parishes that were devoid of evangelical ministry, and occasionally founded revival-based churches, of which they became the first pastors (*see* Grant,

Alexander). Under such circumstances the great sacramental occasions of the CofS were no more than a temporary means of retaining the allegiance of its Highland evangelical wing, which began to show early signs of a propensity towards nonconformity, brought to a head in the Disruption* of 1843.

Until the 1830s Scottish revivals were predominantly associated with the rural areas, and with rural villages or small towns. By the mid-century, however, revival interest was manifesting itself in the cities. After 1839, in the wake of the revival at Kilsyth, William Chalmers Burns* was preaching in several large towns and cities in the Lowlands, including Dundee (where he was assistant to Robert Murray M'Cheyne*), Perth and Edinburgh. The volume of addresses on *The Revival of Religion* (E, 1840) contains contributions by prominent ministers who were almost all in city charges. The '1859 Revival' represented a series of movements which operated powerfully in cities, towns and rural areas, and introduced new features such as wide-ranging itinerant evangelists who preached throughout the land, in the Highlands and the Lowlands. In the later nineteenth century, the larger towns and cities assumed increasing importance as centres which were likely to be frequented by major visiting evangelists, such as the American, D. L. Moody. The impact of Moody's preaching in Glasgow in 1874, which attracted 7,000 people on the final evening in the Kibble Palace, was felt as far afield as the Inner Hebridean island of Tiree, where a strong revival affected the local Baptist church in that year (D. E. Meek, *Island Harvest: Tiree Baptist Church 1838–1988*, E, 1988).

The American connections apparent in the presence of Moody had consequences for the theological base of nineteenth-century revivals, especially in the development of 'revivalism', in which 'revivalist techniques' become prominent. Rather than emphasize the sovereignty of God in sending waves of revival as he willed, it became popular to believe that revival could be expected and achieved regularly, provided that certain conditions were fulfilled. The main figure in this development was Charles Grandison Finney (K. J. Hardman, *Charles Grandison Finney*, Syracuse, NY, 1987), whose *Lectures on the Revivals of Religion* (NY, 1835) had an immediate effect on James Morison* in 1839. Preaching 'for revival' became an acknowledged form of evangelism, and flourished strongly, especially in some dissenting circles. Finney's influence struck Scotland when the CofS was undergoing the Ten Years' Conflict* preceding the Disruption, and the prelude to the emergence of the FCS was marked by revival movements in the Highlands and the Lowlands, in both town and country.

In the twentieth century revivals associated with the cities have been relatively rare. Some, however, have affected individual urban churches, such as Charlotte Baptist Chapel in Edinburgh, which was dramatically revitalised through the ministry of Joseph Kemp* after 1905 (W. Whyte, *Revival in Rose Street*, E, n.d.). Kemp, who was influenced by the views of Finney, visited South Wales during the 1904–5 Revival, and transmitted his enthusiasm to his church, which grew rapidly from fifty to 900 members. Nevertheless, the prevailing pattern after 1900 has tended to show revivals emerging on the coastal or island fringes of Scotland, within rural or seafaring communities. Strong revival movements were prominent among the fisherfolk of the north-west in the late nineteenth century, and emerged periodically after 1900. In 1921 the Wick-born cooper-turned-evangelist, Jock Troup,* was at the centre of a revival movement among the fishermen stationed at Yarmouth during a poor herring season. Troup returned to Fraserburgh to preach, fishermen brought the revival impulses back from Yarmouth, and a significant movement gripped the Moray Firth coast (*see* Fisherfolk, Missions to). The Inner Hebrides were also affected by revivals in this period (*see* Taylor, Francis William), and the crofters of Lewis experienced a powerful movement in 1949–53 (*see* Campbell, Duncan).

SPIRITUAL AND SOCIAL CONTEXTS OF REVIVALS. Given the spread and variety of revival movements throughout Scotland since the 1620s, it is difficult to provide a picture of their spiritual and social contexts in a comprehensive manner. It is, however, apparent that a recurrent feature of revival is the centrality of prayer and of preaching. The beginnings of revivals are frequently traced to faithful intercession by small bands of people or even by individuals; the development of revivals stimulates further prayer, and can result in the creation of prayer-chains which cross oceans and continents. Preaching is pre-eminent, and it would seem that Old Testament texts, especially from the Prophets, assume considerable importance as people seek God to 'come down' among them. Behind this lies the equation of Church and people with Israel in its backslidden and parlous state prior to the Exile, and there is an emphasis on the need to renew the individual's covenant with God. The post-millennial expectation that the 'earth would be filled with the glory of God' is apparent in preaching and writing until the middle of the nineteenth century, and revivals before 1850 can often be seen as part of a wider movement which issued in missionary* endeavour and anticipated the future glory of the Church (I. Murray, *The Puritan Hope*, E, ^{2}1975; *see* Millennialism).

After 1850 the abandoning of post-millennialism in favour of pre-millennialism may have dulled the eschatological perceptions of Evangelicalism, with the result that revivals came to be regarded as occasional rays of light in a darkening world, rather than as harbingers of the final effulgence of the Church. Nevertheless, the central issues of revival have remained unchanged: spiritual lostness and the danger of eternal damnation are primary concerns in most revivals, with a strong focus on the mediatorial role and substitutionary atonement of Christ. In the twentieth century, the emphasis on revival has been maintained most consistently by bodies which have links with the Holiness movement of the late nineteenth century, such as the Salvation Army* and, more noticeably, the Faith

Mission.* It needs to be observed, however, that revivals have no particular links with specific denominations, and that they frequently operate beyond the normal conventions of religious structures. In the course of a revival individuals may find themselves confronted with spiritual issues while they are in the middle of their normal business, and conversions can occur beyond the church walls and even beyond the reach of preaching. The impact of conversions among peer groups may lead to what may seem to be a contagion, as the spirit of revival spreads throughout a community.

Historical awareness of past revivals and the desire to experience similar movements at regular periods are also noticeable contributory factors. An expectancy that God can and will revive his Church is central to revival, although the 'means' may vary. The influential addresses on *The Revival of Religion* were published in 1840, almost exactly a century after the series of revivals beginning with that at Cambuslang in 1742, and the wave of Scottish revivals beginning in 1839 reached its peak before 1846. It was common for preachers to refer to revivals of an earlier day, and locations which had been the scene of particularly strong movements were sometimes visited at intervals by evangelists who alluded to previous happenings in the hope of encouraging similar results. When preaching at Kilsyth in 1839, William Chalmers Burns referred directly and effectively to the revival at the Kirk of Shotts in 1630; when preaching at Moulin, Perthshire, in 1840, he reminded his audience of the revival in the parish in 1799, during the ministry of Alexander Stewart* (W. C. Burns, *Revival Sermons*, E, 1869; rp. 1980, 173). In certain churches, expectation of regular revivals produced a 'revival cycle', which repeated itself after a number of years; the Baptist church in Tiree, for example, experienced significant movements on an approximate ten-year cycle, from 1839 to 1940.

Secular circumstances which affect society in general can create a desire for deeper spiritual experience and thus help to stimulate revivals. The revivals of the seventeenth century occurred at a time of political and ecclesiastical uncertainty, and it is noticeable that several revivals (including that at Cambuslang) took place within the five years prior to the Jacobite* Rising* of 1745. The wave of revivals which began in the Highlands after 1800 occurred against a background of great social instability. The failure of crops, especially the potato, in the period 1836–46 was influential in making people look for 'the bread which perisheth not', and they were therefore more responsive to the Christian message (D. E. Meek, 'Evangelicalism and Emigration: Aspects of the Role of Dissenting Evangelicalism in Highland Emigration to Canada', in G. MacLennan (ed.), *Proceedings of the First North American Congress of Celtic Studies*, Ottawa, 1988, 15–35). Disease too gave cause for the consideration of eternal issues. The cholera epidemic of 1832, for instance, led to spiritual movements in different localities in the British Isles, including the Highlands. It is also possible that an inherent interest in the supernatural in rural (agricultural) and coastal (fishing) communities has intensified perceptions in times of revival (*cf.* S. Bruce, 'Social Change and Collective Behaviour; the Revival in Eighteenth-Century Ross-shire', *British Journal of Sociology* 34 (1983), 554–72).

Revivals can be opposed by forces within society, most frequently individuals, and sometimes Churches, that are unsympathetic to their aims. A community experiencing a religious revival may become strongly polarized, with vigorous expressions of disapproval from the opposing camp. The revival at Stewarton in 1623 was dubbed 'the Stewarton sickness' by 'the profane rabble of that time' (Fawcett, *Cambuslang Revival*, 53–4). During the Cambuslang Revival of 1742, there was strong opposition from the Secession* Church for theological reasons, and landlords and employers tried to prevent attendance by the ordinary people. 'Popular religion', with its associated field-preaching,* was a threat to the structures of the Est.C, and was believed to induce idleness by enticing workers, especially young people, from their labours (T. C. Smout, 'Born Again at Cambuslang; New Evidence on Popular Religion and Literacy in Scotland', *Past and Present* 97 (1982), 114–27). Revivals have also attracted accusations of emotionalism and licence. In the nineteenth century, especially after the introduction of revivalist 'techniques', preachers often went out of their way to emphasize their dislike of uncontrolled expressions of emotional release. Peter Grant,* of Grantown-on-Spey, stressed that the revival which came to his church in 1848 was not a display of 'enthusiasm', but involved only serious and sober-minded people, 'going about the concerns of their immortal souls' (letter to *The Baptist Magazine*, 1848).

RESULTS OF REVIVALS. One of the most obvious results of a revival is that it leads to the conversion of a significantly greater number of people than would usually profess faith through normal church activities. Spiritual interest within a community or an identifiable peer group (often young people in their late teens or early twenties) appears to erode the distinctiveness, or even the embarrassment, of individual response. It is, however, difficult to obtain accurate statistics which show the fruit of a revival in numerical terms. For several revivals, there are extant estimates of the number attending the service and sometimes there is some estimate of the number of converts. For example, at the Kirk of Shotts 'near five hundred had at that time a discernible change wrought on them, of whom most proved lively Christians afterwards', and this resulted in the 'sowing of a seed through Clydesdale' (Gillies, *Historical Collections*, 198). It was believed that about 3,000 people professed faith at the time of the Cambuslang Revival; in 1751 it was reported that communicant membership in Glasgow had increased by 1,200 after 1742, and had remained steady (Fawcett, *Cambuslang Revival*, 172). The period of revivals in 1859–61 probably produced a 10 per cent gain in membership in Presbyterian Churches (Orr, *Second Evangelical Awakening*, 77).

Besides substantial gains in membership,

Churches can experience a strengthening of leadership and of evangelistic activity as the result of revivals. The revivals of the early nineteenth century produced some of the most prominent ministers of the post-1843 FC, among them the brothers Archibald and Finlay Cook,* who were converted during the Arran revival of 1812. Other FC leaders, like John MacDonald of Ferintosh, were closely associated with Highland revivals. Lay leadership was also strengthened, especially in the 1859–61 revivals, when men like Brownlow North* and Hay MacDowall Grant* exercised powerful itinerant ministries. The supply of Gaelic-speaking pastors for Highland Baptist churches was heavily dependent upon revivals, and terminated when revivals in Baptist localities diminished in strength and number after the Second World War. This suggests that 'revival dependency', while productive at certain periods, can cause serious problems if it becomes exclusive of other methods of evangelism and recruitment.

If revivals are productive of converts and leaders, they can also create division within Churches, and contribute to the growth and formation of new ecclesiastical bodies. Thomas Gillespie,* founder of the Relief Church in 1761, was one of the preachers at the Cambuslang and Kilsyth revivals. Following the Cambuslang Revival of 1742, parishioners were not prepared to accept a Moderate minister presented to them by the Duke of Hamilton after the death of McCulloch in 1771, and many defected to the Relief congregation at Bellshill in 1774. Kilsyth also produced a Relief body, because of dissatisfaction with James Robe's* successor. In 1839 James Morison,* dismissed from the USec.C because of his espousal of Finneyite views, founded the Evangelical Union* of churches in Scotland, strongly committed to the application of new revival techniques. The FC itself emerged during a period of revival fervour, which reached its climax in Skye in 1842–3. It is also arguable that the Baptist and Congregational movements in Scotland owed their strength in large measure to a current of revival which centred on the work of James and Robert Haldane*. The 1859–61 revivals led to the establishment of the Brethren* movement in Scotland; prior to 1860 only four assemblies are known to have existed, but the foundations of many were laid in the decade before 1870, with at least a dozen in Lanarkshire alone (N. Dickson, 'Scottish Brethren: Division and Wholeness 1838–1916', *Christian Brethren Review Journal* 41, 1990, 5–41).

The evidence therefore suggests that revivals have brought ferment and considerable dislocation to Church life in Scotland. The view that 'denominational prejudices are forgotten during revivals' is also contradicted by the evidence. While co-operation between denominations and their ministers is commonly attested during revivals, and 'sectarianism' can be temporarily buried (as allegedly happened in Perth in 1860), the assertion of doctrinal or ecclesiological distinctiveness when bringing converts into the Churches can cause acrimony. The emergent Brethren movement of the 1860s recruited strongly from Baptist churches, and continued to do so thereafter, with accompanying accusations of proselytizing. This demonstrates that revivals may cause a weakening of commitment to existing ecclesiastical structures, with a tendency to create more 'personalized' groupings of like-minded individuals. New-found faith may cross old barriers, but it may also erect fresh ones.

Revivals have an effect on society beyond the Churches, most noticeably in the area of moral and social improvement. A recurrent theme of revivals is their impact on behavioural patterns, especially in relation to the consumption of alcohol. Converts forsake public-houses, and for a time these lose trade. Crime rates decline, and there is concern for the social condition of the poor and the underprivileged, leading to the establishment of missions such as Carrubbbers' Close in Edinburgh, which was instituted in 1858. Other bodies, like Aberdeen Sailors' Mission, founded in 1862, distributed tracts, sold Bibles, and provided elementary schooling. Although some people who are converted in times of revival may already have a familiarity with the Bible, revivals stimulate widespread interest in the Scriptures; in the nineteenth century many non-literate converts expressed a strong desire to read the Bible, and achieved literacy, frequently through Sunday schools* and, in the Highlands, the Gaelic School Societies.* Revival movements, which are often populist and egalitarian, may also help to create a sense of group solidarity which strengthens social and political action; thus the reaction against landlordism in the Highlands after 1880 owed much to previous spiritual awakenings (*see* Clearances).

Revivals influence the 'internal' lives of Churches as well as the 'external' community. While some revivals may be doctrinally conservative, others may lead to the erosion of doctrinal distinctiveness; the overall impact of Finney's 'methods' has been to stress the centrality of the human will in making 'decisions', in contrast to the doctrines of total depravity and effectual calling within orthodox Reformed theology. The Moody campaigns of the 1870s altered Scottish patterns of worship with regard to music.* The methods of Moody's soloist, Ira D. Sankey, had a formative effect on the diet of hymnology and music which came to prevail among dissenters after 1880, and influenced trends more generally, noticeably in the use of organs in churches (*see* Musical Instruments in Worship). Personal spiritual experience is an important feature of revivals, and often finds expression in new hymns (*see* Hymnology, English and Gaelic). In due time these 'revival hymns' become an integral part of normal worship within certain denominations.

Overall, revivals have contributed greatly to the changing complexion of the Scottish Protestant Churches since 1600, and their results have been by no means ephemeral. They are a constant reminder that even the most rigid ecclesiastical structures can be radically altered by spiritual forces which lie beyond their control. In times of lethargy, complacency and listlessness, revival movements have brought a healthy, and often very necessary, discomfort to those who are 'at ease in Zion' or heedless of spiritual concerns.

General background can be found in D. W. Bebbington, *Evangelicalism in Modern Britain* (L, 1989) and C. G. Brown, *The Social History of Religion in Scotland since 1730* (L, 1987). See also D. W. Bebbington (ed.), *The Baptists in Scotland* (G, 1988). There are numerous descriptions of Scottish revivals, but relatively few critical works. Most of the major accounts have been cited above; the most useful general compendia are Gillies, *Historical Collections*; Couper, *Scottish Revivals*; and MacRae, *Revivals in the Highlands and Islands in the Nineteenth Century*. Properly critical analyses exist mainly in academic articles; see especially I. A. Muirhead, 'The Revival as a Dimension of Scottish Church History', *RSCHS* 20 (1980), 179–96. Fawcett's *Cambuslang Revival* remains a landmark of sober, evangelical scholarship in this underworked field. Note also L. E. Schmidt, *Holy Fairs. Scottish Communions and American Revivals in the Early Modern Period* (Princeton, 1989); M. J. Crawford, *Seasons of Grace: Colonial New England's Revival Tradition in Its British Context* (NY, 1991).

D. E. Meek

Revolution, French *see* French Revolution.

Riccaltoun, Robert (1691–1769), minister in Hobkirk, Roxburghshire. Born near Jedburgh, Riccaltoun was educated there and at the University of Edinburgh. Though licensed in 1717, he was not ordained until 1725, to Hobkirk, where he served until his death, his only son John being called as assistant (and successor) in 1765.

Riccaltoun is best known for his anonymously published contributions to the Marrow controversy.* *The Politick Disputant: choice Instructions for Quashing a Stubborn Adversary. Gathered from, and exemplified in, the Learned Principal Hadow's Conduct in His late Appearances against The Marrow of Modern Divinity and its Friends* (E, 1722) was a devastating piece of satire combined with a penetrating analysis of James Hadow's* method and doctrine in *The Antinomianism of the Marrow of Modern Divinity Detected*. It was not only not answered, but was never so much as mentioned in print by the *Marrow*'s opponents. It possibly served as a model for John Witherspoon's* later *Ecclesiastical Characteristics*.

Riccaltoun published two further works relating to the controversy, *A Review of an Essay upon Gospel and Legal Preaching* (E, 1723) against a work by James Bannatine, an Edinburgh minister, which inculcated a moderate legalism, and *A Sober Enquiry into the Grounds of the Present Differences in the Church of Scotland* (E, 1723), an extensive examination of the controversy with particular attention to Hadow's *Antinomianism*. Riccaltoun attempted to mediate, though making it clear that the Marrow Brethren had the better argument and faulting Hadow for widening breaches rather than seeking peace. John Macleod* (*Scottish Theology*, E, ³1974, 158) refers to the *Sober Enquiry* 'as perhaps as able a piece of writing as was called forth in the whole of the controversy'.

Riccaltoun's son published a three-volume posthumous edition of his unprinted works (*The Works*, E, 1771–2), including essays on human nature, the nature of revelation and 'Notes and Observations upon Galatians'.

FES II, 119; *An Inquiry into . . . Letters on Theron and Aspasio* (L, G, E, 1762); D. C. Lachman, *The Marrow Controversy* (E, 1988).

D. C. Lachman

Richard (*d.*1178), Bishop of St Andrews. He was a chaplain in the household of King Malcolm IV (1141–65) when the King appointed him bishop in succession to Arnald (*d.*1162), previously abbot of Kelso. Richard was elected in 1163 and consecrated in 1165 at St Andrews by bishops of the Scottish Church in the King's presence. Unlike his predecessor, he was not granted legatine status in Scotland, probably due to strenuous lobbying at the papal court by the Archbishop of York and his agents. He died in the infirmary of the canons of St Andrews.

Little is known of Richard's episcopate. He was active in the building of the great cathedral church founded by Arnald, as his *acta* show; these also show a developing elaboration in the episcopal household as a body distinct from the priory of St Andrews. He came from a clerical family (his uncle was abbot of Holyrood), but he owed his promotion to service in the King's household. He consented to the Treaty of Falaise,* but must have benefited by Pope Alexander III's angry reaction to it.

Surviving *acta* in *Liber . . . Sancti Andree* (Bannatyne Club, E, 1841); mentioned in Chronicles of Melrose* and of Wyntoun* and Bower*; Dowden, 7–8; A. A. M. Duncan, *Scotland: the Making of the Kingdom* (E, 1975), 261–2, 270.

A. Macquarrie

Richard of St Victor (*d.*1173), medieval mystical writer and Trinitarian theologian. He was born in Scotland (according to a fourteenth-century epitaph) during the first quarter of the twelfth century. At a young age he became an Augustinian* canon regular in the famous Abbey of St Victor in Paris sometime before the death of the Abbot Gilduin in 1155. He became subprior by 1159 and prior in 1162. Highly reputed for piety and erudition, he answered many letters seeking advice and was visited by such notables as Pope Alexander III and Thomas Becket. St Victor was not only a contemplative abbey but also a school in close touch with intellectual trends in Paris, and possessed a rich library of biblical, patristic and medieval learning. He was influenced by the use, by his predecessor, Hugh of St Victor (*d.*1141), of allegorical exegesis of Scripture for moral, contemplative purposes, as well as by Anselm's theological methodology of seeking to understand profound truth 'by necessary reasons'.

Although a mystic, he was a very practical theologian, constantly correlating knowledge and virtue.

His scriptural interpretation, for all its allegorical weakness, has a Christological centre and practical end. He generally follows the medieval threefold interpretation of Scripture as history (what happened), allegory (what it signifies), and tropology (our duty). Sometimes he added a fourth category, 'mystical' (usually a Christological resolution of the problem). Although he was allegorical, he believed that the historical sense provided the basis for a deeper meaning and that the biblical story depicted spiritually significant events in the life of the believer, especially that it demonstrated the Christian's ascent from fear to joyful love of God. He composed numerous works, among them *The Twelve Patriarchs* (or *Benjamin Minor*), a 'tropological' interpretation of the significance of the twelve sons and one daughter of Jacob, concerned with mental and spiritual discipline, and *Benjamin Major* (or *The Mystical Ark*) concerned with meditation ('earnest mental concentration carefully confined to the object studied') and the six types of contemplation ('the mind's clear and untrammelled survey dispersed in all directions'). Contemplation is meant to advance the soul in a fruitful knowledge arising out of love.

In *The Trinity*, following the Anselmian methodology, he contemplates the three-in-oneness of the Trinity in terms of God's ultimate nature of love. He shows that love is never selfish, but is outgoing and must be shared with a worthy equal and thus requires two. But to be true charity, it must not only be given and received, but shared in community, on the analogy of family life, and so requires three. He derived a definition of personality from the Trinity. Rejecting Boethius' definition of 'individual substance of rational nature', he proposed God as a person-constituting being as three persons coinhering in the same substantial community of love yet with particular, inviolable 'incommunicable existence'.

Works in J. P. Migne (ed.), *Patrologia Latina*, vol. 196; *De Trinitate*, ed. J. Ribaillier (Paris, 1958), French tr. G. Salet (*Sources Chrét.* 63; Paris, 1969); selected works tr. G. A. Zinn in *Classics of Western Spirituality* series (L, 1979).

G. S. M. Walker, 'Richard of St Victor: An Early Scottish Theologian?', *SJT* 11 (1958), 37–52; J. Leclercq et al. (eds), *The Spirituality of the Middle Ages* (L, 1968).

D. F. Kelly

Richardson, Charles (1861–1942), Congregational* minister. Born in Wishaw, Lanarkshire, he received his religious formation in Wishaw's Evangelical Union* Church. After business experience followed by Glasgow University (MA, 1889), he trained at Glasgow's Evangelical Union Theological Hall and became pastor at Bathgate EU (1888–92), Duke Street EU, Leith (1892–8) and Montrose Street Congregational, Glasgow (1898–1924). It was, however, as Secretary to the Scottish Congregational Union, part-time and honorary 1900–18, full time 1924–41, that he became best known beyond his denomination. For most of those years his manse was his office. With his dislike of clerical dress and his manifest pastoral sense, he characterized the Congregational spirit, while his administrative ability held Congregationalism together in years of economic difficulty and insistently centralizing pressure. Richardson was to contemporary Scottish Congregationalism what Greville Ewing* had been a century earlier. As part-time Secretary, his chief contribution was to fuse the Congregational and Evangelical Union traditions; as full-time Secretary it lay in tighter organization. He bridged the two with his advocacy and co-ordination of the denomination's Central Fund, adopted in principle in 1913, introduced from 1916 and completed in 1926 with the attainment of its target of £50,000. His second period as Secretary saw the ordination of Vera Findlay,* Scotland's first woman minister ordained to a pastoral charge (*see* Sharpe, Jane), in 1929, and a permanent office in Glasgow from 1936. By now he was Scottish Congregationalism's representative figure, servicing its burgeoning committees, and twice serving as its President (1916–17, 1939–40), active in the Scottish Churches' Council from its inception (1926), and recipient of an honorary DD from Glasgow (1930). He was also a member of the BBC's Religious Advisory Committee (*see* Religious Broadcasting) and Honorary Secretary of the Scottish Temperance* Alliance.

Congregational Year Book (L, 1943), 453; H. Escott, *A History of Scottish Congregationalism* (G, 1960).

W. D. McNaughton

Richardson (Richardinus), Robert (1491–1572), early Protestant. He was born in Edinburgh and studied at St Andrews, being taught by John Major.* He became an Augustinian* canon at Cambuskenneth,* near Stirling, and published *Exegesis in Canonem divi Augustini...*, a Latin commentary on St Augustine's monastic rule (Paris, 1530). He was patronized by Thomas Cromwell, and canvassed Italian universities on behalf of Henry VIII's divorce. He became a naturalized Englishman (1540), and held a small Lincolnshire benefice. He was active against northern English religious uprisings. He was a popular preacher at Protestant funerals, and died as parson of St Matthew's, Friday Street, London.

J. Durkan, 'Scottish "Evangelicals" in the Patronage of Thomas Cromwell', *RSCHS* 21 (1982), 134–7; id., 'Robertus Richardinus and STC 21021', *Edinburgh Bibliogr. Soc. Trans.* 3 (1948–55), 83–4; G. G. Coulton (ed.), *Commentary on the Rule of St Augustine* (SHS, E, 1935).

J. Durkan

Riding Committees, committees of Synod* or General Assembly* in the CofS, 1729 to 1752, sent to a parish to induct a patron's* presentee when the local presbytery refused to do so, so called because the committee had to ride to the parish from outwith the bounds of the presbytery. Although patronage had previously been almost universally condemned in the Presbyterian CofS, its restoration in 1712 came increasingly to be accepted. Settlements against the will of the people became more common (see Concurrence/Congregational Assent) and in 1729 the device of a Riding Committee was first used. Many objected to such forced settlements, seeing them as undermining the rights of congregations to choose their own ministers, as taught in the *First** and *Second* Books of Discipline* (see Call). Ebenezer Erskine's* public opposition led to the Secession of 1733 (see Associate Presbytery), which in turn led the Church to rethink, for a time, its attitude towards Riding Committees. In 1736 an Act was passed by the General Assembly against the intrusion of ministers in parishes contrary to the wishes of the congregation. This Act was something of a desperate attempt to win back the Seceders. When it became clear that the Secession's break with the national Church was final the Act was by and large ignored. Between 1740 and 1752 more than fifty ministers were inducted into their parishes by Riding Committees. From 1752, when the Assembly decided to compel presbyteries to do the work on pain of deposition and made Thomas Gillespie* an example (see Relief Church), the practice was abandoned.

N. Morren, *Annals of the General Assembly of the Church of Scotland, from the Final Secession in 1739 to the Origin of the Relief in 1752* (E, 1837).

I. Hamilton

Ridpath, George, see *Scotch Presbyterian Eloquence*.

Rising of 1715. Of all the Jacobite* risings the 1715 was the most likely to be successful. Both its prospects for success and its failure owed much to religious factors. Its failure resulted in repressive religious legislation.

Although Elector George of Hanover had no difficulty in succeeding Queen Anne in 1714, the Jacobite cause enjoyed considerable popularity, especially in Scotland where the recent acts of the Parliament of Great Britain restoring patronage* in the CofS and extending toleration to Episcopalians* whose worship was led by 'qualified' clergy were resented as breaches of the Treaty of Union* of 1707. The Episcopalian clergy who refused to 'qualify' by taking the oaths abjuring the exiled Stuarts and recognizing the House of Hanover (see Non-Jurors) were very active in promoting the Jacobite cause, especially in the north-east where they still had possession of many parish churches and manses. When the Pretender, or James VIII, came to Scotland he landed at Peterhead and the minister of Fraserburgh led his congregation in thanksgiving for the king's safe arrival. At Fetteresso, near Stonehaven, a deputation of clergy headed by James* and George Garden* presented an address of loyalty. James then moved on to Glamis where in the castle chapel he touched for the King's Evil, a skin disease which could be cured, it was thought, by the touch of the rightful king. Tradition says that all the patients recovered.

James' own adherence to RCism had enlisted the sympathy of the RC powers of Europe, especially France, but it was a dissuasive in Scotland, and Jacobites argued that their cause had nothing to do with religion. RCs were a minority of the Jacobite following. The majority of the population of Scotland proved unwilling to jeopardize the 1689–90 religious settlement by supporting the Rising of 1715.

The failure of the rising meant that immediate steps were taken against 'unqualified' ministers and twenty-one in Edinburgh were fined for not praying for King George. Thirty-six in the diocese of Aberdeen were ejected from their parishes. In 1719 Parliament passed an act forbidding anyone to officiate in any Episcopal meeting-house or congregation where nine or more persons were present in addition to the members of the household, without praying for King George and the royal family and without having taken the oaths of abjuration and allegiance. The penalty prescribed was six-months' imprisonment for the clergyman and the closure of the meeting-house for the same period. Some congregations decided to appoint clergy willing to take the oaths, but these were not recognized by the Scottish bishops.

B. Lenman, *The Jacobite Risings in Britain 1689–1746* (L, 1980); C. Sinclair-Stevenson, *Inglorious Rebellion* (L, 1971).

H. R. Sefton

Rising of 1745. The coming of the Young Pretender, Princes Charles Edward Stuart (1720–88), to Scotland had much to do with the initial success of the Rising of 1745 and its continuing romantic appeal. Its failure had much to do with religious factors.

Although Charles declared on behalf of his father James VIII *de jure* that it was his intention 'not to impose upon any a religion which they dislike, but to secure them all in the enjoyment of those which are respectively at present established among them, either in Scotland, England or Ireland', the ministers of the CofS fully deserved the praise of the Duke of Cumberland and his thanks for their 'very steady and laudable conduct'. The ministers of Edinburgh were active in preparations to defend the city against Charles and some of them actually took up arms. Ebenezer Erskine,* the Seceder, formed a voluntary force at Stirling and is said to have acted as a captain.

Many Episcopalians* were still Jacobite* at heart and wanted to see the Stuarts restored, but few openly supported the rising. Only two clergymen followed Charles' army and both were executed. Despite this, Cumberland's march north from the Tay to the Spey was notable for the number of Episcopal chapels he destroyed. In June 1746 all Episcopal chapels in Edinburgh were ordered to be closed.

In the summer of 1746 an act of Parliament was passed requiring the imprisonment and, for a second offence, the transportation of all Episcopal ministers who after 1 September should officiate to five or more persons (in addition to the family if in a house), without having taken the oaths of allegiance and abjuration and registered their letters of orders and without praying for the King by name. A supplementary act passed in 1748 declared that only letters of orders granted by the bishops of the CofE or Church of Ireland would qualify a clergyman to officiate. This legislation, passed in response to the rising of 1745 reduced the EpCS, in the words of Scott, to a 'shadow of a shade'.

A. J. Youngson, *The Prince and the Pretender* (L, 1985); Sir J. Fergusson, *Argyll in the Forty-five* (L, 1951); H. Kemp, *The Jacobite Rebellion* (L, 1975); J. Prebble, *Culloden* (L, 1961).

H. R. Sefton

Ritchie, John (1878–1952), missionary statesman. Ritchie was a native of Kilmarnock. Converted through the ministry of D. J. Findlay* and supported by Quarrier's* Homes, he sailed for Peru in 1906 with the Regions Beyond Missionary Union. A member of the Evangelical Union of South America from 1912 to 1927, Ritchie became, in 1932, the Secretary of the Upper Andes Agency of the American Bible Society. He was involved in the struggle for religious liberty in Peru in 1912–16, and became a founder of the '*Iglesia Evangélica Peruana*' in 1922. An initiator of the National Evangelical Council of Peru 1940, he was also a prolific author, and editor and publisher of Christian magazines in Spanish, e.g.: *El Heraldo* (1911–18); *El Cristiano* (1916–21); and *Renacimiento* (1921–52: Lima). His main missiological work is *Indigenous Church Principles in Theory and Practice* (NY, 1946).

G. S. McIntosh, *The Life And Times of John Ritchie* (Tayport, 1988).

G. S. McIntosh

Robb, Alexander (1825–1901), UP missionary and scholar. Born in Aberdeen, Robb was educated at Aberdeen University. Posted to Jamaica in 1852, he and his wife went to Calabar six years later. A distinguished Hebrew scholar, Robb excelled as teacher and translator. Well-argued reasons for his form of evangelism were offered in *The Gospel To The Africans* (E, 1861) and *The Heathen World And The Duty Of The Church* (E, 1863). In 1868, *Mbuk Asana Usun Heun*, an Efik version of Bunyan's *Pilgrim's Progress*, appeared, co-authored with Esien E. Ukpabio. In 1869 Aberdeen University awarded Robb a DD. Four years later his translation of the Efik *Akani (Old) Testament* was published.

As a literary giant he rivalled Hugh Goldie*, and he encouraged Efik writers. He prepared Ukpabio, Nigeria's first Presbyterian minister, for ordination in 1872. He had a fine awareness of nuance, and went far beyond literal translations, putting European concepts into African terms.

By 1875 his health had deteriorated (West Africa was 'the white man's grave') and he returned to the Caribbean, where, as Professor of Theology at Kingston, Jamaica, he continued translating, teaching and evangelizing. He retired to Australia, where he died at Cowes, Victoria.

MRUFCS 1 (1901), 165–6; A. Gammie, *Cruickshank of Calabar* (L, n.d.).

W. H. Taylor

Robe, James (1688–1753), evangelical CofS minister. Born in Cumbernauld, Dunbartonshire, and educated at the University of Glasgow, he was licensed by the Presbytery of Linlithgow in 1709 and ordained to the parish of Kilsyth, Stirlingshire, in 1713, where he remained until his death. In 1733 he received a call from the parish of Kirkintilloch, Dunbartonshire, but the Presbytery, believing him to be well situated, refused to effect the translation. The wisdom of the Presbytery was confirmed when a religious awakening of similar proportions to the revival* of Cambuslang* broke out in the parish of Kilsyth beginning in April 1742. Industrious and methodical in temperament, Robe set out in great detail an account of the events of the revival in his *Narrative of the Extraordinary Work of the Spirit of God at Kilsyth* (E, 1742; r.p. *When the Wind Blows*, G, 1985).

Robe's assessment of the revivals as a genuine work of God was attacked by James Fisher,* a leading minister of the Associate Presbytery.* A series of letters were exchanged in which Robe defended the revivals against charges of delusion and enthusiasm. During the controversy over William Leechman's* sermon on prayer, Robe wrote a defence of the actions of the Presbytery and General Assembly in *The Remarks . . . upon Mr Leechmann's Sermon on Prayer . . .* (E, 1744).

In November 1743 Robe began the religious periodical *The Christian Monthly History* (1–6, E, 1743–6). Similar to its New England counterpart, *Christian History*, it was designed to disseminate revival news from Scotland and abroad, and served to increase the already considerable flow of correspondence and news between Scotland and the American colonies. Among those with whom Robe carried on an extensive correspondence was the celebrated New England minister and theologian Jonathan Edwards.* Robe was instrumental in the formation and promotion of the Concert of Prayer which significantly contributed to the rise of the missionary enterprise of the late eighteenth century.

A Short Narrative of the Extraordinary Work at Cambuslang (G, 1742); *Counsels and Comforts to Troubled Christians* (G, 1749); *Sermons*, 2 vols (1: E, 1750; 2: G, 1756).

A. Fawcett, *Cambuslang Revival* (L, 1971); P. Anton, *Kilsyth: A Parish History* (G, 1893), 121–42; *FES* III, 479; *DNB* XLVIII, 341–2.

C. W. Mitchell

Robert I (the Bruce) (1274–1329), the son of Robert Bruce and Marjorie Countess of Carrick, and grandson of Robert Bruce 'the Competitor', and thus heir to the Bruce claim to the Scottish throne after the death of Margaret ('Maid of Norway') in 1290. During the years 1296–1305 he was intermittently associated with the patriotic party, but was unable to give them full support because

ROBERT I (THE BRUCE)

they fought in the name of the rival Balliol claimant. In 1306, however, after the murder of John Comyn, he asserted his own kingship and rallied support to his leadership in spite of early reverses; from 1307 he won victories both against the English and over his enemies within Scotland. After Bannockburn (1314), he was undisputed master of the kingdom, but despite repeated successes against the English was unable to secure a final peace until 1328. He was buried in Dunfermline Abbey.

Throughout his life Robert displayed conventional piety and respect for the Church. Robert Wishart,* Bishop of Glasgow, was a loyal supporter of the Bruce cause from the start, and from 1306 most of the Scottish clergy supported him as the best defence of the liberties of the Scottish Church against Edward I's encroachments. At Robert's first parliament, at St Andrews in March 1309, the 'bishops, abbots, priors and other clergy' issued an impressive declaration of support for the King; they asserted the validity of the Bruce family claim, denounced the rival Balliol claim as having been intruded *de facto* by Edward I against the wishes and judgment of the Scots, and declared their willingness to support and defend him in time to come. A parallel letter from the barons, issued at the same time, has not survived.

That most of the clergy did in fact support King Robert is clearly shown by the denunciations of Scottish bishops and other clergy brought before the pope by the English crown; these accused the clergy of asserting that it was just as meritorious to fight for King Robert against the English as to go to the Holy Land to fight against Turks and Saracens. Chief among Robert's clerical supporters were the Bishops of St Andrews and Glasgow and the abbots of Inchaffray and Arbroath, the last named being the King's chancellor Bernard (*d.* 1331). His office drafted the famous Declaration of Arbroath* (1320) and other important chancery documents of the reign.

Throughout his life Robert wished to go on crusade, as his father and grandfather had done in 1270, but was prevented by the wars against the English. On his deathbed he instructed Sir James Douglas (*c.* 1286–1330) to carry his heart to the Holy Sepulchre and in battle against the Saracens; Sir James died fighting against the Moors in Spain. This expression of conventional chivalrous piety helped to rehabilitate Robert, denounced by the pope as a sacrilegious rebel and excommunicated for the murder of Comyn; after long supporting the English against him, Pope John XXII (a native of the English fief of Gascony) confirmed the treaty of 1328, and allowed to Robert and his successors the right of coronation and anointing when they were made king.

King Robert's reign is important to the Church because he prevented the intrusion of Englishmen into Church office in Scotland, and identified ecclesiastical liberty with national freedom.

Acta in *The Acts of Robert I: Regesta Regum Scottorum*, V, ed. A. A. M. Duncan (E, 1988); verse life by John Balfour, *The Bruce*, ed. W. M. Mackenzie (L,

ROBERTSON, ALEXANDER

1909); G. W. S. Barrow, *Robert Bruce* (E, 1965).

A. Macquarrie

Roberts, Alexander (1826–1901), FC minister and scholar. Born at Marykirk, Kincardineshire, he graduated MA from King's College, Aberdeen, in 1847, and studied theology at New College,* Edinburgh. He was ordained to Stonehaven FC, Kincardineshire, in 1852, moving in 1857 to Carlton Hill Church in London. In 1870 he was appointed Professor of Humanity in St Andrews Unviersity, resigning in 1899.

In 1870–84 Roberts was a member of the revision company which produced the Revised Version of the New Testament. He acted as co-editor and part translator of the *Ante-Nicene Christian Library*, 25 vols (E, 1867–97). He was best known for his argument that Christ and the apostles habitually spoke Greek (see his *Greek the Language of Christ and His Apostles*, L, 1888, and *A Short Proof that Greek was the Language of Christ*, L, 1893).

Other works include: *Discussions on the Gospels* (L, 1864); *The Words of the New Testament* (with W. Milligan, E, 1873); *Inquiry into the Original Language of St Matthew's Gospel* (L, 1859); *The Bible of Christ and His Apostles* (L, 1879).

Roberts received a DD from Edinburgh University in 1864.

AFCS I, 300; *DNB Second Suppl.* III, 209.

N. R. Needham

Robertson, Alexander (1846–1933), minister in Italy and writer. Born in Edinburgh and educated at its Royal High School and University (1866–9), after mission work there he was ordained to the UP Church on South Ronaldsay, Orkney, in 1875. His wife's ill-health led him to move to the UP station at San Remo on the Italian Riviera in 1882. There he encountered a large and influential foreign – and Protestant – community. With the backing of the UPC Foreign Mission Board, from 1882 he set about building a UP church. Good progress was made, and the project received a charter from the Italian crown, but funding difficulties compounded by a serious earthquake (1887) left it unfinished.

Robertson, probably no longer supported by the UPC, moved to Venice in 1890 where he acted as an independent *pastore scozzese* until recognized by the CofS in 1900. Until World War I, he seasonally attracted large numbers to his services, held in premises owned by an American-supported Protestant church near the Piazza San Marco. In the 1920s, services for a dwindling congregation were held at his home, the Ca' Struan, near S. Maria della Salute. In 1931 he resigned his charge, but was granted a CofS pension and the title of honorary chaplain.

Through his second wife, Julia Dawson (1885), Robertson became associated with movements for internal reform of the RC Church (although his writing can be violently anti-papal), and the education of poor children in the Romagna. He was engaged by the Hope Trust* of Edinburgh in speaking tours. He also met and corresponded with

ROBERTSON, JAMES

a wide circle of people: Gladstone; Ruskin; Count Enrico Campello (founder of the Italian Reformed Church); Andrew White (American academic, diplomat and associate of Andrew Carnegie*); Ezra Pound; Benito Mussolini.

Above all he was a prolific writer, supplying copy to a large number of journals and newspapers in the Protestant, English-speaking world, including *The Scotsman*. His widely circulated books reflected his extensive interests and involvement in some of the leading issues of the day. Two works inspired by Ruskin drew moral and religious lessons from the Basilica of St Mark and the city of Venice. Enthusiastic biographies of Victor Emmanuel III and Mussolini saw them as champions of Italy determined to resist the influence of papacy and priesthood.

When the extent and nature of Robertson's journalism are better known his career will be better understood. He certainly attracted criticism and even ridicule, but he reached a wide audience, was fondly remembered in Venice, and received formal recognition for his work. He was awarded a DD by the Presbyterian College of Montreal (1894), and was made a knight of the Order of SS. Maurizio and Lazaro by Umberto II (1898) and a *commendatore* of Italy by Victor Emmanuel III (1930).

Count Campello and Catholic Reform in Italy (L, 1891); *Fra Paolo Sarpi, the Greatest of the Venetians* (L, 1893); *The Bible of St Mark: St Mark's Church, the Altar and Throne of Venice* (L, 1898); *The Roman Catholic Church in Italy* (L, 1903); *Venetian Sermons drawn from the History, Art and Customs of Venice* (L, 1905); *Papal Conquest, Italy's Warning: 'Wake up John Bull'* (L, 1909); *Victor Emmanuel III King of Italy* (L, 1925); *Mussolini and the New Italy* (L, 1929).

A. G. Mackinnon, *Beyond the Alps* (L, E, 1937); A. L. Drummond, *The Kirk and the Continent* (E, 1956); Small II, 501; *FES* VII, 555, VIII, 729; *Who Was Who, 1929–40*, 1152–3.

J. E. Law

Robertson, James (1803–60), leading Moderate.* Born in Pitsligo (Aberdeenshire), he studied with distinction at Marischal College, Aberdeen, and took up school-teaching, becoming Master of Gordon's Hospital in the city. Ordained in 1832 to Ellon (Aberdeenshire), he wrote the account of the parish for the *NSA* (vol. XII, 1841). Despite suspension (1842) for maintaining communion with the deposed ministers of Strathbogie* (on which case he published two pamphlets), Aberdeen made him DD (1843). After the Disruption* he succeeded David Welsh* in the chair of Ecclesiastical History at Edinburgh (1844). A man of many parts, but not church history, he mugged up his lectures by the midnight oil. None of his numerous publications was devoted to it, and distinction passed with Welsh to the FC and New College.*

His greatest achievement was as convener ('Endowment Robertson') of the CofS Committee on the Endowment of Chapels of Ease* (from 1847), raising £500,000 and erecting sixty-four churches.

ROBERTSON LECTURES

'Robertson of Ellon' contributed powerfully to General Assembly debates (becoming its Moderator in 1856), served on the Poor Law Commission (1843–4), and championed Indian missions* (writing also an *Appeal for the Advancement of Female Education in India*, E, 1846). *Free Trade in Corn* (E, 1825) illustrates his economic interests, on which he addressed the Association for the Advancement of Social Science. In Ellon he even pioneered the application of dissolved bones to fertilize soil. He was buried in St Cuthbert's churchyard, Edinburgh.

FES VI, 191–2; *DNB* XLVIII, 410–11; A. H. Charteris, *Life of the Rev. James Robertson, D.D.* (E, 1863; abridged, *A Faithful Churchman*, E, 1897); obituary by E. B. Ramsay in *Proc. of Royal Soc. of Edinb.* 4 (1857–62), 497–500; appreciation by G. Wilson, in *Scottish Divines, 1505–1872* (St Giles Lectures, 3; E, 1883).

D. F. Wright

Robertson, James (Gallus) (1758–1820), Catholic missioner. Born in Aberdeenshire, nephew of Marianus Brockie,* he entered the Scots College* at Dinant 1771, then the Ratisbon (*see* Schottenklöster) seminary. Professed as a Benedictine* in 1778 as Brother Gallus, ordained priest 1782, he was a missioner in Scotland 1784–1800. He edited John Austin's *Devotions* (E, 1789) and the NT (1792), and campaigned to introduce hymn-singing and other liturgical innovations.

Endowed with initiative rather than steadiness, he obtained from Napoleon in 1803 a decree preserving Ratisbon monastery and thereafter worked in England and Ireland. In 1808–9, at great personal risk, he obtained for Wellington the services of a Spanish army detained in Denmark. His account was published: *Narrative of a Secret Mission to the Danish Islands* (L, 1863). From 1813 he again worked for Wellington. Returning to Ratisbon 1816, he founded a deaf school and a blind asylum there, both short-lived. His last achievement was the re-opening of the Ratisbon seminary.

M. Dilworth

Robertson Lectures, a series established in defence of the Christian faith by the will of Alexander Robertson, a probationer of the FCS (*d.* 1899). The lectureship is in the gift of Glasgow University Court, on the nomination of a committee comprising the Divinity professors and the University principal. It is open to members of any Church. The first series, *New Ideas in India During the Nineteenth Century* (L, 1907), was also delivered as the Gunning Lectures,* by John Morrison, (1856–1932; see *FES* VII, 703, for his service in India and theological education). Later series have included John Baillie,* *Invitation to Pilgrimage* (L, 1942); E. Brunner, *The Scandal of Christianity* (L, 1951); A. R. Vidler, *Twentieth Century Defenders of the Faith* (L, 1965). Other eminent lecturers have included F. Gogarten, H. Richard Niebuhr, J. Hromadka and G. Bornkamm.

List of lecturers to date in *University of Glasgow*

Calendar 1976-77, lxvii-lxviii; details in CofS Year Book (annual), 1930-62.

D. F. Wright

Robertson, William (1705-83), one of the key figures in the early Unitarian* movement. Born in Dublin of a Scottish father, he studied there under Francis Hutcheson* and then took arts (MA, 1724) and divinity (under John Simson*) at Glasgow University. He played a leading role in the conflict between the students and Principal John Stirling which led to the appointment of a Royal Commission in 1726.

In the course of the Royal Commission, which owed its existence to Robertson's expulsion from the university and his subsequent appeal to the second Duke of Argyll, he gained the patronage of the Earl of Islay, who introduced him to Anglican circles. He abandoned Presbyterianism, took Anglican orders, becoming a curate in Ireland in 1728, and then obtained plural livings in 1729 and 1738, as well as other preferments. After 1759 he felt unable to subscribe to the use of all parts of the *Book of Common Prayer* and in 1764 resigned his benefices. In 1766 he published anonymously *An Attempt to explain the words, Reason, Substance . . . .* He presented a copy to Glasgow University and received its DD in 1768. He then became a schoolmaster until 1778 he agreed to become Theophilus Lindsey's colleague at the latter's Unitarian chapel at Essex Street, London, but did not take up the appointment. He died at Wolverhampton.

In the *Attempt*, Robertson advocated an establishment based only on subscription to the Bible and with a non-controversial service book. Although the *Attempt* was seen as having a key role in the beginnings of English Unitarianism, in it Robertson denied both the Socinian (*see* Unitarians) and Arian positions. It has been suggested that in fact he adopted Unitarian positions under the influence of Joseph Priestley and Lindsey.

DNB XLVIII, 423-5 (with references to other literature).

J. R. McIntosh

Robertson, William (1721-93), ecclesiastical and academic statesman and distinguished historian. Robertson guided the business of the General Assembly for twenty-eight years as leader of the Moderate* party in the CofS.

The son of William Robertson, minister at Borthwick, Midlothian, he was educated at the parish schook in Borthwick, the grammar school of Dalkeith and the University of Edinburgh. He was licensed in 1743 by the Presbytery of Dalkeith and presented by the Earl of Hopetoun to Gladsmuir, East Lothian, to which he was ordained by the Presbytery of Haddington in 1744. During the 1745 Jacobite rising* Robertson offered his services to General Cope but was refused.

Robertson first came to prominence in connection with the disputed settlement at Torphichen, West Lothian 1748-51. He was a member of the riding committee* which ordained and inducted James Watson to that parish when the Presbytery of Linlithgow failed to do so. But he determined that this should be the last occasion when a presbytery was excused the painful duty of settling an unpopular but legally presented minister. In 1752 he was successful in persuading the General Assembly to insist on the Presbytery of Dunfermline's settling an unpopular presentee at Inverkeithing, Fife. This led to the deposition of Thomas Gillespie* and the founding of the Relief Church,* but also confirmed Robertson's position as a leading ecclesiastical politician.

His translation to Edinburgh in 1758, first to Lady Yester's and then to Old Greyfriars, and his appointment as Principal of the University of Edinburgh in 1762, gave him a secure basis for the influence he exercised in the councils of the Church until 1780. Honours were showered upon him. He became a DD of Edinburgh University in 1758 and chaplain of Stirling Castle in 1759. He was appointed a chaplain to the King in 1761 and Historiographer Royal for Scotland in 1763, the year in which he was Moderator of the General Assembly.

When in 1755 Robertson was invited to preach the annual sermon of the SSPCK,* he chose to speak on the situation of the world at the time of Christ's appearance. He pointed out that God gave Christianity to the world at the precise historical moment 'when the world stood most in need of such a revelation and was best prepared to receive it'. The sermon went through several editions and was translated into German.

But it is as an historian rather than as a preacher that Robertson is remembered. The breadth of his writing is astonishing: Scotland during the reigns of Queen Mary and James VI, the reign of the Emperor Charles V, the colonizing of America and ancient India. *The History of Scotland* proved an instant success (2 vols, L, 1759) and had been through seventeen editions by 1806 when Robertson's last emendations were incorporated in a three-volume version. *The History of America* (2 vols, L, 1777; 4 vols, 1808) was published when Britain was in process of losing its American colonies and is remarkably frank about the destructiveness of much of the Spanish colonization. Its translation into Spanish was far advanced when stopped by order of the Spanish government. *An Historical Disquisition concerning Ancient India* (L, 1791; ²1794) was written to counteract the prejudice that the peoples of India were 'an inferior race' and to make known the achievements of Indian civilization.

Although Robertson insisted that the rights of patrons in presenting ministers to parishes must be respected, he did not himself have a 'patron' such as Patrick Cuming and Robert Wallace had had in Islay and Tweeddale. He owed his position to his own remarkable ability and to the fact that as Principal of Edinburgh University he was able to represent the university in the General Assembly each year.

There have been many explanations of Robertson's sudden withdrawal from Church affairs in 1780. These include his support of a plan

ROBERTSON, WILLIAM BRUCE

to extend penal relief to RCs in Scotland which sparked off 'No Popery' riots, his failing health, and the strained relationships between him and Henry Dundas,* who was emerging as the dominant force in Scottish political management.

The Situation of the World at the time of Christ's Appearance and its Connection with the Success of His Religion Considered (E, 1755); *The History of Scotland during the reigns of Queen Mary and King James VI till his Accession to the Crown of England* (2 vols, L, 1759); *The History of the Reign of the Emperor Charles V* (3 vols, L, 1769; 4 vols, 1866).

FES I, 41–2; *DNB* XLVIII, 425–30; Lives by Dugould Stewart (E, 1801–2) and George Gleig (E, 1812); Andrew Hook (ed.), *The History of Scottish Literature*, vol. 2: *1660–1800* (A, 1987); Richard B. Sher, *Church and University in the Scottish Enlightenment* (E, 1985).

H. R. Sefton

Robertson, William Bruce (1820–86), USec.C minister and author. He was born at Greenhill (Stirlingshire) in the parish of St Ninians, and educated at the University of Glasgow. From 1837 to 1841 he was a student at the Secession Theological Hall in Edinburgh; thereafter he studied at the University of Halle, Germany. He was ordained in December 1843 to the Secession church in Irvine. In 1854 he published a collection of hymns for Sunday school use, and six years after his death three of his lectures were published (see A. Guthrie, ed., *Passages from Sermons and Addresses by W. B. Robertson*, Ardrossan, 1897). He was awarded the degree of DD by Glasgow University in 1869.

DNB XLVII, 431–2; Small II, 301–2; J. Brown, *Life of William B. Robertson* (G, 1889).

S. D. Gill

Robinson, Alexander (1861–1907), CofS minister deposed for his heretical views in 1897. A graduate of the University of Glasgow (MA, 1883; BD, 1886), he served as an assistant at Dunoon, Argyll, before becoming the minister of Kilmun, Argyll, in 1894. Controversy was aroused by the publication of *The Saviour in the Newer Light* (E, 1895), in which he radically restated the doctrine of Christ's divinity. His Presbytery instituted libel proceedings against him and the case came before the General Assembly of 1896. It was found that he had denied the authenticity and truthfulness of the Gospels, the divine inspiration and integrity of the Gospel writers, and the divinity, miracles and resurrection of Christ. Having been suspended from his charge for a year he refused to repudiate his views at the following assembly and was deposed from the ministry of the Kirk. He was the minister of Crieff Congregational Church from 1899 to 1907. He wrote *The Story of the Kilmun Case* (G, 1907).

FES IV, 33; A. L. Drummond and J. Bulloch, *The Church in Late Victorian Scotland, 1874–1900* (E, 1978), 286–7; D. M. Murray, 'Doctrine and Worship', *Liturgical Review* 7:1 (1977), 31; C. L.

ROLFE, FREDERICK WILLIAM

Warr, *Alfred Warr of Rosneath* (Paisley, 1917), 213–44.

D. M. Murray

Robson, John (1836–1908), UP missionary and Moderator. The son of the minister of Wellington UP Church, Glasgow, he studied at the UP theological hall in Edinburgh from 1854, and in 1860 was ordained to serve as a missionary at Ajmer, India. After twelve years' ministry there, illness kept him in Scotland. In 1876 he was awarded Glasgow's DD and inducted to St Nicholas UP Church, Aberdeen, becoming senior minister in 1899. He was Moderator of the last regular UP Synod in 1900, and also spoke at the closing of the UP theological hall in April that year. He was an active writer, of both journal articles and books. While recognizing parallels between religions, he affirmed Christianity's distinctiveness. Unlike other sacred texts, the Bible's inspiration did not annihilate its human authors' personalities.

Hinduism and Its Relations to Christianity (E, 1874; ³L, 1905); *The Bible. Its Revelation, Inspiration and Evidence* (L, 1883); *Outlines of Protestant Missions* (E, 1885); *The Holy Spirit the Paraclete* (E, L, 1894); *Our Last Synod and the Last of Our Theological Hall* (E, 1900); *The Resurrection Gospel* (E, L, 1908); *Christ's Great Commission and the Work in Jamaica...* (Kingston, Jam., 1899).

Small I, 14.

D. F. Wright

Rognvald (d.1159), Jarl (i.e. Earl) of Orkney.* He was sister's son of St Magnus,* in whose honour he began the building of the cathedral in Kirkwall soon after his accession to the earldom (c.1137). He fostered religious and secular contacts with the Scottish kingdom of David I* and Malcolm IV;* c.1138 he entertained a Scottish bishop called John, possibly the bishop of Glasgow of that name (d.1147). In 1151–3 he went on pilgrimage to the Holy Land and Constantinople, possibly influenced by tales of the Second Crusade (1147–8); but he declined Manuel Comnenus' invitation to serve as a 'Varangian' mercenary captain at Constantinople. During his pilgrimage he emulated many of the feats of King Sigurd of Norway, who had visited Jerusalem in 1107 and earned the name *Jorsalafara*. St Magnus Cathedral was unfinished at his death in 1159, but the Romanesque central section represents Rognvald's work.

See bibliography to Magnus, Saint.

A. Macquarrie

Rolfe, Frederick William (1860–1913). Born in London, he taught in a succession of schools, became a RC 1886 and for a few months directed the Marquess of Bute's* choir school in Oban. In 1888, at a seminary in England, he received the clerical tonsure before being asked to leave. He entered the Scots College,* Rome, in late 1889 as a probationary candidate but was expelled some months later.

Thereafter he was seldom settled, often destitute, writing and endeavouring to publish, until his death in Venice. He used other names, notably Baron Corvo. Although talented, he was paranoic and vindictive, amoral with money, homosexually inclined. He always asserted his priestly vocation;* in his celebrated *roman à clef, Hadrian the Seventh* (L, 1904; many reprints), Rolfe, being elected Pope, redresses the ills of the RCC and his personal injuries, particularly his expulsion from the Scots College.

M. J. Benkovitz, *Frederick Rolfe: Baron Corvo* (L, 1977); A. S. MacWilliam, 'Fr. Rolfe and the Scots College, Rome', *IR* 21 (1970), 124–39.

M. Dilworth

Rollock, Robert (*c*.1555–99), first Principal of Edinburgh University and biblical commentator. The son of a laird of Powis, not far from Stirling, Rollock went to St Salvator's College, St Andrews, and passed through Andrew Melville's* innovative educational programme there. Rollock was made a regent (or tutor) in the college, and in 1580 the director of the faculty of arts. Edinburgh minister James Lawson* in 1583 brought Rollock to the notice of the Edinburgh town council, which then appointed the young man the regent of the college of James VI, created in the town in that year. Texts by Aristotle were used in teaching logic, ethics and physics, and the course also embraced mathematics, anatomy, geography and Greek. Scholars were trained in the Heidelberg Catechism, which the king's printer published at Edinburgh in 1591, and Rollock gave lectures in religion based on the *Quaestiones* by Theodore Beza (1519–1605), Calvin's successor at Geneva.

Rollock became Principal in 1585, and in 1587 began preaching at the East Kirk of Edinburgh and was authorized by the Presbytery as the college's Professor of Theology. Prominent in his preparation of men for ministerial labours was counsel concerning conduct in the pastoral office, exposition of the Pauline epistles, discourses on the commonplaces of theology, and a discussion of the points of controversy with RCism. Out of his public preaching and college instruction grew his nine published commentaries and five volumes of sermons. Between 1590 and 1634 at least forty printings of his writings issued from presses in Edinburgh, Geneva, and Heidelberg and Herborn in Germany. Rollock fell in with the policies of James VI* toward the Church, and was Moderator of the General Assembly which the King attended at Dundee in May 1597. Rollock became minister of the Upper Tolbooth and then of Magdalen Church in Edinburgh in 1598.

Rollock was a seminal early exponent of covenant theology* in Scotland. In his treatises of 1596–7 he contends that every part of Scripture pertains to some covenant, for God speaks nothing to humankind outside a covenant. Rollock argued that RC teaching about justification* was a covenant of works, that such teaching underestimated the depravity which prevails after Adam's fall, and that it encouraged a vain hope that human free will could rise to a meritorious ethical performance. Only Adam with a holy nature in its original integrity in Eden could have complied with the requirements of the law written on his heart. Restoration must come by a second covenant, of which Christ will be the mediator, subjecting himself to the law and thus providing a righteousness which fulfilled the terms of the original covenant. The only condition of the covenant of grace is faith in the mediator, which accentuates the freeness of the divine gift of a vicariously performed righteousness. Preaching is seen as the proclamation of this covenant, whose blessings are appropriated only by the elect, for in them the Holy Spirit creates faith by their effectual calling, so that they may respond with the condition of the covenant. Rollock used the dialectic of Peter Ramus (1515–72) to get at the meaning of the biblical text; passages were interpreted by restating them in syllogistic demonstrations, with the intention of removing ambiguity through a discrimination of the individual units of thought in each discourse.

See also Exegesis, Biblical.

Tractatus De Vocatione Efficaci (E, 1597; ET, *A Treatise of God's Effectual Calling*, L, 1603); *Quaestiones et Responsiones Aliquot De Foedere Dei* (E, 1596); *Analysis Dialectica in Epistolam ad Romanos* (E, 1594); *In Epistolam ad Ephesios* (E, 1590); *In Librum Danielis* (E, 1591); *De Aeterna Mentis Divinae Approbatione et Improbatione* (E, 1594); *In Epistolam ad Thessalonicenses* (E, 1598); *Certaine Sermons Upon Several Places of the Epistles of Paul* (E, 1599, 1616); *In Evangelium secundum Sanctum Johannem* (Geneva, 1599); *In Selectos Aliquot Psalmos Davidis* (Geneva, 1599; *An Exposition Upon Some Select Psalmes of David*, E, 1600); *In Epistolam ad Colossenses* (E, 1600); *Analysis Logica in Epistolam ad Galatas* (L, 1602); *Lectures Upon Colossians* (L, 1603); *Analysis Logica in Epistolam ad Hebraeos* (E, 1605); *Lectures Upon the Epistles to the Thessalonians* (E, 1606); *Lectures Upon the History of the Passion, Resurrection and Ascension* (E, 1616); *Five and Twentie Lectures Upon the Last Sermon and Conference of Christ* (E, 1619); *Select Works of Rollock*, 2 vols (ed. W. M. Gunn, E, 1844–9).

DNB XLIX, 171–3; T. M'Crie, *Life of Andrew Melville* (E, 1819, ²1824); G. Robertson and H. Charteris, *De Vita et Morte Roberti Rollok* (E, 1826); J. K. Cameron, *Letters of John Johnston and Robert Howie* (E, 1963); Calderwood; I. Backus, 'Piscator Misconstrued?' *Journal of Medieval and Renaissance Studies* 14 (1984), 113–19.

S. Isbell

Roman Catholicism, the religion of those in communion with the pope. In the eyes of its adherents the RCC is the true Catholic (universal) Church, possessing the fulness of doctrine and sacramental life, which it transmits to ensuing generations. It became separate from the Eastern Orthodox Church in the schism conventionally dated to 1054. Protestants however distinguish modern RCism from the undivided early Church, and consider that, after the corruptions of the later Middle Ages against which the Reformers protested, it consolidated its distinctive character in the Counter-Reformation* of the later sixteenth century. The RC doctrinal response to the Reformation was defined particularly by the Council of Trent (1545-63), which among other things upheld transubstantiation and the role of the RCC as the interpreter of Scripture. The Council repudiated Protestant views of justification.* Also of great importance at this period was the establishment of the Jesuits* in 1534.

In subsequent centuries there has been further definition of RC doctrine, partly in reaction to variation within the Church. Thus Jansenism* was condemned by the papal bull *Unigenitus* of 1713. Gallicanism, in effect the assertion of the independence of national Churches from papal authority, occurred in various countries, particularly in France, and brought a response in the growth of Ultramontanism, which asserted the authority of Rome. The ascendancy of the Ultramontanes was clinched by the declaration of papal infallibility at the First Vatican Council of 1870. Meanwhile doctrines regarding the Blessed Virgin Mary were receiving clearer definition: the Immaculate Conception in 1854 and the Assumption in 1950. In recent years the Second Vatican Council of 1962-5 has led to substantial changes in RC life and a more open attitude to other Christian Churches. This, in summary, is the background against which the history of RCism in Scotland should be viewed.

THE ORIGINS OF THE SCOTTISH MISSION 1560-1694. The Reformation Parliament* of 1560 brought to an end the state support of the medieval Scottish Church. Its institutional structure quickly collapsed, a development which Mary, Queen of Scots,* despite her continued personal loyalty to Rome, made little effort to prevent. The bishops did not offer any sustained resistance, although several, notably Archbishop James Beaton* of Glasgow, refused to conform. With Beaton's death in exile in 1603 the old hierarchy became extinct. At the grass roots in the later sixteenth century there were significant pockets of recusancy, especially in rural areas, where the authorities were weaker than in the towns, and above all where RCism had the protection of a local magnate. The most notable were in the north-east (Aberdeenshire and Banffshire) and the south-west, where Gilbert Brown* was supported by the Maxwells. Although there was some persecution, this was not systematic or intense, and RCs, on the whole, did not defy the Protestant government in any organized fashion. Catholicism lost ground steadily, while political initiatives on its behalf had little success.

By the early seventeenth century Scottish RCism had lost its internal cohesion. The pre-Reformation priests had died out and the role of missionary priests, facilitated by a few aristocratic and gentry families, was now of crucial importance. The Jesuits had commenced a mission in the 1580s and Irish Franciscans* began to work in the Highland west from 1619 (*see* Irish Missions to Highlands). The Church was able to consolidate its position in a number of regions, notably in Gaelic-speaking areas: the Western Isles, the western districts of mainland Inverness-shire and parts of the eastern Highlands, remote regions in which the authority of the Kirk was weak. A further important centre was Enzie in Banffshire, where RCs were protected by the marquesses of Huntly (later dukes of Gordon). The early Scottish mission was dominated by the regular clergy (religious orders), but a missionary organization of secular clergy gradually emerged, assisted by the formation in Rome in 1622 of the Congregation of *Propaganda Fide*.* Propaganda (as it was usually called) set up a Scottish mission under a prefect-apostolic in 1653 and was to remain responsible for the Church in Scotland until 1908. A key role was played by William Leslie* (1620-1707), the mission's agent in Rome. However, strong rivalry with the Jesuits precluded the development of any overall strategy. During this period an important contribution to keeping alive the traditions of Scottish RCism was made by the Scots Colleges* abroad, which were essential for the supply of priests. There were also Scottish Benedictine* communities at Ratisbon, Würzburg and Erfurt (*see* Schottenklöster).

The modest RC presence in seventeenth-century Scotland was sustained against a background of turbulent national politics and official attitudes that veered from persecution to limited encouragement. In particular the reign of James VII* (1685-8) saw a false dawn for Scottish RCism. The King, himself a RC, granted qualified toleration to his co-religionists and established a public chapel at Holyrood,* together with a printing press and Jesuit college. Such actions, however, provoked a widespread Protestant backlash, which, in conjunction with James's general political failure, led to his deposition in 1688. For RCs this meant a return to obscurity, while Protestant suspicion of them had been reinforced.

STRUGGLE AND CONFLICT, 1694-1789. In 1694 Thomas Nicholson* was appointed vicar-apostolic for Scotland, the first RC prelate to reside in the country since the old bishops died. The Scottish mission thus acquired a co-ordinated structure, in which the Jesuits worked under the bishops. For almost two centuries Scottish RCs were to be ruled by vicars-apostolic, missionary bishops responsible to Propaganda for the district (vicariate) entrusted to them. In 1727 the country was divided into two vicariates, Lowland and Highland. Meanwhile small seminaries were set up, most notably at Scalan in Glenlivet in 1716, which enabled priests to be trained on Scottish soil (*see* Colleges and Seminaries, Roman Catholic).

The bishops and their clergy faced considerable difficulties from geography, lack of money, Protestant competition and actual persecution. In the mid-eighteenth century the Scottish SPCK* made efforts to convert 'papists', and the close identification of Catholics with Jacobites* led to vigorous attacks on them, especially after 1745. Anti-Catholic feeling was still running high in the late 1770s (see Catholic Emancipation; Anti-Catholic Societies). There were also self-inflicted wounds, notably from the controversies over alleged Jansenism.* The significance of these is a matter of some debate among scholars, but it has been suggested that they were the result of continuing suspicions between regular and secular clergy, particularly those educated at Paris, and were exacerbated by the tensions between Lowland and Highland priests. The Scottish RCC, despite its smallness and remoteness, thus reflected wider European movements.

Despite these difficulties the islands of Barra, South Uist, Eigg and Canna, and the west mainland districts of Moidart, Knoydart and Morar remained very predominantly RC. There were also important pockets in Glengarry, Brae-lochaber, Badenoch, Strathglass, Glengairn and Braemar. In the Lowland vicariate (which included some Gaelic-speaking areas in the eastern Highlands, e.g. Glenlivet, Strathavon), Catholics were generally thinly dispersed, but were a significant presence in Aberdeenshire, Banffshire and Galloway. Evidence on the numbers of RCs at this period is very problematic: in 1755 Alexander Webster gave a figure of 16,490, but some modern scholars would maintain that there were more than 30,000 in the 1760s.

THE TRANSFORMATION OF SCOTTISH CATHOLICISM, 1789–1878. The leadership of Bishop George Hay* in the late eighteenth century saw recovery from the long-term effects of the failure of the Jacobite rising* of 1745 and the laying of foundations for a period of spectacular expansion. RCs abandoned their allegiance to Jacobitism and openly professed allegiance to the Hanoverian dynasty. After 1789 the attack of the French revolutionaries on the Church meant that RCism now appeared to be arrayed on the side of order rather than subversion, and a period of greater sympathy towards RCs ensued. This was reinforced by the arrival of refugee priests and the subsequent wars against Napoleon, in which RCs were clearly aligned with their fellow-countrymen. The Relief Act of 1793 followed by Emancipation in 1829 marked the beginning of greater legal security for RCs in Scottish society. Protestant hostility continued and even became stronger during the early Victorian period, but it was increasingly represented by unofficial anti-Catholic societies rather than the direct action of government and the law.

From around 1790, too, social changes affected RCs profoundly. People were uprooted in some Highland districts where RCs were numerous; most emigrated, but others moved south to the cities of central Scotland. Glasgow received its first resident priest, Alexander MacDonnell,* in 1792. Numbers were also being swelled, particularly on Clydeside, by the flow of immigration* from Ireland; by 1828 there were 70,000 RCs in the newly-formed Western district, 25,000 of them in Glasgow itself. Thus the Church, hitherto scattered over rural Scotland, now became predominantly urban in character and had to face the pastoral problems arising from the concentration of the migrants in the industrializing cities.

Already before 1789 chapels built as such were replacing the former unsatisfactory, even crude, places of worship. In the 1790s music was introduced into worship and gradually more elaborate services, such as High Mass, were held. Then, to cater for the influx of immigrants, large chapels were built in the Lowland towns. Meanwhile the Scots Colleges abroad ceased to operate in the aftermath of the French Revolution, and two were never to be reopened. It was accordingly vitally necessary to train more priests at home. The tiny Scalan seminary moved in 1799 to Aquhorties near Inverurie; then, in 1829, this and the Highland seminary joined to form the much larger Blairs College near Aberdeen. RCism was also strengthened by the religious orders* which returned to Scotland from 1834 onwards.

In 1827 the two vicariates were reorganized into three, Eastern, Western and Northern, with the Highlands divided between the latter two. In the north of Scotland, largely rural apart from Aberdeen, conservative RCism continued under Bishop James Kyle,* with a gradual improvement in church buildings in both Highland and Lowland areas, despite ongoing depopulation. In Edinburgh, seat of the Eastern vicariate, there was a steady expansion in numbers, especially under Bishop James Gillis,* and the Church maintained a high profile with some spectacular public ceremonies. There was a receptivity to foreign devotional influences, as derived from the continent and the English Catholic 'second spring' (see Worship and Devotion, Catholic (post-Reformation)).

It was, however, in the west that developments were most rapid and extensive. Immigration from Ireland increased and, in the 1840s especially, RCs flooded in, though almost half the incomers were Protestants. The problems thus created, particularly on Clydeside, were enormous. The pastoral challenge stemmed not only from the sheer numbers of the immigrants, but also, according to some scholars, from the initially ambivalent attitude of the Irish to the Church: they identified strongly with it, but arrived in Scotland without a commitment to regular devotional observance. The dedication of the clergy (both Scottish and Irish) and the religious orders bore fruit in drawing the bulk of the immigrants into active church life. RCs were set apart from their Protestant neighbours by the development of strong parochial identities, in which considerable social as well as spiritual support was given to the urban poor, and loyalties were reinforced by the provision of elementary education. By 1878 RCs numbered 325,000 (9 per cent of the population) and of these roughly two-thirds were in the Lowland west.

In the mid-nineteenth century there was great tension within the RC body in the west. The immigrants resented the tight control of all church affairs exercised by Scottish priests and bishops, while the native clergy, for their part, were worried by the political overtones of popular Irish Catholicism.

The division grew until in the 1860s schism seemed a real possibility, but Charles Eyre,* an Englishman brought to Glasgow as bishop in 1869, restored a sufficient measure of unity.

ROMAN CATHOLICISM SINCE 1878. The troubles in the Western vicariate led to the establishment (or, in RC eyes, restoration) of a normal episcopal hierarchy in 1878. St Andrews and Edinburgh became a metropolitan see, with suffragan dioceses of Aberdeen, Argyll and the Isles, Dunkeld, and Galloway. Glasgow, as archbishopric, was to become fully metropolitan by acquiring suffragan sees at Motherwell and Paisley in 1947.

During the last century RCism, though faced with the continued hostility of staunch Protestants, and worried about the leakage of its own faithful, has consolidated a position at the centre of Scottish religion. RC numbers were estimated at 817,000, or 15.7 per cent of the population, in the 1960s, though immigration from Ireland has virtually ceased. The Education Act* of 1918 was important in maintaining and, in some respects extending, the Church's social influence. By giving state support to RC education it not only assisted the upbringing of the younger generation, but also increased the numbers of teachers, who played an important role in the development of the community, which thus acquired a growing middle-class element. RCs also became significantly involved in politics, most notably under the leadership of John Wheatley (1869–1930), an important figure in early socialism. They have, however, been slow to find a place in the mainstream of intellectual and cultural life, partly because of a certain anti-intellectualism in Scottish RCism until after the Second Vatican Council, and partly because of the initially overwhelmingly working-class composition of its adherents, who have been under-represented in secondary and higher education.

The importance of the RCC in modern Scotland was underlined by the visit of Pope John Paul II in 1982. It has the highest attendances of any single church, although these are now falling, as are other indices, such as baptisms and numbers of clergy. Nevertheless, the contrast between the strength of present-day RCism and the ostracism and weakness of the seventeenth and eighteenth centuries could hardly be more striking.

See also Celibacy; Emigration; Fort Augustus Abbey; Gaelic, RC Publications; Geddes, John; Innes, Thomas; Papacy; Worship, Catholic; York, Cardinal Duke of.

General
A. Bellesheim, *History of the Catholic Church of Scotland*, vols 3 and 4 (E, L, 1889–90);
O. Blundell, *The Catholic Highlands of Scotland*, 2 vols (E, L, 1907–17); J. Darragh, 'The Catholic Population of Scotland Since the Year 1680', *IR* 4 (1953), 49–59; J. F. S. Gordon, *The Catholic Church in Scotland* (A, 1874); P. F. Anson, *Underground Catholicism in Scotland 1622–1878* (Montrose, 1970); C. G. Brown, *The Social History of Religion in Scotland since 1730* (L, 1987);
M. Dilworth, 'Roman Catholic Worship' in D. B. Forrester and D. M. Murray (eds), *Studies in the History of Worship in Scotland* (E, 1984). The *Innes Review* is a key source of information on Scottish Catholic history. The Scottish Catholic Archives have had a complex history, but are now kept at Columba House, Edinburgh. They are described by D. McRoberts in *IR* 28 (1977), 54–118.

Reformation to Eighteenth Century
M. Dilworth, 'The Counter-Reformation in Scotland: a Select Critical Bibliography', *RSCHS* 22 (1986), 85–100; M. H. B. Sanderson, 'Catholic Recusancy in Scotland in the Sixteenth Century', *IR* 21 (1970), 87–107; I. B. Cowan, 'The Roman Connection: Prospects for Counter-Reformation during the Personal Reign of Mary, Queen of Scots', *IR* 38 (1987), 105–19; J. F. McMillan, 'Jansenists and anti-Jansenists', *IR* 39 (1988), 12–45; W. Forbes-Leith (ed.), *Narratives of Scottish Catholics* (E, 1885); *id.*, *Memoirs of Scottish Catholics*, 2 vols (L, 1909); J. F. McMillan, 'Money and the Scottish Mission in the Eighteenth Century', *Studies in Church History* 24 (1987), 267–82; M. McHugh, 'The Religious Condition of the Highlands and Islands in the Mid-Eighteenth Century', *IR* 35 (1984), 12–21.

Late Eighteenth Century Onwards
C. Johnson, *Developments in the Roman Catholic Church in Scotland 1789–1829* (E, 1983); *id.*, *Scottish Catholic Secular Clergy 1879–1989* (E, 1991); J. E. Handley, *The Irish in Scotland* (Cork, 1945); *id.*, *The Irish in Modern Scotland* (Cork, 1947); B. Aspinall, 'The Formation of the Catholic Community in the West of Scotland', *IR* 33 (1982), 44–57; D. McRoberts (ed.), *Modern Scottish Catholicism 1878–1978* (G, 1979) = *IR* 29 (1978); T. Gallagher, *Glasgow: the Uneasy Peace* (Manchester, 1987); J. Cooney, *Scotland and the Papacy* (E, 1982); W. M. Walker, 'Irish Immigrants in Scotland', *Historical Journal* 15 (1972), 649–67; J. H. Treble, 'The Working of the 1918 Education Act in Glasgow Archdiocese', *IR* 31 (1980), 27–44.

J. R. Wolffe

Ronan, *see* Celtic Saints.

Rose (Ross) Alexander (*c.* 1647–1720), Bishop of Edinburgh. Bishop at the time of the Glorious Revolution of 1688–9, Rose is chiefly remembered for his reply to William of Orange which ensured the Parliamentary abolition of prelacy: 'Sir, I will serve you so far as law, reason or conscience shall allow me.'

The second son of Alexander Rose, minister of Monymusk, Aberdeenshire, Rose was educated at King's College, Aberdeen, and the University of Glasgow. Licensed by the Presbytery of Glasgow in 1670, he was ordained at Perth in 1672, where he served until 1683. After brief spells as Professor of Divinity at Glasgow and Principal of St Mary's College, St Andrews, he was consecrated as Bishop of Moray in 1687 and translated to Edinburgh in 1688, being deprived in 1689.

Described as a sweet-natured man by Bishop George Keith,* Rose was ill-suited to the position of leadership which was forced upon him by the inability of the two Archbishops at the time of the Revolution. He seems to have been taken by surprise at William's challenge: 'I hope you will be kind to me and follow the example of England.' His evasive reply associated Scottish Episcopalians with Jacobitism* for a century.

Rose seems to have assumed that the ecclesiastical changes of 1689-90 would only be temporary and that the exiled Stuarts would return and restore episcopal government. His main concern was therefore to ensure the continuity of the episcopate rather than to make diocesan appointments and thus usurp the prerogative of the exiled King. He was the only diocesan bishop at his death in 1720. He also acted as pastor to those who left St Giles' Edinburgh at the Revolution and formed the congregation of Old St Paul's, Carrubbers Close.

DNB XLIX, 252-4; FES IV, 230, 234, VII, 342-3; J. P. Lawson, *History of the Scottish Episcopal Church* (E, 1843); M. E. Ingram, *A Jacobite Stronghold of the Church ... Old St Paul's, Edinburgh* (E, 1907).

H. R. Sefton

Rose, Charles, (d.1791), bishop, last of the regular EpCS non-juring* succession. Son of James Rose, College Bishop and then Bishop of Fife under the 1731 Concordate, and nephew of Bishop Alexander Rose* of Edinburgh, he was chaplain to Lord Arbuthnott, then incumbent at Doune (1755-91) and Bishop of Dunblane (1774-91) with Dunkeld (1776-86). 'Most Jacobite* of all Jacobites', he successfully blocked the consecration of the moderate Abernethy Drummond to Brechin in 1781, and in 1784 opposed the consecration of Samuel Seabury* because he derived his orders from 'the Schismatical Church of England'. Following the other bishops' 1788 acceptance of the Hanoverians, he irregularly consecrated James Brown* to continue the non-juring succession.

G. T. S. Farquhar, *Three Bishops of Dunkeld: Alexander, Rose and Watson 1743-1808* (Perth, 1915); W. Walker, *The Life and Times of John Skinner, Bishop of Aberdeen and Primus of the Scottish Episcopal Church* (A, 1887); J. Skinner, *Annals of Scottish Episcopacy* (E, 1818); G. Grub, *An Ecclesiastical History of Scotland* (E, 1861), IV; T. Stephen, *The History of the Church of Scotland* (L, 1845), IV.

R. J. Angus

Roslin (Rosslyn) Chapel, in Midlothian, one of the most remarkable monuments of ecclesiastical architecture* in Scotland. It was founded in 1446 by William St Clair, Earl of Caithness and Orkney, and formally received collegiate* status in 1523-4. Dedicated to St Matthew, it is now an independent chapel within the Scottish Episcopal Church.* It comprises only choir and sacristy, with no nave, but survives almost unaltered, distinguished by the extravagant sumptuousness of its ornamentation, both internal and external, exemplified by the Prentice Pillar. The eccentricities, idiosyncrasies and crudities of the building suggest the inspiration and oversight of its single founder.

[R. Forbes], *An Account of the Chapel of Roslin* (E, 1778); S. Cruden, *Scottish Medieval Churches* (E, 1986), 187-96; D. MacGibbon and T. Ross, *The Ecclesiastical Architecture of Scotland*, 3 vols (E, 1896-7), III, 149-79; C. McWilliam, *Lothian (Buildings of Scotland*; Harmondsworth, 1978), 409-17.

D. F. Wright

Ross, Donald (1824-1903), pioneer evangelist. He was born at Alness, Ross-shire, converted in his teens, and joined the FC in 1843. He was then a schoolmaster, but his gifts and calling were those of an evangelist. Moving to Edinburgh about 1850, he was given charge of a church-sponsored mission near the West Port. In 1857 he became a missionary to coal-miners at New Mains, Lanarkshire. He was active in the 1859 revival,* and became superintendent of one of its offshoots, the North-East Coast Mission, with headquarters in Aberdeen. After ten years he resigned this office because of tension with its directorate, and with some like-minded associates founded the Northern Evangelistic Society, to evangelize the landward population of northeastern Scotland. The organ of this Society, the *Northern Intelligencer*, developed later into *The Witness*, a leading Brethren* periodical. About 1871 Ross and his converts became integrated in the Brethren movement; that movement in northeastern Scotland still exhibits traits inherited from those days.

In 1876 Ross visited the USA, where he found so many opportunities for evangelism that he moved his family there in 1879. From headquarters in Chicago, San Francisco and Kansas City, he conducted gospel campaigns in many parts of North America. He died at Savannah, Georgia.

See also Fisherfolk, Missions to.

C. W. Ross (ed.), *Donald Ross* (Kilmarnock, 1904).

F. F. Bruce

Ross, James (1837-1912), historian and one of the Congregational Union's most revered statesmen and leaders in the last quarter of the nineteenth century. A native of Elgin, Ross was a reporter with the *Banffshire Journal* prior to commencing his studies for the ministry in the Theological Hall of the Congregational Churches in Scotland, 1857, and Edinburgh University. He was ordained pastor of Linlithgow Congregational Church in 1862. Leaving Linlithgow in 1864, he subsequently held the following pastorates: Stirling (1864-70), Union Chapel, Calcutta (1870-6), Baltic Street, Montrose (1876-81), Eglinton, Glasgow (colleague, 1881-9, sole pastor, 1889-1906). He was Secretary of the Congregational Union of Scotland, 1877-83, Chairman, 1887, and Editor of *The Scottish Congregationalist*. Taking a prominent

ROSS, JOHN

part in the movement which brought the Evangelical Union* and the Congregational Union together in 1896, Ross was made Chairman of the enlarged Union, 1898-9. He was awarded a DD by Edinburgh University in 1905.

A History of Congregational Independency in Scotland (G, 1900); *W. Lindsay Alexander, D.D., LL.D.: His Life and Work, with Illustrations of His Teaching* (L, 1877); ed. *A System of Biblical Theology* by W. Lindsay Alexander, 2 vols (E, 1888).

T. H. Walker, *Fellow-Labourers* (Greenock, 1916).

W. D. McNaughton

Ross, John (1842-1915), missionary. Born in Rarichie, Nigg, Easter Ross, on 6 July 1842, the son of a tailor, he studied at the UP Divinity Hall in Edinburgh 1865-9, and at Glasgow University, and was licensed in 1870. As student and probationer he served in several Highland appointments (notably Lismore). Though attracted to Gaelic* ministry he offered for the UP's newly opened field. Initially appointed to Cheefoo in 1872, under the eye of Alexander Williamson* of the National Bible Society, he quickly moved to open new work in Manchuria, first in the port of Newchwang (now Ying k'ou), then in Mukden. His work involved itinerancy and the training of an indigenous evangelistic and pastoral ministry. He held that Christian teaching did not conflict with Confucian (his first school provided free teaching, using only Chinese classics), asserted the existence of a monotheistic strand in ancient Chinese religion, denied that Chinese ancestral rites were idolatrous (while insisting that adjudication on traditional customs was the local church's province) and believed Buddhist ascetics to be the most earnest seekers, and, when converted, the most dynamic evangelists. As early as 1874 he saw possibilities of Christian penetration into the closed neighbouring land of Korea. Persuading Korean visitors to be his first teachers, he worked at the language, produced a primer (Shanghai, 1877) and a grammar (Shanghai, 1882) and directed the first Korean translation of the NT. Though the UP never gave Korea much priority, Ross's work produced the earliest Korean protestant churches.

Ross also wrote on East Asian history and culture, naturally influenced by the perspective and the sources available in his Manchurian base: *Chinese Foreign Policy* (Shanghai, 1877), *History of Corea* (Paisley, 1879) and *The Manchus* (Paisley, 1880). Thereafter, in addition to his Korean works he published a study of the evangelist *Old Wang* (L, 1889), Bible commentaries in Chinese and many articles. Retiring through ill-health in 1900, he continued to write: *The Boxers of Manchuria* (Shanghai, 1901), the influential *Mission Methods in Manchuria* (E, 1903), *The original Religion of China* (E, 1909) and the posthumous *Origin of the Chinese People* (E, 1916). He received the DD of Glasgow University in 1894.

FUFCS 551 (inaccuracies); D. Christie, *LW* n.s.s. (1934), 76-8; S. I. Choi, 'John Ross (1842-1915)

ROSS, WILLIAM

and the Korean Protestant Church' (PhD, Edinburgh University, 1992); J. H. Grayson, 'The Manchurian Connection', in C. Chung and J. E. Hoare (eds), *Essays in Celebration of the Centenary of Korean-British Diplomatic Relations* (Seoul, 1984), 53-68.

A. F. Walls

Ross, Thomas (1768-1843), CofS minister who superintended the publication of the 1807 edition of the Gaelic* Bible (*see* Bible (Versions, Gaelic)). Born in Creich, Sutherland, educated at Edinburgh University, and licensed by the Presbytery of Edinburgh (1802), he served briefly in the Scots Church, Rotterdam. Admitted to the parish of Lochbroom in 1808, he maintained a strong interest in Bible translation, and, objecting to the dialectal forms in the existing Gaelic version, reputedly made his own new translation. In 1820 the Synod of Ross unsuccessfully petitioned the General Assembly for its use 'in those districts of the country where it shall be best understood, or otherwise preferred'. Ross 'amended' Alexander MacFarlane's revision of the Gaelic Psalter (*see* Psalms, Psalter (Gaelic)), and published a Gaelic version of Ossian's poems (L, 1807).

FES VII, 158-9; D. MacKinnon, *The Gaelic Bible and Psalter* (Dingwall, 1930), 66-71.

D. E. Meek

Ross, William (1836-1904), FC and UFC minister and evangelist. Born at Allt-a-Chliabhan, near Latheron, Caithness, he studied at Moray House, Edinburgh, to become a teacher in a FC school, but then went to Edinburgh University, where he excelled at maths and moral philosophy, and took theology at New College. In 1867 he was ordained to Chapelhill Free Gaelic Church, in Rothesay, Bute. He taught the Gaelic class at the FC College, Glasgow (*see* Trinity College), from 1881 till his death. In 1883 he moved to Cowcaddens FC, Glasgow, where he became famous for his evangelistic work. In 1901 he was appointed to a special position as evangelist to the Highlands.*

Ross was noted for his advocacy of temperance* and prohibition - as secretary of the FC Total Abstinence Society (1874-); a founder of the Highland Temperance League (1880); chaplain (1876 -) and president (1877-9) of the Scottish Lodge of the Independent Order of Good Templars (an international temperance body).

Ross's evangelistic ministry in Cowcaddens provided a striking example of the Church's effective outreach to the socially deprived and religiously antagonistic. His evangelistic strategy had four central principles: (i) the Church must aim at the spiritual, not the temporal, well-being of the unevangelized; (ii) the local congregation, not a para-Church body, must be the agent of evangelism; (iii) the congregation must have a clearly defined target area for its activities - the 'territorial principle'; (iv) the church building must be in constant use as a centre of outreach, with daily evangelistic meetings.

Ross was conservative in doctrine, progressive in

worship (he used hymns and choirs), an ardent Voluntary (see Voluntaryism, Voluntary Controversy), and a radical Liberal in politics. He was keenly devoted to the language, culture and spiritual welfare of the Highlands.

J. M. E. Ross, *William Ross of Cowcaddens* (L, 1905); *AFCS* I, 307; *FUFCS* 216.

N. R. Needham

Rough, John (d.1557), Protestant martyr.* He was a Dominican* friar in Stirling who entered St Andrews University in 1520 and was later chosen as a chaplain for Governor Arran's (see Hamilton, James, d.1575) household during Arran's Protestant phase in 1543. He left court for Kyle in Ayrshire when inhibited from preaching as a consequence of Arran's reconciliation with Cardinal David Beaton.* He later preached in St Andrews (inaugurating Knox* to his ministry in the Castle in 1547) and Dumfries. Gaining Somerset's patronage, he was licensed to preach in England and served at Carlisle, Newcastle (where he married an Englishwoman), Berwick and Hull. There he recognized the two dominical sacraments,* not seven, repudiated transubstantiation and the papacy, criticized auricular confession and approved the doctrines of Archbishop Cranmer and Bishops Ridley and Latimer, and the content of the second, more radical, Edwardine *Book of Common Prayer*. On Mary Tudor's accession he left for Friesland, but on a visit to London was arrested, condemned for heresy and burned at Smithfield.

J. Foxe, *Acts and Monuments* (L, 1868), VIII, 443-51; Knox, *History* I, 42-43, 48, 81-3, 87; *DNB* XLIX, 313.

J. Kirk

Row, John (c.1525-80), Reformer and minister of Perth. Said to have been born at Row near Dunblane, he was educated at Stirling grammar school and St Leonard's College, St Andrews, where he matriculated in 1544. As clerk of Dunblane diocese, he served as procurator at the papal court at Rome in the 1550s, and was a prolific benefice-hunter. Created a licentiate in civil and canon law at Rome in 1557, he is said by his son to have graduated doctor in both laws at Padua and also to have had a knowledge of Hebrew. He appears to have been in Rome at the end of 1559. Returning home, he joined the Reformers, reputedly through the influence of Lord James Stewart (d.1570),* John Knox* and Christopher Goodman.* He was evidently considered sufficiently reformed to help compose the *FBD** and the (Scots) Confession* in 1560, and to be appointed in 1560 minister of Perth, a charge he held till his death in 1580. In 1561, he agreed with Knox that subjects might lawfully restrain their Queen from attending mass. Appointed by the General Assembly to act as its commissioner for Galloway and Nithsdale, Row was chosen four times as the Assembly's Moderator (July and December 1567, April 1576 and June 1578) and participated in drafting the *SBD*.* He died at Perth. One of his ten sons, John (d.1646),*

minister of Carnock, produced the *History of the Kirk of Scotland* from 1558 to 1637, to which in turn his son, also John (d.1672),* Principal of King's College, Aberdeen, supplied a continuation to 1639.

Vatican Archives, Register of Supplications; J. Row, *The History of the Kirk of Scotland* (E, 1842); *BUK*; Calderwood; *FES* IV, 229; *DNB* XLIX, 327-9.

J. Kirk

Row, John (1568-1646), Covenanting* minister and historian. A younger son of John Row (1525-80),* he is said to have been precocious, mastering Hebrew by the age of seven and subsequently teaching it to his schoolmaster in Perth. Certainly he became, after his father's death, a schoolmaster himself at the age of fifteen, at Kennoway in Fife. Later he attended Edinburgh University, graduating in 1590, and then became a schoolmaster at Aberdour, Fife. In 1592 he was appointed minister of Carnock, Fife, where he remained for the rest of his life. He was an opponent of the Crown's religious policies, protesting at the introduction of episcopacy* in 1606 and being summoned before the Court of High Commission* in 1619 and 1622 for refusing to conform to the Five Articles of Perth.* He enthusiastically supported the revolt against Charles I,* and was an active member of the Glasgow Assembly.* In his later years he compiled a historical account of the tribulations of the Church of Scotland from 1558 to 1637 for the use of young ministers.

The History of the Kirk of Scotland (Wodrow Soc., E, 1842), including D. Laing's 'Account of the Life of Mr John Row', vii-xxxviii; *DNB* XLIX, 329-30; *FES* V, 7-8.

D. Stevenson

Row, John (1598-1672), Principal of King's College, Aberdeen. A younger son of John Row* (1568-1646), he graduated from St Andrews University (MA, 1617) and became Master of the Grammar School of Kirkcaldy two years later. He resigned c.1628, becoming tutor to the son of the Earl of Kinnoull. He was appointed Rector of the Grammar School of Perth in 1632, and in 1641 was ordained to the third charge in Aberdeen. In 1642 he agreed to give lectures on Hebrew in Marischal College, Aberdeen,* and in 1644 his Hebrew grammar and vocabulary were published in Glasgow. After the English conquest (see Commonwealth and Protectorate), Row was appointed Principal of King's College* in 1652, his energies being devoted especially to rebuilding and to revising college regulations. Although previously an active Covenanter,* for some years he became an Independent,* but eventually returned to Presbyterianism. He was forced to resign in 1661, after the Restoration,* and for a time ran a school in Aberdeen.

'A Supplement of the Historie of the Kirk of

Scotland', 1637–9, in J. Row, *History of the Kirk of Scotland* (E, 1842), 481–525.

DNB XLIX, 330–1; *FES* VI, 14, VII, 366; D. Laing, 'Notice respecting the Life and Writings of John Row' in J. Row, *History*, xxxix–liv; G. D. Henderson, *Religious Life in Seventeenth-Century Scotland* (C, 1937), esp. 108–10.

D. Stevenson

Royal Bounty, an annual sum of money (originally £1,000) first given by the king in 1725, and administered by the Royal Bounty Committee of the Est.C.* The money was used initially to strengthen the Presbyterian presence in 'the popish parts' of the Highlands,* by employing itinerant catechists, probationers and missionary-ministers. Later it helped to provide more adequate ministry in over-large Highland parishes (*see* Scottish SPCK). The Royal Bounty agents operated in remote parts which were usually inaccessible to parish ministers and in areas with significant concentrations of people (such as garrisons, industrial sites and fishing ports). The missionary-ministers frequently had neither manse nor church, and were characterized by evangelical zeal, manning *ad hoc* 'preaching stations' under difficult conditions. Some served at long-standing mission stations, like that of Achreny in Caithness. Achreny was supplied by a succession of men who later became leaders of Highland Evangelicalism* and the FC,* including John MacDonald* of Ferintosh and Finlay Cook* of Reay. Some of the missionaries became the ministers of Parliamentary Churches* after 1824.

John MacInnes, *The Evangelical Movement in the Highlands of Scotland* (A, 1951), 198–211.

D. E. Meek

Royal, Chapel. The name 'Chapel Royal' has been applied to several church buildings within or beside royal residences, but especially to the chapels at Stirling Castle and Holyrood. That at Stirling was rebuilt by James III* and in 1501 became collegiate,* with a dean, sub-dean, canons and song-school. The deanery was well endowed from teinds* and, later, feu duties (*see* Feuing), the appointment being held by a notable churchman, e.g., the Bishop of Whithorn or Galloway. About 1503 King James IV built a palace beside Holyrood Abbey, on the south side of which was a chapel. In 1571 the chapel at Stirling, where James VI* was baptized, was despoiled by Protestants and then little used. The chapel at Holyrood then became the Chapel Royal until the Revolution of 1689.

The emoluments of the deanery fell to the Crown and were used to supplement the salaries of some University principals and professors. Principals William Carstares* and John Lee* and many others were granted 'a deanery of the Chapels Royal'. Of this arrangement only a financial allocation to certain divinity professors remains.

The Dean of the Chapel Royal today is the appointed senior of the Chaplains in Ordinary to the Queen in Scotland.

C. Rogers, *History of the Chapel Royal of Scotland* (Grampian Club, L, 1882); T. B. S. Thomson, *The Chaplain in the Church of Scotland* (E, 1947).

A. I. Dunlop

Rule (Regulus), *see* Celtic Saints.

Rule, Gilbert (*c*.1629–1701), minister and Principal of Edinburgh University. Born probably in Edinburgh (possibly in Elgin in 1628), Rule was educated at Glasgow University, after which he served as regent there and, in 1651, as sub-principal at King's College, Aberdeen. He was then settled in (and apparently ordained to) Alnwick and, though harassed for not using the *Book of Common Prayer*, ministered there until ejected in 1662. After study in France and Holland, he obtained an MD at Leiden and returned to Berwick, where he practised medicine and preached to dissenters. He accepted the Indulgence* of 1679, but on baptizing a child in Edinburgh, though with the permission of the Episcopalian incumbent, he was convicted of breaking the law against conventicles* and sent to the Bass Rock.* Freed on condition of his departing Scotland, he returned to Berwick. Although he was later granted permission to practice in Scotland as a doctor of medicine, provided he kept no conventicles, he accepted a call to Dublin. In 1688 he was called to be one of the ministers of the Presbyterians in Edinburgh and subsequently to Greyfriars. In 1690 he was appointed Principal, in which position, with his ministerial duties, he remained until his death.

A leading Presbyterian minister at the Revolution, he counselled moderation in dealing with Episcopalian incumbents. He was part of a delegation sent by the General Assembly to the court and, it is said, was received with particular favour by King William.

Although his learning was impugned by the Episcopalian party, A. Bower (*The History of the University of Edinburgh*, E, 1817, 319–21) says that Rule's talents were respectable and describes his *An Answer to Dr Stillingfleet's Irenicum* (L, 1680) as 'at least as formidable as the work to which it is intended as a reply'. Of *The Good Old Way Defended* (E, 1697), James Walker* (*The Theology and Theologians of Scotland*, E, ²1888, 113–14) says: 'Read the Principal's work, if you wish to see what sort of man a true-blue Presbyterian of the old school was, who believed in the divine right of his Church system, who hated ceremonies and holidays, and perhaps would have died rather than practise them. You will see what room his ideas left him for a generosity and expansiveness to which his prelatic antagonists were, I should think, utter strangers.'

FES I, 39–40; E. Calamy, *The Nonconformist's Memorial*, ed. S. Palmer (L, 1802), III, 52–5; R. Wodrow, *The History of the Sufferings of the Church of Scotland* (²G, 1828), III, 194–5; J. Anderson, 'The Martyrs of the Bass', in *The Bass Rock* (E, 1847), 291–313.

D. C. Lachman

Rullion Green (the Pentland Rising), a Covenanter* insurrection in November 1666. In the context of repressive measures designed to compel obedience on recalcitrant Covenanters, four fugitives encountered and captured four soldiers who had arrested a farmer charged with absenting himself from church. The news reached a conventicle* nearby and those assembled, fearing they would be blamed for the affair, attacked and captured a local garrison. This rash reaction led to their taking prisoner Sir James Turner, who had charge of the government troops. They decided to enlist support and march on Edinburgh to present their grievances. At their strongest they numbered some thousand men, about half mounted, commanded by James Wallace, an experienced soldier. A much larger government force was sent to pursue them, under Lieutenant-General Thomas Dalyell. After being exposed to sleet and snow while marching overnight, and without expected reinforcements, the Covenanters were forced to face their pursuers on the Pentland Hills, just outside Edinburgh at Rullion Green. After a bloody battle they were defeated and dispersed under cover of darkness. In addition to those killed, some 120 were captured, tried for rebellion and executed. Haphazard decisions and lack of preparation doomed the rising from the start and further oppressive measures followed.

J. K. Hewison, *The Covenanters*, 2 vols (G, ²1913), II, 190–207.

J. A. Dickson

Russel, John (1740–1817), CofS preacher of great power, and nationally known Evangelical.* He was minister of Kilmarnock (High) (1774–99), and of Stirling (Second Charge) (1799–1817). He was the 'Black Russel' of Robert Burns's* 'Twa Herds' and 'The Holy Fair'. In the former, the poet wrote: 'What herd like Russel tell'd his tale, / His voice was heard through muir and dale'; in the latter: 'His piercing words like Highland swords, / Divide the joints an' marrow; / His talk o' Hell, whare devils dwell, / Our verra sauls does harrow.' He led the attack on 'Socinianism'* in the Synod of Glasgow and Ayr in the later eighteenth century, and his sermon on *The Reasons for our Lord's Agony in the Garden, and the Influence of Just Views of them on Universal Holiness* (Kilmarnock, 1787), was a detailed rebuttal of William McGill's* *Practical Essay on the Death of Christ*. He wrote a preface to James Fraser of Brea's* *Sermons on Sacramental Occasions* (Kilmarnock, 1785).

The Nature of the Gospel Delineated . . . (Ayr, 1796); *True Religion the Foundation of True Patriotism* (Stirling, 1801).

D. Sage, *Memorabilia Domestica* (E, 1889), 23–5; *FES* IV, 326.

J. R. McIntosh

Russell, David (1779–1848), Congregational minister. Born in Glasgow, Russell never attended university, but taught himself Latin, Greek and theology while tending cattle or weaving. He came to the attention of Greville Ewing,* in whose church he worshipped. This led in 1803 to his entering the Edinburgh Theological Academy established by the Haldanes.*

After supply preaching and a brief pastorate in Aberdeen, in 1809 Russell became minister of the Sailors' Hall Independent Church in Dundee, which in 1810 merged with another congregation to form West Port Chapel. Russell ministered there for the rest of his life. (The church moved to different premises in 1833, and was thereafter known as Ward Chapel.)

Russell conducted a powerful expository ministry, under which Ward Chapel grew hugely in size and began a 'long and glorious history' in Scottish Congregationalism (H. Escott, *A History of Scottish Congregationalism*, G, 1959, 268). Russell's theology was that of a moderate Calvinist. His writings were prized in their day, particularly his *Letters, Chiefly Practical and Consolatory* (E, 1821), which continued to be reprinted up to the end of the nineteenth century. His *Catechism on the First Principles of Holy Scripture* (²D, 1822, many further editions) was used throughout Scotland and translated into several foreign languages.

Russell received a DD from Vermont University in 1834.

A Compendious View of the Original Dispensation Established with Adam and of the Mediatorial Dispensation Established through Christ (E, 1824); *A Familiar Survey of the Old and New Covenants* (E, 1824; ²G, 1843); *The Duties of the Christian Pastor* (E, 1812); *An Essay on the Salvation of All Dying in Infancy* (E, 1823).

R. Kinniburgh, *Fathers of Independency in Scotland* (E, 1851), 377–92; W. L. Alexander, *The Good Man's Grave* (G, 1848); C. M. Falconer and J. C. Low, *A Hundred Years of Congregationalism: The Story of Ward Chapel* (Dundee, 1934).

N. R. Needham

Rutherford House, Edinburgh, evangelical research and publishing centre opened in 1983 for the scholarly defence and promotion of orthodox Christianity. Its foundation was the work of leading CofS Evangelicals associated with the Crieff Fraternal.* The House is both a residential library and a publisher with special interests in systematic, practical and historical theology. Christian approaches to medical ethics emerged as a subsidiary concern. The House has initiated a range of research groups and conferences involving scholars and churchmen from Britain and overseas. Nigel Cameron (*Who's Who in Scotland 1986*, 66) was Warden from the outset until 1991, succeeded in 1993 by David C. Searle (*FES* X, 41, 336).

Publications have included the journals, *Evangel*, a quarterly for ministers, *Scottish Bulletin of Evangelical Theology** (published in association with the Scottish Evangelical Theology Society*), and *Ethics and Medicine*. In 1988 two dissertation publishing series were begun. Projects bringing scholars and publishers together include a new translation of

RUTHERFORD, JOHN

Calvin's Old Testament Commentaries and this *Dictionary*.

The House's developing ministry is increasingly concerned with the continuing education and formation of ministers and elders, the promotion of evangelical church life and the maintenance of an evangelical testimony in national church debates.

N. M. de S. Cameron

Rutherford, John (*c.* 1520–77), philosopher. The son of an Augustinian* canon at Jedburgh (and possibly of the same family as Samuel Rutherford*), he studied (with Patrick Buchanan) under George Buchanan* and Nicholas de Grouchy at Bordeaux and from 1547 at Coimbra in Portugal. He lectured briefly there before moving to Paris in 1551. In 1555 he was tutoring in the Montaigne household near Bordeaux (and may have influenced Montaigne's intellectual formation), but in 1556 responded to Archbishop John Hamilton's* call to teach humanity in his refounded St Mary's College, St Andrews. From 1560 until shortly before his death he was Provost of St Salvator's College there.

Rutherford became a Protestant, perhaps abroad but perhaps not much before 1560, when the Reformation Assembly declared him qualified for the ministry. In 1563 he was ordained to Cults (near Cupar, Fife), but was later rebuked by the Assembly for neglect. His only published work, *Commentariorum de Arte Disserendi...* (Paris, 1557; ²E, 1577), is a commentary on Aristotle's logic. His unpublished reply to John Davidson's* *Dialogue betwixt ... a Clerk and ane Courteour* (E, 1574) displeased the Assembly. Rutherford opposed John Knox* amid the Protestant quarrels in St Andrews in 1572 (Knox, *Works* VI, 622–31), and also rejected the Ramism and radical church polity of Andrew Melville.* He sought a return to Aristotle, but as a humanist, not a scholastic.

DNB L, 6; *FES* V, 138, VII, 411, VIII, 441; J. Durkan, 'John Rutherford and Montaigne...', *Bibliothèque d'Humanisme et Renaissance* 41 (1979), 115–22; J. MacQueen (ed.), *Humanism in Renaissance Scotland* (E, 1990).

D. F. Wright

Rutherford (or Rutherfurd), Samuel (1600–61), one of Scotland's greatest theologians, political theorists and devotional writers. He was born the son of a gentleman at Nisbet near Roxburgh, and educated at Jedburgh and Edinburgh University (graduated 1621). From 1623 he acted as regent of humanity, with responsibilities as a Latin tutor. He underwent a religious change and began reading theology at Edinburgh under Andrew Ramsay,* and in 1627 was presented to the scattered charge of Anwoth in Galloway. In 1630 he was directed to appear before the Court of High Commission* in Edinburgh for nonconformity to the Perth Articles.* Further proceedings against him by the Episcopalian party arose from the publication of his book *Exercitationes Apologeticae Pro Divina Gratia* (Amsterdam, 1636), which sought to discomfit the Arminian* theology that William Laud* was

RUTHERFORD, SAMUEL

patronizing in Scotland. In July 1636 the High Commission brought Rutherford's nine-year ministry in Anwoth to an end, barring him from preaching in Scotland and exiling him to Aberdeen for the duration of the King's pleasure. There he was required to debate with Robert Barron, one of the Aberdeen Doctors,* about Arminianism and ceremonies, and proved himself an able disputant.

After the Covenanters'* revolution in 1638 Rutherford returned to Anwoth and was a commissioner to the Glasgow Assembly.* The commission of that Assembly designated him Professor of Divinity at St Mary's College,* St Andrews. He consented to the office with the stipulation that he be permitted to preach regularly, and was made a colleague of Robert Blair* in the city pulpit. In 1642 he issued the first of several books in defence of Presbyterian Church government against the views of the emerging Independents* and Separatists.* In November 1643 he left for London as one of the Scottish Commissioners to the Westminster Assembly.* He remained in the city four years, preached before the Long Parliament, took a prominent part in the Assembly's debates on theology and Church polity, and published five major books. *Lex, Rex* (E, 1644) was at once received in the CofS as an authoritative successor to the political writing of George Buchanan;* Rutherford denied that a limitless sovereignty belonged to the King, and contended that the Crown is bestowed by the voluntary consent of the people, who are at liberty to resist a tyrant.

In November 1647 he resumed his duties at St Andrews and was soon made Principal of St Mary's. In 1651 he became Rector of the university. His writing brought him an international reputation in the Reformed Churches: he declined invitations to professorships at Harderwyck in Holland in 1648, Edinburgh in 1649, and Utrecht in 1651. When Charles II* visited St Andrews in 1650, Rutherford gave a speech before him on the duty of kings. When the Scots crowned the King the next year, they were obliged to support him with arms, and for the country's defence many wished to restore some who had previously offered support to the King under the terms of the Engagement.* Rutherford opposed the rehabilitation of the eschewed 'malignants', and was an outspoken Protester* against the resolutions (*see* Resolutioners) brought to the General Assembly of 1651. The two parties in the Church maintained a bitter schism for ten years, and during this time Rutherford's colleagues at St Mary's were against him. At the Restoration* of Charles II in 1661 the Committee of Estates ordered the burning of *Lex Rex*, deprived Rutherford of his offices, and cited him to come before Parliament* to answer a charge of treason. Rutherford was already terminally ill and replied, 'I have got summons already before a Superior Judge and Judicatory, and I behove to answer to my first summons, and ere your day come, I will be where few kings and great folks come.'

In *The Divine Right of Church Government and Excommunication* (L, 1646) Rutherford asserts that there is delineated in the New Testament a form

RUTHERFORD, SAMUEL

of Church government by elders* and Presbyteries which is of permanent obligation; moreover, that discipline* and suspension from the sacraments are vested with Church officers rather than with the Christian civil magistrate. The book also expounds the Westminster* Assembly's principle that the mode of acceptable worship is regulated by the will of Christ as king speaking in the Scriptures; the Church is not at liberty to alter or invent anything in worship or government which goes beyond the pattern in God's Word. Rutherford's writings during the London years provide a significant commentary on the theology of the Westminster Confession and Catechisms. In *Christ Dying and Drawing Sinners to Himself* (L, 1647), Rutherford elaborately scrutinizes the Antinomian notion that the law has no obligation for the Christian.

The *Examen Arminianismi* (Utrecht, 1668) is based on the lectures Rutherford delivered to his students at St Andrews. In his *Letters* (originally published as *Joshua Redivivus*, Rotterdam, 1664; best edit. by A. A. Bonar,* 2 vols, E, 1863; rp. slightly rev. in 1 vol, 1891; rp. 1986), most of which were written from exile in Aberdeen, Rutherford pictures himself as a Joshua sent ahead to spy out the land and send back word of the rich comforts Christ gives to his bride, the persecuted Church. Easily his most popular work, though not intended by him for publication (they were collected and published by his former student Robert MacWard*), the *Letters* have been frequently reprinted to the present day.

Disputatio Scholastica De Divina Providentia (E, 1649); *The Covenant of Life* (E, 1655); *The Due Right of Presbyteries* (L, 1644); *A Peaceable and Temperate Plea for Pauls Presbyterie in Scotland* (L, 1642); *Trial and Triumph of Faith* (L, 1645, E, 1845); *A Free Disputation Against pretended Liberty of Conscience* (L, 1649); *Influences of the Life of Grace* (L, 1659); *A Survey of the Survey of that Summe of Church Discipline Penned by Mr. Thomas Hooker* (L, 1658); *A Survey of the Spiritual Antichrist* (L, 1648); *Fourteen Communion Sermons* (G, 1877); *Quaint Sermons* (L, 1885).

T. Murray, *Life of Rev. Samuel Rutherford* (E, 1827; ²1828); R. Gilmour, *Samuel Rutherford, A Study Biographical and Somewhat Critical* (E, 1904); A. Thomson, *Samuel Rutherford* (L, 1889); A. Taylor Innes, 'Samuel Rutherford' in *The Evangelical Succession*, 2nd Series (E, 1883), 125–72; A. Whyte, *Samuel Rutherford and some of his Correspondents* (E, 1894); C. N. Button, 'Scottish Mysticism in the 17th Century, with special reference to Samuel Rutherford' (PhD, Edinburgh University, 1927); W. Campbell, 'Samuel Rutherford: Exponent of Scottish Presbyterianism' (PhD, Edinburgh University, 1937); D. R. Strickland, 'Union with Christ in the Theology of Samuel Rutherford' (PhD, Edinburgh University, 1972); R. Flinn, 'Samuel Rutherford and Puritan Political Theory', in *Journal of Christian Reconstruction* 5:2 (1978–9), 49–74; A. Grosart, *Representative Nonconformists* (L, 1879); M. Loane, *Makers of Religious Freedom in the Seventeenth Century* (L, 1960); J. Walker, *The Theology and Theologians of Scotland* (E, ²1988).

S. Isbell

Ruthven Raid, an attempt by Protestant nobles led by William Ruthven, the first Earl of Gowrie (c.1541–84), to control the government of the young James VI.* It ended the ascendancy of Esmé Stewart, first Duke of Lennox (c.1542–83), which raised a 'Popish Scare' and provoked the King's* or Negative Confession. James was invited to Ruthven Castle (Perthshire) in August 1582 and detained there until his escape in June 1583. Pro-Presbyterian policies prevailed, and John Durie* was able to return to Edinburgh. After the final rout of the Ruthven alliance in April 1584, and the flight of its leaders to England, the Earl of Arran (see Stewart, James, d.1596) exercised an 'anti-Presbyterian dictatorship' (1584–5; see Black Acts), until James began to direct policy himself.

G. Donaldson, *The Scottish Reformation* (C, 1960), 208–11; Calderwood III.

D. F. Wright

Ruthwell Cross, a standing stone cross erected as a preaching cross probably in the early eighth century, depicting scenes from Christ's life with identifying Latin inscriptions in Roman and Runic letters. It was reconstructed in the nineteenth century and moved back into the church at Ruthwell, Dumfriesshire, after being broken up following an iconoclastic decree by the General Assembly of the CofS in 1642.

It is a magnificent example of the standing cross, an art form unique to the British Isles, and perhaps originating in the Anglian kingdom of Northumbria, which embraced Ruthwell. Strong Eastern influence on the Western Church of that period is seen in the iconography of the sculptured panels on the shaft. Inhabited vine scrolls ornament the East and West faces, representing the tree of life, and are surrounded by an Anglo-Saxon poetic text in runes, in which the cross describes its experience as both victim and murderer at the crucifixion. These sixteen lines of poetry appear to be a quotation from a variant and perhaps earlier poem, 'The Dream of the Rood', preserved in the late tenth-century Vercelli Book. The anonymous author of this longer poem has a vision of a bejewelled, bleeding tree spanning the heavens which reveals itself as the cross and urges him to cling to the cross for protection from the coming judgment. This moving panegyric and the phenomenon of standing stone crosses testify to the strong influence of the cult of the cross in the British Isles.

M. Swanton (ed.), *The Dream of the Rood* (Manchester, 1970); B. Cassidy (ed.), *The Ruthwell Cross* (Princeton, NJ, 1992).

R. J. Meek

S

Sabbatarianism, the conception of Sunday as the Christian 'Sabbath' of the fourth commandment. Its distinguishing feature is the idea of 'rest for worship' – abstention from secular employment (and, usually, recreation) to devote the entire day to the public and private worship of God.

PRE-REFORMATION SCOTLAND. The *Céli Dé* (Culdee*) reform movement in the Celtic Church* was characterized by a strongly sabbatarian attitude to Sunday. This finds lucid expression in the *Cain Domnaig*, the 'Law of the Lord's Day' (ET in D. Maclean, *The Law of the Lord's Day in the Celtic Church*, E, 1926). This Old Irish (*see* Gaelic) document probably originated in the seventh or eighth century. Its prohibition of all manner of servile work, travel and recreation extends from Saturday vespers to Monday matins, and its high tone can be gauged from its threat that 'Whoever violates the sanctity of the Lord's day, there shall be lasting death to his soul and to his children after him, and he shall have no portion in heaven with Christ and His apostles.' Maclean argues that the sabbatarian legislation of the Carolingian Renaissance ultimately derived through Alcuin from the Celtic tradition, but this is debatable (see K. Hughes, *The Church in Early Irish Society*, L, 1966, 178–9).

The Scottish Church remained theoretically sabbatarian through the Middle Ages. Kings William,* Alexander III and (particularly) James IV* all supported sabbatarian practice, by laws or personal example. General practice, however, as elsewhere in Christendom, fell conspicuously below the ideal, and the status of Sunday was relativized by the prominence given to other 'holy days' of ecclesiastical origin.

REFORMATION AND COVENANTING TIMES. The Scottish Reformation* initiated a movement towards a purer sabbatarianism. This was largely indirect at first, consisting in the abolition of the medieval 'holy days' and the exaltation of Sunday as the national day for Reformed worship and teaching. The *First Book of Discipline** emphasized the ecclesiastical nature of Lord's Day observance, demanding that 'Sunday must be straitly kept both before and after noon in all towns', by enforced attendance at the morning sermon and afternoon catechizing. The General Assembly in 1562 petitioned Queen Mary* for the punishment of those who held markets on Sunday, and in 1579 Parliament prohibited Sunday markets and labouring, and playing and drinking during the appointed time for the sermon. These moves, however, were probably pragmatic in design, to facilitate attendance at worship, rather than principled enactments of the fourth commandment as such.

The Scottish Reformers bequeathed no fully developed sabbatarian theory of Sunday to the Reformed Kirk. Nothing of this nature is found in the Scots Confession,* *FBD*, or the various authorized catechisms,* *e.g.* the Genevan and Heidelberg. However, sentiment in favour of a strict sabbatarian theology grew as the sixteenth century drew to its close, probably reflected in the increasing sweep and severity of disciplinary actions taken by Kirk Sessions* and magistrates against 'sabbath desecration'. Some have detected English Puritan influence here. At any rate, the movement came of age in the General Assembly of 1596, where commissioners lamented the nation's profanation of the fourth and other commandments, and resolved to promote sabbath piety. John Davidson* was particularly outspoken on the issue.

The seventeenth century saw the blossoming of a native Scottish sabbatarian literature. Three seminal works were published in the 1630s: John Wemyss's* (or Weemse) *Exposition of the Laws of Moses* (1632), a section in David Calderwood's* *A Re-examination of Five Articles Enacted at Perth* (1636), and Thomas Young's* *Dies Dominica* (1639). The Westminster* Confession and Catechisms' sabbatarian doctrine of the Lord's Day simply articulated what Scottish Presbyterians had now universally embraced. By contrast, the Scottish episcopate in the pre-Covenanting* era was associated with anti-sabbatarianism, through the influence of James VI* and Charles I,* and particularly William Laud.*

Other important seventeenth-century writers who advocated sabbatarianism included John Brown of Wamphray,* James Durham* and Robert Leighton.* Leighton's sabbatarianism evinces the doctrine's ultimate acceptance across the Presbyterian-Episcopalian divide. The post-Covenanting Scottish Parliament enacted severe sabbath laws in 1661, 1672, 1693, 1695 and 1701.

EIGHTEENTH AND NINETEENTH CENTURIES. The eighteenth century produced relatively little sabbatarian literature (but *see* Wilson, John), and probably saw some slackening in strictness of Sunday observance under the influence of Moderatism.* However, the older view lived on, especially among Seceders,* and James Fisher's* *Catechism Explained* (G, 1753, 1760) contains in its second part an exposition of sabbatarianism of which James Gilfillan (below) pronounced that there was no account 'clearer, more satisfactory, or more adapted for general usefulness'.

The nineteenth century was a great age for Scottish sabbatarianism, both for volume of publications and concerted attempts to bring national life into harmony with the fourth commandment. This was due to the resurgence of Evangelicalism, flowing from the Haldane* revival of the 1790s. Evangelicalism and sabbatarianism were closely linked, and the Scottish MP Sir Andrew Agnew's* efforts at piloting sabbatarian legislation through Parliament stimulated public awareness. In 1839 the Scottish Society for Promoting the Due Observance of the Lord's Day (usually called the Lord's Day Observance Society) was established in Edinburgh. Proponents of sabbatarianism included Thomas Chalmers* (CofS and FC), John Brown of Edinburgh* (USec.C), Gavin Struthers* (Relief) James and Robert Haldane* (Baptist), Ralph Wardlaw* (Congregationalist), and D. T. K. Drummond* (EpCS) – an impressive cross-Church consensus. One of the richest treasuries of information on sabbatarian theology and literature was produced by James Gilfillan, UPC minister at Stirling, in his *The Sabbath* (E, 1861; ³1863).

The Voluntary Controversy,* however, divided Scottish sabbatarians in their tactics. The more Voluntary a person's views, the less likely he was to accept the propriety of state legislation as a means of enforcing sabbath-keeping. Wardlaw, for instance, wrote powerfully on the sabbatarian nature of Sunday, but finally repudiated all attempts to compel observance by statute. He preferred to rely on moral persuasion.

Several years of heated debate and polemic literature (the 'Sabbath War') commenced in 1865 when the North British Railway Company proposed to run trains on Sunday between Glasgow and Edinburgh (R. D. Brackenridge, 'The "Sabbath War" of 1865–66 . . .', *RSCHS* 16, 1966, 23–34; C. J. A. Robertson, 'Early Scottish Railways and the Observance of the Sabbath', *SHR* 57, 1978, 143–67). A previous attempt at running Sunday trains had been defeated in 1845. The CofS Glasgow Presbytery instructed its ministers to read a pastoral letter on the sanctity of the Lord's Day, but Norman Macleod (1812–72)* refused. He made a speech to his Presbytery justifying his refusal in which he propounded an alternative theology of Sunday, denying the obligation of the fourth commandment on Christians. Presbytery merely admonished him, but he had to endure a storm of popular abuse and clerical ostracism. W. C. Smith* of the FC uttered similar views, leading to his appearance before the General Assembly of 1867, where he was censured but (to the dismay of conservatives) not deposed.

MODERN PERIOD. Sabbatarianism declined in the closing decades of the nineteenth century, and suffered the same fate as other Christian beliefs and practices in society's progressive secularization in the twentieth century. The Highlands* have retained a more traditional sabbatarian Sunday, but the rest of Scotland has drifted from social sabbatarianism, both legally and in practice, even more noticeably than England. Shopping, mail, public transport and recreation are now accepted features of a typical Scottish Sunday. Campaigns for a return to a more traditional Sunday observance, e.g. by the 'Keep Sunday Special' lobby, do not always share the sabbatarian theology which motivated their nineteenth-century predecessors.

F. N. Lee, *The Covenantal Sabbath* (L, 1969); D. A. Carson (ed.), *From Sabbath to Lord's Day* (Grand Rapids, 1982); P. K. Jewett, *The Lord's Day* (Grand Rapids, 1971); J. MacGregor, *The Sabbath Question* (E, 1866); R. Cox, *The Literature of the Sabbath Question*, 2 vols (E, 1865); J. R. Fleming, *A History of the Church in Scotland 1843–1874* (E, 1927); J. Wigley, *The Rise and Fall of the Victorian Sunday* (Manchester, 1980); A. H. Lewis, *A Critical History of Sunday Legislation* (NY, 1888); Burleigh.

N. R. *Needham*

Sacraments, the common designation for certain rites or ceremonies of the Church which have both an outward and visible aspect (the sign) and a corresponding inward and spiritual reality (the thing signified). The word is not used in the Bible, and it was not until the later medieval era that the Catholic Church categorically distinguished its seven sacraments, claimed to have been instituted by Christ, from other rites. The Protestant Reformers insisted that Christ had instituted only two gospel sacraments – baptism* and the Lord's Supper* (Luther for a time recognized penance as well). They differed little on baptism, but they had to defend infant baptism against its rejection by reforming radicals.* The Lord's Supper, on the other hand, occasioned deep disagreement, most sharply between Luther and Zwingli. Although chiefly influenced by later Reformers, especially Calvin, who moved beyond earlier disputes, the Scottish Reformation still reflected continental controversies.

The Scots Confession* sets out the fundamentals of Reformed sacramental theology: right administration of the sacraments is one of the 'notes' of the true Kirk, which requires that they be always associated with God's Word and promise, and be administered only by 'lawful ministers' and in the elements and manner appointed in God's Word; they were certainly not 'nothing else than naked and bare signs' (probably an allusion to Zwinglian views); like their Old Testament counterparts, circumcision and Passover, their purpose was to distinguish God's people from outsiders, to exercise faith and to seal the assurance of the divine promise and of union with Jesus Christ.

The *First Book of Discipline** made very much the same points, insisting on administration in the vernacular (i.e. not Latin). The characteristic Reformed annexation of the sacraments to the Word was stressed; they could not be rightly ministered 'by him in whose mouth God has put no Sermon of exhortation'. This emphasis has sometimes led to the Lord's Supper being viewed as part of the ministry of the Word, just as the centrality of the latter has from time to time fostered a quasi-sacramental understanding of it.

Neither the Scots Confession nor the *FBD* deals precisely with the relation between the sign and the thing signified – what the Westminster Confession calls a 'spiritual relation' or a 'sacramental union'. Robert Bruce's* celebrated sermons on the Supper began with sacraments in general. He taught that the signs are 'instruments to deliver and exhibit the things that they signify', and the latter is nothing less than 'the whole Christ with his whole gifts, benefits and graces, applied and given to my soul'. While we receive no more in the sacraments than in the Word, we 'get a better hold of Christ than we get in the simple Word'.

Bruce's exposition reveals the difficulty of speaking at length about both sacraments at once. In particular, the baptizing of infants cannot satisfy in any obvious sense the Reformation axiom that faith is necessary for the recipient to benefit from a sacrament. In Scotland, among Presbyterians, it is probably fair to say that a higher view of the Lord's Supper has prevailed than of baptism. The former has been fenced around by infrequency of observance, the solemnity of the Communion season* and restrictions on, and scruples against, participation, whereas the latter has often been given much less carefully to infants. Much less of baptism than of the rare and dignified Presbyterian Communion, have Scottish churchmen found it congenial to confess that the sensible signs actually convey and confer what they signify – not of themselves, of course, but by the gift of Christ, who is the true minister of the sacraments, through the power of the Spirit. To that extent the notion of a sacrament remains a problematic one for Reformed and Presbyterian theology.

Other Protestants prefer to talk of 'ordinances' rather than 'sacraments', without thereby implying any devaluation of them. Baptists* and Brethren* in Scotland have generally avoided the 'occasional' nature of Communion by administering it as a part of the weekly diet of worship, sometimes before or after the main service. For these bodies, the Communion is an ordinance that demonstrates their visible Christian unity as gathered congregations, and combines commemoration of the Lord's death with celebration of his resurrection.

For Brethren, the 'breaking of bread' is probably more significant than baptism by immersion; for Baptists, however, baptism by immersion takes precedence in terms of Church order, and is frequently (but by no means always) a prerequisite of full membership. Most Scottish Baptist churches now practice 'open Communion', but in the past there have been conflicts between this position and a restriction to baptized members of the local church or churches known to be in fellowship with it. Within the Baptist movement, lay preachers (*see* Laity) can preside at communion, and lay elders or deacons can administer baptism, although 'good order' would normally favour the involvement of ordained men where available.

Some Christian bodies, especially the Salvation Army* and the Society of Friends,* observe neither of the sacraments, yet are full members of ecumenical groupings such as Action of Churches Together in Scotland.

D. M. Baillie, *The Theology of the Sacraments* (L, 1957); H. J. Wotherspoon and J. M. Kirkpatrick, *A Manual of Church Doctrine according to the Church of Scotland* (^{2}L, 1960); H. J. Wotherspoon, *Religious Values of the Sacraments* (E, 1928).

D. F. Wright

Sage, Donald (1789–1869), minister and author. Sage was a grandson of Aeneas Sage (1694–1774), the first Presbyterian minister of Lochcarron (Wester Ross) after the Revolution, and a man noted as much for his great physical strength as for his eminent spirituality. His father, Alexander Sage (1753–1824), was for many years minister of Kildonan, in Sutherland, where Sage himself was born and received much of his early education. In 1804 he enrolled at Marischal College, Aberdeen (MA, 1808), and thereafter studied divinity at Aberdeen and Edinburgh. In 1815 he was licensed by the Presbytery of Lochcarron, within whose bounds he served for some time as a private tutor. In the following year he was ordained to the missionary charge of Achness in Sutherland. His ministry there was brief, ending two years later with the wholesale eviction of his parishioners in the Strathnaver clearances.* In 1819 he became minister of the Gaelic Chapel in Aberdeen, but his stay here too was short, and in 1822 he removed to Resolis, in the Black Isle, where he spent the remaining forty-six years of his ministry. At the Disruption* he entered the FC, with the great majority of his congregation.

Sage is chiefly noted for his *Memorabilia Domestica*, edited by his son, and first published in 1889. Largely autobiographical, it provides a fascinating insight into the social and ecclesiastical life of the time, with many interesting anecdotes and asides. Sage was a keen observer of people and events, combining a vivid attention to detail with a highly accomplished literary style. Perhaps his most celebrated passage is his description of the clearances, which he himself witnessed, and which he relates with a particular poignancy. The book abounds in character sketches of individuals, ranging from the professors under whom he studied in his early days to his fellow-ministers in later life. Some of these are drawn with a frankness which occasioned no little controversy when the book was published, notwithstanding his son's careful emendations. To all his work, however, Sage brought a transparent sincerity, which is nowhere more evident than in his accounts of his own spiritual experience. His preaching drew forth from John Kennedy* of Dingwall the commendation: 'Few preachers have ever laboured more to exalt their theme and to abase themselves.'

Memorabilia Domestica, or Parish Life in the North of Scotland (Wick, 1889; rp. E, 1975).

J. Greig (ed.), *Disruption Worthies of the Highlands* (E, 1877), 45–52; *FES* VII, 19–20, 90, 160–1.

M. Grant

Sage, John (1652–1711), non-juring* Bishop. His father was captain in Lord Duffus's regiment. He was born at Creich, Fife, where he was educated in the parish school. After graduating MA at St. Andrews in 1669, he first served as schoolmaster in Ballingry and then became a private tutor. He was ordained in 1684 at Glasgow and served as Synod Clerk. After the Revolution he opened a meeting house in Edinburgh, but was banished by the Privy Council. He spent the remainder of his life as a tutor and domestic chaplain. He was consecrated a Bishop in 1705 in Edinburgh.

Although he had a considerable reputation as a patristic scholar, because of his adherence to Episcopacy and the Stewart cause Sage forfeited a chair at St Andrews, to which he had been nominated, but not installed, just prior to the Revolution. Sage is best known for his controversial works, in which he attempted to demonstrate a primitive diocesan episcopacy (*see* Rule, Gilbert; Jameson, William).

The Works ... with Memoir and Notes (E, 1844–6); *The Fundamental Charter of Presbytery* (L, 1695); *The Principles of the Cyprianic Age* (L, 1695); *A Vindication of ... The Principles of ... The Principles of the Cyprianic Age* (L, 1701); *An Account of the Late Establishment of Presbyterian-Government by the Parliament of Scotland Anno 1690* (L, 1693).

J. Gillan, *The Life of John Sage* (L, 1714); J. Skinner, *Ecclesiastical History of Scotland*, 2 vols (L, 1788); G. Grub, *Ecclesiastical History of Scotland* 4 vols (E, 1861); *DNB* L, 115–16; *FES* III, 452.

A. E. Nimmo

St Andrew Press, *see* Publishing, Religious.

St Andrews Priory. The episcopacy (1124–59) of Robert, former prior of Scone,* led to the establishment in 1144 of a house of Augustinian* canons in St Andrews. They constituted the cathedral chapter and in 1147 were given the right to elect the bishop. A Culdee* community (*see* Early Ecclesiastical Sites), which they were intended to replace, continued to co-exist and eventually became a secular collegiate body. The Augustinians had a dual role, being a religious house but also responsible, with the bishop, for the cathedral (which Robert began to build) and its services. Their consent in chapter was needed for various diocesan transactions and they administered the diocese when the see was vacant, with the prior acting as vicar general. The bishop ceded to them the right to elect their own prior and freely conduct their community affairs themselves.

They were the most important religious corporation in Scotland and their prestige grew in the later Middle Ages as St Andrews became a metropolitan see (1472) and the location of the first Scottish university.* In 1512 St Leonard's College was founded within the priory confines, endowed and controlled by them. Though only a prior, the Augustinian superior took precedence over all Scottish abbots and in 1418 was granted *pontificalia* (episcopal insignia). The right of electing bishop and prior was, however, replaced by agreement between king and pope. The priory was the wealthiest religious house in Scotland and had the largest community: twenty-four canons died in the Black Death of 1349 and there were over thirty in 1560.

St Andrews had two dependent houses: Loch Leven (Portmoak), where Augustinians replaced Culdees c.1150, and Pittenweem, where Augustinians had replaced the Benedictines* of Isle of May by 1318. Both were in Fife/Kinross, not far from St Andrews. Loch Leven had no community after the early fifteenth century, but Pittenweem, having been granted to bishops of St Andrews in the fifteenth century, regained its monastic status and in 1541–2 had nine resident canons. Authors are mistaken in claiming that Pittenweem merged with St Andrews and that Monymusk* in Aberdeenshire was a dependency of St Andrews.

Many canons attained high office or celebrity, including the chroniclers Andrew of Wyntoun* and Walter Bower,* abbot of Inchcolm in the Firth of Forth. St Andrews priors were never pluralists, this unique position being incompatible with other offices. The last regular prior was Patrick Hepburn,* later Bishop of Moray. In 1538 James Stewart,* natural son of James V and later Regent of Scotland, became commendator.* The priory made an outstanding contribution to the Reformation:* Gavin Logie* taught Protestantism at St Leonard's College (see J. Herkless and R. K. Hannay, *The College of St Leonard*, E and L, 1905, *passim*), Alesius* was an early Reformer, John Winram* was one of the first superintendents, twenty canons became ministers or readers,* and David Peebles* (*d*.1579) composed music for the Scottish Psalter (*see* Psalms).

Liber Cartarum Prioratus Sancti Andree in Scotia (Bannatyne Club, E, 1841); J. H. Baxter (ed.), *Copiale Prioratus Sanctiandree* (O, 1930); G. W. S. Barrow, *The Kingdom of the Scots* (L, 1973), 171–2, 212–32; M. Dilworth, 'The Augustinian Chapter of St Andrews', *IR* 25 (1974), 15–30; *id.*, 'The Dependent Priories of St Andrews' in D. McRoberts (ed.), *The Medieval Church of St Andrews* (G, 1976), 157–66; *FESMA*, 299–302; Easson-Cowan, *passim*.

M. Dilworth

ST COLM'S COLLEGE

St Colm's College, CofS training college in Edinburgh, since 1984 called St Colm's Education Centre and College. It was founded in 31 George Square in 1894 as the FC Women's Missionary Training Institute, with Annie Small* as principal until 1913 (*PGAFCS 1895*, Women's For. Miss. Rep. 12–15). Students attended some lectures at New College.* In 1897 it moved to 16 Atholl Crescent and in 1910 (now UFC) to purpose-built premises at 23 Inverleith Terrace (extended in 1921).

After the 1929 Union, the CofS women's training programme based in Deaconess House in 27 George Square (founded under Alice Maxwell* in 1888 at 33 Mayfield Gardens but soon moved to George Square) was merged with the UFC Institute. Now known as the CofS Women's Missionary College (St Colm's), it would prepare women for service abroad and at home (*PGACS 1934*, 347–50). From 1951 men were also accepted for training for overseas service.

As missionary personnel have decreased, the College's role has expanded, to cater not only for CofS overseas mission and diaconate* but also for Presbyterian Church in Ireland deaconesses, lay ministries, some overseas churches' personnel, and church members seeking deeper training. Distance learning has also been developed. The Christian Science church next door was acquired in 1988 and developed as the Annie Small Centre.

Among teachers at St Colm's have been Elizabeth Hewat,* Kenneth Mackenzie* and Mary Lusk (Levison).*

O. Wyon, *The Three Windows* (L, 1953), 57–83; A. H. Small *et al.*, ... *Memories of Fifty Years 1894–1944* (E, 1944); id. (ed.) *Missionary College Hymns* (E, 1914).

D. F. Wright

St Giles', the parish church of medieval Edinburgh. The first, Romanesque, cruciform building was probably begun soon after the founding of the burgh in 1130 and survived until its rebuilding, by stages, in the fourteenth and fifteenth centuries. The growing significance of the town was reflected both in the new Gothic building and in its collegiate status, granted by the Pope at the Town Council's request in 1467. Thereafter it was administered by a chapter, directly responsible to Rome, under a provost (one notable provost being Gavin Douglas*). The crown spire was built around 1500. Between 1560 and 1572 John Knox,* as minister of Edinburgh, had St Giles' as his church. The many ornaments and altars were removed, and towards the end of the sixteenth century walls were built dividing the building into separate places of worship. The divisions were removed when the church was designated, in 1633, the cathedral of the new diocese of Edinburgh, but were re-created after the episcopal period, and remained, to some extent, until the unifying restoration of 1881–3, when the congregation of the High Church, which had worshipped in the medieval choir as the 'town church' of Edinburgh, occupied the entire building. An earlier restoration of 1829–33 covered the external walls in new stone in a manner which has been widely regarded as unfortunate. Monuments, largely military, were added in the early twentieth century. The CofS General Assembly has attended worship annually in St Giles'. The Thistle Chapel* was added in 1909–11, and the Knights of the Thistle attend service there annually on the Sunday on or following St Andrew's Day.

J. Cameron Lees, *St Giles', Edinburgh* (E, 1889); J. Gifford, C. McWilliam and D. Walker, *Edinburgh* (Harmondsworth, 1984), 102–18.

G. I. Macmillan

St Mary's College, theological faculty in the University of St Andrews. Founded under a papal bull by Archbishop James Beaton* in 1539, the 'College of the Assumption of the Blessed Virgin Mary' was intended primarily for the training of secular clergy. Until the nineteenth century it was commonly known as 'New College', in distinction from the older College of St Salvator.

Although taken over by Beaton's nephew and successor, Cardinal David Beaton,* St Mary's foundation was not secure until Archbishop John Hamilton's* reorganization in 1554–5. The first principal had been Robert Bannerman, succeeded by Archibald Hay (1546–7), whose humanism aspired to a trilingual college on the Louvain or Paris pattern, and then by John Douglas* (1547–74), who carried through Hamilton's re-foundation designed to serve Catholic reform by promoting biblical theology and improving the parish clergy.

Principal Douglas sided with Protestantism from 1560, and his College retained its leading position in the University. The Reformers' plans for the universities (*FBD* 137–55) stipulated that one St Andrews college be devoted solely to divinity, which was enacted for St Mary's by Parliament in 1579. Five masters (professors) were envisaged in Hebrew, Old Testament (two), New Testament and Systematic Theology, the last coupled with the principalship, now assumed by Andrew Melville* (1580–1606). This outstanding scholar and educationalist made St Mary's one of the leading theological schools of Protestant Europe.

Robert Howie's* long principalship (1607–46) outlasted the years of episcopacy.* As befitted Scotland's ecclesiastical capital, James VI* intended St Mary's to be the country's principal school of divinity, and it survived the 1621 revocation of the 1579 Act little changed. But a reform Commission during the Covenanting* era in 1643 assigned appointments to the four surviving chairs to the General Assembly. Alexander Henderson* was well disposed to the University, and Samuel Rutherford* was professor (from 1639) and principal (1648–60).

The Revolution of 1689, when St Andrews finally lost ecclesiastical primacy, and economic changes, which the Union of 1707 intensified, brought decline to the University and St Mary's. Controversy troubled James Hadow,* principal 1707–47 and opponent of the *Marrow*,* and Archibald Campbell,

Professor of Ecclesiastical History 1730–56 (*DNB* VIII, 340–1; *AGACS* 638–9, 644–5). As Professor of Divinity from 1772 and Principal of St Mary's 1791–1819, the leading Moderate George Hill* dominated a later generation. His nepotism proverbially popularized Psalm 121!

Under Hill's principalship Thomas Chalmers* became a young Divinity student in 1795, returning as Professor of Moral Philosophy 1823–8. His successor in the chair, George Cook,* was his chief opponent during the Ten Years' Conflict.* Sir David Brewster,* Principal of the United College, openly joined the FC, but none of the Divinity professors supported the Disruption,* unlike some of the students. In consequence, alone of the Scottish Divinity faculties, St Mary's was not confronted by a rival FC college.

A. F. Mitchell* proved a distinguished Church History professor (1868–94), and another long-serving principal, John Tulloch* (1854–86), did much to restore the standing of St Mary's, although his concern for the CofS led him to consider transplanting the College to Edinburgh, to counter the pre-eminence of the FC's New College.* Even into the twentieth century, St Mary's sometimes seemed a bastion of Auld Kirk* Moderatism.* Yet its stars have included Donald Baillie,* G. S. Duncan* and E. P. Dickie.* Among its most erudite professors was the enduring if eccentric James Houston Baxter (1894–1973; *FES* VII, 434, VIII, 719, IX, 768, X, 428), who held the Ecclesiastical History chair 1922–70. John Herkless*, later Principal of the University, had held the chair 1894–1915.

Although St Andrews had no UF college, St Mary's was included in the reorganization of theological education after the 1929 Union. The three offices of professor of Divinity, Dean of Faculty and principal of St Mary's, combined since Andrew Melville's day, were separated. The latter two became University appointments, with professors (of Divinity, Biblical Criticism, Hebrew and Oriental Languages, Ecclesiastical History) selected by joint University–Church nominating boards. The Church also founded and financed two new chairs of Systematic Theology and Practical Theology and Christian Ethics, open only to CofS ministers. More recent changes have removed this restriction and effected other reorganization. The Faculty has also been particularly successful in extending theology to non-ordinands, and in hosting a Summer School popular with US ministers.

See also Education, Theological.

R. G. Cant, *The University of St Andrews* (E, 1946); id., *The New Foundation of 1579 in Historical Perspective* (E, 1979); J. K. Cameron, in D. W. D. Shaw (ed.), *In Divers Manners. A St Mary's Miscellany* (St Andrews, 1990), 29–72; H. R. Sefton, 'St Mary's College, St Andrews, in the Eighteenth Century', *RSCHS* 24 (1991), 161–80; J. H. Baxter, 'The Theological Society 1760–1960', *St Mary's College Bulletin* 3 (1961), 11–18.

D. F. Wright

St Ninian's, Crieff, CofS training centre. Founded in 1959 by D. P. Thomson,* Evangelist of the CofS, St Ninian's had its origins in 'Work and Witness', a lay training organization established by Thomson, and found its home in the redundant West Church of Crieff, adapted by volunteer labour for its new use.

Thomson was succeeded as Warden in 1967, and in 1970 the church building was imaginatively reconstructed to provide the facilities of a modern conference centre within the walls of the old church. At this time also the properties were transferred to the CofS, although the Centre's operation continued under the supervision of an interdenominational Board of Management. Succeeding years have seen continuing development. A chapel was provided in 1984 and the renovated and extended annexe was re-opened as Thomson House in 1987.

Redesignated in 1984 as a Training and Resource Centre for mission and renewal, the Centre seeks to witness through its life and ministry to the renewing power of the Holy Spirit and God's missionary purpose for his people. Training resources are provided at the Centre and in parishes, and continuing research is carried out in the work of mission and the state of the Scottish Church.

RGACS, Home Board Reports, 1959–1988; D. F. Wright and A. H. Gray (eds), *Local Church Evangelism* (E, 1987).

P. T. Bisset

Saints. The saints, in scriptural terms, are the body of the faithful in Christ. In the early Christian period, the term 'saints' included all Christians, to distinguish them from non-Christians. With the growth of Christianity, *sanctus* (Greek *hagios*) came to be used to describe men and women who had shown great virtue in their lifetime and were believed to be intercessors with God in heaven. In the Roman Catholic Church,* saints are those persons who, by tradition or by formal process, have been declared to be in heaven, and to be holy and exemplary models for public veneration, through a life of virtue or a death by martyrdom.* Beatification, whereby a person is declared to be 'Blessed' and in heaven, is a half-way stage towards canonization. The formal procedure for canonization developed after the twelfth century. It was elaborated especially by Urban VIII (1623–44) and Benedict XIV (1740–58), restricted to Rome, and made very stringent.

A medieval saint's holiness was manifested in miracles which were often related in his or her written Life, and attestation of miracles remains integral to canonization. The Lives of the early saints of the Church are mostly legendary; they were written to eulogize the saints' heroic Christian qualities and to inspire devotion to their cults. During the Middle Ages, the cult of the saints was, and in Latin countries still is, an important part of religious devotion. Saints' tombs became places of pilgrimage and worship; their relics continue to be revered as sacred objects, since their use increases the expectation that the saint is interceding, and/ or that God will honour that saint.

SAINTS, MEDIEVAL

The RCC continues to declare saints by formal canonization. The saints of the early Christian period in Scotland are retained by that Church and in the nomenclature and calendars of the EpCS and (informally) the CofS, although the invocation of saints was banned by the Reformers*. *See* Anglo-Saxon Saints; Celtic Saints.

H. Delehaye, *The Legends of the Saints*, trans. D. Attwater (L, 1962); *id.*, *Sanctus: Essai sur les cultes des saintes dans l'antiquité* (Brussels, 1927); P. Brown, *The Cult of the Saints* (L, 1981); *New Catholic Encyclopedia* XII, 852–3; R. Aingrain, *L'hagiographie* (Paris, 1953).

D. A. Bray

Saints, Medieval, *see* Andrew; Gilbert of Perth; Magnus; Margaret.

Salmond, Stewart Dingwall Fordyce (1837–1905), FC and UFC divine. Born and educated in Aberdeen, he was ordained in 1865 as minister of Barry FC, Angus. He returned to Aberdeen in 1876 on his appointment as Professor of Systematic Theology at the FC College, becoming Principal in 1898 (Professor of Dogmatics, 1910). He founded the Aberdeenshire Theological Club in 1882 to encourage ministers to keep up their study of theology. Aberdeen University awarded him a DD.

Salmond is chiefly notable for his editorship of the International Theological Library, along with Charles A. Briggs of Union Theological Seminary, New York. He is also known for his translations of patristic writers and his commentaries in the Century Bible and other series. His *magnum opus* was *The Christian Doctrine of Immortality* (Cunningham lectures,* E, 1895; ³1897), a learned and lucid tome which among other things offers a penetrating critique of eschatological universalism and annihilationism, and broadly endorses the traditional doctrine of eternal punishment.

AFCS I, 58; *FUFCS* 582; J. S. McEwen, 'Aberdeenshire Theological Club 1882–1982', *AUR* 50 (1983–4), 351–8.

H. R. Sefton

Saltire (Cross), *see* Andrew, Saint.

Salvation Army, worldwide evangelistic and charitable organization run on military principles. In 1865, twenty-one years after his conversion, William Booth (1829–1912) resigned from his Methodist (New Connexion) ministry and in partnership with his wife established the East London Christian Mission to evangelize the destitute. In 1878 this became the Salvation Army, when cumbersome consensus government was replaced by the autocratic control of Booth, now designated 'General' for life in a hierarchical structure modelled on the British army. In 1929 the generalship became elective and ceased to be a lifelong appointment.

Aggressive evangelism, extensive use of music, informality and simplicity of worship, with a disregard of the sacraments, characterized the movement.

SALVATION ARMY

Booth's *Orders and Regulations* established strict principles of conduct and organization for Salvationists, who were given military ranks, and organized in corps, divisions and territories. By December 1879 the Christian Mission's thirty stations had increased to 130 Salvation Army corps, with almost 200 officers nationwide.

The first Scottish corps was established in Anderston, Glasgow, in 1879, with assistance from Thomas Robinson, JP, of Paisley, who provided financial backing for much of the early work. By the end of 1880 further corps had been established in Bridgeton, Aberdeen, Coatbridge and Kilsyth. Slow progress thereafter was attributed by Booth, paradoxically, to the strength of conventional religion in Scotland, where the Churches' prejudice and suspicion turned church-going people against the Army. In 1881 Booth appointed American-born Henry Edmonds, aged twenty, to expand the sluggish Scottish work. In 1883 the CofS first admitted publicly that the new movement could no longer be ignored; by 1888 seventy-eight corps had been established under Edmonds' leadership.

The Army's uncompromising moral stance and robust evangelism aroused opposition not only from street mobs, but also from procurers, the liquor trade and local authorities, which often turned a blind eye to mob attacks on Army meetings. In January 1882 the newly-formed Dumfries Corps, having been thrown into the River Nith in a mob attack, was then arraigned by the town magistrates for breach of the peace. In 1890 fifty Kirkcaldy ratepayers petitioned the council to take action against the Army's 'noisy demonstrations', and in 1907, after 20,000 had met illegally in Motherwell in defiance of a magistrates' ban on open-air meetings, twenty-five Army supporters were imprisoned briefly.

Yet the Army gained in credibility as its practical evangelism was seen to cater for both bodies and souls. In 1883 it opened its first female rescue home in Glasgow, and also worked among city street children and in rural communities. In 1890 the publication of Booth's social welfare manifesto, *In Darkest England* (L), inaugurated a tripartite scheme to rehabilitate the 'submerged tenth' of Britain's population in city refuges, farm colonies and an overseas settlement. Despite its title, the programme was not confined to England. Male and female hostels, prison visitation and prisoners' aid, eventide homes* and labour bureaux were established in several Scottish cities and towns, and the first Glasgow hostel incorporated an emigration department alongside its labour bureau.

Although no overseas colony was implemented as part of the 'Darkest England' scheme, from the 1890s to the 1920s the Salvation Army was Britain's leading emigration* agency, supervising the departure of many thousand emigrants, not least Scots, to destinations all over the Empire. Meanwhile the domestic welfare programme became – and continues to be – the best-known aspect of the Salvationists' international work, involving the provision of aid and counsel to victims of disaster, food and shelter depots for the destitute, rescue and rehabilitation programmes for prostitutes, alcoholics and discharged prisoners, hospitals and daycare centres, and a much-used lost persons' department.

Salvation Army, *Marching as to War* (L, 1979); R. Sandall, A. Wiggins, F. Coutts, *The History of the Salvation Army*, 7 vols (L, 1947–86); W. Booth, *Orders and Regulations for Soldiers of the Salvation Army* (L, 1907).

M. Harper

Sandeman, Robert (1718–71), author and Glasite elder. Robert Sandeman was born in Perth in a linen merchant's family which was drawn early into the Glasite movement. In 1734, while a student in Edinburgh, Sandeman joined the church, returned to business in Perth, and in 1737 married John Glas's* daughter Katherine. In 1744 he was appointed an elder and was able to devote his whole time to the church. By his books and extensive correspondence Sandeman became the chief publicist of the Glasite, or, as they are called outside Scotland, Sandemanian churches. His main work, *Letters on Theron and Aspasio* (E, 1757), controverting James Hervey, was widely influential in England, Wales and New England. In 1764 Sandeman accepted an invitation to Boston, Massachusetts, where he had sympathizers, and settled in Danbury, Connecticut, where he died.

Sandeman developed and promulgated Glas's views in theology and Church practice. Sandemanianism, which for some years disturbed Baptists and Congregationalists on both sides of the Atlantic, is characterized by a search for primitive Christianity, free of the corruptions that even the Reformers allowed. 'Let the people take the whole of scripture for their law and guide' was Glas's motto, and since Christendom had fallen from truth, the New Testament Church must be re-established. Each local congregation is subject to 'no other judicatory under heaven', and must be furnished with elders and deacons. Extraordinary offices, such as evangelists, have ceased. Baptism is administered to infants by pouring, and the Lord's Supper is observed weekly. Worship consists of metrical psalms, sung by rotation, prayers led by elders and brethren, several chapters of Scripture read in succession so that the whole Bible is read in public, and at the love feast the singing of hymns (first edition of *Christian Songs*, compiled by Glas, Dundee, 1749). The kiss of charity is enjoined, there is potential community of goods, there must be unanimity in decisions, the lot is sacred, and believers must abstain from eating blood. Sandemanians were exclusive in Church fellowship, but have been notably generous to secular charities. The basic theology of the movement is Calvinist. Evangelism is by answers to enquiries and by the written word. Worship is unemotional and sermons are largely in the words of Scripture, as are prayers. Sandeman insisted that faith be not confused with its effects. It is a simple act of belief in the resurrection of Christ and must never be seen as a work. This intellectualist view led to Sandemianism's reputation as a cold mechanical religion. Elegies and other private writings witness to an inner warmth belied by the attempt to avoid Pharisaism, but such an exclusive system carried in it the seeds of its own decay. Only a handful of Sandemanians survive in Scotland.

Epistolary Correspondence with S. Pike (G, 1762), *An Essay on Preaching* (E, 1763); *The Honour of Marriage* (L, 1777); ed., *Supplementary Volume of Letters and Other Documents...* (Perth, 1865) by John Glas.

L. A. McMillan, *Restoration Roots* (Dallas, TX, 1983); A. Fuller, *Strictures on Sandemanianism* (L, 1820).

D. B. Murray

Sandford, Daniel (1766–1830), Bishop of Edinburgh 1806–30. The second son of D. Sandford of Sandford Hall, Shropshire, and born near Dublin, Sandford was later educated in Bath and at Christ Church, Oxford (BA, 1787; MA, 1791; DD, 1802). He was ordained deacon in 1790 and served a curacy at Hanworth. His connections with Scotland arose from his marriage in 1790 to Helen, eldest daughter of Erskine Douglas. In 1792, probably at the request of his Scottish relatives, he moved to Edinburgh where he opened an Episcopal chapel. At first his congregation worshipped in a room in West Register Street, then in a chapel in Rose Street, the site later of Charlotte Chapel (1797–8), and finally in St John's Church, Princes Street (1818). In 1806 he was consecrated Bishop of Edinburgh. The *Remains of the Late Right Reverend Daniel Sandford...* (3 vols, E, 1830) contain a memoir, a diary, letters (1813–29), fifteen sermons and two tracts on the union of qualified chapels* with the EpCS and the claims of the Scottish bishops.

Sandford was the first Englishman to serve as a bishop in the EpCS. As such he played a leading part in the reconciliation of the qualified clergy and congregations with the EpCS, a project which had become possible after the repeal of the Penal Laws (1792). He was one of the first in English orders to place himself and his congregation under the jurisdiction of the Scottish bishops and wrote an influential pamphlet on the subject (1804). He was active in rebuilding diocesan administration, and held regular visitations and confirmations. Fife was added to his jurisdiction in 1807 and Glasgow diocese in 1809. During his episcopate six new churches were consecrated and the number of clergy in the Edinburgh diocese increased from seven to twenty-five.

DNB L, 268–9; R. Foskett, 'The Episcopate of Daniel Sandford 1806–30', *RSCHS* 15 (1965), 141–52.

G. D. Duncan

Sands, Lord (Christopher Nicholson Johnston) (1857–1934), judge and prominent CofS elder. The second son of James Johnston of Sands (in Fife), he was educated at St Andrews, at Madras College and the University, and then at Edinburgh, where he graduated in arts before going on to Heidelberg. Admitted to the Faculty of Advocates in 1880 he soon established a good junior practice, acting for the Board of Trade and the Department of Woods and Forests and being appointed advocate depute in 1892. His profound interest in farming was to result later in the production of standard works on agricultural holdings. In 1902 he took silk, three years later became Sheriff of Perthshire, and was elevated to the bench in 1917, taking his judicial title of Lord Sands from his father's estate. Of his career on the bench it has been said: 'His judgments are noted for a sound knowledge of law and a vast amount of common sense. No other judge of his day could be said to so well combine law and equity. But there is more. His pawkiness had to find outlet even in the most unpromising and barren regions of law. These judgments are read with no less interest and appreciation today.'

Lord Sands' interests outside the court were varied. He had considerable literary gifts (he wrote, for example, a life of Archibald Scott;* E, L, 1919), and his concern for sport was based upon a close commitment, as a younger man, to tennis, cricket and rugby. His consuming interest, however, was the CofS, to which he gave the most valuable service in its pulpits and more especially around its conference tables. He was Procurator* 1907–18. His was the unusual distinction for an elder of receiving a DD from the University of Edinburgh (1928), St Andrews (1909) and Glasgow (1930) having already honoured him with the LLD. He played a quite outstanding part in the Union* of the CofS and UFC in 1929, his first major contribution lying in his production in 1912 of 'The Memorandum' which formed the constructive basis of all the subsequent discussion and debate. The terms of the Declaratory Articles* of 1921 owed much to his genius. Above all, he was implicitly trusted by both sides. From the UF angle, Principal Alexander Martin* said of him, 'The spirit of controversy had been mastered in him by the nobler spirit of conciliation, by that wisdom from above which is peaceable and without partiality, full of mercy and good fruits.' From the other side John White* wrote of his insistence that, when reunion comes, the Churches should not merely declare their adherence to the catholic creeds, but should 'with equal solemnity declare their acceptance of the evangelical message which the Church is to promulgate to the world'.

DNB 1931–40, 490–1; *Who Was Who, 1929–1940*, 1195; R. Sjölinder, *Presbyterian Reunion in Scotland 1907–1921* (E, n.d.).

A. Herron

Sanquhar Declaration (1680), a Covenanting* statement renouncing allegiance to Charles II.* Drawn up by Richard Cameron,* who headed a band of twenty horsemen, it was delivered at Sanquhar on the first anniversary of the battle of Bothwell Bridge.* Thanking God for a remnant that continued the work of Reformation* in Scotland, and acknowledging their respect for good government, they rejected Charles Stuart as king for his tyranny, perjury and covenant-breaking, and held themselves culpable for having tolerated him so long. They also disowned the Duke of York ('that professed papist') as heir-presumptive to the Crown, and expressed the hope that 'none will blame us for or offend at our rewarding those that are against us, as the Lord gives opportunity', unless the offenders had a change of heart.

Following up an earlier Covenanting principle that the character of the authority determines the extent of the subject's obedience, the Declaration makes it clear that Charles was rejected for civil as well as for ecclesiastical tyranny. This was none the less the first time the Covenanters had officially renounced the king because of his claimed supremacy over the Kirk. Regarded at the time as an audacious but futile gesture by a tiny minority, the Sanquhar Declaration's main thesis was nine years later to reflect the mind of Great Britain as a whole, and to become the basis of the Revolution Settlement.

J. C. Johnston, *Treasury of the Scottish Covenant* (E, 1887), 141–3 – text.

J. D. Douglas

Santalia, *see* MacPhail, James Merry; Missions.

Saphir, Aaron Adolph (1831–91), Hebrew Christian minister. He attended a school in Budapest where in 1843 (with his parents) he converted to Christianity under the influence of 'Rabbi' Duncan,* who now became his mentor. Leaving Budapest with another Jewish convert, Alfred Edersheim,* he enrolled at the Berlin gymnasium (1844–8) and later at Glasgow University (MA, 1854), studying theology at Aberdeen and New College, Edinburgh. In 1854 he was licensed and ordained by the FC as a missionary to the Jews of Hamburg, although he soon resigned because of organizational restraints. He later ministered to English Presbyterian congregations in South Shields (1856–61), Greenwich (1861–72), Notting Hill (1872–80) and Belgravia (1882–8).

Saphir was peculiarly well qualified to expound the Jewish origins of Christianity, and his books on biblical subjects were deservedly popular, especially with Brethren* (he could say, 'I am enough of a Plymouthist to . . . feel very lonely among the Presbyterians'. He happily accepted an anti-paedobaptist, Henry Brooke, as his assistant). Always an enthusiastic supporter of Jewish missions, he sympathized with various initiatives for the establishment of a national Jewish Church and his writings were later used by Arno Gaebelein in his American magazine *Our Hope*, which was specifically addressed to a Jewish readership. As a conservative he strenuously opposed much German 'rationalism', though ready to recognize the faith of a scholar like 'dear Schleiermacher'.

Expository Lectures on the Epistle to the Hebrews, 2 vols (L, 1874–5); *Christ and the Scriptures* (L, 1867); *Christ and Israel*, ed. D. Baron (L, 1890).

G. Carlyle, *'Mighty in the Scriptures', a Memoir of Adolph Saphir* (L, 1893); *DNB* L, 299; Fr. Stolle, 'Dr Aaron Adolf [sic] Saphir', in A. Frank (ed.),

Witnesses from Israel (E, 1903), 78–89; D. A. Rausch, 'Our Hope: Proto-fundamentalism's Attitude towards Zionism 1894–1897', *Jewish Social Studies* 40 (1978), 246; L. Meyer (ed.), *Eminent Hebrew Christians of the Nineteenth Century*, ed. D. A. Rausch (Lewiston, NY, 1983).

T. C. F. Stunt

Scalan, *see* Colleges and Seminaries, Roman Catholic.

Scandinavia, *see* Gau, John; Missions; Henderson, Ebenezer; Paterson, John (1776–1855); Scott, George.

Schism Overture. The General Assembly of 1765 received an overture* requesting it to consider the remarkable progress of 'schism' in the Church and 'provide remedies' for this 'alarming evil'. The Assembly appointed a committee to consider it. The committee's report recommended presbyteries 'to inquire into the truth of this fact' of the dangerous consequences from 'the increase of Secession' to the Est.C. It also identified patronage* as the cause of the Secession* and proposed that the Assembly set up a committee to discuss with Presbyteries and the 'landed interest' the matter of how to reform the abuse. This proposal, rejected by ninety-nine votes to eighty-five, marked the emergence within the CofS of a coherent ecclesiastical and secular polemic against patronage. Advocates of the proposals rejected arguments that schism was a necessary evil and that they were persecutors of the Seceders. They distinguished between 'the rights of the people' to choose their own pastors, and the right to call 'a parochial minister upon an Establishment'. The former was undeniable, the latter was asserted by no one. They went on to attempt to detach heritors* from patrons by asserting that the wishes of men of rank and influence in the parishes were being disregarded in the choice of ministers, and argued that the setting up of dissenting congregations would deprive the landlords of rents and be detrimental to the poor funds. The appeal to the landed classes was justified on the grounds that no relief from patronage could be obtained but with their concurrence. The secular arguments were probably the result of the influence of Andrew Crosbie.*

N. Morren, *Annals of the General Assembly of the Church of Scotland . . . 1752 . . . 1766* (E, 1841), 305–8, 311, 329–47; *Scots Magazine* 27–8 (1765–6).

J. R. McIntosh

Schools, *see* Education (Scotland) Acts, 1872 and 1918; *First Book of Discipline*; Gaelic School Societies; Ragged Schools; Renaissance; Roman Catholicism; Scottish School Book Association; Scottish SPCK; Scripture Union; Stow, David; Welsh, David.

Schottenklöster. Ten Irish Benedictine* monasteries, including an abbey in Ratisbon (Regensburg), were founded in the South German lands 1075–1232. Known as Schottenklöster (Scots monasteries), they were united under the Ratisbon abbot but declined in the fifteenth century. Several ceased to exist or, like that in Vienna, fell into other hands. Those remaining were taken over by Scottish monks in 1515. Scottish administration was consolidated under Ninian Winzet,* and three monasteries survived into the nineteenth century: Ratisbon, Würzburg, Erfurt. Much was destroyed by the Swedish invasions 1631–5, but Würzburg monks, including Alexander Baillie,* brought about recovery. Erfurt became a dependent priory of Ratisbon. Placid Fleming* raised Ratisbon to a position of influence and in 1713 founded a seminary there for Scottish youths. Attempts to unite the Scots monasteries constitutionally were unsuccessful.

Ratisbon and Würzburg sent priests to Scotland. In the eighteenth century, all three monasteries contributed greatly to German cultural life. Monks teaching in Erfurt university, particularly Andrew Gordon,* were influential for science and philosophy and Ildephonse Kennedy* was important in the Academy movement. Marianus Brockie* and Gallus Robertson* were well-known in Germany and Britain. Würzburg and Erfurt were secularised 1803–19; Ratisbon and its seminary, despite efforts to revitalize them, were finally terminated in 1862. Fort Augustus* was constituted successor to Ratisbon.

M. Dilworth, *The Scots in Franconia* (E, 1974); T. A. Fischer, *The Scots in Germany* (E, 1902), 137–63, 217–19, 289–305; M. Dilworth, 'Two Necrologies of Scottish Benedictine Abbeys in Germany', *IR* 9 (1958), 173–203; *Records of the Scots Colleges* (New Spalding Club, A. 1906); Easson-Cowan, 240–4.

M. Dilworth

Science and Religion. Science and religion have had a fruitful interaction in Scottish history. The names of eminent Scots stalk the history of science – such as John Napier,* James Hutton (1729–97), Joseph Black (1728–99), W. J. M. Rankine (1820–72), James Clerk Maxwell,* William Thomson (*see* Kelvin, Lord), and James Y. Simpson.* Modern science found the general intellectual climate provided in the lands of the Reformation* conducive to its advance, and Scotland was no exception. The Reformation gave a central belief in God as lawgiver – and therefore of 'laws of nature' to be disclosed. It also brought together hand and head, experiment and theory. Scotland was a happy blend of the more theoretical tendencies of continental Europe and the empiricism of England. It is difficult to contain this subject within the narrow confines of a national perspective. Scientific activity has national trends – but science has for the past 400 years been an international adventure.

It is a matter for debate to what extent Reformational ideas stimulated modern science. But there is a widespread acknowledgement today that the Reformation provided the milieu in which experimental science could and did flourish. In the

SCIENCE AND RELIGION

sixteenth and seventeenth centuries the relationship between science and Reformed theology was reasonably happy. However, there arose an apparently deepening conflict between the two disciplines. This reached a climax in the wake of the Darwinian controversy of the nineteenth century. This led to various viewpoints concerning the basic roles of science and theology. Some saw the two disciplines in fundamental conflict. Others divorced the two realms – science dealing with the physical world of nature, theology with the spiritual world of grace. Science took over more and more of what had been mysterious and unexplained; while increasingly theology was left to fill in the decreasing gaps in man's knowledge.

In our century, attempts were made to rehabilitate theology with science by seeing the two disciplines as complementary – explaining different aspects of the one reality. In the last fifteen to twenty years another view has sought a more radical unity of the two disciplines. This has been called the 'symbiotic' view.

The educational dream of Knox* is perhaps important within the Scottish context. Scotland was swift to bring the new disciplines of science within its educational purview. As one general history of science puts it: 'The universities of Presbyterian Scotland, like the Nonconformist Academies of England, were noted for the teaching of the sciences during the eighteenth century; in fact Edinburgh became famous for her medical school at that time' (S. F. Mason, *A History of the Sciences*, NY, 1962, 287). The Scottish universities left 'Oxbridge' far behind in the pursuit of science right up until the twentieth century.

Edinburgh was the focal point of one of the great geological controversies, involving among many others, Black, Hutton and Hugh Miller*. Joseph Black was professor of chemistry at Edinburgh and eventually advised James Watt, one of his better students. James Hutton, disillusioned by controversy, became a chemical manufacturer. Hugh Miller,* a member of the Free Church,* wrote several works on geology which became best sellers. His *Testimony of the Rocks* (E, 1857), for example, sold some 42,000 copies.

Certainly, cultural and scientific pursuits were more avidly pursued by the Moderates* than the Evangelicals – but even the latter evidenced a continuing interest in scientific pursuits. Thomas Chalmers* was keenly interested in mathematics, and even after his conversion, though his priorities altered, he did not lose his appetite for knowledge on that wider canvas. George Matheson* – partially blind minister and hymn-writer – was elected a Fellow of the Royal Society of Edinburgh on account of his work in archaeology and anthropology.

Towards the end of the nineteenth century, running in to the twentieth, the dominant names in Scottish science are Rankine, Maxwell, Ernest Rutherford (1871–1937) and Thomson. They were at the forefront of the development of the electro-dynamic unity which saw the greatest strides forward since Newton. These men of science were often devout Christians.

Clerk Maxwell,* for example, was a convinced Christian. In Corsock Kirk in Kirkcudbrightshire there is a stained glass window to his memory. The inscription reads: 'This window is erected by admirers of a genius that discovered the kinship between electricity and light and was led through the mystery of nature to the fuller knowledge of God.' From a youth Maxwell had been encouraged by his mother to 'look up through nature to nature's God'. Thomas F. Torrance in *Transformation and Convergence in the Frame of Knowledge* (Belfast, 1984) devotes a chapter to Maxwell. There he cites Maxwell's reply on being invited to join the Victoria Institute in 1875: 'I think men of science as well as other men need to learn from Christ, and I think Christians whose minds are scientific are bound to study science that their view of the glory of God may be as extensive as their being is capable of.'

In Scotland, the leading proponent of a unified understanding of the universe is Thomas F. Torrance,* who has sought to expound the unity of the two realms. He has championed a fresh understanding of the coherence of science with biblical revelation, and has written extensively to that end. The very title of the book cited above is testimony to the direction of his thinking. There is no fundamental contradiction between any of the sciences and God's revelation in his Word; no divergence between a biblical theology (itself a science) and the other fields of human investigations.

Scottish Academic Press is currently publishing a series reflecting upon the theological and scientific unification of thought, with Torrance as general editor. This indicates two things. First, it points to a direction that is being taken by our understanding of the relationship between science and theology. Second, it is perhaps significant that this series is edited by a leading Scottish minister and academic and published by a Scottish publisher.

H. T. Pledge, *Science Since 1500* (L, 1966); C. C. Gillispie, *Genesis and Geology* (NY, 1959); C. A. Russell in S. B. Ferguson and D. F. Wright (eds), *New Dictionary of Theology* (Leicester, 1988), 625–7; C. A. Russell (ed.), *Science and Religious Belief: A Selection of Recent Historical Studies* (L, 1973); J. Y. Simpson, *Landmarks in the Struggle Between Science and Religion* (L, 1925); R. Hooykaas, *Religion and the Rise of Modern Science* (E, 1973).

J. C. Sharp

SCLATER, JOHN ROBERT PATERSON

Sclater, John Robert Paterson (1876–1949), Presbyterian writer and preacher prominent in Canada. Born at Manchester and educated there and at Cambridge (Emmanuel College and Westminster Theological College; BA, 1898; MA, 1900; President of the Union, 1899), he was ordained to Greenhill Presbyterian Church of England, Derby (1902–7), before moving to New North UF, Edinburgh, 1907–23 (war service 1914–17). Thereafter he achieved distinction in Canada and the USA, as minister in Toronto (Parkdale Presbyterian Church, 1923–4, and Old St Andrew's, 1924 to his death), and as a college preacher. Virtually all his publications were sermons, addresses or lectures: *The Sons of Strength* (E, 1909, based on George Meredith's poems), *The Enterprise of Life* (L, 1911), *The River of Content* (L, 1913, expanded from a children's talk, with illustrations), *The Eve of Battle. Addresses at Church Parade* (L, 1915), *God and the Soldier* (L, 1917 – with Norman MacLean;* addresses given at a camp in France), *Modernist Fundamentalism* (L, 1926 – arguing that criticism is no enemy of evangelical faith), *The Public Worship of God* (L, 1927 – the Lyman Beecher lectures at Yales, and partly repeating his Warrack lectures* of 1922), and *The Priesthood of All Believers* (n.p., n.d. – the Dudleian lecture for 1936–7 at Harvard). Having joined the United Church of Canada at its inception in 1925, he was Moderator 1942–4 and chairman of its Commission on Reunion from 1943. He won the DD of St Andrews (1917), Queen's University, Kingston, Ontario (1935), and Victoria University, Toronto (1942), and the LLD of the University of Toronto (1944). He died on a visit to Edinburgh.

FUFCS 21; *Canadian Who's Who*, volumes for 1936–48.

D. F. Wright

Scone, Augustinian* abbey near Perth. It was the first Augustinian foundation in Scotland c.1120, when Alexander I* brought canons from Nostell, Yorkshire. Scone was important in Scottish history, being a royal residence from early times and the place where kings were enthroned. Even after the coronation stone (Stone of Destiny) was removed to Westminster in 1296, Scone continued to be used for royal coronations and for meetings of council and Parliament. Robert, prior of Scone, having become Bishop of St Andrews* in 1123–4, was instrumental in founding the priory and cathedral chapter there. Scone became an abbey c.1164 and its abbot was granted *pontificalia* (episcopal insignia) in 1395. The head of St Fergus (*see* Celtic Saints) was venerated at Scone.

Sacked by the English in 1298, the abbey underwent restoration. James Kennedy,* Bishop of Dunkeld, was its commendator* 1439–47 (the first such appointment in Scotland). Scone was again ruled by commendators from 1518, the last being Patrick Hepburn,* Bishop of Moray. In 1559 the abbey was severely damaged by a Protestant mob; there were then sixteen canons. Robert Carver,* canon of Scone, composed polyphonic music, which has enjoyed a revival in recent times.

Liber Ecclesie de Scon (E, 1843); G. W. S. Barrow, *The Kingdom of the Scots* (L, 1973), 169–72; J. Wilson, 'Foundation of the Austin Priories of Nostell and Scone', *SHR* 7 (1910), 141–59; Easson-Cowan, 88–98.

M. Dilworth

Scot (Scott), John of Scotstarvet (1585–1670), lawyer, statesman and Covenanter.* His family came from Knightspottie, Perthshire. He bought Tarvet in Fife in 1611, when he succeeded his father as Director of Chancery. In 1632 he became Lord of Session, and later a Privy Councillor. He had a European reputation as a patron of letters, endowed the chair of humanity at St Andrews (where he had studied), and was prominent in national life until the Cromwellian era. He had been one of many lawyers and lairds who accepted the 1638 Covenant, and as an elder was active in the church courts in the 1640s. He was closely involved in the nobles' negotiations with Charles I* over church properties. He has been called 'a kind of prototype of the serious church layman or influential elder of later days who stands forth as a champion of honesty in public office and virtue in private character' (Snoddy).

The Staggering State of the Scots Statesmen . . . 1550 to 1650 (E, 1754).

DNB LI, 39–41; C. Rogers, memoir in E 1872 edit. of Scot's *The Staggering State of the Scots Statesmen*; T. G. Snoddy, *Sir John Scot Lord Scotstarvit* (E, 1968).

D. F. Wright

Scotch Baptists, sometimes called Sandemanian* or MacLeanite Baptists, are one of the minor contributing streams of British Baptist* life. Archibald MacLean* was their chief theologian, publicist and best known elder, serving from 1767–1812 in the Edinburgh church known until 1927 as Bristo Place Scotch Baptist Church, and setting in order churches in Glasgow (1769), Dundee (1769), Montrose (1770), Largo (1791), Kirkcaldy (1798), Paisley (1795), and in England, at Wooler, Hull, Beverley, Nottingham and London. McLean's writings influenced J. R. Jones of Ramoth, whose followers formed Scotch Baptist churches in North Wales, ten of which still exist. A group of Lancashire churches based on Haggate, Burnley, came into the movement in 1834. Church teaching and practice derived much from John Glas* and Robert Sandeman,* although McLean deplored the coldness and worldliness he perceived in Sandemanianism. The connection was beset by successive controversies, and in 1810 there was a major division over the question of partaking of the Lord's Supper without elders. A second division on the same point in 1834 severely weakened the churches. Those who were more liberal and willing to tolerate change formed closer links with other Baptist churches, although they were reluctant to join the Baptist Union of Scotland* until this century. The strict party, helped by William Jones of Liverpool and London, author and publisher of a succession of journals dedicated to primitive Christianity, and by James Everson of Beverley, stood by the earlier discipline, lost many members in the 1840s to the Campbellites (*see* Churches of Christ), and developed even greater exclusiveness.

A. M'Lean, 'A Short Account of the Scots Baptists', in *The Baptist Annual Register 1794–7* (L, 1797), 361–76; T. W. Davies, 'The McLeanist (Scotch) Baptist and Campbellite Baptists of Wales', *Transactions of the Baptist Historical Society* 7 (1920–1), 147–81; P. Wilson, *The Origin and Progress of the Scotch Baptist*

Churches, 1765–1834 (E, 1844); D. B. Murray, 'The Scotch Baptist Tradition in Great Britain', *BQ* 33 (1989–90), 186–98; D. W. Bebbington (ed.), *The Baptists in Scotland* (G, 1988), 19–24.

D. B. Murray

Scotch Presbyterian Eloquence, a scurrilous pamphlet, first published in London in 1692, lampooning Presbyterianism in general and Scottish Presbyterian preachers in particular. It appeared under the name 'Jacob Curate', which is generally believed to be a pseudonym for Gilbert Crockat. Its main design was to prejudice Episcopalians in England against the Scottish Presbyterians, in the hope of securing the re-establishment of episcopacy in Scotland. The author spares no pains to blacken his victims' character, and to pour scorn on the cause they represented. Starting with the premise that Presbyterian principles are antinomian, he rehearses instances of alleged loose living on the part of pastors and people, which he maintains are the result of their flawed creed. He goes on to quote copious extracts from the writings and preaching of Presbyterian ministers, all designed to render them ridiculous in the eyes of his readers. Many of the quotations – such as those from Samuel Rutherford's* *Letters* – merely serve to highlight the author's lack of spiritual perception in quoting them; others are no more than homely turns of phrase or quaint expressions of thought. In some cases the author has recorded some gems which might otherwise have perished: an example is Rutherford's remark at Jedburgh: 'In these twenty-eight years the grass is grown long betwixt Jedburgh and heaven.' The work called forth an *Answer*, in considerably more lurid terms, by George Ridpath (styling himself William Laick) in which he ruthlessly exposed the immorality of the Episcopalian clergy. Ridpath (d.1726) was a journalist who had been imprisoned in 1681 for burning an effigy of the pope in Edinburgh.

See Preaching: Themes and Styles, Seventeenth Century.

M. Grant

Scotch Sermons, a controversial volume published in London, 1880, by thirteen CofS ministers 'to show the direction in which thought is moving'. Somewhat like *Essays and Reviews* (1860) in England, it was a manifesto of broad-church theology. The editor was William A. Knight* of St Andrews, and contributors included John Caird* and R. H. Story.* It evoked a sharp response, including *Notes* . . . (E, 1880) by 'A Parish Minister', John Storie's *The Scotch Sermons Analysed and Tested* (E, 1881), and *The Teaching of 'Scotch Sermons' Exhibited and Examined* (E, 1881) by 'A Layman' (Robert Gossip). Proceedings were taken only against W. L. McFarlan of Lenzie (*FES* III, 486). In the General Assembly of 1881, Robert Flint* insisted that McFarlan give satisfaction of his allegiance to the fundamental doctrines of the faith, which he gave by an apology the following day (*PAGACS 1881*, 43–5, 47).

H. F. Henderson, *The Religious Controversies of Scotland* (E, 1905), 194–206; A. L. Drummond and J. Bulloch, *The Church in Late Victorian Scotland 1874–1900* (E, 1978), 240–3; D. MacMillan, *The Life of Robert Flint* (L, 1914), 371–8.

D. F. Wright

Scotland. An ancient European nation, the country forms the northern part of Britain, now within the United Kingdom of Great Britain and Northern Ireland. The Christian faith and Church have been part of its national life from the earliest period down to the present.

Christian missions to the tribes of northern Britain (*see* Ninian, Columba, Celtic Church) preceded the gradual formation of one Scottish kingdom uniting these different peoples between the ninth and eleventh centuries. Out of such diverse races under a single crown, a common sense of Scottish nationhood emerged by the thirteenth century, in part out of the recognition by the papacy* of the separate province of the Ecclesia Scoticana, or Scottish Church, granted by 1200, and in part out of the political struggle in the Wars of Independence from England, 1296–1314. During that period the Scottish Church supported the cause of Scottish independence and its leader Robert the Bruce.* A Scottish churchman drafted the Declaration of Arbroath,* 1320, in which a Christian and national appeal was made to Rome by the Scottish nobility, requiring the pope to urge the English king to make peace with the free nation of Scots (*see* Roman Catholicism). This nationalist sentiment took further root in the medieval Church in the fifteenth and sixteenth centuries. Influenced by continental developments, there was a deliberate cultivation of devotion to Scottish saints* in the liturgy and pilgrimages,* and a patriotic pride that new Scottish churches and universities enhanced the nation as well as the Church.

The Scottish Reformation* of 1560 meant a shift of national alliances, away from RC France and towards Protestant England, as well as the reform of the national Church. From 1560 until 1707, the year of parliamentary union* with England (following the union of the crowns in 1603), the Reformed Kirk provided Scotland with a new, Calvinist identity (*see* Calvinism; Social Concern) but also with an ambivalent attitude to national autonomy. John Knox* himself, although a patriot, was not a Scottish nationalist and would seem to have favoured a British union with England under a Protestant crown. Among the complex factors that may have made the Kirk less nationalistic in outlook than its medieval predecessor is the importance it gave to biblical rather than nationalist models in the life of Church and nation. The notion of Scotland as a covenanted nation (*see* National Covenant) may have made the preservation of a Protestant, Presbyterian national Church seem more important for the nation's identity than the retention of a Scottish Parliament. In the negotiations leading to the Union of Parliaments* in 1707, the security of the established national Church was seen as an essential condition of a British union and Scottish nationhood within it. After the loss of the Scottish Parliament and statehood, the CofS remained a key national institution, along with the separate Scottish legal and educational systems.

For that autonomous post-Union Scottish civil society, the Disruption* of the national Church in 1843 was a crisis from which it did not recover. Already weakened by the various secessions* in the previous century, after 1843 the divided CofS no longer functioned as a unifying national institution in a pluralist society, even after reunion in 1929, although the Christian ethic remained part of the secular national identity. The increasing involvement of the nineteenth- and twentieth-century British state in Scottish civil society met with demands for greater Scottish control of its own affairs within the UK. Political autonomy came to be seen as vital to the nation's wellbeing, just as the autonomy of the national Church had been up to 1843. Scottish churchmen like James Begg* and James Barr* were prominent figures in the Home Rule cause in the period from the 1850s to the 1920s. But the Churches played little part in the history of the twentieth-century Scottish nationalist movement. While the CofS consistently supported Scottish devolution within the UK from the late 1940s onwards, secular, cultural and political developments lay behind the survival of Scottish nationhood in the late twentieth century. Yet in the 1980s there was some indication of renewed interest in the Christian influence on Scottish culture and identity (see C. Beveridge and R. Turnbull, *The Eclipse of Scottish Culture* (E, 1989), 91–111).

G. Donaldson, *Scotland, Church and Nation through Sixteen Centuries* (E, 1972); A. H. Williamson, *Scottish National Consciousness in the Age of James VI* (E, 1979); D. McRoberts, 'The Scottish Church and Nationalism in the Fifteenth Century', *IR* 19 (1968), 3–14; R. L. Greaves, *Theology and Revolution in the Scottish Reformation* (Grand Rapids, 1980), 203–16; S. Mews (ed.), *Religion and National Identity* (Studies in Church History 18; O, 1982), 465–518; G. Donaldson, *Scottish Church History* (E, 1985), 220–38; H. J. Hanham, *Modern Scottish Nationalism* (L, 1969); J. Brand, *The National Movement in Scotland* (L, 1978), 127–35; K. Webb, *The Growth of Nationalism in Scotland* (Harmondsworth, 1978), 55–8; M. Fry, *Patronage and Principle* (A, 1987), 30–58; I. Henderson, *Power Without Glory* (L, 1967).

W. F. Storrar

Scotland, Church of, *see* Church of Scotland.

Scoto-Catholics, the name given to high churchmen in the CofS by W. P. Paterson* of Edinburgh. At first referring to those who were influenced by the Tractarianism* of the CofE, in Scotland it came to refer to all those who wished to recover what they believed to be the catholic tradition of the Kirk. Scoto-Catholics gave expression to their concerns in the founding of the Scottish Church Society* in 1892. They wished to affirm the place of catholic doctrine in relation to the Church, the ministry and the sacraments. Scoto-Catholicism was a parallel movement to the Oxford Movement in England. Both were reactions to liberalism: both stressed the importance of doctrine in the life of the Church, recalled the Church to its catholic tradition, and sought to revive its life and faith and not just to introduce certain novel practices in worship. But the traditions to which they appealed were fundamentally different. With the notable exception of James Cooper,* Scoto-Catholics were not influenced by Anglicanism to any great extent. Rather they wished to recover the catholic tradition of the Kirk as they found it in the Scots Confession,* and expressed more recently in the teaching of John McLeod Campbell* and the writings of William Milligan.* The chief emphasis among Scoto-Catholics was thus 'traditionally Presbyterian', and their doctrinal position is set out in H. J. Wotherspoon* and J. M. Kirkpatrick, *A Manual of Church Doctrine* (L, 1919; 2nd edn revised and enlarged by T. F. Torrance* and R. S. Wright, L, 1960). Scoto-Catholics wished to safeguard what they considered to be the fundamental doctrines of the Christian faith in relation to the change in the subscription* of ministers and elders* to the Westminster* Confession and in the union* negotiations with the UFC. They stressed the divine nature of the Church, sharing in the ministry of Christ to the Father and to the world. The unity of the Church was also of fundamental importance and they were among the most enthusiastic supporters of the ecumenical movement.* They defended the ministerial orders of the Kirk as a succession of presbyters from the Reformation and stressed the importance of ordination.* But they also wished to emphasize the ministry of the whole Church as the priesthood of all believers. These fundamental doctrines of the faith they believed to be also vital in worship, and they advocated the saying of the Creed* and the use of the Christian year.* They wished the Lord's Supper* to be celebrated every week as the main service of the Lord's Day. Scoto-Catholics, although relatively small in numbers, have exercised a considerable influence within the CofS.

See also Catholic Revival in Worship (Nineteenth Century); Church Service Society; Leishman, Thomas; Macleod, John; Sprott, George W.

H. J. Wotherspoon, *James Cooper* (L, 1926); J. F. Leishman, *Linton Leaves* (E, 1937); D. M. Murray, 'Disruption to Union', in D. B. Forrester and D. M. Murray (eds), *Studies in the History of Worship in Scotland* (E, 1984), 79–85; A. C. Cheyne, *The Transforming of the Kirk* (E, 1983).

D. M. Murray

Scots Colleges. The Council of Trent in 1563 decreed the setting up of seminaries for the spiritual and intellectual training of priests. As such were impossible in Scotland, colleges for Scots were established on the continent.

DOUAI. Founded at Paris in 1580 with the assistance

of James Beaton* and a subsidy from Mary, Queen of Scots,* the college moved several times before settling at Douai (Flanders) in 1608-9. It was staffed by Jesuits* and subject to the local Jesuit provincial; from 1632 the rector was Scottish. Students were not ordained priest at the college; many entered Jesuit noviciates. In 1765, after Jesuits were expelled from France, Scots secular priests staffed the college, which produced priests for Scotland until suppressed by the revolutionaries in 1793.

PARIS. In 1325 bursaries at Paris university were founded for four students from Moray diocese; the foundation, having declined sadly, was rehabilitated after 1560. James Beaton and Mary, Queen of Scots, supported Scottish clerical students at Paris and in 1603 Beaton bequeathed a house and endowment for them. The two foundations were united 1639-40. Though staffed by Scots secular priests and having as superior the local Carthusian* prior, it was not exclusively a seminary. Under Innes priests (see Innes, Thomas) the college flourished; James VII* made it the depository for Jacobite* court archives. It supplied many missioner priests, though suspected for a time of Jansenism.* In 1793 the college was sequestrated; in 1798 Paul MacPherson* brought to Scotland what remained of the Glasgow muniments and diplomatic correspondence deposited by Beaton, the Stuart papers and college archives. All are now in Columba House, Edinburgh.

ROME. Established by Clement VIII in 1600, the college received its first students 1602. From 1615 the rectors were Jesuits, mostly Scots but interspersed with Italians; from 1724, Italian Jesuits; then, after Jesuits were suppressed in 1773, Italian secular priests. Despite struggles between Jesuits and seculars, and between Scots and Italians, the college supplied priests steadily for Scotland; the Scots clergy agents (notably William Leslie*), Propaganda Fide* and cardinal protectors endeavoured to ensure this. In 1798, when French troops seized Rome, Paul MacPherson* convoyed students and archives to safety. He returned as rector in 1800, and all rectors since have been Scottish secular priests. In 1964 the college moved to a site outside Rome.

SPAIN. In 1627 Colonel William Semple (Sempill, 1546-1633) founded a college in Madrid; the first students arrived 1632. Staffed by Scottish or Spanish Jesuits, the college was often in jeopardy; under Spanish superiors, in 1681-1714 and from 1734, there were no students. Many students became Jesuits and very few ever worked in Scotland. Jesuits were expelled from Spain 1767 and in 1771 John Geddes* refounded the college in Valladolid. Under Scottish secular priests, it has continued to train priests for Scotland. In 1988 the college moved to Salamanca.

Two other colleges made a contribution. The monastic seminary at Ratishon (see Schottenklöster) was used increasingly by the vicars-apostolic in the nineteenth century. In 1864-74 Irish religious conducted a Scottish seminary at Rockwell, Co. Tipperary. Until recently some Scots seminarians were educated in France, in compensation for the loss of the French colleges, and at Propaganda College in Rome.

See also Colleges and Seminaries, Roman Catholic.

Records of the Scots Colleges (A, New Spalding Club, 1906); J. F. S. Gordon (ed.), *The Catholic Church in Scotland* (A, 1874), 66-75, 90-6, 191-209, 247-53; H. Chadwick, 'The Scots College, Douai, 1580-1613', *English Historical Review* 56 (1941), 571-85; W. A. McNeill, 'Documents Illustrative of the History of the Scots College, Paris', *IR* 15 (1964), 66-85; W. J. Anderson (ed.), 'Abbé Paul MacPherson's History of the Scots College, Rome', *IR* 12 (1961), 1-172; M. Taylor, *The Scots College in Spain* (Valladolid, 1971); *Rockwell College Annual: Centenary 1864-1964* (Cashel, Co. Tipperary, 1964).

M. Dilworth

Scots Confession, the formal religious and theological testimony of what the Scottish Reformers believed. It was accepted by the Reformation Parliament* in 1560 and then by the reconstituted CofS. Acquiring full legal status in 1567, it was the chief subordinate doctrinal norm (after the Apostles' Creed) of the CofS, Presbyterian* or Episcopalian,* until superseded, but not abrogated, by the acceptance of the Westminster* Confession in 1647.

Confessions* of faith were literary media employed by various Reformation Churches throughout Europe since 1530. Their basic function was to indicate what beliefs were shared with the pre-Reformation Church and those beliefs establishing unambiguous lines of demarcation from it. In the latter, the distinctiveness and peculiarity of Reformation doctrines are found. All such confessions claimed to be grounded exclusively on Scripture,* and to be free from extra-biblical accretions and traditions. The secondary theological hue of the Scots Confession classifies it among confessions of the Reformed tradition,* and so it is more akin to the doctrinal consensus incorporating the theological perspectives of Geneva and Zürich than to Lutheran* tradition. There is nothing distinctively Scottish in the content of the Confession, except perhaps in its aggressive, cordial and evangelical style of presentation.

The Scots Confession, along with the (First) *Book of Discipline*,* represents the climax of varying degrees of Reformation agitation during the previous forty years. Its sudden official acceptance is explained by the political and religious *putsch* which occurred in 1559/60, enabling the Scottish Reformation* to be instituted during the reign of a RC sovereign. Decisive was the intervention of Protestant England in favour of the Reformation party in Scotland, though its motivation was as much diplomatic as religious. At the request of English diplomats the Confession was drawn up at short notice by a committee of churchmen, the 'six Johns', namely Knox,* Willock,* Winram,* Spottiswoode,* Row,* and Douglas.* It was presented to and accepted, though not quite unanimously, by Parliament, more as a *fait accompli* than the consequence of serious debate.

The Confession is composed of twenty-five articles. The first ten are non-controversial, embodying the doctrinal tradition of the early Church. The rest reflect the controversial theology of the age on topics like justification,* sanctification, faith, Scripture, the offices of Christ, the civil power, the Church, its authority and sacraments.* Comparatively unusual are the combination of systematic and biblical theology, the stress placed on ecclesiology and the sacramental eating of Christ's flesh and blood, and the explicit treatment of Christian ethics. Though the 'Papistical Kirk' is denounced, the papacy is not mentioned.

While the most discernible basic theological influence on the Confession is Calvin's* *Institutes*, his voice in it is less exclusive than many maintain. Theologically the document is relatively syncretistic. A Latin translation was published in 1572. Alongside this Confession, the General Assembly* also sanctioned the Genevan English Confession, the 'orthodox faith and Catholic doctrines' of the Second Helvetic (Swiss) Confession in 1566, and the Negative Confession* of 1581.

The Confession of Faith Professit, and belevit, be the protestantes within the realme of Scotland (E, 1561); LT, *Confessio fidei* (St Andrews, 1572).

W. Niesel (ed.), *Bekenntnisschriften und Kirchenordnungen...* (²Zürich, 1938), 79–117; Knox, *History* I, 338–9; G. D. Henderson (ed.), *Scots Confession, 1560...* (E, 1937); W. I. P. Hazlett, 'The Scots Confession 1560: Context, Complexion and Critique', *ARG* 78 (1987), 287–320; K. Barth, *The Knowledge of God... Recalling the Scots Confession* (L, 1938); M. Robinson, 'Language Choice in the Reformation. The Scots Confession of 1560' in J. D. McClure (ed.), *Scotland and the Lowland Tongue* (A, 1983), 59–78.

W. I. P. Hazlett

Scots Kirks, overseas congregations of the CofS. They have existed since the seventeenth century, but the majority date from the nineteenth century.

Over the centuries, seamen, soldiers, traders and settlers from Scotland have reached many parts of the world, and the Church of their origin has gone with them. Often through their own initiative, with the help of some Presbytery or even single congregation in Scotland, and with the good will and co-operation of the indigenous Church where such existed, they established congregations – in mainland Europe, the Indian sub-continent and Sri Lanka, Africa, the Caribbean and the Southern cone of South America.

Links with Europe naturally pre-date those with the rest of the world, so it is not surprising that the oldest surviving overseas congregations are in Amsterdam, established in 1607, and in Rotterdam, established in 1643 – unless one counts Geneva where the congregation's origins are with John Knox* and his fellow religious refugees in the mid-sixteenth century. By the nineteenth century such congregations were widely scattered over the continent. The later colonial expansion saw the formation of congregations in the Southern hemisphere, and the records contain names like Calcutta, Bombay, Madras, Colombo, Nairobi, Dar es Salaam, Nassau, Port of Spain, Buenos Aires and Valparaiso. Both the CofS and the FCS/UFC had such overseas involvements.

There was a separation of this 'colonial and continental' work in the Southern hemisphere from that of 'foreign mission'. Administratively they were distinct, and sadly in some places where both worked there was little co-operation between them. Since then there have been major changes. Most congregations beyond Europe have become part of the now independent, indigenous Churches with which the CofS is in partnership, e.g. the Churches of South India and North India, the Presbyterian Church of East Africa, the United Church of Jamaica and Grand Cayman. Only half a dozen have not been thus integrated. At home, the CofS's former Foreign Mission Committee and Colonial and Continental Committee in 1964 became the Overseas Council, and in 1984 united with the Inter-Church Relations Committee to become the Board of World Mission and Unity.

The congregations in Europe continue to be part of the CofS, but in several cases are also part of the Reformed Church of the country. In 1990 there were congregations in Amsterdam, Rotterdam, Brussels, Paris, Geneva, Lausanne, Fribourg, Lisbon, Gibraltar, Fuengirola, Malta and Budapest, with the prospect of some new congregations, for example in Prague.

The most dramatic change however is that these are no longer congregations solely of Scots or of members of the CofS. They use the English language, follow the Reformed tradition and are staffed by ministers of the CofS, but in their membership they are international and interdenominational; at a recent count in one congregation there were forty-three nations and fourteen Churches represented. They also have great opportunities of contact with people outside normal membership of the Church, and so are important agents of mission.

See also Chaplains, Colonial.

Records in *FES* VII, 534–684 (bibliography 754–61), VIII, 726–38, IX, 721–66, X, 412–14; and histories of individual Kirks, *e.g. The Scots Kirk, Lausanne...* (E, 1963).

A. R. Morton

Scott, Alexander John (1805–66), pioneering theological opponent of Westminster confessionalism. Reared in the Middle Parish manse, Greenock, his father was John Scott, a prominent minister in the national Kirk (1763–1836; *FES* III, 202). Educated at Glasgow University, Scott was licensed to preach in 1827, but already questioned his Church's doctrine of particular redemption. Over the next few years Scott, Thomas Erskine,* John McLeod Campbell* and Edward Irving* formed a small band of theological reformers, increasingly incurring the opposition of Scottish orthodoxy. Scott's *On the Divine Will* (Greenock, 1830) articulated the theological foundations of this reforming movement. God's saving love was to be understood in terms of the compassion Christ displayed for sinners, and therefore was not limited to the elect. In 1830 Scott accepted a call to the Scots Church, Woolwich, but his conscientious refusal to sign the Westminster* Confession obstructed the ordination proceedings and ultimately resulted in unanimous deposition from the ministry by the 1831 General Assembly. Scott's theology of the Spirit, as put forward in *Neglected Truths* (L, 1830), also created controversy. His pneumatology influenced Irving and the Catholic Apostolics* and gave rise to the first appearance of modern 'Pentecostal' phenomena, which, however, Scott rejected as inauthentic. He now pursued an independent ministry in England, and in 1848, with F. D. Maurice, became one of the founders of Christian Socialism. Translating his theological convictions into sociopolitical concerns he committed himself to the higher education of women and workers. He spent his final years as the first Principal of Owens College, later Manchester University. His closest disciple, George MacDonald,* was to reproduce much of Scott's theology in works of literature.

Discourses (L, 1866); *The Social Systems of the Present Day* (L, 1841).

DNB LI, 12–13; *FES* VII, 502–3; J. P. Newell, 'A. J. Scott and His Circle' (PhD, Edinburgh University, 1981); id., ' "Unworthy of the Dignity of the Assembly": the Deposition of Alexander John Scott', *RSCHS* 21 (1983), 249–62; J. Hunter, 'Alexander John Scott', *Exp* (8th series) 21 (1921), 386–400, 450–62; N. R. Needham, *Thomas Erskine of Linlathan* (E, 1990).

J. P. Newell

Scott, Andrew (fl. 1761–91), dissenting Antiburgher (*see* General Associate Synod). From Abernethy, Perthshire, he was ordained in 1761 to Bell Street Antiburgher Church, Dundee. A paper of 'scruples' submitted to the 1767 Synod listed his disagreements with Secession and Antiburgher positions. Adam Gib* pursued the case against him and he was suspended, and deposed next year. He argued that Antiburghers eroded the distinction between the kingdoms of Christ and the world. Dissenting from commitment to a 'covenanted reformation', he refrained from covenanting* in the congregation on the grounds of the hypocrisy of taking oaths on issues not understood by members. Archibald Bruce* regarded the episode as symptomatic of the drift towards New Light* views.

Scott's congregation split, but he and his supporters had to vacate the building after a significant court case in 1771 (F. Lyall, *Of Presbyters and Kings*, A, 1980, 87–8) and moved to Barrack Street. Dundee still had a congregation of 'Scottites' in 1803, although, after being found guilty of immorality in 1791, he disappeared, reputedly to London.

An Account of . . . the Late Difference between the Antiburgher-Seceders, and Andrew Scott . . . (E, 1770); *The Peculiar Scheme of the Antiburgher-Seceders Unmasked . . .* (E, 1770).

Small I, 287–8; *ASUPC*, 160–1.

D. F. Wright

Scott, Andrew (1772–1846), promoter of RC resurgence in west Scotland. Born in Banffshire and educated at Scalan (*see* Colleges and Seminaries, Roman Catholic) and Scots College,* Douai, he was ordained in 1795 and served in Aberdeenshire until 1805 and then in Glasgow (1805–27). Appointed coadjutor in 1827, he succeeded as vicar apostolic of the Western district 1832, resigning because of ill health in 1845.

In Glasgow he built St Andrew's Chapel, the first neo-Gothic church in Scotland, and eleven other chapels in his district to cope with massive Irish Catholic immigration.* He promoted Sunday schools, established an orphanage and began the first Glasgow Catholic school – using the Protestants' Bible and Protestant financial aid.

Scott's vigorous zeal provoked controversy. He won a libel action against William McGavin's* persistent character assassination in *The Protestant* (1818–22), and he faced a prolonged battle with Irish laymen of the local Catholic Association (1823). Such a clash of attitudes bedevilled the Western District until 1868 (*see* Eyre, Charles).

Scottish Catholic Directory 1831–48; J. F. S. Gordon, *The Catholic Church in Scotland* (A, 1874), 465–74; J. E. Handley, *The Irish in Scotland, 1798–1845* (Cork, 1943); B. Aspinwall, 'The Formation of the Catholic Community in the West of Scotland'; *IR* 33 (1982), 44–57.

B. Aspinwall

Scott, Archibald (1837–1909), CofS minister. Born in Cadder, in north-west Lanarkshire, the son of a farmer, he was educated at the University of Glasgow (BA, 1855). He became minister of the East Church in Perth in 1860, of Abernethy, Perthshire, in 1863, of Maxwell Church in Glasgow in 1865, of Linlithgow in 1869 and of Greenside in Edinburgh in 1871, before moving to St George's in Edinburgh in 1880. He was appointed convener of the Business Committee of the General Assembly and 'Leader' of the house in 1888 – a position in which he showed his skills as an administrator and debater. He took a leading role in the discussions which led to the legislation which changed the terms of subscription* of ministers and elders of the CofS to the Westminster Confession of Faith,* and in beginning the negotiations for the Union* between the CofS and the UFC.

Buddhism and Christianity (Croall lectures,* E, 1890); *Sacrifice: its Prophecy and Fulfilment* (Baird lectures,* E, 1894).

DNB Second Suppl. III, 275–6; *FES* I, 107; Lord Sands (C. N. Johnston), *Dr Archibald Scott of St George's, Edinburgh, and His Times* (E and L, 1919).

D. M. Murray

Scott, David Clement Rufelle (1853-1907), head of the CofS Mission, Blantyre, Malawi (1882-98) and Kikuyu, Kenya (1901-7). Born at Edinburgh and educated at the Royal High School, when apprenticed to an insurance firm, he resolved to become a missionary. He was a brilliant student at Edinburgh University, graduating MA (1878) and BD (1881). He was almost immediately licensed, then ordained and appointed to head the Blantyre Mission of the CofS. The mission was situated in the territory, at that time free of any European control, later to be called British Central Africa, then Nyasaland and now Malawi. In 1898 he resigned, and in 1901 he was appointed to head the mission at Kikuyu in Kenya, where he died.

Scott had to restart the mission at Blantyre after the dismissal or resignation of all the staff, and began a new era of close co-operation with the local people. He used his outstanding linguistic ability to master Chinyanja and to achieve a profound understanding of African culture, unusual in an era when European thought was dominated by social Darwinism.

In 1898 he resigned, ill and saddened by the Foreign Missions Committee's siding with his white-settler critics. He left behind the beautiful Blantyre church and a large body of devoted African converts, the founders of both Christianity and nationalism in southern Malawi.

His years in Kenya were dogged by ill-health and were relatively ineffective. His one achievement in Kenya was that he attracted to the mission a group of families who were later to play a vital role in the creation of the Presbyterian Church of East Africa.

A Cyclopaedic Dictionary of the Mang'anja Language... (E, 1892; enlarged edit., A. Hetherwick, *Dictionary of the Nyanja Language*..., L, 1930).

FES VII, 705-6; *Life and Work in British Central Africa* (ed. Scott), 1886-99, *passim*; A. C. Ross, 'The Origins and Development of the Church of Scotland Mission, Blantyre, Nyasaland, 1875-1926' (PhD, Edinburgh University, 1968).

A. C. Ross

Scott, George (1804-74), evangelical figure in Sweden. Born in Edinburgh, after some time in commerce he entered the Wesleyan ministry in 1830 and was appointed to Stockholm, where British workers were engaged in building Sweden's heavy industry (a devout Methodist had begun the project). Scott had a powerful ministry in the British community (among those converted was the head of the diplomatic mission, Lord Bloomfield), but he aimed more widely at revival in the Swedish national church. He spoke Swedish, and avoided specifically Methodist institutions such as the class meeting. His preaching, coinciding with burgeoning aspirations for a new political and social order, attracted great attention, and made a large church building necessary. The Swedish church authorities wanted this restricted to Sunday worship in English for foreigners only. Government permission to build without such restrictions was greeted as an advance for religious liberty (membership of the national church was obligatory in Sweden until 1860). Scott went to raise money for the chapel in Britain and America; reports of his speeches about the state of Swedish religion caused such outrage in Sweden as to lead to physical attack. He was recalled, and the Methodist mission abandoned, in 1842. Scott's evangelical preaching was, however, a catalyst for evangelical developments, as he discovered in a return visit in 1859, after controversy had died down. His chapel became Bethlehem Church, the centre for the Evangelical National Society for Home and Foreign Mission (EFS), and his influence was acknowledged by such figures as Free Church leader C. O. Rosenius (who described himself as 'G. Scott's successor in Swedish labour') and the Lappland missionary Carl Tellström (Scott helped to found a missionary society and was active for the Bible societies). His later ministry in Britain included periods in Aberdeen (where he developed good relations with the FC, revived a flagging cause, and began a slum mission) and Glasgow, and he became Wesleyan district chairman in Scotland. In 1866 he was appointed by the British Conference to preside over both the Canadian and Eastern British America conferences, preparatory to their union. He died in Glasgow.

Tellström and Lapland, with an Introductory Sketch of the Stockholm mission... (L, 1841, 1868); *A Coronet Laid at the Feet of Jesus* [on Lord Bloomfield] (L, 1856).

Minutes of the Wesleyan Methodist Conference 1860, 347-52; 1866, 616-21, 642-9; 1874, 305 (obituary); G. Westin, *George Scott och hahs verksamet i Sverige* (Stockholm, 1929; contains speeches and letters); *id.*, *Den kristna friförsamlingen i Norden* (Stockholm, 1956); G. G. Findlay and W. W. Holdsworth, *History of the Wesleyan Methodist Missionary Society* (L, 1922), 424ff; A. F. Walls, *Some Personalities of Aberdeen Methodism* (A, 1973).

A. F. Walls

Scott, Peter Cameron (1867-96), founder of the Africa Inland Mission (*see* Missions). Born in humble circumstances in Glasgow, he was reared in the Evangelicalism* of Bethany Hall. In 1879 his family emigrated to Philadelphia, where he joined a Presbyterian* church. Weak health required a temporary return to Scotland. Back in the USA he had some part-time college training and in 1890 was sent by the Missionary Alliance to the Congo. Illness soon recalled him to the USA, via London, where he rededicated his service at Livingstone's* tomb. In a fresh sense of call to East Africa he inspired supporters, including A. T. Pierson, to found the Africa Inland Mission as a 'faith mission'. In 1895 Scott led a party to Kenya and began work at Nzawi, north-east of Kilimanjaro, where others, including a product of the Bible Training Institute,* Glasgow, joined him before his early death of blackwater fever. Under new leadership the AIM soon went from strength to strength.

SCOTT, (SIR) WALTER

C. S. Miller, *Peter Cameron Scott* (L, 1955).

D. F. Wright

Scott, (Sir) Walter (1772–1832). There is some uncertainty as to the religious views of Sir Walter Scott. Both the CofS and the EpCS have claimed his allegiance, and doubt has been expressed (by James Hogg*) as to whether Scott had any vital Christian faith.

There is no documentary evidence of Scott's baptism, but it is improbable that his parents, who were regular attenders at Old Greyfriars and the Tron Kirk in Edinburgh, neglected to have him baptized by a minister of the CofS. In 1806 he was ordained to the eldership* at Duddingston Kirk and represented the royal burgh of Selkirk in the General Assemblies of 1806 and 1807.

The main source of information as to Scott's connection with the EpCS is his son-in-law and biographer, J. G. Lockhart (1794–1854), but the only documentary evidence in records of the EpCS refers to Mrs Scott paying seat rents in St George's Chapel, York Place, Edinburgh.

James Hogg asserts that Scott was 'no great favourer of sects, and seldom or never went to church'. On the other hand he read the English liturgy to his family every Sunday and actually wrote two sermons to help a young probationer minister who was cataloguing the library at Abbotsford. He considered having a domestic chaplain at Abbotsford, but the man he had in mind was a RPC minister (*see* Societies, United), the uncle of his factor.

On his death-bed Scott declined the ministrations of an Episcopal clergyman in Edinburgh, but asked the nurse attending him to read aloud some metrical psalms. After his death, services at Abbotsford were conducted by three CofS ministers, but the burial service at Dryburgh was conducted by Archdeacon Williams at the request of Lockhart.

See also Literature, Religion in Scottish.

H. R. Sefton, 'Scott as Churchman', in J. H. Alexander and D. Hewitt (eds), *Scott and his Influence* (A, 1983), 234–42.

H. R. Sefton

Scot, William (1558–1642), Presbyterian writer. Having graduated from the University of St Andrews in 1586, Scott's first ministerial charge was at Kennoway in his native Fife before his translation to nearby Cupar where he remained 1604–42. As a leading opponent of James VI's* innovations* in church government and worship he was briefly imprisoned in London in 1606–7, confined to his parish 1609–14, and the government refused to permit his translation to Edinburgh in 1620. He lived to see the triumph of the Covenanters.*

An Apologetical Narration of the State of the Kirk of Scotland, in D. Laing (ed.), *Scot's Narration and Forbes' Records* (Wodrow Society, E, 1846); *The Course of Conformitie* (n.p., 1622).

FES V, 142.

K. M. Brown

Scottish Bible Society, *see* Bible Societies.

SCOTTISH CHURCH HISTORY SOCIETY

Scottish Book of Common Prayer, *see* Scottish Prayer Book.

Scottish Catholic Herald, *see* Periodicals, Religious.

Scottish Christian Herald, *see* Periodicals, Religious.

Scottish Christian Journal, *see* Periodicals, Religious.

Scottish Christian Social Union, interdenominational body advocating social reform. Set up in 1901, the Scottish Union was modelled on the existing Christian Social Union in England, founded in 1889 by liberal Anglican churchmen to stimulate Christian social thought and criticism of the social effects of industrial capitalism. The aim of the Scottish Union was to assert that social practice should be shaped by Christian social teaching; to affirm and encourage the social mission of the church; to research social problems and the application of Christian social principles to them; and to act in support of specific reforms.

The moving force behind the founding of the Union was David Watson,* a leading CofS advocate of the social implications of Christianity and a prolific writer on social questions. He won support for the idea from prominent churchmen and laymen in both the established Church and the recently formed United Free Church,* including George Adam Smith* and A. H. Charteris,* who both served as vice-presidents. Local branches were set up in the major Scottish towns, and annual summer schools held, to study social problems. While local activities had largely ceased by 1914, the national organization remained active until the late 1930s. The Union did not realize its founding vision, nor did it offer radical analysis of social problems. But it was an important pioneer influence in the twentieth-century growth of social concern in the Scottish Churches, and enabled Presbyterians from different Churches to work together on social issues before church reunion.

D. Watson, *The Scottish Christian Social Union and How It Came to be Formed* (G, 1901); *id.*, *Chords of Memory* (E, 1936); D. C. Smith, *Passive Obedience and Prophetic Criticism* (NY, 1987); D. J. Withrington, 'The Churches in Scotland c.1870–c.1900; Towards a New Social Conscience?' *RSCHS* 19 (1977), 155–68; B. Aspinwall, *Portable Utopia* (A, 1984).

W. F. Storrar

Scottish Church and University Almanac, *see* Periodicals, Religious.

Scottish Church History Society, founded in 1922 to promote the study of the history of all branches of the Church in Scotland. William J. Couper (*AFCS* I, 125; *FUFCS* 225; *FES* IX, 280) was largely instrumental in its foundation and became the first Honorary Secretary. The *Records* of the Society were first published in 1923 and in the

SCOTTISH CHURCH SOCIETY

preface to Volume I the first President, Principal Alexander Martin,* outlined the reason for the foundation of the society: 'The field, in a word, is one in which unsifted data abound, problems await solution at every step, and "gaps" in the record, as designed to satisfy the standards of modern method, are innumerable. To aid, as far as may be, in supplying these lacunae is the object with which the S.C.H.S. has been formed.'

The Society is non-sectarian and began with a membership of sixty individuals and eight libraries. This has grown to a worldwide membership of about 200 individuals and eighty libraries. It continues to encourage historians, both professional and amateur, ministerial and lay, to present the fruits of their research at its meetings in New College, Edinburgh, and seeks to provide, through the annual publication of these papers in the *Records*, ever more exact and reliable details of the Scottish people's religious past. Recent volumes of the *Records* contain a series of select critical bibliographies which will, in time, cover all periods of Scottish church history.

C. G. F. Brockie

Scottish Church Society. Founded in 1892 by members of the CofS, its general purpose was defined as 'to defend and advance Catholic Doctrine as set forth in the Ancient Creeds and embodied in the Standards of the Church of Scotland; and generally to assert Scriptural principles in all matters relating to Church Order and Policy, Christian Work and Spiritual Life, throughout Scotland.'

The Society has never been as large as the Church Service Society,* with which it is sometimes confused, but it has a much wider remit than worship and has exercised an influence out of all proportion to its numbers. This has been due to the distinction of many of its members, several of whom have served as Moderator of the General Assembly. Prominent among them were William Milligan* and John Macleod.*

The Society is committed to ecumenism, but has been critical of some of the schemes for reunion. During the negotiations for union between the CofS and the UFC, two members of the society, James Cooper* and Arthur Wotherspoon,* strongly criticized the proposed doctrinal basis and secured the special status of the doctrinal first article of the Articles Declaratory* of the Constitution of the Church of Scotland in Matters Spiritual, adherence to which is essential to the continuity and corporate life of the Church.

One of the special objects of the Society has been 'the consideration of social problems with a view to their adjustment on a basis of Christian justice and brotherhood'. In this regard it anticipated the witness of the Iona Community.*

Scottish Church Society Conferences (E, 1894–); A. C. Cheyne, *The Transforming of the Kirk* (E, 1983), 102–7; W. Milligan, *The Scottish Church Society: Some Account of its Aims* (E, 1893); A. K. Robertson, 'The Revival of Church Worship in the Church of Scotland' (PhD, Edinburgh University, 1956).

H. R. Sefton

Scottish Church Theology Society. The CofS has since the Reformation taken biblical theology very seriously. In the turmoil of the 1940s it was felt by many that the issues confronting the Church were basically theological. A series of conferences were held in the town of Crieff in Perthshire, and out of these the Society was founded in 1943. T. F. Torrance* was among the initiators.

The Society is primarily for CofS ministers, though other interested people are welcomed. It meets in area groups for papers, discussion and fellowship. For its Annual Conference it has met every January at Crieff Hydro Hotel since it reopened after World War II. The Honorary Presidential Address each year is given by a theologian of distinction, and is followed by other papers by members and discussion.

It is the Society's concern to explore the deep truths of the Word of God in Reformed theology as they bear practically upon the present day, in the conviction that (as its original Constitution declared) 'the main issue confronting the Church in all its practical problems is basically theological'. Recent subjects include the interplay of theology and worship, the Gospel according to St Matthew, questions raised by ecumenism, and the nature of the good news for the twenty-first century.

W. D. Brown

Scottish Churches Act (1905), settling the property dispute between the UFC and FC. A legal judgement of 1904 found that the name, title and property of the former FC belonged to the small minority which had declined to enter the Union of 1900. Protests from the UFC secured from the government a Royal Commission which recommended the appointment of an Executive Commission to divide the funds and property between the contending parties. The Act accepted and embodied this recommendation, though with the provision that priority be given to meeting the material needs of the continuing FC. The Act also gave the General Assembly of the CofS the right to alter the formula for Confessional subscription.

See also House of Lords Decision, 1904; Free Church of Scotland, post-1900; United Free Church of Scotland.

H. Morrison (ed.), *Manual of the Church Question in Scotland* (E, 1905); A. Stewart and J. K. Cameron, *The Free Church of Scotland 1843–1910* (E, 1910), 276–314; P. C. Simpson, *The Life of Principal Rainy* (L, 1909), II, 441–67.

K. R. Ross

Scottish Churches Council, *see* Ecumenical Movement; Action of Churches Together in Scotland.

Scottish Churches Ecumenical Association/Committee, *see* Ecumenical Movement.

Scottish Churches House, *see* Ecumenical Movement.

Scottish Clergy Society. Founded at Dundee in 1888 (originally the Scotch ...), it can be regarded as the EpCS equivalent of the Wodrow Society.* It was concerned to assert the Scottishness of the EpCS at a time when English influence seemed to predominate (*e.g.* by encouraging 'a native Ministry' and 'a healthy national sentiment among Churchmen'), and to print historical material relating to the Church at and after the Revolution of 1689-90.

Publications: James Gordon, *A Sermon Preached to the Clergy of Aberdeen 1692*, ed. J. T. F. Farquhar (E, 1901); Robert Forbes, *A Catechism Dealing Chiefly with the Holy Eucharist*, ed. J. Dowden (E, 1904); W. W. Hawdon and G. Sutherland (eds), *Sidelights on the Church in Revolution Times. Aberdeen Movement 1688-1695* (E, 1907); John A. Philip (ed.), *Records of the Church in Kirriemuir* (E, 1909).

Scottish Episcopal Church Directory/Year Book, for 1891ff.

H. R. Sefton

Scottish Colportage Society. The progenitor of the Scottish Colportage Society was the Edinburgh Religious Tract and Book Society, founded in 1793 by John Campbell (1766-1840), Edinburgh ironmonger and from 1804 minister of Kingsland Chapel, London. Financed chiefly by donations and annual subscriptions, the Society printed and distributed many tracts, including some in Gaelic, and gave moral and financial support to tract societies in London and Dublin. By 1855, renamed the Religious Tract and Book Society of Scotland, the Society was becoming more commercial, and developing a network of colporteurs (travelling salesmen) to reach country districts and poorer quarters of the cities. By 1879, 251 were working throughout Scotland; in 1885 their extensive sales included 137,000 Bibles and Testaments. Local Societies were established in Glasgow and Aberdeen, and a bookshop opened in Edinburgh. In 1890 this shop sold 20,000 copies of works by the novelist Annie S. Swan.* The commercial and spiritual aspects of the work sometimes co-existed uneasily: booksellers complained that the Society, financed by public donations, was underselling them. The Society was renamed the Tract and Colportage Society of Scotland by 1908, and in 1925 was reconstituted as the Scottish Colportage Society, a modest organization in comparison with the Religious Tract and Book Society of Scotland. In 1939, although preserving its separate identity, it was incorporated with the Stirling Tract Enterprise,* and in 1957 merged with the Scottish Evangelistic Council.* The aim of tract societies has always been to promote spiritual transformation and social amelioration: it is, however, notoriously difficult to quantify their effectiveness.

See also Bible Societies.

A. Macdonald (ed.), *Colportage, What Is It?* (G, 1968); R. Philip, *Life of Mr Campbell* (L, 1841); W. G. Blaikie, *John Campbell Founder of the Tract Society of Scotland* (E, 1886); K. G. Rendell, *Out and About with the Bible. The Story of Two Centuries of Colportage in Scotland* (G, 1993).

Scottish Ecclesiastical Journal, *see* Periodicals, Religious.

Scottish Ecclesiological Society, *see* Ecclesiological Societies.

Scottish Episcopal Church, *see* Episcopalianism.

Scottish Episcopal Church Society. In 1838 the EpCS's General Synod enacted that a society should be organized whose objects were to give financial aid to poor and aged clergymen and to poor congregations, to assist candidates for the ministry, and to further the cause of education. This was the Scottish Episcopal Church Society. It was widely supported, so much so that between 1838 and 1858 churches increased from seventy-three to 150, and clergymen from seventy-eight to 163. The growing Church soon required a broader financial and administrative system, and in 1876 the Representative Church Council was created, which absorbed the Society.

G. Grub, *Ecclesiastical History of Scotland* (E, 1861), vol. IV; F. Goldie, *A Short History of the Episcopal Church in Scotland* (E, 1976).

G. N. Pennie

Scottish Evangelical Theology Society, an evangelical forum for serious theological study and discussion with a pastoral orientation. Founded in 1958 as the Scottish Tyndale Fellowship, it has links with the Tyndale Fellowship for Biblical and Theological Research, a branch of the Inter-Varsity Fellowship.* In 1981 it changed its name, but remains affiliated to the IVF (now the Universities and Colleges Christian Fellowship). The society aims to promote evangelical theology in Scotland, to encourage research and to foster evangelical perspectives on current issues. Its membership is open to ministers, theological teachers and other theologically literate evangelical Christians. The society holds an annual theological conference, which includes a lecture in honour of the late Professor R. A. Finlayson,* its first chairman. There are also some local group meetings.

The *Scottish Bulletin of Evangelical Theology* is published jointly with Rutherford House.* It contains conference papers and other articles.

Scottish Tyndale Bulletin, 1-2 (1978-9); *SBET*, 1ff (1981ff.).

G. W. Grogan

Scottish Evangelistic Council, begun in 1929, formally constituted in 1930 and restructured 1953, to foster prayer and evangelism in Scotland. Especially active during and after the Second World War, it was instrumental in organizing Bible rallies with such speakers as David Martyn Lloyd-Jones, who later made an annual visit to Scotland under its auspices. In 1957 the Scottish Colportage Society* became part of the SEC, followed in 1962 by a merger with the Caravan Mission. Its work continues.

K. G. Rendell, *Fifty Years of Evangelical Witness by Scottish Evangelistic Council* (G, 1980).

A. T. B. McGowan

Scottish Guardian, see Periodicals, Religious.

Scottish Hymnal, see Hymnology.

Scottish Journal of Theology, one of the world's leading journals for systematic theology. Under H. R. Mackintosh,* and through the influence of Karl Barth,* in 1935–6 there began a revival of dogmatic theology in Scotland, and a determination to refound Scottish theology. Emerging from this renewal, immediately after the Second World War, T. F. Torrance* promoted the Scottish Church Theology Society.* Prominent in that group were T. M. Murchison,* John Heron, James McEwen, R. S. Wallace, J. K. S. Reid and G. S. Hendry. The group met a number of times for study. Torrance had definite plans to found a journal, eventually going to Oliver and Boyd, the Edinburgh publishers, where Douglas Grant and Ainslie Thin took the project on. Torrance invited Reid to join him as Editor, and they formed a comittee with Murchison as Secretary, John McFadden as Treasurer and Hendry as Chairman of the Directors. The first number was published in June 1948.

This renewed interest in dogmatic theology had a parallel movement in England. Immediately preceding the War, a group in Oxford founded the SCM Theological Club. It included Daniel Jenkins, Alec Whitehouse, Charles Cranfield, Philip Watson, Gordon Rupp, D. Whiteley, T. F. Torrance, Gordon Hewitt, and A. Raymond George. With the support of this group there emerged the Society for the Study of Theology, which had its first meeting at Queens' College, Cambridge, in 1952, organized by Torrance, with Henry Chadwick as the first Secretary of the Society. Some of the early proceedings of the Society were then published by *SJT*. The *Journal* was, then, outward-looking and international from the beginning, and determined to publish theology of value, not being merely a platform for the current fashion. And so it has remained. The *Journal* was a major organ for the reception of the theology of Karl Barth in the English-speaking world, and also that of Brunner, Bonhoeffer, Tillich and Rahner. It was critical of *The Myth of God Incarnate* (ed. John Hick, L, 1977) because it was such a repetition of the nineteenth century, but has encouraged studies on Moltmann, Jüngel and Pannenberg. Originally, the *Journal* published more biblical material, but biblical theology has latterly lost confidence. Nevertheless, the *Journal* has emphasized the shift in Pauline studies precipitated by E. P. Sanders. The *Journal* always sees as one of its principal aims the promotion of theology from Scotland, but the *Journal* now looks more widely for its material.

The first twenty-two volumes were published by Oliver and Boyd, and the next five by Cambridge University Press. With volume 28, the *Journal* returned to Edinburgh, to the Scottish Academic Press and Douglas Grant. T. and T. Clark of Edinburgh took over publication with volume 45. With volume 35 Torrance and Reid became Editors Emeriti. A. I. C. Heron and J. Houston (earlier Associate Editors) became Editors. From volume 38 A. E. Lewis and I. R. Torrance (earlier Associate Editors) joined Heron as Editors.

I. R. Torrance

Scottish Missionary Society, see Missions.

Scottish Paraphrases, see Paraphrases.

Scottish Prayer Books (Episcopalian). Some desire for 'a uniform order in form of common prayer' appears to have been felt in Scotland as early as 1584, when a commission so reported to Archbishop Patrick Adamson,* but for a variety of reasons nothing came out of it. Until his accession to the throne of England in 1603, James VI* himself gave no impression of wanting liturgical change, but at a Conference at Hampton Court in January 1604, to which the King agreed out of his love for debate, a draft Prayer Book (which was essentially the 1559 Prayer Book of Elizabeth I of England) was prepared with the co-operation of some from all parties in the Church. Once again, the climate for such changes was not right in Scotland and the King did not persist on his new course. His campaign for liturgical reform did not start in earnest until after a compromise between Presbytery and Episcopacy was reached at the 1610 General Assembly and approved by Parliament in 1612. A draft for a revised morning service appeared in 1616 and a second draft, this time for a complete Prayer Book, in 1617. Permission to print a third, revised version was given in 1619. However, after the stormy reception of the Five Articles he had imposed on the 1618 General Assembly at Perth,* the King quietly dropped the entire project and the Book never saw the light.

The project was revived by Charles I,* who never equalled his father in political acumen. In 1634, Charles commanded the Scottish bishops, who much preferred to have a liturgy of their own, to 'draw up a liturgy as near to that of England as might be'. After much controversy, a Scottish Prayer Book was authorized by royal warrant and promulgated by Act of the Scottish Privy Council* and royal proclamation. Neither ministers nor General Assembly were consulted or their attitude considered. In consequence, the attempt to introduce the book in Scotland, which was made on 23 July 1637, met with disastrous results. The Book was silenced by popular tumult: braver than most, the Bishop of Brechin had to read the Book under the protection of loaded pistols.

The 1637 Scottish Prayer Book, the introduction of which was a presage of the civil war,* was not revived at the Restoration. During the reigns of Charles II* and James VII,* the Scottish Church had no liking for liturgical forms. After the disestablishment in 1688, the 1662 English *Book of Common Prayer** became the basis of matins, evensong and the occasional services in the EpCS. From 1724 onwards, the Communion Office of 1637, which Scottish Episcopalians tended to prefer, was printed separately, with or without variations, in a succession of 'wee bookies', starting thereby a process of revision which, thanks to the scholarship of Thomas Rattray,* culminated in the production of the 1764 Scottish Communion Office. In 1849, Patrick Torry* authorized single-handedly the printing of a Prayer Book which sanctioned actual use of what was substantially that of Charles I, apart from the inclusion of the Communion Office of 1764. In 1912 *The Book of Common Prayer (Scotland)* limited itself to the incorporation and authorization of a limited number of deviations from the English services already in use by the clergy. A more radical revision was attempted with the publication in 1929 of *The Scottish Book of Common Prayer*, which – among other sources – drew its inspiration from the failed English Book of 1928 and is still now the official Prayer Book of the EpCS.

See also Laud, William.

G. Donaldson, *The Making of The Scottish Prayer Book of 1637* (E, 1954); W. Perry, *The Scottish Prayer Book, Its Value and History* (C, 1929); A. C. Don, *The Scottish Book of Common Prayer 1929* (L, 1949); J. Dowden, *The Scottish Communion Office of 1764* (O, 1922); G. Donaldson, 'Reformation to Covenant', in D. Forrester and D. Murray (eds.), *Studies in the History of Worship in Scotland* (E, 1984), 33–51; G. W. Sprott, *Scottish Liturgies of the Reign of James VI* (1901); A. Maclean, 'Episcopal Worship in the Nineteenth and Twentieth Centuries', in D. Forrester and D. Murray (eds.), *Studies in the History of Worship in Scotland* (E, 1984), 96–112.

G. Tellini

Scottish Pulpit, *see* Periodicals, Religious.

Scottish Realism, a movement sometimes known as 'Scottish common-sense philosophy' or 'the Scottish School' that took its rise principally from the reaction of Thomas Reid (1710–96) to the scepticism of David Hume,* particularly his scepticism about the self and the external world. James M'Cosh,* himself a Scottish Realist, and a historian of Scottish philosophy, claimed to discern a 'Scottish Philosophy' over a longer period of time, identifying it as much with the distinctive Scottish intellectual temper as with a set of philosophical positions.

Born at Strachan, Kincardineshire, and educated at Marischal College, Aberdeen, Reid was librarian of Marischal (1733–6), minister of New Machar, Aberdeenshire (1737–51), regent at King's College, Aberdeen (1751–64), and Professor of Moral Philosophy of Glasgow (1764–96). Reid was brought up under the influence of Locke and Berkeley, but abandoned his early Berkeleian views after reading Hume's *Treatise* in 1739. Besides *An Inquiry into the Human Mind on the Principles of Commonsense* (E, 1764) he wrote two other books, *Essays on the Intellectual Powers of Man* (E, 1785) and *Essays on the Active Powers of Man* (E, 1788).

MAIN THEMES. The common-sense tenets to which Reid appealed were not gathered by induction or by polling men and women in the street. They were claimed to be intuitive beliefs. For some, *e.g.* Frances Hutcheson,* these beliefs were a 'sense'. For others, as Reid, they were a matter of common sense. Later Scottish Realists thought of them in more definitely *a priori* ways, as fundamental laws of thought (Dugald Stewart*) or *a priori* forms (Sir William Hamilton*). 'All who are truly of the Scottish school agree in maintaining that there are laws, principles, or powers in the mind anterior to any reflex observation of them, and acting independently of the philosopher's classification or explanation of them' (M'Cosh, *The Scottish Philosophy*, L, 1874, 7).

Such an appeal enabled the Scottish Realists to resist the 'theory of ideas' of Locke and his followers which culminated in Hume's scepticism (even though Hume was granted a place by M'Cosh in the panoply of distinctively Scottish philosophers). Reid resisted the view that what we know directly or immediately are our own sensations, which we take to represent an inaccessible external reality. Hence 'realism', the view that fundamental matters are known directly.

Appeals to common sense or to intuition harbour special dangers. The denial of such powers leads to a loss of innocence. For if their existence is denied – and has to be defended – then how can they ever again be treated as intuitive or obvious matters of common sense? But Reid attempts a defence by pointing to the absurdity of making a denial, the paradoxical difficulties arising from such denials, and the way in which such denials are literally unworkable. He tries to let the common-sense principles speak for themselves. No one can live as if there is no external world, or as if he had no memory, or as if there is no other person in the universe besides himself. And so the theoretical repudiators of common sense must live a lie. (But only if they regard common sense as a *theoretical* alternative to their preferred theory, which they may not.)

Another way of interpreting Scottish Realism is to think of 'common sense' not as a way of knowing certain truths, but rather as describing those particular matters which are known. So a person may know that there has been a past not because his 'common sense' tells him, but because he is more certain of this fact than of any general theory that might overthrow it, and any general theory must also depend, presumably, upon trusting to the validity of memory.

ADVANTAGES. Despite its philosophical weaknesses, the advantages of common-sense Realism were judged to be considerable. It cohered with theism, since God is both the source of the common-sense principles, for he has implanted them in our nature, and, on some accounts at least, is himself one of those principles. 'God exists' is a necessary, self-evident truth, one that any rational person not blinded by prejudice or pernicious philosophical views would at once accept.

Realism has other advantages; besides providing an answer to scepticism, it gave a grounding to morality and to a version of mind-body dualism. Equally importantly, appealing to common sense enabled the onus to be placed on the sceptic, and it cohered well with the temper of the Moderate* party in the CofS, though Evangelicals such as Thomas Chalmers* readily adopted common-sense principles.

Through his personal influence and that of his writings, Reid gained a number of disciples: James Oswald,* James Beattie (1735–1802; *DNB* IV, 22–5), Dugald Stewart* and most notably Sir William Hamilton,* though in Hamilton the principles of common sense and those of post-Kantian idealism are held in uneasy alliance. Hamilton's views were subjected to sustained criticism from the standpoint of radical empiricism by J. S. Mill in *An Examination of Sir William Hamilton's Philosophy* (L, 1865).

Scottish Realism is important less for its philosophical originality and power than for the influence it wielded over the minds of countless Scottish and American ministers, who were introduced to its tenets by such gifted teachers as Stewart, Chalmers and later, M'Cosh. They found in it an attractive, philosophically-endorsed option between scepticism and materialism. It also enabled busy preachers to maintain a largely non-theoretical stance in the pulpit, while at the same time vindicating certain metaphysical positions widely believed to be endorsed by Scripture.

Scottish Realism was exported to America by John Witherspoon,* who emigrated from Scotland to become the President of the College of New Jersey (Princeton University*) in 1768 and there attracted large numbers of students. This influence was later reinforced by other less well-known immigrants. Scottish Realism became staple fare in numerous Presbyterian colleges and seminaries from New Jersey to South Carolina, eclipsing the influence of Jonathan Edwards* everywhere, except perhaps in New England.

DECLINE. Although the influence of Scottish Realism waned after about 1850 under the impact of continental idealism, and came to be regarded as both provincial and unphilosophical, it continued to be maintained in a recognizable form by philosophers such as Henry Calderwood,* John Veitch (1829–94; *DNB* LVIII, 199–200), and A. C. Fraser.* But it ceased to be the 'national' philosophy of Scotland, though some of its characteristic positions have enjoyed something of a minor renaissance in the twentieth century through the influence of the English philosopher G. E. Moore (1873–1958) and the American Roderick Chisholm (1916–).

Reid: *DNB* XLVII, 436–9; *FES* VI, 66–7; lives by A. C. Fraser (E, 1898) and Dugald Stewart (E, 1803); *The Works...*, ed. Sir W. Hamilton and H. C. Mansel, 2 vols (E, 1846–63); *Essays on the Intellectual Powers of Man...*, ed. A. D. Woozley (L, 1941); M. Dalgarno (ed.), *The Philosophy of Thomas Reid* (Dordrecht, 1989); K. Lehrer, *Thomas Reid* (L, 1989).

J. Beattie, *An Essay on the Nature and Immutability of Truth* (E, 1770); H. Laurie, *Scottish Philosophy in its National Development* (G, 1902); S. A. Grave, *The Scottish Philosophy of Common Sense* (O, 1960); M. Kuehn, *Scottish Common Sense in Germany, 1768–1800* (Kingston, Ont., 1987).

P. Helm

Scottish Reformation Society, the principal Scottish anti-Catholic* society. It was formed at a meeting in the Edinburgh Music Hall on 5 December 1850, called to protest at the formation of a territorial RC hierarchy in England, a perceived 'Papal Aggression' that stirred intense anti-Catholicism on both sides of the Border. The Society's stated objectives were 'to resist the aggressions of Popery – to watch the designs and movements of its promoters and abettors – and to diffuse sound and Scriptural information on the distinctive tenets of Protestantism and Popery'. Its constitution was interdenominational, although in practice it was dominated by members of the FC,* particularly James Begg* and James Aitken Wylie.*

Initially the Scottish Reformation Society was primarily a political pressure group, concerned to resist further concessions to RCs on matters such as the provision of chaplains* in prisons. Above all, it campaigned for the repeal of the state endowment to Maynooth College, the Irish RC seminary. In the mid-1850s it took a leading role in attempts to develop combined action with the English anti-Catholic societies in fruitless efforts to achieve their common political objectives.

It was recognized from the outset that successful political action would require the mobilization of public opinion at the grass roots. Energetic deputation work has always been a prominent feature of the Society's activities and in the 1850s this helped to establish branches throughout Scotland. There has also been extensive publishing activity, and the Society's journal, *The Bulwark*, has appeared continuously since 1851. In the early 1860s the SRS took a leading part in the formation in Edinburgh of the Protestant Institute of Scotland, which provided instruction in Protestant theology and history for students and other young people. Classes were also held in a number of other Scottish towns and missionary efforts among RCs were supported. In the 1860s operations were extended to England and Protestant Educational Classes were held in London.

As the years passed, the political side of the work receded and the promotion of a consciousness of the importance of the Reformation heritage became the most prominent part of the Society's activities. Negative anti-Catholicism was less apparent and the constitution was amended in 1964 to emphasize the positive propagation of evangelical Protestantism and the diffusion of scriptural teaching.

This change has provided a basis for growth during the last quarter of a century. The Society thus continued active with an office on George IV Bridge, Edinburgh, in the original Protestant Institute building. The Scottish Protestant Alliance was absorbed in 1911, the Scottish Women's Protestant Union in 1950 and the Protestant Institute of Scotland in 1963. The SRS's main activities are now the production and distribution of appropriate literature and the organization of tours to sites with Reformation associations in Scotland and abroad. It is financed mainly by the subscriptions of its members, including some from overseas, and also receives support from the Hope Trust.* It owns Magdalen Chapel,* Edinburgh.

The Scottish Reformation Society: Its Origins, Its Objects and Its Work (E, 1951); J. R. Wolffe, *The Protestant Crusade in Great Britain, 1829–1860* (O, 1991); S. Bruce, *No Pope of Rome* (E, 1985). Further information from the Society's publications including its Annual Reports, *The Bulwark* and its Newsletter.

J. R. Wolffe

Scottish School Book Association. Presbyteries of the CofS* persuaded Parliament to allow them to set up a fund for the relief of widows and children of burgh and parochial schoolmasters. In 1818, some members of the fund founded the Scottish School Book Association to produce and sponsor school text books of better quality and variety, and of a more reliable 'religious tendency' than those available at the time. By mid-century, the SSBA listed fifty-five separate publications (including maps). By 1881, the number had nearly trebled.

From the beginning, the Association provided bursaries for the education of the children of needy members and assisted individual schoolmasters involved in battles with their employers, the results of which were considered to affect the interests of the whole profession. Throughout its existence, the SSBA sought to maintain the constitution and management of the parish school system with its intimate connection with the CofS and the land-owning classes. It also sought to protect the parish school as an avenue to university education for any boy of whatever social class, who had the necessary intellectual gifts.

That the SSBA became a model political pressure group in defence of its objectives was due largely to one man, William Knox (1799–1874), schoolmaster of St Ninians, Stirlingshire. Knox was treasurer of the SSBA from 1844 to 1871, and although he became the second president of the Educational Institute of Scotland (1848), his sole aim was to guard the interests of the parish schools, principally through the SSBA. Knox dominated all the activities of the Association on a day-to-day basis and largely determined policies in all its activities. He immersed the SSBA in Scottish educational politics, using with great flair and energy every available method of influencing parliamentary and public opinion.

Educational change was becoming inevitable. Extension of the franchise provided by the Reform Bill (1832), the Disruption* and the consequent proliferation of FC schools, upheavals abroad in the late 1840s, the growing educational chaos in the industrial centres (particularly Glasgow), all increased agitation for a national, integrated system. In his evidence to the Argyll Commission in 1864, Knox had to concede the inadequacies of the parish school system, but he hoped that the schools might remain unchanged within a larger structure. Although nearly every parish schoolmaster was a member of the CofS and had subscribed to the Westminster* Confession, Knox insisted that the parish schools were national and non-sectarian, being open to all. In his view, they taught the 'basic truths' of Christianity, albeit these truths led inevitably to Protestantism rather than RCism. The General Assembly of the CofS had declared as far back as 1849 that the parish school was 'part and parcel of the national Church' and that parochial schoolmasters were 'ecclesiastical persons', but spokesmen for the SSBA clung forcibly to Knox's view.

The Burgh and Schoolmasters Act of 1861 significantly weakened the connection between the parish schools and the CofS. Although the determined efforts of the SSBA helped to delay change, the final battle was lost with the Education Act* of 1872. Membership of the SSBA nevertheless increased, as more and more schoolmasters struggled with the new School Boards, which often exceeded their powers due to the ambiguities of the Act. However, under the new national system, the Educational Institute of Scotland came to be seen as better able to defend all teachers, and the SSBA was dissolved, in spite of opposition, in 1881.

Despite its prominence in the educational politics of Scotland in the middle decades of the century, the SSBA and Knox have passed almost into oblivion in the history of Scottish education.

M. P. Scholan, 'A Study of the Scottish School Book Association 1818–1891, with Special Reference to William Knox, Treasurer, 1844–1871' (MEd, Edinburgh University, 1972).

M. P. Scholan

Scottish SPCK (Society in Scotland for Propagating Christian Knowledge), an Edinburgh-based benevolent society which sought to promote Protestantism, chiefly in its Presbyterian form, among Scottish Highlanders and (after 1730) among the North American Indians. Its roots lie in a 'Society for the Reformation of Manners', established in Edinburgh in 1701 on the foundations of an earlier praying society. This Society made an unsuccessful attempt to erect a school 'in the paroch of Abertarff, in the shyre of Inverness, being the center of a countrey where Popery and Ignorance did much abound'. Although this venture failed, it established the concept of a society which operated through charity schools. The concept was supported by James Kirkwood,* apparently the author of *Proposals concerning the Propagation of Christian Know-*

ledge in the Highlands and Islands of Scotland and Forraign Parts of the World (E, 1706). Money was gathered, and the Scottish SPCK was founded by royal charter in May 1709. It soon began to erect charity schools in the Highlands,* many of which were located on the eastern and southern edges of the Highlands, although it was also active in the central Highlands and the Hebrides, planting a school in St Kilda in 1710 (C. W. Withers, *Gaelic in Scotland*, E, 1984, 120-33).

Schools were funded by means of interest on capital investments, and their number increased slowly, from five in 1711, to 176 in 1758 and 229 in 1795. Schoolmasters, who were to be persons 'of loyalty, prudence, gravity, competent knowledge and literature', were carefully selected by the Society, and had to commit themselves to the eradication of 'popery'. The teaching of Latin was forbidden, doubtless because of its association with Roman Catholicism, and so too, initially and for similar reasons, was the teaching of Gaelic.* English was to be the pre-eminent language, taught to Protestant and RC pupils alike. Gradually, however, the Society had to resign itself to the use of Gaelic in its schools, and in 1767 it published the Scottish Gaelic New Testament (*see* Bible, Versions, Gaelic). The schools were rigorously supervised, the use and training of pupil-teachers was encouraged, and schoolmasters frequently acted as catechists, in co-operation with the Royal Bounty* during 1729-58. Some teachers, such as Dugald Buchanan,* became influential figures in their localities, leading the Presbyterian thrust against 'incivility' and Jacobitism.* The opposite development is apparent in the career of the Gaelic poet, Alexander MacDonald, who became a RC and an ardent Jacobite after a period as an SSPCK schoolmaster in Ardnamurchan. MacDonald compiled a Gaelic-English vocabulary (E, 1741) for the Society (R. Black, *Mac Mhaighstir Alasdair*, Coll, 1986).

The Society was active in the provision of religious means for Highlanders who had migrated to the Lowlands; it supplied a catechist for the Gaelic Chapel erected in Edinburgh in 1769. The North American interests of the Society began after 1730, in fulfilment of its commitment to evangelize 'Popish and Infidel parts of the World'. Through Commissioners in Boston and New York, it supported several missionaries to the North American Indians, including the celebrated David Brainerd and his brother, John. Its concern for the spiritual welfare of both emigrant Highlanders and Indians was underlined in 1735, when it sent 'Mr John Macleod, a native of the Isle of Skye', to minister to a settlement of Gaelic speakers in Georgia; Macleod was also to act as one of the Society's 'missionaries for instructing the native Indians'.

By 1800, the role and influence of the Scottish SPCK as an active evangelistic body had diminished significantly, and in the Highlands after 1810 its work came to be modified in the light of the principles of the Gaelic School Societies.* Nevertheless, it still maintained 134 schools in Gaelic-speaking parishes in 1824.

J. MacInnes, *The Evangelical Movement in the Highlands of Scotland* (A, 1951), 236-50; *An Account of the Society in Scotland for Propagating Christian Knowledge* (E, 1774); H. R. Sefton, 'The Scotch Society in the American Colonies in the Eighteenth Century', *RSCHS* 17 (1972), 169-84; V. E. Durkacz, *The Decline of the Celtic Languages* (E, 1983), 45-72; D. E. Meek, 'Scottish Highlanders, North American Indians and the SSPCK', *RSCHS* 23 (1989) 378-96.

D. E. Meek

Scottish Sunday School Union, *see* Sunday School Movement.

Scottish Tyndale Fellowship, *see* Scottish Evangelical Theology Society.

Scougal, Henry (1650-78), Professor of Divinity in King's College, Aberdeen. Scougal was born at Leuchars, Fife, the second son of Patrick Scougal (1607?-82; *DNB* LI, 121—2; *FES* VII, 331). Patrick served the Fife parishes of Dairsie and then Leuchars. In 1658 he was transferred to Saltoun (E. Lothian), where he developed a close friendship with Robert Leighton.* In 1664 he became Bishop of Aberdeen. He was an able minister, esteemed by both dissenters and conformists. At the age of fifteen, Henry entered King's College, Aberdeen. He graduated in 1668 and the next year, at the age of nineteen, he was made a tutor. It is thought that he was the first in Scotland to teach Baconian philosophy. He was ordained in 1672 and served as minister of the parish of Auchterless in Aberdeenshire. In 1674 he was recalled to Aberdeen as Professor of Divinity.

Scougal belonged to the school of Leighton in stressing personal holiness as well as theological learning. He died at the age of twenty-eight, telling his friends: 'When you have the charity to remember me in your prayers, do not think me a better man than I am; but look on me, as indeed I am, a miserable sinner.' Scougal produced several minor writings, mainly sermons, but above all *The Life of God in the Soul of Man* (L, 1677). This became a classic of Christian devotional literature, valued by Presbyterians as well as Episcopalians. In part one, Scougal defines true religion as 'a union of the soul with God' and 'a divine life'. The 'root' of this life is faith; and its 'chief branches are love to God, charity to men, purity, and humility'. The author then describes how these qualities were 'perfectly exemplified in the holy life of our blessed Saviour'. Part two sets forth 'the excellency and advantages' of true religion, and part three 'the difficulties and duties of the Christian life'. We are encouraged in our pursuit of holiness by God's love toward his people, the effectual work of God's Son, and the life-giving activity of the Holy Spirit. Scougal urges his readers to abstain from sin, watch continually, and strive toward godliness. The purpose in this effort is 'not to appear better than we are', he writes, 'but that we may really become so'. 'Fervent and hearty prayer' and 'frequent and conscientious use' of the sacrament of the Lord's Supper are two other means 'for begetting a holy and religious disposition by faith', since they concentrate on true and vital religion as contrasted with outward forms and sectarian commitment. John Wesley* gave a copy of the book to his friend George Whitefield,* who later wrote in his journal that 'he never knew what true religion was' until he read 'that excellent treatise'. Whitefield learned that it did not consist in good works but was 'union of the soul with God, and Christ formed in us'. He wrote: 'A ray of Divine light was instantaneously darted in upon my soul, and from that moment, but not till then, did I know that I must be a new creature.'

The Works of Mr Henry Scougal (^{2}A, 1765), ed. J. Cooper, with 'Life' (A, 1892); appreciations by many editors of *Life of God*; *DNB* LI, 120–1; *FES* VII, 371; D. Butler, *Henry Scougal and the Oxford Methodists* (E, 1899); W. Anderson, *Scottish Nation* (E, 1877), III, 423–4; Chambers-Thomson III, 335.

D. B. Calhoun

Scripture Union, a worldwide movement engaged in evangelism among young people and the encouragement of Bible reading by people of all ages.

In 1859 a young man Payson Hammond studying at the FC College in Edinburgh conducted a children's mission in nearby Musselburgh. Moved by the opportunities he saw there, he decided to devote his life to evangelism among children. It was through seeing Hammond at work in London in 1867 that Josiah Spiers decided to begin gathering together boys and girls for home meetings. The work grew, and in 1868 a committee was formed to organize these, adopting the name the Children's Special Service Mission (CSSM). At the prompting of a young Sunday School teacher in Keswick, Annie Marston, who wished to help her class read the Bible regularly, the Children's Scripture Union was begun in 1879 as another activity of CSSM. Within ten years circulation of the readings card which was produced had risen to 470,000 in twenty-eight languages.

It was not, however, until 1902 that a committee was formed to develop CSSM in Scotland, although it is known that a seaside mission took place at Seamill in Ayrshire before 1900 under the CSSM banner. A worker was appointed in 1904 to visit girls' private schools, and a camp was held for these girls in the same year – a bold step in those days. The first camp for private-school boys took place in 1922. Camps for state-school children did not begin, however, until 1938. The pioneers of these, and of the formation of Scripture Union (SU) groups in state schools, were Philip W. Petty (*FES* IX, 746, X, 106) and James W. Meiklejohn (the latter first employed by the Glasgow United Evangelistic Association* and then on the CSSM staff from 1939, for thirty-four years).

The work grew steadily throughout the years after World War II, under the leadership of James Beveridge, and included the formation of the Scottish Caravan Mission, which sought to reach children in remote areas. In 1962 responsibility for the Caravan Mission was accepted by the Scottish Evangelistic Council.* Beveridge died in 1954, Meiklejohn filled the interregnum until Peter Campbell was appointed in 1957, and John Butler served as General Secretary from 1965 to 1988. He was followed by CofS minister Colin Sinclair.

In 1975, the implementation of the Wheatley report on local government provided the opportunity to reorganize the work, and offices and bookshops have subsequently been acquired in most Regions in Scotland. The name of the worldwide movement was changed in 1960 to Scripture Union. The Scottish organization became autonomous in 1972, and is one of over 100 similar national movements with common aims and basic philosophy, and a conservative evangelical basis of faith, linked together by Regional Councils and an International Council. The movement is aligned to no denomination. Although most of its work is among Protestant Churches, it welcomes children of all faiths and of none. It strongly supports the Churches, and all involved in its activities are encouraged to become active church members. Worldwide Bible-reading membership is about two million.

There are currently in Scotland some 600 groups in schools, camps organized for 4,000 children each year, twenty summer seaside missions, training activities for Sunday School teachers and extensive circulation of Bible Reading notes, Sunday School teaching materials and related publications. Twenty-one field and executive staff and some thirty-five other staff are employed in Scotland.

J. C. Pollock, *The Good Seed* (L, 1959); J. B. Taylor *et al.*, *Evangelism among Children and Young People* (L, 1967); N. Sylvester, *God's Word in a Young World* (L, 1984); J. Findlay *et al.*, *A Place to Pitch Your Tents* (G, 1988).

J. M. F. Butler

Scroggie, William Graham (1877–1958), Baptist preacher and writer. Born in Malvern, Worcestershire, of Scottish parents from Aberdeenshire, Scroggie trained for the Baptist ministry at Spurgeon's College, London. His first pastorate was in Leytonestone (1899–1902), and thereafter he served at Trinity Church, Halifax (1902–5), Bethesda Free Church, Sunderland (1907–16), Charlotte Chapel, Edinburgh (1916–33) and Spurgeon's Tabernacle, London (1938–44). The period 1933–7 was devoted to ministry in New Zealand, Australia, Canada, South Africa and the United States of America.

Scroggie looked back to his years at Charlotte Chapel as the most fruitful period of his ministry, 'the crown of my pastoral career'. While he was there, thirty-two men entered the ministry, and fifty-one missionaries were sent. His Thursday evening Bible school attracted great crowds from a wide spectrum of churches, including many theological students. In 1927 the University of Edinburgh bestowed upon him its honorary DD for the unusual influence he had exercised in Edinburgh as a preacher and missioner. Special reference was made to his devotion to 'the study and teaching of the Bible in its twofold character of a Divine

Revelation and a great Literature' and to the correspondence courses he conducted 'for three thousand pupils through a four year Course of Systematic Bible Study'.

He made distinctive contributions to the work of the Keswick Convention and the Scripture Union.* He gave the Bible readings at Keswick on no less than twelve occasions, and he provided the daily SU notes continuously for more than six years. Identifying himself with the moderate conservatives within Evangelicalism, Scroggie helped to prevent the emergence of schism over the issue of fundamentalism in the 1920s. Although a premillennialist, he was anxious to avoid rigid dogmatism in eschatological understanding, and in this too he steadied the course of British Evangelicals before 1945.

Besides books arising from his Keswick Bible readings, he wrote numerous other pamphlets and books, prominent among which are *The Book of Psalms* (L, 1948–51), *Know Your Bible* (L, G, 1940), *The Unfolding Drama of Redemption* (L, 1953) and *A Guide to the Gospels* (L, 1948).

W. Graham Scroggie (ed.), *The Story of a Life in the Love of God* (L, 1938).

R. G. Turnbull, *A Treasury of W. Graham Scroggie* (L, 1974); W. Whyte, *Revival in Rose Street: A History of Charlotte Baptist Chapel* (E, n.d.); D. Bebbington, *Evangelicalism in Modern Britain* (L, 1989), 222–3, 227; *Who Was Who, 1951– 1960*, 979.

D. Prime

Seabury, Samuel (1729–96), first Bishop of the Protestant Episcopal Church in the USA, consecrated by three bishops of the EpCS in November 1784 in Aberdeen.

Seabury was no stranger to Scotland and the EpCS, for he had studied medicine in Edinburgh during 1752. The following year he received deacon's and priest's orders from English bishops, as had all the other episcopal clergy in the American colonies. During the American War of Independence Seabury supported the British government and served as a chaplain to the King's American regiment.

After the war the need for a resident American bishop was felt more keenly, and Seabury was elected Bishop by the clergy of Connecticut in 1782. He was then sent to London to seek consecration from the English bishops. This was refused on the grounds that the form of service contained an oath of allegiance to the King which Seabury could not now take; the oath could not be omitted without authority of Parliament. The Scottish bishops laboured under no such difficulty, and agreed to consecrate Seabury.

As part of a concordat of friendship between the Scottish and American churches, Seabury agreed to commend the adoption of the Scottish Communion Office used at his consecration to the clergy of Connecticut. He was as good as his word, and the American Prayer Book still contains a Communion office based on the Scottish service.

A. W. Rowthorn, *Samuel Seabury* (NY, 1983); B. E. Steiner, *Samuel Seabury . . . A Study in the High Church Tradition* (Athens, OH, 1971).

H. R. Sefton

Seamen's Missions, organized efforts to promote the spiritual and social welfare of seamen. The Naval and Military Bible Society (1779) and small Marine Bible Societies (from 1813) distributed Bibles to sailors. Shipboard prayer meetings advertised by a flag proclaiming 'Bethel' (1817) heralded the foundation of seamen's missions proper. Among them were the British and Foreign Sailors' Society (1833, though absorbing earlier bodies), the Seamen's Christian Friend Society (1846), which maintained an evangelistic emphasis, and the Missions to Seamen (1856), an Anglican body. In Scotland Seamen's Friend Societies were launched in Greenock, Leith, Aberdeen, Glasgow and Dundee (1820–2), there was a Scottish Sailors' and Soldiers' Bethel Flag Union (1835), and Scottish Coast Missions (founded 1850–8) promoted evangelism. There followed the Royal National Mission to Deep Sea Fishermen (1881) and Agnes Weston's Sailors' Rests for the navy (from the 1870s). American societies had existed since 1812, and after 1864 Protestant equivalents were established elsewhere. The worldwide RC Apostleship of the Sea (1920– 70) was commenced by Glasgow laymen.

See also Fisherfolk, Missions to.

R. Kverndal, *Seamen's Missions* (Pasadena, CA, 1986); P. F. Anson, *The Church and the Sailor* (L, 1948); L. A. G. Strong, *Flying Angel* (L, 1956); K. Heasman, *Evangelicals in Action* (L, 1962), 246– 58.

D. W. Bebbington

Secession Church, *see* Associate Presbytery; Associate Synod; General Associate Synod; Original Secession Church; United Presbyterian Church; United Secession Church.

Secessions. Although the 'First Secession' did not occur until 1733, the unity of the Church in Scotland had been ruptured by the refusal of both Episcopalians* and Cameronians (*see* Societies, United) to accept the restoration of Presbyterianism* in 1690. The separate identity of these bodies has been maintained to the present day in the Scottish Episcopal Church and the Reformed (Covenanting) Presbyterian Church.*

The Secession of 1733 was the first major secession from the national Church. Led by Ebenezer Erskine,* a small number of ministers objected to an overture approved by the 1731 General Assembly to give elders* and heritors* the right to fill a vacancy in cases where the Presbytery had responsibility. Although a majority of Presbyteries opposed this proposal, it was moved at the 1732 Assembly to pass it as an act. Erskine's vehement opposition led to his being formally rebuked at the 1733 Assembly. Erskine submitted a protest signed by himself, Alexander Moncrieff,* James Fisher* and William Wilson.* For refusing to withdraw

SECESSIONS

their protest they were first suspended, and later removed from their charges. They refused to accept the sentence and seceded from ministerial communion. On 5 December 1733 they met at Gairney Bridge, Kinross-shire, to form the Associate Presbytery.* In 1740 they were formally deposed and the secession made definitive.

Soon after, in 1761, a further secession took place. Thomas Gillespie,* minister of Carnock, near Dunfermline, along with five others, presented a 'Humble Representation' to the Assembly of 1752, protesting at the intrusion of ministers contrary to the wishes of congregations, and the Act of 1736. When Gillespie made a further statement he was subsequently deposed from the ministry. Gillespie accepted his deposition but continued his ministry. In 1761, along with two others, he formed the Presbytery of Relief* 'for Christians oppressed in their church privileges'.

The Secession, meanwhile, had itself split in 1747 over the rightness of church members taking the Burgess oath.* The Burghers (Associate Synod),* led by Ebenezer and Ralph* Erskine, and Antiburghers (General Associate Synod)* were each in turn split over the Westminster Confession's* teaching regarding the role of the civl magistrate in religion. In 1799 the Associate Synod was divided into New Lichts (Lights),* who rejected all intolerant and persecuting principles in religion, and the Auld Lichts, who wanted to maintain the teaching of the Confession as it stood. A similar split occurred in the ranks of the General Associate Synod in 1806. (1820 witnessed a reversal in this trend when the New Light Burghers and the New Light Antiburghers united to form the United Secession Church.* This in turn united with the Relief Church in 1847 as the United Presbyterian Church, bringing together most of the Secessionists into one body.)

The major secession of the nineteenth century occurred in 1843, when over 450 ministers left the CofS to form the Free Church.* This secession was preceded by a bitter Ten Years' Conflict* centring on the Church's relation with the state. The evangelical* party, led by Thomas Chalmers,* having assumed a majority in the Assembly in 1834, endeavoured to assert the Church's spiritual independence of the state by passing a Veto Act* which gave parishioners the right to veto the ministerial nominee of parish patrons. In 1838 the Court of Session declared the Act to be *ultra vires*. The debate now focused upon the question of the Church's spiritual independence, in particular its sovereignty in spiritual matters. The Crown's rejection of the Claim of Right* in January 1843 inevitably led to the Disruption* of that year. This new ecclesiastical body was joined in 1852 by a majority of the Original Secession Church.* The Original Burgher (Old Light) Synod (properly, the Associate Synod) had joined the CofS in 1839. The FC was further increased by the majority of the Reformed Presbyterians (Cameronians) joining in 1876.

In 1892, two ministers and about 4,000 members, mainly from the Highlands, seceded from the FC in protest over the passing of a Declaratory Act* which allowed ministers 'liberty of opinion on matters not entering the substance of the faith'. This newly constituted Free Presbyterian Church* continues to the present day.

In 1900, 150 mainly Highland, congregations refused to enter the union of the FC and UPC to form the UFC because of supposed doctrinal laxity. The continuing FC exists to the present day, though mainly confined to its Highland and Island heartlands (*see* Free Church of Scotland, post-1900).

The present ecclesiastical situation was in substance arrived at in 1929, when the UFC merged with the CofS. Again a small minority refused to enter the union, this time in protest against the Church's connection with the state, and formed the continuing United Free Church.* The remnant of the Original Secession Church joined the CofS in 1956, but in 1989 roughly half of the ministers and a smaller proportion of members left the Free Presbyterian Church over a disciplinary case, forming the Associated Presbyterian Churches.*

Secessions have occupied a significant place in the development of the Scottish Church. They have fragmented the Church's witness and internalized its energies, but paradoxically stimulated the Church's convictions and initiated national and international mission.

J. M'Kerrow, *History of the Secession Church* (G, 1841); W. Wilson, *Defence of Reformation Principles* (E, 1739); J. H. Leckie, *Secession Memories* (E, 1926); A. Gib, *The Present Truth: A Display of the Secession Testimony*, 2 vols (E, 1774); A. C. Cheyne, *The Transforming of the Kirk* (E, 1983).

K. R. Ross

SECOND BOOK OF DISCIPLINE

Second Book of Discipline (1578), the product of the General Assembly's decision by 1576 to abandon the experiment in episcopacy* introduced in 1572 at the Convention of Leith* and to devise a fresh statement of the Church's constitution. This would be modelled more firmly on the principles enunciated in the *FBD*,* from which the Church had seemed in danger of departing in the early 1570s under the Regent Morton's policy of 'conformity with England' (*see* Douglas, James). The Assembly's dissatisfaction with the operation of the Leith arrangements from 1572 resulted in its decision by 1576 to entrust oversight to discussions on securing 'a perfect polity' for the kirk. In 1576 the Regent Morton finally conceded to the Assembly that if the Church were not prepared to adhere to the Leith settlement of 1572 a revised formulation should be prepared. This marked the start of drafting the 'Heads and Conclusions of the Policy of the Kirk' or *SBD*, which was completed by 1578. Authorship of the work belonged to no one individual or group of individuals. Andrew Melville* was merely one of thirty or so participants in its composition, most of whom belonged to the earlier generation of Reformers who had accepted the Reformation* principles of 1560. Under the

Assembly's authority, regional committees were established in Glasgow, Edinburgh, St Andrews, Montrose and Aberdeen. Their deliberations were revised by further committees of the Assembly, then debated within the Assembly, before the final work was ready for inspection by a wider public.

A much more terse and orderly document than the somewhat untidy *FBD*, the *SBD* began by defining the Church and by distinguishing ecclesiastical from secular government. The substance of the Church's polity was identified as doctrine, discipline and distribution, from which there was understood to arise a threefold permanent order of office-bearers elected to serve within the Church, first, the ministers, bishops or preachers; secondly, elders* or governors; and thirdly, deacons (*see* Diaconate) or distributors. Yet from this threefold order, there emerged four distinct offices of minister, doctor,* elder and deacon, for both ministers and doctors (or teachers) had a role in expounding doctrine and interpreting Scripture. In keeping with the General Assembly's statements of 1565 and 1575, the term 'bishop' was identified with the minister of the congregation, the overseer of the flock; and the practice of permitting bishops to serve as 'pastors of pastors, pastors of many flocks and yet without a certain flock' of their own was declared contrary to Scripture. Visitation was understood to reside not in individuals but in the 'elderships' or courts of the Church, as manifestations of the whole Church, which might commission temporary visitors to discharge supervisory duties.

As all office-bearers were recognized to have a vocation and therefore ought to serve for life, it was thought appropriate that at their admission to office they should receive ordination* by 'the imposition of hands of the eldership'. Elders and deacons elected from congregations to serve respectively as 'governors' in disciplinary matters and as financial officers were seen to exercise a 'ministry' by virtue of the spiritual duties they discharged; and the *SBD*'s description of the elder as occupying 'a function spiritual, as is the ministry', is wholly consistent with St Andrews kirk session's recognition from 1561 that the elder formed part of 'the ministry'. Although they were to be elected for life, elders and deacons were not expected to serve continuously without a break from their duties; they had their own livelihoods to earn; and the earlier practice that elders should submit themselves for re-election persisted.

Government of the Church through courts* or 'elderships' was reaffirmed, and three of the four office-bearers (ministers, doctors and elders but not the deacons, whose role was purely financial) were accorded a seat on the courts: all three were understood to be comprehended under the term 'elder', and therefore eligible to sit on the eldership, which might be of four sorts, the eldership of one congregation or of several adjacent congregations; the eldership of a province, or provincial synod; the eldership of a nation, the national or General Assembly; and the eldership or assembly representing all Christendom, an international ecumenical assembly organized on presbyterian lines. The Latinized term 'presbytery'* occurred in three passages and was used as a synonym of the vernacular eldership, which, in turn, by the 1580s came to denote both the local kirk session and the new district presbytery. But of a district presbytery intermediate between kirk session and synod there is only a vague glimmering in the *SBD*, which seemed to favour a common eldership or presbytery of several contiguous churches to kirk sessions of individual congregations. Voting membership in the general assembly was restricted to 'ecclesiastical persons', that is, ministers, doctors and elders attending as commissioners from towns, shires and universities, but others interested in attending were eligible to express their views in debates.

The theory of the Church and its relationship to the secular authorities expounded in the *SBD* was consistent with much earlier thinking. The offices of minister and magistrate, with distinct and separate jurisdictions, were seen to be complementary, the one reinforcing the authority of the other. Magistrates were required to ensure that ministers performed their duties according to the Word, and ministers were to 'teach' the magistrates to discharge their duties as directed in scripture. In language reminiscent of the Scots Confession* of 1560, kings, to whom it 'chiefly' pertained to 'advance the kingdom of Jesus Christ', were acknowledged protectors, nourishers and defenders of the Church, which hardly suggests that the authors intended to exclude the magistracy from authority in the Church; but what could not be conceded was the Crown's claim to supremacy over the Church. Ecclesiastical authority was understood to derive immediately from God and not intermediately through the prince. More embarrassing, however, were the renewed claims for a restoration of the Church's patrimony in support of the ministry, education and poor relief. Such a programme, which went even further than the *FBD*, threatened Crown and nobility with a loss of their rights to ecclesiastical property and patronage. As a consequence, the *SBD*, like the *FBD*, failed to be submitted for parliamentary recognition. It did, however, gain the General Assembly's approval in 1578, and when discussions were held with the King at Stirling, agreement was forthcoming on most issues except on patrimony and episcopacy.

On failing to secure from the government full endorsement of the *SBD*, the General Assembly pressed ahead as best it could to give effect to the programme of 1578, and in April 1581 formally registered the *SBD* among the acts of Assembly. Copies were to be distributed to presbyteries which were then being established, and despite political setbacks in the 1580s the Assembly renewed its efforts for subscription to it by presbyteries in the early 1590s. By 1592, Parliament ratified the Church's Presbyterian constitution, but the *SBD* was still denied statutory recognition by Crown and Parliament.

J. Kirk (ed.), *The Second Book of Discipline* (E, 1980).

J. Kirk

Second Reformation (1638–60), a period later regarded in popular thought as a 'Golden Age' of Scottish Reformed theology, when it enjoyed a series of distinguished writers and when the CofS implemented an historic paradigm of Presbyterian government and worship (see Presbyterianism). Commencing with the Glasgow Assembly's* work of reconstruction after the impositions of episcopacy,* and culminating in the work of the Westminster Assembly* to which the CofS sent commissioners, the constitutional documents, the theological definitions and church practices of this period provided standards (see Subscription) for later generations. Less enduring was the practice of national covenanting,* by which the people entered a bond for their maintenance of the Reformed religion. Primary architects of the Church settlement where Alexander Henderson* and Sir Archibald Johnston,* and the most eminent theological writers were Samuel Rutherford,* George Gillespie,* David Dickson,* and James Durham.* The turmoil of war and the conflicts between Resolutioners* and Protesters* are generally forgotten in more glowing evaluations of the period.

J. K. Hewison, *The Covenanters*, 2 vols (G, ²1913); F. N. McCoy, *Robert Baillie and the Second Scots Reformation* (Berkeley, CA, 1974); Robert Baillie, *Letters and Journals*, 3 vols (E, 1841–2); J. MacLeod, *Scottish Theology* (E, ³1974); J. Walker, *The Theology and Theologians of Scotland* (E, ²1888).

S. Isbell

Second World War (1939–45). Unlike the First,* World War II propelled the Scottish Protestant churches into crises of membership, church-building and ideology. Although the Presbyterian churches (CofS* and UFC*) gained members during the 1914–18 War, the CofS lost 22 per cent of communicants during 1938–43. Losses were also experienced by the Baptist Union,* the Congregationalists* and the EpCS.* The membership crisis arose in part because of severe dislocation of the civil population through city evacuation early in the War, and in part through the completion of state-subsidized housing estates. One CofS estimate was that 21,000 communicants were lost during 1940–1 alone, largely through migration to new housing areas. Shortage of funds for Church Extension,* a problem lingering since the Union* of 1929, and inhibitions on fund-raising during the conflict, made it impossible to provide sufficient church accommodation to maintain membership amongst the re-housed population. Evacuation increased the damage to congregational life. Some of this was permanent, particularly in relation to Sunday schools* which in the CofS lost one fifth of their scholars. To exacerbate difficulties, many church buildings were damaged through bombing. This applied particularly to Clydebank, where the 'blitz' of 1941 struck nearly every place of worship in the burgh.

As for combatants, it is apparent that the Churches played a less prominent part in military life. Religious ceremonial gave way to secular entertainment (in the form of concert shows, for example). Certainly, ministers reported in the late 1940s that many returning servicemen were not inclined to resume church attendance. This ideological challenge to religious values was equally apparent on the 'home front'. The CofS General Assembly Temperance* Committee campaigned forlornly against the government's change from its pro-temperance policy of the 1914–18 War to the pro-beer policy of 1939–45, and criticized BBC radio's light entertainment shows. The War crystallized the liberalization of popular culture and values. Though some Churches (notably the CofS) experienced a recovery of membership figures between 1944 and 1953, the War marked an important watershed for the Churches, introducing a keener sense of social responsibility and bringing secular organizing methods (e.g. Christian Commandos) to evangelizing work.

See also Huts and Canteens.

C. G. Brown, *The Social History of Religion in Scotland* (L, NY, 1987), 210–13; A. Muir, *John White* (L, 1958), 335–58; L. L. L. Cameron, *A Badge to Be Proud Of* (E, 1972); C. G. Brown, 'Religion 1914–45', in J. Hood (ed.), *The History of Clydebank* (Carnforth, 1988).

C. G. Brown

Security Act, 1707. Properly the Protestant Religion and Presbyterian Church Act 1706, 1707 c.6, this Act, one of the last of the Scottish Parliament, was part of the legislative steps taken to protect the position of the CofS and of its Presbyterian government in the union with England 1707 (see Union of Parliaments 1707). It narrates the prior Acts on such questions and, requiring that 'the true Protestant religion as presently professed' should be 'effectually and unalterably' secured, establishes and confirms 'the said true Protestant Religion and Worship, Discipline and Government of the Church to continue without any alteration to the people' in Scotland 'in all succeeding generations'. The Confession of Faith Ratification Act 1690 c.7 and all relative Acts are ratified and confirmed and, after other detailed provision as to universities and colleges, and as to oaths, future sovereigns are required by oath* to preserve inviolable this settlement of the Protestant religion and Presbyterian church government. Finally, the Act was required to be inserted into the legislation dealing with the Union, and duly appears in the Union with England Act 1706 c.7 of the Scots Parliament as s.2 of the Union with England Act 1706, 6 Anne c.11, its English counterpart.

Despite the absolute nature of the terms of the Act of Security and other elements of the Union Agreement, the new Parliament and the new 'British' government soon entrenched somewhat on its terms, for example by passing the Scottish Episcopalians Act 1711 (10 Anne c.10) and the Church Patronage* (Scotland) Act 1711 (10 Anne c.21), and through the House of Lords hearing an appeal in a Scottish case, which concerned licensing of preachers, *Greenshields* v Magistrates of Edinburgh*, (1710) Robertson's Appeals 12.

F. Lyall, *Of Presbyters and Kings* (A, 1980), 21–2.

F. Lyall

Separatists, Highland* dissenting movement, c.1797–1875. The abuse of patronage* and the advent of Moderatism* which in the Lowlands gave rise to the Secession churches, in the Highlands resulted in a separatist movement which stopped short of formal secession. Highly critical of the 'corruptions' of the EstC, the Separatists withdrew from the parish churches. Yet they considered themselves still to belong to the true CofS and depended on ministers of the Establishment for the sacraments. The movement began late in the eighteenth century in three centres: Kildonan, Inverness and Assynt. It was led entirely by 'the Men'* such as John Grant, Joseph Mackay and Alexander Gair. Added impetus was given by the missionary work of Robert and James Haldane,* which was hostile to the CofS. Staunch Calvinists, the Separatists were distinguished for their zealous piety. However, their censorious and vituperative descriptions of Established ministers made them less attractive to some. The movement spread widely until separation from the EstC became endemic throughout the Highlands in the first half of the nineteenth century. While some of the Separatist leaders kept their distance even from the 'purified' FC of 1843, most dissenting groups found a congenial home in her communion. By 1875 the movement was finished; but the mentality remained. The ideal of a pure Church had a strong hold and contributed to the support attracted by the secession of the FPC* from the later liberalizing FC and by the post-1900 continuation of the FC.

J. Macleod, *By-paths of Highland Church History* (E, n.d.), 78–162; D. Sage, *Memorabilia Domestica* (Wick, 1899); J. MacInnes, *The Evangelical Movement in the Highlands of Scotland* (A, 1951).

K. R. Ross

Serf, *see* Celtic Saints.

Seventh-day Adventists, a conservative evangelical Church with headquarters in Washington, DC, which emerged from the religious revivals of the first half of the nineteenth century in the northeastern USA. The leaders of the original nucleus of the SDA Church were part of the Adventist movement led by William Miller (1782–1849), which disintegrated after the failure of Miller's prediction of the Second Advent in 1844.

By 1848, SDA pioneers had consolidated their distinctive beliefs, in particular, observance of the seventh-day sabbath (adopted through Seventh-day Baptist influence in New England) and anticipation of the imminent return of Christ, without the time-setting of the Millerites. A further theological distinctive is the belief in conditional immortality.

At the end of 1989 world membership numbered 6.2 million. Seventh-day Adventism is noted for its medical and educational work. It operates hospitals and sanatoriums, and over 750,000 students, from primary to doctoral level, study at the Church's schools and colleges.

The SDA Church began work in Scotland in 1886. After extensive advertising, S. H. Lane and R. F. Andrews held public meetings in a hall in Lochmaben (Dumfriesshire) and, according to reports, thousands of pieces of literature were sent to various parts of Scotland in the hope of arousing interest in the seventh-day sabbath. The first congregation of SDAs was formed in Glasgow in 1901 by Harry E. Armstrong, who became the first superintendent of the Scottish SDA Church the next year.

There are presently nine SDA congregations in Scotland. The Church also operates Roundelwood Health Centre and Nursing Home in Crieff, Perthshire, and a retirement home at Lundin Links, Leven, Fife.

General Conference of Seventh-day Adventists, *Seventh-day Adventists Believe...* (Hagerstown, MD, 1988); *Seventh-day Adventist Encyclopedia* (Washington, DC, 1976); E. S. Gaustad (ed.), *The Rise of Adventism* (NY, 1974) – bibliography, 207–317; D. Porter, *A Century of Adventism in the British Isles* (Watford, 1974); N. Barham, 'The Progress of the Seventh-day Adventist Church in Great Britain, 1878–1974' (PhD, Michigan University, 1976).

A. G. Mustard

Sharp, James (1618–79), Archbishop of St Andrews. Born in Banff, he graduated from King's College, Aberdeen, and became in 1648 professor of philosophy at St Andrews, and in 1649 minister of nearby Crail. His ambition, Episcopalian tendencies, and rumours of a scandalous private life made him suspect among the more zealous Covenanters,* but in 1657 the Resolutioner* party sent him to London to safeguard the Kirk's position and privileges. He sent back to Scotland reports which (it was claimed later) were far from accurate, while all the time he was 'loosing the pins of Presbyterian government' and planning the restoration of Episcopacy. Whatever the truth of this, at the end of 1661 (the year after the return of Charles II*) Sharp and three others of 'known loyalty' to the government were summoned to London and given episcopal consecration, with Sharp himself becoming primate and Archbishop of St Andrews. There began a relentless persecution of his former colleagues, to help which policy he revived the notorious Court of High Commission* in 1664, with himself as its president. It had absolute power, could and did hand out death sentences, and there was no appeal from its verdicts (the King himself intervened to suppress the Court in 1666). When later Gilbert Burnet* suggested that the low moral state of Scotland might not be unconnected with the advent of the bishops, Sharp would have deposed and excommunicated the culprit if Burnet had not had connections among the highly-placed in government.

Sharp opposed the various Indulgences* offered to dissenters,* and continued to implement harsh measures against them. An attempt on his life in 1668 intensified the persecution. Finally in 1679 the Archbishop's coach was stopped on Magus Muir, near St Andrews, by a group of nine zealots, and he was brutally assassinated. Though the deed was swiftly repudiated by Covenanting leaders it precipitated the second major rebellion of Charles's reign.

The very fulsome inscription in Latin to be seen in Holy Trinity Church, St Andrews, would not have been endorsed by many of Sharp's contemporaries. Oliver Cromwell, after an interview, had labelled Sharp an atheist, and even Charles II regarded him as 'one of the worst of men', according to Burnet. The view of him as 'that mitred ruffian' has been challenged chiefly by Episcopalian writers (e.g. J. B. Craven, *Scots Worthies 1560–1688*, E, 1894, 98–101).

T. Stephen, *Life and Times of Archbishop Sharp* (L, 1839); I. B. Cowan, *The Scottish Covenanters 1660–88* (L, 1976), 35–48; *DNB* LI, 404–7; J. Buckroyd, *The Life of James Sharp, Archibishop of St Andrews* (E, 1987).

J. D. Douglas

Sharp, John (Scharpius, Joannes) (*c.* 1572–*c.* 1647), Professor of Divinity, Edinburgh. After graduating at St Andrews University in 1592, Sharp became minister of Kilmany, Fife, in 1601. He acted as clerk of the General Assembly held in Aberdeen in 1605 in defiance of James VI.* On being summoned before the Privy Council he and five other ministers declined to recognize its authority in ecclesiastical matters. For this they were imprisoned in Blackness Castle (West Lothian) and in 1606 tried by the Court of Justiciary and found guilty of treason. They were then banished for life. Sharp travelled to France and in 1608 became Professor of Theology at Die University (near Grenoble). Archbishop Spottiswoode* alleged in 1618 that Sharp had written to him, begging to be allowed to return and offering to submit, but this was denied by his friends – though the fact that he dedicated his *Cursus Theologicus* (Geneva, 1618; ²1622) to James VI at this time suggests that he was seeking a return to favour. In 1626 Sharp can be traced acting as minister to a Huguenot* congregation, but in 1630 he was expelled from France by Cardinal Richelieu, evidently because of his growing reputation as a Protestant theologian. He was permitted to return to Scotland, and the same year became Professor of Divinity at Edinburgh University, in which position he served the rest of his life.

Tractatus de Justificatione (Geneva, 1609; ²1612); *Tractatus de Misero Hominis Statu sub Peccato* (Geneva, 1610); *Symphonia Prophetarum et Apostolorum* (Geneva, 1625, ²1629).

Calderwood; R. Pitcairn (ed.), *Ancient Criminal Trials in Scotland*, 3 vols (Bannatyne Club, E, 1833), II, 494–502; *DNB* LI, 407–8; *FES* VI,

160–1, VII, 382; A. Bower, *History of the University of Edinburgh*, 3 vols (E, 1817–30), I, 176–7.

D. Stevenson

Sharp, Patrick (*d.* 1615), Principal and Professor of Divinity at Glasgow (1586–1614) and accommodating churchman. Of his early life little is known: he was probably related to the Sharps (Shairps) of Houston in W. Lothian. While master of the Glasgow grammar school 1574–82, he associated with and became deeply indebted to Andrew Melville.* In 1882 he was made a regent of the University (having been Dean of the Faculty 1577, and probably University examiner), and as such was imprisoned by the Earl of Arran in 1583. In 1584 he was acting as minister at Paisley. On Arran's downfall the King appointed him Principal and Divinity Professor (1586 – no replacement had been possible on Thomas Smeaton's* death in 1583), and for almost three decades his conciliatory moderation shielded the university from political interference and undue pressure from the town council.

Sharp played an increasingly prominent role in ecclesiastical affairs. As schoolmaster he already enjoyed recognition as a doctor* of the Church and hence eligibility for Church courts, and as Principal he was minister of Govan. (He was also an elder in the Glasgow session.) Until *c.* 1596 he maintained a pro-Presbyterian stance, but that year attended the Perth Assembly and increasingly inclined to the side of James VI's* pro-episcopal policy, but without forsaking his moderation. With other doctors he was appointed to a commission to resolve the question of ministers' votes in Parliament, and he was twice unsuccessfully nominated as Moderator of General Assembly.

At the Hampton Court Conference in 1606 he opposed the Melvilles, Andrew and James,* in denying the lawfulness of the Aberdeen Assembly, in 1607 agreed to become constant moderator (bishop-substitute) of Glasgow Presbytery, in 1609 argued at the Falkland Conference for accommodation with episcopacy, and in 1610 was made a member of the Court of High Commission.* Yet his principalship was not an unqualified success, and in 1614 he resigned to avoid disgrace in a royal visitation. He was succeeded by Robert Boyd* of Trochrigg.

As a teacher Sharp appears to have been thorough rather than sparkling, but among his pupils were future lights like John Cameron* and David Dickson.* Although spoken of in lofty terms, the erudition of his only extant work, *Doctrinae christianae brevis explicatio...*, E, 1599), which is a digest of his lectures, is modest, although its doctrine is securely Reformed.

DNB LI, 412–13; *FES* III, 410; H. M. B. Reid, *The Divinity Principals in the University of Glasgow* (G, 1917), 106–14; J. Durkan and J. Kirk, *The University of Glasgow 1451–1577* (G, 1977); Glasgow University Library MS Gen. 1209/71 (Wodrow's* Collections).

T. G. Addington

Sharpe, Jane Brayton (1865–1943), probably the first Scottish woman to be ordained in Scotland. Born in Motherwell, Jane Rose was the daughter of a builder. The family emigrated to New York state in 1884. In 1887 she married George Sharpe (also from Motherwell) who entered the Methodist ministry. Without any formal theological education, she was persuaded to preach during her husband's absence. The Sharpes returned to Scotland in 1901 and founded the Pentecostal Church of Scotland (a Wesleyan 'holiness' church opposed to speaking in tongues) which united with the Church of the Nazarene* in 1915. Mrs Sharpe, whose preaching made a considerable impact, was ordained at the Parkhead Church of the Nazarene in Glasgow on 7 April, 1917, five years after the first woman ordained in Scotland, the American, Olive M. Winchester.* Her daughter, Agnes Kanema Hynd (the wife of David Hynd*), was ordained in the same Parkhead Church in 1924.

See also Findlay, Vera Mary Muir.

G. Sharpe, *This is My Story* (G, 1948); Jack Ford, *In the Steps of John Wesley* (Kansas City, 1968).

T. A. Noble

Shaw, Geoffrey (1927–78), Christian social activist. Dux of Edinburgh Academy in 1944, Shaw originally studied law at Edinburgh University, changing to divinity after a period of military service. In 1953, while engaged in post-graduate study at Union Theological Seminary, New York, he came in contact with the experimental East Harlem Protestant Parish. The encounter with severe deprivation, drug abuse, racial prejudice and powerlessness radically changed his life. On his return to Scotland, he helped found the Gorbals Group – a Christian community living in one of Glasgow's most notorious slums. His home in Cleland Street, Gorbals, became a refuge for disadvantaged and despairing young people, and his ministry was marked by a refusal to reject anyone, no matter how anti-social. Shaw's concern with the plight of the disadvantaged led him into politics, and in 1970 he was elected Labour Councillor for Govanhill. Within three years he became leader of the administration of the city of Glasgow, and in 1974 was elected first Convener of the new Strathclyde Regional Council. As Convener, he helped promote programmes which gave special assistance to deprived areas. He was a notable member of the Labour Party's Scottish Executive, and with the expectation that a Scottish Assembly would be established by Parliament in the late 1970s, Shaw was widely forecasted as its first leader, and effectively the first Chief Minister of Scotland. After his premature death in 1978, he was described by Prime Minister James Callaghan as 'one of Scotland's foremost sons'.

R. Ferguson, *Geoff: The Life of Geoffrey M. Shaw* (Gartocharn, Dunbartonshire, 1979); J. Harvey, *Bridging the Gap* (E, 1987).

R. Ferguson

Shaw, Robert (1795–1863), theologian. A native of Perth, he was educated at Edinburgh University and under Archibald Bruce* at the divinity hall of the Associate Presbytery* in Whitburn, W. Lothian. In 1817 he was ordained to follow Bruce in Whitburn, where he remained until his death. He was synod clerk for the Original Secession Church* from 1834 until he and the majority of the synod joined the FC* in 1852. His *Exposition of the Westminster* Confession* (E, 1845) is the most thorough commentary by a Scottish Presbyterian. Writing in sympathy with its writers, Shaw elucidates the opposing views against which the Confession was framed. Shaw wrote articles for the *Biblical Repertory and Princeton Review*, and received the DD from the College of New Jersey (Princeton) in 1851. Other publications include *Reflections on the Translation of Elijah* (E, 1835); and *The New Theology Examined* (E, 1843), on the nature and extent of the atonement.

ASOSC; AFCS II, 313.

S. Isbell

Shaw, William (1749–1831), Gaelic grammarian, lexicographer and Ossianic controversialist. He was minister at Ardclach, 1779–80, and rector of Chelvey, Somerset, 1795–1831.

Born at Clachaig, Arran, and educated at Glasgow University, he spent some time as schoolmaster and tutor, eventually arriving in London where, in 1774, he met Samuel Johnson, who encouraged him to publish his rudimentary Gaelic* grammar, *An Analysis of the Galic Language* (L, 1778). Johnson also assisted him in the more ambitious plan to publish a Gaelic dictionary. Shaw undertook a collecting tour in Scotland and Ireland, 1778–9, and thereafter published his *A Gaelic and English Dictionary* (L, 1780). He had to pursue a lengthy, and eventually successful, legal action against some subscribers who argued that the finished work did not live up to the encyclopaedic promise of the published *Proposals*. His brief incumbency at Ardclach was vigorously opposed by some of the parishioners, who found fault with his moral character and his Gaelic dialect.

He entered the pamphlet war over the authenticity of James MacPherson's alleged translations of the poems of Ossian, taking a strongly anti-MacPherson stance. After his admission to the CofE, he engaged in further controversy, attacking Hannah More and her plan for Sunday schools.

DNB LI, 448; *FES* VI, 431; K. D. MacDonald, 'The Rev. William Shaw – Pioneer Gaelic Lexicographer', *TGSI* 50 (1979), 1–19.

K. D. MacDonald

Shepherd, James (1847–1926), UP and UFC medical missionary to India. Born in Aberdeen, Shepherd studied arts and medicine at Aberdeen before attending the UP Theological Hall in Edinburgh 1867–71. There followed further medical study at Berlin. In May 1872 he was set apart as a missionary by the UP Synod and sent to India. Shepherd's mission field was Udaipur, a native

SHEPHERD, ROBERT HENRY WISHART

state in Rajputana in north-western India. He established a dispensary here in 1877 after several years of running a hospital in nearby Ajmer. His medical skill soon brought him popularity and made Indians tolerant of his daily street-preaching. (He was ordained in 1880.) A small church of twenty-four was formed in 1881, and a building for worship completed and opened in 1891. The work was hampered, however, by the fact that the price of embracing Christianity was losing one's job; this meant that many of Shepherd's converts had to leave Udaipur to find work in territory under British control.

A new hospital was built in Udaipur in 1886, and from 1907 Shepherd had a permanent missionary colleague in J. W. Runciman. Shepherd's most notable Indian colleague was Isa Das, a converted Hindu sorcerer and indefatigable evangelist.

Shepherd retired in 1920 and spent his remaining years in Aberdeen, worshipping in East Belmont Street UFC. He received Aberdeen's DD in 1898.

See also Missions.

FUFCS 547–8; G. Carstairs, *Shepherd of Udaipur* (L, 1926).

N. R. Needham

Shepherd, Robert Henry Wishart (1888–1971), UFC and CofS missionary. Born at Invergowrie, near Dundee, he left school at fourteen and worked in a mill and as a railway clerk. He gained university entrance in 1911 and began the arts course at St Andrews but finished it at Edinburgh, where he then studied at New College.* In May 1918, immediately after licensing, he was ordained by the UFC Presbytery of Dundee for service in South Africa. From 1920 until 1927 he worked among Xhosa-speaking people. From 1927 until his retirement in 1955 he was associated with the Lovedale Institution, first as Chaplain and Director of the Press, then from 1942 as Principal. In 1942 the University of the Witwatersrand awarded him a DLitt, and in 1947 Edinburgh a DD. The General Assembly of the CofS called him to be its Moderator in 1959.

As well as a fine educator and administrator, Shepherd was a skilful writer. In addition to his own publications, he was editor of *The Outlook* (1942–63), a journal of Christian opinion open to black as well as white writers.

Lovedale 1841–1941 (Lovedale, 1941); *Where Aloes Flame* (L, 1948); *A South African Medical Pioneer* (Lovedale, 1952).

FUFCS 556; FES IX, 748–9; G. C. Oosthuizen, *Shepherd of Lovedale* (Johannesburg, 1970).

A. C. Ross

Shetland, Christianity in. Some archaeologists surmise, from lamentably incomplete material, that Christianity came to Shetland well after 700, a generation after it arrived in Orkney,* others that Shetland has an older Christian inheritance. The archaeological evidence is by no means easy to interpret. Charles Thomas has proposed that the

SHETLAND, CHRISTIANITY IN

pioneer Christian sites in Shetland may well have included small monasteries and communal and eremitic hermitages. He suggests that Papil, in the island of Burra, where cross-marked slabs and sculptured stones have occasionally come to light, may have been a monastery. Papil is on good farming land, and its denizens no doubt farmed and fished there. On the other hand, there is a series of as yet undated 'stack' sites around the coast of Shetland – some of them 'on the summits of veritable pillars of rock' – where ascetics prayed and lived on seabirds.

Pagan colonists from Scandinavia arrived in the islands from about 800. The fact that the natives left no trace of their language suggests that the Vikings achieved linguistic and cultural dominance. There is a possibility, however, that some ecclesiastical institutions survived the invasions. The *Papa* place-names in Shetland and Orkney are Norse, deriving from *papi*, pl. *papar*, the Norse word for 'priest'. These 'priests' were Irish anchorites (Old Irish, *pápa*) of the Celtic Church,* who were inclined to travel to isolated locations to pursue their religious ideals. The survival of such nomenclature suggests that some ecclesiastics, for a time at least, were permitted to retain their possessions. It was not long before the colonists themselves became Christian: there have been very few finds of Norse pagan graves in Shetland, and it is now thought that the islands were substantially a Christian society long before the official Christianization of Shetland and Orkney by Olaf Trygvason in 995.

From the eighth century until 1195 Shetland was part of the Earldom of Orkney. Half-way through that period, secular and ecclesiastical institutions in the islands became more formal and sophisticated. Around 1050 Earl Thorfinn Sigurdson established an episcopal seat at Birsay in Orkney, and in 1137 Earl Rognvald Kolson, who had special interest in Shetland, began to build a cathedral in Kirkwall. Around 1200 we first find references to an archdeaconry of Shetland, whose incumbent acted as president of the cathedral chapter, and, of course, oversaw the organization of the Church (and collected revenues) in Shetland. By that time Shetland had been separated politically from Orkney, and her secular affairs were henceforth in the hands of the Kings of Norway. It may have been during this late-medieval period, when Shetland's institutions were moulded by royal chamberlains, Orcadian (and gradually Scottish) ecclesiastics, and locally elected tribunes of the people called 'lawmen', that Shetland's parish organization took its relatively final form.

In 1468 and 1469 the King of Denmark mortgaged his royal rights in Orkney and Shetland to the King of Scotland. Ecclesiastical structures in the islands remained unaltered until the 1540s, when the archdeacons of Shetland ceased to be *ex officio* heads of the cathedral chapter. Soon afterwards the Reformation* took its course in Shetland without major upheaval; Adam Bothwell,* who had become Bishop of Orkney in 1559, aided by Patrick Cheyne of Essilmont, Archdeacon of Shetland, staffed eleven of Shetland's parishes with two ministers and nine readers.*

The seventeenth century in Shetland was a period of economic and social crisis, and there is no evidence that the clergy played an inspiring part in local affairs. Following the Revolution Settlement of 1689-90, a Commission of the General Assembly established a Presbytery of Shetland, comprising at first only four ministers. In 1700 John Brand, a commissioner, discovered that 'in the matter of God and religion the body of the people are said to be very ignorant', and found widespread dereliction of church property. During the eighteenth century the Church slowly pulled itself together, and created the normal disciplinary structures and machinery of poor relief.* In some parishes there were the beginnings of an education system.

Religious revival,* commencing during the Napoleonic Wars, was for the first time largely local in inspiration. In the first decade of the nineteenth century Independent* congregations sprang up in Lerwick and Bixter, following a crisis in the Lerwick kirk session. Baptists* came on the scene in 1816, and Methodists* in 1821. In each case the driving force behind the movement was a Shetlander: James Tulloch of Bixter, Sinclair Thomson* of Spiggie and John Nicolson* of Quenster. Ronald Cant remarks that such 'indigenous leadership and support' were 'almost without parallel elsewhere', although broadly similar patterns can be detected with Independents and Baptists in the Highlands.* Visiting preachers, especially Methodists like Adam Clarke, John Raby and Samuel Dunn, attracted enormous and enthusiastic congregations, often out of doors.

It is possible, however, to exaggerate the strength of dissent* in Shetland. Statistics produced by the Commissioners of Religious Instruction (Scotland) in 1838, and in the *New Statistical Account** (1845), showed that, outside Lerwick, 88 per cent of church adherents were still members of the Kirk. In Lerwick three-quarters of churchgoers remained faithful. Ironically the dissent, insignificant as it was, was sufficiently powerful to blunt appeals for followers by FC ministers in the 1840s. 'The life', one of them remarked in 1845, 'has escaped to dissent in all its varieties.' Only in one or two parishes, for specific historical reasons, did the FC make any headway. 'The Shetlanders', wrote Robert Cowie in 1871, 'have ... always in religious matters "sailed with the running stream". . . . Shetland at the present day is the stronghold of the Establishment.'

The period from the 1870s onwards produced no alteration in this pattern. Socialist and rationalist philosophies of a rather unorthodox kind flourished in Lerwick before the First World War, much as dissent had flourished a century previously. Temperance,* especially via the Rechabite movement, became popular as well. But this sceptical twist in the Shetland character tends to be mild and 'intellectual' rather than practical. In 1986 70 per cent of Shetland church members outside Lerwick were still members of the CofS (although only 19 per cent of the population remained church members). In Lerwick and environs some charismatics* and several other denominations meet, but in small numbers.

A. Small, C. Thomas and D. M. Wilson (eds), *St Ninian's Isle and its Treasure* I (O, 1973); R. Lamb, 'Coastal Settlements of the North', *Scottish Archaeological Forum* 5 (1973), 76-98; B. Crawford, *Scandinavian Scotland* (Leicester, 1987); R. Lamb, 'Carolingian Orkney and its Transformation', *Proceedings of the 11th Viking Congress*, forthcoming; R. Cant, 'The Church in Orkney and Shetland and its Relations with Norway and Scotland in the Middle Ages', *Northern Scotland* 1 (1972), 1-18; G. Donaldson, 'Some Shetland Parishes at the Reformation', in B. Crawford (ed.), *Essays in Shetland History* (Lerwick, 1984), 143-60; J. Brand, *A Brief Description of Orkney, Zetland, Pightland-Firth and Caithness* (E, 1701); R. Cant, 'Church Life in Shetland in the Nineteenth Century', in B. Crawford (ed.), *Essays in Shetland History* (Lerwick, 1984), 208-23; A. MacWhirter, 'The Early Days of Independentism and Congregationalism in the Northern Islands of Scotland', *RSCHS* 16 (1969), 63-87; R. Cowie, *Shetland: Descriptive and Historical* (E, 1871); G. Fitzgibbon, *An Introduction to Shetland's Christian Heritage* ([Lerwick], n.d.).

B. Smith

Shields, Alexander (1660-1700), Covenanter* preacher and political theorist. Born in the parish of Earlston, Berwickshire, the son of a tenant farmer, he graduated from Edinburgh University in 1675, and remained to read theology under Lawrence Charteris.* He early sided with the more radical Covenanters,* and enrolled as a theological student at Utrecht in 1680. In London he became amanuensis to the English Puritan John Owen, and was licensed to preach by the Scottish Presbyterians of that city. He was arrested at a conventicle* there in 1685, was returned to Scotland for imprisonment on Bass Rock* off the East Lothian coast, but escaped the next year. He then sought out James Renwick* and as a close companion aided Renwick in revising *The Informatory Vindication.** In 1687 Shields took to Holland the manuscript for Renwick's book, and also the manuscript for his own *A Hind Let Loose*. Both were printed in Utrecht in 1687. Upon his return to Scotland, he preached to field meetings of the Cameronians (*see* Societies, United) after the arrest of Renwick. Following the accession of William III,* Shields concluded that continued separation from the CofS was inadmissible, and made his reconciliation to the Church. He elected to leave the country as chaplain of the Cameronian regiment serving in Flanders in the war against France, and was ordained to this work by Edinburgh Presbytery in 1691. William III sought out the author when he visited the regiment. Shields was admitted to his only settled pastorate in 1697 as colleague to Thomas Forrester* in St Andrews. In 1699 he was sent by the General Assembly as one of the CofS's first foreign missionaries on the second expedition to establish a Scottish mercantile station at the Darien* colony in Central America. Inability to converse with the Indians, and the licentious living of the colonists frustrated the mission. Shields died of a fever at Port Royal, Jamaica (*see* Missions).

In *A Hind Let Loose*, Shields justified the Cameronian resistance to royal absolutism and the divine right of kings.* He argued that government is divinely ordained, but the people are entitled to bring a king to judgment for wrongdoing. Parliament is commissioned by the people to oversee the nation's affairs, but the compact between the people and their rulers does not entail a forfeiture of the people's power to depose tyrants and confer authority on someone else. Government is by consent, and must justify itself to the consciences of the people. God has given men the right of self-defence, and this extends to a right not only passively to resist, but also to kill relentless persecutors.

A True and Faithful Relation of the Sufferings of Alexander Shields (E, 1715); *Church Communion Enquired Into* (E, 1706, 1747); *The Life of James Renwick* (E, 1724); *A Short Memorial of the Sufferings of the Presbyterians in Scotland* (E, 1690).

H. MacPherson, *The Cameronian Philosopher: Alexander Shields* (E, 1932); J. D. Douglas, *Light in the North* (L, 1964); *DNB* LII, 21–3; J. Howie, *Sermons Delivered in Times of Persecution in Scotland* (E, 1880).

S. Isbell

Signal, The, *see* Periodicals, Religious.

Simeon, Charles (1759–1836), leading Anglican Evangelical who visited Scotland in 1796, 1798, 1815 and 1819. Born at Reading, he was educated at Eton and at King's College, Cambridge, where he remained as Fellow. As vicar of Holy Trinity, Cambridge, from 1783 to his death, he survived fierce opposition to become the uncrowned king of evangelical Anglicanism. As preacher, counsellor, patron and animator (especially of new initiatives like the Church Missionary Society and British and Foreign Bible Society), he made a huge impact, not least in building up a body of evangelical ministers in the Church of England.

Simeon's introduction to Scotland came from Walter Buchanan of Canongate, Edinburgh (*FES* I, 29), who visited Cambridge in 1796 (preceded in 1795 by 'two young Scotch ministers'). In 1796 and 1798 he travelled widely as far north as Inverness and the Hebrides, preaching frequently in pulpits of the CofS, which, as the Est.C, he regarded as differing from the CofE only in church-government, and occasionally, as an Episcopalian, in Episcopal chapels. He cited royal precedent – 'where the king *must* attend a clergyman *may* preach' – and also took Communion in the CofS. His activities alarmed not only stiffer CofE spirits (cf.C. H. Smyth, *Simeon and Church Order*, C, 1940) but also CofS Moderates* unhappy with the Haldanites'* itinerancy* and viewing Simeon, who as-

sociated with James Haldane,* as a bad example. In 1799 the General Assembly effectively barred its pulpits to all but its licensed and ordained clergy.

In Edinburgh Simeon companied with leading ministers such as Andrew Hunter,* John Colquhoun,* John Erskine,* John Kemp of Tolbooth, Secretary of SSPCK* (*FES* I, 124), and David Dickson of St Cuthberts, Secretary of the Scottish Missionary Society (*FES* I, 102–3). In Perthshire he preached with Rowland Hill,* and transformed the ministry of Alexander Stewart* of Moulin (who in turn freshly influenced the parents of Alexander Duff* in the congregation). Simeon's response varied from deep emotion at a Communion in Stirling to criticism of dry formalism and physical exhaustion from four-hour services. He returned south with a renewed appreciation of Anglican liturgy. Simeon's final visit in 1819 was to promote Jewish missions. He also had correspondence with other Scottish churchmen such as Thomas Chalmers*.

W. Carus (ed.), *Memoirs...* (L, ²1847), 112–36, 152–64, 406–7, 414–15, 502–3, 511–13.

DNB LII, 255–7; H. C. G. Moule, *Charles Simeon* (L, 1892), 150–66; H. E. Hopkins, *Charles Simeon of Cambridge* (L, 1977).

D. F. Wright

Simony, the offence of buying and selling of ecclesiastical office. The name derives from the attempt of Simon Magus to purchase the power to confer the Holy Spirit (Acts 8:9–24). Simony became scandalously common in the medieval Church in the West, and was frequently condemned by councils and reformers, including the sixteenth-century Scottish Reformers. Nor did abuse die out with the Reformation, though it persisted in a subtler form. When the national Church in Scotland was maintained at the expense of heritors,* who in turn enjoyed a right of presentation to the charge, there was considerable scope for candidate and patron to enter into a tacit agreement that the former if presented would not press for augmentation of stipend,* the building of a new manse, an extension to the church or other cause of expense to the latter.

An Act against Simoniacal Practices was passed in 1759. An Act of 1888 referred to 'the great danger' arising to the Church from bargains betwixt titular and candidate and appointed deposition as the appropriate sentence. The 1759 Act (of considerable length) was to be read in full at all services of licensing* and of induction.* By 1903, patronage* having been abolished, the reading of the Act was discontinued, but the successful candidate, with his letter to the Presbytery accepting the call,* was required to enclose a statement that the Act was known to him and that he had done nothing at variance with it. Today all that is required is what is generally called 'a letter giving the usual assurances' – that is to say, affirming that he has used no undue influence either by himself or others to secure the call.

See also Barratry.

A. Herron, *A Guide to the Ministry* (E, 1987), 82;

SIMPSON, ELSPETH BUCHAN

A. Mair, *A Digest of Laws and Decisions . . . Church of Scotland* (4E, L, 1923), 542-4.

A. Herron

Simpson, Elspeth Buchan, *see* Buchanites.

Simpson, (Sir) James Young (1811–70), obstetrician. He was the seventh son of a village baker of Bathgate, West Lothian. He entered Edinburgh University in 1825 to study arts, changed to medicine in 1827, qualified MRCSE at age eighteen (1829) and graduated MD in 1832. He remained in Edinburgh teaching pathology and became interested in midwifery. In 1840 he was elected Professor of Midwifery at Edinburgh against stiff opposition. He transformed obstetrics and gynaecology by the improvements in diagnosis and treatment he introduced, and acquired an international reputation and an immense clinical practice amongst rich and poor. In November 1847 he discovered the anaesthetic effect of chloroform and promoted its use in childbirth, meeting some religious opposition based on Genesis 3:16. He was a man of vigorous and enquiring mind who engaged in numerous controversies and wrote extensively on medical, theological and archaeological topics.

He belonged to the evangelical tradition in the CofS, came out at the Disruption,* and in 1861 had a deep spiritual experience. Created a baronet (1866), he chose *Victo dolore* as his motto. Indefatigable to the end, he died at home of coronary heart disease aged fifty-eight. Although interment in Westminster Abbey was offered, he was buried in Edinburgh amid national mourning. The Simpson Memorial Hospital, Edinburgh, is his lasting monument.

J. Duns, *Memoir of Sir James Y. Simpson* (E, 1873); E. B. Simpson (his daughter), *Sir James Young Simpson* (E, 1896); H. L. Gordon, *Sir James Young Simpson and Chloroform* (L, 1897); M. Simpson, *Simpson the Obstetrician* (L, 1972) *DNB* LII, 272–3.

J. Wilkinson

Simpson, James Young (1873–1934), UFC scientist and religious thinker. Born in Edinburgh, the grand-nephew of Sir James Young Simpson,* he studied arts at Edinburgh University 1891–4, and then the life sciences (BSc, 1897). He spent two summers at Cambridge as a research student and received a DSc from Edinburgh in 1901. In 1899 he had been appointed Lecturer in Natural Science at the FC (later UFC) College, Glasgow. In 1904 the UF General Assembly made him Professor of Natural Science, with a remit to lecture in Edinburgh and Glasgow. Simpson remained in this position the rest of his life, with a break during the First World War* when he worked in Intelligence and took part in the Paris Peace Conference of 1919.

The greatest influence on Simpson's life was Henry Drummond,* whose biography he wrote (*The Life of Henry Drummond*, E, 1901), and whose synthesizing approach to science and theology he developed. In particular he made Drummond's concept of evolution in the natural and spiritual realms the key to the relationship between God and creation. He interpreted Christ as the perfect man, the omega-point of human evolution, although not a mere natural product of evolution. 'The most significant fact in the Universe is process, and the most significant fact in the process is Jesus Christ' (*The Garment of the Living God*, L, 1934). Simpson had little use for classic Christology; he preferred to speak of Christ as 'the incarnation in human life of that which God is in Himself – Creative Love', rather than as God incarnate.

Simpson donated his property of 52 Queen Street ('Simpson House'), Edinburgh, to the UFC for Church use in 1916. It now belongs to the CofS.

G. F. Barbour, 'Memoir' prefixed to Simpson's *The Garment of the Living God*; *FUFCS*, 583; H. Watt, *New College Edinburgh* (E, 1946), 57–8, 248–50 (bibliography); *Who Was Who, 1929–1940*, 1239.

N. R. Needham

Simpson, Patrick Carnegie (1865–1947), Presbyterian minister and writer. Born in Belfast, Victoria (Australia), he was educated at George Watson's College, Edinburgh, Edinburgh University, and New College, Edinburgh. He was ordained in the Presbyterian CofE at Wallington, Surrey, in 1895. He served as minister of Renfield Street UFC, Glasgow (1899–1911) and Egremont Presbyterian CofE, Cheshire (1911–14), and as Professor of Church History, Westminster College, Cambridge (1914–38). He was Moderator of the Federal Council of the Free Churches of England in 1926 and 1927 and Moderator of the General Assembly of the Presbyterian CofE in 1928.

His most influential work was *The Fact of Christ* (L, 1900), a persuasive presentation of the person and claims of Christ, which enjoyed a wide circulation for over half a century (last issued in 1952). A sort of sequel to it, *The Facts of Life in Relation to Faith* (L, 1913), did not attain the same popularity. His two-volume *Life of Principal Rainy* (L, 1909) is not only a distinguished essay in biography (with a flavour of hagiography in places) but also an authoritative (if sometimes partisan) survey of Scottish Church history from the Disruption* to the Churches (Scotland) Act of 1905. His Chalmers Lectures* were published as *The Evangelical Church Catholic* (L, 1934).

Recollections: Mainly Ecclesiastical but Sometimes Human (L, 1943).

AFCS I, 376; *FUFCS* 243; *Who Was Who, 1941–1950*, 1057.

F. F. Bruce

Simson, Alexander (*c.*1570–1639), CofS minister. The son of Andrew Simson, minister of Dunbar, Dalkeith, etc. (*see* Simson, Archibald), he graduated from Glasgow University and became minister in turn of Muckhart, Perthshire (1591), Alva, Stirlingshire (1592) and Mertoun, Berwickshire (1597). In 1621 he preached a sermon in Edinburgh denouncing the King and the country's rulers in general. As a result he was imprisoned in Dumbarton Castle for a time, and thereafter confined to his parish. He resigned his charge in or before 1632.

The Destruction of Inbred-Corruption (L, 1644).

RPCS, *1619–22*, 577; *DNB* LII, 282–3; *FES* II, 158; IV, 296; V, 68.

D. Stevenson

Simson, Andrew, *see* Simson, Archibald.

Simson, Archibald (1564–1628), CofS minister. He was the son of Andrew Simson (*d.c.*1590; *DNB* LII, 282–3; *FES* I, 314, 406; IV, 268), who was a schoolmaster, author of a Latin grammar, and minister successively of Dunning and Cargill (Perthshire), Dunbar (East Lothian) and Dalkeith (Midlothian). Archibald graduated at St Andrews University in 1585. He became assistant to his father in 1586, and on his death succeeded him as minister of Dalkeith. An opponent of James VI's* policies, he meant to attend the General Assembly which met in 1605 in defiance of the King's orders, but reached Aberdeen too late. He declared his support for those who had attended, but escaped punishment by promising to act more moderately in future. In 1617 he acted as secretary to ministers who protested to the King about a proposed act giving him power to alter the government of the Church. The act was abandoned, but the Court of High Commission* deposed Simson and confined him to Aberdeen. However, he admitted his offence and was restored to Dalkeith. He had some reputation as a poet and his writings include a life of his brother Patrick,* poems, sermons and a variety of other religious works. His works on the history of the Church in Scotland remain unpublished.

Christes Testament Unfolded (E, 1620); *A Sacred Septenarie . . . on the Seven Psalmes of Repentance* (L, 1623); 'True Record of the Life and Death of Master Patricke Simsone', in W. K. Tweedie (ed.), *Select Biographies*, 2 vols (Wodrow Soc., E, 1845–7), I, 63–111.

DNB LII, 283–4; *FES* I, 314–15; W. J. Couper, 'The Levitical Family of Simson', *RSCHS* 4 (1932), 119–37, 208–66.

D. Stevenson

Simson, John (1667–1740), Professor of Divinity in the University of Glasgow, subject of two extended heresy* trials. His father was Patrick Simson (1628–1715).* He studied at Edinburgh (MA, 1692), Glasgow (divinity, also serving as librarian) and Leiden (under Johannes Marckius, whose *Medulla* he later used as a text). He was ordained to Troqueer (Traquair, Peebleshire) in 1705 and appointed Professor of Divinity in 1708. In 1714 James Webster* raised charges of Socinianism (*see* Unitarians) and Arminianism* against Simson before the Presbytery of Glasgow, without success. Eventually, after extended discussion in the 1716 General Assembly, the 1717 Assembly found Simson guilty of venting 'some opinions not necessary to be taught in divinity' (e.g., sin will cease in hell after the Last Judgment; the moon may be inhabited), using doubtful expressions and adopting hypotheses tending 'to attribute too much to natural reason and the power of corrupt nature' (*AGACS 1717*, 518).

Simson was again accused before the 1726 Assembly of Arianism and Socinianism, reputedly having said, for example, that 'the proposition, *Christus est summus Deus*, is to be taken *cum grano salis*' (R. Wodrow, *The Correspondence* (E, 1843), III, 268). He was suspended for a year by both the 1727 and 1728 Assemblies. Despite considerable pressure for deposition, the suspension was made permanent in 1729; without exercising his office he remained on the Glasgow faculty until his death.

Simson's views apparently developed without reaching the deism* and rationalism so characteristic of the eighteenth century. Although some were active against him in the first trial (e.g., John Flint* and John McLaren,* both of whom wrote against him), many who were neutral then (e.g., Wodrow,* who said 'His being my father's successor makes me decline dipping into that affair', *Correspondence* II, 158, and James Hadow*) took an active role in the second. Thomas Boston* believed the Assembly's leniency dishonouring to Christ. But Simson's family connections, particularly in the first trial, and friends, including those who had studied under him, as well as the Glasgow faculty, shielded him from higher censure.

FES VII, 400; John Dundas, *State of the Processes Depending against Mr John Simson* (E, 1728); H. M. B. Reid, *The Divinity Professors in the University of Glasgow* (G, 1923).

D. C. Lachman

Simson, Patrick (1556–1618), Presbyterian minister. The son of Andrew Simson, schoolmaster of Perth, then of Dunbar and afterwards minister at Dalkeith (*see* Simson, Archibald), Simson entered St Mary's College, St Andrews by 1571. On graduating in 1575 he intended further study at Cambridge but progressed no further than Brigstock, near Kettering, where he gained access to a library of Greek authors. Returning home, he entered the ministry at Spott near Dunbar by 1577, offered instruction in Greek, and was translated to Cramond near Edinburgh in 1582, and to Stirling in 1590.

Throughout his career, Simson sided with the Presbyterians against the Crown's claims for supremacy over the Church. He refused to sign the subscription demanded by the Crown of ministers in 1584 enjoining acceptance of episcopacy* and the royal supremacy, and lost his stipend as a consequence. In 1600, he argued against 'anti-christian and Anglican episcopal dignities', continued to oppose James VI's* efforts at introducing episcopacy, and disallowed 'this new imposed government as that which is not agreeable to the word of God'. Justifying the legality of the General Assembly which met at Aberdeen in 1605 in defiance of the King's instructions, Simson protested at the trial in Linlithgow of those ministers imprisoned by the Crown for attending the Aberdeen assembly, and was prominent in drawing up a formal protest to Parliament against episcopacy in 1606. He refused, when nominated in 1607, to be appointed to the newly devised office of 'constant moderator' of Presbyteries, declined to accept a bishopric and defended in 1608 the earlier Presbyterian polity. In later life, he resolutely refused to change his views on Church government, holding that the 'episcopal seat in Scotland has a similitude with the chair of Rome'.

Simson's *magnum opus* was *The Historie of the Church* (^{3}L, 1634).

Calderwood, IV-VI; J. Melville, *Autobiography and Diary*, ed. R. Pitcairn (E, 1842); *Select Biographies*, ed. W. K. Tweedie (E, 1845), I, 65-111; *FES* I, 10, 418, IV, 318; W. J. Couper, 'The Levitical Family of Simson', *RSCHS* 4 (1932), 128-37.

J. Kirk

Simson, Patrick (1628-1715), minister. Grandson of Patrick Simson* and son of Adam (of New Abbey, Kirkcudbrightshire; *FES* II, 293; W. J. Couper in *RSCHS* 4, 1932, 208-11), he was reared, after his father's death in 1642, by George Gillespie.* He probably studied at Edinburgh University, and spent four years (1649-53) as chaplain and tutor to the Marquis of Argyll at Inveraray, where he also acted as scribe for David Dickson* and James Durham.* (*The Sum of Saving Knowledge* was dictated to him.)

He was ordained to Renfrew in 1653 but ejected in 1662. Granted an indulgence and appointed to Kilmacolm 1672, he was declared a rebel in 1678 for failing to appear before the Privy Council on a charge of preaching outside his parish. He eluded arrest, and the royal indulgence* of 1687 returned him to Renfrew, although he did not take possession until 1690.

Simson was Moderator of the 1695 General Assembly, and Dean of the Faculty in the University of Glasgow 1690-1701. Wodrow,* who knew him well, called him 'the most digested and distinct master of the Scripture that ever I met with'. He compiled *Spiritual Songs or, Holy Poems. A Garden of True Delight* (E, 1685), being mediocre versified translations of all the Bible's songs apart from the Psalms. After much discussion the Assembly of 1708 authorized a revised selection for congregational use, but it was never issued.

FES III, 186; W. J. Couper, 'The Levitical Family of Simson, II', *RSCHS* 4 (1932), 211-27; J. Warrick, *The Moderators of the Church of Scotland from 1690 to 1740* (E, L, 1913), 71-91.

D. F. Wright

Simson (Symson), William (*c.*1580-*c.*1625), early Presbyterian Hebraist. The son of Andrew Simson (*see* Simson, Archibald) and member of an extensive ministerial family, he was by 1597 the minister of Burntisland, Fife. Lack of stipend there justified his translation to Dumbarton in 1601, where he was still minister in late 1624. In 1607 he withdrew from the Synod of Clydesdale in protest against the appointment of the Archbishop of Glasgow as Moderator. His work on Hebrew accents (*De Accentibus Hebraicis Breves et Perspicuae Regulae*, L, 1617) was the first book on Hebrew literature produced (but not published) in Scotland. Now rare, whether it was known to later writers on the subject, *e.g.* Thomas Boston,* who does not refer to it (on whose work see D. M. G. Stalker, in *RSCHS* 9, 1947, 61-8), has not been ascertained.

FES III, 341; V, 81; W. J. Couper, 'The Levitical Family of Simson - Final Records', *RSCHS* 5 (1935), 126-8.

D. F. Wright

Sinclair, Dugald (1777-1870), a pioneer of Baptist* home mission in the West Highlands* and Hebrides. Born in Mid-Argyll, Sinclair was baptized (1801) in Glasgow, and became a member of Bellanoch Baptist Church (near Lochgilphead, Argyll). Training at Bradford Baptist Academy in 1806-10, he joined the itinerant* society of Christopher Anderson* and George Barclay.* In 1810-15 he was engaged in full-time itinerant preaching throughout the West Highlands, chiefly in the Inner Hebrides and mainland Argyll, as described in his *Journals of Itinerating Exertions*, 6 vols (E, 1814-17). His work laid the foundation of Colonsay Baptist Church (1814), and encouraged the growth of Baptist witness in Islay, Mull and Tiree. About 1815 he became the pastor of the Bellanoch church, moving it to its present-day location in Lochgilphead, Argyll. He continued his preaching tours, and by ordaining pastors and exercising general oversight he strengthened the Baptist cause in the islands (*see* Baptist Home Missionary Society for Scotland).

In 1831 Sinclair emigrated to Lobo, Middlesex Co., Ontario, in response to the persistent requests of earlier Argyll emigrants. In Lobo he became the elder (*i.e.*, pastor) of a Baptist church formed by emigrants, and was soon a strong leader of the Scottish Baptist community in the area. He again exercised general oversight of several churches, which were temporarily labelled 'Sinclair-Baptist' churches. By 1850 he was under the sway of Alexander Campbell,* and encouraged his churches to identify with the Disciples of Christ. He is recognized as a 'pioneer preacher' of the Disciples in Ontario.

D. Bebbington (ed.), *The Baptists in Scotland* (G, 1988), 36, 283-4, 289, 295; D. E. Meek, 'Evangelical Missionaries in the Early Nineteenth-Century Highlands', *SS* 28 (1987), 3-4, 16-17; *id.*, 'Evangelicalism and Emigration: Aspects of the Role of Dissenting Evangelicalism in Highland Emigration to Canada', in G. MacLennan (ed.), *Proceedings of the First North American Congress of Celtic Studies* (Ottawa, 1988), 28-9, 31; *id.*, 'Dugald Sinclair', *SS* 30 (1991), 59-91.

D. E. Meek

SINCLAIR, HENRY

Sinclair, Henry (1508–65), bishop of Ross. The younger son of Sir Oliver Sinclair of Roslin, he studied at St Andrews, and was incorporated in St Leonard's College in 1521. He found preferment in the Church acting as a canon of Glasgow, official of Moray and treasurer of Brechin. Appointed a lord of session by James V in 1537, he obtained provision as commendator* of Kilwinning Abbey (see Tironensions), 1542, but had difficulty in obtaining provision, receiving a lease of revenues in 1545 and finally exchanging it for the deanery of Glasgow in 1550. He was employed in various public matters abroad and acted as vice-president of the Court of Session, of which he became lord president in 1558. Granted the temporality of the see of Ross, November 1558, following the death of David Paniter, the onset of the Reformation* appears to have delayed his provision until June 1561. In May 1563, having refused to conform and heavily taxed with infirmities and weakness, he received licence to pass to parts of France, dying in Paris after an operation for stone.

Dowden, 228–9; G. Brunton and D. Haig, *An Historical Account of the Senators of the College of Justice* (E, 1832), 58–60.

I. B. Cowan

Sinclair, James Steven (1868–1921), FP minister. He was born in Wick and studied at Edinburgh University and at New College, Edinburgh, with a view to entering the ministry of the FC. He and several other students left New College in 1892 over the FC Declaratory Act,* completing their studies in Belfast under Professor Robert Watts. Sinclair became one of the first ministers in the new FPC and was a major figure in that denomination for nearly thirty years. He founded, and edited, the *Free Presbyterian Magazine*, and for many years was a powerful and effective Clerk of the Church's Synod. His lifelong ministry was at John Knox's Tabernacle in Glasgow.

A. McPherson (ed.), *History of the Free Presbyterian Church of Scotland* (Inverness, 1974); *Free Presbyterian Magazine*; *Free Presbyterian Pulpit* (Inverness, 1961); D. Beaton, *Memoir, Diary and Remains of Revd Donald Macfarlane, Dingwall* (Inverness, 1929); D. Macfarlane, *Memoir and Remains of the Revd Donald Macdonald, Shieldaig* (G, ²1957).

J. L. MacLeod

Sinclair, Margaret (1900–25), RC nun. Born in Edinburgh and baptized in St Patrick's RC Church, she attended St Anne's School, which was under the care of the Sisters of Mercy. In August 1914 she began work as an apprentice french polisher; later she worked in a biscuit factory and gained certificates in domestic economy. In her early twenties she was for a time engaged to be married.

Feeling called to the religious life, she entered a convent of Poor Clares (Franciscans) in London and made her vows as an extern sister in February 1925. Soon afterwards she contracted tuberculosis of the throat and died that November after a long

SKINNER, JOHN, OF LINSHART

and painful illness. She was buried in London but was later re-interred in Mount Vernon Cemetery, Edinburgh.

Her short life was marked by holiness, serenity and happiness, as many who knew her testified. The process for her beatification was begun, and in 1978 she was given the title of Venerable (a stage on the way).

F. A. Forbes, *Margaret Sinclair* (L, ²1928); T. A. Agius, *Margaret Sinclair* (G, 1952); D. E. Barry, *Margaret Sinclair: 'The Kind Girl'* (n.p., 1979).

S. McGrath

Sinclair, (Sir) William (*d.*1767), second baronet of Dunbeath and Baptist pioneer. He was born around the end of the seventeenth century into one of the litigious families of Sinclair lairds of Caithness. Much about him is conjectural, but he may have been a soldier in England and there become a Baptist. Certainly he founded a church at Keiss* on his estate in 1750, for which he composed a hymnbook and found a meeting place. Complex debts drove him to Edinburgh in 1763, and from there he corresponded with his flock. He worshipped for a time with the Glasites,* and carried on a correspondence with Robert Sandeman,* arguing with him on the obedience of Christ and the law of liberty. He was somewhat eccentric, and was reputed to have instituted a Passover meal before Communion, and obligatory foot-washing.

G. Yuille (ed.), *History of Baptists in Scotland* (G, 1926); F. Johnstone,* in *The Evangelist*, Vol. 1 (G, 1846/7); D. Beaton, *Ecclesiastical History of Caithness* (Wick, 1909).

D. B. Murray

Skinner, John, of Linshart (1721–1807), scholar and poet. Skinner graduated at Marischal College, Aberdeen, when only seventeen, and became a teacher. Though brought up a Presbyterian, at nineteen he became an Episcopalian,* and studied for holy orders. In 1742 he was ordained, and appointed to the congregation of Longside, Aberdeenshire, where he ministered almost until his death. The EpCS's official political stance was Jacobite,* but Skinner swore allegiance to George II, and prayed for him publicly, for which he earned his Bishop's displeasure. Nevertheless in 1746 government soldiers invaded Linshart (Longside, NE Aberdeenshire) and burnt his house, his chapel and all his possessions, leaving him and his family homeless. In 1748 the final Penal Act against the EpCS disqualified the clergy and proscribed their public worship. In 1753 Skinner was imprisoned for six months for defying the Act.

Skinner used his wide biblical and theological knowledge to train for the ministry many of the Aberdeenshire and Brechin diocesan clergy in the latter part of the eighteenth century. In 1784, largely through his influence, his son John,* Coadjutor (i.e. assistant) Bishop of Aberdeen, and two other Bishops consecrated Samuel Seabury* as Bishop for Connecticut.

From early life Skinner wrote verse in Latin, English and Scots, the last being highly praised by Robert Burns. Of his considerable literary work the most significant is *An Ecclesiastical History of Scotland* (L, 1788). It informed English readers of the EpCS's sufferings between 1688 and 1788, and helped to prepare for the repeal of the Penal Acts in 1792.

Theological Works, 2 vols (A, 1809).

W. Walker, *John Skinner of Linshart* (L, 1883); id., *The Life and Times of John Skinner* (A, 1887).

G. N. Pennie

Skinner, John (1744–1816), Bishop of Aberdeen 1782–1816 and Primus* of the EpCS 1788–1816. Skinner was a leading figure in the recovery of the Church after the troubles of the eighteenth century.

The second son of John Skinner of Linshart,* well known as a writer of Scottish verse, Skinner entered Marischal College, Aberdeen in 1757. He was ordained in 1763 and given the charge of Episcopal congregations in nearby Ellon, but soon after removed to Aberdeen, where he gathered a congregation in his house at Longacre. Elected by the clergy of Aberdeen as coadjutor and successor of Bishop Robert Kilgour, he was consecrated in 1782.

Skinner played a leading part in the negotiations which led to the consecration in 1784 of Samuel Seabury* as the first Bishop of the Episcopal Church in the United States of America. The Seabury consecration brought the existence of the EpCS to the notice of many who had not heard of it and began the process which made possible the worldwide Anglican Communion. It also gave Skinner at the threshold of his career a commanding authority which he never lost, and greatly facilitated the success of his long and eventful episcopate.

It was Skinner who first suggested that the death of Prince Charles Edward Stuart in January 1788 made it possible for the Episcopal clergy in good conscience to pray for King George III and the royal family. When both his own synod and the EpCS Synod agreed, Skinner was able to embark on the protracted negotiations which led to the repeal of the Penal Acts in 1792.

The corollary of this was a reconsideration of the position of the clergy who had previously 'qualified' by taking the oath of abjuration and allegiance but who had had no relationship with the Scottish bishops. It was Skinner who persuaded the EpCS to adopt the Thirty-nine Articles of the CofE as its own Articles and thus effected a reconciliation between the two groups of Episcopalians.

Primitive Truth and Order Vindicated . . . A Defence of Episcopacy . . . (A, 1803).

DNB LII, 344–6; W. Walker, *The Life and Times of John Skinner* (A, 1887); John Skinner, *Annals of Scottish Episcopacy . . .* (incl. memoir of Bishop Skinner) (E, 1818).

H. R. Sefton

Slessor, Mary Mitchell (1848–1915), missionary. She was born in Aberdeen. Poverty and the increasing alcoholism of her shoemaker father induced a family move in 1859 to Dundee, where she worked as a mill-weaver. She offered for missionary service under the UP and was accepted as a teacher for the Calabar mission, where, after a short period of preparation in Edinburgh, she arrived in 1876, and was placed under the tutelage of William and Louisa Anderson.* It became clear that, despite the mission's reservations about women working independently, she would be better in a 'sphere of her own'. After a time in charge in Old Town she was in 1888 established in Okoyong, hitherto only spasmodically visited by the mission. In this period the mission was beginning to break from its long restriction to the Calabar townships. Okoyong was in danger of social collapse, its institutions unable to cope with economic and social changes. Slessor became in effect a reforming chief, settling disputes acceptably, encouraging outside trade, establishing the social changes long associated with the mission within Calabar – protection of twins, avoidance of witchcraft ordeals and ritual killings at major funerals, and introducing Western education. In 1898, when British authority was being enforced locally, she was made Vice-Consul in Okoyong, arguably the first woman magistrate in the British Empire. Her presbytery deprecated this as potentially confusing the temporal and spiritual spheres; in practice, the appointment probably did not greatly alter either her methods or her local status. She was not primarily an evangelist (the first Communion occurred only in 1903, and even then there was no organized congregation), but her work made subsequent church growth possible.

She was vociferous on the need for new missionary activity following the British destruction of Aro power in 1901. In default of other provision for extension she spent the home furlough due to her in 1903 in reconnaissance on the Enyong Creek, winning the important assistance of an influential chief, Onoyom Iya Nya. She urged, ultimately with success, the strategic importance of establishing the mission at Itu and Arochukwu. In 1905 she was assigned to Okot Obong, within the new area of evangelism, and the same year was appointed Vice-President of the Itu Native Court. Later she removed to Use, where she died after years of illness and disability.

Mary Slessor was a complex character; strongly assertive and painfully shy; flouting the conventions of European life in the tropics (she went hatless and barefoot, and never boiled her drinking water), yet anxious to introduce 'refinement' into African domestic life; unique in her personal authority, expressed in vivid vernacular, within African traditional society, but often a difficult missionary colleague. She was pre-eminently a groundbreaker who constantly argued and acted for mission extension; yet she was also a proponent of the type of industrial education eventually realized in the Hope Waddell* Training Institution, as well as an apologist for education for girls. She adopted various African children (twins, orphans and other rejects); her practice of bringing them on furlough contributed to the colourful impression she made in Scotland and to her position as perhaps, after David Livingstone,* the best known Scottish missionary.

See Missions: Nigeria.

There is no first-class biography: *DNB Miss. Pers.* 609–10; W. P. Livingstone, *Mary Slessor of Calabar, Pioneer Missionary* (L, 1917); J. Buchan, *The Expendable Mary Slessor* (E, 1980); shrewd assessments in G. Johnston, *Of God and Maxim Guns* (Waterloo, Ontario, 1988).

A. F. Walls

Sloan, John Morrison (1835–1915), translator of German hymns. The son of John Sloan of Stairard, Ayrshire, he studied at the Universities of Glasgow, Edinburgh (MA, 1859) and Erlangen. He was a FC minister successively at Dalkeith, Aberdeen, Glasgow and the Grange FC, Edinburgh. He translated German hymns for *The Service of Praise* (E, 1865) and *Songs of Zion* (²E, 1876), both compiled by J. H. Wilson of the Barclay FC, Edinburgh.

The only translation still used is one of J. A. Schlegel's 'Wie herrlich strahlt der Morgenstern', recast from Philipp Nicolai's earlier hymns. Sloan's 'How brightly shines the morning star!' appeared in both of Wilson's collections and, revised, in *The FC Hymn Book* (Paisley, 1882). The 1882 version was included in *Hymns of the Kingdom*, Student Christian Movement ed. (L, 1923).

See also Hymnology, English.

J. Julian, *Dictionary of Hymnology* (²L, 1907); *AFCS* I, 318; *FUFCS*, 9; J. S. Andrews, *Survey of German Hymns in Current English Hymnals* (Berne, 1981), 40–4, 161, 215–21.

J. S. Andrews

Sloan, William Gibson (1838–1914), pioneer evangelist to the Faroe Islands. A weaver's son from Dalry (Ayrshire), Sloan was store manager at Baird's Ironworks, Airdrie, in 1860 when he trusted Christ for salvation. He served as a colporteur with the Edinburgh Religious Tract and Book Society (*see* Tract Societies) from 1863–5, when he sailed to Faroe and settled there. After fifteen years of home visitation, his faithfulness was rewarded when a young Faroese man confessed his allegiance to Christ by being baptized in the harbour at Torshavn. Despite strong opposition from the islanders his sister, Elsebeth, and a few others followed his example. William married Elsebeth in Glasgow in October 1881, and returned to set up home in Torshavn. His quiet, consistent witness during thirty-five years won others to Christ, so that, when he died, there were six assemblies of 'brethren' scattered throughout the islands. Today there are thirty such gatherings.

Personal diaries of William Gibson Sloan (in family possession in Torshavn); F. H. Kelling, *William Gibson Sloan: Fisherman of Faroe* (forthcoming).

F. H. Kelling

Small, Annie Hunter (1857–1945), missionary, author and educationist. Born in Redding, Falkirk, she was the daughter of John Small, missionary in India. She lived in India in 1864–8 and was educated at the School for the Daughters of Missionaries, Walthamstow. In 1876 she returned to India as a FC missionary herself, serving in Chindwara and Pune, where she took charge of the Girls School. Publications relating to this period are *Yeshu-das* (⁴L, 1938) and *Light and Shade in Zenana Missionary Life* (Paisley, 1890). In 1892 she was invalided back to Scotland, and from 1894 to 1913 was first Principal of the FC/UFC Women's Missionary Training Institute (later St Colm's College*), established in permanent premises in Inverleith Terrace, Edinburgh in 1909. Small believed that the calling of a missionary of Jesus Christ is to a life, not a mere life-work. Training was given in the context of community living, in which worship, work, meal fellowship and leisure all had their essential places. Her teaching laid special emphasis on personal prayer, the world religions (see her books, *Buddhism* and *Islam*, L, 1905) and practical preparation for service (see her *Letters to Missionary Friends*, E, 1908).

The Psalter and the Life of Prayer (E, 1914).

O. Wyon, *The Three Windows* (L, 1953).

R. G. Brown

Smeaton, George (1814–89), eminent FC scholar. He was born in Berwickshire, and after studies at Edinburgh University was ordained to the charge of Falkland in the Presbytery of Cupar in 1839. In 1843 Smeaton signed the Deed of Separation at the Disruption,* and later that year was inducted to Auchterarder FC. In 1853 he was appointed by the FC to the Chair of Divinity at its Aberdeen College, and in 1857 was transferred to New College as Professor of New Testament Exegesis, a post he held until his death.

During the 1860s, Smeaton was a vigorous opponent of the proposed union between the FC and the UPC. In 1871 he published a pamphlet, *National Christianity and Scriptural Union*, in which he questioned the theological laxity of the UPC. Commenting on that Church's proposed Declaratory Statement (*see* Declaratory Acts) in 1878, Smeaton declared, 'There are good Calvinists in the United Presbyterian Synod, but I should not find it difficult to prove that in its Declaratory Statement the Synod has taken up Arminian ground.'

In 1861, on the death of his colleague William Cunningham,* Smeaton became Editor of the *British and Foreign Evangelical Review*.* Smeaton is probably best known for two volumes which continue in print to the present day: his Cunningham Lectures,* *The Doctrine of the Holy Spirit* (E, 1882; ²1889), and *The Doctrine of the Atonement* (E, 1868, 1870). B. B. Warfield considered Smeaton's work on the Holy Spirit one of the finest books on the subject ever published. James MacGregor (1830–94; *AFCS* I, 57), a fellow FC Professor, considered Smeaton to possess 'the best constituted theological intellect in Christendom'.

SMEATON, THOMAS

FES V, 154; *AFCS* I, 58; *FCSR* Sept. 1889, 279–80.

I. Hamilton

Smeaton, Thomas (1536–83), Principal of Glasgow University. He was born at Gask near Perth and educated at Perth Grammar School and St Salvator's College, St Andrews, where he matriculated in 1554. At the Reformation,* Smeaton left his college, where he served as regent, for France and entered the Collège de Clermont, the Jesuits' college in Paris. On a visit to Rome, he met Andrew Melville* in Geneva; by 1572 he quit the Society of Jesus, and with the Massacre of St Bartholomew gained refuge in the home of Francis Walsingham, the English ambassador in Paris, then left for England where he taught as schoolmaster in Colchester before returning to Scotland as a convinced Calvinist.* He resumed his friendship with Melville, agreed to serve as minister at Paisley by 1577, was elected Dean of the Arts Faculty at Glasgow University in 1578 and was appointed Principal as Melville's successor in January 1581. At Melville's suggestion, he published a reply in 1579 to Archibald Hamilton's* attack on Scottish Calvinism. He was esteemed 'a man learned in the languages' and well versed in patristic writings. In Church controversy, he and his students demonstrated in the cathedral at the intrusion of Robert Montgomery* as Archbishop of Glasgow in 1582. He was elected Moderator of the General Assembly in July 1579 and April 1583.

BUK; Calderwood, III; Spottiswoode, II, 319–20; J. Melville, *Autobiography and Diary*, ed. R. Pitcairn (E, 1842); J. Durkan and J. Kirk, *The University of Glasgow, 1451–1577* (G, 1977); H. M. B. Reid, *The Divinity Principals in the University of Glasgow* (G, 1917), 83–105; *DNB* LII, 404–5; *FES* III, 162, 410.

J. Kirk

Smellie, Alexander (1857–1923), Original Secession Church* minister and writer. Born at Stranraer, he graduated at Edinburgh, and after theological studies was ordained and inducted to Stranraer in 1880. During 1892–4 he edited the *Sunday School Chronicle* in London, but returned to minister in Thurso (1894–1900) and Carluke (1900–23). Smellie always had the vision of 'a reunited Evangelical and Presbyterian Church of Scotland', and retained cordial relations with those in other Churches. For some years he contributed weekly to the *Sunday School Times* of Philadelphia. He wrote biographies of R. M. M'Cheyne* and Evan Hopkins, and a number of devotional works, but is chiefly remembered for his beautifully-written *Men of the Covenant* (L, 1903), the 1924 edition of which was reproduced in 1975, and which has been translated into several languages.

Who Was Who, 1916–1928, 968; *Original Secession Magazine*, 4th. ser. 21 (1923), 259–65, 291–304, 339–45, 367–74.

J. D. Douglas

SMITH, GEORGE ADAM

Smith, George Adam (1856–1942), Presbyterian Old Testament scholar. Born in India where his father was editor of the *Calcutta Review*, Smith moved to Edinburgh in 1858. At eighteen he took a degree in arts from the University of Edinburgh and three years later graduated from New College, Edinburgh, where he was influenced by A. B. Davidson.* Summer vacations were spent in Germany studying under Franz Delitzsch, Adolf Harnack and others. Following New College, Smith made the first of several trips to the Middle East. Upon his return he was assistant FC minister in Brechin, until appointed to teach Hebrew and Old Testament in the FC College, Aberdeen, as a temporary replacement for the recently deposed William Robertson Smith.* From 1882–92 Smith was minister in Queen's Cross Church, Aberdeen, and from 1892–1909 Professor of Old Testament Language and Literature in the FC and then UFC College, Glasgow. From Glasgow he moved back to Aberdeen to become Principal and Vice-Chancellor of the University, a post he held until his retirement in 1935.

Smith wrote commentaries on Deuteronomy (C, 1918), Isaiah (NY, 1927), Jeremiah (NY, 1929) and the minor prophets (NY, 1928), numerous articles, several collections of sermons and what is doubtless his best work, the more technical *Historical Geography of the Holy Land* (L, 1894; ^{25}1931) and *Jerusalem . . . From the Earliest Times to 70 AD* (2 vols, L, 1907–8).

Regarding himself first and foremost as a 'modernizer', Smith said his real ability was 'to interpret to the present age the messages of the ancient prophets', and this could be done best, he urged, by means of modern critical approaches to the Bible. His views on the relationship of criticism and preaching were set out in *Modern Criticism and the Preaching of the Old Testament* (L, 1901). The book was the cause of a near-trial for heresy in the UFC General Assembly of 1901. Smith was accused of, among other things, undermining the truthfulness, inspiration and authority of large sections of Scripture. On a motion by Robert Rainy* the case was dismissed.

Smith opposed what he called 'dogmas of verbal inspiration' and was influenced by evolutionary views of the progress of biblical religion from Israel's primitive barbarity through the ethical teaching of the prophets, culminating in the person and work of Christ. For Smith this meant that the latter superseded and annulled the former rather than fulfilled it, so that the death of Christ, for instance, must be interpreted not as sacrificial but as ethical, giving Smith's Christianity an essentially moralistic character, as he put it, 'clear, practical and without mystery'.

Four Psalms (L, 1896); *Life of Henry Drummond* (L, 1899); *Early Poetry of Israel* (L, 1912); *Syria and the Holy Land* (L, 1918).

L. A. Smith, *George Adam Smith* (L, 1943); R. A. Riesen, *Criticism and Faith in Late Victorian Scotland . . . George Adam Smith* (Lanham, MD, and L, 1985); S. A. Cook, 'George Adam Smith

1856–1942', *Proceedings of the British Academy* 28 (1942), 325–46; S. A. Cook, 'George Adam Smith', *ExT* 54 (1942–3), 33–7; *DNB 1941–50*, 192–4.

R. A. Riesen

Smith, James (of Newburn) (1708–75), one of the founders of the Old Scots Independents.* Smith was educated at Aberdeen University and ordained to Newburn, Fife, in 1735. Together with Robert Ferrier* of Largo he came under the influence of the writings of John Glas.* Converted to a Congregational view of Church polity and a separatist view of Church–state relations, Smith left the CofS in 1768. He and Ferrier opened a meeting house in Balchrystie, Fife, which became the first Old Scots Independent congregation. They were its first elders.

Smith expounded his conception of Church government in *A Compendious Account ... of the Form and Order of the Church of God* (E, 1765), and wrote a polemic against the Covenanting* ideals of the RPC (*see* Societies, United) and the Secession Churches in his *Defence of National Covenanting by Mr Flocker Insufficient* (E, 1767).

J. Smith and R. Ferrier, *The Case of James Smith ... and Robert Ferrier* (E, 1768).

FES V, 224–5; H. Escott, *A History of Scottish Congregationalism* (G, 1959), 25–7.

N. R. Needham

Smith, James (*d*.1736), successor of William Hamilton* from 1732 first as Professor of Divinity at Edinburgh University, later also Principal from 1733. Smith offered his services to the Earl of Hay, later third Duke of Argyll, and 'managed' the Church in the government's interest. He was minister at Morham, E. Lothian (1706–12), and Cramond near Edinburgh (1712–32), and New North Church, Edinburgh (1730–2, 1733–6) and is said to have been distinguished 'for easiness of speaking and distinctiveness of thought'. He gained popularity for supporting the suspension of John Simson* and the deposition of John Glas,* but strongly favoured the imposition of a patron's* nominee upon an unwilling congregation. He was Moderator of the General Assembly in 1723 and 1731, and published a few sermons.

FES I, 143–4; J. Warrick, *The Moderators of the Church of Scotland 1690–1740* (E, 1913).

H. R. Sefton

Smith, James (1782–1867), known as 'Smith of Jordanhill', geologist and writer on biblical subjects. Born in Glasgow, he studied at the University, and became a sleeping partner in a mercantile firm. His chief interest, however, was geology; most of his work was collected in his *Researches in Newer Pliocene and Post-Tertiary Geology* (G, 1862). But his most celebrated work was in the area of biblical history, *The Voyage and Shipwreck of St Paul* (L, 1848; ¹1880), in which he argued that the island of Acts 28:1 was Malta, not Melida in the Adriatic.

He also wrote a *Dissertation on the Origin and Connection of the Gospels* (E, 1853), where he argued that Luke was dependent on Matthew and an Aramaic original translated into Greek by Mark. He also wrote *Letters to an English Peer on the Present State of the Church of Scotland* (G, 1843).

DNB LIII, 59–60.

N. R. Needham

Smith, John (1747–1807), one of the translators of the Gaelic* Bible (*see* Bible (Versions, Gaelic)). Born in Glenorchy, Argyll, Smith became assistant parish minister in Kilbrandon and Kilchattan (1777–81), where his Gaelic translation of Alleine's *Alarm to the Unconverted* (E, 1781) stimulated a revival* (*see* Douglas, Niel). Moving to Campbeltown (1781–1807), he translated the fourth part of the Gaelic Old Testament, the prophets (1786), later revised by Alexander Stewart.* Smith also revised the Gaelic Psalter, and made a new Gaelic translation of the Paraphrases (1787). His wide scholarly interests embraced Hebrew verse, Ossianic poetry and farming.

D. MacKinnon, *The Gaelic Bible and Psalter* (Dingwall, 1930), 15–17, 34–8, 60–2; *FES* IV, 50–1.

D. E. Meek

Smith, Ronald Gregor (1913–68), 'secular' theologian. Pastor (CofS minister, Selkirk, 1939–44), publisher (Editor, SCM Press, 1950–6), professor (Glasgow, 1956–68) and creative teacher, Gregor Smith was a fastidious stylist, whose complex thought was influenced by Bonhoeffer, Buber, Bultmann, Hamann and Kierkegaard. These he made more familiar or introduced to the English-speaking world. In his view, the process of secularization had its more immediate origins in the European Renaissance, or earlier in the songs of the troubadours (esp. Bernard de Ventadour). Its final origins are biblical, and to be located in the 'de-demonization of the world' in the synoptic Gospels and in the Pauline transition from 'slave' to 'son'. This process is to be welcomed by the Christian, whom the gospel sets free to live responsibly in what is, at one and the same time, man's history and 'God's history with man'.

The New Man (L, 1956); *J. G. Hamann 1730–1788* (L, 1960); *Secular Christianity* (L, 1966); *The Free Man* (L, 1969); Smith and A. D. Galloway (eds), *The Doctrine of God* (L, 1970).

E. T. Long (ed.), *God, Secularization, and History* (Columbia, SC, 1974); K. W. Clements, *The Theology of Ronald Gregor Smith* (Leiden, 1986, with full bibliography).

D. A. Templeton

Smith, Walter Chalmers (1824–1908), FC poet and broad Evangelical. Born in Aberdeen, he studied there at Marischal College and at New College, Edinburgh. He was minister at Chadwell St, Pentonville, London (1850), Orwell, Kinross-shire (1854), Roxburgh, Edinburgh (1858), Tron, Glasgow (1862), and Edinburgh High (1876-96). He published several volumes of simple, unpretentious verse (complete edition, L, 1902). He represented a somewhat liberal, post-Calvinist Evangelicalism, supporting William Robertson Smith,* and also Norman Macleod* on the sabbath* question. His views on the latter were censured by the FC Assembly in 1867 (*PAGAFCS 1864-68*, 349-51). He was Moderator of the FC's jubilee Assembly (1893), and was made DD by Glasgow (1869) and LLD by Aberdeen (1876) and Edinburgh (1893).

The Sermon on the Mount (E, 1867); *Sermons* (G, 1909).

AFCS I, 322; *FUFCS* 11; *DNB Second Suppl.* III, 350.

D. F. Wright

Smith, (Sir) William Alexander (1854-1914), founder of the Boys' Brigade.* Smith was born at Pennyland House, Thurso, the son of a businessman and ex-army officer. After education at Thurso's Miller Institution, Smith joined his uncle, a Glasgow clothing wholesaler, setting up his own export business in 1878. His main influences in these years were Glasgow YMCA,* the Volunteer Movement, George Reith's College Free Church and its North Woodside Mission, inspired by D. L. Moody* and Ira D. Sankey's visit to Glasgow. There Smith was impressed by the need for creatively disciplined work among boys of pre-YMCA age. The Boys' Brigade was founded as a result (1883). He became its first secretary in 1885, working full-time from 1888. Thereafter Smith's life and the Brigade's were indistinguishable. A diplomatic administrator and persuasive writer, he was the model of deceptively diffident pragmatism, sustaining his concept of a boys' movement centred in local congregations and Sunday schools. Distinguishing clearly between method (the Brigades' uniform and discipline doubtless coloured by his Volunteers' patriotism) and aim (never militaristic), Smith opposed all attempts to incorporate the Brigade into a Cadet Force. Despite the Brigade's international spread he travelled little except in the States, where his manner was at variance with American style, and Canada, where he was more successful.

Knighted in 1909, Smith died in London. A service in St Paul's Cathedral preceded the funeral in Glasgow; 160,000 people lined the route from College and Kelvingrove United Free Church to the Western Necropolis.

Who Was Who, 1897-1916, 661; John Springhall, Brian Fraser, Michael Hoare, *Sure and Stedfast: A History of the Boys' Brigade 1883-1983* (L, 1983); F. P. Gibbon, *William A. Smith of the Boys' Brigade* (L, 1934); R. S. Peacock, *Pioneer of Boyhood; Study of Sir William A. Smith...* (G, 1954).

J. C. G. Binfield

Smith, William Robertson (1846-94), orientalist, OT scholar and minister of the FC. Born in the Aberdeenshire parish of Keig and Tough,

Smith was educated largely by his talented FC minister father. Intellectually precocious as a child, at fifteen he entered Aberdeen University. In 1866 he moved to New College,* Edinburgh, to train for the ministry of the FC, and came under the special influence of A. B. Davidson,* though his interests extended to mathematics and natural science (he published on both). In 1867 and 1869 he paid important summer visits to Germany, where he was deeply impressed by Rothe and Ritschl ('I never heard anything so interesting on a theological subject as Ritschl's lectures'). At twenty-three he was elected by the FC General Assembly of 1870 to the chair of Hebrew in the Church's Aberdeen college. Smith's tenure of the chair proved brief and turbulent, as his brilliance, pugnacity and growing engagement with contemporary German theology and biblical criticism plunged him into a series of controversies with the conservatives in the FC, which took the form of an extended 'case' (strictly, two) in the courts of the Church. He never married.

The influence of the German 'middle school' is already evident in Smith's letters and early (then unpublished) papers, although, as Nelson has demonstrated, his conversion to the 'advanced' critical conclusions of German OT scholarship did not take place until some time after his arrival in Aberdeen. His initial sympathies were with the relatively conservative approach taken by Ewald, but he was evidently deeply influenced by the Graf-Wellhausen analysis during the early 1870s. By 1875 he had submitted a series of articles to the *Encyclopaedia Britannica* (⁹E, 1875-89), and it was the appearance of his article 'Bible' in volume three on 7 December 1875, which initiated the five-year controversy which was to end his career in the FC and, ironically, to be a turning-point in popularizing the new approach to the Bible which he represented – not only in Scotland, but throughout the English-speaking world.

After the appearance in early 1876 of critical reviews of 'Bible', the matter was raised with the FC's College Committee, who invited Smith to an informal discussion with James Candlish* and Robert Rainy.* The Committee expressed disquiet, in particular over Smith's views on Deuteronomy, but did not 'find sufficient ground to support a process for heresy'. Meanwhile, the first of many pamphlets appeared, and Smith replied trenchantly in the press. The matter was raised in August at the Commission of Assembly,* which referred it to the Presbytery of Aberdeen. The Presbytery questioned Smith, passed the question to the Assembly of 1877, and (under pressure from Smith to formalize proceedings) presented in February 1878 a 'libel' founded on the doctrine of Scripture set forth in the Westminster* Confession of Faith. It maintained that to deny, to tend to deny, or to adopt a neutral attitude towards this doctrine, 'are severally offences, especially in a Professor of Divinity'. These three offences were each alleged to have been committed in eight particulars. Smith responded in a vigorous sixty-four-page pamphlet, *Answer to the Form of Libel* (A, 1878).

The Presbytery debated the case, and Smith won

the rejection of each particular under the first general charge of denying the Confession. The third charge of 'neutrality' was dismissed. Smith objected to the second general charge of 'tendency' as unconstitutional, but lost by a majority of one. On appeal to the Synod* this verdict was overthrown, and appeals in each matter passed up to the General Assembly. Meanwhile a second pamphlet had been in preparation and, like the first, was laid before Presbytery, the *Additional Answer to the Libel* (A, 1878).

The General Assembly sustained the appeal on the second particular under the first general charge, that Smith's views on Deuteronomy contradicted the Confession. Appeals on other charges were either withdrawn or rejected, except for that on the relevancy of the second general charge of 'tendency', which was effectively upheld but referred back to Presbytery in re-drafted form. Aberdeen Presbytery rejected all eight particulars under 'tendency', and referred the decision on Deuteronomy back once more to the Assembly. The Synod referred ensuing appeals under the 'tendency' charges to the Assembly also.

The General Assembly of 1879 set aside the 'tendency' charge to focus on the more important second particular of the first charge, and voted to serve the libel on Smith by 321 to 320. A special committee was set up to report to the following Assembly. In May 1880 a compromise was put to the Assembly: the libel would be abandoned, Smith would be removed from his chair on the grounds that he no longer commanded the confidence of the Church, and he would retain his ministerial status. Despite support from leaders on both sides, the Assembly rejected the proposal and opted for a more liberal conclusion, with an admonishment from the Moderator and an unusually contrite response from Smith. It had been a 'weighty lesson'. 'I hope that by His grace I shall not fail to learn by it.'

On the day the Assembly rose a further controversial article appeared, and seven days later his piece on 'Hebrew Language and Literature' appeared in the eleventh volume of *Britannica*. In June a memorial* and petition* to the College Committee had been laid before the Presbytery of Edinburgh, which resolved to send them instead to the Commission of Assembly. The Commission met in August, appointed a committee to report to its October meeting, and called Smith to appear then 'for his own interest'; after which he was suspended from his academic duties. In May 1881 the process of litigation finally came to an end. Smith was dismissed from his post, on the ground that the article on 'Hebrew Language and Literature' contained 'statements which are fitted to throw grave doubt on the historical truth and divine inspiration of several books of Scripture', and that the manner in which he had dealt with the subject showed 'a singular lack of sympathy with the reasonable anxieties of the Church as to the bearing of critical speculations on the integrity and authority of Scripture'. His ministerial status remained unaffected, though he ceased to exercise it.

Smith's later career was brilliant though tragically brief. Two major works appeared at this point – *The Old Testament in the Jewish Church* (E, 1881) and *The Prophets of Israel* (E, 1882), both based on popular lectures delivered during the years of the case; but he then turned increasingly from the OT to comparative studies. His final book, *Lectures on the Religion of the Semites* (E, 1889), sets the OT firmly in such a context. He was considered, formally or informally, for chairs of Mathematics (Glasgow) and Logic (Aberdeen), as well as in areas closer to his current interests (Harvard and Johns Hopkins). He became co-editor of *Britannica* (1881), but soon moved to Cambridge where he was appointed Lord Almoner's Reader in Arabic (1883–6), Fellow of Christ's College (from 1885), University Librarian (1886–9), and finally Sir Thomas Adams Professor of Arabic (1889), in which post he died at the age of forty-seven. This last alone is recorded on the austere obelisk that marks his grave at Keig.

Lectures and Essays, ed. J. S. Black and G. W. Chrystal (L, 1912).

J. S. Black and G. W. Chrystal, *The Life of William Robertson Smith* (L, 1912); R. R. Nelson, *The Life and Thought of William Robertson Smith, 1846–1894* (Ann Arbor, MI, 1980); R. A. Riesen, *Criticism and Faith in Late Victorian Scotland, A. B. Davidson, William Robertson Smith and George Adam Smith* (Lanham MD, 1985); N. M. de S. Cameron, *Biblical Higher Criticism and the Defense of Infallibilism in Nineteenth Century Britain* (Lewiston, NY, 1987); *AFCS* I, 59.

N. M. de S. Cameron

Snodgrass, John (1744–97), CofS minister of Dundee South Parish (1774–81) and of Paisley Middle Parish (1781–97), and theological writer. He proposed the more careful selection of presbytery commissioners to the General Assembly as a means of ending the Moderate* domination there, attacked the luxury and dissipation of the upper classes as a major cause of impiety, and defended Calvinist doctrinal orthodoxy. He also maintained an evangelical emphasis in matters of faith and stressed the importance of personal holiness. Princeton awarded him a DD degree in 1793.

An Effectual Method for Recovering our Religious Liberties (G, 1770); *Prospects of Providence respecting the Conversion of the World to Christ* (Paisley, 1796); *The Leading Doctrines of the Gospel Stated and Defended* (E, 1795) in J. Brown (ed.), *Theological Tracts*, III (E, 1854); *A Commentary ... on ... Revelation...* (Paisley, 1799).

FES III, 179.

J. R. McIntosh

Social Concern, arising out of the mission and service of the church. From the earliest healing stories associated with St Columba* and the Celtic Church* in the sixth century, concern for those in need has been a recorded part of Scottish Christianity. The successor Catholic Church in the early medieval period held its churches and religious houses responsible for local poor relief*, supplemented by a range of institutions and religious orders serving the destitute and sick. Over a hundred almshouses, hospices, leper-houses and hospitals* had been set up by 1560. Mendicant orders of Friars* were active in caring for the poor and sick from the thirteenth century in Scotland.

Such caring work was part of a broader concern to maintain the social fabric of Scotland as a Christian community. In the corporate piety of parish worship and the disciplinary machinery of its courts, the church sought to reconcile those in dispute within marriage, the family or community. The late-medieval Church stressed the communal nature of Christianity and the collective responsibility of a society bound by ties of kinship and local loyalties to live in social peace. The failure to share ecclesiastical wealth with the poor, or to protect their interests, is one of the contemporary criticisms made of the late-medieval church in works like *Ane Satyre of the Thrie Estaitis* by Sir David Lindsay;* a failure recognized by the Church's own provincial councils* in the years before the Reformation.*

This tradition of communal Christianity and corporate social responsibility continued after the Reformation* of the church in 1560. This is reflected in the social thought of leading reformers like John Knox* and in the *First Book of Discipline*.* The care of the poor by the church and community was seen as a Christian duty requiring both relief work and an end to unjust social and economic practices. Poor relief* was to have been financed by income from the patrimony of the pre-Reformation church. Such aid was to be administered by the local parishes and kirk sessions,* with a distinction being made between dependent recipients like widows and orphans, and able-bodied paupers or beggars, who were to be excluded from assistance. Underpinning this welfare system was the Reformers' teaching on the social obligation of Christians to provide for the needy and to ensure a just social order. However, the practice of the Reformed Kirk fell far short of its social ideal. Secular interests appropriated the old Church's wealth and constrained the new Kirk's social criticism. Poor relief had to be financed out of voluntary giving for that purpose in each parish. Local poor funds were seldom adequate to meet the extent of poverty in Scotland. Despite this failure, the CofS* retained its concern for the social as well as the spiritual welfare of the nation.

The social problems created in the wake of industrialization and urbanization in nineteenth-century Scotland placed the historic system of parish poor relief administered by the established CofS under enormous strain. Thomas Chalmers* sought to adapt this system to the social conditions of an industrial society by establishing new parishes in urban areas, which would have sole responsibility for meeting the needs of the urban poor without state intervention. While his own parish ministry pioneered methods of social work, its voluntary and parochial approach to poverty proved inadequate to tackle the scale and causes of urban deprivation. The Disruption* of the national Church in 1843 ended the possibility of comprehensive social care through its parish system. While the tradition of voluntary or church-supported social conern continued after Chalmers' death, for example, in the work of James Begg* to improve working class housing, central and local government bodies increasingly took over responsibility for the provision of public welfare, including poor relief from 1845. Christian social concern was often channelled into popular campaigns for moral reform, like the Temperance movement,* or mission and charitable work in poor areas. In the twentieth century the churches developed their own social work agencies and projects; with many of them, such as the CofS Board of Social Responsibility,* drawing on government funding or concerned with particular issues, like the anti-abortion work of the RC Church. The charitable work of many independent churches, individual church members and voluntary groups, continued a tradition going back to the medieval Catholic laity and later Christian philanthropists like David Dale.*

The voice of social criticism within the churches' social concern was rarely heard until the twentieth century, except from individuals like Patrick Brewster.* Criticism of the existing social and economic order as the cause of social problems grew among many churchmen in the 1900s, partly in response to the rise of the labour and socialist movements, and leading to the formation of social research bodies like the Scottish Christian Social Union;* to the establishing of denominational committees concerned with social issues, such as the CofS Church and Nation Committee,* set up in 1919; and to Church reports calling for a new social order, such as the Baillie Commission's reports (*see* Baillie, John) to the CofS General Assembly during the Second World War, which advocated a post-war welfare state. By the 1980s this social concern included an ecumenical dialogue on social issues among bodies such as the Church and Nation Committee*, the RC Justice and Peace Commission, and the Scottish Churches Council and its successor, Action of Churches Together in Scotland*.

S. Mechie, *The Church and Scottish Social Development 1780–1870* (L, 1960); D. C. Smith, *Passive Obedience and Prophetic Protest* (NY, 1987); S. J. Brown, *Thomas Chalmers and the Godly Commonwealth* (O, 1982); R. L. Greaves, *Theology and Revolution in the Scottish Reformation* (Grand Rapids, MI, 1980), 185–202; A. L. Drummond and J. Bulloch, *The Scottish Church 1688–1843* (E, 1973), 161–79; *id.*, *The Church in Victorian Scotland 1843–74* (E, 1975), 79–84; A. C. Cheyne, *The Transforming of the Kirk* (E, 1983), 110–56; T. C. Smout, *A History of the Scottish People 1560–1830* (L, 1972), 67–93; *id.*, *A Century of the Scottish People 1830–1950* (L, 1986), 133–80; R. Nicholson, *Scotland: The Later Middle Ages* (E, 1978), 8–14; A. Grant, *Independence and Nationhood* (L, 1984), 116–19; J. Durkan, 'Care of the Poor: Pre-Reformation Hospitals', *IR* 10 (1959), 268–80; D. McRoberts (ed.), *Modern Scottish Catholicism 1878–1978* (G, 1979), 92–109; D. J.

SOCIAL RESPONSIBILITY, BOARD OF

Withrington, 'The Churches in Scotland, c.1870–1900: Towards a New Social Conscience?', *RSCHS* 19 (1977), 155–68; D. Forrester, *Christianity and the Future of Welfare* (L, 1985), 38–43; J. Harvey, *Bridging the Gap* (E, 1987).

W. F. Storrar

Social Responsibility, Board of, CofS department that is the largest voluntary organization providing residential care in Scotland. Its mission statement – 'In Christ's name we seek to retain and regain the highest quality of life which each individual is capable of experiencing at any given time' – reflects the Christian basis on which all its work is done.

The Board's work has two main branches, in practical rehabilitative residential care and in Christian ethics and moral issues. The Board came into being in 1976 to unify the work of the Committees on Social Service and Moral Welfare and the Women's Committee on Social and Moral Welfare. From 1963 the Department of Social and Moral Welfare had combined the spheres of Social Service and of Temperance and Morals. The Committee on Social Service was formed in 1945 out of the earlier Committee on Christian Life and Social Work dating from 1936. The Committee on Social Work went back to 1904 (Lord Polwarth* was its convener 1905–26), and the Committee on Christian Life and Work to 1869. It was one of A. H. Charteris'* many initiatives.

The present Board's remit from the CofS General Assembly is as follows: (i) to provide specialist resources to further the caring work of the Church; (ii) to identify existing and emerging areas of need, and to guide the Church in pioneering new approaches to relevant problems; (iii) to study and present essential Christian judgements on social and moral issues arising within the area of the Committee's concern.

The Board seeks to co-operate with local churches in their caring for their community and also in providing specialist services, such as those for sufferers from senile dementia or addiction to alcohol or drugs. It currently works in all the Scottish Regions and runs seventy-one residential and care establishments, including over forty Eventide homes.* As a voluntary organization, the Board seeks to respond to emerging needs and is currently engaged in providing imaginative ways of helping those who have been in long-term psychiatric wards be integrated into local communities.

In building up the Board's distinguished record of wide-ranging social service, Lewis Cameron,* Director of Social Service 1937–63, has an honoured place.

See also Temperance.

M. B. MacGregor, *Towards Scotland's Social Good* (E, 1948); L. L. L. Cameron, *The Challenge of Need. A History of Social Service by The Church of Scotland 1869–1969* (E, 1971).

J. M. Carswell

Societies, United, the general gathering of the

SOCIETIES, UNITED

'Society people', often called 'Cameronians', those Covenanters* largely in the south-west of Scotland who were hearers of field-preachers* such as Donald Cargill* and Richard Cameron.* Patrick Walker* dates the first use of the name 'Cameronians' after Cameron's death, with little use until after the Revolution, and thinks 'Cargillites' more appropriate if a nickname must be given, as Cargill 'was of the same principles and practice a little after Mr Cameron was born' (*Six Saints of the Covenant*, ed. D. H. Fleming, E, 1901, I, 241).

From the beginning of the period of persecution societies sprang up, partly for fellowship and prayer and partly to give 'their testimony in that day against the tyranny and defections of all kinds' (*ibid.* II, 66). Walter Smith, a well-known field-preacher, drew up 'Rules and Directions anent private Christian Meetings, for Prayer and Conference to mutual edification, and to the right management of the same' (*ibid.* II, 83–96).

From 1681, shortly after Cargill and Smith were hanged, there was a movement to unite these separate societies in a 'General Correspondence' for mutual consultation and aid in giving a public testimony against the Test Act* and other targets. The first of the General Meetings was held in December 1681. Although some who managed the affairs of the societies were described by Michael Shields, who served as clerk to the United Societies, as having 'more zeal than knowledge, more honesty than policy, and more single-hearted simplicity than prudence', yet nevertheless they maintained their cause as best they could through 'the time's darkness and confusions' (*Faithful Contendings displayed*, ed. J. Howie, G, 1780, 6–9).

The societies denied the lawfulness of hearing the curates and those presbyterians who had taken the Indulgence,* denied the authority of the uncovenanted king, characterizing the regime as tyrannical (and in the Sanquhar Declaration* and elsewhere taking much the same ground as did the majority of Scots in rejecting James VII* and recognizing William* and Mary in 1689), rejected the imposition of unlawful oaths and justified field-meetings and their self-defence (see Alexander Shields,* *A Hind let loose*, 1687, in which a careful vindication of these positions is given).

James Renwick* was executed early in 1688 and the last Covenanter martyr was killed that July. With the Revolution the societies raised a regiment (the famous Cameronian regiment) which played a significant part in repelling the forces loyal to James VII. In 1690 the societies first met at Leadhills, Lanarkshire, in April and subscribed a petition lamenting defections and demanding a vindication of the covenants. In June they drew up a list of grievances for the consideration of the forthcoming General Assembly. The societies' three ministers, Alexander Shields,* Thomas Linning (*FES* III, 314) and William Boyd (*FES* II, 408), considered this testimony sufficient to exonerate their consciences and, believing the reconstituted CofS a true church, applied to join and were received by it. Though some followed them in this, a substantial number refused to join an uncovenanted, Erastian Church. The continuing society people were thus left without a minister until John Macmillan* eventually joined them. When he in turn was joined by Thomas Nairn* they together formed a presbytery which in time became the RPC.

M. Hutchison, *The Reformed Presbyterian Church in Scotland* (Paisley, 1893).

D. C. Lachman

Society for Propagating the Gospel at Home, late eighteenth-century home missionary body. Formed in Edinburgh in January 1798 by James Haldane,* John Campbell* and a group of fellow members of the Est.C, the privately funded SPGH appeared in part as a response to the challenge of domestic unbelief issued by Moderate* critics of overseas missions. The Society derived considerable impetus from the influence of David Bogue* and the new wave of evangelical activity in England which had already espoused the cause of home and overseas missions. At its inception it declared its undenominational and non-political character, indicating as its principal concerns itinerant preaching,* Sunday schools* and the private reading of the Bible and devotional literature. It employed its own preachers and catechists (*see* Haldane Preachers), while encouraging settled ministers to extend their preaching to neighbouring communities. Using young men trained in the academies financed by Robert Haldane,* the Society extended its influence in Fife, north-east Scotland, Caithness and Orkney, and among the Gaelic-speaking communities of Perthshire, the Spey valley and mid-Argyll. Its use of unordained persons as preachers and catechists, its disregard for parish boundaries and its criticism of ministers whom it believed to be neglecting the gospel or disseminating heretical ideas, provoked hostility from the CofS and from the Antiburgher* and Relief* synods. The most forceful opposition came in 1799 with the promulgation by the General Assembly* of the largely ineffectual Pastoral Admonition.* By 1808, when the conversion to Baptist* principles of Robert and James Haldane led to the Society's demise, it had laid the foundations of Scottish Independency* in the form of its converts and hearers, and had contributed to the resurgence of Evangelicalism within the CofS.

The Missionary Magazine (E, 1796–1813); *An Account of the Proceedings of the Society for Propagating the Gospel at Home* (E, 1799); A. Haldane, *The Lives of Robert Haldane of Airthrey, and of his brother, James Alexander Haldane* (L, 1852).

D. W. Lovegrove

Socinianism, *see* Unitarians.

Soga, Tiyo (*c.* 1829–71), missionary, Bible translator and first African ordained to the Christian ministry in South Africa. He was born near the Mgwali river to a councillor of the great Xhosa chief Ngqika. His mother, Nosuthu, was a Christian of the people of Tshatsu, one of the first converts among the Xhosa. Tiyo attended a Church school, and in 1844 entered Lovedale, the Scottish missionary High School and Training College. William Govan, its principal, took him to Scotland at the end of the war of 1846–7. In Glasgow he was trained as a missionary by the UPC and sent back to Cape Colony as a catechist. In June 1851 he began studies for the ministry at the UP college in Edinburgh and was ordained in 1856. The next year he married Janet Burnside and returned with his Scottish wife to the Cape where he opened a new station among the people of Ngqika.

He translated *Pilgrim's Progress* as well as the four Gospels into Xhosa. He wrote on Xhosa traditional culture and composed several hymns. He was an outstanding preacher in English as well as Xhosa. Despite chronic throat trouble he refused to retire, and when the Gcaleka chief Sarili asked for a mission to be established among his people, Soga went to begin the work at what is now the town of Somerville. He died there at the early age of forty-two. All four of his sons and one daughter studied in Scotland. His eldest son, William, became the first African doctor in South Africa and his second, James Henderson, was a distinguished minister and historian of the Xhosa people.

D. Williams, *Umfundisi; a Biography of Tiyo Soga* (Lovedale, 1978); J. A. Chalmers, *Tiyo Soga* (L, 1878); H. T. Cousins, *From Kaffir Kraal to Pulpit* (L, 1899).

A. C. Ross

Solemn League and Covenant, a religious covenant and civil league between the Scots and English, agreed and ratified in mid-1643. In the context of a worsening military situation in England and fears that a Royalist victory would threaten the Reformed religion and civil liberty in both countries, many desired closer co-operation. However the Scottish Covenanters* primarily wanted religious uniformity, whereas the English preferred civil, and particularly military, co-operation. As Robert Baillie expressed it, 'The English were for a civill League, we for a religious Covenant' (*Letters and Journals* II, 90). But the English were willing to make concessions to obtain military aid. They extended an invitation to the Scots to send commissioners to the newly-called Westminster Assembly,* and approved the draft of a league and covenant drawn up by Alexander Henderson.* This was then approved by the General Assembly and the convention of estates, which was essentially acting on behalf of the Scottish Parliament. A treaty for sending an army to England, in English pay, was approved shortly afterward.

The Solemn League and Covenant, as thus agreed, was first of all a religious covenant. After noting that they had one king and one Reformed religion and expressing their concern about the estate of both Church and kingdom in England and Scotland, the signatories swear to preserve 'the Reformed Religion in the Church of Scotland' and the Reformation of religion in England and to bring the churches to the 'nearest Conjunction and Uniformity in Religion', confession, government and worship. They also bound themselves to extirpate popery and prelacy as well as superstition, heresy and whatever is contrary to sound doctrine.

Only after these religious points did they proceed to the civil, binding themselves to preserve the 'Rights and Priviledges of the Parliaments and the Liberties of the Kingdoms and to Preserve and Defend the King's Majesty's Person and Authority', to bring to trial all who hinder such reformation of religion or divide the king from his people and to continue such 'to all Posterity' and not suffer themselves to be withdrawn from 'this blessed Union and Conjunction'. They desire to be humbled for their sins and look to God to turn away his wrath and strengthen them in their work.

The English Parliament made some alterations to the draft before approving it, particularly in a desire to avoid a commitment to use the Scottish Presbyterian model in reforming the Church of England. They also included Ireland in a document which had previously referred only to Scotland and England. But the urgency of the situation overcame any further misgivings, both theirs, and the Scots' on receiving the amended document. Though the English believed a door was left open for Independency,* the Scots were confident that 'Reformation of Religion ... according to the Word of God' involved Presbyterianism.* And all looked for God to bless their armies with success in the continuing conflict.

Records of the Kirk of Scotland, ed. A. Peterkin (E, 1838), 362–4; D. Stevenson, *The Scottish Revolution 1637–1644* (Newton Abbot, 1973); J. K. Hewison, *The Covenanters*, 2 vols (²G, 1913).

D. C. Lachman

Somerville, Alexander Neil (1813–89), parish minister and evangelist. He was born in Edinburgh and attended the University there. Minister of Anderston (CofS and FC) Church, Glasgow, 1837–89 (senior minister from 1878), he was also convener of several important church committees and involved in organizational labours on behalf of local missionary societies. Appointed a director of the Glasgow Bible Society, Somerville went on to become a co-founder of the National Bible Society of Scotland in 1860 (*see* Bible Societies). As convener of the Mission Committee he promoted the cause of missions within the FC and was responsible for securing the establishment of a chair in Evangelistic Theology for the Free Church Colleges. He was much interested in prophecy related to the future of the Jews.

The visit to Scotland of D. L. Moody* and I. D. Sankey in 1873 prompted a profound change in Somerville's mission practice. Sponsored by the Glasgow United Evangelistic Association,* he eventually became a full-time evangelist at the age of 64. His most effectual campaigns were conducted in the English-speaking world, *i.e.* India, North America, Australia, New Zealand and South Africa. His evangelistic labours in France, Italy, Greece, Russia, Germany and Eastern Europe were notably less productive, often arousing considerable clerical opposition. His appointment as Moderator of the FC General Assembly in 1886 was, in part, a recognition of this work. Within the broad ecclesiological spectrum of the FC of the late nineteenth century, Somerville's combination of Calvinist* theology with the evangelistic techniques of Moody and Sankey stands in contrast to the principles and practice of the more conservative 'constitutionalist'* party. He received Glasgow's DD in 1877.

The Churches of Asia (Paisley, 1885); *Evangelization for the World: Addresses Delivered at the General Assembly of the Free Church of Scotland* (G, 1886).

G. Smith, *A Modern Apostle: Alexander N. Somerville, DD* (²L, 1891); memoir by W. F. Somerville (son) in Somerville, *Precious Seed Sown in Many Lands* (L, 1890), ix–xlvii; *DNB* LIII, 249; *AFCS* I, 323; *FES* III, 390.

I. D. Maxwell

Somerville, Thomas (1741–1830), CofS Moderate* minister and historian. Born at Hawick, Roxburghshire, he entered Edinburgh University in 1756. The death of his father in 1757 compelled him to teach privately to support his family. He continued training for the ministry, and was ordained to Minto, in Roxburghshire, in 1766. In 1772 he was appointed to Jedburgh against the opposition of the congregation, remaining there until his death. To supplement his income. Somerville took to writing, producing works on the American and French revolutions and on British history. He was offered the chair of church history in Edinburgh University in 1798, but declined it.

Somerville received a DD from St Andrews in 1789, and was made one of the king's chaplains for Scotland in 1793.

My Own Life and Times 1741–1814 (E, 1861).

DNB LIII, 255–6; *FES* II, 127–8.

N. R. Needham

Souter, Alexander (1873–1949), classicist, New Testament linguistic and perhaps Scotland's finest patristic scholar. He was born at Perth but educated at Aberdeen (Robert Gordon's College and the University's distinguished classics school) and Cambridge, where J. E. B. Mayor deeply influenced him. (Souter and T. R. Glover alone attended his lectures on Tertullian's *Apology*. Souter later translated some Tertullian.) After teaching Aberdeen students (1897–1903) he became Yates Professor of New Testament Greek and Exegesis at Mansfield College, Oxford (1903–11); like his devout father, Souter was a Congregationalist,* and served as a director of the London Missionary Society.* He returned to Aberdeen to succeed his teacher W. M. Ramsay* as Regius Professor of Humanity (1911–37).

Souter worked extensively on the Greek New Testament, producing *A Pocket Lexicon to the Greek New Testament* (O, 1916) and *The Text and Canon of the New Testament* (L, 1913), as well as on early Latin

New Testament MSS. To students of the Greek New Testament he is best known as editor of the widely used *Novum Testamentum Graece* (O, 1910), which is noteworthy for the evidence from the Latin church Fathers in its critical apparatus (see B. M. Metzger, *The Text of the New Testament*, O, ²1968, 138–9). But his most lasting contributions came from the study of Latin patristic commentaries on Paul, with *A Study of Ambrosiaster* (C, 1905), an edition of Ps-Augustine's *Questions on the Old and New Testament* which he showed to be by Ambrosiaster (Vienna, 1908), *The Earliest Latin Commentaries on the Epistles of St Paul* (O, 1927, the Stone Lectures at Princeton), and his establishment of the original text of Pelagius' *Expositions of Thirteen Epistles of St Paul* (C, 1922–31). He was aware of the irony of 'an all-wise Providence, in decreeing that an Augustinian should spend a large portion of his life in studying Pelagius'. In addition to other aids he produced a *Glossary of Later Latin to 600 A.D.* (O, 1949). He won numerous honours, including DLitt (Aberdeen, 1905), DD (St Andrews, 1925, and Dublin, 1932), FBA (1926), and LLD (Aberdeen, 1938).

Memoir by R. J. Getty in *AUR* 33 (1949–50), 117–24, revised and expanded in *Proceedings of British Academy* 38 (1952), 255–68; *Who Was Who, 1941–1950*, 1082.

D. F. Wright

South Africa, *see* Emigration; Dutch Reformed Church; Missions.

Spalding, John (*c.*1631–*c.*1699), minister in Dundee. Educated at St Andrews (MA, 1651), Spalding was ordained to Dreghorn (Ayrshire) in 1656. Deprived in 1662, he returned in 1670 after the Indulgence of 1669.* Removed again in the 1680s (possibly a result of the Test Act*), he returned in 1687 with the Toleration. In 1689 he removed to Kirkcudbright and in 1691 to the South Church in Dundee. He was held in sufficiently high esteem to serve as clerk to the general meeting of Presbyterian ministers which met after the Toleration.

His *Synaxis Sacra; or, A Collection of Sermons preached at several Communions* (E, 1703) is as John Macleod (*Scottish Theology*, E, ³1974, 112) terms it, a representative collection for the period. Also published posthumously was *The Oeconomy of the Holy Trinity about Man's Salvation* (E, 1720).

FES V, 320; D. C. Lachman, *The Marrow Controversy* (E, 1988).

D. C. Lachman

Spang, William (*c.*1607–64), Scots minister in Holland. Born in Glasgow and an MA of its University (1625), he studied divinity at Edinburgh and taught at its High School until 1630, when the Convention of Royal Burghs nominated him as a minister of the Scots congregation at Campvere (Veere), Walcheren, in south Holland. He was translated to nearby Middleburg in 1652. He is best known as the correspondent of his cousin Robert Baillie,* some eighty of whose letters to Spang during 1637–62 survive, but only three from Spang to him. Spang was 'a considerable theologian, an acute observer and an assiduous correspondent ... Their knowledge of current theology, preaching, polemics, and ecclesiastical gossip was phenomenal' (A. L. Drummond, *The Kirk and the Continent*, E, 1956, 82–4, 132–6). Spang helped in the editing and publishing of Scottish works in Holland (e.g. Baillie's *Operis Historici et Chronologici Libri Duo...*, Amsterdam, 1668; Arthur Johnston(e)'s *Poemata Omnia*, Middleburg, 1642), assisted John Forbes (*d.*1648)* in exile, and wrote his own account of recent Scottish history (*Historia Motuum in Regno Scotiae*, Danzig, 1640; much expanded, 1641). He attended the 1642 Assembly.

FES VII, 541, 547–8; J. Davidson and A. Gray, *The Scottish Staple at Veere* (L, 1909), 278–300; *The Letters and Journals of Robert Baillie*, ed. D. Laing, 3 vols (Bannatyne Club, E, 1841–2), esp. III, App. cxii–cxvi.

D. F. Wright

Special Commission on Baptism, *see* Baptism.

Spottiswoode, John (1510–85), Superintendent* of Lothian. Second son of William Spottiswoode of that Ilk and educated at Glasgow University, Spottiswoode intended a clerical career but was disturbed by the prosecution of heretics,* so left for England where he came under Archbishop Cranmer's influence. Returning home in 1543, he associated himself with the reforming circle of the Earls of Glencairn* and Lennox, Sir James Sandilands of Torphichen and his brother Sir John Sandilands of Calder (E. Lothian), who presented him to the parsonage of Calder-Comitis in 1547. A friend of Lord James Stewart,* whom he may have tutored, Spottiswoode accompanied Stewart to France in 1558 to witness Queen Mary's* marriage contract to the Dauphin. At the Reformation,* he was selected as one of six contributors to the *First Book of Discipline*.* With John Knox's* refusal to accept the office of superintendent, Spottiswoode was appointed Superintendent of Lothian in March 1561, an office whose duties he discharged while retaining his parish ministry at Mid-Calder. He repeatedly sought to be relieved of the work of a superintendent but was exhorted by the General Assembly to continue for a further spell. Though a regular and prominent attender at General Assemblies, Spottiswoode was never elected Moderator. In 1566, at the Assembly's bidding, he congratulated Queen Mary on the birth of Prince James, but the Kirk's request which he conveyed that James be baptized according to Reformed practice was refused. After Mary's enforced abdication he officiated at the coronation of the infant James VI* at Stirling in 1567, and during the ensuing civil war he actively supported the King's party. He attended the Convention of Leith* in 1572 which sought a settlement for the Church's finances. In 1576 he admitted his fault when the General Assembly censured him for inaugurating Alexander

Hepburn as the Bishop of Ross at Holyrood. In 1574, he identified the superintendent's office with that of commissioner or visitor; but he seems to have played no part in the preparation of the *Second Book of Discipline** of 1578. In his old age, his elder son John,* the future Archbishop, served as his colleague at Mid-Calder. His younger son, James, became Bishop of Clogher in Ireland.

J. Kirk, *Patterns of Reform* (E, 1989); K. Hewat, *Makers of the Scottish Church at the Reformation* (E, 1920), 272-307; *FES* I, 175-6.

J. Kirk

Spottiswoode, John (1565-1639), Archbishop of Glasgow (1603-15) and St Andrews (1615-38). The son of John Spottiswoode,* and educated at Glasgow University under Andrew Melville's* regime, Spottiswoode graduated in 1581 and entered the ministry as assistant to his father at Mid-Calder in 1583. He seems to have sided with the stricter Presbyterian ministers in opposing Archbishop Patrick Adamson's* release from excommunication in 1586, and was charged with the task of re-establishing Linlithgow Presbytery. He was also returned by Presbytery and Synod as commissioner to the General Assembly in 1590 and 1593, and elected Moderator of the Synod of Lothian in October 1594. In 1597, he supported Robert Bruce's* refutation of the King's charge that ministers had instigated a riot in the capital, and in 1599 defended the Church's jurisdiction. By 1600, however, he approved the King's plans for 'parliamentary bishops', and his father-in-law, David Lindsay,* was then advanced to the bishopric of Ross. In 1601, he acted as the Duke of Lennox's chaplain in France and is said to have witnessed the celebration of mass in Paris. Returning home, he accompanied James VI* on his journey to London in 1603, and was advanced to the archbishopric of Glasgow in July. The office at that point entailed no episcopal duties apart from voting in parliament; he therefore remained parish minister at Mid-Calder and a member of Linlithgow Presbytery. But with James's scheme for 'constant moderators' and the restitution of the estate of bishops in 1606, the restoration of the bishops' consistorial jurisdiction in 1609, and the creation of two Courts of High Commission* in St Andrews and Glasgow in 1610, Spottiswoode (who was consecrated by three English bishops in 1610) came to exercise the government both of his archdiocese and of the western province, and to hold office as Chancellor of the university. At the King's will he proceeded against Presbyterian nonconformists as well as RC recusants and was active in the trial for treason of the Jesuit John Ogilvie.* As James' devoted servant in the church, Spottiswoode moved from Glasgow* to the archbishopric of St Andrews in 1615. He took the Moderator's chair at the General Assembly in Perth in 1618 which was persuaded to approve the King's programme for liturgical innovation, the Five Articles of Perth.* On James' death in 1625, Spottiswoode continued to enjoy the favour of Charles I* who appointed him Chancellor of the kingdom, and revived James' project for liturgical changes. The new *Book of Common Prayer** and Book of Canons marked the beginnings of the revolt. The Covenanting* General Assembly at Glasgow in 1638 declared episcopacy to be abolished, and Spottiswoode, who had already retreated to England, remarked how 'all that we have been doing these thirty years past is thrown down at once'. He died in London and was buried in Westminster Abbey. His best known work was *The History of the Church of Scotland* (L, 1655), undertaken at James' request.

Spottiswoode; *BUK*; Calderwood; *Spottiswoode Miscellany*, ed. J. Maidment (E, 1844); J. F. S. Gordon, *Scotichronicon* (G, 1867), I; J. Kirk, *Archbishop Spottiswoode and the See of Glasgow* (G, 1988); *FESMA*, 151, 299; *FES* I, 176; *DNB* LIII, 42-3.

J. Kirk

Spottiswoode Society, founded in Edinburgh in 1843 to publish historical material of the periods when the CofS was governed episcopally – works of bishops and clergy, books, manuscripts, pamphlets, etc. The name came from John Spottiswoode,* Archbishop of St Andrews 1615-38. There were six publications, some having several volumes: 1. Robert Keith's* *History*; 2. Works of John Sage;* 3. and 3a. Miscellany of Spottiswoode's works, etc.; 4. Funeral sermons on death of Bishop Patrick Forbes;* 5. Works of Bishop William Forbes* of Edinburgh; 6. Spottiswoode's *History of the CofS*. The last volume was published in 1851.

D. and W. B. Stevenson (eds), *Scottish Texts and Calendars* (SHS 4th ser. 23; E, 1987), 169.

A. I. Dunlop

Sprott, George Washington (1829-1919), minister of the Cof S and liturgical scholar. Born and brought up in Nova Scotia, Canada, the son of a Scottish minister, he was educated at the University of Glasgow. He served as a minister in Canada and then in Ceylon until he returned to Scotland to become minister of Chapel of Garioch, Aberdeenshire, in 1866, and then of North Berwick in East Lothian from 1874 to 1904. He was the Lecturer in Pastoral Theology to divinity students in 1878 (*The Worship and Offices of the Church of Scotland*, E, 1882). It was while he was ministering in Ceylon, alongside churches of different traditions, that he examined the basis of Presbyterian worship. People in the colonies, in his opinion, were often attracted to the worship of the Anglican Church when the worship of a Presbyterian church was not available. To renew the worship of the CofS, Sprott studied the Reformation* period in Scotland, since he wished any changes to be in harmony with the Reformed traditions* of the Kirk. Along with Thomas Leishman* he produced a new edition of *The Book of Common Order and the Westminster Directory* (E, 1868). His Lee Lecture, *The Worship of the CofS during the Covenanting Period, 1638-1661* (E, 1893), remains a standard work on that subject. Sprott's first publication, *The Worship, Rites and*

SPURGEON, CHARLES HADDON

Ceremonies of the CofS (E, 1863), suggested the formation of a society which might foster the renewal of worship in the Kirk, and the Church Service Society* was founded in 1865. Sprott served on its editorial committee, as a vice-president, 1899–1907, and as president in 1907. As one who wished to recover the Catholic tradition of the Kirk, Sprott emphasized the centrality of the Lord's Supper* in worship. He was also instrumental in the formation of the Scottish Church Society* of which he was second president. Other Scoto-Catholics* said that Sprott and Leishman had been the original 'foster-fathers' of the movement, since they had long witnessed to high church principles and their work had provided the basis for the study of Catholic doctrine.

(Ed.), *Scottish Liturgies of the Reign of James VI* (E, 1871); (ed. with H. J. Wotherspoon), *The Second Prayer Book of King Edward the Sixth* (E, 1905); *The Doctrine of Schism* (E, 1902).

FES I, 393; *DNB Suppl.* II, 373–5; J. C. Saunders, 'George Sprott and the Revival of Worship in Scotland', in *Liturgical Review* 7:1 (1977), 45–54, and *ibid.*, 8:1 (1978), 11–22; 'A Sprott Bibliography' in *ibid.*, 7:2 (1977), 44–8; D. M. Murray, 'Disruption to Union', in D. B. Forrester and D. M. Murray (eds), *Studies in the History of Worship in Scotland* (E, 1984), 79–95.

D. M. Murray

Spurgeon, Charles Haddon (1834–92), Baptist pastor. He was the son and grandson of Essex Independent ministers. Converted and baptized as a believer in 1850, he acted as pastor of Waterbeach Baptist Church, Cambridgeshire (1851–4). As pastor of New Park Street Baptist Church, London, from 1854, he drew vast congregations. From 1861 to 1891 he preached in the specially erected Metropolitan Tabernacle that held nearly 6,000. In 1887 he left the Baptist Union during the 'Down-Grade Controversy', criticizing the liberalism* of certain younger ministers. His numerous publications included: *Lectures to my Students*, 3 vols (L, 1875–99); *Commenting and Commentaries* (L, 1876); *The Treasury of David*, 6 vols (L, 1870–85), a commentary on the Psalms; and weekly sermons appearing as *The New Park Street Pulpit* (1856–62) and then *The Metropolitan Tabernacle Pulpit* (1863–1917).

From 1855 onwards he frequently visited Scotland. In 1866 he addressed the General Assemblies of the FC and the UPC. Four years later he opened a new church building for John Kennedy,* one of many Presbyterian ministers with whom he enjoyed friendship. Between 1876 and 1878 his summer holidays were spent in Scotland. The Calvinist framework of his theology earned him a wide readership. His sermons, which were translated into Gaelic, were said to be more popular in Scotland than anywhere else. Several students from his Pastor's College came to Scottish Baptist pulpits. Gifted with a powerful voice and an ebullient wit, Spurgeon was the greatest preacher of the nineteenth century.

STATISTICAL ACCOUNT OF SCOTLAND

The Early Years, 1834–1859 (L, 1962); *The Full Harvest, 1860–1892* (E, 1973).

P. S. Kruppa, *Charles Haddon Spurgeon* (NY, 1982); G. H. Pike, *The Life and Work of C. H. Spurgeon*, 3 vols (L, 1892–3); E. A. Payne, 'The Down Grade Controversy', *BQ* 28 (1979), 146–58.

D. W. Bebbington

Stalker, James (1848–1927), FC minister and professor. He was born in Crieff, educated in the University of Edinburgh, and served as minister of St Brycedale, Kirkcaldy (1874) and St Matthew's, Glasgow (1887). From 1902 to 1924 he was Professor of Church History in the FC College, Aberdeen, adding the chair of Christian Ethics in 1905, until his retirement in 1924. His books included *The Life of Jesus* (E, 1879); *The Life of St Paul* (E, 1884); *The Trial and Death of Jesus Christ* (L, 1894); *The Christology of Jesus* (Cunningham lectures,* L, 1899).

Stalker was widely read. His works were mainly devotional expositions of Scripture characterized by an orthodox, evangelical outlook. He was aware of contemporary critical theories but preferred to write on a less scholarly level.

FUFCS 583; *Who Was Who, 1916–1928*, 987; MRUFCS n.s. 27 (1927), 102–3.

I. H. Marshall

Stark, Mark Young (1799–1866), one of the Fathers of the Disruption* in British North America. Born in Dunfermline, he was educated privately in Essex and at the University of Glasgow, where he graduated MA in classics in 1821 and then undertook his theological studies for the CofS. He was licensed by the Presbytery of Glasgow in 1824 but was a 'stickit minister'* until September 1833, when he moved to Canada under the sponsorship of the Glasgow Colonial Society* and was ordained and inducted to the charge of Dundas in Upper Canada. In 1844 he was elected Moderator of the Canadian Synod and presided over their Disruption meeting at Kingston in July 1844. He became the first Moderator of the Synod of the Presbyterian Church of Canada (Free Church), and helped to establish, and sat on the board of, Knox College, Toronto.

A. L. Farris, 'Mark Young Stark', *Called to Witness*, vol. I (Toronto, 1980), 11–21.

S. D. Gill

Statistical Account of Scotland, a parish-by-parish description of Scotland, 1791–9. In May 1790 Sir John Sinclair of Ulbster announced to the General Assembly* in Edinburgh his scheme for compiling and collecting parish-by-parish accounts, which would 'examine with anatomical exactness and minuteness the internal structure of society' in Scotland, giving government the opportunity to legislate on the basis of fact and not mere surmise, ascertaining 'the quantum of happiness enjoyed by its inhabitants as the means of its future improvement'.

The General Assembly directed the parish ministers to respond to Sinclair's approach, and they did not let him down. Within two years over half had sent in replies to his queries (over 160 of them) and by the end of 1794 nearly 800 out of 938. Certainly, it took another four years to bring in the remaining reports, but these latecomers were by no means all dilatory or recalcitrant; many had delayed as they laboured diligently to produce elaborate, deeply-informed and often very perceptive replies. Sinclair had, at first, intended only to abstract and summarize the parish reports into a shorthand, national analysis; but he was so impressed by the sheer quality of the ministers' responses that he determined to issue them in full as they came in – eventually in twenty-one fat bound volumes.

Sinclair bequeathed to us an unparalleled historical source, a uniquely full view of the state of Scottish society in the later eighteenth century. The authors often showed themselves to be men of some independence of mind, very critical of heritors* and patrons* or of government itself in their commentaries. The vast majority approached their task with both energy and commitment, often taking advantage of Sinclair's suggestion that they 'consider the queries merely as a key to inquiry' to provide illuminating observations on such topics as population movements, agricultural and industrial developments, on the state of religion and the poor and schooling, on work-practices, wages and prices, etc.

As early as February 1791 George Dempster of Dunnichen wrote to Sinclair that his *Account* would be more read and quoted than any work since Doomsday Book, and 'the older it gets, the more valuable it will prove'. Other nations tried, and generally failed, to emulate Sinclair's survey, usually because their clergy could not or would not cooperate in the enterprise. The *Statistical Account of Scotland* is a remarkable testimony not only to one man's enlightened vision and 'unwearied perseverance' but also to the public-spiritedness and informed ingelligence of the ministers who collaborated with him.

The original *Account* (21 vols, E, 1791–9) has been reprinted in a new format, bringing together the parish returns into their county-groupings in 20 volumes (general editors, D. J. Withrington and I. R. Grant: Wakefield, 1973–8), each with a new introduction. The introductory essay to volume I contains an account of the making and management of Sinclair's undertaking. See also R. Mitchison, *Agricultural Sir John* (L, 1962); J. Sinclair, *Analysis of the Statistical Account of Scotland*, 2 vols (E, 1825–6).

D. J. Withrington

Stevenson, George (1772/3–1841), Secession theologian. From Morebattle in Roxburghshire, he was minister of Ayr Antiburgher (*see* General Associate Synod) Church from 1797. On the committee for union with the New Light* Burghers (*see* Associate Synod), he resisted making covenanting* non-essential (cf. *A Plea for the Covenanted Reformation* . . . , E, 1822), and with his congregation was prominent among the Protesters against the USec.C of 1820. He was moderator of the Protesters' Synod (*see* United Secession Church) in 1823 and 1827 and of the Original Secession* Synod in 1829 and 1840, having contributed the doctrinal part of the Original Secession Testimony* in 1827.

Stevenson was 'one of the best-equipped theologians of his day' (J. Macleod, *Scottish Theology*, E, ^{3}1974, 252). The College of New Jersey (Princeton) made him a DD in 1836.

A Dissertation on the Nature and Necessity of the Atonement (E, 1817); *A Treatise on the Offices of Christ* (E, 1834); 'The Grace of Christ Illustrated', in *Sermons on Miscellaneous Subjects*, by Ministers of the General Associate Synod, I (E, 1820).

Small II, 328; *ASUPC*, 406; *ASOSC*; J. M'Kerrow, *History of the Secession Church* (G, ^{2}1841).

D. F. Wright

Stevenson, John Wright (1903–73), minister, writer, and journalist. He was editor of the Kirk magazine *Life and Work** from 1945 to 1965. Previously he was CofS Press Secretary and editor of an independent weekly, *Scots Observer*, and then minister at Culter (1932–45). A man of practical piety, Stevenson's sympathies lay with the ecumenical movement and a moderate centre-left social approach, with emphasis on distinctive Scottish identity. He expressed at its best the liberalism and social concern of the Kirk in its confident post-war phase. In retirement he lived at Leighton House, Dunblane, which he restored and gave to the Scottish Churches Council.* His books included *Incredible Church* (L, 1936) and *God in my Unbelief* (L, 1960).

FES IX, 801, X, 456.

R. D. Kernohan

Stevenson, Marion Scott (1871–1930), CofS missionary in Kenya. She was born in Forfar, where her father was minister. When he died the family moved to Edinburgh. She was head girl and dux at both John Watson's College and Esdaile,* and attended classes organized by the Edinburgh Association for the University Education of Women. She went to Germany to study music and language, but returned to Scotland with the poor health which plagued her for years. She was drawn into activities supporting the foreign missions of the CofS, and eventually decided to dedicate herself to work in the field. In 1907 she travelled to Kenya as a self-supporting missionary.

Her great achievement was in the organization of education, of which she took charge at the new station of Tumutumu in 1910. By 1924, the Phelps-Stokes Commission stated 'We can assure the Government that they will travel far and wide throughout the world to find a better educational worker. Considering the time that the mission has been organized, it would hardly be possible to discover a more brilliant system of village education' (quoted in H. E. Scott's biography, *A Saint in Kenya*, L, 1932).

Towards the end of her service, Stevenson was able to delegate this work in order to concentrate on her abiding concern – work with women and girls. Most of her last days in Africa were spent under canvas as she travelled around scattered villages to visit women. Mrs. H. E. Scott speaks of her 'intellectual grasp, allied to spiritual power, dedication and reliability', and claims that 'without doubt, Marion Scott Stevenson will rank as one of the greatest missionaries of the Church' (*LW* n.s. 1, 1930, 355–7).

L. O. *Macdonald*

Stewardship. The Christian understanding of stewardship has a deeper source than the occasional use of the Hebrew and Greek words which are translated by 'steward'. This source is the whole biblical witness to the revelation of God as Creator, Lord, Father, Saviour and Spirit. In response to this revelation Christians are called to look on the universe as God's creation, to treat the earth and its resources as God's provision for the needs of all people, to regard life, personal abilities and possessions as gifts from God to be enjoyed and used in his service, to be stewards of the gospel and to share in Christ's mission to the world.

Despite its range and importance, the biblical teaching on stewardship has not found much place in the teaching of the Churches until the twentieth century. Before this, in Scotland and elsewhere, the Churches which seceded from the Established Churches were the first to rely on the practice of stewardship by their people for the support of their work. The provision made, after the Disruption* in 1843, by the members and adherents of the FC* for the building of churches and schools and the support of ministers, teachers and missionary work was a remarkable achievement in practical stewardship.

A new emphasis on the biblical teaching on stewardship came to Scotland in the twentieth century from Churches in North America, Australia and New Zealand. Because of the Churches' pressing need for financial support, the application of stewardship has often been concentrated too much on the stewardship of money. In a time when the need for care of the environment, the wise use of financial and economic power and the fair sharing of resources has also become evident and urgent, it is essential that the wider relevance of Christian stewardship should be recognized and applied within the Churches and in the world.

D. J. Hall, *The Steward* (NY, 1982); BCC Report, *Christian Stewardship in the 1980s* (L, 1980); J. H. MacNaughton, *Stewardship – Myth and Methods* (NY, 1975); R. Moss, *The Earth in our Hands* (L, 1982).

G. *Elliot*

Stewart, Alexander (*c.*1493–1513), Archbishop of St Andrews and Chancellor of Scotland. An illegitimate son of James IV, he was directed into the Church by his father at a very early age. Dispensed by Pope Alexander VI from the impediment of his illegitimacy, by 1502 he was already archdeacon of St Andrews. He was elevated to the archbishopric of St Andrews in 1504 but was merely administrator until he could be consecrated when he became twenty-seven. The see was vacant by the death of James Stewart, the king's brother, who had likewise been appointed while under age and still unconsecrated. Such appointments boded ill for the Scottish Church. James IV paid careful attention to his son's education, his early tutors being James Watson, Dean of the Faculty of Arts of St Andrews University, and the King's secretary, Patrick Paniter, and in 1507 he was sent to Italy to study rhetoric and Greek under Erasmus at Siena. Appointed Chancellor of the kingdom in 1509, he returned to Scotland in 1510 and quickly assumed the duties of his several offices. As Chancellor, he sat regularly on the King's daily Council, the Judicial Council, and as an Auditor of the Exchequer. As Chancellor of the University of St Andrews, he wanted to raise its pedagogy into a centre of humanist teaching, and in 1512 he was the joint founder, with the prior of St Andrews,* of St Leonard's College. He had already been granted the abbey of Dumferline *in commendam* in 1509, to which was added the priory of Coldingham in 1510. He was killed with his father at Flodden on 9 September 1513, a loss sharply mourned by Erasmus in his *Adages*. He had shown high promise and he took his duties seriously and conscientiously.

L. J. Macfarlane, 'The Primacy of the Scottish Church 1472–1521', *IR* 20 (1969), 111–29; R. L. Mackie and A. Spilman (eds), *The Letters of James IV 1505–1513* (E, 1953); A. I. Dunlop (ed.), *Acta Facultatis Artium Universitatis S. Andree 1413–1588*, 2 vols (E, 1964); J. Herkless and R. K. Hannay, *The Archbishops of St Andrews* (E, 1907), I; M. M. Phillips, *The 'Adages' of Erasmus* (C, 1946), 300–8.

L. J. *Macfarlane*

Stewart, Alexander (1764–1821), noted Gaelic* scholar and evangelical CofS minister. Born in the parish of Blair Atholl, Perthshire, he was CofS minister of Moulin, Perthshire (1786–1805), Dingwall, north of Inverness (1805–20) and the Canongate, Edinburgh (1820–1). Influenced by the evangelical revival* which emerged in Scotland in the 1790s, he was affected deeply by an evening exhortation given by the Anglican Evangelical, Charles Simeon,* when Simeon visited his manse in 1796 in the company of James Haldane.* 'I never was alive till then', Stewart wrote later. Thereafter he preached with new power, and a quiet but significant awakening took place in Moulin, resulting in the conversion of about seventy parishioners, mainly between March and August 1799. Among them were the parents of Alexander Duff.* Stewart extensively revised John Smith's* translation of the

STEWART, ALEXANDER

Prophets for the 1807 edition of the Gaelic Bible (see Bible (Versions, Gaelic)). A Gaelic translation of Isaac Watts' *Protection for the Young* (E, 1795) is ascribed to him, but he is best known for his popular *Gaelic Grammar* (E, 1801).

Account of a Late Revival of Religion in a Part of the Highlands of Scotland (E, 1800).

J. Sievewright, *Memoirs of the Late Alexander Stewart* (²E, 1882); D. MacKinnon, *The Gaelic Bible and Psalter* (Dingwall, 1930), 77–8.

D. E. Meek

Stewart, Alexander (1794–1847), evangelical CofS and FC minister. He was the son of Alexander Stewart* (of Moulin), and was ordained to Cromarty, a village north-east of Inverness, in 1824, continuing in the FC there. Despite its relative obscurity, he became known throughout Scotland for his preaching, especially for his typological interpretations of the Old Testament. He was influential in the conversion of Hugh Miller.* Stewart died shortly after being called to succeed R. S. Candlish* as minister of Free St George's in Edinburgh.

The Tree of Promise, with a Biographical Notice by C. Stewart and A. Beith (E, 1864); *The Mosaic Sacrifices* (E, 1883).

FES VII, 6; *AFCS* I, 327; *Disruption Worthies*, 455–62.

D. A. Currie

Stewart, David (1378–1402), Duke of Rothesay, and Lieutenant of Scotland 1399–1402. He was the eldest son of King Robert III. Owing to Robert's age and incapacity, his reign was presided over by lieutenants, first his brother Robert until 1398, then his son David 1399–1402, then Robert again. Robert and David were created Dukes of Albany and Rothesay respectively in 1398. Rothesay relied for support on his mother Annabella Drummond, Archibald 'the Grim' Earl of Douglas, and the scholarly Walter Trail,* Bishop of St Andrews. The death of these three in 1400–1 left him isolated, as did his jiltings of noblemen's daughters. Early in 1402 he was arrested by his uncle Albany, and died in obscure circumstances at Falkland Castle in Fife.

His oath of office as Lieutenant pledged him to restrain heretics;* but he was not as notably hostile to Lollards* as was Albany. He continued Scotland's loyalty to Pope Benedict XIII after France had withdrawn its allegiance in 1398. After the death of Bishop Trail in 1401, the chapter of St Andrews* elected Thomas Stewart, a bastard son of Robert II and associate of Albany, but he resigned before receiving papal confirmation; perhaps Rothesay opposed him.

Rothesay appears to have been rash and intemperate, and corrupt in his private life. In Church matters, the main features of his brief lieutenancy are loyalty to Benedict XIII and opposition to heresy; but there is no evidence of the persecution which Albany practised.

STEWART, DUGALD

Chronicles* of Wyntoun* and Bower;* records of his councils in *APS* I; R. Nicholson, *Scotland: the Later Middle Ages* (E, 1974); A. Grant, *Independence and Nationhood: Scotland, 1306–1469* (L, 1984).

A. Macquarrie

Stewart, Dugald (1753–1828), eighteenth-century Scottish philosopher. Stewart had early experience as a mathematical teacher, assisting and later succeeding his father who was Professor of Mathematics at the University of Edinburgh. For a time Stewart lectured in place of Adam Fergusson (1723–1816) and eventually (1785) was appointed to the chair of moral philosophy when Fergusson resigned. Early in his career Stewart had come under the influence of Thomas Reid (see Scottish Realism), and he came to wield considerable authority, due to his personal influence and to his gifts as a teacher, as a gifted proponent of Reid's philosophy.

In the development of Scottish philosophy it is possible to detect an increasing emphasis upon the part played by the character of the mind in the acquisition of knowledge. What started out in the writings of Reid as principles of common sense, came in the writings of Sir William Hamilton* to be *a priori* forms of intuition. Stewart adopted a mid-point in this swing of emphasis, disliking the phrase 'common sense' and appealing, against empiricism, to what he called the fundamental laws of thought. There is some unclarity as to the number of such laws, and also some confusion between claims about the conceptual structure of human knowledge and contingent psychological facts. There is more than a suggestion of parochialism about Stewart, for he seems to have had little appreciation of general, i.e. non-Scottish, philosophy after Leibniz. His grand, orotund style is evidence that he had little taste for the detail of philosophical argument or the nuances of philosophical scholarship.

Stewart stressed the need for an inductive, Baconian approach to the philosophy of the mind or psychology, based upon introspection. Presupposing the 'fundamental laws' we are, by an inductive procedure, to arrive at general psychological laws, which provide the framework of a science of the mind. The fundamental laws – e.g. I exist, I am the same person today as I was yesterday, the material world exists independently of my mind – have the status of axioms. Hovering in the background here is the idea of the unity of all science, very influential in positivist programmes in the twentieth century, but Stewart did very little with it.

As with Reid, the philosophical positions favoured by Stewart in turn favoured theism, both evangelical theism and the less demanding theism of the Moderates.* Thus the immutability of the mind establishes a presumption in favour of immortality. Moral values are objective. The argument from design for the existence of God is cogent. As did Reid, Stewart had considerable influence both in America and also in France, through the work of Victor Cousin.

Stewart retired from the Edinburgh chair in moral

philosophy in 1809, when Thomas Brown (1778–1820) became his successor. On Brown's death in 1820 Stewart again became the Professor, but shortly thereafter retired for good.

During his lifetime his home was a philosophical and literary centre in Edinburgh. He had liberal political views, and at first gave support to the early movements of the French Revolution,* but later repudiated it when its excesses became apparent.

Collected Works, ed. Sir W. Hamilton, with a memoir by J. Veitch (11 vols, E, 1854–60).

J. McCosh, *The Scottish Philosophy* (L, 1875); H. Laurie, *Scottish Philosophy in its Natural Development* (G, 1902); S. A. Grave, *The Scottish Philosophy of Common Sense* (O, 1960).

P. Helm

Stewart, James (*c*.1531–70), Earl of Moray and commendator* of St Andrews priory. He was an illegitimate son of King James V,* and therefore half-brother of Mary, Queen of Scots.* He received from James V the lands of Tantallon (E. Lothian) in 1536, and though a minor was presented to St Andrews priory in 1538. He matriculated at St Leonard's College, St Andrews in 1545. In 1549 he attended the Church's provincial council,* took his seat on the Privy Council* by 1550 and attended the burning of Adam Wallace* for heresy in 1550. A visitor to France, where he was prior of Mâcon, Stewart was a party to the marriage contract of Queen Mary to the Dauphin in 1558. For whatever motives, he embraced Protestantism, became a leader of the Lords of the Congregation,* was an active iconoclast, welcomed English intervention and attended the Reformation Parliament* in 1560. With Mary's return home in 1561 to rule in person, Stewart became the Queen's chief adviser till 1565. He gained the earldom of Moray in 1562 but fell from power with Mary's marriage to Henry, Lord Darnley, which he opposed by force. With Mary's enforced abdication in 1567, Stewart served as Regent for young James VI* until his murder at Linlithgow by James Hamilton of Bothwellhaugh.

M. Lee, *James Stewart, Earl of Moray* (NY, 1953); *DNB* LIV, 297–307.

J. Kirk

Stewart (Steuart), (Sir) James, of Goodtrees (1635–1713), Covenanter* lawyer and writer. The son of Sir James of Allanton, an Edinburgh banker and Lord Provost, a prominent Covenanter who had Hugh M'Kail* as his family chaplain, Stewart studied law and was called to the bar in 1661. But his work throughout the 1660s was almost entirely a defence of his father, who was both fined repeatedly by the rapacious Lauderdale* and imprisoned. Stewart corresponded with the Pentland insurgents (*see* Rullion Green) and co-authored with James Stirling of Paisley (*FES* III, 168), *Naphtali, or The Wrestlings of the Church of Scotland For the Kingdom of Christ; . . . with The last Speeches and Testimonies of some who have died for the Truth since the Year 1660* (E, 1667; ²1680, frequently reprinted). Stewart wrote the defence of the Covenanters and the (Presbyterian) CofS, justifying their position historically and legally. That the book was ordered to be burned, and a £10,000 fine imposed on any possessing it, only increased its popularity.

A reply having been written to *Naphtali* by Andrew Honyman* (*A Survey Of the Insolent and Infamous Libel, entituled Naphtali, &c.*, E, 1668), Stewart replied in turn with *Jus Populi Vindicatum, or The People's Right to defend themselves and their Covenanted Religion, vindicated* (L, 1669). Stewart then went to Rouen as a merchant, under the name 'Graham'; returning after a few years to Scotland, he wrote *An Accompt of Scotland's Grievances* (L, 1674), after which he fled to London. Again in Scotland in 1679, he went to Holland after the Test Act* of 1681. He wrote the *Declaration and Apology* (E, 1685) issued when Argyll came to Scotland and was sentenced to death *in absentia*. He was nevertheless invited by James VII (II) to try to persuade Presbyterians to petition for a general toleration. While in England he gave information to William of Orange regarding the general state of affairs there.

After the Revolution he was first appointed Prosecutor and then, in 1692, Lord Advocate in Scotland. He wrote the Act by which patronage* was abolished, appeared for the prosecution in the trial of Thomas Aikenhead* for blasphemy* and prepared a Habeas Corpus Act for Scotland (1701). A man universally recognized as of great ability, he remained true to the principles for which he had suffered. He was influential in the Church: 'In the affair of the Tolleration and Patronages, and I must say generally since the Revolution, most of the publick papers of this Church are his draught'. Wodrow* goes on to characterize him as 'a great Christian, ane able Statesman, one of the greatest Lawyers ever Scotland bred, of universall learning, of vast reading, great and long experience in publick business' (*Analecta* II, 205).

The Index of Abridgement of the Acts of Parliament . . . 1424 [to] *1707, before the union* (E, 1707); *The Oath of Abjuration Set in its True Light* (E, 1712).

G. W. T. Omond, *The Lord Advocates of Scotland* (E, 1888), I, 243–80; J. C. Johnston, *Treasury of the Scottish Covenant* (E, 1887), 375–6.

D. C. Lachman

Stewart, James (1831–1905), FC missionary educationalist. Born in Edinburgh, he worked to support himself through the arts course at Edinburgh University (MA, 1854). In 1855 he began theology at New College* and in 1859 the medical course at the University. During 1862–4 he was in Africa with David Livingstone's* Zambesi Expedition at the behest of a committee of Scots contemplating a mission in the area. This came to nothing, and he returned to complete his medical course in 1866. He was ordained by the FC Presbytery of Glasgow in 1865. In 1867 he joined the staff of Lovedale Institution in the Cape Colony. He made it clear that he believed advance for Africans would come

STEWART, JAMES ALEXANDER

through technical and general education for the many rather than the advanced education of the academically gifted few. When the Church authorities in Scotland refused to back him, the then principal, William Govan, resigned and Stewart replaced him in 1870. The Institution rapidly increased in size but did continue high level academic work along with Stewart's new developments.

Throughout his principalship, Lovedale was both co-educational and multi-racial. A group of very distinguished white South Africans received part of their education there alongside some of the men who were to found the African National Congress in 1912.

Despite a strong paternalist element in his character, Stewart consistently supported the legal equality of people of all racial groups in the Cape Colony, for which John Philip* had fought so tirelessly. In 1870 he founded a magazine, *The Kaffir Express*, later *The Christian Express* and now *The South African Outlook*, a vehicle for African and 'Cape liberal' opinion in which some of his best writing can be found. In 1887 he answered the many critics of 'liberal' education for Africans in a large volume, *Lovedale: Past and Present* (E, 1884), in which he detailed the careers of the 2,000 African and several hundred white pupils of the school. In his later years he devoted himself to the planning of a university for Africans, University College, Fort Hare. During two periods of leave from Lovedale, he did pioneering work in the founding of the Livingstonia Mission, Malawi, and the mission in Kenya which later became the Kikuyu Mission of the CofS. He was Moderator of the General Assembly of the FC in 1899.

The Christian Express, 1872–1906, passim.

DNB Second Suppl. III, 416–19; AFCS I, 329; FUFCS 557; J. Wells, *Stewart of Lovedale* (L, 1908); H. Davies, *Great South African Christians* (Cape Town, 1951); J. P. R. Wallis (ed.), *The Zambesi Journals of James Stewart, 1862–1863* (L, 1952); S. M. Brock, 'James Stewart and Lovedale...' (PhD, Edinburgh University, 1974).

A. C. Ross

Stewart, James Alexander (1910–75), evangelist in Europe. He was the product of devout Northern Irish parents in the fervent evangelical ethos of Glasgow. Forsaking a promising soccer career, and after only basic education, he soon became widely known as 'the boy preacher' for his street evangelism and tract distribution. He joined the Open Air Mission, but in 1934 obeyed a missionary call by promptly setting out for Riga, Latvia (of which he had heard from a Latvian student in London). There, and in Tallinn, Estonia, his preaching evoked revival,* and he was now launched on a remarkable independent evangelistic ministry in several E. European countries, most fruitfully in Hungary (where in 1938 he married an American Baptist, Ruth Mahan).

World War II compelled withdrawal to the USA, frustrating plans for a Bible School in central Europe (even though Stewart had no formal training, recognition or authorization). After the War, E. Europe was soon again closed, and the Stewarts and their associates turned to W. Europe. Their European Evangelistic Fellowship (1938) became in 1944 the European Evangelistic Crusade, with its first base in Buffalo, NY. It soon had a hundred workers in a dozen W. European countries. Stewart found structured organization irksome and withdrew from leadership, and the EEC broke up from 1958, giving birth in Britain in 1959 to the European Missionary Fellowship, led until 1988 by T. Omri Jenkins. The EMF in several respects reflects Stewart's emphases – on prayer, Bible distribution and low-key preaching evangelism, in association with independent evangelical groups in the main. Stewart himself, always dependent on interpreters, deployed in preaching powerful untutored gifts. His numerous writings are distributed by Revival Literature of Asheville, NC, where he died.

R. Stewart, *James Stewart Missionary* (Asheville, NC, 1977); T. O. Jenkins, *Five Minutes to Midnight. James Stewart and Mission to Europe* (Darlington, 1989); E. S. Watt, *Dynamite in Europe* (L, 1940).

D. F. Wright

Stewart, James Stuart (1896–1990), perhaps the most outstanding modern Scottish preacher. His father was YMCA Secretary, Dundee, and ran an influential Bible Class. As a boy he heard James Denney* preach. He was educated at Dundee High School, the University of St Andrews (classics and divinity), and after war service, at New College, Edinburgh (1918–21), proceeding to the University of Bonn (1921–2) as Cunningham Fellow. As minister he served at Auchterarder St Andrews UFC (1924–8), Aberdeen Beechgrove UFC then CofS (1928–35), and North Morningside, Edinburgh (1935–46). He collaborated with H. R. Mackintosh* in the translation of Schleiermacher's *The Christian Faith* (E, 1928), wrote the Bible Class Handbook *Life and Teaching of Jesus Christ* (L, 1933, ²1957, reissued E, 1977), gave the Cunningham Lectures* (1934) published as *A Man in Christ: The Vital Elements of St Paul's Religion* (L, 1935), and the Warrack Lectures* at Edinburgh and St Andrews (1944), *Heralds of God* (L, 1946, reissued as *Teach Yourself Preaching*, L, 1955) – all during his time as a parish minister.

While Professor of New Testament Language, Literature and Theology, University of Edinburgh (1947–66), he served as Moderator of the General Assembly, CofS (1963–4), and gave the Hoyt Lectures, Union Theological Seminary, New York (1949), Lyman Beecher Lectures, Yale (1952) published as *A Faith to Proclaim* (L, 1953), Duff Missionary Lectures* (1953) published as *Thine is the Kingdom* (E, 1956), and Stone Lectures, Princeton (1962). He published several collections of sermons: *The Gates of New Life* (E, 1937), *The Strong Name* (E, 1940), *The Wind of the Spirit* (L, 1968), *River of Life* (L, 1972), *King for Ever* (L, 1974).

His preaching was based on a carefully worked out theology of the New Testament. Stewart, following Deissmann, taught that union with Christ was the centre of Paul's doctrine. Union happened when the sinful soul was confronted with the sacrifice of the Father and the Son and abandoned itself to that love. Self-abandonment is faith. Participation in the death and resurrection of Christ brought the possession of the new status and carried with it life. There is no separation of justification and sanctification. A socialist, he did not preach socialism. He was shy, but an assiduous writer of warm pastoral letters.

Malcolm McDow, 'The Study of the Preaching of James Stewart', (PhD, New Orleans Baptist Theological Seminary, 1968); William M. Pinson and Clyde E. Fant, *Twenty Centuries of Great Preaching*, vol. 13 (Waco, TX, 1971); appreciation by R. A. S. Barbour (New College, 1990).

J. C. O'Neill

Stewart, John (d.1579), fourth Earl of Atholl, Chancellor of Scotland. As a staunch RC, Atholl remained loyal to Mary of Guise* throughout her regency, and in 1560 opposed the Protestant legislation of the Reformation Parliament.* He was also close to Mary Queen of Scots,* being appointed to her Privy Council* in 1561, but was alienated by her marriage to the Earl of Bothwell in 1567. During the civil war he changed sides twice, ending it in 1573 as one of the victorious King's Party. In the first week of March 1578 Atholl participated in a coup at Stirling which prematurely ended the regency of James Douglas,* fourth Earl of Morton.* Atholl was appointed Chancellor, but was forced to come to an accommodation with Morton when the latter seized the King back on 27 April.

DNB LIV, 323–5; *Scots Peerage* I, 444–5; G. Donaldson, *All The Queen's Men* (L, 1983).

K. M. Brown

Stewart, Robert (c.1521–86), bishop-elect of Caithness. A younger son of John, third Earl of Lennox, he pursued an ecclesiastical career as provost of Dumbarton collegiate* kirk (from 1539) and as bishop-elect of Caithness, which he administered from 1542. For supporting the unsuccessful rising of his brother, Matthew fourth Earl of Lennox, at Henry VIII's instigation, in 1544, he was deprived of his bishopric. He was incorporated in St Andrews University in 1548, regained his bishopric, and visited France with Mary of Guise* in 1550. He attended the burning of Walter Milne* for heresy in 1558 but conformed to the Reformation* and served the Kirk as commissioner in Caithness. In his later years, he retired to St Andrews where he gained the commendatorship* of the priory on the death of Lord James Stewart,* the Earl of Moray, in 1570. He acquired the earldom of Lennox in 1578, which he subsequently relinquished for the earldom of March in 1580.

Dowdon 249–51; *FES* VII, 336; J. Kirk, *Patterns of Reform* (E, 1989).

J. Kirk

Stewart, Robert (c.1550–1633), reader* and parish minister in Orkney. Stewart probably owed his initial appointment (c.1567) as reader in the parishes of Birsay and Harray to the reforming bishop, Adam Bothwell.* Then, in an extraordinarily long ministry apparently of about sixty-six years, he was successively minister of the parishes of Orphir, Hoy and Graemsay, and Holm. Stewart was Episcopalian in his sympathies, and was a consistent supporter of Bishops James Law (1605–15) and George Grahame (1615–38; *FES* VII, 353). He was described by the historian J. B. Craven (himself an Episcopalian) as 'standing far beyond all others in learning, godliness and sincerity'.

J. B. Craven, *History of the Church in Orkney, 1558–1662* (Kirkwall, 1893); id., *Scots Worthies* (E, 1894); A. Goodfellow, *Birsay Church History* (Kirkwall, 1903); J. Smith, *The Church in Orkney* (Kirkwall, 1907).

W. P. L. Thomson

Stewart, William (1479–1545), churchman. The son of Sir Thomas Stewart of Minto, Roxburghshire, he was born in Glasgow. He held a number of benefices (parson of Lochmaben, 1528, Prebendary of Glasgow as rector of Ayr, Provost of Lincluden, Kirkcudbrightshire, 1529–36, Dean of Glasgow, 1530–3) before becoming Bishop of Aberdeen in 1532. He was also High Treasurer of Scotland 1530–7. In 1533–4 he served on embassies to England and France, while with Cardinal David Beaton* and others he tried Sir John Borthwick* at St Andrews in 1540. He built the library at King's College, Aberdeen, and enlarged the College with other benefactions.

FESMA 4, 155, 365; Dowden 139–41; C. Innes, *Registrum Episcopatus Aberdonensis* I (Maitland and Spalding Club; E, 1845), lvi–lviii.

D. F. Wright

Stewarton Case, dispute focusing on conflict between Church and state.* The judgment in this case may be seen as the last milestone on the road to the Disruption* (see Auchterarder Cases; Strathbogie Cases). In 1839 the 'Auld Licht' Burghers (see New Light) returned to the fellowship of the Kirk. One of their charges was a new cause established in the town of Stewarton, Ayrshire, whose minister was James Cleland (*FES* III, 127). The Presbytery of Irvine welcomed the new body, granted Cleland a seat, and resolved to carve out a parish for the new cause, erecting it into a parish *quoad sacra*.* William Cuninghame of Lainshaw* and some other of the heritors* objected, claiming that new parishes could be created only by the Court of Teinds* (the Court of Session* wearing another hat) and also that Cleland as a chapel minister had no right to sit or vote in the Presbytery. They raised a successful action in the courts. The Presbytery decided to contest the matter, which went to a bench of the whole Court of Session, where it was decided by eight votes to five in favour of Cuninghame. This meant in effect that the Chapels Act* had been declared illegal. Such a decision reached at such a time (January 1843) made the Disruption practically inevitable.

F. Lyall, *Of Presbyters and Kings* (A, 1980), 43-6.

A. Herron

Stickit Minister, a Scots term of disparagement for a minister who fails to 'make the grade' in his profession, and has to turn to other employment (*e.g.* school-teaching). The adjective 'stickit' is the past participle of the verb 'stick'; it can be applied to any object which has 'stuck' in its growth, so that it is incomplete (of a task), stunted (of crops, plants or persons), insufficiently qualified or unsuccessful (of persons). In nineteenth-century literature the epithet 'stickit' was sometimes applied to a minister who was unable to complete his first sermon, and 'stuck' in the middle of the discourse (see, for example, Walter Scott's *Guy Mannering*). This reflects the strong Scottish emphasis on 'correct' delivery in preaching, but it is probably fanciful. The term was apparently adopted by Gaelic* speakers, who related it to 'stick, piece of wood', and coined the phrase *ministear maide* ('wooden minister'). Conveying 'woodenness' in style and lack of evangelical spontaneity, the Gaelic term was used initially of allegedly time-serving Moderate* ministers of the Established Church,* especially after the Disruption,* but came to be applied more generally to 'worldly' non-evangelical ministers.

W. Grant and D. Murison (eds), *The Scottish National Dictionary*, 10 vols (E, 1931-76), IX, 38-9; N. Dickson, *The Kirk and its Worthies* (L, 1912), 29-32.

D. E. Meek

Still, William (1911-), minister of Gilcomston South CofS, Aberdeen (1945-) and spearhead of conservative Evangelicalism in the CofS from the 1950s. Born in Aberdeen and raised in the Salvation Army,* he was a gifted musician, serving as organist at Crown Street Methodist Church, Aberdeen, during Vincent Taylor's ministry. After studies at Aberdeen University, he became Assistant Minister, Springburn Hill CofS, Glasgow (1944-5).

Distinctive elements in his lengthy ministry at Gilcomston South include: systematic biblical exposition (in which he was a pioneer followed by large numbers of evangelical ministers), the centrality of corporate prayer, and what he once called 'unstarching the church' (creating a simple congregational lifestyle uncluttered by non-essential organizations). In his hands *The Gilcomston Record* (congregational bulletin) developed into a widely-distributed and eagerly-read monthly magazine, containing a vigorous and wide-ranging pastoral letter, pages of current news of Christian work and daily Bible study notes.

Central emphases of his teaching include: the graciousness of the gospel, the humanity (human-ness) of the divine Christ, Scripture as the 'Spirit's sword' (cf. Eph. 6:17), union with Christ (cf. Rom. 6:1ff.) as the heart of the Christian life understood as warfare against Satan (Bunyanesque in its rigour). As a pastor, he early saw his bachelor status as a God-given means for devoting himself to developing the family character of life in the church and to encouraging students and young people in Christian discipleship.

He founded the Crieff Fraternal* in 1971. In 1974 he declined Aberdeen University's offer of a DD. He served as Honorary President of British IVF (UCCF) in 1975 (*see* Inter-Varsity Fellowship).

Dying to Live (autobiography) (Fearn, Ross-shire, 1991); *Collected Writings* (ed. N. M. de S. Cameron, S. B. Ferguson), 3 vols (E, 1990-); *History of Gilcomston South Church*, 3 vols (A, 1968-85); *Towards Spiritual Maturity* (G, 1986); *Letters of William Still* (E, 1984).

N. M. de S. Cameron and S. B. Ferguson (eds), *Pulpit and People. Essays in Honour of William Still on his 75th Birthday* (E, 1986); *FES* IX, 561, X, 326.

S. B. Ferguson

Stipend, the 'living' allowance received by a full-time minister in most Churches. In the CofS it goes with a parish* and is paid to a minister in virtue of his having been inducted to a charge.* At one time it was the only payment the minister received and out of it he had to meet all the outlays incurred in the discharge of his office. Today it is, for all practical purposes, equivalent to a salary, paid monthly in arrears to the minister concerned, out of funds generally supplied by his congregation and supplemented by payment of expenses incurred in travelling and in other ways.

Under the old system in Scotland stipend was paid out of teind* - the tithes of Old Testament times. It was paid by the heritors* out of the fruits of the soil, and originally consisted of such fruits, being specific amounts of victual, that is, so much of each of the crops native to the parish. Stipend was vested in the minister who was in the charge at Michaelmas in each year, and was payable at Whitsunday and Michaelmas. It took no account of how long he had been in the charge. It was subject to ann,* an arrangement whereby six months' stipend of a deceased minister went not into his estate but direct to his widow (cf. Cox 291-2, 671).

In terms of an Act of 1808 it became obligatory to pay stipend in currency, and to enable the conversion to be made a system of fixing Fiars' Prices* operated. In 1925, in virtue of the Church of Scotland (Property and Endowments) Act of that year, a system of standardization was imposed whereby on the first occurrence of a vacancy the obligation was converted into a fixed charge, being collected by the CofS General Trustees* who held it, not necessarily wholly for the minister, but for the parish and its neighbourhood. As a result of inflation these moneys which once represented a generous income are now, in almost every case, a small endowment towards the stipend provided for the minister by the congregation.

The amount of the stipend of each CofS charge is today fixed by the Presbytery concerned with concurrence of the relevant General Assembly committee; and when this is beyond the resources of the congregation(s) concerned a system of 'aid' comes to the rescue so that no stipend falls below a 'minimum' declared at the previous General Assembly.

Part-time ministers are in some churches, such as the EpCS, identified as 'non-stipendiary' (cf. Auxiliary Ministry*).

A. J. H. Gibson, *Stipend in the Church of Scotland* (E, 1961); A. Herron, *A Guide to Ministerial Income* (E, 1987); N. V. Hope, 'Ministerial Stipends in the Church of Scotland from 1560 to 1833' (PhD, Edinburgh University, 1944).

A. Herron

Stirling Tract Enterprise. It was founded by Peter Drummond (1799–1877), seed-merchant, active Free Churchman, and uncle of Henry Drummond.* The response to a first tract, issued in 1848, was so encouraging that Drummond rapidly expanded his activities: three million pieces of literature had been distributed by the end of 1851. In 1853, now committed full-time to the Enterprise, Drummond launched the monthly *British Messenger*: it was followed by other periodicals, foreign language material and, from the 1880s, by books. All these publications aimed to promote spiritual revival and to uphold Christian values. Their effectiveness is difficult to assess: the development of the railway network and reforms in the postal service made widespread distribution possible for the first time, and Drummond despatched a staggering volume of literature – sixty million items by 1872. But the work of the Enterprise was largely funded by donations, many tracts being issued freely in bulk for distribution to the final audience, and it is open to question how many were actually read. In 1863, the Drummond Trust* was established to run the Enterprise: Drummond himself retired in 1872. A high level of output continued until the 1950s, after which inflation and the supplanting of the tract by more potent media led to the decline and eventual closure of the Enterprise in 1980.

See also Publishing, Religious; Scottish Colportage Society.

J. Birkbeck, *Peter Drummond* (Stirling, 1984); M. J. Cormack, *The Stirling Tract Enterprise and the Drummonds* (Stirling, 1984).

J. A. H. Dempster

Stool of Repentance. In Reformed Churches it was believed that discipline* of the congregation in moral behaviour must accompany preaching and sacraments. Minister and Kirk Session were to supervise the order and morality of the parish and punish breaches of the Ten Commandments. Sinners had to sit or stand in a prominent place in the church for one or more Sundays, according to the magnitude of the offence, sometimes clad in sackcloth or linen sheet. Repentance had to be declared before absolution. Normally the prominent place was before a pillar but most often it was at a stool before the pulpit, called the stool of repentance or cutty (low, short) stool. Sabbath-breaking, any social disorder, but most commonly sexual misbehaviour brought this punishment in the seventeenth and eighteenth centuries. In the nineteenth, practice died out, being replaced by private Kirk Session* or ministerial action. Then and in earlier days, it was sometimes possible to have the punishment commuted to money payment for the poor.

A. Edgar, *Old Church Life in Scotland* (Paisley, 1885); W. Steuart of Pardovan, *Collections and Observations Methodiz'd* (E, 1709).

A. I. Dunlop

Story, Robert (1790–1859), CofS minister, an Evangelical who stayed in the Est.C at the Disruption.* Born in Yetholm, Roxburgh, Story attended Edinburgh University 1805–11, and then taught privately for four years. In 1815, after being licensed by the Presbytery of Haddington, he became assistant to George Drummond, Minister of Rosneath on the Gareloch, Dunbartonshire. In 1818 Story succeeded him. His ensuing ministry wrought a profound moral reformation in the parish.

When McLeod Campbell* became minister of Row (adjoining Rosneath), Story became his fast friend; during Campbell's trial for heresy, Story defended him almost single-handed before Presbytery and Synod. He escaped deposition himself only because he rejected Campbell's obnoxious phraseology of 'universal pardon'. Story was also involved at this time in the rise of 'Irvingism' (*see* Irving, Edward), since Mary Campbell* lived in his parish. When she spoke in tongues in 1830 Story initially inclined to believe in the authenticity of the phenomenon. He soon lost faith, however, and attempts to persuade him to join the Catholic Apostolic Church* met with no success.

At the Disruption, half Story's flock left him for the FC. He remained, however, on good terms with several FC ministers (e.g. Thomas Chalmers,* an old friend), despite the fact that he drifted latterly from the Calvinism of his youth in favour of the teachings of F. D. Maurice and F. W. Robertson. He retained to the end, however, his ethical fervour and Christ-centred preaching and spirituality.

Story was the father of R. H. Story.*

Peace in Believing: A Memoir of Isabella Campbell of Fernicarry (Greenock, 1829; new ed., L. 1854).

R. H. Story, *Memoir of the Life of the Rev. Robert Story* (C, 1862); *DNB* LIV, 430; *FES* III, 364.

N. R. Needham

Story, Robert Herbert (1835–1907), eminent CofS divine and Scoto-Catholic* pioneer. Born in Rosneath, Argyll, the son of Robert Story,* he studied arts at Edinburgh University 1849–54, and then divinity at Edinburgh and St Andrews 1854–7. Licensed in 1858 by the Presbytery of Dunbarton, in 1859 he was assistant minister in St Andrew's Church, Montreal, Canada, and ordained by the Presbytery of Montreal, before returning to Scotland to succeed his father as minister of Rosneath in 1860, where he remained for twenty-six years.

During that period, Story's influence and stature as a Church court debater and public figure steadily grew, and he was rewarded in 1886 with three appointments, as Junior Clerk to the General Assembly, chaplain to Queen Victoria and Professor of Church History at Glasgow University. In 1894 he acted as Moderator of the General Assembly, and the following year became its Principal Clerk. In 1898 he was appointed Principal of Glasgow University, a position he held till his death.

Story was instrumental in the founding of the Church Service Society* in 1865, the aim of which was to make the worship of the CofS more seemly and liturgical (*see* Liturgy). Accordingly Story introduced into Rosneath Church a choir, an organ, stained glass windows and Christmas day services. Accusations of Romanizing fell somewhat wide of the mark, since his theology was that of a staunchly Protestant liberal who detested Anglo- and Roman Catholicism as much as he did the traditional Calvinism of his own Church. Rejecting biblical infallibility, substitutionary atonement and the Reformed doctrine of election, Story preached a gospel of God's universal Fatherhood and a conception of Christ's death which owed not a little to John McLeod Campbell.* The deity of Christ, however, proved a sticking point, and in 1897 he supported the deposition from the ministry of Alexander Robinson* of Kilmun, who had broached deistic* views in his book *The Saviour in the Newer Light* (E, 1895).

Story's liberalism led him to champion the abolition of religious tests in university theological appointments, and the relaxation of subscription to the Westminster* Confession by ministers and elders. However, he remained deeply committed to the ideal of a national Church, and spared no effort in promoting the work of the Church Defence Association in the struggle against Voluntaryism* and disestablishment.

Story received a DD from Edinburgh University in 1874, and an LLD from Michigan University in 1897 and St Andrews University in 1900.

Memoir of the Life of the Rev. Robert Story (C, 1862); *The Apostolic Ministry in the Scottish Church* (Baird lectures* for 1897, G, 1897); *Life and Remains of Robert Lee* (L, 1870); *William Carstares* (L, 1874); *The Reformed Ritual in Scotland* (Lee lecture* for 1886, E, 1886). Story edited *The Scottish Church*, later called *The Scots Magazine*, 1885–9, and *The Church of Scotland, Past and Present*, 5 vols (L, 1890–1).

Memoir of Robert Herbert Story (G, 1909) – by daughters; FES VII, 398–9; *DNB Second Suppl.* 431–3.

N. R. Needham

Stow, David (1793–1864), educational reformer. He was born in Paisley, son of a merchant there, and educated at Paisley Grammar School. His major publications are *Moral Training, Infant and Juvenile* (G, 1834), *The Training System* (G, 1836).

A devoted elder in Thomas Chalmers'* Tron parish in Glasgow, and an early member of Chalmers' Tron Sabbath School Society (1816), David Stow shared his mentor's view that the only sure way to reclaim Scotland (especially urban Scotland) from religious indifference, immorality and criminality, and secularist radicalism was through the inculcation of faith and morality through early religious instruction. Stow was convinced that simple Bible exposition, attractively presented as the core of an infant-training system, could counteract the worst environmental influences of Glasgow, in and out of home and at all social levels. His training system was to incorporate a novel pedagogy, emphasizing observation and activity-methods in a school atmosphere marked out by sympathy and kindly exploration. Stow founded the Glasgow Infant School Society in 1826, and by 1832 his own school was effectively also a 'normal college' for the professional training of teachers and a very important influence in the development of state-supported teacher-training in Britain in and after 1839.

Stow shared also Chalmers' fierce dedication to the idea of a national Est.C supported by the state and responsible to state and people for the supervision and control of national schooling. He developed his infant-training system at the height of the Voluntary Controversy,* when the Voluntaries violently attacked the principle of Church establishment and particularly government financing of Church-related schooling. Stow reacted, in conjunction with George Lewis (editor of the *Scottish Guardian*, a newspaper founded in order to support Church endowments) and the newly-arrived Robert Buchanan* at the Tron, by setting up the Glasgow Educational Society as an agency for Church defence. Almost the first action of the society was to publish *Scotland, a Half-Educated Nation* (ed. G. Lewis; G, 1834), an extreme and violent attack on Voluntaryism* in Scotland for having caused a sad decline in both the quantity and quality of Scottish education, especially the quality of teachers, and claiming that only a revived and much-extended parochial system under the aegis of the national Church could meet the rightful demands of the people. Melbourne's Liberals declined to act; but Peel's new Conservatives gave the CofS more money for school-extension in 1839 and in 1841 offered a lifeline to Stow's Dundas Vale training college and school (opened 1836), then in deep financial troubles, by making an outright grant of £5,000 and £500 annually on condition that it was made over to the General Assembly of the CofS. Paradoxically, this new arrangement was quickly to be followed by the Disruption.* When Stow and his teachers and students, and the vast bulk of the schoolchildren, left the Est.C, they abandoned Dundas Vale and the immediate prospect of government support, and were to be dependent on the voluntary contributions of the new FC through which to set up new schools and colleges.

M. Cruikshank, *A History of the Training of Teachers in Scotland* (L, 1970); W. Fraser, *Memoir of the Life of David Stow* (L, 1868); D J Withrington, '"Scotland a Half-Educated Nation" in 1834?

Strachan, Douglas (1875–1950), artist in stained glass. Strachan was born in Aberdeen, the son of a solicitor. He was educated at Robert Gordon's College and Gray's School of Art in Aberdeen and at the Royal Scottish Academy. After gaining experience as a newspaper artist and cartoonist he continued his studies in Europe and the Middle East and he eventually found an opening for his gifts in the art of stained glass. His designs displayed an awe-inspiring power of expressing in brilliant colour biblical imagery, mystic symbolism, historical events and heroic challenge.

His work is found in St Giles' Cathedral; in Glasgow and Dunblane Cathedrals; in St John's Church, Perth; St Paul's, Greenock; Holy Trinity, St Andrews; St Modan's, Rosneath; and the East Kirk of St Nicholas, Aberdeen. He designed the windows in the War Memorial Shrine in Edinburgh Castle but, splendid as they are, he did not regard them as among his finest work.

Outside Scotland, he gained recognition by his designs for the windows contributed by Great Britain to the Peace Palace at the Hague. He designed the splendid series of windows in Westminster College, Cambridge (the gift of Lord Kirkley), and in the Church of St Thomas the Martyr, Winchelsea (the gift of Lord Blanesburgh). Both series span the whole Christian scheme of salvation from the creation to the completion of the new creation in the communion of saints in heaven.

He was elected an honorary member of the RSA in 1920 and he received the degree of LLD from Aberdeen University in 1923.

The Times and *The Scotsman*, 21 November 1950; *DNB 1941–50*, 845–6; C. L. Warr, *The Glimmering Landscape* (L, 1960); R. B. Knox, *Westminster College, Cambridge* (C, 1980); M. Saville, *The Story of Winchelsea Church* (St. Leonards-on-sea, *c.*1980); A. C. Russell, *Stained Glass Windows of Douglas Strachan* (Aberlemno, 1972).

R. B. Knox

Strachan, George (*c.*1572–*c.*1640), orientalist. Born probably at Thornton, Kincardineshire, he was a student in Paris by 1592, and thereafter at several French universities, including Pont-à-Mousson (attracted by William Barclay*) and Carpentras, in the diocese of William Chisholm, nephew and successor of his namesake (*d.*1593).* A tribute by Strachan appeared in Chisholm's *Examen Confessionis Fidei Calvinianae* (Avignon, 1601). In the early 1600s visits to Scotland (where his family had turned Protestant) alternated with sojourns in Rome, where he was an early student at the Scots College.* A courier between Rome and Scottish RCs, he published a verse celebration of Paul V's election (1605). After teaching in Paris (1604–7) and serving the Duke of Guise, he turned to the East. By 1610 he was resident on the Euphrates, and for three decades or so he travelled widely, mastered languages, collected manuscripts and worked for the East India Company. His surviving manuscripts are now mostly in the Vatican and Naples. For his years in the East the Italian Pietro Della Valle (1586–1652) is an important source, as Thomas Dempster* is for his earlier life. His writings, in Latin, mostly deal with the classics.

G. L. Dellavida, *George Strachan. Memorials of a Wandering Scottish Scholar . . .* (Third Spalding Club; A, 1956); D. McRoberts, 'George Strachan of the Mearns, An Early Scottish Orientalist', *IR* 3 (1952), 110–28; J. F. K. Johnstone, *The Alba Amicorum of George Strachan . . .* (A, 1924), 1–17.

D. F. Wright

Strachan, Harry (1872–1945), founder of the Latin American Mission. Born to Scottish Presbyterians in Ontario, Canada, he was brought up in Aberdeen, Scotland, after 1879. He ran away from home to England, where he was much influenced by independent Evangelicals. After gaining evangelistic experience he prepared, in London, for mission in the Congo. However, he left for Argentina (with the Regions Beyond Missionary Union) in 1902. Known as 'a hard-driving Scotchman' he pioneered bold evangelistic forays far and wide. After arriving in New York in 1918 he founded 'the Latin America Evangelistic Campaign' (1921). Based in San José, Costa Rica, it became the Latin America Mission in 1938. His interdenominational, evangelistic campaigns throughout the sub-continent prepared the way for the launching of the Evangelism-in-Depth movement by his son, R. Kenneth Strachan.

[Anon] 'Missionary to a Continent. The Life Story of Dr Harry Strachan', *The Latin American Evangelist* 24 (Jan.–Apr. 1945), 3–7, 25–6; E. Elliott, *Who Shall Ascend? The Life of R. Kenneth Strachan of Costa Rica* (L, 1968).

A. C. Smith

Strachan, John (1778–1867), Anglican Bishop of Toronto. Born in Aberdeen of an Episcopalian father and Secessionist Presbyterian mother, he became a schoolteacher and attended St Andrews University part-time. In 1799 he accepted a position as tutor at Kingston in Upper Canada (Ontario). In 1803 he sought Anglican ordination and became incumbent of the St Lawrence river town of Cornwall. In this situation he was distinguished for conducting a school which produced some of the colony's leading citizens. In 1812 he began his association with York (Toronto), which would last for the rest of his life, and in which he would be successively rector, archdeacon, and bishop.

Strachan was an ecclesiastical statesman who sought the expansion and maintenance of the Church of England as the religious establishment of British North America. In order to fulfil this vision he particularly worked for Anglican control of education, especially at the university level, and the endowment of the Church through what were known as the Clergy Reserves. Aware that Anglicans were a decided minority of the population, Strachan engaged in herculean labors to defend his 'ancient Christendom' view of Church and society. He secured appointment to both the Executive Council and the Legislative Council, where he was heart and soul of the Tory Family Compact. He was also president of the Board for the General Superintendance of Education. He made trips to Britain seeking support. He attacked the burgeoning Methodists, whose enthusiastic evangelism he detested, accusing them spitefully of disloyalty. On this level Strachan's work was a failure, as by mid-century the inevitable forces of North American pluralism and egalitarianism made an Anglican establishment impossible of realization.

At the same time Strachan was one of the builders of Canada* in Church and state. Under his leadership Anglican congregations were erected throughout the colony to care for English and Irish immigrants, while educational institutions such as Trinity College, Toronto were also brought into being. He also helped to create a society which stressed the co-operation of Church and state.

A. N. Bethune, *Memoir of the Right Reverend John Strachan, first Bishop of Toronto* (Toronto and L, 1870); *Dictionary of Canadian Biography* IX, 751–66; J. L. H. Henderson, *John Strachan 1778–1867* (Toronto, 1969); S. Boorman, *John Toronto: A Biography of Bishop Strachan* (Toronto, 1969).

I. S. Rennie

Straiton (Stratoun), David, of Woodstone (*d.* 1534), Protestant martyr.* He was burnt in Edinburgh for heresy* after refusing to pay fishing teinds* (tithe) – he had each tenth fish thrown back for the Prior of St Andrews to collect personally. Following excommunication for non-payment, he was indicted for heresy.

Knox* records that Straiton discussed his beliefs with John Erskine of Dun* and had portions of the Scriptures read to him. Refusing to recant, he became one of the few lairds to suffer for his faith. His nephew Andrew Straiton of Laurieston (Kincardineshire) supported the Reformation in 1560 as anti-clericalism in the Mearns developed over thirty years to full Protestantism.

Knox, *History* I, 24–5; F. D. Bardgett, *Scotland Reformed* (E, 1989); J. M. Scott, *Martyrs of Angus and Mearns* (Arbroath, 1885), 78–98; M. Sanderson, *Cardinal of Scotland* (E, 1986).

F. D. Bardgett

Strang, John (1584–1654), Principal of Glasgow University. The son of William Strang, minister of Irvine, Ayrshire, he graduated from St Andrews University in 1600, and afterwards taught in St Leonard's College there as a regent. He was appointed minister of Errol, Perthshire, in 1614. From the first he seems to have rejected both extremes in the disputes about the relationship of the Crown and the Church. On the one hand he was in favour sufficiently to be one of the first to be awarded the degree of DD (by St Andrews University) when it was revived on the King's orders in 1616; to be appointed a member of the Court of High Commission* in 1618; and to be appointed Principal of Glasgow University in 1626. But on the other hand he opposed the Five Articles of Perth* in the 1617 General Assembly, and opposed the introduction of the new Scottish Prayer Book* in 1637. As the quarrel with Charles I* grew, opinions tended to polarize, and John found that increasingly his moderate stance offended both extremes. He opposed the National Covenant* at first, but later accepted it. As the 1638 Glasgow Assembly* approached he and others in Glasgow University drew up a protest at elders taking part in elections to the Assembly and sitting as members of it, but in the face of threats from the Covenanters* first his colleagues and then Strang himself withdrew. Subsequently charges of heresy were brought against him. After scrutinizing his statements, the Assembly of 1647 found in favour of his orthodoxy. This decision, Wodrow said, masked the real complaint and was in large degree the result of personal friendships. Many remained dissatisfied and in 1650 Strang resigned his office, though at his request he was given a certificate of orthodoxy, particularly in regard to Arminianism.* As Reid puts it, this represented a victory for the Covenanters and a defeat for Robert Baillie,* his son-in-law. He devoted his last years to preparing his works for publication, but failed to complete the task, entrusting this work to Baillie in his will.

De Voluntate et Actionibus Dei circa Peccatum (Amsterdam, 1657); *Tractatus de Interpretatione et Perfectione Scripturae* (Rotterdam, 1663), with Life by Baillie.

DNB LV, 18; *FES* IV, 206, VII, 394; note on Strang by D. Laing in R. Baillie, *Letters and Journals*, 3 vols (E, 1841), I, ci–cii; H. M. B. Reid, *The Divinity Principals of the University of Glasgow* (G, 1917), 252–302.

D. Stevenson

Strathbogie Cases, legal processes reflecting the conflict between Church and state that led to the Disruption.* The parish of Marnoch, near Huntly, Aberdeenshire, fell vacant in 1837 and John Edwards (1791–1848) was duly presented. The local inn-keeper alone signed the call* while 261 heads of families exercised the veto. Presbytery sought guidance from the Synod, who passed the issue to the Commission of Assembly, who emphatically said 'Reject', as the Presbytery did. This the patron accepted, but not so Edwards, who raised an action to be taken on trials. By a majority the Presbytery resolved to await the judgment of the civil court. For this they were censured by the Commission. Scarcely had the censure been passed when the Court of Session decreed that the Presbytery was to proceed, and, the House of Lords having found the Veto Act* illegal, the Presbytery took Edwards on trials, sustained them, and proposed to have him inducted. The Commission of Assembly met specifically to deal with the situation. They annulled

STRATHPEFFER

all the Presbytery had done and suspended from office the seven ministers who formed the Presbytery majority, ordaining that intimation of sentence was to be made by the four remaining (minority) ministers. Four days after this sentence the seven met as the Presbytery of Strathbogie, applying (successfully) to the Court of Session for interdict against the others entering their parishes and officiating therein. Edwards now raised an action to be inducted or paid damages, the former part of his crave being granted. On a bleak January day five ministers appeared at Marnoch and amid scenes of considerable uproar and unhappiness Edwards was admitted as minister of the parish. To the following Assembly commissioners were sent both by the majority, who claimed that having been improperly suspended they were the Presbytery, and by the minority, who claimed to be now the whole Presbytery. The latter (though under interdict of the civil court) were accepted. This of course led to questions about the legality of the Assembly itself.

See also Auchterarder Cases; Stewarton Case.

FES VI, 323-4; F. Lyall, *Of Presbyters and Kings. Church and State in the Law of Scotland* (A, 1980), 37-41.

A. Herron

Strathpeffer, see Conventions.

Strong, Charles (1844-1942), CofS minister and liberal theologian. Strong was educated at Glasgow University (1859-67) and deeply influenced by John Caird.* He was ordained and inducted to the Old West Kirk, Greenock, in 1868, moved to Anderston, Glasgow, in 1871, and on Caird's advice was called to Scots' Church, Melbourne, Victoria, in 1875. His deviation from orthodox theology and sympathy with Unitarianism* attracted notice from 1877 onwards, and formal processes against him were begun in 1880. The case came to a climax in 1883, when the General Assembly declared him no longer a Presbyterian minister and dissolved the pastoral tie. In 1885 Strong became minister of the 'Australian Church' which his supporters founded. Initially it was a flourishing congregation of liberal theological persuasion, but difficulties soon emerged. The new Church lost support because of Strong's radical political views, which included campaigns against the Boer War, imperialism and conscription for World War I. The Church finally terminated in 1957. Its assets were applied to create a memorial trust whose main aim is to promote liberal Christian religion. Strong was also known for his ardent social concern for underprivileged people.

FES III, 390. VII, 598-9; C. R. Badger, *The Reverend Charles Strong and the Australian Church* (Melbourne, 1971); *Australian Dictionary of Biography* VI, 208-9.

A. M. Harman

Struthers, Gavin (1791-1858), Relief* Church minister and writer. Born in Udstonhead, Lanark-

STRUTHERS, JOHN PATERSON

shire, he was educated at Glasgow University. Licensed by the Relief Presbytery of Glasgow in 1817, he was ordained the same year to Anderston, Glasgow, where he spent his entire ministry.

Although not a great preacher, by the 1830s Struthers had become the leading figure in the Relief Church, by virtue of his intellectual abilities and pastoral wisdom. He played a prominent part in the movement which issued in the union of the Relief and USec.C in 1847 (*see* United Presbyterian Church). Throughout his career he championed Relief principles, particularly free communion and Voluntaryism.* He was also a zealous supporter of missions, acting as a secretary of the Glasgow Missionary Society from 1824.

Struthers' enduring literary monument is his *History of the Rise, Progress and Principles of the Relief Church* (G, 1843). A somewhat diffuse work, it is nevertheless a treasury of useful information about Relief history and more generally Scottish religious history. Although published in the year of the Disruption,* Struthers' book is characterized by the polemical antagonism which the Campbeltown case* aroused between the Relief and CofS Evangelicals.

Struthers received a DD from Glasgow University in 1843, and was Moderator of the UP Synod in 1848.

A Treatise on Scriptural Terms of Communion (G, 1836); *An Explanation of the Shorter Catechism* (G, 1845).

'Sketch...' in *UP Magazine*, new ser., 2 (1858), 455-62.

N. R. Needham

Struthers, John Paterson (1851-1915), Reformed Presbyterian* minister. Born in Glasgow, he attended Glasgow University from 1866, graduating MA, and then studied theology at the University under John Caird,* supplemented by classes at the FC College and the Divinity Hall of the United Original Sec.C. A distinguished student of Greek, he declined the offer of a Greek professorship in an Australian university in order to become a RPC minister. The majority of Reformed Presbyterians merged with the FC in 1876, but Struthers continued with the small non-uniting minority. Licensed that year, he pastored a congregation at Whithorn in Wigtownshire from 1878, then at Greenock, Renfrewshire, from 1882 until his death. He declined Glasgow University's DD in 1895.

Despite continuing in the RPC, Struthers had a broad mind. He was a close friend and admirer of James Denney* and sympathized with the UFC in their dispute with the FC. He was an ardent advocate of temperance;* his two great hatreds, according to his wife, were drink and RCism.

Struthers edited *The Morning Watch*, a halfpenny children's magazine. H. R. Mackintosh* is said to have remarked to theology students about secondhand copies of this magazine, 'Buy it and have a complete set in your library.'

Pilgrim Cheer (L, 1924); *Stories Twice Told* (L,

1923); *Windows in Heaven* (L, 1926); *The Word and the Road* (L, 1922).

A. L. Struthers, *Life and Letters of John Paterson Struthers* (L, n.d.); T. Cassels, *Men of the Knotted Heart* (Greenock, 1915).

N. R. Needham

Stuart, Alexander Moody (1809–98), Edinburgh FC preacher. Born at Paisley, the son of the chief magistrate of the burgh, and educated at Glasgow and Edinburgh Universities, he served as missionary at Holy Island (1833–5) and territorial assistant in St George's, Edinburgh (1835–7) before being ordained to St Luke's, Edinburgh in 1837. From 1843 to 1887 he was minister of Free St Luke's. He was Moderator of the FC General Assembly in 1875, and convener of the FC Jewish Committee 1847–88.

Stuart was the product of the evangelical revival spearheaded by Andrew Thomson* in the 1820s. His ministry in St Luke's was a distinctive one. He was an expert in 'case divinity', and his preaching* was intensely religious, subjective, searching, experimental and introspective. This style of preaching and piety was welcomed and adopted in the 1830s by a number of men who were to be very influential on the religious side of the Disruption* movement, including Robert Murray M'Cheyne,* Andrew* and Horatius Bonar,* Alexander Somerville* and John Milne.* Taylor Innes described him as 'a man who was the first and earliest of a well-defined and very remarkable school of preaching; who was also its patriarch and survivor; and who, besides being the originator, was himself the most original man not only in that school but, according to my judgement, in the whole Scottish pulpit during the long span of his ministerial career.' Published transcripts of his sermons fail to convey the effect of his deeply biblical and conscience-searching preaching. A better impression is given by the report that 'Rabbi' John Duncan* often broke down and was seen to be sobbing during the sermon. (Stuart compiled *Recollections of the late John Duncan*, E, 1872.) Though experimental religion was his absorbing interest and first concern, it is wrong to describe him as pietistic. He was a notable figure in the ecclesiastical and theological controversies of his day; he took part in the Disruption;* he opposed the proposed union of the Free and UP Churches; and he took the conservative side in the Robertson Smith* case, producing learned and able speeches and pamphlets.

His writings include: *The Song of Songs An Exposition of the Song of Solomon* (²L, 1860); *The Three Marys* (L, 1862); *Capernaum* (L, 1862); *The Union Overture: is it wise or right?* (E, 1870); *Israel's Lawgiver: his narrative true and his laws genuine* (L, 1882).

FES I, 110–11; *AFCS* I, 333; K. Moody Stuart, *Alexander Moody Stuart* (L, 1899).

K. R. Ross

Stuart, Charles, of Dunearn (1745–1826), Calvinistic Baptist theologian and physician. Trained in Edinburgh for the CofS ministry, Stuart was ordained to Cramond, near Edinburgh, in 1773. However, he had already embraced anti-establishment principles during time spent at a dissenting academy in London. This, coupled with his espousal of believers' baptism, led to his demitting his charge in 1776. After a failed attempt to found a Baptist church in Edinburgh, he commenced a new and lifelong career in medicine.

Stuart was widely involved with the evangelical world of his day, particularly with Andrew Fuller's* missionary enterprise and the Haldane revival.* He zealously promoted the Society for the Support of Gaelic Schools (*see* Gaelic Schools Societies), which helped to evangelize the Highlands.* He co-founded with Greville Ewing* Edinburgh's first evangelical periodical, *The Missionary Magazine*,* in 1796. From 1798 to 1800 Stuart edited the *Edinburgh Quarterly Magazine* and from 1803 to 1805 he ran his own periodical, the *Edinburgh Evangelical Magazine*.

An incisive and combative theologian, Stuart numbered among his friends Andrew Fuller (see his *A Short Memoir of the Late Mr Andrew Fuller*, n.p., 1815), James Haldane,* Thomas M'Crie,* Thomas Chalmers* and Thomas Erskine.* His first wife was a daughter of John Erskine (1721–1803).* One of his sons was the Whig politician James Stuart.

Stuart derived his agnomen from his estate in Dunearn, Fifeshire.

J. P. Wood, *The Antient and Modern State of the Parish of Cramond* (E, 1794); N. R. Needham, *Thomas Erskine of Linlathen* (E, 1990), 112ff.; *FES* I, 12.

N. R. Needham

Stuart, James (1701–89), translator of the New Testament into Scottish Gaelic (1767) (*see* Bible (Versions, Gaelic)). A native of Glen Finglas, Perthshire, Stuart studied at St Andrews University, and became parish minister of Killin, Perthshire, in 1737. He held the charge until his death, fifty-two years later. Remembered as a man of great learning and an eminent Gaelic preacher, he passed on his scholarly interests to his son, John Stuart,* who was a major contributor to the translation of the Gaelic Old Testament.

D. MacKinnon, *The Gaelic Bible and Psalter* (Dingwall, 1930), 57–9; D. W. MacKenzie, *The Worthy Translator* (Killin, 1992); *FES* IV, 185.

D. E. Meek

Stuart, John (1743–1821), one of the translators of the Gaelic Old Testament (*see* Bible (Versions, Gaelic)). Son of James Stuart* of Killin, and a graduate of Edinburgh University, he was successively assistant minister of Arrochar (1773–4) and minister of Weem, near Aberfeldy (1774–7) and Luss, Dunbartonshire (1777–1821). Stuart translated the third part of the Old Testament (2 Chronicles to the Song of Solomon) into Gaelic. At the very least, he also acted as reviser of the first two parts (Genesis to 1 Chronicles), but he probably contributed much more than the surviving evidence suggests. He revised the 1796 edition of

STUART, JOHN PATRICK CRICHTON

the New Testament. Stuart also had botanical interests. He discovered many Alpine plants in the Breadalbane hills, and contributed his knowledge to John Lightfoot's *Flora Scotica* (L, 1777).

D. MacKinnon, *The Gaelic Bible and Psalter* (Dingwall, 1930), 59–60, 76; D. W. MacKenzie, *The Worthy Translator* (Killin, 1992); *FES* III, 360.

D. E. Meek

Stuart, John Patrick Crichton (1847–1900), third Marquis of Bute, succeeding to the title in 1848. He was born at Mountstuart, Isle of Bute. Brought up as a Presbyterian, he travelled extensively in Europe with his mother until her death in 1859. He was educated at Harrow and Christ Church, Oxford, where he became acquainted with Charles Scott Murray and his chaplain, the RC preacher and controversialist, Thomas W. Capel. But his interest in things medieval was even more influential in his sensational conversion to RCism in 1868, which provided the basis for Benjamin Disraeli's *Lothair* (3 vols, L, 1870). He subsequently married Gwendoline Fitzalan, the daughter of Baron Howard of Glossop and niece of the Duke of Norfolk, and by her had four children.

A staunch conservative, he inherited immense family wealth drawn from estates in Scotland and south Wales. In 1868 his annual income was reputed to be £150,000. Secure in his considerable inheritance, he was a deeply religious man, committed to education and a scholar in his own right. At the same time he warmly endorsed Scottish and Welsh home rule. His Scottish restorations included Falkland Palace, Pluscarden,* Mochrum, and Crichton Peel, Sanquhar. His *Scottish Review* originally published his much reprinted 'Parliament in Scotland'. His many Scottish historical publications included *The Arms of the Royal and Parliamentary Burghs of Scotland* (E, 1897). A Welsh speaker himself, he contributed significantly to the Welsh revival. Conversant with Hebrew, Coptic and Arabic, he warmly sympathized with Jewish aspirations. He also bought lands in Palestine and Syria.

His scholarly interest in medievalism found expression in many ways: in establishing an ill-fated choir school at Oban cathedral, whose teachers briefly included Frederick Rolfe;* acquiring and restoring ancient monuments; publishing his English translation of the Roman breviary; reintroducing the Premonstratensians* into Scotland. The cross carried at the opening of the First Vatican Council was his gift. His learning in liturgy, architecture and language was immense.

His educational concerns were considerable. A member of the Scottish Universities Commission, he was also President of University College, Cardiff. At St Andrews, where he was Rector 1892–8, he made generous endowments. At Glasgow, he gave the Bute Hall. Three Scottish universities gave him honorary degrees. His charitable work was equally substantial: many churches in south-west Scotland and Wales owed their existence to him. He served as Mayor of Cardiff, 1890, Provost of

STUDENT CHRISTIAN MOVEMENT

Rothesay, 1896–9 and received the freedom of Glasgow in 1891.

DNB LV, 92–8; William Knight, *Some Nineteenth Century Scotsmen* (E, 1903), 406–12; D. Hunter Blair, *John Patrick, Third Marquess of Bute* (L, 1921); John Davies, *Cardiff and the Marquesses of Bute* (Cardiff, 1981); R. Macdonald, 'The "Tin" Cathedral at Oban 1886–1934', *IR* 15 (1964), 47–55.

B. Aspinwall

Stuart, Kenneth Moody (1842–1904), FC and UFC minister and writer, son of Alexander Moody Stuart.* Born in Edinburgh, he studied at Edinburgh University and New College.* He was ordained in 1868 to Moffat St Mary's, in Annandale, Dumfriesshire. He wrote lives of his father, *Alexander Moody Stuart* (L, 1899), and of the evangelist of the 1859 revival, Brownlow North* (*Brownlow North*, L, 1878).

Stuart's father had played a prominent part in opposing union between the FC and UPC in the first union controversy of 1863–72, but Stuart himself came to support this cause, and entered the UFC in 1900. See his *Letter to a Friend . . .* (Moffat, 1892); *The New Declaratory Act* (Moffat, 1893).

Light from the Holy Hills (L, 1900); *Why We Do Not Mean to Change Our Confession of Faith* (E, 1889).

AFCS I, 334; *FUFCS* 99.

N. R. Needham

Student Christian Movement, an organization for the support of Christian witness in universities and colleges. The origins of the Student Christian Movement can be traced back to initiatives taken in the second half of the nineteenth century in Edinburgh and Glasgow, and then Cambridge and Oxford Universities. In 1865 the Edinburgh Medical Students' Christian Association was founded, followed shortly afterwards by the Glasgow University Students' Christian Association. The American evangelist, D. L. Moody,* visited Edinburgh for the first time in 1873 (*see* Revivals) and had a profound impact on the student community. He particularly influenced a young New College student, Henry Drummond,* whose evangelistic meetings in the succeeding decades challenged the university world throughout Britain as well as in the USA. A major revival occurred in 1884 during the tercentenary celebrations of Edinburgh University, and important gatherings of student leaders took place in Bonskeid House, Perthshire, under the auspices of R. W. Barbour, a friend of Drummond. The Cambridge Inter-Collegiate Christian Union (CICCU) was founded in 1878, and the Oxford equivalent a year later. In 1893 the Inter-University Christian Union was established, and in 1909 it changed its name to the Student Christian Movement. The following year the CICCU, followed by a number of other Christian Unions, voted to disaffiliate from SCM on the grounds that it was moving away from evangelical orthodoxy. This was the origin of the

SUBSCRIPTION, CONFESSIONAL

Inter-Varsity Fellowship* (IVF), now Universities and Colleges Christian Fellowship (UCCF).

From the beginning SCM has emphasized the importance of Christian unity and has been a vanguard of the ecumenical movement,* producing several generations of ecumenically-minded Church leaders. At its peak it was one of the largest of British student organizations, with branches in all British universities and most colleges. Since the 1960s it has declined numerically, and is now far smaller than the UCCF.

Steve Bruce, 'The Student Christian Movement and the Inter-Varsity Fellowship: A Sociological Study of Two Student Movements' (PhD, Stirling University, 1980); Eric Fenn, *Learning Wisdom* (L, 1939); J. Davis McCaughey, *Christian Obedience in the University* (L, 1958); Ruth Rouse, *The World's Student Christian Federation* (L, 1948); Tissington Tatlow, *The Story of the Student Christian Movement of Great Britain and Ireland* (L, 1933).

D. B. Forrester

Subscription, Confessional. Prior to 1560, the Apostles' Creed was the universally acknowledged symbol of faith in the Scottish Church. In that year the Scots Confession* was 'voted and ratified' by Parliament as 'the Confession of Faith of the only true and holy Kirk of Jesus Christ within this realm'. There is no record of subscription to this Confession being required until 1572, when two Acts were passed (Acts 46 and 47) requiring that all within the nation 'give their confession, and make their profession of the said true religion'. The General Assembly also gave approval to other confessions, such as the (English) Genevan Confession* and the Second Helvetic Confession (*see also* Catechisms).

The Scots Confession continued to be the standard that all 'ecclesiastical persons' were required to subscribe *simpliciter*, until the CofS adopted the Westminster Confession* in 1647. Only oral subscription was required during the period 1647–90. However, confessional subscription was ignored during the reign of Charles II.*

The advent of William of Orange (*see* William II) to the throne led in 1690 to the re-establishing of Presbyterian Church government, including recognition of the Westminster Confession as 'the public and avowed confession of this Church'. An Act was passed by the General Assembly of 1690 requiring all probationers, ministers, and elders, 'to subscribe their approbation of the Confession of Faith'. In 1693 the Scottish Parliament passed an Act, approved by the General Assembly of that year, 'That no person be admitted ... to be a minister ... within this Church, unless that he ... do subscribe the Confession of faith ... Declaring the same to be the Confession of his Faith, and that he owns the Doctrine therein contained to be the true doctrine which he will constantly adhere to.' The following year a new Formula* of Subscription was enacted by the General Assembly. Each individual seeking ordination was required to subscribe the Westminster Confession as the confession of his faith, and to 'own the doctrine therein contained to be the true doctrine, which I will constantly adhere to'.

This Formula held until 1711 when a 'stricter' version was adopted with the aim of excluding Episcopalians from the ministry. At their ordination, ministers were required to sign the following Formula: 'I do hereby declare, that I do sincerely own and believe the whole doctrine contained in the Confession of faith ... to be the truths of God; and I do own the same as the confession of my faith.' Although it has been argued that the Church subsequently allowed ministers 'a certain measure of liberty to depart from the Confessional standard' (C. G. M'Crie), there is no evidence to suggest this was a matter of policy.

The first breach in the requirement of unqualified subscription to the Westminster Confession occurred in 1796, when the General Associate Synod* (Antiburgher) effectively qualified its commitment to the Confession by declaring that it approved solely of spiritual means for bringing men and women into the Church: 'the power of the gospel not the sword of the civil magistrate'. This reservation was further highlighted in the first Synod of the United Secession Church* in 1820. Question 2 of the newly revised Formula asked ordinands only to acknowledge that the Confession was 'expressive of the sense' in which they understood the Scriptures. This 'relaxed' Formula was in no small measure due to the arguments advanced by John Brown of Edinburgh,* who argued that it was 'very difficult' for licentiates and ministers to give a 'rational assent' to every proposition in the Confession. But ministers were still required to acknowledge the Confession as the confession of their faith. This changed, however, with the formation of the UPC in 1847. For the first time since 1690, ministers were not required to own the Westminster Confession as the confession of their faith. The revised Formula of 1847 put the following question to ordinands: 'Do you acknowledge the Westminster Confession of Faith ... as an exhibition of the sense in which you understand the Holy Scriptures ... ?' A. T. Innes* was of the opinion that the UPC had abolished the Formula of Subscription by this revised wording.

However, the most significant revision of confessional subscription occurred in 1879. The UPC Declaratory Act* allowed ministers 'liberty of opinion ... on such points in the Standards not entering the substance of the faith'. In its new Formula subscription was no longer to a defined corpus of doctrine, but to an undefined 'substance of the faith'. In 1892 the FC followed the lead given by the UPC in re-defining its commitment to the Westminster Confession. In 1905, by the Churches (Scotland) Act, Parliament gave the National Church the power to amend its Formula of Subscription to the Westminster Confession. A new Formula was enacted in 1910: 'I hereby subscribe the Confession of Faith, declaring that I accept it as the Confession of this Church, and that I believe the fundamental doctrines of the Christian Faith contained therein.' What was meant by 'fundamental doctrines' was not specified.

The Union of 1929 of the CofS and the UFC consolidated the confessional position both Churches had held for the previous thirty years. Other Presbyterian Churches – FC and FPC – continue to require from ordinands an unqualified subscription to the Westminster Confession.

See also Formula; Declaratory Acts; King's Confession; Confessions of Faith; Catechisms.

BUK; C. G. M'Crie, *Confessions of the Church of Scotland* (E, 1907); *id.*, *The Church of Scotland: Her Divisions and Reunions* (E, 1901); A. T. Innes, *The Law of Creeds in Scotland* (E, L, 1867); J. M'Kerrow, *History of the Secession Church*, (E, 1841); A. C. Cheyne, *The Transforming of the Kirk* (E, 1983); I. Hamilton, *The Erosion of Calvinist Orthodoxy: Seceders and Subscription in Scottish Presbyterianism* (E, 1990).

I. Hamilton

Sum of Saving Knowledge, see Dickson, David; Durham, James.

Sunday School movement. The movement began in the 1780s in response to the growth of child labour in industry (especially textiles). Though Sunday communicants' classes had existed previously, it was the work of Robert Raikes of Gloucester from 1780 that proved inspirational. Through articles in papers like *The Scots Magazine*, his idea of using Sabbath classes for educating children employed six days a week in industry, and for reducing lawlessness and burglary of worshippers' homes, became very popular with Scottish burgh administrators and élites. The first major Sunday school operations began in 1786–7 in Aberdeen, Glasgow and Edinburgh, spreading to smaller Lowland towns and villages, often organized by societies composed of CofS ministers, town councillors, elders and general subscribers, and using salaried teachers. Meeting for up to six hours on a Sunday, with additional church services, the curriculum included Bible lessons, psalmody, reading and writing. But from 1796–7 James and Robert Haldane,* Greville Ewing* and the Society for Propagating the Gospel at Home* encouraged dissenters to copy another English innovation – *gratis* Sabbath schools using volunteer teachers. During the revolutionary wars of the 1790s, Moderates* in the CofS objected to them vociferously, culminating in the CofS General Assembly's 'Pastoral Admonition' of 1799, which described Sabbath school organizers as 'persons notoriously disaffected to the Constitution'. Because of Moderate* hostility, the majority of new schools until the 1820s were formed by Independents* (*see* Congregationalists), Methodists* and Seceders,* providing in many communities the principal education for millworking children of between five and twelve years of age. Several CofS Evangelicals like Thomas Chalmers* and William Collins (senior), the publisher, also started them. District and national unions were formed after 1814, and by 1819 the Sabbath School Union for Scotland claimed the affiliation of 567 schools and 39,000 scholars.

The most significant growth of the movement occurred between 1830 and 1850 with the formation of the FC* and the UPC.* In the Census, Religious 1851,* total scholars stood at 292,549, of which 31 per cent were attached to the FC, 26 per cent to the CofS and 19 per cent to the UPC. In urban districts, more children attended Sunday than day schools, and until *c.*1890 growth of scholars exceeded population growth. By 1891, Scottish Sunday school enrolment represented 52 per cent of children aged five to fifteen.

With the arrival of compulsory state education in 1873, the secular education rôle of Sunday schools, already diminishing through sabbatarian* pressure, was effectively removed, and the curriculum became more devotional. At the same time, Sunday school teachers had developed new evangelical 'agencies' like penny savings banks and young men's societies. But with the rise of competing secular leisure and sport from 1870, churches started to offer alternative pursuits. Within congregations, the interest of the young started to shift from Sunday schools to more 'secular' activities: the Boys' Brigade* and temperance* organizations like the Band of Hope. As a result of these factors, Sunday school enrolments started to fall from the 1890s: CofS + FC + UPC + UFC falling from 494,790 peak in 1896 to 369,115 in 1931, and to 273,746 in 1962. The revolution in youth culture since the 1960s, coupled with increasing religious alienation amongst younger parents, has led to even more rapid decline. By 1985, Presbyterian enrolment (CofS) stood at only 98,012, and the fall continues.

The movement started to centralize in 1899 with the powerful Glasgow Sabbath School Union (formed 1816, lapsed *c.*1820, re-formed 1837) becoming the Scottish National SSU, and then in 1925 drawing official Protestant Church representation to become the Scottish Sunday School Union for Christian Education. Later disagreements with CofS have somewhat splintered the movement's leadership.

C. G. Brown, 'The Sunday-school Movement in Scotland, 1780–1914', *RSCHS* 21 (1981), 3–26; *id.*, *The Social History of Religion in Scotland since 1730* (L and NY, 1987); *id.*, 'Religion, Class and Church Growth', in W. H. Fraser and R. J. Morris (eds), *People and Society in Scotland*, vol. 2, *1830–1914* (E, 1989); R. Currie *et al.*, *Churches and Churchgoers* (O, 1977); T. W. Laquer, *Religion and Respectability* (New Haven and L, 1976).

C. G. Brown

Superintendent, an office which the Reformers* introduced almost as an afterthought in the *First Book of Discipline*, designed to remedy the shortage of ministers and to further the work of evangelization throughout the land. Repudiating the traditional ecclesiastical hierarchy, the Reformers placed their emphasis on the pastoral ministry which, they considered, might be exercised within the context of a congregation or more widely over a whole district. The reasons adduced for making 'difference between preachers at this time' by introducing superintendent ministers were entirely practical, not theological. To meet the emergency confronting them at the Reformation,* the Reformers decided not to restrict the ablest ministers to individual congregations but to distribute the ministry across the nation, as best they could, by selecting as 'a thing most expedient for this time' ten or twelve ministers as superintendents, whose task was 'to plant and erect kirks, to set, order and appoint ministers', so that all who had 'never heard Jesus Christ truly preached shall come to some knowledge'. Because of inadequate finance and political instability, only five superintendents were appointed: John Spottiswoode* for Lothian in March 1561; John Winram* for Fife in April 1561; John Willock* for Glasgow and the West by September 1561; John Erskine of Dun* for Angus by January 1562, and John Carswell* for Argyll (whose appointment cannot be dated); elsewhere oversight was entrusted by the General Assembly to ministers who acted for a spell as commissioners or visitors (in whose ranks were placed the three conforming bishops of Galloway, Caithness and Orkney; see Bothwell, Adam; Gordon, Alexander; Stewart, Robert). Superintendence, in short, was to be exercised not by a district order or degree of bishops (see Episcopacy) but by ministers who received a commission from the Church to exercise supervisory duties, for a shorter or longer interval (though not for life). One superintendent is on record as accepting office 'only for a time', and all five repeatedly sought release from their duties. The superintendent's subordination to the ministry and to the wider Church was spelt out both in the FBD and in the Form and Order for the election of superintendents in 1561, and was put to the test in the General Assembly's disciplinary proceedings. Not only were they accountable to the graded series of Church courts, the superintendents were expected to act collegiately where practicable, both during visitations and when resident in the chief towns of their provinces. Besides preaching, appointing ministers and readers* and examining congregations, superintendents played their part in convening synods, selecting certain categories of commissioner to the General Assembly, and in giving collation to benefices.

The novelty of the superintendent's office lay in its freedom from traditional concepts of superiority and lordship; and the ample continental precedents available to the Scots for appraisal strongly suggest that the example of employing superintendents as administrators was borrowed from no single country. The appearance of bishops, so recognized by the Kirk, after the Convention of Leith* in 1572, complicated the machinery for oversight which had developed in the 1560s; it displaced the jurisdiction of superintendents in those dioceses where bishops were immediately appointed (though the Convention itself recognized that the new bishops should exercise no greater ecclesiastical powers than the existing superintendents), and it held the prospect that the superintendent's office would disappear, as the old diocesan organization took final form. In practice, however, it was the new bishops, and not the superintendents, who came under attack as the General Assembly in 1576 returned to its earlier device of commissioning ministers to serve as visitors. The surviving superintendents, as well as some bishops and other ministers, continued to act in this capacity. The original five superintendents had no successors, and with their deaths the office fell into disuse.

J. Kirk, *Patterns of Reform* (E, 1989), 154–231 – 'The Superintendent: Myth and Reality'.

J. Kirk

Swan, Annie Shepherd (1859–1943), (Mrs Burnett Smith), writer. Born and educated in Edinburgh, she grew up in Evangelical Union* congregations in Leith and Dalkeith. In 1883 she married James Burnett Smith, a schoolteacher who later trained at Edinburgh to become a doctor, practising for many years in London and Hertford. From 1927 she lived in Gullane, E. Lothian.

Throughout her life Swan was a prolific author of novels (on middle-class *mores* and romance), and of articles and serials for papers and magazines, especially *The People's Friend*, the *British Weekly* (for which she wrote stories on the Boer War as 'David Lyall') and *The Woman at Home* (originally *Annie Swan's Magazine*), founded and edited by her close friend W. R. Nicoll.* Her first successful book was *Aldersyde* (E, 1883), one of her best *The Gates of Eden* (E, 1887).

She retained an ardent Christian faith, and associated with leading churchmen of several denominations (*e.g.* Robert Flint* and Rowntree Clifford) as well as eminent literary figures. An active supporter of the Temperance movement* and home missions, she helped found St Andrew's Presbyterian Church in Hampstead (which called Roderick Macleod* as its first minister), stood as Liberal candidate in Glasgow in 1922 (being much influenced by Sir Donald MacLean, 1864–1932, the Liberal MP), and worked for the Food Ministry in the Second World War.

My Life (L, 1934).

M. R. Nicoll (ed.), *The Letters of Annie S. Swan* (L, 1945); T. Royle, *The MacMillan Companion to Scottish Literature* (L, 1983), 294.

D. F. Wright

Swanston, John (1720–67), Associate Synod* minister, Professor of Divinity. Born at Hume in Berwickshire, he studied arts at Edinburgh University, and then theology at the Secession Divinity Hall in Perth. He was licensed to preach in 1743. Adhering to the Burghers in the dispute over the Burgess oath,* he was called to the Associate congregation in Kinross, Perthshire, in 1748. This was a new and small congregation, but its numbers greatly increased under Swanston's ministry. In 1764 he succeeded James Fisher* as the Associate Synod's* Professor of Divinity. He died suddenly and unexpectedly, however, a few years later.

Swanston published nothing during his lifetime, but a posthumous collection of his sermons was issued in 1773 (*Sermons on Several Important Subjects*, G). The volume also contains a memoir by John Smith of Dunfermline.

Swanston left behind him a remarkable reputation for sanctity. In the words of one of his congregation, 'Mr Swanston was like a god amongst us.'

J. M'Kerrow, *History of the Secession Church* (G, 1841), 850–2; Small I, 385–6.

N. R. Needham

Swedenborgians, *see* New Jerusalem Church.

Sydserff, Thomas (1581–1663), Bishop of Brechin, Galloway and Orkney. Sydserff was ordained to St Giles, Edinburgh, 1611, translated to Trinity, Edinburgh, 1626, and became Dean of Edinburgh, 1634. That year, he was consecrated Bishop of Brechin and was translated to Galloway, 1635. He promoted the so-called English Liturgy and Canons* of 1636, and was among those excommunicated at the Glasgow Assembly* of December 1638. He was in exile in England and Paris until the Restoration. As the only surviving Scottish bishop, he became Bishop of Orkney, 1662.

FES VII, 353–4; *DNB* LV, 255; D. G. Mullan, *Episcopacy in Scotland* (E, 1986); J. B. Craven, *Scots Worthies, 1560–1688* (E, 1894).

J. M. Mcluckie

Symington, Andrew (1785–1853), RP divine. Born and schooled in Paisley (like his younger brother William*), he carried off the prizes at Glasgow University (MA, 1803) before studying with John Macmillan of Stirling for the RP ministry. He was ordained to the Paisley congregation in 1809, and in addition appointed the Church's Professor of Theology, succeeding Macmillan in 1820. His death followed a railway accident.

Apart from tracts and sermons, Symington's publications were few. His distinction lay not in 'pre-eminence of learning and talent' but in the balanced biblical influence he exercised at a formative period on a generation of RP ministers – and on Irish and American students too. (He received the DD degree not only of Glasgow, 1840, but also of the Western University of Pennsylvania, 1831.) He was 'never misled by any crotchety fondness for a particular doctrine'. He taught the whole span of theological disciplines, but his strength was in systematics. He prepared various formularies and standards for his Church, in worship, discipline and doctrine, and thereby further contributed to denominational harmony, but never gave undue prominence to RP distinctives. His support for charitable and evangelical causes (sabbath* observance, temperance,* Bible Society,* home and foreign missions) made him widely known and respected, and he was an enthusiastic leader in the Evangelical Alliance.* His contemporaries attested to his 'benignity', displaying neither 'the contractedness of the bigot' nor 'the moroseness of the cynic'.

The Martyrs' Monument: A Brief View of the Principles and Character of the Scottish Martyrs (Paisley, 1847); *The Principles of the Second Reformation* (G, 1841).

DNB LV, 268–9; preface to his *Elements of Divine Truth: A Series of Lectures . . . to Sabbath-School Teachers* (E, 1854); W. Symington, *Departed Worth and Greatness Lamented: A Sermon on the Death of The Rev. Andrew Symington, D.D.* . . . (Paisley, 1853); Blackwood (listed under William Symington*).

D. F. Wright

Symington, William (1795–1862), RP theologian. He was born in Paisley and ordained in the RPC in Stranraer in South West Scotland, serving as pastor there 1819–39 and then in Great Hamilton Street Church, Glasgow, 1938–62. He published two theological works, *On the Atonement and Intercession of Jesus Christ* (E, 1834) and *Messiah the Prince* (E, 1839 ²L, 1881 with a memoir). The latter was his most important contribution to Scottish theology; it expounds a basis in the theology of Christ's kingship and kingdom for Church–state* relationships.

The RP Synod elected him Professor of their Theological Hall after the death of his brother, Andrew Symington* in 1853, and once described the two brothers as 'the most distinguished ministers who have been raised up to us since the martyrdom of James Renwick'.* They led the RPC out of an attitude of narrow provincialism focused on self-preservation and into a sense of missionary responsibility for the Church in Scotland and throughout the world.

Symington was pre-eminently a Covenanter* Evangelical. He once described how, at the age of seventeen, 'I gave myself away to the Lord in a solemn, personal covenant.' He insisted that the only basis for Scotland's national covenants* was the covenant of grace. He became deeply involved in social reform because he saw intemperance, ignorance of the Scriptures, illiteracy, slavery, bad working conditions and corruption in government as moral sins in a nation committed to God in public covenant. He was recognized as one of Scotland's most powerful and eloquent preachers and frequently spoke to these issues in other churches and on public platforms. What Thomas Chalmers* and Andrew Thomson* were to Glasgow and Edinburgh, Symington was to south-west Scotland. In Glasgow he focused on the thousands drawn into deplorable living conditions by the Industrial Revolution. The church (which seated a thousand people) went to three services, then formed two mission churches and a school system involving over 900 students and fifty teachers. In 1838 the University of Edinburgh recognized his leadership by granting him the degree of DD. His life motto was (in Greek) 'To God Alone be Glory'.

DNB LV, 270; complete bibliography in

R. Blackwood, *Wm. Symington, Churchman and Theologian, 1795–1862* (Indianapolis, 1985); J. Smith, *Our Scottish Clergy* (E, 1848), 78–84; Wm. M. Taylor, *The Scottish Pulpit* (L, 1887), 222–4.

R. Blackwood

Symson (Simson), Andrew (1638–1712), minister, printer and editor. He was probably born in England. (On his father, Andrew, the son of Alexander Simson,* see W. J. Couper in *RSCHS* 4, 1932, 244–7.) At Edinburgh University (MA, 1661) he became a friend of Alexander Stewart, the Earl of Galloway. After teaching Latin at Stirling Grammar School, 1661–3 (his brother Matthias was minister there; Couper, *ibid.*, 247–53; *FES* IV, 319), he became minister of Kirkinner, Wigtownshire, 1663–86. A government supporter in Covenanting* territory, he needed the shelter provided by the Earl of Galloway, yet had leisure for literary pursuits, producing *Tripatriarchicon* (E, 1705), a mediocre material account of Abraham, Isaac and Jacob, and his best-known work, *A Large Description of Galloway* (first published E, 1823, ed. T. Maitland, with biographical introduction). A list of local troublemakers he submitted in 1684 included Margaret McLauchlan, one of the Wigtown Martyrs.*

He transferred to Douglas in 1686 but left in contested circumstances after three years, and thereafter lived mostly in Edinburgh as a printer and bookseller in the Cowgate, near the present Guthrie Street. He took over the press his son Matthias (Couper, *ibid.*, 259–64) had started while a student in Edinburgh. He produced Jacobite* tracts, legal works (including the second edition of George Mackenzie's *Laws and Customs of Scotland in Matters Criminal*, E, 1699), curiosities (including *Octupla*, E, 1696 – eight Latin versions of Psalm 104) and short-lived newspapers. Among still unpublished material is *Ane Alphabetical Account of all the Churches or Paroch Kirks in Scotland*. The sale catalogue of his library, *Bibliotheca Symsoniana* (E, 1712), listed several thousand books.

W. J. Couper, 'Andrew Symson. Preacher, Printer and Poet', *SHR* 13 (1915), 47–67; *id.*, 'The Levitical Family of Simson, III', *RSCHS* 4 (1932), 253–8; *DNB* LII, 283; *FES* II, 365, III, 301–3.

D. F. Wright

Synod, one of the courts* of the Church in Presbyterian polity. The term is in common use (Provincial Synod is the full title) for that court of the CofS which, from the sixteenth century (*see SBD*) until 1992, stood between Presbytery* and General Assembly.* (Other Presbyterian Churches have no such intermediate court, or make the Synod the supreme court.) Its membership latterly consisted of all who were members of its constituent Presbyteries, as well as 'correspondents', *i.e.* a minister and an elder appointed by each of the neighbouring Synods. There were twelve Synods and the Presbyteries of Orkney and Shetland enjoyed synodical powers. The Synod was bound to meet at least once a year, but most met twice – in spring and autumn. It had no power to legislate, but by an Act of 1592 had 'power to handle, ordour and redress all things omitted or done amiss', and so appeals against decisions of Presbytery went first to the Synod and overtures from Presbyteries addressed to the General Assembly were first considered by Synods, which, however, were bound to transmit them to the Assembly. The Presbyteries' maintenance of records and fulfilment of duties generally were subject to Synod review.

Of late there was a strong movement to have the CofS Synods discontinued, since meetings generally were poorly attended. Although constitutional difficulties prevented speedy action, their fate is now sealed. They were dissolved as from 1 January 1993, by a decision (*RGACS 1992*, 547–8) involving the first ever amendment to the Articles Declaratory.*

Cox 185–92; *RGACS 1978*, 2, 8–9, 25–7, *RGACS 1990*, 4, 15–18.

A. Herron

Synod Hall, Edinburgh. The Synod Hall's name derived ultimately from the court in the post-Reformation CofS intermediate between the General Assembly and the Presbyteries (*see* Synod). Church bodies seceding from the national Church in the eighteenth century gave the name 'Synod' to their highest court. The UPC,* formed in 1847 by the union of the United Secession and Relief Churches, met in its Synod Hall at 5 Queen Street, Edinburgh, and there its students for the ministry came for teaching. The Queen Street buildings were prepared by John Dick Peddie; behind the class rooms was a 'noble' hall with 'coved' ceiling, fondly remembered as a comfortable and easy debating chamber.

About 1875, the Synod rearranged its provision for divinity students. More room was required and opportunity came in the purchase, for £50,000, of a building in Castle Terrace built by James Gowans in 1875 as a theatre. (R. H. Wyndham's theatre had become bankrupt.) It was one of the largest halls in Europe. By 1880 it was ready for use and there for twenty years the Synod met and ministers were taught. The word 'Hall' was equally applicable to the building and the training college.

After the union with the FC* in 1900, the Hall was bought by the City Council and let as a bowling alley, a rifle range and dancing schools. The Royal Scottish Geographical Society met there. In 1906 a 'diorama' was installed, and later it became Poole's cinema. In 1965–9 it was demolished to make room for an opera house which was never built.

Edinburgh Evening Express, 15 May 1882; *PUPS*.

A. I. Dunlop

Systematic Theology. Theology, broadly considered, is a result of God's self-disclosure. The category of systematic theology reflects only the academic need to classify, to apportion various aspects of the God-given remit to different experts. It draws heavily on biblical theology, historical theology and dogmatic theology but is distinguished from all of them by four peculiar features: (i) it is *thematic*. Its interest is not in particular books or distinct *genres* of biblical literature or individual authors but in the doctrinal themes of Scripture; (ii) it is *comprehensive*. It seeks to cover all the theological topics of Scripture, and it draws on the insights of all other related disciplines; (iii) it is *normative*. The teaching of particular prophets, apostles and Church fathers may be transitional. Systematic theology tries to ascertain the overall teaching of Scripture, and the last word of Scripture; (iv) it is *systematic*. It sets out to arrange individual topics in the best possible order, to clarify them and to relate them to the life of the Church and the needs of the world as coherently as possible.

One problem besetting this process is that systematic theology can easily become the prisoner of philosophy. Some co-operation between theologian and philosopher is obviously inevitable, if only because any classification of subject-matter presupposes a philosophical standpoint. Philosophy also helps to clarify theological concepts; and of course philosophers ask questions which theologians cannot ignore. What is unacceptable is that theology should allow philosophy to set its agenda, that theologians should use philosophical rather than theological methods (metaphysical speculation rather than exegesis), and that philosophical prejudices should prevent us hearing what God is saying in his Word. The most notorious example of this is the way that the notion of *apatheia* (passionlessness), derived from Stoicism, has precluded our seeing God in the light of the incarnation. It became a fixed dogma that the Almighty was emotionally inert and totally immune to pain. Within Scotland, there is no doubt that nineteenth-century theologians were both reacting to the empiricism of David Hume* and influenced by the common-sense philosophy of Thomas Reid (*see* Scottish Realism), Dugald Stewart* and Thomas Brown (Stewart's colleague at Edinburgh University from 1810). Thomas Chalmers,* for example, wrote the preface to Brown's *Lectures on Ethics* (E, 1846). However, the extent of this influence is often exaggerated. Other philosophical influences (notably the necessitarianism of Jonathan Edwards* and the empiricism of Joseph Butler) were at least equally important for men like Chalmers. Furthermore, some Scottish divines were dismissive of the common-sense philosophy. John Duncan,* for example, commented: 'Common sense I believe in, but not in a philosophy of common sense ... You tell me that this or that is the voice of Nature, and that we can't help believing it. But does this Reidist solution really satisfy any man? The belief may be false, though we cannot help believing it. May not some malign being, a *kakodaimon*, have created us, or such a demiourgos as the Gnostics believed in? Can't-help-myself-ism is to me a very shallow philosophy' (*Colloquia Peripatetica*, 1871, 63,2).

It is also very difficult to distinguish between the 'common sense' of the philosophers and the theistic presuppositionalism of Calvin and St Paul. Whatever the influence of common-sense philosophy, nineteenth-century Calvinists on both sides of the Atlantic remained faithful to Calvin's insistence that the foundation of theistic belief was the *notitia Dei insita* ('the implanted knowledge of God') or the *sensus Deitatis* ('awareness of deity') engraven on every human heart.

The Reformed church in Scotland has produced many experts in systematic theology, from Samuel Rutherford* to Thomas Boston* to Thomas Crawford.* But few of them produced compendia of theology. According to James MacGregor,* the greatest systematic theologian Scotland produced was William Cunningham* (*The British and Foreign Evangelical Review* 20, 1871, 786) but we have only his *Historical Theology* (2 vols, E, 1862) to prove it. The reason for this apparent lack of productivity on the part of Scottish theologians was probably their conviction that they could not improve on the work of the seventeenth-century continental Reformed dogmaticians.

The most influential Scottish compendium was undoubtedly that of George Hill,* Professor of Theology at St Andrews University. His lectures, edited by his son in three volumes (E, 1821), are models of order and lucidity. The subject-matter is arranged in six books which deal successively with Christian evidences, general view of the Scripture system, the Trinity, the nature and extent of redemption, the application of redemption, and ecclesiology. The most striking feature of Hill's work (especially to those familiar with the corresponding works of American theologians) is the amount of space devoted to Christian evidences. In this respect Hill set a precedent for other Scottish systematicians. Thomas Chalmers used Hill as a class text-book and extolled his virtues, particularly his lucid arrangement of topics. But he was also aware of his faults. He noted Hill's 'frigidity' and lamented 'the want of a *sal evangelicum*, even though it be an evangelical system of truth which is ably and on the whole correctly expounded' (*Selected Works*, E, 1856, VIII, 263).

A year before the publication of Hill's *Lectures* John Dick* was appointed Professor of Theology to the USec.C. His *Lectures on Theology* were published in four volumes (E, 1834; ²1838). The arrangement is generally similar to Hill's, without the division into books. The first fifteen lectures deal with Prolegomena, including Christian evidences and the doctrine of Scripture. The remainder deal with the divine attributes, the Trinity, the decrees, the execution of the decrees (creation, providence and the fall), the covenant of grace, the Mediator, the application of redemption, eschatology and ecclesiology. The doctrine of the Mediator occupies 300 pages and follows the traditional analysis of Prophet, Priest and King. There is an extensive discussion of the means of grace; and the concluding chapters deal with the Decalogue.

One fascinating feature of Dick's work is his distinction between natural and supernatural theology. The supernatural, obviously, is that which is derived from Scripture. The natural is 'the knowledge of God which the light of nature teaches, or which is acquired by our unassisted powers, by the exercise of reason, and the suggestions of conscience'. But he was anxious not to be misunderstood: 'It is not meant that there is in the human mind an innate idea of God ... but that man, by contemplating the objects around him, is led to infer the existence of an invisible Being by whom they were created.'

Doubts have been expressed about Dick's views on inspiration (see John Macleod, *Scottish Theology*, E, ³1974, 253; and J. Bannerman, *Inspiration*, E, 1865, 141, 249). Such doubts could have resulted only from misunderstanding. Dick distinguished three levels of inspiration: superintendence, elevation and suggestion. These distinctions had already been drawn by Hill, and should not be confused with the idea of partial inspiration. Dick believed in the inspiration of the whole of the Scriptures: they are the Word of God 'because all the parts of which they consist have been written by persons moved, directed and assisted by his Holy Spirit'. He distinguished between different degrees of inspiration only because he wished to note that 'the same degree of divine assistance was not necessary in the composition of every part of it'. In this, Dick was surely correct. Ezra, transcribing the genealogies of the children of the Captivity (2:1-58) and Paul writing Romans 8 were both 'borne' by the Spirit (2 Peter 1:21). But the two activities were not equally 'elevated'. As William Cunningham was to point out years later, 'The doctrine of the plenary verbal inspiration does not by any means imply that everything stated in Scripture proceeded from the supernatural agency of the Holy Spirit' (*Theological Lectures*, L, 1878, 350). Dick also conceded that the inspiration of the Scriptures did 'not mean that all the sentiments contained in them are just, and all the examples are worthy of imitation'. His concern here, however, was only to alert people to the fact that Scripture records the words and actions of wicked as well as good, and does not always endorse what it records.

Hill and Dick exercised a wide influence, not least in America. The Southern Presbyterian theologian, R. L. Dabney, referred to them constantly in his *Lectures in Systematic Theology* (Richmond, VA, 1878); J. H. Thornwell was also aware of Dick's work (*Collected Writings* ... II, NY, 1871, 532); and Archibald Alexander of Princeton endorsed the judgement that it had no equal in the English language (see preface to the 1838 edition of Dick's *Lectures*).

Thomas Chalmers, as we have seen, used Hill's *Lectures* as his text-book. His own *Institutes of Theology* were published as Volumes VII and VIII of his *Select Works* (E, 1856). Some of the defects of the *Institutes* were the direct result of his use of Hill. In 'Chalmers' Thinking Habits' (*The Practical and the Pious*, ed. A. C. Cheyne, E, 1985), Friedhelm Voges comments that it is 'hardly a coincidence that even at the end of his life, the chapter on the Trinity is only an appendix in the *Institutes of Theology*'. This overlooks the fact that the whole of Book III of Hill's *Lectures* (over 300 pages) is devoted to this subject; and that Chalmers commented extensively on these chapters in his class (see 'Notes on Hill's *Lectures in Divinity*', Vol. VIII, 302-54).

In fact, the *Institutes* presuppose Hill throughout and follow his order closely. There are two main sections, the first dealing with Prolegomena and the second with the 'Subject-Matter of Christianity'. These sections in turn are carefully divided. The Prolegomena occupy three books: 'General and Introductory', 'Natural Theology' and 'Christian Evidences'. The second section consists merely of Part I, on the disease for which the gospel remedy is provided; Part II, on the nature of the gospel remedy; and Part III, on the extent of the gospel remedy. There is nothing on eschatology, the Decalogue, the sacraments or ecclesiology, probably because these had been adequately treated by Hill.

There was nothing original in the content of Chalmers' theology. According to his colleague, John Duncan,* he was neither a widely-read divine nor a speculative thinker (*Colloquia Peripatetica*, 27f.). His unmodified confessionalism was distinguished only by such minor peculiarities as his emphasis on philosophical necessity (Vol. VIII, 86ff.). What is original in Chalmers is the arrangement. When he came to discuss the 'Subject-Matter of Christianity', he abandoned the traditional order and began instead with the human plight: 'The Disease ...'. He then went on to expound the remedy. This order reflects again the influence of Hill, who entitled the opening chapter of Book IV, 'Disease for which the remedy is Provided'. It also reflects Chalmers' own life-long conviction of the practical importance of the doctrine of total depravity. But above all it reflects his awareness that his task was to train preachers. His treatment of the disease concludes with a lecture 'On the Practical and Pulpit Treatment of this Subject', just as his treatment of the atonement concludes with one 'On the Preaching of Christ Crucified'; and one of the Supplementary Lectures is 'On the Distinction between the Mode in which Theology should be Learned at the Hall and the Mode in which it should be Taught from the Pulpit'. Chalmers' concern throughout was to give the students exactly what Hill could not give them: practical guidance and evangelical enthusiasm. As John Duncan said, 'he was especially great in all questions where the heart aids the intellect' (*ibid.*, 28).

Since Chalmers' day Scottish theologians have remained as reluctant as before to produce compendia of systematic theology. Three attempts deserve a brief mention.

The United Presbyterian theologian, James Orr,* published his Kerr Lectures,* *The Christian View of God and the World as centring in the Incarnation* (E, 1893). Orr's aim was to present not merely a systematic theology but a world-view (*Weltanschauung*), using the incarnation as his unifying principle. *The Christian View* is a work of massive erudition, not least in the field of continental theology, but Orr's own theology exists in tension with that of the scholars he quotes (notably I. A. Dorner). He borrowed, debated, re-phrased and synthesized, but never moved far away from the evangelical orthodoxy of his roots. It is difficult to think of a single original idea attributable to James Orr.

James Denney* said of his *Studies in Theology* (L, 1894), 'They do not amount to a system of theology, but the writer believes they are consistent with each other, and would find their place in a system.' The *Studies* are robustly evangelical on such topics as the atonement, but there is already evidence of hesitancy on the doctrine of Scripture: 'It is by no means necessary that we should know everything that is in the gospels to be true, or that we should be bound to the accuracy of every detail before they begin to do for us what God designs them to do.'

Like Orr, David S. Cairns* (best known for *The Faith That Rebels*, L, 1928) had his roots in the UPC. His book, *A System of Christian Doctrine*, was published in 1979, thirty-three years after his death, under the editorship of his son. It consists of only 200 pages but within that brief compass it traverses all the main *loci* of theology. The result is certainly not the theology of the old Seceders. Indeed, it is impossible to categorize, because while most articulate in its repudiations, it is much less confident in its affirmations. The work of a Scot in exile, John Macquarrie (b.1919), *Principles of Christian Theology* (L, 1966, ^{2}1977), has been much used. In its reinterpretations of central Christian doctrines it is heavily indebted to existentialism and to Paul Tillich. Whether the greatest of twentieth-century Scottish theologians, T. F. Torrance,* will produce a systematic theology, remains to be seen.

D. Macleod

T

Tait, Archibald Campbell (1811–82), Archbishop of Canterbury. He was the ninth and youngest child of a Scots Presbyterian landowner. He was educated at the Royal High School Edinburgh, Glasgow University and Balliol College Oxford, where he was confirmed in 1830, became a Fellow in 1834, and was ordained an Anglican clergyman in 1836. A firm liberal Protestant, he drafted the Four Tutors' protest against Newman's *Tract 90*, and in 1842 succeeded the liberal Protestant Thomas Arnold as Headmaster of Rugby. He became dean of Carlisle in 1849 and supported University reform. As Bishop of London from 1856, he encouraged popular evangelism and laboured in the cholera epidemic of 1866. He held a difficult middle ground between the defenders and assailants of the radical *Essays and Reviews*, and liberalized the terms on which the clergy subscribed to the Thirty-nine Articles. As Archbishop of Canterbury from 1868, he won the best possible settlement for the Church of Ireland (disestablished in 1869), and tried, ineffectively, to curb ritualism through the Public Worship Regulation Act of 1874. He presided at the second Lambeth Conference of 1878. A consummate and principled politician, his anti-ecclesiastical temper reflected his conception of a non-Roman national Christianity.

R. T. Davidson and W. Benham, *Life of Archibald Campbell Tait*, 2 vols (L, 1891); W. Benham (ed.), *Catharine and Craufurd Tait. A Memoir* (L, 1879); *DNB* LV, 292–9; P. T. Marsh, *The Victorian Church in Decline* (L, 1969).

S. Gilley

Tallach, John (1890–1955), FP missionary. After service with the Seaforth Highlanders during the First World War, he studied to become a missionary with the FPC in Rhodesia. In October 1924 he sailed there as the first Scottish missionary to work alongside John Radasi,* the founder of the FP mission. Radasi's untimely death, however, meant that Tallach began his work with very limited help. Within two years he was conducting services in Xhosa, and he worked energetically on the ministerial, educational and agricultural aspects of the mission. He laboured in Africa for twenty-four years, returning home in 1946. He died in Oban.

A. McPherson (ed.), *History of the Free Presbyterian Church of Scotland* (Inverness, 1974); id., *James Fraser* (L, 1967).

J. L. MacLeod

Taylor, Alfred Edward (1869–1945), philosopher. Born in Oundle, Northamptonshire, brought up as a Wesleyan Methodist and educated at Oxford, Taylor spent the bulk of his university teaching career in St Andrews (1908–24) and Edinburgh (1924–41) as Professor of Moral Philosophy. Previously he had taught at Oxford, Manchester, and in Canada. During his years in Oxford and Manchester he was particularly influenced by F. H. Bradley and Samuel Alexander.

Taylor had an international reputation as a Plato scholar. His wide and deep knowledge of the history of Western thought flavoured his more directly philosophical writings. Besides the work on Plato and Greek philosophy, his published writings were chiefly in moral philosophy and the philosophy of religion. His developed religious thought found expression in *The Faith of a Moralist*, 2 vols (L, 1930: Gifford lectures* given at St Andrews in 1926–8), and, at a more popular level, in *The Christian Hope of Immortality* (L, 1938) and *Does God Exist?* (L, 1943).

Taylor adopted the familiar post-Kantian idealist view that morality requires and finds its fulfilment in religion. This is because morality points beyond a mere succession of temporal goods to that which is eternal. For Taylor, morality is grounded in the undeniable facts of human experience. Unlike some idealists, Taylor did not scorn 'ecclesiastical faith', and he was in fact a strong Anglo-Catholic.

Embedded in Taylor's idealism was a marked strand of Augustianism. For in his view, the experience of human sin and guilt prevents a natural and automatic ascending of the human to the divine. It

TAYLOR, FRANCIS WILLIAM

is only divine grace which enables a person to fulfil himself as a moral being and so to find God and immortality.

DNB 1941–1950, 864–5; W. D. Ross in *Proceedings of British Academy* 31 (1945), 407–22.
P. Helm

Taylor, Francis William (1877–1957), Baptist* pastor and revivalist* preacher in the Inner Hebrides. Taylor was born at Ardchrishnish Farm in the Ross of Mull, where his father was farm manager. Although named after F. W. Clark, the landlord of Ulva noted for his severe policy of clearance,* Taylor identified fully with the crofting population of the Inner Hebrides. Following his conversion through Baptist preaching, he studied at Dunoon Baptist College (1906–10) (*see* MacGregor, Duncan), becoming pastor successively of the churches at Bowmore in Islay (1910–13), Bunessan on Mull (1913–20), Broadford in Skye (1920–7) and Tiree (1928–39). Well known as a powerful evangelist, Taylor was a central figure in the Tiree revival of 1922–4. Trained in the years immediately after the Welsh Revival (1904–5), he was one of the last Gaelic*-speaking revivalist preachers in the Baptist churches.

D. E. Meek, *Island Harvest: Tiree Baptist Church 1838–1988* (E, 1988), 35–8; D. W. Bebbington (ed.), *The Baptists in Scotland* (G, 1988), 297–304.
D. E. Meek

Taylor, (Sir) Thomas Murray (1897–1962), distinguished Presbyterian Principal of Aberdeen University. Born at Keith, Banffshire, he studied at Aberdeen, graduating MA in 1919 in classics. He then studied law (LLB, 1922), and was called to the bar in 1924. In 1929 he became Advocate-Depute, in 1934 Home Advocate-Depute, and in 1935 Professor of Law in Aberdeen University. In 1948 he was appointed Principal and Vice-Chancellor. He served on the Executive Committee of the World Council of Churches 1948–54.

Murray was brought up in the UFC, and went with most of his Church into the CofS in 1929. He addressed the special sitting of the CofS General Assembly in 1960 commemorating the 400th anniversary of the Scottish Reformation with a speech marked by 'bold adherence to Reformation truths ... combined with an equally vehement call for closer co-operation and understanding with the Roman Catholics' (obituary in *LW*, September 1962, 226). His 'The Rock Whence Ye are Hewn' is an eloquent defence of the Scottish Reformation (in his *Where One Man Stands*, E, 1960, 88–99).

Taylor received a DD from Edinburgh University and an LLD from St Andrews and Glasgow. He delivered the Riddell lectures in the University of Durham in 1954.

The Discipline of Virtue (L, 1954); *Christians and the Prevention of War in an Atomic Age* (with R. S. Bilheimer, L, 1961).

Who Was Who, 1961–70, 1104; *DNB 1961–1970*,

TEINDS

1001–2; memoir in his *Speaking to Graduates* (E, 1965), ed. A. M. Hunter and W. Lillie.
N. R. Needham

Teinds, or tithes, the 'tenths' of produce provided for uses such as the maintenance of clergy, the upkeep of church property and relief of the poor. With the development of a parish* structure in Scotland in the twelfth and thirteenth centuries, patrons,* on building churches, endowed them with land, and the priest appointed as parson ('rector', in Latin), besides the rents he gained from his kirkland, had the right to the teinds of the parish. As a levy on the produce of the land, teinds were payable by the farmers who reaped the crops. With the appropriation of the major part of parsonage revenues by religious houses, cathedrals and other ecclesiastical institutions in the course of the Middle Ages, vicarage settlements resulted, permitting a vicar, as substitute for the parson, to serve a parish with an income derived in part from a share of the teinds.

Teinds were divided into personal and predial. Personal teinds were levied on wages, the fruits of men's labour, but soon fell into disuse because of difficulties in estimation and collection, and offerings were regarded as a substitute. Predial, or real, teinds were leviable on produce renewed by nature from year to year, and were subdivided into the greater or garbal or parsonage teinds levied on cereal crops, and the lesser or vicarage teinds which included all other farm produce from hay to animals and dairy produce. Teinds might be commuted into a sum of money. They might also be leased, along with lands, for a single annual payment representing both rent and teind. This process meant that temporality (consisting of lands and their rents) and spirituality (essentially the teinds) were confused. Teind rights might be included in charters conveying property and so might pass into lay hands, to the church's ultimate loss. Whereas a resident vicar holding his own teinds might seek to collect them personally from parishioners, non-resident teind-holders, who might be bishops, abbots, canons or laymen, found it useful to free themselves from the burden connected with the direct lifting of the sheaves by leasing the teinds to tacksmen as middlemen in return for an annual rent. The tacksmen, in turn, might sublet their leases.

All this contributed to the Reformers' difficulties at the Reformation* in seeking to claim the teinds as the church's proper patrimony. The *FBD*'s* solution in 1560 of separating teinds from other ecclesiastical revenues stood untested; the ancient system of benefices, far from being dissolved as the Reformers intended, remained in being; and funds for ministers' stipends* were forthcoming in 1562 when a levy of a third of the revenues from benefices was assigned (in unequal measure) to the Crown and Reformed ministry (*see* Thirds of Benefices); from 1566 ministers gained access to vacant parochial benefices as a means of further sustenance; then, at the Convention of Leith* in 1572 the greater benefices were placed at the disposal of the kirk and Crown. At that point, too, it was agreed that benefice holders should be liable to a levy of a tenth of their income derived from teinds for support of the poor. Efforts were also made then to secure adequate stipends from the teinds for ministers who served churches appropriated to religious houses, where the temporality and title usually lay with a lay commendator.*

In 1578, the *SBD** reiterated the ideal that every man should have his own teinds, and urged a reform of the practice of leasing teinds and of confusing teinds with lands and their rents, but the problem of extricating the teinds still awaited a comprehensive solution. In 1596, Lindsay of Menmuir's 'constant platt' recognized the minister's right to teinds locally assigned; then in 1617 and 1621 James VI* appointed commissioners to assign at their discretion local stipends from the teinds, which increased the share tacksmen of the teinds contributed to ministers' stipends; but it was left to Charles I, in his Revocation scheme, to embark on a thorough-going programme for improving stipends by recovering patrimony previously alienated. In the process, nobles were threatened with a loss of their teinds; and machinery was established for valuing and commuting teinds, and for providing ministers' stipends, fixed at a minimum of 800 merks, with augmentations where necessary. This machinery endured with minor modifications till 1925, when Parliament passed the CofS Properties and Endowments Act,* ending the system of maintaining parish ministers from the teinds.

J. Connell, *A Treatise on the Law of Scotland Respecting Tithes* (E, 1830); W. Buchanan, *Treatise on the Law of Scotland on the Subject of Teinds or Tithes* (E, 1862); A. A. Cormack, *Teinds and Agriculture in Scotland* (O, 1930).

J. Kirk

Tell Scotland (1952–65), a major missionary movement of the Scottish churches that originated in a deeply held concern to reach the unchurched of the nation for Christ. Its immediate occasion was the encouragement given to the cause of mission by the Radio Missions of 1950 and 1951–2 (*see* Religious Broadcasting) and the subsequent challenge to the Churches to accept the responsibility and respond to the opportunities discovered.

The Movement was inter-Church, embracing the main denominations apart from the RCC. Mission was seen as the Church's essential task, in which the role of the laity was decisive. Two years, 1953–4, were planned as years of recruitment and training. Within congregational groups lay people would learn to incarnate and articulate their faith. 1955 would be the year of outreach.

The year of climax 1955 became also the year of crisis. On the commendation of Tom Allan,* first Secretary of the Movement, Billy Graham* was invited to conduct the 'All Scotland Crusade'. Controversy surrounded the decision before and after. There were fears that the crusade model and the personality focus would seriously prejudice the essential principles of the Movement.

Tell Scotland never recovered from the trauma of 1955. Tom Allan, whose vision had largely inspired the Movement, returned to the parish ministry, and his successors, Ian McTaggart (1955–61) and Colin Day (1962–5), continued the work of its four Commissions on the Bible, the Laity, the Community, and Evangelism. Kirk Weeks* modelled on the German Kirchentag became the main points of focus. In 1965 Tell Scotland was subsumed within the operation of the Scottish Churches' Council (*see* Ecumenical Movement), with which it had become increasingly identified.

RGACS, Home Board Reports, 1953–66; R. H. Falconer, *The Kilt Beneath My Cassock* (E, 1978); J. Highet, *The Scottish Churches* (L, 1960).

P. T. Bisset

Temperance Movement. The temperance movement originated in North America in the 1820s, and was first introduced to Britain through two working-class societies in Greenock and Maryhill in 1828–9. It spread throughout Britain, aided by the lecturing work of middle-class patrons like John Dunlop* of Greenock and William Collins (senior), the Glasgow publisher. It was dedicated initially to individual abstinence from spirits (in Scotland principally whisky), but by 1836 anti-spirits activity had ceased in Scotland; it re-emerged in the late 1830s under the banner of total abstinence from alcohol (or 'teetotallism'). The pledge committed members to renouncing alcohol and refusing to offer it to others. During 1839–50 the movement developed a strong connection with political radicalism and Chartism* (especially in the west of Scotland), and was shunned by the political and religious establishment. Although quickly attracting Baptist,* Evangelical Union* and Congregationalist* support, most Presbyterian ministers opposed it for offering a substitute for Christian salvation. But support grew during the 1840s, mostly in the UPC* and FC.* In 1845, a Personal Abstinence Society was formed by Secession* and Relief* Church ministers, continuing in the UPC, with 180 ministers by 1858. The FC Temperance Society was formed with thirty-three ministers in 1849 (191 by 1858), and the FC emerged in 1861 as the main teetotal denomination, with 320 pledged ministers, a very active Assembly committee, and with FC members strong in the Scottish Temperance League and in agitation on licensing boards. In the UPC, an overture to Synod in 1854 called for the expulsion of members who 'traffic in intoxicating liquor', but when a Temperance Committee was formed in 1859 it was specifically instructed to conduct its work 'without pronouncing any judgment on the question of abstinence ... or infringing on the liberties of the members of the Church on this point'. Yet the UP Synod adopted a more radical stance from 1870, but the CofS, known disparagingly as the 'Whisky Kirk', remained distanced from the movement; its Committee on Intemperance was formed only in 1867 and its Temperance Society in 1876.

By 1900, the temperance movement was becoming

TEMPERANCE MOVEMENT

dominated by the Churches, and by women's and children's sections. Youth campaigning had started in the late 1840s in temperance friendly societies like the Rechabites, but by the 1880s the Band of Hope dominated amongst Protestant children; Scottish membership rose from perhaps 2,000 in 1870 to 147,000 in 1908. For Catholic adults and children, the League of the Cross grew slowly from the 1860s to have by the 1890s over 30,000 members in the Glasgow Archdiocese alone. Other organizations also promoted teetotallism: the Glasgow Foundry Boys' Religious Society, the Boys' Brigade* and the Good Templars.

The movement's strategies were often the cause of division. The Presbyterian Churches debated the use of fermented or unfermented wine in communion. More fundamentally, division arose between reliance on 'moral suasion' ('converting' individuals by the pledge) and demanding 'moral force' (legal restriction or prohibition of the drinks trade). The trend was toward the latter. The Temperance (Scotland) Act 1913 allowed local-veto plebiscites with a 55 per cent voter majority to secure either prohibition of, or a reduction in, public houses and off-licenses. The Act came into force in June 1920, giving rise to frenetic campaigning in which Bands of Hope, Women's and Young Men's Guilds and home missionaries were deployed in canvassing. But only around forty of 584 wards polled went 'dry' in the first year and re-polls reduced that number by half by 1927.

This proved to be the turning point. In the mid-1920s adult pledge-taking fell dramatically, the Labour Movement portrayed the Temperance Act as 'class legislation' (in part because it did not affect middle-class restaurant licenses), and the Band of Hope started to lose members and branches. The main Churches continued their temperance committees, but the cause became progressively geographically isolated to the Highlands,* Hebrides and Northern Isles, and to some fishing and industrial villages. Even there, local prohibition was mostly reversed by 1950, with notable exceptions like Kilsyth (which remained 'dry' until the repeal of the 1913 Act in 1976) and the Presbyterian Hebrides, where licensing is less liberal than elsewhere. Though the Scottish Band of Hope Union and other temperance organizations survive, the Licensing (Scotland) Act 1976 and general social liberalization have severely diminished the popularity of teetotallism and the prohibition cause.

D. C. Paton, 'Temperance and the Churches in Scotland 1829–1927', *Scottish Records Association Conference Report* 7 (1987), 22–9; *id.*, 'Drink and the Temperance Movement in Nineteenth Century Scotland' (PhD, Edinburgh University, 1977); C. G. Brown, 'Religion and the Development of an Urban Society: Glasgow 1780–1914' (PhD, Glasgow University, 1982), II, 143–90; E. King, *Scotland Sober and Free* (G, 1979); T. C. Smout, *A Century of the Scottish People* (L, 1986), 133–48.

C. G. Brown

TEN YEARS' CONFLICT

Ten Years' Conflict (1834–43), events leading up to the Disruption.* When the Veto Act* was passed in 1834, Moderates* dissented on the ground that the congregational 'veto' granted by the General Assembly was a violation of the civil rights of the patron and of the entitlement of the presentee. On this basis Robert Young, a presentee rejected through the 'veto', appealed to the Court of Session for redress. The result of the Auchterarder* case was that in March 1838 the Court of Session, by a vote of eight judges to five, found in favour of Young and declared the Veto Act incompetent. The Non-Intrusionists* took exception to the judgment not only because it overbore the conscientious opposition of the people, but primarily because, they alleged, the civil courts were interfering with the strictly ecclesiastical business of ordination. The General Assembly of 1838 affirmed that 'in all matters touching the doctrine, government or discipline of this Church her judicatories possess an exclusive jurisdiction founded on the Word of God'. As the number of cases going through the courts multiplied, it became apprent that the judges were intent on rejecting this claim to an independent jurisdiction and on asserting the Church's subordination to the legislature and the courts. The General Assembly resisted these judgments with vigour and upheld the Veto Act. The conflict intensified when John Edwards, a presentee rejected under the Veto Act in the parish of Marnoch, obtained an interdict from the Court of Session instructing the Presbytery of Strathbogie* to take him on trials. When seven ministers submitted to the interdict they were suspended and later deposed by the General Assembly. The alternative would have been to defy the Court of Session and risk imprisonment. To satisfy the demands of both civil and ecclesiastical law was impossible.

With its Non-Intrusionist majority ever more militant, by 1842 the General Assembly was petitioning for the abolition of patronage and in the Claim of Right* demanded from the government an unequivocal acknowledgement of the spiritual independence of the Church. However, the Erastian Peel had taken office in 1841: his government was unsympathetic to Non-Intrusion in principle and considered it insignificant in practice. The government placed great faith in the 'Middle Party'* which emerged in 1842 – men of evangelical sympathy who were nevertheless determined not to split the Church – but it remained small. The large majority of the evangelical party met in Convocation* late in 1842, to make practical preparations for Disruption.* Early in 1843 the government made it known that it would not act. At the same time the Court of Session, in the Stewarton* judgment, declared the Chapels Act* incompetent. By depriving 'chapel' ministers of their seats in church courts, Evangelicals alleged that the Court of Session had committed the further intrusion of claiming jurisdiction over the composition of the Church's organs of government and discipline. In order to vindicate the principle of spiritual independence the Non-Intrusionists were prepared to give up Establishment and, at the Assembly in May 1843, 451 ministers seceded to form the Church of Scotland Free.

The conflict unfortunately distracted the Church from the urgent task of addressing the industrialization of Scotland. Could it have been avoided? Sir James Graham, the Home Secretary, later expressed his regret that the government did not do more to avert the calamity of the Disruption. It was probably true that the Court of Session took pleasure in 'winging wild churchmen'. Had the young evangelical leaders been more experienced and the old leader, Chalmers,* less determined, then in 1838 the Church might not have joined issue on a point of such high principle that any compromise was impossible from the start. However, even superior tactical manoeuvring may only have delayed the collision. The conflict involved fundamental principles of political and social organization, reaching down to questions regarding the nature and location of sovereignty within the State. The Church's recovery of the 'two kingdoms' teaching of the sixteenth and seventeenth centuries coincided with a time when the pretensions of the State were expanding so as to make rapprochement very unlikely. At any rate, the basic position taken by the General Assembly in 1838 has come to be regarded as essential to the freedom and integrity of the Church.

AGACS, 1832–42; *PGAFC*, 1843; *The Witness*, 1840–3; R. Buchanan, *The Ten Years Conflict*, 2 vols (L, 1849); J. Bryce, *Ten Years of the Church of Scotland*, 2 vols (E, 1850); H. Watt, *Thomas Chalmers and the Disruption* (E, 1943), 115–314; J. Hope, *Letter to the Lord Chancellor* (E, 1839); A. M. Dunlop, *Letter to the Earl of Aberdeen* (E, 1840).

K. R. Ross

Ternan, *see* Celtic Saints.

Terrot, Charles Hugh (1790–1872), Episcopal Bishop of Edinburgh. Terrot was born in India, and reared by his uncle, priest at Haddington. He achieved the Cambridge BA in 1812. Ordained priest in 1814, and elected Bishop in 1841, he became Primus of the Episcopal College in 1857. He was a moderate high churchman.

Terrot was also Pantonian Professor at the Episcopal Theological College*, Edinburgh. A man of high ability, especially in mathematics, he anticipated the discovery of 'Quaternions'. He upheld Scottish Realism* in philosophy. He mixed in the high circles of the Royal Society of Edinburgh, but also had an avid concern for the poor. He addressed himself to the debates of the time, such as the Disruption* and Newman's secession.

Terrot composed poetry and won the Seatonian Prize. He wrote papers on mathematics, and penned pastoral letters and sermons which were published in the 1830s and 1840s. He is known for his *Exposition of the Epistle to the Romans* (L, E, 1828) and his translation of Ernesti's *Institutio Interpretis* (E, 1832).

DNB LVI, 83; W. Walker, *Three Churchmen* (E, 1893).

A. E. Nimmo

Test Act (1681), an Act of Parliament entitled 'Act anent Religion and the Test', passed on 31 August, 1681. Part of the more rigorous policy against the Covenanters* initiated by the appointment of James, Duke of York and Albany, as Lord High Commissioner, it required all office-holders in Church and state to accept the Scots Confession* of 1560 and royal supremacy in both civil and ecclesiastical government, and to renounce the Covenants.

The Act, which demanded absolute allegiance 'without any equivocation, mental reservation or any manner of evasion whatsoever', had the effect of producing a variety of equivocating and explanatory responses, the ejection of over sixty ministers from their parishes and the exile or deprivation of a variety of nobles and office-holders, from the Duke of Argyll down. Moreover it had the effect of stimulating the various societies of Covenanters to form a union or General Correspondence (*see* Societies, United), thus considerably polarizing the situation.

I. B. Cowan, *The Scottish Covenanters* (L, 1976); J. K. Hewison, *The Covenanters*, 2 vols (G, ²1913).

H. R. Sefton

Testimonies, declarations issued by the Secession* churches or the Reformed Presbyterian Church, consisting of historical narrative and theological statements applying the principles of the subordinate standards (*see* Subscription) to contemporary questions at issue. Testimonies were not regarded as carrying the constitutional obligation which was accorded to the documents of the Westminster Assembly.* They were used to vindicate a Church's separation from other Churches, and to bear witness against errors which had recently arisen.

The Associate Presbytery* published in 1733 a testimony enumerating the reasons for their departure from the national Church; their Judicial Testimony of 1736 gave a more elaborate indictment of the CofS's defections from former principles, and served to confirm the division which had occurred. The Old Light/New Light* Controversy was the occasion for the General Associate Synod* and the Associate Synod* to revise their testimonies, and these revisions led to divisions in both bodies. The Original Secession Church* was created in 1827 with the adoption of a testimony composed by ministers from both of the uniting Churches. The Reformed Presbyterian testimony of 1761 contested the claim of the Seceders to be the true representatives of a covenanted Second Reformation,* and the New Testimony of 1839 expounded the same principles with a more moderate tone.

J. M'Kerrow, *History of the Secession Church* (E, 1854); M. Hutchison, *The Reformed Presbyterian Church in Scotland* (Paisley, 1893).

S. Isbell

Theatre, Christian attitudes to the. Only titles and fragments survive from Scottish medieval church drama but the vigour and scale of David Lindsay's 1540 morality play, *Ane Pleasant Satyre of the Thrie Estaitis*, indicates the strength of the dramatic tradition, while burgh records indicate that it was also widespread. The aim of the mystery and miracle plays was to entertain and at the same time instruct a largely illiterate population on the occasion of major Christian festivals.

At first drama was used to further the cause of the Reformation, with plays such as *The Beheading of John the Baptist*, by James Wedderburn,* and propagandistic pageants such as the one that John Knox* is recorded as attending in St Andrews in 1571. The Protestant spirit of Lindsay's *Thrie Estaitis* is also evident in the Latin plays of George Buchanan.*

There was, however, a close connection between drama and social life in Scotland, and the drive to order and 'discipline' town life, which began before the Reformation, inevitably affected the theatre. The Robin Hood plays and other folk revels associated with the seasonal feasts were banned in 1555, before the Reformation,* by the Queen Regent, Mary of Guise.* In 1575 the General Assembly* of the Reformed Church banned 'canonical' or scriptural plays. Drama was now solely connected with the court and royal patronage (a factor that increased Presbyterian antagonism), and, with the loss of the court to London in 1603, the theatre was effectively silenced. Drama as a literary concept survived in the classroom, but the imaginative impulse went underground in ballads and folktales.

The next play of note is Archibald Pitcairne's *The Assembly* (1692), a satire on the General Assembly which was performed in London in 1722 and did nothing to reconcile Presbyterianism to theatrical entertainment. Further conflict ensued when the theatre, despite severe legal restrictions, began again in Edinburgh. The performance in 1756 of *The Douglas* (*see* Douglas Affair) in the Canongate Playhouse provoked an uproar because its author, John Home,* was a minister.

Although Home was forced to resign, there was a progressive diminishing of hostility as the theatre gained in respectability, and dramatizations in the early nineteenth century of Sir Walter Scott's* novels did much to popularize the theatre throughout Scotland.

It was only in the twentieth century, however, following the huge changes in church worship in the latter part of the previous century (*see* Arts, Churches and the), that the attitude of the Christian Churches became one of support rather than tolerance. From the 1930s, dramatic performances became more frequent in Presbyterian as well as Episcopal churches, and many of the new community drama groups were based in church halls. In 1946 the CofS renovated the Gateway Theatre in Edinburgh, and played a valuable role in encouraging indigenous Scottish drama of all kinds. Controversy could still occur, as with the proposed production – subsequently cancelled – of Aristophanes' *Lysistrata* in 1960, but the General Assembly of 1961 affirmed the CofS's support for theatre and its own commitment to the arts (*RGACS 1961*, 311–21), which, after the sale of the Gateway, was continued through the Netherbow Arts Centre in Edinburgh and the Iona Community.*

J. Stuart, *A Scots Gospel* (E, 1985); T. Royle, *The Macmillan Companion to Scottish Literature* (L, 1983); T. Fleming et al., *The Twelve Seasons of The Edinburgh Gateway Company* (E, 1965); id., *Miracle at Midnight* (L, 1959); A. Reid, *Kirk and Drama* (E, 1958); D. Hutchison, *The Modern Scottish Theatre* (G, 1977); J. Dibdin, *Annals of Edinburgh Stage* (E, 1888); A. J. Mill, *Mediaeval Plays in Scotland* (E, 1927); S. Carpenter, 'The Bible in Mediaeval Verse and Drama', in D. F. Wright (ed.), *The Bible in Scottish Life and Literature* (E, 1988), 65–78.

D. Smith

Theological Education, *see* Education, Theological.

Theology, *see* Education, Theological; Practical Theology; Systematic Theology.

Thirds of Benefices, a scheme to finance the ministry of the Kirk after the Reformation.* The *First Book of Discipline*'s* designs on the patrimony of the old Church (*FBD* 156–64) were impracticable, and in late 1561 a compromise arrangement decreed that one-third of the revenues of all ecclesiastical benefices be collected by the Crown for its own needs and for the new Reformed ministry. The division of the thirds between Crown and Kirk was left unspecified, and Knox (*History* II, 28–30) and the General Assembly* (100–4) protested at the inadequacy of provision. On Mary's* deposition in 1567 it was decided that the Church should have a prior claim on the thirds, to be collected now by the General Assembly's agents, but this proved ineffective and the Crown resumed collection in 1573. Accounts of the collector-general survive for 1561–97. The scheme remained in force into the seventeenth century, but well before then the Reformed Church was on its way to a complete takeover of ecclesiastical revenues.

Knox, *History* II, 326–32; G. Donaldson, *The Scottish Reformation* (C, 1960), 68–72, 90–4, 151–4; id., *Accounts of the Collectors of Thirds of Benefices 1561–1572* (SHS, E, 1949); *SBD* 16–18.

D. F. Wright

Thistle, Chapel and Dean of. The first reference to the thistle as a Scottish emblem is probably in William Dunbar's* *The Thistle and the Rose*, celebrating the marriage of James IV* to Margaret Tudor in 1503. Little is known about the origin of the Order of the Thistle. It may be that the precedent of the Orders of the Garter, St Michael and the Golden Fleece, suggested that Scotland should have its own order of chivalry. The date 1540 has been postulated. However, two years later James V* died and nothing is heard of the Order until

THOM, WILLIAM

James VII* promulgated a new body of statutes in 1687 and ordered the nave of Holyrood Abbey Church to be fitted out as a Chapel for the Order, with throne and stalls for eight knights. An altar, images and vestments for RC worship infuriated the Edinburgh populace, which ransacked the building, and it eventually became a ruin.

Queen Anne revived the Order in 1703 and George II increased the number of knights to sixteen. Thanks to the benevolence of the family of Leven and Melville, a very fine Chapel, designed by Robert Lorimer, was erected at the south-east corner of St Giles' Cathedral,* and inaugurated by King George V in 1911. The Queen is Sovereign of the Most Noble Order and there is a Chancellor and a Dean, who has sometimes, but not always, been the Dean of the Chapel Royal.*

C. L. Warr, 'The Order of the Thistle', and F. J. Grant, 'The Chapel', in *Trans. of Scott. Ecclesiological Society* 14 (1948), 26–8; C. and H. Burnett, *The Green Mantle* (E, 1989); R. J. Malloch, 'The Order of the Thistle', *Journal of the Heraldry Society of Scotland* 1 (1977–78), 35–46.

A. I. Dunlop

Thom, William (1751–1811), co-founder of the Methodist New Connexion. Born in Aberdeen, where he had a good education (colleagues were struck by his knowledge of mathematics, Latin and Hebrew), he became one of Wesley's preachers in 1774, serving with distinction in Lincolnshire and Yorkshire. Wesley made him one of the Legal Hundred in 1784, despite his lack of seniority. In the controversies following Wesley's death he sided with those who desired clear distinction from the Church of England (symbolized in administration of the sacrament by Methodist preachers) and effective lay participation in the government of Methodism. In 1795 he signed Alexander Kilham's* petition seeking clarification of the Plan of Pacification; and after Kilham's expulsion Thom was one of only three preachers (another, Alexander Cummin or Cumming, was probably also a Scot) to leave the Methodist Conference of 1797 for Kilham's 'New Itinerancy' (later, the Methodist New Connexion). The connexion incorporated lay participation in a form not dissimilar to the Presbyterianism from which Thom came. He was its first President, serving six presidential terms in all, and with Kilham's early death was regarded as the Connexion's father. He died in harness at Shooter's Hill, Staffs.

Methodist New Connexion Minutes, 1812 (obituary); O. A. Beckerlegge, *United Methodist Ministers and their Circuits* (L, 1968); W. J. Townsend, H. B. Workman and G. Eayrs (eds), *A New History of Methodism* (L, 1909) I, 481ff; G. Packer (ed.), *The Centenary of the Methodist New Connexion* (L, 1897), 71ff; R. E. Davies, A. R. George and G. Rupp (eds), *A History of the Methodist Church in Great Britain*, II (L, 1878), 276ff.

A. F. Walls

Thomas, Rosie, *see* Fisherfolk, Missions to.

THOMSON, ANDREW MITCHELL

Thompson, Christina, *see* Women in Presbyterian Missions.

Thomson, Alexander (1798–1868), Laird of Banchory (Devenick), near Aberdeen, descendant of John Knox,* theologian and ecclesiastical controversialist, educational and penal reformer, diarist, letter-writer, archaeologist, traveller and bibliophile.

Thomson was educated at the Grammar School and Marischal College in Aberdeen (MA, 1816) and thereafter studied law at Edinburgh University. The early death of his father meant that Thomson assumed the duties of a country gentleman immediately on attaining his majority. He made a grand tour of Europe 1826–9 and kept a careful diary of his travels. He was appointed a Deputy Lieutenant of both Aberdeenshire and Kincardineshire and on several occasions was elected Dean of Faculty at Marischal College. As Dean he played an important part in the negotiations for the union of King's College and Marischal College in 1860.

A devout Evangelical* in theology, Thomson actively supported the Non-Intrusionists* in the Ten Years' Conflict* and joined the FC in 1843. He was a generous benefactor to the FC College in Aberdeen (*see* Christ's College) and strenuously supported its recognition by the FC General Assembly. Thomson made the arrangements for the British Association to meet in Aberdeen in 1859 and was host to the Prince Consort when he visited the Association.

He bequeathed his diaries, museum and library to the FC College. (Christ's College has deposited the diaries and library in Aberdeen University Library.) In 1878 the College instituted in his memory an annual Thomson Lectureship in Natural Science and Theology, which was held without a break until *c.*1935.

George Smeaton, *Memoir of Alexander Thomson of Banchory* (E, 1869); R. A. Lendrum *et al.*, *The Church College in Aberdeen* (A, 1936) – includes list of Thomson Lecturers; MS papers also in New College Library, Edinburgh.

H. R. Sefton

Thomson, Andrew Mitchell (1779–1831), leading Evangelical* in the CofS and editor of the *Edinburgh Christian Instructor.** Born in Sanquhar (Dumfriesshire), the son of John Thomson (*FES* I, 34–5), he studied at Edinburgh University. He was ordained to Sprouston (in the Presbytery of Kelso) in 1802, translated in 1808 to the East Church, Perth, and in 1810 to New Greyfriars, Edinburgh. In 1814 he was called to the newly-opened St George's, Edinburgh, in which charge his reputation as a preacher flourished. A large and eminent congregation was attracted and Thomson remained there until his sudden death.

Thomson took an active part in both Presbytery and General Assembly and was noted for both his mastery of Church law and his ability in debate. The great champion of the evangelical party in the CofS in his day, he was described by Thomas Chal-

mers* as a man of 'colossal mind', 'wielding the weapons of spiritual warfare' vigorously, with 'an arm of might, and voice of resistless energy', carrying 'as if by storm the convictions of his people'. When William Cunningham* first spoke in the Assembly, it was said of him that it was Andrew Thomson come again to hammer the Moderates!*
In 1810, with others of like mind, Thomson started the *Edinburgh Christian Instructor,* both serving as editor and contributing a substantial number of articles and reviews. From its inception, the *Instructor* served to foster the growth of the evangelical party* in the CofS from a fairly small minority in the General Assembly to a majority. The Moderates* resented the *Instructor* greatly and in 1820 had the Assembly censure it as 'highly injurious and calumnious'. Not at all intimidated, it took a vigorous stand on the issues of the day. Patronage,* which ultimately led to the formation of the FC,* was opposed, as Thomson championed the right of Christian people to call their own pastor. In the Little Dunkeld case, he prevented the settlement of a presentee who knew no Gaelic in a parish four-fifths Gaelic-speaking; Thomson observed that 'Little Dunkeld is the mouth of the Highlands, and ought certainly to have a Gaelic tongue in it'. He prevailed by a majority of eight.

The inclusion of the Apocrypha in editions of the Bible issued by the British and Foreign Bible Society on the continent led to the Apocrypha Controversy* and Thomson's championing of a Bible free from all human addition. The formation of the Edinburgh Bible Society (*see* Bible Societies), of which Thomson became secretary, resulted. He also energetically opposed the continuation of slavery in the British West Indies, arguing that slavery violated basic scriptural principles. He urged immediate emancipation and persuaded the Edinburgh Anti-Slavery Society* to adopt his views, but did not live to see this objective accomplished.

In *The Doctrine of Universal Pardon Considered and Refuted* (E, 1830), Thomson examined the doctrine of Thomas Erskine of Linlathen* and the similar opinions expressed by John McLeod Campbell.* In this he maintained the orthodox position against the universalism they propounded. He also wrote a trenchant reply to Andrew Marshall's* *Ecclesiastical Establishments Considered* (G, 1829), but died before the Voluntary Controversy* reached its peak.

A diligent pastor in spite of all his other activities, in addition to regular congregational visitation he devoted considerable attention to catechizing.* He catechized the youth of the church on Sabbath afternoons between the worship services and wrote a pamphlet for prospective communicants (*A Catechism for the Instruction of Communicants in the Nature and Uses of the Sacrament of our Lord's Supper* (E, 1807, ³E, n.d.). Conscious of the needs of his parish, he started a week-day school for the children of the lower classes and, for a time, served both as teacher and superintendent.

He had considerable musical talent and gathered and revised a collection of psalm tunes and added to them several compositions of his own (*Sacred Harmony*, E, 1820). Among his many friends were numbered various Secession* Church ministers, including Thomas M'Crie* (the elder), who wrote regularly for him in the *Instructor*. Thomson received a DD from Aberdeen in 1823.

Lectures on Portions of the Psalms (E, 1826); *Sermons on Various Subjects* (E, 1829); *Sermons and Sacramental Exhortations* (E, 1831) includes a memoir.

FES I, 105–6; *DNB* LVI, 234–5; memorial sermons by David Dickson, *The Remembrance of the Righteous*... (E, 1831), and Thomas Chalmers, *A Sermon*... (E, 1831); J. L. Watson, *Life of Andrew Thomson, D.D.* (E, 1882); T. M'Crie in *Blackwood's Magazine* 29 (1831), 577–8.

D. C. Lachman

Thomson, David Patrick (1896–1974), CofS evangelist. Born in Dundee, he went to schools there and in St Andrews. Commissioned as an army officer during the First World War, he found his first ministry in witness among his men. Invalided out of the army, the sole survivor of three brothers and five cousins who had gone to war, his survival gave him an awesome awareness of some special purpose for which he had been spared, and developing experience confirmed his calling to be an evangelist. From that date onwards evangelism was the passion of his life. Studies at Glasgow University and UF College (1919–25; MA, 1922) were almost incidental to the enterprise of mission. Experience of revival meetings in the north east of Scotland in 1921 brought a new experience of the Holy Spirit's working. Out of the experience was born the Glasgow Students' Evangelistic Union. 1921 saw also his first ventures in Christian publishing.

His first call to a regular pastorate came from Gillespie UF Church, Dunfermline (1928–34). There he embarked upon his customary vigorous ministry, and out of a deep concern for the development of lay training (*see* Laity) founded his first conference centre at Glassiebarns in 1931, moving to a slightly larger centre at Lassodie in 1933.

Appointed Evangelist by the Home Board of the CofS (1934–9, 1945–66), he began the work to which his life would be committed (apart from ministry in Trinity Church, Cambuslang, during the Second War 1939–45). Seaside Missions, launched pre-War, developed most fully in the post-War years until in 1974 some thousand young people were sharing in team witness. Closely related were the area missions engaging evangelism teams in door-to-door visitation, with a publication setting the mission in local context, and lay training schools to carry the work forward.

These enterprises had a special significance in the Kirk's missionary advance in the post-War years and helped prepare for the Tell Scotland* movement. Later, the need for effective leadership became pressing, and in 1958 led to the founding of St Ninian's, Crieff,* where D.P. (as he was widely known) was Warden until he retired in 1966.

Writing continued prolifically during the years of retirement, with a growing concern for congregational re-appraisal. Evangelism had led to the perceived need for lay training. Lay training pointed to the need of a Church re-formed for mission.

FUFCS 348; FES IX, 323, 460, X, 456; J. Highet, *The Scottish Churches* (L, 1960).

P. T. Bisset

Thomson, George Thomas (1887–1958), theological professor. Born in Edinburgh, he studied there and at Oxford and Berlin. After varied wartime service, he was minister of Tain (Ross-shire, 1920–4) and St Boswells (Roxburghshire, 1924–8), before becoming Professor of Systematic Theology at Aberdeen, 1928–36, and then of Christian Dogmatics at Edinburgh, 1936–52. He translated Barth (*Church Dogmatics* I: 1, and *Dogmatics in Outline*), and H. Heppe's *Reformed Dogmatics*, and jointly exegeted Romans in the IVF's* *New Bible Commentary* (ed. F. Davidson *et al.*, L, 1953). His vigorous defence of orthodoxy (he used Heppe in lectures) had something of a military flavour.

FES VII, 74, VIII, 714, IX, 775; *Who Was Who, 1951–1960*, 1083.

D. F. Wright

Thomson, James (1768–1855), CofS minister and editor of the *Encyclopaedia Britannica*. Born in Crieff, Perthshire, he attended Edinburgh University and was licensed by the Presbytery of Haddington in 1793. In 1795 he became co-editor with George Gleig,* Bishop of Brechin, of the third edition of the *Britannica*. He himself wrote the articles on 'Scripture', 'Septuagint' and 'Superstitition'; that on Scripture was retained in later editions. He resigned in 1796 to become a private tutor. In 1805 Thomson was ordained to Eccles, Berwickshire. He retired in 1847.

Thomson published *Expository Lectures on St Luke* (3 vols, L, 1849–51) and *Expository Lectures on the Acts of the Apostles* (L, 1854), the former of which received Charles Spurgeon's highest commendation.

He gained a DD from St Andrews in 1842.

DNB LVI, 255–6; FES II, 14–15.

N. R. Needham

Thomson, James or Diego (1788–1854), missionary. He was born in Creetown, Kirkcudbright. After theological studies in Glasgow, he was co-pastor of the Leith Walk Tabernacle, Edinburgh, with James Haldane.* In 1818, he went to South America, partly supported by Haldane churches. In Argentina (1818–21), Chile (1821–2) and Peru (1822–4) he organized public education on the Lancasterian model, and distributed Scriptures, largely through RC clergy. (He differed from the Haldanes on the Apocrypha* question.)

He married in 1826, and as BFBS (*see* Bible Societies) agent went with his wife to Mexico (1827–30), where their two daughters died in infancy, Venezuela (1831–2), the Caribbean (1832–8), Canada (1838–42) and Mexico and Yucatan (1842–4). In 1842 he graduated MD from McGill University. Throughout this period he coupled BFBS work with his educational interests. In 1845 he represented the BFBS in Scotland, and later went to Spain (1847–9). The death of his wife in Madrid in 1848 led to his involvement in the debate over religious liberty in Spain. In 1849 he left BFBS to encourage Protestant work in Portugal and Spain. He died in London. The Spanish Evangelization Society, founded in 1855, resulted from his initiatives.

Thomson's interest in the Bible and education brought personal contact with significant political leaders and intellectuals of Latin America – Bolivar, O'Higgins, San Martin, Mora – though BFBS was often uncomfortable with his political interests. His concern for minority groups involved him in Bible translation into the vernacular languages of Peru, Mexico, Canada and Spain. His life was characterized by a deep piety and an evangelistic zeal that established churches in Buenos Aires, Lima, Mexico and Madrid. In Latin America today he is regarded as both the pioneer of Evangelicalism and the forerunner of public education.

Letters on the Moral and Religious State of South America (L, 1827); *Spain, Its Position and Evangelization* (L, 1853).

A. Canclini, *Diego Thomson: Apóstol de la enseñanza y distribución de la Biblia en America y España* (Buenos Aires, 1987); R. Mitchell, 'The Evangelical Contribution of James Thomson to South American Life (1818–1825)' (PhD, Princeton Theological Seminary, 1972).

W. Mitchell

Thomson, Sinclair (1784–1864), Baptist* missionary in Shetland. A crofter's son, after a brief education he became a whaler, and then returned to farming in Dunrossness. He was led through Independency to Baptist principles, and was baptized by an itinerant evangelist in 1814. He founded a church at Dunrossness in 1816, and from his croft at Spiggie he travelled throughout the Shetlands, founding churches on Burra Isle, at Sandsting, Scalloway, and in 1840, in Lerwick. The last public act of his career was to buy at an auction a building for the Lerwick church. To finance his work and the building of churches, Thomson for many years went on tours both in Scotland and in England, where he became well known as the 'Shetland Apostle'. He was also able to provide pastors for the churches, and opened schools, including one on the Out Skerries, for which he received help from R. S. Candlish* of Edinburgh. Although Thomson was a fervent Evangelical, he came to see closed Communion as the only way for his churches. The work he did in Shetland has endured to the present.

See also Baptist Home Missionary Society for Scotland.

J. A. Smith, *Sinclair Thomson, the Shetland Apostle* (reprinted Lerwick, 1969); W. Fotheringham, *Sinclair Thomson* (Lerwick, 1917); D. W.

Bebbington (ed.), *The Baptists in Scotland* (G, 1988), 327-30.

D. B. Murray

Thomson, William, *see* Kelvin, Lord.

Thorfinn the Mighty, Earl of Orkney (1014-c.1065). Thorfinn succeeded to an earldom only recently converted to Christianity and still lacking the institutions of a fully Christian society. The early part of his reign was spent in warfare in Scotland and the north of England, and in a bitter power struggle with his brothers and nephew, from which he emerged as sole Earl. In his last twenty years Thorfinn brought Orkney into full membership of Western Christendom (*see* Orkney, Early Christianity in). It was probably during his visit to Rome (*c*.1050) that arrangements were made for the appointment of Orkney's first Bishop, Turolf, whom Thorfinn installed in his new cathedral of Christchurch adjacent to his own residence in Birsay. The *Orkneyinga Saga* describes how Thorfinn spent his latter peaceful years in making 'new laws'. These new laws possibly brought Norse society into conformity with Christian practice.

B. E. Crawford, *Scandinavian Scotland* (Leicester, 1987); H. Palsson and P. Edwards, *Orkneyinga Saga* (L, 1981); W. P. L. Thomson, *History of Orkney* (E, 1987).

W. P. L. Thomson

Tironensians, monastic order. St Bernard of Tiron (*c*.1046-1117), after many years as a Benedictine* monk and prior, lived in a colony of hermits in Brittany. Elected abbot at Poitiers, he resisted the claims of Cluny (*see* Cluniacs) and again became a leader of solitaries. In 1109 he founded a monastery at Tiron near Chartres, which flourished and soon became the head of many houses, mostly in France. This was a time of remarkable monastic ferment, characterized by a desire to follow the traditional *Rule* of Benedict, but in a radical and often literal way. Monks following the *Rule* strictly were in great demand. There was also a reaction against the authoritarianism and elaborate choir offices of Cluny.

Tiron was somewhat overshadowed by the contemporary and very similar Cistercian* reform. They had in common a love of simplicity, with accretions in choir office removed and manual work restored. The Tironensian emphasis was not on agriculture, however, but on arts and crafts. Strong links with daughter houses and discipline were maintained by annual general chapters and regular visitations. The habit was grey. Having flourished as a centralized congregation, Tironensians eventually grew more like black Benedictines, and in 1629 Tiron became a Maurist house. It was suppressed in 1790.

The first foundation in Britain by any of these reforming groups was at Selkirk, founded from Tiron in 1113, during Bernard's lifetime. David I* himself visited Tiron. Though Tironensians hardly existed in England, they flourished in Scotland and had four abbeys with dependent priories. The Selkirk house, having moved to Kelso* 1128, established priories at Lesmahagow and Fogo. From Kelso were founded also abbeys at Kilwinning (after 1162), Arbroath* (1178), which set up its own priory at Fyvie, Aberdeenshire, and Lindores* (1191). Attendance at the general chapter in Tiron was obligatory, in theory at least, every three years. All four abbeys retained substantial communities until the Reformation, having made a distinctive contribution to Scottish monasticism.

New Catholic Encyclopedia II, 343, XIV, 171; D. Knowles, *The Monastic Order in England* (C, 1950), 191-207; G. W. S. Barrow, *The Kingdom of the Scots* (L, 1973), 174-7, 199-211; Easson-Cowan, 66-71; S. Cruden, *Scottish Medieval Churches* (E, 1986), 42-64.

M. Dilworth

Tithes, *see* Teinds.

Toleration. Religious toleration first became official policy in Scotland through a declaration of the English Parliament (agreed in 1651 but not published until 1652) in which Scotland's conquerors promised 'countenance and encouragement' to those who served and worshipped God 'according to his mind revealed in his word'. Though vague, in practice this did provide a degree of toleration among Protestants – though Episcopalians as well as RCs were excluded. Small numbers of Scots took advantage of the declaration, by joining English-inspired groups such as Quakers,* Baptists* and Independents.* But the great majority were opposed to even this modest degree of toleration, and it lapsed with the Restoration* in 1660. The resistance of many Presbyterians to the re-imposition of episcopacy* in the 1660s led to discussion of the possibility of offering them limited toleration, but this did not become official policy until the Third Declaration of Indulgence* of 1679, which suspended the laws enforcing conformity so as to permit dissidents to attend 'house conventicles'* (meetings for worship in private houses) – though only south of the Tay and not in the larger towns, and the preachers had to be officially approved. In 1686 the Scottish Parliament reluctantly accepted James VII's* demand that his RC co-religionists be allowed to worship privately. In February 1687 an indulgence issued by James allowed 'moderate Presbyterians' to worship in private houses, and RCs and Quakers to worship in houses and chapels. Moreover, RCs were to be as free as Protestants to hold public offices. Another indulgence a few months later suspended all laws against indoor worship by non-conformists, provided sedition was not taught. Most Protestants, however, remained suspicious, regarding (with some justification) this offer of general toleration as being designed to make official favour to RCism palatable, James's ultimate ambition being the re-imposition of RCism on the country. After the 1688-9 Revolution and the Restoration of Presbyterianism in 1690, the CofS sought to reassert its religious monopoly, but this soon crumbled, largely due to the reluctance of the state to support persecution. The rights of the Presbyterian establishment were guaranteed at the time of the Union of Parliaments,* but political union with Episcopalian England inevitably weakened its position. In 1711 an appeal against imprisonment, by James Greenshields,* an Episcopalian preacher, to the House of Lords was decided in his favour, and in 1712 a Toleration Act followed. The immediate effect of this was limited by the fact that it specified that Scots Episcopalians must use the English liturgy and make explicit their allegiance to the regime. Thus the many 'nonjuror'* Episcopalians loyal to the Jacobite* cause were still liable to persecution – as were RCs. None the less, the 1712 Act confirmed that the state had no intention of trying to force everyone into the Est.C. Without such civil support the establishment lacked the means to enforce conformity, and a changing intellectual climate eroded the will to pursue it. Thus when the mid-eighteenth century Secessions* took place, it was accepted that there was no possibility of suppressing them forcibly. The sporadic persecution of RCs and non-juror Episcopalians declined after the harsh aftermath of the final (1745–6) Jacobite rebellion, as it gradually became clear that they no longer represented a political threat. The most oppressive penal laws against RCs in Ireland and England were repealed in 1777 and 1778 respectively, but an attempt to introduce a similar measure for Scotland led to such serious rioting that, though the Moderates* of the Est.C initially declared their approval of the bill, it was withdrawn from parliament. However, most of the penal laws relating to Scotland's RCs were repealed in 1793. The remaining disabilities affecting Episcopalians were removed in the same decade. By that time the main ideological threat to the status quo was seen as that posed by the French Revolution* rather than by rival brands of Christianity, and Bishop George Hay* took advantage of the situation to persuade the government to act. Full RC emancipation,* granting RCs the right to sit in Parliament, came in 1829.

C. Brown, *Social History of Religion in Scotland since 1730* (L, 1987), ch. 2; Burleigh, 231–2, 274–7, 306, 325.

D. Stevenson

Tonsure (from Latin *tondere*), the ceremonial cutting of hair performed when entering a religious order. The early Roman Church prescribed a shaven circle on the crown of the head, leaving a fringe of hair (a symbol of the Crown of Thorns). The monks of the Celtic Church* shaved their heads at the front from ear to ear, leaving the hair long at the back. One theory states that this style may have been derived from the druids.* The Roman Church condemned it as the tonsure of Simon Magus, and it was one of the points of controversy between the Celtic and Roman factions which culminated in the Synod of Whitby.*

B. Colgrave and R. A. B. Mynors (eds), *Bede's Ecclesiastical History of the English People*

(O, ²1992); *New Catholic Encyclopedia* XIV, 199–200; J. T. McNeill, *The Celtic Churches* (Chicago, 1974).

D. A. Bray

Torphichen Case, dispute over patronage.* In 1749 and 1750 the Presbytery of Linlithgow failed to obey the General Assembly's instructions to induct to the parish of Torphichen, W. Lothian, James Watson, the presentee of the patron, Lord Torphichen, in the face of overwhelming popular opposition (N. Morren, *Annals of the General Assembly of the Church of Scotland* I, E, 1838, 156, 181–2). A long debate in the 1751 Assembly ended with a censure of the Presbytery and the (last ever) appointment of a riding committee* to act if the Presbytery remained recalcitrant (as it did). The proposal of John Home* and William Robertson,* in their maiden Assembly speeches, to suspend the disobedient presbyters was heavily defeated. Home and Robertson were part of a group forming the emerging Moderate* party who used the case to take a stand on strict obedience to Church courts (R. B. Sher, *Church and University in the Scottish Enlightenment*, E, 1985, 50ff.). The Assembly's judgment evoked a dissent led by William Wishart* which appealed to conscience ('in the Lord') for a limitation to ecclesiastical obedience (Morren, 198–212, 367).

A similar disputed settlement to Inverkeithing, Fife, in 1751–2 led not only to the Moderate and 'Popular'* parties in the Kirk 'coming into more direct and violent collision' than ever before (each in effect laying out a manifesto; Morren, 231–42, 242–60), but also to the deposition of Thomas Gillespie* and the formation of the Relief* Church.

D. F. Wright

Torphichen, Preceptory of, headquarters in Scotland (near Bathgate in West Lothian), of the Knights Hospitallers,* granted to them by King David I.* The surviving remains date from the twelfth to the sixteenth centuries, and consist of a central tower and transepts, with a romanesque chancel arch now west of the crossing. The eighteenth-century parish church occupies the site of the nave, and there are foundations of other buildings. The preceptory had important rights of sanctuary in the Middle Ages.

Royal Commission on Ancient and Historical Monuments of Scotland: Inventory of Midlothian and West Lothian (E, 1929), 236ff.; *Knights of St John of Jerusalem in Scotland*, I. B. Cowan, P. H. R. Mackay, and A. Macquarrie (eds) (SHS, E, 1983).

A. Macquarrie

Torrance, Thomas Forsyth (1913–), distinguished CofS theologian. He was born the son of missionary parents in Western China, and studied at Edinburgh, taking philosophy under A. E. Taylor,* Norman Kemp Smith (1872–1958) and John Macmurray* and theology at New College* under H. R. Mackintosh.* Postgraduate work was pursued with Karl Barth. After ten years as a parish minister, at Alyth in Perthshire (1940–7) and Beechgrove, Aberdeen (1947–50), and as chaplain to British forces in North Africa and Italy, he returned to New College as Professor of Church History (1950–2), then Professor of Christian Dogmatics, 1952–79. He served as Moderator of the General Assembly of the CofS in 1976 and received the Templeton Prize for Progress in Religion in 1978. He was a founding editor of the *Scottish Journal of Theology** and a joint editor of the English edition of Barth's *Church Dogmatics* and of an edition of Calvin's *New Testament Commentaries*.

His major works on theological and scientific method include *Theological Science* (L, 1969), *Transformation and Convergence in the Frame of Knowledge* (Belfast, 1984), and *Reality and Scientific Theology* (E, 1985). A good introduction to his own theology is found in the Introduction to *The School of Faith* (L, 1959), in *The Mediation of Christ* (Exeter, 1983), and in his exposition of the theology of the fourth-century Fathers, *The Trinitarian Faith* (E, 1988).

THEOLOGY AND SCIENCE. Torrance's major thesis is that Christian theology is a positive science and that its scientific method, particularly as practised by such major doctors of the Church as Athanasius, Cyril of Alexandria, John Calvin and Karl Barth, is analogous to the scientific method of modern physics since James Clerk Maxwell* and Albert Einstein (1879–1955), a method illuminated in the writings of Michael Polanyi (1891–1976). Such a bold thesis is based first on Torrance's understanding of the classical theologians, whom he approaches as a 'historical theologian' interested in the profound convergence of thought, rather than as a 'theological historian' concerned with cultural relativities, and secondly, on his grasp (unique among theologians) of the philosophy of science.

REALISM, RATIONALITY AND OBJECTIVITY. He identifies himself as a Scottish Realist* in a tradition 'which goes back at least to Duns Scotus'* (see *Divine and Contingent Order*, O, 1981). Both theological and natural science begin with intelligible reality, divine or natural, disclosing itself to us. The human mind apprehends reality and, under its impact, in an intuitive, heuristic leap which cannot be formally analysed, discerns its basic coherent structure and pattern. This is then expressed in the great scientific 'dogmas', such as Einstein's theory of relativity in natural science, or the doctrines of Trinity and incarnation in theological science. The beginning of all scientific activity, and indeed of all rationality (see *God and Rationality*, L, 1971), is therefore belief, which is an acknowledgement, or confession, or 'epistemic awareness', of what is really there (see 'The Framework of Belief' in Torrance (ed.), *Belief in Science and in Christian Life*, E, 1980). It is foolish to contrast faith and reason, for such faith is integral to all knowledge and is irrefutable and unprovable. True objectivity therefore lies not in a supposed detachment from reality, but in an engagement with reality in which it is sovereign and our notions of it are therefore relativized and revisable. It is in this detachment from our own culturally conditioned ideas that Torrance sees the ecumenical role of a scientific theology; see *Conflict and Agreement in the Church* (2 vols, L, 1959, 1960), *Theology in Reconciliation* (L, 1975), and *Theological Dialogue Between Orthodox and Reformed Churches* (E, 1985).

TRINITY, INCARNATION AND ATONEMENT. Natural science arose from the Judaeo-Christian belief in a contingent and orderly universe, created out of nothing and held in being by the faithfulness of the triune God. He has irrevocably united it to himself in the incarnation of the Son (see *Space, Time and Incarnation*, L, 1969) and will recreate it through his resurrection (see *Space, Time and Resurrection*, E, 1976). In the incarnate Son, Jesus Christ, we apprehend and know God himself, for the Son is consubstantial (*homoousion*) with the Father, as the Nicene Creed declares, but so to know God demands a *metanoia*, a transformation or conversion of the mind. Thus revelation and knowledge of God are inseparable from personal reconciliation. Reconciliation between God and humanity is already completed from both sides (scientifically, actuality always proceeds possibility), for in Christ God has irrevocably laid hold of our fallen humanity in 'unconditional grace' to heal and save us, and in Christ also (in his 'vicarious humanity') humanity has responded in reconciling faith and obedience.

Theology in Reconstruction (L, 1965); *Christian Theology and Scientific Culture* (Belfast, 1980); *The Ground and Grammar of Theology* (Belfast, 1980); *Reality and Evangelical Theology* (Philadelphia, 1982); *The Mediation of Christ* (^{2}E, 1992).

FES IX, 524, 775–6, X, 432–3; T. A. Langford, 'T. F. Torrance's *Theological Science*: A Reaction', SJT 25 (1972), 155–70; A. I. C. Heron, *A Century of Protestant Theology* (L, 1980), 209–14; D. W. Hardy, 'Thomas F. Torrance,' *The Modern Theologians*, D. F. Ford (ed.), vol. I (O, 1989), 87–91; R. W. A. McKinney (ed.), *Creation, Christ and Culture: Studies in Honour of T. F. Torrance* (E, 1976); I. R. Torrance, 'A Bibliography ... 1941–1989', SJT 43 (1990), 225–62.

T. A. Noble

Torry, Patrick (1763–1852), Bishop of Dunkeld, Dunblane and Fife. The son of a cloth-manufacturer at the Wauk Mill of Garneston, Forfarshire, he was brought up in the CofS. Without the benefit of a formal education, he learnt Latin, Greek, Hebrew and mathematics and taught at Haddington Grammar School and Lonmay Parish School. In 1782 he was ordained in the EpCS and served at Arradoul, N-W Banffshire (1782–91), and Peterhead. In 1808 he became Bishop of Dunkeld and Dunblane and, in 1838, also of Fife.

In a bid to preserve the independence and traditions of his Church at a time when anglicization was the fashion, Torry gave his authority to the printing of a Prayer Book (1849) which, except for the eucharist where it followed the rite of 1764, was no more than a reprint of the Scottish Prayer Book* of 1637. Disavowed by his fellow bishops before the entire Anglican world, Torry constantly

TORWOOD DECLARATION

refused to withdraw his authority and is reputed to have exclaimed on his death-bed: 'Firm to the last!'

J. M. Neale, *The Life and Times of Patrick Torry, D.D.* (L, 1856); M. Lochhead, *Episcopal Scotland in the Nineteenth Century* (L, 1966), 63ff.; *The Book of Common Prayer* (E, 1849); J. Dowden, *The Scottish Communion Office 1764* (O, 1922); J. Skinner, *Annals of Scottish Episcopacy* (E, 1818), 472ff.; W. Walker, *The Life of George Gleig* (E, 1878).

G. Tellini

Torwood Declaration (1680), the 'Action of Excommunication' at Torwood, near Stirling, pronounced by Donald Cargill* on Charles II,* the Dukes of York and Monmouth, the Earl of Rothes, Sir George Mackenzie and General Thomas Dalziel. It was preceded by a worship service conducted by the veteran Covenanter.* The Duke of Lauderdale (*see* Maitland, John), inadvertently omitted in the morning, was formally added to the list by Cargill that afternoon. The Declaration logically followed the Sanquhar Declaration's* civil disowning of the King. The Torwood pronouncement was repeated in other parts of western Scotland. Charles was condemned for perjury in renouncing the Solemn League and Covenant* he had sworn to uphold, for his persecution of Covenanters, and for his immoral life-style. After the Torwood Declaration the government increased to 5000 merks the reward for Cargill's capture.

J. D. Douglas

Tract and Colportage Society of Scotland, *see* Scottish Colportage Society.

Tract Societies. Following the establishment of the Edinburgh Religious Tract and Book Society* in 1793, the sale and distribution of tracts proliferated throughout Scotland, and tract societies multiplied. In 1832, for example, there were in Glasgow no fewer than five distinct societies sharing a broadly common aim, including the Glasgow Religious Tract Society. These societies were founded by middle-class Evangelicals, whose chief motivation was a desire to spread the gospel. They aimed also, through the 'circulation of pure literature among the masses', to counteract what they saw as the pernicious influence of morally questionable chapbooks and other reading material available through itinerant hawkers to the increasingly literate working classes. The weapon they chose was the tract: most tracts were brief pamphlets designed to be sold cheaply or freely distributed.

The years after 1850 seem to have seen a resurgence of activity, possibly in response to the evangelical revivals.* The Aberdeen Book Agent and Colporteur Society was established in 1857, while the Glasgow Committee for Colportage was formed in 1866. Most of these organizations had links with the parent Edinburgh body and by 1859 distribution under the general auspices of that society was taking place in all but five of the Scottish counties.

TRACT SOCIETIES

The tracts these societies distributed included biblical excerpts, 'cautionary tales', and 'pious exhortation': they were always moralistic in their content, and evangelical in their theology. Although some tracts dealt with issues such as temperance (*see* Temperance Movement) and sabbath* observance, by far the majority presented the gospel. The Aberdeen Religious Tract Society, instituted in 1811, quoted with approval a document issued by the London Religious Tract Society, which contended that 'A good tract contains the words of eternal life. It is the gospel in miniature. It contains the very essence of revelation, and presents in a form the most simple and striking, the radical truths and precepts of Christianity.'

The tract societies, while occasionally printing their own tracts, or re-printing material which had been effective elsewhere, concentrated for the most part on distributing literature from bodies specializing in tract production, some of which were run as charitable organizations, others more as commercial businesses. The tract producers included the Religious Tract Society, the Stirling Tract Enterprise,* W. R. McPhun of Glasgow, and, at the end of the nineteenth century the two foremost Brethren* publishers, John Ritchie of Kilmarnock, and Pickering and Inglis of Glasgow. The first three groups also produced Gaelic* tracts, commonly translations of English originals (*see* Gaelic, Protestant Prose Publications in).

The early nineteenth-century tract societies were in most cases groups of like-minded individuals who came together to support and encourage their own personal tract distribution, financing this work out of their own pockets. Some such societies emphasized the lending, rather than the distribution of tracts. For example, the aim of members of the early nineteenth-century Aberdeen Tract Lending Society was systematically and conscientiously to visit working-class homes lending tracts, and exchanging them on a regular basis. These societies also sold tracts to travelling hawkers, who included them among their wares, and to itinerant preachers and home missionary societies. Thus the Aberdeen Religious Tract Society sold some of their tracts to 'chapmen'.

Later in the century, the societies were more highly organized. They were financed by income from sales, by public subscription, and by grants. The Glasgow Committee, for example, received financial aid from the National Bible Society of Scotland (*see* Bible Societies), and grants of tracts from the English Religious Tract Society. The societies employed 'agents' or colporteurs, who were more than mere literature salesmen. They were instructed to 'act as missionaries as opportunity afforded' and were normally paid a fixed salary rather than a commission, to encourage them to spend time distributing tracts freely and talking to those perceived to be in moral and spiritual need, rather than simply concentrating on their best customers. As well as tracts, their stock included books and periodicals. By 1859, for example, the Aberdeen Book Agent and Colportage Society employed five agents: in that year they sold goods to the value of

£305, including 28,491 periodicals; while by 1876, the Glasgow Committee had thirty-one colporteurs who in that year sold 138,821 periodicals and 185,500 tracts, whose value totalled £3,149. That year marked the zenith of the Glasgow Committee's activities, and the high-water mark of tract distribution in Scotland had been reached before the end of the nineteenth century. As new technology and more effective distribution had increased the quantity and availability of general reading material, and as the periodical increasingly replaced the pamphlet as the normal non-book mode of publication, the acceptability of the tract declined. The Tract Societies were largely a nineteenth-century phenomenon, although the actual production and distribution of tract literature continued at high (though decreasing) levels for several decades thereafter.

The extent to which tracts were actually read is frequently questioned by those who view them merely as a means of social control exercised by the middle classes. But in the early years of the nineteenth century, when tracts were frequently sold, it is likely that they were also read by those who took the trouble to purchase them, even to improve their reading skills. Where tracts were freely distributed there was inevitably some wastage – the schoolmaster at Gartsherrie in the 1830s persisted in distributing 800 tracts monthly for the Glasgow Society even though he believed only 20 per cent of them were read. But the annual reports of the societies are full of accounts of those who claimed to have derived spiritual and moral benefit from tracts and from the counsel of the colporteurs who, like themselves, were working-class people. While there is little independent testimony to the effectiveness of tract distribution, it would seem from this evidence that the societies had a significant role in affecting the religious perceptions of ordinary people in nineteenth-century Scotland.

Aberdeen Religious Tract Society (Pamphlet) (A, *c.*1812); J. Cleland, *Enumeration of the Inhabitants of the City of Glasgow* . . . (G, 1832); *Report of the Glasgow Committee for Colportage . . . for the year 1876* (G, 1877); Annual Reports of the *Aberdeen Book Agent and Colportage Society* (A, 1857, 1859, 1861); *Rules of the Aberdeen Tract-Lending Society* (A, n.d.); A. R. Thompson, 'An Enquiry into the Reading Habits of the Working Classes of Scotland from 1830–1840' (BLitt, Glasgow University, 1961).

J. A. H. Dempster

Tractarianism, alternatively known as the Oxford Movement. The original Tractarians, including John Keble (1792–1866), John Henry Newman (1801–90) and Edward Pusey (1800–82), were the authors of a series of ninety tracts published in Oxford between 1833 and 1841. The immediate origin of the movement lay in the hostile responses of Anglican high churchmen to the Whig* reforms of the early 1830s. The tracts asserted the doctrine of apostolic succession* and sought to encourage Anglican devotion, informing their readers about the discipline and liturgy of the CofE. The series came to an end with Tract 90 which appeared in February 1841. This was an ingenious attempt by Newman to argue that the Thirty-nine Articles of the CofE could be interpreted in a RC sense. It provoked furious controversy. The initial phase of the movement is generally considered to have ended with Newman's conversion to RCism in 1845, but it marked a crucial phase in the development of Anglo-Catholicism.*

There were three immediate implications of Tractarianism for Scotland. The EpCS, like the CofE, was deeply divided by the movement, most notably in relation to the Drummond schism of 1842 (*see* Drummond, D. T. K.*). Secondly, the English Tractarians, for their part, generally revered the EpCS and were attracted to the Scottish Communion Office, leading to a simplistic identification between Episcopalianism* and Tractarianism in Scotland and to consequent Protestant antagonism to the EpCS. Thirdly, there is a parallel to be drawn between Tractarianism in England and the contemporary Non-Intrusion* controversy in the CofS; although very different in their theological character, they reflected a common concern for a revival of ecclesiastical purity in the face of perceived corrupt Erastian influence.

See also Anglicanism.

O. Chadwick, *The Victorian Church*, I (L, 1966), chs I, III; R. W. Church, *The Oxford Movement* (L, 1891); P. B. Nockles, 'Continuity and Change in Anglican High Churchmanship in Britain' (DPhil, Oxford University, 1982), ch. 7; G. White, 'New Names for Old Things: Scottish Reactions to early Tractarianism', *Studies in Church History* 14 (1977), 329–37; W. Perry, *The Oxford Movement in Scotland* (C, 1933).

J. R. Wolffe

Trail, Ann (Sister Agnes Xavier) (1798–1872). Daughter of David Trail, CofS minister of Panbride (Angus), she showed early signs of deep spirituality and a talent for painting. She pursued artistic studies in London 1824–6, then Rome 1826–9, where she was received into the RCC in June 1828. In October 1833, encouraged by James Gillis,* she entered the Ursuline noviciate at Chavagnes (Vendée), taking the name of Sister Agnes Xavier. She was a founder member of St Margaret's Covent, Edinburgh, in December 1834 (*see* Religious Orders) and lived there until her death in 1872.

History of St Margaret's Convent, Edinburgh (E, 1886), 1–40, 245–371; *The Story of Panbride* (Carnoustie, n.d.), 28–38.

M. Dilworth

Trail, Walter (*d.*1401), Bishop of St Andrews. He studied at Paris and Orleans in the 1360s and 1370s, and had degrees in arts and in canon and civil law. Before becoming bishop he held a number of Church offices, including official and treasurer of Glasgow, vicar of Monifieth (Angus), parson of Fetteresso (Stonehaven), Canon of Aberdeen,

Moray and Ross, and Dean of Moray. In 1380 he came to enjoy the favour of anti-pope Clement VII at Avignon and was appointed papal chaplain and judge of the sacred palace of causes. He was loyal to the Avignon popes during the Great Schism. In 1385, on the death of William Landallis, he was elected bishop of St Andrews and provided by the pope. He held an important diocesan council at St Andrews c.1400. During the reign of Robert III (1390–1406) he was influential with the Queen, Annabella Drummond, and with Archibald 'the Grim' Earl of Douglas. Contemporary writers call Bishop Trail 'a very solid pillar of the church, a vessel of eloquence, a treasury of wisdom, and a defender of the church'. He died in St Andrews Castle, which he had built.

Contemporary notices in Wyntoun* and Bower;* frequently mentioned in *Calendar of Papal Letters to Scotland of Clement VII and Benedict XIII* (SHS, E, 1976), and *Calendar of ... Petitions of the Pope*, ed. W. H. Bliss (L, 1896), I; Dowden, 27–8; R. Nicholson, *Scotland: the Later Middle Ages* (E, 1974); D. Patrick (ed.), *Statutes of the Scottish Church, 1225–1559* (SHS, E, 1907).

A. Macquarrie

Traill (Trail), Robert (1642–1716), Presbyterian pastor and theologian. Traill was born at Elie in Fife where his father, Robert (1603–78; *FES* I, 38), was minister. A zealous Presbyterian, the elder Traill served as chaplain with the Scottish army in 1644 and was present at the battle of Marston Moor. He later served the Greyfriars Church in Edinburgh, until at the Restoration,* with eleven other former protesters, he presented an address to Charles II, congratulating him on his return but reminding him of the obligations of the Covenant*. He was prosecuted, imprisoned for ten months, and then banished. His son Robert studied at the University of Edinburgh, and then prepared himself for the ministry. He was present when his father's friend James Guthrie* was executed in 1661. With his brother and mother he was obliged to conceal himself when John Brown's (of Wamphray)* *Apologeticall Relation* (1665) was found in their house. He lived under constant threat of arrest until, after the Pentland Rising in 1666 (see Rullion Green), he was branded a traitor and fled to Holland early in 1667, where he joined his father. He continued to study theology and assisted in the reprinting of Samuel Rutherford's* *Examen Arminianismi* (Utrecht, 1668). By 1669 he was in England, where in 1670 he was ordained by Presbyterian ministers in London. He then was called to a church at Cranbrook in Kent. During a visit to Edinburgh in 1677 he preached in a private house and was arrested and, on his refusal to deny attending field conventicles*, was imprisoned on the Bass Rock* for several months. On his release, which was contingent on his engagement to 'live orderly in obedience to law' (*i.e.*, to abstain from keeping conventicles), he returned to Cranbrook. Subsequently he moved to London, where after the Revolution he was called as colleague to Nathaniel Mather in the Independent congregation meeting in Paved Alley, Lime Street. After Mather's death he pastored a separate congregation, which he gathered.

Although a Presbyterian, Traill joined with most of the Independents* against Richard Baxter, Daniel Williams and the majority of the Presbyterians in the Neonomian Controversy, occasioned by the republication of the works of Tobias Crisp (1600–43). He defended the Reformed doctrines of grace both against the charges of antinomianism and against the legalism of his opponents, publishing *A Vindication of the Protestant Doctrine concerning Justification ... from the Unjust Charge of Antinomianism* (L, 1692). His other writings include a short account of William Guthrie,* a recommendation of Walter Marshall's *Gospel-Mystery of Sanctification* (L, 1692), and several series of sermons: *The Throne of Grace* (thirteen sermons on Hebrews 4:16) (L, 1696), sermons on 'the Lord's Prayer' (sixteen on John 17:24), *A Stedfast Adherence to the Profession of our Faith* (twenty-one sermons on Hebrews 10:20–4) (L, 1718), 'Righteousness in Christ' (six sermons on Galatians 2:21), and eleven sermons on 1 Peter 1:1–4. A single sermon on 1 Timothy 4:16 was entitled 'By What Means May Ministers Best Win Souls?' His theological writings were admired by many, such as Thomas Boston*, and his sermons, devout and plain, were widely read. Traill wrote in the preface to his *Throne of Grace*: 'I know no true Religion but Christianity; No true Christianity but the doctrine of Christ; of his Divine Person...; of his Divine Office...; of his Divine Righteousness...; and of his Divine Spirit... I know no true Ministers of Christ, but such as make it their business, in their Calling, to commend Jesus Christ in his Saving fulness of Grace and Glory, to the faith and love of Men. No true Christian, but one united to Christ by Faith, and abiding in him by Faith and Love, unto the glorifying of the Name of Jesus Christ, in the Beauties of Gospel-Holiness. Ministers and Christians of this spirit, have for many years been my Brethren and Companions, and, I hope, shall ever be, withersoever the Hand of God shall lead me.'

Best edition of *Works*, 4 vols (G, 1806), with brief 'Life' in vol. I, and another in *Select Practical Writings* (E, 1845); *Twenty Nine Sermons* (E, 1731).

DNB LVII, 150; Walter Wilson, *The History and Antiquities of Dissenting Churches ... in London ...*, 4 vols (L, 1808–14), I, 236–40; T. M'Crie, *Memoirs of William Veitch and George Brysson* (E, 1825), 205; W. Anderson, *Scottish Nation* (E, 1877), III, 575; Chambers-Thomson III, 1161–2; J. Wylie, *Scots Worthies* (L, 1875), 728–9.

D. B. Calhoun

Training for the Ministry, see Education, Theological.

Translations and Paraphrases, see Paraphrases.

Travelling People, often popularly referred to as gypsies or tinkers (names they themselves would decline as derogatory), of diverse origins. Their numbers, estimated by a 1969 census as over 2,000, include people from England, from the Scottish Highlands* (tinsmiths, freshwater pearl-fishers, basket-weavers and others, with their distinctive Highland religious and cultural ethos) and from Ireland (often horse-dealers, both RC and Protestant). Many of them travel widely throughout Britain. In Scotland they concentrate chiefly on sites in the central belt, especially the Uddingston –Coatbridge–Larkhall area, and engage in various forms of work, including tarmacking, housepainting and hawking, especially of carpets. Although they are isolated in many ways from society, the provision of supervised and equipped sites by some local authorities (which the Scottish Churches have strongly encouraged) has made them less inclined to roam, not least since unlicensed sites have become more difficult to find.

Individual congregations have from time to time made contact with the travelling people's camps, but the Christian Church has generally tended to keep them at arm's length. The RC travellers commonly maintain attendance at mass. From c.1917 the CofS and the UFC, soon joined by the FC and EpCS, shared in a Central Committee on the Welfare of Tinkers. Miss E. Campbell Colquhoun was its agent on behalf of travellers, chiefly around Perth, and in 1921 Miss Helen L. Hardie become its missionary agent, ministering more directly among them. Kintyre around Campbeltown was another focus of effort, e.g. to provide housing. After the 1929 Union,* the Churches divided up responsibility, with the FC taking the north, the EpCS the north-east and the CofS the rest. The Central Committee was replaced in 1930 by a Central Advisory Council, which proved ineffective and ceased c.1940. The CofS Mission to Tinkers took over until 1958 with a range of activities largely in Perthshire.

A series of agents, mostly women, were appointed to evangelize and provide welfare. Denis Sutherland (*FES* X, 1972) worked among travellers as a CofS agent from a base in Perth 1964–73, and Miss Tilly Wilson, herself one of the travelling people, has more recently ministered among them as a CofS deaconess and minister with Woman's Guild* backing. In 1988 the Church and Nation Committee produced a report on 'Scotland's Travelling People – The Church's Contribution' (*RGACS 1988*, 91–4), which estimated their numbers to be perhaps twice the 1969 count.

The Gypsies and Travellers Evangelical Movement (known as Gypsies for Christ), which started on the continent in the mid-1950s, came to the UK c.1981. From its base in Darlington it has become increasingly active in Scotland through its summer campaigns. It belongs to the Pentecostal* (Assemblies of God) tradition, and has tended to encourage a self-conscious exclusiveness among travelling folk, even identifying them with the lost tribes of Israel. Its activities have been somewhat divisive.

In recent years the Edinburgh City Mission has supported a minister to visit travellers' sites in the central belt of Scotland, to provide them with customary ministerial services as required and to share the gospel with them through a befriending ministry.

Travelling people remain conservative and traditional in their ways. They maintain a respect for parents and reverence for Christian ministers decreasingly in evidence in contemporary society. The elderly are invariably cared for in their own community, and generation gaps and conflicts are largely avoided by giving children their full place at an early age. Illiteracy among men and women is still considerable, but most children now have schooling until eleven or twelve. The travelling people continue to show an openness to Christian teaching. Those who can, read the Bible to others, and memories are often very retentive, containing a rich store of traditions and tales generally lost in literate society. Yet the association of travelling folk with routine Church life remains largely an unsolved challenge, and their isolation leaves them vulnerable to religious influences alien to orthodox Christianity, although a number in west central Scotland and the north (including Lewis) have joined local evangelical congregations in recent years. Christian and non-Christian travellers alike offer a salutary example in sitting light to material possessions.

H. Gentleman and S. Swift, *Scotland's Travelling People* (E, 1971), esp. 14–18.

N. MacDonald and D. Sutherland

Travers, Walter (1548–1635), the foremost literary advocate of a Presbyterian polity for the late Elizabethan CofE. Born the son of a goldsmith at Nottingham and educated at Cambridge, he was deeply influenced there by Thomas Cartwright's divinity lectures and advocacy of Presbyterian polity. Travers followed him to Geneva after his dismissal in 1570. While at Geneva Travers published, anonymously, his *Ecclesiasticae Disciplinae* (1574; ET by Cartwright, Heidelberg, 1574), the first attempt by an English divine to apply Presbyterian polity to the CofE. It accepted the Anglican ministerial framework while interpolating into it a parity of ministers and a distinction between elder and deacon. Copies of the work circulated in Scotland while the *Second Book of Discipline** was in preparation. Subsequently, both Travers and Cartwright were offered Divinity chairs in St Andrews at the suggestion of Andrew Melville,* himself a Genevan returnee. The offers were not accepted. The Scottish interest in Travers ought not to be understood as indicating significant dependence upon his thought. Scotland's Reformed polity was already more aligned with French and Genevan models than the transitional one Travers proposed for England. The 1587 treatise edited by Travers, *Disciplina Ecclesiae ... Descripta*, itself conforms to these models and reflects an abandonment of his former strategy. This 'Book of Discipline' was never printed, surviving only in MS copies, but was published in ET by authority of the Westminster Assembly* under the title *A Directory of Church-Government* (L, 1644).

S. J. Knox, *Walter Travers* (L, 1962); A. F. S. Pearson, *Thomas Cartwright and Elizabethan Puritanism, 1535–1603* (C, 1925); P. Collinson, *The Elizabethan Puritan Movement* (L, 1967).

K. J. Stewart

Triduanna, see Celtic Saints.

Trinitarians. This order, founded in France by St John of Matha (and, less certainly, St Felix of Valois) received papal approval in 1198. Its primary purpose was the redemption of Christians held captive by infidels; the habit was white, with a red and blue cross on the breast. Though classed as friars* and known in Scotland as Red Friars, they were not mendicant and held corporate possessions. Only a third of their revenues was allotted to their own upkeep, the remainder being divided equally between the ransom of captives and alms for the poor and travellers. Initially each house was for seven friars, namely minister (prior), three priests and three lay-brothers, but in 1267 this was changed to a minister and five brethren. The order declined in the late Middle Ages and suffered later from internal divisions, but it still exists in some European and American countries. Following the general abolition of slavery, its role is now wider.

The official complement was occasionally exceeded, but several Scottish houses consisted of only a single member. In all, eight houses were founded in Scotland. Of these Berwick (before 1240–8) may have been the earliest although Aberdeen (attested *c.*1274, with earlier traditions) may possess an equal claim. However, Dunbar (1240–8); Scotlandwell in Kinross-shire (1250–1); Houston in E. Lothian (*c.*1270); Peebles (1296); and Fail in Ayrshire, with an associated hospital* (*c.*1335), all appear to have been of later provenance. Dirleton in E. Lothian, usually considered the eighth foundation, does not appear on record until 1507 and was annexed to Scotlandwell in 1540, by which date Peebles had annexed the revenues of Berwick (*c.*1477), Dunbar (1529) and Houston (1531). The remaining four houses survived with small communities until the Reformation.

New Catholic Encyclopedia XIV, 293–5; Easson-Cowan, 107–12, 179; P. J. Anderson (ed.), *Aberdeen Friars: Red, Black, White, Grey* (A, 1909); J. Bain, 'Notes on the Trinitarian or Red Friars in Scotland', *PSAS* 22 (1887–8), 26–32; D. McRoberts, 'Three Bogus Trinitarian Pictures', *IR* 11 (1960), 52–67.

I. B. Cowan

Trinity College, Glasgow, the name since the Union* of 1929 of what was earlier the FC's and then the UFC's Glasgow theological college. Since 1929 the CofS college has been identified with the University Divinity Faculty.

The Disruption* of 1843 was followed by disagreement between the 'Limitarians', led by William Cunningham,* who thought that New College,* Edinburgh, should be built up to meet all the FC's needs for theological education, and 'Extensionists' like R. S. Candlish,* who wanted colleges also in Aberdeen and Glasgow. The Aberdeen foundation (see Christ's College) opened the way for Glasgow also. Financial support was volunteered (already in 1844, a £5000 legacy was earmarked for this purpose), and the College began in 1856 under Patrick Fairbairn* (Principal 1857–74) and James Gibson,* joined next year by G. C. M. Douglas* (Principal 1875–1902) and W. M. Hetherington.* The College's distinguished building in Lynedoch Street, designed by Charles Wilson, was opened in 1857. Its tall Lombard tower with a companile made it a prominent landmark. The adjoining Free College Church, later converted into the College Library, had two similar smaller towers.

Despite some early problems (Gibson was charged with heresy in 1858) and student numbers smaller than New College's (the intake in 1856 was over thirty, peaked at forty in 1882 and after 1900 varied between ten and twenty-five), its teaching staff in the later 1800s and early 1900s enjoyed world standing, including T. M. Lindsay,* James Denney,* A. B. Bruce,* Henry Drummond* (part-time; the College had a lectureship in Natural Science since 1858), George Adam Smith,* James Orr,* James Moffatt,* and many other luminaries. The College had somewhat more liberal tendencies than its Edinburgh counterpart (although heresy proceedings against Bruce and Smith were abortive). The contrast became more marked after World War II, when Ian Henderson* and Ronald Gregor Smith* taught in Glasgow. Yet Trinity's best-known teacher in the mid-twentieth century was William Barclay.* It has latterly trained far more CofS ministerial candidates than the other Scottish Faculties.

The 1973 General Assembly resolved to sell the Trinity College building and gift its Library to the University (cf. *RGACS 1973*, 581–3). Although now housed wholly in University premises, Trinity College lives on under its Principal and Senate.

See also Education, Theological.

S. Mechie, *Trinity College, Glasgow 1856–1956* (G, 1956); W. M. MacGregor, *A Souvenir of the Union in 1929, With An Historical Sketch of the United Free Church College, Glasgow* (G, 1930).

D. F. Wright

Troup, John, always 'Jock' (1896–1954), Salvationist, lay evangelist, city missioner. Born at Dallachie in Morayshire, he was brought up in Wick, where he worked as a cooper. After joining the Royal Naval Patrol Service in the 1914–18 War, he was converted at the Dublin YMCA.* After the War he joined the Salvation Army* in Wick. In 1920, on his way to Yarmouth, at the Aberdeen Fishermen's Mission he felt 'a deeper commitment and fuller cleansing'. Thus prepared he held open-air meetings in the Lowestoft Market Place late on Saturday nights, and soon every night during that disastrous herring season. Fervent converts took home revival zeal, and Troup, summoned by a vision to Fraserburgh, led with others the widely-publicized 1921 revival.* This spread rapidly to every fishing community and most denominations from Eyemouth to Wick. D. P. Thomson* as a ministerial student briefly continued Troup's rôle in Fraserburgh, regarding him as a formative influence in his own evangelistic endeavours. Troup gave an account of the revival to the CofS General Assembly. After study at the Glasgow Bible Training Institute* Troup became for some ten years a travelling evangelist, and, from 1932-45, Missioner at the Tent Hall in Glasgow. Despite ill-health he then travelled widely, including ministry in America, where he died during an evangelistic campaign in Spokane, Washington, after announcing his text, 'You must be born again'.

J. A. Steward, *Our Beloved Jock* (Philadelphia, 1964); Jackie Ritchie, *Floods upon the Dry Ground* (Peterhead, 1983); Paul Thompson, *Living the Fishing* (L, 1983); D. P. Thomson, *The Road to Dunfermline* (Dunfermline, 1951); S. C. Griffin, *A Forgotten Revival. East Anglia and NE Scotland – 1921* (Bromley, 1992).

H. R. Bowes

Trumwine, see Anglo-Saxon Saints.

Tulchan Bishops, the derisive name given to the titular bishops who were appointed in terms of the Concordat of Leith 1572.* A tulchan was a stuffed calf-skin placed beside a cow to persuade it to yield its milk and the Tulchan bishops were a device to milk the ancient bishoprics of Scotland in the interests of the nobility.

The reforming legislation of 1560 and 1567 did not deal specifically with the bishoprics. Existing incumbents of any benefice were left undisturbed provided they did not say mass. They were however expected to hand over a third of the revenues to collectors for the purposes of government and the Reformed Church. The prototype of the Tulchan bishop was John Campbell, who was granted the bishopric of Brechin by Queen Mary in 1566. Campbell made over much of the revenues to his kinsmen and used the rest to further his education and maintain himself for the next forty years. He was never consecrated and rarely visited Brechin.

It was the vacancy in the archbishopric of St Andrews caused by the execution of John Hamilton* in 1571 that gave rise to the Concordat of Leith. The Regent Morton appointed John Douglas,* one of the six Johns who compiled the Scots Confession* and the *First Book of Discipline*,* to the vacant see. This was strongly contested by the General Assembly. A confrontation was averted by the Concordat of Leith, which provided a procedure whereby ministers of the Reformed Church could be nominated by the crown and elected by chapters of the ministers of the cathedral town to fill a vacant bishopric. The minister was to be inaugurated as bishop to give him a legal title to the revenues of the bishopric. On the advice of John Knox* the General Assembly agreed to this arrangement as a temporary expedient. It was hoped that this would make available to the Reformed Church the revenues necessary to realize the schemes planned in the *Book of Discipline*. When it became plain that the revenues were being diverted to the pockets of the nobility the General Assembly, on the advice of Andrew Melville,* denounced the Tulchans and in 1580 called for the abolition of the office of bishop.

D. G. Mullan, *Episcopacy in Scotland . . . 1560-1638* (E, 1986).

H. R. Sefton

Tulloch, John (1823-86), leading CofS divine in the post-Disruption* era. Born in Dron, Perthshire, the son of a CofS minister who remained in the Est.C in 1843, Tulloch studied arts in the United College of St Andrews 1837-41, and then theology at St Mary's College 1841-3. He took his final year of theology at Edinburgh University. Licensed by Perth Presbytery in 1844, in 1845 he became minister of St Paul's Church, Dundee; in 1849 he moved to Kettins, Forfarshire; in 1854 he was appointed Professor of Theology and Principal of St Mary's College, St Andrews, positions he held until his death. He became depute-clerk to the CofS General Assembly in 1862, and chief clerk in 1875. In 1859 Queen Victoria made him one of her royal chaplains; in 1882 he was appointed Dean of the Chapel Royal* and of the Order of the Thistle*.

After Norman MacLeod's death in 1872, Tulloch was the CofS's best-known spokesman. Theologically, he pioneered a new school of thought, which aimed to transcend the traditional Scottish Presbyterian quarrel between Moderate* and Evangelical.* In place of the moralism of the old Moderates, Tulloch emphasized that Christianity was a divine and spiritual life in the soul; against Evangelicals, he never tired of insisting that human understanding of divine truth is always fallible, and that all theology is therefore an historically conditioned enterprise. It was this latter aspect of Tulloch's thought, coupled with his positive attitude to biblical criticism, which in his own day drew upon him accusations of scepticism.

Tulloch's distinction between religion and theology enabled him to admire the Reformers, the Cambridge Platonists, Pascal and the Puritans, on all of whom he produced notable works – 'not that their ideas are any longer serviceable', as he said of the last named, 'but that they have a grip of spiritual profundities' (quoted in M. Oliphant, *A Memoir of the Life of John Tulloch*, E, 1888, 355). Tulloch, in fact, was most at home and at his best in the sympathetic exposition of other people's thoughts from an historical point of view. His most enduring literary monument is his *Movements of Religious Thought in Britain During the Nineteenth Century* (L, 1885; ²NY, 1971), in which he performs this exercise brilliantly in relation to his own age. Almost all subsequent accounts of nineteenth-century British theology have started from Tulloch's assessment. His other publications included: *Rational Theology and Christian Philosophy in England in the Seventeenth Century*, 2 vols (E, 1872); *The*

Christ of the Gospels and the Christ of Modern Criticism (L, 1864); *Leaders of the Reformation* (E, 1859; 3-1883); *English Puritanism and its Leaders* (E, 1861); *The Christian Doctrine of Sin* (E, 1876; Croall lectures* for 1876).

Tulloch spent his last years mobilizing supporters of the CofS against what he feared was Gladstone's* purpose to disestablish it. The Church's surest defence, he felt, lay in a broad popular and theological base; he wished his Church to emulate the CofE, whose comprehensiveness and liturgy he increasingly admired.

Tulloch was Moderator of the CofS General Assembly in 1878. He received a DD from St Andrews in 1854, and an LLD from Glasgow University in 1879 and from Edinburgh in 1884.

A. C. Cheyne, introduction to Tulloch's *Movements of Religious Thought in Britain During the Nineteenth Century* (NY, 1971), 1–34; *id.*, 'Church Reform and Church Defence: the Contribution of Principal John Tulloch', *RSCHS* 23 (1989), 397–416; *FES* VII, 423–4; *DNB* LVII, 307–10.

N. R. Needham

Tulloch, William (1776–1861), a pioneer missionary with the Independents* and later with the Baptists.* Born in Pityoulish (Abernethy parish, Strathspey), Tulloch was initially employed in the timber trade. His spiritual awakening owed much to Lachlan MacKenzie* of Lochcarron, whom he heard preaching at Communion services in the Inverness area. Following his conversion, Tulloch met James Haldane,* who encouraged him to attend classes in Edinburgh. He then moved to Killin, Perthshire, where he was associated with the Independent church as an itinerant preacher (1801–3). He later became co-pastor of the similar church at Lawers, on Loch Tay, which had grown during the revival* under John Farquharson.*

While at Lawers Tulloch became a Baptist in 1808, and established a Baptist church. Moving briefly to Renfrewshire during 1815, he returned to Perthshire with the support of a Baptist church in Glasgow. Stationed for some time at Aberfeldy (1816–19), he then settled long-term in the parish of Blair Atholl (where his son William* was born), building a meeting-house at Kilmaveonaig, and replacing it with another at Balentoul (1836). He continued to itinerate extensively throughout Perthshire, the north-west Highlands and the Hebrides.

Tulloch's journals drew the attention of other Baptists to the spiritual destitution of the Highlands, and as a result the Baptist Highland Mission was formed in 1816. This was supported by Baptists in Perth and Glasgow (chiefly the Scotch Baptist church at John Street). Latterly financing six itinerant missionaries, it was one of the forerunners of the Baptist Home Missionary Society for Scotland.*

W. Tulloch, 'Memoir of the late Mr Wm. Tulloch, Minister of the Gospel, Blair-Athole', *Reports of the Baptist Home Missionary Society for Scotland*, 1861, 19–24; D. W. Bebbington (ed.), *The Baptists in Scotland* (G, 1988), 36, 284–9.

D. E. Meek

Tulloch, William (1822–98), Baptist* pastor. The second son of William Tulloch (1776–1861),* he was born in Blair Atholl, Perthshire, educated at Edinburgh University and settled as pastor in Elgin in 1843. There he was remembered as 'a strong man physically. He was strong as a preacher, for he had a passion for God's book. He was strong in counsel, always manifesting denominational loyalty' (J. Dunlop, *History of the Baptist Church in Elgin*, Elgin, 1908). In 1855 he was called to Edinburgh to minister to the remnants of Haldane's* Tabernacle Church, whose move to its present home in Duncan Street he superintended. In 1869 he became Secretary of the newly-formed Baptist Union of Scotland,* and in 1872 resigned his pastorate to become Superintendent of the Baptist Home Missionary Society* and evangelist of the Union. In 1883 he settled in Long Wynd Church, Dundee, where he ministered with success until in 1889 he returned to Duncan Street, where he remained until he retired in 1893. Secretary of the Union in its formative period, when he relinquished office in 1880 he handed to his successor a well-established body. He was President of the Baptist Union of Scotland in 1882, and died an honoured elder statesman.

G. Yuille (ed.), *History of the Baptists in Scotland* (G, 1926); obituary in *Scottish Baptist Magazine*, August 1898.

D. B. Murray

Turgot (*d.* 1115), prior of Durham, Bishop of St Andrews and probable author of the *Life of St Margaret,* Queen of Scotland*. He was the son of a landed Saxon family in Lincolnshire, and became a monk under the direction of Aldwin at Jarrow in the see of Durham about 1074. Later Aldwin took Turgot and others to establish a Benedictine* chapter at Melrose* in Scotland, where they ran into conflict with King Malcolm III* over their oath of allegiance. Bishop Walcher of Durham advised them to return to Wearmouth and still later, in 1083, Walcher's successor transferred them to become his chapter at Durham. When Aldwin died in 1087, Turgot became prior for some twenty years. During this time he apparently paid visits to the Court of Malcolm III at Dunfermline, where he seems to have served as spiritual director to Queen Margaret. Six months before her death in 1093, she asked Turgot to care for her children. By this time he was on good terms with Malcolm, who was present that year at the laying of the foundation of the Cathedral of Durham along with Turgot.

When Malcolm's younger son, Alexander I,* became King of Scots in 1107, he decided to fill the long vacant bishopric of St Andrews by appointing Turgot. This set off a long conflict related to the European struggle of lay investiture and to new ecclesiastical rules dating from the Norman Conquest. In 1072 Lanfranc, Archbishop of Canterbury under William the Conqueror, had ruled that all churches in Britain (including York) were under the primacy of Canterbury, but that York had metropolitan authority over churches in the north, including Scotland. Thus, by these rules Turgot was supposed to profess obedience to York and seek consecration there, which Alexander I forbade. Through the influence of Henry I of England, however, Turgot was finally consecrated by Thomas, Bishop of York, in 1109, with St Andrews still reserving its own episcopal rights, leaving the question of jurisdiction unsettled.

During his tenure he appears to have held a reforming council dealing with issues similar to those raised earlier by Queen Margaret (such as the time of Lent, infant communion and confession to laymen, reflecting practices of the Eastern-influenced old Celtic Church). He died at Wearmouth and probably wrote the *Life of Margaret* before 1107.

A. A. M. Duncan, *Scotland: The Making of the Kingdom* (E, 1975), ch. 6; *DNB* LVII, 326–7; Burleigh, 64–70.

D. F. Kelly

Turnbull, William (*c.*1400–54), Bishop of Glasgow 1447–54, and founder of its University in 1451. Born at Bedrule near Jedburgh, Roxburghshire, he studied under Laurence of Lindores* at the University of St Andrews *c.*1416–20. After various appointments he studied canon law at Louvain 1431–3 (BCL, 1434), and became papal chamberlain and procurator of James I at the Roman Curia 1433. He attended the Council of Basle 1435, and after further studies in canon law at Pavia *c.*1427–9 (DCL, 1439), the Council of Florence 1439. He returned to Scotland 1439 and was Keeper of the Privy Seal 1440–8, Secretary to James II 1441–2 and vicar of St Giles, Edinburgh, *c.*1445. Provided to the see of Dunkeld, he transferred before consecration to the see of Glasgow in 1447. He founded the University of Glasgow under the papal bull of Nicholas V, 7 January 1451.

Like other able Scottish churchmen trained abroad in the fifteenth century, Turnbull played a full part in the political, religious and cultural life of his country. The opportunity came early when he was chosen to represent the King's interests at the Roman Curia. Pope Eugenius IV was in deep trouble with the conciliarists* at the Council of Basle (1431–49) who, following the mandates of the Council of Constance (1414–18), wished to curb papal nominations to higher benefices, limit papal taxation, and place the authority of the pope under that of the Council. James I, however, although anxious to exercise greater control over the Scottish Church, had no desire to fall in with the more extreme demands of the conciliarists. Trusted both by his king and the pope, Turnbull was therefore able to exercise a moderating influence at the Council of Basle, and later at the Council of Florence. Given the political unrest which followed the murder of James I in 1437, Turnbull strove to restore order to a fractious baronage, extend truces and peace treaties with neighbouring states, and issue legislation designed to stabilize the country's fragile economy and improve its overseas trade.

As Bishop of Glasgow he was a reformer: watchful over his clergy, a friend of the religious orders within his diocese, and, if supportive of crown rights, actively protective of the liberties of the Church. His founding of the University of Glasgow was, however, his lasting achievement. His training and teaching at St Andrews, Louvain and Pavia, and contacts with leading humanists in Italy, gave him an acute understanding of the intellectual and cultural needs of his country, and provided him with the vision and careful preparation required to draft its first constitution, to select its early teachers, and avoid a collegiate system. The philosophical content of his Arts Faculty was that of a moderate realism. His Divinity Faculty was intended to provide a buttress against Lollardy.* And if his Faculties of Law and Medicine were initially under-endowed, the fault lay in the political uncertainty then current in the kingdom.

J. Durkan, 'William Turnbull, Bishop of Glasgow', *IR* 2 (1951), 5–61; J. Durkan and J. Kirk, *The University of Glasgow 1451–1577* (G, 1977); J. H. Burns, *Scottish Churchmen and the Council of Basle* (G, 1962); R. Nicholson, *Scotland: The Later Middle Ages* (E, 1974).

J. Durkan

Tweedie, William King (1803–63), FC minister and writer. Born at Ayr, he studied at the Universities of Glasgow, Edinburgh and St Andrews, and was licensed to preach by the CofS Presbytery of Arbroath in 1828. In 1832 he became minister of the Scots Church at London Wall; in 1836 he moved to South Parish, Aberdeen, and in 1842 to the Tolbooth Church in Edinburgh, whose name his congregation retained when they became part of the FC in 1843.

As a FC minister, Tweedie was Convener of the Sustentation Fund Committee 1845–7, the Foreign Mission Committee 1848–62, and the Committee on Popery. He was also Secretary of the Society for the Relief of the Destitute Sick from 1843 until his death. He received a DD from St Andrews in 1852.

Tweedie was a voluminous author. His publications included: *Man by Nature and Grace* (E, 1850); *The Atonement of Christ* (E, 1843); *The Parables of our Lord* (L, 1861); *Satan as Revealed in Scripture* (E, 1862); *Select Biographies* (2 vols ed. for Wodrow Society, E, 1845–7). He had a particular interest in Calvin, and planned a biography of the Reformer, but delivered his materials to Thomas M'Crie* (the elder) when he discovered that he too was working on such a biography. Tweedie translated into English Rilliet's *Calvin and Servetus* (E, 1846).

The Life of John MacDonald (E, 1849); *Light and Shadows in the Life of Faith* (E, 1852); [5]L, 1860, entitled *Pathways of Many Pilgrims*); *The Sacrament of Baptism* (E, 1845); *The Hand of God in War* (E, 1854); *The Psalms of David in Metre* (L, 1865).

Disruption Worthies 481–8; *FES* I, 121; *AFCS* I, 347.

N. R. Needham

Twopenny Faith, the traditional nickname for a brief exhortation on the mass issued by Archbishop John Hamilton* with the approval of the provincial council* in spring 1559. (The price seems high for a four-page leaflet!) It is generally regarded as exemplifying the inadequacy – too little, too late – of Catholic reform measures prior to the Reformation itself. One copy survives, formerly in Blairs College Library, now in the National Library of Scotland.

D. Patrick, *Statutes of the Scottish Church* (SHS, E, 1907), 188–91 (text); A. F. Mitchell (ed.), *The Catechism Set Forth by Archbishop Hamilton* (E, 1882), (facsimile); Knox, *History* I, 139, *Works* VI, 676–8; W. J. Anderson, 'Some Documents of the Scottish Reformation', in D. McRoberts (ed.), *Essays on the Scottish Reformation* (G, 1962), 359–61.

D. F. Wright

Tyrie, James (1543–97), Jesuit*. Born at Drumkilbo (Perthshire), he studied at St Salvator's College, St Andrews (1557). After the failure of a Jesuit mission to Scotland, he matriculated at Louvain (1563) and the same year joined the Jesuits at Rome. In 1567 he was sent to the Jesuit College de Clermont in Paris, whence he dispatched a treatise to his Protestant brother, David. It elicited *An Answer*... (St Andrews, 1572) from Knox,* and Tyrie responded with *The Refutation* (Paris, 1573). In Paris he lectured mainly on moral theology. In logic he supported Jacques Charpentier (1524–74) against the Protestant Peter Ramus (1515–72) championed by Andrew Melville,* with whom Tyrie disputed in 1574. Later Tyrie became Professor of Scripture (1590) and Rector of the Scots College* of Pont-à-Mousson (near Metz). On returning to Rome (1592), he assisted in the restoration of the Scots hospice and helped to draw up the Jesuits' educational charter *Ratio... Studiorum...* (Rome, 1586). Tyrie enjoyed the respect of Scots Protestant opponents.

MSS of works in Paris and elsewhere; Selections, ed. T. G. Law, *Catholic Tractates of the Sixteenth Century* (STS 45, E, 1901).

DNB LVII, 436–7; Knox, *Works* VI, 474–8; J. Durkan, 'The identity of George Thomson, Catholic Controversialist', *IR* 31 (1980), 45–6; J. Feyer (ed.), *Defuncti Primi Saeculi Societatis Jesu*, pt 1 (Rome, 1982).

J. Durkan

U

Ulster, *see* Ireland.

Union of Parliaments (1707), the uniting of the legislatures of Scotland and England following upon the Articles of Union between England and Scotland signed in 1706 and passed with minor amendment by the Scots Parliament in January and by the English Parliament in March 1707. The complete Union Agreement which comprises the Articles of Union, the Acts of Union of the respective Parliaments and the associated Union legislation, came into force on 1 May 1707, the two prior legislatures being superseded by the united Parliament of Great Britain. Sixteen of the peers of Scotland were elected by their number to serve in the House of Lords, with a new election every fresh Parliament until the Peerage Act 1963, when all surviving Scottish peers were admitted. Scottish membership of the House of Commons has followed the vagaries of the electoral system since 1707, there now being seventy-two Scottish constituencies.

In the Union Agreement, the position of the CofS and its Presbyterian government were safeguarded by the Scottish Commissioners who negotiated the Articles of Union being specifically barred from treating of religion by the Scots Act 1705 c.50, and by the passing of the Act of Security 1706 c.6 confirming the 'true Protestant religion as presently professed' and ratifying and confirming the Confession of Faith Ratification Act 1690 c.7 (*see* Security Act (1707)). The Act of Security was inserted into the Union with England Act 1706 c.7 of the Scottish Parliament, and appears as s.2 of the Union with Scotland Act 1706 (6 Anne c.11) of the English Parliament. (England secured the Church of England similarly by the Maintenance of the Church of England Act 1706 (6 Anne c.8)).

Under the Union Agreement, Scots law and the Scottish legal system were also secured, with no appeal being permitted to 'any court sitting in Westminster Hall', and no alteration to public law save for the 'evident utility' of the Scots was to be permitted. However, the fragility of such protection was soon indicated when in 1710 the House of Lords took an appeal in a religious case, allowing an appeal against a decision of the Court of Session not to overturn an order by the Magistrates of Edinburgh to imprison one Greenshields* for preaching without a licence from the Presbytery of Edinburgh: *Greenshields v Magistrates of Edinburgh* (1710) Robertson's Appeals 12. Greenshields was an Episcopalian. Further, the Scottish Episcopalians Act 1711 afforded toleration to that denomination in Scotland, and the Church Patronage (Scotland) Act 1711 re-established patronage (*see* Patron, Patronage, Patronage Acts). The effective removal of the Scottish legislature to London did not work satisfactorily, particularly in days of bad communications and times when Scotland might be considered to be in rebellion (e.g. 1715 and 1745).

It remains a question whether, or to what extent, the Union Agreements limit the power of the Parliament of the United Kingdom, as the Union Parliament has become, and if so how that restriction may be enforced. Regrettably the Union Parliament followed the traditions of the English Parliament and behaved as if it were that parliament continuing, with a Scottish addition. Parliamentary (and governmental) intervention in Scottish Church matters has often been inept, notably at the time of the Disruption* controversy, though matters have improved since the Church of Scotland Act 1921.*

F. Lyall, *Of Presbyters and Kings* (Aberdeen, 1980); E. C. S. Wade and A. W. Bradley, *Constitutional and Administrative Law* (L, [10]1985); T. B. Smith, 'Fundamental Law', sec.2 and 'Parliament', sec.3 of 'Constitutional Law', vol. 5 of *The Stair Memorial Encyclopedia of the Laws of Scotland*, 1987; A. V. Dicey and R. S. Rait, *Thoughts on the Scottish Union* (L, 1920).

F. Lyall

Union Theological Seminary, New York, an interdenominational college with close associations with Presbyterianism and Scotland. It was founded in 1836 and incorporated by the New York State

Legislature in 1839. Although all the founders were Presbyterians, the charter provided that 'equal privileges of admission and instruction, with all the advantages of the Institution, shall be allowed to students of every denomination of Christians'. Until 1870 the Seminary was autonomous, but in that year it agreed to allow the General Assembly of the Presbyterian Church, USA, to confirm the appointment of its professors. When in 1893 Charles A. Briggs was suspended from the ministry on the grounds of heresy by the General Assembly, the Seminary refused to dismiss him and resumed its autonomy.

The founders believed 'that large cities furnish many peculiar facilities and advantages for conducting theological education' and hoped to recruit most of the students from the cities of New York and Brooklyn, but the majority of students have come from all over the United States and from many other countries. Most of its presidents have been Presbyterians, but the faculty and students have come from many different denominations.

Several Scots, including John Baillie,* Hugh Black* and James Moffatt,* have served as professors and since 1919 a generous provision of fellowships has enabled many Scots to undertake postgraduate study in the Seminary.

H. S. Coffin, *A Half Century of Union Theological Seminary* (NY, 1954); G. L. Prentiss, *Fifty Years of the Union Theological Seminary* (NY, 1889); R. T. Handy, *A History of Union Theological Seminary in New York* (NY, 1987).

H. R. Sefton

Unions and Readjustments. The Church in Scotland has since the eleventh century considered that it has a territorial responsibility for the whole country. In the days when the population was relatively static, this was progressively achieved by the creation of the parish system.* From 1707 any changes were made by the Court of Teinds. In the nineteenth century the movement of population to cities and towns made necessary the creation of chapels of ease* and parishes *quoad sacra*.* After the Union of 1929 adjustment has been done by the General Assembly of the CofS through Presbyteries and the Committee on Unions and Readjustments. The attempt is made to see that parish areas, each with its own minister, are readjusted so that no part of the country is without the ordinances of the gospel of Christ and so that undue duplication of ministry does not occur. This sensitive task can often entail the disturbance of old fellowships and the loss of beloved places of worship.

At the time of the 1929 Union* of the CofS and the UFCS (which had been formed by the Union of the FCS and the UPC in 1900), there were, in many communities, three churches, all thereafter CofS. Since ministers are normally inducted *ad vitam aut culpam** (for life or retiral or until a serious fault), it took a long while before consideration could be given to whether or how reduction in the number of churches should be made. The size of congregations, the population in the parishes, financial viability, state of buildings etc., together with the need to serve the area reasonably well, have all to be taken into account.

Since 1929, the growing shortage of ministers available for parishes – there are now less than half the total number available in 1929 – together with the greatly increased cost of building maintenance and a smaller membership, means that readjustment must go on. In some country areas this is particularly difficult and it is necessary to link together two or three former parish areas, each with its own church, under the care of one minister. Such readjustment is seldom popular, nor is it easy for the minister appointed.

In cities and towns, the usual form of readjustment is by union under the care of one minister, when a vacancy occurs by the death, demission or translation of the other, or when both become vacant. It is possible to appoint a minister for a terminable period until a vacancy in another church permits permanent change.

One other possibility is dissolution of the congregation and the distribution of its area and assets, when its members join other congregations. A legal document – a Basis and Plan of Union or Dissolution – is prepared and has to be approved by congregation(s), Presbytery and the General Assembly's Committee, and there is always the right of congregations to appeal to the General Assembly, the Church's supreme court.

Cox, 748–60; *RGACS 1984*, pt I, 301–21, pt II, 44–50.

A. I. Dunlop

Unions, Church, in Scotland. It was firmly established by the Reformers that there should be 'ane face of the kirk in the land'. For well over 100 years the idea of a visible catholic Church in Scotland held sway. When broken, it was not lightly and not without careful justification. Even then the Cameronian secession (*see* Societies, United; Reformed Presbyterian Church) was not numerous. With the Secession of 1733 (*see* Associate Presbytery) the ideal was maintained: the separation was not from the CofS as such, but rather from those who had usurped power in it. Much the same position was taken by the FC.* However, even before 1843, a movement of reunion had begun which from 1820 to 1929 steadily pieced together much of the fragmented national Church. It is to the Secession* that the origins of the movement are to be traced.

UNION OF THE NEW LIGHT BURGERS AND NEW LIGHT ANTIBURGHERS TO FORM USEC.C, 1820. Following the softening of attitudes discernible in the Secession after the dawning of 'New Light'* in the 1790s, it was widely felt that the Burgess Oath,* which had split the Associate Synod* (*see also* General Associate Synod) into two streams in 1747, lacked relevance in the new century. Negotiations were opened and led to the formation of the United Secession Church* with 280 congregations. This Union heralded the advent of a new forbearance by allowing for differing views on the Burgess Oath and on public covenanting. Another very significant departure was a slight loosening of the terms of Confessional subscription* which had been imposed in the CofS in 1711, the more so since the Burgher Synod had received a protest from a group of younger ministers who considered the compass of the Church's Confessional commitment to be too wide.

UNION OF PROTESTING NEW LIGHT ANTIBURGHERS AND OLD LIGHT ANTIBURGHERS TO FORM THE ASSOCIATE SYNOD OF ORIGINAL SECEDERS, 1827. Following the 1820 Union some conservative Antiburghers, unhappy with the theological tone and direction of the new Church, separated to form the Associate Synod of Protesters (see Original Secession Church) which soon found a congenial home among the Old Light Antiburghers.

OLD LIGHT BURGHERS RECEIVED INTO THE COFS, 1839. The Old Light Burghers recognized in the Est.C of the 1830s the 'free, faithful and reforming' General Assembly to which the Secession fathers had appealed. They were warmly received but were soon to leave the Establishment again at the Disruption* of 1843.

UNION OF UNITED SECESSION CHURCH AND RELIEF CHURCH TO FORM THE UNITED PRESBYTERIAN CHURCH, 1847. The Relief Church* had a very different ethos from the Secession, being non-covenanting and holding free and open Communion. From the 1820s the Relief was interested in Union with the USec, and when it was achieved in 1847 it resulted in the United Presbyterian Church of 518 congregations. The relative theological liberalism of the Relief had been matched in the 1840s by a movement away from thoroughgoing Calvinism in the USec. The Union was the occasion of a further distancing of the Church from the Westminster Standards – no longer were office-bearers obliged to own them as 'the confession of *their* faith' and the teaching on the civil magistrate was explicitly disowned. Positive Voluntaryism,* the duty to give, was strongly accented.

UNION OF FC AND ORIGINAL SECESSION CHURCH, 1852. The small number of Old Light Burghers who declined to enter the CofS in 1839, three years later united with the Original Secession Synod to form the Synod of United Original Seceders (the Original Secession Church). Following the FC's 'Act and Declaration' of 1851 which displayed its continuity with the Reformers and Covenanters, the majority of the Original Secession Church entered a Union with the FC. They were specifically permitted to hold their distinctive views within the united Church. Nevertheless a minority remained apart on the ground that the perpetual obligation of the National Covenants* was not a term of communion.

UNION OF FC AND RPC, 1876. The Reformed Presbyterian Church* took part in the tripartite Union negotiations of 1863–73 and when these failed they determined to unite with the FC. They entered on condition that they held their own position but agreed not to press the continuing obligation of the Covenants. One minister and twelve congregations remained apart.

UNION OF FC AND UPC TO FORM THE UFC, 1900. The Voluntary Controversy* of the 1830s caused a deep rift between the Secession and the Establishment Evangelicals who subsequently formed the FC, so that at the Disruption* it did not seem conceivable that Scottish dissent could be formed into one ecclesiastical body. However, it was not long before the softening of Voluntaryism in the UPC and the practical Voluntaryism of the FC raised the question of whether the two bodies should be kept apart by a purely theoretical difference as to Establishment. When official discussions began in 1863 the UPs were practically unanimously in favour of Union. Initially the situation in the FC appeared similar, but a hardening of loyalty to the 1843 constitution among a Constitutionalist* minority finally dashed the Union hopes of the majority. However, when negotiations were abandoned in 1873, the principle was clearly laid down that the majority considered Union to be their duty as soon as was expedient.

During the next twenty years the FC anti-Union party was greatly depleted and confined almost entirely to the Highlands*, the Disestablishment* campaign gave a common perspective on the wider ecclesiastical situation and the Declaratory Acts* loosened the ties of both Churches to the Confession of Faith. These developments meant that when Union was formally proposed again in 1896 the circumstances were much more auspicious. The UPs remained unanimous and in the process of the negotiations many former Constitutionalists were won over. Irresistible momentum gathered behind 'Union on the basis of the Standards'. Maximum liberty was allowed for different views to be held on non-essential points and innumerable matters of detail were left to be settled by the united Church. The prominence of the Declaratory Acts* in the new constitution distanced the united Church from the Confession while maintaining historical continuity. A separate FC continued, mainly in the Highlands, protesting loyalty to the Establishment principle and the Confession of Faith, but the vast majority of Presbyterian seceders were in 1900 gathered into one ecclesiastical body.

UNION OF COFS WITH UFC, 1929. At the time of the 1900 Union the hope was expressed that the remaining major ecclesiastical division in Scotland could be taken down 'by hands working on both sides of the wall'. All attempts at conference between the Established and non-Established Churches had hitherto been frustrated, because the CofS was not prepared to consider any terms which involved Disestablishment and the Free and UP Churches were not prepared to consider anything else. By the turn of the century the beginnings of a more open and concessive spirit could be traced. The House of Lords decision* of 1904 had a galvanizing effect as it strengthened the CofS argument that only by concordat with the state could spiritual independence be achieved. Another favourable development was the demise of the Disestablishment cause. Above all, a new urgency was born of a sense of the religious needs of the nation, which cried out for a rationalization of ecclesiastical resources.

When representatives of the two Churches met in conference in 1909 the determination was growing to find a way forward which would accommodate both profound belief in the Establishment principle and jealous upholding of spiritual independence. A Memorandum brought forward by the CofS Committee in 1912 drafted a new constitution. Spiritual independence was set in the forefront and the possibility of state interference was obviated. It would be no longer 'the Church by law established', but national recognition was preserved. Both Churches accepted these proposals and Articles Declaratory* were formulated which were given statutory ratification by Parliament in 1921. The state thus finally accepted the ecclesiastical claims advanced in 1843 and 1906. Four years later Parliamentary legislation settled the vexed question of endowments by vesting the patrimony of the Church in a central body of trustees. The way to Union was clear and when the reconstituted CofS was formed in 1929, only a small UF minority remained separate, protesting loyalty to Voluntaryism and theological liberty. The growing desire to stress Presbyterian catholicity and unity and to allow maximum liberty on nonfundamentals had led to the rebuilding of one national Church. Designed along UF lines to be a relatively broad Church with ample freedom to develop, it was able to accommodate all but the most strict. Five separate strands of Presbyterianism remained: one of these, the United Original Secession, acceded to the CofS in 1954.

C. G. M'Crie, *The Church of Scotland: her Divisions and Reunions* (E, 1907); J. R. Fleming, *The Church in Scotland 1875–1929* (E, 1933); id., *The Story of Church Union in Scotland* (L, 1929); A. J. Campbell, *Two Centuries of the Church of Scotland* (Paisley, 1930); J. M'Kerrow, *History of the Secession Church* (G, 1841); J. Cairns, *John Brown* (E, 1860); P. C. Simpson, *Principal Rainy* (L, 1909), II, 188–268; J. K. Cameron, *Scottish Church Union of 1900* (Inverness, 1923); A. Muir, *John White* (L, 1958), 191–267; J. Barr, *The Scottish Church Question* (L, 1920); R. Sjölinder, *Presbyterian Reunion in Scotland 1907–1921* (Stockholm, 1962); J. Walker, *The Theology and Theologians of Scotland* (E, ²1888).

K. R. Ross

Unitarians. Unitarians regard faith as a matter of personal responsibility. They draw not only on Jewish and Christian teachings about responding to God's love by loving our neighbours as ourselves, but also on wisdom from other world religions, insights from science and humanism and personal experience.

Unitarians adopt a critical stance towards the Trinity, election and human depravity. The corresponding Unitarian positions are that God is one and Jesus 'a man approved of God' (Acts 2:22) (Unitarianism), that God's love is effective for all (Universalism), and that human nature is worthy. Unitarians distinguish between essential and non-essential Christian teachings, and adopt a position of strict non-subscription to creeds and confessions of faith.

The earliest known incident of Unitarianism in Scotland is that of Thomas Aikenhead* (c. 1678–97), hanged in Edinburgh for mocking the Trinity in the last execution for heresy (strictly, blasphemy*) in Britain. The General Assembly of the CofS in 1704 condemned Socinianism (*i.e.* Unitarianism) as error.

CofS Moderates* with distinct Unitarian tendencies included John Simson,* Francis Hutcheson* and William Leechman,* all professors at Glasgow College, and the Ayrshire ministers William McGill* and William Dalrymple (1723–1814). Robert Burns* also held a Unitarian position. Scottish common-sense philosophy (*see* Scottish Realism) at Harvard University directly influenced the growth of American Unitarianism.

Organized Unitarianism in Scotland derives from two influences. First was a native reaction against strict Calvinism initiated by the posthumous 1749 publication of James Fraser of Brea's* *A Treatise on Justifying Faith* (E,), which split the Reformed Presbytery (*see* Reformed Presbyterian Church) and resulted in a number of small Universalist societies in the Borders. The Edinburgh church (1776) began as one of these societies. The preaching of Niel Douglas* led to a later wave of Universalist societies; and the present Dundee church is a memorial to Henry Williamson (1839–1925), a Universalist who re-founded the Unitarian church there in 1860. The Universalist Church of America operated a Scottish mission during the nineteenth century.

The second influence came from English Unitarians. William Christie (1748–1823), disciple of Joseph Priestley (1703–1804), the Unitarian apologist and scientist, started the first distinctly Unitarian congregation in Scotland at Montrose in 1781. Christie also enticed Thomas Fyshe Palmer* to Scotland, where he founded the earlier Dundee congregation in 1785.

The present Glasgow church (1791) is a response to both influences. Universalist societies were numerous in the west, and many English Unitarians studied at Glasgow College since English universities were closed to them. The Aberdeen church (1833) is a tribute to the energy of Glasgow minister George Harris (1794–1859) in propagating Unitarianism in a wide variety of Scottish centres.

Unitarian congregations are sovereign in their own affairs, including the calling of ministers, who may be of either sex. There is a Scottish Unitarian Association. The Scottish churches are affiliated to the (British) General Assembly of Unitarian and Free Christian Churches, which is itself a member of the International Association for Religious Freedom, which links globally Unitarian and other liberal religious organizations, both Christian and non-Christian.

E. M. Wilbur, *A History of Unitarianism*, 2 vols (Cambridge, MA, 1945); C. G. Bolam et al., *The English Presbyterians* (L, 1968); L. B. Short, *Pioneers of Scottish Unitarianism* (Swansea, 1963); *Transactions of the Unitarian Historical Society* (1916–); G. Rowell, 'The Origins and History of Universalist Societies in Britain, 1750–1850', *JEH* 22 (1971), 35–56; R. E. Miller, *The Larger Hope: the Second Century of the Universalist Church in America 1870–1970* (Boston, 1984), 400–11; Martin Fitzpatrick, 'Varieties of Candour: Scottish and English Style', *Enlightenment and Dissent* 7 (1988), 35–56; R. K. Webb, *The English Unitarians* (NY, forthcoming).

A. M. Hill

United Free Church, Presbyterian Church formed in 1900 by the Union* between the UPC and FC. Five hundred and ninety-three UP congregations united with 1,068 from the FC, giving an initial total membership of some half a million.

THE ORIGINAL UFC, 1900–1929. The first decade of the UFC's existence was clouded by its legal and political struggle with the continuing FC for the property of the pre-1900 FC. This was eventually settled by the intervention of Parliament in the Churches (Scotland) Act 1905 (*see* Scottish Churches Act), which appointed an Executive Commission to distribute the property between the FC and UFC in accordance with criteria specified in the Act. The Commission completed its work in 1909, but the legacy of ill feeling between the two Churches was enduring. (*See* Free Church Case; Free Church of Scotland, 1843–1900; Free Church of Scotland, post-1900.)

The UFC was a broadly evangelical body. Its theological and practical ethos was that of liberal Evangelicalism, blending a moderate higher criticism (*see* Believing Criticism), an acceptance of the findings of contemporary science, and a commitment to evangelism and missions.* One outstanding characteristic of the UFC was its attitude to confessions of faith and Church constitutions. The conflict in the FC between Unionists and Constitutionalists,* and its legal fall-out in 1904, prompted the UFC to pass in 1906 its Act Anent Spiritual Independence of the Church, which gave the UF General Assembly plenary power 'to alter, change, add to, or modify, her constitution and laws, Subordinate Standards, and Formulas, and to determine and declare what these are, and to unite with other Christian Churches'. This was revolutionary; the Church was now master of, not subject to, its creed.

Within this basically non-confessional, liberal evangelical spectrum there were varying doctrinal hues, as can be gauged from the presence of both George Adam Smith* and James Orr* within the UFC.

The UFC's only approach to heresy* proceedings occurred in 1902, when George Adam Smith appeared before its General Assembly, charged by some with denying the Bible's inspiration and authority in his *Modern Criticism and the Preaching of the Old Testament* (L, 1901). The UFC College, Glasgow, where Smith was Old Testament Professor, had already declined to institute proceedings against him. Robert Rainy* submitted a motion to the Assembly recommending acceptance of the College's findings; James Wells (*AFCS* I, 354; *FUFCS*, 241) submitted an alternative, seeking further consultation with Smith. Rainy's motion was adopted by 534 votes to 263. What could have become another Robertson Smith* case was thus swiftly terminated, securing safety and freedom in the new Church for liberal critics like G. A. Smith. It proved to be 'the last of the heresy hunts', as George Reith called it.

At the other end of the theological spectrum from Smith was James Orr, contributor to *The Fundamentals*, whose writings were (and are) highly esteemed by the international Reformed community (*e.g.* by Abraham Kuyper). Yet it seems typical of the UFC's ethos that Orr voted for Rainy's motion in the 1902 Smith case.

The UFC was gifted with a wealth of notable biblical and theological scholars and teachers, including James Denney,* H. R. Mackintosh,* James Hastings,* David S. Cairns,* James Moffatt,* J. E. McFadyen,* A. C. Welch* and H. A. A. Kennedy.* Others, such as John and Donald Baillie,* were trained in the UFC but achieved academic prominence only in the CofS after the Union of 1929.

As its early years had been preoccupied with the legal aftermath of the 1900 Union, so the UFC's latter years were increasingly dominated by the coming Union* with the CofS. The essential problem was the CofS's status as an established Church, which conflicted with the UFC's Voluntaryism.* Discussions began as early as 1909, but proved complex. The main obstacles, however, were deemed by a majority in the UFC to have been removed by two notable parliamentary statutes. The first was the Church of Scotland Act* of 1921, recognizing the CofS's right to adopt its Articles Declaratory* of 1919 as part of its basic constitution. The second was the Church of Scotland (Properties and Endowments) Act* of 1925, which transferred to Church commissioners the administration of the CofS's secular patrimony. These Acts satisfied all but a few intransigent UFC Voluntaries that all objectionable vestiges of Church–state entanglement in the CofS had been abolished, and the way was paved for the Union of October 1929. When the Basis and Plan of Union was submitted by the UF Assembly to the whole Church, 1,298 congregations approved and 101 dissented. In the uniting UF Assembly of May 1929 only 39 voted against the Union.

THE CONTINUING UFC, 1929–. Voluntaryist opposition to the Union within the UFC was led by James Barr,* minister of Govan, Glasgow and Labour MP for Motherwell from 1925, and was carried on through the United Free Church Association (*see* National Church Defence Association). When the Union came some 14,000 UFC members remained outside, calling themselves the United Free Church Continuing (the 'Continuing' was

UNITED FREE CHURCH ASSOCIATION

dropped in 1934). To avoid the legal problems created by the 1900 Union of the FC and UPC, an arrangement was agreed whereby local UFC property would remain with the majority of each congregation, whether they entered the Union or not. £25,000 was also paid from pre-Union UFC funds to the UFC Continuing. This obviated most of the inter-Church bitterness of 1900, although many local property disputes still occurred.

The ongoing UFC continued the traditions of liberal Evangelicalism, with a fresh accent on the 'liberal'. It was the first Scottish Presbyterian Church to ordain a female minister (Elizabeth Barr* of Auchterarder UFC, in 1935), and the first British Presbyterian Church to elect a female Moderator (Barr again, 1960).

The modern UFC is committed to the ecumenical movement,* and is a member of the World Council of Churches and ACTS. At the time of writing it has seventy-five Scottish congregations, thirty parish ministers and several others in other appointments (e.g. lecturing and overseas mission). Its headquarters are in Newton Place, Glasgow, and it publishes a monthly magazine, *Stedfast*. It has no theological seminary of its own.

J. Barr, *The United Free Church of Scotland* (L, 1934); id., *The Scottish Church Question* (L, 1920); J. R. Fleming, *The Story of Church Union in Scotland* (L, n.d.); G. Reith, *Reminiscences of the United Free Church General Assembly (1900–1929)* (E, 1933); G. N. M. Collins, *The Heritage of Our Fathers* (E, 1976), 96–156; A. Stewart and J. K. Cameron, *The Free Church of Scotland 1843–1910* (E, 1910); Burleigh 394–408; *FUFCS*; K. R. Ross, *Church and Creed in Scotland* (E, 1988).

N. R. Needham

United Free Church Association, see National Church Defence Association.

United Original Seceders, see Original Secession Church.

United Pentecostal Mission, see Missions: West Africa.

United Presbyterian Church, 1847–1900. On 13 May 1847 the USec.C and the Relief Church* united to form the UPC. They brought together the two elements from both the first (1733) and second (1761) Secessions from the CofS, and their different traditions, particularly in matters of Church discipline, did not make the union an easy one. In terms of polity, the UPC had a synod which had in effect the powers of a General Assembly, with ministers and representative elders from every congregation. This differed from the representation in both the CofS and the FC and gave the appearance of being more democratic.

The Basis of Union held to the Westminster* Confession of Faith and the Larger and Shorter Catechisms* along with three important additions. The first disapproved of anything contained in these documents which taught 'persecuting and in-

UNITED PRESBYTERIAN CHURCH

tolerant principles in religion'. This recognized the stand that both Churches had made for civil and religious liberty. Secondly, there was an article on free Communion, which was the traditional practice of the Relief Church. Finally, a declaration on the importance of generosity in giving reflected both Churches' belief in Voluntaryism.* The new Church was distinguished by its Voluntary principles, its active promotion of overseas missions, and its openness to 'enlightened' theological opinions.

During the latter decades of the nineteenth century the UPC departed from the position and character of the early Secession. The Church came to be largely concentrated in the lowland cities of Scotland, where developments in liberal theology within the Church gave expression to a radical political and social outlook (see D. C. Smith, *Passive Obedience and Prophetic Protest* (NY, 1987), 257–66). Despite this more liberal approach to both the Bible and theology, it also had such men in its ranks as James Orr* who were to defend orthodox Evangelicalism with a 'modified Calvinism'.

CHURCH AND STATE. The UPC was at the forefront of the movement to disestablish the CofS. The first UP Synod minutes described Voluntaryism as 'the obligation and the privilege of its members, influenced by regard to the authority of Christ, to support and extend by voluntary contribution the ordinances of the Gospel' (*United Presbyterian Synod Minutes* (E, 1847), 9). This stand on Voluntaryism held back negotiations for union with the FC for twenty years and led the Church to object to religious education in schools. The main battle over disestablishment* was fought out in the period 1875 to 1895. In 1874 an anti-patronage act was introduced into Parliament and the UP Synod formed a committee headed by George Hutton* of Paisley in order to push for the disestablishment of the CofS. The FC also formed a committee and a joint campaign drew the two Churches closer together.

MISSIONS. From the very beginning the UPC had a missionary character. Both uniting Churches had initiated missions of their own and had given strong support to independent missionary societies like the London Missionary Society.* The UPC did not aspire to be a national Church in the same sense as the FC and the CofS. The union of 1847 led to consolidation of congregations rather than expansion at home. Consequently, the UPs were able to put more money into overseas missions. The result of this can be clearly seen. In the mid-eighteenth century missions had been started in the North American Provinces and in Nova Scotia and, from 1802, in Upper and Lower Canada, present-day Ontario and Quebec. The new Church also inherited a Jamaican mission which in turn commenced work in Calabar, West Africa, in 1846. In 1847 the Church took over from the Glasgow Missionary Society (see Missions) the mission in Kaffraria in South Africa which had begun in 1821. The challenge of India was taken up by the Synod in 1858 and the following year it sent its first

UNITED PRESBYTERIAN CHURCH

missionaries. The last mission that was established by the Church was in China at Ningpo in 1863. The best known UP missionary is Mary Slessor* who went to Calabar in 1876.

THEOLOGY. In 1877 the UPC appointed a committee to consider revising the Westminster Confession of Faith. This was in response to changes in theology that were affecting all the Scottish Churches. In the UPC it manifested itself in a movement that wanted either to amend the Confession or to write a new and simpler creed. Subscription* to the Confession had always allowed a certain liberty allowed in non-essentials, but there was no qualifying statement in print. The committee appointed in 1877 consisted of James Harper,* John Cairns,* James Orr and Fergus Ferguson.* The last-named was accused in 1878 of heresy particularly because of his views on the atonement. However, the Synod, in light of the forthcoming Declaratory Statement, chose to acquit him.

In 1879 the Synod adopted the Declaratory Act.* Among its more controversial articles were those that dealt with the doctrine of redemption, the divine decrees, total depravity, the ultimate destiny of the heathen and the salvation of children who die in infancy. The final clause provided for liberty of conscience on matters of faith and worship. This Declaratory Act was the first passed by any Presbyterian Church in Scotland, and pointed the way in which the others were not slow to follow. The changes instituted, especially those affecting the divine decrees, had, according to Cairns, brought the UPC closer to John Wesley* than to the Westminster Divines.

Theological training within the UPC was provided during attendance by the students on two-month courses in the Edinburgh Divinity Hall during the summer. In 1847 there were five professors at the UP Hall, Neil McMichael and William Lindsay* from the Relief Church and the better known John Brown,* James Harper, and John Eadie.* Later John Ker, Cairns and Orr would each serve as professors at the Hall. The Hall was remodelled in 1878 and the professors were employed full-time in order to relieve them of the burden of pastoring a congregation.

While the other Presbyterian Churches in Scotland were being rocked by the issue of higher criticism* the UPC remained comparatively unaffected. There was a long-standing tradition of relatively liberal biblical interpretation, but in general the UPs remained indifferent to the controversy and out of the major debates.

WORSHIP. One of the most important innovations* in Presbyterian worship* during the nineteenth century was the introduction of organs. The first conflict over the use of organs arose in the UPC in 1856 with a request to the Synod from the Claremont Church in Glasgow. The Synod forbade the organ on the grounds that it would lead to disharmony in the Church. The issue reappeared in 1858 and 1867 and the reply of the Synod was as in 1856. Finally in 1872 official sanction was given to the use of instrumental music* in worship services.

UNITED REFORMED CHURCH

The UPC was the first Presbyterian Church in Scotland to allow this innovation in worship. In 1851 a new hymn book was introduced and as the century wore on exclusive psalmody* no longer dominated worship (see Hymnology, English).

UNION. No sooner had union taken place in 1847 than some began to talk of union with the FC. However, formal negotiations did not commence until 1863, when committees were formed by the UP Synod and the FC General Assembly to investigate areas of co-operation and ultimately union. Cairns was the leader of the union movement in the UPC; he wrote 'that the only divergence between the two Churches, a different view of the Civil Magistrate's duties in regard to religion, need not be a hindrance, as neither Church made this a term of communion' (A. R. MacEwan, *Life and Letters of John Cairns*, L, 1896), 502. The biggest stumbling block was, as Cairns rightly discerned, the divergent views on the establishment principle. The initial enthusiasm in both Churches waned after ten years of stormy negotiations. In 1873 union negotiations were brought to an end as the FC faced a potential disruption over the issue.

In 1896 union again became a live issue in the UPC and in 1897, having co-operated on the disestablishment campaign of the 1880s, the FC agreed to renew negotiations. The conviction that union was right had never been doubted by the UP Synod and they merely waited for the same conviction to dawn upon the FC. The Churches were similar in doctrine, worship and church government, and they had moved closer in doctrine with the move away from Calvinism among many of the younger ministers. The UPC voted unanimously in favour of union and it took place in Edinburgh on 31 October 1900, when the UFC was formed.

D. Woodside, *The Soul of a Scottish Church* (E, n.d.); *Memorial of the Jubilee Synod of the UPC* (E, 1897); Small; G. Struthers, *Historical Sketch of the Origin of the Secession Church* (E, 1848); J. M'Kerrow, *History of the Foreign Missions of the Secession and UPC* (E, 1867); J. H. Leckie, *Secession Memories* (E, 1926); D. C. Smith, *Passive Obedience and Prophetic Protest* (NY, 1987); A. C. Cheyne, *The Transforming of the Kirk* (E, 1983); A. L. Drummond and J. Bulloch, *The Church in Late Victorian Scotland* (E, 1978).

S. D. Gill

United Reformed Church, belonging to the Reformed family of churches (and hence to the World Alliance of Reformed Churches*) that resulted from the union in 1972 of the Congregational Church in England and Wales and the Presbyterian Church of England. (A number of Congregational churches did not join, and two Presbyterian congregations – in the Channel Islands* – were admitted into the CofS instead.) By further union in 1981 with most of the Churches of Christ* it came to have congregations in Scotland also (there were thirteen in Scotland at the time). 'The United Reformed Church in the United Kingdom' in 1990 had about 1800 churches, 1100 ministers and

120,000 members. Its Northern Province includes its six Scottish churches, with about 300 members.

As the first union in Britain of churches with divergent ecclesiastical polities across denominational lines, the URC maintains a strong ecumenical witness, though numerically it has been experiencing sharp decline. Following the assimilation of the Churches of Christ it has been distinctive in observing both infant and believers' baptism* as equally acceptable alternatives.

Year Book, annually (L).

D. F. Wright

United Secession Church (properly, the United Associate Synod of the Secession Church), formed in 1820 by the union of the Associate Synod* and the General Associate Synod,* the two New Light* branches of the Secession* which had originally parted from the CofS in 1733. The first rupture in the Secession occurred in 1747 over a disagreement whether a Seceder's taking the Burgess oath* should be a term of Communion. This split led to the forming of the Associate Synod (Burgher), and the General Associate Synod (Antiburgher). Both were noted for godly piety and evangelistic zeal, as well as a penchant for controversy. Towards the end of the eighteenth century a further split was precipitated by a dispute in both Synods regarding the teaching of the Westminster* Confession of Faith on the duties of the civil magistrate in relation to church affairs. Both Synods disavowed all 'compulsory and persecuting principles' in religion, and included this statement in their respective Testimonies.* This disavowal was, however, opposed by small minorities in both Synods. This resulted in 1799 in the Burghers being split into the 'New Lichts' (who supported the revision; *see* New Light), and the 'Auld Lichts' (who were opposed to any change in the Synod's relation to the Confession of Faith). A similar split among the Antiburghers occurred in 1806.

The union of the (New Light) Associate Synod and General Associate Synod originated in the missionary, Bible and religious societies which sprang up all over early nineteenth-century Scotland, bringing together members of all churches in common efforts. Apparently union was proposed first in a reading society in Mid- and East Calder, which on being publicized, met with enthusiastic reception in the two Churches throughout Scotland. The 1819 Synods received numerous petitions from congregations urging union and took appropriate action, resulting in the 1820 union. There was some dissent. In the General Associate Synod, George Paxton,* the theological professor, and six others protested and refused to join the union, joining instead the Constitutional Associate Presbytery, and forming, in 1827, the Associate Synod of Original Seceders (*see* Original Secession Church). All ministers of the Associate Synod joined in the union.

The United Secession Church continued the emphases and institutions of its parent bodies, including zeal for missionary activity. Thus the second article of the new Church's Basis of Union canonized its opposition to intolerant and persecuting principles in religion: 'We do not approve or require an approbation of any thing in those books [the Westminster Standards] which teaches, or may be thought to teach, compulsory or persecuting and intolerant principles in religion.'

Within the ranks of this new ecclesiastical body, which comprised some 280 congregations, three future professors, John Brown* (*d.* 1858), Robert Balmer,* and James Harper,* levelled criticism against the new Church's relation to the Confession of Faith. In 1821 they presented a document criticizing the terms of the formula of subscription. They argued that 'it must be very difficult for ministers, and still more for licentiates and elders, to examine every proposition in these standards with such care, as to be qualified to give a rational assent to it with the solemnity of an oath. Besides, it will be universally admitted that these standards contain some things, the belief of which are not essential as qualifications for office in the Church of Christ.' This action precipitated a further separation when seven ministers and five elders seceded from the united Church in 1821, unhappy with its 'new' theological emphases. In 1827 the Church issued a new testimony* reflecting its distinctive theological positions (*Testimony of the United Associate Synod of the Secession Church*, E, 1827). The United Secession Church was troubled in the 1840s by the Atonement Controversy.* This crystallized the growing dissatisfaction of traditional Westminster Calvinists with what appeared to them the increasing questioning within the Church of the Confession's teaching. Chief among the theologians of the United Secession Church were John Brown, whose exegetical works continue to be reprinted, and John Dick,* whose systematic theology* had considerable influence at home and abroad.

In 1847, the United Secession Church joined with the Relief Church* to form the United Presbyterian Church,* with 518 congregations.

J. M'Kerrow, *History of the Secession Church* (E, 1848); Small; C. G. M'Crie, *The Confessions of the Church of Scotland* (E, 1907); I. Hamilton, *The Erosion of Calvinist Orthodoxy. Seceders and Subscription in Scottish Presbyterianism* (E, 1990).

I. Hamilton

Uniting Act (1900), act of FC General Assembly approving union of FC and UP Churches. Avoiding the mistaken policy of earlier negotiations when prior agreement had been sought on every point, the principle of the 1900 Uniting Act was that each Church would take the other as it found it. The Westminster Confession,* under the qualifications of the Declaratory Acts,* defined the common doctrinal commitment; all points not covered in the Confession were to be regarded as 'open questions'. A special FC General Assembly was called in October 1900 to pass the Act on the same day as a special Synod of the UPC, which approved the Union almost without dissent. A dissident Constitutionalist* minority argued that the Act was a violation of the FC constitution. It was passed by a majority of 643 to 27, the majority entered the Union and the minority continued the separate existence of the FC.*

See also Free Church of Scotland, 1843–1900; Unions, Church, in Scotland.

J. K. Cameron, *Scottish Church Union of 1900* (Inverness, 1923); P. C. Simpson, *The Life of Principal Rainy* (L, 1909), II, 188–268; K. R. Ross, *Church and Creed in Scotland* (E, 1988).

K. R. Ross

Universalism, *see* Unitarians.

Universities are a unique creation of the medieval world, autonomous institutions which have survived the constant transformations imposed by the varying needs of different ages and the recurrent crises engendered by conflict with external authority, secular and ecclesiastical. Despite the 'ivy-leaf' campus image presented by some American models harking back to schools in scholastic townlets like Oxford and Cambridge, the earlier universities, Paris and Bologna, were typically urban outgrowths. Monastic and cathedral schools could not meet the demands of the new breed of questioning city-dweller or assist the isolated masters competing outside cathedral closes or monastic precincts – men like Theobald of Etampes, correspondent of Queen Margaret of Scotland,* a pre-university Oxford master.

The new universities aspired to be *studia generalia*, international schools, the foundations of popes and emperors who alone could grant their students the privilege and professional teaching licence (*ius ubique docendi*) of Europe-wide authority. The new foundations of friars,* springing up in towns rather than set in pastoral landscapes, orders themselves committed to higher studies, helped the 'university' or corporation of masters and students to assert its independence of local church and city officials. But, in addition to the reservations that Reformed Franciscans, as later Andrew Melville,* had with the acceptance of degree-styles, they had to overcome problems set by the introduction of philosophical and scientific texts from the Islamic and late Greek worlds, seemingly intractable problems like those set by a pagan ethic or by Aristotle's view of the world as eternal. There already existed a tradition of 'faith seeking understanding' inherited from St Anselm and the pre-university schools, but ethics teaching won a more precarious recognition – *si placet* ('if it please'), to cite the customary formula. Clashes led to scholarly migrations, as to Cambridge from Oxford, out of which new universities emerged. Clashes demanded solidarity among the members, for a university was a sworn society, any promotion in which was safeguarded by fresh oaths of reciprocal obligation. The Glasgow statutes described one of its models, Bologna, as 'freest of universities'; such liberties principally envisaged freedom from taxation and juridical process rather than academic freedoms, especially in an increasing number of local universities with mostly local importance. Yet opinions banned elsewhere could, it was accepted, be aired in universities. Even so, society's priorities continued often to conflict with those of the university – hence the late sixteenth-century visitations by state officials and the nineteenth-century commissions.

Up to 1400, Scots students were obliged to study abroad. The first native university, St Andrews, emerged in 1411 from local initiative (*see* Wardlaw, Henry) and took its foundation bull from the Avignon pope, Benedict XIII, during the Great Schism. Under Laurence of Lindores,* a teacher of repute in Central Europe, Inquisitor and opponent of followers of John Wyclif (*see* Lollards), St Andrews adopted in its foundation faculty (arts) and in its foundational subject, whose linguistic techniques even penetrated theology (logic), the so-called *via moderna*, 'modern approach', of nominalism. Wyclif's adhesion to realism, the *via antiqua* followed by the more ancient doctors like Thomas Aquinas and John Duns Scotus,* would be an additional motive for the intolerance of Lindores, so that its Scots followers found Cologne (1388) and Louvain (1426) more congenial. Paris, apart from the short prohibition of nominalism by Louis XI, tolerated both approaches.

Cologne was another acknowledged model for Glasgow, Scotland's second university (1451). Renaissance* humanism allied to a moderate scholasticism inspired the foundation at Aberdeen (1495); the first principal of King's College, Hector Boece,* employed Renaissance rhetoric in his history of Scotland while also producing a serviceable text-book of logic that can be linked to the formidable logical output of the so-called 'School of John Major'.* Another new approach was that of the Reformation university exemplified in Edinburgh's Town College (1583). Many new Reformation universities styled themselves Academies on the Athenian model (*e.g.* Strasbourg and Geneva), and that title differentiated university-type Academies like Saumur from other French colleges entitled *de plein exercice*.

The first medieval colleges were no more than dormitory buildings, but St Salvator's College in St Andrews (1450) had resident teaching, and St Leonard's (1512), initially a 'college of the poor', was normalized in Cardinal Beaton's* time. St Mary's College at St Andrews aimed, at least in Archbishop James Hamilton's* revised foundation (1554), to produce trained pastors, which was the main concern of Protestant foundations for some time to come. The Renaissance* stress on eloquence and declamation for a time threatened the hold of disputation and therefore of logic as foundational subjects, and even emptied some universities of students for a period, at a time when not only divines studied arts, but medical men and lawyers as well. The philological revival in Greek and Hebrew, particularly espoused by Andrew Melville at Glasgow and subsequently in St Mary's, was aided by the Reformation principle of 'Scripture alone'. This reform was supported by the *FBD*.*

The scientific revolution brought its own problems, to which universities were slow to respond, and more followed the Enlightenment's* raising of new secular issues. The trials of John Simson* and others mirrored an intense concern with the relationship of human reasoning, especially in moral matters, to Christian faith, a concern reminiscent of medieval confrontations, like Melville's doubts about Aristotle. The Scots remained philosophers through all these theoretical storms until the nineteenth-century commissioners began to undermine the national devotion to general studies.

The eighteenth-century displacement of Latin as the vehicle of teaching made a universal licence to teach more unreal and created a rupture with Leiden and mainland Europe, although Latin's dethronement is a more modern phenomenon, with some signs of its revitalization outside of Britain. The replacement of regent teaching by that of specialist professors meant a narrowing as well as a deepening of outlook, and probably a weakening of institutional solidarity, with professors intent on defending their specialisms rather than broader corporate interests. By 1730 the largest university in Scotland, Edinburgh, took 600 students, but expansion lay ahead. Often it was planned. In Geneva the Academy saw a need to include more secular subjects, the Company of Pastors becoming less resistant to the project of a civic university. Edinburgh underwent massive changes, moving from an Erasmian ideal of 'learned piety', tied for a time to a methodical pedagogy based on Petrus Ramus, to one of corrosive reasoning coupled with an ideal of civilized good manners. Pluralism is the mark of the modern university, visible in new foundations: Strathclyde (1964), Heriot-Watt (1966), Stirling and Dundee (both 1967). The earlier fusions of Marischal* and King's in Aberdeen (1860), and of St Leonard's and St Salvator's at St Andrews (1747) are warning signs that a common inheritance constantly benefitting from the access of new participants is also constantly threatened by the very society it nourishes.

See also Education, Theological.

H. Rashdall, F. M. Powicke, A. B. Emden, *The Universities of Europe in the Middle Ages*, 3 vols (O, 1936); R. S. Rait, *The Universities of Aberdeen* (A, 1895); R. G. Cant, *The University of St Andrews* (E, ²1970); J. Durkan and J. Kirk, *The University of Glasgow 1451–1577* (G, 1977); D. E. R. Watt, *A Biographical Dictionary of Scottish Graduates to AD 1410* (O, 1977); D. B. Horn, *A Short History of the University of Edinburgh*, 1967); M.-M. Compère and D. Julia, *Les Collèges Français 16e–18e Siècles*, 2 vols (Paris, 1984–8); J. Durkan, 'The Universities of Scotland in the Middle Ages' (PhD, Edinburgh University, 1959); A. Broadie, *The Tradition of Scottish Philosophy* (E, 1990); J. MacQueen, *Humanism in Renaissance Scotland* (E, 1990).

J. Durkan

Universities and Colleges Christian Fellowship, see Inter-Varsity Fellowship.

Urquhart, John (1808–27), student missionary leader. Born in Perth, Urquhart was a precocious child who excelled in school and developed spiritually under the direction of the Congregationalist minister, William Orme*. At the University of St Andrews he was known for his learning, piety, and missionary enthusiasm. Inspired by the example of the Cambridge students in the previous generation, he led his fellow students – including Alexander Duff,* John Adam, Robert Nesbit,* William Sinclair Mackay,* and David Ewart* – in the formation of the St Andrews University Missionary Association in 1824. Urquhart's address to the association on 3 April 1826 has been described by missions scholar O. G. Myklebust, as 'an eloquent appeal, one of the ablest on record, to . . . students on the subject of foreign missions'. Urquhart died at the age of eighteen, before he could become a missionary, but his single-minded crusade for missions at the university motivated others to missionary careers.

W. Orme, *Memoirs of John Urquhart*, 2 vols (L, 1828); S. Piggin and J. Roxborogh, *The St Andrews Seven* (E, 1985).

D. B. Calhoun

Urquhart, William Spence (1877–1964), distinguished missionary educationist, appointed Professor of Philosophy in Duff College, Calcutta, in 1902 and Principal in 1928. He also served as Professor of Philosophy in Calcutta University, and was Vice-Chancellor 1928–30. He edited the *Calcutta Review* for some years, and in his retirement taught systematic theology in Aberdeen and in Knox College, Toronto. His main publications were useful but now dated studies in Hinduism (*The Upanishads and Life* (Calcutta, 1913), *Pantheism and the Value of Life* (L, 1919), *Theosophy and Christian Thought* (L, 1922), *The Vedanta and Modern Thought* (L, 1928)). A sound and careful scholar, he did not achieve the eminence as an interpreter of Hinduism of Nicol MacNicol* or J. N. Farquhar*.

Who Was Who, 1961–1970, 1143; *FUFCS* 537; *FES* IX, 752, X, 426.

D. B. Forrester

Usages, liturgical practices which divided Scottish Episcopalians* especially in the 1720s. The four main ones were eucharistic – the dilution of wine with water, prayers for the dead, epiclesis and prayer of sacrifice – but others included chrism in confirmation and for the sick and immersion in baptism. They mostly found support in the Scottish Prayer Book* of 1637, reprinted in 1712 (see Laud, William), but not in the 1662 *BCP** then commonly used in Scotland. A similar dispute divided English non-jurors,* with some favouring the 1549 *BCP*. The Scottish dispute, in the years after the Toleration Act* of 1712 and the first Jacobite* rising of 1715,* saw the bishops at loggerheads, with James Gadderar of Aberdeen (1655–1733) and Thomas Rattray* the most ardent Usagers. Rattray provided a scholarly defence from early Christian practice. Concordats of 1724 and 1731 effected a compromise, allowing a form of the 1637 Book to be used.

A similar controversy involving the 1637 Book broke out in the episcopate of A. P. Forbes.*

G. Grub, *An Ecclesiastical History of Scotland*, III (E, 1861), 386–95; T. Lathbury, *A History of the Nonjurors* (L, 1845), 464–73; J. Dowden, *The Scottish Communion Office 1764*, ed. H. A. Wilson (O, 1922), 49–65.

D. F. Wright

V

Valliscaulians, a medieval monastic order.* The order of Val des Choux (*Vallis Caulium* or *Vallis Oleorum*) was instituted at the place of that name in the diocese of Langres in Burgundy by Viard, a former lay-brother of the Carthusian* monastery of Louvigny, towards the end of the twelfth century. Its rule, confirmed by Pope Innocent III in 1205, has affinities with the rules of the Cistercians* and the Carthusians, and placed each daughter house in a relation of direct dependence on the mother house. The order is said to have been introduced into Scotland in 1230 by William de Malvoisin, Bishop of St Andrews, and Alexander III, King of Scots, who thereafter founded for its monks the priory of Pluscarden* in his forest of Elgin (1230 or 1231). In the same period Duncan McCowll (or McDougall) endowed a priory at Ardchattan, while John Byset, possibly in association with the King, founded another at Beauly. All three, which are sometimes described as Cistercian, lie in isolated regions in the north and west of the kingdom (*see* Highlands). Pluscarden remained Valliscaulian until its six remaining monks became Benedictine* on its separation from Val des Choux and subsequent union with the priory of Urquhart in 1454. The prior of Val des Choux continued to claim jurisdiction over Beauly, whose prior was summoned in 1506 to the next general chapter of the order and was also commissioned to visit Ardchattan. The Beauly priory nevertheless became Cistercian in 1510, when a papal bull directed to the prior and convent of Beauly extinguished the order of Vallis Caulium there, leaving Ardchattan with some four to six monks as the sole survivor of the Valliscaulian order in Scotland at the Reformation (Easson-Cowan, 83-5).

E. C. Batten (ed.), *The Charters of the Priory of Beauly* (L, 1877); S. R. MacPhail, *History of the Religious House of Pluscardyn* (E, 1881).

I. B. Cowan

Veto Act, 1834, granting congregations power of veto in ministerial appointment. The evangelical party within the CofS had long believed that the law of the Church allowed that no presentee should be 'intruded' by a patron on any congregation contrary to the will of the people. Accordingly, when the Evangelicals began to gain the ascendancy in the General Assembly in the early 1830s, one of their first actions was to draw up a measure designed to restrict the practice of patronage* so as to ensure that no congregation would have an unwanted minister thrust upon it. The Veto Act provided a ballot for church members on the appointment of their ministers (though only male heads of family could vote). They could not freely elect their minister, but they did have the right by majority vote to veto the appointed presentee of the patron. Congregational rights were further safeguarded by the provision that members did not have to give reasons for their veto, providing that it was conscientious. It seemed to the Evangelicals a modest measure. They did not seek the abolition of patronage but merely attempted to regulate it so that unhappy settlements could be avoided. The Act was first proposed by Thomas Chalmers* in 1833, but his motion was narrowly defeated. The following year it was proposed by its drafter, Lord (later Sir) Henry Wellwood Moncrieff, and was passed by 184 votes to 139. The Moderates* opposed the measure and John Hope, Dean of the Faculty of Advocates, dissented on the grounds of the Assembly's incompetence to deprive a patron of his civil rights or a presentee of his entitlement to the benefice. On these grounds the civil courts later took issue with the Church in the conflict which led to the Disruption* (*see* Ten Years Conflict).

AGACS, 1037-40; R. Buchanan, *The Ten Years' Conflict* (L, 1849), I, 289-316; H. Watt, *Thomas Chalmers and the Disruption* (E, 1943), 129-34.

K. R. Ross

Video. The development of religious video in Scotland was pioneered when Ronald Falconer,* formerly head of BBC religious broadcasting* in

Scotland, took the leading role in the CofS's publicity work. Helped by the Baird Trust* and the Woman's Guild,* the CofS put considerable resources into the formation of a video unit before the full impact of video as a social and commercial phenomenon had been realised. A video unit was set up and won a number of awards, later moving into television production work, under the direction of Ralph Smith (*FES* X, 283; cf. his *Video in the Service of the Congregation*, E, 1988).

R. D. Kernohan

Vincentian Mission to Scotland. Vincentians (known also as Lazarists and Congregation of the Mission), founded by St Vincent de Paul (1580?–1660), are secular priests under simple vows. In 1650 two Irish Gaelic-speakers, Dermot Duggan (*c.*1620–57) and Francis White (*c.*1620–79), were sent to the Highlands. Both were extraordinarily successful. Duggan ministered in the Islands and Western mainland, and White, apart from some months' imprisonment in 1655 and visits to Paris 1660–2 and 1665–8, in the Highlands until his death. A Scot, Thomas Lumsden, worked in north-east Scotland 1653–63. Various Irish priests ministering in the Highlands until the eighteenth century were apparently, if not Vincentians, recruited by Vincentians in Paris.

M. Purcell, *The Story of the Vincentians* (Dublin, 1973), 42–66; P. Boyle, *St Vincent de Paul and the Vincentians in Ireland, Scotland and England* (L, 1909), 77–95, 113.

M. Dilworth

Vocation. In its more general and scriptural sense, vocation (or calling) is a reality for all Christians, whatever their state of life. By baptism all are called to holiness and Christian witness and to share in the Church's mission to spread the Good News. Thus marriage too is a true form of Christian vocation.

In its restricted sense, particularly in RC spirituality, vocation is the call of certain individuals to the priesthood or religious life. After the pattern of biblical callings it originates in God's initiative, but it operates according to God's usual dealings with men and women, mediated by their individual characteristics and circumstances. Although an intensively spiritual and personal reality, vocation in this sense is also ecclesial and will be discerned, in the case of priesthood, by the bishop and his delegates, normally in the context of seminary* formation; and in the case of religious life, by the aspirant's superiors.

In post-Reformation Scotland the apartness of priests was emphasized by years of formation in remote seminaries at home (*see* Colleges and Seminaries, Roman Catholic) and Scots Colleges* abroad. Today, although Vatican II* has stressed the call of all the baptized to holiness and witness, particularly in the constitution *Lumen Gentium* (Light of the Nations), 'Scottish vocations directors' are active in promoting recruitment to the priesthood and religious life.

The Protestant Reformers rejected the superiority of the vocation of the 'religious', insisting on the holiness of all callings and ways of life in society (cf. Henry Balnaves,* in Knox, *Works* III, 519–31). Yet vocation to church ministry remained important, with a distinctive emphasis on the church's calling: 'Ordinarie Vocation consisteth in Election, Examination and Admission' (*FBD* 96), although God's 'extraordinary vocation' was not excluded (*FBD* 207). The Reformed understanding of vocation to special ministries has preserved a marked concern for 'lawful calling' by the church (cf. *SBD* 65–73, 178–82; Westminster *Form of Presbyterial Church Government*; and *see* Call).

New Catholic Encyclopedia XIV, 735–40; J. L. Ainslie, *The Doctrines of Ministerial Order in the Reformed Churches of the 16th and 17th Centuries* (E, 1940).

P. Tartaglia and D. F. Wright

Voluntary Church Association, set up in Edinburgh in 1832 to promote dissent* during the early years of the Voluntary Controversy.* It held 'that a compulsory support of Religious Institutions is inconsistent with the nature of religion, the Spirit of the Gospel, the express appointment of Jesus Christ and the civil rights of man'. Dozens of similar associations followed in its wake and in 1833 the Glasgow branch published a monthly magazine, under the editorship of Andrew Marshall,* which became a major tool of the dissenters in their attack on the Establishment and their campaign for the disestablishment* of the Church. Though slow at first to respond, those who defended the Est.C eventually set up, in 1833, the Glasgow Society to promote the cause of the CofS. The *Church of Scotland Magazine*, the major anti-Voluntary review, was as vituperative in its language as the *Voluntary Church Magazine*, and the various associations, with their respective magazines, pamphlets and local meetings, divided Scottish Christians, especially in missionary endeavours (*see* Periodicals, Religious). Opinion was polarized, especially over the appeal of the Est.C for additional parliamentary endowments to enable church extension work to go ahead. The Voluntaries, on the other hand, wanted a more pluralistic society in which Church and state* would be separated. In 1833 they defined their purpose as 'to induce civil governments to let religion alone, and to allow every man, and every body of men, while they conducted themselves as good citizens, to manage their own concerns in the way they think most agreeable to the Will of God'.

S. Brown, *Thomas Chalmers and the Godly Commonwealth in Scotland* (O, 1982), ch. 5; A. B. Montgomery, 'The Voluntary Controversy in the Church of Scotland, 1829–1843' (PhD, Edinburgh University, 1953).

G. F. C. Jenkins

Voluntary Controversy, initiated in 1829 by a proposed government bill to provide relief for RCs in Northern Ireland. Andrew Marshall,* among others, saw this as the first step towards the re-establishment of the RCC by the state. Until then the Seceders had largely adhered to the Westminster* Confession and had refused to follow English dissenters in their views on the separation of Church and state*. But in the 1830s the CofS faced a challenge from a radical and aggressive Voluntaryism* in a concerted campaign for disestablishment*. Three main reasons have been suggested for this: the dramatic rise of dissent*, the triumphs of liberal political reform and the concern among dissenters over the evangelical trend within a revitalized Est.C, especially after the passing of the Veto* and Chapel Acts* in 1834. These two Acts enabled Thomas Chalmers* from the Est.C side to counteract the aggressive Voluntaryism of the dissenters with his own brand of internal Voluntaryism, in which he called on the middle classes to support his scheme for church extension* and to press for increase in the numbers of ecclesiastical endowments. Whereas Chalmers' programme was based on the need for ample provision of religious ordinances through parochial endowments and church extension, the Voluntaries maintained that religion ought to be regulated by the law of supply and demand and churches set up by 'private enterprise'.

S. Brown, *Thomas Chalmers and the Godly Commonwealth in Scotland* (O, 1982); A. B. Montgomery, 'The Voluntary Controversy in the Church of Scotland 1829–1843' (PhD, Edinburgh University, 1953); P. Chalmers, *Strictures of Some Sayings and Doings of the Dunfermline Voluntaries* (G, 1835); J. Law, *Reply to the Strictures of the Revd T. Chalmers on Some Recent Sayings and Doings of the Dunfermline Voluntaries* (Dunfermline, 1835); A. Marshall, *Ecclesiastical Establishments Farther Considered* (G, 1831).

G. F. C. Jenkins

Voluntaryism, the belief that 'every congregation should support its own minister' by voluntary contributions, rather than relying on parochial endowments by the state. Churches with a Congregationalist* policy, such as Glasites (*see* Glas, John), Baptists* and Independents,* were all Voluntary from the outset. The emergence of Voluntaryism within Presbyterian Churches was more gradual. While the Relief* Church adopted Voluntaryism almost from its inception, it is more difficult to ascertain when it became part of the belief of the Secession* Churches. Though Voluntaryism as a religious ideal was entertained in Scotland before the end of the eighteenth century, it became a political issue around 1829 (*see* Marshall, Andrew; Voluntary Controversy).

Voluntaryism was opposed to the concept of a national Church upheld by the state (*see* Church and state) and also insisted that the oversight of the poor (*see* Poor Relief) and of the schools (*see* Education) should be taken out of the hands of the Church. It became an important issue in the Ten Years' Conflict* and in the campaign for disestablishment.* Though Thomas Chalmers* had stated in his opening address at the 1843 Assembly that those who formed the FC were 'unwilling Voluntaries', many in the new Church soon adopted Voluntaryism as the norm. The question of the FC's relationship to the state remained unresolved for most of the nineteenth century, when it was seen by those in the northern part of the country as a major stumbling-block to union with the UPC.

A. L. Drummond and J. Bulloch, *The Scottish Church 1686–1843* (E, 1973); C. Leckie, *The Substance of Two Lectures on the Effects of Voluntaryism* (n.p., 1835); J. A. Haldane, *The Voluntary Question Political not Religious* (E, 1839).

G. F. C. Jenkins

Vows, *see* Oaths; Ordination Vows.

W

Waddell, Hope Masterton (1804–95), missionary. Born in Dublin, he spent twenty years with the Scottish Missionary Society in Jamaica before accepting an Efik invitation to start a mission in Calabar, eastern Nigeria. In his voluminous writings he describes the school as the Church's nursery and claims that his greatest love was to teach children. But he was primarily a politician, regularly concerned with affairs of state. Convinced that the Efik economy's future lay in international commerce, he stressed English literacy and numeracy as school subjects. Keen to consolidate, he encouraged a special Efik-Presbyterian relationship, agreeing not to expand beyond Efik frontiers.

Although he admitted to being a slow learner of Efik, he frequently recorded his indignation at the 'absence' of certain words (e.g. none for 'chastity'). He often condemned what he saw as widespread immorality in Efik traditions. Always authoritarian, he became so crotchety that the Mission Council forced his resignation in 1854. He is commemorated by one of Nigeria's greatest schools, which still bears his name.

Twenty-nine Years in the West Indies and Central Africa ... 1829–1858 (L, 1863).

D. M. McFarlan, *Calabar* (L, E, ²1957).

W. H. Taylor

Waddell, Peter Hately (1817–91), minister and man of letters. Born at Balquhatston, Slamannan, in Stirlingshire, he studied at Glasgow University and joined the FC as a divinity student in 1843. He was called in 1844 to the new FC in Girvan, Ayrshire, but when he refused to subscribe (*see* Subscription, Confessional) the confession on account of his voluntaryist* views, his licence was withdrawn. Taking many of his congregation with him, he established an independent chapel which he called 'the Church of the Future' (see *The Church of the Future*, G, 1861). In 1862 he moved to Glasgow, preaching in the city hall, and gathered a large congregation. He joined the CofS in 1888, but held no charge. His son and namesake (1854–1922) was minister of Whitekirk, E. Lothian, and a noted author (*FES* VIII 113; J. C. Gibson, *P. Hately Waddell*, G, 1925).

Waddell was an outstanding pulpit orator. His poetic aptitude found expression in a devotion to Robert Burns,* a new edition of whose poems he issued (G, 1867–9). He edited and annotated Sir Walter Scott's* Waverley novels in 1882–5. He himself wrote verse, e.g. *Behold the Man* (G, 1872), and skilfully translated the Psalms into Scots in *The Psalms: frae Hebrew intil Scottis* (E, 1871) and later Isaiah in *Isaiah: frae Hebrew intil Scottis* (E, 1879). His *Ossian and the Clyde* (G, 1875) presented a topographic justification of the genuineness of the Ossianic poems of James Macpherson.

The Sojourn of a Sceptic in the Land of Darkness and Uncertainty (E, 1847).

DNB LVIII, 405–6; G. Tulloch, *A History of the Bible in Scots* (A, 1989), 37–47; *AFCS* II, 57.

N. R. Needham

Waldef (d. 1159), abbot of Melrose*, 1148–59. He was the second son of Simon de Senlis, Earl of Northampton, and of Maud, daughter of Judith, niece of William the Conqueror. He was named after his grandfather, Earl Waltheof, who had been executed by the Conqueror in 1076. After his father's death, his mother married Earl David of Scotland (the future David I*), c.1113. David, therefore, was Waldef's stepfather. His date of birth is unknown, probably c.1095.

Waldef early showed signs of piety, and entered the Augustinian priory of St Oswald at Nostell, near Pontefract (Yorkshire). By c.1130 he had been elected prior of Kirkham (Lancashire). His name was canvassed during the York election dispute of 1140–3, and he took part in the negotiations which led to its settlement. About the same time he met St Malachi, became influenced by the Cistercian* ideal, and entered the abbey of Rievaulx c.1143. In 1148 he was elected second abbot of Melrose. He held this office until 1159, when he was elected

Bishop of St Andrews; but age and infirmity prevented him from taking up this office.

His advancement to high office and his posthumous reputation for sanctity may owe much to the nobility of his family connections. Jocelin of Furness wrote a *Life of Waldef* c.1206–7, which is the only authority for this reputation, which may have been exaggerated.

J. P. B. Bulloch, 'St Waltheof', *RSCHS* 11 (1955), 105–32; G. McFadden, 'The *Life of Waldef* and its Author, Jocelin of Furness', *IR* 6 (1955), 5–13; D. Baker, 'Legend and Reality: the Case of Waldef of Melrose', *Studies in Church History* 12 (1975), 59–82.

A. Macquarrie

Wales. The earliest extant literature in Welsh (c.AD 600) is attributed to Aneurin, the court poet of Mynyddawg Mwynfawr, king of Gododdin, whose seat was in Edinburgh, while Taliesin sang to Urien, the king of Rheged, in the western Lowlands. After the disruption of these Brythonic kingdoms, the connections between Wales and Scotland have been sporadic.

During the Evangelical Revival in Wales, there was a lively interest in similar events in Scotland. Howel Harris (1714–72), for example, avidly sought news of the 1742 revival* at Cambuslang. His correspondence with the minister, William McCulloch,* extended from 1742 to 1745. James Erskine, Lord Grange (1679–1754; *DNB* XVII, 413–14), whom Harris first introduced to Lady Huntingdon, was another frequent correspondent between 1743 and 1746, and in the summer of the latter year they were in each other's company at London. James Erskine was a family relation of Ebenezer and Ralph Erskine.* Although he told Harris that he considered the two to be 'bigots', that did not diminish Harris's admiration for them. He insisted that the Welsh Methodists put 'great value' on their books and some of them were translated into Welsh. Harris was also acquainted with Henry David Erskine, tenth earl of Buchan (d.1767) and his daughter, Lady Anne (d.1804).

The teaching of John Glas* and his son-in-law, Robert Sandeman,* was introduced into Wales by John Popkin (*fl.*1759–1824), the well-to-do Methodist exhorter. He embraced Sandeman's views about 1760 and campaigned vigorously in support of them. He founded Sandemanian churches at Swansea, Llangadog and Carmarthen. Up to about 1768 he published translations into Welsh of books by Glas and Sandeman. But his views were rejected by the Calvinistic Methodists and he was excommunicated.

The Baptist churches were convulsed from 1791 onwards by supporters of the teachings of Archibald M'Lean.* In that year William Richards (1749–1818), the Baptist minister of King's Lynn, Norfolk, launched campaigns in his native Wales in support of M'Lean's views. He met with no immediate success, but in 1794 M'Lean's books were drawn to the attention of John Richard Jones (1765–1822), the very gifted minister of Ramoth Baptist Church, Merionethshire. He was completely won over and persuaded his church to adopt M'Lean's principles. At first Jones was supported by the distinguished preacher Christmas Evans (1766–1838), but his enthusiasm soon evaporated. Jones, however, persisted. He began to correspond with M'Lean and in 1798 he announced that his church was severing its links with the Welsh Baptists and entering into communion with the so-called 'Scotch Baptists'.* By 1801 seven churches, all in north Wales, had joined the new denomination and it still remains in existence.

The most striking example of Scottish influence on Welsh religious life occurred amongst the Welsh Calvinistic Methodists. That influence was mediated primarily through Lewis Edwards (1809–87), who was a student at the University of Edinburgh from 1833 to 1836. John Phillips (1810–67), later to be the first principal of Bangor Normal College, accompanied him there. Edwards was deeply influenced by John Brown (1784–1858)* and by what he saw of the life of the Secession Church* to which Brown ministered. But what made an even deeper impression upon him was studying under Thomas Chalmers.* Edwards became convinced that, although the Calvinistic Methodist communion in Wales was a child of the Evangelical Revival, it should align itself with the Presbyterian family of Churches. Others besides him were educated at Edinburgh and were to assist him in promoting this conviction. Such were Owen Thomas (1812–91), John Parry (1812–74), David Charles Davies (1826–91), David Rowlands (1827–1917), Josiah Thomas (1830–1905) and David Lloyd Jones (1843–95).

The ways in which the Scottish influence can be seen amongst Welsh Methodists were the following: the instituting of the General Assembly in 1864; the resolve to create a learned ministry, the main instrument being the college at Bala, of which Edwards was the founder and first principal; the campaign to establish a settled ministry to replace the older itinerant pattern; the creation of a sustentation fund on the model of that set up by Thomas Chalmers. In addition, Lewis Edwards pioneered in the literary field by emulating *Blackwood's Magazine*, and his own Welsh literary style was beneficially influenced by that of his teacher, John Wilson ('Christopher North', 1785–1854; *DNB* LXII, 107–12). It was in harmony with these developments that Lewis Edwards and his colleagues worked consistently to secure a place for the Calvinistic Methodists of Wales in the international organizations created by the Presbyterian churches. In this way, a church that had its historical roots in the revival enthusiasm of the eighteenth century came to see itself as part of the Reformed tradition. It was a fitting culmination to the transformation that the denomination adopted, as an alternative title for itself, the name 'Presbyterian Church of Wales' in 1933.

Of the individual contacts between Wales and Scotland, the most noteworthy were, first, John Williams (1792–1858), who tutored Sir Walter Scott's son, and who became in 1824 the first principal of the Edinburgh Academy and in 1848 the first principal of Llandovery School, Dyfed; and second, Sir Henry Jones (1852–1922), professor successively at Bangor (1884), St Andrews (1891) and Glasgow (1894), a man whose influence was as extensive in Wales as it was in Scotland.

All the Welshmen named are in the *Dictionary of Welsh Biography* (L., 1959); E. G. Bowen, *Saints, Seaways and Settlements in the Celtic Lands* (Cardiff, 1977); Thomas Parry, *A History of Welsh Literature* (trans. H. Idris Bell, O, 1955); J. Idwal Jones, *J. R. Jones, Ramoth* (Llandysul, 1966); G. F. Nuttall, *Howel Harris* (Cardiff, 1965); G. M. Roberts, *Selected Trevecka Letters, 1742–1747* (Caernarvon, 1956); *id.*, *Selected Trevecka Letters, 1747–1794* (Caernarvon, 1962); T. Lloyd Evans, *Lewis Edwards* (Abertawe, 1967).

R. Tudur Jones

Walker, James (c.1770–1841), Bishop of Edinburgh (1830–41) and Primus of the EpCS (1837–41). Walker was born in Fraserburgh and educated at Marischal College, Aberdeen, and St John's College, Cambridge (BA, 1793; MA, 1796; DD, 1826). He was ordained deacon in 1793 and priest in 1805 and was appointed to the charge of St Peter's Chapel, Edinburgh, in 1807. By 1811, he was Dean of Edinburgh. He was consecrated Bishop of Edinburgh in 1830, and elected Primus in 1837.

Walker's life spanned the period of the penal laws (he knew clergy who had suffered under them), their repeal, and the union of the non-juring* and qualified* elements in the EpCS (*see* Episcopalianism). He was keenly aware and proud of the history of a persecuted and disestablished Church, but he also believed in the centrality of the Anglican* tradition to its life and worship. He called Richard Hooker 'the great defender of the faith and polity of our church' (*A Serious Expostulation*, E, 1826, 28), and claimed that 'to the Church of England we naturally refer on all subjects, especially which respect polity, discipline, doctrine and worship...', for the Episcopal Church 'has ever regarded the Church of England with the most devoted and grateful respect' (*A Charge delivered to the ... Episcopal Communion*, E, 1833, 12). He was a firm defender of traditional Episcopalian principles in the Caroline and non-juring tradition, as in his maintenance of baptismal regeneration (see *A Serious Expostulation*), but he constantly tried to present these principles as entirely 'respectable', at one with the CofE and no threat to the Est.C (see especially *The Conditions and Duties of a Tolerated Church*, E, 1806).

Walker was the first Pantonian Professor, a post endowed for the training of young men for the ministry of the EpCS (*see* Episcopal Theological College). In this capacity he taught students in his Edinburgh home from 1824 until his death. His teaching and literary work were combined with pastoral care. As a parish priest in Edinburgh and later as a Bishop he laid great emphasis on systematic catechizing.

Walker said of himself that few men had had 'equal opportunities of examining the present state of the Christian church as it exists in the various nations of Europe' (*Conditions and Duties*). He travelled extensively on the continent, both as tutor to Sir John Hope of Craighall in the early years of the nineteenth century and later on his own account. His earlier travels reinforced his horror of the French Revolution, but also produced an article on Kant for the supplement of the *Encyclopedia Britannica*, a work which he had sub-edited under Bishop George Gleig.* In 1817–18 he organized the first Anglican services in Rome.

Walker was particularly close to Bishop Sandford* of Edinburgh and to Bishop Jolly.* There is little reason to doubt that he 'long held a position of unique and exceptional influence not only in Edinburgh, but also in the whole of the little church' (W. Walker, *The Life of the Right Revd Alexander Jolly D.D., Bishop of Moray*, ²E, 1976, 159). His published work consists mainly of sermons.

Papers of British Churchmen 1780–1940 (L., 1987), 82; *DNB* LIX, 68; J. P. Lawson, *History of the Scottish Episcopal Church from the Revolution to the Present Time* (E, 1843); T. Stephen, *The History of the Church of Scotland from the Reformation to the Present Time*, 4 vols (L., 1843–5), IV; F. Goldie, *A Short History of the Episcopal Church in Scotland* (²E, 1976).

G. D. Duncan

Walker, James (1821–91), FC minister and writer. Born at Carnwath, Lanarkshire, the son of the parish minister, he studied arts and divinity at Edinburgh University. Throwing in his lot with the FC in 1843, he was licensed by Edinburgh FC Presbytery that year and ordained to Carnwath FC.

In the debate over union with the UPC in 1863–73 Walker was strongly pro-union. He was made a member of the FC Committee on Union in 1867, and at the Committee's request drafted a reply to the anti-union statement put out by James Begg* and his supporters (*The Union Question and the Minority of the Last Assembly*, E, 1868). In 1869 he successfully proposed William Robertson Smith* for the Hebrew Chair in Aberdeen FC College (*see* Christ's College), although he had no sympathy with the critical views Robertson later expressed. Walker's Cunningham lectures* (1870–1) were published as *The Theology and Theologians of Scotland, Chiefly of the Seventeenth and Eighteenth Centuries* (E, 1872, ²1988), and are the standard work on the subject.

Walker's health broke down in 1871, and he never recovered; he was 'a shattered invalid during the last twenty years of his life' (W. G. Blaikie,* quoted in R. Logan's 'Memoir', preface to *James Walker, D.D. of Carnwath Free Church. Essays, Papers and Sermons*, E, 1898, xlix).

His great love was Church history, especially patristic and Scottish. The volume cited above contains valuable studies of Tertullian, the Eastern Church and Sir William Lockhart.* Walker received a DD from Edinburgh University in 1871. He was the brother of Norman Walker.*

WALKER, JOHN

AFCS I, 349.

N. R. Needham

Walker, John (1731–1803), geologist. After training in Edinburgh for the CofS ministry (and attending William Cullen's lectures on chemistry) Walker served in the parishes of Glencorse, Midlothian (1758) and Moffat (1762). Devoting all his spare time to botany and geology, in 1764 he was appointed by the General Assembly to make a survey of the Hebrides, also being commissioned to report to the SSPCK and being sponsored by Lord Kames. Appointed to the Regius chair of Natural History at Edinburgh (1779), he became 'the father of geological education', teaching James Hall (1761–1532; *DNB* XXIV, 68–9, Robert Jameson (1774–1854; *DNB* XXIX, 234–5) and John Playfair (1748–1819; *DNB* XLV, 413–14). A correspondent of Linnaeus, he did much unpublished work in botany (especially on the genus *Salix*). He continued in the ministry, and though the Presbytery of Lochmaben found his holding the charge of Moffat incompatible with a teaching career in Edinburgh (some sixty miles apart), the Moderate*-dominated synod reversed the decision. He ministered from 1783 at Colinton (near Edinburgh) and in 1790 was Moderator of the General Assembly.*

Classes Fossilium (E, 1787); *An Economical History of the Hebrides and Highlands of Scotland*, 2 vols (E, 1808, ²L, 1812).

FES I, 4; *DNB* LIX, 74; *Dictionary of Scientific Biography* XIV, 131–3; H. W. Scott, biographical chapter in reprint of Walker's *Lectures on Geology* (Chicago, 1965), xvii–xlvi, and with bibliography; G. Taylor, 'John Walker DD, FRSE, 1731–1803', *Trans. Bot. Soc. Edinburgh* 38 (1959), 180–203; W. Jardine, *The Birds of Great Britain and Ireland* III (L, 1842), 3–50 ('Memoir of J. Walker, DD').

C. A. Russell

Walker, Norman MacDonald Lockhart (1826–1905), FC minister and writer. Born at Carnwath, Lanarkshire, he studied at Edinburgh University and New College, and was ordained to Dysart FC, Kirkcaldy, in 1850, where he ministered until his retirement in 1892. Walker was a strong proponent of union between the FC and UPC, and edited the pro-union magazine *The Presbyterian** during the controversy of 1863–73. He entered the UFC in 1900. Prior to that he was editor of the FC *Monthly Record** 1869–1900; under him its circulation rose from 30,000 to 82,000.

Walker wrote several significant works, including a biography of Robert Buchanan* (L, 1887). *Chapters in the History of the Free Church of Scotland* (E, 1895) has been described as the best book on that subject and period, and *Christ at Sychar* (E, 1864) as his best book.

Walker received a DD from Edinburgh University in 1889. He was the brother of James Walker.*

Our Church Heritage (L, 1875; revised ed., *Scottish Church History*, 1882); *Religious Life in Scotland: From the Reformation to the Present Day* (ed., L,

WALKER, PATRICK

1888); *The New Lines and the Old* (L, 1881); *Life in the Spirit: A Memorial of the Rev. Alex. Anderson* (L, 1859); *Jesus Christ and His Surroundings* (L, 1898); *David Maclagan, FRSE* (L, 1884); *The Ritualistic Movement* (L, 1874); *Thomas Chalmers: His Life and its Lessons* (L, 1880); *The Scottish Churches: On What Basis Can They Be Reunited?* (L, 1896); *The Church Standing of the Children* (E, 1897).

Obituary in *MRUFCS* no. 56, August 1905, 358–60; *AFCS* I, 350; *FUFCS* 359.

N. R. Needham

Walker, Patrick (c.1666–1745), Covenanter and author. Born of Covenanting parents, possibly in Carnwath, Lanarkshire, he heard Covenanter* preachers from his infancy. As a boy of thirteen he was apparently at the battle of Bothwell Bridge.* Listed a fugitive in 1684, he was captured and sentenced to be banished to America. Accused of complicity in the death of trooper Francis Garden, he was tortured and imprisoned in Dunnottar Castle. After fourteen months he escaped and threw in his lot with James Renwick* and his party. He took an active part in ejecting Episcopalian* incumbents at the time of the Revolution, a work he never regretted.

Respected by his peers in the United Societies*, he was one of five appointed to draw up a paper listing grievances and protesting defections against the first General Assembly after the Revolution. Although dissatisfied with much in the re-established CofS, he welcomed William II* as a great deliverer. He disapproved of the Union of 1707,* restoration of patronage,* toleration of the Episcopalians and the Oath of Abjuration.* He nevertheless shunned what to him were 'right-hand extremes' as well as 'left-hand defections'. Thus he disapproved of John Macmillan's* position, espoused the cause of the Marrow* brethren and was even willing to forgo his own good rather than injure the 'serious gracious souls' who had subscribed the Oath. But he denounced Professor Simson* and deplored the backsliding spirit of his day.

Although many have described him as a 'packman' or itinerant peddlar, it is not clear what he did for a living (though apparently he sold books). He was buried in Greyfriars' Churchyard, Edinburgh.

Walker's fame rests on his 'Lives' of various Covenanters and martyrs,* many of whom he had known personally. Having travelled over 1,000 miles in collecting information, he began with the *Life of Alexander Peden** in 1724 (E, often reprinted, 1728 with additions), and followed it with *Some Remarkable Passages of the Life and Death of ... John Semple ... John Welwood ... Richard Cameron* (E, 1727) and *Some Remarkable Passages in the Life and Death of ... Daniel [Donald] Cargill* ...* (E, 1732). From the first, Walker's accuracy and judgment have been attacked. Attempts were made to keep him from publishing or at least to have him submit his work to revision by men of 'sound judgment', but all in vain. Robert Wodrow* criticizes him for inadequate documentation and an unChristian spirit. Nevertheless, though without a formal education, in a simple style, his command of language was most effective and, though depreciated by some, has been held in esteem by others, including Sir Walter Scott* and Robert Louis Stevenson. His expressions are pithy and often strong: bishops are 'graceless graces' and Archbishop James Sharp* a 'compend of wickedness'.

In so far as his work can now be verified, his quotations are substantially accurate and his facts and dates correct. D. H. Fleming* characterizes his writings as occupying 'a unique position among the histories of that stirring period through which he lived', supplying 'a series of vivid realistic pictures drawn by an untrained but born artist... no one who studies that period can afford to neglect him' ('Introduction', xxxiii, in *Six Saints of the Covenant*, 2 vols, L, 1901, an edition of Walker's works. An earlier collected edition is *Biographia Presbyteriana*, 2 vols, E, 1827).

D. C. Lachman

Walker, William Lowe (1845–1930), Congregational minister. Born at Inverarity, Forfarshire, he studied in Edinburgh at the University and the Congregational Theological Hall. He held pastorates at Hawick (1873–8), Thurso (1878–80), Great Hamilton Street, Glasgow (1880–6), and Laurencekirk (1894–1905), with a final spell at a Unitarian* Church in Glasgow. He enjoyed some repute as a progressive theologian. Both Edinburgh and Glasgow made him DD. He wrote a dozen books, including *The Spirit and the Incarnation* (E, 1899) and *What About the New Theology?* (E, 1907), a response to R. J. Campbell. A man of 'pilgrim temperament', he read widely, wrote often obscurely and had a humanitarian interest in missions. He was President of the Congregational Union of Scotland in 1913–14.

Who Was Who, 1929–1940, 1404; H. Wallace, in *The Scottish Congregationalist* n.s. 26 (Dec. 1930), 14.

D. F. Wright

Wallace (alias Fean), Adam (*d.* 1550), Protestant martyr.* Born at Fail in Ayrshire, and depicted as 'a simple poor man in appearance' but 'zealous in godliness', Wallace was arrested at Winton Castle, Lord Seton's home, in East Lothian, where he had served as tutor to Cockburn of Ormiston's children. Tried for heresy* before the ecclesiastical judges in Edinburgh in 1550, he admitted that 'sometimes at the table and sometimes in other privy places, he would read and had read the Scriptures and had given such exhortation as God pleased to give to him and to such as pleased to hear him'. Holding Scripture as the test of sound doctrine, he admitted he had little Latin but had 'read the Bible and word of God in three tongues' and had 'understood them so far as God gave me grace'. At his waist, he carried a Bible in French, Dutch and English. He sought assurance of his salvation in the Bible, condemned the bishops as 'dumb dogs and unsavoury salt', open enemies to the doctrine he professed, repudiated transubstantiation, affirmed the mass was not only unscriptural but idolatrous and blasphemous, denied Christ's natural body could be in two places at once, stressed the memorial aspect of the Lord's Supper, rejected belief in purgatory and claimed that 'to pray to saints and for the dead is idolatry and a vain superstition'. He also admitted to having baptized his own child. Condemned for his beliefs, Wallace was burned on Castlehill in Edinburgh, despite protests from the Earl of Glencairn*.

Knox, *History* I, 114–16; J. Foxe, *Acts and Monuments* (L, 1858), V, 636–41; J. Kirk, 'The Religion of Early Scottish Protestants', in *Humanism and Reform*, ed. J. Kirk (O, 1991).

J. Kirk

Wallace, Robert (1696–1771), Moderate* divine and mathematician. Wallace was particularly interested in population statistics (sharing the credit for Alexander Webster's* 1755 census) and made the calculations on which the annuities and regulations were based in the setting up of the Widows and Orphans Fund* for the Church and Universities of Scotland (1744).

During the administration of the Marquess of Tweeddale (1742–6), Wallace was 'leader' of the CofS and by extensive consultations ensured the harmonious operation of the patronage* system. His Synod sermon attacking deism* (1731) led to his translation from Moffat to Edinburgh, where he ministered at New Greyfriars (1733–8) and West St Giles (1738–71). He was Moderator of the General Assembly in 1743, a Dean of the Chapel Royal*, and the author of several publications.

DNB LIX, 103; *FES* I, 33, 144 (for further literature); J. B. Dow, 'Early Actuarial Work in Eighteenth Century Scotland', *Transactions of the Faculty of Actuaries* 33 (1975), 193–229; H. R. Sefton, 'Rev. Robert Wallace: An Early Moderate', *RSCHS* 16 (1966), 1–22.

H. R. Sefton

Wallace, Robert (1831–99), CofS minister, professor, and advocate of 'ritual reform and doctrinal expansion' (R. H. Story). He was born at Kincaple (Fife) and educated at St Andrews (MA, 1853) and – partly while teaching classics at Cupar – Edinburgh (Divinity). In 1857 he was ordained to Newton-on-Ayr, moved in 1860 to Trinity College Church, Edinburgh, and then to Old Greyfriars (1868); in 1872 he was also appointed Professor of Ecclesiastical History in Edinburgh. His inaugural, *The Study of Ecclesiastical History, in its Relation to Theology* (E, 1873), declared the concern of his discipline to be not the truth of theology but 'the truth of its history'. His work on *George Buchanan* (E, 1899) was completed on his death by J. C. Smith. In 1876, Wallace demitted charge, chair and orders (but not his DD, given by Glasgow in 1869) and became editor of the *Scotsman*. He resigned in 1880, moved to London, studied law, was called to the English bar and was elected a radical MP for East Edinburgh from 1886 until his death.

Wallace had a 'Calvinistic upbringing' which he later satirized, especially the sabbath. He moved sufficiently far from his evangelical roots to decide, with admirable honesty, 'not to take a Church's pay while he assailed that Church's creed'. He first attracted criticism for his support of 'the Greyfriars rebellion' in worship initiated by Robert Lee,* his predecessor at Greyfriars. His appointment to the chair provoked an ill-focused heresy trial in which he was attacked, inter alia, for his essay 'Church Tendencies in Scotland' (Recess Studies, ed. Sir Alexander Grant, E, 1870, 187–239) – a perceptive survey of the ecclesiastical scene (much taken, not surprisingly, by Episcopalian growth) that went beyond description, but in prediction more than confession, concluding that 'If ... the religious thought of the country is moving towards a new point of view, the Church must go there also to meet it, if it means to be instrumental in preserving a living faith within the mind of the nation.' This questionable prescription reflected Wallace's predilection for theological free-thinking, as also for the liturgical liberty of the individual minister. The CofE came nearest to his religious ideals.

FES I, 43–4; DNB Suppl. III, 504; R. Lawson, Reminiscences of the late Robert Wallace, Esq., M.P. (Paisley, 1899); J. C. Smith and W. Wallace, Robert Wallace. Life and Last Leaves (L, 1903 – including autobiographical material).

D. F. Wright

Walpole, George Henry Somerset (1854–1929), theological writer and Episcopal Bishop of Edinburgh (1910–29). After distinguished ministries in Truro, Cornwall (1877–82), and New Zealand (1882–9), he was Professor of Dogmatic Theology at General Theological Seminary, New York (1889–96), Principal of Bede College, Durham (1896–1903), and Rector of Lambeth, South London (1904–10).

Walpole combined a deep spirituality with unrivalled ability to communicate the gospel. Well known for his leadership of missions and retreats, he also wrote or edited some forty books, such as The People's Psalter (L, 1903), Vital Religion (L, 1902, and many reprints), The Kingdom of Heaven (Paddock lectures, New York; L, 1909), and The Undiscovered Country (L, 1925). In Edinburgh he is remembered for the completion of the western spires of St Mary's Episcopal Cathedral in 1917, and by the Walpole Hall, opened by his elder son, the novelist Sir Hugh Walpole, in 1933.

The Scotsman, 5 March 1929 – obituary and photograph; Who Was Who, 1929–1940, 1408; R. Hart-Davis, Hugh Walpole (L, 1952).

J. V. Howard

Ward, Cornelius (fl.1634), see Irish Missions.

Ward, Valentine (1781–1834), one of the most influential Methodist* preachers to be stationed in Scotland in the early nineteenth century. In 1811 he was sent to Glasgow for three years, then Edinburgh (1814–16); Aberdeen (1817–19); Glasgow (1820–2); Edinburgh (1823) and finally Glasgow (1827–8). For thirteen of these years, Ward was Chairman of one or other of the (then) two Scottish Districts (Aberdeen and Edinburgh). He was an eloquent preacher, an inveterate pamphleteer, a powerful advocate of Sunday Schools and a protagonist of the mission field, especially in relation to the emancipation of slaves. However, his passion during his Scottish ministry was the erection of new chapels, building or buying at least fourteen between 1813 and 1819. His zeal exceeded the bounds of common sense since, although a number were sited in major towns (e.g. Nicolson Square, Edinburgh; Tradestown, Glasgow), others were imposed on small Methodist Societies (e.g. Haddington, Gourock), which suddenly found themselves in possession of large buildings and correspondingly large debts. These 'chapel speculations', plus Ward's inability to account for his building loans in any rational way, did much to inhibit the spread of Methodism in Scotland in the second quarter of the nineteenth century. Further, the resumption of the gold standard in 1822, whereby debts could no longer be paid off by inflation, led eventually to acute financial embarrassment in the whole Methodist Connexion. Nevertheless, the view remains that, had Ward been properly supported by his ministerial colleagues, his schemes might have been more successful (see also Bunting, Jabez; Methodism). In 1834 Ward was appointed special representative of the Missionary Committee and the Conference in the West Indies; he died in Jamaica after a few months' service.

A Brief Statement of Facts (E, 1815); Free and Candid Strictures on Methodism (A, 1818); The Two Great Duties of the Christian Minister (A, 1819).

A. J. Hayes, 'Valentine Ward – A Reassessment', Journal of the Scottish Branch of the Wesley Historical Society (1976), 2–19; A. J. Hayes and D. A. Gowland, Scottish Methodism in the Early Victorian Period (E, 1980); W. F. Swift, Methodism in Scotland (E, 1947).

A. J. Hayes

Wardlaw, Henry (d.1440), Bishop of St Andrews and founder of Scotland's first university there (see Universities). He was nephew of Walter Wardlaw,* Bishop of Glasgow and cardinal. After studying at Paris and Orleans, he was at various times Canon, Precentor and Archdeacon of Glasgow, parson of Cavers Magna, Canon of Aberdeen, and Prebendary of Belhelvie, Deer, and Old Roxburgh. He was elected Bishop in 1403. The foundation of St Andrews University in 1411 was necessitated by the withdrawal of France's allegiance from the antipope Benedict XIII, whom Scotland continued to recognize; so French universities were closed to Scottish scholars, as English ones had long been. Teaching began in 1410, and bulls of foundation were issued by Benedict XIII in 1413. One of the motivations in the foundation was the combating of heresy, which indicates that Lollardy* was prevalent in Scotland at the time. In 1418 the University persuaded the Bishop and the Governor, the Duke of Albany, to abandon Benedict and follow the obedience of Pope Martin V.

On the return of James I to Scotland in 1424, Wardlaw as Chancellor found his influence at the University threatened; the King even petitioned the Pope to have it removed to Perth in 1426. When this move failed, James promoted the influence of Laurence of Lindores,* a renowned philosopher and enemy of heresy, against that of Bishop Wardlaw and his associate James Haldenstone, Dean of the faculty of Theology. As a consequence, relations between Wardlaw and the King were strained for much of the 1420s and 1430s. The deaths of the King and Lindores in 1437 eased Wardlaw's position considerably, but he was by now an old man.

Dowden, 30–1, supplemented by D. E. R. Watt, *Biographical Dictionary of Scottish Graduates to 1410* (O, 1977), 564–9; J. M. Anderson, 'The Beginnings of St Andrews University', *SHR* 8 (1911), 225–48, 333–60; H. Rashdall, *Universities of Europe in the Middle Ages*, eds. F. M. Powicke and A. B. Emden (O, 1936), II, 301–11; E. M. W. Balfour Melville, *James I* (L, 1936).

A. Macquarrie

Wardlaw, Ralph (1779–1853), outstanding Congregationalist* divine. Born in Dalkeith, Midlothian, Wardlaw spent his youth in Glasgow, attending the University from 1791. Then from 1795 he studied for the ministry of the Burgher Secession* Church (to which his father belonged) at its theological hall in Selkirk (*see* Associate Synod; Lawson, George).

The Burgher Seceders were at that time troubled by disputes about Church–state relations (*see* Church and State; New Light) which influenced Wardlaw to adopt Voluntary and Congregational principles in 1800 (*see* Voluntary Controversy; Voluntaryism). He associated himself with the Haldane* brothers and their movement and preached frequently in the Edinburgh Tabernacle.

In 1803 Wardlaw became pastor of a new Independent* church in North Albion Street, Glasgow. This was formed specially for Wardlaw by members of Greville Ewing's* Jamaica Street congregation, some sixty of whom transferred membership to the new church to form its nucleus. The church prospered under Wardlaw's ministry, and a new chapel had to be built in 1819 in West George Street to accommodate the expanded congregation.

Wardlaw's theology remained stable throughout his career. He was the most distinguished Scottish champion of 'Moderate, or what may be designated modern Calvinism, as held and ably elucidated by the late Dr Andrew Fuller,* Dr Edward Williams, and others, and now embraced by a growing proportion of Calvinistic ministers and professing Christians', which he contrasted with 'Calvinism as more generally held by the orthodox' (*Systematic Theology*, 3 vols, E, 1856, II, 439). This principally involved holding the 'moral government' view of the atonement. Wardlaw maintained that Christ had endured sin's penalty not as a legal satisfaction for the sins of the elect, but as a divine governmental expedient to display graphically what all sin deserves, so that God might pardon the penitent without fostering in them a light attitude to transgression. Wardlaw rejected the traditional 'double payment' argument, that God cannot justly punish the elect since Christ paid their penalty: 'I confess myself, with Andrew Fuller, more than disposed to doubt whether we should consider "the Moral Governor of the world as laid under a kind of obligation to show mercy to sinners as a creditor is under to discharge a debtor, on having received full satisfaction at the hands of a surety"' (*ibid.*, 451). The atonement made it possible for God to forgive any on condition of repentance; divine election simply determined who would repent. These views brought Wardlaw into conflict with orthodox Calvinists such as William Symington.* Latterly, however, Wardlaw resisted Arminianizing* tendencies among Scottish Congregationalists with regard to God's sovereignty in election and regeneration.

Wardlaw was a staunch Congregationalist and paedobaptist. His first publication in 1807 was a defence of infant baptism; its main argument, expanded in his *Dissertation on the Scriptural Authority, Nature and Uses of Infant Baptism* (G, 1825), was the spiritual identity of the Abrahamic with the New Covenant and the consequent inclusion of believers' offspring in Church membership. In 1839 he tested his mettle against Thomas Chalmers* by lecturing in London against Chalmers' views on Church–state relations and the establishment principle (*National Church Establishments Examined*, L, 1839). The lectures were well received, but Wardlaw was criticized by some fellow Independents for seeming to divorce the state from any obligation to submit to Scripture.

Together with Greville Ewing, Wardlaw pioneered the Glasgow Theological Academy, a Congregational seminary, where he taught theology from 1811 till his death in 1853 without relinquishing his pastoral charge. His lectures were posthumously published as three volumes of systematic theology. These are a storehouse of acutely argued and limpidly expressed views on Christian doctrine and ethics, mostly orthodox although including a lengthy denial of the eternal Sonship of Christ and procession of the Spirit. His expositions of Scripture were highly regarded and widely influential: *Christian Ethics* (L, 1832); *Congregational Independency* (G, 1848); *Discourses on the Nature and Extent of the Atonement* (G, 1844); *Discourses on the Principal Points of the Socinian Controversy* (G, 1814); *Lectures on the Book of Ecclesiastes*, 2 vols (G, 1821).

Wardlaw received a DD from Yale College, Connecticut, in 1818.

See also Calvinism, Moderate.

W. L. Alexander, *Memoirs of the Life and Writings of Ralph Wardlaw* (E, 1865); Chambers-Thomson III, 491–3; *DNB* LIX, 353–4.

N. R. Needham

Wardlaw, Walter (*d.* 1387), Bishop of Glasgow and Scotland's first cardinal. He studied at Paris, graduating in 1340, and taught there in the 1340s and 1350s, being for part of that time procurator of the English nation. He entered the service of David II,* becoming his secretary by 1364. Like others of David's clerical servants he was well rewarded, becoming archdeacon of Lothian and in 1367 Bishop of Glasgow. On the outbreak of the Great Schism in 1378 Scotland sided with the Avignon anti-popes, and in 1383 Wardlaw was rewarded for his loyalty to Clement VII by being made Cardinal without title. In the following year he was appointed papal legate *a latere* to Scotland and Ireland; there were many supporters of the Roman Pope Urban VI in the latter country. It has been observed that 'the death of Scotland's first cardinal in September 1387 ended a shrewd move that might have promoted in Ireland both the ecclesiastical interests of the Avignonese papacy and the political interests of the Scottish monarch' (R. Nicholson, *Scotland: the Later Middle Ages*, E, 1974, 192).

Dowden, 314–16; *Calendar of Papal Letters to Scotland of Clement VII* (SHS, E, 1976); *The Acts of David II*, ed. B. Webster (*Regesta Regum Scottorum* VI, E, 1982); D. E. R. Watt, *Biographical Dictionary of Scottish Graduates before 1410* (O, 1977).

A. Macquarrie

Wariston, Archibald Johnston, *see* Johnston.

Warr, Charles Laing (1892–1969), minister of St Giles,* Edinburgh (1926–62), and Dean of the Chapel Royal* and Dean of the Thistle* (1926–69). He held these three offices for longer than any before him. Though associated with national ceremonies and linked with prestigious historic societies, he ministered continuously to a large city congregation, devoted himself to orderly and 'catholic' worship, and published articles, biographies, sermons and other material. He introduced weekly Communion (and held early services 'for cyclists' in the 1930s). His sermons were frequently reported in the press. He opposed capital punishment, and defended the atom bomb. He promoted Church unity, while asserting the highest claims of the post-Reformation CofS within Catholic Christianity. He both reflected the Edinburgh of the second quarter of the twentieth century and served it as pastor and priest with wisdom, piety, dignity and care.

Alfred Warr of Rosneath (Paisley, 1917) – father; *The Glimmering Landscape* (L, 1960) – autobiography.

FES III, 204, VIII, 11, IX, 16, X, 10; *Who Was Who, 1961–1970*, 1170; *DNB 1961–1970*, 1053–4.

G. I. Macmillan

Warrack, or Preachers', Lectures, a series established in 1920 in the UFC by Frank Warrack of Kersewell, Carnwath, Lanarkshire. The Preachers' Lectureship (its original title) had as its main topic 'the Sermon and methods of effective preaching', but could deal instead with 'the seemly and orderly conduct of public worship'. To it were to be elected, from the UFC, CofS 'or any of the evangelical churches at home or abroad', 'the Preachers most noted for their power to attract and hold the people'; it must not become a reward for services, however eminent, in other fields – or 'a Consolation prize for comparative failure in all'! At least five lectures were to be given in each of the Aberdeen, Glasgow and Edinburgh UF Colleges. The appointment is now in the hands of a CofS (formerly UFC) committee.

The first lecturer was John A. Hutton, *That the Ministry Be Not Blamed* (NY, 1921). Others of note have included: J. M. Black,* *The Mystery of Preaching* (L, 1924); A. J. Gossip,* *In Christ's Stead* (L, 1925); Henry S. Coffin, *What to Preach* (L, 1926); G. F. Macleod,* *Speaking the Truth – In Love* (L, 1936); H. H. Farmer, *The Servant of the Word* (L, 1941); J. S. Stewart,* *Heralds of God* (L, 1946); D. H. C. Read,* *The Communication of the Gospel* (L, 1952); Ian Pitt-Watson, *A Kind of Folly. Towards a Practical Theology of Preaching* (E, 1976).

With the continuing loss of confidence in preaching, the lectureship has of late given a somewhat uncertain sound.

Details in *CofS Year Book* (annual), 1930–62.

D. F. Wright

Watchword, The. Two nineteenth-century periodicals bore this title. The first appeared monthly immediately prior to the Disruption,* between October 1842 and March 1843. Published by John Menzies (1808–79) of Edinburgh, it espoused an anti-patronage* position and had as motto a quotation from Samuel Rutherford,* 'I stand to my testimony'.

The second appeared monthly between April 1866 and July 1873 during the controversy over moves towards union between the FC and the UPC. It was edited by Free Churchman James Begg* who, while in theory favouring union, had concluded that it could not be attained without fatally compromising certain fundamental 'Disruption principles', notably those relating to the Atonement* and the relationship between Church and state.* Begg and the anti-unionist lobby established *The Watchword* since they considered that the rest of the Scottish press was heavily influenced by the pro-unionists. They in turn founded their own pro-union journal, *The Presbyterian.** Contributors to *The Watchword*, chief among them Hugh Martin,* defended their position with a vigorous directness which was said to have brought 'many reproaches and much obloquy' upon the editor. *The Watchword* was published initially by the Edinburgh firm of James Nichol (1806–66) and later by John Menzies.

J. A. H. Dempster

Waterston, Jane Elizabeth (1843–1933), FC missionary, pioneer educationalist and physician in South Africa. Born and educated in Inverness, she joined the FC (though her family remained CofS) and offered her services to the Foreign Mission Committee. In 1866 she travelled to Lovedale, South Africa, to initiate work with girls at the mission there. She was head of Lovedale Girls School until 1873. 'From the start, she began to impress on the school her own vigorous and original personality' (R. W. H. Shepherd, *Lovedale, South Africa*, Lovedale, 1941). Although her aim was to educate African girls primarily as Christian housekeepers and wives, she was also proud of their academic achievements.

Her own lifestyle was at odds with the Victorian ideal of womanhood: she was forthright in expression of her opinions, ambitious, and would defer to no man. At Lovedale, and subsequently, she was known as '*Noqataka*', 'the mother of activity'. In 1873 she resigned in order to take up medical studies, so that she could serve 'up country' in Central Africa. No British university allowed women to study and take exams, so she trained in London and qualified in Dublin, later as MD in Belgium. By 1878 she was on the medical register, and the FC Livingstonia committee appointed her as female medical assistant at the new mission to be run by Robert Laws.* After only four months she resigned and returned, disheartened, to Lovedale. There she established a dispensary and also treated the pupils. But failure to get her medical work officially recognized and funded by the Foreign Mission Committee meant that she had to give up her mission work.

In 1883 she established a private general practice in Cape Town. For fifty years her medical, philanthropic and political activities made her a legend. She received an honorary LLD from the University of Cape Town, and in 1925 was elected a fellow of the Royal College of Physicians in Ireland.

Waterston was able, innovative, strong-minded and unconventional. Her good working relationship with James Stewart* of Lovedale contrasted with the personality clash between her and Laws at Livingstonia. She resented the subordinate role expected of her there, and also the innuendos that she was primarily looking for a husband. The committee did not look kindly on her unilateral decision to return to Lovedale. Her eventual departure to Cape Town 'was a keen disappointment and a cause of the deepest regret ... The action of the Committee which necessitated the step has never ceased to be deplored' (R. M. Young, *African Wastes Reclaimed*, L, 1902).

L. Bean and E. van Heyningen (eds), *Letters of Jane Elizabeth Waterston 1866–1905* (Cape Town, 1983); S. Brock, 'A Broad, Strong Life', in *Enterprising Scot: Scottish Adventure and Achievement* (E, 1986); D. P. Thomson, *Women of the Scottish Church* (Perth, 1975), 251–63.

L. O. Macdonald

Watson, David (1859–1943), minister and social reformer. He was educated at Alva Academy and University of Glasgow (which also gave him a DD in 1913). As the first minister of St Clement's Church, a working-class congregation in Glasgow (1888–1938), Watson was an exponent of the new social liberalism that permeated both the CofS and the UFC in the first decades of this century. While an initiator of the CofS's Social Work Committee (he was convener or vice-convener 1904–35), Watson did not believe that social work was a substitute for social reform and social criticism. So he strongly promoted the creation of the Church and Nation Committee* established in 1919. Watson was his Church's most prolific writer on social questions. He was also the founder of the Scottish Christian Social Union* in 1901. His best-known works were: *Social Problems and the Church's Duty* (L, 1908); *The Social Expression of Christianity* (L, 1919); his Gunning lectures*, *Social Advance – Its Meaning, Method and Goal* (L, 1911); and his autobiography *Chords of Memory* (L, 1935).

FES III, 436; D. C. Smith, *Passive Obedience and Prophetic Protest*... (NY, 1987).

D. C. Smith

Watson, John, see Maclaren, Ian.

Watson, Jonathan (1795–1878), Baptist* minister. He was born in Montrose. He became a druggist and pharmacist in Dundee, where he was baptized in the Scotch Baptist church. He moved to Cupar in 1815, and moving from Scotch Baptist* views, began a 'new' church in Cupar in 1816, being set apart by William Innes* and Robert Aitkenhead. After a successful ministry he was called to Elder Street, Edinburgh, to be colleague and successor to Innes in 1841. His ministry to students was especially valuable, and he was accused by the wealthy of the church of caring too much for the poor. He was a founding member of the Edinburgh Medical Missionary Society,* and co-operated widely in Christian work. He was chosen first President of the Baptist Union of Scotland* in 1869, when his address was 'Ecclesiastical Liberty, Equality and Fraternity'. He published many tracts, including *Bethel, the Blessedness of Frequenting the House of God* (L, ⁷1852).

Obituary, *SBM*, December 1878; A. M. Baines, *History of Dublin Street Baptist Church, Edinburgh, 1858–1958* (E, 1958).

D. B. Murray

Watt, Hugh (1879–1968), church historian. He was born of farming stock at Kilmaurs, Ayrshire, and reared in the UPC. After studying at Glasgow (MA, 1901; BD, 1905), Marburg, Berlin and Halle, he was UF minister at Waterbeck, Dumfriesshire (1907–12), and the Glasgow suburb of Bearsden North (1912–19), and did war service in France, the Middle East and Germany (1915–19), during which his skills at bridge and soccer attracted comment. From 1919–50 he was Professor of Church History in New College, Edinburgh, and latterly Dean and Principal (1946–50). He was an important figure in the expansion of New College's postgraduate work and in maintaining its North American links. He was honoured with Glasgow's DD (1926) and the DLitt of Muskingum College,

Ohio (1949), and made Moderator of the CofS General Assembly in 1950.

Watt had a detailed knowledge of Scottish Churches and ministers, and inclined towards the study of the great personalities of history. His main works were *Representative Churchmen of Twenty Centuries* (L, 1927), *Thomas Chalmers and the Disruption* (E, 1943; the Chalmers Lectures*), *Recalling the Scottish Covenants* (L, 1946); *New College, Edinburgh: A Centenary History* (E, 1946), and *John Knox in Controversy* (L, 1950; the Stone Lectures at Princeton). Of these his chronicle of New College remains of greatest value.

FUFCS 584; FES IX, 776; *Who Was Who, 1961–1970*, 1177; *LW* Nov. 1968, 16; appreciation by R. L. Small in D. Shaw (ed.), *Reformation and Revolution: Essays Presented to ... Hugh Watt ... on the Sixtieth Anniversary of His Ordination* (E, 1967), 11–16 – the first such *Festschrift* in the Church of Scotland.

D. F. Wright

Watt, Lauchlan MacLean (1867–1957), pastor, preacher and scholar. Born at Grantown, he was minister of Turriff, Aberdeenshire (1897–1901), Alloa and Tullibody (1901–11), St Stephen's, Edinburgh (1911–23), and Glasgow Cathedral (1923–34). He was Moderator of the CofS General Assembly* in 1933. A prolific writer in prose and poetry, he contributed to newspapers and periodicals on many aspects of religion and literature. His religious poems include *By Still Waters* (E, 1904), and his books of a devotional nature and on pastoral work, such as *Prayers for Public Worship* (L, 1924) and *The Minister's Manual* (²L, 1934), are still useful. His mother being a native of Skye, he had a particular interest in Celtic subjects.

FES VIII, 305; *Scottish Biographies 1938* (L, 1938), 776–7, with bibliography.

R. MacLeod

Watts, Robert (1820–95), Irish Presbyterian theologian. Born in Co. Down, Ireland, he was educated in Belfast and in the USA, where he graduated at Washington College, VA, in 1849. He studied theology at Princeton where he became a disciple of Charles Hodge. Ordained in 1853 he had ministries in Philadelphia and Dublin, and from 1866 to his death in 1895 he was Professor of Theology in the Presbyterian College, Belfast.

In lectures, books and controversies, he defended the inerrancy of the original biblical texts and held the Bible to be the only Rule of Faith for all true believers. He defended the Westminster documents* as the clear declaration of the Rule of Faith, 'the fundamental principles of the economy of redemption'. He was a critic of the teaching of W. Robertson Smith,* Marcus Dods,* Henry Drummond,* A. B. Bruce,* A. M. Fairbairn,* John Tyndall and Herbert Spencer.

He shaped the outlook of many Irish Presbyterian ministers and of the many Scottish students who were drawn by his repute to study in Belfast. He was Moderator of the Irish General Assembly, 1879–80.

An Examination of Herbert Spencer's Biological Hypothesis (Belfast, 1875); *The New Apologetic, or the Downgrade in Criticism* (E, 1879); *The Newer Criticism, and the Analogy of Faith* (a reply to lectures by W. Robertson Smith on the Old Testament in the Jewish Church) (E, 1881); *The Rule of Faith and the Doctrine of Redemption* (L, 1885).

DNB LX, 73; Robert Allen, *The Presbyterian College, Belfast 1853–1953* (Belfast, 1954); A. F. P. Sell, 'An Englishman, an Irishman, and a Scotsman', *SJT* 38 (1985), 41–83.

R. Buick Knox

Wauchope, Robert (c.1500–51), Archbishop of Armagh. He was the son of Gilbert Wauchope of Niddrie Marischal, near Edinburgh. Despite defective eyesight he was an able student and by 1526 was lecturing in the University of Paris. He was known as *Doctor caecus* (the blind doctor). Among his pupils was Reginald (Cardinal) Pole. Due to Pole's influence, the Pope in 1539 made Wauchope the administrator of the diocese of Armagh, where the Archbishop, George Cromer, had been accused of heresy. Henry VIII kept him out of Ireland, but Wauchope sent two Jesuits* on an undercover and ineffectual visit.

The spread of the Reformation made Wauchope an early advocate of the calling of a general council and he was a supporter of the Jesuits. He urged a reform of the lives of Church members. He was a papal theologian at the Colloquy of Worms in 1540 and at the Colloquy of Ratisbon in 1541. He worked zealously to recover Germany to the papal obedience.

He was made Archbishop of Armagh in 1545 and in that year was at the Council of Trent, where his formidable erudition was valued in discussions and in drafting the canons on Scripture, tradition and justification. In 1550 he set out for Ireland to claim his see. After travelling through Scotland he reached Derry, but received a cool reception and withdrew after a month. Having set out in 1551 in another attempt to reach Ireland, he died in Paris.

His best known book is *Conclusiones de Sacrosancto Missae Sacrificio et Communione Laica* (Mainz, 1544).

John Durkan, 'Robert Wauchope, Archbishop of Armagh', *IR* 1 (1950), 48–66; H. Jedin, 'The Blind Doctor Scotus', *JEH* 1 (1950), 76–84; Benignus Millett, 'The Pastoral Zeal of Robert Wauchope', *Seanchas Ardmhacha* 2 (1956), 32–60; Farge 437–41.

R. Buick Knox

Waugh, Percival (1854–1934), civil servant and elder/co-pastor of Bristo Place Scotch Baptist* Church, Edinburgh. He was born into an Anglican family in Galway, and educated in Dublin. He entered the Inland Revenue Office in Edinburgh in 1872, and rose to be Assistant Secretary to the Board of Inland Revenue and Registrar of Death Duties in 1915. He joined the Scotch Baptist

WEBSTER, ALEXANDER

Church in Bristo Place in the 1880s and served as lay elder 1903–23. From 1889 to 1923 he was Secretary of the Baptist Home Missionary Society for Scotland,* gaining a unique knowledge of the churches and pastors in the Highlands and Islands. He was for a time editor of the *SBM*, and, with George Yuille,* co-editor of the *History of the Baptists in Scotland* (G, 1926). He had an unrivalled collection of Baptist historical material.

Obituary, *SBM*, May 1934; M. I. Smith, *Bristo Baptist Church Bicentenary, 1965* (E, 1965).

D. B. Murray

Webster, Alexander (1707–84), prominent CofS Evangelical. He was the son of James Webster* and brother-in-law of Ebenezer Erskine.* For long minister of Edinburgh Tolbooth (1737–84), he was Moderator of the 1753 General Assembly and awarded the DD of Edinburgh, 1760. An eminent statistician, he compiled the 1755 *Census of the Population of Scotland* and performed the actuarial calculations for the Ministers' Widows and Orphans Fund* of which he was a leading promoter in 1742. He was an enthusiastic supporter of spreading both the gospel and industry in the Highlands,* and a leading defender of the Cambuslang revival.* He was a strong Hanoverian, becoming one of HM Chaplains for Scotland and a Dean of the Chapel Royal*. He was also one of the few ministers who remained in Edinburgh in 1745 during the Jacobite* occupation. It is thought that he suggested the construction of the Edinburgh New Town to Lord Provost Drummond. He was known for evangelical orthodoxy and fervour, intellectual ability, love of conviviality, and a capacity for claret, the combination of which both nonplussed and infuriated his Moderate* opponents.

Divine Influence the True Spring of the Extraordinary Work at Cambuslang (E, 1742); *Zeal for the Civil and Religious Interests of Mankind Recommended* (E, 1754).

DNB LX, 114–15; *FES* I, 119–20; A. Carlyle, *Autobiography* (L, 1910); id., *Anecdotes and Characters of the Times* (L, 1973); R. B. Sher, *Church and University in the Scottish Enlightenment* (E, 1985).

J. R. McIntosh

Webster, James (c.1659–1720), CofS minister and prosecutor of Professor John Simson* in his first trial. Born in Fife and educated at St Andrews, Webster was a Covenanter* of fiery temperament who was imprisoned for a time on the Bass Rock.* He was ordained to Liberton, near Edinburgh, in 1688, translated to Whitekirk, E. Lothian, in 1691 and to the second charge of the Tolbooth Church in Edinburgh in 1693. His friendship with James Hog* (who edited Webster's *Select Sermons*, E, 1723) included a full endorsement of Marrow* theology. He is best known for his initiation and tenacious prosecution of the first process against Simson.

Webster's publications included *Sacramental Sermons and Discourses at the Lords Table* (E, 1705),

WEDDERBURN, JAMES

and various pamphlets, on Church government (*A Discourse, demonstrating that the Government of the Church is Fixed, and not Ambulatory*, E, 1701), against Episcopalians (*An Essay on Toleration*, E, 1703), against the 1707 Union* (*Lawful Prejudices against the Union*, E, 1707), and on the covenants (*The Covenants of Redemption and Grace Displayed*, E, 1707; *The Two Great Promises of the Covenant of Grace*, E, 1720). Though he did not write against it, he refused to take the Oath of Abjuration.*

FES I, 123–4; *Threnodia A Funeral Poem to The Memory of... James Webster* (E, 1720).

D. C. Lachman

Wedderburn, James (c.1495–c.1553), Protestant sympathizer and dramatist. He was the son of James Wedderburn, merchant at West Kirk stile of Dundee. He was admitted burgess of Dundee 1517, and educated at St Andrews, but does not seem to have taken a degree. Because of the large number of Wedderburns (of various families) in Dundee in the early sixteenth century, it is not easy to determine exactly the biography of this James. He is said by Calderwood,* however, to have been the eldest of three literary-minded brothers (I, 141–2); the others were John Wedderburn,* who is connected with the *Gude and Godlie Ballatis*,* and Robert (c.1515–57), to whom the *Complaynt of Scotland* (c.1550) has been attributed.

Wedderburn is reported to have studied at St Leonard's College, under Gavin Logie, Regent and later Acting Principal, and said to be an early secret supporter of the Lutheran* movement. After leaving St Andrews, Wedderburn appears to have spent some time in France – possibly in Rouen or Dieppe – and may well have engaged in mercantile activity there; he is known, however, to have been in Dundee during the periods 1521–3 and 1531–7. On returning to Dundee, then something of a hotbed of Lutheran sentiment, Wedderburn's religious sympathies were encouraged by James Hewat, a Dominican friar. Possibly under the latter's influence, Wedderburn began to compose anti-clerical propaganda. In this he was also following the example of the Dominican friar Kyllour, author of a passion play performed in Stirling on Good Friday 1535 in the presence of King James V, which, according to Knox* (*History* I, 26), roused the spectators to condemn the clergy (Kyllour was burned for heresy three years later). Calderwood ascribes three works to Wedderburn: (i) a tragedy on the subject of the decollation of John the Baptist, acted at the West Port of Dundee; (ii) a comedy, 'The Historie of Dyonisius the Tyranne', performed in the playfield of Dundee; and (iii) a parody of the exorcism carried out by friar Laing (James V's confessor) at Kinghorn. These provocative pieces – none of which has survived – resulted in Wedderburn's having to go into exile (1540); he returned to Dieppe, and worked there as a factor until his death (in 1550 he sent a cargo of wine from Dieppe to Dundee). Although other members of the Scottish community denounced him to the Bishop of Rouen, no proceedings for heresy seem to have

WEDDERBURN, JAMES

been undertaken against Wedderburn, who must therefore have conformed at least outwardly to the RCC. There is no apparent ground for Mitchell's attribution (xxi–ii) to him of the poem. 'The Bischop of Hely brak his neck', in the *Gude and Godlie Ballatis*.

A Compendious Book [etc.] (*The Gude and Godlie Ballatis*), ed. A. F. Mitchell (STS, E, 1897); *A Compendious Book [etc.]* (*The Gude and Godlie Ballatis*), ed. D. Laing (E, 1868); Calderwood; T. M'Crie, *Life of John Knox* 2 vols (E, ²1813); *Essays on the Scottish Reformation 1513–1625*, ed. D. McRoberts (G, 1962); *The Complaynt of Scotland*, ed. A. M. Stewart, (STS, E, 1979).

A. A. MacDonald

Wedderburn, James (1585–1639), Bishop of Dunblane 1636–8 and a Scottish 'Canterburian', or admirer of William Laud,* Archbishop of Canterbury. A liturgical perfectionist, his amendments to the *Book of Common Prayer* of 1637 (Laud's Liturgy) made the book even less acceptable in Scotland.

A member of a famous Dundee family, Wedderburn was educated at St Andrews University (MA, 1608) and after a brief ministry in England was appointed Professor of Divinity at St Mary's College, St Andrews, in 1617. He returned to England in 1628 and held benefices in the dioceses of Ely and Bath and Wells. His appointment as Dean of the Chapel Royal* at Stirling in 1635 and his promotion to Dunblane were seen as a change from the moderate policies advocated by the senior Scottish bishops. It was Wedderburn who persuaded Laud to omit the second sentence in the words of administration in the Communion service, thus returning to the form in the *BCP* of 1549. Wedderburn regarded the sentence, 'Take and eat this in remembrance that Christ died for thee and feed on him in thy heart by faith with thanksgiving', and the corresponding sentence about the cup, as seeming to 'relish somewhat of the Zwinglian tenet that the sacrament is a bare sign taken in remembrance of Christ's passion'. He was deprived and excommunicated by the Glasgow General Assembly* of 1638 because he 'had been the confidential correspondent and agent of Archbishop Laud in introducing the new liturgy and popish ceremonies'. He went to England, where he died at Canterbury.

DNB LX, 137–8; *FES* VII, 338; G. Donaldson, *The Making of the Scottish Prayer Book of 1637* (E, 1954).

H. R. Sefton

Wedderburn, John (c.1508–56), Protestant sympathizer and poet. The son of James Wedderburn, merchant at West Kirk stile of Dundee, he was educated at St Andrews (incorporated 1525 in the Paedagogy – later St Mary's College – BA, 1526, MA, 1528). He was thus a student at the time of the execution of Patrick Hamilton* outside St Salvator's College, which he may have witnessed. At the Paedagogy Wedderburn would have studied under John Major;* Calderwood* (I, 141–2), how-

WELCH, ADAM CLEGHORN

ever, declares him, like his brothers James* and Robert, to have come under the influence of Gavin Logie*, of St Leonard's College, who, unlike Major, is said to have been receptive to Lutheran* ideas.

After graduation, Wedderburn entered the ministry and a record of 1533 shows him to be the chaplain of St Matthew's chapel in Dundee. By 1539 he had been summonsed on a charge of heresy* and his goods confiscated; in the same year a king's messenger was despatched to Dundee to search his goods and those of James Rollok. It is possible that, as Mitchell states, Wedderburn's crime was that of possessing heretical books; at any rate, the accused seems to have fled before being brought to trial.

Wedderburn moved to Germany and became a disciple of Luther and Melanchthon. In 1539 a 'Joannes Scotus' is recorded in the university registers at Wittenberg, and it is possible that this name may designate Wedderburn. In Germany Wedderburn, in Calderwood's words, 'Turned manie bawdie songs and rymes in godlie rymes': this statement is the basis of the ascription of the *Gude and Godlie Ballatis** to him. In 1542, following the death of James V,* he returned to Scotland, at a more hopeful time, when, under the Governor, the Earl of Arran (*see* Hamilton, James *d.*1575), it was made legal to read the Scriptures in the vernacular (*see* Bible (Versions, English)). Subsequently, however, Wedderburn was pursued by Cardinal David Beaton.* He fled to England, where he died in exile, according to John Johnston* (M'Crie, II, 440), in 1556.

A Compendious Book [etc.] (*The Gude and Godlie Ballatis*), ed. A. F. Mitchell, (STS, E, 1897); *A Compendious Book [etc.]* (*The Gude and Godlie Ballatis*), ed. D. Laing (E, 1868); Calderwood; T. M'Crie, *Life of John Knox*, 2 vols(E, ²1813); *Essays on the Scottish Reformation 1513–1625*, ed. D. McRoberts (G, 1962); J. Durkan, 'Henry Scrimgeour, Renaissance Bookman', *Edinburgh Bibliographical Society Transactions* 5 (1971–4), 1–31; B. Murdoch, 'The Hymns of Martin Luther in the *Gude and Godlie Ballatis*', *Studies in Scottish Literature* 12 (1974–5), 92–109.

A. A. MacDonald

Wee Frees, *see* Free Church of Scotland.

Welch, Adam Cleghorn (1864–1943), biblical scholar. Welch was born at Goschen, Jamaica. After the death of his parents in 1870, he was brought to Scotland and cared for by relatives. He graduated MA at Edinburgh, then studied at the UP Divinity Hall. There followed strenuous ministerial service at Waterbeck, Dumfriesshire (1887–92), Helensburgh (1892–1902), and Claremont, Glasgow (1902–13). During this period he published *Anselm and His Work* (E, 1901). His stature as an Old Testament scholar was indicated by *The Religion of Israel under the Kingdom* (E, 1912), and in 1913 he was appointed to the chair of Hebrew and Old Testament Exegesis at New College,* Edinburgh, which he held until 1934. Welch published

WELLWOOD, (SIR) HENRY MONCRIEFF

several highly original works challenging generally accepted hypotheses, *e.g. The Work of the Chronicler* (O, 1939), *Post-Exilic Judaism* (E, 1935), and his books on Deuteronomy (*The Code of Deuteronomy*, L, 1924, and *Deuteronomy: The Framework to the Code*, O, 1932). In New College he lectured with insight and power, as is reflected in the posthumous volume, *Kings and Prophets of Israel*, ed. N. W. Porteous (L, 1952).

Small I, 57, 237, II, 100; *FUFCS* 584; *FES* IX, 777; *DNB 1941-1950*, 943-4; G. S. Gunn, 'Memoir' in *Kings and Prophets of Israel*, 13-44.

G. W. Anderson

Wellwood, (Sir) Henry Moncrieff (Moncreiff) (1750-1827), leader of the Evangelicals* ('Popular party'*) in the CofS. He was minister of Blackford (1771-5) and St Cuthbert's, Edinburgh (1775-1827), Moderator of the General Assembly in 1785, and won the DD (Glasgow) in 1785. One of the most influential churchmen of his day, he appears in J. G. Lockhart's *Peter's Letters to his Kinsfolk* (III, 45, 74). His intellectual eminence, skill in debate, and mastery of Church law enabled him and Henry Erskine,* the Dean of the Faculty of Advocates, to seize the initiative in the General Assembly from the Moderates* in the 1780s. Ecclesiastically, this as much as anything else marked the beginnings of Moderate decline at the Assembly. He supported the Test Act overture in 1790 and the appointment of John Leslie* to the Chair of Mathematics at Edinburgh University in the famous Leslie Case of 1805.

Four volumes of his *Sermons* appeared between 1805 and 1831, in addition to various single sermons between 1799 and 1839. Several of his works related to issues of Church government and patronage* and were to become virtual handbooks for the Non-Intrusion party* in the Ten Years' Conflict* between 1834 and 1843. A close friend of John Erskine,* he edited the latter's *Discourses* for publication in 1804, and his *Account of the Life and Writings of John Erskine* (E, 1818), as well as being an impressive piece of ecclesiastical biography, is an important source for the history of the CofS in the latter half of the eighteenth century. His theological writings were slighter, though in one of his earlier works, *The Connexion between Natural and Revealed Religion* (E, 1777), he adopted a view of natural religion which accorded it greater theological value than was common among many of his evangelical contemporaries. His lasting reputation rests on his practical sermons, his biography of Erskine, his extensive work on Church government, and his role in the General Assembly.

Remarks on Chapels of Ease, (n.p., 1797); *Remarks on a Pamphlet, entitled 'Substance of Principal Hill's Speech in the General Assembly, May 23, 1807'* (E, 1807); *Discourses on the Evidence of the Jewish and Christian Revelations* (E, 1815); *A Brief Account of the Constitution of the Established Church of Scotland* (E, 1833).

DNB XXXVIII, 167-8; *FES* I, 98; memoir by J. W. Moncrieff in *Sermons*, vol. III (E, 1831).

J. R. McIntosh

WELSH, DAVID

Welsh, David (1793-1845), Professor of Church History and FC pioneer. Born in Covenanting* country (Braefoot, near Moffat), he was educated at Edinburgh - the High School, arts and divinity. He relished moral philosophy with Thomas Brown (*DNB* VII, 31-3) and later wrote an *Account of the Life and Writings of T. Brown, M.D.* (E, 1825; abridged in editions of Brown's *Lectures on the Philosophy of the Human Mind* from E, 1828, on). Composition and literature also became life-long loves. (He was the *North British Review*'s first editor in 1844, and Chalmers* likened him to a walking epitome of the University library.) Ordained to Crossmichael (Kirkcudbrightshire) in 1821, he moved to St David's, Glasgow, in 1827, and in 1831 assumed the chair of Ecclesiastical History at Edinburgh. Single-mindedness led him not only to revise his lectures thoroughly each session but to decline ministerial labours (not a fluent preacher, he found preaching physically taxing), and to visit Germany in 1834. *Elements of Church History*, I (E, 1844), on the first three centuries, was the first Church history published by an Edinburgh professor. (No more was published; a student's notes as far as the Reformation are in MS in New College Library.) Students and peers alike attested his reinvigoration of an undervalued discipline. He made the study of original sources a priority.

Moderator in 1842, Welsh presided over the General Assembly whose adoption of the Claim of Right* presaged the Disruption.* A long-standing opponent of patronage* and, from student days, associate of leading Evangelicals like Andrew Thomson,* Welsh read the 'Protest' at the 1843 Assembly prior to the departure. He lost not only his chair but also the Secretaryship of the infant Bible Board* (1839). He was soon convener of the new FC committee 'On the Education of Students for the Ministry, and the Establishment of a System of Schools'. Schools for infants had concerned him since Glasgow (and Germany). Now the foundation of elementary and secondary (normal) schools engaged his efforts, as well as the construction of New College, Edinburgh (inaugurated 1846). Meanwhile, he was Professor of Church History and Librarian in its temporary premises; on his death his books greatly enriched the library. Welsh's piety, learning and culture represented the FC at its best.

Practical Subjects (E, 1834); *The Limits and Extent of the Right of Private Judgment* (E, 1843 - also in *Sermons*); articles on 'Jesus' and 'Jews' in *Encyclopedia Britannica* (⁷E, 1841).

FES VII, 390; *AFCS* I, 59; *DNB* LX, 237-8; Memoir by A. Dunlop in his *Sermons* (E, 1846), 1-138; *Disruption Worthies*, 489-96; James Dodds, 'On the Study of Church History', in *Edinburgh Academic Annual for MDCCCXL* (E, 1840), 1-28; D. Masson, *Memories of Two Cities, Edinburgh and Aberdeen* (E, 1911), 96-107.

D. F. Wright

Welsh, John (c.1570–1622), Reformed minister of Ayr. Welsh was son of the laird of Collieston in Nithsdale. In his youth, he joined a band of Border reivers before reforming his ways and entering Edinburgh University, where he graduated in 1588. Appointed minister first of Selkirk in 1589, then at Kirkcudbright in 1594, Welsh incurred King James VI's* displeasure for a fiery sermon delivered in St Giles* shortly after a riot in the capital in December 1596. Welsh's ministry in the second charge at Ayr (from 1600) was long highly regarded. For approving a General Assembly at Aberdeen in 1605, which the King had forbidden, he was imprisoned in Blackness Castle and then banished, with other ministers, for treason in 1606. Arriving at Bordeaux, he became minister to Reformed congregations, first at Jonsac in 1608, then at Nerac in 1614 and finally at St Jean d'Angely in Saintonge from 1617. With renewed religious warfare, Welsh left his charge in 1620 and reached Zealand where, through his wife Elizabeth, daughter of John Knox,* he petitioned King James for permission to return home. James' condition that Welsh should submit to Episcopacy* was declined by Elizabeth; lifting the corners of her apron she said she would 'sooner kep [catch] his head there' than have him submit. Welsh's failing health persuaded James to let him come to London in 1622, where he died after preaching a sermon.

Forty Eight Select Sermons (E, 1744); *A Reply against M. Gilbert Browne Priest* (E, 1602), rp. as *Popery Anatomized* (G, 1672), and again as *'The Morning Star': or, Where was the Protestant Religion before Luther?* (L, 1878); *L'Armegeddon de la Babylon Apocalyptique* (Jonsac, 1612).

Wodrow Society Miscellany, ed. D. Laing (E, 1844), I, 541–63; Calderwood; *Select Biographies*, ed. W. K. Tweedie (E, 1845), I, 1–61; *FES* III, 5–7; *DNB* LX, 154–5; James Young, *Life of John Welsh* (E, 1866).

J. Kirk

Welsh (Welch), John (of Irongray) (?1624–81), Covenanting* field-preacher.* The grandson of John Welsh* of Ayr and a great-grandson of John Knox,* Welsh studied at Glasgow (MA, 1647) and was ordained to Kirkpatrick-Irongray (Dumfriesshire) in 1653. With all but two of his brethren in the Presbytery of Dumfries he was ejected in 1662. Almost immediately, with Gabriel Semple, he began preaching in the fields, holding conventicles* even in his former parish. He preached not only throughout the south-west of Scotland but in Perthshire and in Fife, where in 1674 he gathered as many as ten thousand hearers. For a time he lived in Northumberland, even preaching on the frozen River Tweed. He attended the debacle at Rullion Green,* and was at Drumclog and Bothwell Bridge,* where he counselled moderation. Although not in agreement with them, he refused to hold meetings in the parishes of those ministers who had accepted the Indulgence.* In spite of his reputation, the frequency, duration and public nature of his preaching, and a large price on his head, Welsh was never apprehended and, retiring to London after Bothwell Bridge, died in peace.

Fifty and Two Directions . . . to his Paroch of Irongray (E, 1703); 'Two Sermons' in Michael Shields, *Faithful Contendings Displayed . . .* , ed. John Howie (G, 1780), and other single, posthumously published, sermons.

FES II, 187–8; John Howie, *The Scots Worthies*, ed. W. M'Gavin (G, 1838); R. Wodrow, *The History of the Sufferings of the Church of Scotland*, II, III (G, 1828).

D. C. Lachman

Wemyss (Weemse), John (c.1579–1636), minister and Hebrew scholar. Born at Lathocker, East Fife, and educated at St Andrews (MA, 1600), he was appointed minister of Hutton, Berwickshire, in 1608, and translated to Duns in 1613. For several years he acted as a representative of Presbyterian* ministers in altercations with champions of episcopacy,* e.g. at the Falkland Conference (1609) and the Perth Assembly of 1618 which issued the Five Articles.* After appearing before the Court of High Commission* in 1620 for disobeying the Articles, he apparently gave up ecclesiastical affairs and devoted himself to study and writing. His commitment to Presbyterianism also gave way to Episcopalian* sympathies; Charles I appointed him a prebendary of Durham in 1634.

His writings were all devoted to the interpretation of Scripture to aid preaching and teaching. Three expositions dealt with the parts of the Mosaic law, judicial, ceremonial and moral (L, 1632). *The Portraiture of the Image of God in Man* (L, 1627) is a biblical anthropology and psychology, and *The Christian Synagogue* (L, 1623) a kind of Bible handbook, while *Exercitations Divine* (L, 1634) resolve issues and questions touching on the right understanding of Scripture. Wemyss stressed the value of 'arts and sciences' and the original languages. The prominence he gave to Hebrew and to Jewish writings, from the Midrash through the medievals, to the early moderns, made him one of the pioneers in Scotland of the study of Jewish life and learning.

See Sabbatarianism.

Works, 4 vols (L, 1636).

FES II, 8–9; *DNB* LX, 249–50; Calderwood VII; D. M. G. Stalker, 'John Weemse of Lathocker . . .', *RSCHS* 8 (1944), 150–66.

D. F. Wright

Wesley, John (1703–91), CofE clergyman, itinerant evangelist and one of the founders of Methodism.* Wesley first preached in Scotland in 1751 at the invitation of Captain Gallatin, an English soldier quartered at Musselburgh. He went despite George Whitefield's* warning, 'You have no business there, for your principles are so well known that if you spoke like an angel, none would hear you.' The 'principles' in question were Wesley's Arminianism.* Whitefield's prediction may have conditioned Wesley's strategy, for Wesley determined to limit his Scottish preaching to a proclamation of the essential gospel, and never to attack Calvinism. In Wesley's words, 'From the first hour that I entered the kingdom, it was a sacred rule with me never to preach on any controverted point – at least, not in a controversial way.' He rebuked one of his Scottish preachers in 1770 as 'lost to all common sense' for having preached against the doctrine of perseverance.

In one sense, Wesley's strategy succeeded. He made twenty-two visits to Scotland, and was generally accorded a friendly reception, preaching in both Presbyterian and Episcopal churches at a time when CofE pulpits were closed to him. His warmest ministerial supporter was John Gillies* of the College Church, Glasgow; his most influential disciple Lady Maxwell* of Pollok. The governing classes treated him well, and he was given the freedom of the city at Perth and Arbroath in 1772. At grassroots level, Wesley himself frequently testified that the common people of Scotland heard him more gladly than their English counterparts did. As he put it during his 1764 visit, 'O what a difference there is between North and South Britain! Every one here at least loves to hear the Word of God and none takes it into his head to speak one uncivil word to any for endeavouring to save their souls.' In striking contrast to his English experience, Wesley suffered violence only once when preaching in Scotland – a minor incident in 1768 at Aberdeen, where an unruly element disrupted his sermon and threw potatoes at him.

However, despite Wesley's favourable reception by large audiences, he won few followers for his 'societies'. During his 1784 visit he lamented, 'I am amazed at this people. Use the most cutting words, and apply them in the most pointed way, still they hear but feel no more than the seats they sit upon.' There were only 468 Methodists in Scotland by 1767, and 1,079 by the time of Wesley's death in 1791. Adam Clarke, who organized Methodist missions in the Shetland Islands,* said that Methodism had no hold in Scotland save in Glasgow and Edinburgh. It was as late as 1785 that Wesley commenced ordaining preachers for Scotland; John Pawson, Thomas Hanby and Joseph Taylor were the first three. Others followed. In 1788 Wesley ordained Alexander Mather* as the first Scottish superintendent.

Wesley's failure to attract many disciples in Scotland can be explained in large measure by hostility to his Arminian theology on the part of influential Scottish Calvinists. The opposition was spearheaded by John Erskine* of Edinburgh, leader of the CofS Evangelicals, who published James Hervey's *Eleven Letters . . . to the Rev. Mr John Wesley* (L, 1765) and his own *Mr Wesley's Principles Detected* (E, 1765). Erskine paid tribute to Methodist sincerity and piety, but saw grave danger in Wesley's leadership; despite his reticence in Scotland, Wesley was a propagandist of 'Arminian, Antinomian, and enthusiastic errors' in England. Wesley felt his Scottish work was seriously undermined: 'O the precious convictions those letters destroyed!' Another blow fell in 1771 when Lady Glenorchy* threw the weight of her influence against Wesley and barred Methodist preachers from her chapel.

Other factors which contributed to the meagre success of Methodism in Scotland were Wesley's refusal to provide a settled (as opposed to an itinerant) ministry, his centralized administration of affairs from England, and the relatively high standard of popular religious education in Scotland, which disposed Scottish audiences to hear Wesley more as judges than docile learners.

See also McAllum, Duncan.

H. D. Rack, *Reasonable Enthusiast* (L, 1989); D. Butler, *John Wesley and George Whitefield in Scotland* (E, 1898); S. J. Rogal, *John Wesley's Mission to Scotland, 1751–1790* (NY, 1988), with extensive bibliography; S. J. Royal, 'John Wesley at Edinburgh: 1751–1790', *Trinity Journal* 4 (1983), 18–34.

N. R. *Needham*

West Indies, *see* Missions.

West Port Scheme (Edinburgh). After the Disruption,* Thomas Chalmers,* the evangelical clergyman and social reformer, soon became disillusioned with the new FC,* to the extent that it was not demonstrating enthusiasm for his conviction that only territorial churches could create a sense of community and elevate the labouring poor in industrial society. In 1844, he announced a new interdenominational church and community building campaign for Scotland's cities. As a model operation, he devised a scheme for the West Port, one of the poorest districts in Edinburgh. He promised to create a self-supporting working-class Christian community with only modest initial doses of middle-class money and voluntary effort. Within a few years, he managed to establish a church, schools, laundry, lending library, reading rooms, and savings bank. The operation, however, cost far more than he had estimated, and it remained dependent on salaried professionals and extraparochial subsidies. The scheme's impact on the district, moreover, was limited, and it did not revive public enthusiasm for Chalmers's social ideal.

S. J. Brown, 'The Disruption and Urban Poverty', *RSCHS* 20 (1978), 65–89; *id.*, *Thomas Chalmers* (O, 1982), 350–66; W. Hanna, *Memoirs of Dr Chalmers*, 4 vols (E, 1849–52), IV, 391–415.

S. J. *Brown*

Westminster Assembly and Documents. On 12 June 1643, the English Parliament 'thought fit and necessary to call an Assembly of learned, godly, and judicious Divines . . .' (Ordinance calling the Assembly). Three aims were in view: (i) a reformation of liturgy, discipline and government in the Church of England; (ii) the promotion of church unity with Scotland and the continent; (iii) the clarification and revision of the Thirty-nine Articles. The Assembly was convened in Henry VII's Chapel at Westminster Abbey, on 1 July 1643. William Twisse (1578?–1646) was named as Prolocutor (being succeeded on his death by Charles Herle, 1598–1659). Members of the Assembly were to be remunerated at a *per diem* rate of four shillings.

BACKGROUND. The Assembly convened against the background, and indeed as part of, the ongoing struggle between King Charles I* and the Long Parliament (convened in 1640, the same year as the 'Root and Branch' petition urging the abolition of episcopacy, and only dissolved, forcibly, by Cromwell in 1652). Already, in 1641, the General Assembly* of the CofS had urged greater ecclesiastical uniformity, specifically mentioning a Confession, Catechisms and Directory for worship. That same year a parliamentary Grand Remonstrance had also petitioned Charles for such an Assembly. In April 1642 a list of potential participants was drawn up (two divines from each English county, the two English universities, one for each Welsh county, four from the City of London, plus some fourteen others named by the Lords). In addition twenty lay representatives from the Commons and ten from the Lords were chosen.

Despite a royal proclamation prohibiting the Assembly (22 June 1643), Parliament proceeded with its own Ordinance, and the Assembly was opened on 1 July with a sermon by Twisse. It was, therefore, a gathering under parliamentary, not ecclesiastical authority, in R. Baillie's* words, 'no proper Assemblie, but a meeting called by Parliament to advyse them in what things they are asked' (*Letters and Journals*, ed. D. Laing, 3 vols, E, 1841–2, II, 186).

MEETINGS. Regular meetings of the Assembly began on 6 July 1643, in Henry VII's Chapel, with the revision of the Thirty-nine Articles. The venue for plenary sessions soon moved, with the onset of winter, to the Jerusalem Chamber. Throughout the Assembly a strict procedure for preparation and debating of material was followed.

Draft materials for discussion were prepared by three committees which met regularly in the afternoons of the Assembly (each member being assigned to one without being barred from attendance at the others). Mornings were then devoted to plenary debates. In addition to the documents prepared by the Divines, the duties of an ecclesiastical 'watch-dog' committee, including the examination of ministers, were assigned to them.

The Assembly was punctuated by regular, lengthy spiritual exercises, but such minuted items as the forbidding of the private (clandestine!) reading of books and papers safeguard against a mistaken hagiographic view of the Divines.

By October 1643, the Assembly had worked on fifteen of the Thirty-nine Articles (giving special attention to Article Eleven, 'On Justification'), when Parliament ordered a discussion of the more pressing questions of the government and discipline of the Church. In order to secure the Parliamentary cause, appeal had been made to the Scots, and had led to the drawing up of the Solemn League and Covenant.* On 19 August 1643, the General Assembly of the CofS deputed eight Commissioners 'to propone, consult, treat and conclude' with the Assembly. Five were ministers: Alexander Henderson,* Robert Douglas,* Samuel Rutherford,* Robert Baillie* and George Gillespie.* At the instigation of Baillie (*Letters*, II, 478–9), three ruling elders were also appointed, John, Earl of Cassilis (1595–1668 – he was never present at the Assembly), John, Lord Maitland,* later to become Duke of Lauderdale, and Sir Archibald Johnston,* Lord Wariston. Other Scottish Commissioners visited the Assembly on occasion, including John, Earl of Loudoun (1598–1663) and Archibald Campbell (*d.*1661)*, Marquis of Argyll.

The Scots Commissioners refused to be members of the Assembly, but served as an advisory body, with considerable *de facto* powers, and met frequently with a committee from the Assembly and Parliament to discuss the acceptability to the Scottish Kirk and nation of the work in progress.

The Solemn League and Covenant was subscribed by the Assembly and the Commons (25 September 1943), and by the Lords (15 October 1643). Consequently the Divines' work was now redirected to the preparation of 'one Form of Kirkgovernment, one Confession of Faith, one Catechism, one Directory for the worship of God'.

The progress of the Assembly, recorded in the minutes, in Robert Baillie's correspondence, and in the writings of George Gillespie (*Notes of the Debates and Proceedings of the Assembly of Divines and other Commissioners at Westminster*..., ed. D. Meek, E, 1845) and John Lightfoot (1602–75, *The Journal of the Proceedings of the Assembly of Divines*..., *Works*, XIII, ed. R. Pitman, L, 1824), was marked by constant tension among the various ecclesiastical parties (Presbyterians of various stripes, Independents, Erastians).

Questions of the government of the Church, the relationship of congregations to one another, the role (if any) of presbyteries, synods and assemblies, carried weighty political as well as religious overtones. The Independent authors of *An Apologeticall Narration* (L, 1643), Thomas Goodwin (1600–80), Philip Nye (1596?–1672), Sidrach Simpson (1600?–55), William Bridge (1600?–70) and the milder Jeremiah Burroughes (1599–1646), proved to be a thorn in the flesh to the Scots Presbyterians. Baillie in particular found their devotion to detailed argument a drain on his patience ('nothing in any Assemblie that was in the world except Trent, like to this in prolixitie', *Letters*, II, 164), and prescribed his panacea: 'No people had so much need of a Presbyterie' (*ibid.*, 177. For full discussion see R. S. Paul, *The Assembly of the Lord*, E, 1985; J. R. de Witt, *Jus Divinum*, Kampen, 1969).

The Assembly debates also indicate some of the growing tensions in international Reformed theology in the seventeenth century over such questions as the extent of the atonement* (*see* Cameron, John, *c.*1579–1625). 'Unhappily Amyraut's questions are brought in on our Assemblie', writes Baillie. 'Many more love their fancies here than I did expect ... Amyraut's treatise goes in the Assemblie from hand to hand' (*ibid.*, 324). In some matters, we find indications that the Divines were concerned to express a generic Reformed theology in such a way that a certain latitude of interpretation would be possible (see, *e.g.*, A. F. Mitchell, J. Struthers (eds), *Minutes of the Sessions of the Assembly of Divines*, E, 1874, 150–1). Whether the a-Presbyterian character of the Confession of Faith is further evidence of this may be questioned, although the General Assembly of the CofS did not leave the issue itself in doubt, in stating that 'the not mentioning in this Confession the several sorts of ecclesiastical officers and assemblies shall be no prejudice to the truth of Christ in these particulars, *to be expressed fully in the Directory of Government*' (Act approving the Confession, 1647, emphasis added). The same Assembly qualified the interpretation of Chapter XXXI, Of Synods and Councils, understanding it to apply only to 'kirks not settled'.

DOCUMENTS OF THE ASSEMBLY. *The Directory for Public Worship* was intended to produce a more uniform ethos in worship. It covered such matters as the behaviour of the congregation, conduct of worship, prayers, forms of administration of baptism and Communion, marriage, pastoral visiting of the sick, burial of the dead, fasting, thanksgiving and praise. Behind its production lay extensive discussion of the proper application of the Puritan regulative principle reducing elements of acceptable worship to what is prescribed or necessarily deducible from Scripture alone. One of its most enduring sections is its discussion of preaching (the drafting of which was originally committed to Stephen Marshall, 1594?–1655). It contains perhaps the finest brief description of expository preaching to be found in the English language. The *Directory* was finally approved by Parliament in January 1645.

The Form of Church Government outlines the distinctive roles of pastors, teachers or doctors (seen as a distinct calling within the ministry of the Word), 'other church governors' which 'reformed churches commonly call elders', and deacons. It also argued for 'congregational, classical, provincial, and national assemblies' in church government. Ordination to the ministry of Word and sacraments is seen as an act of presbytery, following examination (the details of which are included and remain of interest as a testimony to the seventeenth century's concern for an educated and articulate ministry). The *Form* was sent to Parliament for approval on 7 July 1645.

The Larger Catechism and the Shorter Catechism both provide exposition of Christian duties as well as doctrines. Indeed, more than half of the former is devoted to detailed instruction in Christian living, and has consequently been subject to the accusation of legalism. From the authors' point of view, however, such attention to detail had a pastoral motivation and simply underlined their conviction that the whole of Scripture must be applied to the whole of life. It was completed by 15 October 1647.

The Shorter Catechism, notable for its opening question and answer on 'the chief end of man' and its many succinct theological definitions, has had an enduring influence on Presbyterianism. While lacking the quality of personal engagement which enhances, *e.g.*, the Heidelberg Catechism (1563), it possessed great strength in the production of *systematic* thinking. It is sometimes suggested that its chief architect was Anthony Tuckney (1599–1670), later Regius Professor of Divinity at Cambridge. Completed by 25 November 1647, along with the Larger Catechism, it was presented to Parliament in final form on 14 April 1648 (*see* Catechisms; Catechizing).

The composition of the Confession of Faith constitutes the central accomplishment of the Assembly. Calvinistic* in emphasis, its theology is covenantal* in orientation, and its soteriology evangelical. Only a few representative features of its teaching can be mentioned here. The Confession opens with an extensive and carefully-worded chapter on Scripture* (cf. First Helvetic, 1536; Formula of Concord, 1576; Irish Articles, 1615). Following Calvin, it stresses the *testimonium internum Spiritus Sancti*, emphasizes the perspicuity and preservation of Scripture, justifies translations, and underlines the Reformed hermeneutical principle that 'The infallible rule of interpreting Scripture is Scripture itself' (I.ix).

Chapter II, Of God and of the Holy Trinity, accused on occasion of setting forth a scholastic *definition* of God, in fact is quarried out of Scripture itself and has its antecedents in the language of the early Christian Fathers. Significantly absent are the Thomistic proofs. Teaching on the divine decree follows (ch. III), expounding and defending the principles of the sovereignty, righteousness and freedom of God, including his will of election and reprobation. Here the Divines seek to retain both Christological focus (III.v) and pastoral consciousness (III.viii). More thoroughly than Leith admits, but perhaps less obviously than Warfield states (see bibliography), the Confession gives expression to the mature covenant theology* of the seventeenth century. A twin covenant structure is specified, of works and of grace (VII.ii, iii), albeit even the former is the result of 'voluntary condescension on God's part'. The covenant of grace is seen as the unifying structure of all redemptive history.

The Confession presents a classical Christology* (VIII), briefly refuting a wide variety of heresies.* Its exposition of a *communio idiomatum* in Christ, but not a *communicatio*, is distinctively Calvinian. The chapter on free will (IX) outlines the pattern of humanity's 'fourfold state' (innocence, sin, grace, glory) which would later be worked out in detail in Thomas Boston's* famous book. It also prepares the ground for the treatment of the application of redemption which follows (chs X–XVIII). It is noteworthy that this entire section is structured covenantally (God's activity/human response) rather than by an *ordo salutis** which might reduce every soteriological element to a series of one-dimensional causes and effects. Equally striking is the way in which the exposition of the law *follows* at this point (XIX), leading to the various areas of Christian responsibility (use of liberty, religious worship, oaths, magistracy, marriage, XX–XXIV). The role of the magistrate includes furthering both the defence and the prosperity of the people specifically for the glory of God (XXIII.i). In a much discussed section, the magistrate is also said to be responsible to 'take order' (perhaps in the limited sense of 'provide for', since the Latin translation of 1656 renders by *providere*) to preserve unity and peace, orthodoxy in doctrine and practice, and to call synods to that end (XXIII.iii. Cf. the General Assembly's qualification above).

The Divines equated the Church, in some sense, with the kingdom of Christ (XXV.ii). He himself is exclusively its head, not the Roman pontiff, who (following the Scots Confession*) is identified with the Antichrist (XXV.vi). Children of believers are recognized as members of the Church and are baptized accordingly (XXVIII.vi. cf. the wording of the *Directory*: 'they are Christians, and federally holy before baptism, and therefore are they baptized'). The efficacy of baptism* is, however, not caused by the act itself as such, nor is it tied to the moment of administration (XXVIII.v, vi). The treatment of the Lord's Supper* denies both transubstantiation and the re-presentation of the sacrifice of Christ (XXIX. ii), but affirms the reality of the presence of the exalted Christ, and communion with (feeding on) him by faith (vi). The final chapters deal with church discipline,* synods* and councils* (XXX, XXXI) and the last things (XXXII–XXXIII).

The Confession expresses a characteristically seventeenth-century Reformed theology, frequently criticized in nineteenth- and twentieth-century scholarship for its scholasticism and its distance from Calvin himself. While some of the Divines in their personal writings are capable of employing the scholastic methodology, later studies in the history and development of Reformed theology have increasingly raised damaging questions against rigid forms of this widely-held thesis. It is clear that too much has been made of the supposed differences between Calvin and Westminster on, *e.g.* the relation between faith and assurance*. Again, insufficient attention has been given to the fact that a separate exposition of adoption (definitive of Christian experience for Calvin) is given a place in a major Christian confession for the first time in the history of the Church. No doctrine is less scholastic in nature.

On the other hand, there appear to be (minor) occasions where the Westminster Standards are not wholly consistent with themselves and evidence the committee structure which lies behind their production. Furthermore, even Churches committed to the generic Calvinism of the Confession (*e.g.* in the USA, the Orthodox Presbyterian and the Presbyterian Church in America), have detected a too specifically seventeenth-century orientation in its identification of the pope as the Antichrist. It may be asked whether such a specific interpretation of a biblical prophecy is not itself an application of Scripture which goes beyond the doctrinal substance of Scripture and therefore is not only unique in the Confession (the fulfilment of no other New Testament prophecy receives such specific identification), but also transgresses the Confession's own basic intention.

Despite the decision of Parliament to change the title of the Confession to 'Articles of Christian Religion', in view of its non-confessional format, the title has remained. Ironically, however, Parliament did overcome the resistance of the Divines to adding 'proof texts' to the Confession. This, in itself, suggests that the accusation of a 'proof text mentality', commonly levelled at the Divines, fails to recognize their own vision for a more biblical and theological approach. The Confession itself was completed by 26 November 1646, and the proof texts by the following April.

The Divines were also responsible for approving the version of the Psalter produced by Francis Rous (1579–1659).

On the completion of its more formal work, the Assembly continued to meet to June 1648, discussing queries on *jus divinum* issues, seeking to answer the Dissenting Brethren, and dealing with questions of accommodation. The last numbered session (1163) was held on 22 February 1648, but the Assembly continued to meet with less frequency, as a committee for examining ministers, until 25 March 1652.

The political context in which the Assembly met meant that the original vision for a closer unity among the Churches was virtually doomed to failure. It was only within Scottish Presbyterianism and its international derivatives that the Standards it produced would play a formative role. Nevertheless, the Westminster Assembly of Divines was, beyond question, one of the most significant gatherings in the history of the post-Reformation Churches. Its documents have exercised an unparalleled Christian influence on the people of Scotland and on the history of Scottish theology.

B. B. Warfield, *The Westminster Assembly and its Works* (NY, 1931); A. F. Mitchell, *The Westminster Assembly. Its History and Standards* (L, 1883); J. H. Leith, *Assembly at Westminster* (Atlanta, 1973); S. W. Carruthers, *The Everyday Work of the Westminster Assembly* (Philadelphia, 1943); J. B. Rogers, *Scripture in the Westminster Confession* (Grand Rapids, MI, 1967); I. Hamilton, *The Erosion of Calvinist Orthodoxy: Seceders and Subscription in Scottish Presbyterianism* (E, 1990); R. M. Norris, 'The Thirty-Nine Articles at the Westminster Assembly' (PhD, St Andrews University, 1977); W. Spear, 'Covenanted Uniformity in Religion: The Influence of the Scots Commissioners on the Ecclesiology of the Westminster Assembly' (PhD, Pittsburgh University, 1976).

S. B. Ferguson

Whigs, Covenanters,* later a political group. The term Whig has changed its meaning several times since it was first used in the mid-seventeenth century to denote a Presbyterian* adherent of the National Covenant* of 1638. After 1660, 'Whigs' accordingly became a colloquial word for Covenanters and hence more generally for rebels.

In the early 1680s the term was appropriated by English political polemicists as an abusive epithet for the faction that sought to exclude the Duke of York (later James VII and II*) from the throne because he was a RC, while his supporters were known as Tories. After the Revolution of 1688 resulted in the deposition of James and the accession of William III,* Whigs were the key supporters of the constitutional settlement of limited monarchy, aristocratic government and the Establishment* of Presbyterianism* in Scotland. Tories, associated with Episcopalianism* in Scotland and the High Church Party in England, continued to oppose them. The Tories, however, were tainted by their supposed links with the Jacobite* Risings* of 1715 and 1745, and Whigs dominated British politics from 1715 until the accession of George III (1738–1820) in 1760.

The seventy years after 1760 were a period of political flux during which a number of men with Whig backgrounds gravitated to a revised Tory party now free of subversive links and coming to appear representative of conservatism. The Whigs themselves advocated the moderate reform expressed in the Reform Act of 1832. They were in power, from 1830 to 1841, as conflict grew in the CofS.* The Erastian attitudes of the Whigs made them unsympathetic to Non-Intrusionism* and probably contributed to the onset of the Disruption.* After the mid-nineteenth century Whigs generally became subsumed in the emerging Liberal Party.

Oxford English Dictionary; R. Willman, 'The Origins of "Whig" and "Tory" in English Political Language', Historical Journal 17 (1964), 247–64; B. W. Hill, The Growth of Parliamentary Parties 1689–1742 (L, 1985); id., British Political Parties 1742–1832 (L, 1985); G. I. T. Machin, Politics and the Churches in Great Britain 1832 to 1868 (O, 1977).

J. R. Wolffe

Whitby, Synod of (664), an ecclesiastical council held in Northumbria to settle a dispute over the best method for calculating the date of Easter and related festivals. The monks of Lindisfarne, following the leadership of their motherhouse at Iona,* used Easter-tables based on a pseudo-Anatolian eighty-four-year cycle; the majority of the Western Church, including the Roman mission to Britain sent by Pope Gregory the Great in 597, used a more modern nineteen-year cycle devised by Dionysius Exiguus in the sixth century. The controversy arose with the arrival in Northumbria of a Romanizing party led by Wilfrid under the patronage of Alhfrith, son of King Oswy; the king himself was under the influence of the Lindisfarne monks led by Abbot Colman (see Celtic Saints). At the synod Wilfrid and Colman both presented their arguments before Oswy and his court, and Oswy decided in favour of the Roman way on the basis of the Petrine commission in the New Testament. Colman and many of his monks withdrew from Lindisfarne and went back to Iona, and the influence of Iona in the Northumbrian Church was much reduced. The Synod also discussed the matter of the correct shape of the monastic tonsure,* again deciding in favour of the Roman practice.

The significance of the Synod of Whitby is debatable. Bede* gives the Easter question great prominence, but that may reflect his own preoccupations and expertise; other writers, such as Adomnán,* have much less to say about it. It has been suggested that underlying the Synod was a private quarrel between Oswy and Alhfrith, who may have been trying to embarrass his father. One account of the Synod states that Oswy gave his answer in favour of the Roman practice 'with a smile', implying a less than serious approach to the issue. But during the half-century following Whitby, Roman practice continued to spread through Britain and Ireland, and was accepted by the Picts* c.715 and imposed by them on Iona itself.

See also Celtic Church; Christian Year.

Bede's Ecclesiastical History of the English People III:25, ed. B. Colgrave and R. A. B. Mynors (O, ^{2}1992), 294–309, and Eddius' Life of Wilfrid 10, ed. B. Colgrave (C, 1927), 20–23; H. Mayr-Harting, The Coming of Christianity to Anglo-Saxon England (L, 1972).

A. Macquarrie

White, John (1867–1951), ecclesiastical politician, architect of Church Union and campaigner for church extension. He was the dominant figure in the CofS from the mid-1920s to the late 1940s, working to restore the national Church to a position of leadership in Scottish society and to re-create a sense of Christian commonwealth in a secular era.

White was the son of a flour miller from Kilwinning, Ayrshire. After a distinguished student career at Glasgow University, where he was strongly influenced by the neo-Hegelianism of Edward Caird,* he became in 1893 the CofS minister of Shettleston, Glasgow. In 1904 he was transferred to South Leith, and in 1911 called to the prestigious Barony Church in Glasgow, where he remained until his retirement in 1934. During the First World War he was a zealous patriot, delivered fierce anti-German sermons, assisted with recruitment, and served for over a year as a chaplain on the Western Front.

White's major contributions were made within the 1908–29 movement to unite the CofS and UFC. Through his capacity to master detail and his power in debate he quickly emerged as a leader in the Union movement. He asserted his dominance over the movement, and over the two Churches, after the War. Parliamentary action was required to guarantee the spiritual independence of the CofS, which the UFC defined as a necessary condition for Union. Through White's influence with leading Conservative politicians the Church secured the legislation between 1921 and 1925, and Union was achieved in 1929. His contributions were recognized when he was made Moderator of the first General Assembly of the newly united CofS.

In 1932 White inaugurated a church extension* campaign with the motto 'The Church in the Midst'. The aim was to respond to Scotland's shifting population by erecting churches in new housing areas being created on urban peripheries. Despite the economic depression of the 1930s, White experienced modest success in collecting voluntary donations and gaining state co-operation, and about forty churches were eventually built.

White was a controversial figure. A staunch Tory, he condemned pacifism* and opposed socialism. During the 1920s he worked unsuccessfully (through his position as co-convener of the Church and Nation Committee*) to convince the government to halt Irish RC immigration* into Scotland and to deport Scoto-Irish RCs receiving state relief. His ascendancy over the Church was increasingly challenged by more liberal churchmen such as John Baillie,* who believed White's social conservatism was perpetuating working-class alienation from religion.

Who Was Who, 1951–1960, 1159–60; FES III, 395, VIII, 289–90, IX, 256; A. Muir, John White (L, 1958); A. Gammie, John White (L, 1929).

S. J. Brown

White, John Campbell (1843–1908), first Baron Overtoun, Presbyterian philanthropist. Born at Hayfield, near Rutherglen, Lanarkshire, he studied logic and natural philosophy at Glasgow University 1859–64. Deeply influenced by the 1859 revival* he acquired a lifelong commitment to evangelism and missions. He joined his father's chemical manufacturing firm, later becoming principal partner, and devoted vast sums of money to Christian causes, particularly the Livingstonia mission. He was president of the Glasgow United Evangelistic Association.*

White was a zealous member of the FC, and supported the 1900 union with the UPC. In the legal dispute between the UFC and the dissident FC minority he was principal defender of the former, and was at the forefront of its emergency fund and in aiding dispossessed ministers and congregations after the House of Lords decision against the UFC in 1904 (see Free Church Case).

White was a Liberal in politics, and on Gladstone's* recommendation was created Baron Overtoun (the name of his estate near Dumbarton) in 1893. Criticisms of the conditions in his Rutherglen chemical factory made by an Independent Labour Party investigation led to adverse publicity (1899). Overtoun House has more recently been the home of an independent evangelical congregation.

The Scottish Covenanters: Civil and Religious Freedom (priv., 1903); introd. to W. A. Elmslie, Among the Wild Ngoni (E, L, 1899).

DNB Second Suppl. III, 649–50; Who Was Who, 1897–1916, 542; D. Carswell, Brother Scots (L, 1927), 191–211.

N. R. Needham

Whitefield, George (1714–70), preacher and evangelist. Born in Gloucester, in 1732 he went to Oxford University. After his conversion in 1735, partly through reading Henry Scougal's* The Life of God in the Soul of Man, Whitefield became intimately associated with the Wesleys in the Holy Club. In 1736 he was ordained a deacon of the CofE. In 1737 he travelled to Georgia, where he began a life-long work caring for orphans. Soon after his return to England in 1738 Whitefield began open-air preaching in Bristol, a ministry he encouraged John Wesley* to undertake. Whitefield's disregard for ecclesiastical conventions brought him notoriety, and he was often refused permission to preach in churches. One of his main supporters was Selina, Countess of Huntingdon.

In 1741, after a further visit to America, Whitefield came to Scotland at the invitation of Ralph Erskine.* Soon a dispute arose which effectively severed Whitefield's links with the Secession. Whitefield was urged to agree that episcopacy was not in harmony with God's Word, and that Presbyterianism was the only form of Church government agreeable to the Word of God, but he argued for mutual toleration. Thereafter the Secession resolved neither to hear Whitefield nor to be identified with his ministry. A number of CofS ministers also refused to hold communion with him because he was an Anglican. The pamphlet war which followed was full of bitter recriminations. Whitefield was, however, warmly welcomed by the majority of Evangelicals in the CofS, and visited Scotland fourteen times, most notably during the revival* in 1742 at Cambuslang and Kilsyth. Whitefield's affection for Scotland is evident in his correspondence. Writing in 1761 to John Gillies, his first biographer, Whitefield declared, 'I have thoughts of seeing Scotland ... that will be a desirable place to go to heaven from. I love, I love that dear people.'

Whitefield was an indefatigable preacher. During his 1759 visit to Scotland he preached one hundred times in seven weeks. He was probably the greatest of the preachers raised up during the revival of religion in the middle decades of the eighteenth century. He died in America.

See Revivals.

A. Dallimore, George Whitefield, 2 vols (L, E, 1970, 1980); J. M'Kerrow, History of the Secession Church (G, 1841); A. L. Drummond and J. Bulloch, The Scottish Church 1688–1843 (E, 1973), 51–5; D. Butler, John Wesley and George Whitefield in Scotland (E, L, 1898).

I. Hamilton

Whitelaw, Thomas (1840–1917), UP and UFC divine. Born at Perth, he graduated MA from St Andrews University in 1859, and then studied theology at the UP Divinity Hall in Edinburgh. Licensed by Perth Presbytery in 1863, in 1864 he was ordained to Mile-end Road Church, South Shields, in Durham. In 1867 he moved to the UP church in Glasgow's Cathedral Street, and in 1877 to King Street, Kilmarnock, where he remained until his retirement in 1914. He received a DD from St Andrews University in 1883.

Whitelaw read widely in theology, including contemporary German thought. He had a conservative view of Scripture in the face of the higher critical movement, and an orthodox Christology, lucidly presented in his How is the Divinity of Jesus depicted in the *Gospels and Epistles?* (L, 1883). Of special interest to modern theology is his denial of God's impassibility.

The Gospel of St John (G, 1888); *A Homiletical Commentary on the Acts of the Apostles* (NY, 1896); *Old Testament Critics* (L, 1903); *Genesis* (L, 1897); *The Patriarchal Times* (L, 1887); *The Old Lamp* (L, 1912).

Small II, 292; *FUFCS* 141.

N. R. Needham

Whithorn (archaeology). Whithorn Priory* is the traditional site of the church built by St Ninian.* Historians still debate the character and chronology of his foundation and the location of his church and missionary activities. The earliest records of Whithorn belong to the period of Northumbrian supremacy in S. Scotland in the eighth and ninth centuries. These include Bede's* brief accounts in *Hist. Eccl.* II:iv and V:xxiii, a verse Life of St Ninian and metrical hymn, a letter from Alcuin and entries in annals recording the accession and death of bishops of the Northumbrian see of Whithorn. These sources clearly suggest the existence of a monastery and reflect the Northumbrians' propagation, for whatever pious or political reasons, of the cult of St Ninian. There are no further records until the twelfth century, when the bishopric was restored (if, indeed it had ever fully lapsed), a new cathedral was built and a community of Premonstratensian* canons established.

There has been intermittent archaeological excavation at Whithorn Priory since the late 1880s, with four principal campaigns:

(i) Clearance and restoration work at the east end of the Priory Church on behalf of the Marquis of Bute in the 1880s and 1890s. An important collection of sculptured stones was recovered including a mid-fifth-century memorial (the Latinus stone) and crosses of the so-called Whithorn School of the tenth/eleventh centuries.

(ii) Research by C. A. R. Radford in 1949 and 1950 included excavations in the high-medieval church, at St Ninian's Cave and St Ninian's Chapel at the Isle of Whithorn. The depleted remains of a rectangular stone-founded building underlying the east end of the Priory Church were re-examined. Secured by clay bonding, the outer wall face bore traces of dirty white clay plaster, suggesting an identification as St Ninian's *Candida Casa*.

(iii) Excavation in 1958–67 by R. Ritchie within the east end of the Priory Church revealed the graves of the late medieval bishops and priors of Whithorn associated with rich ritual objects (a crozier, pyx, patens and rings). Earlier oriented burials have been ascribed to the early Christian period and cremated human bone has been advanced as evidence of a late Roman cremation cemetery.

(iv) Continuing excavations (1986–) by the Whithorn Trust on ground to the south of the high-medieval church has produced rich evidence of developments from *c.*500 (or slightly earlier) to the present day. Remains of the early Christian period (fifth–seventh centuries) are still under examination and relatively little is known. A settlement of insubstantial wattle roundhouses of the fifth or sixth century at the foot of the slope was approximately coeval with the mid-fifth-century Latinus stone. Scattered sherds of imported late Roman amphorae attest direct mercantile contact with the eastern Mediterranean. There is, as yet, no certain evidence of the late Roman (third/fourth century) settlement inferred by some authorities, nor is there anything overtly ecclesiastical in the remains uncovered.

The settlement was deserted by the late sixth/early seventh century when the ground at the foot of the hill was cultivated. At roughly the same time the crown of the hill was girdled by a shallow ditch. A cemetery of long cist graves lying over and beyond this ditch had developed around an earlier focal grave. The principal buildings probably occupied the crown of the hill with burials and fields on the periphery.

Rich remains of the period of Northumbrian supremacy (later seventh to mid-ninth century) include a range of ecclesiastical buildings, comprising a long-lived timber church, a stone-founded, clay-walled burial chapel, and an enclosed children's graveyard. A regular terrace of large timber halls occupied level ground beyond the ecclesiastical buildings and smaller timber buildings extended over the lower ground beyond.

The church had developed around a stone monument apparently enclosed within a shrine. The earliest timber church was built immediately west of this shrine and was later extended eastwards to enclose it completely. The enlarged building measured some 20m × 5m and was substantially refurnished at least three times before it was destroyed by fire in the early ninth century. It was rebuilt with timber walls resting on low dry-stone sills and eventually demolished in the mid-ninth century. This is the only large timber church of the early historic period known from Scotland and there are no close parallels in the British Isles. It gives the first true insight to the timber churches built in the 'Scottish style' which prevailed before the introduction of stone buildings.

The stone foundations of the burial chapel supported clay walls protected from damp by limewash. An enduring local architectural tradition of lime-washed, clay-walled buildings could account for the name *Candida Casa* and its possible precursor on Ptolemy's map, *Leucophibia*. Both names – and indeed the Old English *Hwit Aerne* (Whithorn) – translate as shining, brilliant or fair; shed, building or place. This has never been a particularly appropriate name for a church. Its attribution to the church built by St Ninian was perhaps a retrospective conceit of Northumbrian hagiographers creating a false popular icon which survives today.

Despite its clay walls the chapel was an important building, with stained glass windows. The east end contained the graves of four tall adults (including at least one female) buried in wooden coffins with iron fittings. An enclosed graveyard immediately to the east of the chapel contained the remains of more than fifty infants and young children. Most were too young to have entered the monastery. These burials indicate an undocumented lay community and the burial chapel possibly contained the remains of secular rather than ecclesiastical potentates.

The function of the timber buildings is less clear. The terrace of large structures could have been feasting halls, barns or even byres. The smaller buildings were probably houses. It is uncertain whether they formed part of the monastery or an immediately adjacent lay settlement. These buildings had been abandoned by the early ninth century.

Coin finds show that the ecclesiastical buildings were abandoned in the mid-ninth century probably during the first reign of Aethelred II of Northumbria. The reigns of the ninth-century Northumbrian monarchs are not precisely dated but the abandonment may well date to the 840s, when Viking raiders pushed northwards through Ireland and western Britain. Whatever the political circumstances, the archaeological record was dramatically transformed, probably reflecting the physical destruction of much or all of the Northumbrian monastery.

Renewed settlement in the period from c.850 to 1000 is represented by small rectangular buildings lying on both sides of a road leading towards the crown of the hill. We can infer tentatively that this was the site of a church, possibly a surviving Northumbrian building. A rich collection of cross-slabs of the Whithorn School date to this period. These indicate that Whithorn continued to be the focus of ecclesiastical activity in the Machars district where the distribution of cross-slabs corresponds broadly with the pattern of medieval parishes.

The settlement expanded c. 1000, apparently functioning as a trading post, processing raw materials from the Galloway hinterland and importing commodities and luxuries from Ireland and beyond. The inhabitants were probably Hiberno-Norse entrepreneurs and Whithorn clearly formed part of a trade network linking the territories around the Irish Sea. The role of the church is undocumented, but its continuing importance is indicated by the location of a trading post at this otherwise undistinguished inland site.

The restoration of the bishopric c. 1125 and the construction of a new cathedral made no immediate impact on the settlement. A major re-organization of the ecclesiastical precinct in the mid-thirteenth century probably reflects the final defeat of the Lords of Galloway in 1234. New land boundaries were erected and the settlement was relocated, probably on the site of the present town. The area to the south of the church was now used as a graveyard and the ground to the east was cultivated. There was a further reorganization c.1500. The graveyard went out of use and a road was laid over it leading from the west door of the church to a new gatehouse on the main street of the town. The road continued in use after the Reformation and was eventually abandoned when a manse was built in the late seventeenth century. This building survived as a school after a new manse was built to the north in the early nineteenth century. It was demolished at the end of the century and its site was subsequently used as a market garden.

See also Early Ecclesiastical Sites.

P. H. Hill, *Excavations at Bruce Street, Whithorn 1984* (E, 1984); *id.*, *Whithorn 1 [2/3/4] . . . Interim Report* (Whithorn, 1987 [1988/90/92]); *id.*, 'Whithorn: the Missing Years' in Oram and Stell (below); J. and W. MacQueen, *St Nynia* (E, 1990); D. Pollock, *Whithorn 5 . . . Interim Report* (Whithorn, 1993); J. MacQueen, 'The Literary Sources for the Life of St Ninian', in Oram and Stell (below); R. D. Oram and G. P. Stell (eds), *Galloway: Land and Lordship* (E, 1991); C. A. R. Radford, 'Excavation at Whithorn, 1949', *TDGAS* 27 (1950), 85–126; *id.*, 'St Ninian's Cave', *ibid.* 28 (1951), 96–8; *id.*, 'Excavations at Whithorn (Final Report)', *ibid.* 34 (1957), 131–94; *id.*, 'The Early Church in Strathclyde and Galloway', *Medieval Archaeology 11* (1967), 105–26; C. Thomas, *The Early Christian Archaeology of North Britain* (O, 1971); *id.*, *Christianity in Roman Britain to AD 500* (L, 1985); *id.*, *Whithorn's Christian Beginnings* (Whithorn, 1992); P. A. Wilson, 'St Ninian and Candida Casa: Literary Evidence from Ireland', *TDGAS* 41 (1964), 156–85.

P. Hill

Whithorn, cathedral priory. Fergus of Galloway (*d.* 1161) is recorded as founder, but Premonstratensian* canons regular were apparently introduced from the SE (Wigtownshire) c. 1177, possibly replacing Augustinians* or a community of clergy (*see* Early Ecclesiastical Sites). They formed the cathedral chapter of Galloway diocese. As at St Andrews,* they were a religious community, but also intimately involved in the affairs of the diocese and cathedral, whose building began early in the twelfth century, when continuity of the episcopal line also becomes clearer. Only seven such Premonstratensian chapters existed. The canons enjoyed the right of electing the bishop, though possibly not exclusively. This occasioned disputes, and only one prior became Bishop (Michael de Mackenlagh in 1355). The prior ranked immediately after the bishop. In 1451 priors were granted limited *pontificalia* (episcopal insignia), thus becoming the only mitred Premonstratensian prelates in Scotland or England. The abbey of Fearn (Ross-shire) was founded from Whithorn c. 1222.

Whithorn's popularity as a place of pilgrimage in honour of St Ninian* continued, James IV (1466–1513) being a frequent visitor. Commendators* held the priory for a time after 1516, but were followed by two regular priors belonging to the powerful local family of Fleming. There were twenty-five canons in 1508 and eighteen are recorded in the late 1550s. Of these, eight served in the Reformed Church, though Prior Malcolm Fleming was imprisoned in 1563 for exercising his priesthood. Part

WHYTE, ALEXANDER

of the church was used for Protestant worship until 1822.

R. C. Reid (ed.), *Wigtownshire Charters* (SHS, E, 1960); C. A. R. Radford and G. Donaldson, *Whithorn* (E, 1984); N. Backmund, 'The Premonstratensian Order in Scotland', *IR* 4 (1953), 25-40; G. Donaldson, 'The Bishops and Priors of Whithorn', *TDGAS* 27 (1950), 127-54; Easson-Cowan, 51-2, 100-3, 211-12; *FESMA*, 133-5; Dowden, 353-75.

M. Dilworth

Whyte, Alexander (1836-1921), minister of Free St George's Church, Edinburgh, and often described as 'the last of the Puritans'. He was born at Kirriemuir and brought up by a godly though unmarried mother. He overcame poor circumstances and deficiencies of early education to go to King's College, Aberdeen (MA, 1862), and then for divinity studies to the FC's New College, Edinburgh. He received invaluable training as assistant minister to John Roxburgh at Free St John's, Glasgow (1866-70) before accepting a call to be colleague and successor (1870-3) to R. S. Candlish* at Free St George's, Edinburgh, where he was to minister until 1916. From 1909 he carried a double load as Principal of New College, where he taught New Testament literature and from which he did not retire until 1918. He was Moderator of the General Assembly in 1898.

Whyte was, however, essentially a preacher and pastor. Even in a nation of preachers his drawing power, impact and appeal were probably unparalleled, not least for what has been called his 'acute and often morbid anatomy of sin'. His sermons were the outcome of meticulous preparation. His mornings were spent in the study. He always read with pencil in hand, which practice he commended to students, also urging them to have regular habits of prayer. He exploited a lively imagination in preaching so that the words and the dramatic intensity with which they were delivered could pass the defences of even the hardened or most sophisticated listener.

His reading and correspondence ranged over a wide field, and among those of other traditions with whom he kept in touch was Cardinal Newman. Whyte disliked controversy among Christians, but did not hesitate to speak his mind if the gospel were being diluted or basic Christian doctrines attacked. At the same time he believed that the Bible had nothing to fear from higher criticism. He contributed significantly to the 1900 Union* between the FC and UPC and prophesied an even greater one within thirty years. He regarded the true Catholic as 'the well-read, the open-minded, the hospitable-hearted, the spiritually exercised Evangelical'. He gained a wider audience when for more than twenty years his evening sermons were published by the *British Weekly**. Declared J. M. Barrie, himself a native of Kirriemuir, 'To know Dr Whyte was to know what the Covenanters were like in their most splendid hours.'

Whyte's numerous books included *Bible Charac-* ters, 6 vols (E, 1896-1902) and *Bunyan Characters* (4 vols, L, 1893-1908); *A Commentary on the Shorter Catechism* (E, 1883); *Father John of the Greek Church* (E, 1908); *The Apostle Paul* (E, 1903); *Four Temperaments* (L, 1895); *The Walk, Conversation and Character of Jesus Christ* (E, 1905). Other biographical works, reflecting Whyte's diversity of interest, included J. H. Newman, James Fraser* of Brea, Samuel Rutherford,* St Teresa, Lancelot Andrewes, William Law, Thomas Shepard, and Thomas Goodwin.

AFCS I, 355; *FUFCS* 28; *DNB 1912-1921*, 576-7; G. F. Barbour, *The Life of Alexander Whyte* (L, 1923; ^{8}1925, rev.).

J. D. Douglas

Whytock, George (1750-1805), Old Light (*see* New Light) General Associate (Antiburgher) Synod* minister. Influenced by the ministry of Alexander Troup (Small I, 623; II, 546), the Antiburgher minister in Perth, Whytock studied under William Moncrieff.* In 1776 he was ordained to the Associate Church in Dalkeith, where he spent the whole of his ministry. He did not share the Synod's change of principles in regard to the relationship between Church and state (*see* Church and State (theological questions)), but died before he could join with Thomas McCrie* and Archibald Bruce* in the formation of the Constitutional Presbytery the following year. His *A Short Vindication of Presbyterial Church-Government* (E, 1799; reprinted E, 1843, with the addition of twelve 'Essays on the Church') presents in concise form the leading arguments for presbytery against Independency.

A Defence of Covenanting (G, 1780).

Small I, 557; *ASOSC*, 521-2.

D. C. Lachman

Widows and Orphans Fund. In the eighteenth century, ministers became concerned about provision for their widows, who would receive only one payment of what was called 'ann',* one year's stipend,* and then might thereafter be destitute.

In 1744, at the request of the General Assembly, Parliament passed an Act making it compulsory for ministers of the Church and professors of the four old universities to pay one of three rates, with corresponding benefits, to a fund which would provide pensions for their widows and orphans. The scheme had been prepared by three Edinburgh ministers, Robert Wallace,* Alexander Webster* and George Wishart (1703-85),* using data provided by parish ministers. The calculations were checked by Colin MacLaurin, Professor of Mathematics; the only other guidance they had being from Halley's 'Death Tables' of Breslau.

This was, probably, the first annuity scheme on sound principles and was soon followed by similar annuity schemes in England and America and then by all life assurance of today.

The scheme was amended as the years passed to suit changing circumstances and requirements.

WIGTOWN MARTYRS

The so-called 'maximum' scheme became based on actuarial principles in the middle of nineteenth century. It is still, as The Churches and Universities (Scotland) Widows and Orphans Fund, operating under an Act of 1954 (as amended in 1967 and 1981) and acting on actuarial advice, providing for widows and orphans of ministers of the CofS, FCS and some professors of the old universities. There are twenty trustees.

A. Ian Dunlop, *The Scottish Ministers' Widows' Fund 1743–1993* (E, 1992).

A. I. Dunlop

Wigtown Martyrs, two women executed on 2 May 1685 by drowning. Instructions had been given to Commissions of Justiciary to enforce the laws enacted against the Covenanters* and conventicles.* Before such a commission in Wigtown, Margaret Lauchlison, an elderly widow, Margaret and Agnes Wilson, girls of eighteen and thirteen respectively, and Margaret Maxwell, a servant, were tried and condemned on 13 April for rebellion, attending conventicles, not disowning James Renwick's* Apologetical Declaration (justifying resort to measures of self-defence), and refusing an oath abjuring the same. Commissions had been instructed that any persons not disowning Renwick's principles should be hanged immediately; but women 'are to be drowned'.

Maxwell was flogged and put in the jougs (a kind of pillory) for three days. Gilbert Wilson, the girls' father, paid a bond of £100 for Agnes, who was then set free. But despite petitions issued for the other two, both were taken to the Solway Firth, just below the parish church, and tied to stakes driven in the sand, where they would be drowned by the tide. The older woman was apparently tied farther out so that her struggles might influence the younger to take the oath. But she steadfastly refused, saying of her companion, 'What do I see but Christ wrestling there?' Both were drowned. Quite appropriately, much has been made of this as illustrating the barbarity of the government of Charles II* in repressive measures against the Covenanters.

In the nineteenth century Mark Napier attacked the veracity of the account in *The Case for the Crown in re The Wigtown Martyrs proved to be myths* (E, 1863), and defended his views in *History Rescued* (E, 1870). He was answered by Archibald Stewart, *History Vindicated in the Case of the Wigtown Martyrs* (E, 1869), who ably presents and evaluates the evidence. John Tulloch* ('The Wigtown Martyrs' in *Macmillan's Magazine*, Cambridge, December 1862, 152) aptly characterizes Napier: 'sense, impartiality, and critical sagacity are not only entirely lacking – the writer has no perception of such qualities'.

See also Martyrs.

R. Wodrow, *The History of the Sufferings of the Church of Scotland*, 4 vols (²G, 1828), IV, 246–9;

WILKINSON, GEORGE HOWARD

A Cloud of Witnesses,* ed. J. H. Thomson (E, 1871).

J. A. Dickson

Wilkie, Arthur West (1878–1958), missionary educationalist. Born in Cheshire, he studied at Glasgow University (MA, 1896; BD, 1900) and at the UP Divinity Hall in Edinburgh. Ordained by the UF Presbytery of Perth in 1901, he served at Calabar 1901–18, then in the Gold Coast at Accra 1918–30, and finally as Principal of Lovedale* in S. Africa 1931–41. He took part in the Edinburgh World Missionary Conference (1910)* and the first meeting of the International Missionary Council at Lake Mohonk, New York, 1921. He was called to lead the Scottish Missionary Society's work in the Gold Coast following the British exclusion in 1917 of the Basel and Bremen missions, and skilfully promoted harmony in assimilating their legacies. He was prominent in educational affairs and in negotiations with the government.

He and his wife (the sole woman) served on the first Phelps-Stokes Commission on African education in 1920–1. Although it was financed and inspired by American Protestants, the Commission's influential recommendations (T. J. Jones, ed., *Education in Africa. A Study of West, South, and Equatorial Africa...*, NY, 1922) not surprisingly echoed central features of the Calabar school system, including systematic inspection, positive discrimination in enrolling girls, school gardening and local crafts in the curriculum. The Scots mission schools used schooling to serve African rather than colonial needs.

At Lovedale Wilkie developed especially the Bible School and Lovedale Press. The *Memorandum by Lovedale...* (1935) that was the Institution's submission to the Inter-Departmental Committee on Native Education (1935–6) was largely Wilkie's work. Wilkie was honoured (CBE, 1926; DD of Glasgow, 1927) for his work on the Phelps-Stokes Commission, but remains little known despite his significant contribution to the advance of 'western' education in anglophone Africa, through its influence on the shaping of the British government's first African educational policies (*Educational Policy in British Tropical Africa*, L, 1922; *Memorandum on the Education of African Communities*, L, 1935).

FUFCS 561; FES IX, 753; *Who Was Who, 1951–1960*, 1168; *LW* 13 (1958), 146; R. H. W. Shepherd, *Lovedale... 1841–1941* (Lovedale, n.d.), 381–507.

A. F. Walls

Wilkinson, George Howard (1833–1907), Anglican priest and Bishop of St Andrews. Born in Durham, he went to Brasenose College, Oxford University, in 1851, and was elected a fellow of Oriel (MA, 1859). Ordained an Anglican curate and priest in 1857 and 1858 respectively, he occupied a variety of incumbencies before becoming Bishop of Truro in 1883. Though he resigned through illness in 1891, his health had recovered sufficiently for him to be elected Bishop of St

WILLIAM I ('THE LION')

Andrews in 1893. In 1904 he was elected Primus.* Wilkinson's early Evangelicalism gave way before the inspiration of the Oxford movement (*see* Tractariansism), and his mature outlook was Anglo-Catholic. A man of intense energy, he promoted foreign missions (particularly in South Africa), open-air preaching and closer relations between bishop and priests. As Bishop of Truro he founded the Community of the Epiphany, an Anglican sisterhood; as Bishop of St Andrews he raised £14,000 for the construction of a chapter-house for St Ninian's Cathedral, Perth. He was the author of a large number of minor devotional writings, including *The Communion of Saints* (L, 1908); *Pentecost* (L, 1866); *In Spirit and in Truth* (L, 1917); *Instructions in the Devotional Life* (L, 1871); *Prayers for Children* (L, 1885).

A. J. Mason, *Memoir of George Howard Wilkinson*, 2 vols (L, 1909); *DNB Second Suppl.* III, 667–8.

N. R. Needham

William I ('the Lion') (1143–1214), King of Scotland (1165–1214). Grandson of David I,* he succeeded his brother Malcolm IV* and reigned nearly fifty years. His main achievement in the ecclesiastical sphere was the freeing of the Scottish Church from English claims of overlordship. This arose, however, out of adversity, for by the terms of the Treaty of Falaise* in 1174 the Scottish Church was forced to acknowledge such subjection, from which it was freed by Pope Alexander III and confirmed in its liberty by his successors. In 1178 William founded the great Tironensian* abbey of Arbroath* and dedicated it to Thomas Becket, murdered eight years earlier for his defiance of Henry II's attacks on Church freedom. But in the same year William provoked a serious ecclesiastical dispute by quashing an election to the bishopric of St Andrews and intruding his own candidate, his chaplain Hugh. The dispute between Hugh and the chapter's elected candidate, John Scot, came before Pope Alexander, who forbade compromise when it was suggested that John should accept another vacant bishopric; the height of the dispute came in 1181–2, when William was excommunicated by a papal legate and the kingdom placed under interdict. The dispute dragged on until 1188, when Hugh died and John accepted another bishopric (Dunkeld). In 1192 William secured for the Church the papal bull *Cum universi*, declaring the Scottish Church to be a special daughter of the Holy See without intermediary. When he died at an advanced age, William was buried before the high altar of his abbey at Arbroath.

Less notably devout than his grandfather or elder brother, William was not above manipulating the Scottish Church for his own ends; the dedication of Arbroath Abbey to St Thomas may reflect antipathy to Henry II more than admiration for Becket's stand. For most of his reign, however, resistance to English demands and the freedom of the Scottish Church went together, and (except for 1178–88) relations between crown and Church were largely harmonious.

WILLIAM II (III)

Acta, ed. G. W. S. Barrow in *The Acts of William I: Regesta Regum Scottorum*, ii (E, 1971); A. A. M. Duncan, *Scotland: the Making of the Kingdom* (E, 1975), esp. chapters 8 and 10.

A. Macquarrie

William II (III) (1650–1702), Prince of Orange, Statholder of the United Provinces of the Netherlands from 1672, and King of England, Ireland and Scotland 1689–1702. After the flight of James VII (II)* in December 1688, Scottish representatives met William of Orange in London where an agreement was made that he should administer Scotland's affairs until a national convention determined the future shape of its government. In March 1689 William summoned the Scottish Estates; 'Williamites' outnumbered Jacobites,* and on the withdrawal of the latter the convention followed England's example and on 11 April offered the Scottish Crown to William and Mary (his wife, James VII's daughter) in a document called the 'Claim of Right'.

In June William recalled the convention as his first Scottish Parliament (another was never elected during his reign – he simply kept the convention in being for nine successive sessions). The King was guided by William Carstares* in the ensuing religious legislation. Episcopacy* was abolished, but Presbyterianism* was not established until Parliament's second session in 1690, by which time the unpopularity of the Episcopalian clergy and their Jacobite sympathies had overcome William's hesitations about Presbyterianism. Patronage* was abolished, as was the Act of Supremacy (1669) which had declared the monarch supreme in ecclesiastical affairs. William's Presbyterian settlement, however, was not based on the National Covenant,* so many Cameronians remained outside the restored Presbyterian CofS (*see* Societies, United).

Armed Jacobite resistance to William in 1689 was successful at Killiecrankie (Perthshire, 27 July), but defeated at Dunkeld (Perthshire, 21 August). Jacobite sympathies among Highland* clans simmered on, providing fuel for the Risings* of 1715 and 1745.

William was more tolerant in religion than the triumphant Presbyterians wished. He refused to interpret a clause in the Scottish coronation oath binding him 'to root out all heretics and enemies to the true worship of God' in a persecuting sense, and issued indulgences* to a hundred Episcopalian clergy who acknowledged him as King (only nonjurors* were excluded).

Despite certain autocratic tendencies in William's political conduct, his re-establishment of Protestantism (in Presbyterian form) at home, and relentless championship of its cause internationally against Louis XIV of France, guaranteed the loyalty of the majority of his Scottish subjects. He was a popular Protestant hero to the common people, although their sentimental enthusiasm was not shared by the ruling classes.

P. W. J. Riley, *King William and the Scottish*

Politicians (E, 1979); W. L. Mathieson, *Politics and Religion in Scotland, 1550-1695* (G, 1902); *id.*, *Scotland and the Union, 1965-1747* (G, 1905); W. Ferguson, *Scotland: 1689 to the Present* (E, 1968); *id.*, *Scotland's Relations with England* (E, 1977).

N. R. Needham

William of Perth, also known as William of Rochester (*d.*1201), saint* and martyr*. He was born in Perth. Little is known of his early life from the medieval sources, but they record that he abandoned his livelihood as a fisherman in order to devote himself to the relief of the destitute and to the welfare of orphans and foundlings. Deciding later to make a pilgrimage* to Jerusalem by way of Canterbury and Dover, and taking with him as companion one of his earlier foundlings, he was robbed and murdered just outside of Rochester. He was buried in the nearby Cathedral Priory of St Andrew. Miracles soon began to be recorded at his tomb. The Bishop of Rochester, Lawrence of St Martin, took these attested depositions to the Roman curia in order to seek his canonization, which was granted in 1256 by Alexander IV (feast day, 23 May). His shrine thereafter became a centre of pilgrimage throughout the remainder of the Middle Ages. Edward I of England gave a votive offering there of seven shillings on 18 February 1300, and the same amount the next day, while in 1398 Pope Boniface IX granted an indulgence to penitents visiting the altar of St William the Martyr. His cult was suppressed at the Henrician Reformation, but traces of his shrine are still visible in the north transept of Rochester Cathedral.

Acta Sanctorum Maii V, ed. F. Baertis and C. Ianniago (Rome, 1866), 270-1; T. E. Bridgett, 'St William of Perth and Rochester', *The Month* 72 (1891), 501-8; W. St John Hope, *The Cathedral and Monastery of St Andrew at Rochester* (Rochester, 1910); L. E. Boyle, *Bibliotheca Sanctorum* VII, ed. F. Caraffa (Rome, 1966), 481-2.

L. J. MacFarlane

William of Rochester, *see* William of Perth.

William, Alexander (1829-90), *see* Missions: East Asia.

Williamson, Andrew Wallace (1856-1926), prominent CofS minister. Born at Thornhill, Dumfriesshire, he studied at Edinburgh University (MA, 1878) and was ordained to North Leith (1882), moving the next year to St Cuthbert's, Edinburgh, and in 1910 to St Giles,* retiring in 1925. He collected several distinctions: DD (Edinburgh) 1900, a chaplain to Edward VII in 1907 (and later to George V), Croall Lecturer* 1907-8 (*The Person of Christ in the Faith of the Church*, E, 1920; he published little else of substance apart from *Ideals of Ministry*, E, 1901), President of the (Samuel) Johnson Society 1911, Moderator 1913, Dean of the Order of the Thistle* and of the Chapel Royal* from 1913. His high churchmanship was lower than the mainstream within the Scottish Church Society* and he was chiefly influenced by John Macleod* of Govan, who did not think the Society should seek to act as a party within the Church. He resigned over the stance it took on the relaxation of subscription* to the Westminster Confession.* He was asked to succeed Macleod at Govan in 1898 and gave the first of the Macleod Memorial Lectures, *Dr John Macleod, his Work and Teaching* (E, 1901).

FES I, 63, VIII, II; *Who Was Who, 1916-1928*, 1131; C. N. Johnston, *The Life of Andrew Wallace Williamson* (E, L, 1929); R. Sjölinder, *Presbyterian Reunion in Scotland 1907-1921* (E, 1962).

D. F. Wright

Williamson, John (*d.*1740), one of the twelve Marrow* brethren. The son of David Williamson, a Covenanter* denounced as a rebel in 1674 for holding conventicles* and one of the commissioners to the 1690 General Assembly after the Revolution (*FES* I, 100, 96), Williamson studied at Edinburgh (MA, 1697) and was ordained to Inveresk (Musselburgh) in 1702. He joined the defenders of the *Marrow* just prior to the 1721 Assembly, having taken no previous part in drafting the *Representation and Petition*. But, being of 'a clear head, a ready wit, and very forward' (Thomas Boston,* *A General Account of My Life*, E, 1908, 255), he made himself useful and published two works in defence of the *Marrow: The Scope and Substance of the Marrow* (E, 1722), a running commentary on the debate which shed more heat than light, and *The Second Part of the Marrow* (E, 1722), with an extensive introduction and appendix.

From 1720 to 1722 he and Robert Bonaly, ordained in 1719 as a colleague, were involved in a process before the Presbytery of Dalkeith on account of a 'deplorable breach' between them. They were both suspended indefinitely, but ultimately restored after repentance and a promise to work together in harmony. Williamson's participation in the Marrow Controversy* served if anything to shield him from action against him individually (D. C. Lachman, *The Marrow Controversy*, E, 1988, 352-6).

After the Secession,* Williamson strongly objected to the position of the Associate Presbytery* and wrote two pamphlets against his former friends: *Seasonable Testimony* (E, 1738) and *Plain Dealing for the Conviction of the Seceding Brethren* (E, 1739).

The Gospel Method of Conquering Sinners (E, 1721); *Gospel Truth and Holiness Considered* (E, 1726); *Gospel Preaching and Gospel Conversation* (E, 1727); *Reasons against the Restoration of Prof. Simson* (E, 1729); *Reasons why Several Ministers of the Church of Scotland did not Read the Act of Parliament relating to the Murderers of Captain Porteous* (E, 1737).

FES I, 326.

D. C. Lachman

Willison, John (1680-1750), influential evangeli-

WILLISON, JOHN

cal CofS minister and author. He was minister of Brechin (1703–16) and of Dundee South (1716–50). His devotional works were among the most widely read during the century; his support of and participation in the Cambuslang and Kilsyth revivals* (which latter commenced after his sermon on the way back from Cambuslang) were regarded by many as a guarantee of their evangelical orthodoxy; and he launched a reasoned and systematic attack on the system of ecclesiastical patronage* which he saw as leading to a corrupt ministry and the rise of those theological trends which have come to be known as Moderatism.*

His earlier ministry was preoccupied with struggles against Episcopalians* and Jacobites.* He was actively engaged in countering the position of the Glasites*, against whom he published his *Defence of National Churches against the Cavils of Independents* (E, 1729). Sympathetic to the Seceders* and an admirer of their stern opposition to patronage, and commitment to scriptural principles, which he felt were being neglected in many quarters in the Est.C, he fought unsuccessfully for their restoration, though he felt their secession to be misguided. In 1744 he published his *A Fair and Impartial Testimony* (E) against what he saw as the defections of the Est.C, the schism begun by the Seceders, the adoption of RC liturgical innovation* by the Scottish Episcopalians, and the increase of heresy. In his last years, he came increasingly to link the growth of infidelity with the failure of the CofS to preserve its purity of doctrine and worship, to act against heretical opinions, clerical laxity and immorality, to encourage and ensure evangelical preaching, and to guard against 'legal doctrine' and the failure to preach Christ to sinners. These failings, for which he blamed the Moderates,* precluded God's blessing on the Church.

Willison's reputation, however, derives mainly from his devotional works, the most notable of which were his *A Sacramental Directory* (E, 1716), greatly enlarged and issued in two parts as *A Sacramental Directory: or, A Treatise concerning the Sanctification of a Communion Sabbath* (^{3}E, 1741) and *A Treatise Concerning the Sanctifying the Lord's Day* (^{2}E, 1722), *A Sacramental Catechism; or, A Familiar Instructor for Young Communicants* (E, 1720), *The Mother's Catechism* (E, 1731), *The Afflicted Man's Companion* (E, 1737), and *The Balm of Gilead* (E, 1742). He saw faith essentially as an act of the understanding and believed that it could be defended on rational grounds. Assurance* of salvation came not from any inward experience of the individual, but from the united testimony of Christians to the operation of the Holy Spirit. Willison's writings provide a major starting point for the understanding of the theological and spiritual preoccupations of evangelical thought in the later eighteenth-century Scottish Church.

W. M. Hetherington, *The Practical Works of the Rev. John Willison* (G, 1844), with life.

J. Macleod, *Scottish Theology* (E, ^{3}1974); *DNB* LXII, 27–8; *FES* V, 320–2.

J. R. McIntosh

WILSON, GABRIEL

Willock, John (*d.*1585), superintendent* of Glasgow. He was a former Dominican* friar at Ayr who fled to England in the mid-1530s to escape charges of heresy.* Appointed a curate in London by 1539, he was imprisoned in the Fleet for preaching against confession and the use of holy water, against praying to saints and for the souls of the departed and against purgatory and for holding that priests might marry. He later became a chaplain to the Marquis of Dorset. The Zürich divine Henry Bullinger dedicated the fifth book of his *Decades* to Dorset and Willock, who, after studying at Oxford, moved to preach near the Scottish borders by 1552. A supporter of the claims of Lady Jane Gray (Dorset's daughter) to the throne on Edward VI's death in 1553, Willock took part in attempts to overturn Mary Tudor's accession, was declared a rebel and fled to Emden in Friesland. In 1555 he received a commission from the Duchess of East Friesland to negotiate with Mary of Guise,* who had become regent, in Edinburgh.

While in Scotland he encouraged the growth of 'privy kirks'* for Protestant worship and attended John Knox's* sermon on the need for Christians to absent themselves from mass; and home again in 1558 he resumed his preaching in Dundee, Edinburgh, Ayr and elsewhere, was ordered by Mary of Guise to stand trial for heresy in 1559, and was ready to conduct a disputation with abbot Quintin Kennedy* of Crossraguel. For a spell, Willock deputized for Knox in 1559 as minister of St Giles* in Edinburgh, where he administered the Lord's Supper. He argued for the deposition of Mary of Guise, and after a visit to England in 1560 he gained an interview with Mary of Guise on her deathbed. A contributor to the *First Book of Discipline** and Confession of Faith (see Scots Confession), Willock moved to Glasgow by October 1560, and was admitted in September 1561 superintendent of Glasgow, an office he agreed to hold 'only for a time'. Recognition of his abilities as a leader in the Church is forthcoming, too, in his appointment as Moderator in the General Assemblies of December 1563, June 1564, June 1565, July 1568 and December 1568. In 1565, with the Earl of Moray's exile (see Stewart, James *d.*1570), Willock left for England, was active as a preacher at Paul's Cross in London in December 1565, and returned to Scotland only in 1568, after Mary's enforced abdication, at the Assembly's invitation. He died at Loughborough in Leicestershire.

J. Foxe, *Acts and Monuments* (L, 1858), V, 448; Knox, *History*; Calderwood; *BUK*; J. Kirk, *Patterns of Reform* (E, 1989); *Reformation and Revolution*, ed. D. Shaw (E, 1967), 42–69; K. Hewat, *Makers of the Scottish Church at the Reformation* (E, 1920), 130–65; *DNB* LXII, 30–1.

J. Kirk

Wilson, Gabriel (*c.*1679–1750), one of the Marrow brethren. After completing his studies at Edinburgh (MA, 1697), Wilson was ordained to Maxton (near Selkirk) in 1709. One of Thomas Boston's* intimate friends, he took an active part in the Marrow Controversy.* He published an anonymous letter (*A Letter to a Gentleman in Edinburgh*, E, 1721) criticizing the 1720 General Assembly and its Act against the *Marrow* in fairly harsh terms. He extended and completed Boston's draft of the Marrow brethren's *Answers* (E, 1722) to the queries of the General Assembly's Commission, relying on what Boston described as his 'great collection of books'. In 1721 charges were brought against him for teaching Marrow doctrine in a sermon (printed as *The Trust ...*, E, 1723) preached before the Synod of Merse and Teviotdale. The case was ultimately heard by the 1723 Assembly, which merely admonished him and prohibited him from using like expressions in the future, his failure to give 'satisfaction' and his protest notwithstanding.

In the mid-1730s he and Henry Davidson (of Galashiels) turned to practical Independency,* forming an essentially congregational church which met at Maxton and frequently observed the Lord's Supper on sabbath evenings. He continued, however, to minister in his parish unimpeded by Presbytery until his death.

FES II, 185; H. Davidson, *Letters to Christian Friends* (E, 1811); T. Boston, *A General Account of My Life*, ed. G. Low (E, 1908); D. C. Lachman, *The Marrow Controversy* (E, 1988), 291-4, 342-51.

D. C. Lachman

Wilson, John (1804-75), *see* Bayne, Margaret; Missions: India.

Wilson, Margaret (*d*.1685), *see* Wigtown Martyrs.

Wilson, Margaret (*d*.1835), *see* Bayne, Margaret.

Wilson, William (1690-1741), one of the founders of the Secession* Church. Born in Glasgow of parents who had suffered for their faith in the period of persecution,* Wilson studied at Glasgow University (MA, 1707). Disdaining to embrace Episcopacy* as the condition of inheriting his uncle's estate, he studied divinity. Though without encouragement from the Presbytery of Glasgow, which objected to his unwillingness to take the Oath of Abjuration,* he was licensed in 1713 by the Presbytery of Dunfermline, with Ralph Erskine* as moderator. He was called to Dalry (Ayrshire), but not settled there, apparently due to opposition in presbytery and synod, perhaps stemming from his willingness to testify against his teacher, John Simson.* In 1716 he was called to a newly created third charge in Perth.

Wilson joined with the ministers who met to consider how to respond to the 1720 General Assembly's act against the *Marrow* (*see* Marrow Controversy), but due to what his biographer termed 'unavoidable circumstances' took no further part in the controversy. Later he expressed firm support for the *Marrow*'s theology.

From the first Wilson was involved in the events which led to the founding of the Secession Church. After the October 1732 sermon by Ebenezer Erskine,* Wilson joined in the disssent, protest and appeal against the Synod's sentence finding Erskine censurable. When the 1733 Assembly rebuked Erskine, Wilson joined with him, Alexander Moncrieff* and James Fisher* in a protest. He and Moncrieff submitted a representation to the Commission, inquiring if subscription to Acts of Assembly was to be made a term of ministerial communion. He was suspended in August and loosed from his charge in November. In December he joined in the meeting at Gairney Bridge in which the four constituted themselves into the Associate Presbytery.* Although he was encouraged by the 1734 Assembly and was the one most inclined to return to the CofS, he found the course of subsequent Assemblies justified a continuation of the Secession. He had the chief hand in preparing the testimony the Presbytery issued in 1737 and took the lead in an itinerant ministry throughout Scotland, so much so that he could be called 'the tongue of the Associate Presbytery'. In 1737 Wilson began to train men for the ministry, using the *Medulla* of Johannes Marckius as his text. His students spoke of him with high regard. With his brethren Wilson was deposed by the 1740 Assembly, but a large congregation adhered to him and soon constructed an appropriate building, in which he ministered until his death.

It has been said of Wilson that he was the 'masterspring' of the Secession and that 'all their public papers were of his concoction'. He had several sermons published (*e.g., The Blessedness lost in The first Adam, To be found in Christ the second Adam*, E, 1735) and controversial works (*e.g., A Vindication and Defence of the Christian Peoples Divine Right To choose their own Ministers*, E, 1739). But his chief work was *A Defense of the Reformation-Principles of the Church of Scotland* (E, 1739; greatly enlarged, G, 1739) in which he expounded the nature of Church communion and replied to those who had attacked the Secession, particularly John Currie* (*An Essay on Separation: or A Vindication of the Church of Scotland* E, 1738). Like many contemporaries, Wilson kept a short-hand diary, including an account of his religious experiences. This was transcribed and partly incorporated in Andrew Ferrier, *Memoirs of ... William Wilson* (G, 1830).

FES IV, 237; *DNB* LXII, 145-6; J. Eadie, *Life and Times of ... William Wilson* (E, 1849); J. M'Kerrow, *History of the Secession Church* (E, 1848).

D. C. Lachman

Wilson, William (1808-88), FC divine. Born at Blawearie, Bassendean, in Berwickshire, he studied arts and theology at Edinburgh University 1825-33. Licensed by the CofS Presbytery of Earlston in the Borders in 1833, he was a parochial missionary in Glasgow until 1837, and was editor (1835-7) of the *Scottish Guardian* (*see* Periodicals, Religious). In 1837 he was ordained to Carmylie in Forfarshire. He was a zealous Non-Intrusionist* in the 'Ten Years' Conflict.' His FC congregation was without a building for several years.

WINCHESTER, OLIVE MARY

Wilson became minister of the Mariners' Church (afterwards St Paul's) in Dundee in 1848. He was convener of the FC Home Mission Committee (1863–73), and in 1868 was appointed Junior Clerk of the General Assembly. In 1877 he resigned his charge at St Paul's to become secretary to the Sustentation Fund Committee, of which he was also joint-convener. He was Moderator of the General Assembly in 1866, and received a DD from Edinburgh University in 1870.

Wilson wrote the standard biography *Memorials of R. S. Candlish** (E, 1880).

The Kingdom of Our Lord Jesus Christ (E, 1859); *Christ Setting His Face Towards Jerusalem* (D, 1878); *Statement of the Scriptural Argument Against Patronage* (E, 1842).

Disruption Worthies, 505–10; *DNB* LXII, 148; *AFCS* I, 359.

N. R. Needham

Winchester, Olive Mary (1880–1947), thought to be the first woman ordained in Scotland (*see* Findlay, Vera Mary Muir; Sharpe, Jane). Born in Monson, Maine, she took her first degree in classics at Harvard University and taught at a college in Rhode Island before being the first woman to be admitted to divinity studies at Glasgow University in 1909. After graduation with the BD degree (*see* Melville, Frances), she was ordained on 11 May, 1912, in Parkhead in Glasgow to the ministry of the newly formed Pentecostal Church of Scotland (*see* Church of the Nazarene). She taught at their Bible College in Kelvinside, returning to the United States in 1914. In 1925 she was awarded the degree of Doctor of Theology, by Drew Theological Seminary in New Jersey. She became Vice-President of Northwest Nazarene College in Idaho and was then Dean of the Graduate School at Pasadena College in California until her death. She was a productive writer.

Christ's Life and Ministry (Kansas City, 1932); *Crisis Experiences in the Greek New Testament* (Kansas City, 1953).

T. L. Smith, *Called Unto Holiness* (Kansas City, 1962); J. Ford, *In the Steps of John Wesley* (Kansas City, 1968).

T. A. Noble

Winram, John (c.1492–1582), superintendent* of Fife and Strathearn. A kinsman of the Winrams of Ratho, he was educated at St Andrews University where he matriculated at St Leonard's College in 1515. He entered the Augustinian* priory of St Andrews,* became a Bachelor of Divinity by 1532, and was sub-prior in 1536. He also held office as prior of the dependent house of Portmoak at Lochleven, and so was entitled to a seat in Parliament. By 1540 he took his doctorate in theology, was a member of the Arts faculty in 1541, and Professor of Sacred Letters in 1541. He took part in the condemnation for heresy* of Sir John Borthwick* in 1540, preached at the trial of George Wishart* in 1546, yet was criticized by John Hamilton,* the Archbishop of St Andrews, for not opposing strenuously the heresies preached by John Rough* and John Knox* in 1547. He participated at the Church's provincial councils* of 1549 and 1559, and was active preaching in Fife in 1559. In 1550 he attended the burning for heresy of Adam Wallace* and as late as 1558 was present at the trial and execution for heresy of Walter Milne.* During 1559, Winram cast in his lot with his prior, Lord James Stewart (d.1570),* who declared for Protestantism. In 1560 he attended the Reformation Parliament,* and approved the Protestant Confession of Faith (*see* Scots Confession) he had helped draft. He also contributed to the *First Book of Discipline.** In December 1560 he was adjudged fit to serve as minister by the General Assembly, and in April 1561 was admitted superintendent of Fife and Strathearn. He overturned in 1561 the earlier sentence of heresy passed against Borthwick in 1540, to which he had been a signatory, on the grounds that the judges were 'ignorant of God's Word and laws, and plain enemies to his truth'. In 1564 he married Margaret Stewart, and continued to live in the precincts of the priory. He agreed in 1564 that the nobility and estates might legitimately oppose Mary, Queen of Scots,* but doubted whether force might be used to prevent the Queen from attending mass. He participated in the Convention of Leith* in 1572, and was assigned a role in inaugurating John Douglas,* Provost of St Mary's College, as the first Protestant Archbishop of St Andrews. Though active in the General Assembly, he was never elected Moderator. His service in the Reformed Church extended over two decades.

BUK; Calderwood; Knox, *History*; J. Kirk, *Patterns of Reform* (E, 1989); K. Hewat, *Makers of the Scottish Church at the Reformation* (E, 1920), 166–222; *DNB* LXII, 200–1.

J. Kirk

Winzet, Ninian (c.1518–92). Born in Renfrew, he was ordained priest c.1541, and in 1551, though not a graduate, became a master in Linlithgow grammar school. When Protestant teaching and worship were introduced into Linlithgow in 1559, he debated publicly with John Knox* on the eucharist. He also debated on prayer for the dead and in 1561 disputed, again on the eucharist, with the minister, Patrick Kinlochy (*FES* I, 214), and the superintendent, John Spottiswoode.* Having refused to subscribe to the (Scots) Confession* of Faith, he was expelled from Linlithgow in summer 1561.

Winzet found a place at the court of Mary, Queen of Scots.* Already his controversial 'questions' circulated in manuscript and in May 1562 he published *Certane Tractatis*, consisting of texts he had delivered to various parties, including John Knox. In July his *The Last Blast of the Trompet . . . aganis the usurpit auctoritie of Iohne Knox* (E) was impounded and in September he fled abroad. In late 1563 *The Buke of Fourscoir-Thre Questions*, with an open letter to Knox, and his translation of Vincent of Lerins' *Commonitorium* were published at Antwerp. His translation in 1565 of a Latin controversial work has not survived.

Winzet now studied at Paris university, supported financially by Archbishop James Beaton.* He graduated in arts 1566, was elected procurator of the German 'nation' 1567, sat on its Council 1568-9 and, according to Thomas Dempster,* taught philosophy. In 1571, however, he was 'Scottish secretary' and confessor to the captive Queen Mary at Sheffield, then lived with John Leslie* in England. In late September he visited Linlithgow. He was again teaching and procurator of his 'nation' at Paris 1572-3. In 1574 the Scottish Privy Council* named him a traitor and rebel.

Having graduated as bachelor, then master, of theology at Douai 1574-5, Winzet was with Leslie in Rome 1575-7 and assisted in producing Leslie's Latin *History*. Provided abbot of Ratisbon in 1577, he resided there until his death. Though he had limited success in recovering other Schottenklöster,* his community gradually increased. The college he established, and taught in himself, had almost a hundred pupils by 1583. In 1582 he published two works of controversy: *Flagellum Sectariorum* (Scourage of heretics) and *Velitatio* (Dispute) with George Buchanan.*

Winzet, before studying at Paris, was no academic theologian but rather an upholder of tradition, outraged by unwarranted change. He therefore demanded by what authority the Reformers, Knox in particular, acted. An independent thinker, writing (he said) on behalf of the lower clergy and laity betrayed by their superiors, he castigated his own clergy for their sloth, ignorance and avarice and blamed kings and nobles for appointing unworthy clerics. His first work was written 'for reformation of doctrine and manners'.

J. K. Hewison (ed.), *Certaine Tractates* (Winzet's Scots works) (STS, E, 1888-90); J. H. Burns, *Ninian Winzet* (G, 1959); *id.*, 'Catholicism in Defeat: Ninian Winzet 1519-92', *History Today* 16 (1966), 788-95; M. Dilworth, *The Scots in Franconia* (E, 1974); *id.*, 'Ninian Winzet: Some New Material', *IR* 24 (1973), 125-32; M. Taylor, 'The Conflicting Doctrines of the Scottish Reformation' in D. McRoberts (ed.), *Essays on the Scottish Reformation 1513-1625* (G, 1962), 259-72.

M. Dilworth

Wishart, George (c.1513-1546), Protestant Reformer and martyr.* Related to the Wisharts of Pittarrow, near Montrose, he was a student at Louvain where he graduated in arts in 1532. John Leslie* described him as a clerk, and Alexander Petrie* depicted him as schoolmaster in Montrose where he taught the New Testament in Greek until pursued by the Bishop of Brechin when he fled the country in 1538. By 1539 he appeared in Bristol as the 'stiff-necked Scot' who came to the notice of Thomas Cromwell for the radical tenets, verging on Socinianism, which he was reported to have uttered in a lecture in St Nicholas Church. After examination by Archbishop Cranmer and other divines, he recanted some utterances, and may have left England to visit Germany. By 1542, he seems to have entered 'Benet's college', or Corpus Christi, in Cambridge, where he was considered 'well travelled', 'glad to teach, desirous to learn' and ready to give to the poor. Returning to Edinburgh in 1543 in the company of Scottish commissioners (who were friends of reform) sent south to negotiate a treaty with Henry VIII, he stayed for a spell at Pittarrow, then rented a house adjacent to the kirk of Montrose and expounded the Scriptures to all who showed interest. This was the prelude to his preaching tours which took him to Dundee and west to Ayr, Galston, Barr and Mauchline. Returning to Dundee and Montrose (escaping attempts on his life), from Invergowrie he made his way to Perth, Fife and Leith, and on to East Lothian, where John Knox* accompanied him. He visited Brunstane, Longniddry, Ormiston, Inveresk, Tranent, Haddington, preaching as he went, sometimes in kirks, until his arrest at Ormiston on the orders of Cardinal David Beaton* and his execution by burning as a heretic* at St Andrews in March 1546. It is unclear whether he was the 'Scottish man called Wishart' implicated in English plots in 1544 against the cardinal; and it was for heresy, not conspiracy to attempted murder, that Wishart stood condemned in 1546.

Wishart's evangelism during 1544-5 helped popularize the doctrines of the Swiss Reformers in Scotland, and he translated into English the first Helvetic Confession of Faith of 1536. He is known to have preached on Paul's Epistle to the Romans (with its affirmation of justification* by faith) and to have taught the Ten Commandments, the Twelve Articles of Faith (i.e. the Apostles' Creed) and the Lord's Prayer in the vernacular; and at his trial in 1546 he declined to accept that auricular confession was a sacrament, adhered solely to the two dominical sacraments,* denied free will and the claim that he was a 'soul sleeper', recognized the priesthood of all believing Christians, and maintained that as God was infinite he could not be 'comprehended in one place' between 'the priest's hands'. In characteristically Protestant fashion, he discerned the true Church by faithful preaching of the Word and lawful administration of the sacraments.

Knox, *History* I, 60-74; II, 233-45; C. Rogers, 'Memoir of George Wishart', *Transactions of the Royal Historical Society* 4 (1876), 260-3; J. Durkan, 'George Wishart: his Early Life', *SHR* 32 (1953), 98-9; J. Kirk, 'The Religion of Early Scottish Protestants', in *Humanism and Reform*, ed. J. Kirk (O, 1991); *DNB* LXII, 248-51.

J. Kirk

Wishart, George (1599-1671), Bishop of Edinburgh. Born in East Lothian and educated, it appears, at the universities of Edinburgh and St Andrews, Wishart was ordained to Monifieth (near Dundee) in 1624 and translated to St. Andrews in 1626. An Episcopalian of the Laudian school, he fled to England in 1637 and, after the Covenanters* gained power, was deposed in 1639 for desertion of his parish. He was appointed to two lectureships in Newcastle churches. In October 1644 he was captured by the Scottish army and imprisoned in Edinburgh, where he remained almost a year. He was released following the victory of James Graham*, the Earl of Montrose, at Kilsyth on 15 August 1645. Wishart then joined the royalist army and was appointed chaplain to Montrose. From this time he was constantly with the army and wrote an eye-witness narrative of the campaign. After the battle of Philiphaugh, he fled Scotland with Montrose and accompanied him on the continent. After Montrose's death, Wishart may have received protection and favour from Elizabeth, Queen of Bohemia, sister of Charles I.* At the Restoration* he returned to England and became rector of Newcastle upon Tyne. He was consecrated Bishop of Edinburgh in 1662.

He published an elegant Latin history of the wars of Montrose (*De rebus auspiciis*, n.p., 1647; ET, *The History of the Kings Majesties Affairs in Scotland*, The Hague, 1648), which was hung by a cord from the neck of Montrose at his execution in 1650. The second part of this work, down to the death of Montrose, was not published in its original form, though a number of translations of the whole work were later published (A Complete History..., L?, 1720; *Memorials of Montrose and his Times*, 2 vols, G, 1848–50). Wishart was buried in a magnificent tomb in Holyrood Abbey. Evaluations of his character differ widely: from a 'drunkard' who wrote lascivous poems (Wodrow*) to a 'person of great religion' (Keith*).

DNB LXII, 251–3; *FES* V, 238, 362, VII, 342; R. Keith, *Catalogue of the Bishops of Scotland* (E, 1755); W. Anderson, *Scottish Nation* (E, 1877), III, 665; Chambers-Thomson III, 553–5. J. C. Craven, *Scots Worthies, 1560–1688* (E, 1894).

D. B. Calhoun

Wishart, George (1703–85), Moderate* divine. His entire ministry was spent in Edinburgh, at St Cuthbert's (1726–30) and at the Tron (1730–85), first charge, in which he was successor to his father and, from 1745, colleague to his brother. It was said that few equalled him 'in an easy, fluent, neat and elegant style'. He accompanied Robert Wallace* in an application to Parliament for an Act to set up the Widows and Orphans Fund.* He supported his brother William* against William Robertson* over the strict enforcement of patronage.* He was Principal Clerk (from 1746) and Moderator (1748) of the General Assembly, and Dean of the Chapel Royal*, 1765–85. Alexander Carlyle* described Wishart as 'the Tillotson of the Church of Scotland'.

FES I, 97, 136; H. Sefton, 'The Early Development of Moderatism in the Church of Scotland' (PhD, Glasgow University, 1962).

H. R. Sefton

Wishart, Robert (*d.* 1316), Bishop of Glasgow. He was a member of a prominent ecclesiastical family – his uncle was Bishop of St Andrews, and a cousin archdeacon of Lothian. He was elected Bishop of Glasgow in 1271 and consecrated in 1273. He was named as one of the guardians of Scotland on the death of Alexander III in 1286, and occupied a prominent place in public affairs thereafter; he was instrumental in negotiations with Edward I both before and after the death of the 'Maid of Norway' in 1290. For the most part he seems to have favoured the claims of Robert Bruce, Lord of Annandale, and his family, and as such counterbalanced the influence of William Fraser,* Bishop of St Andrews. During the years 1296–1306 he was frequently in rebellion against Edward I, made several submissions to him, and was harshly imprisoned 1297–1300. He seems to have been privy to the conspiracy of Robert Bruce* in 1306, and quickly absolved Bruce of the sacrilegious murder of John Comyn in February of that year. He was not present at Bruce's enthronement in March, but was apparently in the west awaiting Irish reinforcements for Bruce's cause; and by his preaching he encouraged many to join the king. He was captured by the English at Cupar in the summer of 1306, and kept in prison in England for eight years. He was released after Bannockburn (1314) as part of an exchange of prisoners and allowed to return to his diocese; he was by now very old and allegedly blind. He is buried in his cathedral at Glasgow, and a recumbent effigy in the crypt (not *in situ*) has been identified as his.

For his courage and consistent loyalty to the cause of Scottish independence, Robert Wishart emerges as one of the heroic figures of the Scottish struggle after 1286. Throughout a career spanning some forty-five years, he tenaciously maintained the view that national and ecclesiastical freedom were identical.

Some *acta* in *Glasgow Registrum*; E. L. G. Stones and G. G. Simpson, *Edward I and the Throne of Scotland* (O, 1978); Dowden, 306–9; *DNB* LXII, 255–6; and see bibliography for Robert I (the Bruce).

A. Macquarrie

Wishart (Wisheart), William (1660–1729), CofS minister, Principal of the University of Edinburgh and five times Moderator of the General Assembly (between 1706 and 1728). Educated at the Universities of Edinburgh (MA, 1680) and Utrecht, and subsequently imprisoned like his father before him for Covenanting* principles, he first ministered to a congregation gathered in South Leith under his father and was ordained there in 1688. He was translated to the Tron Church, Edinburgh, in 1707 and, in conjunction, was appointed Principal in 1716. His son George* succeeded him in the Tron and his son William,* in 1737, in the Principalship.

He published a variety of undistinguished sermons. His largest work, *Theologia, or Discourses of God* (2 vols, E, 1716) was, Wodrow reported (*Analecta*, E, 1843, IV, 61), 'reaconed a compend of Charnock on the Attributes'. This is an overstatement, though there is a noticeable resemblance at points. Wishart's ministry was held in considerable regard. Elizabeth West gives a favourable account of his preaching. He 'was zealous in his opposition to Mr [John] Simson's innovation' (Wodrow, *ibid.*; *see* Simson, John).

FES I, 136, 163; J. Warrick, *Moderators of the Church of Scotland* (E, 1913), 180–95.

D. C. Lachman

Wishart, William (*d.* 1753), Principal of Edinburgh University 1737–53. Eldest son of the preceding, he was educated in Edinburgh (MA, 1709), licensed in 1717 and appointed by the magistrates preacher in Skinners Close Chapel for three years. He was minister of Glasgow Tron 1724–30, then Scots Church (Founders' Hall), London 1730–7, Edinburgh (New Greyfriars) 1739–44 and (Tron, second charge) 1745–53. He had a significant influence on the theology of later eighteenth-century Scottish ministers as a result of his University teaching. Although his importance is perhaps greatest as a forerunner of Moderatism,* his stress on such concepts as divine benevolence as the key to the understanding of the divine nature and love did influence the Church as a whole, as did his promotion of the Enlightenment*-inspired conception of God as 'Universal Governor' at the head of a rational system. He espoused a sanguine view of human nature which limited the impact of the Fall on man. In 1737, on the basis of *A Sermon preached before the Society for Reformation of Manners in London* (L, 1732), he was charged with heresy* before the Presbytery of Edinburgh for alleged propagation of the ideas of Lord Shaftesbury, but eventually acquitted by the General Assembly of 1738. Despite suspicion of him by Evangelicals, he supported the 'Popular' party* on patronage,* notably in 1757 when he dissented from the resolution of the General Assembly censuring the Presbytery of Linlithgow in the Torphichen Case.* The social and political thought of many in the CofS owed much to Wishart, who also wrote perceptively on such issues as population growth, the rise of crime, and entrepreneurial activity. His thinking on liberty of conscience was increasingly accepted in the 1740s and 1750s. He was Moderator of the General Assembly in 1745.

Charity the End of the Commandment: or, Universal Love the Design of Christianity. A Sermon (L, 1731); *The Certain and Unchangeable Difference betwixt Moral Good and Evil* (L, 1732); *Discourses on Several Subjects* (L, 1753); *Public Virtue Recommended* (E, 1746).

FES I, 33, 140, III, 474–5, VII, 381, 442.

J. R. McIntosh

Witchcraft. The Witchcraft Act was passed in 1563, as part of a package whereby the government took responsibility for matters formerly dealt with by the pre-Reformation Church. It was short and to the point: practising witchcraft or consorting with witches was a capital crime. In 1735 it was repealed, along with the English Witchcraft Act. Between these dates around 1,500 women died as witches (not, as used to be thought, thousands), a number which (compared to *c.* 1,000 in England with its substantially larger population) puts Scotland among the leading witch-persecuting societies of early modern Europe – France, the German principalities, Switzerland and Poland. There were five great outbreaks, 1591–2, 1597, 1628–30, 1649 and 1661–2. Only after the last did the general pursuit of witches decline and the number of convictions fall; the last execution was that of Janet Horne in 1727 at Dornoch.

Witches certainly practised their arts in Scotland, but not only between 1563 and 1735. The wise woman with a knowledge of healing learned from her mother and transmitted to her daughter was not a new figure; and, even before 1563, the few known cases of witchcraft (such as at St Andrews in 1542) indicate that such skills were not always employed as 'white magic'. The change came when all magic, whether used for good or ill, was declared by authority to be black and diabolically inspired. Not surprisingly, however, witch-hunting was much more effective in the Lowlands. Apart from a few cases in the Highland/Lowland borders, the 'wise woman' survived unharmed in the Highlands. It was the Lowlands, especially Lothian and Fife, the eastern borders and the area round Aberdeen, which were repeatedly terrorized by Satan's creatures. Yet that practical consideration explains only the geographic limits of the persecution.

For the persecution itself there is no single explanation. The involvement of the scholar-king James VI* in the 1590–1 outbreak at North Berwick suggests an obvious reason for both panic and the development of the theory of the demonic pact. But neither hunt nor theory began with King James; and no king was necessary for the later great persecutions. Nor was it a peculiarly Calvinist phenomenon. The scene was set by Innocent VIII's bull against black magic in 1484 and the handbook of witchcraft (*Malleus Maleficarum*, the 'hammer of witches') provided by the Dominicans Jacob Sprenger and Heinrich Krämer in 1487; and Catholic France anticipated Protestant Scotland in witch-hunting. Certainly it was the Reformed Kirk which underwrote the Scottish persecution; its continual onslaught on the evil which stalked the earth was translated into outbursts of intensive hunting when the state provided the machinery to deal with the witches which Kirk Sessions* were all too willing to find. More generally, this was the age of deep religious and social dislocation, among élites and local communities alike. Traditional beliefs and forms of service were abruptly and dramatically altered; rituals and symbols of spiritual comfort were thrown, by Protestants and Catholics, on to the dungheap of 'superstition'; and the war between a vengeful God and his great enemy the Devil, both directly intervening in human lives, was hammered home from the pulpit. Meanwhile, the role-model of the godly and pious woman was superimposed on the traditional image of the emotionally irrational and sexually voracious female; the first was God's servant, the second an obvious target for the Devil. And the healing woman, practising 'magical arts', readily became the curser and practiser of *maleficium*, especially when in disturbed communities *maleficium* was indeed practised. 'Thou shalt not suffer a witch to live' had a long run. Only when the ruling élite began to question whether accused witches were actually consorting with the Devil, and then question the very existence of witchcraft, did local communities – give or take the odd lynching – follow suit, and the panic and the persecution die out.

C. J. Larner, *Enemies of God* (L, 1981); *id.*, *Witchcraft and Religion: the Politics of Popular Belief* (O, 1984); C. J. Larner, C. Hyde and H. McLachlan, *A Source Book of Scottish Witchcraft* (G, 1977); S. Clark, 'King James's *Daemonologie*', in S. Anglo (ed.), *The Damned Art* (L, 1977), 156–81; B. P. Levack, *The Witchhunt in Early Modern Europe* (NY, 1987); K. V. Thomas, *Religion and the Decline of Magic* (L, 1971).

J. Wormald

Witherspoon, John (1723–94), evangelical CofS minister and later president of the College of New Jersey (now Princeton University) and signer of the Declaration of Independence. He was born in the manse of Yester in Haddingtonshire, according to some traditions a descendant through his mother of John Knox. He attended Edinburgh University (MA, 1739), where he had as classmates John Erskine* and Moderates* such as William Robertson,* Alexander Carlyle,* Hugh Blair* and John Home,* all later prominent leaders in Church and society. He was ordained to Beith in Ayrshire in 1745, which prospered under his preaching.

In 1753 Witherspoon attacked the Moderate party of the CofS by an anonymous satire, *Ecclesiastical Characteristics*, which effectively made fun of the cultured 'nature religion' of the ruling party which tended towards deism* and avoided traditional doctrines of sin and grace. He was called to the large Leigh Kirk in Paisley in 1757, where he became a leader of the evangelical* party of the Church, opposing Moderate policies, particularly the excesses of patronage*. Not fearful of controversy, he wrote vehemently against stage plays and was sued for libel for preaching against the irreverent behaviour of a drunken lawyer.

The College of New Jersey called him as its sixth president (following Jonathan Edwards* and Samuel Davies) in 1768. He travelled to raise funds for the needy institution and introduced the Scottish lecture system in place of the old recitation method based on examining students in set texts. He had an empirical approach in line with Scottish common-sense Realism (*see* Scottish Realism), which assumes direct perception of objects, against both idealism and scepticism. Witherspoon taught a moral philosophy which emphasized representative government, checks and balances and constitutional restraints. He taught one future US President (James Madison, architect of the Constitution), ten cabinet members, twelve state governors, sixty congressmen and three Supreme Court Justices. Siding with America during the War of Independence, he was elected to the continental congress in Philadelphia, and was the only minister signing the Declaration of Independence. From 1776 to 1782 he served in Congress, and helped negotiate an alliance with France. He encouraged economic free enterprise and a hard money standard.

Though more a man of action than a theologian, his *Practical Treatise on Regeneration* (L, 1764) and his *Essay on Justification* (L, 1756) have been frequently reprinted. He preached at the first General Assembly of the Presbyterian Church in America at Philadelphia in 1789 and encouraged its adoption of the Westminster* Standards (with minor modifications concerning the civil magistrate).

Collected Works, ed. A. Green, 4 vols (NY, 1800–1); 9 vols (E, 1804–5).

A. Green, *The Life of the Revd John Witherspoon* (Princeton, 1973); V. L. Collins, *President John Witherspoon: A Biography*, 2 vols (Princeton, 1925); D. W. Woods, *John Witherspoon* (Chicago, 1906); M. L. L. Stohlman, *John Witherspoon, Parson, Politician, Patriot* (Philadelphia, 1976); A. L. Drummond, 'Witherspoon of Gifford and American Presbyterianism' in *RSCHS* 12 (1958), 185–201; G. L. Tait, 'John Witherspoon, American Intellectual Leader', *Journal of Religious Studies* 12 (1986), 1–13.

D. F. Kelly

Witness, The. Two journals bore this title. The first was a bi-weekly newspaper established in 1840 at the height of the Ten Years' Conflict* to further the evangelical, Non-Intrusionist* cause, at a time when (with some exceptions such as the *Scottish Guardian*, founded in 1832) the Scottish press roundly supported the Moderates*. *The Witness* was launched and partly financed by a group of leading Evangelicals, including Robert Candlish,* published by John Johnstone and Robert Fairly, and edited by Hugh Miller,* who for months produced it almost single-handed, and contributed extensively to its columns.

While the main objective of *The Witness* was initially to publicize and promote the cause of the evangelical party within the CofS and later of the fledgling FC* – an objective which its racy, crusading style achieved with massive effectiveness – it was never merely a religious newspaper. Miller, who enjoyed almost complete editorial autonomy, dealt freely with political, educational and international issues from a Liberal standpoint in his powerful, closely-reasoned editorials. The circulation figures emphasize its impact: 600 in 1840, 1,800 by late 1841, reaching a peak of 3,657 and temporarily outselling the rival *Scotsman*.

After 1844, Miller survived attempts to undermine his independence, assuming financial responsibility for *The Witness*, and continuing to uphold FC principles as he saw them. After his death, circulation declined under various editors, despite a brief (and disastrous) attempt at daily publication. *The Witness* faced a crisis of identity, having outlived both the situation which gave it birth, and the founder-editor in whose image it was fashioned, and went out with a whimper in February 1864.

The second *Witness*, one of the periodicals springing from the Brethren* movement in Scotland, assumed that title in 1887, although its antecedents date back to 1870. Issued in Glasgow by George Turner until 1893, it then passed to Pickering* and Inglis, who remained its publishers until its demise in 1980.

On the first *Witness*: J. W. Scott, 'A Bibliography of Edinburgh Periodical Literature', *Scottish Notes and Queries* (August 1893), 35–7; R. M. W. Cowan, *The Newspaper in Scotland* (G, 1946).

On the second *Witness*: J. A. H. Dempster, 'Aspects of Brethren Publishing Enterprise in late Nineteenth-Century Scotland', *Publishing History*, 20 (1986), 61–101.

J. A. H. Dempster

Wodrow, Robert (1679–1734), minister, church historian and antiquary. The youngest son of James Wodrow, he was born while his father was being hunted for keeping conventicles.* He studied at Glasgow University (MA, 1697); while a student of divinity there (under his father, who served as Professor of Divinity from 1692 to his death in 1707 and was influential in shaping the thought of some 900 students; *FES* VII, 399–400), he served for four years as librarian to the college. In this position he was able to begin to exercise the wide range of interests which he pursued throughout his life. After serving as chaplain to Sir John Maxwell of Nether-Pollock, one of the Senators of the College of Justice, he was licensed and called to Eastwood (near Paisley), where Sir John lived. Declining calls to other charges (Glasgow, and Stirling twice), he served in Eastwood the rest of his life.

Although faithful in his parochial duties, the lighter demands of a small parish enabled him to carry on the researches which were his delight. He was interested in the natural history of Scotland and frequently visited Edinburgh to examine records and documents. He attended meetings of Presbytery, Synod and General Assembly regularly, the last even when not a commissioner, and took considerable interest in the proceedings. He was in the habit of sending regular letters to his wife, detailing and analysing the proceedings; the letters were passed on and were perhaps of more interest to Sir John. He carried on an extensive correspondence, begun in his youth, both at home and abroad, including among his correspondents Cotton Mather and Benjamin Colman in New England. A large selection, edited by The younger Thomas M'Crie* (*The Correspondence of the Rev. Robert Wodrow*, 3 vols, E, 1842–3) was published from the larger MS collection in the Advocates' Library (now in the NLS); it sheds much light on the events of the time. Equally candid and informative is a collection amassed by Wodrow for his own use, edited for the Maitland Club: *Analecta: or Materials for a History of Remarkable Providences; mostly relating to Scotch Ministers and Christians* (4 vols, E, 1843).

Although always an interested observer, sometimes more so than many participants, as was the case with the Marrow Controversy,* Wodrow took an active part in the controversies of his day. He refused to sign the Oath of Abjuration,* remained neutral in the first process against Professor John Simson* ('His being my father's successor makes me decline dipping into that affair', *Correspondence*, II, 158), but opposed him in the second. He opposed patronage,* but was willing to take part in the drawing up of the Act of the 1731 Assembly on Planting Vacant Churches, which did not require the consent of the people and did not guard against intrusion against their will.

Wodrow's great work was *The History of the Sufferings of the Church of Scotland from the Restoration to the Revolution*, 2 vols (E, 1721–2; 2nd edition, ed. Robert Burns, 4 vols, G, 1828). The result of years of research, it was dedicated to George I, which elicited a disbursement of £105 sterling from the royal purse. Although not without numerous critics, some exceedingly bitter ('facts', as Wodrow said in one of his letters, 'are ill-natured things' and the truth was unwelcome to many), Wodrow's history is essentially a reliable account and Wodrow himself, in Andrew Lang's words, 'a candid, as well as an industrius historian' (cf. W. J. Couper, 'Robert Wodrow and His Critics', *RSCHS* 5 (1935), 238–50). D. H. Fleming* said: 'Its reliability and honesty will not be questioned by anyone who has examined the sources from which it is drawn' (*Critical Reviews*, L, 1912, 307).

Wodrow intended, at the solicitation of friends, to write a more comprehensive history of the Church in Scotland and to that end began to collect material. *The Collections upon the Lives of the Reformers and Most Eminent Ministers of the Church of Scotland*, 3 vols (G, 1834–48) and *Selections from Wodrow's Biographical Collection: Divines of the North-East of Scotland* (A, 1890) represent a considerable portion of his endeavours to this end prior to his death. A substantial collection of MS material, written or gathered by Wodrow, is located in the NLS.

FES III, 135–6; *DNB* LXII, 280–1; additional volume issued by the SHS as *Early Letters of Robert Wodrow, 1698–1709*, ed. L. W. Sharp (E, 1937).

D. C. Lachman

Wodrow Society, 'for the publication of the works of the fathers and early writers of the Reformed Church of Scotland'. Instituted in May 1841, and named after the early eighteenth-century CofS historian and antiquary, Robert Wodrow,* by June 1845 the Society had something over 2,000 members. But by 1849 David Laing* found it necessary to apologize for having to 'avoid all unnecessary expense' in producing the index volume of David Calderwood's* *History* due to 'the state of the funds' of the Society. Although a final volume was published in 1850, the Society was unable to complete its other projects, including the final four volumes of Knox (published later by T. G. Stevenson), a further volume of biographies and further volumes of miscellaneous pieces. The following volumes were published, in Edinburgh, by the Society: John Row, *The History of the Kirk of Scotland, ... 1558 ... 1637*, ed. D. Laing, 1842; *The Autobiography and Diary of Mr James Melvill*, ed. R. Pitcairn, 1842; *The Correspondence of the Rev. Robert Wodrow*, ed. T. M'Crie, 3 vols, 1842–3; David Calderwood, *The History of the Kirk of Scotland*, ed. T. Thomson, 8 vols, 1842–9; *Sermons by The Rev. Robert Bruce ... with Collections for his life* [by] Robert Wodrow, ed. W. Cunningham, 1843; *The Miscellany* Vol. I, ed. D. Laing, 1844; *Select Works of Robert Rollock*, ed. W. M. Gunn, 2 vols, 1849–4; *Select Biographies*, ed. W. K. Tweedie, 2 vols, 1845–7; W. Scot, *An Apologetical Narration* [and] John Forbes, *Certain Records*, ed. D. Laing, 1846; *The Life of Mr Robert Blair*, ed. T. M'Crie, 1848; Charles Ferme, *A Logical Analysis of ... Romans*, transl. W. Skene, [and] Andrew Melville, *Commentarius in ... Romanos*, ed. W. L. Alexander, 1850; *The Works of John Knox*, ed. D. Laing, 2 vols, 1846.

Laws and List of the Members... (E, 1842); C. S. Terry, *A Catalogue of the Publications of Scottish Historical ... Societies* (G, 1909), 196–9.

D. C. Lachman

Woman's Guild, the organization that unites the women of the CofS. It was founded in 1887 by the General Assembly on the initiative of A. H. Charteris,* then Professor of Biblical Criticism in the University of Edinburgh. Women* were already widely involved in service for the Church and Charteris believed there was 'need to develop and organize them as an official working unit within the Church'. Within ten years there were 400 branches with a membership of 29,000. In the 1950s this peaked at over 160,000, but at the time of the Guild Centenary in 1987 it had dropped to around 80,000, which still made it the largest voluntary organization for women in Scotland.

From the Young Women's Groups which the Guild formed in the 1950s emerged its other section – Young Woman's Groups. With Guild branches these Groups share the continuing aim of the Guild – 'to unite the women of the Church in the dedication of their lives to the Lord Jesus Christ through Worship, Fellowship and Service' – and its associated motto – 'Whose I am and Whom I serve'. The result is that women of all ages in congregations throughout Scotland, the Presbytery of England and some expatriate congregations, meet regularly for Christian worship, fellowship and service, and to develop Christian faith, share in the wider Church and face contemporary issues from a Christian perspective. Leadership training is offered and a wide variety of resource material is made available.

Members are invited to support a special project annually for an area of work suggested by one of the Boards of the Church, for which other funds do not exist. Previous projects have included the provision of an irrigation system for a teacher training college in Zambia, funding for work among young drug-addicted prostitutes, and supporting research and development work on sharing Christian faith with mentally handicapped people.

Members are encouraged to build local programmes around an annual theme, for which a guide is published, and to include opportunity for members to consider the annual discussion topic which seeks to develop Christian perspectives on topical issues. Recent topics have included Christian lifestyle, the debt crisis and media awareness.

Through its delegate system the Guild has close links with, and is involved in, the work of several of the Boards of the Church. It is represented also on various other Church and ecumenical committees and on a number of outside organizations, including the government-sponsored Women's National Commission.

The Guild reports annually to the General Assembly,* which approves its constitution (published as part of the *Guild Handbook*; cf. Cox 762–5, for 1975 constitution).

In all its activities the Guild tries to present its members with challenges: of Christ's authority in its wholeness; of the Guild's aim, which may not always be reflected in its practice; of the need to embrace a wide age-range of women in the organization and to make it an important factor in the outreach and growth of congregations; and to pray – as a vital part of the Guild's commitment. Where these challenges are being seriously addressed there are signs of new life and growth. Despite tendencies for some branches to provide little more than social activities, the Guild remains by far the most significant body in the CofS apart from the Church courts.

L. M. Paterson

Women in Highland Churches. Women have played a very important role in the life of Highland* churches since the Middle Ages. In the pre-Reformation period there were several nunneries* in the Hebrides. Reginald, son of the Somerled, 'king of Argyll', founded a house of Augustinian* canonesses at Iona* about 1203, and it appears to have been occupied continuously until at least the time of the Reformation.* Gaelic* place names preserve record of a nunnery (Taigh nan Cailleachan Dubha, 'The House of the Black-robed, Veiled Women') at Uig in Lewis and at Nunton (Baile nan Cailleach, 'The Township of the Nuns') in South Uist. Well-to-do Highland ladies sometimes took the veil; for example, Euphemia, heiress to the earldom of Ross, resigned her title in 1415 and apparently entered a nunnery thereafter.

Specific examples of female devotion are difficult to trace in the Highlands in the years immediately following the Reformation, but there is some later evidence that it was maintained within both the RC and Protestant Churches. Women, as the custodians of hearth and home, combined devotion with practical application in hymns and prayers, some of which have survived. Sìleas MacDonald, known in Gaelic as *Sìleas na Ceapaich* ('Sìleas of Keppoch'), composed a number of hymns* within the RC tradition *c.*1700 (Colm Ó Baoill, ed., *Bàrdachd Shilis*

WOMEN IN HIGHLAND CHURCHES

na Ceapaich, E, 1972). After 1750 there is clear evidence of a strong vein of Gaelic hymnology* composed by women associated with the evangelical movement. One of its earliest exponents was Mrs Mary Clark (née MacPherson), Bean Torra Dhamh ('The Wife from Torr Dhamh'), from Badenoch. Her hymn, *M'anam imich thusa sàmhach* ('My soul, walk thou in quietness') was published as a broadside in 1785 (A. MacRae, ed., *Mary MacPherson*, G, n.d., 11, 49–51). The nineteenth century produced several important female composers, including Mary MacDonald* from Mull, and the contribution of women to Gaelic hymnology, especially within the Protestant churches, continues to the present (e.g. in the compositions of Catherine MacDonald, Staffin, Skye: see her book, *Na Bannan Gràidh* ('The Bonds of Love'), Stornoway, 1987).

Within Highland Evangelicalism there was also a strong tradition of female spirituality which was much respected as a source of wise counsel. 'The women', although unrecognized as an 'order' like 'The Men',* were among those who shared 'the secret of the Lord'. Most districts preserve records of women who enjoyed a particularly close relationship with God, had facility in pithy spiritual utterance and penetrated the mysteries of providence. Of these 'elect ladies', the best known is Mrs Peggy MacKay (*d.* 1841) of Sutherland, celebrated as *Bean a' Chreidimh Mhòir* ('The Woman of the Great Faith'), whose reply to an admirer of her 'great faith' is still quoted: 'I am merely the woman of the little faith in the great God.'

Highland women have sometimes exercised roles of spiritual leadership within their communities. In west-coast communities, women would conduct informal worship (e.g., in the home and the wider community) while menfolk were absent at the fishing and at seasonal labour in the Lowlands. The fishing, and especially the need for Biblewomen to minister to fishergirls (*see* Fisherfolk, Missions to), also provided opportunities for female leadership to emerge. For long-term female ministry, however, the most important channel has probably been the Faith Mission,* which has allowed Highland and other women to serve as itinerant preachers and evangelists.

Only very occasionally and exceptionally have Highland women become the pastors of churches. Miss Mary Flora MacArthur (*d.* 1981), a native of Tiree, acted as pastor (without formal ordination) in the Baptist* churches in Tobermory (1938–41) and Colonsay (1945–7). Her role was probably a reflection of the decline in the number of male candidates for Baptist charges in the Highlands and Islands, but it is noteworthy that she also served as a missionary with the Baptist Home Missionary Society for Scotland,* being stationed at Eday and Sanday in Orkney (1943–5). Formally recognized ministry by women in Highland churches has been encouraged only within Congregationalism* and the CofS, and has been implemented mainly in southern districts (*e.g.*, in Oban and Islay). In August 1992, Mairi Byers, a Gaelic speaker, was inducted to the CofS charge in the island of Jura, Argyll. The appointment of women as elders or deacons in the Highlands follows a broadly similar pattern.

A. Macquarrie, *Iona through the Ages* (Coll, 1983), 25–6; R. Nicholson, *Scotland: The Latter Middle Ages* (E, 1974); M. Campbell, *Gleanings of Highland Harvest* (²Tain, 1989), 43–52; A. Auld, *Ministers and Men of the Far North* (Wick, 1868), 281–4.

D. E. Meek

Women in Presbyterian Churches. Prior to the Scottish Reformation, the relationship of women to the Church took various forms. Many women found value and purpose in a conventual life – living in female communities and exercising intellectual, spiritual and practical gifts (*see* Nunneries). For most ordinary women that was not an option. The Church's theology, while acknowledging the necessity of marriage for procreation, also emphasized the 'natural' inferiority and sinfulness of women.

Outside RC orthodoxy, women seem to have been prominent among the Lollards,* who opposed the clericalism and privilege of the institutional Church. According to John Knox,* the sect was particularly strong in Ayrshire, and women were among the thirty 'Lollards of Kyle' who were brought before James IV in 1494 on charges of heresy.

Many women were valued and consulted for their healing gifts and practical wisdom, and acted, if not in direct opposition to the Church, certainly outside its jurisdiction. St Margaret* was an outstanding exception.

THE REFORMATION. When the Scottish Reformers challenged and broke the control exercised by the Roman Church, preaching the doctrine of the priesthood of all believers, the possibility for women of equal status in this life, as well as its promise for the life to come, might have seemed nearer. But the new society which Knox envisaged for Scotland denied women any status in its shaping (but see D. P. Thomson, *Women of the Scottish Church*, Perth, 1975, chs 1–2). They were no longer allowed the opportunity to join religious orders and societies. The prescribed role within the new dispensation was largely domestic and subservient – as obedient wife and mother. Knox himself condemned the rule and authority of women in Church and nation in no uncertain terms. By nature they were 'weak, frail, impatient, feeble and foolish, and experience hath declared them to be unconstant, variable, cruel and lacking the spirit of counsel and regiment' (*The First Blast of the Trumpet Against the Monstrous Regiment of Women*, 1558). Moreover, he declared unequivocally: 'Hereof it is plain – that the administration of the grace of God is denied to all women' (*ibid.*).

In Protestant Scotland, ecclesiastical courts* – and Kirk Sessions* in particular – assumed the right to legislate on the social and sexual lives of the people, including women. Although never universally successful in achieving its end, Kirk discipline* had some truly unfortunate consequences (*e.g.* the practice of infanticide of illegitimate children).

COVENANTING WOMEN. However, Scottish women also found opportunities to affirm their religious principles and personal dignity within Presbyterianism. The Covenanting* movement of the seventeenth century was well supported by women. Indeed, some of their tactics (as reported in J. Anderson, *Ladies of the Covenant*, G, 1857) suggest a determined female guerrilla war against the imposition of episcopacy! Women were so persistent in their opposition that the government decreed that husbands would be held responsible for the religious sentiments and activities of their wives. This attempt at control seems to have been a failure. A man complained to the Privy Council in 1666: 'Many husbands here who yield to the full length are punished by fining, cess and quarter, for their wives' non-obedience, and ye know, Sir, that is hard. There are many wives who will not be commanded by their husbands in lesser things than this' (*ibid*., xxvi).

Covenanting ranks included numerous well-educated, faithful and resolute women, many of whom became martyrs: 'Under examination, Helen Campbell displayed a dignity of bearing and a superior intelligence which struck her adversaries with conviction, and the judges with admiration... Her uncompromising fortitude stands favourably contrasted with the timidity of most men brought before the commissioners' (*ibid*.). (*See also* Wigtown Martyrs.)

In the seventeenth and eighteenth centuries – and beyond – women fulfilled the traditional supportive roles ascribed to them as daughter, sister, wife or mother. Although the institutions, structures and official work of the Presbyterian Churches were the exclusive province of men, women often showed independence of mind and spirit and took responsibility not only for their own salvation but also exercised considerable influence. Ebenezer Erskine,* for example, owed much to his wife, Alison Turpie, for his own 'acquaintance with the power and comfort of religion' (*The Life and Diary of ... Ebenezer Erskine*, ed. Donald Fraser, E, 1831, 63). He described her life with him as 'most savoury, edifying and helpful' and her 'judgment in religion' as being of 'a great reach ... beyond many women ...' (288, 286). Alison Turpie's theological literacy and personal convictions were no doubt shared by many more Presbyterian women.

Those whose names have been recorded, by virtue of their membership of the aristocracy and their achievements, include Lady Glenorchy,* who founded new churches, chose ministers, and drew up their rules, Lady Maxwell* and Lady Leven, who knew John Wesley* and George Whitefield* and were involved in charitable and philanthropic activities. Other women were at the centre of charismatic offshoots of Scottish Presbyterianism (*see* Buchanites; Campbell, Isabella and Mary).

VICTORIAN WOMAN. During the reign of Victoria, in Scotland as elsewhere in Protestant Christendom the notion that women and men, by virtue of their radical differences, had rigidly separate spheres of activity became a basic tenet. Christians utilized arguments from nature and Scripture to create a veritable cult of true womanhood, for 'Had not reason and revelation both affirmed that woman's one duty in the world was to efface herself, so far as any other sphere of action is concerned than that circumscribed by the four walls of her home?' (J. Corbett, in *UP Magazine* 11, 1894, 70).

However, as the nineteenth century progressed, women were increasingly encouraged to believe that their own 'feminine' characteristics were the very ones required to make the grimy world a godly place. They were not simply meekly subordinate, passive providers of solace and bearers of offspring: they were individuals with a special and sacred vocation: 'If you are a pure, chaste, noble Christian woman, you will be a blessed central power in the household, mighty to raise all around you ... If you are a base, impure, unchaste, ungodly woman, your power will be equally great to pollute and pull down to the level of your own degradation ... Cultivate and perfect your womanhood ... to brighten and bless our homes' ('A Word to the Town-Servant Women', *LW* 12, 1890, 51–2). Presbyterian men and women began to make the connection between the innate (as they thought) female inclination towards moral righteousness and religion, and the call to Christianize society both at home and abroad in the mission fields (*see* Women and Scottish Presbyterian Missions). The 'blessed power' of women was to be exerted in an entirely 'womanly' extension of domestic virtues into Church and world.

The development of women's work was one of the most significant and enduring factors in Church life of the period. From tentative beginnings women organized and became directly involved in philanthropic work at home and in the mission fields. Up to the 1880s women were increasingly engaged in three kinds of activity:

(i) Spare-time involvement in a range of congregational and parish societies. A. H. Charteris* noted, on the basis of long experience and observation, that 'When one looks closely at the work done by a congregation in aid of the minister, women obviously get most of it to do ... The Sunday School ... The Clothing Society and Mothers' Meeting ... The District-visiting – hardest, most trying, but most effective of all mission agencies – is as a rule entirely done by the minister and his "lady visitors"' (*LW* 6, 1884, 33).

(ii) Full-time employment of Bible-women and female missionaries. In 1862, the *CSHFMR* (n.s. 1, 27) declared that '"Bible women, in the homes of the poor", have become an important auxiliary to the parish minister', and reported on the Dundee East Church Female Domestic Mission, established in 1859 'to reach, through means of a female missionary, a class of destitute and degraded females by the influence of religion'.

(iii) Associations organized within towns and cities, and nationally, for various philanthropic, educational and religious purposes, and connected in some way with the Churches. From the 1830s, societies for foreign and Jewish missions* were paralleled by those for, *e.g.*, Gaelic Schools,* Female Industrial Schools, missions to RCs, and for the abolition of slavery. By and large, these associations were auxiliary, fund-raising bodies. They did have committees and prayer meetings, but they were always ultimately under male supervision and direction.

Until the 1880s, women's work was widespread, but far from being universally condoned. Male disapproval was common, as was female apathy. But by the 1870s the upsurge of the movement for women's rights in many areas of life was beginning to make an impact on the Church: 'In all other departments of work the conviction is gaining ground that men and women were meant to stand side by side – that while they have different and distinct qualifications, both are equally needed for the work to be done in God's world. Are our churches to be the last to say that woman's work, as well as man's, should enter in their calculation? Is there no place for their *organized* Christian service unless they retire into sisterhoods and convents, or force their way into the pulpit?' (*CSHMFR* n.s. 10, 1877, 424).

NEW STRUCTURES. In the late nineteenth and early twentieth centuries, the Presbyterian Churches implemented schemes whereby women's work was indeed organized and co-ordinated within their national structures. In 1887, the CofS Woman's Guild,* including the revived order of Deaconesses (*see* Diaconate), was established. In 1894 the CofS Women's Association for Home Mission was formed 'to provide the means requisite for the supply of trained female missionaries to go down to the slums of our cities, to labour in the crowded mining districts' (*CSHFMR* n.s. 19, 1893, 3). From 1904 women were also involved in CofS Social Work.

In 1901, the new UFC instigated the Women's Home Mission, of which it was claimed that 'This is no new creation. It is only sought to organize work already in existence, to give it greater visibility, and to throw upon the women workers of the Church a greater sense of responsibility towards Home Mission work' (*PGAUFCS 1901*, 155).

All these organizations sought to utilize the skills, enthusiasm, time and means of women at local, Presbyterial and national levels. Women worked full-time as Deaconesses, Parish Sisters and Church Sisters. They ran hospitals, training institutions, rescue homes and orphanages. They did pioneering mission and healing work in the slums. They led meetings and worship, and travelled all over Scotland to encourage other women to work for the Church. Women like Katharine Davidson,* Alice Maxwell,* and Mary Lamond* gave their services gratuitously. At local level, women engaged voluntarily in an amazing range of activities – Sunday schools, Bible classes, Bands of Hope (*see* Temperance Movement), Girls' Guildry*, Mothers' Meetings, visitation schemes, study circles, New Year Temperance Cafés, sewing bees, bazaars and endless fund-raising. They were responding to a new message – one which seemed to contradict what the Church had been preaching for centuries. 'That a woman should never be seen out of her own house was ... a heathen idea; that a woman should be a fellow-worker with Christ Himself and with His apostles and ministers, is the teaching of the New Testament' (*LW* 18, 1896, 69).

Even so, the advent of women workers in the Presbyterian Churches hardly signalled a new era of equality and power within Church structures. The rhetoric of separate spheres exalted the 'female' qualities, and declared that Christian women were 'angels of peace, whose unique and glorious mission is to elevate and purify and save'. In doing so, it effectively denied women the possibility that they could exercise any of the peculiarly 'male' offices of the Church. Miss Martin, editor of the *LW WG Supplement*, was clear about this: 'It would seem that Christ from the very beginning intended a definite place in the Christian Church to be accorded to woman, a ministry of service to the poor, the suffering, the dying, and to the children, in which her gentler nature will supply the elements of sympathy and tenderness which would be lacking in man's service. Woman's place in Church, then, is clearly intended to *supplement*, never to *supplant* man's' (*LW Guild Supplement* 20, 1906, 73).

Women were the indispensable work force of every congregation; the most loyal worshippers; the most enthusiastic fund-raisers. Their efforts were regarded as increasingly vital as the Church struggled to confront and overcome its isolation from, and apparent irrelevance to, the poor. But they had no official participation in the courts and decision-making of the Church.

WOMEN'S CHURCH RIGHTS. Nevertheless, the growth of women's work and organizations opened up new possibilities for women of talent and resourcefulness. And it unleashed, especially in the second and third decades of the twentieth century, the frustration and grievances of a significant minority, who began (in parallel with the height of the women's suffrage* movement) to assert their right to responsibility within Church structures. A leading article in the April 1914 edition (n.s. 160) of the *UFC Missionary Record* stated that 'The claim of women is beginning to make itself felt within the Church. Many are restless and dissatisfied with their position ... They have hitherto been content to do what might be called the drudgery of Church work ... But apparently the time is coming when they will no longer be satisfied to do this work, fine as it is, without some ampler responsibility than they have at present ... The assumption is that they will wish some sort of say in the government of the Church' (151–2).

In fact the issue of women's rights was exercising the Secession Church as early as 1736, when it was declared that office-bearers were to be chosen by the call and consent of the majority of communicant members. But when pressed as to whether this gave women the right of call, it was explained that women were not sustained as electors. That privilege was reserved for male heads of families, while 'wives and children might take part therein by influencing with religious and rational arguments their husbands and fathers' (Small I, 711–6). From the 1747 Breach (*see* Burgess Oath) till the 1820 Union the Burghers (*see* Associate Synod) allowed the female vote, while the Antiburghers (*see* General Associate Synod) did not. After 1820 the right of women to vote became the general practice, although some ministers continued to object. J. Smith of Whithorn (*ibid*., II, 10), in 1821, craved to have it recorded that 'He could not help expressing his disapprobation of female members ... being admitted to vote and subscribe a call, it being in his opinion contrary to the appointed rule, as well as to the law of nature manifested in the constitution of human society' (*ibid*., I, 715).

At the first General Assembly of the FC* in October 1843 the same question was raised. Opponents of female voters claimed that the innovation would take woman away from her proper sphere; that 'she must be protected from the hazards of public debate and collision'; that 'ungodly and flippant women would elect ministers, and a silly sentimentality, a drawing room theology, would come to fill our pulpits'. But women had supporters too: 'They have shown throughout [the Disruption] more power and vigour and steadfastness in maintaining our principles. I say that we owe much to the powerful agency of our female adherents' (see *PGAFCS October 1843*, 136–44). The right to vote in a call was conceded to women. In the UPC, women were entitled to serve on boards of management.

In the twentieth century this process continued. In 1914 the General Assembly of the UFC appointed a special committee on 'the Recognition of the Place of Women in the Church's Life and Work'. As a result, the office of Church Sister was regularized, and provision made for the co-option to certain General Assembly committees of women to a maximum of a sixth of their membership. More significant was the debate about the proposal to ordain women as deacons (a managerial rather than ruling or pastoral office). Opponents declared their unwillingness, on grounds of Scripture and tradition, to accept the ordination of women. A. R. MacEwen,* who left the Moderator's chair to contribute to the 1915 debate, disputed the validity of these grounds: 'Let us thank God that the position of women is not what it was in New Testament times. Dr Henderson is quite right in saying that the Reformers gave women no place in Church life ... (They) held to the old domineering idea of the authority of males. But in this they were quite wrong, and it is fantastic to appeal to them as arbiters' (cf. *PGAUFCS 1915*, 68–9, 79–80).

Although under the Barrier Act* both Presbyteries and Kirk Sessions gave majority support to the proposal, the UFC eventually (in 1919) agreed to enact an overture* that the office of deacon should be tenable either by men ordained for life or by men and women appointed for three years, thus sidestepping the controversy about the ordination of women.

The issue would not disappear. Years of war work and wages, and the prospect of enfranchisement, had given women a new sense of power, and the Churches were beginning to realize that they might have to fight to hold on to them. As the *UF Record* of May 1918 (n.s. 205) observed, 'Having tested and proved their capabilities, they will continue to seek every opportunity for employing whatever talents they possess in the various branches of public labour ... The difficulty may be that many of the finest women, with special aptitude for the work, may be lost to Church service because of the demand elsewhere for competent and well-paid workers' (79–80).

In 1926, an effort was made to open all offices of the UFC to women, to meet the aspirations of missionaries and others who were now studying theology. Although G. A. F. Knight (*FUFCS* 216) berated his colleagues for their 'curious lack of appreciation of the significance of the revolution of thought that Jesus Christ had produced on this subject', the UFC Assembly debate remained on the level of discussing whether 'admission of women to the ministry ... would discourage a certain class of men of a virile type from entering the profession' (*PGAUFCS 1926*, 233–4; *Proceedings and Debates ... 1926*, 224–30), and it was decided that the time was not opportune to consider the matter further.

FIRST ORDINATIONS. In 1929, the ordination of the first UFC woman minister in a mainstream denomination was recognized by the Congregational Union (*see* Findlay, Vera). The small minority of the UFC who refused to accept union with the CofS passed an Act at the first General Assembly of the continuing UFC, that 'Any member of the Church in full communion shall be eligible to hold any office within the UFC.' Elizabeth Barr* and Edith Martin were the first women to be ordained, and in 1960, Barr became the first female Moderator of any British Presbyterian Church.

In the reunited CofS, women could be members of Committees of Management (ex-UP); of Congregational Boards (ex-UF); and members of ex-FC Deacons Courts, only where deacons were appointed without ordination. In 1930, there were sixty-two deaconesses and around 100 Church Sisters. There were 1,176 branches of the Women's Guild, with around 68,000 members. Twenty-eight assembly committees had a combined membership of 1,752, of which 160 were women. In Foreign Mission, 510 out of 788 agents (including wives) were women. The feminization of the Church was notable, measured largely in terms of work done, not status bestowed.

In 1931 the first of a series of attempts was made to give women official equality. The Marchioness of Aberdeen* and 335 others petitioned the General Assembly in these terms: '[We] believe that the continued exclusion of women from [ordination to the ministry, the eldership, and the diaconate] is contrary to the mind and teaching of Christ, and that it limits the operation of the Spirit of God. [We] are convinced that women no less than men are called to the ministry of the Church, and that the Church is the poorer by reason of women being debarred from the ministry ...' They entreated the assembly not to discourage those who heard this call, and placed their petition for the privilege of full service to the Church in the assembly's hands (*APCS 1931*, 63–4).

As a result of this plea, a special committee recommended that women should be admitted to the diaconate* and eldership* on the same terms as men but not to the ministry of Word and sacrament. In fact, under the Barrier Act,* only admission to the diaconate was enacted, in 1935. Other discussions took place concerning the constitution of the Women's Guild and the Order of Deaconesses, but the next significant recommendation about the role of women was made by the Baillie Commission* in 1943, based on concern for the efficiency of the Church. It called for the ordination of women as elders. The majority of Presbyteries voted in favour, but most unusually the 1945 Assembly refused to convert the overture into law. Consultation with Kirk Sessions and congregations led to a reversal of the proposal.

In 1946 John White* asked the Assembly to consider a scheme whereby women could have a definite place on the courts of the Church without raising doctrinal questions about ordination. His suggestion was defeated.

In 1949 it was decided to amalgamate Church Sisters with the Order of Deaconesses, and in 1956 that suitably trained deaconesses should be licensed as preachers. However, it was not until 1990 that an Act was passed to enable deaconesses to become members of Presbyteries and other Church courts.

In 1957 the Assembly received a further overture anent women in the eldership, as the result of which a Committee on the Place of Women in the Church was appointed. It reported in 1959 and 1960, and the whole issue was passed on to the Panel on Doctrine when it was formed in 1962. Because there had been an indecisive vote on the question of women elders, the panel asked for permission to widen its remit, to include, yet again, the wider question of women in the Church.

In 1963, Mary Lusk (Levison*), a deaconess and divinity graduate, petitioned the Assembly on the grounds that her appointment as assistant chaplain at Edinburgh University constituted a call to the ordained ministry: '... and humbly begs that the Church will ... test her call, and if satisfied proceed to make possible her ordination' (*APCS 1963*, 103). After further reports, and consultation with Presbyteries, women were admitted to the eldership in 1966. In 1967 a report dealing solely with the theological questions raised by the issue of female ordinations was sent to Presbyteries, and in 1968, a law was enacted to allow the ordination of women to the ministry of Word and sacrament on the same terms as men.

Although all offices of the CofS are now open to both women and men, the decision-making bodies are still dominated by men. For example, in 1986–7 Glasgow Presbytery had a membership of 462. Of that number, forty-five were women (six ministers and thirty-nine elders). At the 1990 General Assembly about 15 per cent of commissioners were women. On committees women are also in a small minority, though centrally appointed members maintain a balance between women and men. However, in 1990 more than 50 per cent of all newly ordained elders in congregations were women.

ATTITUDES. Within Scottish Presbyterianism, over the past hundred years, attitudes towards the greater participation of women have varied widely. On the one hand, there are those, both male and female, who hold that women are forbidden by Scripture from holding any public office, or position of authority, within the Church. In 1960, Glasgow CofS Presbytery asserted: 'It may be observed that every religion which has instituted priestesses or otherwise afforded office to women has become degenerate and corrupt' (special committee to comment on Assembly Report on Place of Women). There are still CofS ministers and congregations which refuse to consider ordaining women as elders. This stance is not consistent with the intention of the law, since the law is declaratory, confirming both the eligibility of women and theological recognition of their status.

On the other hand, there are those, both male and female, who assert that equality of office and opportunity is a fundamental expression of the Christian faith. So, in 1986, the 'Community of Women and Men in the Church' Group (within the Board of World Mission and Unity) stated that 'It is no longer possible to avoid this underlying problem of patriarchy .... The concern for a genuine community of women and men in place of patriarchy can therefore no longer be regarded as an extra, as though it mattered only to the few, and had no integral connection with the agenda of the Church's courts and committees. It must be recognized as a matter of central importance for the life of the Church, its unity, its mission and faithfulness to the gospel' (*RGACS 1986*, 322).

It is clear that a minority of Church members are dissatisfied with the very structures and institutions of the CofS, and are seeking, often across denominational boundaries, completely different patterns of church life. One such group claimed in 1989 that 'Conforming to male criteria and patterns is a tacit acceptance of the validity, appropriateness and "rightness" of the present structures and systems. Instead, women in the proposed Network of Ecumenical Women in Scotland (NEWS) should be probing and searching for alternative forms, contexts, new styles of leadership and partnership' (discussion paper for the women's lobby to Action of Churches Together in Scotland*).

It is probably true to say that most members of the CofS occupy a middle ground between these two poles. They have no strong objections to the present structures, and have adopted a pragmatic acceptance of the gradual increase in female participation, based primarily on the fact that women form the majority of active members. They are not particularly concerned either about the apostle Paul's injunctions restricting female ministry or about questions of patriarchy and 'sexist' language in the Church. While the Woman's Guild generally fails to attract younger women because of its image as a traditional and ageing organization, women are increasingly exercising their gifts in all aspects of Church life. It remains to be seen to what extent the present framework will be stretched or even broken by the long-term impact of feminization. In 1931, writing in support of the ordination of women, Annie H. Small* nevertheless expressed concern that this would tend further to conventionalize the Church: 'Formal equal status with men through admission to the eldership and ministry is a minor concern. Far more important, because fundamental, will be that we attain throughout the Church, to the understanding and the practice of those principles so evidently founded in our common humanity, so graciously hinted at in the gospels ... Should we not serve the Church and the world better by becoming explorers ... ?' (*LW* n.s. 2, 1931, 144).

L. O. *Macdonald*

Women in Presbyterian Missions. From the beginning of the Victorian era, a small but increasing number of Scottish Presbyterian women responded to their religious convictions and their circumstances by choosing to work in the foreign mission field. This female missionary movement was of significance both to the women directly involved (and those with whom they came into contact in India, Africa, China and the Caribbean), and to women belonging to the organizations which supported them. It was central to an evangelical female culture which gradually pushed some women beyond the strictly prescribed woman's sphere of private and domestic concerns, by offering opportunities to acquire new skills, confidence and authority in an acceptable environment. Both in Scotland and overseas, female endeavour became increasingly important, numerically and strategically, to the whole missionary enterprise. Women were key workers in promotion and fund-raising at home, and by 1900 outnumbered men in the mission stations.

In the early years of the nineteenth century, pioneering Scots missionaries went to Africa and India with non-denominational societies. They often took wives or sisters with them. From the beginning, Scottish women supported this new evangelical movement with money and prayers. As early as 1820, the *Scots Missionary Magazine* carried reports of Ladies Auxiliary Missionary Associations in towns like Peebles and Lanark. But even in 1797, a female reader of the magazine was pleading for a more active involvement: 'Why are females alone excluded from all ostensible share in these labours of love? It cannot be denied, that some among them possess both ability and inclination suited to the purpose. Nor let it be argued that their own familiar and domestic concerns afford the only sphere of their exertions. Here they ought undoubtedly to begin, but they are not called to stop there, when circumstances allow them to do otherwise.'

FIRST SOCIETIES. However, it was not until 1837 that the direct participation of Scottish Presbyterian women began. Captain St Clair Jameson, a Scottish soldier in India, who had admired the work of Margaret Bayne,* wrote to a woman friend in Fife: 'I am in hopes soon to send you a very strong appeal on behalf of native female education in Bombay ... Some few friends of the cause here are in hopes of getting ladies in Edinburgh to form themselves into an association to aid in promoting Female Education in India' (quoted in *Women's Work*, 1885). In 1837 the Edinburgh Association of Ladies for the Advancement of Female Education in India was constituted, and in 1839 the Glasgow Ladies Association for Promoting Female Education in Kaffraria. Thus began the societies which, through many changes of name and constitution, employed women as missionaries on behalf of the Presbyterian churches until separate women's associations ceased to exist after the 1929 Union.*

In 1838, Miss Reid was the first agent from Scotland to India. The first woman to Africa was Christina Thompson in 1842. The tentative beginnings of 'women's work for women' were complicated by two early afflictions which befell several agents – death and marriage! Those who succumbed to the latter were lost to the Ladies Associations, though most continued their missionary labours unpaid, as wives.

The 1843 Disruption* divided the Scottish Ladies Association. Most of the office-bearers and missionaries joined the FC,* and a new Female Society was formed under its auspices. Thereafter, women served in the Scottish mission fields on behalf of the three main Presbyterian denominations – although the UPC* did not have a separate female society until 1881. The FC Society always supported more agents than the others, and was notable for its creative thinking, forward planning and practical initiatives. Indeed, it was among the first of all Western agencies in the development of female caste schools and boarding schools, and in securing entry into zenanas (the prison-like homes to which Indian wives were confined from a very early age). The CofS Association, on the other hand, was often unable to find suitable female agents from within the Est.C. The UP missionaries often came from working class backgrounds (e.g. Mary Slessor,* Euphemia Miller, and Christina Thompson).

'WOMEN'S WORK FOR WOMEN'. From 1837 to 1929, the work of Scottish women missionaries developed in a great variety of circumstances; but their goal and purpose remained constant, in rhetoric if not always in practice. 'Women's work for women' was the rallying cry – and the associations took great pride in their responsibility for carrying out a distinctive and special mission. Education, healing and Christian exhortation were acceptable because they were directed at women and children.

A Mrs Parker of the UPC's Zenana Mission in Benares told a meeting in 1895: 'In order to reach the poor and down-trodden amongst the despised daughters of India, Christian women preach every day in religious festivals, in the streets, and amongst the villages ... low and outcaste women ... The emancipation of Hindu and Mohammedan women can come only through the Gospel of Him who has done so much to elevate woman, and to place her in the position she occupies in Christian lands as equal and helpmeet of man' (*UP Magazine*, 12, 1895, 446–9). The importance of female conversion was seen to lie not only in its inherent redemptive value for individuals, but also because only *Christian* women would be able to influence potential *male* converts. They would be providers of the domestic environment which was central to the Victorian vision of Christian civilization. Christina Rainy (sister to Robert*), reporting on her 1887 Jubilee Tour of the FC Society's work in India, wrote: 'The progress of Christianity will elevate and purify the tone of Indian society ... at least we are raising up Christian wives and mothers who may become a power for good' (*Women's Work*, 1887). And Jane Waterston,* the pioneer educationalist and doctor, spoke thus of the situation in South Africa: 'Our main aim is not to turn out school girls but *women* ... Homes are what are wanted in Kaffirland, and young women will never be able to make homes unless they understand and see what a home is ... If religion is to advance, a great social reform in habits and customs is required' (1868, quoted by R. Young, *African Wastes Reclaimed*, L, 1902).

J. W. Jack, author of *Daybreak in Livingstonia* (E, 1901), 333, expressed well the prevailing wisdom about the appropriate missionary spheres of men and women: 'To men belongs the task of opening a way for the Gospel ... striking vigorous blows at the citadel of heathendom, superintending various agencies ... and accomplishing other deeds of strength and wisdom. But to women belongs the quiet, patient labour in the homes of the natives, striving to win the hearts of the wives and mothers, and to gain the love of the children. Let women hear the tender call of Christ to the foreign field!'

PIONEERS AND INNOVATORS. It is true that many men and women saw their roles in this highly differentiated way, and also that a main aim of mission work was to build Christian communities which would replicate the values and arrangements of Scottish Presbyterian culture. But there were also missionaries who were never circumscribed by such attitudes, either in their own lifestyle and work or in their approach to those among whom they laboured. Their service was innovative and unconventional, as well as compassionate. Within the remit of 'women's work for women', forms of care and outreach were pioneered which would have been impossible for men. In the process, missionaries also pioneered the involvement of women in educational, pastoral, and especially medical professions.

From fitful and difficult beginnings, Scottish women established a network of day-schools, orphanages, boarding schools and training centres. The first recipients of such education had to contend with deep-seated prejudices. But within fifty years, a few women in India and Africa had moved from positions of enforced ignorance to a situation in advance of their Scottish sisters. For by the mid-1880s they were able to take university degrees.

Chundra Mukki Bose, a pupil at the FC Society female school in Calcutta, was the first Indian woman to graduate MA. Three of her colleagues from the school were already, in 1885, studying medicine.

But in India, it was work in the zenanas which became the truly distinctive form of women's mission. They seemed an impenetrable obstacle to the aims of the Ladies Associations. But the FC Society in Calcutta, and later the CofS Association in Poona, were among the pioneers of zenana missions. In 1855, two agents of the FC Society, after protracted negotiations, were admitted to a zenana with a view to teaching the enclosed girls and women: 'Many thought we were attempting the impossible, but we told ourselves, "This is the beginning of a new era for India's daughters"' (Mrs Fordyce, quoted in *Women's Work*, 1887). In September 1885, the Bengal Missionary Conference passed the following resolution: 'They rejoice in the hopeful commencement of the zenana school scheme, both as a sign of progress, and as a NEW MEANS for the elevation of women in India' (*ibid.*).

Zenana work was taken up by all the main societies, and it captured the imagination of women in Scotland (and elsewhere in the West). It was work which only women could do; it brought them into close and often intimate contact with their pupils, and it gave rise to the female medical missions. Zenana women suffered appalling health problems. Their environment was enclosed and airless; they had a poor diet and little exercise; and their treatment during pregnancy and childbirth was at best negligent and at worst dangerous. Male doctors could do nothing, because they simply were not allowed access to women. The *Free Church Monthly*, March 1889, recounts the development of female medical missions in India (80–2). In 1860, Mrs Smith, based in Serampore, began educational work in zenanas, but 'experience led her to develop into a medical mission, also to women, so far as that was possible without a fully qualified co-worker ... [Mrs Smith] gave up her little leisure to plead for the one hundred and twenty-seven million women of India that they might have Christian physicians of their own sex.'

Alexander Duff* added his considerable weight to the case: 'If a female missionary knew something of medical science and practice, readily would *she* find access, and while applying medical skill to the healing of the body, would have precious opportunities of applying the balm of spiritual healing to the worst diseases of the soul. Would to God we had such an agency ready for work! Soon might India be moved in its innermost recesses!' (to Edinburgh Medical Missionary Society,* quoted by J. Lowe, *Medical Missions: Their Place and Power*, L, 1886, 178).

The CofS was the first Scottish society to appoint a woman medical doctor – Letitia Bernard went to Poona in 1884. Matilda MacPhail* of Madras began work for the FC Society in 1888. Other notable early medical missionaries included Agnes Henderson of Nagpur, Jean Grant of Ajmer, Jeannie Grant of Seoni, and Jane Waterston,* who, working in the rather different circumstances of South Africa, was the first Scottish woman missionary to qualify as a physician. These pioneers not only practised medicine, but established dispensaries, raised funds to build hospitals, taught and advised. Scottish doctors were noted for their training of nurses, and their encouragement to local women to qualify in medicine.

If, in India, the major concern was to offer possibilities to those confined in zenanas, in Africa there was much more emphasis on the need to restrain and domesticate women who were spoken of as 'savages'. As early as 1839, the Glasgow Missionary Society declared that they hoped to 'raise the female character above mere animal propensities and brute labour, to make them acquainted with their high destinies in another world, and so to give them a sense of self-respect.' The courage, commitment and commonsense of women such as Mary Slessor,* Christina Thompson, Christina Forsyth, Jane Waterston and Marion Stevenson* won them affection and respect. Their most unusual lifestyle was eloquent testimony to the benefits of the gospel they preached, although it was a cause of recurring confusion that women who spoke so highly of the model Christian wife and mother, were themselves neither!

The China mission field, with its unique cultural and political challenges, demanded perseverance and courage in the face of ancient customs, difficult languages and complex crises. Among the Scotswomen who served with honour were Elizabeth Macgregor, who trained female evangelists, Dr Jean McMinn, Nurse Helen Wilson and Meta Pirrie. In the 1920s, the Church in Manchuria made women eligible for election to the Church's courts – many years before the same privileges were granted in Scotland.

As the Scottish missionary enterprise grew in scope and numbers, there was a marked feminization of its agency, although this was not reflected in the relative incomes of the Women's Associations and the Foreign Mission Committees of the Churches. By 1900, the CofS Association had fifty staff (plus twenty-five missionary wives who worked voluntarily) and an income of £13,626. The Foreign Mission Committee had forty agents and an income of £24,576. In 1909, the Women's Foreign Mission of the UFC had 158 agents, plus 142 wives, and an income of £38,345 (compared with the FMC income of £91,571). In 1930, the total female agency in the united CofS was 449 (256 single women, 193 married women). The total male agency was 253.

It is not surprising that Christian women of strong character and independent spirit felt called to mission work: 'The inspiration of Miss Slessor has fired the women of the Church, and many intrepid spirits have followed her into the wilds ... women missionaries are to be found, doing the work of men; teaching, healing, preaching, laying foundations of new industries, introducing new forms of agriculture, and renewing the life of people through their homes. The Church at home debates whether women may rightly serve as deacons, while the Church abroad thrusts almost the whole office of ministry upon (them) ... Some are lonely, in danger, all are weary and overstrained, but none is timid or regretful of their choice of life-work. "I had far rather be building mud houses out here than doing deputation work at home – a thousand times more! it is the people at home who ought to have the sympathy"' (*UFC Women's Missionary Magazine*, Aug./Sept. 1918).

HOME DEVELOPMENTS. Missionaries on furlough or returned home from service were often in the vanguard of moves to achieve equality of office and status for women in the Church (and several were prominent suffragists too; *see* Women's Suffrage). Some, like Annie H. Small* and Elizabeth Hewat,* brought their radical influence to bear in institutions such as the Women's Missionary College (St Colm's),* and the Woman's Guild.*

At home, the missionary societies, as they grew and developed, provided scope for women to learn new skills and confidence, to enjoy a sense of purpose and achievement beyond domestic confines, and to discover some measure of female autonomy and solidarity. Women used their traditional gifts, and discovered new ones, as they held meetings, wrote letters, sewed and knitted, studied and prayed, edited magazines and ran bazaars, for the spreading of the gospel. In structural terms, the associations came to mirror the presbyterial institutions of the Churches. Thus they retained their independence (until 1929), while maintaining close administrative ties with the 'official' Foreign Mission Committees.

The boom in female service required increasingly sophisticated levels of organization and fundraising by thousands of women operating locally and nationally – a fact scarcely appreciated by many men. While some were supportive and encouraging, others were scornful and derisory. Competence was not readily accepted as a female attribute: 'People failed to remember that one half of the mission field was the work among women. He dared say that as this work was in the hands of the ladies, there might be a polite feeling on the part of the male classes – (laughter) – that the work could not be very complete or well done' (Robet Rainy,* *PGAFCS 1884*, 93).

But the significance of the home societies was well expressed by Miss Adam, addressing the Jubilee Conference of the UPC in 1897. She spoke with pride about the success of the Zenana Mission in giving women a share in the management of a concern which they had always supported generously, and concluded: 'The work at home is important. Women's work has brought a fuller life into many a heart ... "I am conscious of my relations to the whole world. I feel that with my own hand I am unlocking forces which will speedily bring the world to its Lord and Christ"' (Report of the UPC Jubilee Conference, 1897).

Women's foreign mission in Scotland, then, contributed to a definite change and expansion in the role of women. That change was direct and often dramatic in the experience of women missionaries. It was indirect in the romance and example of their lives, and the possibilities they opened up for others. It had an impact on men and on the structures of the Presbyterian Churches – not because they were directly challenged or contradicted, but because women gradually assumed for themselves greater responsibility and authority. The transforming power of mission was felt not only in the lives of converts in the field, but in the lives of women who helped shape a positive and changing view of woman's sphere, by their involvement in 'women's work for women'.

In addition to denominational papers (*RGACS* etc.) and magazines, note also: reports of CofS Women's Association for Foreign Mission, UPC Zenana Mission (1881–1900), and UFC Women's Foreign Mission (1900–29); *Women's Work* (1880s) and *The Helpmeet* (1891–1900), both FC Society journals; *UFC Women's Missionary Magazine* (1901–29); *LW Women's Supplements* (1891–1929); E. Hewat, *Vision and Achievement 1796–1956* (E, 1960); A. S. Swan, *Seedtime and Harvest* (L, 1937); E. A. C. Walls, *Pages of Life* (E, 1987); D. P. Thomson, *Women of the Scottish Church* (Perth, 1975).

L. O. Macdonald

Women's Suffrage and the Churches. Between 1909 and 1914 the movement for the enfranchisement of women was a passionately fought campaign in which all possible allies were enlisted. It was believed by many that if women could vote for their representatives in Parliament this would help to put right much that was wrong with Edwardian society, from drunkenness and prostitution to the exploitation of women in the sweated industries. The 'religious aspect' of the women's movement was frequently stressed.

In view of the crucial part which women played in the Scottish churches (*see* Women in the Presbyterian Churches) it was inevitable that the aid of those churches should have been enlisted. Many ministers fully appreciated the work done by their wives, sisters, mothers and daughters, and supported their claim for a voice in the nation's affairs. Others, however, believed in 'separate spheres' – that helping the poor and needy was woman's function but politics was not.

The first official support from members of various churches came in 1912 when the Scottish Churches League for Women's Suffrage was formed, with Lady Frances Balfour* as president. Literature was sent to secretaries of Woman's Guilds and other societies connected with the churches in Scotland that summer, resulting in numerous applications for membership.

The women's suffrage movement in Britain at this time had two distinct wings, militant and non-militant. The militant wing was headed by Emmeline Pankhurst. In March 1913, when Mrs Pankhurst was on bail and due to stand trial for incitement to violence, she addressed a public meeting in Glasgow. On the platform were some fourteen ministers of different denominations (with their wives). Their presence on that platform was roundly condemned by many, but was defended by the ministers themselves and applauded by women supporters.

During the closing months of 1913 and opening months of 1914 every CofS and UF presbytery in the country was approached by a non-militant organziation, the Northern Men's Federation for Women's Suffrage, asking them to overture* their respective General Assembly. Discussions within the presbyteries were reported at length, revealing all shades of opinion, but only two CofS presbyteries – Glasgow and Irvine – voted in favour of taking action. The UF presbyteries all agreed that it would be injudicious or incompetent to send an overture to the General Assembly on the subject.

The militant wing of the movement believed in more direct action. Their tactics were to interrupt church services – normally after the intercessory prayer – by chanting their own prayer for women who were fasting or being forcibly fed in prison because of their actions on behalf of women's suffrage. Such interruptions occurred in Presbyterian and Episcopal churches in Edinburgh, Glasgow, Dundee, Aberdeen and Perth. In some cases the women were simply ignored; in other cases they were removed from the church with some violence; in most cases they were asked to leave and did so quietly. Their conduct invariably caused a great stir (which was, of course, the intention). In March 1914 seven women who interrupted a service at St Giles* in Edinburgh were arrested and charged with committing a breach of the peace.

Militant suffragettes and non-militant suffragists in Scotland (both male and female) believed that the women's suffrage movement was a force for moral purity, and that the churches should therefore give it their full support. That support was never more than patchy, but it did exist, and by forcing church members to confront the issue, fighters for the suffrage ensured that women's concerns gained a good deal of prominence in the years leading up to the First World War.

E. King, *The Scottish Women's Suffrage Movement* (G, 1978) – brief; *Glasgow Herald* and other papers; L. Leneman, *Guid Cause: Women's Suffrage Movement in Scotland* (A, 1991); *id.*, 'The Scottish Churches and "Votes for Women"', *RSCHS* 24 (1991), 237–52.

L. Leneman

Wood, James (1609–64), Covenanter,* Professor and Principal in St Andrews. Son of a St Andrews merchant, Wood studied there as well. He was apparently brought up an Episcopalian* and an Arminian* until, while serving as regent in the university, he was convinced otherwise through Alexander Henderson* and the reading of David Calderwood's* *Altare Damascenum*. He was ordained to nearby Dunino in 1640. In 1644 he was elected Professor of Divinity at Marischal College, Aberdeen, and minister of Greyfriars Church there, but was not settled. In 1645 he was translated to the

WOOD (WODE), THOMAS

third charge (Ecclesiastical History) at St Mary's College (the New College), St Andrews.

Wood was one of the commissioners sent by the CofS to Charles II* at The Hague in 1649 and again in 1650, resulting in the Treaty of Breda. He defended the commission's dealings with the King and accepted his word, as given at his coronation in Scone, that he took the Covenants* sincerely. A zealous Resolutioner,* Wood maintained against James Guthrie* that none should be hindered from fighting an invading enemy. He took 'a most active and instrumental' part in the debates which followed (*A Vindication of The Freedom & Lawfulnes of the late Generall Assembly Begun at St Andrews and Continued at Dundee* (L., 1652); *A Review and Examination of a Pamphlet lately published Bearing the Title of Protestors No Subverters* (E., 1659)). He wrote with a vigour and sharpness (Robert Baillie, *The Letters and Journals*, E., 1842, III, 354) which were not helpful to reconciliation.

In the same period he wrote his major published work: *A Little Stone Pretended to be Out of the Mountain, Tried, and Found to be a Counterfeit* (E., 1654), a refutation of the English Independent Nicholas Lockyer. James Walker characterizes it as perhaps the best Scottish discussion of church authority and ranks Wood 'among our ablest men' (*The Theology and Theologians of Scotland*, E., ²1888, 18–19).

In 1656 Wood recommended James Sharp* as most fit to be sent to London to maintain the Resolutioners' cause to Cromwell, a recommendation he lived to regret. The following year, partly to escape the contentions resulting from working in the college of which Samuel Rutherford* was Principal, he accepted the position of Principal of the Old College. Wood's character was such that Rutherford nevertheless believed him an honest man, unlike his colleague Andrew Honyman,* whom he characterized as 'a knave' (R. Wodrow, *Analecta*, E., 1842, II, 118). Wood, Wodrow further reports, 'preached the Gospell, and practicall truths, and medled litle with publick matters in his sermons' (*ibid.*, II, 325). Wood continued in St Andrews, preaching until 1662, when Sharp, now Archbishop, silenced him for not conforming to the new situation. He held his post as Principal until 1663, when, at Sharp's desire, he was removed by the Privy Council* and confined to Edinburgh. Sharp, after visiting him on his deathbed, spread a rumour that he had professed himself amenable to Episcopacy. Wood, hearing of this lie, drew up a testimony to the contrary (R. Wodrow, *The History of the Sufferings of the Church of Scotland*, G, 1828, I, 403–6; Blair, *op. cit.*, 464).

Wood was said to have left a refutation of Arminianism in manuscript (Wodrow, *History*, I, 370).

FES V, 196, VII, 411.

D. C. Lachman

Wood (Wode), Thomas (*fl.* 1560–92) compiler of the St Andrews Psalter (1562–6), the first metrical Psalter of the Reformed Church (*see* Psalms). A canon of Lindores Abbey,* Fife, before the Reformation,* he joined the Reformers and was resident in St Andrews by 1562. He appears frequently in the Kirk Session* register until 1592. He spent the early 1560s collecting and copying in a very fine hand the contents of Wood's Psalter, as it is often called. It comprised five parts. Although not extant in its entirety, most sections of two copies survive divided between Edinburgh University Library, the British Library and Trinity College, Dublin. They contain, in addition to David Peebles'* psalm-settings, canticles, anthems, psalms, songs and instrumental pieces by other composers from the period 1566–92.

The rest of Wood's life is obscure. He may have lived in Dunbar at some stage.

M. Patrick, *Four Centuries of Scottish Psalmody* (L, 1949), 58–64; S. Sadie (ed.), *The New Grove Dictionary of Music and Musicians* (L., 1980), XX, 519; K. Elliott (ed.), *Music of Scotland 1500–1700* (*Musica Britannica* 15; L, ²1964); *id.*, 'Scottish Music of the Early Reformed Church', *Trans. of Scott. Ecclesiological Soc.* 15:2 (1961), 18–32.

D. F. Wright

WORDSWORTH, CHARLES

Wordsworth, Charles (1806–92), CofE clergyman, Bishop of St Andrews and nephew of the poet William. Born at Lambeth, south London, he entered Christ Church, Oxford University, in 1825, graduating with a classics first in 1830. After several years as a private tutor he was ordained in the CofE (deacon, 1834; priest, 1840). From 1835–46 second master of Winchester College, England's oldest public school, in 1847, he accepted the invitation of W. E. Gladstone* to be first warden of Trinity College in Glenalmond, Perthshire, a new establishment, both a public school for boys and a seminary for training Scottish Episcopal clergy.

In 1852 Wordsworth was elected Bishop of St Andrews, Dunblane and Dunkeld by his own casting vote in an evenly divided contest. This aroused controversy, but he was consecrated to the office in 1853, resigning as warden of Trinity in 1854. His episcopate was marred by an estrangement between himself and the clergy of St Ninian's Cathedral in Perth (where he resided until 1876), and by other controversies such as that caused in his own Church by his conciliatory attitude towards Scottish Presbyterianism (cf. *A Discourse on Scottish Church History*, E, 1881; *A Discourse on the Scottish Reformation*, E, 1861).

Wordsworth's churchmanship was of the older high Anglican school, leavened by evangelical sympathies. He consistently opposed what he saw as Romanizing tendencies within Scottish Episcopalianism (cf. *Is the Church of Rome the Babylon of Revelation?*, L, 1851).

Annals of My Early Life 1806–46 and *Annals of My Life 1847–56*, 2 vols (L, 1891–3).

J. Wordsworth, *The Episcopate of Charles Wordsworth, 1853–1892* (L, 1899); A. E. Nimmo, 'Charles Wordsworth, Bishop of St Andrews, 1853–1892; Reconciler or Controversialist?' (MPhil, Edinburgh University, 1983); *DNB* LXIII, 1–7.

N. R. Needham

WORLD ALLIANCE

World Alliance of Reformed Churches. The Alliance, which resulted from the union in 1970 of the World Presbyterian Alliance (1875) with the International Congregational Council (first meeting, 1891; constitution 1948), comprised in 1993 175 member churches in more than eighty countries: a total community of some seventy millions. The following Scottish churches are currently members of the Alliance: CofS, Congregational Union of Scotland, UFC. The withdrawal of a founding member, the FC, was reported with regret at the General Council of 1959.

Constitutionally, 'Any Church which accepts Jesus Christ as Lord and Saviour; holds the Word of God given in the Scriptures of the Old and New Testaments to be the supreme authority in matters of faith and life; acknowledges the need for the continuing reformation of the Church catholic; whose position in faith and evangelism is in general agreement with that of the historic Reformed confessions,* recognizing that the Reformed tradition* is a biblical, evangelical and doctrinal ethos, rather than any narrow and exclusive definition of faith and order, shall be eligible for membership.'

Under this rubric gathers a wide diversity of Churches: Presbyterian, Congregational; established, free; transconfessionally united (as in Canada, Zambia, North India, Australia); theologically 'conservative' and 'liberal'. Historically, their roots are variously in pre-Reformation reforming movements, the Zwingli-Calvin Reformation, English dissent, modern missions and revival* movements, ecumenism,* and secession.*

James MacGregor (1830–94)* and James M'Cosh* were among those who proposed a regular Presbyterian International Council in the 1860s. The first WPA President was William Garden Blaikie* (1888–92). In 1874 Hastings Ross called for an ecumenical Council of Congregational Churches, and Henry Martyn Dexter and Alexander Hannay were prominent early advocates of the idea. In addition to Blaikie, J. Marshall Lang,* J. N. Ogilvie,* W. A. Curtis,* and E. J. Hagan served as WPA Presidents, while the second, third and fourth WPA General Secretaries were R. D. Shaw (1913–18), J. R. Fleming (1918–27) and W. H. Hamilton (1927–48). W. L. Walker,* J. G. Drummond and C. S. Duthie were among Scots who participated in the ICC.

In recent years D. W. D. Shaw has served on the WARC Executive Committee, and as President of the European Committee and Council. J. K. S. Reid, D. W. Torrance, J. B. Torrance, T. F. Torrance,* A. I. C. Heron, A. D. Falconer and G. M. Newlands are among those Scots who have contributed to the Alliance's theological work.

The WPA held nineteen Councils prior to 1970, the ICC, ten. There followed a Centennial Consultation (1977), the twenty-third Council at Ottawa, Canada, in 1982, and the twenty-fourth at Seoul, S. Korea, in 1989.

The Alliance holds a General Council every five to seven years; its Executive Committee normally meets annually. There is a European Committee, and a Caribbean and North American Area Council.

WORLD MISSIONARY CONFERENCE

The General Secretariat is concerned with policy and public relations, membership and finance. The Department of Theology maintains contact with some 300 theological faculties, seminaries and church-related colleges; organizes consultations (e.g. Reformed theology and the Jewish people; Confessing the Faith today); and participates in international bilateral dialogues (with the RCC, the Anglican Communion, the Baptist World Alliance, the Mennonite World Conference, the Disciples Ecumenical Consultative Council, the Lutheran World Federation, and the Orthodox Churches). The Department of Co-operation and Witness disseminates news and information, and is concerned with questions of human rights, religious and civil liberties, etc., as these affect member Churches.

Among significant recent acts were the declaring that apartheid is a sin, and its attempted theological justification a heresy; the calling for a covenant for peace and justice; and the launching of a major study-programme, *Called to Witness to the Gospel Today*.

The Alliance maintains contact with the World Council of Churches, the Reformed Ecumenical Synod, and the International Congregational Fellowship.

WARC Constitution (Geneva, 1970/1982); WPA, ICC and WARC Council *Proceedings*; *The Reformed World* (and predecessors); *World Congregationalism* (1959–65) and *Congregational Studies* (1965–70); M. Pradervand, *A Century of Service* (E, 1975); A. Peel and D. Horton, *International Congregationalism* (L, 1949); A. P. F. Sell, *A Reformed Evangelical Catholic Theology. The Contribution of the Theological Publications of the World Alliance of Reformed Churches, 1875–1982* (Grand Rapids, 1991).

A. P. F. Sell

World Council of Churches, see Ecumenical Movement.

World Missionary Conference, held in Edinburgh 14–23 June, 1910, the most representative consultation to date and a powerful stimulus to the ecumenical movement.* Compared with earlier international missionary conferences (Liverpool, 1860; London, 1885; New York, 1900; William Carey had proposed such gatherings, at roughly ten-yearly intervals, to start in 1810 or so), 'Edinburgh 1910' (as it came to be known) was marked by thoroughness of preparation (progress was tracked by a *Monthly News Sheet* from October 1909 to May 1910), range of participants (no longer very largely Evangelicals), quality of reports and addresses, and its influence as 'a fountain head of international and inter-Church co-operation on a depth and scale never before known'. It may deserve to be called 'one of the most creative events in the long history of the Christian Church' (Martin).

Whereas previous conferences had been non-denominational, participants at Edinburgh rep-

denominational, participants at Edinburgh represented missionary societies (not churches) across virtually the whole Protestant spectrum, but without RC or Orthodox involvement. Places were allocated in proportion to societies' incomes. Consequently attendance was overwhelmingly Anglo-American, with less than a score from the 'younger churches'. Of 1355 delegates, 560 came from 46 societies in the British Isles, 594 from 60 in N. America, 175 from 40 in continental Europe and 26 from 12 in S. Africa and Australasia. As for Scotland, 16 represented three CofS agencies and 35 four UFC ones, with one from the Edinburgh Medical Missionary Society,* two from the EpCS and four from the National Bible Society. SCM advocacy helped to secure an Anglo-Catholic presence, but at the price of Latin America's absence, as an RC preserve, from agenda and representation.

The Conference met in the UF (now CofS) Assembly Hall adjacent to New College.* The 'central act' of daily proceedings was 'the mid-day half-hour devoted to intercession', the greatest service the Conference could render to its cause of promoting Christian missions. A parallel programme for visitors and the local community was provided in the Synod Hall,* to bring home to the Church 'the true nature, difficulty and glory of the missionary enterprise'. Separate meeting for schoolboys and schoolgirls were held in the CofS Assembly Hall (latterly Highland-Tolbooth Church). And during 20–21 June a supplementary (early morning and evening) programme focussed on medical aspects of missionary work. Burroughs Wellcome & Co. sponsored an exhibition of medical equipment used by celebrated pioneers (and its adverts filled out *A Brief History of Missionary Enterprise in Antient and Modern Times* (E, 1910), compiled as 'lecture memoranda' for delegates).

The planning committee (largely Scottish) ensured that the Conference would be a carefully prepared consultation, by engaging eight international commissions to prepare reports, subsequently published in full (E, NY, 1910): I. *Carrying the Gospel to all the Non-Christian World* (led by John Mott, the Conference chairman, with George Robson, editor of the *MRUFCS* (*FUFCS* 333) as a vice-chairman; this commission also produced a *Statistical Atlas of Christian Missions* (E, 1910) a detailed directory of missionary societies); II. *The Church in the Mission Field* (chaired by J. Campbell Gibson (*see* Missions: S. China)); III. *Education in Relation to the Christianisation of National Life* (led by Bishop Charles Gore); IV. *The Missionary Message in Relation to the Non-Christian Religions* (under D.S. Cairns* with W. P. Paterson* participating; MS submissions are kept in the Centre for the Study of Christianity in the Non-Western World, New College); V. *The Preparation of Missionaries* (commission members included Henry Cowan*, A. R. MacEwen* and Annie Small*); VI. *The Home Base of Missions*; VII. *Missions and Governments* (chaired by the Conference president, Lord Balfour of Burleigh*); VIII. *Co-operation and the Promotion of Unity* (led by Sir Andrew Fraser of Glenisla, Perthshire, late of Bengal). Among those delivering evening addresses (published in volume IX, *The History and Records . . .*) were Archbishop Randall Davidson,* W. P. Paterson,* H. A. A. Kennedy,* A. R. MacEwen* and James Denney.*

All agreed that John Mott (1865–1955; President of the World Student Christian Federation) in the chair and J. H. Oldham* as secretary were masterful – hence their appointment to the same roles in the continuation committee, the key innovative organ whose creation was the sole resolution passed by the Conference. (Later, as Oldham's theology became more liberal, he came to view 1910's vision as 'too limited'; 'Fifty years After', *Intern. Rev. of Missions* 49, 1960, 257–72.) Among the stewards (organized by SCM) were several destined for distinction, including William Temple, John Baillie,* William Manson* and John A. Mackay.* It was at Edinburgh that the American Bishop Charles Brent got his call to ecumenical activism. The Conference led more or less directly to a number of co-operative enterprises, including the *International Review of Missions* (1912, edited by Oldham), the International Missionary Council (1921), uniting the network of national and regional councils that were formed after 1910, including the Conference of British Missionary Societies (1911–12; based in Edinburgh House, London), and the Faith and Order movement, first convened at Lausanne in 1927 (*see* Edinburgh Conference 1937).

Yet if Edinburgh 1910 opened a new era in ecumenical endeavour (though unity was not on the agenda, aspirations repeatedly surfaced, even for the inclusion of RC and Orthodox), it marked perhaps the apogee of the modern missionary movement (to Kenneth Latourette 'the Great Century' ended in 1914), at any rate as a Western Protestant movement. Europe's Christian nations would soon be locked in devastating war (1914–18). Despite its restricted representative character, the Conference stimulated a shift in Protestantism's centre of gravity from the old West to the emerging South and East. It also presaged the ecumenical captivity of 'mission', and the need for the later Lausanne Congress (1974) movement to carry forward the Conference's fundamental concern with 'the evangelisation of the world'.

World Missionary Conference 1910–official handbook (E, 1910); W. H. T. Gairdner, *Edinburgh 1910 . . .* (E, 1910); H. Martin, *Beginning at Edinburgh . . . A Jubilee Assessment . . .* (L, 1960); T. Tatlow, *The Story of the Student Christian Movement* (L, 1933), 404–11; S. C. Neill, *A History of Christian Missions* (Harmondsworth, ²1986), 331–4; R. Rouse and S. C. Neill (eds), *A History of the Ecumenical Movement 1517–1948* (L, 1954), 355–62; *Addresses and Papers of John R. Mott*, vol. 5: *The International Missionary Council* (NY, 1947), 1–178; C. H. Hopkins, *John R. Mott 1865–1955* (Geneva, 1979), 343–429; A. W. Schreiber, *Die Edinburger Welt-Missions-Konferenz* (Basel, 1910).

D. F. Wright

Worship. There is virtually no evidence as to forms of worship in the early Christian centuries in Scotland. The idea that there was a 'Celtic Church'* aware of distinctiveness from Rome and nurturing its own liturgical forms and practices is unsubstantiated. There is no doubt that the Church in Scotland from the beginning preached the gospel, baptized, confirmed, celebrated the eucharist and nurtured people by prayer and worship in monasteries, homes and churches. In all probability there were in Scotland, as elsewhere, local variations of ritual and formulae. But although there might be variations in regard to ecclesiastical organization, the date of Easter (see Christian Year), and such matters, worship was not in any serious way a matter of contention. Furthermore it seems certain that Christians in the territory that later became Scotland regarded themselves as fully part of the *una sancta* and believed that their worship was at one in all essentials with the worship of the rest of Christendom.

In Iona* and associated monastic foundations, as elsewhere in Europe, the divine office centred on the recitation of the Psalms at the canonical hours. Mass was said only on Sundays and feast days, and there were services for the sick. The evidence is very scanty – the Book of Deer,* the Stowe Missal (ninth century), the Bangor Antiphony (seventh century) and the *Liber Hymnorum* (eleventh century) – only the first of Scottish provenance – but it all suggests that the Christian worship of early Scotland was in all important respects the same as that of the rest of Europe and particularly close to that of Gaul and Spain.

The 'Romanization' of the Scottish Church under Queen Margaret* in the eleventh century probably included some pressure for greater liturgical uniformity: Margaret's chaplain, Turgot,* wrote of her Scots subjects celebrating mass in 'I know not what barbarous rite'. Scottish liturgical usage was commonly close to that of Sarum, although the Wars of Independence and the Great Schism (in which Scotland and England took different sides) encouraged the Scots to adopt continental rather than English uses. For reasons of national identity it became important to assert not only that York and Canterbury had no jurisdiction in Scotland, but that Scotland had its own distinctive liturgical use, its own variant of the liturgical practices of Western Christendom. This was particularly developed by William Elphinstone* of Aberdeen and his colleagues in the early sixteenth century.

REFORMATION. With the coming of the Reformation* there was a strong sense of discontinuity, of the need to abolish the relics of a sullied past and make a new beginning, in which there could be a return to the purity in worship of the New Testament Church. Images, stained glass windows, special ceremonies, relics, feasts, shrines and pilgrimages* were to be swept away along with the central 'idolatry of the mass', to be replaced with a very different system of simple, biblically authorized worship centring on the preaching* of the Word and the administration of the two dominical sacraments* of baptism* and the Lord's Supper.* There was to be a radical break with the past, a new beginning.

Yet there was in fact also a certain continuity. The same buildings were used, cleared of altars, statues and other relics of the old dispensation, and with modifications in their layout and furnishing. Many priests and monks who conformed to the Reformed faith were made ministers or readers.* Some of them intelligently and wholeheartedly embraced the Reformation; others were differently motivated, and willing quietly to continue to perform the old rituals. There must have been some continuity in the practice of worship, particularly perhaps in rites of passage such as funerals and other points where Christian worship and folk religion came together. Popular feeling in Lowland Scotland, inflamed to an extraordinary degree against Romanism, still had continuities of prejudice and of superstition. Some people continued to observe saints' days, reverence holy places, and resist the suggestion of the Reformers that Christian people should receive the Lord's Supper frequently.

Such continuities are, by the nature of things, hard to demonstrate. However, granted that people are conservative in matters of worship, it would have been surprising if there had not been some carry-over. What is notable is that in Scotland such far-reaching changes in worship were accepted so quickly and so generally. This must partly have derived from the widespread corruption of the late medieval Church and resulting anticlericalism so vividly portrayed in Sir David Lindsay's* *Ane Satyre of the Thrie Estaits* (E, 1602).

Whatever continuities there were with the immediate or more remote past, it is clear that the reformation of worship in sixteenth-century Scotland was greatly affected by outside influences flowing from Germany, England and Geneva, in ascending order of significance.

Early Reformers such as Patrick Hamilton* (martyred 1528) brought distinctively Lutheran* doctrines to Scotland, and we may assume that their understanding of worship was shaped by the same influences. Still, there is no evidence that what we might call specifically Lutheran forms of worship ever took root in Scotland. Yet the Reformation in Scotland, as in Germany, was born in song, and much of this music at the beginning was derived from Germany. This was especially true of the *Gude and Godlie Ballatis** compiled by the Wedderburn* brothers of Dundee and published for the first time between 1542 and 1546. This collection includes metrical Psalms,* metrical versions of the Creed and the Lord's Prayer, a catechism in metre, popular spiritual songs set to ballad tunes, carols and anti-Romanist taunt songs such as 'The paip that pagane full of pryde', and 'God send everie priest ane wyfe, and everie nunne ane man'. Many items were direct translations from the German, and the doctrine of the catechism was slightly Lutheran.

English influence was continuous from the beginning. The Reformation party in Scotland fairly consistently sought closer relations with England, and there was considerable flow of ministers and others between the two countries. Knox* himself had a small part in the production of the second English *Book of Common Prayer* of 1552, and as a result he was prepared to think well of the book and recommended it to the congregation at Berwick. It was widely used in Scotland for a period.

CALVINIST INFLUENCE. The third and most significant influence on Scottish worship in the Reformation period was Calvinism.* The *First Book of Discipline** and other sources suggest that about 1560 there was a fear that there would be confusion and disorder in the worship of the Reformed Kirk. It was Calvinism that gave it shape. In the Scots Confession* two of the marks of the true Kirk were the faithful preaching* of the Word of God and the right administration of the sacraments* of Jesus Christ 'quhilk man be annexed unto the word and promise of God, to seale and confirme the same in our hearts'. Sacraments were not to be regarded as 'naked and baire signes', but in baptism 'we ar ingrafted in Christ' and in the Supper Jesus Christ becomes 'very nurishment and fude of our saules'. The Sacrament 'is nothing else but a visible Word', but 'even if you get the same thing which you get in the Word, yet you get that same thing better' (Robert Bruce,* *The Mystery of the Lord's Supper*). The *FBD* lays down particularly clearly the regulative principle – nothing is to be done in worship save what is authorized or sanctioned in the Bible.

The Book of Common Order* of 1564, sometimes rather misleadingly called 'Knox's Liturgy', shows how the theology of the Scots Confession* and the regulations of the *FBD* were expressed in the practice of worship. It is not a prayer book but is nevertheless more than a directory. It provided the norm for Reformed worship in Scotland until well into the seventeenth century.

Initiatives for further changes in worship came at first from the King. James VI* raised the issue as early as 1584, but nothing seems to have happened at that stage. From 1614, having established a constitutional episcopate* in Scotland, James turned his attention to the introduction of certain changes in practice and the development of a more elaborate liturgy. The Five Articles of Perth* (1618) enjoin kneeling to receive Communion, private Communion for the sick, confirmation, and the observance of the major festivals. But a draft prayer book was abandoned, and it was left to Charles I,* backed by Archbishop Laud,* to press matters. Initially they wanted the English prayer book to be adopted, but they settled for a Scottish prayer book which made various concessions to Scottish feeling, while at the same time in several ways expressing Laud's liturgical views more adequately than the English book. This so-called 'Laud's Liturgy' was authorized and introduced in 1637 but met strong resistance, and in the confused political situation of the time it was almost immediately abandoned. It remains however a significant source for the later liturgical work of the EpCS.

WESTMINSTER DIRECTORY. A major task for the Westminster Assembly* of Divines, which convened in 1643, was the preparation of a *Directory of Public Worship* for the united Church of the three kingdoms. One of the Scottish commissioners, Robert Baillie,* saw the intention as being 'to abolish the great Idol of England, the Service Book, and to erect in all the parts of worship a full conformity to Scotland in all things worthy to be spoken of'. Although the Scots played a major role in drafting the *Directory*, they did not always get their way. In 1645 the *Directory* was authorized by the London Parliament for England and Ireland, and in the same year the General Assembly enacted it as the standard for worship in the CofS – a status it retains at least nominally to this day.

The *Directory* is in some parts, particularly in relation to the sacraments, quite specific, giving detailed prayers and rubrics. In other parts it offers general guidance to the minister. The chapter 'Of the Preaching of the Word' has a classic quality, and the sections on baptism and the Lord's Supper have attracted favourable comment from liturgists of many traditions. The *Directory* is a rather didactic, minister-centred document. The people's part in worship is 'wholly to attend upon it' and to abstain from 'all private whisperings, conferences, salutations, ... as also from all gazing, sleeping and other indecent behaviour, which may disturb the minister or people, or hinder themselves or others in the service of God'.

The fifty years following the promulgation of the Directory was a time of great turmoil and confusion in politics and in the life of the Church. The Commonwealth* period was followed by the Restoration* and the times of persecution. After the Revolution, with the establishment of Presbyterianism,* the General Assembly once again enjoined the observance of the *Directory*. The eighteenth century and the early part of the nineteenth century were a period when Presbyterian worship was markedly didactic, long sermons being supplemented by almost equally lengthy 'lectures' or biblical expositions. The annual, or occasionally twice-yearly, Communion seasons* were the high point in most parishes. The devout would move from one parish to another so that they in fact received Communion frequently, particularly in the period between May and October. A Communion season lasted from Thursday until Monday, and often the main services took place in the open, so great was the throng. But while Communion services and preaching could be uplifting, by the mid-nineteenth century Presbyterian worship was increasingly criticized, with not a little justification, for being long-winded, formless and repetitive. There was scant interest in the history of Christian worship, and there were relatively few efforts to measure the practice of worship against either Scripture or the earlier standards of Presbyterian Scotland. Much energy was invested in resisting 'innovations'.*

NEW STYLES OF WORSHIP. Various developments sparked off a renaissance of liturgical worship in the second half of the nineteenth century. The romantic movement, personified in Scotland above all by Sir Walter Scott,* led to a new consciousness of the importance of the past and fresh interest in the older documents such as 'Knox's Liturgy'. In theology there was some questioning of the adequacy of the inherited Calvinism, while Evangelicals* saw the need for warmth in worship as against the dry moralism of the Moderates.* Partly as a result of education in English private schools, an increasing proportion of the aristocracy abandoned the parish kirk, whose worship they felt lacked dignity and taste, and became Episcopalians or even RCs.

The Church Service Society,* founded in 1865, spearheaded the reform of the worship of Presbyterian Scotland. The Society's leaders included G. W. Sprott,* H. J. Wotherspoon,* R. H. Story,* T. Leishman* and James Cooper* – an able and influential group. The Society's pioneering work gradually transformed the worship of the CofS and of the UFC, basing the orders of worship included in successive editions of *Euchologion** on a new and extensive liturgical understanding (*see* Catholic Revival in Worship).

The EpCS established its own liturgical tradition in the eighteenth century, blending together material from Anglican sources, from Laud's Liturgy of 1637, and from early Eastern liturgies. Thomas Rattray* was particularly responsible for the distinctive shape of the Scottish Episcopal eucharistic prayer, including a strong epiclesis after the narration of the institution. After Seabury's* consecration in 1784, this liturgical tradition became influential in the USA, and far later it found sympathetic echoes in Scottish Presbyterianism (*see* Scottish Prayer Books (Episcopalian)).

RC worship until the late eighteenth century tended rather to reflect a Presbyterian norm, the Sunday service consisting of a sermon, long prayers in the vernacular, and low mass. Irish immigration* in the nineteenth century led to a large increase in the size of the RCC, a new confidence, the introduction of more elaborate forms of worship, and the coming of modern forms of devotion from Ireland and elsewhere in Europe (*see* Worship and Devotion Catholic (post-Reformation)).

TWENTIETH CENTURY. The twentieth century has been a period of remarkable change and ecumenical convergence in worship in Scotland. This has been most marked in the RCC, which after introducing various significant reforms in the first half of the century, such as encouraging the faithful to receive Communion frequently rather than at most once a quarter, implemented the liturgical changes of Vatican II, putting the revised liturgy into the vernacular, moving altar tables from the east wall to a position where the people could gather around, and emphasizing the central place of the Scriptures in worship. The EpCS, like the CofE, increasingly emphasized the centrality of the eucharist, and produced a lively series of liturgical revisions culminating in the outstanding *Scottish Liturgy 1982*. Things moved more slowly in the CofS, but the reunited Church produced in the *Book of Common Order* of 1940* a standard for worship which expressed both the tradition nurtured by the Church Service Society and the more recent insights of the liturgical movement. In many ways the Iona Community* became a pacemaker for the reform of worship in the CofS. And the process of liturgical reform common to all the major Churches was also a process of convergence for different traditions, as too to some extent was the experience of charismatic* renewal of worship.

G. B. Burnet, *The Holy Communion in the Reformed Church of Scotland, 1560–1960* (E, 1960); Duncan Forrester and Douglas Murray (eds), *Studies in the History of Worship in Scotland* (E, 1984); D. H. Hislop, *Our Heritage in Public Worship* (E, 1935); C. G. M'Crie, *The Public Worship of Presbyterian Scotland* (E, 1892); W. M. McMillan, *The Worship of the Scottish Reformed Church, 1550–1638* (L, 1931); W. D. Maxwell, *A History of Worship in the Church of Scotland* (L, 1955); H. J. Wotherspoon, *Religious Values in the Sacraments* (E, 1928).

D. B. Forrester

Worship and Devotion, Catholic (post-Reformation). A description of RC worship must be wide enough to include the whole of the Church's liturgy and sacraments. Devotion denotes a state of mind and soul, implying some warmth in the performance of one's religious duties; by extension it means doing more than the compulsory minimum, or attachment to a particular form of prayer or religious practice. Particular non-liturgical formulas of prayer are termed devotions. There can be no rigid delineation between worship and devotion.

The central act of RC worship is the eucharist. It is usually termed 'mass', while the word 'Communion' denotes the reception (consumption) of the consecrated bread and wine. Going forward to receive these is optional for the laity attending mass, but the consecrated bread can be preserved for administering later, usually to the sick. Of the other six sacraments, penance (confession) was commonly used, though less so now, to prepare for Communion. There are two sacraments of initiation: baptism, usually conferred in infancy, and confirmation, usually in pre-adolescence. The last anointing (unction) is for the seriously ill. Matrimony and holy orders consecrate persons to certain states of life.

The following account describes RC worship in late medieval times and indeed until the Second Vatican Council (1962–5). Only a priest could say mass (and thus provide Communion for the laity), hear confessions or anoint the sick. Even for baptism and marriage, as for funerals (non-sacramental), only a priest could provide the various ceremonies. Only a bishop could administer confirmation, bless the oil for anointing the sick or ordain a priest. In sharp contrast with Reformed practice, RC worship was fundamentally sacramental and priest-centred, with the bishop implicated too.

Contrast with Reformed worship was seen most sharply in the matter of ritual. Texts for mass and the other sacraments were in Latin, making a missal (mass book) and *Rituale* (ritual book) essential. Priestly vestments were also required, and so was a certain amount of equipment: chalice, candles, blest oil and so on. Ritual actions and postures (sign of the cross, kneeling, standing, etc.) were prescribed for the laity as well as the priest. A crucifix (with figure) would be on the altar, while almost every chapel would have pictures or statues to stimulate devotion. Much church adornment fulfilled the function of what we now call visual aids, in an age when literacy and even printed books were scarce.

The cycle of the liturgical year provided much variety. The date of Easter changed each year, and other feasts and seasons with it. Penitential or festive days and seasons alternated, bringing changes in the colour of vestments and altar trappings. Christmas and Easter were preceded by Advent and Lent respectively. The days before Easter were given over to elaborate ceremonies seen at no other time; on certain other days there were litanies and processions. Some of the ritual had lost its point through the passage of time, and the degree of solemnity differed widely from ordinary days to minor and major feasts. There would also be the widest variation in what was practicable in cathedrals, monasteries and collegiate churches at one end of the scale and in small parish churches and chapels at the other. In the former, too, the full choir office would be sung or recited in public, whereas the ordinary priest would read his office privately from a breviary. The lay person was obliged to very little of all this, but merely had to attend mass on Sundays and certain feasts and receive Communion (the bread alone) once a year. There is no clear evidence as to how well these obligations were fulfilled in late medieval Scotland, and active participation in a Latin, priest-centred liturgy would be fairly minimal.

The void was filled by voluntary devotional practices and 'popular' religion. RC practice was 'incarnated' into daily life, with the liturgical year, popular devotion and folk customs inextricably bound together. Evergreens and Christmas and the winter solstice went together, as did eggs and Easter and spring. Local saints and fairs, local holy places and wells, local customs and stories and sayings, embodied worship and belief into everyday life. Some of the customs were pagan survivals and the border-line with superstition was no doubt frequently overstepped. People were also much attached to religious objects, kept in the house or worn on the person. The Reformers were vehemently opposed to these visible, tangible embodiments of religion as well as to their extension into local folk custom.

In the decades after 1560, when all RC practices were forbidden, the authorities took action against defaulting priests and destroyed mass gear. As only a handful of new priests came into Scotland, RC worship steadily withered away. Only in the south-west, where Gilbert Brown* was influential, and in the north-east, did mass in public survive. Less successful was the campaign against practices such as praying for the dead in kirkyards or observing particular festivals.

Much the same is true of the seventeenth century. Official policy was to banish priests and destroy their gear, to prevent gatherings on feast-days and to extirpate religious objects and popular practices. This was the period of exceptionally sharp contrast between baroque RCism and austere Protestantism. In noble households sheltering Jesuit* chaplains, worship and devotion flourished; elsewhere RCs were dependent on the scanty ministration of an itinerant priest, though family prayers were encouraged and prayer-books were in use. As no bishop was available, the sacrament of confirmation was in abeyance and the blest oil for anointing the sick was often lacking. The remarkably successful Franciscan* missionary priests (*see* Irish Mission to Highlands) were hampered by lack of gear and also by somewhat unintelligent legalism concerning the trappings of worship.

At the end of the century, RC worship underwent dramatic vicissitudes: toleration under James VII (1685-8) with a public chapel in Holyrood* attempting elaborate services, then the disaster of the Revolution and in 1697 the arrival of Bishop Thomas Nicolson.* Confirmation was again available, and priests and bishops began to be ordained in Scotland. Regulations were drawn up for feast-days on which mass was obligatory (thirteen in addition to Sundays) and for fast-days (twenty-three in addition to the forty days of Lent). In the early eighteenth century, Jansenism* affected RC spirituality by making attitudes to God and worship more sin-conscious and rigoristic. The results are still observable today.

The defeat of the Jacobite* rising* of 1745, though disastrous for RCs, freed them from being politically alienated. As their rehabilitation continued, chapels were built, the blessed sacrament (consecrated bread) was kept in them as a focus for devotion, a *Rituale* for Scottish priests was produced, and lay people went to confession and received Communion more often than was obligatory. Devotional books in English and Gaelic* became freely available and, in the 1790s, a Scottish RC edition of the Bible. The revival went further and faster than its principal architect, Bishop George Hay,* thought prudent, but even he could not hold back the pressure to introduce music into worship.

In the early nineteenth century, as industrialization and immigration* swelled the congregations in Lowland towns, larger and more imposing chapels were built and choirs and organs became commonplace. Benediction of the blessed sacrament was introduced and even, on special occasions, a solemn high mass. In 1829 the annual publication of the Scottish liturgical calendar began. Sung vespers on Sunday afternoons became quite common.

About this time, the build-up of RC urban congregations, due mostly to Irish immigration, together with the founding of religious communities (*see* Religious Orders, modern), led to development in another direction, that of experiential piety, with a wealth of devotions centred on, for instance, the suffering Christ, the eucharist and Our Lady (Mary). They encouraged a warm and even sentimental piety and were accompanied by visual trappings, such as the fourteen Stations of the cross and the Christmas crib. There was great devotion to the blessed sacrament: Benediction remained popular and _Quarant' Ore_ (Forty Hours' adoration) was introduced, with the altar banked by massed flowers and candles. Processions of the blessed sacrament took place at Corpus Christi, a feast which usually fell in June. May was the month for honouring Mary, and June for honouring Christ's sacred heart, as a statue was carried in procession to the singing of hymns. Statues or pictures of Christ, Mary and the saints were placed in churches; Robert Monteith,* a notable benefactor of the Church, imported and presented a great number. Evening devotions replaced sung vespers on Sunday. Parish missions (a week or more of special services and visitation of houses, aimed at recalling the lapsed and stimulating the regular) became common. Parish societies embodying different devotions proliferated; well-loved, rather sentimental hymns were frequently sung. It was all somewhat Italianate and went with a growing ultramontane, pro-papal outlook and a loyalty to one's parish and priests that could be almost ghetto-like. Until well into this century, Scottish RCism, particularly in the central belt, was marked by a popular 'culture' very different from Protestantism.

Very little modified this pattern of somewhat passive attendance at Sunday mass and a wide choice of optional devotions. The full office in choir could be heard in a few religious houses. From the 1890s, Scottish saints were included in the calendar and pilgrimages were organized, both in Scotland and abroad. A pilgrimage centre set up at Carfin* in the 1920s drew worshippers in amazing numbers. The most far-reaching change was to introduce the frequent reception of Communion after 1904, until gradually it became the accepted norm to receive Communion at mass. Gradually, too, a revival of interest in Scripture took place, while liturgy came to be considered as parish-based rather than a prerogative of religious houses. RCs began to attend reformed Holy Week ceremonies in fair numbers.

All this was a slow build-up to the changes introduced by the Second Vatican Council. Reforms were swift and comprehensive, embracing every area of sacramental and liturgical practice. The most radical changes included the replacement of Latin by the vernacular, the removal of accretions and obsolete ritual, and the much greater use of Scripture. As regards mass in particular, the priest now faced the people, who played a more active part. Lay persons could read lessons and distribute communion and, after centuries of receiving the consecrated bread alone, could now be offered the chalice also. Priests were permitted to administer confirmation to adult converts and bless the oil for anointing the sick. The removal of the requirement of fasting from midnight made evening mass possible, which led to the demise of evening devotional services. Devotion is now much more centred on the eucharist, based on Scripture and aimed at spiritual renewal of the Church. There is more lay involvement and more social and global concern. Charismatic renewal* has been influential in making liturgy less formal and inhibited, while the traditional popular devotion of the rosary has suffered eclipse. The conservative separatist movement headed by Archbishop Lefebvre made practically no impact in Scotland. RC worship, though fundamentally different in various ways, is now closer to Protestant ideals than at any time since 1560.

D. B. Forrester and D. M. Murray (eds), _Studies in the History of Worship in Scotland_ (E, 1984), 113–31, 165–8; M. H. B. Sanderson, 'Catholic Recusancy in Scotland in the Sixteenth Century', _IR_ 21 (1970), 87–107; W. J. Anderson, 'Catholic Family Worship on Deeside in 1691', _IR_ 18 (1967), 151–6; D. McRoberts, 'The Rosary in Scotland', _IR_ 23 (1972), 81–6; C. Johnson, _Developments in the Roman Catholic Church in Scotland 1789–1829_ (E, 1983), 152–69; B. Aspinwall, 'The Formation of the Catholic Community in the West of Scotland', _IR_ 33 (1982), 44–57; _Catholic Directory for Scotland_ (annually, 1829–).

B. Aspinwall

Wotherspoon, Arthur Wellesley (1853–1936), CofS minister and hymn-writer, son of William L. Wotherspoon, minister of Kilspindie, and brother of Henry J. Wotherspoon.* Educated at the universities of St Andrews (MA, 1872) and Edinburgh, he was the minister of Oatlands, a church extension charge in the parish of Govan, Glasgow, 1883–1923. One of the founding members of the Scottish Church Society,* he was its president 1908–9, and gave papers at its conferences. He was sub-editor of the _Scottish Mission Hymnbook_ (1912), to which he contributed three hymns and two tunes. One of the hymns, 'O Christ, who sinless art alone', was included in _Church Hymnary_ (1973). He was a member of the Church Union Committee in negotiation with the UFC and along with James Cooper* held out for the inclusion, in the first of the Articles Declaratory,* of a statement of the doctrines of the Trinity and the incarnation which they considered to be in harmony with the catholic creeds.

See also Scoto-Catholics.

FES III, 428; VIII, 298; IX, 284; Scottish Church Society, _Annual Reports_, 1909–10, 1935–6.

D. M. Murray

Wotherspoon, Henry Johnstone (1850–1930), CofS minister, liturgical scholar and theologian, son of William L. Wotherspoon, minister of Kilspindie, and brother of Arthur W. Wotherspoon.* He was educated at the universities of St Andrews (MA, 1871; DD, 1913) and Edinburgh. He became minister of Burnbank near Hamilton in 1880, and of St Oswald's, Edinburgh in 1894. He was a founding member of the Scottish Church Society* and its president, 1904–5 and 1921–4. He contributed many papers to its conferences which expounded the significance of the incarnation and of

Pentecost for the doctrines of the Church, the ministry and the sacraments. *The Manual of Church Doctrine* (L, 1919) which he wrote with J. M. Kirkpatrick* was intended as a clear statement of the Society's doctrinal position. His major book, *Religious Values in the Sacraments* (E, 1928), was described by D. M. Baillie* as 'the best book Scotland has produced on the sacraments for a long time' (*The Theology of the Sacraments*, L, 1957, 96).

See also Scoto-Catholics.

The Divine Service (G, 1893); *The Ministry in the Church* (L, 1916); *What Happened at Pentecost?* (E, 1937); ed. with G. W. Sprott, *The Second Prayer Book of Edward VI* (E, 1905).

Scottish Church Society, *Annual Reports 1929–30*; J. F. Leishman, *Linton Leaves* (E, 1937); *FES* I, 115.

D. M. Murray

Wycliffitism, see Lollards.

Wylie, James Aitken (1808–90), minister and noted author. Born at Kirriemuir, Angus, he studied in Aberdeen and St Andrews before proceeding to the divinity hall of the Original Secession* Synod where George Paxton* was then the professor. In 1831 he was ordained to Dollar (near Stirling), but in 1846 his demission from the charge was accompanied by an expression of regret from the congregation that, due to their small numbers, they were unable to provide him an adequate stipend on which to live. He had already accepted the assistant editorship of the *Witness*,* for which he wrote the leading article alternately with the editor, Hugh Miller,* until the newspaper's demise. Having been admitted into the FC* in 1852, he served as editor of the *Free Church Record** 1853–60. He was then appointed Professor to the Protestant Institute of Scotland (*see* Scottish Reformation Society) by his presbytery. The remainder of his life was fully occupied with writing, speaking and travelling. He received Aberdeen's LLD in 1856.

Wylie was a prolific and influential author. His 3-volume *History of Protestantism* (L, 1874–7), frequently reprinted in America as well as London and translated into German and Dutch, was perhaps his most influential work. Many of his writings in one way or another supported Protestantism against the dangers of Roman Catholicism. They included *The Papacy; its History, Dogmas, Genius, and Prospects: being the Evangelical Alliance First Prize Essay on Popery* (E, 1851), *Pilgrimage from the Alps to the Tiber: or the influence of Romanism on Trade, Justice and Knowledge* (E, 1855), *The Jesuits* (L, 1881) and *Words to the Protestants of Scotland on the Projected Establishment of the Popish Hierarchy* (E, 1878). His writings on prophecy had similar focus (*e.g. The Seventh Vial; being an Exposition of the Apocalypse* (L, 1848)), as did a goodly portion of the books which grew out of his extensive travels, which included most of Europe and Palestine, and frequent speaking engagements: *e.g. Wanderings and Musings in the Valleys of the Waldenses* (E, 1858) and *Over the Holy Land* (L, 1883). His various other writings included such editorial labours as a new edition of John Howie's* *Scots Worthies* (L, 1875) and a historical introduction to *Disruption Worthies* (E, 1881). From his departure from Dollar until his death he lived in Edinburgh.

ASOSC; *AFCS* I, 361–2; Small II, 712; *DNB* LXII, 237.

D. C. Lachman

Wyntoun, Andrew of (*c.*1355–1422), chronicler. An Augustinian* canon of St Andrews,* and prior of St Serf's, Lochleven (Kinross-shire), 1395–1413, he compiled *c.*1400, at the request of Sir John Wemyss, an *Orygynale Cronykil of Scotland*, a metrical history from creation to 1406 (the accession of James I). It is a valuable source for events around his own era, especially where he used sources now lost. It was first edited by D. Macpherson (2 vols, L, 1795), and later by D. Laing (3 vols, *Historians of Scotland* II, III, IX, E, 1872–9) and F. J. Amours (6 vols, STS, E, 1903–14).

D. F. Wright

X

Xavier, Sister Agnes, *see* Trail, Ann.

Y

YMCA (Young Men's Christian Association), an inter-denominational and inter-confessional lay movement (*see* Laity). It was formed by George Williams (1821–1905) in London in 1844 out of his meetings for prayer and Bible study. The oldest association in Scotland is in Glasgow. 'The Glasgow Young Men's Society for Religious Improvement' was founded in 1824, by the evangelist David Naismith (who later founded the London City Mission). In 1877 it united with a society called 'The Young Men's Christian Institute' to form the Glasgow United YMCA. In 1832 Naismith conducted an evangelistic campaign in Paisley which resulted in the formation of 'Paisley Young Men's Sabbath Morning Association for Prayer and Religious Improvement'. In 1875 this association united with other similar associations to form the present Young Men's Christian Association of Paisley.

The World Alliance of YMCAs was founded in 1855. The YMCA is now to be found in ninety-six countries of the world with over 23 million members. Scotland has one of four National Councils of YMCAs in the British Isles. The basis of union is as follows: 'The Young Men's Christian Association seeks to unite those who, regarding Jesus Christ as their God and Saviour, according to the Holy Scriptures, desire to be his disciples in their faith and in their life, and to associate their efforts for the extension of his Kingdom.'

The YMCA in Scotland has forty-five local associations. They work in partnership with Churches, local education authorities, and government bodies. The YMCA is involved in youth work, housing homeless persons, and helping drug addicts and the unemployed. It engages in membership training, health/fitness, sport, and Christian Education.

Y Care International is the world development wing of the Great Britain and Ireland YMCA movements.

C. P. Shedd *et al.*, *History of the World's Alliance of Young Men's Christian Associations* (L, 1955); C. Binfield, *George Williams and the Y.M.C.A.* (L, 1973); National Council of YMCAs, *The YMCA in Focus* (rev. ed., L, 1987); *Jubilee of the Y.M.C.A.: Fifty Years' Work Among Young Men In All Lands 1844–1894* (L, 1895).

R. King

York, Cardinal Duke of (1725–1807). Prince Henry Benedict Stuart, younger brother of Bonnie Prince Charlie, was born at Rome. Given the title Duke of York by his father James (VIII and III), the Old Pretender, he grew up to be both pious and studious. He never set foot in Britain, and on the failure of the last Jacobite* rising (1745)* he decided to enter the priesthood. He was created a cardinal in 1747, ordained priest 1748, received episcopal consecration 1758 and made cardinal-bishop 1761. At his see of Frascati near Rome he became known as a benefactor of the poor and a patron of the arts, reforming the local seminary, equipping it with a printing-press and theatre and assembling a splendid library. Upon the death of his brother in 1788, the Cardinal, as the last of the Stuarts, assumed the title 'Henry IX, King of Great Britain and Ireland'. He was vice-chancellor of the RCC from 1763. The invasion of Italy in 1798 by the French forced him into temporary exile and poverty, but a timely pension from the British government enabled him to live out his last years in peace and comfort, and he died at Frascati.

B. Fothergill, *The Cardinal King* (L, 1958).

A. Cherry

Young, George Armstrong (1898–1991), Baptist missionary. He was born in Leicester, the son of a carpet dyer from Langholm, Dumfriesshire. After being gassed in the trenches of Passchendaele during 1917, he dedicated himself to Christian work. He studied at Rawdon Baptist College, Yorkshire. He served with the Baptist Missionary Society in the north-western Chinese province of Shensi from 1924 to 1951, an acutely troubled period, first in rural evangelism and then (from 1932) in the capital of Sian. From 1952 to 1968 he was minister of Adelaide Place Baptist Church in central Glasgow, leading it in visitation evangelism and in hosting a Chinese Christian Fellowship. Young was warm-hearted and optimistic, an unobtrusive pacifist and socialist who passionately believed that Christianity was more revolutionary than Communism. He wrote *The Living Christ in Modern China* (L, 1947) and *The Fish or the Dragon* (Kippen, 1985).

D. W. Bebbington

Young, John, of Hawick (d.1806), Associate Synod* minister. Born in Kinross-shire, he studied philosophy and various languages at Edinburgh University, and then theology under William Moncrieff* of Alloa. In 1766 he was licensed by Sanquhar Presbytery, and in 1767 ordained to the First Associate Church of Hawick, Roxburghshire, where he ministered until his death. Paralysis, however, rendered him largely incapable of performing his duties for the last few years of his life.

Young was best known for his *Essays on Government, Revolution, etc.* (G, 1794), a fervent exposition and defence of Tory principles against the ideas of the French Revolution*. The work swiftly went through several editions, and he was rewarded with a DD from King's College, Aberdeen.

Sermons, 2 vols (E, 1780); *Sermons*, 3 vols (E, 1797); *A History of the Late War between Great Britain and France*, 2 vols (E, 1802); *Three Letters concerning the Covenants* (n.p., 1799); *The True State of the Unhappy Controversy about the Burgess Oath* (Hawick, 1783).

J. M'Kerrow, *History of the Secession Church* (G, 1841), 876–8.

N. R. Needham

Young, Patrick (latinized, Patricius Junius) (1584–1652), biblical and patristic scholar. He was born at Seaton, East Lothian. After graduation at St Andrews (1603), he became librarian to the bishop of Chester. He was incorporated MA at Oxford (1605) and took Anglican orders. He was royal librarian (from 1620) under James VI and I* and Charles I*. He examined the Codex Alexandrinus when it was placed in the royal library in 1628; his transcription of it survives in the British Library (Harl. 7522), while his *Annotationes* on it were published in vol. 6 of Walton's *Biblia Sacra Polyglotta* (L, 1657). His reputation rests mainly on his *editio princeps* (O, 1633) of *I Clement*, the text of which first became known in the west from its inclusion in Codex Alexandrinus (along with a fragment of the homily called *II Clement*, which Young also edited). In 1637 he published a catena of Greek commentators on Job.

He was rector of Hayes, Middlesex, 1623–47; in 1649 he retired to Broomfield, Essex, where he died.

DNB LXIII, 385.

F. F. Bruce

Young, Robert (1822–88), FC orientalist and textual critic. Born in Haddington, East Lothian, he was apprenticed to a printing business in 1838, becoming a printer and bookseller in 1847. He joined the FC in 1843, and from 1856–61 was literary missionary and superintendent of the Mission Press at Surat, India. From 1864–74 he conducted the Missionary Institute.

Young's true gift, however, was linguistic; in his own time he mastered Hebrew, Greek, Latin, Syriac, Chaldee, Arabic, Samaritan, and many modern languages. He put his philological skills to use in a plethora of works, such as his *Shorter Catechism, translated into French, Italian, Portuguese, Hebrew and Samaritan* (E, 1855). His belief in verbal inspiration led him to publish his own translation of the Bible, *The Holy Bible ... literally and idiomatically translated* (E, 1863; rev. ed. 1898). This employed a strict verbal equivalence, and was based on the *textus receptus*, although Young disavowed belief in its perfection. His most popular and enduring work was his *Analytical Concordance to the Bible* (E, 1879; ⁸L, 1939).

Dictionary and Concordance of Bible Words and Synonyms (E, 1883); *A Commentary on the Holy Bible, as literally and idiomatically translated out of the original languages* (E, 1863); *Hyper-criticism: An Answer to Dr Kennedy's 'Hyper-evangelism'* (E, n.d.); *Variations of the Alexandrian, Vatican and Sinaitic MSS of the New Testament* (E, 1912).

Schaff-Herzog Encyclopaedia of Religious Knowledge (³NY, 1891), IV, 247–8; *DNB* LXIII, 390.

N. R. Needham

Young, Thomas (1587–1655), Westminster divine. Born at Luncarty in Perthshire, he graduated MA from St Andrews University in 1606. He probably gained his theological education in Germany. He went on to distinguish himself by a long career outside his native Scotland, which he may have abandoned due to his opposition to episcopacy.

After assisting the Puritan Thomas Gataker in a private school in London, in 1622 Young became chaplain to the English merchants in Hamburg. In 1628 he returned to England and was appointed Anglican minister of St Peter and St Mary in Stowmarket, Suffolk, where he evaded conformity to disagreeable Anglican practices such as wearing a surplice. In 1639 he had published, possibly abroad, anonymously in Latin, a weighty defence of sabbatarianism* entitled *Dies Dominica* (ET, *The Lord's Day*, L, 1672).

When Charles I's* government collapsed, Young was the moving spirit behind the celebrated antiepiscopal manifesto, *An Answer to an Humble Remonstrance by Joseph Hall* (L, 1641). The treatise claimed to be written by 'Smectymnuus', a name composed of the initials of five Puritans. The 'TY' was Young, who according to Robert Baillie* wrote most of the treatise. The ensuing pamphlet warfare is known as the Smectymnuan controversy, made famous by the contributions of John Milton, an old pupil of Young's.

In 1643 Young was appointed a member of the Westminster* Assembly, where he argued for the divine institution of the ruling elder* and helped

YOUNG, THOMAS CULLEN

prepare the *Directory for the Publick Worship of God*. In 1644 he became Master of Jesus College, Cambridge, but was dismissed in 1650 for refusing to swear loyalty to the new republican government.

D. Laing, *Biographical Notices of Thomas Young* (E, 1870); *DNB* LXIII, 392–3; J. Reid, *Memoirs of the Westminster Divines*, 2 vols (Paisley, 1811–15), II, 267–8.

N. R. Needham

Young, Thomas Cullen (1880–1955), missionary and anthropologist. Born in Edinburgh (where his father was a UP minister), he trained in accountancy. Involvement with the Student Volunteer movement was followed by years at the Glasgow and Edinburgh (New College) UF colleges and appointment as accountant to Livingstonia (*see* Missions). Between 1904 and 1931 he served at several places in modern Malawi, chiefly Livingstonia and Loudon. He married Jessie Fiddes on furlough in 1908 (and attended New College again), and in 1914 was (without call*) ordained in Edinburgh.

Young was influenced by the serious interest in African customs and beliefs shown by other missionaries such as W. A. Elmslie* and Donald Fraser.* He became fluent in Tumbuka, and published *Notes on the Speech and History of the Tumbuka-Henga Peoples* (Livingstonia, 1923) and *Notes on the Customs and Folklore of the Tumbuka-Kamanga Peoples* (Livingstonia, 1931). He increasingly viewed Christianity as the fulfilment of African traditions, and opposed racial segregation and inequality of treatment in mission and church. African education was a major concern; he was head of the Overtoun Institute at Livingstonia 1920–5.

His wife's illness hastened his departure from Africa in 1931, never to return. He worked in London with the Religious Tract Society, promoting literature for Africa, and helped to form in 1935 the United Society for Christian Literature, of which he became General Secretary (1940–6). He was active in the Royal Anthropological Institute and similar circles, and published steadily on 'Africanity' and related concerns. His religious outlook moved towards Quakerism.

In 1946 he retired to Scotland and helped to translate the Tumbuka Old Testament. Edinburgh University made him an honorary MA in 1950. He died at Kirknewton, Midlothian. A USCL bookshop at Kitwe, Zambia, became his memorial.

FUFCS 564; P. G. Forster, *T. Cullen Young: Missionary and Anthropologist* (Hull, 1989).

D. F. Wright

Yuille, George (*c.*1845–1935), Baptist minister. Born in Irvine (Ayrshire), baptized in Hope Street Church, Glasgow, and educated at Glasgow University and the theological classes conducted for the Baptist Association by James Paterson (*d.* 1880; minister of what became Adelaide Place Church,

YWCA

Glasgow from its foundation in 1829 to his death), he was minister at Stirling (1870–1913), building up the church and beginning the local Baptist Association. From 1880 to 1919 he was secretary of the Baptist Union of Scotland* and from 1913 to 1916 Superintendent of its Home Mission (*see* Baptist Home Missionary Society for Scotland). In the last years of the nineteenth century he edited the *Scottish Baptist Magazine*. He was the main architect of the modern Baptist Union, and its historian (he edited *History of the Baptists in Scotland*, G, 1926), linking in himself the early days of George Barclay* with the modern world, and attending every Union Assembly from the beginning in 1869 until 1935. Described as 'orthodox but fair', he contended for historic Christology at the Union's one heresy* trial in 1932. He was a fervent evangelist, deeply influenced by the awakening of 1859 and the Welsh revival of 1905 (*see* Revivals).

Obituary in *Scottish Baptist Magazine*, 1936, and *Scottish Baptist Yearbook 1937*, 161; *Irvine Baptist Church, 1803–1928* (Irvine, 1928), 25; D. B. Murray, *The First Hundred Years* (G, 1969), 82.

D. B. Murray

YWCA (Young Women's Christian Association), an interdenominational and inter-confessional lay movement. Its twofold British origins in 1855 sprang from the Protestant missionary thrust and evangelical revival of that period. Concerned for young women's spiritual well-being, Miss Emma Robarts formed a Prayer Union whose members prayed for young women in changing social conditions. Prayer circles spread rapidly, Scotland's earliest YWCA presence being a Prayer Union in Kelso in 1859. The second origin came through the practical Christian response of Mary Jane Kinnaird (later Lady Kinnaird) by providing a hostel for Florence Nightingale's nurses. In 1876 these two movements united.

In 1894 the World YWCA was formed. Though Protestant in origin, in 1914 its Basis was revised in response to appeals from leaders in Greek Orthodox and RC cultures. Since then the YWCA has fulfilled a significant part in the ecumenical movement.

More liberal theology and changed social conditions for women brought challenge to the British YWCA between 1919 and 1924, leading to a division in Scotland in 1924. The seceders, retaining the original aims and emphasis, formed the YWCA of Scotland. Those who remained, the Scottish Divisional Council of the British YWCA, felt that the gospel must be expressed more openly. Such openness has continued and shows in a diversity of work and witness shared with the world movement whose members experience ecumenical awareness, fellowship and common purpose.

E. Kinnaird, *Reminiscences* (L, 1925); J. Duguid, *The Blue Triangle* (L, 1955).

S. A. Moyes

Z

Zwinglianism, the teaching of Huldrych Zwingli (1484–1531), sometimes simply his understanding of the sacraments,* usually as distinct from Calvinism* and Lutheranism.* The Reformation* in Switzerland and the Reformed tradition* began with him in Zürich, where he ministered from 1519 to his death at the battle of Kappel, when he was succeeded by Bullinger. His initial influence was strongest in Switzerland and South Germany, but soon spread to include England and Scotland.

Zwingli's theology is strongly theocentric, with a stress on the creator (over against the creature), the divinity of Christ (over against the humanity), providence and predestination* (over against chance and merit), and God's Word (over against man's). The sovereignty of God shapes all his teaching, not least its most controversial areas – the sacraments and Church–state relations.

The Bible was at the heart of the Zwinglian Reformation – in preaching,* in disputations, and in the 'prophecy'. Zwingli preached consecutively through books of the Bible (NT and OT) from 1519 onwards. He regarded Scripture as the judge at disputations. In the almost daily prophecy or prophesying (based on 1 Cor. 14; *see* Exercise), he developed a team exposition of the Bible (in Hebrew, Greek, and Latin) for ministers and students, the study concluding with a public sermon.

In salvation the stress was on faith, contrasted not with works (as Luther), but with faith in the creature, which is idolatry. Faith in the sacraments rather than Christ and his atoning death, is also idolatry. Faith is in Christ as God, not as man. Zwingli's emphasis on the distinction of the two natures in Christ was one factor in the eucharistic* controversy with Luther. Christ is not absent. He is present in his divine nature, but his human nature is in heaven. His presence is spiritual, not bodily. Moreover bodily eating cannot affect the soul. Zwingli stressed John 6:63, Luther the words of institution. Zwingli distinguished the sign from what it signified, and understood 'This is' as 'This signifies'. Remembrance and thanksgiving are prominent. Zwingli's order is Spirit and Word rather than Word and Spirit, as in his stress on the new life it is gospel and law, not Luther's law and gospel.

Controversy with Anabaptists led him to develop his understanding of predestination, the argument that there is one covenant in the OT and NT, and the analogy from circumcision in support of infant baptism.*

He did not separate Church and state. The whole of society is under the rule of God (theocracy). He argued from both NT and OT that the Christian magistrate has a role in the Church in reform and discipline. The magistrate is not autonomous but acts in obedience to the Word and with the consent of the Church. He can be deposed. The minister has a prophetic role and is more necessary than the magistrate. In the churchly role of the magistrate Zwingli went further than some, including Calvin.

In Scotland, as in England, the initial impulse in the Reformation was Lutheran rather than Reformed, although it was the Reformed influence that prevailed. The natural dominance of Calvin and Geneva has often obscured the part played by the Zwinglian tradition in the first decades, and indeed the persistence of a Zwinglian standpoint in many quarters, particularly in the sacraments.

The influence came through the writings of Zwingli, Bullinger, and others, but also through visits to Switzerland and correspondence. The writings would have been read usually in Latin, but two of Zwingli's works were translated into English in 1543 and 1550, and Bullinger's *Decades* were published in English in 1577, with many parts much earlier. Rudolf Gualther's 1545 Zürich Latin edition of Zwingli's works was in the libraries of Clement Little* and Adam Bothwell.* Moreover works by Bullinger, Oecolampadius, and several others with Zwinglian views were in Scottish libraries before 1560. Besides the reading of books there was correspondence, some of which (John Willock* and Bullinger in 1552 and George Buchanan* and Gualther 1577–9) survives.

Opposition to books is one pointer to their influence. In England in 1526 and 1531 Zwingli's and

Oecolampadius' writings were in lists of prohibited books, and Richard Smith (1500–63), later to move to Scotland, attacked their eucharistic views in writings in 1546 and 1547. There was an attack by Ninian Winzet* in 1562 on 'Oecolampadius, Zwingli, and Calvin'.

Of the early Reformers, Patrick Hamilton* was clearly Lutheran, but not George Wishart.* He visited Germany and Switzerland in 1539–40 and translated the First Helvetic Confession. He may have introduced a Zwinglian order of Holy Communion. John Knox,* his disciple, was in the Zwinglian tradition till his time in Geneva in 1554, though Zwinglian accents remained (covenant, attacks on idolatry, political concern). John Willock was also Zwinglian.

The most easily identifiable Zwinglian contributions are in the sacraments, the covenant, and the prophecy.

The emphasis on John 6, the stress on faith and spiritual eating, and the opposition to a bodily presence are generally signs of Zwinglian sacramental views, which were frequently described by opponents as 'sacramentarian'. There is evidence of such views in 1539 when Thomas Forret* of Dollar was executed for sacramentarianism. Attacks on sacramentarians persisted in the following years and in 1550 Adam Wallace* was burnt for Zwinglian views of the Lord's Supper. In Knox there is a characteristically Zwinglian stress on faith, Christ's presence in our hearts and not the bread, receiving Christ spiritually, and the Church as the body of Christ. The *BCO* (1564)* emphasized John 6, while Communion four times a year in the *FBD** (1561) was Zwingli's pattern in Zürich. The Scots Confession* (1560) rejected the idea of sacraments as 'bare signs', thereby implicitly attacking Zwingli's view of the eucharist.

The covenant* ideas of Zwingli developed into a covenant theology in Bullinger. Joined with already existing forms of covenant and band it had great importance in politics and religion in Scotland. Knox had covenant ideas in the 1550s. The General Assembly in 1590 mentioned 'a band of mainteaning religion and confession'. Robert Rollock* developed the relation of covenant and eucharist in 1596 and impressed ideas of making one's covenant with God.

The prophecy as developed in Zürich, widely used in England, was introduced to Scotland, perhaps by Wishart and others. The prophesying or interpretation of Scriptures, as it was called, is in the *FBD* (1561) and the *BCO*, where the biblical reference for it includes 1 Corinthians 14. It was intended as a corporate weekly Bible study for the whole congregation. (*See* Exercise.)

Other elements could also be Zwinglian: the strong hostility to and removal of images (or idols) from the 1530s onwards (*e.g.* Walter Stewart in Ayr in 1533), the opposition to ceremonies, the reserve about music* in worship and the removal of organs, the continuous exposition of biblical books in preaching* (practised by Zwingli from 1519), the presentation of election in article 8 of the Scots Confession, the close relation of Church and society, the prophetic role of the minister (as with Knox), and the view that rulers can be deposed.

S. M. Jackson, *The Selected Works of Huldreich Zwingli* (Philadelphia, 1901, rp. 1972); *id.*, *The Latin Works and the Correspondence of Huldreich Zwingli*, Vol. I: *1510–1522* (New York, 1912); W. J. Hinke, *The Latin Works of Huldreich Zwingli*, Vol. II (Philadelphia, 1922, rp. as *Zwingli on Providence and Other Essays*, Durham, NC, 1983); C. N. Heller, *The Latin Works of Huldreich Zwingli*, Vol. III (Philadelphia, 1929, rp. as *Commentary on True and False Religion*, Durham, NC, 1981); G. W. Bromiley, *Zwingli and Bullinger* (L, 1953); E. J. Furcha, *Huldrych Zwingli Writings: The Defense of the Reformed Faith* (Allison Park, PA, 1984); H. W. Pipkin, *Huldrych Zwingli Writings: In Search of True Religion* (Allison Park, PA, 1984).

G. R. Potter, *Zwingli* (C, 1976); G. W. Locher, *Zwingli's Thought* (Leiden, 1981) – ch. 15 on England and Scotland; W. P. Stephens, *The Theology of Huldrych Zwingli* (O, 1986); D. Shaw, 'Zwinglian Influences on the Scottish Reformation', *RSCHS* 22 (1985), 119–39.

W. P. *Stephens*